lonely

Italy

Trentino &
South Tyrol
p300

Friuli
Venezia Giulia
p401

Milan &
the Lakes
p239

Venice &
the Veneto
p333

Turin,
Piedmont & the
Italian Riviera
p164

Emilia-Romagna
& San Marino
p430

Florence &
Tuscany
p475

Umbria &
Le Marche
p576

Rome &
Lazio
p62

Abruzzo &
Molise
p633

Naples &
Campania
p652

Sardinia
p847

Puglia, Basilicata
& Calabria
p719

Sicily
p781

Gregor Clark, Peter Dragicevich, Hugh McNaughtan,
Brendan Sainsbury, Donna Wheeler, Nicola Williams,
Cristian Bonetto, Kerry Christiani, Marc Di Duca, Duncan Garwood,
Paula Hardy, Virginia Maxwell, Kevin Raub, Regi

May 2018

Contents

PLAN YOUR TRIP

ST PETER'S BASILICA, VATICAN CITY P110

BILL PERRY/SHUTTERSTOCK ©

SELINUNTE, SICILY P840

KUBAIS/SHUTTERSTOCK ©

ON THE ROAD

Contents

ON THE ROAD

SVILUPPO/SHUTTERSTOCK ©

BAKERY, NAPLES P653

Contents

Welcome to Italy

Home to many of the world's greatest works of art, architecture and gastronomy, Italy elates, inspires and moves like no other place.

Cultural Riches

Epicentre of the Roman Empire and birthplace of the Renaissance, this European virtuoso groans under the weight of its cultural cachet: it's here that you'll stand in the presence of Michelangelo's *David* and Sistine Chapel frescoes, Botticelli's *Birth of Venus* and *Primavera* and da Vinci's *The Last Supper*. In fact, Italy has more Unesco World Heritage cultural sites than any other country on Earth. Should you walk in the footsteps of ancient Romans in Pompeii, revel in Ravenna's glittering Byzantine treasures or get breathless over Giotto's revolutionary frescoes in Padua? It's a cultural conundrum as thrilling as it is overwhelming.

Inimitable Style

In few places do art and life intermingle so effortlessly. This may be the land of Dante, Titian and Verdi, but it's also the home of Prada, Massimo Bottura and Renzo Piano. Beauty, style and flair furnish every aspect of daily life, from those immaculately knotted ties and seamless espressos to the flirtatious smiles of striking strangers. The root of Italian psychology is a dedication to living life well, and effortless as it may seem, driving that dedication is a reverence for the finer things. So slow down, style up and indulge in a little *vita all'italiana* (life, Italian style).

Endless Feasts

It might look like a boot, but food-obsessed Italy feels more like a decadently stuffed Christmas stocking. From delicate *tagliatelle al ragù* to velvety *cannoli*, every bite can feel like a revelation. The secret: superlative ingredients and finely tuned know-how. And while Italy's culinary soul might prefer simplicity, it's also ingenious and sophisticated. Expect some of the world's top fine-dining destinations, from San Pellegrino 'World's Best 50' hot spots to Michelin-starred musts. So whether you're on a degustation odyssey in Modena, truffle hunting in Piedmont or swilling powerhouse reds in the Valpolicella wine region, prepare to loosen that belt.

Spectacular Landscapes

Italy's fortes extend beyond its galleries, wardrobes and dining rooms. The country is one of mother nature's masterpieces, with extraordinary natural diversity matched by few. From the north's icy Alps and glacial lakes to the south's fiery craters and turquoise grottoes, this is a place for doing as well as seeing. One day you're tearing down Courmayeur's powdery slopes, the next you could be galloping across the marshes of the Maremma, or diving in coral-studded Campanian waters. Not bad for a country not much bigger than Arizona.

Why I Love Italy

By Cristian Bonetto, Writer

Italy's 20 regions feel more like 20 independent states, each with its own dialects, traditions, architecture and glorious food. From nibbling on *knödel* in an Alto Adige chalet to exploring souk-like market streets in Sicily, the choices are as diverse as they are seductive. Then there's the country's incomparable artistic treasures, which amount to more than the rest of the world put together. It's hard not to feel a little envious sometimes, but it's even harder not to fall madly in love.

For more about our writers, see p992

Above: Mercato di Ballarò (p789), Palermo, Sicily

Italy

Gran Paradiso
Hike across high-altitude passes (p237)

Lago di Como
Cruise Lombardy's VIP Alpine lake (p270)

Dolomites
Scale Italy's most awesome granite peaks (p322)

Venice
Count millions of mosaic tesserae at San Marco (p336)

Emilia-Romagna
Tuck into Italy's culinary epicentre (p431)

Piedmont
Indulge in a gourmand's Valhalla (p199)

Italian Riviera
Village-hop along the Cinque Terre (p184)

ELEVATION

2500m
2000m
1500m
1000m
500m
300m
100m
0

200 km
100 miles

SWITZERLAND
AUSTRIA
HUNGARY
SLOVENIA
CROATIA
BOSNIA & HERCEGOVINA
SERBIA
MONTENEGRO

BERN
VADUZ
Zürich
Geneva
Courmayeur
Briançon
Modane
Valtournenche
Varallo
Aosta
Parco Nazionale del Gran Paradiso
Milky Way
Nice
Turin
PIEDMONT
LIGURIA
Genoa
Nice
Gulf of Genoa
Riviera di Ponente
Riviera di Levante
Gorgona
Capraia
Pianosa
Montecristo
Elba
Marittima
Massa
Livorno
Pisa
Lucca
Volterra
Siena
Arezzo
Florence
TUSCANY
Orvieto
Todi
Viterbo
LAZIO
Spoleto
Norcia
Assisi
UMBRIA
Perugia
Gubbio
Urbino
Pesaro
Ancona
Macerata
Parco Del Conero
Sarnano
Ascoli Piceno
Pescara
Chieti
Isole Tremiti
Adriatic Sea
Bologna
SAN MARINO
Ravenna
EMILIA ROMAGNA
Parco Nazionale delle Cinque Terre
Garfagnana
Cremona
Brescia
Bergamo
LOMBARDY
Milan
Parco Nazionale dello Stelvio
Valtellina
Lago di Como
Merano
Bolzano
Trento
Rovereto
Lago di Garda
Verona
Mantua
VENETO
Vicenza
Padua
Venice
Po Delta
Po
Innsbruck
Tarvisio
Tolmezzo
Alpe di Siusi
Dolomites
Pordenone
Udine
Gorizia
Palmanova
Lignano
Grado
Trieste
Rijeka
LJUBLJANA
ZAGREB
Graz
Pécs
Osijek
Banja Luka
SARAJEVO
Dubrovnik
PODGORICA
Danube

43°N

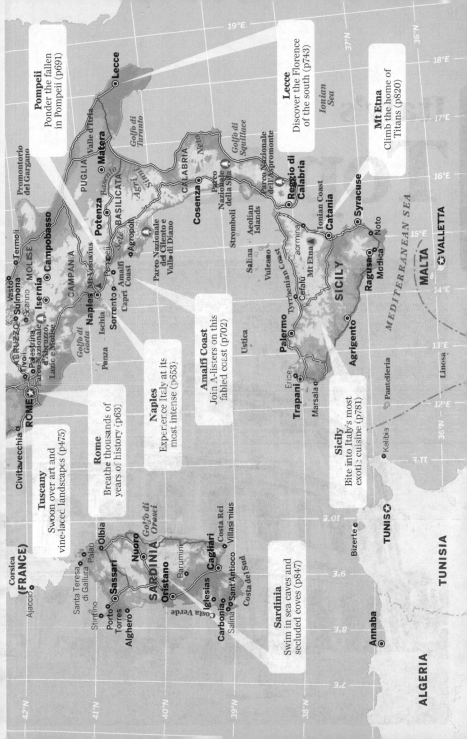

Tuscany
Swoon over art and vine-laced landscapes (p475)

Rome
Breathe thousands of years of history (p63)

Naples
Experience Italy at its most intense (p553)

Amalfi Coast
Join A-listers on this fabled coast (p702)

Pompeii
Ponder the fallen in Pompeii (p691)

Lecce
Discover the Florence of the south (p743)

Mt Etna
Climb the home of Titans (p820)

Sicily
Bite into Italy's most exotic cuisine (p781)

Sardinia
Swim in sea caves and secluded coves (p847)

Italy's
Top 18

Eternal Rome

1 Once *caput mundi* (capital of the world), Rome (p63) was legendarily spawned by a wolf-suckled boy, grew to be Western Europe's first superpower, became the spiritual centrepiece of the Christian world and is now the repository of over two millennia of European art and architecture. From the Pantheon and the Colosseum to Michelangelo's Sistine Chapel and countless works by Caravaggio, there's simply too much to see in one visit. So, do as countless others have done before you: toss a coin into the Trevi Fountain and promise to return. Left: Colosseum (p70)

Virtuoso Venice

2 An Escher-esque maze of skinny streets and waterways, Venice (p336) straddles the middle ground between reality and sheer fantasy. This is a city of ethereal winter fogs, fairy-tale domes and Gothic arches fit for the set of an opera. Look beyond its sparkling mosaics and brooding Tintorettos and you'll discover the other Venice: a living, breathing organism studded with secret gardens, sleepy *campi* (squares) and well-worn *bacari* (small bars) filled with the fizz of *prosecco* (sparkling wine) and the sing-song lilt of the Venetians' local dialect.

JAROSLAW PAWLAK/SHUTTERSTOCK ©

Touring Tuscany

3 Italy's most romanticised region, Tuscany (p475) is tailor-made for fastidious aesthetes. Home to Brunelleschi's Duomo and Masaccio's Cappella Brancacci frescoes, Florence, according to Unesco, contains 'the greatest concentration of universally renowned works of art in the world'. Beyond its blockbuster museums, elegant churches and Renaissance streetscapes sprawls a landscape of sinuous cypress trees, olive groves and coveted regional treasures, from the Gothic majesty of Siena and Manhattanesque skyline of medieval San Gimignano to the vineyards of Italy's most famous wine region, Chianti.

Amalfi Coast

4 Italy's most celebrated coastline (p702) is a gripping strip: coastal mountains plunge into creamy blue sea in a prime-time vertical scene of precipitous crags, sunbleached villages and lush woodland. Between sea and sky, mountain-top hiking trails deliver Tyrrhenian panoramas fit for a god. While some may argue that the peninsula's most beautiful coast is Liguria's Cinque Terre or Calabria's Costa Viola, it is the Amalfi Coast that has seduced and inspired countless greats, from Wagner and DH Lawrence to Tennessee Williams, Rudolf Nureyev and Gore Vidal.

Ghostly Pompeii

5 Frozen in its death throes, the timewarped ruins of Pompeii (p692) hurtle you 2000 years into the past. Wander through chariotgrooved Roman streets, lavishly frescoed villas and bathhouses, food stores and markets, theatres, even an ancient brothel. Then, in the eerie stillness, your eye on ominous Mt Vesuvius, ponder Pliny the Younger's terrifying account of the town's final hours: 'Darkness came on again, again ashes, thick and heavy. We got up repeatedly to shake these off; otherwise we would have been buried and crushed by the weight.'

OLEG VORONISCHE/SHUTTERSTOCK ©

LAURADIBI/SHUTTERSTOCK ©

Mighty Masterpieces

6 A browse through any art-history textbook will highlight seminal movements in Western art, from classical, Renaissance and mannerist to baroque, futurist and metaphysical. All were forged in Italy by a red-carpet roll call of artists (p909) including Giotto, da Vinci, Michelangelo, Botticelli, Bernini, Caravaggio, Carracci, Boccioni, Balla and de Chirico. Find the best of them in Rome's Museo e Galleria Borghese and Vatican Museums, Florence's Uffizi, Venice's Gallerie dell'Accademia, Milan's Museo del Novecento and Naples' hilltop Palazzo Reale di Capodimonte. Top: Botticelli's *La Primavera*

Devouring Emilia-Romagna

7 They don't call Bologna 'La Grassa' (the fat one) for nothing. Many of Italy's belt-busting classics call this city home, from *mortadella* and tortellini to its trademark *tagliatelle al ragù*. Shop the deli-packed Quadrilatero and take a side trip to the city of Modena for world-famous aged balsamic vinegar. Just leave room for a trip to Parma, hometown of *parmigiano reggiano* cheese and the incomparable *prosciutto di Parma*. Wherever you plunge your fork, toast with a glass or three of Emilia-Romagna's (p431) renowned Lambrusco or sauvignon blanc.
Bottom: Bologna tortellini

PAUL FEARN/ALAMY STOCK PHOTO ©

GIORGIO MORARA/SHUTTERSTOCK ©

Tackling the Dolomites

8 Scour the globe and you'll find plenty of taller, bigger and more geologically volatile mountains, but few can match the romance of the pink-hued, granite Dolomites (p322) Maybe it's their harsh, jagged summits, the vibrant skirts of spring wildflowers or the rich cache of Ladin legends. Then again, it could just be the magnetic draw of money, style and glamour at Italy's most fabled ski resort, Cortina d'Ampezzo (p399). Whatever the reason, this tiny pocket of northern Italy takes seductiveness to dizzying heights. Above left: Cortina d'Ampezzo (p399)

Murals & Mosaics

9 Often regarded as just plain 'dark', the Italian Middle Ages had an artistic brilliance that's hard to ignore. Perhaps it was the sparkling handcut mosaic of Ravenna's Byzantine basilicas that provided the guiding light, but something inspired Giotto di Bondone to leap out of the shadows with his daring naturalistic frescoes in Padua's Cappella degli Scrovegni (p378) and the Basilica di San Francesco in Assisi. With them he gave the world a new artistic language, and from then it was just a short step to Masaccio's Trinity and the dawning light of the Renaissance. Top right: Cappella degli Scrovegni (p378), Padua

Neapolitan Street Life

10 Nowhere else in Italy are people as conscious of their role in the theatre of everyday life as in Naples (p653). And in no other Italian city does daily life radiate such drama and intensity. Naples' ancient streets are a stage, cast with boisterous matriarchs, bellowing *baristi* and tongue-knotted lovers. To savour the flavour, dive into the city's rough-and-tumble Porta Nolana market, a loud, lavish opera of hawking fruit vendors, wriggling seafood and the irresistible aroma of just-baked *sfogliatelle* (sweetened ricotta pastries).

Hiking the Italian Riviera

11 For the sinful inhabitants of the Cinque Terre's (p184) five sherbet-coloured villages – Monterosso, Vernazza, Corniglia, Manarola and Riomaggiore – penance involved a lengthy and arduous hike up the vertiginous cliffside to the local village sanctuary to appeal for forgiveness. You can scale the same trails today, through terraced vineyards and hillsides smothered in *macchia* (shrubbery). They may give your glutes a good workout, but as the heavenly views unfurl, it's hard to think of a more benign punishment. Count your blessings. Below: Vernazza (p188)

Sardinian Shores

12 The English language fails to accurately describe the varied blue, green and – in the deepest shadows – purple hues of the sea surrounding Sardinia (p847). While models, ministers and perma-tanned celebrities wine, dine and sail along the glossy Costa Smeralda, much of Sardinia remains a wild, raw playground. Slather on that sunscreen and explore the island's rugged coastal beauty, from the tumbledown boulders of Santa Teresa di Gallura and the wind-chiselled cliff face of the Golfo di Orosei to the windswept beauty of the Costa Verde's dune-backed beaches. Top right: Golfo di Orosei (p888)

11

MARCO SIMONI/ALAMY STOCK PHOTO ©

Living Luxe on Lago di Como

13 If it's good enough for the Clooneys, it's good enough for mere mortals. Nestled in the shadow of the Rhaetian Alps, dazzling Lago di Como (p270) is the most spectacular of the Lombard lakes, its Liberty-style villas home to movie moguls, fashion royalty and Arab sheikhs. Surrounded on all sides by lush greenery, the lake's siren calls include the gardens of Villa Melzi d'Eril, Villa Carlotta and Villa Balbianello, which blush pink with camellias, azaleas and rhododendrons in April and May. Left: Villa Melzi d'Eril (p275)

Piedmont on a Plate

14 Piedmont (p199) is one of Italy's gastronomic powerhouses, a mouth-watering, knee-weakening Promised Land of culinary decadence. At its best in the autumn, this is the place to trawl through woods in search of prestigious fungi and to nibble on cocoa concoctions in gilded cafes, not to mention swill cult-status reds in Slow Food villages. Stock the larder at Turin's sprawling food emporium Eataly, savour rare white truffles in Alba and compare the nuances of vintage Barolo and Barbaresco wines on the vine-graced slopes of the Langhe. Top: White truffles

Scaling Mt Etna

15 Known to the Greeks as the 'column that holds up the sky', Mt Etna (p820) is not only Europe's largest volcano, it's one of the world's most active. The ancients believed the giant Tifone (Typhoon) lived in its crater and lit the sky with spectacular pyrotechnics. At 3329m it literally towers above Sicily's Ionian Coast. Whether you tackle it on foot or on a guided 4WD tour, scaling this time bomb rewards with towering views and the secret thrill of having come cheek-to-cheek with a towering threat.

MAURIZIO MILANESIO/SHUTTERSTOCK ©

IOANNIS DOUKAS/EYEEM/GETTY IMAGES ©

Savouring Sicily

16 Sour, spicy and sweet, the flavours of Sicily (p781) reflect millennia of cross-cultural influences – Greek, Arab, Spanish and French.No other regional Italian cuisine is quite as complex and intriguing. Tuck into golden *panelle* (chickpea fritters) in Palermo, fragrant couscous in Trapani and chilli-spiked chocolate in Modica. From Palermo's Mercato di Ballarò to Catania's Pescheria, market stalls burst with local delicacies: Bronte pistachios, briny olives, glistening swordfish and nutty Canestrato cheese. Just leave room for a fluffy, ricotta-filled *cannolo,* not to mention a slice of oh-so-sweet Sicilian *cassata.*
Top left: *Cannoli*

Baroque Lecce

17 There's baroque, and then there's *barocco leccese* (Lecce baroque), the hyper extravagant spin-off defining many a Puglian town. Making it all possible was the local stone, so impossibly soft it led art historian Cesare Brandi to claim it could be carved with a penknife. Craftspeople vied for ever greater heights of creativity, crowding facades with swirling vegetal designs, gargoyles and strange zoomorphic figures. Queen of the architectural crop is Lecce's Basilica di Santa Croce (p744), so insanely detailed the Marchese Grimaldi said it made him think a lunatic was having a nightmare. Top right: Detail, Basilica di Santa Croce (p744)

Escaping to Paradiso

18 If you're pining for a mind-clearing retreat, wear down your hiking boots on the 724km of marked trails and mule tracks traversing 'Grand Paradiso'. Part of the Graian Alps and the very first of Italy's national parks, Gran Paradiso's (p237) pristine spread encompasses 57 glaciers and Alpine pastures awash with wild pansies, gentians and alpenroses, not to mention a healthy population of Alpine ibex, for whose protection the park was originally established. The eponymous Gran Paradiso (4061m) is the park's only peak, accessed from tranquil Cogne. Bottom right: Alpine ibex

Need to Know

For more information, see Survival Guide (p947)

Currency
Euro (€)

Language
Italian

Visas
Generally not required for stays of up to 90 days (or at all for EU nationals); some nationalities need a Schengen visa.

Money
ATMs are widespread in Italy. Major credit cards are widely accepted, but some smaller shops, trattorias and hotels might not take them.

Mobile Phones
Local SIM cards can be used in European, Australian and some unlocked US phones. Other phones must be set to roaming.

Time
Central European Time (GMT/UTC plus one hour)

Room Tax
Visitors may be charged an extra €1 to €7 per night. This is known as a 'tourist tax' or 'room occupancy tax'.

When to Go

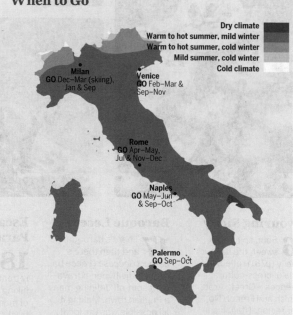

Dry climate
Warm to hot summer, mild winter
Warm to hot summer, cold winter
Mild summer, cold winter
Cold climate

Milan
GO Dec–Mar (skiing), Jan & Sep

Venice
GO Feb–Mar & Sep–Nov

Rome
GO Apr–May, Jul & Nov–Dec

Naples
GO May–Jun & Sep–Oct

Palermo
GO Sep–Oct

High Season
(Jul–Aug)

➡ Queues at big sights and on the road, especially in August.

➡ Prices also rocket for Christmas, New Year and Easter.

➡ Late December to March is high season in the Alps and Dolomites.

Shoulder
(Apr–Jun & Sep–Oct)

➡ Good deals on accommodation, especially in the south.

➡ Spring is best for festivals, flowers and local produce.

➡ Autumn provides warm weather and the grape harvest.

Low Season
(Nov–Mar)

➡ Prices up to 30% less than in high season.

➡ Many sights and hotels closed in coastal and mountainous areas.

➡ A good period for cultural events in large cities.

Useful Websites

Lonely Planet (www.lonely planet.com/italy) Destination information, hotel bookings, traveller forum and more.

Trenitalia (www.trenitalia.com) Italian railways website.

Agriturismi (www.agriturismi.it) Guide to farm accommodation.

ENIT (www.italia.it) Official Italian-government tourism website.

The Local (www.thelocal.it) English-language news from Italy, including travel-related stories.

Important Numbers

From outside Italy, dial your international access code, Italy's country code (⌨39) then the number (including the '0').

Country code	⌨39
International access code	⌨00
Ambulance	⌨118
Police	⌨112, 113
Fire	⌨115

Exchange Rates

Australia	A$1	€0.67
Canada	C$1	€0.67
Japan	¥100	€0.81
New Zealand	NZ$1	€0.64
Switzerland	Sfr1	€0.92
UK	UK£1	€1.14
US	US$1	€0.89

For current exchange rates, see www.xe.com.

Daily Costs

Budget: Less than €100

➡ Dorm bed: €20–35

➡ Double room in a budget hotel: €60–130

➡ Pizza or pasta: €6–12

Midrange: €100–250

➡ Double room in a hotel: €110–200

➡ Local restaurant dinner: €25–45

➡ Admission to museum: €4–15

Top End: More than €250

➡ Double room in a four- or five-star hotel: €200 plus

➡ Top restaurant dinner: €45–150

➡ Opera ticket: €40–210

Opening Hours

Opening hours vary throughout the year. We've provided high-season opening hours; hours will generally decrease in the shoulder and low seasons. 'Summer' times generally refer to the period from April to September or October, while 'winter' times generally run from October or November to March.

Banks 8.30am–1.30pm and 2.45pm–4.30pm Monday to Friday

Restaurants noon–3pm and 7.30–11pm or midnight

Cafes 7.30am–8pm, sometimes until 1am or 2am

Bars and clubs 10pm–4am or 5am

Shops 9am–1pm and 4–8pm Monday to Saturday, some also open Sunday

Arriving in Italy

Rome Leonardo da Vinci The express train (€14) takes 30 minutes and runs between 6.23am and 11.23pm. Buses (€6) take an hour and run between 5am and 12.30am; night services run at 1.15am, 2.15am and 3.30am. Taxis (set fare €48) complete the journey in 45 to 60 minutes.

Malpensa Airport (Milan) The express train (€13) takes 50 minutes and runs between 5.40am and 10.40pm. Buses (€10) take 50 minutes and run between 5am and 1.20am. Taxis (set fare €90) take 50 minutes.

Marco Polo Airport (Venice) The ferry (€15) takes 45 to 90 minutes and runs between 6.15am and 1.15am. Buses (€8) take 20 minutes and run between 5.20am and 12.50am. Water taxis (from €110) take 30 minutes.

Naples International Airport (Capodichino) Shuttle buses (€4) take 20 to 45 minutes and run between 6am and 11.40pm. Taxis (set fare €16 to €23) take 20 to 35 minutes.

Getting Around

Transport in Italy is affordable, quick and efficient.

Train Reasonably priced, with extensive coverage and frequent departures. High speed trains connect major cities.

Car Handy for travelling at your own pace, or for visiting regions with minimal public transport. Not a good idea for travelling within major urban areas.

Bus Cheaper and slower than trains. Useful for more remote villages not serviced by trains.

For much more on **getting around**, see p963

First Time Italy

For more information, see Survival Guide (p947)

Checklist

➡ Ensure your passport is valid for at least six months past your arrival date

➡ Check airline baggage restrictions

➡ Organise travel insurance

➡ Make bookings (for popular museums, entertainment and accommodation)

➡ Inform your credit- or debit-card company of your travels

➡ Check you can use your mobile (cell) phone

➡ Check requirements for hiring a car

What to Pack

➡ Good walking shoes for those cobblestones

➡ Hat, sunglasses, sunscreen

➡ Electrical adapter and phone charger

➡ A detailed driving map for Italy's rural back roads

➡ A smart outfit and shoes

➡ Patience: for coping with inefficiency

➡ Phrasebook: for ordering and charming

Top Tips for Your Trip

➡ Visit in spring and autumn – good weather and thinner crowds.

➡ Always carry some cash. Some restaurants and hotels only accept cash, while unattended petrol (gas) stations don't always accept foreign credit cards.

➡ If you're driving, head off the main roads: some of Italy's most stunning scenery is best on secondary or tertiary roads.

➡ Don't rely solely on a GPS, which can occasionally lead you too far off the beaten track; cross-check your route on a printed road map.

➡ Speak at least a few Italian words. A little can go a long way.

➡ Queue-jumping is common in Italy: be polite but assertive.

➡ Avoid restaurants with touts and the mediocre *menu turistico* (tourist menu).

What to Wear

Appearances matter in Italy. Milan, Italy's fashion capital, is rigidly chic. Rome and Florence are marginally less formal, but with big fashion houses in town, sloppy attire won't do. In the cities, suitable wear for men is generally trousers (including stylish jeans) and shirts or polo shirts, and for women skirts, trousers or dresses. Shorts, T-shirts and sandals are fine in summer and at the beach, but long sleeves are required for dining out. For evening wear, smart casual is the norm. A light sweater or waterproof jacket is useful in spring and autumn, and sturdy shoes are good for archaeological sites.

Sleeping

Hotels All prices and levels of quality, from cheap-and-charmless to sleek-and-exclusive boutique.

Farm stays Perfect for families and for relaxation, *agriturismi* range from rustic farmhouses to luxe country estates.

B&Bs Often great value, can range from rooms in family houses to self-catering studio apartments.

Pensions Similar to hotels, though *pensioni* are generally of one- to three-star quality and family-run.

Hostels You'll find both official HI-affiliated and privately run *ostelli*, many also offering private rooms with bathroom.

Money

Credit and debit cards can be used almost everywhere with the exception of some rural towns and villages.

Visa and MasterCard are widely recognised. American Express is only accepted by some major chains and big hotels; few places take Diners Club.

ATMs are everywhere but be aware of transaction fees. Some ATMs in Italy reject foreign cards. Try a few before assuming your card is the problem.

Change money at banks, post offices or a *cambio* (exchange office). Post offices and banks tend to offer the best rates.

Bargaining

Gentle haggling is common in markets. Haggling in stores is generally unacceptable, though good-humoured bargaining at smaller artisan or craft shops in southern Italy is not unusual if making multiple purchases.

Tipping

Italians are not big tippers. Use the following as a rough guide:

Taxis Optional, but most people round up to the nearest euro.

Hotels Tip porters about €5 at high-end hotels.

Restaurants Service (*servizio*) is generally included in restaurants – if it's not, a euro or two is fine in pizzerias, 10% in restaurants.

Bars Optional, though many Italians leave small change on the bar when ordering coffee (usually €0.10 per coffee). If drinks are brought to your table, a small tip is generally appreciated.

Phrases to Learn Before You Go

You can get by with English, but you'll improve your experience no end by mastering a few basic words and expressions. This is particularly true in restaurants where menus don't always have English translations and some places rely on waiters to explain what's on. For more on language, see p968.

 What's the local speciality?
Qual'è la specialità di questa regione?
kwa-le la spe-cha-lee-ta dee kwes-ta re-jo-ne

A bit like the rivalry between medieval Italian city-states, these days the country's regions compete in speciality foods and wines.

 Which combined tickets do you have?
Quali biglietti cumulativi avete?
kwa-lee bee-lye-tee koo-moo-la-tee-vee a-ve-te

Make the most of your euro by getting combined tickets to various sights; they are available in all major Italian cities.

 Where can I buy discount designer items?
C'è un outlet in zona? che oon owt-let in zo-na

Discount fashion outlets are big business in major cities – get bargain-priced seconds, samples and cast-offs for *la bella figura*.

 Let's meet at 6pm for pre-dinner drinks.
Ci vediamo alle sei per un aperitivo.
chee ve-dya-mo a-le say per oon a-pe-ree-tee-vo

At dusk, watch the main piazza get crowded with people sipping colourful cocktails and snacking the evening away. Join your new friends for this authentic Italian ritual!

Etiquette

Italy is a surprisingly formal society; the following tips will help avoid awkward moments.

Greetings Greet people in shops, restaurants and bars with a '*buongiorno*' (good morning) or '*buonasera*' (good evening); kiss both cheeks and say '*come stai*' (how are you) to friends.

Asking for help Say '*mi scusi*' (excuse me) to attract attention; use '*permesso*' (permission) to pass someone in a crowded space.

Dress Cover shoulders, torso and thighs when visiting churches and dress smartly when eating out.

At the table Eat pasta with a fork, not a spoon; it's OK to eat pizza with your hands.

Gifts If invited to someone's home, traditional gifts are a tray of *dolci* (sweets) from a *pasticceria* (pastry shop), a bottle of wine or flowers.

What's New

New & Renewed Landmarks, Rome

The Spanish Steps (p104) are wowing once more after a major restoration. Further south in the EUR district, heads are turning thanks to La Nuvola (p99), a new, cutting-edge convention centre designed by Massimiliano and Doriana Fuksas.

Tuscan Gastronomy 2.0, Tuscany

Tuscan gastronomy is finding new-school verve at Florence's Essenziale (p507), stomping ground of bold, young chef Simone Cipriani. In Pietrasanta, Lorenzo Barsotti's Filippo Mud Bar (p571) is redefining the region's cocktails and fusion fare.

Cutting-Edge Architecture, Milan

Milan has reaffirmed its 'Design Capital' status with Herzog & de Meuron's conservatory-like Fondazione Feltrinelli. Home to a bookstore and bar, it's one of several striking new developments in town, among them CityLife. (p242)

Museo Archeologico Nazionale, Naples

Italy's foremost archaeological museum (p660) is showcasing its ancient Egyptian artefacts in impressive new galleries. Improvements are also visible at Palazzo Reale di Capodimonte (p668), with rehabilitated parkland and a museum shuttle bus.

'Gate of Heaven' Tour, Siena

Exploring Siena's iconic Romanesque-Gothic Duomo is now even more breathtaking thanks to its Porta del Cielo tour, which takes visitors up to the cathedral's roof and dome for a close-up inspection. (p517)

Top Budget Digs, Lago di Como

The latest trend to sweep across northern Italy's A-list lake is top-notch budget accommodation. Live the high life *sans* breaking the bank at Ostello Bello (p250) and Locanda Barchetta (p275).

A Week of Glass, Venice

Murano's glass masters have wowed the world with their alchemy for centuries. September's new Venice Glass Week festival showcases their finest work, with behind-the-scenes insight. (p32)

Messner Mountain Museum Kronplatz

Reinhold Messner's final museum of mountain culture in the South Tyrol, with 360-degree Alpine views and sublime architecture from the late Zaha Hadid. (p331)

Museo Archeologico Regionale, Palermo

Palermo's magnificent museum has reopened, with new exhibition spaces worthy of its extraordinary ancient treasures, uncovered across Sicily. (p790)

For more recommendations and reviews, see lonelyplanet.com/italy

If You Like...

Masterpieces

Sistine Chapel Michelangelo's ceiling fresco aside, Rome's famous chapel also features work by Botticelli, Ghirlandaio and Perugino. (p112)

Galleria degli Uffizi Cimabue, Botticelli, da Vinci, Raphael, Titian: Florence's alpha art museum delivers a who's who of artistic deities. (p485)

Museo e Galleria Borghese A digestible serve of Renaissance and baroque masterpieces in an elegant villa in Rome. (p118)

Cappella degli Scrovegni See just how much Giotto revolutionised art in Padua's Cappella degli Scrovegni and Assisi's Basilica di San Francesco. (p378)

Basilica di San Vitale Witness early Christian mosaics at Ravenna's Basilica di San Vitale and Basilica di Sant'Apollinare Nuovo. (p464)

Cenacolo di Sant'Apollonia Home to Andrea del Castagno's 15th-century *Last Supper*, pioneering for its effective application of Renaissance perspective. (p496)

Pompeii The Dionysiac frieze in the Villa dei Misteri is one of the world's largest ancient frescoes. (p696)

Palazzo Grassi French billionaire François Pinault's contemporary collection is showcased against Tadao Ando interior sets in Venice. (p356)

Museion Bolzano's contemporary art space highlights the ongoing dialogue between Alto Adige, Austria and Germany. (p312)

Pinturicchio Perugia and Spello showcase the work of Umbria's home-grown Renaissance talent, Pinturicchio. (p580)

Fabulous Food

Bologna Bologna straddles Italian food lines between the butter-led north and the tomato-based cuisine of the south. (p439)

Truffles Sniff around Piedmont, Tuscany and Umbria for the world's most coveted fungi. (p217)

Osteria Francescana Rave about Massimo Bottura's ingenious flavour combinations at one of the world's hottest restaurants. (p449)

Seafood So fresh you can eat it raw in Venice, home to the seafood-heaving Rialto Market. (p350)

Sicily Buxom eggplants (aubergines), juicy raisins and velvety marzipan – cross-cultural Sicily puts the fusion in Italian cuisine. (p789)

Pizza Eat Italy's most famous export at its birthplace in Naples. (p653)

Parmigiano Reggiano Parma's cheese is the most famous; just leave room for Lombardy's Taleggio, Campania's buffalo mozzarella and Puglia's creamy burrata. (p454)

Tuscan T-Bone Carnivores drool over Florence's iconic *bistecca alla fiorentina*, hailing from Tuscany's prized Val di Chiana. (p503)

Eataly Feast and shop at Turin's showcase of quality Italian gastronomy, flagship of the Eataly empire. (p214)

Medieval Hill Towns

Umbria & Le Marche Medieval hill towns galore: start with Spello and Spoleto, and end with Todi and Urbino. (p576)

Montalcino A pocket-sized Tuscan jewel lined with wine bars pouring the area's celebrated Brunello *vini*. (p540)

Erice Splendid coastal views from the hilltop Norman castle make this western Sicily's most photogenic village. (p845)

San Gimignano A medieval Tuscan Manhattan, studded with skyscraping towers from centuries past. (p533)

Ravello Lording it over the Amalfi Coast, Campania's cultured jewel has wowed the best of them, including Wagner. (p710)

Maratea A 13th-century *borgo* (medieval town) with pint-sized piazzas, winding alleys and startling views across the Gulf of Policastro. (p767)

Puglia From the Valle d'Itria to the sierras of the Salento, Puglia is dotted with whitewashed hilltop villages. (p722)

Pitigliano One of Tuscany's most dramatic hilltop treasures, with Escher-like streets and Jewish flavours. (p547)

Wine Tasting

From Etna's elegant whites to Barolo's complex reds, Italian wines are as varied as the country's terrain. Sample them in cellars, over long, lazy lunches or dedicate yourself to a full-blown tour.

Tuscan Wine Routes Discover why Chianti isn't just a cheap table wine left over from the 1970s. (p525)

Festa dell'Uva e del Vino In early October, food and vino stalls take over the Lombard wine town of Bardolino. (p288)

Museo del Vino a Barolo Explore the history of *vino* through art and film at Barolo's wine museum. (p221)

Friuli Venezia Giulia Oenophiles revere the Colli Orientali and Il Carso areas for their Friuliano and blended 'superwhites'. (p401)

Valpolicella and Soave Wine tastings in these two Veneto regions include blockbuster drops both white and red. (p390 and p391)

Top: San Gimignano (p533), Tuscany
Bottom: Vineyards in Chianti (p525)

South Tyrol Weinstrasse Here native grapes Lagrein, Vernatsch and Gewürztraminer thrive alongside imports pinot blanc, sauvignon, merlot and cabernet. (p318)

Cantine Aperte Private wine cellars throughout the country open their doors to the public on the last weekend in May.

Villas & Palaces

Reggia di Caserta As seen in *Star Wars* and *Mission Impossible*; the Italian baroque's spectacular epilogue. (p697)

Rome Grapple with real-estate envy at Galleria Doria Pamphilj, Palazzo Farnese and Palazzo Barberini. (p63)

Palazzo Ducale The doge's Venetian palace comes with a golden staircase and interrogation rooms. (p337)

Villa di Maser Andrea Palladio and Paolo Veronese conspired to create the Veneto's finest country mansion. (p396)

Reggia di Venaria Reale Piedmont's sprawling Savoy palace inspired French rival Versailles. (p203)

Palazzi dei Rolli A collection of 42 Unesco-protected lodging palaces in Genoa. (p168)

Villa Romana del Casale See where the home decor obsession began with this Roman villa's 3500-sq-metre mosaic floor in Sicily. (p833)

Il Vittoriale degli Italiani Gabriele d'Annunzio's Lombard estate would put a Roman emperor to shame. (p285)

Palazzo Ducale A crenellated, 500-room palace lavished with frescoes in medieval Mantua. (p295)

Markets

Rialto Market Shop for lagoon specialities at Venice's centuries-old produce market. (p350)

Mercato di Ballarò Spices, watermelons and giant swordfish under striped awnings down cobbled alleys: Palermo's market recalls an African bazaar. (p789)

La Pescheria A loud, wet, action-packed citadel of fresh fish, seafood and more in central Catania. (p814)

Mercato di Porta Nolana Elbow your way past bellowing fishing folk, fragrant bakeries and bootleg CD stalls for a slice of Neapolitan street theatre. (p664)

Fiera Antiquaria di Arezzo Arezzo's monthly antiques fair is the region's most famous. (p573)

Porta Palazzo Turin's outdoor food market is the continent's largest. (p215)

Islands & Beaches

Counting all its offshore islands and squiggly indentations, Italy's coastline stretches 7600km from the sheer cliffs of the Cinque Terre, down through Rimini's brash resorts to the bijou islands in the Bay of Naples and Puglia's sandy shores.

Sardinia Take your pick of Italy's most spectacular beaches, including the Aga Khan's personal favourite, Spiaggia del Principe. (p847)

Puglia Superb sandy sweeps, including the Baia dei Turchi near Otranto and the cliff-backed beaches of the Gargano. (p722)

Aeolian Islands Sicily's seven volcanic islands sport hillsides of silver-grey pumice, black lava beaches and lush green vineyards. (p798)

Borromean Islands Graced with villas, gardens and wandering peacocks, Lago Maggiore's trio of islands are impossibly refined. (p265)

Procida A sleepy Campanian island made famous in a string of celebrated films. (p685)

Rimini Trade high culture for thumping beats and party crowds on the Adriatic coast. (p407)

Elba An island of the Parco Nazionale Arcipelago Toscano, Europe's largest marine park. (p556)

Gardens

Italy's penchant for the 'outdoor room' has been going strong since Roman emperors landscaped their holiday villas. Renaissance princes refined the practice, but it was 19th-century aristocrats who really went to town.

Villa Carlotta An extraordinary oasis on the Italian lakes, whose other botanical wonders include Villa Balbianello. (p279)

Villa d'Este Tivoli's superlative High Renaissance garden, dotted with fantastical fountains and cypress-lined avenues. (p154)

Ravello Applaud classical-music concerts in Villa Rufolo's romantic, sky-high gardens. (p710)

Reggia di Venaria Reale Amble in elegant gardens at Turin's World Heritage–listed former royal pad. (p203)

La Mortella A tropical and Mediterranean paradise inspired

Ravello (p710), Amalfi Coast

by the gardens of Granada's Alhambra. (p682)

Giardini Pubblici Venice's first green space and the home of the celebrated Biennale with its avant-garde pavilions. (p345)

Unspoilt Wilderness

Parco Nazionale del Gran Paradiso Spectacular hiking trails, Alpine ibex and a refresh-

ing lack of ski resorts await at Valle d'Aosta's mountainous wonderland. (p237)

Parco del Conero Hit this protected pocket of Le Marche for fragrant forest, gleaming white cliffs and pristine bays. (p621)

Selvaggio Blu Sardinia's toughest trek doesn't shortchange on rugged beauty – from cliffs and caves to hypnotic coastal scenery. (p887)

Parco Nazionale dei Monti Sibillini Head for the border

between Umbria and Le Marche for woodland and subalpine meadows dotted with peregrine falcons, wolves and wildcats. (p630)

Northern Lagoon, Venice Take a boat tour of Europe's largest coastal wetland, home to a bounty of migrating birds from September to January. (p359)

Riserva Naturale dello Zingaro Dip in and out of picturesque coves along the wild coastline of Sicily's oldest nature reserve. (p841)

Month by Month

January

Following hot on the heels of New Year is Epiphany. In the Alps and Dolomites it's ski season, while in the Mediterranean south winters are mild and crowd-free, although many resort towns are firmly shut.

🚣 Regata della Befana

Witches in Venice don't ride brooms: they row boats. Venice celebrates Epiphany on 6 January with the Regatta of the Witches, complete with a fleet of brawny men dressed in their finest *befana* (witch) drag.

🏃 Ski Italia

Italy's top ski resorts are in the northern Alps and the Dolomites, but you'll also find resorts in Friuli, the Apennines, Le Marche and even Sicily. The best months of the season are January and February.

February

'Short' and 'accursed' is how Italians describe February. In the mountains the ski season hits its peak in line with school holidays. Further south it's chilly, but almond trees blossom and herald the carnival season.

🎭 Carnevale

In the period leading up to Ash Wednesday, many Italian towns stage pre-Lenten carnivals, with whimsical costumes, confetti and festive treats. Venice's Carnevale (www.carnevale.venezia.it) is the most famous, while Viareggio's version (http://viareggio.ilcarnevale.com) is well known for its giant papier-mâché floats.

🍴 Nero Norcia

An early-spring taste of truffles in the gastronomic Umbrian town of Norcia, this fair usually runs over two to three weekends in late February and early March. Thousands of visitors sift through booths focusing on all things fungi, alongside other specialty produce. (p609)

🎭 Sa Sartiglia

Masqueraded horse riders, fearless equestrian acrobatics, and grandly costumed drummers and trumpeters define this historic event (www.sartiglia.info), held in the Sardinian town of Oristano on the last Sunday before Lent and on Shrove Tuesday.

March

The weather in March is capricious: sunny, rainy and windy all at once. The official start of spring is 21 March, but the holiday season starts at Easter.

🍴 Taste

For three days in March, gourmands flock to Florence for Taste (www.pittimmaginc.com), a bustling food fair held inside industrial-sleek Stazione Leopolda. The program includes culinary-themed talks, cooking demonstrations and the chance to sample food, coffee and liquor from more than 300 Italian artisan producers.

🎭 Settimana Santa

The Pope leads a candlelit procession to the Colosseum on Good Friday and blesses from St Peter's

Square on Easter Sunday. Fireworks explode in Florence's Piazza del Duomo, with notable processions taking place in Procida and Sorrento (Campania), Taranto (Puglia), Trapani (Sicily) and Iglesias (Sardinia).

April

Spring has sprung and April sees the Italian peninsula bloom. The gardens of northern Italy show off their tulips and early camellias, and as April edges towards May, the mountains of Sicily and Calabria begin to fill with wildflowers.

⊙ Salone Internazionale del Mobile

Held annually in Milan, the world's most prestigious furniture fair (www.salone-milano.it) is held at Fiera Milano, with satellite exhibitions in Zona Tortona. Running alongside it is the Fuorisalone (www.fuori salone.it), serving up design-related exhibits, events and parties across the city.

⊙ Settimana del Tulipano

Tulips erupt in spectacular bloom during the Week of the Tulip, held at Lago Maggiore's Villa Taranto (www. villataranto.it); the dahlia path and dogwood are also in bloom in what is considered one of Europe's finest botanical gardens.

☆ Maggio Musicale Fiorentino

Established in 1933, Italy's oldest art festival (www.

operadifirenze.it) brings world-class performances of theatre, classical music, jazz, opera and dance to Florence's opera house and other venues across the city. Events run from April to June.

May

The month of roses, early summer produce and cultural festivals makes May a perfect time to travel. The weather is warm but not too hot, and prices throughout Italy are good value. An especially good month for walkers.

☆ Maggio dei Monumenti

As the weather warms up, Naples rolls out a mammoth, month-long program of art exhibitions, concerts, performances and tours around the city. Many historical and architectural treasures usually off-limits to the public are open and free to visit.

🍷 Wine & the City

A three-week celebration (www.wineandthecity.it) of regional *vino* in Naples, with free wine degustations, *aperitivo* sessions and cultural events in venues as diverse as museums and castles, art galleries, boutiques and restaurants.

⊙ La Biennale di Venezia

Held from mid-May to late November, Europe's premier arts showcase (www. labiennale.org) is actually held annually, though the spotlight alternates between art (odd-numbered years) and architecture

(even-numbered years). Running alongside the two main events are annual showcases of dance, theatre, cinema and music.

☆ Piano City

In mid-May, Milan dedicates a long weekend to extraordinary piano concerts (www.pianocitymilano.it) held in the city's museums, courtyards, stations, parks and markets. Classical music aside, ears are also treated to jazz, rock and world music tunes. Book tickets early.

June

The summer season kicks off in June. The temperature cranks up quickly, *lidi* (beaches) start to open in earnest and some of the big summer festivals commence. Republic Day, on 2 June, is a national holiday.

☆ Napoli Teatro Festival Italia

Naples celebrates all things performative with one month of theatre, dance and literary events. Using both conventional and unconventional venues, the program (www.napoliteat rofestival.it) ranges from classic works to specially commissioned pieces from both local and international talent. Held from early June to early July.

🎆 Estate Romana

From June to October, Rome puts on a summer calendar of events that turn the city into an outdoor stage. Dubbed Estate Romana (www.estateromana. comune.roma.it), the program encompasses music, dance, literature and film, with events staged in some of Rome's most evocative venues.

✨ Giostra del Saracino

A grandiose affair deep-rooted in neighbourhood rivalry, this medieval jousting tournament (www.giostradelsaracinoarezzo.it) sees the four *quartieri* (quarters) of Arezzo put forward a team of knights to battle on one of Tuscany's most beautiful and unusual city squares, Piazza Grande; third Saturday in June and first Sunday in September.

☆ Spoleto Festival

Held in the Umbrian hill town of Spoleto from late June to mid-July, the Spoleto Festival (www.festivaldispoleto.it) is a world-renowned arts event, serving up 17 days of international theatre, opera, dance, music and art.

July

School is out and Italians everywhere are heading away from the cities and to mountains or beaches for their summer holidays. Prices and temperatures rise. While the beach is in full swing, many cities host summer art festivals.

✨ Il Palio di Siena

Daredevils in tights thrill the crowds with this chaotic bareback horse race around the Siena's world-famous medieval piazza. Preceding the race is a dashing medieval-costume parade. Held on 2 July and 16 August.

✨ Sagra della Madonna della Bruna

A week-long celebration (www.festadellabruna.it) of Matera's patron saint that culminates on 2 July with a colourful procession that sees the Madonna della Bruna escorted around town in a papier-mâché-adorned chariot. The chariot is ultimately torn to pieces by the crowd, who take home the scraps as souvenirs.

✨ Festa di Sant'Anna

The Campanian island of Ischia celebrates the feast day of Sant'Anna to spectacular effect on 26 July. Local municipalities build competing floats to sail in a flotilla, with spectacular fireworks and a symbolic 'burning' of Ischia Ponte's medieval Castello Aragonese.

☆ Giffoni Film Festival

Europe's biggest children's film festival (www.giffonifilmfestival.it) livens up the town of Giffoni Valle Piana, east of Salerno, Campania. The nine-day event includes screenings, workshops, seminars and big-name guests such as Oscar-winning director Gabriele Salvatores and award-winning actor Bryan Cranston.

August

August in Italy is hot, expensive and crowded. Everyone is on holiday, and while not everything is shut, many businesses and restaurants do close for part of the month.

✨ Ferragosto

After Christmas and Easter, Ferragosto, on 15 August, is Italy's biggest holiday. It marks the Feast of the Assumption, but even before Christianity the Romans honoured their gods on Feriae Augusti. Naples celebrates with particular fervour.

☆ Venice International Film Festival

The Venice International Film Festival (www.labiennale.org) is one of the world's most prestigious silver-screen events. Held at the Lido from late August to early September, it draws the international glitterati with its red-carpet premieres and paparazzi glamour.

September

This is a glorious month to travel in Italy. Summer warmth lingers in much of the country and the start of the harvest season sees lots of local *sagre* (food festivals) spring up. September is also the start of the grape harvest.

✨ Regata Storica

In early September, gondoliers in period dress work those biceps in Venice's Historic Regatta (www.regatastoricavenezia.it). Period boats are followed by gondola and other boat races along the Grand Canal.

🍷 Festival delle Sagre

On the second Saturday and Sunday in September

more than 40 communes in the Piedmontese province of Asti put their wines and local gastronomic products on display at this appetite-piquing, waist-expanding culinary fest (www.festival dellesagre.it).

Expo del Chianti Classico

There is no finer opportunity to taste Tuscany's Chianti Classico than at Greve in Chianti's annual Chianti Classico Expo (www.expochianticlassico.com), on the second weekend in September. All of the major producers are represented, with supporting events including musical performances.

Couscous Fest

The Sicilian town of St Vito celebrates multiculturalism and its famous fish couscous at this 10-day event (www.couscousfest.it) in mid to late September. Highlights include an international couscous cook-off, tastings and live world-music gigs.

Venice Glass Week

This recently established festival (www.thevenice glassweek.com) in Venice showcases the work of Murano's finest glass-blowers. The week-long event also offers visitors a peek into what were previously off-limits furnaces.

October

October is a fabulous time to visit the south, when the days still radiate with late-summer warmth and the *lidi* (beaches) are

emptying. Further north the temperature starts to drop and festival season comes to an end.

RomaEuropa

From late September to late November or early December, top international artists take to the stage for Rome's premier festival (www.romaeuropa.net) of theatre, opera and dance. Performances are held at numerous venues across the city.

Salone Internazionale del Gusto

Hosted by the home-grown Slow Food Movement, this biennial food expo (www.salonedelgusto.it) takes place in Turin in even-numbered years. Held over five days, mouth-watering events include workshops, presentations and tastings of food, wine and beer from Italy and beyond.

Eurochocolate

Over a million chocoholics pour into Perugia in mid-October for the city's 10-day celebration of the cocoa bean. The festival (www.eurochocolate.com) includes exhibitions and chocolate sculptures, cooking classes and no shortage of free samples.

November

Winter creeps down the peninsula in November, but there's still plenty going on. For gastronomes, this is truffle season. It's also the time for the chestnut harvest, mushroom picking and All Saints' Day.

Ognissanti

Celebrated all over Italy as a national holiday, All Saints' Day on 1 November commemorates the Saint Martyrs, while All Souls' Day, on 2 November, is set aside to honour the deceased.

Opera Season

Italy is home to four of the world's great opera houses: La Scala in Milan, La Fenice in Venice, Teatro San Carlo in Naples and Teatro Massimo in Palermo. The season traditionally runs from mid-October to March, although La Scala opens later on St Ambrose Day (7 December).

Truffle Season

From the Piedmontese towns of Alba (www.fiera deltartufo.org) and Asti, to Tuscany's San Miniato and Le Marche's Acqualagna, November is prime truffle time, with local truffle fairs, events and music.

December

The days of alfresco living are firmly at an end. December is cold and Alpine resorts start to open for the early ski season, although looming Christmas festivities keep life warm and bright.

Natale

The weeks preceding Christmas are studded with religious events. Many churches set up nativity scenes known as *presepi*. Naples is especially famous for these. On Christmas Eve the Pope serves midnight mass in St Peter's Square.

Itineraries

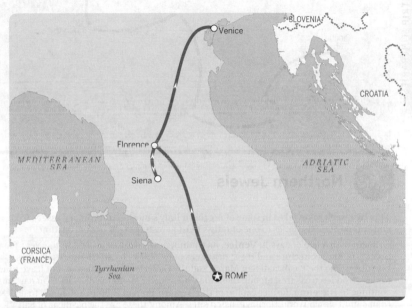

9 DAYS Italian Highlights

A perfect introduction to Italy, this easy tour ticks off some of the country's most seductive sights, including Roman ruins, Renaissance masterpieces and the world's most beautiful lagoon city.

Start with three days in mighty **Rome**, punctuating blockbuster sights like the Colosseum, Palatino (Palatine Hill) and Sistine Chapel with market grazing in the Campo de' Fiori, boutique-hopping in Monti and late-night revelry in Trastevere.

On day four, head to Renaissance **Florence**. Drop in on Michelangelo's *David* at the Galleria dell'Accademia and pick your favourite Botticelli at the Galleria degli Uffizi. For a change of pace, escape to the Tuscan countryside on day six for a day trip to Gothic **Siena**, home of the biannual Palio horse race.

The following day, continue north for three unforgettable days in **Venice**. Check off musts like the mosaic-encrusted Basilica di San Marco, art-slung Gallerie dell'Accademia and secret passageways of the Palazzo Ducale, then live like a true Venetian, scouring seafood-laden stalls at the Rialto Market, noshing on the city's famous *cicheti* (Venetian tapas) and toasting with a Veneto *prosecco* (sparkling wine).

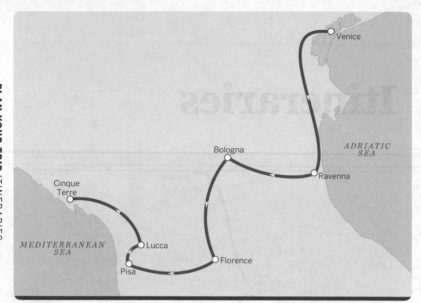

Northern Jewels

This two-week route takes in some of northern Italy's most extraordinary assets, from cultural-powerhouse cities to one of Italy's most arresting stretches of coastline.

Begin with a trio of days in **Venice**, its trading-port pedigree echoed in the Near East accents of its architecture and the synagogues of its 500-year-old Ghetto. Don't miss big-hitters like the Basilica di San Marco and the Gallerie dell'Accademia, but leave time for less-trodden treasures, among them the Chiesa della Madonna dell'Orto. On day four, continue to **Ravenna**, former capital of the Western Roman Empire and home to no less than eight Unesco World Heritage–listed sites. Among these are the basilicas of San Vitale and Sant'Apollinare Nuovo, both adorned with extraordinary Byzantine mosaics.

Spend days six and seven in erudite **Bologna**, home to the world's fifth-largest church and its oldest university. The university district is the location of the Pinacoteca Nazionale, its powerhouse art collection including works by regional master Parmigianino. One of Bologna's fortes is gastronomy, a fact not lost on its Quadrilatero district, an area smothered with produce stalls, fragrant delis, restaurants and an appetite-piquing food hall.

Burn off those excess calories with three days of pavement pounding in **Florence**. It's here that you'll find many of Western art's most revered works, including Michelangelo's chiselled *David* and Botticelli's ethereal paintings *Primavera* and *La nascita di Venere*. The city's Renaissance credentials extend to its architecture, which includes Filippo Brunelleschi's show-stopping Duomo dome. Even the city's gardens are manicured masterpieces, exemplified by the supremely elegant Giardino di Boboli.

On day 11, pit-stop in **Pisa** to eye-up the architectural ensemble that makes up the Piazza dei Miracoli, then continue to nearby Renaissance show pony **Lucca**. Spend the following day exploring Lucca's elegant streets, picnicking on its centuries-old ramparts and meditating on Tintoretto's soul-stirring *Last Supper* in the Cattedrale di San Martino. Human ingenuity and natural beauty merge on Liguria's World Heritage–listed **Cinque Terre**, where five colourful villages seemingly defy their precarious natural setting. This is your final stop, with two days to explore its medieval village streets, remarkable terraced gardens, *muretti* (dry stone walls) and breathtaking coastal walks.

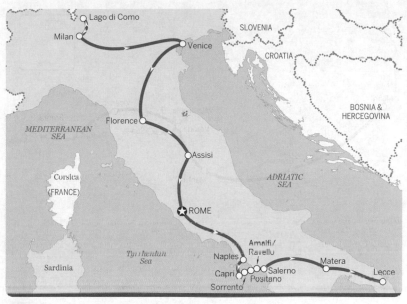

The Grand Tour

From elegant northern cities and lakes to ancient southern coasts and dwellings, this grand tour encapsulates Italy's inimitable natural and cultural diversity.

Start in style with two days in **Milan**. Shop among coveted boutiques, dine at hot-spot restaurants and demand an encore at the gilded La Scala. Come day three, continue to **Lago di Como** (Lake Como), basing yourself in Como or Bellagio and spending two romantic days among its sublime waterside villas and villages. If you haven't been wooed by Hollywood royalty, continue to **Venice** on day five, where the following trio of days burst with Titians and Tintorettos, artisan studios and convivial *bacari* (bars). On day eight, shoot southwest to **Florence**, allowing three days to tackle its heavyweight art collections and sink your teeth into its *bistecca alla fiorentina* (T-bone steak). Glutton-ous acts are forgiven on day 11 as you travel to the pilgrimage city of **Assisi**, its Gothic basilica lavished with Giotto frescoes. Head southwest to **Rome** on day 13 and spend three full days exploring its two-millennia-worth of temples, churches, piazzas and artis-tic marvels.

On day 17, slip south to **Naples** and its explosion of baroque architecture and subter-ranean ruins. Day-trip it to the ruins of Pompeii on day 19, then sail to **Capri** on day 20 for three seductive days of boating, hikes and piazza-side posing. If it's high season, catch a ferry directly to laid-back **Sorrento** on day 23, spending a night in town before hitting the hairpin turns of the glorious Amalfi Coast. Allow two days in chi-chi **Posi-tano**, where you can hike the heavenly Sentiero degli Dei (Walk of the Gods). Spend day 26 in historic **Amalfi** before continuing to sky-high **Ravello**, long-time haunt of composers and Hollywood stars. Stay the night to soak up its understated elegance, and spend the following morning soaking up its uber-romantic gardens. After an evening of bar-hopping in upbeat **Salerno**, shoot inland to **Matera** on day 28 to experience its World Heritage–listed *sassi* (former cave dwellings) and dramatic Matera Gravina gorge. Come day 30, continue through to architecturally astounding **Lecce**, the 'Florence of the South' and your final cross-country stop.

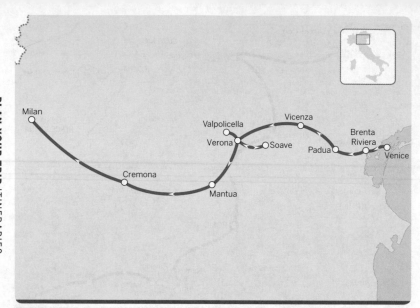

2 WEEKS Venice to Milan

Aristocratic villas, renegade frescoes, star-struck lovers and cult-status wines; this easy two-week journey serves up a feast of northern assets.

Begin with a couple of days in **Venice**, sampling the city's enviable art, architecture and seafood. In the 16th century the Venetian summer began early in June, when every household loaded onto barges for a summer sojourn along the nearby **Brenta Riviera**. You too can make like a Venetian on a boat trip along the Riviera, marvelling at the Tiepolo frescoes of Villa Pisani Nazionale and snooping around Palladio's Villa Foscari. Boat trips along the Brenta Riviera end in **Padua** where you can overnight overlooking the Basilica di Sant'Antonio. With advance booking, you can see Padua's crowning glory, Giotto's frescoed Capella degli Scrovegni.

On day six hop on the train to **Vicenza**. Spend the afternoon watching sunlight ripple across the soaring facades of Palladio's *palazzi* (mansions) and illuminate the Villa Valmarana 'ai Nani', covered floor-to-ceiling with frescoes by Giambattista and Giandomenico Tiepolo, then head on to **Verona** for three or four days. Here you can view Mantegnas at Basilica di San Zeno Maggiore, ponder modern art at the Galleria d'Arte Moderna Achille Forti, and find tranquillity in the 16th-century oasis of Giardino Giusti. It's also here that you can listen to opera in the Roman Arena and wander balconied backstreets where Romeo wooed Juliet.

From Verona, consider a day trip northwest to **Valpolicella** to sip highly prized Amarone (red wine), or back east to **Soave** for a sampling of its namesake DOC white wine.

On day 11 dip southwest to **Mantua** for an impressive display of dynastic power and patronage at the Gonzagas' fortified family pad, the Palazzo Ducale. Finish up with a two-day stop in **Cremona**, where you can chat with artisans in one of the 100 violin-making shops around Piazza del Comune before hearing the instruments in action at the Teatro Amilcare Ponchielli. Done, shoot northwest to wrap up your tour in Italy's financial and fashion epicentre, **Milan**. On-trend shopping and dining aside, the city is home to a string of artistic treasures, among them Leonardo da Vinci's iconic *The Last Supper*.

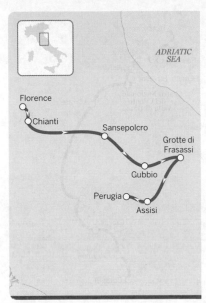

Central Italian Escape

10 DAYS

Revered vineyards, medieval hilltop towns and Unesco-lauded artwork: this trip takes in evocative landscapes, from well-trodden Tuscany to lesser-known Umbria and Le Marche.

Begin with two cultured days in **Florence**, then enjoy a pair of decadent days in **Chianti**, toasting to the area's *vino* and indulging in lazy lunches and countryside cycling. On day five, head east, pit-stopping in tiny **Sansepolcro** to meditate on Pietro della Francesca's trio of masterpieces and calling it a night in the Umbrian hilltop town of **Gubbio**. Spend the following day exploring the town's Gothic streets, then drive into Le Marche on day seven for a guided tour of the incredible **Grotte di Frasassi** cave system. The same day, head back into Umbria to **Assisi**, one of Italy's most beautiful medieval towns. Stay two nights, taking in the frescoes of the Basilica di San Francesco and finding peace on the hiking trails flanking Monte Subasio. Come day nine, make your way to the lively university city of **Perugia**, where your adventure ends with brooding Gothic architecture and world-famous Bacio chocolates.

Northeastern Interlude

2 WEEKS

Laced with cross-cultural influences, hot-list wines, world-famous charcuterie and stunning Alpine landscapes, this lesser-known corner of the country is ripe for discovery.

After three days in **Venice**, head east to Trieste via the Roman ruins of **Aquileia** and the medieval heart of **Grado**. Take two days in **Trieste** for its gilded cafes, literary heritage and central European air, then catch a ferry to **Muggia**, the only Italian settlement on the Istrian peninsula. On day seven, head inland for celebrated whites in the **Collio** wine region. Spend two days in **Udine**, dropping in on the Museum of Modern and Contemporary Art and sidestepping to **Cividale dei Friuli**, home to Europe's only surviving example of Lombard architecture and artwork. On day 10, pit-stop in **San Daniele del Friuli** for Italy's best prosciutto before hitting breathtaking mountain scenery on your way to ski town **Cortina d'Ampezzo**. Allow two days to hit the slopes, on winter skis or in summer hiking boots. Either way, head south on day 14, stopping for afternoon bubbles in the *prosecco* heartland of **Conegliano** before wrapping things up in Venice.

A Lakes Tour

Southern Coastal Route

Tickling the snowcapped Alps, Italy's glacial lakes have lured romantics for centuries, from European royalty to American silver-screen pin-ups. Live the dream, if only for a week.

A short drive northwest of Malpensa airport, **Milan**, and you're on the edge of Lago Maggiore. Start with three nights in belle époque **Stresa** and visit the lavish **Borromean Islands**: Isola Madre for its romantic gardens and wisteria-clad Staircase of the Dead; and Isola Bella for its priceless art collection, vast ballrooms and shell-encrusted grotto. Take the funicular up to **Monte Mottarone** and day-trip to **Lago d'Orta** and bijou **Isola San Giulio**. On day four head north from Stresa to **Verbania**, picnicking at Villa Taranto before gliding east across the lake to **Laveno** and straight on to celebrity haunt **Como**. Amble the flower-laden lakeside to view art exhibits at Villa Olmo before finding a sun lounge at the Lido di Villa Olmo. You could spend days in Como, hiring out boats or hiking the mountainous Triangolo Lariano. If you're ambitious you can walk to chic **Bellagio**. Otherwise, take the lake road and lunch on a perch in **Lezzeno** before one last romantic night lakeside.

Graeco-Roman ruins, a Bourbon palace and some of Italy's most beautiful coastline: crank up the romance on this two-week journey through the sun-baked south.

Rev things up with three days in exhilarating **Naples**, day-tripping it to **Caserta** to explore Italy's largest royal palace. On day four, head south to the Amalfi Coast, allowing for two nights in **Positano**, followed by a day in **Amalfi** and **Ravello** on your way to **Salerno**. Come day seven, continue to the World Heritage–listed temples of **Paestum**, then through the **Parco Nazionale del Cilento e Vallo di Diano** to cognoscenti coastal jewel **Maratea**. Spend two nights in town, followed by lunch in **Tropea** (one of Calabria's most beautiful coast towns) on your way to **Villa San Giovanni**. Catch the ferry across to Sicily and treat yourself to three nights in fashionable **Taormina**, Sicily's former Byzantine capital and home to the world's most spectacularly located Greek amphitheatre. Sun-kissed and relaxed, continue to **Catania** on day 13, taking two days to soak up the city's ancient sites, extraordinary baroque architecture and vibrant market life.

Spaghetti alle vongole (spaghetti with clams)

Plan Your Trip
Eat & Drink Like a Local

Gastronomy is one of Italy's raisons d'être. In fact, the country feels like one gargantuan kitchen, jam-packed with superlative produce, irresistible bites and finely tuned culinary know-how. Locals are fiercely proud of their regions' specialities, and devouring them is an essential part of any Italian sojourn.

The Year in Food

While *sagre* (local food festivals) go into overdrive in autumn, there's never a bad time to raise your fork in Italy.

Spring (March–May)

Asparagus, artichokes and Easter specialities, plus a handful of festivals like Turin's Cioccolatò and Ascoli Piceno's Fritto Misto all'Italiana.

Summer (June–August)

Eggplants, peppers and berries. Tuck into tuna at Carloforte's Girotonno tuna catch in June and beat the heat with gelato and Sicilian *granita* (crushed ice with fruit, nuts or coffee).

Autumn (September–November)

Food festivals, chestnuts, mushrooms and game. Truffle hunters head to Piedmont, Tuscany and Umbria, while wine connoisseurs hit Elba's wine harvest and Merano's wine festival.

Winter (December–February)

Christmas and Carnevale treats. Fishers serve up sea urchins and mussels on Sardinia's Poetto beach, while Umbria celebrates black truffles with the Mostra Mercato del Tartufo Nero.

Food Experiences

So much produce, so many specialities, so little time! Fine-tune your culinary radar with the following edible musts.

Meals of a Lifetime

Osteria Francescana, Modena Emilia-Romagna's produce gets seriously experimental at the world's second-best restaurant, as voted in the 2017 San Pellegrino World's Best 50 Restaurants. (p449)

President, Pompeii One of Italy's best-priced Michelin-starred restaurants, serving whimsical re-interpretations of Campanian cuisine. (p697)

Piazza Duomo, Alba Langhe produce and Japanese technique fuse to spectacular effect at Enrico Crippa's Michelin-starred blockbuster, rated number 15 in the world by San Pellegrino. (p220)

Essenziale, Florence Rising culinary star Simone Cipriani is making waves with extraordinary modern takes on classic Tuscan flavours. (p507)

Dal Pescatore, Mantua The first female Italian chef to hold three Michelin stars, Nadia Santini is a self-taught culinary virtuoso. (p298)

Il Frantoio, Puglia Long, legendary Sunday lunches at an olive-grove-fringed *masseria* (working farm) in Italy's deep south. (p740)

Cheap Treats

Pizza al taglio 'Pizza by the slice' is the perfect piazza-side nibble.

Arancini Deep-fried rice balls stuffed with *ragù* (meat sauce), tomato and vegetables.

Porchetta rolls Warm sliced pork (roasted whole with fennel, garlic and pepper) in a crispy roll.

Pane e panelle Palermo chickpea fritters on a sesame roll.

Gelato The best Italian gelato uses seasonal ingredients and natural colours.

Dare to Try

Pajata A creamy Roman pasta dish made with calves' entrails containing the mothers' congealed milk.

Missoltini Como's sun-dried fish cured in salt and bay leaves.

Lampredotto Cow's stomach boiled, sliced, seasoned and bunged between bread in Florence.

Pani ca meusa A Palermo sandwich of beef spleen and lungs dipped in boiling lard.

Zurrette Sardinian black pudding made of sheep's blood, cooked in a sheep's stomach with herbs and fennel.

Local Specialities

The Italian term for 'pride of place' is *campanilismo,* but a more accurate word would be *formaggismo:* loyalty to the local cheese. Clashes among medieval city-states involving castle sieges and boiling oil have been replaced by competition in producing speciality foods and wines.

Emilia-Romagna

Emilia-Romagna claims some of Italy's most famous exports. Bologna piques appetites with *mortadella* (pork cold cut), *stinco di maiale al forno con porcini* (roasted pork shanks with porcini mushrooms) and *tagliatelle al ragù* (pasta with white wine, tomato, oregano, beef and pork belly). It's also famous for soothing *tortellini in brodo* (pasta stuffed with ground meats in a thin meat broth). While Parma is world-famous for *parmigiano reggiano* cheese (Parmesan) and *prosciutto di Parma* (cured ham), lesser-known claims include *pesto di cavallo* (raw minced horse meat with herbs and Parmesan).

Lombardy

Lombardy is all about *burro* (butter), risotto and gorgonzola cheese. Milan serves up *risotto alla milanese* (saffron and bone-marrow risotto), *panettone* (a yeast-risen sweet bread), uberfashionable restaurants and food emporium Peck. Renaissance Mantua remains addicted to *tortellini di zucca* (pumpkin-stuffed pasta), wild fowl and its *mostarda mantovana* (apple relish). The Valtenesi area is home to some of Italy's finest emerging olive oils, including Comincioli's award-winning Numero Uno.

Naples & Campania

Procida lemons get cheeky in *limoncello* (lemon liqueur), while the region's vines create intense red Taurasi and the dry white Fiano di Avellino. Naples is home to superlative street food, including *pizza fritta* (fried pizza dough stuffed with salami, dried lard cubes, smoked *provola* cheese, ricotta and tomato). The town of Gragnano produces prized pasta, perfect for *spaghetti alle vongole* (spaghetti with clam sauce). Leave room for a *sfogliatella* (sweetened ricotta pastry) and *babà* (rum-soaked sponge cake). Both Caserta and the Cilento produce prime *mozzarella di bufala* (buffalo mozzarella).

Piedmont

The birthplace of the Slow Food Movement. Guzzle Lavazza and Caffè Vergnano coffee in Turin, a city also famed for vermouth, nougat and its buzzing *aperitivo*

Parmesan and Grana Padano cheeses

scene (pre-dinner drinks). Leave room for *gianduja* (a chocolate hazelnut spread) and a *bicerin* (a chocolate, coffee and cream libation). Alba treats taste buds to white truffles, hazelnuts, and pedigreed Barolo and Barbaresco reds, while Cherasco is celebrated for its *lumache* (snails).

Puglia

Head southeast for peppery olive oil and honest *cucina povera* (peasant cooking). Breadcrumbs lace everything from *strascinati con la mollica* (pasta with breadcrumbs and anchovies) to *tiella di verdure* (baked vegetable casserole), while snacks include *puccia* (bread with olives) and ring-shaped *taralli* (pretzel-like biscuits). In Salento, linger over lunch at a *masseria* and propose a toast with hearty reds like Salice Salentino and Primitivo di Manduria.

Rome & Lazio

Carb-up with *spaghetti alla carbonara*, *bucatini all'amatriciana* (with bacon, tomato, chilli and *pecorino* cheese) and

Fried polenta

spaghetti cacio e pepe (with *pecorino* cheese and black pepper). Head to Rome's Testaccio neighbourhood for nose-to-tail staples like *trippa alla romana* (tripe cooked with potatoes, tomato, mint and *pecorino* cheese), and to the Ghetto for kosher deep-fried *carciofi* (artichokes). Southeast of the city in Frascati, tour the vineyards and swill the area's eponymous, delicate white *vino*.

Sicily

Channel ancient Arab influences with fish couscous and spectacular sweets like *cannoli* (crisp pastry shells filled with sweet ricotta). In Palermo, snack on *sfincione* (spongy, oily pizza topped with onions and *caciocavallo* cheese), and feast on *pasta con le sarde* (pasta with sardines, pine nuts, raisins and wild fennel) and *involtini di pesce spada* (thinly sliced swordfish fillets rolled up and filled with breadcrumbs, capers, tomatoes and olives). In Catania, tackle *pasta alla norma* (pasta with basil, eggplant, ricotta and tomato). Further south, taste-test Modica's spiced chocolate.

Tuscany

In Florence, drool over *bistecca alla fiorentina* (T-bone steak), made with Chianina beef from the Val di Chiana valley. The valley is also famous for *ravaggiolo* (sheep's-milk cheese wrapped in fern fronds). Head to Castelnuovo di Garfagnana for autumnal porcini and chestnuts, and to San Miniato for white truffles (from October to December). These prized *fungi* are celebrated at San Miniato's white-truffle fair (Mostra Mercato Nazionale del Tartufo Bianco di San Miniato), held in November. Savour *cinta senese* (indigenous Tuscan pig), *pecorino* (sheep's-milk cheese) and prized extra-virgin olive oils in Montalcino, a place also known for its Brunello and Rosso di Montalcino reds. Montepulciano is the home of Vino Nobile red, its equally quaffable second-string Rosso di Montepulciano, and Terre di Siena extra-virgin olive oil. Just leave time for Chianti's world-famous vineyards.

Wine, Montalcino (p540)

Umbria

Uncork a bottle of Sagrantino di Montefalco red and grate a black truffle from Norcia over fresh *tagliatelle* (ribbon pasta) or *strozzapreti* (an elongated pasta literally meaning 'priest-strangler'). Black truffles aside, Norcia is Italy's capital of pork. Another popular meat is wild boar. In Lago Trasimeno, freshwater fish flavours dishes like *regina alla porchetta* (roasted carp stuffed with garlic, fennel and herbs) and *tegemacchio* (fish stew made with garlic, onions, tomatoes and a medley of underwater critters). Meanwhile, on the Strada dei Vini del Cantico wine trail, the town of Torgiano celebrates wine and olives with two dedicated museums.

Venice & the Veneto

It's not all bubbly *prosecco* (local sparkling wine) and fiery grappa; Italy's northeast peddles *risotto alle seppie* (cuttlefish-ink risotto) and *polenta con le quaglie* (polenta with quails), as well as the odd foreign spice – think *sarde in saor* (grilled sardines in a sweet-and-sour sauce). Sail into Venice for *cicheti* (Venetian bar snacks) at local *bacari* (bars) and to scour Rialto Market produce such as lagoon seafood (look for tags reading *nostrano,* meaning 'ours'). The prime wine region of Valpolicella is celebrated for Amarone, Valpolicella Superiore, Ripasso, Recioto, and inspired renegade *Indicazione geografica tipica* (IGT) red blends from winemakers like Giuseppe Quintarelli and Zýmē.

Sardinia

The waters off Sardinia provide *ricci di mare* (sea urchins) and *bottarga* (salted, pressed and dried mullet roe), while its interior delivers *porchetta* (roast suckling pig, often served on a bed of myrtle leaves). Pasta classics here include *culurgiones* (pasta pockets stuffed with potato and *casu de fitta* cheese), *fregola* (granular pasta similar to couscous) and *malloreddus* (a gnocchi-pasta hybrid), while its cheeses include top-notch *pecorino.* A lesser-known *formaggio* (cheese) is *casu marzu* (rotten maggoty cheese), though this can be hard to find unless you know a farmer with a stash in the Nuoro region.

CAFFÈ ITALIAN-STYLE

➡ Caffè latte and cappuccino are considered morning drinks, with espresso and macchiato the preferred post-lunch options.

➡ Baristas may offer a glass of water, either *liscia* (still) or *frizzante* (sparkling), with your espresso. Many (especially southern Italians) drink it before their coffee to cleanse the palate.

➡ Take the edge off the day with a *caffè corretto*, a shot of espresso spiked with liqueur (usually grappa).

➡ Coffee with dessert is fine, but ordering one with your main meal is a travesty.

How to Eat & Drink

Now that your appetite is piqued, it's time for the technicalities of eating *all'italiana*.

When to Eat

Colazione (Breakfast) Often little more than an espresso and a *cornetto* (Italian croissant) or brioche.

Pranzo (Lunch) Traditionally the main meal of the day. Standard restaurant times are noon to 3pm, though most locals don't lunch before 1pm.

Aperitivo Post-work drinks usually take place between 5pm and 8pm, when the price of your drink includes a buffet of tasty morsels.

Cena (Dinner) Traditionally lighter than lunch, though still a main meal. Standard restaurant times are 7.30pm to around 11pm, with southern Italians generally eating later than their northern cousins.

Where to Eat

Ristorante Formal service and refined dishes.

Trattoria Cheaper than a restaurant, with more-relaxed service and regional classics.

Osteria Historically a tavern focused on wine; the modern version is often an intimate trattoria or wine bar offering a handful of dishes.

Enoteca A wine bar often serving snacks to accompany your tipple.

Agriturismo A working farmhouse offering food made with farm-grown produce.

Pizzeria Cheap grub, beer and a convivial vibe. The best pizzerias are often crowded: be patient.

Tavola calda Cafeteria-style spots serving cheap premade food such as pasta and roast meats.

Friggitoria A simple joint selling freshly fried local street food and snacks to go.

Menu Decoder

Antipasto A hot or cold appetiser; for a tasting plate of different appetisers, request an *antipasto misto* (mixed antipasto).

Contorno Side dish; usually *verdura* (vegetable).

Dolce Dessert; including *torta* (cake).

Frutta Fruit; usually the epilogue to a meal.

Menù alla carta Choose whatever you like from the menu.

Menù di degustazione Degustation menu; usually consisting of six to eight 'tasting size' courses.

Menù turistico The 'tourist menu' usually signals mediocre fare – steer clear!

Nostra produzione Made in-house.

Piatto del giorno Dish of the day.

Primo First course; usually a substantial pasta, rice or *zuppa* (soup) dish.

Secondo Second course; often meat or fish.

Surgelato Frozen; usually used to denote fish or seafood not freshly caught.

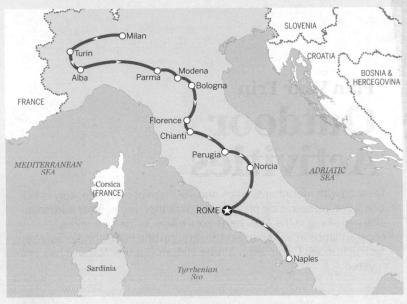

Italian Food Odyssey

3 WEEKS

Kick off your cross-country feast with two days in **Milan** (p242), famed for its hearty *risotto alla milanese* (saffron and marrow-bone risotto), *panettone* (a yeast-risen sweet bread) and gourmet deli Peck. Hit hot-spot restaurants and tuck into Lombard classics at Trattoria Milanese. Spend two days in **Turin** (p202), shopping at Eataly, sipping at 18th-century Al Bicerin and indulging in high-end *aperitivi* (pre-dinner drinks) at slinky Bar Cavour. Annual events in town include Slow Food expo Salone del Gusto (October) and chocolate festival Cioccolatò (November).

Next, base yourself for three days in **Alba** (p217), famed for its white truffles. Include day trips to the wine-growing towns of Barolo and Barbaresco, then continue east to **Parma** (p452) for *prosciutto di Parma* (cured ham) and *parmigiano reggiano* at Ristorante Cocchi, and dine at world-famous Osteria Francescana (book months ahead). Then dedicate two days to food obsessed **Bologna** (p431); deli-hop in the Quadrilatero district and take a pasta-making course at La Vecchia Scuola Bolognese.

Spend days 12 and 13 in appetite-piquing **Florence** (p478), hunting down prized olive oils at Mercato Centrale, tucking into succulent *bistecca alla fiorentina* (T-bone steak) at Trattoria Mario and noshing on standout modern Tuscan at Essenziale. Full, slow down the pace with two days of vineyard-hopping and cycling in Tuscany's **Chianti** (p525) wine region. Come day 16, shoot east to **Perugia** (p577) to tour (or take a chocolate-making course) at Casa del Cioccolato Perugina before pushing on to **Norcia** (p608) the following day, a town renowned for its black truffles and *norcinerie* (butcher shops).

Days 18 and 19 see you in **Rome** (p63). Whet the appetite at alfesco Mercato di Campo de' Fiori, sample Jewish-Roman cuisine in the Ghetto and dine nose-to-tail in the Testaccio district. Shoot south for two gut-rumbling days in **Naples** (p653), getting acquainted with local seafood and vegetables at the raucous Mercato di Porta Nolana, chowing down Italy's best pizza at Pizzeria Starita, and savouring its world-famous buffalo mozzarella. Conclude with one final feast at Eccellenze Campane, a sprawling showcase for Campanian gastronomy before a parting *sfogliatella* (sweet, ricotta-filled pastry) at stalwart bakery Pintauro.

Plan Your Trip

Outdoor Activities

Blessed with mountains, lakes and 7600km of coastline, Italy is like one giant, pulse-racing playground. Whether you're after adrenalin-charged skiing in the Alps, hard-core hiking in the Dolomites, coastal climbs in Sardinia, white-water rafting in Calabria or low-key cycling through Piedmont – Madre Natura (Mother Nature) has you covered.

Best Activities

Best Outdoor Experiences

Hiking The Dolomites, Piedmont's Gran Paradiso, Trentino's Stelvio and Calabria's Pollino parks, Umbria's Piano Grande and the coastal tracks of the Cinque Terre, the Amalfi Coast, Sicily and Sardinia.

Cycling The Po Delta and Bolzano offer good networks, as do the wine regions of Franciacorta, Barolo, Barbaresco and Chianti. Urban options include Rome's Via Appia Antica, Ferrara, Lucca, Bologna and Lecce.

Skiing Cross-border into Slovenia at Sella Nevea; skiing and snowboarding in Courmayeur; downhill and cross-country in Cortina d'Ampezzo, the Valle d'Aosta and Sella Ronda.

Diving Best marine parks are off the Cinque Terre, the Gargano Promontory, Elba, the Sorrento Peninsula, the Aeolian Islands, Ustica and Sardinia.

Best Times to Go

April to June Walk among wildflowers.

July & September Water sports and warm-water diving without the August crowds.

December, February & March Best ski months for atmosphere, snow and value respectively.

On Land

From the skyscraping Alps to the soft undulations of the Tuscan hills, Italy's diverse geography provides a plethora of land-locked diversions. The Alps are alive with the sound of skiing, snowboarding and mountain biking, while the vine-laced landscapes of Tuscany and Piedmont put the romance into cycling, with gentle inclines and mile after glorious mile of country routes. Further south, the precipitous peaks of the Amalfi Coast harbour an ancient network of shepherds' paths, making for heavenly hikes.

Hiking & Walking

Italy is laced with thousands of kilometres of *sentieri* (marked trails). Most local and regional tourist office websites have information about walking in their area. Italian Parks (www.parks.it) lists walking trails through each of the country's 25 national parks, and provides updates on Italy's marine parks and other protected areas. Another useful website is that of Italy's major walking club, the Club Alpino Italiano (www.cai.it) – follow the *rifugi* (mountain huts) link for information about trail routes and accommodation (members of organisations such as the New Zealand Alpine Club, Fédération Française des Clubs

Alpins et de Montagne and Deutscher Alpenverein can enjoy discounted rates for accommodation and meals).

Bear in mind that most Italians take their summer holidays in August, so this is when the trails are at their most crowded and the *rifugi* are often jam-packed – you'll need to book weeks, if not months, in advance. On lower terrain, August's intense heat can be oppressive. Sidestep this month if you can. Also note that backcountry or wild camping is not permitted in Italy; if you want to pitch a tent, you'll have to do so at a private campsite.

For detailed information on hiking routes in specific regions, check out the reliable Cicerone (www.cicerone.co.uk) series of walking guides.

The Alps & Dolomites

Italy's wild, lushly wooded Alps stretch from France in the west, via the southern borders of Austria and Switzerland, to Slovenia in the east. For hikers, they offer heady mountain vistas, swooping forested valleys and views over large glacial lakes such as Garda, Como and Maggiore.

In the far west, dropping into Piedmont and Liguria, are the Graian, Maritime and Ligurian Alps, which take in the full sweep of the Valle d'Aosta (p230), the vast Gran Paradiso (p237) park and the lesser-known Parco Naturale delle Alpi Marittime, before making a sharp and dramatic descent to the Cinque Terre (p184) and Portofino park on the Ligurian coastline.

To the east in Friuli Venezia Giulia, you'll find the Giulie and Carnic Alps, where you can hike in pursuit of lynx, marmots and eagles amid supercute Tyrolean villages. Heading west, the white ridges pass through Trento's Parco Nazionale dello Stelvio (p321), northern Italy's (and the Alps') largest national park, and spill into Lombardy. Lombardy's great lakes – encompassing Garda, Como, Iseo, Maggiore and Orta – are prime hiking territory, mixing mountain and lake vistas. Particularly scenic is the crumpled ridge of mountains in Como's Triangolo Lariano and Garda's Monte Baldo.

Soaring across the borders of the Veneto, Trentino and Alto Adige, the enormous limestone fangs of the Dolomites (p322) have the edge when it comes to wild beauty. The Unesco World Heritage–listed mountain range offers some of Italy's most dramatic and vertiginous hiking trails.

The multi-day, hut-to-hut Alte Vie (High Routes) that slice through the heart of the range are among the most stunning in Europe. To up the ante somewhat, the region is laced with *vie ferrate*, fixed routes that snake and ladder up the peaks and allow would-be mountaineers to flirt with rock climbing with the security of a cable to hook onto.

Accommodation in the mountains is in huts (*rifugi*) or chalets, which should be booked ahead in high season. For serious hiking you'll need to bring appropriate equipment and get detailed trail maps. Tourist offices and visitor centres provide some information, resources and basic maps for easier tourist routes.

Central Italy

Abruzzo's national parks are among Italy's least explored. Here, you can climb Corno Grande, the Apennines' highest peak at 2912m, and explore vast, silent valleys. A top hike here is the three- to four-day trek through the Majella (p640) mountains, which follows an old POW escape route from Sulmona to Casoli.

In neighbouring Umbria, the glacier-carved valleys, beech forests and rugged mountains of Monti Sibillini (p630) and the Piano Grande, a 1270m-high plain flanked by the peaks of the Apennines, are well off the trodden path and beg to be discovered on foot. Both are spattered with a painter's palette of vibrant wildflowers in spring and early summer.

Tuscany's only significant park with good walking trails is in the southern Maremma (p550), where you can sign up for walks of medium difficulty. The tower-topped medieval town of San Gimignano is also a fine base for guided nature walks into the hills. The Apuane Alps and the stunning Garfagnana valleys are for serious hikers, with hundreds of trails encompassing everything from half-day hikes to long-distance treks. For most people, though, an easy amble through the picturesque vineyards of Chianti (p525) suits just fine – with a little wine tasting thrown in for good measure, naturally. Autumn, when the wine and olive harvests start, has a particularly mellow appeal.

Edging northwest, Cinque Terre (p184) is postcard stuff, with its collection of five rainbow-bright villages pasted precariously to the clifftops, looking as though the slightest puff of wind would make them topple into the Ligurian Sea any second. The area is honeycombed with terrific trails that teeter through the vines and along the precipitous coastline. The star trek is undoubtedly the serpentine Sentiero Azzuro linking all five villages, while the Sentiero Rosso (p184) presents a highly scenic alternative.

The South

For spectacular sea views hit the Amalfi Coast (p702) and Sorrento Peninsula, where age-old paths such as the Sentiero degli Dei (Path of the Gods) disappear into wooded mountains and ancient lemon groves. Across the water, Capri (p675) subverts its playboy image with a series of bucolic walking trails far from the crowds.

Crossing the border between Calabria and Basilicata is the Parco Nazionale del Pollino (p768), Italy's largest national park. Claiming the richest repository of flora and fauna in the south, its varied landscapes range from deep river canyons to alpine meadows. Calabria's other national parks – the Sila (p771) and Aspromonte (p774) – offer similarly dramatic hiking, particularly the area around Sersale in the Sila, studded with waterfalls and the possibility of trekking through the **Valli Cupe** (☑334 9174699, 333 8342866; www.vallicupe. it) canyon.

Close to the heel of the stiletto in the sun-baked region of Puglia, the Parco della Murgia Materana, part of the Matera (p757) Unesco World Heritage site, is full of fascinating cave churches and is great for birdwatching.

Sicily & Sardinia

With their unique topographies, Sicily and Sardinia provide unforgettable walking opportunities. Take your pick of volcano hikes in Sicily: the mother of them all is Mt Etna (p820), but there's a whole host of lesser volcanoes on the Aeolian Islands, from the slumbering Vulcano (p803), where you can descend to the crater floor, to a three-hour climb to the summit of Stromboli (p807) to see it exploding against the night sky. On Salina, you can clamber up extinct volcano Monte Fossa delle Felci (p806) for staggering views of symmetrically aligned volcanic peaks. From Etna you can also trek across into the Madonie (p798) park, or on Sicily's northwest coast, you can track the shoreline in the Riserva Naturale dello Zingaro (p841).

Hiking Sardinia's granite peaks is more challenging. The Golfo di Orosei e del Gennargentu (p888) park offers a network of old shepherds' tracks on the Supramonte plateau and incorporates the prehistoric site of Tiscali (p886) and the Gola Su Gorropu (p885) canyon, which requires a guide and a little rock climbing. Arguably the toughest trek in Italy, the island's seven-day Selvaggio Blu (p887) is not for

---

TOP TRAILS

Alpe di Siusi, Alto Adige (p325) Europe's largest plateau ends dramatically at the base of the Sciliar Mountains. Average stamina will get you to Rifugio Bolzano, one of the Alps' oldest mountain huts. The more challenging peaks of the Catinaccio group and the Sassolungo are nearby.

Val Pusteria, Alto Adige (p329) This narrow Tyrolean valley runs from Bressanone to San Candido. At the far end of the valley are the Sesto Dolomites, criss-crossed with spectacular walking trails, including moderate trails around the iconic Tre Cime di Lavaredo (Three Peaks).

Val Gardena, Alto Adige (p324) One of only five valleys where the Ladin heritage is still preserved. Located amid the peaks of the Gruppo del Sella and Sassolungo, there are challenging *alte vie* (high-altitude) trails and easier nature walks such as the Naturonda at Passo di Sella (2244m).

Brenta Dolomites, Trentino (p308) The Brenta group is famed for its sheer cliffs and tricky ascents, which are home to some of Italy's most famous *vie ferrate* (trails with permanent steel cables and ladders), including the Via Ferrata delle Bocchette.

Parco Nazionale delle Dolomiti Bellunesi, Veneto (p398) A Unesco Heritage park offering trails amid wildflowers. This park also harbours the high-altitude Alte Vie delle Dolomiti trails, accessible between June and September.

ITALY'S BEST PARKS & RESERVES

PARK	FEATURES	ACTIVITIES	BEST TIME TO VISIT
Abruzzo, Lazio e Molise (p644)	granite peaks, beech woods, bears, wolves	hiking, horse riding	May-Oct
Appennino Tosco-Emiliano (p451)	mountains, forests, lakes	skiing, cycling, hiking, horse riding	Feb-Oct
Arcipelago di La Maddalena (p881)	rocky islets, beaches, translucent sea	sailing, diving, snorkelling	Jun-Sep
Asinara (p873)	albino donkeys, former prison	cycling, boat tours, snorkelling	Jun-Sep
Aspromonte (p774)	coniferous forests, high plains, vertiginous villages	hiking	May-Oct
Circeo (p162)	sand dunes, rocky coastline, woods and wetlands	hiking, birdwatching	Apr-Jun & Sep-Oct
Cilento e Vallo di Diano (p716)	Greek temples, dramatic coastline, caves	hiking, swimming, birdwatching	May-Oct
Cinque Terre (p184)	colourful fishing villages, terraced hillsides	hiking, diving	Apr-Oct
Delta del Po (p467)	marshes, wetlands	cycling, birdwatching	May-Oct
Dolomiti Bellunesi (p398)	rock spires, highland meadows, chamois	skiing, hiking, mountain biking	Dec-Oct
Dolomiti di Sesto (p330)	jagged mountains, Tre Cime di Lavaredo (Three Peaks)	hiking, mountain biking, rock climbing	Jun-Sep
Etna (p820)	active volcano, lava fields, forests	hiking, horse riding	May-Oct
Gargano (p728)	ancient forests, limestone cliffs, grottoes	diving, hiking, cycling, snorkelling	Jun-Sep
Golfo di Orosei e del Gennargentu (p888)	sheer cliffs, granite peaks, prehistoric ruins	hiking, sailing, rock climbing, canyoning	May-Sep
Gran Paradiso (p237)	Alpine villages, mountains, meadows, ibex	skiing, snowboarding, hiking, climbing, mountain biking	Dec-Oct
Gran Sasso e Monti della Laga (p636)	ragged peaks, birds of prey, wolves	skiing, hiking, climbing	Dec-Mar
Madonie (p798)	Sicily's highest peaks, wooded slopes, wolves, wildflowers	hiking, horse riding	May-Jun & Sep-Oct
Majella (p640)	mountains, deep gorges, bears	hiking, cycling	Jun-Sep
Maremma (p550)	reclaimed marshes, beaches	hiking, horse riding, birdwatching	May-Oct
Monti Sibillini (p630)	ancient hamlets, mountains, eagles	hiking, mountain biking, paragliding	May-Oct
Pollino (p768)	mountains, canyons, forest, Larico pines, rare orchids	rafting, canyoning, hiking	Jun-Sep
Prigionette (p873)	forest paths, albino donkeys, Giara horses, wild boar	hiking, cycling	May-Oct
Sciliar-Catinaccio (p325)	pasture lands, valleys, storybook alpine villages	hiking, cycling	Jun-Sep
Sila (p771)	wooded hills, lakes, remote villages, mushrooms	skiing, hiking, canyoning, horse riding	Dec-Mar & May-Oct
Stelvio (p321)	Alpine peaks, glaciers, forests	year-round skiing, hiking, cycling, mountain biking	Dec-Sep

the faint-hearted. Stretching 45km along the Golfo di Orosei, the trek traverses wooded ravines, gorges and cliffs and a string of stunning coves. It's not well signposted (a deliberate decision to keep it natural), there's no water en route and some climbing and abseiling is involved.

Cycling

Whether you're after a gentle ride between trattorias, a 100km road race or a teeth-rattling mountain descent, you'll find a route to suit. Tourist offices can usually provide details on trails and guided rides, and bike hire is available in most cities and key activity spots.

Tuscany's rolling countryside has enduring appeal for cyclists, with gentle rides between achingly pretty villages, vines and olive groves. The wine-producing Chianti (p525) area south of Florence is a particular favourite. In Umbria, the Valnerina (p608) and Piano Grande at Monte Vettore have beautiful trails and quiet country roads to explore. Further north, the flatlands of Emilia-Romagna and the terraced vineyards of Barolo (p221), Barbaresco (p222) and Franciacorta are also ideally suited to bike touring, as are the trails rimming Lake Como (p270) and Lake Maggiore (p263). Cycling meets architecture on the Veneto's Brenta Riviera, which offers 150km of bike routes past glorious Venetian villas. In the south, Puglia's flat

countryside and coastal paths are also satisfying.

In summer, many Alpine ski resorts offer wonderful cycling. Mountain bikers are in their element whizzing among the peaks around Lake Garda (p281), Lake Maggiore and the Dolomites (p322) in Trentino-Alto Adige. Another challenging area is the granite landscape of the Supramonte (p884) in eastern Sardinia.

A useful first port of call for two-wheel adventures is Italy Cycling Guide (http://italy-cycling-guide.info), which gives the lowdown on major national and international routes in Italy, as well as route options (including maps and GPS files) for a number of regions.

Rock Climbing

The huge rock walls of the Dolomites set testing challenges for rock climbers of all levels, with everything from simple, single-pitch routes to long, multi-pitch ascents, many of which are easily accessible by road. To combine rock climbing with high-level hiking, clip into the *vie ferrate* in the Brenta Dolomites (p308).

Climbs of all grades are found in the Trentino town of Arco, home to the world-famous Rock Master Festival, from short, single-pitch sport routes to lengthier, Dolomite-style climbs.

For hard-core mountaineering, alpinists can pit themselves against Western

---

BIKE TOURS

I Bike Tuscany (p526) Year-round one-day bike tours for riders of every skill level. Transport to Chianti and a support vehicle are provided. It also offers electric-bike tours. Multi-day tours are available through US-based **We Bike Tuscany** (www.webiketuscany.com).

Iseobike (p281) Tours around the Franciacorta wine region, with wine tastings.

Bicisì (http://bicisi.wix.com/bicisi) Bike rental and themed foodie tours. Will deliver to accommodation in the Valtenesi.

Kayak Cardedu (☎348 9369401, 0782 7 51 85; www.cardedu-kayak.com; Località Perda Rubia, SS125, Km 121.6, Cardedu) Organises scenic half-day mountain-bike excursions and downhill rides on old mule tracks in Ogliastra, Sardinia.

Colpo di Pedale (www.colpodipedale.it) Trips for all levels on racers, mountain bikes and city bikes around Piedmont's Langhe wine region.

Ciclovagando (p742) Organises full-day tours of 20km, departing from various Puglian towns including Ostuni and Brindisi.

Guti Bike Rent (☎389 5539775; www.gutibikerent.com; Via Spluga 5, Argegno; bike hire per half-day €25-35, full day €35-50; ☺9am-12.30pm & 2-7pm) Run by a Spanish National Champion, this outfit arranges daily bike tours on and around Lake Como.

Europe's highest peaks in the Valle d'Aosta (p230). Courmayeur and Cogne, a renowned ice-climbing centre, make good bases.

To the south, the Gran Sasso (p636) massif is a favourite. Of its three peaks, Corno Grande (2912m) is the highest and Corno Piccolo (2655m) the easiest to get to.

Other hot spots include Monte Pellegrino outside Palermo in Sicily, and Domusnovas, Ogliastra and the Supramonte (p884) in Sardinia.

The best source of climbing information is the Club Alpino Italiano (www.cai.it). Another good information source is the website Climb Europe (www.climb-europe.com), which also sells rock-climbing guidebooks covering Italy.

Skiing & Snowboarding

Most of Italy's top ski resorts are in the northern Alps, where names like Sestriere (p228), Cortina d'Ampezzo (p399), Madonna di Campiglio (p310) and Courmayeur (p234) are well known to serious skiers. Travel down the peninsula and you'll find smaller resorts dotted throughout the Apennines, in Lazio, Le Marche and Abruzzo. The Apennines often receive mega snowfalls and fewer crowds (so shorter lift queues), and historic villages such as Scanno (p642) and Pescocostanzo (p641) are far more charming than some of the bigger resorts found elsewhere. Even Sicily's Mt Etna (p820) is skiable in winter.

Two snowboarding hot spots are Trentino's Madonna di Campiglio and Valle d'Aosta's Breuil-Cervinia (p231). Madonna's facilities are among the best in the country and include a snowboard park with descents for all levels and a dedicated boarder-cross zone. Breuil-Cervinia, situated at 2050m in the shadow of the Matterhorn, is better suited to intermediate and advanced levels.

Facilities at bigger centres are generally world-class, with pistes ranging from nursery slopes to tough black runs. As well as *sci alpino* (downhill skiing), resorts might offer *sci di fondo* (cross-country skiing) and *sci alpinismo* (ski mountaineering).

The ski season runs from December to late March, although there is year-round skiing in Trentino-Alto Adige and on Mont Blanc (Monte Bianco) and the Matterhorn in the Valle d'Aosta. Generally, January and February are the best, busiest and priciest months. For better value, consider

FLIGHT OF THE ANGEL

How do angels fly? At the speed of light, apparently. Il Volo dell'Angelo (p765) in Basilicata is one of the world's longest (1452m) and fastest (120kmh) zip lines, racing you between two villages: Castelmezzano and Pietrapertosa! If you want to amp up the adventure, this is the ultimate high-wire thrill.

Friuli's expanding Sella Nevea (p427) runs or Tarvisio (p427), one of the coldest spots in the Alps, where the season is often extended into April.

The best bargain of the ski year is the *settimana bianca* (literally 'white week'), a term used by resorts that generally refers to an all-inclusive ski package that covers accommodation, food and ski passes.

Skiing Resources

Click on the following websites for detailed information about Italy's ski resorts, including facilities, accommodation, updated snow reports, webcams and special offers.

J2Ski (www.j2ski.com)

Iglu Ski (www.igluski.com)

On the Snow (www.onthesnow.co.uk)

If You Ski (www.ifyouski.com)

On Water

On the coast, sport goes beyond posing on packed beaches. Sardinia's cobalt waters and Sicily's Aeolian Islands claim some of Italy's best diving. Windsurfers flock to Sardinia, Sicily and the northern lakes, while adrenalin junkies ride rapids from Piedmont to Calabria.

Diving

Diving is one of Italy's most popular summer pursuits, and there are hundreds of schools offering courses, dives for all levels and equipment hire.

Most diving schools open seasonally, typically from about June to October. If possible, avoid August, when the Italian coast is besieged by holidaymakers and peak-season prices.

Sailing

Italy has a proud maritime tradition and you can hire a paddle boat or sleek sailing yacht almost anywhere in the country. Sailors of all levels are catered for: experienced skippers can island-hop around Sicily and Sardinia, or along the Amalfi, Tuscan, Ligurian or Triestino coasts on chartered yachts; weekend boaters can explore hidden coves in rented dinghies around Puglia, in the Tuscan archipelago and around Sorrento (p698); and speed freaks can take to the Lombard lakes in sexy speedboats.

Down south, on the Amalfi Coast (p702), prime swimming spots are often only accessible by boat. It's a similar story on the islands of Capri, Ischia, Procida and Elba.

In Sicily, the cobalt waters of the Aeolian Islands (p798) are perfect for idle island-hopping. Across in Sardinia, the Golfo di Orosei (p888), Santa Teresa di Gallura (p879) and the Arcipelago di La Maddalena (p881) are all top sailing spots. Sardinia's main sailing portal is www.sailingsard inia.it.

Italy's most prestigious sailing regattas are Lake Garda's September Centomiglia (www.centomiglia.it), which sails just south of Gargnano, and the Barcolana (p407) held in Trieste in October. The latter is the Med's largest regatta.

Reputable yacht charter companies include Bareboat Sailing Holidays (www. bareboatsailingholidays.com).

TOP SKI RESORTS

Spread across the north of the country in the Alps and Dolomites, Italy has a bumper crop of ski resorts, which range from the fast and fashion-conscious to the low key and affordable. Here's our pick of them at a glance.

Courmayeur

Dominated by spectacular Mont Blanc, Courmayeur (p234) has access to legendary runs like the Vallée Blanche. Besides 100km of downhill skiing is geared towards confident intermediates, there's good off-piste, heliskiing and a pumping après-ski scene.

Cortina d'Ampezzo

In the Veneto Dolomites, Cortina d'Ampezzo (p399) has some serious downhill and cross-country skiing on Italy's most glamorous slopes, including the legendary Staunies black mogul run, and uplifting views of the Dolomites all around.

Breuil-Cervinia

In Matterhorn's shadow and within skiing distance of Zermatt over the mountain in Switzerland, Breuil-Cervinia (p231) in Aosta is a fine choice for late-season snow, intermediate runs and family facilities.

Monte Rosa

Straddling three valleys, the Monte Rosa (p229) ski area has a nicely chilled atmosphere, pretty Walser villages and white-knuckle off-piste skiing and heli-skiing, which figures among Europe's best.

Via Lattea

Italy's Via Lattea (p227), or 'Milky Way', covers a staggering 400km of pistes and links five ski resorts, including one of Europe's most glamorous, Sestriere, which is snow-sure thanks to its 2035m elevation.

Madonna di Campiglio

The Dolomites form a spectacular backdrop to the ultra-fashionable Madonna di Campiglio (p310), which attracts the Italian A-list to its swanky slopes. There's 150km of manicured runs and a snowboarding park to play on.

TOP DIVE SITES

For divers ready to take the plunge, Italy delivers on all fronts, with everything from sea caves, the remnants of old volcanoes and abundant marine life underwater. Most of the best diving centres on the clear waters surrounding the country's islands and islets.

Sicily makes an exceptional base, especially the cobalt waters of the Unesco-protected Aeolian Islands (p798), where you can dive in sea grottoes around the remains of old volcanoes. The volcanic island of Ustica (p796), Italy's first marine reserve, is also rich with underwater flora and fauna.

Over on Sardinia, the diving is equally outstanding. Dangling off the northwest coast, Capo Caccia (p872) is the dive site for Sardinia's coral divers and features the largest underwater grotto in the Mediterranean. In the north, the Maddalena marine park boasts translucent waters and diving around 60 islets.

On the craggy shores of the Italian Riviera in Liguria, Cinque Terre Marine Reserve is a good base for diving in the north of the country.

Heading further south, Capri (p675), Ischia (p682) and Procida (p685) in Campania are three islands in the Bay of Naples with exceptional diving amid sun-struck sea caves. In the southeast, the Isole Tremiti (p734) are wind-eroded islands off Puglia's Gargano Promontory, pock-marked with huge sea caves.

White-Water Action

A mecca for water rats, the Sesia river in northern Piedmont (p199) is Italy's top white-water destination. At its best between April and September, it runs from the slopes of Monte Rosa (p229) down through the spectacular scenery of the Valsesia. Operators in Varallo (p229) offer various solutions to the rapids: there's canoeing, kayaking, white-water rafting, canyoning, hydrospeed and tubing.

In Alto Adige, the Val di Sole (p311) is another white-water destination, as is Lake Ledro in Trentino, where you can canyon beneath invigorating waterfalls. Further south, Monti Sibillini (p630) in Umbria is another good choice for white water adventures.

On the southwest coast, **Kayak Napoli** (☏331 9874271; www.kayaknapoli.com; tours €20-30; ☐140 to Via Posillipo) ✆ offers great tours of the Neapolitan coastline for all levels, ticking off often-inaccessible ruins, neoclassical villas, gardens and grottoes from the water.

At the southern end of the peninsula, the Lao river rapids in Calabria's Parco Nazionale del Pollino (p768) provide exhilarating rafting, as well as canoeing and canyoning. Trips can be arranged in Scalea.

The compelling red granite coastline of Ogliastra in Sardinia is best seen on a relaxed paddle with Kayak Cardedu (p50).

Windsurfing

Considered one of Europe's prime windsurfing spots, Lake Garda (p281) enjoys excellent wind conditions: the northerly *peler* blows in early on sunny mornings, while the southerly *ora* sweeps down in the early afternoon as regular as clockwork. The two main centres are Torbole, home of the World Windsurfing Championship, and Malcesine (p287), 15km south.

For windsurfing on the sea, head to Sardinia. In the north, Porto Pollo, also known as Portu Puddu, is good for beginners and experts – the bay provides protected waters for learners, while experts can enjoy the high winds as they funnel through the channel between Sardinia and Corsica. To the northeast, there's good windsurfing on the island of Elba (p556), off the Tuscan coast. Competitions such as the Chia Classic are held off the southwest coast in June.

An excellent guide to windsurfing and kitesurfing spots across Italy and the rest of Europe is Stoked Publications' *The Kite and Windsurfing Guide: Europe*. Equipment hire is widely available.

Plan Your Trip
Travel with Children

Be it kid-friendly capital, smouldering volcano or beach-laced coast, Italy spoils families with its rich mix of historical and cultural sights, staggering portfolio of outdoor activities and stunning natural land-scapes. To get the most out of exploring as a family, plan ahead.

Best Regions for Kids

Rome & Lazio

Ancient Roman ruins and world-class museums make Rome interesting for older children.

Naples & Campania

Gold for every age: subterranean ruins in Naples, gladiator battlefields in Pompeii and Hercula-neum, and natural high drama – think volcanoes, thermal pools and coastal caves.

Puglia, Basilicata & Calabria

Beautiful seaside scapes and towns, islands loaded with swashbuckling adventure and an unembellished cuisine most kids love.

Sicily

Volcano climbing for sporty teens and beachside fun for sand-loving tots, alongside ancient ruins, hilltop castles and traditional 18th-century puppet theatre to inspire and entertain all ages.

Sardinia

Alfresco paradise overflowing with dazzling beaches, water-sports action, horseriding and scenic hikes suitable for all ages and abilities.

Trentino & South Tyrol

Ski or snowboard in some of Italy's best family-friendly winter ski resorts. Summer ushers in mountain hiking and biking for all ages.

Italy for Kids

Italian family travels divide into two camps: urban and rural. Cities in Italy are second to none in extraordinary sights and experiences, and with the aid of audio-guides, smartphone apps and and some inventive guided tours, parents can find kid-appeal in almost every museum and monument.

Away from urban areas the pace slows and good, old-fashioned fresh air kicks in. Sandcastles, sea swimming and easy beachside ambles are natural elements of coastal travel (beach-rich Puglia, the Amalfi Coast, Sardinia and Sicily sizzle with family fun on and off the sand), while mountains and lakes inland demand im-mediate outdoor action from kids aged five and over – the older the child, the more daredevil and adrenalin-pumping the ac-tivity gets.

Museums & Monuments

When it comes to learning about art and history, Italy's wealth of museums beat school textbooks hands down. Few or-ganise specific tours and workshops for children (there are dazzling exceptions in Florence), but an increasing number cater to younger-generation minds with multi-media displays, touchscreen gadgets and audio guides.

In Rome, time visits to the Vatican to coincide with the weekly papal address – kids love guessing which of the many windows the Pope will pop out of. Kill queue time for St Peter's Basilica by penning postcards home complete with a rare Vatican City postage stamp.

Dining

Children are welcomed in most eateries, especially in casual trattorias and *osterie* – often family-owned with overwhelmingly friendly, indulgent waiting staff and a menu featuring simple pasta dishes as well as more elaborate items. A *menù bambini* (children's menu) is fairly common. It's also acceptable to order a *mezzo piatto* (half-portion) or a simple plate of pasta with butter or olive oil and Parmesan.

Italian families eat late. Few restaurants open their doors before 7.30pm or 8pm, making pizzerias – many open early – more appealing for families with younger children. High chairs are occasionally available; if your toddler absolutely needs to be strapped in, bring your own portable cloth seat.

In cities look out for branches of sustainable Slow Food champion Eataly (the impressive, hugely creative force behind Italy's dazzling new food theme park in Bologna), which serves meals all day using local, organic produce.

Pizza al taglio (pizza by the slice), *panini* from delicatessens and gelato are tasty on-the-run snacks. Markets everywhere burst with salami, cheese, olives, bread, fruit and other inspiring picnic supplies.

Baby requirements are easily met (except on Sundays when most shops are closed). Pharmacies and supermarkets sell baby formula, nappies (diapers), ready-made baby food and sterilising solutions. Fresh cow's milk is sold in cartons in supermarkets and in bars with a *'Latteria'* sign.

Children's Highlights

Outdoor Fun

Sardinia (p847) Albino donkey spotting, horse riding, water sports on some of Italy's top beaches (including excellent bubblemaker diving courses for kids), rock climbing and caving adventures.

Aeolian Islands (p798) Seven tiny volcanic islands off Sicily with everything from spewing lava to black-sand beaches.

The Dolomites Hit Alto Adige's Alpe di Siusi (p325) and Kronplatz (p331) for abundant blue and red ski runs, or cycle through orchards and farmland on a Dolomiti di Brenta bike tour.

Venice (p336) Glide across Venetian waters on a customised sailing or kayaking tour, or learn to row standing up like a bona fide gondolier.

Lago Maggiore (p263) **& Lago di Garda** (p281) Lakeside beaches, water sports, climbing, mountain hiking, canyoning (from Riva del Garda), paragliding (from Monte Baldo), swimming, horse riding, easy cycling etc.

History Trips

Colosseum, Rome (p70) Throw yourself into Ancient Rome with tales of brave gladiators and wild beasts in the Roman Empire's biggest, mightiest stadium.

Pompeii (p692) **& Herculaneum** (p687), **Campania** Evocative ruins with ancient shops and houses, chariot-grooved streets, swimming pools and a gladiator battlefield.

Castello Sforzesco, Milan (p247) Massively cool castle, with guided rampart and subterranean family tours with tour operator Ad Artem.

ADMISSION PRICES

Discounted admission for children is available at most attractions, although there is no fixed rule as to how much – or not – children pay. State-run museums and archaeological sites usually offer free entry to EU citizens under the age of 18. Otherwise, museums and monuments offer a reduced admission fee (generally half the adult price) for children, usually from the ages of 6 to 18. Many offer money-saving family tickets covering admission for two adults and two children or more.

Planning a family visit to museum-laden cities such as Rome and Florence on the first weekend of the month cuts costs dramatically: admission to state-run museums and monuments countrywide is free for everyone on the first Sunday of each month.

Palazzo Comunale & Torre Grossa, San Gimignano (p534) Slip on augmented-reality glasses in this Tuscan town to learn about frescoes and its medieval past.

Matera, Basilicata (p757) One of the world's oldest towns with epic biblical scenery peppered with *sassi* (habitable caves).

Palazzo del Podestà, Bergamo (p289) High-tech gadgetry, animated maps and interactive gizmos bring Bergamo's Venetian age vividly to life.

Cool Climbs

St Peter's Basilica, Rome (p110) Climbing up inside the dome of Italy's largest, most spectacular church is undeniably cool.

Duomo, Florence (p478) Repeat the dome-climbing experience with Brunelleschi's dome in Italy's favourite Renaissance city (for kids over five years of age).

Catacombe dei Cappuccini, Palermo (p789) Climb down to Palermo's creepy catacombs, packed with mummies in their Sunday best. Find more catacombs beneath Via Appia Antica in Rome and Naples (for kids over 12 years).

Napoli Sotterranea, Naples (p668) A secret trap door, war-time hideouts, sacred catacombs and ghoulish cemeteries make this guided tour of subterranean Naples gripping (for kids over eight years).

Leaning Tower, Pisa (p560) The bare interior of this pearly-white icon is accessible to children from ages eight and up; otherwise snap your kids propping up the tower.

Torre dell'Orologio, Venice (p342) Climb inside the world's first digital clock to examine its Renaissance mechanisms and the two bronze Moors hammering out the hour (for kids over six years).

Stromboli, Aeolian Islands (p807) A guided ascent to the firework-spitting crater of this volcano is a total thrill for active teenagers.

Rainy Days

Museo Nazionale della Scienza e della Tecnologia, Milan (p247) Italy's best science and technology museum makes budding inventors go gaga.

Museo Nazionale del Cinema, Turin (p206) Multimedia displays and movie memorabilia make this museum a winner for kids and adults alike.

Museo Archeologico dell'Alto Adige, Bolzano (p312) Drop in on Iceman Ötzi, Europe's oldest natural human mummy.

MAV, Ercolano (p690) Multimedia installations at this virtual archaeological museum bring famous ancient ruins back to life.

Palazzo Vecchio, Florence (p481) Theatrical tours for children and families through secret staircases and hidden rooms, led by historical figures.

Culinary Experiences

Pasta Challenge your child to taste different shapes and colours of pasta while in Italy: *strozzapreti* ('priest strangler' pasta) is an Umbrian highlight, while in southern Italy Puglia's *orecchiette con cima di rape* (small ear-shaped pasta with turnip greens) is the perfect way of ensuring your kids eat some vegetables.

Pizza in Naples Hands-down the best in Italy. Favourite addresses include Starita (p671) and Pizzeria Gino Sorbillo (p671).

Gelato Museum Carpigiani, Anzola (📱051 650 53 06; www.gelatomuseum.com; Via Emilia 45, Anzola; adult/reduced €7/5, classes €20-50; 🕙9am-6pm Tue-Sat; 🚶) Gelato-themed tours with lots of tasting, or make your own with masters from the neighbouring Gelato University; 30 minutes from Bologna in Anzola.

Cook in Venice (www.cookinvenice.com; tours €35-60, courses €185-225) Kid-friendly food tours and cooking classes by Venetian *mamma* of two, Monica Cesarato.

Casa del Cioccolato Perugina, Perugia (p581) Wonka-esque chocolate-making workshops and tours at the Baci Perugina chocolate factory.

Eataly Tonrio Lingotto, Turin (p214) Dining with Italy's biggest champion of sustainable and Slow Food dining allows every member of the family to dine on a different cuisine.

Florence Town, Florence (p500) Gelato classes or pizza-making with a professional *pizzaiolo* for all the family.

Regions at a Glance

Rome & Lazio

History
Art
Scenery

History
Rome's ancient centre is history in 3D. Romulus killed Remus on the Palatino (Palatine Hill), Christians were fed to lions in the Colosseum and rulers soaked at the Terme di Caracalla. Ponder the remains of the great and the good in the catacombs along Via Appia Antica.

Art
The breadth of cultural treasures housed in Rome's museums and galleries is, quite frankly, embarrassing. If you plan on hitting several of them, consider one of the various discount cards available.

Scenery
Often upstaged by the urban must-sees of Rome, the Lazio region harbours lesser-known delights, from the classic Mediterranean beauty of the Isole Pontine to the extraordinary stone village of Civita di Bagnoregio.

p62

Turin, Piedmont & the Italian Riviera

Activities
Villages
Food & Wine

Activities
From the slopes of Piedmont's Milky Way and the Valle d'Aosta to wild coastal hikes along the Cinque Terre, this northwest corner of the country is a pulse raising paradise.

Villages
With chic medieval fishing villages along the Cinque Terre, quaint wine-growing villages on Langhe hilltops and secret villages in the Valle d'Aosta, it's not hard to find your ideal storybook refuge.

Food & Wine
Birthplace of the Slow Food Movement, Piedmont has an embarrassment of culinary riches, from the truffles of Alba to the *vini* of the Langhe region.

p164

Milan & the Lakes

Shopping
Gardens
Food & Wine

Shopping
Every style maven knows that Milan takes fashion and design as seriously as others take biotech or engineering. Best of all, topnotch discount outlets mean that even mere mortals can make a *bella figura* (good impression).

Gardens
Framed by gazebos, blushing bushes of camellias, artfully tumbling terraces and world-class statuary, Lombardy's lakeside villas knock the socks off the 'luxury getaway' concept.

Food & Wine
Bergamo, Brescia, Cremona and Mantua, the cultured cities of the Po Plain, combine wonderful art and architecture with a slew of sophisticated, regional restaurants.

p239

Trentino & South Tyrol

Activities
Wellness
Food & Wine

Activities

Ski, hike, ice-climb, sledge-ride or Nordic walk in the Sella Ronda and the remote Parco Nazionale dello Stelvio. Real adrenalin junkies will want to scale the WWI-era *vie ferrate* (trails with permanent cables and ladders).

Wellness

Attend to your wellness in the thermal baths at Terme Merano, then stock up on tisane and cosmetics infused with Alpine herbs, grapes, apples and mountain pine.

Food & Wine

Bolzano beer halls, strudels, Sachertorte, sourdough breads and buckwheat cakes are just some of the region's Austro-Italian specialities. Combine with regional wines such as Gewürztraminer and riesling.

p300

Venice & the Veneto

Art
Architecture
Wine

Art

Canvases by Titian and Veronese, stirring frescoes by Tintoretto and Tiepolo, all illuminating the path to the modern creativity showcased at Punta della Dogana, Peggy Guggenheim Collection and the Venice Biennale.

Architecture

Formidable castles, gracious country villas and an entire city of palaces on the water, many of the Veneto's architectural landmarks admire their own reflections in glassy, historic waterways.

Wine

A wine-growing heavyweight, this region is home to Valpolicella's cult-status Amarone, Soave's mineral whites and Conegliano's *prosecco* (sparkling wine), not to mention dozens of innovative blends.

p333

Friuli Venezia Giulia

Culture
Wine
Activities

Culture

The geographic proximity of *Mitteleuropa* (Central Europe) is echoed in the region's earthy Slavic flavours, Austrian cakes and minority languages, not to mention the cosmopolitan other-worldliness of oft-overlooked Trieste.

Wine

Italy's northeast corner is home to an ever-growing number of small, innovative and often natural wine producers; their products are swilled by locals well-known for their love of fine libations.

Activities

Dramatic, unspoilt Alpine wilderness sets the scene for laid-back winter skiing, sublime summertime hikes and wildlife sightings, from foxes and deer to chamois and lynx.

p401

Emilia-Romagna & San Marino

Food
Architecture
Activities

Food

Indulge in Modena's aged balsamic vinegar, Parma's coveted *prosciutto* (ham) and cheese, Ferrara's *cappellacci di zucca* (pumpkin pasta dumplings) and Bologna's comforting *ragù* (meat and tomato sauce).

Architecture

Tour the churches for a quick art-history lesson, from Ravenna's dazzling Byzantine mosaics and Modena's Romanesque cathedral to Bologna's Gothic-Renaissance blockbuster Basilica di San Petronio.

Activities

It's time to hit the pedal. Bologna's cobbled streets recall a continental Oxford, while smaller Modena and Ferrara, the latter with 9km of old city walls, are two of Italy's most bicycle-friendly locales.

p430

Florence & Tuscany

Art
Food & Wine
Scenery

Art

Read the story of the evolving Renaissance within the vibrant frescoes and paintings adorning Florence, Siena, Arezzo and San Gimignano. Notable mavericks include Giotto, Masaccio, Ghirlandaio, Lippi and Botticelli.

Food & Wine

Intoxicating white truffles and juicy Chianina *bistecche* (steaks) – few regions whet the appetite so lasciviously. Add a glass of Montepulciano's Vino Nobile or Montalcino's world-famous Brunello, and rediscover bliss.

Scenery

Cypress-lined gardens in Florence, terraced hills in Chianti, the Unesco-lauded beauty of the Val d'Orcia and Val di Chiana: Tuscany's landscapes seem sketched by its artistic greats.

p475

Umbria & Le Marche

Villages
Scenery
Food & Wine

Villages

Perched snugly on their peaks like so many storks on chimneys, Umbria's hill towns – Perugia, Assisi, Gubbio, Urbino, Spoleto, Todi – are the postcard-pretty protectors of local traditions.

Scenery

Mountainous and wild, views come at you from all angles. Shoot up the *funivia* (cable car) in Gubbio or strike out into the snowcapped ranges of Monti Sibillini and the wildflower-flecked Piano Grande.

Food & Wine

Richly forested and deeply rural, the Umbrian larder is stocked with robust flavours, from wild boar and pigeon to Norcia's *cinta senese* (Tuscan pig) salami and black truffles.

p576

Abruzzo & Molise

Scenery
Activities
Wilderness

Scenery

Vintage Italy lives on in the isolated mountain villages of Pescocostanzo, Scanno and Sulmona. En route from Sulmona to Scanno, the untamed scenery of the Gole di Sagittario gorge will bewitch you.

Activities

From Corno Grande (2912m) to Monte Amaro (2793m), Abruzzo's parks offer hiking and skiing without the northern hordes. The best-loved route: the ascent of Corno Grande.

Wilderness

These regions excel in outstanding natural beauty. Traced with walking trails, the ancient forests of three national parks still rustle with bears, chamois and wolves.

p633

Naples & Campania

Scenery
History
Food & Wine

Scenery

From Ischia's Med-tropical gardens and Capri's vertiginous cliffs, to the citrus-scented panoramas of the Amalfi Coast, the views from this sun drenched coastline are as famous as the stars who holiday here.

History

Sitting beneath Mt Vesuvius, the Neapolitans abide by the motto carpe diem. And why not? All around them – at Pompeii, Herculaneum, Cuma and the Phlegraean Fields – are vivid reminders that life is short.

Food & Wine

Campania produces powerhouse coffee, pizzas, tomato pasta, *sfogliatelle* (sweetened ricotta pastries) and an incredible panoply of seafood, eaten every which way you can.

p652

Puglia, Basilicata & Calabria

Beaches
Wilderness
Food & Wine

Beaches

Lounge beneath white cliffs in the Gargano, gaze on violet sunsets in Tropea and soak up summer on the golden beaches of Otranto and Gallipoli.

Wilderness

A crush of spiky mountains, Basilicata and Calabria are where the wild things are. Burst through the clouds in mountain-top Pietrapertosa, pick bergamot in the Aspromonte and swap pleasantries with quietly curious locals.

Food & Wine

Puglia has turned its poverty into a culinary art: sample vibrant, vegetable-based pasta dishes like *orecchiette con cima di rape* (pasta with broccoli rabe) and wash it down with a Salento red from Italy's heel.

p719

Sicily

Food & Wine
History
Activities

Food & Wine

Sicilian cuisine seduces seafood lovers and sets sweet teeth on edge. Tuna, sardines, swordfish and shellfish come grilled, fried or seasoned with mint or wild fennel. Desserts are lavished with citrus, ricotta, almonds and pistachios.

History

A Mediterranean crossroads for centuries, Sicily keeps history buffs busy with Greek temples, Roman and Byzantine mosaics, Phoenician statues, Norman-Romanesque castles and art-nouveau villas.

Activities

Outdoor enthusiasts can swim and dive in Ustica's pristine waters, hike the Aeolian Islands' dramatic coastlines or watch the volcanic fireworks of Stromboli and Etna.

p781

Sardinia

Beaches
Activities
History

Beaches

Surfers, kitesurfers, sailors and divers from Italy and beyond flock to the Costa Smeralda, Porto Pollo, the Golfo di Orosei and the Archipelago di La Maddalena.

Activities

Sardinia's rugged, awe-inspiring mountains leave hikers and free climbers breathless. Climbs deliver stunning views of the sea, while Supramonte hikes traverse old, atmospheric shepherd routes.

History

The island's grey-granite landscape is littered with strange prehistoric dolmens, menhirs, wells and *nuraghi,* the latter huge, mysterious stone towers built by the island's earliest inhabitants.

p847

On the
Road

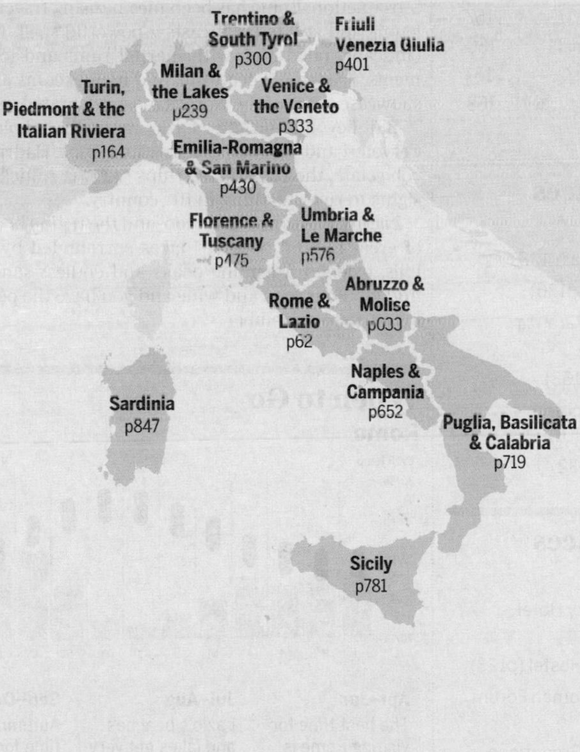

Turin, Piedmont & the Italian Riviera p164

Milan & the Lakes p239

Trentino & South Tyrol p300

Venice & the Veneto p333

Friuli Venezia Giulia p401

Emilia-Romagna & San Marino p430

Florence & Tuscany p475

Umbria & Le Marche p576

Rome & Lazio p62

Abruzzo & Molise p633

Naples & Campania p652

Puglia, Basilicata & Calabria p719

Sardinia p847

Sicily p781

Rome & Lazio

Best Places to Eat

→ Pianostrada (p129)

→ Pizzarium (p136)

→ La Nostra Paranza (p162)

→ Gli Archi (p163)

→ Antico Ristorante Pagnanelli (p161)

→ Sbanco (p132)

Best Places to Sleep

→ Palm Gallery Hotel (p128)

→ Generator Hostel (p123)

→ Inn at the Roman Forum (p122)

→ Residenze Gregoriane (p155)

→ Villa Ersilia (p163)

Why Go?

From ancient treasures and artistic gems to remote hilltop monasteries, sandy beaches and volcanic lakes, Lazio is one of Italy's great surprise packages. Its epic capital needs no introduction. Rome has been mesmerising travellers for millennia and still today it casts a powerful spell. Its romantic cityscape, piled high with martial ruins and iconic monuments, is achingly beautiful, and its museums and basilicas showcase some of the world's most celebrated masterpieces.

But beyond the city, Lazio more than holds its own. Cerveteri and Tarquinia's Etruscan tombs, Hadrian's vast Tivoli estate, the remarkable ruins of Ostia Antica – these are sights to rival anything in the country.

Nature has contributed too, and the region boasts pockets of great natural beauty – lakes surrounded by lush green hills, wooded Apennine peaks and endless sandy beaches. Add fabulous food and wine and you have the perfect recipe for a trip to remember.

When to Go
Rome

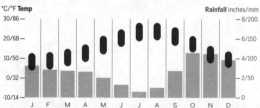

Apr–Jun
The best time for visiting Rome is spring. Easter is busy in Rome and peak rates apply

Jul–Aug
Lazio's beaches and lakes get very busy in the peak summer months.

Sep–Oct
Autumn is a good time for visiting regional sites. Festivals and outdoor events are on.

ROME

⏸ 06 / POP 2.86 MILLION

History

Rome's history spans three millennia, from the classical myths of vengeful gods to the follies of Roman emperors, from Renaissance excess and papal plotting to swaggering 20th-century fascism. Everywhere you go in this remarkable city, you're surrounded by the past. Martial ruins, Renaissance *palazzi* (mansions) and flamboyant baroque basilicas all have tales to tell – of family feuding, historic upheavals, artistic rivalries, intrigues and dark passions.

Ancient Rome, the Myth

Rome's original myth-makers were the first emperors. Eager to reinforce the city's status as *caput mundi* (capital of the world), they turned to writers such as Virgil, Ovid and Livy to create an official Roman history. These authors, while adept at weaving epic narratives, were less interested in the rigours of historical research and frequently presented myth as reality. In the *Aeneid,* Virgil brazenly draws on Greek legends and stories to tell the tale of Aeneas, a Trojan prince who arrives in Italy and establishes Rome's founding dynasty. Similarly, Livy, a writer celebrated for his monumental history of the Roman Republic, makes liberal use of mythology to fill the gaps in his historical narrative.

Ancient Rome's rulers were sophisticated masters of spin and under their tutelage, art, architecture and elaborate public ceremony were employed to perpetuate the image of Rome as an invincible and divinely sanctioned power. Monuments such as the Ara Pacis, the Colonna di Traiano and the Arco di Costantino celebrated imperial glories, while gladiatorial games highlighted the Romans' physical superiority. The Colosseum, the Roman Forum and the Pantheon were not only sophisticated feats of engineering, they were also impregnable symbols of Rome's eternal might.

Legacy of an Empire

Rising out of the bloodstained remains of the Roman Republic, the Roman Empire was the Western world's first great superpower. At its zenith under the emperor Trajan (r AD 98–117), it extended from Britannia in the north to North Africa in the south, from Hispania (Spain) in the west to Palestina (Palestine) and Syria in the east. Rome itself had more than 1.5 million inhabitants and the city sparkled with the trappings of imperial splendour: marble temples, public baths, theatres, circuses and libraries. Decline eventually set in during the 3rd century, and by the latter half of the 5th century, the city was in barbarian hands.

Emergence of Christianity

Christianity entered Rome's religious cocktail in the 1st century AD, sweeping in from Judaea, a Roman province in what is now Israel and the West Bank. Its early days were marred by persecution, most notably under Nero (r 54–68), but it slowly caught on, thanks to its popular message of heavenly reward and the evangelising efforts of Sts Peter and Paul. However, it was the conversion of the emperor Constantine (r 306–37) that really set Christianity on the path to European domination. In 313 Constantine issued the Edict of Milan, officially legalising Christianity, and later, in 378, Theodosius (r 379–95) made it Rome's state religion. By this time, the Church had developed a sophisticated organisational structure based on five major sees: Rome, Constantinople, Alexandria, Antioch and Jerusalem. At the outset, each bishopric carried equal weight, but in subsequent years Rome emerged as the senior party. The reasons for this were partly political – Rome was the wealthy capital of the Roman Empire – and partly religious – early Christian doctrine held that St Peter, founder of the Roman Church, had been sanctioned by Christ to lead the universal Church.

New Beginnings, Protest & Persecution

Bridging the gap between the Middle Ages and the modern era, the Renaissance (*Rinascimento* in Italian) was a far-reaching intellectual, artistic and cultural movement. It emerged in 14th century Florence but quickly spread to Rome, where it gave rise to one of the greatest makeovers the city had ever seen. Not everyone was impressed though, and in the early 16th century the Protestant Reformation burst into life. This, in turn, provoked a furious response by the Catholic Church, the Counter-Reformation.

The Counter-Reformation

The Counter-Reformation, the Catholic response to the Protestant Reformation, was marked by a second wave of artistic and architectural activity as the Church once again turned to bricks and mortar to restore its

Continued on p68

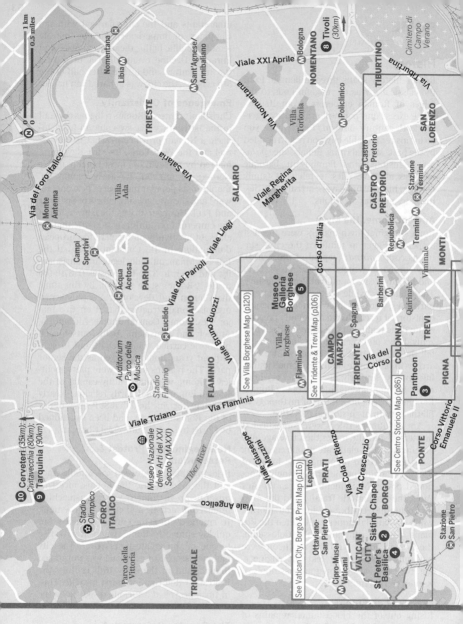

Rome & Lazio Highlights

1 Colosseum
(p70) Getting your first spine-tingling glimpse of Rome's great gladiatorial arena.

2 Sistine Chapel
(p115) Marvelling at Michelangelo's legendary frescoes in the heart of the Vatican Museums.

3 Pantheon
(p84) Gazing heavenwards in this extraordinary Roman temple.

4 St Peter's Basilica (p110)
Being blown away by the super-sized opulence of the Vatican's showpiece church.

5 Museo e Galleria Borghese
(p118) Going face to face with sensational baroque sculpture.

6 Palatino
(p72) Enjoying fabulous views from Rome's mythical birthplace.

7 Scavi Archeologici di Ostia Antica (p152) Strolling the fossilised streets of ancient Rome's main seaport.

8 Villa Adriana (p153) Poking around the monumental ruins of Hadrian's vast Tivoli estate.

9 Necropoli di Tarquinia (p156) Delving into frescoed Etruscan tombs in Tarquinia.

10 Necropoli di Banditaccia (p155) Exploring rows of grass-capped tombs at Cerveteri's haunting city of the dead.

NEIGHBOURHOODS AT A GLANCE

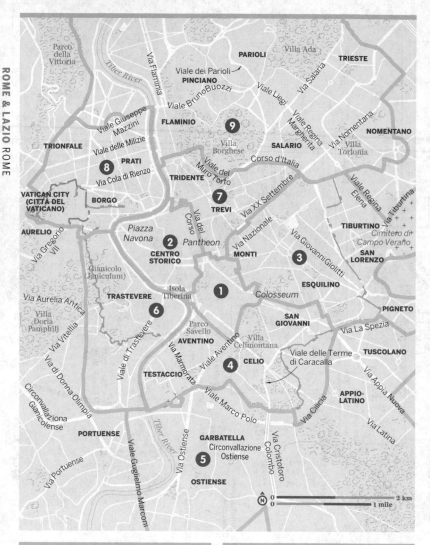

❶ Ancient Rome (p68)

In a city of extraordinary beauty, Rome's ancient heart stands out. It's here you'll find the great icons of the city's past: the Colosseum; the Palatino; the forums; and the Campidoglio (Capitoline Hill), the historic home of the Capitoline Museums. Touristy by day, it's quiet at night with few after-hours attractions.

❷ Centro Storico (p82)

A tangle of piazzas, alleys, Renaissance *palazzi* and baroque churches, the historic centre is the Rome many come to find. Its streets teem with boutiques, cafes, restaurants and bars, while market traders and street artists work the crowds on the squares. The Pantheon and Piazza Navona are the star turns, but you'll also find a host of monuments, museums and art-laden churches.

❸ Monti, Esquilino & San Lorenzo (p89)

Centred on transport hub Stazione Termini, this is a large and cosmopolitan area which, upon first glance, can seem busy and overwhelming. But hidden among its traffic-noisy streets are some beautiful churches, Rome's best unsung art museum at Palazzo Massimo alle Terme, and any number of trendy bars and restaurants in the fashionable Monti, student-loved San Lorenzo and bohemian Pigneto districts.

❹ San Giovanni & Testaccio (p93)

Encompassing two of Rome's seven hills, this sweeping, multifaceted area offers everything from barnstorming basilicas and medieval churches to ancient ruins, colourful markets and popular clubs. Its best-known drawcards are the Basilica di San Giovanni in Laterano and Terme di Caracalla, but there are heavenly views to be had on the Aventino and Villa Celimontana is a lovely, tranquil park. Down by the river, Testaccio is a trendy district known for its nose-to-tail Roman cuisine and thumping nightlife.

❺ Southern Rome (p97)

Boasting a wealth of diversions, this huge area extends to Rome's southern limits. Glorious ancient ruins lounge amid pea-green fields and towering umbrella pines along the cobbled Via Appia Antica, one of the world's oldest roads and pot holed with subterranean catacombs. By contrast, post industrial Ostiense blasts visitors straight back to the 21st century with its edgy street art, dining and nightlife. Then there's EUR, an Orwellian quarter of wide boulevards and linear buildings, which risks being the new fashionista hot spot with the arrival of Italian fashion house Fendi.

❻ Trastevere & Gianicolo (p99)

With its cobbled lanes, ochre *palazzi*, ivy-clad facades and boho vibe, ever-trendy Trastevere is one of Rome's most vivacious and Roman neighbourhoods – its very name, 'across the Tiber' (tras tevere), evokes both its geographical location and sense of difference. Outrageously photogenic and pleasurably car-free, its labyrinth of lanes heaves after dark as crowds swarm to its restaurants, cafes and bars. Rising up behind all this, Gianicolo Hill offers a breath of fresh air and a superb view of Rome laid out at your feet.

❼ Tridente, Trevi & the Quirinale (p102)

With the dazzling Trevi Fountain and Spanish Steps among its A-lister sights, this central part of Rome is glamorous, debonair and tourist-busy. Designer boutiques, fashionable bars, swish hotels and a handful of historic cafes and trattorias lace the compelling web of streets between Piazza di Spagna and Piazza del Popolo in Tridente, while the Trevi Fountain area south swarms with overpriced eateries and ticky tacky shops. Lording over it all, the presidential Palazzo del Quirinale exudes sober authority – and wonderful views of the Rome skyline at sunset.

❽ Vatican City, Borgo & Prati (p109)

The Vatican, the world's smallest sovereign state, sits over the river from the historic centre. Centred on the domed bulk of St Peter's Basilica, it boasts some of Italy's most revered artworks, many housed in the vast Vatican Museums (home of the Sistine Chapel), as well as batteries of overpriced restaurants and souvenir shops. Nearby, the landmark Castel Sant'Angelo looms over the Borgo district and upscale Prati offers excellent accommodation, eating and shopping.

❾ Villa Borghese & Northern Rome (p118)

This moneyed area encompasses Rome's most famous park (Villa Borghese) and its most expensive residential district (Parioli). Concert-goers head to the Auditorium Parco della Musica, while art lovers can choose between contemporary installations at MAXXI, Etruscan artefacts at the Museo Nazionale Etrusco di Villa Giulia, or baroque treasures at the Museo e Galleria Borghese.

Continued from p63

authority. But in contrast to the Renaissance, the Counter-Reformation was also a period of persecution and official intolerance. With the full blessing of Pope Paul III, Ignatius Loyola founded the Jesuits in 1540, and two years later the Holy Office was set up as the Church's final appeals court for trials prosecuted by the Inquisition. In 1559 the Church published the *Index Librorum Prohibitorum* (Index of Prohibited Books) and began to persecute intellectuals and freethinkers. Galileo Galilei (1564–1642) was forced to renounce his assertion of the Copernican astronomical system, which held that the earth moved around the sun. He was summoned by the Inquisition to Rome in 1632 and exiled to Florence for the rest of his life. Giordano Bruno (1548–1600), a freethinking Dominican monk, fared worse. Arrested in Venice in 1592, he was burned at the stake eight years later in Campo de' Fiori.

Despite, or perhaps because of, the Church's policy of zero tolerance, the Counter-Reformation was largely successful in re-establishing papal prestige. And in this sense it can be seen as the natural finale to the Renaissance that Nicholas V had kicked off in 1450. From being a rural backwater with a population of around 20,000 in the mid-15th century, Rome had grown to become one of Europe's great 17th-century cities.

◉ Sights

◉ Ancient Rome

Arco di Costantino   MONUMENT
(Map p80; Via di San Gregorio; Ⓜ Colosseo) On the western side of the Colosseum, this monumental triple arch was built in AD 315 to celebrate the emperor Constantine's victory over his rival Maxentius at the Battle of the Milvian Bridge (AD 312). Rising to a height of 25m, it's the largest of Rome's surviving triumphal arches.

Carcere Mamertino   HISTORIC SITE
(Carcer Tullianum; Map p80; ☑ 06 6989 6375; www.operaromanapellegrinaggi.org; Clivo Argentario 1; adult/reduced €10/5; ⊙ 8.30am-4.30pm; ◳ Via dei Fori Imperiali) Hidden beneath the 16th-century Chiesa di San Giuseppe dei Falegnami, the Mamertine Prison was ancient Rome's maximum-security jail. St Peter did time here and, while imprisoned, supposedly created a miraculous stream of water to baptise his jailers.

On its bare stone walls you can make out traces of medieval frescoes depicting Jesus, the Virgin Mary and Sts Peter and Paul.

Imperial Forums   ARCHAEOLOGICAL SITE
(Fori Imperiali; Map p80; Via dei Fori Imperiali; ◳ Via dei Fori Imperiali) Visible from Via dei Fori Imperiali and, when it's open, Via Alessandrina, the forums of Trajan, Augustus, Nerva and Caesar are known collectively as the Imperial Forums. These were largely buried when Mussolini bulldozed Via dei Fori Imperiali through the area in 1933, but excavations have since unearthed much of them. The standout sights are the **Mercati di Traiano** (Trajan's Markets), accessible through the Museo dei Fori Imperiali, and the landmark **Colonna Traiana** (Trajan's Column).

Little recognisable remains of the **Foro di Traiano** (Trajan's Forum), except for some pillars from the **Basilica Ulpia** and the Colonna Traiana, the minutely detailed reliefs of which celebrate Trajan's military victories over the Dacians (from modern-day Romania).

To the southeast, three temple columns arise from the ruins of the **Foro di Augusto** (Augustus' Forum), now mostly under Via dei Fori Imperiali. The 30m-high wall behind the forum was built to protect it from the fires that frequently swept down from the nearby Suburra slums.

The **Foro di Nerva** (Nerva's Forum) was also buried by Mussolini's road-building, although part of a temple dedicated to Minerva still stands. Originally, it would have connected the Foro di Augusto to the 1st-century **Foro di Vespasiano** (Vespasian's Forum), also known as the Foro della Pace (Forum of Peace). On the other side of the road, three columns on a raised platform are the most visible remains of the **Foro di Cesare** (Caesar's Forum).

★ Mercati di Traiano
Museo dei Fori Imperiali   MUSEUM
(Map p80; ☑ 06 06 08; www.mercatiditraiano. it; Via IV Novembre 94; adult/reduced €11.50/9.50; ⊙ 9.30am-7.30pm, last admission 6.30pm; ◳ Via IV Novembre) This striking museum brings to life the **Mercati di Traiano**, Emperor Trajan's great 2nd-century complex, while also providing a fascinating introduction to the Imperial Forums with multimedia displays,

explanatory panels and a smattering of archaeological artefacts.

Sculptures, friezes and the occasional bust are set out in rooms opening onto what was once the Great Hall. But even more than the exhibits, the real highlight here is the chance to explore the echoing ruins of the vast complex. The three-storey hemicycle was originally thought to have housed markets and shops – hence its name – but historians now believe it was largely used to house the forum's administrative offices.

Rising above the markets is the **Torre delle Milizie** (Militia Tower; Map p80; 🚇 Via IV Novembre), a 13th-century red-brick tower.

Piazza del Campidoglio
PIAZZA

(Map p80; 🚇 Piazza Venezia) This hilltop piazza, designed by Michelangelo in 1538, is one of Rome's most beautiful squares. There are several approaches but the most dramatic is via the graceful **Cordonata** staircase up from Piazza d'Aracoeli.

The piazza is flanked by **Palazzo Nuovo** and **Palazzo dei Conservatori**, together home to the Capitoline Museums, and **Palazzo Senatorio**, the seat of Rome city council. In the centre is a copy of an **equestrian statue** of Marcus Aurelius. The original, which dates to the 2nd century AD, is in the Capitoline Museums.

Chiesa di Santa Maria in Aracoeli
CHURCH

(Map p80; Scala dell'Arce Capitolina; ⊙ 9am-6.30pm summer, to 5.30pm winter; 🚇 Piazza Venezia) Atop the steep 14th-century Aracoeli staircase, this 6th-century Romanesque church marks the highest point of the Campidoglio. Its rich interior boasts several treasures including a wooden gilt ceiling, an impressive Cosmatesque floor and a series of 15th-century Pinturicchio frescoes illustrating the life of St Bernardine of Siena. Its main claim to fame, though, is a wooden baby Jesus that's thought to have healing powers.

Vittoriano
MONUMENT

(Victor Emanuel Monument; Map p80; Piazza Venezia; ⊙ 9.30am-5.30pm summer, to 4.30pm winter; 🚇 Piazza Venezia) **FREE** Love it or loathe it (as many Romans do), you can't ignore the Vittoriano (aka the Altare della Patria, Altar of the Fatherland), the massive mountain of white marble that towers over Piazza Vene-

zia. Begun in 1885 to honour Italy's first king, Vittorio Emanuele II – who's immortalised in its vast equestrian statue – it incorporates the **Museo Centrale del Risorgimento** (📞 06 679 35 98; www.risorgimento.it; adult/reduced €5/2.50; ⊙ 9.30am-6.30pm), a small museum documenting Italian unification, and the **Tomb of the Unknown Soldier**.

For Rome's best 360-degree views, take the **Roma dal Cielo** (Map p80; adult/reduced €7/3.50; ⊙ 9.30am-7.30pm, last admission 7pm) lift to the top.

Housed in the monument's eastern wing is the **Complesso del Vittoriano** (📞 06 871 51 11; www.ilvittoriano.com; Via di San Pietro in Carcere; admission fee variable; ⊙ 9.30am-7.30pm Mon-Thu, to 10pm Fri & Sat, to 8.30pm Sun; 🚇 Via dei Fori Imperiali), a gallery space that regularly hosts major art exhibitions.

Palazzo Venezia
HISTORIC BUILDING

(Map p80; Piazza Venezia; 🚇 Piazza Venezia) Built between 1455 and 1464, this was the first of Rome's great Renaissance palaces. For centuries it served as the embassy of the Venetian Republic – hence its name – but it's most readily associated with Mussolini, who installed his office here in 1929, and famously made speeches from the balcony. Nowadays, it's home to the tranquil **Museo Nazionale del Palazzo Venezia** (📞 06 6999 4283; www.museopalazzovenezia.beniculturali.it; Via del Plebiscito 118; adult/reduced €5/2.50; ⊙ 8.30am-7.30pm Tue-Sun) and its eclectic collection of Byzantine and early Renaissance paintings, ceramics, bronze figures, weaponry and armour.

Basilica di San Marco
BASILICA

(Map p80, Piazza di San Marco 48; ⊙ 10am-1pm Tue-Sun & 4-6pm Tue-Fri, 4-8pm Sat & Sun; 🚇 Piazza Venezia) The early-4th-century Basilica di San Marco stands over the house where St Mark the Evangelist is said to have stayed while in Rome. Its main attraction is the golden 9th-century apse mosaic showing Christ flanked by several saints and Pope Gregory IV.

Bocca della Verità
MONUMENT

(Mouth of Truth; Map p80; Piazza Bocca della Verità 18; ⊙ 9.30am-5.50pm; 🚇 Piazza Bocca della Verità) A bearded face carved into a giant marble disc, the *Bocca della Verità* is one of Rome's most popular curiosities. Legend has

Continued on p82

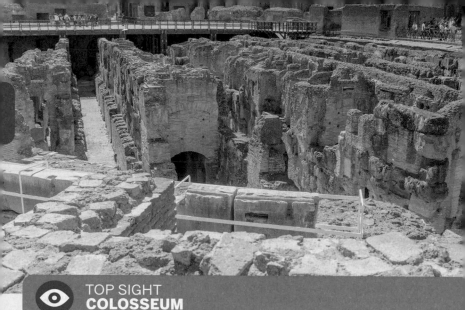

◉ TOP SIGHT
COLOSSEUM

An awesome, spine-tingling sight, the Colosseum is the most thrilling of Rome's ancient monuments. It was here that gladiators met in mortal combat and condemned prisoners fought off wild beasts in front of baying, bloodthirsty crowds. Two thousand years on and it's one of Italy's top tourist attractions, drawing more than six million visitors a year.

The Exterior

The outer walls have three levels of arches, framed by decorative columns topped by capitals of the Ionic (at the bottom), Doric and Corinthian (at the top) orders. They were originally covered in travertine and marble statues filled the niches on the 2nd and 3rd storeys. The upper level, punctuated with windows and slender Corinthian pilasters, had supports for 240 masts that held the awning over the arena, shielding the spectators from sun and rain. The 80 entrance arches, known as *vomitoria*, allowed the spectators to enter and be seated in a matter of minutes.

The Arena

The stadium originally had a wooden floor covered in sand – *harena* in Latin, hence the word 'arena' – to prevent combatants from slipping and to soak up spilt blood.

From the floor, trapdoors led down to the hypogeum, a subterranean complex of corridors, cages and lifts beneath the arena floor.

DON'T MISS
→ The stands
→ The arena
→ The hypogeum

PRACTICALITIES
→ Colosseo
→ Map p80
→ ☏ 06 3996 7700
→ www.coopculture.it
→ Piazza del Colosseo
→ adult/reduced incl Roman Forum & Palatino €12/7.50
→ ⊙ 8.30am-1hr before sunset
→ Ⓜ Colosseo

Hypogeum

The hypogeum served as the stadium's backstage area. It was here that stage sets were prepared and combatants, both human and animal, would gather before showtime.

'Gladiators entered the hypogeum through an underground corridor which led directly in from the nearby Ludus Magnus (gladiator school)', explains the Colosseum's Technical Director, Barbara Nazzaro.

A second gallery, the so-called Passaggio di Commodo (Passage of Commodus), was reserved for the emperor, allowing him to avoid the crowds as he entered the stadium.

To hoist people, animals and scenery up to the arena, the hypogeum had a sophisticated network of 80 winch-operated lifts, all controlled by a single pulley system.

The Seating

The *cavea,* or spectator seating, was divided into three tiers: magistrates and senior officials sat in the lowest tier, wealthy citizens in the middle and the plebs in the highest tier. Women (except for Vestal Virgins) were relegated to the cheapest sections at the top. And as in modern stadiums, tickets were numbered and spectators were assigned a precise seat in a specific sector – in 2015, restorers uncovered traces of red numerals on the arches, indicating how the sectors were numbered.

The podium, a broad terrace in front of the tiers of seats, was reserved for the emperor, senators and VIPs.

TOP TIPS

➡ Visit in the early morning or late afternoon to avoid the crowds.

➡ If queues are long, get your ticket at the Palatino, about 250m away at Via di San Gregorio 30.

➡ Other queue-jumping tips: book your ticket online at www.coopculture.it (plus a €2 booking fee); get the Roma Pass; or join an official English-language tour (€5 on top of the regular ticket price).

➡ The hypogeum, along with the top tier, can be visited on a guided tour. This must be booked in advance and costs €9 plus the normal Colosseum ticket.

THE NAME

The arena was originally known as the Flavian Amphitheatre (Anfiteatro di Flavio) in honour of Vespasian's family name, and although it was Rome's most fearsome arena, it wasn't the biggest – the Circo Massimo could hold up to 250,000 people. The name Colosseum, when introduced in the Middle Ages, wasn't a reference to its size but to the Colosso di Nerone, a giant statue of Nero that stood nearby.

⊙ TOP SIGHT
PALATINO

Sandwiched between the Roman Forum and the Circo Massimo, the Palatino (Palatine Hill) is an atmospheric area of towering pine trees, majestic ruins and memorable views. It was here that Romulus supposedly founded the city in 753 BC and Rome's emperors lived in unabashed luxury.

Historical Development

Roman myth holds that Romulus founded Rome on the Palatino after he'd killed his twin Remus in a fit of anger. Archaeological evidence clearly can't prove this, but it has dated human habitation on the hill to the 8th century BC.

As the most central of Rome's seven hills, and because it was close to the Roman Forum, the Palatino was ancient Rome's most exclusive neighbourhood. The emperor Augustus lived here all his life and successive emperors built increasingly opulent palaces. But after Rome's fall, it fell into disrepair and in the Middle Ages churches and castles were built over the ruins. Later, wealthy Renaissance families established gardens on the hill. Most of the Palatino as it appears today is covered by the ruins of Emperor Domitian's vast complex, which served as the main imperial palace for 300 years. Divided into the Domus Flavia, Domus Augustana, and a *stadio* (stadium), it was built in the 1st century AD.

Stadio

On entering the Palatino from Via di San Gregorio, head uphill until you come to the first recognisable construction, the *stadio*. This sunken area, which was part of the main imperial palace, was used by the emperor for private games. A path to the side of the *stadio* leads

DON'T MISS

- ➡ Stadio
- ➡ Domus Augustana
- ➡ Orti Farnesiani

PRACTICALITIES

- ➡ Palatine Hill
- ➡ Map p80
- ➡ ☑ 06 3996 7700
- ➡ www.coopculture.it
- ➡ Via di San Gregorio 30, Piazza di Santa Maria Nova
- ➡ adult/reduced incl Colosseum & Roman Forum €12/7.50
- ➡ ⊙ 8.30am-1hr before sunset
- ➡ Ⓜ Colosseo

to the towering remains of a complex built by Septimius Severus, comprising baths (**Terme di Settimio Severo**) and a palace (**Domus Severiana**) where, if they're open, you can visit the **Arcate Severiane** (Severian Arches; admission incl in Palatino ticket; ⊘8.30am-4pm Tue, Thu & Fri), a series of arches built to facilitate further development.

Casa di Livia & Casa di Augusto

Among the best-preserved buildings on the Palatino is the **Casa di Livia** (incl Casa di Augusto visit/guided tour €4/9; ⊘visits 12.45pm daily, pre-booking necessary), northwest of the Domus Flavia. Home to Augustus' wife Livia, it was built around an atrium leading onto fres coed reception rooms. Nearby, the **Casa di Augusto** (incl Casa di Livia visit/guided tour €4/9; ⊘visits 12.45pm daily, reservations necessary), Augustus' private residence, features some superb frescoes in vivid reds, yellows and blues.

Domus Augustana & Domus Flavia

Next to the *stadio* are the ruins of the Domus Augustana, the emperor's private quarters in the imperial palace. This was built on two levels, with rooms leading off a *peristilio* (peristyle or porticoed courtyard) on each floor. You can't get down to the lower level, but from above you can see the basin of a big, square fountain and beyond it rooms that would originally have been paved in coloured marble.

North of the Museo Palatino is the Domus Flavia, the public part of the palace. This was centred on a grand columned peristyle off which the main halls led: the emperor's audience chamber (*aula Regia*); a basilica where the emperor judged legal disputes; and a large banqueting hall, the triclinium.

Museo Palatino

The grey building next to the Domus houses the **Museo Palatino** (admission incl in Palatino ticket; ⊘8.30am-1½hr before sunset; Ⓜ Colosseo), a small museum dedicated to the history of the area. Archaeological artefacts on show include a beautiful 1st-century bronze, the *Erma di Canefora*, and a celebrated 3rd-century graffito depicting a man with a donkey's head being crucified.

Orti Farnesiani

Covering the Domus Tiberiana (Tiberius' palace) in the northwest corner of the Palatino, the Orti Farnesiani is one of Europe's earliest botanical gardens. Named after Cardinal Alessandro Farnese, who had it laid out in the mid-16th century, it commands breathtaking views over the Roman Forum.

TOP TIPS

➜ Enjoy stunning views over the Roman Forum from the viewing balcony in the Orti Farnesiani.

➜ You'll need to book if you want to visit the Casa di Livia and Casa di Augusto. English-language guided tours run at 1.45pm Saturday and Sunday.

ROMULUS & REMUS

Rome's mythical founders were supposedly brought up on the Palatino by a shepherd, Faustulus, after a wolf had saved them from death. Their shelter, the 8th-century-BC **Capanne Romulee** (Romulean Huts), is situated near the Casa di Augusto.

In 2007 the discovery of a mosaic-covered cave 15m beneath the Domus Augustana reignited interest in the legend. According to some scholars, this was the *Lupercale*, the cave believed by ancient Romans to be where Romulus and Remus were suckled by a wolf.

TOP SIGHT
ROMAN FORUM

The Roman Forum was ancient Rome's showpiece centre, a grandiose district of temples, basilicas and vibrant public spaces. Nowadays, it's a collection of impressive, if sketchily labelled, ruins that can leave you drained and confused. But if you can get your imagination going, there's something wonderfully compelling about walking in the footsteps of Julius Caesar and other legendary figures of Roman history.

Via Sacra Towards Campidoglio

Entering from Largo della Salara Vecchia – you can also enter from the Palatino or via an entrance near the Arco di Tito – you'll see the **Tempio di Antonino e Faustina** (pictured above) ahead to your left. Erected in AD 141, this was transformed into a church in the 8th century, the Chiesa di San Lorenzo in Miranda. To your right, the 179 BC **Basilica Fulvia Aemilia** was a 100m-long public hall with a two-storey porticoed facade.

At the end of the path you'll come to **Via Sacra**, the Forum's main thoroughfare, and the **Tempio di Giulio Cesare** (also known as the Tempio del Divo Giulio). Built by Augustus in 29 BC, this marks the spot where Julius Caesar was cremated.

Heading right up Via Sacra brings you to the **Curia**, the original seat of the Roman Senate. This barn-like construction was rebuilt on various occasions and what you see today is a 1937 reconstruction of how it looked in the reign of Diocletian (r 284–305).

DON'T MISS

➜ Curia

➜ Arco di Settimio Severo

➜ Tempio di Saturno

➜ Chiesa di Santa Maria Antiqua

➜ Casa delle Vestali

➜ Basilica di Massenzio

➜ Arco di Tito

PRACTICALITIES

➜ Foro Romano

➜ Map p80

➜ ☑ 06 3996 7700

➜ www.coopculture.it

➜ Largo della Salara Vecchia, Piazza di Santa Maria Nova

➜ adult/reduced incl Colosseum & Palatino €12/7.50

➜ ⊙ 8.30am-1hr before sunset

➜ 🚇 Via dei Fori Imperiali

In front of the Curia, and hidden by scaffolding, is the **Lapis Niger**, a large piece of black marble that's said to cover the tomb of Romulus.

At the end of Via Sacra, the 23m-high **Arco di Settimio Severo** is dedicated to the eponymous emperor and his sons, Caracalla and Geta. Close by are the remains of the **Rostri**, an elaborate podium where Shakespeare had Mark Antony make his famous 'Friends, Romans, countrymen...' speech. Facing this, the **Colonna di Foca** rises above what was once the Forum's main square, **Piazza del Foro**.

The eight granite columns that rise behind the Colonna are all that survive of the **Tempio di Saturno**, an important temple that doubled as the state treasury. Behind it are (from north to south): the ruins of the **Tempio della Concordia**, the **Tempio di Vespasiano** and the **Portico degli Dei Consenti**.

Via Sacra Towards Colosseum

Returning to Via Sacra you'll come to the **Casa delle Vestali**, home of the virgins who tended the flame in the adjoining Tempio di Vesta.

Further on, past the **Tempio di Romolo**, is the **Basilica di Massenzio**, the largest building on the Forum. Started by the emperor Maxentius and finished by Constantine in 315, it originally measured approximately 100m by 65m.

Beyond the basilica, the **Arco di Tito** was built in AD 81 to celebrate Vespasian and Titus' victories against rebels in Jerusalem.

Chiesa di Santa Maria Antiqua

The 6th-century **Chiesa di Santa Maria Antiqua** is the oldest Christian monument in the Forum. A treasure trove of early Christian art, it boasts exquisite 6th- to 9th-century frescoes and a hanging depiction of the Virgin Mary with child, one of the earliest icons in existence.

In front of the church is the **Rampa imperiale** (Imperial Ramp), a vast underground passageway that allowed the emperors to access the Forum from their Palatine palaces without being seen.

THE VESTAL VIRGINS

Despite privilege and public acclaim, life as a Vestal Virgin was no bed of roses. Every year, six physically perfect patrician girls aged between six and 10 were chosen by lottery to serve Vesta, goddess of hearth and household. Once selected, they faced a 30-year period of chaste servitude at the Tempio di Vesta. Their main duty was to ensure the temple's sacred fire never went out. If it did, the priestess responsible would be flogged. If a priestess were to lose her virginity, she risked being buried alive as the offending man was flogged to death.

ROMAN TRIUMPH

The Forum's main drag, Via Sacra was the principal route of the Roman Triumph. This official victory parade, originally awarded by the Senate to a victorious general but later reserved for emperors, was a huge spectacle involving a procession from the Porta Triumphalis (Triumphal Gate) through the Forum to the Temple of Jupiter Capitolinus on the Capitoline Hill.

Roman Forum

A HISTORICAL TOUR

In ancient times, a forum was a market place, civic centre and religious complex all rolled into one, and the greatest of all was the Roman Forum (Foro Romano). Situated between the Palatino (Palatine Hill), ancient Rome's most exclusive neighbourhood, and the Campidoglio (Capitoline Hill), it was the city's busy, bustling centre. On any given day it teemed with activity. Senators debated affairs of state in the **1 Curia**, shoppers thronged the squares and traffic-free streets and crowds gathered under the **2 Colonna di Foca** to listen to politicians holding forth from the **2 Rostri**. Elsewhere, lawyers worked the courts in basilicas including the **3 Basilica di Massenzio**, while the Vestal Virgins quietly went about their business in the **4 Casa delle Vestali**.

Special occasions were also celebrated in the Forum: religious holidays were marked with ceremonies at temples such as **5 Tempio di Saturno** and **6 Tempio di Castore e Polluce**, and military victories were honoured with dramatic processions up Via Sacra and the building of monumental arches like **7 Arco di Settimio Severo** and **8 Arco di Tito**.

The ruins you see today are impressive but they can be confusing without a clear picture of what the Forum once looked like. This spread shows the Forum in its heyday, complete with temples, civic buildings and towering monuments to heroes of the Roman Empire.

TOP TIPS

➡ Get grandstand views of the Forum from the Palatino and Campidoglio.

➡ Visit first thing in the morning or late afternoon; crowds are worst between 11am and 2pm.

➡ In summer it gets hot in the Forum and there's little shade, so take a hat and plenty of water.

Colonna di Foca & Rostri

The free-standing, 13.5m-high Column of Phocus is the Forum's youngest monument, dating to AD 608. Behind it, the Rostri provided a suitably grandiose platform for pontificating public speakers.

Campidoglio (Capitoline Hill)

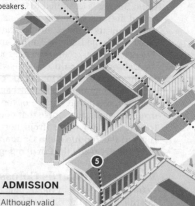

ADMISSION

Although valid for two days, admission tickets only allow for one entry into the Forum, Colosseum and Palatino.

Tempio di Saturno

Ancient Rome's Fort Knox, the Temple of Saturn was the city treasury. In Caesar's day it housed 13 tonnes of gold, 114 tonnes of silver and 30 million sestertii worth of silver coins.

IASCIC/SHUTTERSTOCK ©

VIACHESLAV LOPATIN/SHUTTERSTOCK ©

Tempio di Castore e Polluce

Only three columns of the Temple of Castor and Pollux remain. The temple was dedicated to the Heavenly Twins after they supposedly led the Romans to victory over the Latin League in 496 BC.

Arco di Settimio Severo

One of the Forum's signature monuments, this imposing triumphal arch commemorates the military victories of Septimius Severus. Relief panels depict his campaigns against the Parthians.

Curia

This big barn-like building was the official seat of the Roman Senate. Most of what you see is a reconstruction, but the interior marble floor dates to the 3rd-century reign of Diocletian.

Basilica di Massenzio

Marvel at the scale of this vast 4th-century basilica. In its original form the central hall was divided into enormous naves; now only part of the northern nave survives.

JULIUS CAESAR

Julius Caesar was cremated on the site where the Tempio di Giulio Cesare now stands.

Via Sacra

Templo di Giulio Cesare

Arco di Tito

Said to be the inspiration for the Arc de Triomphe in Paris, the well-preserved Arch of Titus was built by the emperor Domitian to honour his elder brother Titus.

Casa delle Vestali

White statues line the grassy atrium of what was once the luxurious 50-room home of the Vestal Virgins. The virgins played an important role in Roman religion, serving the goddess Vesta.

TOP SIGHT
CAPITOLINE MUSEUMS

Housed in two stately *palazzi* on Piazza del Campidoglio, the Capitoline Museums are the world's oldest public museums. Their origins date to 1471, when Pope Sixtus IV donated a number of bronze statues to the city, forming the nucleus of what is now one of Italy's finest collections of classical sculpture. There's also a formidable picture gallery with works by many big-name Italian artists.

Entrance & Courtyard

The entrance to the museums is in **Palazzo dei Conservatori**, where you'll find the original core of the sculptural collection on the 1st floor, and the Pinacoteca (picture gallery) on the 2nd floor.

Before you head up to start on the sculpture collection proper, take a moment to admire the marble body parts littered around the ground-floor **courtyard**. The mammoth head, hand, and feet all belonged to a 12m-high statue of Constantine that once stood in the Basilica di Massenzio in the Roman Forum.

Palazzo dei Conservatori

Of the permanent sculpture collection on the 1st floor, the Etruscan *Lupa Capitolina* (Capitoline Wolf) is the most famous piece. Standing in the **Sala della Lupa**, this 5th-century-BC bronze wolf stands over her suckling wards, Romulus and Remus, who were added to the composition in 1471.

DON'T MISS

- ➡ *Lupa Capitolina*
- ➡ *Spinario*
- ➡ *La Buona Ventura*
- ➡ *Galata Morente*
- ➡ *Venere Capitolina*

PRACTICALITIES

- ➡ Musei Capitolini
- ➡ Map p80
- ➡ ☑ 06 06 08
- ➡ www.museicapitolini.org
- ➡ Piazza del Campidoglio 1
- ➡ adult/reduced €11.50/9.50
- ➡ ⊙ 9.30am-7.30pm, last admission 6.30pm
- ➡ ▢ Piazza Venezia

Other crowd-pleasers include the *Spinario,* a delicate 1st-century-BC bronze of a boy removing a thorn from his foot in the **Sala dei Trionfi**, and Gian Lorenzo Bernini's *Medusa* bust in the **Sala delle Oche**.

Also on this floor, in the modern wing known as the **Esedra di Marco Aurelio**, is an imposing bronze **equestrian statue** of the emperor Marcus Aurelius – the original of the copy that stands in the piazza outside. Here you can also see the foundations of the Temple of Jupiter, one of the ancient city's most important temples that once stood on the Capitoline Hill.

Palazzo Nuovo

This *palazzo* is crammed to its elegant 17th-century rafters with classical Roman sculpture.

From the lobby, where the curly-bearded **Mars** glares ferociously at everyone who passes by, stairs lead up to the main galleries where you'll find some real showstoppers. Chief among them is the *Galata Morente* (Dying Gaul) in the **Sala del Gladiatore**. One of the museum's greatest works, this sublime piece, actually a Roman copy of a 3rd-century-BC Greek original, movingly captures the quiet, resigned anguish of a dying Gaul warrior.

Next door, the **Sala del Fauno** takes its name from the red marble statue of a faun.

Another superb figurative piece is the sensual yet demure portrayal of the *Venere Capitolina* (Capitoline Venus) in the **Gabinetto della Venere**, off the main corridor.

Also worth a look are the busts of philosophers, orators and poets in the **Sala dei Filosofi** – look out for likenesses of Homer, Pythagoras, Socrates and Cicero.

Pinacoteca

The 2nd floor of Palazzo dei Conservatori is given over to the Pinacoteca, the museum's picture gallery. Dating to 1749, the collection is arranged chronologically with works from the Middle Ages through to the 18th century.

Each room harbours masterpieces but two stand out: the **Sala Pietro da Cortona**, which features Pietro da Cortona's famous depiction of the *Ratto delle sabine* (Rape of the Sabine Women; 1630), and the **Sala di Santa Petronilla**, named after Guercino's huge canvas *Seppellimento di Santa Petronilla* (The Burial of St Petronilla; 1621–23). This airy hall boasts a number of important canvases, including two by Caravaggio: *La Buona Ventura* (The Fortune Teller; 1595), which shows a gypsy pretending to read a young man's hand but actually stealing his ring, and *San Giovanni Battista* (John the Baptist; 1602), an unusual nude depiction of the youthful New Testament saint with a ram.

TOP TIPS

➡ Note that ticket prices increase, typically to around €15/13, when there's an exhibition on.

➡ Don't leave it too late – the museums are open until 7.30pm but last admission is an hour earlier at 6.30pm.

➡ Have a camera handy for the views over the Roman Forum from the Tabularium.

TREATY OF ROME

With frescoes depicting episodes from ancient Roman history and two papal statues – one of Urban VIII by Bernini and one of Innocent X by Algardi – the **Sala degli Orazi e Curiazi** provided the grand setting for one of modern Europe's key events. On 25 March 1957 the leaders of Italy, France, West Germany, Belgium, Holland and Luxembourg gathered here to sign the Treaty of Rome and establish the European Economic Community, the precursor of the European Union.

THE CONSERVATORI

Palazzo dei Conservatori takes its name from the *Conservatori* (elected magistrates) who used to hold their public hearings in the *palazzo* in the mid-15th century.

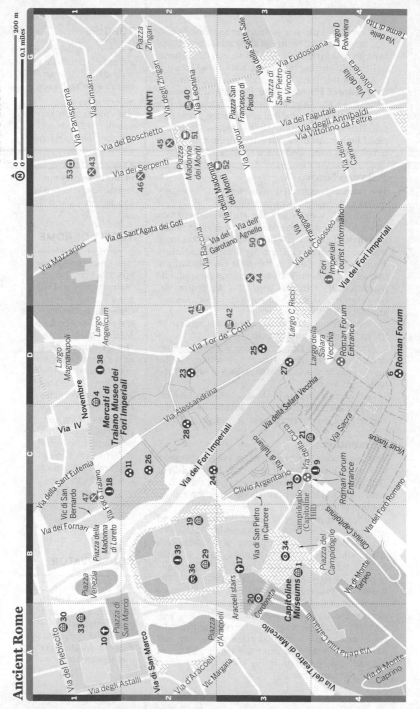

Ancient Rome

MONTI

Piazza Zingari

Via Panisperna

Via Cimarra

Via del Boschetto

Via dei Serpenti

Via degli Zingari

Via Leonina

Piazza San Francesco di Paola

Via delle Sette Sale

Via di San Pietro in Vincoli

Via Eudossiana

Largo D Polveriera

Via delle Terme di Tito

Via della Polveriera

Via del Fagutale

Via degli Annibaldi
Via Vittorino da Feltre

Piazza Madonna dei Monti

Via della Madonna dei Monti

Via Cavour

Via delle Carine

Via di Sant'Agata dei Goti

Via Mazzarino

Via Baccina

Via del Garotano Agnello

Via dell' Agnello

Via del Colosseo

Fori Imperiali Tourist Information

Via dei Fori Imperiali

Largo Angelicum

Largo Magnanapoli

Largo C Ricci

Via Tor de' Conti

Via Alessandrina

Largo della Salara Vecchia

Roman Forum Entrance

Roman Forum

Largo Novembre

Via IV Novembre

Mercati di Traiano Museo dei Fori Imperiali

Via della Sant'Eufemia

Via Foro Traiano

Via dei Fornari

Piazza della Madonna di Loreto

Via dei Fori Imperiali

Via della Salara Vecchia

Via della Curia

Via Sacra

Clivio Argentario

Roman Forum Entrance

Vicus Tuscus

Via del Foro Romano

Via di Tulliano

Clivus Capitolinus

Via di San Pietro in Carcere

Campidoglio (Capitolino Hill)

Piazza del Campidoglio

Clivius Capitolinus

Via di Monte Tarpeo

Via del Plebiscito

Piazza Venezia

Piazza di San Marco

Via di San Marco

Via degli Astalli

Via d'Aracoeli

Piazza d'Aracoeli

Vic Margana

Via Margana

Aracoeli stairs

Cordonata

Capitoline Museums

Via del Teatro di Marcello

Via della Villa Caffarelli

Via di Monte Caprino

Via IV Novembre

Via di San Bernardo

Vic di San Bernardo

30 33 10 4 38 53 43 46 45 40 51 52 50 44 41 42 47 18 11 26 28 23 25 27 13 9 21 6 24 19 39 36 29 17 20 34 1

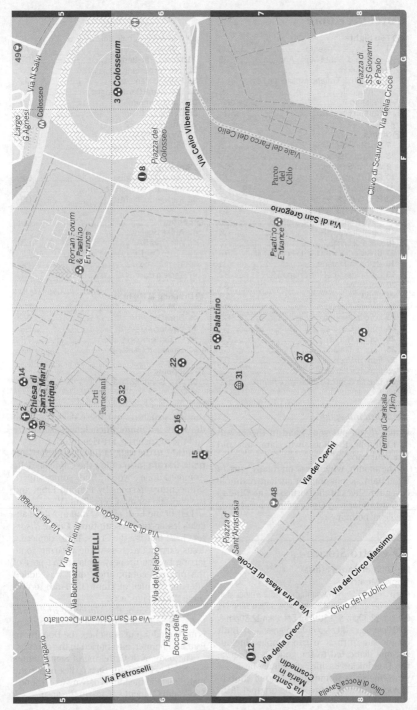

Colosseum

Largo
G Agnesi

Via N Salvi

49

Via del Colosseo

3 Colosseum

8

Piazza del
Colosseo

Via Celio Vibenna

Piazza di
SS Giovanni
e Paolo

Via della Croce

Viale del Parco del Celio

Clivo di Scauro

Roman Forum
& Palatine
Entrance

Parco
del Celio

Via di San Gregorio

Palatino
Entrance

14
2 Chiesa di
Santa Maria
Antiqua
35

5 Palatino

22

32

Orti
Farnesiani

31

37

7

16

15

Via dei Cerchi

Terme di Caracalla
(1km)

48

Via del Fienili

CAMPITELLI

Via del Velabro

Via di San Teodoro

Piazza d'
Sant'Anastasia

Via d Ara Mass di Ercole

Via del Circo Massimo

Clivo dei Publici

Vic Jungario

Via Bucimazza

Via di San Giovanni Decollato

Piazza
Bocca della
Verità

Via della Greca

12

Via Santa
Maria in
Cosmedin

Clivo di Rocca Savella

Via Petroselli

Ancient Rome

Continued from p69

it that if you put your hand in the mouth and tell a lie, the Bocca will slam shut and bite your hand off.

The mouth, which was originally part of a fountain, or possibly an ancient manhole cover, now lives in the portico of the **Chiesa di Santa Maria in Cosmedin**, a handsome medieval church.

◎ Centro Storico

Basilica di Santa Maria
Sopra Minerva   BASILICA
(Map p86; www.santamariasopraminerva.it; Piazza della Minerva 42; ☺ 6.40am-7pm Mon-Fri, 6.40am-12.30pm & 3.30-7pm Sat, 8am-12.30pm & 3.30-7pm Sun; ☐ Largo di Torre Argentina) Built on the site of three pagan temples, including one dedicated to the goddess Minerva, the Dominican Basilica di Santa Maria Sopra Minerva is Rome's only Gothic church. However, little remains of the original 13th-century structure and these days the main drawcard is a minor Michelangelo sculpture and the magisterial, art-rich interior.

Inside, to the right of the altar in the **Cappella Carafa** (also called the Cappella della Annunciazione), you'll find some superb 15th-century frescoes by Filippino Lippi and the majestic tomb of Pope Paul IV.

Left of the high altar is one of Michelangelo's lesser-known sculptures, *Cristo Risorto* (Christ Bearing the Cross; 1520), depicting Jesus carrying a cross while wearing some jarring bronze drapery. This wasn't part of the original composition and was added after the Council of Trent (1545–63) to preserve Christ's modesty.

An altarpiece of the *Madonna and Child* in the second chapel in the northern transept is attributed to Fra' Angelico, the Dominican friar and painter, also buried in the church.

The body of St Catherine of Siena, minus her head (which is in Siena), lies under the high altar, and the tombs of two Medici popes, Leo X and Clement VII, are in the apse.

⭐**Galleria Doria Pamphilj**　　　GALLERY
(Map p86; ☑06 679 73 23; www.doriapamphilj.
it; Via del Corso 305; adult/reduced €12/8; ⊙9am-
7pm, last entry 6pm; 🚇Via del Corso) Hidden
behind the grimy grey exterior of Palazzo Doria Pamphilj, this wonderful gallery
boasts one of Rome's richest private art collections, with works by Raphael, Tintoretto,
Titian, Caravaggio, Bernini and Velázquez,
as well as several Flemish masters. Masterpieces abound, but the undisputed star is
Velázquez' portrait of an implacable Pope
Innocent X, who grumbled that the depiction was 'too real'. For a comparison, check
out Gian Lorenzo Bernini's sculptural interpretation of the same subject.

Chiesa di Sant'Ignazio di Loyola　　CHURCH
(Map p86; www.santignazio.gesuiti.it; Piazza di
Sant'Ignazio; ⊙7.30am-7pm Mon-Sat, 9am-7pm
Sun; 🚇Via del Corso) Flanking a delightful
rococo piazza, this important Jesuit church
boasts a Carlo Maderno facade and two celebrated trompe l'oeil frescoes by Andrea Pozzo (1642–1709). One cleverly depicts a fake
dome, while the other, on the nave ceiling,
shows St Ignatius Loyola being welcomed
into paradise by Christ and the Madonna.

⭐**Chiesa di San Luigi
dei Francesi**　　　　　　CHURCH
(Map p86; Piazza di San Luigi dei Francesi
5; ⊙9.30am-12.45pm & 2.30-6.30pm Mon-Fri,
9.30am-12.15pm & 2.30-6.45pm Sat, 11.30am-
12.45pm & 2.30-6.45pm Sun; 🚇Corso del Rinascimento) Church to Rome's French community
since 1589, this opulent baroque *chiesa*
is home to a celebrated trio of Caravaggio
paintings: the *Vocazione di San Matteo*
(The Calling of Saint Matthew), the *Mar-
tirio di San Matteo* (The Martyrdom of
Saint Matthew) and *San Matteo e l'angelo*
(Saint Matthew and the Angel), known collectively as the St Matthew cycle.

These three canvases, housed in the
Cappella Contarelli to the left of the main
altar, are among the earliest of Caravaggio's
religious works, painted between 1600 and
1602, but they are inescapably his, featuring
a down-to-earth realism and the stunning
use of chiaroscuro (the bold contrast of light
and dark).

Before you leave the church, take a
moment to enjoy Domenichino's faded
17th-century frescoes of St Cecilia in the
second chapel on the right. St Cecilia is also
depicted in the altarpiece by Guido Reni,
which is a copy of a work by Raphael.

⭐**Museo Nazionale Romano:
Palazzo Altemps**　　　　MUSEUM
(Map p86; ☑06 3996 7700; www.coopculture.it;
Piazza Sant'Apollinare 44; adult/reduced €7/3.50;
⊙9am-7.45pm Tue-Sun; 🚇Corso del Rinascimento) Just north of Piazza Navona,
Palazzo Altemps is a beautiful late-15th-
century *palazzo* housing the best of the
Museo Nazionale Romano's formidable collection of classical sculpture. Many pieces
come from the celebrated Ludovisi collection, amassed by Cardinal Ludovico Ludovisi in the 17th century.

Prize exhibits include the beautiful
5th-century *Trono Ludovisi* (Ludovisi
Throne), a carved marble block whose central relief depicts a naked Venus (Aphrodite)
being modestly plucked from the sea. In the
neighbouring room, the *Ares Ludovisi*, a
2nd-century-BC representation of a young,
clean-shaven Mars, owes its right foot to a
Gian Lorenzo Bernini restoration in 1622.

Another affecting work is the sculptural
group *Galata Suicida* (Gaul's Suicide), a
melodramatic depiction of a Gaul knifing
himself to death over a dead woman.

The building itself provides an elegant
backdrop with a grand central courtyard
and frescoed rooms. These include the **Sala
delle Prospettive Dipinte**, which was
painted with landscapes and hunting scenes
for Cardinal Altemps, the rich nephew of
Pope Pius IV (r 1560–65) who bought the
palazzo in the late 16th century.

The museum also houses the Museo Nazi-
onal Romano's Egyptian collection.

⭐**Piazza Navona**　　　　PIAZZA
(Map p86; 🚇Corso del Rinascimento) With
its showy fountains, baroque *palazzi* and
colourful cast of street artists, hawkers and
tourists, Piazza Navona is central Rome's
elegant showcase square. Built over the
1st-century **Stadio di Domiziano** (Domitian's
Stadium; ☑06 4568 6100; www.stadiodomiziano.
com; Via di Tor Sanguigna 3; adult/reduced €8/6;
⊙10am-7pm Sun-Fri, to 8pm Sat), it was paved
over in the 15th century and for almost
300 years hosted the city's main market. Its
grand centrepiece is Bernini's **Fontana dei
Quattro Fiumi** (Fountain of the Four Rivers), a
flamboyant fountain featuring an Egyptian
obelisk and muscular personifications of the
rivers Nile, Ganges, Danube and Plate.

Legend has it that the Nile figure is
shielding his eyes from the nearby **Chiesa**

Continued on p88

TOP SIGHT
PANTHEON

A striking 2000-year-old temple, now a church, the Pantheon is Rome's best-preserved ancient monument and one of the most influential buildings in the Western world. Its greying, pockmarked exterior might look its age, but inside it's a different story, and it's a unique and exhilarating experience to pass through its vast bronze doors and gaze up at the largest unreinforced concrete dome ever built.

History

In its current form the Pantheon dates to around AD 125. The original temple, built by Marcus Agrippa in 27 BC, burnt down in AD 80, and although it was rebuilt by Domitian, it was struck by lightning and destroyed for a second time in AD 110. The emperor Hadrian had it reconstructed between AD 118 and 125, and it's his version you see today.

Hadrian's temple was dedicated to the classical gods – hence the name Pantheon, a derivation of the Greek words *pan* (all) and *theos* (god) – but in 608 it was consecrated as a Christian church after the Byzantine emperor Phocus donated it to Pope Boniface IV. It was dedicated to the Virgin Mary and all the martyrs and took on the name by which it is still officially known, the Basilica di Santa Maria ad Martyres.

Thanks to this consecration, it was spared the worst of the medieval plundering that reduced many of Rome's ancient buildings to near dereliction. But it didn't escape entirely unscathed – its gilded-bronze roof tiles were removed and, in the 17th century, Pope Urban VIII had the portico's bronze ceiling melted down to make 80 canons for Castel Sant'Angelo and to provide Bernini with bronze for the baldachin at St Peter's Basilica.

During the Renaissance, the building was much admired – Brunelleschi used it as inspiration for his cupola in Florence and Michelangelo studied it before designing the dome

DON'T MISS

→ The entrance doors

→ The dome

→ Raphael's tomb

PRACTICALITIES

→ Map p86

→ www.pantheonroma.com

→ Piazza della Rotonda

→ ⊘ 8.30am-7.15pm Mon-Sat, 9am-5.45pm Sun

→ 🚊 Largo di Torre Argentina

at St Peter's Basilica – and it became an important burial chamber. Today, you'll find the tomb of the artist Raphael here alongside those of kings Vittorio Emanuele II and Umberto I.

Exterior

Originally, the Pantheon was on a raised podium, its entrance facing onto a rectangular porticoed piazza. Nowadays, the dark-grey pitted exterior faces onto busy, cafe-lined Piazza della Rotonda. And while its facade is somewhat the worse for wear, it's still an imposing sight. The monumental entrance **portico** consists of 16 Corinthian columns, each 11.8m high and each made from a single block of Egyptian granite, supporting a triangular **pediment**. Behind the columns, two 20-tonne bronze doors – 16th century restorations of the original portal – give onto the central rotunda.

Little remains of the ancient decor, although rivets and holes in the brickwork indicate where marble-veneer panels were once placed.

Interior

Although impressive from outside, it's only when you get inside that you can really appreciate the Pantheon's full size. With light streaming in through the **oculus** (the 8.7m diameter hole in the centre of the dome), the cylindrical marble-clad interior seems vast, an effect that was deliberately designed to cut worshippers down to size in the face of the gods.

Opposite the entrance is the church's main **altar**, over which hangs a 7th century icon of the *Madonna col Bambino* (Madonna and Child). To the left (as you look in from the entrance) is the tomb of Raphael, marked by Lorenzetto's 1520 sculpture of the *Madonna del Sasso* (Madonna of the Rock). Neighbouring it are the tombs of King Umberto I and Margherita of Savoy. Over on the opposite side of the rotunda is the tomb of King Vittorio Emanuele II.

The Dome

The Pantheon's dome, considered the Romans' most important architectural achievement, was the largest dome in the world until the 15th century when Brunelleschi beat it with his Florentine cupola. Its harmonious appearance is due to a precisely calibrated symmetry – its diameter is exactly equal to the building's interior height of 43.4m. At its centre, the oculus, which symbolically connected the temple with the gods, plays a vital structural role by absorbing and redistributing the dome's huge tensile forces.

Radiating out from the oculus are five rows of 28 coffers (indented panels). These were originally ornamented but more importantly served to reduce the cupola's immense weight.

THE INSCRIPTION

For centuries the Latin inscription over the entrance led historians to believe that the current temple was Marcus Agrippa's original. Certainly, the wording suggests this, reading: 'M.AGRIPPA.L.F.COS. TERTIUM.FECIT' or 'Marcus Agrippa, son of Lucius, in his third consulate built this'. However, excavations in the 19th century revealed traces of an earlier temple and scholars realised that Hadrian had simply placed Agrippa's original inscription over his new temple.

PENTECOST AT THE PANTHEON

Each Pentecost, tens of thousands of red petals are rained down on the Pantheon through the oculus. This centuries-old tradition represents the Holy Spirit descending to earth.

BARBERINI & THE BARBARIANS

The stripping of the Pantheon's bronze by the Barberini pope Urban VIII gave rise to the saying, still in use today: 'What the barbarians didn't do, the Barberini did.'

Centro Storico

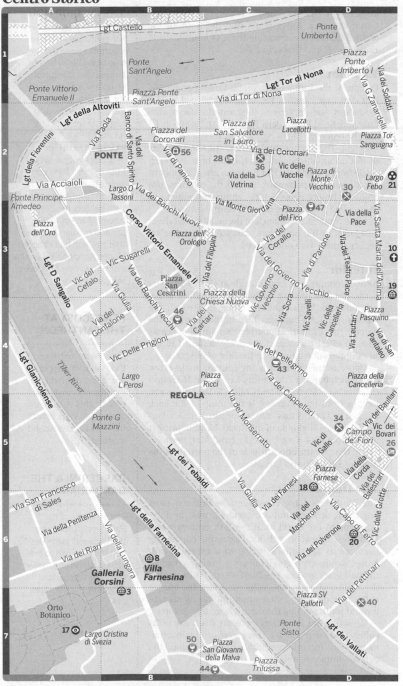

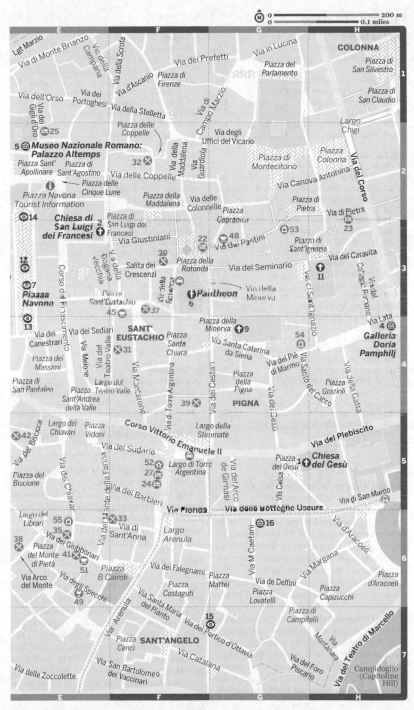

0 ——— 200 m
0 ——— 0.1 miles

COLONNA

Piazza di
San Silvestro

Lgt Marzio

Via di Monte Brianzo

Vic della Campana

Via della Scrofa

Via d'Ascanio

Via dei Prefetti

Via in Lucina

Piazza del
Parlamento

Piazza di
Firenze

Via dell'Orso

Via dei
Portoghesi

Via della Stelletta

Via di Campo Marzio

Piazza di
San Claudio

Via dei Gigli d'Oro

25

Piazza delle
Coppelle

Via degli
Uffici del Vicario

Largo
Chigi

5 **Museo Nazionale Romano:
Palazzo Altemps**

32

Via della Maddalena

Piazza di
Montecitorio

Piazza
Colonna

Via del Corso

Piazza Sant'
Apollinare

Piazza di
Sant'Agostino

Via delle Coppelle

Via Canova Antonina

Piazza delle
Cinque Lune

Piazza della
Maddalena

Via della
Colonnelle

Via
Guardiola

Piazza
Capranica

Piazza di
Pietra

Via di Pietra

Piazza Navona
Tourist Information

14 **Chiesa di
San Luigi
dei Francesi**

2

Piazza di
San Luigi dei
Francesi

Via Giustiniani

22   48

Via dei Pastini

53

Piazza di
Sant'Ignazio

23

Via del Caravita

12

Corso del Rinascimento

Via della
Dogana Vecchia

30

Salita dei
Crescenzi

Piazza della
Rotonda

Via del Seminario

11

7

**Piazza
Navona**

Piazza
Sant'Eustachio

45   37

Via della Rotonda

Pantheon
6

Via della
Minerva

Via di Sant'Ignazio

Via del Collegio Romano

Via Lata

4

13

Via dei
Canestrari

Via dei Sediari

**SANT'
EUSTACHIO**

31

Piazza della
Minerva   9

Piazza
Santa
Chiara

Via Santa Caterina
da Siena

54

**Galleria
Doria
Pamphilj**

Piazza dei
Massimi

Via del
Teatro Valle

Via Melone

Via Monterone

Via dei Cestari

Piazza
della
Pigna

Via del Piè
di Marmo

Via Santa del Caccio

Piazza
Grazioli

Via della Gatta

Piazza di
San Pantaleo

Piazza
Sant'Andrea
della Valle

Largo del
Teatro Valle

Via d. Torre Argentina

39

PIGNA

Via del Gesù

42

Via del Biscione

Largo dei
Chiavari

Piazza
Vidoni

Corso Vittorio Emanuele II

Largo della
Stimmate

Via del Plebiscito

Piazza
del Biscione

Via dei Chiavari

Via del Sudario

52
27
24

Largo di Torre
Argentina

Via dell'Arco
de Ginnasi

Piazza
del Gesù

**Chiesa
del Gesù**

Via Celsa

Via di San Marco

55

35

Via di
Sant'Anna

Via Florida

Via delle Botteghe Oscure

Largni dei
Librari

33

Via del Monte della Farina

Largo
Arenula

16

Via M Caetani

Via d'Aracoeli

38

Piazza
del Monte
di Pietà

Via dei Giubbonari

41

51

Piazza
B Cairoli

Via dei Falegnami

Piazza
Mattei

Via de Delfini

Via Margana

Piazza
d'Aracoeli

Via Arco
del Monte

Via degli Specchi

49

Via Santa Maria
del Pianto

Piazza
Costaguti

Piazza
Lovatelli

Piazza
Capizucchi

Piazza di
Campitelli

Via Montanara

15

Piazza
Cenci

SANT'ANGELO

Via del Portico d'Ottavia

Via Catalana

Via del Foro
Piscario

Via del Teatro di Marcello

Via delle Zoccolette

Via San Bartolomeo
dei Vaccinari

Campidoglio
(Capitoline
Hill)

Centro Storico

Continued from p83

di Sant'Agnese in Agone (Map p86; ☑ 06 6819 2134; www.santagneseinagone.org; Piazza Navona; concerts €13; ⊗ 9.30am-12.30pm & 3.30-7pm Tue-Sat, 9am-1pm & 4-8pm Sun; ⊡ Corso del Rinascimento) designed by Bernini's hated rival, Francesco Borromini. In truth, Bernini completed his fountain two years before his contemporary started work on the church's facade and the gesture simply indicated that the source of the Nile was unknown at the time.

The **Fontana del Moro** at the southern end of the square was designed by Giacomo della Porta in 1576. Bernini added the Moor holding a dolphin in the mid-17th century, but the surrounding Tritons are 19th-century copies. At the northern end of the piazza, the 19th-century **Fontana del Nettuno** depicts Neptune fighting with a sea monster, surrounded by sea nymphs.

The piazza's largest building is **Palazzo Pamphilj** (http://roma.itamaraty.gov.br/it; Piazza Navona; ⊗ by reservation only), built for Pope Innocent X between 1644 and 1650, and now home to the Brazilian embassy.

Palazzo Farnese   HISTORIC BUILDING
(Map p86; www.inventerrome.com; Piazza Farnese; €9; ⊗ guided tours 3pm, 4pm & 5pm Mon, Wed & Fri; ⊡ Corso Vittorio Emanuele II) Home of the French embassy, this formidable Renaissance *palazzo*, one of Rome's finest, was started in 1514 by Antonio da Sangallo the Younger, continued by Michelangelo and finished by Giacomo della Porta. Inside, it boasts a series of frescoes by Annibale and Agostino Carracci that are said by some to

rival Michelangelo's in the Sistine Chapel. The highlight, painted between 1597 and 1608, is the monumental ceiling fresco *Amori degli Dei* (The Loves of the Gods) in the Galleria dei Carracci.

Palazzo Spada HISTORIC BUILDING

(Palazzo Capodiferro; Map p86; ☑ 06 683 2409; http://galleriaspada.beniculturali.it; Piazza Capo di Ferro 13; adult/reduced €5/2.50; ⊙ 8.30am-7.30pm Wed-Mon; ☐ Corso Vittorio Emanuele II) With its stuccoed ornamental facade and handsome courtyard, this grand *palazzo* is a fine example of 16th-century Mannerist architecture. Upstairs, a small four-room gallery houses the Spada family art collection with works by Andrea del Sarto, Guido Reni, Guercino and Titian, while downstairs Francesco Borromini's famous optical Illusion, aka the *Prospettiva* (Perspective), continues to confound visitors.

★ Chiesa del Gesù CHURCH

(Map p86; ☑ 06 69 7001; www.chiesadelgesu. org; Piazza del Gesù, ⊙ 7am 12.30pm & 4-7.45pm, St Ignatius rooms 4-6pm Mon-Sat, 10am-noon Sun, ☐ Largo di Torre Argentina) An imposing example of Counter-Reformation architecture, Rome's most important Jesuit church is a fabulous treasure trove of baroque art. Headline works include a swirling vault fresco by Giovanni Battista Gaulli (aka Il Baciccia), and Andrea del Pozzo's opulent tomb for Ignatius Loyola, the Spanish soldier and saint who founded the Jesuits in 1540. St Ignatius lived in the church from 1544 until his death in 1556 and you can visit his private rooms to the right of the main building in the Cappella di Sant'Ignazio.

The church, which was consecrated in 1584, is fronted by an impressive and much-copied facade by Giacomo della Porta. But more than the masonry, the real draw here is the church's lavish interior. The cupola frescoes and stucco decoration were designed by Baciccia, who also painted the hypnotic ceiling fresco, the *Trionfo del Nome di Gesù* (Triumph of the Name of Jesus).

In the northern transept, the **Cappella di Sant'Ignazio** houses the tomb of Ignatius Loyola. The altar-tomb, designed by baroque maestro Andrea Pozzo, is a sumptuous marble-and-bronze affair with lapis lazuli-encrusted columns and, on top, a lapis lazuli globe representing the Trinity. On either side are sculptures whose titles neatly encapsulate the Jesuit ethos: to the left, *Fede*

che vince l'Idolatria (Faith Defeats Idolatry); and on the right, *Religione che flagella l'Eresia* (Religion Lashing Heresy).

Museo Nazionale Romano: Crypta Balbi MUSEUM

(Map p86; ☑ 06 3996 7700; www.coopculture. it; Via delle Botteghe Oscure 31; adult/reduced €7/3.50; ⊙ 9am-7.45pm Tue-Sun; ☐ Via delle Botteghe Oscure) The least known of the Museo Nazionale Romano's four museums, the Crypta Balbi sits over the ruins of several medieval buildings, themselves set atop the Teatro di Balbo (13 BC). Archaeological finds illustrate the urban development of the surrounding area, while the museum's underground excavations, which can currently be visited only by guided tour, provide an interesting insight into Rome's multilayered past.

Jewish Ghetto AREA

(Map p86; ☐ Lungotevere de' Cenci) Centred on lively Via Portico d'Ottavia, the Jewish Ghetto is a wonderfully atmospheric area studded with artisan studios, vintage clothes shops, kosher bakeries and popular trattorias.

Rome's Jewish community dates back to the 2nd century BC, making it one of the oldest in Europe. The first Jews came as business envoys, with many later arriving as slaves following the Roman wars in Judaea and Titus' defeat of Jerusalem in AD 70. Confinement to the Ghetto came in 1555 when Pope Paul IV ushered in a period of official intolerance that lasted, on and off, until the 20th century. Ironically, though, this confinement meant that Jewish cultural and religious identity survived intact.

⊙ Monti, Esquilino & San Lorenzo

★ Basilica di Santa Maria Maggiore BASILICA

(Map p90; ☑ 06 6988 6800; Piazza Santa Maria Maggiore; basilica free, adult/reduced museum €3/2, museum & loggia €5/4; ⊙ 7am-7pm, loggia guided tours 9.30am-5.45pm; ☐ Piazza Santa Maria Maggiore) One of Rome's four patriarchal basilicas, this monumental 5th-century church stands on the summit of the Esquiline Hill, on the spot where snow is said to have miraculously fallen in the summer of AD 358. To commemorate the event, every year on 5 August thousands of white petals are

Monti, Esquilino & San Lorenzo

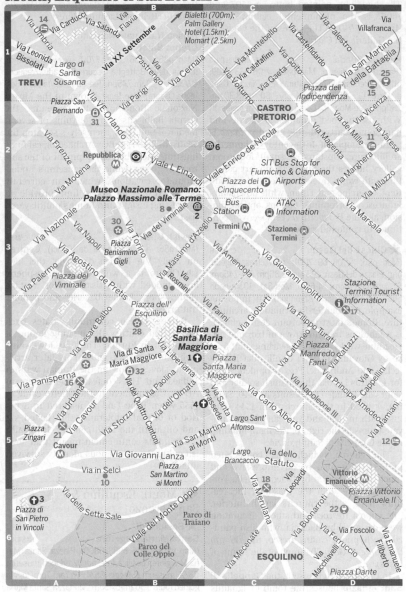

released from the basilica's coffered ceiling. Much altered over the centuries, it's an architectural hybrid with 14th-century Romanesque belfry, 18th-century baroque facade, largely baroque interior and a series of glorious 5th-century mosaics.

Outside, the exterior is decorated with glimmering 13th-century mosaics, protected by Ferdinand Fuga's baroque loggia (1741). Rising behind, the belfry – Rome's tallest – tops out at 75m.

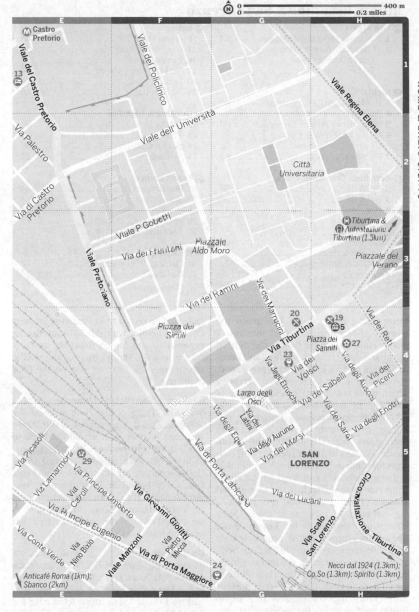

The vast interior retains its original structure, despite the basilica's many overhauls. Particularly spectacular are the 5th-century mosaics in the triumphal arch and nave, depicting Old Testament scenes. The central image in the apse, signed by Jacopo Torriti, dates from the 13th century and represents the coronation of the Virgin Mary. Beneath your feet, the nave floor is a fine example of 12th-century Cosmati paving.

The baldachin over the high altar is heavy with gilt cherubs; the altar is a porphyry

Monti, Esquilino & San Lorenzo

sarcophagus, which is said to contain the relics of St Matthew and other martyrs. A plaque embedded in the floor to the right of the altar marks the spot where Gian Lorenzo Bernini and his father Pietro are buried. Steps lead down to the *confessio* (a crypt in which relics are placed), where a statue of Pope Pius IX kneels before a reliquary containing a fragment of Jesus' manger.

The sumptuously decorated Cappella Sistina, last on the right, was built by Domenico Fontana in the 16th century and contains the tombs of Popes Sixtus V and Pius V.

Through the souvenir shop on the right-hand side of the church is the **Museo del Tresoro** (Treasury Museum) with a glittering collection of religious artefacts. Most interesting, however, is the **Loggia delle Benedizioni** (upper loggia), accessible only by 30-minute guided tours (in English; book at the basilica entrance), the extraordinary creation of Ferdinando Fuga. Here you can get a close look at the facade's iridescent 13th-century mosaics created by Filippo Rusuti, and Bernini's magnificent baroque helical staircase.

Basilica di Santa Prassede   CHURCH
(Map p90; ☑06 488 24 56; Via Santa Prassede 9a; ⊙7am-noon & 4-6.30pm; ☐Piazza Santa Maria Maggiore) Famous for its brilliant Byzantine mosaics, this tiny gem of a 9th-century church is dedicated to St Praxedes, an early Christian heroine who hid Christians fleeing persecution and buried those she couldn't save in a well. The position of the well is now marked by a marble disc on the floor of the nave.

Basilica di San Pietro in Vincoli   BASILICA
(Map p90; Piazza di San Pietro in Vincoli 4a; ⊙8am-12.30pm & 3-7pm summer, to 6pm winter; Ⓜ️Cavour) Pilgrims and art lovers flock to this 5th-century basilica for two reasons: to marvel at Michelangelo's colossal *Moses* (1505) sculpture and to see the chains that supposedly bound St Peter when he was imprisoned in the Carcere Mamertino (near the Roman Forum). Access to the church is via a flight of steps through a low arch that leads up from Via Cavour.

Domus Aurea   ARCHAEOLOGICAL SITE
(Golden House; ☑06 3996 7700; www.coopculture. it; Viale della Domus Aurea; adult/under 6yr €14/ free; ⊙9am-4.45pm Sat & Sun; Ⓜ️Colosseo) Nero had his Domus Aurea constructed after the fire of AD 64 (which he is rumoured to have started to clear the area). Named after the gold that lined its facade and interiors, it was a huge complex covering up to a third of the city. Making full use of virtual reality, superb state-of-the-art guided tours shed light on just how grand the Golden House –

a lavish villa with porticoes – was. Advance online reservations are obligatory.

Piazza della Repubblica

(Map p90; M Repubblica) Flanked by grand 19th-century neoclassical colonnades, this landmark piazza was laid out as part of Rome's post-unification makeover. It follows the lines of the semicircular *exedra* (benched portico) of Diocletian's baths complex and was originally known as Piazza Esedra.

★ Museo Nazionale Romano: Palazzo Massimo alle Terme

(Map p90; ☑ 06 3996 7700; www.coopculture. it; Largo di Villa Peretti 1; adult/reduced €7/3.50; ⊘ 9am-7.45pm Tue-Sun; M Termini) One of Rome's great unheralded museums, this is a fabulous treasure trove of classical art. The ground and 1st floors are devoted to sculpture with some breathtaking pieces – check out the *Pugile* (Boxer), a 2nd-century-BC Greek bronze; the graceful 2nd-century-BC *Ermafrodite dormiente* (Sleeping Hermaphrodite); and the idealised *Il discobolo* (Discus Thrower). It's the magnificent and vibrantly coloured frescoes on the 2nd floor, however, that are the undisputed highlight.

These vibrantly coloured panels were originally used as interior decor and provide a vivid picture of the inside of a grand ancient Roman villa. There are intimate *cubicula* (bedroom) frescoes focusing on nature, mythology, domestic and erotic life; and delicate landscape paintings from a dark-painted winter triclinium.

Particularly breathtaking are the frescoes (dating from 30 BC to 20 BC) from Villa Livia, one of the homes of Augustus' wife Livia Drusilla. These cover an entire room and depict a paradisiacal garden full of a wild tangle of roses, pomegranates, irises and camomile under a deep-blue sky. They once decorated a summer triclinium, a large living and dining area built half underground to provide protection from the heat.

The 2nd floor also features some exquisitely fine floor mosaics and rare inlay work. That these mosaics carpeted the floors of plush villas of aristocratic Romans in the 13th and 14th centuries is really quite extraordinary.

In the basement, the unexciting-sounding coin collection is far more absorbing than you might expect, tracing the Roman Empire's propaganda offensive through its coins. There's also jewellery dating back several millennia, and the disturbing remains of a mummified eight-year-old girl, the only known example of mummification dating from the Roman Empire.

Note that the museum is one of four that collectively make up the Museo Nazionale Romano. The ticket, which is valid for three days, also gives admission to the other three sites: the Terme di Diocleziano, Palazzo Altemps and the Crypta Balbi. Count €5 for an audio guide.

Museo Nazionale Romano: Terme di Diocleziano

(Map p90; ☑ 06 3996 7700; www.coopculture. it; Viale Enrico de Nicola 78; adult/reduced €7/3.50; ⊘ 9am-7.30pm Tue-Sun; M Termini) The Terme di Diocleziano was ancient Rome's largest bath complex, covering about 13 hectares and able to accommodate some 3000 people. Today its ruins house a branch of the impressive Museo Nazionale Romano. Exhibits, which include memorial inscriptions, bas-reliefs and archaeological artefacts, provide a fascinating insight into Roman life. Outside, the vast cloister, constructed from drawings by Michelangelo, is lined with classical sarcophagi, headless statues and huge sculpted animal heads, thought to have come from the Foro di Traiano.

◉ San Giovanni & Testaccio

★ Basilica di San Giovanni in Laterano

(Map p94; Piazza di San Giovanni in Laterano 4; basilica/cloister free/€5 with audio guide; ⊘ 7am-6.30pm, cloister 9am-6pm; M San Giovanni) For a thousand years this monumental cathedral was the most important church in Christendom. Commissioned by Constantine and consecrated in AD 324, it was the first Christian basilica built in the city and, until the late 14th century, was the pope's main place of worship. It's still Rome's official cathedral and the pope's seat as the bishop of Rome.

The basilica has been revamped several times, most notably by Borromini in the 17th century, and by Alessandro Galilei, who added the immense white facade in 1735.

Surmounted by 15 7m-high statues – Christ with St John the Baptist, John the Evangelist and the 12 Apostles – Galilei's **facade** is an imposing example of late-baroque classicism. The **central bronze doors** were moved here from the Curia in the Roman Forum, while, on the far right, the **Holy Door** is only opened in Jubilee years.

San Giovanni & Celio

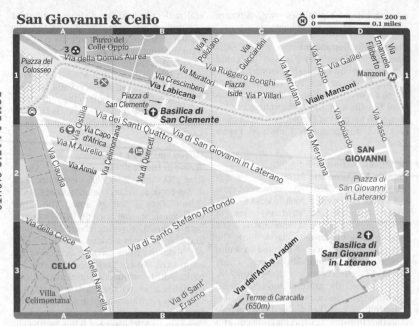

San Giovanni & Celio

The cavernous interior owes much of its present look to Francesco Borromini, who redecorated it for the 1650 Jubilee. It's a breathtaking sight with a golden gilt **ceiling**, a 15th-century **mosaic floor**, and a wide central **nave** lined with muscular 4.6m-high sculptures of the apostles.

At the head of the nave, the Gothic **baldachin** over the papal altar is said to contain the relics of the heads of Sts Peter and Paul. In front, a double staircase leads down to the **confessio** and the Renaissance tomb of Pope Martin V.

Behind the altar, the massive **apse** is decorated with sparkling mosaics. Parts of these date to the 4th century, but most were added in the 1800s.

At the other end of the basilica, on the first pillar in the right-hand aisle, is an incomplete Giotto fresco. While admiring this, cock your ear towards the next column, where a monument to Pope Sylvester II (r 999–1003) is said to sweat and creak when the death of a pope is imminent.

To the left of the altar, the beautiful 13th-century **cloister** is a lovely, peaceful place with graceful twisted columns set around a central garden.

★ Basilica
di San Clemente   BASILICA
(Map p94; www.basilicasanclemente.com; Piazza San Clemente; excavations adult/reduced €10/5; ◷ 9am-12.30pm & 3-6pm Mon-Sat, 12.15-6pm Sun; ⊠ Via Labicana) Nowhere better illustrates the various stages of Rome's turbulent past than this fascinating multilayered church. The ground-level 12th-century basilica sits atop a 4th-century church, which, in turn, stands over a 2nd-century pagan temple and a 1st-century Roman house. Beneath

everything are foundations dating from the Roman Republic.

The street-level *basilica superiore* features a marvellous 12th-century apse mosaic depicting the *Trionfo della Croce* (Triumph of the Cross) and some wonderful 15th-century frescoes by Masolino in the Cappella di Santa Caterina showing a crucifixion scene and episodes from the life of St Catherine.

Steps lead down to the 4th-century *basilica inferiore,* mostly destroyed by Norman invaders in 1084, but with some faded 11th-century frescoes illustrating the life of San Clement. Follow the steps down another level and you'll come to a 1st-century Roman house and a dark, 2nd-century temple to Mithras, with an altar showing the god slaying a bull. Beneath it all, you can hear the eerie sound of a subterranean river flowing through a Republic-era drain.

Basilica di Santa Sabina
BASILICA

(Map p96; ☎06 57 94 01; Piazza Pietro d'Illiria 1; ☺8.15am-12.30pm & 3.30-6pm; 🚇Lungotevere Aventino) This solemn basilica, one of Rome's most beautiful early Christian churches, was founded by Peter of Illyria around AD 422. It was enlarged in the 9th century and again in 1216, just before it was given to the newly founded Dominican order – note the tombstone of Muñoz de Zamora, one of

---

STREET ART IN THE SUBURBS

Street art in Rome is edgy, exciting, progressive and a fabulous excuse to delve into the city's gritty southern suburbs when Ancient Rome's tourist crowds and top-billing sights tire. Tourist kiosks have maps marked up with key street-art works, and online street-art itineraries can be found at www.turismoroma.it and www.ostiensedistrict.it.

With over 30 works, ex-industrial and alternative Ostiense is one of the best parts of Rome to lap up the outdoor gallery of wall murals. Highlights include the murals at Caserma dell'Aeronautica (Via del Porto Fluviale; Ⓜ Piramide), a former military warehouse where Bolognese artist Blu (www.blublu.org) painted a rainbow of sinister faces across the entire building in 2014. He transformed the 48 arched windows into eyes, apparently to represent the evils of homelessness on a building that has been a long-term squat. Walk around the side of the building to admire a mural of a boat topped by cranes and robots.

Further up Via Ostiense is another work by Blu, depicting interlocking yellow cars, that covers the entire facade of a now-derelict building. Known as Alexis (Via Ostiense 122; 🚇Via Ostiense), the mural immortalises Alexis Grigoropoulos, the 15-year-old student who was killed, allegedly by a police bullet, during demonstrations in Greece in 2008 – the mural incorporates his portrait and the date of his death.

The signature stencil art of well-known Italian street artists, Sten & Lex (http://stenlex.com) is well represented in Ostiense with a B&W wall mural of an anonymous student at Via delle Conce 14 (neighbouring a menacing bald gangster spray-painted by French artist MTO, guarding the entrance to the now-closed Rising Love nightclub next door at No 12) and the giant Peassagio Urbano XVIII (2016) emblazoning the pedestrian entrance to Stazione Roma-Ostiense next to Eataly on Piazzale XII Ottobre. Nearby, on Via dei Magazzini Generali, a line-up of larger-than-life portraits by Sten & Lex provide an admiring audience for the iconic *Wall of Fame* by Rome's very own JBRock (www.jbrock.it).

Two experimental museums give Rome's street-art scene instant street cred and bags of buzz. East of the Appian Way, in the off-beat district of Quadraro, M.U.Ro (Museo di Urban Art di Roma; www.muromuseum.blogspot.it; Via dei Lentuli, Quadraro; walking/bicycle tour €10/20; Ⓜ Porta Furba Quadraro) runs highly recommended guided tours – on foot or by bicycle – of the wealth of murals, many by big-name international artists, decorating its streets. More recently, in 2017 the ruins of 19th-century soap factory Mira Lanza (1899) in Ostiense opened its doors as a museum (☎351 031 75 63; www.999contemporary.com/exmiralanza; Via Amedeo Avogadro; ☺24hr; Ⓜ Stazione Trastevere) FREE, the result of a public-art project by 999Contemporary which invited French globe-painter Seth (www.seth.fr) to spruce up the site in 2016 with a series of large-scale art installations and murals. Home to a handful of squatters today, the ruined factory-turned-museum is open 24 hours and free guided tours with museum curator Stefan Antonelli can be reserved in advance. The advertised address: Via Amedeo Avogadro, first hole in the net behind garbage bins.

Aventino & Testaccio

ROME & LAZIO SIGHTS

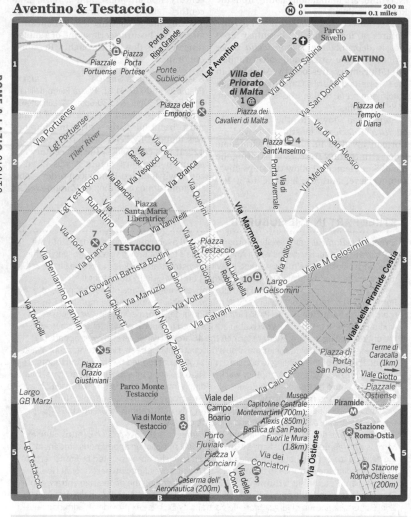

N 0 ——————— 200 m
0 ——————— 0.1 miles

Aventino & Testaccio

the order's founding fathers, in the nave floor. A 20th-century restoration returned it to its original look.

★ Villa del Priorato di Malta
HISTORIC BUILDING

(Map p96; Villa Magistrale; Piazza dei Cavalieri di Malta; Lungotevere Aventino) Fronting an ornate cypress-shaded piazza, the Roman headquarters of the Sovereign Order of Malta, aka the Cavalieri di Malta (Knights of Malta), boasts one of Rome's most celebrated views. It's not immediately apparent, but look through the keyhole in the villa's green door and you'll see the dome of St Peter's Basilica perfectly aligned at the end of a hedge-lined avenue.

★ Terme di Caracalla
ARCHAEOLOGICAL SITE

(06 3996 7700; www.coopculture.it; Viale delle Terme di Caracalla 52; adult/reduced €6/3; 9am-1hr before sunset Tue-Sun, 9am-2pm Mon; Viale delle Terme di Caracalla) The remains of the emperor Caracalla's vast bathhouse complex are among Rome's most awe-inspiring ruins. Inaugurated in AD 216, the original 10-hectare site, which comprised baths, gyms, libraries, shops and gardens, was used by up to 8000 people daily.

Most of the ruins are what's left of the central bathhouse. This was a huge rectangular edifice bookended by two **palestre** (gyms) and centred on a **frigidarium** (cold room), where bathers would stop after spells in the warmer **tepidarium** and dome-capped **caldarium** (hot room).

But while the customers enjoyed the luxurious facilities, below ground hundreds of slaves sweated in a 9.5km tunnel network, tending to the complex plumbing systems.

The baths remained in continuous use until AD 537, when the Visigoths cut off Rome's water supply. Excavations in the 16th and 17th centuries unearthed some important sculptures, many of which found their way into the Farnese family's art collection.

In summer, the ruins are used to stage spectacular opera and ballet performances.

◉ Southern Rome

Museo Capitoline Centrale Montemartini
MUSEUM

(Museums at Centrale Montemartini; 06 06 08; www.centralemontemartini.org; Via Ostiense 106; adult/reduced €7.50/6.50, incl Capitoline Museums €16/14, ticket valid 7 days; 9am-7pm Tue-Sun; Via Ostiense) Housed in a former power station, this fabulous outpost of the Capitoline Museums (Musei Capitolini) boldly juxtaposes classical sculpture against diesel engines and giant furnaces. The collection's highlights are in the Sala Caldaia, where ancient statuary strike poses around the giant furnace. Beautiful pieces include the *Fanciulla Seduta* (Seated Girl) and the *Musa Polimnia* (Muse Polyhymnia), and there are also some exquisite Roman mosaics, depicting favourite subjects such as hunting scenes and foodstuffs.

★ Basilica di San Paolo Fuori le Mura
BASILICA

(06 6988 0803; www.basilicasanpaolo.org; Via Ostiense 190; adult/reduced €4/3; 7am-6.30pm; Basilica San Paolo) The largest church in Rome after St Peter's (and the world's third-largest), this magnificent basilica stands on the site where St Paul was buried after being decapitated in AD 67. Built by Constantine in the 4th century, it was largely destroyed by fire in 1823 and much of what you see is a 19th-century reconstruction.

However, many treasures survived, including the 5th-century **triumphal arch**, with its heavily restored mosaics, and the Gothic marble **tabernacle** over the high altar. This was designed around 1285 by Arnolfo di Cambio together with another artist, possibly Pietro Cavallini. To the right of the altar, the elaborate Romanesque Paschal candlestick was fashioned by Nicolò di Angelo and Pietro Vassalletto in the 12th century and features a grim cast of animal-headed creatures. St Paul's tomb is in the nearby **confessio**.

Looking upwards, doom-mongers should check out the papal portraits beneath the nave windows. Every pope since St Peter is represented here, and legend has it that when there is no longer room for the next portrait, the world will fall.

Also well worth a look is the stunning 13th-century Cosmati mosaic work that decorates the columns of the **cloisters** of the adjacent Benedictine abbey.

★ Via Appia Antica
HISTORIC SITE

(Map p98; Appian Way; 06 513 53 16; www.parcoappiaantica.it; Via Appia Antica) Named after consul Appius Claudius Caecus, who laid the

Appia Antica

Appia Antica

first 90km section in 312 BC, ancient Rome's *regina viarum* (queen of roads) was extended in 190 BC to reach Brindisi on Italy's southern Adriatic coast. Via Appia Antica has long been one of Rome's most exclusive addresses, a beautiful cobbled thoroughfare flanked by grassy fields, Roman structures and towering pine trees. Most splendid of the ancient houses was **Villa dei Quintili** (☑ 06 3996 7700; www.coopculture.it; Via Appia Nuova 1092; adult/reduced incl Terme di Caracalla & Mausoleo di Cecilia Metella €6/3; ☉ 9am-before sunset Tue-Sun; ☐ Via Appia Antica), so desirable that Emperor Commodus murdered its owner and took it for himself.

The Appian Way has a dark history – it was here that Spartacus and 6000 of his slave rebels were crucified in 71 BC, and it was here that the early Christians buried their dead in 300km of **underground catacombs**. You can't visit all 300km, but three major catacombs – San Callisto, San Sebastiano and **Santa Domitilla** (☑ 06 511 03 42; www.domitilla.info; Via delle Sette Chiese 282; adult/reduced €8/5; ☉ 9am-noon & 2-5pm Wed-Mon mid-Jan–mid-Dec; ☐ Via Appia Antica) – are open for guided exploration.

The most pleasurable way of exploring the Appian Way is by bicycle. Rent a set of wheels (with helmet and lock) and pick up maps (€1.50) at the **Info Point Appia Antica** (☑ 06 513 53 16; www.parcoappiaantica.it; Via Appia Antica 58-60; ☉ 9.30am-sunset summer, 9am-1pm & 2-5pm Mon-Fri, 9.30am-5pm Sat & Sun winter; ☐ Via Appia Antica) at the northern end of the road. Alternatively book a guided tour by bike, on foot or by electric golf cart. The Info Point also sells the **Appia Antica Card** (€6), valid seven days and covering admission to three key sights along the way (Villa dei Quintili, Mausoleo di Cecilia Metella and Terme di Caracalla).

★ **Catacombe di San Sebastiano**   CATACOMB
(Map p98; ☑ 06 785 03 50; www.catacombe. org; Via Appia Antica 136; adult/reduced €8/5; ☉ 10am-5pm Mon-Sat Jan-Nov; ☐ Via Appia Antica) Extending beneath the **Basilica di San Sebastiano** (Via Appia Antica 136; ☉ 8am-1pm & 2-5.30pm; ☐ Via Appia Antica), these underground burial chambers were the first to be called catacombs – the name was derived from the Greek *kata* (near) and *kymbas*

(cavity), because they were located near a cave. They were heavily developed from the 1st century and during the persecutory reign of Vespasian they provided a safe haven for the remains of Saints Peter and Paul.

The 1st level is now almost completely destroyed, but frescoes, stucco work and epigraphs can be seen on the 2nd level. There are also three perfectly preserved mausoleums and a plastered wall with hundreds of invocations to Peter and Paul, engraved by worshippers in the 3rd and 4th centuries.

Above the catacombs, the basilica, a much-altered 4th-century church, preserves one of the arrows allegedly used to kill St Sebastian, and the column to which he was tied.

Catacombe di San Callisto
CATACOMB

(Map p98; ☑ 06 513 01 51; www.catacombe.roma. it; Via Appia Antica 110-126; adult/reduced €8/5; ☺ 9am-noon & 2-5pm Thu-Tue Mar-Jan; ☐ Via Appia Antica) These are the largest and busiest of Rome's catacombs. Founded at the end of the 2nd century and named after Pope Calixtus I, they became the official cemetery of the newly established Roman Church. In the 20km of tunnels explored to date, archaeologists have found the tombs of 16 popes, dozens of martyrs and thousands upon thousands of Christians.

Villa di Massenzio
RUINS

(Map p98; ☑ 06 06 08; www.villadimassenzio. it; Via Appia Antica 153; ☺ 10am-4pm Tue-Sun; ☐ Via Appia Antica) FREE The outstanding feature of Maxentius' enormous 4th century palace complex is the Circo di Massenzio, Rome's best-preserved ancient racetrack – you can still make out the starting stalls used for chariot races. The 10,000-seat arena was built by Maxentius around 309, but he died before ever seeing a race here. Above the arena are the ruins of Maxentius' imperial residence. Near the racetrack, the Mausoleo di Romolo (Tombo di Romolo; ☺ 10am-4pm Tue-Sun; ☐ Via Appia Antica) FREE was built by Maxentius for his 17-year-old son Romulus.

Rome Convention Centre La Nuvola
ARCHITECTURE

(☑ 06 5451 3710; www.nellanuvola.it; Viale Asia, entrance cnr Via Cristoforo Colombo; Ⓜ EUR Fermi) Contemporary architecture buffs will appreciate Rome's brand-new congress centre, designed by Italian architects Massimiliano and Doriana Fuksas, and unveiled with much pomp and ceremony in late 2016. The striking building comprises a transparent, glass-and-steel box (40m high, 70m wide and 175m long) called Le Theca ('The Shrine'), inside of which hangs organically shaped La Nuvola ('The Cloud') containing an auditorium and conference rooms seating up to 8000 people. A separate black skyscraper called La Luma ('The Blade'), with a 439-room hotel, spa and restaurant, completes the ambitious €270 million ensemble.

EUR District
AREA

(Ⓜ EUR Palasport) This Orwellian quarter of wide boulevards and linear buildings was built for an international exhibition in 1942, and although war intervened and the exhibition never took place, the name stuck. Esposizione Universale di Roma ('Roman Universal Exhibition') or EUR. The area's main interest lies in its rationalist architecture, which finds perfect form in the iconic Palazzo della Civiltà Italiana (Palace of Italian Civilisation; ☑ 06 33 45 01; www.fendi.com; Quadrato della Concordia; ☺ 8am-6pm Mon-Sat, 10am-7pm Sun; Ⓜ EUR Magliana) FREE, aka the Square Colosseum, where Italian fashion house Fendi has had its global headquarters since 2015.

☉ Trastevere & Gianicolo

★ Basilica di Santa Maria in Trastevere
BASILICA

(Map p100; ☑ 06 581 4802; Piazza Santa Maria in Trastevere; ☺ 7.30am-9pm Sep-Jul, 8am-noon & 4-9pm Aug; ☐ Viale di Trastevere, ☐ Viale di Trastevere) Nestled in a quiet corner of Trastevere's focal square, this is said to be the oldest church dedicated to the Virgin Mary in Rome. In its original form, it dates to the early 3rd century, but a major 12th-century makeover saw the addition of a Romanesque bell tower and glittering facade. The portico came later, added by Carlo Fontana in 1702. Inside, the 12th-century mosaics are the headline feature.

In the apse, look out for Christ and his mother flanked by various saints and, on the far left, Pope Innocent II holding a model of the church. Beneath this are six mosaics by Pietro Cavallini illustrating the life of the Virgin (c 1291).

According to legend, the church stands on the spot where a fountain of oil miraculously

Trastevere & Gianicolo

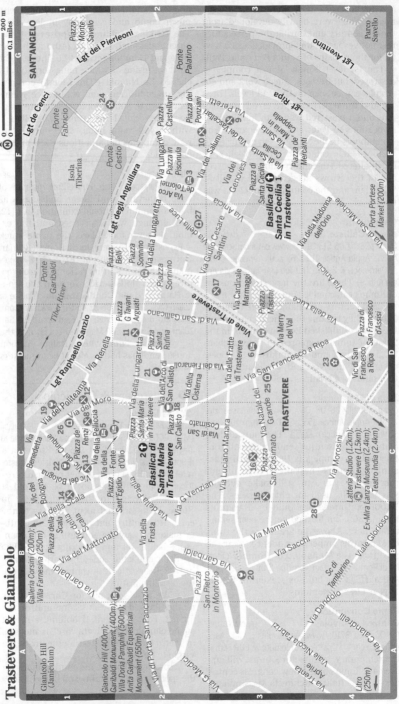

Galleria Corsini (200m);
Villa Farnesina (250m)

Gianicolo Hill (400m);
Garibaldi Monument (400m);
Villa Doria Pamphilj (500m);
Anita Garibaldi Equestrian
Monument (550m)

SANT'ANGELO

Piazza Monte Savello

Parco Savello

Lgt dei Pierleoni

Lgt de Cenci

Lgt de Cenci

Ponte Fabricio

Ponte Cestio

Ponte Palatino

Isola Tiberina

Lgt Aventino

Lgt degli Anguillara

Lgt Ripa

Piazza dei Castellani

Piazza dei Ponziani

Piazza in Piscinula

Via Lungarina

Via dei Salumi

Via dei Vascellari

Via di Santa Cecilia

Via Santa Maria in Cappella

Piazza de' Mercanti

Via Anicia

Via di San Michele

Porta Portese Market (200m)

Basilica di Santa Cecilia in Trastevere

Via Arco de' Tolomei

Via della Luce

Via di San Michele

Via Genovesi

Piazza di Santa Cecilia

Ponte Garibaldi

Tiber River

Ponte Garibaldi

Piazza Belli

Piazza Sonnino

Via della Lungaretta

Piazza Sonnino

Via Giulio Cesare Santini

Via Anicia

Via della Luce

Lgt Raphaello Sanzio

Via Rienella

Piazza G Tavani Arguati

Piazza Santa Rufina

Via della Lungaretta

Via di San Gallicano

Viale di Trastevere

Via Cardinale Marmaggi

Piazza Mastai

Piazza di San Francesco d'Assisi

Via Merry del Val

Via della Luce

Via del Moro

Piazza de' Renzi

Via della Pelliccia

Piazza Santa Maria in Trastevere

Piazza San Calisto

Via dell'Arco di San Calisto

Via della Cisterna

Via delle Fratte di Trastevere

Via di San Francesco a Ripa

Via San Francesco a Ripa

Vic di San Francesco a Ripa

Piazza di San Francesco d'Assisi

Via Benedetta

Via del Cinque

Vic del Bologna

Piazza de' Renzi

Via Fonte d'Olio

Piazza Sant'Egidio

Via della Fonte d'Olio

Via della Paglia

Basilica di Santa Maria in Trastevere

Via della Scala

Vic del Cinque

Piazza della Scala

Via della Scala

Via G Venzian

Via Luciano Manara

Via di San Cosimato

Piazza San Cosimato

Via Natale del Grande

TRASTEVERE

Via Morosini

Latteria Studio (1.2km);
Trastevere (1.5km);
Ex-Mira Lanza Museum (2.4km);
Teatro India (2.4km)

Via Garibaldi

Via del Mattonato

Via della Frusta

Piazza San Pietro in Montorio

Via di Porta San Pancrazio

Via G Medici

Via Dandolo

Via Calandrelli

Viale Nicola Fabrizi

Via Trenta Aprile

Via Goffredo Mameli

Via Sacchi

Via Mameli

Sc di Tamburino

Viale Glorioso

Litro (250m)

SANT'ANGELO

0 200 m
0 0.1 miles

Trastevere & Gianicolo

ROME & LAZIO SIGHTS

sprang from the ground. It incorporates 21 ancient Roman columns, some plundered from the Terme di Caracalla, and boasts a 17th-century wooden ceiling.

★ **Villa Farnesina**   HISTORIC BUILDING
(Map p86; ☑ 06 6802 7268; www.villafarnesina.it; Via della Lungara 230; adult/reduced €6/5, guided tour €4; ⊗ 9am-2pm Mon-Sat, to 5pm 2nd Sun of the month; ☒ Lungotevere della Farnesina) The interior of this gorgeous 16th-century villa is fantastically frescoed from top to bottom. Several paintings in the Loggia of Cupid and Psyche and the Loggia of Galatea, both on the ground floor, are attributed to Raphael. On the 1st floor, Peruzzi's dazzling frescoes in the Salone delle Prospettive are a superb illusionary perspective of a colonnade and panorama of 16th-century Rome.

★ **Galleria Corsini**   GALLERY
(Palazzo Corsini; Map p86; ☑ 06 6880 2323; www.barberinicorsini.org; Via della Lungara 10; adult/reduced €5/2.50, incl Palazzo Barberini €10/5; ⊗ 8.30am-7.30pm Wed-Mon; ☒ Lungotevere della Farnesina) Once home to Queen Christina of Sweden, whose richly frescoed bedroom witnessed a steady stream of male and female lovers, the 16th-century Palazzo Corsini was designed by Ferdinando Fuga in grand Versailles style, and houses part of Italy's national art collection. Highlights include Caravaggio's mesmerising *San Giovanni Battista* (St John the Baptist), Guido Reni's unnerving *Salome con la Testa di San Giovanni Battista* (Salome with the Head of John the Baptist), and Fra' Angelico's Corsini Triptych, plus works by Rubens, Poussin and Van Dyck.

Orto Botanico   GARDENS
(Botanical Garden; Map p86; ☑ 06 4991 7107; Largo Cristina di Svezia 24; adult/reduced €8/4; ⊗ 9am-6.30pm Mon-Sat Apr-Oct, to 5.30pm Nov-Mar; ☒ Lungotevere della Farnesina, Piazza Trilussa) Formerly the private grounds of Palazzo Corsini, Rome's 12-hectare botanical gardens are a little-known, slightly neglected gem and a great place to unwind in a tree-shaded expanse covering the steep slopes of the Gianicolo. Plants have been cultivated here since the 13th century and the current gardens were established in 1883, when the grounds of Palazzo Corsini were given to the University of Rome. They now contain up to 8000 species, including some of Europe's rarest plants.

★ **Basilica di Santa Cecilia in Trastevere**   BASILICA
(Map p100; ☑ 06 589 9289; www.benedettinesantacecilia.it; Piazza di Santa Cecilia; fresco & crypt each €2.50; ⊗ basilica & crypt 10am-1pm & 4-7pm, fresco 10am-12.30pm Mon-Sat; ☒ Viale di Trastevere, ☒ Viale di Trastevere) The last resting place of the patron saint of music features Pietro Cavallini's stunning 13th-century fresco, in the nuns' choir of the hushed convent adjoining the church. Inside the church itself, Stefano Maderno's mysterious sculpture depicts

STUMBLING STONES

Watch your footing when meandering Trastevere's impossibly quaint, old-world lanes and alleys. Among the uneven, well-worn, square-shaped cobblestones (dangerously slippery in rain), you will occasionally stumble across a *pietri d'inciampo* (literally 'stumbling stone' in Italian) glinting in the sunlight. Each one of these polished brass stones, shaped square like a Roman cobble and engraved with the name of a local Jewish resident, marks the exact spot where the Holocaust victim was rounded up by Nazi soldiers during WWII and deported to Auschwitz or other death camp. Most stumbling blocks are embedded in pavements in front of private homes and invariably count more than one – a stone for each member of entire Jewish families deported.

The stumbling stones are part of a Europe-wide memorial project initiated by German artist Gunter Demning. Some 200 pave the historic streets of Rome to date, predominantly in Trastevere and the old Jewish Ghetto directly across the river.

St Cecilia's miraculously preserved body, unearthed in the Catacombs of San Callisto in 1599. You can also visit the excavations of Roman houses, one of which was possibly that of Cecilia.

Villa Doria
Pamphilj
MONUMENT, PARK

(⊙ sunrise-sunset; 🚇 Via di San Pancrazio) Lorded over by the 17th-century Villa Doria Pamphilj is Rome's largest landscaped park – many a Roman's favourite place to escape the city noise and bustle. Once a vast private estate, it was laid out around 1650 for Prince Camillo Pamphilj, nephew of Pope Innocent X. It's a huge expanse of rolling parkland, shaded by Rome's distinctive umbrella pines. At its centre is the prince's summer residence, Casino del Belrespiro (used for official government functions today), with its manicured gardens and citrus trees.

Gianicolo Hill
HILL

(Janiculum) The verdant hill of Gianicolo is dotted by monuments to Garibaldi and his makeshift army, who fought pope-backing French troops in one of the fiercest battles in the struggle for Italian unification on this spot in 1849. The Italian hero is commemorated with a massive **monument** (Piazzale Giuseppe Garibaldi; 🚇 Passeggiata del Gianicolo) in Piazzale Giuseppe Garibaldi, while his Brazilian-born wife, Anita, has her own **equestrian monument** about 200m away in Piazzale Anita Garibaldi; she died from malaria, together with their unborn child, shortly after the siege.

◉ Tridente, Trevi & the Quirinale

Keats-Shelley House
MUSEUM

(Map p106; ☎ 06 678 42 35; www.keats-shelley-house.org; Piazza di Spagna 26; adult/reduced €5/4; ⊙ 10am-1pm & 2-6pm Mon-Sat; Ⓜ Spagna) The Keats-Shelley House is where Romantic poet John Keats died of tuberculosis at the age of 25, in February 1821. Keats came to Rome in 1820 to try to improve his health in the Italian climate, and rented two rooms on the 3rd floor of a townhouse next to the Spanish Steps, with painter companion Joseph Severn (1793–1879). Watch a film on the 1st floor about the Romantics, then head upstairs to see where Keats and Severn lived and worked.

★ Villa Medici
PALACE

(Map p106; ☎ 06 676 13 11; www.villamedici.it; Viale Trinità dei Monti 1; 1½hr guided tour adult/reduced €12/6; ⊙ 10am-7pm Tue-Sun; Ⓜ Spagna) This sumptuous Renaissance palace was built for Cardinal Ricci da Montepulciano in 1540, but Ferdinando de' Medici bought it in 1576. It remained in Medici hands until 1801, when Napoleon acquired it for the French Academy. Guided tours take in the wonderful landscaped gardens, cardinal's painted apartments, and incredible views over Rome – tours in English depart at noon. Note the pieces of ancient Roman sculpture from the Ara Pacis embedded in the villa's walls.

The villa's most famous resident was Galileo, imprisoned here between 1630 and 1633 during his trial for heresy; Keith Richards and Anita Pallenberg stayed here in the 1960s. There are up to 19 resident French-speaking artists and musicians, with exhibitions and performances at the end of February and June. There's a lovely, high-ceilinged cafe (open from 8am) that serves reasonably priced *panini* and *prosecco*-fuelled lunches. You can also overnight at the villa, for a price.

★ **Piazza del Popolo**   PIAZZA

(Map p106; M Flaminio) This dazzling piazza was laid out in 1538 to provide a grandiose entrance to what was then Rome's main northern gateway. It has since been remodelled several times, most recently by Giuseppe Valadier in 1823. Guarding its southern approach are Carlo Rainaldi's twin 17th-century churches, **Chiesa di Santa Maria dei Miracoli** (Map p106; Via del Corso 528; ⊙ 6.45am-12.30pm & 4.30-7.30pm Mon-Sat, 8am-1.15pm & 4.30-7.45pm Sun; M Flaminio) and **Chiesa di Santa Maria in Montesanto** (Chiesa degli Artisti; Map p106; www.chiesadegli artisti.it; Via del Babuino 198; ⊙ 5.30-8pm Mon-Fri, 11am-1.30pm Sun, M Flaminio). In the centre, the 36m-high **obelisk** was brought by Augustus from ancient Egypt; it originally stood in Circo Massimo.

On the northern flank, the **Porta del Popolo** was created by Bernini in 1655 to celebrate Queen Christina of Sweden's defection to Catholicism, while rising to the east is the viewpoint of the Pincio Hill Gardens.

★ **Basilica di Santa Maria del Popolo**   BASILICA

(Map p106; www.smariadelpopolo.com; Piazza del Popolo 12; ⊙ 10.30am-12.30pm & 4-6.30pm Mon-Thu, 10.30am-6.30pm Fri & Sat, 4.30-6.30pm Sun; M Flaminio) A magnificent repository of art, this is one of Rome's earliest and richest Renaissance churches. Of the numerous works of art on display, it is the two Caravaggio masterpieces that draw the most onlookers – the *Conversion of Saul* (1601) and the *Crucifixion of St Peter* (1601), in a chapel to the left of the main altar – but it contains other fine works, including several by Pinturicchio and Bernini.

The first chapel was built here in 1099 to exorcise the ghost of Nero, who was secretly buried on this spot and whose ghost was thought to haunt the area. It had since been overhauled, but the church's most important makeover came when Bramante renovated the presbytery and choir during the early 16th

Continued on p107

OFF THE BEATEN TRACK

FLEE THE CROWDS: HIDDEN CURIOSITIES

When the camera-wielding Trevi Fountain crowd gets too much, nip up the church steps and into Chiesa di Santissimi Vincenzo e Anastasio (p105). Originally known as the 'Papal church' due to its proximity to the papal residence on Quirinal Hill, this 17th-century church overlooking Rome's most spectacular fountain safeguards the hearts and internal organs of dozens of popes – preserved in amphorae in a tiny gated chapel to the right of the apse. This practice began under Pope Sixtus V (1585–90) and continued until the 20th century when Pope Pius X (1903–1914) decided it was not for him.

Traditionally, before the body of the deceased pontiff was embalmed in preparation for the solemn and elaborate funeral ceremony that would last for several days, the precordia – heart, stomach, intestines and other less-fragrant internal organs – were removed and brought to Chiesa di Santissimi Vincenzo e Anastasio for sacred safekeeping. Two marble tombstones on the apse wall, to the right of the altar, list the 23 popes whose precordia are preserved here.

To admire another hidden treasure *senza* crowds, meander west from Trevi Fountain, along pedestrian Via delle Muratte, and duck a block south to **Galleria Sciarra** (Map p106; Via Marco Minghetti 9-10; ⊙ 9am-8pm Mon-Fri; M Barberini), a stunning interior courtyard with art nouveau glass roof and vibrant frescoes depicting the late 19th-century aristocratic Roman woman in all her feminine guises: as wife, mother, musician and so on. Further frescoes evoke the female virtues of strength, patience, modesty, kindness etc. Hidden away inside 16th-century Palazzo Sciarra Colonna di Carbognano on Via Marco Minghetti, the frescoes and unusual glass roof date to 1890 when the courtyard was remodelled and spruced up by the wealthy Sciarra family. Spot the single man in the frescoes: late Romantic writer Gabriele d'Annunzio.

TOP SIGHT
PIAZZA DI SPAGNA & THE SPANISH STEPS

A magnet for visitors since the 18th century, the Spanish Steps (Scalinata della Trinità dei Monti) rising up from Piazza di Spagna provide a perfect people-watching perch: think hot spot for selfies, newly-wed couples posing for romantic photos etc. In the late 1700s the area was much loved by English visitors on the Grand Tour and was known to locals as the *ghetto de l'inglesi* (the English ghetto).

Spanish Steps

Piazza di Spagna was named after the Spanish Embassy to the Holy See, but the staircase – 135 gleaming steps designed by the Italian Francesco de Sanctis and built in 1725 with a legacy from the French – leads up to the hilltop French Chiesa della Trinità dei Monti. The dazzling sweep of stairs reopened in September 2016 after a €1.5 million clean-up job funded by luxury Italian jewellery house Bulgari.

Chiesa della Trinità dei Monti

This landmark **church** (Piazza Trinità dei Monti 3; ⊘ 7.30am-8pm Tue-Fri, 10am-5pm Sat & Sun) was commissioned by King Louis XII of France and consecrated in 1585. Apart from the great city views from its front steps, it has some wonderful frescoes by Daniele da Volterra.

Fontana della Barcaccia

At the foot of the steps, the fountain of a sinking boat, the **Barcaccia** (1627), is believed to be by Pietro Bernini, father of the more famous Gian Lorenzo. It's fed from an aqueduct, the ancient Roman Acqua Vergine, as are the fountains in Piazza del Popolo and the Trevi Fountain. Here there's not much pressure, so it's sunken as a clever piece of engineering. It was damaged in 2015 by Dutch football fans, and the Dutch subsequently offered to repair the damage.

DON'T MISS

➡ City views from the top of the Spanish Steps

➡ Fontana della Barcaccia

➡ Chiesa della Trinità dei Monti

PRACTICALITIES

➡ Map p106

➡ Ⓜ Spagna

TOP SIGHT
TREVI FOUNTAIN

Rome's most famous fountain, the iconic Fontana di Trevi in Tridente is a baroque extravaganza – a foaming white-marble and emerald-water masterpiece filling an entire piazza. The flamboyant baroque ensemble, 20m wide and 26m high, was designed by Nicola Salvi in 1732 and depicts sea-god Oceanus' chariot being led by Tritons with seahorses – one wild, one docile – representing the moods of the sea.

Coin-tossing

The famous tradition (since the 1954 film *Three Coins in the Fountain*) is to toss a coin into the fountain, thus ensuring your return to Rome. Up to €3000 is thrown into the Trevi each day. This money is collected daily and goes to the Catholic charity Caritas, with its yield increasing significantly since the crackdown on people extracting the money for themselves.

Chiesa di Santissimi Vincenzo e Anastasio

After tossing your lucky coin into Trevi Fountain, nip into this 17th-century church (Map p106; www.santivincenzoeanastasio.it; Vicolo dei Modelli 73; ⏱9am-1pm & 4-8pm; Ⓜ Barberini) overlooking Rome's most spectacular fountain. Originally known as the 'Papal church' due to its proximity to the papal residence on Quirinal Hill, the church safeguards the hearts and internal organs of dozens of popes – preserved in amphorae in a tiny gated chapel to the right of the apse. This practice began under Pope Sixtus V (1585–90) and continued until the 20th century when Pope Pius X (1903-14) decided it was not for him.

DON'T MISS

➡ The contrasting sea horses, or moods of the sea

➡ Throwing a coin or three into the fountain

➡ Papal innards in Chiesa di Santissimi Vincenzo e Anastasio

PRACTICALITIES

➡ Fontana di Trevi

➡ Map p106

➡ Piazza di Trevi

➡ Ⓜ Barberini

Tridente & Trevi

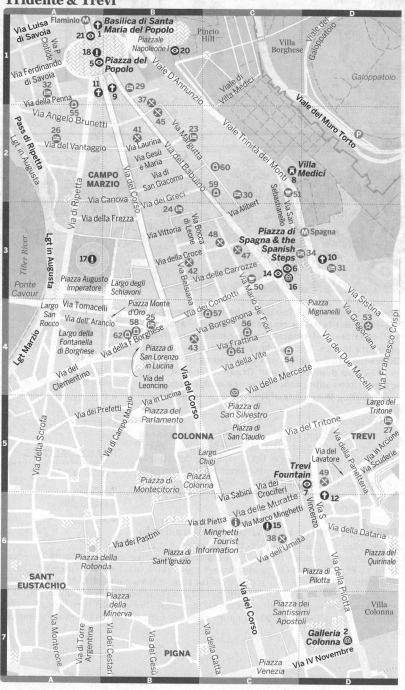

Continued from p103

century and Pinturicchio added a series of frescoes. Bernini further reworked the church in the 17th century.

Look out for Raphael's **Cappella Chigi**, which was completed by Bernini some 100 years later.

★**Galleria Colonna** GALLERY
(Map p106; ☎06 678 43 50; www.galleriacolonna.it; Via della Pilotta 17; adult/reduced €12/10; ⊙9am-1.15pm Sat, closed Aug; 🚍Via IV Novembre) The only part of Palazzo Colonna open to the public, this opulent 17th-century gallery houses the Colonna family's private art collection. It's not the capital's largest collection but with works by Salvatore Rosa, Guido Reni, Guercino and Annibale Carracci, it's well worth the ticket price (which includes an optional guided tour in English at noon).

The gallery's six rooms are crowned by glorious ceiling frescoes, all dedicated to Marcantonio Colonna, the family's greatest ancestor, who defeated the Turks at the naval Battle of Lepanto in 1571. Works by Giovanni Coli and Filippo Gherardi in the Great Hall, Sebastiano Ricci in the Landscapes Room and Giuseppe Bartolomeo Chiari in the Throne Room commemorate his efforts. Of the paintings on display, Annibale Carracci's *Mangiafagioli* (The Bean Eater) is generally considered the outstanding masterpiece. Note also the cannonball lodged in the gallery's marble stairs, a vivid reminder of the 1849 siege of Rome. Another wing includes the sumptuous **Chapel Hall** and the rich 17th-century Artemisia tapestries collection. From May to October a terrace cafe is open.

★**Palazzo del Quirinale** PALACE
(Map p106; ☎06 3996 7557; www.quirinale.it; Piazza del Quirinale; 1¼hr tour €1.50, 2½hr tour adult/reduced €10/5; ⊙9.30am-4pm Tue, Wed & Fri-Sun, closed Aug; Ⓜ Barberini) Overlooking Piazza del Quirinale, this immense palace is the official residence of Italy's head of state, the President of the Republic. For almost three centuries it was the pope's summer residence, but in 1870 Pope Pius IX begrudgingly handed the keys over to Italy's new king. Later, in 1948, it was given to the Italian state. Visits, by guided tour only, should be booked at least five days ahead by telephone (collect your tickets at the nearby **Infopoint** at Salita di Montecavallo 15) or buy online at www.coopculture.it.

Shorter tours visit the reception rooms; longer tours include the gardens and

Tridente & Trevi

carriage collection. Tours (only in Italian) use the tradesmen entrance on Via del Quirinale; arrive 15 minutes before your allotted time. On the other side of the piazza, the palace's former stables, the **Scuderie al Quirinale** (Map p106; ☏ 06 3996 7500; www.scuderiequirinale.it; Via XXIV Maggio 16; adult/reduced €12/9.50; ⊙ 10am-8pm Sun-Thu, to 10.30pm Fri & Sat; ◻ Via Nazionale), host excellent art exhibitions.

Piazza del Quirinale　　　PIAZZA
(Map p106; ⓂBarberini) A wonderful spot to enjoy a glowing Roman sunset, this piazza, which is dominated by the imposing presidential palace of Palazzo del Quirinale (p107), marks the summit of Quirinal Hill. The central obelisk was moved here from the **Mausoleo di Augusto** (Map p106; Piazza Augusto Imperatore; ◻ Piazza Augusto Imperatore) in 1786 and is flanked by 5.5m statues of Castor and Pollux reining in a couple of rearing horses. Catch the weekly changing of the (young and very fidgety) guards on Sunday at 6pm in summer, 4pm the rest of the year.

★**Palazzo Barberini**　　　GALLERY
(Galleria Nazionale d'Arte Antica; Map p106; ☏ 06 481 45 91; www.barberinicorsini.org; Via delle Quattro Fontane 13; adult/reduced €5/2.50, incl Palazzo

Corsini €10/5; ⊙8.30am-7pm Tue-Sun; Ⓜ Barberini) Commissioned to celebrate the Barberini family's rise to papal power, Palazzo Barberini is a sumptuous baroque palace that impresses even before you clap eyes on the breathtaking art. Many high-profile architects worked on it, including rivals Bernini and Borromini; the former contributed a large square staircase, the latter a helicoidal one. Amid the masterpieces, don't miss Pietro da Cortona's *Il Trionfo della Divina Provvidenza* (Triumph of Divine Providence; 1632–39), the most spectacular of the *palazzo* ceiling frescoes in the 1st-floor main salon.

Other must-sees include Hans Holbein's famous portrait of a pugnacious Henry VIII (c 1540); Filippo Lippi's luminous *Annunciazione e due devoti* (Annunciation with two Kneeling Donors); and Raphael's *La Fornarina* (The Baker's Girl), a portrait of his mistress, who worked in a bakery in Trastevere. Works by Caravaggio include *San Francesco d'Assisi in meditazione* (St Francis in Meditation), *Narciso* (Narcissus; 1571–1610) and the mesmerisingly horrific *Giuditta e Oloferne* (Judith Beheading Holophernes; c 1597–1600).

Convento dei Cappuccini   MUSEUM
(Map p106; ☎ 06 487 11 85; www.cappucciniviaveneto.it; Via Vittorio Veneto 27; adult/reduced €8.50/5; ⊙9am-7pm; Ⓜ Barberini) This church and convent complex safeguards what is possibly Rome's strangest sight: crypt chapels where everything from the picture frames to the light fittings is made of human bones. Between 1732 and 1775 resident Capuchin monks used the bones of 3700 of their departed brothers to create this macabre *memento mori* (reminder of death) – a 30m-long passageway ensnaring six crypts, each named after the type of bone used to decorate (skulls, shin bones, pelvises etc).

⊙ Vatican City, Borgo & Prati

St Peter's Square   PIAZZA
(Piazza San Pietro; Map p116; Ⓜ Ottaviano-San Pietro) Overlooked by St Peter's Basilica, the Vatican's central square was laid out between 1656 and 1667 to a design by Gian Lorenzo Bernini. Seen from above, it resembles a giant keyhole with two semicircular colonnades, each consisting of four rows of Doric columns, encircling a giant ellipse that straightens out to funnel believers into the basilica. The effect was deliberate – Bernini described the colonnades as representing 'the motherly arms of the church'.

The scale of the piazza is dazzling: at its largest it measures 320m by 240m. There are 284 columns and, atop the colonnades, 140 saints. The 25m **obelisk** in the centre was brought to Rome by Caligula from Heliopolis in Egypt and later used by Nero as a turning post for the chariot races in his circus.

Leading off the piazza, the monumental approach road, **Via della Conciliazione**, was commissioned by Mussolini and built between 1936 and 1950.

★ Castel Sant'Angelo   MUSEUM, CASTLE
(Map p116; ☎ 06 681 91 11; www.castelsantangelo.beniculturali.it; Lungotevere Castello 50; adult/reduced €10/5; ⊙9am-7.30pm, ticket office to 6.30pm; 🚌 Piazza Pia) With its chunky round keep, this castle is an instantly recognisable landmark. Built as a mausoleum for the emperor Hadrian, it was converted into a papal fortress in the 6th century and named after an angelic vision that Pope Gregory the Great had in 590. Nowadays, it houses the **Museo Nazionale di Castel Sant'Angelo** and its eclectic collection of paintings, sculpture, military memorabilia and medieval firearms.

Many of these weapons were used by soldiers fighting to protect the castle, which, thanks to a secret 13th-century passageway

Continued on p118

DON'T MISS

LEAVES OF STONE
....
In a city essentially known for its extraordinary ancient art and architecture, contemporary art installations in public spaces are a rare breed in conservative Rome. Enter *Foglie di Pietra* (2016), a sensational new sculpture outside the Fendi flagship store on posh shopping strip Largo Carlo Goldoni in Tridente. Donated to the city of Rome by the homegrown Fendi fashion house and unveiled in spring 2017, the sculpture by Italian artist Giuseppe Penone comprises two life-sized bronze trees supporting an 11-tonne marble block with their interlocked branches. The trees tower 18m and 9m high into the sky and represent a definite breath of contemporary fresh air in Rome's art scene.

TOP SIGHT
ST PETER'S BASILICA

In a city of outstanding churches, none can hold a candle to St Peter's, Italy's largest, richest and most spectacular basilica. A monument to centuries of artistic genius, it boasts many spectacular works of art, including three of Italy's most celebrated masterpieces: Michelangelo's *Pietà*, his soaring dome, and Bernini's 29m-high baldachin over the papal altar.

Interior – The Nave

Dominating the centre of the basilica is Bernini's 29m-high **baldachin**. Supported by four spiral columns and made with bronze taken from the Pantheon, it stands over the **papal altar**, also known as the Altar of the Confession. In front, Carlo Maderno's **Confessione** stands over the site where St Peter was originally buried.

Above the baldachin, Michelangelo's **dome** soars to a height of 119m. Based on Brunelleschi's design for the Duomo in Florence, it's supported by four massive stone **piers**, each named after the saint whose statue adorns its Bernini-designed niche. The saints are all associated with the basilica's four major relics: the lance **St Longinus** used to pierce Christ's side; the cloth with which **St Veronica** wiped Jesus' face; a fragment of the Cross collected by **St Helena**; and the head of **St Andrew**.

At the base of the **Pier of St Longinus** is Arnolfo di Cambio's much-loved 13th-century bronze **statue of St Peter**, whose right foot has been worn down by centuries of caresses.

Behind the altar, the tribune is home to Bernini's extraordinary **Cattedra di San Pietro**. A vast gilded bronze throne held aloft by four 5m-high saints, it's centred on a wooden seat that was once thought to have been St Peter's but in fact dates to the 9th century.

DON'T MISS

➡ *Pietà*

➡ Statue of St Peter

➡ The dome

➡ The baldachin

➡ *Cattedra di San Pietro*

PRACTICALITIES

➡ Basilica di San Pietro

➡ Map p116

➡ ☎ 06 6988 5518

➡ www.vatican.va

➡ St Peter's Square

➡ ⊙ 7am-7pm summer, to 6.30pm winter

➡ 🚇 Piazza del Risorgimento, Ⓜ Ottaviano-San Pietro

Above, light shines through a yellow window framed by a gilded mass of golden angels and adorned with a dove to represent the Holy Spirit.

To the right of the throne, Bernini's **monument to Urban VIII** depicts the pope flanked by the figures of Charity and Justice.

Interior – Right Aisle

At the head of the right aisle is Michelangelo's hauntingly beautiful **Pietà**. Sculpted when he was only 25 (in 1499), it's the only work the artist ever signed – his signature is etched into the sash across the Madonna's breast.

Nearby, a **red floor disc** marks the spot where Charlemagne and later Holy Roman emperors were crowned by the pope.

On a pillar just beyond the *Pietà,* Carlo Fontana's gilt and bronze **monument to Queen Christina of Sweden** commemorates the far-from-holy Swedish monarch who converted to Catholicism in 1655.

Moving on, you'll come to the **Cappella di San Sebastiano**, home of Pope John Paul II's tomb, and the **Cappella del Santissimo Sacramento**, a sumptuously decorated baroque chapel with works by Borromini, Bernini and Pietro da Cortona.

Beyond the chapel, the grandiose **monument to Gregory XIII** sits near the roped-off **Cappella Gregoriana**, a chapel built by Gregory XIII from designs by Michelangelo.

Much of the right transept is closed off but you can still make out the **monument to Clement XIII**, one of Canova's most famous works.

The Facade

Built between 1608 and 1612, Maderno's immense facade is 48m high and 115m wide. Eight 27m-high columns support the upper attic on which 13 statues stand representing Christ the Redeemer, St John the Baptist and the 11 apostles. The central balcony is known as the **Loggia della Benedizione**, and it's from here that the pope delivers his *Urbi et Orbi* blessing at Christmas and Easter.

Running across the entablature is an inscription, 'IN HONOREM PRINCIPIS APOST PAVLVS V BVRGHESIVS ROMANVS PONT MAX AN MDCXII PONT VII' which translates as 'In honour of the Prince of Apostles, Paul V Borghese, Roman, Pontiff, in the year 1612, the seventh of his pontificate'.

In the grand atrium, the **Porta Santa** (Holy Door) is opened only in Jubilee years.

WORLD'S LARGEST CHURCH

Contrary to popular opinion, St Peter's Basilica is not the world's largest church – the Basilica of Our Lady of Peace in Yamoussoukro on the Ivory Coast is bigger. Still, its measurements are pretty staggering – it's 187m long and covers more than 15,000 sq metres.

Bronze floor plates in the nave indicate the respective sizes of the 14 next-largest churches.

FACE IN THE BALDACHIN

The frieze on Bernini's baldachin contains a hidden narrative that begins at the pillar to the left (looking with your back to the entrance). As you walk clockwise around the baldachin note the woman's face carved into the frieze of each pillar. On the first three pillars her face seems to express the increasing agony of childbirth; on the last one, it's replaced by that of a smiling baby. The woman was a niece of Pope Urban VIII, who gave birth as Bernini worked on the baldachin.

◉ TOP SIGHT
VATICAN MUSEUMS

Visiting the Vatican Museums is a thrilling and unforgettable experience. With some 7km of exhibitions and more masterpieces than many small countries can call their own, this vast museum complex boasts one of the world's greatest art collections. Highlights include a spectacular collection of classical statuary in the Museo Pio-Clementino, a suite of rooms frescoed by Raphael, and the Michelangelo-decorated Sistine Chapel.

Pinacoteca

Often overlooked by visitors, the papal picture gallery displays paintings dating from the 11th to 19th centuries, with works by Giotto, Fra' Angelico, Filippo Lippi, Perugino, Titian, Guido Reni, Guercino, Pietro da Cortona, Caravaggio and Leonardo da Vinci.

Look out for a trio of paintings by Raphael in Room VIII – the *Madonna di Foligno* (Madonna of Folignano), the *Incoronazione della Vergine* (Crowning of the Virgin), and *La Trasfigurazione* (Transfiguration), which was completed by his students after his death in 1520. Other highlights include Filippo Lippi's *L'Incoronazione della Vergine con Angeli, Santo e donatore* (Coronation of the Virgin with Angels, Saints, and donors); Leonardo da Vinci's haunting and unfinished *San Gerolamo* (St Jerome); and Caravaggio's *Deposizione* (Deposition from the Cross).

DON'T MISS

➡ Sistine Chapel

➡ Stanze di Raffaello

➡ *Apollo Belvedere* and *Laocoön,* Museo Pio-Clementino

➡ *La Trasfigurazione,* Pinacoteca

PRACTICALITIES

➡ Musei Vaticani

➡ Map p116

➡ ☎ 06 6988 4676

➡ www.museivaticani.va

➡ Viale Vaticano

➡ adult/reduced €16/8, last Sun of month free

➡ ⊙ 9am-6pm Mon-Sat, 9am-2pm last Sun of month, last entry 2hr before close

➡ 🚌 Piazza del Risorgimento, Ⓜ Ottaviano-San Pietro

Museo Chiaramonti & Braccio Nuovo

This museum is effectively the long corridor that runs down the lower east side of the Palazzetto di Belvedere. Its walls are lined with thousands of statues and busts representing everything from immortal gods to playful cherubs and ugly Roman patricians.

Near the end of the hall, off to the right, is the Braccio Nuovo (New Wing), which contains a celebrated statue of the Nile as a reclining god covered by 16 babies.

Museo Pio-Clementino

This stunning museum contains some of the Vatican's finest classical statuary, including the peerless *Apollo Belvedere* and the 1st-century-BC *Laocoön*, both in the Cortile Ottagono (Octagonal Courtyard).

Before you go into the courtyard, take a moment to admire the 1st century *Apoxyomenos*, one of the earliest known sculptures to depict a figure with a raised arm.

To the left as you enter the courtyard, the *Apollo Belvedere* is a 2nd-century Roman copy of a 4th-century BC Greek bronze. A beautifully proportioned representation of the sun god Apollo, it's considered one of the great masterpieces of classical sculpture. Nearby, the *Laocoön* depicts the mythical death of the Trojan priest who warned his fellow citizens not to take the wooden horse left by the Greeks.

Back inside, the Sala degli Animali is filled with sculpted creatures and some magnificent 4th-century mosaics. Continuing on, you come to the Sala delle Muse (Room of the Muses), centred on the *Torso Belvedere*, another of the museum's must-sees. A fragment of a muscular 1st-century-BC Greek sculpture, this was found in Campo de' Fiori and used by Michelangelo as a model for his *ignudi* (male nudes) in the Sistine Chapel.

The next room, the Sala Rotonda (Round Room), contains a number of colossal statues, including a gilded-bronze *Ercole* (Hercules) and an exquisite floor mosaic. The enormous basin in the centre of the room was found at Nero's Domus Aurea and is made out of a single piece of red porphyry stone.

Museo Gregoriano Egizio

Founded by Pope Gregory XVI in 1839, this Egyptian museum displays pieces taken from Egypt in ancient Roman times. The collection is small but there are fascinating exhibits, including a fragmented statue of the pharaoh Ramses II on his throne, vividly painted sarcophagi dating from around 1000 BC, and a macabre mummy.

BLUE SKY ABOVE

One of the striking features of the *Giudizio Universale* is the amount of ultramarine blue in the painting – in contrast with the ceiling frescoes, which don't have any. In the 16th century, blue paint was made from the hugely expensive stone lapis lazuli, and artists were reluctant to use it unless someone else was paying. In the case of the *Giudizio Universale*, the pope picked up the tab for all Michelangelo's materials; on the ceiling, however, the artist had to cover his own expenses and so used less costly colours.

MICHELANGELO SELF-POTRAITS

Hidden amid the mass of bodies in the Sistine Chapel frescoes are two of Michelangelo's self-portraits. On the *Giudizio Universale* look for the figure of St Bartholomew, holding his own flayed skin beneath Christ. The face in the skin is said to be Michelangelo's, its anguished look reflecting the artist's tormented faith. His stricken face is also said to be that of the prophet Jeremiah on the ceiling.

Museo Gregoriano Etrusco

At the top of the 18th-century Simonetti staircase, this fascinating museum contains artefacts unearthed in the Etruscan tombs of northern Lazio, as well as a superb collection of vases and Roman antiquities. Of particular interest is the *Marte di Todi* (Mars of Todi), a black bronze of a warrior dating to the late 5th century BC.

Stanze di Raffaello

These four frescoed chambers, currently undergoing partial restoration, were part of Pope Julius II's private apartments. Raphael himself painted the **Stanza della Segnatura** (1508–11) and the **Stanza d'Eliodoro** (1512–14), while the **Stanza dell'Incendio di Borgo** (1514–17) and **Sala di Costantino** (1517–24) were decorated by students following his designs.

The first room you come to is the **Sala di Costantino**, originally a ceremonial reception room, which is dominated by the *Battaglia di Costantino contro Maxentius* (Battle of the Milvian Bridge) showing the victory of Constantine, Rome's first Christian emperor, over his rival Maxentius.

Leading off the *sala,* but often closed to the public, the **Cappella Niccolina**, Pope Nicholas V's private chapel, boasts a superb cycle of frescoes by Fra' Angelico.

The **Stanza d'Eliodoro**, which was used for the pope's private audiences, takes its name from the *Cacciata d'Eliodoro* (Expulsion of Heliodorus from the Temple), reflecting Pope Julius II's policy of forcing foreign powers off Church lands. To its right, the *Messa di Bolsena* (Mass of Bolsena) shows Julius paying homage to the relic of a 13th-century miracle at the lakeside town of Bolsena. Next is the *Incontro di Leone Magno con Attila* (Encounter of Leo the Great with Attila), and, on the fourth wall, the *Liberazione di San Pietro* (Liberation of St Peter), a brilliant work illustrating Raphael's masterful ability to illustrate light.

The **Stanza della Segnatura**, Julius' study and library, was the first room that Raphael painted, and it's here that you'll find his great masterpiece, *La Scuola di Atene* (The School of Athens), featuring philosophers and scholars gathered around Plato and Aristotle. The seated figure in front of the steps is believed to be Michelangelo, while the figure of Plato is said to be a portrait of Leonardo da Vinci, and Euclide (the bald man bending over) is Bramante. Raphael also included a self-portrait in the lower right corner – he's the second figure from the right in the black hat. Opposite is *La Disputa del Sacramento* (Disputation on the Sacrament), also by Raphael.

The most famous work in the **Stanza dell'Incendio di Borgo**, the former seat of the Holy See's highest court and later a dining room, is the *Incendio di Borgo* (Fire in the Borgo). This depicts Leo IV extinguishing a fire by making the sign of the cross. The ceiling was painted by Raphael's master, Perugino.

From the Raphael Rooms, stairs lead to the **Appartamento Borgia** and the Vatican's collection of modern religious art.

Sistine Chapel

The jewel in the Vatican crown, the Cappella Sistina (Sistine Chapel) is home to two of the world's most famous works of art – Michelangelo's ceiling frescoes and his *Giudizio Universale* (Last Judgment).

SISTINE CHAPEL CEILING

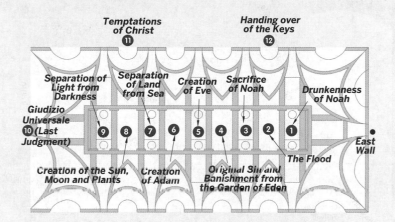

Museum Tour: Sistine Chapel

LENGTH 30 MINUTES

On entering the chapel head over to the main entrance in the far (east) wall for the best views of the ceiling.

Michelangelo's design, which took him four years to complete, covers the entire 800-sq-metre surface. With painted architectural features and a colourful cast of biblical figures, it centres on nine panels depicting stories from the Book of Genesis.

As you look up from the east wall, the first panel is the ❶ **Drunkenness of Noah**, followed by ❷ **The Flood**, and the ❸ **Sacrifice of Noah**. Next, ❹ **Original Sin and Banishment from the Garden of Eden** famously depicts Adam and Eve being sent packing after accepting the forbidden fruit from Satan, represented by a snake with the body of a woman coiled around a tree. The ❺ **Creation of Eve** is then followed by the ❻ **Creation of Adam**. This, one of the most famous images in Western art, shows a bearded God pointing his finger at Adam,

thus bringing him to life. Completing the sequence are the ❼ **Separation of Land from Sea**; the ❽ **Creation of the Sun, Moon and Plants**; and the ❾ **Separation of Light from Darkness**, featuring a fearsome God reaching out to touch the sun. Set around the central panels are 20 athletic male nudes, the so-called *ignudi*.

Straight ahead of you on the west wall is Michelangelo's mesmeric ❿ **Giudizio Universale** (Last Judgment), showing Christ – in the centre near the top – passing sentence over the souls of the dead as they are torn from their graves to face him. The saved get to stay up in heaven (in the upper right) while the damned are sent down to face the demons in hell (in the bottom right).

The chapel's side walls also feature stunning Renaissance frescoes, representing the lives of Moses (to your left) and Christ (to the right). Look out for Botticelli's ⓫ **Temptations of Christ** and Perugino's great masterpiece, the ⓬ **Handing over of the Keys**.

Vatican City, Borgo & Prati

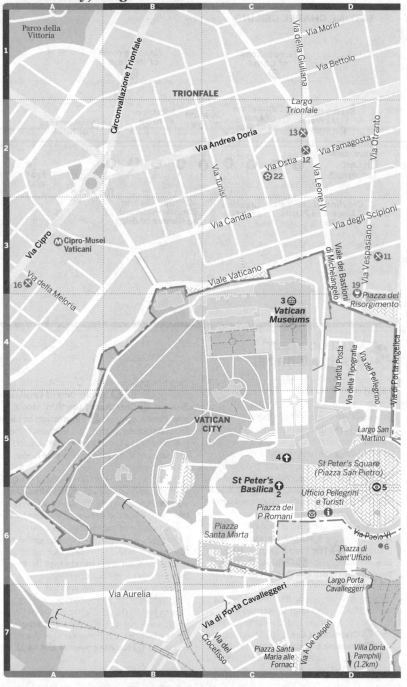

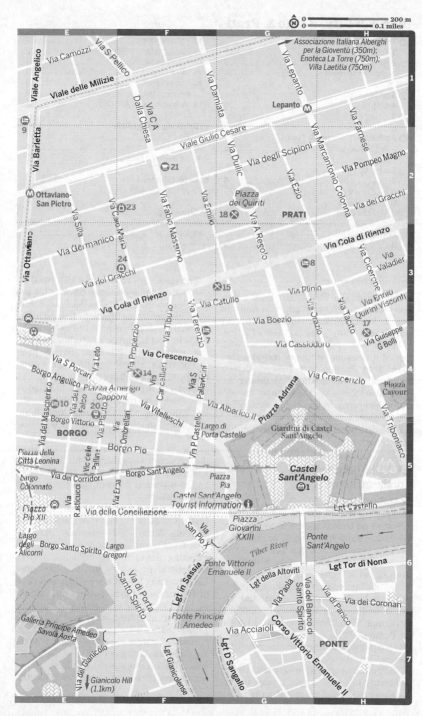

ROME & LAZIO

0 — 200 m
0 — 0.1 miles

Associazione Italiana Alberghi
per la Gioventù (350m);
Enoteca La Torre (750m);
Villa Laetitia (750m)

Via Camozzi
Via S Pellico
Viale Angelico
Viale delle Milizie
Via Barletta
Via Lepanto
Via Damiata
Lepanto M
Via C A Dalla Chiesa
Viale Giulio Cesare
Via Duilic
Via degli Scipioni
Via Marcantonio Colonna
Via Farnese
Via Pompeo Magno
9
21
M Ottaviano-
San Pietro
Via Sila
Via Capo Mario
23
Via Fabio Massimo
Via Emilio
Via A Resolo
Piazza
dei Quiriti
18
PRATI
Via Ezio
Via dei Gracchi
Via Ottaviano
Via Germanico
24
Via dei Gracchi
Via Cola di Rienzo
Via Cicerone
Via Valadier
Via Cola di Rienzo
Via Plinio
8
Via Tacito
Via Ennio Quirini Visconti
15
Via Catullo
Via Tibulo
Via Terenzio
Via Boezio
Via Orazio
17
Via Guiseppe G Belli
7
Via Cassiodoro
Via S Porcari
Via Propezio
Via Crescenzio
14
Borgo Angelico
Via del Falco
Via Leto
Piazza Amerigo
Capponi
Via Carcelieri
Via S Pallavicini
Via Crescenzio
Piazza Adriana
Via Crescenzio
Piazza
Cavour
Via del Mascherino
10
20
Via Plauto
Via Vitelleschi
Via Alberico II
Via Tribuniaz
Borgo Vittorio
BORGO
Via P Castello
Largo di
Porta Castello
Giardini di Castel
Sant'Angelo
Piazza della
Città Leonina
Vic cele
Pallini
Borgo Pio
Via Erba
Via della Conciliazione
Castel
Sant'Angelo
1
Largo
Colonnato
Via dei Corridori
Borgo Sant'Angelo
Piazza
Pia
Castel Sant'Angelo
Tourist Information
Lgt Castello
Piazza
Pio XII
Via Rusticucci
Piazza
Giovanni
XXIII
Ponte
Sant'Angelo
Largo
degli
Alicorni
Borgo Santo Spirito
Largo
Gregori
Via
San Pio X
Tiber River
Lgt Tor di Nona
Ponte Vittorio
Emanuele II
Lgt Sassia
Lgt della Altoviti
Via Paola
Via di Panico
Via dei Coronari
Galleria Principe Amedeo
Savoia Aosta
Via di Porta
Santo Spirito
Ponte Principe
II Amedeo
Via Acciaioli
Lgt D Sangallo
Corso Vittorio Emanuele II
PONTE
Via del Gianicolo
Gianicolo Hill
(1.1km)
Lgt Gianicolense

Vatican City, Borgo & Prati

Continued from p109

to the Vatican (the *Passetto di Borgo*), provided sanctuary to many popes in times of danger. Most famously, Pope Clemente VI holed up here during the 1527 sack of Rome.

The castle's upper floors are filled with elegant Renaissance interiors, including the lavish **Sala Paolina** with frescoes depicting episodes from the life of Alexander the Great. Two storeys up, the **terrace**, immortalised by Puccini in his opera *Tosca,* offers unforgettable views over Rome.

Note that ticket prices may increase during temporary exhibitions.

◎ Villa Borghese & Northern Rome

★**Museo e Galleria Borghese**　MUSEUM
(Map p120; ☎06 3 28 10; www.galleriaborghese. it; Piazzale del Museo Borghese 5; adult/reduced €15/8.50; ☉9am-7pm Tue-Sun; 🚇Via Pinciana) If you only have the time (or inclination) for one art gallery in Rome, make it this one. Housing what's often referred to as the 'queen of all private art collections', it boasts paintings by Caravaggio, Raphael and Titian, as well as some sensational sculptures by Bernini. Highlights abound, but look out for Bernini's *Ratto di Proserpina* (Rape of Proserpina) and Canova's *Venere vincitrice* (Venus Victrix).

To limit numbers, visitors are admitted at two-hourly intervals, so you'll need to prebook your ticket and get an entry time.

The museum's collection was formed by Cardinal Scipione Borghese (1579–1633), the most knowledgeable and ruthless art collector of his day. It was originally housed in the cardinal's residence near St Peter's but in the 1620s he had it transferred to his new villa just outside Porta Pinciana. And it's here, in the villa's central building, the Casino Borghese, that you'll see it today.

Over the centuries, the villa has undergone several overhauls, most notably in the late 1700s when Prince Marcantonio Borghese added much of the lavish neoclassical decor.

The museum is divided into two parts: the ground-floor gallery, with its superb sculptures, intricate Roman floor mosaics and over-the-top frescoes, and the upstairs picture gallery.

From the basement entrance, stairs lead up to **Sala IV**, home of Gian Lorenzo Bernini's *Ratto di Proserpina* (1621–22). This flamboyant sculpture, one of a series depicting pagan myths, brilliantly reveals the artist's virtuosity – just look at Pluto's hand pressing into the seemingly soft flesh of Persephone's thigh. Further on, in **Sala III**, he captures the exact moment Daphne's hands start morphing into leaves in *Apollo e Dafne* (1622–25).

Another statuesque scene-stealer is Antonio Canova's daring depiction of Napoleon's sister, Paolina Bonaparte Borghese, reclining topless as *Venere vincitrice* (1805–08) in **Sala I**.

Caravaggio dominates **Sala VIII**. There's a dissipated-looking *Bacchino malato* (Young Sick Bacchus; 1592–95), the strangely beautiful *La Madonna dei Palafenieri* (Madonna with Serpent; 1605–06), and *San Giovanni Battista* (St John the Baptist; 1609–10), probably Caravaggio's last work. There's also the much-loved *Ragazzo col Canestro di Frutta* (Boy with a Basket of Fruit; 1593–95), and the dramatic *Davide con la Testa di Golia* (David with the Head of Goliath; 1609–10) – Goliath's severed head is said to be a self-portrait.

Beyond Sala VIII, a **portico** flanks the grand **entrance hall**, decorated with 4th-century floor mosaics of fighting gladiators and a 2nd-century *Satiro Combattente* (Fighting Satyr). High on the wall is a gravity-defying bas-relief of a horse and rider falling into the void (*Marco Curzio a Cavallo*) by Pietro Bernini (Gian Lorenzo's father).

Upstairs, the **pinacoteca** offers a wonderful snapshot of Renaissance art. Don't miss Raphael's extraordinary *La Deposizione di Cristo* (The Deposition; 1507) in **Sala IX**, and his *Dama con Liocorno* (Lady with a Unicorn; 1506). In the same room is Fra Bartolomeo's superb *Adorazione del Bambino* (Adoration of the Christ Child; 1495) and Perugino's *Madonna con Bambino* (Madonna and Child; first quarter of the 16th century).

Other highlights include Correggio's erotic *Danae* (1530–31) in **Sala X**, Bernini's self-portraits in **Sala XIV**, and Titian's great masterpiece, *Amor Sacro e Amor Profano* (Sacred and Profane Love; 1514) in **Sala XX**.

Villa Borghese   PARK

(Map p120, www.soyrmintendenzaroma.it; entrances at Piazzale San Paolo del Brasile, Piazzale Flaminio, Via Pinciana, Via Raimondo, Largo Pablo Picasso; ☺ sunrise-sunset; 🚊 Via Pinciana) Locals, lovers, tourists, joggers – no one can resist the lure of Rome's most celebrated park. Originally the 17th-century estate of Cardinal Scipione Borghese, it covers about 80 hectares of wooded glades, gardens and grassy banks. Among its attractions are several excellent museums, the landscaped **Giardino del Lago** (boat hire per 20min €3; ☺ 7am-9pm summer, to 6pm winter), **Piazza di Siena**, a dusty arena used for Rome's top equestrian event in May, and a panoramic terrace on the **Pincio Hill** (Map p106; Ⓜ Flaminio).

★ Museo Nazionale
Etrusco di Villa Giulia   MUSEUM
(Map p120; ☎ 06 322 65 71; www.villagiulia.beni culturali.it; Piazzale di Villa Giulia; adult/reduced €8/4; ☺ 8.30am-7.30pm Tue-Sun; 🚊 Via delle Belle Arti)

Pope Julius III's 16th-century villa provides the charming setting for Italy's finest collection of Etruscan and pre-Roman treasures. Exhibits, many of which came from tombs in the surrounding Lazio region, range from bronze figurines and black *bucchero* tableware to temple decorations, terracotta vases and a display of sophisticated jewellery.

Must-sees include a polychrome terracotta statue of Apollo from a temple in Veio, and the 6th-century-BC *Sarcofago degli Sposi* (Sarcophagus of the Betrothed), found in 1881 in Cerveteri.

Further finds relating to the Umbri and Latin peoples are housed in the nearby **Villa Poniatowski** (Map p120; ☎ 06 322 65 71; Piazzale di Villa Giulia; incl in Museo Nazionale Etrusco di Villa Giulia ticket; ☺ 10am-1pm Thu, 3 6pm Sat; 🚊 Via delle Belle Arti).

★ La Galleria Nazionale   GALLERY
(Map p120; ☎ 06 3229 8221; http://lagallerianazi onale.com; Viale delle Belle Arti 131, accessible entrance Via Antonio Gramsci 71, adult/reduced €10/5; ☺ 8.30am-7.30pm Tue-Sun; 🚊 Piazza Thorvaldsen) Housed in a vast belle-époque palace, this oft-overlooked modern art gallery, known locally as GNAM, is an unsung gem. Its superlative collection runs the gamut from neoclassical sculpture to abstract expressionism with works by many of the most important exponents of 19th- and 20th-century art.

There are canvases by the *macchiaioli* (Italian Impressionists) and futurists Boccioni and Balla, as well as sculptures by Canova and major works by Modigliani, de Chirico and Guttuso. International artists represented include Van Gogh, Cézanne, Monet, Klimt, Kandinsky, Mondrian and Man Ray.

Museo Nazionale
delle Arti del XXI Secolo   GALLERY
(MAXXI; ☎ 06 320 19 54; www.fondazionemaxxi.it; Via Guido Reni 4a; adult/reduced €12/8, permanent collection free Tue-Fri & 1st Sun of month; ☺ 11am-7pm Tue-Fri & Sun, to 10pm Sat; 🚊 Viale Tiziano) As much as the exhibitions, the highlight of Rome's leading contemporary art gallery is the Zaha Hadid–designed building it occupies. Formerly a barracks, the curved concrete structure is striking inside and out with a multilayered geometric facade and a cavernous light-filled interior full of snaking walkways and suspended staircases.

There is a permanent collection of 20th- and 21st-century works, of which a selection are on free display in Gallery 4, but more interesting are its international exhibitions.

ROME & LAZIO COURSES

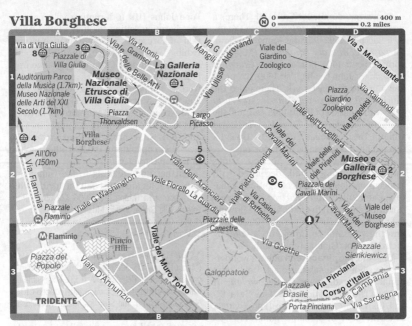

Villa Borghese

🎓 Courses

🍴 Cooking & Wine Tasting

Vino Roma WINE
(Map p90; ☑ 328 487 44 97; www.vinoroma.com;
Via in Selci 84g; 2hr tastings per person €50; Ⓜ Cavour) With beautifully appointed century-
old cellars and a chic tasting studio, Vino
Roma guides novices and experts in tasting
wine under the knowledgeable stewardship
of sommelier Hande Leimer and her expert
team. Also on offer is a wine-and-cheese dinner (€60) with snacks, cheeses and cold cuts
to accompany the wines, and bespoke three-
hour food tours. Book online.

Latteria Studio COOKING
(☑ 835 29 990; https://latteriastudio.com; Via
di Ponziano 29; 🚊 Viale di Trastevere, 🚊 Viale di Trastevere) Highly personalised market tours and
cooking classes in a stylish food photography studio in backstreet Trastevere. Prices
vary, depending on the course. Count on
around €75 for a day's fresh pasta-making
class with lunch.

🍴 Language

**Torre di Babele Centro
di Lingua e Cultura Italiana** LANGUAGE
(☑ 06 4425 2578; www.torredibabele.com; Via
Cosenza 7; 🚊 Via Bari) As well as language lessons, this school offers courses on cooking,
art, architecture and several other subjects.
Individual language lessons start at €39,
with an enrolment fee of €80.

🍴 Arts & Crafts

Art Studio Lab ART
(Map p116; ☑ 348 6099758, 344 0971721; box@
savellireligious.com; Via Paolo VI 27-29, c/o Savelli
Arte e Tradizione; ⊙ 9.30am-7pm; 🚊 Lungotevere
in Sassia) This mosaic school, operating out
of the Savelli Arte e Tradizione shop, offers
individually tailored workshops and courses. In a basic three-hour workshop, which

includes a bite to eat, you'll learn how to cut marble and enamels and make your own frames, mirrors or tiles. Reckon on €90/80 per adult/child for a group of one to three people.

Tours

Casa Mia   TOURS
(📱346 800 17 46; www.italyfoodandwinetours. com; 3hr tour with tastings 2/4 people €360/420) Serious food and wine tours, including a Trastevere and Jewish Quarter neighbourhood tour, with tastings and behind-the-scene meetings with local shopkeepers, producers, chefs and restaurateurs. Bespoke tours, dining itineraries and reservations can also be arranged.

Roman Guy   TOURS
(https://theromanguy.com) A professional set-up that organises a wide range of group and private tours. Packages, led by English-speaking experts, include skip-the-line visits to the Vatican Museums (US$89), foodie tours of Trastevere and the Jewish Ghetto (US$84), and an evening bar hop through the historic centre's cocktail bars (US$225).

A Friend in Rome   TOURS
(📱340 501 92 01; www.afriendinrome.it) Silvia Prosperi and her team offer a range of private tours covering the Vatican and main historic centre as well as areas outside the capital. They can also organise kid-friendly tours, food and wine itineraries, vintage car drives and horse rides along Via Appia Antica. Rates start at €165 for a basic three hour tour for up to eight people; add €55 for every additional hour.

GT Food & Travel   TOURS
(📱320 720 42 22; www.gtfoodandtravel.com; 3hr tour with tastings per person around €120) Small-group food-lover tours, including a themed 'Cucina Povera & Roman Cuisine' tour in Monteverde. Gelato tours (with the option of an add-on gelato-making class), half- and full-day custom tours, cooking classes and in-home dining experiences are also on offer.

Bici & Baci   TOURS
(Map p90; 📱06 481 40 64; www.bicibaci.com; Via Rosmini 26; bike tours from €30, Vespa tours from €145; ⏰8am-7pm Mon-Sat; M Termini) The flagship branch of two-wheeled specialists Bici & Baci is the place to sign up for a daily bike tour or organise a tour on the back of a Vespa, in a classic Fiat 500 or three-wheeled Ape. It has a second branch at Via del Viminale (Map p90; 📱06 482 84 43; www.bicibaci.com; Via del Viminale 5; bike tours from €30, Vespa tours from €145; ⏰8am-7pm; M Repubblica).

Festivals & Events

Natale di Roma   CULTURAL
(⏰21 Apr) Rome celebrates its birthday with music, historical re-enactments and fireworks. Action is centred on Via dei Fori Imperiali and the city's ancient sites.

Easter   RELIGIOUS
(⏰Mar/Apr) On Good Friday, the pope leads a candlelit procession around the Colosseum. At noon on Easter Sunday he blesses the crowds in St Peter's Square.

Carnevale Romano   CARNIVAL
(www.carnevaleroma.com; ⏰Feb) Rome goes to town for Carnival with horse shows, costumed parades, street performers, fireworks and crowds of kids in fancy dress. Action is centred on Piazza del Popolo, Via del Corso, Piazza di Spagna and Piazza Navona.

Concerti del Tempietto   MUSIC
(www.tempietto.it; ⏰mid-Jul–mid-Oct) The Teatro di Marcello and Basilica di San Nicola in Carcere are among the atmospheric venues used to stage performances during this summer concert series.

Festa dei Santi
Pietro e Paolo   RELIGIOUS
(⏰29 Jun) On 29 June Rome celebrates its two patron saints, Peter and Paul, with flower displays on St Peter's Square, fireworks at Castel Sant'Angelo, and festivities near the Basilica di San Paolo Fuori-le-Mura.

Estate Romana   CULTURAL
(www.estateromana.comune.roma.it; ⏰Jun-Oct) Rome's big summer festival involves everything from concerts and dance performances to book fairs, puppet shows and late-night museum openings.

Romaeuropa   PERFORMING ARTS
(http://romaeuropa.net; ⏰late-Sep–early Dec) From late September to early December, top international artists take to stages across town for Rome's autumn festival of theatre, opera and dance.

Primo Maggio   MUSIC
(Piazza di San Giovanni in Laterano; ⏰1 May) Rome's May Day rock concert attracts huge

crowds and big-name Italian performers to Piazza di San Giovanni in Laterano.

Romaeuropa
MUSIC

(☑box office 06 4555 3050; www.romaeuropa. net; Via dei Magazzini Generali 20a; tickets €15-40; ☉late Sep-early Nov; Ⓜ Piramide) Rome's premier dance and drama festival takes to the stage in various venues around the city from late September to early November. Think avant-garde dance performances, contemporary art installations, multimedia shows, recitals and readings.

Mostra delle Azalee
CULTURAL

(Piazza di Spagna; ☉mid-Apr–May; Ⓜ Spagna) As per an 80-year-old tradition, the Spanish Steps are decorated with hundreds of vases of blooming, brightly coloured azaleas from mid-April to early May.

Festa del Cinema di Roma
FILM

(www.romacinemafest.it; Viale Pietro de Coubertin 10, Auditorium Parco della Musica; ☉late Oct; ⓖ Viale Tiziano) Held at the Auditorium Parco della Musica in late October, Rome's film festival rolls out the red carpet for big-screen big shots.

🛏 Sleeping

Rome is expensive and busy; book ahead to secure the best deal. Accommodation ranges from palatial five-star hotels to hostels, B&Bs, *pensioni* and private rooms. Hostels are the cheapest, with dorm beds and private rooms: around Stazione Termini several budget hotels also offer 'dorm beds', meaning you can book a bed in a shared double, triple or quad hotel room. B&Bs and hotels cover every style and price range.

Rental in Rome
ACCOMMODATION SERVICES

(☑06 322 00 68; www.rentalinrome.com) Good selection of midrange and top-end apartments in the historic centre and surrounds.

Sleep in Italy
ACCOMMODATION SERVICES

(☑334 3583338; www.sleepinitaly.com) A reliable rental operator with midrange to top-end listings.

Cross Pollinate
ACCOMMODATION SERVICES

(☑06 9936 9799; www.cross-pollinate.com) Has budget B&Bs, private apartments and guesthouses.

🛏 Ancient Rome

★Residenza Maritti
GUESTHOUSE €€

(Map p80; ☑06 678 82 33; www.residenzamaritti.com; Via Tor de' Conti 17; s/d/tr €120/170/190; ❄ ☎; Ⓜ Cavour) Boasting stunning views over the nearby forums and Vittoriano, this hidden gem has rooms spread over several floors. Some are bright and modern, others are more cosy in feel with antiques, original tiled floors and family furniture. There's a fully equipped kitchen and a self-service breakfast is provided.

Room rates drop considerably in low season and for longer stays.

★Inn at the Roman Forum
BOUTIQUE HOTEL €€€

(Map p80; ☑06 6919 0970; www.theinnattheromanforum.com; Via degli Ibernesi 30; d €228-422; Ⓜ Cavour) Hidden behind a discreet entrance in a quiet street near the Imperial Forums, this chic boutique hotel is pure gold. From the friendly welcome to the contemporary-styled rooms and panoramic roof terrace, it hits the jackpot. It even has its own ancient ruins in the form of a small 1st-century BC tunnel complex.

🛏 Centro Storico

Hotel Pensione Barrett
PENSION €€

(Map p86; ☑06 686 8481; www.pensionebarrett.com; Largo di Torre Argentina 47; s/d/tr €115/135/165; ❄ ☎; ⓖ Largo di Torre Argentina) This exuberant pension is quite unique. Boasting a convenient central location, its decor is wonderfully over the top with statues, busts and vibrant stucco set against a forest of leafy potted plants. Rooms are cosy and come with thoughtful extras like foot spas, coffee machines and fully stocked fridges.

Argentina Residenza
GUESTHOUSE €€

(Map p86; ☑06 6819 3267; www.argentinaresidenza.com; Via di Torre Argentina 47, 3rd fl; d €170-240; ❄ ☎; ⓖ Largo di Torre Argentina) A classy boutique guesthouse, Argentina Residenza provides a stylish bolthole in the heart of the historic centre. Its six rooms, fresh from a recent facelift, cut a contemporary dash with their white and pearl-grey palettes, parquet floors, design touches and sparkling bathrooms.

Albergo Cesàri
HISTORIC HOTEL €€

(Map p86; ☑06 674 9701; www.albergocesari. it; Via di Pietra 89a; s €130-170, d €145-280; ❄ ☎;

Via del Corso) This friendly three-star has been welcoming guests since 1787 and both Stendhal and Mazzini are said to have slept here. Modern-day visitors can expect traditionally attired rooms, complete with creaky parquet floors, a stunning rooftop terrace, and a wonderful central location.

The panoramic terrace bar (6pm to 11.30pm) is also open to non-guests.

Relais Palazzo Taverna BOUTIQUE HOTEL €€
(Map p86; 06 2039 8064; www.relais palazzotaverna.com; Via dei Gabrielli 92; s/d/tr €140/210/240; ❄ 🛜; Corso del Rinascimento) Housed in a 15th-century *palazzo*, this six-room boutique hotel is just off Via dei Coronari, an elegant cobbled street north of Piazza Navona. Its rooms are simply furnished but come alive thanks to imaginative design touches, wood-beamed ceilings and dark-wood flooring. There's no dining area so breakfast is served in your room.

★ Hotel Campo de' Fiori BOUTIQUE HOTEL €€€
(Map p86; 06 6880 6865; www.hotelcampo defiori.com; Via del Biscione 6; r €280-430, apt €230-350; ❄ @ 🛜; Corso Vittorio Emanuele II) This rakish four-star has got the lot – enticing boudoir decor, an enviable location, professional staff and a fabulous panoramic roof terrace. The interior feels delightfully decadent with its boldly coloured walls, low wooden ceilings, gilt mirrors and crimson damask. Also available are 13 apartments, each sleeping two to five people.

Gigli D'Oro Suite BOUTIQUE HOTEL €€€
(Map p86; 06 6839 2055; www.giglidoro suite.com; Via dei Gigli d'Oro 12; r €215-410; ❄ 🛜; Corso del Rinascimento) This classy hideaway offers six suites in a 15th-century *palazzo* that once belonged to Pope Sixtus V. Traces of the original building have been kept intact so you'll find stone doorways, antique fireplaces and, in the top-floor executive suite, a sloping wood-beamed ceiling. The suites, all named after roads that once crisscrossed the area, boast a chic white look and designer bathrooms.

Argentina Residenza Style Hotel BOUTIQUE HOTEL €€€
(Map p86; 06 6821 9623; www.argentinaresi denzastylehotel.com; Via di Torre Argentina 47, 1st fl; r €180-280; Largo di Torre Argentina) This discreet boutique hotel offers a prime central location and nine stylish rooms, each decorated in sleek contemporary style. High beds

with big padded headsteads are set against largely unadorned white walls while parquet and original wood-beamed ceilings add colour and character. Reception and most rooms are on the 1st floor but there's also a family apartment one floor up.

Albergo Abruzzi HOTEL €€€
(Map p86; 06 679 2021; www.hotelabruzzi.it; Piazza della Rotonda 69; d €227-340, tr €295-400, q €295-450; ❄ 🛜; Largo di Torre Argentina) As far as locations go, the Abruzzi's tops the charts, smack bang opposite the Pantheon. But there's more to the place than its views. Its pristine rooms, while small, are good-looking with blown-up photos printed on white walls and modern dark-wood flooring. Kettles are provided with tea- and coffee-making kit, and smartphones are available for guests to use.

🛏 Monti, Esquilino & San Lorenzo

★ Generator Hostel HOSTEL €
(Map p90; 06 492 330; https://generator hostels.com; Via Principe Amedeo 257; dm €17-70, d €50-200; ❄ @ 🛜; M Vittorio Emanuele) Hostelling just got a whole lot smarter in Rome thanks to this designer hostel which, quite frankly, is more uber-cool hotel in mood – 72% of the 174 beds here languish in bright white private rooms with sharp bathrooms, and dorms max out at four beds. Check in at the zinc-topped bar, linger over a cappuccino in the stylish lounge, chill on the sensational rooftop lounge.

There are connecting doubles for families, the bar opens from 6pm to 2am every day, and DJs spin sets Friday and Saturday evenings.

★ **Yellow Hostel** HOSTEL €
(Map p90; ☑06 446 35 54; www.the-yellow.com; Via Palestro 51; dm €20-35, d €90-120, q €100-150; ❋@🛜; Ⓜ Castro Pretorio) This sharp, 300-bed party hostel, with designer dorms, play area sporting comfy beanbags, escape room and kitchen you'd actually want to hang out in, is rapidly colonising the entire street – aka the 'Yellow Square' – with its top-notch facilities aimed squarely at young travellers.

What with the bike tours, cooking classes, rooftop yoga, burlesque classes and stacks of other social events it hosts – not to mention DJs every night in its stylish **bar** (Map p90; Via Palestro 40; ⏱24hr; 🛜; Ⓜ Castro Pretorio) across the street – guests have little time to actually sleep.

★ **Beehive** HOSTEL €
(Map p90; ☑06 4470 4553; www.the-beehive. com; Via Marghera 8; dm €35-40, d without bathroom €80, s/d/tr €70/100/120; ⏱reception 7am-11pm; ❋🛜; Ⓜ Termini) 🌿 More boutique chic than backpacker dive, the Beehive is a small and stylish hostel with a glorious summer garden. Dynamic American owners Linda and Steve exude energy and organise cooking classes, storytelling evenings, weekly hostel dinners around a shared table, pop-up dinners with chefs, and so on. Pick from a spotless eight-bed dorm (mixed), a four-bed female dorm, or private rooms with ceiling fan and honey-based soap.

Hotel des Artistes HOTEL €
(Map p90; ☑06 445 43 65; www.hoteldes artistes.com; Via Villafranca 20; s/d/tr/q from €95/115/135/155; ❋@🛜; Ⓜ Castro Pretorio) The wide range of rooms here (including triples and family rooms) are decked out in wood and gold, with faux-antique furniture, heavy gold-framed oil paintings and gilt lamps. In contrast to all this period kitsch is the light and airy contemporary lobby with rose-shaped lamps and the meaning of 'true love' written in several languages on the wall.

Hotel Artorius HOTEL €€
(Map p106; ☑06 482 11 96; www.hotelartorius rome.com; Via del Boschetto 13; d €165-185, tr €220; ❋@🛜; Ⓜ Cavour) With an art-deco lobby and 10 neat, if plain and dated, rooms, this two-star hotel is a rare budget choice in increasingly trendy Monti. Find it at home in a 19th-century *palazzo* on one of Monti's key dining and drinking strips. Book well ahead to snag the best room in the house –

terrace-clad No 109. Check online for discounted rates.

Hotel Duca d'Alba HOTEL €€
(Map p80; ☑06 48 44 71; www.hotelducadalba. com; Via Leonina 14; d from €180; ❋🛜; Ⓜ Cavour) This appealing four-star hotel with attractive ochre-coloured facade has 27 small but charming rooms, many with fabric-covered walls, wood-beamed ceilings and travertine marble bathrooms. Breakfast is served beneath red-brick vaults and the best rooms have gorgeous little balconies overlooking the Monti rooftops.

★ **Villa Spalletti Trivelli** BOUTIQUE HOTEL €€€
(Map p106; ☑06 4890 7934; www.villaspalletti. it; Via Piacenza 4; d €625; Ⓟ❋@🛜; Ⓜ Spagna) This glorious boutique hotel resides in a mansion fitted out with 16th-century tapestries, antique books and original period furnishings. It was built by Gabriella Rasponi, niece of Carolina Bonaparte (Napoleon's sister), and much of the family's art collection remains. Its 14 romantic suites are elegantly decorated, with lovely green garden views. But nothing beats the rooftop terrace with sunloungers and bubbling Jacuzzis.

🛏 San Giovanni & Testaccio

★ **Althea Inn** B&B €
(Map p96; ☑06 9893 2666, 339 4353717; www. altheainn.com; Via dei Conciatori 9; d €120; ❋🛜; Ⓜ Piramide) In a workaday apartment block near the Aurelian Walls, this friendly B&B offers superb value for money and easy access to Testaccio's bars, clubs and restaurants. Its spacious, light-filled rooms sport a modish look with white walls and tasteful modern furniture, and each has its own small terrace.

Hotel Lancelot HOTEL €€
(Map p94; ☑06 7045 0615; www.lancelothotel. com; Via Capo d'Africa 47; s €120-128, d €180-216, f €250-278; ❋🛜; 🚌 Via di San Giovanni in Laterano) A great location near the Colosseum, striking views and super-helpful English-speaking staff – the family-run Lancelot scores across the board. The lobby and communal areas gleam with marble and crystal while the spacious rooms exhibit a more modest classic style. The best, on the 6th floor, also come with their own terrace.

In high season, three-course dinners (€25) are available and served at the hotel's communal tables.

★ **Hotel Sant'Anselmo**   HOTEL €€€
(Map p96; ☑ 06 57 00 57; www.aventinohotels.com; Piazza Sant'Anselmo 2; s €135-265, d €155-285; ❄ 🛜; 🚇 Via Marmorata) A ravishing romantic hideaway in the hilltop Aventino district. Housed in an elegant villa, its individually named rooms are not the biggest but they are stylish, juxtaposing retro four-poster beds, Liberty-style furniture and ornate decorative flourishes with modern touches and contemporary colours.

🛏 Southern Rome

Hotel Pulitzer   DESIGN HOTEL €€
(☑ 06 59 85 91; www.hotelpulitzer.it; Via Guglielmo Marconi 905; d €150; ❄ @ 🛜 ✖; Ⓜ Marconi) One of several business hotels in the 1930s EUR 'hood, the 83-room Pulitzer stands out for its classic Italian design, spoiling rooftop pool and proximity to the metro (a five-minute walk away). Its summertime garden bar is a joy to lounge in after a hard day's sightseeing (as are those poolside sunloungers on the 7th floor roof terrace from where there are great EUR views).

Hotel Abitart   HOTEL €€
(☑ 06 454 31 91; www.abitarthotel.com; Via Pel legrino Matteucci 10-20; d €140; 🚇 Via Ostiense; Ⓜ Piramide) Changing contemporary art exhibitions by local Roman artists decorate this art hotel in gritty Ostiense. Standard doubles are a riot of bright colours and themed suites evoke different art periods (cubism, 1970s, pop art) and genres (poetry, photography). Pluses include the hotel restaurant-bar **Estrobar** (☑ 06 5728 0141; www.estrobar.com; Via Pellegrino Matteucci 20; menu/meals €27/40; ☺ 9am-midnight; Ⓜ Piramide, 🚇 Via Ostiense) with attractive summertime terrace, and garage parking (€24 per night) right next door.

🛏 Trastevere & Gianicolo

★ **Relais Le Clarisse**   HOTEL €€
(Map p100; ☑ 06 5833 4437; www.leclarisse trastevere.com; Via Cardinale Merry del Val 20; d €80-250; ❄ 🛜; 🚇 Viale di Trastevere, 🚇 Viale di Trastevere) Set hacienda-style around a pretty internal courtyard with an 80-year-old olive tree, orange trees and a scattering of summertime breakfast tables, this is a peaceful 18-room oasis in Trastevere's bustling core. In contrast to the urban mayhem outside, the hotel is a picture of farmhouse charm with rooms, each named after a plant, decorated in rustic style with wrought-iron

bedsteads and wood-beamed ceilings, and equipped with kettle.

★ **Arco del Lauro**   GUESTHOUSE €€
(Map p100; ☑ 06 9784 0350; www.arcodellauro. it; Via Arco de' Tolomei 27; d €95-135, q €135-175; ❄ @ 🛜; 🚇 Viale di Trastevere, 🚇 Viale di Trastevere) Perfectly placed on a peaceful cobbled lane in the 'quiet side' of Trastevere, this ground-floor guesthouse sports six gleaming white rooms with parquet floors, a modern low-key look and well-equipped bathrooms. Guests share a kettle, a fridge, a complimentary fruit bowl and cakes, and breakfast is served in a nearby cafe. Daniele and Lorenzo, who run the place, could not be friendlier or more helpful.

★ **Villa Della Fonte**   B&B €€
(Map p100; ☑ 06 580 37 97; www.villafonte.com; Via della Fonte dell'Olio 8, s €120-140, d €150-190; ❄ 🛜; 🚇 Viale di Trastevere, 🚇 Viale di Trastevere) A lovely terracotta-hued, ivy-shrouded gem in a 17th-century townhouse, Villa della Fonte is precisely what Rome's la dolce vita is about. Five pretty rooms, some with original red brick and wood-beam ceilings, exude old-world charm. But the crowning glory is the trio of rooftop gardens, strewn with sunloungers, potted pomegranate trees and fragrant citrus plants.

★ **Hotel Santa Maria**   HOTEL €€€
(Map p100; ☑ 06 5894 626; www.hotelsanta maria.info; Vicolo del Piede 2; d/tr/q €240/295/325; P ❄ @ 🛜; 🚇 Viale di Trastevere, 🚇 Viale di Trastevere) Squirreled away behind a wall in the heart of Trastevere is this old convent, today an idyllic 20-room hotel arranged around a gravel courtyard peppered with orange trees. An alley of potted lemon trees leads up to the modern, low-lying building and functional, if dated, rooms evoke the sun with terracotta floors and Provencal colour schemes. Quads with bunk beds cater to families. Free bicycles available for guests.

★ **Hotel Donna Camilla Savelli**   HOTEL €€€
(Map p100; ☑ 06 588 861; www.hoteldonnacamilla savelli.com; Via Garibaldi 27; d €270; P ❄ @ 🛜; 🚇 Viale di Trastevere, 🚇 Viale di Trastevere) It's seldom you can stay in a 16th-century convent designed by baroque genius Borromini. This four-star hotel is exquisitely appointed – muted colours complement the serene concave and convex curves of the architecture – and the service is excellent. The best rooms

overlook the cloister garden or have views of Rome; otherwise, head up to the chic roof garden for a drink with a view in the bar.

🛏 Tridente, Trevi & the Quirinale

La Controra
HOSTEL €

(Map p90; ☎ 06 9893 7366; Via Umbria 7; dm €20-40, d €80-110; ✴ @ 🛜; ⓜ Barberini, ⓜ Repubblica) Quality budget accommodation is thin on the ground in the upmarket area north of Piazza Repubblica, but this great little hostel is a top choice. It has a friendly laid-back vibe, cool staff, double rooms and bright, airy mixed dorms (for three and four people), with parquet floors, air-con and private bathrooms. Minimum two-nights stay at weekends.

★ Casa Fabbrini
B&B €€

(Map p106; ☎ 329 947 01 53; www.casafabbrini.it; Vicolo delle Orsoline 13; d €150; ✴ 🛜; ⓜ Spagna) In a part of Rome nicknamed 'Piccolo Londra' (Little London), Casa Fabbrini is a stunning art nouveau villa with an interior straight out of the glossy pages of *Elle Decoration* – host and owner Simone Fabbrini is, funnily enough, an interior designer. Weathered antique doors are upcycled as uberchic bedheads; coloured glass lamps light up rooms to romantic perfection; and rich fabrics make bold use of colour.

Hotel Modigliani
HOTEL €€

(Map p106; ☎ 06 4281 5226; www.hotelmodigliani.com; Via della Purificazione 42; d/tr/q €195/260/340; ✴ 🛜; ⓜ Barberini) Run by Italian writer Marco and musician Giulia, this three-star hotel is all about attention to detail. Twenty-three modern, spacious rooms sport a soothing, taupe-and-white palette and some have balconies. Room 602 steals the show with a St Peter's view from its romantic rooftop terrace. Oh, and the pretty courtyard patio garden for summer drinks beneath the stars is rather lovely too.

Hotel Locarno
HOTEL €€

(Map p106; ☎ 06 361 08 41; www.hotellocarno.com; Via della Penna 22; d from €200; ◒ ✴ @ 🛜; ⓜ Flaminio) With its stained-glass doors and rattling cage-lift, this 1925 hotel is an art-deco classic – the kind of place Hercule Poirot might stay if he were in town. Many rooms have silk wallpaper, period furniture, marble bathrooms and are full of vintage charm, if in need of a little TLC. Roof gar-

den, wisteria-draped courtyard, restaurant and fin de siècle **cocktail bar** (⊙ 7pm-1am) with wintertime fireplace too.

Giuturna Boutique Hotel
BOUTIQUE HOTEL €€

(Map p106; ☎ 06 6228 9629; www.giuturnaboutiquehotel.com; Largo del Tritone 153; d from €180; ⊙ reception 7am-9pm; ✴ @ 🛜; ⓜ Barberini) A hop, skip and coin's throw from Trevi Fountain, this stylish boutique hotel is a peaceful and elegant retreat from the madding crowds. Rooms mix parquet flooring and original architectural features like polished 18th-century beams and exposed brickwork with soft taupe walls, beautiful fabrics and contemporary furniture. Reception doubles as a drawing room and lounge, with complimentary coffee.

Hotel Forte
HISTORIC HOTEL €€

(Map p106; ☎ 06 320 7625; www.hotelforte.com; Via Margutta 61; d/tr €180/230; ✴ @ 🛜; ⓜ Spagna) At home in elegant 18th-century Palazzo Alberto, this three-star hotel from 1923 is a fabulous midrange choice for those seeking peace, quiet and a room with a view on one of Rome's prettiest ivy-draped streets, peppered with art galleries and car-free to boot. Its 20 classical rooms are comfortable, and spacious quads make it a sterling family choice.

BDB Luxury Rooms
GUESTHOUSE €€

(Map p106; ☎ 06 6821 0020; www.bdbluxuryrooms.com; Via Margutta 38; d from €160; ✴ 🛜; ⓜ Flaminio) For your own designer pied-à-terre on one of Rome's prettiest and most peaceful pedestrian streets, reserve yourself one of seven chic rooms on Via Margutta. The ground-floor reception is, in fact, a contemporary art gallery and bold wall art is a prominent feature of the stylish rooms inside the 17th-century *palazzo*. Minimum two-night stay.

First
DESIGN HOTEL €€€

(Map p106; ☎ 06 4561 7070; www.thefirsthotel.com; Via del Vantaggio 14; d from €450; ✴ @ 🛜; ⓜ Flaminio) Noble 19th-century *palazzo* turned 'luxury art hotel' is the essence of this boutique, five-star hotel. From the magnificent white cow in the lobby to the contemporary artworks exhibited (and for sale), this is one stylish urban retreat. The rooftop garden (with restaurant and cocktail bar) is one of Rome's best and guests can rent an electric car (half/full day €74/104) to cruise silently around town.

In the hotel's ground-floor, Michelin-starred restaurant **Aquolino** (menus around €100), chef Alessandro Narduccio cooks up sensational gourmet seafood cuisine.

Fendi Private Suites
DESIGN HOTEL €€€

(Map p106; ☑ 06 9779 8080; www.fendipri vatesuites.com; Via della Fontanella di Borghese 48, Palazzo Fendi; d from €900; P❄@🛜; 🚇 Via del Corso) Comfortably at home on the 2nd floor of Palazzo Fendi (the Roman fashion house's flagship store is right below), this exclusive boutique hotel is pure class. Original artworks, photographs of the city snapped by Fendi creative director Karl Lagerfeld, Fendi Casa furniture and haute-couture fabrics in soothing greys and blues dress the seven exquisite suites. Dress the part.

Il Palazzetto
BOUTIQUE HOTEL €€€

(Map p106; ☑ 06 699 341 000; www.ilpalazzetto roma.com; Vicolo del Bottino 8; d €360; ❄@🛜; 🚇Spagna) Something of a secret retreat, this luxury four-room hotel in a 16th-century *palazzo* treats guests to four beautifully appointed doubles with classical décor and spectacular views of the neighbouring Spanish Steps. Luxurious bathrooms are marble, guests share the glorious roof terrace, and breakfast is served in the historic Hotel Hassler, Il Palazzetto's big sister, up the hill; guests can also use its spa and business centre.

Hotel Hassler
HOTEL €€€

(Map p106; ☑ 06 69 93 40; www.hotelhassler roma.com; Piazza della Trinità dei Monti 6; s/d from €415/550; ❄@🛜; 🚇Spagna) Surmounting the Spanish Steps, the historic Hassler is a byword for old-school luxury. A long line of VIPs have stayed here, enjoying the ravishing views and sumptuous hospitality. Its Michelin-starred restaurant **Imàgo** (☑06 6993 4726; www.imagorestaurant.com; tasting menus €120-150; ⊘7-10.30pm Feb-Dec) has one of the finest city views. Under the same management is nearby boutique hotel Il Palazzetto, with views over the Spanish Steps.

🛏 Vatican City, Borgo & Prati

Colors Hotel
HOTEL €

(Map p116; ☑ 06 687 40 30; www.colorshotel. com; Via Boezio 31; s €53-90, d €62-122, q €98-150; ❄🛜; 🚇Via Cola di Rienzo) Popular with young travellers, this welcoming hotel impresses with its fresh, artful design and clean, colourful rooms. These come in various shapes and sizes, including two or three cheaper ones with shared bathrooms and, from June to August, dorms for guests under 38 years. Buffet breakfast on request costs €6.50.

★ Le Stanze di Orazio
B&B €€

(Map p116; ☑ 06 3265 2474; www.lestanzedi orazio.com; Via Orazio 3; d €110-135; ❄🛜; 🚇Via Cola di Rienzo, 🚇Lepanto) This friendly boutique B&B makes for an attractive home away from home in the heart of the elegant Prati district, a single metro stop from the Vatican. It has five bright, playfully decorated rooms – think shimmering rainbow wallpaper, lilac accents and designer bathrooms – and a small breakfast area.

Quod Libet
GUESTHOUSE €€

(Map p116; ☑347 1222642; www.quodlibetroma .com; Via Barletta 29, 4th fl; d €120-150; ❄🛜; 🚇Ottaviano-San Pietro) A friendly family-run guesthouse offering big colourful rooms and a convenient location near Ottaviano-San Pietro metro station. Rooms are spacious with hand-painted watercolours, parquet and homey furnishings, and there's a kitchen for guest use. Host Gianluca extends a warm welcome and is always happy to help.

Vatican Style
GUESTHOUSE €€

(Map p116; ☑ 06 687 63 36; www.vaticanstyle. com; Via del Mascherino 46, 6th fl; d €142-199; 🚇Piazza del Risorgimento) A short hop from St Peter's, this stylish bolthole has 12 rooms spread over two floors of a large residential building. There's a hushed air about the place with its white, light-filled rooms, modern décor and occasional rooftop view. Cheaper rates are available without breakfast.

★ Villa Laetitia
BOUTIQUE HOTEL €€€

(☑06 322 6776; www.villalaetitia.com; Lungotevere delle Armi 22; r €179-390; ❄🛜; 🚇Lungotevere delle Armi) Villa Laetitia is a stunning boutique hotel in a riverside art nouveau villa. Its 20 rooms and mini-apartments, spread over the main building and a separate Garden House, were all individually designed by Anna Venturini Fendi of the famous fashion house. The result are interiors which marry modern design touches with family furniture, vintage pieces and rare finds, such as a framed Picasso scarf in the Garden Room.

Also in the hotel is the Enoteca La Torre, one of Rome's Michelin-starred fine-dining restaurants.

🛏 Villa Borghese & Northern Rome

⭐ Palm Gallery Hotel
HOTEL €€

(📞 06 6478 1859; www.palmgalleryhotel.com; Via delle Alpi 15d; s €130-160, d €150-210; 🅿🛜❄; 🚌 Via Nomentana, 🚌 Viale Regina Margherita) Housed in a 1905 Liberty-style villa, this gorgeous hotel sports an eclectic look that effortlessly blends African and Middle Eastern art with original art deco furniture, exposed brickwork and hand-painted tiles. Rooms are individually decorated, with the best offering views over the wisteria and thick greenery in the surrounding streets. In an adjacent building, a small swimming pool provides a welcome respite from the summer heat.

✖ Eating

This is a city that lives to eat. Food feeds the Roman soul, and a social occasion would be nothing without it. Cooking with local, seasonal ingredients has been the norm for millennia. Over recent decades the restaurant scene has become increasingly sophisticated, but the city's traditional no-frills trattorias still provide some of Rome's most memorable gastronomic experiences.

✖ Ancient Rome

Terre e Domus
LAZIO CUISINE €€

(Map p80; 📞 06 6994 0273; Via Foro Traiano 82-4; meals €30; ⏰ 9am-midnight Mon & Wed-Sat, 10am-midnight Sun; 🚌 Via dei Fori Imperiali) This modern white-and-glass restaurant is the best option in the touristy Forum area. With minimal decor and large windows overlooking the Colonna di Traiano, it's a relaxed spot to sit down to traditional local staples, all made with ingredients sourced from the surrounding Lazio region, and a glass or two of regional wine.

✖ Centro Storico

⭐ Forno Roscioli
PIZZA, BAKERY €

(Map p86; 📞 06 686 4045; www.anticoforno roscioli.it; Via dei Chiavari 34; pizza slices from €2, snacks €2; ⏰ 6am-8pm Mon-Sat, 9am-7pm Sun; 🚌 Via Arenula) This is one of Rome's top bakeries, much loved by lunching locals who crowd here for luscious sliced pizza, prize pastries and hunger-sating *supplì* (risotto balls). The pizza *margherita* is superb, if messy to eat, and there's also a counter serving hot pastas and vegetable side dishes.

Tiramisù Zum
DESSERTS €

(Map p86; 📞 06 6830 7836; www.facebook. com/zumroma; Piazza del Teatro di Pompeo 20; desserts €2.50-6; ⏰ 11am-11.30pm Sun-Thu, to 1am Fri & Sat; 🚌 Corso Vittorio Emanuele II) The ideal spot for a mid-afternoon pick-me-up, this fab dessert bar specialises in tiramisu, that magnificent marriage of mascarpone and liqueur-soaked ladyfinger biscuits. Choose between the classic version with its cocoa powdering or one of several tempting variations – with pistachio nuts, blackberries and raspberries, and Amarena cherries.

I Dolci di Nonna Vincenza
PASTRIES, CAFE €

(Map p86; www.dolcinonnavincenza.it; Via Arco del Monte 98a; pastries from €2.50; ⏰ 7.30am-8.30pm Mon-Sat, 8am-8.30pm Sun; 🚌 Via Arenula) Bringing the flavours of Sicily to Rome, this pastry shop is a real joy. Browse the traditional cakes and tempting *dolci* (sweet pastries) in the old wooden dressers, before adjourning to the adjacent bar to tear into the heavenly selection of creamy, flaky, puffy pastries and ricotta-stuffed *cannoli*.

Gelateria del Teatro
GELATO €

(Map p86; 📞 06 4547 4880; www.gelateria delteatro.it; Via dei Coronari 65; gelato €2.50-5; ⏰ 10.30am-8pm winter, 10am-10.30pm summer; 🚌 Via Zanardelli) All the ice cream served at this excellent gelateria is prepared on-site – look through the window and you'll see how. There are about 40 flavours to choose from, all made from thoughtfully sourced ingredients such as hazelnuts from the Langhe region of Piedmont and pistachios from Bronte in Sicily.

Forno di Campo de' Fiori
PIZZA, BAKERY €

(Map p86; www.fornocampodefiori.com; Campo de' Fiori 22; pizza slices around €3; ⏰ 7.30am-2.30pm & 4.45-8pm Mon-Sat, closed Sat dinner Jul & Aug; 🚌 Corso Vittorio Emanuele II) This buzzing bakery on Campo de' Fiori, divided into two adjacent shops, does a roaring trade in *panini* and delicious fresh-from-the-oven *pizza al taglio* (pizza by the slice). Aficionados swear by the pizza *bianca* ('white' pizza with olive oil, rosemary and salt), but the *panini* and pizza *rossa* ('red' pizza, with olive oil, tomato and oregano) taste plenty good too.

Caffetteria Chiostro del Bramante
CAFE €

(Map p86; ☑ 06 6880 9036; www.chiostrodel bramante.it; Via Arco della Pace 5; meals €15-25; ⊙ 10am-8pm Mon-Fri, to 9pm Sat & Sun; ☏; ☐ Corso del Rinascimento) Many of Rome's galleries and museums have in-house cafes but few are as beautifully located as the Caffetteria Chiostro del Bramante on the 1st floor of Bramante's elegant Renaissance cloister. With outdoor tables overlooking the central courtyard and an all-day menu offering everything from cakes and coffee to baguettes, risottos and Caesar salads, it's a great spot for a break.

★ Pianostrada
RISTORANTE €€

(Map p86; ☑ 06 8957 2296; Via delle Zoccolette 22; meals €40; ⊙ 1-4pm & 7pm-midnight Tue-Fri, 10am-midnight Sat & Sun; ☐ Via Arenula) Hatched in foodie Trastevere but now across the river in a mellow white space with vintage furnishings and glorious summer courtyard, this bistro is a fashionable must. Reserve ahead, or settle for a stool at the bar and enjoy big bold views of the kitchen at work. Cuisine is refreshingly creative, seasonal and veg-packed, including gourmet open sandwiches and sensational homemade focaccia as well as full-blown mains.

The warm smiles and chit-chat of the charismatic, all-female team – best friends Chiara and Paola, and Paola's daughters Flaminia and Alice – cap off the relaxed, uber-hip dining experience.

★ Emma Pizzeria
PIZZA €€

(Map p86; ☑ 06 6476 0476; www.emmapizze ria.com; Via Monte della Farina 28-29; pizzas €8-18, mains €35; ⊙ 12.30-3pm & 7-11.30pm; ☐ Via Arenula) Tucked in behind the Chiesa di San Carlo ai Catinari, this smart, modern pizzeria is a top spot for a cracking pizza and smooth craft beer (or a wine from its pretty extensive list). It's a stylish set-up with outdoor seating and a spacious, art-clad interior, and a menu that lists seasonal, wood-fired pizzas alongside classic Roman pastas and mains.

★ La Ciambella
ITALIAN €€

(Map p86; ☑ 06 683 2930; www.la-ciambella. it; Via dell'Arco della Ciambella 20; meals €35-45; ⊙ bar 7.30am-midnight, wine bar & restaurant noon-11pm Tue-Sun; ☐ Largo di Torre Argentina) Central but largely undiscovered by the tourist hordes, this friendly wine-bar-cum-restaurant beats much of the neighbour-hood competition. Its spacious, light-filled interior is set over the ruins of the Terme di Agrippa, visible through transparent floor panels, and its kitchen sends out some excellent food, from tartares and chickpea pancakes to slow-cooked beef and tradition-al Roman pastas.

Armando al Pantheon
ROMAN €€

(Map p86; ☑ 06 6880 3034; www.armandoal pantheon.it; Salita dei Crescenzi 31; meals €40; ⊙ 12.30-3pm Mon-Sat & 7-11pm Mon-Fri; ☐ Largo di Torre Argentina) With its cosy wooden interi-or and unwavering dedication to old-school Roman cuisine, Armando al Pantheon is a regular go-to for local foodies. It's been on the go for more than 50 years and has served its fair share of celebs, but it hasn't let fame go to its head and it remains as popular as ever. Reservations essential.

Ginger
ITALIAN €€

(Map p86; ☑ 06 6830 8559; www.gingersaporie salute.com; Piazza Sant'Eustachio 54; meals €30; ⊙ 8am-midnight; ☐ Corso del Rinascimento) Boasting a white, casually contemporary interior and al fresco seating on a charac-teristic piazza, this is one of Rome's new breed of all day eateries. It serves everything from coffee and fresh fruit juices to gourmet *panini* and a full restaurant menu featuring the likes of *tonnarelli con polpa* (square spaghetti with octopus) and a killer choco-late orange cake.

Casa Coppelle
RISTORANTE €€€

(Map p86; ☑ 06 6889 1707; www.casacoppelle. it; Piazza delle Coppelle 49; meals €65, tasting menu €85; ⊙ noon-3.30pm & 6.30-11.30pm; ☐ Corso del Rinascimento) Boasting an enviable setting near the Pantheon and a plush, theatrical look – think velvet drapes, black lacquer ta-bles and bookshelves – Casa Coppelle sets a romantic stage for high-end Roman-French cuisine. Gallic trademarks like snails and onion soup feature alongside updated Ro-man favourites such as pasta *amatriciana* (with tomato sauce and pancetta) and *cacio e pepe* (pecorino and black pepper), here re-invented as a risotto with prawns. Book ahead.

Salumeria Roscioli
DELI, RISTORANTE €€€

(Map p86; ☑ 06 687 5287; www.salumeriarosci oli.com; Via dei Giubbonari 21; meals €55; ⊙ 12.30-4pm & 7pm-midnight Mon-Sat; ☐ Via Arenula) The name Roscioli has long been a byword for foodie excellence in Rome, and this luxuri-ous deli-restaurant is the place to experience

VEGETARIANS, VEGANS & GLUTEN-FREE

Vegetarians eat exceedingly well in Rome, with a wide choice of bountiful antipasti, pasta dishes, *insalate* (salads), *contorni* (side dishes) and pizzas. Some high-end restaurants such as **Imàgo** (p127) even serve a vegetarian menu, and slowly but surely, exclusively vegetarian and/or vegan eateries and cafes are cropping up: try **Babette** (Map p106; ☑ 06 321 15 59; www.babetteristorante.it; Via Margutta 1d; meals €50; ☉ 1-3pm & 7-10.45pm Tue-Sun, closed Jan; ☑; Ⓜ Spagna, Flaminio) and **Il Margutta** (Map p106; ☑ 06 3265 0577; www.ilmargutta.bio; Via Margutta 118; lunch buffet weekdays/weekends €15/25, meals €15-40; ☉ 8.30am-11.30pm; ☑; Ⓜ Spagna, Flaminio) near the Spanish Steps, or **Vitaminas 24** (☑ 331 204 5535; Via Ascoli Piceno 40-42; meals €15; ☉ 11am-midnight Tue-Sun, to 4pm Mon; 🛜☑; 🚇 Circonvallazione Casilina) 🏃 in edgy Pigneto.

Be mindful of hidden ingredients not mentioned on the menu – for example, steer clear of anything that's been stuffed (like zucchini flowers, often spiced up with anchovies) or check that it's *senza carne o pesce* (without meat or fish). To many Italians, vegetarian means you don't eat red meat.

Vegans are in for a tougher time. Cheese is used universally, so you must specify that you want something *senza formaggio* (without cheese). Also remember that *pasta fresca*, which may also turn up in soups, is made with eggs. The safest bet is to self-cater or try a dedicated vegetarian restaurant, which will always have some vegan options.

Most restaurants offer gluten-free options, as there is a good awareness of coeliac disease here: one of the city's top restaurants, **Aroma** (☑ 06 9761 5109; www.aromarestaurant.it; Via Labicana 125; meals €120-150; ☉ 12.30-3pm & 7.30-11.30pm; 🚇 Via Labicana), has a four-course, gluten-free menu (€115). Just say *lo sono celiaco* or *senza glutine* when you sit down, and usually the waiters will be able to recommend suitable dishes.

---

it. Tables are set alongside the deli counter, laden with mouth-watering Italian and foreign delicacies, and in a small bottle-lined space behind it. The sophisticated food is top notch and there are some truly outstanding wines to go with it.

Casa Bleve
RISTORANTE €€€

(Map p86; ☑ 06 686 59 70; www.casableve.it; Via del Teatro Valle 48-49; meals €55-70; ☉ 12.30-3pm & 7.30-11pm Mon-Sat; 🚇 Largo di Torre Argentina) Ideal for a special occasion dinner, this palatial restaurant-wine-bar dazzles with its column-lined dining hall and stained-glass roof. Its wine list, one of the best in town, accompanies a refined menu of creative antipasti, seasonal pastas and classic main courses.

✖ Monti, Esquilino & San Lorenzo

★ Panella
BAKERY, CAFE €

(Map p90; ☑ 06 487 24 35; www.panellaroma.com; Via Merulana 54; meals €7-15; ☉ 8am-11pm Mon-Thu, to midnight Fri & Sat, 8.30am-4pm Sun; Ⓜ Vittorio Emanuele) Pure heaven for foodies, this enticing bakery is littered with well-used trays of freshly baked pastries loaded with confectioner's custard, wild-cherry fruit

tartlets, *pizza al taglio, arancini* (rice balls) and focaccia – the smell alone is heavenly. Grab a bar stool between shelves of gourmet groceries inside or congratulate yourself on scoring a table on the flowery, sun-flooded terrace – one of Rome's loveliest.

Breakfast, full-blown lunch menus and evening *aperitivo* are also on offer.

Aromaticus
HEALTH FOOD €

(Map p90; ☑ 06 488 13 55; www.aromaticus.it; Via Urbana 134; meals €10-15; ☉ 11am-3pm & 6-8.30pm; 🛜; Ⓜ Cavour) Few addresses exude such a healthy vibe. Set within a shop selling aromatic plants and edible flowers, this inventive little cafe is the perfect place to satisfy green cravings. Its short but sweet menu features lots of creative salads, soups and gazpacho, tartare and carpaccio, juices and detox smoothies – all to stay or go.

Order at the bar, set your own table and collect your food when it's ready.

Zia Rosetta
SANDWICHES €

(Map p90; ☑ 06 3105 2516; www.ziarosetta.com; Via Urbana 54; salads €4.50-6, panini mini €2-3.50, regular €4.50-7; ☉ 11am-4pm Mon-Thu, to 10pm Fri & Sat; Ⓜ Cavour) Grab a pew at a marble-topped table and brace your taste buds for a torturous choice of 25-odd different gourmet *panini* and another dozen monthly specials – all creatively stuffed with unexpected combinations, and with catchy names like Amber Queen, Strawberry Hill and Lady Godiva. If you really can't decide, pick a trio of mini *panini*. Freshly squeezed juices (€3.50) too. Glam and gluten-free.

Alle Carette   PIZZA €
(Map p80; ☑ 06 679 27 70; www.facebook. com/allecarrette; Via della Madonna dei Monti 95; pizza €5.50-8; ☺ 11.30am-4pm & 7pm-midnight; ✤; ⓂCavour) Honest pizza, super-thin and swiftly cooked in a wood-burning oven, is what this traditional Roman pizzeria on one of Monti's prettiest car-free streets has done well for decades. Tobacco-coloured walls give the place a vintage vibe and Roman families pile in here at weekends. Begin your local feast with some battered and deep-fried zucchini flowers or *baccalà* (salted cod).

Pasta Chef   FAST FOOD €
(Map p80; ☑ 06 488 31 98; www.pastachef roma.it; Via Baccina 42; pasta €5-8; ☺ 12.30-9.30pm Mon-Sat; ⓂCavour) 'Gourmet street food' is the strapline of this fast-food pasta joint where chefs Mauro and Leopoldo whip up steaming bowls of perfectly cooked pasta laced with carbonara, *pomodoro e basilico* (tomato and basil), bolognese and other classic sauces for a discerning, budget-conscious crowd. There's a veggie lasagne and other vegetarian options. The dynamic duo also runs pasta-cooking classes.

Mercato Centrale   FOOD HALL €
(Map p90; www.mercatocentrale.it/roma; Via Giolitti 36, Stazione Termini; snacks/meals from €3/10; ☺ 7am-midnight; 🛜; ⓂTermini) A gourmet oasis for hungry travellers at Stazione Termini, this dazzling three-storey food hall is the latest project of Florence's savvy Umberto Montano. You'll find breads, pastries, cakes, veggie burgers, fresh pasta, truffles, pizza and a whole lot more beneath towering vaulted 1930s ceilings, as well as some of the city's most prized producers, including Gabriele Bonci (breads, focaccia and pizza), Roberto Liberati (salami) and Marcella Bianchi (vegetarian).

Grab something quick to eat from one of the many stalls on the ground floor, or head upstairs to 1st-floor **La Tavola** (meals €40), an appealing restaurant with a menu signed off by Rome-based Michelin-starred chef Oliver Glowig and Salvatore De Gennaro.

★Ai Tre Scalini   WINE BAR €€
(Map p80; ☑ 06 4890 7495; www.aitrescalini. org; Via Panisperna 251; meals €25; ☺ 12.30pm-1am; ⓂCavour) A firm favourite since 1895, the 'Three Steps' is always packed, with crowds spilling out of the funky violet-painted door and into the street. Tuck into a heart-warming array of cheeses, salami and dishes such as *polpette al sugo* (meatballs with sauce), washed down with superb choices of wine or beer.

Temakinho   SUSHI €€
(Map p80; ☑ 06 4201 6656; www.temakinho. com; Via dei Serpenti 16; meals €40; ☺ 12.30-3.30pm & 7pm-midnight; ⓂCavour) In a city where most food is still resolutely (though deliciously) Italian, this Brazilian-Japanese hybrid serving up sushi and ceviche makes for a sensationally refreshing change. As well as delicious, strong caipirinhas, which combine Brazilian *cachaça*, sugar, lime and fresh fruit, there are 'sakchinhas' made with sake. It's very popular; book ahead.

Pastificio San Lorenzo   ITALIAN €€
(Map p90; ☑ 06 9727 3519; www.pastificio sanlorenzo.com; Via Tiburtina 196; lunch/dinner €25/40, ☺ 12.30-3pm & 8-11.30pm Mon-Fri, 8-11.30pm Sat; 🛜; 🚊 Via Tiburtina, 🚊 Via dei Reti) With a vintage horse vault serving as a bench, saggy ginger-leather armchairs in the *salotto* (salon), a white ceramic-tiled bar and edgy brasserie-style seating, this restaurant is a stylish place to hang out. It is the dining arm of the **Pastificio Cerere art gallery** (Map p90; ☑ 06 4542 2960; www. pastificiocerere.com; Via degli Ausoni 7; ☺ 3-7pm Mon-Fri, 4-8pm Sat; 🚊 Via Tiburtina), in an old pasta factory around the corner, and cuisine is predictably creative.

End with chocolate and caramel *baba al rum* or tiramisu served in a coffee cup. Reservations recommended.

Da Valentino   TRATTORIA €€
(Map p106; ☑ 06 488 06 43; Via del Boschetto 37; meals €30; ☺ 12.30-2.45pm & 8-11pm Mon-Sat; 🚊 Via Nazionale) The 1930s sign outside says 'Birra Peroni' and its enchanting vintage interior feels little changed. Come to this mythical dining address for delicious bruschetta, grilled meats, the purest of hamburgers and *scamorza*, a type of Italian cheese that is grilled and melted atop myriad ingredients: tomato and rocket, artichokes, wafer-thin slices of aromatic *lardo di*

colonnata (pork fat) from Tuscany and porcini mushrooms. No coffee.

L'Asino d'Oro
ITALIAN €€
(Map p106; ☑06 4891 3832; www.facebook.com/asinodoro; Via del Boschetto 73; weekday lunch menu €16, meals €45; ☉12.30-2.30pm & 7.30-11pm Tue-Sat; Ⓜ Cavour) This fabulous restaurant was transplanted from Orvieto, and its Umbrian origins resonate in Lucio Sforza's exceptional cooking. Unfussy yet innovative dishes feature bags of flavourful contrasts, like lamb meatballs with pear and blue cheese. Save room for the equally amazing desserts. Intimate, informal and classy, this is one of Rome's best deals – its lunch menu is a steal.

★Antonello Colonna Open
ITALIAN €€€
(Map p106; ☑06 4782 2641; www.antonellocolonna.it; Via Milano 9a; lunch/brunch €16/30, meals €16-100; ☉12.30-3.30pm & 8-11pm Tue-Sat, 12.30-3.30pm Sun; ✳; ☐ Via Nazionale) Spectacularly set at the back of Palazzo delle Esposizioni, super-chef Antonello Colonna's Michelin-starred restaurant lounges dramatically under a dazzling all-glass roof. Cuisine is new Roman – innovative takes on traditional dishes, cooked with wit and flair – and the all-you-can-eat lunch buffet and weekend brunch are unbeatable value. On sunny days, dine al fresco on the rooftop terrace.

★Said
ITALIAN €€€
(Map p90; ☑06 446 92 04; www.said.it; Via Tiburtina 135; meals €50; ☉6pm-12.30am Mon, 10am-12.30am Tue-Fri, to 1.30am Sat, to midnight Sun; ☎; ☐ Via Tiburtina, ☐ Via dei Reti) Housed in an early 1920s chocolate factory, this hybrid cafe-bar, restaurant and boutique is San Lorenzo's coolest hipster haunt. Its Japanese pink-tea pralines, indulged in with a coffee or bought wrapped to take home, are glorious, and dining here is urban chic, with battered sofas, industrial antiques and creative cuisine. Reservations for lunch and dinner, served from 12.30pm and 8pm, are recommended.

✖ San Giovanni & Testaccio

★Trapizzino
FAST FOOD €
(Map p96; ☑06 4341 9624; www.trapizzino.it; Via Branca 88; trapizzini from €3.50; ☉noon-1am Tue-Sun; ☐ Via Marmorata) The original of what is now a growing countrywide chain, this is the birthplace of the *trapizzino*, a kind of

hybrid sandwich made by stuffing a cone of doughy focaccia with fillers like *polpette al sugo* (meatballs in tomato sauce) or *pollo alla cacciatore* (stewed chicken). They're messy to eat but quite delicious.

Mordi e Vai
STREET FOOD €
(Map p96; www.mordievai.it; Box 15, Nuovo Mercato di Testaccio; panini €3.50-5; ☉8am-3pm Mon-Sat; ☐ Via Galvani) Chef Sergio Esposito's critically acclaimed and much frequented market stall – 'Bite and Go' in English – is all about the unadulterated joy of traditional Roman street food. That means *panini* such as his signature *allesso di scottona*, filled with tender slow-cooked beef, and plastic plates of no-nonsense meat-and-veg dishes.

★Romeo e Giulietta
RISTORANTE, PIZZA €€
(Map p96; ☑Giulietta 06 4522 9022, Romeo 06 3211 0120; https://romeo.roma.it; Piazza dell'Emporio 28; pizzas €6.50-12, meals €40; ☉Romeo 10am-2am, Giulietta 7pm-midnight daily, noon-3pm Sat-Sun; ☐ Via Marmorata) Occupying a former car showroom, this contemporary multi-space food hub is the latest offering from top Roman chef, Cristina Bowerman. The centre of operations is Romeo Chef & Baker, a designer deli, cocktail bar and restaurant offering modern Italian and international fare, but there's also Giulietta Pizzeria (https://giuliettapizzeria.it) dishing up sensational wood-fired pizzas and, a short hop away, Frigo, an artisanal gelateria.

★Sbanco
PIZZA €€
(☑06 78 93 18; Via Siria 1; pizzas €7.50-12.50; ☉7.30pm-midnight; ☐ Piazza Zama) With its informal warehouse vibe and buzzing atmosphere, Sbanco is one of the capital's hottest pizzerias. Since opening in 2016, it has quickly made a name for itself with its creative, wood-fired pizzas and sumptuous fried starters – try the carbonara *supplì* (risotto balls). To top things off, it serves some deliciously drinkable craft beer.

✖ Southern Rome

★Eataly
ITALIAN €
(www.eataly.net; Piazzale XII Ottobre 1492; meals €10-50; ☉shops 9am-midnight, restaurants typically noon-3.30pm & 7-11pm; ☎; Ⓜ Piramide) Be prepared for some serious taste-bud titillation in this state-of-the-art food emporium of gargantuan proportions. Four shop floors showcase every conceivable Italian food

product (dried and fresh), while multiple themed food stalls and restaurants offer plenty of opportunity to taste or feast on Italian cuisine.

Savour paper-thin slices of raw ostrich, horse, fish or shellfish in the 2nd-floor Ristorantino del Crudo specialising in raw cuisine; lunch on Sicilian and Roman classics in Fattoria delle Torri on the same floor; taste five Italian craft beers on tap in the 1st-floor Birreria (Beer Hall) or different coffee beans in the cafe. There are also cooking classes, demonstrations and wine tastings too.

★ **Doppiozeroo** ITALIAN €

(☑06 5730 1961; www.doppiozeroo.com; Via Ostiense 68; meals €15; ☺7am-2am; Ⓜ Via Ostiense, Ⓜ Piramide) This easygoing bar was once a bakery, hence the name ('double zero' is a type of flour). But today the sleek, modern interior attracts hungry, trendy Romans who pile in here for its cheap, canteen-style lunches, famously lavish *aperitivo* (6pm to 9pm) and abundant weekend brunch (12.30pm to 3.30pm).

Verde Pistacchio VEGETARIAN, VEGAN €

(☑06 4547 5965; www.facebook.com/verde pistacchioroma; Via Ostiense 181; lunch menu €14; ☺10am-3.30pm & 5.30pm-midnight Mon-Thu, 10am-3.30pm & 5.30pm-2am Fri, 6pm-2am Sat, 6pm-midnight Sun; ☞; Ⓜ Via Ostiense, Ⓜ Garbatella) Camilla, Raffaele and Francesco are the trio of friends behind Green Pistachio, a stylish bistro and cafe with a minimalist, vintage interior and streetside tables in the sun in summer. The kitchen cooks up fantastic vegetarian and vegan cuisine, and the lunchtime deal is a steal. Lunch here before or after visiting Rome's second-largest church, a stone's throw away on the same street.

★ **L'Archeologia**
Ristorante ITALIAN €€

(Map p98; ☑06 788 04 94; www.larcheologia.it; Via Appia Antica 139; meals €50; ☺12.30-3pm & 8-11pm; Ⓜ Via Appia Antica) At home in an old horse exchange on the Appian Way, this 19th-century inn exudes vintage charm. Dining is elegant, with white-tablecloth-covered tables beneath age-old beams or in front of the fireplace. In summer, dining is al fresco and fragrant with the blooms of a magnificent 300-year-old wisteria. Cuisine is traditional Roman, and the wine list exemplary. Reservations recommended.

Seacook SEAFOOD €€€

(☑06 5730 1512; www.seacook.it; Via del Porto Fluviale 7d-e; meals €60; ☺noon-3pm & 7pm-midnight; ☞; Ⓜ Piramide) For stylish seafood dining in a chic aquatic ambience, look no further than this glorious Scandinavian-styled space in Ostiense with sea-blue bar-stool seating, potted plants in white ceramic jugs and bamboo lampshades. *Cuochi e Pescatori* (Cooks and Fishermen) is the strapline and fish is fresh from seafaring Salento in southern Italy. Kick off your fishy feast with the fish carpaccio of the day with papaya and lime.

✕ Trastevere & Gianicolo

★ **La Prosciutteria** TUSCAN €

(Map p100; ☑06 6456 2839; www.laprosciutteria. com/roma-trastevere; Via della Scala 71; taglieri €5 per person; ☺11am-11.30pm; Ⓜ Piazza Trilussa) For a gratifying taste of Tuscany in Rome, consider lunch or a decadent *aperitivo* at this Florentine *prosciutteria* (salami shop). Made-to-measure *taglieri* (wooden chopping boards) come loaded with different cold cuts, cheeses, fruit and veg and are best devoured over a glass of Brunello di Montalcino or simple Chianti Classico. Bread comes in peppermint-green tin saucepans and dozens of hams and salami dangle overhead.

Well-stuffed *panini* too, to eat in or take away. Clear your own table before leaving.

★ **Da Augusto** TRATTORIA €

(Map p100; ☑06 580 37 98; Piazza de' Renzi 15; meals €25; ☺12.30-3pm & 8-11pm; Ⓜ Viale di Trastevere, Ⓜ Viale di Trastevere) Bag one of Augusto's rickety tables outside and tuck into some truly fabulous mamma style cooking on one of Trastevere's prettiest piazza terraces. Hearty portions of all the Roman classics are dished up here as well as lots of rabbit, veal, hare and *pajata* (calf intestines). Winter dining is around vintage Formica tables in a bare-bones interior, unchanged for decades. Be prepared to queue. Cash only.

★ **Da Enzo** TRATTORIA €

(Map p100; ☑06 581 22 60; www.daenzoal29.com; Via dei Vascellari 29; meals €30; ☺12.30-3pm & 7-11pm Mon-Sat; Ⓜ Viale di Trastevere, Ⓜ Viale di Trastevere) Vintage buttermilk walls, red-checked tablecloths and a traditional menu featuring all the Roman classics: what makes this staunchly traditional trattoria exceptional is its careful sourcing of local, quality products, many from nearby farms in Lazio. The seasonal, deep-fried Jewish artichokes and the *pasta cacio e pepe* (cheese-and-black-pepper pasta) in particular are among the best in Rome.

Le Levain
BAKERY €

(Map p100; ☑ 06 6456 2880; www.lelevainroma.it; Via Luigi Santini 22-23; meals €5.50-10; ⊙ 8am-8.30pm Tue-Sat, 9am-7.30pm Sun; ☐ Viale di Trastevere, ☐ Viale di Trastevere) Many a foreigner living in Rome swears by this *pâtisserie au beurre fin* for their daily dose of rich and creamy butter, albeit it in the guise of authentic croissants, *pains au chocolat* and other irresistible French pastries. Traditional French cakes – colourful cream-filled macarons, flaky millefeuilles, miniature *tartes aux pommes* (apple tarts) – are equally authentic.

Well-stuffed baguettes, quiches and soups make the French bakery a popular lunchtime spot too. Find it around the corner from the San Cosimato **outdoor market** (Map p100; Piazza San Cosimato; ⊙ 7am-2pm Mon-Sat; ☐ Viale di Trastevere, ☐ Viale di Trastevere).

Fior di Luna
GELATERIA €

(Map p100; ☑ 06 6456 1314; http://fiordiluna.com; Via della Lungaretta 96; gelato from €1.70; ⊙ 11.30am-11.30pm Easter-Oct, to 9pm Tue-Sun Nov-Easter; ☐ Viale di Trastevere, ☐ Viale di Trastevere) For many Romans this busy little hub makes the best handmade gelato and sorbet in the world. It's produced in small batches using natural, seasonal ingredients – a few flavours are even made from donkeys' milk. Favourites include walnut and honey, blueberry yoghurt, kiwi (complete with seeds) and pistachio (the nuts are ground by hand).

The late spring–early summer strawberry gelato is to die for, while chocolate aficionados will enjoy the sweet crepes doused in homemade chocolate sauce.

Forno La Renella
BAKERY €

(Map p100; ☑ 06 581 72 65; www.panificiolarenella.com; Via del Moro 15-16; pizza slices from €2.50; ⊙ 7am-2am Tue-Sat, to 10pm Sun & Mon; ☐ Piazza Trilussa) Watch urban pizza masters at work behind glass at this historic Trastevere bakery, a fantastic space to hang out in with its wood-fired ovens, bar-stool seating and heavenly aromas of pizza (€9 to €18 per kilo), bread and biscuits baking throughout the day. Piled-high toppings (and fillings) vary seasonally, to the joy of everyone from punks with big dogs to old ladies with little dogs. It's been in the biz since 1870.

Panattoni
PIZZA €

(Map p100; Ai Marmi; ☑ 06 580 09 19; Viale di Trastevere 53; pizzas €6.50-9; ⊙ 6.30pm-1am Thu-Tue; ☐ Viale di Trastevere, ☐ Viale di Trastevere) Also called 'ai Marmi' or *l'obitorio* (the morgue) because of its vintage marble-slab tabletops, this is Trastevere's most popular pizzeria. Think super-thin pizzas, a clattering buzz, testy waiters, a street terrace and some fantastic fried starters – the *supplì* (risotto balls), *baccalà* (salted cod) and zucchini flowers are all heavenly.

Litro
ITALIAN €€

(☑ 06 4544 7639; http://vinerialitro.it; Via Fratelli Bonnet 5, Monteverde; meals €25; ⊙ 12.30pm-3.30am & 5.30-midnight Mon-Fri, 12.30pm-12.30am Sat; ☎; ☐ Via Fratelli Bonnet) Crunchy brown bread comes in a paper bag and the 1950s clocks on the wall – all three dozen them – say a different time at this understated vintage-styled bistro-bar in wonderfully off-the-beaten-tourist-track Monteverde. The creative Roman kitchen is predominantly organic, with ingredients sourced from small local producers, and the choice of natural and biodynamic wines is among the best in Rome.

Da Teo
TRATTORIA €€

(Map p100; ☑ 06 581 83 55; www.trattoriadateo.it; Piazza dei Ponziani 7; meals €30; ⊙ 12.30-3pm & 7.30-11.30pm Mon-Sat; ☐ Viale di Trastevere, ☐ Viale di Trastevere) One of Rome's classic trattorias, Da Teo buzzes with locals digging into steaming platefuls of Roman standards, such as carbonara, *pasta cacio e pepe* and the most fabulous seasonal artichokes – both Jewish (deep-fried) and Roman-style (stuffed with parsley and garlic, and boiled). In keeping with hardcore trattoria tradition, Teo's homemade gnocchi is only served on Thursday. Reservations essential.

In warm weather dine al fresco, on a pretty car-free piazza.

Glass Hostaria
ITALIAN €€€

(Map p100; ☑ 06 5833 5903; www.glass-restaurant.it; Vicolo del Cinque 58; menus €85-140, meals €90; ⊙ 7.30-11.30pm Tue-Sun; ☐ Piazza Trilussa) Trastevere's foremost foodie address, Michelin-starred Glass cooks up innovative cuisine in a contemporary, sophisticated space with mezzanine. Law-graduate-turned-chef Cristina Bowerman creates inventive, delicate dishes that combine seasonal ingredients with traditional elements to delight and surprise the palate – best experienced with her tasting menu. There's also a vegetarian menu, too.

✗ Tridente, Trevi & the Quirinale

★Bistro del Quirino   ITALIAN €

(Map p106; ☑06 9887 8090; www.bistrotquirino. com; Via delle Vergini 7; brunch €10, à la carte €25; ⊙noon-3.30pm & 4pm-2am; ☑Via del Corso) For unbeatable value near Trevi Fountain, reserve a table at this artsy bistro adjoining Teatro Quirino. Theatre posters add bags of colour to the spacious interior, where a banquet of a 'brunch' buffet – fantastic salads, antipasti, hot and cold dishes – is laid out for knowing Romans to feast on.

From 4pm, the bistro morphs into a cafe – until 6.30pm when the sacrosanct *aperitivo* spread kicks in.

★Pastificio   FAST FOOD €

(Map p106; Via della Croce 8; pasta, wine & water €4; ⊙1-3pm Mon-Sat; ☑Spagna) A brilliant budget find, this old-fashioned pasta shop (1918), with a kitchen hatch, serves up two choices of pasta at lunchtime. It's fast food, Italian style – freshly cooked (if you time it right) pasta, with wine and water included. Grab a space to stand and eat between shelves packed with packets of dry pasta, or take it away.

Fatamorgana Corso   GELATERIA €

(Map p106; ☑06 3265 2238; www.gelateria fatamorgana.com; Via Laurina 10; 2/3/4/5 scoops €2.50/3.50/4.50/5; ⊙noon-11pm; ☑Flaminio) The wonderful all-natural, gluten-free gelato served at Fatamorgana is arguably Rome's best artisanal ice cream. Innovative and classic tastes of heaven abound, including flavours such as pear and caramel, all made from the finest seasonal ingredients. There are several branches around town.

Pompi   DESSERTS €

(Map p106; www.barpompi.it; Via della Croce 82; tiramisu €4; ⊙10.30am-9.30pm; ☑Spagna) Rome's most famous vendor of tiramisu (which literally means 'pick me up') sells takeaway cartons of the deliciously yolky yet light-as-air dessert. As well as classic, it comes in pistachio, strawberry, hazelnut and banana-chocolate variations. Eat on the spot (standing) or buy frozen portions that will keep for a few hours until you're ready to tuck in at home.

★Fiaschetteria Beltramme   TRATTORIA €€

(Map p106; ☑06 6979 7200; Via della Croce 39; meals €40; ⊙12.15-3pm & 7.30-10.45pm; ☑Spagna) A super spot for authentic Roman dining near the Spanish Steps, Fiaschetteria (meaning 'wine-seller') is a hole-in-the-wall, stuck-in-time place with a short menu. Fashionistas with appetites dig into traditional Roman dishes made using recipes unchanged since the 1930s when a waiter at the 19th-century wine bar (from 1886 to be precise) started serving food. Seeking the perfect carbonara? This is the address.

These days more creative dishes run alongside the timeless classics.

Hostaria Romana   TRATTORIA €€

(Map p106; ☑06 474 52 84; www.hostariaroma na.it; Via del Boccaccio 1; meals €40; ⊙12.30-3pm & 7.15-11pm Mon-Sat; ☑Barberini) A highly recommended address for lunch or dinner near Trevi Fountain, Hostaria Romana cooks up meaty, traditional classics like grilled goat chops, veal cutlets, roast suckling pig and T-bone steaks to a mixed Roman and tourist crowd. Busy, bustling and noisy, this is everything an Italian trattoria should be. Sign your name on the graffiti-covered walls before leaving.

Ginger   BRASSERIE €€

(Map p106; ☑06 9603 6390; www.ginger.roma. it; Via Borgognona 43; sandwiches €7-10, salads €9-14, meals €50; ⊙10am-11.30pm; ☑Spagna) 🍴 This buzzy white-tiled space is a fantastic all-day dining spot near the Spanish Steps. The focus is on organic 'slow food' dishes using seasonal Appellation d'Origine Protégée (AOP) ingredients, and all appetites are catered for with gourmet, French baguette-style sandwiches, steamed 'baskets', meal-sized salads and healthy mains like salmon with orange mayonnaise.

There are smoothies, shakes, cold-pressed juices (the 100% pomegranate is superb) and magnificent fresh fruit platters presented like floral displays to share. Spacious pavement terrace with winter heaters too.

Vineria Il Chianti   TUSCAN €€

(Map p106; ☑06 679 24 70; www.vineriailchianti. com; Via del Lavatore 81-82a; meals €45; ⊙10am-1am; ☑Via del Tritone) With a name like Il Chianti, this pretty ivy-clad wine bar can only be Tuscan. Cosy up inside its bottle-lined interior or grab a table on the street terrace and dig into superb Tuscan dishes like *stracotto* al *Brunello* (beef braised in Brunello wine) or handmade pasta laced with *lardo di Colonnata* (aromatic pork fat aged in Carrara marble vats). Florence's iconic T-bone steak is also fantastic here.

★ **Colline Emiliane** ITALIAN €€€
(Map p106; ☑ 06 481 75 38; www.collineemiliane. com; Via degli Avignonesi 22; meals €45; ⊙ 12.45-2.45pm & 7.30-10.45pm Tue-Sun, closed Sun dinner & Mon; M Barberini) Sensational regional cuisine from Emilia-Romagna aside, what makes this small white-tablecloth dining address so outstanding is its family vibe and overwhelmingly warm service. It's been a stronghold of the Latini family since the 1930s, and today son Luca runs the show with his mother Paola (dessert queen), aunt Anna (watch her making fresh pasta each morning in the glassed-off lab) and father Massimo.

The kitchen flies the flag for Emilia-Romagna, the well-fed Italian province that has blessed the world with Parmesan, balsamic vinegar, bolognese sauce and Parma ham. Winter ushers white truffles with eggs, pasta or gooey Fontina cheese onto the menu. Whatever you do, don't scrimp on *dolci* – Anna's warm caramelised hazelnut and walnut tart is out of this world.

✗ Vatican City, Borgo & Prati

★ **Pizzarium** PIZZA €
(Map p116; ☑ 06 3974 5416; Via della Meloria 43; pizza slices €5; ⊙ 11am-10pm; M Cipro-Musei Vaticani) When a pizza joint is packed at lunchtime on a wet winter's day, you know it's something special. Pizzarium, the takeaway of Gabriele Bonci, Rome's acclaimed pizza king, serves Rome's best sliced pizza, bar none. Scissor-cut squares of soft, springy base are topped with original combinations of seasonal ingredients and served on paper trays for immediate consumption. Also worth trying are the freshly fried *supplì* (risotto balls).

★ **Fa-Bio** SANDWICHES €
(Map p116; ☑ 06 6452 5810; www.fa-bio.com; Via Germanico 43; sandwiches €5; ⊙ 10.30am-5.30pm Mon-Fri, to 4pm Sat; ☐ Piazza del Risorgimento; M Ottaviano-San Pietro) ✈ Sandwiches, wraps, salads and fresh juices are all prepared with speed, skill and fresh organic ingredients at this friendly takeaway. Locals, Vatican tour guides and in-the-know visitors come here to grab a quick lunchtime bite and if you can

find room in the tiny interior, you'd do well to follow suit.

★ **Fatamorgana** GELATO €
(Map p116; www.gelateriafatamorgana.it; Via Leone IV 52; gelato €2.50-5; ⊙ noon-11pm summer, to 9pm winter; M Ottaviano-San Pietro) The Prati branch of hit gelateria chain. As well as all the classic flavours there are some wonderfully left-field creations, including a strange but delicious *basilico, miele e noci* (basil, honey and hazelnuts).

Mo's Gelaterie GELATO €
(Map p116; ☑ 06 687 43 57; Via Cola di Rienzo 174; gelato €2.50-6; ⊙ 11am-8pm; ☐ Piazza del Risorgimento) Chocoholics should make a beeline for Mo's, a small gelateria nestled between the shops on Via Cola di Rienzo. The choice of flavours is limited, but the artisanal gelato really hits the mark. The dark chocolate is wonderful, and the banana is packed with taste.

Il Sorpasso ITALIAN €€
(Map p116; ☑ 06 8902 4554; www.sorpasso.info; Via Properzio 31-33; meals €20-35; ⊙ 7am-1am Mon-Fri, 9am-1am Sat; ☐ Piazza del Risorgimento) A bar-restaurant hybrid sporting a vintage cool look – vaulted stone ceilings, exposed brick, rustic wooden tables – Il Sorpasso is a Prati hotspot. Open throughout the day, it caters to a fashionable crowd, serving everything from salads and pasta specials to *trapizzini* (pyramids of stuffed pizza), cured meats and cocktails.

Velavevodetto Ai Quiriti ROMAN €€
(Map p116; ☑ 06 3600 0009; www.ristorante velavevodetto.it; Piazza dei Quiriti 5; meals €30-35; ⊙ 12.30-3pm & 7.45-11pm; M Lepanto) This welcoming restaurant wins you over with its unpretentious, earthy food and honest prices. The menu reads like a directory of Roman staples, and while it's all pretty good, standout choices include *fettuccine con asparagi, guanciale e pecorino* (pasta ribbons with asparagus, guanciale and pecorino cheese) and *polpette di bollito* (meatballs).

Hostaria Dino e Toni ROMAN €€
(Map p116; ☑ 06 3973 3284; Via Leone IV 60; meals €25-30; ⊙ 12.30-3pm & 7-11pm, closed Sun & Aug; M Ottaviano-San Pietro) A bustling old-school trattoria, Dino e Toni offers simple, no-frills Roman cooking. Kick off with its house antipasto, a minor meal of fried *supplì*, olives and pizza, before plunging into its

signature pasta dish, *rigatoni all'amatriciana* (pasta tubes with bacon-like *guanciale*, chilli and tomato sauce). No credit cards.

Enoteca La Torre
RISTORANTE €€€

(☑06 4566 8304; www.enotecalatorreroma.com; Villa Laetitia, Lungotevere delle Armi 22; fixed-price lunch menu €60, tasting menus €95-120; ⊙12.30-2.30pm Tue-Sat & 7.30-10.30pm Mon-Sat; ☐Lungotevere delle Armi) The romantic art nouveau Villa Laetitia provides an aristocratic setting for this refined Michelin-starred restaurant. Since opening in 2013, it has firmly established itself on Rome's fine-dining scene with its sophisticated brand of contemporary creative cuisine and a stellar wine list.

Ristorante L'Arcangelo
RISTORANTE €€€

(Map p116; ☑06 321 09 92; www.larcangelo.com; Via Giuseppe G Belli 59; meals €50; ⊙1-2.30pm Mon-Fri & 8-11pm Mon-Sat; ☐Piazza Cavour) Styled as an informal bistro with wood panelling, leather banquettes and casual table settings, L'Arcangelo enjoys a stellar local reputation. Dishes are modern and creative yet still undeniably Roman in their use of traditional ingredients such as sweetbreads and *baccalà* (cod). A further plus is the wine list, which boasts some interesting Italian labels.

✖ Villa Borghese & Northern Rome

Neve di Latte
GELATO €

(☑06 320 84 85; Via Poletti 6; gelato €2.50-5; ⊙noon-11pm Sun-Thu, to midnight Fri & Sat; ☐Viale Tiziano) Behind the MAXXI gallery, this out of the way gelateria is one of Rome's best. There are few exotic flavours, rather the onus is on the classics, all prepared with high-quality seasonal ingredients. The pistachio, made with nuts from the Sicilian town of Bronte, is excellent, as is the crème caramel.

All'Oro
RISTORANTE €€€

(☑06 9799 6907; www.ristorantealloro.it; Via Giuseppe Pisanelli 23-25; tasting menus €78-130; ⊙7-11pm daily & 1-2.45pm Sat & Sun; ☐Flaminio) This Michelin-starred restaurant, recently relocated to the five-star H'All Tailor Suite hotel, is one of Rome's top fine-dining tickets. At the helm is chef Riccardo Di Giacinto whose artfully presented food is modern and innovative while still being recognisably Italian. Complementing the cuisine, the decor strikes a contemporary club look with dark-wood ceilings, brass lamps and a fireplace.

Metamorfosi
RISTORANTE €€€

(☑06 807 68 39; www.metamorfosiroma.it; Via Giovanni Antonelli 30; tasting menus €100-130; ⊙12.30-2.30pm & 8-10.30pm, closed Sat lunch & Sun; ☐Via Giovanni Antonelli) This Michelin-starred Parioli restaurant is one of Rome's top dining tickets offering international fusion cuisine and a contemporary look that marries linear clean-cut lines with warm earthy tones. Chef Roy Carceres' cooking is eclectic, often featuring playful updates of traditional Roman dishes, such as his signature Uovo 65° carbonara antipasto, a deconstruction of Rome's classic pasta dish.

☗ Drinking & Nightlife

Often the best way to enjoy nightlife in Rome is to wander from restaurant to bar, getting happily lost down picturesque cobbled streets. There's simply no city with better backdrops for a drink: you can savour a Campari overlooking the Roman Forum or sample some artisanal beer while watching the light bounce off baroque fountains.

☗ Ancient Rome

BrewDog Roma
CRAFT BEER

(Map p80; ☑392 9308655; www.brewdog.com/bars/worldwide/roma; Via delle Terme di Tito 80; ⊙noon-1am Sun-Thu, to 2am Fri & Sat; ☐Colosseo) This new bar by Scottish brewery BrewDog has proved a hit with Rome's craft-beer lovers since opening in the shadow of the Colosseum in late 2015. With a stripped-down grey-and-brick look, and up to 20 brews on tap, it's a fine spot to kick back after a day on the sights.

0,75
BAR

(Map p80; ☑06 687 57 06; www.075roma.com; Via dei Cerchi 65; ⊙11am-2am; ☎; ☐Via dei Cerchi) This welcoming bar overlooking the Circo Massimo is good for a lingering evening drink, an *aperitivo* or casual meal (mains €6 to €16.50). It's a friendly place with a laid-back vibe, an international crowd, attractive wood-beam look, and cool tunes.

Cavour 313
WINE BAR

(Map p80; ☑06 678 54 96; www.cavour313.it; Via Cavour 313; ⊙12.30-3.15pm daily & 6-11.30pm Mon-Thu, 6pm-midnight Fri & Sat, 7-11pm Sun, closed Aug; ☐Cavour) Close to the Forum, Cavour 313 is a historic wine bar, a snug, wood-panelled retreat frequented by everyone from tourists to actors and politicians.

It serves a selection of salads, cold cuts and cheeses (€9 to €12), but the headline act here is the wine. And with more than 1000 labels to choose from, you're sure to find something to please your palate.

Centro Storico

★ Open Baladin
BAR

(Map p86; ☑06 683 8989; www.openbaladin roma.it; Via degli Specchi 6; ⊘noon-2am; ⓢ; ⓠVia Arenula) For some years, this cool, modern pub near Campo de' Fiori has been a leading light in Rome's craft-beer scene, and with more than 40 beers on tap and up to 100 bottled brews (many from Italian artisanal microbreweries), it's still a top place for a pint. There's also a decent food menu with *panini*, gourmet burgers and daily specials.

★ Barnum Cafe
CAFE

(Map p86; ☑06 6476 0483; www.barnumcafe. com; Via del Pellegrino 87; ⊘9am-10pm Mon, to 2am Tue-Sat; ⓢ; ⓠCorso Vittorio Emanuele II) A laid-back *Friends*-style cafe, evergreen Barnum is the sort of place you could quickly get used to. With its shabby-chic vintage furniture and white bare-brick walls, it's a relaxed spot for a breakfast cappuccino, a light lunch or a late-afternoon drink. Come evening, a coolly dressed-down crowd sips seriously good cocktails.

Roscioli Caffè
CAFE

(Map p86; ☑06 8916 5330; www.rosciolicaffe. com; Piazza Benedetto Cairoli 16; ⊘7am-11pm Mon-Sat, 8am-6pm Sun; ⓠVia Arenula) The Roscioli name is a sure bet for good food and drink in this town: the family runs one of Rome's most celebrated delis (p129) and a hugely popular bakery (p128), and this cafe doesn't disappoint either. The coffee is wonderfully luxurious, and the artfully crafted pastries, petits fours and *panini* taste as good as they look.

Caffè Sant'Eustachio
COFFEE

(Map p86; www.santeustachioilcaffe.it; Piazza Sant'Eustachio 82; ⊘8.30am-1am Sun-Thu, to 1.30am Fri, to 2am Sat; ⓠCorso del Rinascimento) This small, unassuming cafe, generally three deep at the bar, is reckoned by many to serve the best coffee in town. To make it, the bartenders sneakily beat the first drops of an espresso with several teaspoons of sugar to create a frothy paste to which they add the rest of the coffee. It's superbly smooth

and guaranteed to put some zing into your sightseeing.

La Casa del Caffè Tazza d'Oro
COFFEE

(Map p86; ☑06 678 9792; www.tazzadoro coffeeshop.com; Via degli Orfani 84-86; ⊘7am-8pm Mon-Sat, 10.30am-7.30pm Sun; ⓠVia del Corso) A busy, stand-up affair with burnished 1940s fittings, this is one of Rome's best coffee houses. Its espresso hits the mark nicely and there's a range of delicious coffee concoctions, including a cooling *granita di caffè,* a crushed-ice coffee drink served with whipped cream. There's also a small shop and, outside, a coffee *bancomat* for those out-of-hours caffeine emergencies.

Etablì
WINE BAR, CAFE

(Map p86; ☑06 9761 6694; www.etabli.it; Vicolo delle Vacche 9a; ⊘cafe 7.30am-6pm, wine bar 6pm-1am; ⓢ; ⓠCorso del Rinascimento) Housed in a 16th-century *palazzo,* Etablì is a rustic-chic lounge-bar-restaurant where you can drop by for a morning coffee, have a light lunch or chat over an *aperitivo.* It's laid-back and good-looking, with original French-inspired country decor – leather armchairs, rough wooden tables and a crackling fireplace. It also serves full restaurant dinners (€45) and hosts occasional live music.

Escosazio
JUICE BAR

(Map p86; ☑06 6476 0784; www.escosazio.it; Via dei Banchi Vecchi 135; ⊘8.30am-8pm Mon-Sat; ⓠCorso Vittorio Emanuele II) Rome is discovering juice bars right now and this friendly bolthole is a good bet for a refreshing smoothie or juice extract. Keep it simple with a freshly squeezed OJ, or spice things up with a *digestivo* made from orange, pineapple, fennel and ginger. If you're hungry, stop by at lunch for a tasty risotto or made-to-order *panino.*

❶ Monti, Esquilino & San Lorenzo

★ Spirito
COCKTAIL BAR

(☑327 2983900; www.club-spirito.com; Via Fanfulla da Lodi 53; ⊘7.30pm-3am Wed-Mon; ⓠVia Prenestina) A fashionable address only for those in the know, Spirito is spirited away behind a simple white door at the back of a sandwich shop in edgy Pigneto. This New Yorker Prohibition–style speakeasy has expertly mixed craft cocktails (around €10), gourmet food, live music and shows, roulette at the bar and a fun-loving crowd.

LOCAL KNOWLEDGE

ROME AFTER DARK

Night-owl Romans tend to eat late, then drink at bars before heading off to a club at around 1am. Like most cities, Rome is a collection of districts, each with its own character, which is often completely different after dark. The *centro storico* (historic centre) and Trastevere pull in a mix of locals and tourists as night falls. Ostiense and Testaccio are the grittier clubbing districts, with clusters of clubs in a couple of locations – Testaccio has a parade of crowd-pleasing clubs running over the hill of Monte Testaccio. There are also subtle political divisions. San Lorenzo and Pigneto, to the south of Rome, are popular with a left-leaning, alternative crowd, while areas to the north (such as Ponte Milvio and Parioli) attract a more right-wing, bourgeois milieu.

The *bella figura* (loosely translated as 'looking good') is important. The majority of locals spend evenings checking each other out, partaking in gelato, and not drinking too much. However, this is changing and certain areas – those popular with a younger crowd – can get rowdy with drunk teens and tourists (for example, Campo de' Fiori and parts of Trastevere).

★ Il Sorì
WINE BAR

(Map p90; ☑ 393 4318661; www.ilsori.it; Via dei Volsci 51; ⊙ 7.30pm-2am Mon-Sat; ☐ Via Tiburtina) Every last salami slice and chunk of cheese has been carefully selected from Italy's finest artisanal and small producers at this gourmet wine bar and *bottega* (shop), an unexpected pearl of a stop for dedicated foodies in student-driven San Lorenzo. Interesting and unusual wine tastings, theme nights, 'meet the producer' soirées and other events cap off what is already a memorable drinking (and dining) experience.

★ Gatsby Café
BAR, CAFE

(Map p90; ☑ 06 6933 9626; Piazza Vittorio Emanuele II 106; cocktails €7-10; ⊙ 8am-midnight Mon-Thu, to 2am Fri & Sat; Ⓜ Termini) There's good reason why the friendly bar staff here all wear flat caps, feather-trimmed trilbys and other traditional gents' hats: this fabulous 1950s-styled space with salvaged vintage furniture and flashes of funky geometric wallpapering was originally a milliner's shop called Galleria Venturini. Brilliant rhubarb or elderflower *spritz,* craft cocktails, gourmet *panini* (€5) and *taglieri* (salami and cheese platters) make it a top *aperitivo* spot.

★ La Casetta a Monti
CAFE

(Map p80; ☑ 06 482 7756; www.facebook. com/lacasettadeimonti; Via della Madonna dei Monti 62; ⊙ 9.30am-8pm Mon-Thu, to 10pm Fri & Sat, 8.30am-9pm Sun; ☏; Ⓜ Cavour) Delicious cakes, pastries and the finest chocolate salami in town is the name of the game at this uber-cute cafe, doll's house in size, run with much love and passion by Eugenio and Alessandro. Find the cafe, all fresh and sassy after a 2017 restyle, in a low-lying house with big windows and foliage-draped facade in the cobbled heart of Monti. There's breakfast, lunch, drinks and music too.

★ Co.So
COCKTAIL BAR

(☑ 06 4543 5428; Via Braccio da Montone 80; ⊙ 7pm-3am Mon-Sat; ☐ Via Prenestina) The chicest bar in Pigneto, tiny Co.So (meaning 'Cocktails & Social') is run by Massimo D'Addezio (a former master mixologist at Hotel de Russie) and is hipster to the hilt. Think Carbonara Sour cocktails (with pork-fat-infused vodka), bubblewrap coasters, and popcorn and M&M bar snacks. Check its Facebook page for the latest happenings.

★ Necci dal 1924
CAFE, BAR

(☑ 06 9760 1552; www.necci1924.com; Via Fanfulla da Lodi 68; ⊙ 8am-2am; ☏⊕; ☐ Via Prenestina) An all-round hybrid in edgy Pigneto, iconic Necci opened as a gelateria in 1924 and later became a favourite of film director Pier Paolo Pasolini. These days, with English chef and owner Ben Hirst at its helm, Necci caters to a buoyant hipster crowd with its laid-back vibe, retro interior and food served all day. Huge kudos for the fabulous summertime terrace.

Vicious Club
CLUB

(Map p90; ☑ 345 845 65 91; www.viciousclub. com; Via Achille Grandi 7a; ⊙ 10pm-late Mon-Sat; ☐ Piazza di Porta Maggiore) This hugely trendy, gay-friendly club and cocktail bar near Termini station is the hottest kid on the block (not to mention a little wild around the edges) on Rome's fairly conservative clubbing scene. Expect an underground vibe, unfamiliar to Romans, with its dark-black interior covered almost entirely in mirrors, sultry twinset of DJ booths, and smoking room.

La Bottega del Caffè
CAFE

(Map p80; ☑ 06 474 15 78; Piazza Madonna dei Monti 5; ☺ 8am-2am; ☂; Ⓜ Cavour) On one of Rome's prettiest squares in Monti, La Bottega del Caffè – named after a comedy by Carlo Goldoni – is the hot spot in Monti for lingering over coffee, drinks, snacks and lunch or dinner. Heaters in winter ensure balmy al fresco action year-round.

🍷 San Giovanni & Testaccio

Anticafé Roma
CAFE

(☑ 06 7049 4442; Via Veio 4B; ☺ 9am-10pm; ☂; Ⓜ San Giovanni) Something of a novelty in Rome, Anticafé doesn't charge for its drinks. Instead you pay for the time you spend there – €4 for the first hour, then €3 for successive hours. With that you're free to hang out and do pretty much whatever – use the wi-fi, play board games, read on the sofa, drink. You can BYO or there's a bar with free drinks and snacks.

Bibenda Wine Concept
WINE BAR

(Map p94; ☑ 06 7720 6673; www.wineconcept.it; Via Capo d'Africa 21; ☺ noon-3pm & 6pm-midnight Mon-Thu, to 2am Fri & Sat, closed Sat lunch & Sun; 🚇 Via Labicana) Wine buffs looking to excite their palate should search out this smart modern *enoteca* (wine bar). Boasting a white, light-filled interior, it has an extensive

---

GAY & LESBIAN ROME

There is only a smattering of dedicated gay and lesbian clubs and bars in Rome, though many nightclubs host regular gay and lesbian nights. For local information, pick up a copy of the monthly magazine *AUT*, published by Circolo Mario Mieli (www.mariomieli.org). There's also info at AZ Gay (www.azgay. it). Lesbians can find out more about the local scene at Coordinamento Lesbiche Italiano (www.clrbp.it).

Most gay venues (bars, clubs and saunas) require you to have an **Arcigay** (☑ 06 6450 1102; www.arcigayroma. it; Via Nicola Zabaglia 14) membership card. These cost €15/8 per year/three months and are available from any venue that requires one.

---

list of Italian regional labels and European vintages, as well as a small daily food menu. Wines are available to drink by the glass or buy by the bottle.

🍷 Southern Rome

★ Circolo Illuminati
CLUB, BAR

(☑ 327 7615286; www.circolodegliilluminati.it; Via Libetta 1a; ☺ midnight-late; Ⓜ Garbatella) Tech house, hip-hop and chill music revs up clubbers at this wildly popular Ostiense club on the international DJ club circuit. The vibe is very much underground, and its courtyard garden with potted plants and olive trees is a gorgeous space in which to kick-start the evening beneath the stars.

★ Goa
CLUB

(☑ 06 574 82 77; www.goaclub.com; Via Libetta 13; ☺ 11.30pm-4.30am Thu-Sat; Ⓜ Garbatella) At home in a former motorbike repair shop down a dead-end alley in industrial-style Ostiense, Goa is Rome's serious super-club with exotic India-inspired decor and international DJs mixing house and techno. Expect a fashion-forward crowd, podium dancers, thumping dance floor, sofas to lounge on and heavies on the door.

Vinile
CLUB

(☑ 06 5728 8666; www.vinileroma.it; Via Libetta 19; ☺ 8pm-2am Tue & Wed, to 3am Thu, to 4am Fri & Sat, 12.30-3pm & 8pm-2am Sun; Ⓜ Garbatella) On weekends a mixed bag of Romans of all ages hit the dance floor at Vinyl, a buzzing bar and club cooking up food, music and party happenings on the southern fringe of Ostiense. Inside its huge cavernous interior – with part-vegetal, part-frescoed ceiling – the night starts with an *aperitivo* banquet from 8pm; DJ sets start at 11.30pm. On Sunday students pile in here for the unbeatable-value brunch.

🍷 Trastevere & Gianicolo

★ Rivendita Libri, Cioccolata e Vino
COCKTAIL BAR

(Map p100; ☑ 06 5830 1868; www.facebook.com/cioccolateriatrastevere; Vicolo del Cinque 11a; shot €3-5; ☺ 7pm-2am Mon-Fri, 2pm-2am Sat & Sun; 🚇 Piazza Trilussa) There is no finer – or funnier – spot in the whole of Rome for a swift French Kiss, Orgasm or One Night Stand than this highly inventive cocktail bar, packed every night from around 10pm with a fun-loving, post-dinner crowd. Cocktails are served in miniature chocolate cups, filled with various types of alcohol and topped with whipped cream.

★ Keyhole
COCKTAIL BAR

(Map p100; Via Arco di San Calisto 17; ⏱10pm-2am; 🚊Viale di Trastevere, 🚊Viale di Trastevere) The latest in a growing trend of achingly hip, underground speakeasies in Rome, Keyhole ticks all the boxes: no identifiable name or signage outside the bar; a black door smothered in keys; and Prohibition-era decor including leather Chesterfield sofas, dim lighting and an electric craft cocktail menu. Not sure what to order? Ask the talented mixologists to create your own bespoke cocktail (around €10).

★ Pimm's Good
BAR

(Map p86; ☎06 9727 7979; www.facebook.com/pimmsgood; Via di Santa Dorotea 8; ⏱10am-2am; 🛜; 🚊Piazza Trilussa) 'Anyone for Pimm's?' is the catchline of this eternally popular bar with part red-brick ceiling that does indeed serve Pimm's – the classic way or in a variety of cocktails (€10). The party-loving guys behind the bar are serious mixologists and well-crafted cocktails is their thing. Look for the buzzing street-corner pavement terrace – lit up in winter with flaming outdoor heaters.

★ Freni e Frizioni
BAR

(Map p100; ☎06 4549 7499; www.freniefrizioni. com; Via del Politeama 4-6; ⏱7pm-2am; 🚊Piazza Trilussa) This perennially cool Trastevere bar is housed in an old mechanic's workshop – hence its name ('brakes and clutches') and tatty facade. It draws a young spritz loving crowd that swells onto the small piazza outside to sip superbly mixed cocktails (€10) and seasonal punches, and fill up on its lavish early-evening aperitivo buffet (7pm to 10pm). Table reservations are essential on Friday and Saturday evenings.

★ Bar San Calisto
CAFE

(Map p100; Piazza San Calisto 3-5; ⏱6am-2am Mon-Sat; 🚊Viale di Trastevere, 🚊Viale di Trastevere) Those in the know head to 'Sanca' for its basic, stuck-in-time atmosphere and cheap prices (beer from €1.50). It attracts everyone from intellectuals to keeping-it-real Romans, alcoholics and foreign students. It's famous for its chocolate – come for hot chocolate with cream in winter, and chocolate gelato in summer. Try the sambuca con la mosca ('with flies' – raw coffee beans). Expect occasional late-night jam sessions.

Il Baretto
BAR

(Map p100; ☎06 589 60 55; www.ilbarettoroma. com; Via Garibaldi 27; ⏱7am-2am Mon-Sat; 🚊Via Garibaldi) Venture a little way up the Gianicolo, up a steep flight of steps from Trastevere - go on, it's worth it. Because there you'll discover this good-looking cocktail bar where the basslines are meaty, the bar staff hip, and the interior a mix of vintage and pop art.

Bir & Fud
CRAFT BEER

(Map p86; ☎06 589 40 16; www.birandfud.it; Via Benedetta 23; ⏱noon-2am; 🚊Piazza Trilussa) On a narrow street lined with raucous drinking holes, this brick-vaulted bar-pizzeria wins plaudits for its outstanding collection of craft bir (beer), many on tap, and equally tasty fud (food) for when late-night munchies strike. Its Neapolitan-style wood-fired pizzas are particularly excellent.

🍷 Tridente, Trevi & the Quirinale

★ Zuma Bar
COCKTAIL BAR

(Map p106; ☎06 9926 6622; www.zumarestau rant.com; Via della Fontanella di Borghese 48, Palazzo Fendi; ⏱6pm-1am Sun-Thu, to 2am Fri & Sat; 🛜; 🚊Via del Corso) Dress up for a drink on the rooftop terrace of Palazzo Fendi of fashion-house fame – few cocktail bars in Rome are as sleek, hip or achingly sophisticated as this. City rooftop views are predictably fabulous; cocktails mix exciting flavours like shiso with juniper berries, elderflower and prosecco; and DJ sets spin Zuma playlists at weekends.

★ Antico Caffè Greco
CAFE

(Map p106; ☎06 679 17 00; Via dei Condotti 86; ⏱9am-9pm; Ⓜ Spagna) Rome's oldest cafe, open since 1760, is still working the look with the utmost elegance: waiters in black tails and bow tie, waitresses in frilly white pinnies, scarlet flock walls and age-spotted gilt mirrors. Prices reflect this amazing heritage: pay €9 for a cappuccino sitting down or join locals for the same (€2.50) standing at the bar.

★ Il Palazzetto
CAFE, COCKTAIL BAR

(Map p106; ☎06 6993 41000; Vicolo del Bottino 8; ⏱noon-8.30pm Tue-Sun, closed in rain; Ⓜ Spagna) No terrace proffers such a fine view of the comings and goings on the Spanish Steps over an expertly shaken cocktail (€10 to €13). Ride the lift up from the discreet entrance on narrow Via dei Bottino or look for steps leading to the bar from the top of the steps. Given everything is al fresco, the bar is only open in warm, dry weather.

Pepy's Bar   CAFE
(Map p106; ☑ 06 4040 2364; www.pepysbar. it; Piazza Barberini 53; ⊘ 7am-2am; ☎; Ⓜ Barberini) Play the Roman: sit at a bistro table on the narrow pavement terrace and watch the fountains gush and *motorini* whizz by on Piazza Barberini at this down-to-earth, neighbourhood cafe in Trevi. It is a perfect spot for a relaxed drink any time of day, and its all-day sandwiches – made with perfectly square, crustless white bread – are almost too beautiful to eat.

Caffè Ciampini   CAFE
(Map p106; ☑ 06 678 56 78; www.caffeciampini. com; Viale Trinità dei Monti; ⊘ 8am-11pm Mar-Oct; Ⓜ Spagna) Hidden away a short walk from the top of the Spanish Steps towards the Pincio Hill Gardens, this graceful seasonal cafe has a vintage garden-party vibe, with green wooden latticework and orange trees framing its white-clothed tables. There are lovely views over the backstreets behind Spagna, and the gelato – particularly the *tartufo al cioccolato* (chocolate truffle) – is renowned. Serves food too.

Stravinskij Bar   BAR
(Map p106; ☑ 06 3288 8874; Via del Babuino 9, Hotel de Russie; ⊘ 9am-1am; Ⓜ Flaminio) Can't afford to stay at the celeb-magnet Hotel de Russie? Then splash out on a drink at its swish bar. There are sofas inside, but best is a drink in the sunny courtyard, with sun-shaded tables overlooked by terraced gardens. Impossibly romantic in the best dolce vita style, it's perfect for a pricey cocktail or beer accompanied by appropriately posh bar snacks.

Vatican City, Borgo & Prati

★ Sciascia Caffè   CAFE

(Map p116; ☑ 06 321 15 80; Via Fabio Massimo 80/A; ⊘ 7am-8.30pm Mon-Sat, 8am-8pm Sun; Ⓜ Ottaviano-San Pietro) There are several contenders for the best coffee in town but in our opinion, nothing tops the *caffè eccellente* served at this polished old-school cafe. A velvety smooth espresso served in a delicate cup lined with melted chocolate, it's nothing short of magnificent.

Be.re   CRAFT BEER
(Map p116; ☑ 06 9442 1854; www.be-re.eu; Piazza del Risorgimento, cnr Via Vespasiano; ⊘ 10am-2am; ⬜ Piazza del Risorgimento) Rome's craft-beer fans keenly applauded the opening of this contemporary bar in late 2016. With its copper beer taps, exposed brick decor and high vaulted ceilings, it's a good-looking spot for an evening of Italian beers and cask ales. And should hunger strike, there's a branch of hit takeaway Trapizzino right next door.

Makasar Bistrot   WINE BAR, TEAHOUSE
(Map p116; ☑ 06 687 46 02; www.makasar.it; Via Plauto 33; ⊘ noon-midnight Mon-Thu, to 2am Fri & Sat, 5pm-midnight Sun; ⬜ Piazza del Risorgimento) Recharge your batteries with a quiet drink at this bookish *bistrot*. Pick your tipple from the 250-variety tea menu or opt for an Italian wine and sit back in the softly lit earthenware-hued interior. For something to eat, there's a small menu of salads, bruschetta, baguettes and hot dishes.

Villa Borghese & Northern Rome

Momart   CAFE
(☑ 06 8639 1656; www.momartcafe.it; Viale XXI Aprile 19; ⊘ noon-2am, to 3am Sat & Sun; ⬜ Viale XXI Aprile) A modish restaurant-cafe in the university district near Via Nomentana, Momart serves one of Rome's most bountiful spreads of *apericena* (an informal evening meal involving *aperitivi* and tapas-style food). A mixed crowd of students and local professionals flocks here to fill up on the ample buffet and kick back over cocktails on the pavement terrace.

☆ Entertainment

Watching the world go by in Rome is often entertainment enough, but don't overlook the local arts and sports scene. As well as gigs and concerts in every genre, there are fantastic arts festivals, especially in summer, performances with Roman ruins as a backdrop, and football games that split the city.

☆ Classical Music

★ Auditorium
Parco della Musica   CONCERT VENUE
(☑ 06 8024 1281; www.auditorium.com; Viale Pietro de Coubertin; ⬜ Viale Tiziano) The hub of Rome's thriving cultural scene, the Auditorium is the capital's premier concert venue.

Its three concert halls offer superb acoustics, and together with a 3000-seat open-air arena, stage everything from classical music concerts to jazz gigs, public lectures and film screenings.

The Auditorium is also home to Rome's world-class **Orchestra dell'Accademia Nazionale di Santa Cecilia** (www.santacecilia.it).

Teatro Palladium THEATRE
(☑ box office 06 5733 2772; http://teatropalladium.uniroma3.it; Piazza Bartolomeo Romano; Ⓜ Garbatella) Once at risk of being turned into a bingo hall, the historic Teatro Palladium (1926), with a beautifully renovated 1920s interior, stages a rich repertoire of theatre, classical music concerts, cinema and art exhibitions.

☆ Opera

Teatro Argentina THEATRE
(Map p86; ☑ 06 68400 0311; www.teatrodiroma.net; Largo di Torre Argentina 52; tickets €12-32, ☑ Largo di Torre Argentina) Founded in 1732, Rome's top theatre is one of the two official homes of the Teatro di Roma – the other is the **Teatro India** (☑ 06 68400 0311; www.teatrodiroma.net; Lungotevere Vittorio Gassman 1; Ⓜ Stazione Trastevere) in the southern suburbs. Rossini's *Barber of Seville* premiered here in 1816, and these days the theatre stages a wide-ranging program of drama (mostly in Italian), high-profile dance performances and classical music concerts.

Teatro dell'Opera di Roma OPERA, BALLET
(Map p00; ☑ 06 48 16 01; www.operaroma.it; Piazza Beniamino Gigli 1; ⊙ box office 10am-6pm Mon-Sat, 9am-1.30pm Sun; Ⓜ Repubblica) Rome's premier opera house boasts a plush gilt interior, a Fascist 1920s exterior and an impressive history: it premiered Puccini's *Tosca*, and Maria Callas once sang here. Opera and ballet performances are staged between September and June.

☆ Jazz, Blues, Indie & Rock

Blackmarket LIVE MUSIC
(Map p90; www.blackmarketartgallery.it/monti; Via Panisperna 101; ⊙ 7.30pm-2am; Ⓜ Cavour) A bit outside the main Monti hub, this charming, living-room-style bar filled with eclectic vintage furniture is a small but rambling place, great for sitting back on mismatched armchairs and having a leisurely, convivial drink. It hosts regular acoustic indie and folk gigs, which feel a bit like having a band in your living room.

ConteStaccio LIVE MUSIC
(Map p96; ☑ 06 5728 9712; www.contestaccio.com; Via di Monte Testaccio 65b; ⊙ 8pm-4am Thu-Sun; ☑ Via Galvani) With an under-the-stars terrace and buzzing vibe, ConteStaccio is one of the top venues on the Testaccio clubbing strip. It's something of a multipurpose outfit with a cocktail bar, pizzeria and restaurant, but is best known for its free live music. Gigs by emerging groups set the tone, spanning indie, rock, acoustic, funk and electronic genres.

Caffè Letterario LIVE MUSIC
(☑ 06 5730 2842; www.caffeletterarioroma.it; Via Ostiense 95; ⊙ 10am-2am Tue-Sat, 4pm-2am Sun; ☑ Via Ostiense, Ⓜ Piramide) Caffè Letterario is an intellectual hang-out housed in the funky converted, post-industrial space of a former garage. It combines designer looks, a bookshop, gallery, co-working space, performance area and lounge bar. There are regular gigs from 10pm to midnight, ranging from soul and jazz to Indian dance.

Big Mama BLUES
(Map p100; ☑ 06 581 25 51; www.bigmama.it; Vicolo di San Francesco a Ripa 18; ⊙ 9pm-1.30am, shows 10.30pm, closed Jun-Sep; ☑ Viale di Trastevere, ☑ Viale di Trastevere) Head to this cramped Trastevere basement for a mellow night of Eternal City blues. A long-standing venue, it also stages jazz, funk, soul and R&B acts, as well as popular cover bands.

Gregory's Jazz Club JAZZ
(Map p106; ☑ 06 679 63 86; www.gregorysjazz.com; Via Gregoriana 54d; obligatory drink €15-20;

TICKETS

Tickets for concerts, live music and theatrical performances are widely available across the city. Prices range enormously depending on the venue and artist. Hotels can often reserve tickets for guests, or you can contact the venue or organisation directly – check listings publications for booking details. Otherwise you can try the following:

Vivaticket (☑ 892 234; www.vivaticket.it)

Orbis (Map p90; ☑ 06 482 74 03; Piazza dell'Esquilino 37; ⊙ 9.30am-1pm & 4-7pm Mon-Sat; ☑ Via Cavour)

⊘8pm-2am Tue-Sun; Ⓜ Barberini, Spagna) If Gregory's were a tone of voice, it'd be husky: unwind over a whisky in the downstairs bar, then unwind some more on squashy sofas upstairs to slinky live jazz and swing, with quality local performers who also like to hang out here.

Alexanderplatz JAZZ
(Map p116; ☑06 8377 5604; www.facebook. com/alexander.platz.37; Via Ostia 9; ⊘8.30pm-1.30am; Ⓜ Ottaviano-San Pietro) Intimate, underground, and hard to find – look for the discreet black door – Rome's most celebrated jazz club draws top Italian and international performers and a respectful cosmopolitan crowd. Book a table for the best stage views or to dine here, although note that it's the music that's the star act, not the food.

☆ Cinema

Isola del Cinema OUTDOOR CINEMA
(Map p100; www.isoladelcinema.com; Isola Tiberina; tickets €6) From mid-June to September, the Isola Tiberina sets the stage for a season of outdoor cinema, featuring Italian and international films, some shown in their original language.

Nuovo Cinema Palazzo ARTS CENTER
(Map p90; www.nuovocinemapalazzo.it; Piazza dei Sanniti 9a; ⊘hours vary; 🚇 Via Tiburtina) Students, artists and activists are breathing new life into San Lorenzo's former Palace Cinema with a bevy of exciting creative happenings: think film screenings, theatre performances, DJ sets, concerts, live music, breakdance classes and a host of other artsy events. In warm weather, the action spills outside onto the street terrace, overlooked by a B&W stencil mural by Rome street artists Sten & Lex. Check its Facebook page for the monthly calendar.

☆ Sport

Stadio Olimpico STADIUM
(☑06 3685 7563; Viale dei Gladiatori 2, Foro Italico; 🚇 Lungotevere Maresciallo Cadorna) A trip to Rome's impressive Stadio Olimpico offers an unforgettable insight into Rome's sporting heart. Throughout the football season (September to May) there's a game on most Sundays featuring one of the city's two Serie A teams (Roma or Lazio), and during the Six Nations rugby tournament (February to March) it hosts Italy's home games.

Tickets cost from €20 depending on the match and can be bought at Lottomatica (lottery centres), the stadium, ticket agencies, www.listicket.it or one of the many Roma or Lazio stores around the city.

☆ Comedy

Teatro Ambra Jovinelli THEATRE
(Map p90; ☑06 8308 2884; www.ambrajovinelli. org; Via G Pepe 43-47; Ⓜ Vittorio Emanuele) A home away from home for many famous Italian comics, the Ambra Jovinelli is a historic venue for alternative comedians and satirists. Its program is still geared towards comedians today, although it also stages the odd drama, musical and contemporary work.

🏠 Shopping

Rome enthrals with a fabulous portfolio of department stores, specialist shops, independent boutiques and artisan workshops – guaranteed to please the most hedonist of shoppers. 'Retro' is among the Roman shopping scene's many unique qualities, with jewel-like boutiques run by third-generation artisans, dusty picture-framing and basket-weaving workshops, historic department stores all oozing an impossibly chic, old-school glamour. Meander, explore backstreets, enjoy.

🏠 Centro Storico

★**Confetteria**
Moriondo & Gariglio CHOCOLATE
(Map p86; ☑06 699 0856; Via del Piè di Marmo 21-22; ⊘9am-7.30pm Mon-Sat; 🚇 Via del Corso) Roman poet Trilussa was so smitten with this historic chocolate shop – established by the Torinese confectioners to the royal house of Savoy – that he was moved to mention it in verse. And we agree, it's a gem. Decorated like an elegant tearoom, with crimson walls, tables and glass cabinets, it specialises in delicious handmade chocolates, many prepared according to original 19th-century recipes.

★**Ibiz –**
Artigianato in Cuoio FASHION & ACCESSORIES
(Map p86; ☑06 6830 7297; www.ibizroma.it; Via dei Chiavari 39; ⊘9.30am-7.30pm Mon-Sat; 🚇 Corso Vittorio Emanuele II) In her diminutive family workshop, Elisa Nepi and her team craft exquisite, soft-as-butter leather wallets, bags, belts and sandals, in simple but classy

designs and myriad colours. You can pick up a belt for about €35, while for a bag you should bank on at least €110.

Marta Ray   SHOES
(Map p86; ☑06 6880 2641; www.martaray.it; Via dei Coronari 121; ⊘10am-8pm; 🚇Via Zanardelli) Women's ballet flats and elegant, everyday bags, in rainbow colours and butter-soft leather, are the hallmarks of the emerging Marta Ray brand. At this store, one of three in town, you'll find a selection of trademark ballerinas and a colourful line in modern, beautifully designed handbags.

Salumeria Roscioli   FOOD & DRINKS
(Map p86; ☑06 687 5287; www.salumeriaroscioli.com; Via dei Giubbonari 21; ⊘8.30am-8.30pm Mon-Sat; 🚇Via Arenula) The rich scents of cured meats, cheeses, conserves, olive oil and balsamic vinegar intermingle at this top-class deli, one of Rome's finest. Alongside iconic Italian products, you'll also find a vast choice of wines and a range of French cheeses, Spanish hams and Scottish salmon.
You can also dine here at the deli's excellent in-house restaurant (p129).

Bartolucci   TOYS
(Map p86; www.bartolucci.com; Via dei Pastini 98; ⊘10am-10.30pm; 🚇Via del Corso) It's difficult to resist going into this magical toyshop where everything is carved out of wood. By the main entrance, a Pinocchio pedals his bike robotically, perhaps dreaming of the full-size motorbike parked nearby, while inside there are all manner of ticking clocks, rocking horses, planes and more Pinocchios than you're likely to see in your whole life.

🔒 Monti, Esquilino & San Lorenzo

Tina Sondergaard   FASHION & ACCESSORIES
(Map p80; ☑334 385 07 99; Via del Boschetto 1d; ⊘3-7.30pm Mon, 10.30am-1pm & 1.30-7.30pm Tue-Sat, closed Aug; Ⓜ Cavour) Sublimely cut and whimsically retro-esque, Tina Sondergaard's handmade threads for women are a hit with fashion cognoscenti, including Italian rock star Carmen Consoli and the city's theatre and TV crowd. You can have adjustments made (included in the price); dresses cost around €150.

Feltrinelli International   BOOKS
(Map p90; ☑06 482 78 78; www.lafeltrinelli.it; Via VE Orlando 84-86; ⊘9am-8pm Mon-Sat, 10.30am-1.30pm & 4-8pm Sun; Ⓜ Repubblica) The

international branch of Italy's ubiquitous bookseller has a splendid collection of books in English, Italian, Spanish, French, German and Portuguese. You'll find everything from recent bestsellers to dictionaries, travel guides, DVDs and an excellent assortment of maps.

🔒 San Giovanni & Testaccio

Volpetti   FOOD & DRINKS
(Map p96; www.volpetti.com; Via Marmorata 47; ⊘8.30am-2pm & 4.30-8.15pm Mon-Wed, 8.30am-8.15pm Thu-Sat; 🚇Via Marmorata) This superstocked deli, considered by many the best in town, is a treasure trove of gourmet delicacies. Helpful staff will guide you through the extensive selection of smelly cheeses, homemade pastas, olive oils, vinegars, cured meats, veggie pies, wines and grappas. It also serves excellent sliced pizza.

🔒 Trastevere & Gianicolo

★Benheart   FASHION & ACCESSORIES
(Map p100; ☑06 5832 0801; www.benheart.it; Via del Moro 47; ⊘11am-11pm; 🚇Piazza Triussa) From the colourful resin floor papered with children's drawings to the vintage typewriter, dial-up telephone and old-fashioned tools decorating the interior, everything about this artisanal leather boutique is achingly cool. Benheart, a young Florentine designer, is one of Italy's savviest talents and his fashionable handmade shoes (from €190) and jackets for men and women are glorious.

★Antica Caciara Trasteverina   FOOD & DRINKS
(Map p100; ☑06 581 28 15; www.anticacaciara.it; Via San Francesco a Ripa 140; ⊘7am-2pm & 4-8pm Mon-Sat; 🚇Viale di Trastevere, 🚇Viale di Trastevere) The fresh ricotta is a prized possession at this century-old deli, and it's all usually snapped up by lunchtime. If you're too late, take solace in the to-die-for *ricotta infornata* (oven-baked ricotta), 35kg wheels of famous, black-waxed *pecorino romano* DOP (€16.50 per kilo), and aromatic garlands of *guanciale* (pig's jowl) begging to be chopped up, pan-fried and thrown into the perfect carbonara.

★Biscottificio Innocenti   FOOD
(Map p100; ☑06 580 39 26; www.facebook.com/biscottificioInnocenti; Via delle Luce 21; ⊘8am-8pm Mon-Sat, 9.30am-2pm Sun; 🚇Viale di Trastevere, 🚇Viale di Trastevere) For homemade biscuits,

bite-sized meringues and tiny fruit tarts, there is no finer address in Rome than this vintage *biscottificio* with ceramic-tiled interior, fly-net door curtain and a set of old-fashioned scales on the counter to weigh out biscuits (€16 to €24 per kilo). The shop has been run with much love and passion for several decades by the ever-dedicated Stefania.

Les Vignerons　　　　　　　　WINE
(Map p100; ☑06 6477 1439; www.lesvignerons.it; Via Mameli 61; ⊙4-9pm Mon, 11am-9pm Tue-Thu, 11am-9.30pm Fri & Sat; ☒Viale di Trastevere, ☒Viale di Trastevere) If you're looking for some interesting wines to take home, search out this lovely Trastevere wine shop. It boasts one of the capital's best collections of natural wines, mainly from small Italian and French producers, as well as a comprehensive selection of spirits and international craft beers.

🔒 Tridente, Trevi & the Quirinale

⭐**Re(f)use**　　　　　　　　DESIGN
(Map p106; ☑06 6813 6975; www.carmina campus.com; Via della Fontanelle di Borghese 40; ⊙11am-7pm; ☒Via del Corso) Fascinating to browse, this clever boutique showcases unique Carmina Campus pieces – primarily bags and jewellery – made from upcycled objects and recycled fabrics. The brand is the love child of Rome-born designer Ilaria Venturini Fendi (of the Fendi family), a passionate advocate of ethical fashion, who crafts contemporary bracelets from beer and soft-drink cans, and bold bags from recycled materials.

⭐**Manila Grace**　　　FASHION & ACCESSORIES
(Map p106; ☑06 679 78 36; www.manilagrace. com; Via Frattina 60; ⊙10am-7.30pm; Ⓜ Spagna) An essential homegrown label for dedicated followers of fashion, Manila Grace mixes bold prints, patterns and fabrics to create a strikingly unique, assertive style for women who like to stand out in a crowd. Think a pair of red stiletto shoes with a fuchsia-pink pom-pom on the toe, a striped jacket or a glittering gold bag with traditional tan-leather trim. Alessia Santi is the talented designer behind the brand.

⭐**Artisanal Cornucopia**　　　　DESIGN
(Map p106; ☑342 871 4597; www.artisanalcornu copia.com; Via dell'Oca 38a; ⊙10am-7pm; Ⓜ Flaminio) One of several stylish independent boutiques on Via dell'Oca, this chic concept store showcases exclusive handmade pieces by Italian designers: think a trunk full of Anthony Peto hats, bold sculpture-like lamps by Roman designer Vincenzo Del Pizzo, and delicate gold necklaces and other jewellery crafted by Giulia Barela. It also sells artisan bags, shoes, candles, homewares and other lovely handmade objects.

⭐**Gente**　　　　　FASHION & ACCESSORIES
(Map p106; ☑06 320 7671; www.genteroma.com; Via del Babuino 77; ⊙10.30am-7.30pm Mon-Thu, to 8pm Fri & Sat, 11.30am-7.30pm Sun; Ⓜ Spagna) This multi-label boutique was the first in Rome to bring all the big-name luxury designers – Italian, French and otherwise – under one roof and its vast emporium-styled space remains an essential stop for every serious fashionista. Labels include Dolce & Gabbana, Prada, Alexander McQueen, Sergio Rossi and Missoni.

Flumen Profumi　　　　　PERFUME
(Map p106; ☑06 6830 7635; www.flumenpro fumi.com; Via della Fontanella di Borghese 41; ⊙11am-2pm & 3.30-8pm Mon-Sat, 11am-2pm & 3-7.30pm Sun; ☒Via del Corso) Unique 'made in Rome' scents is what this artisan perfumery on Tridente's smartest shopping strip is all about. Natural perfumes are oil-based, contain four to eight base notes and evoke la dolce vita in Italy. Incantro fuses pomegranate with white flower, while Ritrovarsi Ancora is a nostalgic fragrance evocative of long, lazy, family meals around a shared countryside table (smell the fig!).

Federico Buccellati　　　　JEWELLERY
(Map p106; ☑06 679 03 29; www.buccellati. com; Via dei Condotti 31; ⊙3-7pm Mon, 10am-1.30pm & 3-7pm Tue-Fri, 10am-1.30pm & 2-7pm Sat; Ⓜ Spagna) Run today by the third generation of one of Italy's most prestigious silver- and goldsmiths, this historical shop opened in 1926. Everything is handcrafted and often delicately engraved with decorative flowers, leaves and nature-inspired motifs. Don't miss the Silver Salon on the 1st floor showcasing some original silverware and jewellery pieces by grandfather Mario.

Anglo American Bookshop　　BOOKS
(Map p106; ☑06 679 52 22; www.aab.it; Via della Vite 102; ⊙3.30-7.30pm Mon, 10.30am-7.30pm Tue-Sat; Ⓜ Spagna) Particularly good for university reference books, the Anglo American Bookshop is well stocked and well known. It has an excellent range of literature, travel

guides, children's books and maps, and if it hasn't got the book you want, staff will order it in.

Fendi FASHION & ACCESSORIES
(Map p106; ☑06 33 45 01; www.fendi.com; Largo Carlo Goldoni 420, Palazzo Fendi; ⊙10am-7.30pm Mon-Sat, 10.30am-7.30pm Sun; Ⓜ Spagna) With travertine walls, stunning contemporary art and sweeping red-marble staircase, the flagship store of Rome's iconic fashion house inside 18th-century Palazzo Fendi is dazzling. Born in Rome in 1925 as a leather and fur workshop on Via del Plebiscit, this luxurious temple to Roman fashion is as much concept store as *maison* selling ready-to-wear clothing for men and women (including its signature leather and fur pieces).

La Bottega del Marmoraro ART
(Map p106; ☑06 320 76 60; Via Margutta 53b, ⊙8am-7.30pm Mon-Sat; Ⓜ Flaminio) Watch *marmoraro* (marble artist) Sandro Fiorentini chip away in this enchanting Aladdin's cave filled, floor to ceiling, with his decorative marble plaques engraved with various inscriptions: la dolce vita, *la vita é bella* (life is beautiful) etc. Plaques start at €10 and Sandro will engrave any inscription you like (from €15). On winter days, warm your hands with Sandro in front of the open log fire.

Fausto Santini SHOES
(Map p106; ☑06 678 41 14; www.faustosantini.com, Via Frattina 120; ⊙11am-7.30pm Mon-Sat, to 7pm Sun; Ⓜ Spagna) Rome's best-known shoe designer, Fausto Santini is famous for his beguilingly simple, architectural shoe designs, with beautiful boots and shoes made from butter-soft leather. Colours are beautiful, and the quality impeccable. Seek out the end-of-line discount shop (Map p90; ☑06 488 09 34; Via Cavour 106; ⊙10am-1pm & 3.30-7.30pm Tue-Fri, 10am-1pm & 3-7.30pm Sat; Ⓜ Cavour) if the shoes here are out of your price range.

Vatican City, Borgo & Prati

★**Il Sellaio** FASHION & ACCESSORIES
(Map p116; ☑06 321 17 19; www.serafinipelletteria.it; Via Caio Mario 14; ⊙9.30am-7.30pm Mon-Fri, 9.30am-1pm & 3.30-7.30pm Sat; Ⓜ Ottaviano-San Pietro) During the 1960s Ferruccio Serafini was one of Rome's most sought-after artisans, making handmade leather shoes and bags for the likes of John F Kennedy, Liz Taylor and Marlon Brando. Nowadays, his daughter Francesca runs the family shop where you can pick up beautiful hand-stitched bags, belts and accessories. You can also have your own designs made to order.

★**Rechicle** VINTAGE
(Map p116; ☑06 3265 2469; Piazza dell' Unità 21; ⊙10.30am-2pm & 3.30-7.30pm Mon-Sat; ☑Via Cola di Rienzo) Lovers of vintage fashions should make a beeline for this fab boutique. Furnished with antique family furniture and restored cabinets, it's full of wonderful finds such as Roger Vivier comma heels (with their original box), iconic Chanel jackets, Hermès bags, Balenciaga coats and much more besides.

Villa Borghese & Northern Rome

Bialetti HOMEWARES
(Via Salaria 52; ⊙10am-8pm; ☑Via Salaria) In 1933 Alfonso Bialetti revolutionised domestic coffee-making by creating his classic *moka caffettiera*. His design has by now become a household staple, as ubiquitous in Italian kitchens as kettles in British homes. Here at this gleaming shop you'll find a full range as well as all manner of cool kitchenware.

ℹ Information

EMERGENCY

Ambulance	☑118
Fire	☑115
Police	☑112, 113

INTERNET ACCESS

➡ Free wi-fi is widely available in hostels, B&Bs and hotels, though with signals of varying quality. Some also provide laptops/computers.

➡ Many bars and cafes offer wi-fi.

➡ There are many public wi-fi hotspots across town run by **Roma Wireless** (https://captivik.uni.it/romawireless) and **WiFimetropolitano** (www.cittametropolitanaroma.gov.it/wifimetropolitano). To use these you'll need to register online using a credit card or an Italian mobile phone.

MEDIA

Newspapers Key national dailies include centre-left *la Repubblica* (www.repubblica.it) and its right-wing rival *Corriere della Sera* (www.corriere.it). For the Vatican's take on affairs, *L'Osservatore Romano* (www.osservatoreromano.va) is the Holy See's official paper.

Television The main terrestrial channels are RAI 1, 2 and 3 run by Rai (www.rai.it), Italy's state-owned national broadcaster, and Canale 5, Italia 1 and Rete 4 run by Mediaset (www.mediaset.it), the commercial TV company founded and still partly owned by Silvio Berlusconi.

Radio As well as the principal Rai channels (Radiouno, Radiodue, Radiotre), there are hundreds of commercial radio stations operating across the country. Popular Rome-based stations include Radio Capital (www.capital.it) and Radio Città Futura (www.radiocittafutura.it). Vatican Radio (www.radiovaticana.va) broadcasts in Italian, English and other languages.

MEDICAL SERVICES

Italy has a public health system that is legally bound to provide emergency care to everyone. EU nationals are entitled to reduced-cost, sometimes free, medical care with a European Health Insurance Card (EHIC), available from your home health authority; non-EU citizens should take out medical insurance.

For emergency treatment, you can go to the *pronto soccorso* (casualty) section of an *ospedale* (public hospital). For less serious ailments call the **Guardia Medica Turistica** (🖉 06 7730 6650; Via Emilio Morosini 30; ⊘ 8am-8pm Mon-Fri; 🚊 Viale di Trastevere, 🚊 Viale di Trastevere).

To arrange a (paid) home visit by a private doctor call the **International Medical Centre** (🖉 06 488 23 71; www.imc84.com/roma; Via Firenze 47; GP call-out & treatment fee €140, 8pm-9am & weekends €200; ⊘ 24hr; Ⓜ Repubblica).

If you need an ambulance, call 🖉 118.

In the Vatican, **Farmacia Vaticana** (🖉 06 6988 9806; Palazzo Belvedere; ⊘ 8.30am-6pm Mon-Fri Sep-Jun, 8.30am-3pm Mon-Fri Jul & Aug, plus 8.30am-1pm Sat year-round; 🚊 Piazza del Risorgimento, Ⓜ Ottaviano-San Pietro) sells certain drugs that are not available in Italian pharmacies, and will fill foreign prescriptions (something local pharmacies can't do).

There's also a **pharmacy** (🖉 06 474 54 21; Via Marsala 29; ⊘ 7am-10pm; Ⓜ Termini) in Stazione Termini, next to platform 1, open 7.30am to 10pm daily.

MONEY

ATMs are widespread. Major credit cards are widely accepted but some smaller shops, trattorias and hotels might not take them.

POST

Italy's postal system, **Poste Italiane** (🖉 803 160; www.poste.it), is reasonably reliable, though parcels do occasionally go missing.

Stamps (*francobolli*) are available at post offices and authorised tobacconists (look for the official *tabacchi* sign: a big 'T', usually white on black).

Opening hours vary but are typically 8.30am to 6pm Monday to Friday and 8.30am to 1pm on Saturday. All post offices close two hours earlier than normal on the last business day of each month.

Main Post Office (Map p106; 🖉 06 6973 7205; Piazza di San Silvestro 19; ⊘ 8.20am-7pm Mon-Fri, to 12.35pm Sat; 🚊 Via del Tritone)

Vatican Post Office (Map p116; 🖉 06 6989 0400; St Peter's Square; ⊘ 8.30am-6.45pm Mon-Fri, 8am-1.45pm Sat Sep-Jun, 8am-1.45pm Jul & Aug) Letters can be posted in yellow Vatican postboxes only if they carry Vatican stamps.

TOURIST INFORMATION

There are tourist information points at **Fiumicino** (International Arrivals, Terminal 3; ⊘ 8am-8.45pm) and **Ciampino** (Arrivals Hall; ⊘ 8.30am-6pm) airports, and locations across the city:

Piazza delle Cinque Lune (Map p86; ⊘ 9.30am-7pm; 🚊 Corso del Rinascimento) Near Piazza Navona.

Stazione Termini (Map p90; 🖉 06 06 08; www.turismoroma.it; Via Giovanni Giolitti 34; ⊘ 9am-5pm; Ⓜ Termini) In the hall adjacent to platform 24.

Imperial Forums (Map p80; Via dei Fori Imperiali; ⊘ 9.30am-7pm; 🚊 Via dei Fori Imperiali)

Via Marco Minghetti (Map p106; 🖉 06 06 08; www.turismoroma.it; ⊘ 9.30am-7pm; 🚊 Via del Corso) Between Via del Corso and the Trevi Fountain.

Via Nazionale (Map p106; 🖉 06 06 08; www.turismoroma.it; Via Nazionale 184; ⊘ 9.30am-7pm; 🚊 Via Nazionale) In front of the Palazzo delle Esposizioni.

Castel Sant'Angelo (Map p116; Piazza Pia; ⊘ 9.30am-7pm; 🚊 Piazza Pia)

For information about the Vatican, contact the **Ufficio Pellegrini e Turisti** (Map p116; 🖉 06 6988 1662; St Peter's Square; ⊘ 8.30am-6.30pm Mon-Sat; 🚊 Piazza del Risorgimento, Ⓜ Ottaviano-San Pietro).

The **Comune di Roma** (🖉 06 06 08; www.060608.it; ⊘ 9am-9pm) runs a free multi-lingual tourist-information phone line providing info on culture, shows, hotels, transport etc. Its website is also an excellent source of information.

More practical information, for example, the nearest hospital, car park, etc can be answered by phoning the Comune di Roma's **ChiamaRoma** (🖉 06 06 06; ⊘ 24hr) call centre.

USEFUL RESOURCES

060608 (www.060608.it) Great for practical details on sights, transport, upcoming events and more.

Coopculture (www.coopculture.it) Information and ticket booking for Rome's monuments.

Lonely Planet (www.lonelyplanet.com/rome) Destination information, hotel bookings, traveller forum and more.

Tavole Romane (www.tavoleromane.it) An Italian-language site covering the city's food scene.

Turismo Roma (www.turismoroma.it) Rome's official tourist website with inspirational and practical information.

Vatican Museums (www.museivaticani.va) Book tickets and guided tours to the museums and other Vatican sites.

ⓘ Getting There & Away

AIR

Rome's main international airport, **Leonardo da Vinci** (☑ 06 6 59 51; www.adr.it/fiumicino), aka Fiumicino, is 30km west of the city. It's divided into four terminals: Terminals 1, 2 and 3 are for domestic and international flights; Terminal 5 is for American and Israeli airlines flying to the US and Israel.

Ciampino (☑ 06 6 59 51; www.adr.it/ciampino), 15km southeast of the city centre, is used by **Ryanair** (☑ 895 5895509; www.ryanair.com) for European and Italian destinations. It's not a big airport but there's a steady flow of traffic and at peak times it can get extremely busy.

BOAT

The nearest port to Rome is at Civitavecchia, about 80km north of town. Ferries sail here from Barcelona and Tunis, as well as Sicily and Sardinia. Check www.traghettiweb.it for route details, prices, and to book.

Bookings can also be made at the Termini-based **Agenzie 365** (☑ 06 4782 5179; www.agenzie365.it; Stazione Termini, Via Giolitti 34; ☺8am-9pm; Ⓜ Termini), at travel agents or directly at the port.

From Civitavecchia there are half-hourly trains to Stazione Termini (€5 to €16, 45 minutes to 1½ hours). Civitavecchia's station is about 700m from the entrance to the port.

BUS

Long-distance national and international buses use **Autostazione Tiburtina** (Tibus; Largo Guido Mazzoni; Ⓜ Tiburtina). Get tickets at the bus station or at travel agencies.

From the bus station, cross under the overpass for the Tiburtina train station, where you can pick up metro line B and connect with Termini for onward buses, trains and metro line A.

Bus operators include the following:

Interbus (☑ 091 34 25 25; www.interbus.it) To/from Sicily.

Marozzi (☑ 080 579 02 11; www.marozzivt.it) To/from Sorrento, Bari and Puglia.

SENA (☑ 0861 199 19 00; www.sena.it) To/from Siena, Bologna and Milan.

Sulga (☑ 800 099661; www.sulga.it) To/from Perugia, Assisi and Ravenna.

CAR & MOTORCYCLE

Rome is circled by the Grande Raccordo Anulare (GRA) to which all autostradas (motorways) connect. The main autostradas serving Rome are the following:

A1 The principal north–south artery which runs from Milan to Naples, via Bologna, Florence and Rome.

A12 Runs to/from Civitavecchia and connects with the A91 Rome–Fiumicino Airport.

Car & Scooter Hire

To hire a car you'll require a driving licence (plus International Driving Permit if necessary) and credit card. Age restrictions vary but generally you'll need to be 21 or over.

Car hire is available at both Rome's airports and Stazione Termini. Reckon on at least €40 per day for a small car. Note also that most Italian hire cars have manual gear transmission.

Avis (☑ 06 45210 8391; www.avisautonoleggio.it)

Europcar (☑ 199 307030; www.europcar.it)

Hertz (☑ Stazione Termini office 06 488 39 67; www.hertz.it)

Maggiore National (☑ Termini office 06 488 00 49, central reservations 199 151120; www.maggiore.it; Via Giolitti 34, Stazione Termini; Ⓜ Termini)

To hire a scooter, prices range from about €30 to €120 depending on the size of the vehicle. Reliable operators:

Eco Move Rent (☑ 06 4470 4518; www.ecomoverent.com; Via Varese 48-50; bike/scooter/Vespa hire per day from €8/40/110; ☺8.30am-7.30pm; Ⓜ Termini)

On Road (☑ 06 481 56 69; www.scooterhire.it; Via Cavour 80a; bicycle & scooter rental per day from €12/45; ☺10am-2pm & 2.30-6.30pm; Ⓜ Termini)

Treno e Scooter (☑ 06 4890 5823; www.trenoescooter.com; Piazza dei Cinquecento; per day €28; ☺9am-2pm & 4-7pm)

TRAIN

Rome's main station and principal transport hub is **Stazione Termini** (www.romatermini.com; Piazza dei Cinquecento; Ⓜ Termini). It has regular connections to other European countries, all major Italian cities and many smaller towns.

Train information is available from the Customer Service area on the main concourse to the left of the ticket desks. Alternatively, check www.trenitalia.com or phone ☑89 20 21.

From Termini, you can connect with the metro or take a bus from Piazza dei Cinquecento out front. Taxis are outside the main entrance/exit.

Left Luggage (Stazione Termini; 1st 5hr €6, 6-12hr per hour €0.90, 13hr & over per hour €0.40; ☉6am-11pm; Ⓜ Termini) is available by platform 24 on the Via Giolitti side of the station.

ⓘ Getting Around

TO/FROM THE AIRPORT
Fumicino

The easiest way to get into town is by train, but there are also buses and private shuttle services.

Leonardo Express (one way €14) Runs to/from Stazione Termini. Departures from the airport every 30 minutes between 6.23am and 11.23pm, and from Termini between 5.35am and 10.35pm. Journey time is 30 minutes.

FL1 (one way €8) Connects to Trastevere, Ostiense and Tiburtina stations, but not Termini. Departures from the airport every 15 minutes (half-hourly on Sundays and public holidays) between 5.57am and 10.42pm, from Tiburtina every 15 minutes between 5.01am and 7.31pm, then half-hourly to 10.01pm.

SIT Bus (☑06 591 68 26; www.sitbusshuttle. com; one way/return €6/11) Regular departures to Stazione Termini (Map p90; Via Marsala 5) from 8.30am to 12.30am; from Termini between 5am and 8.30pm. All buses stop near the Vatican (Via Crescenzio 2) en route. Tickets are available on the bus. Journey time is approximately one hour.

Taxi The set fare to or from the city centre is €48, which is valid for up to four passengers including luggage. Note that taxis registered in Fiumicino charge more, so make sure you catch a Comune di Roma taxi – these are white with a taxi sign on the roof and Roma Capitale written on the door along with the taxi's licence number. Journey time is approximately 45 to 60 minutes depending on traffic.

Campino

Schiaffini Rome Airport Bus (☑06 713 05 31; www.romeairportbus.com; Via Giolitti; one way/return €4.90/7.90) Regular departures to/from Via Giolitti outside Stazione Termini. From the airport, services are between 4am and 10.50pm; from Via Giolitti, buses run from 4.50am to midnight. Buy tickets on board, online, at the airport, or at the bus stop. Journey time is approximately 40 minutes.

SIT Bus (☑06 591 68 26; www.sitbusshuttle. com; to/from airport €6/5, return €9) Regular departures from the airport to Via Marsala outside Stazione Termini between 7.45am and 11.15pm, and from Termini between 4.30am and 9.30pm. Get tickets on the bus. Journey time is 45 minutes.

Atral (www.atral-lazio.com) Runs buses between Ciampino Airport and Anagnina metro station (€1.20) and Ciampino train station (€1.20), where you can get a train to Termini (€1.50).

Taxi The set rate to/from the airport is €30. Journey time is approximately 30 minutes depending on traffic.

CAR & MOTORCYCLE
Access

➨ Driving around Rome is not recommended. Riding a scooter or motorbike is faster and makes parking easier, but Rome is no place for learners, so if you're not an experienced rider, give it a miss. Hiring a car for a day trip out of town is worth considering.

➨ Most of Rome's historic centre is closed to unauthorised traffic from 6.30am to 6pm Monday to Friday, from 2pm to 6pm (10am to 7pm in some places) Saturday, and from 11pm to 3am Friday and Saturday. Evening restrictions also apply in Trastevere, San Lorenzo, Monti and Testaccio, typically from 9.30pm or 11pm to 3am on Fridays and Saturdays (also Wednesdays and Thursdays in summer).

➨ All streets accessing the Limited Traffic Zone (ZTL) are monitored by electronic-access detection devices. If you're staying in this zone, contact your hotel. For further information, check www.agenziamobilita.roma.it.

Parking

➨ Blue lines denote pay-and-display parking – get tickets from meters (coins only) and *tabacchi* (tobacconist's shops).

➨ Expect to pay up to €1.20 per hour between 8am and 8pm (11pm in some places). After 8pm (or 11pm) parking is free until 8am the next morning.

➨ Traffic wardens are vigilant and fines are not uncommon. If your car gets towed away, call the **traffic police** (☑06 67691).

➨ There's a comprehensive list of car parks on www.060608.it – click on the transport tab then car parks.

Useful car parks are located at:

Piazzale dei Partigiani (per hr €0.77; ☉6am-11pm; Ⓜ Piramide)

Stazione Termini (Map p90; Piazza dei Cinquecento; per hr/day €2.20/18; ☉6am-1am; 🚇 Piazza dei Cinquecento)

Villa Borghese (Map p106; ☑06 322 59 34; www.sabait.it; Viale del Galoppatoio 33; per hr/day €2.20/18; ☉24hr; 🚇 Via Pinciana)

ℹ TICKETS & PASSES

Public-transport tickets are valid on all of Rome's bus, tram and metro lines, except for routes to Fiumicino airport. They come in various forms:

BIT (*biglietto integrato a tempo*, a single ticket valid for 100 minutes; in that time it can be used on all forms of transport but only once on the metro) €1.50

Roma 24h (valid for 24 hours) €7

Roma 48h (valid for 48 hours) €12.50

Roma 72h (valid for 72 hours) €18

CIS (*carta integrata settimanale*, a weekly ticket) €24

Abbonamento mensile (a monthly pass) a pass restricted to a single user €35; a pass that can be used by anyone €53

➡ Children under 10 travel free.

➡ Buy tickets at *tabacchi* (tobacconist's shops), newsstands and from vending machines at main bus stops and metro stations. They must be purchased before you start your journey and validated in the machines on buses, at the entrance gates to the metro, or at train stations. Ticketless riders risk a fine of at least €50.

➡ The Roma Pass (two/three days €28/38.50) comes with a two/three-day travel pass valid within the city boundaries.

PUBLIC TRANSPORT
Metro

➡ Rome has two main metro lines, A (orange) and B (blue), which cross at Termini. A branch line, 'B1', serves the northern suburbs, and line C runs through the southeastern outskirts, but you're unlikely to need those.

➡ Trains run between 5.30am and 11.30pm (to 1.30am on Fridays and Saturdays).

➡ All stations on line B have wheelchair access and lifts except Circo Massimo, Colosseo and Cavour. On line A, Cipro and Termini are equipped with lifts.

➡ Take line A for the Trevi Fountain (Barberini), Spanish Steps (Spagna) and St Peter's (Ottaviano–San Pietro).

➡ Take line B for the Colosseum (Colosseo).

Bus

➡ Rome's bus service is run by **ATAC** (📞 06 5 70 03; www.atac.roma.it).

➡ The **main bus station** (Map p90; Piazza dei Cinquecento) is in front of Stazione Termini on Piazza dei Cinquecento, where there's an **information booth** (Map p90; Piazza dei Cinquecento; ⊙ 8am-8pm; Ⓜ Termini).

➡ Other important hubs are at Largo di Torre Argentina and Piazza Venezia.

➡ Buses generally run from about 5.30am to midnight, with limited services through the night.

➡ Rome's night bus service comprises more than 25 lines, many of which pass Termini and/ or Piazza Venezia. Buses are marked with an 'n' before the number and bus stops have a blue owl symbol. Departures are usually every 15 to 30 minutes, but can be much slower.

The most useful routes:

n1 Follows the route of metro line A

n2 Follows the route of metro line B.

n7 Piazzale Clodio, Piazza Cavour, Via Zanardelli, Corso del Rinascimento, Corso Vittorio Emanuele II, Largo di Torre Argentina, Piazza Venezia, Via Nazionale and Stazione Termini.

Tram

Rome has a limited tram network. For route maps see www.atac.roma.it.

TAXI

➡ Official licensed taxis are white with an ID number and Roma Capitale on the sides.

➡ Always go with the metered fare, never an arranged price (the set fares to and from the airports are exceptions).

➡ In town (within the ring road) flag fall is €3 between 6am and 10pm on weekdays, €4.50 on Sundays and holidays, and €6.50 between 10pm and 6am. Then it's €1.10 per km. Official rates are posted in taxis and at https://roma mobilita.it/it/servizi/taxi/tariffe.

➡ You can hail a taxi, but it's often easier to wait at a rank or phone for one. There are taxi ranks at the airports, Stazione Termini, Piazza della Repubblica, Piazza Barberini, Piazza di Spagna, Piazza Venezia, the Pantheon, the Colosseum, Largo di Torre Argentina, Piazza Belli, Piazza Pio XII and Piazza del Risorgimento.

➡ To book, call the automated **taxi line** (📞 in Italian 06 06 09), which sends the nearest car

WORTH A TRIP

MONTECASSINO'S MOUNTAINTOP MONASTERY

Dramatically perched on a mountaintop near the regional border with Campania, the **Abbazia di Montecassino** (☎0776 31 15 29; www.abbaziamontecassino.org; abbey free, museum adult/reduced €5/3; ⊙8.45am-7pm daily summer, 9am-4.45pm Mon-Sat & 8.45am-5.15pm Sun winter) was one of the most important Christian centres in the medieval world. St Benedict founded it in 529 AD, supposedly after three ravens led him to the spot, and lived there until his death in 547.

Its history, which is illustrated in the abbey's small museum, has been turbulent and it has been destroyed and rebuilt several times, most recently after WWII.

During the war, it was at the centre of heavy fighting as the Germans sought to stop the Allied push north. After almost six months of bloody deadlock, the Allies bombed it to rubble in May 1944 in a desperate bid to break through German defences.

To reach the abbey from Rome, take one of the half-hourly trains from Stazione Termini to Cassino (€8.20, 1½ to two hours) and then one of the three daily buses that run up from the station.

available; a taxi company direct; or use the Chiama Taxi app.

➡ The website www.060608.it has a list of taxi companies – click on the transport tab, then 'getting around' and 'by taxi'.

➡ Note that when you call for a cab, the meter is switched on straight away and you pay for the cost of the journey from wherever the driver receives the call.

Pronto Taxi (☎06 66 45; www.6645.it)
Radiotaxi 3570 (☎06 35 70; www.3570.it)
Samarcanda (☎06 55 51; www.samarcanda.it)
Taxi Tevere (☎06 41 57; www.taxitevere.it)

LAZIO

Ostia Antica

An easy train ride from Rome, Ostia Antica is one of Italy's finest and most under-appreciated archaeological sites.

Founded in the 4th century BC, the city started life as a fortified military camp guarding the mouth of the Tiber – hence the name: Ostia is a derivation of the Latin word *ostium* (mouth). It quickly grew, and by the 2nd century AD was a thriving port with a population of around 50,000.

Decline set in after the fall of the Roman Empire, and by the 9th century the city had largely been abandoned, its citizens driven off by barbarian raids and outbreaks of malaria. Over subsequent centuries, it was plundered of marble and building materials and its ruins were gradually buried in river silt, hence their survival.

◉ Sights

★ Scavi Archeologici di Ostia Antica
ARCHAEOLOGICAL SITE

(☎06 5635 0215; www.ostiaantica.beniculturali.it; Viale dei Romagnoli 717; adult/reduced €8/4, free 1st Sun of month, exhibitions €3; ⊙8.30am-6.15pm Tue-Sun summer, shorter hours winter) One of Lazio's prize sights, the ruins of ancient Rome's seaport are wonderfully complete, like a smaller version of Pompeii. Highlights include the Terme di Nettuno (Baths of Neptune), a steeply stacked amphitheatre, and an ancient cafe, complete with a bar and traces of the original menu frescoed on the wall.

Note that the site is pretty large and you'll need a few hours to do it justice. Also, it gets busy at weekends, but is much quieter on weekdays.

Near the entrance, **Porta Romana** gives onto the **Decumanus Maximus**, the site's central strip, which runs over 1km to **Porta Marina**, the city's original sea-facing gate.

On the Decumanus, the **Terme di Nettuno** is a must-see. This baths complex, one of 20 that originally stood in town, dates to the 2nd century and boasts some superb mosaics, including one of Neptune driving his sea-horse chariot. In the centre of the complex are the remains of an arcaded **Palestra** (gym).

Next to the *terme* is the **Teatro**, an amphitheatre originally built at the end of the 1st century BC by Agrippa and later enlarged to hold 4000 people.

The grassy area behind the amphitheatre is the **Piazzale delle Corporazioni** (Forum of the Corporations), home to the offices of

Ostia's merchant guilds. The mosaics that line the perimeter – ships, dolphins, a lighthouse, an elephant – are thought to represent the businesses housed on the square: ships and dolphins indicated shipping agencies, while the elephant probably referred to a business involved in the ivory trade.

The **Forum**, Ostia's main square, is overlooked by what remains of the **Capitolium**, a temple built by Hadrian and dedicated to Jupiter, Juno and Minerva.

Nearby is another highlight: the **Thermopolium**, an ancient cafe, complete with a bar, frescoed menu, kitchen and small courtyard where customers would have relaxed by a fountain. Just to the north of the Thermopolium are two of the site's so-called case decorate. These **frescoed houses** are off-limits to unaccompanied visitors but can be visited on a guided tour at 10.30am each Sunday – book a place via email (ss-col.do musostia@beniculturali.it).

Over on the other side of the Decumanus are the remains of the 2nd-century **Terme del Foro**, originally the city's largest baths complex. Here, in the *forica* (public toilet), you can see 20 well-preserved latrines set sociably in a long stone bench.

For more modern facilities, there's a cafeteria-bar complex with toilets and a gift shop to the north of the Decumanus (head up Via dei Molini). Also at this complex is a small **museum** displaying statues and sarcophagi excavated at the site.

✕ Eating

Ristorante Monumento   RISTORANTE **€€**
(☑ 06 565 00 21; www.ristorantemonumento.it; Piazza Umberto I 8; meals €30-35; ☺ 12.30-3.30pm & 8-11pm Tue-Sun) In Ostia's small medieval centre, this long-standing restaurant started life in the 19th century, catering to the men working on reclaiming the local marshlands. Nowadays, it does a brisk business serving homemade pastas and seafood dishes to sightseers fresh out of the nearby ruins. Bookings recommended at weekends.

ⓘ Getting There & Away

From Rome, take the Ostia Lido train from Stazione Porta San Paolo (next to Piramide metro station), getting off at Ostia Antica (25 minutes, every 15 minutes). The trip is covered by a standard Rome public transport ticket (€1.50).

By car, take Via del Mare, which runs parallel to Via Ostiense, and follow signs for the *scavi* (ruins).

Tivoli
☑ 0774 / POP 56,500 / ELEVATION 235M

A summer retreat for ancient Romans and the Renaissance rich, the hilltop town of Tivoli is home to two Unesco World Heritage Sites: Villa Adriana, the sprawling estate of Emperor Hadrian, and the 16th-century Villa d'Este, a Renaissance villa famous for its landscaped gardens and lavish fountains.

◉ Sights

★ Villa Adriana   ARCHAEOLOGICAL SITE
(☑ 0774 38 27 33; www.villaadriana.beniculturali.it; Largo Marguerite Yourcenar 1; adult/reduced €8/4; ☺ 9am-1hr before sunset) The ruins of Hadrian's vast country villa, 5km outside of Tivoli proper, are quite magnificent, and easily on a par with anything you'll see in Rome. Built between AD 118 and 138, the villa was one of the largest in the ancient world, encompassing more than 120 hectares – of which about 40 are now open to the public. You'll need up to three hours to explore it fully.

Must-sees include the canopo, a landscaped canal overlooked by a *nymphaeum* (shrine to the water nymph), and the **Teatro Marittimo**, Hadrian's personal refuge.

Hadrian, a great traveller and enthusiastic architect, designed much of the villa himself, basing his ideas on buildings he'd seen around the world. The **pecile**, the large pool area near the walls, is a reproduction of a building in Athens. Similarly, the *canopo* is a copy of a sanctuary in the Egyptian town of Canopus, with a narrow 120m-long pool flanked by sculptural figures. At its head, the **Serapaeum** is a semi-circular *nymphaeum* that was used to host summer banquets. Flanking the water, the **antiquarium** is used

---

ⓘ TIVOLI IN A DAY

Tivoli makes an excellent day trip from Rome but to cover its two main sites you'll have to start early. The best way to see both is to visit Villa d'Este first, then have lunch up in the centre, before heading down to Villa Adriana. To get to Villa Adriana from the centre, take local CAT bus 4 or 4X (€1.30, 10 minutes, half-hourly) from Piazza Garibaldi. After you've visited Villa Adriana, pick up the Cotral bus back to Rome.

Lazio

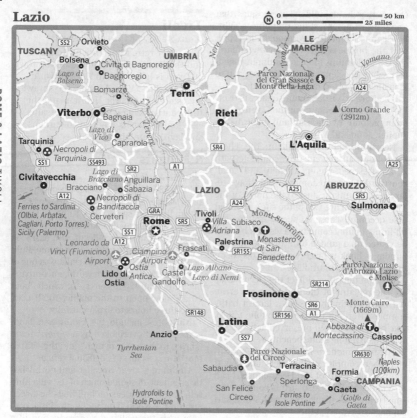

to stage temporary exhibitions (note that when these are on, admission to the villa costs slightly more than usual).

To the northeast of the *pecile*, the Teatro Marittimo is one of the villa's signature buildings, a mini-villa built on an island in an artificial pool. Originally accessible only by swing bridges, it's currently off-limits due to ongoing restoration.

To the east, **Piazza d'Oro** makes for a memorable picture, particularly in spring, when its grassy centre is cloaked in wild yellow flowers.

There are also several bath complexes, temples and barracks.

Parking (€3) is available at the site.

Villa d'Este   HISTORIC BUILDING
(☑ 0774 33 29 20; www.villadestetivoli.info; Piazza Trento; adult/reduced €8/4; ☉ 8.30am-1hr before sunset Tue-Sun) In Tivoli's hilltop centre, the steeply terraced grounds of Villa d'Este are a superlative example of a Renaissance gar-

den, complete with monumental fountains, elegant tree-lined avenues and landscaped grottoes. The villa, originally a Benedictine convent, was converted into a luxury retreat by Lucrezia Borgia's son, Cardinal Ippolito d'Este, in the late 16th century. It later provided inspiration for composer Franz Liszt, who stayed here between 1865 and 1886 and immortalised it in his 1877 piano composition *The Fountains of the Villa d'Este*.

Before heading out to the gardens, take time to admire the villa's rich mannerist frescoes. Outside, the manicured park features water-spouting gargoyles and shady lanes flanked by lofty cypress trees and extravagant fountains, all powered by gravity alone. Look out for the Bernini-designed **Fountain of the Organ**, which uses water pressure to play music through a concealed organ, and the 130m-long **Avenue of the Hundred Fountains**.

🛏 Sleeping

★ Residenze Gregoriane
BOUTIQUE HOTEL €€€

(☑ 347 7136854; www.residenzegregoriane.it; Via Domenico Giuliani 92; ste €230-250; ✷ 🛜 ❄) For a night to remember, the Residenze Gregoriane is steeped in history. Its three spacious suites, all decorated in classic antique style, occupy the fabulous 15th-century Palazzo Mancini-Torlonia. Frescoes adorn the historic building, many by the same artists who worked on Villa d'Este, and there's a magnificent internal courtyard. Room rates also cover use of a small pool in the vaulted cellar.

🍴 Eating

Sibilla
RISTORANTE €€€

(☑ 0774 33 52 81; www.ristorantesibilla.com; Via della Sibilla 50; meals €50; ☺ 12.30-3pm & 7.30-10.30pm Tue-Sun, 6-8pm Mon) With tables set out by two ancient Roman temples and water cascading down the green river gorge below, this historic restaurant sets a romantic stage for seasonally driven food and superlative wine. In summer, look out for its Monday evening music and cocktails event.

ℹ Information

Tourist Information Point (☑ 0774 31 35 36; Piazzale delle Nazioni Unite; ☺ 10am-1pm & 4-6pm Tue-Sun) Information is available from this kiosk, near where the bus arrives.

ℹ Getting There & Away

Tivoli, 30km east of Rome, is accessible by **Cotral** (☑ 800 174471, from a mobile 06 7205 7205; www.cotralspa.it) bus (€1.30, 50 minutes, at least twice hourly) from Ponte Mammolo metro station.

By car you can either take Via Tiburtina or the quicker Rome–L'Aquila autostrada (A24).

Trains run from Rome's Stazione Tiburtina to Tivoli (€2.60, one hour, at least hourly).

Cerveteri

☑ 06 / POP 37,500 / ELEV 81M

A quiet provincial town 35km northwest of Rome, Cerveteri is home to one of Italy's great Etruscan treasures – the Necropoli di Banditaccia. This ancient burial complex, now a Unesco World Heritage Site, is all that remains of the formidable Etruscan city that once stood here.

Founded in the 9th century BC, the city that the Etruscans knew as Kysry, and Latin speakers called Caere, was a powerful member of the Etruscan League, and, for a period between the 7th and 5th centuries, one of the Mediterranean's most important commercial centres. It eventually came into conflict with Rome and, in 358 BC, was annexed into the Roman Republic.

⊙ Sights

★ Necropoli di Banditaccia
ARCHAEOLOGICAL SITE

(☑ 06 994 06 51; www.tarquinia-cerveteri.it; Piazzale Mario Moretti 32; adult/reduced €8/5, incl museum €10/6; ☺ 8.30am-1hr before sunset) This haunting 12-hectare necropolis is a veritable city of the dead, with streets, squares and terraces of *tumuli* (circular tombs cut into the earth and capped by turf). Some tombs, including the 6th-century-BC **Tomba dei Rilievi**, retain traces of painted reliefs, many of which illustrate endearingly domestic household items, as well as figures from the underworld.

Another interesting tomb is the 7th-century BC **Tumulo Mengarelli**, the plain interior of which shows how the tombs were originally structured.

Museo Nazionale Cerite
MUSEUM

(☑ 06 994 13 54; www.tarquinia-cerveteri.it; Piazza Santa Maria 1; adult/reduced €8/5, incl necropolis €10/6; ☺ 8.30am-7.30pm Tue-Sun) Housed in a medieval fortress on what was once ancient Caere's acropolis, this splendid museum charts the history of the Etruscan city, housing archaeological treasures unearthed at the necropolis.

Exhibits, which are displayed chronologically, include the *Euphronios Krater*, a celebrated 1st century-BC vase that was returned to Cerveteri in 2015 after an extended period in New York and Rome.

🍴 Eating

Mille800 Stazione del Gusto
RISTORANTE €€

(☑ 329 4970782, 06 9955 1565; Via Antonio Ricci 9; meals €30-35; ☺ noon-5pm & 6.30pm-12.30am Tue-Sun) Near the tourist information kiosk, this welcoming restaurant is styled as an old train station with brick arches, signs for *binari* (platforms) and leather suitcases as decor. Food-wise it's a cut above your average trattoria, serving a mixed menu of pizzas, fail-safe pastas and creative main courses.

LAZIO'S NORTHERN LAKES

North of Rome, Lazio's verdant landscape is pitted with volcanic lakes. The closest to the capital is **Lago di Bracciano**, a beautiful blue expanse surrounded by picturesque medieval towns. There's a popular lakeside beach at **Anguillara Sabazia** and you can visit a 15th-century castle, **Castello Odescalchi** (☑06 9980 4348; www. odescalchi.it; Via del Lago 1; adult/reduced €8.50/6; ⊙10am-6pm Mon-Fri, to 7pm Sat & Sun), at **Bracciano**.

Both towns are accessible by half-hourly trains from Roma Ostiense (Anguillara €2.60, 55 minutes; Bracciano €3, one hour).

In the north of the region, **Lago di Bolsena** is one of Europe's largest volcanic lakes. Its main town is **Bolsena**, a charming place with a hilltop medieval centre and a famous 13th-century miracle story.

Hourly Cotral buses serve Bolsena from Viterbo (€2.20, 45 minutes).

ℹ Information

Tourist Information Point (☑06 9955 2637; Piazza Aldo Moro; ⊙9.30am-12.30pm & 5.30-7.30pm Mon-Sat & 10am-1pm Sun Apr, May, Jul & Aug, 9.30am-12.30pm Mon-Sat & 10am-1pm Sun Oct-Mar, Jun & Sep) A kiosk by the entrance to the historic centre.

ℹ Getting There & Away

Cerveteri is easily accessible from Rome by Cotral bus (€2.80, one hour, up to twice hourly Monday to Saturday, 10 daily Sunday) from the Cornelia metro station (line A).

To get to the necropolis from the town centre, take bus G from Piazza Aldo Moro (€1.10, five minutes, approximately hourly).

By car, take either Via Aurelia (SS1) or the Civitavecchia autostrada (A12) and exit at Cerveteri–Ladispoli.

Tarquinia

☑0766 / POP 16,500 / ELEV 133M

Some 90km northwest of Rome, Tarquinia is the pick of Lazio's Etruscan towns. The highlight is the magnificent Unesco-listed necropolis and its extraordinary frescoed tombs, but there's also a fantastic Etruscan museum (the best outside of Rome) and an atmospheric medieval centre.

Legend holds that Tarquinia was founded towards the end of the Bronze Age in the 12th century BC. It was later home to the Tarquin kings of Rome, reaching its peak in the 4th century BC, before a century of struggle ended with surrender to Rome in 204 BC.

◉ Sights

★ **Necropoli di Tarquinia** ARCHAEOLOGICAL SITE
(Necropoli dei Monterozzi; ☑0766 84 00 00; www. tarquinia-cerveteri.it; Via Ripagretta; adult/reduced €6/3, incl Museo €8/4; ⊙8.30am-7.30pm Tue-Sun summer, to 1hr before sunset winter) This remarkable 7th-century-BC necropolis is one of Italy's most important Etruscan sites. At first sight, it doesn't look like much – a green field littered with corrugated huts – but once you start ducking into the tombs and seeing the vivid frescoes, you'll realise what all the fuss is about.

Some 6000 tombs have been excavated in this area since digs began in 1489, of which 140 are painted and 20 are currently open to the public.

For the best frescoes search out the **Tomba della Leonessa**; the **Tomba della Caccia e della Pesca**, which boasts some wonderful hunting and fishing scenes; the **Tomba dei Leopardi**; and the **Tomba della Fustigazione**, which is named after a scratchy scene of an S&M threesome.

To get to the necropolis, which is about 1.5km from the centre, take the free shuttle bus B from near the tourist office. Alternatively, it's about 20 minutes on foot – head up Corso Vittorio Emanuele, turn right into Via Porta Tarquinia and continue along Via Ripagretta.

Museo Archeologico Nazionale Tarquiniense MUSEUM
(☑0766 85 00 80; www.tarquinia-cerveteri.it; Via Cavour 1; adult/reduced €6/3, incl necropoli €8/4; ⊙8.30am-7.30pm Tue-Sun) This charming museum, beautifully housed in the 15th-century Palazzo Vitelleschi, is a treasure trove of locally found Etruscan artefacts. Highlights include the *Cavalli Alati*, a magnificent frieze of two winged horses, and, in the next room, the *Mitra Tauroctono*, a striking sculpture of the headless, handless god Mithras killing a bull.

🛏 Sleeping

Camere Del Re   HOTEL €
(☑ 327 7639742, 0766 85 58 31; www.cameredelre.
com; Via San Pancrazio 41; s €53-70, d €54-99, q
€99-129; ❄ 🛜) Just off the historic centre's
main strip, this quiet hotel has spacious
rooms decorated in simple, monastic style
with tiled floors and wrought-iron bedsteads. The best also sport original vaulted
ceilings and the occasional fresco.

🍴 Eating

Il Cavatappi   LAZIO €€
(☑ 0766 84 23 03; www.cavatappirestaurant.it;
Via dei Granari 2; meals €25-30; ⊙ 12.30-2pm Fri-
Sun & 7-10pm Wed-Mon) Tarquinia has several
decent eateries, including this family-run
restaurant in the *centro storico*. Bag a table
in the tastefully cluttered interior, or on the
summer terrace, and get into satisfying helpings of earthy regional food – bruschette and
pâté starters, flavoursome grilled steaks and
unctuous, creamy desserts.

ℹ Information

Tourist Office (☑ 0766 84 92 82; www.tar
quiniaturismo.it; Barriera San Giusto; ⊙ 9am-
1pm & 4-7pm summer, 9.30am-12.30pm &
3-6pm winter) In the town's medieval gate
(Barriera San Giusto).

ℹ Getting There & Away

The best way to reach Tarquinia from Rome is
by train from Termini (€6.90, 1½ hours, hourly).
From Tarquinia station, catch the hourly BC bus
to the hilltop historic centre.

By car, take the autostrada for Civitavecchia
and then Via Aurelia (SS1).

Viterbo

☑ 0761 / POP 67,200 / ELEV 326M
The largest town in northern Lazio, Viterbo
is a much overlooked gem with a handsome
medieval centre and a relaxed, provincial
atmosphere.

Founded by the Etruscans and later tak-
en over by the Romans, it developed into
an important medieval centre, and in the
13th century became the seat of the popes. It
was bombed heavily in WWII, but much of
its historic core survived and is today in remarkably good nick. This, together with its
good bus connections, makes it a pleasant
base for exploring Lazio's rugged north.

◎ Sights

★ Palazzo dei Papi   HISTORIC BUILDING
(☑ 320 7911328; www.archeoares.it; Piazza San
Lorenzo; incl Cattedrale & Museo Colle del Duomo
€9; ⊙ guided tours only) This handsome Gothic
palazzo was built for the popes who lived in
Viterbo from 1257 to 1281. To go inside you'll
have to sign up for a tour at the Museo Colle del Duomo, but you can pop up the stairs
to the **loggia** (colonnade) and peer into the
Sala del Conclave, scene of the first and
longest ever papal conclave.

Cattedrale
di San Lorenzo   CATHEDRAL
(www.archeoares.it; Piazza San Lorenzo; ⊙ 10am-1pm
& 3-7pm Tue-Sun, to 6pm winter) With its black-
and-white bell tower, Viterbo's 12th-century
duomo looms over Piazza San Lorenzo, the
religious nerve centre of the medieval city.
Originally built to a simple Romanesque design, it owes its current Gothic look to a 14th-
century makeover and a partial post-WWII
reconstruction. Inside, look out for *Redentore
e Santi* by the 15th-century artist Gerolamo
da Cremona and the tomb of Pope Giovanni XXI. A second pope, Alessandro IV, is also
buried in the cathedral but the location of
his body remains a mystery. Next door, the
Museo Colle de Duomo (☑ 320 7911328; www.
museocolledelduomo.com, €3, incl Cattedrale & Palazzo dei Papi €9) displays a small collection of
archaeological artefacts and religious art.

Museo
Nazionale Etrusco   MUSEUM
(☑ 0761 32 59 29; Piazza della Rocca; adult/re-
duced €6/3; ⊙ 8.30am-7.30pm Tue-Sun) Housed
in the Albornaz fortress, this modest museum is the place for a shot of ancient culture.
Reconstructions and locally found artefacts
illustrate the Etruscan lifestyle, while a series of life-sized statues hark back to the
city's Roman past.

Palazzo dei Priori   HISTORIC BUILDING
(Piazza del Plebiscito, Via Ascenzi 1; ⊙ 9am-1pm &
3-6.30pm Mon-Fri, 9am-noon & 4-7pm Sat, 9am-
noon Sun) **FREE** Viterbo's 15th-century city
hall overlooks Piazza del Plebiscito, the
elegant Renaissance square that has long
been the city's political and social hub. It's
not all open to the public but you can visit a
series of impressively decorated halls whose
16th-century frescoes colourfully depict Viterbo's ancient origins. During the week, the
entrance is at Via Ascenzi 1; at weekends it's
on Piazza del Plebiscito.

Viterbo

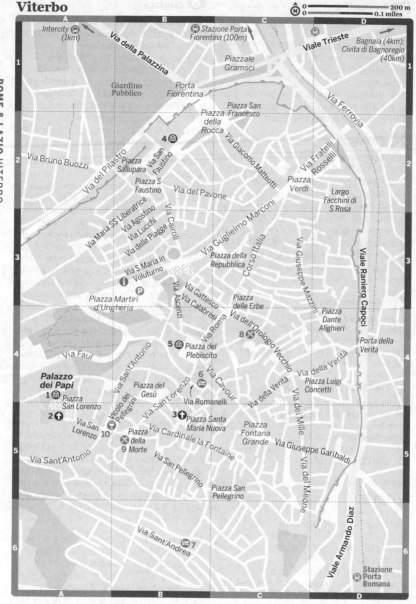

0
200 m
0
0.1 miles

Intercity (1km)

Via della Palazzina

Stazione Porta Fiorentina (100m)

Viale Trieste

Bagnaia (4km); Civita di Bagnoregio (40km)

Piazzale Gramsci

Giardino Pubblico

Porta Fiorentina

Piazza della Rocca

Piazza San Francesco

Via Ferrovia

Via Bruno Buozzi

Via del Pilastro

4

Piazza Sallupara

Via San Faustino

Via Giacomo Matteotti

Via Fratelli Rosselli

Piazza Verdi

Largo Facchini di S.Rosa

Piazza S Faustino

Via del Pavone

Via Maria SS Liberatrice

Via Agostino

Via Lucchi

Via delle Piagge

Via Cairoli

Via Guglielmo Marconi

Corso Italia

Piazza della Repubblica

Via Giuseppe Mazzini

Via S Maria in Voluturno

Via Ascenzi

Piazza Martiri d'Ungheria

Via Gattesco

Via Calabresi

Via Roma

Piazza delle Erbe

Via dell'Orologio Vecchio

8

Piazza Dante Alighieri

Porta della Verità

Viale Raniero Capoci

Via Faul

Via Sant'Antonio

5

Piazza del Plebiscito

Via Cavour

Via della Verità

Piazza Luigi Concetti

Via della Verità

Via dei Mille

Palazzo dei Papi

1

Piazza San Lorenzo

2

Vicolo dei Pellegrini

Piazza del Gesù

Via San Lorenzo

6

Via Romanelli

3

Piazza Santa Maria Nuova

Piazza Fontana Grande

Via San Lorenzo

10

Piazza della Morte

Via Cardinale la Fontaine

Via Giuseppe Garibaldi

Via del Meone

Via Sant'Antonio

9

Via San Pellegrino

Piazza San Pellegrino

Via Sant'Andrea

7

Viale Armando Diaz

Stazione Porta Romana

Chiesa di Santa Maria Nuova CHURCH
(Piazza Santa Maria Nuova; ⊙church 7am-7pm, cloisters 10am-noon & 4-7pm) This 11th-century Romanesque church, the oldest in Viterbo, was restored to its original form after sustaining bomb damage in WWII. A series of freshly restored 13th- to 16th-century frescoes line the solemn, grey interior, while outside you can see a stone pulpit where St Thomas Aquinas preached in 1266. Also of note is the church's cloister, the so-called **Chiostro Longobardo**.

Viterbo

◎ **Top Sights**
1 Palazzo dei Papi A4

◎ **Sights**
2 Cattedrale di San Lorenzo A5
3 Chiesa di Santa Maria Nuova B5
4 Museo Nazionale Etrusco B2
5 Palazzo dei Priori B4

◎ **Sleeping**
6 B&B Centro Storico B4
7 Medieval House B6

◎ **Eating**
8 Al Vecchio Orologio C4
9 Il Gargolo Ristorantino B5

◎ **Drinking & Nightlife**
10 Magnamagna A5

🛏 Sleeping

**B&B Centro
Storico** B&B €
(☑389 2386283; www.bebcentrostoricoviterbo.
com; Via Romanelli 24; d €69-85, q €85-120; ❋ ☎) A great little bolthole in the heart of the historic centre. Its cool, tastefully attired rooms, including a mini-apartment for four, are up a steep set of stairs on the 1st floor of a 14th-century *palazzo*, about 200m from Piazza del Plebiscito. The only disappointing note is the breakfast, which is just a selection of packaged snacks.

Medieval House B&B €
(☑393 4501586; www.bbmedievalhouse.com; Via Sant'Andrea 78; s/d €50/65; ❋ ☎) Run by the gregarious Matteo, this welcoming B&B near the medieval walls makes for a wonderful base – it's within easy walking distance of all the main sights but is far enough out to offer a quiet night's sleep. The look is exposed brick, timbered ceilings and homey furniture, while breakfast is a feast of *cornetti* (croissants) and cured meats.

🍴 Eating

★ **Il Gargolo
Ristorantino** LAZIO €€
(☑0761 32 45 99; www.ilgargolo.com; Piazza della Morte 14; meals €25-30; ⊙noon-3pm & 7.30-11pm, closed Tue winter) Young, friendly people, excellent food and a prime setting on an atmospheric *centro storico* piazza, Il Gargolo scores across the board. Its al fresco tables, shaded by leafy trees, are a wonderful place to tuck into scrumptious pastas – try the *tonnarelli* (thick square spaghetti) with pecorino, *guanciale* (cured pig's cheek) and black truffle – and rich cheesecake desserts.

**Al Vecchio
Orologio** RISTORANTE, PIZZA €€
(☑335 337754; www.alvecchioorologio.it; Via dell'Orologio Vecchio 25; pizzas €8-10, meals €30; ⊙12.30-2.30pm Wed-Sun & 7.30-10.30pm Mon & Wed-Sun) This much-lauded eatery hits the bullseye with its charming setting – in a vaulted *centro storico palazzo* – and creative local cuisine. There's a full range of pizzas but to get the best out of the kitchen, opt for the main menu and dishes like saffron-flavoured pasta with zucchini and perch from Lake Bolsena or lamb ribs with ginger and pink pepper.

🍷 Drinking & Nightlife

Magnamagna BAR
(☑329 8054913; Vicolo dei Pellegrini 2; ⊙11am-1am Tue-Fri, 8am-1am Sat & Sun) Join the buzzing crowds for a glass of wine in the atmospheric setting of Piazza della Morte. The bar, which also serves craft beers and local foodie specialities, is standing room only, but there's seating outside in the piazza and in a vaulted hall known as the Winter Garden, where you can kick back to the occasional gig or DJ set.

ℹ Information

Tourist Office (☑0761 22 64 27; www.visit.
viterbo.it; Piazza Martiri d'Ungheria; ⊙10am-1pm & 3-7.30pm Tue-Sun) By the Piazza Martiri d'Ungheria car park.

ℹ Getting There & Away

From Rome, **Cotral** (☑800 174471, from a mobile 06 7205 7205; www.cotralspa.it) buses serve Viterbo from Saxa Rubra station (€4.50, 1½ hours, every 20 minutes) – get to Saxa Rubra by Ferrovia Roma-Nord train from Piazzale Flaminio.

In Viterbo, make sure to get off at Porta Romana, not the intercity bus station at Piazza Giordano Bruno, which is a kilometre or so northwest of Porta Fiorentina.

By car, Viterbo is about a 1½-hour drive up Via Cassia (SR2). Once in town, the best bet for parking is Piazza Martiri d'Ungheria.

Trains from Rome's Ostiense station to Viterbo Porta Romana (€5, 1¾ hours) depart hourly from Monday to Saturday and every two hours on Sundays.

OFF THE BEATEN TRACK

AROUND VITERBO

Largely overlooked by travellers, the lush, emerald-green countryside around Viterbo hides some wonderful treasures. Chief among them is **Palazzo Farnese** (☑ 0761 64 60 52; Piazza Farnese 1, Caprarola; adult/reduced €5/2.50; ☉ 8.30am-7.30pm Tue-Sun, garden entry 10am, 11am, noon, 3pm & 4pm Tue-Fri winter, plus 5pm summer), 20km southeast of Viterbo in Caprarola. A 16th-century Renaissance *palazzo*, it features a distinct pentagonal design and, inside, an internal circular courtyard and extraordinary columned staircase. Visits take in the richly frescoed rooms and, on weekdays, the beautiful hillside gardens.

For more horticultural splendours, head to Bagnaia and **Villa Lante** (☑ 0761 28 80 08; Via Jacopo Barozzi 71, Bagnaia; adult/reduced €5/2.50; ☉ 8.30am-1hr before sunset Tue-Sun), whose 16th-century mannerist gardens feature monumental fountains and an ingenious water cascade.

Some 30km north of Viterbo, Bagnoregio is home to one of Lazio's most dramatic apparitions, the **Civita di Bagnoregio** (€1.50; ☉ ticket office 8am-8pm), aka *il paese che muore* (the dying town). This medieval village, accessible by footbridge only, sits atop a huge stack of slowly crumbling rock in a dramatic deep-cut valley.

The best way to get around the area is by car, although you can also get to all the places listed here by **Cotral** (www.cotralspa.it) bus from Viterbo.

Castelli Romani

A pretty pocket of verdant hills and volcanic lakes 20km southeast of Rome, the Colli Albani (Alban Hills) and their 13 towns are collectively known as the Castelli Romani. Since ancient times they've provided a green refuge from the city and still today Romans flock to the area on hot summer weekends. Highlights include the famous wine town of Frascati, hilltop Castel Gandolfo, and the scenic Lago Albano.

❶ Getting There & Away

Regular trains run from Rome's Stazione Termini to Frascati (€2.10, 30 minutes) and Castel Gandolfo (€2.10, 40 minutes) – for Castel Gandolfo, take the Albano Laziale train.

If travelling by car, exit Rome on Via Tuscolana (SS215) for Frascati or Via Appia (SS7) for Castel Gandolfo and Lago Albano.

Frascati

☑ 06 / POP 22,100

An easy train ride from Rome, the elegant and well-to-do wine town of Frascati makes for a refreshing day trip with its compact historic centre and delicious food and drink.

The town is also famous for its aristocratic villas, built as summer retreats by rich Roman families in the late Renaissance and early baroque period.

◉ Sights

Villa Aldobrandini
Gardens
GARDENS

(☑ 06 942 25 60; Via Cardinal Massai 18; ☉ 8.30am-5.30pm Mon-Fri) **FREE** Looming over Frascati's main square, Villa Aldobrandini is a haughty 16th-century villa designed by Giacomo della Porta and built by Carlo Maderno. It's closed to the public, but you can visit its impressive baroque gardens during the week.

Scuderie Aldobrandini
MUSEUM

(☑ 06 941 71 95; Piazza Marconi 6; adult/reduced €3/1.50, plus exhibition €5.50/3; ☉ 10am-6pm Tue-Fri, to 7pm Sat & Sun) The former stables of Villa Aldobrandini, restored by architect Massimiliano Fuksas, house Frascati's single museum of note, the **Museo Tuscolano**. Dedicated to local history, its collection includes ancient Roman artefacts and several interesting models of local villas.

✖ Eating

Cantina Simonetti
OSTERIA €

(Piazza San Rocco 4; meals €25; ☉ 1-4pm Sat & Sun, 7.45pm-midnight Wed-Sun, longer hours summer) For an authentic *vino e cucina* (wine and food) experience, search out this traditional *cantina* and sit down to a meal of *porchetta*, cold cuts and cheese, accompanied by jugs of local white wine. In keeping with the traditional food, the decor is rough-and-ready rustic with plain wooden tables and simple white tablecloths. No credit cards.

Cacciani

RISTORANTE €€€

(☑06 942 03 78; www.cacciani.it; Via Armando Diaz 13; fixed-price lunch menu €25, meals €50; ⊙1-2.30pm Tue-Sun & 8-10.30pm Tue-Sat) One of Frascati's most renowned restaurants, Cacciani offers fine food and twinkling terrace views of Rome. The menu lists various creative dishes, but it's the classics like *tonnarello a cacio e pepe* (egg spaghetti with pecorino cheese and black pepper) that really stand out. There's also a weighty wine list and a fixed-price lunch menu, available Tuesday through to Friday.

ⓘ Information

Frascati Point Tourist Office (☑06 9418 4406; Piazza Marconi 5; ⊙9am-7pm Mon-Fri, 10am-7pm Sat & Sun) As well as town information, can provide details about tours of local vineyards.

Castel Gandolfo

☑06 / POP 9000

One of the Castelli's prettiest towns, Castel Gandolfo is a refined hilltop *borgo* (medieval town). Its best-known sight is the Palazzo Apostolico, a 17th-century palace that was for centuries the pope's summer residence. Formerly off limits to the public, it now houses a small museum.

Once you've visited the *palazzo* and explored the papal gardens, you can hang out on Piazza della Libertà and enjoy gorgeous views over Lago Albano.

◎ Sights

Giardini di Villa Barberini

GARDENS

(Villa Barberini Gardens; www.museivaticani.va; Via Carlo Rosselli; adult/reduced €20/15, incl guided tour €26/15; ⊙8.30am-3pm Mon-Sat) Since 2014, the papal gardens in Castel Gandolfo have been open to guided visits. The regular one-hour tours involve a mini-train ride through the extensive gardens, taking in Roman ruins, artful flower displays, woods, fruit and veg patches, and the papal helipad. Guided tours on foot are also available but need to be booked in advance.

✕ Eating

Antico Ristorante Pagnanelli

RISTORANTE €€€

(☑06 936 00 04; www.pagnanelli.it; Via Antonio Gramsci 4; meals €60; ⊙noon-3.30pm & 6.30-11.45pm) Housed in a colourful wisteria-clad villa, this celebrated restaurant is a great place for a romantic meal. It's no casual trattoria, erring on the formal side, but the seasonally driven food is excellent. There's a colossal wine list (and an amazing cellar carved into tufa rock) and the terrace views over Lago Albano are unforgettable.

Palestrina

☑06 / POP 21,700

Archaeology buffs should make a beeline for Palestrina. In ancient times the town, then known as Praeneste, was home to a spectacular terraced temple, the Santuario della Fortuna Primigenia, which covered much of what is now the *centro storico*. The sanctuary has long since been built over but you can see a model in the Museo Archeologico Nazionale di Palestrina, the town's excellent hilltop museum.

Palestrina stands on the slopes of Monte Ginestro about 40km east of Rome.

◎ Sights

★**Museo Archeologico Nazionale di Palestrina**

MUSEUM

(☑06 953 81 00; Piazza della Cortina; admission incl sanctuary €5; ⊙9am-8pm, sanctuary 9am-1hr before sunset) This delightful museum occupies Palazzo Colonna Barberini, a Renaissance palace built atop the 2nd-century-BC Santuario della Fortuna Primigenia. Its airy halls display an interesting collection of ancient sculpture and funerary artefacts, as well as some huge Roman mosaics. But the crowning glory is the breathtaking *Mosaico Nilotico*, a detailed 2nd-century-BC mosaic depicting the flooding of the Nile and everyday life in ancient Egypt.

ⓘ Getting There & Away

Cotral (☑800 174471, from a mobile 06 7205 7205; www.cotralspa.it) buses run to Palestrina from Rome's Ponte Mammolo metro station (€2.80, 55 minutes, hourly).

By car, follow Via Prenestina (SR155) for approximately 40km.

South Coast

Lazio's southern coast boasts its best beaches and tracts of beautiful, unspoilt countryside, particularly around Monte Circeo, a rocky promontory that rises to 541m as it juts into the sea.

The main centres of interest are Anzio, a cheerful port known for its fish restaurants; Sabaudia, a popular beach destination; and Sperlonga, a lovely seafront town with a whitewashed medieval centre.

Anzio

📍 06 / POP 54,200

Anzio, 40km south of Rome, was at the centre of ferocious WWII fighting in the wake of a major Allied landing on 22 January 1944. Nowadays, it's a likeable port town popular with day trippers who come to eat at its seafood restaurants and hang out on its sandy beaches.

✗ Eating

★ **La Nostra Paranza**   SEAFOOD €
(📞 338 2303844; Via Porto Innocenziano 23; set menu €20; ⊙ noon-3pm & 7-11pm, closed Wed & Sun dinner) One of a string of seafood eateries on the port, this bustling trattoria is a real find. The menu is fixed but you won't be short of choice as the multi-dish antipasto gets the four-course feast off to a superlative start. Continue with pasta before digging into freshly fried calamari and a dessert of lemon sorbet. Booking essential for weekends.

Sabaudia

📍 0773 / POP 20,400

Set in the heart of the Parco Nazionale del Circeo, Sabaudia boasts one of southern Lazio's finest beaches, a glorious, unspoilt stretch of sand backed by low-lying dunes. The town itself was founded in 1934 by Mussolini and features some striking works of rationalist architecture.

◉ Sights

Parco Nazionale del Circeo   NATIONAL PARK
(www.parcocirceo.it) Encompassing around 85 sq km of sand dunes, rocky coastline, forests and wetlands, the Circeo National Park offers a range of activities including hiking, fishing, birdwatching and cycling. Further information is available at the **visitor centre** (📞 0773 51 50 46; Via Carlo Alberto 188; ⊙ 9am-1pm & 2-4.30pm) in Sabaudia.

🛏 Sleeping

Agriturismo I Quattro Laghi   AGRITURISMO €€
(📞 3382894796, 0773 59 31 35; www.quattrolaghi.it; Strada Sacramento 32, Sabaudia; half-board per person €52-77; P ❄ 🛜) This friendly year-round *agriturismo* (farm-stay accommoda-tion) sits in green farmland about 800m inland from the beach. It's an authentic set-up with basic guest rooms and a large restaurant serving filling farmhouse fare. Meals, open to all, cost €25 to €32. No credit cards.

ℹ Information

Tourist Office (📞 0773 51 50 46; www.prolocosabaudia.it; Piazza del Comune 18; ⊙ 9.15am-12.30pm & 4.30-7.30pm Mon-Sat, 9.15am-12.30pm Sun) Can provide town maps and accommodation lists.

ℹ Getting There & Away

From Laurentina metro station in Rome, **Cotral** (www.cotralspa.it) buses cover the 90km to Sabaudia (€5, two hours, nine daily Monday to Friday).

On Sundays (and Saturdays in winter) you'll need to get a train from Termini to Priverno-Fossanova (€5, one hour, hourly) and then a connecting Cotral bus.

Sperlonga

📍 0771 / POP 3300

The pick of Lazio's southern coastal towns, Sperlonga is a fashionable summer spot, much frequented by weekending Romans and Neapolitans. It has two sandy beaches either side of a rocky promontory and a steeply stacked medieval centre whose narrow whitewashed lanes are lined with boutiques, cafes and restaurants.

◉ Sights

Museo Archeologico di Sperlonga e Villa di Tiberio   MUSEUM
(📞 0771 54 80 28; Via Flacca, Km 16.3; adult/reduced €5/2.50; ⊙ 8.30am-7.30pm) Other than the beach – and the great views from the historic centre – Sperlonga's main attraction is this archaeological museum. Here you can admire ancient sculptures and poke around the ruins of Villa Tiberio, Emperor Tiberius' seafront villa set around a gaping sea cave, the Grotta di Tiberio.

🛏 Sleeping

Hotel Mayor   HOTEL €€
(📞 0771 54 92 45; www.hotelmayor.it; Via 1 Romita 4; s €45-110, d €55-180, q €105-290; ⊙ Mar-Oct; P ❄ 🛜) Within easy walking distance of the beach and historic centre, the three-star Mayor is an old-school, family-run hotel with simple, sunny rooms and its own patch of private beach. Note that there's a three-night minimum stay in summer.

Eating

★ Gli Archi
SEAFOOD €€

(☑ 0771 54 83 00; www.gliarchi.com; Via Ottaviano 17; meals €40; ☺ 12.30-3pm & 7.30-11pm Thu-Tue) One of several restaurants in the medieval centre, Gli Archi provides a lovely setting for fresh seafood. Sit down in the coolly elegant arched interior or go al fresco on the terrace and dig into sautéed clams followed by pasta with squid, asparagus and tomatoes.

❶ Getting There & Away

To get to Sperlonga, take the train from Termini to Fondi-Sperlonga (€6.90, 1¼ hours, hourly) and then a connecting **Piazzoli** (☑ 0771 51 90 67; www.piazzoli.it) bus to Sperlonga (€1.50, 10 minutes, up to 12 daily).

By car, Sperlonga is 112km from Rome. Take Via Pontina (SS148) and follow signs to Terracina and then Sperlonga.

Isole Pontine

Off the southern Lazio coast, this group of volcanic islands serves as an Italian Hamptons. Between mid-June and the end of August, **Ponza** and **Ventotene** – the only two inhabited islands – buzz with holidaymakers and weekenders who descend in droves to eat shellfish at terrace restaurants, swim in emerald coves and cruise around the craggy coast. Outside of summer, the islands are very quiet, and, although expensive, a joy to explore.

Action centres on colourful Ponza town where you'll find the usual array of souvenir shops, cafes and restaurants, as well as a small sandy beach.

⌕ Tours

Cooperativa Barcaioli Ponzesi BOATING
(☑ 0771 80 99 29; www.barcaioliponza.it; Sotto il Tunnel di S Antonio; ☺ 9am-10.30pm) Cooperativa Barcaioli is one of several outfits in Ponza offering cruises around the island (€27.50 to €35 including lunch and a swimming stop) and boats to the beach at Frontone (€5 return).

⌂ Sleeping

★ Villa Ersilia
B&B €€

(☑ 328 7749461; www.villaersilia.it; Via Scotti 2, Ponza; d €85-160; ❋ 🛜) Housed in a panoramic villa a short but steep walk up from the harbour (follow the signs), this friendly place wins you over with its simple sunny rooms, manicured gardens and tasty breakfast. What stands out more than anything, though, is the blissful view that unfurls before you from the terrace.

Eating

Tutti Noi
SEAFOOD €€

(☑ 0771 82 00 44; Via Dante 5, Ponza; fixed-price menu €22, meals €30; ☺ 12.30-3pm & 6pm-midnight daily Jun-Aug, closed Sun dinner Sep-May) A casual trattoria opposite the beach in Ponza town. What you'll eat will depend on the morning catch, but you can depend on excellent pasta and simply cooked fish mains. The €22 fixed-price menu includes a mixed seafood starter and a daily pasta, perhaps with eggplant and swordfish, along with water and wine.

❶ Information

Tourist Office (☑ 0771 8 00 31; www.proloco diponza.it; Via Molo Musco; ☺ 9am-1pm & 4-8pm) Has island maps and accommodation lists.

❶ Getting There & Away

Ponza and Ventotene are accessible from Anzio, Terracina, Naples and Formia. Some services run year-round, including daily ferries from Terracina, but most operate from June to September.

The major ferry companies:

Laziomar (☑ 0771 70 06 04; www.laziomar. it) Services to Ponza from Terracina (ferry €10 one way, 2½ hours), Formia (ferry €15 one way, 2½ hours; fast ferry €22.50 one way, 1¼ hours), and Anzio (fast ferry €23.40 one way, 1½ hours).

Navigazione Libera del Golfo (NLG; ☑ 081 552 07 63; www.navlib.it) Hydrofoils from Terracina to Ponza (€46 return, 50 minutes) and Ventotene (€51 return, 1¾ hours).

Vetor (☑ 06 984 50 83; www.vetor.it) Hydrofoils from Anzio to Ponza (€25 to €44 one way, 70 minutes).

❶ Getting Around

Autolinee Schiaffini (www.schiaffini.com) runs buses from the port to points across the island. Tickets cost €1.50; bags are an extra €0.50. Timetables are posted at the tourist office.

To get your own set of wheels, **Noleggio Pilato** (☑ 0771 83 16 45, 360 730166; Via Dante, Ponza) rents scooters (€30 per day including helmet and petrol) and mini-mokes (€50 per day).

Turin, Piedmont & the Italian Riviera

Why Go?

The beauty of northwestern Italy is its diversity. Piedmont's capital, Turin, is an elegant, easy city of baroque palaces, cutting-edge galleries and fittingly fabulous dining. While the region has been one of Italy's 20th-century industrial success stories, it has also retained deep, lasting links to the soil, its wines and culinary offerings earning it the name of the 'new Tuscany'.

To the south, Liguria's slim, often vertical, sliver is home to Italy's Riviera, the fabled port city of Genoa and the beguiling villages of Cinque Terre. Expect dramatic coastal topography, beautifully preserved architecture and one of Italy's most memorable cuisines.

Head north and you'll soon hit the Alps and the semi-autonomous region of Aosta, where you can ski or hike beneath Europe's highest mountains while discovering its delightful French-tinged traditions along the way.

Best Places to Eat

➡ La Piola (p220)

➡ Banco vini e alimenti (p210)

➡ Il Marin (p175)

➡ Gaudenzio (p210)

➡ La Cucina di Nonna Nina (p180)

➡ Dandelion (p236)

Best Places to Sleep

➡ DuParc Contemporary Suites (p208)

➡ Palazzo Grillo (p173)

➡ Villa Rosmarino (p180)

➡ Via Stampatori (p208)

➡ La Sosta di Ottone III (p188)

When to Go
Turin

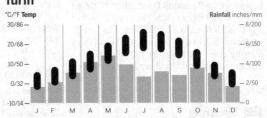

Jan–Mar Most reliable snow cover for skiing in the Alps.

Apr Fewer crowds and fine days on the Ligurian coast.

Sep & Oct Autumn food festivals in Turin and the Langhe.

THE ITALIAN RIVIERA

Italy's famed crescent of Mediterranean coast, where the Alps and the Apennines cascade into the sea, is defined by its sinuous, giddy landscapes. The region of Liguria is shaped by its extreme topography – its daily life is one of ascents and descents, always in the presence of a watery horizon.

Anchored beside the region's best natural harbour is noble Genoa. Known as La Superba (the Superb One) to biased locals, it's a city that ruled over one of the finest maritime empires in medieval Europe. Fanning out on either side is the Riviera (western 'Ponente', eastern 'Levante'), including the Portofino peninsula, along with legendary Cinque Terre.

This is both a deeply historic destination and a fabulously in-the-moment pleasure-seeking one, where you can explore lavish *palazzi* or humble village churches and then simply swim, eat, walk or stare at the sea.

Genoa

☑ 010 / POP 594,750

Italy's largest sea port is indefatigably contradictory, full at once of grandeur, squalor, sparkling light and deep shade. But a gateway to the Riviera for many travellers today, a weighty architectural heritage speaks of its former glory – the Most Serene Republic of Genoa ruled over the Mediterranean waves during the 12th to the 13th centuries – and history feels alive in Genoa. No more is this true than in its extensive old city, an often confronting reminder of pre-modern life with its twisting maze of narrow *caruggi* (streets), largely intact. Emerge blinking from this thrillingly dank heart to Via Garibaldi and the splendid Enlightenment-era gold-leaf halls of the Unesco-listed Palazzi dei Rolli.

The city's once-tatty port area now hosts museums and a number of eating and drinking options. Its old town, too, has had its own far more organic revitalisation, with a bright new crop of fashionable shops, restaurants and bars lighting the way.

◉ Sights

Old City AREA

(Centro Storico) The heart of medieval Genoa – bounded by ancient city gates Porta dei Vacca and Porta Soprana, and the streets of Via Cairoli, Via Garibaldi and Via XXV Aprile – is famed for its *caruggi* (narrow lanes). Looking up at the washing pegged on lines everywhere, it becomes obvious that these dark, cave-like laneways and blind alleys are still largely residential, although the number of fashionable bars, shops and cafes continues to grow.

Parts of the *caruggi* can feel somewhat unnerving, especially after dark. Although it's not particularly dangerous, do take care in the zone west of Via San Luca and south to Piazza Banchi, where most street prostitution and accompanying vice concentrates. East of the piazza is Via Orefici, where you'll find **market** stalls.

★ **Musei di Strada Nuova** MUSEUM
(Palazzi dei Rolli; ☑ 010 557 21 93; www.museidigenova.it; Via Garibaldi; combined ticket adult/reduced €9/7; ⊙ 9am-7pm Tue-Fri, 10am-7.30pm Sat & Sun summer, to 6.30pm winter) Skirting the northern edge of what was once the city limits, pedestrianised Via Garibaldi (formerly called the Strada Nuova) was planned by Galeazzo Alessi in the 16th century. It quickly became the city's most sought-after quarter, lined with the palaces of Genoa's wealthiest citizens. Three of these *palazzi* – Rosso, Bianco (p168) and Doria-Tursi (p168) – today comprise the Musei di Strada Nuova. Between them, they hold the city's finest collection of old masters. Whether you visit the actual museums or not, the street is a must to wander.

Buy tickets to the Musei di Strada Nuova at the bookshop inside Palazzo Doria-Tursi.

Palazzo Rosso MUSEUM
(www.museidigenova.it; Via Garibaldi 18; combined ticket adult/reduced €9/7; ⊙ 9am-7pm Tue-Fri, 10am-7.30pm Sat & Sun summer, to 6.30pm winter) Lavishly frescoed rooms in Palazzo Rosso, part of the Musei di Strada Nuova, provide the backdrop for several portraits by Van Dyck of the local Brignole-Sale family. Other standouts include Guido Reni's *San Sebastiano* and Guercino's *La morte di Cleopatra* (The Death of Cleopatra), as well as works by Veronese, Dürer and Bernardo Strozzi.

Franco Albini Apartment ARCHITECTURE
(www.museidigenova.it; Palazzo Rosso, Via Garibaldi 18) One of Italy's best-loved 20th-century architects, Franco Albini was a key figure in the restoration of Genova's *palazzi* in the post-war period. The third floor of the Palazzo Rosso hides an Italian mid-century gem – an apartment Albini designed for the

Turin, Piedmont & the Italian Riviera Highlights

1 Museo Egizio (p202) Exploring the largest collection of Egyptian history outside of Cairo.

2 Palazzi dei Rolli (p165) Discovering the art and architecture of Genoa's once-great maritime empire.

3 Barolo (p221) Discussing terroir, tannins and tenacity with some of the world's most revered winemakers.

4 Cinque Terre (p184) Hiking the blue trail, the red trail, the sanctuary trails – in fact, any trail.

5 Funivie Monte Bianco (p235) Jumping the border aboard the state-of-the-art cable-car in Valle d'Aosta.

6 Truffle festival (p217) Braving the crowds of truffle-snorting high rollers in Alba in October.

7 Tellaro (p194) Swimming in the Golfo di Poeti and remembering Shelley and Byron.

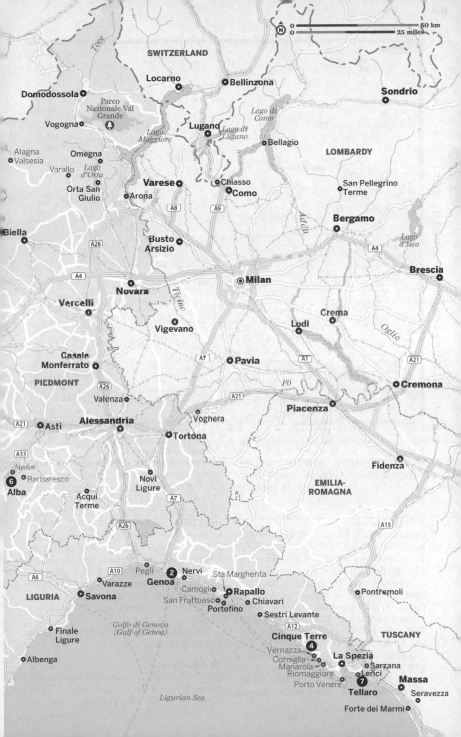

Liguria

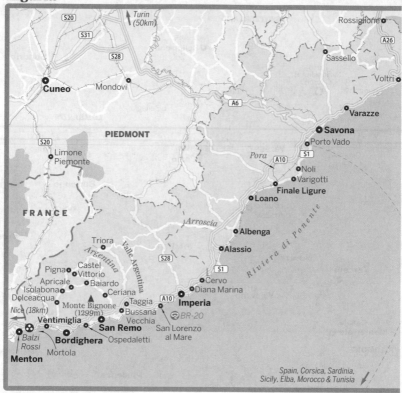

museum's director, now open to the public. Its mix of signature Albini furniture, clean modern lines and Genovese excess, will delight design fans (the city views aren't bad either).

Palazzo Bianco   MUSEUM

(www.museidigenova.it; Via Garibaldi 11; combined ticket adult/reduced €9/7; ⊘9am-7pm Tue-Fri, 10am-7.30pm Sat & Sun summer, to 6.30pm winter) Flemish, Spanish and Italian artists feature at Palazzo Bianco, the second of the triumvirate of *palazzi* that are together known as the Musei di Strada Nuova. Rubens' *Venere e Marte* (Venus and Mars) and Van Dyck's *Vertumna e Pomona* are among the highlights, which also include works by Hans Memling, Filippino Lippi and Murillo, as well as 15th-century religious icons. Beyond the art itself, architect Franco Albini's mid-century refit is particularly lovely here.

Palazzo Doria-Tursi   MUSEUM

(www.museidigenova.it; Via Garibaldi 9; combined ticket adult/reduced €9/7; ⊘9am-7pm Tue-Fri, 10am-7.30pm Sat & Sun summer, to 6.30pm winter) This palace, one of three that together make up the Musei di Strada Nuova, features a small but absorbing collection of legendary violinist Niccolò Paganini's personal effects. In the Sala Paganiniana, pride of place goes to his Canone violin, made in Cremona in 1743. One lucky musician gets to play the maestro's violin during October's Paganiniana festival. Other artefacts on show include letters, musical scores and his travelling chess set.

The palace has also housed Genoa's town hall since 1848.

★ Palazzo Reale   PALACE

(☑ 010 271 02 36; www.palazzorealegenova.beni culturali.it; Via Balbi 10; adult/reduced €4/2; ⊘9am-7pm Tue-Sat, 1.30-7pm Sun) If you only

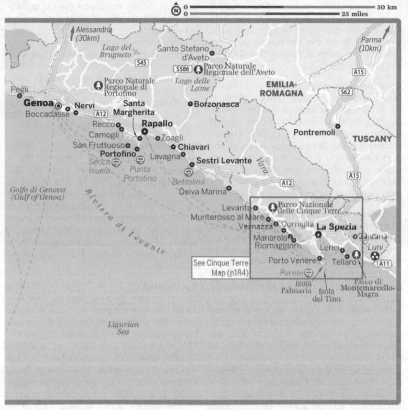

get the chance to visit one of the Palazzi dei Rolli (a group of palaces belonging to the city's most eminent families), make it this one. A former residence of the Savoy dynasty, it has terraced gardens, exquisite furnishings, a fine collection of 17th-century art and a gilded Hall of Mirrors that is worth the entry fee alone.

★ **Primo Piano**   GALLERY
(www.hotelpalazzogrillo.it; Vico alla Chiesa delle Vigne 18r; ⊘4-8pm Wed-Sun) FREE A beautiful historical space that runs a program of modern and contemporary shows along interesting curatorial themes. The focus is often on photography. It's part of Palazzo Grillo (p173) hotel but has a separate backstreet entrance.

Santa Maria di Castello   ABBEY
(☑347 995 67 40, 010 86 03 90; www.santama riadicastello.it; Salita di Santa Maria di Castello 15; ⊘10-1pm & 5-6pm) Built on the site of the original settlement, and sheltering under the 11th century Embriaci Tower, this Romanesque church and convent, itself built before AD 900, is an extraordinary and little visited historic site. Its walls are covered with treasures that were commissioned by the noble families of Genoa from the earliest times, though some of the notable frescoes also date to the 16th-and 17th centuries. Private tours, by coin donation, are possible.

La Lanterna   LIGHTHOUSE
(www.lanternadigenova.it; Via alla Lanterna; adult/reduced €5/4; ⊘2-6.30pm Sat & Sun) The port may have changed radically since its '90s rebirth, but its emblematic sentinel hasn't moved an inch since 1543. Genoa's lighthouse is one of the world's oldest and tallest – and it still works, beaming its light over 50km to warn ships and tankers. Visitors can climb 172 steps and ponder exhibits in an adjacent museum of lamps, lenses and related history.

La Lanterna is best accessed via a special 800m walking trail that starts at the ferry terminal. It's surrounded by a pleasant park. On the last Sunday of the month there are guided tours (meet at Palazzo San Giorgio; €15 per person).

Casa della Famiglia Colombo   MUSEUM

(www.coopculture.it; Piazza Dante; admission €6; ⊘11am-5pm Tue-Sun) Not the only house claiming to be the birthplace of the navigator Christopher Columbus (Calvi in Corsica is another contender), this one probably has the most merit, as various documents inside testify. Curiously, it stands just outside the old city walls in the shadow of the Porta Soprana gate (built in 1155).

Cattedrale di San Lorenzo   CATHEDRAL

(Piazza San Lorenzo; ⊘8am-noon & 3-7pm) Genoa's zebra-striped Gothic-Romanesque cathedral owes its continued existence to the poor quality of a British WWII bomb that failed to ignite here in 1941; it still sits on the right side of the nave like an innocuous museum piece.

The cathedral, fronted by three arched portals, twisting columns and crouching lions, was first consecrated in 1118. The two bell towers and cupola were added later in the 16th century.

Inside, above the central doorway, there's a great lunette with a painting of the *Last Judgment,* the work of an anonymous Byzantine painter of the early 14th century. In the sacristy, the **Museo del Tesoro** (⊠010 247 18 31; Piazza San Lorenzo; adult/child €6/4.50; ⊘9am-noon & 3-6pm Mon-Sat) preserves various dubious holy relics, including the medieval *Sacro Catino,* a glass vessel once thought to be the Holy Grail. Other artefacts include the polished quartz platter upon which Salome is said to have received John the Baptist's head, and a fragment of the True Cross.

Acquario   AQUARIUM

(www.acquariodigenova.it; Ponte Spinola; adult/reduced €22/17; ⊘9am-8pm Mon-Fri, to 9pm Sat & Sun summer, from 9.30am winter; ⊛) Genoa's much-vaunted aquarium is one of the largest in Europe, with more than 5000 sea creatures, including sharks. Moored at the end of a walkway is the ship *Nave Blu,* a unique floating display, specialising in exhibits of coral reefs. The aquarium's 'cetaceans pavilion' may concern some visitors: while the dolphins do not perform tricks and the aquarium fulfils its international legal requirements, including rehousing abused

dolphins, animal welfare groups claim keeping dolphins in enclosed tanks such as these is harmful.

Buy tickets online to avoid long, hot queues (and harassment from street traders) in summer; a combination ticket (adult/reduced €49/40) gives you access to other port attractions, the Galata Museo del Mare, the Biosphere and the panoramic lift. During August, it's open until 10.30pm; note last entrance is two hours before closing.

Galata Museo del Mare   MUSEUM

(www.galatamuseodelmare.it; Calata de Mari 1; admission €11; ⊘10am-7.30pm, closed Mon Nov-Feb) Genoa was rivalled only by Barcelona and Venice as a medieval and Renaissance maritime power, so its 'museum of the sea' is, not surprisingly, one of its most relevant and interesting. High-tech exhibits trace the history of seafaring, from Genoa's reign as Europe's greatest dockyard to the ages of sail and steam.

Boccadasse   VILLAGE

When the sun is shining, do as the Genovese do and decamp for a *passeggiata* along the oceanside promenade, Corso Italia, which begins around 3km east of the city centre. This broad 2.5km-long pavement lined with Liberty villas leads to Boccadasse, a once separate fishing village that appears like a sawn-off chunk of Cinque Terre. Its pebble beach is a perfect gelato-licking location by day and its gaggle of small bars serve up *spritzes* to happy crowds on summer evenings.

Galleria Nazionale   GALLERY

(www.palazzospinola.beniculturali.it; Piazza Superiore di Pellicceria 1; adult/reduced €4/2; ⊘8.30am-7.30pm Tue-Sat, from 1.30pm Sun) This gallery's paintings are wonderfully displayed over four floors of the 16th-century **Palazzo Spinola**, once owned by the Spinola family, one of Genoa's most formidable dynasties. The main focus is Italian and Flemish Renaissance art of the so-called Ligurian School (look out for Van Dyck, Rubens and Strozzi), but it's also worth visiting to gape at the decorative architecture.

Palazzo Ducale   MUSEUM

(www.palazzoducale.genova.it; Piazza Giacomo Matteotti 9; price varies by exhibition; ⊘hours vary) Once the seat of the independent republic, this grand palace was built in the mannerist style in the 1590s and was largely refurbished after a fire in the 1770s. Today it hosts high-profile temporary art exhibitions, several smaller galleries and occasional markets in its lofty atrium. The *palazzo* also has a bookshop and cafe.

Chiesa del Gesù   CHURCH
(Piazza Giacomo Matteotti; ⊙ 4.30-7pm) Half-hidden behind the Cattedrale di San Lorenzo but emulating it in its ecclesial brilliance, this former Jesuit church dating from 1597 has an intricate and lavish interior. The wonderfully frescoed walls and ceiling are anchored by two works by the great Dutch artist Rubens. *Circoncisione* (Circumcision) hangs over the main altar, and *Miracoli di San Ignazio* is displayed in a side chapel.

Porto Antico   AREA
(www.portoantico.it; ⛵) The port that once controlled a small empire is now one of the most popular places to enjoy a *passeggiata* (evening stroll). Super yacht-fanciers are particularly well catered for and those with kids will love the aquarium, the futuristic Bigo (lookout), the small public swimming pool and the pirate ship.

Piazza de Ferrari   PIAZZA
Genoa's fountain-embellished main piazza is ringed by magnificent buildings that include the art nouveau **Palazzo della Borsa**, which was once the country's stock exchange, and the hybrid neoclassical-modernist Teatro Carlo Felice (p177), bombed in WWII and not fully rebuilt until 1991.

🏃 Activities

Genoa-Casella Railway   RAIL
(www.ferroviagenovacasella.it; one way €4.50, family one way/return €20) Spectacular views of Genoa's forts can be seen from this 1929 narrow-gauge railway, which snakes 25km north from the cute Stazione Genova to the village of **Casella** in the Valle Scrivia. Stazione Genova is 1.3km north of Stazione Brignole: it's 15 minutes by foot or you can catch bus 33.

Ring of Forts   WALKING
(www.visitgenoa.it; €14) The tourist office (p178) organises this four-hour walking tour to the city's 'new walls' – built in the 1600s – and its ring of forts, with an expert guide. As well as these evocative historical structures, there are amazing views and protected mountain flora to be seen along the way. Tours leave at 9.15am and run monthly; check the website for dates and details.

Piscina Porto Antico   SWIMMING
(☑ 345 298 37 44; www.piscinaportoantico.it; Piazzale Penne; half/full day €6.50/8; ⊙ 9am-7pm) Right on the water by the super yachts, this bijou public pool is just the thing if you've not got enough time to escape to the beach. It might not be great for swimming laps but the location is hard to beat.

🎉 Festivals & Events

Slow Fish   FOOD & DRINK
(http://slowfish.slowfood.it; ⊙ May) 🍴 Every odd-numbered year in early May, this festival celebrates seafood with a fish market and tastings. Affiliated with the Slow Food movement, it also runs free workshops focusing on water pollution, good fishing practices and aquaculture.

Salone Nautico Internazionale   SAILING
(http://salonenautico.com; Fiera di Genova; ⊙ Oct) One of the world's biggest and best boat shows, with over one thousand boats to covet, including yachts, outboard engines and inflatable boats, and motor boats.

🛏 Sleeping

La Superba   B&B €
(☑ 010 869 85 89; www.la-superba.com; Via del Campo 12; s/d €80/90; ❄ 🛜) This lovingly cared-for, well-equipped place at a bargain price has rooms spread over the two top floors of an old *palazzo*. Top-floor rooms have pretty mansard ceilings and one a tiny terrace with spectacular port and city views (along with the Genovese soundtrack of crosstown traffic). There's also generous lounge and breakfast areas.

Palazzo Cambiaso   APARTMENT €
(☑ 010 856 61 88; www.palazzocambiaso.it; Via al Ponte Calvi 6; d €110, apt €120-180; 🛜) A real attention to design is evident in these rooms and apartments, set on the upper floor of a stately *palazzo*. The larger ones (sleeping up to six) come with full marble kitchens, long dining tables and laundries, but even the cheapest double is spacious, soothing and has the signature Frette linen.

Hotel Meuble Suisse   HOTEL €
(☑ 010 54 11 76; www.meublesuisse.com; 3rd fl, Via XX Settembre 21; s/d €55/70; 🛜) Clean, uncluttered rooms, service with a smile and your own personal chandelier. What more could you want? Climb the stairs to the 3rd floor of this strapping Genoa building near Stazione Brignole for a bit of faded fin-de-siècle magic.

Genoa

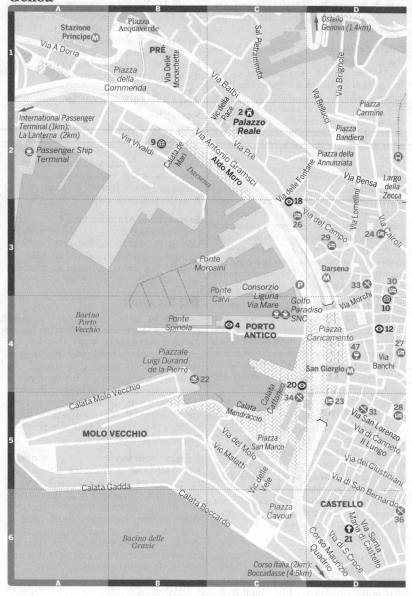

B&B Palazzo Morali   B&B €
(📞 010 246 70 27; www.palazzomorali.com;
Piazza della Raibetta; s/d €75/85; ❋ 📶) Stay in
rarefied splendour at this antique-clad bed
and breakfast that is located near the Porto Antico (p171). Situated on the top two
floors of a lofty building, its palatial rooms
(some of which have a shared bathroom)
are embellished with ornate gold-leafed
four-poster beds, gilt-framed mirrors and
magnificent Genovese art.

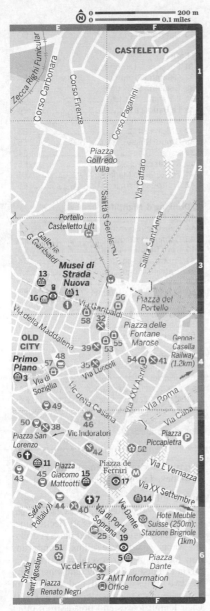

themed on modern artists and feature works inspired by the likes of Mondrian, Dorazio and Alexander Calder. Add in a library, chill-out area, internet point, small gym and terrace, and you have the ideal bolthole.

Cheaper rates are also available without breakfast.

The hotel also has several apartments, sleeping up to eight people.

Hotel Cristoforo Colombo
HOTEL €

(☏ 010 251 36 43; www.hotelcolombo.it; Via di Porta Soprana 27; s/d €80/100; 🖝) A totally charming family-run hotel ideally situated near Cattedrale di San Lorenzo, Cristoforo Colombo has 18 colour-accented rooms with eclectic furnishings. Breakfast is served on an inviting 6th-floor rooftop terrace.

★ Palazzo Grillo
DESIGN HOTEL €€

(☏ 010 247 73 56; www.hotelpalazzogrillo.it; Piazza delle Vigne 4; d €160-250; ✲🖝) Genovese locals Matteo and Laura have created the extraordinary place to stay that Genoa has been crying out for in a once derelict *palazzo*. Stunning public spaces are dotted with spot-on contemporary design pieces, character-filled vintage finds and – look in any direction – original 15th-century frescoes. Rooms are simple but super stylish with Vitra TVs and high ceilings.

Best of all, most of the entire 2nd floor is given over to a private guest salon, where you can lounge around by the windows overlooking the piazza, browse the art and design library, or just gaze at the befrescoed walls.

Le Nuvole
BOUTIQUE HOTEL €€

(☏ 010 251 00 18; www.hotellenuvole.it; Piazza delle Vigne 6; d €130-160; ✲@🖝) A lovely small hotel where smart modern furniture and slick bathrooms make the most of an ancient *palazzo*'s original architecture and its knockout lofty ceilings, lovingly restored plaster mouldings and beautiful tilework. Owners are hands-on and helpful; breakfast is taken in the beautiful rooftop space at neighbouring Palazzo Grillo.

Locanda di Palazzo Cicala
BOUTIQUE HOTEL €€

(☏ 010 251 88 24; www.palazzocicala.it; Piazza San Lorenzo 16; d/ste €150/195; ✲@🖝) In stark contrast to its grand 18th-century stucco exterior, the six minimalist rooms include pieces by Jasper Morrison and Philippe Starck. Great stuff, but don't expect TLC and do make sure you get a firm confirmation of where exactly you'll sleep, as guests are

Hotel Cairoli
HOTEL €

(☏ 010 246 14 54; www.hotelcairoligenova.com; Via Cairoli 14/4; d €65-105; tr €85-125; q €90-150; ✲@🖝) For five-star service at three-star prices, book at this artful hideaway. Rooms, on the 3rd floor of a towering *palazzo*, are

Genoa

often palmed out to adequate but far less appealing apartments in the surrounding streets.

Quarto Piano B&B €€
(☎ 348 7426779; www.quarto-piano.it; Piazza Pellicceria 2/4; d/ste €130/165; ❇ 🎧) Four elegant, cosy modern rooms share the 4th floor here, complete with a terrace for breakfast or a hot tub dip.

✕ Eating

La Botega Del Gusto LIGURIAN €
(Vico Superiore del Ferro 3; dishes €4-8.50; ⏱ 11.30am-4.30pm Mon-Sat) Genovese fast food done in the most authentic, and moreish, of ways can be had at this backstreet hole in the wall. Come for a quick and easy plate of *pansotti* (filled pasta with wild greens), pes-

to pasta, quiche-like spinach-and-artichoke *torta*, baked rabbit or steamed salt cod.

Pane e Tulipani BAKERY €
(☎ 010 817 88 41; Via dei Macelli di Soziglia 75; pizza €6.50; ⏱ 6am-7.30pm Mon-Sat) Hectic times rule at this poetically named bakery: everyone wants what they're selling. Drop by any time for one of their several varieties of focaccia or make a Saturday date when there are two drops (10.30am and 3.30pm) of half-price pizza margherita, a steal at €6.50. Their kamut loaves and breads from other ancient grains are also worth trying.

Rooster FAST FOOD, LIGURIAN €
(☎ 010 899 69 14; Piazza Giacomo Matteotti 41; sandwiches €6-8; ⏱ 10.30am-9.30pm Mon-Sat, to 3pm Sun) A cute little hole in the wall place that breathes new life into the traditional

rotisserie chicken. Birds are all free range and local; buy them whole for a picnic or eat in for one of their special *panino*, which may come with grilled peppers, as a schnitzel or with apple and walnuts.

Gelateria Profumo
GELATO €

(www.villa1827.it; Vico Superiore del Ferro 14; cones from €2.20; ⊙noon-7.30pm Tue-Sat) A wonderfully old-fashioned place, with fragrant scoops appearing from under metal-topped vats. The *panera* (a Genovese coffee-and-cream blend), creamy Sorento lemon and bitter orange flavours are standouts.

Gelateria San Luca
GELATO €

(Via San Luca 88; cones from €2; ⊙noon-7pm) A selection of beautiful traditional gelato flavours are complemented by a creative menu of semifreddo-filled cups, ice-cream sandwiches and chocolate-coated popsicles. If you have a gelato emergency out of hours, the sweet owner has been known to dish out a mercy cone if you knock and ask nicely.

Trattoria Da Maria
TRATTORIA €

(☑ 010 58 10 80; Vico Testadoro 14r; meals €10-18; ⊙11.45am-3pm Mon-Sat, 7-9.30pm Thu & Fri) Brace yourself for lunchtime mayhem. This is a totally authentic, if well touristed, workers' trattoria and there's much squeezing into tiny tables, shouted orders and a fast and furious succession of plates plonked on tables. A daily hand-scrawled menu is a roll call of elemental favourites that keep all comers full and happy, along with the jugs of ridiculously cheap wine.

Cross your fingers you're there on a minestrone alla Genovese, pesto lasagne or donkey *ragù* day – pure Ligurian bliss. Dinner hours are slightly less hectic, but still fun.

Focaccia e Dintorni
BAKERY €

(Via Canneto Il Curto 7-8; focaccia from €1; ⊙7am-8pm) Punt a football anywhere in Genoa and you're bound to hit somewhere that sells focaccia. This *focacceria* sells a range of focaccia slices, pizza, *farinata* and sweet treats.

Mangiabuono
LIGURIAN €

(Vico Vegetti 3; meals €19-23; ⊙noon-2.30pm & 7-9pm Mon-Sat) While there are photos of the NZ All Blacks team enjoying a slap-up meal here (Genoa is Italy's great rugby city), this remains one of the city's fabulously unfancy trattorias. Come and eat the glorious staples: pesto lasagna, *corzetti* (disc-shaped pasta) with *salsa di noce* (walnut sauce), rabbit stew or simply done seafood.

★ Trattoria Rosmarino
TRATTORIA €€

(☑ 010 251 04 75; www.trattoriarosmarino.it; Salita del Fondaco 30; meals €32-38; ⊙12.30-2.30pm & 7.30-10.30pm Mon-Sat) Rosmarino cooks up the standard local specialities, yes, but the straightforwardly priced menu has an elegance and vibrancy that sets it apart. With two nightly sittings, there's always a nice buzz (though there are also enough nooks and crannies that a romantic night for two isn't out of the question). Call ahead for an evening table.

La Berlocca
TRATTORIA €€

(☑ 010 796 33 33; www.laberlocca.com; Via Soziglia 45r; meals €30; ⊙12.30-3pm & 7.30-11pm Tue-Sun) On one of the old city's nicest streets, this one-time *farinata* shop has a hand-written menu of Ligurian standards – tripe, stockfish with pine nuts and potatoes – as well as fresh and inventive dishes like smoked gnocchi. Lunch deals here start at €10 and top at €18 for an all in feast that includes a quarter litre of wine.

Officina 34
MODERN ITALIAN €€

(☑ 010 302 71 84; www.officina34.it; Via di Ravecca 34; meals €30, ⊙6pm-midnight Mon-Sat) Genoa is a long way from Berlin or Brooklyn, but that urban aesthetic is in full force at Officina 34. Subway tile jokes aside, it's a beautifully fitted-out space in a pretty location, and has a simple, gently innovative menu that shows the kitchen cares about quality ingredients. A young, good-looking crowd come for raw plates and *aperitivo* and often end up staying late.

Ombre Rosse
ITALIAN €€

(☑ 010 275 76 08; Vico Indoratori 20; meals €35; ⊙12.30-10pm Mon-Fri, 7.45-10.30pm Sat) Encased in one of the oldest medieval houses in the city, dating from the early 13th century, Ombre Rosse has a dark but romantic interior, full of books, posters and interesting nooks. There's also alfresco seating in a delightful small park opposite (one of the few in Genoa's dense urban grid) not to mention good Ligurian dishes and thoughtful service.

★ Il Marin
SEAFOOD €€€

(Eataly Genova; ☑ 010 869 87 22; www.eataly. net; Porto Antico; meals €50; ⊙noon-3pm & 7-10.30pm) Eating by the water often means a compromise in quality, but Eataly's 3rd-floor fine-dining space delivers both panoramic port views and Genoa's most innovative seafood menu. Rustic wooden tables, Renzo Piano–blessed furniture and an open

LOCAL KNOWLEDGE

LIGURIAN FOOD

Pesto A viridian green blend of basil leaves, pine nuts, extra virgin olive oil and, later, Parmesan. Garlic is controversial with some swearing it's not pesto without it, while others claim it's an upstart addition – if you buy a fresh tub in the supermarket, it comes both with or without.

Focaccia The ubiquitous olive-oil-laden bread, sold in squares; variations include those topped with sweet onion or stuffed with straccino cheese.

Farinata: a chickpea flour pancake, like the *Niçoise panisse* and *socca*; usually made in dedicated shops where you can buy by the slice, though often found on restaurant menus, too.

Polpettone Yes, this sounds like meatballs, but is in fact totally meat-free, rather a bubble-and-squeak like slice of potato, green beans or other seasonal vegetables and eggs, scented with marjoram, baked and topped with breadcrumbs and cheese.

Corzetti Handmade disc-shaped pasta, often embossed with a stamp and traditionally 'flavoured' with a few drops of the local white wine, Pigato.

Salsa di noce A pesto-like pasta sauce made from ground walnuts, olive oil, garlic and soaked bread as a thickener; usually served either with *corzetti* or with ravioli filled with bitter wild greens.

Torta pasqualina An Easter-time special that's also served year-round, a quiche-like mix of eggs, cheese and sautéed spring artichokes baked in a short pastry crust.

Minestrone A vegetable and pulse soup that's not a wholly Ligurian dish, but one that the region has made its own by omitting the tomatoes and adding a dollop of pesto which it's then cooked in.

Cappon magro A celebratory layered salad of eggs, green beans, celery and other vegetables on top of dry olive oil biscuits and topped with lobster, prawns and other seafood, as well as green olives and artichokes.

kitchen make for an easy, relaxed glamour, while dishes use unusual Mediterranean-sourced produce and look gorgeous on the plate.

This is the destination restaurant the city has long needed. Book ahead.

Drinking & Nightlife

Aperitivo spritzes can be had anywhere, but never underestimate the lure of the *caruggi* (narrow lanes) later on. You'll find a number of new drinking spots intermingled with old-time favourites throughout the city, particularly in the streets just northwest of Piazza de Ferrari. Piazza delle Erbe pulls the city's young for cheap and cheerful *aperitivi* and occasionally gets rowdy well into the night.

★**Cantine Matteotti** WINE BAR
(☏010 868 70 00; www.facebook.com/Cantine-Matteotti; Archivolto Baliano 4-6/r; ⊙5pm-1am Tues-Sun) The Puccini wafting up the laneway gives you some clue that this is a special little place. The owners here have a passion for good music and for good

wine, and will pour you some amazing local drops and stave off your hunger with a plate of fresh raw broad beans and Sardinian cheese or a beef tartare made before your eyes.

★**Les Rouges** COCKTAIL BAR
(☏010 246 49 56; www.lesrouges.it; 1st fl, Piazza Campetto 8a; ⊙5.30-11pm Tue-Thu & Sun, to 12.30am Fri & Sat) One of Genoa's surfeit of crumbling *palazzi* is being put to excellent use in this atmospheric cocktail bar. Three bearded, vest-wearing, red-headed brothers – the 'rouges' of the name – man the floor and shake up one of the city's only new-wave cocktails, using top-shelf ingredients and herbal or floral flavours such as chamomile and kaffir lime.

Bar Gio.Si BAR
(Via Canneto il Lungo 78; ⊙5pm-2am Mon, Tue & Thu-Sat) If you've been yearning for some late-night drinking fun, this *antica*-is-the-new-black place is your answer. A completely untouched old-school backstreet bar,

along with its elderly owners, have become the darlings of the city's cool kids, who come to throw back €3 negronis or the totally local *asinello* – a somewhat challenging local fortified wine that's the princely sum of €1 a *spritz*.

Enoteca Pesce
WINE BAR

(Via Sottoripa; ⊗ 8.30am-7.30pm Mon-Sat) Tiny wine bars dot Genoa's old city, although this one, under the arches by the port, is particularly characteristic and full of colourful locals. They are serious about their wine, though glasses hover around the €2 mark so it's a good place to get to know Liguria's unusual grapes.

Cavo Cafe
BAR

(www.cavoristorante.it; Via Falamonica 9; ⊗ noon-3pm & 5-11pm Mon-Sat) Admire the exquisite 17th-century frescoes of Bernardo Strozzi while sipping on your *aperitivo spritz* or wine in this spectacular bar-cafe (it also serves lunch and dinner) encased in an old Doria palace. For somewhere so elegantly storied, staff are friendly and welcoming and while you'll pay a (gentle) premium for drinks, a meal-sized plate of savoury delights is served to your table.

Fratelli Klainguti
CAFE

(Via di Soziglia; ⊗ 8am-8pm) Pre-dating cappuccinos, Klainguti opened in 1828 and its Mittel European charms, and presumably its strudel and pastries, had Verdi and Garibaldi coming back for more. Waiters in bow ties toil under an impressive chandelier and the decor is a fabulous, if tatty, mid-century historical pastiche.

Café degli Specchi
CAFE

(Via Salita Pollaiuoli 43r; ⊗ 7am-9pm Mon-Sat) A bit of Turin disconnected and relocated 150km to the south, this tiled art deco showpiece was (and is) a favourite hang-out of Genoa's intellectuals. You can sink your espresso at street level or disappear upstairs among the velvet seats and mirrors for coffee, cake and an *aperitivo* buffet.

Scurreria Beer & Bagel
BEER HALL

(http://scurreria.com; Via di Scurreria 22r; ⊗ 6pm-2am) A little bit of Brooklyn or Melbourne in the *caruggi*, this brewpub packs out Genoese black-clad young. There's two taps of local and imported beers and an extensive by-the-bottle list. And, yes, they do bagels, stuffed in a way that only an Italian can do, along with other belly-liners.

☆ Entertainment

Teatro Carlo Felice
THEATRE

(☑ 010 538 12 24; www.carlofelice.it; Passo Eugenio Montale 4) Genoa's stunning four-stage opera house with a seasonal opera program that's worth booking ahead for.

Giardini Luzzati
ARTS CENTRE

(www.giardiniluzzati.it; Piazzetta Rostango) A multi-function alternative space that hosts live music, street festivals, archaeological walks, debates, workshops and other performances. A full program can be found online, or just drop by for a weekend beer and see what's on.

🛍 Shopping

★ Via Garibaldi 12
HOMEWARES

(☑ 010 253 03 65; www.viagaribaldi12.com; Via Garibaldi 12; ⊗ 10am-2pm & 3.30-7pm Tue-Sat) Even if you're not in the market for designer homewares, it's worth trotting up the noble stairs just to be reminded how splendid a city Genoa can be. There's an incredibly canny collection of contemporary furniture and objects, as well as 'interventions' by contemporary artists such as Damian Hirst and Sterling Ruby, with works occasionally loaned from New York's Gagosian gallery.

Lipstick Vintage
VINTAGE

(☑ 010 247 42 56; www.facebook.com/Lipstick Genova; Via 25 Aprile 62; ⊗ 4-7.30pm Mon, 10am-1pm & 4-7.30pm Tue-Sat) A treasure trove of upmarket vintage fashion with pieces from classic Italian designers such as Ferragamo, Prada, Pucci and Gucci, with some fashion-forward pieces from internationals such as Vivienne Westwood and YSL. If you're on a budget or like a bargain, check out their discount back rooms where you can uncover Milanese fashion house samples and beautiful dressmaker items.

Mimì e Cocò
CHILDREN'S CLOTHING

(☑ 010 403 32 97; www.mimi-coco.it; Piazza del Ferro 21; ⊗ 3.30-7.30pm Mon, 10am-1pm & 3.30-7.30pm Tue-Sat) A wonderful find in a country increasingly dominated by big budget labels, everything here is handmade in Genoa. Smocks, shirts, shorts, cardigans and playsuits for babies and to five-year-olds are crafted from natural fibres, and their simple, traditional cuts also have a very contemporary appeal.

Butteghetta Magica di Tinello Daniela
HOMEWARES

(☎ 010 247 42 25; Via della Maddalena 2; ⊙ 3-7pm Mon, 10am-1pm & 3-7pm Tue-Sat) Stock your kitchen from a selection of brightly glazed traditional ceramics and beautiful contemporary kitchenware. This is also the place to buy a *corzetti*, a carved wooden stamp that is used to make a local pasta speciality of the same name. If you're here during the Christmas season, the *'magica'* of the title comes into play with spectacular nativity scenes to admire.

Pasticceria Profumo
PASTRIES, CHOCOLATE

(www.villa1827.it; Via del Portello 2; ⊙ 9am-1pm & 3.30-7.30pm Tue-Sat) A traditional *pasticceria* and chocolate shop that follows the seasons – chocolate, chestnuts and cream dominate in winter, fresh stone fruit and berries in summer – this is also one of Genoa's most pretty, with bright, stylish packaging that makes for fantastic take-home gifts.

Pietro Romanengo fu Stefano
CHOCOLATE

(www.romanengo.com; Via Soziglia 74r; ⊙ 3.30-7.30pm Mon, 9am-1pm & 3.15-7.15pm Tue-Sat) An intriguing historic chocolate shop (est. 1780) that specialises in candied flowers and floral waters: it really does feel as if nothing has changed since *long* before the Risorgimento.

❶ Information

Ticket Booths
(Ponte Spinola; ⊙ 9.30am-6.30pm Sep-Jun, 9am-8pm Jul & Aug) Information and tickets for boat trips around the port and destinations further afield are available from the ticket booths beside the aquarium at Porto Antico (p171).

Tourist Office
(☎ 010 557 29 03; www.visit genoa.it; Via Garibaldi 12r; ⊙ 9am-6.20pm) Helpful office in the historic centre.

❶ Getting There & Away

AIR

Regular domestic and international services, including Ryanair flights to London Stansted, use **Cristoforo Colombo Airport** (☎ 010 6 01 51; www.airport.genova.it), 6km west of the city in Sestri Ponente.

The airport service, AMT **Volabus** (☎ 848 000 030; www.amt.genova.it; one way €6), runs hourly between 5.15am and 10.10pm to the airport, 5.50am to 11.05pm from the airport. It departs from Stazione Principe, with a stop also in Piazza de Ferrari. Tickets can be bought from the driver and include a 60-minute window of use on other public transport.

A taxi to or from the airport will cost around €20 to €30.

BOAT

From June to September, **Golfo Paradiso SNC** (www.golfoparadiso.it) operates boats from Porto Antico to Camogli (one way/return €10/16), Portofino (€12/20) and Porto Venere (€20/35).

Consorzio Liguria Via Mare (www.liguriavia mare.it) runs a range of seasonal trips to Camogli, San Fruttuoso and Portofino; Monterosso in Cinque Terre; and Porto Venere.

Only cruise ships use the 1930s Ponte dei Mille terminal while ferries sailing to Spain, Sicily, Sardinia, Corsica, Morocco and Tunisia use the neighbouring international **passenger terminals** or the **Terminal Traghetti** (Ferry Terminal; Via Milano 51).

Fares listed here are for one-way, high-season deck-class tickets. Ferry operators include the following:

Grandi Navi Veloci (GNV; ☎ 010 209 45 91; www.gnv.it) Ferries to Sardinia (Porto Torres, €78) and Sicily (Palermo, €85). Also to Barcelona (Spain, €85) and Tunis (Tunisia, €120).

Moby Lines (☎ 199 30 30 40; www.mobylines. it) Ferries to the Sardinian ports of Olbia (€55) and Porto Torres (€50).

Tirrenia (☎ 89 21 23; www.tirrenia.it) To/from Sardinia (Porto Torres €55; Olbia from €50).

TRAIN

Genoa's Stazione Principe and Stazione Brignole are linked by very frequent trains to Milan (€14, 1½ hours), Pisa (€16, two hours), Rome (€51.50, five hours) and Turin (€12.50, 1¾ hours).

Stazione Principe tends to have more trains, particularly going west to San Remo (€114, two hours, five daily) and Ventimiglia (€16.10, 2¼ hours, six daily).

❶ Getting Around

AMT (www.amt.genova.it) operates buses throughout the city and there is an **AMT information office** (Via d'Annunzio 8; ⊙ 7.15am-6pm Mon-Fri, 7am-7pm Sat & Sun) at the bus terminal. Bus line 383 links Stazione Brignole with Piazza de Ferrari and Stazione Principe. A ticket valid for 90 minutes costs €1.50. Tickets can be used on main-line trains within the city limits, as well as on the metro (www.genovametro.com).

Riviera di Levante

Beyond Genoa's claustrophobic eastern sprawl, this narrow strip of coast between the deep blue waters of the Mediterranean and the ruggedly mountainous Ligurian hinterland is home to some of Italy's most elite resorts, including jet-set favourite

Portofino and the gently faded Santa Margherita. Anything but off the beaten track, this glittering stretch of coast is hugely popular, but retains pockets of extreme natural beauty and profound authenticity.

Nervi

010 / POP 10,900

A former fishing village engulfed by Genoa's urban sprawl, modern Nervi serves as Genoa's summer playground with a string of resort-style beach clubs and seasonal bars along the waterfront. Its bounty of museums and galleries, and the 2km cliffside promenade, the Passeggiata Anita Garibaldi, make for a pleasant, evocative day trip, whatever the season.

★ Wolfsoniana   MUSEUM
(www.wolfsoniana.it; Via Serra Gropallo 4; adult/reduced €5/4; 11am-6pm Tue-Fri, noon-7pm Sat & Sun summer, 11am-5pm Tue-Sun winter) Some 18,000 items from the period 1880–1945 are displayed in the Wolfson Collection, including paintings, sculptures, furniture, decorative arts, propaganda, everyday objects and industrial design. Absolute eye-candy for 20th century design and interiors fans, they also form an incredibly rich, and sometimes troubling, document of post-Risorgimento Italy's cultural complexity.

Galleria d'Arte Moderna   GALLERY
(Via Capolungo 3; adult/reduced €5/4; 11am-6pm Tue-Fri, noon-7pm Sat & Sun summer, 11am-5pm Tue-Sun winter) Set in the 16th-century Villa Saluzzo, this museum displays the collection of the former Prince Odone di Savoia, mostly works by 19th- and early-20th-century artists such as futurist Fortunato Depero, semi-official fascist sculptor Arturo Martini and the lyrical eccentric Filippo De Pisis.

Museo Giannettino Luxoro   MUSEUM
(Via Mafalda di Savoia 3; adult/reduced €5/4; 9am-2pm Tue-Sat) This early-20th-century villa has a huge collection of decorative objects: 18th-century clocks, silverware, ceramics and furniture. Don't expect modern lines – the cliffside former holiday home was built in a Historicist style specifically to house the collection.

Bagni Blue Marlin   SEAFOOD €
(349 6413692; Passeggiata Anita Garibaldi 25; snacks €10-15, meals €20-30; 10am-9pm April-Sep) Part natural rock formation, part whitewashed concrete, this little place juts right out into the Med, making for an utterly magical spot to *spritz* a sunset away or snaffle up snap-fried anchovies in a paper cone. It morphs from daytime bathing spot into a restaurant and laid-back beach bar as the sun sets.

Camogli

0185 / POP 5500

Camogli, 25km east of Genoa, is most famous for its sheer number of trompe l'oeil villas, its photogenic terraced streets winding down to a perfect cove of pebble beach amid a backdrop of umbrella pines and olive groves. While tourists flock to Portofino, this is where many of northern Italy's intellectuals and creatives have their summer apartments. Still, as pretty as the town is, it remains a working fishing hub – the town's name means 'house of wives', hailing from the days when the womenfolk ran the show while the husbands were away at sea. Come the second weekend in May, the town celebrates its maritime heritage with the **Sagra del Pesce** (Fish Festival) and a huge fish fry – hundreds are cooked in 3m-wide pans along the waterfront.

🏃 Activities

Punta Chiappa   SWIMMING
(www.golfoparadiso.it; boats hourly in summer, 3-5 times per day rest of year) From the main esplanade, Via Garibaldi, boats sail to the Punta Chiappa (one way/return €6/11), a rocky outcrop on the Portofino promontory where you can swim and sunbathe like an Italian. By sea it's a 5 minute trip; otherwise it's an easy 3km walk along the trail that begins at the end of Via San Bartolomeo.

San Rocco Trail   WALKING
A trail from the train station leads along Via Nicolò Cuneo and up countless steps to the church of San Rocco di Camogli: follow the two red dots. From here the path continues 3km to the clifftop battery, a WWII German anti-aircraft gun emplacement.

🛌 Sleeping

La Rosa Bianco   B&B €
(0185 77 66 66; www.larosabiancodiportofino. com; Via Mortola 37; d €110-135;) Gorgeously sited on the slopes of San Rocco di Camogli, inside the Portofino park amid olive and lemon trees, La Rosa Bianco is a genuine B&B in the home of Marco and Laura. Rooms are furnished in a friendly, family

style with plenty of personal touches, while breakfast is served in the old mill room with its enormous grinding stone.

★ Villa Rosmarino
B&B **€€€**

(☎0185 77 15 80; www.villarosmarino.com; Via Figari 38; d €230-290; ☀Mar-Nov; **P**❅☎⊛) Villa Rosmarino's motto is 'you don't stay, you live' and it's apt. Simply taking in the views here is life affirming. This elegant pink 1907 villa is a typical Ligurian beauty on the outside, a calming oasis of modernity on the inside.

Mario and Fulvio's collection of 20th-century furniture and contemporary artworks is scattered throughout the lounge, library and light-filled rooms. Despite the haute design credentials, there's a sensual warmth to it all. Even breakfasts – taken around the dining table – pop with colour and texture. The setting is sublimely tranquil but Camogli's bustle, and the beach, is just a 15-minute walk down a picturesque lane. Note prices in March and October drop substantially.

Hotel Cenobio dei Dogi
HOTEL **€€€**

(☎0185 72 41; www.cenobio.com; Via Cuneo 34; s €195, d €265-375; **P**❅☎⊛) The Cenobio's name means 'gathering place of the doges', and yes, the Genovese dukes used to holiday here aeons ago. A private beach and waterfront saltwater swimming pool signal you're in the Riviera, as do the 105 refined, if old-fashioned, rooms. Note, you'll pay a premium for a sea view.

✗ Eating & Drinking

Revello
BAKERY **€**

(☎0185 77 07 77; www.revellocamogli.com; Via Garibaldi 183; ☀8am-1pm & 3.30-7.30pm Mon-Fri, 8am-7.30pm Sat & Sun) If you're not on a mission to taste-test every town's *focacceria*, Revello is a suitably respectable choice if you had to choose just one. Pick up slices of their *focaccia di Recco* – a slightly flaky variety stuffed with stracchino cheese – or others topped with anchovies, fresh tomatoes and Ligurian olives, or go for the plainer sage or onion topped loaves.

★ La Cucina di Nonna Nina
TRATTORIA **€€**

(☎0185 77 38 55; www.nonnanina.it; Viale Franco Molfino 126, San Rocco di Camogli; meals €35-50; ☀12.30-2.30pm & 7.30-10pm Thu-Tue) 🖉 In the leafy heights of San Rocco di Camogli you'll find the only Slow Food–recommended restaurant along the coast, named for grand-

mother Nina, whose heirloom recipes have been adapted with love by Paolo Delphin. Your culinary odyssey will include fabulous traditional dishes such as air-dried cod stewed with pine nuts, potatoes and local Taggiasca olives, and *rossetti* (minnow) and artichoke soup.

Da Paolo
SEAFOOD, LIGURIAN **€€**

(☎0185 77 35 95; www.ristorantedapaolocamogli. com; Via San Fortunato 14; meals €40-48; ☀noon-2.30pm & 7.30-10.30pm Wed-Sun, 7.30-10.30pm Tue) Up a back lane from the waterfront, stylish Da Paolo has the town's best fish and seafood, all fresh off the boats and done in a variety of simple local styles. Order fish by the *etto* (100g) or plates of scampi or squid. Pastas include a fabulous fish ravioli.

La Mancina
BAR

(Via al Porto Camogli; ☀5pm-2am Thu-Tue) A couple of stools outside will give you a sea view, but the real action here is inside, where books line the walls and locals chat with the welcoming owner over *spritzes* or local wines.

ⓘ Information

Tourist Office (☎0185 77 10 66; www.camogliturismo.it; Via XX Settembre 33; ☀9.15am-12.15pm & 3.30-6.30pm Tue-Sat, from 10am Mon, 9.15am-12.15pm Sun) Has a list of diving schools and boat-rental operators.

ⓘ Getting There & Away

Camogli is on the Genoa–La Spezia train line, with regular connections to Santa Margherita (€2.55, five minutes), Rapallo (€2.55, 10 minutes) and Genoa (€3.60, 45 minutes).

The **Golfo Paradiso SNC** (☎0185 77 20 91; www.golfoparadiso.it; Via Piero Schiaffino 14) runs boats year-round to Punta Chiappa (one way/return €6/11) and San Fruttuoso (€9/14). Between April and September there are services to Genoa's Porto Antico (€15/23), Portofino (€11/19) and Cinque Terre (€20/31).

Portofino

☎0185 / POP 440

Even the trees are handsome in Portofino, a small but perfectly coiffured coastal village that sits on its own peninsula, seemingly upping the exclusivity factor by mere geography. Hotels here are hushed and heavily priced, but a drink by Portofino's yacht-filled harbour or a stroll around its designer shops can be easily enjoyed on a day trip from Genoa.

WORTH A TRIP

SAN FRUTTUOSO

San Fruttuoso is a slice of ancient tranquillity preserved among some of Italy's busiest coastal resorts. Its blissful isolation means you have only two transport options: foot or sea.

Come here with the lucky Ligurians to swim, sunbake and eat a seafood lunch in the sun. You can also wander the hamlet's sensitively restored Benedictine abbey. The **Abbazia di San Fruttuoso di Capodimonte** (www.visitfai.it/sanfruttuoso; adult/reduced €6.50/3; ⊙10am-5.45pm summer, to 3.45pm winter) was built as a final resting place for Bishop St Fructuosus of Tarragona, martyred in Spain in AD 259, then rebuilt in the mid-13th century with the assistance of the Doria family. The abbey fell into decay with the decline of the religious community; by the 19th century it was divided into small living quarters. Today it has a calm simplicity and its charming everyday collection of ancient monkish things feels touchingly close and human. It's also the only place you can sleep here. One rustic apartment, the **Casa de Mar** (Foresteria dell'Abbazia, ✆041 522 24 81; www.landmarktrust.org.uk/italia; 4-bed apt 4 nights €785), is located within the Abbey compound. Once the last boat leaves you're pretty much alone; basic pantry items are provided, although nightly meals can be arranged in advance with one of the beach-side restaurants. There's a thrilling sense of isolation, unbroken silence and gentle beauty. Bookings are done via email only (four-night minimum) or through the English Landmark organisation.

Walk in from Camogli (a tricky, rocky hike with metal hand supports) or Portofino, a steep but easier 5km cliffside walk. Both hikes take about 2½ hours one way. Alternatively, you can catch a boat from Camogli (one way/return €9/14), Punta Chiappa (€6/11) and, in summer, Genoa (€12/21).

◉ Sights & Activites

Castello Brown CASTLE
(www.castellobrown.com; Via alla Penisola 13a; admission €5; ⊙10am-7pm summer, to 5pm Sat & Sun winter) A flight of stairs signposted 'Salita San Giorgio' leads from the harbour and past the **Chiesa di San Giorgio** to Portofino's unusual castle, a 10-minute walk altogether (do confirm it's open with the tourist office (p182) before setting out, as the castle often closes for private events). The Genoese-built bulwark saw action against the Venetians, Savoyards, Sardinians and Austrians, and later fell to Napoleon.

**Parco Naturale
Regionale di Portofino** HIKING
(www.parks.it/parco.portofino) The Portofino peninsula's 60km of narrow trails are a world away from the sinuous sports-car-lined road from Santa Margherita. Many of them are absolutely remote and all of them free of charge. The tourist office (p182) has maps.

A good but tough day hike (there are some super-exposed sections) is the 18km coastal route from Camogli to Santa Margherita via San Fruttuoso and Portofino. There are handy train connections at both ends.

🛏 Sleeping

**Eight Hotels
Paraggi** HOTEL €€€
(✆0185 28 99 61; http://paraggi.eighthotels.it; Via Paraggi a Mare 8; d €480-750; 🖭🖥) This low-key hotel has simple, luxurious rooms, but its real appeal is the location. Right on the perfect crescent of Paraggi beach, there's a sense of calm here that can be elusive around the cove in Portofino proper. Such beauty doesn't come cheap, however: rooms with balconies start at €690 per night.

Eden BOUTIQUE HOTEL €€€
(✆0185 26 90 91; www.hoteledenportofino.com; Vico Dritto 18; s €80-160, d €180-250; 🅿🖭) Pretty and unpretentious Eden feels like it slipped out of an EM Forster novel or a grunge fashion spread. Its floral wallpaper residence-hotel appeal is coupled with a great location, 100m up a quiet cobbled side street from the harbour.

🍴 Eating & Drinking

Pizzeria El Portico PIZZA €
(✆0185 26 92 39; Via Roma 21; meals €25; ⊙noon-10pm Wed-Mon) Wander a block from the harbour and pizzas can be procured for under €10. You can also enjoy dishes such as

octopus salad, *vongole* (clams) and Genovese favourites on chequered tablecloths outside.

Ristorante Puny
LIGURIAN €€

(☑ 0185 26 90 37; Piazza Martiri dell'Olivetta; meals €38-45; ⊘ noon-3pm & 7-11pm Wed-Fri) Puny's harbourside location is the one you've come to Portofino for and the owners treat *everyone* like they're a visiting celeb. The food sticks loyally to Ligurian specialities, especially seafood.

Caffè Excelsior
LIGURIAN €€

(☑ 0185 26 90 05; www.excelsiorportofino.it; Piazza Martiri dell'Olivetta 54; meals €28-35; ⊘ 8am-11pm Wed-Mon) A fashionable eatery overlooking the port, Caffè Excelsior is a good perch with romantic outdoor booths – where Greta Garbo used to hide behind dark glasses – serving up octopuses and prawns.

Winterose
WINE BAR

(☑ 0323 207 09 65; www.winteroseportofino. it; Calata Marconi 42; ⊘ 10am-8pm) A serious wine shop with simple tables right on the waterfront for your nightly *aperitivo*. It's a yachties' favourite.

ℹ️ Information

Tourist Office (www.marinadiportofino.com; Via Roma 35; ⊘ 10am-6pm summer, 10am-1pm & 2-4.30pm Tue-Sun winter) Has free trail maps for the Parco Naturale Regionale di Portofino (p181) and information on mountain-bike rental, as well as seasonal sail- and motorboat-rental.

ℹ️ Getting There & Away

ATP (www.atp-spa.it) bus 882 runs to Portofino from outside the tourist office in Santa Margherita (€1.80, every 30 minutes), but by far the best way is to walk. A designated path tracks the gorgeous coastline for 3km.

From April to October, **Servizio Marittimo del Tigullio** (www.traghettiportofino.it) runs daily ferries from Portofino to/from San Fruttuoso (one way/return €8.50/12), Rapallo (€9/13) and Santa Margherita (€7/11). Golfo Paradiso (www. golfoparadiso.it) also has a regular service from Camogli (€11/19).

Motorists can only park in the car park at the village entrance, with fees starting from €8 per hour (cash only).

Santa Margherita

☑ 0185 / POP 10,100

Santa Margherita materialises like a calm Impressionist painting. You wouldn't want to change a single detail of its picture-perfect seaside promenade, where elegant hotels with Liberty facades overlook yachts in this fishing village turned retirement spot. It's decidedly less bling than Portofino, with some affordable hotel options and a surprisingly workaday town behind the waterfront.

Villa Durazzo
VILLA, GARDEN

(www.villadurazzo.it; Piazzale San Giacomo 3; ⊘ 9am-1pm & 2.30-6.30pm) FREE This exquisitely turned-out mansion and gardens, part of a 16th-century castle complex, overlooks the sea. You can take an aromatic stroll among lemon trees, hydrangea and camellia hedges, and other flora typical of the town's mild climate in the lavish Italian gardens, or wander among its recently restored collection of 17th-century paintings.

Santuario di Nostra Signora della Rosa
CHURCH

(Piazza Caprera) You'll gasp audibly when entering Santa Margherita's small yet lavish baroque church, not just at the truly dazzling array of gold leaf, frescoes, chandeliers and stained glass, but also at the sheer serendipity of it being here at all.

★ Blu di Te House
BOUTIQUE HOTEL €€€

(☑ 0185 28 71 87; www.bludite.com; Via Favale 30; s/d €250/320; P❄🖥) Once a rambling old Ligurian villa, the Blu di Te now has 20 clean-lined rooms. Colours echo the Ligurian landscape and there is a combination of mid-century classics and more traditional pieces scattered across the hotel. A rooftop terrace overlooks a baroque church and treetops to the blue of the gulf.

Grand Hotel Miramare
HISTORIC HOTEL €€€

(☑ 0185 28 70 13; www.grandhotelmiramare.it; Via Milite Ignoto 30; s/d €310/430; P❄🖥🏊) The Miramare, which looks back over to the town across the Gulf of Tigullio, feels from another time, the antithesis of vulgarity. Staff are gracious, public spaces are elegant, facilities are plentiful and rooms are soothing. While it's much in the grand European tradition, it also has a friendly, relaxed vibe and a surprisingly youthful clientele, including families.

Pasticceria Oneto
CAFE €

(Via Partigiani d'Italia 3; cakes from €1.50; ⊘ 8am-8pm) Busy *pasticceria* (pastry shop) and cafe populated by locals who pop in for brioche and seasonal tarts, and linger with an espresso.

L'Altro Eden
SEAFOOD €€

(☑ 0185 29 30 56; www.laltro.ristoranteeden.com; Calata del Porto 11; meals €40-55; ⊙ noon-11.30pm Mon-Fri, noon-2.30pm & 7-11.30pm Sat & Sun) A seafood place right on the docks, yes, but this grey-and-white streamlined vaulted space is a maritime kitsch-free zone. Romantic and cosy on colder evenings, outside tables are right by the boats in summer. Fish is done by weight and to order, but they are best known for *crudo* and risotto with fresh prawns or, in season, squid ink.

❶ Information

Parco Naturale Regionale di Portofino (www.parks.it/parco.portofino; Viale Rainusso 1; ⊙ 9am-1pm Mon-Fri) Maps and information on hiking.

Tourist Office (www.lamialiguria.it; Piazza Vittorio Veneto; ⊙ 9.30am-noon & 2.30-5.30pm Mon-Sat) Keeps lots of information about water sports along the gulf.

❶ Getting There & Away

ATP Tigullio Trasporti (www.atpesercizio.it) runs buses to/from Portofino (every 20 minutes) and Camogli (every 30 minutes), both with the Portofino Pass one way/return €4/6.

By train, there are fast hourly services to/from Genoa (€8.50, 30 minutes) and La Spezia (€10, one hour).

Servizio Marittimo del Tigullio (www.traghettiportofino.it) runs seasonal ferries to/from Cinque Terre (one way/return €22.50/34), Porto Venere (€22.50/34), San Fruttuoso (€11/16), Portofino (€8.50/12) and Rapallo (€4.50/5.50).

Rapallo

☑ 0185 / POP 30,750

WB Yeats, Max Beerbohm and Ezra Pound all garnered inspiration in Rapallo and it's not difficult to see why. With its bright-blue changing cabins, palm-fringed beach and diminutive 16th-century castle perched above the sea, the town has a poetic and nostalgic air. It's at its busiest on Thursdays, when market stalls fill central Piazza Cile.

✈ Activities

Cable Car
CABLE CAR

(☑ 0185 5 23 41; http://doganaccia2000.it; Piazzale Solari 2; one way/return €7/10; ⊙ 9am-12.30pm & 2-6pm) When you've had your fill of the promenade poseurs, rise above them in a 1934-vintage cable car up to **Santuario Basilica di Montallegro** (612m), built on the spot where, in 1557, the Virgin Mary was reportedly sighted. Walkers and mountain bikers can follow an old mule track (5km, 1½ hours) to the hilltop site.

🛏 Sleeping

Europa Hotel Design Spa 1877
HOTEL €€

(☑ 0185 66 95 21; www.gruppoplinio.it/europahotel; Via Milite Ignoto 2; s €95-180, d €160-225; 🅿 ❄ 🌐) Close to the beach and with its own spa facilities – a thermal bath and steam room – this recently refurbished place is super relaxing. Whitewashed rooms are pretty but modern while public areas do the shiny Italian glam thing.

✕ Eating

Bansin
TRATTORIA €

(☑ 0185 23 11 19; www.trattoriabansin.it; Via Venezia 105; meals €17-25; ⊙ noon-2pm & 7.15-10.30pm, closed Sun lunch summer & Mon lunch winter) Ligurian comfort food – salt cod fritters, chickpea soup, spinach-stuffed pasta with walnut sauce, mussels gratin – gets served up here with a minimum of fuss and not just a little bit of love. Lunch menus, with two courses and house wine or water, are €10 or with just a first course and side for €5, and there's a garden courtyard in summer.

★ uGiancu
OSTERIA, LIGURIAN €€

(☑ 0185 26 05 05; www.ugiancu.it; Via San Massimo 78; meals €32-45; ⊙ 7.30-10.30pm Thu-Tue, noon-3pm Sun Dec-Oct) About 5km inland in the hamlet of San Massimo di Rapallo, this cult restaurant is run by comic-book collector Fausto Oneto, and half of his collection decorates the walls. Away from the coast, the cooking focuses on meat and vegetables, including an incredibly succulent herb-battered suckling lamb with field greens from the kitchen gardens.

Vecchia Rapallo
SEAFOOD €€

(☑ 0185 5 00 53; www.vecchiarapallo.com; Via Cairoli 20/24; meals €30-45; ⊙ noon-2.30pm & 6-11pm summer, shorter hours winter) Seafood is the star here, and it's done well with the occasional creative touch. House-made stuffed pastas have particular appeal – snapper ravioli comes with beetroot and prawn sauce, while a chard-filled variety is shaved with truffles. There's a cocktail and wine bar if you're just after a drink, too.

ⓘ Information

Tourist Office (☏ 0185 23 03 46; www. lamialiguria.it; Lungomare Vittorio Veneto 7; ⊙ 9.30am-12.30pm & 2.30-5.30pm Mon-Sat) Details of walks in the area, plus maps.

Cinque Terre

Set amid some of the most dramatic coastal scenery on the planet, these five ingeniously constructed fishing villages can bolster the most jaded of spirits. A Unesco World Heritage Site since 1997, Cinque Terre isn't the undiscovered Eden it once was but, frankly, who cares? Sinuous paths traverse seemingly impregnable cliffsides, while a 19th-century railway line cut through a series of coastal tunnels ferries the footsore from village to village. Thankfully cars were banned over a decade ago.

Rooted in antiquity, Cinque Terre's five villages date from the early medieval period and while much of this fetching vernacular architecture remains, Cinque Terre's unique historical draw is the steeply terraced cliffs bisected by a system of fields and gardens that have been hacked, chiselled, shaped and layered over the course of nearly two millennia. The extensive *muretti* (low stone walls) can be compared to the Great Wall of China in their grandeur and scope.

🏃 Activities

Since the 2011 floods, many of Cinque Terre's walking paths have been in a delicate state and prone to periodic or permanent closure. At the time of writing only half of the iconic Sentiero Azzurro was open. However, Cinque Terre has a whole network of spectacular trails and you can still plan a decent village-to-village hike by choosing from any of 30 numbered paths, although bear in mind that this can add quite a few kilometres onto your walk. Check ahead for the most up-to-date trail information at www. parconazionale5terre.it/sentieri_parco.asp.

★ Sentiero Rosso   HIKING

Just a few kilometres shy of a full-blown marathon, the 38km Sentiero Rosso (Red Trail; marked No 1 on maps) – which runs from Porto Venere to Levanto – dangles a tempting challenge to experienced walkers who aim to complete it in nine to 12 hours.

For every 100 people you see on the Sentiero Azzurro, there are less than a dozen up here plying their way along a route that is mainly flat, tree-covered and punctuated with plenty of shortcuts. An early start is assured by an efficient train and bus connection to Porto Venere (via La Spezia), while refreshments en route are possible in a liberal smattering of welcoming bars and restaurants.

Cinque Terre

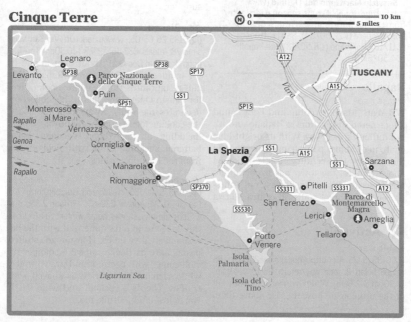

★ **Sentiero Azzurro**   WALKING

(Blue Trail; admission with Cinque Terre card) The Sentiero Azzurro (Blue Trail; marked No 2 on maps), a 12km old mule path that once linked all five oceanside villages by foot, is Cinque Terre's blue-riband hike, narrow and precipitous. The trail dates back to the early days of the Republic of Genoa in the 12th and 13th centuries and, until the opening of the railway line in 1874, it was the only practical means of getting from village to village.

At the time of writing, the path between Riomagiorre and Manarola (the famed via dell'Amore) and that between Manarola and Corniglia were closed and will possibly remain so until at least 2019. Only very experienced and well-equipped hikers should attempt the current alternative route from Manarola to Corniglia via Volastra.

ℹ Information

Parco Nazionale Offices (www.parconazion alebterre.it; ☺ 8am-8pm summer, 8.30am-12.30pm & 1-5pm winter) Offices in the train stations of all five villages and La Spezia station; has comprehensive information about hiking trail closures.

ℹ Getting There & Away

BOAT

In summer the **Golfo Paradiso SNC** (☏ 0185 77 20 91; www.golfoparadiso.it) runs boats to Cinque Terre from Genoa (one way/return €21/36). Seasonal boat services to/from Santa Margherita (€22.50/34) are handled by the Servizio Marittimo del Tigullio (www.traghetti portofino.it).

CAR & MOTORCYCLE

Private vehicles are not allowed beyond village entrances and during high volume days roads between villages can be closed. If you're arriving by car or motorcycle, you'll need to pay to park in designated car parks (€12 to €25 per day) though these are often full. In some villages, minibus shuttles depart from the car parks (one way/return €1.50/2.50) – park offices have seasonal schedules.

TRAIN

Between 6.30am and 10pm, one to three trains an hour trundle along the coast between Genoa and La Spezia, stopping at each of Cinque Terre's villages (Trenitalia has renamed its usual service the Cinque Terre Express in summer). Unlimited 2nd-class rail travel between Levanto and La Spezia is covered by the Cinque Terre

---

ℹ THE CINQUE TERRE CARD

The best way to get around Cinque Terre is with a **Cinque Terre card**.

Two versions of the card are available: with or without train travel. Both include unlimited use of walking paths and electric village buses, as well as cultural exhibitions. The basic one-/two-day card for those aged over four years costs €7.50/14.50. With unlimited train trips between the towns, the card costs €12/23. A one-day family card for two adults and two children (under 12) costs €31.50/19.60 with/without train travel.

Both versions of the card are sold at all Cinque Terre park information offices and each of Cinque Terre's train stations. For those not interested in hiking, an all-day train ticket between villages is also good value at €4.

Train card (one/two day €16/29), or you can buy a €4 ticket for travel between any two villages. The IC train from La Spezia is €8 to €10 one way; the slower regional €3.10.

Monterosso

♫ 0187 / POP 1500

The most accessible village by car and the only Cinque Terre settlement to sport a proper stretch of beach, the westernmost Monterosso is the least quintessential of the quintet. The village, known for its lemon trees and anchovies, is delightful. Split in two, its new and old halves are linked by an underground tunnel that burrows beneath the blustery San Cristoforo promontory.

◉ Sights & Activites

Convento dei Cappuccini   CHURCH

(Salita San Cristoforo) Monterosso's most interesting church and convent complex is set on the hill that divides the old town from the newer Fegina quarter. The striped church, the **Chiesa di San Francesco**, dates from 1623 and has a painting attributed to Van Dyck *(Crocifissione)* to the left of the altar. The convent welcomes casual visitors but also has a program of spiritual retreats and workshops.

1. Terraced fields, Manarola (p190) **2.** Vernazza (p188)
3. Manarola **4.** Riomaggiore (p191)

SERGIOET/SHUTTERSTOCK ©

2 # Cinque Terre

Climb above the crowds on Cinque Terre's terraced cliffs and you might have to pinch yourself to check that you're still in the 21st century. Rooted in antiquity and bereft of modern interferences, these five historic fishing villages have embellished the Ligurian coastline with subtle human beauty and a fascinating medieval heritage.

Terraced Fields

Cinque Terre's cleverly cultivated cliff terraces are so old no one truly knows who built them. Held in place by hundreds of kilometres of dry stone walls, they add a strange human beauty to a stunning natural landscape.

Manarola

Grapes grow abundantly on Cinque Terre's terraced plots, especially around the village of Manarola (p190). The area's signature wine is the sweet white Sciacchetrà, a blend of Bosco, Albarola and Vermentino grapes best sampled with cheese or sweet desserts.

4

Riomaggiore

The pleasantly peeling medieval houses of the unofficial capital (p191) are tucked into a steep ravine. Jump on a boat to best experience one of the Cinque Terre's most iconic views: the warm pastel glow of Riomaggiore's pastel facades as the sun sets.

Vernazza

Sporting the best natural harbour of the five towns, Vernazza (p188) rises tightly from its central square. Its tightly clustered streets and lanes are a labyrinth of steep, switchback stairs rewarding the strong of thigh with stunning sea views from a cluster of handkerchief-sized terraces.

TURIN, PIEDMONT & THE ITALIAN RIVIERA CINQUE TERRE

Monterosso to Santuario della Madonna di Soviore   WALKING

From Via Roma in the village, follow trail 9 up through forest and past the ruins of an old hexagonal chapel to an ancient paved mule path that leads to Soviore, Liguria's oldest sanctuary dating from the 11th century. Here you'll find a bar, restaurant and views as far as Corsica on a clear day. It's a two-hour trip.

🛏 Sleeping

Hotel La Spiaggia   HOTEL €€

(☎0187 81 75 67; www.laspiaggiahotel.com; Via Lungomare 98; d €175-195; ❄️🖥️📶) Welcoming La Spiaggia is right on Monterosso's *spiaggia* (beach) and its 20 largish rooms are popular – book early (up to six months in advance). If you don't get lucky with the fabulous views of the sea-facing rooms, console yourself with a back one with terraces instead. The 1st floor rooms have been recently refurbished.

La Poesia   B&B €€

(☎0187 81 72 83; www.lapoesia-cinqueterre.com; Via Genova 4; d €170; ❄️📶) Shoehorned up a backstreet in the older part of town, La Poesia's three rooms occupy an early-17th-century house, where breakfast is served on a terrace surrounded by lemon trees. It's very old-fashioned but it remains open over the winter.

★ La Sosta di Ottone III   BOUTIQUE HOTEL €€€

(☎0187 81 45 02; www.lasosta.com; Località Chiesanuova 39, Levanto; d €220-250; ⊙Apr-Oct; 🅿️📶) Up in the hills between the beautiful, almost Cinque Terre, beach town of Levanto and Monterosso, La Sosta di Ottone III is a lovely hideaway that's also in prime position for striking out to Cinque Terre by foot or car. The owners have revitalised a village house with extreme attention to detail that also feels effortless.

Six rooms all have delicious hill and sea views but each is different. Four have rich painterly tones and beams, two are airy and minimal. Everything here is hyper-local, from the beautiful patchwork curtains in the lobby made of local damask and the Chiavari chairs to other antiques and even the marble used in the stylish, sexy bathrooms. You can eat here too – there's a perfectly sitting-ed small restaurant that serves simple but carefully prepared Ligurian classics.

Hotel Pasquale   HOTEL €€€

(☎0187 81 74 77; www.hotelpasquale.it; Via Fegina 4; s/d/tr €170/255/340; ⊙Mar-Nov; ❄️📶) Offering soothing views and 15 unusually stylish, modern guest rooms, this friendly seafront hotel is built into Monterosso's medieval sea walls. To find it, exit the train station and go left through the tunnel towards the *centro storico* (historic centre). Room prices drop outside the main summer months to a far more reasonable €140 for a double.

🍴 Eating

Trattoria da Oscar   TRATTORIA €€

(Via Vittorio Emanuele 67; meals €25-30; ⊙noon-2pm & 7-10pm) Behind Piazza Matteoti, in the heart of the old town, this vaulted dining room is run by a young, friendly team and attracts a strong local crowd. The town's famed anchovies dominate the menu; whether you go for the standard fried with lemon, with a white wine sauce or deep fried, they are all good. There's some lovely laneway tables too. No credit cards.

Ristorante Belvedere   SEAFOOD €€

(☎0187 81 70 33; www.ristorante-belvedere.it; Piazza Garibaldi 38; meals €30; ⊙noon-3pm & 6.15-10.30pm Wed-Mon) With tables overlooking the beach, this unpretentious seafood restaurant is a good place to try the local bounty. Start with *penne con scampi* (pasta tubes with scampi) before diving into a rich *zuppa di pesce* (fish soup). Or partake of their speciality, the amphora Belvedere, where lobsters, mussels, clams, octopus and swordfish are stewed in a herb-scented broth in traditional earthenware.

Miky   SEAFOOD €€€

(☎0187 81 76 08; www.ristorantemiky.it; Lungomare Fegina 104; meals €45-65; ⊙noon-2.30pm & 7-10pm Wed-Mon summer) If you're looking for something a little more elegant than a seafront fry-up, Miky does a seasonal fish menu in a moody, modern dining room. Booking ahead is advised. If you miss out on a table, casual beach-side tables are available at its *cantina* (wine bar); ask for directions.

Vernazza

 0187 / POP 1000

Vernazza's small harbour – the only secure landing point on the Cinque Terre coast – guards what is perhaps the quaintest, and steepest, of the five villages. Lined with little cafes, a main cobbled street (Via Roma) links seaside Piazza Marconi with the train station. Side streets lead to the village's trademark Genoa-style *caruggi* (narrow lanes), where sea views pop at every turn.

⊙ Sights & Activties

Castello Doria
CASTLE
(entrance fee €1.50; ⊙10am-7pm summer, to 6pm winter) This castle, the oldest surviving fortification in Cinque Terre, commands superb views. Dating to around 1000, it's now largely a ruin except for the circular tower in the centre of the esplanade. To get there, head up the steep, narrow staircase by the harbour.

Chiesa di Santa Margherita d'Antiochia
CHURCH
(Piazza Matteotti) The waterfront is framed by this small Gothic-Ligurian church, built in 1318, part of a murky legend about the bones of St Margaret being found in a wooden box on a nearby beach. It is notable for its 40m-tall octagonal tower.

Vernazza Winexperience
WINE
(Deck Giani Franzi; ☑331 3433801; www.vernazzawinexperience.com; Via San Giovanni Battista 41; ⊙5-9pm Apr-Oct) Sommelier Alessandro Villa's family have lived in Vernazza for over six generations. Let him take you through the rare, small-yield wines that come from the vineyards that tumble down the surrounding hills. While the wine and stupendous sunset view will be pleasure enough, knowing you're also helping keep a unique landscape and culture alive feels good.

Vernazza to Santuario della Madonna di Reggio
WALKING
From underneath Vernazza's railway bridge, follow trail 8 up numerous flights of steps and past 14 sculpted Stations of the Cross to an 11th-century chapel with a Romanesque facade. It's approximately a 45-minute walk.

🛏 Sleeping

★La Mala
BOUTIQUE HOTEL €€
(☑334 2875718; www.lamala.it; Via San Giovanni Battista 29; d €160-220; ❋🅰) These four rooms are some of Cinque Terre's nicest. Up in the cliffside heights of the village, they are in a typical Ligurian house that's run by the grandson of the original owner. The fit out is a clean-lined contemporary one, providing both comfort and a place to soak in some fabulous sea views, either from bed or a sunny terrace.

Gianni Franzi Rooms
B&B €€
(☑0187 82 10 03; www.giannifranzi.it; Via San Giovanni Battista 41; d €130; 🅰) Spread over two locations, one above the attached restaurant, the other up the hill, rooms here are an atmospheric mix of antique furniture and simple traditional architecture, all kept with care. Breakfast on their deck delivers not just *cornetti* (Italian croissant) and cappuccino, but sublime sea-drenched views; there's a small garden under the Doria castle for guest use.

🍴 Eating & Drinking

Batti Batti
FAST FOOD €
(Via Visconti 3; focaccia €3.50-6, seafood €9-14) Batti Batti knocks out the best focaccia slices in the village (some would say in all of Cinque Terre), along with bountifully topped pizza. Their *friggitoria*, a few shops down, turns out *fritto misto* (fried seafood) to take away in paper cones.

Gianni Franzi
SEAFOOD €€
(☑0187 82 10 03; www.giannifranzi.it; Piazza Matteotti 5; meals €22-35; ⊙mid-Mar–early Jan) Traditional Cinque Terre seafood (mussels, seafood, ravioli and lemon anchovies) has been served up in this harbourside trattoria since the 1960s. When it comes to seafood this fresh, if it's not broken, don't fix it.

Gambero Rosso
SEAFOOD €€
(☑0187 81 22 65; www.ristorantegamberorosso.net; Piazza Marconi 7; meals €35-45; ⊙noon-3pm & 7-10pm Fri-Wed) If you've been subsisting on focaccia, Gambero's house specials – *tegame di Vernazza* (anchovies with baked potatoes and tomatoes), skewered baby octopus or stuffed mussels – will really hit the spot. Bookings recommended.

Burgus Bar
WINE BAR
(Piazza Marconi 4; ⊙7am-1am) A charming hole-in-the-wall, with only a couple of ringside benches looking over Piazza Marconi to the little beach, this bar serves up glasses of the fragrant, ethereal mix of local Albarola, Bosco and Vermentino grapes that is Cinque Terre DOC. They also do breakfast pastries, sandwiches and *aperitivo*, and stock a range of local produce to take away.

Corniglia

☑0187 / POP 150

Corniglia is the 'quiet' middle village that sits atop a 100m-high rocky promontory surrounded by vineyards. It is the only Cinque

TURIN, PIEDMONT & THE ITALIAN RIVIERA CINQUE TERRE

Terre settlement with no direct sea access, although steep steps lead down to a rocky cove. Narrow alleys and colourfully painted four-storey houses characterise the ancient core, a timeless streetscape that was name-checked in Boccaccio's *Decameron*. To reach the village proper from the railway station you must first tackle the **Lardarina**, a 377-step brick stairway, or jump on a shuttle bus (one way €2.50, free with the Cinque Terre card).

◉ Sights & Activities

Belvedere di Santa Maria   VIEWPOINT
Enjoy dazzling 180-degree sea views at this heart-stopping lookout in hilltop Corniglia. To find it, follow Via Fieschi through the village until you eventually reach the clifftop balcony.

Guvano Beach   BEACH
This hard-to-find, clothing-optional beach is situated between Cornigla and Vernazza. Getting there involves walking through an abandoned railway tunnel; best ask a local for directions.

Santuario della
Madonna delle Grazie   WALKING
This sanctuary can be approached from either Corniglia (on trail 7b) or Vernazza (trail 7), both take around an hour. The latter is considered more scenic. Branch off the Sentiero Azzurro and ascend the spectacular Sella Comeneco to the village of San Bernardino, where you'll find the church with its adored image of Madonna and child above the altar.

⌒ Sleeping

★ 3 Passi dal Mare   B&B €
(www.vernazzani5terre.it/it/camere-corniglia; Via Fieschi 204; s/d €70/90; 🛜) Four appealingly simple, rustic rooms all have spectacular views, including the single room, and two have terraces. Private bathrooms are new, if basic, and breakfast is taken in the town's best bar La Scuna. A rare find.

Case di Corniglia   APARTMENT €
(☑ 0187 81 23 42; www.casedicorniglia.eu; Via alla Stazione 19; apt €90-180; 🅿🛜) These rent-a-rooms are spread over two buildings in the village's main street. All have kitchens; they're good for families or groups. Some of them are cutely called 'nonna 1', 'nonna 2' etc – which gives you an idea of the decor. If you

can snare one with a terrace, you're in for some great views.

Ostello di Corniglia   HOSTEL €
(☑ 0187 81 25 59; www.ostellocorniglia.com; Via alla Stazione 3; dm/d €24/60; 🛜) One of only two hostels in Cinque Terre, Ostello di Corniglia is perched at the top of the village and has two eight-bed dorms and four doubles (with private bathroom). Prices are negotiable. There's a lockout from 1pm to 3pm. No breakfast.

🍸 Drinking & Nightlife

★ La Scuna   BAR
(☑ 347 7997527; Via Fieschi 185; ⊘ 9am-1am late-March–Nov) Vinyl, beer *and* a panoramic terrace? This bastion of hipsterdom comes as a surprise in this most traditional of regions but the welcome is warm and the beers on tap are both cold and a cut way above bottled Peroni.

Manarola
☑ 0187 / POP 850

Bequeathed with more grapevines than any other Cinque Terre village, Manarola is famous for its sweet Sciacchetrà wine. It's also awash with priceless medieval relics, supporting claims that it is the oldest of the five. The spirited locals here speak an esoteric local dialect known as Manarolese. Due to its proximity to Riomaggiore (852m away), the village is heavily trafficked, especially by Italian school parties along with the regular tourists.

◉ Sights & Activities

Punta Bonfiglio   VIEWPOINT
Manarola's prized viewpoint is on a rocky promontory on the path out of town towards Corniglia where walkers stop for classic photos of the village. A rest area, including a kids' playground, has been constructed here and there's also a bar just below. Nearby are the ruins of an old chapel once used as a shelter by local farmers.

Manarola to Santuario
della Madonna delle Salute   WALKING
The pick of all the sanctuary walks is this breathtaking traverse (trail 6) through Cinque Terre's finest vineyards to a diminutive Romanesque-meets-Gothic chapel in the tiny village of Volastra. It takes around 30 minutes.

🛏 Sleeping

Ostello 5 Terre
HOSTEL €

(📞0187 92 00 39; www.hostel5terre.com; Via Riccobaldi 21; dm/d/f €28/80/120; ⊙closed mid-Jan–mid-Feb; @📶) Manarola's hostel sits at the top of the village next to the Chiesa di San Lorenzo. It has single-sex, six-bed dorms, each with their own bathroom and great views, and several double and family rooms. It has its own bright and stylish little restaurant and a terrace for evening drinks.

Hotel Marina Piccola
BOUTIQUE HOTEL €€

(📞0187 92 07 70; www.hotelmarinapiccola.com; s/d/tr €125/145/190, ste €160; ❄📶) This choice Manarola hotel has 12 big, comfortable, contemporary rooms, with a few looking over the sea. The lovely lobby and lounge area, which sports a surprisingly on-trend interior, is a welcome respite from the busy day-time streets. A real find at this price, although there is a minimum two-day stay in summer.

Hotel Ca' d'Andrean
HOTEL €€

(📞0187 92 00 40; www.cadandrean.it; Via Doscovolo 101, Manarola; s €100, d €140-160; ⊙Mar–mid-Nov; ❄📶) An excellent family-run hotel in the upper part of Manarola. Rooms are large with soothing, stylish white-grey tones and slick bathrooms; some have private terraces. Breakfast (€7) is optional. No credit cards.

★ La Torretta Lodge
BOUTIQUE HOTEL €€€

(📞0187 92 03 27; www.torrettas.com; Vico Volto 20; d/ste €250/550; ❄❄) Sitting high up above the village, a collection of both private and public terraces command spectacular views while decor differs in each of the rooms, with a seductive Italian maximalist mash of contemporary pieces, mosaic tiles, antiques, murals and unexpected surprises such as a dedicated toilet TV.

🍴 Eating

Il Porticciolo
SEAFOOD €€

(📞0187 92 00 83; www.ilporticciolo5terre.it; Via Renato Birolli 92; meals €28-37; ⊙11.30am-11pm) One of several restaurants lining the main route down to the harbour, this is a popular spot for an alfresco seafood feast. Expect seaside bustle and a fishy menu featuring classic crowd-pleasers such as spaghetti with mussels and crispy fried squid.

Marina Piccola
SEAFOOD €€

(📞0187 76 20 65; www.hotelmarinapiccola.com; Via Lo Scalo 16; meals €30; ⊙noon-10.30pm Wed-Mon; ❄📶) A number of fish dishes, including some tasty antipasti such as *soppressata di polpo* (sliced boiled octopus) are served up here along with right-by-the-sea views. There's a great list of Cinque Terre DOCs from both the vines above and Vernazza, as well as some excellent Vermentinos.

Riomaggiore

📞 0187 / POP 1600

Cinque Terre's easternmost village, Riomaggiore, is the largest of the five and acts as its unofficial HQ (the main park office is based here). Its peeling pastel buildings march down a steep ravine to a tiny harbour – the region's favourite postcard view – and glow romantically at sunset. If you are driving, the hills between here and La Spezia are spectacular to explore.

👁 Sights & Activities

Fossola Beach
BEACH

This small pebbly beach is immediately southeast of Riomaggiore marina. It's rugged and delightfully secluded. Swimmers should be wary of currents here.

Riomaggiore to Santuario della Madonna di Montenero
WALKING

Trail 3 ascends for around an hour from the top of the village, up steps and past walled gardens to a restored 18th-century chapel with a frescoed ceiling, which sits atop an astounding lookout next to the park's new cycling centre.

Via dell'Amore
WALKING

This beautiful coastal path that links Riomaggiore to Manarola in a leisurely 20-minute stroll was, until rockslides caused its closure in 2012, Cinque Terre's most popular. The name is a nod to the number of marriages the opening of the path engendered between villagers of the once geographically divided hamlets.

The first 200m of the path, from Manarola's train station to Bar Via dell'Amore, has reopened and it's worth the brief stroll it allows. It's uncertain when the rest will be completed, with 2018 to 2019 a vaguely mooted date (much to the consternation of locals; the path is not just a scenic thoroughfare for them, but an integral part of village social life).

Cooperative Sub 5 Terre
DIVING

(📞0187 92 00 11; www.5terrediving.it; Via San Giacomo; ⊙10am-4pm Apr-Oct) To dive or snorkel in the translucent waters of the protected marine park, contact this outfit in the subway at the bottom of Via Colombo. It also rents out canoes and kayaks, but book ahead by phone as the office is not always attended.

🛏 Sleeping

Due Gemelli
HOTEL €

(✆0187 92 06 78; www.duegemelli.it; Via Litoranea 1; d €90, with half-board €130; P 🌐 🛜) Up the hill, 4km out of town on the way to La Spezia, this '60s hotel is in an utterly stunning location. Rooms are old-fashioned but clean and rather charming. The panoramic terrace is just that, there's a restaurant and bar, and you've got access to extraordinary hiking trails. Ask for a seafront, air-con room at no additional charge.

Hotel Zorza
HOTEL €€

(www.hotelzorza.com; Via Colombo 231; d €130; 🛜) Basic but well-kept rooms are spread across the sinuous 17th-century house of a former wine-grower.

Riomaggiore
Reservations
ACCOMMODATION SERVICES

(✆0187 76 05 75; www.riomaggiorereservations.com; Via Colombo 181) If you're looking for help with reservations, this company, run by a local and his American wife, has a large number of simple, but well-vetted properties and are super helpful and efficient to deal with.

🍴 Eating & Drinking

La Lampara
MODERN ITALIAN €

(Via Malborghetto 2; meals €20-28; ⊙10am-3pm, & 6.30-11pm Wed-Mon) There are always lots of tourists here but you won't feel like one as the service is so genuinely personable. Fish dishes predominate, though the pizza and pasta *al pesto* are also made with care.

Colle del Telegrafo
LIGURIAN €€

(✆0187 76 05 61; Località Colle del Telegrafo; meals €35-45; ⊙8am-8.30pm) Perched on a ridge south of Riomaggiore, where the old telegraph line used to be strung, the views from the Colle del Telegrafo are spectacular. But they don't overshadow the carefully prepared dishes of pasta with Cinque Terre cooperative pesto, white bean soup and super-fresh whitebait. During the day, join hikers for bolstering rounds of cake and espresso.

Dau Cila
SEAFOOD €€

(✆0187 76 00 32; www.ristorantedaucila.com; Via San Giacomo 65; meals €40-45; ⊙12.30-3pm & 7-10.30pm) Perched within pebble-lobbing distance of Riomaggiore's wee harbour, Dau Cila is a smart, kitsch-free zone, and specialises in classic seafood and hyper-local wines. Pair the best Cinque Terre whites with cold plates such as smoked tuna with apples and lemon, or lemon-marinated anchovies.

★ La Conchiglia
BAR

(✆0187 92 09 47; Via San Giacomo 149; ⊙8am-midnight) A fantastic find: down-to-earth, friendly and unflustered staff; a fantastic well-priced local wine list; absolute waterfront positions and a menu of big, healthy salads, *panini* and burgers if you've missed lunch or dinner service elsewhere. The shaded waterfront terrace upstairs is a delight.

Golfo dei Poeti
✆0187

Back when Cinque Terre was but a collection of remote hardscrabble fishing villages, the Golfo dei Poeti (Gulf of Poets) was drawing an it-crowd. Renamed for the English poets Lord Byron and Percy Bysshe Shelley, who escaped here in the 1820s, its natural beauty had inspired writers and artists as far back as Petrarch and Dante.

The port of La Spezia, Italy's largest naval base, is the main town and makes for a nicely urban, if supremely easygoing, base. Around each side of the bay, mountains loom on the horizon and cliffs plummet into the sea, and there's a deliciously remote feeling to the many forest-fringed sandy coves. Bumping up against Tuscany, there are the ridiculously beautiful, discrete resort towns of Lerici, San Terenzo and Tellaro, while at the other sits the historic sentinel village of Porto Venere. Each has its own charm, but all share the evocative vertiginous tumble of pastel houses.

La Spezia
✆0187 / POP 94,000

It's an understandable oversight. Situated minutes to the east of Cinque Terre by train, and sidling up to the exquisite Lerici and Tellaro, this hard-working port town and home to Italy's largest naval base is routinely overlooked. But it's not only an affordable place to overnight if you're heading to Cinque Terre, it's really worthy of at least a wander – the winding streets of the old town are hugely atmospheric and there are plenty of cosy trattorias showcasing the Ligurian kitchen's finest.

La Spezia's bustle peaks on 19 March, the **feast day** of the city's patron saint, San Giuseppe (St Joseph). Celebrations see a giant market fill the port and surrounding streets, and the naval base (off-limits the rest of the year) opens to the public.

◉ Sights

Museo Amedeo Lia   MUSEUM
(http://museolia.spezianet.it; Via Prione 234; adult/reduced €7/4.50, with temporary exhibition €10/7; ☉10am-6pm Tue-Sun) This fine-arts museum in a restored 17th-century friary is La Spezia's star cultural attraction. The collection spans from the 13th to 18th centuries and includes paintings by masters such as Tintoretto, Montagna, Titian and Pietro Lorenzetti. Also on show are Roman bronzes and ecclesiastical treasures, such as Limoges crucifixes and illuminated musical manuscripts.

⌂ Sleeping

Alta Marea   GUESTHOUSE €
(☑377 5448365; www.affittacamerealtamarea.it; Via Torino 70; d €110; ✳☎) Friendly Andrea will be there to greet you at this small B&B and can be counted on for his local knowledge and restaurant tips. Rooms are spotless, airy and bright, with wooden floors and signature graphic design, and the location is handy for making an early morning train to the Cinque Terre.

Albergo Birillo   HOTEL €
(☑0187 73 26 66; www.albergobirillo.it; Via Dei Mille 11/13; s/d €75/110; ☎) This haven has rather tight-fitting rooms, which are more than made up for by the ultrafriendly owners. It's a few blocks from Via Prione and near plenty of good places to eat.

✕ Eating & Drinking

Vicolo Intherno   MODERN ITALIAN €€
(www.vicolointherno.it; Via della Canonica 20; meals €28-36; ☉noon-3pm & 7pm-midnight Tue-Sat) 🌿 Take a seat around chunky wooden tables beneath beamed ceilings at this buzzing Slow Food–affiliated restaurant and wash down the *torte di verdure* (Ligurian vege-

table pie), stockfish or roast beef with local vintages.

Odioilvino   WINE BAR
(☑392 2141825; www.facebook.com/Odioilvino; Via Daniele Manin 11; ☉12.30-3.30pm & 6-11.30pm) A dark, bohemian, elegantly dishevelled wine bar on a pretty street in the pedestrian centre, Odioilvino is a fine place to relax with locals over a French or local wine. Small plates such as a fish tartare or octopus salad are on offer, too.

ⓘ Information

Cinque Terre Park Office (☑0187 74 35 00; ☉7am-8pm) Inside La Spezia's train station.
Tourist Office (www.myspezia.it; La Spezia Central Station; ☉9am-1pm)

ⓘ Getting There & Away

Buses run by Azienda Trasporti Consortile (www.atclaspezia.it) are the only way to reach Porto Venere (€2.50, approximately every 30 minutes) and Lerici (€2.50, approximately every 15 minutes); catch from Via Domenico Chiodo. Daily tickets (€7.50) are available.

La Spezia is on the Genoa–Rome railway line and is also connected to Milan (€26.50, three hours, four daily), Turin (€27.50, 3½ hours, several daily) and Pisa (€5.20, 50 minutes, almost hourly). Cinque Terre and other coastal towns are easily accessible by train and boat.

Porto Venere
☑0187 / POP 4100

Perched on the dreamy Golfo dei Poeti's western promontory, the historic fishing port's sinuous seven- and eight-storey harbourfront houses form an almost impregnable citadel around the muscular Castello Doria.

The Romans built Portus Veneris as a base en route from Gaul to Spain, and in later years the Byzantines, Lombards, Genovese and Napoleon all passed through here and made the most of its spectacular natural defences. Its appeal is, however, not just strategic, its beauty drawing the poet Byron who famously swam from the now collapsed Grotta Arpaia's rocky cove to San Terenzo to visit fellow poet Percy Shelley (it was to be renamed Grotta di Byron for him). The town remains a romantic, scenic place for a day trip, or a relaxing base for exploring the coast. Serene by comparison to its Cinque Terre neighbours, weekends and summer evenings do bring Ligurians from far and wide for the *passeggiata*.

★ Grotta di Byron   VIEWPOINT

(Grotta Arpaia) At the end of the quay, a Cinque Terre panorama unfolds from the rocky terraces of a cave formerly known as Grotta Arpaia. Lord Byron once swam across the gulf from here to Lerici to visit the resident Shelleys and despite the cave's collapse, the rocky terraces remain stunningly beautiful and suitably dishevelled and affecting.

To add to the frisson, know that traces of a pagan temple dedicated to Venus (hence a suggestion to the name 'Venere') have been uncovered here, as well as inside the black-and-white-marble Chiesa di San Pietro. Just off the promontory, you can see the tiny islands of **Palmaria**, **Tino** and **Tinetto**.

Chiesa di San Pietro   CHURCH

(www.parrocchiaportovenere.it) This stunning wind- and wave-lashed church, built in 1198 in Gothic style, stands on the ruins of a 5th-century palaeo-Christian church, with its extant floor still partially visible. Before its Christianisation, it was a Roman temple dedicated to the goddess Venus, born from the foam of the sea, from whom Porto Venere takes its name.

La Lanterna   B&B €

(☑ 0187 79 22 91; www.lalanterna-portovenere.it; Via Capellini 109; d/tr €100/150; ❄) Down by Porto Venere's picturesque harbourfront, this little guesthouse has just two homey rooms (there's also an option of a four-person apartment on request).

Anciua   STREET FOOD €

(☑ 331 7719605; Via Cappellini 40; snacks from €6; ⊙ 10am-7pm) A perfect spot to pick up something to snack on while dangling your feet in the drink, this is Ligurian street food made with love. Grab a *panini* stuffed with anchovies or cod and olive paste, or pick up a whole spinach pie (aka *torta*) for a picnic. The slabs of sweet, fragrant rice-pudding cake are also highly recommended.

❶ Information

Tourist Office (www.prolocoportovenere. it; Piazza Bastreri 7; ⊙10am-noon & 3-8pm Jun-Aug, to 6pm Thu-Tue Sep-May) Sells a couple of useful maps and has walking guides in English.

❶ Getting There & Away

Porto Venere is served by daily buses from La Spezia. Note that you can't park in the town during summer; a parking area is located just outside the town and a shuttle service (€1 per person) operates all day.

From late March to October, **Consorzio Maritimo Turistico Cinque Terre Golfo dei Poeti** (☑ 0187 73 29 87; www.navigazionegolfodeipoeti.it) sails from Porto Venere to/from Cinque Terre villages (all day, all stops €33, one way €24, afternoon-only ticket €25) and runs three-hour excursions to the islands of Palmaria, Tino and Tinetto (€13).

Lerici, San Terenzo & Tellaro

Magnolia, yew and cedar trees grow in the 1930s public gardens at Lerici, an exclusive retreat of terraced villas clinging to the cliffs along its beach, and in another age Byron and Shelley sought inspiration here.

From Lerici, a scenic 3km coastal stroll leads northwest to San Terenzo, a seaside village with a sandy beach and Genoese castle. The Shelleys lived in the waterfront Villa Magni (sadly closed to visitors) in the early 1820s and Percy drowned here when his boat sank off the coast in 1822, on an ill-fated return trip from Livorno.

Another coastal stroll or drive, 4km to the southeast, takes you past magnificent little bays to Tellaro, a fishing hamlet with pink-and-orange houses cluttered about narrow lanes and tiny squares. Sit on the rocks at the Chiesa San Giorgio and imagine an octopus ringing the church bells – which, according to legend, it did to warn the villagers of a Saracen attack.

⌶ Sleeping

Hotel Fiascherino   HOTEL €€

(☑ 0187 96 60 32; www.hotelfiascherino.it; Via Byron 13, Tellaro; d €140-170; P ❄ ☎ ☀) There's nothing remotely Riviera-fancy about this place, but there's an old-fashioned grace and charm that's beguiling. Rooms are simple with many vintage pieces and the location is a knockout. Breakfast overlooking a peaceful, forest-clad beach is a special treat.

Eco Del Mare   RESORT €€€

(☑ 0187 96 86 09; www.ecodelmare.it; Via Fiascherino 4, Tellaro; d €280-400; ⊙ May-Sep; P ☎) One of the Riviera's loveliest beaches is home to this exclusive, remote-seeming hotel and beach club. An insouciant boho glamour pervades here; rooms are deeply romantic, filled with an idiosyncratic mix of decor, muted crumpled linen and classical chairs, while the restaurant, despite the prices, gives off beach shack vibes.

Day guests are welcome: for €60 to €100 for two people, depending on the month, you'll get sun loungers and umbrellas.

✖ Eating & Drinking

RedFish Cafe   LIGURIAN €
(☑0187 966 86 68; Via Gramsci 22, Tellaro; meals €18-25; ⊙noon-2.15pm & 7.20-10pm Wed-Mon) You can sit in the little dining room of this busy place, but if it's a warm day try to snare one of their outside tables, half a block down the street on the port. There's a short menu of pastas – squid ink, seafood, pesto – and a far longer list of seafood dishes that can be had either as mains or tapas style.

These include octopus in creamed chickpeas, fried sardines and grilled prawns. Service is sweetly amicable.

Dei Pescatori   TRATTORIA, SEAFOOD €€
(☑0187 96 55 34; Via Andrea Doria 6, Lerici; meals €35; ⊙noon-2.30pm & 7.30-10.30pm Tue-Sun) Located in an alley that leads on to the hiking trail to Montemarcello, Dei Pescatori is devoted to fresh seafood, hence the lack of a menu as you simply get what's fresh that day. Pace yourself though for the multicourse onslaught, which features a wonderful selection of clams and shrimp with gnocchi, grilled fillet of fish and fried fish platters.

Bar la Marina   BAR
(Piazza 4 Novembre 2, Tellaro; ⊙8am-10pm) A simple tiny bar dispenses *spritzes* and wine to tables on the tiny port's cobblestones. Time your visit for sunset and you'll understand what so enchanted Byron and Shelley.

ℹ Information

Tourist Office (Via Biaggini 35, Lerici; ⊙9am-1pm & 3-5.30pm Mon-Sat, to 1pm Sun) Can advise on walking and cycling in the area, as well as accommodation.

ℹ Getting There & Away

Regular **Azienda Trasporti Consortile** (www.atclaspezia.it) buses run to Lerici and Tellaro from La Spezia's train station, a 35-minute trip.

Riviera di Ponente
☑0184

Curving west from Genoa to the French border, the Ponente stretch of the Ligurian coast is more down-to-earth than the flashy Rivieria di Levante. As a result, it shelters some relatively well-priced escape hatches, particularly along the stretch of coast from Noli to Finale Ligure.

Savona
☑019 / POP 61,400

Behind Savona's sprawling port facilities, the city's unexpectedly graceful medieval centre is well worth a stop. Among the old-town treasures to survive destruction by Genoese forces in the 16th century are the baroque Cattedrale di Nostra Signora Assunta and the lumbering Fortezza del Priamàr. There's also a nice urban buzz, with lots of new shops, bars and restaurants regenerating the old centre.

◎ Sights

Fortezza del Priamàr   FORTRESS
(Piazza Priamar) This imposing fortress guards a couple of sculpture museums and the Civico Museo Storico Archeologico.

Pinacoteca Civica Savona   GALLERY
(www.comune.savona.it; Piazza Chabrol 1/2; admission €8; ⊙10am-1.30pm daily, 3.30-6.30pm Thu-Sat) The city pinacoteca has an important collection of religious paintings dating from the 14th to 15th centuries, including a Madonna and child by Taddeo di Bartolo, along with two Picassos.

🛏 Sleeping & Eating

Villa de' Franceschini   HOSTEL €
(☑019 26 32 22; www.ostello-de-franceschini.com; Via alla Strà 'Conca Verde' 29; dm/s/d €16/22/38; ⊙mid-Mar–Oct; ℗ @) Savona has one of Liguria's few hostels, a big place set in a sprawling park, 3km from the train station.

Mare Hotel   HOTEL €€
(☑019 26 32 77; www.marehotel.it; Via Nizza 41; d €160; ❄@🤝🏊) The four-star seafront Mare with its infinity pool, private beach and candle-lit open-air restaurant is Italian beach bling in action. New rooms adopt a Milanese nightclub aesthetic, while older rooms (around €100 a night) are comfortable, if a little frumpy. It's 2km west along

the beach from the station – regular buses run there.

Casa della Panizza
LIGURIAN, FAST FOOD €

(Vico dei Crema 4; €1.50-4; ⊙9am-8pm) This is the real deal – a perpetually busy back alley kitchen where salt cod or *borage fritelle* (fritters), *panizza* and *farinata* from both chickpea and chestnut flour are fried before your eyes and the banter flies as thick as the salt. You order by weight but can just request a cone or box if you're unsure.

Wine is dispensed into plastic cups if you want to make a night of it.

Vino e Farinata
ITALIAN €

(Via Pia 15; meals €18-25; ⊙noon-2pm & 6-10pm Tue-Sat) To enter this place in the cobbled centre, you'll have to walk past the two busy chefs: one shovelling fish into a wood-fired oven and the other mixing up batter in a barrel-sized whisking machine. The result: Ligurian *farinata*, the menu staple in this *very* local restaurant that also pours some excellent local wines.

ℹ Information

Tourist Office (www.rivieraculture.it; Via dei Maestri d'Ascia 7; ⊙9am-12.30pm & 3-6pm Mon-Sat, to 1pm Sun) A short stroll from Savona's sandy beach.

ℹ Getting There & Away

ACTS (www.tpllinea.it) bus services, departing from Piazza del Popolo and the train station while trains run along the coast to Genoa's Stazione Brignole (€5.10, 45 minutes, almost hourly) and San Remo (€12.50, 1¼ hours, eight daily).

Corsica Ferries (www.corsica-ferries.fr) runs up to three boats daily between Savona's Porto Vado and Corsica.

Finale Ligure

☑ 019 / POP 11,650

Set amid lush Mediterranean vegetation, this township comprises several districts. Finale Ligure has a wide, fine-sand beach. The walled medieval centre, known as **Finalborgo**, is a knot of twisting alleys set 1km back from the coast on the Pora river. **Finale Marina** sits on the waterfront, the more residential **Finale Pia** runs along the Sciusa river and the **Finalese** rises up into the hinterland.

🛏 Sleeping & Eating

★ Valleponci
AGRITURISMO €

(☑329 3154169; www.valleponci.it; Val Ponci 22, Localita Verzi; d/apt €85/165) Only 4km from the beach, Val Ponce feels deliciously wild, tucked away in a rugged Ligurian valley. Horses graze, grapevines bud and the restaurant turns out fresh Ligurian dishes, with vegetables and herbs from a kitchen garden. On weekend evenings and Sunday lunch, there's live music or classic vinyl. Rooms are simple but show the keen eye of the Milanese escapee owners.

There are some wonderful hiking and mountain-biking paths around here: ask the knowledgeable Giorgio for a map and tips on the historical and archaeological sites to look out for.

Paradiso di Manù
HOTEL €€

(☑019 749 01 10; www.paradisodimanu.it; Via Chiariventi 35, Noli; d €120-160; P @ ≋) Overlooking the Gulf of Spotorno, this 'diffusion' hotel is a revitalised hamlet with six elegant Provençal-style rooms located in a variety of stone buildings overlooking florid terraces, one with a large, inviting pool.

Hotel Florenz
HOTEL €€

(☑019 69 56 67; www.hotelflorenz.it; Via Celesia 1; s/d €86/132; ⊙closed Nov & Feb; P @ ≋) This rambling 18th-century former convent just outside Finalborgo's village walls (800m from the sea) is simple and homey but one of the area's most atmospheric spots to sleep.

Salumeria Chiesa
DELI, TRATTORIA €

(☑019 69 25 16; Via Pertica 15; ⊙11am-2.30pm & 6-8.30pm May-Oct, closed Sun Nov-Apr) Presided over by Laura Chiesa, this delicatessen offers a huge array of seafood salads, salamis, cheeses and gnocchi with pesto, of course. Order what you like in the shop and eat it at the *tavola calda* ('warm table', a casual eatery) round the corner on Vico Gandolino.

Osteria ai Cuattru Canti
OSTERIA €

(Via Torcelli 22; set menus €20; ⊙noon-2pm & 8-10pm Tue-Sun) Simple and good Ligurian specialities are cooked up at this rustic place in Finalborgo's historic centre.

ℹ Information

Tourist Office (Via San Pietro 14; ⊙9am-12.30pm & 3-6pm Mon-Sat year-round, 9am-noon Sun Jul & Aug) From the train station on Piazza Vittorio Veneto, at Finale Marina's western end, walk down Via Saccone to the sea and this office.

ⓘ Getting There & Away

TPL (☑0182 2 15 44; www.tpllinea.it) buses run every 30 minutes to/from Savona (€2.50, 50 minutes).

San Remo

☑0184 / POP 57,000

Fifty kilometres east of Europe's premier gambling capital lies San Remo, Italy's own Monte Carlo, a sun-dappled Mediterranean resort with a casino, a clutch of ostentatious villas and lashings of Riviera-style grandeur. Known colloquially as the City of Flowers for its colourful summer blooms, San Remo also stages an annual music festival (the supposed inspiration for the Eurovision Song Contest) and the world's longest professional one-day cycling race, the 298km Milan–San Remo classic.

During the mid-19th century the city became a magnet for regal European exiles, such as Empress Elisabeth of Austria and Tsar Nicola of Russia, who favoured the town's balmy winters. Swedish inventor Alfred Nobel maintained a villa here, and an onion-domed Russian Orthodox church reminiscent of Moscow's St Basil's Cathedral still turns heads down along the seafront.

◎ Sights & Activites

Il Casinò Municipale
CASINO
(www.casinosanremo.it; Corso degli Inglesi; ⊘24hr) San Remo's belle époque casino, one of only four in Italy, was dealing cards when Vegas was still a waterhole in the desert. The building dates from 1905 and was designed by Parisian architect Eugenio Ferret. Slot machines (more than 400 of them) open at 10am; other games (roulette, blackjack, poker etc) kick off at 2.30pm. Dress smart-casual and bring ID.

Chiesa Russa Ortodossa
CHURCH
(Via Nuvoloni 2; admission €1; ⊘9.30am-noon & 3-6pm) Built for the Russian community that followed Tsarina Maria to San Remo in 1906, the Russian Orthodox church – with its onion domes and heavenly pale-blue interior – was designed by Alexei Shchusev, who later planned Lenin's mausoleum in Moscow. These days it's used as an exhibition space for Russian icons.

WORTH A TRIP

BUSSANA VECCHIA

Ten kilometres northeast of San Remo lies an intriguing artists' colony. On Ash Wednesday 1887, an earthquake destroyed the village of Bussana Vecchia. It remained a ghost town until the 1960s, when artists and counterculture devotees moved in and began rebuilding the ruins using the original stones from the rubble. A thriving community of international artists remains in residence today. To get there, take a bus to Bussana, 5km east of San Remo, and walk up (30 minutes).

Museo Civico
MUSEUM
(Palazzo Borea d'Olmo; Corso Matteotti 143; adult/reduced €3/2; ⊘9am noon & 2 7pm Tue Sat) Housed in a 15th-century *palazzo*, several rooms in this museum, some with fine frescoed ceilings, display local prehistoric and Roman archaeological finds, paintings and temporary exhibitions. Highlights include Maurizio Carrega's 1808 homage, *Gloria di San Napoleone*, and bronze statues by Franco Bargiggia.

Parco Costiero della Riviera dei Fiori
CYCLING
(www.pistaciclabile.com) As befits a city that hosts professional cycling's greatest Spring Classic, San Remo has a 25km *pista ciclabile* (cycling path) through what is known as the Parco Costiero della Riviera dei Fiori. The path – which runs along the route of a former railway line – connects Ospedaletti to San Lorenzo al Mare via San Remo and eight other seaside towns.

Bike hire outlets and refreshment/rest stops are set up along the route, including at San Remo's old train station, Stazione Vecchia.

✨ Festivals & Events

Festival di San Remo
MUSIC
(⊘Mar) Celebrating Italian popular music, this festival has been going strong since 1951, and attracts top Italian and international talent.

🛏 Sleeping

Pisolo Resort
B&B €
(☑340 8748323; www.pisoloresort.it; Piazza Colombo 29; s/d €70/90; ❋ 🅕) Hard to find despite being in San Remo's main square,

San Remo

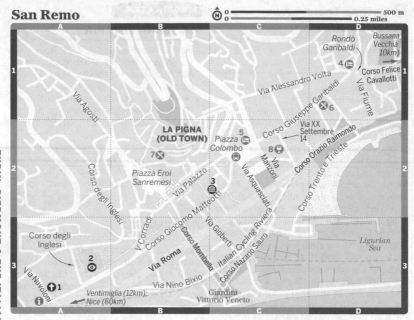

San Remo

⊙ Sights
1 Chiesa Russa Ortodossa A3
2 Il Casinò Municipale.........................A3
3 Museo Civico C2

🛏 Sleeping
4 Hotel Liberty.......................................D1
5 Pisolo Resort C2

✕ Eating
6 Cuvèa..D1
7 Ristorante Urbicia Vivas B2

🍷 Drinking & Nightlife
8 Cafe' Du Centre.................................C2

Pisolo offers five modern rooms. There's no reception but you'll get a basket of breakfast snacks and a coffee machine, and staff are on call.

Hotel Liberty　　　　　　　HOTEL €
(☑ 0184 50 99 52; www.hotellibertysanremo.com; Rondò Garibaldi 2; s €60, d €90-110; P ❄) A 10-room hotel is set in a Liberty-style villa off a small traffic circle about 100m from the train station. It's quiet, clean and run by helpful young owners.

✕ Eating & Drinking

Cuvèa　　　　　　　ITALIAN €
(Corso Giuseppe Garibaldi 110; meals €22; ⊙ noon-2.30pm & 7-10pm) This cosy, brightly lit place lined with wine bottles overflows with locals tucking into homemade traditional dishes such as pesto-doused pasta; it also has the most genial host in town.

Ristorante Urbicia Vivas　　　　　　　LIGURIAN €€
(☑ 0184 57 55 66; Piazza Dolori 5; meals €32; ⊙ 10.30am-midnight) Basking in a quiet medieval square in San Remo's remarkable old town, Urbicia is slavishly faithful to old Ligurian recipes with a strong bias towards seafood. There's a €12 lunch deal and Friday night is risotto night.

Cafe' Du Centre　　　　　　　WINE BAR
(☑ 0184 50 72 11; Via XX Settembre 14; ⊙ noon-midnight Tue-Sun) A lively if sophisticated bar once you've had enough seaside fun for the day. Friendly staff, excellent wines and great *aperitivo* snacks draw the locals.

ℹ Information

Tourist Office (www.visitrivieradeifiori.it; Largo Nuvoloni 1; ⊙ 9am-7pm Mon-Sat, 9am-1pm Sun)

ℹ Getting There & Away

Riviera Trasporti buses leave regularly from the **bus station** (Piazza Colombo 42) for the French border, and destinations east along the coast and inland.

From San Remo's underground train station there are trains to/from Genoa (€9.80, 2½ hours, hourly), Ventimiglia (€2.70, 15 minutes, hourly) and stations in between.

Ventimiglia

📋 0184 / POP 25,700

Bordertown Ventimiglia once harboured a stoic Roman town known as Albintimulium, which survived until the 5th century AD, when it was besieged by the Goths. These days it's besieged by a weekly horde of French bargain hunters who cross the border each market day.

◉ Sights

Giardini Botanici Hanbury   GARDENS

(www.giardinihanbury.com; Corso Montecarlo 43; adult/reduced €9/7.50; ⊙ 9.30am-6pm) Established in 1867 by English businessman Sir Thomas Hanbury, the 18-hectare Villa Hanbury estate is planted with 5800 botanical species from five continents, including cacti, palm groves and citrus orchards. Today it's a protected area, under the care of the University of Genoa.

Market   MARKET

(Piazza della Libertà; ⊙ 8am-3pm Fri) Ventimiglia is best known for its huge Friday market when hundreds of stalls sell food, clothes, homewares, baskets and everything else under the sun. The market is concentrated on Piazza della Libertà, near the river.

✕ Eating

Pasta & Basta   LIGURIAN €

(📋 0184 23 08 78; www.pastaebastaventimiglia.com; Via Marconi 20; meals €20; ⊙ noon-3pm & 7-10pm Tue-Sun, noon-3pm Mon) Duck into the underpass near the seafront on the border side of town to the perpetually redeveloping port area where you'll find Pasta & Basta. Various house-made fresh pasta can be mixed and matched with a large menu of sauces, including a good pesto or *salsa di noci* (walnut purée), and washed down with a carafe of pale and refreshing Pigato, a local white.

OFF THE BEATEN TRACK

LA DOLCEAQUA

Up a narrow, dead-end valley from Ventimiglia lies Dolceaqua, a serene medieval town whose beauty once inspired Monet. Its original, steeply sited heart is watched over by a recently restored castle, while its new town, a typical 19th-century affair, sits across a fast-flowing river, joined by an ancient humpback stone bridge. Well away from the mayhem of the coast, it's a lovely place to simply wander the *caruggi* (narrow streets) then have a leisurely lunch at **Casa e Bottega** (📋 340 5665339; www.ristocasaebottega.it; Piazza Garibaldi 2; meals €25; ⊙ noon-3pm daily & 6-10pm Fri-Sun).

ℹ Information

Tourist Office (Lungo Roja Rossi; ⊙ 9am-12.30pm & 3.30-7pm Mon-Sat Jul & Aug, 9am-12.30pm & 3-6.30pm Mon-Sat Sep-Jun) Just steps from the train station.

ℹ Getting There & Away

Train Station (Via della Stazione)

PIEDMONT

Italy's second-largest region is arguably its most elegant: a purveyor of Slow Food and fine wine, regal *palazzi* and an atmosphere that is superficially more *français* than *italiano*. But dig deeper and you'll discover that Piedmont has 'Made in Italy' stamped all over it. Emerging from the chaos of the Austrian wars, the unification movement first exploded here in the 1850s, when the noble House of Savoy provided the nascent nation with its first prime minister and its dynastic royal family.

Most Piedmont journeys start in stately Turin, famous for football and Fiats. Beyond the car factories, Piedmont is also notable for its food – everything from rice to white truffles – and pretty pastoral landscapes not unlike nearby Tuscany.

The region's smaller towns were once feuding fiefdoms that bickered over trade and religion. Today the biggest skirmishes are more likely to be over recipes and vintages as they vie for the gourmet traveller euro.

Piedmont

0 25 miles
0 50 km

Parco della Grigna Settentrionale

Milan

Pavia

Como

Lugano

Varese

Vigevano

Bellinzona

A9

A8

A7

LOMBARDY

Malpensa Airport

Locarno

Cannobio

Lago Maggiore

Borromean Islands

Stresa

Novara

A4

Verbania

Monte Mottarone (1491m)

Arona

A26

Borgomanero

River Sesia

Parco della Val Grande

Omegna

Lago d'Orto

Varallo

Vercelli

Domodossola

Macugnaga

Sacro Monte di Varallo

Balmuccia

Borgosesia

A4

Parco Naturale Alta Valle Sesia

Alagna Valsesia

Valsesia

Rassa

Biella

Ivrea

A5

Monte Rosa (4633m)

Punta Indren (3260m)

Lessolo

Caselle Airport

SWITZERLAND

Matterhorn (Monte Cervino) (4478m)

Dora Baltea

Orco

VALLE D'AOSTA

A5

Cogne

Val Soana

Orco

Val di Ala

Allein

Aosta

Pila

Parco Nazionale del Gran Paradiso

Valle Orco

Val Grande

Courmayeur

A5

FRANCE

Chamonix

Mont Blanc (4810m)

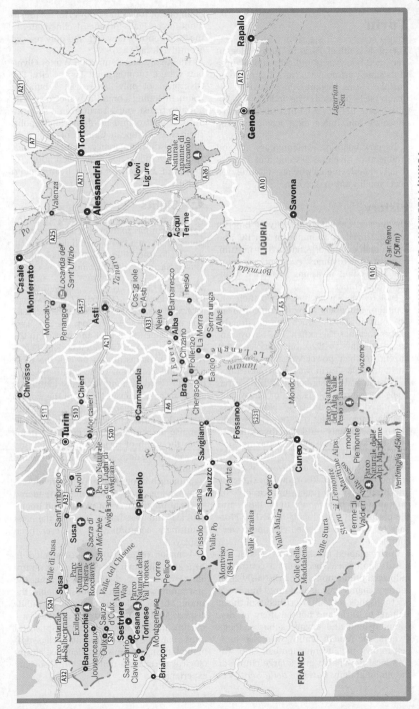

Turin

📱 011 / POP 892.650 / ELEV 240M

There's a whiff of Paris in Turin's elegant tree-lined boulevards and echoes of Vienna in its stately art nouveau cafes, but make no mistake – this elegant, Alp-fringed city is utterly self-possessed. The industrious Torinese gave the world its first saleable hard chocolate and Italy's most iconic car, the Fiat.

Its now booming contemporary art and architecture, live-music scene and innovative food and wine culture are definitely aspects you'll want to discover.

History

The ancient Celtic-Ligurian city of Taurisia was destroyed by Hannibal in 218 BC and the Roman colony of Augusta Taurinorum, established here almost two centuries later, saw succeeding invasions of Goths, Lombards and Franks.

In 1563 the Savoys abandoned their old capital of Chambéry (now in France) to set up court in Turin, which shared the dynasty's fortunes thereafter. The Savoys annexed Sardinia in 1720, but Napoleon put an end to their power when he occupied Turin in 1798. Turin was then controlled by Austria and Russia before Vittorio Emanuele I restored the House of Savoy and re-entered Turin in 1814. Nevertheless, Austria remained the true power throughout northern Italy until the Risorgimento in 1861, when Turin became the nation's inaugural capital. Piedmont, with its wily president, the Count of Cavour, was the engine room of the Risorgimento (literally 'the Resurgence', or Italian unification). Its capital status lasted only until 1864, and the parliament had already moved to Florence by the time full-sized chambers were completed.

Turin adapted quickly to its loss of political significance, becoming a centre for industrial production during the early 20th century. Giants such as Fiat lured hundreds of thousands of impoverished southern Italians to Turin and housed them in vast company-built and -owned suburbs. Fiat's owners, the Agnelli family (who also happen to own the Juventus football club, Turin's local newspaper and a large chunk of the national daily *Corriere della Sera*), remain one of Italy's most powerful establishment forces. Fiat's fortunes declined later in the 20th century, however, and only revived around a decade ago.

The highly successful 2006 Winter Olympics were a turning point for the city. The Olympics not only ushered in a building boom, including a brand-new metro system, but also transformed Turin from a staid industrial centre into a vibrant metropolis. Turin was European Capital of Design in 2008, hosting conferences and exhibitions, and the national focus of celebrations of the 150th anniversary of the Risorgimento in 2011.

◉ Sights

Got a week? You might need it to see all the sights Turin has to offer. The time-poor can concentrate on a trio of highlights: the Museo Egizio, the Mole Antonelliana and the Museo Nazionale dell'Automobile.

★ **Museo Egizio**   MUSEUM
(Egyptian Museum; 📱011 561 77 76; www.museoegizio.it; Via Accademia delle Scienze 6; adult/reduced €15/11; ⊙9am-6.30pm Tue-Sun, 9am-2pm Mon) Opened in 1824 and housed in the austere Palazzo dell'Accademia delle Scienze, this Turin institution houses the most important collection of Egyptian treasure outside Cairo. Among its many highlights are a statue of Ramses II (one of the world's most important pieces of Egyptian art) and the world's largest papyrus collection. There are also 500 funerary and domestic items from the tomb of royal architect Kha and his wife Merit, dating to 1400 BC and found in 1906.

Both anthropomorphic coffins are incredibly moving, but Merit's image, rendered in *cartonnage* (layers of plaster and linen), gold leaf and glass inlays, is one of the most hauntingly beautiful that has ever been displayed.

A major renovation was completed in 2015 and, although the old museum's rambling rooms had their dusty charm, the new minimalist spaces almost double the amount of the collection available for public display. Modern museological techniques – splicing in documentary photographs and films about the early 20th-century digs, dramatic lighting and a well-articulated chronological narrative – make for an absorbing experience.

★ **Museo Casa Mollino**   ARCHITECTURE

(☑011 812 98 68; cm@carlomollino.org; Via Napione 2; 1-2hr tour €30; ⊘by appointment) Architect-designer-artist Carlo Mollino is perhaps Turin's most intriguing son, a quintessentially 20th-century Torinese. The little-known Museo Casa Mollino is a testament to his deliriously lush aesthetic, his skill as a craftsman, as well as his manifold obsessions. It was also where many of his theatrical, erotically-charged Polaroid portraits were shot. Father and son Fulvio and Napoleone Ferrari are dedicated keepers of his legacy and compelling interpreters and storytellers.

For those with a passion for 20th-century art and architecture, it's a profoundly rewarding experience. The tours must be pre-arranged by email.

★ **Castello di Rivoli**   GALLERY

(Museo d'Arte Contemporanea; www.castellodirivoli.org; Piazza Mafalda di Savoia; adult/reduced €6.50/4.50, Tue free; ⊘10am-5pm Tue-Fri, to 7pm Sat & Sun) Castello di Rivoli Museum of Contemporary Art's establishment in 1984 came about as the canny Torinese realised contemporary art could help build a new identity for the city. Its ambition and reach, not to mention healthy regional funding, has since been the envy of Milan, Venice and Rome's art worlds. The permanent collection has a sizeable number of Arte Povera works which are beautifully displayed in the historical setting, along with pieces from the Transavanguardia, Minimal, Body and Land Art movements.

★ **Museo Nazionale dell'Automobile**   MUSEUM

(☑011 67 76 66; www.museoauto.it; Corso Unità d'Italia 40; adult/reduced €12/8; ⊘10am-7pm Wed, Thu & Sun, to 9pm Fri & Sat, to 2pm Mon, 2-7pm Tue; Ⓜ Lingotto) As the historic birthplace of one of the world's leading car manufacturers – the 'T' in Fiat stands for Torino – Turin is the obvious place for a car museum. This dashing modern museum, located roughly 5km south of the city centre, doesn't disappoint with its precious collection of over 200 automobiles – everything from an 1892 Peugeot to a 1980 Ferrari 308 (in red, of course).

The museum – rather than leaving you to gawp helplessly at boring engines – takes you on a rollercoaster journey spread over three floors; the first part a car chronology, the second a more technical look at car design, and the third a self-critical assessment of issues such as pollution and congestion.

Fondazione Merz   GALLERY

(☑011 1971 9437; http://fondazionemerz.org; Via Limone 24; adult/reduced €6/3; ⊘11am-7pm Tue-Sun) The Arte Povera powerhouse, Mario Merz, was born in Milan but spent most of his creative life in Turin. This foundation space, a reworking of the former Lancia heating plant, holds regular exhibitions of his work and an astute program of Italian contemporary art. It also plays host to an internationally significant emerging artist prize.

Fondazione Sandretto re Rebaudengo   GALLERY

(FSRR; ☑011 2799 7600; www.fsrr.org; Via Modane 16; adult/reduced €5/3, free Thu; ⊘8-11pm Thu, noon-7pm Fri-Sun) This classic white-cube contemporary gallery space was created with Italian super curator Francesco Bonami and runs a great exhibition program, with big-name Italians such as Maurizio Cattelan often making an appearance and provocative thematic shows that bring mid-career Europeans together with their younger peers.

Juventus Museum   MUSEUM

(www.juventus.com; Strada Comunale di Altessano 131; museum €15, incl stadium visit €22; ⊘10.30am-6.30pm Mon & Wed-Fri, to 7.30pm Sat & Sun) The state-of-the-art Juventus Stadium has a museum that will blind you with its silverware (32 Serie A titles – and the rest!) and proudly recount how it was all amassed. On match days your museum visit can include viewing the team's match prep behind the scenes (€30).

Reggia di Venaria Reale   PALACE

(☑011 499 23 33; www.lavenaria.it; Piazza della Re pubblica; admission incl exhibitions €25, Reggia & gardens €16, gardens only €5; ⊘9am-5pm Tue-Fri, to 6.30pm Sat & Sun) OK, it may not enjoy the weighty publicity of its French counterpart, but this is one of the largest royal residences in the world, rescued from ruin by a €235 million 10-year-long restoration project. Humongous, ostentatious, regal, yet strangely under-publicised, this Unesco-listed baroque palace complex was built as a glorified hunting lodge in 1675 by the frivolous Duke of Savoy, Carlo Emanuele II.

Basilica di Superga   BASILICA

(www.basilicadisuperga.com; Strada della Basilica di Superga 75; adult/reduced €5/4; ⊘10am-1.30pm & 2.30-7pm summer, to 6pm winter) Vittorio Amedeo II's 1706 promise, to build a basilica to honour the Virgin Mary if Turin was saved from besieging French and Spanish armies,

Turin

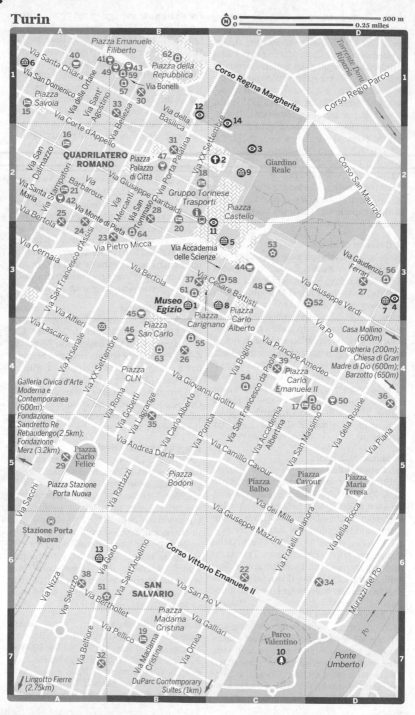

N
0 — 500 m
0 — 0.25 miles

Piazza Emanuele Filiberto

Via Santa Chiara
Via San Domenico

Piazza
Savoia

Via Corte d'Appello

QUADRILATERO
ROMANO

Piazza
Palazzo
di Città

Piazza della
Repubblica
Via Bonelli

Via della
Basilica

Corso Regina Margherita

Corso Regio Parco

Torrente Dora Riparia

Corso San Maurizio

Giardino
Reale

Piazza
Castello

Via Pietro Micca

Via Accademia
delle Scienze

Museo
Egizio

Piazza
Carignano

Piazza
Carlo
Alberto

Via Cesare Battisti

Via Giuseppe Verdi

Via Gaudenzio
Ferrari

Casa Mollino
(600m)

La Drogheria (200m);
Chiesa di Gran
Madre di Dio (600m);
Barzotto (650m)

Piazza
San Carlo

Via Giovanni Giolitti

Piazza
Carlo
Emanuele II

Galleria Civica d'Arte
Moderna e
Contemporanea
(600m);
Fondazione
Sandretto Re
Rebaudengo(2.5km);
Fondazione
Merz (3.2km)

Piazza
CLN

Via XX Settembre

Via Roma

Piazza
Carlo Felice

Piazza Stazione
Porta Nuova

Stazione Porta
Nuova

Via Andrea Doria

Piazza
Bodoni

Piazza
Balbo

Piazza
Cavour

Piazza
Maria
Teresa

Via dei Mille

Via Giuseppe Mazzini

SAN
SALVARIO

Corso Vittorio Emanuele II

Piazza
Madama
Cristina

Via Madama
Cristina

Via Pellico

Parco
Valentino

Ponte
Umberto I

Murazzi del Po

Lingotto Fierre
(2.75km)

DuParc Contemporary
Suites (1km)

Turin

resulted in this wedding cake edifice, built on a hill across the Po river.

Cattedrale di San Giovanni Battista
CATHEDRAL

(www.duomoditorino.it; Via XX Settembre 87; ⊙9am-12.30pm & 3-7pm) Turin's cathedral was built between 1491 and 1498 on the site of three 14th-century basilicas and, before that, a Roman theatre. Plain interior aside, as home to the **Shroud of Turin** (still alleged to be the burial cloth in which Jesus' body was wrapped, despite years of controversy), this is a highly trafficked church. A copy of the famous cloth is on permanent display to the left of the cathedral altar.

Museo Nazionale del Risorgimento Italiano
MUSEUM

(☑011 562 11 47; www.museorisorgimentotorino.it; Via Accademia delle Scienze 5; adult/reduced €10/8; ⊙10am-6pm Tue-Sun) After extensive renovations, this significant museum re-opened in 2011 to coincide with the centenary of the Risorgimento (reunification period). An astounding 30-room trajectory illustrates the creation of the modern Italian state in the very building (the baroque Palazzo Carignano) where many of the key events happened. Not only was this the birthplace of Carlo Alberto and Vittorio Emanuele II, but it was also the seat of united Italy's first parliament from 1861 to 1864.

Pinacoteca Giovanni
e Marella Agnelli
GALLERY

(Lingotto; www.pinacoteca-agnelli.it; Via Nizza 230; adult/reduced €10/8; ⊘10am-7pm Tue-Sun; Ⓜ Lingotto) On the rooftop of the Lingotto Fiere, 3km south of the centre, this intimate gallery houses the personal collection of late Fiat head Gianni Agnelli, with masterpieces by Canaletto, Renoir, Manet, Matisse and Picasso, among others. Apart from the paintings, your ticket grants you access to the Lingotto's famous rooftop test track.

It also has an attached bookshop, full of wonderful art and design titles. When there's no temporary exhibition showing, the gallery admission is €8.

Piazza Castello
PIAZZA

Turin's central square is lined with museums, theatres and cafes. The city's Savoy heart, although laid out from the mid-1300s, was mostly constructed from the 16th to 18th centuries. Dominating it is the part-medieval, part-baroque **Palazzo Madama**, the original seat of the Italian parliament. To the north, is the exquisite facade of the **Palazzo Reale**, the royal palace built for Carlo Emanuele II in the mid-1600s.

Galleria Civica d'Arte
Moderna e Contemporanea
GALLERY

(GAM; ☎011 442 95 18; www.gamtorino.it; Via Magenta 31; adult/reduced €10/8; ⊘10am-6pm Tue-Sun) GAM was one of Italy's first modern art museums and has an astounding 45,000 works in its vaults dedicated to 19th- and 20th-century European artists, including Giorgio De Chirico, Otto Dix and Paul Klee. It's a great place to expand your knowledge of Italy's post-war period: Paolini, Boetti, Anselmo, Penone and Pistoletto are all well represented.

Private View Gallery
GALLERY

(☎011 668 68 78; www.privateviewgallery.com; Via Goito 16; ⊘3-7pm Tue-Sat, or by appointment) Silvia and Mauro's San Severino space is possibly Turin's most interesting commercial contemporary gallery. Exhibitions might be by a local artist or a hot new New Yorker.

Museo Ettore Fico
GALLERY

(MEF; ☎011 85 30 65; www.museofico.it; Via Francesco Cigna 114; adult/reduced €10/5; ⊘2-7pm Wed-Fri, from 11am Sat & Sun) This exciting new space joins Turin's already stellar collection of contemporary art foundations. Set in an old factory in a rapidly hipsterising, post-industrial neighbourhood north of the Dora River, MEF has three major shows per year, with high-profile monographic exhibitions as well as installation work by contemporary artists, along with design, fashion or film-based shows. Work by Ettore Fico, the late Torinese painter to whom the museum is dedicated, also features.

Porta Palatina
ROMAN SITE

(Piazza Cesare Augusto) The low-key and little-visited Porta Palatina is, in fact, one of the best preserved 1st-century BC Roman gateways in the world. Together with the remains of the Roman city walls, it forms a small but lovely open-air archaeological park.

Roman Amphitheatre
ROMAN SITE

Razed to the ground by Napoleon's armies, little remains of this 1st-century amphitheatre, but it's still an atmospheric spot to stroll around.

Palazzo Reale
MUSEUM

(www.ilpalazzorealeditorino.it; Piazza Castello; adult/reduced €12/6, 1st Sun of month free; ⊘9am-7pm Tue-Sun) Statues of the mythical twins Castor and Pollux guard the entrance to this eye-catching palace and, according to local hearsay, they also watch over the magical border between the sacred and diabolical halves of the city. Built for Carlo Emanuele II around 1646, its lavishly decorated rooms house an assortment of furnishings, porcelain and other decorative objects. The **Giardino Reale** (Royal Garden; ⊘9am-1hr before sunset) FREE, north and east of the palace, was designed in 1697 by André Le Nôtre, who also created the gardens at Versailles.

The Palazzo Reale ticket allows you to view the **Galleria Sabauda**, the personal art collection of the Savoy monarchy, which was amassed over 400 years and includes gems by Van Dyck, Rubens and Lippi. Since 2012, the collection has been housed in the Manica Nuova, the newer wing of the Palazzo Reale. On Thursdays in August and September, you can visit until 10pm for €2.

Museo Nazionale del Cinema
MUSEUM

(☎011 813 85 60; www.museocinema.it; Via Montebello 20; adult/reduced €10/8, incl lift €14/11; ⊘9am-8pm Sun, Mon & Wed-Fri, to 11pm Sat) Housed in the Mole Antonelliana, this enjoyable museum takes you on a fantastic tour through cinematic history. Memorabilia on display includes Marilyn Monroe's black lace bustier, Peter O'Toole's robe from *Lawrence of Arabia* and the coffin used by Bela Lugosi's Dracula. At the heart of the museum, the vast Temple Hall is surrounded by 10 interactive 'chapels' devoted to various film genres.

There's also a cinema that often shows version-original English-language art-house films.

Lingotto Fiere   LANDMARK
(www.lingottofiere.it; Via Nizza 294; M Lingotto) Turin's former Fiat factory, one of Italy's most praised examples of early-20th-century industrial architecture, is 5km south of the city centre. It was redesigned by architect Renzo Piano in the 1980s to house an exhibition centre, a university campus and hotels. While still starkly beautiful, the shopping mall that occupies much of its accessible space is less than inspiring.

Lingotto is on the M1 metro line and easily accessible from the city centre

**Museo Civico
d'Arte Antica**   MUSEUM
(Palazzo Madama; ☑ 011 443 35 01; www.palazzomadamatorino.it; Piazza Castello; adult/reduced €10/8; ☑ 10am-6pm Wed-Mon) A part-medieval, part-baroque castle built in the 13th century on the site of the old Roman gate, this *palazzo* is named after Madama Reale Maria Cristina, the widow of Vittorio Amedeo I (Duke of Savoy, 1630–37). Today, much of the building houses this expansive museum, which contains four floors of mostly decorative arts from medieval to the post-unification period, along with temporary exhibitions of contemporary art.

Museo della Sindone   MUSEUM
(www.sindone.org; Via San Domenico 28; adult/reduced €6/5; ☑ 9am-noon & 3-7pm) Encased in the crypt of Santo Sudario church, this fascinating museum documents one of the most studied objects in human history: the Holy Shroud. Despite the shroud's dubious authenticity, its story unfolds like a gripping suspense mystery, with countless plots, subplots and revelations. Note the shroud itself is not on display here; it's kept in the Duomo and shown occasionally by decree of the Pope.

Mole Antonelliana   LANDMARK
(www.gtt.to/it/cms/turismo/ascensore-mole; Via Montebello 20; lift adult/reduced €7/5, incl Museo €14/11; ☑ lift 10am-8pm Sun, Mon & Wed-Fri, to 11pm Sat) The symbol of Turin, this 167m tower with its distinctive aluminium spire appears on the Italian two-cent coin. It was originally intended as a synagogue when construction began in 1862, but was never used as a place of worship, and nowadays houses the Museo Nazionale del Cinema. For dazzling 360-degree views, take the **Panoramic Lift** up to the 85m-high outdoor viewing deck.

**Chiesa di Gran
Madre di Dio**   CHURCH
(Piazza Gran Madre di Dio) A grand backdrop across the Po from Piazza Vittorio Veneto, this church was built in the style of a mini Pantheon from 1818 to 1831 to commemorate the return of Vittorio Emanuele I from exile. It's small and rounded inside; some claim it's yet another secret repository for the Holy Grail.

In 1969 the church was memorably featured in the film *The Italian Job* when Michael Caine and his gang drove their Mini Coopers down the front staircase.

🖝 Tours

Somewhere   WALKING
(www.somewhere.it) Turin's alleged 'black and white magic' is illuminated on a quirky walking tour, Torino Magica (€25), and its underbelly examined during Underground Turin (€29.50). You can opt for more traditional food or royal palace tours, or even a vintage Fiat 500 driving tour (€100 per car), if the dark arts aren't your cup of chocolate. Confirm departure points when booking.

🎊 Festivals & Events

Torino Film Festival   FILM
(www.torinofilmfest.org) Well-respected international festival with main screenings at the Mole Antonelliana during the last weeks of November.

**Salone del Gusto
& Terre Madre**   FOOD & DRINK
(www.salonedelgusto.com; ☑ late Sep) Held each even-numbered year in venues across Turin, Slow Food's global symposium features producers, chefs, activists, restaurateurs, farmers, scholars, environmentalists, epicureans and food lovers from around the world...not to mention the world's best finger food. Events from €7 to €100, day passes around €25.

Cioccolatò
FOOD & DRINK

(www.cioccola-to.it) Turin celebrates chocolate and its status as a world chocolate capital in late November; from 2017 the focus has returned to artisan producers.

🛏 Sleeping

⭐ Via Stampatori
B&B €

(☎ 339 2581330; www.viastampatori.com; Via Stampatori 4; s/d €90/110; 🛜) This utterly lovely B&B occupies the top floor of a frescoed Renaissance building, one of Turin's oldest. Six bright, stylish and uniquely furnished rooms overlook either a sunny terrace or a leafy inner courtyard. The owner's personal collection of 20th-century design is used throughout, including in the two serene common areas. It's central but blissfully quiet.

⭐ Tomato Backpackers Hotel
HOSTEL €

(☎ 011 020 94 00; www.tomato.to.it; Via Pellico 11; dm/s/d/tr €24/44/59/85; 🛜) 🏄 This eco-friendly hostel in the boozy San Salvario area is one of the few central places that caters to budget travellers. And it does so with style and soul, offering pristine dorms, smart private rooms, a kitchen and communal lounge. There's a relaxed, inclusive vibe and a long list of extras including laundry facilities and luggage storage.

San Giors
BOUTIQUE HOTEL €

(☎ 011 521 63 57; www.hotelsangiors.it; Via Borgo Dora 3; s €75, d €90-110; 🛜) If you're not perturbed by a still-gentrifying neighbourhood, this welcoming family-run place offers individual artist-decorated rooms that are basic but often include beautiful vintage design pieces and a witty, bohemian eye. The restaurant comes highly recommended, and come Saturday, you're in the thick of the Balon (p214), one of Italy's best flea markets.

Ostello Torino
HOSTEL €

(☎ 011 660 29 39; www.ostellotorino.it; Via Giordano Bruno 191; dm/s/d without bathroom €17/25/42; ✳@) Turin's neat 76-bed HI hostel, 1.8km from Stazione Porta Nuova, is around 10 minutes' walk from Lingotto station or can be reached by bus 52. Facilities include free breakfast, computer use and wi-fi; towels and AIG/HI membership are extra. If you're in town for a live act or DJ at Hiroshima Mon Amour (p213), it's close by. Check for annual closing dates if visiting in December or January.

⭐ DuParc
Contemporary Suites
DESIGN HOTEL €€

(☎ 011 012 00 00; www.duparcsuites.com; Corso Massimo D'Azeglio 21; r/ste from €120/140; P✳🛜) A business-friendly location doesn't mean this isn't a great choice for all travellers. Staff are young, clued-up and friendly, the building's iconic modern lines are matched with a fantastic contemporary art collection and tactile, comfortable furnishing along with stunning Italian lighting. Best of all, even the cheapest rooms here are sumptuously large, with king beds, ample cupboard space, huge baths and floor-to-ceiling windows.

There's a gym and basement spa area with saunas and a large whirlpool. Note that the location puts you in walking distance of the bars and restaurants of San Salvario and elegant green avenues of Parco Valentino.

Palazzo Chiablese
B&B €€

(☎ 333 8862670; www.bbpalazzochiablese.com; Vicolo San Lorenzo 1; s €110-120, d €120-130; 🛜) Marta and Riccardo's two B&B rooms are the epitome of pared back Torinese elegance, and mix warm mid-century Italian design with contemporary paintings, beautiful linen, design-centric bathrooms and large white draped windows. Breakfast is taken in the apartment's stylish kitchen, adding to the feeling you're staying with friends, rather than at a hotel.

Le Due Matote
B&B €€

(www.leduematote.com/en/torino/home; Via Garibaldi 31; s/d €110/135; ✳🛜) Perched above Turin's favourite *passeggiata* (evening stroll) parade, this elegant B&B is a bastion of calm. Three classically decorated rooms come with features that are rare at this price: Nespresso machines in all rooms, marble-topped baths in two, and one with its own lushly planted terrace.

NH Lingotto Tech
BUSINESS HOTEL €€

(☎ 011 664 20 00; www.nh-hotels.com; Via Nizza 262; d €130-200; P✳🛜) A unique perk awaits you at this hotel: the 1km running track on the roof is Fiat's former testing track and featured in the film *The Italian Job*. Twentieth-century industrial bones also mean rooms are huge and bright, while the fit-out is high-2000s designer slick, with an industrial edge. A corporate favourite, facilities are comprehensive and include a 24-hour gym.

Ai Savoia
BOUTIQUE HOTEL €€

(☑ 339 1257711; www.aisavoia.it; Via del Carmine 1b; d €95-125; P) Occupying an 18th-century town house, this little treasure seems like something you'd find in a small village. The classical decor of each of its three rooms is kitsch-ornate but staff are friendly and obliging.

NH Piazza Carlina
DESIGN HOTEL €€€

(☑ 848 39 02 30; www.nh-hotels.com; Piazza Carlo Emanuele II; s/d €180/220; P ❋ 🛜) Situated on one of Turin's most beautiful squares, this sprawling property occupies a 17th-century building, once the Albergo di Virtù, a Savoy charitable institution (and home to the famous political theorist Antonio Gramsci). The decor is cutting edge, highly atmospheric and deeply luxurious. There's a great downstairs bar and guests have access to rooftop terraces and a gym.

Breakfast is served in a stately courtyard among the hotel's own lemon trees.

Art Hotel Boston
BOUTIQUE HOTEL €€€

(☑ 011 50 03 59; www.hotelbostontorino.it; Via Massena 70; s €90-115, d €115-300; ❋ 🛜) The Boston's austere classical facade gives no inkling of the interiors that await inside. Public areas are filled with original works by Warhol, Lichtenstein and Aldo Mondino, while individually styled guest rooms are themed on subjects as diverse as Lavazza coffee, Ayrton Senna and Pablo Picasso.

Townhouse 70
BOUTIQUE HOTEL €€€

(☑ 011 1970 0003; www.townhouse.it; Via XX Settembre 70; d €190-230; @ 🛜) The Turin outpost of a Milanese boutique hotel chain, there's attitude here in spades but the large and comfortable rooms, a stellar location and a peaceful internal terrace make up for it.

🍴 Eating

Turin is blessed with a hinterland fabulously rich in produce and tradition. Both can be found in its deliciously ancient grand cafes and dining rooms as well as its booming new bar and restaurant scene.

The Quadrilatero Romano has a concentrated clutch of small casual places or for pizza, tapas or cheap eats, head to San Salvario in the city's south.

⭐ Hafastorie
MOROCCAN, PIEDMONTESE €

(☑ 011 1948 6765; http://hafastorie.it; Galleria Umberto I 10; meals €17-22; ⊙ 11am-3pm & 4pm-midnight Tue-Fri, 9am-midnight Sat, 11.30am-4.30pm Sun) A bright, stylish beacon in a beautiful, entirely un-revamped old arcade, Hafastorie is a passion project of its well-travelled owner. One side of the menu is a neat Maghrebi homage, with tagines, seven-vegetable couscous and spiced herb salads, while the other a beautifully edited list of Piedmontese favourites. Half serves are a rare bonus for those of more delicate appetites.

Ruràl Pizza
PIZZA €

(☑ 011 235 9179; www.ruralpizza.it; Via Mantova 27; pizza €18-22; ⊙ 12.30-2.30pm & 7.30-10.30pm Mon, Tue, Thu & Fri, 7.30-10.30pm Sat & Sun) This happy, pretty pizzeria set in an old glassworks, does Sicilian-style pizza using good quality ingredients, along with rather fancy desserts.

Société Lutéce
FRENCH, BAR €

(☑ 011 88 76 44, www.societelutece.it, Piazza Carlo Emanuele II 21, meals €25, ⊙ noon-2am Mon-Sat, to 3pm Sun) One of surprisingly few French places in the once Savoy city, Société Lutéce proudly flies the French flag – at least its menu does. Come for well-prepared French classics, from tartare to coq au vin to *moules* (mussels), salads and quiches for lunch, or just drop in for a spot of local conviviality and a glass of rosé or muscadet.

Host
BISTRO, CAFE €

(☑ 011 765 33 76; Via Porta Palatina 13; meals €14-20; ⊙ noon-3pm & 5-11pm Tue-Sat, noon-3pm Mon; 🖉) A bright, friendly spot for a simple pasta lunch or dinner, or an extended *aperitivo*. While not a vegetarian place, it's a favourite with many Torinese veggies, who come for the internationally-inflected meatless dishes.

Eataly Incontra
PIEDMONTESE, SUPERMARKET €

(☑ 011 037 32 21; www.eataly.net; Via Lagrange 3; meals €18-25; ⊙ noon-10.30pm, cafe from 8am, shop from 10am) Perfect for a casual lunch or dinner, this mini-Eataly has shaded tables on the lovely pedestrian stretch of Lagrange. Food is fresh, simple and quick – think octopus and potato salad, *cruda* (raw minced steak) or linguine with pistachio pesto and *stracciatella* cheese – and the drinks list includes sulphur-free wines and artisan beers.

Perino Vesco
BAKERY €

(☑ 011 068 60 56; www.perinovesco.it; Via Cavour 10; snacks from €5; ⊙ 7.30am-7.30pm Mon-Sat) 🍞 Cult Slow Food baker Andrea Perino turns out the city's best *grissini* (bread sticks) along with dense, fragrant *torta langarola* (hazelnut cake), naturally yeasted *panettone* and focaccia that draws sighs from homesick Ligurians. Join the queues for takeaway pizza and focaccia slices or head out the back and nab a seat for sandwiches, pizza slices, savoury tarts and coffee.

È Cucina
MODERN ITALIAN €

(☏ 011 562 90 38; www.cesaremarretti.com; Via Bertola 27a; meals €12-35; ⊗ 12.30-3pm & 8-11pm) Northern Italians are fond of a 'concept' and Bolognese chef Cesare Marretti's concept here is *sorpesa* (surprise). Beyond the choice of meat, fish or vegetables and the number of courses you want, it's up to the kitchen. What *is* certain is the innovative cooking and excellent produce that will arrive. Local's tip: don't be tempted to over order.

Gofri Piemontéisa
FAST FOOD €

(www.gofriemiassepiemontesi.it; Via San Tommaso 7; gofri €4.40-5; ⊗ 11.30am-7.30pm Mon-Sat) *Gofri*, thin waffles snap cooked in hot irons, are a traditional dish from the mountainous regions of northern Piedmont and have been reinvented here by a local chef as tasty fast food. Try the house *gofre* with ham, *toma* (alpine cheese) and artichokes or one of the equally delicious *miasse*, a corn-based variation, also adapted from ancient recipes.

Grom
GELATO €

(www.grom.it; Piazza Pietro Paleocapa 1d; cones/cups from €2.50; ⊗ 11am-11pm Sun-Thu, to midnight Fri & Sat winter, to 1am Fri & Sat summer) 🍦 At the vanguard of the gourmet gelato trend, the Grom chain founded their first store here in 2003, eschewing syrups and embracing sustainably sourced fresh ingredients. You can now lick a Grom cone in Paris or New York, but it's sweeter grabbing one in their home town. Look out for original Piedmontese flavours like *gianduja* (hazelnut chocolate) and lemon-scented cream.

Alberto Marchetti
GELATO €

(☏ 011 839 08 79; www.albertomarchetti.it; Corso Vittorio Emanuele II 24; scoop €3; ⊗ noon-midnight Tue-Sat, 1-11pm Sun) Riding in the slipstream of the Grom phenomenon, Alberto Marchetti is a master of quality, managing every part of his gelato-making process, from fruit selection to the type of milk used. Scoops to seek out include mandarin and the interesting *farina bona*, a childhood pudding comfort flavour. Is it better than Grom? You decide.

★ Gaudenzio
GASTRONOMY, PIEDMONTESE €€

(☏ 011 869 92 42; www.gaudenziovinoecucina. it; Via Gaudenzio Ferrari 2h; cichetti €5-12, meals €45; ⊗ 6-11pm Tue-Sat, noon-3.30pm Sun) Meet the gang who are intent on breaking down Italy's beloved course structure. It's small plates here – although there is a sliding scale of small to large – and the innovative but sublimely local dishes are some of the city's best. All wine is natural and/or from small producers and in lieu of a list, you and the sommelier will have a chat.

The space is small, smart and unfussy and although everything – produce, technique, wine, service – is thoughtful, serious even, there's something of a party vibe as the night wears on, with lots of fellow wine or food people popping in for a drink or snack at the bar.

★ Banco vini e alimenti
PIEDMONTESE €€

(☏ 011 764 02 39; www.bancovinialimenti.it; Via dei Mercanti 13f; meals €25-30; ⊗ 6.30pm-12.30am Mon, 12.30pm-12.30am Tue-Sat) A hybrid restaurant-bar-deli, this smartly designed but low-key place does clever small-dish dining for lunch and dinner. While it might vibe casual wine bar, with young staff in T-shirts and boyfriend jeans, don't underestimate the food: this is serious Piedmontese cooking. Open all day, you can also grab a single-origin pour-over here in the morning, or a herbal house *spritz* late afternoon.

Consorzio
PIEDMONTESE €€

(☏ 011 276 76 61; http://ristoranteconsorzio.it/; Via Monte di Pietà 23; mains €30-40, set menu €34; ⊗ 12.30-2.30pm Mon-Fri, 7.30-11pm Mon-Sat) A Quadrilatero Romano institution, it can be almost impossible to secure a table here. Do book ahead, don't expect flash decor and pay the not-always-chummy staff no mind. Everyone is here for the pristinely sourced, spot-on Piedmontese cooking that's so traditional it's innovative.

The wine list, too, is thoughtful and occasionally provocative, and some of it is sourced from a family vineyard near Asti, and all of it is natural.

Scannabue
PIEDMONTESE €€

(☏ 011 669 66 93; www.scannabue.it; Largo Saluzzo 25h; meals €30-40; ⊗ 12.30-2.30pm & 7.30pm-midnight) Scannabue, housed in a former corner garage, is a retro-fitted bistro that has a touch of Paris in its cast iron doors and tiled floors. There's a casual feel, but the cooking is some of Turin's most lauded.

Staples like *baccalà* (cod) are freshly matched with Jerusalem artichoke purée and crisped leeks, a starter reworks the French *tarte Tatin* into a thoroughly modern onion pie, and there's a club sandwich on offer if you miss service.

La Sartoria
PIEDMONTESE €€

(☑ 011 046 16 83; www.ristorantelasartoria.com; Via Sant'Anselmo 27a; meals €35; ⊗ 1-2pm Tue-Fri, 8-11pm Mon-Sat) A forward-thinking chef runs this diminutive San Salvario place with much attention to detail and plenty of whimsical touches, both in his cooking and in the sweetly evocative tailor-shop decor. The pace is leisurely, the wine list good and dishes can be had as starters or mains. The menu, mostly creative takes on the Piedmont kitchen, makes occasional strides into the international (fish and chips! green curry!).

L'Acino
PIEDMONTESE €€

(☑ 011 521 70 77; Via San Domenico 2a; meals €35-40; ⊗ 7.30-11.30pm Mon-Sat) Half a dozen tables and a legion of enamoured followers mean this inviting restaurant is hard to get into. Book ahead or arrive at the stroke of 7.30pm for snails, tripe and *ragù* (meat stew) cooked in Roero wine, or classic Piedmontese pasta staples such as *plin* (ravioli). Their *bonet* (chocolate pudding) is considered one of the city's best.

Oinos
SUSHI, FUSION €€

(☑ 011 83 50 84; www.oinosristorante.it; Via della Rocca 39g; dishes €12-18; ⊗ 12.30-3pm & 8pm-midnight Mon-Sat) Turin's sushi obsession runs possibly only second to Milan's. Yes, like many of its counterparts, Oinos offers top-quality traditional Japanese raw plates, but also has a 'susciliano' menu that fuses Japanese technique with the ingredients of Italy's Mediterranean ports, especially those of Sicily. Raw fish teamed with citrus oils and capers, basil powder and almonds or spicy *caponata*? Genius.

Porto di Savona
TRATTORIA €€

(☑ 011 817 35 00; www.foodandcompany.com; Piazza Vittorio Veneto 2; meals €28; ⊗ 12.30-2.30pm & 7.30-10.30pm) An unpretentious trattoria that dates to Turin's capital days (ie the 1860s), it has a deserved reputation for superb *agnolotti al sugo arrosto* (Piedmontese ravioli in a meat gravy), and *gnocchi di patate al gorgonzola*. The mains – including *bollito misto alla piemontese* (boiled meat and vegetable stew) – are equally memorable.

DON'T MISS

APERICENA HOUR

Who needs *cena* (dinner) when you've got bar snacks the size of...well...dinners? Turin's answer to the aperitif is the *apericena*, where bar-side buffets resemble full-blown meals. Turin's most groaning, if not always the best quality, apericenas can be had along Via Po and in Piazza Vittorio Veneto. Here, places such as **La Drogheria** serve up brimming bowls of pasta, artichoke pies and risotto along with meats, cheese and bread. The Quadrilatero quarter is another buffet wonderland – **Pastis** and **Boka** (Piazza Emanuele Filiberto 7c; ⊗ 5pm-1am) on Piazza Filiberto do a full carb-heavy spread, or keep it classy with just cheese at I Tre Galli (p212). Expect to pay between €6 to €12 for an apericena hour drink.

Piano 35
GASTRONOMY €€€

(☑ 011 438 78 00; www.grattacielointesasanpaolo.com/en/ristorante; Corso Inghilterra 3; meals €70, degustation €85/110; ⊗ 12.30-2.30pm & 8-10.30pm Tue-Sat, dinner only Mon) Much of Turin's fine dining is done in hallowed old Savoy surrounds, but Piano 35 is defiantly different. Its setting, atop the new Renzo Piano-designed Grattacielo Intesa San Paolo (at 166m, the city's second-tallest building), is the loftiest restaurant in Italy and, as you might imagine, light and super contemporary as well as being fringed with a small forest of indoor plants.

Food is big-occasion dining which is brought back to earth by its extensive use of wild herbs, heritage vegetables and traditional favourites.

Ristorante Del Cambio
GASTRONOMY €€€

(☑ 011 54 66 90; www.delcambio.it; Piazza Carignano 2; set menus from €60; ⊗ 7.30-10.30pm Tue, 12.30-2.30pm & 7.30-10.30pm Wed-Sat, 12.30-2.30pm Sun) Crimson velvet, glittering chandeliers, baroque mirrors and a timeless air greet you at this grande dame of the Turin dining scene, regularly patronised by Count Cavour in his day. It first opened its doors in 1757, and classic Piedmont cuisine still dominates the menu, although you'll eat in the company of some great contemporary art now, too. Bookings and smart dress are advised.

🍷 Drinking & Nightlife

Nightlife – including the nightly *aperitivo* crawl – concentrates in the riverside area around Piazza Vittoria Veneto, the Quadrilatero Romano district and, with a younger crowd, the southern neighbourhood of San Salvarino. The Po-side enclaves of Vanchiglia and Dora are the city's new cool zone – both have some excellent wine bars and great live venues and club nights.

★ I Tre Galli   WINE BAR
(www.3galli.com; Via Sant'Agostino 25; ⊗ 12.30pm-2.30pm & 6.30pm-midnight Mon-Wed, to 2am Thu-Sat) A Quadrilatero favourite that's been here for over two decades, spacious and rustic, cool but warm, Tre Galli is a fabulous spot for a drink at any time, but at its most local when the gourmet *aperitivi* appears around 6pm. The dinner menu is also worth investigating if you've not gorged on cheese already.

Bar Cavour   COCKTAIL BAR
(⊘ 011 54 66 90; http://delcambio.it; Piazza Carignano 2; ⊗ 7pm-1.30am Tue-Sat) Named for its most famous barfly, the ubiquitous Count Cavour, this beautiful historical room combines a magical, mirrored setting with a great collection of contemporary art and design savvy. Upstairs from Del Cambio (p211), a Michelin-starred restaurant, the *aperitivo* here doesn't come cheap but is an elegant respite from pizza slices.

Da Emilia   WINE BAR
(Corso San Maurizio 47; ⊗ 11am-3am Mon-Fri, from 6pm Sat & Sun) This Vanchiglia local is everything you could want in a neighbourhood bar: come for coffee, have a bite to eat, drop in for a good wine or nicely made cocktail in the early evening then end up hanging out to the small hours with bands playing late most nights of the week.

Luogo Divino   WINE BAR
(⊘ 011 1932 3530; www.luogodivino.com; Via San Massimo 13; ⊗ 6-11.30pm Tue-Sat, noon-3pm & 7-10.30pm Sun) The excellent, and not ridiculously priced, wines here are poured after a discussion about your likes, mood and whims. While wine is the raison d'être, it's hard not to mention the food too, which comes small-plate style, and is hugely creative but well-rooted in the Piedmontese landscape and ethos.

GRAND CAFES

While Turin's contemporary food and wine scene booms, some things – namely its classic cafes – stay the same.

Al Bicerin (www.bicerin.it; Piazza della Consolata 5; ⊗ 8.30am-7.30pm Thu-Tue, closed Aug) Founded in 1763, with an exquisitely simple boiserie interior dating to the early 1800s, this one-room cafe takes its name from its signature drink, a potent combination of chocolate, coffee and cream. Fuelling the likes of Dumas, Puccini, Nietzsche and Calvino, along with Savoy royalty and Turin's workers, the price didn't rise for a century to ensure no one missed out.

Caffè Mulassano (Piazza Castello 15; ⊗ 7.30am-10.30pm) Elbow your way to the bar or hope for a seat at one of the five wee tables at this art nouveau gem, where regulars sink espresso *in piedi* (standing) while discussing Juventus' current form with the bow-tied baristas.

Caffè San Carlo (Piazza San Carlo 156; ⊗ 8am-midnight Tue-Fri, to 1am Sat, to 9pm Mon) Perhaps the most gilded of the gilded, this glittery cafe dates from 1822. You'll get neckache admiring the weighty chandelier and pay for the privilege (€4 and upwards for coffee), but the service is the most genial of the old-school cafe clique.

Fiorio (Via Po 8; ⊗ 8.30am-1am Tue-Sun) Garner literary inspiration in Mark Twain's old window seat as you contemplate the gilded interior of a cafe where 19th-century students once plotted revolutions and the Count of Cavour deftly played whist. The bittersweet hot chocolate remains inspirational.

Caffè Torino (Piazza San Carlo 204; ⊗ 7.30am-1am) This chandelier-lit showpiece opened in 1903. A brass plaque of the city's emblem, a bull (Torino in Italian means 'little bull'), is embedded in the pavement out front; rub your shoe across it for good luck (you won't have to queue like in Milan).

Farmacia Del Cambio BAR
(☑011 1921 1250; www.delcambio.it/farmacia; Piazza Carignano 2; ☺9am-9.30pm) Cambio Corner – home to one of Turin's best restaurants, not to mention bars – now has this 'informal' but glamorous all-day space, situated within an old pharmacy that dates back to 1833. Pop in for morning coffee or to pick up deli goods, but do come back for *aperitivo*, either beneath the dark shelves, by the theatrically open kitchen or out on the piazza.

Enoteca Botz WINE BAR
(☑340 2150497; www.facebook.com/enoteca botz; Via Santa Giulia 48; ☺6pm-3am Tue-Sat, to midnight Sun & Mon) A Vanchiglia triangle stalwart, come here for good wine served by serious wine pros at reasonable prices. Plus you get to hang out with some of the neighbourhood's cool kids at the same time. A good choice when you're too old (or tired) for clubs, but too young (or excited) to go home.

Barolino Cocchi BAR, CAFE
(☑011 436 76 41; Via Bonelli 16c; ☺8.30am-5pm Mon-Fri, 7.30pm-1am Fri & Sat) A beautifully decorated neighbourhood bolthole with excellent coffee during the week and convivial little *amaro*-fuelled (a dark liqueur prepared from herbs) sessions on Friday and Saturday nights.

Caffè-Vini
Emilio Ranzini WINE BAR
(☑011 765 04 77; Via Porta Palatina 9g; ☺9:30am-8.30pm Mon-Fri, 10:30am-5pm Sat) Location scouts looking for a neighbourhood bar from Turin's mid-century glory days would jump on this little place. A crew of local shopkeepers, creatives and students frequently prop up its dark wooden bar and loll about the summer courtyard with wines by the glass, €1 boiled eggs and small plates.

Bazaaar BAR
(www.bazaaar.it; Via Stampatori 9; ☺7am-2am) This big, bright corner space offers up everything from breakfast espressos to gelato to cocktails, all day, every day. A relaxing place to while away a few hours, you can also stay busy here with a calendar of musical acts on Saturday nights, and weekly events, including themed 'cook & roll' music and cooking nights.

La Drogheria BAR
(www.la-drogheria.it; Piazza Vittorio Veneto 18; ☺10am-2am) Occupying an old pharmacy, La Drogheria's vintage sofas are coveted by a laid-back, studenty crowd who enjoy drinks and a groaning, and unusually healthy, *aperitivi* buffet before hitting the clubs down by the Po.

Pastis WINE BAR
(Piazza Emanuele Filiberto 9; ☺9am-3.30pm & 6pm-2am) A cute take on Paris in the '60s, this day-night bar has a loyal local following. Young Torinese come for big weekend brunches, a nightly *aperitivo* spread or a late-night *amaro* or three.

Hiroshima
Mon Amour CLUB
(www.hiroshimamonamour.org, Via Bossoli 83; admission free-€15; ☺hours vary) This legendary dance club features everything from folk and punk to tango and techno. Check the website for specific opening hours and details on the weekend night bus.

☆ Entertainment

Most live-music venues are out of the centre either south in Lingotto and San Salvario or to the north in Vanchiglia and Dora.

Teatro Regio Torino THEATRE
(☑011 881 52 41; www.teatroregio.torino.it; Piazza Castello 215; ☺ticket office 10.30am-6pm Tue-Fri, to 4pm Sat & 1hr before performances) Sold-out performances can sometimes be watched free on live TV in the adjoining Teatro Piccolo Regio, where Puccini premiered *La Bohème* in 1896, and it's always worth popping into the box office to see what might not be sold out. Sadly, some of Carlo Mollino's visionary mid-century fit-out did not survive subsequent renovations, but the seductive red, rhythmic foyer is still a treat. Tickets start at €55.

Astoria LIVE MUSIC, CLUB
(☑345 4483156; www.astoria-studios.com; Via Berthollet 13; ☺7pm-4am Thu-Sat) A street-side cocktail bar hides a basement venue that showcases some excellent international and local indie talent as well as club nights. Kicks Up on a Saturday is the most long running of these and pushes into psych and hip-hop from a rock and roll base. Tickets for larger shows can be bought online and picked up at the venue on the night.

Bunker
LIVE MUSIC

(www.variantebunker.com; Via Niccolò Paganini 0/200) A multi-disciplinary collective that organises one of winter's best electronic and techno club nights as well as live concerts. Also worth checking out for their street-art exhibitions and various other hard-hitting cultural activities.

Blah Blah
LIVE MUSIC

(☑ 392 7045240; www.blahblahtorino.com; Via Po 21; ⊙ 7am-2am Mon-Thu, to 3am Fri, 8am-3am Sat, 9am-2am Sun) An intriguing, and very Torinese, venue that will feed you breakfast or lunch, surprise you with an alternative cinema screening pre-*aperitivo*, have a cult international music act serenade you (say ex-Bad Seed Hugo Race and the Fatalists) after dinner and then keep you dancing to 3am.

Spazio 211
LIVE MUSIC

(☑ 011 1970 5919; www.spazio211.com; Via Cigna 21) This long-established live-music venue, a 10-minute taxi ride north of the city centre, is the city's main venue for international indie acts, interesting theme nights, as well as big Italian names like Guida. Book tickets on the website.

🔒 Shopping

★ Laboratorio Zanzara
ARTS & CRAFTS

(☑ 011 026 88 53; www.laboratoriozanzara.it; Via Bonelli 3a; ⊙ 10am-12.30pm & 2-4pm Mon-Fri, 10am-12.30pm & 3.30-7pm Sat) A delightfully eccentric collection of handmade objects, light fittings, posters, textiles, cards and calendars fills this bright shop, which is run as a non-profit cooperative, employing people with intellectual disabilities. It's a noble enterprise, yes, but its wares are the model of Torinese cool, with the co-op's director, Gianluca Cannizzo, also one of the city's most celebrated creatives.

Giorgio Maffei
BOOKS

(www.giorgiomaffei.it; Via San Francesco da Paola 13; ⊙ by appointment) Giorgio Maffei was one of the world's most dedicated collectors of books by 20th-century visual and literary avant-garde artists, including Futurist, Dadaist and Surrealist work but also by conceptual artists from the 1960s onwards. His wife and son lovingly tend the collection and are happy to arrange viewings and sales for those with an interest in 20th-century and conceptual art; by appointment only.

Balon
MARKET

(www.balon.it; Via Borgo Dora; ⊙ 7am-7pm Sat) This sprawling flea market has brought street merchants to the north of Porta Palazzo for over 150 years. It's both fascinating and overwhelming, but can turn up some splendid vintage finds for the persistent and sharp of eye. The pace settles down come mid-afternoon and there are plenty of artfully dishevelled cafes and bars at which to grab a coffee or *spritz*.

The Gran Balon, with more specialised antique and vintage dealers, happens on the second Sunday of the month, from 8am.

Eataly Torino Lingotto
FOOD & DRINKS

(www.eataly.net; Via Nizza 230; ⊙ 10am-10.30pm) 🖋 The global Slow Food phenomenon began here in Lingotto. Set in a vast converted factory, the Eataly mothership houses a staggering array of sustainable food and drink, along with beautiful affordable kitchenware and cook books. Specialist counters that correspond to their produce area – bread and pizza, cheese, pasta, seafood, Piedmontese beef – serve lunch from 12.30pm to 2.30pm. Food lovers heaven!

JUVENTUS FOREVER

If paying your respects to the Holy Shroud has little appeal, you might prefer to tap into Italy's other religion: *calcio* (football). Its cathedral is the **Juventus Stadium**, inaugurated in 2011 as the home ground to the legendary *bianconeri*, Italy's most successful football club. The state-of-the-art ground has a Juventus Museum (p203) that will blind you with its silverware (28 league titles – and the rest!) and proudly recount how it was all amassed.

On the other side of town, the **Stadio Olimpico** (which hosted the 2006 Winter Olympics) is home to Turin's other team, Torino FC. Until 2011, Torino shared their ground with Juventus, but now they've got the place to themselves except when they play the *bianconeri* in the hotly fought *Derby della Mole*.

To get to the Juventus Stadium from the city centre, catch bus 72 from the corner of Via XX Settembre and Via Bertola. To get to the Stadio Olimpico, take tram 4 from Porta Nuova train station and get off after eight stops.

Porta Palazzo MARKET
(http://scopriportapalazzo.com; Piazza della Repubblica; ⊙7am-1pm Mon-Fri, to 7pm Sat) Europe's largest food market has hundreds of stalls, including a large open-air market with a separate undercover local and organic produce area, and a large covered fish and meat hall. It's frantic, fabulously multicultural and fun.

La Belle Histoire FASHION & ACCESSORIES
(⊘011 813 61 99; www.labellehistoire.it; Via Montebello 15; ⊙10am-1pm & 3.30-7.30pm Tue-Sat, 3.30-7.30pm Mon) Torinese women have a very particular version of the Italian *bella figura* and the mostly Italian designers here (with Japan and France also occasionally represented, too) really epitomise the pared-back, if far from casual, style of the city. Upstairs you'll find an equally special range for homewares including pure linen sheets and tableware and a line of Tuscan terracotta pottery.

Magnifica Preda VINTAGE
(⊘334 7335553; www.magnificapreda.it; Via Sant'Agostino 28; ⊙3.30-7pm Mon-Thu, to 11pm Fri, 11am-11pm Sat) This huge vintage shop has both high-end collectable pieces and good quality everyday finds if you're willing to put in the leg work. There's also a cute attached bar for coffee or *spritzes*.

Via Stampatori Perfumeria PERFUME
(⊘339 2581330; Via Stampatori 4) Elena Boggio, who owns the Via Stampatori (p208) B&B upstairs, has a passion for natural perfumes, which she considers have their own life force. She grows many of the botanical elements that go into her range of scents (which can be both worn on the skin or used as room sprays) herself.

Parrot and Palm CLOTHING, PERFUME
(⊘011 817 78 62; www.parrotandpalm.it; Via Maria Vittoria 28g; ⊙3.30-7.30pm Mon, 10am-1pm & 3.30-7.30pm Tue-Thu, 10am-7.30pm Fri & Sat) Two pretty rooms are packed here with beautiful women's clothes, accessories and a select number of perfumes and homewares. There are locally made items as well as an eclectic range of labels sourced from the peripatetic owner's travels.

Sapori di Tassinari FOOD & DRINKS
(⊘011 53 03 47; Via San Tommaso 12; ⊙9am-7.30pm Tue-Sat) This neighbourhood pasta shop and *rosticceria* (delicatessan) has been run with love by Maurizio and Iva for 30 years. Choose from the brimming window of prepared dishes sold by weight that include roast salmon, meatballs, Russian salad and gratiné leeks or artichokes: perfect picnic or hotel-room fare.

San Carlo dal 1973 FASHION & ACCESSORIES
(San Carlo 1; ⊘011 511 41 11; www.sancarlodal1973. com; Piazza San Carlo 201; ⊙10.30am-7pm Tue-Sat, from 3pm Mon) This Torinese fashion institution – the city's first 'concept store' – stocks a tightly curated selection of Italian and European high fashion, along with a selection of perfumes and candles. It's Turin at its most edgily elegant.

Guido Gobino CHOCOLATE
(www.guidogobino.it; Via Lagrange 1; ⊙10am-8pm Tue-Sun, 3-8pm Mon) Guido Gobino's extreme attention to detail, flair and innovation have made him Turin's favourite modern chocolatier. Have a box of his tiny tile-like ganache chocolates made to order; highly evocative flavours include vermouth, Barolo, and lemon and clove, or grab a bag of his classic *gianduiotto* (triangular chocolates made from *gianduja* – Turin's hazelnut paste).

There's also a slim back cafe where you can order hot chocolates and a chocolate tasting plate.

Libreria Luxemburg BOOKS
(Via Battisti 7; ⊙9am-7.30pm Mon-Sat, 10am-1pm & 3-7pm Sun) This dark, rambling Anglophone bookshop is well stocked with literary fiction, light reading, international magazines and a full stash of travel guides, including Lonely Planet. They also carry British news papers. Just don't expect an Inglese-style chat about the weather.

Pepino CHOCOLATE
(Piazza Carignano 8; ⊙8.30am-8pm Sun-Thu, to midnight Fri & Sat) Chocolate in all its guises is available at Pepino, where ice cream dipped in chocolate on a stick was invented in 1937. Longer opening hours in summer.

❶ Information

Ospedale Mauriziano Umberto I (⊘011 5 08 01; www.mauriziano.it; Largo Turati 62)

Piazza Castello Tourist Office (⊘011 53 51 81; www.turismotorino.org; Piazza Castello; ⊙9am-6pm) Central and multilingual.

Police Station (⊘011 5 58 81; Corso Vinzaglio 10)

Post Office (Via Alfieri 10; ⊙8.30am-7pm Mon-Fri, to 1pm Sat)

Around Turin

N 0 ——— 5 km
0 ——— 2.5 miles

Turin Airport
(Caselle)

Basilica di
Superga

Reggia di
Venaria Reale

Juventus
Museum

Museo
Casa
Mollino

See Turin Map (p204)

Castello
di Rivoli

Galleria Civica
d'Arte Moderna e
Contemporanea

Chiesa di
Gran Madre
di Dio

Lingotto
Fiere

Museo Nazionale
dell'Automobile

TURIN, PIEDMONT & THE ITALIAN RIVIERA LANGHE

ℹ Getting There & Away

AIR

Turin's **Caselle** (☎ 011 567 63 61; www.aeropor
toditorino.it; Strada Aeroporto 12) airport, 16km
northwest of the city centre in Caselle, has connections to European and national destinations.
Budget airline Ryanair operates flights to Bari,
Palermo, London Stansted, Barcelona, Dublin
and Ibiza.

TRAIN

Regular daily trains connect Turin's **Stazione
Porta Nuova** (Piazza Carlo Felice) to the following destinations.

DESTINATION	FARE (€)	DURATION (HR)	FREQUENCY
Milan	12.45	1¾	28
Aosta	9.45	2	21
Venice	70	4½	17
Genoa	12.40	1¾	16
Rome	96	7	11

Some international trains also depart from **Stazione Porta Susa** (Corso Inghilterra) terminal.

BUS

Most international, national and regional buses
terminate at the **bus station** (Corso Castelfidardo), 1km west from Stazione Porta Nuova along
Corso Vittorio Emanuele II, including services to
Milan's Malpensa airport.

ℹ Getting Around

PUBLIC TRANSPORT

The city boasts a dense network of buses,
trams, a metro system and a cable car, all run
by the **Gruppo Torinese Trasporti** (GTT; www.
gtt.to.it/en; Piazza Castello; ⊙10am-6pm).
It has an **information office** (GTT; ☎ 011 562
89 85; www.gtt.to.it; Porta Nuova, via Sacchi;
⊙7.15am-7pm Mon-Fri, 8.30am-7pm Sat, to
6pm Sun) at Stazione Porta Nuova, if you're
happy to take a ticket and wait in line for minimal
information. Buses and trams run from 6am to
midnight and tickets cost €1.50 (90 minutes),
€3 (four hours), €5 (one-day pass) or €17.50 for
a 15-ticket carnet. **Taxis** (☎ 011 57 30; www.rad
iotaxi.it) can be ordered online or by phone.

TRAIN

Turin's single-line metro runs from Fermi to
Lingotto. It first opened for the Winter Olympics
in February 2006 and reached Lingotto in 2011.
The line will extend south to Piazza Bengasi, two
stations south of Lingotto, at some time late
2017 or in 2018. Ordinary tickets cost €1.50 and
allow 90-minute connections with bus and tram
networks.

BICYCLE

Turin's ever-expanding bike-sharing scheme,
[To]Bike (www.tobike.it; 1-/2-day pass €8/13),
is one of the largest in Italy. Tourist passes for
either one day (four hours) or two days (eight
hours) use of the bright-yellow *biciclette* can be
bought at the Piazza Castello tourist office. For
longer subscriptions, see the website.

The Langhe

☎ 0173

Gourmets get ready to indulge: the rolling
hills, valleys and townships of southern
Piedmont are northern Italy's most redolent
pantry, weighed down with sweet hazelnuts,
rare white truffles, arborio rice, delicate veal,
precious cheeses and Nebbiolo grapes that
metamorphose into the magical Barolo and
Barbaresco wines. Out here in the damp Po
river basin, the food is earthy but sublime,
steeped in traditions as old as the towns that
foster them. There's Alba, the region's vibrant, pretty capital; Bra, home of the Slow
Food Movement; Pollenzo, host to the University of Gastronomic Sciences and the con-
stellation of charming villages that includes
La Morra, Neive, Barolo and Barbaresco.

Alba

🌿 0173 / POP 31,700 / ELEV 172M

A once-powerful city-state – its centre had more than 100 towers – Alba is considered the capital of the Langhe and has big-city confidence and energy while retaining all the grace and warmth of a small rural town. Alba's considerable gastronomic reputation comes courtesy of its white truffles, dark chocolate and wine. Its annual autumn truffle fair draws huge crowds and the odd truffle-mad celebrity (Jay Z, we're looking at you). The *vendemmia* (grape harvest) remains refreshingly local and low key, if ecstatic in its own way.

The vine striped Langhe Hills radiate out from the town like a giant undulating vegetable garden, replete with grapes, hazelnut groves and wineries. Exploring Alba's fertile larder on foot or with two wheels is a delicious pleasure.

👁 Sights & Activities

Centro Culturale
San Giuseppe
CULTURAL CENTRE

(🌿 0173 29 61 63; www.centroculturalesangiuseppe.it; Piazza Vernazza 6; ⏰ church 2.30-6.30pm Tue-Sun, exhibitions vary) A converted church turned cultural centre, this is a lovely place to catch a choral or chamber music performance, or undertake a bracing hike up 134 steps to the 36m belltower (€1). In the basement, 2nd-century archaeological remains from the vanquished Roman Empire have been uncovered, and they also host temporary art exhibitions here.

Consorzio Turistico
Langhe Monferrato Roero
TOUR

(🌿 0173 36 25 62; www.booking-experience.tartufoevino.it; Piazza Risorgimento 2) This Alba-based consortium organises a wide variety of tours and courses unique to the Alba region. Truffle hunting can be arranged seasonally for white (September to December) or black (May to September) for €65 per person. Year-round, you can tour a hazelnut farm for €30 or take part in a four-hour cooking course for €130.

✨ Festivals & Events

Fiera del Tartufo
FOOD & DRINK

(Truffle Festival; www.fieradeltartufo.org; ⏰ Oct-Nov) October's precious white truffle crop is bought, sold and celebrated at this annual festival, held every weekend from mid-October to mid-November. Come and watch princely sums exchanged and sample autumn's bounty. Book accommodation, and restaurants, well ahead.

🛏 Sleeping

Hotel Langhe
HOTEL €

(🌿 0173 36 69 33; www.hotellanghe.it; Strada Profonda 21; s/d €85/110; 🅿 ❋ 🛜) Two kilometres from the city centre, Hotel Langhe sits on the edge of vineyards that push up against Alba's not entirely unpleasant suburban sprawl. Staff are friendly and the pace relaxed, with a wine conservatory, a bright breakfast area and downstairs rooms with French windows that open onto a sunny forecourt.

Casa Bona
B&B, APARTMENT €

(🌿 0173 29 05 35; www.casa-bona.it; Corso Nino Bixio 22; d €95; 🅿 🛜) Disregard the unremarkable building. This collection of several apartments with modern bedrooms and bathrooms is thoughtfully equipped (you get your own stovetop espresso maker), along with an owner who will drop by with homemade cakes. No credit cards and slightly out of town.

L'Orto delle Rose
B&B €€

(🌿 333 2614143; http://ortodellerose.weebly.com; Via Cuneo 5; s/d €100/120, 🅿 ❋ 🛜) High ceilings and beautiful original bones make this one-room family-run B&B a real find. Bonus points come from the fact it puts you in the historic centre but has a small garden *and* a car space.

Casa Dellatorre
B&B €€

(🌿 0173 44 12 04; Via Elvio Pertinace 20; s/d €135/160; ❋) Three sisters run this central, upmarket B&B, once their family home, with love. The three classically decorated, antique filled rooms share a flowery internal courtyard. Breakfast is served in the courtyard in summer, and in the sisters' pretty cafe in winter.

🍴 Eating

Dolcemente Alba
PASTRIES €

(🌿 0173 36 14 26; www.facebook.com/pg/dolcementealba; Piazza Savona 9; ⏰ 8am-12.30pm & 3.30-7.30pm) Pastry chef Luca Montersino's Golosi di Salute brand is known throughout northern Italy for its biscuits, cakes, tarts and spreads that variously avoid gluten, dairy or sugar; these days his produce is available as far afield as New York. He is an Alba local (with a killer gluten-free *torta di*

ANDERSPHOTO/SHUTTERSTOCK ©

1. White Alba truffles **2.** Truffle hunting, Norcia (p609)
3. Digging up truffles **4.** Black truffle and Parmesan pasta

Truffles: Food of the Gods

One of the world's most mystical, revered foodstuffs, truffles are Italy's gastronomic gold. Roman emperor Nero called them the 'food of the gods', while composer Rossini hailed them as the 'mushrooms of Mozart'.

Hunting them out is a specialist activity. Truffles – subterranean edible fungi, similar to mushrooms, that colonise the roots of certain tree species – are notoriously hard to find. The most prized variety is the white truffle from the Alba region in Piedmont. Other slightly less aromatic white truffles are found in Tuscany, while black truffles are most prevalent in Umbria and Le Marche. White truffles are harvested from early October to December; black truffles are available from November to March.

Italy's biggest truffle festival is held in Alba every weekend for a month from mid-October to mid-November, while other notable events are the Tuscan towns of San Miniato and San Giovanni d'Asso, near Siena, during the second half of November. The season is crowned in a boisterous celebration of the black truffle in the Umbrian town of Norcia during late February and early March.

JOINING A TRUFFLE HUNT

Alba Tourist Office (www.langheroero. it) Organises truffle hunts and lists local restaurants offering truffle menus.

Tartufo e Vino (www.tartufocvino.it) From Alba, hit the woods with an expert *trifulau* for white truffles in autumn and winter, black in spring and summer.

Assotartufi San Giovanni (www.asso tartufi.it) Organises hunts year-round in San Giovanni d'Asso, southern Tuscany.

Barbialla Nuova (www.barbiallanuova.it) An organic truffle farm *agriturismo* known for its hunts near the town of San Miniato in Tuscany.

Love Umbria (www.love-umbria.com) Agency offering culinary tours of Umbria, including truffle-hunting weekends around Norcia.

nocciole – hazelnut cake – to prove it) and this, his flagship, carries a large range.

Osteria dei Sognatori
OSTERIA €€

(Via Macrino 8b; meals €18-28; ⏲noon-2pm & 7-11pm Thu-Tue) Menu? What menu? You get whatever's in the pot at this dimly lit place. Munch on the theatrically large breadsticks while you wait for an array of antipasti to arrive, then try to keep up as the dishes mount up. Walls are bedecked with football memorabilia and B&W snaps of bearded wartime partisans look over rowdy tables of locals. Bookings advised.

★ La Piola
PIEDMONTESE €€

(⏲0173 44 28 00; www.lapiola-alba.it; Piazza Risorgimento 4; meals €25-45; ⏲noon-2.30pm & 7-10pm Mon-Sat, closed Mon in summer) Part of the Ceretto family's small empire, La Piola offers a faithful menu of traditional Piedmontese dishes but at the same time manages to be stylish, modern and relaxed (let's put it down to *sprezzatura* – the Italian art of studied nonchalance), with a kitchen overseen by one of Italy's most respected chefs, Enrico Crippa, from gastronomic Piazza Duomo upstairs.

Expect wonderful produce – the vegetables and herbs all come from the Cerettos' own garden – and technique, along with a sense-grabbing flair. Engaged young staff and great contemporary artwork (including specially commissioned 'show' plates) make the experience a special one. Don't miss their version of *vitello tonnato* (sliced cold veal and tuna sauce) and *bonet* (chocolate pudding): both the apotheosis of their respective genres. Check the website for details of their monthly dinners that celebrate Piedmontese classics often too difficult to do for single diners.

Osteria della Rosa Rossa
OSTERIA €€

(⏲0172 48 81 33; Via San Pietro 31, Cherasco; set menus €30-35; ⏲noon-2pm & 7-11pm Wed-Mon) This lovely rustic dining room in Cherasco, with shady terrace for summer days, specialises in dishes made with the town's signature produce, snails. Advance reservations are required.

Piazza Duomo
GASTRONOMY €€€

(⏲0173 44 28 00; www.piazzaduomoalba.it; Piazza Risorgimento 4; meals €150, degustation €200/240; ⏲12.30-2pm & 7.30-10pm Tue-Sat) Enrico Crippa's Michelin-starred restaurant is now in its second decade and considered one of Italy's best. Dreamlike frescoes by Francesco Clemente fill the fleshy pink dining room, which is otherwise a bastion of elegant restraint. On the plate, expect the high concept play beloved of Italian fine-dining chefs, along with spectacular super-local, and some homegrown, produce (this *is* white truffle country).

Four elegant rooms (from €240 a night) are available for restaurant guests who just want to fall in a heap after a long night of degustation dining.

Restaurant Larossa
GASTRONOMY €€€

(⏲0173 06 06 39; www.ristorantelarossa.it; Via Alberione 10; meals €70, set menus €60-110; ⏲7-10pm Wed, noon-3pm & 7-10pm Thu-Mon) Young chef Andrea Larossa has been wowing them from this unusual basement space for a few years now. This is Italian gastronomy with all its flourishes but with a nice, earthy Piedmontese touch. If you're keen to try his cooking on a budget, he caters the summertime *aperitivo* at the Contratto winery in nearby Canelli – check the website for details.

🍷 Drinking & Nightlife

I LOVE BA
WINE BAR

(⏲327 3276081; Via Alberione 1; ⏲8am-9pm) BA here stands for Barbaresco and this bright and welcoming little *enoteca* is a relaxed *aperitivo* favourite, with a good range of local wines and knowledgeable staff. Located on the historic centre's perimeter road, it's also convenient for grabbing supplies for a picnic or last-minute gourmet gifts on the way out of town.

Bistrot dei Sognatori
BAR

(Piazza San Giovanni 5; ⏲8am-1am Tue-Sun, from 2pm Mon) This nondescript corner bar packs in the *ragazzi* (guys) every night: perfect if you're done with fine dining and upmarket *enoteca*. Wine choices are still excellent, as are the *spritzes*, cocktails and late night soundtrack.

Pensavo Peggio
BREWERY, BAR

(Corso Langhe 59; ⏲8am-10.30pm Tue-Sat) A 15-minute walk from the old town, this '*microbirrificio e ristoro*', brewery and restaurant, is also one of the city's liveliest places to drink. Join Alba's younger set here for excellent microbrews and interesting wines, including Nascetta, a local white. The kitchen dishes up hearty belly liners – tortellini or roast beef – and offers a lunchtime 'worker's menu' for €10.

Vincafé WINE BAR

(www.vincafe.com; Via Vittorio Emanuele II 12; ⊘7am-midnight) Squeeze through the door and sift through a list of over 350 varieties or, if in doubt, have a Barolo. Downstairs, in a cool vaulted stone cellar, the Veg Cafe restaurant serves up huge healthy salads and pasta.

ℹ Information

Tourist Office (☑ 0173 3 58 33; www.langhe roero.it; Piazza Risorgimento 2; ⊘9am-6pm Mon-Fri, from 9.30am Sat & Sun) In the town's historic centre, this office sells walking maps and can advise on a huge range of food and wine tours.

ℹ Getting There & Away

From the **bus station** (Corso Matteotti 10) there are frequent buses to/from Turin (two hours, €4.95, up to 10 daily) and infrequent buses to/from Barolo (25 minutes, €3.10, two daily) and other surrounding villages.

From Alba's **train station** (Piazza Trento e Trieste) regular trains run to/from Turin via Bra/Asti (1¼ hours, €5.75, hourly).

The irregularity of buses to the surrounding villages makes touring the Langhe better by car or bike. For bike hire (from €20 a day) book through the tourist office. Car hire goes from about €35 per day or the tourist office can hook you up with a driver (prices vary).

Barolo

☑ 0173 / POP 700

The tiny, 1800-hectare parcel of undulating land immediately around this hilltop village knocks out what is arguably the finest *vino* in Italy and currently the next big thing with Anglophone collectors. No flash in the pan, Barolo has been a viticultural hub for at least four centuries and is far too deeply rooted in the soil and the seasons to have wine-snob attitude. The ancient streets are delightful enough themselves to warrant a stroll even if wine is not your thing, but being able to taste its precious, aromatic wines in a relaxed and welcoming tasting room makes visiting a sublime experience indeed.

◉ Sights & Activities

Museo del Vino a Barolo MUSEUM

(www.wimubarolo.it; Castello Comunale Falletti di Barolo; adult/reduced €8/6; ⊘10.30am-7pm, closed Jan & Feb) A capricious jaunt through the history of viticulture via light, film and installations, care of the imagination of Swiss designer François Confino (who also designed Turin's cinema museum; p206). It's set over three floors of the village's stunning medieval castle and best braved *after* a tasting session, when it all will seem to make sense.

Marchesi di Barolo WINE

(☑ 0173 56 44 91; www.marchesibarolo.com; Via Roma 1; ⊘10.30am-6pm) A venerable winery that was first established by the fascinating Juliette Colbert de Maulévrier, a French noblewoman and social reformer, in the early years of the 19th century. You can pop in to buy a bottle, but better to book for a tour and guided tasting (if you're lucky, you'll be taken around the sprawling, historic cellars by 6th-generation Barolo-makers Valentina or Davide Abbona).

🏃 Activities

Gianni Gagliardo WINE

(☑ 0173 5 08 29; www.gagliardo.it; Via Roma 35; ⊘11am-7pm) Gianni Gagliardo is known as the 'father of Favorita', the man responsible for bringing that native white grape back from obscurity in the 1970s. Favorita forays aside, this shop and tasting room is yet another temple to the Nebbiolo grape. There's some extreme vintages represented, along with 'collectors' prices to match.

You can also buy Nebbiolo and Favorita seedlings (€10) here to DIY at home.

Enoteca Regionale del Barolo WINE

(www.enotecadelbarolo.it; Piazza Falletti; ⊘10am-12.30pm & 3-6.30pm Fri-Wed) A huge and well organised, if rather formal, tasting room and shop. A great starting point before striking out to the various cellars and vineyards.

🛏 Sleeping

Casa Svizzera AGRITURISMO €

(☑ 0173 56 64 08; www.casasvizzera.com; Via Roma 65; d €100-130; P 🗢) Five minutes from the Germano family's vines, these three pretty, balconied rooms sit above their central *enoteca* and former bottling plant. It's quiet and ridiculously atmospheric, but also puts you in toddling distance of all the village's tasting rooms and restaurants. Kind staff will happily make local recommendations and reservations for you.

Hotel Barolo HOTEL €

(☑ 0173 5 63 54; www.hotelbarolo.it; Via Lomondo 2; s €80-90, d €100-150; P @ 🗢) Overlooked by the famous *enoteca*-castle, Hotel Barolo is an old-school place; sit back on the terrace with a glass of you-know-what, contemplating the 18th-century Piedmontese architecture that guards its shimmering swimming pool. Follow up with a meal at the in-house Brezza restaurant (it's been serving up truffles and the like for three generations, and making wine since 1885).

Eating & Drinking

La Cantinetta
PIEDMONTESE €
(☑ 0173 5 61 98; Via Roma 33; meals €22-35; ⊙ 12.30-3pm & 7-10pm Fri-Wed) A sunny outside terrace is the big draw here, although you'll be far from unhappy with the menu of local dishes: Ligurian rolled rabbit, risotto with radicchio, veal tongue with salsa verde. Don't miss the antipasto dish of egg in pasta (€7), one of those better-than-the-sum of its parts culinary experiences.

Barolo Friends
PIEDMONTESE €
(☑ 0173 56 05 42; www.barolofriends.it; Piazza Castello 3; meals €20-30; ⊙ 11am-11pm Thu-Tue) An easy, contemporary place that does Piedmontese staples but, helpfully, doesn't keep to rigid service hours or menu formats. Need a quick *vitello tonnato* (cold sliced veal with tuna sauce) or soup? Fancy a late afternoon glass of something special as the sun dips over the vines? Here's your place.

★ La Vita Turchese
WINE BAR
(☑ 366 4556744; www.laviteturchese.com; Via Alba 5; ⊙ 11am-9.30pm Wed-Sat, to 7.30pm Mon) This friendly *enoteca* is run by passionate young staff who will talk you through their good stock of local wines – from a cheap and cheerful Nebbiolo or Arneis to a '74 Barolo at €59 a glass – and they also branch out to some other Italian regions. Daily cheese and *salumi* (cured meats/charcuterie) choices are sourced with love and it's a local favourite for *aperitivo*.

Barbaresco

☑ 0173 / POP 650

Delightful Barbaresco is surrounded by vineyards and characterised by its 30m-high, 11th-century tower, visible from miles around. There are more than 40 wineries and two *enotecas* (wine shop/bars) in the area. Only a few kilometres separate Barolo from Barbaresco; a rainier microclimate, nutrient-rich soil and fewer ageing requirements have made the latter's eponymous wine into a softer, more ethereal red that plays 'queen' to Barolo's 'king'. The village itself is similarly a little softer, less in your face than Barolo. The hilltop hamlet of Treiso, 15 minutes' drive away, also produces Barbaresco.

Activities

★ Le Rocche dei Barbari
WINE
(☑ 0173 63 51 38; Via Torino 62; ⊙ 10am-6pm) This historic winery has a moody tasting room and cellar, with wines that are not retailed elsewhere. Generous complimentary tastings are conducted by the owner, cheese and hazelnuts are offered on pewter platters and the stories of each vintage are enchanting. A quiet Langhe highlight.

Enoteca Regionale del Barbaresco
WINE
(www.enotecadelbarbaresco.it; Piazza del Municipio 7; tower (with wine tasting) €5/4; ⊙ 10am-7pm) Fittingly for a wine that conjures such reverence, this intimate *enoteca* is housed inside a deconsecrated church, with wines lined up where the altar once stood. It costs €2 per tasting glass; six Barbaresco wines are available to try each day, or climb the ancient tower and taste with a view.

Sentiero dei Barbaresco
HIKING
Various trails surround the village, including this 13km loop through the undulating vineyards. The Enoteca Regionale has maps.

Sleeping

Casa Boffa
PENSION €
(☑ 0173 63 51 74; www.boffacarlo.it; Via Torino 9a; s €70, d €85-125; ☎) In a lovely house in the centre of the village, Boffa offers four modern rooms and one suite above a stunning terrace with limitless Langhe valley views. Boffa's cellars are open for tasting daily except Wednesday.

Eating

Ristorante Rabayà
ITALIAN €€
(☑ 0173 63 52 23; Via Rabayà 9; set menus €30-45; ⊙ noon-2pm & 7-10pm Tue-Sat, noon-2pm Sun) Rabayà, on the fringe of the village, has the ambience of dining at a private home. The signature rabbit in Barbaresco works better in its antique-furnished dining room in front of a roaring fire, but its terrace set high above the vineyards is perfect for a summer

evening, even if it's just for a plate of cheese. A snail menu also makes the occasional appearance.

Antinè   PIEDMONTESE €€€
(☑0173 63 52 94; www.antine.it; Via Torino 34; meals €45-55; ☉12.30am-2.30pm & 7.30-10pm Thu-Tue) Sigh-worthy meals are to be had at this justifiably well-regarded restaurant, upstairs in what used to be the village prison. They do the Piedmontese favourites but also push the envelope a tad with dishes such as gnocchi with tripe and *cima di rapa* (bitter greens) and pigeon or sweetbreads for mains. Book ahead.

Bra & Pollenzo
☑0172 / POP 29,850

Bra seems like a small, unassuming Piedmontese town, but as the place where the Slow Food movement first took root in 1986, it's also something of a gastronomic pilgrimage site. There are defiantly no supermarkets in the historic centre, where small, family-run shops are replete with organic sausages, handcrafted chocolates and fresh local farm produce. Naturally, shops shut religiously for a 'slowdown' twice a week. Just down the hill sits Pollenzo, a slightly less picturesque but still pretty town, with the Slow Food movement's very own University of Gastronomic Sciences at its heart.

🍴 Activities

Banca del Vino   WINE
(☑0172 45 80 45; www.bancadelvino.it; Piazza Vittorio Emanuele II 13, Pollenzo; tour & tastings €3-20; ☉10.30am-1pm & 3.30-7.30pm Tue-Sat, 10.30am-1pm Sun) Slow Food's Università di Scienze Gastronomiche oversees this extensive wine cellar/'library' of Italian wines. Free guided tastings are available by reservation.

Università di Scienze Gastronomiche
(University of Gastronomic Sciences; www.unisg.it; Piazza Vittorio Emanuele 9, Pollenzo) 🖉 Another creation of Carlo Petrini, founder of the Slow Food Movement, this university, established in the village of Pollenzo in 2004, occupies a former royal palace and offers three-year courses in gastronomy and food management. Its Banca del Vino conducts free guided tastings by appointment, but it's a nice place to just wander, too.

🛏 Sleeping & Eating

★**Albergo Cantine Ascheri**   DESIGN HOTEL €€
(☑0172 43 03 12; www.ascherihotel.it; Via Piumati 25, Bra; s/d €115/125; ❋❋@) Built around the Ascheri family's 1880-established winery, incorporating wood, steel mesh and glass, this ultra-contemporary hotel includes a mezzanine library, 27 sun-drenched rooms and a vine-lined terrace overlooking the rooftops. From the lobby you can see straight down to the vats in the cellar (guests get a free tour). It's just one block south of Bra's train station.

Albergo Dell'Agenzia   HOTEL €€
(☑0172 45 86 00; www.albergoagenzia.it; Via Fossano 21, Pollenzo; s/d €115/190; ❋❋❋❋) Part of the same sprawling complex that houses Pollenzo's Università di Scienze Gastronomiche, the rooms are spacious and elegantly furnished, with huge beds, walk-in wardrobes, marble bathrooms and the occasional roof terrace that looks over village rooftops. With a restaurant run by people who really know their business, a well-stocked wine cellar and a park, its ever-so-slight corporate edge soon melts away.

Osteria del Boccondivino   OSTERIA €€
(☑0172 42 56 74; www.boccondivinoslow.it; Via Mendicità Istruita 14, Bra; meals €25-32, set menus €19-21; ☉noon-2.30pm & 7-10pm Tue-Sat) 🖉 On the 1st floor of the Slow Food movement's utterly typical courtyard headquarters, this bottle-lined dining room was the first to be opened by the emerging organisation back in the 1980s. Service can be rather humourless, but the menu, which changes daily, is, as you'd expect, a picture of precise providence and seasonality, with dishes that are beautifully prepared.

Guido Ristorante   GASTRONOMY €€€
(☑0173 62 61 62; www.guidoristorante.it; Via Alba 15, Serralunga d'Alba; tasting menus €80-110; ☉7.30-10.30pm Tue-Sat, 12.30-2.30pm Sat & Sun, closed Jan & Aug) The acclaimed fairytale-like space that is the Guido Ristorante is a place that people have been known to cross borders to visit, especially for the veal with truffled cream.

🛈 Information

Tourist Office (☑0172 43 01 85; www.langhe roero.it; Piazza Caduti della Liberta 20, Bra; ☉8.30am-12.30pm & 3-6pm Mon-Fri, 9am-noon Sat & Sun) Has information on both towns and the region.

La Morra

🎵 0173 / POP 2650

Atop a hill surrounded by vines with the Alps as a backdrop, La Morra is bigger and quieter than Barolo, though no less beguiling. The village's *cantina comunale* (communal wine seller) provides lists of places to do tastings.

◉ Sights

★ Cappella del Barolo — PUBLIC ART

(www.ceretto.com/en/experience/art-design/the -chapel-of-barolo; Borgata Cerequio) Alba's wine-making, restaurateuring Ceretti family has commissioned a number of site-specific artworks in the region and this (never consecrated) chapel is one of the most wonderful. Its Sol Lewitt exterior and David Tremlett interiors were added in 1999. Lewitt's playful intervention is visible from across the vines, but don't miss Tremlett's work inside, which is both serene and enlivening. It's always open, just push the door.

🛏 Sleeping

★ Brandini — AGRITURISMO €€

(www.agriturismolamorra.com; Borgo Brandini 16; s €95, d €135-200; P ✻ 🛜 ⛵) 🅿 A five-minute drive below La Morra, this vineyard restaurant and cellar has five cosy, modern rooms. Each is named for a writer and graced with appropriate quotes and reading material, along with equally inspiring views of the Alps. All fittings, from paint to wood to bedding, are made from sustainable, non-toxic materials in line with their organic agricultural practices.

Cooking classes that explore the specialities of the Langhe can be organised for groups or individuals in English or Italian.

Uve Rooms & Wine Bar — BOUTIQUE HOTEL €€

(📞 333 7137892; www.uve.info; Via Umberto I 13; s/d €180/200; ✻ 🛜) A stylish newcomer to La Morra, eight rooms and a couple of suites are Italian flash rather than rustic. Set around an original courtyard of a former monastery, there's rest and contemplation on offer here, or you can worship the grape downstairs at the purple-themed *enoteca*. Guest bikes or bespoke tours will get you out into the countryside.

Arborina Relais — BOUTIQUE HOTEL €€€

(📞 0173 50 03 51; www.arborinarelais.it; Frazione Annunciata 27; d €220-300; P ✻ 🛜 ⛵) A gorgeous, contemporary design is a departure from the usual stately traditional upmarket hotels of this region. The look throughout is dark glamour, with extensive use of grey and dark wood. Beds are large and luxuriously made-up, there's a variety of terraces and vineyard-side gardens to loll about in and both an on-site restaurant and a wine/produce shop at reception.

Note that the smaller 'suites' are more standard-room-size but with benefits, ie coffee machines, mini-kitchens and terraces.

🍴 Eating

★ More e Macine — PIEDMONTESE €

(📞 0173 50 03 95; Via XX Settembre 18; meals €25; ⏰ noon-3pm & 6-11pm) A rambunctious, casual and seemingly chaotic place that turns out some of the town's best food. This is the Piedmontese kitchen at its most essential: come for a mountainous swirl of the signature fine *tajarin* pasta with *ragù*, risotto with whatever vegetable's in season, spicy sauced tongue or sliced octopus. But the star of the menu here is the Barolo by-the-glass list.

You can sample widely and well across producers and vintages from €12 to €30, but if that's not your thing there's a less lofty blackboard with local and pan-Italian whites and 'starter' Barolo, as well as other local reds from €3.50 to €8.

Fontanazza — PIEDMONTESE €

(📞 0173 5 07 18; www.locandafontanazza.it; Strada Fontanazza 4; meals €25; ⏰ noon-2.30pm & 7.30-10pm Tue, Wed, Fri-Sun, dinner only Mon; 🅿) You can take the sun on the terrace in summer or warm up by the open fire on chilly days and enjoy simple, traditional dishes like *tajarin al ragù di arrosto di vitello* (pasta with veal stew) along with a number of vegetable-focused options and whimsical desserts. All pasta, bread and *grissini* are homemade.

Brandini — PIEDMONTESE €€

(📞 0173 5 02 66; www.agriturismolamorra.com; Borgo Brandini 16; meals €28-38; ⏰ 12.30-2.30pm & 7-10pm Wed-Sun, daily for B&B guests) There's a stunning view across vineyards to a wall of snow-capped mountains from the rustic farmhouse tables that grace the light open space at Brandini, while the food is similarly a coming together of tradition and fresh ideas using local produce and organic vegetables from their own gardens. Ask about the cooking classes if you're keen to reproduce the Piedmontese kitchen at home.

Osteria Aborina
GASTRONOMY €€€

(☑0173 500 340; www.osteriarborina.it; Fratzione Annunziata 27; meals €48-55, degustation 5-/6-courses €55/65; ☉dining room 7-10pm Tue-Sat, bar & grill noon-10pm Wed-Mon) Part of the Arborina Relais hotel, this very smart dining room offers gastronomic menus that either rework Piedmontese standards in surprising ways or go for complete culinary poetry and use the global influences that the widely-travelled chef has gathered. The sommelier is one of the region's most revered and overall service is extremely attentive and personal.

In summer, head to the rooftop terrace if you'd prefer a casual grill or plate of *crudo* (they do both raw fish and beef).

Neive

☑0173 / POP 3000

Ping-ponged between Alba and Asti during the Middle Ages, Neive is a quieter proposition these days, its hilltop medieval layout earning it a rating as one of Italy's *borghi più belli* (most beautiful towns). Come here to taste the village's four legendary wines – Dolcetto d'Alba, Barbaresco, Moscato and Barbera d'Alba – among sun-dappled squares and purple wisteria.

🛏 Sleeping

Al Palazzo Rosso
B&B €

(☑333 1179127; http://al-palazzo-rosso.it; Piazza Italia 6; d/ste €110/140; ❄️🛜) Looking out to Piazza Italia, this cute, rather modern place has four stylish rooms. Some are decked out in grey, white and black tones, while others come with wood and earthy-toned accents. The suite has huge windows, some have fireplaces and all have wooden floorboards.

Borgo Vecchio
APARTMENT €€

(☑377 4911705; www.borgovecchioneive.it; Via Borgese 10; ste €170-250; ❄️🛜) These large, luxuriously furnished and very pretty apartment-style suites can sleep two to four and have espresso machines, terraces and, in the largest, a Jacuzzi. No breakfast. There are amazing views and a garden, too.

✗ Eating & Drinking

Osteria del Borgo Vecchio
VEGETARIAN, PIEDMONTESE €

(☑377 4911705; www.borgovecchioneive.it; Via Borgese 10; meals €20-25, set menus €20-33; ☑) A sweet surprise in meat-centric Piedmont, Osteria del Borgo Vecchio does parallel vegetarian and meat menus, with all organic ingredients and all pasta made in-house. Despite these 21st-century conceits, you could still be in your Piedmontese nonna's dining room with delightful tiled floors, farmhouse chairs and a deep red, green and brown palette.

Rather ironically, the steak here is sensational, but so too are the meat-less meatballs.

Donna Selvatica
PIEDMONTESE €€

(☑335 8008282; www.borgovecchioneive.it; Via Rocca 13; meals €38-50, set menu €45; ☉12-3pm & 7-10pm) On the Barbaresco hills overlooking the village, the name Donna Selvatica honours the local grappa producer Romano Levi for whom the 'wild woman' was a symbol. This is an upmarket but still pleasantly rustic dining room with a rooftop terrace to enjoy the view in summer. Dishes are carefully prepared using top-quality ingredients like Fassone beef, snails and truffles.

Al Nido Della Cinciallegra
WINE BAR

(☑0173 67367; www.alnidodellacinciallegra.com; Piazza Cocito 8; ☉8am-10pm) Join Neive's winemakers and restaurateurs here for a wine and a generous *aperitivo* plate; if the weather's warm, you'll all boisterously spill out onto the pretty square. This is the Langhe at its unpretentious best: on one side of the shop buy a brilliant Barolo, on the other, batteries or a ballpoint pen (it's both *enoteca* and village corner shop).

ℹ Information

Tourist Office (www.langheroero.it; Via Borgese 1; ☉8am-1pm, 2-6pm Mon & Thu, 8am-2pm Tue, Wed & Fri, 8am-1pm Sat)

Asti

☑0141 / POP 75,800 / ELEV 123M

Just 30km apart, Asti and Alba were fierce rivals in medieval times, when they faced off against each other as feisty, independent strongholds ruled over by feuding royal families. These days the two towns maintain a friendly rivalry – stately but workaday Asti sniffs at Alba's burgeoning glamour – but are united by viticulture. Asti produces the sparkling white Asti Spumante wine made from white muscat grapes. It's also the best way to access the Monferrato region, a land of literary giants (contemporary academic and novelist Umberto Eco and 18th-century dramatist Vittorio Alfieri hail from here) and yet another classic wine (the intense

OFF THE BEATEN TRACK

MONFERRATO BOLTHOLE

A great find in not-always-budget-friendly Piedmont, **Cascina Rosa** (☑ 0141 92 52 35; www.cascinarosa33.it; Viale Pininfarina 33; s/d €50/80; P ❄ 🛜 🏊) farmhouse B&B stands on a hilltop and enjoys a 360-degree panorama of the lush Monferrato countryside. Switched-on owners really want you to unwind and enjoy the region and besides providing simple, stylish and suitably rustic rooms, offer up a host of ideas for rides, walks and other leisurely pursuits.

Barbera del Monferrato). Vineyards fan out in all directions interspersed with castles and celebrated restaurants.

◉ Sights & Activities

Torre Troyana o Dell'Orologio
LANDMARK

(☑ 0141 39 94 89; www.comune.asti.it; Piazza Medici; adult/reduced €3/1.60; ⊙ 10am-1pm & 4-7pm Sat & Sun Apr-Sep) **FREE** During the late 13th century the region became one of Italy's wealthiest, with 150-odd towers springing up in Asti alone. Of the 12 that remain, only this one can be climbed. Troyana is a 38m-tall tower that dates from the 12th century. The clock was added in 1420.

Enoteca Boero di Boero Mario
WINE

(Piazza Astesano 17; ⊙ 9am-noon & 3-8pm Tue-Fri, 3-8pm Sat-Mon) Roll up your sleeves and get down to Asti's most pleasurable activity – wine tasting. This small, unassuming *enoteca* lines up the glasses morning and afternoon. It's all good, but you're here for the Barbera d'Asti and the sparkling Moscato.

🎉 Festivals & Events

Palio d'Asti
SPORTS

(www.astiturismo.it/en/content/palio-asti) Held on the third Sunday of September, this bareback horse race commemorates a victorious battle against Alba during the Middle Ages and draws over a quarter of a million spectators from surrounding villages. Cheeky Alba answers with a donkey race on the first Sunday in October.

🛏 Sleeping

★ Villa Pattono
BOUTIQUE HOTEL €€

(☑ 0141 96 20 21; www.villapattono.com; Strada Drotte, Costiglione d'Asti; d €144-180; ⊙ late-Mar–Dec; P ❄ 🛜 🏊) Around a 15-minute drive south of the city, surrounded by vineyards and rolling hills, Villa Pattono is a painstakingly restored 18th-century country mansion with frescoed ceilings, dark wood floors and marble bathrooms. There are just nine plush rooms located in the main house, a couple more in the annexed farm buildings and a magnificent three-floor suite in a neo-medieval tower.

Hotel Palio
HOTEL €€

(☑ 0141 3 43 71; www.hotelpalio.com; Via Cavour 106; s/d €110/160; P ❄ @ 🛜) Wedged between the train station and the old town, the Palio's utilitarian exterior belies comfortable facilities inside and its rather charming rooms. The owners also run the Ristorante Falcon Vecchia, one of Asti's oldest, which opened in 1607.

🍴 Eating

CasaMàr
SEAFOOD €€

(☑ 0141 35 11 00; http://casamar.it; Vicolo GB Giuliani 3; meals €28-35; ⊙ 12.30-2pm & 7.30-11.30pm Tue-Fri, lunch only Sat & Sun) A fabulous surprise: a bright, modern seafood place in the heart of tradition-bound, landlocked Piedmont. Some of the international-leaning dishes can be a little ambitious but locals, who obviously need the occasional break from the earthy Langhe flavours, come for the tasty seafood pastas and citrus-spritzed fish tartares. There's also a concise but nice vegetarian menu.

Pompa Magna
PIEDMONTESE €€

(Via Aliberti 65; set menu €20-30; ⊙ 10am-2pm & 6-10pm Tue-Sat, 10am-3pm Sun) This split-level brasserie is a great spot for a bruschetta and glass of very good wine (they also own an *enoteca* at Corso Alfieri 332). But the chef-prepared menus and *bonet* (chocolate pudding) are also worthwhile.

ℹ Information

Tourist Office (www.astiturismo.it; Piazza Alfieri 29; ⊙ 9am-1pm & 2-6pm Mon-Sat, to 5.30pm Sun) Has details of September's flurry of wine festivals.

❶ Getting There & Away

Asti is on the Turin–Genoa railway line and is served by hourly trains in both directions. Journey time is 30 to 55 minutes to/from Turin (€5.25), and 1¾ hours to/from Genoa (€9.45).

The Milky Way

Neither a chocolate bar nor a galaxy of stars, Piedmont's Milky Way (Via Lattea) consists of two parallel valleys just west of Turin that offer top-notch skiing facilities. The more northern of the two, **Valle di Susa**, meanders past a moody abbey, the old Celtic town of Susa and pretty mountain villages. Its southern counterpart, the **Valle di Chisone**, is pure and simple ski-resort territory. The valleys hosted many events at the 2006 Winter Olympics, and the facilities and infrastructure remain state of the art.

◉ Sights

Sacra di San Michele   ABBEY
(www.sacradisanmichele.com; Via alla Sacra 14, Avigliana; adult/reduced €8/6; ⊙ 9.30am-12.30pm & 2.30-6pm summer, to 5pm winter Tue-Sun) This Gothic-Romanesque abbey, brooding above the road 14km from Turin, has kept sentry atop Monte Pirchiriano (962m) since the 10th century. It housed a powerful, bustling community of Benedictine monks for over 600 years and was a staging point for high social level pilgrims. Look out for the whimsical 'Zodiac Door', a 12th-century doorway sculpted with *putti* (cherubs) pulling each other's hair.

Parco Naturale dei Laghi di Avigliana   STATE PARK
(www.parks.it/parco.laghi.avigliana) This nature reserve, a lovely natural amphitheatre, is located on Avigliana's western fringe and includes protected lakes and marshlands.

🏃 Activities

Via Lattea   SKIING
(www.vialattea.it) The Via Lattea ski domain embraces 400km of pistes and five interlinked ski resorts: Sestriere (2035m), Sauze d'Oulx (1509m), Sansicario (1700m), Cesana Torinese (1350m) and Claviere (1760m) in Italy; and Montgenèvre (1850m) in neighbouring France. A single daily ski pass costing €37 covers the entire Milky Way, or €48 including the French slopes.

🛏 Sleeping

Casa Cesana   HOTEL €
(☑ 0122 8 94 62; www.hotelcasacesana.com; Viale Bouvier, Cesana Torinese; s/d €55/110, weekly only in ultra-high season; ℗ ❄) Right across from Cesana Torinese's ski lift, this timber chalet was built for the 2006 Olympics. Its rooms are light-filled and spotless, there's a bustling restaurant open to non-guests (set menus from €20) and its bar is one of the area's liveliest.

Chalet Chez Nous   CHALET, B&B €€
(☑ 0122 85 97 82; www.chaletcheznous.it; Frazione Jouvenceaux 41; s/d €60/120; ⊙ Dec-Jul; ℗ 🛜) Located in Jouvenceaux, the old part of Sauze, barely five minutes from the chair lift, Chalet Chez Nous is not only superbly located but warm and friendly. Rooms are simple, with exposed oak beams and traditional furnishings, and staff are on hand to help with shuttles and ski hire.

❶ Information

Cesana Torinese Tourist Office (☑ 0122 8 92 02; Piazza Vittorio Amedeo 3, Cesana Torinese; ⊙ 9am-1pm & 2-6pm)

WORTH A TRIP

ROMAN SUSA

Susa has a palpable sense of confidence that dates back millennia. It was an important Gaulish city that agreed to be Romanised in the 1st-century BC, then continued as a cosmopolitan trading post during the medieval and Renaissance periods. Its Roman ruins make for an interesting stop on the way to the western ski resorts and it can make a very pleasant base for exploration, hiking or a cheaper alternative to the resorts in winter.

The pristine and impressive triumphal **Arch of Augustus** (Via Impero Romano), dating to 9 BC, sits just outside the centre of town. It marks the transition of power between the Celtic-Ligurian Marcus Julius Cottius and Roman Emperor Augustus, who in fact inaugurated it on his way home from Gaul. Its beautifully peaceful position makes it all the more enthralling, plus you'll often get it all to yourself.

Sauze d'Oulx Tourist Office (☎0122 85 80 09; www.consorziofortur.it; Viale Genevris 7, Sauze d'Oulx; ⊙9am-noon & 3-6pm)

Sestriere

☎0122 / POP 900

Built in the 1930s by the Agnelli clan of Fiat fame, Sestriere ranks among Europe's most glamorous ski resorts due to its enviable location in the snowy eastern realms of the vast Milky Way ski area (you'll either love or hate the architecture).

✖ Eating & Drinking

Pinky PIZZA€
(☎0122 43 21 47; Piazza Fraiteve 5n; pizzas €4-6; ⊙noon-2am) The perennially popular pizzeria Pinky is a skiers' favourite, not to mention a post-bar pitstop. During the season, they also have live music.

L'Officina PUB
(Piazza Fraiteve; ⊙5pm-1am Thu-Tue) A nicely urban-feeling pub located up in the shopping mall that stays open later than some and has good wine and cocktails, as well as a super-cheap tapas menu if you're carb loading.

ℹ Information

Sestriere Tourist Office (☎0122 75 54 44; www.turismotorino.org; Via Pinerolo 19; ⊙9am-1pm & 2-6pm)

Cuneo

☎0171 / POP 56,000 / ELEV 543M

There is a raft of reasons why you should drop by stately Cuneo, not least being the food, the bike friendliness, the hiking possibilities nearby, and, last but certainly not least, the city's signature rum-filled chocolates.

Sitting on a promontory of land between two rivers, Cuneo also provides excellent Alpine views framed by the high pyramid-shaped peak of Monte Viso (3841m) in the Cottian Alps.

◉ Sights

Piazza Galimberti PIAZZA
Arriving in Cuneo's gargantuan main piazza, you'd think you'd just touched down in a capital city. Finished in 1884, it sits aside an older portico-embellished town founded in 1198.

Museo Civico di Cuneo MUSEUM
(Via Santa María 10; adult/reduced €3/2; ⊙3.30-6.30pm Tue-Sun) Cuneo has some wonderfully dark and mysterious churches. The oldest is the deconsecrated San Francisco convent and church, which today hosts this museum tracking the history of the town and province.

🛏 Sleeping

Hotel Ligure HOTEL €
(☎0171 63 45 45; www.ligurehotel.com; Via Savigliano 11; s/d €60/75; P✳☎) In the heart of the old town, this two-star hotel is run by a charming, elegant family and has simple but spotless rooms and self-catering apartments for longer stays.

Hotel Palazzo Lovera HOTEL €€
(☎0171 69 04 20; www.palazzolovera.com; Via Roma 37; s/d €105/130; P✳☎) A French king and an Italian pope have stayed here, hinting at the Loverna's stately past. Rooms are comfortable and the hotel offers rare small-town Italian extras, such as a gym, sauna and two affiliated restaurants, including the Michelin-starred Delle Antiche Contrade.

✖ Eating

★Arione SWEETS, CAFE €
(www.arione-cuneo.com; Piazza Galimberti 14; cake €2-5; ⊙8am-8pm Tue-Sat, 8am-1pm & 3.30-8pm Sun) This 1920s-vintage chocolatier and cafe invented the *Cuneesi al Rhum*, a large, rum-laced praline wrapped in cellophane. The chocolates came to the attention of Hemingway, who made a detour from Milan en route to Nice in 1954 to try them and there's a photograph of his visit in the window. We're with Hemingway: buy a bag. Actually, buy two.

★4 Ciance PIEDMONTESE €
(☎0171 48 90 27; www.4cianceristorante.it; Via Dronero 8c; meals €25, degustation €32; ⊙7.45-10pm Mon, noon-2pm & 7.45-10pm Tue-Sat) A warm, unpretentious place that makes everything from scratch, including the bread. Local specialities (beef cheek in Nebbiolo wine) are requisitely earthy but plated with an unexpected elegance for such a well-priced restaurant.

Bove's STEAK, PIEDMONTESE €
(☎0171 69 26 24; www.boves1929.it; Via Dronero 2; meals €24; ⊙noon-3pm & 6.30-midnight Thu-Tue) This dark corner bar may seem like a Brooklyn transplant with its tiles and high stools, but it's the real deal, serving up high

quality Piedmontese *cruda* (raw minced beef) and steaks since 1929. These days they've added an ever-so-slightly international burger menu: the smoked beef with crunchy pancetta (€11.50) comes highly recommended.

Delle Antiche Contrade GASTRONOMY €€€
(☑0171 48 04 88; www.antichecontrade.it; Via Savigliano 11; meals €55-120; ☺12.15-2.15pm & 7.15-9.15pm Thu-Mon) This former 17th-century postal station is the culinary workshop of Ligurian chef Bruno Zambon, who melds the fish of his home region with the meat and pasta of his adopted one. There's an express two-course lunch deal for €13, which even includes sparkling water.

❶ Information

Tourist Office (www.comune.cuneo.it; Via Roma 28; ☺8.30am-10pm & 2.30-6pm Mon-Fri, 10am-1pm & 2-5pm Sat)

❶ Getting There & Away

Regular trains run from Cuneo's central train station, at Piazzale Libertà, to Turin (€7, 1¼ hours, up to eight daily) and Ventimiglia (€8.30, 2½ hours, at least six daily) from where you can continue over the border to Nice.

Limone Piemonte & the Maritime Alps

☑0171 / ELEV 1525M

Shoehorned between the rice-growing plains of Piedmont and the sparkling coastline of Liguria lie the brooding Maritime Alps – a small pocket of dramatically sculpted mountains that rise like stony-faced border guards along the frontier of Italy and France. Smaller yet no less majestic than their Alpine cousins to the north, the Maritimes are speckled with mirror-like lakes, foraging ibexes and a hybrid cultural heritage that is as much southern French as northern Italian.

There's a palpable wilderness feel to be found among these glowering peaks. Get out of the populated valleys and onto the imposing central massif and you'll quickly be projected into a high-altitude Shangri-La. Whistling marmots scurry under rocky crags doused in mist above a well-marked network of mountain trails where the sight of another hiker – even in peak season – is about as rare as an empty piazza in Rome. This is Italy at its most serene and serendipitous.

🏃 Activities

Maritime Alps Circuits HIKING
(www.limonepiemonte.it) The Lago di Valscura Circuit (21km) starts in the airy spa of Terme di Valdieri and follows an old military road via the Piano del Valasco to a lake near the French border. It loops back past the Rifugio Questa before descending via the same route.

Limone Piemonte SKIING
(www.limonepiemonte.it) Limone Piemonte, 20km south of Cuneo, has been a ski station since 1907 and maintains 15 lifts and 80km of runs, including some put aside for Nordic skiing. The town (population 1600) has numerous hotels and ski-hire shops.

🛏 Sleeping

Borgo Fantino APARTMENT €
(☑019 838 72 11; www.borgofantino.it; Corso Nizza 54; 4-person apt €110-140; Ⓟ�) These brand new apartments in a low-slung structure of wood and stone are both stylish and comfortingly rustic. There's a communal games room, a spa and a shuttle service to town and the lifts. Apartments sleep up to four people.

Hotel Marguareis HOTEL €
(☑0171 92 75 67; www.hotelmarguareis.com; Via Genova 30; d €65-80) A family run hotel in the centre of Limone, well located for an early morning start on the Marguareis Circuit. Rooms are neat and retro-Alpine in style.

Varallo & the Valsesia

Situated 66km northwest of Vercelli in northern Piedmont, this wild, remote region is a place for either contemplation or for adventure along the lines of black skiing, rafting, canyoning or fishing. Varallo is home to the occasionally macabre pilgrimage site of the Sacro Monte di Varallo, while beyond here, the Sesia river heads spectacularly north to the foot of the Monte Rosa massif. Alpine slopes climb sharply, offering numerous walking, cycling and white-water rafting possibilities. The valley's last village, **Alagna Valsesia**, is an ancient Swiss-Walser settlement turned ski resort, which is part of the Monte Rosa Ski Area.

Monte Rosa Ski Area SKIING
(www.monterosa-ski.com) The Monte Rosa ski area consists of three valleys. Champoluc anchors the Valle d'Ayas, Gressoney

lights up the Val de Gressoney and Alagna Valsesia is the focal point in the Valsesia. These valleys have a less manic resort scene and harbour some quiet Walser villages. The skiing, however, is white-knuckle, with some of Europe's best off-piste and heli-skiing possibilities, particularly in the Valsesia.

Corpo Guide Alagna   OUTDOORS
(📞0163 9 13 10; www.guidealagna.com; Piazza Grober 1, Alagna) From Alagna, the Corpo Guide Alagna organises a smorgasbord of winter and summer activities. A highlight is its summer two-day trip up to the highest *rifugio* in Europe, the Capanna Regina Margherita perched atop Punta Gnifetti on the Swiss–Italian border at an astounding 4554m. Guided ascents cost €290 to €400 per person depending on group size.

🛏 Sleeping

Capanna Regina Margherita   CHALET €
(📞0163 9 10 39; www.rifugimonterosa.it; dm with breakfast/half-board €70/100) If you're confident in your Alpine fitness, set out for the highest *rifugio* in Europe from the top cable car stop at Punta Indren (3260m). Perched atop Punta Gnifetti on the Swiss–Italian border, it's an ascent that requires glacier travel.

Those without high-altitude equipment or mountaineering experience will need to hire an IFMGA (International Federation of Mountain Guide Associations) guide.

Rifugio Camparient   CHALET €
(www.rifugiocamparient.com; Via alla Chiesa 4, Alpe di Mera; d €80; 🅿🛜) Beautifully sited family-run place that's a great base for exploring the region, both in winter or summer.

ℹ Getting There & Away

This region is in fact closer to Milan than to Turin, although it's an easy two or so hours' drive from the Piedmontese capital. The closest train station is Vercelli, from there it's a two- to three-hour bus ride to Alagna Valsesia (€9.40, three daily).

VALLE D'AOSTA

📞0165 / POP 128,500
While its Dolomite cousins tend to the Tyrolean, Aosta's nuances are French. The result is a hybrid culture known as Valdostan, a long-ago mingling of the French Provençal and northern Italian that is notable in the local architecture, the dining table and in the survival of an esoteric local language, Franco-Provençal or Valdôtain.

Comprising one large glacial valley running east–west, bisected by several smaller valleys, the semi-autonomous Valle d'Aosta is overlooked by some of Europe's highest peaks, including Mont Blanc (4810m), the Matterhorn (Monte Cervino; 4478m), Monte Rosa (4633m) and Gran Paradiso (4061m). Not surprisingly, the region offers some of the best snow facilities on the continent: descend hair-raisingly into France and Switzerland over glaciers or via cable cars.

The hiking is just as extraordinary, with access to the 165km Tour du Mont Blanc, Parco Nazionale del Gran Paradiso, and Aosta's two blue-riband, high-altitude trails: the Alte Vie 1 and 2.

Aosta

📞0165 / POP 34,600 / ELEV 565M
Jagged Alpine peaks rise like marble cathedrals above the regional capital Aosta, a once-important Roman settlement that retains a charming historic centre, while also sprawling rather untidily across the valley floor. Bounced around between Burgundy (France) and Savoy (Italy) in the Middle Ages, the modern town remains bilingual, with a Valdostan culture that can be heard in its musical local dialect and simple but hearty cuisine.

👁 Sights

Museo Archeologico Regionale   MUSEUM
(Piazza Roncas 12; ⏰10am-1pm & 2-6pm Tue-Sun) FREE Aosta's little city museum does an excellent job of detailing the city's Roman history with a scale model of Aosta's Roman layout plus various antediluvian remains and some fascinating finds from a necropolis discovered at the gates of the Roman city.

Chiesa di Sant'Orso   CHURCH
(Via Sant'Orso; ⏰9am-5.30pm) This intriguing church is part of a still-operating monastery. The church dates back to the 10th century but was altered on several occasions, notably in the 15th century, when Giorgio di Challant of the ruling family ordered the original frescoes to be painted over and a new, lower roof installed.

All was not lost: the renovations left the upper levels of the frescoes intact above the new roofline. You can ask the warden to unlock the door, letting you clamber up a narrow flight of wooden steps into the cavity between the original and the 15th-

Valle d'Aosta

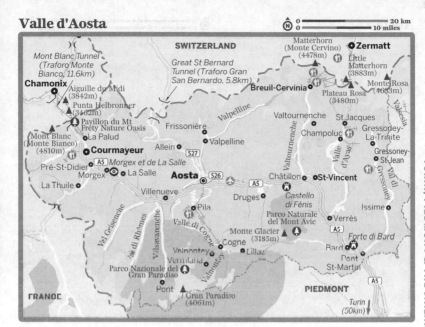

century ceilings to view the well preserved remnants.

Cattedrale Santa Maria Assunta CATHEDRAL

(Piazza Giovanni XXIII; ⊙ 6.30am-noon & 3-7pm) The neoclassical facade of Aosta's cathedral belies the impressive Gothic interior. Inside, the carved 15th-century walnut-wood choir stalls are particularly beautiful. Two mosaics on the floor, dating from the 12th to the 13th centuries, are also notable, as are the treasures displayed in the lovingly attended **Museo del Tesoro**.

🏃 Activities

The Valle d'Aosta allows access to three of Europe's most prestigious ski areas – Courmayeur, Breuil-Cervinia and Monte Rosa – plus numerous smaller runs. A lift pass covering the entire Valle d'Aosta costs €138/293 for three/seven days; seven-day pass holders can choose an international option which gives you two ski days in Zermatt for €346. For up-to-date prices and pass variations see www.skivallee.it.

The best of the smaller resorts is Pila, easily accessible by **cable car** (one way/return €3/5; ⊙ 9am-5.30pm mid-Jun–early Sep) from Aosta town, while the pristine **Valle di Cogne**, in Parco Nazionale del Gran Paradiso, is an idyllic place to enjoy cross-country skiing in relative solitude.

Breuil-Cervinia SKIING

(www.cervinia.it) Breuil-Cervinia, in the shadow of the Matterhorn, is set at a high altitude and has more reliable late-season snow. There are good intermediate runs and kids' facilities here, but the resort is rather tacky in places. On the brighter side, you can ski across into Zermatt in Switzerland.

Pila SKIING

(www.pila.it; half-/full-day pass €28/37; ⊙ mid Dec–mid-Apr) The 1800m-high resort of Pila is accessible by the Aosta–Pila cable car or a zigzagging 18km drive south of Aosta. Its 70km of runs, served by 13 lifts, form one of the valley's largest ski areas. Its highest slope, in the shadow of Gran Paradiso, reaches 2700m and sports an ace snow park with a half-pipe, jump and slide, and freestyle area for boarders and freestyle skiers.

Cave Mont Blanc de Morgex et La Salle WINE

(www.cavemontblanc.com; Chemin des Iles 31; ⊙ 10am-noon & 3.30-6.30pm Mon-Sat) The Valle d'Aosta is home to vineyards producing sought-after wines that are rarely available outside the region, including those from

Aosta

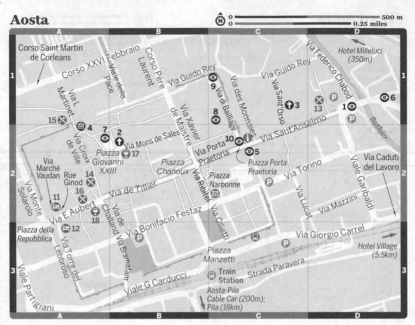

Aosta

◉ Sights

1 Arco di Augusto D1
2 Cattedrale Santa Maria
   Assunta B2
3 Chiesa di Sant'Orso C1
4 Museo Archeologico
   Regionale A2
5 Porta Praetoria C2
6 Roman Bridge D1
7 Roman Forum A2
8 Roman Theatre C1
9 Torre dei Balivi C1
10 Torre dei Fromage C2

🛏 Sleeping

11 Le Rêve Charmant A2
12 Maison Colombot A3

✦ Eating

13 Bataclan D1
14 Croix de Ville A2
15 Il Vecchio Ristoro A1
16 Trattoria degli Artisti A2

Drinking & Nightlife

17 Ad Forum B2
18 In Bottiglieria A2

Europe's highest vineyard, named after the two villages that are strung together by its vines. Aosta's tourist office (p234) has a free, comprehensive booklet in English with information on cellars you can tour and do tastings at. The vineyard is 25km west of Aosta.

🛏 Sleeping

Hotel Village
HOTEL €

(📞 0165 77 49 11; www.hotelvillageaosta.it; Torrent de Maillod 1; d/cabin €80/115) Don't let the proximity to the highway and suburban surrounds put you off, the Village has got so much else going for it. Cabins are set among tall trees and have a contemporary dark-hued style with lots of space and rustic balconies, while rooms in the main building are pure Scando cool.

Maison Colombot
GUESTHOUSE €

(📞 0165 23 57 23; www.aostacamere.com; Via Torre del Lebbroso 3; s/d €55/90) This sweetly old-fashioned place has six rooms with rustic furniture and beamed ceilings overlooking the pretty main pedestrian street or a rustic courtyard. Breakfast here is delivered to your door on a tray – so cosy.

★ **Le Rêve Charmant**   GUESTHOUSE €€
(☑ 0165 23 88 55; www.lerevecharmant.com; Via Marché Vaudan 6; d €130; ![P][❄][📶]) Tucked away in a quiet historic alley, this 12-room hotel is full of traditional Aostan furniture and decoration but keeps it simple and rather stylish. A warm, welcoming lounge leads to surprisingly spacious rooms that have beautiful modern bathrooms and high ceilings. The young owners are charming and service is top rate.

Le Coffret Design Suites   BOUTIQUE HOTEL €€
(www.lecoffret.it; Lieu-dit Jayer, Saint Marcel; d €145; ![P][❄][📶]) Around 20 minutes' drive from the city, this upmarket little hotel is a redolent combination of solid Aostan stone, heavy wooden beams, lots of glass and contemporary furniture. The lofts under the beams are particularly cosy. Some rooms have spa baths or there's a spa area for all guests to enjoy.

Hotel Milleluci   HOTEL €€€
(☑ 0165 4 42 74; www.hotelmilleluci.com; Loc Porossan 15; d €180-270; ![P][❄][@][♨]) Old wooden skis, traditionally carved wooden shoes, claw-foot baths, indoor and outdoor pools, a Jacuzzi, sauna and gym, and sumptuous skiers' breakfasts make this large, family-run converted farmhouse seem more like a luxury resort. Set on a hillside above town, its balconied rooms look out to the eponymous 'thousand lights' twinkling from Aosta below.

✗ Eating & Drinking

Bataclan   PIZZA €
(☑ 393 3026153; www.facebook.com/ristorante bataclan; Piazza Arco D'Augusto 15; pizza €7-12, meals €18-27; ⊙ noon-3pm & 7.30-midnight) You might be lured here by the pizza (which is good), but you'll stay on for the atmosphere, with convivial staff, happy locals and a wonderful position by the Roman ruins.

Croix de Ville   MODERN ITALIAN €
(☑ 0165 23 07 38; Via Croix de Ville 25; dishes €15-18; ⊙ 11am-3pm & 6-10.30pm Sun-Thu, 11am-10.30pm Fri & Sat) This smart, bustling dining room serves up contemporary Italian favourites such as tartares, beef *tagliata* (rare slices) with rocket and Parmesan, and Mediterranean-tinged pastas, dispensing with the strict first- and second-course format. Similarly, the wine list takes it pan-Italian and international, though there's no reason to stray from the beautiful Aostan drops on offer.

Trattoria degli Artisti   TRATTORIA €€
(Via Maillet 5-7; meals €22-30; ⊙ 12.30-2.30pm & 7-10pm Tue-Sat) Fabulous Valdostan cuisine is dished up at this dark and cosy trattoria, tucked down an alleyway off Via E Aubert. Antipasti such as puff pastry filled with Valdostan fondue, cured ham and regional salami are followed by dishes such as roe venison with polenta, and beef braised in Morgex et de La Salle white wine.

Il Vecchio Ristoro   GASTRONOMY €€€
(☑ 0165 3 32 38; www.ristorantevecchioristoro.it; Via Tourneuve 4; meals €50, menu degustazione €80; ⊙ 12.30-2.30pm & 7.30-10.30pm Tue-Sat) Originating from the Valtellina, Alfio Fascendini knows a thing or two about good food and wine. Sample the chestnut bread, the saffron-creamed pearl barley with crispy artichokes and the smoked fillet of bream.

In Bottiglieria   WINE BAR
(☑ 0165 4 08 85; www.inbottiglieria.com; Via E Aubert 15; ⊙ 10.30am-10pm Tue-Sat) Hidden down an alley, a young, well-dressed local crowd fills this stone-vaulted cellar for *aperitivo* and later on weekends. The wine selection is great and they also are known for their huge list of champagne and Italian sparklings.

DON'T MISS

1ST CENTURY AD AOSTA

Aosta's 2000-year-old centre is awash with Roman ruins. The grand triumphal arch, **Arco di Augusto** (Piazza Arco di Augusto), has been strung with a crucifix in its centre since medieval times. From the arch, head east across the Buthier river bridge to view the cobbled **Roman bridge** – in use since the 1st century AD.

Backtracking west 300m along Via Sant'Anselmo brings you to **Porta Praetoria**, the main gate to the Roman city. Heading north along Via di Bailliage and down a dust track brings you to Aosta's **Roman theatre** (Via Porta Praetoria; ⊙ 9am-7pm Sep-Jun, to 8pm Jul & Aug). Part of its 22m-high facade is still intact. Further north, the 12th-century **Torre dei Balivi**, a former prison, marks one corner of the Roman wall and peers down on the smaller **Torre dei Fromage** – named after a family rather than a cheese. The city's **Roman forum** was another couple of blocks west, beneath what's now Piazza Giovanni XXIII.

FORTE DI BARD

A fort has existed here for millennia and the current 1830s Savoy edifice is an imposing one, set high up upon a rocky escarpment at the jaws of the Valle d'Aosta. **Forte di Bard** (www.fortedibard.it; fort entrance free, single museum adult/reduced €15/12; ⊙ 10am-6pm Tue-Fri, to 7pm Sat & Sun) makes for a great day's diversion from skiing or hiking at around 70 minutes from Aosta by bus.

Ride up a series of super-modern panoramic lifts, where you can admire the inspiring Alpine views and visit the Vallée Culture rooms, which offer interesting nuggets of information on Aosta's history and traditions.

The **Museo delle Alpi**, a clever, interactive museum, takes you on an journey across the entire Alps – children love the Flight of the Eagle, a cinematic simulation of a bird's flight over valleys, villages, lakes and snow-capped peaks. The newest museum, **Il Ferdinando**, **Museo delle Fortificazioni e delle Frontiere** details the region's military history. The fort's prisons, which were still in use right up until the end of WWII, can also be visited (adult/reduced €4/3), and there's an excellent program of big-ticket 20th-century art and photography shows in another space.

Overnight at **Hotel Ad Gallias** (🖉 0125 80 98 78; www.hoteladgallias.com; Via Vittorio Emanuele 5/7, Bard; d €140; P ﹡ 🕸) which occupies a couple of village houses at the entrance to the village. This stylish hotel has views of the fort and fabulous wellness area built around a Roman wall with a hot tub, sauna, steam room and treatments.

Ad Forum   WINE BAR
(🖉 0165 4 00 11; Via Mons de Sales 11; ⊙ noon-2.30pm & 7-10.45pm Tue-Sun) A stylish garden and indoor-outdoor rooms are built on part of the remains of the Roman forum and fill up with locals at *aperitivo* hour. They have a great list of local wines.

❶ Information

Aosta Tourist Office (www.lovevda.it; Piazza Porta Praetoria 3; ⊙ 9am-7pm; 🕸) Housed in the old Roman gateway to the city, this helpful office has good maps, lists of wine and cheese producers in the region as well as extensive listings of farmstays and B&Bs.

❶ Getting There & Away

Buses operated by Savda (www.savda.it) run to Milan (€17, 1½ hours to 3½ hours, two daily), Turin (€9, two hours, up to 10 daily) and Courmayeur (€3.50, one hour, up to eight daily), as well as to French destinations, including Chamonix. Services leave from Aosta's **bus station** (Via Giorgio Carrel), almost opposite the train station. To get to Breuil-Cervinia, take a Turin-bound bus to Châtillon (€1.50, 30 minutes, eight daily), then a connecting bus (€2.90, one hour, seven daily) to the resort.

Aosta's train station, on Piazza Manzetti, is served by trains from most parts of Italy. All trains to Turin (€9.45, two to 2½ hours, more than 10 daily) change at Ivrea.

Aosta is on the A5, which connects Turin with the Mont Blanc tunnel and France. Another exit road north of the city leads to the Great St Bernard tunnel and on to Switzerland.

Courmayeur

🖉 0165 / POP 2900 / ELEV 1224M

Flush up against France and linked by a dramatic cable-car ride to its cross-border cousin in Chamonix, Courmayeur is an activity-oriented Aosta village that has grafted upmarket ski facilities onto an ancient Roman bulwark. Its pièce de résistance is lofty Mont Blanc, Western Europe's highest mountain – 4810m of solid rock and ice that rises like an impregnable wall above the narrow valleys of northwestern Italy, igniting awe in all who pass.

In winter Courmayeur is a fashion parade of skiers bound for the high slopes above town that glisten with plenty of late-season snow. In summer it wears a distinctly different hat: the Società delle Guide Alpine di Courmayeur is bivouacked here and the town is an important staging post on three iconic long-distance hiking trails: the Tour du Mont Blanc (TMB), Alta Via 1 and Alta Via 2.

◉ Sights

Giardino Botanico
Alpino Saussurea   GARDENS
(www.saussurea.it; admission €3, free with cable-car ticket in high summer; ⊙ 9am-5pm Jul-Sep) Walk through this flower-filled Alpine garden in summer (it's blanketed by snow in winter) and enjoy numerous other trails,

including the Sentiero Francesco e Giuditta Gatti, where you have a good chance of spotting ibexes, marmots and deer.

Pavillon du Mt Fréty
Nature Oasis   NATURE RESERVE
A protected zone of 1200 hectares tucked between glaciers, this nature oasis is accessible from the Pavillon du Mt Fréty. Enjoy numerous trails, including the Sentiero Francesco e Giuditta Gatti.

Museo Alpino Duca degli Abruzzi   MUSEUM
(☑0165 84 20 64; Piazza Henry 2; adult/reduced €3/1.50; ⊙9am-12.30pm & 4-7pm Thu-Tue) Courmayeur guiding association's history unfolds in this small but inspiring museum that tracks the heroic deeds of erstwhile alpinists.

🏃 Activities

Courmayeur offers some extraordinary skiing in the spectacular shadow of Mont Blanc. The two main ski areas – the Plan Chécrouit and Pré de Pascal – are interlinked by various runs (100km worth) and a network of chairlifts. Three lifts leave from the valley floor: one from Courmayeur itself, one from the village of Dolonne and one from nearby Val Veny. They are run by **Funivie Courmayeur Mont Blanc** (www.courmayeur-montblanc.com; Strada Regionale 47). Daily ski passes (€48) give you access to Courmayeur and Mont Blanc, 3-day passes and above include all of Aosta's resorts (3-/7-day pass €128/265). Queues are rarely an issue.

★ Funivie Monte Bianco   CABLE CAR
(Skyway; www.montebianco.com; Strada Statale 26; return €48, Pavillon du Mt Fréty return €27; ⊙8.30am-4pm) The Mont Blanc cable car might not be the world's highest, but it's surely the most spectacular. This astounding piece of engineering reaches three-quarters of the way up Western Europe's highest mountain before heading across multiple glaciers into France. New stations, with glass surfaces and futuristic cantilevers, opened in summer 2015, along with the introduction of state-of-the-art 360-degree rotating cabins. It departs every 20 minutes from the village of **La Palud**, 15 minutes from Courmayeur's main square by a free bus.

First stop is the 2173m-high midstation **Pavillon du Mt Fréty**, while at the top of the ridge is **Punta Helbronner** (3462m). All three stations have restaurants and other facilities; there's a sparkling wine cellar at the Pavilion and, in summer, the Giardino Botanico Alpino Saussurea and a crystal display at Helbronner. Take ample warm clothes and sunglasses for the blinding snow, and head up early in the morning to avoid the heavy weather that often descends in the early afternoon.

From Punta Helbronner another cable car (from late May to late September, depending on weather conditions, €33.50) takes you on a breathtaking 5km transglacial ride across the Italian border into France to the **Aiguille du Midi** (3842m), from where the world's highest cable car transports you down to Chamonix (€77). The return trip from Chamonix to Courmayeur by bus is €15. Not a cheap day out, but a spectacular one.

Plan Chécrouit Swimming Pool   SWIMMING
(half-day/day lift and pool admission €18/25; ⊙10.30am-5pm mid-Jul–Aug) Yes, there's a highest heated swimming pool in Europe, and, at 1700m, this is it. Take the Dolonne cable car for a dip with a view and a laze among lush green surrounds, or hike up from Courmayeur in around an hour.

Terme di Pré-Saint-Didier   SPA
(☑0165 86 72 72; www.termedipre.it; Allée des Thermes; admission €35-50; ⊙9.30am-9pm Mon-Thu, 8.30am-11pm Fri & Sat, to 9pm Sun) Bubbling up a natural 37°C from the mountains' depths, the thermal water at Pré-Saint-Didier, a 10-minute drive south of Courmayeur, has been a source of therapeutic treatments since the bath-loving Romans marched into the valley. A spa opened here in 1838, with the newest addition dating to the 1920s. Admission includes use of a bathrobe, towel and slippers, plus water and herbal teas.

In addition to saunas, whirlpools and toning waterfalls, there's an indoor outdoor thermal pool. It's lit by candles and torches at night, and is spectacular amid the snow and stars in wintertime. The older of the two spa buildings, accessed by a tunnel, has stunning high ceilings and fabulous views from its relaxation areas. Historical bonus: there's a little **Roman bridge** arcing over a trout-filled river, 50-odd metres beyond the car park in the opposite direction to the village.

Tour du Mont Blanc   WALKING
For many walkers (some 30,000 each summer), Courmayeur's trophy hike is the Tour du Mont Blanc (TMB). This 169km trek cuts across Italy, France and Switzerland, stopping at nine villages en route. Snow makes it impassable for much of the year. The

TURIN, PIEDMONT & THE ITALIAN RIVIERA COURMAYEUR

average duration is anything from one week to 12 days; smaller sections are also possible.

You can undertake the hike solo, but if you're unfamiliar with the area, hooking up with a local guide is a good idea as the route traverses glacial landscapes. Easy day hikes will take you along the TMB as far as the Rifugio Maison Vieille (6.6km, one hour and 50 minutes) and Rifugio Bertone (4.5km, two hours). Follow the yellow signposts from the Piazzale Monte Bianco in the centre of Courmayeur.

Vallée Blanche   SKIING

This is an exhilarating off-piste descent from Punta Helbronner across the Mer de Glace glacier into Chamonix, France. The route itself is not difficult – anyone of intermediate ability can do it – but an experienced guide is essential to steer you safely round the hidden crevasses.

All up, the 24km Vallée Blanche takes around four to five hours, allowing time to stop and take in the view.

Toula Glacier   SKIING

Only highly experienced, hard-core skiers need apply for this terrifying descent, which also takes off from Punta Helbronner and drops for six sheer kilometres to La Palud. A guide is essential; it's usually easy to join a group.

Società delle Guide
Alpine di Courmayeur   OUTDOORS

(☑ 0165 84 20 64; www.guidecourmayeur.com; Strada del Villair) Founded in 1859, this is Italy's oldest guiding association. In winter, guides lead adventure seekers off-piste, up frozen waterfalls and on heli-skiing expeditions. In summer, rock climbing, canyoning, canoeing, kayaking and hiking are among its many outdoor activities. Excursions start at €110 for single day climbs and ascents and range up to €965 for a four-day Alpinist course.

Scuola di Sci Monte Bianco   SKIING

(www.scuolascimontebianco.com; Strada Regionale 51) Founded in 1922, this veritable ski school offers instructors for downhill and snowboarding (one hour/day €48/360), along with specialist courses in freeride, telemark and cross-country.

🛏 Sleeping

Hotel Svizzero   HOTEL €€

(☑ 0165 84 81 70; www.hotelsvizzero.com; Strada Statale 26/11; d €145; P ❄ 🛜) On the road just outside of the town's pedestrian centre, the

family-run Svizzero has 27 rustic-contemporary rooms, as well as a chalet that can be rented on a weekly basis. The lovely old recycled wood and stone used throughout makes for loads of atmosphere, and the hotel provides the Alpine essentials of a steam room and lift shuttle.

Hotel Triolet   HOTEL €€

(☑ 0165 84 68 22; www.hoteltriolet.com; Strada Regionale 63; s/d €100/170; P ❄ 🛜 🛎) Triolet is a tad smaller than your average ski digs, with only 20 rooms, allowing service to remain personal as well as affable. Aside from the usual tick-list, there's a pleasant spa (Jacuzzi, steam room, sauna), ski lockers and a vista-laden breakfast room.

Hotel Bouton d'Or   HOTEL €€

(☑ 0165 84 67 29; www.hotelboutondor.com; Strada Statale 26/10; s/d €95/180; P ❄ @ 🛜) Charmingly folksy Bouton d'Or is in the centre of Courmayeur and not only has incredible views of the imposing hulk of Mont Blanc, but also a sauna, a lounge full of interesting Alpine paraphernalia and, in summer, a peaceful garden.

★Grand Hotel
Courmayeur Mont Blanc   SPA HOTEL €€€

(☑ 0165 84 45 42; www.grandhotelcourmayeur montblanc.it; Strada Grand Ru 1; d €270-360; P ❄ 🛜 🛎) This new 72-bed luxury place hits all the right notes, with exquisitely comforting yet Alpine-sleek rooms with soft wool blankets, light wood and dark furniture. There's everything you need here, from a spa and pool, to restaurants and après-ski, and of course Alpine views. But you're also close to the lifts and the town's happy bustle.

🍴 Eating

★Dandelion   ALPINE €€

(☑ 0165 185 11 83; www.dandelionlapalud.com; Via San Bernardo 3, La Palud; meals €35-45; ⏲ 12.30-2.30pm & 7.30-10pm) Up the hill in the hamlet of La Palud, Dandelion does 'cuisine de montagne' – a proudly Aostan menu that's both rustic and sophisticated. Come for salt cod lasagne, baby goat and artichokes in a garlic cream or Aostan beef fillet with green pepper and foie gras. There's a cosy dining room with fireplace or book a terrace table in summer.

La Padella   AOSTAN, PIZZA €€

(☑ 0165 84 19 77; www.lapadella.eu; Vicolo Dolonne 7; meals €25; ⏲ noon-2.30pm & 6.30-10.30pm Fri-Wed) Friendly, cosy and popular, there's a huge menu of polenta and *fontina* cheese dishes – add your topping of mushroom, sausage or various other meats. They also run a takeaway prepared-meal place, Mmmartine, a good option for lazy self-caterers or picnicking.

La Chaumière
ITALIAN €€

(☑ 392 9585987; www.lachaumiere.it; Località Planchecrouit 15; meals €25-40; ☺ 9am-5pm) Set on the slopes above Courmayeur, within walking distance of the cable car, is the fabulous sun-kissed terrace of La Chaumière. Views straight down the Aosta valley are accompanied by superlative polenta and 38 carefully sourced wines.

ℹ Information

Centro Traumatologico (☑ 0165 84 46 84; Strada dei Volpi 3) Medical clinic. The nearest hospital is in Aosta.

Tourist Office (☑ 0165 84 20 60; www.lovecourmayeur.com; Piazzale Monte Bianco 13; ☺ 9am-12.30pm & 3-6.30pm)

ℹ Getting There & Away

Three trains a day from Aosta terminate at Pré-Saint-Didier, with bus connections (20 to 30 minutes, eight to 10 daily) to **Courmayeur bus station** (Piazzale Monte Bianco), outside the tourist office. There are up to eight direct Aosta–Courmayeur buses daily (€3.50, one hour). long-haul buses serve Milan (€19.50, 4½ hours, three to five daily) and Turin (€10, 3½ to 4½ hours, two to four daily).

Immediately north of Courmayeur, the 11.6km Mont Blanc tunnel leads to Chamonix in France (one way/return €43.50/54.30). At the Italian entrance, a plaque commemorates Pierlucio Tinazzi, a security employee who died while saving at least a dozen lives during the 1999 disaster when a freight truck caught fire in the tunnel.

Parco Nazionale del Gran Paradiso

☑ 0165

Italy's oldest national park, the Gran Paradiso, was created in 1922 after Vittorio Emanuele II gave his hunting reserve to the state, ostensibly to protect the endangered ibex. The park preceded the rise of the modern ski resort and has so far resisted the lucrative mass tourist trade. Its tangible wilderness feel is rare in Italy.

Gran Paradiso incorporates the valleys around the eponymous 4061m peak (Italy's 7th highest), three of which are in the Valle

d'Aosta: the Valsavarenche, Val di Rhêmes and the beautiful Valle di Cogne. On the Piedmont side of the mountain, the park includes the valleys of Soana and Orco.

The main stepping stone into the park is tranquil **Cogne** (population 1481, elevation 1534m), a refreshing antidote to overdeveloped Breuil-Cervinia on the opposite side of the Valle d'Aosta. Aside from its plethora of outdoor opportunities, Cogne is known for its lace-making, and you can buy local products at several craft and antique shops.

◉ Sights & Activities

Giardino Alpino Paradisia
GARDENS

(☑ 0165 7 53 01; www.pngp.it; Frazione Valnontey 44, Cogne; adult/reduced €3/1.50; ☺ 10am-5.30pm mid-Jun–mid-Sep, to 6.30pm Jul & Aug) The park's amazing biodiversity, including butterflies and Alpine flora, can be seen in summer at this fascinating Alpine botanical garden in the tiny hamlet of Valnontey (1700m), 3km south of Cogne. Guided nature walks are available from July to September.

Le Traineau Equestrian Tourism Centre
HORSE RIDING

(☑ 333 3147248; Frazione Valnontey, Cogne) This group in Valnontey organises horse riding and 45-minute horse-and-carriage rides through the mountain meadows.

Società Guide Alpine di Cogne
SKIING

(☑ 0165 7 40 50; www.guidealpinecogne.it; Piazza Chanoux 1) The Società Guide Alpine di Cogne provides guides and offers climbing excursions and pro skiing lessons.

Associazione Guide della Natura
WALKING

(www.cogneturismo.it; Rue Bourgeois 33, Cogne; ☺ 9am-noon Mon, Wed & Sat) Guided nature walks from July to September are organised by the Associazione Guide della Natura.

⌂ Sleeping

Rifugio Sella
CHALET €

(☑ 0165 7 43 10; www.rifugiosella.com; Località Lauson, Cogne; dm €26; ☺ Apr, Jun-Sep) The Rifugio Sella is a former hunting lodge of King Vittorio Emanuele II and offers standard mountain hut accommodation. From the town bridge follow the Alta Via 2 uphill for 8km, around a two- to three-hour walk, or park halfway at Valnontey.

Camping Lo Stambecco
CAMPGROUND €

(☑ 0165 7 41 52; www.campeggiolostambecco.it; Frazione Valnontey 6; campsite €24; ☺ May-Sep; P) Pitch up under the pine trees in the heart of the park at this well-run and friendly site. Its sister hotel, La Barme, rents bikes to explore the mountains. No tent? Ask about if one of their caravans are available (€40 per night).

Hotel Sant'Orso　　　　　HOTEL €€
(☑ 0165 7 48 21; www.hotelsantorso.com; Via Bourgeois 2; d €140-180; ☺ spring & autumn closures vary; P ☒) Cogne personified (ie tranquil, courteous and understated), the Sant'Orso is nonetheless equipped with plenty of hidden extras, including a wellness area and huge gardens. Further kudos is gained by the fact that you can start your cross-country skiing pretty much from the front door. The owners also run the Hotel du Gran Paradis nearby.

★ **Hotel Bellevue**　　　HERITAGE HOTEL €€€
(☑ 0165 7 48 25; www.hotelbellevue.it; Rue Grand Paradis 22; s €220, d €190-290, 2-person chalet €270-330; ☺ mid-Dec–mid-Oct; P ☒) Overlooking meadows, this green-shuttered mountain hideaway evokes its 1920s origins with romantic canopied timber 'cabin beds', weighty cowbells strung from old beams, claw-foot baths and the occasional open fire (it's definitely not for minimalists). Afternoon tea is included in the price, as is use of the health spa, and you can also rent mountain bikes and snowshoes.

Its four restaurants include a Michelin-starred gourmet affair, a wonderful cheese restaurant (goat raclette!) with produce from the family's own cellar, a lunchtime terrace restaurant and a dark, historic brasserie on the village's main square, a few moments' stroll away.

✘ Eating

Lou Ressignon　　　　　VALDOSTAN €€
(☑ 0165 7 40 34; www.louressignon.it; Via des Mines 23, Cogne; meals €28-40; ☺ 12-3pm & 6-10pm Tue-Sun) In a wood-panelled dining room with red curtains bunched at the windows, David and Elizabeth Allera keep Valdostan traditions alive, serving bowls of belly-filling *seupetta á la cogneintze*, a dish of rice and toasted bread slathered in *fontina* cheese. They also offer five well-priced chalet rooms (doubles €75 to €100).

Hotel Ristorante Petit Dahu　　ITALIAN €€
(☑ 0165 7 41 46; www.hotelpetitdahu.com; Frazone Valnontey 27; meals €35; ☺ 7-9pm, closed May & Oct; P) Straddling two traditional stone-and-wood buildings, this friendly, family-run spot has a wonderful restaurant (also open to

nonguests; advance bookings essential) preparing rustic mountain cooking using wild Alpine herbs. It also has pretty rooms to stay in (single/double half-board €80/140).

🛍 Shopping

Le Marché Aux Puces　　ARTS & CRAFTS, ANTIQUES
(Rue Grand Paradis 4; ☺ 9.30am-12.30pm & 3.30-7pm Wed, Sat & Sun) Cogne is known for its lace-making; you can buy the local fabrics at this charming craft and antique shop.

ℹ Information

Tourist Office (www.cogneturismo.it; Rue Bourgeois 33, Cogne; ☺ 9am-12.30pm & 2.30-5.30pm Mon-Sat) Has detailed information on all aspects of the park and a list of emergency contact numbers.

ℹ Getting There & Away

Up to 10 buses run daily to/from Cogne and Aosta (€2.90, 50 minutes). Cogne can also be reached by cable car from Pila.

Valtournenche
☑ 0166

One of Europe's most dramatic – and deadly – mountains, the Matterhorn (4478m) frames the head of Valtournenche. Byron once stood here and marvelled at 'Europe's noble rock'. Today he'd also get an eyeful of one of the Alps' most architecturally incongruous ski resorts, Breuil-Cervinia. But, ugly or not, Cervinia's ski facilities are second to none; you can hit the snow year-round and even swish across into Zermatt, Switzerland.

Società Guide del Cervino　　　　SKIING
(www.guidedelcervino.com; Via J Antoine Carrel 20) Contact Breuil-Cervinia's mountain-guide association to make the most of the Matterhorn's wild off-piste opportunities.

Mollino Rooms　　　　　　B&B €€
(☑ 0166 94 93 51; Strada Funivie 9, Breuil-Cervinia; d €195; P ☀ 🛜) A modern refit yes, but lovely Alpine-style rooms of slate and patinated wood, make this an atmospheric choice. It's just near the lifts and offers the occasional glimpse of the Matterhorn.

ℹ Getting There & Away

Savda (www.savda.it) operates buses from Breuil-Cervinia to Châtillon (€2.90, one hour, seven daily), from where there are connecting buses to/from Aosta.

Milan & the Lakes

Best Places to Eat

➡ Ratanà (p254)
➡ Cracco (p254)
➡ Seta (p254)
➡ Casabella (p266)
➡ Materia (p279)

Best Places to Sleep

➡ Lido Palace (p286)
➡ Atellani Apartments (p251)
➡ Hotel Silvio (p275)
➡ Hotel Garni Villa Maria (p286)
➡ Da Vittorio (p292)

Why Go?

Wedged between the Alps and the Po valley, the lakes of Lombardy (Lombardia) were formed at the end of the last ice age, and have been a popular holiday spot since Roman times. At the region's heart is Milan, capital of the north and Italy's second-largest city. Home to the nation's stock exchange, one of Europe's biggest trade-fair grounds and an international fashion hub, it is also Italy's economic powerhouse.

Beyond Milan pretty countryside unfolds, dotted with patrician towns including Pavia, Monza, Bergamo, Cremona and Mantua; all are steeped in history, hiding Unesco monuments and world-class museums. To the north a burst of Mediterranean colour and a balmy microclimate awaits around lakes Orta, Maggiore, Como, Garda and Iseo. Ringed by hot-pink oleanders in tiered gardens, the lakes are powerfully seductive. No wonder European aristocrats, Arab princes and Hollywood celebrities choose to call this home.

When to Go
Milan

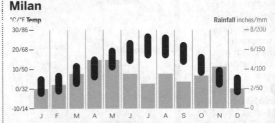

Spring (Mar–Jun)	Summer (Jul & Aug)	Winter (Nov–Feb)
Peak season – delightful weather, Salone (Furniture Fair) and Fashion Weeks are in progress.	Low season in Milan. The city is hot and everyone heads to the lakes and mountains.	Opera season starts (December); followed by Christmas fairs.

Milan & the Lakes Highlights

1 The Last Supper (p247) Pondering the power of Leonardo Da Vinci's ageless painting.

2 Il Duomo (p243) Climbing Milan's marble cathedral for views of spires and flying buttresses.

3 Museo del Novecento (p243) Discovering the modernists who shaped Milan.

4 Accademia Carrara (p291) Coming face to face with Old Masters in Bergamo's newly renovated gallery.

5 Isola Bella (p265) Strolling in Lago Maggiore's most spectacular island garden.

6 Lago di Como (p270) Touring this famous lake James Bond–style, in your own cigarette boat.

7 Riva del Garda (p285) Sailing, surfing and kayaking beneath the snowcapped peaks.

8 Palazzo Ducale (p295) Marvelling at sumptuous Renaissance frescoes in this Mantuan palace.

9 Orta San Giulio (p268) Discovering lake-side bliss in this enchanting town on Lago d'Orta.

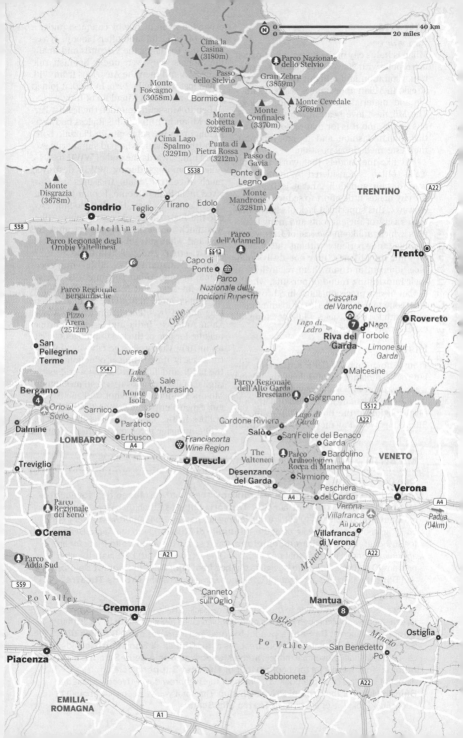

MILAN

POP 1.35 MILLION

Milan is Italy's city of the future, a fast-paced metropolis with New World qualities: ambition, aspiration and a highly individualistic streak. In Milan appearances really do matter and materialism requires no apology. The Milanese love beautiful things, luxurious things, and it is for that reason perhaps that Italian fashion and design maintain their esteemed global position.

But like the models that work the catwalks, Milan is considered by many to be vain, distant and dull. And it is true that the city makes little effort to seduce visitors. However, this superficial lack of charm disguises a city of ancient roots and many treasures, which, unlike in the rest of Italy, you'll often get to experience without the queues. So while the Milanese may not always play nice, jump in and join them regardless in their intoxicating round of pursuits, whether that means precision-shopping, browsing edgy contemporary galleries or loading up a plate with local delicacies while downing an expertly mixed negroni.

History

From its founding as a Celtic settlement, Milan (or Mediolanum – Middle of the Plain) was always an important crossroads. It was here that Christianity was declared the official religion of the Roman Empire in AD 313. As a powerful medieval city-state, Milan expanded its influence by conquest under a series of colourful (and often bloody) dynasties – the Torrianis, the Viscontis and finally the Sforzas. However, under Spanish rule from 1525 and then the Austrians from 1713, Milan lost some of its *brio*. In 1860, it joined the nascent, united Kingdom of Italy.

Benito Mussolini founded the Fascist Party in Milan in 1919 and his lifeless body was strung up in the same city, in Piazzale Loreto, by the partisans who had summarily executed him towards the end of WWII in 1945. Allied bombings during WWII destroyed much of central Milan. Treasures that survived include the Duomo, Leonardo da Vinci's *Il Cenacolo* (just), the Castello Sforzesco and the Teatro alla Scala opera house. Milan was quick to get back on its feet after the war and what still sets it apart today is its creative streak and can-do attitude.

At the vanguard of two 20th-century economic booms, Milan cemented its role as Italy's financial and industrial capital. Immigrants poured in from the south and were later joined by others from China, Africa, Latin America, India and Eastern Europe, making for one of the least homogenous cities in Italy. Culturally, the city was the centre of early Italian film production, and in the 1980s and '90s it ruled the world as the capital of design innovation and production. Milan's self-made big shot and media mogul, Silvio Berlusconi, made the move into politics in the 1990s and was then elected prime minister three more times – scandal

---

MILAN IN ...

One Day

Rise early to beat the crowds at the **Duomo**, then head into the **Museo del Novecento** for a blast of 20th-century art. Lunch at **Trattoria Milanese** then make for the imposing **Castello Sforzesco** to admire Michelangelo's moving *Rondanini Pietà*. After examining Milan's design pedigree at the **Triennale di Milano**, climb the **Torre Branca** for 360-degree views of **Parco Sempione**, then head to the **Arco della Pace** for an *aperitivo* at one of the bars that ring its base. Dine at (pre-booked) **La Brisa**, then hop on tram 10 and whizz down to Navigli to bar hop from **Mag Café** to **Rebelot del Pont** and **Bar Rita**. If you've got anything left, catch some blues at the **Nibada Theatre**.

Two Days

Devote your second morning to the masterpiece-packed halls of the **Pinacoteca di Brera**, then wander through **Brera's** chic, cobbled lanes heading south towards the **Quad**. After lunch at **De Santis**, ponder the medieval treasures of the **Basilica di Sant'Ambrogio**, Bernardino Luini's frescoes at the **Chiesa di San Maurizio** and Leonardo da Vinci's inventive models at the **Museo Nazionale della Scienza e Tecnologia**. Then head for a (prebooked) tour of **The Last Supper** before an elegant dinner at La Brisa (also pre-booked). Finish off this highbrow day with cocktails at the **Bulgari Hotel** or the **Armani Privé** nightclub. That, or if you've been wise enough to book ahead, join the opera buffs at **Teatro alla Scala**.

and financial Armageddon finally forced him from office in 2011.

Since that nadir, leading up to the Expo2015 World Fair, Milan has undergone a series of sweeping redevelopments. New districts such as Porta Nuova and CityLife have been constructed, the enormous exhibition centre now has an even bigger new home at Rho, museums have been modernised, the city's infrastructure has been improved, and the old dock area has been rehabilitated. The mood in the city is buoyant and, for now, the Milanese are quietly pleased with the forward-looking, confident modern city that is emerging.

⊙ Sights

Milan's runway-flat terrain and monumental buildings are defined by concentric ring roads that trace the path of the city's original defensive walls. Although very little remains of the walls, ancient *porta* (gates) act as clear compass points. Almost everything you want to see, do or buy is contained within these city gates.

★ Duomo   CATHEDRAL

(Map p248; ⌂02 /202 3375; www.duomomilano.it; Piazza del Duomo; adult/reduced Duomo €2/3, roof terraces via stairs €9/4.50, lift €13/7, archaeological area €7/3; ⊙Duomo 8am-7pm, roof terraces 9am-7pm; ⓜDuomo) A vision in pink Candoglia marble, Milan's extravagant Gothic cathedral, 600 years in the making, reflects the city's creativity and ambition. Its pearly white facade, adorned with 135 spires and 3400 statues rises like the filigree of a fairy-tale tiara, wowing the crowds with its extravagant detail. The interior is no less impressive, punctuated by the largest stained-glass windows in Christendom, while in the crypt saintly Carlo Borromeo is interred in a rock-crystal casket.

Begun by Giangaleazzo Visconti in 1386, the cathedral's design was originally considered unfeasible. Canals had to be dug to transport the vast quantities of marble to the centre of the city and new technologies were invented to cater for the never-before-attempted scale. There was also that small matter of style. The Gothic lines went out of fashion and were considered 'too French', so it took on several looks as the years, then centuries, dragged on. Its slow construction became the byword for an impossible task ('fabrica del Dom', in the Milanese dialect). Indeed, much of its ornament is 19th-century neo-Gothic, with the final touches only applied in the 1960s. The most spectacular view is through the innumerable marble spires and pinnacles that adorn the rooftop. Crowning it all is a gilded copper statue of the Madonnina (Little Madonna), the city's traditional protector.

Il Grande Museo del Duomo   MUSEUM

(Map p248; www.museo.duomomilano.it; Piazza del Duomo 12; adult/reduced €6/4; ⊙10am-6pm Thu-Tue; ⓜDuomo) Stepping through Guido Canali's glowing spaces into the Duomo's museum is like coming upon the sets for an episode of *Game of Thrones*. Gargoyles leer down through the shadows; shafts of light strike the wings of heraldic angels; and a monstrous godhead, once intended for the high altar, glitters awesomely in copper. It's an exciting display, masterfully choreographed through 26 rooms, which tell the 600-year story of the cathedral's construction through priceless sculptures, paintings, stained glass, tapestries and bejewelled treasures.

Palazzo Reale   MUSEUM, PALACE

(Map p248; ⌂02 87 56 72; www.palazzorealemilano.it; Piazza del Duomo 12; admission varies; ⊙2.30-7.30pm Mon, 9.30am-7.30pm Tue, Wed, Fri & Sun, to 10.30pm Thu & Sat; ⓜDuomo) Empress Maria Theresa's favourite architect, Giuseppe Piermarini, gave this town hall and Visconti palace a neoclassical overhaul in the late 18th century. The supremely elegant interiors were all but destroyed by WWII bombs; the **Sala delle Cariatidi** remains unrenovated as a reminder of war's indiscriminate destruction. Now the once opulent palace hosts blockbuster art exhibits, attracting serious crowds to shows featuring artists as diverse as Escher, Caravaggio and Arnaldo Pomodoro.

★ Museo del Novecento   GALLERY

(Map p248; ⌂02 8844 4061; www.museodelnovecento.org; Via Marconi 1; adult/reduced €10/8; ⊙2.30-7.30pm Mon, 9.30am-7.30pm Tue, Wed, Fri & Sun, to 10.30pm Thu & Sat; ⓜDuomo) Overlooking Piazza del Duomo, with fabulous views of the cathedral, is Mussolini's Arengario, from where he would harangue huge crowds in his heyday. Now it houses Milan's museum of 20th-century art. Built around a futuristic spiral ramp (an ode to the Guggenheim), the lower floors are cramped, but the heady collection, which includes the likes of Umberto Boccioni, Campigli, de Chirico and Marinetti, more than distracts.

Gallerie d'Italia   MUSEUM

(Map p248; www.gallerieditalia.com; Piazza della Scala 6; adult/reduced €10/8; ⊙9.30am-7.30pm Tue-Wed

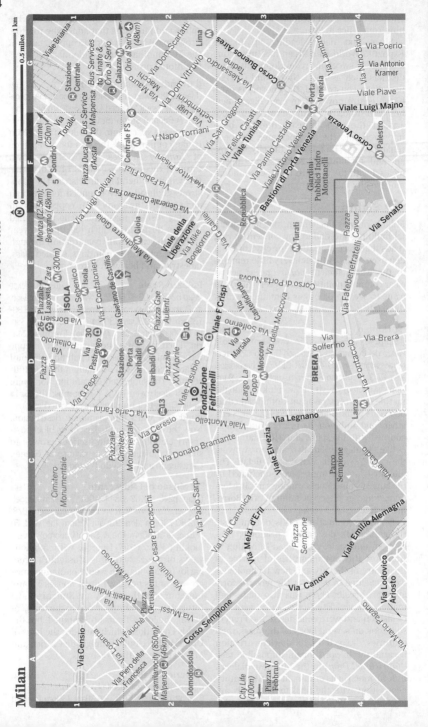

Milan

244

MILAN & THE LAKES

Via Censio

Via Losanna

Via Fratelli Induno

Via Mussi

Via Giulio Cesare Procaccini

Piazza Gerusalemme

Via Morivione

Via Fauchè

Via Piero della Francesca

Fieramilanocity (850m);
Malpensa (46km)

Domodossola

City Life
(100m)

Piazza VI
Febbraio

Corso Sempione

Via Paolo Sarpi

Via Luigi Canonica

Via Melzi d'Eril

Piazza
Sempione

Via Canova

Via Lodovico
Ariosto

Viale Emilio Alemagna

Via Mario Pagano

Cimitero
Monumentale

Piazzale
Cimitero
Monumentale

20

Via Donato Bramante

Viale Elvezia

Parco
Sempione

Piazza
Fidia

Via G Pepe

Via Carlo Farini

Stazione
Porta
Garibaldi

Garibaldi

Piazzale
XXV Aprile

13

Viale Pasubio

1
Fondazione
Feltrinelli

Viale Montello

Via Legnano

BRERA

Via Solferino

Via Brera

Via Pontaccio

Via Fatebenefratelli

Lanza

Viale Gadio

Piazzale
Lagosta
Zara

26

Via Borsieri

Via Pollaiuolo

30

Via
Pastrengo

19

ISOLA

Via Sebenico

Via F Confalonieri

Via Gaetano de Castillia

17

Piazza Gae
Aulenti

10

27

Viale F Crispi

21

Via
Marsala

Via
Castelfidardo

Via della Moscova

Via Moscova

Largo La
Foppa

Corso di Porta Nuova

Via Senato

Piazza
Fatebenefratelli Cavour

Viale della
Liberazione

Via Mike
Bongiorno

Via G Galilei

Via Melchiorre Gioia

Via Gioia

Via Luigi Galvani

Tunnel
(250m)

Sondrio

Piazza Duca
d'Aosta

Via Tonale

Monza (22.5km);
Bergamo (48km)

Stazione
Centrale

Bus Services
to Linate &
Orio al Serio

Bus Service
to Malpensa

Centrale FS

Orio al Serio
(48km)

Caiazzo

Via Alessandro
Tadino

Via Dom Scarlatti

Lima

Corso Buenos Aires

Via Dom Vitruvio

Via Mauro
Macchi

Via Luigi
Settembrini

Via Fabio Filzi

Via Generale Gustavo Fara

Via Vittor Pisani

V Napo Torriani

Via San Gregorio

Via Felice Casati

Viale Tunisia

Republica

Turati

Via Panfilo Castaldi

Viale Vittorio Veneto

Bastioni di Porta Venezia

Porta
Venezia

7

Viale Luigi Majno

Corso Venezia

Giardini
Pubblici Indro
Montanelli

Palestro

Viale Piave

Via Antonio
Kramer

Via Nino Bixio

Via Poerio

Via Lambro

1 km

0.5 miles

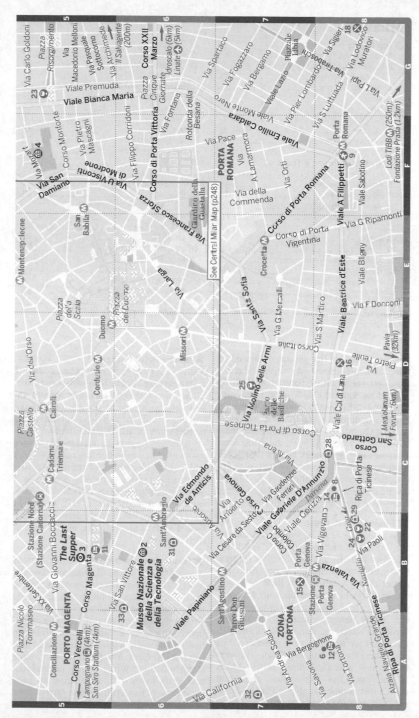

PORTO MAGENTA

Corso Vercelli

Piazza Nicolò Tommaseo

Conciliazione Ⓜ

Via XX Settembre

Lampugnano Ⓜ (4km); San Siro Stadium (4km)

Stazione Nord (Stazione Cadorna) Ⓜ

Via Giovanni Boccaccio

The Last Supper 3

Corso Magenta

Via San Vittore

Museo Nazionale della Scienza e della Tecnologia 2

Viale Papiniano

Sant'Agostino Ⓜ

Parco Don Giussani

ZONA TORTONA

Via Andrea Solari

Via Bergognone

Via Savona

Via California

Via Tortona

Piazza Castello

Cadorna Triennale Ⓜ

Cairoli Ⓜ

Cordusio Ⓜ

Via dell'Orso

Piazza della Scala

Duomo Ⓜ

Piazza del Duomo

Via Larga

Missori Ⓜ

Via Edmondo de Amicis

Via Ausonia

Via Arioorto

Via Cesare da Sesto

Sant'Ambrogio Ⓜ

Via Molino delle Armi

Parco delle Basiliche

Corso di Porta Ticinese

Via Ariena

Viale Gabriele D'Annunzio

Corso Colombo

Corso Genova

Via Vigevano

Via Valenza

Porta Genova Ⓜ

Stazione Porta Genova Ⓜ

Naviglio Grande

Ripa di Porta Ticinese

Alzaia Naviglio Grande

Darsena

Viale Col di Lana

Corso San Gottardo

Ripa di Porta Ticinese

Viale Gorizia

Montenapoleone Ⓜ

San Babila Ⓜ

Via Francesco Sforza

Via U Visconti di Modrone

Via San Damiano

Corso Monforte

Via Mozart

Via Pietro Mascagni

Corso di Porta Vittoria

Via Filippo Corridoni

Via Fontana

Giardini della Guastalla

See Central Milan Map (p248)

Via Santa Sofia

Via G Mercalli

Corso Italia

Via S Martiro

Crocetta Ⓜ

Corso di Porta Vigentina

Via della Commenda

Corso di Porta Romana

PORTA ROMANA

Via Pace

Rotonda della Besana

Piazza Cinque Giornate

Viale Premuda

Viale Bianca Maria

Piazza Risorgimento

Via Carlo Goldoni

Via Macedonio Melloni

Via Pasquale Sottocorno

Via Archimede

Il Salvagente (200m)

Corso XXII Marzo

Idroscalo (6km); Linate (5km)

Via Spartaco

Via Fogazzaro

Via Bergamo

Viale Lazio

Via Pier Lombardo

Piazzale Libia

Via Tiraboschi

Via Sigieri

Via Lodovico Muratori

Via S Luttuada

Via dei Papi

Porta Romana Ⓜ

Viale Montenero

Viale Emilio Caldara

Via A Lamarmora

Via Orti

Viale A Filippetti

Viale Sabotino

Viale Beatrice d'Este

Viale Bligny

Viale F Dondoni

Via G Ripamonti

Fondazione Prada (1.2km); Lodi TIBB Ⓜ (250m)

Pavia (32km)

Medolanum Forum (6km)

Via Pietro Teulié

Via Gaudenzio Ferrari

Via Paoli

Porta Genova

Via California

4

23

11

33

3

2

31

32

6

12

15

24

22

29

14

8

28

16

25

9

Milan

& Fri-Sun, to 10.30pm Thu; Ⓜ Duomo) Housed in three fabulously decorated palaces, the enormous art collection of Fondazione Cariplo and Intesa Sanpaolo bank pays homage to 18th- and 19th-century Lombard painting. From a magnificent sequence of bas-reliefs by Antonio Canova to luminous Romantic masterpieces by Francesco Hayez, the works span 23 rooms and document Milan's significant contribution to the rebirth of Italian sculpture, the patriotic romanticism of the Risorgimento (reunification period) and the birth of futurism at the dawn of the 20th century.

★ Pinacoteca di Brera GALLERY

(Map p248; ☑ 02 72 26 31; www.pinacotecabrera. org; Via Brera 28; adult/reduced €10/7; ⊙ 8.30am-7.15pm Tue-Wed & Fri-Sun, to 10.15pm Thu; Ⓜ Lanza, Montenapoleone) Located upstairs from the centuries-old Accademia di Belle Arti (still one of Italy's most prestigious art schools), this gallery houses Milan's impressive collection of Old Masters, much of it 'lifted' from Venice by Napoleon. Rubens, Goya and Van Dyck all have a place in the collection, but you're here for the Italians: Titian, Tintoretto, Veronese and the Bellini brothers. Much of the work has tremendous emotional clout, most notably Mantegna's brutal *Lamentation over the Dead Christ*.

★ Museo Poldi Pezzoli MUSEUM

(Map p248; ☑ 02 79 48 89; www.museopoldipezzoli. it; Via Alessandro Manzoni 12; adult/reduced €10/7; ⊙ 10am-6pm Wed-Mon; Ⓜ Montenapoleone) Inheriting his fortune at the age of 24, Gian Giacomo Poldi Pezzoli also inherited his mother's love of art. During extensive European travels, he was inspired by the 'house museum' that was to become London's V&A and had the idea of transforming his apartments into a series of themed rooms based on the great art periods (the Middle Ages, early Renaissance, baroque etc). Crammed with big-ticket Renaissance artworks, these **Sala d'Artista** are exquisite works of art in their own right.

★ Fondazione Feltrinelli ARCHITECTURE

(Map p244; ☑ 02 495 83 41; www.fondazionefeltri nelli.it; Viale Pasubio 5; Ⓜ Monumentale) Herzog & de Meuron's first public building in Italy is a combination of two elongated, slanted structures that look reminiscent of a greenhouse. That's not a coincidence as they are built on the site of a former nursery and take inspiration from Milan's historic *cascine* (farm buildings). With a steeply pitched roof and shark-tooth edge, they bring an awesome dose of modernity to the surrounding neighbourhood.

Villa Necchi Campiglio   MUSEUM
(Map p244; ☑02 7634 0121; www.visitfai.it/villanec chi; Via Mozart 14; adult/child €9/4; ⊙10am-6pm Wed-Sun; Ⓜ San Babila) This exquisitely restored 1930s villa was designed by rationalist architect Piero Portaluppi for heiresses Nedda and Gigina Necchi, and Gigina's husband Angelo Campiglio. The trio were proud owners of one of Milan's only swimming pools, as well as terrarium-faced sunrooms and streamlined electronic shuttering. Portaluppi's mingling of art deco and rationalist styles powerfully evokes Milan's modernist imaginings while at the same time remaining anchored to a past that was rapidly slipping away.

⭐**Castello Sforzesco**   CASTLE
(Map p248; ☑02 8846 3703; www.milanocastello it; Piazza Castello; adult/reduced €5/3; ⊙9am-5.30pm Tue-Sun; ⊞; Ⓜ Cairoli) Originally a Visconti fortress, this iconic red-brick castle was later home to the mighty Sforza dynasty, who ruled Renaissance Milan. The castle's defences were designed by the multitalented da Vinci; Napoleon later drained the moat and removed the drawbridges. Today, it houses seven specialised museums, which gather together intriguing fragments of Milan's cultural and civic history, including Michelangelo's final work, the *Rondanini Pietà*, now housed in the frescoed hall of the castle's Ospedale Spagnolo (Spanish Hospital).

Of the museums, the most interesting is the **Musei d'Arte Antica** (Museum of Ancient Art), which is displayed in the ducal apartments, some of which are frescoed by Leonardo da Vinci. Included in the collection are early paleo-Christian sculptures, the superb equestrian tomb of Bernabò Visconti and sculpted reliefs depicting Milan's triumph over Barbarossa. The exhibit eloquently tells the story of the birth of Italy's first city *comune* through murderous dynastic and regional ambitions, which made this one of the most powerful courts in Europe.

On the 1st floor, the **Museo dei Mobile** (Furniture Museum) and **Pinacoteca** (Picture Gallery) lead you from ducal wardrobes and writing desks through to a collection of Lombard Gothic art.

Triennale di Milano   MUSEUM
(Map p248; ☑02 7243 4208; www.triennaledesign museum.it; Viale Emilio Alemanga 6; adult/reduced €10/6.50; ⊙10.30am-8.30pm Tue-Sun; Ⓟ; Ⓜ Cadorna) Italy's first Triennale took place in 1923 in Monza. It aimed to promote Italian design and applied arts, and its success

led to the construction of Giovanni Muzio's **Palazzo d'Arte** in Milan in 1933. Since then, this exhibition space has championed design in all its forms, although the triennale formula has been replaced by long annual exhibits and international shows.

⭐**The Last Supper**   ARTWORK
(Map p244; Il Cenacolo; ☑02 9280 0360; www. cenacolovinciano.net; Piazza Santa Maria delle Grazie 2; adult/reduced €10/5, plus booking fee €2; ⊙8.15am-6.45pm Tue-Sun; Ⓜ Cadorna) Milan's most famous mural, Leonardo da Vinci's *The Last Supper*, is hidden away on a wall of the refectory adjoining the **Basilica di Santa Maria delle Grazie** (☑02 467 61 11; www. legraziemilano.it; Piazza Santa Maria delle Grazie; ⊙7am-noon & 3.30-7.30pm Mon-Sat, 7.30am-12.30pm & 4-9pm Sun; Ⓜ Cadorna, 🚋16). Depicting Christ and his disciples at the dramatic moment when Christ reveals he's aware of his betrayal, it's a masterful psychological study and one of the world's most iconic images. To see it you must book in advance or sign up for a guided city tour.

⭐**Museo Nazionale della Scienza e della Tecnologia**   MUSEUM
(Map p244; ☑02 48 55 51; www.museoscienza.org; Via San Vittore 21; adult/child €10/7.50, submarine tours €8, flight simulator €10; ⊙9.30am-5pm Tue-Fri, to 6.30pm Sat & Sun; ⊞; Ⓜ Sant'Ambrogio) Kids and would-be inventors will go goggle-eyed at Milan's science museum, the largest of its kind in Italy. It is a fitting tribute in a city where arch-inventor Leonardo da Vinci did much of his finest work. The 16th-century monastery where it is housed features a collection of more than 10,000 items, including models based on da Vinci's sketches, and outdoor hangars housing steam trains, planes and Italy's first submarine, *Enrico Toti*. More recently, the museum added a helicopter flight simulator, in which you can swoop over Milan in a real AW109 cockpit. The museum's fabulous **MUST Shop** (Map p244; ☑02 4855 5340; www.mustshop.it; Via Olona 6; ⊙10am-7pm Tue-Sun; 🌐⊞; Ⓜ Sant' Ambrogio) is the place for all manner of science-inspired books, design items, gadgets and games. Access it through the museum or from Via Olona.

⭐**Chiesa di San Maurizio**   CHURCH
(Map p248; ☑02 8844 5208; Corso Magenta 15; ⊙9.30am-7.30pm Tue-Sun; Ⓜ Cadorna) This 16th-century royal chapel and one-time Benedictine convent is Milan's hidden crown

Central Milan

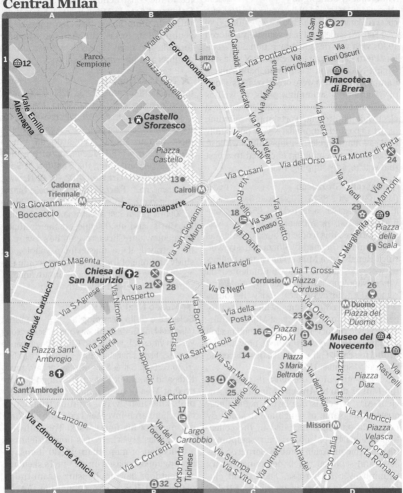

jewel, every inch of it covered in breathtaking frescoes, most of them executed by Bernardino Luini, who worked with Leonardo da Vinci. Many of the frescoes immortalise Ippolita Sforza, Milanese literary maven, and other members of the powerful Sforza and Bentivoglio clans who paid for the decoration.

Basilica di Sant'Ambrogio BASILICA
(Map p248; ☑02 8645 0895; www.basilicasant
ambrogio.it; Piazza Sant'Ambrogio 15; ☉10am-noon
& 2.30-6pm Mon-Sat, 3-5pm Sun; Ⓜ Sant'Ambrogio)
St Ambrose, Milan's patron saint and onetime superstar bishop, is buried in the crypt of this red-brick cathedral, which he founded

in AD 379. It's a fitting legacy, built and rebuilt with a purposeful simplicity that is truly uplifting: the seminal Lombard Romanesque basilica. Shimmering altar mosaics and a biographical golden altarpiece (835), which once served as the cladding for the saint's sarcophagus, light up the shadowy vaulted interior.

Fondazione Prada GALLERY
(☑02 5666 2611; www.fondazioneprada.org; Largo Isarco 2; adult/reduced €10/8; ☉10am-7pm Sun-Mon, Wed & Thu, to 8pm Fri & Sat; Ⓜ Lodi)
Conceived by author and architect Miuccia Prada and Rem Koolhaas, this museum is as innovative and creative as the minds that

MILAN & THE LAKES MILAN

gave it shape. Seven renovated buildings and three new structures have transformed a dilapidated former brandy factory into 19,000 sq metres of exciting, multilevel exhibition space. The buildings, including a four-storey Haunted House tower clad in gold leaf, work seamlessly together, presenting some stunning visual perspectives.

🏃 Activities

Navigli Lombardi BOATING
(Map p244; ☏ 02 667 91 31; www.navigliLombardi. it; Alzaia Naviglio Grande 4; adult €14; ⊙ Apr-Sep; Ⓜ Porta Genova, 🚌 3) Canals were once the

autostradas of medieval Milan, transporting timber, marble, salt, oil and wine into town. The largest of them, the Naviglio Grande, grew from an irrigation ditch to one of the city's busiest thoroughfares by the 13th century. Four cruises run from April to September; the most popular, the Conche Trail, loops round the Naviglio Grande and Naviglio Pavese back through the dock.

QC Terme Milano
SPA

(Map p244; ☑ 02 5519 9367; www.termemilano. com; Piazzale Medaglie d'Oro 2; day ticket weekdays/weekend €45/50; ⊙ 9.30am-midnight Mon-Fri, from 8.30am Sat & Sun; M Porta Romana) Pad down the hallways of Milan's former public transport headquarters and make yourself comfortable in a pine-clad railway carriage for a bio sauna session. Such is the ingenuity of this remodelled spa, which has turned the art deco building into a luxurious wellness centre. Outside, the garden is dotted with Jacuzzi pools around which fatigued Milanese office workers snooze.

⌲ Tours

Autostradale Viaggi
TOURS

(Map p248; ☑ 02 3008 9900; www.autostradale viaggi.it; Piazza Castello 1; tours €75; ⊙ 9am-6pm Mon-Fri, 9am-2pm Sat & Sun; ♿; M Cairoli) Autostradale's three-hour city bus tours include admission to *The Last Supper*, Castello Sforzesco and the Teatro alla Scala (La Scala) museum. Tours run Tuesday to Sunday and depart either from the Central Station at 9am or from the taxi rank on the western side of Piazza del Duomo at 9.30am.

Ad Artem
CULTURAL

(Map p244; ☑ 02 659 77 28; www.adartem.it; Via Melchiorre Gioia 1; adult/child €13/8; ♿; M Sondrio) Unusual cultural tours of Milan's museums and monuments with qualified art historians and actors. Highlight tours include a walk around the battlements of Castello Sforzesco; explorations of the castle's subterranean Ghirlanda passageway; and family-friendly tours of the Museo del Novecento, where kids are invited to build and design their own artwork.

Bike & the City
CYCLING

(Map p244; ☑ 393 8032968; www.bikeandthecity. it; day/sunset tours €40/35; ⊙ tours 10am, 3.30pm & 6.30pm; ♿; M Porta Venezia) Make friends while you get the inside scoop on city sights during these leisurely, four-hour cycle tours. Tours start from Via Melchiorre Gioia 73.

☆⁂ Festivals & Events

Carnevale Ambrosiano
RELIGIOUS

Lent comes late to Milan, with Carnevale sensibly held on the Saturday that falls after everyone else's frantic February Fat Tuesday.

Cortili Aperti
CULTURAL

(www.adsi.it) Over the last weekend in May, the gates to some of the city's most beautiful private courtyards are flung open. Print a map and make your own itinerary, or sign up for tours with **Città Nacosta Milano** (Map p248; ☑ 347 3661174; www.cittanascostamilano.it; Via del Bollo 3; membership adult €20-40, under-28 €7; ⊙ 9am-1pm & 2-6pm Mon-Fri; M Duomo, Missori).

MiArt
FAIR

(www.miart.it) Milan's annual modern and contemporary art fair held in April may not be Basel, but it attracts more than 30,000 art lovers, but more than 200 exhibitors and increasing amounts of international attention.

Salone Internazionale del Mobile
FAIR

(International Furniture Fair; www.salonemilano.it) The world's most prestigious furniture fair is held annually in April at **Fiera Milano** (www.fieramilano.it; Strada Statale del Sempione 28, Rho; M Rho), with satellite exhibitions in Zona Tortona. Alongside the Salone runs the **Fuorisalone** (http://fuorisalone.it; literally, the outdoor lounge), which incorporates dozens of spontaneous design-related events, parties, exhibits and shows that animate the entire city.

Festa di Sant'Ambrogio & Fiera degli Obej Obej
RELIGIOUS

The feast day of Milan's patron saint, St Ambrose, is celebrated on 7 December with the opening of the opera season at Teatro alla Scala (La Scala). In conjunction, a large Christmas Fair sets up in Castello Sforzesco with stalls selling regional foods, sweets and seasonal handicrafts.

⊨ Sleeping

★ Ostello Bello
HOSTEL €

(Map p248; ☑ 02 3658 2720; www.ostellobello.com; Via Medici 4; dm/d/tr €45/129/149; ✳❄☎✉; ◻ 2, 3, 14) A breath of fresh air in Milan's stiffly suited centre, this is the best hostel in town. Entrance is through its lively bar-cafe, open to nonguests, where you're welcomed with a smile and a complimentary drink. Beds are in mixed dorms or spotless private rooms, and there's a kitchen, a small terrace, and a basement lounge equipped with guitars, board games and table football.

Casa Base
DESIGN HOTEL €

(Map p244; http://base.milano.it; Via Bergognone 34; dm with/without bathroom €55/35, d €90; ✳❄☎; ◻ 14, 68) Hot on the heels of the co-working trend is this co-living artists' residence and guesthouse styled by Stella Orsini who's given it a super cool 1950s vibe. With just 10 rooms (some with shared bathrooms) it has the feel of a house, but you also have access to the Base co-working space, bar and events in the renovated Ansaldo steelworks.

★ **Atellani Apartments** APARTMENT €€

(Map p244; ☑340 951 9126; www.atellaniapart ments.com; Corso Magenta 65; 1-bed apt €180-247, 2-bed apt €332; ℗ 🛜; 🛗16) Now you can bed down in the 15th-century palace where Leonardo lodged whilst he painted *The Last Supper*. But unlike him, you won't have to deal with rudimentary plumbing. Instead you'll enjoy Portaluppi-inspired modernist design, parquet floors and slick contemporary kitchens, as well as unique views over Santa Maria delle Grazie. Breakfast is provided in the chic cafe downstairs.

★ **Maison Borella** BOUTIQUE HOTEL €€

(Map p244; ☑02 5810 9114; www.hotelmaison borella.com; Alzaia Naviglio Grande 8; d €160-215; ✱ @ 🛜; 🄼Porta Genova) With geranium-clad balconies overhanging the Naviglio Grande and striking period decor, this canalside hotel offers a touch of class in a dedicated bohemian neighbourhood. Converted from an old apartment block, the hotel's rooms are arranged around an internal courtyard and mix mid-century and contemporary furnishings with charming decorative features such as parquet floors, beamed ceilings and elegant *boiserie* (sculpted panelling).

★ **LaFavia Four Rooms** B&B €€

(Map p244; ☑347 7842212; www.lafavia4rooms. com; Via Carlo Farini 4; s €90-105, d €100-125; ✱ 🛜; 🄼Garibaldi) Marco and Fabio's fourroom bed and breakfast in the former Rabarbaro Zucca factory is a multicultural treat with rooms inspired by their travels through India, Mexico and Europe. Graphic wallpapers by Manuela Canova in zippy greens and oranges are complemented by lush window views onto plant-filled verandas. Best of all is the rooftop garden, where an organic breakfast is served in summer.

Hotel Gran Duca di York HOTEL €€

(Map p248; ☑02 87 48 63; www.ducadiyork.com; Via Moneta 1; d €190; ✱ @ 🛜; 🄼Duomo) This lemon yellow palazzo, literally a stone's throw from the Duomo, was once a residence for scholars working in the nearby Ambrosiana library. Now it offers solid service and 33 small rooms (some with balconies), plump beds and neat, marble bathrooms. Our advice is to skip the rather dull breakfast.

Palazzo Segreti DESIGN HOTEL €€€

(Map p248; ☑02 4952 9250; www.palazzosegreti. com; Via San Tomaso 8; d €275, ste €350; ✱ 🛜; 🄼Cairoli, Cordusio) This 19th-century 'palace of secrets' hides a shockingly modern interior and 18 subdued rooms with raw concrete finishes, rough antique wooden floorboards and shadowy chiaroscuro lighting effects. It appeals to design buffs who favour its minimal furnishings, open-plan bathrooms and achingly hip bar where folk gather in the evening to gossip over goldfish-bowl-sized wine glasses.

Armani Hotel Milano DESIGN HOTEL €€€

(Map p248; ☑02 8883 8381; www.armanihotelmilano.com; Via Alessandro Manzoni 31; d €440-1200; ✱ 🛜 ✽; 🄼Montenapoleone) Armani's new flagship hotel rises above Via Manzoni like a new-age temple, attracting acolytes who slip into its branded lifestyle as easily as into one of his trouser suits. Let your personal Lifestyle Manager escort you to one of the 98 leather-lined rooms, book you a spa session or design you a personal itinerary of the city.

3Rooms B&B €€€

(Map p244; ☑02 62 61 63; www.3rooms-10corso como.com; Corso Como 10; d €270-340; ℗ ✱ @ 🛜; 🄼Garibaldi) Can't drag yourself away from concept shop Corso Como? You don't have to – the villa's three guestrooms (mini-apartments with bedroom, bathroom and sitting room) let you sleep between Eames bedspreads, lounge on Arne Jacobsen chairs and dine off Eero Saarinen's iconic tables. Thrown in are some vintage items and a few eye-catching artworks.

✗ Eating

Milan's dining scene is much like its fashion scene, with new restaurant openings hotly debated and seats at Michelin-starred tables hard to come by. All restaurants should be reserved in advance Friday to Sunday.

Gattullo PASTICCERIA €

(Map p244; ☑02 5831 0497; www.gattullo.it; Piazzale di Porta Lodovico 2; pastries from €1.50; ⊙7am-9pm Tue-Sun, ✱ ✚, 🚇3, 9) Hailing from that great southern baking town, Ruvo di Puglia, in 1961, Joseph Gattullo built his small bakery into a pastry empire. The historic store and cafe is still located in its 1970s premises, resplendent with sci-fi Murano chandeliers and an elegant veneered wooden bar. Come for breakfast, lunch or *aperitivo;* it's all fantastic.

De Santis SANDWICHES €

(Map p248; ☑02 7209 5124; www.paninidesantis. it; Corso Magenta 9; sandwiches €6-8; ⊙noon-11.30pm Sun-Thu, to 12.30am Fri & Sat; ✚; 🄼Cadorna) Sandwiches here are so damn good you may eschew restaurant dining just to sample that *panini* with prosciutto, spicy goat cheese, pepperoni, aubergine and

MILAN & THE LAKES MILAN

Design

Better living by design: what could be more Italian? From the cup that holds your morning espresso to your bedside light, there's a designer responsible and almost everyone in Milan will know their name. Design here is a way of life.

Modern Italian Design

The roots of Italian design stretch back to early-20th-century Milan, with the development of the Fiera trade fair, the rebuild of the Rinascente department store (Giorgio Armani started there as window dresser), the founding of architectural and design magazines *Domus* and *Casabella* and the opening of the Triennale in 1947. Where elaborate French rococo and ornate Austrian art nouveau had captured the imagination of a genteel prewar Europe, the dynamic deco style of Italian futurism was a perfect partner for the industrial revolution and Fascist philosophies.

Fascist propaganda co-opted the radical, neoclassical streamlining that futurism inspired and Italy implemented these ideas into architecture and design. Modern factories had to aid the war effort and Fascist tendencies towards centralised control boosted Italian manufacturing. Through an inherent eye for purity of line, modern Italian design found beauty in balance and symmetry. This refreshing lack of detail appealed to a fiercely democratising war-torn Europe where minimalism and utility came to represent the very essence of modernity.

1. Cassina furniture
2. 1964 Alfa Romeo Giulietta Spider
3. Alessi corkscrew

'From the Spoon to the City'

Milan's philosopher-architects and designers – Giò Ponti, Vico Magistretti, Gae Aulenti, Achille Castiglioni, Ettore Sottsass and Piero Fornasetti – saw their postwar mission as not only rebuilding the bombed city but redesigning the urban environment. A defining statement came from Milanese architect Ernesto Rogers, who said he wished to design 'everything, from the spoon to the city'.

Far from being mere intellectual theorists, this cadre of architect-designers benefited from a unique proximity to artisanal businesses located in Brianza province, north of Milan. This industrial district grew from rural society and thus retained many specialist peasant craft skills. While these production houses remained true to the craft aspect of their work, they were able to use modern sales and production techniques via the central marketplace of the Triennale. This direct connection between craftsman, producer and marketplace allowed for a happy symbiosis between creativity and commercialism, ultimately fine-tuning Italian design to achieve the modernist ideal of creating beautiful, *useful* objects.

DESIGN CLASSICS

Alessi Crafted kitchen utensils designed by big-name architect-designers.

Vespa 1946 Piaggio mini-motor scooter that transformed the lives of urbanites.

Cassina 'Masters' collection furniture by Le Corbusier, Frank Lloyd Wright and Giò Ponti.

Alfa Romeo This legendary roadster, launched in 1910, is the most famous product from Milanese petrolheads.

artichokes. There are 200 variations on the menu and De Santis' decades of experience are good reasons why punters are prepared to queue at this tiny venue. Beer is served on tap to the lucky few who find seating.

Luini
FAST FOOD €

(Map p248; ☑ 02 8646 1917; www.luini.it; Via Santa Radegonda 16; panzerotti €2.70; ⊗ 10am-3pm Mon, to 8pm Tue-Sat; ⓐ; Ⓜ Duomo) This historic joint is the go-to place for *panzerotti,* delicious pizza-dough parcels stuffed with a combination of mozzarella, spinach, tomato, ham or spicy salami, and then fried or baked in a wood-fired oven.

★ Ratanà
MILANESE €€

(Map p244; ☑ 02 8712 8855; www.ratana.it; Via Gaetano de Castillia 28; meals €35-45; ⊗ 12.30-2.30pm & 7.30-11.30pm; Ⓜ Gioia) Located in a lovely Liberty building that once belonged to the railway, Cesare Battisti's neo-bistro turns out authentic Milanese flavours. Drawing his produce from Slow Food artisans, the menu offers up classics such as roasted pumpkin with robiola, risotto with turnip greens and crispy veal tongue with mash. There's a small bar, which locals mob at *aperitivo* time for tasty tapas and local wines.

★ Un Posto a Milano
MODERN ITALIAN €€

(Map p244; ☑ 02 545 77 85; www.unpostoamilano. it; Via Cuccagna 2; meals €15-35; ⊗ 12.30-3pm & 7.30-11pm; ⓐⓐ; Ⓜ Porta Romana) A few years ago this country *cascina* (farmhouse) was a derelict ruin until a collection of cooperatives and cultural associations returned it to multifunctional use as restaurant, bar, social hub and hostel. Delicious salads, homemade foccacia, soups and snacks are served throughout the day at the bar, while the restaurant serves simple home cooking using locally sourced ingredients.

Trattoria Milanese
MILANESE €€

(Map p248; ☑ 02 8645 1991; Via Santa Marta 11; meals €35-45; ⊗ noon-2.45pm & 7-10.45pm Mon-Sat; ⓐ 2, 14) Like an old friend you haven't seen in years, this trattoria welcomes you with generous goblets of wine, hearty servings of traditional Milanese fare and convivial banter over the vegetable buffet. Regulars slide into their seats, barely needing to order as waiters bring them their usual: meatballs wrapped in cabbage, minestrone or the sinfully good *risotto al salto* (refried risotto).

★ Il Luogo di Aimo e Nadia
MODERN ITALIAN €€€

(☑ 02 41 68 86; www.aimoenadia.com; Via Montecuccoli 6; meals €95-145; ⊗ 12.30-2pm & 7.30-10.30pm Mon-Fri, 7.30-10.30pm Sat; Ⓜ Primaticcio) For the Milanese, food should be like clothing: excellent, imaginative, seasonal and suitable for all occasions. Not surprisingly, all adore this two-Michelin starred restaurant, which offers seasonal dishes such as tagliolini with truffles and turnips in winter, and prawns in pistachio crust with artichokes in spring. The wine list delights all year round.

★ Seta
GASTRONOMY €€€

(Map p248; Mandarin Oriental; ☑ 02 8731 8897; www.mandarinoriental.com; Via Andegari 9; meals €120; ⊗ 12.30-2.30pm & 7.30-10.30pm Mon-Fri, 7.30-10.30pm Sat; ⓟⓐⓐ; Ⓜ Montenapoleone) Smooth as the silk after which it is named, Seta is Michelin-starred dining at its best: beautiful, inventive and full of flavour surprises. Diners sit on the edge of their teal-coloured velvet chairs in keen anticipation of Antonio Guida's inspired dishes such as plum-coloured roe deer with a dazzling splash of mango salsa. It's both solidly traditional and subtly daring, just like Milan.

★ La Brisa
MODERN ITALIAN €€€

(Map p248; ☑ 02 8645 0521; www.ristorantelabrisa. it; Via Brisa 15; meals €50-70; ⊗ 12.45-2.30pm & 7.45-10.30pm Mon-Fri, 7.45-10.30pm Sun; ⓐ; Ⓜ Cairoli, Cordusio) Discreet, elegant and exquisitely romantic. Push open the screened door and the maître d' will guide you to a table beneath centuries-old linden trees in a secluded courtyard, where ivy climbs the walls and pink hydrangeas bob in the breeze. Chef Antonio Facciolo's seasonal menus are similarly elegant; his signature dish is a mouthwatering roast pork in a myrtle-berry drizzle.

★ Basara
SUSHI €€€

(Map p244; ☑ 02 8324 1025; www.basaramilano.it; Via Tortona 12; meals €50-70; ⊗ 8.30am-3.30pm & 7pm-12.30am Mon-Sat; Ⓜ Porta Genova) Making a name for yourself in Milan's sophisticated sushi scene isn't easy, but chef Hiro's lobster maki roll sings a siren song that packs this place out for two sittings every evening. The raw-fish plates are superb, particularly the pretty block of red Sicilian shrimps served on a black slate slab with a sprinkle of sea salt.

Cracco
MODERN ITALIAN €€€

(Map p248; ☑ 02 87 67 74; www.ristorantecracco. it; Via Victor Hugo 4; meals €130-160; ⊗ 12.30-2pm & 7.30pm-12.30am Tue-Fri, 7.30-11pm Mon & Sat; Ⓜ Duomo) Two Michelin-star chef Carlo Cracco keeps the Milanese in thrall with his off-the-wall inventiveness. The *risotto al sedano, rapa, tartufo nero e caffè* (risotto with celery, turnip, black truffle and coffee) is unlike any northern Italian rice dish you may have stumbled across elsewhere. Let the waiters do the thinking by ordering one of the tasting menus (€130 and €160).

Drinking & Nightlife

Drinking is a stylish affair in Milan and an opportunity to make *la bella figura* (a good impression). Wine and cocktail bars abound, particularly in Navigli, Brera and Corso Como, and many stay open until 2am, while clubs stay open until 5am. Zero's (http://zero.eu/milano) fortnightly guide and online info is useful, as is 2night (www.2night.it).

★ Botanical Club
BAR

(Map p244; ☑ 02 3652 3846; www.thebotanical club.com; Via Pastrengo 11; meals €25-30; ⊗ 12.30-2.30pm & 6.30-10.30pm Mon-Fri, 6.30-10.30pm Sat; ⍟, Ⓜ Isola) This bar, bistro and gin distillery is Italy's first foray into the micro-distillery trend. Behind a bar festooned with greenery, mixologist Katerina Logvinova has over 150 gins to play with, including the house brand, Spleen & Ideal, which experiments with interesting botanicals such as Serbian juniper and tonka beans. To accompany divine concoctions like Chinese Dusk (London Dry Gin, sake, plum bitter and fruit liqueur) are contemporary plates of veal tartare and crab salad with green apple.

Ceresio 7
BAR

(Map p244; ☑ 02 3103 9221; www.ceresio7.com; Via Ceresio 7; aperitivo €15, meals €60-80; ⊗ 12.30pm-1am; ⍟; 🚋 2, 4) Heady views match the heady price of *aperitivo* at Milan's coolest rooftop bar, sitting atop the former 1930s Enel (electricity company) HQ. Two pools, two bars and a restaurant under the guidance of former Bulgari head chef Elio Sironi make this a hit with Milan's beautiful people. In summer you can book a whole day by the pool from €110, which includes food and drinks.

★ Pasticceria Marchesi
CAFE

(Map p248; ☑ 02 86 27 70; www.pasticceriamarch esi.it; Via Santa Maria alla Porta 11/a; ⊗ 7.30am-8pm Tue-Sat, 8.30am-1pm Sun; Ⓜ Cardusio, Cairoli) Coffee that's perfect every shot since 1824, accompanied by a delectable array of sweets, biscuits and pastries.

Mag Café
BAR

(Map p244; ☑ 02 3956 2875; Ripa di Porta Ticinese 43; cocktails €7-9, brunch €10; ⊗ 7.30am-2am Mon-Fri, 9am-2am Sat & Sun; 🚋 2, 9) A Milanese speakeasy with wingback armchairs in whisky-coloured velvet, marble-topped tables,

FEELING PECKISH?

Milan's historic deli **Peck** (Map p248; ☑ 02 802 31 61; www.peck.it; Via Spadari 9; ⊗ 3-8pm Mon, 9am-8pm Tue-Sat, 10am-5pm Sun; ⍟; Ⓜ Duomo) is a bastion of the city's culinary heritage with three floors below ground dedicated to turning out the fabulously colourful display of foods that cram every counter. It showcases a mind-boggling selection of cheeses, chocolates, pralines, pastries, freshly made gelato, seafood, meat, caviar, pâté, fruit and vegetables, olive oils and balsamic vinegars.

The in-house cafe is certainly worth a lunch or tea stop to sample some of the stunning array, particularly the selection of freshly made cakes. Peck also runs an all-day restaurant, **Peck Italian Bar** (Map p248; ☑ 02 869 30 17; Via Cantù 3; meals €40-45; ⊗ 8am-10pm Mon-Fri, to 9pm Sat; ⍟⍟; Ⓜ Duomo), which appeals to a banking and business lunch crowd. Like the clientele, the food is traditional and the service efficient.

a patchwork of Persian rugs and huge lampshades that look like bird's nests. Like the decor, the drinks are creatively crafted, utilising interesting herbs and syrups, and served in vintage glassware. Mag also does a popular brunch on weekends.

Nottingham Forest
COCKTAIL BAR

(Map p244; www.nottingham-forest.com; Viale Piave 1; cocktails €10; ⊗ 6.30pm-2am Tue-Sat, 6pm-1am Sun; 🚋 9, 23) If Michelin awarded stars for bars, Nottingham Forest would have one. This eclectically decorated Asian-cum-African tiki bar named after an English football team is the outpost of molecular mixologist Dario Comino, who conjures smoking cocktails packed with dry ice and ingenuity. Unique cocktails include the Elite, a mix of vodka, ground pearls and sake – supposedly an aphrodisiac.

Camparino in Galleria
BAR

(Map p248; ☑ 02 8646 4435; www.camparino.it; Piazza del Duomo 21; drinks €12-24; ⊗ 7.15am-8.40pm Tue-Sun; Ⓜ Duomo) Open since the inauguration of the Galleria Vittorio Emanuele II arcade in 1867, this art nouveau bar has served drinks to the likes of Verdi, Toscanini, Dudovich and Carrà. Cast-iron chandeliers and huge mirrored walls trimmed with mosaics of birds and flowers set the tone for a classy

Campari-based cocktail. Drink at the bar for one of the cheapest *aperitivo* in town.

Dry
COCKTAIL BAR

(Map p244; ☑ 02 6379 3414; www.drymilano.it; Via Solferino 33; cocktails €8-13, meals €20-25; ⏱7pm-1.30am; 🛜; Ⓜ Moscova) The brainchild of Michelin-starred chef Andrea Berton, Dry pairs its cocktails with gourmet pizzas. The inventive cocktail list includes the Corpse Reviver (London Dry gin, cointreau, Cocchi Americano and lemon juice) and the Martinez (Boompjes genever, vermouth, Maraschino liqueur and Boker's bitters), the latter inspired by French gold hunters in Martinez, the birthplace of barman Jerry Thomas.

N'Ombra de Vin
WINE BAR

(Map p248; ☑ 02 659 96 50; www.nombradevin.it; Via San Marco 2; ⏱10am-2am; 🛜; Ⓜ Lanza, Moscova) This *enoteca* (wine bar) is set in a one-time Augustine refectory. Tastings can be had all day and you can also indulge in food such as *carpaccio di pesce spade agli agrumi* (swordfish carpaccio prepared with citrus) from a limited menu. Check the website for occasional cultural events and DJ nights.

★ Rebelot del Pont
COCKTAIL BAR

(Map p244; ☑ 02 8419 4720; www.rebelotdelpont. com; Ripa di Porta Ticinese 55; ⏱6pm-2am Mon-Sat, noon-midnight Sun; 🚌2, 9, 14, 19) *Rebelot* means 'pandemonium' in Milanese dialect and this place certainly pushes out the culinary and cocktail boat. You can expect taste sensations such as the Marrakech Souk (blended whisky and spiced honey) and the Garden Sazerac (Monkey 47 gin, cherry liqueur, absinthe and a homemade 'perfume'). Pair with small plates of salted codfish and Tuscan black pork.

BEHIND THE SCENCES AT LA SCALA

To glimpse the inner workings of La Scala, visit the **Ansaldo Workshops** (Map p244; ☑ 02 4335 3521; www.teatroallascala. org; Via Bergognone 34; per person €10; ⏱9am-noon & 2-4pm Tue & Thu; Ⓜ Porto Genova), where the stage sets are crafted and painted, and where some 800 to 1000 new costumes are handmade each season. Tours on Tuesdays and Thursdays must be booked in advance and are guided in conjunction with the heads of each department.

★ VOLT
CLUB

(Map p244; ☑ 345 2285157; www.voltclub.it; Via Molino delle Armi 16; €15-20; ⏱11.30pm-5am; 🚌3) Milan's youngest club is also its hippest, and has its sights firmly set on the European Top Club's chart. Fully renovated, it now has a lighting and sound system designed in Berlin, a slick all-black interior and a line-up of top-notch DJs. Expect house music on Saturday, while other nights alternate different electronic-based genres, as well as hip-hop and dance.

☆ Entertainment

The tourist office stocks several entertainment guides in English: *Hello Milano* (www. hellomilano.it) and *Easy Milano* (www. easymilano.it). For club listings, check out ViviMilano (http://vivimilano.corriere.it), which comes out with the *Corriere della Sera* newspaper on Wednesday; *La Repubblica* (www.repubblica.it) is also good on Thursday. Another source of inspiration is 2night (www.2night.it).

Most big events and names that play Milan do so at major venues outside the city centre, which run shuttle buses for concerts. They include **Mediolanum Forum** (☑ 02 48 85 71; www.mediolanumforum.it; Via Giuseppe di Vittorio 6; Ⓜ Assago Milanofiori) and the San Siro Stadium.

Teatro alla Scala
OPERA

(Map p248; La Scala; ☑ 02 7200 3744; www.teatro allascala.org; Piazza della Scala; tickets €30-300; Ⓜ Duomo) One of the most famous opera stages in the world, La Scala's season runs from early December through July. You can also see theatre, ballet and concerts here year-round (except August). Buy tickets online or by phone up to two months before the performance, or from the central box office. On performance days, tickets for the gallery are available from the box office at Via Filodrammatici 2 (one ticket per customer). Queue early.

Blue Note
JAZZ

(Map p244; ☑ 02 6901 6888; www.bluenotemilano. com; Via Borsieri 37; tickets €22-40; ⏱7.30pm-midnight Tue-Sun Sep-Jun; Ⓜ Isola, Zara) Top-class jazz acts from around the world perform here at the only European outpost for New York's Blue Note jazz club. If you haven't prebooked, you can buy tickets at the door from 7.30pm. It also does an easy-listening Sunday brunch (€35 per adult, or €70 for two adults and two children under 12).

Teatro Gerolamo
THEATRE

(Map p248; ☑02 4538 8221; www.teatrogerolamo.it; Piazza Cesare Beccaria 8; ⓂDuomo) Built in 1868, this miniature theatre modelled on La Scala was built for the purpose of staging puppet shows in Milanese dialect. In danger of dereliction, it was closed in 1957. Recent renovations have restored its pretty painted *palchi* (boxes) and stucco ceiling beneath which you'll enjoy intimate classical music and jazz concerts, as well as recitals and puppet shows.

San Siro Stadium
FOOTBALL

(Stadio Giuseppe Meazza; ☑02 4879 8201; www. sansiro.net; Piazzale Angelo Moratti; tickets from €20; ; ⓂSan Siro Stadio) San Siro Stadium wasn't designed to hold the entire population of Milan, but on a Sunday afternoon amid 80,000 football-mad citizens it can certainly feel like it. The city's two clubs, AC Milan and FC Internazionale Milano (aka Inter), play on alternate weeks September to May.

🅾 Shopping

Milan is an industry town that lives and breathes fashion and design and takes retail as seriously as it does biotech or engineering. Beyond the just seen-on-the-runway collections and heart-fluttering price tags of the Quad, the rest of the city abounds with vintage stores, discount outlets, concept shops, multi-brand retailers, cute boutiques and artisanal ateliers.

★ Spazio Rossana Orlandi
HOMEWARES

(Map p244; ☑02 467 44 71; www.rossanaorlandi. com; Via Matteo Bandello 14; ☺10am-7pm Mon-Sat; ⓂSant'Ambrogio) Installed in a former tie factory in the Magenta district, this iconic interior design studio is a challenge to find. Once inside, though, it's hard to leave the dream-like treasure trove stacked with vintage and contemporary limited-edition pieces from young and upcoming artists.

★ NonostanteMarras
FASHION & ACCESSORIES

(Map p244; ☑393 8934340; Via Cola di Rienzo 8; ☺10am-7pm Mon-Sat, noon-7pm Sun; 🚊14) Brainchild of Sardinian fashion designer Antonio Marras, this eccentric concept store hidden in an ivy-draped courtyard is full of magpie artefacts, books and Marras' creative, colourful clothes. Come here to find something unique, have a cup of tea or simply to enjoy the magical space.

Monica Castiglioni
JEWELLERY

(Map p244; ☑02 8723 7979; www.monicacastiglioni.com; Via Pastrengo 4; ☺11am-8pm Thu-Sat Sep-Jul; ⓂGaribaldi) Daughter of famous designer Achille Castiglioni, Monica Castiglioni has a deep understanding of materials and proportions. To this she adds her own unique vision, turning out organic, industrial-style jewellery in bronze, silver and gold using an ancient lost-wax casting technique.

Wait and See
FASHION & ACCESSORIES

(Map p248; ☑02 7208 0195; www.waitandsee.it; Via Santa Marta 14; ☺3.30-7.30pm Mon, 10.30am-7.30pm Tue-Sat; ⓂDuomo, Missori) With collaborations with international brands and designers such as Missoni, Etro and Anna Molinari under her belt, Uberta Zambeletti launched her own collection in 2010. Quirky Wait and See indulges her eclectic tastes and showcases unfamiliar brands alongside items exclusively designed for the store, including super-fun Lana Bi striped pant suits and Lisa C pop-art earrings.

★ Eataly
FOOD

(Map p244; ☑02 4949 7301; www.eataly.net/it_it/negozi/milano-smeraldo/; Piazza XXV Aprile 10; ☺8.30am-midnight; ; ⓂMoscova, Garibaldi) A cult destination dedicated to Italian gastronomy, this 5000-sq-metre emporium showcases the best, locally sourced products over four huge floors, including small craft

---

VINTAGE FINDS

Il Salvagente (☑02 7611 0328; www.salvagentemilano.it; Via Fratelli Bronzetti 16; ☺10am-7.30pm Tue-Sat, 11am-2pm & 3-7pm Sun, 3-7.30pm Mon; 🚊60, 62 & 92) The grim basement courtyard of Il Salvagente gives scant indication of the big brands inside. Prada, Dolce & Gabbana, Versace and Alberta Ferretti are just a few of the names discounted on the tightly packed racks. Payment is cash only.

Cavalli e Nastri (Map p248; ☑02 7200 0449; www.cavallienastri.com; Via Brera 2; ☺10.30am-7.30pm Mon-Sat, noon-7.30pm Sun; ⓂMontenapoleone) This gorgeously colourful shop is known for its vintage clothes and accessories. It specialises in lovingly curated frocks, bags, jewellery and even shoes, sourced from early- and mid-20th-century Italian fashion houses, and priced accordingly. You'll find its **menswear store** (☑02 4945 1174; www.cavallienastri.com; Via Gian Giacomo Mora 3; ☺10.30am-7.30pm Mon-Sat, noon-7.30pm Sun; 🚊2, 14) at Via Mora 3.

Fashion

Northern Italian artisans and designers have been dressing and adorning Europe's affluent classes since the early Middle Ages. At that time Venetian merchants imported dyes from the East and Leonardo da Vinci helped design Milan's canal system, connecting the wool merchants and silk weavers of the lakes to the city's market places. Further south, Florence's wool guild grew so rich they were able to fund a Renaissance.

Global Powerhouses

In the 1950s Florence's fashion houses, which once produced only made-to-measure designs, began to present seasonal collections to a select public. But Milan literally stole the show in 1958, hosting Italy's first Fashion Week. With its ready factories, cosmopolitan workforce and long-established media presence, Milan created ready-to-wear fashion for global markets.

Recognising the enormous potential of mass markets, designers such as Armani, Missoni and Versace began creating and following trends, selling their 'image' through advertising and promotion. In the 1980s Armani's power suits gave rise to new unisex fashions, Dolce & Gabbana became a byword for Italian sex appeal and Miuccia Prada transformed her father's ailing luxury luggage business by introducing democratic, durable totes and backpacks made out of radical new fabrics (like waterproof Pocono, silk faille and parachute nylon).

Fashion Mecca Milan

Milan's rise to global fashion prominence was far from random. No other Italian

1. Versace store, Milan
2. Perla lingerie
3. Prada shoes

city, not even Rome, was so well suited to take on this mantle. First, thanks to its geographic position, the city had historically strong links with European markets. It was also Italy's capital of finance, advertising, television and publishing, with both *Vogue* and *Amica* magazines based there. What's more, Milan always had a fashion industry based around the historic textile and silk production of upper Lombardy. And, with the city's postwar focus on trade fairs and special events, it provided a natural marketplace for the exchange of goods and ideas.

As a result, by 2011 Milan emerged as Italy's top (and the world's fourth-biggest) fashion exporter. The Quadrilatero d'Oro, that 'Golden Quad', is now dominated by more than 500 fashion outlets in an area barely 6000 sq metres. Such is the level of display, tourists now travel to Milan to 'see' the fashion. Helping them do just that, in 2015 King Giorgio opened Armani Silos, a museum dedicated to over 40 years of Armani success showcasing 600 couture outfits and 200 accessories

FASHION WEEKS

The winter shows are held in January (men) and February (women) and the spring/summer events are in June (men) and September (women). You'll enjoy the full carnival effect as more than 100,000 models, critics, buyers and producers descend on the city to see 350-plus shows.

For a full timetable check out www.cameramoda.it or http://milanfashionweeklive.com.

beer producers, specialist gelato from Làit and mozzarella from Miracolo a Milano. In addition, there are 19 different eateries, rooms for food workshops and a Michelin-starred restaurant, Alice. It's housed in the revamped Teatro Smeraldo so live music, readings and recitals are a part of the experience.

La Rinascente   DEPARTMENT STORE
(Map p248; ☏02 8 85 21; www.rinascente.it; Piazza del Duomo; ⊙9.30am-9pm Mon-Thu & Sun, to 10pm Sat; Ⓜ Duomo) Italy's most prestigious department store doesn't let the fashion capital down – come for Italian diffusion lines, French lovelies and LA upstarts. The basement also hides a 'Made in Italy' design supermarket, and chic hairdresser Aldo Coppola is on the top floor. Take away edible souvenirs from the 7th-floor food market (and peer across to the Duomo while you're at it).

10 Corso Como   FASHION & ACCESSORIES
(Map p244; ☏02 2900 2674; www.10corsocomo.com; Corso Como 10; ⊙10.30am-7.30pm Fri-Tue, to 9pm Wed & Thu; Ⓜ Garibaldi) This might be the world's most hyped 'concept shop', but Carla Sozzani's selection of desirable things (Lanvin ballet flats, Alexander Girard wooden dolls, a demicouture frock by a designer you've not read about *yet*) makes 10 Corso Como a fun window-shopping experience. There's a bookshop upstairs with art and design titles, and a hyper-stylish bar and restaurant in the main atrium and picture-perfect courtyard.

NAVIGLI MARKETS

Mercato Comunale (Map p244; Piazza XXIV Maggio; ⊙8.30am-1pm & 4-7.30pm Tue-Sat, 8.30am-1pm Mon; 🚋3, 9, 10, 14) Overlooking the revitalised Darsena, where boats once docked in medieval Milan, the city's main food market now has a swish new glass-and-steel enclosure. Inside, myriad stalls sell meat, cheese, fresh fruit and veg.

Mercatone dell'Antiquariato (Map p244; www.navigliogrande.mi.it; Naviglio Grande; ⊙last Sun of month; Ⓜ Porta Genova) This antiques market is the city's most scenic market, and sets up along a 2km stretch of the Naviglio Grande. With more than 400 well-vetted antique and secondhand traders, it provides hours of treasure-hunting pleasure.

ⓘ Information

American International Medical Centre (AIMC; ☏02 5831 9808; www.aimclinic.it; Via Mercalli 11; ⊙9am-5.30pm Mon-Fri; Ⓜ Crocetta) Private, international health clinic with English-speaking staff.

Lloyds Farmacia (☏02 498 4165; www.lloydsfarmacia.it; Piazza de Angeli 1; ⊙24hr; Ⓜ Angeli) Convenient 24-hour pharmacy close to the De Angeli metro stop.

Ospedale Maggiore Policlinico (☏24hr 02 5 50 31; www.policlinico.mi.it; Via Francesco Sforza 35; Ⓜ Crocetta) Milan's main hospital; offers an outpatient service.

Police Station (Questura; ☏02 6 22 61; http://questure.poliziadistato.it/milano; Via Fatebenefratelli 11; ⊙8am-2pm & 3-6pm Mon-Fri; Ⓜ Turati) Milan police headquarters.

Milan Tourist Office (☏02 8845 5555; www.turismo.milano.it; Galleria Vittorio Emanuele II 11-12; ⊙9am-7pm Mon-Fri, to 6pm Sat, 10am-6pm Sun; Ⓜ Duomo) Centrally located in the Galleria with helpful English-speaking staff and tonnes of maps and brochures.

ⓘ Getting There & Away

AIR

In addition to its own airports, Milan has direct links to Bergamo's Orio al Serio airport (p293).

Aeroporto Linate (LIN; ☏02 23 23 23; www.milanolinate-airport.com) Located 7km east of Milan city centre; domestic and European flights only.

Aeroporto Malpensa (MXP; ☏02 23 23 23; www.milanomalpensa-airport.com; 🚆 Malpensa Express) Northern Italy's main international airport is about 50km northwest of Milan city. Services include car rental, banks, a VAT refund office and free wi-fi with the ViaMilano app.

BUS

Buses converge on Milan from most major European cities. Most services depart from and terminate in **Lampugnano Bus Terminal** (Via Giulia Natta; Ⓜ Lampugnano).

TRAIN

Milan is a major European rail hub. High-speed services arrive from across Italy, and from France, Switzerland and Germany. An overnight sleeper train also runs from Barcelona (Spain). For train timetables and fares, check out www.trenitalia.com, www.sbb.ch and www.bahn.de.

ⓘ Getting Around

TO/FROM THE AIRPORTS

Aeroporto Malpensa

Malpensa Express (☏02 7249 4949; www.malpensaexpress.it; one way €13) trains run to the city centre (50 minutes) every 30 minutes from 5.40am to 10.40pm; the **Malpensa**

Shuttle (☑02 5858 3185; www.malpensa shuttle.it; one way/return €10/16; Ⓜ Centrale) continues a limited services between 10.45pm and 5.30am. Taxis are a €90 set fare (50 minutes).

Aeroporto Linate

Airport Bus Express (☑02 3391 0794; www.air portbusexpress.it; one way/return €5/9; Ⓜ Centrale) coaches run to Central Station (25 minutes) every 30 minutes between 5.30am and 10pm; ATM city bus 73 departs to Piazza San Babila (€1.50, 25 minutes) every 10 minutes between 5.35am and 12.35am. Taxis cost between €20 and €30, depending on your destination.

Aeroporto Orio al Serio

The **Orio al Serio Bus Express** (☑02 3008 9300; www.airportbusexpress.it; one way/return €5/9; Ⓜ Centrale) runs to Central Station (one hour) every 30 minutes from 4.25am to 10.20pm; **Autostradale** (☑02 3008 9300; www.autostradale.It) also runs a half-hourly service to Central Station (one way €5) between 7.45am and 12.15am.

BICYCLE

BikeMi (☑02 4860 7607; www.bikemi.it; 🚲) is a public bicycle system with stops all over town. Get passes online or by dropping into the ATM Info Point at the Duomo, Cadorna or Centrale metro stops.

CAR & MOTORCYCLE

It simply isn't worth having a car in Milan. Many streets have restricted access and parking is a nightmare. A congestion zone, AreaC, is now enforced in the city centre between 7.30am and 7.30pm Monday to Wednesday and Friday (to 6pm on Thursday). To enter you need to buy a daily pass costing €5. You can purchase it online at www.muoversi.milano.it.

In the centre, street parking costs between €1.50 and €3 per hour. To pay, buy a SostaMilano card from a tobacconist, scratch off the date and hour, and display it on your dashboard.

Underground car parks charge between €25 and €40 for 24 hours.

PUBLIC TRANSPORT

ATM (Azienda Trasporti Milano; ☑02 4860 7607; www.atm.it) runs the metro, buses and trams. The metro is the most convenient way to get around and consists of four underground lines (red M1, green M2, yellow M3 and lilac M5) and a suburban rail network, the blue Passante Ferroviario. Services run from 6am to 12.30am. A ticket costs €1.50 and is valid for one metro ride or up to 90 minutes' travel on buses and trams.

TAXI

Taxis cannot be hailed, but must be picked up at designated ranks, usually outside train stations,

DON'T MISS

QUADRILATERO D'ORO

A stroll around the world's most famous shopping district, the **Quadrilatero d'Oro** (Golden Quad; Ⓜ Monte Napoleone), is a must. This quaintly cobbled quadrangle of streets – bounded by Via Monte Napoleone, Via Sant'Andrea, Via della Spiga and Via Alessandro Manzoni – has always been synonymous with elegance and money (Via Monte Napoleone was where Napoleon's government managed loans). Even if you don't have the slightest urge to sling a swag of glossy carriers, the window displays and people-watching are priceless.

large hotels and in major piazze. You can call a cab on ☑02 40 40, 02 69 69, 02 85 85 or 02 77 77. English is spoken.

Be aware that when you call for a cab, the meter runs from receipt of call, not pick up. The average short city ride costs €10.

AROUND MILAN

Pavia

POP 72,580

Founded by the Romans as a military garrison, Pavia has long been a strategic city both geographically and politically It sits at the centre of an agricultural plain (hence its ugly periphery), it is an important provincial political player with strong Lega Nord leanings, and its university is considered one of the best in Italy. Pavia's historic centre preserves a clutch of worthwhile sights including, to the north of the city, the fabulous Carthusian monastery Certosa di Pavia.

⊙ Sights

★ **Certosa di Pavia** MONASTERY
(☑0382 92 56 13; www.certosadipavia.com; Viale Monumento; entry by donation; ⊙9-11.30am & 2.30-5.30pm Tue-Sun summer, to 4.30pm winter) **FREE** One of the Italian Renaissance's most notable buildings is the splendid Certosa di Pavia. Giangaleazzo Visconti of Milan founded the monastery, 10km north of Pavia, in 1396 as a private chapel and mausoleum for the Visconti family. Originally intended as an architectural companion piece to Milan's Duomo, the same architects worked on its design; the final result, however, completed

more than a century later, is a unique hybrid between late-Gothic and Renaissance styles.

✕ Eating

★ La Torre degli Aquila ITALIAN €€
(☏0382 2 63 35; www.latorredegliaquila.it; Corso Strada Nuova 20; meals €30-40; ☉noon-2.30pm & 8-10.30pm Mon-Sat) It is almost worth a trip to Pavia just to eat in Dimo and Maria's medieval tower. Although rooted in tradition, the sensational cooking is highly creative. Homemade pistachio bread is followed by tender black bean and potato gnocchi with prawns and sliced sirloin with prunes and *lardo di Colonnata* (lard from Colonnata).

❶ Getting There & Away

Pavia-Milan Trasporti (☏0382 46 92 93; www.pmtsrl.it) Frequent buses link Pavia bus station and Certosa di Pavia (€1.80, 15 minutes, every 30 minutes).

Monza
POP 122,700

Known to many as the home of a classic European Formula One track (where high-speed races have been held annually in September since 1950), Monza is sadly overlooked by visitors to Milan. Aside from the racetrack, which you can actually drive on most days in winter, history and architecture buffs will also be amply rewarded with an excursion to this elegant provincial town.

◉ Sights & Activities

★ Villa Reale PALACE
(☏039 578 34 27; www.villarealedimonza.it; Piazza della Repubblica 30; royal apartments adult/reduced €10/8, royal apartments & exhibitions €19/16; ☉9am-6pm Mon-Fri, 9am-noon Sat) Built between 1777 and 1780 as a viceregal residence for Archduke Ferdinand of Austria, Giuseppe Piermarini's vast Villa Reale was modelled on Vienna's Schönbrunn Palace. It served as the summer home for Italian royalty, but was abandoned following the murder of Umberto I. Years of restoration have revived its glorious 3500-sq-metre frescoed, stuccoed and gilded interior which is used for a variety of exhibitions and cultural events.

Duomo CATHEDRAL
(☏039 38 94 20; www.duomomonza.it; Piazza del Duomo; Corona Ferrea adult/reduced €4/3; ☉9am-6pm) The Gothic *duomo*, with its white-and-green-banded facade, contains a key early-medieval treasure, the **Corona Ferrea** (Iron Crown), fashioned according to legend with one of the nails from the Crucifixion. Charlemagne, King of the Franks and the first Holy Roman Emperor, saw it as a symbol of empire, and he was not alone. Various other Holy Roman emperors, including Frederick I (Barbarossa) and Napoleon, had themselves crowned with it. It's on show in the chapel (from Tuesday to Sunday) dedicated to the Lombard queen Theodolinda.

Museo e Tesoro del Duomo MUSEUM
(☏039 32 63 83; www.museoduomomonza.it; Piazza del Duomo; adult/reduced €6/4, incl Corona Ferrea €8/6; ☉9am-1pm & 2-6pm Tue-Sun) Monza's cathedral museum contains one of the finest collections of religious art in Europe. It's split into two parts: the first section, displaying treasures from the original Palatine Chapel founded by Lombard queen Theodolinda; the second containing masterpieces intended for the 'new' cathedral. Among the highlights are a unique collection of Carolingian art, Palestinian ampullae, a priceless collection of Lombard gold and a stunning, 15th-century rose window. Admission includes viewing the Corona Ferrea (Iron Crown) in the *duomo*'s chapel.

Parco di Monza PARK
(www.reggiadimonza.it; Porta Monza, Viale Cavriga; ☉7am-9.30pm summer, to 8.30pm winter; P🅿♿🚺) **FREE** This enormous park is the green lung of the city; it's also one of the largest enclosed parks in Europe, with some 295 hectares of *bello bosco* (charming woodland). It sits on the Lambro river and incorporates the Autodromo di Monza race course, a horse-racing track, a golf course, tennis courts, a 50m Olympic **swimming pool** (☏039 248 22 32; Porta Santa Maria delle Selve, Via Vedano; full-/half-day €8/6; ☉10am-7pm Jun-Aug; ♿) and miles of cycle paths. You can hire bikes at Cascina Bastia (single/tandem €3/6 per hour).

Autodromo Nazionale Monza CAR RACING
(☏039 2 48 21; www.monzanet.it; Via Vedano 5, Parco di Monza; ☉7am-7pm) Monza's racetrack with its long straights, tricky chicane and sweeping Curva Parabolica is one of the most famous racetracks in the world. In addition to glitzy race days, the track hosts year-round events including cycle races, bike fests and even marathons. In winter, you can roll up in your own vehicle and tool around the infamous chicane; or go all out and take a spin in a Ferrari (from €299; www.puresport.it).

ℹ Getting There & Away

Monza is 23km northeast of Milan, making this an easy day trip. You can practically reach Monza on Milan's metro system. Ride the M1 (red line) to Sesto 1st Maggio and then it's just one stop on the suburban rail network. Other frequent trains connect from Milan's Stazione Centrale (€2.20 to €9.90, 10 to 30 minutes).

THE LAKES

Writers from Goethe and Stendhal to DH Lawrence and Hemingway have lavished praise on the Italian Lakes, a dramatic region of vivid-blue waters ringed by snow-powdered peaks. Curling Lago Maggiore is home to the bewitching Borromean Islands and offers a blast of the belle époque. Mountain-fringed Lago di Como delivers extravagant villas and film-star glamour. Families find fun in the southern amusement parks of Lago di Garda while adrenaline junkies are drawn to the spectacular mountains in the north. Little Lago d'Iseo serves up soaring slopes while the villages and islands of diminutive, often bypassed Lago d'Orta are laced with laid-back charm.

Lago Maggiore

If Lake Maggiore is your first impression of Italy, you're in for a treat. By train or by road, travellers traversing the Alps from Switzerland at the Simplon Pass wind down from the mountains and sidle up to this enormous finger of blue beauty. The star attractions are the Borromean Islands, which, like a fleet of fine vessels, lie at anchor at the entrance to the Borromean Gulf (Golfo Borromeo), an incursion of water between the lake's two main towns, Stresa and Verbania.

ℹ Information

The website www.illagomaggiore.com features lake-wide information.

ℹ Getting There & Around

BOAT

Navigazione Lago Maggiore (☑ 800 551801; www.navigazionelaghi.it) Operates passenger ferries and hydrofoils around the lake; its ticket booths are next to embarkation quays. Services include those connecting Stresa with Arona (€6.20, 40 minutes), Angera (€6.20, 35 minutes) and Verbania Pallanza (often just called Pallanza; €5, 35 minutes). Day passes include a ticket linking Stresa with Isola Superiore, Isola

Bella and Isola Madre (€16.90). Services are drastically reduced in autumn and winter.

BUS

SAF (☑ 0323 55 21 72; www.safduemila.com) The daily Verbania Intra–Milan service links Stresa with Arona (€2.70, 20 minutes), Verbania Pallanza (€2.70, 20 minutes), Verbania Intra (€2.70, 25 minutes) and Milan (€10.50, 1½ hours). SAF also runs the Alibus, a pre-booked shuttle bus linking the same towns with Malpensa airport (€15).

TRAIN

Maggiore is well connected by rail, with trains running the length of the east bank and up the west bank to Stresa before continuing on to Domodossola.

Stresa

POP 5000

Perhaps more than any other Lake Maggiore town, Stresa, with a ringside view of sunrise over the lake, captures the lake's prevailing air of elegance and bygone decadence. This is most evident in the string of belle époque confections along the waterfront, a legacy of the town's easy access from Milan, which has made it a favourite for artists and writers since the late 19th century.

◎ Sights & Activities

Giardino Botanico Alpinia　　　GARDENS
(☑ 0323 92 71 73; Viale Mottino 26; adult/reduced €4/3.50; ⊙ 9.30am-6pm mid-Apr–early-Oct) More than 1000 alpine and subalpine species flourish in this 4-hectare botanical garden set part-way up Monte Mottarone. It was

---

DON'T MISS

SANTA CATERINA DEL SASSO

One of northern Italy's most spectacularly sited monasteries, **Santa Caterina del Sasso** (www.santacaterinadelsasso.com; Via Santa Caterina 13; ⊙ 9am-noon & 2-6pm Apr-Oct, to 5pm Mar, closed weekdays Nov-Feb) FREE clings to the high rocky face of Lago Maggiore's southeast shore. The buildings span the 13th and 14th centuries; the porticoes and chapels are packed with frescoes; the views from the tiny courtyards are superb. The monastery is reached either by climbing up 80 steps from the Santa Caterina ferry quay, or by clattering down a 268-step staircase from the car park (there's also a lift for €1 each way).

founded in 1934 and profiles trees and shrubs from as far away as China and Japan against a backdrop of fine lake views. If the Stresa–Mottarone cable car is operating, the easiest access is via the Alpino midstation. Otherwise, the gardens are a 10km drive from Stresa; check whether the bus is running from the tourist office (single €3; 30 minutes).

Parco della Villa Pallavicino ZOO
(🖉 0323 3 15 33; www.parcozoopallavicino.it; SS33/Via Sempione Sud, Stresa, Lake Maggiore; adult/reduced €9.50/6.50; ⏰ 9am-7pm mid-Mar–Oct; 🖰) Barely 1km southeast of central Stresa along the SS33 main road, exotic birds and animals roam relatively freely in the woods and meadows of this child-friendly 20 hectare park. Some 40 species of wildlife, including llamas, Sardinian donkeys, zebras, flamingos and toucans, keep everyone amused. The park was closed for long-term maintenance when we last passed by.

Funivia Stresa–Mottarone CABLE CAR
(🖉 0323 3 02 95; www.stresa-mottarone.it; Piazzale della Funivia; return adult/reduced €19/12, to Alpino station €13.50/8.50; ⏰ 9.30am-5.40pm Apr-Oct, 8.10am-5.20pm Nov-Mar) Captivating lake views unfold during a 20-minute cable-car journey to the top of 1491m-high Monte Mottarone. On a clear day you can see Lago Maggiore, Lago d'Orta and Monte Rosa on the Swiss border. At the Alpino midstation a profusion of alpine plants flourish in the Giardino Botanico Alpinia (p263). The mountain itself offers good hiking and biking trails.

Alpyland AMUSEMENT PARK
(🖉 0323 199 10 07; www.alpyland.com; Mottarone; adult/child €5/4; ⏰ 10am-5pm Mon-Fri, to 6pm Sat & Sun Apr-Oct, weekends only Dec-Mar, closed Nov; 🖰) For an adrenaline rush, this 1200m-long bobsled descent has adjustable speeds that make it ideal for families.

🛏 Sleeping

Hotel Saini Meublè HOTEL €
(🖉 0323 93 45 19; www.hotelsaini.it; Via Garibaldi 10; d €95-125, tr €130-160; 🛜) With their warm tones, and wooden cabinets and floors, the rooms in Hotel Saini have a timeless feel – fitting for a house that's some 400 years old. Spacious bedrooms, a swirling spiral staircase and a location in the heart of Stresa's old town add to the appeal.

Hotel Elena HOTEL €
(🖉 0323 3 10 43; www.hotelelena.com; Piazza Cadorna 15; s/d/tr/q €65/90/110/120; 🛜) Adjoin-

ing a cafe, the old-fashioned Elena is slap-bang on Stresa's central pedestrian square. Comfortable rooms feature simple furnishings and balconies, many overlooking the piazza. There's a lift, and wheelchair access is possible.

Casa Kinka B&B €€
(🖉 0323 3 00 47; www.casakinka.it; Strada Comunale Lombartino 21, Magognino; d €200; ⏰ Mar-Oct; 🅿🛜) It's hard to imagine a more appealing midrange hilltop hideaway: wood-framed mirrors, stately furniture and artfully arranged antiques define cosy bedrooms; birdsong and flowers fill the garden; most of the windows feature bewitching lake views. It's just over 1km southeast of Stresa, off the A26.

Grand Hotel des Iles Borromees HISTORIC HOTEL €€€
(🖉 0323 93 89 38; www.borromees.it; Corso Umberto I 67; r €308-451, ste €583; 🅿✳@🛜🏊) One of Lake Maggiore's most celebrated hotels (it makes an appearance in Ernest Hemingway's A Farewell to Arms), this place exudes an extravagant, old-world charm with luxurious rooms, attentive service and and a front-row perch overlooking the lake.

🍴 Eating & Drinking

While Stresa is packed with restaurants, it's wise to book a table – even at lunchtime – if arriving on the weekend.

★ Ristorante Il Vicoletto RISTORANTE €€
(🖉 0323 93 21 02; www.ristorantevicoletto.com; Vicolo del Pocivo 3; meals €30-45; ⏰ noon-2pm & 6.30-10pm Fri-Wed) One of the most popular restaurants in Stresa, Il Vicoletto has a delectable regional menu including lake trout, wild asparagus, and traditional risotto with radicchio and Taleggio (cheese). The dining room is modestly elegant with bottle-lined dressers and linen-covered tables, while the local clientele speaks volumes in this tourist town. Reservations essential.

Taverna del Pappagallo TRATTORIA €€
(🖉 0323 3 04 11; www.tavernapappagallo.com; Via Principessa Margherita 46; meals €25-35; ⏰ noon-2pm & 6.30-10pm) It's not fancy and doesn't take itself too seriously but this welcoming trattoria is where you'll find Stresa's families tucking into tasty regional dishes, ranging from pizzas cooked in an old wood-fired oven to perch fillet with butter and sage.

La Botte TRATTORIA €€
(🖉 0323 3 04 62; Via Mazzini 6; meals €25-35; ⏰ noon-2.05pm & 6.50-10pm Thu-Tue) Regional

dishes are at the heart of this tiny trattoria's business, so expect grilled lake fish, boar fillets and plenty of polenta (the version with sauteed mushrooms is superb). The decor is old-style *osteria* (casual tavern or eatery presided over by a host) with dark timber furniture and decades of accumulated knick-knacks.

Piemontese   PIEDMONTESE €€€

(📞0323 3 02 35; www.ristorantepiemontese.com; Via Mazzini 25; meals €40-55; ⊗noon-3pm & 7-11pm Tue-Sun) The name gives a huge clue as to the focus of this refined dining room. Regional delights include gnocchi with gorgonzola and hazelnuts, and baked perch with black venere rice. The Lake Menu (€39) features carp, trout, perch and pike, while the *menù degustazione* (€55) takes things up a notch with a decadent spread of *lumache* (snails), *cupesante* (scallops) and foie gras.

Il Clandestino   ITALIAN €€€

(📞0323 3 03 99; www.ristoranteilclandestino. com; Via Roamini 5; meals €50-65; ⊗7.30-10pm Wed-Sun) An elegant, corner dining room with parquet floors, creamy white linen, soft music and a largely seafood menu, Il Clandestino is worth searching out. Some dishes have a Sicilian touch, with Sicilian prawns a recurring theme. It does some excellent lake-fish dishes, too, but acknowledges the existence of red meat only occasionally.

**Grand Hotel des
Iles Borromées**   COCKTAIL BAR

(📞0323 93 89 38; www.borromees.it; Corso Umberto I 67; ⊗6pm-late) Following his WWI stint on the Italian front, Ernest Hemingway checked in here to nurse his battle scars, and to write *A Farewell to Arms*. The passionate antiwar novel featured this sumptuous hotel. You might baulk at room prices (guests have included Princess Margaret and the Vanderbilts) but you can still slug back a Manhattan on the terraces with cinematic views.

ⓘ Information

Stresa Tourist Office (📞0323 3 13 08; www. stresaturismo.it; Piazza Marconi 16; ⊗10am-12.30pm & 3-6.30pm summer, closed Sat afternoon & Sun winter) Has brochures and tips on activities in the area. Located at the ferry dock.

Borromean Islands

Forming Lake Maggiore's most beautiful corner, the Borromean Islands (Isole Borromee) can be reached from various points

---

ⓘ LAGO MAGGIORE EXPRESS

The **Lago Maggiore Express** (📞091 756 04 00; www.lagomaggioreexpress. com; adult/child 1-day tour €34/17, 2-day tour €44/22) is a picturesque day trip you can do under your own steam. It includes train travel from Arona or Stresa to Domodossola, from where you get the charming Centovalli (Hundred Valleys) train to Locarno in Switzerland, before hopping on a ferry back to Stresa. Tickets are available from the Navigazione Lago Maggiore (p263) ticket booths at each port.

---

around the lake, but Stresa and Verbania offer the best access. Three of the four islands – Bella, Madre and Superiore (aka Isola dei Pescatori) – can all be visited, but tiny San Giovanni is off limits.

ISOLA BELLA

The grandest and busiest of the islands – the crowds can get a little overwhelming on weekends – Isola Bella is the centrepiece of the Borromeo Lake Maggiore empire. The island took the name of Carlo III's wife, the bella Isabella, in the 17th century, when its centrepiece, Palazzo Borromeo, was built for the Borromeo family.

⦿ Sights

Palazzo Borromeo   PALACE

(📞0323 3 05 56; www.isoleborromee.it; Isola Bella; adult/child €16/8.50, incl Palazzo Madre €21/10; ⊗9am-5.30pm mid-Mar–mid-Oct) Presiding over 10 tiers of spectacular terraced gardens roamed by peacocks, this baroque palace is arguably Lake Maggiore's finest building. The grounds and 1st floors reveal guestrooms, studies and reception halls. Particularly striking rooms include the Sala di Napoleone, where the emperor Napoleon stayed with his wife in 1797; the grand Sala da Ballo (Ballroom); the ornate Sala del Trono (Throne Room); and the Sala delle Regine (Queen's Room). Paintings from the 130-strong Borromeo collection hang all around.

✕ Eating

Elvezia   ITALIAN €€

(📞0323 3 00 43; Via de Martini 35; meals €32-42; ⊗9am-6pm Tue-Sun Mar-Oct, Fri-Sun only Nov-Feb) With its rambling rooms, fish-themed portico and upstairs pergola and balcony dining area, this is the best spot on Isola

Bella for home cooking. Dishes include ricotta-stuffed ravioli, various risottos and lake fish such as *coregone alle mandorle* (lake whitefish in almonds). Elvezia also opens on Saturday nights (from 7pm) during the summer. Reservations essential.

ISOLA SUPERIORE (ISOLA DEI PESCATORI)

Tiny 'Fishermen's Island,' with a permanent population of around 50, retains much of its original fishing-village atmosphere. Apart from an 11th-century apse and a 16th-century fresco in the charming Chiesa di San Vittore, there are no real sights. Many visitors make it their port of call for lunch, but stay overnight and you'll fall in love with the place

🛏 Sleeping & Eating

★ Albergo Verbano   HOTEL €€

(📞 0323 3 04 08; www.hotelverbano.it; Via Ugo Ara 2; d €140-210; ⊙ Mar-Dec; 🕲) Set at the southern tip of enchanting Isola Superiore, Albergo Verbano has been putting up guests in this idyllic spot since 1895. Dishes from a fish-focused menu are served on the tree-shaded waterside terrace, and bedrooms are a study in sunny elegance – choose one looking out towards Isola Bella or Isola Madre; the views are exquisite either way.

Albergo Ristorante Belvedere   HOTEL €€

(📞 0323 3 22 92; www.belvedere-isolapescatori.it; Isola Superiore; d €120-190; ⊙ Apr-Oct) Perfectly located towards the quieter northern end of Isola Superiore, this cheerful little hotel-restaurant has eight simply styled bedrooms, most with a balcony or terrace giving superb views of the lake, Isola Madre and the mountains beyond.

★ Casabella   RISTORANTE €€€

(📞 0323 3 34 71; www.isola-pescatori.it; Via del Marinaio 1; meals €30-50, five-course tasting menu €55; ⊙ noon-2pm & 6-8.30pm Feb-Nov) The setting is bewitching – right by the shore – and the food is acclaimed. The admirably short menu might feature home-smoked beef with spinach, blanched squid with ricotta or perfectly cooked lake fish. Leave room for dessert; the pear cake with chocolate fondant is faultless.

VERBANIA

POP 30,800

Verbania, the biggest town on Lake Maggiore, makes a good base for exploring the west bank. The town is strung out along the lakeshore and consists of three districts.

Verbania Pallanza, the middle chunk, is the most interesting of the three, with a pretty waterfront and a ferry stop.

◎ Sights

Villa Taranto   GARDENS

(📞 0323 55 66 67; www.villataranto.it; Via Vittorio Veneto 111, Verbania Pallanza; adult/reduced €10/5.50; ⊙ 8.30am-6.30pm Apr-Sep, 9am-4pm Oct; 🅿) The grounds of this late-19th-century villa are one of Lake Maggiore's highlights. A Scottish captain, Neil McEacharn, bought the Normandy-style villa from the Savoy family in 1931 after spotting an ad in the *Times*. He planted some 20,000 plant species over 30 years, and today it's considered one of Europe's finest botanic gardens. Even the main entrance path is a grand affair, bordered by lawns and a cornucopia of colourful flowers. It's a short walk from the Villa Taranto ferry stop.

🛏 Sleeping

Aquadolce   HOTEL €

(📞 0323 50 54 18; www.hotelacquadolce.eu; Via Cietti 1, Verbania Pallanza; d €85-105, tr €120; 🕸🕲) Ask for a room at the front of this bijou waterfront address and your window will be filled with a glittering lake backed by the mountains rearing up behind. Inside it's a beautifully lit, genteel affair, with all the quiet assurance of a well-run hotel.

Hotel Belvedere   HOTEL €€

(📞 0323 50 32 02; www.pallanzahotels.com; Viale Magnolie 6, Verbania Pallanza; d €120-180; 🕸🕲) Set in a gracious 19th-century building right across from the Verbania Pallanza boat landing, the Belvedere is a fine Lago Maggiore base. The service is at once friendly and professional, while the refined rooms are well sized – it's worth paying extra for a lake view.

🍴 Eating

★ Osteria Castello   OSTERIA €€

(📞 0323 51 65 79; www.osteriacastello.com; Piazza Castello 9, Verbania Intra; meals €25-35; ⊙ 11am-2.30pm & 6pm-midnight Mon-Sat) Its 100-plus years of history run like a rich seam through this enchanting *osteria,* where archive photos and bottles line the walls. Order a glass of wine from the vast selection; sample some ham; or tuck into the pasta or lake fish of the day.

Osteria dell'Angolo   PIEDMONTESE €€

(📞 0323 55 63 62; Piazza Garibaldi 35, Verbania Pallanza; meals €32-42; ⊙ noon-2.30pm & 7-9.30pm Tue-Sun) Greenery drapes a terrace dotted with only eight tables at this *osteria,* and well-presented dishes showcase creative Piedmontese cuisine. The lake fish is particularly fine (try the trout carpaccio), while the well-chosen wine list means it could turn into a very long lunch indeed.

★ **Ristorante Milano**　　MODERN ITALIAN €€€
(☑ 0323 55 68 16; www.ristorantemilanolagomaggiore.it; Corso Zanitello 2, Verbania Pallanza; meals €68-80, menus €55-75; ⊙ noon-2pm & 7-9pm Wed-Mon; ✱) The setting really is hard to beat: Milano directly overlooks Pallanza's minuscule horseshoe-shaped harbour (200m south of the ferry jetty), with a scattering of tables sitting on lakeside lawns amid the trees. It's an idyllic spot to enjoy lake fish, local lamb and some innovative Italian cuisine, such as pigeon with paté and red-currant reduction.

ℹ Information

Verbania Tourist Office (☑ 0323 50 32 49; www.verbania-turismo.it; Via Ruga 44, Verbania Pallanza; ⊙ 9.30am-12.30pm & 3-5pm Mon-Sat) The tourist office is located in the same complex as the **Museo del Paesaggio** (☑ 0323 55 66 21; www.museodelpaesaggio.it; €5; ⊙ 10am-6pm Tue-Fri, to 7pm Sat, Sun & holidays).

CANNOBIO
POP 5200

Just 5km south of the Swiss border, Cannobio's toy-town cobblestone streets are delightfully quaint. Nicely set apart from the busier towns to the north and south, it's a dreamy place that makes for a charming lake base. There's a public beach at the north end of town, which is also the departure point for a scenic walk along the Cannobino River.

🏃 Activities

Tomaso Surf & Sail　　WATER SPORTS
(☑ 333 7000291; www.tomaso.com; Via Nazionale 7; ⊙ 9.30am-7pm Jun-Sep, 11am-6pm Oct-May) This recommended outfitter has all the essentials for a day out on the water. You can hire SUP boards (per one/two hours €25/40), windsurfing gear (per one/four hours from €25/80), sailing dinghies (two hours €65), catamarans and motorboats. If you lack the know-how, Tomaso also offers lessons in windsurfing (per hour €80), sailing (per hour from €110) and waterskiing (per half-hour €85).

🍽 Sleeping & Eating

★ **Hotel Pironi**　　HOTEL €€
(☑ 0323 7 06 24; www.pironihotel.it; Via Marconi 35; s €120, d €160-195; P 🛜) Set in a 15th-century mini-monastery (later home of the noble Pironi family) high in Cannobio's cobbled maze, Hotel Pironi is a charming choice. Thick-set stone walls shelter interiors evocative of another era; it's full of antiques, frescoed vaults, exposed timber beams and stairs climbing off in odd directions.

Lo Scalo　　MODERN ITALIAN €€€
(☑ 0323 7 14 80; www.loscalo.com; Piazza Vittorio Emanuele III 32; meals €45-55; ⊙ noon-2.30pm & 7-11pm Wed-Sun, 7-11pm Tue) Cannobio's best restaurant, Lo Scalo serves cuisine that is sophisticated and precise, featuring dishes such as a suckling pig with spring onions and black garlic, and ricotta and tomato gnocchi with clams. The two-course lunch (€25) and five-course *menù degustazione* (€55) are both great value treats, best enjoyed at a table on the waterfront promenade.

WALKING TO ORRIDO DI SANT'ANNA

The 3km walk to **Orrido di Sant'Anna** is a splendid way to see some of Cannobio's natural beauty. From the beach just north of the centre, follow the Cannobino River inland, crossing the second bridge (a bouncy pedestrian-only suspension bridge), and take the well-marked trail along the northern bank. This passes besides woods (meandering paths lead closer to the rushing mountain stream), and finally to tranquil shallows at the base of a cliff topped by a small church (the 17th-century Chiesa di Sant'Anna). The rocky beach here makes a fine spot for a dip on warm days. Just past the church is the Orrido di Sant'Anna, a tight ravine where the rushing water has carved a path through the mountains on its descent to the lake. From here, you can retrace your steps back to town, or loop back to Cannobio by taking the road from here. Take the trail leading uphill off to the right near the Camping Valle Romantica, which offers pretty views on the return trip to Cannobio.

Allow about two hours for the walk – though it's worth timing your arrival at Orrido di Sant'Anna to allow a lunchtime stop at the **Grotto Sant'Anna** (☑ 0323 7 06 82; Via Sant'Anna 30; meals €35-45; ⊙ noon-1.45pm & 7-9.45pm Tue-Sun Apr-Oct), right next to the ravine (reserve ahead). Though the trail is easy to follow, you can pick up a map and get other walking suggestions at the tourist office (p268).

MAGGIORE'S FABULOUS FRESCOES

Among the best-kept secrets of the Lake Maggiore area are the fabulous frescoes, artistic remnants with centuries of history, some remarkably well preserved. The best range from pre-Romanesque to wonderful Florentine Renaissance. Our favourites include the following:

Basilica di San Giulio The 12th-century church on Lake Orta's island is jammed with vibrant frescoes depicting saints.

Museo della Collegiata (www.museocollegiata.it; Via Cardinal Branda 1, Castiglione Olona; adult/reduced €6/4; ⊘10am-1pm & 3-6pm Tue-Sun Apr-Sep, 9.30am-12.30pm & 2.30-5.30pm Tue-Sat & 10am-1pm & 3-6pm Sun Oct-Mar) Florentine master Masolino da Panicale carried out a series on the life of St John the Baptist in 1435.

Chiesa di Santa Maria Foris Portas (Holy Mary Outside the Gates; Castelseprio; ⊘8.30am-7pm Tue-Fri, 8.30am-2.30pm & 5.30-7pm Sat, 9.45am-2.30pm & 5.30-6pm Sun Feb-Nov, shorter hours Dec & Jan) FREE A modest Lombard church contains extraordinary pre-Romanesque frescoes that may date to the 7th century.

Santa Caterina del Sasso (p263) The church in this former monastery is filled with well-preserved frescoes.

ℹ️ Information

Tourist Office (☑ 0323 7 12 12; www.pro cannobio.it; Via Giovanola 25; ⊘9am-noon & 4-7pm Mon-Sat, 9am-noon Sun) Hands out brochures and provides town info. Located next to the Romanesque bell tower.

Arona

POP 14,200

Some 20km south of Stresa, Arona is a lakeside town whose lanes are lined with shops and eateries, and its piazzas draw a wide cross section of Maggiorean society in the evenings. Arona was the birthplace of the son of the Count of Arona and Margherita de' Medici, who would go on to be canonised San Carlo Borromeo (1538–84). Arona's biggest attraction is a massive statue of San Carlo that looms on a hilltop north of town.

👁 Sights

Sacro Monte di San Carlo   LANDMARK
(☑0322 24 96 69; www.statuasancarlo.it; Piazza San Carlo; €6, to exterior only €3.50; ⊘9am-12.30pm & 2.30-6.15pm mid-Mar–mid-Oct, to 4.30pm Sun Nov-Dec and Mar 1-15, closed Jan & Feb) When Milan's superstar bishop San Carlo Borromeo was declared a saint in 1610, his cousin Federico ordered the creation of a *sacro monte* in his memory, featuring 15 chapels lining a path to a church. The church and three of those chapels were built, along with a special extra: a hollow 35m bronze-and-copper statue of the saint. Commonly known as the Sancarlone (Big St Charles) you can climb up inside it to discover views through the giant's eyes (and even ears).

🍴 Eating

Taverna del Pittore   RISTORANTE €€€
(☑0322 24 33 66; www.ristorantetavernadel pittore.it; Piazza del Popolo 39; meals €50-70; ⊘noon-2.30pm & 7.30-10pm Fri-Wed) What is possibly Largo Maggiore's most romantic restaurant has a waterside terrace and views of the illuminated **Rocca di Angera fortress** (www.isoleborromee.it; Via Rocca Castello 2; adult/child €9.50/6, combined ticket incl Isola Bella & Isola Madre €25/13.50; ⊘9am-5.30pm) at night. The refined food is no less fabulous, with squid, duck and octopus transformed into exquisitely arranged dishes featuring ravioli, broth, risotto and gnocchi.

Lago d'Orta

Enveloped by thick, dark-green woodlands, tranquil Lake Orta (aka Lake Cusio) could make a perfect elopers' getaway. Measuring 13.4km long by 2.5km wide, it's separated from its bigger and better-known eastern neighbour, Lake Maggiore, by Monte Mottarone. The focal point of the lake is the captivating medieval village of Orta San Giulio, often referred to simply as Orta.

👁 Sights

Orta San Giulio   VILLAGE
Overlooking the forest-lined banks of the shimmering Lake Orta, this tiny village has abundant allure. There's something magical about rising early and heading for a coffee on **Piazza Mario Motta**, gazing across

at the sun-struck Isola San Giulio in the early-morning quiet.

At the north end of the square, a squat, fresco-enlivened structure sitting atop pillars like giant stilts, the **Palazzotto**, was once the seat of a local council and now occasionally opens for temporary exhibitions. The square burbles with local life on **market day** (Wednesday).

Basilica di San Giulio — CHURCH
(⊙9.30am-6pm Tue-Sun, 2-5pm Mon Apr-Sep, 9.30am-noon & 2-5pm Tue-Sun, 2-5pm Mon Oct-Mar) This atmospheric church is the main attraction on the tiny Isola San Giulio and was built over various periods dating back to the 9th century. Its bell tower and medieval pulpit date from the 12th century. Frescoes (from the 14th to 19th centuries) cover the walls, though the church's most surprising feature is in the sacristy. From the vault hangs a large fossilized vertebra, which according to legend belonged to one of the terrible dragons San Giulio vanquished from the island.

Sacro Monte di San Francesco — CHAPEL, PARK
Beyond the lush gardens and residences that mark the hill rising behind Orta is a kind of parallel 'town' – the *sacro monte,* where 20 small chapels dedicated to St Francis of Assisi dot the hillside. The views down to the lake are captivating, and meandering from chapel to chapel is a wonderfully tranquil way to pass a few hours.

🛏 Sleeping

Locanda di Orta — BOUTIQUE HOTEL €
(☑0322 90 51 88; www.locandaorta.com; Via Olina 18; s €70, d €80-95, ste €150-160; 🕾) Teaming white leather and bold pink with medieval grey stone walls is a bold design choice – but it works. Because of the age and size of the building, the cheaper rooms are tiny, but still delightful. Suites are roomier; each features a Jacuzzi and a pocket-sized balcony overlooking the cobbled lane.

Hotel Leon d'Oro — HOTEL €€
(☑0322 91 19 91; www.albergoleondoro.it; Piazza Mario Motta 42; r €110-200; ⊙Feb-Dec; ❉🕾) At this 200-year-old hotel, a red carpet leads you through the front door of the lakefront beauty. Sunny yellows and deep blues dominate the decor, with heavy window curtains, timber furniture and tiled floors; though you should avoid the cramped standard rooms. It also has some smallish suites. The waterfront terrace offers gorgeous Isola San Giulio views. Wi-fi costs extra (€2 per 24 hours).

Villa Crespi — HISTORIC HOTEL €€€
(☑0322 91 19 02; www.hotelvillacrespi.it; Via Giuseppe Fava 18; d €365, ste €525-765; ⊙Apr-Dec; 🅿❉@🕾💺) Staying at this Moorish extravaganza, which is topped with an aqua-coloured onion-dome spire, is to enter the madcap design dream of the family (a rich textile clan) that built this caprice. Think velvet walls, four-poster beds in some rooms and otherwise opulent interiors and sprawling gardens, all designed for cotton trader Benigno Crespi in 1879.

🍴 Eating

Enoteca Al Boeuc — PIEDMONTESE €
(☑339 5840039; http://alboeuc.beepworld.it; Via Bersani 28; meals €18-25; ⊙11.30am-3pm & 6.30pm-midnight Wed-Mon) This candlelit stone cavern has been around since the 16th century. These days it offers glasses of fine wines (try the velvety Barolo) and snacks including mixed bruschette with truffles and mushrooms, meat and cheese platters, and that Piedmontese favourite. *bagna caüda* (a hot dip of butter, olive oil, garlic and anchovies in which you bathe vegetables).

★ Cucchiaio di Legno — AGRITURISMO €€
(☑339 5775385; www.ilcucchiaiodilegno.com; Via Prisciola 10, Legro; set menu €30; ⊙6-9pm Thu-Sun, noon-2.30pm Sat & Sun; 🅿❉) Delicious home cooking emerges from the kitchen of this honest-to-goodness *agriturismo* (farmstay accommodation); expect fish fresh from the lake, and salami and cheese from the local valleys. When eating al fresco on the patio it feels rather like you're dining at the house of a friend. Bookings required.

Venus — TRATTORIA €€
(☑0322 9 03 62; www.venusorta.it; Piazza Motta 50; meals €30-45; ⊙noon-3pm & 6-10pm Tue-Sun) Although the food doesn't quite match the views, this lakeside charmer always draws a crowd. The menu of local dishes features rich plates of creamy risotto with scallops, lamb chops in a pistachio crust and fillet of perch with a butter, spinach and citrus reduction.

★ Locanda di Orta — MODERN ITALIAN €€€
(☑0322 90 51 88; www.locandaorta.com; Via Olina 18; meals €55-80, menus €75-90; ⊙noon-2.30pm & 7.30-9pm) Some of Orta's most creative cooking is served up in the wisteria-draped Locanda di Orta, squeezed into the heart of the old town. It's a supremely stylish, intimate affair (it only seats around 17 people) where culinary alchemy converts traditional Lake Orta ingredients into works of art.

ALESSI OUTLET STORE

Established in the small town of Omegna on Lago d'Orta in 1921, Alessi went on to transform modern kitchens with humorous, ultracool utensils designed by a pantheon of great-name architect-designers, including Achille Castiglioni, Philippe Starck, Massimiliano Fuksas and, most recently, Zaha Hadid. Go mad in this huge factory **outlet** (📋0323 86 86 48; www.alessi.com; Via Privata Alessi 6, Omegna; ⊗9.30am-6pm Mon-Sat, 2.30-6pm Sun), where the whole range sits alongside special offers and end-of-line deals.

ⓘ Information

Main Tourist Office (📋 0322 91 19 72; www.distrettolaghi.it; Via Panoramica; ⊗10am-1pm & 2-6pm Wed-Mon) This small info house on the road into Orta San Giulio can provide information on the whole of Lake Orta.

Pro Loco (📋 339 5267436; Via Bossi 11; ⊗11am-1pm & 2-4pm Mon, Tue & Thu, 10am-1pm & 2-4pm Fri-Sun) In the town hall, this is a handy office for all things Lake Orta related. The small public garden behind the office has pretty lake views.

ⓘ Getting There & Away

BOAT

Navigazione Lago d'Orta (📋345 5170005; www.navigazionelagodorta.it) Operates ferries from its landing stage on Piazza Motta to places including Isola San Giulio (return €3.15), Omegna, Pella and Ronco. A day ticket for unlimited travel anywhere on the lake costs €9.

TRAIN

The main destination for most visitors is **Orta-Miasino** (Via Stazione), located 3km outside of Orta San Giulio. From Milan's Stazione Centrale trains go to Orta-Miasino every two hours or so – change at Novara – (from €9, two hours).

Lago di Como

Set in the shadow of the snow-covered Rhaetian Alps and hemmed in on both sides by steep wooded hills, Lake Como (aka Lake Lario) is the most spectacular of the region's three major lakes. Shaped like an upside-down Y (or an armless wanderer), its winding shoreline is dotted with ancient villages and exquisite villas.

The lake's main town, Como, sits where the southern and western shores converge.

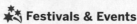

✈ Festivals & Events

Lake Como Festival MUSIC
(www.lakecomofestival.com) Several times a month from May through September, musical concerts are held at some of Lago di Como's finest villas.

ⓘ Information

The website www.lakecomo.it features information covering the whole lake.

ⓘ Getting There & Around

BOAT

Ferries and hydrofoils operated by Como-based **Navigazione Lago di Como** (📋 800 551801; www.navigazionelaghi.it; Lungo Lario Trento) criss-cross the lake, departing year-round from the jetty at the north end of Piazza Cavour. Single fares range from €2.50 (Como–Cernobbio) to €12.60 (Como–Lecco or Como–Gravedona). Return fares are double. Hydrofoil fast services entail a supplement of €1.40 to €4.90, depending on the trip.

BUS

ASF Autolinee (📋 031 24 72 47; www.sptlinea.it) Operates regular buses around Lago di Como, which in Como depart from the **bus station on Piazza Matteotti** (Piazza Matteotti). Key routes include Como to Colico (€6.10, two hours, three to five daily), via all the villages on the western shore, and Como to Bellagio (€3.40, 70 minutes, hourly).

TRAIN

Como's main train station, **Como San Giovanni** (Via Corrado e Giulio Venini), is served from Milan's Stazione Centrale or Porta Garibaldi (€4.80 to €13.50 depending on type of train, 37 to 90 minutes, at least hourly) by trains that continue into Switzerland. Trains from Milan's Stazione Nord (€4.80, one hour, hourly) use Como's lakeside **Como Nord Lago** (Stazione FNM; Via A Manzoni). When heading for Bellagio, it's best to continue on the train to Varenna and make the short ferry crossing from there.

Como

POP 84,500

With its charming historic centre, the town of Como sparkles year-round. Within its remaining 12th-century city walls, the beautiful people of this prosperous city whisk about from shop to cafe, sweeping by the grandeur of the city's cathedral, villas and the loveliness of its lakeshore with admirable insouciance. The town is a lovely spot for an aimless wander, punctuated with coffee and drink stops, especially in Piazzas Cavour, Alessandro Volta and San Fedele.

⊙ Sights

Passeggiata Lino Gelpi
WATERFRONT

One of Como's most charming walks is the lakeside stroll west from Piazza Cavour. Passeggiata Lino Gelpi leads past the **Monumento ai Caduti** (Memorial; Viale Puecher 9), a 1931 memorial to Italy's WWI dead. Next you'll pass a series of mansions and villas, including **Villa Saporiti** (Via Borgovico 148) and **Villa Gallia**, both now owned by the provincial government and closed to the public, before arriving at the garden-ringed Villa Olmo.

Villa Olmo
HISTORIC BUILDING

(☑031 25 23 52; www.villaolmocomo.it; Via Cantoni 1; gardens free, villa entry varies by exhibition; ⊙villa during exhibitions 10am-6pm Tue-Sun, gardens 8am-11pm Apr-Sep, to 7pm Oct-Mar) Set facing the lake, the grand creamy facade of neoclassical Villa Olmo is one of Como's biggest landmarks. The extravagant structure was built in 1728 by the Odescalchi family, related to Pope Innocent XI. If there's an art exhibition showing, you'll get to admire the sumptuous *stile Liberty* (Italian art nouveau) interiors. Otherwise, you can enjoy the Italianate and English gardens.

★ Duomo
CATHEDRAL

(Cattedrale di Como; ☑031 3 31 22 75; Piazza del Duomo; ⊙10.30am-5pm Mon-Sat, 1-4.30pm Sun) Although largely Gothic in style, elements of Romanesque, Renaissance and baroque can also be seen in Como's imposing, marble-clad *duomo*. The cathedral was built between the 14th and 18th centuries, and is crowned by a high octagonal dome.

★ Basilica di San Fedele
BASILICA

(Piazza San Fedele; ⊙8am-noon & 3.30-7pm) With three naves and three apses, this evocative basilica is often likened to a clover leaf. Parts of it date from the 12th century while the facade is the result of a 1914 revamp. The 16th-century rose window and 16th- and 17th-century frescoes enhance the appeal. The apses are centuries-old and feature some eye-catching sculpture on the right.

Basilica di Sant'Abbondio
BASILICA

(Via Regina; ⊙8am-6pm summer, to 4.30pm winter) About 500m south of Como's city walls is the remarkable 11th-century Romanesque Basilica di Sant'Abbondio. Aside from its proud, high structure and impressive apse decorated with a geometric relief around the outside windows, the highlights are the extraordinary frescoes inside the apse.

Museo della Seta
MUSEUM

(Silk Museum; ☑031 30 31 80; www.museosetacomo.com; Via Castelnuovo 9; adult/reduced €10/7; ⊙10am-6pm Tue-Fri, to 1pm Sat) Lake Como's aspiring silk makers still learn their trade in the 1970s-built Istituto Tecnico Industriale di Setificio textile technical school. It's also home to the Museo della Seta, which draws together the threads of the town's silk history. Early dyeing and printing equipment features amid displays that chart the entire fabric production process.

🏃 Activities

★ Lido di Villa Olmo
SWIMMING

(☑031 3 38 48 54; www.lidovillaolmo.it; Via Cernobbio 2; adult/reduced €9/5; ⊙9am-7pm mid-May–Sep) What a delight: a compact *lido* (beach) where you can plunge into open-air pools, sunbathe beside the lake, rent boats, sip cocktails at the waterfront bar and soak up mountain views. Bliss. Bring a swim cap or purchase one here if you want to use the pool.

Aero Club Como
SCENIC FLIGHTS

(☑031 57 44 95; www.aeroclubcomo.com; Viale Masia 44; 30min flight €180) For a true touch of glamour, take one of these seaplane tours and buzz about the skies high above Como. The often-bumpy take-off and landing on the lake itself is thrilling, as are the views down onto the villages dotted far below. Flights are popular; in summer book three or four days ahead.

THE KILOMETRE OF KNOWLEDGE (& BEAUTY)

On Sundays, the interconnected grounds of three Como villas open to the public (from about 10am to 6pm). Dotting the shore just northwest of the centre, a 1km promenade connects the Villa Olmo, the **Villa del Grumello** (www.villadelgrumello.it; Via Cernobbio 11; ⊙grounds 10am-7pm Sun year-round, daily in Aug) and the **Villa Sucota** (☑031 338 49 76; www.fondazioneratti.org; Via Cernobbio 19; ⊙gardens 10am-6pm Sun year-round, daily in Aug; museum hours vary). Sometimes referred to as the Chilometro della Conoscenza (Kilometre of Knowledge), this scenic stroll takes in lush trails, fragrant gardens and hilltop views with lovely Lake Como ever in the background. Be sure to stop in the Villa Olmo and the Villa Sucota, which often host temporary art exhibitions.

Como

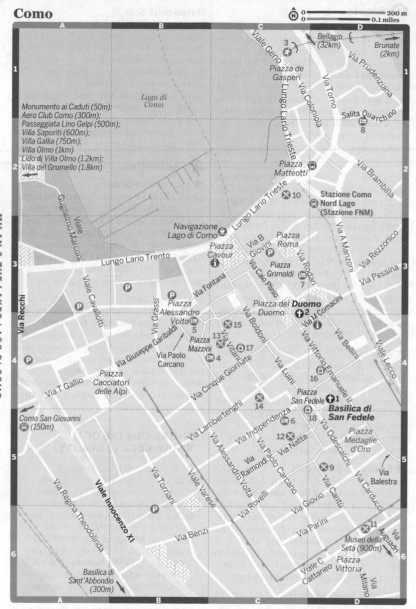

0   200 m
0   0.1 miles

Bellagio (32km)
Brunate (2km)

Lago di Como

Monumento ai Caduti (50m);
Aero Club Como (300m);
Passeggiata Lino Gelpi (500m);
Villa Saporiti (600m);
Villa Gallia (750m);
Villa Olmo (1km);
Lido di Villa Olmo (1.2km);
Villa del Grumello (1.8km)

Piazza de Gasperi

Via Prudenziana

Via Geno

Via Torno

Via Colonicla

Salita Quarchino
8

Lungo Lario Trieste

Via Brambilla

Piazza Matteotti

Viale Guglielmo Marconi

Navigazione Lago di Como

Lungo Lario Trieste

10

Stazione Como
Nord Lago
(Stazione FNM)

Via A Manzoni

Via Rezzonico

Via Pessina

Lungo Lario Trento

Piazza Cavour

Piazza B Giovini

Piazza Roma

Via Recchi

Via Cavallotti

Via Grassi

Via Caio Plinio

Piazza Grimoldi
7

Piazza Fontana

Piazza Alessandro Volta
5

Piazza del Duomo

Duomo

Via M Comacini

Via Bellini

Viale Lecco

Via Giuseppe Garibaldi

13   15

Piazza Mazzini

Via Vitani

17

Via Boldoni

Via Vittorio Emanuele II

Via Paolo Carcano
4

Via Cinque Giornate

Via Luini

16

Via T Gallio

Piazza Cacciatori delle Alpi

14

Piazza San Fedele
1

18

Basilica di San Fedele

Como San Giovanni
(150m)

Via Lambertenghi

Via Indipendenza

6

12

Via Odescalchi

Piazza Medaglie d'Oro

Via Alessandro Volta

Via Raimondi

Via Paolo Carcano

Via Natta

9

Via Cantù

Via Balestra

Via Regina Theodolinda

Viale Innocenzo XI

Via Torriani

Viale Varese

Via Rovelli

Via Giovio

Via Parini

11

Via Carducci

Via Auguadri

Museo della Seta (900m)

Via Benzi

Via C Cattaneo

Piazza Vittoria

Via Milano

Basilica di Sant'Abbondio
(300m)

Funicolare Como–Brunate   CABLE CAR
(☎031 30 36 08; www.funicolarecomo.it; Piazza de
Gasperi 4; adult one way/return €3/5.50, reduced
€2/3.20; ◷half-hourly departures 6am-midnight
summer, to 10.30pm winter) Prepare for some
spectacular views. The Como–Brunate ca-

ble car (built in 1894) takes seven minutes
to trundle up to the quiet hilltop village of
Brunate (720m), revealing a memorable
panorama of mountains and lakes. From
there a steep 30-minute walk along a stony
mule track leads to **San Maurizio** (907m),

Como

where 143 steps climb up to the top of a lighthouse.

🛏 Sleeping

Quarcino
HOTEL €

(📞031 30 39 34; www.hotelquarcino.it; Salita Quarchino 4; s/d/tr/q €53/80/105/120; P❄🐾🌐) You'll struggle to find a more appealing, central budget hotel in Como. The modern decor is simple but appealing; the bathrooms are pristine; and there are lake glimpses from some of the front rooms. Parking is free, but breakfast costs extra (€7 per person).

Le Stanze del Lago
APARTMENT €

(📞031 30 11 82; www.lestanzedellago.com; Via Rodari 6; apt €110-150; ❄🌐) For loft living Como-style, check into one of these five serviced apartments, where sloping wooden ceilings and rough stone walls meet bright furnishings. The ample space (including a kitchenette and a dining area) and the location in the heart of Como make these a great deal.

★ Avenue Hotel
BOUTIQUE HOTEL €€

(📞031 27 21 86; www.avenuehotel.it; Piazzolo Terragni 6; d €190-280, ste €280-310; P❄🌐) An assured sense of style at this delightful hotel sees ultramodern, minimalist rooms team crisp white walls with shots of purple or fuchsia-pink. Breakfast is served in a chic courtyard, service is warm but discreet, and you can borrow a bike for free.

Albergo del Duca
HOTEL €€

(📞031 26 48 59; www.albergodelduca.it; Piazza Mazzini 12; s/d €80/140; ❄🌐) The setting is an attractive one (on the edge of a pedestrianised square); the atmosphere is all friendliness; and the rooms are as neat as a pin, with polished wooden floors. There's a good restaurant with terrace at the entrance.

Albergo Firenze
HOTEL €€

(📞031 30 03 33; www.hotelfirenzecomo.it; Piazza Volta 16; s €120-160, d €130-170, tr €170-200; ❄💻) Overlooking the Piazza Volta a few blocks south of the waterfront, this smart hotel has bright, spotless rooms. Don't be put off by the somewhat gloomy reception area, but do consider paying extra for a superior room with a piazza view, as the rooms at the back can be a little dark.

🍴 Eating

Como's **food market** (Viale C Battisti; ⊗8.30am-1pm Tue & Thu, to 6.30pm Sat) is held outside **Porta Torre**.

★ Cascina Respaù
ITALIAN €

(📞031 52 36 62; www.cascinarespau.it; Via Santa Brigide e Respaù; meals €15-25; ⊗noon-3pm & 7-10pm Sat & Sun) 🌿 Amid the lush greenery high above Como, this small rustic eatery feels like an idyllic escape from the sometimes maddening crowds along the lake. Charming hosts, delicious homemade dishes and a cosy setting (with outdoor seating on warm days) add to the appeal – as does the attention to locally sourced ingredients, like fall-off-the-bone pork and organic wines from small producers.

Gelateria Ceccato
GELATO €

(📞031 2 33 91; Lungo Lario Trieste 16; gelato €2-4; ⊗noon-midnight summer, hours vary winter) For generations *comaschi* (Como residents) have turned to Ceccato for their Sunday-afternoon gelato and then embarked on a ritual *passeggiata* (stroll) with their dripping cones along the lake shore. You can do no better than imitate them: order a creamy *stracciatella* (chocolate chip) or perhaps a mix of fresh fruit flavours and head off for a relaxed promenade.

MILAN & THE LAKES LAGO DI COMO

★ **Natta Café**　　　　　　　CAFE €€

(📱031 26 91 23; www.facebook.com/nattacafecomo; Via Natta 16; meals €20-35; ⏰12.30-3pm & 7.30-11pm Tue-Sun; 🛜) 🍴 In an atmospheric stone-arched dining room, this *osteria* (tavern) has a proud focus on superb local ingredients and classic wines, while also remaining remarkably warm and inviting. It's a particularly good spot for a light meal, with delectable cheese platters, creative bruschetta and *piadine* (flat-bread sandwiches) and excellent salmon tartare – though pastas and daily specials provide more filling options.

★ **Crotto del Sergente**　　　TRATTORIA €€

(📱031 28 39 11; www.crottodelsergente.it; Via Crotto del Sergente 13; meals €35-45; ⏰noon-2pm & 7.30-10pm Sun-Fri, 7.30-10pm Sat) Although it's a bit of a trek (4km southeast of Como's centre), the delectable Slow Food cooking at this rustic eatery makes it well worth the effort. Set in a barrel-vaulted brick dining room, Crotto del Sergente serves excellent grilled meats and seafood (including a flavoursome bouillabaisse), best matched with a fine glass of Nebbiolo. Reserve ahead.

★ **Osteria del Gallo**　　　　ITALIAN €€

(📱031 27 25 91; www.osteriadelgallo-como.it; Via Vitani 16; meals €26-32; ⏰12.30-3pm Mon, to 10pm Tue-Sat) An ageless *osteria* that looks exactly the part. In the wood-lined dining room, wine bottles and other goodies fill the shelves, and diners sit at small timber tables to tuck into traditional local food. The menu is chalked up daily and might include a first course of *zuppa di ceci* (chickpea soup), followed by lightly fried lake fish.

Pane e Tulipani　　　　　　CAFE €€

(📱031 26 42 42; www.pane-e-tulipani.com; Via Lambertenghi 3; meals €28-45; ⏰10am-11pm Tue-Sun) With its vast number of grappa bottles, shabby-chic furniture and huge vases of flowers, this sweet eatery – which is part-cafe, part-bistro and part–flower shop – has a bohemian air. This means you get to sample creative twists on Italian standards (don't expect big portions) or linger in the afternoon over drinks and snacks surrounded by a profusion of blooms.

Ristorante da Rino　　　　TUSCAN €€

(📱031 27 30 28; www.ristoranterino.com; Via Vitani 3; meals €35-45; ⏰12.30-2pm & 7.30-10pm Tue-Sat, 12.30-2pm Sun) When the (acclaimed) specialities of the house all involve truffles, you tend to be onto a good thing. There's a stellar range of *primi* and *secondi*, and you'll find truffles with *tagliolini* (thin ribbon pasta), risotto and eggs. The pick is *filetto alla medici* – a tender beef fillet steeped in truffles and red wine.

Castiglioni　　　　　　　　TRATTORIA €€

(📱031 26 33 88; www.castiglionistore.com; Via Cantù 9; meals €25-30; ⏰deli 8am-2pm & 4-7pm Mon-Fri, 9am-7.30pm Sat, restaurant noon-2.30pm Mon-Sat) Going strong since 1958, Castiglioni's wonderful deli has evolved to include a wine bar and now a restaurant. Sample dozens of local vintages with plates of sweet prosciutto, or take lunch on the pleasant outdoor patio. The menu, which includes all manner of charcuterie plates, lake fish and mountain meat dishes, is surprisingly refined and great value.

🛍 Shopping

A craft and antiques **market** (Piazza San Fedele; ⏰9am-7pm Sat) fills the piazza beside the Basilica di San Fedele.

Lopez Vintage　　FASHION & ACCESSORIES

(📱031 24 20 43; Via Vitani 32; ⏰10am-12.30pm & 3.30-7pm Tue-Sat) On Como's most atmospheric street, Lopez Vintage lures you in with its whimsical window displays of curios from a bygone era. Inside, the tiny jewel box of a shop has elegant vintage pieces – slim-fitting dresses, oversized sunglasses, hats, accessories and other eye candy. Prices can be high, but you'll discover unique apparel you won't find elsewhere.

A Picci　　　　　　　　GIFTS & SOUVENIRS

(📱031 26 13 69; Via Vittorio Emanuele II 54; ⏰3-7.30pm Mon, 9am-12.30pm & 3-7.30pm Tue-Sat) First opened in 1919, this is the last remaining silk shop in town dedicated to selling Como-designed-and-made silk ties, scarves, throws and sarongs. Products are grouped by price category (starting at €15 for a tie), reflecting the skill and workmanship involved.

ℹ Information

Main Tourist Office (📱031 26 97 12; www.visitcomo.eu; Piazza Cavour 17; ⏰9am-1pm & 2.30-6pm Mon-Sat year-round, 9.30am-1pm Sun Jun-Sep) Como's main tourist office.

Tourist Office (📱342 0076403; www.visitcomo.eu; Como San Giovanni, Piazzale San Gottardo; ⏰9am-5pm summer, 10am-4pm Wed-Mon winter) Inside San Giovanni train station.

Tourist Office (📱031 26 42 15; www.visitcomo.eu; Via Comacini; ⏰10am-6pm) Beside the *duomo*.

Bellagio

POP 3100

Bellagio's waterfront of bobbing boats, its maze of steep stone staircases and its gardens filled with rhododendrons are a true joy. Inevitably these draw the summer crowds – stay overnight for a more authentic feel and the full magical effect.

◉ Sights

Before setting out to explore Bellagio, pick up the three self-guided walking tour brochures from the tourist office. They range from one-hour (*Historical Tour & Itinerary of the Central Part of Town*) to a three-hour walk that takes in neighbouring villages, including **Pescallo**, a small one-time fishing port about 1km from the centre, and **Loppia**, with the 11th-century **Chiesa di Santa Maria**, which is only visitable from the outside.

Villa Melzi d'Eril   GARDENS

(☑339 4573838; www.giardinidivillamelzi.it; Lungo Lario Manzoni; adult/reduced €6.50/4; ☺9.30am-6.30pm Apr-Oct) The grounds of neoclassical Villa Melzi d'Eril are a highlight among Lake Como's (many) delightful places. The villa was built in 1808 for one of Napoleon's associates and is coloured by flowering azaleas and rhododendrons in spring. The statue-studded garden was the first English-style park on the lake.

Villa Serbelloni   GARDENS

(☑031 95 15 55; Piazza della Chiesa 14; adult/child €9/5; ☺tours 11.30am & 3.30pm Tue-Sun mid-Mar–Oct) The lavish gardens of Villa Serbelloni cover much of the promontory on which Bellagio sits. The villa has been a magnet for Europe's great and good, including Austria's emperor Maximilian I, Ludovico il Moro and Queen Victoria. The interior is closed to the public, but you can explore the terraced park and gardens, by guided tour only. Numbers are limited; tickets are sold at the PromoBellagio (p278) info office near the church.

🏃 Activities

Lido di Bellagio   SWIMMING

(☑031 95 11 95; www.lidodibellagio.com; Via Carcano 1; per half/full day €6/10; ☺10.30am-6.30pm Tue-Sun May, Jun & Sep, daily Jul & Aug) With its sand-covered decking, diving platforms and gazebos, Bellagio's *lido* is a prime place to laze or plunge into the lake.

Bellagio Water Sports   WATER SPORTS

(☑340 394 93 75; www.bellagiowatersports.com; Pescallo Harbour; rental per 2/4hr €18/30, tours €35; ☺8.30am-4.30pm Mon-Sat, to 2.30pm Sun) You can hire sit-on-top kayaks and SUP boards at this experienced outfitter based in Pescallo, on the east side of the Bellagio headland. Bellagio Water Sports also offers five different kayaking tours, from a one-hour paddle taking in nearby historical villas to a 3½-hour trip to scenic Varenna.

Barindelli's   BOATING

(☑338 211 03 37; www.barindellitaxiboats.it; Piazza Mazzini; tours per hour €150) For a touch of film-star glamour, take a tour in one of Barindelli's chic mahogany cigarette boats. The group offers hour-long sunset tours around the Bellagio headland and can also tailor-make outings around the lake.

🍴 Courses

★ Bellagio Cooking Classes   COOKING

(☑333 7060090; www.gustoitalianobellagio.com; Salita Plinio 5; per person €90) A wonderful way to really get to know Bellagio, these cooking classes have a personal touch – they take you to the village shops to buy the food and then local home-cooks lead the sessions. Classes are small (a minimum of three, maximum of seven). Payment in cash only.

🛏 Sleeping

Locanda Barchetta   B&B €

(☑031 95 10 30; www.ristorantebarchetta.com; Via Centrale 13; d €90-100; ☎) A great-value, central hideaway tucked into Bellagio's maze of cobbled streets. Barchetta provides small, unfussy but spruce rooms and a fabulous breakfast.

Hotel Silvio   HOTEL €€

(☑031 95 03 22; www.bellagiosilvio.com; Via Carcano 10; d €135-190, meals €32-42; P🅿❄🛜🏊) Located above the fishing hamlet of Loppia a short walk from the village, this family-run hotel is one of Bellagio's most relaxing spots. Here you can wake up in a contemporary Zen-like room and gaze out over the gardens of some of Lago di Como's most prestigious villas, then spend the morning at Bellagio's *lido;* it's free for hotel guests.

Residence La Limonera   APARTMENT €€

(☑031 95 21 24; www.residencelalimonera.com; Via Bellosio 2; r €110-180; ❄@🛜) It's a steep but supremely picturesque hike up cobbled lanes to this elegant villa, set high up in Bellagio in an old lemon grove. Once there you'll discover 11 spacious and thoughtfully furnished self-catering apartments for two to four people.

ALEXANDRE ROTENBERG/SHUTTERSTOCK ©

1. Lago di Como (p270)

Hemmed in by wooded hills, the shores of Lago di Como are dotted with villas.

2. Lago di Garda (p281)

The lake's prettiest village, Sirmione, has hot springs, Roman ruins and a castle.

3. Varenna (p279)

Pastel-coloured houses rise steeply up the hillside in Varenna on Lago di Como's eastern shore.

4. Lago Maggiore (p263)

Isola Bella is the highlight of Lago Maggiore, with spectacular terraced gardens and a baroque palace.

Il Borgo
APARTMENT €€

(☑ 031 95 24 97; www.borgoresidence.it; Salita Plinio 4; r €105-135; ❄❂🖥) With their blond-wood beams and sleek lines, these stylish apartments make it easy to imagine living in Bellagio full time. Especially as you're just a minute's walk down a picturesque lane to the lake and are surrounded by countless eateries and bars.

🍴 Eating & Drinking

⭐ Ristorante Silvio
ITALIAN €€

(☑ 031 95 03 22; www.bellagiosilvio.com; Via Carcano 12; meals €28-38; ⊘ noon-3pm & 6.30-10pm Mar–mid-Nov & Christmas week) Operating since 1919, this place must be getting something right to achieve seemingly unanimous acclaim. Simple food at reasonable prices combines with lovely views over the lake. You might start with a *riso e filetto di pesce* (rice with lemon juice and Parmesan, topped by fillets of the day's lake catch), followed by a *frittura leggera di luccio* (fry-up of pike chunks).

⭐ Ittiturismo da Abate
SEAFOOD €€

(☑ 031 91 49 86; www.ittiturismodaabate.it; Frazione Villa 4, Lezzeno; meals €28-38; ⊘ 7-10.30pm Tue-Sun, noon-2.30pm Sun; P 🚗) Most dishes at Slow Food–focused Da Abate feature fish that's been caught that day in the lake (the restaurant will only open if they've caught enough), so you can sample *lavarello* (white fish) in balsamic vinegar, linguine with perch and black olives, and the robust *missoltino* (fish dried in salt and bay leaves).

⭐ Enoteca Cava Turacciolo
WINE BAR

(☑ 031 95 09 75; www.cavaturacciolo.it; Salita Genazzini 3; ⊘ 10.30am-1am Thu-Tue Apr-Oct, shorter hours Nov, Dec & Mar, closed Jan & Feb) A contender for Bellagio's most charming address, this cosy wine bar occupies a candlelit, stonewalled space tucked down a lane near the waterfront. The encyclopedic wine list covers every region in Italy, and there's excellent charcuterie and cheese boards on offer – as well as a few pasta and fish plates.

🔒 Shopping

Alimentaria Gastronomia
FOOD

(Via Bellosio 1; ⊘ 7.30am-9pm) The smells wafting out from this deli will surely tempt you to step inside. Among the piled-high Larian goodies are dried porcini mushrooms, DOP Laghi Lombardi-Lario olive oil, *missoltini* (dried fish) and some rather irreverently shaped bottles of limoncello.

ℹ️ Information

PromoBellagio (☑ 031 95 15 55; www.bellagiolakecomo.com; Piazza della Chiesa 14; ⊘ 9.30am-1pm Mon, 9-11am & 2.30-3.30pm Tue-Sun Apr-Oct) A consortium of local businesses that provides useful information. This is also the place to book guided tours to visit Villa Serbelloni (p275).

Tourist Office (☑ 031 95 02 04; www.bellagiolakecomo.com; Piazza Mazzini; ⊘ 9am-1pm & 2-6pm Mon-Sat, 10.30am-12.30pm & 1.30-5.30pm Sun, reduced hours winter) Bellagio's official tourist office, next to the boat landing stage, is quite helpful. Can provide information on walks in the area, water sports, mountain biking and other activities.

Cernobbio to Lenno

The sunny, western lake-front stretch from Cernobbio to Lenno is one of Lago di Como's most glamorous. The big draws here are the blockbuster villas; some are open to the public (such as bewitching Villa Balbianello); some are definitely closed (including George Clooney's place, Villa Oleandra, in Laglio).

👁 Sights

⭐ Villa Balbianello
VILLA, GARDENS

(☑ 0344 5 61 10; www.fondoambiente.it; Via Comoedia 5, Località Balbianello; villa & gardens adult/reduced €20/10, gardens only adult/reduced €10/5; ⊘ gardens 10am-6pm Tue & Thu-Sun mid-Mar–mid-Nov) A 1km walk along the (partially wooded) lake shore from Lenno's main square, Villa Balbianello has cinematic pedigree: this was where scenes from *Star Wars Episode II* and the 2006 James Bond remake of *Casino Royale* were shot. The reason? It is one of the most dramatic locations anywhere on Lake Como, providing a genuinely stunning marriage of architecture and lake views.

🛏 Sleeping

Villa d'Este
HISTORIC HOTEL €€€

(☑ 031 34 81; www.villadeste.it; Via Regina 40; d €970-1430, ste €1530-1850; P ❄ @ 🖥 🏊) Much of Lago di Como draws the rich and glamorous; this hotel draws the richest and most glamorous of the lot. The 16th-century palace is beyond luxury: rich brocades drape beside marble bathrooms; balconies are bigger than some hotel rooms; fountains burble beside statues gazing onto exquisite lake views.

Villa Regina Teodolinda
LUXURY HOTEL €€€

(☑ 031 40 00 31; www.villareginateodolinda.com; Via Vecchia Regina 58, Laglio; r €190-450; ⊘ Mar-

Oct; ▣❋@🛜🏊) For a taste of the A-lister lifestyle, head for this sumptuous villa, slightly north of the village of Laglio (sometime residence of Mr and Mrs Clooney). Elegant and deliciously tasteful rooms, many with lake views, emit refined sophistication; the welcome is discretion itself. Approach by the lake road or by boat via the private landing stage; you'll pass through delightful gardens either way.

✖ Eating

★ Antica Trattoria del Risorgimento
ITALIAN €€

(📞0344 4 17 89; Via San Abbondio 8, Mezzegra; meals €30-38; ⏰7-10.30pm Tue-Sun & noon-2.30pm Sat & Sun; 🛜📄) Tucked down a narrow lane in the tiny village of Mezzegra, this charming spot cooks up beautifully prepared regional dishes. The small menu, which changes by day, features three different starters, three first courses and three second courses, and might include delicacies like lake trout cooked on a stone, risotto with wild nettle, and roast suckling pig. Reserve ahead.

★ Materia
ITALIAN €€€

(📞031 207 55 48; www.ristorantemateria.it; Via Cinque Giornate 32; meals €45-55, menus €50-90; ⏰noon-2.30pm Wed-Sun & 7-10.30pm Tue-Sun) The talk of the town is this enticing Zen-like space, a 10-minute walk from the waterfront. Materia sources many herbs (including unusual varieties) and vegetables from its own greenhouse, and its daring menu pushes flavour notes you won't find elsewhere. Think marinated trout with horseradish and fermented kiwi; pearl barley with sage, bacon and potatoes; and lamb with wild garlic.

Tremezzo
POP 1260

Tremezzo draws fleets of ferries thanks to the 17th-century Villa Carlotta and spectacular Lago di Como views.

👁 Sights

★ Villa Carlotta
HISTORIC BUILDING

(📞034 44 04 05; www.villacarlotta.it; Via Regina 2; adult/reduced €10/8; ⏰9am-7.30pm Apr-Sep, 9.30am-5pm mid-Mar & Oct) Waterfront Villa Carlotta sits high on Como's must-visit list. The botanic gardens are filled with colour from orange trees interlaced with pergolas, while some of Europe's finest rhododendrons, azaleas and camellias bloom. The 8-hectare gardens also contain a lush fern

valley, a bamboo grove, a Zen-style rock garden, towering cedars and a high-up lookout fringed by olive trees. The 17th-century villa, strung with paintings, sculptures (some by Antonio Canova) and tapestries adds an artful element to the beauty.

🛏 Sleeping & Eating

★ Hotel La Perla
HOTEL €€

(📞0344 4 17 07; www.laperlatremezzo.com; Via Romolo Quaglino 7; d €125-160, with lake views €165-180, family ste €250; ▣❋🛜🏊) It's rare that hotels are so universally acclaimed as this one. Rooms are immaculate; service is warm and friendly; and the vantage point from the hillside setting is one of Lago di Como's loveliest. All this is housed in an artful conversion of a 1960s villa. It's worth paying extra for a room with a view.

★ Al Veluu
RISTORANTE €€€

(📞0344 4 05 10; www.alveluu.com; Via Rogaro 11; meals €45-75; ⏰noon-2.30pm & 7-10pm Wed-Mon; 🅿) Situated on a steep hillside with panoramic lake views from its terrace, this excellent restaurant serves up home-cooked dishes that are prepared with great pride. They also reflect Lake Como's seasonal produce, so expect butter-soft, milk-fed kid with rosemary at Easter or wild asparagus and polenta in spring.

ℹ Information

Tremezzo Tourist Office (📞0344 4 04 93; Via Statale Regina; ⏰9am-noon & 3.30-6.30pm Wed-Mon Apr-Oct) By the boat jetty.

Varenna
POP 780

Varenna, a beguiling village bursting with florid plantlife, exotic flowery perfumes and birdsong, is a short ferry ride away from its rival in postcard beauty, Bellagio. Its pastel-coloured houses defy the standard laws of physics, seeming to grip for all they're worth to the steep slopes that rise from the lake.

👁 Sights

Castello di Vezio
CASTLE

(📞348 8242504; www.castellodivezio.it; Vezio, near Varenna; adult/reduced €4/3; ⏰10am-6pm Apr-Sep, to 5pm Mar & Oct) High above the terracotta rooftops of Varenna, the imposing Castello di Vezio offers magnificent views over Lake Como. The 13th-century building was once part of a chain of early-warning medieval watchtowers. Get there by taking a steep cobblestone path (about a half-hour hike) from Olivedo (the northern end of Varenna) to Vezio. You can also take a path (around 40-minutes' walk) along the Sentiero Scabium, reached by taking the uphill ramp just opposite the Villa Monastero.

Villa Cipressi   GARDENS
(☑0341 83 01 13; www.hotelvillacipressi.it; Via IV Novembre 22; adult/child €4/2; ☺10am-6pm Mar-Oct) In Villa Cipressi's gardens cypress trees, palms, magnolias and camellias fill terraces that descend to the lake. Even getting here is picturesque: from the square next to the boat jetty (Piazzale Martiri della Libertà), follow the narrow lakeside promenade around the shore then bear left (inland) up the steps to central Piazza San Giorgio. The villa is signposted from there.

🛏 Sleeping

Albergo Milano   HOTEL €€
(☑0341 83 02 98; www.varenna.net; Via XX Settembre 35; s €130, d €150-210; ☺Mar-Oct; ✳@🤶) In the middle of Varenna on the pedestrian main street (well, lane), hillside Albergo Milano opens onto a terrace with magnificent lake vistas. Most of the 12 rooms have some kind of lake view and balcony – they're also tastefully appointed, with gaily painted iron bedsteads, dark-wood wardrobes and creamy-white linen.

🍴 Eating

Il Cavatappi   ITALIAN €€
(☑0341 81 53 49; www.cavatappivarenna.it; Via XX Settembre 10; meals €30-40; ☺noon-2pm & 6.30-9pm Thu-Tue, closed Jan & Feb; 🍴) Set along a narrow pedestrian lane in the upper part of Varenna, Il Cavatappi is an intimate spot with just seven tables set amid arched ceilings and stone walls, as opera plays quietly in the background. The cooking is outstanding, with creative twists on traditional recipes.

Osteria Quatro Pass   ITALIAN €€
(☑0341 81 50 91; www.quattropass.com; Via XX Settembre 20; meals €28-42; ☺noon-2pm & 7-10pm, closed Mon-Wed winter) Places that don't have a lake view in Varenna are at a distinct disadvantage, which is why this place works just that bit harder with the food and service. Cured meats, lake fish and other local specialities are perfectly prepared and presented.

Cavallino   TRATTORIA €€
(☑0341 81 52 19; www.cavallino-varenna.it; Piazza Martiri della Libertà 5; meals €32-42; ☺noon-2.30pm & 7-9.30pm Thu-Tue; 🍴) Lake-fish specialities pack the menu of this Slow Food eatery set on Varenna's quay. Among the highlights are *crostoni* topped with a fish and calvados pâté; ravioli filled with *lavarello* (white fish) in a radicchio sauce; and a risotto of perch, Parmesan, butter and sage.

Vecchia Varenna   ITALIAN €€
(☑0341 83 07 93; www.vecchiavarenna.it; Contrada Scoscesa 14; meals €35-45; ☺12.30-2pm & 7.30-9.30pm Tue-Sun) You can't get closer to Lake Como than these 15 or so tables set on a terrace suspended over the water. Which means you can dine on lake fish, duck breast or little gnocchi cooked in goat cheese, cream and truffle oil while gazing over towards Como's western shore.

🍸 Drinking & Nightlife

Il Molo   BAR
(☑0341 83 00 70; www.barilmolo.it; Via Riva Garibaldi 14; ☺9am-1am Apr-Oct) The terrace of Bar Il Molo is Varenna's most sought-after *aperitivi* spot. It's raised above the water with views north right up the lake. It also offers pizzas, sandwiches and other light fare.

ℹ Information

Tourist Office (☑0341 83 03 67; www.varenna italy.com; Via 4 Novembre 3; ☺10am-3pm Mon, 10am-1pm & 2-6pm Tue-Sun Jul, shorter hours rest of year) Varenna's tourist office can provide information on the lake's entire eastern shore. Located on the main road in town, just west of Villa Monastero.

Lago d'Iseo

Cradled in a deep glacial valley and shut in by soaring mountains, little-known Lake Iseo (aka Sebino) is a magnificent sight. The main town, picturesque Iseo (population 9200), is tucked into the southwest shore. To the west, the lovely old town of Sarnico (population 6640) features Liberty villas, while in the north Lovere (population 6630) is a working harbour with a higgledypiggledy old centre and a wealth of walking trails. Lago d'Iseo is less than 50km from both Bergamo and Brescia. To its north stretches the Valle Camonica, renowned for its prehistoric rock carvings; to the south sits the rolling Franciacorta wine region.

👁 Sights & Activities

Monte Isola   ISLAND
Monte Isola towers from the south end of Lake Iseo, making it easily the lake's most

intriguing feature. It's Europe's largest lake island, at 4.28 sq km, and today remains dotted with fishing villages. From Carzano, in the northeast – where many ferries land – you can climb rough stairs to the scattered rural settlements and follow a path to the top of the island (599m).

Accademia Tadini GALLERY
(☑035 96 27 80; www.accademiatadini.it; Via Tadini 40, Lovere; adult/reduced €7/5; ☉3-7pm Tue-Sat, 10am-noon & 3-7pm Sun May-Sep, weekends only Apr & Oct) A considerable art collection with works by Jacopo Bellini, Giambattista Tiepolo and Antonio Canova set in a neoclassical palace on the lakefront in Lovere.

Iseobike CYCLING
(☑340 3962095; www.iseobike.com; Via per Rovato 26, Iseo; bike rental per 2hr/day €5/20, helmet €3; ☉9.30am-12.15pm & 2.30-7pm Apr-Sep) Iseobike hires out bikes and can put together tailor-made cycling tours around the lake into the Franciacorta wine region.

🛏 Sleeping & Eating

Hotel Milano HOTEL €
(☑030 98 04 49; www.hotelmilano.info; Lungolargo Marconi 4, Iseo; s/d €47/90, with lakeviews €50/104; ✳@🅟🛜) One of several hotels in the centre of Iseo, the two-star, lakefront Milano is an excellent deal. It's definitely worth paying extra for the lake-view rooms (one-week minimum stay from mid-July to mid-August), so you have a front-row seat for the sunset behind the mountains over the lake.

★Locanda al Lago ITALIAN €€
(☑030 988 64 72; www.locandaallago.it; Località Carzano 38, Monte Isola; meals €27-37; ☉noon-2.30pm & 7-9pm Wed-Sun) The Soardi family has been serving up local dishes since 1948, perfecting deceptively simple treatments of lake fish. It means you can sit on their waterside terrace and feast on trout carpaccio or the day's catch combined with *trenette* (a flat pasta) and lashings of extra virgin Monte Isola olive oil. It's near the quay where ferries from Sale Marasino stop.

Gös TRATTORIA €€
(☑030 982 18 18; www.trattoriagos.it; Viale Repubblica 6, Iseo; meals €25-35; ☉6pm-midnight daily, 11.30am-2pm Sat & Sun) Behind Gös' nondescript front sits a gleaming microbrewery where happy locals tuck into meat-rich, homemade pasta dishes – try the beef, butter and cheese *casoncelli* (stuffed pasta). It's all best washed down with a glass or two of Gös' own zesty unfiltered brew.

La Tana dell'Orso RISTORANTE €€
(☑030 982 16 16; Vicolo Borni 19, Iseo; meals €32-42; ☉7-9.30pm Mon, Tue & Thu, noon-2pm & 7-9.30pm Fri-Sun) For an intimate ambience and fine local fare head to this excellent catery where a barrel ceiling sits above rough stone walls. 'The Bear's Den' is hidden away down a cobbled *vicolo* off Piazza Garibaldi. The gnocchi with mussels and clams, beef with polenta, and *casoncelli* (stuffed pasta) are all crowd-pleasers.

❶ Information

Iseo Tourist Office (☑030 374 87 33; www.iseolake.info; Lungolago Marconi 2, Iseo; ☉10am-12.30pm & 3.30-6.30pm May-Sep, shorter hr winter) Facing the waterfront, the helpful Iseo Tourist Office can give you the lowdown on the region. Ask here about vineyards open for wine tasting in Franciacorta.

❶ Getting There & Away

Iseo Train Station (Via XX Settembre) Iseo train station links Iseo with Brescia (€3.30, 30 minutes, one to two hourly), where you can connect to Bergamo (from €6.70, 90 minutes)

Navigazione sul Lago d'Iseo (☑035 97 14 83; www.navigazionelagoiseo.it) Navigazione sul Lago d'Iseo ferries zigzag their way along the length of the lake with stops around Monte Isola. There are also fairly regular runs between Lovere and Pisogne in the north.

SAB (☑035 28 90 11; www.arriva.it) Regular buses run between Sarnico and Bergamo (€3.80, 50 minutes).

Lago di Garda

Poets and politicians, divas and dictators, they've all been drawn to Lago di Garda. At 370 sq km it is the largest of the Italian lakes, straddling the border between Lombardy and the Veneto, with soaring mountains

OFF THE BEATEN TRACK AROUND LAKE GARDA

Ponale Road (p287) Hike from Riva del Garda for a bird's-eye view of Lake Garda.

Avemaria (p297) Barge and cycle down the Mincio river.

Rocca di Manerba Cycle through the evergreen woods around.

Scuderia Castello (☎0365 64 41 01; www.scuderiacastello.it; Via Castello 10, Gaino; s/d €55/110; P) Scale the Alto Garda plateau on horseback.

to the north and softer hills to the south. Everywhere villages line a string of natural harbours, and vineyards, olive groves and citrus trees range up the slopes.

Information

The website www.visitgarda.com is a good source of lake-wide information.

Getting There & Around

AIR

Verona Villafranca Airport (☎045 809 56 66; www.aeroportoverona.it)

BOAT

Navigazione Lago di Garda (☎030 914 95 11; www.navigazionelaghi.it) Lake Garda has a surprisingly extensive ferry network. One-day, unlimited-travel foot-passenger tickets include: lake-wide (adult/reduced €34.30/17.60); lower lake (€23.40/12.40); and upper lake (€20.50/11). Sample single passenger fares include Sirmione to Salò (adult/reduced €9.80/5.90) and Riva del Garda to Sirmione (adult/reduced €15.10/8.60). Car ferries link Toscolano-Maderno with Torri del Benaco and (seasonally) Limone with Malcesine.

There are no ferries in winter; services are reduced in spring and autumn.

BUS

ATV (☎045 805 79 22; www.atv.verona.it) Runs buses up the lake's west side, including regular connections between Desenzano del Garda train station and Riva del Garda, via Salò and Gardone. ATV also runs shuttles along the lake's east shore with regular services between Riva del Garda and Verona, via Garda.

SIA (☎840 620001; www.arriva.it) Operates regular buses from Brescia up the western side of the lake to Riva del Garda (€9, three hours, two-hourly). It also runs hourly buses linking Brescia with Desenzano, Sirmione, Peschiera and Verona along the southern shore.

Trentino Trasporti (☎0461 82 10 00; www.ttesercizio.it) Connects Riva del Garda with Trento (€4, one hour, every two hours).

CAR

Car is the best way to get to Lake Garda, the A4 motorway skirting the southern shores on its way between Verona and Brescia.

TRAIN

There are two railway stations on the southern shores of Lake Garda – one in Desenzano, the other in Peschiera. Both are served by direct trains from Verona and Brescia.

Sleeping

Hotel Elda LODGE €
(☎0464 59 10 40; www.hotelelda.com; Via 3 Giugno 3, Frazione Lenzumo, Ledro; s/d from €50/100; P@☒) This ultra-modern, glass-and-timber ecolodge 3km north of Lake Ledro is a real treat with its balconies affording views of the Val di Ledro and eco and bio deluxe rooms. The hotel has its own sauna and Turkish baths as well as a restaurant where ingredients are sourced from organic and cruelty-free farms.

Entertainment

Medieval Show THEME PARK
(adult/reduced dinner & show €30/20; ⏲2 shows daily May–mid-Sep) There are two daily medieval shows at CanevaWorld (p284). The dinner and show session begins every day in the summer at 7.30pm.

Sirmione

POP 7650

Built on the end of an impossibly thin, appendix-like peninsula sticking out from the southern shore, pretty Sirmione has drawn the likes of Catullus and Maria Callas to its banks over the centuries, and today millions of visitors follow in their footsteps for a glimpse of Lake Garda's prettiest village and a dip in its only hot spring.

Sights & Activities

★Grotte di Catullo ARCHAEOLOGICAL SITE
(☎030 91 61 57; www.grottedicatullo.beniculturali.it; Piazzale Orti Manara 4; adult/reduced €6/3, with Rocca Scaligera €10/5; ⏲8.30am-7.30pm Tue-Sat & 9.30am-6.30pm Sun summer, 8.30am-5pm Tue-Sat & 8.30am-2pm Sun winter) Occupying 2 hectares at Sirmione's northern tip, this ruined 1st century AD Roman villa is a picturesque complex of teetering stone arches

and tumbledown walls, some three storeys high. It's the largest domestic Roman villa in northern Italy and wandering its terraced hillsides offers fantastic views.

Rocca Scaligera
CASTLE

(Castello Scaligero; ☑ 030 91 64 68; adult/reduced €5/2.50, with Grotte di Catullo €10/5; ☺ 8.30am-7.30pm Tue-Sat, to 1.30pm Sun) Expanding their influence northwards, the Scaligeri of Verona built this enormous square-cut castle right at the entrance to old Sirmione. Rising out of the still waters of the lake it guards the only bridge into town, looming over the scene with impressive crenellated turrets and towers. There's not a lot inside, but the climb up 146 steps to the top of the tower affords beautiful views over Sirmione's rooftops and the enclosed harbour.

★ Aquaria
SPA

(☑ 030 91 60 44; www.termedisirmione.com; Piazza Piatti; pools per 90min/day €19/53, treatments from €30; ☺ pools 9am-10pm Sun-Wed, to midnight Thu-Sat Mar-Jun & Sep-Dec, 9am-midnight daily Jul & Aug, hours vary Jan & Feb) Sirmione is blessed with a series of offshore thermal springs that pump out water at a natural 37°C. They were discovered in the late 1800s and the town's been tapping into their healing properties ever since. At the Aquaria spa you can enjoy a soothing wallow in two thermal pools – the outdoor one is set right beside the lake.

🛏 Sleeping & Eating

★ Meublé Grifone
HOTEL €

(☑ 030 91 60 14; www.gardalakegrifonehotel.eu; Via Gaetano Bocchio 4; s €50-80, d €70-110) The location is superb: set right beside the shore, Grifone's many bedrooms directly overlook the lake and Sirmione's castle. With this family-run hotel you get five-star views for two-star prices. Inside it's all old-school simplicity, but very spick and span. Breakfast and a balcony cost €10 extra each.

Hotel Marconi
HOTEL €€

(☑ 030 91 60 07; www.hotelmarconi.net; Via Vittorio Emanuele II 51; s €45-75, d €80-150; P❄🐶🛜) Blue-and-white-striped umbrellas line the lakeside deck at this stylish, family-run hotel. The quietly elegant, light-filled rooms, some with balconies and lake views, sport subtle shades and crisp fabrics, while the breakfasts involving freshly baked bread and cakes in an elegant dining room are a treat.

★ La Rucola 2.0
GASTRONOMY, GARDESE €€€

(☑ 030 91 63 26; www.ristorantelarucola.it; Vicolo Strentelle 7; meals €75-120; ☺ noon-2.30pm &

7-11pm Sat-Wed, 7-11pm Fri) Boasting a Michelin star, Sirmione's best eatery is a refined affair. A recent makeover lends modern freshness to the experience while the chefs add a touch of class to a menu strong on sea and lake fish. Expect sea bass, prawns and the catch of the day to feature in risottos, pastas and grilled guises, combined with flavour-enhancing confits, pâtés and marinades.

ℹ Information

Tourist Office (☑ 030 91 61 14; iat.sirmione@provincia.brescia.it; Viale Marconi 8; ☺ 10am-12.30pm & 3-6.30pm daily summer, 10am-12.30pm & 3-6pm Mon-Fri, 9.30am-12.30pm Sat winter) Efficient if visitor-weary office on the main road into Sirmione, just before the castle.

Valtenesi

The Valtenesi stretches languidly between Desenzano and Salò, its rolling hills etched with vine trellises and flecked with olive groves. The main lake road heads inland, allowing for gentle explorations of an array of wineries and small towns, including Padenghe sul Garda, Moniga del Garda, Manerba del Garda and San Felice del Benaco.

👁 Sights & Activities

★ Parco Archeologico
Rocca di Manerba
NATURE RESERVE

(☑ 0365 55 25 33; www.parcoroccamanerba.net; Via Rocca 20, Manerba del Garda; ☺ 10am-8pm Apr-Sep, to 6pm Thu-Sun Oct-Mar) **FREE** Protected by Unesco, the gorgeous 'rock of Minerva' juts out scenically into the lake just north of Moniga del Garda. The park contains the remaining low rubble walls of a medieval castle, a restful nature reserve of evergreen woods, orchid meadows and walking trails, and some of the best beaches on the lake.

Santuario della Madonna
del Carmine
MONASTERY

(☑ 0365 6 20 32; www.santuariodelcarmine-san felice.it; Via Fontanamonte 1, San Felice del Benaco; ☺ 7am-noon & 3-6pm; P) The sanctuary of the Madonna del Carmine dates from 1452. Its simple Gothic-Romanesque exterior does little to prepare you for the technicolour frescoes inside, depicting images of Christ and the Virgin and scenes resonant with the Carmelite Order.

Cicli Mata
CYCLING

(☑ 0365 55 43 01; www.matashop.it; Via Nazionale 63, Raffa di Puegnago; half/full day €20/27; ☺ 9am-1pm & 2.30-7.30pm Tue-Sat, 2.30-7.30pm Sun &

Mon) The Valtenesi is perfect cycling country, so pick up a bike from Cicli Mata in Raffa di Puegnago.

La Basia HORSE RIDING
(☑ 0365 55 59 58; www.labasia.it; Via Predefitte 31, Puegnago del Garda; per hour €25) At this rambling vineyard and riding school you can have a formal riding lesson or head out for a trot among the vines, before sampling wines and wild honey on the terrace. Between March and September you can also bed down in one of the family-sized apartments (from €345 to €550 per week).

🛏 Sleeping & Eating

★ **Campeggio Fornella** CAMPGROUND €
(☑ 0365 6 22 94; www.fornella.it; Via Fornella 1, San Felice del Benaco; camping per person/car & tent €14/23.50; P ❄ ⊜) This luxury, four-star campground boasts a private beach, lagoon pool, Jacuzzi, children's club, boat centre, restaurant, bar and pizzeria. You pay considerably more for a lakeside pitch.

★ **Agriturismo i Vegher** AGRITURISMO €€
(☑ 0365 65 44 79; www.agriturismovegher.it; Via Mascontina 6, Puegnago del Garda; meals €25-35; ⊙ 7-10pm Wed-Sat & Mon, noon-2.30pm Sun; P ⛖) Well worth the journey along unsurfaced roads and the long booking lead times (book at least a month in advance for holiday weekends, otherwise about two weeks),

---

LAKE GARDA FOR KIDS

Lago di Garda features two top theme parks, which offer enough rides and stunt shows to thrill all day long.

Gardaland (☑ 045 644 97 77; www.garda land.it; Via Dema 4, Castelnuovo del Garda; adult/reduced €40.50/34; family €102-170; ⊙ 10am-11pm mid-Jun–mid-Sep, 10am-6pm Apr–mid-Jun) At Lake Garda's most touted attraction expect larger-than-life dinosaurs, pirate ships and roller coasters, and an aquarium with a glass tunnel where sharks swim overhead.

CanevaWorld (☑ 045 696 99 00; www. canevaworld.it; Località Fossalta 58) CanevaWorld contains two theme parks: **Aquaparadise** (www.canevapark.it; adult/child €28/22; ⊙ 10am-7pm Jul & Aug, 10am-6pm mid-May–Jun & Sep) features plenty of exhilarating water slides, while **Movieland Studios** (www.movieland.it; adult/reduced €28/22) has stunt-packed action shows. Check the website for details.

I Vegher is a place you'll want to arrive at hungry. Awaiting you are numerous and delicious antipasti courses, homemade pasta and the unrivalled meat *secondi*.

Salò

Wedged between the lake and the foothills of Monte San Bartolomeo, Salò exudes an air of courtly grandeur, a legacy of its days as Garda's capital when the Venetian Republic held sway over the lake. Devoid of any singular sights, Salò's lovely historic centre is lined with fine *stile Liberty* buildings and small, ordinary shops and restaurants. In 1901 an earthquake levelled many of its older *palazzi*, although a few fine examples remain: the Torre dell'Orologio (the ancient city gate), the late Gothic *duomo* (cathedral) with its Renaissance facade and the grand porticoed Palazzo della Magnifica Patria.

◉ Sights

★ **Isola del Garda** ISLAND
(☑ 328 6126943; www.isoladelgarda.com; tour incl boat ride €27.50-33.50; ⊙ Apr-Oct) It's not often you get to explore such a stunning private island, villa and grounds. Anchored just off Salò, this speck of land is crowned with impressive battlements, luxuriant formal gardens and a sumptuous neo-Gothic Venetian villa. Boats depart from towns including Salò, San Felice del Benaco, Gardone Riviera and Sirmione, but in typical Italian fashion they only leave each location one or two times a week, so plan ahead. See the website for the precise timetable.

Republic of Salò AREA
In 1943 Salò was named the capital of the Social Republic of Italy as part of Mussolini and Hitler's last efforts to organise Italian Fascism in the face of advancing American forces. This episode, known as the Republic of Salò, saw more than 16 public and private buildings in the town commandeered and turned into Mussolini's ministries and offices. Strolling between the sites is a surreal tour of the dictator's doomed mini-state. Look out for the multilingual plaques scattered around town.

🛏 Sleeping & Eating

Hotel Laurin HISTORIC HOTEL €€
(☑ 0365 2 20 22; www.hotellaurinsalo.com; Viale Landi 9; d €155-300; P ❄ 🕸 ⛖) An art-nouveau treat with some real history behind it, the Hotel Laurin (formerly the Villa Simonini) was the Foreign Ministry during Mussolini's

short-lived Republic. Downstairs salons retain wonderful details: frescoes by Bertolotti, intricate parquet floors, and wood inlay and wrought-iron volutes. Rooms are stylish and very well equipped.

★ **Villa Arcadio**   VILLA €€€
(☑ 0365 4 22 81; www.hotelvillaarcadio.it; Via Navelli 2; d €150-270, ste €300-450; 🅿 ❋ @ 🛜 ⛾ 🏊) Perched above Salò and surrounded by olive groves, this converted convent is the essence of lakeside glamour. Enjoy the vista of glassy lake and misty mountains from the panoramic pool or retreat inside to frescoed rooms and ancient wood-beamed halls. There's a pricey restaurant on the premises and a programme of massage, yoga and beauty treatments to enjoy.

★ **Al Cantinone**   TRATTORIA €€
(☑ 0365 2 02 34; Piazza Sant'Antonio 19; meals €25 30; ⊙ noon 2.30pm & 7-10pm Fri-Wed) It's well worth heading just a few streets back from the waterfront to track down this friendly neighbourhood trattoria, home to gingham tablecloths, fabulous cooking smells and a clutch of regulars playing cards in the corner. The dishes draw on Salò's lake-meets-mountains setting.

Gardone Riviera
POP 2700

Once Lake Garda's most prestigious corner, Gardone is flush with belle-époque hotels, opulent villas and extravagant gardens. They tumble down the hillside from the historic centre, Gardone Sopra, complete with tiny chapel and piazza, to the cobbled lungolago (lake front) of Gardone Sotto, which is lined with cafes and other tourist paraphernalia. Although the haute glamour of Gardone's 19th-century heyday is long gone it is a pleasant enough place for a stroll and drink, although you'll probably want to base yourself elsewhere on the lake.

👁 Sights

★ **Il Vittoriale degli Italiani**   MUSEUM
(☑ 0365 29 65 11; www.vittoriale.it; Piazza Vittoriale; gardens & museums adult/reduced €16/13; ⊙ 9am-8pm Apr-Oct, to 5pm Tue-Sun Nov-Mar; 🅿) Poet, soldier, hypochondriac and proto-Fascist, Gabriele d'Annunzio (1863–1938) defies easy definition, and so does his estate. Bombastic, extravagant and unsettling, it's home to every architectural and decorative excess imaginable and is full of quirks that help shed light on the man. Visit and you'll take in a dimly lit, highly idiosyncratic villa,

WORTH A TRIP

ROMAN VILLA

Before the Clooneys and Versaces, wealthy Roman senators and poets had holiday homes on Italy's northern lakes. One survivor is Desenzano's now-ruined **Villa Romana** (☑ 030 914 35 47; Via Crocifisso 2; adult/reduced €2/1; ⊙ 8.30am-7pm mid-Mar–mid-Oct, to 4.30pm mid-Oct–mid-Mar, closed Mon), which once extended over a hectare of prime lakeside land. Today, wooden walkways snake through the villa above a colourful collage of black, red, olive and orange mosaics, many depicting hunting, fishing and chariot riding, garlanded by fruits and flowers.

a war museum and tiered gardens complete with full-sized battleship.

★ **Giardino Botanico Fondazione André Heller**   GARDENS, SCULPTURE
(☑ 336 410877; www.hellergarden.com; Via Roma 2; adult/reduced €11/5; ⊙ 9am-7pm Mar-Oct) Gardone's heyday was due in large part to its mild climate, which benefits the thousands of exotic blooms that fill artist André Heller's sculpture garden. Laid out in 1912 by Arturo Hruska, the garden is divided into pocket-sized climate zones, with tiny paths winding from central American plains to African savannah, via swathes of tulips and bamboo.

🛏 Sleeping & Eating

★ **Locanda Agli Angeli**   B&B €€
(☑ 0365 2 09 91; www.agliangeli.biz; Via Dosso 7; s €80, d €90-180; 🅿 ❋ 🏊) It's a perfect hillside Lago di Garda bolt-hole: a beautifully restored, rustic-chic *locanda* (inn) with a pint-sized pool and a terrace dotted with armchairs. Ask for room 29 for a balcony with grandstand lake and hill views, but even the smaller bedrooms are full of charm.

❶ Information

Tourist Office (☑ 0365 374 87 36; Corso della Repubblica 8; ⊙ 9am-12.30pm & 2.15-6pm Mon-Sat) Stocks information on activities.

Riva del Garda & Around
POP 16,850

Officially in the Alpine region of Trentino-Alto Adige, stunning and very popular Riva is encircled by towering rock faces and a looping landscaped lake front. Its appealing

DON'T MISS

THE GOOD OIL

Comincioli (☑ 0365 65 11 41; www.comincioli.it; Via Roma 10, Puegnago del Garda; ⊙ 9.30am-noon & 2.30-7pm Mon-Sat by reservation) produces some of Italy's best olive oils – its Numero Uno is legendary. The family has been harvesting olives for nearly 500 years. Get an insight into that complex process and indulge in a tutored tasting at their farm-vineyard deep in the Valtenesi hills.

historic core is arranged around handsome Piazza III Novembre.

◎ Sights

★ Cascata del Varone   WATERFALL

(☑ 0464 52 14 21; www.cascata-varone.com; Via Cascata 12; adult/reduced €5.50/2.50; ⊙ 9am-7pm May-Aug, to 6pm Apr & Sep, to 5pm Mar & Oct, 10am-5pm Jan & Feb) This 100m waterfall thunders down sheer limestone cliffs through an immense, dripping gorge. Spray-soaked walkways snake 50m into the mountain beside the torrent, and ambling along them is like walking in a perpetual downpour. It's well signposted 3km northwest of Riva's centre.

Museo Alto Garda   MUSEUM

(La Rocca; ☑ 0464 57 38 69; www.museoaltogarda.it; Piazza Cesare Battisti 3; adult/reduced €5/2.50; ⊙ 10am-6pm Tue-Sun mid-Mar–May & Oct, daily Jun-Sep) In Riva's compact medieval castle, the civic museum features local archaeology, frescoes from Roman Riva, documents and paintings. In light of Riva's much fought-over past, perhaps the most revealing exhibits are the antique maps dating from 1579 and 1667, and a 1774 *Atlas Tyrolensis,* which evocatively convey the area's shifting boundaries.

🛏 Sleeping

★ Hotel Garni Villa Maria   HOTEL €

(☑ 0464 55 22 88; www.garnimaria.com; Viale dei Tigli; s €40-75, d €70-115; 🅿✳🛜) Beautifully designed, uber-modern rooms make this small family-run hotel a superb deal. Pristine bedrooms have a Scandinavian vibe, with all-white linens, sleek modern bathrooms and accents of orange and lime green. There's a tiny roof garden, and bedrooms with balconies offer impressive mountain views.

Villa Angelica   VILLA €€

(☑ 0464 55 67 91; www.villaangelicariva.com; Via San Giacomo 48; d €100-270, q €130-450; 🅿🛜)

Located 1.6km outside Riva, the Angelica is classified as one of Lake Garda's historic villas. Inside, the handsome apartments sleeping up to four seem almost too good to be true. Your hostess, Angelica, is happy to share the house's history with you or you can simply wander the English-style garden like Franz Kafka did when he came to stay.

Lido Palace   HISTORIC HOTEL €€€

(☑ 0464 02 18 99; www.lido-palace.it; Viale Carducci 10; d/ste from €300/450; 🅿✳@🛜☀) If you're flush with euros, Riva's captivating Lido Palace is the place to offload them. The exquisite building dates back to 1899 when it opened as a resort for holidaying Austrian royalty. Sensitive renovations mean modern bedrooms with muted colour schemes now sit in the grand Liberty-style villa, offering peerless views over lawns and lake.

✗ Eating

Cristallo Caffè   GELATO €

(☑ 0464 55 38 44; www.cristallogelateria.com; Piazza Catena 17; cones €2.50; ⊙ 7am-1am, closed Nov-Mar) More than 60 flavours of artisanal gelato are served up in this seasonal lakeside cafe, all of it crafted by the Pancieras, a Belluno gelato-producing family since 1892. It's also a top spot to sip a *spritz* (cocktail made with *prosecco*) while enjoying lake views.

★ Osteria Le Servite   OSTERIA €€

(☑ 0464 55 74 11; www.leservite.com; Via Passirone 68, Arco; meals €30-45; ⊙ 7-10.30pm Tue-Sun Apr-Sep, 7-10.30pm Wed-Sat Oct-Mar; 🅿🚻) Tucked away in Arco's wine-growing region, this elegant little *osteria* (tavern) serves dishes that are so seasonal the menu changes weekly. You might be eating mimosa gnocchi, tender *salmerino* (Arctic char) or organic ravioli with *stracchino* cheese.

★ Restel de Fer   ITALIAN €€

(☑ 0464 55 34 81; www.resteldefer.com; Via Restel de Fer 10; meals €40-60; ⊙ noon-2.30pm & 7-11pm daily Jul & Aug, Thu-Tue Sep, Oct & Dec-Jun; 🅿🛜) Going to the restaurant at this family-run *locanda* (inn) feels like dropping by a friend's rustic-chic house: expect worn leather armchairs, copper cooking pots and glinting blue glass. The menu focuses on seasonal, local delicacies such as rabbit wrapped in smoked mountain ham, char with crayfish, and veal with Monte Baldo truffles.

❶ Information

Tourist Office (☑ 0464 55 44 44; www.gardatrentino.it; Largo Medaglie d'Oro; ⊙ 9am-7pm daily May-Sep, to 6pm Mon-Fri Oct-Apr)

Can advise on everything from climbing and paragliding to wine tasting and markets.

Malcesine

POP 3647

With the lake lapping right up to the tables of its harbourside restaurants and the vast, snow-capped ridge of Monte Baldo behind, Malcesine is quintessential Lake Garda. Alas, its picturesque setting attracts thousands of holidaymakers and day trippers, who flood the town's tiny streets. However, Malcesine hasn't completely sold its soul to tourism and locals still inhabit the tangle of alleyways, hanging their washing between houses in typical Italian fashion and filling the place at mealtimes with mouth-watering aromas.

🏃 Activities

Funivia Malcesine–Monte Baldo   CABLE CAR
(📞 045 740 02 06; www.funiviedelbaldo.it; Via Navene Vecchia 12; adult/reduced return €22/15; ⊗ 8am-7pm Apr-Sep, to 5pm Oct-Mar) Jump aboard this cable car and glide 1760m above sea level for spectacular views – circular ro-

tating cabins reveal the entire lake and surrounding mountains. For the first 400m the slopes are covered in oleanders, and olive and citrus trees – after that, oak and chestnut take over. Mountain-bike trails wind down from the summit.

Xtreme Malcesine   CYCLING
(📞 045 740 01 05; www.xtrememalcesine.com; Via Navene Vecchia 10; road/mountain bike per day €15/25; ⊗ 8am-7pm) Rents bikes from its shop at the base of the Monte Baldo cable car. There's also a bike cafe and the owners run mountain-bike tours into the hills.

Consorzio Olivicoltori di Malcesine   FOOD
(📞 045 740 12 86; www.oliomalcesine.it; Via Navene 21; ⊗ 9am-12.30pm & 3.30-6.30pm Mon-Sat, 9am-1pm Sun, shorter hours winter) FREE Olives harvested around Malcesine are milled into first-rate extra-virgin olive oil by this local consortium. You can sample the product here. Known as 'El nos Oio' (Our Oil), it's a gold-green liquid that's low in acidity and has a light, fruity, slightly sweet taste. Prices of the cold-pressed extra virgin DOP oil start at €8.50 for 0.25l.

ACTIVITIES AROUND RIVA DEL GARDA

Riva makes a natural starting point for a host of activities, including hiking and biking trails around Monte Rocchetta (1575m), climbing in Arco and canyoning in the Val di Ledro. One of the town's top highlights is the easy 7km hike along **La Strada del Ponale** (www.ponale.eu).

Canyoning

Thanks to glacial meltwaters, which have worn smooth the limestone mountains surrounding Riva and the Val di Ledro, canyoning here is a fantastic experience offering lots of slides, jumps and abseiling. Both **Canyon Adventures** (📞 334 8698666; www.canyon adv.com; ⊗ May-Oct) and **Arco Mountain Guide** (📞 330 567285; www.arcomoun tainguide.com) arrange trips to the Palvico and Rio Nero gorges in the Val di Ledro and the Vione canyon in Tignale.

Climbing

Surrounded by perfect waves of limestone, Arco is one of Europe's most popular climbing destinations and is the location of the Rockmaster festival in late August.

With hundreds of routes of all grades to choose from, Arco climbs are divided between short, bolted, single-pitch sports routes and long, Dolomite-style climbs, some extending as much as 1400m. The 300m **Zanzara** is a world classic, a 7a+ climb directly above the Rockmaster competition wall. For information on climbing courses and routes contact Arco Mountain Guide.

Lakefront Activities

Along the gorgeous landscaped lakefront gentle pursuits are possible such as swimming, sunbathing and cycling the 3km lakeside path to Torbole. The water here is safe for small children, and there are numerous play areas set back from the water. Like its neighbour Torbole, Riva is well known for windsurfing and has several schools that hire out equipment on Porfina Beach.

Fleets of operators provide equipment hire and tuition along the lakefronts in Riva and Torbole. One of the largest is **Surfsegnana** (📞 0464 50 59 63; www.surfsegnana.it; Foci del Sarca, Torbole), which operates from Lido di Torbole and Porfina Beach in Riva.

Eating

Speck Stube
BARBECUE €

(☑ 045 740 11 77; www.speckstube.com; Via Navene Vecchia 139; meals €15-25; ⊙ noon-11pm Mar-Oct; P) Catering for northern European tourists, the specialities at this family-friendly place 2.5km north of Malcesine are wood-roast chickens, sausages and pork on the bone. Help yourself to hearty portions and mugs of beer at tables beneath the olive trees, while the kids let off steam in the play park.

★ Vecchia Malcesine
GASTRONOMY €€€

(☑ 045 740 04 69; www.vecchiamalcesine.com; Via Pisort 6; meals €55-110; ⊙ noon-2pm & 7-10pm Thu-Tue) The lake views from the terrace at hillside Vecchia Malcesine do their best to upstage the food. But the Michelin-starred menu wins; its exquisitely presented, creative dishes might include trout with horseradish, smoked caviar and white chocolate, or risotto with lake fish, apple and raspberry.

❶ Information

Tourist Office
(☑ 045 740 00 44; www.tourism.verona.it; Via Gardesana 238; ⊙ 9.30am-12.30pm & 3-6pm Mon-Sat, 9.30am-12.30pm Sun) Malcesine's tourist office is set back from the lake beside the bus station, on Via Gardesana, the main road through town.

Punta San Vigilio

Picturesque Punta San Viglio is a popular destination for beach-goers.

◉ Sights

Punta San Vigilio
BEACH

(adult/reduced incl Parco Baia delle Sirene €12/6; P) The leafy headland of Punta San Vigilio curls out into the lake 3km north of Garda. An avenue of cypress trees leads from the car park towards a gorgeous crescent of bay backed by olive groves. There the **Parco Baia delle Sirene** (☑ 045 725 58 84; www.parcobaiadellesirene.it; Punta San Vigilio; adult/reduced incl Punta San Vigilio €12/6, cheaper after 4.30pm; ⊙ 10am-7pm Apr & May, 9.30am-8pm Jun-Aug; P) offers sun loungers beneath the trees; there's also a children's play area.

🛏 Sleeping & Eating

★ Locanda San Vigilio
BOUTIQUE HOTEL €€€

(☑ 045 725 66 88; www.punta-sanvigilio.it; Punta San Vigilio; d €270-375, ste €440-900; P ❄ @ ≋) This enchanting 16th-century *locanda* (inn) feels just like a luxurious English manor house: discreet, understated and effortlessly elegant. Dark wood, stone floors and plush furnishings ensure an old-world-meets-new luxury feel. The excellent restaurant (lunch/dinner €40/55) sits right beside the water, offering memorable food and views.

❷ Drinking & Nightlife

★ Taverna San Vigilio
CAFE €

(☑ 045 725 51 90; Punta San Vigilio; meals €20-30; ⊙ 10am-5.30pm; P) With an olive-tree-shaded garden and tables strung out along a tiny crab-claw harbour, the Taverna San Vigilio is one of the most atmospheric bars on the lake. Nibbles include lobster, veal and *prosciutto crudo* (cured ham).

Bardolino

POP 6700

Gathered around a tiny harbour, prosperous Bardolino is a town in love with the grape. More than 70 vineyards and wine cellars grace the gentle hills that roll east from Bardolino's shores, many within DOC and the even stricter DOCG quality boundaries. They produce an impressive array of pink Chiaretto, ruby classico, dry superiore and young novello. In October, the popular **Festa dell'Uva e del Vino** celebrates the region's exceptional food and wine.

◉ Sights & Activities

Pieve di San Zeno
CHURCH

(Corte San Zeno) Flee the gelato and Aperol brigade for a pilgrimage to this ancient miniature church, concealed in a picturesquely shabby courtyard north of the main road. Dating from the 9th century, it's one of the finest pieces of Carolingian architecture to have survived in northern Italy, and its almost windowless form and moody interior give visitors a good impression of how early Christian worship must have felt.

Museo del Vino
MUSEUM

(☑ 045 622 83 31; www.museodelvino.it; Via Costabella 9; ⊙ 9am-12.30pm & 2.30-7pm mid-Mar–Sep, hours vary Oct–mid-Mar) **FREE** Just off the main lake road, the Museo del Vino is set within the Zeni winery and rarely has a museum smelt this good. Rich scents waft around displays of wicker grape baskets, cooper's tools, drying racks and gigantic timber grape presses. Tastings of Zeni's red, white and rosé wines are free, or pay to sample pricier vintages, including barrel-aged Amarone.

Zeni Winery
WINE

(☑ 045 721 00 22; www.zeni.it; Via Costabella 9; ⊙ 2.30-7pm daily, 9am-12.30pm Sat & Sun) Zeni has been crafting wines from Bardolino's morainic hills since 1870. Get an insight into that process with an hour-long winery tour that ends with a mini-tasting in the *cantina* (cellar). Reservations aren't necessary.

🛏 Sleeping & Eating

Corte San Luca   APARTMENT €
(☑345 8212906; www.cortesanluca.com; Piazza Porta San Giovanni 15; d €90, 4-person apt from €200; P❈🛜) Someone with a flair for design has created 11 smart central apartments – expect suspended furniture, moulded chairs and glass-topped tables. With their fully kitted-out kitchens, laundries and 32in TVs, the apartments are a particularly smart home away from home. There's a minimum stay of a week in July and August.

★ Il Giardino delle Esperidi   OSTERIA €€
(☑045 621 04 77; Via Goffredo Mameli 1; meals €35 50; ⊙7-10pm Mon & Wed-Fri, noon-2.30pm & 7-10pm Sat & Sun) Holidaying gourmets should head for this intimate little *osteria*, where sourcing local delicacies is a labour of love for its sommelier owner. The intensely flavoured baked truffles with *parmigiano reggiano* (Parmesan) are legendary, and the highly seasonal menu may feature rarities such as red grouse or bull meat marinaded in Garda olive oil.

🍷 Drinking & Nightlife

La Bottega del Vino   WINE BAR
(☑348 6041800; Piazza Matteotti 46; ⊙10.30am-2pm & 5-10pm Sun-Thu, to midnight Fri & Sat) To experience some authentic Bardolino atmosphere head to this no-nonsense bar in the centre of town. Inside, a stream of lively banter passes between locals and staff beside walls lined with bottles four deep.

❶ Information

Tourist Office (☑045 721 00 78; www. tourism.verona.it; Piazzale Aldo Moro 5; ⊙9am-noon & 3-6pm Mon-Sat, 10am-2pm Sun) Operates a hotel booking service and can advise on the surrounding wine region.

THE PO PLAIN

Stretching from the foot of the pre-Alps to low-lying, lake-fringed plains, this is a region that's overlooked by many but is itching to spring a surprise. In the north, edged by mountains and encircled by defensive walls, you'll find Bergamo, an ancient hill town rich in architecture and art. Nearby, Brescia showcases gutsy cuisine and impressive fragments of its Roman past. In unique Cremona, home to Antonio Stradivari, discover a vibrant musical heritage and old-town vibe. And in the far east comes captivating Mantua, surrounded by lakes, enriched by art-packed palaces and ready to delight with the architectural harmony of its interlocking squares.

Bergamo

POP 121,000

This eastern Lombard city offers a wealth of art and medieval Renaissance and baroque architecture, a privileged position overlooking the southern plains, breathtaking views and some fine dining. Bergamo is one of northern Italy's most beguiling cities.

The city's defining feature is a double identity. The ancient hilltop Città Alta (Upper Town) is a tangle of tiny medieval streets, embraced by 5km of Venetian walls. It lords it over the largely (but not entirely) modern Lower Town (Città Bassa). A funicular connects the two.

◎ Sights

The Upper Town's beating heart is the cafe-clad Piazza Vecchia, lined by elegant architecture that is a testament in stone and brick to Bergamo's long and colourful history. Le Corbusier apparently described it as the 'most beautiful square in Europe'.

★ Torre del Campanone   TOWER
(☑035 24 71 16; Piazza Vecchia; adult/reduced €3/free; ⊙9.30am-6pm Tue-Fri, to 8pm Sat & Sun Apr-Oct, reduced hours winter) Bergamo's colossal, square-based Torre del Campanone soars 52m above the city. It still tolls a bell at 10pm, the legacy of an old curfew. Taking the lift to the top of the tower reveals sweeping views down onto the town, up to the pre-Alps and across to the Lombard plains.

★ Palazzo del Podestà   MUSEUM
(Museo Storico dell'Età Veneta; ☑035 24 71 16; www.palazzodelpodesta.it; Piazza Vecchia; adult/reduced €7/5; ⊙9.30am-1pm & 2.30-6pm Tue-Sun) On the northwest side of Piazza Vecchia, the fresco-dappled Palazzo del Podestà was traditionally home to Venice's representative in Bergamo. Today, the medieval building houses a small imaginative museum with audiovisual and interactive displays that tell the story of Bergamo's Venetian age. Admission also includes access to the Torre del Campanone, with superb views over Bergamo.

Bergamo

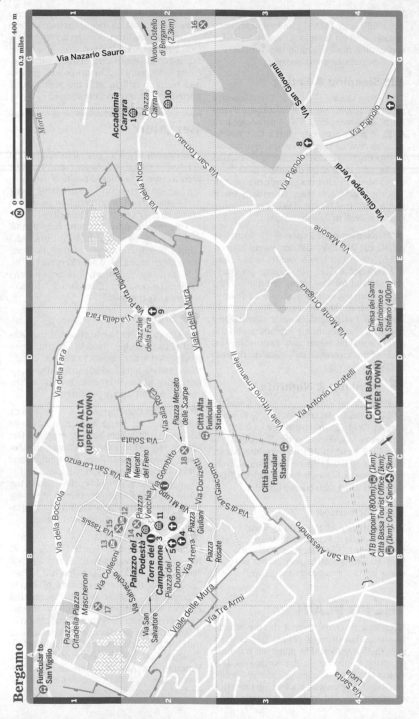

Bergamo

★**Accademia Carrara**　　GALLERY
(☑ 035 23 43 96; www.lacarrara.it; Piazza Carrara 82; adult/reduced €10/8; ◎ 10am-7pm May-Nov, 9.30am-5.30pm Dec-Apr) Just east of the old city walls is one of Italy's great art repositories. Founded in 1780, it contains an exceptional range of Italian masters. Raphael's *San Sebastiano* is a highlight, and other artists represented include Botticelli, Canaletto, Mantegna and Titian.

Cattedrale di Bergamo　　CATHEDRAL
(☑ 035 21 02 23; www.cattedraledibergamo.it; Piazza del Duomo; ◎ 7.30am-noon & 3-6.30pm Mon-Fri, 7am 6.30pm Sat & Sun) Roman remains were discovered during renovations of Bergamo's baroque cathedral, with an interior dating to the 17th century. A rather squat building, it has a brilliant white facade (completed in the 19th century). Among the relics in a side chapel is the one-time coffin of the beatified Pope John XXII. The church also contains paintings by Moroni and Tiepolo.

Palazzo della Ragione　　HISTORIC BUILDING
(Piazza Vecchia) The imposing arches and columns of the Palazzo della Ragione sit at the southern end of Piazza Vecchia. Built in the 12th century, it bears the lion of St Mark – a reminder of Venice's long reign here. The animal is actually an early 20th-century replica of the 15th-century original, which was torn down when Napoleon took over in 1797. Note the sun clock in the pavement beneath the arches and the curious Romanesque and Gothic animals and busts decorating pillars.

Basilica di Santa Maria Maggiore　　BASILICA
(Piazza del Duomo; ◎ 9am-12.30pm & 2.30-6pm Mon-Fri, 9am-6pm Sat & Sun Apr-Oct, shorter hours Nov-Mar) Bergamo's most striking church, begun in 1137, is quite a mishmash of styles. To its whirl of Romanesque apses (on which some external frescoes remain visible), Gothic additions were added. Influences seem to come from afar, with dual-colour banding (black and white, and rose and white) typical of Tuscany and an interesting *trompe l'œil* pattern on part of the facade. Highlights include wooden marquetry designed by Lorenzo Lotto and the funerary tomb of the great Bergamo-born composer Gaetano Donizetti.

Cappella Colleoni　　CHAPEL
(Piazza del Duomo; ◎ 9am-12.30pm & 2-6.30pm Mar-Oct, 9am-12.30pm & 2-4.30pm Tue-Sun Nov-Feb) The Cappella Colleoni was built between 1472 and 1476 as a magnificent mausoleum-cum-chapel for the Bergamese mercenary commander Bartolomeo Colleoni (c 1400–75), who led Venice's armies in campaigns across northern Italy. He lies buried inside in a magnificent tomb.

Galleria d'Arte Moderna e Contemporanea　　GALLERY
(GAMeC; ☑ 035 27 02 72; www.gamec.it; Via San Tomaso 53; Permanent/temporary exhibition free/€6; ◎ 10am-1pm & 3-6pm Wed-Mon) The modern works by Italian artists displayed here include pieces by Giacomo Balla, Giorgio Morandi, Giorgio de Chirico and Filippo de Pisis. A contribution from Vassily Kandinsky lends an international touch.

🛏 Sleeping

Albergo Il Sole　　HOTEL €
(☑ 035 21 82 38; www.ilsolebergamo.com; Via Colleoni 1; s/d/tr €65/85/110; P ⏏) Bright rugs and throws bring bursts of the modern to this traditional, family-run *albergo* (hotel) in the heart of the Città Alta; cheerfully painted walls and picture windows add to the quaint feel. The best room is 107, where the balcony offers mountain glimpses and roof-top views.

Hotel Piazza Vecchia　　HOTEL €€
(☑ 035 25 31 79; www.hotelpiazzavecchia.it; Via Colleoni 3; s €135, d €172-300; ✳ @ ⏏) The perfect

IN SEARCH OF LORENZO LOTTO

One of the great names of the late Venetian Renaissance, Lorenzo Lotto worked for 12 years in and around Bergamo from 1513. Today, three of his works remain in situ in three churches scattered about the city. Seeing them is largely a matter of luck, as finding these churches open is a hit-and-miss affair. Just off Via Porta Dipinta at the eastern end of the Città Alta, the diminutive **Chiesa di San Michele al Pozzo** (St Michael at the Well; Via Porta Dipinta; ⊙ 9am-noon & 2-6pm) is home to a chapel filled with a cycle of paintings known as the *Storie della vergine* (Stories of the Virgin Mother), starting with her birth and culminating with the scene of her visiting Elisabeth (her cousin and soon-to-be mother of St John the Baptist). In two churches in the Città Bassa, the **Chiesa del Santo Spirito** (Church of the Holy Spirit; Via Tasso 100; ⊙ 8-11am & 3-6pm Thu-Tue) and **Chiesa di San Bernardino** (Via Pignolo 59; ⊙ 9.30-10.30am Sun), you can observe how Lotto treats the same subject in quite different fashion in altarpieces dedicated to the *Madonna in trono e santi* (The Madonna Enthroned with Saints). The latter is done with great flair and freedom, full of vivid colour, while the former seems more subdued.

Città Alta bolt-hole, this 14th-century townhouse oozes atmosphere, from the honey-coloured beams and exposed stone to the tasteful art on the walls. Rooms have parquet floors and bathrooms that gleam with chrome; the deluxe ones have a lounge and a balcony with mountain views.

★ **Da Vittorio** BOUTIQUE HOTEL €€€
(☑ 035 68 10 24; www.davittorio.com; Via Cantalupa 17, Brusaporto; s €300-350, d €400-450; P✳🕸) Da Vittorio is not only a noteworthy gourmet hideout 9km east of town, but also offers 10 quality suites in its low-slung country estate. Each of the generous rooms enjoys its own sumptuous decor, with beautifully woven fabrics and marble bathroom. Indulge in a tasting menu breakfast, with a series of miniportions of various sweet and savoury options.

✖ Eating

Polentone ITALIAN €
(☑ 348 8046021; Piazza Mercato delle Scarpe 1; polentas €6-9; ⊙ 11.30am-3.30pm & 6.30-10.30pm Mon-Fri, 11.30am-1am Sat, to 10pm Sun; ✐) Styling itself as Italy's first polenta takeaway, Polentone serves up steaming bowls of polenta in the sauce of your choice, including wild boar or vegetarian. Choose between *gialla* (simple corn polenta) or *taragna* (with Taleggio cheese and butter).

Il Fornaio PIZZA, BAKERY €
(Via Colleoni 1; pizza slices around €3-4; ⊙ 8am-9pm) Join the crowds that mill around this local favourite for coffee that packs a punch and pizza slices with delicious ingredients: spinach laced with creamy mozzarella or gorgonzola studded with walnuts. Take it away or compete for a table upstairs.

★ **Noi** ITALIAN €€
(☑ 035 23 77 50; www.noi-restaurant.it; Via Alberto Pitentino 6; meals €35-45; ⊙ 7.30pm-midnight Mon, 12.30-2.30pm & 7.30pm-midnight Tue-Sat; 🕸) Thirty-something chef Tommaso Spagnolo learned his craft at celebrated restaurants in London and New York (including the top-rated Eleven Madison Park) before returning to his hometown to open this creative *osteria* in 2016. The seasonally driven menu features beautifully prepared dishes, including a tender grilled octopus with sweet potato and radicchio, sashimi with horseradish, and the juiciest ribeye for miles around.

Osteria della Birra OSTERIA €€
(☑ 035 24 24 40; www.elavbrewery.com; Piazza Mascheroni 1; meals €25-30; ⊙ noon-3pm & 6pm-2am Mon-Fri, noon-2am Sat & Sun) Being the official *osteria* (tavern) of craft brewers, this convivial eatery ensures there's a top selection on tap; the tangy Indie Ale tastes particularly fine. Squeeze in at a tiny table or lounge in the courtyard and chow down on platters piled high with local meats, or polenta stuffed with Taleggio (cheese) and porcini mushrooms.

Colleoni & Dell'Angelo ITALIAN €€€
(☑ 035 23 25 96; www.colleonidellangelo.com; Piazza Vecchia 7; meals €55-65; ⊙ noon-2.30pm & 7-10.30pm Tue-Sun) Grand Piazza Vecchia provides the ideal backdrop to savour truly top-class creative cuisine. Sit at an outside table in summer or opt for the noble 15th-century interior; either way expect to encounter dishes such as risotto with white truffle, or venison medallions with chestnut purée and pumpkin.

⭐ **Da Vittorio** GASTRONOMY €€€

(☑ 035 68 10 24; www.davittorio.com; Via Canta-lupa 17, Brusaporto; set menu lunch €70, dinner €180-280; ⊗ 12.30-2.30pm & 7-10pm Thu-Tue Sep-Jul) Bergamo's acclaimed Vittorio is set in a country house 9km east of town and is up there with the best restaurants in Italy, thanks to the celebrated talents of Bergamo-born chef Enrico Cerea. The guiding thought behind the cuisine is the subtle use of the freshest possible seasonal products to create local dishes with inventive flair.

❶ Information

Airport Tourist Office (☑ 035 32 04 02; www.visitbergamo.net; arrivals hall; ⊗ 8am-8pm Mon-Sat, 10am-6pm Sun) Useful first point of contact in the arrivals hall.

Città Alta Tourist Office (☑ 035 24 22 26; www visitbergamo net; Via Gombito 13; ⊗ 9am-5.30pm) Helpful multilingual office in the heart of the Upper Town.

❶ Getting There & Away

AIR

Orio al Serio (☑ 035 32 63 23; www.sacbo.it) Low-cost carriers link Bergamo airport with a wide range of European cities. It has direct transport links to Milan.

BUS

Bus Station (☑ 800 139392; www.bergamo trasporti.it) Located just off Piazza Marconi. **SAB** (☑ 035 28 90 11; www arriva it) Part of the Arriva group, operates regular services from Bergamo to Brescia, Mantua and the lakes.

TRAIN

Train Station (☑ 035 24 79 50; Piazza Marconi) Services to Milan (€5.50, one hour), Lecco (€3.80, 40 minutes) and Brescia (€4.80, one hour, with connections for Lake Garda and Venice).

❶ Getting Around

TO/FROM THE AIRPORT

ATB (☑ 035 23 60 26; www.atb.bergamo.it) buses to/from Orio al Serio airport depart every 20 minutes from Bergamo bus and train stations (€2.30, 15 minutes). Direct buses also connect the airport with Milan and Brescia.

PUBLIC TRANSPORT

ATB bus 1 connects the train station with the **funicular** (☑ 035 23 60 26; www.atb.bergamo.it; ⊗ 7.30am-11.45pm) to the Upper Town and Colle Aperto (going the other way not all buses stop right at the station but at the Porta Nuova stop). From Colle Aperto, either bus 21 or a funicular continues uphill to San Vigilio. Buy tickets, valid for 75 minutes' travel on buses, for €1.30 from machines at the train and funicular stations or at newspaper stands.

There's a taxi rank at the train station.

Brescia

POP 196.800

Brescia's core takes the form of a fascinating old town, which more than compensates for the city's rather unappealing urban sprawl. The old town's narrow streets are home to some of the most important Roman ruins in Lombardy, and a circular Romanesque church. While many visitors stop in only for a day, there's much to see here, from a sprawling collection of 2000-year-old architecture to the fresco filled corridors of a medieval monastery.

⊙ Sights & Activities

⭐ **Santa Giulia** MUSEUM, MONASTERY

(Museo della Città; ☑ 030 297 78 33; www.bresciamusei.com; Via dei Musei 81; adult/reduced €10/5.50, combined ticket incl Tempio Capitolino €15/10; ⊗ 9.30am-5.30pm Tue-Sun Oct–mid-Jun, 10.30am-7pm Tue-Sun mid-Jun–Sep) The jumbled Monastero di Santa Giulia and Basilica di San Salvatore is Brescia's most intriguing sight. Inside this rambling church and convent complex, the Museo della Città houses collections that run the gamut from prehistory to the age of Venetian dominance. Highlights include Roman mosaics and medieval jewels.

Tempio Capitolino RUINS

(www.bresciamusei.com; Via dei Musei; adult/reduced €8/6, combined ticket incl Santa Giulia €15/10; ⊗ 9.30am-5.30pm Wed-Sun Oct–mid-Jun, 10.30am-7pm mid-Jun–Sep) Brescia's most impressive Roman relic is this temple built by Emperor Vespasian in AD 73. Today, six Corinthian columns stand before a series of cells. A ticket gets you admission to the temple chambers, where you can see original coloured marble floors, frescoed walls, altars in Botticino limestone and religious statues.

Teatro Romano RUINS

(Roman Theatre; off Via dei Musei; adult/reduced €8/6; ⊗ 9.30am-5.30pm Wed-Sun Oct–mid-Jun, 10.30am-7pm mid-Jun–Sep) At the height of the Roman era the theatre of Brescia (then Brixia) could seat 15,000 spectators. You can see the somewhat overgrown surviving ruins from outside the gate off cobbled Vicolo del Fontanon. To walk around inside, buy a ticket to the Tempio Capitolino.

MILAN & THE LAKES BRESCIA

Duomo Vecchio
CHURCH

(Old Cathedral; Piazza Paolo VI; ☺9am-noon & 3-6pm Tue-Sat, 9-10.45am & 3-7pm Sun) The most compelling of all Brescia's religious monuments is the 11th-century Duomo Vecchio, a rare example of a circular-plan Romanesque basilica, built over a 6th-century church. The inside is surmounted by a dome borne by eight sturdy vaults resting on thick pillars.

Duomo Nuovo
CATHEDRAL

(New Cathedral; Piazza Paolo VI; ☺7.30am-noon & 4-7pm Mon-Sat, 8am-1pm & 4-7pm Sun) The Duomo Nuovo was begun in 1604 but wasn't finished until 1825. Repeated alterations over the centuries make it a bit of a mishmash; the lower part of the facade is baroque; the upper part showcases the classical flourishes of the later 1700s.

Museo Mille Miglia
MUSEUM

(☑030 336 56 31; www.museomillemiglia.it; Viale della Rimembranza 3; adult/reduced €8/6; ☺10am-6pm) The original Mille Miglia (Thousand Miles) ran between 1927 and 1957 and was one of Italy's most legendary endurance car races – it started in Brescia and took some 16 hours to complete. The race's colourful museum is loaded with some of the greatest cars to cross the finish line, as well as old-style petrol pumps and archived race footage.

Brescia Underground
WALKING

(☑349 0998697; www.bresciaunderground.com; tour per person from €10) For a different view of Lombardy, sign up for a tour with Brescia Underground. True to name, this outfit takes you into the earth, on a ramble through the underground canals and waterways that still course beneath Brescia and its environs. Excursions range from 30-minute highlight tours to 2½-hour walks – some of which happen outside the city centre. Call or email for upcoming tours and meeting points.

🛏 Sleeping & Eating

Risotto, beef dishes and *lumache alla Bresciana* (snails cooked with Parmesan and fresh spinach) are common in Brescia.

★ Albergo Orologio
HOTEL €

(☑030 375 54 11; www.albergoorologio.it; Via Beccaria 17; s €74-90, d €84-104; 🏧@🛜🅿) Just opposite its namesake clock tower and just steps away from central Piazza Paolo VI, the medieval Albergo Orologio boasts fragrant rooms dotted with antiques. Bedrooms feature terracotta floors, soft gold, brown and olive furnishings, and snazzy modern bathrooms.

La Vineria
ITALIAN €€

(☑030 28 05 43; www.lavineriabrescia.it; Via X Giornate 4; meals €28-40; ☺noon-3pm & 7-11pm Tue-Sat, noon-3pm Sun) Near the Piazza della Loggia, La Vineria serves up delectable regional cuisine at al fresco tables in the portico or in the classy downstairs dining room with vaulted ceilings. Try dishes like chestnut gnocchi with creamy Bagoss cheese, leeks and walnuts, or polenta prepared three different ways. True to name, 'the winery' has good wine selections.

ⓘ Information

Main Tourist Office (☑030 240 03 57; www.turismobrescia.it; Via Trieste 1; ☺9am-7pm) Brescia's main tourist office, on the edge of Piazza Paolo VI, can advise on exploring the city's churches and Roman sites. There's another, smaller tourist office at the **train station** (☑030 306 12 40; www.turismobrescia.it; Piazzale Stazione; ☺9am-7pm).

ⓘ Getting There & Around

Bus Station (☑030 288 99 11; Via Solferino) Near the main train station. Buses operated by SIA (☑030 288 99 11; www.arriva.it) serve destinations throughout the province including Desenzano del Garda and Mantua. Some services leave from another station off Viale della Stazione.

Train Station (☑030 4 41 08; Viale della Stazione 7) Brescia is on the Milan–Venice line, with regular services to Milan (€7.30 to €20, 45 minutes to 1¼ hours) and Verona (€6.75, 40 minutes). There are also secondary lines to Cremona (€5.50, one hour), Bergamo (€4.80, one hour) and Parma (€7.65, two hours). A smart new metro (one ride €1.40) links the train station with Piazza della Vittoria (one stop) in the heart of the old town.

Bike Station (Il Parcheggio Biciclette; ☑030 306 11 00; Piazzale Stazione; ☺7am-7.30pm Mon-Fri, 7.30am-1.40pm Sat) You can hire a bicycle (€1 for two hours, €4 a day) from the bike storage building in front of the train station.

Mantua

POP 46,670

As serene as the three lakes it sits beside, Mantua (Mantova) is home to sumptuous ducal palaces and a string of atmospheric cobbled squares. Settled by the Etruscans in the 10th century, it has long been prosperous. The Latin poet Virgil was born just outside the modern town in 70 BC, Shakespeare's Romeo heard of Juliet's death here and Verdi set his tragic, 19th-century opera, *Rigoletto*, in its melancholy fog-bound streets.

Sights

★ Palazzo Ducale
PALACE

(☑ 041 241 18 97; www.ducalemantova.org; Piazza Sordello 40; adult/reduced €12/7.50; ⊘ 8.15am-7.15pm Tue-Sat, from 1.45pm Sun) For more than 300 years the enormous Palazzo Ducale was the seat of the Gonzaga – a family of wealthy horse breeders who rose to power in the 14th century to become one of Italy's leading Renaissance families. Their 500-room, 35,000-sq-metre palace is vast; a visit today winds through 40 of the finest chambers. Along with works by Morone and Rubens, the highlight is the witty mid-15th-century fresco by Mantegna in the **Camera degli Sposi** (Bridal Chamber).

★ Palazzo Te
PALACE

(☑ 0376 36 58 86; www.palazzote.it; Viale Te 13; adult/reduced €12/8; ⊘ 1-6.30pm Mon, 9am-6.30pm Tue-Sun) Palazzo Te was where Frederico II Gonzaga escaped for love trysts with his mistress Isabella Boschetti, and it's decorated in playboy style with stunning frescoes, playful motifs and encoded symbols. A Renaissance pleasure-dome, it is the finest work of star architect Giulio Romano, whose sumptuous Mannerist scheme fills the palace with fanciful flights of imagination.

Rotonda di San Lorenzo
CHURCH

(Piazza delle Erbe; ⊘ 10am-1pm & 2.30-6.30pm Mon-Fri, 10am-7pm Sat & Sun) **FREE** The weather-worn 11th-century, Lombard Romanesque Rotonda di San Lorenzo is sunk below the level of the square, its red-brick walls still decorated with the shadowy remains of 12th- and 13th-century frescoes. The two-level church was 'rediscovered' in 1907 when houses were being demolished on Piazza delle Erbe to make way for a road. This is thought to be the erstwhile site of a Roman temple dedicated to Venus – today's church is still a Dominican place of worship.

Teatro Bibiena
THEATRE

(Teatro Scientifico; ☑ 0376 28 82 08; Via dell'Accademia 47; adult/reduced €2/1.20; ⊘ 10am-1pm & 3-6pm Tue-Fri, 10am-6pm Sat & Sun) If ever a theatre were set to upstage the actors, it's the 18th-century Teatro Bibiena. Dimly lit and festooned with velvet, its intimate bell-shaped design sees four storeys of ornate, stucco balconies arranged around curving walls. It was specifically intended to allow its patrons to be seen – balconies even fill the wall behind the stage. You can wander round at will during the day or come to an evening performance to see the building come alive.

Just a few weeks after it opened in 1769 the theatre hosted a concert by a 14-year-old prodigy – one Wolfgang Amadeus Mozart.

Basilica di Sant'Andrea
BASILICA

(Piazza Mantegna; ⊘ 8am-noon & 3-7pm) This towering basilica safeguards the golden vessels said to hold earth soaked by the blood of Christ. Longinus, the Roman soldier who speared Christ on the cross, is said to have scooped up the earth and buried it in Mantua after leaving Palestine. Today, these containers rest beneath a marble octagon in front of the altar and are paraded around Mantua in a grand procession on Good Friday.

Piazza Broletto
PIAZZA

Once home to the city's highest official and adorned with a coat of arms, the **Palazzo del Podestà** is located between Piazza Broletto and Piazza delle Erbe. The square also features a white stone shrine dedicated to Virgil, depicting the poet sitting at his desk. The brick arch to the left, the **Arengario** (Via Roberto Ardigò), bears evidence of medieval Mantuan punishments. Prisoners were suspended from the iron rings in the ceiling and the ropes pulled taught, a torture known as *squassi di corda*.

Activities

La Rigola
CYCLING

(☑ 0335 605 49 58; Via Trieste 5; per day from €10; ⊘ 9.30am-12.30pm & 2.30-7.30pm) Rent bikes by the day to explore the surrounding lakes, the Po river and the Parco del Mincio (www.parcodelmincio.it). The shortest route (a couple of hours) takes cyclists around Lago Superiore to the Santuario di Santa Maria delle Grazie, while longer routes meander south to the abbey of San Benedetto Po and the Gonzaga town of Sabbioneta.

Tours

★ Visit Mantua
WALKING

(☑ 347 4022020; www.visitmantua.it; tours per 2 people 90min/5hr €100/300) Get the insider view of Renaissance dukes and duchesses – what they ate for breakfast, how they conspired at court and the wardrobe crises of the day – with Lorenzo Bonoldi's fascinating conversational tours of Mantua's highlight palaces. Tours leave from Piazza Sordello 40.

Motonavi Andes
BOATING

(☑ 0376 32 28 75; www.motonaviandes.it; Via San Giorgio 2) Organises frequent boat tours of Mantua's lakes (starting from €9 for 1½ hours) as well as other occasional cruises along the Po and to the Parco del Mincio.

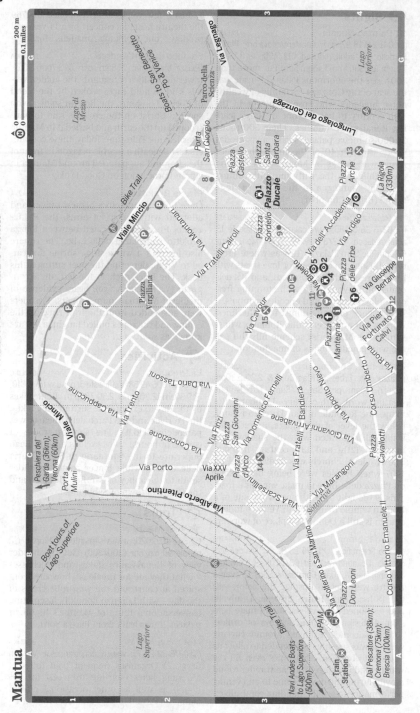

Mantua

Mantua

🛏 Sleeping

★ La Zucca Guesthouse B&B €

(☑ 392 382 7503; www.lazucca.mn.it; Via Spagnoli 10; s €45-50, d €65-80; @ 🛜) This three-room B&B up an ancient staircase off Via Spagnoli is pure delight. Rooms flutter in bright fabrics, beds are comfortable and pleasant aromas fill the air throughout. Breakfast is self-service and laid out all day, and the wi fi is speedy. The only downside is the shared bathroom. Prior booking essential.

★ Armellino B&B €

(☑ 346 3148060; www.beharmellino.it; Via Cavour 67; s €60-65, d €75-85; @ 🛜) Enjoy a touch of ducal splendour in Antonella and Massimo's fabulous *palazzo*. Grand rooms are furnished with 18th-century antiques and retain their original wooden floors, fireplaces and ceiling frescoes. Not all bedrooms have a bathroom, but this place has the feel of an exclusive private apartment rather than a B&B.

★ C'a delle Erbe B&B €€

(☑ 0376 22 61 61; www.cadelleerbe.it; Via Broletto 24; d €120-150; ❄ 🛜) In this gorgeous 16th-century townhouse historic features have undergone a minimalist remodelling: exposed stone walls surround pared-down furniture; whitewashed beams cohabit with lavish bathrooms and modern art. The pick of the bedrooms must be the one with the balcony overlooking the iconic Piazza delle Erbe, a candidate for the town's best room.

🍴 Eating & Drinking

With its pumpkin ravioli and apple relish, spiced-pork risotto and cinnamon-flavoured *agnoli* (ravioli stuffed with capon, cinnamon and cloves), Mantua has a marvellous culinary tradition dating back to the Renaissance when sweet-and-sour flavours were de rigeur.

Osteria delle Quattro Tette OSTERIA €

(☑ 0376 32 94 78; Vicolo Nazione 4; meals €10-15; ⏱ 12.30-2.30pm Mon-Sat) Queue then grab a pew at rough-hewn wooden tables and order up pumpkin pancakes, pike in sweet salsa or *risotto alla pilota*. It's spartan but extremely well priced, which is why half of Mantua is here at lunchtime. Lingering after your meal is not the done thing.

Fragoletta LOMBARD €€

(☑ 0376 32 33 00; www.fragoletta.it; Piazza Arche 5, meals €35; ⏱ noon-3pm & 8pm-midnight Tue-Sun) Wooden chairs scrape against the tiled floor as diners eagerly tuck into Slow Food–accredited *culatello di Zibello* (lard) at this friendly local trattoria. Other Mantuan specialities feature, such as *risotto alla pilota* (rice studded with sausage meat) and pumpkin ravioli with melted butter and sage.

★ Il Cigno MODERN ITALIAN €€€

(☑ 0376 32 71 01; Piazza d'Arco 1; meals €60; ⏱ 12.30-1.45pm & 7.30-9.45pm Wed-Sun) The building is as beautiful as the food: a yellow facade dotted with faded reen shutters. Inside, Mantua's gourmets graze on delicately steamed risotto with spring greens, poached cod with polenta or gamey guinea fowl with spicy Mantuan *mostarda*.

Bar Caravatti BAR

(☑ 0376 32 78 26; Portici Broletto 16; ⏱ 7am-8.30pm Sun-Thu, to midnight Fri & Sat) All of Mantua

---

HOLIDAY AFLOAT

Peek out of your porthole at banks of wildflowers and cormorants sunning themselves on branches as you glide down the Mincio and Po rivers all the way to Venice. Barging hotel **Avemaria Boat** (☑ 0444 127 84 30; www.avemariaboat.com; Via Conforto da Costozza 7, Vicenza; 7 days per person €990; 🚤) offers four-day or week-long itineraries exploring the peaceful nooks and crannies of the delta.

WORTH A TRIP

DAL PESCATORE RESTAURANT

Petals of egg pasta frame slices of guinea fowl caramelised in honey saffron; silky tortellini are stuffed to bursting with pumpkin, nutmeg, cinnamon and candied *mostarda* (fruit in a sweet-mustard sauce). You practically eat the Mantuan countryside in Nadia Santini's internationally acclaimed restaurant, **Dal Pescatore** (☑0376 72 30 01; www.dalpescatore. com; Località Runate, Canneto sull'Oglio; meals €160-260; ☺noon-4pm & 7.30pm-late Thu-Sun, 7.30pm-late Wed). What's even more surprising is that the triple-Michelin-starred chef is entirely self-taught and has only ever cooked here, in what was originally the modest trattoria of her husband's family. It is 40km west of Mantua in a green glade beside the Oglio river. Nearby, **9 Muse B&B** (☑335 8007601; www.9muse.it; Via Giordano Bruno 42a, Canneto sull'Oglio; s €45-55, d €73-90; P❋@) provides charming accommodation.

passes through Caravatti at some point during the day for coffee, *spritz* or a 19th-century *aperitivo* of aromatic bitters and wine.

ℹ Information

Tourist Office (☑0376 43 24 32; www.turismo. mantova.it; Piazza Mantegna 6; ☺9am-5pm Sun-Thu, to 6pm Fri & Sat)

ℹ Getting There & Away

APAM (☑0376 23 03 39; www.apam.it)
Bus Station (Piazza Don Leoni)
Train Station (Piazza Don Leoni)

Cremona

POP 72,000

A wealthy, independent city-state for centuries, Cremona boasts some fine medieval architecture. The Piazza del Comune, the heart of the city, is where Cremona's historic beauty is concentrated. It's a wonderful example of how the religious and secular affairs of cities were divided neatly in two. The city is best known around the world, however, for its violin-making traditions.

◉ Sights

Piazza del Comune   PIAZZA
This beautiful, pedestrian-only piazza is considered one of the best-preserved medieval squares in all Italy. To maintain divisions between Church and state, buildings linked to the Church were erected on the eastern side and those linked to secular affairs were constructed on the west.

Cattedrale di Cremona   CATHEDRAL
(Duomo; www.cattedraledicremona.it; ☺10.30am-noon & 3.30-5pm Mon-Sat, noon-12.30pm & 3-5pm Sun) Cremona's cathedral started out as a Romanesque basilica, but the simplicity of that style later gave way to an extravagance of designs. The interior frescoes are overwhelming, with the *Storie di Cristo* (Stories of Christ) by Pordenone perhaps the highlights. One of the chapels contains what is said to be a thorn from Jesus' crown of thorns.

Torrazzo   TOWER
(Piazza del Comune; adult/reduced €5/4, incl Baptistry €6/5; ☺10am-1pm & 2.30-6pm, closed Mon winter) Cremona's 111m-tall *torrazzo* (bell tower, although 'torrazzo' translates literally as 'great, fat tower') soars above the city's central square. A total of 502 steps wind up to the top. The effort is more than repaid with marvellous views across the city.

Chiesa di Sant'Agostino   CHURCH
(Piazza Sant'Agostino; ☺8am-noon & 2.30-6pm Mon-Sat, noon-12.30pm & 3.30-6pm Sun) Head for the third chapel on the right, the **Cappella Cavalcabò**, which features a stunning late-Gothic fresco cycle by Bonifacio Bembo and his assistants. One of the altars is graced with a 1494 painting by Pietro Perugino, *Madonna in trono e santi* (The Madonna Enthroned with Saints).

✯ Festivals & Events

**Festival di Cremona
Claudio Monteverdi**   MUSIC
(☺May) A month-long series of concerts centred on Monteverdi and other baroque-era composers, held in the **Teatro Amilcare Ponchielli** (☑0372 02 20 01; www.teatroponchielli.it; Corso Vittorio Emanuele II 52).

Stradivari Festival   MUSIC
(www.stradivarifestival.it; ☺mid-Sep–mid-Oct) Focusing on music for string instruments, organised by the **Museo del Violino** (☑0372 08 08 09; www.museodelviolino.org; Piazza Marconi 5; adult/reduced €10/7; ☺10am-6pm Tue-Sun).

Festa del Torrone   FOOD & DRINK
(www.festadeltorronecremona.it; ☺Nov) Weekend full of exhibitions, performances and tastings dedicated to the toffee-tough Cremona-made Christmas sweet: *torrone* (nougat).

CREMONA'S VIOLINS

It was in Cremona that Antonio Stradivari lovingly put together his first Stradivarius violins, helping establish a tradition that continues today. Other great violin-making dynasties that started here include the Amati and Guarneri families.

Some 100 violin-making workshops occupy the streets around Piazza del Comune but few accept casual visitors. To visit, you generally need to be looking to buy a violin, but the **Consorzio Liutai Antonio Stradivari** (☑0372 46 35 03; www.cremonaliuteria.it; Piazza Stradivari 1; ☺11am-1pm & 4-6.30pm Tue-Fri), which represents the workshops, can make appointments for visits. Count on €60 to €80 per group for a one-hour visit.

The **Triennale Internazionale degli Strumenti ad Arco** (International Stringed Instrument Expo; www.entetriennale.com) is held in Cremona every third year in September/October; if you're in town in 2018 or 2021, don't miss it. If you really want to learn about the intricacies of Cremona's musical legacy, the best place is the state-of-the-art Museo del Violino. To hear Cremona's violins in action, the season at the 19th-century Teatro Amilcare Ponchielli runs from October to June.

🛏 Sleeping

Hotel Continental
HOTEL €

(☑0372 43 41 41; www.hotelcontinentalcremona.it; Piazza della Libertà 26; s/d from €67/95; P❋🛜) A short stroll outside the historic centre, this hotel has modern, carpeted rooms set in neutral tones. An attractive lobby, a rooftop bar and a main floor restaurant add to the value. The single rooms are on the small side – but still good value for solo travellers.

L'Archetto
HOSTEL €

(☑0372 80 77 55; www.ostellocremona.com; Via Brescia 9; dm/s/d €30/45/60; ❋@🛜) Cost-conscious musicians love this luxurious hostel where cheerful, modern bedrooms and four-bed dorms are pristine and thoughtfully furnished. Sadly, the limited reception hours (8am to 10am and 5pm to 9pm) – and no option to leave luggage – might be inconvenient.

Dellearti Design Hotel
DESIGN HOTEL €€

(☑0372 2 31 31; www.dellearti.com; Via Bonomelli 8; s €90-135, d €135-210; ❋🛜) A firm favourite with fashion-minded guests, Cremona's hippest hotel is a high-tech blend of glass, concrete and steel. Stylish bedrooms feature clean lines, bold colours and artful lighting. There are also some whimsical flourishes: undulating gold, corrugated corridors, and a bowl of liquorice allsorts on the front desk.

🍴 Eating

Hosteria '700
LOMBARD €€

(☑0372 3 61 75; www.hosteria700.com; Piazza Gallina 1; meals €33-40; ☺noon-2.45pm Wed-Mon, 7-11pm Wed-Sun) Behind the dilapidated facade lurks a sparkling gem. Some of the vaulted rooms come with ceiling frescoes, dark timber tables come with ancient wooden chairs, and the hearty Lombard cuisine comes at a refreshingly competitive cost.

Il Violino
ITALIAN €€

(☑0372 46 10 10; www.ilviolino.it; Via Vescovo Sicardo 3; meals €40-50; ☺12.30-2pm daily & 7.30-10pm Mon-Sat) Il Violino is Cremona's timeless class option. Smooth service is key to this elegant spot, where you might start with one of a number of risotto options or the *tortelli alle erbette al burro spumoso* (stuffed pasta in herbs and frothy hot butter), then move on to roast meat dishes and fresh fish of the day with polenta.

Kandoo
JAPANESE €€

(☑0372 2 17 75; Piazza Luigi Cadorna 11; meals €30-45; ☺11.30am-2.30pm & 6-11pm Tue-Sun) For a break from risottos and pastas, this elegant Japanese spot makes a fine destination. Amid vaulted brick ceilings and flickering candles, Kandoo serves beautifully prepared sashimi platters, mouth-watering sushi rolls, crispy tempura and satisfying bowls of miso soup. For a broad selection, opt for a *barca* (boat-shaped platter), with a mix of sushi, sashimi and nigiri (for one/two persons €20/40).

ℹ Information

Tourist Office (☑0372 40 70 81; www.turismocremona.it; Piazza del Comune 5; ☺9.30am-1pm & 1.30-4.30pm Mon-Fri, 10am-1pm & 2-5pm Sat & Sun) Helpful staff in an office across from the cathedral.

ℹ Getting There & Away

Train Station (Via Dante) Trains to Brescia (€5.50, one hour), Mantua (€6.10, 40 to 80 minutes), Milan (€7.30, one to two hours) and Piacenza (€4.80, 40 to 80 minutes) run roughly hourly.

Trentino & South Tyrol

Best Places to Eat

➡ Zur Kaiserkron (p316)
➡ Paradeis (p318)
➡ Restaurant Ladinia (p329)
➡ St Hubertus (p329)
➡ Locanda Margon (p307)
➡ Pur Südtirol (p332)

Best Places to Stay

➡ Ottmanngut (p320)
➡ Niedermairhof (p332)
➡ Park Hotel Azalea (p323)
➡ Das Wanda (p318)
➡ Le Pedevilla (p332)
➡ Miramonti (p320)

Why Go?

Home to Italy's most spectacular mountains, the Dolomites, the two semi-autonomous provinces of Trentino and South Tyrol (Südtirol or Alto Adige) offer up a number of stunning wilderness areas where adventure and comfort can be found in equal measure. The region has had a faithful fan club of skiers, hikers, climbers, poets and fresh-air fanciers for at least the last few centuries; today the region's ridiculously scenic Sella Ronda is one of the world's most iconic ski circuits.

Wooden farmhouses dot vine- and orchard-covered valleys and the region's cities – the southerly enclave of Trento, the Austro-Italian Bolzano and the very Viennese Merano – are easy to navigate, cultured and fun. From five-star spa resorts to the humblest mountain hut, multigenerational hoteliers combine genuine warmth with extreme professionalism.

Nowhere are the oft-muddled borders of Italy's extreme north reflected more strongly than on the plate: don't miss out on tasting one of Europe's most fascinating, and tasty, cultural juxtapositions.

When to Go
Bolzano

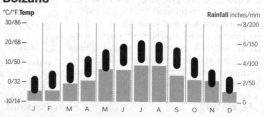

Jan Grab a bargain on the slopes between the Christmas and February highs.

Jul Hit the high-altitude trails and mountain huts of the Alte Vie.

Dec Get festive at Tyrolean Christmas markets in Bolzano, Merano and Bressanone.

TRENTINO

Trento

📱 0461 / POP 117,300 / ELEV 194M

The capital of Trentino is quietly confident, liberal and easy to like. Bicycles glide along spotless streets fanning out from the atmospheric, intimate Piazza del Duomo, students clink *spritzes* by Renaissance fountains and a dozen historical eras intermingle seamlessly among stone castles, shady porticoes and the city's signature medieval frescoes. While there's no doubt you're in Italy, Trento does have its share of Austrian influence: apple strudel is ubiquitous and beer halls not uncommon. Set in a wide glacial valley guarded by the crenellated peaks of the Brenta Dolomites, amid a patchwork of vineyards and apple orchards, Trento is a perfect jumping-off point for hiking, skiing or wine tasting. And road cycling is huge: 400km of paved cycling paths fan out from here. Those with an interest in early-modern history will also find Trento fascinating: the Council of Trent convened here in the 16th-century, during the tumultuous years of the Counter-Reformation, dishing out far-reaching condemnations to uppity Protestants.

◎ Sights

★ MUSE
MUSEUM

(Museo della Scienze; 📱 0461 27 03 11; www.muse. it, Corso del Lavoro e della Scienza 3; adult/reduced €10/8, guided tours (in English by appointment) €3; ⊙ 10am-6pm Tue-Fri, to 9pm Wed, to 7pm Sat & Sun; ♿) A stunning new architectural work, care of Renzo Piano, houses this 21st-century science museum and cleverly echoes the local landscape. Curatorially, the museum typifies the city's brainy inquisitiveness, with highly interactive exhibitions that explore the Alpine environment, biodiversity and sustainability, society and technology. Highlights are a truly amazing collection of taxidermy, much of it suspended in a multistorey atrium, along with a fabulous experiential kids' area. During the week the museum's working laboratories are open to visitors – check the website for session times.

★ Civica
GALLERY

(Galleria Civica di Trento; 📱 0461 98 55 11; www. mart.tn.it/galleriacivica; Via Belenzani 44; €2; ⊙ 10am-1pm & 2-6pm Tue-Sun) This city gallery–project space is the current Trento campus of MART (Museo di Arte Moderna e Contemporanea di Trento e Rovereto; p308) and focuses on 20th-century and contemporary art, architecture and design of the region. The small space's seasonal program is always fascinating and tightly curated and there's an interesting little merchandise **shop** in the entrance.

Villa Margon
HISTORIC BUILDING

(📱 0461 972 416; www.ferrraritrento.it; Via Margone; ⊙ 9am-4pm Wed-Sat Apr-Oct, by appointment) Built by a Venetian family as a summer house in the 1540s, Villa Margon is one of the most beautiful historic sites in Trentino. Frescoes documenting the life of Holy Roman Emperor Charles V line a series of reception rooms and are both startling for their narrative content and for their vivid, and entirely unretouched, colour. The setting is no less lovely with a backing of mountains and a tight circle of forest making it feel far more remote than it actually is.

Duomo
CATHEDRAL

(Cattedrale di San Vigilio; 📱 0461 23 12 93; www.cattedralesanvigilio.it; Piazza del Duomo; archaeological area adult/reduced €1.50/1; ⊙ 6.30am-6pm) Once host to the Council of Trent, Romanesque cathedral displays fragments of medieval frescoes inside its transepts. Two colonnaded stairways flank the nave, leading, it seems, to heaven. Below is a paleo Christian **archaeological area**, which includes the 4th-century temple devoted to San Vigilio, patron saint of Trento, and a number of Christian martyrs murdered by pagans in the nearby Val di Non.

Piazza del Duomo
PIAZZA

Trento's heart is this busy yet intimate piazza, dominated, of course, by the *duomo*, but also host to the **Fontana di Nettuno**, a flashy late-baroque fountain rather whimsically dedicated to Neptune. Intricate, allegorical frescoes fill the 16th-century facades of the **Casa Cazuffi-Rella**, on the piazza's northern side.

Museo Diocesano Tridentino
MUSEUM

(Palazzo Pretorio; 📱 0461 23 44 19; www.museodiocesanotridentino.it; Piazza del Duomo 18; adult/reduced incl archaeological area €5/3; ⊙ 10am-1pm & 2-6pm Wed-Mon summer, 9.30am-12.30pm, 2-5.30pm Mon, Wed-Sat winter) Sitting alongside the Duomo, this former bishop's residence dates from the 11th century. It now houses one of Italy's most important ecclesiastical collections with enormous documentary paintings of the Council of Trent, along with Flemish tapestries, exquisite illustrated manuscripts,

Trentino & South Tyrol Highlights

1 Sella Ronda (p322) Working up a high-altitude appetite on the slopes, then hitting the fine-dining hot spots of Alta Badia.

2 Alpe di Siusi (p325) Riding across the enchanting high pastures on a pretty local horse.

3 Brenta Dolomites (p308) Testing your mettle on a vertiginous, historic *via ferrata* climb.

4 Terme Merano (p319) Floating away at this modern spa beneath palm trees and snowy peaks.

5 Südtirol Weinstrasse (p318) Tasting Italy's most elegant white wines along this gourmet route.

6 Museo Archeologico dell'Alto Adige (p312) Meeting Ötzi the iceman and uncovering his Copper Age lifestyle.

7 MART (p308) Uncovering the excellent modern and contemporary art collections in Rovereto.

8 Val Pusteria (p329) Feasting on schnitzel and *spätzle*, strudel and *knödel* in this traditional valley.

9 Ferrari (p304) Discovering Trento DOC sparklings at this Trentino legend.

10 Val di Sole (p311) Mountain biking apple-clad hills.

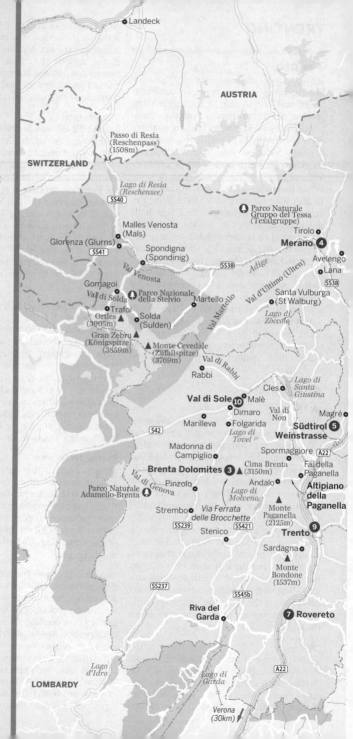

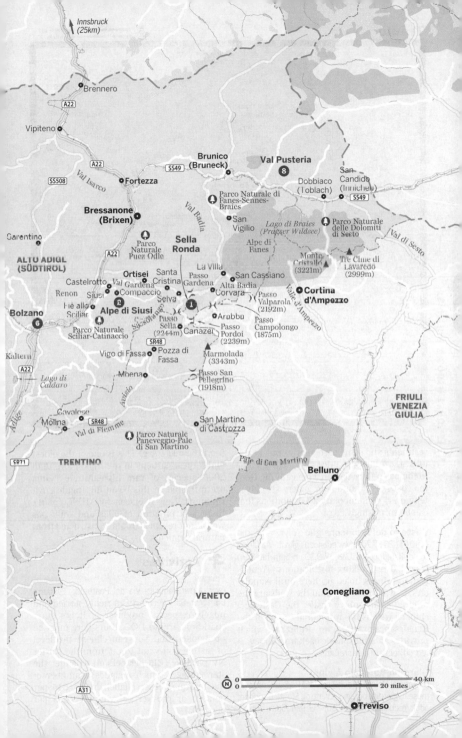

Trento

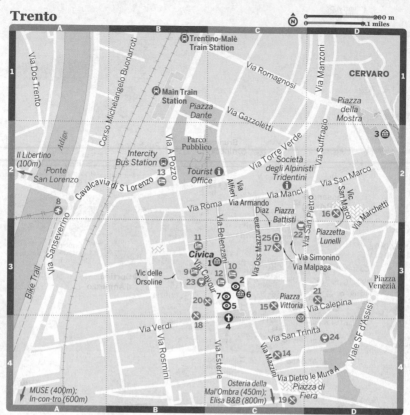

vestments and some particularly opulent reliquaries. Admission price also include entry to the paleo-Christian area beneath the Duomo (p301). A ground-floor gallery also hosts temporary contemporary-art exhibitions that can be surprisingly edgy.

Castello del Buonconsiglio   MUSEUM
(☎ 0461 23 37 70; www.buonconsiglio.it; Via Clesio 5; adult/reduced €10/8; ☺ 9.30am-5pm Tue-Sun) Guarded by hulking fortifications, Trento's bishop-princes holed up here until Napoleon's arrival in 1801. Behind the walls are the original 13th-century castle, the Castelvecchio, as well as the residential rooms of the Renaissance-era **Magno Palazzo**, which provides an atmospheric backdrop for a varied collection of artefacts.

Giardino Botanico Alpino   GARDENS
(Botanical Alpine Gardens; ☎ 0461 94 80 50; www2. muse.it/giardinobotanico; Viote de Monte Bondone; adult/reduced €3.50/2.50; ☺ 9am-5pm Jun &

Sep, to 6pm Jul & Aug) This is one of the oldest and largest gardens in the Alps; more than 2000 species of rare high-altitude plants are nurtured in this beautiful, fragile environment. Now overseen by MUSE (p301), there is a program of talks and walks, as well as a forest playground constructed from natural elements.

🏃 Activities

Ferrari   WINE
(www.ferraritrento.it; Via del Ponte 15; ☺ 10am-6pm Mon-Sat) Ferrrari is a richly storied and hugely respected producer of Italy's other sparkling, Trento DOC. Tours here must be pre-booked and you can choose the level of tasting you want to do, from the starter NV package (€15 per person) to either the star vintages which includes a number of the marque's reserve-label drops (€45 per person) or pro vertical vintages (€65 per person).

Trento

It's a 5min drive south of the city centre, though not accessible by public transport.

Funivia Trento–Sardagna　　　CABLE CAR
(☑0461 23 21 54; www.ttesercizio.it/Funivia; Via Montegrappa 1; one-way/return €3.50/6; ⊙7am–10pm) A brief but spectacular cable-car ride from Trento's valley floor delivers you to the pretty village of Sardagna – admire the vista over a grappa or two. You can take bicycles on board, too. There's a pdf timetable online.

**Vaneze di Monte &
Monte Bondone**　　　SKIING
(www.montebondone.it; ski pass 1/3/7 days €33/85/153) The small, down-to-earth ski station of Vaneze di Monte (1350m) is a 17km drive from Trento and is connected by cable car to its higher counterpart, Vasòn, and the gentle slopes of Monte Bondone (1537m), criss-crossed by 37km of cross-country ski trails and nine downhill runs in winter. On weekends between December and March, Skibus Monte Bondone, run by Trentino Trasporti, wends its way from Trento to Vason and Viote (free with Trentino Guest Card, one way €3, 7-day pass €15).

🛏 Sleeping

Al Cavour 34　　　B&B €
(www.alcavour34.it; Via Cavour 34; s/d €75/110; ❋ 🕏) This little B&B is run by a young couple, both five-star hospitality veterans, who infuse all with a wonderful mix of genuine warmth and absolute professionalism. Rooms are large and decorated in a con-

temporary style; breakfast is taken around a large table with daily home-baked treats like cookies or apple crumble or surprises from the local artisan baker.

Al Palazzo Malfatti　　　B&B €
(☑0461 92 21 33; www.bbpalazzomalfatti.it; Via Belenzani 47; s/d €70/100; ❋ 🕏) Perched on a rooftop, this beautifully designed B&B is a calm and airy retreat that's bang smack in Trento's centre. Upstairs rooms are super private but it retains the feeling of a welcoming home with an elegant living area to relax in and a terrace when it's warm. The charming, caring hosts dispense organic breakfasts, along with invaluable local tips

Elisa B&B　　　B&B €
(☑0461 92 21 33; www.bbelisa.com; Viale Rovereto 17; s/d €65/90; ❋ 🕏) This is a true B&B in an architect's beautiful family home, with two private, stylish rooms and breakfasts that are a feast of home-baked cakes, freshly squeezed juice and artisanal cheese. It's located in a smart residential neighbourhood, a pleasant stroll from Trento's city centre, with lots of eating, shopping and drinking options along the way.

Hotel Venezia　　　HOTEL €
(☑0461 23 41 14; www.hotelveneziatn.it; Piazza del Duomo 45; s/d €61/84, without bathroom €48/€64; 🕏) Rooms in this friendly place overlook the Piazza del Duomo, pretty Via Belanzani or a quiet inner courtyard. The hotel has been recently remodelled, including rather flash bathrooms, while prices remain the same.

TRENTINO & SOUTH TYROL TRENTO

Ostello Giovane Europa
HOSTEL €

(☑ 0461 26 34 84; www.gayaproject.org; Via Torre Vanga 9; dm/s/d/q €26/40/80/100; ⊗ reception closed 10am-2pm; ☎) Clean rooms are comfortable and upper floors have mountain views; the mansard-roofed family room on the top floor is particularly spacious. While it's conveniently located, it can get noisy.

Albergo Accademia
HOTEL €€

(☑ 0461 23 36 00; www.accademiahotel.it; Vicolo Colico 4/6; s/d €95/140; ℗ ✳ @) Elegant small hotel in a historic medieval house with rooms that are modern and airy (if a little on the staid side). Suites are luxuriously spacious, including one with a large private terrace and sauna.

✖ Eating

Gusto Giusto
BURGERS €

(www.gustogiusto-trento.it; Piazza Vittoria Alessandro 1; burgers €5-10; ⊗ 11.30am-2.30pm Mon-Sat, 7.30-10.30pm Wed-Sat) Great burger shack that serves up a variety of burgers from New York style to local varieties such as the wurst burger and one that pairs a beef patty with cream of zucchini, radicchio and tomino cheese. Beers are, of course, artisan too.

Moki
MODERN ITALIAN €

(☑ 347 0431426; www.moki-trento.it; Via Malpaga 20; meals €28, Sat brunch €18; ⊗ 9am-8pm Mon, 9am-10pm Tue-Sat) A warren of bright white rooms, welcoming staff, new ideas and a stack of great magazines make Moki a perfect choice for breakfast, lunch or an *aperitivo* (if there's a bottle of the pink Revi Trento DOC open, don't say no). Dinners on Friday and Saturday nights begin with 'tapas'-style platters and the fresh, tasty mains always include a vegetarian option. Their cutely kitschy cocktails, at €4 to €6, are also worth popping in for.

Pedavena
PUB FOOD €

(☑ 0461 98 62 55; Piazza di Fiera 13; meals €22-35; ⊗ Wed-Mon 9am-midnight, Fri & Sat to 1am) Proudly crowd-pleasing and perennially popular, this sprawling 1920s beer hall (complete with fermenting brew in the corner) serves up the comfort food you'd expect in a studenty mountain town: bratwurst, schnitzel and steaming plates of polenta with mushroom stew and slabs of melty white *tosella* cheese.

★ Ai Tre Garofani
TRENTINO €€

(☑ 0461 23 75 43; www.aitregarofani.com; Via Mazzini 33; meals €38-45; ⊗ Mon-Sat 12.30-2pm & 7.30-10pm) While the low-beamed ceiling and deep drapery give a traditional vibe, the staff here deliver a dining experience full of new ideas and local flavours. Diners are welcomed with an *amuse-bouche* (perhaps a deer-and-yoghurt mousse) and house-made breads – milk and potato, spelt and seeded.

Mountain pine mugo scents a tagliatelle, while a hazelnut-crusted hare is accompanied by a dark cocoa sorbet and bitter-sweet roots and leaves. Wines are well chosen and, of course, local.

Il Libertino
ALPINE €€

(☑ 0461 26 00 85; www.ristoranteillibertino.com; Piazza Piedicastello 4-6; meals €30-38; ⊗ noon-2.30pm & 6.30-10.30pm Wed-Mon) Stroll the bridge over the fast-flowing Adige to this woody, hushed restaurant for carefully prepared traditional dishes. Think venison, chestnuts, radicchio, boar sausage and river trout, along with an encyclopedic wine list of Trentino DOCs.

Il Cappello
TRENTINO €€

(☑ 0461 23 58 50; www.osteriailcappello.it; Piazzetta Lunelli 5; meals €34-40; ⊗ noon-2.30pm & 7-10pm Tue-Sat, noon-3pm Sun) This intimate dining room has an unexpectedly rustic feel, with wooden beams and a terrace set in a quiet courtyard. The menu is Trentino to the core, and simple presentation makes the most of beautiful artisan produce. Wines, too, are local and rather special.

Scrigno del Duomo
GASTRONOMY, WINE BAR €€

(☑ 0461 22 00 30; www.scrignodelduomo.com; Piazza del Duomo 29; meals €35, degustation menus from €55; ⊗ wine bar 11am-2.30pm & 6-11pm, dining room 12.30-2.30pm & 7.30-10pm Tue-Sun, dinner only Sat) Trento's culinary and social epicentre is discreetly housed in a building dating back to the 1200s. For degustation dining take the stairs down to the formal restaurant, with its glassed-in Roman-era cellar. Or stay upstairs underneath the beautiful painted wooden ceiling, where there are simple, stylishly done local specialities.

Terra Mia
SEAFOOD €€

(☑ 0461 26 26 66; www.terramiaristorante.eu; Via Calepina 39; meals €35; ⊗ noon-3pm, 6.30-10.30pm Mon-Sat) A little escape to the Med in the mountains, this Sicilian-run restaurant is a friendly place. There's a trolley of freshly transported fish that you can choose to have grilled or fried or make a meal from the interesting menu of antipasti – say fish-stuffed eggplant – and seafood pastas.

★ **Locanda Margon** GASTRONOMY, TRENTINO €€€
(☑ 0461 34 94 01; www.locandamargon.it; Via Margone 15, Ravina; meals €40-70, gourmet degustation 4-/6-course €80/170) The Lunelli family who make Trento's Ferrari sparkling wines (p304) are also responsible for this gourmet eyrie perched among the vines in the Brenta Dolomites foothills. It's a thrilling drive up and a rather heady experience once you're there. Choose between the tiny, darkly glamorous gastronomic salon or the informal 'verandah', or just come for a suitably refined *aperitivo* with a view.

★ **Osteria a**
le Due Spade GASTRONOMY, TRENTINO €€€
(☑ 0461 234343; www.leduespade.com; Via Don Arcangelo Rizzi 11; meals €55, tasting menu €60, 2-course lunch menu €30; ⊙ 7.30-10pm Mon-Sat, noon-2pm Tue-Sat) You usually have to book ahead to secure a table at this tiny, vaulted place, but it's always worth braving the heavy door and drapes to see if they have a spare spot. The kitchen here really celebrates the local as well as giving you the options of a fish tasting menu with a great value two-course lunch deal, too.

🍷 **Drinking & Nightlife**

Locanda Gatto Gordo BAR
(www.facebook.com/locandadelgattogordo; Via Cavour 40; ⊙ 11.30am-midnight Tue-Thu, to 2am Fri & Sat) A central but very neighbourly bar which attracts a young, relaxed but not so studenty crowd. *Spritzes* and wine by the glass are well priced and there is a wide selection of 0km artisan beers.

Roccaforte BEER HALL
(☑ 0461 26 00 72; www.roccafortetrentina.com; Piazza Garzetti 20; ⊙ 10am-2am) There's a handful of German-style beers on tap as well as an extensive list by the bottle in this evocatively austere basement beer hall beneath the medieval Torre del Massarello. You also won't go hungry with a big menu of porky, cheesy, carby, meaty favourites.

Osteria della
Mal'Ombra BAR
(☑ 392 9932564; www.facebook.com/andrea. massarelli.56; Corso III Novembre 43; ⊙ 8.30am-12.30pm & 3.30pm-midnight Mon-Fri, 4pm-1am Sat) Join the university set for good wine and grappa, possibly some spirited political debate, and music on Tuesdays or other random nights.

Casa del Caffe CAFE
(☑ 0461 98 51 04; www.casadelcaffetn.it; Via San Pietro 38; ⊙ 7.30am-12.30pm & 3-7.30pm Mon-Sat) Follow your nose to this coffee bar and chocolate shop for Trento's best espresso. Beans are roasted on the premises and the crowded shelves feature some of the country's best boutique chocolates, sweets and biscotti.

🛍 **Shopping**

In-con-tro FASHION & ACCESSORIES
(☑ 0461 230 130; www.in-con-tro.com; Viale della Costituzione 37, MUSE area; ⊙ 3-7pm Mon, 11am-7pm Tue-Sat) The Trentini have a particular pared-back, intellectual elegance and this shop – the latest in three branches – encapsulates that style. It stocks global conceptual fashion from Marni, Martin Margela, Comme des Garçons et al, but come for the more interesting independent Italian labels or just a peek at its whimsical displays and enjoy a slice of torta and espresso in the in-store cafe.

Raccolta Differenziata FASHION & ACCESSORIES
(☑ 0461 26 12 92; Via Malpaga 16-18; ⊙ 3-7pm Mon, 11am-7pm Tue-Sat) Luigi Andreis has long been Trento's superstylist and it's worth seeking out his shop, tucked away in a quiet courtyard of an ancient palazzo from the 1400s, to experience his fascinating eye and treat yourself to one of the beautiful pieces from mostly Italian, or a few Belgian, designers.

ℹ **Information**

Società degli Alpinisti Tridentini (SAT; ☑ 0461 98 28 04; www.sat.tn.it; Palazzo Saracini Cresseri, Via Manci 57; ⊙ 9am-noon & 2-6pm Mon-Fri, to 7pm Thu, often afternoons only in winter) For walking information, including itineraries and *rifugi* in Trentino, contact the local Società degli Alpinisti Tridentini.

Tourist Office (☑ 0461 21 60 00; www.apt. trento.it; Piazza Dante 24; ⊙ 9am-7pm)

ℹ **Getting There & Away**

Trento is situated on the A22, which runs north from Verona to the Austrian border at the Brenner Pass. Regular trains leave from the main **train station** (Piazza Dante) for the following destinations:

Bologna (€23.75, 3¼ hours, every two hours)
Bolzano (€6.40, 30 minutes, every 20 minutes)
Venice (€11.20, 2½ hours, hourly)
Verona (€14.90, one hour, every 30 minutes)
Next door to the main station, the Trento–Malè–Marilleva train line connects the city with Cles in the Val di Non.

From the **InterCity bus station** (Via Andrea Pozzo), local bus company **Trentino Trasporti** (☑ 0461 82 10 00; www.ttesercizio.it) runs buses to and from Madonna di Campiglio, San Martino di Castrozza, Molveno, Canazei and Rovereto.

Rovereto

☑ 0464 / POP 37,550

In the winter of 1769, Leopold Mozart and his soon-to-be-famous musical son visited Rovereto and found it to be 'rich in diligent people engaged in viticulture and the weaving of silk'. The area is no longer known for silk, but still produces some outstanding wines, including the inky, cherry-scented Marzemino (the wine's scene-stealing appearance in *Don Giovanni* suggests it may have been a Mozart family favourite). Those on a musical pilgrimage come for the annual Mozart Festival in August and the town that Mozart knew still has its haunting, tightly coiled historic-centre streets. But it's the shock of the new that now lures most: Rovereto is home to one of Italy's best contemporary and 20th-century art museums.

★ **Museo di Arte Moderna e Contemporanea Rovereto**   GALLERY
(MART; ☑ 0464 43 88 87; http://english.mart.trento.it; Corso Bettini 43; adult/reduced €11/7, incl Casa del Depero and Civica Trento €14/10; ⊙ 10am-6pm Tue-Thu, Sat & Sun, to 9pm Fri) The four-floor, 12,000-sq-m steel, glass and marble behemoth, care of the Ticinese architect Mario Botta, is both imposing and human in scale, with mountain light gently filling a central atrium from a soaring cupola. It's home to some huge 20th-century works, including Warhol's *Four Marilyns* (1962), several Picassos and a clutch of contemporary art stars, including Bill Viola, Kara Walker, Arnulf Rainer and a whopping great Anselm Keifer.

Italian work is, naturally, also well represented, with excellent pieces from Giacomo Balla, Giorgio Morandi, Giorgio de Chirico, Lucio Fontana and Piero Manzoni. Temporary exhibitions cast a broad net, from easygoing shows of Monet or Modigliani to cutting-edge contemporary surveys.

Casa del Depero   MUSEUM
(☑ 0464 43 18 13; www.mart.trento.it/casadepero; Via Portici 38; adult/reduced €7/4, incl MART & Civica Trento €14/10; ⊙ 10am-6pm Tue-Sun) Those Futurists were never afraid of a spot of self-aggrandisement and local lad Fortunato Depero was no exception. This self-designed museum was first launched shortly before his death in 1960, and was then restored and reopened by MART in recent years. The obsessions of early-20th-century Italy mix nostalgically, somewhat unnervingly, with a historic past – bold tapestries and machine-age-meets-troubadour-era furniture decorate a made-over medieval townhouse.

WAM International Mozart Festival   MUSIC
(www.wamrovereto.com; ⊙ May) The town's annual Mozart festival has become a reference point in the European classical-music scene over its two decades and attracts some stellar performers. Performances are held across Rovereteo, in homes, churches and gardens as well as the usual concert halls.

Osteria del Pettirosso   WINE BAR €€
(www.osteriadelpettirosso.com; Corso Bettini 24; snacks €5-9, meals €25; ⊙ 11am-3pm, 6pm-1am Mon-Sat) There's a moody downstairs dining room for evenings but during the day join locals for a blackboard menu of small-producer wines by the glass, a plate of cheese, a couple of *crostone all lardo* (toast pieces with cured pork fat), a big salad or one of the beautifully prepared local dishes such as fillet of pork perfumed with thyme and Garda lemon.

ⓘ Information

Tourist Office (☑ 0464 43 03 63; www.visitrovereto.it; Piazza Rosmini 16; ⊙ 9am-1pm & 2-6pm Mon-Sat, 10am-4pm Sun) The tourist office has lots of information on Rovereto, town maps and details of cycling trails.

Brenta Dolomites

The Brenta group lies like a rocky island to the west of the main Dolomite range. Protected by the Parco Naturale Adamello Brenta, these sharp, majestic peaks are well known among mountaineers for their sheer cliffs and tricky ascents. They are home to some of the world's most famous *vie ferrate* (trails with permanent cables and ladders), including the Via Ferrata delle Bocchette, pioneered by trailblazing British climber Francis Fox Tuckett in the 1860s.

On the densely forested western side of the Brenta group is the popular resort of Madonna di Campiglio, while on the eastern side is the Altipiano della Paganella, a high plateau offering some skiing and a huge range of outdoor adventures. The wiggly S421, S237 and S239 linking the two make for some scenic driving.

Parco Naturale
Adamello Brenta   PARK

(www.pnab.it; Casa del Parco, Lago Rosso, Tovel; ⊙10am-1pm 2-6pm Jun-Oct) FREE Parco Naturale Adamello Brenta is a wild and beautiful park encompassing more than 80 lakes and the vast Adamello glacier, which was once home to the Alps' only brown bears. Although this became a protected area in 1967, by then bear numbers had dwindled to just three. Beginning in 1999, park authorities set about reintroducing Alpine brown bears from Slovenia. The first cubs were born in the park in 2002 and more are born every winter.

Bears aside, the 620-sq-km park – Trentino's largest protected area – is home to ibexes, red deer, marmots, chamois and 82 bird species, along with 1200 different mountain flowers, including two (*Nigritella buschmannie* and *Erysimum auranthiacum*) that are unique to the area. This wildlife thrives around the banks of Lago di Tovel, set deep in a forest some 30km north of Spormaggiore in the park's heart. An easy one-hour walking trail encircles the once red lake. The lakeside visitors centre has extensive information on other walks.

ℹ Getting There & Away

Ferrovia Trento–Malè (☑ 0463 90 11 50; www.ttesercizio.it) Ferrovia Trento-Malè has frequent services to Cles (€3.30, 45 minutes) and Malè (€5.10, 1½ hours, eight daily), which continue to Dimaro and Marilleva (€5.50).

Altipiano della Paganella

ELEV 2098M

Less than an hour's drive northwest of Trento, this dress-circle plateau looks out onto the towering Brenta Dolomites. The Altipiano incorporates five small villages: ski resort **Fai della Paganella**, touristy **Andalo**, lakeside **Molveno** and little **Cavedago** and **Spormaggiore**.

⊙ Sights & Activities

Paganella Ski Area   SKIING

(www.paganella.net; Cima Paganella) The Paganella ski area is accessible from Andalo by cable car and Fai della Paganella by chairlift. It has two cross-country skiing trails and 50km of downhill ski slopes, ranging from beginner-friendly green runs to the heart-pounding black.

Casa Museo
del Parco Orso   ANIMAL SANCTUARY

(☑ 0461 65 36 22; www.parcofaunistico.tn.it/sito/museo-parco-orso; Spormaggiore; adult/reduced €3/2; ⊙9am-12.30pm & 2-6pm Tue-Sun Jul-Sep, openings for other periods on website) Part of the larger **Parco Faunistico**, this is *the* place to see the Parco Naturale Adamello Brenta's 20-odd population of brown bears. There are cute displays for kids, and you can book to see the bears in winter dormancy via infrared camera. It's 15km northeast of Molveno.

🛏 Sleeping

★ Agriturismo Florandonole   FARMSTAY €

(☑ 0461 58 10 39; www.florandonole.it; Via ai Dossi 22, Fai della Paganella; d €110; P🐾) ⟋ This modern farmhouse may look like every other from the outside. Inside, however, smart local-wood furniture and crisp goosedown duvets give this place a luxury feel. If the views over fields towards the Brenta Dolomites or Paganella ranges beckon, grab a complimentary mountain bike. This is also a working **honey farm**, with hives, production facilities and a shop to explore.

Camping Spiaggia   CAMPGROUND €

(☑ 0461 58 69 78; www.campingmolveno.it; Via Lungolago 25, Molveno; camping €45-52, bungalow €80-144; ⊙reception 9am-noon & 2-7pm year-round; P@☀) These pleasant sites on the shores of Lago di Molveno come with free use of the neighbouring outdoor pool, tennis court and table tennis. It's an easy stroll into Molveno's bustling village centre, and entertainment and water sports are on tap in high summer.

🍽 Eating

Al Penny   TRENTINO, PIZZA €€

(☑ 0461 58 52 51; Viale Trento 23, Andalo; meals €30; ⊙11am-2.30pm & 5pm-midnight) First impressions may clock the decor as a little too Alpine-for-dummies, but this is a genuinely cosy spot. A glass of warming Marzemino sets the scene, then out come authentic and tasty Trentino specialities – venison *ragù* (meat and tomato sauce) with pine nuts, *taiadele smalzade* (pan-fried fat noodles) or mushroom *canederli*, all served with homemade bread. The pizza also rates.

ℹ Information

Andalo Tourist Office (☑ 0461 58 58 36; www.visitdolomitipaganella.it; Piazza Dolomiti 1,

Andalo; ⊘ 9am-12.30pm & 3-6.30pm Mon-Sat, 9.30am-12.30pm Sun) The main office on the Altipiano della Paganella, with good information for both winter and summer activities.

Madonna di Campiglio & Pinzolo

Welcome to the Dolomites' bling belt, Madonna di Campiglio, where ankle-length furs are standard après-ski wear and the formidable downhill runs often a secondary concern to the social whirl and Michelin-starred dining. Austrian royalty set the tone in the 19th century, in particular Franz Joseph and wife Elisabeth (Sissi). This early celeb patronage is commemorated in late February, when fireworks blaze and costumed pageants waltz through town for the annual **Habsburg Carnival**.

Despite the traffic jams and mall-like hotel complexes, the town is still charming, overlooked by a pretty stone church and the jutting battlements of the Brenta Dolomites beyond. In summer this is an ideal base for hikers and *via ferrata* enthusiasts.

Pinzolo (population 2000, elevation 800m), in a lovely valley 16km south, misses out on the most spectacular views but has a lively historic centre and quite a lot fewer tickets on itself.

◉ Sights & Activities

Val di Genova   AREA
North of Pinzolo is the entrance to the Val di Genova, often described as one of the Alps' most beautiful valleys. It's great walking country, lined with a series of spectacular waterfalls. Four mountain huts strung out along the valley floor make overnight stays an option – Pinzolo's tourist office has details.

Chiesa di San Vigilio   CHURCH
(Via San Vigilio; ⊘ 9.30-11.30am & 3.30-5pm Tue-Sat, 3.30-5pm Sun, Jun-Oct) Pinzolo's beautifully sited 16th-century Chiesa di San Vigilio merits a visit for its setting, yes, but even more for its *danza macabra* (dance of death) decor.

Funivie Madonna di Campiglio   CABLE CAR
(☑ 0465 44 77 44; www.funiviecampiglio.it; round-trip summer €8.80-13.40, various single-run and pass prices winter) A network of cable cars takes skiers and boarders from Madonna to its numerous ski runs and a snowboarding park in winter and to walking and mountain-biking trails in summer. In Campo Carlo Magno, 2km north of Madonna, the

Cabinovia Grostè takes walkers to the Passo Grostè (2440m), and Brenta's most famous *via ferrata*, the **Via Bocchetta di Tuckett** (trail No 305), leaves from its upper station.

Funivia Pinzolo   CABLE CAR
(☑ 0465 50 12 56; www.doss.to; Via Nepomuceno Bolognini 84; one-way/return summer €6.50/10; ⊘ 8.30am-12.30pm & 2-6pm mid-Dec–Apr & Jun–mid-Sep) This cable car climbs to the 2100m-high **Doss del Sabion**, stopping at midstation **Pra Rodont** en route. Mountain-bike hire is available.

🛌 Sleeping

Camping Parco Adamello   CAMPGROUND €
(☑ 0465 50 17 93; www.campingparcoadamello.it; Localita Magnabò, Pinzolo; camping €40, apt s/d €45/90; ⊘ year-round; ℗) Beautifully situated within the national park 1km north of Pinzolo, this campground is a natural starting point for outdoor adventures such as skiing, snowshoeing, walking and biking. Weekly rates are cheaper and 5-day stays obligatory in July and August.

Chalet Fogajard   AGRITURISMO €€
(www.chaletfogajard.it; Località Fogajard 36, Madonna di Campiglio; d €195; 🕿) 🥾 If you're looking for a mountain retreat, this six-room Alpine idyll will fit the bill. Its remote location, down a steep dirt track way south of Madonna's resort row, is stupefyingly beautiful and blissfully silent. Rooms have a craft ethos that seems from another era and an atmospheric dining room delivers hearty, wholesome, locally sourced meals.

DV Chalet   DESIGN HOTEL €€€
(☑ 0465 44 31 91; www.dvchalet.it; Via Castelletto Inferiore 10, Madonna di Campiglio; d €320; ℗ ✳ 🛜 🐾) The most fashionable of Madonna's ultraluxe hotels, DV is a surprisingly relaxed place with friendly staff and a quiet, wooded setting. The bar keeps the Milanese fashion set happy come *aperitivo* hour, there's a worthy Michelin-starred restaurant, Dolomieu, and once upstairs guests are cocooned in beautiful, earthy rooms.

🍴 Eating & Drinking

Le Roi   ALPINE €
(☑ 0465 44 30 75; www.ristoranteleroicampiglio.com; Via Cima Tosa 40, Madonna di Campiglio; meals €25, pizza €6-13; ⊘ noon-3pm & 6-11pm) Touristy, tick, loud and raucous, tick. Yes, this is a typical ski-town restaurant, but it's fun, friendly and affordable. The polenta,

mushrooms and fried-cheese platter won't win any prizes for presentation, either, but it is an unbeatable post-piste belly warmer and served with good cheer.

Il Convivio
GASTRONOMY €€€
(☑ 0465 44 01 00; www.alpensuitehotel.it; Viale Dolomiti di Brenta 84; meals €65, set menu €85; ☺ 7-9.30pm Mon-Sat) Places like Convivio are what Madonna is all about – return guests and long-held traditions – and while it won't win any prizes for the decor, the food here is carefully prepared and a great showcase of local produce. Risotto comes scented with pine, there are eggs done with pumpkin and truffle, and even the beef in the carpaccio is the Trentini Rendena breed.

ℹ Information

Madonna Tourist Office (☑ 0465 44 75 01, www.campigliodolomiti.it; Via Pradalago 4; ☺ 9am-12.30pm & 2-7pm; reduced hours low season) Madonna's tourist office teams up with the Parco Naturale Adamello-Brenta in high summer to run guided thematic walks.
Pinzolo Tourist Office (☑ 0465 50 10 07; www.campigliodolomiti.it; Piazza S Giacomo; ☺ 9am-12.30pm & 2-7pm)

ℹ Getting There & Away

Madonna di Campiglio and Pinzolo are accessible by **Trentino Trasporti** (☑ 0461 82 10 00; www.ttesercizio.it) bus from Trento (€7.10, 1½ hours, five daily), Brescia (€13.90, 1½ hours, one daily) and Milan (€25, 3¾ hours, one daily).

From mid-December to mid-April, the **Flyski** (☑ 0461 39 11 11; www.flyskishuttle.com; transfers from €35) shuttle runs weekly services to Madonna and Pinzolo from Verona, Bergamo, Treviso and Venice airports, as well as Trento's train station.

Val di Non

The first thing you notice about Val di Non is the apple trees – their gnarly, trellised branches stretch for miles, and in spring their fragrant blossoms scent the air. Craggy castles dot the surrounding rises, including the stunning Castel Thun. The valley is centred on **Cles**, whose tourist office is just off the main road through town.

Italy's apple giant, Melinda, is a valley girl. A couple of villages on from Cles, near Mollaro, Melinda Mondo conducts tours of the orchards and processing plants and has a cheery shop selling apples and all sorts of apple-related products. Look out also for the big cheese next door, the home of Trentin-

grana, Trentino's sweet, subtle 'Parmesan-style' Grana.

Castel Thun
CASTLE
(☑ 0461 49 28 29; www.buonconsiglio.it; Vigo di Ton; adult/reduced €8/6; ☺ 10am-5pm Tue-Sun) This stunning Gothic castle, some of it dating to the 1250s, occupies a panoramic position and typifies the region's architectural style.

Melinda Mondo
ORCHARD, SHOP
(☑ 0463 46 92 99; www.melinda.it; Via della Cooperazione 21; ☺ 8.30am-12.30pm & 3-7pm, guided visits Oct-Jun) On Val di Non's southern limits, you can watch videos, taste apples, take cooking lessons and tour the apple-processing plant of Melinda Mondo, famed for its golden delicious apples. Or you can just pick up some of the fruity products in the cheerful factory shop.

ℹ Information
Val di Non Tourist Office (☑ 0463 42 28 83; Corso Dante 30, Cles; ☺ 9am-12.30pm & 3-6pm Mon-Sat, 9am-noon Sun Jul & Aug)

Val di Sole

Leaving Cles in the rearview mirror, the apple orchards draw you west into the aptly named Val di Sole (Valley of the Sun) tracing the course of the foaming river Noce, with its charming main town of **Malè**. This valley is renowned for the full complement of outdoor pursuits and is popular with young Trentini. The Noce offers great rafting and fishing.

Dolomiti di Brenta Bike
CYCLING
(☑ 0465 70 26 26; www.dolomitibrentabike.it; €15 per stage) Val di Sole guards a flattish 35km section of the Brenta Dolomite Bike Loop and there is a special bike train June to September, allowing cyclists to step on and alight when they wish.

Cicli Andreis
CYCLING
(☑ 0463 90 28 22; www.andreissnc.com; Via Conci 19, Malè; ☺ 8.30am-noon & 3-7pm Mon-Sat) Offering a huge range of bikes for hire, and friendly, knowledgeable service, Cicli Andreis is handily located just off Malè's main street. Daily/weekly mountain-bike rental costs from €20/55.

Dolomiti Camping Village
CAMPGROUND €
(☑ 0463 97 43 32; www.campingdolomiti.com; Via Gole 105, Dimaro; camping €48, d apt €90;

⊗mid-May–mid-Oct & Dec-Easter; P@⊠) Riverside and adjacent to the rafting centre, the well-kept campsites and bungalows come with access to a wellness centre, indoor and outdoor pools, volleyball courts and trampolines.

Agritur il Tempo delle Mele FARMSTAY €€
(⊠0463 95 58 401; www.agriturdellemele.it; Via Strada Provinciale 65, Caldes; s/d €95/150; P⊠) ✈ This family-owned farm offers both bright, comfortable, modern rooms and easy access to the Folgarida-Marilleva and Pejo 3000 ski areas, from where you can ski on to Madonna di Campiglio. Prices drop out of winter high season.

ℹ Information

Malè Tourist Office (⊠0463 90 12 80; www. valdisole.net; Piazza Regina Elena 19; ⊗3-7pm Mon-Sat) Has good information on the entire Val di Sole and can advise you on ski facilities and walking trails in nearby Stelvio (p321).

Val di Rabbi

POP 1450

Narrow, deep green Val di Rabbi is a refreshingly tranquil and picturesquely rustic Alpine valley that provides the best southern entry into Parco Nazionale dello Stelvio (p321). Europeans come here for the supposedly curative Antica Fonte spring waters; the Terme di Rabbi offers a wide range of traditional treatments and is administered by the suitably grand **Grand Hotel Rabbi** (⊠0463 98 30 50; www.grandhotelrabbi. it; Fonti di Rabbi 153; half-board d €85; ⊗May-Sep; P⊠). Next door is a small visitors centre and the starting point for a network of paths into Stelvio, some of which connect to Val Martello in Alto Adige.

Terme di Rabbi THERMAL BATHS
(⊠0463 98 30 00; www.termedirabbi.it; Località Fonti di Rabbi 162; baths from €32; ⊗8.30am-noon & 4-7pm Mon-Sat, 5-7pm Sun Jul & Aug) Europeans come to his remote spa to take the supposedly curative Antica Fonte spring waters; a wide range of traditional treatments are available.

ℹ Information

Val di Rabbi Visitors Centre (⊠0463 98 51 90; www.valdirabbi.com; Località Còler; ⊗8.30am-1pm & 3-7pm Thu-Tue Jun-Sep, 9am-noon & 2-5pm Oct-May)

SOUTH TYROL (SÜDTIROL)

Bolzano (Bozen)

⊠0471 / POP 105,700 / ELEV 265M

Bolzano, the provincial capital of South Tyrol (known within the province as Südtirol, or in Italy as Alto Adige), is anything but provincial. Once a stop on the coach route between Italy and the flourishing Austro-Hungarian Empire, this small city is worldly and engaged, a long-time conduit between cultures. Its quality of life – one of the highest in Italy – is reflected in its openness, youthful energy and an all-pervading greenness. A stage-set-pretty backdrop of grassy, rotund hills sets off rows of pastel-painted townhouses, while bicycles ply riverside paths and wooden market stalls are laid out with Alpine cheese, *speck* (cured ham) and dark, seeded loaves. German may be the first language of 95% of the region, but Bolzano is an anomaly. Today its Italian-speaking majority – a legacy of Mussolini's brutal Italianisation program of the 1920s and the more recent siren call of education and employment opportunities – looks both north and south for inspiration.

◉ Sights

★**Museo Archeologico dell'Alto Adige** MUSEUM
(⊠0471 32 01 00; www.iceman.it; Via Museo 43; adult/reduced €9/7; ⊗10am-6pm Tue-Sun) The star of the Museo Archeologico dell'Alto Adige is Ötzi, the Iceman, with almost the entire museum being given over to the Copper Age mummy. Kept in a temperature-controlled 'igloo' room, he can be viewed through a small window (peer closely enough and you can make out faintly visible tattoos on his legs). Ötzi's clothing – a wonderful get-up of patchwork leggings, rush-matting cloak and fur cap – and other belongings are also displayed.

Museion GALLERY
(⊠0471 22 34 13; www.museion.it; Via Dante 2; adult/reduced €7/3.50, from 6pm Thu free; ⊗10am-6pm Tue-Sun, to 10pm Fri) Bolzano's contemporary art space is housed in a huge multifaceted glass cube, a brave architectural surprise that beautifully vignettes the old-town rooftops and surrounding mountains from within. There's an impres-

Bolzano

Bolzano

sive permanent collection of international art work and it's especially strong on photography; temporary shows are a testament to the local art scene's vibrancy, or often highlight an ongoing dialogue with artists and institutions from Austria and Germany. The river-facing cafe has a terrace perfect for a post-viewing *spritz*.

BZ '18-'45   MUSEUM
(☎324 5810106; www.monumenttovictory.com; Piazza Vittoria; ⊙11am-1pm & 2pm-5pm Tue & Wed, Fri-Sun, 3-9pm Thu summer, 10.30am-12.30pm & 2.30-4.30pm Tue-Sun winter) **FREE** This dense but visually seductive museum explores Bolzano's turbulent interwar years via the history of the Fascist Monument to Victory, where it is sited. It's a thoughtful and

overdue examination of a highly complex time in the city's past and covers the city's post-WWI handover to Italy and the later Nazi occupation. The displays on the radical urban transformation of the 1920s – the enduring face of Mussolini's 'Italianisation' project – are particularly fascinating.

Messner Mountain Museum Firmian
MUSEUM

(MMM Firmian; ☑0471 63 12 64; www.messner-mountain-museum.it; Via Castel Firmiano 53; adult/reduced €10/8; ⊙10am-6pm Fri-Wed late-Mar–mid-Nov) The imposing Castel Firmiano, dating back to AD 945, is the centrepiece of mountaineer Reinhold Messner's six museums. Based around humankind's relationship with the mountains across all cultures, the architecture itself suggests the experience of shifting altitudes, and requires visitors to traverse hundreds of stairs and mesh walkways. The collection is idiosyncratic, but when it works, it's heady stuff. Messner's other museums are scattered across the region, including his newest, at Corones (p331), and his most remote, at Ortles (p321).

Castel Roncolo
CASTLE

(Schloss Runkelstein; ☑0471 32 98 08; www.runkelstein.info; Via San Antonio 15; adult/child €8/5.50; ⊙10am-6pm Tue-Sun, to 5pm Nov-Mar) This stunningly located castle was built in 1237 but is renowned for its vivid 14th-century frescoes. These are particularly rare, with themes that are drawn from secular literature, including the tale of Tristan and Isolde, as well as depictions of day-to-day courtly life. In summer a free shuttle runs from Piazza Walther – ask at the tourist

office (p318) for the schedule – or catch suburban bus 12 or 14.

Chiesa dei Domenicani
CHURCH

(Piazza Domenicani; ⊙9.30am-6pm Mon-Sat) **FREE** The cloisters and chapel here feature touching, vibrant 14th-century frescoes by school-of-Giotto artists.

🏃 Activities

Bolzano's trio of *funivie* (cable cars) whisk you up out of the city, affording spectacular views over the city and valley floor, then of terraced vineyards, tiny farms, ancient mountain chapels and towering peaks beyond. The respective villages might be delightful destinations in themselves but they are also a great jumping off point for rambles or serious hikes. Walks can also be done from the city centre – ask at the tourist office (p318) for a comprehensive map marked with all the easily accessible routes.

★Salewa Cube
CLIMBING

(☑0471 188 68 67; www.salewa-cube.com; Via Waltraud-Gebert-Deeg, Bolzano Sud; adult/reduced €13/10; ⊙9am-11pm) Part of the outdoor-clothing empire's HQ, this is Italy's largest indoor-climbing centre. There are over 2000 sq m of climbing surface and 180 different routes. In good weather the enormous entrance is open, so climbing has an outdoor feel. Take bus 10A/B from the centre or ask at the tourist office (p318) for details of the summer shuttle.

Funivia del Renon
CABLE CAR

(Rittner Seilbahn; www.ritten.com; Via Renon; one way/return €6/10; ⊙6.30am-10.45pm) The long journey over the Renon (Ritten) plateau to

---

MEET ÖTZI THE ICEMAN

When Austrian hikers stumbled upon a human corpse wedged into a melting glacier on Hauslabjoch pass in 1991, they assumed they'd found the remains of an unfortunate mountaineer caught in a winter storm. But when the mummified body was removed and taken to a morgue, it was discovered to be more than 5300 years old.

The male corpse – subsequently nicknamed Ötzi, or the Iceman – is the oldest mummified remains ever found in Europe, dating from an ancient Copper Age civilisation that lived in the Dolomites around the same time as ancient Egypt's founding. What Ötzi was actually doing 3200m up a glaciated mountainside, 52 centuries before alpinism became a serious sport, is still a matter of some debate.

Though initially claimed by the Austrian government, it was later ascertained that Ötzi had been unearthed 100m inside the Italian border on the Schnalstal (Val Senales) glacier. After a brief diplomatic impasse and stabilisation work in Innsbruck, the mummy was returned to Italy, where it has been on display in Bolzano's Museo Archeologico dell'Alto Adige (p312) since 1998.

Soprabolzano (Oberbozen) runs along the world's longest single track, stretching for 4.56km, passing over eerie red-earth pyramids and farm-, vine- and spire-dotted valleys.

Funivia San Genesio CABLE CAR
(Seilbahn Jenesien; www.sii.bz.it; Via Sarentino; one-way/return €3/5; ⊙8am-7pm) An ultra-steep ascent takes you to the beautiful terraced village of San Genesio (Jenesien), where there are roof-of-the-world views and forest trails to follow.

Funivia del Colle CABLE CAR
(Kohlererbahn; Via Campegno 4; one way/return €4/6.50; ⊙7-11am, noon-7pm Mon-Fri, to 5pm Sat) This is the world's oldest cable car, dreamt up by a canny inn-keeper in 1908, with a pristine village awaiting at the top. Check website for Sunday and holiday running times.

Bike Rental CYCLING
(☑0471 99 75 78; Via della Stazione 2; ⊙7.30am-7.45pm Mon-Sat Easter-Oct) FREE Bicycles can be picked up at the open-air bike rental stall near the train station. Rental is free, but bikes must be returned overnight and you'll need cash for a deposit plus ID.

Alpine Information Office WALKING
(Alpenverein Südtirol; ☑0471 81 41 55; www.alpen verein.it; Via Giotto 3; ⊙9am-noon, 1-5pm Mon-Thu, 9am-noon Fri) A mountaineering and serious hiking organisation that provides information about various routes and mountain huts, and can direct you to guides and equipment suppliers.

🛏 Sleeping

Villa Anita GUESTHOUSE €
(www.villaanitabolzano.it; Via Castel Roncolo 16; d/family without bathroom €70/79; P 🖥) Although it's just a short walk from the historic centre, the surrounding gardens make this beautiful 1905 villa seem like you're already out in the countryside. Rooms are spacious and light, the shared bathrooms are modern and spotlessly maintained and the owner is gracious and kind. You can pay a little extra for a room with a balcony or for their spacious self-catering apartment.

Goethe Guesthouse GUESTHOUSE €
(☑335 8258599, 070 58 38 346; www.booking bolzano.com; Via Goethe 28; s €75-90, d €85-110, no breakfast) If you don't mind hopping down the stairs to a *pasticceria* or the market for breakfast and don't need front desk or

other hotel facilities, Ivan and Marco's historic townhouse rooms are super stylish. Contemporary furnishings are minimal but comfortable, while floorboards, subtle lighting and dramatic exposed stone adds atmosphere. Check-in is DIY or at Booking Bolzano's central office.

Youth Hostel Bolzano HOSTEL €
(Jugendherberge Bozen; ☑0471 30 08 65; www.bozen.jugendherberge.it; Via Renon 23; dm/s €23.50/32; 🖥) The three- and four-bed dorms in this airy and friendly hostel are well designed and configured for privacy. Single rooms can squeeze in a fold-out if needed. Rooms at the back have balconies, but sadly no longer any view.

Hotel Greif DESIGN HOTEL €€
(☑0471 31 80 00; www.greif.it; Piazza Walther; s/d €100/195; 🖥🖥) Tumbling golden text courtesy of the troubled poet Ezra Pound greets you in the stairwell (this was, it seems, an 'art hotel' long before its modern makeover). Rooms here are generously proportioned, full of light and richly draped; all include a bath. Guests can use the lush gardens at parent Parkhotel Laurin (p315), just down the lane, for cocktails or a swim.

Lauben Haus APARTMENT €€
(www.bookingbolzano.com; Via Portici 53; apt €150-210) High above the city's ancient arcaded-shopping street, these apartments combine interesting historical-architectural details with comfortable and stylish contemporary furniture in soothing natural tones. There's a variety of views, sizes and configurations; check the website for individual photos. Check-in is at the central Booking Bolzano office.

Booking Bolzano ACCOMMODATION SERVICES €€
(☑0471 98 00 23; www.bookingbolzano.com; Via Piave 7b) An ever-expanding local alternative to both hotels and Airbnb, Booking Bolzano has a growing collection of stylish, pristinely maintained apartments scattered through the historic centre of town. Staff are consummate professionals and, while prices, sizes and decor differ, they are all great value.

★Parkhotel Laurin HOTEL €€€
(☑0471 31 10 00; www.laurin.it; Via Laurin 4; s €95-125, d €130-250; P 🖥🖥🖥) Set in its own lush gardens in the centre of town, this five-star hotel has large rooms endowed with a weighty, old-fashioned opulence and staff

TRENTINO & SOUTH TYROL BOLZANO (BOZEN)

that mesh haute-professionalism with relaxed Alpine charm. There's a distinct individual style and contemporary sensibility throughout, though, with an idiosyncratic mix of original artworks, Tyrolean antiques and 1980s Memphis pieces.

The splendid ground floor is home to what's considered one of Bolzano's best **restaurants** and a dark baronial **bar** that bustles from early morning to late at night; beyond the window is a park-like garden for summer drinks or a dip.

Hotel Belvedere HOTEL €€€
(📞0471 35 41 27; www.belvedere-hotel.it; Pichl 15, San Genesio; d half-board €300) Ten minutes from Bolzano by cable car, the location of this stylish but unpretentious 'hiking hotel' is otherworldly. It offers a number of wellness-themed programs (stays of three nights plus are cheaper, too) but you could just hole up with a book, eat yourself silly, with the occasional swim in the infinity pool, hike or massage to break the exquisite monotony.

✕ Eating

Redolent of rural mountain life one minute, Habsburg splendour the next, Bolzano's restaurants – often in the guise of a traditional wood-panelled dining room called a *stube* – are a profound reminder of just how far north of Rome you've come.

★ Stars BURGERS €
(📞0471 324 507; www.stars-burgers.com; Piazza della Erbe 39; ⊙noon-10pm Mon-Fri, to 11pm Fri & Sat, to 6pm Sun) ⦿ This may look like another of the world's hipster burger places but the people behind this (and its Merano sibling) have serious culinary credentials, including local Michelin-starred chef Theodor Falser. Burgers are made with beef from one local farmer-butcher, minced twice daily, vegetables are all '0km', sauces are house-made and the bread is long-risen and all soft drinks and beers are from artisan producers.

Vögele ALPINE €
(📞0471 97 39 38; Via Goethe 3; meals €25-40; ⊙noon-4pm & 6-11pm) Dating back to 1277 and owned by the same family since 1840, this multilevel antique-stuffed restaurant is well loved for its schnitzels and steaks along with local favourites risotto with rabbit *ragù* and rosemary, or jugged venison with polenta. There are some good vegetarian options and much of the produce is organic. The attached bar is pleasantly rowdy, too.

Gasthaus Fink ALPINE €
(📞0471 97 50 47; Via della Mostra 9; meals €20-25; ⊙noon-2pm & 7-9.30pm Thu-Mon, noon-2pm Wed) Fink's dining room is a calm, contemporary take on *stube* style where you can fill up on local comfort food that's cooked with care, including a €15 nightly special. A great lunch choice, with pasta and *canederli* (dumplings) under €12.

★ Zur Kaiserkron ALPINE €€
(📞0471 98 02 14; www.kaiserkron.bz; Piazza della Mostra 2; meals €45-50, lunch special 2/3 courses €30/35; ⊙noon-2.30pm & 7-9.30pm Mon-Sat) Refined but unfussy takes on regional favourites fill the menu at this calm and elegant dining room, and excellent produce is allowed to shine. It's tempting to just choose a selection from the interesting starters – say, spelt ravioli with fresh curd-cheese or mountain-lentil soup with *speck* chips – but the meaty mains are also particularly well executed.

Sweetly efficient staff are happy to guide you, as well as provide excellent advice on the wine list's hyperlocal labels.

Anita ALPINE €€
(📞0471 97 37 60; Piazza delle Erbe 5; meals €36; ⊙noon-2.30pm Mon-Sat, 6.30-9.30pm Mon-Fri) A super-traditional place with a two cosy wood-clad rooms that has become the ironic favourite with Bolzano's cool kids. Come for all the South Tyrol standards: goulash, dumplings, roasts and a killer spinach *spätzle*.

Löwengrube
ALPINE €€

(☑0471 970032; www.loewengrube.it; Piazza Dogana 3; meals €40, 6-course tasting menu €60; ⊙11am-midnight Mon-Sat) A 16th-century *stube* is the surprise design element in an otherwise super-modern, glamorous fit-out. The menu ranges across local and Mediterranean dishes, and its combinations and presentation push boundaries, as well as borders.

The wine list is extensive and very well priced, but don't miss a peek at the cellar (dating back to 1280). It holds a vast collection that honours international-name vineyards as well as local micro-producers (drink in with a modest corkage of €10).

🍷 Drinking & Nightlife

Bolzano after dark may come as a surprise. The pristine city centre is often hushed at 8pm, but it's a different story round midnight. Follow the locals heading for Piazza delle Erbe's bar strip or the beer halls – including local Forst and the Bavarian Paulaner along Via Argentieri and Via Goethe. A younger local crowd frequents the bars across the river in the 'Italian town'.

★Thaler Champagne Bar
WINE BAR

(☑0471 31 30 30; www.thaler.bz.it; Via Portici 69; ⊙10am-8pm Mon-Sat) On the top floor of Bolzano's luxe perfumerie and skincare department store, this dark and glamorous little bar is a great place to celebrate a good day on the slopes or up a mountain. There are wines by the glass and sparklings from both France and local producers in Trentino and Franciacorta.

★Franzbar
WINE BAR

(☑0471 30 02 52; Via Leonardo da Vinci 1; ⊙8am-1pm Mon-Sat) A local favourite that straddles the wine-bar/beer-hall and student/grown-up divides. Come for a groaning *stuzzichini* (snack) at lunch or the same at *aperitivo* hour, or pop in late for a rowdier scene.

Temple Bar
IRISH PUB

(☑388 3684746; www.facebook.com/templebar bz; Piazza Domenicani 20; ⊙10.30am-1am Tue-Sat, 3pm-1am Sun & Mon) Tanya and Stephen's little slice of Dublin has been awarded a coveted 'best Irish pub outside Ireland' title. While it's Irish to the core with welcoming staff, pints and big matches on the big screen, it's also quintessentially Bolzanino, with great *spritzes*, wine and a gang of hiking-, skiing- and sports-mad locals ready to offer up tips and advice to visitors.

Batzen-bräu
PUB

(☑0471 05 09 50; www.batzen.it; Via Andreas Hofer 30; ⊙10am-midnight) A mash of traditional and contemporary architecture makes for many different moods as you elbow your way from one end to the next. A beer garden is welcome during flash Bolzano heatwaves and a basement theatre space turns into a nightclub on weekends. You can also eat suitably beery dishes here at lunch or dinner.

Enovit
WINE BAR

(☑0471 97 04 60; Via Dott Streiter 30; ⊙10am-1pm & 3.30-8.30pm Mon-Fri, 10am-1pm Sat) An older, well-dressed lot frequents this warm, woody corner bar and shop for expertly recommended, generously poured local wine by the glass. If there's a crowd – and on Fridays there *always* is – it kicks on past demarcated closing.

Il Baccaro
WINE BAR

(☑0471 97 14 21; Via Argentieri 17; ⊙8am-2pm Mon-Sat, 7-9pm Mon-Fri) Scurry down the cobbled passageway and poke your nose into this wonderful wine burrow, with delightful hosts and a good blackboard selection of regional and pan-Italian wines. *Stuzzichini* (snacks) are a euro or two and made to order.

Fischbänke
WINE BAR

(☑340 5707468; Via Dott Streiter 26; ⊙noon-sunset Mon-Fri) Local wines and bruschetta (from €7) care of bon vivant Cobo at the old outdoor fish market; pull up a stool at one of the original marble-slab counters.

Sunrise
WINE BAR

(☑0471 97 52 61; Piazza delle Erbe 46; ⊙4pm-1am Tue-Sat) A grown-up alternative to the more raucous Piazza delle Erbe usuals, but one that's also open late. Kind and welcoming staff ply you with local wines and cheese under vaulted ceilings.

Nadamas
BAR

(☑0471 98 06 84; www.ristorantenadamas.it; Piazza delle Erbe 43; ⊙Mon-Sat 9am-1am) Bolzano's party reputation got started at this Piazza delle Erbe veteran. If you can make it through the animated front-bar crowd, there are tables and a tapas menu out back.

Hopfen & Co
PUB

(☑0471 30 07 88; Piazza delle Erbe 17; ⊙9.30am-1am Mon-Sat) The dark bar is the perfect stage for sampling the cloudy, unfiltered beer that's brewed on the premises. This 800-year-old inn also serves up hearty portions of traditional dishes like sauerkraut and sausages cooked in ale (meals €16 to €24).

ⓘ Information

Tourist Office (☑ 0471 30 70 00; www. bolzano-bozen.it; Via Alto Adige 60; ☺9am-7pm Mon-Fri, 9.30am-6pm Sat year-round, 10am-3pm Sun summer)

ⓘ Getting There & Away

Bolzano's tiny **airport** (Aeroporto di Bolzano; ☑ 0471 25 52 55; www.abd-airport.it; Via Baracca 1) is served by twice-daily flights from Rome on Etihad Regional and, seasonally, from Olbia.

Local **SAD** (☑ 840 000471, 0471 45 01 11; www.sad.it) buses leave from the **bus station** (Via Perathoner) for destinations throughout the province, including hourly routes to Val Gardena, Brunico and Merano. SAD buses also run to Cortina d'Ampezzo.

Bolzano's train station is connected by hourly or half-hourly trains with Merano (€5.60, 40 minutes), Trento (€7.10, 30 minutes) and Verona (€12.35, 2½ hours), with slightly less frequent connections to Bressanone (€6.95, 25 minutes) and Brunico (€12.35, 1½ hours) in the Val Pusteria. All regional trains within South Tyrol and right down to Trento are covered by the Museumobil card. Deutsche Bahn trains run to Innsbruck and Munich via Brennero and south to Venice.

Südtirol Weinstrasse

☑ 0471

You might only be an hour or so south of the Brenner pass, but there's no mistaking the Mediterranean vibe along South Tyrol's Weinstrasse, or the Strada del Vino. It begins northwest of Bolzano in Nals, meanders past Terlano (Terlan) through Upper Adige (Überetsch) and Lower Adige (Unterland) until it reaches Salorno (Salurn). Grapevines cover gentle rolling hills, fringed with palm trees and apple orchards. It's a gentle, relaxed place where you can taste the region's world-famous white wines made from native grape varieties (Lagrein, Vernatsch and Gewürztraminer) along with well-adapted imports pinot blanc, sauvignon, merlot and cabernet, or you can swim, windsurf or sun-worship at its central lake the Kalterer See, the warmest body of water in the region. Of course, glimpses of the mighty Dolomites at every turn will remind you that you're still in the Alps.

Kalterer See   LAKE
(Lago di Caldaro) The Weinstrasse's little Lake Kaltern may look rather small compared to Northern Italy's splendid collection of lakes, but up close it's a stunningly pretty little pond, fringed with old-style boat sheds, with walkways skirting over water lilies and lots of lakeside spots for lunch or a drink.

Summa   WINE
(☑ 0471 80 95 00; www.summa-al.eu; Piazza Santa Geltrude 10, Magrè; ☺ early Apr) ⏺ Possibly the world's most joyful, scenic and welcoming wine event, Alois Lageder's annual Summa is a must-do for both enthusiastic amateur imbibers and wine professionals alike. Held across several of the Lageder family's properties in a beautiful Weinstrasse village, it's both a treat for the eyes and for the palate. Producers are all from organic or biodynamic vineyards across Europe.

Seehotel Ambach   DESIGN HOTEL €€
(☑ 0471 96 00 98; www.seehotel-ambach.com; Campi al Lago 3, Kaltern; s/d half-board €140/240; ☺Apr-Oct; ⓟ ✳ ☎ ☞ ☲) This Othmar Barth-designed hotel dates to 1973 and is remarkably intact. Gentle revamping has not altered its fabulous 20th-century charm. All rooms from single to suite offer a view of the lake and feature design classics from 1920s Eileen Gray lamps to '60s Magistretti for FLOS to contemporary Italian and Scando pieces.

★ Das Wanda   BOUTIQUE HOTEL, B&B €€€
(☑ 0471 66 90 11; www.das-wanda.com; Via Garnellen 18, Kaltern; d €230-300, adults only; ⓟ ✳ ☎ ☲) Verena Huf is a third-gen hotelier and her gorgeous 12-suite place combines that rich lineage with youthful enthusiasm and a relaxed style. Rooms are spacious, clean-lined but deliciously cosy and all have huge bathrooms, balconies (some two) overlooking the vines, palm-clad gardens and Dolomite peaks beyond. Swim laps or sauna with vine views in the dramatically low-lit spa area, or laze by the outdoor pool in summer.

★ Paradeis   WINE BAR
(Alois Lageder; ☑ 0471 80 95 80; www.aloislageder.eu/a-place-of-encounter/alois-lageder-paradeis; Piazza Geltrude 5, Magrè; meals €40-65; ☺10am-6pm summer Mon-Sat, to 5pm winter) ⏺ Take a seat at the long communal table, crafted from the wood of a 250-year-old oak tree, at fourth-generation winemaker Alois Lageder's biodynamic *weinschenke/vineria* (winery), and start tasting. Book for lunch in the stunning dining room where simple, 'meat-light' dishes are prepared with biodynamic produce, or linger over a bottle and plate of cheese in the pretty courtyard.

Merano (Meran)

☎ 0473 / POP 38,200 / ELEV 325M

With its leafy boulevards, birdsong, oleanders and cacti, Merano feels like you've stumbled into a valley Shangri-La. Long lauded for its sunny microclimate, this poignantly pretty town (and one-time Tyrolean capital) was a Habsburg-era spa and the hot destination of its day, favoured by the Austrian royals plus Freud, Kafka and Pound. The Jugendstil (art nouveau) villas, recuperative walks and the grand riverside Kurhaus fan out from its intact medieval core. The city's therapeutic traditions have served it well in the new millennium, with spa hotels drawing a new generation of health-conscious visitors and a booming organics movement in the surrounding valleys. German is spoken almost exclusively here, sausage and beer stalls dot the streets and an annual open-air play celebrates Napoleonic-era Tyrolean freedom fighter Andreas Hofer. Despite the palm trees, you're far closer to Vienna than Rome. Apart from its old-fashioned charms, it also makes an urban base for skiing or hiking nearby Merano 2000.

◉ Sights & Activites

★ Castel Trauttmansdorff   GARDENS
(www.trauttmansdorff.it; Via San Valentino 51a; garden & museum adult/reduced €13/10.50; ⏰9am-7pm Apr-Nov, to 11pm Fri Jun-Aug) You could give an entire day to these beautiful botanical gardens a little outside Merano (and they do suggest it). Exotic cacti and palms, fruit trees and vines, beds of lilies, irises and tulips all cascade down the hillside surrounding a mid-19th-century castle where Sissi – Empress Elisabeth – spent the odd summer. Inside, Touriseum charts two centuries of travel in the region, exploring the changing nature of our yearning for the mountains. There's a restaurant and a cafe by the lily pond.

Castel Tirolo
Bird Care Centre   WILDLIFE RESERVE
(www.gufyland.com; Via del Castello, Tirolo; adult €10; ⏰10.30am-5pm Apr-Nov, shows 11.15am & 3.15pm) Just below Castel Tirolo's entrance, this wildlife-rescue centre rehabilitates injured birds of prey. There is a collection of eagles, vultures, hawks, owls and buzzards to see, but the real attraction are the twice-daily shows spectacularly sited with the valley below.

Kunst Meran   GALLERY
(☎0473 21 26 43; www.kunstmeranoarte.org; Via Portici 16; adult/reduced €6/5; ⏰10am-6pm Tue-Sat, from 11am Sun) Shows of high-profile international and regional artists are installed in this contemporary gallery, a thoughtful refiguring of a skinny medieval townhouse. Ask about the monthly talks over *aperitivo*.

★ Terme Merano   THERMAL BATHS
(☎0473 25 20 00; www.thermemeran.it; Piazza Terme 1; bathing pass 2hr/all-day €13/19, with sauna $18/25; ⏰9am-10pm) Bolzano-born Matteo Thun's dream commission – a redevelopment of the town's thermal baths – reopened in 2005. Its 13 indoor pools sit within a massive glass cube; there are another 12 outdoor pools in summer. Swim through the sluice and be met by a vision of palm-studded gardens and snow-topped mountains beyond.

Promenades   WALKING
The promenade or *passeggiata* (evening stroll) has long been a Merano institution. Fin-de-siècle-era walks trace the river, traverse pretty parks and skirt Monte Benedetto (514m). A winter and summer pair follow opposing sides of the river, one shady, one sunny. The Gilfpromenade follows 24 poems carved on wooden benches (also handy for a breather). The particularly evocative Tappeiner meanders above the town for 4km.

Merano 2000   SKIING
(www.hafling-meran2000.eu; Hafling) Some 6km east of town, a cable car carries wintersports enthusiasts up to Piffling in Merano 2000, with 30km or mostly beginner but very pleasant slopes. A great choice for families with ski kindergartens, designated children's ski areas and nature-based playgrounds. Local bus 1A and the SAD (p321) Meran-Hafling-Falzeben bus links Merano with the Naif valley station (€4, 15 minutes).

🛏 Sleeping

Youth Hostel Merano   HOSTEL €
(☎0473 20 14 75; www.meran.jugendherberge. it; Via Carducci 77; dm/s €24.50/27; 🅿@🛜) A five-minute stroll from both Merano's train station and the riverside promenade, this hostel is bright and modern, with a sunny terrace and other down-time extras. It has 59 beds, either singles or en-suite dorms.

Hotel Aurora   HOTEL €€
(☎0473 21 18 00; www.hotelaurora.bz; Passeggiata lungo Passirio 38; s €120, d €130-190; 🅿❄🛜)

A family hotel, just across the river from the Terme, works some fresh ideas. 'New' rooms are Italian designed, bright and slick, but the parquetry-floored '60s to '80s originals have their own vintage charm, along with some river-facing balconies. The corridors, too, are littered with original but pristine mid-century pieces. Service is attentive and kind.

★ **Miramonti** BOUTIQUE HOTEL €€€
(☑0473 27 93 35; www.hotel-miramonti.com; Via Santa Caterina 14, Avelengo; d €190-240; P ❄ ☒) ✔ This extraordinary small hotel, 15 minutes' drive from Merano, nestles on the side of a mountain at 1230m. Run by an incredibly vibrant young couple, the whole place exemplifies Südtirolean hospitality, relaxed but attentive to every detail. Deeply comfortable original rooms have been joined by a new batch of clean-lined design suites, including some very glamorous lofts.

★ **Ottmanngut** BOUTIQUE HOTEL €€€
(☑0473 44 96 56; www.ottmanngut.it; Via Verdi 18; s €125, d €250-300; ☎) ✔ This boutique hotel encapsulates Merano's beguiling mix of stately sophistication, natural beauty and gently bohemian backstory. The remodelled townhouse has nine rooms scattered over three floors, and is set among terraced vineyards a scant five-minute walk from the arcades of the centre. Individually furnished, antique-strewn rooms evoke different moods, each highlighting the different landscape glimpsed from the window.

San Luis Hotel BOUTIQUE HOTEL €€€
(☑0473 27 95 70; www.sanluis-hotel.com; Vöranerstrasse 5, Avelengo; ☺half-board s/d €365/630; P ☎ ☒) In what's fast becoming a five-star enclave up in Avelengo, the San Luis' luxe-rustic wooden chalets are either by a small lake or nestled 'tree house' style deep in the forest, including a family suite. The spa area includes both an outdoor and indoor pool, the latter housed in a loft barn.

✗ Eating

★ **Pur Südtirol** DELI €
(www.pursuedtirol.com; Corso della Libertà 35; plates from €9; ☺9am-7.30pm Mon-Fri, to 2pm Sat; ⌕) ✔ This stylish regional showcase – now a chain with branches in Bolzano and Brunico – has an amazing selection of farm produce: wine, cider, some 80 varieties of cheese, *speck* and sausage, pastries and breads, tisanes and body care. Everything is hyperlocal (take Anton Oberhöller's chocolate, flavoured with apple, lemon balm or dark bread crisps).

Sigmund ALPINE €€
(☑0473 23 77 49; www.restaurantsigmund.com; Corso Libertà 2; meals €35-40; ☺noon-2.30pm, 6-10pm Thu-Tue) This intimate place is what Merano is all about: gentility and tradition. A few Italian dishes (steak *tagliata*, *tagliatelle alla bolognese*) sit side-by-side with Tyrolean classics (schnitzel, boiled calf's head with onion) and more innovative dishes such as pork in a black-bread crust with local asparagus or risotto with wild-garlic pesto. The terrace is lovely in summer, too.

Hellweger ALPINE, PIZZA €€
(☑0473 21 25 81; Piazza Duomo 30; meals €28-35; ☺11.30am-2:30pm, 6-9pm) This big, bustling place does both pizza and a menu of traditional dishes, including good risottos and pastas. It's nestled away in what appears to be a 14th-century shopping mall but you'll be able to follow your nose to the spot.

Forsterbräu ALPINE, PUB FOOD €€
(☑0473 23 65 35; Corso della Libertà 90; meals €35; ☺10.30am-midnight Tue-Sun, 7-11pm Mon) This brewery restaurant has a huge beer garden and a number of beautifully designed and cosy dining rooms. Come for a pint or heaped plates of trout, roast boar or calf's head with pickled onions, cabbage and potatoes. Or really bring it home with the Forst plate: pork leg, spare ribs, sausage, *knödel* (dumplings) and sauerkraut.

Sissi GASTRONOMY €€€
(☑0473 23 10 62; www.sissi.andreafenoglio.com; Via Galilei 44; meals €57, degustation menu €80/90, lunch special €40) Andrea Fenoglio is one of the region's best-loved chefs and his big personality fills this small early-20th-century room. The food here is inventive, for sure, but the experience is warm and refreshingly relaxed. Even the most experimental dish retains a connection to the traditional, or what Fenoglio calls 'memory food'.

♀ Drinking & Nightlife

Why Not? COCKTAIL BAR
(☑338 8015278; Corso Libertà 15; ☺8.30am-1am Tue-Sun) Loud, shiny but lots of fun. Stefano loves what he does and most of the cocktail ingredients are homemade. If you're more interested in an *aperitivo*, there's an interesting *spritz* menu to choose from.

Café Kunsthaus
BAR

(www.kunstmeranoarte.org; Via Portici 16; ⊙8.30am-8pm Mon-Thu, to 1am Fri & Sat, 10am-6pm Sun) You can while away the hours in this gallery-cafe, then find yourself still here when the DJs begin and the beer and pizzas are doing the rounds. Note, evening access is from the back lane off Via Risparmio.

🛍 Shopping

Meraner Weinhaus
WINE

(www.meranerweinhaus.com; Via Roma 76; ⊙8.30am-1pm, 2-7pm Mon-Fri, 8.30am-12.30pm Sat) A stylish but very serious wine shop, a few minutes' walk from Merano's centre. It's a great place to discover the region's best producers in one place and there's parking at the front if you're *really* stocking up.

❶ Information

Tourist Office (📞 0473 27 20 00; www.mer aninfo.it; Corso della Libertà 45; ⊙9am-6pm Mon-Fri, to 4pm Sat, 10am-12.30pm Sun summer, 9am-12.30pm & 2-5pm Mon-Fri, 9.30am-12.30pm Sat winter)

❶ Getting There & Away

SAD (📞 840 000471, 0471 45 01 11; www.sad.it; ⊙6am-8pm Mon-Sat, 7.30am-8pm Sun) buses leave Merano **bus station** (Piazza Stazione) for surrounding mountain villages and the Parco Nazionale dello Stelvio.

By train, Bolzano (€5.90, almost hourly) is an easy 40-minute trip from Merano **train station** (Piazza Stazione), while the Venosta/Vinschgau line heads west to Malles, from where you can catch buses to Switzerland or Austria.

❶ Getting Around

Hire a bike and helmet next door to Merano's train station; the **bikemobil card** (www.suedti rolbike.it; 1/3/7 days €24/30/34, children half price) includes both bike rental and unlimited regional train travel, or there are city bikes for €5 per day, opposite the bikemobil shed or on Via Piave near the Terme Merano. Bike trails run between Bolzano, Merano and Malles.

Parco Nazionale dello Stelvio

It's not quite Yellowstone, but 1346-sq-km **Parco Nazionale dello Stelvio** (📞 0473 83 04 30; www.parks.it/parco.nazionale.stelvio) FREE is the Alps' largest national park, spilling into Lombardy and bordering Switzerland's Parco Nazionale Svizzero.

It's primarily the preserve of walkers who come for the extensive network of well-organised mountain huts and marked trails that, while often challenging, don't require the mountaineering skills necessary elsewhere in the Dolomites. Stelvio's central massif is guarded over by **Monte Cevedale** (3769m) and **Ortles** (3905m), protecting glaciers, forests and numerous wildlife species, not to mention many mountain traditions and histories.

❶ Getting There & Away

The park is reached via the SS38 from Merano. From June to September, subject to late or early snowfall, you can travel to and from Bormio in Lombardy via the Passo di Stelvio (2757m), the second-highest pass in the Alps and one of Europe's most spectacular roads. The excellent **Vinschgau rail service** between Merano and Mals – 100% owned and operated by South Tyrol – makes much of this region easily accessible, as do numerous bike trails.

Val di Solda & Val d'Ultimo

The village of **Solda** (Sulden; 1906m), reached by winding your way up the deep, dark valley of the same name, is surrounded by 14 peaks over 3000m high. This low-key ski resort becomes a busy base for walkers and climbers in summer. The narrow **Val d'Ultimo** is home to a string of picturesque traditional villages where you can partake in winter or summer sports (including great fishing) or just soak up the beauty and silence.

Messner Mountain Museum
MUSEUM

(MMM Ortles; 📞 0473 61 32 66; www.mess ner-mountain-museum.it; adult/reduced €7/6; ⊙1-7pm Wed-Mon summer, 2-6pm Wed-Mon winter, closed May & mid-Oct–Nov) Located – quite literally – inside a hill, the unique Messner Mountain Museum Ortles articulates the theme of 'ice' with artistically displayed exhibits on glaciers, ice-climbing and pole expeditions, all at 1900m.

Eggwirt
GUESTHOUSE €€

(📞 0473 79 53 19; www.eggwirt.it; Frazione Santa Valburga 112; half-board d €136; 🅿❄🐾) The Schwienbacher's welcoming inn has beautifully designed contemporary rooms with dreamlike valley views, a free sauna and a wonderful historic *stube* to eat your hearty (included) dinner. It's the kind of place that has had repeat guests who've been enjoying the place since childhood.

TRENTINO & SOUTH TYROL PARCO NAZIONALE DELLO STELVIO

Yak & Yeti ALPINE €€

(☑0473 61 35 77; Località Solda 55; meals €30; ☺Wed-Mon 3-9pm) The Yak & Yeti is a 17th-century farmhouse that Messner has transformed into a restaurant, yak farm and 'bio-homestead'; dishes are typical food of the Solda valley – slow-cooked meats, dumplings, pasta – rather than that of the Himalayas, FYI.

Val Venosta (Vinschgau)

The northwestern valley of Val Venosta is prettily pastoral, dotted with orchards, farms and small-scale, often creative, industries including marble quarries and workshops. It may feel remote, nestled as it is within the embrace of towering, snowy peaks, but for much of its history it was a vibrant border zone, long on the road to somewhere. Come and enjoy its gentle way of life, the excellent bike trails – part of the ancient **Via Claudia Augusta** forms an easy, intriguing, 80km bicycle trail from Merano to Malles – and easy access to some interesting local ski areas.

◉ Sights

Lago di Resia LAKE

Just before the Passo di Resia and Austrian border is the deep blue Lago do Resia, a result of 1950s dam projects. The drowned Romanesque church tower in the lake here might be the region's de rigueur roadside photo op, but is still oddly, and deeply, affecting. Besides the view, it's a popular destination for sailing and kiteboarding in summer and ice-fishing and snowkiting in winter, and is also a gateway to the Skiparadies Reschenpass area.

Glorenza VILLAGE

(Glurns) A walled medieval town, Glorenza was once a kingpin in the region's salt trade. Its pristine burgher houses, colonnaded shops, town gates, fortifications and ramparts were faithfully restored in the 1970s, and while it's certainly picturesque, it retains a comforting normalcy, with the road to Switzerland passing through its very centre.

Marienberg MONASTERY

(www.marienberg.it; Schlinig 1, Malles; museum adult/reduced €5/2.50; ☺10am-5pm Mon-Sat, mid-Mar-Oct, late-Dec–early Jan) The beautiful Benedictine monastery of Marienberg, perched up some 1340m above Malles, has a museum dedicated to its eight centuries of monastic life, though the view and architecture are worth the drive up alone.

🛏 Sleeping

★**Gasthof Grüner Baum** BOUTIQUE HOTEL €€

(☑0473 83 12 06; www.gasthofgruenerbaum. it; Piazza della Città 7, Glorenza; d €140; 🅿❄🛜) Gracious Gasthof Grüner Baum combines arresting contemporary architecture, authentic charm and quiet luxury – free-standing baths, antiques and handcrafted furniture are standard issue in the rooms. For as little as €10 extra per person, the half-board option is great as the upstairs dining room is as beautiful as the rest of the hotel.

Josephus LODGE €€

(☑335 348299; www.josephus.it; Madonna 42, Senales; 2-/4-person apt €150/220; 🅿🛜) Using the historical furniture of the original farm house along with beautiful contemporary design and the wools and wood of the region, these apartments are incredibly evocative and thoroughly South Tyrolean. Up another hidden valley arm, there are magnificent views of Val Senales. They are also very well equipped with full cooking facilities, espresso machines and lovely homewares.

THE DOLOMITES

The jagged peaks of the Dolomites, or Dolomiti, span the provinces of Trentino and South Tyrol, jutting into neighbouring Veneto. Europeans flock here in winter for highly hospitable resorts, sublime natural settings and extensive, well-coordinated ski networks. Come for downhill, cross-country and snowboarding or get ready for *sci alpinismo*, an adrenalin-spiking mix of skiing and mountaineering, freeride and a range of other winter adventure sports, including on the legendary circuit, the Sella Ronda. It's also a beautiful summer destination, with excellent hiking, sublime views and lots of fresh, fragrant air.

★**Sella Ronda** SKIING

(http://sellaronda.info) One of the Alps' most iconic ski routes, this 40km circumnavigation of the Gruppo di Sella range (3151m, at Piz Boé) – linked by various cable cars and chairlifts – takes in four passes and their surrounding valleys: Alto Adige's **Val Gardena**, **Val Badia** (in the Veneto) and Trentino's **Val di Fassa**. Experienced skiers can complete the clockwise (orange) or anticlockwise (green) route in a day.

Val di Fiemme

In a region where few valleys speak the same dialect, let alone agree on the same cheese recipe, the Val di Fiemme's proud individualism is above and beyond. In the 12th century, independently minded local noblemen even set up their own quasi-republic here, the Magnificent Community of Fiemme, and the ethos and spirit of the founders lives on, with the modern-day headquarters in the wonderfully frescoed Palazzo Vescovile in Cavalese.

Come here for relaxed skiing at Cermis or for access to other Dolomiti Superski resorts, or for the more adventurous, high-altitude ski excursions and summertime ascents on the gnarly Pale di San Martino and other extraordinary peaks.

🛏 Sleeping & Eating

Agritur la Regina dei Prati   AGRITURISMO €
(www.lareginadeiprati.it; Via Margherita Dellafior 17, Masi di Cavalese; s/d €65/100; [P][❄][🐾]) Across the river in a village 'suburb' of Cavalese, this is a relaxed, family-run place with surprisingly spacious rooms that have nice extras like heated floors and balconies. The rustic setting is magnificent and is ski-in during winter.

★ Park Hotel Azalea   SPA HOTEL €€
([☎]0462 34 01 09; www.parkhotelazalea.it; Via delle Cesure 1; d €180-210; [P][🐾]) 🅿 This hotel combines impeccable eco-credentials, super-stylish interiors and a warm, welcoming vibe. Rooms are individually decorated and make use of soothing, relaxing colours; some have mountain views, others look across the village's pretty vegetable gardens.

Children's facilities eschew plastic and tat for wood and natural textiles, and there are little daily extras like an afternoon tea spread (all organic, of course). Vegetarians and vegans are welcomed and well catered for.

★ El Molin   GASTRONOMY €€€
([☎]0462 34 00 74; www.alessandrogilmozzi.it; Piazza Battisti 11, Cavalese; meals €60, degustation menus €120; ⊗Wed-Mon noon-2.30pm & 7-11pm) A legend in the valley, this Michelin-starred old mill sits at the historic heart of Cavalese. Downstairs, next to the old waterwheels, you will find playful gastronomic dishes featuring ultralocal, always seasonal ingredients. Streetside, the wine bar does baked-to-order eggs with Trentingrana or truffles, burgers, hearty mains and creative desserts from €15. Its G&T is also known throughout the valley.

ⓘ DOLOMITI SUPERSKI

Dolomiti Superski (www.dolomitisuperski.com; ⊗high season 3/6 days €147/258) gives you access to 450 lifts and some 1200km of ski runs, spread over 12 resorts in the Dolomites.

ⓘ Information

Val di Fiemme Tourist Office ([☎]0462 24 11 11; www.visitfiemme.it; Via Bronzetti 60; ⊗9am-noon & 3.30-7pm Mon-Sat)

ⓘ Getting There & Away

A pre-booked shuttle bus **Transfer Fiemme** ([☎]328 1696199; www.transferfiemme.it) links Cavalese and Ora, Bolzano and Trento.

Val di Fassa

Val di Fassa is Trentino's only Ladin-speaking valley, framed by the stirring peaks of the **Gruppo del Sella** to the north, the **Catinaccio** to the west and the **Marmolada** to the southeast. The valley has two hubs: **Canazei**, beautifully sited but verging on overdeveloped, and the pretty riverside village of Moena, more down to earth and increasingly environmentally conscious. Fassa is the nexus of Italy's cross-country skiing scene. Italian cross-country champ Cristian Zorzi hails from Moena and the town also plays host to the annual Marcialonga.

⭐ Festivals & Events

Marcialonga   SPORTS
(www.marcialonga.it; ⊗late Jan) Moena hosts skiing's most illustrious mass-participation race, the annual **Marcialonga**, a 70km march through the snow to Canazei and back through Cavalese in the adjoining Val di Fiemme. It's had up to 7570 participants in recent years, and between 2007 and 2017 it's been won by either a Norwegian or a Swede.

⊙ Sights

Museo Ladin de Fascia   MUSEUM
([☎]0462 76 01 82; museo@istladin.net; Via Milano 5, Vigo di Fassa; ⊗10am-noon & 3-7pm Jul & Aug, 3-7pm Tue-Sat Sep-Jun) **FREE** One of the Ladin valley's fascinatingly kooky cultural museums, with beautiful wood carvings and quotidian objects.

💤 Sleeping

Garnì Ladin   B&B €
(📞0462 76 44 93; www.ladin.it; Strada de la Piazedela 9, Vigo di Fassa; s/d €70/100; 🅿️🛜) Right in the middle of villagey Vigo di Fassa, midway between Moena and Canazei, the rooms here are full of sweetly kitsch Ladin-alia but have ultramodern bathrooms.

Villa Kofler   DESIGN HOTEL €€
(📞0462 75 04 44; www.villakofler.it; Via Dolomiti 63, Campitello di Fassa; d €170-220; 🅿️🛜) 🏊 An intimate hotel in a valley of giants, just outside of the Canazei bustle; choose from rooms that range across various current design trends and tastes. There's a little gym, a library and, bliss, in-room infrared saunas.

🍴 Eating & Drinking

Sausage Stand   FAST FOOD €
(Piazza Marconi, Canazei; sausages €4; ⏱️11am-7pm Sep-Jun, 10am-10pm Jul & Aug) The fork-wielding Ladin sausage cooks are a Canazei institution, with this roadside stall just by the bus stop drawing queues of ravenous skiers all winter long and keeping hikers happy into the night in summer.

El Paél   ALPINE €€
(📞0462 60 14 33; www.elpael.com; Via Roma 58, Canazei; meals €30; ⏱️noon-2.30pm & 6.30-10pm Tue-Sun) This *osteria tipica trentina* was known for its traditional Ladin specialities of the valley, but now mixes this up with a contemporary Italian slickness. Luckily for the old fans this works: dishes are carefully prepared and always tasty.

Malga Panna   GASTRONOMY €€€
(📞0462 57 34 89; www.malgapanna.it; Via Costalunga 29, Moena; degustation €65-75; ⏱️12.30-2pm & 7.30-10pm) Fine-dining interpretations of mountain food stay true to their culinary roots and are served in an evocatively simple setting. Expect to encounter the flavours of Alpine herbs and flowers and lots of game.

Kusk La Locanda   BAR
(📞0462 57 46 27; Via dei Colli 7, Moena; ⏱️8am-2am Wed-Mon) Legendary throughout Val di Fassa for après-ski, this four-way split between a pizzeria, American bar, trash disco and Italian restaurant still manages to maintain a Ladin cosiness.

ℹ️ Information

Canazei Tourist Office (📞0462 60 96 00; www.fassa.com; Piazza Marconi 5; ⏱️8.30-12.30pm & 3-7pm daily Jul-Mar, 8.30am-12.30pm & 2.30-6.30pm Mon-Sat Apr-Jun)

Moena Tourist Office (📞0462 60 97 70; www.fassa.com; Piazza del Navalge 4; ⏱️8.30-12.30pm & 3-7pm daily Jul-Mar, 8.30am-12.30pm & 2.30-6.30pm Mon-Sat Apr-Jun)

ℹ️ Getting There & Away

SAD (📞840 000471, 0471 45 01 11; www.sad.it) buses serve Val di Fassa from Bolzano (€6, 1½ hours, six a day) and **Trentino Trasporti** (📞0461 82 10 00; www.ttesercizio.it) runs buses to Val di Fassa from Trento year-round (€6.80, 1½ to 2½ hours, three to four a day).

Val Gardena

Despite its proximity to Bolzano, Val Gardena's historical isolation among the turrets of Gruppo del Sella and Sassolungo has ensured the survival of many pre–mass tourism traditions. Ladin is a majority tongue and this linguistic heritage is carefully maintained. The pretty and bustling villages are full of reminders of this distinct culture too, with folksy vernacular architecture and a profusion of woodcarving shops.

In recent times, the valley, part of Dolomiti Superski (p323), has become an 'everyman' ski area, with the emphasis firmly on classic runs and fine powder. The valley's main trilingual towns, **Ortisei** (St Ulrich; population 6000, elevation 1236m), **Santa Cristina** (population 1900, elevation 1428m) and **Selva** (Wolkenstein; population 2580, elevation 1563m) all have good facilities.

⦿ Sights & Activites

Museum de Gherdëina   MUSEUM
(📞0471 79 75 54; www.museumgherdeina.it; Via Rezia 83, Ortisei; adult/reduced €7/5.50; ⏱️10am-12.30pm & 2-6pm Mon-Fri, 2-6pm Sat winter, closed Mon winter) Ortisei's fabulously folky Museum de Gherdëina has a particularly exquisite collection of wooden toys and sculptures.

Scuola di Alpinismo Catores   OUTDOORS
(📞0471 79 82 23; www.catores.com; ⏱️8.30-11.30am & 4.30-6.30pm) Offers botanical walks, climbing courses, glacier excursions and treks.

💤 Sleeping

⭐ **Saslong Smart Hotel**   HOTEL €
(📞0471 77 44 44; www.saslong.eu; Strada Palua, Santa Christina; d/tr €60/85, breakfast €11; 🛜) Rooms are small but comfortable and slick

(Antonio Citterio had a hand in the design), staff are friendly and the restaurant is great. The 'smart' concept keeps rates low by making daily cleaning and breakfast optional, and the longer you stay the cheaper the rate.

Charme Hotel Uridl
HOTEL €€

(☏ 0471 79 32 15; www.uridl.it; Via Chemun 43, Santa Christina; s/d half-board €100/180; P ✴ @) Nestled behind the church in the original 'high' village, this is a friendly, character-filled hotel with bright, simple rooms, a heritage *stube* and beautiful views back over the valley from its sunny garden. They provides daily free transport to the Sella Ronda lifts in winter.

Chalet Gerard
HOTEL €€€

(☏ 0471 79 52 74; www.chalet-gerard.com; Plan de Gralba; half-board s €180, d €280-350; 🛎) Stunning modern chalet with panoramic views, 10 minutes' drive from Selva proper. There are lots of spots for cosy lolling by the (architect-designed) fire, a steam room and the option to ski in, and, naturally, supercute rooms. The restaurant is beautiful and romantic – all pine, felt and candlelight – but also soothingly down to earth.

ℹ Information

Ortisei Tourist Office (☏ 0471 77 76 00; www.valgardena.it; Via Rezia 1, Ortisei; ⊙ 8.30am-12.30pm & 2.30-6.30pm Mon-Sat, 9am-noon & 4-6.30pm Sun, reduced hrs Apr & May, Oct & Nov)

ℹ Getting There & Away

The Gardena Pass links Selva to Corvara in Alta Badia and is open year-round but subject to avalanche-risk closures. The Val Gardena is accessible from Bolzano and Bressonone by **SAD** (☏ 840 000471, 0471 45 01 11; www.sad.it) buses year-round.

Alpe di Siusi & Parco Naturale Sciliar-Catinaccio

There are few more jarring or beautiful juxtapositions than the undulating green pastures of the Alpe di Siusi – Europe's largest plateau – ending dramatically at the base of the towering Sciliar Mountains. To the southeast lies the jagged Catinaccio range, its German name, 'Rosengarten', an apt description of the eerie pink hue given off by the mountains' dolomite rock at sunset. Both areas fall within the Parco Naturale Sciliar-Catinaccio. While great skiing and hiking is a huge draw, the villages that dot the valleys – including **Castelrotto** (Kastelruth), **Fiè allo Sciliar** (Völs am Schlern) and **Siusi** – signposted by their onion-domed churches, are lovingly maintained, unexpectedly sophisticated and far from mere resorts. Horses are a big part of local life and culture here, and there's nothing more picturesque than a local chestnut Haflinger pony galloping across endless pastureland.

◉ Sights & Activites

Parco Naturale Sciliar-Catinaccio
PARK

This 7291-hectare park takes in the Sciliar and Catinaccio massifs as well as pine forests, pasture land and lakes.

Alpe di Siusi Cableway
CABLE CAR

(Seiser Alm; www.seiseralmbahn.it; one way/return €11/17; ⊙ 8am-6pm mid-Dec–Mar & mid-May–Oct, to 7pm summer) A dizzying 15-minute, 4300m trip (800m ascent) from Siusi to Compaccio. The road linking the two is closed to normal traffic when the cableway is open.

Panorama Chairlift
CABLE CAR

(one way/return €6/8.50) Take the Panorama chairlift from Compaccio to the Alpenhotel, followed by paths S, No 5 and No 1 to the Rifugio Bolzano; from here it is an easy walk to **Monte Pez** (2564m; three hours total).

🛏 Sleeping & Eating

Rifugio Bolzano
CHALET €

(☏ 0471 61 20 24; www.schlernhaus.it; dm/s/d €25/30/60, breakfast €9; ⊙ Jun Oct) The Rifugio Bolzano is one of the Alps' oldest mountain huts, which rests at 2457m, just under Monte Pez, the Sciliar's summit.

★ Hotel Heubad
SPA HOTEL €€

(☏ 0471 72 50 20; www.hotelheubad.com; Via Sciliar 12, Fiè allo Sciliar; d €180-250; P ✴ @ ✇) As if the views, pretty garden and lounge areas here weren't relaxing enough, the hotel's spa is known for its typically Tyrolean hay baths, which have been on offer since 1903 and give the hotel its name. Delightful service is courtesy of the founder's great- and great-great-grandchildren, while the hotel rooms are modern, light and spacious.

LUC KOHNEN/SHUTTERSTOCK ©

EZIO HSU/SHUTTERSTOCK ©

LUCA LORENZELLI/SHUTTERSTOCK ©

3

1. Val di Non (p311)
Famed for its apples, the valley is filled with fragrant blossoms in the springtime.

2. Alpe di Siusi (p325)
Horses graze in an idyllic green landscape overlooked by the Sciliar Mountains.

3. Merano (p319)
The sunny, pretty town of Merano boasts art nouveau villas, beautiful walks and thermal baths.

4. Brenta Dolomites (p308)
This majestic range is home to some of the world's most famous *vie ferrata* (trail with cables and ladders) climbs.

Alpina Dolomites

HOTEL €€€

(☎0471 79 60 04; www.alpinadolomites.it; d half-board €500-600; P ❋ 🛜 ⛶) A suitably high-style super-luxe lodge for one of the world's most beautiful high-altitude plateaus. A stunning contemporary building of wood, stone and glass houses calming, cosy rooms and suites, a wellness centre and restaurant, bar and lounging areas. Views are in abundance.

Gostner Schwaige

ALPINE €€

(☎347 8368154; footpath No 3 from Compaccio; meals €35-50; ⊗ Jun-Oct & Dec-Apr) Chef Franz Mulser gives new meaning to the tag 'locally sourced' at his mountain refuge (elevation 1930m). The butter and cheese come from the barn next door, and herbs from the garden outside. Boards of salami, steaming broth and slow-cooked stews are the order of the day.

ⓘ Information

Castelrotto Tourist Office (☎0471 70 63 33; www.alpedisiusi.info; Piazza Kraus 1; ⊗9am-noon & 2-6pm Mon-Fri, 10am-noon Sat)

ⓘ Getting There & Away

This region is accessed from the A22. **SAD** (☎840 000471, 0471 45 01 11; www.sad.it) runs buses to the Alpe di Siusi from Bolzano, the Val Gardena and Bressanone.

Val Badia & Alpe di Fanes

For centuries potent Ladin legends have resonated across this mystical landscape, which inspired the fantasies of JRR Tolkien. Not surprisingly, the Badia valley and the adjoining high plains of Fanes are often touted as one of the most evocative places in the Dolomites. Since 1980 they have been protected as part of the Parco Naturale di Fanes-Sennes-Braies. **Colfosco** (1645m), **Pedraces** (1324m), **La Villa** (1433m), **San Cassiano** (St Kassian; 1537m) and **Corvara** (1568m) form the Alta Badia ski area. While undoubtedly upmarket, they remain relatively low key and retain something of their original, and highly individual, village character.

◉ Sights & Activities

Museo Ladin

MUSEUM

(☎0474 52 40 20; www.museumladin.it; Tor 65, St Martin de Tor; adult/reduced €8/6.50; ⊗10am-5pm Tue-Sat, 2-6pm Sun summer, 3-7pm Thu-Sat

winter) Atmospherically set in a castle 15km south of Brunico and full of folk treasures.

Alta Badia Guides

GUIDES

(☎0471 83 68 98; www.altabadiaguides.com; Via Col Alt 94, Corvara; ⊗office 5-7pm) Freeride, ski circuits and ice-climbing courses and tours, as well as snowshoe walks in winter. In summer they organise climbs, including *vie ferrate*, trekking and excursions to the natural parks and WWI sites.

🛏 Sleeping

Garni Ciasa Urban

HOTEL €

(www.garniurban.it; Via Pantansarè 35, Badia; d €98, 4-bed apt €150; P 🛜) A simple, welcoming, family-run place, set in a blissfully peaceful spot right at the top of Badia village. The uncluttered, spacious rooms have spectacular views of Santa Croce and home-cooked dinners can be arranged. Note, the Urban of the name is the house saint, not a style or attitude!

★ Berghotel Ladinia

BOUTIQUE HOTEL €€

(☎0471 83 60 10; www.berghotelladinia.it; Pedecorvara 10, Corvara; s/d half-board €95/200; P ❋ 🛜) Hotel La Perla's family owners have taken over this traditional small hotel just up the hill from their luxurious place. Rooms are exquisitely simple and rustic and the location is sublime. Included dinners are in the hotel **restaurant** or a food credit (€40 per person per day) can be used at any of La Perla's restaurants instead.

Dolomit B&B

B&B €€

(☎0471 84 71 20; www.dolomit.it; Via Colz 9, La Villa; d €150-180; P ❋ @ 🛜 ⛶) Rooms here are very prettily decorated, as well as surprisingly spacious (baths! walk-in wardrobes!). You might be right in the middle of town, but the mountain views are still something to behold. The attached **La Tor** restaurant does Ladin dishes and pizza; its popularity with locals makes it a fun spot year-round.

Lagacio Mountain Residence

APARTMENT, HOTEL €€€

(☎0471 84 95 03; www.lagacio.com; Strada Micurá de Rü 48, San Cassiano; apt €300-370; P ❋ 🛜) 🌱 A stylish residence-hotel with young, happy staff and a casual vibe. Pared-back apartments are decorated with wood, wool and leather; all have heated floors, big baths and balconies. Attention to detail is keen: kitchens come with top-of-the-line equipment, Nespresso machines and filtered mountain water. There is a guest-only bar and lavish all-organic breakfast served in a traditional *stube*.

✕ Eating

Rifugio Scotoni
ALPINE €

(☑ 0471 84 73 30; www.scotoni.it; Alpe Lagazuoi 2, San Cassioano; meals €25; ☺ year-round) At 1985m there are stunning views, and the traditional food and mountain hospitality make this a quintessential Badia experience. Book ahead to stay in one of the cosy, blonde-wood bunkrooms.

Delizius
DELI €

(☑ 0471 84 01 55; www.delizius.it; Strada Micurà de Rü 51, San Cassiano; ☺ 8am-noon & 3-7pm Mon-Sat) Specialist cheese and *speck* counters, well-priced local wine and grappa, plus an excellent selection of prepared meals – *canederli*, goulash, lasagne – perfect for self-catering diners.

Restaurant Ladinia
ALPINE €€

(☑ 0471 83 60 10; www.berghotelladinia.it; Pedecorvara 10, Corvara; meals €35, 4-course menu €48; ☺ noon-2pm & 7-9pm May Oct, Dec-early Apr) The Berghotel Ladinia'sdining room is appealingly cosy, or you can soak up the sun on a protected terrace on warmer days. Mountain-style food is done in a fresh but unpretentious way: trout carpaccio with chicory, *paccheri* (pasta) with freshwater crayfish, salmon with mashed purple carrots and artichokes, and a yoghurt-mousse dessert will wake up stew-and-dumpling-dulled palates.

Piz Arlara
ALPINE €€

(☑ 0471 83 66 33; www.pizarlara.it; Prè Ciablun; meals €20-30; ☺ 8am-5.30pm mid-Jun–Sep, Dec-early Apr) A social hub at 2040m; stop by for a *spritz* with a view or settle in for a lunch of *schlutzkrapfen* (ravioli), beef goulash or the Tyrolean favourite *gröstl* (a tasty Alpine bubble and squeak). *Kaiserschmarren* (scrambled pancakes) and apple fritters are great afternoon revivers, too. Accessible only by the Arlara chairlift from Corvara, or in summer on foot.

La Siriola
GASTRONOMY €€€

(Hotel Ciasa Salares; ☑ 0471 84 94 45; www.ciasasalares.it; Pré de Ví 31, Armentarola; meals €75; ☺ Tue-Sun 7.15-9.30pm) A whitewashed pine room nestles in a wonderful setting just outside San Cassiano, and offers a menu that ranges from crowd-pleasers to the more creative. The wine-by-the-glass selection is broader than most fine-dining places, and

there is a dessert degustation if you feel like you simply can't look another dish involving deer or pork. Chocolate is also a speciality.

Stüa de Michil
GASTRONOMY €€€

(Hotel La Perla; ☑ 0471 83 10 00; www.hotel-laperla.it; Col Alt 105, Corvara; meals €110; ☺ 7-9.30pm Mon-Sat) Stuffed with Alpine antiques and built entirely from wood, Stüa de Michil is intimate and ridiculously atmospheric. Beautifully presented dishes rework Ladin or Tyrolean traditions and use biodynamic ingredients. Rare wines are also a speciality.

St Hubertus
GASTRONOMY €€€

(Hotel Rosa Alpina; ☑ 0471 84 95 00; www.rosalpina.it; Strada Micurá de Rü 20, San Cassiano; 3-/4-/5-course degustation €120/145/170; ☺ 7-10pm Wed Mon) Part of the luxurious Rosa Alpina Hotel & Spa, this two-Michelin starred restaurant has a quiet elegance. The mountain beef cooked in salt and hay is a menu stalwart, as is crispy suckling pig (most recently served with a parsnips and a pig's-head sandwich). Many of Norbert Niederkofler's dishes take a whimsical turn while desserts are pared back to essentials.

ℹ Information

Corvara Tourist Office (☑ 0471 83 61 76; www.altabadia.org; Via Col Alt 36; ☺ 9am noon & 3-6pm)

San Cassiano Tourist Office (☑ 0471 84 94 22; Strada Micurá de Rü 24; ☺ 8.30am-noon & 3-6.30pm Mon-Sat, 10am-noon & 4 6pm Sun)

ℹ Getting There & Away

SAD (☑ 840 000471, 0471 45 01 11; www.sad.it) buses link the Alta Badia villages with Bolzano (2½ hours) and Brunico (1¼ hours) roughly hourly. Summer services link Corvara with the Val Gardena and Canazei.

Val Pusteria

Running from the junction of the Valle Isarco at Bressanone (Brixen) to **San Candido** (Innichen) in the far east, the narrow, verdant Val Pusteria is profoundly Tyrolean and almost entirely German speaking and is a gentle, traditional alternative to the more glamorous Dolomites resorts during the ski season, with plenty to do in summer, too.

Dobbiaco (Toblach), where Gustav Mahler once holed up and wrote his troubled but ultimately life-affirming *Ninth Symphony*, is the gateway to the ethereal **Parco Naturale**

HOTEL PRAGSER WILDSEE

This beautiful historic **hotel** (www.lago dibraies.com; St Veit 27, Prags; half-board d €140) situated on the Lago di Braies still has some rooms fitted out with original furnishing from 1899–1930. Serious walkers might like to tackle part of the Alta Via No 1 that begins here, but it's an equally charming place to stay put and watch the lake's many moods. Beyond its architectural appeal, it's a richly story-filled place for those with an interest in 20th-century history. Grand Duke Franz Ferdinand was a frequent guest in the years just before his assassination, while at the end of WWII it housed a group of high-profile politicians, diplomats, royalty, artists and writers, who were rescued from the SS after being transported to South Tyrol from the Dachau concentration camp.

delle Dolomiti di Sesto, home of the much-photographed **Tre Cime di Lavaredo** ('Three Peaks' or, in German, Drei Zinnen). Down yet another deeply forested valley twist are the jewel-like **Lago di Braies** (Pragser Wildsee) and its serious Alta Via No 1 walking route.

Bumping the Austrian and Veneto borders in the far northeast is a vast, wild territory, the **Sesto Dolomiti**, which is criss-crossed with spectacular walking and cross-country ski trails.

Bressanone (Brixen)

📞0472 / POP 21,500 / ELEV 560M

Alto Adige's oldest city, dating to 901, might be the picture of small-town calm, but has a grand ecclesiastical past and a lively, cultured side today. Stunning baroque architecture is set against a beguiling Alpine backdrop, a stately piazza leads into a tight medieval core and pretty paths trace the fast-moving Isarco river. Come for excellent hiking in summer, or the spectacular views and beautiful 11km ski run at town mountain **Plose** in winter or, by all means, just stay, eat, drink and shop.

⊙ Sights & Activities

Cathedral of Santa Maria Assunta and San Cassiano   CATHEDRAL
(Piazza del Duomo; ⊙6am-6pm Apr-Oct & Dec, 6am-noon & 3-6pm Nov, Jan-Mar) The lofty two-

spired Baroque beauty you see today was built on top of the AD 980 Gothic-Romanesque original in 1745. While the bishop decamped to Bolzano some years back, this remains Südtirol's most important church. Interiors feature Michelangelo Unterberger's altar work depicting the death of Mary, and ceilings by Paul Troger.

Museo Diocesano   MUSEUM
(☑0472 83 05 05; www.hofburg.it; Piazza Palazzo Vescovile 2; €8; ⊙10am-5pm Tue-Sun Mar-Oct, daily Dec-early Jan) This museum is far more interesting than most of its ilk, its magnificent *palazzo* home testament to Bressanone's once-important religious standing. It's popular when the Christmas Market crowds arrive, due to its extensive, and rather bonkers, 'crib' collection – nativity figures and dioramas.

Brixen Plose Ski Area   SKIING
(www.plose.org) A south-orientated (that is, sunny) ski area at 2500m, 7km from Bressanone, Plose offers more than 40km of slopes for both skiers and snowboarders, with 19km blue, 14km red and 10km of black runs including **Trametsch**, the longest in South Tyrol. From the top of the mountain, there are spectacular Dolomites views.

Funpark Plose also has a 10km toboggan run, one of the longest in Europe.

🛏 Sleeping

⭐**Hotel Elephant**   HISTORIC HOTEL €€
(☑0472 83 27 50; www.hotelelephant.com; Via Rio Bianco 4; s €95-125, d €160-220; 🅿✹🛜🌊) This 15th-century inn marks the entrance to old Bressanone, and as the name suggests, once gave shelter to an Indian elephant, a gift on its way to Archduke Maximilian of Austria. The quince-toned exterior hints at what's inside: extremely comfortable rooms and serenely professional service, exquisite historic *stufas* (tiled stoves) in the dining room and museum-worthy paintings lining the stairs.

Hotel Pupp   BOUTIQUE HOTEL €€€
(☑0472 26 83 55; www.small-luxury.it; Via Mercato Vecchio 36; d €250; 🅿✹🛜) Things take a totally contemporary turn at this small and fun hotel, even if its hospitality lineage reaches way back (the owners have branched out from the venerable bakery opposite). Fabulously designed rooms are suite-sized and come with Nespresso machines and wine-

stocked fridges; some include a terrace with hot tub and one has its own private pool. Adults only.

Eating

Vitis
ITALIAN €€

(☎0472 83 53 43; www.vitis.bz; Vicolo Duomo 3; meals €35-50; ⊙10am-3pm, 5pm-midnight Tue-Sat) Downstairs from its parent restaurant, the venerable Oste Scuro, Vitis occupies a vaulted, whitewashed shopfront and a pretty vineclad courtyard. The menu is as much a departure as its Alpine-contemporary look, with a menu of light, modern Italian-influenced dishes with global flavours and a light touch. There's a special tartare menu and an extensive cellar to sample.

Oste Scuro
ALPINE €€€

(Restaurant Finsterwirt; ☎0472 83 53 43; www. ostescuro.com; Vicolo del Duomo 3; meals €50-55; ⊙11.45am-2.15pm & 6.45-9.15pm Tue-Sat, noon-3pm Sun) This place would be worth a visit for the decor alone – a wonderful series of dark-wooded rooms strewn with moody mountain paintings and Alpine curios – but the food here is very good, if seriously rich. Don't pass up the postprandial nut-infused digestives, even if you skip dessert. Tip: lunch menus are a steal at €20.

Drinking & Nightlife

Pupp Konditorei Cafe
CAFE

(www.pupp.it; Via Mercato Vecchio 37; ⊙7am-7pm Tue-Sat, 7am-noon Sun) In the Pupp family for almost a hundred years, this is a Bressanone favourite. The cosy velvet booths of this oh so-'80s cafe are perpetually filled with locals scoffing great coffee and cake. The poppyseed or walnut *potize* (stuffed brioche) is known throughout the valley.

Peter's Weinbistro
WINE BAR

(Vinus; www.vinothekvinus.it; Via Mercato Vecchio 6; ⊙10am-1pm & 4-10pm Mon & Tue, to midnight Wed-Fri, 10am-6pm Sat) A classy, dark, low-ceilinged space with an extensive wine-by-the-glass list. Peter – yes, that's him – offers a nightly *tavola calda* (a limited hot menu; mains €22) on Wednesdays and Fridays and Saturday lunch, and sometimes keeps pouring local drops until midnight.

La Habana
WINE BAR

(☎0472 83 66 00; www.facebook.com/HabanaBX; Via Portici Maggiore 14; ⊙8am-1pm & 2pm-midnight Mon-Sat) Smart hole-in-the-wall bar that caters equally well to workers sipping morning espresso, ladies who *spritz* mid-morning and students nursing a *hugo* (elderflower and sparkling wine) late into the night.

ℹ Getting There & Away

On the main Bolzano–Innsbruck line (25 minutes, €8.80, times vary), the town is connected by regionals half-hourly. Regional Val Pusteria trains connect to this line a little north at Fortezza (Franzensfeste).

Brunico (Bruneck)

☎0474 / POP 13,700 / ELEV 835M

As Val Pusteria's big smoke, Brunico is often relegated to a quick stop on the way to the slopes. But its quintessentially Tyrolean historic centre offers a delightful detour and a great local eating and drinking scene, not to mention easy access to good skiing and hiking, making longer stays a very attractive option.

◉ Sights & Activites

Kronplatz
SKIING

(Plan de Corones; www.kronplatz.com) This family-friendly ski area is covered by Dolomiti Superski (p323) and is easily accessible by public transport from Brunico, 4km to the north, or by the Ski Pustertal Express, a train that connects directly to the lift at Percha. The ample green and blue runs are still spectacularly set, a rare treat for beginners.

★ Messner Mountain Museum Kronplatz
MUSEUM

(MMM Corones; ☎0471 63 12 64; www.messner-mountain-museum.it; €8 (cash only), ⊙10am-4pm June-Oct, Dec–mid-Apr) Reinhold Messner's sixth and final mountain museum also sadly happened to be one of the final projects of star architect Zaha Hadid before her untimely death in 2016. Located at 2275m (access is only via the Kronplatz cable car), its buried concrete forms are both architecturally thrilling and spectacularly sited. Inside there's a touching, inspiring collection of objects that accompanied some of the world's most accomplished mountaineers on legendary ascents, displayed in descending galleries and spliced with views out to the peaks and valleys beyond.

War Cemetery
CEMETERY

(Via Riscone) This pristinely maintained cemetery is set in a forest on Kühbergl just behind the town and has graves of soldiers from the nearby WWI front as well as a section of WWII dead. Most of the WWI soldiers buried here are from the Slavic regions of the old Austro-Hungarian empire and there are Christian, Muslim and Jewish graves. It's a peaceful if solemn place.

🛏 Sleeping

⭐ La Pedevilla
APARTMENT €€

(☎0474 50 10 74; www.lapedevilla.it; Strada Pliscia 13, Enneberg; 2br apt €300; P✷🛜) It's only 20 minutes drive from Bruneck, but this stylish black-clad chalet – next to the architect-owner's home – feels deliciously remote. Two pine-floored bedrooms sit above an open living space that's both calmingly simple and super cosy. Huge windows make everyday cinema of the extraordinary, every-changing mountain and valley views and there's a design-focused library, big TV and a well-equipped kitchen.

⭐ Niedermairhof
B&B, BOUTIQUE HOTEL €€

(☎348 2476761; www.nmhof.it; Via Duca Teodone 1; ste €195-238; P✷🛜) Niedermairhof is a delightful meeting of family B&B and stylish boutique hotel, set in a rambling old 13th-century farmhouse on Kathrin Mair and Helmuth Mayr's working vegetable farm. There are eight spacious, beautifully designed rooms here, all different and all utterly charming. They variously feature balconies, big baths or mountain views and there's an airy guest loft for relaxing or kids' play.

🍴 Eating & Drinking

Acherer Patisserie & Blumen
PASTRIES €

(☎0474 41 00 30; www.acherer.com; Via Centrale; ⏲8am-12.30pm & 2.30-7pm Mon-Fri, 8am-1pm & 2-6pm Sat) Right by the town gate, Acherer Patisserie & Blumen sells strudel and Sachertorte that may just be the region's best; the young owner reopened his grandfather's former bakery after apprenticing in Vienna. His inventive, rather fancy cakes, chocolates and seasonal preserves now grace many of the region's five-starred pillows and breakfast buffets and you can pick them up here.

Pur Südtirol
CAFE, BAR €

(☎0474 05 05 00; www.pursuedtirol.com; Via Duca Sigismondo 4A; dishes €5-12; ⏲7.30am-7.15pm Mon-Fri, to 2pm Sat) Merano's local gourmet shop has a bustling Brunico outlet and sit-down lunches here are a great option, especially if you're in need of a break from goulash or schnitzel. There's a huge sandwich menu but follow the locals' lead and order one of the smoked fish or vegetarian

salads, washed down with a glass of small-producer white or local apple juice.

Rienzbräu Bruneck
ALPINE €€

(☎0474 53 13 07; www.facebook.com/rienz braeubruneck; Via Stegona 8; meals €20-27; ⏲10am-midnight) It would be sad to stop at this backstreet brewery for just a beer. Join big tables of locals by the vats for a sample of Oma's – grandma's – kitchen, with no-frills dishes ranging from drinking food like smoked beef and cheese plates and barley minestrone to simple pastas, schnitzels and steaks. They also do a rather good pizza.

Capuzina
BAR

(☎342 6834597; www.capuzina.com; Piazza Cappuccini 1; ⏲5pm-1am Tue-Sat) Fire pits and art school–style video projections give this bar a big-town feel although it's beloved by locals and staff are faulously welcoming. The *aperitivo* scene is also the town's best and there's some nice kicking on and a weekly *aperitivo lungo* – ie a big buffet – on Thursday evenings. Weekends are all about cocktails and there are Saturday-night DJs or live acts.

🛍 Shopping

Horvat Alimentari
FOOD & DRINKS

(☎0474 55 53 97; www.horvat.it; Via Centrale 5; ⏲8.30am-1.30pm, 3-7pm Mon-Fri, to 6pm Sat) Jars, tins and bottles of delicious things to take home line this redolently traditional deli. Self-caterers could do worse than a jar of their boar *ragù* or there are fascinating local herbal syrups, cordials and schnapps. And of course, *speck* and cheese in all its local forms.

Moessmer
FASHION & ACCESSORIES

(☎0474 53 31 11; www.moessmer.it; Via Vogelweide 6; ⏲9am-12.30pm & 2.30-6pm Mon-Fri, 9am-2.30pm Sat) Visit local wool manufacturer Moessmer for cashmere and Tyrolean tweeds from its outlet shop on the town's outskirts, or just for an interesting slice of early-20th-century industrial architecture.

ℹ Getting There & Away

SAD (☎840 000471, 0471 45 01 11; www.sad. it) buses connect Brunico (45 minutes, hourly) and Cortina (one hour, four daily) to San Candido. Brunico is easily accessible by train from both Bolzano (€6.90, 1½ hours, hourly; via Fortezza (€5.30, 1 hour, half-hourly)) and from Lienz in Austria. All regional trains are covered by the **HolidayPass** that most hotels offer to guests or can be bought from tourist offices.

Venice & the Veneto

Best Places to Eat

→ Antiche Carampane (p368)

→ Belle Parti (p381)

→ Gelateria Dassie (p397)

→ Locanda 4 Cuochi (p389)

→ Ristorante Quadri (p366)

Best Places to Sleep

→ Cima Rosa (p364)

→ Al Ponte Antico (p364)

→ Oltre Il Giardino (p364)

→ Agriturismo San Mattia (p388)

→ Hotel Gabbia d'Oro (p388)

Why Go?

Venice really needs no introduction. This incomparable union of art, architecture and lagoon-based living has been a fabled destination for centuries. No matter how many photographs, films or paintings you've seen, the reality is more surprising and romantic than you could ever imagine. Many of the world's most famous writers and artists have visited to admire the mosaics of San Marco, the masterpieces in the Accademia and the city's maze of *calle* (lanes) and canals. They've written and painted Venice into the world's imagination, so it is no wonder that tourists outnumber locals by two to one on summer days.

Beyond Venice, the remainder of the Veneto region is often overlooked, but it is no less enticing. Giotto's spectacular frescoes in Padua, Palladio's elegant architecture in Vicenza, Verona's romantic riverside location and the Unesco-designated landscapes of the Dolomites would be unmissable anywhere else. So take our advice: love Venice then leave her. You won't regret it.

When to Go
Venice

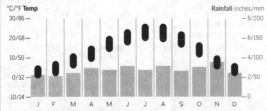

°C/°F Temp — Rainfall inches/mm

Dec–Feb Snow-covered gondolas, skiers in the Dolomites and Carnevale parties.

Apr–Jun Warming weather, canalside dining and Biennale openings.

Sep–Nov Venice International Film Festival, wild duck pasta and palatial accommodation for less.

Venice & the Veneto Highlights

1 Venice (p336)
Finally realising what all the fuss is about in this extraordinary city of canals, churches and palaces.

2 Padua (p378)
Gazing in awe at the Cappella degli Scrovegni then kicking back with the students in statue-lined Prato della Valle.

3 Verona (p382)
Experiencing opera in the astonishing 1st-century amphitheatre, right in the heart of the city centre.

4 Treviso (p396)
Tasting some of Italy's best gelato in this pretty mid-sized city.

5 La Strada del Prosecco (p398)
Taking a wine-fuelled tour of the vineyards strung out between Conegliano and Valdobbiadene.

6 Valpolicella (p390) Sampling one of Italy's boldest red wines, Amarone, at cutting-edge wineries.

7 Vicenza (p392)
Indulging in art and Palladian architecture in one of Italy's most underrated cities.

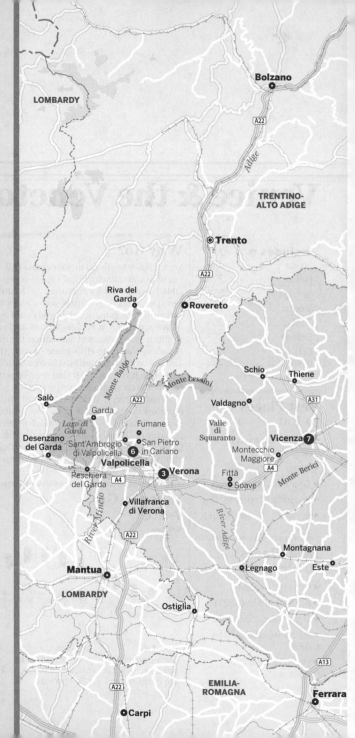

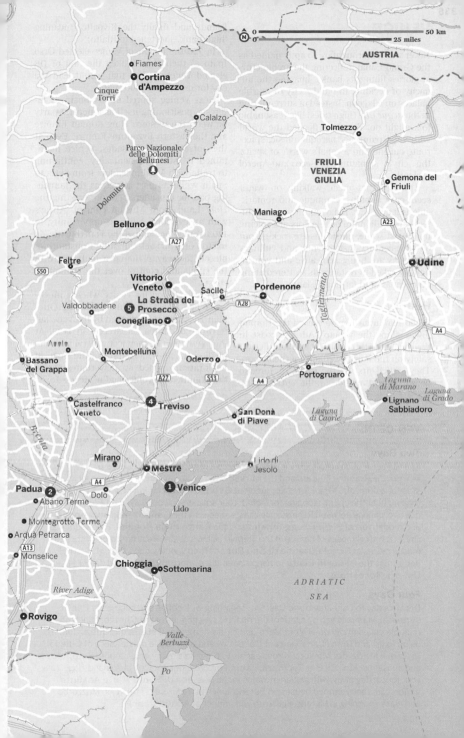

VENICE

POP 76,700

Never was a thoroughfare so aptly named as the Grand Canal, reflecting the architectural glories lining its banks. Imagine the audacity of deciding to build a city of marble palaces on a lagoon. Instead of surrendering to the *acque alte* (high tides) like reasonable folk might do, Venetians flooded the world with vivid paintings, baroque music, spice-route cuisine and a canal's worth of spritz, the city's signature prosecco-and-Aperol cocktail.

The city that made walking on water seem easy remains as unique and remarkable as it ever was. Today, cutting-edge architects and billionaire benefactors are spicing up the art scene, musicians are rocking out on 18th-century instruments, and culinary traditions are being kept alive and continually tweaked in restaurants scattered along quiet canals and far-flung islands.

History

When barbarian hordes sacked the Roman towns along the Veneto's Adriatic coast in the 5th and 6th centuries, refugees fled to safety on the murky wetlands of the lagoon. They settled first on the island of Torcello before spreading out to the surrounding islands and finally the Rivoalto (meaning 'high bank', shortened to Rialto).

In 726 the people of Venice elected Orso Ipato as their *doge* (duke), the first of 118 elected Venetian dogi that would lead the city for more than 1000 years.

Next Venice shored up its business interests, positioning itself as a neutral party between the western Holy Roman Empire and the eastern Byzantine Empire. Even at the outset of the Crusades, Venice maintained its strategic neutrality, continuing to trade with Muslim leaders from Syria to Spain while its port served as the launching pad for crusaders bent on wresting the Holy Land from Muslim control. Always with an eye for a business opportunity, in 1203 Venice persuaded the Fourth Crusade to stop off and sack Christian Constantinople on the way, claiming a hefty share of the spoils and control over the Dalmatian coast.

This backfired for Venice when a much-weakened Constantinople fell to the Ottoman Turks in 1453, followed by the Venetian territory of Morea (in Greece) in 1499. At the same time as they lost control over the Mediterranean trade routes, the Age of Exploration opened up new routes across the Atlantic that Venice had no access to.

VENICE & THE VENETO VENICE

VENICE IN...

Two Days

Spend your first day exploring Piazza San Marco's big hitters: the **Basilica di San Marco**, the **Palazzo Ducale** and the **Museo Correr**. When sensory overload kicks in, stop for a drink at **Caffè Florian** or lunch at **Osteria da Carla**. Put on your glad rags for a night at the opera, stopping for *cicheti* (bar snacks) on your way to **La Fenice**. On day two, choose between Renaissance masterpieces at the **Gallerie dell'Accademia** and modern art at **Peggy Guggenheim** and the **Punta della Dogana**. Follow lunch at **Riviera** with glimpses of heaven in the Tiepolo ceilings at **Ca' Rezzonico** or Tintoretto's masterpieces at **Scuola Grande di San Rocco**. Then window-shop through San Polo and across the **Ponte di Rialto** to happy hour at **Un Mondo di Vino** and dinner at **Osteria Boccadoro**.

Four Days

Devote a day to Cannaregio and Castello, beginning with coffee and pastries at **Pasticceria dal Mas** followed by a tour of the historic synagogues of the **Ghetto**. Lunch on multiple plates of *cicheti* at **Vino Vero** or a sit-down meal at **Osteria da Rioba**. Continue on to art and Grand Canal views at **Ca' d'Oro** and the marble masterpiece of **Chiesa di Santa Maria dei Miracoli**. Cross canals to Castello's many-splendoured **Zanipolo** and sunset cocktails at **Bar Terrazza Danieli** before dinner at **CoVino**. Island-hop your fourth day away, with golden mosaics in the **Basilica di Santa Maria Assunta** on Torcello, candy-striped houses on Burano, lunch at **Venissa Osteria** on Mazzorbo and glass shopping in Murano. Finish up with dinner at **Acquastanca**..

Once it could no longer rule the seas, Venice changed tack and began conquering Europe by charm. Venetian art was incredibly daring, bringing sensuous colour and sly social commentary even to religious subjects. By the end of the 16th century, Venice was known across Europe for its painting, catchy music and 12,000 registered prostitutes.

Venice's reputation did nothing to prevent Napoleon from claiming the city in 1797 and looting its art. By 1817, now under Austrian rule, one quarter of Venice's population was destitute. When Venice rallied to resist the Austrian occupation in 1848–49, a blockade left it wracked by cholera and short on food. Venetian rebels lost the fight but not the war: they became early martyrs to the cause of Italian independence, and in 1866 Venice joined the newly minted Kingdom of Italy.

In the 19th and early 20th centuries, Venice started to take on an industrious workaday aspect, with factories springing up on its fringes and a road connecting it to the mainland built by Mussolini. Venice emerged from WWII relatively unscathed from Allied bombing – but the mass deportation of Venice's Jewish population in 1943 had all but annihilated that historic community. Postwar, many Venetians left for Milan and other centres of industry.

On 4 November 1966 unprecedented floods struck the city, inundating 16,000 Venetian homes. But Venice's cosmopolitan charm was a saving grace: assistance from admirers poured in and Unesco coordinated international charities to redress the ravages of the flood.

It was decided to commission a system of barriers MoSE at the three mouths of the lagoon, which could be raised to prevent flooding during high tides. Initial costs were estimated at €1.5 billion with a completion date set for 1995. After a high-profile corruption scandal which claimed the scalp of the mayor, MoSE is not expected to be fully completed until 2022 and the price tag has risen to over €5 billion.

Just as public opinion questions the efficacy of MoSE as a solution to rising sea levels and a sinking city, Venice faces another rising tide – the boom in tourism – which threatens to overwhelm the city. Grassroots activists are demanding immediate measures to tackle the lack of affordable housing, a complete ban on cruise ships entering the

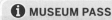

ⓘ MUSEUM PASS

The **Civic Museum Pass** (adult/reduced €24/18) is valid for six months and covers single entry to 11 civic museums, including Palazzo Ducale, Ca' Rezzonico, Ca' Pesaro, Palazzo Mocenigo, Museo Correr, the Museo del Vetro (Glass Museum) on Murano and the Museo del Merletto (Lace Museum) on Burano.

lagoon and the creation of a sustainable, long-term tourism strategy.

◉ Sights

As Tiziano Scarpa observed, the Rialto islands really do look like a fish, made up of the six *sestieri* (neighbourhoods): San Marco, San Polo, Santa Croce, Dorsoduro, Cannaregio and Castello, with the island of Giudecca underscoring it like a wavy tilde. So many world-class attractions are concentrated here that some visitors never leave. But Venice's past lies northeast on the glass manufacturing island of Murano, the fishing island of Burano and historic Torcello. East are the barrier islands of Lido and Pellestrina, where you'll find Venice's few beaches.

◉ San Marco

★ **Palazzo Ducale**   MUSEUM
(Ducal Palace; Map p342; ☑041 271 59 11; www.palazzoducale.visitmuve.it; Piazzetta San Marco 1; adult/reduced incl Museo Correr €19/12, with Museum Pass free; ◷8.30am-7pm Apr-Oct, to 5.30pm Nov-Mar; ⛴San Zaccaria) Holding pride of place on the waterfront, this pretty Gothic confection is an unlikely setting for the political and administrative seat of a great republic, but an exquisitely Venetian one. Beyond its dainty colonnades and geometrically patterned facade of white Istrian stone and pale pink Veronese marble lie grand rooms of state, the Doge's private apartments and a large complex of council chambers, courts and prisons.

The Doge's official residence probably moved to this site in the 10th century, although the current complex only started to take shape around 1340. In 1424, the wing facing the Piazzetta was added and the palace assumed its final form, give or take a few major fires and refurbishments.

Venice

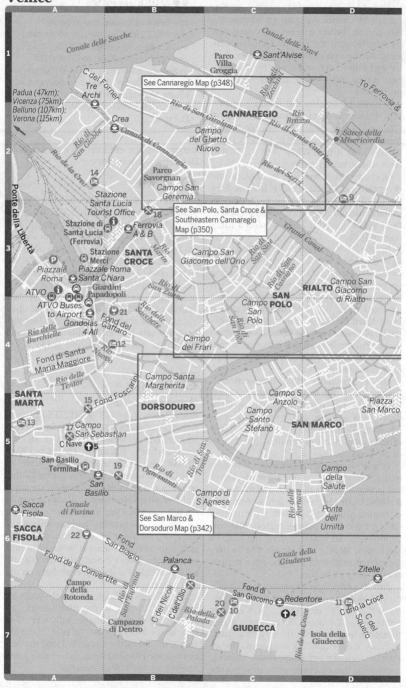

VENICE & THE VENETO

Padua (47km);
Vicenza (75km);
Belluno (107km);
Verona (115km)

To Ferrovia &

Canale delle Sacche

Canale delle Navi

Parco Villa Groggia

Sant'Alvise

C del Forner

Tre Archi

See Cannaregio Map (p348)

CANNAREGIO

Rio di San Girolamo

Rio dei Tre Archi

Rio Brazzo

Rio di Santa Caterina

Crea

7 Sacca della Misericordia

Campo del Ghetto Nuovo

Rio di San Giobbe

Canale di Cannaregio

Rio dei Serri

9

Rio de la Crea

14

Parco Savorgnan

Stazione Santa Lucia Tourist Office

Campo San Geremia

See San Polo, Santa Croce & Southeastern Cannaregio Map (p350)

18

Ferrovia A & B

Grand Canal

Stazione di Santa Lucia (Ferrovia)

SANTA CROCE

Rio Marin

Campo San Giacomo dell'Orio

Rio di San Stae

Stazione Merci

Santa Chiara

Piazzale Roma

Campo San Giacomo di Rialto

Piazzale Roma

RIALTO

Giardini Papadopoli

Rio di San Zuane

Rio di San Cassiano

ATVO

ATVO Buses to Airport

Gondolas 4 All

21

Rio delle Sacchere

SAN POLO

Campo San Polo

Rio di San Polo

Fond del Gaffaro

Rio delle Burchielle

12

Rio Novo

Campo dei Frari

Fond di Santa Maria Maggiore

Rio delle Tentor

Campo Santa Margherita

SANTA MARTA

15

Fond Foscarini

DORSODURO

Campo S Anzolo

Piazza San Marco

13

17

Campo San Sebastian

Campo Santo Stefano

SAN MARCO

C Nave

5

San Basilio Terminal

19

Rio di Ognissanti

Rio di San Trovaso

Campo della Salute

San Basilio

Rio delle Fornace

Ponte dell' Umiltà

Sacca Fisola

Canale di Fusina

Campo di S Agnese

SACCA FISOLA

22

Fond San Biagio

See San Marco & Dorsoduro Map (p342)

Fond de le Convertite

Rio di Sant'Eufemia

Palanca

Canale della Giudecca

Zitelle

Campo della Rotonda

16

Fond di San Giacomo

Redentore

11

C drio la Croce

C del Nicoli

C dell'Olio

20

10

4

C del Squero

Campazzo di Dentro

Rio della Palada

GIUDECCA

Isola della Giudecca

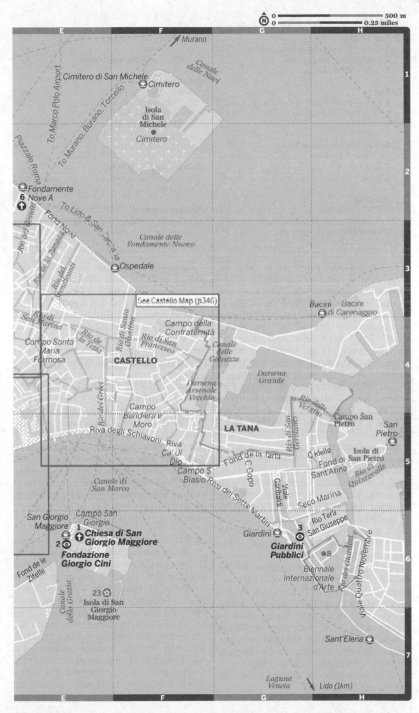

Venice

A standard ticket allows you access to the grand central **courtyard**, a display of historic masonry (**Museo dell'Opera**) on the ground floor and a circuit of the main part of the palace that leads through the state rooms, armoury, prisons and institutional rooms. The **Doge's Apartments** are now used for temporary art exhibitions, which are ticketed separately (around €10 extra). Further rooms, too small for the masses, can be visited on the 1¼-hour **Secret Itineraries Tour** (🗗 041 4273 0892; adult/reduced €20/14; ⊙ in English 9.55am, 10.45am & 11.35am, in Italian 9.30am & 11.10am, in French 10.20am & noon).

The most impressive parts of the palace are at the top. Ascend Sansovino's 24-carat gilt stuccowork **Scala d'Oro** (Golden Staircase) and emerge into rooms covered with gorgeous propaganda. In the Palladio-designed **Sala delle Quattro Porte** (Hall of the Four Doors), ambassadors awaited ducal audiences under a lavish display of Venice's virtues by Giovanni Cambi, Titian and Tiepolo.

Few were granted an audience in the Palladio-designed **Collegio** (Council Room), where Veronese's 1575–78 *Virtues of the Republic* ceiling shows Venice as a bewitching blonde waving her sceptre like a wand over Justice and Peace. Father-and-son team Jacopo and Domenico Tintoretto attempt similar flattery, showing Venice keeping company with Apollo, Mars and Mercury in their *Triumph of Venice* ceiling for the **Sala del Senato** (Senate Hall).

Government cover-ups were never so appealing as in the **Sala Consiglio dei Dieci** (Chamber of the Council of Ten), where Venice's star chamber plotted under Veronese's *Juno Bestowing Her Gifts on Venice,* a glowing goddess strewing gold ducats. Over the slot where anonymous treason accusations were slipped into the **Sala della Bussola** (Compass Room) is his *St Mark in Glory* ceiling.

The cavernous 1419 **Sala del Maggior Consiglio** (Grand Council Hall) provides the setting for Domenico Tintoretto's swirling *Paradise,* a work that's more politically correct than pretty: heaven is crammed with 500 prominent Venetians, including several Tintoretto patrons. Veronese's political posturing is more elegant in his oval *Apotheosis of Venice* ceiling, where gods marvel at Venice's coronation by angels, with foreign dignitaries and Venetian blondes rubbernecking on the balcony below.

★ **Basilica di San Marco**   CATHEDRAL
(St Mark's Basilica; Map p342; 🗗 041 270 83 11; www.basilicasanmarco.it; Piazza San Marco; ⊙ 9.45am-5pm Mon-Sat, 2-5pm Sun summer, to 4pm Sun winter; ⛴ San Marco) **FREE** With a profusion of domes and over 8000 sq metres of luminous mosaics, Venice's cathedral is an unforgettable sight. It was founded in the 9th century to house the corpse of St Mark after wily Venetian merchants smuggled it out of Egypt in a barrel of pork fat. When the original building burnt down in 932 Venice rebuilt the basilica in its own cosmopolitan image, with Byzantine domes, a Greek cross

layout and walls clad in marbles from Syria, Egypt and Palestine.

Unbelievably this incredibly sumptuous church was the Doge's private chapel. It only officially became Venice's cathedral in 1807 following the demise of the republic, replacing the considerably less grand Basilica di San Pietro in Castello.

The front of St Mark's ripples and crests like a wave, its five niched portals capped with shimmering mosaics and frothy stonework arches. It's especially resplendent just before sunset, when the sun's dying rays set the golden mosaics ablaze. The oldest mosaic on the facade, dating from 1270, is in the lunette above the far-left portal, depicting St Mark's stolen body arriving at the basilica. The theme is echoed in three of the other lunettes, including the 1660 mosaics above the second portal from the right, showing turbaned officials recoiling from the hamper of pork fat containing the sainted corpse. Grand entrances are made through the central portal, under an ornate triple arch featuring Egyptian purple porphyry columns and intricate 13th- to 14th-century stone reliefs.

There's no charge to enter the church and wander around the roped-off central circuit, although you'll need to dress modestly (ie knees and shoulders covered) and leave large bags around the corner at the **Ateneo San Basso Left Luggage Office** (free for maximum 1hr; ⊘9.30am-5pm). Those simply wishing to pray or attend Mass can enter from the **Porta dei Fiori**, on the north side of the church.

Blinking is natural upon your first glimpse of the basilica's glittering ceiling mosaics, many made with 24-carat gold leaf fused onto the back of the glass to represent divine light. Just inside the vestibule are the basilica's oldest mosaics: **Apostles with the Madonna**, standing sentry by the main door for more than 950 years. Inside the church proper, three golden domes vie for your attention. The images are intended to be read from the altar end to the entry, so the first dome you see is actually the last: the **Pentecost Cupola**, with the Holy Spirit represented by a dove shooting tongues of flame onto the heads of the surrounding saints. In the central 13th-century **Ascension Cupola**, angels swirl around the central figure of Christ hovering among the stars.

The **Cupola of the Prophets** is best seen from behind the main altar which houses the simple **sarcophagus** containing St

Mark's body. But the main reason visitors fork out €2 to enter this space is to see the stupendous **Pala d'Oro**, a gold altarpiece studded with 2000 emeralds, amethysts, sapphires, rubies, pearls and other gemstones. The screen's most priceless treasures, however, are biblical figures in vibrant cloisonné, begun in Constantinople in 976 AD and elaborated by Venetian goldsmiths in 1209. The embellished saints have wild, unkempt beards and wide eyes fixed on Jesus.

Other holy bones and booty from the Crusades fill the **Tesoro** (treasury; admission €3) and there are more treasures on show in the **museum** (adult/reduced €5/2.50; ⊘9.45am-4.45pm) upstairs, accessed from the vestibule. A highlight is the **Quadriga of St Mark's** (also known as the Triumphal Quadriga), a group of four bronze horses plundered from Constantinople and later carted off to Paris by Napoleon before being returned to the basilica. The originals are now kept inside but a door leads out to where they were originally placed on the **Loggia dei Cavalli**, where reproductions of the horses gallop off the balcony over Piazza San Marco.

Between mid-September and October, the diocese offers free **guided tours** (☑041 241 38 17; www.basilicasanmarco.it; ⊘11.30am Mon-Sat) explaining the theological messages in the mosaics. They're given in different languages on different days; check online for details.

Campanile   TOWER
(Bell Tower; Map p342; www.basilicasanmarco.it; Piazza San Marco; adult/reduced €8/4; ⊘8.30am-9.30pm summer, 9.30am-5.30pm winter, last entry 45min prior; ⛴San Marco) The basilica's 99m-tall bell tower has been rebuilt twice since its initial construction in AD 888. Galileo Galilei tested his telescope here in 1609, but today visitors head to the top for 360-degree lagoon views and close encounters

---

ⓘ CHURCH PASS

The association of Venice churches offers a **Chorus Pass** (adult/student under 29 years €12/8) for single entry to 16 historic Venice churches any time within one year (excluding I Frari). Otherwise, admission to these individual churches costs €3. Passes are for sale at church ticket booths; proceeds support restoration and maintenance of churches throughout Venice.

San Marco & Dorsoduro

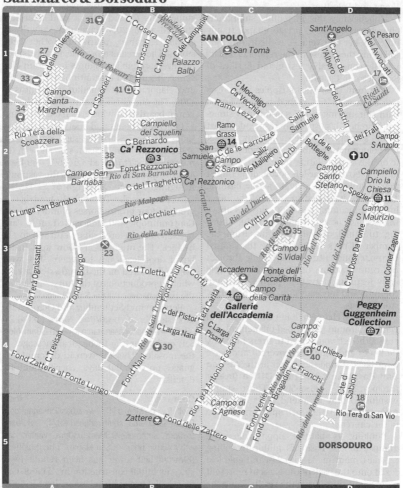

with the **Marangona**, the booming bronze bell that originally signalled the start and end of the working day for the artisans *(marangoni)* at the Arsenale shipyards. Today it rings twice a day, at noon and midnight.

Torre dell'Orologio
LANDMARK

(Clock Tower; Map p342; ☎041 4273 0892; www.museiciviciveneziani.it; Piazza San Marco; adult/reduced €12/7; ⊗tours by appointment; ☷San Marco) The two hardest-working men in Venice stand duty on a rooftop around the clock, and wear no pants. No need to file workers' complaints: the 'Do Mori' (Two Moors) exposed to the elements atop the Torre dell'Orologio are made of bronze, and their bell-hammering mechanism runs like, well, clockwork. Below the Moors, Venice's gold-leafed, 15th-century timepiece tracks lunar phases. Visits are by guided tour; bookings essential.

★ Museo Correr
MUSEUM

(Map p342; ☎041 240 52 11; www.correr.visit muve.it; Piazza San Marco 52; adult/reduced incl Palazzo Ducale €19/12, with Museum Pass free; ⊗10am-7pm Apr-Oct, to 5pm Nov-Mar; ☷San

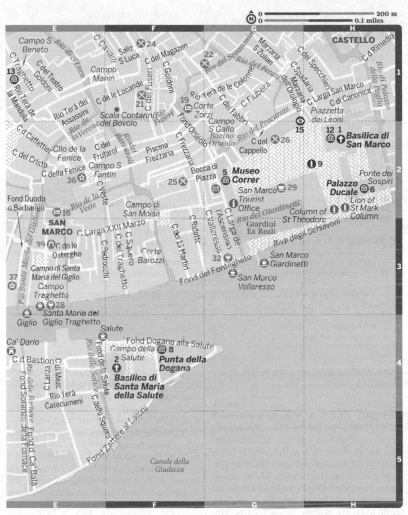

Marco) Napoleon bowled down an ancient church to build his royal digs over Piazza San Marco and then filled them with the riches of the doges while taking some of Venice's finest heirlooms to France as trophies. When Austria set up shop the Empress Sissi remodelled the palace, adding ceiling frescoes, silk cladding and brocade curtains. It's now open to the public and full of many of Venice's reclaimed treasures, including ancient maps, statues, cameos and four centuries of artistic masterpieces.

Scala Contarini del Bovolo NOTABLE BUILDING
(Map p342; ☑ 041 309 66 05; www.scalacontarini delbovolo.com; Calle Contarini del Bovolo 4299; adult/reduced €7/6; ☉10am-6pm; ☑ Sant'Angelo) Under the republic, only the church and state were permitted to erect towers, as they could conceivably be used for military purposes. In around 1400 the Contarini family, eager to show off their wealth and power, cheekily built this non-tower instead. Combining Venetian Gothic, Byzantine and Renaissance elements, this romantic 'staircase' looks even higher than its 26m due to the

San Marco & Dorsoduro

simple trick of decreasing the height of the arches as it rises.

Museo Fortuny MUSEUM
(Map p342; ☑041 520 09 95; www.fortuny.visit muve.it; Campo San Beneto 3958; adult/reduced €12/10; ☉10am-6pm Wed-Mon; ☺Sant'Angelo) Find design inspiration at the palatial home studio of art nouveau designer Mariano Fortuny y Madrazo (1871–1949), whose shockingly uncorseted Delphi goddess frocks set the standard for bohemian chic. First-floor salon walls are eclectic mood boards: Fortuny fashions and Isfahan tapestries, family portraits and artfully peeling plaster. Interesting temporary exhibitions spread from the basement to the attic, the best of which use the general ambience of grand decay to great effect.

Chiesa di Santo Stefano CHURCH
(Map p342; ☑041 522 50 61; www.chorusvenezia .org; Campo Santo Stefano; museum €4, with Chorus Pass free; ☉10.30am-4.30pm Mon-Sat; ☺Sant'Angelo) FREE The free-standing bell tower, visible from the square behind, leans disconcertingly, but this brick Gothic church has stood tall since the 13th century. Credit

for shipshape splendour goes to Bartolomeo Bon for the marble entry portal and to Venetian shipbuilders, who constructed the vast wooden *carena di nave* (ship's keel) ceiling that resembles an upturned Noah's Ark.

It's well worth visiting the sacristy museum to see three extraordinary and brooding 1575–80 Tintorettos: *The Last Supper,* with a ghostly dog begging for bread; the gathering gloom of *The Agony in the Garden;* and the mostly black, surprisingly modern, *Washing of the Feet.* There's also a small cloister.

◎ Castello

The vast crenellated walls of the Arsenale still dominate Venice's largest *sestiere* (district), but where it was once the secret preserve of highly skilled artisans feeding Venice's naval war machine, it is now thrown open annually to alternating throngs of art and architecture luvvies during the famous Biennale. The Riva degli Schiavoni is Venice's prime waterfront promenade, but step back into the maze of lanes and you'll still find washing lines strung between buildings and little neighbourhood cafes on sunny squares.

★ **Giardini Pubblici** GARDENS

(Map p338; ⊠ Giardini) Begun under Napoleon as the city's first public green space, these leafy gardens are now the main home of the Biennale. Only around half of the gardens is open to the public all year round as the rest is given over to the permanent **Biennale pavilions**, each representing a different country. Many of them are attractions in their own right, from Carlo Scarpa's daring 1954 raw-concrete-and-glass Venezuelan Pavilion to Denton Corker Marshall's 2015 Australian Pavilion in black granite.

Porta Magna GATE

(Map p346; Campo de l'Arsenal; ⊠ Arsenale) Capped by the lion of St Mark, the Arsenale's land gate is considered by many to be the earliest example of Renaissance architecture in Venice; it was probably executed in 1460. A plaque on the wall celebrates the 1571 victory at Lepanto, and at the foot of the gate is a row of carved lions; the biggest one, regally seated, was taken as booty by Francesco Morosini from the Greek port of Piraeus.

★ **Scuola Dalmata di San Giorgio degli Schiavoni** CHURCH

(Map p346; ☑ 041 522 88 28; Calle dei Furlani 3259a; adult/reduced €5/3; ⊙ 1.30-5.30pm Mon, 9.30am-5.30pm Tue-Sat, 9.30am-1.30pm Sun; ⊠ San Zaccaria) This 15th-century Dalmatian religious-confraternity house is dedicated to favourite Slavic saints George, Tryphon and Jerome, whose lives are captured with precision and glowing, early Renaissance grace by 15th-century master, Vittore Carpaccio.

Chiesa di San Zaccaria CHURCH

(Map p346; Campo San Zaccaria 4693; ⊙ 10am-noon & 4-6pm Mon-Sat, 4-6pm Sun; ⊠ San Zaccaria) **FREE** When 15th-century Venetian girls showed more interest in sailors than saints, they were sent to the convent adjoining San Zaccaria. The wealth showered on the church by their grateful parents is evident. Masterpieces by Bellini, Titian, Tintoretto and Van Dyck crowd the walls.

Palazzo Grimani MUSEUM

(Map p346; ☑ 041 520 03 45; www.palazzogrimani.org; Ramo Grimani 4858; adult/reduced €5/2.50; ⊙ 8.15am-7pm Tue-Sat, 2-7pm Sun; ⊠ San Zaccaria) The Grimani family built their Renaissance *palazzo* (mansion) in 1568 to showcase their extraordinary Graeco-Roman collection, which was destined to become the basis of the archaeological museum now housed in the Museo Correr (p342). Unusually for Venice, the palace has a Roman-style courtyard, which shed a flattering light on the archaeological curiosities. These days, the halls are mainly empty, though their bedazzling frescoed interiors are reason enough to visit.

★ **Zanipolo** BASILICA

(Basilica di San Giovanni e Paolo; Map p346; ☑ 041 523 59 13; www.basilicasantigiovanniepaolo.it; Campo Zanipolo; adult/reduced €2.50/1.25;

BRIDGES OF WOOD, STONE & SIGHS

Ponte dell'Accademia (Map p342; btwn Campo di San Vidal & Campo della Carità; ⊠ Accademia) The wooden Ponte dell'Accademia was built in 1933 as a temporary replacement for an 1854 iron bridge, but this span, arched like a cat's back, remains a beloved landmark. Engineer Eugenio Miozzi's notable works include the Lido Casino, but none has lasted like this elegant little footbridge – and recent structural improvements have preserved it for decades to come.

Ponte di Rialto (Map p350; ⊠ Rialto-Mercato) A superb feat of engineering, Antonio da Ponte's 1592 Istrian stone span took three years and 250,000 gold ducats to construct. Adorned with stone reliefs depicting St Mark, St Theodore and the Annunciation, the bridge crosses the Grand Canal at its narrowest point, connecting the neighbourhoods of San Polo and San Marco. Interestingly, it was da Ponte's own nephew, Antonio Contino, who designed the city's other iconic bridge, the Ponte dei Sospiri (Bridge of Sighs).

Ponte dei Sospiri (Bridge of Sighs; Map p342; ⊠ San Zaccaria) One of Venice's most photographed sights, the Bridge of Sighs connects the Palazzo Ducale to the 16th-century Priggione Nove (New Prisons). Its improbable popularity is due to British libertine Lord Byron (1788–1824), who mentioned it in his narrative poem *Childe Harold's Pilgrimage*. Condemned prisoners were said to sigh as they passed through the enclosed bridge and glimpsed the beauty of the lagoon. Now the sighs are mainly from people trying to dodge the snapping masses as they attempt to cross the neighbouring bridges.

Castello

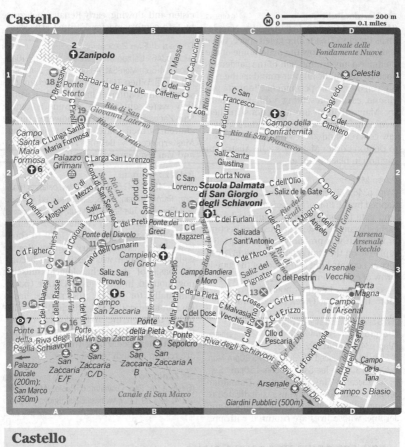

Castello

◎ Top Sights

◷ 9am-6pm Mon-Sat, noon-6pm Sun; ⊠ Ospedale) Commenced in 1333 but not finished until the 1430s, this vast church is similar in style and scope to the Franciscan Frari in San Polo which was being raised at the same time. Both oversized structures feature red-brick facades with high-contrast detailing in white stone. After its completion, Zanipolo quickly became the go-to church for ducal funerals and burials.

🎯 Cannaregio

Anyone could adore Venice on looks alone, but in Cannaregio you'll fall for its personality. A few streets over from bustling Strada Nova, footsteps echo along moody Fondamenta de la Misericordia, and there's not a T-shirt kiosk in sight. Between the art-filled Chiesa della Madonna dell'Orto, the Renaissance miracle of Chiesa di Santa Maria dei Miracoli and the tiny island Ghetto, a living monument to the outsized contributions of Venice's Jewish community, are some of Venice's top casual eateries and *cicheti* (Venetian tapas) bars.

★Chiesa di Santa Maria
dei Miracoli   CHURCH
(Map p350; Campo dei Miracoli 6074; adult/reduced €3/1.50, with Chorus Pass free; ⏰10.30am-1.30pm Mon Sat; 🚤Fondamento Novo) When Nicolò di Pietro's *Madonna* icon started miraculously weeping in its outdoor shrine around 1480, crowd control became impossible. With public fundraising and marble scavenged from San Marco slag heaps, this magnificent church was built (1481–89) to house the painting. Pietro and Tullio Lombardo's design dropped grandiose Gothic in favour of human-scale harmonies, introducing Renaissance church architecture to Venice.

I Gesuiti   CHURCH
(Santa Maria Assunta; Map p338; 🚤041 528 65 79; Salizada dei Specchieri 4882; €1; ⏰10am-noon & 3.30-5.30pm; 🚤Fondamente Nove) Giddily over the top even by rococo standards, this glitzy 18th-century Jesuit church is difficult to take in all at once, with staggering white-and-green intarsia (inlaid marble) walls that look like a version of Venetian flocked wallpaper, marble curtains draped over the pulpit and a marble carpet spilling down the altar stairs. While the ceiling is a riot of gold-and-white stuccowork, gravity is provided by Titian's uncharacteristically gloomy *Martyrdom of St Lawrence,* on the left as you enter the church.

★Galleria Giorgio
Franchetti alla Ca' d'Oro   MUSEUM
(Map p350; 🚤041 520 03 45; www.cadoro.org; Calle di Ca' d'Oro 3932; adult/reduced €8.50/4.25; ⏰8.15am-2pm Mon, to 7.15pm Tue-Sun; 🚤Ca' d'Oro) One of the most beautiful buildings on the Grand Canal, 15th-century Ca' d'Oro's lacy arcaded Gothic facade is resplendent even without the original gold leaf details that gave the palace its name (Golden House). Baron Franchetti (1865–1922) bequeathed this treasure-box palace to Venice, packed with his collection of masterpieces, many of which were originally plundered from Veneto churches during Napoleon's

---

ISLAND ESCAPE: LIDO DI VENEZIA

The **Lido** (🚤Lido SME) is no longer the glamorous bolt-hole of Hollywood starlets and European aristocracy that it once was, but its groomed beaches, scattering of art nouveau buildings and summering Venetians sipping *prosecco* (sparkling white wine) beneath candy-striped awnings make it an interesting diversion on a hot day. However, the presence of cars and suburban sprawl can be jarring after the lost-in-time nature of central Venice, and in winter even fading glamour is in short supply

Beaches

A near-continuous stretch of sand is spread out alongside the seaward side of the Lido. The shallow gradient makes it ideal for toddlers but not great for adults and, despite its somewhat murky appearance, it has been granted Blue Flag status, certifying that the water quality is of a high standard for swimming.

There are only six 'free' beaches open to the public: the **spiaggia comunale** accessed through the **Blue Moon complex** (Piazzale Bucintoro 1; ⏰10am-6.30pm summer; 🚹; 🚤Lido SME), two north of here, one a little further south and two near the **Pineta degli Alberoni** (Lido; 🚌A) at the southern end of the island.

The rest of the shoreline is occupied by *stabilimenti:* privately managed areas lined with wooden *capannas* (cabins), a relic of the Lido's 1850s bathing scene. Many of them are rented by the same families year in, year out or reserved for guests of seafront hotels. The *stabilimenti* also offer showers, sun loungers and umbrellas (€13 to €18) and small lockers. Rates drop a few euros after 2.30pm.

Cannaregio

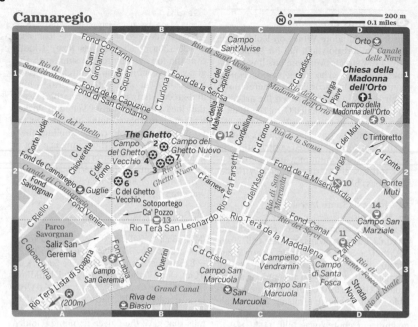

Cannaregio

conquest of Italy. The baron's ashes are interred beneath an ancient purple porphyry column in the magnificent open-sided, mosaic-floored court downstairs.

★ **Chiesa della Madonna dell'Orto** CHURCH
(Map p348; Campo de la Madonna dell'Orto 3520; adult/reduced €3/2; ◎10am-5pm Mon-Sat; ☉Orto) This elegantly spare 1365 brick Gothic church remains one of Venice's best-kept secrets. It was the parish church of Venetian Renaissance painter Tintoretto (1518–94), who filled the church with his paintings and is buried in the chapel to the right of the altar.

★ **The Ghetto** JEWISH SITE
(Map p348; ☉Guglie) In medieval times this part of Cannaregio housed a *getto* (foundry). But it was as the designated Jewish quarter from the 16th to 19th centuries that the word acquired a whole new meaning. In accordance with the Venetian Republic's 1516 decree, Jewish lenders, doctors and clothing merchants were allowed to attend to Venice's commercial interests by day, while at night and on Christian holidays, they were locked into the gated island of the **Ghetto Nuovo** (New Foundry). When Jewish merchants fled the Spanish Inquisition for Venice in 1541, there was no place to go in the Ghetto but up. Around the Campo del Ghetto Nuovo, upper storeys housed new arrivals, synagogues and publishing houses. A plain wooden cupola in the corner of

the *campo* marks the location of the **Schola Canton** (Corner Synagogue; Map p348; Campo del Ghetto Nuovo; ⊙ entry by guided tour via Museo Ebraico). Next door is the **Schola Tedesca** (German Synagogue; Map p348; Campo del Ghetto Nuovo; ⊙ entry by guided tour via Museo Ebraico), while the rooftop **Schola Italiana** (Italian Synagogue; Map p348; Campo del Ghetto Nuovo; ⊙ entry by guided tour via Museo Ebraico) is a simple synagogue built by newly arrived and largely destitute Italian Jews, who had fled from Spanish-controlled southern Italy.

As numbers grew, the Ghetto was extended into the neighbouring **Ghetto Vecchio** (Old Foundry), creating the confusing situation where the older Jewish area is called the New Ghetto and the newer is the Old Ghetto. Sephardic Jewish refugees raised two synagogues in the Campo di Ghetto Vecchio that are considered among the most beautiful in northern Italy, which were lavishly rebuilt in the 17th century. The **Schola Levantina** (Levantine Synagogue; Map p348; Campo del Ghetto Vecchio), founded in 1541, has a magnificent 17th-century woodworked pulpit, while the **Schola Spagnola** (Spanish Synagogue; Map p348; Campo del Ghetto Vecchio; ⊙ entry by guided tour via Museo Ebraico), founded around 1580, shows just how Venetian the community had become, with a flair for Venetian architectural flourishes: repeating geometric details, high-arched windows, and exuberant marble and carved-wood baroque interiors.

After Venice fell to Napoleon in 1787 the city's Jews experienced six months of freedom before the Austrian administration restricted them to the Ghetto once again. It wasn't until Venice joined with Italy in 1866 that full emancipation was gained, but even that was short lived. Many of Venice's Jews fled before the Nazi occupation but 246 were arrested and sent to the camps between 1943 and 1944; only eight survived. A **memorial** consisting of harrowing bas reliefs and the names and ages of those killed now lines two walls facing Campo del Ghetto Nuovo.

Although you can stroll around this peaceful precinct day and night, the best way to truly experience the Ghetto is to take one of the guided tours of three of the synagogues offered by the Museo Ebraico, departing hourly from 10.30am.

Museo Ebraico   MUSEUM
(Jewish Museum; Map p348; ☏ 041 71 53 59; www.museoebraico.it; Campo del Ghetto Nuovo 2902b; adult/reduced €8/6, incl tour €12/10; ⊙ 10am-7pm Sun-Fri Jun-Sep, to 5.30pm Sun-Fri Oct-May; ☒ Guglie) This museum explores the history of Venice's Jewish community and showcases its pivotal contributions to Venetian, Italian and world history. Opened in 1955, it has a small collection of finely worked silverware and other objects used in private prayer and to decorate synagogues, as well as early books that were published in the Ghetto during the Renaissance.

⊙ San Polo & Santa Croce

Heavenly devotion and earthly delights co-exist in San Polo and Santa Croce, where divine art rubs up against the ancient red-light district, now home to artisan workshops and *osterie* (taverns).

Museo di Storia
Naturale di Venezia   MUSEUM
(Fondaco dei Turchi, Museum of Natural History; Map p350; ☏ 041 275 02 06; www.visitmuve.it; Salizada del Fontego dei Turchi 1730, Santa Croce; adult/reduced €8/5.50; ⊙ 10am-6pm Tue-Sun Jun-Oct, 9am-5pm Tue-Fri, 10am-6pm Sat & Sun Nov-May; ☒ San Stae) Never mind the doge: insatiable curiosity rules Venice, and inside the Museo di Storia Naturale it runs wild. The adventure begins upstairs with dinosaurs and prehistoric crocodiles, then dashes through evolution to Venice's great age of exploration, when adventurers like Marco Polo fetched peculiar specimens from distant lands.

Palazzo Mocenigo   MUSEUM
(Map p350; ☏ 041 72 17 98, tour reservations 041 270 03 70; www.visitmuve.it; Salizada di San Stae 1992, Santa Croce; adult/reduced €8/5.50; ⊙ 10am-5pm Tue-Sun Apr-Oct, to 4pm Nov-Mar; ☒ San Stae) Venice received a dazzling addition to its property portfolio in 1945 when Count Alvise Nicolò Mocenigo bequeathed his family's 17th-century *palazzo* to the city. While the ground floor hosts temporary exhibitions, the *piano nobile* (main floor) is where you'll find a dashing collection of historic fashion, from duchess *andrienne* (hip-extending dresses) to exquisitely embroidered silk waistcoats. Adding to the glamour and intrigue is an exhibition dedicated to the art of fragrance – an ode to Venice's 16th-century status as Europe's capital of perfume.

San Polo, Santa Croce & Southeastern Cannaregio

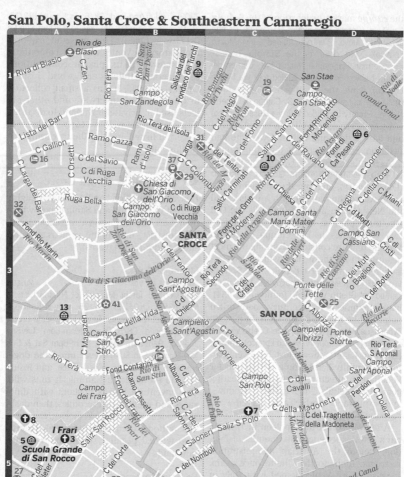

Ca' Pesaro
MUSEUM

(Galleria Internazionale d'Arte Moderna e Museo d'Arte Orientale; Map p350; ☑041 72 11 27; www.visitmuve.it; Fondamenta di Ca' Pesaro 2070, Santa Croce; adult/reduced €14/11.50; ⏱10am-6pm Tue-Sun summer, to 5pm winter; ⛴San Stae) Like a Carnevale costume built for two, the stately exterior of this Baldassare Longhena-designed 1710 *palazzo* hides two intriguing museums: **Galleria Internazionale d'Arte Moderna** and **Museo d'Arte Orientale**. While the former includes art showcased at the Venice Biennale, the latter holds treasures from Prince Enrico di Borbone's epic

1887–89 souvenir-shopping spree across Asia. Competing with the artworks are Ca' Pesaro's fabulous painted ceilings, which hint at the power and prestige of the Pesaro clan.

★ Rialto Market
MARKET

(Map p350; ☑041 296 06 58; San Polo; ⏱7am-2pm; ⛴Rialto-Mercato) Venice's Rialto Market has been whetting appetites for seven centuries. To see it at its best arrive in the morning with trolley-toting shoppers and you'll be rewarded with pyramids of colourful seasonal produce like Sant'Erasmo

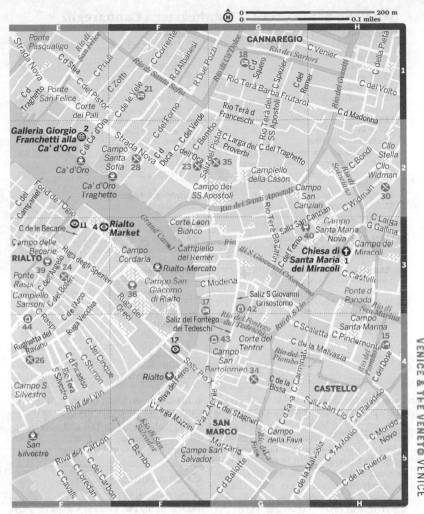

castraure (baby artichokes), *radicchio trevisano* (bitter red chicory) and thick, succulent white asparagus. If you're in the market for picnic provisions, vendors may offer you samples. Nearby is the **Pescaria** (Fish Market; Map p350; Rialto, San Polo; ⊙7am-2pm Tue-Sun; ⏹Rialto-Mercato).

★**I Frari** CHURCH
(Basilica di Santa Maria Gloriosa dei Frari; Map p350; ☑041 272 86 18; www.basilicadeifrari. it; Campo dei Frari 3072, San Polo; adult/reduced €3/1.50; ⊙9am-6pm Mon-Sat, 1-6pm Sun; ⏹San Tomà) A soaring Gothic church, I Frari's

assets include marquetry choir stalls, Canova's pyramid mausoleum, Bellini's achingly sweet *Madonna with Child* triptych in the sacristy, and Longhena's creepy Doge Pesaro funereal monument.

Upstaging them all, however, is the small altarpiece. This is Titian's 1518 *Assunta* (Assumption), in which a radiant red-cloaked Madonna reaches heavenward, steps onto a cloud and escapes this mortal coil. Titian himself – lost to the plague in 1576 – is buried near his celebrated masterpiece.

San Polo, Santa Croce & Southeastern Cannaregio

Chiesa di San Rocco CHURCH
(Map p350; ☎ 041 523 48 64; Campo San Rocco 3053, San Polo; ◷9.30am-1pm & 2.30-5.30pm; ⛴San Tomà) FREE Originally built between 1489 and 1508, Bartolomeo Bon's creation received a baroque facelift in 1765–71, which included a grand portal flanked by Giovanni Marchiori statues. Bon's rose window was moved to the side of the church, near the architect's original side door. Inside the church's Sala dell'Albergo are a couple of comparatively quiet Tintorettos, including *St Rocco Healing the Animals*.

★Scuola Grande di San Rocco MUSEUM
(Map p350; ☎ 041 523 48 64; www.scuolagrande sanrocco.it; Campo San Rocco 3052, San Polo; adult/reduced €10/8; ◷9.30am-5.30pm; ⛴San Tomà) Everyone wanted the commission to paint this building dedicated to the patron saint of the plague-stricken, so Tintoretto cheated: instead of producing sketches like rival Veronese, he gifted a splendid ceiling panel of patron St Roch, knowing it couldn't be refused, or matched by other artists. The artist documents Mary's life story in the assembly hall, and both Old and New Testament scenes in the Sala Grande Superiore, upstairs.

◉ Dorsoduro

★Ca' Rezzonico MUSEUM
(Museum of the 18th Century; Map p342; ☎041 241 01 00; www.visitmuve.it; Fondamenta Rezzonico 3136, Dorsoduro; adult/reduced €10/7.50; ◷10am-6pm Wed-Mon summer, to 5pm winter; ⛴Ca' Rezzonico) Baroque dreams come true at Baldassare Longhena's Grand Canal palace, where a marble staircase leads to gilded ballrooms, frescoed salons and sumptuous boudoirs. Giambattista Tiepolo's Throne Room ceiling is a masterpiece of elegant social climbing, showing gorgeous Merit ascending to the Temple of Glory clutching the Golden Book of Venetian nobles' names – including Tiepolo's patrons, the Rezzonico family.

★ Gallerie dell'Accademia GALLERY

(Map p342; ☎041 520 03 45; www.gallerieac cademia.org; Campo della Carità 1050, Dorsoduro; adult/reduced €12/6, 1st Sun of month free; ☺8.15am-2pm Mon, to 7.15pm Tue-Sun; ⛴Accademia) Venice's historic gallery traces the development of Venetian art from the 14th to 18th centuries, with works by Bellini, Titian, Tintoretto, Veronese and Canaletto, among others. The former Santa Maria della Carità convent complex housing the collection maintained its serene composure for centuries until Napoleon installed his haul of Venetian art trophies here in 1807. Since then there's been non-stop visual drama on its walls.

★ Peggy Guggenheim Collection MUSEUM

(Map p342; ☎041 240 54 11; www.guggen heim-venice.it; Palazzo Venier dei Leoni 704, Dorsoduro; adult/reduced €15/9; ☺10am-6pm Wed-Mon; ⛴Accademia) After losing her father on the *Titanic,* heiress Peggy Guggenheim became one of the great collectors of the 20th century. Her palatial canalside home, Palazzo Venier dei Leoni, showcases her stockpile of surrealist, futurist and abstract expressionist art with works by up to 200 artists, including her ex-husband Max Ernst, Jackson Pollock (among her many rumoured lovers), Picasso and Salvador Dalí.

★ Basilica di Santa Maria della Salute BASILICA

(La Salute; Map p342; www.basilicasalutevenezia.it; Campo della Salute 1b, Dorsoduro; basilica free, sacristy adult/reduced €4/2; ☺basilica 9.30am-noon & 3-5.30pm, sacristry 10am-noon & 3-5pm Mon-Sat, 3-5pm Sun; ⛴Salute) Guarding the entrance to the Grand Canal, this 17th-century domed church was commissioned by Venice's plague survivors as thanks for their salvation. Baldassare Longhena's uplifting design is an engineering feat that defies simple logic; in fact, the church is said to have mystical curative properties. Titian eluded the plague until age 94, leaving 12 key paintings in the basilica's art-slung sacristy.

★ Punta della Dogana GALLERY

(Map p342; ☎041 271 90 39; www.palazzograssi.it; Fondamente della Dogana alla Salute 2, Dorsoduro; adult/reduced €15/10, incl Palazzo Grassi €18/15; ☺10am-7pm Wed-Mon Apr-Nov; ⛴Salute) Fortuna, the weathervane atop Punta della Dogana, swung Venice's way in 2005, when bureaucratic hassles in Paris convinced art collector François Pinault to showcase his works in Venice's long-abandoned customs

---

ℹ ACCADEMIA TIPS

➡ There's free admission to the gallery on the first Sunday of each month.

➡ To skip ahead of the queues in high season, book tickets in advance online (booking fee €1.50).

➡ Queues are shorter in the afternoon; last entry is 45 minutes before closing, but a proper visit takes at least 1½ hours.

➡ The audio guide (€6) is mostly descriptive and largely unnecessary – avoid the wait and follow your bliss and the explanatory wall tags.

➡ Bags larger than 20x30x15cm need to be stored in the lockers, which require a refundable €1 coin.

---

warehouses. Built by Giuseppe Benoni in 1677 to ensure no ship entered the Grand Canal without paying duties, the warehouses reopened in 2009 after a striking reinvention by Tadao Ando. The dramatic space now hosts exhibitions of ambitious, large-scale contemporary artworks from some of the world's most provocative creative minds.

◉ Giudecca

Chiesa del Santissimo Redentore CHURCH

(Church of the Most Holy Redeemer; Map p338; www.chorusvenezia.org; Campo del SS Redentore 194, Giudecca; adult/reduced €3/1.50, with Chorus Pass free; ☺10.30am-4.30pm Mon-Sat; ⛴Redentore) Built to celebrate the city's deliverance from the Black Death, Palladio's *Il Redentore* was completed under Antonio da Ponte (of Rialto Bridge fame) in 1592. Inside there are works by Tintoretto, Veronese and Bassano, but the most striking is Paolo Piazza's 1619 *Venice's Offering for Liberation from the Plague of 1575–77*, near the door.

◉ Isola di San Giorgio Maggiore

★ Chiesa di San Giorgio Maggiore CHURCH

(Map p338; ☎041 522 78 27; www.abbaziasan giorgio.it; Isola di San Giorgio Maggiore; bell tower adult/reduced €6/4; ☺8.30am-6pm; ⛴San Giorgio Maggiore) FREE Solar eclipses are only marginally more dazzling than Palladio's white Istrian stone facade at this abbey church. Begun in 1565 and completed in 1610, it owes more to ancient Roman temples than the bombastic baroque of Palladio's day. Inside, ceilings billow over a generous nave, with

VENICE & THE VENETO VENICE

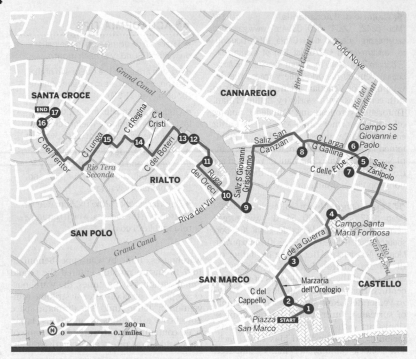

City Walk
Venice Labyrinth

START PIAZZA SAN MARCO
END CAMPO SAN GIACOMO DELL'ORIO
LENGTH 6KM; TWO HOURS, EXCLUDING
LUNCH AND DRINKS

This adventure begins with a salute to
1 Basilica di San Marco (p340). Duck under the **2 Torre dell'Orologio** (p342) and
follow the *calle* veering right into **3 Campo
della Guerra**. Pass over the bridge along Calle
de la Guerra into **4 Campo Santa Maria
Formosa**. Straight ahead is Calle Lunga Santa
Maria della Formosa; follow it and bear left
across two bridges to Salizada San Zanipolo,
then turn left to appear beside the massive
Gothic basilica, **5 Zanipolo** (p345), and the
beautiful facade of the **6 Scuola Grande di
San Marco**. This is a good pitstop for a *spritz*
or gelato at popular *campo* cafe **7 Rosa
Salva**.

Facing Zanipolo, Calle Larga Gallina leads
over a bridge; follow along and bear left to the
marble-clad **8 Chiesa di Santa Maria dei
Miracoli** (p347). Backtrack over the last
bridge and continue west through Campo
Santa Maria Nova towards Salizada San Canzian, which you'll follow around to Salizada
San Giovanni Grisostomo and down to skinny
9 Campo San Bartolomeo, lined with souvenir stalls. To the west is **10 Ponte di Rialto**
(p345); stay on the right as you cross and
duck towards **11 Campo di San Giacomo di
Rialto**. Continue along the Grand Canal to the
produce-piled **12 Rialto Mercato** (p350)
and the covered seafood market, **13 Pescaria**
(p351).

Head up to Calle dei Boteri and follow it
along to boutique-lined Calle dei Cristi, where
you'll come to **14 Campo San Cassian**, the
site of the world's first public opera house.
Cross the bridge to Calle de la Regina, turn left
and then head right across another bridge to
15 Campo di Santa Maria Mater Dominii,
with its cafes and ancient neighbourhood well.
Turn left down Calle Lunga and over a bridge
until it dead-ends, then right to Rio Terà Seconda, left and right again onto Calle del Tentor.
Ahead, you'll see the medieval church, **16 San
Giacomo dell'Orio**, and your pick of Italy's
best natural-process wines at **17 Al Prosecco**
(p371).

high windows distributing filtered sunshine. Two of Tintoretto's masterworks flank the altar, and a lift whisks visitors up the 60m-high bell tower for stirring panoramas – a great alternative to queuing at San Marco's *campanile*.

★**Fondazione Giorgio Cini** CULTURAL CENTRE
(Map p338; ☑ 347 338 64 26; www.cini.it; Isola di San Giorgio Maggiore; adult/reduced €10/8; ⏰ tours 10am-5pm Sat & Sun; ☒ San Giorgio Maggiore) In 1951, industrialist and art patron Vittorio Cini – a survivor of Dachau – acquired the monastery of San Giorgio and restored it in memory of his son, Giorgio Cini. The rehabilitated complex is an architectural treasure incorporating designs by Palladio and Baldassare Longhena. Weekend tours allow you to stroll through a garden labyrinth and contemplate the tranquil Cypress Cloister, the oldest extant part of the complex (1526). Check the website for exhibitions, events and performances in the open-air **Teatro Verde**.

◉ Isola di San Lazzaro degli Armeni

Once the site of a Benedictine hospice for pilgrims and then a leper colony, this tiny island was given to Armenian monks fleeing Ottoman persecution in 1717. The entire island is still a working **monastery** (☑ 041 526 01 04; Isola di San Lazzaro degli Armeni; adult/reduced €6/4.50; ⏰ tours 3.25pm; ☒ San Lazzaro), so access is by tour only.

◉ Isola di San Michele

This picturesque walled islet, positioned between Murano and the city, is Venice's main cemetery. *Vaporetti* 4.1 and 4.2 stop here, en route between Fondamente Nove and Murano.

Cimitero di San Michele CEMETERY
(Map p338; Isola di San Michele; ⏰ 7.30am-6pm Apr-Sep, to 4.30pm Oct-Mar; ☒ Cimitero) FREE
Until Napoleon established a city cemetery on this little island, Venetians had been buried in parish plots across town – not an ideal solution in a watery city. Today, goths, incorrigible romantics and music lovers pause here to pay respects to Ezra Pound, Joseph Brodsky, Sergei Diaghilev and Igor Stravinsky. Pick up a map from the information point near the entrance and join them, but be aware, the map pinpointing of the famous graves isn't accurate.

◉ Murano

Venetians have been working in glass since the 10th century, but due to the fire hazards of glass-blowing, the industry was moved to the island of Murano in the 13th century. Woe betide the glass-blower with wanderlust: trade secrets were so jealously guarded that any glass worker who left the city was guilty of treason and subject to assassination. Today, glass artisans continue to ply their trade at workshops all over the island, but particularly on Fondamenta dei Vetrai.

Murano is less than 10 minutes from Fondamente Nove by *vaporetto* and services are frequent.

Museo del Vetro MUSEUM
(Glass Museum; ☑ 041 527 47 18; www.museovetro. visitmuve.it; Fondamenta Giustinian 8, Murano; adult/reduced €10/7.50, free with Museum Pass; ⏰ 10am-5pm; ☒ Museo) Since 1861, Murano's glass-making prowess has been celebrated in Palazzo Giustinian (the seat of the Torcello bishopric from 1659 until its dissolution in 1818) and renovations finally do justice to the fabulous collection. On entry a video geeks out on the technical processes innovated on Murano, while upstairs eight rooms have beautifully curated displays of objects dating back to the 5th century BC.

Basilica del SS Maria e Donato CHURCH
(www.sandonatomurano.it; Campo San Donato, Murano; ⏰ 9am-6pm Mon-Sat, 12.30-6pm Sun; ☒ Museo) FREE Fire-breathing is the unifying theme of Murano's medieval church, with its astounding 12th-century gilded-glass apse mosaic of the Madonna made in Murano's *fornaci* (furnaces) and the bones of a dragon hanging behind the altar. According to tradition, this beast was slayed by St Donatus of Arezzo, whose mortal remains also rest here. The other masterpiece here is underfoot: a Byzantine-style 12th-century mosaic pavement of waving geometric patterns and peacocks rendered in porphyry, serpentine and other precious stones.

◉ Burano & Mazzorbo

Once Venice's lofty Gothic architecture leaves you feeling overwhelmed, Burano brings you back to your senses with a reviving shock of colour. The 50-minute ferry ride on line 12 from the Fondamente Nove is packed with amateur photographers preparing to bound into Burano's backstreets, snapping away at pea-green stockings hung to dry between hot-pink and royal-blue houses.

Grand Canal

A WATER TOUR

The 3.5km route of vaporetto (passenger ferry) No 1, which passes some 50 palazzi (mansions), six churches and scene-stealing backdrops featured in four James Bond films, is public transport at its most glamorous.

The Grand Canal starts with controversy: ❶ **Ponte di Calatrava** a luminous glass-and-steel bridge that cost triple the original €4 million estimate. Ahead are castle-like ❷ **Fondaco dei Turchi**, the historic Turkish trading-house; Renaissance ❸ **Palazzo Vendramin**, housing the city's casino; and double-arcaded ❹ **Ca' Pesaro**. Don't miss ❺ **Ca' d'Oro**, a 1430 filigree Gothic marvel.

Points of Venetian pride include the ❻ **Pescaria**, built in 1907 on the site where fishmongers have been slinging lagoon crab for 600 years, and neighbouring ❼ **Rialto Market** stalls, overflowing with island-grown produce. Cost overruns for 1592 ❽ **Ponte di Rialto** rival Calatrava's, but its marble splendour stands the test of time.

The next two canal bends could cause architectural whiplash, with Sanmicheli-designed Renaissance ❾ **Palazzo Grimani** and Mauro Codussi's ❿ **Palazzo Corner-Spinelli** followed by Giorgio Masari-designed ⓫ **Palazzo Grassi** and Baldassare Longhena's baroque jewel box, ⓬ **Ca' Rezzonico**.

Wooden ⓭ **Ponte dell'Accademia** was built in 1930 as a temporary bridge, but the beloved landmark remains. Stone lions flank the ⓮ **Peggy Guggenheim Collection**, where the American heiress collected ideas, lovers and art. You can't miss the dramatic dome of Longhena's ⓯ **Chiesa di Santa Maria della Salute** or ⓰ **Punta della Dogana**, Venice's triangular customs warehouse reinvented as a contemporary art showcase. The Grand Canal's grand finale is pink Gothic ⓱ **Palazzo Ducale** and its adjoining ⓲ **Ponte dei Sospiri**.

Palazzo Grassi
French magnate François Pinault scandalised Paris when he relocated his contemporary art collection here, to be displayed in galleries designed by Gae Aulenti and Tadao Ando.

Ca' Rezzonico
See how Venice lived in baroque splendour at this 18th-century art museum with Tiepolo ceilings, silk-swagged boudoirs and even an in-house pharmacy.

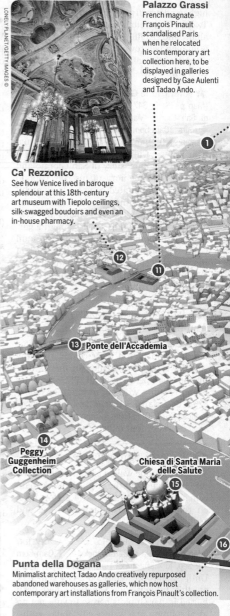

Ponte dell'Accademia

Peggy Guggenheim Collection

Chiesa di Santa Maria delle Salute

Punta della Dogana
Minimalist architect Tadao Ando creatively repurposed abandoned warehouses as galleries, which now host contemporary art installations from François Pinault's collection.

Ponte di Calatrava
With its starkly streamlined fish-fin shape, the 2008 bridge was the first to be built over the Grand Canal in 75 years.

Fondaco dei Turchi
Recognisable by its double colonnade, watchtowers, and dugout canoe parked at the Museo di Storia Naturale's ground-floor loggia.

Ca' d'Oro
Behind the triple Gothic arcades are priceless masterpieces: Titians looted by Napoleon, a rare Mantegna and semiprecious stone mosaic floors.

Palazzo Vendramin

Pescaria

Rialto Market

Palazzo Crimani

Palazzo Corner-Spinelli

Ponte di Rialto

Ponte dei Sospiri

Palazzo Ducale

Ponte di Rialto
Antonio da Ponte beat out Palladio for the commission of this bridge, but construction costs spiralled to 250,000 Venetian ducats – about €19 million today.

Ca' Pesaro
Originally designed by Baldassare Longhena, this palazzo was bequeathed to the city in 1898 to house the Galleria d'Arte Moderna and Museo d'Arte Orientale.

Burano is famed for its handmade lace, which once graced the décolletage and ruffs of European aristocracy. Unfortunately the ornate styles and expensive tableware fell out of vogue in lean post-WWII times and the industry has since suffered a decline. Some women still maintain the traditions, but few production houses remain; with a couple of notable exceptions, most of the lace for sale in local shops is of the imported, machine-made variety.

If you fancy a stroll, hop across the 60m bridge to Burano's even quieter sister island, Mazzorbo. Little more than a broad grassy knoll, Mazzorbo is a great place for a picnic or a long, lazy lunch. Line 12 also stops at Mazzorbo, and line 9 runs a shuttle between Burano and Torcello.

◉ Torcello

On the pastoral island of Torcello, sheep outnumber the 14 or so human residents. This bucolic backwater was once a Byzantine metropolis of 20,000, but rivalry with its offshoot Venice and a succession of malaria epidemics systematically reduced its population. Of its original nine churches and two abbeys, all that remain are the Basilica di Santa Maria Assunta and the 11th-century Chiesa di Santa Fosca.

GLIDE TIME: GONDOLA RIDES

A gondola ride offers a view of Venice that is anything but pedestrian. Official daytime rates are €80 for 40 minutes (€100 for 35 minutes from 7pm to 8am), not including songs or tips. Additional time is charged in 20-minute increments (day/night €40/50). You may negotiate a price break in overcast weather or around noon. Agree on a price, time limit and singing in advance to avoid unexpected surcharges.

Gondolas cluster at *stazi* (stops) along the Grand Canal and near major monuments and tourist hot spots, but you can also book a pick-up by calling Ente Gondola (📞041 528 50 75; www.gondolavenezia.it). Gondolas 4 All (Map p338; 📞328 243 13 82; www.gondolas4all.com; Fondamente Cossetti, Santa Croce), supported by the Gondoliers Association, offers gondola rides to wheelchair users in a specially adapted gondola. Embarkation is from a wheelchair-accessible pier at Piazzale Roma.

Not all line 12 *vaporetto* services stop at Torcello, but those that do provide a direct link to Burano, Mazzorbo, Murano and Fondamente Nove. The more frequent line 9 shuttles to and from Burano.

★ **Basilica di Santa Maria Assunta** CHURCH
(📞041 73 01 19; Piazza Torcello, Torcello; adult/reduced €5/4, incl museum €8/6, incl museum, audio guide & campanile €12/10; ⊙10am-5pm; 🚤Torcello) Life choices are presented in no uncertain terms in the dazzling mosaics of this former cathedral. Look to a golden afterlife amid saints and a beatific Madonna, or turn your back on her and face the wrath of the devil gloating over lost souls in an extraordinary *Last Judgement* scene. In existence since the 7th century, the church is the lagoon's oldest Byzantine Romanesque structure.

Chiesa di Santa Fosca CHURCH
(Piazza Torcello, Torcello; ⊙10am-4.30pm; 🚤Torcello) Literally overshadowed by Torcello's famous basilica, to which it's connected by a colonnaded walkway, this interesting little round Byzantine-style church dates from the 11th century. It's relatively unadorned inside, with plain brick walls, a domed wooden roof and Corinthian columns in grey marble.

🏃 Activities

Row Venice BOATING
(Map p338; 📞347 725 06 37; www.rowvenice.org; Fondamenta Gasparo Contarini; 90min lessons 1-2 people €85, 3/4 people €120/140; 🚤Orto) The next best thing to walking on water: rowing a traditional *batellina coda di gambero* (shrimp-tailed boat) standing up like gondoliers do. Tours must be pre-booked and commence at the wooden gate of the Sacca Misericordia boat marina.

SUP in Venice WATER SPORTS
(Map p348; 📞339 565 92 40; www.supinvenice.com; Fondamenta Contarini 3535; lesson from €60; ⊙Apr-Oct; 🚤Orto) Try your hand at stand-up paddleboarding in the Cannaregio canals; swimming is prohibited, so try to stay upright. More experienced boarders can join an island-to-island tour or paddle to a bar for a *spritz*.

Venice Kayak KAYAKING
(📞346 477 13 27; www.venicekayak.com; Vento di Venezia, Isola della Certosa; half-/full-day tours €90/120) Of all Venice's watery pursuits, kayaking is probably the best fun you can have without a licence or the pirouetting skill of a gondolier. Well-planned tours take you

into the warren of Venice's canals alongside police boats, fire boats and floating funeral hearses, or out to remote islands in the broad garden of the lagoon.

Brussa Is Boat
BOATING

(Map p348; ☎041 71 57 87; www.brussaisboat.it; Fondamenta Labia 331; 7m boat per hr/day incl fuel €43/196; ⏱7.30am-5.30pm Mon-Fri, to 12.30pm Sat & Sun; ⛴Ferrovia) Aspiring sea captains can take on the lagoon (not the Grand Canal or canals in the historic centre) in a rented boat from Brussa. You don't need a licence, but you will be taken on a test run to see if you can manoeuvre and park; ask staff to point out the refuelling stations on a map.

☞ Tours

Venice Urban Adventures
FOOD & DRINK

(☎348 980 85 66; www.veniceurbanadventures. com; tours €36-180, ⏱tours 11.30am & 5.30pm Mon-Sat) Knowledgable, enthusiastic, local foodies lead tours around bakeries and *cicheti* (bar snacks), some of which involve a short stint on a *traghetto* (gondola ferry) or *aperitivo* (pre-dinner drink) on a water taxi. They also offers day trips to wineries around Treviso.

See Venice
CULTURAL

(☎349 084 83 03; www.seevenice.it; tours per hr €75) Intimate and insightful cultural tours are offered by Venetian native Luisella Romeo, whose love and enthusiasm for the city is infectious. She covers all the grand-slam sights, as well as offering off-the-beaten path itineraries, guided tours of contemporary art museums, visits to artisan studios, design shops and musical venues, which expand visitors' experiences of the city.

Context Travel
CULTURAL

(☎800 691 60 36; www.contexttravel.com; group tours €315-409) Context offers scholarly tours for the curious minded. Groups are small and subjects range from politics to art, history and ecology. Families should try the Art Tour, Lion Hunt, Daily Life in Venice and, for older kids, the Science and Secrets of the Lagoon – led by a marine biologist.

Monica Cesarato
CULTURAL

(www.monicacesarato.com; tours €35) With her mesmerising storytelling skills, Monica's tours are a whirlwind of cultural, social and epicurean information punctuated by generous glugs of wine and excellent plates of *cicheti*. She's so persuasive that she's been known to convince die-hard fish-phobics to

THE BUDGET GONDOLA

A *traghetto* is the gondola service locals use to cross the Grand Canal between its widely spaced bridges. *Traghetti* rides cost just €2 for non-residents and typically operate from 9am to 6pm, although some routes finish by noon. You'll find *traghetto* crossings at Campo San Marcuola, the Rialto Market, Riva del Vin, San Tomà, Ca' Rezzonico and beside the Gritti Palace, though note that service can be spotty at times at all crossings.

mop up a plate of octopus. Kids will love her cleverly conceived ghost tours, full of grizzly murders and plague deaths.

Eolo Cruises
BOATING

(www.cruisingvenice.com; per person €350-450 for 4-6 people) Eolo Cruises covers the lagoon on a double-masted 1946 fishing *bragozzo* (flat bottomed fishing boat) for one to eight day trips (for six to 10 people), including onboard cooking tours. Guests sleep in select villas and *palazzi* (mansions), spend the day sailing and eat seafood lunches on board.

🐾 Courses

Venice Italian School
LANGUAGE

(Map p350; ☎347 963 51 13, 340 751 08 63; www. veniceitalianschool.com; Campo San Stin 2504, San Polo; group course 1-/2-weeks €290/530, individual lessons per person €65; ⛴San Tomà) Founded by Venetian brother and sister Diego and Lucia Cattaneo, this language school offers excellent, immersive courses for adults and children between the ages of five and 13 years old. Teaching is based on the communicative Dogme technique and additional cultural lessons use associative physical activities (such as food and wine tasting, cooking and rowing lessons) to encourage students to practise what they've learnt.

Painting Venice
ART

(☎340 544 52 27; www.paintingvenice.com; Cannaregio; 2hr private lessons €100, 2-day workshops €280) Sign up for a session with professionally trained and practising artists Caroline, Sebastien and Katrin and you'll strike out into tranquil *campi* (squares) in the tradition of classic Venetian *vedutisti* (outdoor artists). Beginners learn the basic concepts of painting 'en plein air', while those with more advanced skills receive tailormade

VENICE & THE VENETO VENICE

Venetian Artistry

Glass

Venetians have been working in crystal and glass since the 10th century, though fire hazards prompted the move of the city's furnaces to Murano in the 13th century. Trade secrets were so closely guarded that any glass-worker who left the city was considered guilty of treason. By the 15th century Murano glassmakers were setting standards that couldn't be equalled anywhere in the world. They monopolised the manufacture of mirrors for centuries, and in the 17th century their skill at producing jewel-bright crystal led to a ban on the production of false gems out of glass. For a short course in Murano's masterly skill, head to the Museo del Vetro (p355).

Today, along Murano's Fondamenta dei Vetrai, centuries of tradition are upheld in Cesare Toffolo's winged goblets and Davide Penso's lampworked glass beads, while striking modern glass designs by Nason Moretti at ElleElle, Marina e Susanna Sent and Venini keep the tradition moving forward.

Paper

Embossing and marbling began in the 14th century as part of Venice's burgeoning publishing industry, but these bookbinding techniques and *ebru* (Turkish marbled paper) endpapers have taken on lives of their own. Artisan Rosanna Corrò of Cárte uses bookbinding techniques to create marbled, bookbound handbags and even furniture, while Cartavenezia turns hand-pulped paper into embossed friezes and free-form lamps. Gianni Basso uses 18th-century book symbols to make letter-pressed business cards with old-world flair, and you can watch a Heidelberg press in

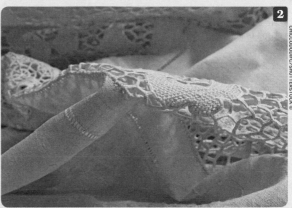

1. Glass sculpture, Murano **2.** Lace embroidery, Burano **3.** Marbled paper

action at Veneziastampa, churning out menus and ex-libris (bookplates).

Textiles

Anything that stands still long enough in this city is liable to end up swagged, tasselled and upholstered. Venetian lace from Burano (p358) was a fashion must for centuries, and Bevilacqua still weaves luxe tapestries (and donates scraps to nonprofit Banco Lotto 10 to turn into La Fenice costumes and handbags).

But the modern master of Venetian bohemian textiles is Fortuny, whose showroom on Giudecca features hand-stamped wall coverings created in strict accordance with top-secret techniques. But though the methods are secret, Fortuny's inspiration isn't: it covers the walls of his home studio, from Persian armour to portraits of socialites who tossed aside their corsets for Fortuny's Delphi gowns – now available for modern boho goddesses at Venetia Studium.

TOP FIVE NON-TOURISTY SOUVENIRS

➡ Customised business cards at **Gianni Basso**.

➡ Lilac smoking jacket with handprinted scarlet skulls from **Fiorella Gallery**.

➡ Blown-glass soap-bubble necklaces from **Marina e Susanna Sent**.

➡ Lux, hand-stamped velvet evening bags in gold and mulberry from **Venetia Studium**.

➡ Bold, funky, cardboard-and-paper handbags from **Cárte**.

tuition. It's a great way to slow down and really appreciate the colour and composition of each view.

Venice Photo Tour
PHOTOGRAPHY

(☎ 041 963 73 74; www.venicephototour.com; 2/3/6hr walking tours for up to 4 people €210/300/600) Throughout San Marco you'll be tripping over iPhone touting tourists. Everyone, it seems, wants to capture the perfect Venetian scene. Getty photojournalist Marco Secchi will show you how during an in-depth tutorial exploring the secret corners of the city. In particular, you'll learn how to capture the nuances of light and how to frame that masterpiece for the mantle.

🎇 Festivals & Events

Carnevale
CARNIVAL

(www.carnevale.venezia.it; ⊘ Jan/Feb) Masquerade madness stretches over two weeks in January or February before Lent. A Cannaregio Canal flotilla marks the outbreak of festivities that feature masked balls, processions, public parties in every *campo* (square), and all manner of dressing up.

Vogalonga
CULTURAL

(www.vogalonga.com) A show of endurance each May or June, this 32km 'long row' starts with over 1500 boats launching outside the Palazzo Ducale, looping past Burano and Murano, and ending with cheers, sweat and enough *prosecco* to numb blisters at Punta della Dogana.

Venice Biennale
ART

(Map p338; www.labiennale.org; Giardini della Biennale; ⊘ mid-May–Nov; 🚤 Giardini Biennale) Europe's premier arts showcase since 1907 is something of a misnomer: the Venice Biennale is now actually held every year, but the spotlight alternates between the art (odd-numbered years) and architecture (even-numbered years). Running alongside the two main events are annual showcases of dance, theatre, cinema and music.

Festa del Redentore
RELIGIOUS

(Feast of the Redeemer; Map p338; http://events.veneziaunica.it; ⊘ Jul) Walk on water across the Giudecca Canal to Il Redentore via a wobbly pontoon bridge on the third Saturday and Sunday in July, then watch the fireworks from the Zattere.

Venice International Film Festival
FILM

(Mostra Internazionale d'Arte Cinematografica; www.labiennale.org/en/cinema; Lido; ⊘ Aug-Sep)

The only thing hotter than a Lido beach in August is the Film Festival's star-studded red carpet, usually rolled out from the last weekend in August through to the first week of September.

Regata Storica
CULTURAL

(www.regatastoricavenezia.it) Sixteenth-century costumes, eight-oared gondolas and ceremonial barques feature in this historical procession (usually held in early September) along the Grand Canal, which re-enacts the arrival of the Queen of Cyprus and precedes gondola races.

🛏 Sleeping

🛏 San Marco

⭐ Rezidenza Corte Antica
B&B €€

(Map p342; ☎ 335 186 35 55; www.residenza corteantica.com; Calle Frutarol 2876; r from €119; ❉🤶; 🚤 Accademia) A tasteful renovation showcases the ancient wooden beams and stone staircases of this historic Venetian house, hidden down a small lane at the far end of the San Marco quarter. Each of the three romantic guest rooms is decorated with white walls and linen, and antique-style beds – including one four-poster.

⭐ B&B Al Teatro
B&B €€

(Map p342; ☎ 333 918 24 94; www.bedandbreak fastalteatro.com; Fondamenta de la Fenice 2554; r from €165; 🤶; 🚤 Giglio) With La Fenice for your neighbour and a chorus of singing *gondolieri* passing beneath your windows, you'll need to book early to nab one of the three rooms in Eleonora's 15th-century family home. Inside, old-world elegance meets a minimalist style with white linen and Murano chandeliers. Eleonora hosts breakfast every morning tossing, out recommendations over freshly brewed coffee.

⭐ Corte di Gabriela
HOTEL €€€

(Map p342; ☎ 041 523 50 77; www.cortediga briela.com; Calle dei Avvocati 3836; r from €270; ❉🤶; 🚤 Sant'Angelo) Yes, Corte di Gabriela is a 19th-century *palazzo,* but there's nothing old or traditional about its 11 rooms, which inventively play with the palace's historic features, combining frescoed ceilings and terrazzo floors with contemporary design pieces, high-spec finishes and a modern colour palette. The views are undeniably romantic, and the atmosphere sophisticated.

Locanda Orseolo
B&B €€€

(Map p342; ☑041 520 48 27; www.locandaorseo lo.com; Corte Zorzi 1083; r from €200; ✳☎; ⚐San Marco) Hide out behind Piazza San Marco: no one will know but the *gondolieri*, who regularly row past the lobby. Consistently warm greetings and cosy wood-trimmed rooms – some with vintage-kitsch Carnevale murals – make this the ideal launch pad.

🛏 Castello

B&B San Marco
B&B €

(Map p346; ☑041 522 75 89; www.realvenice.it; Fondamente San Giorgio dei Schiavoni 3385l; r with/ without bathroom €135/105; ✳; ⚐San Zaccaria) Alice and Marco welcome you warmly to their home overlooking Carpaccio's frescoed Scuola Dalmata. The 3rd-floor apartment (no lift), with its parquet floors and large windows, is furnished with family antiques and offers photogenic views over the terra-cotta rooftops and canals. The hosts live up-stairs, so they're always on hand with great recommendations.

Residenza de L'Osmarin
B&B €€

(Map p346; ☑347 450 14 40; www.residenza delosmarin.com; Calle Rota 4960; r from €170; ✳☎; ⚐San Zaccaria) This B&B is good value, especially considering it is barely 300m from Piazza San Marco. Rooms – one with a roof terrace and another with a courtyard-facing terrace – are quaintly decorated with quilt-ed bedspreads, painted wardrobes and peri-od furnishings. The hosts make guests feel warmly welcome with slap-up breakfasts of homemade cakes, brioche and platters of ham and cheese.

Hotel le Isole
HOTEL €€

(Map p346; ☑041 522 89 11; www.hotel-leisole. it; Campo San Provolo 4661; r from €185; ▦◉⚐; ⚐San Zaccaria) Barely a stone's throw from San Marco, this small, friendly hotel offers good value. Arranged around a vine-clad central courtyard, rooms are understated and elegant with wooden floors, Venetia Studium lamps, Fortuny-style fabrics, cable TV and gleaming marble bathrooms. Break-fast is similarly generous: a buffet loaded with cold cuts, fruit and cakes, with eggs to order from the kitchen.

Ca' dei Dogi
BOUTIQUE HOTEL €€

(Map p346; ☑041 241 37 51; www.cadeidogi.it; Corte Santa Scolastica 4242; s/d from €95/165; ✳☎; ⚐San Zaccaria) Even the nearby Bridge of Sighs can't dampen the high spirits of the sunny Ca' dei Dogi, with guest room windows sneaking peeks into the convent cloisters next door. Streamlined, modern rooms look like ship cabins, with tilted wood-beamed ceilings, dressers that look like steamer trunks, and compact mosaic-covered bathrooms – ask for the one with the terrace and Jacuzzi.

Ai Cavalieri di Venezia
HOTEL €€€

(Map p350; ☑041 241 10 64; www.hotelaicav alieri.com; Calle Borgolocco 6108; r from €315; ✳☎; ⚐Rialto) Venetian glam is dialled up to the max in this luxurious *palazzo* hotel, yet it somehow avoids slipping into tackiness. Rooms are dripping in gilt, silk damask wall coverings and sparkling Murano chande-liers – and with canals on two sides, you've got an excellent chance of a watery view.

🛏 Cannaregio

⭐ Allo Squero
B&B €

(Map p350; ☑041 523 69 73; www.allosquero.it; Corte dello Squero 4692; r from €100; ☎; ⚐Fon-damente Nove) Dock for the night at this his-toric gondola *squero* (shipyard), converted into a garden retreat. Gondolas float right by the windows of two of the rooms. All have their own bathrooms, although one is accessed from the corridor. Hosts Andrea and Hiroko offer Venice-insider tips over cappuccino and pastry breakfasts in the fra-grant, wisteria-filled garden. Cots and cribs available.

ℹ APARTMENT RENTALS

For longer stays and groups of three or more, renting an apartment is an eco-nomical option that gives you the free-dom to cook your own meals. To rent a studio for yourself, expect to pay €800 to €1200 per month.

Venice Prestige (www.veniceprestige. com) The crème de la crème of Venetian apartments to rent in aristocratic *pala-zzi* (mansions) in the best locations in town. Add-on services include private chefs, guides, boat trips and water taxis.

Views on Venice (☑041 241 11 49; www. viewsonvenice.com) A comprehensive selection of apartments picked for their personality, character and view, of course. Rentals start at around €900 per week.

★**Locanda Ca' Le Vele** B&B €€
(Map p350; ✆041 241 39 60; www.locandalevele. com; Calle de le Vele 3969; r/ste from €130/183; ✳🛜; 🚢Ca' d'Oro) The lane may be quiet and the house might look demure but inside it's Venetian glam all the way. The six guest rooms are a surprisingly stylish riot of terrazzo floors, damask furnishings, Murano glass sconces and ornate gilded beds with busy covers. Pay a little extra for a canal view.

★**Venice Halldis Apartments** APARTMENT €€
(Map p338; ✆024 795 22 00; www.venicehalldis apartments.com; Calle Priuli dei Cavalletti 96t; apt from €189; ✳🛜; 🚢Ferrovia) Modern apartment blocks are a rarity in central Venice, but this converted factory offers spacious, chic, well-equipped units that are surprisingly quiet, despite being just across a canal from the train station. Treats include laundry facilities, spacious wardrobes and showers with adjustable mood lighting which double as Turkish baths. The only downsides are the hard beds and no reception.

3749 Ponte Chiodo B&B €€
(Map p338; ✆041 241 39 35; www.pontechiodo. it; Calle de la Racchetta 3749; r from €130; ✳🛜; 🚢Ca' d'Oro) This charming little B&B offers six sweet rooms with period furnishings, views over the canal and a private front garden. It takes its name from the bridge at the back door – the only remaining one without parapets. All bridges in Venice were once like this before too many drunks took the plunge and the government decreed new safety measures.

★**Al Ponte Antico** BOUTIQUE HOTEL €€€
(Map p350; ✆041 241 19 44; www.alponteantico. com; Calle dell'Aseo 5768; r from €320; ✳🛜; 🚢Rialto) Like a courtesan's boudoir, this 16th-century *palazzo* is swathed in damask wall coverings, heavy silk curtains and thick, plush carpets. A smiling host greets you at the padded, golden reception desk and whisks you up to large, unabashedly lavish rooms with enough gilt to satisfy Louis XIV. In the evening, romance blossoms on the terrace, framed by views of Rialto Bridge.

🛏 **San Polo & Santa Croce**

Al Gallion B&B €
(Map p350; ✆380 4520466, 041 524 47 43; www. algallion.com; Calle Gallion 1126, Santa Croce; d €75-110; 🛜; 🚢Riva de Biasio) A couple of bridges away at train station hotels, weary tourists wait at front desks – but at this 16th-century

family home, you'll be chatting and sipping espresso in the living room. The whitewashed guest room (which can be divided in two and turned into a quad) is handsomely furnished with walnut desks, cheerful yellow bedspreads, terrazzo floors and host Daniela's family art collection. Breakfasts are homemade spreads; tasty, affordable restaurants abound nearby.

★**Oltre Il Giardino** BOUTIQUE HOTEL €€
(Map p350; ✆041 275 00 15; www.oltreilgiardino -venezia.com; Fondamenta Contarini 2542, San Polo; d €180, ste €230-280; ✳🛜; 🚢San Tomà) Live the dream in this garden villa, the 1920s home of Alma Mahler, the composer's widow. Hidden behind a lush walled garden, its six high-ceilinged guest rooms marry historic charm with modern comfort: marquetry composers' desks, candelabras and 19th-century poker chairs sit alongside flatscreen TVs and designer bathrooms, while outside, pomegranate trees flower.

★**Hotel Palazzo Barbarigo** DESIGN HOTEL €€€
(Map p350; ✆041 74 01 72; www.palazzobarbarigo. com; Grand Canal 2765, San Polo; d €240-440; ✳🛜; 🚢San Tomà) Brooding, chic and seductive, Barbarigo delivers 18 plush guest rooms combining modern elegance and intrigue – think dark, contemporary furniture, sumptuous velvets, feathered lamps and the odd fainting couch. Whether you opt for a suite overlooking the Grand Canal (get triple-windowed Room 10) or a standard room overlooking Rio di San Polo, you can indulge in the sleek bathrooms, positively royal breakfasts and smart, attentive service.

★**Cima Rosa** B&B €€€
(Map p350; ✆373 749 50 41; www.cimarosavenezia. com; Calle Tron 1958, Santa Croce; d €245-385; 🛜; 🚢San Stae) Although many B&Bs promise a 'living in Venice' experience, Cima Rosa, in the northern reaches of Santa Croce, delivers it in spades. There are just three suites and two doubles in this 15th-century *palazzo*, all with beamed ceilings, romantic pastel wall washes and stunning Grand Canal views. Breakfast in the stylish downstairs lounge and let owner Brittany plan you an insider's itinerary.

🛏 **Dorsoduro**

★**Le Terese** B&B €
(Map p338; ✆041 523 17 28; www.leterese.com; Campiello Tron 1902, Dorsoduro; d €80-100; 🛜; 🚢San Basilio) Join architectural duo Antonel-

la and Mauro in their 18th-century granary on the Rio Terese for a dose of local living. There are just two rooms overlooking the canal and both are furnished in understated style with comfortable beds, Persian rugs and modernist furniture. The large, marble-tiled bathroom is shared, which just adds to the home-away-from-home feeling.

Locanda Ca' del Brocchi B&B €
(Map p342; 041 522 69 89; www.cadelbrocchi. it; Rio Terà San Vio 470, Dorsoduro; d €100-200; P ✿ 🗟; Accademia) A colourful character inhabiting a quiet side street in Dorsoduro's museum district, Ca' del Brocchi has small yet over-the-top baroque-styled rooms – tasselled, gilt to the hilt and upholstery padded, with matching scrollwork wallpaper. Lower-level rooms have porthole-sized windows; better options have garden views, balconies and/or Jacuzzi tubs. Babysitting and cradles are available for families.

★ **Hotel Moresco** BOUTIQUE HOTEL €€€
(Map p338; 041 244 02 02; www.hotelmoresco venice.com; Fondamente del Passamonte 3499, Dorsoduro; d €280-390; ✿; Piazzale Roma) A complimentary glass of *prosecco* (sparkling white wine) at check-in and a daily *aperitivo* (pre-dinner drinks) hour in the walled garden will give you an idea of the welcoming and friendly service you'll encounter at this lovely hotel. Rooms are similarly well cared for with fine fabrics, elaborate wallpapers, plush sofas and sleek modern bathrooms. Staff can help with all manner of things, and do.

🛏 Giudecca

Generator HOSTEL €
(Map p338; 041 877 82 88; www.generator hostels.com; Fondamenta de la Croce 86, Giudecca; dm/r from €35/155; ✿ @ 🗟; Zitelle) Generator rocks a sharp, contemporary interior including a fabulous kooky-kitsch bar-restaurant with crazy wallpaper, Murano chandeliers and a pool table. Try to score a bunk by the window – you might even wake up to a San Marco view. Sheets, blanket and a pillow are provided; breakfast is an additional €4.50.

★ **Al Redentore di Venezia** APARTMENT €€
(Map p338; 041 522 94 02; www.alredentore divenezia.com; Fondamenta del Ponte Longo 234a, Giudecca; apt from €167; ✿; Redentore) These fully serviced apartments blend modern facilities with antique-style furnishings, and then throw in travertine bathrooms, top-quality

pillows, high-end bath products and divine views across the water to San Marco.

🛏 Murano

★ **Murano Palace** HOTEL €€
(041 73 96 55; www.muranopalace.com; Fondamenta dei Vetrai 77, Murano; d €110-180; ✿ 🗟; Colonna) Come here for designer fabulousness at an outlet price. Jewel-toned colour schemes and (naturally) Murano glass chandeliers illuminate high-ceilinged, woodfloored rooms, and there are free drinks and snacks in the minibar. Expect canal views and unparalleled art-glass shopping in the vicinity, but eerie calm descends once the shops close around 6pm.

★ **Villa Lina** B&B €€
(041 527 53 58; www.villalinavenezia.com; Calle Dietro gli Orti 12, Murano; s/d from €110/170; Mar-Dec; ✿ 🗟; Colonna) Finding 16th-century Villa Lina in the grounds of the Nason Moretti glassworks is like chancing upon a wonderful secret. The home of Carlo Nason and his wife Evi has a mod 1950s vibe and is scattered with Carlo's glass designs. Bedrooms are large, comfortable and contemporary, and the flower-filled garden backs directly on to the Serenella Canal.

✗ Eating

Even in unpretentious Venetian *osterie* and *bacari*, most dishes cost a couple of euros more than they might elsewhere in Italy – not a bad mark-up, considering all that fresh seafood and produce brought in by boat. *Cicheti* are fresh alternatives to fast food worth planning your day around, but you'll also want to treat yourself to a leisurely sitdown meal while you're in town. If you stick to tourist menus you're bound to be disappointed, but adventurous diners who order seasonal specialities are richly rewarded, and often spend less, too.

✗ San Marco

★ **Marchini Time** BAKERY €
(Map p342; 041 241 30 87; www.marchinitime.it; Campo San Luca 4589; items €1.20-3.50; 7.30am-8.30pm; Rialto) Elbow your way through the morning crush to bag a warm croissant filled with runny apricot jam or melting Nutella. Everything here is freshly baked, which is why the crowd hangs around as croissants give way to focaccia, *pizette* (mini pizzas) and generously stuffed *panini*.

★ **Ai Mercanti**   ITALIAN €€

(Map p342; ☑ 041 523 82 69; www.aimercanti.it; Corte Coppo 4346a; meals €34-38; ⊙ 11.30am-3pm & 7-10pm Tue-Sat, 7-11pm Mon; 🖄 Rialto) With its pumpkin-coloured walls, gleaming golden fixtures and jet-black tables and chairs, Ai Mercanti effortlessly conjures up a romantic mood. No wonder dates whisper over glasses of wine from the vast selection before tucking into modern bistro-style dishes. Although there's a focus on seafood and secondary cuts of meat, there are some wonderful vegetarian options as well.

Osteria da Carla   VENETIAN €€

(Map p342; ☑ 041 523 78 55; www.osteriadacarla.it; Corte Contarina 1535a; meals €43-48; ⊙ 8.30am-11pm Mon-Sat; 🖄 San Marco) Diners in the know duck into this hidden courtyard, less than 100m from Piazza San Marco, to snack on *cicheti* (Venetian tapas) at the counter or to sit down to a romantic meal. The surroundings are at once modern and ancient, with exposed brick and interesting art.

★ **Ristorante Quadri**   MODERN ITALIAN €€€

(Map p342; ☑ 041 522 21 05; www.alajmo.it; Piazza San Marco 121; meals €110-138; ⊙ 12.30-2.30pm & 7.30-10.30pm Tue-Sun; 🖄 San Marco) When it comes to Venetian glamour, nothing beats this historic Michelin-starred restaurant overlooking Piazza San Marco. A small swarm of servers greets you as you're shown to your table in a room decked out with silk damask, gilt, painted beams and Murano chandeliers. Dishes are precise and delicious, deftly incorporating Venetian touches into an inventive modern Italian menu.

★ **Bistrot de Venise**   VENETIAN €€€

(Map p342; ☑ 041 523 66 51; www.bistrotdevenise.com; Calle dei Fabbri 4685; meals €47-78; ⊙ noon-3pm & 7pm-midnight; 🖋; 🖄 Rialto) Indulge in some culinary time travel at this fine-dining bistro where they've revived the recipes of Renaissance chef Bartolomeo Scappi. Dine like a doge in the red-and-gilt dining room on braised duck with wild apple and onion pudding, or enjoy the Jewish recipe of goose, raisin and pine-nut pasta. Even the desserts are beguilingly exotic.

✗ **Castello**

★ **CoVino**   VENETIAN €€

(Map p346; ☑ 041 241 27 05; www.covinovenezia.com; Calle del Pestrin 3829; 3-course menu €39; ⊙ 12.30-3.30pm & 7pm-1am Thu-Mon; 🖘; 🖄 Arsenale) Tiny CoVino has only 14 seats but demonstrates bags of ambition with its inventive, seasonal menu inspired by the Venetian terroir. Speciality products are selected from Slow Food Presidia producers, and the charming waiters make enthusiastic recommendations from the interesting wine list. Only the set menu is available at dinner, but there's an à la carte selection at lunch.

Met   MODERN ITALIAN €€€

(Map p346; ☑ 041 524 00 34; www.metrestaurantvenice.com; Riva degli Schiavoni 4149; 3-/5-/6-course meal €100/150/200; ⊙ 7-10.30pm Tue-Fri, 12.30-2.30pm & 7-10.30pm Sat & Sun; 🖄 San Zaccaria) The Hotel Metropole's Michelin-starred restaurant offers an intriguing proposition: at each stage of its multicourse menu you can order a traditional Venetian

---

VENICE'S BEST GELATO

Suso (Map p350; ☑ 348 564 65 45; www.gelatovenezia.it; Calle de la Bissa 5453; scoops €1.60; ⊙ 10am-midnight; 🖄 Rialto) Indulge in gelato as rich as a doge, in original seasonal flavours like marscapone cream with fig sauce and walnuts. All Suso's gelati are locally made and free of artificial colours; gluten-free cones are available.

Gelato di Natura (Map p350; ☑ 340 286 71 78; www.gelatodinatura.com; Calle Larga 1628, Santa Croce; 1 scoop €1.50; 🖄; 🖄 Riva di Biasio, San Stae) Along with a dozen other things, Marco Polo is said to have introduced ice cream to Venice after his odyssey to China. At this gelato shop the experimentation continues with vegan versions of your favourite flavours, Japanese rice cakes and the creamiest, small-batch gelato incorporating local ingredients such as Bronte pistachios, Piedmontese hazelnuts and Amalfi lemons.

Gelateria Ca' d'Oro (Map p350; ☑ 041 522 89 82; Strada Nova 4273b; scoops €1.80; ⊙ 10am-10pm; 🖄 Ca' d'Oro) Foot traffic stops here for spectacularly creamy gelato made in-house daily. For a summer pick-me-up, try the *granita di caffe con panna* (coffee shaved ice with whipped cream).

dish or a theatrical modern interpretation using the same ingredients. The enthusiastic staff will ably assist you in your decision but, either way, you can't go wrong. Jellyfish-like Murano chandeliers add whimsy to an otherwise formal room.

Il Ridotto
MODERN ITALIAN €€€

(Map p346; ☑ 041 520 82 80; www.ilridotto.com; Campo SS Filippo e Giacomo 4509; meals €70-87; ⊙ 6.45-11pm Thu, noon-3pm & 6.45-11pm Fri-Tue; ⓢ San Zaccaria) When the octopus starter looks so beautiful that it elicits gasps, there's no questioning how this small, elegant restaurant gained its Michelin star. Head chef Gianni Bonaccorsi is ably complemented by his Bangladeshi offsider Murshedul Haque, creating a menu that broadens the bounds of Italian cuisine. Tables spill out onto the square but the brick-lined interior is equally appealing.

Al Covo
VENETIAN €€€

(Map p346; ☑ 041 522 38 12; www.ristorantealcovo.com; Campiello de la Pescaria 3969; meals €42-67; ⊙ 12.45-3.30pm & 7.30pm-midnight Fri-Tue; ❄; ⓢ Arsenale) Chef-owner Cesare Benelli has long been dedicated to the preservation of heritage products and lagoon recipes. Only the freshest seasonal fish gets the Covo treatment, accompanied by artichoke, eggplant (aubergine), cipollini onions and mushrooms from the lagoon larders of Sant'Erasmus, Vignole, Treporti and Cavallino. Meat is also carefully sourced and much of it is Slow Food accredited.

✗ Cannaregio

★ Pasticceria Dal Mas
BAKERY €

(Map p338; ☑ 041 71 51 01; www.dalmaspasticceria.it; Rio Terà Lista di Spagna 150; pastries €1.30-6.50; ⊙ 7am-9pm; ❄; ⓢ Ferrovia) Our favourite Venetian bakery-cafe sparkles with mirrors, marble and metal trim, providing a fitting casket for the precious pastries displayed within. Despite the perpetual morning crush, the efficient team dispense top-notch coffee and cornetti (croissants) with admirable equanimity. Come mid-morning for mouth-watering, still-warm quiches. The hot chocolate is also exceptional – hardly surprising given its sister chocolate shop next door.

Trattoria da Bepi Già "54"
VENETIAN €€

(Map p350; ☑ 041 528 50 31; www.dabepi.it; Campo SS Apostoli 4550; meals €24-37; ⊙ noon-3pm & 7-10pm Fri-Wed; ⓢ Ca' d'Oro) Much better

than it looks, Da Bepi is a traditional trattoria in the very best sense. The interior is a warm, wood-panelled cocoon, and the service is efficient and friendly. Take their advice on the classic Venetian menu and order spaghetti col nero di seppia (with cuttlefish ink), grilled fish and a tiramisu that doesn't disappoint.

Ai Promessi Sposi
VENETIAN €€

(Map p350; ☑ 041 241 27 47; Calle d'Oca 4367; meals €29-37; ⊙ 6.30-11.30pm Mon & Wed, 11.30am-3pm & 6.30-11.30pm Tue & Thu-Sun; ⓢ Ca' d'Oro) Bantering Venetians thronging the bar are the only permanent fixtures at this neighbourhood osteria (casual tavern), where ever-changing menus feature fresh Venetian seafood and Veneto meats at excellent prices. Seasonal standouts include seppie in umido (cuttlefish in rich tomato sauce) and house-made pasta, but pace yourself for cloudlike tiramisu and excellent semifreddo.

★ Osteria Boccadoro
VENETIAN €€€

(Map p350; ☑ 041 521 10 21; www.boccadoro venezia.it; Campiello Widmann 5405a; meals €40-55; ⊙ noon-3pm & 7-10pm Tue-Sun; ⓢ Fondamente Nove) Birds sweetly singing in this campo are probably angling for your leftovers, but they don't stand a chance. Chef-owner Luciano's creative crudi (raw seafood) are two-bite delights and cloudlike gnocchi and homemade pasta is gone entirely too soon. Save room for luxuriant desserts.

Osteria da Rioba
VENETIAN €€€

(Map p348; ☑ 041 524 43 79; www.darioba.com; Fondamenta de la Misericordia 2553; meals €46-49; ⊙ 12.30-2.30pm & 7.30-11pm Tue-Sun; ⓢ Orto) Taking the lead with fresh seafood and herbs pulled from the family's Sant'Erasmo farm, Da Rioba's inventive kitchen turns out exquisite plates as colourful and creative as the artwork on the walls. This is prime date-night territory. In winter, cosy up in the wood-beamed interior; in summer sit canalside. Reservations recommended.

✗ San Polo & Santa Croce

★ All'Arco
VENETIAN €

(Map p350; ☑ 041 520 56 66; Calle dell'Ochialer 436, San Polo; cicheti from €2; ⊙ 8am-2.30pm Mon, Tue & Sat, to 7pm Wed-Fri summer, 8am-2.30pm Mon-Sat winter; ⓢ Rialto-Mercato) Search out this authentic neighbourhood osteria (casual tavern) for the best cicheti in town. Armed with ingredients from the nearby Rialto Market, father-and-son team Francesco and Matteo serve miniature masterpieces such as *cannocchia* (mantis shrimp) with pumpkin and roe, and *otrega crudo* (raw butterfish) with mint-and-olive-oil marinade. Even with copious *prosecco,* hardly any meal here tops €20.

★ Dai Zemei
VENETIAN €

(Map p350; ☏ 041 520 85 96; www.ostariadaize mei.it; Ruga Vecchia San Giovanni 1045, San Polo; cicheti from €1.50; ☺ 8.30am-8.30pm Mon-Sat, 9am-7pm Sun; ☻ San Silvestro) Running this small *cicheti* counter are *zemei* (twins) Franco and Giovanni, who serve loyal regulars small meals with plenty of imagination: gorgonzola lavished with *peperoncino* (chilli) marmalade, duck breast drizzled with truffle oil, or chicory paired with leek and marinated anchovies. A gourmet bargain for inspired bites and impeccable wines – try a crisp *nosiola* or invigorating *prosecco* brut.

★ Osteria Trefanti
VENETIAN €€

(Map p350; ☏ 041 520 17 89; www.osteriatrefanti. it; Fondamenta Garzotti 888, Santa Croce; meals €40; ☺ noon-2.30pm & 7-10.30pm Tue-Sun; ☏; ☻ Riva de Biasio) ✦ La Serenissima's spice trade lives on at simple, elegant Trefanti, where a dish of marinated prawns, hazelnuts, berries and caramel might get an intriguing kick from garam masala. Furnished with old pews and recycled copper lamps, it's the domain of the competent Sam Metcalfe and Umberto Slongo, whose passion for quality extends to a small, beautifully curated selection of local and organic wines.

Osteria La Zucca
MODERN ITALIAN €€

(Map p350; ☏ 041 524 15 70; www.lazucca.it; Calle del Tentor 1762, Santa Croce; meals €35-40; ☺ 12.30-2.30pm & 7-10.30pm Mon-Sat; ☏; ☻ San Stae) With its menu of seasonal vegetarian creations and classic meat dishes, this cosy, woody restaurant consistently hits the mark. Herbs and spices are used to great effect in dishes such as cinnamon-tinged pumpkin flan and chicken curry with yoghurt, lentils and rice. The small interior can get toasty, so reserve canalside seats in summer.

★ Antiche Carampane
VENETIAN €€€

(Map p350; ☏ 041 524 01 65; www.antichecar ampane.com; Rio Terà delle Carampane 1911, San Polo; meals €50; ☺ 12.45-2.30pm & 7.30-10.30pm Tue-Sat; ☻ San Stae) Hidden in the once shady lanes behind Ponte delle Tette, this culinary indulgence is a trick to find. Once you do, say goodbye to soggy lasagne and hello to a market-driven menu of silky *crudi* (raw

fish/seafood), surprisingly light *fritto misto* (fried seafood) and *caramote* prawn salad with seasonal vegetables. Never short of a smart, convivial crowd, it's a good idea to book ahead.

✕ Dorsoduro

★ Pasticceria Tonolo
PASTRIES €

(Map p350; ☏ 041 532 72 09; Calle dei Preti 3764, Dorsoduro; pastries €1-4; ☺ 7.45am-8pm Tue-Sat, 8am-1pm Sun, closed Sun Jul; ☻ Ca' Rezzonico) Long, skinny Tonolo is the stuff of local legend, a fact confirmed by the never-ending queue of customers. Ditch packaged B&B croissants for flaky *apfelstrudel* (apple pastry), velvety *bignè al zabaione* (marsala cream pastry) and oozing *pain au chocolat* (chocolate croissants). Devour one at the bar with a bracing espresso, then bag another for the road.

Pane, Vino e San Daniele
ITALIAN €

(Map p338; ☏ 041 523 74 56; www.panevinoesan daniele.net; Calle Lunga San Barnaba 2861, Dorsoduro; meals €15-30; ☺ 9am-11pm Thu-Tue; ☻ Ca' Rezzonico) Artists can't claim they're starving any more after a meal in this wood-beamed trattoria, a favourite of art students and professors alike. Settle in to generous plates of gnocchi with truffle cheese, Veneto game such as roast rabbit and duck, lavish appetisers featuring the namesake San Daniele cured ham, and Friulian house wines made by the Fantinel family owners.

★ Estro
VENETIAN, WINE BAR €€

(Map p350; ☏ 041 476 49 14; www.estrovenezia. com; Calle dei Preti 3778, Dorsoduro; meals €35; ☺ 11am-midnight Wed-Mon; ☀; ☻ San Tomà) Estro is anything you want it to be: wine bar, *aperitivo* pit stop, or sit-down degustation restaurant. The 500 wines – all of them naturally processed – are chosen by young-gun owners Alberto and Dario, whose passion for quality extends to the grub, from *cicheti* (Venetian tapas) topped with house-made *porchetta* (roast pork) to roasted guinea fowl and a succulent burger dripping with Asiago cheese.

Da Codroma
VENETIAN €€

(Map p338; ☏ 041 524 67 89; www.osteriada codroma.it; Fondamenta Briati 2540, Dorsoduro; meals €30-35; ☺ 10am-4pm & 6-11.30pm Tue-Sat; ☻ San Basilio) In a city plagued by high prices and indifferent eating experiences, da Codroma wears its Slow Food badge of approval with pride. Chef Nicola faithfully maintains Venetian traditions here, serving up boiled baby octopuses with a spritz of lemon, and buckwheat *bigoli* pasta with anchovy sauce. It's a local favourite thanks to the quiet location and democratic prices.

★Riviera   VENETIAN €€€
(Map p338; ☑041 522 76 21; www.ristoranterivi era.it; Fondamenta Zattere al Ponte Lungo 1473, Dorsoduro; meals €70-85; ⊘12.30-3pm & 7-10.30pm Fri-Tue; ⛴Zattere) Seafood connoisseurs concur that dining at GP Cremonini's restaurant is a Venetian highlight. A former rock musician, GP now focuses his considerable talents on delivering perfectly balanced octopus stew, feather-light gnocchi with lagoon crab, and risotto with langoustine and hop shoots. The setting, overlooking the Giudecca Canal, is similarly spectacular, encompassing views of Venetian domes backed by hot-pink sunsets.

Enoteca Ai Artisti   ITALIAN €€€
(Map p342; ☑041 523 89 44; www.enoteca artisti.com; Fondamenta della Toletta 1169a, Dorsoduro; meals €45; ⊘noon-3pm & 7-10pm Mon-Sat; ⛴Ca' Rezzonico) Indulgent cheeses, exceptional *nero di seppia* (cuttlefish ink) pasta, and tender *tagliata* (sliced steak) drizzled with aged balsamic vinegar atop rocket are paired with exceptional wines by the glass by your gracious oenophile hosts. Sidewalk tables for two make for great people-watching, but book ahead for indoor tables for groups; space is limited. Note: only turf (no surf) dishes on Monday.

✖ Giudecca

★Trattoria Altanella   VENETIAN €€
(Map p338; ☑041 522 77 80; Calle de le Erbe 268, Giudecca; meals €38-47; ⊘12.30-2.30pm & 7.30-10.30pm Wed-Sun; ⛴; ⛴Redentore) Founded by a fisherman and his wife in 1920 and still run by the same family, this cosy restaurant serves fine Venetian fare such as potato gnocchi with cuttlefish and perfectly grilled fish. Inside, the vintage interior is hung with artworks, reflecting the restaurant's popularity with artists, poets and writers, while outside a flower-fringed balcony hangs over the canal.

★La Palanca   VENETIAN €€
(Map p338; ☑041 528 77 19; Fondamenta Sant'Eufemia 448, Giudecca; meals €25-33; ⊘7am-8pm Mon-Sat; ⛴Palanca) Locals of all ages pour into this humble bar for *cicheti*,

coffee and *spritz*. However, it's at lunchtime that it really comes into its own, serving surprisingly sophisticated fare like swordfish carpaccio with orange zest alongside more rustic dishes, such as a delicious thick seafood soup. In summer, competition for waterside tables is stiff.

✖ Murano

★Acquastanca   MODERN ITALIAN €€
(☑041 319 51 25; www.acquastanca.it; Fondamenta Manin 48, Murano; meals €40-44; ⊘10am-11pm Mon & Fri, 9am-8pm Tue-Thu & Sat summer, 10am-10pm Mon & Fri, 10am-4pm Tue-Thu & Sat winter; ⛴Faro) A modern sensibility imbues both the decor and the menu at this wonderful little restaurant. A knowing array of old-fashioned Murano mirrors adorns a wall, while birds perch on artfully arranged twigs on another. Seafood features prominently on a menu that includes fresh flavour-filled takes on the classic Venetian bean soup, octopus with chickpeas and a panoply of pasta.

✖ Burano & Mazzorbo

★Venissa Osteria   VENETIAN €€
(☑041 527 22 81; www.venissa.it; Fondamenta Santa Caterina 3, Mazzorbo; meals €40-47; ⊘noon-6pm Wed, Thu, Sun & Mon, noon-midnight Fri & Sat Apr-Oct; ⛴Mazzorbo) A more affordable companion piece to its Michelin-starred sister, this upmarket *osteria* offers updates on Venetian classics such as marinated fish, duck pasta and *bigoli* (thick wholemeal pasta with anchovies). For an extra treat, splash out on a glass of Dorona, the prestigious golden-hued wine varietal only grown here. Make sure you save room for some of Venice's best desserts.

✖ Torcello

★Locanda Cipriani   VENETIAN €€€
(☑041 73 01 50; www.locandacipriani.com; Piazza Torcello 29, Torcello; meals €53-69; ⊘noon-3pm Wed-Mon Mar-Dec, plus 6-11pm Fri & Sat Apr-Sep; ⛴Torcello) Run by the Cipriani family since 1935, the Locanda is Harry's Bar gone rustic, with a wood-beamed dining room opening onto a pretty country garden. But standards are standards, so staff buzz about in dapper bow ties, theatrically silver serving every dish – even the pasta! The kitchen is just as precise, delivering pillowy gnocchi, perfectly cooked fish and decadent chocolate mousse.

Drinking & Nightlife

The happiest hour (or two) in Venice begins around 6pm at booze and *cicheti* (Venetian tapas) *bacari* (hole-in-the-wall bars). If you're prompt, you might beat the crowds to the bar for *un'ombra* (a 'shade'; a small glass of wine), which can go for as little as €0.60 at cupboard-sized Bacareto Da Lele. Heading in early also means grabbing *cicheti* while they're fresh. *Osterie* (taverns) and *enoteche* (wine bars) are also renowned for their *vino*-friendly bites.

San Marco

★ Caffè Florian   CAFE
(Map p342; ☑041 520 56 41; www.caffeflorian. com; Piazza San Marco 57; ⊗9am-11pm; ⊜San Marco) The oldest still-operating cafe in Europe and one of the first to welcome women, Florian maintains rituals (if not prices) established in 1720: besuited waiters serve cappuccino on silver trays, lovers canoodle in plush banquettes and the orchestra strikes up as the sunset illuminates San Marco's mosaics. Piazza seating during concerts costs €6 extra, but dreamy-eyed romantics hardly notice.

★ Grancaffè Quadri   CAFE
(Map p342; ☑041 522 21 05; www.alajmo.it; Piazza San Marco 121; ⊗9am-midnight; ⊜San Marco) Powdered wigs seem appropriate inside this baroque bar-cafe, serving happy hours since 1638. During Carnevale, costumed Quadri revellers party like it's 1699 – despite prices shooting up to €15 a *spritz*. Grab a seat on the piazza to watch the best show in town: the sunset sparking the basilica's golden mosaics ablaze.

★ Bar Longhi   COCKTAIL BAR
(Map p342; ☑041 79 47 81; www.hotelgrittipal acevenice.com; Campo di Santa Maria del Giglio 2467; ⊗11am-1am; ⊜Giglio) The Gritti's beautiful Bar Longhi may be hellishly expensive, but if you consider the room – with its Fortuny fabrics, intarsia marble bar, 18th-century mirrors and million-dollar Piero Longhi paintings – its signature orange martini (the work of art that it is) starts to seem reasonable. In summer you'll have to choose between the twinkling interior and a spectacular Grand Canal terrace.

★ Harry's Bar   BAR
(Map p342; ☑041 528 57 77; www.harrysbarven ezia.com; Calle Vallaresso 1323; ⊗10.30am-11pm; ⊜San Marco) Aspiring auteurs hold court at tables well scuffed by Ernest Hemingway, Charlie Chaplin, Truman Capote and Orson Welles, enjoying the signature €22 bellini (Giuseppe Cipriani's original 1948 recipe: white peach juice and *prosecco*) with a side of reflected glory.

Castello

★ Bar Dandolo   COCKTAIL BAR
(Map p346; ☑041 522 64 80; www.danielihotel venice.com; Riva degli Schiavoni 4196; ⊗9.30am-1.15am; ⊜San Zaccaria) Dress to the nines and swan straight past the 'hotel guests only' sign to the glamorous bar filling the grand hall of the 14th-century Palazzo Dandolo. Sparkles from Murano chandeliers reflect off the gilt edges and silk furnishings, while snappily dressed staff effortlessly descend with signature Vesper martinis and bottomless bowls of snacks.

Bar Terrazza Danieli   BAR
(Map p346; ☑041 522 64 80; www.danielihotel venice.com; Riva degli Schiavoni 4196; ⊗3-7pm May-Sep; ⊜San Zaccaria) Gondolas glide in to dock along the quay, while across the lagoon the white-marble edifice of Palladio's San Giorgio Maggiore turns from gold to pink in the waters of the canal: the late-afternoon scene from the Hotel Danieli's top-floor balcony bar definitely calls for a toast. Linger over a *spritz* or cocktail.

Cannaregio

★ Vino Vero   WINE BAR
(Map p348; ☑041 275 00 44; www.facebook.com/ vinoverovenezia; Fondamenta de la Misericordia 2497; ⊗11am-midnight Tue-Sun, from 6pm Mon; ⊜San Marcuola) Lining the exposed-brick walls of this superior wine bar are interesting small-production wines, including a great selection of natural and biodynamic labels. However, it's the *cicheti* that really lifts this place beyond the ordinary, with arguably the most mouth-watering display of continually replenished, fresh *crostini* (open-face sandwiches) in the entire city. In the evenings the crowd spills out onto the canal.

★ Timon   WINE BAR
(Map p348; ☑041 524 60 66; Fondamenta dei Ormesini 2754; ⊗6pm-1am; ⊜San Marcuola) Find a spot in the wood-lined interior or, in summer, on the boat moored out front along the canal and watch the motley parade of drinkers and dreamers arrive for seafood *crostini* and quality wines by the *ombra*

(half-glass) or carafe. Musicians play sets canalside when the weather obliges.

★ **Torrefazione Cannaregio** CAFE
(Map p348; ☑041 71 63 71; www.torrefazione cannaregio.it; Rio Terà San Leonardo 1337; ⊘7am-7.15pm; 🚢Guglie) Venetians can't catch a train without a pit stop at this aromatic shopfront lined with brass-knobbed coffee bins. Since 1930, Venice's Marchi family has been importing speciality beans, roasted fresh daily in a washtub-size roaster behind the marble bar and ground to order. Service is as perky and efficient as you'd hope from such a well-caffeinated place.

★ **Il Santo Bevitore** PUB
(Map p348; ☑335 841 57 71; www.ilsantobevitore pub.com; Calle Zancani 2393a; ⊘4pm-2am; 🛜; 🚢Ca' d'Oro) San Marco has its glittering cathedral, but beer lovers prefer pilgrimages to this shrine of the 'Holy Drinker' for 20 brews on tap, including Trappist ales and seasonal stouts – alongside a big range of speciality gin, whisky and vodka. The faithful receive canalside seating, footy matches on TV, free wi-fi and the occasional live band.

★ **Un Mondo di Vino** BAR
(Map p350; ☑041 521 10 93; www.unmondo divinovenezia.com; Salizada San Canzian 5984a; ⊘11am-3pm & 5.30-11pm Tue-Sun; 🚢Rialto) Get here early for first crack at marinated artichokes and *sarde in saor* (sardines in tangy onion marinade), and to claim a few square inches of ledge for your plate and wineglass. There are dozens of wines offered by the glass, so take a chance on a freak blend or obscure varietal.

🍷 **San Polo & Santa Croce**

★ **Al Prosecco** WINE BAR
(Map p350; ☑041 524 02 22; www.alprosecco. com; Campo San Giacomo dell'Orio 1503, Santa Croce; ⊘10am-8pm Mon-Fri, to 5pm Sat Nov-Mar, to 10.30pm Apr-Oct; 🚢San Stae) 🌿 The urge to toast sunsets in Venice's loveliest *campo* is only natural – and so is the wine at Al Prosecco. This forward-thinking bar specialises in *vini naturi* (natural-process wines) – organic, biodynamic, wild-yeast fermented – from enlightened Italian winemakers like Cinque Campi and Azienda Agricola Barichel. So order a glass of unfiltered 'cloudy' *prosecco* and toast to the good things in life.

★ **Al Mercà** WINE BAR
(Map p350; ☑346 834 06 60; Campo Cesare Battisti 213, San Polo; ⊘10am-2.30pm & 6-8pm

OFF THE BEATEN TRACK

Stretching south of Lido and repeating its skinny shape, **Pellestrina** reminds you what the lagoon might have been like if Venice had never been dreamed of. The 11km-long island is home to three tight-knit fishing communities strung out along the water's edge. There are no hotels or sun loungers here, just elderly women sitting on their porches and fisherfolk mending their nets. Bus 11 travels from the Lido SME *vaporetto* stop to Pellestrina via a short hop on a ferry.

Mon-Thu, to 9.30pm Fri & Sat; 🚢Rialto-Mercato) Discerning drinkers flock to this cupboard-sized counter on a Rialto Market square to sip on top-notch *prosecco* and DOC wines by the glass (from €3). Edibles usually include meatballs and mini *panini* (€1.50), proudly made using super-fresh ingredients.

Bacareto Da Lele BAR
(Map p338; Campo dei Tolentini 183, Santa Croce; ⊘6am-8pm Mon-Fri, to 2pm Sat; 🚢Piazzale Roma) Pocket-sized Da Lele is never short of students and workers, stopping for a cheap, stand-up *ombra* (small glass of wine; from €0.60) on their way to and from the train station. Scan the blackboard for the day's wines and pair them with bite-sized *panini* (€1), stuffed with freshly shaved cured meats and combos like pancetta and artichoke. The place closes for much of August.

Cantina Do Spade BAR
(Map p350; ☑041 521 05 83; www.cantinado spade.com; Calle delle Do Spade 860, San Polo; ⊘10am-3pm & 6-10pm; 🛜; 🚢Rialto-Mercato) Famously mentioned in Casanova's memoirs, cosy, brick-lined 'Two Spades' continues to keep Venice in good spirits with its bargain Tri-Veneto wines and young, laid-back management. Come early for market-fresh *fritture* (batter-fried seafood) or linger longer with satisfying, sit-down dishes like *bigoli in salsa* (pasta in anchovy and onion sauce).

Basegò BAR
(Map p350; ☑041 850 02 99; www.basego.it; Campo San Tomá, San Polo; ⊘9am-11pm; 🚢San Tomà) Focusing on three essential ingredients – good food, good wine and good music – newly opened Basegò has rapidly formed a dedicated group of drinkers. Indulge in a *cicheti* feast of lagoon seafood, Norcia prosciutto, smoked tuna and Lombard cheeses, and on Friday night enjoy live music from the likes of Alessia Obino and Simone Massaron.

CAMPO SANTA MARGHERITA

Even in the dead of winter or the scorching heat of summer, you can count on action at Campo Santa Margherita, Venice's nightlife hub. The oblong, unruly square features a bevy of beverage temptations, including veteran **Il Caffè Rosso** (Map p342; ☑ 041 528 79 98; www.cafferosso.it; Campo Santa Margherita 2963, Dorsoduro; ☺7am-1am Mon-Sat; ☎; ☻Ca' Rezzonico) and hipsterish **Bakarò** (Map p342; ☑ 041 241 27 58; Calle della Chiesa 3665, Dorsoduro; ☺10am-1am; ☻Ca' Rezzonico). The nightly happy-hour scene unfolds like a live-action, 21st-century Veronese painting, with an animated, eclectic crowd of Italian architecture and foreign exchange students, gay and straight international hipsters, wise-cracking Venetian grandmothers and their knitwear-clad pugs. It also hosts a produce market Monday to Saturday (no fish or seafood on Monday), as well as the odd political protest.

☝ Dorsoduro

Residents of down-to-earth Dorsoduro convene nightly in Campo Santa Margherita or along the Zattere boardwalk for mandatory happy-hour *spritz* and pretty pink sunsets. Other areas that attract a drinking crowd include Fondamenta Nani, which overlooks the San Trovaso boat shed, dinky Campo San Barnaba and Calle San Pantalon, where the party regularly spills out into the street.

★ Cantinone Già Schiavi BAR
(Map p342; ☑ 041 523 95 77; www.cantinaschiavi.com; Fondamenta Nani 992, Dorsoduro; ☺8.30am-8.30pm Mon-Sat; ☻Zattere) Regulars gamely pass along orders to timid newcomers, who might otherwise miss out on smoked swordfish *cicheti* (bar snacks) with top-notch house Soave, or *pallottoline* (mini-bottles of beer) with generous *sopressa* (soft salami) *panini*. Chaos cheerfully prevails at this legendary canalside spot, where Accademia art historians rub shoulders with San Trovaso gondola builders without spilling a drop.

El Sbarlefo BAR
(Map p342; ☑ 041 524 66 50; www.elsbarlefo.it; Calle San Pantalon 3757, Dorsoduro; ☺10am-midnight; ☻San Tomà) If you're looking to escape the raucous student scene on Campo Santa

Margherita, head to this grown-up bar with its chic industrial look, sophisticated rock and blues soundtrack, and live music at weekends. Aside from the long list of regional wines, there's a serious selection of spirits here. Accompany with plates of high-brow *cicheti* such as swordfish wrapped in *robiola* (soft-ripened) cheese.

Osteria alla Bifora BAR
(Map p342; ☑ 041 523 61 19; Campo Santa Margherita 2930, Dorsoduro; ☺noon-3pm & 5pm-2am Wed-Mon; ☻Ca' Rezzonico) Other bars around this *campo* cater to *spritz*-pounding students, but this chandelier-lit medieval wine cave sets the scene for gentle flirting over a big-hearted Veneto merlot. Cured-meat platters are carved to order on that Ferrari-red meat slicer behind the bar, and there are placemats to doodle on and new-found friends aplenty at communal tables.

☝ Giudecca

★ Skyline ROOFTOP BAR
(Map p338; ☑ 041 272 33 11; www.skylinebarvenice.com; Fondamenta San Biagio 810, Giudecca; ☺5pm-1am; ☻Palanca) From white-sneaker cruise passengers to the €300-sunglasses set, the rooftop bar at the Hilton Molino Stucky wows everyone with its vast panorama over Venice and the lagoon. DJs spin tunes on Friday night year-round and on additional nights in summer, when the action moves to the deck and pool. There's occasional live music, too.

☆ Entertainment

★ La Fenice OPERA
(Map p342; ☑ 041 78 66 72; www.teatrolafenice.it; Campo San Fantin 1977; restricted view from €30; ☻Giglio) One of Italy's top opera houses, La Fenice stages a rich roster of opera, ballet and classical music. The cheapest seats are in the boxes at the top, nearest the stage. The view is extremely restricted, but you will get to hear the music, watch the orchestra, soak up the atmosphere and people-watch.

★ Palazzetto Bru Zane CLASSICAL MUSIC
(Centre du Musique Romantique Française; Map p350; ☑ 041 521 10 05; www.bru-zane.com; Palazzetto Bru Zane 2368, San Polo; adult/reduced €15/5; ☺box office 2.30-5.30pm Mon-Fri, closed late Jul–mid-Aug; ☻San Tomà) Pleasure palaces don't get more romantic than Palazzetto Bru Zane on concert nights, when exquisite harmonies tickle Sebastiano Ricci angels

tumbling across stucco-frosted ceilings. Multi-year restorations returned the 1695–97 Casino Zane's 100-seat music room to its original function, attracting world-class musicians to enjoy its acoustics from late September to mid-May.

Scuola Grande di San Giovanni Evangelista
OPERA

(Map p350; ☏041 426 65 59; www.scuolasangiovanni.it; Campiello della Scuola 2454, San Polo; adult/reduced from €20/5; ⛴San Tomà) Drama comes with the scenery when Italian opera favourites – Puccini's *Tosca,* Verdi's *La Traviata,* Rossini's *Il Barbiere di Seviglia* – are performed in the lavish hall where Venice's secretive Council of Ten socialised. Stage sets can't compare to the *scuola:* sweep up Mauro Codussi's 15th-century staircase into Giorgio Massari's 1729 hall, and take your seat amid Giandomenico Tiepolo paintings.

Musica a Palazzo
OPERA

(Map p342; ☏340 971 72 72; www.musicapalazzo.com; Palazzo Barbarigo Minotto, Fondamenta Duodo o Barbarigo 2504; ticket incl beverage €85; ☉from 8pm; ⛴Giglio) Hang onto your *prosecco* and brace for impact: in historic salons, the soprano's high notes imperil glassware, and thundering baritones reverberate through inlaid floors. During performances of opera

from Verdi or Rossini, the drama progresses from receiving-room overtures to parlour duets overlooking the Grand Canal, followed by second acts in the Tiepolo-ceilinged dining room and bedroom grand finales.

Interpreti Veneziani
CLASSICAL MUSIC

(Map p342; ☏041 277 05 61; www.interpretiveneziani.com; Chiesa San Vidal, Campo di San Vidal 2862; adult/reduced €29/24; ☉performances 8.30pm; ⛴Accademia) Hard-core classical fans might baulk at the idea of Vivaldi being played night after night for decades, but it truly is a fitting soundtrack to this city of intrigue. You'll never listen to *The Four Seasons* again without hearing summer storms erupting over the lagoon, or snow-muffled footsteps hurrying over footbridges in winter's-night intrigues.

 ## Shopping

Fondaco dei Tedeschi
DEPARTMENT STORE

(Map p350; www.dfs.com/en/venice; Calle del Fontego dei Tedeschi 5350; ☉10am–8pm; ⛴Rialto) Occupying one of the Grand Canal's most imposing buildings, a 16th-century German trading house, this branch of the DFS chain is worth visiting whether you're in the market for a handbag with a four-digit price tag or not. Four floors of colonnaded galleries

---

WORTH A TRIP

LIDO DI JESOLO

This 13km strand of golden sand on the mainland east of Venice is far and away Venetians' preferred beach – if they can be bothered with the travel time. Unlike its island namesake, this Lido looks to be booming, with upmarket apartments, shops selling designer eyewear, a water park, a large aquarium complex, and a stretch of colourful buildings housing kebab shops, pizzerias, bars and the odd top-notch restaurant, the best of which is **Ristorante da Omar** (☏042 19 36 85; www.ristorantedaomar.it; Via Dante Alighieri 21; meals €33-63; ☉noon-3.30pm & 7.30-10.30pm Thu-Tue).

Aside from the beach, the other attraction of Lido di Jesolo is its summertime nightclubs. Keep an eye out for flyers around Venice advertising club nights and beach concerts, often featuring international acts. Note that the main clubs are set back from the beach, about an hour's walk west from the bus station.

For more information on things to do and see in Jesolo, call into the **Casa del Turismo** (☏041 37 06 01; www.jesolo.it; Via XIII Martiri; ☉8.30am-6.30pm; ☒23a).

Getting to Lido di Jesolo takes about an hour by car. If you plan to come by public transport, ATVO has buses departing from Piazzale Roma roughly hourly from 6am until about 11pm (€8 return, 70 minutes). Another option is to catch a *vaporetto* (small passenger ferry) to Punta Sabbioni on the tip of the peninsula (lines 14, 15, 17 and 22) and then catch bus 23A (€3, 38 minutes).

If you're planning a club night, the problem is getting back. Taxis cost upwards of €80, so you might want to wait for the first buses. The 23A to Punta Sabbioni stops near the main clubs from around 5.20am.

rise up to line the vast central void, leading to sublime views from the rooftop.

★ Coin
DEPARTMENT STORE

(Map p350; ☑041 520 35 81; www.coinexcelsior. com; Ponte de l'Ogio 5787; ⏰10am-8pm; 📶; 🚢Rialto) Its glitzy neighbour, Fondaco dei Tedeschi, gets all the attention these days but non-oligarchs will find Coin much more accessible. It's expensive but not stupidly so (especially during the legendary sales), and the range includes streetwear, famous brands and lesser known but top-quality local fashion.

★ L'Armadio di Coco Luxury Vintage
VINTAGE

(Map p342; ☑041 241 32 14; www.larmadiodi coco.it; Campo di Santa Maria del Giglio 2516a; ⏰10.30am-7.30pm; 🚢Giglio) Jam-packed with pre-loved designer treasures from yesteryear, this tiny shop is the place to come for classic Chanel dresses, exquisite cashmere coats and limited-edition Gucci shoulder bags.

Libraria Aqua Alta
BOOKS

(Map p346; ☑041 296 08 41; Calle Lunga Santa Maria Formosa 5176b; ⏰9am-8pm; 🚢Ospedale) Precarious stacks of books look at constant danger of collapse at this wonderfully ragtag secondhand bookshop. Some books are displayed in a gondola – which must come in handy during floods – and you can even climb a stack for views over the back canal.

★ Oh My Blue
JEWELLERY, HANDICRAFTS

(Map p350; ☑041 243 57 41; www.ohmyblue. it; Campo San Tomà 2865, San Polo; ⏰11am-1pm & 2.30-7.30pm; 🚢San Tomà) In her white-on-white gallery, switched-on Elena Rizzi showcases edgy, show-stopping jewellery, accessories and decorative objects from both local and international talent like Elena Camilla Bertellotti, Ana Hagopian and Yoko Takirai. Expect anything from quartz rings and paper necklaces to sculptural bags and ceramics.

Gmeiner
SHOES

(Map p350; ☑338 896 21 89; www.gabriele gmeiner.com; Campiello del Sol 951, San Polo; ⏰by appointment 9am-1pm & 3-7pm Mon-Fri; 🚢Rialto-Mercato) Paris, London, Venice: Gabriele Gmeiner honed her shoemaking craft at Hermès and John Lobb, and today jet-setters fly to Venice just for her ultra-sleek Oxfords with hidden 'bent' seams and her minutely hand-stiched brogues, made to measure for men and women (around €3000, including hand-carved wooden last).

★ Paolo Olbi
ARTS & CRAFTS

(Map p342; ☑041 523 76 55; http://olbi.atspace. com; Calle Foscari 3253a, Dorsoduro; ⏰10.30am-12.40pm & 3.30-7.30pm Mon-Sat, 11.30am-12.40pm & 4-7.30pm Sun; 🚢Ca' Rezzonico) Thoughts worth committing to paper deserve Paolo Olbi's keepsake books, albums and stationery, whose fans include Hollywood actors and NYC mayors (ask to see the guestbook). Ordinary journals can't compare to Olbi originals, handmade with heavyweight paper and bound with exquisite leather bindings. The €1 watercolour postcards of Venice make for beautiful, bargain souvenirs.

Ca' Macana
ARTS & CRAFTS

(Map p342; ☑041 277 61 42; www.camacana.com; Calle de le Botteghe 3172, Dorsoduro; ⏰10am-7.30pm Sun-Fri, to 8pm Sat; 🚢Ca' Rezzonico) Glimpse the talents behind the Venetian Carnevale masks that impressed Stanley Kubrick so much he ordered several for his final film *Eyes Wide Shut*. Choose your papier-mâché persona from the selection of coquettish courtesan's eye-shades, chequered Casanova disguises and long-nosed plague doctor masks – or invent your own at Ca' Macana's mask-making workshops (one hour per person €49, two hour per person from €80).

★ ElleElle
GLASS

(☑041 527 48 66; www.elleellemurano.com; Fondamenta Manin 52, Murano; ⏰10.30am-1pm & 2-6pm; 🚢Faro) Nason Moretti has been making modernist magic happen in glass since the 1950s, and the third-generation glass designers are in fine form in this showroom. Everything is signed, including an exquisite range of hand-blown drinking glasses, jugs, bowls, vases, tealight holders, decanters and lamps.

★ Cesare Toffolo
GLASS

(☑041 73 64 60; www.toffolo.com; Fondamenta dei Vetrai 37, Murano; ⏰10am-6pm; 🚢Colonna) Mind-boggling miniatures are the trademarks of this Murano glass-blower, but you'll also find some dramatic departures: chiselled cobalt-blue vases, glossy black candlesticks that look like minarets, and drinking glasses so fine that they seem to be made out of air.

Marina e Susanna Sent Studio
GLASS

(☑041 527 46 65; www.marinaesusannasent.com; Fondamenta Serenella 20, Murano; ⏰10am-5pm Mon-Fri; 🚢Colonna) This striking space dedicated to the work of the pioneering Sent sisters is as sleek as their jewellery: white walls and huge picture windows flood the room with light, setting their signature bubble necklaces ablaze. The collection is displayed in colour groups and neatly stashed in drawers – don't be too shy to ask for assistance; there's a lot to see.

Other shops, with a more highly curated selection, can be found in **Dorsoduro** (Map p342; ☑ 041 520 81 36; Campo San Vio 669; ⏰ 10am-1pm & 1.30-6.30pm; 🛳 Accademia), San Polo and San Marco.

ℹ Information

MEDICAL SERVICES

First Aid Point (Piazzale Roma; ⏰ 8am-8pm; 🛳 Piazzale Roma) Dedicated to serving out-of-town visitors, this first-aid point performs diagnostics and minor surgery, issues drug prescriptions and referrals for further hospital treatment

Guardia Medica (☑ 041 238 56 48) This service of night-time call-out doctors in Venice operates from 8pm to 8am on weekdays and from 10am the day before a holiday (including Sunday) until 8am the day after.

Ospedale dell'Angelo (☑ 041 965 71 11; www.ulss12.ve.it; Via Paccagnella 11, Mestre) Vast modern hospital on the mainland.

Ospedale SS. Giovanni e Paolo (☑ 041 529 41 11; www.ulss12.ve.it; Campo Zanipolo 6777, Castello; 🛳 Ospedale) Venice's main hospital for emergency care and dental treatment. The entrance is on the water near the Ospedale vaporetto stop.

POST

There are a couple of post offices in every Venetian *sestiero* (district), with addresses and hours online at www.poste.it.

Post Office (Map p342; www.poste.it; Calle Larga de l'Ascension 1241; ⏰ 8.20am-1.35pm Mon-Sat; 🛳 San Marco) A convenient regional branch located behind Piazza San Marco.

TOURIST INFORMATION

Airport Tourist Office (☑ 041 24 24; www.veneziaunica.it; Arrivals Hall, Marco Polo Airport; ⏰ 8.30am-7pm)

Piazzale Roma Tourist Office (Map p338; ☑ 041 24 24, lost & found 041 272 21 79; www.veneziaunica.it; ground fl ASM car park, Piazzale Roma; ⏰ 7.30am-7.30pm; 🛳 Piazzale Roma)

San Marco Tourist Office (Map p342; ☑ 041 24 24; www.veneziaunica.it; Piazza San Marco 71f; ⏰ 9am-7pm; 🛳 San Marco)

Stazione Santa Lucia Tourist Office (Map p338; ☑ 041 24 24; www.veneziaunica.it; ⏰ 7am-9pm; 🛳 Ferrovia)

ℹ Getting There & Away

AIR

Most flights to Venice fly in to **Marco Polo Airport** (☑ flight information 041 260 92 60; www.veniceairport.it; Via Galileo Gallilei 30/1, Tessera), 12km outside Venice, east of Mestre. Ryanair and some other budget airlines also use Treviso airport (p397), about 4km southwest of Treviso and a 26km, one-hour drive from Venice.

BUS

Urban, regional and long-distance buses arrive at the bus station (Map p338) in Piazzale Roma, from where *vaporetti* connect with the rest of the city. Services include:

ATVO (Map p338; ☑ 0421 59 46 71; www.atvo.it; Piazzale Roma 497g, Santa Croce; ⏰ 6.40am-7.45pm) Operates buses from Piazzale Roma to destinations all over the eastern Veneto, including airport connections.

ACTV (Azienda del Consorzio Trasporti Veneziano; ☑ 041 272 21 11; www.actv.it) Venice's public transport company. Runs buses to Mestre and surrounding areas.

Eurolines (www.eurolines.com) Operates a wide range of international routes.

CAR & MOTORCYCLE

To get to Venice by car or motorcycle, take the often-congested Trieste–Turin A4, which passes through Mestre. From Mestre, take the 'Venezia' exit. Once over Ponte della Libertà from Mestre, cars must be left at a car park in Piazzale Roma or on the Isola del Tronchetto. Be warned: you'll pay a hefty price in parking fees, and traffic backs up at weekends.

TRAIN

Direct intercity services operate out of Venice to most major Italian cities, as well as points in France, Germany, Austria, Switzerland, Slovenia and Croatia.

ℹ Getting Around

TO/FROM THE AIRPORT
Bus

ACTV runs bus 5 between Marco Polo Airport and Piazzale Roma (€8, 30 minutes, four per hour) with a limited number of stops en route. Alternatively, a bus+*vaporetto* ticket covering the bus journey and a one-way *vaporetto* trip within a total of 90 minutes costs €14.

ATVO runs a direct bus service between the airport and Piazzale Roma (Map p338; €8, 25 minutes, every 30 minutes from 8am to midnight). At Piazzale Roma you can pick up the ACTV *vaporetti* to reach locations around Venice.

Ferry

Alilaguna (☑ 041 240 17 01; www.alilaguna. it; airport transfer one way €15) operates four water shuttles that link the airport with various parts of Venice at a cost of €8 to Murano and €15 to all other landing stages. Passengers are permitted one suitcase and one piece of hand luggage. All further bags are charged at €3 per piece. Expect it to take 45 to 90 minutes to reach most destinations; it takes approximately 1¼ hours to reach Piazza San Marco. Lines include the following:

Linea Blu (Blue Line) Stops at the Lido, San Marco, Stazione Marittima and points in between.

Linea Rossa (Red Line) Stops at Murano and the Lido.

Linea Arancia (Orange Line) Stops at Stazione Santa Lucia, Rialto and San Marco via the Grand Canal.

Linea Gialla (Yellow Line) Stops at Murano and Fondamente Nove.

Taxi

A taxi from the aiport to Piazzale Roma costs €50; the taxi rank (Map p338) is located by the bus station (p375). From there you can either hop on a *vaporetto* or pick up a water taxi (Map p338) at the nearby Fondamente Cossetti.

Water Taxi

The dock for water transfers to the historic centre is a 10-minute walk from the arrivals hall via a raised, indoor walkway accessed on the 1st floor of the terminal building. Luggage trolleys (requiring a €1 deposit) can be taken to the dock.

Private water taxis can be booked at the **Consorzio Motoscafi Venezia** (☑ 041 240 67 12; www.motoscafivenezia.it; ⊙ 9am-6pm) or **Veneziataxi** (☑ information 328 238 96 61; www.veneziataxi.it) desks in the arrivals hall, or directly at the dock. Private taxis cost from €110 for up to four passengers and all their luggage. Extra passengers (up to a limit of 12 or 16) carry a small surcharge.

If you don't have a large group, there is also the option of a shared **Venice Shuttle**. This is a shared water taxi and costs from €25 per person with a €6 surcharge for night-time arrivals. Seats should be booked online at www.venice-link.com. Boats seat a maximum of eight people and accommodate up to 10 bags. Those opting for a shared taxi should be aware that the service can wait for some time to fill up and has set drop-off points in Venice; only private transfers will take you directly to your hotel.

PUBLIC TRANSPORT

ACTV (p375) runs all public transport in Venice, including the waterborne. Although the service is efficient and punctual, boats on main lines get full fast and can be overcrowded during Carnevale and in peak season. One-way tickets cost €7.50.

Inter-island ferry services to Murano, Torcello, the Lido and other lagoon islands are usually provided on larger *motonave*.

WATER TAXI

Licensed water taxis are a costly way to get around Venice, though they may prove handy when you're late for the opera or have lots of luggage. Fares can be metered or negotiated in advance. Official rates start at €15 plus €2 per minute, €5 extra if they're called to your hotel. There's a €10 surcharge for night trips (10pm to 6am), a €5 surcharge for additional luggage (above five pieces) and a €10 surcharge for each extra passenger above the first four. Note: if you order a water taxi through your hotel or a travel agent, you will be subject to a surcharge. Tipping isn't required.

Make sure your water taxi has the yellow strip with the licence number displayed. There are official water-taxi ranks at the airport, outside the train station, in front of Piazzale Roma and at Tronchetto.

Even if you're in a hurry, don't encourage your taxi driver to speed through Venice – this kicks up *motoschiaffi* (motorboat wakes) that expose Venice's ancient foundations to degradation and rot.

THE VENETO

Most visitors to the Veneto devote all their time to Venice, which is understandable – until you discover the rich variety of experiences that await just an hour or two away.

First, there are the city-states Venice annexed in the 15th century: Padua (Padova), with its pre-Renaissance frescoes; Vicenza, with Palladio's peerless architecture; and Verona, with its sophisticated bustle atop Roman foundations. All are easily reached by train from Venice.

Then there are the wines, in particular, Valpolicella's bold Amarones. In a party

---

ⓘ VAPORETTO PASSES

The ACTV Tourist Travel Cards allow for unlimited travel on *vaporetti* (small passenger ferries) and Lido buses within the following time blocks:

24 hours €20

48 hours €30

72 hours €40

One week €60

mood? The hills around Conegliano produce Italy's finest bubbly: Prosecco Superiore. For harder stuff, Bassano del Grappa provides its eponymous firewater.

When the Adriatic wipes Venice clean of its mists, you can catch glimpses of the snowcapped Dolomites – in less than two hours you can go from canals to the crisp Alpine clarity of Belluno and Cortina d'Ampezzo: a land of idyllic hikes, razor-sharp peaks and the world's most fashion-conscious skiing.

Brenta Riviera

Every 13 June for 300 years, summer officially kicked off with a traffic jam along the Grand Canal, as a flotilla of fashionable Venetians headed to their villas along the banks of the Brenta. Every last ball gown and poker chair was loaded onto barges for dalliances that stretched until November. The annual party ended when Napoleon arrived in 1797, but 80 villas still strike elegant poses along the Brenta, and six of them are now open to the public at various times of the year.

◉ Sights

Villa Foscari　　　HISTORIC BUILDING
(☏041 520 39 66; www.lamalcontenta.com; Via dei Turisti 9, Malcontenta; €10; ⊘9am-noon Tue & Sat Apr-Oct) The most romantic Brenta villa, the Palladio-designed, Unesco-listed Villa Foscari (built 1555–60) got its nickname La Malcontenta from a grande-dame of the Foscari clan who was reputedly exiled here for cheating on her husband – though these bright, highly sociable salons hardly constitute a punishment. The villa was abandoned for years, but Giovanni Zelotti's frescoes have now been restored to daydream-inducing splendour.

Villa Widmann Rezzonico Foscari　　　HISTORIC BUILDING
(☏041 547 00 12; Via Nazionale 420, Mira; €10; ⊘9am-noon Tue & Sat May-Oct) To appreciate both gardening and Venetian-style social engineering, stop just west of Oriago at Villa Widmann Rezzonico Foscari. Originally owned by Persian-Venetian nobility, the 18th-century villa captures the Brenta's last days of rococo decadence, with Murano sea-monster chandeliers and a frescoed grand ballroom with upper viewing gallery. Head to the gallery to reach the upstairs ladies' gambling parlour where, according to local lore, villas were once gambled away in high-stakes games.

Villa Pisani Nazionale　　　HISTORIC BUILDING
(☏049 50 20 74; www.villapisani.beniculturali.it; Via Doge Pisani 7, Stra; adult/reduced €7.50/3.75, park only €4.50/2.25; ⊘9am-8pm Tue-Sun Apr-Sep, to 6pm Oct, to 5pm Nov-Mar) To keep hard-partying Venetian nobles in line, Doge Alvise Pisani provided a Versailles-like reminder of who was in charge. The 1774, 114-room Villa Pisani Nazionale is surrounded by huge gardens, a labyrinthine hedge-maze, and pools to reflect the doge's glory. Here you'll find the bathroom with a tiny wooden throne used by Napoleon; the sagging bed where new king Vittorio Emanuele II slept; and, ironically, the reception hall where Mussolini and Hitler met in 1934 under Tiepolo's ceiling depicting the Geniuses of Peace.

🏃 Activities

★ Il Burchiello　　　CRUISE
(☏049 876 02 33; www.ilburchiello.it; adult/reduced half-day cruise from €55/45, full day €99/55) Watch 50 villas drift by on this modern barge. Full-day cruises run between Venice and Padua, stopping at Malcontenta, Widmann (or Barchessa Valmarana) and Pisani villas. From Venice, cruises depart from Pontile della Pietà pier on Riva degli Schiavoni (Tuesday, Thursday and Saturday). From Padua, cruises depart from Pontile del Portello pier (Wednesday, Friday and Sunday).

Veloce　　　CYCLING
(☏346 847 11 41; www.rentalbikeitaly.com; touring/mountain/racing bicycle per day €20/25/35; ⊘8am-8pm) The scenic Brenta Riviera plains make an easy, enjoyable bicycle ride, and you can speed past those tour boats along 150km of cycling routes. Rental Bike Venice is a friendly bike-rental outlet with branches in many Veneto towns offering mountain and city bikes, plus pre-loaded GPS units (€10), guided tours (€80 per person), roadside assistance and advice in English on itineraries and local restaurants.

🍴 Eating

Osteria Da Conte　　　VENETIAN €€
(☏049 47 95 71; www.osteriadaconte.it; Via Caltana 133, Mira; meals €25-35; ⊘noon-2.30pm & 8-10.30pm Tue-Sat, noon-2.30pm Sun) An unlikely bastion of culinary sophistication lodged practically underneath an overpass, Da

Conte has one of the most interesting wine lists in the region, plus creative takes on regional cuisine, from shrimps with black sesame and pumpkin purée to gnocchi in veal-cheek *ragù*. If it's on the menu, end your meal with the faultless *zabaglione* (egg and Marsala custard).

⊕ Getting There & Away

ACTV's Venezia–Padova Extraurbane bus 53 leaves from Venice's Piazzale Roma about every half hour, stopping at key Brenta villages en route to Padua.

Local Venice–Padua train services stop at Dolo (€3.40, 25 minutes, one to three per hour).

By car, take SS11 from Mestre-Venezia towards Padua and take the A4 autostrada towards Dolo/Padua.

Padua

POP 212.500

Though under an hour from Venice, Padua (Padova in Italian) seems a world away with its medieval marketplaces, Fascist-era facades and hip student population. As a medieval city-state and home to Italy's second-oldest university, Padua challenged both Venice and Verona for regional hegemony. A series of extraordinary fresco cycles recalls this golden age – including in Giotto's blockbuster Cappella degli Scrovegni, Menabuoi's heavenly gathering in the baptistry and Titian's *St Anthony* in the Scoletta del Santo. For the next few centuries, Padua and Verona challenged each other for dominance over the Veneto plains. But Venice finally settled the matter by occupying Padua permanently in 1405.

As a strategic military-industrial centre, Padua became a parade ground for Mussolini speeches, an Allied bombing target and a secret Italian Resistance hub (at its university).

⊙ Sights

★**Cappella degli Scrovegni**   CHAPEL
(Scrovegni Chapel; ☑049 201 00 20; www.cappelladegliscrovegni.it; Piazza Eremitani 8; adult/reduced €13/8, night ticket €8/6; ⊙9am-7pm, night ticket 7-10pm) Padua's version of the Sistine Chapel, the Cappella degli Scrovegni houses one of Italy's great Renaissance masterpieces – a striking cycle of Giotto frescoes. Dante, da Vinci and Vasari all honour Giotto as the artist who ended the Dark Ages with these 1303–05 paintings, whose humanistic depiction of biblical figures was especially well suited to the chapel Enrico Scrovegni commissioned in memory of his father (who as a moneylender was denied a Christian burial).

It's a simple brick building, with little indication from the outside of what lies within. It took Giotto two years to finish the frescoes, which tell the story of Christ from Annunciation to Ascension. Scrovegni's chapel once adjoined the family mansion (demolished in 1824) – the city of Padua acquired the chapel in 1881.

Giotto's moving, modern approach helped change how people saw themselves: no longer as lowly vassals, but as vessels for the divine, however flawed. And where before medieval churchgoers had been accustomed to blank stares from saints perched on high thrones, Giotto introduced biblical figures as characters in recognisable settings. Onlookers gossip as middle-aged Anne tenderly kisses Joachim, and Jesus stares down Judas as the traitor puckers up for the fateful kiss. He also used unusual techniques such as impasto, or building paint up into 3D forms. A 10-minute introductory video provides some helpful insights before you enter the church itself.

Book tickets at the Musei Civici agli Eremitani, where you access the chapel, or at the tourist office. Chapel visits last 15 to 20 minutes (depending on the time of year), plus another 10 minutes for the video. Arrive at least 15 to 30 minutes before your tour starts, or an hour before if you want to get around the Musei Civici agli Eremitani beforehand.

LOCAL KNOWLEDGE

SUPER MARKETS

One of the most enjoyable activities in Padua (Padova) is browsing the markets in **Piazza delle Erbe** and **Piazza della Frutta**, which operate very much as they've done since the Middle Ages. Dividing them is the Gothic Palazzo della Ragione, whose arcades – known locally as **Sotto il Salone** (www.sottoilsalone.it) – rumble with specialist butchers, cheesemakers, fishmongers, *salumerie* and fresh pasta producers. The markets are open all day, every day, except Sunday, although the best time to visit is before midday.

HEAD TO THE HILLS: COLLI EUGANEI

Southwest of Padua, the Euganean Hills feel a world away from the Veneto's cities. To help you explore the region's walled hilltop towns, misty vineyards and bubbling hot springs, visit www.parcocollieuganei.com or grab information at the Padua tourist offices.

Just south of Padua lie the natural hot-spring resorts of **Abano Terme** and **Montegrotto Terme**. They have been active since Roman times, when the Patavini built their villas on Mt Montirone. The towns are uninspiring, but the waters do cure various ailments.

In the medieval village of Arquà Petrarca, look for the elegant little **house** (☑ 0429 71 82 94; www.arquapetrarca.com; Via Valleselle 4, Arquà Petrarca; adult/reduced €4/2; ☺ 9am-12.30pm & 3-7pm Tue-Sun Mar-Oct, 9am-12.30pm & 2.30-5.30pm Tue-Sun Nov-Feb) where the great Italian poet Petrarch spent his final years in the 1370s.

At the southern reaches of the Euganei, you'll find Monselice, with its remarkable medieval **castle** (☑ 0429 7 29 31; www.castellodimonselice.it; Via del Santuario 11, Monselice; adult/reduced €8/6; ☺ 1hr guided tours 9am, 10am, 11am, 3pm & 4pm Tue-Sun Apr-Nov); Montagnana, with its magnificent 2km defensive perimeter; and Este, with its rich architectural heritage and important **archaeological museum** (☑ 0429 20 85; www.atestino. beniculturali.it, Via Guido Negri 9c, Este; adult/reduced €4/2; ☺ 8.30am 7.30pm). Este is also home to **Este Ceramiche Porcellane** (☑ 0429 22 70; www.esteceramiche.com; Via Zanchi 22a, Este; ☺ 8am-noon & 2-6pm Mon, to 5.30pm Tue-Fri, by appointment Sat), one of the oldest ceramics factories in Europe.

Located in the town of Galzignano Terme, **Villa Barbarigo Pizzoni Ardemani** (☑ 340 082 58 44; www.valsanzibiogiardino.it; adult/reduced €11/6.50; ☺ 10am-1pm & 2pm-sunset summer) is home to one of the finest historical gardens in Europe, shot through with streams, fish ponds and Bernini fountains. It's near Padova Golf Club, southwest of the city.

Palazzo del Bò
HISTORIC BUILDING

(☑ 049 827 30 47; www.unipd.it/en/guidedtours; Via VIII Febbraio; adult/reduced €7/4; ☺ see website for tour times) This Renaissance *palazzo* (mansion) is the seat of Padua's history-making university. Founded by renegade scholars from Bologna seeking greater intellectual freedom, the university has employed some of Italy's greatest and most controversial thinkers, including Copernicus, Galileo, Casanova and the world's first female doctor of philosophy, Eleonora Lucrezia Cornaro Piscopia (her statue graces the stairs). Admission is on a 45-minute guided tour only, which includes a visit to the world's first **anatomy theatre**.

Palazzo della Ragione
HISTORIC BUILDING

(☑ 049 820 50 06; Piazza delle Erbe; adult/reduced €6/4; ☺ 9am-7pm Tue-Sun Feb–Oct, to 6pm Nov-Jan) Ancient Padua can be glimpsed in the elegant twin squares (one the fruit market, the other the vegetable market) separated by the triple-decker Gothic Palazzo della Ragione, the city's tribunal dating from 1218. Inside Il Salone (the Great Hall), frescoes by Giotto acolytes Giusto de' Menabuoi and Nicolò Miretto depict the astrological theories of

Padovan professor Pietro d'Abano, with images representing the months, seasons, saints, animals and noteworthy Paduans (not necessarily in that order).

Duomo
CATHEDRAL

(☑ 049 65 69 14; Piazza del Duomo; baptistry €3; ☺ 7.30am noon & 4 7.30pm Mon Sat, 7.30am-1pm & 4-7.30pm Sun & holidays, baptistry 10am-6pm) Built from a much-altered design of Michelangelo's, the rather industrial facade and whitewashed symmetry of Padua's cathedral is a far cry from its rival in Piazza San Marco. Pop in quickly for Giuliano Vangi's contemporary chancel crucifix and sculptures before visiting the adjoining 13th-century **baptistry**, a Romanesque gem frescoed with luminous biblical scenes by Giusto de' Menabuoi. Hundreds of saints congregate in the cupola, posed as though for a school graduation photo, exchanging glances and stealing looks at the Madonna.

Basilica di Sant'Antonio
CHURCH

(Il Santo; ☑ 049 822 56 52; www.basilicadel santo.org; Piazza del Santo; ☺ 6.20am-6.45pm Mon-Sat, to 7.45pm Sun) `FREE` A pilgrimage site and the burial place of St Anthony of Padua (1193–1231), this huge church was

Padua

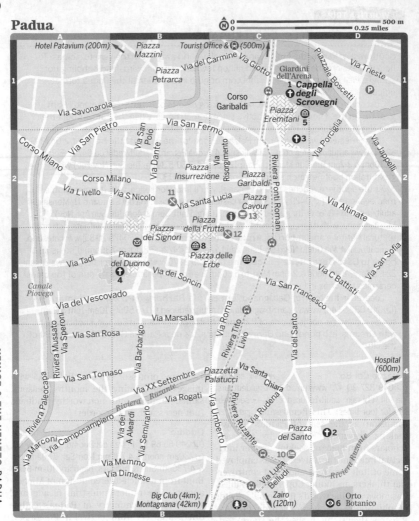

begun in 1232, its polyglot style incorporating rising eastern domes atop a Gothic brick structure crammed with Renaissance treasures. Behind the high altar, nine radiating chapels punctuate a broad ambulatory homing in on the Cappella delle Reliquie (Relics Chapel), where the relics of St Anthony reside.

Orto Botanico   GARDENS
(📞049 827 39 39; www.ortobotanicopd.it; Via dell'Orto Botanico 15; adult/reduced €10/8; ⏰9am-7pm daily Apr & May, 9am-7pm Tue-Sun Jun-Sep, to 6pm Tue-Sun Oct, to 5pm Tue-Sun Nov-Mar) Planted in 1545 by Padua University's medical faculty to study the medicinal properties of rare plants, Padua's World Heritage–listed Orto Botanico served as a clandestine Resistance meeting headquarters in WWII. The oldest tree is nicknamed 'Goethe's palm'; planted in 1585, it was mentioned by the great German writer in his *Italian Journey*. A much more recent addition is the high-tech Garden of Biodiversity, five interconnected greenhouses that recreate different climate zones and explore botanical and environmental themes via multimedia displays.

Padua

Prato della Valle   PARK

At the southern edge of the historical centre, this odd, elliptical garden was long used as a communal sportsground. Today it's a popular spot for locals wanting to soak up some summer rays and students swotting for exams. Framing the space is a slim canal lined by 78 statues of sundry great and good of Paduan history, plus 10 empty pedestals. Ten Venetian doges once occupied them, but Napoleon had them removed after he took Venice in 1797.

🛏 Sleeping

Belludi37   BOUTIQUE HOTEL €€

(☑ 049 66 56 33; www.belludi37.it; Via Luca Belludi 37; s €80, d €140-180; 🅿 ❋ 🛜) Graced with Flos bedside lamps and replica Danish chairs, the neutrally toned rooms at Belludi37 feature high ceilings, queen-sized beds and free minibar. Extra perks include a central location and helpful staff always on hand with suggestions for biking itineraries and walking tours.

Hotel Patavium   HOTEL €€

(☑ 049 72 36 98; www.hotelpatavium.it; Via B Pellegrino 106; s €60-120, d €75-140; ❋ 🛜) Smart, carpeted rooms with wide beds, flat-screen TVs and modern bathrooms define Patavium, a quick walk northwest of the city centre. Suites come with Jacuzzis, while the breakfast room is a middle-class affair of candlesticks, chandeliers and corner lounge with communal TV.

🍴 Eating & Drinking

Dalla Zita   STREET FOOD €

(☑ 049 65 49 92; Via Gorizia 12; snacks €2-5, coffee €1; ⊙ 9am-8pm Mon-Fri) So small that around five people fill the place standing, this unmarked street-food bar is Padua's best spot when you need to eat on the hop. Choose from the large menu of sandwiches stuck to the wall on multicoloured sticky notes, or if your Italian and patience is up to it, customise your very own *panini*. Gets very busy at lunchtime.

⭐ **Belle Parti**   ITALIAN €€€

(☑ 049 875 18 22; www.ristorantebelleparti.it; Via Belle Parti 11; meals €50; ⊙ 12.30-2.30pm & 7.30-10.30pm Mon-Sat) Prime seasonal produce, impeccable wines and near-faultless service meld into one unforgettable whole at this stellar fine-dining restaurant, resplendent with 18th-century antiques and 19th-century oil paintings. Seafood is the forte, with standout dishes including an arresting *gran piatto di crudità di mare* (raw seafood platter). Dress to impress here, and book ahead.

⭐ **Caffè Pedrocchi**   CAFE

(☑ 049 878 12 31; www.caffepedrocchi.it; Via VIII Febbraio 15; ⊙ 8am-midnight Sun-Thu, to 1am Fri & Sat) This unmissable piece of olde worlde European cafe culture takes you back to the days when Stendhal held court here. The cafe is divided into three rooms, each one sporting huge maps of the world, high ceilings, simple tables and waiters scurrying central Europe–style. A white grand piano completes the scene.

ℹ Information

Hospital (☑ 049 821 11 11; Via Giustiniani 1) Main public hospital.

Post Office (Via Monte di Pietà 4; ⊙ 8.20am-1.35pm Mon-Fri, to 12.35pm Sat)

Tourist Office (☑ 049 201 00 80; www.turismopadova.it; Vicolo Pedrocchi; ⊙ 9am-7pm Mon-Sat) Ask about the PadovaCard (p382) here. There is a second **tourist office** (☑ 049 201 00 80; Piazza di Stazione; ⊙ 9am-7pm Mon-Sat, 10am-4pm Sun) at the train station.

ℹ Getting There & Away

Train is by far the easiest way to reach Padua from virtually anywhere. The station is about

ℹ PADOVACARD

A **PadovaCard** (€16/21 per 48/72 hours) gives one adult and one child under 14 free use of city public transport and access to almost all of Padua's major attractions, including the Cappella degli Scrovegni (plus €1 booking fee; reservations essential). PadovaCards are available at Padua tourist offices, Musei Civici agli Eremitani and the hotels listed on the PadovaCard section of the tourist office website (www.turismopadova.it).

500m north of Cappella degli Scrovegni and linked to the centre by Padua's odd monorail tram-bus. Connections include:

Venice €4.15 to €14.90, 25 to 50 minutes, one to nine per hour.

Verona €7.10 to €22, 40 to 80 minutes, one to four per hour.

Vicenza €4.15 to €14.90, 15 to 25 minutes, one to five per hour.

ℹ Getting Around

It is easy to get to all the sights by foot from the train and bus stations, but the city's unusual single-branch monorail tram-bus running from the train station passes within 100m of all the main sights. Tickets (€1.30) are available at tobacconists and newsstands.

Verona

POP 260,000

Best known for its Shakespeare associations, Verona attracts a multinational gaggle of tourists to its pretty piazzas and knot of lanes, most in search of Romeo, Juliet and all that. But beyond the heart-shaped kitsch and Renaissance romance, Verona is a bustling centre, its heart dominated by a mammoth, remarkably well-preserved 1st-century amphitheatre, the venue for the city's annual summer opera festival. Add to that countless churches, a couple of architecturally fascinating bridges over the Adige, regional wine and food from the Veneto hinterland and some impressive art, and Verona shapes up as one of northern Italy's most attractive cities. And all this just a short hop from the shores of stunning Lake Garda.

History

Shakespeare placed star-crossed lovers Romeo Montague and Juliet Capulet in Verona for good reason: romance, drama and fatal family feuding have been the city's hallmark for centuries. From the 3rd century BC Verona was a Roman trade centre with ancient gates, a forum (now Piazza delle Erbe) and a grand Roman arena, which still serves as one of the world's great opera venues. In the Middle Ages the city flourished under the wrathful della Scala clan, who were as much energetic patrons of the arts as they were murderous tyrants. Their elaborate Gothic tombs, the **Arche Scaligere**, are just off Piazza dei Signori.

Under Cangrande I (1308–28) Verona conquered Padua and Vicenza, with Dante, Petrarch and Giotto benefitting from the city's patronage. But the fratricidal rage of Cangrande II (1351–59) complicated matters, and the della Scala family was run out of town in 1387. Venice took definitive control in 1404, ruling until Napoleon's arrival in 1797.

The city became a Fascist control centre from 1938 to 1945, a key location for Resistance interrogation and transit point for Italian Jews sent to Nazi concentration camps. Today, the city is a Unesco World Heritage Site and a cosmopolitan crossroads, especially in summer when the 2000-year-old arena hosts opera's biggest names.

◉ Sights

★ **Museo di Castelvecchio**　　MUSEUM
(📞 045 806 26 11; https://museodicastelvecchio. comune.verona.it; Corso Castelvecchio 2; adult/reduced €6/4.50; ⊙ 1.30-7.30pm Mon, 8.30am-7.30pm Tue-Sun) Bristling with fishtail battlements along the River Adige, Castelvecchio was built in the 1350s by Cangrande II. Severely damaged by Napoleon and WWII bombings, the fortress was reinvented by architect Carlo Scarpa, who constructed bridges over exposed foundations, filled gaping holes with glass panels, and balanced a statue of Cangrande I above the courtyard on a concrete gangplank. The complex is now home to a diverse collection of statuary, frescoes, jewellery, medieval artefacts and paintings.

Ponte Scaligero　　BRIDGE
(Corso Castelvecchio) From the battlements of the Castelvecchio you can look down on this asymmetrical, brick-built bridge that takes just three leaps to span the River Adige. It links the Castelvecchio with some pretty public gardens on the other side of the water.

★ **Roman Arena** RUINS
(☑ 045 800 32 04; Piazza Brà; adult/reduced €10/7.50; ⏲ 8.30am-7.30pm Tue-Sun, from 1.30pm Mon) Built of pink-tinged marble in the 1st century AD, Verona's Roman amphitheatre survived a 12th-century earthquake to become the city's legendary open-air opera house, with seating for 30,000 people. You can visit the arena year-round, though it's at its best during the summer opera festival. In winter months, concerts are held at the **Teatro Filarmonico** (☑ 045 800 28 80; www. arena.it; Via dei Mutilati 4; opera €23-60, concerts €25-50). From January to May and October to December, admission is €1 on the first Sunday of the month.

The eighth biggest amphitheatre in the Roman Empire and predating the Colosseum in Rome, nothing of the incredible inside is visible from outside. Pass through the dingy ancient corridors, wide enough to drive a gladiator's chariot down, to re-emerge into the massive, sunlit stone arena, at least 50 levels of seating rising from the mammoth, oval showground. Note the amphitheatre is completely open so this is not a great place to visit in the rain.

Chiesa di San Fermo CHURCH
(Stradone San Fermo; admission €2.50, combined Verona church ticket €6 or with VeronaCard free; ⏲ 10am-6pm Mon-Sat, 1-6pm Sun Mar-Oct, 10am-1pm & 1.30-5pm Mon-Sat, 1-5pm Sun Nov-Apr) At the river end of Via Leoni, Chiesa di San Fermo is actually two churches in one. Franciscan monks raised the 13th-century Gothic church right over an original 11th-century Romanesque structure. Inside the main Gothic church, you'll notice a magnificent timber *carena di nave*, a ceiling reminiscent of an upturned boat's hull. In the right transept are 14th-century frescoes, including some fragments depicting episodes in the life of St Francis. Stairs from the cloister lead underground to the spare but atmospheric Romanesque church below.

Piazza delle Erbe SQUARE
Originally a Roman forum, Piazza delle Erbe is ringed with buzzing cafes and some of Verona's most sumptuous buildings, including the elegantly baroque **Palazzo Maffei**, which now houses several shops at its northern end. Just off the piazza, the monumental arch known as the **Arco della Costa** is hung with a whale's rib. Legend holds that the rib will fall on the first just person to walk beneath it. So far, it remains intact, despite visits by popes and kings.

★ **Galleria d'Arte Moderna Achille Forti** GALLERY
(Palazzo della Ragione; ☑ 045 800 19 03; www. palazzodellaragioneverona.it; Cortile Mercato Vecchio; adult/reduced €4/2.50, incl Torre dei Lamberti €8/5; ⏲ 10am-6pm Tue-Fri, 11am-7pm Sat & Sun) In the shadow of the Torre dei Lamberti, the Romanesque Palazzo della Ragione is home to Verona's jewel-box Gallery of Modern Art. Reached via the Gothic **Scala della Ragione** (Stairs of Reason), the collection of paintings and sculpture spans 1840 to 1940 and includes influential Italian artists such as Giorgio Morandi and Umberto Boccioni. Among the numerous highlights are Francesco Hayez' arresting portrait *Meditazione* (Meditation), Angelo Dall'Oca's haunting *Foglie cadonti* (Falling Leaves) and Ettore Berladini's darkly humourous *I vecchi* (Old Men).

Torre dei Lamberti TOWER
(☑ 045 927 30 27; Via della Costa 1; adult/reduced incl Galleria d'Arte Moderna Achille Forti €8/5, with VeronaCard €1; ⏲ 10am-7pm) One of Verona's most popular attractions, this 84m-high watchtower provides panoramic views of Verona and nearby mountains. Begun in

---

ROMEO & JULIET IN VERONA

Shakespeare had no idea what he'd start when he set his (heavily derivative) tale of star-crossed lovers in Verona, but the city has seized the commercial possibilities with both hands – everything from *osterie* and hotels to embroidered kitchen aprons get the R&J branding. While the play's depiction of feuding families has genuine provenance, the lead characters themselves are fictional.

Undaunted, in the 1930s the authorities settled on a house in Via Cappello (think Capulet) as Juliet's and added a 14th-century-style balcony and a bronze statue of our heroine. You can squeeze onto the balcony itself at the altogether underwhelming **Casa di Giulietta** (Juliet's House; ☑ 045 803 43 03; Via Cappello 23; adult/reduced €6/4.50, free with VeronaCard; ⏲ 1.30-7.30pm Mon, 8.30am-7.30pm Tue-Sun), or – more sensibly – see the circus from the square below, a spot framed by a slew of lovesick sticky notes.

Verona

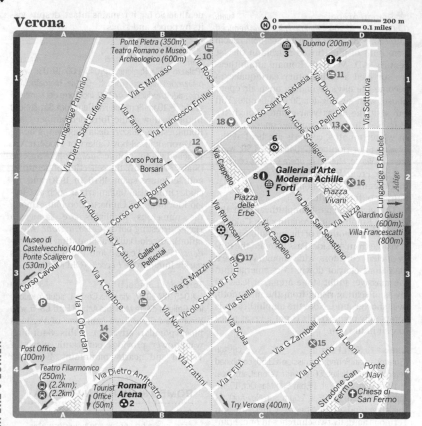

the 12th century and finished in 1463 – too late to notice invading Venetians – it sports an octagonal bell tower whose two bells retain their ancient names: Rengo once called meetings of the city council, while Marangona warned citizens of fire. A lift whisks you up two-thirds of the way but you have to walk the last few storeys.

Piazza dei Signori   SQUARE

Verona's beautiful open-air salon is ringed by a series of elegant Renaissance *palazzi*. Chief among these are the **Palazzo degli Scaligeri** (aka Palazzo Podestà), the 14th-century residence of Cangrande I Della Scala; the arched **Loggia del Consiglio**, built in the 15th century as the city council chambers; and the brick and tufa stone **Palazzo della Ragione**. In the middle of the piazza is a famous statue of **Dante**, who was given refuge in Verona after he was exiled from Florence in 1302.

Most of the piazza's buildings are off limits to the public, but you can visit the 12th-century **Palazzo della Ragione**, on your left as you enter from the Arco della Costa, which has housed a modern art gallery since April 2014. Next door, the **Palazzo del Capitano** is fronted by a cobbled square with two huge round windows in the ground, which reveal the excavated Roman and medieval basements beneath. To the northeast loom the **Arche Scaligere**, the ornate, Gothic funerary monuments of the Della Scala family.

Basilica di Sant'Anastasia   BASILICA

(www.chieseverona.it; Piazza di Sant'Anastasia; €2.50; ⊙9am-6pm Mon-Sat, 1-6pm Sun Mar-Oct, 10am-1pm & 1.30-5pm Mon-Sat, 1-5pm Sun Nov-Feb) Dating from the 13th to 15th centuries and featuring an elegantly decorated vaulted ceiling, the Gothic Basilica di Sant'Anastasia is Verona's largest church

Verona

and a showcase for local art. The multitude of frescoes is overwhelming, but don't overlook Pisanello's story-book-quality fresco *St George and the Princess* above the entrance to the Pellegrini Chapel, or the 1495 holy water font featuring a hunchback carved by Paolo Veronese's father, Gabriele Caliari.

Arena Museo Opera –
AMO   MUSEUM
(⌖ 045 80 30 461; www.arenamuseopera.com; Palazzo Forti, Via Massalongo 7; adult/reduced €10/8; ⊙ 2.30-7.30pm Mon, 9.30am-7.30pm Thu-Sun) Opera fans shouldn't miss this under-visited multimedia museum dedicated entirely to the great Italian opera culture. Exhibits include scores, letters and notes by big names such as Bellini, Rossini, Donizetti, Verdi and Puccini as well as costumes, sets and photographs of great operatic events of grander times gone by.

Duomo   CATHEDRAL
(⌖ 045 59 28 13; Piazza Duomo; €2.50, combined Verona church ticket €6 or with Verona

Card free; ⊙ 10am-5.30pm Mon-Sat, 1.30-5.30pm Sun Mar-Oct, 10am-1pm & 1.30-5pm Mon-Fri, to 4pm Sat, 1.30-5pm Sun Nov-Feb) Verona's 12th-century cathedral is a striking Romanesque creation, with bug-eyed statues of Charlemagne's paladins Roland and Oliver, crafted by medieval master Nicolò, on the west porch. Nothing about this sober facade hints at the extravagant 16th- to 17th-century frescoed interior with angels aloft amid *trompe l'œil* architecture. At the left end of the nave is the **Cartolari-Nichesola Chapel**, designed by Renaissance master Jacopo Sansovino and featuring a vibrant Titian *Assumption*.

Ponte Pietra   ARCHAEOLOGICAL SITE
At the northern edge of the city centre, this bridge is a quiet but remarkable testament to the Italians' love of their artistic heritage. Two of the bridge's arches date from the Roman Republican era in the 1st century BC, while the other three were replaced in the 13th century. The ancient bridge remained largely intact until 1945, when retreating German troops blew it up. Locals fished the fragments out of the river, and painstakingly rebuilt the bridge stone by stone in the 1950s.

The views from the bridge of the River Adige are some of Verona's most photogenic.

Teatro Romano e
Museo Archeologico   ARCHAEOLOGICAL SITE
(⌖ 045 800 03 60; Regaste Redentore 2; adult/reduced €4.50/3, or with VeronaCard free; ⊙ 8.30am-7.30pm Tue-Sun, 1.30-7.30pm Mon) Just north of the historic centre you'll find a **Roman theatre**. Built in the 1st century BC, it is cunningly carved into the hillside at a strategic spot overlooking a bend in the river. Take the lift at the back of the theatre to the former convent above, which houses an interesting collection of Greek and Roman pieces.

★ **Giardino Giusti**   GARDENS
(⌖ 045 803 40 29; Via Giardino Giusti 2; adult/reduced €8.50/5; ⊙ 9am-8pm Apr-Sep, to 7pm Oct-Mar) Across the river from the historic centre, these sculpted gardens are considered a masterpiece of Renaissance landscaping, and named after the noble family that has tended them since opening them to the public in 1591. The vegetation is an Italianate mix of the manicured and natural, graced by soaring cypresses, one of which the German poet Goethe immortalised in his travel writings.

Shakespeare's Veneto

There is much debate about whether Shakespeare ever visited Italy, but his Italian plays are full of local knowledge. Venetian writer, architect and presenter Francesco da Mosto spoke to *Lonely Planet Traveller* magazine about the playwright's favourite Italian cities.

Verona

Verona was not thought of as a city of romance before *Romeo and Juliet* – in fact, not many people would have heard of it as it was very much in the shadow of Venice at that time. We don't know whether Romeo and Juliet existed, although Italian poet Dante did mention two feuding families, called the Montecchi and the Cappelletti. The famous balcony where Romeo is said to have declared his love to Juliet is close to Verona's main promenade – although since the balcony was apparently added to a suitably old house in 1936, it's doubtful it is the original! My favourite site in Verona is Juliet's tomb. People go there to pay tribute to Juliet and Shakespeare – even Dickens visited.

Padua

The University of Padua was one of the first in the world, and in Shakespeare's time, the city was very well known throughout Europe as a centre of learning – Galileo (of telescope fame) and Casanova (of sexual-conquest fame) are both alumni. Shakespeare used its reputation, rather than actual locations,

1. Basilica di San Marco (p340) and Palazzo Ducale (p337), Venice 2. Juliet's balcony, Casa di Giulietta (p383), Verona 3. University of Padua (p378)

as a backdrop for *The Taming of the Shrew* apart from the university, he rarely mentions specific sites. The best way to experience Shakespeare's Padua is by having a stroll around the university. It feels like a little world unto itself, detached from the rest of the city. There is a marvellous wooden anatomical amphitheatre in the Medical School that was built in the 16th century, where they dissected humans and animals for the students. The life of the university runs through the city. It's lovely to walk through the portico walkways that run under the houses, and into the Prato della Valle, one of the main city squares.

Venice

Shakespeare set *Othello* in Venice, and *The Merchant of Venice* mentions the Rialto Market area several times. He even talked about gondolas and 'the tranect', which could refer to the *traghetto* ferry, which transported people from Venice to the mainland. If he did visit, Shakespeare would have spent his time wandering the streets, eavesdropping on people's conversations and observing the goings-on in shops and at the market. A walk to the Rialto is certainly evocative of that time. The Palazzo Ducale, with its magnificent Gothic facades and huge council hall, is probably what Shakespeare had in mind as the setting for the final courtroom scene in *The Merchant of Venice*, while the two bronze figures on top of the Torre dell'Orologio clock tower in Piazza San Marco are known as 'i Mori', or 'the Moors', which is a key reference in *Othello*.

ℹ️ VERONACARD

The **VeronaCard** (€18/22 per 24/48 hours; www.tourism.verona.it), available at tourist sights, tobacconists and numerous hotels, offers access to most major monuments and churches, unlimited use of town buses, and discounted tickets to selected concerts and opera and theatre productions.

Basilica di San Zeno Maggiore   BASILICA
(www.basilicasanzeno.it; Piazza San Zeno; €2.50; ⏰ 8.30am-6pm Mon-Sat, 12.30-6pm Sun Mar-Oct, 10am-1pm & 1.30-5pm Mon-Sat, 12.30-5pm Sun Nov-Feb) A masterpiece of Romanesque architecture, the striped brick-and-stone basilica was built in honour of the city's patron saint. Enter through the flower-filled cloister into the nave – a vast space lined with 12th- to 15th-century frescoes. Painstaking restoration has revived Mantegna's 1457–59 *Majesty of the Virgin* altarpiece, painted with such astonishing perspective that you actually believe there are garlands of fresh fruit hanging behind the Madonna's throne.

👣 Tours

Try Verona   TOURS
(www.tryverona.com; Via Pallone 16) This superb outfit runs myriad tours focusing on anything from local cuisine and shopping to Romeo and Juliet. It also runs tours to neighbouring towns and out to Lake Garda, many of them themed.

Pagus Wine Tours   WINE
(📱327 796 53 80, 340 083 07 20; www.pagus valpolicella.net; half-/full-day group tour €60-80) If you don't want to rent a car, Pagus offers tours of Valpolicella and Soave, leaving regularly from Verona. Tours include visits to unusual, rural sites, impromptu rambles, lunches in local restaurants and, of course, wine tastings. The tours can also be customised.

🎉 Festivals & Events

Verona's Opera Festival   OPERA
(📱045 800 51 51; www.arena.it; Via Dietro Anfiteatro 6; ⏰ late Jun–late Aug) Around 14,000 music lovers pack the Roman Arena on summer nights during the world's biggest open-air lyrical music event, which draws international stars. Performances usually start at

8.45pm or 9pm. Tucking into a pre-show picnic on the unreserved stone steps is fine, so decant that wine into a plastic bottle (glass and knives aren't allowed), arrive early, rent a cushion and prepare for an unforgettable evening.

🛏️ Sleeping

Agriturismo San Mattia   AGRITURISMO €€
(📱045 91 37 97; www.agriturismosanmattia.it; Via Santa Giuliana 2a; s €70-110, d €90-140, apt from €160; 🅿️❄️🛜) Make friends with the chickens, ducks and horses as you wander through San Mattia's olive groves, orchards and vineyards, then sit back on the patio and soak up the stunning views of Verona. Host Giovanni Ederle is the tour de force behind this 14-room farm, its popular Slow Food–focused restaurant and Valpolicella vintages. It's located around 2km north of the city centre.

Corte delle Pigne   B&B €€
(📱333 758 41 41; www.cortedellepigne.it; Via Pigna 6a; s €60-110, d €90-150, tr €110-170, q €130-190; 🅿️❄️🛜) In the heart of the historic centre, this tiny three-room B&B is set around a quiet internal courtyard. It offers tasteful rooms and plenty of personal touches: sweets jars, luxury toiletries and even a Jacuzzi for one lucky couple.

Anfiteatro B&B   B&B €€
(📱347 248 84 62; www.anfiteatro-bedandbreakfast .com; Via Alberto Mario 5; s €60-90, d €80-130, tr €100-150; 🛜) Opera divas rest up steps from the action in this 19th-century townhouse, one block from the Roman Arena and just off boutique-lined Via Mazzini. Spacious guest rooms have high wood-beamed ceilings, antique armoires for stashing purchases, and divans for resting after shows.

Hotel Gabbia d'Oro   HOTEL €€€
(📱045 59 02 93; www.hotelgabbiadoro.it; Corso Porta Borsari 4; d from €200; ❄️🛜) One of the city's top addresses and also one of its most romantic, the Gabbia d'Oro features luxe rooms inside an 18th-century *palazzo* that manage to be both elegant and cosy. The rooftop terrace and central location are the icing on the proverbial cake.

Due Torri Hotel   HOTEL €€€
(📱045 59 50 44; http://hotelduetorri.duetorri hotels.com/en; Piazza di Sant'Anastasia 4; s/d €430/486-750, ste €850; 🅿️❄️@🛜) This former Della Scala palace exudes luxury from

the velvet-clad sofas in the cavernous lobby to walls clad in tapestries. Suites for the deep-of-pocket feature burnished antiques, embossed leather books and monogrammed towels. Significant discounts (up to 70%) apply if you book online, in advance.

✕ Eating

Hostaria La Vecchia Fontanina TRATTORIA €
(☑ 045 59 11 59; www.ristorantevecchiafontanina. com; Piazzetta Chiavica 5; meals €20-25; ⊘ 10.30am-3.30pm & 6.30-midnight Mon-Sat) With tables on a pint-sized piazza, cosy indoor rooms and excellent food, this historic, knick-knack-filled eatery stands out from the crowd. The menu features typical Veronese dishes alongside a number of more unusual creations such as *bigoli con ortica e ricotta affumicata* (thick spaghetti with nettles and smoked ricotta) and several heavenly desserts. Queuing to get in is normal.

★ Locanda 4 Cuochi MODERN ITALIAN €€
(☑ 045 803 03 11; www.locanda4cuochi.it; Via Alberto Mario 12; meals €40, 3-course set menu €25; ⊘ 12.30-2.30pm & 7.30 10.30pm, closed lunch Mon-Wed; 🍴) With its open kitchen, urbane vibe and hotshot chefs, you're right to expect great things from Locanda. Culinary acrobatics play second fiddle to prime produce cooked with skill and subtle twists. Whether it's perfectly crisp suckling pig lacquered with liquorice, or an epilogue of *gianduja* ganache with sesame crumble and banana, expect to to be gastronomically impressed.

Osteria da Ugo VENETIAN €€
(www.osteriadaugo.com; Vicolo Dietro Sant'Andrea 1b; meals €25-30; ⊘ noon-2.30pm & 7.30-10.30pm, closed Sun dinner) Lost in a backstreet away from the tourists, this *osteria* is a popular treat typically frequented at mealtimes by whole families. Surrounded by stained glass, elegantly laid tables and hundreds of wine bottles, enjoy a menu of Italian favourites as well as Vicenza-style codfish and tortellini with Lessinia truffles. Be prepared to queue to get a table during busy periods.

★ Pescheria I Masenini SEAFOOD €€€
(☑ 045 929 80 15; www.imasenini.com; Piazzetta Pescheria 9; meals €40-50; ⊘ 12.40-2pm & 7.40-10pm, closed Sun evening & Mon) Located on the piazza where Verona's Roman fish market once held sway, softly lit Masenini quietly serves up Verona's most imaginative, modern fish dishes. Inspired flavour combinations might see fresh sea bass carpaccio paired with zesty green apple and pink pepper, black-ink gnocchi schmoozing with lobster *ragù,* or sliced amberjack delightfully matched with crumbed almonds, honey, spinach and raspberries.

🍷 Drinking & Nightlife

Archivio COCKTAIL BAR
(☑ 345 816 96 63; Via Rosa 3; ⊘ 8am-midnight Mon-Fri, from 9am Sat, from 11am Sun) Fragrant with aromatic cocktail ingredients, this sidestreet micro-bar is one of the best places for a night-launching drink. Imaginative mixology combines with craft beers to give a lot of choice to drinkers, and the friendly owner knows his tipples.

Antica Bottega del Vino WINE BAR
(☑ 045 800 45 35; www.bottegavini.it; Vicolo Scudo di Francia 3; ⊘ 11am-1am) Wine is the primary consideration at this historic, baronial-style wine bar (the cellar holds around 18,000 bottles), the linen-lined tables promise a satisfying feed. Ask the sommelier to recommend a worthy vintage for your braised donkey, Vicenza-style codfish or Venetian liver – some of the best wines here are bottled specifically for the *bottega.*

Cafe Borsari COFFEE
(☑ 045 803 13 13; Corso Porta Borsari 15d; ⊘ 7.30am-8.15pm) It might look like a ceramics shop from the outside, but open the door and you'll discover this magically minuscule coffee house that's been roasting its own coffee and supplying hot chocolate to tables since 1969. It also sells quirky Christmas gifts year-round.

🔒 Shopping

Sunday Flea Market MARKET
(Piazza San Zeno; ⊘ 8am-5pm Sun) The flea market that fills Piazza San Zeno and the surrounding streets is a real feast of art nouveau light fittings, gramophone players, fascist-era bike parts and lots of alarm clocks – a mix of antiques and junk that you could spend all day browsing.

ℹ Information

Guardia Medica (☑ 045 761 45 65; ⊘ 8pm-8am Mon-Fri, 10am-8pm Sat, 8am-8pm Sun) A locum doctor service – doctors usually come to you.
Ospedale Borgo Trento (☑ 045 812 11 11; Piazza A Stefani; ⊘ 24hr) Hospital northwest of Ponte Vittoria.

Ospedale Civile Maggiore (☎045 807 11 11; Piazzale Stefani 1; ⊙24hr)

Post Office (Via C Cattaneo 23; ⊙8.20am-7.05pm Mon-Fri, to 12.35pm Sat)

Tourist Office (☎045 806 86 80; www.tourism.verona.it; Via degli Alpini 9; ⊙10am-7pm Mon-Sat, to 3pm Sun)

ℹ Getting There & Away

AIR

Verona-Villafranca Airport (☎045 809 56 66; www.aeroportoverona.it) is 12km outside town and accessible by ATV Aerobus to/from the train station (€6, 15 minutes, every 20 minutes 6.30am to 11.30pm). A taxi costs between €25 and €30, depending on the time of day. Flights arrive from all over Italy and some European cities, including Amsterdam, Barcelona, Berlin, Brussels, Dusseldorf, London and Paris.

BUS

The main intercity bus station is in front of the train station in the Porta Nuova area. Buses run to Padua, Vicenza and Venice.

ATV (Azienda Trasporti Verona; www.atv.verona.it) city buses 11, 12 and 13 (bus 92 or 93 on Sundays and holidays) connect the train station with Piazza Brà. Buy tickets from newsagents, tobacconists, ticket machines or the ATV office within the train station before you board the bus (tickets valid for 90 minutes, €1.30).

TRAIN

Verona Porta Nuova station is a major stop on the Italian rail network with direct services to numerous northern Italian towns and cities, including:

Venice €8.85 to €27, 70 minutes to 2¼ hours, one to four hourly.

Padua €7.10 to €22, 40 to 80 minutes, one to four hourly.

Vicenza €5.55 to €20, 25 to 55 minutes, one to four hourly.

Milan €12.75 to €25, 1¼ to two hours, one to three hourly.

There are also direct international services to Austria, Germany and France.

Valpolicella

The 'valley of many cellars', from which Valpolicella gets its name, has been in the business of wine production since the ancient Greeks introduced their *passito* technique (the use of partially dried grapes) to create the blockbuster flavours we still enjoy in the region's Amarone and Recioto wines.

Situated in the foothills of Monte Lessini, the valleys benefit from a happy microclimate created by the enormous body of Lake Garda to the west and cooling breezes from the Alps to the north. No wonder Veronese nobility got busy building weekend retreats here. Many of them, like the extraordinary Villa della Torre, still house noble wineries, while others have been transformed into idyllic places to stay and eat.

⊙ Sights

★Massimago   WINERY

(☎045 888 01 43; Via Giare 21, Mezzane di Sotto; wine tastings from €10, 2-person apt €120-150, 4-person apt €220-250; ⊙9am-6pm Mon-Fri, by appointment Sat & Sun; ℗) Presiding over the cutting-edge of Valpolicella viticulture is the dynamic Camilla Chauvenet, who took over this winery when she was just 20 years old, and has since been turning out lighter, more modern versions of the classics, including an unusual rosé and sparkling variety. The on-site four-room *relais* is as elegant and refined as the wines. Call or email ahead for wine tastings, which are preferred in the afternoon.

Allegrini   WINERY

(☎045 683 20 11; www.allegrini.it; Via Giare 9/11, Fumane; wine tasting & cellar tour €20, tour of villa €10, tour of villa with wine tasting & snack €30-40; ⊙cellar tour & wine tasting 10.30am & 3.30pm Mon-Fri by appointment, villa tours 11am & 4pm Mon-Sat by appointment; ℗) The Allegrini family have been tending vines in Fumane, Sant'Ambrogio and San Pietro since the 16th century, and this has been one of the leading wineries of the Valpolicella region. Pride of place goes to the *cru* wines produced from Corvinia and Rondinella grapes grown on the La Grola hillside (La Poja, La Grola and Palazzo della Torre). Wine tastings in the historic 16th-century **Villa della Torre** are a fabulous experience.

⌨ Sleeping & Eating

Villa Spinosa   APARTMENT €€

(☎045 750 00 93; www.villaspinosa.it; Via Colle Masua 12, Negrar; apt per 2 people €90-130, minimum 2-night stay; ℗🛜) This *agriturismo* (farmstay accommodation) and winery is located at the foot of the Masua hills just south of the centre of Negrar. Accommodation is in two split-level apartments in the main farmhouse, both of which come with two double bedrooms, a fully equipped kitchen and wonderful views over the Valpolicella Classico valley.

★ **Enoteca della Valpolicella** VENETIAN €€
(☑ 045 683 91 46; www.enotecadellavalpolicella.it; Via Osan 47, Fumane; meals €25; ☺ noon-2.30pm Sun, noon-2.30pm & 7.30-10pm Tue-Sat) Gastronomes flock to the town of Fumane, just a few kilometres north of San Pietro in Cariano, where an ancient farmhouse has found renewed vigour as a rustically elegant restaurant. Put your trust in gracious owners Ada and Carlotta, who will eagerly guide you through the day's menu, a showcase for fresh, local produce.

★ **Osteria Numero Uno** OSTERIA €€
(☑ 045 770 13 75; www.osterianumero1.com; Via Flaminio Pellegrini 2, Fumane; meals €15-30; ☺ noon-2.30pm & 7-10.30pm Thu-Mon, noon-2.30pm Tue) The archetypal *osteria* with a wooden bar packed with overall-clad vintners and delicious aromas wafting out of the kitchen. Glasses of Valpolicella (around 120 types) range from just €2 to €5 for a good Amarone. Pair them with salty speck and belly-filling duck with wild garlic and gnocchi.

ℹ Information

Valpolicella Tourist Office (☑ 045 770 19 20; www.valpolicellaweb.it; Via Ingelheim 7, San Pietro in Cariano; ☺ 9am 1pm Mon-Sat)

ℹ Getting There & Away

To get the most out of the Valpolicella area, you really need a hire car. From Verona, take the SP1 northwest out of the city. This changes into the SP12; all the villages in the wine region can be found off this road.

Soave

POP 6900

Southeast of Verona and an easy day trip, Soave serves its namesake DOC (Denominazione di Origine Controllate) white wine in a story-book setting. The town is entirely encircled by medieval fortifications, including 24 bristling watchtowers guarding a medieval castle. Wine is the main reason to come here, with tastings available throughout the year.

◉ Sights

Castello di Soave HISTORIC BUILDING
(☑ 045 768 00 36; www.castellodisoave.it; adult/ reduced €7/4; ☺ 9am-noon & 3-6.30pm Tue-Sun

Apr-Oct, 9am-noon & 2-4pm daily Nov-Mar) Built on a medieval base by Verona's fratricidal Scaligeri family, the Castello complex encompasses an early Renaissance villa, grassy courtyards, the remnants of a Romanesque church and the Mastio (the defensive tower apparently used as a dungeon): during restoration, a mound of human bones was unearthed here. The highlight for most, however, will be the panoramas of the surrounding countryside from the many rampart viewing points.

★ **Suavia** WINERY
(☑ 045 767 50 89; www.suavia.it; Via Centro 14, Fittà; ☺ 9am-1pm & 2.30-6.30pm Mon-Fri, 9am-1pm Sat & by appointment; ℙ) Soave is not known as a complex white, but this trailblazing winery, located 8km outside Soave via the SP39, has been changing the viticultural landscape in recent years. Don't miss its Monte Carbonare Soave Classico, with its mineral, ocean-breeze finish.

✗ Eating

★ **Locanda Lo Scudo** MODERN ITALIAN €€
(☑ 045 768 07 66; www.loscudo.vr.it; Via Covergnino 9, Soave; meals €35; ☺ noon-2.30pm & 7.30-10.30pm Tue-Sat, noon-2.30pm Sun; ☎) Just outside the medieval walls of Soave, Lo Scudo is half country inn and half high-powered gastronomy. Cult classics include a risotto of scallops and porcini mushrooms, though – if it's on the menu – only a fool would resist the extraordinary dish of tortelloni stuffed with local pumpkin, Grana Padano, cinnamon, mustard and Amaretto, and topped with crispy fried sage.

Above the restaurant, the owners rent out four bright, lovely rooms (single/double €85/95) that continue the theme of countrified sophistication.

ℹ Information

Soave's **tourist office** (☑ 045 619 07 73; www.soaveturismo.it; Piazza Foro Boario I, Soave; ☺ 10am-5pm Mon, 9am-6pm Tue-Fri, 9am-3pm Sat & Sun Apr-Oct, 9am-5pm Tue-Fri, to 2pm Sat & Sun Nov-Mar) is just outside the medieval wall, in front of the central bus stop.

ℹ Getting There & Away

To reach Soave from Verona, take ATV bus 130 (€3.40, around one hour) from Corso Porta Nuova (the main road that links Verona's city centre to its train station). Buy tickets from the machines on the platforms. If driving, exit the A4 autostrada at San Bonifacio and follow the Viale della Vittoria 2km north into town.

Vicenza

POP 116,000

When Palladio escaped an oppressive employer in his native Padua, few would have guessed the humble stonecutter would, within a few decades, transform not only his adoptive city but also the history of European architecture. By luck, a local count recognised his talents in the 1520s and sent him to study the ruins in Rome. When he returned to Vicenza, the autodidact began producing his extraordinary buildings, structures that marry sophistication and rustic simplicity, reverent classicism and bold innovation. His genius would turn Vicenza and its surrounding villas into one grand Unesco World Heritage Site. And yet, the Veneto's fourth-largest city is more than just elegant porticoes and balustrades – its dynamic exhibitions, bars and restaurants provide a satisfying dose of modern vibrancy.

◉ Sights

★ **Palazzo Leoni Montanari**　　MUSEUM

(☑ 800 57 88 75; www.gallerieditalia.com; Contrà di Santa Corona 25; adult/reduced €10/8, or with MuseumCard free; ◷ 9.30am-7.30pm Tue, Wed & Fri-Sun, to 10.30pm Thu) An extraordinary collection of treasures await inside Palazzo Leoni Montanari, among them ancient pottery from Magna Graecia and grand salons filled with Canaletto's misty lagoon landscapes and Pietro Longhi's 18th-century satires. A recent addition is Agostino Fasolato's astounding *The Fall of the Rebel Angels,* carved from a single block of Carrara marble and featuring no less than 60 angels and demons in nail-biting battle. Topping it all off is a superb collection of 400 Russian icons.

★ **Teatro Olimpico**　　THEATRE

(☑ 0444 96 43 80; www.teatrolimpicovicenza.it; Piazza Matteotti 11; adult/reduced €11/8, or with MuseumCard free; ◷ 9am-5pm Tue-Sun, to 6pm early Jul-early Sep) Behind a walled garden lies a Renaissance marvel: the Teatro Olimpico, which Palladio began in 1580 with inspiration from Roman amphitheatres. Vincenzo Scamozzi finished the elliptical theatre after Palladio's death, adding a stage set modelled on the ancient Greek city of Thebes, with streets built in steep perspective to give the illusion of a city sprawling towards a distant horizon.

Today, Italian performers vie to make an entrance on this extraordinary stage; check the website for opera, classical and jazz performances.

Palazzo Chiericati　　MUSEUM

(☑ 0444 22 28 11; www.museicivicivicenza.it; Piazza Matteotti 37/39; adult/reduced €7/5; ◷ 9am-5pm Tue-Sun, 10am-6pm Tue-Sun early Jul-early Sep) Vicenza's civic art museum occupies one of Palladio's finest buildings, designed in 1550. The ground floor, used for temporary exhibitions, is where you'll find the **Sala dal Firmamento** (Salon of the Skies) and its blush-inducing ceiling fresco of Diana and an up-skirted Helios by Domenico Brusasorci. Highlights in the upstairs galleries include Anthony Van Dyke's allegorical *The Four Ages* and Alessandro Maganza's remarkably contemporary *Portrait of Maddalena Campiglia.*

Another floor up is the private collection of the late marquis Giuseppe Roi, including drawings by Tiepolo and Picasso.

Basilica Palladiana　　GALLERY

(☑ 0444 22 21 22; www.museicivicivicenza.it; Piazza dei Signori; temporary exhibitions €10-13) Now a venue for world-class temporary exhibitions, the Palladian Basilica is capped with an enormous copper dome reminiscent of the hull of an upturned ship. The building, modelled on a Roman basilica, once housed the law courts and Council of Four Hundred. Palladio was lucky to secure the commission in 1549 (it took his patron 50 years of lobbying the council), which involved radically restructuring the original, 15th-century *palazzo* and adding an ambitious double order of loggias, supported by Tuscan and Ionic columns topped by soaring statuary.

The building is also home to the elegant **Museo del Gioiello** (www.museodelgioiello.it; Piazza dei Signori; adult/reduced €6/4; ◷ 3-7pm Mon-Fri, 11am-7pm Sat & Sun) and its dazzling collection of historic and contemporary jewellery.

★ **La Rotonda**　　HISTORIC BUILDING

(☑ 049 879 13 80; www.villalarotonda.it; Via della Rotonda 45; villa/gardens €10/5; ◷ villa 10am-noon & 3-6pm Wed & Sat mid-Mar–Oct, 10am-noon & 2.30-5pm Wed & Sat Nov–mid-Mar, gardens 10am-noon & 3-6pm Tue-Sun mid-Mar–Oct, 10am-noon & 2.30-5pm Tue-Sun Nov–mid-Mar) No matter how you look at it, this villa is a showstopper: the namesake dome caps a square base, with

Vicenza

Vicenza

◎ **Top Sights**

1 Palazzo Leoni Montanari.....................C1
2 Teatro Olimpico.....................................D1

◎ **Sights**

3 Basilica Palladiana..............................C2
4 Chiesa di Santa Corona.......................C1
5 Museo del Gioiello...............................C2
6 Palazzo Chiericati................................D1
7 Palladio Museum..................................B2
8 Roman Criptoportico............................B3

🛌 **Sleeping**

9 Hotel Palladio......................................C2
10 Relais Santa Corona............................C1

🍽 **Eating**

11 Al Pestello...C1
12 Gastronomia Il Ceppo..........................C2
13 Osteria Il Cursore................................C3
Sòtobotega.....................................(see 12)

identical colonnaded facades on all four sides. This is one of Palladio's most admired creations, inspiring variations across Europe and the USA, including Thomas Jefferson's Monticello. Inside, the circular central hall is covered from the walls to the soaring cupola with *trompe l'œil* frescoes. Catch bus 8 (€1.30, €2 on board) from in front of Vicenza's train station, or simply walk (about 25 minutes).

Villa Valmarana 'ai Nani'　HISTORIC BUILDING
(☎0444 32 18 03; www.villavalmarana.com; Stradella dei Nani 8; adult/reduced €10/7; ☺10am-6pm) From La Rotonda, a charming footpath leads about 500m to the neoclassical elegance of Villa Valmarana 'ai Nani', nicknamed after the 17 statues of gnomes ('ai

Nani') around the perimeter walls. Step inside for 1757 frescoes by Giambattista Tiepolo and his son Giandomenico. Giambattista painted the Palazzina wing with his signature mythological epics, while his offspring executed the rural, carnival and Chinese themes adorning the *foresteria* (guesthouse).

🛌 Sleeping

Hotel Palladio　HOTEL €€
(☎0444 32 53 47; www.hotel-palladio.it; Contrà dei Servi 25; s/d €100/160; ❄️🐾) The top choice in central Vicenza, this friendly four-star hotel delivers crisp, whitewashed rooms with earthy accents and contemporary bathrooms, many of which feature generously

sized showers. The lobby's stone column and rustic ceiling beams attest to the *palazzo's* Renaissance pedigree.

Relais Santa Corona   HOTEL €€

(☑ 0444 32 46 78; www.relaissantacorona.it; Contrà di Santa Corona 19; s/d €119/135; ✲⊛) A boutique bargain, offering stylish stays in an 18th-century palace located on a street dotted with landmarks. The six rooms and two suites are soothing and soundproofed, with excellent mattresses, flat-screen TVs and uncluttered chic.

✖ Eating

★ Osteria Il Cursore   OSTERIA €

(☑ 0444 32 35 04; www.osteriacursore.it; Stradella Pozzetto 10; meals €25; ⊙11am-3pm & 6pm-2am Mon & Wed-Sat, 11am-1pm & 6pm-2am Sun) A short walk from the city centre, behind a stained-glass door, this local institution serves up a thoroughly local scene where walls are hung with family photos, and Tiffany & Co lamps illuminate the bar. Local diners keep one eye on the televised football match as they tuck into simple, tasty fare that includes local Vicenza dishes and pan-Italian favourites.

★ Sòtobotega   VENETIAN €

(☑ 0444 54 44 14; www.gastronomiailceppo.com; Corso Palladio 196; meals €25, set tasting menus €26; ⊙11.30am-3pm) Drop into cult-status deli **Gastronomia Il Ceppo** (prepared dishes per 100g from around €2.50; ⊙8am-7.45pm Tue-Sat, 9am-2pm Sun) for picnic provisions, or head down into its cellar for sensational sit-down dishes like expertly crafted *bigoli* (a type of pasta) with the sauce of the day, or the star of the show, *bacalà alla vicentina*, Vicenza's signature codfish dish. Some 500 mostly Italian wines line the walls and transparent floor panels reveal an ancient Roman footpath and the foundations of an 11th-century dwelling.

★ Al Pestello   VENETIAN €€

(☑ 0444 32 37 21; Contrà San Stefano 3; meals €32; ⊙7.30-10pm Mon, Wed & Thu, noon-2pm & 7.30-10pm Fri-Sun; ⊛) Homely, brightly lit Al Pestello dishes out intriguing, lesser-known *cucina vicentina* such as *la panà* (bread soup), red-wine braised donkey and *bresaola* 'lollies' filled with grappa-flavoured Grana Padano and mascarpone. The kitchen is obsessed with local ingredients, right down to the Colli Berici truffles, while the collec-

tion of harder-to-find *digestivi* makes for an enlightening epilogue. Book ahead.

❶ Information

Post Office (Contrà Garibaldi 1; ⊙8.20am-7.05pm Mon-Fri, to 12.35pm Sat) Large office near the cathedral.

Tourist Office (☑ 0444 32 08 54; www.vicenzae.org; Piazza Matteotti 12; ⊙9am-5.30pm) Ask the helpful staff about the excellent-value MuseumCard, a pass (adult/reduced €15/12) valid for a whole week that offers admission to numerous city museums.

❶ Getting There & Away

BUS

FTV (☑ 0444 22 31 11; www.ftv.vi.it) buses leave for outlying areas from the bus station, located next to the train station.

CAR

There are several larger car parks skirting the historic centre, including the underground Park Verdi just north of the train station (enter from Viale dell'Ippodromo). For real-time updates on available parking spaces, see www.muoversiavicenza.it/it/parcheggi-auto.php (in Italian).

TRAIN

Vicenza has the following connections:

Padua €4.15 to €14.90, 15 to 25 minutes, up to five hourly.

Venice €4.15 to €16, 45 to 80 minutes, up to five hourly.

Verona €5.55 to €20, 25 to 55 minutes, up to four hourly.

Bassano del Grappa

POP 43,100

Bassano del Grappa sits with charming simplicity on the banks of the River Brenta as it winds its way free from Alpine foothills. The town is famous above all for its namesake spirit, grappa – a fiery distillation made from the discarded skins, pulp, seeds and stems from wine-making. But the town isn't all about its most famous tipple – there are a couple of interesting sights to explore, making it an easy-going day trip from Treviso, Padua or Venice.

❂ Sights

Ponte degli Alpini   BRIDGE

Spanning the river is Palladio's photogenic 1569 covered bridge, the Ponte degli Alpini. Fragile as the wooden structure seems, it is cleverly engineered to withstand the rush of spring melt waters from Monte Grappa. It's always been critical in times of war: Napoleon bivouacked here for many months and during the Great War, the Alpine brigades adopted the bridge as their emblem.

Poli Museo della Grappa MUSEUM
(☑0424 52 44 26; www.poligrappa.com; Via Gamba 6; admission free, distillery guided tours €5; ☺museum 9am-7.30pm, distillery guided tours 8.30am-1pm & 2-6pm Mon-Fri) Explore four centuries of Bassano's high-octane libation at this interactive museum, which includes tastings and the chance to tour the distillery of esteemed producer Poli (book tours online). Although grappa is made all over Italy, and indeed inferior versions are distilled well beyond the peninsula, the people of the Veneto have been doing it since at least the 16th century. In fact, an institute of grappa distillers was even created in Venice in 1601!

🛏 Sleeping

★ **B&B Via Museo** B&B €
(☑320 725 44 07; Via Museo 61; s/d €58/72; 🛜) Centrally located in the old part of town, the Via Museo is a real mix of the old and new – IKEA furniture sits next to antiques, and modern air-con units chill exquisite parquet floors. It receives much praise for its breakfast, and for its welcoming owners.

🍴 Eating & Drinking

Osteria alla Caneva VENETIAN €
(☑335 542 35 60; Via G Matteotti 34, Bassano del Grappa; dishes €20-30; ☺9am-3pm Wed-Mon, 5.30pm-midnight Wed-Sun) Behind the yellow-tinted glass lies this old-school favourite, with its pots, worn wooden tables and inter-generational regulars washing down rustic regional grub with a glass or three of *vino* from local wineries like Vigneto Due Santi di Zonta. Food options lean towards cured meats and pasta dishes like fettuccine with artichokes. For a light bite, don't miss the *baccala cicchetti* (salted cod tapas).

Nardini BAR
(www.nardini.it; Ponte Vecchio 2, Bassano del Grappa; ☺8.30am-9.30pm) Flanking Bassano del Grappa's 16th-century Ponte degli Alpini, this historic distillery is a great place to grab a few bottles of Nardini's famous grappa, or to simply kick back with a glass of bitter-sweet *mezzo e mezzo*, a unique *aperitivo* made with Rabarbaro Nardini, Rosso Nardini, Cynar and soda water.

ⓘ Getting There & Away

Train is the easiest way to reach Bassano del Grappa. The train station is 150m east of the centre. The town has the following connections:
Venice €6.10, 90 minutes, twice hourly.
Padova €4.90, one hour, hourly.
Trento €7.05, two hours, hourly.

Asolo
POP 9100

Known as the 'town of 100 vistas' for its panoramic hillside location, the medieval walled town of Asolo has long been a favourite of literary types. Robert Browning bought a house here, but the ultimate local celebrity is Caterina Corner, the 15th-century queen of Cyprus, who was given the town, its castle (now used as a theatre) and the surrounding county in exchange for her abdication. She promptly became queen of the literary set, holding salons that featured writer Pietro Bembo.

ⓞ Sights

Museo Civico di Asolo MUSEUM
(☑0423 95 23 13; www.asolo.it; Via Regina Cornaro 74; adult/reduced €5/4; ☺9.30am-12.30pm & 3-6pm Sat & Sun) In the Museo Civico you can explore Asolo's Roman past and wander through a small collection of paintings, including a pair of Tintoretto portraits. The museum also includes rooms devoted to Eleanora Duse (1858–1924) and British traveller and writer Freya Stark (1893–1993), who retreated to Asolo between Middle Eastern forays.

Rocca RUINS
(☑329 850 85 12; €2; ☺10am-7pm Sat & Sun Apr-Jun, Sep & Oct, 10am-noon & 3-7pm Sat & Sun Jul & Aug, 10am-5pm Sat & Sun Nov-Mar) Perched on the summit of Monte Ricco and looking down on central Asolo are the hulking ruins of a fortress dating back to the 12th to early 13th centuries. The still-visible cistern well was constructed between the 13th and 14th centuries, while the heavily restored buttresses offer a breathtaking panorama that takes in soft green hills, snowcapped mountains and the industrious Po Valley.

🍴 Eating

Villa Cipriani MODERN ITALIAN €€€
(☑0423 52 34 11; www.villaciprianiasolo.com; Via Canova 298, Asolo; meals €60; ☺12.30-2.30pm & 8-10.30pm; ℗) The Ciprianis behind this

---

WORTH A TRIP

ART & ARCHITECTURE AROUND ASOLO

The area's most intriguing attractions are a little out of Asolo, such as the Villa di Maser, 8km to the east, and the Museo Canova, 8km to the north.

Villa di Maser (Villa Barbaro; ☑0423 92 30 04; www.villadimaser.it; Via Cornuda 7, Maser; adult/reduced €9/7; ☉10am-6pm Tue-Sat, from 11am Sun Apr-Oct, 11am-5pm Sat & Sun Nov-Mar; P)
A World Heritage Site, the 16th-century Villa di Maser is a spectacular monument to the Venetian *bea vita* (good life). Designed by the inimitable Andrea Palladio, its sublimely elegant exterior is matched by Paolo Veronese's wildly imaginative trompe l'œil architecture inside. Vines crawl up the Stanza di Baccho; a watchdog keeps an eye on the painted door of the Stanza di Canuccio (Little Dog Room); and in a corner of the frescoed grand salon, the painter has apparently forgotten his spattered shoes and broom.

Museo Canova (☑0423 54 43 23; www.museocanova.it; Via Canova 74, Possagno; adult/reduced €10/6; ☉9.30am-6pm Tue-Sun) Antonio Canova was Italy's master of neoclassical sculpture. He made marble come alive, but mastery didn't always come easy: you can see Canova's rough drafts in plaster at the **Gipsoteca**, in a building completed by modernist master Carlo Scarpa in 1957.

Renaissance villa are the same as those in Venice, and they are just the latest in a long line of illustrious owners including the Guinnesses, the Galantis, and English poet Robert Browning. Now you, too, can enjoy the perfumed rose garden, not to mention the kitchen's seasonal, market-driven menus; the pasta dishes are particularly seductive.

🛍 Shopping

★ **Mercatino dell'Antiquariato** ANTIQUES
(Antiques Market; ☑0423 52 46 75; www.asolo.it; Piazza Garibaldi; ☉2nd Sun of month) Taking over the town's main piazza and surrounding streets, Asolo's monthly antiques market is one of the region's finest, peddling anything and everything from 18th century clocks and furniture, to vintage lithographs, ceramics, cufflinks, and books.

❶ Getting There & Away

The best way to reach Asolo if you don't have your own car is to take the train to Treviso where you change onto local bus 112 (€3.50, one hour, hourly).

Treviso

POP 82,500

Treviso has everything you could want from a mid-sized Veneto city: medieval city walls, lots of pretty canals, narrow cobbled streets and frescoed churches. Despite this, it receives few visitors, eclipsed by its more impressive neighbours. If you want to experience authentic Veneto life away from the

tourist crowds, this is a great place to come, especially when the weather is bad as almost the entire centre is arcaded.

One reason foreigners may find their way here is due to the city's rugby links. Benetton Rugby Treviso plays in the highest European competitions, and international matches are held at their stadium.

◎ Sights

Chiesa di Santa Lucia CHURCH
(Piazza San Vito; ☉8am-noon Mon-Fri, 8am-noon & 4-6.30pm Sat, 9am-12.30pm & 4-6.30pm Sun) **FREE** The small Chiesa di Santa Lucia adjoins the larger **Chiesa di San Vito** and is an absolute beauty. Its vaulted ceiling and walls are covered with colourful 14th- and 15th-century frescoes, including the *Madonna del Pavejo* (c 1450) by Tommaso da Modena.

Fontana delle Tette STATUE
(Calle del Podestà 9) Treviso's best-known piece of statuary is the 16th-century naked female torso called the *Fontana delle Tette*, a snigger-worthy translation coming in as 'Tits Fountain'. Essentially created as a free wine dispenser (white wine flowed from one breast, red from the other) for the celebrating masses during autumn wine festivals, it now stands in a courtyard off Calle del Podestà – the wine has, sadly, long since been replaced with water.

Chiesa di San Nicolò CHURCH
(Via San Nicolò; ☉8.30am-noon & 3.30-6pm) **FREE** This glorious 14th-century Gothic

church towers over you. Outside it seems preposterously tall with vertical lines drawing the eye upwards, while inside an enormous fresco of Jesus reinforces the effect.

🍴 Sleeping & Eating

Maison Matilda　　　　　　B&B €€€
(📞 0422 58 22 12; www.maisonmatilda.com; Via Riccati 44; d €160-350; 🅿🛜) This darkly beautiful townhouse is the perfect display of contemporary Italian design, from its Carrara marble bathrooms and art deco bedrooms to its sleek modernist furniture. There are only six rooms, so book ahead.

⭐Gelateria Dassie　　　　　GELATO €
(www.stefanodassie.it; Via Sant'Agostino 42; servings from €1.50; ⊘10.30am-midnight Tue-Sun) No one should leave Treviso without savouring an award-winning gelato by Stefano Dassie, one of Italy's top *gelatisti*. The Dassie family has a 45-year tradition of gelato production, but Stefano has taken things to new levels, grabbing prize after international prize at ice cream competitions. Ingredients are meticulously sourced from around the world.

⭐Osteria Dalla Gigia　　　　OSTERIA €
(Via Barberia 20; snacks €1.30-3; ⊘9.30am-2pm & 4-8.30pm Mon-Sat) This friendly and authentic snack bar is a great place to rub shoulders with locals. Everyone crams in to enjoy the legendary *mozzarella alla Gigia*, a tiny deep-fried sandwich filled with molten mozzarella and either prosciutto or sardines, washed down with an equally tiny beer. Made with the freshest locally sourced ingredients, it's dangerously moreish and one is never enough.

Antico Morer　　　　　　SEAFOOD €€
(📞 0422 59 03 45; www.ristoranteanticomorer treviso.com; Via Riccati 28; meals €35-45; ⊘noon-2.30pm & 7.30-10.30pm Tue-Sun) Named after an old mulberry tree, this classy restaurant serves some of Treviso's finest seafood. Chef Gaetano selects the finest ingredients from the fish market each day for his grand platters, including crab ravioli and tuna in pistachio crust.

ℹ Information

Tourist Office (📞 0422 54 76 32; www.marca treviso.it; Via Fiumicelli 30; ⊘10am-1pm Mon, to 5pm Tue-Sat, to 4pm Sun)

ℹ Getting There & Away

AIR

Treviso's **airport** (📞 0422 31 51 11; www.tre visoairport.it; Via Noalese 63) serves Ryanair flights from across Europe and some Wizz Air services. It is located around 5km west of Treviso. ACTT **buses** (📞 0422 58 83 11; www. mobilitadimarca.it) (line 6) run from the airport to the train station in Treviso (€2.80, 15 minutes, at least two per hour from 6am to 11pm).

TRAIN

Treviso Centrale station, located just south of the city centre, has at least hourly connections with Venice (€3.40, 30 minutes) and Vicenza (€6.60, one hour).

Conegliano

POP 35,400

At the foothills of the Alps, Conegliano is one of the Veneto's drowsier settlements with only a handful of worthwhile sights. However, the surrounding hillsides produce *prosecco*, a dry, crisp white wine made from *prosecco* grapes in *spumante* (bubbly), *frizzante* (sparkling) or still varieties. Conegliano's *prosecco* was promoted to DOCG status in 2009, Italy's highest oenological distinction. The town is the starting point for a tasting detour along the Strada di Prosecco (Prosecco Rd) from Conegliano to the Valdobbiadene.

⊙ Sights

Castello　　　　　　　　CASTLE
(Piazza San Leonardo; ⊘24hr) **FREE** Head up steep Calle Madonna della Neve, following an intact section of 13th-century defensive walls all the way to a summit, where the last remaining tower of Conegliano's 10th-century castle dominates an attractive set of gardens. The tower is home to a small museum, but the real joy here is the views across the surrounding hills. It's also a superb place to unfurl the picnic blanket, or to spend a sleepy afternoon in the company of a good book.

🍴 Sleeping & Eating

Hotel Canon d'Oro　　　　HISTORIC HOTEL €€
(📞 0438 3 42 46; www.hotelcanondoro.it; Via XX Settembre 131; s/d €85/125; 🅿🛜) If you decide to spend the night in town, Hotel Canon d'Oro provides classic elegance and modern

DON'T MISS

PROSECCO COUNTRY

La Strada del Prosecco (Prosecco Road; www.coneglianovaldobbiadene.it) Running through a landscape of rolling vineyards, this driving route takes you from Conegliano to Valdobbiadene via some of the region's best wineries. The website provides an itinerary, background information on *prosecco*, and details about stops along the way.

Agriturismo Da Ottavio (☑ 0423 98 11 13; Via Campion 2, San Giovanni di Valdobbiadene; meals €15-20; ⊘ noon-3pm Sat, Sun & holidays, closed Sep; ℗) *Prosecco* is typically drunk with *sopressa*, a fresh local salami, as the sparkling *spumante* cleans the palate and refreshes the mouth. There's no better way to test this than at Da Ottavio, where everything on the table, *sopressa* and *prosecco* included, is homemade by the Spada family.

comforts in a 15th-century *palazzo*. Rooms are plush, and the breakfast is good.

Al Castello   CAFE €€
(☑ 0438 22 379; www.ristorantealcastello.it; Piazzale San Leonardo 7, Conegliano; meals €30-40; ⊘ 8am-midnight Wed-Sun, to 2.15pm Mon) In the grounds of the Castello, the combination of well-executed pan-Italian food and the incredible views across the surrounding hills make this place a winner and well worth the hike uphill from the centre. Go for a full-blown meal involving duck *tagliata* (sliced grilled meat) with orange sauce or codfish Vicentina, or just for a coffee and cake stop to admire the Veneto panorama.

ℹ Information

APT Tourist Office (☑ 0438 2 12 30; Via XX Settembre 132, Conegliano; ⊘ 9am-1pm Tue & Wed, 9am-1pm & 2-6pm Thu-Sun)

ℹ Getting There & Away

The easiest way to reach Conegliano is by train. The town has the following connections:
Treviso €3.40, 20 minutes, at least twice hourly.
Belluno € 4.90, one hour, hourly.
Venice €5.55, one hour, at least twice hourly.

Belluno

POP 35,400 / ELEV 390M

Perched on high bluffs above the Piave River and backed majestically by the snow-capped Dolomites, Belluno makes a scenic and strategic base to explore the surrounding mountains. The historical old town is its own attraction, mixing stunning views with Renaissance–era buildings. And you'll be happy to fuel up for hikes in the nearby mountains on the city's hearty cuisine, including Italy's most remarkable cheeses: Schiz (semi-soft cow's-milk cheese, usually fried in butter) and the flaky, butter-yellow Malga Bellunese.

◉ Sights

Parco Nazionale delle
Dolomiti Bellunesi   NATIONAL PARK
(☑ 0437 2 70 30; www.dolomitipark.it; Piazza Piloni; ⊘ 7am-9pm Mon, Tue & Thu, to 2.30pm Wed, to midnight Sat, 10.30am-7pm Sun) Northwest of Belluno, this magnificent national park offers trails for hikers at every level, wildflowers in spring and summer and restorative gulps of crisp mountain air year-round. Between late June and early September, hikers walking six **Alte Vie delle Dolomiti** (high-altitude Dolomites walking trails) pass Belluno en route to mountain *rifugi*. The excellent info centre in Belluno can help with maps and routes.

Piazza dei Martiri   SQUARE
Belluno's main pedestrian square is the Piazza dei Martiri (Martyrs' Sq), named after the four partisans hanged here in WWII. On the north side various bars, restaurants and shops seek shade under arcading; the rest of the square is pleasant parkland.

🍽 Sleeping & Eating

Parco Dolomiti Fisterre B&B   B&B €
(☑ 339 229 16 68; Via Michele Cappellari 55; s/d €39/76; ℗ 🛜) This three-room B&B has one of the warmest welcomes in the Dolomites with extremely friendly and helpful owners, tasty breakfasts and a tranquil location just next to the Ardo River, 10 minutes on foot from the train station. Bathrooms are shared and the check-in time is a little late (5pm) but these are small irritations.

Al Borgo   ITALIAN €€
(☑ 0437 92 67 55; www.alborgo.to; Via Anconetta 8; meals €30-40; ⊘ noon-2.30pm Mon, noon-2.30pm

& 7.30-10.30pm Wed-Sun) If you have a car or strong legs, seek out this delightful restaurant in an 18th-century villa in the hills about 3km south of Belluno. Considered the area's best, the kitchen produces everything from homemade salami and roast lamb to artisanal gelato. Wines are also skillfully chosen, and the grappa is locally sourced.

❶ Information

Tourist Office (☑ 334 281 32 22; Piazza Duomo 2; ☺ 9am-12.30pm daily, 3.30-6.30pm Mon-Sat)

❶ Getting There & Away

CAR

By car, take the A27 from Venice (Mestre) – it's not the most scenic route, but avoids traffic around Treviso.

TRAIN

The train station is around 700m northwest of the central Piazza del Martiri. Belluno has the following connections:

Conegliano €5, one hour, hourly.

Treviso €7.10, one hour 50 minutes, hourly.
Venice €8.20, two hours 10 minutes, hourly (change in Conegliano).

Cortina d'Ampezzo

POP 6100 / ELEV 1224M

The Italian supermodel of ski resorts, Cortina d'Ampezzo is icy, pricey and undeniably beautiful. The town's stone church spires and pleasant cascading piazzas are framed by magnificent alps. It doubles as a slightly less glamorous but still stunning summertime base for hiking, biking and rock climbing.

🏃 Activities

Winter crowds arrive in December for top-notch downhill and cross-country skiing and stay until late March or April, while from June until October summertime adventurers hit Cortina for climbing and hiking. Two cable cars whisk skiers and walkers from Cortina's town centre to a central departure point for chairlifts, cable cars and

---

WORTH A TRIP

CINQUE TORRI

At the heart of the Dolomites, just 16km west of Cortina at the confluence of the Ampezzo, Badia and Cordevole Valleys, is the gorgeous area of Cinque Torri (www.5torri.it). Hard though it is to believe, some of the fiercest fighting of WWI took place in these idyllic mountains between Italian and Austro-Hungarian troops. Now you can wander over 5km of restored trenches in an enormous open-air museum between Lagazuoi and the Tre Sassi fort. Guided tours are offered by the Gruppo Guide Alpine, and in winter you can ski the 80km **Great War Ski Tour** with the Dolomiti Superski ski pass. En route mountain refuges provide standout meals and beds with spectacular views.

Rifugio Nuvolau (☑ 0436 86 79 38; www.nuvolau.com; 2575m; dm €20) Established in 1883, this is one of the Dolomites' oldest mountain huts and little has changed since those days. This 24-bed *rifugio* is perched atop a huge chunk of rock overlooking several trails, has no hot water or showers and serves only very basic food. However it offers a much more authentically spartan experience than the sometimes rather pampering modern-day *rifugi*.

Rifugio Averau (☑ 0436 46 60; www.rifugioaverau.com; Forcella Averau, 2416m; meals €35-50, half-board dm/s/d €63/100/170; ☺ 9am-10pm) The Rifugio Averau, a rough-hewn cabin tucked dramatically under the rocky spears of the Averau peak, has a hostel-style dormitory where guests can spend the night and an excellent restaurant. With views of the pink-tinged peaks settle down by the wood-burning stove for a dinner of house-made pasta, succulent lamb chops, speck-fried potatoes and deeply perfumed mountain bread.

Rifugio Scoiattoli (☑ 333 814 69 60; www.rifugioscoiattoli.it; Località Potor, 2255m; dm/d €60/130; ☺ 9am-9pm) In 1969 Alpine guide Lorenzo Lorenzi built this *rifugio* and it is still managed by his family today. Accessible by foot from the Cinque Torri chairlift, the terrace offers gorgeous panoramic views to accompany the typical Ampezzo dishes the *rifugio* serves, such as pasta with wild blueberries. The outdoor hot tub is a bonus.

trails. Lifts usually run from 9am to 5pm daily mid-December to April and resume June to October.

Ski Pass Cortina
SKIING

(☑0436 86 21 71; www.skipasscortina.com; Via Marconi 15; 1-/3-/7-day Valley Pass €47/135/252; ☺8.30am-12.30pm & 3.30-7pm Mon-Sat, 8.30am-12.30pm & 5-7pm Sun winter only) Ski and snowboard runs range from bunny slopes to the legendary Staunies black mogul run, which starts at 3000m. The Dolomiti Superski pass provides access to 12 runs in the area, or you can opt for a Valley Pass that includes San Vito di Cadore and Auronzo/Misurina; both are sold at the Ski Pass Cortina office.

Olympic Ice Stadium
SKATING

(☑0436 88 18 11; Viale Bonacossa 1; adult/reduced incl skate rental €10/9; ☺10.30am-12.30pm & 3.30-5.30pm Dec-Apr) During white-outs, take a spin around this beautiful ice-skating rink built for the 1956 Winter Olympics. The venue also hosts ice hockey matches, curling and figure-skating competitions.

Sleeping

Hotel Montana
HOTEL €

(☑0436 86 21 26; www.cortina-hotel.com; Corso Italia 94; s €52-87, d €82-168; ☏) Right in the heart of Cortina, this friendly, vintage 1920s Alpine hotel offers simple but well-maintained rooms. In winter, there is a seven-night minimum (€310 to €570 per person), but call for last-minute cancellations. Reception areas double as gallery space for local artists.

★ Rifugio Ospitale
CHALET €€

(☑0436 45 85; www.ristoranteospitale.com; Via Ospitale 1; d €125; ☺closed Jun; ☏) A 15-minute forest-clad drive from Cortina, this serene and stylish place is astoundingly good value, with spectacular mountain views from its large rooms. The well-regarded restaurant has an unexpected elegance: choose from a modern communal dining table or cosy traditional *stuben* (traditional dining room). Make sure to ask the owner for the key to the beautiful fresco-filled 13th-century church that nestles below the hotel.

✖ Eating

★ Agriturismo El Brite de Larieto
VENETO €

(☑368 700 80 83; www.elbritedelarieto.it; Passo Tre Croci, Località Larieto; meals €25-35; ☺noon-3pm & 7-10pm, closed Thu out of season; 🅿 🍃 Located 5km northwest of Cortina off the SS48 towards Passo Tre Croci, this idyllic farm enjoys a sunny situation amid thick larch forest. It produces all its own dairy products, vegetables and much of the meat on the menu, and its *canederli* (dumplings) are a highlight.

Ristorante Da'Aurelio
GASTRONOMY €€

(☑0437 72 01 18; www.da-aurelio.it; Passo Giau 5, Colle Santa Lucia; meals €45-55; ☺noon-2pm & 6.30-10pm; 🅿) Located at an altitude of 2175m, on the road between Cortina and Selva (SP638), elegant Da'Aurelio serves haute mountain cuisine in a classic chalet-style restaurant. Luigi 'Gigi' Dariz produces startling flavours from the freshest mountain ingredients, such as his rich, yellow egg with fragrant *finferlo* mushrooms and a rack of lamb crusted with mountain herbs. The restaurant also offers two comfortable rooms.

ⓘ Information

Tourist Office (☑0436 86 90 86; www.dolomiti.org; Corso Italia 81; ☺9am-1pm & 2-7.30pm Mon-Sat, 10am-1pm Sun)

ⓘ Getting There & Away

The nearest train station is in Calalzo di Cadore, 35km south of Cortina. A convenient bus service departs every hour from outside the station, taking you straight to the centre of Cortina. The following companies also operate out of Cortina's **bus station** (Via G Marconi).

Cortina Express (☑0437 86 73 50; www.cortinaexpress.it) Daily direct services to Mestre train station (€27, 2¼ hours) and Venice airport (two hours).

Dolomiti Bus (☑0437 21 71 11; www.dolomitibus.it) For smaller mountain towns.

SAD Buses (☑0471 45 01 11; www.sad.it) Services to Bolzano and other destinations in Alto Adige (Südtirol).

Friuli Venezia Giulia

Best Places to Eat

➡ La Frasca (p422)

➡ La Subida (p422)

➡ Osteria Salvagente (p409)

➡ Al Bagatto (p410)

➡ Caffe 'Tomaso (p422)

➡ Maanja Restaurant (p427)

➡ Orsone (p425)

Best Places to Sleep

➡ Seven Historical Suites (p408)

➡ Mercatovecchio Luxury Suites (p421)

➡ Palazzo Lantieri (p415)

➡ Maanja Suites (p426)

➡ Borgo Eibn (p427)

➡ Hotel Riviera & Maximilian's (p408)

➡ Forvm Boutique Hotel (p407)

Why Go?

With its triple-barrelled moniker, Friuli Venezia Giulia's multifaceted nature should come as no surprise. Cultural complexity is cherished in this small, little-visited region, tucked away on Italy's far northeastern borders with Austria and Slovenia. Friuli Venezia Giulia's landscapes offer profound contrasts too, with the foreboding, perpetually snowy Giulie and Carnic Alps in the north, idyllic grapevine-filled plains in the centre, the south's beaches, Venetian-like lagoons and the curious, craggy karst that encircles Trieste.

While there's an amazing reserve of often uncrowded historical sights, from Roman ruins to Austro-Hungarian palaces, this is also a fine destination for simply kicking back with the locals, tasting the region's world-famous wines and discovering a culinary heritage that will broaden your notions of the Italian table. Serene, intriguing Trieste and friendly, feisty Udine make for great city time – they're so easy and welcoming you'll soon feel as if you're Friulian, Venezian or Giulian too.

When to Go
Trieste

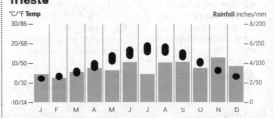

Feb Discover the uncrowded slopes of the Carnic and Giulie Alps.

Jun Feast on prosciutto at San Daniele's Aria di Festa.

Oct Watch sails fill the horizon at Trieste's Barcolana Regatta.

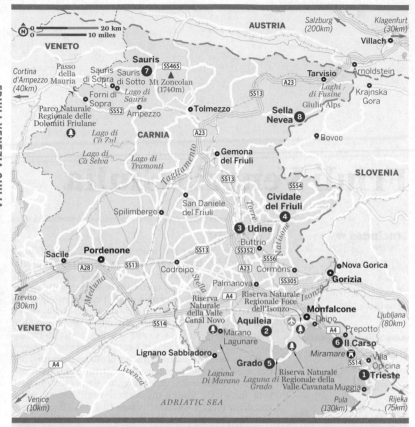

Friuli Venezia Giulia Highlights

1 Trieste (p403) Communing with the literary ghosts in this extraordinary city.

2 Basilica di Santa Maria Assunta (p416) Being enthralled by the extraordinary 4th-century mosaic floors of this Aquileia church.

3 Frasca di Citta (p423) Relaxing Udinese-style, with late-night wine and *frico* (fried cheese).

4 Tempietto Longobardo (p424) Marvelling at the 8th-century Lombard chapel in Cividale del Friuli.

5 Grado (p417) Strolling the lively old town of this sun-drenched beach resort.

6 Zidarich (p414) Tasting your way through the wild and wonderful wines of the Carso.

7 Sauris (p426) Discovering the lakes, forests, peaks and prosciutto of this little-visited region.

8 Sella Nevea (p427) Skiing some of Europe's snowiest and least crowded slopes.

History

The semi-autonomous region of Friuli Venezia Giulia came into being as recently as 1954; its new capital, Trieste, had already traded national allegiances five times since the beginning of the century. Such is the region's history, a rollicking, often blood-stained one of boom, bust and conquest that began with the Romans in Aquileia, saw Cividale rise to prominence under the Lombards, and witnessed the Venetians do their splendid thing in Pordenone and Udine. It was Austria, however, that established the most lasting foothold, with Trieste as its main, and free, seaport. While the region today is a picture of quiet prosperity, much of the 20th century was another story. War, poverty, political uncertainty and a devastating earthquake saw Friulians become the north's largest migrant population, most bound for Australia and Argentina.

ℹ️ Getting There & Away

Most of the region's major destinations can be reached by train or road from Venice in around two hours. **Friuli Venezia Giulia airport** (No-Borders; www.triesteairport.it; Via Aquileia 46, Ronchi Dei Legionari), aka Ronchi dei Legionari or Trieste No-Borders, is 33km northwest of Trieste, near Monfalcone, with daily flights from Rome, London, Munich and Frankfurt, and less-frequent services from Belgrade (Serbia) and Tirana (Albania). The Austrian cities of Salzburg and Graz are around four hours' drive from Udine while Slovenia's capital Ljubljana is just over an hour from Gorizia.

Trieste

📞 040 / POP 235,500

Trieste, as travel writer Jan Morris once opined, 'offers no unforgettable landmark, no universally familiar melody, no unmistakable cuisine', yet it's a city that enchants, its 'prickly grace' inspiring a cult-like roll-call of writers, exiles and misfits.

Tumbling down to the Adriatic from a wild, karstic plateau and almost entirely surrounded by Slovenia, the city is physically isolated from the rest of the Italian peninsula. From as long ago as the 1300s, Trieste has indeed faced east, later becoming a free port under Austrian rule. The city blossomed under the 18th- and 19th-century Habsburgs; Vienna's seaside salon was also a fluid borderland where Italian, Slavic, Jewish, Germanic and even Greek culture intermingled.

Devotees come to think of its glistening belle époque cafes, dark congenial bars and buffets and even its maddening Bora wind as their own; it's also a great base for striking out into the surrounding Carso and Collio wine country.

👁️ Sights

Most of Trieste's sights are within walking distance of the city's centre, the vast Piazza dell'Unità d'Italia, or can be accessed by Trieste's efficient bus network.

★**Castello di Miramare**   CASTLE
(📞040 22 41 43; www.castello-miramare.it; Viale Miramare; adult/reduced €8/5; ⊙9am-7pm) Sitting on a rocky outcrop 7km from town, Castello di Miramare is Trieste's elegiac bookend, the fanciful neo-Gothic home of the hapless Archduke Maximilian of Austria. Maximilian originally came to Trieste in the 1850s as the commander-in-chief of Austria's imperial navy, an ambitious young aristocrat who was known for his liberal ideas. But in 1867 he was shot by a republican firing squad in Mexico, after briefly, and rather foolishly, taking up the obsolete crown.

The castle's decor reflects Maximilian's wanderlust and the various obsessions of the imperial age: a bedroom modelled to look like a frigate's cabin, ornate orientalist salons and a red silk-lined throne room. Upstairs, a suite of rooms used by the military hero Duke Amadeo of Aosta in the 1930s is also intact, furnished in the Italian Rationalist style. The duke's fate was also a tragic one: he died in a POW camp in Kenya during WWII.

Maximilian was a keen botanist and the castle boasts 22 hectares of **gardens** (⊙8am-7pm summer, to sunset winter), which burst with the colour and scent of rare and exotic trees. To get to the castle from the city centre, take bus 6 to Grignano, from which it's a 15-minute walk.

Piazza dell'Unità d'Italia   PIAZZA
This vast public space – Italy's largest sea-facing piazza – is an elegant triumph of Austro-Hungarian town planning and contemporary civil pride. Flanked by the city's grandest *palazzi* (mansions), including Palazzo del Municipio, Trieste's 19th-century city hall, it's a good place for a drink or a chat, or simply for a quiet moment staring out at ships on the horizon.

Borgo Teresiano   AREA
Much of the graceful city-centre area north of Corso Italia dates to the 18th-century reign of Empress Maria Theresa, including the photogenic **Canal Grande**. Reflecting centuries of religious tolerance, it's here you'll also find the mosaic-laden 1868 Serbian Orthodox Chiesa di Santo Spiridione (p406) juxtaposed with the neoclassical 1842 Catholic Chiesa di Sant'Antonio Taumaturgo (p407). On the Via Roma bridge stands a life-sized statue of James Joyce;

Trieste

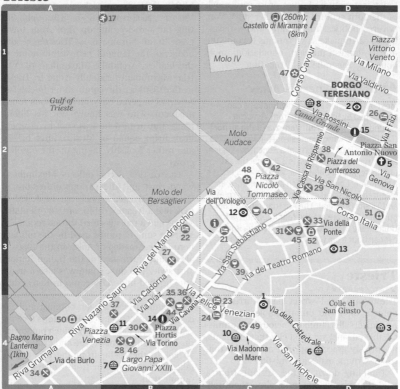

Piazza Hortis is home to a similar bronze of Italo Svevo (p406).

Civico Museo Sartorio
MUSEUM
(☏040 30 14 79; www.museosartoriotrieste.it; Largo Papa Giovanni XXIII 1; ⊙10am-1pm Tue-Thu, 2-5pm Fri & Sat, 10am-6pm Sun) FREE Yet another significant city villa, stuffed with art, ceramics and jewellery, and featuring beautiful ceiling frescoes – some dating to the late 18th century – and a basement Roman mosaic. Don't miss the room of superb **Tiepolo drawings**, virtuous and intimate in turns, or the **Triptych of Santa Chiara**, an exquisitely detailed, extremely intimate wooden altarpiece from the 14th century.

Synagogue
SYNAGOGUE
(☏040 37 14 66; www.triestebraica.it; Via San Francesco d'Assisi 19; adult/reduced €4/3; ⊙guided tours 3.45pm, 4.45pm & 5.45pm Mon & Wed, 9.30am, 10.30am & 11.30am Tue) This imposing and richly decorated neoclassical synagogue, built in 1912, is testament to Trieste's once significant Jewish community. Heavily damaged during WWII, it has been meticulously restored and remains one of the most important, and profoundly beautiful, synagogues in Italy.

Val Rosandra
NATURE RESERVE
(☏040 832 64 35) An extraordinary natural wilderness, just south of Trieste towards the border with Slovenia, the Val Rosandra is a wonderful spot to hike or picnic. Its unique flora also attracts botany enthusiasts. The village-suburb of Bagnoli is the best access place and can be reached by buses 40 or 41, direction Dolina, from central Trieste.

Statue of James Joyce
PUBLIC ART
James Joyce's presence in the city is palpable (see p410), but if you're not feeling it, this bronze statue will help. He's often

N 0 — 400 m
0 — 0.2 miles

Piazza Oberdan

(550m)

18 54

32

20

19

16

41

Via San Francesco d'Assisi

Via Cesare Battisti

Via Della Zonta

Via San Lazzaro

Viale XX Settembre

4

25

Via Carducci

Via Ginnastica

Via Slataper

Via Martini

Via Santa Caterina da Siena

Piazza Carlo Goldoni

Piazza dell' Ospedale

9

Via Capitolina

Largo della Barriera Vecchia

53

Via del Monte

Via Oriani

Via San Giusto

Piazza Garibaldi

surrounded by Irish visitors and his scenic home on the Grand Canal makes for great selfies. Don't miss the companion statue of his great friend and fellow writer, Italo Svevo (p406).

Museo Joyce & Svevo
MUSEUM

(☑040 675 81 70; www.museojoycetrieste.it; 2nd fl, Via Madonna del Mare 13; ☺9am-1pm Mon-Sat & 3-7pm Wed-Fri) FREE Joyce would enjoy the irony: his museum really belongs to friend and fellow literary great, Italo Svevo, housing a significant collection of the Triestini's first editions, photos and other memorabilia. Joyce is dealt with ephemerally, with a wall map of his haunts and homes and a Bloomsday bash in June (Svevo's birthday is also celebrated, on 19 December).

Staff can give you suggestions for a DIY walking tour of Joyce sites.

Museo Revoltella
MUSEUM

(☑040 675 43 50; www.museorevoltella.it; Via Diaz 27; adult/reduced €7/5; ☺10am-7pm Wed-Mon) This city museum was founded in 1872 and now spills rather confusingly over two neighbouring buildings. Baron Revoltella's original mid-19th-century house throbs with conspicuous consumption; his cup runneth over with chandeliers, ornate gilded plaster work and flamboyant silk wallpaper. The modern Palazzo Brunner has an interesting collection of 19th- and 20th-century works by Triestine artists, including some arresting early-20th-century portraiture and busts. There's also a pretty rooftop cafe and a good bookshop.

Civico Museo di Storia ed Arte ed Orto Lapidario
MUSEUM

(History & Art Museum & Stone Garden; ☑040 31 05 00; www.museostoriaeartetrieste.it; Piazza della Cattedrale 1; ☺10am-1pm & 4-7pm Tue-Sat, 10am-5pm Sun) FREE This creaky old museum houses Roman antiquities unearthed in and around Trieste and Aquileia, including the impressive iron hoard of the Necropolis of Reka from the Slovenian border. The Orto Lapidario (Stone Garden) has a pot-luck assembly of weather-resistant stone finds scattered among flowers and fruit trees.

Arco di Riccardo
ROMAN SITE

(Via del Trionfo) The Arco di Riccardo is one of the Roman town gateways, dating from 33 BC, and overlooks a pretty residential square. The gate is named for the English King Richard, who was supposed to have passed through en route from the Crusades.

Risiera di San Sabba
MEMORIAL

(☑040 82 62 02; www.risierasansabba.it; Via Palatucci 5; ☺9am-7pm) FREE This former rice-husking plant became a concentration camp in 1943 and has been a national monument and museum since the 1960s. The site commemorates the 5000 people who perished here and the many thousands more who passed through on the way to Nazi forced labour and death camps. These included a great many of the city's Jewish population along with Triestine and Slovenian resistance fighters. Tours cost €3.

Museo della Comunità Ebraica Carlo e Vera Wagner
MUSEUM

(☑040 63 38 19; www.triestebraica.it; Via del Monte 5 & 7; adult/reduced €5/3; ☺10am-1pm Wed, 4-7pm Tue & Thu) A small, highly prized collection of liturgical items, textiles, documents

Trieste

and photographs, including a touching number of personal items stolen by Nazi troops in 1945. It's been under renovation for several years; call ahead to confirm opening hours.

Civico Museo Teatrale Carlo Schmidl   MUSEUM
(☑040 675 40 72; www.museoschmidl.it; Via Rossini 4; adult/reduced €4/3; ◎9am-5pm Tue-Sun) Trieste's long-standing cultural cred is documented at this museum, housed inside the grand Palazzo Gopcevich, with a collection that traces the city's rich musical and theatrical heritage from the 18th century onwards.

Chiesa di Santo Spiridione   CHURCH
(☑040 63 13 28; www.comunitaserba.org; Via F Filzi; ◎9am-6pm Mon-Sat) The striking Serbian Orthodox Chiesa di Santo Spiridione

was completed in 1868 and sports glittering mosaics.

Statue of Italo Svevo   PUBLIC ART
(Piazza Hortis) Triestine modernist writer Italo Svevo is celebrated in this touching bronze, a companion piece to his great friend, James Joyce (p410).

Castello di San Giusto   MUSEUM
(☑040 30 93 62; www.castellodisangiustotrieste. it; Piazza della Cattedrale 3; adult/reduced €3/2; ◎10am-7pm summer, to 5pm Tue-Sun winter) Once a Roman fort, this sturdy 15th-century castle was begun by Frederick of Habsburg and finished off by blow-in Venetians. The city museum is housed here, with temporary exhibitions and a well-stocked armoury. Wander around the walls for magnificent views. Bus 24 can help out if you can't face the hill.

Roman Theatre ROMAN SITE

(Via del Teatro Romano) Behind Piazza dell'Unità d'Italia rise remains of the Roman theatre, which was built between the 1st and 2nd centuries AD. Concerts are held here occasionally during summer.

Chiesa di Sant'Antonio Taumaturgo CHURCH

(Via Della Zonta) The east end of Piazza San Antonio Nuovo is dominated by the enormous neoclassical Catholic Chiesa di Sant'Antonio Taumaturgo (1842).

Activities & Tours

Any hint of sun sees the Triestini flock to the concrete platforms along the waterfront **Viale Miramare** (it's more pleasant than it sounds).

La Diga BEACH

(☎0345 908 98 90; www.ladigaditrieste.it; ⊙9am-7pm, bar to 11pm Jun-Sep) La Diga – 'the dam' – is not exactly a swimming beach but it's Trieste's idea of a perfect beach club, moored just off the waterfront, opposite Mole Audace. Prebook a chair and umbrella (€6 to €15) or just sail over for some briny air, a gelato or a yoga-flow class. In the evenings it becomes more club than beach. A free shuttle leaves Mole Audace half-hourly.

Bagno Marino Lanterna SWIMMING

(El Pedocìn; ☎040 30 59 22; Molo Fratelli Bandiera 3; adult €1; ⊙7.30am-7.30pm Jun-Sep, open year-round for sunbathing) For sun-worshipping and a dip in town, head to Bagno Marino Lanterna, tucked away behind the city's disused 19th-century lighthouse (it's often referred to as *'el pedocìn'* by locals). A living piece of Austro-Hungarian history, this pebbly beach is still genteelly gender-segregated.

No 2 Tram TOURS

(www.triestetrasporti.it; Piazza Oberdan; hourly/daily €1.50/4.35; ⊙departures every 20min 7am-8pm) For wonderful views, jump on this vintage tram to Villa Opicina. For most of the 5km journey from Piazza Oberdan it's a regular tram, but a funicular section tackles the steep gradient as it heads up into the Carso. It's a short but significant trip – Villa Opicina was once almost entirely Slovenian-speaking and today retains a decidedly un-Italian feel.

Old Railway Cycling Trail CYCLING

(www.turismofvg.it) This bike route takes you from the city centre to the picturesque Val Rosandra and the Slovenian border, all along a disused railway line. It's a very pleasant cycle and also takes in some 19th-century industrial architecture, including nine toll houses and two railway stations. The route map can be downloaded from the tourist office website or the office has copies.

Walking Tours WALKING

(www.discover-trieste.it; €9, free with FVG card; ⊙10.30am Sun Mar-Jan) Themed tours of the city centre in English. Book through the tourist office (p412), or ask about self-guided tours for other times.

Festivals & Events

Barcolana Regatta SPORTS

(www.barcolana.it) Barcolana is a major sailing spectacle with thousands of sailing boats filling the gulf on the second Sunday in October.

Sleeping

Trieste's mid-range to high-end places often slash rates on weekends and can be astonishingly good value, especially compared with other Italian cities. There's also a large number of well-run B&Bs.

★**B&B Lidia Polla Trieste** B&B €

(☎033 47150231; www.atelierlidiapolla.com; Via del Coroneo 1; s/d €60/90) A very special B&B where you'll find exquisite parquetry floors, antique furniture and objects set against contemporary textiles and a simple sensibility. The quality of the linens, duvets, towels and bathrobes is a rare find at this price. Bathrooms *are* in the hall, but are exclusive to each room, plus one has a claw-foot bath and all are beautiful.

Forvm Boutique Hotel BOUTIQUE HOTEL €

(☎040 372 08 93; www.forvmboutiquehotel.it; Via Valdirivo 30; s/d €90/110; ❄📶) Occupying an upper floor of a nondescript 19th-century office building, the hushed, dramatically lit lounge of this small hotel immediately soothes the weary traveller. Well that, and the complimentary welcome *aperitivo*. Rooms aren't large but they are comfortable, plush and rather sexy; elegant staff are ever on hand when you need city tips or an espresso or herbal tea. Breakfast costs €10 extra.

Residenzale 6a BOUTIQUE HOTEL €

(☎040 672 67 15; www.residenzale6a.it; Via Santa Caterina 7; s/d €75/105; ❄📶) Upstairs in an imposing Borgo Teresiano building, this

---

ⓘ DISCOUNT CARDS

The FVGCard (48 hours/72 hours/ seven days €18/21/29) provides free admission to all civic museums; free transport in Udine, Lignano and on the Udine–Cividale del Friuli train; and free audio tours plus numerous discounts in the region's shops, spas, beaches and parks. The cards are available from all FVG tourist offices, some hotels and online (www.turismofvg.it).

---

small, cosy hotel mixes traditional furnishings with bright, modern bathrooms, a large lounge and an internal courtyard. Poetically, each of the elegant rooms is named and decorated for one of Italo Svevo's female characters.

Residence del Mare   APARTMENT €
(☏ 040 30 73 46; www.residencedelmare.it; Via della Madonna del Mare 4; apt 1/2 people €75/97; ❄ 🛜) If you're not after high design or pots of atmosphere, these apartments are large, very well equipped and brilliantly located. Upper floors have city views and the young staff are helpful.

★ Seven Historical Suites   BOUTIQUE HOTEL €€
(☏ 040 760 08 17; www.seventrieste.com; Via F Filzi 4; apt s/d €160/180; ❄ 🛜) Yes, there are seven suites and they are, indeed, historical, nestled on the beamed attic floor of a grand 1884 commercial building. Still, their lavish size, a slick contemporary way with glass, marble, stone and iron, and finally, their incredible collections of Sicilian objects and antique furniture, are a surprise departure from Trieste's usual haute Habsburg style.

Apart from the absolute luxury of the spaces themselves, each suite has a fully equipped kitchen stocked with beautiful ceramics, pewter and stemware, plus 24/7 access to a personal concierge. There's also an exquisite two-bedroom 'owners' suite' up for rent, lined with museum-quality artworks and with beautiful views.

L'Albero Nascosto   BOUTIQUE HOTEL €€
(☏ 040 30 01 88; www.alberonascosto.it; Via Felice Venezian 18; s €90, d €135-170; ❄ 🛜) A delightful little hotel in the middle of the old town, Nascosto is a model of discreet style. Rooms are spacious and tastefully decked out with parquet floors, original artworks, books and a vintage piece or two; most also

have a small kitchen corner. Breakfasts are simple but thoughtful, with local cheeses, top-quality preserves and Illy coffee.

Rooms here get snapped up; book well ahead if you can.

Grand Hotel Duchi d'Aosta   LUXURY HOTEL €€
(☏ 040 760 00 11; www.grandhotelduchidaosta.com; Piazza dell'Unità d'Italia 2; d €140-275; ❄ 🛜 ♒) There's been a hotel of sorts on this prime site since Roman times, and the Duchi remains Trieste's grand dame. Public spaces are hushed and intimate, and the rooms are opulently traditional – the way repeat visitors like them. The bathrooms might be a tad frumpy for some five-star tastes, but the moody basement pool is a good trade-off.

Hotel Vis a Vis   HOTEL €€
(☏ 040 760 00 11; www.hotelvisavis.net; Piazza dello Squero Vecchio 1; s/d €105/150; ❄ 🛜) Vis a Vis is the Duchi's slickly modern offshoot, with small-ish but luxurious, all mod-con rooms. A great choice if your tastes tend towards the contemporary, but you'd like in on the Duchi facilities.

Hotel Savoia Excelsior Palace   HOTEL €€
(☏ 040 7 79 41; http://savoiaexcelsiorpalace.starhotels.com; Riva del Mandracchio 4; d €190; ❄ 🛜) This glamorous 'newcomer' to Trieste's hotel scene, a classic but contemporary (and ever so slightly camp) refit of the great-boned Habsburg-era Grand Hotel, is giving the city's famed Duchi a run for its money. Grand it still is, with more than 100 light-filled luxurious rooms, first-rate public areas, sea views and reasonable prices.

Hotel Miramare   HOTEL €€
(☏ 040 224 70 85; http://hotelmiramaretrieste.it; Viale Miramare 325; d €150-200; 🅿 ❄ 🛜) There are beautiful sea views from all the rooms, a simple beachy design and a well-priced but stylish – love those Cassina leather chairs – restaurant and summery bar.

★ Hotel Riviera & Maximilian's   HISTORIC HOTEL €€€
(☏ 040 22 45 51; www.rivieramax.eu; Strada Costiera 22; d €230-310; 🅿 ❄ 🛜 ♒) Along the coast from the city, just north of Castello di Miramare, this hotel has the feel of a gracious Habsburg summer resort, but with light, if classically decorated, rooms and modern spa facilities. Its absolute waterfront position is rare and views are accordingly a knockout.

Eating

★ Osteria Salvagente SEAFOOD €
(☑040 260 66 99; Via dei Burlo 1; mains €22)
After meeting Marco and Valentina, the 80-something couple who owned this old seafood place finally felt comfortable passing on their life's work. It's indeed in good hands. The young team have changed little of the original maritime-themed decor but have instead relaxed the menu to include a huge array of Venetian-style mix and match *cicheti* (bar snacks).

Take a spritz (*prosecco* cocktail) and a spread of those to an outside bench or bag a table and choose from mains such as octopus steamed in paper or crumbed sardines. Or kick on later with Trieste's hipster set with house Malvasia and lots of convivial chat.

★ SaluMare SEAFOOD €
(www.facebook.com/SaluMare; Via di Cavana 13a; meals €12-20; ☺11.30am-3pm & 6.30-10.30pm Mon-Sat) This bright, buzzing reinvention of the Triestine buffet features fish and seafood. Order at the bar from a menu of small dishes: white polenta and *baccalà mantecato* (salt-cod purée) or *seppie bolito* (cuttlefish stew), prawn ceviche, anchovy butter tartines. Wash it down with a well-chosen Friulian or Veneto white and a good sparkling.

Buffet Da Pepi BUFFET €
(www.buffetdapepi.it; Via Cassa di Risparmio 3; meals €20; ☺8.30am-10pm Mon-Sat) The counter here is a site of porcine carnage: legs, necks, bellies, tongues and testicles, all awaiting a slap of relish from the huge ceramic mustard jars and a final grate of snowy *kren* (horseradish). At lunchtime there are hot, takeaway brisket or pork rolls (€4), best devoured by the nearby waterfront.

Buffet da Siora Rosa BUFFET, SEAFOOD €
(☑040 30 14 60; Piazza Hortis 3; meals €25; ☺8am-10pm Tue-Sat) Opened before WWII, the family-run Siora Rosa is one Trieste's best-loved traditional buffets (bar-restaurants). Sit outside or in the wonderfully retro interior and tuck into boiled pork, sauerkraut and other Germanic and Hungarian offerings, or opt for something fishy like *baccalà* (salted cod) with polenta.

Buffet Rudy BUFFET €
(Via Valdirivo 32; meals €20; ☺9am-1am Mon-Sat) Rudy has been concocting traditional boiled meats, cold cuts and beer since, oh, 1897.

Come for the pork joints, served up with the house sauerkraut or just drinks and snacks at the bar (this being the beer-iest of all the buffets).

L'Osteria del Vento FRIULIAN, ITALIAN €
(Eataly; ☑040 246 57 01; www.eataly.net; Riva Tommaso Gulli 1; meals €25, pizza €6-15; ☺noon-2.30pm & 7-10.30pm) For the city's best table with harbour views, head to Eataly's upstairs *osteria*. Clean and serene tones and nice use of wood offset the bustle, and the menu manages to be both crowd-pleasing and flawless in execution. Pasta, burgers, steaks, pizzas and a daily fish are done with flair and precision and Friuli's finest (often organic) drops come by the glass.

Genuino CAFFETERIA €
(www.genuino.com; Via delle Beccherie 13; dishes €6.50-16; ☺noon-10pm Mon-Sat) Perpetually busy Genuino packs them in for big salads, fish, wild rice and roast vegetable combination plates, seasonal soup and chicken burgers. It's fast and furious and on fastfood-style plates and trays, but rest assured everything has eco-credentials, and there are local wines by the glass and artisan beers to help slow things down.

Gelateria Soban GELATO €
(☑391 4617405; www.gelateriasoban.com; Via Cicerone 10; gelato €3-4.50; ☺11am-10pm) Chiara

DON'T MISS

BUFFET, TRIESTE-STYLE

You'll be sure to eat well, in fact extremely well, at a Triestine buffet, but banish any thought of all-you-can-eat meal deals. These rowdy bar restaurants are yet another legacy of the city's Austro Hungarian past; if Trieste's bakeries conjure up Vienna, its buffets are Budapest all over. Usually all-day, and night, affairs, small snacks – cod or zucchini fritters, topped toasts and *panini* – are available from early morning and gobbled over lunch or at *aperitivo* time. But, hey, who's here for zucchini? Beef brisket may be a stalwart, but pork – baked, boiled, cured, stuffed into a sausage or fried – is the star attraction. Fresh grated *kren* (horseradish), *capuzi* (sauerkraut) and *patate in tecia* (mashed potatoes) are traditional accompaniments.

Soban is from a family of artisan gelato makers originally from the Veneto. They have three gelaterias in Piedmonte but she has brought the first to Trieste. This is a Gambero Rosso–ordained operation, so expect only the best: minimal, pure and ultra-seasonal ingredients, the best local milk and eggs and slow, flavour-enhancing technique.

Viezzoli   PASTRIES €

(Via Cassa di Risparmio 7; cakes €3-4; ☉7am-8pm Mon-Sat, 8am-2pm Sun) Brave the battalion of Illy-gulping locals at this cafe-bakery and try a slice of *putizza* or another Triestine specility, most usually sold only as whole cakes or loaves.

Ristorante Ai Fiori   SEAFOOD €€

(☑040 30 06 33; www.aifiori.com; Piazza Hortis 7; meals €38; ☉12.30-2.30pm & 7.30-11pm Tue-Sat, 7.30-11pm Sun) As the pretty name might suggest (*fiori* means 'flower'), there's a dedication to the seasons at this discreet little restaurant and an emphasis on freshness. In summer that might be a surprise cold spaghetti with spanner crab or one of the darker, tastier fish dishes with horseradish, apple and potatoes in winter. The wine list includes a few rarities and celebration-priced French drops.

Chimera di Bacco   FRIULIAN, SEAFOOD €€

(☑040 36 40 23; Via del Pane 2; meals €37, tasting menu 4/7 courses €52/72; ☉noon-2.30pm & 7.30-11pm) Much more than the *'picolo enotect'* that they describe themselves, Chimera di Bacco does a very interesting regional menu

of both local seafood and meat. Don't miss the Istrian-style *fusi* pasta (hand-cut and rolled diamonds served with a meat ragú) if it's on the menu, or do the literary tasting menu composed of small dishes from the book *Italo Svevo's Table*.

Trattoria Nerodiseppia   SEAFOOD €€

(☑040 30 13 77; www.trattorianerodiseppia.com; Via Luigi Cadorna 23; meals €28-32; ☉noon-2.30pm & 7-11pm Tue-Sat) A simple place that's full of youthful enthusiasm. The menu keeps it simple – fish ragù, fish tartares, risotto with local clams, *fritto misto* of both fish and vegetables – but is not afraid to roam further into the Italian kitchen than is usual in these parts. Pesto, aubergine, mozzarella and capers pop up all over the place, adding welcome colour and punch.

Angry Diamond   MODERN ITALIAN €€

(☑329 3241750; www.facebook.com/angrydia mondrestaurant; Via Torino 32; meals €32, hamburgers €8-15; ☉6pm-1am Wed-Sun) Despite its high glamour clubby interior, Angry Diamond is welcoming, serious about the food it serves and great value. Taking Trieste's meaty obsession in an entirely different direction, the menu is a pan-global celebration of beef (with a little pork and fish thrown in for the non-believers). Even the hamburger menu lists several varieties of beef to choose from.

Al Bagatto   SEAFOOD €€€

(☑040 30 17 71; www.albagatto.it; Via Cadorna 7; meals/degustation €52/59; ☉7.30-11pm Mon-

---

THE DUBLINER

Think you're escaping and run into yourself. Longest way round is the shortest way home.
– James Joyce, *Ulysses*

Stifled by the gloom and obligations of Dublin, James Joyce escaped to Trieste in 1905 with a contract to teach English at the local Berlitz language school. Along with lover (and soon wife) Nora Barnacle, the precocious but still unpublished 22-year-old arrived in a city that epitomised the twilight years of the Austro-Hungarian Empire.

Trieste was a booming, brilliantly cosmopolitan place, with a polyglot creative class and no shortage of dissolute aristocrats. The gregarious Irishman wasted no time immersing himself in this fertile scene and quickly picked up the floral Triestine dialect. In between his teaching commitments, failed business ventures, family life and all-night benders, he set about drafting the text of his first two ground-breaking novels, *Dubliners* and *Portrait of the Artist as a Young Man*. Perennially poor, he spent the bulk of his writing hours in the city's fin de siècle cafes, Trieste life all about him.

The Joyces remained in the city until 1915, when the outbreak of WWI forced them to relocate to neutral Zürich. Joyce returned after the war, but he was unimpressed by the brash new order and quickly made tracks for Paris. *Ulysses* may have been given form in the City of Light, but its genesis was undoubtedly in the multilingual melting pot that was pre-WWI Trieste.

Sat) This old-timer, with its dark, brooding dining room, does a Triestine seafood *degustazione* – a *crudo* (raw fish) and something involving squid ink will invariably play a part – that's daunting but delicious. The 'seasonal creative' menu is just that, or you can try ordering like the suited regulars: the freshest of fish by the *etto* (100g), weighed and filleted at the table.

Drinking & Nightlife

Trieste's historic cafes conjure times past, but remain a thriving and satisfying part of daily city life (the Triestini drink twice as much coffee as the national average). Cafes, bars and buffets blur, as does what constitutes *aperitivo*. Evenings out are a refined, relaxed mix of young and old, and early-evening drinks often stretch well into the night with the help of hearty buffet snacks. Via San Nicolo's bars cater to a smart after-work set, while the old town's cluster of bars are of a more boho bent. In summer there are come-and-go outdoor places along the Viale Miramare.

★ Caffè San Marco   CAFE
(📞040 064 17 24; www.caffesanmarcotrieste.eu; Via Battisti 18; ☺8.30am-11pm Tue-Sun) Opening just before WWI, and a favourite of writers Svevo, Saba and Joyce, this Viennese Secession giant is spectacularly decorated with theatrical mask paintings, coffee-leave themed gilt and dark chocolate walls, and miles of red marble tables. Saved from demolition in 2013, it's no longer a place of melancholy nostalgia, but instead a vibrant cultural hub with beautifully restored decor, young staff and an in-cafe bookshop.

There are both local and Slovenian wines by the glass, *prosecco* or Champagne, and sandwiches, snacks and pastries or a more substantial menu in the evenings.

Osteria da Marino   WINE BAR
(Via della Ponte 5; ☺11am-3pm & 7pm-1am Mon-Thu, to 2.30am Fri & Sat, 7pm-midnight Sun) If you can't make it to the Carso wine region, get the owner here to ply you with indigenous grape varieties (the Vitovska selection is encyclopedic). Or just settle in with a Franciacorte sparkling or a Tuscan red and wait for the little meatballs to appear. It also has a menu of good local dishes that can be eaten out the back or at the bar.

Romi Jass Kaffee   BAR
(www.facebook.com/kaffeehausromi; Via Torino 30; ☺7.45am-2.30pm Mon, to 11pm Tue-Thu, to

NERO? CAPO? LATTE?

This coffee capital has its own, often confounding, terminology. For an espresso ask for *un nero*, for a cappuccino, order a caffe latte, for a macchiato order a *capo* – a cappuccino – and, for either in a glass, specify '*un b*' – the 'b' short for *bicchiere*, a glass.

midnight Fri & Sat) This daytime bakery and cafe morphs into a bar come evening. It's an intriguing, gently ironic tribute to a bygone Trieste, with portraits of Imperial rulers casting their gaze over a gaggle of bearded or black-clad Triestini boys and girls. Live music happens out the back on weekends; the Facebook page has details. It's great.

Al Ciketo   BAR
(📞348 6444034; www.facebook.com/alciketo; Via San Sebastiano 6a; ☺10am-midnight Mon-Sat) Trieste does do glamour and this bar, which convivially spills out into the alley beside it, attracts a slightly older, well-put-together crowd come Friday and Saturday evening. There are lots of bottles of sparkling doing the rounds, and this being Trieste, the big wooden platters of *stuzzicini* – bread topped with all kinds of pork – are not far behind.

Cantina del Vescovo   WINE BAR
(📞344 1820600; Via Torino 32; ☺noon-12.30am Tue-Sun) Trieste's cosmopolitan gaze usually faces east, but here we have a bar that feels like you've been transported to an ultra-hip neighbourhood of Madrid. The city's most fashionable pack out this moody industrial space for bold Spanish wines, *pintxos* (tapas plates) of piquillo peppers, *jamón* or *patatas bravas* and late-night burgers.

Caffè Torinese   CAFE
(Corso Italia 2; ☺7am-midnight) The smallest and, dare we say, friendliest of the historic bunch, this is an exquisite room that's just as nice for an evening tipple as a morning *capo un' b* (macchiato in a glass).

Caffè degli Specchi   CAFE
(📞040 66 19 73; www.caffespecchi.it; Piazza Unità d'Italia 7; ☺8am-9pm) This veritable hall of mirrors *(specchi)* first opened its doors back in 1839 and has more recently been taken over by the chocolatiering Faggiotto from Pordenone (although the matriarch is a local; in fact, she was Miss Trieste 1982). This

is the ultimate Piazza Unità front-row seat, whatever the weather, and the coffee has returned to its once former glory.

Chocolat
CAFE

(Via Cavana 15b; ☉7.30am-8pm Tue-Sat) This lovely cafe and chocolate shop makes everything in-house, including the hot chocolate slowly simmering in a great pot behind the counter and, in summer, gelato. Happily there's no surcharge for sitting at the big communal table outside on the square.

Caffè Tommaseo
BAR

(☑040 36 26 66; www.caffetommaseo.it; Riva III Novembre; meals €30; ☉9am-10pm) Virtually unchanged since its 1830 opening, the rich ceiling reliefs, primrose-yellow walls and Viennese mirrors here couldn't be any more evocative. Take coffee at the bar or sit down in the prim but very pretty dining room for some *fritto misto* (fried seafood) and a chance to linger among the ghosts.

☆ Entertainment

Tetris
LIVE MUSIC

(www.gruppotetris.org; Via della Rotonda 3) One of Trieste's iconic alternative cooperative venues, Tetris has an impressive line-up of international and local live acts and DJs, with electronica and indie being well represented. It's also just a nice, friendly place to drop in for a beer and there's a monthly Sunday vintage clothing and vinyl market.

Teatro Miela
CABARET

(☑040 36 51 19; www.miela.it; Piazza Duca degli Abruzzi 3) It's always worth checking the Miela calendar for its legendary Pupkin Kabarett nights, but the regular live music program is also a nice way to tap into alternative Triestine life. Good times.

Teatro Verdi
OPERA

(☑040 672 21 11; www.teatroverdi-trieste.com; Riva III Novembre 1) Trieste's opera house is a little bit Scala and a little bit Fenice (thanks to a pair of duelling architects), but wears the mix well. Don't miss a chance to see a performance here; the Triestini are passionate opera lovers and make a great audience.

🛍 Shopping

Eataly
FOOD & DRINKS

(☑040 246 57 01; www.eataly.net; Riva Tommaso Gulli 1; ☉9am-10.30pm Sun-Thu, to midnight Fri & Sat) Possibly the most beautiful of the Eataly family of food and wine superstores, set in a beautiful old dockside warehouse, with two floors of windows overlooking the marina and lighthouse. The usual great lineup of pan-Italy produce is here, along with some excellent Friulian specialities and wine.

Pirona
FOOD, CHOCOLATE

(Largo Barriera Vecchia 12; ☉7.30am-7.30pm Tue-Sat, 8am-1.30pm Sun) This jewel-box pastry shop and cafe was one of Joyce's favourites. Its nutty, spicy, boozy Triestine speciality cakes – *putizza*, *presnitz* and *pinza* – are particularly good.

Francesco Tagliente
ANTIQUES

(☑347 4449108; Via del Ponte 7; ☉3-7.30pm Tue-Sat) The streets of Trieste's Jewish ghetto once were filled with antique shops and a few remain among the bars and cafes that have sprung up more recently. Francesco Tagliente, a kind and welcoming specialist, has a good mix of traditional Habsburg-era pieces and those from the 20th-century, including some rare Luciano Florio Paccagnella vases from the Memphis era.

Ts360
BOOKS

(☑040 36 34 94; Piazza Oberdan 7; ☉10am-7pm Tue-Sat) Part bookshop, part Slovenian cultural hub, this is a fascinating place to explore the cultural fluidity of Trieste; it has a particularly engaging children's reading corner. The shop's design, by Slovenian firm SoNo Arhitekti, has design fans from around the world coming to have a look too.

Eppinger
FOOD

(☑040 63 78 38; www.eppingercaffe.it; Via Dante Alighieri 2; ☉8am-9pm) Eppinger does the usual, if ever compelling, pantheon of Triestine cakes, but best of all it can do the favourite nut-filled pastries *presnitz* and *putizza* sealed and in boxes which make them easy to pack. It also happens to be one of the city's best.

ℹ Information

Hospital (Ospedale Maggiore Di Trieste; ☑040 399 11 11; Piazza dell'Ospedale 2)

Police Station (☑040 323 58 00; Via Hermet 7)

Tourist Office (☑040 347 83 12; www.turismo fvg.it; Via dell'Orologio 1; ☉9am-6pm)

ℹ Getting There & Away

AIR

Friuli Venezia Giulia airport (p403) has direct daily flights to and from Rome, London, Munich and Frankfurt, and less-frequent services for Belgrade and Tirana. Venice's Marco Polo airport is around 1½ hours away by car or you can catch the train to Mestre (two to three hours) and then bus it from there.

BOAT

From mid-June to late September motor-boat services run to and from Grado, Lignano and points along the Istrian coast in Slovenia and Croatia; check with the tourist office for the current operator.

BUS

National and international services operate from the **bus station** (☑ 040 42 50 20; www.auto stazionetrieste.it; Via Fabio Severo 24).

APT (☑ 800 955957; www.aptgorizia.it) Buses link Udine and Friuli Venezia Giulia airport (€4.75, one hour, hourly).

Florentia Bus (☑ 040 42 50 20; www.florentia bus.it) Services international destinations such as Ljubljana (€17, 2¾ hours, daily Monday to Saturday), Zagreb (€30, five hours, daily Monday to Saturday), Belgrade (€55, 10 hours, two days a week) and Sofia (€65, 16½ hours, daily).

SAF (☑ 0432 60 81 11; www.saf.ud.it) Operates buses to and from Udine (€7.50, 1¼ hours, hourly), Aquileia (€3.30, one to 1¼ hours, up to eight daily), Lignano Sabbiadoro (€5.75, 1½ hours, eight to 11 daily) and Grado (€4.75, 1¼ hours, 12 daily).

TRAIN

The **train station** (Piazza della Libertà 8) serves Gorizia (€4.75, 50 minutes, hourly), Udine (€8.75, one hour, at least hourly), Venice (€19.30, two hours, at least hourly) and Rome (€99, 6½ to 7½ hours; most require a change at Mestre).

❶ Getting Around

BOAT

Shuttle boats operated by **Trieste Trasporti** (☑ 800 016675; www.triestetrasporti.it) depart from the Stazione Marittima to Muggia year-round (one way/return €4.25/7.90, 30 minutes, six to 10 times daily). Check for other seasonal services with the tourist office.

BUS

Trieste Trasporti (p413) bus 30 connects the train station with Via Roma and the waterfront; bus 24 runs from the station to Castello di San Giusto; bus 36 links Trieste bus station with Miramare. One-hour tickets cost €1.50 (€1.35 pre-purchased); all-day €4.35.

TAXI

Radio Taxi Trieste (☑ 040 30 77 30; www. radiotaxitrieste.it) operates 24 hours; from the train station to the centre will cost around €10, and there's a flat fee of €58 to the airport.

MUGGIA

The fishing village of Muggia, 5km south of Trieste, is the only Italian settlement on the historic Istrian peninsula. Slovenia is just 4km south and Croatia (the peninsula's main occupant) a score more. With its 14th-century castle and semi-ruined walls, the port has a Venetian feel and its steep hills make for lovely views back towards Trieste.

Locals gather over jugs of wine and groaning platters of deer or boar salami at **Pane, Vine e San Daniele** (Piazza Marconi 5, Muggia; salumi €8-15; ⊗8am-2pm & 8pm-2am Mon Sat) on the main square behind the port, or there are a number of same-ish seafood restaurants along the waterfront. Ferries shuttle between Muggia and Trieste.

Il Carso

If Trieste is known for its cultural idiosyncrasy, its hinterland is also fittingly distinct. Dramatically shochorned between Slovenia and the Adriatic, the Carso (*Karst* in German, *kras* in Slovenian) is a windswept calcareous tableland riddled with caves and sinkholes. This wild landscape has long inspired myths and legend, while its geology has lent its name – karst – to geologically similar terrain around the world. It's a compelling place to visit in any season but is particularly pretty in spring, when the grey-green hills are speckled with blossom, or in autumn, when the vines and *ruje* (smoke trees) turn crimson and rust.

◉ Sights

Castello di Duino CASTLE

(☑ 040 20 81 20; www.castellodiduino.it; Frazione di Duino 32, Duino; adult/reduced €8/6; ⊗ 9.30am-5.30pm Wed-Mon Apr-Sep, to 4pm Sat & Sun Mar, Oct & Nov) Fourteen kilometres northwest along the coast from Miramare, this 14th-and 15th-century bastion picturesquely marches down the cliff, surrounded by a verdant garden and mind-blowing views. Poet Rainer Maria Rilke was a guest here during the winter of 1911–12, a melancholy and windswept stay that produced the *Duino Elegies*. The castle is still in private hands and the collection is idiosyncratic to say the least, but delightfully so. To get here, take bus 41 from Trieste's Piazza Oberdan.

OZMIZE: THE CARSO'S POP-UP WINE CELLARS

Osmize (or *osmice*) predate the trendy retail pop-up phenomena by a few centuries, care of an 18th-century Austrian law that gave Carso farmers the right to sell surplus from their barns or cellars once a year (the term *osmiza* comes from the Slovenian word for 'eight', the number of days of the original licence). It's mainly vineyards that hold *osmize* today, and farm cheeses and cured meats are always on offer too. While the Carso is known for its gutsy, innovative winemakers, these old traditions still hold sway. Don't try asking for a list: finding an *osmiza* is part of the fun. Look first, along Carso roads, for the red arrows. Then look up, to gates or lintels bearing a *frasca* – a leafy branch hung ceremoniously upside down announcing that an *osmiza* is open for business. Don't forgo the chance to try the Carso's native wines: the complex, often cloudy, sometimes fierce, white Vitovska; or Terrano, aka Teran, a berry-scented red. Internationally known winemakers **Zidarich** (☑ 040 20 12 23; www.zidarich.it; Prepotto 23) and **Skerk** (☑ 040 20 01 56; www.skerk.com; Prepotto 20, Prepotto) do, in fact, announce *osmiza* dates on their websites, as do smaller producers **David Sardo** (☑ 040 22 92 70; www.osmize.com/samatorza/sardo-david; Samatorza 5, Samatorza) and **Le Torri di Slivia** (☑ 338 3515876; www.letorridislivia.net; Aurisina Cave 62, Duino). And, OK, there is now an online calendar: www.osmize.com. That said, you can't miss the *frasca* clustering at every cross roads in spring and autumn, and cellar visits are also usually possible by appointment year-round.

Grotta Gigante
CAVE

(☑ 040 32 73 12; www.grottagigante.it; Località Borgo Grotta Gigante 42, Sgonico; adult/reduced €12/9; ⊙ 50min guided tours hourly 10am-6pm daily summer, 10am-4pm Tue-Sat winter) The area's big-ticket attraction is near Villa Opicina, 5km northeast of Trieste. At 120m high, 280m long and 65m wide, it's one of the largest and most spectacular caves that's accessible on the continent. It's easily reached from Trieste on bus 42, or by tram 2 and bus 42 in the other direction.

Casa Carsica
MUSEUM

(☑ 040 32 72 40; www.kraskahisa.com; Rupingrande 31, Monrupino; ⊙ 11am-12.30pm & 3-5pm Sun Apr-Oct) **FREE** This house museum in Rupingrande re-creates life in the premodern Slovenian-speaking Carso. It also organises the plateau's most important folk festival, Nozze Carsiche (*Kraška ohcet;* Karstic Wedding), held every two years for four days at the end of August in a 16th-century fortress in Monrupino.

🛏 Sleeping

Da Rosy
B&B €

(www.darosy.it; Sistiana 59L, Sistiana; s/d/tr €60/75/100) A friendly young couple run this bright, happy B&B with four smart bedrooms. There are two bathrooms shared between them, as well as a living room, guest kitchen and garden. It's a short stroll to the waterfront or a short drive up to the vineyards.

Gorizia

☑ 0481 / POP 36,000 / ELEV 86M

Gorizia's appeal lies in the aristocratic ambience of its centre, its unique Friulian-Slovenian cooking and its easy access to the surrounding countryside, famed for its wine and rustic restaurants. Considering this serene modern incarnation, you'd never guess the turmoil of Gorizia's past. An oft-shifting border zone throughout much of its history and the scene of some of the most bitter fighting of WWI's eastern front, it was most recently an Iron Curtain checkpoint.

The town's name is unmistakably Slovenian in origin and before the outbreak of WWI it was not uncommon to hear conversations in several different languages – German, Slovenian, Friulian, Italian, Venetian and Yiddish – in the main square.

◉ Sights

Borgo Castello
CASTLE

(☑ 0481 53 51 46; Borgo Castello 36; adult/reduced €6/3; ⊙ 10am-7pm Tue-Sun, 9.30-11.30am Mon) Gorizia's main sight is its castle, perched atop a knoll-like hill. It has some convincing re-creations and a fine wood-panelled great hall. Beneath the main fortress huddle two oddly paired museums. The tragic, gory history of Gorizia's WWI Italian-Austrian front is explored at the **Museo della Grande Guerra** (☑ 0481 53 39 26; Borgo

Castello 13-15; admission with Borgo Castello; ⊘9am-7pm Tue-Sun), including a to-scale re-creation of a trench. Then there's fashion: 19th- and early-20th-century finery at the **Museo della Moda e delle Arti Applicate** (☑0481 53 39 26; Borgo Castello 13-15; admission with Borgo Castello; ⊘9am-7pm Tue-Sun).

Piazza Transalpina HISTORIC SITE

One for Cold War kids. The Slovenian border – a mere formality since December 2007 – bisects the edge of Gorizia, and you can celebrate Schengen with a bit of border hopscotch at this piazza's centre, while contemplating the now crumbling fences, border posts and watchtowers.

Palazzo Coronini Cronberg PALACE

(☑0481 53 34 85; www.coronini.it; Viale XX Settembre 14; adult/reduced €5/3; ⊘10am-1pm & 3-6pm Wed-Sun) This 16th-century residence is jammed with antiquities and is surrounded by lush gardens, which are free to visit on their own and open until 9pm in summer.

🛏 Sleeping

★**Palazzo Lantieri** B&B €€

(☑0481 53 32 84; www.palazzo-lantieri.com; Piazza Sant'Antonio 6; s/d €100/140; P 🕸) This *palazzo*-stay offers light, spacious rooms in the main house or self-catering apartments in former farm buildings, all overlooking a glorious Persian-styled garden. Goethe, Kant and Empress Maria Theresa were repeat guests back in the day. Antiques fill both public and private spaces, but the charming Lantieri family are far from stuck in the past.

Their contemporary art commissions mean there's a Michelangelo Pistoletto on the ceiling and a Jannis Kounellis in the attic. Non-guests can arrange guided tours.

🍴 Eating & Drinking

Cafes and bars can be found on Corso Italia and Via Terza Armata, while the old-town streets below the castle and around the covered **food market** (Via Verdi 30) are the best places to find casual restaurants.

Majda GORIZIAN €

(☑0481 3 08 71; Via Duca D'Aosta 71; meals €25; ⊘noon-3pm & 7.30-11pm Mon-Sat) With a courtyard bar, friendly staff and colourful decor, Majda is a happy place to sample local specialities such as ravioli filled with potato (Slovenian-style) or beetroot and local herbs,

wild boar on polenta and interesting sides like steamed wild dandelion.

Pasticceria Centrale PASTRIES €

(Via Garibaldi 4a; pastries €2-4; ⊘7.30am-7.30pm) No visit to Gorizia would be complete without tasting the town's signature pastry, *gubana*, a fat snail of shortcrust filled with nuts, sultanas and spices.

Rosenbar GORIZIAN €€

(☑0481 52 27 00; www.rosenbar.it; Via Duca d'Aosta 96; meals €30; ⊘noon-3pm & 7.30-10pm Tue-Sat) Rosenbar is a traditional dining room set in an airy shop front. It's known for attention to detail, in both preparation and in the always local and mostly organic produce it uses. Along with dishes capturing Gorizia's cross-border culinary spirit, there are also a few Adriatic fish and seafood options on the menu.

Bierkeller BEER HALL

(☑0481 53 78 91; Via Lantieri 4; ⊘5pm-midnight Fri Wed) Venture down into this ancient vaulted cellar for a little piece of Bavaria, with pretzels, football on the big screen or DJs on weekends. Staff are delightful and in summer there's a pretty walled beer garden.

ℹ Information

Tourist Office (☑0481 53 57 64; Corso Italia 9; ⊘9am-6pm Mon-Sat, to 1pm Sun)

ℹ Getting There & Away

The **train station** (Piazzale Martiri Libertà d'Italia), 2km southwest of the centre, has regular connections to and from Udine (€3.20, 30 minutes, at least hourly) and Trieste (€3.80, 50 minutes, hourly). **APT** (☑800 955957; www.aptgorizia.it) runs buses from the train station across to Slovenia's **Nova Gorica bus station** (€1.30, 25 minutes).

Palmanova

☑0432 / POP 5340

Shaped like a nine-pointed star – although you'd need an aeroplane to check – Palmanova is a defensively designed town-within-a-fortress built by the Venetians in 1593. Once common throughout Europe, these military monoliths were known as 'star forts' or *trace italienne*. So impregnable were the town's defences that Napoleon used and extended them in the late 1700s, as did the Austrians during WWI. To this day the Italian army maintains a garrison here.

◉ Sights

From hexagonal Piazza Grande, at the star's centre, six roads radiate through the old town to the defensive walls. An inviting grassy path connects the bastions and three main *porte* (gates): Udine, Cividale and Aquileia.

Civico Museo Storico   MUSEUM
(☑0432 91 91 06; Borgo Udine 4; adult/reduced €2/1.50; ⊙9.30am-12.30pm Tue-Sun summer, or by appointment) Head along Borgo Udine to uncover local history and weaponry from the Venetian and Napoleonic eras in the Civico Museo Storico, inside **Palazzo Trevisan**. The museum also acts as a tourist office and has information on secret-tunnel tours that wind beneath the city walls.

Museo Storico Militare   MUSEUM
(☑0432 92 81 75; Piazza Grande 21; ⊙10am-4pm Mon, Tue & Thu, 10am-12pm Fri-Sun) FREE The Museo Storico Militare is inside Porta Cividale. The military museum traces the history of troops stationed in Palmanova from 1593 to WWII.

✕ Eating

La Campana d'Oro   FRIULIAN €€
(☑0432 92 87 19; Borgo Udine 25b; meals €35; ⊙noon-2pm Wed-Mon, 7.30-9.30pm Wed-Sat) Besides its goulash, La Campana d'Oro prepares delicate dishes such as smoked goose breast, fish soup, and fettucine with wine-soused clams, as well as simply grilled fish caught in nearby Marano.

❶ Information

Tourist Office (☑0432 92 48 15; Borgo Udine 4; ⊙10am-noon)

The Friulian Coast

Friuli's marshy, lagoon-filled Adriatic coast combines seaside charm and some of the least visited Roman sites in the country, while sandwiched between the beach resorts of Grado and Lignano, the Laguna di Marano succumbs to nature, in particular birdlife.

The beaches may not be Italy's prettiest, though its resorts do have the only sand beaches in the region. But there's a lovely timeless quality to the towns and nature reserves, and brilliant views and excellent seafood restaurants to be enjoyed.

Aquileia

☑0432 / POP 3500

Aquileia, off the beaten track? It certainly wasn't 2000 years ago. Colonised in 181 BC, Aquileia was once one of the largest and richest cities of the Roman Empire, at times second only to Rome, with a population of at least 100,000 at its peak. After the city was levelled by Attila's Huns in AD 452, its inhabitants fled south and west where they founded Grado and then Venice. A smaller town rose in Roman Aquileia's place in the early Middle Ages, and with the construction of the present basilica, it went on to become the largest and a hugely significant Christian diocese in Europe. Conferred with a Unesco World Heritage listing in 1998, this now charming rural town and living museum still, rather thrillingly, lies above one of the most complete, unexcavated Roman sites in Europe. But there's plenty to see above ground too.

◉ Sights

Guided tours of the extraordinary Roman sights are organised by the tourist office; otherwise, wander at will.

⭐**Basilica di
Santa Maria Assunta**   CHURCH
(www.basilicadiaquileia.it; Piazza Capitolo; crypts adult/reduced €4/3, bell tower €2; ⊙9am-7pm Apr-Sep, shorter hours winter, bell tower summer only) The entire floor of the Latin cross-shaped basilica, rebuilt after an earthquake in 1348, is covered with one of the largest and most spectacular Roman-era mosaics in the world. The 760-sq-metre floor of the basilica's 4th-century predecessor is protected by glass walkways, allowing visitors to wander above the long-hidden tile work, which includes astonishingly vivid episodes from the story of Jonah and the whale, the Good Shepherd, exacting depictions of various lagoon wildlife, and portraits of wealthy Roman patrons and their quotidian business interests.

Museo Archeologico Nazionale   MUSEUM
(☑0431 9 10 16; www.museoarcheo-aquileia.it; Via Roma 1; adult/reduced €4/2; ⊙8.30am-7.30pm Tue-Sun) A daunting number of statues, pottery, glassware and jewellery, all locally excavated, are displayed in this museum, representing one of northern Italy's most important collections of Roman-era treasures.

Porto Fluviale
ROMAN SITE

(River Port; Via Sacra; ☉8.30am-1hr before sunset)
Scattered remnants of the Roman town include extensive ruins of the Porto Fluviale, the old port, which once linked the settlement to the sea. Also free to visit are the partially restored remains of houses, roads and the standing columns of the ancient Forum on Via Giulia Augusta.

Museo
Paleocristiano
MUSEUM

(☑0431 9 11 31; Piazza Pirano, Località Monastero; adult/reduced €4/2, incl Museo Archeologico Nazionale; ☉8.30am-1.30pm Thu-Sun) Part of the Museo Archeologico Nazionale, this museum houses Early Christian–era mosaics and funerary monuments gathered from the surrounding ruins.

🛏 Sleeping

Camping Aquileia
CAMPGROUND €

(☑0431 9 10 42; www.campingaquileia.it; Via Gemina 10; camping €28, d cabin €46, 4-bed bungalow €78; P🖙🛜🌊) This well-maintained campground is set beside pretty fields; its comfortable new bungalows look towards the basilica and old Roman port.

Ostello Domus Augusta
HOSTEL €

(☑0431 9 10 24; www.ostelloaquileia.it; Via Roma 25; s/d €28/46; P🛜) A spotless if rather institutional hostel with two- to six-bed rooms and private bathrooms down the hall. Friendly, relaxed staff are helpful and happy to dole out maps and timetables.

❶ Information

Tourist Office (☑0431 91 94 91; Via Giulia Augusta; ☉9am-6pm summer, 9am-1pm & 2-6pm winter)

❶ Getting There & Away

Regular SAF buses link Aquileia with Grado (€1.55, 10 minutes) and buses run between here and Udine (€4.75, one hour, 12 daily). Trains to Venice and Trieste run to nearby Cervignano.

Grado

☑0431 / POP 8650

A Friulian surprise, the tasteful beach resort of Grado, 14km south of Aquileia, spreads along a narrow island backed by lagoons and is linked to the mainland by a causeway. Behind the less-than-spectacular beaches you'll find a mazelike medieval centre, criss-crossed by narrow *calli* (lanes).

OFF THE BEATEN TRACK

LAGUNA DI MARANO

Beyond the workaday docks and medieval streets of old Roman fishing port Marano Lagunare, peace and quiet is ensured by two nature reserves: the 14-sq-km **Riserva Naturale della Foci dello Stella**, protecting the marshy mouth of the Stella river and reached by boat, and the **Riserva Naturale della Valle Canal Novo**, a 121-hectare reserve in a former fishing valley. A **visitor centre** (☑0431 6 75 51; www.parks.it/riserva.valle.canal.novo; Via delle Valli 2, Marano Lagunare; adult/reduced €3.50/2.50; ☉9am-5pm Tue-Sun), in a characteristic reed hut, is shared by the two reserves.

Belle époque mansions, beach huts and thermal baths line the cheerful seafront – the greyish local sand is considered curative and used in treatments. Grado comes alive from May to September, but is also prime *passeggiata* (evening stroll) territory on any sunny Sunday.

Beyond Grado's perpetual holiday bustle lie two picturesque nature reserves; a scant 15-minute drive will take you into a dreamlike watery landscape of marsh and reeds, rich in local fauna and with intriguing examples of traditional coastal life.

◎ Sights

Santuario di Barbana
CHURCH

(☑0431 8 04 53; www.santuariodibarbana.it) On the first Sunday in July, a votive procession sails to the Santuario di Barbana, an 8th-century church on a lagoon island. Fishers have done this since 1237 when the Madonna of Barbana was claimed to have miraculously saved the town from the plague. Boats link the sanctuary with Grado. Contact **Motoscafisti Gradesi** (☑0431 8 01 15; www.motoscafistigradesi.it; Riva Scaramuzza; ☉daily summer, Sun only winter) for specific departures and prices.

Basilica di
Sant'Eufemia
BASILICA

(Campo dei Parriarchi; ☉8am-6pm) Grado's beautiful historic core is dominated by this lovely Romanesque basilica, dating back to AD 579; the adjoining lapidary contains 4th- to 5th-century mosaics as well as some 3rd-century Roman sarcophagi facades.

LOCAL KNOWLEDGE

LAGOON LIFE

The final stretch of the Isonzo river's journey into the Adriatic flows through the **Riserva Naturale Regionale Foce dell'Isonzo** (⌨ 0432 99 81 33; www.parks.it/riserva.foce.isonzo; Isola della Cona; adult/reduced €5/3.50; ⊙9am-5pm Fri-Wed), a 23.5-sq-km nature reserve where visitors can birdwatch, horse ride, cycle or walk around salt marshes and mudflats. The visitor centre also has a cafe. Close by, the **Riserva Naturale Regionale della Valle Cavanata** (⌨ 0431 8 82 72; www.vallecavanata.it; ⊙9am-3.30pm Mon, Wed & Fri, noon-6pm Sat & Sun summer, 10.30am-3.30pm Wed-Fri & Sun winter) FREE protects a 1920s fish-farming area and extraordinary birdlife in the east of the lagoon. More than 230 bird species have been observed, including the greylag goose and many wading birds.

Mosaics ARCHAEOLOGICAL SITE
(Piazza Biagio Marin) A corner of Grado's busy town square is home to the mosaic floors of a paleo-Christian basilica. Uncovered during roadworks in 1902, they have, more recently, been made more accessible with a glass footbridge and atmospheric flood lighting in the evening.

🛏 Sleeping

Albergo Alla Spiaggia HOTEL €€
(⌨ 0431 8 48 41; www.albergoallaspiaggia.it; Via Mazzini 2; s/d €110/150; ⊙Apr-Oct; P❄@) The Spiaggia sports a South Beach look, set in a lovely prewar modernist building, with a fresh maritime-toned fit out. It's in a great position, wedged between pedestrian zone, historic centre and beach. Rates outside summer are great value.

🍴 Eating & Drinking

Max'in Botega de Mar SEAFOOD €
(www.maxingrado.it; Piazza Duca d'Aosta 7; share plates €8; ⊙11am-midnight) Snack on a tartine from the extensive menu of seafood-themed toasts (€2.50 to €3.50 each) while downing a few lemon-infused white-wine spritzers at one of the pavement tables. Still hungry? There are fish *polpettone* (meatballs) and large *crudo* plates as well. No bookings, so arrive early.

Trattoria de Toni SEAFOOD €€
(⌨ 0431 8 01 04; www.trattoriadetoni.it; Piazza Duca d'Aosta 37; meals €37; ⊙noon-2.30pm & 6.30-10pm Thu-Tue) This place is undeniably old school and charmingly so, matching genial service with the best local seafood. Sample Grado's signature *boreto,* a lagoon fish stew served with white polenta, or stick with the brimming seafood pasta dishes and super fresh whole grilled fish by the gram, filleted at the table.

Di Sandra WINE BAR
(⌨ 0431 87 60 14; Campo San Niceta 16; ⊙10am-11pm Tue-Sun) Cute hole-in-the-wall bar that attracts a local crew for an early-evening spritzer or three on an old-town corner. Has an excellent chilled white selection available for purchase if you're considering a picnic.

ℹ Information

Tourist Office (⌨ 0431 87 71 11; Viale Dante Alighieri 66; ⊙9am-7pm summer)

ℹ Getting There & Away

Regular **SAF** (⌨ 0432 60 81 11; www.saf.ud.it) buses link Aquileia with Grado (€1.55, 10 minutes) and Palmanova (€3.30, 45 minutes, up to eight daily); buses run between Grado and Udine (€4.75, 1¼ hours, 12 daily) via Aquileia. Trains to Venice and Trieste run to the Cervignano-Aquileia-Grado station, in Cervignano, around 15km away.

Udine

⌨ 0432 / POP 100.500 / ELEV 114M
While reluctantly ceding its premier status to Trieste in the 1950s, this confident, wealthy provincial city remains the spiritual and gastronomic capital of Friuli. Udine gives little away in its sprawling semi-rural suburbs, but encased inside the peripheral ring road lies an infinitely grander medieval centre: a dramatic melange of Venetian arches, Grecian statues and Roman columns. The old town is pristine, but also very lively: bars here are not just for posing, for the Udinese, kicking on is the norm.

As well as its culinary and vinous pleasures, the city also has a handful of excellent museums; this was the second home of Tiepolo and there's a number of his works spread over a few sites. You'll often get to see these marvellous works in only your own company.

Udine

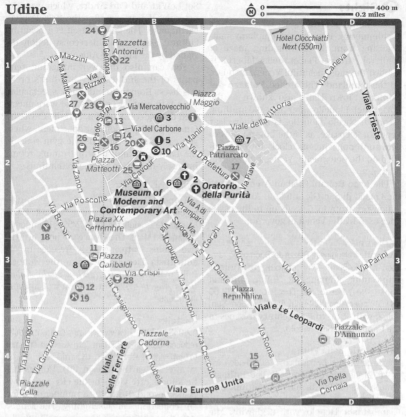

Udine

◎ Top Sights

1 Museum of Modern and Contemporary Art	B2
2 Oratorio della Purità	B2

◎ Sights

3 Castello	B2
4 Cathedral	B2
Galleria d'Arte Antica	(see 3)
5 Loggia di San Giovanni	B2
6 Museo del Duomo	B2
7 Museo Diocesano & Tiepolo Galleries	C2
8 Museo Etnografico del Friuli	A3
9 Palazzo del Comune	B2
10 Piazza della Libertà	B2

⊜ Sleeping

11 Albergo Vechhio Tram	A3
12 Hotel Allegria	A3
13 Locanda Al Cappello	B2
14 Mercatovecchio Luxury Suites	B2
15 Stop & Sleep	C4

⊗ Eating

16 Antica Maddalena	B2
17 Caffe 'Tomaso	C2
18 Fred	A3
19 La Bottega del Borgo	A3
20 Laboratorio del Dolce	B2
21 L'Alimentare	A1
Oggi	(see 13)
22 Trattoria ai Frati	B1

⊖ Drinking & Nightlife

Al Cappello	(see 13)
23 Birreria Gambrinus	A1
24 Caffè Caucigh	A1
25 Caffè Contarena	B2
26 Frasca di Citta	A2
27 Leon d'Oro	A1
28 Osteria al Barnabiti	B3
29 Osteria delle Mortadele	B1

◉ Sights

Piazza della Libertà   PIAZZA

A shimmering Renaissance epiphany materialising from the surrounding maze of medieval streets, Piazza della Libertà is dubbed the most beautiful Venetian square on the mainland. The arched **Palazzo del Comune** (Town Hall), also known as the Loggia del Lionello after its goldsmithing architect, Nicolò Lionello, is another clear Venetian keepsake, as is the **Loggia di San Giovanni** opposite, its clock tower modelled on the one gracing Venice's Piazza San Marco.

The **Arco Bollani** (Bollani Arch), next to the Loggia di San Giovanni, an Andrea Palladio work from 1556, leads up to the castle once used by the Venetian governors.

Cathedral   CATHEDRAL

(www.cattedraleudine.it; Piazza del Duomo; ⊗7am-noon & 4-6.45pm) The chapels of Udine's 13th-century Romanesque-Gothic cathedral house the **Museo del Duomo** (✆0432 50 68 30; ⊗9am-noon & 4-6pm Tue-Sat, 4-6pm Sun) **FREE**, with 13th- to 17th-century frescoes in the Cappella di San Nicolò.

★Oratorio della Purità   CHURCH

(Piazza del Duomo; by donation; ⊗10am-noon, ask for key at the cathedral if closed) The intimate Oratorio della Purità has a beautiful, dramatic ceiling painting of the Assumption by Giambattista Tiepolo, with a glowing Madonna framed by tumbling, rather mischievous looking cherubs. It's a wondrous work. Eight biblical scenes in far more sombre chiaroscuro on the walls are by his son, Giandomenico. The building opened as a theatre in 1680 but the patriarch of Aquileia ordered its transformation 80 years later, repulsed that such a devilish institution existed so close to a cathedral.

★Museum of Modern and Contemporary Art   GALLERY

(Casa Cavazzini; ✆0432 41 47 72; www.civicimuseiudine.it; Via Cavour 14; adult/reduced €5/2.50; ⊗10.30am-7pm Tue-Sun summer, to 5pm winter) Udine's modern and contemporary hub brings together a number of bequests, creating a substantial collection of 20th-century Italian artists, including De Chirico, Morandi, Campigli and Mušič. There's also a surprise stash of notable 20th-century American work, including a Donald Judd, Sol LeWitt and Carl Andre, which were donated by the artists after the 1976 Friulian earthquake. The gallery itself is a beautiful cultural asset, its bold reconstruction designed by the late Gae Aulenti.

You can also discover intriguing remnants of the 16th-century building's previous lives: Roman foundations, spectacular, vivid 14th-century frescoes that were uncovered during construction, and the Cavazzini family's 1930s Rationalist apartment, where you can peek at the old-style gym rings in the bathroom and a formal dining room's intensely-hued folk-art inspired murals.

Museo Diocesano & Tiepolo Galleries   GALLERY

(✆0432 2 50 03; www.musdioc-tiepolo.it; Piazza Patriarcato 1; adult/reduced €7/5; ⊗10am-1pm & 3-6pm Wed-Mon) The drawcard here are the two rooms featuring early frescoes by Giambattista Tiepolo, including the wonderfully over-the-top *Expulsion of the Rebellious Angels* (1726) at the apex of a grand staircase.

Castello   MUSEUM

(✆0432 27 15 91; www.civicimuseiudine.it; adult/reduced €8/4; ⊗10.30am-7pm Tue-Sun summer, to 5pm winter) Rebuilt in the mid-16th century after an earthquake in 1511, Udine's castle affords rare views of the city and snowy peaks beyond. It houses a number of different collections, all fascinating. The **Museo del Risorgimento** is both compellingly designed and set in a series of beautiful rooms, while the **Museo Archeologico** highlights both locally found objects as well as the region's archaeological heyday of the late 19th century.

The sprawling upper floors are given to the **Galleria d'Arte Antica**, which has significant works by Caravaggio (a portrait of St Francis in room 7), Carpaccio (with a work showing the adoration of Christ's blood in room 3) and Tiepolo (several works in room 10). The bulk of the collection is dedicated to lesser-known Friulian painters and religious sculpture.

Museo Etnografico del Friuli   MUSEUM

(✆0432 27 19 20; www.civicimuseiudine.it; Via Grazzano 1; €1; ⊗10.30am-5pm Tue-Sun, to 7pm summer) A small but engrossing museum of daily life, with various exhibitions devoted to the Friulian hearth, unusual spiritual practices, folk medicine, furniture production and dress. The building itself features soaring ceilings, intricate 19th-century woodwork with carved Friulian forest scenes, and its own little canal gurgling by the entrance.

🛌 Sleeping

Central Udine has a number of small, smart midrange hotels, and a couple of notable budget places. If you're driving, there are some good B&Bs and farm-stays in the surrounding suburbs or countryside. The tourist office has online listings.

Locanda Al Cappello GUESTHOUSE €
(www.osteriaalcappello.it; Via Paolo Sarpi 5; s/d €70/110; 🕸🛜) Upstairs from the stalwart spritzers are six cosy bedrooms, all individually decorated with antiques and rich colours; beautiful original beams and fireplaces feature in the larger ones. Bathrooms are both modern and atmospheric and staff give you a genuine Friulian welcome.

Stop & Sleep B&B €
(🕿 339 7561610; www.stopsleepudine.com; Viale Europa Unita 101; s/d €45/65; 🕸🛜) Don't be put off by the unprepossessing locale, this is a rare find. Five colourful, cutely decorated rooms occupy a top-floor apartment and have mosaic-tiled bathrooms, a full kitchen with DIY breakfast supplies and self-catering facilities, and you'll be greeted by the caring, knowledgable owner. One room is en suite, while the other four rooms share two (spotless) bathrooms.

Hotel Allegria BOUTIQUE HOTEL €
(🕿 0432 20 11 16; www.hotelallegria.it; Via Grazzano 18; s/d €75/105; 🅿🕸@) 🍴 This hotel occupies a historic townhouse opposite one of Udine's loveliest little churches. The rooms are large and what might be described as Udinese-organic in style, with lightwood beams, parquetry floors and shuttered windows. Quirk factor points: the hotel has a *bocciofila* (bowling area) on-site.

★ Mercatovecchio Luxury Suites BOUTIQUE HOTEL €€
(🕿 0432 50 00 27; www.mercatovecchio.it; Via del Carbone 1; s €120, d €140-160) Artist Antonella Arlotti has created Udine's ultimate place to stay. Six elegantly designed suites are packed with various extras, from full kitchens in some to coffee machines and luxe linen throughout. A stylish, simple breakfast spread of sweet and savoury pastries, juice

and DIY coffee can be taken at a big table in reception or whisked back to your room.

Albergo Vechhio Tram HOTEL €€
(🕿 0432 50 71 64; www.hotelvecchiotram.com; Via Brenari 28; s/d €80/150; 🕸🛜) This is a small, friendly business-oriented place in a corner townhouse. Rooms are streamlined and contemporary, though the larger ones retain the mansard lines and rafters of the original townhouse. There's a bijou bar and courtyard, and staff are friendly.

Hotel Clocchiatti Next DESIGN HOTEL €€
(🕿 0432 50 50 47; www.hotelclocchiatti.it; Via Cividale 29; s/d classic €80/130, design €150/190; 🅿🕸🛜🏊) Two properties, one location: older-style classic rooms are in the original villa, while the contemporary steel-and-glass 'Next' rooms line up around a pool and outdoor bar in the garden. It's a pleasant 15-minute walk from the centre, with easy access out of the city if you're driving. Breakfasts include luxurious extras like homemade cakes and Mariage Frères teas.

🍴 Eating

Udine's flavours are as intriguing as the city itself. Look out for country-style cheeses (smoked ricotta and Montasio), game, San Daniele and D'Osvaldo prosciutto and delicious gnocchi and dumplings. Open-air cafes and restaurants are dotted around Piazza Matteotti and the surrounding pedestrian streets. Via Paolo Sarpi and its surrounding streets are lined with lively bars, all with bountiful enough snacks to make a meal of.

★ L'Alimentare ITALIAN, DELI €
(🕿 0432 150 37 27; www.lalimentare.it; Via D'Aronco 39; meals €22; ⊙10am-2.30pm Mon, 10am-2.30pm & 4.30-10pm Tue-Sat) A bright, young, cool, casual and friendly addition to Udine's dining scene, L'Alimentare serves up eat in or takeaway meals that strike out beyond the borders. Vegetable curries sit beside Piedmontese meatballs and there's a number of healthy vegetable sides. Friuli's not forgotten though, with excellent local *salumi* and cheese and great Collio wines like Bastianich's Vespa Bianco on offer.

Laboratorio del Dolce PASTRIES €
(🕿 0432 29 93 75; www.laboratoriodeldolce.it; Vicolo Sottomonte 2; cakes €3-20; ⊙8am-12.30pm & 3.30-5.30pm Tue-Sat, 8am-12.30pm Sun) This hidden-away *pasticceria* is one of Udine's

DON'T MISS

RUSTIC TABLES

Friuli's rural cuisine makes the most out of each season's earthy ingredients with bold flavours and traditional *miseria* (poverty) techniques, even when it's taken way upmarket, as it increasingly is.

The game game is strong, while root vegetables and wild greens enhance pastas and sides. The local Montasio cheese turns up in *frico* (which turns up everywhere), be that a cheese-enhanced potato pancake or as chip-like crispy fried, well, cheese.

These much-lauded country restaurants are all within an hour's drive of Udine, either in the Colli Orientali or south towards the coast. Here you'll discover the best of Friulian produce done with exceptional flair.

La Frasca (☑ 0432 67 51 50; Viale Grado 10, Pavia di Udine; meals €35; ⊘ noon-3pm & 7-10pm Thu-Tue) A *frasca* is similar to an *osmize,* a rustic place serving *salumi* (cured meats) and wine, and takes its name from the same practice of hanging a branch out as a shingle. Walter Scarbolo's relaxed roadside dining room has retained the *frasca* experience, and his fans gather for his artisan cured meats, menus that highlight a single seasonal crop, and, naturally, the wonderful Scarbolo wines.

La Subida (☑ 0481 6 05 31; www.lasubida.it; Via Subida, Cormòns; meals €50; ⊘ noon-2.30pm & 7-11pm Sat & Sun, 7-11pm Mon, Thu & Fri) A famous family-run inn, with border-crossing dishes and ingredients – rabbit, boar, flowers and berries – that bring the landscape to the plate in a very modern way. Stay over in one of the stunning forest houses and wake to birdsong and rustling leaves. Across the way there is a casual grill and terrace, with great natural orange wines (skin-contact whites) from Paraschos.

Terre e Vini (☑ 0481 6 00 28; www.terraevini.it; Via XXIV Maggio, Brazzano di Cormons; meals €52; ⊘ noon-2.30pm Tue-Sun, 7-10pm Tue-Sat) The Felluga family are Friulian wine royalty and their cosy 19th-century *osteria* looks out over the plantings. Feast on tripe on Thursdays, salt cod on Fridays and goose stew or herbed frittata any day of the week. Book ahead for Sunday lunch.

best, supplying many restaurants and shops as well as Udinese in the know. There are cakes, pastries and biscuits from the standard Italian repertoire but also a good range of Friulian specialities such as the *gubana*, a yeasted brioche-like cake stuffed with a nutty, boozy, spiced filling.

Oggi   GELATO €

(www.oggigelato.it; Via Paolo Sarpi 3a; cones & cups €2.50-3.50; ⊘ 11am-10pm) If you're lucky, one of the owners of this fabulous Friulian startup, Andrea, will be on hand to take you through Oggi's 0km ethos. Gelato here is made entirely from Friulian milk and local eggs and while there's concessions to favourite flavours and ingredients from across Italy, there's always a local special: try the *biscotto di mais* (cornmeal biscuit) and chocolate.

La Bottega del Borgo   DELI €

(☑ 0432 159 09 73; www.labottegadelborgo.com; Via Grazzano 26; snacks €6-12, meals €15-22; ⊘ 7am-3pm & 4-10.30pm, bar to 11pm Mon-Sat, 8am-1pm Sun) This busy corner deli and wine bar has such a winning way it will make you want to up sticks and settle in Udine.

Locals drop in for morning coffee, pastries and bread, grab supplies for quick at-home dinners, or have things plated up to eat at the back bar area. Wine here represents Friuli's finest and there's always an elegant sparkling on offer.

Caffe 'Tomaso   FRIULIAN €€

(☑ 0432 50 43 87; www.fvgusto.it; Via della Prefettura 16; meals €25-32; ⊘ noon-2.30pm & 7.30-10.30pm Mon-Sat) Local produce and fresh takes on Friulian standards are served in this dark and highly atmospheric dining room filled with bright wooden furniture under a canopy of vintage lamps. Smart young Friulians come here for dishes that are highly in sync with the seasons with lots of vegetable options for pork-overloaded palates. In summer there are tables overlooking a beautiful garden.

Fred   FRIULIAN €€

(☑ 0432 50 50 59; www.enotecafredudine.com; Via del Freddo 6; meals €25-28; ⊘ 11am-3pm & 6-11.30pm Mon-Sat) Fred's dark wood and produce-lined shelves are of the stylish variety but there's a very traditional attention to detail here at what is at heart a serious wine purveyor. Meals will be seasonal and often light and fresh: think a salad of shaved raw asparagus or a simple baked chicken breast.

Trattoria ai Frati
FRIULIAN €€

(☑ 0432 50 69 26; Piazzetta Antonini 5; meals €25-30; ☺ 10am-11pm Mon-Sat) A popular old-style eatery on a cobbled cul-de-sac where you can expect local specialities such as *frico* (fried cheese), pumpkin gnocchi with smoked ricotta, or, in season, white asparagus and fish stew. It's loved by locals, including the university set, for its whopper steaks and its raucous front bar.

Antica Maddalena
FRIULIAN €€

(☑ 0432 50 05 44; Via Pelliccerie 4; meals €25; ☺ noon-3pm & 6-10pm Tue-Sat, 6-10pm Mon) This low-key restaurant, spread over two floors, is known for its quality produce. This is a great place to try *frico* (fried cheese). It's served both ways: *morbido*, a cheese-and-potato omelette, and *croccante*, its snackier crispy-fried form. At *aperitivo* time, Venetian-style seafood *stuzzichini* (snacks) can be devoured at a laneway table.

♉ Drinking & Nightlife

The Udinese have a reputation for being fond of a drink or three, and with such stellar wines produced in their backyard, who can blame them? Wine bars here are unpretentious though serious about even the simplest wine by the glass and *stuzzichini* (bar snacks, usually bread with various toppings) are plentiful. Don't miss the particularly lively cluster of bars around Largo del Pecile.

★ Frasca di Citta
WINE BAR

(Corte Giacomelli 4; ☺ 8am-11pm Tue-Sat) With its '50s terrazzo floors and vintage wooden furniture, you'll feel like you've stumbled into a neighbourhood house party. Hang with the locals at the bar or find a quiet spot in one of many rooms lined with overstuffed bookshelves and black-and-white photographs. There's beer on tap, ridiculously good wines and a menu of stomach-liners like *frico* and polenta.

Birreria Gambrinus
BREWERY

(☑ 0432 50 90 06; www.facebook.com/gambrinus-birreria; Via Paolo Sarpi 18; ☺ 5pm-1am Tue-Sun) Hidden in a small courtyard off the Paolo Sarpi strip, this dark little brewery has a welcoming vibe and some great local artisan beers on tap, including the delicious Gjulia brews from nearby Cividale.

Leon d'Oro
BAR

(☑ 0432 50 87 78; 2 Via dei Rizzani; ☺ 10am-3pm & 6pm-midnight Mon-Sat) A particularly good choice if the weather is balmy (or in any way warm) and the young, good-looking crowd spills out onto the corner terrace, giving it a street-party vibe. Look out for the complimentary plates of fried potatoes doing the rounds: perfect for sopping up the extra *spritz* you're bound to have here.

Caffè Caucigh
BAR

(www.caucigh.com; Via Gemona 36; ☺ 7am-11pm Tue-Sun, to 1am Fri) This ornate, dark-wooded bar is a perfect Udinese compass point – it feels far more like Prague than points south. Regulars take glasses of red to the pavement for a chat with passing strangers. A calendar of jazz acts – Friuli's finest and some international surprises – play from 10pm on Friday nights.

Osteria delle Mortadele
WINE BAR

(Riva Bartolini 8; ☺ 10am-10pm Mon-Sat) Yes, there's a popular restaurant out back, but it's the spill-onto-the-road front bar that will hold your interest. A rock-and-roll soundtrack, excellent wine by the glass, bountiful *stuzzichini* and great company make this a one-drink-or-many destination.

Caffè Contarena
CAFE

(Via Cavour 11; ☺ 8am-9pm Sun-Thu, to 2am Fri & Sat) Beneath the arcades of Palazzo d'Aronco, Contarena's soaring domed ceilings glitter with gold leaf and other Liberty fancy. Designed by Raimondo d'Aronco, a master of the genre and one-time local, it's a glamorous espresso stop or late-night cocktail venue, and beloved by everyone from senior citizens to students.

Al Cappello
WINE BAR

(Via Paolo Sarpi 5; ☺ 10.30am-3pm & 5.30-11pm Tue-Fri, to midnight Sat, 10am-3pm & 5.30-9pm Sun winter) Follow the locals' lead and order what may be northern Italy's most reasonably priced *spritz* (€1 to €2.50) through the window. *Stuzzichini* here are generous enough to constitute dinner, or you can eat well at one of the tables.

Osteria al Barnabiti
BAR

(☑ 347 1747850; www.barnabiti.com; Piazza Garibaldi 3a; ☺ 10am-midnight Mon-Thu, 10am-1am Fri & Sat) Fabulously eccentric decor makes this place rather memorable in a city of atmospheric bars. Great wines, grappa and cheese and meat platters complete the picture.

ℹ Information

Hospital (📞 0432 55 21; Piazza Santa Maria della Misericordia 15) About 2km north of the centre.

Tourist Office (📞 0432 29 59 72; www.turismo fvg.it; Piazza I Maggio 7; ⊙ 9am-7pm Mon-Sat, 10am-1.30pm & 2-6pm Sun) Super helpful office; can book you onto local wine tours.

ℹ Getting There & Away

From the **bus station** (📞 0432 50 69 41; Viale Europa Unita 31), services operated by **SAF** (📞 0432 60 81 11; www.saf.ud.it) go to and from Trieste (€5.75, 1¼ hours, hourly), Aquileia (€3.30, one to 1¼ hours, up to eight daily), Lignano Sabbiadoro (€5.75, 1½ hours, eight to 11 daily) and Grado (€4.05, 1¼ hours, 12 daily). Buses also link Udine and Friuli Venezia Giulia airport (€4.05, one hour, hourly).

From Udine's **train station** (Viale Europa Unita) services run to Trieste (€8.75, one to 1½ hours), Venice (€12.30, 1¾ to 2½ hours, several daily) and Gorizia (€4.05, 25 to 40 minutes, hourly).

Cividale del Friuli

📞 0432 / POP 11,600 / ELEV 138M

Cividale del Friuli, 15km east of Udine, is hauntingly picturesque. Rambling around its dark stone streets makes for a rewarding morning or, better still, stay to enjoy its hearty table and cracking bars. It may be a small country town these days, but in terms of Friulian history and identity it remains hugely significant. Founded by Julius Caesar in 50 BC as Forum de Lulii (ultimately condensed into 'Friuli'), the settlement reached its apex under the Lombards, who arrived in AD 568 and usurped Roman Aquileia a couple of hundred years later. The well-preserved Lombard church here is unique in Europe.

◉ Sights & Activities

Tempietto Longobardo   CHAPEL
(Oratorio di Santa Maria in Valle; 📞 0432 70 08 67; www.tempiettolongobardo.it; Via Monastero Maggiore 34; adult/reduced €4/3; ⊙ 10am-1pm & 3-6pm Mon-Fri, 10am-6pm Sat & Sun summer, to 5pm winter) Cividale's most important sight is this stunning complex that houses the only surviving example of Lombard architecture and artwork in Europe. Its stucco reliefs and choir stalls of the darkest wood are unusual and extremely intimate and moving; some elements date as far back as the 8th century.

Ponte del Diavolo   BRIDGE
(Corso Paolino d'Aquileia) Splitting the town in two is the Devil's Bridge that crosses the emerald green Natisone river. The 22m-high bridge was first constructed in the 15th century with its central arch supported by a rock said to have been thrown into the river by the devil. It was rebuilt post-WWI, after it was blown up by retreating Italian troops.

Cathedral & Museo Cristiano   CATHEDRAL
(Piazza del Duomo; museo adult/reduced €4/3; ⊙ museo 10am-1pm & 3-6pm Wed-Sun) This 16th-century cathedral houses the Museo Cristiano in a small annexe. Its main treasure, the 8th-century stone Altar of Ratchis is a stunning Lombard relic. Sharp-etched carvings, including a be-quiffed oddly modern Jesus with one very piercing stare, dramatically pop against the smooth white background.

Bastianich   WINE
(📞 0432 70 09 43; www.bastianich.com; Via Darnazzacco 44/2, Gagliano) Joe Bastianich is a certified celebrity in the US, but his Italian vineyards, a few minutes' drive from Cividale, remain all about the wine and gracious Friulian hospitality. Pull up a stool at the new tasting room and sniff and swirl your way through drops made from the surrounding plantings and the Bastianich holdings in nearby Buttrio.

🛏 Sleeping

Orsone   B&B €€
(📞 0432 73 20 53; www.orsone.com; Via Darnazzacco 63; s/d €80/150) A short drive from town, Orsone has a handful of simple, smart rooms upstairs from its vineyard restaurant. Dark wood furniture and beams contrast with crisp white linen and an otherwise contemporary sensibility. It's a fabulously peaceful spot and you won't go hungry or thirsty either.

🍴 Eating & Drinking

Al Duomo   GELATO €
(Piazza Duomo 2; cones & cups €1.30-2.50; ⊙ 10.30am-1pm & 2.30-9.30pm) Cividale is made for gelato-licking strolls and this cute artisan gelateria is the the town's best. You'll find all your favourite flavours but also some Friulian specialities, including the *gubana* (from the nut-filled Slovenian-style cake of the same name) and a deeply woodsy dark honey and walnut.

Osteria alla Terrazza   FRIULIAN €
(📞 338 3957303; www.facebook.com/osteria.alla-terrazza; Via Stretta Cornelio Gallo 3; meals €20; ⊙ 8am-7.30pm Wed-Mon) A self-appointed champion of all things Friulian, this street-

food style *osteria* and its laneway 'terrace' serves up little trays of *salumi*, meat balls, polenta and *frico*, with well-priced wines by the glass. It also has a range of vac-packed *frico* to take away.

Antico Leon d'Oro
FRIULIAN €

(☑ 0432 73 11 00; Via Borgo di Ponte 24; meals €20-25; ☺ 12-2.30pm & 7-10.30pm Thu-Tue) Eat in the courtyard of this friendly, festive place, just over the Ponte del Diavolo, and, if you're in luck, watch a polenta cook stir the pot. Dishes here couldn't be more regional: sublime d'Osvaldo *proscuitto crudo*, seasonal pasta enlivened with asparagus and *sclupit* (a mountain herb), a Friulian tasting plate of *frico*, salami and herbed frittata, and roast venison.

Orsone
FRIULIAN, BURGERS €€

(☑ 0432 73 20 53; www.orsone.com; Via Darnazzacco 63, Fraz, Gagliano; meals €35, burgers €10-13; ☺ 12-2.30pm & 7-10.30pm Wed-Sun) Nestled among the vines, Joe Bastianich's once fine diner has gone casual. Come here for a mouthwatering menu of local comfort-food dishes – slow cooked eggs and truffles, ravioli, tartare – alongside Italian-American favourites, like spaghetti and meatballs, a veal chop and crab cakes. There's also a stellar list of burgers and sandwiches.

Elliott
FRIULIAN €€

(☑ 0432 75 13 83; www.elliothotel.it; Via Orsaria 50, Buttrio; meals €25-30; ☺ 10am-3pm & 5pm midnight) Beautiful seafood dishes (using produce from nearby Grado) are a surprise here but there's also a good range of bold-flavoured, prettily plated risottos, pastas, steaks and duck dishes on offer at this smart restaurant, wine bar and hotel.

Shopping

Tirare
CERAMICS

(Via Ristori 12; ☺ 9.30am-12.30pm & 3.30-7pm Tue-Sat) Working with ancient Roman and Middle Eastern techniques, local ceramic artist Stefania Zurchi creates sculptures, reliefs and beautifully decorated utilitarian objects. Her palette evokes the Friulian landscape, moody indigos and olives cut through with a flash of bright oxide yellow and dusty pinks. Her 'girl' figures representing the seasons are highly sought after, as are her touching Madonna-and-child reliefs.

ℹ Information

Tourist Office (☑ 0432 71 04 60; Piazza Paolo Diacono 10; ☺ 10am-1pm & 3-5pm, later in summer) Info on walks around the medieval core.

ℹ Getting There & Away

Private (and cute) trains run by **Ferrovie Udine Cividale** (☑ 0432 58 18 44; www.ferroviciudine-cividale.it) connect Cividale with Udine (€2.75, 20 minutes), at least hourly.

San Daniele del Friuli
☑ 0432 / POP 8200

Hilltop San Daniele sits above an undulating landscape that comes as a relief after the Venetian plains, with the Carnic Alps jutting up suddenly on the horizon. While ham is undoubtedly the town's raison d'être, there's a broad gastronomic bent in play, with a ridiculous number of good *alimentari* (grocery stores), as well as a number of new culinary industries springing up, such as sustainably farmed local trout.

HAMMING IT UP

There are two world-revered prosciuttos manufactured in Italy: the lean, deliciously nutty (and more famous) ham from Parma, and the dark, exquisitely sweet Prosciutto di San Daniele. It might come as a surprise to find that the latter – Friuli Venezia Giulia's greatest culinary gift to the world – comes from a village of only 8000 people, where it is salted and cured in 27 *prosciuttifici* (ham-curing plants) safeguarded by EU regulations.

Standards are strict. San Daniele's prosciutto is made only from the thighs of pigs raised in a small number of northern Italian regions. Salt is the only method of preservation allowed – no freezing, chemicals or other preservatives can be used. The X factor is, of course, *terroir*, the land itself. Some *prosciuttifici* claim it's the cool, resinous Alpine air meeting the Adriatic's humid, brackish breezes that define their product, others argue that it's about San Daniele's fast-draining soil: such effective ventilation makes for perfect curing conditions.

In late June, the town holds the Aria di San Daniele Festa (p426), a multiday annual ham festival. San Daniele's tourist office (p426) has a list of *prosciuttifici* that also welcome visitors year-round; call ahead to book your tasting.

⊙ Sights

Chiesa di San Antonio Abate　　CHURCH
(Via Garibaldi) Frescoes are one of San Daniele's other fortes besides porky products and you'll find some colourful examples etched by Pellegrino da San Daniele, aka Martino da Urbino (1467–1547), in the small Romanesque Chiesa di San Antonio Abate.

✿ Festivals & Events

Aria di San Daniele　　FOOD & DRINK
(Le Festa; www.ariadisandaniele.it; ☉ late Jun) San Daniele holds the Aria di Festa, a four-day feeding frenzy each summer. *Prosciuttifici* do mass open house tours and tastings, musicians entertain and everyone tucks in.

✕ Eating & Drinking

Ai Bintars　　ITALIAN €
(☑ 0432 95 73 22; www.aibintars.com; Via Trento Trieste 67; mains €15-25; ☉ 9am-11pm Fri-Tue, 9am-3pm Wed; P) No menu, no fuss, no kerbside appeal, Ai Bintars simply serves the best prosciutto and salami alongside small plates of marinated vegetables, local cheeses and generous hunks of bread.

Osteria di Tancredi　　FRIULIAN €€
(☑ 0432 94 15 94; www.osteriaditancredi.it; Via Sabotino 10; plates €8-10, meals €30; ☉ noon-10pm Thu-Tue) Serves up Friulian classics, *cjalcions* (filled pasta), *frico* and apple gnocchi in a cosy room that pares back the rustic touches to a pleasing simplicity.

Enoteca la Trappola　　WINE BAR
(☑ 0432 94 20 90; Via Cairoli 2) Head to dark and moody Trappola for crowd-pleasing platters of prosciutto (from €6), cheese (€6 to €8) or smoked trout (€8) and well-priced wine by the glass with a very local, very vocal crowd.

Il Michelaccio　　BAR
(Piazza Vittorio Emanuele 1; ☉ 10am-1am) This is the bar that's open when all the genteel wine bars are shuttered (and where all the hospitality staff head after their shifts are done), but it's also a great all day hang out with good coffee, great spritzes and a none-too-shabby list of wines by the glass.

ⓘ Information

Tourist Office (☑ 0432 94 07 65; www.turismofvg.it; Via Roma 3; ☉ 9am-1pm & 2.30-6.30pm Mon-Fri, 10am-1pm & 3.30-6.30pm Sat & Sun)

ⓘ Getting There & Away

Regular buses run to San Daniele from Udine (€4.75, 45 minutes), 25km to the southeast.

The Carnic Alps

Stretching as far west as the Veneto Dolomites and as far north as the border with Austria, Carnia is intrinsically Friulian – the language is widely spoken here in lieu of Italian – and named after its original Celtic inhabitants, the Carnics. Geographically, it contains the western and central parts of the Carnic Alps and presents both down-to-earth ski areas, wild and beautiful walking country, and curious, pristinely rustic villages.

Sauris

☑ 0433 / POP 430 / ELEV 1212M
Up towards Friuli's far northwest border, a twisted road takes you past the plunging Lumiei Gorge to emerge at the intensely blue **Lago di Sauris**. Another 4km west is the village of **Sauris di Sotto** and another 4km on, eight switchbacks and a few dripping rock tunnels included, is the breathtakingly pretty **Sauris di Sopra**. These twin hamlets (in German, Zahre) are an island of unique dark timber houses and German-speakers, and are known for their fine hams, sausages and locally brewed beer. There are also lots of good walking trails, much fresh air and exquisite silence, plus in winter you're close to good, uncrowded local ski runs.

⌂ Sleeping

Albergo Diffuso Sauris　　APARTMENT €
(www.albergodiffusosauris.com; 2-6 bed apt €80-180) Part of the larger *alberghi diffusi* (or scattered hotels) movement in the Carnic region, the Albergo Diffuso Sauris offers various apartments in a collection of refurbished village houses, all constructed in the unusual local vernacular style, with deep verandahs screened with horizontal slats.

★**Maanja Suites**　　BOUTIQUE HOTEL €€
(☑ 0433 8 62 27; www.sauris811.it; Località La Maina 10; ste €150-210; P @ 🖾) Overlooking the bright aqua Lago di Sauris and surrounded by dark pine forests and Alpine peaks, this new addition to a traditional mountain has a handful of stylishly sparse but comfortable suites. Most have full kitchens and some come with whirlpools and covered balconies.

Borgo Eibn LODGE €€€
(✆ 392 0027191; Stavoli Ander Eibn 80, Sauris di Sotto; ste €250-290) In a secluded location, up a steep winding road from the village, Borgo Eibn has created a folk-luxe playground. Three large chalets of reclaimed timber and local stone house 15 apartments and suites which have traditional stufa fireplaces, wooden furniture and contemporary textiles.

✗ Eating

Speck Stube DELI, FRIULIAN €
(Via Sauris di Sopra 44, Sauris di Sopra; meals €8-12; ⊙ bar 7.30am-12.30pm Mon & Thu, to 8.30pm Fri-Sun & Wed, shop 7.30am-12.30pm Mon-Sat, 4-7pm Tue, Wed, Fri & Sat) On one side, this village epicentre will sell you cheese, wine, the fabulous local Wolf-brand prosciutto or a bottle of wine, on the other grab your morning espresso, afternoon beer or settle in for a hearty dinner of local meats, cheese, *frico* and polenta.

Maanja Restaurant FRIULIAN €€
(✆ 0433 86 227, www.sauris811.it, Località La Maina 10; meals €25-32) Part of the small Maanja hotel, this is a surprisingly urban space, with dramatic black slate floors, long rustic-modern fir tables and contemporary Italian chairs, with an equally dramatic view out floor to ceiling windows. The food too has a casual sophistication.

ℹ Getting There & Away

There is no direct public transport connection to Sauris, rather buses run from Tolmezzo or Gemona, usually with a change at Ampezzo. By car it's an hour to an hour and a half via the A23 to Ampezzo and then by regional roads.

The Giulie Alps

Named after Julius Caesar, the Giulie Alps' dramatic limestone monoliths bear more than a passing resemblance to their more famous Dolomite cousins. These rugged, frigid peaks are shared with Slovenia, with the Triglavski Narodni Park just across the border. Though there's been some recent development of the region, including a cross-border ski lift, the area is still relatively pristine and retains a wildness often lacking in the west.

It has excellent hiking terrain with some of the loneliest, most scenic trails in Italy. As the area stands at the meeting point of three different cultures, multilingual skills can come in handy. Hikers should get ready to swap their congenial *salve* (Italian) for a *grüss gott* (German) or *dober dan* (Slovenian).

Tarvisio

Tarvisio (Tarvis in Friulian and German) is 7km short of the Austrian border and 11km from Slovenia. Down to earth and prettily wedged into the Val Canale between the Giulie and eastern Carnic Alps, it's a good base for both winter and summer activities.

Tarvisio is famous for its historic Saturday market, which has long attracted day trippers from Austria and Slovenia and is now open during the week too. It has a definite border-town buzz, though since the advent of Schengen, the trade is mostly in dubious-looking leather jackets.

Sella Nevea SKIING
(www.sellanevea.net) The Sella Nevea resort has a number of satisfying red runs and respected freeride and backcountry skiing.

Laghi di Fusine HIKING
The Fusine lakes lie within mirror-signalling distance of the Slovenian border and are perennially popular with hikers in summer and cross-country skiers and snowshoers in winter. The two lakes – Lago Superiore and Lago Inferiore – are ringed by paths and encased in the Parco Naturale di Fusine.

No Borders Music Festival MUSIC
(www.nobordersmusicfestival.com; ⊙ Jul) Indie-ish music festival with at least one big-name headliner each year. There are good-value hotel and ticket deals (€50 to €60).

Hotel Edelhof HOTEL €€
(✆ 0428 4 00 81; www.hoteledelhof.com; Via Armando Diaz 13; s/d €75/140; P 🕏) Situated by the lifts with large rooms furnished with hand-painted wooden furniture and a spa. Seven-night minimum in high season.

ℹ Information

Tourist Office (✆ 0428 21 35; Via Roma 14; ⊙ 9am-1pm & 3-7pm Mon-Sat, 9am-1pm Sun winter, reduced hours summer) The helpful tourist office has trekking maps and details on Alpine conditions.

ℹ Getting There & Away

Trains connect Tarvisio with Udine (€9.65, 1¼ hour, up to seven daily).

Coffee Culture

From Trapani to Tarvisio, every day begins with coffee. A quick cup from a stove-top Moka pot might be the first, but the second (third, fourth and fifth) will inevitably be from a neighbourhood bar. Italians consider these visits a moment to pause, but rarely linger. It's a stand-up sniff, swirl and gulp, a *buon proseguimento* to the barista, and on your way.

Origins

Coffee first turned up in mid-16th-century Venice, then a few years later in Trieste, care of the Viennese. While basic espresso technology made an appearance in the early 19th century, it wasn't until 1948 that Gaggia launched the first commercial machines. These reliably delivered full-bodied espresso shots with the characteristic aromatic *crema*: Italy was hooked. The machines, in fact the whole espresso ritual, spoke of a hopeful modernity as Italy reimagined itself as an urban, industrial postwar nation.

Today's Cup

Italy's superior coffee-making technology took seed around the world, carried by postwar immigrants. Global coffee culture today may embrace latte art and new brewing technologies, but in Italy tradition holds sway. Italians still overwhelmingly favour Arabica and Robusta blends with a dense *crema*, high caffeine jolt and, crucially, a price point everyone can afford. Roasts remain dark and often bitter – Italians routinely sweeten coffee – but Italian baristas use far less coffee per

1. Espresso coffee being made
2. Streetside cafe, Rome
3. Coffee beans from Trieste's Illy brand

shot and ultra smooth blends. Espresso is the overwhelming order of choice and takeaway cups uncommon. Why? Clutching a coffee on the move misses coffee's dual purpose for Italians: contemplation and social belonging.

Bean Hunting

Finding your ultimate Italian espresso is trial and error, albeit enjoyable and inexpensive. Best-of lists will only get you so far: Rome's famed Caffè Sant'Eustachio, Florence's Gilli and Naples' Caffè Gambrinus will almost certainly get it right, but so too will many small town bars. Take note of *torrefazionie* (bean roasters): global giants like Trieste's Illy and Turin's Lavazza are reliable, but do seek out regional favourites, such as Verona's Giamaica, Parma's Lady, Piemonte's Caffè Vergnano and Pascucci from Le Marche.

BARISTA BASICS

➡ **Caffè, espresso** Short shot of black coffee.

➡ **Ristretto** Short espresso.

➡ **Lungo** Long espresso.

➡ **Americano** Espresso with added hot water.

➡ **Macchiato** Espresso 'stained' with a little milk.

➡ **Cappuccino** Espresso with steamed milk.

➡ **Cappuccino scuro** Strong (dark) cappuccino.

➡ **Marochino** Small cappuccino with cocoa.

➡ **Latte macchiato** Dash of coffee in steamed milk.

➡ **Deca** Decaf.

➡ **Corretto** Spiked espresso, usually with grappa.

Emilia-Romagna & San Marino

Best Places to Eat

➡ Trattoria da Amerigo (p442)

➡ All'Osteria Bottega (p441)

➡ Ca' de Vèn (p466)

➡ Tratorria di Via Serra (p441)

➡ Antica Corte Pallavicina (p457)

Best Places to Sleep

➡ Prendiparte B&B (p439)

➡ B&B Pio (p453)

➡ Bologna nel Cuore (p438)

➡ Alchimia B&B (p461)

➡ Foresteria San Benedetto (p451)

Why Go?

Sweeping north from the Apennines to the fertile Po valley, Emilia-Romagna boasts some of Italy's most hospitable people, some of its most productive land, some of its fastest vehicles (Ferrari, Ducati, Maserati and Lamborghini call Emilia-Romagna home) and most soul-satisfying food. Since antiquity, the verdant Po lowlands have sown enough agricultural riches to feed a nation and finance an unending production line of lavish products: luxury cars, regal *palazzi* (mansions), Romanesque churches, prosperous towns and a gigantic operatic legacy (Verdi and Pavarotti, no less).

You can eat like a Roman emperor here, in the birthplace of *tagliatelle al ragù*, pumpkin-filled *cappellacci* pasta, Parma prosciutto, balsamic vinegar and *parmigiano reggiano* (Parmesan). And then there's Emilia-Romagna's treasure trove of oft-neglected destinations: Bologna with its photogenic porticoes, Ravenna with its mosaics, posh Parma and the wealthy micronation of San Marino. Wherever you go, you'll be welcomed with the warmth of Emilia-Romagna's people.

When to Go
Bologna

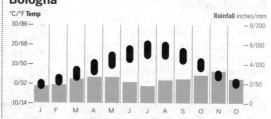

May Enjoy pleasant cycling weather on the Po plains and avoid summer crowds on Rimini's beaches.

Jun–Aug Summer music festivals fill the agenda from Bologna to Ravenna.

Sep Ideal hiking conditions in Parco Nazionale dell'Appennino Tosco-Emiliano.

EMILIA-ROMAGNA

Bologna

📞 051 / POP 380,000

Fusing haughty elegance with down-to-earth grit and one beautifully colonnaded medieval grid, Bologna is a city of two intriguing halves. One side is a hard-working, hi-tech city located in the super-rich Po valley where suave opera-goers waltz out of regal theatres and into some of the nation's finest restaurants. The other is a bolshie, politically edgy city that hosts the world's oldest university and is famous for its graffiti-embellished piazzas filled with mildly inebriated students swapping Gothic fashion tips.

No small wonder Bologna has earned so many historical monikers. *La Grassa* (the fat one) celebrates a rich food legacy (*ragù* or bolognese sauce was first concocted here). *La Dotta* (the learned one) doffs a cap to the city university founded in 1088. *La Rossa* (the red one) alludes to the ubiquity of the terracotta medieval buildings adorned with miles of porticoes, as well as the city's longstanding penchant for left-wing politics.

👁 Sights

⭐ **San Colombano –
Collezione Tagliavini**   MUSEUM

(📞 051 1993 6366; www.genusbononiae.it; Via Parigi 5; adult/reduced €7/5; ⏱ 11am-7pm Tue-Sun) An absolutely stunningly restored church with original frescoes and a medieval crypt rediscovered in 2007, the San Colombano hosts a wonderful collection of over 80 musical instruments amassed by the octogenarian organist Luigi Tagliavini. Many of the assembled harpsichords, pianos and oboes date from the 1500s and, even more surprisingly, are still in full working order. Listen out for regular free concerts and charge up your phone – this is one of Bologna's most photogenic museums.

⭐ **Museo della Storia di Bologna**   MUSEUM

(📞 051 1993 6370; www.genusbononiae.it; Via Castiglione 8; adult/reduced €10/8; ⏱ 10am-7pm Tue-Sun) Walk in a historical neophyte and walk out an A-grade honours student in Bologna's golden past. This magnificent interactive museum, opened in 2012 and skillfully encased in the regal Palazzo Pepoli, is – in a word – an 'education'. Using a 3D film, a mock-up of an old Roman canal and super-modern presentations of ancient relics, the innovative displays start in a futuristic open-plan lobby and progress through 35 chronologically themed rooms that make Bologna's 2500-year history at once engaging and epic.

There are many hidden nuggets (who knew Charles V was crowned Holy Roman Emperor in the city?). The only glaring omission is much talk of Mussolini, who was born 'down the road' in Forlì.

⭐ **Basilica di Santo Stefano**   CHURCH

(www.abbaziasstefano.wixsite.com/abbaziasstefano; Via Santo Stefano 24; ⏱ 8am-7pm) Bologna's most unique religious site is this atmospheric labyrinth of interlocking ecclesiastical structures, whose architecture spans centuries of Bolognese history and incorporates Romanesque, Lombard and even ancient Roman elements. Originally there were seven churches – hence the basilica's nickname Sette Chiese – but only four remain intact today: Chiesa del Crocefisso, Chiesa della Trinità, Chiesa del Santo Sepolcro and Santi Vitale e Agricola.

Entry is via the 11th-century **Chiesa del Crocefisso**, which houses the bones of San Petronio and leads through to the **Chiesa del Santo Sepolcro**. This austere octagonal structure probably started life as a baptistery. Next door, the **Cortile di Pilato** is named after the central basin in which Pontius Pilate is said to have washed his hands after condemning Christ to death. In fact, it's an 8th-century Lombard artefact. Beyond the courtyard, the **Chiesa della Trinità** connects to a modest cloister and a small **museum**. The fourth church, the **Santi Vitale e Agricola**, is the city's oldest. Incorporating recycled Roman masonry and carvings, the bulk of the building dates from the 11th century. The considerably older tombs of two saints in the side aisles once served as altars.

⭐ **Basilica di San Petronio**   CHURCH

(www.basilicadisanpetronio.org; Piazza Galvani 5; photo pass €2; ⏱ 7.45am-6.30pm) Bologna's hulking Gothic basilica is Europe's sixth-largest church, measuring 132m by 66m by 47m. Work began on it in 1390, but it was never finished and still today its main facade remains incomplete. Inside, look for the huge sundial that stretches 67.7m down the eastern aisle. Designed in 1656 by Gian Cassini and Domenico Guglielmi, this was instrumental in discovering the anomalies of the Julian calendar and led to the creation of the leap year.

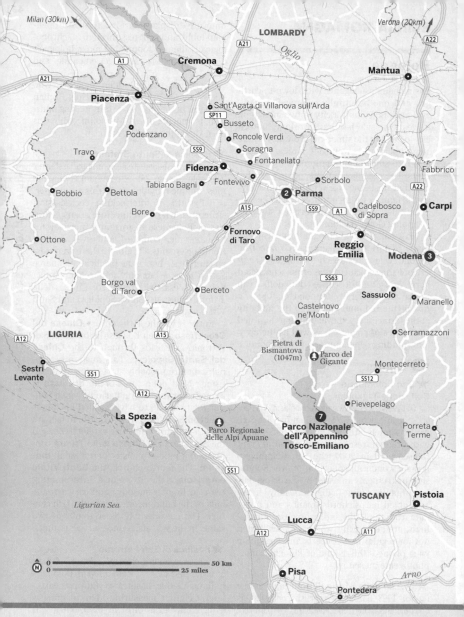

Emilia-Romagna & San Marino Highlights

1 **Ravenna** (p462) Basking in the reflected glow of Italy's most gorgeous mosaics.

2 **Parma** (p452) Soothing your senses with opera or an early-evening *aperitivi* among spectacular religious sights and iconic gastronomy.

3 **Modena** (p446) Savouring a long, slow and delicious lunch at one of the city's down-to-earth eateries.

4 **Bologna** (p431) Strolling under the graceful porticoes, climbing the tilted towers and indulging in the fabled gastronomy of this vibrant university city.

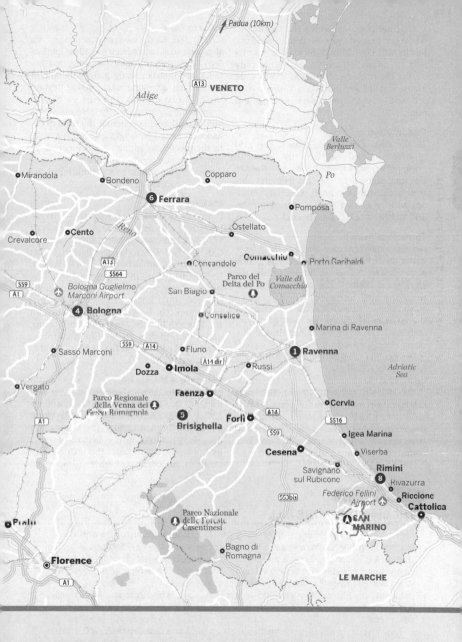

Original plans called for the basilica to be larger than Rome's St Peter's Basilica, but in 1561 Pope Pius IV blocked construction by commissioning a new university on the basilica's eastern flank. If you walk along Via dell'Archiginnasio you can still see semi-constructed apses poking out oddly.

Quadrilatero
AREA

To the east of Piazza Maggiore, the grid of streets around Via Clavature (Street of Locksmiths) sits on what was once Roman Bologna. Known as the Quadrilatero, this compact district is a great place for a wander with its market stalls, happening cafes and lavishly stocked gourmet delis.

Torre degli Asinelli
TOWER

(www.duetorribologna.com; Piazza di Porta Ravegnana; €5; ⊘ 9.30am-7.30pm summer, to 5.30pm winter) Bologna's two leaning towers are the city's main symbol. The taller of the two, the 97.2m-high Torre degli Asinelli, is open to the public, though it's not advisable for the weak-kneed (there are 498 newly re-stabilised steps) or for superstitious students (local lore says if you climb it you'll never graduate). Built by the Asinelli family between 1109 and 1119, it today leans 2.2m off vertical.

Its shorter twin, the 47m-high **Torre Garisenda** is sensibly out of bounds given its drunken 3.2m tilt. Tickets must be purchased in advance in 45-minute increments from the official web site or at Bologna Welcome (no tickets are sold on site).

Palazzo Fava
GALLERY

(☑051 1993 6305; www.genusbononiae.it; Via Manzoni 2; adult/reduced €13/9; ⊘10am-7pm Tue-Sun) This exhibition space encased in a Renaissance mansion is frequently the site of blockbuster temporary art shows. Beyond these special exhibits, the palace's biggest draw is the group of heavily frescoed rooms on the 1st floor, in particular the **Sala di Giasone**, painted in bright naturalistic style by the precocious young Carraccis (brothers Annibale and Agostino and their cousin Ludovico) in the 1580s (to say nothing of the stunning coffered ceiling).

MAMbo
MUSEUM

(Museo d'Arte Moderna di Bologna; www.mambo-bologna.org; Via Don Minzoni 14; adult/reduced €6/4, with temporary exhibitions €10/8; ⊘10am-6pm Tue, Wed & Sun, to 7pm Thu, Fri & Sat) Avant-gardes, atheists and people who've had their fill of dark religious art can seek solace in one of Bologna's newer museums (opened 2007) housed in a cavernous former municipal bakery. Its permanent and rotating exhibits showcase the work of up-and-coming Italian artists. Entrance to the permanent collection is free the first Sunday of every month.

Pinacoteca Nazionale
GALLERY

(www.pinacotecabologna.beniculturali.it; Via delle Belle Arti 56; adult/reduced €6/3; ⊘8.30am-7.30pm Tue-Sun Sep-Jun, 8.30am-2pm Tue-Wed & 1.45-7.30pm Thu-Sun Jul-Aug) The city's main art gallery has a powerful collection of works by Bolognese artists from the 14th century onwards, including a number of important

---

DON'T MISS

THE CHURCH ON THE HILL

About 3.5km southwest of the city centre, the hilltop **Basilica Santuario della Madonna di San Luca** (www.santuariobeataverginesanluca.org; Via di San Luca 36; ⊘7am-12.30pm & 2.30-6pm) occupies a powerful and appropriately celestial position overlooking the teeming red-hued city below. The church houses a black representation of the Virgin Mary, supposedly painted by St Luke and transported from the Middle East to Bologna in the 12th century. The 18th-century sanctuary is connected to the city walls by the world's longest portico, held aloft by 666 arches, beginning at Piazza di Porta Saragozza.

The most direct way to reach the basilica is on the **San Luca Express** (☑051 35 08 53; www.cityredbus.com; adult/reduced €10/5), a tourist 'train' that leaves Piazza Maggiore six times daily, four days a week during peak tourist season. Alternatively, take bus 20 from the city centre to Villa Spada, where you can catch minibus 58 up to the sanctuary, or continue one more stop on bus 20 to the Meloncello arch and walk the remaining 2km under the arches.

canvases by the late 16th-century Carraccis (brothers Annibale and Agostino and their cousin Ludovico). Among the founding fathers of Italian baroque art, the Carraccis were deeply influenced by the Counter-Reformation sweeping through Italy in the latter half of the 16th century. Much of their work is religious and their imagery is often highly charged and emotional.

Palazzo Comunale
HISTORIC BUILDING

(Piazza Maggiore 6) **FREE** The palace that forms the western flank of Piazza Maggiore has been home to the Bologna city council since 1336. A salad of architectural styles, it owes much of its current look to makeovers in the 15th and 16th centuries. On the 2nd floor you'll find the *palazzo*'s **Collezioni Comunali d'Arte** (051 219 39 98; adult/reduced €5/3; 9am-6.30pm Tue-Fri, from 10am Sat & Sun) with its interesting collection of 13th- to 19th-century paintings, sculpture and furniture. Don't miss the city scale model of medieval Bologna in Room 9, with hundreds of offensive/defensive towers, similar to today's Torre degli Asinelli, jutting above rooftops all over the city.

Palazzo Poggi
PALACE

(www.museopalazzopoggi.unibo.it; Via Zamboni 33; adult/reduced €5/3; 10am 4pm Tue Fri, 10.30am 5.30pm Fri & Sat) Three university museums are housed inside this 14th-century palace. At **Museo di Palazzo Poggi**, you can peruse waxwork uteri in the Obstetrics exhibition, giant tortoise shells in the Natural Sciences collection and impressive exhibitions dedicated to ships and old maps, military architecture and physics.

At the guided-tour-only **Observatory Museum** (adult/reduced €5/3), you can climb Bologna's first tower built for scientific study (as opposed to defences), which was erected in 1726. Reserve ahead for three daily tours Tuesday through Friday (10.45am, 12.15pm and 3pm) and two on weekends (11am and 3pm). The free **European Student Museum (MeuS)** covers student life from medieval times to the 1960s.

Teatro Anatomico
HISTORIC BUILDING

(www.archiginnasio.it/teatro.htm; Piazza Galvani 1; admission €3; 10am-6pm Mon-Fri, to 7pm Sat, 10am-2pm Sun) Housed in Palazzo dell'Archiginnasio, the fascinating 17th-century Teatro Anatomico is where public body dissections were held under the sinister gaze of an Inquisition priest, ready to intervene if proceedings became too spiritually compromising. Cedar-wood tiered seats surround a central marble-topped table while a sculptured Apollo looks down from the ceiling. The canopy above the lecturer's chair is supported by two skinless figures carved into the wood.

Down the hall, and covered by the same entrance ticket, is the **Aula Magna di Stabat Mater**, a grand former classroom.

Basilica di San Domenico
CHURCH

(Piazza San Domenico 13; 9am-noon & 3.30-6pm) Built in 1238, this basilica shelters the remains of San Domenico, the founder of the Dominican order. Along the right aisle, the **Cappella di San Domenico** houses the saint's elaborate sarcophagus, designed by Nicola Pisano and later added to by a host of artists. Famous ghosts present here include Michelangelo, who carved the angel on the right of the altar when he was only 19, and Mozart, who spent a month at Bologna's music academy and occasionally played the church's organ.

Oratorio di Santa Cecilia
CHURCH

(Via Zamboni 15; 10am-1pm & 2-6pm, to 7pm summer) This is one of Bologna's unsung gems. Inside, the magnificent 16th-century frescoes by Lorenzo Costa depicting the life and technicolour death of St Cecilia and her husband Valeriano are in remarkably good nick, their colours vibrant and their imagery bold and unabashed.

Tours

Curious Appetite's La Grassa Food Tour
FOOD & DRINK

(www.thecuriousappetite.com; 3hr tours €95) Created by authoritative Italian American foodie (and food critic) Coral Sisk, who started in Florence (p500), these excellent themed food tours (cocktails, markets, progressive dining crawls etc) closely follow all the movements (slow, artisan, farm-to-table) and take no more than six on culinary journeys through several of Emilia-Romagna's 40-plus consortium-protected DOP traditional products. Tours depart at 10am Monday to Friday. Skip breakfast.

Courses

Bologna Cucina
COOKING

(335 217893; www.cookingschoolbologna.com; Via Castiglione 4) A top-rated Bologna cooking

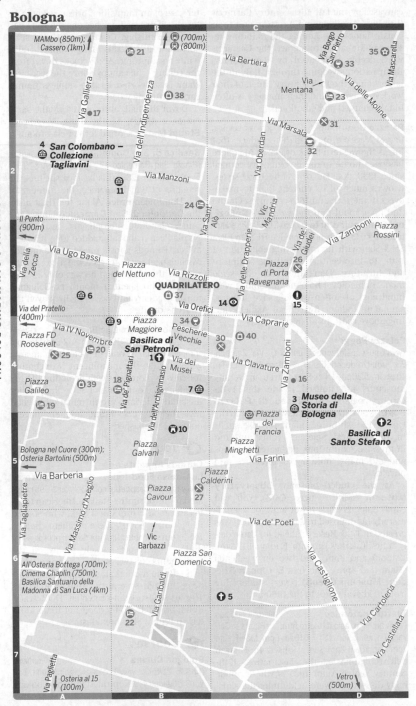

MAMbo (850m);
Cassero (1km)

21

(700m);
(800m)

Via Bertiera

Via Borgo
San Pietro

35

33

Via Galliera

17

Via
Mentana

Via delle Moline

38

23

Via Mascarella

**4 San Colombano –
Collezione
Tagliavini**

Via dell'Indipendenza

Via Oberdan

Via Marsala

31

32

Il Punto
(900m)

11

Via Manzoni

Via Sant'Alò

Vic
Mandria

Via Zamboni

Piazza
Rossini

Via della Zecca

Via Ugo Bassi

24

Via de'
Giudei

Piazza
del Nettuno

Via Rizzoli

Piazza
di Porta
Ravegnana

26

Via del Pratello
(400m)

6

QUADRILATERO

37

Via delle Draperie

14

15

Piazza FD
Roosevelt

Via IV Novembre

9

Piazza
Maggiore

Via Orefici

Via Caprarie

25

20

**Basilica di
San Petronio**

34

Pescherie
Vecchie

40

30

Piazza
Galileo

39

1

Via dei
Musei

Via Clavature

Via Zamboni

16

19

18

Via de' Pignattari

7

Via dell'Archiginnasio

**3 Museo della
Storia di
Bologna**

Bologna nel Cuore (300m);
Osteria Bartolini (500m)

10

Piazza
del
Francia

2

**Basilica di
Santo Stefano**

Piazza
Galvani

Piazza
Minghetti

Via Barberia

Via Farini

Via Tagliapietre

Via Massimo d'Azeglio

Piazza
Cavour

Piazza
Calderini

27

Via de' Poeti

Vic
Barbazzi

Piazza
Cavour

Via de' Poeti

All'Osteria Bottega (700m);
Cinema Chaplin (750m);
Basilica Santuario della
Madonna di San Luca (4km)

Piazza San
Domenico

5

Via Garibaldi

Via Castiglione

Via Cartoleria

22

Via Castellata

Via Paglietta

Osteria al 15
(100m)

Vetro
(500m)

school with classes in English. Three-hour introductory courses range from €45 to €98 per person depending on the size of the class; pricier courses with professional chefs start at €175.

La Vecchia Scuola Bolognese COOKING
(☑ 051 649 15 76; www.lavecchiascuola.com; Via Galliera 11) It stands to reason: Bologna is a good place to learn to cook and this is one of several schools that offer courses for English speakers. Prices range from €65 for various three-hour courses to €325 for a five-day pasta course.

★★ Festivals & Events

Bologna Estate ART
(www.bolognaestate.it; ⏱ mid-Jun–mid-Sep) A three-month program of concerts, film projections, dance performances and much more held in open-air venues throughout the city. Many events are free. Head to the tourist office for details.

🛏 Sleeping

Accommodation in Bologna is geared to the business market, with a glut of mid-range to top-end hotels in the convention zone situated to the north of the city. If possible, avoid the busy spring and autumn trade-fair seasons when hotels get heavily booked, advance reservations are essential, and standard prices can literally double or triple. There is a city tax levied on top of room rates that runs between €1 and €5 per person per night depending on the rack rate.

We Bologna HOSTEL €
(☑ 051 039 79 00; www.we-gastameco.com; Via de' Carracci 69/14; dm €15-25, tw €35-60; P 🌀 @ 🛜) On the suburb side of the ring road 1km north of the train station, this massive new hostel is a world unto itself, with 92 rooms made up of excellent four-bed dorms with private bathrooms and colourful twin private rooms with huge desks, minibars, closets and hot water kettles.

You can rent a bike, watch a movie in the mini-cinema or whip up some *tagliatelle* in the modern kitchen. From October to July, half the rooms are turned over to university students, so there's always a great vibe. To get here, catch bus 30 from Via Rizzoli just near Le Due Torri, which drops you within a few hundred metres.

Bologna

Dopa Hostel   HOSTEL €
(☎ 051 095 24 61; www.dopahostel.com; Via Ir-
nerio 41; dm from €19-28, d €60-80, tr without
bathroom €60-80; ❄@◉) Situated barely
a kilometre from the train station, this
stylish new hostel features all manner of
recycled design touches (Mason-style jars
as light covers, beer crates reincarnated as
wall shelving), classy tiled bathrooms and
a communal kitchen that's above and beyond with an induction stovetop (it's Italy,
after all!). Four, six and eight-bed dorms offer lockers, privacy curtains and individual
electrical sockets.

Hotel University
Bologna   HOTEL €
(☎ 051 22 97 13; www.hoteluniversitybologna.
com; Via Mentana 7; d €65-110; ❄◉) Student
digs never felt so good. This low-key hotel
received a modern makeover in 2017 and
offers a hospitable welcome in its newly
slicked-out lobby and ramped-up three-
star rooms in muted grey tones, some with
king-size beds, in the heart of the university
district.

★ **Bologna nel Cuore**   B&B €€
(☎ 051 26 94 42; www.bolognanelcuore.it; Via Cesare Battisti 29; s €75-100, d €95-140, apt €125-130;
P❄◉) This centrally located, immaculate
and well-loved B&B features a pair of bright,
high-ceilinged rooms with pretty tiled bathrooms and endless mod cons, plus two comfortable, spacious apartments with kitchen
and laundry facilities. Owner and art historian Maria generously shares her knowledge
of Bologna and serves breakfasts featuring
jams made with fruit picked near her childhood home in the Dolomites.

Hotel Touring   BOUTIQUE HOTEL €€
(☎ 051 58 43 05; www.hoteltouring.it; Via dè Mat-
tuiani 1; s €80-280, d €100-350; P❄@◉) It's
overpriced at the high end, but other times
of year this family-run, three-star superior
hotel is a real gem, mainly for its panoramic terrace, which affords extraordinary city
views to Torre degli Asinelli, San Luca and
San Domenico churches (and everything
else). The newly remodelled 2nd floor offers
subtly city-themed rooms marrying modern
wall-mounted flat-screen TVs with rustic
working desks.

Hotel Metropolitan
BOUTIQUE HOTEL €€

(☑ 051 22 93 93; www.hotelmetropolitan.com; Via dell'Orso 6; d €130-300, ste €180-220; P ❄ @ 🛜) One of Bologna's few design hotels, the 45-room Met mixes functionality with handsome modern furnishings, injecting peace and tranquillity into its frenetic city-centre location with unexpected touches such as the superior rooms upstairs surrounding a small courtyard with olive trees and new slate-toned deluxe 4th floor rooms with terraces. The new rooftop courtyard is superb sundowner territory.

Arthotel Orologio
DESIGN HOTEL €€

(☑ 051 745 74 11; www.bolognarthotels.it; Via IV Novembre 10; s €118-158, d €170-218, ste €225-397; P ❄ @ 🛜) Affiliated with the upmarket Bologna Art Hotels mini-chain, this refined pile with a prime location just off Piazza Maggiore seduces guests with its slick service, smart rooms furnished in elegant gold, blue and burgundy, swirling grey-and-white marble bathrooms, antique clocks and complimentary chocs. It also sponsors rotating art shows on the hotel walls and in the sweet piazzetta out front.

Two sister hotels within a two-block radius of the Orologio offer similarly enticing amenities: the **Arthotel Commercianti** (☑ 051 745 75 11; Via de' Pignattari 11; s €98-140, d €137-216, ste €235-347; P ❄ @ 🛜) and the more modern **Arthotel Novecento** (☑ 051 745 73 11; Piazza Galileo Galilei 4/3; s €107-370, d €163-410, ste €235-610; P ❄ @ 🛜). Free bicycles for guests.

★ Prendiparte B&B
B&B €€€

(☑ 335 5616858, www.prendiparte.it; Piazzetta Prendiparte 5; r €500; 🛜) You will never – repeat, never – stay anywhere else like this. Forget the B&B tag: you don't just get a room here, you get an entire 900-year-old tower (Bologna's second tallest). The living area (bedroom, kitchen and lounge with newly renovated bathroom) is spread over three floors and there are nine more levels to explore, with outstanding views from the terrace up top.

The price includes breakfast, a welcome drink on the panoramic terrace and a personal tour of the tower with owner convivial Matteo Giovanardi. For another couple of hundred euros, you can have a private dinner catered by a professional chef or a private jazz concert. Find a millionaire to shack up with and pretend you're an errant medieval prince(ss) for the night!

🍴 Eating

Bologna is the kind of city where you can be discussing Chomsky with a leftie newspaper-seller one minute, and eating like an erstwhile Italian king in a fine restaurant the next. And as if the city wasn't an already agonising example of too many restaurants, too little time, the city centre exploded with culinary options between 2011 and 2016, jumping from 471 to nearly a thousand. Two meals into your Bologna stay and you'll start to understand why the city's known as La Grassa.

★ Vetro
VEGETARIAN €

(☑ 370 3336439; www.vetro.kilowatt.bo.it; Via Castiglione 134; meals €15-22; ⊙ 8am-8pm Mon, to 1am Tue-Fri, 9am-1am Sat, 9am-8pm Sun; 🛜 ☑) 🍴 Bologna's best time: Parking yourself down with an Aperol spritz in hand among the cool kids and digital nomads at these formerly abandoned city greenhouses that have been transformed into an immensely cool and highly recommended co-working space, vegetarian/vegan restaurant, bar and community gardens in the heart of Giardini Margherita, the city's largest greenspace.

It's a potpourri of hipsters with dogs, vegan anarchists, skateboarding economists and expat artists. Reserve ahead for the restaurant.

Osteria al 15
OSTERIA €

(☑ 051 33 18 06; Via Mirasole 13; meals €20-25; ⊙ 7.30pm-1am Mon-Sat) Just far enough off the culinary beaten track to feel like a find, this rustic osteria (tavern) caters more to locals than tourists – for now! Start with the wonderful tigelle with salumi misti paired with a creamy squacquerone cheese and wash it all down with a local Sangiovese.

Then go for perfectly al dente garganelli – this veggie version with basil pesto and zucchini is superb and you'll have had get your fill of meat with the salumi, anyway. Either way, the restaurant retains an air of Bolognese authenticity that's often hard to find at more famous places.

Cremeria Funivia
GELATO €

(☑ 051 656 93 65; www.cremeriafunivia.com; Piazza Cavour 1d; small/medium/large €2.50/3/3.50; ⊙ noon-11.30pm Mon-Sat, from 11am Sun) Ask Bologna residents to name the best gelateria in town, and this place often comes out on top. Its newest branch sits directly opposite pretty Piazza Cavour. Fill a cone (or a focaccia sandwich!) with house-special flavours

LOCAL KNOWLEDGE

SPAGHETTI BOLOGNESE

If you came to Emilia-Romagna in search of 'authentic' spaghetti bolognese, you're out of luck. The name is a misnomer. Spaghetti bolognese is about as Bolognese as roast beef and Yorkshire pudding, and Bologna's fiercely traditional trattorias never list it. Instead, the city prides itself on a vastly superior meat-based sauce called *ragù*, consisting of slow-cooked minced beef simmered with pancetta, onions and carrots, and enlivened with liberal dashes of milk and wine. Calling the city's signature meat sauce 'spaghetti bolognese' is like calling Champagne 'fizzy wine'.

So why the misleading moniker? Modern legend suggests that *ragù* may have acted as spaghetti bolognese's original inspiration when British and American servicemen passing through Emilia in WWII fell in love with the dish. Returning home after the war, they subsequently asked their immigrant Italian chefs to rustle up something similar. Details clearly got lost in translation. The 'spaghetti bolognese' eaten in contemporary London and New York is fundamentally different to Bologna's centuries-old *ragù*. First there's the sauce. Spaghetti bolognese is heavy on tomatoes while *ragù* is all about the meat. Then there's the pasta. Spaghetti bolognese is served with dry durum-wheat spaghetti from Naples taken straight from a packet. *Ragù* is spread over fresh egg-based *tagliatelle* (ribbon pasta), allowing the rich meat sauce to stick to the thick al dente strands.

Ever keen to safeguard their meat sauce from mediocrity, Bologna's chamber of commerce registered an official *ragù* recipe in 1982, although, ironically, it's still nigh on impossible to find two Bologna *ragù* that taste the same.

like Alice (mascarpone and chocolate) or Leonardo (pine-nut ice cream with toasted pine nuts), then head across the street and cool off under the trees.

Mercato di Mezzo
FOOD HALL €

(Via Clavature 12; ⊙9am-midnight; 🛜) Trade the packed-like-sardine Quadrilatero chaos for comparative calm in this newly opened gourmet food hall, which was the town's original market after reunification, though it sat abandoned for many years in recent times. The three-storey pavilion houses a cavalcade of top purveyors hawking pizza, craft beer, espresso, cheese and charcuterie, including stalls from Bologna's most famous bakery (Forno Calzolari) and patisserie (Centrale del Gusto).

Bottega Portici
ITALIAN €

(www.bottegaportici.it; Piazza di Porta Ravegnana 2; meals €5-9; ⊙7.30am-10pm) Upstart and trendy, this bustling 2017 opener under the shadow of the towers is a great pit stop for high-quality Bologna specialities (tortellini in *brodo* or with sage and butter, *tagliatelle al ragú*) up lightning fast or to go.

It doubles as a gourmet provisions shop (pick up the famous Bolognese broth to go) and its impressive, hi-tech Faema E71 espresso machine (which costs significantly more than most Fiats!) means it's a great choice for a stunning *caffè* as well.

Osteria Bartolini
SEAFOOD €

(☑051 26 21 92; www.osteriabartolinibologna.com; Piazza Malpighi 16; mains €8.50-16.50; ⊙noon-2.30pm & 7-10.30pm; 🛜) Landlocked Bolognese flock to this city seafooder that sources its wares daily from Milano Marittima on the Romagna coast. Standouts on the snarky menu include anything fried and a tasty and delicate white seafood *tagliolini ragú*, but no matter what you fancy, dine al fresco in one of the city's loveliest courtyards under a massive sycamore tree. Reservations not accepted.

Botanica Lab
VEGAN €

(☑342 8606026; www.botanicalab.com; Via Battibecco 4c; meals €20-30; ⊙noon-4pm Mon, noon-11pm Tue-Fri, 11am-11pm Sat; 🛜🚲) 🌿 Bologna's first plant-based bistro sits defiantly in the heart of *ragú* wonderland just off Piazza Maggiore. Vegan or not, it's a wonderful place for a respite from the rich recipes of traditional Bolognese cuisine, a culinary detox fuelled by clean, fresh seasonal dishes like beetroot spaghetti with marinated asparagus and cashew cream or tomato ravioli with macadamia ricotta and arugula pesto.

Osteria dell'Orsa
ITALIAN €

(☑051 23 15 76; www.osteriadellorsa.com; Via Mentana 1; meals €10-20; ⊙noon-1am) If you were to make a list of the great wonders of Italy, hidden amid Venice's canals and Rome's Colosseum would be cheap, pretension-free *osterie* (casual taverns) like Osteria dell'Orsa, where the food is serially sublime and the prices are giveaway cheap.

It's wildly popular with students, who mob the place for daily specials and a long list of panini, crostini other quick eats.

Cremeria Santo Stefano

GELATO €

(www.facebook.com/CremeriaSantoStefano; Via Santo Stefano 70; small/medium/large €2.50/3/3.50; ⊙11am-11.30pm) Offering a welcoming rustic-chic ambience, this locally recommended, family-run gelateria shakes things up among the usual Italian artisanal suspects and brings imported ingredients to the mix, like Turkish pistachios (for the absolutely excellent salted pistachio) and Venezuelan chocolate.

★ All'Osteria Bottega

OSTERIA €€

(☑051 58 51 11; Via Santa Caterina 51; meals €35-45; ⊙12.30-2.30pm & 8pm-1am Tue-Sat) At this Bologna institution truly worthy of the name, owners Daniele and Valeria lavish attention on every table between trips to the kitchen for plates of *culatello di Zibello* ham, tortellini in capon broth, Petroniana-style veal cutlets (breaded and fried, then topped with Parma ham and *parmigiano reggiano* and pan-sauteed in broth) and other Slow Food delights.

★ Trattoria di Via Serra

TRATTORIA €€

(☑051 631 23 30; www.trattoriadiviaserra.it; Via Luigi Serra 9b; meals €30-40; ⊙7-10pm Wed-Thu, noon-2pm & 7-10pm Fri-Sun; 🐾) 🍴 Book at least three weeks in advance at this seemingly unassuming trattoria in Bolognina, just a step outside the city centre. Flavio and Tommaso came down from their established destination restaurant in the mountains in Zocca five years ago wielding recipes that forge a bridge between classic Emilian and hilltop twists, carefully outlined on their short menu.

So you get *tagliatelle,* for example, but with *ragù* that minces guinea fowl, duck, rabbit, pork and chicken together; or *gramigna* pasta with a natural-fed mountain pork white *ragù* (phenomenal!), all of which washes down quite nicely with the biodynamic house wines. The experience here is made most memorable by Flavio's passionate dedication to the ingredients (all farm-to-table), which carries over into his lengthy tableside menu explanations. It's a magnificent Slow Food winner.

★ Drogheria della Rosa

TRATTORIA €€

(☑051 22 25 29; www.drogheriadellarosa.it; Via Cartoleria 10; meals €35-40; ⊙1-3pm & 7.30-11.45pm; 🐾) With its wooden shelves and apothecary jars, it's not difficult to picture this place as the pharmacy it once was. Nowadays it's a charming, high-end trattoria, run by a congenial owner who gets round to every table to explain the day's short, sweet menu of superbly prepared Bolognese classics, and often bestows roses upon guests at evening's end.

🍷 Drinking & Nightlife

Hit the graffiti-strewn streets of the university district after sunset and the electrifying energy is enough to make any jaded 30- or 40-something feel young again. For a more upmarket, dressier scene head to the Quadrilatero; or try the more down-to-earth Via del Pratello for the city's overall coolest concentration of bars.

★ Ranzani 13

CRAFT BEER

(☑051 849 37 43; www.ranzani13.it; Via Camillo Ranzani 5; beers €5-6; ⊙11am-3pm & 7pm-1am Tue-Fri, 7pm-1am Sat & Sun; 🐾) Ditch the city centre and venture just outside the Viali (Bologna's ring road) to a distinctly unremarkable apartment block where the city's best craft-beer bar and gastropub awaits. Twelve rotating taps fuel a delectable section of gourmet pizzas like Happy Pork (slow-cooked pork shoulder, burrata, basil and Parmesan) and burgers (try the Magali, with bacon, pecorino, caramelised onions and balsamic vinegar).

Il Punto

CRAFT BEER

(www.puntobologna.com; Via San Rocco 1g; draught beers €3.50-6; ⊙5.30pm-1.30am Sun-Thu, to 2am Fri & Sat; 🐾) Bologna's best craft-beer bar offers eight taps of local *birra artigianale* (including one hand-pump) and over 150 mostly Italian and Belgian choices by the bottle, which you can take at the bar or one of the informal hardwood tables inside or out.

Baladin Bologna

CRAFT BEER

(www.baladin.it; Via Clavature 12; draught beers €4.50; ⊙11.30am-midnight Sun-Thu, til 2.30am Fri & Sat; 🐾) Part of a homegrown, sustainably focused brewpub chain born in Piozzo, Bologna's Baladin sits inside the Quadrilatero's newly opened Mercato di Mezzo. Eight proprietary beers (as well as Baladin's full line of bottles) rotate across 12 taps over two floors, a market hallway space and a more

EMILIA-ROMAGNA & SAN MARINO BOLOGNA

WORTH A TRIP

TRATTORIA DA AMERIGO

....

Emilia-Romagna's best dining experience awaits in truffle territory. In the small village of Savigno, a 30km detour west of Bologna, the fantastic **Trattoria da Amerigo** (☑ 051 670 82 36; www.amerigo1934.it; Via Marconi 14-16, Savigno; meals €40-50; ☉ 7.30-10.30pm Tue-Fri, noon-2.30pm & 7.30-10.30pm Sat-Sun), armed with a Michelin star (but lacking any pretension), is the domain of legendary pastamaker Nonna Giuliana Vespucci (you wish she was *your* grandmother!), executive chef Alberto Bettini and his talented young apprentice, Orlando Giacomo.

Together, their traditional takes and seasonal creations (*tortelli* stuffed with *parmigiano reggiano* and wood-fired prosciutto, gnocchi with regional truffles, Parmesan basket-cradled poached egg with regional mushrooms and shaved truffles – we could go on and on) are the Italian dishes of your culinary dreams. You could drop a paycheque on the in-house provisions at the attached gourmet shop. Book a bed, too (singles/doubles from €50/70). You'll want breakfast!

atmospheric lounge area rife with vintage furniture.

Caffè Rubik
COFFEE

(Via Marsala 31d; coffee from €1.10; ☉ 7am-1am Mon-Sat, 8am-1pm Sun; 🕾) This little bohemian pop-art coffee shop packs a wallop of soul into a tiny space. Cassette tapes and old school lunch boxes line the walls and the exquisite espresso – some of Bologna's best – is unexpectedly served in Japanese porcelain. The hippie-blue sidewalk seating is great for pairing caffeine (or a stiff drink) with early-evening people-watching.

Osteria del Sole
BAR

(www.osteriadelsole.it; Vicolo Ranocchi 1d; ☉ 10.30am-10pm Mon-Sat) The sign outside this ancient Quadrilatero dive bar tells you all you need to know – '*vino*' (wine). Bring in your own food, and elbow past the cacophony of smashed students, mildly inebriated grandpas and the occasional Anglo tourist for a sloppily poured glass of chianti, Sangiovese or Lambrusco. It's a spot-on formula that's been working since 1465.

Cassero
CLUB

(www.cassero.it; Via Don Minzoni 18; ☉ 7pm-midnight Mon, Tue, Thu & Sun, to 5am Wed, Fri & Sat) Wednesday, Friday and Saturday are the big nights at this legendary gay-and-lesbian (but not exclusively) club, home of Italy's Arcigay organisation. Evenings kick off with happy hour (7pm to 8pm) at the club's Queer Garden Bar seven nights a week.

Le Stanze
WINE BAR

(www.lestanzecafe.it; Via Borgo San Pietro 1; ☉ 11am-1am Tue-Sun) For sheer atmosphere, former private chapel of the Bentivoglio family boasts four interior rooms with original paintings. The *aperitivo* buffet is top-notch here, with paellas, pastas and chicken drumsticks to accompany your wine or cocktail.

☆ Entertainment

Bologna, courtesy of its large student population, knows how to rock – but it also knows how to clap politely at the opera. The most comprehensive listings guide is *Bologna Spettacolo* (www.bolognaspettacolo.it; in Italian), available at newsstands or online. During the summer, Cineteca di Bologna hosts films in Piazza Maggiore on the biggest open-air cinema screen in Europe. Grab a beer and a pizza and join the masses for one of the city's best summer pastimes.

Cantina Bentivoglio
JAZZ

(☑ 051 26 54 16; www.cantinabentivoglio.it; Via Mascarella 4b; cover €4.50; ☉ 8pm-1.30am Sun-Mon, to 2am Tue-Sat) Bologna's top jazz joint, the Bentivoglio is a jack of all trades. Part wine bar (choose from over 600 labels), part restaurant and part jazz club (there's live music six nights a week most of the year), this much-loved institution oozes cosy charm with its labyrinth of chambers sporting ancient brick floors, arched ceilings and shelves full of wine bottles.

In summer, it joins with three other neighbouring venues to host the annual **Salotto di Jazz**, during which revellers pour out into pedestrianised Via Mascarella for six weeks of live jazz under the stars.

Covo Club
LIVE MUSIC

(www.covoclub.it; Viale Zagabria 1) The city's best alternative rock club, located about 5km northeast of the centre. It has drawn the likes of Franz Ferdinand, the Mars Volta, the Decemberists, Modest Mouse and the XX in recent years.

Oratorio di Santa Cecilia · LIVE MUSIC
(www.sangiacomofestival.it; Via Zamboni 15; ⊙Mar-Sep) The annual San Giacomo Festival brings regular free chamber-music recitals to this lovely space. Check the website or the board outside for upcoming events.

Cinema Chaplin · CINEMA
(www.cinemachaplin.it; Piazza di Porta Saragozza 5a; tickets €6-8) Screens films in English from September through May. Tickets are reduced to €5 on Mondays and Wednesdays.

Teatro Comunale · THEATRE
(☑051 52 90 19; www.tcbo.it; Largo Respighi 1; ⊙box office 2-6pm Tue-Fri, 11am-3pm Sat) This venerable theatre, where Wagner's works were heard for the first time in Italy, is still Bologna's leading opera and classical music venue.

Villa Serena · LIVE MUSIC
(www.villaserena.bo.it; Via della Barca 1; ⊙10pm-late Thu-Sat) Three floors of film screenings and music, live and canned, plus a garden for outdoor chilling.

🛍 Shopping

If you came for the food, head for the Quadrilatero, a haven of family-run delis and speciality food shops. You'll find myriad Italian boutiques and upscale shopping along main avenues like Via Rizzola, Via Ugo Bassi and Via dell'Indipendenza.

New Dandy · CLOTHING
(www.newdandy.it; Via Marescalchi 4; ⊙10am-2pm & 3-8pm Mon-Sat) For those looking for a true made-to-measure Italian suit, an exquisite experience awaits at this fiercely artisanal tailor, where Leonardo and Gianluca will take you (and your suit) on a journey of old school craftsmanship that forges a creative bridge between classic Napolese tailoring and English sensibility.

Paolo Atti · FOOD
(http://paoloatti.com/; Via delle Drapperie 6; ⊙10am-7.15pm Mon-Thu, to 7.30pm Fri & Sat, 10.30am-1.30pm Sun) This shop in Bologna's famed Quadrilatero neighbourhood specialises in beautifully packaged boxes of traditional Bolognese tortellini stuffed with prosciutto, *mortadella* (pork cold cut), fresh Parmesan and nutmeg. Decorative boxes run €10 or €18

empty, and then can be filled with as much as 1kg or 3kg of pasta (per kg €37.40).

Enoteca Italia · WINE
(☑051 23 59 89; www.enoteca-italiana.it; Via Marsala 2; ⊙8am-9pm) Pick up a bottle of Lambrusco and so much more at Bologna's award-winning and most authentic wine shop, with over 4000 different Italian labels and a knowledgeable staff.

Cineteca di Bologna · GIFTS & SOUVENIRS
(☑051 219 48 26; www.cinetecadibologna.it; Voltone del Podestà; ⊙10am-7pm) Bang in the city centre, this art-house historical film preservation shop sells original vintage Italian movie posters and newly restored DVDs of classic films. Its cinema, located at Via Azzo Gardino 65, screens classic Italian and original language films in its hi-tech Cinema Lumière daily (Wednesday screenings are €5).

ℹ Information

Bologna Welcome (Tourist Office; ☑051 658 31 11; www.bolognawelcome.it; Piazza Maggiore 1e; ⊙9am-7pm Mon-Sat, 10am-5pm Sun) Bologna's official tourist information hub offers daily, two-hour afternoon walking tours (€15), among other excursions; can help with bookings; puts out a handy daily news and events brochure in English and sells the Bologna Welcome Card (48/72hr card €20/30) and 24-hour bus passes (€5). Also has an office at the airport (☑051 647 22 01; Via Triumvirato 84; ⊙9am-7.30pm Mon-Fri, to 5pm Sun).

Ospedale Maggiore (☑051 647 81 11; Largo Nigrisoli 2) West of the city centre.

Poste Italiane (Post Office; www.poste.it; Piazza Minghetti 4; ⊙8.20am-7.05pm Mon-Fri, to 12.35pm Sat) Postal services.

ℹ Getting There & Away

AIR

Bologna's **Guglielmo Marconi airport** (☑051 647 96 15; www.bologna-airport.it; Via Triumvirato 84) is 8km northwest of the city. It's served by over 40 dozen airlines including Ryanair, easyJet and British Airways.

BUS

Intercity buses leave from the **main bus station** (☑051 24 54 00; www.tper.it; ⊙4.30am-11.30pm) off Piazza XX Settembre, just southeast of the train station. However, for nearly all destinations, the train's a better option.

Like...? Try...

Like Florence? Try Bologna

Climb the 498 steps of medieval Torre degli Asinelli and the city unfurls before you like a map. There were once more than 100 such towers here, but only some 20 remain. Massimo Medica, director of Bologna's Musei Civici d'Arte Antica, explains. 'In the Middle Ages Bologna was an important city. Its university was comparable to Paris'. There wasn't the space to have a castle, so every tower belonged to a powerful family – the height showed the extent of their power. When a family was defeated, their tower would be cut.'

In the central square, Piazza Maggiore, locals and tourists recline as if at the beach. They're probably considering Bologna's other great achievement, its food. This is the home of yolky pasta: fine ribbons of *tagliatelle* entwined with *ragù* (meat sauce), *tortellini in brodo* (pork pasta parcels in a thin soup), and the artisanal ice cream of 1950s parlour La Sorbetteria Castiglione.

Like the Dolomites? Try Monti Sibillini

'On a clear day you can see Croatia from here,' says affable Maurizio Fusari, zoologist and trekking guide in the Monti Sibillini, gesturing out at the views that stretch off into the Adriatic. In this weathered mountain range, split between Umbria and Le Marche, the predominant sounds are birdsong and the swirl of the breeze, yet the wild hills are appealingly approachable. 'It's possible to reach even

1. Peschici (p733), Promontorio del Gargano
2. Piazza Maggiore, Bologna (p431)
3. Monti Sibillini (p630)

the tallest without Alpine equipment. These are mountains for everyone.'

Walks range from gentle afternoon strolls through mountain valleys to night-time hikes to watch the sunrise, or a nine-day trek on the Grande Anello trail (120km). En route, look out for wildlife Maurizio reels off a list: 'Wild boar, roe deer, wolves, golden eagles, peregrine falcons. Oh, and one bear. He has come here from Abruzzo. It seems he's looking for a mate.'

Like the Amalfi Coast? Try the Gargano Promontory

The Gargano, the sea-thrusting spur of the Italian boot, was once connected to what is now Dalmatia, Croatia, across the Adriatic Sea. Knowing this makes sense of the place. It feels a region apart, with a skirt of sea so blue it makes you blink. The land is a tumultuous mix: bleached sea cliffs, dense dark-green scrub, wild orchids, pine forests and silver beaches, all of it protected and treasured as a national park. The area's uniqueness extends well into the sea, its waters punctuated with curious-looking *trabucchi*, ancient fishing traps whose origins reputedly stretch back to Phoenician times.

Vieste and Peschici are the main coastal towns, bunched-up clusters of narrow lanes and heavy limestone houses. Their pale, Arabesque buildings seem to grow out of the sea cliffs, with fierce-blue views in every direction.

In high summer, it can feel like everyone in Italy is here. Come in June and September, however, and you will experience the Gargano in its finest months, a time when the weather is seductively warm, many businesses are still open, and the carnival-like crowds are nowhere to be seen.

CAR & MOTORCYCLE

Bologna is linked to Milan, Florence and Rome by the A1 Autostrada del Sole. The A13 heads directly to Ferrara, Padua and Venice, and the A14 to Rimini and Ravenna. Bologna is also on the SS9 (Via Emilia), which connects Milan to the Adriatic coast. The SS64 goes to Ferrara.

Major car-hire companies are represented at Guglielmo Marconi airport and outside the train station. City offices include **Budget** (✐ 051 634 16 32; www.budget.com; Via Nicolo dall'Arca 2d; ⊙ 8am-8pm Mon-Fri, to 6pm Sat, 8.30am-12.30pm Sun) and **Hertz** (✐ 344 1908587; www.hertz.it; Via Boldrini 4; ⊙ 8am-7pm Mon-Sat).

TRAIN

Bologna is a major transport junction for northern Italy, with most trains arriving at **Bologna Centrale station** (✐ 199 89 20 21; www.trenitalia.com; Piazza Medaglie d'Oro 2; ⊙ 24hr, ticket windows 6am-9pm). The high-speed train to Florence (from €15 takes only 37 minutes. Other lightning-quick Frecciarossa links include Venice (from €15, 1¼ hours), Milan (from €20, 1¼ hours), Rome (from €19.90, 2¼ hours) and Naples (from €30, 3½ hours). Slower, less expensive trains also serve these destinations. Do as locals do and ask taxis to drop you directly at the underground high-speed platforms ('Stazione Alta Velocità') at the station (though occasionally Freccia trains are moved elsewhere).

Frequent trains connect Bologna with cities throughout Emilia-Romagna, including Modena, Parma, Ferrara, Ravenna and Rimini.

❶ Getting Around

BICYCLE

BikeinBo (✐ 347 0017996; www.bikeinbo.it; Via Indipendenza 69a; bike rental per day/week €16/60; ⊙ 8am-8pm) will deliver a rental bike to your door anywhere in Bologna. Rates include helmet, lock, maps and front basket; an optional child seat costs €2 extra.

CAR & MOTORCYCLE

Much of the city centre is off-limits to vehicles. If you're staying downtown, your hotel can provide a ticket (€6 per 24-hour period) that entitles you to enter the ZTL (Zona a Traffico Limitato) and park in designated spaces marked with blue lines.

PUBLIC TRANSPORT

Bologna has an efficient bus system, run by **TPER** (✐ 051 29 02 90; www.tper.it), with information booths at Bologna Centrale train station and the nearby bus station. Minibus A is the most direct of several buses that connect the train station with the city centre. A single costs €1.30; a 24-hour ticket is €5.

Modena

⬀ 059 / POP 186,000

If Italy were a meal, Modena would be the main course. Here, on the flat plains of the slow-flowing Po, lies one of the nation's great gastronomic centres, the creative force behind *real* balsamic vinegar, giant tortellini stuffed with tantalising fillings, sparkling Lambrusco wine and backstreets crammed with some of the best restaurants no one's ever heard of (and one, Osteria Francescana, that everybody was awarded the top spot on the coveted 'World's 50 Best Restaurants' list in 2016, the first Italian restaurant to nab the honour).

For those with bleached taste buds, the city has another equally lauded legacy: cars. The famous Ferrari museum is situated in the nearby village of Maranello. Modena is also notable for its haunting Romanesque cathedral and as the birthplace of the late Italian opera singer Pavarotti, whose former home is now a worthwhile museum just outside town.

◉ Sights

Several of Modena's museums and galleries, including Galleria Estense and Musei Civici, are conveniently housed together in the Palazzo dei Musei on the western fringes of the historic centre. A new Unesco World Heritage Site combo ticket, which includes admission to Torre Ghirlandina, Musei del Duomo, Palazzo Comunale and Acetaia Comunale, can be purchased for €6.

★ **Duomo** CATHEDRAL
(www.duomodimodena.it; Corso Duomo; ⊙ 7am-7pm Tue-Sun, 7am-12.30pm & 3.30-7pm Mon) Modena's celebrated cathedral combines the austerity of the Dark Ages with throwback traditions from the Romans in a style known as Romanesque. The church stands out among Emilia-Romagna's many other ecclesial relics for its remarkable architectural purity. It is, by popular consensus, the finest Romanesque church in Italy, and in 1997 was listed as a Unesco World Heritage Site.

While not as large or spectacular as other Italian churches, the cathedral – dedicated to the city's patron saint, St Geminianus – has a number of striking features. The dark, brick-walled interior is dominated by the huge Gothic **rose window** (a 13th-century addition) that shoots rays of light down the grand central apse. On the exterior facade,

Modena

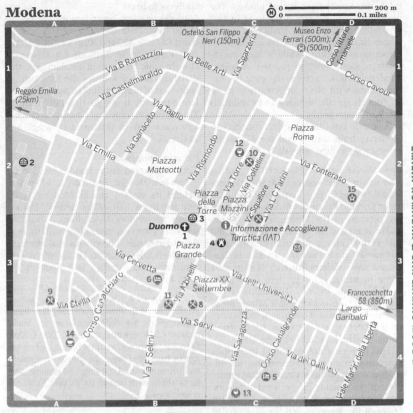

Modena

⊙ Top Sights

EMILIA-ROMAGNA & SAN MARINO MODENA

a series of vivid bas-reliefs depicting scenes from Genesis are the work of the 12th-century sculptor Wiligelmo. Interior highlights include an elaborate rood screen decorated by Anselmo da Campione and, in the crypt, Guido Mazzoni's *Madonna della pappa*, a group of five painted terracotta figures.

Museo Enzo Ferrari MUSEUM

(www.museomodena.ferrari.com; Via Paolo Ferrari 85; adult/reduced €15/13, incl Maranello museum €26/22; ☉ 9.30am-7pm Apr-Oct, to 6pm Nov-Mar) While Maranello's Ferrari museum focuses on the supersonic cars, this museum near Modena's train station, inaugurated in 2012, celebrates Signor Enzo Ferrari himself. The memorabilia is cleverly juxtaposed in two separate buildings. The traditional house where Enzo was born in 1898 includes the Museum of Engines, while a slick curvaceous modern building painted in bright 'Modena yellow' acts as a gigantic car showroom, with plenty of Ferraris to gawp at, though specific vehicles and exhibition themes change yearly.

A shuttle bus (day pass €12) connects to Modena's train station and the Maranello museum six to nine times daily.

Casa Museo Luciano Pavarotti   MUSEUM

(www.casamuseolucianopavarotti.it; Stradello Nava 6; adult/reduced €8/6; ⊙10am-6pm) Legendary tenor Luciano Pavarotti's final home is prettily perched in the Modenese countryside 8.5km southeast of the city. The building was turned into a museum in 2015; 40-minute self-guided audio tours in nine languages take visitors through the modest home in which Pavarotti lived from 2004 until his death in 2007. Highlights of the tour include access to intimate private areas like his bedroom and bathroom; his buttery yellow kitchen and personal letters from Frank Sinatra, Bono and Princess Di.

The 12 rooms are dedicated to various aspects of the singer's extraordinary life, including stage costumes, Grammy and Emmy Awards and plenty of personal artefacts. Bus 820 (direction Pavullo) gets you within 1.6km of the museum, but the best way to reach it is on a combo Discover Ferrari and Pavarotti Land tour (adult/child €48/24; www.ferraripavarottiland.it) bookable at the Modena tourist office (p451) or the Enzo Ferrari Museum.

Museo del Duomo/
Museo Lapidario   MUSEUM

(www.duomodimodena.it/musei-del-duomo; Via Lanfranco 6; adult/child €4/3; ⊙9.30am-12.30pm & 3.30-6.30pm Tue-Sun) Tucked down an alley along the left side of the cathedral, these side-by-side museums operate like two exhibitions within the same space. **Museo del Duomo** focuses on religious artefacts belonging to San Geminianus, the patron saint of Modena, including his portable altar dating to 1106. **Museo Lapidario** displays more captivating stonework by famed 12th-century sculptor Wiligelmo as well as eight monstrous metopes by an unidentified sculptor who likely worked in Wiligelmo's workshop, which graced the Duomo's rooftop until 1948.

Galleria Estense   GALLERY

(www.gallerie-estensi.beniculturali.it; Palazzo dei Musei, Largo Porta Sant'Agostino 337; adult/reduced €4/2; ⊙8.30am-7.30pm Tue-Sat, 2-7.30pm Sun) Reopened in 2015 after a three-year closure (due to earthquake damage), this delightful gallery features the Este family's collection of northern Italian paintings from late medieval times to the 18th century. There are also some fine Flemish works and a canvas or two by Velázquez, Correggio and El Greco.

Palazzo Comunale   PALACE

(Corso Duomo; admission Mon-Sat free, Sun €2; ⊙9am-7pm Mon-Sat, 9am-noon & 3-7pm Sun) Behind its elegant facade, Modena's 17th-century town hall offers several historic rooms for visitors to explore; if possible, schedule your visit to coincide with tours of the palace's balsamic-vinegar-making facility, which take place on Friday afternoons, Saturdays and Sundays (€2; book at the tourist office; p451).

Museo Civico Archeologico   MUSEUM

(☑051 275 72 11; www.comune.bologna.it/museo archeologico; Via dell'Archiginnasio 2; adult/reduced €5/3; ⊙9am-3pm Tue-Fri, 10am-6.30pm Sat & Sun) Impressive in its breadth of coverage of historical eras, this museum displays well-documented Egyptian and Roman artefacts along with one of Italy's best Etruscan collections.

☞ Tours

Emilia Delizia   FOOD & DRINK

(www.emiliadelizia.com; tours from €119) It's undeniably pricey, but this UK-based foodie tour company and its wonderful, Modena-based guide, Paolo, will take you on a wonderful and comprehensive gastronomic adventure fuelled by artisanal balsamic vinegar, *parmigiano reggiano* and Parma ham with generous tastings, intimate interactions with producers and invaluable insight.

🛏 Sleeping

Canalgrande Hotel   HISTORIC HOTEL €

(☑059 21 71 60; www.canalgrandehotel.it; Corso Canal Grande 6; s €74-89, d €84-114; P❄🔊) Though not as elegant as its former life as a palace and monastery dating to 1530 suggest, there is a pleasant air of aged European elegance at Canalgrande that strikes the right balance between history, location, value and friendliness. Original 17th and 18th century canvases pepper the lobby halls while comfortable rooms feature pleasant surprises like linen hand towels.

Ostello San Filippo Neri
HOSTEL €

(☑ 059 23 45 98; www.ostellomodena.it; Via Santa Orsola 48-52; dm/s/d/tr €19/38/44/52; P@🛜) Modena's businesslike HI hostel has 76 beds in single-sex dorms and family units. Pluses include the convenient location between the train station and downtown Modena, a guest kitchen and bar, disabled access, capacious lockers, spacious, uncrowded rooms (maximum three beds per dorm) and a bike-storage area. Each room also has a private bathroom (though not inside the room).

Hotel Cervetta 5
HOTEL €€

(☑ 059 23 84 47; www.hotelcervetta5.com; Via Cervetta 5; s €80-120, d €125-160; 🌀🛜) Cervetta is about as posh as Modena gets without pandering to the convention crowd. Adjacent to the intimate Piazza Grande, it has quasi-boutique facilities, including 15 (of 22) recently renovated rooms that are now better complement the wonderfully soothing, candle-lit lobby with rustic-chic additions like African iron light covers, unfinished concrete bathrooms and roped Edison lighting.

✗ Eating

Modena would easily make a top-10 list of best Italian culinary towns. Its beauty lies not just in the food, but in the way it is presented in simple, unpretentious eateries shoehorned up blind alleys or hidden inside faceless office blocks, often without signage.

Modena's outstanding municipal market has its main entrance on Via Albinelli.

★ Gelateria Bloom
GELATO

(www.facebook.com/gelateriabloom; Via Luigi Carlo Farini 23; small/medium/large €2.40/2.90/3.30; ⊙12.30-11pm) 🍴 Dare we call this Emilia-Romagna's best gelateria? Yes, we dare. Owner Gianluca Degani is fiercely devoted to chemical and additive-free gelato and achieves his creamy magic by adhering to a farm-to-table philosophy, working directly with farmers who specialise in ancient fruits (such as Monettina and Buttina pears or 147 types of as-yet-unnamed apples).

Mercato Albinelli
MARKET

(www.mercatoalbinelli.it; Via Luigi Albinelli 13; ⊙6.30am-2.30pm Mon-Sat year-round, plus 4.30-7pm Sat Oct-May) Modena's covered municipal market cradles a cornucopia of local delights. Foodies should head straight here for Bible-size hunks of *parmigiano reggiano*, bottles of Vecchia Modena Lambrusco or aged balsamic vinegar, just-stuffed tortellini and tortelloni, piles and piles of fresh produce, and a million other things you will be dying to try. You can assemble a picnic of Last Supper proportions here.

Trattoria Aldina
TRATTORIA €

(☑ 059 23 61 06; Via Albinelli 40; meals €15-25; ⊙noon-2.30pm Mon-Thu, noon-2.30pm & 8-10.30pm Fri & Sat) Cloistered upstairs in a utilitarian apartment block, Aldina feels like a precious secret guarded loyally by local shoppers from the adjacent produce market. The menu features the kind of no-nonsense homemade grub that only an Italian *nonna* raised on hand-shaped pasta could possibly concoct. Despite a written menu, you'll be offered what's in the pot and revel in the people-watching potential.

FERRARI FANTASIES & LAMBORGHINI LEGENDS

Fiats might be functional, but to appreciate the true beauty of Italian artisanship you must visit the small triangle of land between Modena and Bologna – sometimes called 'Motor Valley' – where the world's finest luxury cars, namely Ferraris and Lamborghinis, are constructed. Here, serious aficionados can bliss out for a day or two touring the region's four automotive museums, two devoted to Ferraris – including the Museo Enzo Ferrari (p447) in Modena – and two to Lamborghinis.

Museo Ferrari (www.museomaranello.ferrari.com; Via Ferrari 43, Maranello; adult/reduced €15/13; ⊙9.30am-7pm Apr-Oct, to 6pm Nov-Mar)

Lamborghini Museum (☑ 051 681 76 11; www.lamborghini.com/en/museum; Via Modena 12, Sant'Agata Bolognese; adult/reduced €15/12, with factory tour €75/50; ⊙9.30am-7.30pm)

Museo Ferruccio Lamborghini (☑ 051 86 33 66; www.museolamborghini.com; Via Galliera 319, Argelato; adult/reduced €15/10, 1hr guided tour €8; ⊙10am-1pm & 2-6pm Tue-Sat, 3-6pm Sun May-Jun, otherwise by appointment only)

> **WORTH A TRIP**
>
> ## DOZZA WINE TASTING
>
> Whose idea of shopping for wine in Italy doesn't involve a 13th-century medieval castle and a rigorous, six-member blind tasting board? The worth-a-detour **Enoteca Regionale Emilia Romagna** (☑ 0542 36 77 00; www.enotecaemilia romagna.it; Piazza Rocca Sforzesca, Dozza; ⊙ 9.30am-1pm & 3-7pm Tue-Fri, 10am-1pm & 3-7pm Sat-Sun) wine shop is set in the former icehouse of the Rocca di Dozza in Dozza and represents 250 of Emilia-Romagna's best producers, counting nearly 1000 labels in its inventory. Lambrusco, Sangiovese, Pignoletto – it's all here.
>
> You can taste as well, either from the self-serve Winemotion automatic dispensers (€1.20 to €6) or, if you're travelling with a gaggle of oenophiles, you can book a three-wine (or more) tasting with a professional sommelier (€100 plus €11 per person). Dozza is off the Via Emilia (SS9) 40km southeast of Bologna.

If the lasagna is in the pot, don't miss it.

★ **Ristorante da Danilo** ITALIAN €€
(☑ 059 21 66 91; www.ristorantedadanilomodena. it; Via Coltellini 31; meals €25-30; ⊙noon-3pm & 7pm-midnight Mon-Sat) Speedy waiters glide around balancing bread baskets, wine bottles and pasta dishes in this deliciously traditional dining room where first dates mingle with animated families and office groups on a birthday jaunt. Folks mob the antipasti of salami, *pecorino* and fig marmalade, but don't overdo it – the tortelloni of ricotta and spinach in a bacon cream sauce is nothing short of transcendent.

Osteria Francescana GASTRONOMY €€€
(☑ 059 22 39 12; www.osteriafrancescana.it; Via Stella 22; tasting menus €220-250, with wine €350-420; ⊙12.30-1.30pm & 8-9.30pm Mon-Fri, 8-9.30pm Sat) Reserve months in advance (or pray for a waiting list miracle) at this fabled 11-table restaurant, where reimagined Italian fare is art and tasting menus top out at €250. Owner Massimo Bottura is onto his third Michelin star (earned in 2011), and in 2016 the restaurant leap-frogged into the number one spot on *the* influential 'World's 50 Best Restaurants' list.

Though it fell to No 2 in 2017, it remains Italy's most coveted reservation. For creative international cuisine with a more moderate price tag, try Bottura's equally diminutive bistro **Franceschetta 58** (☑ 059 309 10 08; www. franceschetta58.it; Via Vignolese 58; 4-/6-course tasting menu €48/65; ⊙12.30-3pm & 7.30pm-midnight Mon-Sat; ☎), 1km southeast of the centre.

DRINKING & NIGHTLIFE

A youthful bar-hopping crowd congregates along Via dei Gallucci. There's also a cluster of bars along Via Emilia near the cathedral. *Birra artigianale* – craft beer – is the latest trend to take hold in the city.

★ **Menomoka** COFFEE
(www.facebook.com/menomoka; Corso Canal Chiaro 136a; ⊙7am-10pm Sun-Thu, to midnight Fri & Sat; ☎) Step up your coffee game at this trendy, barista-driven cafe that produces Modena's best espresso, pulled from 100% Arabica specialty blends from around the world. Coffee connoisseurs will also find siphon and V60 methods served here, along with wine and craft beer.

Archer WINE BAR
(www.facebook.com/archermodena; Via Cesare Battisti 54; ⊙10am-midnight Tue-Sun) Though she has no formal certification, renegade wine expert Marina Bersani has been slinging juice since the age of 15 and Archer – named after *The Portrait of a Lady's* free-spirited Isabel Archer – is her unpretentious wine bar with a serious soul. Thirty or so wines, served in top Riedel stemware, are available at any given time (€6 to €10).

Maltomania CRAFT BEER
(Via Saragozza 99; beer €3.50-5; ⊙5-10pm Mon-Sat; ☎) This divey rock-and-roll craft-beer bar is the perfect marriage of Megadeth and malt, drawing a legion of leather-bound hopheads and visiting suds seekers, who trample around well-worn hardwoods tanned with spillage. There are 25 taps – a heavy focus on Belgian and Italian sour and funk but always a well-rounded selection – and a small bottle shop.

☆ Entertainment

During July and August, outdoor concerts and ballets are staged on Piazza Grande.

Teatro Comunale Luciano Pavarotti THEATRE
(☑ 059 203 30 10; www.teatrocomunalemodena.it; Corso Canalgrande 85) It will come as no sur-

prise that the birthplace of Pavarotti has a decent opera house. The Comunale opened in 1841 and has 900 seats and 112 boxes. Following the death of the city's exalted native son in September 2007, it was renamed in his honour.

ⓘ Information

Informazione e Accoglienza Turistica (IAT; ☑059 203 26 60; www.visitmodena.it; Piazza Grande 14; ⊘2.30-6pm Mon, 9.30am-1.30pm & 2.30-6pm Tue-Sun) Provides city maps and a wealth of information about the surrounding area, book hotels, and sells tickets to attractions and excursions among medieval Palazzo Comunale ruins. It also offers Unersco World Heritage Site audio guides in English, German, Spanish and French (€4).

Poste Italiane (Post Office; www.poste.it; Via Modonella 8; ⊘8.20am-7.05pm Mon-Fri, 8.20am-12.35pm Sat) Postal services.

ⓘ Getting There & Away

By car, take the A1 Autostrada del Sole if coming from Rome or Milan, or the A22 from Mantua and Verona.

The **train station** (☑06 6847 5475; www. ferroviedellostato.it; Piazza Dante Alighieri) is north of the historic centre, fronting Piazza Dante. Destinations include Bologna (€3.85, 30 minutes, half-hourly), Parma (€5.40, 30 minutes, half-hourly) and Milan (regional €15.55, 2¼ hours, hourly; express €27.50, 1¾ hours, every two hours).

Parco Nazionale dell'Appennino Tosco-Emiliano

In the late 1980s Italy had half a dozen national parks. Today it has 25. One of the newest additions is Parco Nazionale dell' Appennino Tosco-Emiliano (www.appennino reggiano.it), a 260-sq-km parcel of land that straddles the border between Tuscany and Emilia-Romagna. Running along the spine of the Apennine mountains, the park is notable for its hiking potential, extensive beech forests and small population of wolves.

◎ Sights & Activities

Of the park's many majestic peaks, the highest is 2121m Monte Cusna, easily scalable from the village of Civago, near the Tuscan border, on a path (sentiero No 605) that passes the region's best mountain hut, the

Rifugio Cesare Battisti (☑0522 89 74 97; www.rifugio-battisti.it; Ligonchio; dm incl half-board €46). The *rifugio* sits alongside one of Italy's great long-distance walking trails: the three-week, 375km-long Grande Escursione Appennenica (GEA), which bisects the park in five stages from Passo della Forbici (near the Rifugio Cesare Battisti) up to its termination point just outside the park's northwest corner in Montelungo. Sections of the GEA can be done as day walks. *Trekking in the Apennines* by Gillian Price provides an excellent detailed guide of the whole route.

Day-hikers should take on the 5km trek to 1047m Pietra di Bismantova (Castelnovo ne' Monti), which is reachable from the parking lot situated in front of Foresteria San Benedetto or from tiny Eremo di Dismantova monastery, which dates from 1400. From here various paths fan out to the rock's summit (25 minutes). You can also circumnavigate the rock on the lovely 5km Anello della Pietra or even tackle it on a difficult *via ferrata* (trail with permanent cables and ladders), with the proper equipment.

🛏 Sleeping

⭐ **Foresteria San Benedetto**　　　　　LODGE €
(☑0522 61 17 52; www.foresteriasanbenedetto.it; Castelnovo ne' Monti; ⊘s/d/tr/q €45/80/105/140, half board/full board per person extra €15/25) Picturesquely set at the foot of the dramatic Pietra di Bismantova, this simple but cosy lodge offers rooms housing up to six people, along with hearty meals for hikers.

ⓘ Information

Tourist Office (☑0522 81 04 30; www.app enninoreggiano.it; Via Roma 79e, Castelnovo ne' Monti; ⊘9am-noon & 3.30-6.30pm Mon & Wed-Sat, 9am-noon Sun Apr-Sep, 9am-noon Mon, Fri & Sat Oct-Dec) The large village of Castelnovo ne' Monti has an ultrahelpful tourist office that stocks stacks of free information and sells cheap maps of the region for hikers, cyclists and equestrians.

ⓘ Getting There & Away

One of the best gateways to the park is the village of Castelnovo ne' Monti, about 40km south of Reggio Emilia along the winding SS63 on a delightfully scenic ACT bus route. To reach Castelnovo ne' Monti via public transport, take bus 3B44 from Reggio Emilia (€4.50, 1½ hours, seven to 15 daily), operated by **SETA** (☑ 840 000216; www.setaweb.it).

Parma

☑ 0521 / POP 187,000

If reincarnation ever becomes an option, pray you come back as a Parmesan. Where else do you get to cycle to work through streets virtually devoid of cars, lunch on fresh-from-the-attic prosciutto and aged *parmigiano reggiano,* quaff full-bodied Sangiovese wine in regal art-nouveau cafes, and spend sultry summer evenings listening to classical music in architecturally dramatic opera houses?

Smarting from its position as one of Italy's most prosperous cities, Parma has every right to feel smug. More metropolitan than Modena, yet less clamorous than Bologna, this is the city that gave the world Lamborghinis, a composer called Verdi and enough ham and cheese to start a deli chain. Stopping here isn't an option, it's a duty.

◉ Sights

★**Duomo** CATHEDRAL

(www.piazzaduomoparma.com; Piazza del Duomo; ◷10am-6pm Mar-Oct, to 5pm Nov-Feb) Another daring Romanesque beauty? Well, yes and no. Consecrated in 1106, Parma cathedral's has a classic Lombard-Romanesque facade, but inside, the gilded pulpit and ornate lamp-holders scream baroque. Take note: there are some genuine treasures here. Up in the dome, Antonio da Correggio's *Assunzione della Vergine* (Assumption of the Virgin) is a kaleidoscopic swirl of cherubs and whirling angels, while down in the southern transept, Benedetto Antelami's *Deposizione* (Descent from the Cross; 1178) relief is considered a masterpiece of its type.

★**Battistero** CHRISTIAN SITE

(www.piazzaduomoparma.com; Piazza del Duomo; adult/reduced incl Museo Diocesano €8/6; ◷10am-6pm Apr-Oct, to 5pm Nov-Mar) Overshadowing even the cathedral, the octagonal pink-marble baptistery on the south side of the piazza is one of the most important such structures in Italy. Its architecture is a hybrid of Romanesque and Gothic, and its construction started in 1196 on the cusp of the two great architectural eras. The interior is particularly stunning, with its interplay of pencil-thin marble columns and richly

coloured 13th-century frescoes in the Byzantine style, interspersed at irregular intervals with statues and bas-reliefs.

Architect and sculptor Benedetto Antelami oversaw the project and it contains his best work, including a celebrated set of figures representing the months, seasons and signs of the zodiac. The baptistery wasn't completed until 1307 thanks to several interruptions, most notably when the supply of pink Verona marble ran out.

★**Galleria Nazionale** GALLERY

(www.parmabeniartistici.beniculturali.it; Piazza della Pilotta 5; adult/reduced incl Teatro Farnese & Museo Archeologico Nazionale €10/5, after 2pm €5; ◷8.30am-7pm Tue-Sat, to 2pm Sun) The Galleria Nazionale displays Parma's main art collection. Alongside works by local artists Correggio and Parmigianino, you'll find paintings by Fra Angelico, Canaletto and sometimes El Greco. Before you get to the gallery, though, you'll pass through the Teatro Farnese, a copy of Andrea Palladio's Teatro Olimpico in Vicenza.

Teatro Farnese THEATRE

(☑0521 23 33 09; www.parmabeniartistici.beniculturali.it; Piazzale della Pilotta 15; adult/reduced incl Galleria Nazionale & Museo Archeologico Nazionale €10/5, after 2pm €5; ◷8.30am-7pm Tue-Sat, to 2pm Sun) Rebuilt to original plans after WWII bombing, this stunning theatre is almost entirely made out of wood. The great Monteverdi, frustrated by the theatre's acoustic problems before its inaugural event in 1628, was forced to put his orchestra in a pit below the stage – long before 19th-century composer Wagner established this modern practice.

Parco della Cittadella PARK

(Viale Delle Rimembranze 5a; ◷7am-9pm Apr-Oct, to 8pm Sep-Mar) Parma's favourite city park is set inside a cinematic 16th-century pentagonal fortress surrounded by an intact 10m-high wall. Restored and made into a park in 2009, it's a great spot for picnics, adventures with kiddos (there is a playground and a giant trampoline) or a workout: a 1.6km jogging trail flanks the ramparts.

Pinacoteca Stuard MUSEUM

(www.comune.parma.it/cultura; Borgo del Parmigianino 2; ◷10am-5pm Mon & Wed-Fri, 10.30am-6pm Sat & Sun) FREE Giuseppe Stuard was a 19th-century Parmese art collector who amassed 500 years worth of epoch-defining art linking the Tuscan masters of the 1300s to the *novecento* romantics. In 2002 the collection was moved into a wing of this 10th-century Benedictine monastery dedicated to St Paul, where it has been artfully laid out over 24 rooms on the site of an old Roman villa.

Museo Bocchi   MUSEUM
(www.museobocchi.it; Via Cairoli; ⊙ 10.30am-1pm Tue-Sun) FREE Don't underestimate Amedeo Bocchi, a 20th-century Parma-born artist whose painting owes a debt to the symbolism of Gustav Klimt. This museum spreads his stirring work over six rooms. Most compelling are the impressionistic studies of his beloved daughter Bianca.

La Casa del Suono   MUSEUM
(www.casadelsuono.it; Piazzale Salvo d'Acquisto; ⊙ 10am-6pm Wed-Sun) FREE Housed in the 17th-century Chiesa di Santa Elisabetta is this funky modern museum that focuses on the history of music technology. Review the 'ancient' 1970s tape recorders, ponder over jazz-age gramophones and stop to listen under a high-tech 'sonic chandelier'. It's a very good time for audiophiles.

Chiesa & Monastero di San Giovanni Evangelista   CHURCH
(www.monasterosangiovanni.com; Piazzale San Giovanni; ⊙ church 8-11.45am & 3-7.45pm daily, monastery 9-11.30am & 3-5.30pm Mon-Wed, Fri & Sat Oct-May, 3-5.30pm Mon-Wed, Fri & Sat Jun-Sep) Situated directly behind the Duomo, this abbey church is noteworthy for its 16th-century mannerist facade and Correggio's magnificent frescoed dome, which was highly influential for its time and inspired many later works. The adjoining monastery is known as much for the oils and unguents that its monks produce as for its Renaissance cloisters. Upstairs, a library is adorned with huge old maps that hang from the walls of a musty reading room.

Piazza Garibaldi   PIAZZA
On the site of the ancient Roman forum, Piazza Garibaldi is Parma's cobbled hub bisected by the city's main east–west artery, Via Mazzini, and its continuation, Strada della Repubblica. On the square's north side, the facade of the 17th-century **Palazzo del Governatore**, these days municipal offices, sports a giant sundial, added in 1829.

Casa Natale di Toscanini   MUSEUM
(www.museotoscanini.it; Borgo R Tanzi 13; ⊙ 9am-1pm Tue, 9am-1pm & 2-6pm Wed-Sat, 10-6pm Sun) FREE At the Parco Ducale's southeast corner, the birthplace of Italy's greatest modern conductor, Arturo Toscanini (1867–1957), retraces his life and travels through relics and records. Of interest are his collaborations with acclaimed Italian tenor Aureliano Pertile.

☞ Tours

Tastybus   FOOD
(☎ 0521 21 88 89; Piazza Garibaldi; adult/child €55/40) Leaving from Piazza Garibaldi Monday to Friday at 9.30am, this minibus tour (maximum 18 people) is the most convenient (read: *not* the most intimate) way to hit both production farms of *parmigiano reggiano* and *prosciutto di Parma* in one tour. For more information, head to Parma's tourist office.

🛌 Sleeping

★ B&B Pio   B&B
(☎ 347 7769065; www.piorooms.it; Borgo XX Marzo 14; s/d €70/80; 🖤) Location, comfort and hospitality all come together at this B&B run by a gregarious owner with a passion for local food and wine. Four lower-floor doubles and a kitchenette-equipped upper-floor suite share attractive features such as beamed ceilings, antique textiles and ultra-modern fixtures.

Al Ducale   B&B €€
(☎ 0521 28 11 71, www.bbalducale.it; Via della Costituente 11; s/d/tr/q from €50/70/90/110, apt €60-150; ❄🖤) Opera-loving, English-speaking Giovanni is a consummate host at this sensible Oltretorrente choice, which offers well-equipped rooms, studios and one-, two- and three-bedroom apartments. All are within pleasant walking distance of the historical centre, yet are far enough removed from the hubbub to make you really feel like a local.

Organic fruits and breads are delivered to your door each morning, along with any city tips you could ever want or need. It's especially popular with composers, actors and singers, whose autographed messages dot the B&B.

Palazzo dalla Rosa Prati   BOUTIQUE HOTEL €€€
(☎ 0521 38 64 29; www.palazzodallarosaprati.co.uk; Piazza del Duomo 7; r €85-130, ste €150-250,

Parma

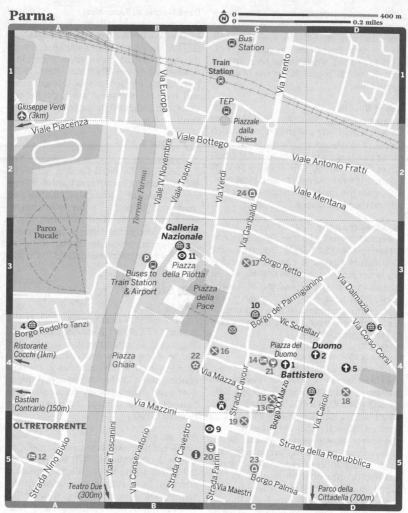

apt €160-280; ❄ 🛜) Kick back like Marie Antoinette in regal digs right next to Parma cathedral. Choose among seven posh and palatial renovated historic suites, 10 modern apartments and two smaller, less expensive doubles. Corner suite 5 is especially alluring, with views into the baptistery's upper window directly across the street (a trade-off for the gaudy pink bedspread).

Downstairs, sip wine or coffee at the modish **T-Cafe** (www.palazzodallarosaprati.it/cafe; Strada Duomo 7; ☺8am-8pm Mon-Wed & Sun, to 3pm Thu, to 9pm Fri & Sat; 🛜). Parking costs €14.

✖ Eating

Most Parma specialities need no introduction to anyone familiar with the food of planet Earth. Both *prosciutto di Parma* (Parma ham) and *parmigiano reggiano* (Parmesean cheese) make excellent antipasto plates, accompanied by a good Sangiovese red. And then there's the horse meat...

Pepèn   SANDWICHES €
(Borgo Sant'Ambrogio 2; sandwiches €2.50-6; ☺8.30am-7.30pm Tue-Thu, 8.30am-3pm & 4.20-7.30pm Fri & Sat) Join the throngs of locals pouring into this buzzing little sandwich

Parma

shop, where *panini* get piled high with *prosciutto di Parma,* cheeses and countless other tasty ingredients. After seven decades, it's a dearly beloved Parma institution.

Borgo 20   MODERN ITALIAN €
(🗷 0521 23 45 65; www.borgo20.it; Borgo XX Marzo 14/16; meals €23; ⏱ 12.15-2.10pm & 7.30-10pm Tue-Sat) A father-son team has taken over from a formerly starred Michelin chef at this wonderful contemporary bistro in the city centre, but the concept – and, more importantly, the food – hasn't skipped a beat. The team continues to serve up inventive culinary treats made from Parma's classic local ingredients.

Ciacco Lab   GELATO €
(www.ciaccolab.it; Via Garibaldi 11; small/medium/large €2/2.50/3.20; ⏱ noon-11.30pm Tue-Thu, to midnight Fri & Sat, to 11pm Sun) 🍦 This experimental farm-to-table gelataria wants nothing to do with additives, preservatives, hydrogenated vegetable oils, added fats or starches, and works directly with Emilian producers to concoct ace flavours. The pistachio is the best we've had in Emilia-Romagna, and surprising choices like green tea matcha or *nero ardente* (with Trinidadian cacao, *añejo* rum and habanero peppers) have some serious bite!

★ **Ristorante Cocchi**   EMILIAN €€
(🗷 0521 98 19 90; www.ristorantecocchi.it; Viale Antonio Gramsci 16a; meals €27-45; ⏱ 12.15-

2.15pm & 7.30-10.15pm Sun-Fri; 🚗) You'll need to venture across the river to Oltretorrente for a traditional Parmigiani experience untainted by the city's influx of culinary tourism. Classy yet unpretentious, father and son duo Corrado and Daniele Cocchi woo you with tradition at this top restaurant.

Anolini in brodo (round pasta pockets stuffed with beef and *parmigiano reggiano* in broth) or *trio di tortelli* (a sampler of square pasta pockets stuffed with ricotta and spinach, pumpkin and potato with Fragno black truffles) – choosing is so painful – and *secondi* specials like sea bass on a bed of blanched artichokes and a touch of olive oil are the reason you have come to Parma. Between October and mid-April, its all about *bolliti* – seven mixed boiled meats served from a traditional cart with numerous sauces. They've been at it since 1925.

Osteria dello Zingaro   OSTERIA €€
(🗷 0521 20 74 83; www.osteriadellozingaro.it; Borgo del Correggio 5b; meals €25-30; ⏱ noon-3pm & 7pm-midnight Mon-Sat; 🚗) Hidden behind the cathedral is this local favourite, a modern bistro clinging to traditional ways. It's most famous for its horse meat (a Parma speciality), but you can also indulge in superb regional classics like *tortelli di erbette* (spinach-and-Parmesan-filled pasta pockets). The personable owner chats up locals while he slices plates of *salumi misti* (six varieties of cured Parma pork).

La Greppia GASTRONOMY €€

(☑ 0521 23 36 86; www.ristorantelagreppia.axelero web.it; Via Garibaldi 39a; meals €30-40; ⊙12.30-2.30pm & 7.30-10.30pm Tue-Sun) A legend in its own lunchtime (and dinnertime, come to that), La Greppia is hallowed ground for the kind of Emilia-Romagna gourmands who know their *ragù* from their bolognese. Sticking tradition and modernity in the same blender, it comes up with sea bass with blanched dandelions, pork confit with pecans and crispy celery and plenty more surprises. Service is impeccable.

🍷 Drinking & Nightlife

★ Bastian Contrario CRAFT BEER

(www.bastiancontrarioparma.it; Strada Inzani 34a; pints €5; ⊙6pm-1am Sun-Thu, to 2am Fri & Sat; 🛜) Owner Marco has done up this cosy neighbourhood bar with a nine-tap distribution system made from recycled farming irrigation piping, with tap handles hand-carved by his father – a retired doctor who surely must harbour an admiration for the monolithic statues of Easter Island – and beer colours displayed in small, hotel-style honey jars.

★ Tabarro BAR

(www.tabarro.net; Strada Farini 5b; wines by the glass from €3.50; ⊙5.30pm-12.45am Sun-Mon & Wed-Thu, to 1.45am Fri, noon-3pm & 5.30pm-1.45am Sat; 🛜) In the heart of Parma's animated Strada Farini drinking scene is this classy but friendly wine bar run by a personable ex-rugby player. In warm weather, aficionados crowd the street out front, sipping fine vintages at barrels draped with tablecloths. For some fine people-watching, grab one of the pavement tables tucked across the street on Borgo Salina.

☆ Entertainment

There are few better places in Italy to see live opera, concerts and theatre. Pick up a copy of Italian-only *Teatri* (www.teatriparma. it) for annual comprehensive theatre and concert listings.

Teatro Regio THEATRE

(☑ 0521 20 39 99; www.teatroregioparma.org; Via Garibaldi 16a; ⊙box office 10.30am-1.30pm & 5-7pm Tue-Sat plus 30min before performances) Offers a particularly rich program of music and opera, even by exacting Italian standards.

Teatro Due THEATRE

(☑ 0521 23 02 42; www.teatrodue.org; Viale Basetti 12a; ⊙box office 10am-1pm & 5-7.30pm Mon-Fri, 10.30am-1pm & 5-7.30pm Sat) Presents the city's top drama.

🛍 Shopping

Salumeria Garibaldi FOOD

(Via Garibaldi 42; ⊙8am-8pm Mon-Sat) Tempting new visitors just steps from the train station is this bountiful delicatessen dating to 1829, with dangling sausages, shelves of Lambrusco wines, slabs of Parma ham and wheel upon wheel of *parmigiano reggiano*.

There's an ever-tempting case of ready-made dishes as well – perfect picnic fodder.

Rural FOOD

(www.rural.it; Borgo Giacomo Tommasini 7; ⊙3.30am-1.30pm & 5-8pm Tue-Sat) ✔ The owners of the former Salumeria Grisenti have gone green: this small but fantastic market now specialises in organic Tuscan-Emilian products direct from farmers whose faces now grace the walls. Pick up sustainably produced black pig *prosciutto*, fresh milk cheeses, delectable olive oils and sauces and other farm-to-table delights.

ℹ Information

Informazione e Accoglienza Turistica (IAT; Tourist Information; ☑ 0521 21 88 89; www. turismo.comune.parma.it; Piazza Garibaldi; ⊙9am-7pm) Parma's helpful tourist information sits handily on Piazza Garibaldi.

Poste Italiane (Post Office; www.poste.it; Strada Melloni 4b; ⊙8.20am-7.05pm Mon-Fri, 8.20am-12.35pm Sat)

ℹ Getting There & Around

Parma is on the A1 connecting Bologna and Milan, and just east of the A15, which runs to La Spezia. Via Emilia (SS9) passes right through town.

Parma's **Giuseppe Verdi Airport** (☑ 0521 95 15 11; www.parma-airport.it; Via Licinio Ferretti 40) is a mere 3km from the city centre. Ryanair (www.ryanair.com) offers service to Trapani and Cagliari; Mistral Air (www.mistralair.it) to Olbia; and FlyOne (www.flyone.md) to Chișinău (Moldova). **Bus 6 (Aeroporto)** (Viale Toschi), best-caught heading north along Viale Toschi near Palazzo della Pilotta, links to both the train station and airport (€1.20).

From the **bus station** (Piazzale dalla Chiesa), attached to the north side of Parma's train station, **TEP** (☑ 0521 21 41; www.tep.pr.it) operates buses throughout the region; and **Flixbus** (www.

flixbus.com) goes to Rome, Milan, Naples and Perugia, among others.

There are trains once or twice hourly from Parma's newly remodelled **train station** (www.trenitalia.com; Piazza Carlo Alberto Dalla Chiesa 11; ⊗ 4.30am-1.30am) to Milan (regional/express €11.10/19.90, 1¼ to 1¾ hours), Bologna (€7.35, one to 1¼ hours), Modena (€5.40, 30 minutes) and Piacenza (€5.40, 40 minutes, half-hourly).

The taxi queue is unsigned and difficult to find on arrival at the train station. It's on level one along Viale Falcone on the west side of the station. A taxi to the airport from the station runs around €10.

Busseto & Verdi Country

During the 'golden age of opera' in the second half of the 19th century, only Wagner came close to emulating Giuseppe Verdi, Italy's operatic genius who was born in the tiny village of Roncole Verdi in 1813. You can discover his extraordinary legacy starting in the town of Busseto (35km northwest of Parma), a pleasant place imbued with history and endowed with some good cafes and restaurants. There are enough sights for a decent musical day out.

◉ Sights

★ Teatro Verdi
THEATRE

(Piazza Verdi; adult/reduced €4/3; ⊗ 9.30am-12.30pm & 3-6pm Tue-Sun Apr-Oct, to 5pm Nov-Mar) This stately theatre on Busseto's aptly named Piazza Verdi was built in 1868, although Verdi himself initially pooh-poohed the idea. It opened with a performance of his masterpiece *Rigoletto*. Guided tours in English (and sometimes German or French) take place every 30 minutes.

Villa Verdi
MUSEUM

(www.villaverdi.org; Via Verdi 22, S Agata di Villanova sull'Arda; adult/reduced €9/5; ⊗ 9.30-11.45am & 2.30-6.15pm Tue-Sun Apr-Oct, shorter hours rest of year) Verdi's 56-room villa, where he composed many of his major works, is 5km northwest of Busseto. Verdi lived and worked here from 1851 onwards and literally willed it to remain just as he left it, leaving behind a fascinating array of furniture, personal artefacts and art, just as it was the day he passed. Guided visits through the five rooms open to the public (descendants of Verdi's second cousin still occupy the rest) start every 30 minutes.

Museo Nazionale Giuseppe Verdi
MUSEUM

(www.museogiuseppeverdi.it; Via Provesi 35; adult/reduced €9/7; ⊗ 10am-6.30pm Tue-Sun Apr-Oct, shorter hours rest of year) Take a trip through the rooms of this fine country mansion turned museum, which cleverly maps out the story of Verdi's life through paintings, music and audio guides (€1; available in English, German and French). As you explore, you'll undoubtedly recognise numerous stanzas from classic operas such as *Il Trovatore* and *Aida*, still fresh after two centuries.

WORTH A TRIP

ANTICA CORTE PALLAVICINA

Picking favourites at the 14th-century **Antica Corte Pallavicina** (☎ 0524 93 65 39; www.anticacortepallavicinarelais.com; Strada Palazzo due Torri 3, Polesine Parmense; 7-course tasting menu €86-94, with wines €115-125; ⊗ noon-2.30pm & 7.30-10pm Tue-Sun; [P][☎]) is excruciating: there's the castle itself, especially when enveloped in cinematic Po river fog; the ageing cave, where 5000 of the world's best *salumi* (cured meats) hang alongside namecards of their owners (Prince Charles, Monaco's Prince Albert II); the 11 rooms with enchanting free-standing bathtubs; or Massimo Spigaroli's one-star Michelin foodgasm.

Luckily, choosing one over the other is not mandatory, which is why this food-focused destination hotel and restaurant makes most for a memorable culinary stopover.

The charcuterie plates include a sampling of the sublime, top-of-the-line *culatello di suico nero di Parma* (made from the free-range black pigs) and nearly everything else on your plate is made in-house (their own aged *parmigiano reggiano*, the butter, the herbs and vegetables – they even make their own wine). And then there's the cheese service. You will never forget that cheese service!

It's 6km from central Busseto.

Casa Natale di Giuseppe Verdi
MUSEUM

(www.casanataleverdi.it; Via della Processione 1, Roncole Verdi; adult/reduced €6/4; ⊙ 9.30am-1pm & 2.30-6pm Tue-Sun Apr-Oct, shorter hours rest of year) The humble cottage where Giuseppe Verdi was born in 1813 is now a small museum. Grab a tablet at the entrance to take advantage of multimedia exhibits highlighting the composer's life and music. It's in the hamlet of Roncole Verdi, 5km southeast of Busseto.

ℹ Information

A combined ticket covering many of the Verdi-related sights costs €14. For more information, contact Busseto's **tourist office** (☑ 0524 9 24 87; www.bussetolive.com; Piazza Verdi 10; ⊙ 9.30am-1pm & 3-6.30pm Tue-Sun Apr-Oct, shorter hours rest of year).

ℹ Getting There & Away

The train from Parma to Busseto (€3.85, 30 to 45 minutes) requires a change in Fidenza. Alternatively, **TEP** (www.tep.pr.it; Piazzale Carlo Alberto della Chiesa) offers direct but slow bus service between the two towns (1½ hours, one to three daily) on route 2106.

Ferrara

☑ 0532 / POP 135,000

A heavyweight Renaissance art city peppered with colossal palaces and still ringed by its intact medieval walls, Ferrara jumps out at you like an absconded Casanova (he once stayed here) on the route between Bologna and Venice. But, like any city situated in close proximity to La Serenissima, it is serially overlooked, despite its UNESCO World Heritage status. As a result, Venice avoiders will find that Ferrara's bike-friendly streets and frozen-in-time *palazzi* relatively unexplored and deliciously tranquil.

Historically, Ferrara was the domain of the powerful Este clan, rivals to Florence's Medici in power and prestige, who endowed the city with its signature building – a huge castle complete with moat positioned slap-bang in the city centre. Ferrara suffered damage from bombing raids during WWII, but its historical core remains intact. Of particular interest is the former Jewish ghetto, the region's largest and oldest, which prevailed from 1627 until 1859.

◉ Sights

Renaissance palaces reborn as museums are Ferrara's tour de force. Also check out the intricate old town with its one-time Jewish ghetto. Note that most museums are closed on Monday.

If you're sticking around for a while, you'll save money with a **MyFE Ferrara Tourist Card** (www.myfecard.it/en; 2-/3-/6-day card €10/12/18), which offers free museum admissions, some exemptions from Ferrara's hotel tourist tax and discounts at some hotels and restaurants.

★ Palazzo dei Diamanti
PALACE

(www.palazzodiamanti.it; Corso Ercole I d'Este 21) Named after the spiky diamond-shaped ashlar stones on its facade, the late-15th-century 'diamond palace' was built for Sigismondo d'Este. It houses Ferrara's Pinacoteca Nazionale (p460), where you can contemplate the genius of the 16th- to 17th-century 'Ferrara school'. High-profile special exhibits are held in the adjacent **Spazio Espositivo** (adult/reduced €13/11; ⊙ 10am-8pm).

★ Castello Estense
CASTLE

(www.castelloestense.it; Viale Cavour; adult/reduced €8/6; ⊙ 9.30am-5.30pm Tue-Sun Jan-Feb & Oct-Dec, 9.30am-5.30pm Mar-Sep.) Complete with moat and drawbridge, Ferrara's towering castle was commissioned by Nicolò II d'Este in 1385. Initially it was intended to protect him and his family from the town's irate citizenry, who were up in arms over tax increases, but in the late 15th century it became the family's permanent residence. Although sections are now used as government offices, a few rooms, including the royal suites, are open for viewing.

Highlights are the **Sala dei Giganti** (Giants' Room), **Salone dei Giochi** (Games Salon), **Cappella di Renée de France** and the claustrophobic **dungeon**. It was here in 1425 that Duke Nicolò III d'Este had his young second wife, Parisina Malatesta, and his son, Ugo, beheaded after discovering they were lovers, providing the inspiration for Robert Browning's *My Last Duchess*.

City Walls
WALLS

Unbroken on their northern and eastern sections, and adorned with a well-marked set of walking and cycling paths, Ferrara's 9km of city walls are among the most impressive in Italy.

Ferrara

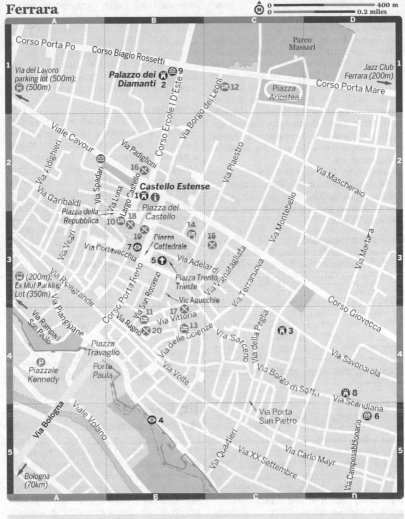

Ferrara

Palazzo Schifanoia
PALACE

(www.artecultura.fe.it/159/museo-schifanoia; Via Scandiana 23; adult/reduced €3/2; ☉9.30am-6pm Tue-Sun) Dating to 1385, the Este's 14th-century pleasure palace suffered significant earthquake damage in May 2012, but its highlight – the **Salone dei Mesi** (Room of the Months) – remains open to visitors. Inside you'll find Ferrara's most famous frescoes, executed by Francesco del Cossa in 1470, which depict the months, seasons and signs of the zodiac and constitute an exceptionally fine and cohesive example of secular Renaissance art.

Covered by the same ticket is the nearby **Museo Lapidario** (Via Camposabbionario; ☉9.30am-6pm Tue-Sun), with its small collection of Roman and Etruscan stelae, tombs and inscriptions.

Pinacoteca Nazionale
GALLERY

(www.gallerie-estensi.beniculturali.it; Corso Ercole I d'Este 21; adult/reduced €4/2; ☉8.30am-2pm Tue-Wed, 8.30am-7pm Thu, 1.30-7pm Fri-Sun) Ferrara's art gallery, housed in the late-15th-century Palazzo dei Diamanti, is the perfect spot to contemplate the genius of the 16th- to 17th-century 'Ferrara school', spearheaded by artists with odd nicknames such as Guercino (the squinter) and Il Maestro degli Occhi Spalancati (master of the wide-open eyes). Free audio guides enhance the experience.

Duomo
CATHEDRAL

(Piazza Cattedrale; ☉7.30am-noon & 3.30-6.30pm Mon-Sat, 7.30am-12.30pm & 3.30-7pm Sun) The outstanding feature of the pink-and-white 12th-century cathedral is its three-tiered marble facade – under renovation at time of research – combining Romanesque and Gothic styles on the lower and upper tiers respectively. Much of the upper level is a graphic representation of *The Last Judgment,* and heaven and hell (notice the four figures clambering out of their coffins). Astride a pair of handsome lions on either side of the main doorway squats an oddly secular duo, mouths agape at the effort of holding up the pillars.

Palazzo Municipale
ARCHITECTURE

(Piazza Municipale 2; ☉9am-1pm Mon, Wed & Fri, 9am-1pm & 3-5pm Tue & Thu) **FREE** Linked to the castle by an elevated passageway, the 13th-century crenellated Palazzo Municipale was the Este family home until they moved next door to the castle in the late 15th century.

Nowadays, it's largely occupied by administrative offices but you can wander around its twin courtyards or ogle 1930s-era frescos in the Sala dell'Arengo (when there isn't an event on). The entrance is watched over by copper statues of Nicolò III and his less-wayward son Borso – they're 20th-century copies but nonetheless imposing.

Casa Romei
PALACE

(Via Savonarola 30; adult/reduced €3/1.50; ☉8.30am-2pm Sun-Wed, 2-7.30pm Thu-Sat) This palace was once owned by Giovanni Romei, a top administrator to the Este clan – and his importance shows in the architecture. The austere brick exterior hides a peaceful inner patio (once part of an adjacent monastery). On the 1st floor is a 16th-century apartment preserved in its original state. There's plenty of art and frescoes dotted around.

★ Festivals & Events

Il Palio
SPORTS

(www.paliodiferrara.it; ☉May) On the last Sunday of May each year, the eight *contrade* (districts) of Ferrara compete in a horse race that momentarily turns Piazza Ariostea into medieval bedlam. Claimed to be the oldest race of its kind in Italy, Ferrara's Palio was first held in 1259, and was officially enshrined as an annual competition in 1279.

⊫ Sleeping

★ Le Stanze di Torcicoda
B&B €

(☑380 9068718; www.lestanze.it; Vicolo Mozzo Torcicoda 9; s €60-70, d €85-110; ✳✳☎) Tucked down a crooked lane in Ferrara's old Jewish quarter, this cosy, long-established B&B offers four rooms of varying sizes in a late 14th-century *cassero* (medieval house). Owner Pietro Zanni keeps things environmentally friendly with outstanding made-from-scratch, organic-leaning breakfasts, green cleaning products and services for cyclists including an enclosed bike garage.

Locanda Borgonuovo
B&B €

(☑0532 21 11 00; www.borgonuovo.com; Via Cairoli 29; s €50-60, d €80-100; ℗✳@☎) Just around the corner from the Duomo, this little gem is Italy's oldest B&B. Four refined rooms and two apartments, each decorated with antiques, come with polished wood floors, minibars, safes, flat-screen TVs and wi-fi. Enjoy breakfast in the elegant upstairs sitting room, or retire to the central patio. Parking costs €10, and guests have free access to bikes.

Albergo degli Artisti
GUESTHOUSE €

(☑0532 76 10 38; www.albergoartisti.it; Via Vittoria 66; s/d €40/60, without bathroom €28/50; 🛜) Ferrara's most economical option, run by a doting ex-Yugoslavian, offers 20 immaculate rooms at an unbeatable price on a back alley within a five-minute walk of the Duomo and Castello Estense. Attractive common spaces include a sunny upstairs terrace and a teeny but cheerful guest kitchen. Book ahead for the three rooms with bathroom. No breakfast.

★ Alchimia B&B
B&B €€

(☑0532 186 46 56; www.alchimiaferrara.it; Via Borgo dei Leoni 122; s €70-90, d €90-130; 🅿🞖🛜) Occupying a lovingly remodelled 15th century home with a spacious, green backyard, this classy six-room B&B seamlessly blends wood-beamed high ceilings with modern comforts such as memory-foam beds, electric tea kettles, state-of-the-art bathrooms, fantastic air-con, rock-solid wi-fi and self-serve wine fridges.

Albergo Annunziata
HOTEL €€

(☑0532 20 11 11; www.annunziata.it; Piazza della Repubblica 5; r €90-200, ste €140-350; 🅿🞖@🛜) At this top-notch, centrally located four-star hotel, romantics can be forgiven for having Casanova apparitions (the man himself once stayed here). Six of the sharp modernist rooms with mosaic bathrooms come with direct views of Castello Estense. Guests enjoy free use of bikes, along with a breakfast that's often described as Italy's best, while kids love the complimentary table football.

✗ Eating

Like all Emilian cities, Ferrara has its gastronomic nuances. Don't leave town without trying *cappellacci di zucca,* a hat-shaped pasta pouch filled with pumpkin and herbs, and brushed with sage and butter.

Salama da sugo is a stewed pork sausage, while *pasticcio di maccheroni* is an oven-baked macaroni pie topped with Parmesan. Even Ferrarese bread is distinctive, shaped into a crunchy twisted knot.

★ Trattoria da Noemi
TRATTORIA €€

(☑0532 76 90 70; www.trattoriadanoemi.it; Via Ragno 31a; meals €28-35; ⊙noon-2.30pm & 7.30-10.30pm Wed-Mon; 🛜) All of Ferrara's classic dishes are delivered *con molto amore* (with much love) at this back-alley eatery named after the hardworking, independent-spirited mother of proprietor Maria Cristina Borgazzi. Arrive early (yes, it's busy) to get some of the city's best *cappellacci di zucca,* grilled meats, macaroni pie and a wonderfully messy and extraordinary *zuppe inglese* finish.

Ca' d' Frara
ITALIAN €€

(☑0532 20 50 57; www.ristorantecadfrara.it; Via del Gambero 4; meals €27-33; ⊙12.15-2pm & 7.15-10pm Thu-Mon, 7.15-10pm Tue-Wed) Looking for a reasonably priced place to sample Ferrara's full gamut of culinary specialities? Step into this classy back-alley trattoria and order the 'Tradizione Ferrarese' menu (€26), a seemingly endless parade of courses that includes antipasti, *cappellacci di zucca, pasticcio di maccheroni, salama da sugo* with mashed potatoes and dessert, all served in a smart modern dining room.

Osteria Savonarola
OSTERIA €€

(☑0532 20 02 14; Piazza Savonarola 18; meals €23-31; ⊙12.30-3.30pm & 7pm-midnight Tue-Sun) Friendly, efficient service and outdoor seating on an arcaded pavement with prime Castello Estense views make this an enjoyable warm-weather spot wildly popular with Ferraresi for lunch or dinner. The menu is classically Ferrarese, and prices are easy on the wallet.

Osteria Quattro Angeli
ITALIAN €€

(☑0532 21 18 69; www.osteriaiquattroangeli.it; Piazza Castello 10; meals €25-30; ⊙8am-1am Tue-Sun) Relax beneath fat, sausage-shaped salamis opposite the castle and demolish enormous portions of Ferrarese classics – there's a divine *cappellacci di zucca al ragù* (pumpkin stuffed pasta with meat sauce) supplemented by cuts of local cured meat. Come 6pm, the tented section out front becomes a busy *aperitivi* bar, upping the noise levels and heightening the atmosphere.

Osteria del Ghetto
OSTERIA €€

(☑0532 76 49 36; www.osteriadelghetto.it; Via Vittoria 26; meals €25-30; ⊙noon-2.30pm & 7.30-10.30pm Tue-Sun) An understated jewel amid the winding streets of Ferrara's old Jewish ghetto, this *osteria* leads you through a nondescript downstairs bar up to a bright upstairs dining room embellished with striking modern murals. The excellent menu mixes Ferrara staples like *cappellacci di zucca* with a less-predictable fish menu.

Il Don Giovanni   GASTRONOMY €€€
(☑ 0532 24 33 63; www.ildongiovanni.com; Corso Ercole I d'Este 1; meals €55-70; ☺ 12.30-2pm & 7.30-10.30pm Tue-Sat, 12.30-2.30pm Sun) This highly acclaimed eatery specialises in fresh-caught fish from the Adriatic, vegetables harvested from the restaurant's own garden, eight varieties of bread baked daily and a wine list featuring over 600 Italian and international labels. The menu is an imaginative feast of unconventional concoctions; guinea-fowl-stuffed pasta and roast eel stand out.

☆ Entertainment

Jazz Club Ferrara   JAZZ
(☑ 0532 171 67 39; www.jazzclubferrara.com; Via 167, Rampari di Belfiore; ☺ 8pm-2am Fri & Sat & Mon) There are few places in the solar system more cinematic than this extraordinary and intimate house of swing and syncopation occupying a restored Renaissance defense tower dating to 1493. Considered one of Europe's top jazz clubs, it draws top talent from around the world – especially the USA and Brazil – and seeing a show here is a privilege indeed.

❶ Information

Informazione e Accoglienza Turistica (IAT; Tourist Information; ☑ 0532 20 93 70; www. ferraraterraeacqua.it; ☺ 9am-6pm Mon-Sat, 9.30am-5.30pm Sun) In Castello Estense's courtyard; very helpful. If there is an extensive line for castle tickets, you don't need to wait to go to IAT – just politely *Scusi* yourself through the line.

Poste Italiane (Post Office; www.poste.it; Viale Cavour 27; ☺ 8.20am-7.05pm Mon-Fri, 8.20am-12.35pm Sat)

❶ Getting There & Away

Ferrara Bus & Fly (☑ 333 2005157; www. ferrarabusandfly.it; €15) offers direct transfers eight times daily between Bologna's Guglielmo Marconi airport and Ferrara (€15, one hour, 4.45am-10.30pm). From Ferrara, buses leave from the train station and Viale Cavour.

From Ferrara's **train station** (www.trenitalia. it; Piazzale della Stazione 28), situated 1.5km west of the centre, regular train services run frequently to Bologna (€4.75, 30 to 50 minutes, half-hourly), Ravenna (€6.65, one to 1½ hours,

hourly) as well as other destinations throughout Emilia-Romagna.

❶ Getting Around

TPER (☑ 0532 59 94 11; www.tper.it) operates frequent local buses along Viale Cavour between the train station and the centre (€1.30, five minutes) – take No 1, 6 or 9. For Castello Estense, get off at Cavour Giardini. **Punto Bus** (☑ 0532 59 94 90; www.tper.it; Piazzale della Stazione 24; ☺ 7am-7pm Mon-Sat, 8am-2pm Sun), inside the train station, provides bus information and tickets. **Buses** (Piazzale della Stazione) leave just across the street from the station.

Most traffic is banned from the city centre. Free 24-hour parking is available at the **Ex Mof** (corner of Corso Isonzo and Via Darsena) and **Via del Lavoro** (Via del Lavoro) parking lots (located south of the *centro storico* and behind the train station, respectively). For a comprehensive list of parking options, see www. ferraratua.com.

Get in the saddle and join the hundreds of other pedallers in one of Italy's most cycle-friendly cities. Many places, such as **Pirani e Bagni** (☑ 0532 77 21 90; Piazzale Stazione 2; bike rental per 1hr/3hr/day €2/5/7; ☺ 4.45am-8pm Mon-Fri, 6.30am-2pm Sat) situated beside the train station and **Ferrara Store** (www.ferrarastore.it; Piazza della Repubblica 23/25; per hour/day €3/12; ☺ 7.30am-7pm Mon-Sat, 9am-6pm Sun) located near Castello Estense, rent bikes – the latter is an in-town representative for **BiciDeltaPo** (www.bicideltapo.it) and must be reserved in advanced. The tourist office can provide information on the region's well-developed network of bike routes; look for the spiral-bound *Bike Book*, which details recommended cycling itineraries throughout Ferrara and the Po Delta.

Ravenna

☑ 0544 / POP 160,000

For mosaic lovers, Ravenna is an earthly paradise. Spread out over several churches and baptisteries around town is one of the world's most dazzling collections of early Christian mosaic artwork, enshrined since 1996 on Unesco's World Heritage list. Wandering through the unassuming town centre today, you would never imagine that for a three-century span beginning in AD 402, Ravenna served as capital of the Western Roman Empire, as well as the chief city of the Ostrogoth Kingdom of Italy and nexus of a powerful Byzantine exarchate. During this prolonged golden

Ravenna

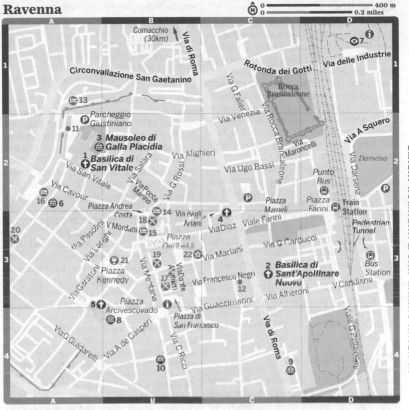

Ravenna

🏛 Top Sights

◎ Sights

◈ Activities, Courses & Tours

🛏 Sleeping

✕ Eating

🍷 Drinking & Nightlife

🎭 Entertainment

age, while the rest of the Italian peninsula flailed in the wake of Barbarian invasions, Ravenna became a fertile art studio for skilled craftsmen, who covered the city's terracotta brick churches in heart-rendingly beautiful mosaics.

⊙ Sights

Ravenna revolves around its eight Unesco World Heritage Sites (seven scattered about town, one 5km to the southeast). A *biglietto cumulativo* (combo ticket, €9.50), good for seven days, grants access to five of the sites: San Vitale, Galla Placidia, Sant'Apollinare Nuovo, Museo Arcivescovile and Battistero Neoniano. Three others (Sant'Apollinare in Classe, Mausoleo di Teodorico and Battistero degli Ariani) require individual tickets. The website www.ravennamosaici.it gives more information.

The city's brilliant 4th- to 6th-century gold, emerald and sapphire masterpieces will leave you struggling for adjectives. A suitably impressed Dante once described them as a 'symphony of colour' and spent the last few years of his life admiring them. Romantic toff Lord Byron added further weight to Ravenna's literary credentials when he spent a couple of years here before decamping to Greece.

Be on the lookout for the impressive new Museo Archeologico di Classe, which is expected to be up and running inside a former sugar factory next door to Basilica di Sant'Apollinare in Classe by 2018.

★ Mausoleo di Galla Placidia
HISTORIC BUILDING

(www.ravennamosaici.it; Via San Vitale; 5-site combo ticket €9.50 plus summer-only surcharge €2; ⊙ 9am-7pm Mar-Oct, 10am-5pm Nov-Feb) In the same complex as Basilica di San Vitale, the small but equally incandescent Mausoleo di Galla Placidia was constructed for Galla Placidia, the half-sister of Emperor Honorius, who initiated construction of many of Ravenna's grandest buildings. The mosaics here are the oldest in Ravenna, probably dating from around AD 430.

★ Basilica di Sant'Apollinare Nuovo
CHURCH

(www.ravennamosaici.it; Via di Roma 52; 5-site combo ticket €9.50; ⊙ 9am-7pm Apr-Sep, 9.30am-5.30pm Mar & Oct, 10am-5pm Nov-Feb) An old legend states that Pope Gregory the Great once ordered the Apollinare's mosaics to be blackened as they were distracting worshippers from prayer. A millennium and a half later, the dazzling Christian handiwork is still having the same effect. It's almost impossible to take your eyes off the 26 white-robed martyrs heading towards Christ with his apostles on the right (south) wall. On the opposite side, an equally expressive procession of virgins bears similar offerings for the Madonna.

The basilica dates originally from the 560s and its architectural fusion of Christian east and west can be seen in its marble porticoes and distinctive conical bell tower.

★ Basilica di San Vitale
CHURCH

(www.ravennamosaici.it; Via San Vitale; 5-site combo ticket €9.50; ⊙ 9am-7pm Mar-Oct, 10am-5pm Nov-Feb) Sometimes, after weeks of strolling around dark Italian churches, you can lose your sense of wonder. Not here! The lucid mosaics that adorn the altar of this ancient church consecrated in 547 by Archbishop Massimiano invoke a sharp intake of breath in most visitors. Gaze in wonder at the rich greens, brilliant golds and deep blues bathed in shafts of soft yellow sunlight.

The mosaics on the side and end walls inside the church represent scenes from the Old Testament: to the left, Abraham prepares to sacrifice Isaac in the presence of three angels, while the one on the right portrays the death of Abel and the offering of Melchizedek. Inside the chancel, two magnificent mosaics depict the Byzantine emperor Justinian with San Massimiano and a particularly solemn and expressive Empress Theodora, who was his consort.

★ Basilica di Sant'Apollinare in Classe
CHURCH

(Via Romea Sud 224; adult/reduced €5/2.50; ⊙ 8.30am-7.30pm Mon-Sat, 1-7.30pm Sun) This signature early Christian basilica, lighter than Ravenna's other churches, is situated 5km southeast of town in the former Roman port of Classe. Its magnificent central apse mosaic, featuring Ravenna's patron Sant'Apollinare flanked by sheep and juxtaposed against a stunningly green landscape, is surmounted by a brilliant star-spangled triumphal arch displaying symbols of the four evangelists.

Other mosaics in the apse depict Byzantine emperor Constantine IV (652–685) and biblical figures such as Abel and Abraham. The basilica – architecturally the city's most 'perfect' – was built in the early 6th century on the burial site of Ravenna's patron saint, who converted the city to Christianity in the 2nd century.

To get here, take a local train to Classe (€1.30, five minutes), one stop in the direction of Rimini, or catch bus 4 opposite the train station. There's free admission on the first Sunday of the month.

Battistero Neoniano
CHRISTIAN SITE

(www.ravennamosaici.it; Piazza del Duomo; 5-site combo ticket €9.50; ⊘9am-7pm Mar-Oct, 10am-5pm Nov-Feb) Roman ruins aside, this is Ravenna's oldest intact building, constructed over the site of a former Roman bathing complex in the late 4th century. Built in an octagonal shape, as was the custom with all Christian baptisteries of this period, it was originally attached to a church (since destroyed). The mosaics, which thematically depict Christ being baptised by St John the Baptist in the River Jordan, were added at the end of the 5th century.

Museo Arcivescovile
MUSEUM

(www.ravennamosaici.it; Piazza Arcivescovado; 5-site combo ticket €9.50; ⊘9am-7pm Mar-Oct, 10am-5pm Nov-Feb) A museum with a difference, this religious gem is on the 2nd floor of the Archiepiscopal Palace. It hides two not-to-be-missed exhibits: an exquisite ivory throne carved for Emperor Maximilian by Byzantium craftsmen in the 6th century (the surviving detail is astounding); and a stunning collection of mosaics in the 5th-century chapel of San Andrea, which has been cleverly incorporated into the museum's plush modern interior.

Battistero degli Ariani
CHRISTIAN SITE

(Via degli Ariani; adult/reduced €1/0.50; ⊘8.30am-7pm) The €1 entry here (unique among Ravenna's Unesco sites) is no reflection of the quality of the artistry inside. The baptistery's breathtaking dome mosaic, depicting the baptism of Christ encircled by the 12 apostles, was completed over a period of years beginning in the 5th century.

Museo TAMO
MUSEUM

(www.tamoravenna.it; Via Nicolò Rondinelli 2; adult/reduced €4/3; ⊘10am-6.30pm) This newer museum doubles-down on Ravenna's extraordinary history of mosaic work by chronicling 12 centuries of history, using technology and multimedia presentations with a particular emphasis on contemporary work. Highlights include a Dante Alighieri–inspired exhibit of 21 thematic works commissioned from great Italian artists in the 1960s. Equally impressive is the setting itself inside the restored 14th-century San Nicolò church, which is covered in frescoes and other historic detail.

Museo d'Arte della Città di Ravenna
GALLERY

(www.mar.ra.it; Via di Roma 13; adult/reduced €6/5; ⊘9am-6pm Tue-Sat) Arranged in a converted 15th-century monastery abutting a public garden, Ravenna's permanent art collection is backed up by regular temporary expos. The ground floor features some rather fetching modern mosaics, first brought together in the 1950s, including one (Le Coq Bleu) based on a design by Marc Chagall.

Domus dei Tappeti di Pietra
MUSEUM

(www.domusdeitappetidipietra.it; Via Gianbattista Barbiani; adult/reduced €4/3; ⊘10am-6.30pm Mar-Sep, shorter hours rest of year) Not nearly as impressive as the Unesco site mosaics, but still worth a look for serious aficionados, these 6th century floor mosaics from a 14-room late-Roman palace were only unearthed in 1993. Restored but incomplete, they show considerable artistic merit, and are decorated with geometric and floral designs.

Mausoleo di Teodorico
TOMB

(Via delle Industrie 14; adult/reduced €4/2; ⊘8.30am-5.30pm Oct-Mar, to 7pm Apr-Sep) Historically and architecturally distinct from Ravenna's other Unesco sites (there are no mosaics here), this two-storey mausoleum was built in 520 for Gothic king Teodorico, who ruled Italy as a Byzantine viceroy. It is notable for its Gothic design features and throwback Roman construction techniques: the huge blocks of stone were not cemented by any mortar. At the heart of the mausoleum is a Roman porphyry basin recycled as a sarcophagus. It's 2km from the city centre; take bus 5.

🍃 Courses

Gruppo Mosaicisti
ART

(www.gruppomosaicisti.it; Via Fiandrini 8; courses from €550) Tucked around the side of San Vitale, this school offers a variety of mosaic-making courses for beginners, experienced artists and those involved in professional restoration work.

Mosaic Art School
ART

(www.mosaicschool.com; Via Francesco Negri 14) Offers five-day intensive mosaic-making courses for all skill levels (€690).

✿ Festivals & Events

Ravenna Festival
MUSIC

(www.ravennafestival.org; tickets €12-80; ⊘ May-Jul) Renowned Italian conductor Riccardo Muti has close ties with Ravenna and is intimately involved with this classical-music festival each year. Concerts are staged at venues all over town, including the **Teatro Alighieri** (☎ 0544 24 92 11; www.teatroalighieri.org; Via Mariani 2; ⊘ box office 10am-1pm Mon-Wed & Fri, 10am-1pm & 4-6pm Thu).

Ravenna Jazz
MUSIC

(www.erjn.it/ravenna; ⊘ May) At this festival dating back to the 1970s, stars of the jazz firmament descend on town.

🛏 Sleeping

★ M Club Deluxe
B&B €

(☎ 333 9556466; www.m-club.it; Piazza Baracca 26; s €58-70, d €75-110; P ❀ 🛜) Two minutes from San Vitale's gorgeous mosaics, industrious young owner Michael Scapini Mantovani has converted this old family home into a luxurious B&B. Historical touches (ancient beamed ceilings, a stuffed crocodile brought from Ethiopia by a great uncle, Michael's father's decades-old collection of *National Geographics*) coexist with countless modern conveniences, including supercomfy beds and wi-fi routers in every room.

Ai Giardini di San Vitale
B&B €

(☎ 0544 3 35 53; www.g-sanvitale.it; Via Don Giovanni Minzoni 63; s €48-88, d €55-118; ❀ 🛜) It's not necessarily about the rooms (simple but spacious) at this family-run, six-room B&B, but rather the jungly back gardens, which sit right next door to Basilica di San Vitale, though you'd never know it – the tourist soundtrack is drowned out by chirping birds in this wonderfully peaceful urban retreat.

Hotel Centrale Byron
HOTEL €

(☎ 0544 21 22 25; www.hotelbyron.com; Via IV Novembre 14; s €58-70, d €75-110; ❀ @ 🛜) You can't beat the friendly Byron's location, in the car-free, wonderfully ingratiating streets of central Ravenna. It's no lie to say you could kick a football from the window of one of the 52 clean, modern rooms into pivotal (and beautiful) Piazza del Popolo.

★ Albergo Cappello
BOUTIQUE HOTEL €€

(☎ 0544 21 98 13; www.albergocappello.it; Via IV Novembre 41; r €99-189; P ❀ @ 🛜) Colour-themed rooms come in three categories at this finely coiffed seven-room boutique hotel smack in the town centre. Murano glass chandeliers, original 15th-century frescoes and coffered ceilings are set against modern fixtures and flat-screen TVs; some rooms boast Venetian silk wallpaper and wood-panelled bathrooms. The ample breakfast features pastries from Ravenna's finest *pasticceria*.

✕ Eating

La Piadina del Melarancio
FAST FOOD €

(www.lapiadina.biz; Via IV Novembre 31; piadinas €3.50-5.50; ⊘ 11.30am-8.30pm Sun-Thu, to 9.30pm Fri & Sat; 🛜) This simple city-centre spot is a great place to try Romagna's classic snack food: a hot, fresh *piadina* (stuffed flatbread). Fillings range from *squacquerone* cheese with caramelised figs to roasted pork and smoked *scamorza* cheese. Place your order at the front counter and wait until your number's called.

★ Ca' de Vèn
RISTORANTE €€

(☎ 0544 3 01 63; www.cadeven.it; Via Corrado Ricci 24; meals €30-35; ⊘ noon-2.30pm & 6-10pm Tue-Sun; 🛜) Old men and their dogs swap oenological tips with wine snobs in this cavernous wine-bar-cum-restaurant beautified with frescoed vaulting and floor-to-ceiling shelves stuffed with bottles, books and other curiosities. Settle in over excellent *aperitivi* and, when the room starts to spin, decamp to the wood-panelled back hall for delectable Romagnola specialities like *squacquerone* cheese pudding with crunchy ham.

Osteria L'Acciuga
SEAFOOD €€

(☎ 0544 21 27 13; www.osterialacciuga.it; Viale Baracca 74; meals €35-45; ⊘ 12.30-2.30pm & 7.30-10.30pm Mon-Sat, 12.30-2.30pm Sun; 🛜) For an inventive change of culinary pace, head to this classy seafooder far enough away from Ravenna's Unesco sites to feel authentic, but close enough to walk. Impressive interiors were forged from a decommissioned submarine, and the changing menu is dependent upon the daily catch.

Osteria dei Battibecchi
OSTERIA €€

(☎ 0544 21 95 36; www.osteriadeibattibecchi.it; Via della Tesoreria Vecchia 16; meals €25-32; ⊘ 12.30-3pm & 7pm-midnight) Simple Romagnola food done right is the hallmark of this Slow Food–recommended local favourite – from the basket of warm *piadina* bread that comes unbidden to your table, through scrumptious plates of pasta, grilled vegeta-

PO DELTA

Italy's greatest river dissolves into the Adriatic Sea in the Po Delta (Foci del Po), an area of dense pine forests and extensive wetlands often doused in an eerie fog, especially in winter. The wetlands, protected in the **Parco del Delta del Po** (www.parcodeltapo.it; Corso Giuseppe Mazzini 200), are one of Europe's largest and are notable for their birdlife – 300 species have been registered here.

The delta's main centre, Comacchio, a picturesque fishing village of canals and brick bridges, harbours a good **tourist office** (📞 0533 31 41 54; www.ferraraterraeacqua.it; Via Agatopisto 2a; ⏰ 9.30am-1pm & 3-6.30pm Mon-Fri, 9.30am-6pm Sat & Sun Apr-Jun & Sep-Mar, 9.30am-6.30pm Jul-Aug) offering reams of information about hiking, cycling, birdwatching, horse riding and boat excursions, and a fascinating new museum, **Museo Delta Antico** (www.museodeltaantico.com; Via Agatopisto 2; adult/reduced €6/3; ⏰ 9.30am-1pm & 3-6.30pm Tue-Sun Mar-Jun, shorter hours rest of year).

bles, meat and fish, to homemade desserts like *zuppa inglese* (liqueur-soaked sponge layered with custard and chocolate sauce).

🍸 Drinking & Nightlife

Fellini ScalinoCinque   COCKTAIL BAR
(www.felliniscalino5.it; Piazza Kennedy 15; cocktails €6-12; ⏰ 11am-2pm Tue-Sun; 🛜) Hip and friendly owner Pepe suffered for a few years while his trendy cocktail bar was cut off from the action by the construction work that transformed a former parking lot into the new and improved Piazza Kennedy in 2017. But his gamble paid off – Fellini ScalinoCinque is now the city centre's most happening lounge.

ℹ️ Information

Tourist Office (📞 0544 3 54 04; www.turismo.ravenna.it; Piazza San Francesco 7; ⏰ 8.30am-/pm summer, shorter hours rest of year) Helpful office with maps and printed material; can also help with booking accommodation. Additional outlets at Mausoleo di Teodorico (📞 0544 4 51 39; Via delle Industrie 14; ⏰ 9.30am-12.30pm & 3.30-6.30pm summer, 9.30am-3.30pm winter) and Basilica di Sant'Apollinare in Classe.

ℹ️ Getting There & Away

Frequent trains connect Ravenna's **train station** (www.trenitalia.com; Viale Stazione) with with Bologna (€7.35, one to 1½ hours), Ferrara (€6.65, 1¼ hours), Rimini (€4.75, one hour) and the south coast. The **bus station** (www.star tromagna.it) is nearby on Piazzale Aldo Moro (helpful for buses to Comacchio).

Ravenna is on a branch (A14 dir) of the main east-coast A14 autostrada. The SS16 (Via Adriatica) heads south to Rimini and on down the coast.

ℹ️ Getting Around

Local buses operated by **START** (www.startromagna.it) depart from Piazza Farini (single/24hr ticket €1.30/3). **Punto Bus** (Piazza Farini; ⏰ 7am-7pm Mon-Sat), inside the train station, provides bus information and tickets. From the train station, it's a 600m walk to the centre along Via Diaz.

In town, cycling is popular (Ravenna finally cut off its city centre from cars in 2016). Rent bikes just outside Ravenna's train station at **Cooperativa San Vitale** (📞 0544 3 70 31; Piazza Farini; bikes per hour/day €1.50/12; ⏰ 7am-7pm Mon-Fri). Alternatively, use the free 'C'entro in Bici' bike-hire service sponsored by Ravenna's main tourist office: simply present photo ID and tourist office staff will provide you with a key to unlock one of the free yellow bikes stored at racks throughout the city. Return the bike at least half an hour before closing time to reclaim your photo ID.

The main car parks are east of the train station and north of the Basilica di San Vitale. **Parcheggio Giustiniano** (Largo Giustiniani; per day €3) is a good place to leave your car in the shadow of San Vitale. For a comprehensive list of parking lots, see www.cesostapervol.it/ragglungi-la-tua-destinazione.

Rimini

📞 0541 / POP 146,000

Roman relics, jam-packed beaches, hedonistic nightclubs and the memory of film director and native son Federico Fellini make sometimes awkward bedfellows in seaside Rimini. Although there's been a settlement here for over 2000 years, Rimini's coast was just sand dunes until 1843, when the first bathing establishments took root next to the ebbing Adriatic. The beach huts gradually morphed into a megaresort that was

Rimini

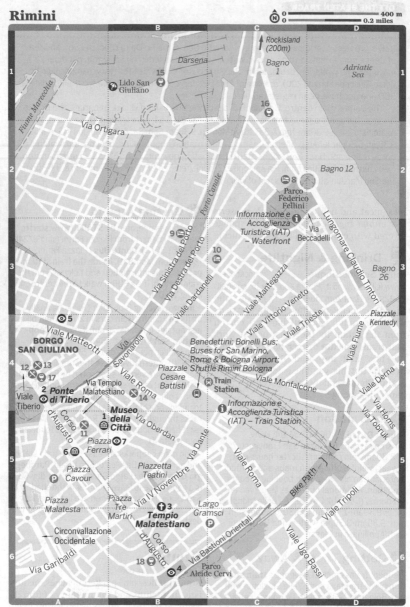

sequestered by a huge nightclub scene in the 1990s. Despite some interesting history, Fellini-esque movie memorabilia and a decent food culture, 95% of Rimini's visitors come for its long, boisterous, sometimes tacky beachfront.

◎ Sights

★ Museo della Città
MUSEUM

(www.museicomunalirimini.it/musei/museo_citta; Via Tonini 1; adult/reduced incl Domus del Chirurgo €7/5, free Wed; ⏱ 9.30am-1pm & 4-7pm Tue-Sat, 10-7pm Sun) This rambling museum is

Rimini

best known for its Roman section. Spread over several rooms, with excellent bilingual (Italian/English) signage, are finds from two nearby Roman villas, including splendid mosaics, a rare and exquisite representation of fish rendered in coloured glass, and the world's largest collection of Roman surgical instruments. Other highlights include the colourful and imaginative doodlings of Federico Fellini, whose *Il libro dei miei sogni* (Book of My Dreams) is on display here.

Museum tickets also include admission to the adjacent **Domus del Chirurgo** (www.domusrimini.com; Piazza Ferrari; ⊙ 9.30am-1pm & 4-7pm Tue-Sat, 10-7pm Sun), a recently excavated Roman villa with several fine floor mosaics still partially intact.

★**Ponte di Tiberio**   LANDMARK
The majestic five-arched Tiberius' Bridge dates from AD 21. In Roman times it marked the start of the Via Emilia – the important arterial road between the Adriatic coast (at Rimini) and the Po river valley (at Piacenza) – which linked up here with the Via Flaminia from Rome. These days, the bridge still connects Rimini's city centre to the old fishing quarter of Borgo San Gi-

uliano and rests on its original foundations consisting of an ingenious construction of wooden stilts.

★**Tempio Malatestiano**   CHURCH
(Via IV Novembre 35; ⊙ 8.30am-12.30pm & 3.30-6.30pm Mon-Fri, 8.30am-12.30pm & 3.30-7pm Sat, 9am-12.30pm & 3.30-6.30pm Sun) Built originally in 13th-century Gothic style and dedicated to St Francis, Rimini's cathedral was radically transformed in the mid-1400s into a Renaissance Taj Mahal for the tomb of Isotta degli Atti, beloved mistress of roguish ruler Sigismondo Malatesta. Sigismondo hired Florentine architect Leon Battista Alberti to redesign the church in 1450, and the resulting edifice, while incomplete, is replete with Alberti's grandiose Roman-inspired touches, along with elements that glorify Sigismondo and Isotta, including numerous medallions bearing the two lovers' initials.

Alberti's grand project was interrupted and eventually abandoned as Sigismondo's popularity and influence waned in the 1460s. Sigismondo, known disparagingly as the 'Wolf of Rimini' thanks to his aggressive military campaigns, came into direct conflict with Pope Pius II, who burned his effigy in Rome and condemned him to hell for a litany of sins that included rape, murder, incest, adultery and severe oppression of the people. Sigismondo lost most of his territory in subsequent battles with Papal forces and died in 1468. His sarcophagus resides near Isotta's inside the church.

Arco di Augusto   LANDMARK
(Corso d'Augusto) This Roman triumphal arch, the oldest of its kind in northern Italy, was commissioned by Emperor Augustus in 27 BC and stands an impressive 17m high on modern-day Corso d'Augusto. It was once the end point of the ancient Via Flaminia that linked Rimini with Rome. Buildings that had grown up around the arch were demolished in 1935 to improve its stature.

Borgo San Giuliano   AREA
Just over the Ponte di Tiberio, Rimini's old fishing quarter has been freshened up and is now a colourful patchwork of cobbled lanes, trendy trattorias, wine bars and trim terraced houses (read: prime real estate). Look out for the numerous murals.

Cinema Fulgor MUSEUM

(Corso d'Augusto 162) Currently undergoing renovation, the top three floors of this historic cinema will reopen in October 2017 as a portion of Rimini's brand new Museo Federico Fellini. Eventually, three more floors will be home to exhibitions on Fellini's poetry told through photographs, drawings, film projects (including films never produced) and interactive and multimedia installations.

🛏 Sleeping

Ironically for a city with more than 1200 hotels, finding accommodation can be tricky. In July and August places can be booked solid and prices are sky-high, especially as many proprietors insist on full board. In winter a lot of places simply shut up shop. Hotels charge a €2.50 per person per night tourist tax.

Sunflower City
Backpacker Hostel HOSTEL €

(🌐 0541 2 51 80; www.sunflowerhostel.com; Viale Dardanelli 102; dm €12-34, s €22-69, d €35-89; @🛜) Run by three ex-backpackers, the Sunflower welcomes travellers with laundry and cooking facilities, retro Austin Powers–style wallpaper, an in-house bar and organised pub crawls. It's in a leafy residential district halfway between the train station and the beach. Exuding an even livelier party vibe, Sunflower's beachside **branch** (🌐 0541 37 34 32; Via Siracusa 25; dm €13-30, s €23-50 d €36-80; ⊙ Mar–mid-Nov; 🅿✳@🛜🎿) has its own stage, with live music in summer.

Up Hotel BOUTIQUE HOTEL €

(🌐 0541 37 88 60; www.uphotel.it; Viale Gubbio 7; s €44-79, d €54-89; 🅿✳@🛜) 🐾 Apologetically dangling the hi-tech carrot to millennials and digital nomads, this new, design-forward 25-room boutique hotel is high-wired (USB ports built into the communal breakfast table, e-Bikes for guests) and prides itself on guest freedom (outside food and drink are welcome, for example). The trendy decor marries recycled bed springs as wall art with contemporary high-design Italian bikes and vintage furniture.

⭐ Grand Hotel HISTORIC HOTEL €€€

(🌐 0541 5 60 00; www.grandhotelrimini.com; Parco Federico Fellini; s €110-470, d €155-655, ste €450-905; 🅿✳@🛜🎿) Rimini's only five-star hotel is as much a monument as a place to stay. Despite a 1920 fire and serious damage incurred during WWII, it has remained true to its 1908 roots with rooms clad in authentic 18th-century Venetian antiques. Beloved by Fellini, the hotel has lured many other celebs with its pool, private beach and elegant communal areas and gardens.

Il Brigitta
B&B B&B €€€

(🌐 339 4816486; ilbrigitta@alice.it; Via Sinestra del Porto 88/90; s/d €130/200; 🛜) Enjoy all that Rimini has to offer without committing to the overwrought beach resort experience at this adorable new three-room B&B overlooking the picturesque Porto Canale. Artist and interior designer Brigitta speaks little English, but her nautical driftwood art and penchant for Provence ensure a cosy, shabby-chic stay. It's all drenched in lavender – a perfectly romantic hideaway.

🍴 Eating

Rimini's cuisine is anchored by the *piadina* and *pesce azzurro* (oily fish), especially sardines and anchovies. The favourite tipple is Sangiovese wine.

NudeCrud SANDWICHES €

(Viale Tiberio 27/29; piadina €4.50-13; ⊙ noon-4pm & 6.30-11.30pm; 🛜🍴) Avoid the tourist onslaught along the waterfront and head to quaint Borgo San Giuliano where locals – including the mayor – go year-round for gourmet *piadine*. Plop down on the colourful patio and dig into stuffed treats ranging from a tasty sardine, chicory, lettuce and spring onion version to grilled vegetables with melted *squacquerone* cheese.

⭐ Abocar
(Due Cucine) FUSION €€

(🌐 0541 2 22 79; www.abocarduecucine.it; Via Farini 13; meals €39-49; ⊙ 7.30-11.30pm Tue-Sun; 🛜) Opened in 2014 by the daughter of fabled local restaurateur Tonino Il Lurido (owner of one of Fellini's former haunts), this Argentine-Italian affair crafts three monthly changing, carefully curated tasting menus – revolving around fish, meat or a combination of the two – and isn't afraid to inject the best of Latin America (Chipotle! Avocados! *Dulce de leche!*) into a firmly Italian pedigree.

★ Osteria De Borg
OSTERIA €€

(☑ 0541 5 60 74; www.osteriadeborg.it; Via Forzieri 12; meals €25-35, pizzas €5-14; ⏲ 12.30-2.30pm & 7.30-11.30pm) A homey *osteria* in the old fishing quarter, this place is all about simple, honest food made with local ingredients and served in unpretentious surroundings. Second courses revolve around meat, from local *mora romagnola* pork to meatballs with stuffed zucchini to steaks grilled on an open fire with rosemary and sea salt. In the evenings there's also wood-fired pizza.

VichyCristina
SEAFOOD €€

(☑ 0541 5 40 13; www.vichycristina.it; Corso Giovanni XXIII 74; meals €30-45; ⏲ noon-3pm & 6pm-midnight Nov-Mar, 6pm-midnight Apr, 8am-midnight May-Oct at the beach; ☎) The food at this eclectic seafooder isn't as avant-garde as the funky Buddha decor would suggest, but it's a creative step up from tossing seafood in a fryer (fresh daily catches, a wealth of tartare and carpaccio, an oyster bar). The trendy, DJ-fueled atmosphere is a good time as well. In summer, it moves to the beach near No 8.

Drinking & Nightlife

Some come to Rimini in search of Roman relics. Others seek out its lavish modern nightclubs. Rimini first garnered a reputation for mega hip nightclubbing in the 1990s when an electric after-dark scene took off in the hills of **Misano Monte** and **Riccione** several kilometres to the south of the city centre. Far from being a tacky re run of Torremolinos or Magaluf, Rimini's new clubs quickly established themselves as modish, fashionable affairs that appealed to a broader age demographic than the 18 to 30 dives of yore. That's not to say they were boring.

Darsena
Sunset Bar
COCKTAIL BAR

(☑ 340 682 58 42; www.darsenasunsetbar.it; Viale Ortigara 78/80; cocktails €8-10; ⏲ 7am-1am Mon-Thu, to 3am Fri-Sun; ☎) It's a good idea to reserve a prime spot in advance at this trendy cocktail bar hidden away in Rimini's marina (Darsena). You have entered the domain of the beautiful people, here to ogle the sunset, groove to loungy, DJ-spun vinyl and sip on exquisitely mixed libations (Instagramming it all along the way).

Enoteca
del Teatro
WINE BAR

(Via Ortaggi 12; wines by the glass €3-6; ⏲ 9.30am-12.45pm & 4.30-9.30pm Mon & Wed-Sat, to 6.30pm Tue) 🍷 In quaint Borgo San Giuliano, this is Rimini's best spot for a sophisticated glass of *vino* without the hubhub that comes along with major European beach resorts. The tiny, standing-room-only candlelit bottleshop features 15 or so choices by the glass, often from small and/or organic producers. Let genial owner Ricky guide to a glass outside your wheelhouse.

Byblos
CLUB

(www.byblosclub.com; Via Pozzo Castello 24, Misano Adriatico; ⏲ 9.30pm-4am Fri & Sat Apr-Sep) Feeling more like a hedonistic Beverly Hills house party than a club, Rimini's top club occupies a converted villa complex with swimming pool, restaurant and highly acclaimed DJs, and fills up with ridiculously beautiful people.

FOB
CRAFT BEER

(www.birreria-fob.it; Via Castracane 17; pints €5-6; ⏲ 5.30pm-2am Mon-Thu, to 3am Fri & Sat, 4.30pm-2am Sun; ☎) FOB, named after the Foam on Beer draught head control system installed above its 34 taps, is Emilia-Romagna's most visually impressive craft-beer drinking den with a long hardwood bar, denim-covered bar seats and its larger, orange-slathered room with chapel-like windows stained not with glass but with colourful beer cans from around the world.

Discoteca
Baia Imperiale
CLUB

(www.baiaimperiale.net; Via Panoramica 36, Gabicce Mare; ⏲ 10.30pm-5am Sat Jun–mid-Sep) With eight dance floors, evergreen Baia Imperiale is one of Europe's largest clubs, and even the stone-cold sober agree that it's one of the world's most beautiful – dripping with marble staircases, pools, and assorted obelisks and statues of Roman emperors.

Disco Bar
Coconuts
CLUB

(www.coconuts.it; Lungomare Tintori 5; ⏲ 6pm-4am mid-May–Sep) This popular nightspot on the Marina Centro waterfront exudes a summer beach-party atmosphere, with palm trees sprouting from its wooden deck.

Cocoricò
CLUB

(www.cocorico.it; Viale Chieti 44, Riccione; ⏲ 12.30am-5.30am Fri & Sat Jun-Sep, Sat only

Oct-Dec & Feb-Apr) Dancing under Cocoricò's glass pyramid, 2000 clammy strangers quickly become friends to the sounds of techno, house and underground. World-famous DJs pop in on Fridays and Saturdays, while drag queens enliven the scene on 'Tunga party' nights. In summer Cocoricò also hosts poolside dance parties at the nearby Aquafàn water park.

❶ Information

Ospedale Infermi (☏0541 70 51 11; www.ausl. rn.it; Viale Settembrini 2) Located 2.5km southeast of the centre.

Tourist Office (☏0541 5 33 99; www.rimini turismo.it) Rimini has two helpful tourist information points, one at the train station (Piazzale Cesare Battisti 1; ⊙8.15am-6.45pm Mon-Sat) and the other at the beach (Piazzale Fellini 3; ⊙8.30am-7pm) near Parco Federico Fellini, as well as a seasonal third that operates at the airport between June and September, depending on flight arrivals.

❶ Getting There & Away

Rimini's **Federico Fellini International Airport** (☏0541 37 98 00; www.riminiairport.com; Via Flaminia 409), 8km south of the city centre, offers direct flights to Scandinavia with Finnair, to Russia with Rossiya and Ural Airlines, and to various other European cities, including with seasonal charter flights.

Benedettini (☏0549 90 38 54; www.bene dettinispa.com) and **Bonelli Bus** (☏0541 66 20 69; www.bonellibus.it) operate 10 buses daily Monday to Saturday from a bus stop outside Rimini's train station to San Marino (8.10am to 7.25pm, €5, 50 minutes) and eight on Sunday (8.10am to 6.10pm). From the same stop, **Shuttle Rimini Bologna** (☏0541 60 01 00; www.shuttleriminibologna.it) runs shuttles direct to Bologna's airport eight times per day (3.30am to 10.15pm, from €20, 1¾ hours). Bonelli buses to Rome (€31, 4¼ hours) also leave from here on Friday (6.50am, 10.15am and noon) and Sunday (2.50pm, 6.55pm and 8.30pm).

By car, you have a choice of the A14 (south into Le Marche or northwest towards Bologna and Milan) or the toll-free but very busy SS16.

Hourly trains run from **Rimini Station** (www.trenitalia.com; Piazzale Cesare Battisti 1; ⊙5am-midnight) down the coast to the ferry ports of Ancona (from €7.30, one to 1¼ hours) and Bari (Intercity/Frecciabianca €19.90/19.90, 4¾ to six hours). Up the line, they serve Ravenna (€4.75, one hour, hourly)

and Bologna (from €9.85, one to 1½ hours, half-hourly).

Brisighella

☏0546 / POP 7660

Romagna's storybook medieval village is cinematically set on the slopes of the Tosco-Romagna Apennines mountains, cradled by pastoral green hills peppered with vineyards and olive plantations. Founded in the 12th century, Brisighella is defined by its trio of iconic hilltop structures: La Rocca (The Rock), La Torre (The Tower) and Il Monticino (The Monticino), the three of which overlook the sunset-hued rooftops of one of Italy's most picturesque villages. In town, one of the country's unique sights: a wonderfully photogenic 700-year-old walkway that evolved from the town's first defensive wall into a commercial thoroughfare used mostly by cart-wielding donkeys – hence its name, the Via degli Assini (Donkey's Street).

Today, Brisighella is best known for its award-winning olive oils which, of course, go down mighty fine alongside the local cuisine, during a scenic weekend getaway in a village not yet overrun by international tourism.

◉ Sights

★**Via Degli Asini**   HISTORIC SITE
Hidden behind a colourful patchwork of warped homes, this low-slung, wood-beamed, delightfully uneven medieval walkway dates to 1290. It's unique in Italy for the fact it began life as a defensive wall that was later incorporated into the town's commercial space (as an elevated pathway for donkeys carrying gypsum from nearby quarries). Today, former donkey stables now hide private homes (and one dental office) that sit atmospherically along 100m of picturesque, non-uniform arches, flanked by at least one surviving guard tower.

★**Rocca di Brisighella**   FORTRESS
(Via Rontana 64; €3; ⊙10am-12.30pm & 3-7pm Sat & Sun May-Sep, shorter hours rest of year) Standing sentinel high above town on a gypsum hilltop, this medieval fortress, along with the Torre dell'Orologio and Santuario del Monticino on neighbouring hilltops, forms the postcard-perfect view of Brisighella. Construction dates to 1310 – with two later

renovations, including the expansion of the western bastion by the Venetians between 1503 and 1506 – and features two watch towers of varying heights. The views from here, both of town and across to the Torre dell'Orologio, are the reason you have come to Brisighella.

✗ Eating

★ Framboise
ITALIAN €

(☑ 329 0740862; www.facebook.com/Framboisecucinina; Via Porta Fiorentina 15; meals €25-30; ⊙ noon-2.30pm & 7-10pm Tue-Sun) A true family affair, where owner Perluigi, along with his wife and personable daughter, will shower you with seasonally changing local delicacies. It's a great spot to try *spoja lorda* (dirty pasta), and the pulled black pork *panino*, cooked *sous-vide* for half a day, is a true delight. It's worth coming in spring for their in-season Moretto artichoke menu (mid-April to mid-May), too.

ⓘ Information

Tourist Office (☑ 0546 8 11 66; www.brisighella.org; Plazzetta Porta Gabolo 5; ⊙ 9.30am-12.30pm & 3.30-5.30pm Mon-Sat, 3.30-6.30pm Sun Apr-Dec, shorter hours rest of year)

ⓘ Getting There & Away

Brisighella sits 12km southwest of Faenza off the SS9. To reach the village by train requires a switch in Faenza (reachable on lines from Bologna, Ancona, Florence and Ravenna), from where there are trains every two hours (€2.20). **Cooperativa Trasporti di Riolo Terme** (www.cooptrasportiriolo.it) also runs five buses per day from Faenza's Stazione della Corriere (€2.10, ½ hour).

SAN MARINO

☑ 0549 / POP 31,800

Of Earth's 196 independent countries, San Marino is the fifth smallest and – arguably – the most curious. How it exists at all is something of an enigma. A sole survivor of Italy's once powerful city-state network, this landlocked micronation clung on long after the more powerful kingdoms of Genoa and Venice folded. And still it clings, secure in its status as the world's oldest surviving sovereign state and its oldest republic (since AD 301). San Marino also enjoys one of the planet's highest GDP per capita, but some say it retains a curious lack of intimacy and lacks soul.

Measuring 61 sq km, the country is larger than many outsiders imagine, being made up of nine municipalities each hosting its own settlement. The largest 'town' is Dogana (on the bus route from Italy), a place 99.9% of the two million annual visitors skip en transit to its Unesco-listed capital, Città di San Marino.

⊙ Sights

Città di San Marino's highlights are its spectacular views, its Unesco-listed streets, and a stash of rather bizarre museums dedicated to vampires, torture, wax dummies and strange facts (pick up a list in the tourist office). Ever popular in summertime is the hourly **changing of the guard** (⊙ hourly 8.30am-12.30pm & 2.30-6.30pm Mon-Fri, 10.30am-5.30pm Sat & Sun summer) in Piazza della Libertà.

A Multimuseo card (€10) is a good bargain for entrance to all of the state museums.

Torre Guaita
CASTLE

(Prima Torre; www.museidistato.sm; Via Salita alla Rocca; adult/reduced €4.50/3.50; ⊙ 8am-8pm summer, 9am-5pm rest of year) The oldest and largest of San Marino's castles, Torre Guaita dates from the 11th century. It was still being used as a prison as recently as 1975.

Torre Cesta
CASTLE

(Seconda Torre; www.museidistato.sm; Via Salita alla Cesta; adult/reduced €4.50/3.50; ⊙ 8am-8pm summer, 9am-5pm rest of year) Dominating the skyline and offering superb views towards Rimini and the coast, the Cesta castle dates from the 13th century and sits atop 750m Monte Titano. Today you can walk its ramparts and peep into its four-room **museum** devoted to medieval armaments.

Museo di Stato
MUSEUM

(www.museidistato.sm/mds; Piazza Titano 1; adult/reduced €4.50/3.50; ⊙ 8am-8pm summer, 9am-5pm rest of year) San Marino's best museum by far is the well laid out if disjointed state museum displaying art, history, furniture and culture.

Don't miss the Domagnano Treasure, a Ostrogothic trove of jewels dating to the 5th/6th centuries.

🛏 Sleeping

Balsimelli 12
B&B €

(☑ 0549 99 01 02; www.balsimelli12.com; Contrada dei Magazzeni 12; s €55-65, d €65-95; 🖥) Well-known Italian actor Fabricio Raggi – along with his two adorable Jack Russells, Rocco and Viola – has renovated his grandfather's historic, late 1800s house into a discerning two-room B&B beautifully tucked away in the centre of everything. Book the attic room – you'll trade a lower ceiling for a stupendous terrace, on which Riggi can arrange an *apertivo* with local wine or in-room massages.

🍴 Eating & Drinking

Osteria
La Taverna
SAMMARINESE €

(☑ 0549 99 11 96; www.ristoranterighi.com; Piazza della Libertà 10; meals €25-30; ⊙ noon-2.30pm & 7.30-10pm; 🖥) Luigi Sartini is San Marino's only Michelin-starred chef and has been championing local cuisine since 1990. His one-star affair, Ristorante Righi, sits above this far more casual *osteria,* where local dishes like *passatelli* (pasta made with breadcrumbs, eggs and grated Parmesan cheese) with clams, shrimp and *stridoli* (a leafy local herb) shine.

Giuletti KmO
BAR

(www.facebook.com/GiuliettiKMO; Piazzale Lo Stradone 3; cocktails €5-13; ⊙ 6.30am-1am; 🖥) 🍴 This restaurant and trendy cocktail lounge prides itself on sticking with local products wherever possible – its menu maps out the 20 or so San Marino producers from whom it sources beer, wine, cheese, cold cuts and other tasty provisions, which help create a long list of *piadine,* sandwiches and *apertivo* tipples.

ℹ Information

Tourist Office (Ufficio del Turismo; ☑ 0549 88 23 90; www.visitsanmarino.com; Contrada Omagnano 20; ⊙ 8.15am-6pm Mon-Fri, 9am-1pm & 2-6pm Sat & Sun) You can get your passport stamped with a San Marino visa for €5 here.

ℹ Getting There & Around

Bonelli Bus (p472) and Benedettini (p472) operate 12 buses daily to/from Rimini (one-way €5, 50 minutes), arriving at Piazzale Calcigni. The SS72 leads up from Rimini.

Leave your car at one of Città di San Marino's numerous car parks and walk up to the *centro storico.* Alternatively, you can park at **car park 11** (Piazzale Campo Della Fiera; per day €8) and take the **funivia** (return €4.50; ⊙ 7.50am-1am Jul-Sep, shorter hours rest of year). In the opposite direction, the *funivia* leaves from next to the tourist office.

Florence & Tuscany

POP 3.74 MILLION

Best Places to Eat

➡ La Leggenda dei Frati (p509)

➡ Essenziale (p507)

➡ Il Leccio (p542)

➡ Osteria del Castello (p533)

➡ L'Osteria di Casa Chianti (p528)

Best Places to Stay

➡ Ad Astra (p503)

➡ Hotel Orto de' Medici (p502)

➡ La Bandita (p541)

➡ Podere Brizio (p541)

➡ Conti di San Bonifacio (p546)

Why Go?

Florence (Firenze in Italian) and Tuscany (Toscana) are the perfect introduction to Italy's famed *dolce vita*. Life is sweet around leading lady Florence, a fashionable urbanite known for her truly extraordinary treasure trove of world-class art and architecture, and a seasonally driven cuisine emulated the world over. Away from the city the pace slows as magnificent landscapes and the gentle heartbeat of the seasons cast their seductive spell.

This part of Italy has been working on its remarkable heritage since Etruscan times, meaning there's mountains to see and do. Explore a World Heritage Site in the morning, visit a vineyard in the afternoon and bunk down in a palatial villa or overwhelmingly rural *agriturismo* (farm stay accommodation) with indigenous black pigs at night. Renaissance paintings and Gothic cathedrals? Check. Spectacular trekking and sensational Slow Food? Yep. Hills laden with vines and ancient olive groves? More than you can possibly imagine.

When to Go
Florence

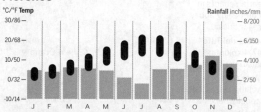

May & Jun Wildflower-adorned landscapes beg outdoor action, be it walking, cycling or horse riding.

Jul Not as madbusy as August (avoid) and with music festivals aplenty.

Sep–Nov Grapes and olives are harvested; forests yield white truffles and porcini mushrooms.

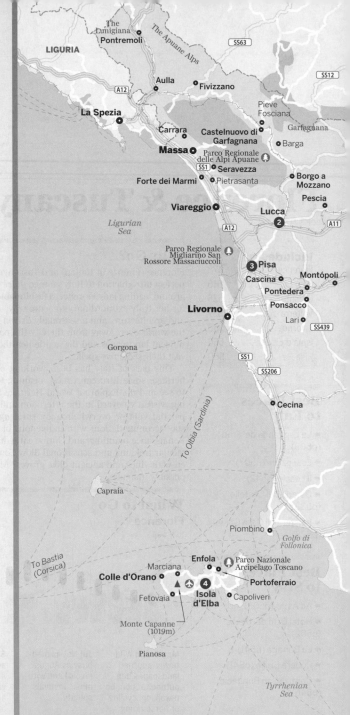

Florence & Tuscany Highlights

❶ Uffizi (p485) Swooning over Florence's treasures: the world's finest collection of Renaissance paintings at the Uffizi and the dome of Brunelleschi's Duomo.

❷ Lucca (p565) Pedalling and picnicking atop stone city walls.

❸ Leaning Tower (p560) Getting lost in medieval Pisa and scaling its iconic tower at sunset.

❹ Elba (p557) Setting sail for the Mediterranean isle and sleeping on an olive estate scented with orange blossoms and olive groves.

❺ Chianti (p525) Vineyard-hopping tand lunching at an Antinori family estate.

❻ Siena (p516) Gorging on Gothic architecture and almond biscuits.

❼ Abbazia di Sant'Antimo (p541) Being spellbound by Gregorian chants in the compelling abbey near Montalcino.

❽ Città del Tufo (p547) Exploring Etruscan heritage.

❾ Arezzo (p571) Marvelling at frescoes in Cappella Bacci and the beautiful Tuscan square Piazza Grande.

FLORENCE

POP 377,600

Return time and again and you still won't see it all. Stand on a bridge over the Arno river several times in a day and the light, mood and view change every time. Surprisingly small as it is, Florence (Firenze) looms large on Europe's 'must-see' list. Host to the tourist masses that flock here to feast on world-class art, Tuscany's largest city buzzes with romance and history. Towers and palaces evoke a thousand tales of its medieval past; designer boutiques and artisan workshops pearl its streets; and the local drinking and dining scene is second to none. Cradle of the Renaissance and home of Machiavelli, Michelangelo and the Medici, Florence is magnetic, romantic and brilliantly absorbing.

◉ Sights

Florence's wealth of museums and galleries house many of the world's most exquisite examples of Renaissance art, and its architecture is unrivalled. Yet don't feel pressured to see everything: combine your personal pick of sights with ample meandering through the city's warren of narrow streets broken by cafe and *enoteca* (wine bar) stops.

Churches enforce a strict dress code for visitors: no shorts, sleeveless shirts or plunging necklines. Photography with no flash is allowed in museums, but leave the selfie stick at home – they are offiicially forbidden.

◉ Piazza del Duomo

★ Duomo   CATHEDRAL

(Cattedrale di Santa Maria del Fiore; Map p482; ☑ 055 230 28 85; www.ilgrandemuseodelduomo. it; Piazza del Duomo; ☺10am-5pm Mon-Wed & Fri, to 4.30pm Thu, to 4.45pm Sat, 1.30-4.45pm Sun) FREE Florence's Duomo is the city's most iconic landmark. Capped by Filippo Brunelleschi's red-tiled cupola, it's a staggering construction whose breathtaking pink, white and green marble facade and graceful *campanile* (bell tower) dominate the medieval cityscape. Sienese architect Arnolfo di Cambio began work on it in 1296, but construction took almost 150 years and it wasn't consecrated until 1436. In the echoing interior, look out for frescoes by Vasari and Zuccari and up to 44 stained-glass windows.

The Duomo's neo-Gothic facade was designed in the 19th century by architect Emilio de Fabris to replace the uncompleted original, torn down in the 16th century. The oldest and most clearly Gothic part of the cathedral is its south flank, pierced by **Porta dei Canonici** (Canons' Door), a mid-14th-century High Gothic creation (you enter here to climb up inside the dome).

After the visual wham-bam of the facade, the sparse decoration of the cathedral's vast interior, 155m long and 90m wide, comes as a surprise – most of its artistic treasures have been removed over the centuries according to the vagaries of ecclesiastical fashion, and many are on show in the Grande Museo del Duomo. The interior is also unexpectedly secular in places (a reflection of the sizeable chunk of the cathedral not paid for by the church): down the left aisle two immense frescoes of equestrian statues portray two *condottieri* (mercenaries) – on the left Niccolò da Tolentino by Andrea del Castagno (1456), and on the right Sir John Hawkwood (who fought in the service of Florence in the 14th century) by Uccello (1436).

Between the left (north) arm of the transept and the apse is the **Sagrestia delle Messe** (Mass Sacristy), its panelling a marvel of inlaid wood carved by Benedetto and Giuliano da Maiano. The fine bronze doors were executed by Luca della Robbia – his only known work in the material. Above the doorway is his glazed terracotta *Resurrezione* (Resurrection).

A stairway located near the main entrance of the cathedral leads down to the cathedral gift shop and **Cripta Santa Reparata** (adult/reduced incl cupola, baptistry, campanile, crypt & museum €15/3; ☺10am-5pm Mon-Wed & Fri, to 4pm Thu, to 4.45pm Sat), the crypt where excavations between 1965 and 1974 unearthed parts of the 5th-century Chiesa di Santa Reparata that originally stood on the site. Should you be visiting on Sunday (when the crypt is closed), know your combined Duomo ticket is valid 48 hours.

★ Cupola del Brunelleschi   LANDMARK

(Brunelleschi's Dome; Map p482; ☑ 055 230 28 85; www.ilgrandemuseodelduomo.it; Piazza del Duomo; adult/reduced incl cupola, baptistry, campanile, crypt & museum €15/3; ☺ 8.30am-7pm Mon-Fri, to 5pm Sat, 1-4pm Sun) A Renaissance masterpiece, the Duomo's cupola – 91m high and 45.5m wide – was built between 1420 and 1436. Filippo Brunelleschi, taking inspiration from the Pantheon in Rome, designed a distinctive octagonal form of inner and outer concentric domes that rests on the drum of the cathedral rather than the roof itself. Over four million bricks were used, laid in consecutive rings according to a vertical herringbone pattern.

When Michelangelo went to work on St Peter's in Rome, he reportedly said: 'I go to build a greater dome, but not a fairer one'. The cupola crowning the Duomo is a feat of engineering and one that cannot be fully appreciated without climbing its 463 interior stone steps.

The climb up the spiral staircase is relatively steep, and should not be attempted if you are claustrophobic. Make sure to pause when you reach the balustrade at the base of the dome, which gives an aerial view of the octagonal *coro* (choir) of the cathedral below and the seven round stained glass windows (by Donatello, Andrea del Castagno, Paolo Uccello and Lorenzo Ghiberti) that pierce the octagonal drum.

Look up and you'll see flamboyant late-16th-century frescoes by Giorgio Vasari and Federico Zuccari, depicting the *Giudizio Universale* (Last Judgement).

As you climb, snapshots of Florence can be spied through small windows. The final leg – a straight, somewhat hazardous flight up the curve of the inner dome – rewards with an unforgettable 360-degree panorama of one of Europe's most beautiful cities.

It is impossible to visit the cupola without an advance reservation, which can be made online or at self-service Ticketpoint machines located inside the Duomo ticket office, opposite the main entrance to the Baptistry at Piazza di San Giovanni 7. Book at least a month in advance in high season; in the low season, a couple of days in advance.

★ **Campanile** TOWER

(Bell Tower; Map p482; ☑ 055 230 28 85; www.il grandemuseodelduomo.it; Piazza del Duomo; adult/ reduced incl campanile, baptistry, cupola, crypt & museum €15/3; ☺ 8.15am-8pm) The 414-step climb up the cathedral's 85m-tall *campanile*, begun by Giotto in 1334, rewards with staggering city views. The first tier of bas-reliefs around the base of its elaborate Gothic facade are copies of those carved by Pisano depicting the Creation of Man and *attività umane* (arts and industries). Those on the second tier depict the planets, cardinal virtues, the arts and the seven sacraments. The sculpted Prophets and Sibyls in the upper-storey niches are copies of works by Donatello and others.

ℹ MUSEUM TICKETS

In July, August and other busy periods such as Easter, unbelievably long queues are a fact of life at Florence's key museums – if you haven't prebooked your ticket, you could well end up standing in line queuing for four hours or so.

For a fee of €3 per ticket (€4 for the Uffizi and Galleria dell'Accademia), tickets to nine *musei statali* (state museums) can be reserved, including the Uffizi, Galleria dell'Accademia (where *David* lives), Palazzo Pitti, Museo del Bargello and the Medicean chapels (Cappelle Medicee). In reality, the only museums where prebooking is vital are the Uffizi and Accademia – to organise your ticket, go online or call **Firenze Musei** (Florence Museums; www.firenzemusei.it), with ticketing desks at the **Uffizi** (Piazzale degli Uffizi; www. uffizi.it; ☺ 8.15am-6.05pm Tue-Sun) (Door 3) and **Palazzo Pitti** (Piazza dei Pitti; ☺ 8.15am-6.05pm Tue-Sun summer, reduced hours winter).

At the Uffizi, signs point prebooked ticket holders to the building opposite the gallery where tickets can be collected; once you've got the ticket you go to Door 1 of the museum (for prebooked tickets only) and queue again to enter the gallery. It's annoying, but you'll still save hours of queuing time overall. Many hotels in Florence also prebook museum tickets for guests.

Admission to all state museums, including the Uffizi and Galleria dell'Accademia, is free on the first Sunday of each month and also on 18 February, the day Anna Maria Louisa de' Medici (1667–1743) died. The last of the Medici family, it was she who bequeathed the city its vast cultural heritage.

EU passport holders aged under 18 and over 65 get into Florence's state museums for free, and EU citizens aged 18 to 25 pay half price. Have your ID with you at all times. Note that museum ticket offices usually shut 30 minutes before closing time.

Florence

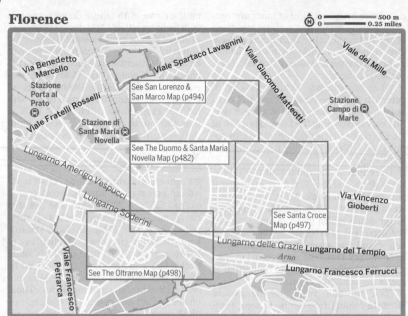

★ **Grande Museo del Duomo** MUSEUM
(Cathedral Museum; Map p482; ☎ 055 230 28 85; www.ilgrandemuseodelduomo.it; Piazza del Duomo 9; adult/reduced incl cathedral bell tower, cupola, baptistry & crypt €15/3; ⊙9am-7.30pm) This awe-inspiring museum tells the magnificent story of how the *duomo* and its cupola were built through art and short films. Among its many sacred and liturgical treasures is Ghiberti's original 15th-century masterpiece, *Porta del Paradiso* (Doors of Paradise; 1425–52) – gloriously golden, 16m-tall gilded bronze doors designed for the eastern entrance to the Baptistry – as well as those he sculpted for the northern entrance (1403–24).

Michelangelo's achingly beautiful *La Pietà*, sculpted when he was almost 80 and intended for his own tomb, is also here. Vasari recorded in his *Lives of the Artists* that, dissatisfied with both the quality of the marble and of his own work, Michelangelo broke up the unfinished sculpture, destroying the arm and left leg of the figure of Christ. A student of Michelangelo's later restored the arm and completed the figure. Fittingly, the sculpture is the only work displayed in the **Tribuna di Michelangelo**.

The museum's spectacular main hall, the **Sala del Paradiso**, is dominated by a life-size reconstruction of the original facade of Florence's Duomo, decorated with some 40 14th- and early-15th-century statues carved for the facade by 14th-century masters. Led by Arnolfo di Cambio, building work began in 1296 but it was never finished and in 1587 the facade was eventually dismantled. This is also where you will find Ghiberti's dazzling twinset of doors.

In Room 8, the **Sala della Maddalena**, it is impossible to miss Donatello's famous wooden representation of a gaunt, desolate Mary Magdalene, a mid-15th-century work completed late in the sculptor's career.

Continuing up to the 1st floor, Rooms 14 and 15 explain in detail just how Brunelleschi constructed the ground-breaking cathedral dome. Look at 15th-century tools, pulleys, tackles and hoisting wagons used to build the cupola, watch a film and admire Brunelleschi's funeral mask (1446). On the 2nd floor, look at a fascinating collection of models of different proposed facades for the cathedral. End on a high with big views of the red-tiled cupola up close from the 3rd-floor, open-air **Terrazza Brunelleschi**.

Battistero di San Giovanni LANDMARK
(Baptistry; Map p482; ☎ 055 230 28 85; www.ilgrandemuseodelduomo.it; Piazza di San Giovanni; adult/reduced incl baptistry, campanile, cupola,

crypt & museum €15/3; ⊙8.15am-10.15am & 11.15am-7.30pm Mon-Fri, 8.15am-6.30pm Sat, 8.15am-1.30pm Sun) This 11th-century baptistry is a Romanesque, octagonal-striped structure of white-and-green marble with three sets of doors conceived as panels illustrating the story of humanity and the Redemption. Most celebrated are Lorenzo Ghiberti's gilded bronze doors at the eastern entrance, the *Porta del Paradiso* (Gate of Paradise). What you see today are copies – the originals are in the Grande Museo del Duomo. Buy tickets online or at the ticket office at Piazza di San Giovanni 7, opposite the main Baptistry entrance.

Andrea Pisano executed the southern doors (1330), illustrating the life of St John the Baptist, and Lorenzo Ghiberti won a public competition in 1401 to design the northern doors, likewise replaced by copies today. Dante counts among the famous dunked in the Baptistry's baptismal font.

◉ Piazza della Signoria & Around

Piazza della Signoria   PIAZZA
(Map p482) The hub of local life since the 13th century – Florentines flock here to meet friends and chat over early-evening *aperitivi* (pre-dinner drinks) at historic cafes. Presiding over everything is Palazzo Vecchio, Florence's city hall, and the 14th-century Loggia dei Lanzi (Map p482) FREE, an open-air gallery showcasing Renaissance sculptures, including Giambologna's *Rape of the Sabine Women* (c 1583), Benvenuto Cellini's bronze *Perseus* (1554) and Agnolo Gaddi's *Seven Virtues* (1384–89).

In centuries past, townsfolk congregated on the piazza whenever the city entered one of its innumerable political crises. The people would be called for a *parlamento* (people's plebiscite) to rubber stamp decisions that frequently meant ruin for some ruling families and victory for others. Scenes of great pomp and circumstance alternated with those of terrible suffering: it was here that vehemently pious preacher-leader Savonarola set fire to the city's art – books, paintings, musical instruments, mirrors, fine clothes and so on – during his famous 'Bonfire of the Vanities' in 1497, and where he was hung in chains and burnt as a heretic, along with two other supporters, a year later.

The same spot where both fires burned is marked by a bronze plaque embedded in the ground in front of Ammannati's

Fontana de Nettuno (Neptune Fountain) with pin-headed bronze satyrs and divinities frolicking at its edges. More impressive are the equestrian statue of Cosimo I by Giambologna in the centre of the piazza, the much-photographed copy of Michelangelo's *David* guarding the western entrance to the Palazzo Vecchio since 1910 (the original stood here until 1873), and two copies of important Donatello works – *Marzocco*, the heraldic Florentine lion (for the original, visit the Museo del Bargello; p490), and *Giuditta e Oloferne* (Judith and Holofernes; c 1455; original inside Palazzo Vecchio).

The Loggia dei Lanzi at the piazza's southern end owes its name to the Lanzichenecchi (Swiss bodyguards) of Cosimo I, who were stationed here.

★ Palazzo Vecchio   MUSEUM
(Map p482; ☑ 055 276 85 58, 055 27 68 22; www.musefirenze.it; Piazza della Signoria; adult/reduced museum €10/8, tower €10/8, museum & tower €14/12, archaeological tour €4, combination ticket €18/16; ⊙ museum 9am-11pm Fri-Wed, to 2pm Thu Apr-Sep, 9am-7pm Fri-Wed, to 2pm Thu Oct-Mar, tower 9am-9pm Fri-Wed, to 2pm Thu Apr-Sep, 10am-5pm Fri-Wed, to 2pm Thu Oct-Mar) This fortress palace, with its crenellations and 94m-high tower, was designed by Arnolfo di Cambio between 1298 and 1314 for the *signoria* (city government). It remains the seat of the city's power, home to the mayor's office and the

---

ℹ CENT SAVER

Firenze Card (www.firenzecard.it, €72) is valid for 72 hours and covers admission to some 72 museums, villas and gardens in Florence, as well as unlimited use of public transport and free wi-fi across the city. Its biggest advantage is reducing queueing time in high season – museums have a seperate queue for card-holders. The downside of the Firenze Card is it only allows one admission per museum, plus you need to visit an awful lot of museums to justify the cost. Buy the card online (and collect upon arrival in Florence) or in Florence at tourist offices or ticketing desks of the Uffizi (Gate 2), Palazzo Pitti, Palazzo Vecchio, Museo del Bargello, Cappella Brancacci, Museo di Santa Maria Novella and Giardini Bardini. If you're an EU citizen, your card also covers family member aged under 18 travelling with you.

The Duomo & Santa Maria Novella

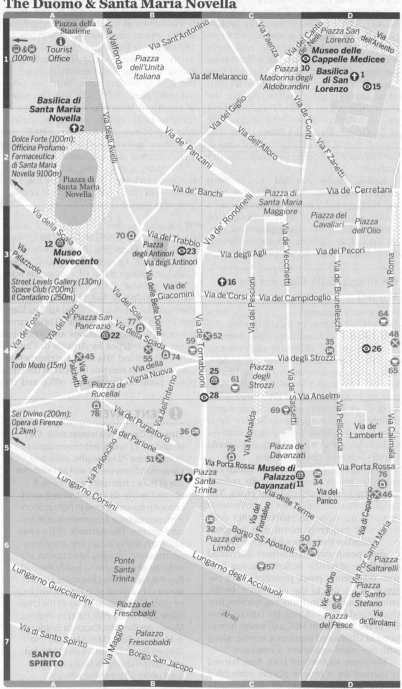

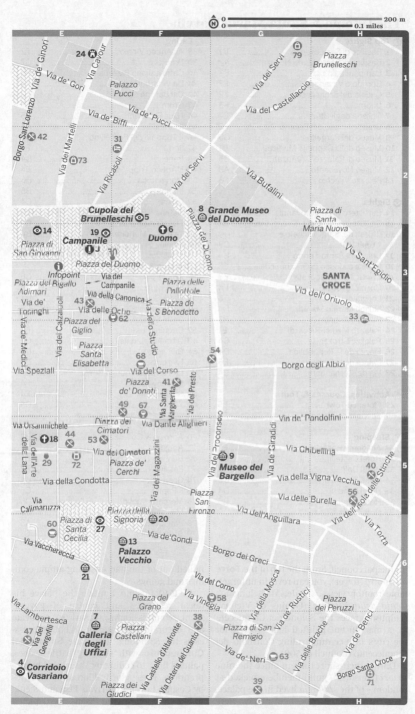

The Duomo & Santa Maria Novella

municipal council. From the top of the **Torre d'Arnolfo** (tower), you can revel in unforgettable rooftop views. Inside, Michelangelo's *Genio della Vittoria* (Genius of Victory) sculpture graces the Salone dei Cinquecento, a magnificent painted hall created for the city's 15th-century ruling Consiglio dei Cinquecento (Council of 500).

During their short time in office the nine *priori* (consuls) – guild members picked at random – of the *signoria* lived in the palace. Every two months nine new names were

pulled out of the hat, ensuring ample comings and goings.

In 1540 Cosimo I made the palace his ducal residence and centre of government, commissioning Vasari to renovate and decorate the interior. What impresses is the 53m-long, 22m-wide **Salone dei Cinquecento** with swirling battle scenes, painted floor to ceiling by Vasari and his apprentices. These glorify Florentine victories by Cosimo I over arch-rivals Pisa and Siena: unlike the Sienese, the Pisans are depicted bare of armour (play 'Spot the Leaning Tower'). To top off this unabashed celebration of his own power, Cosimo had himself portrayed as a god in the centre of the exquisite panelled ceiling – but not before commissioning Vasari to raise the original ceiling 7m in height. It took Vasari and his school, in consultation with Michelangelo, just two years (1563–65) to construct the ceiling and paint the 34 gold-leafed panels. The effect is mesmerising.

Off this huge space is the **Chapel of SS Cosmas and Damian**, home to Vasari's 1557–58 triptych panels of the two saints depicting Cosimo the Elder as Cosmas (right) and Cosimo I as Damian (left). Next to the chapel is the **Sala di Leo X**, the private suite of apartments of Cardinal Giovanni de' Medici, the son of Lorenzo Il Magnifico, who became pope in 1513.

Upstairs, the private apartments of Eleonora and her ladies-in-waiting bear the same heavy-handed decor, blaring the glory of the Medici. The ceiling in the **Camera Verde** (Green Room) by Ridolfo del Ghirlandaio was inspired by designs from Nero's Domus Aurea in Rome. The **Sala dei Gigli**, named after its frieze of fleur-de-lis, representing the Florentine Republic, is home to Donatello's original *Judith and Holofernes*.

The **Sala delle Carte Geografiche** (Map Room) houses Cosimo I's fascinating collection of 16th-century maps charting everywhere in the known world at the time, from the polar regions to the Caribbean.

On rain-free days, end with a 418-step hike up the palace's striking **Torre d'Arnolfo**. No more than 25 people are allowed at any one time and you have just 30 minutes to lap up the brilliant city panorama.

Gucci Museo　　　　　　　　　MUSEUM
(Map p482; www.gucci.com; Piazza della Signoria 10; adult/reduced €7/5; ⊙10am-8pm, to 11pm Fri) Strut through the chic cafe and icon store to reach this museum. It tells the tale of the Gucci fashion house, from the first luggage pieces in Gucci's signature beige fabric emblazoned with the interlocking 'GG' logo to the 1950s red-and-green stripe and beyond. Don't miss the 1979 Cadillac Seville with gold Gs on the hubcaps and Gucci fabric upholstery. Displays continue to the present day.

★ **Galleria degli Uffizi**　　　　GALLERY
(Uffizi Gallery; Map p482; ☑055 29 48 83; www. uffizi.it; Piazzale degli Uffizi 6; adult/reduced €8/4, incl temporary exhibition €12.50/6.25; ⊙8.15am-6.50pm Tue-Sun) Home to the world's greatest collection of Italian Renaissance art, Florence's premier gallery occupies the vast U-shaped Palazzo degli Uffizi, built between 1560 and 1580 to house government offices. The collection, bequeathed to the city by the Medici family in 1743 on condition that it never leave Florence, contains some of Italy's best-known paintings, including Piero della Francesco's profile portaits of the Duke and Duchess of Urbino and rooms full of masterpieces by Sandro Botticelli.

The gallery is undergoing a €65 million refurbishment (the Nuovi Uffizi project) that will eventually see the doubling of exhibition space and possibly a new exit loggia designed by Japanese architect Arato Isozaki. Work is pretty much complete on the permanent collection, which has grown over the years from 45 to 101 revamped rooms split across two floors; but there is much to be done still on areas earmarked for temporary exhibitions. Until the project is completed (date unknown), expect some halls to be closed and the contents of others changed.

The world-famous collection, displayed in chronological order, spans the gamut of art history from ancient Greek sculpture to 18th-century Venetian paintings. But its core is the Renaissance collection.

Visits are best kept to three or four hours maximum. When it all gets too much, head to the rooftop cafe (aka the terraced hanging garden, where the Medici clan listened to music performances on the square below) for fresh air and fabulous views.

➡ *Tuscan Masters: 13th to 14th Centuries*
Arriving in the Primo Corridoio (First Corridor) on the 2nd floor, Rooms 2 to 7 are dedicated to pre- and early Renaissance Tuscan art. Among the 13th-century Sienese works displayed in Room 2 are three large altarpieces from Florentine churches by Duccio di Buoninsegna, Cimabue and Giotto. These clearly reflect the transition from the Gothic to the nascent Renaissance style. Note the overtly naturalistic realism overtones in Giotto's portrayal of the Virgin Mary and saints in *Le Maestà di Ognissanti* (1306–10).

Moving into Siena, Bologna and Pisa in the 14th century, the highlight in Room 3 is Simone Martini's shimmering *Annunciazione* (1333), painted with Lippo Memmi and setting the Madonna in a sea of gold. Also of note is the *Madonna con il bambino in trono e angeli* (Madonna with Child and

The Uffizi
JOURNEY INTO THE RENAISSANCE

Navigating the Uffizi's chronologically-ordered art collection is straightforward enough: knowing which of the 1500-odd masterpieces to view before gallery fatigue strikes is not. Swap coat and bag (travel light) for floor plan and audioguide on the ground floor, then meet 16th-century Tuscany head-on with a walk up the *palazzo's* magnificent bust-lined staircase (skip the lift – the Uffizi is as much about masterly architecture as art).

Allow four hours for this journey into the High Renaissance. At the top of the staircase, on the 2nd floor, show your ticket, turn left and pause to admire the full length of the first corridor sweeping south towards the Arno river. Then duck left into room 2 to witness first steps in Tuscan art – shimmering altarpieces by ❶ **Giotto** et al. Journey through medieval art to room 9 and ❷ **Piero della Francesca's** impossibly famous portrait, then break in the corridor with playful ❸ **ceiling art**. After Renaissance heavyweight ❹ **Botticelli**, meander past the Tribuna (potential detour) and enjoy the daylight streaming in through the vast windows and panorama of the ❺ **riverside second corridor**. Lap up soul-stirring views of the Arno, crossed by Ponte Vecchio and its echo of four bridges drifting towards the Apuane Alps on the horizon. Then saunter into the third corridor, pausing between rooms 25 and 34 to ponder the entrance to the enigmatic Vasari Corridor. End with High Renaissance maestro Michelangelo in the ❻ **San Marco sculpture garden** and with ❼ **Doni Tondo**.

Giotto's Madonna
Room 2
Draw breath at the shy blush and curvaceous breast of Giotto's humanised Virgin (*Le Maestà di Ognissanti*; 1310) – so feminine compared with those of Duccio and Cimabue painted just 25 years before.

Portraits of the Duke & Duchess of Urbino
Room 9
Revel in realism's voyage with these uncompromising, warts-and-all portraits (1472–75) by Piero della Francesca. No larger than A3 size, they originally slotted into a portable, hinged frame that folded like a book.

Start of Vasari Corridor (linking the Palazzo Vecchio with the Uffizi and Palazzo Pitti)

Entrance to 2nd Floor Gallery

Palazzo Vecchio

Piazza della Signoria

Grotesque Ceiling Frescoes
First Corridor
Take time to study the make-believe monsters and most unexpected of burlesques (spot the arrow-shooting satyr outside room 15) waltzing across this eastern corridor's fabulous frescoed ceiling (1581).

The Genius of Botticelli
Room 10–14

The miniature form of *The Discovery of the Body of Holofernes* (c 1470) makes Botticelli's early Renaissance masterpiece all the more impressive. Don't miss the artist watching you in *Adoration of the Magi* (1475), oddly hidden in Room 15.

View of the Arno

Indulge in intoxicating city views from this short glassed-in corridor – an architectural masterpiece. Near the top of the hill, spot one of 73 outer towers built to defend Florence and its 15 city gates below.

Second Corridor

Tribuna

First Corridor

Arno River

Entrance to Vasari Corridor

San Marco sculpture garden
Room 34

A 13-year-old Michelangelo studied classical sculpture as an apprentice at Lorenzo de Medici's sculpture school in San Marco. Admire relief-sculpted sarcophagi that had such a massive influence on this artist.

Third Corridor

Tribuna

No room in the Uffizi is so tiny or so exquisite. It was created in 1851 as a 'treasure chest' for Grand Duke Francesco and in the days of the Grand Tour, the Medici Venus here was a tour highlight.

VALUE LUNCHBOX

Try the Uffizi rooftop cafe or – better value – gourmet *panini* at 'Ino (www.ino-firenze.com; Via dei Georgofili 3-7r).

MATTER OF FACT

The Uffizi collection spans the 13th to 18th centuries, but its 15th- and 16th-century Renaissance works are second to none.

Doni Tondo
Room 35

The creator of *David*, Michelangelo, was essentially a sculptor and no painting expresses this better than *Doni Tondo* (1506–08). Mary's muscular arms against a backdrop of curvaceous nudes are practically 3D in their shapeliness.

THE UFFIZI'S SECRET PASSAGE

Spot the closed door next to Room 25 leading to the Medici's **Corridoio Vasariano** (Vasarian Corridor; Map p482; ☺ by guided tour), a 1km-long covered passageway connecting Palazzo Vecchio (p481) with the Uffizi and Palazzo Pitti (p497) across the river. It was designed by Vasari in 1565 to allow the Medicis to wander between their palaces in privacy and comfort. In the 17th century the Medicis strung it with hundreds of artworks, including self-portraits of Andrea del Sarto, Rubens, Rembrandt and Canova.

The original promenade incorporated tiny windows (facing the river) and circular apertures with iron gratings (facing the street) to protect those who used the corridor from outside attacks. But when Hitler visited Florence in 1941, his chum and fellow dictator Benito Mussolini had big new windows punched into the corridor walls on Ponte Vecchio so that his guest could enjoy an expansive view down the Arno from the famous Florentine bridge.

On the Oltrarno, the corridor passes by **Chiesa di Santa Felicità** (Map p498; Piazza di Santa Felicità; ☺ 9.30am-noon & 3.30-5.30pm Mon-Sat), thereby providing the Medicis with a private balcony in the church where they could attend Mass without mingling with the minions.

Closed for renovation work in 2017, the corridor will be open to a privileged few by guided tour once work is complete. Check the Uffizi website or contact Florence Town (p500) for updated tour details.

Saints; 1340) by Pietro Lorenzetti, which demonstrates a realism similar to Giotto's; unfortunately both Pietro and his artistic brother Ambrogio died from the plague in Siena in 1348.

Masters in 14th-century Florence (Room 4) paid as much attention to detail as their Sienese counterparts: savour the realism of the *Lamentation over the Dead Christ* (1360–65) by gifted Giotto pupil, Giottino.

➡ *Renaissance Pioneers*

Florence's victory over the Sienese at the Battle of San Romano, near Pisa, in 1432, is brought to life with outstanding realism and increased use of perspective in Paolo Uccello's magnificent *Battaglia di San Romano* (1435–40) in Room 8. In the same room, don't miss the exquisite *Madonna con Bambino e due angeli* (Madonna and Child with Two Angels; 1460–65) by Fra' Filippo Lippi, a Carmelite monk who had an unfortunate soft spot for earthly pleasures and scandalously married a nun from Prato. This work clearly influenced his pupil, Sandro Botticelli.

In Room 9, Piero della Francesca's famous profile portraits (1465) of the crooked-nosed, red-robed duke and duchess of Urbino are wholly humanist in spirit: the former painted from the left side as he'd lost his right eye in a jousting accident, and the latter painted a deathly stone-white, reflecting the fact that the portrait was painted posthu-

mously. Don't miss the reverse side featuring the duke and duchess eternalised with the Virtues.

In the same room, the seven cardinal and theological values of 15th-century Florence by brothers Antonio and Piero del Pollaiolo – commissioned for the merchant's tribunal in Piazza della Signoria – radiate energy. More restrained is Piero's *Portrait of Galeazzo Maria Sforza* (1471). The only canvas in the theological and cardinal virtues series not to be painted by the Pollaiolos is *Fortitude* (1470), the first documented work by Botticelli.

➡ *Botticelli Room*

The spectacular **Sala del Botticelli**, numbered as Rooms 10 to 14, but in fact two large light and graceful rooms, is one of the Uffizi's hot spots and is always packed. Of the 18 Botticelli works displayed in the Uffizi in all, the iconic *La nascita di Venere* (The Birth of Venus; c 1485), *Primavera* (Spring; c 1482) and *Madonna del Magnificat* (Madonna of the Magnificat; 1483) are the best known by the Renaissance master known for his ethereal figures. Take time to study the lesser-known *Annunciazione* (Annunciation), a 6m-wide fresco painted by Botticelli in 1481 for the San Martino hospital in Florence.

True aficionados rate his twin set of miniatures depicting a sword-bearing Judith returning from the camp of Holofernes and the discovery of the decapitated Holofernes in his tent (1495–1500) as being among his finest works.

➡ Northern Influences

Don't miss the *Adorazione dei Magi* (Adoration of the Magi; 1475) featuring Botticelli's self-portrait (look for the blond-haired guy, extreme right, dressed in yellow), tucked away in Room 15 alongside Botticelli's *Coronation of the Virgin* (1488–90) and works by Flemish painter Hugo van der Goes (1430–82). Study the altarpiece, painted by the latter for the church inside Florence's Santa Maria Novella hospital, to observe the clear influence artists in northern Europe had on Florentine artists.

➡ La Tribuna

The Medici clan stashed away their most precious masterpieces in this exquisite octagonal-shaped treasure trove (Room 18), created by Francesco I between 1581 and 1586. Designed to amaze and perfectly restored to its original exquisite state, a small collection of classical statues and paintings adorn its walls, upholstered in crimson silk, and 6000 mother-of-pearl shells painted with crimson varnish encrust the domed ceiling.

➡ Elsewhere in Italy: 15th Century

The final rooms in the **Primo Corridoio** (First Corridor), Rooms 19 to 23, delve into the work of painters in Siena, Venice, Emilia-Romagna and Lombardy in the 15th century. As compelling as the art strung on the walls are the ornate vaulted ceilings here, frescoed in the 16th and 17th centuries with military objects, allegories, battles and festivals held on piazzas in Florence.

➡ High Renaissance to Mannerism

Passing through the loggia or **Secondo Corridoio** (Second Corridor), visitors enjoy wonderful views of Florence before entering the **Terzo Corridoio** (Third Corridor).

Rooms 33 and 34, with sage-green painted walls, evoke the artistic environment in which a young Michelangelo lived and worked in Florence. They display sculptures from classical antiquity, of great influence on the aspiring sculptor, and from the Medici-owned sculpture garden in San Marco where Michelangelo studied classical sculpture as an apprentice from the age of 13. The master himself, Michelangelo, dazzles with the *Doni Tondo*, a depiction of the Holy Family that steals the High Renaissance show in Room 35. The composition is unusual – Joseph holding an exuberant Jesus on his muscled mother's shoulder as she twists round to gaze at him, the colours as vibrant as when they were first applied in 1506–08. It was painted for wealthy Florentine merchant Agnolo Doni (who hung it above his bed) and bought by the Medicis for Palazzo Pitti in 1594.

➡ 1st-Floor Galleries

Head downstairs to the 1st-floor galleries where Rooms 46 to 55 display the Uffizi's collection of 16th- to 18th-century works by foreign artists, including Rembrandt (Room 49); Rubens and Van Dyck share Room 55. The next room gives a nod to antique sculpture, before moving back into the 16th century with Andrea del Sarto (Rooms 57 and 58) and Raphael (Room 66), whose *Madonna del cardellino* (Madonna of the Goldfinch; 1505–06) steals the show. Raphael painted it during his four-year sojourn in Florence.

Room 65 is dedicated to Medici portrait artist, Agnolo Bronzino (1503–72), who worked at the court of Cosimo I from 1539 until 1555 (when he was replaced by Vasari). His 1545 portraits of the Grand Duchess Eleonora of Toleto and her son Giovanni together, and the 18-month-old Giovanni alone holding a goldfinch – symbolising his calling into the Church – are considered masterpieces of 16th-century European portraiture. Giovanni was indeed elected a cardinal in 1560, but died of malaria two years later.

As part of the seemingly endless New Uffizi expansion project, four early Florentine works by Leonardo da Vinci are currently displayed in Room 79. (In due course, Leonardo could well be shifted back upstairs to the 2nd floor.) His *Annunciazione* (Annunciation; 1472) was deliberately painted to be admired, not face on (from where Mary's arm appears too long, her face too light, the angle of buildings not quite right), but rather from the lower right-hand side of the painting. The eclectic style of his *Adorazione dei Pastori* (Adoration of the Shepherds; 1495–97) is typical of Florentine figurative painting in the 15th century.

Room 90, with its canary-yellow walls, features works by Caravaggio, deemed vulgar at the time for his direct interpretation of reality. *The Head of Medusa* (1598–99), commissioned for a ceremonial shield, is supposedly a self-portrait of the young artist who died at the age of 39. The biblical drama of an angel steadying the hand of Abraham as he holds a knife to his son Isaac's throat in Caravaggio's *Sacrifice of Isaac* (1601–02) is glorious in its intensity.

★ Museo del Bargello   MUSEUM
(Map p482; www.bargellomusei.beniculturali. it; Via del Proconsolo 4; adult/reduced €8/4; ☉8.15am-1.50pm, closed 2nd & 4th Sun & 1st, 3rd & 5th Mon of month) It was behind the stark walls of Palazzo del Bargello, Florence's earliest public building redecorated in neo-Gothic style in 1845, that the *podestà* (Governing magistrate) meted out justice from the 13th century until 1502. Today the building safeguards Italy's most comprehensive collection of Tuscan Renaissance sculpture with some of Michelangelo's best early works and several by Donatello. Michelangelo was just 21 when a cardinal commissioned him to create the drunken grape-adorned *Bacchus* (1496–97). Unfortunately the cardinal didn't like the result and sold it to a banker.

Other Michelangelo works to look out for in the ground-floor **Sala di Michelangelo e della Scultura del Cinque Cento** (first door on the right after entering the interior courtyard) include the marble bust of *Brutus* (c 1539), the *David/Apollo* from 1530–32 and the large, uncompleted roundel of the *Madonna and Child with the Infant St John* (aka the *Tondo Pitti;* 1505). After Michelangelo left Florence for the final time in 1534, sculpture was dominated by Baccio Bandinelli (his 1551 *Adam and Eve*, created for the Duomo, is also displayed here) and Benvenuto Cellini (look for his playful 1548–50 marble *Ganymede* in the same room).

Back in the interior courtyard, an open staircase leads up to the elegant, sculpture-laced **loggia** (1370) and, to the right, the **Salone di Donatello**. Here, in the majestic Sala del Consiglio where the city council met, works by Donatello and other early-15th-century sculptors can be admired. Originally on the facade of Chiesa di Orsanmichele and now within a tabernacle at the hall's far end, Donatello's wonderful *St George* (1416–17) brought a new sense of perspective and movement to Italian sculpture. Also look for the bronze bas-reliefs created for the Baptistry doors competition by Brunelleschi and Ghiberti.

Yet it is Donatello's two versions of *David,* a favourite subject for sculptors, that really fascinate: Donatello fashioned his slender, youthful dressed image in marble in 1408 and his fabled bronze between 1439 and 1443. The latter is extraordinary – the more so when you consider it was the first free-standing naked statue to be sculpted since classical times.

Criminals received their last rites before execution in the palace's 1st-floor **Cappella del Podestà**, also known as the Mary Magdalene Chapel, where Hell and Paradise are frescoed on the walls, as are stories from the lives of Mary of Egypt, Mary Magdalene and John the Baptist. These remnants of frescoes by Giotto were not discovered until 1840, when the chapel was turned into a storeroom and prison.

The 2nd floor moves into the 16th century with a superb collection of terracotta pieces by the prolific della Robbia family, including some of their best-known works, such as Andrea's *Ritratto idealizia di fanciullo (Bust of a Boy; c* 1475) and Giovanni's *Pietà* (1514). Instantly recognisable, Giovanni's works are more elaborate and flamboyant than either father Luca's or cousin Andrea's, using a larger palette of colours.

Museo Galileo   MUSEUM
(Map p498; ☑055 26 53 11; www.museogalileo. it; Piazza dei Giudici 1; adult/reduced €9/5.50; ☉9.30am-6pm Wed-Mon, to 1pm Tue) On the river next to the Uffizi in 12th-century Palazzo Castellani – look for the sundial telling the time on the pavement outside – is this state-of-the-art science museum, named after the great Pisa-born scientist who was invited by the Medici court to Florence in 1610 (don't miss two of his fingers and a tooth displayed here).

★ Museo di Palazzo Davanzati   MUSEUM
(Map p482; ☑055 238 86 10; www.polomuseale. firenze.it; Via Porta Rossa 13; adult/reduced €6/3; ☉8.15am-2pm, closed 1st, 3rd & 5th Mon, 2nd & 4th Sun of month) This is the address to see precisely how Florentine nobles lived in the 16th century. Home to the wealthy Davanzati merchant family from 1578, this 14th-century *palazzo* with a wonderful central loggia is a gem. Peep at the carved faces of the original owners on the pillars in the inner courtyard and don't miss the 1st-floor **Sala Madornale** (Reception Room) with its painted wooden ceiling, exotic **Sala dei Pappagalli** (Parrot Room) and **Camera dei Pavoni** (Peacock Bedroom).

The 2nd and 3rd floors of the palace can only be visited by guided tours that run daily at 10am, 11am and noon; reservations (by telephone or online) are obligatory. Note the windows in the beautiful **Camera delle Impannate**, not made from glass at all but rather waxed cloth panels tacked to the wooden frame – a luxury only nobles could afford in medieval Florence. The kitchen was always placed on the top floor to ensure living rooms remained cool and free of unsavoury cooking odours.

◉ Around Piazza della Repubblica

Piazza della Repubblica   PIAZZA
(Map p482) The site of a Roman forum and heart of medieval Florence, this busy civic space was created in the 1880s as part of a controversial plan of 'civic improvements' involving the demolition of the old market, Jewish ghetto and slums, and the relocation of nearly 6000 residents. Vasari's lovely Loggia del Pesce (Fish Market) was saved and re-erected on Via Pietrapiana.

**Chiesa e Museo
di Orsanmichele**   CHURCH, MUSEUM
(Map p482; ☑ 055 21 58 52; Via dell'Arte della Lana; ☺ museum 10am-5pm Mon, church 10am-5pm daily, closed Mon Aug) **FREE** This unusual and inspirational church, with a Gothic tabernacle by Andrea Orcagna, was created when the arcades of an old grain market (1290) were walled in and two storeys added during the 14th century. Its exterior is decorated with niches and tabernacles bearing statues. Representing the patron saints of Florence's many guilds, the statues were commissioned in the 15th and 16th centuries after the *signoria* ordered the city's guilds to finance the church's decoration.

Via de' Tornabuoni   LANDMARK
(Map p482) Renaissance palaces and Italian fashion houses border Via de' Tornabuoni, the city's most expensive shopping strip. Named after a Florentine noble family (which died out in the 17th century), it is referred to as the 'Salotto di Firenze' (Florence's Drawing Room). At its northern end is **Palazzo Antinori** in Piazza degli Antinori (1461–69), owned by the aristocratic Antinori family (known for wine production) since 1506. Opposite, huge stone steps lead up to 17th-century **Chiesa dei Santi**

Michele e Gaetano (☺ 7.15am-noon & 1-7.30pm Mon-Sat, 8am-1.15pm & 3.30-8pm Sun).

Chiesa di Santa Trinita   CHURCH
(Map p482; Piazza Santa Trinita; ☺ 8am-noon & 4-5.45pm Mon-Sat, 8-10.45am & 4-5.45pm Sun) Built in Gothic style and later given a Mannerist facade, this 14th-century church shelters some of the city's finest frescoes: Lorenzo Monaco's *Annunciation* (1422) in **Cappella Bartholini Salimbeni** and eye-catching frescoes by Ghirlandaio depicting the life of St Francis of Assisi in **Cappella Sassetti**, right of the altar. The frescoes were painted between 1483 and 1485 and feature portraits of illustrious Florentines of the time; pop a €0.50 coin in the slot to illuminate the frescoes for two minutes.

Palazzo Strozzi   GALLERY
(Map p482; ☑ 055 246 96 00; www.palazzostrozzi.org; Piazza degli Strozzi; adult/reduced €12/9.50, family ticket €22; ☺ 10am-8pm Tue, Wed & Fri-Sun, to 11pm Thu) This 15th-century Renaissance mansion was built for wealthy merchant Filippo Strozzi, one of the Medicis' major political and commercial rivals. Today it hosts exciting art exhibitions. There's always a buzz about the place, with young Florentines congregating in the courtyard **Caffè Strozzi** (☑ 055 28 82 36; www.strozzicaffe.com; ☺ 8am-8.30pm Mon, to 1am Tue-Sun; ☑). Art workshops, tours and other activities aimed squarely at families make the gallery a firm favourite with pretty much everyone.

◉ Santa Maria Novella

★**Basilica di
Santa Maria Novella**   CHURCH
(Map p482; ☑ 055 21 92 57; www.smn.it; Piazza di Santa Maria Novella 18; adult/reduced €5/3.50, ☺ 9am-7pm Mon-Thu, 11am-7pm Fri, 9am-6.30pm Sat, noon-6.30pm Sun summer, shorter hours winter) The striking green-and-white marble facade of 13th- to 15th-century Basilica di Santa Maria Novella fronts an entire monastical complex, comprising romantic church cloisters and a frescoed chapel. The basilica itself is a treasure chest of artistic masterpieces, climaxing with frescoes by Domenico Ghirlandaio. The lower section of the basilica's striped marbled facade is transitional from Romanesque to Gothic; the upper section and the main doorway (1456–70) were designed by Leon Battista Alberti. Book tickets in advance online to cut queuing time.

As you enter, look straight ahead to see Masaccio's superb fresco *Holy Trinity* (1424–25), one of the first artworks to use the then newly discovered techniques of perspective and proportion. Hanging in the central nave is a luminous painted *Crucifix* by Giotto (c 1290).

The first chapel to the right of the altar, **Cappella di Filippo Strozzi**, features spirited late-15th-century frescoes by Filippino Lippi (son of Fra' Filippo Lippi) depicting the lives of St John the Evangelist and St Philip the Apostle.

Behind the main altar is the **Cappella Maggiore** with Domenico Ghirlandaio's frescoes. Those on the right depict the life of John the Baptist; those on the left illustrate scenes from the life of the Virgin Mary. The frescoes were painted between 1485 and 1490, and are notable for their depiction of Florentine life during the Renaissance. Spot portraits of Ghirlandaio's contemporaries and members of the Tornabuoni family, who commissioned them.

To the far left of the altar, up a short flight of stairs, is the **Cappella Strozzi di Mantova**, covered in 14th-century frescoes by Niccolò di Tommaso and Nardo di Cione depicting paradise, purgatory and hell. The altarpiece (1354–57) here was painted by the latter's brother Andrea, better known as Andrea Orcagna.

From the church, walk through a side door into the serene **Chiostro Verde** (Green Cloister; 1332–62), part of the vast monastical complex occupied by Dominican friars who arrived in Florence in 1219 and settled in Santa Maria Novella two years later. The tranquil cloister takes its name from the green earth base used for the frescoes on three of the cloister's four walls. On its north side is the spectacular **Cappellone degli Spagnoli** (Spanish Chapel), originally the friars' chapter house and named as such in 1566 when it was given to the Spanish colony in Florence. The chapel is covered in extraordinary frescoes (c 1365–67) by Andrea di Bonaiuto. The vault features depictions of the Resurrection, Ascension and Pentecost, and on the altar wall are scenes of the *Via Dolorosa, Crucifixion* and *Descent into Limbo*. On the right wall is a huge fresco of *The Militant and Triumphant Church* – look in the foreground for a portrait of Cimabue, Giotto, Boccaccio, Petrarch and Dante. Other frescoes in the chapels depict the *Triumph of Christian Doctrine,* 14 figures symbolising the Arts and Sciences, and the Life of St Peter.

By the side of the chapel, a passage leads into the **Chiostro dei Morti** (Cloister of the Dead), a cemetery existent well before the arrival of the Dominicans to Santa Maria Novella. The tombstones embedded in the walls and floor date to the 13th and 14th centuries.

On the west side of the Chiostro Verde, another passage leads to the 14th-century **Cappella degli Ubriachi** and a large **refectory** (1353–54) featuring ecclesiastical relics and a 1583 *Last Supper* by Alessandro Allori.

Future expansion work costing €3 million at the basilica complex, announced in late 2016, will eventually open up the **Chiostro Grande** (Big Cloister) and **Cappella del Papa** to visitors; the former dormitories will be transformed into a new reception area, bookshop and cafe.

There are two entrances to the Santa Maria Novella complex: the main entrance to the basilica or through the tourist office opposite the train station on Piazza della Stazione. The city-run **Muse Firenze** (☑ 055 276 82 24; http://musefirenze.it) organises fantastic guided tours (€4, 1¼ hours) in English of the basilica complex; reserve in advance by email or phone.

LOCAL KNOWLEDGE

STREET TALK

Take a break from Renaissance art with the pioneering **Street Levels Gallery** (☑ 339 2203607, 347 3387760; www.facebook.com/pg/StreetLevelsGalleriaFirenze; Via Palazzuolo 74r; ⊙ 10am-1pm & 3-7pm). Exhibitions showcase the work of local street artists, including street-sign hacker Clet (p500), the stencil art of Hogre, and ExitEnter, whose work is easily recognisable by the red balloons holding up the matchstick figures he draws. A highlight is the enigmatic Blub, whose caricatures of historical figures wearing goggles and diving masks adorn many a city wall – his art is known as *L'Arte Sa Nuotare* (Art Knows how to Swim).

Check the gallery's Facebook page for workshops, cultural events, *aperitivi* (evening drinks) and other uber-cool happenings.

★ **Museo Novecento** MUSEUM
(Museum of the 20th Century; Map p482; ✆055
28 61 32; www.museonovecento.it; Piazza di Santa
Maria Novella 10; adult/reduced €8.50/4; ☺9am-
7pm Mon-Wed, Sat & Sun, to 2pm Thu, to 11pm Fri
summer, 9am-6pm Fri-Wed, to 2pm Thu winter)
Don't allow the Renaissance to distract from
Florence's fantastic modern art museum,
in a 13th-century *palazzo* previously used
as a pilgrim shelter, hospital and school.
A well-articulated itinerary guides visitors
through modern Italian painting and sculpture from the early 20th century to the late
1980s. Installation art makes effective use
of the outside space on the 1st-floor loggia.
Fashion and theatre get a nod on the 2nd
floor, and the itinerary ends with a 20-
minute cinematic montage of the best films
set in Florence.

Museo Marino Marini GALLERY
(Map p482; ✆055 21 94 32; http://museo
marinomarini.it/; Piazza San Pancrazio 1; adult/
reduced €6/4; ☺10am-7pm Sat-Mon, to 1pm Wed-
Fri) Deconsecrated in the 19th century, Chiesa di San Pancrazio is home to this small
art museum displaying sculptures, portraits
and drawings by Pistoia-born sculptor Marino Marini (1901–80). But the highlight
is the **Cappella Rucellai** with a tiny scale
copy of Christ's Holy Sepulchre in Jerusalem – a Renaissance gem by Leon Battista
Alberti. The chapel was built between 1458
and 1467 for the tomb of wealthy Florentine banker and wool merchant Giovanni
Ruccellai.

◉ San Lorenzo

★ **Museo delle**
Cappelle Medicee MAUSOLEUM
(Medici Chapels; Map p482; www.firenzemusei.
it; Piazza Madonna degli Aldobrandini 6; adult/
reduced €8/4; ☺8.15am-1.50pm, closed 1st, 3rd
& 5th Mon, 2nd & 4th Sun of month) Nowhere is
Medici conceit expressed so explicitly as in
the Medici Chapels. Adorned with granite,
marble, semi-precious stones and some of
Michelangelo's most beautiful sculptures, it
is the burial place of 49 dynasty members.
Francesco I lies in the dark, imposing **Cappella dei Principi** (Princes' Chapel) alongside Ferdinando I and II and Cosimo I, II
and III. Lorenzo il Magnifico is buried in the
graceful **Sagrestia Nuova** (New Sacristy),
which was Michelangelo's first architectural
work.

It is also in the sacristy that you can
swoon over three of Michelangelo's most
haunting sculptures: *Dawn and Dusk* on
the sarcophagus of Lorenzo, Duke of Urbino; *Night and Day* on the sarcophagus of
Lorenzo's son Giuliano (note the unfinished
face of 'Day' and the youth of the sleeping woman drenched in light aka 'Night');
and *Madonna and Child,* which adorns
Lorenzo's tomb.

★ **Basilica**
di San Lorenzo BASILICA
(Map p482; www.operamedicealaurenziana.org;
Piazza San Lorenzo; €6, with Biblioteca Medicea
Laurenziana €8.50; ☺10am-5pm Mon-Sat, plus
1.30-5pm Sun Mar-Oct) Considered one of
Florence's most harmonious examples of
Renaissance architecture, this unfinished
basilica was the Medici parish church
and mausoleum. It was designed by
Brunelleschi in 1425 for Cosimo the Elder
and built over a 4th-century church. In the
solemn interior, look for Brunelleschi's austerely beautiful **Sagrestia Vecchia** (Old
Sacristy) with its sculptural decoration
by Donatello. Michelangelo was commissioned to design the facade in 1518, but his
design in white Carrara marble was never
executed, hence the building's rough, unfinished appearance.

Inside, columns of *pietra serena* (soft
grey stone) crowned with Corinthian capitals separate the nave from the two aisles.
The gilded funerary monument of Donatello
– who was still sculpting the two bronze pulpits (1460–67) adorned with panels of the
Crucifixion when he died – lies in the **Cappella Martelli** (Martelli Chapel) featuring
Filippo Lippi's exquisitely restored *Annunciation* (c 1440).

Donatello's actual grave lies in the basilica crypt, today part of the **Museo del
Tesoro di San Lorenzo** (San Lorenzo
Treasury Museum); the crypt entrance is
in the courtyard beyond the ticket office.
The museum displays chalices, altarpieces,
dazzling altar cloths, processional crucifixes, episcopal brooches and other precious sacred treasures once displayed in
the church. Across from the plain marble
tombstone of Donatello is the tomb of Cosimo the Elder, buried inside the quadrangular pilaster in the crypt supporting the
basilica presbytery – his funerary monument sits directly above, in front of the high
altar in the basilica.

San Lorenzo & San Marco

San Lorenzo & San Marco

◎ Top Sights
1 Galleria dell'Accademia	C2
2 Museo degli Innocenti	D2
3 Museo di San Marco	C1

◎ Sights
4 Cenacolo di Sant'Apollonia	C1

🛏 Sleeping
5 Hotel Azzi	A2
6 Hotel Marine	A1
7 Hotel Orto de' Medici	C1
8 Ostello Archi Rossi	A1

❎ Eating
9 Carabé	C2
10 Da Nerbone	B2
11 La Ménagère	B2
12 Mercato Centrale	B2
13 My Sugar	B2
14 Pugi	C2
15 SimBIOsi	C2
16 Trattoria Mario	B2

🍷 Drinking & Nightlife
17 Ditta Al Cinema	C2
18 Lo Sverso	B2

**Biblioteca Medicea
Laurenziana**   LIBRARY
(Medici Library; Map p482; ☑ 055 293 79 11; www.
bml.firenze.sbn.it; Piazza San Lorenzo 9; €3, incl basilica €8.50; ☉ 9.30am-1.30pm Mon-Sat) Beyond
the Basilica di San Lorenzo ticket office lie
peaceful cloisters framing a garden with orange trees. Stairs lead up the loggia to the
Biblioteca Medicea Laurenziana, commissioned by Giulio de' Medici (Pope Clement
VII) in 1524 to house the extensive Medici
library (started by Cosimo the Elder and
greatly added to by Lorenzo il Magnifico).
The extraordinary staircase in the vestibule,
intended as a 'dark prelude' to the magnificent **Sala di Lettura** (Reading Room), was
designed by Michelangelo.

**Palazzo
Medici-Riccardi**   PALACE
(Map p482; ☑ 055 276 03 40; www.palazzo
-medici.it; Via Cavour 3; adult/reduced €7/4;
☉ 8.30am-7pm Thu-Tue) Cosimo the Elder en-
trusted Michelozzo with the design of the

family's townhouse in 1444. The result was
this palace, a blueprint that influenced the
construction of Florentine family residences
such as Palazzo Pitti and Palazzo Strozzi.
The upstairs chapel, **Cappella dei Magi**,
is covered in wonderfully detailed frescoes
(c 1459–63) by Benozzo Gozzoli, a pupil of
Fra' Angelico, and is one of the supreme
achievements of Renaissance painting.

◎ San Marco

★ **Galleria dell'Accademia**   GALLERY
(Map p494; www.firenzemusei.it; Via Ricasoli
60; adult/reduced €8/4, incl temporary exhibition €12.50/6.25; ☉ 8.15am-6.50pm Tue-Sun) A
queue marks the door to this gallery, built
to house one of the Renaissance's most iconic masterpieces, Michelangelo's *David*. But
the world's most famous statue is worth the
wait. The subtle detail of the real thing – the
veins in his sinewy arms, the leg muscles, the
change in expression as you move around

the statue – *is* impressive. Carved from a single block of marble, Michelangelo's most famous work was his most challenging – he didn't choose the marble himself and it was veined.

And when the statue of the nude boy-warrior, depicted for the first time as a man in the prime of life rather than a young boy, assumed its pedestal in front of Palazzo Vecchio on Piazza della Signoria in 1504, Florentines immediately adopted it as a powerful emblem of Florentine power, liberty and civic pride.

Michelangelo was also the master behind the unfinished *San Matteo* (St Matthew; 1504–08) and four *Prigioni* ('Prisoners' or 'Slaves'; 1521–30), also displayed in the gallery. The Prisoners seem to be writhing and struggling to free themselves from the marble; they were meant for the tomb of Pope Julius II, itself never completed. Adjacent rooms contain paintings by Andrea Orcagna, Taddeo Gaddi, Domenico Ghirlandaio, Filippino Lippi and Sandro Botticelli.

★ **Museo di San Marco** MUSEUM
(Map p494; ☑ 055 238 86 08; Piazza San Marco 3; adult/reduced €4/2; ☉ 8.15am-1.50pm Mon-Fri, 8.15am-4.50pm Sat & Sun, closed 1st, 3rd & 5th Sun & 2nd & 4th Mon of month) At the heart of Florence's university area sits **Chiesa di San Marco** and an adjoining 15th-century Dominican monastery where both gifted painter Fra' Angelico (c 1395–1455) and the sharp-tongued Savonarola piously served God. Today the monastery, aka one of Florence's most spiritually uplifting museums, showcases the work of Fra' Angelico. After centuries of being known as 'Il Beato Angelico' (literally 'The Blessed Angelic One') or simply 'Il Beato' (The Blessed), the Renaissance's most blessed religious painter was made a saint by Pope John Paul II in 1984.

Enter via Michelozzo's **Chiostro di Sant' Antonio** (Saint Antoninus Cloister; 1440). Turn immediately right to enter the **Sala dell'Ospizio dei Pellegrini** (Pilgrims' Hospital Hall) where Fra' Angelico's attention to perspective and the realistic portrayal of nature come to life in a number of major paintings, including the *Deposition from the Cross* (1432).

Giovanni Antonio Sogliani's fresco *The Miraculous Supper of St Domenic* (1536) dominates the former monks' **Refettorio** (Refectory) in the cloister. Fra' Angelico's huge *Crucifixion and Saints* fresco (1441–42), featuring all the patron saints of the convent and city, plus the Medici family who commissioned the fresco, decorates the former **Capitolo** (Chapterhouse). But it is the 44 monastic **cells** on the 1st floor that are the most haunting: at the top of the stairs, Fra' Angelico's most famous work, *Annunciation* (c 1440), commands all eyes.

A stroll around each of the cells reveals snippets of many more religious reliefs by the Tuscan-born friar, who decorated the cells between 1440 and 1441 with deeply devotional frescoes to guide the meditation of his fellow friars. Most were executed by Fra' Angelico himself, with others by aides under his supervision, including Benozzo Gozzoli. Among several masterpieces is the magnificent *Adoration of the Magi* in the cell used by Cosimo the Elder as a meditation retreat (Nos 38 to 39); only 10 people can visit at a time. The frescoes in the cell of San Antonino Arcivescovo (neighbouring Fra' Angelico's *Annunication*) are gruesome: they show Jesus pushing open the door of his sepulchre, squashing a nasty-looking devil in the process.

Contrasting with the pure beauty of these frescoes are the plain rooms (Cell VI) that Savonarola called home from 1489. Rising to the position of prior at the Dominican convent, it was from here that the fanatical monk railed against luxury, greed and corruption of the clergy. Kept as a kind of shrine to the turbulent priest, the three small rooms house a portrait, a few personal items, fragments of the black cape and white tunic Savonarola wore, his rosary beads and the linen banner he carried in processions, and a grand marble monument erected by admirers in 1873.

★ **Museo degli Innocenti** MUSEUM
(Map p494; ☑ 055 203 73 08; www.museo deglinnocenti.it; Piazza della Santissima Annunziata 13; adult/reduced/family €7/5/10; ☉ 10am-7pm) Shortly after its founding in 1421, Brunelleschi designed the loggia for Florence's **Ospedale degli Innocenti**, a foundling hospital and Europe's first orphanage, built by the wealthy silk weavers' guild to care for unwanted children. Inside, a highly emotive, state-of-the-art museum explores its history, climaxing with a sensational collection of frescoes and artworks that once decorated the hospital and a stunning rooftop cafe terrace (fab city views). Brunelleschi's use of rounded arches and Roman capitals marks it as arguably the first building of the Renaissance.

Cenacolo di Sant'Apollonia CONVENT
(Map p494; ☑ 055 238 86 07; www.polomuseale
toscana.beniculturali.it; Via XXVII Apre 1; ⊙ 8.15am-
1.50pm daily, closed 1st, 3rd & 5th Sat & Sun of
month) **FREE** Once part of a sprawling Benedictine monastery, this *cenacolo* harbours
arguably the city's most remarkable *Last
Supper* scene. Painted by Andrea del Castagno in the 1440s, it is one of the first works
of its kind to effectively apply Renaissance
perspective. It possesses a haunting power
with its vivid colours – especially the almost
abstract squares of marble painted above
the apostles' heads – as well as the dark,
menacing figure of Judas.

In season, look for occasional additional
guided tours of the convent on Wednesday
afternoon between 3pm and 5pm; contact
nearby Museo di San Marco (p495) for information and reservations.

FLORENCE & TUSCANY FLORENCE

⊙ Santa Croce

★**Basilica di Santa Croce** CHURCH, MUSEUM
(Map p497; ☑ 055 246 61 05; www.santacroce
opera.it; Piazza di Santa Croce; adult/reduced €8/4;
⊙ 9.30am-5.30pm Mon-Sat, 2-5.30pm Sun) The
austere interior of this Franciscan basilica
is a shock after the magnificent neo-Gothic facade enlivened by varying shades of coloured marble. Most visitors come to see the
tombs of Michelangelo, Galileo and Ghiberti
inside this church, but frescoes by Giotto
in the chapels right of the altar are the real
highlights. The basilica was designed by Arnolfo di Cambio between 1294 and 1385 and
owes its name to a splinter of the Holy Cross
donated by King Louis of France in 1258.

⊙ Oltrarno

The Oltrarno's main sights lie snug on Piazza Santo Spirito and nearby Piazza del Carmine. When you reach museum overload
and need to stretch your legs and see some
sky, meander east towards neighbouring
Boboli where the tiers of parks and gardens
behind Palazzo Pitti entice.

Ponte Vecchio BRIDGE
(Map p498) Dating from 1345, Ponte Vecchio
was the only Florentine bridge to survive destruction at the hands of retreating German
forces in 1944. Above the jewellers' shops on
the eastern side, the **Corridoio Vasariano**
(Vasari Corridor) is a 16th-century passageway between the Uffizi and Palazzo Pitti
that runs around, rather than through, the

medieval **Torre dei Mannelli** at the bridge's
southern end. The first documentation of a
stone bridge here, at the narrowest crossing
point along the entire length of the Arno,
dates from 972.

Floods in 1177 and 1333 destroyed the
bridge, and in 1966 it came close to being
destroyed again. Many of the jewellers with
shops on the bridge were convinced the
floodwaters would sweep away their liveli-
hoods; fortunately the bridge held.

They're still here. Indeed, the bridge has
twinkled with the glittering wares of jewellers, their trade often passed down from
generation to generation, ever since the
16th century, when Ferdinando I de' Medici ordered them here to replace the often
malodorous presence of the town butchers,
who used to toss unwanted leftovers into the
river.

★**Cappella Brancacci** CHAPEL
(Map p498; ☑ 055 238 21 95; http://museici
vicifiorentini.comune.fi.it; Piazza del Carmine 14;
adult/reduced €6/4.50; ⊙ 10am-5pm Wed-Sat
& Mon, 1-5pm Sun) Fire in the 18th century
practically destroyed 13th-century **Basilica
di Santa Maria del Carmine** (Map p498;
Piazza del Carmine), but it spared the magnificent frescoes in this chapel – a treasure of
paintings by Masolino da Panicale, Masaccio
and Filippino Lippi commissioned by rich
merchant Felice Brancacci upon his return
from Egypt in 1423. The chapel entrance is
to the right of the main church entrance.
Only 30 people can visit at a time, limited
to 30 minutes in high season; tickets include
admission to the **Fondazione Salvatore
Romano** (Cenacolo di Santo Spirito; Map p498;
☑ 055 28 70 43; http://museicivicifiorentini.comu
ne.fi.it; Piazza Santo Spirito 29; adult/reduced
€7/5; ⊙ 10am-4pm Sat-Mon).

★**Basilica di Santo Spirito** CHURCH
(Map p498; Piazza Santo Spirito; ⊙ 9.30am-
12.30pm & 4-5.30pm Thu-Tue) The facade of this
Brunelleschi church, smart on Florence's
most shabby-chic piazza, makes a striking
backdrop to open-air concerts in summer.
Inside, the basilica's length is lined with 38
semicircular chapels (covered with a plain
wall in the 1960s), and a colonnade of grey
pietra forte Corinthian columns injects
monumental grandeur. Artworks to look for
include Domenico di Zanobi's *Madonna of
the Relief* (1485) in the Cappella Velutti, in
which the Madonna wards off a little red
devil with a club.

Santa Croce

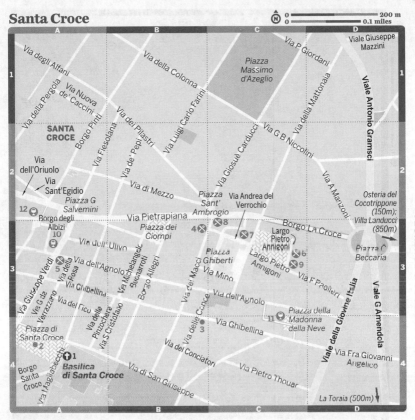

N 0 ——————— 200 m
0 ——————— 0.1 miles

FLORENCE & TUSCANY FLORENCE

Santa Croce

★ **Palazzo Pitti**　　　　　　　　MUSEUM
(Map p498; www.polomuseale.firenze.it; Piazza dei Pitti; ◎8.15am-6.50pm Tue-Sun) Commissioned by banker Luca Pitta and designed by Brunelleschi in 1457, this vast Renaissance palace was later bought by the Medici family. Over the centuries, it served as the residence of the city's rulers until the Savoys donated it to the state in 1919. Nowadays it houses an impressive silver museum, a couple of art museums and a series of rooms re-creating life in the palace during House of Savoy times. Stop by at sunset when its entire vast facade is coloured a vibrant pink.

★ **Giardino di Boboli**　　　　　GARDENS
(Map p498; ☎055 29 48 83; www.polomuseale. firenze.it; Palazzo Pitti, Piazza dei Pitti; adult/

The Oltrarno

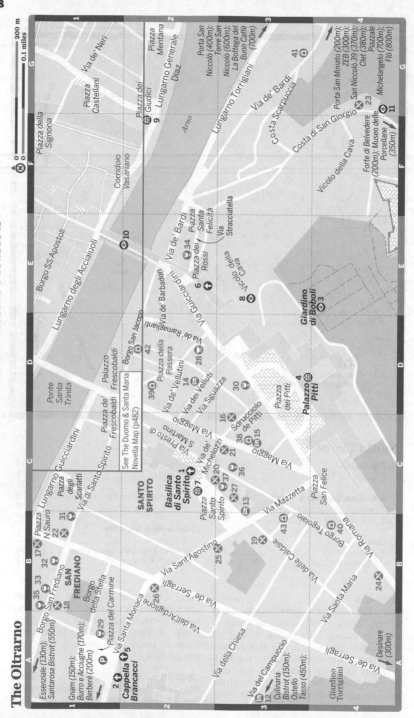

Essenziale (130m); Gnam (150m); Santarosa Bistrot (550m)

Burro e Acciughe (170m); Berberè (200m)

Piazza N Sauro

SAN FREDIANO

Borgo San Frediano

Borgo della Stella

Piazza del Carmine

Via Santa Monaca

Via Sant'Agostino

Via de' Serragli

Via dell'Ardiglione

Culinaria Bistrot (150m); Ostello Tasso (450m)

Via del Campuccio

Via della Chiesa

Giardino Torrigiani

Via de' Serragli

Desinare (300m)

Via Santa Maria

Borgo Tegolaio

Via Romana

Via delle Caldaie

Via Mazzetta

Piazza San Felice

Cappella Brancacci

Piazza degli Scarlatti

Via di Santo Spirito

Via Maffia

Lungarno Guicciardini

Borgo SS Apostoli

Lungarno degli Acciaiuoli

Ponte Santa Trinita

Piazza de' Frescobaldi

Palazzo Frescobaldi

Borgo San Jacopo

Piazza della Signoria

Piazza Castellani

Piazza della Signoria

Corridoio Vasariano

Via de' Neri

Piazza dei Giudici

Piazza Mentana

Lungarno Generale Diaz

Arno

Lungarno Torrigiani

Porta San Niccolò (400m); Torre San Niccolò (600m); La Bottega del Buon Caffè (700m)

Via de' Bardi

Via de' Barbadori

Via de' Ramaglianti

Piazza Santa Felicità

Via Stracciatella

Via de' Guicciardini

Via de' Velluti

Via de' Vellutini

Piazza della Passera

Via dei Velluti

Via dello Sprone

Via Maggio

Via de' Michelozzi

Via Sant'Agostino

SANTO SPIRITO

Basilica di Santo Spirito

Piazza Santo Spirito

Via Mazzetta

Piazza de' Pitti

Palazzo Pitti

Giardino di Boboli

Costa Scarpuccia

Via de' Bardi

Piazza de' Rossi

Vicolo della Cava

Costa di San Giorgio

Forte di Belvedere (200m); Museo delle Porcellane (350m)

Vicolo della Cava

Porta San Miniato (200m); ZEB (300m); San Niccolò 39 (370m); Clet (380m); Piazzale Michelangelo (700m); Flò (800m)

Piazzale Michelangelo (700m)

See The Duomo & Santa Maria Novella Map (p482)

1 Basilica di Santo Spirito
2 Cappella Brancacci
3 Giardino di Boboli
4 Palazzo Pitti
5 Cappella
6
7
8
9
10
11
12
13
14
15
16
17
18
19
20
21
22
23
24
25
26
27
28
29
30
31
32
33
34
35
36
37
38
39
40
41
42
43

The Oltrarno

reduced incl Tesoro dei Granduchi, Museo delle Porcellane & Museo della Moda e del Costume €7/3.50, during temporary exhibition €10/5; ⊙8.15am-7.30pm summer, reduced hours winter, closed 1st & last Mon of month) Behind Palazzo Pitti, the Boboli Gardens were laid out in the mid-16th century to a design by architect Niccolò Pericoli. At the upper, southern limit, beyond the box-hedged rose garden and **Museo delle Porcellane** (Porcelain Museum), beautiful views over the Florentine countryside unfold. Within the lower reaches of the gardens, don't miss the fantastical shell- and gem-encrusted **Grotta del Buontalenti**, a decorative grotto built by Bernardo Buontalenti between 1583 and 1593 for Francesco I de' Medici.

In Spring 2017, much to the joy of many a local Florentine who can be found promenading in Boboli on a Sunday afternoon, Florence's homegrown fashion house Gucci pledged €2 million to restore the gardens and their treasure trove of statues and fountains to their former pristine glory.

Villa e Giardino Bardini   VILLA, GARDENS
(Map p498; ☑055 263 85 99; www.bardinipeyron.it; Costa San Giorgio 2, Via de' Bardi 1r; adult/reduced €8/6; ⊙10am-7pm Tue-Sun) This 17th-century villa and garden was named after 19th-century antiquarian art collector Stefano Bardini (1836–1922), who bought it in 1913 and restored its ornamental medieval garden. It has all the features of a quintessential Tuscan garden, including artificial grottoes, orangery, marble statues and fountains. The villa houses two small museums: **Museo Pietro Annigoni**, with works by Italian painter Pietro Annigoni (1910–88), and **Museo Roberto Capucci**, showcasing Capucci-designed haute couture. End with city views from the romantic **roof terrace**.

Piazzale Michelangelo   VIEWPOINT
(Piazzale Michelangelo; ☑13) Turn your back on the bevy of ticky-tacky souvenir stalls flogging *David* statues and boxer shorts and take in the spectacular city panorama from this vast square, pierced by one of Florence's two *David* copies. Sunset here is particularly dramatic. It's a 10-minute uphill walk along the serpentine road, paths and steps that scale the hillside from the Arno and Piazza Giuseppe Poggi; from Piazza San Niccolò walk uphill and bear left up the long flight of steps signposted Viale Michelangelo.

Or take bus 13 from Stazione di Santa Maria Novella.

Torre San Niccolò
CITY GATE

(☑ 055 276 82 24; http://musefirenze.it; Piazza Giuseppe Poggi; 30min guided visit €4; ☺ 5-8pm daily 24 Jun-Sep) Built in 1324, the best preserved of the city's medieval gates stands sentinel on the banks of the Arno. In summer, with a guide, you can scale the steep stairs inside the tower to enjoy blockbuster river and city views. Visits are limited to 15 people at a time (no children under eight years) making advance reservations essential; book online, by email or by phone. Tours are cancelled when it rains.

Behind the city gate a monumental staircase designed by Giuseppe Poggi winds its way up towards **Basilica di San Miniato al Monte** (☑ 055 234 27 31; www.sanminiatoalmonte.it; Via Monte alle Croci; ☺ 9.30am-1pm & 3-8pm summer, to 7pm winter).

Forte di Belvedere
FORTRESS

(www.museicivicifiorentini.comune.fi.it; Via di San Leonardo 1; ☺ hours vary) **FREE** Forte di Belvedere is a rambling fort designed by Bernardo Buontalenti for Grand Duke Ferdinando I at the end of the 16th century. From the massive bulwark soldiers kept watch on four fronts – as much for internal security as to protect the Palazzo Pitti against foreign attack. Today the fort hosts seasonal art exhibitions, which are well worth a peek if only to revel in the sweeping city panorama that can be had from the fort. Outside of exhibition times, the fort is closed.

Tours

Curious Appetite
TOURS

(www.curiousappetitetravel.com) Private and group food and wine tastings led by Italian-American Coral Sisk and a small team of guides. Tastings last 3½ hours (minimum four people) and are themed: at the market, craft cocktails and *aperitivi*, Italian food and wine pairings, and artisan gelato.

★500 Touring Club
DRIVING

(☑ 346 8262324; www.500touringclub.com; Via Gherardo Silvani 149a) Hook up with Florence's 500 Touring Club for a guided tour in a vintage motor – with you behind the wheel! Every car has a name in this outfit's fleet of gorgeous vintage Fiat 500s from the 1960s. Motoring tours are guided (hop in your car and follow the leader) and themed – families love the picnic trip, couples the wine tasting.

Tuscany Bike Tours
CYCLING

(Map p497; ☑ 055 386 02 53, 339 1163495; www.tuscany-biketours.com; Via Ghibellina 34r; ☺ office 9-10am & 5-7pm Mar-Nov) Offers a fantastic range of cycling tours in and around Florence, including three-hour city tours by bike with a gelato break (adult/reduced €39/35) and a rather cool, Audrey Hepburn–styled one-day Vespa tour from Florence into the Chianti hills (adult/reduced/passenger €125/115/90, including lunch, castle visit and wine and olive-oil tasting). Bike hire too.

Florence Town
WALKING

(Map p482; ☑ 055 28 11 03; www.florencetown.com; Via de' Lamberti 1) Organised tours, activities and workshops in and around Florence.

LOCAL KNOWLEDGE

CLET
....

Should you notice something gone awry with street signs in Oltrarno – on a No Entry sign, a tiny black figure stealthily sneaking away with the white bar for example – you can be sure it is the work of French-born **Clet Abraham** (www.facebook.com/CLET-108974755823172), one of Florence's most popular street artists. In his Oltrarno **studio** (Via dell'Olmo 8) you can buy stickers and postcards featuring his hacked traffic signs and, if you're lucky, catch a glimpse of the rebellious artist at work.

In 2011 Clet created quite a stir in his adopted city by installing, in the black of night, a life-sized figurine entitled *Uomo Comune* (Common Man) on Ponte alle Grazie (to which the city authorities turned a blind eye for a week before removing it). Should you fall completely and utterly head over heels in love with Clet's work, you can either order a reproduction street sign directly from his workshop (from €500) or purchase an original (numbered and signed, from €2500) limited edition from **Mio Concept** (Map p482; ☑ 055 264 55 43; www.mio-concept.com; Via della Spada 34r; ☺ 10am-1.30pm & 2.30-7.30pm Tue-Sat, 3-7pm Mon) – Clet produces only 13 of each design.

Cooking classes, market tours, pizza- and gelato-making courses and Tuscan wine trail tours too.

🎭 Festivals & Events

Festa di Anna Maria Medici   CULTURAL
(⏱18 Feb) Florence's Feast of Anna Maria Medici marks the death in 1743 of the last Medici, Anna Maria, with a costumed parade from Palazzo Vecchio to her tomb in the Cappelle Medicee.

Scoppio del Carro   FIREWORKS
(⏱Mar/Apr) A cart of fireworks is exploded in front of the cathedral in Piazza del Duomo at 11am on Easter Sunday.

Maggio Musicale Fiorentino   PERFORMING ARTS
(www.operadifirenze.it; ⏱Apr–Jun) Italy's oldest arts festival features world class performances of theatre, classical music, jazz, opera and dance. Events are staged at the Opera di Firenze (p512) and venues across town.

Festa di San Giovanni   RELIGIOUS
(⏱24 Jun) Florence celebrates its patron saint, John, with a *calcio storico* (historic football) match on Piazza di Santa Croce and fireworks over Piazzale Michelangelo.

🛏 Sleeping

Florence is unexpectedly small, rendering almost anywhere in the city centre convenient. Advance reservations are essential between Easter and September, while winter ushers in some great deals for visitors – room rates are practically halved.

🛏 Around the Duomo & Piazza della Signoria

Hotel Cestelli   HOTEL €
(Map p482; ☎055 21 42 13; www.hotelcestelli. com; Borgo SS Apostoli 25; d €100, s/d without bathroom €60/80; ⏱closed 2 weeks Jan & 10 days Aug; 🖥) Housed in a 12th-century *palazzo* a stiletto strut from fashionable Via de' Tornabuoni, this intimate eight-room hotel is a gem. Rooms reveal an understated style, tastefully combining polished antiques with spangly chandeliers, vintage art and silk screens. Owners Alessio and Asumi are a mine of local information and are happy to share their knowledge. No breakfast. Ask about low-season discounts for longer stays.

★Hotel Scoti   PENSION €€
(Map p482; ☎055 29 21 28; www.hotelscoti. com; Via de' Tornabuoni 7; d/tr/q €130/160/185; ⏱reception 8am-11.30pm; 🖥) Wedged between designer boutiques on Florence's smartest shopping strip, this hidden *pensione* is a fabulous mix of old-fashioned charm and value for money. Its 16 traditionally styled rooms are spread across the 2nd floor of a 16th-century *palazzo;* some have lovely rooftop views. Guests can borrow hairdryers, bottle openers, plug adapters etc and the frescoed lounge (1780) is stunning. No breakfast.

★Hotel Davanzati   HOTEL €€
(Map p482; ☎055 28 66 66; www.hoteldavanzati.it; Via Porta Rossa 5; s/d/tr €143/215/281; ❄@🖥) Twenty-two steps lead up to this family-run hotel. A labyrinth of enchanting rooms, frescoes and modern comforts, it has bags of charisma – and that includes Florentine brothers Tommaso and Riccardo, and father Fabrizio, who run the show (Grandpa Marcello surveys proceedings). Rooms come with a mini iPad, meaning free wi-fi around town, direct messaging with the hotel and a handy digital city guide.

Hotel Pendini   HISTORIC HOTEL €€
(Map p482; ☎055 2 11 17; www.hotelpendini. it; Via degli Strozzi 2; d €140-210; ❄@🖥) Very much part of city history, the Pendini opened in 1879 as an upmarket *pensione* – hence the giant 'Pensione Pendini' lettering dominating its privileged facade on Piazza della Repubblica. Its 44 comfortable rooms today are up-to-the-minute, with polished parquet floors, antique furnishings, and beautiful floral fabrics and wallpapers. Historic B&W photographs adorn the corridors and classical music plays in the enchanting, vintage-styled lounge.

Hotel Torre Guelfa   HISTORIC HOTEL €€€
(Map p482; ☎055 239 63 38; www.hoteltorre guelfa.com; Borgo SS Apostoli 8; d €270-380, tr €350-390; ❄@🖥) If you want to kip in a real-McCoy Florentine *palazzo* without breaking the bank, this 31-room hotel with fortress-style facade is the address. Scale its 13th-century, 50m-tall tower – Florence's tallest privately owned *torre* – for a sundowner overlooking Florence and you'll be blown away. Rates are practically halved in the low season.

🛏 San Lorenzo & San Marco

★ Academy Hostel HOSTEL €

(Map p482; ☑055 239 86 65; www.academy hostel.eu; Via Ricasoli 9; dm €32-45, d €80-100; ❄@🛜) This classy 13-room hostel – definitely not a party hostel – sits on the 1st floor of Baron Ricasoli's 17th-century *palazzo*. The inviting lobby, with books to browse and computers to surf, was once a theatre and is a comfy spot to chill on the sofa over TV or a DVD. Dorms sport maximum four, five or six beds, high moulded ceilings and brightly coloured lockers.

There is a small kitchen, washing machine and the bijou outdoor terrace is summertime perfect. Rooms are closed for daily cleaning between 11am and 2.30pm.

Hotel Marine HOTEL €

(Map p494; ☑055 26 42 51; www.hotelmarine florence.com; Via Faenza 56; d/tr/q €100/120/140; 🛜) Run by the same team as **Hotel Azzi** (Locanda degli Artisti; Map p494; ☑055 21 38 06; www.hotelazzi.com; Via Faenza 56/88r; d/tr/q €120/140/160; ❄🛜) on the ground floor (the two hotels even share the same reception), 2nd-floor Marine is tip-top value for those on a budget. Its 15 rooms are plain but spotlessly clean and decently sized. The star attraction is breakfast on the summer terrace with dreamy rooftop views, including the Duomo, Capelle Medicee and Palazzo Vecchio.

Ostello Archi Rossi HOSTEL €

(Map p494; ☑055 29 08 04; www.hostelarchi rossi.com; Via Faenza 94r; dm €28-32, s/d/tr/q €60/85/90/120; ⊘closed Dec; @🛜) Guests' paintings and artwork brighten this busy hostel near Stazione di Santa Maria Novella. Bright white dorms have three to nine beds and must be evacuated between 10.30am and 2.30pm for cleaning. Guests can use washing machines, frozen meal dispensers and microwaves. No curfew but guests have to ring the bell after 2am.

★ Hotel Orto de' Medici HOTEL €€

(Map p494; ☑055 48 34 27; www.ortodeimedici. it; Via San Gallo 30; d from €174; ❄@🛜) This three-star hotel in San Marco redefines elegance with its majestic ceilings, chic oyster-grey colour scheme and contemporary furnishings, offset to perfection by the historic *palazzo* in which it languishes. Hunt down the odd remaining 19th-century fresco, and don't miss the garden complete with lemon trees in terracotta pots and rambling ivy. To splurge, go for a room with its own flowery terrace.

🛏 Santa Croce

★ Hotel Dalí HOTEL €

(Map p482; ☑055 234 07 06; www.hoteldali. com; Via dell'Oriuolo 17; d €90, s/d without bathroom €40/70, apt from €95; 🅿🛜) A warm welcome from hosts Marco and Samanta awaits at this lovely small hotel. A stone's throw from the Duomo, it has 10 sunny rooms, some overlooking a leafy inner courtyard, decorated in a low-key modern way and equipped with kettles, coffee and tea. No breakfast, but – miraculous for downtown Florence – free parking in the rear courtyard.

The icing on the cake is a trio of gorgeous self-catering apartments – one with a Duomo view – sleeping three, four or six.

🛏 Oltrarno

Camping Michelangelo CAMPGROUND €

(☑055 681 19 77; Viale Michelangiolo 80; tent site/adult/child €8/11/6.50, bunk bed in dm €10-19, s/d/tr €30/45/60; ⊘Jun–mid-Sep; 🅿🛜🅰) Happy campers roll out of their tents to a panoramic view of Florence at this two-star hilltop campground, equipped with shaded pitches for tents, parking spaces for motorhomes, and comfy prefab tents with bunk beds. On-site grocery, shop, children's playground, pool and bar cooking up breakfast too.

★ Hotel Palazzo Guadagni HOTEL €€

(Map p498; ☑055 265 83 76; www.palazzogua dagni.com; Piazza Santo Spirito 9; d €150-220, tr/q €265/310; ❄🛜) This romantic hotel overlooking Florence's liveliest summertime square is legendary – Zeffirelli shot scenes from *Tea with Mussolini* here. Housed in an artfully revamped Renaissance palace, it has 15 spacious if old-fashioned rooms and an impossibly romantic loggia terrace with wicker chairs and predictably dreamy views.

Palazzo Belfiore APARTMENT €€

(Map p498; ☑055 26 44 15; www.palazzobel fiore.it; Via dei Velluti 8; d €190-315, extra bed €25; 🛜) The smartly painted taupe door with shiny black doorknob reflects the contemporary twist on the historic at this stylish residence, at home in a Renaissance *palazzo* on the Oltrarno. Its seven apartments with fully equipped kitchens sleep two to six, are spacious and swish, and owner Federico goes out of his way to ensure guests feel right at home.

★**SoprArno Suites**   GUESTHOUSE €€€
(Map p498; ☑055 046 87 18; www.soprarnosuites.com; Via Maggio 35; d €300; 🛜) This boutique gem, tucked in a quaint Oltrarno courtyard, creates an intimate home-from-home vibe while making each guest feel special. Eleven designer rooms are exquisitely dressed in vintage objets d'art and collectibles – the passion of Florentine owner Matteo and his talented Florence-born, British-raised wife, Betty Soldi (herself a calligrapher and graphic designer).

★**Ad Astra**   GUESTHOUSE €€€
(Map p498; ☑055 075 06 02; http://adastraflorence.com/; Via del Campuccio 53; d €340; ☑reception 8am-8pm, P🅿🌡@🛜) There is no other address quite like it in Florence. Seductively at home in a 16th-century *palazzo* overlooking Europe's largest private walled garden, this uber-chic guesthouse rocks. Creation of the talented British-Italian duo behind SoprArno Suites, Ad Astra sports 14 beautiful rooms adorned with Betty Soldi's calligraphy, Matteo's vintage collectibles, claw-foot bathtubs and the odd 19th-century fresco or wooden herringbone floor.

✖ Eating

Quality ingredients and simple execution are the hallmarks of Florentine cuisine, climaxing with the *bistecca alla fiorentina*, a huge slab of prime T-bone steak rubbed with tangy Tuscan olive oil, seared on the chargrill, garnished with salt and pepper and served beautifully *al sangue* (bloody). Be it dining in a traditional trattoria or contemporary, designer-chic space, quality is guaranteed.

✖ Around the Duomo & Piazza della Signoria

★**Osteria Il Buongustai**   OSTERIA €
(Map p482; ☑055 29 13 04; Via dei Cerchi 15r; meals €15-20; ⊙8am-4pm Mon-Fri, to 11pm Sat) Run with breathtaking speed and grace by Laura and Lucia, this place is unmissable. Lunchtimes heave with locals who work nearby and savvy students who flock here to fill up on tasty Tuscan home cooking at a snip of other restaurant prices. The place is brilliantly no-frills – expect to share a table and pay in cash; no credit cards.

Trattoria Le Mossacce   TRATTORIA €
(Map p482; ☑055 29 43 61; www.trattorialemossacce.it; Via del Proconsolo 55r; meals €20; ⊙noon-2.30pm & 7-9.30pm Mon-Fri) Strung with legs of ham and garlic garlands, this old-world trattoria lives up to its vintage promise of a warm *benvenuto* (welcome)

BEST PIZZERIE

Santarpia (Map p497; ☑055 24 58 29; www.santarpia.biz; Largo Pietro Annigoni 9; pizza €8.50-11; ⊙7.30pm-midnight Wed-Mon; 🛜) Thin-crust Neapolitan pizza across the street from Mercato di Sant'Ambrogio.

Berberé (☑055 238 29 46; www.berberepizza.it; Piazza del Nerli 1; pizza €6.50-13.50, ⊙12.30-2.30pm & 7pm-midnight Fri-Sun, 7pm-midnight Mon-Thu) Perfect pizza, craft beer and contemporary interior design in San Frediano.

Gustapizza (Map p498; ☑055 28 50 68; Via Maggio 46r; pizza €4.50-8; ⊙11.30am-3pm & 7-11pm Tue-Sun) Student favourite, Neapolitan-style, on the Oltrarno.

SimBIOsi (Map p494; ☑055 064 01 15; www.simbiosi.bio; Via de' Ginori 56r; pizza €6-10, salads €8-9; ⊙noon-11pm; 🛜) Hipster pizzeria cooking organic pizza, with craft beer and wine by small producers.

Caffè Italiano Pizzeria (Map p482; ☑055 28 93 68; www.caffeitaliano.it; Via dell'Isola delle Stinche 11-13r; pizza €8; ⊙7-11pm Tue-Sun) Just three pizza types in a bare-bones setting – or to take away.

Il Pizzaiuolo (Map p497; ☑055 24 11 71; Via dei Macci 113r; pizzas €5-10.50; ⊙12.30-2.30pm & 7.30pm-midnight Mon-Sat, closed Aug) Cosy pizzeria, lovely for an evening out, in Sant'Ambrogio.

and fabulous home cooking every Tuscan nonna would approve of. A family address, it has been the pride and joy of the Fantoni-Mannucci family for the last 50-odd years and their *bistecca alla fiorentina* (T-bone steak) is among the best in town.

Mangiafoco
TUSCAN €€

(Map p482; ☑055 265 81 70; www.mangiafoco.com; Borgo SS Apostoli 26r; meals €40; ☺10am-10pm Mon-Sat) Aromatic truffles get full-page billing at this small and cosy *osteria* with buttercup-yellow walls, cushioned seating and an exceptional wine list. Whether you are a hardcore truffle fiend or a virgin, there is something for you here: steak topped with freshly shaved truffles in season, truffle *taglietelle* (ribbon pasta) or a simple plate of mixed cheeses with sweet truffle honey.

Obicà
ITALIAN €€

(Map p482; ☑055 277 35 26; www.obica.com; Via de' Tornabuoni 16; meals €30-50; ☺noon-4pm & 6.30-11.30pm Mon-Fri, noon-11pm Sat & Sun) Given its exclusive location in Palazzo Tornabuoni, this designer address is naturally uber-trendy – even the table mats are upcycled from organic products. Taste 10 different types of mozzarella cheese in the cathedral-like interior or snuggle beneath

STREET FOOD

'Bringing the countryside to the city' is the driver behind **La Toraia** (☑338 5367198; www.latoraia.com; Lungarno del Tempio; burger €6, with cheese €7; ☺noon-midnight 15 Apr-15 Oct), a cherry-red artisan food truck whose name translates as 'breeding shed'. Parked riverside, a 15-minute stroll east of Piazza di Santa Croce, the truck cooks up sweet 140g burgers, crafted from tender Chianina meat sourced at the family farm in Val di Chiana and topped with melted *pecorino* (sheep's milk cheese). Real-McCoy homemade fries (€4; made from organic Tuscan potatoes grown on the farm, of course), craft beers (€4) from the same valley, and a bunch of table, chairs and comfy loungers by the river cap off the bucolic al fresco experience.

heaters over pizza and salads on sofas in the enchanting star-topped courtyard. At *aperitivo* hour nibble on *taglierini* (tasting boards loaded with cheeses, salami and deep-fried veg).

★ Irene
BISTRO €€€

(Map p482; ☑055 273 58 91; www.roccoforte hotels.com; Piazza della Repubblica 7; meals €60; ☺12.30-10.30pm) Named after the accomplished Italian grandmother of Sir Rocco Forte of the same-name luxury hotel group, Irene (actually part of neighbouring Hotel Savoy) is a dazzling contemporary bistro with a pavement terrace (heated in winter) overlooking iconic Piazza della Repubblica. Interior design is retro-chic 1950s and celebrity chef Fulvio Pierangelini cooks up a playful, utterly fabulous bistro cuisine in his Tuscan kitchen.

✗ Santa Maria Novella

Il Contadino
TRATTORIA €

(☑055 238 26 73; www.trattoriailcontadino.com; Via Palazzuolo 69-71r; meals €11-15; ☺noon-10.30pm) Come the weekend, this no-frills trattoria gets packed with families lunching with gusto on its astonishingly good-value Tuscan cuisine. Lunch, moreover, is served until 3.30pm when the dinner menu kicks in, meaning convenient all-day dining. The day's menu includes 10 or so dishes, including meaty classics like roast rabbit, tripe and oven-roasted pork shank. Two-course lunch/dinner menus start at €9/13.50.

Trattoria Marione
TRATTORIA €€

(Map p482; ☑055 21 47 56; Via della Spada 27; meals €30; ☺noon-3pm & 7-11pm) For the quintessential 'Italian dining' experience, Marione is gold. It's busy, it's noisy, it's 99.9% local and the cuisine is right out of nonna's Tuscan kitchen. No one appears to speak English so go for Italian – the tasty excellent-value traditional fare is worth it. If you don't get a complimentary *limoncello* with the bill, you clearly failed the language test.

Il Latini
TRATTORIA €€

(Map p482; ☑055 21 09 16; www.illatini.com; Via dei Palchetti 6r; meals €30; ☺12.30-2.30pm & 7.30-10.30pm Tue-Sun) A veteran guidebook favourite built around traditional *crostini*, Tuscan meats, fine pasta and roasted meats served at shared tables. There are two dinner seatings (7.30pm and 9pm), with service

BEST PANINI

Semel (Map p497; Piazza Ghiberti 44r; panini €3.50-5; ⊘11.30am-3pm Mon-Sat) Irresistibly creative and gourmet sandwiches to take away in Sant'Ambrogio.

'Ino (Map p482; ☑ 055 21 45 14; www.inofirenze.com; Via dei Georgofili 3r-7r; bruschette/panini €6/8; ⊘noon-4.30pm) 🍴 Made-to-measure, gourmet *panini* by the Galleria degli Uffizi.

Mariano (Map p482; ☑ 055 21 40 67; Via del Parione 19r; panini €3.50; ⊘8am-3pm & 5-7.30pm Mon-Fri, 8am-3pm Sat) Local neighbourhood cafe serving super-fresh *panini* to boot.

Gustapanino (Map p498; www.facebook.com/pages/Gustapanino; Piazza Santa Spirito; focacce from €3.50; ⊘11am-8pm Mon-Sat, noon-5pm Sun) Hole-in-the-wall *enopaninoteca* (wine and sandwich stop) in Santa Croce.

Dal Barone (Map p482; ☑ 366 1479432; https://dalbarone.jimdo.com; Borgo San Lorenzo 30; sandwiches €5-10; ⊘11am-8pm) Hot'n gooey *panini* to take away by San Lorenzo market.

I Due Fratellini (Map p482; ☑ 055 239 60 96; www.iduefratellini.com; Via dei Cimatori 38r; panini €4; ⊘10am-7pm) Memorable vintage kid on the block, around since 1875.

ranging from charming to not so charming. Reservations mandatory.

San Lorenzo & San Marco

★**Mercato Centrale** FOOD HALL €
(Map p494; ☑ 055 239 97 98; www.mercatocentrale.it; Piazza del Mercato Centrale 4; dishes €7-15; ⊘10am-midnight; 🛜) Wander the maze of stalls rammed with fresh produce at Florence's oldest and largest food market, on the ground floor of a fantastic iron-and-glass structure designed by architect Giuseppe Mengoni in 1874. Head to the 1st floor's buzzing, thoroughly contemporary food hall with dedicated bookshop, cookery school and artisan stalls cooking steaks, burgers, tripe *panini,* vegetarian dishes, pizza, gelato, pastries and pasta.

★**Trattoria Mario** TUSCAN €
(Map p494; ☑ 055 21 85 50; www.trattoria-mario.com; Via Rosina 2; meals €25; ⊘noon-3.30pm Mon-Sat, closed 3 weeks Aug; 🗶) Arrive by noon to ensure a stool around a shared table at this noisy, busy, brilliant trattoria – a legend that retains its soul (and allure with locals) despite being in every guidebook. Charming Fabio, whose grandfather opened the place in 1953, is front of house while big brother Romeo and nephew Francesco cook with speed in the kitchen. No advance reservations, no credit cards.

Monday and Thursday are tripe days, and Friday is fish. Whatever the day, local Florentines flock here for a brilliantly blue *bistecca alla fiorentina.*

Pugi BAKERY €
(Map p494; ☑ 055 28 09 81; www.focacceria-pugi.it; Piazza San Marco 9b; per kg €15 to €24; ⊘7.45am-8pm Mon-Sat, closed 2 weeks mid-Aug) The inevitable line outside the door says it all. This bakery is a Florentine favourite for pizza slices and chunks of *schiacciata* (Tuscan flatbread) baked up plain, spiked with salt and rosemary, or topped or stuffed with whatever delicious edible goodies are in season.

Grab a numbered ticket, drool over the sweet and savoury treats demanding to be devoured, and wait for your number to be called. Everything is sold by weight. Should you be queuing to see *David*, Pugi is a perfect two-minute hop from the Galleria dell'Accademia.

Da Nerbone FAST FOOD €
(Map p494; Mercato Centrale, Piazza del Mercato Centrale; meals €10; ⊘7am-2pm Mon-Sat) Forge your way past cheese, meat and sausage stalls on the ground floor of Florence's Mercato Centrale to join the lunchtime queue at Nerbone, in the biz since 1872. Go local and order *trippa alla fiorentina* (tripe and tomato stew) or follow the crowd with a feisty *panini con bollito* (a hefty boiled-beef bun, dunked in the meat's juices before serving). Eat standing up or fight for a table.

★**La Ménagère** INTERNATIONAL €€
(Map p494; 🖉 055 075 06 00; www.lamenagere.
it; Via de' Ginori 8r; meals €15-70; ⏱7am-2am; 🛜)
Be it breakfast, lunch, dinner, good coffee or
cocktails after dark, this bright industrial-
styled space lures Florence's hip brigade.
A concept store, the Housewife is a fashionable one-stop shop for chic china and
tableware, designer kitchen gear and fresh
flowers. For daytime dining and drinking,
pick from retro sofas in the boutique area,
or banquette seating and bar stools in the
jam-packed bistro.

Breakfast – American with pancakes,
bacon and eggs (€22) or continental (€16)
– is cooked up until noon, when the casual
bistro menu and a more formal €55 tasting
menu kicks in. Restaurant dining after dark
is around one very very long shared table
and jazz soirées fill the basement.

✖ Santa Croce

★**All'Antico Vinaio** OSTERIA €
(Map p482; 🖉 055 238 27 23; www.allantico
vinaio.com; Via de' Neri 65r; tasting platters €10-
30; ⏱10am-4pm & 6-11pm Tue-Sat, noon-3.30pm
Sun) The crowd spills out the door of this
noisy Florentine thoroughbred. Push your
way to the tables at the back to taste cheese
and salami in situ (reservations recommended). Or join the queue at the deli
counter for a well-stuffed focaccia wrapped
in waxed paper to take away – the quality is
outstanding. Pour yourself a glass of wine
while you wait.

Koto Ramen JAPANESE €
(Map p497; 🖉 055 247 94 77; http://kotoramen.
it; Via Giuseppe Verdi 42r; meals €20; ⏱12.30-
2.30pm & 7-10.30pm Wed-Fri & Mon, 7-10.45pm
Sat & Sun) When Tuscany's meaty fare tires,
make a beeline for this crisp-cut, contemporary space with huge windows overlooking
the street and the finest bowls of steaming
ramen (Japanese wheat noodles with meat,
veg or tofu) in town. The €13 lunch menu
(€14.50 with water and wine or sake) is unbeatable value.

Brac VEGETARIAN €
(Map p482; 🖉 055 094 48 77; www.libreriabrac.
net; Via dei Vagellai 18r; meals €20; ⏱noon-mid-
night, closed 2 weeks mid-Aug; 🛜🖉) This
hipster cafe-bookshop – a hybrid dining-
aperitivi address – cooks up inventive,
home-style and strictly vegetarian and/or
vegan cuisine. Its decor is recycled vintage

with the occasional kid's drawing thrown in
for that intimate homey touch, and the vibe
is artsy.

★**Il Teatro del Sale** TUSCAN €€
(Map p497; 🖉 055 200 14 92; www.teatrodelsale.
com; Via dei Macci 111r; lunch/dinner/weekend
brunch €15/35/20; ⏱11am-3pm & 7.30-11pm
Tue-Sat, 11am-3pm Sun, closed Aug) Florentine
chef Fabio Picchi is one of Florence's living treasures who steals the Sant'Ambrogio show with this eccentric, good-value,
members-only club (everyone welcome;
membership €7) inside an old theatre. He
cooks up weekend brunch, lunch and dinner,
culminating at 9.30pm in a live performance
of drama, music or comedy arranged by his
wife, artistic director and comic actress
Maria Cassi.

Vivo FISH €€
(Map p497; 🖉 333 1824183; www.ristorantevivo.
it; Largo Pietro Annigoni 9a/b; seafood platters €15-
50, meals €45; ⏱12.30-2.30pm & 7.30-11pm Tue-
Sun; 🛜) Raw fish, shellfish, oysters and other
fishy dishes – all caught in waters around
Italy by the Manno family's 30-strong fleet
of fishing boats – are cooked up by chef
Anna Maria at this fish restaurant, inside a
hangar-styled contemporary space with
a fishing-boat-shaped bar. Everything is
ultra-fresh and the daily changing menu includes many a rare or forgotten fish.

✖ Oltrarno

New places to eat are forever popping up in
this increasingly gentrified neighbourhood
on the 'other side' of the Arno, home to some
outstanding restaurants. Vegetarian, organic
and raw cuisine are also at their Florentine
best here. Several gourmet choices frame Piazza del Passera, an impossibly enchanting
square with no passing traffic.

★**Raw** HEALTH FOOD €
(Map p498; 🖉 055 21 93 79; Via Sant'Agostino
9; meals €7.50; ⏱11am-4pm & 7-10pm Thu & Fri,
11am-4pm Sat, Sun, Tue & Wed; 🛜) Should you
desire a turmeric, ginger or aloe vera shot or
a gently warmed, raw vegan burger served
on a stylish slate-and-wood platter, Raw hits
the spot. Everything served here is freshly
made and raw – to sensational effect. Herbs
are grown in the biodynamic greenhouse of
charismatic and hugely knowledgeable chef
Caroline, a Swedish architect before moving
to Florence.

There are cold-pressed juices, smoothies, soups and wraps too, all to eat here – in a beautifully sleek and soothing, candlelit space – or to take away.

S.Forno BAKERY €
(Map p498; ☑ 055 239 85 80; Via Santa Monaco 3r; ⏱7.30am-7.30pm Mon-Fri, from 8am Sat & Sun) Shop at this hipster bakery, around for at least a century, for fresh breads and pastries baked to sweet perfection in its ancient *forno* (oven). Gourmet dried products stack up on vintage shelves and the local baker Angelo cooks up soups, quiches and bespoke *panini* (€4 to €6) too, to eat in or out.

Carduccio ORGANIC €
(Map p498; ☑ 055 238 20 70; www.carduccio. com; Sdrucciolo de Pitti 10r; meals €15; ⏱8am-8pm Mon-Sat, 10am-5pm Sun; 🐾) With just a handful of tables inside and a couple more al fresco, this *salotto bio* (organic living room) oozes intimacy. Miniature cabbage 'flowers' decorate each table, fruit and veg crates stack up by the bar, and the menu is 100% organic. Knock back a ginger and turmeric shot (€3) or linger over delicious salads, soups, vegan burgers or pumpkin and leek patties.

Gnam BURGERS €
(☑ 055 22 39 52; www.gnamfirenze.it; Via di Camaldoli 2r; burgers €10-12; ⏱7-11pm Tue-Sat,

noon-2.30pm & 7-11pm Sun; 🐾) Bread arrives at the table in a paper bag and fries come in a miniature copper cauldron at this artisanal burger joint in San Frediano. Ingredients are seasonal, locally sourced and organic – and there are vegetarian and gluten-free burgers as well as traditional beef. Delicious soups also (€8), to eat in or take away from Gnam's joint across the street.

Gesto TUSCAN €
(Map p498; ☑ 055 24 12 88; www.gestofailtuo.it; Borgo San Frediano 27r; meals €25; ⏱6pm-2am) Enter hipster Florence: candlelit Gesto is all about eco-sustainability, so much so that all the furniture in the well-scrubbed vintage space is salvaged or upcycled and diners write down their own order on a mini blackboard that subsequently doubles as a plate. Fish, meat and veg dishes (€3.50 to €5) are tapas style – order a few to share for the entire table.

★ **Essenziale** TUSCAN €€
(☑ 055 247 69 56; http://essenziale.me/; Piazza di Cestello 3r; 3-/5-/7-course tasting menu €35/55/75, brunch €28; ⏱7-10pm Tue-Sat, 11am-4pm Sun; 🐾) There's no finer showcase for modern Tuscan cuisine than this loft-style restaurant in a 19th-century warehouse. Preparing dishes at the kitchen bar, in rolled-up shirt sleeves and navy butcher's apron, is dazzling young chef Simone

---

FAST-FOOD FAVOURITE: TRIPE

When Florentines fancy a fast munch-on-the-move, they flit by a *trippaio* – a cart on wheels or mobile stand – for a tripe *panini* (sandwich). Think cow's stomach chopped up, boiled, sliced, seasoned and bunged between bread.

Those great bastions of good old-fashioned Florentine tradition still going strong include **Il Trippaio del Porcellino** (Map p482; ☑ 335 8070240; Piazza del Mercato Nuovo 1; tripe €4.50; ⏱9am-6.30pm Mon-Sat) on the southwest corner of Mercato Nuovo; **L'Antico Trippaio** (Map p482; ☑ 339 7425692; Piazza dei Cimatori; tripe €4.50; ⏱9.30am-8pm); **Trippaio Sergio Pollini** (Map p497; Piazza Sant'Ambrogio; tripe €3.50; ⏱9.30am-3pm Mon, to 8pm Tue-Sat) in Santa Croce; and hole-in-the-wall **Da Vinattieri** (Map p482; Via Santa Margherita 4; panini €4.50; ⏱10am-7.30pm Mon-Fri, to 8pm Sat & Sun) tucked down an alley next to Dante's Chiesa di Santa Margherita. Pay €4.50 for a *panini* with tripe doused in *salsa verde* (pea-green sauce of smashed parsley, garlic, capers and anchovies) or garnished with salt, pepper and ground chilli. Alternatively, opt for a meaty-sized bowl (€5.50 to €7) of *lampredotto* (cow's fourth stomach that is chopped and simmered for hours).

The pew-style seating at staunchly local **Osteria del Cocotrippone** (☑ 055 234 75 27; www.facebook.com/OsteriaCocoTrippone; Via Vincenzo Gioberti 140; meals €25; ⏱noon-3pm & 7-11pm) in the off-centre Beccaria neighbourhood is not a coincidence: Florentines come here to venerate the offal side of their city's traditional cuisine. The *trippa alla fiorentina* (tripe in tomato sauce) and *L'Intelligente* (fried brain and zucchini) are local legends.

BEST GELATERIE

Grom (Map p482; ☑ 055 21 61 58; www.grom.it; Via del Campanile 2; cones €2.60-4.60, tubs €2.60-5.50; ☺10am-10.30pm Sun-Thu, to 11.30pm Fri & Sat) Top-notch gelato, including outstanding chocolate, near the Duomo.

Vivoli (Map p482; ☑ 055 29 23 34; www.vivoli.it; Via dell'Isola delle Stinche 7; tubs €2-10; ☺7.30am-midnight Tue-Sat, 9am-midnight Sun, to 9pm winter) Vintage favourite for coffee and cakes as well as gelato.

My Sugar (Map p494; ☑ 393 0696042; Via de' Ginori 49r; cones €2-2.50, tubs €2-5; ☺1-9pm) Sensational artisan gelateria near Piazza San Marco.

Gelateria La Carraia (Map p498; ☑ 055 28 06 95; Piazza Nazario Sauro 25r; cones & tubs €1.50-6; ☺10.30am-midnight summer, 11am-10pm winter) Florentine favourite on the other side of the river.

Carabé (Map p494; ☑ 055 28 94 76; www.parcocarabe.it; Via Ricasoli 60r; cones €2.50-4; ☺10am-midnight, closed mid-Dec–mid-Jan) Traditional Sicilian gelato and granita in San Marco.

Cipriani. Order one of his tasting menus to sample the full range of his inventive, thoroughly modern cuisine inspired by classic Tuscan dishes.

★ Il Santo Bevitore
TUSCAN €€
(Map p498; ☑ 055 21 12 64; www.ilsantobevitore.com; Via di Santo Spirito 64-66r; meals €40; ☺12.30-2.30pm & 7.30-11.30pm, closed Sun lunch & Aug) Reserve or arrive right on 7.30pm to snag the last table at this ever-popular address, an ode to stylish dining where gastronomes eat by candlelight in a vaulted, whitewashed, bottle-lined interior. The menu is a creative reinvention of seasonal classics: risotto with monkfish, red turnip and fennel; *ribollita* (traditional Tuscan vegetable-and-bread soup) with kale; or chicken liver terrine with brioche and a Vin Santo reduction.

★ Burro e Acciughe
TUSCAN €€
(Butter & Anchovies; ☑ 055 045 72 86; www.burroeacciughe.com; Via dell'Orto 35; meals €35; ☺noon-2pm & 7pm-midnight Fri-Sun, 7pm-midnight Tue-Thu) Carefully sourced, quality ingredients drive this fishy newcomer that woos punters with a short but stylish choice of raw (tartare and carpaccio) and cooked fish dishes. The gnocchi topped with octopus *ragù* (stew) is out of this world, as is the *baccalà* (salted cod) with creamed leeks, turnip and deep-fried polenta wedges. Excellent wine list too.

★ San Niccolò 39
SEAFOOD €€
(☑ 055 200 13 97; www.sanniccolo39.com; Via di San Niccolò 39; meals €40; ☺7-10.30pm Tue, 12.30-2.30pm & 7-10.30pm Wed-Sat; ☺) With a street terrace at the front and hidden summer garden out the back, this contemporary address in quaint San Niccolò is a gem. Fish – both raw and cooked – is the house speciality, with chef Vanni cooking up a storm with his creative salted-cod burgers, swordfish steak with radicchio, and famous *linguine* (fat spaghetti) with squid ink and Cetara anchovy oil.

The two-course lunch menu for €16, or €20 including a glass of wine and water, is fantastic value.

Gurdulù
RISTORANTE €€
(Map p498; ☑ 055 28 22 23; www.gurdulu.com; Via delle Caldaie 12r; meals €40, tasting menu €55; ☺7.30-11pm Tue-Sat, 12.30-2.30pm & 7.30-11pm Sun; ☺) Gourmet Gurdulù seduces fashionable Florentines with razor-sharp interior design, magnificent craft cocktails and seasonal market cuisine with a hint of Balkan spice by Albanian chef Entiana Osmenzeza. A hybrid drink-dine, this address is as much about noshing gourmet *aperitivi* snacks over expertly mixed cocktails – thanks to talented mixologist Sabrina Galloni – as it is about dining exceedingly well.

Osteria dell'Enoteca
TUSCAN €€
(Map p498; ☑ 055 21 27 04; www.osteriadellenoteca.com; Via Romana 70r; meals €30; ☺noon-2.30pm & 7-11pm Wed-Mon) With its vintage red-brick walls, taupe table linen and contemporary designer lighting, this *osteria* near Palazzo Pitti is the perfect fusion of old and new. And then there's the

food and wine: fantastic grilled meats, some of the finest *bistecca* in town and at least 150 wine labels, all carefully sourced by the expert foodies from Enoteca Pitti Gola e Cantina (p511).

Tamerò
ITALIAN €€

(Map p498; ☑ 055 28 25 96; www.tamero.it; Piazza Santa Spirito 11r; meals €25; ☉ noon-3pm & 6.30pm-2am Tue-Sun; ☎) A happening pasta bar on Florence's hippest square: admire chefs at work in the open kitchen while you wait for a table. A buoyant, party-loving crowd flocks here to fill up on imaginative fresh pasta, giant salads and copious cheese and salami platters. Decor is trendy industrial, *aperitivo* 'happy hour' (€9) is 6.30pm to 9pm, and weekend DJs spin sets from 10pm.

★ La Leggenda dei Frati
TUSCAN €€€

(Map p498; ☑ 055 068 05 45; www.laleggenda deifrati.it; Villa Bardini, Costa di San Giorgio 6a; menus €60 & €75; meals €70; ☉ 12.30-2pm & 7.30-10pm Tue-Sun; ☎) Summertime's hottest address. At home in the grounds of historic Villa Bardini, Michelin-starred Legend of Friars enjoys the most romantic terrace with view in Florence. Veggies are plucked fresh from the vegetable patch, tucked between waterfalls and ornamental beds in Giardino Bardini, and contemporary art jazzes up the classically chic interior. Cuisine is Tuscan, gastronomic and well worth the vital advance reservation.

Drinking & Nightlife

Florence's drinking scene covers all bases. Be it historical cafes, contemporary cafes with barista-curated specialist coffee, traditional *enoteche* (wine bars, which invariably make great eating addresses too), trendy bars with lavish *aperitivo* buffets, secret speakeasies and edgy cocktail or craft-beer bars, drinking is fun and varied. Nightlife, less extravagant, revolves around a handful of dance clubs.

◗ Around the Duomo & Piazza della Signoria

★ La Terrazza

Lounge Bar
BAR

(Map p482; ☑ 055 2726 5987; www.lungarno collection.com; Vicolo dell' Oro 6r; ☉ 2.30-11.30pm Apr-Sep) This rooftop bar with wooden-decking terrace, accessible from the 5th floor of the 1950s-styled, design Hotel Continentale, is as chic as one would expect of a fashion-house hotel. Its *aperitivo* buffet is a modest affair, but who cares with that fabulous, drop-dead-gorgeous panorama of one of Europe's most beautiful cities. Dress the part or feel out of place. Count on €19 for a cocktail.

Mayday
COCKTAIL BAR

(Map p482; ☑ 055 238 12 90; Via Dante Alighieri 16; cocktails €8; ☉ 7pm-2am Tue-Sat) Strike up a conversation with passionate mixologist Marco at Mayday. Within seconds you'll be hooked on his mixers and astonishing infusions, all handmade using wholly Tuscan ingredients. Think pancetta-infused whisky, saffron *limoncello* and porcini liqueur. Marco's cocktail list is equally impressive – or tell him your favourite flavours and let yourself be surprised.

Beer lovers will enjoy the pale ales, bitter and other artisanal brews from Tuscany's Birrificio Artigianale Otruo microbrewery.

Coquinarius
WINE BAR

(Map p482; www.coquinarius.com; Via delle Oche 11r; ☉ 12.30-3pm & 6.30-10.30pm Wed-Mon) With its old stone vaults, scrubbed wooden tables and refreshingly modern air, this *enoteca* run by the dynamic Nicolas is spacious and stylish. The wine list features bags of Tuscan greats and unknowns, and outstanding *crostini* and *carpacci* (cold sliced meats) ensure you don't leave hungry. The ravioli stuffed with silky *burrata* cheese and smothered in pistachio pesto is particularly outstanding.

YAB
CLUB

(Map p482; ☑ 055 21 51 60; www.yab.it/en; Via de' Sassetti 5r; ☉ 7pm-4am Mon & Wed-Sat Oct-May) Pick your night according to your age and tastes at this hugely popular nightclub with electric dance floor, around since the 1970s, behind Palazzo Strozzi.

Shake Café
CAFE

(Map p482; ☑ 055 21 59 52; www.shakecafe.bio; Via del Corso 28-32; ☉ 7.30am-8pm) Smoothie bowls with protein powder, kale and goji berries, cold-pressed juices and vitamin-packed elixir shots – to eat in or take away – satisfy wellness cravings at this laid-back cafe on people-busy Via del Corso. International newspapers, mellow music and a relaxed vibe make it a hipster place to hang. All-day wraps, salads and hearty, homemade soups (€6 to €7.50) too.

♀ Santa Maria Novella

★ Todo Modo
CAFE

(☑ 055 239 91 10; www.todomodo.org; Via dei Fossi 15r; ⊙ 10am-8pm Tue-Sun) This contemporary bookshop with hip cafe and pocket theatre at the back makes a refreshing change from the usual offerings. A salvaged mix of vintage tables and chairs sits between book- and bottle-lined shelves in the relaxed cafe, actually called 'UqBar' after the fictional place of the same name in a short story by Argentinian writer Jorges Luis Borges.

Caffè Giacosa
CAFE

(Map p482; ☑ 055 277 63 28; www.caffegiacosa. it; Via della Spada 10r; ⊙ 7.45am-8.30pm Mon-Fri, 8.30am-8.30pm Sat, 12.30-8.30pm Sun; 🕏) This chic cafe with 1815 pedigree was the inventor of the Negroni cocktail and hub of Anglo-Florentine sophistication during the interwar years. Today it is the hip cafe of local hotshot designer Roberto Cavalli, whose flagship boutique is next door. Giacosa is known for its refreshingly unelevated prices, excellent coffee and buzzing street terrace on fashionable Via de' Tournabuoni.

Drink-list standouts include the herbal infusions, ginseng cappuccino and the summertime-cool Caffè de' Medici, a cold shaken espresso topped with whipped cream, chocolate and hazelnuts. Whatever your drink, pay at the cash till first then present your receipt at the bar.

Space Club
CLUB

(☑ 055 29 30 82; www.facebook.com/space firenze2; Via Palazzuolo 37r; admission variable; ⊙ 10pm-4am) Sheer size alone at this vast nightclub in Santa Maria Novella will impress – dancing, drinking, video-karaoke in the bar, and a mixed student-international crowd.

Tenax
CLUB

(☑ 335 5235922; www.tenax.org; Via Pratese 46; admission varies; ⊙ 10pm-4am Thu-Sun Oct-Apr) The only club in Florence on the European club circuit, with great international guest DJs and wildly popular 'Nobody's Perfect' house parties on Saturday night; find the warehouse-style building out of town near Florence airport. Take bus 29 or 30 from Stazione di Santa Maria Novella.

♀ San Lorenzo & San Marco

★ Lo Sverso
COCKTAIL BAR

(Map p494; ☑ 335 5473530; www.facebook. com/losverso.firenze; Via Panicale 7-9r; ⊙ 5pm-1am Mon-Sat, to midnight Sun) In a part of town where drinking holes are unusually scarce, stylish Lo Sverso is a real gem. Bartenders shake cocktails using homemade syrups (any cocktail using their feisty basil syrup is a winner), the craft beers – several on tap – are among the best in Florence, and their home-brewed ginger ale is worth a visit in its own right.

BEST CAFES

Good cafes are a dime a dozen in Florence. Prime squares to sit and people-watch from a pavement terrace are Piazza della Repubblica, Piazza Santo Spirito and Piazza della Signoria. A coffee drunk standing at the bar is dramatically cheaper than one drunk sitting down.

Ditta Artigianale (Map p482; ☑ 055 274 15 41; www.dittaartigianale.it; Via de' Neri 32r; ⊙ 8am-10pm Sun-Thu, 8am-midnight Fri, 9.30am-midnight Sat; 🕏) Hipster coffee roastery and gin bar.

Caffè Giacosa (above) Chic, fashionista cafe with 1815 pedigree by Florence's smartest shopping strip.

Caffè Rivoire (Map p482; ☑ 055 21 44 12; www.rivoire.it; Piazza della Signoria 4; ⊙ 7am-midnight Tue-Sun summer, to 9pm winter) Famous drinking hole with legendary hot chocolate on Piazza della Signoria.

Le Murate Caffè Letterario (Map p497; ☑ 055 234 68 72; www.lemurate.it; Piazza delle Murate Firenze; ⊙ 9am-1am; 🕏) Artsy cafe-bar away from the tourist crowd in the city's former jail.

Gilli (Map p482; ☑ 055 21 38 96; www.gilli.it; Piazza della Repubblica 39r; ⊙ 7.30am-1.30am) Historic cafe at home on Forence's old Roman forum; serious cakes!

★ Ditta Al Cinema   CAFE, BAR

(Map p494; ☑ 055 045 71 63; Via Cavour 50r; ☺ 8am-midnight Mon-Fri, 9am-midnight Sat & Sun; 🛜) At home in Florence's historic La Compagnia cinema, the third and most recent space of iconic coffee roaster and gin bar Ditta Artigianiale doesn't disappoint. Some 150 different labels of gin jostle for the limelight at the bar, while barman Lorenzo's cocktail list plays on the cinema's heritage with drinks named after movie classics. Breakfast, lunch, brunch and all-day tapas too.

🍷 Santa Croce

Blob Club   CLUB

(Map p482; ☑ 324 8043276; Via Vinegia 21r; ☺ 11pm-3am Mon-Wed, to 5am Thu-Sat) This small and edgy Santa Croce club lures an international crowd with its music theme nights – loads of 1960s, hip-hop, alternative rock; all sounds in fact.

Bamboo   CLUB

(Map p497; ☑ 339 4298764; www.bamboolounge club.com; Via Giuseppe Verdi 59r; ☺ 7pm 4am Fri, Sat & Mon, to 3am Thu) A hipster crowd looks beautiful in this Santa Croce lounge and dance club with chintzy red seating, steely grey bar and a mix of hip-hop and R&B on the turntable. Dress up and look good to get in. ('The dress code, if it helps, is 'smart, casual, sexy, chic'.)

Lion's Fountain   IRISH PUB

(Map p497; ☑ 055 234 44 12; www.thelionsfountain. com; Borgo degli Albizi 34r; ☺ 10am-3am) If you have the urge to hear more English than Italian – or to hear local bands play for that matter – this is the place. On a pretty pedestrian square, Florence's busiest Irish pub buzzes in summer when the beer-loving crowd spills across most of the square. Live music and a canary-yellow food 'truck' serving burgers, nachos, clubs, wings and brunch (€5 to €10).

🍷 Oltrarno

★ Mad Souls & Spirits   COCKTAIL BAR

(Map p498; ☑ 055 627 16 21; www.facebook. com/madsoulsandspirits; Borgo San Frediano 38r; ☺ 6pm-2am Thu-Sun, to midnight Mon & Wed; 🛜) A this bar of the moment, cult alchemists Neri Fantechi and Julian Biondi woo a discerning fashionable crowd with their expertly crafted cocktails, served in a tiny aqua-green and red-brick space that couldn't be more spartan. A potted cactus decorates each scrubbed wood table and the humorous cocktail menu is the height of irreverence. Check the 'Daily Madness' blackboard for wild 'n' wacky specials.

★ Le Volpi e l'Uva   WINE BAR

(Map p498; ☑ 055 239 81 32; www.levolpieluva. com; Piazza dei Rossi 1; ☺ 11am-9pm Mon-Sat) This unassuming wine bar hidden away by Chiesa di Santa Felicità remains as appealing as the day it opened over a decade ago. Its food and wine pairings are first class – taste and buy boutique wines by small producers from all over Italy, matched perfectly with cheeses, cold meats and the best *crostini* in town. Wine-tasting classes too.

★ Enoteca Pitti Gola e Cantina   WINE BAR

(Map p498; ☑ 055 21 27 04; www.pittigolaecantina. com; Piazza dei Pitti 16; ☺ 1pm-midnight Wed-Mon) Wine lovers won't do better than this serious wine bar opposite Palazzo Pitti, run with passion and humour by charismatic trio Edoardo, Manuele and Zeno – don't be surprised if they share a glass with you over wine talk. Floor-to-ceiling shelves of expertly curated, small-production Tuscan and Italian wines fill the tiny bar, and casual dining (excellent cured meats and pasta *fatta in casa*) is around a handful of marble-topped tables.

★ Rasputin   COCKTAIL BAR

(Map p498; ☑ 055 28 03 99; www.facebook. com/rasputinfirenze; Borgo Tegolaio 21r; ☺ 8pm-2am) The 'secret' speakeasy everyone knows about, it has no sign outside: disguised as a chapel of sorts, look for the tiny entrance with two-seat wooden pew, crucifix on the wall, vintage pics and tea lights flickering in the doorway. Inside, it's back to the 1930s with period furnishings, an exclusive vibe and bar staff mixing Prohibition-era cocktails. Reservations (phone or Facebook page) recommended.

★ Il Santino   WINE BAR

(Map p498; ☑ 055 230 28 20; Via di Santo Spirito 60r; ☺ 12.30-11pm) Kid sister to top-notch restaurant Il Santo Bevitore two doors down the street, this intimate wine bar with exposed stone walls and marble bar is a stylish spot for pairing cured meats, cheeses and Tuscan staples with a carefully curated selection of wine – many by local producers – and artisan beers.

BEST SUMMER TERRACES

Santarosa Bistrot (☎055 230 90 57; www.facebook.com/santarosa.bistrot; Lungarno di Santarosa; ⊗8am-midnight; 🛜) Hipster garden bistro-bar beneath trees in Santarosa gardens.

Flò (☎055 65 07 91; www.flofirenze.com; Piazzale Michelangelo 84; ⊗7.30pm-4am summer) Summertime terrace bar with dancing, drinks and city views to die for.

La Terrazza (Map p482; La Rinascente, Piazza della Repubblica 1; ⊗9am-9pm Mon-Sat, 10.30am-8pm Sun) Coffee atop the city's central department store.

La Terrazza Lounge Bar (p509) Rooftop chic in 1950s-styled design hotel by the river.

Amblé (Map p482; ☎055 26 85 28; Piazzetta dei del Bene 7a; ⊗10am-midnight Tue-Sat, noon-midnight Sun) Shabby-chic terrace in a back alley, a block from the Arno.

Kawaii COCKTAIL BAR
(Map p498; ☎055 28 14 00; www.ristorante momoyama.it; Borgo San Frediano 8r; ⊗6pm-1am) Head to this smart new Japanese cocktail bar for an inventive Blood Meray (tomato juice, Japanese shochu, fresh ginger, soy sauce and Wasabi) or one of several creative sake-based fusion cocktails in the company of Japanese tapas. Dress smartly and be prepared to try at least a couple of the 30-odd types of sake, 15 Japanese beers and 15 whiskeys.

Volume BAR
(Map p498; ☎055 238 14 60; www.volumefirenze. com; Piazza Santo Spirito 3r; ⊗8.30am-1.30am) Armchairs, recycled and upcycled vintage furniture, books to read, jukebox, crepes and a tasty choice of nibbles with coffee or a light lunch give this hybrid cafe-bar-gallery real appeal – all in an old hat-making workshop with tools and wooden moulds strewn around. Watch for various music, art and DJ events and other happenings.

La Cité BAR
(Map p498; ☎055 21 03 87; www.lacitelibreria. info; Borgo San Frediano 20r; ⊗2pm-2am Mon-Sat, 3pm-2am Sun; 🛜) A hip cafe-bookshop with an eclectic choice of vintage seating, La Cité makes a wonderful, intimate venue for book readings, after-work drinks and fantastic live music – jazz, swing, world music. Check its Facebook page for the week's events.

Ditta Artigianale CAFE, BAR
(Map p498; ☎055 045 71 63; www.dittaartigianale. it; Via dello Sprone 5r; ⊗8am-midnight Mon-Fri, 9am-midnight Sat & Sun; 🛜) The second branch of Florence's premier coffee roaster and gin bar treats its faithful hipster clientele to full-blown dining in a 1950s-styled interior alongside its signature speciality coffees, gin cocktails and laid-back vibe. Think bright geometric-patterned wallpaper, comfy gold and pea-green armchairs, a mezzanine restaurant up top, buzzing ground-floor bar with great cocktails down below, and a tiny street terrace out the back.

Dolce Vita BAR
(Map p498; ☎055 28 45 95; www.dolcevitaflor ence.com; Piazza del Carmine 6r; ⊗7pm-1.30am Sun-Wed, to 2am Thu-Sat, closed 2 weeks Aug) Going strong since the 1980s, this veteran bar with a distinct club vibe is an Oltrarno hot spot for after-work drinks, cocktails and DJ sets. Its chic, design-driven interior gets a new look every month thanks to constantly changing photography and contemporary art exhibitions. In summer, its decked terrace is the place to be seen (shades obligatory). Live bands too.

☆ Entertainment

Opera di Firenze OPERA
(☎055 277 93 09; www.operadifirenze.it; Piazzale Vittorio Gui, Viale Fratelli Rosselli 15; ⊗box office 10am-6pm Tue-Fri, to 1pm Sat) Florence's strikingly modern opera house with glittering contemporary geometric facade sits on the green edge of city park Parco delle Cascine. Its three thoughtfully designed and multifunctional concert halls seat an audience of 5000 and play host to the springtime Maggio Musicale Fiorentino (p501).

🛍 Shopping

Tacky mass-produced souvenirs (boxer shorts emblazoned with *David's* packet) are everywhere, not least at city market **Mercato Nuovo** (Map p482; Piazza del Mercato Nuovo; ⊗8.30am-7pm Mon-Sat), awash with cheap imported handbags and other leather goods. But for serious shoppers keen to delve into a city synonymous with craftsmanship since medieval times, there are plenty of workshops and boutiques to visit.

⭐**Benheart**   FASHION & ACCESSORIES
(Map p482; ☑ 055 046 26 38; www.benheart.it; Via dei Cimatori 25r; ⊙10am-8pm) The flagship store of Benheart, this gorgeous shop showcases the handmade leather designs – shoes, jackets, belts and bags for men and women – of local superstar Ben, a young Florentine fashion designer who set up the business with Florentine schoolmate Matteo after undergoing a heart transplant. The pair swore that if Ben survived, they'd go it alone – which they did with huge success.

The shoes here are to die for – double-lined with soft buffalo leather and stitched before being dyed with natural pigments – and start at €190.

⭐**&Co**   ARTS & CRAFTS
(And Company; Map p498; ☑055 21 99 73; www.andcompanyshop.com; Via Maggio 51r; ⊙10.30am-1pm & 3-7pm Mon-Sat) Souvenir shopping at its best! This Pandora's box of beautiful objects is the love child of a Florence-born, British-raised calligrapher and graphic designer, Betty Soldi, and her vintage-loving husband, Matteo Perduca. Their extraordinary boutique showcases Betty's customised cards, decorative paper products, upcycled homewares and custom fragrances alongside work by other designers (including super-chic leather-printed accessories by the Danish design company Edition Poshette).

⭐**Obsequium**   WINE
(Map p498; ☑055 21 68 49; www.obsequium.it; Borgo San Jacopo 17/39; ⊙10am-10pm Mon, to 9pm Tue & Wed, to midnight Thu-Sat, noon-midnight Sun) Tuscan wines, wine accessories and gourmet foods, including truffles, in one of the city's finest wine shops on the ground floor of one of Florence's best-preserved medieval towers to boot. Not sure which wine to buy? Linger over a glass or indulge in a three-wine tasting with (€20 to €40) or without (€15 to €30) an accompanying *taglieri* (board) of mixed cheese and salami.

⭐**Lorenzo Perrone**   ART
(Map p498; ☑340 274402; www.libribianchi.info; Borgo Tegolaio 59r; ⊙hours vary) Every book tells a different story in this absolutely fascinating artist's workshop, home to Milan-born Lorenzo Perrone, who creates snow-white *Libri Bianchi* (White Books) – aka sublime book sculptures – out of plaster, glue, acrylic and various upcycled objects. His working hours are, somewhat predictably, erratic; call ahead.

⭐**Aquaflor**   COSMETICS
(Map p482; ☑055 234 34 71; www.florencefirenze.com; Borgo Santa Croce 6; ⊙10am-7pm) This elegant Santa Croce perfumery in a vaulted 15th-century *palazzo* exudes romance and exoticism. Artisan scents are crafted here with tremendous care and precision by master perfumer Sileno Cheloni, who works with precious essences from all over the world, including Florentine iris. Organic soaps, cosmetics and body-care products make equally lovely gifts to take back home.

⭐**Street Doing**   FASHION, VINTAGE
(Map p482; ☑055 538 13 34; www.streetdoingvintage.it; Via dei Servi 88r; ⊙2.30-7.30pm Mon, 10.30am-7.30pm Tue-Sat) Vintage couture for men and women is what this extraordinary rabbit warren of a boutique – surely the city's largest collection of vintage – is about. Carefully curated garments and accessories are in excellent condition and feature all the top Italian designers: beaded 1950s Gucci clutch bags, floral 1960s Pucci dresses,

---

BEST SOUVENIRS

Officina Profumo-Farmaceutica di Santa Maria Novella (☑ 055 21 62 76; www.smnovella.it; Via della Scala 16; ⊙9.30am-8pm) Herbal remedies and beauty products in a pharmacy from 1612.

Il Papiro (Map p482; ☑055 21 65 93; http://ilpapirofirenze.eu/en/; Via Porta Rosso 76; ⊙10am-7pm) Florence's signature, hand-marbled paper.

Clet (p500) Hacked street signs: postcards, stickers, limited editions or the real thing.

Lorenzo Villoresi (Map p498; ☑055 234 11 87; www.lorenzovilloresi.it; Via de' Bardi 14; ⊙10am-7pm Mon-Sat) Fragrances of Tuscany by Florence's master perfumer.

Mio Concept (p500) Nifty homeware and fashion accessories, many by local designers, to take home.

Valentino shades from every decade. Fashionistas, *this* is heaven.

Aprosio & Co
ACCESSORIES, JEWELLERY

(Map p482; ☑055 21 01 27; www.aprosio. it; Via del Moro 75-77r; ☺10am-7pm Mon-Fri, 10.30am-7.30pm Sat) Ornella Aprosio fashions teeny-tiny glass and crystal beads into dazzling pieces of jewellery, hair accessories, animal-shaped brooches, handbags, even glass-flecked cashmere. It is all quite magical.

Grevi
FASHION & ACCESSORIES

(Map p482; ☑055 26 41 39; www.grevi.it; Via della Spada 11-13r; ☺10am-2pm & 3-8pm Mon-Sat) It was a hat made by Siena milliner Grevi that actress Cher wore in the film *Tea with Mussolini* (1999); ditto Maggie Smith in *My House in Umbria* (2003). So if you want to shop like a star for a hat by Grevi, this hopelessly romantic boutique is the address. Hats range in price from €30 to possibly unaffordable.

Byørk
FASHION & ACCESSORIES

(Map p498; ☑333 9795839; www.bjorkflorence. com; Via della Sprone 25r; ☺2.30-7.30pm Mon, 10.30am-1.30pm & 2.30-7.30pm Tue-Sat) Cutting-edge fashion plus 'Zines, books, magazines' is what this trendy concept store, incongruously wedged between tatty old artisan workshops on an Oltrarno backstreet, sells. It is the creation of well-travelled Florentine and fashionist Filippo Anzaione, whose taste in Italian and other contemporary European designers is impeccable.

DESIGNER OUTLET MALLS

Mall (www.themall.it; Via Europa 8, Leccio Reggello; ☺10am-7pm, to 8pm Jun-Aug) Find this busy designer outlet 35km from Florence; buses (adult single/ return €7/13) leave from the SITA bus station.

Barberino Designer Outlet (☑055 84 21 61; www.mcarthurglen.it; Via Meucci, Barberino di Mugello; ☺10am-8pm) Previous season's collections by D&G, Prada, Roberto Cavalli, Missoni et al at discounted prices, 40km north of Florence. A shuttle bus (adult single/return €8/15, 30 minutes) departs from Piazza della Stazione 44 (in front of Zoppini) two to four times daily. Check seasonal schedules online.

Eataly
FOOD & DRINKS

(Map p482; ☑055 015 36 01; www.eataly.net; Via de' Martelli 22r; ☺10am-10.30pm; ☎) Eataly is a one-stop food shop for everything Tuscan. Peruse beautifully arranged aisles laden with oils, preserved vegetables, pasta, rice, biscuits and so on. There are fresh bakery and deli counters, fridges laden with seemingly every cheese under the Italian sun, and a coffee bar with outdoor seating. Many products are local and/or organic; most are by small producers.

Upstairs is a wine cellar with 600 labels, a cooking school, summer terrace and the epicurean Osteria di Sopra, serving lunch and dinner.

Pineider
ARTS & CRAFTS

(Map p482; ☑055 28 46 56; www.pineider.com; Piazza de' Rucellai 4-7r; ☺10am-7pm) Stendhal, Byron, Shelley and Dickens are among the literary luminaries who have chosen to purchase top-quality stationery from this company.

Officine Nora
JEWELLERY

(Map p498; www.officinenora.it; Via dei Preti 2-4; ☺11am-1pm, 3.30-7.30pm Mon-Fri) Once a mechanic's shop, this seriously cool workspace for contemporary jewellery-makers brings Florence's rich history of expert goldsmithing right up to date. The large, luminous loft is filled with well-loved desks used by the resident artisans who make a dazzling array of wearable art. Visitors are welcome to watch them at work and purchase pieces, but it's best to email or call in advance.

ⓘ Information

EMERGENCY
Police Station (Questura; ☑055 4 97 71, English-language service 055 497 72 68; http://questure.poliziadistato.it; Via Zara 2; ☺24hr daily) Should you have a theft or other unfortunate incident to report, the best time to visit the city's police station is between 9am and 2pm weekdays when the foreign-language service – meaning someone speaks English – kicks in.

MEDICAL SERVICES
24-Hour Pharmacy (☑055 21 67 61; Stazione di Santa Maria Novella; ☺24hr) Nonstop pharmacy inside Florence's central train station; at least one member of staff usually speaks English.

Dr Stephen Kerr: Medical Service (☑335-836 16 82, 055 28 80 55; www.dr-kerr.com;

Piazza Mercato Nuovo 1; ◷3-5pm Mon-Fri, or by appointment 9am-3pm Mon-Fri) Resident British doctor.

Hospital (Ospedale di Santa Maria Nuova; ☑055 6 93 81; www.asf.toscana.it; Piazza di Santa Maria Nuova 1; ◷24hr)

TOURIST INFORMATION

Airport Tourist Office (☑055 31 58 74; www. firenzeturismo.it; Florence Airport, Via del Termine 11; ◷9am-7pm Mon-Sat, to 2pm Sun)

Infopoint Bigallo (Map p482; ☑055 28 84 96; www.firenzeturismo.it; Piazza San Giovanni 1; ◷9am-7pm Mon-Sat, to 2pm Sun)

Tourist Office (Map p482; ☑055 21 22 45; www.firenzeturismo.it; Piazza della Stazione 4; ◷9am-6.30pm Mon-Sat, to 1.30pm Sun)

Tourist Office (Map p494; ☑055 29 08 32; www.firenzeturismo.it; Via Cavour 1r; ◷9am-1pm Mon-Fri)

❶ Getting There & Away

AIR

Also known as Amerigo Vespucci or Peretola airport, **Florence airport** (Aeroporto Amerigo Vespucci; ☑055 3 06 15, 055 306 18 30; www. aeroporto.firenze.it; Via del Termine 11) is 5km northwest of the city centre and is served by both domestic and European flights.

BUS

Services from the **bus station** (Autostazione Busitalia-Sita Nord; ☑800 373760; Via Santa Caterina da Siena 17r; ◷5.30am-8.30pm Mon-Sat, 6am-8pm Sun), just west of Piazza della Stazione, are limited; the train is better. Destinations operated by Sitabus (www.sitabus.it) include the following:

Siena (€7.80, 1¼ hours, at least hourly)

Greve in Chianti (€4.20, one hour, hourly)

CAR & MOTORCYCLE

Florence is connected by the A1 northwards to Bologna and Milan, and southwards to Rome and Naples. The Autostrada del Mare (A11) links Florence with Pistoia, Lucca, Pisa and the coast, but most locals use the FI-PI-LI – a *superstrada* (dual carriageway, hence no tolls); look for blue signs saying FI-PI-LI (as in Firenze-Pisa-Livorno). Another dual carriageway, the S2, links Florence with Siena. The much more picturesque SS67 connects the city with Pisa to the west, and Forlì and Ravenna to the east.

TRAIN

Florence's central train station is **Stazione di Santa Maria Novella** (Piazza della Stazione). The **left-luggage counter** (Deposito Bagagliamano; Stazione di Santa Maria Novella; 1st

5hr €6, then per hour €0.90; ◷6am-11pm) is located on platform 16. Tickets for all trains are sold in the main ticketing hall, but skip the permanently long queue by buying tickets from the touchscreen automatic ticket-vending machines; they have an English option and accept cash and credit cards.

Florence is on the Rome–Milan line. Services include the following:

DESTINATION	FARE(€)	TIME	FREQUENCY
Bologna	26	1hr-1¾hr	every 15 to 30 minutes
Lucca	7.50	1½hr-1¾hr	twice hourly
Milan	54-64	2¼hr-3½hr	at least hourly
Pisa	8.40	45min-1hr	every 15 minutes
Pistoia	4.40	45min-1hr	every 10 minutes
Rome	45-55	1¾hr-4¼hr	at least twice hourly
Venice	49-54	2¾hr-4½hr	at least hourly

❶ Getting Around

TO/FROM THE AIRPORTS

Bus

ATAF operates a **Volainbus** (☑800 373760; www.fsbusitalia.it) shuttle (single/return €6/10, 30 minutes) between Florence airport and Florence bus station every 30 minutes between 6am and 8.30pm, then hourly from 8.30pm until 11.30pm (from 5.30am to 11.45pm from the airport).

Taxi

A taxi between Florence's airport and the city centre costs a flat rate of €20 (€24 on Sundays and holidays, €25.30 between 10pm and 6am), plus €1 per bag and €1 supplement for fourth passenger. Exit the terminal building, bear right and you'll come to the taxi rank.

Train

Regular trains link Florence's Stazione di Santa Maria Novella with Pisa's central train station, Pisa Centrale (€9.70, 1½ hours, at least hourly from 4.30am to 10.25pm), from where fully automated, super-speedy PisaMover trains (€2.70, five minutes, every five minutes from 6am to midnight) continue to Pisa International Airport.

CENTRAL TUSCANY

When people imagine classic Tuscan countryside, they usually conjure up images of central Tuscany. But there's more to this popular tourist region than gently rolling hills, sun-kissed vineyards and artistically planted avenues of cypress tress. The real gems are the historic towns and cities, most of which are medieval and Renaissance time capsules magically transported to the modern day.

Siena

POP 53,900

Siena is a city where the architecture soars, as do the souls of many of its visitors. Effectively a giant, open-air museum celebrating the Gothic, Siena has spiritual and secular monuments that have retained both their medieval forms and their extraordinary art collections, providing the visitor with plenty to marvel at. The city's historic *contrade* (districts) are marvellous too, being as close-knit and colourful today as they were in the 17th century, when their world-famous horse race, the Palio, was inaugurated. And within each *contrada* lie vibrant streets populated with artisanal boutiques, sweet-smelling *pasticcerie* (pastry shops) and tempting restaurants. It's a feast for the senses and an essential stop on every Tuscan itinerary.

◎ Sights

★**Piazza del Campo**   SQUARE

Popularly known as 'Il Campo', this sloping piazza has been Siena's civic and social centre since being staked out by the ruling Consiglio dei Nove (Council of Nine) in the mid-12th century. Built on the site of a Roman marketplace, its paving is divided into nine sectors representing the number of members of the *consiglio* and these days acts as a carpet on which young locals meet and relax. The cafes around its perimeter are the most popular coffee and *aperitivo* spots in town.

Palazzo Pubblico   HISTORIC BUILDING

(Palazzo Comunale; Piazza del Campo) Built to demonstrate the enormous wealth, proud independence and secular nature of Siena, this 14th-century Gothic masterpiece is the visual focal point of the Campo, itself the true heart of the city. Architecturally clever (notice how its concave facade mirrors the opposing convex curve), it has always housed the city's administration and been used as a cultural venue. Its distinctive bell tower, the **Torre del Mangia** (☑ 0577 29 23 43; www.enjoysiena.it; €10; ☉ 10am-6.15pm summer, to 3.15pm winter), provides magnificent views to those who brave the steep climb to the top.

★**Museo Civico**   MUSEUM

(Civic Museum; ☑ 0577 29 22 32; Palazzo Pubblico, Piazza del Campo 1; adult/reduced €9/8; ☉ 10am-6.15pm summer, to 5.15pm winter) Entered via the Palazzo Pubblico's **Cortile del Podestà** (Courtyard of the Podestà), this wonderful museum showcases rooms richly frescoed by artists of the Sienese school. Commissioned by the city's governing body rather than by the Church, some of the frescoes depict secular subjects – highly unusual at the time. The highlights are two huge frescoes: Ambrogio Lorenzetti's *Allegories of Good and Bad Government* (c 1338–40) and Simone Martini's celebrated *Maestà* (Virgin Mary in Majesty; 1315).

★**Duomo**   CATHEDRAL

(Cattedrale di Santa Maria Assunta; ☑ 0577 28 63 00; www.operaduomo.siena.it; Piazza Duomo; summer/winter €4/free, when floor displayed €7; ☉ 10.30am-7pm Mon-Sat, 1.30-6pm Sun summer, to 5.30pm winter) Consecrated on the former site of a Roman temple in 1179 and constructed over the 13th and 14th centuries, Siena's majestic *duomo* (cathedral) showcases the talents of many great medieval and Renaissance architects and artists: Giovanni Pisano designed the intricate white, green and red marble facade; Nicola Pisano carved the elaborate pulpit; Pinturicchio painted the frescoes in the extraordinary **Libreria Piccolomini** (Piccolomini Library; ☑ 0577 28 63 00; http://operaduomo.siena.it; Piazza Duomo; summer/winter free/€2; ☉ 10.30am-7pm Mon-Sat, 1.30-6pm Sun summer, to 5.30pm winter); and Michelangelo, Donatello and Gian Lorenzo Bernini all produced sculptures.

Battistero di San Giovanni   LANDMARK

(☑ 0577 28 63 00; http://operaduomo.siena.it; Piazza San Giovanni; €4; ☉ 10.30am-7pm Mon-Sat, 1.30-6pm Sun summer, to 5.30pm winter) The Baptistry is lined with 15th-century frescoes and centres around a hexagonal marble font by Jacopo della Quercia, decorated with bronze panels depicting the life of St John the Baptist by artists including Lorenzo Ghiberti (*Baptism of Christ; St John in Prison*) and Donatello (*The Head of John the Baptist Being Presented to Herod*).

Cripta
CHRISTIAN SITE

(☑0577 28 63 00; http://operaduomo.siena.it; Piazza San Giovanni; incl audioguide €6; ☉10.30am-7pm Mon-Sat & 1.30-6pm Sun summer, to 5.30pm winter) Remarkably, this vaulted space under the Duomo's pulpit was totally filled with debris in the late 1300s and was only excavated and restored in 1999. Originally functioning as a cathedral entrance and confessional, it was decorated with 180 sq metres of richly coloured 13th-century *pintura a secco* ('dry' or mural paintings) covering walls, columns, pilasters, capitals and corbels. Fortunately, these managed to survive their ignominious treatment.

Museo dell'Opera
MUSEUM

(☑0577 28 63 00; www.operaduomo.siena.it; Piazza Duomo; €8; ☉10.30am-7pm Mon-Sat & 1.30-6pm Sun summer, to 5.30pm winter) The highlight of this repository of artworks that formerly adorned the Duomo is undoubtedly Duccio (di Buoninsegna)'s striking *Maestà* (1308–11), which was painted on both sides as a screen for the high altar. Duccio portrays the Virgin surrounded by angels, saints and prominent contemporary Sienese citizens; the rear panels (sadly incomplete) show scenes from the Passion of Christ. Entry to the Panorama del Facciatone is included in the entry ticket.

Panorama del Facciatone
TOWER

(☑0577 28 63 00; http://operaduomo.siena.it; Piazza Duomo; ☉10.30am-7pm Mon-Sat & 1.30-6pm Sun summer, to 5.30pm winter) For an unforgettable view of Siena's unique cityscape, head up the 131-step, narrow corkscrew stairway to walk atop the unfinished facade of the Duomo Nuovo (New Cathedral). Entrance is included in the Museo dell'Opera ticket and the entrance is via one of that museum's upstairs floors.

★Museale Santa Maria della Scala
MUSEUM

(☑0577 53 45 11, 0577 53 45 71; www.santamariadellascala.com; Piazza Duomo 1; adult/reduced €9/7; ☉10am-5pm Mon, Wed & Thu, to 8pm Fri, to 7pm Sat & Sun, extended hours in summer) Built as a hospice for pilgrims travelling the Via Francigena, this huge complex opposite

the Duomo dates from the 13th century. Its highlight is the upstairs **Pellegrinaio** (Pilgrim's Hall), featuring vivid 15th-century frescoes by Lorenzo di Pietro (aka Vecchietta), Priamo della Quercia and Domenico di Bartolo. All laud the good works of the hospital and its patrons; the most evocative is di Bartolo's *Il governo degli infermi* (Caring for the Sick; 1440–44), which depicts many activities that occurred here.

There's so much to see in the complex that devoting half a day is barely adequate. Don't miss the hugely atmospheric **Archaeological Museum** set in the basement tunnels; the medieval *fienile* (hayloft) on level three, which showcases Jacopo della Quercia's original 1419 sculptures from Siena's central **Fonte Gaia** (Happy Fountain; Piazza del Campo); and the Sagrestia Vecchia (Old Chapel) of the Chiesa SS Annunziata to the right near the main entrance, which houses di Bartolo's *Madonna della Misericordia* (1444–45) and a fresco cycle by di Pietro illustrating the Articles of the Creed.

There's an excellent gift shop on site, as well as a pleasant cafe that can be accessed from Piazza Duomo.

★Pinacoteca Nazionale
GALLERY

(☑0577 28 11 61; http://pinacotecanazionale.siena.it; Via San Pietro 29; adult/reduced €4/2; ☉8.15am-7.15pm Tue-Sat, 9am-1pm Sun & Mon) An extraordinary collection of Gothic masterpieces from the Sienese school sits inside the once grand but now sadly dishevelled

Siena

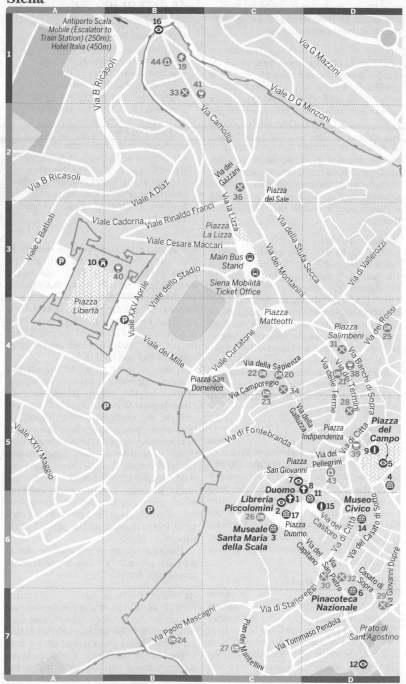

Antiporto Scala Mobile (Escalator to Train Station) (250m); Hotel Italia (450m)

Via B. Ricasoli

Via B Ricasoli

Via G Mazzini

Via Camollia

Viale D G Minzoni

Viale A Diaz

Viale Cadorna

Viale Rinaldo Franci

Viale Cesare Maccari

Via dei Gazzani

Piazza del Sale

Via la Lizza

Via della Stufa Secca

Via dei Montanini

Via di Vallerozzi

Piazza La Lizza

Main Bus Stand

Siena Mobilità Ticket Office

Via C Battisti

Piazza Libertà

Viale XXV Aprile

Viale dello Stadio

Viale dei Mille

Piazza Matteotti

Piazza Salimbeni

Via dei Rossi

Via Banchi di Sopra

Viale Curtatone

Via della Sapienza

Piazza San Domenico

Via Camporegio

Via della Galluzza

Via di Fontebranda

Piazza Indipendenza

Piazza del Campo

Via di Città

Via delle Terme

Via dei Termini

Viale XXIV Maggio

Piazza San Giovanni

Via dei Pellegrini

Via del Castoro

Duomo

Libreria Piccolomini

Museo Civico

Museale Santa Maria della Scala

Piazza Duomo

Via di Città

Via del Casato di Sotto

Via del Capitano

Via San Pietro

Casato di Sopra

Pinacoteca Nazionale

Via Giovanni Duprè

Via Paolo Mascagni

Pian dei Mantellini

Via di Stalloreggi

Via Tommaso Pendola

Prato di Sant'Agostino

Siena

◎ Top Sights
1	Duomo	C6
2	Libreria Piccolomini	C6
3	Museale Santa Maria della Scala	C6
4	Museo Civico	D5
5	Piazza del Campo	D5
6	Pinacoteca Nazionale	D7

◎ Sights
7	Battistero di San Giovanni	C5
8	Cripta	D5
9	Fonte Gaia	D5
10	Fortezza Medicea	A3
11	Museo dell'Opera	D6
12	Orto Botanico	D7
13	Orto de' Pecci	E7
14	Palazzo Chigi Saracini	D6
	Palazzo Pubblico	(see 4)
15	Panorama del Facciatone	D6
16	Porta Camollia	B1
17	Porta del Cielo	C6
18	Torre del Mangia	E5

◉ Activities, Courses & Tours
	Siena Francigena Walking Tour	(see 16)
19	Siena Urban Running	B1

🛏 Sleeping
20	Albergo Bernini	C4
21	Antica Residenza Cicogna	D4
22	Campo Regio Relais	C4
23	Hotel Alma Domus	C4
24	Hotel Athena	B7
25	Hotel Palazzetto Rosso	D4
26	Ostello Casa delle Balie	C6
27	Pensione Palazzo Ravizza	C7

🍽 Eating
28	Enoteca I Terzi	D5
29	La Taverna di San Giuseppe	D7
30	La Vecchia Latteria	D6
31	Morbidi	D4
32	Osteria Boccon del Prete	D6
33	Osteria Il Vinaio	B1
34	Osteria la Chiacchera	C4
35	Ristorante All'Orto de' Pecci	E7
36	Ristorante Enzo	C2
37	Tre Cristi	E4

🍷 Drinking & Nightlife
38	Cacio e Pere	D4
39	Caffè Fiorella	D5
40	Enoteca Italiana	B3
41	Mad in Italy	B1
42	UnTUBO	E5

🛍 Shopping
43	Il Magnifico	D5
44	Il Maratoneta	B1

ℹ️ MUSEUM PASSES

Several combination passes save you money at Siena's major monuments:

OPA SI Pass covers the Duomo, Libreria Piccolomini, Museo dell'Opera, Battistero di San Giovanni and Cripta; €13 March to October, €8 November to February, valid for three days.

OPA SI + Pass covers the list above plus Porta del Cielo tour; €20 March to October, €15 November to February, valid for three days.

Acropoli Pass covers the Duomo, Libreria Piccolomini, Museo dell'Opera, Battistero di San Giovanni, Cripta and Museale Santa Maria della Scala; €18 March to October, €13 November to February, valid for three days.

Acropoli + Pass covers the list above, plus Porta del Cielo tour; €25 March to October, €20 November to February, valid for three days.

14th-century **Palazzo Buonsignori**. The highlights are on the 2nd floor, where magnificent works by Guido da Siena, Duccio (di Buoninsegna), Simone Martini, Niccolò di Segna, Lippo Memmi, Ambrogio and Pietro Lorenzetti, Bartolo di Fredi, Taddeo di Bartolo and Sano di Pietro are housed.

Palazzo Chigi Saracini   MUSEUM
(☑ 333 9180012, 0577 2 20 91; http://eng.chigiana.it; Via di Città 89; adult/student €7/5; ☉ tours 11.30am Mon-Wed & Sat, 11.30am & 4pm Thur & Fri) Few buildings have pedigrees as splendid as this 13th-century palace. Home of the Piccolomini family (of which Pope Pius II was the most prominent member) during the Renaissance, it was acquired by the powerful Saracini family in the 18th century and inherited a century later by a scion of the wealthy Roman Chigi family. Today it houses the **Fondazione Accademia Chigiana** and its art-adorned interiors are a testament to the wealth, erudition and taste of the Saracini and Chigi families.

Orto Botanico   GARDENS
(Botanical Garden; ☑ 0577 23 28 77; www.simus.unisi.it; Via Pier Andrea Mattioli 4; adult/reduced €5/2.50; ☉ 10am-7pm July-Sep, to 5pm Mar-Jun, to 4pm Oct-Feb) The tranquil terraces of this botanical garden, which is spread over 2.5 hectares of the verdant Sant'Agostino Valley, provide a welcome escape from the tourist crowds and gorgeous views across the valley. Owned by the University of Siena, which operates a scientific field here, it features hothouses filled with tropical and sub-tropical species, a genus terrace, fruit trees and gardens planted with aromatic, medicinal and food plants. In total, over 1000 species are found here. Native and endangered species are also represented.

🧭 Tours

Centro Guide Turistiche Siena e Provincia   CULTURAL
(☑ 0577 4 32 73; www.guidesiena.it) This association of accredited guides offers guaranteed daily departures of a two-hour 'Classic Siena' Walking Tour (adult/child under 12 €20/free) at 11am between April and October. This features key historical and cultural landmarks and includes entrance to the Duomo (p516) or Cripta (p517). Tours depart from outside the tourist information office in Santa Maria della Scala (p517) and are conducted in both Italian and English.

Siena Francigena Walking Tour   WALKING
(☑ 347 6137678; www.enjoysiena.it; adult/child under 11yr €20/10; ☉ 9am early May–late Jun & Sep–mid-Oct) Introduced in 2017, this three-to-four-hour guided tour (Italian and English) departs from **Porta Camollia** (Via Camollia) on the northern edge of the historic centre and follows the medieval pilgrim route for 4km to the Duomo before continuing to Porta Romana. The tour stops to visit the Museale Santa Maria della Scala (p517) (ticket price included). Bookings essential.

Siena Urban Running   RUNNING
(☉ 7.45am Mon, Wed & Fri Jul-Oct) Guided 90-minute run through the historic centre organised by **Il Maratoneta** (Maratoneta Sport; ☑ 0577 4 42 77; maratoneta.sport@libero.it; Via Camollia 201; ☉ 9.30am-8pm Mon-Sat) walking and running shop. From November to mid-May there's a two-hour guided run in the early evening on Thursday. Running kits are available for €35.

🛏️ Sleeping

Ostello Casa delle Balie   HOSTEL €
(☑ 347 6137678; ostellosms@operalaboratori.com; Vicolo di San Girolamo 2; dm €18; ❋@⊛) Siena's historic centre sorely lacks backpacker accommodation, so we were thrilled when this hostel just off Piazza Duomo opened in

2017. Though primarily catering to pilgrims walking the Via Francigena, it also welcomes others – book in advance. Rooms have bunk beds and small lockers (sheets and blankets provided); hot showers cost €0.50. Laundry facilities, but no kitchen or lounge.

Note that daytime check-in is at the tourist office in Santa Maria della Scala; the hostel is only staffed between 8pm and 10.30pm.

Hotel Alma Domus
HOTEL €

(☏0577 4 41 77; www.hotelalmadomus.it; Via Camporegio 37; s €55, d €90-140; ❄ @ ⌂) Your chance to sleep in a convent: Alma Domus is owned by the Church and is still home to several Dominican nuns. The economy rooms, although comfortable, are styled very simply and aren't as soundproofed as many would like. But the superior ones are lovely, with a stylish decor and modern fittings; many have mini-balconies with uninterrupted Duomo views.

Albergo Bernini
PENSION €

(☏0577 28 90 47; www.albergobernini.com; Via della Sapienza 15; d €85, without bathroom €65; ⌂) The tiny terrace alone might prompt you to stay at this welcoming, family-run hotel – it sports grandstand views across to the Duomo and is a captivating spot for breakfast (€9) or drinks later in the day. The 10 bedrooms are traditional affairs and only a couple have air-con. Cash payment only.

★ Pensione Palazzo Ravizza
BOUTIQUE HOTEL €€

(☏0577 28 04 62; www.palazzoravizza.it; Pian dei Mantellini 34; s €145-230, d €160-295, ste €250-315; P ❄ ⌂) Occupying a Renaissance-era *palazzo* located in a quiet but convenient corner of Siena, this gorgeous hotel offers rooms perfectly melding heritage features and modern amenities; the best face the large rear garden, which has a panoramic terrace. The breakfast buffet is generous, on-site parking is free and room rates are remarkably reasonable (especially in the low season).

Antica Residenza Cicogna
B&B €€

(☏0577 28 56 13; www.anticaresidenzacicogna. it; Via delle Terme 76; s €90, d €110, ste €150; ❄ @ ⌂) You get a true feel for Siena's history in this 13th-century *palazzo* close to the Campo. Tiled floors, ornate lights and painted ceilings meet tones of yellow ochre and (suitably) burnt sienna. All of the rooms are charming, but we were particularly taken with the Stanza dei Paesaggi, which is named after the frescoed landscapes that decorate it.

Hotel Italia
HOTEL €€

(☏0577 4 42 48; www.hotelitalia-siena.it; Viale Cavour 67; s €70-122, d €85-160, ste €150-190; ❄ @ ⌂ ☼) Close to the busy shopping and eating strip of Via Camollia, this well-priced modern hotel offers a range of accommodation, including worn-but-comfortable standard rooms, renovated superior rooms and swish executive suites. Parking costs €10 per night, the breakfast buffet is generous, and guests can use the swimming pool at a nearby hotel in the same group.

Hotel Athena
HOTEL €€

(☏0577 28 63 13; www.hotelathena.com; Via Paolo Mascagni 55; s €54-380, d €60-420; P ❄ ⌂ ☼) Rooms at this friendly and efficiently run

IL PALIO

Dating from the Middle Ages, this spectacular annual event includes a series of colourful pageants and a wild horse race in Piazza del Campo on 2 July and 16 August. Ten of Siena's 17 *contrade* (town districts) compete for the coveted *palio* (silk banner). Each *contrada* has its own traditions, symbol and colours, plus its own church and palio museum.

From about 5pm on race days, representatives from each *contrada* parade in historical costume, all bearing their individual banners. For scarcely one exhilarating minute, the 10 horses and their bareback riders tear three times around a temporarily constructed dirt racetrack with a speed and violence that makes spectators' hair stand on end.

The race is held at 7.45pm in July and 7pm in August. Join the crowds in the centre of the Campo at least four hours before the start if you want a place on the rails, but be aware that once there you won't be able to leave for toilet or drink breaks until the race has finished. Alternatively, the cafes in the Campo sell places on their terraces; these cost between €350 and €400 per ticket, and can be booked through the tourist office up to one year in advance.

hotel have old-fashioned but pleasant furnishings and plenty of amenities, but vary greatly in size. Opt for a deluxe or executive type if possible, as these are spacious and have wonderful views of cityscapes meeting the fields. There's an in-house **restaurant** and a **summer-only terrace bar** overlooking the Tuscan hills.

⭐**Campo Regio Relais** BOUTIQUE HOTEL **€€€**
(☑0577 22 20 73; www.camporegio.com; Via della Sapienza 25; r €190-450; ☀mid-Mar–early Jan; ❀🛜) Siena's most charming boutique hotel has only six rooms, each individually decorated and luxuriously equipped (opt for deluxe room 5, which has a private terrace). An excellent breakfast is served in the sumptuously decorated lounge or on the main terrace, which has a sensational view across the Fontebranda Valley and across to the Torre del Mangia and the Duomo.

Hotel Palazzetto Rosso DESIGN HOTEL **€€€**
(☑0577 23 61 97; www.palazzettorosso.com; Via dei Rossi 38-42; r €175-270, ste €300-420; ℗❀@🛜🏊) Ooh la la! This French-owned hotel occupies a magnificent 13th-century building and is Siena's only hip hotel, replete with designer furniture and fittings. Nine well-sized rooms have good beds with quality linen, satellite TV and kettle (note that

the ubiquitous shower-nozzle-over-bathtub won't suit everyone). There's a chic breakfast room and bar, attentive service and valet parking (€30 per day).

🍴 Eating

⭐**La Vecchia Latteria** GELATO
(☑0577 05 76 38; Via San Pietro 10; gelato €2-3.50; ☀noon-8pm) Sauntering through Siena's historic centre is always more fun with a gelato in hand. Just ask one of the many locals who are regular customers at this *gelateria artigianale* (maker of handmade gelato) near the Pinacoteca Nazionale. Using quality produce, owners Fabio and Francesco concoct and serve fruity fresh or decadently creamy iced treats – choose from gelato or frozen yoghurt.

Morbidi DELI **€**
(☑0577 28 02 68; www.morbidi.com; Via Banchi di Sopra 75; lunch/aperitivo buffet €12/from €7; ☀8am-8pm Mon-Thu, to 10pm Fri & Sat) A classy deli famed for its top-quality produce, Morbidi's excellent-value basement lunch buffet (€12; 12.15pm to 2.30pm Monday to Saturday) allows you to choose from freshly prepared antipasti, salads, risotto, pasta and dessert. Bottled water is supplied, wine and coffee cost extra. Buy your ticket upstairs before heading down. The cost of the *aperitivo* buffet (6pm to 10pm Friday and Saturday) depends on your choice of drink.

⭐**Osteria Il Vinaio** TUSCAN **€**
(☑0577 4 96 15; Via Camollia 167; antipasti €6-13, pasta €6-7; ☀10am-10pm Mon-Sat) Wine bars are thin on the ground here in Siena, so it's not surprising that Bobbe and Davide's neighbourhood *osteria* is so popular. Join the multi-generational local regulars for a bowl of pasta or your choice from the generous antipasto display, washed down with a glass or two of eminently quaffable house wine.

Osteria la Chiacchera TUSCAN **€**
(☑0577 28 06 31; www.osterialachiacchera.it; Costa di San Antonio 4; €18; ☀12.20-2.30 & 7-10pm Wed-Mon) Forgoing fuss, this unassuming *osteria* has a limited number of shared tables but a lot of charm. The menu (Italian only) offers hearty local dishes – *crostini* and *pici* (a type of pasta) with various sauces are always on offer, as are dishes with *fagioli* (white beans) – and these are enjoyed with the cheap house wine. Book ahead to be sure of snaffling a spot.

FLORENCE & TUSCANY SIENA

ORTO DE'PECCI

Operated by a social cooperative that gives support and employment to people suffering social, intellectual or physical disadvantage, the urban oasis **Orto de'Pecci** (☑0577 22 22 01; www.ortodepecci.it; Via Porta Giustizia; ☀8.30am-10pm summer, reduced hours winter; 🚻) **FREE** is home to public green spaces that are perfect for picnics or an afternoon snooze (locals can often be found here, hiding from the crowds). There's also a small vineyard with clones of medieval vines, a cooperative organic farm that supplies the on-site **restaurant** (☑0577 22 22 01; www.ortodepecci.it; Via di Porta Giustizia, Orto de' Pecci; pizza €5-8, meals €20; ☀noon-2.30pm & 7.30-10pm Tue-Sun) 🌿 with fruit and vegetables, plenty of animals (geese, goats, ducks and donkeys) and a scattering of site-specific contemporary artworks.

Ristorante Enzo
TUSCAN €€

(☑ 0577 28 12 77; www.daenzo.net; Via Camollia 49; meals €40; ⊙ noon-2.30pm & 7.30-10pm Tue-Sun) The epitome of old-fashioned Sienese dining, Da Enzo, as it is popularly called, welcomes guests with a complimentary glass of *prosecco* (sparkling wine) and follows up with traditional dishes made with skill and care. There's fish on the menu, but most locals head here for the handmade pasta and meat dishes. Consider opting for one of the traditional menus (€28 to €35).

Enoteca I Terzi
TUSCAN €€

(☑ 0577 4 43 29; www.enotecaiterzi.it; Via dei Termini 7; meals €35; ⊙ 11am-3pm & 6.30pm-1am Mon-Sat, shorter hours winter) Close to the Campo but off the well-beaten tourist trail, this *enoteca* (wine bar) is located in a vaulted medieval building but has a contemporary feel. It's popular with sophisticated locals, who linger over working lunches, *aperitivi* sessions and slow-paced dinners featuring Tuscan *salumi* (cured meats), delicate handmade pasta, grilled meats and wonderful wines (many available by the glass).

Osteria Boccon del Prete
MODERN ITALIAN €€

(☑ 0577 28 03 88; Via San Pietro 17; meals €25; ⊙ 12.15-3pm & 7.15-10pm Mon-Sat) As popular with locals as it is with tourists, this casual place near the Pinacoteca Nazionale serves Tuscan dishes with a modern twist. The interior features a rich red colour scheme and modern art – very different to most of the city's eateries.

★ La Taverna di San Giuseppe
TUSCAN €€€

(☑ 0577 4 22 86; www.tavernasangiuseppe.it; Via Dupré 132; meals €45; ⊙ noon-2.30pm & 7-10pm Mon-Sat) Any restaurant specialising in beef, truffles and porcini mushrooms attracts our immediate attention, but not all deliver on their promise. Fortunately, this one does. A favoured venue for locals celebrating important occasions, it offers excellent food, an impressive wine list with plenty of local, regional and international choices, a convivial traditional atmosphere and efficient service. Love it.

★ Tre Cristi
SEAFOOD €€€

(☑ 0577 28 06 08; www.trecristi.com; Vicolo di Provenzano 1-7; meals €45, tasting menus €40-65; ⊙ 12.30-2.30pm & 7.30-10pm Mon-Sat) Seafood restaurants are thin on the ground in this meat-obsessed region, so the long existence of Tre Cristi (it's been around since 1830) should be heartily celebrated. The menu

SIENESE SWEETS

Lorenzo Rossi at **Il Magnifico** (☑ 0577 28 11 06; www.ilmagnifico.siena.it; Via dei Pellegrini 27; ⊙ 7.30am-7.30pm Mon-Sat) is Siena's best baker, and his *panforte*, *ricciarelli* (sugar-dusted chewy almond biscuits) and *cavallucci* (chewy biscuits flavoured with aniseed and other spices) are a weekly purchase for most local households. Try them at his bakery and shop behind the Duomo, and you'll understand why.

here is as elegant as the decor, and touches such as a complimentary glass of *prosecco* at the start of the meal add to the experience. Exemplary service.

🍷 Drinking & Nightlife

Via Camollia and Via di Pantaneto are Siena's major bar and coffee strips. Though atmospheric, the bars lining the Campo are expensive if you sit at a table – consider yourself warned.

Caffè Fiorella
CAFE

(Torrefazione Fiorella; www.torrefazionefiorella.it; Via di Città 13; ⊙ 7am-6pm Mon-Sat) Squeeze into this tiny, heart-of-the-action space to enjoy some of Siena's best coffee. In summer, the coffee granita with a dollop of cream is a wonderful indulgence.

Enoteca Italiana
WINE BAR

(☑ 0577 22 88 43; www.enoteca-italiana.it; Fortezza Medicea, Piazza Libertà 1; ⊙ noon-7.30pm Mon & Tue, to midnight Wed-Sat) The former munitions cellar and dungeon of this **Medici fortress** (Piazza Caduti delle Forze Armate; ⊙ 24hr) **FREE** has been artfully transformed into a classy *enoteca* that carries more than 1500 Italian labels. You can take a bottle with you, ship a case home or just enjoy a glass in the attractive courtyard or vaulted interior.

Mad in Italy
WINE BAR

(☑ 0577 4 39 81; Via Camollia 136-138; ⊙ 11am-4pm Mon-Thu, to midnight Fri & Sat) About as hip as Siena gets, this laid-back 'biobar' is popular with the student set. Decor is thrift-shop quirky, the vibe is friendly and there's often live music on Fridays and Saturdays. Choose from a good range of wine and spirits and consider eating, too – many of the imaginatively presented dishes (€6 to €10) are vegetarian and organic.

Cacio e Pere CLUB

(☑ 0577 151 07 27; Via dei Termini 70; ⊙ 7pm-1am)
If you're a university student studying in
Siena, you're likely to be a regular at this
hybrid bar and club, which is known for its
live music, cheapish food and free-flowing
drinks. Those who head here for *aperitivi
musicali* tend to stay on to closing time – it's
that type of place. Check its Facebook page
for events info.

UnTUBO CLUB

(☑ 0577 27 13 12; www.untubo.it; Via del Luparello
2; cover charge varies; ⊙ 6.30pm-3am Tue-Sat)
Live jazz acts regularly take the stage at this
intimate club near the Campo, which is popular with students and the city's boho set.
Check the website for a full events program
– blues, pop and rock acts pop in for occasional gigs too. Note that winter hours are
often reduced.

ⓘ Information

Azienda Ospedaliera Universitaria Senese
(☑ 0577 58 51 11; www.ao-siena.toscana.it;
Strada delle Scotte) Hospital just north of Siena
at Le Scotte.

Police Station (Questura; ☑ 0577 20 11 11;
http://questure.poliziadistato.it/Siena; Via del
Castoro 6; ⊙ 8am-8pm Mon-Sat)

Tourist Office (☑ 0577 28 05 51; www.enjoy
siena.it; Piazza Duomo 1, Santa Maria della
Scala; ⊙ 9am-6pm summer, to 5pm winter)
Siena's tourist information office is located in
the Museale Santa Maria della Scala, and can
provide free maps of the city. The entrance
is on the right (western) side of the museum
building.

ⓘ Getting There & Away

BUS

Siena Mobilità (☑ 800 922984; www.siena
mobilita.it), part of the Tiemme network, links
Siena with the rest of Tuscany. It has a **ticket
office** (⊙ 6.30am-7.30pm Mon-Fri, from 7am
Sat) underneath the main bus station in Piazza
Gramsci; there's also a daytime-only **left-
luggage office** here (⊙ 7am-7pm; per bag
€5.50).

TRAIN

Siena's rail links aren't that extensive; buses
can be a better option. There is a direct *regionale*
service to Florence (from €9.10, 1½ hours,
hourly). Rome requires a change of train at
Chiusi-Chianciano Terme. For Pisa, change at
Empoli.

A free *scala mobile* (escalator) connects the
train station (Piazza Carlo Rosselli) with Viale
Vittorio Emanuele II, near Porta Camollia in the
historic centre.

ⓘ Getting Around

BUS

Within Siena, **Tiemme** (☑ 0577 20 41 11; www.
tiemmespa.it) operates *pollicino* (city centre),
urbano (urban) and *suburbano* (suburban) buses
(€1.20 per one hour). Buses 3 and 9 run between
the train station and Piazza Gramsci.

CAR & MOTORCYCLE

There's a ZTL (Limited Traffic Zone) in Siena's
historic centre, although visitors can often drop
off luggage at their hotel; ask reception to report
your licence number in advance, or risk a hefty
fine.

BUS ROUTES FROM SIENA

DESTINATION	FARE (€)	TIME	FREQUENCY (MON–SAT)	NOTES
Arezzo	6.60	1½hr	8 daily	
Colle di Val d'Elsa	3.40	30min	hourly	Onward connections for Volterra (€2.75, 4 daily)
Fiumicino Airport (Rome)	22	3¾hr	2 daily	
Florence (Corse Rapide/ Express service via the autostrada)	7.80	1¼hr	frequent	'Corse Ordinarie' services don't use the *autostrada* and take at least 20 min extra
Montalcino	4.90	70min	6 daily	Departs train station
Montepulciano	6.80	1½hr	2 daily	Departs train station
Monteriggioni	6.10	75min	frequent	
Pienza	5.50	70min	2 daily	Departs train station
San Gimignano	6	1-1½hr	10 daily	Often changes in Poggibonsi (€4.35, 1 hr, hourly)

There are large car parks operated by **Siena Parcheggi** (☑ 0577 22 87 11) at the Stadio Comunale and around the Fortezza Medicea, both just north of Piazza San Domenico. Hotly contested free street parking (look for white lines) is available in Viale Vittorio Veneto on the Fortezza Medicea's southern edge. The paid car parks at San Francesco and Santa Caterina (aka Fontebranda) each have a free *scala mobile* (escalator) going up into the centre.

Most car parks charge €2 per hour between 7am and 8pm. There's more parking information at www.sienaparcheggi.com.

Chianti

The vineyards in this postcard-perfect part of Tuscany produce the grapes used in namesake Chianti and Chianti Classico: world-famous reds sold under the Gallo Nero (Black Cockerel/Rooster) trademark. It's a landscape where you'll encounter historic olive groves, honey-coloured stone farmhouses, dense forests, graceful Romanesque *pievi* (rural churches), handsome Renaissance villas and imposing stone castles built in the Middle Ages by Florentine and Sienese warlords.

Though now part of the province of Siena, the southern section of Chianti (Chianti Senese) was once the stronghold of the Lega del Chianti, a military and administrative alliance within the city-state of Florence that comprised Castellina, Gaiole and Radda. Chianti's northern part sits in the province of Florence (Chianti Fiorentino) and is a popular day trip from that city. The major wine and administrative centres are Greve in Chianti, Castellina in Chianti and Radda in Chianti.

For regional information, including festivals and special events, see www.wcchianti.com and www.chianti.com.

Greve in Chianti

POP 13,900

The main town in the Chianti Fiorentino, Greve is a hub of the local wine industry and has an amiable market-town air. It's not picturesque (most of the architecture is modern and unattractive), but it does boast an attractive, historic central square and a few notable businesses. The annual wine fair, **Expo del Chianti Classico** (Chianti Classico Expo; www.expochianticlassico.com/en), is held in the second week of September – if visiting at this time, book accommodation here and throughout the region well in advance.

◉ Sights & Activities

Enoteca Falorni   WINE

(☑ 0558 54 64 04; www.enotecafalorni.it; Piazza delle Cantine 6; ⊙10.30am-7.30pm spring & autumn, to 8pm summer, closed Wed winter) This *enoteca* is a perfect place to let your palate limber up before visiting individual wineries. It stocks more than 1000 wines and offers 100 for tasting, including Chianti, Chianti Classico, IGTs, grappa and Vin Santo made by a variety of producers. Buy a prepaid wine card (€5 to €25) and use it to test your tipple of choice.

The *enoteca* also sells bottles to take away or ship home. To get here, head down a staircase opposite the entrance of the Coop supermarket on the main road through Greve.

Castello di Verrazzano   WINE

(☑ 0558 5 42 43; www.verrazzano.com; Via Citille, Greti; tours €18-62; ⊙9.30am-6pm Mon-Sat, 10am-1pm & 3-6.30pm Sun) This hilltop castle 3km north of Greve was once home to Giovanni da Verrazzano (1485–1528), who explored the North American coast and is commemorated in New York by the Verrazano-Narrows Bridge (the good captain lost a 'z' from his name somewhere in the mid-Atlantic). Today it presides over a 225-hectare wine estate offering a wide range of tours.

Vignamaggio   WINERY, GARDEN

(☑ 0558 54 66 24; www.vignamaggio.com; Via Petriolo 5; ⊙Apr-Oct) Mona Lisa Gherardini, subject of Leonardo da Vinci's world-famous painting, married into the family that built this villa in the 14th century. More recently, the villa and its magnificent formal gardens featured in Kenneth Branagh's film adaptation of *Much Ado About Nothing*. Restored in 2017, it offers accommodation, a restaurant, cooking classes, wine tastings (two hours, €27) and a three-hour tour of the gardens, organic vineyard and historic wine cellars (€59 including four-course lunch with wines). Bookings essential.

The estate is located 5km southeast of Greve in Chianti and 9km northeast of Panzano in Chianti.

✗ Eating & Drinking

Bistro Falorni   DELI €

(☑ 0558 53029; www.falorni.it; Piazza Giacomo Matteotti 71; taglieri €7-16, bruschetta €4, panini €5; ⊙10.30am-7pm) Italians do fast food

CYCLING CHIANTI

Exploring Chianti by bicycle is a true highlight. The Greve in Chianti **tourist office** can supply information about local cycling and walking routes, and the town is home to the well-regarded Discovery Chianti, which runs guided cycling and walking tours. It's also possible to rent bicycles from **Ramuzzi** (☑ 055 85 30 37; www.ramuzzi.com; Via Italo Stecchi 23; mountain/hybrid bike per day/week €20/130, scooter €55/290; ⊙ 9am-1pm & 3-7pm Mon-Fri, 9am-1pm Sat) in Greve's town centre.

A number of companies offer guided cycling tours leaving from Florence:

Discovery Chianti (☑ 328 6124658; www.discoverychianti.com; Via I Maggio 32, Greve in Chianti; price on application; ⊙ Mar-Oct)

Florence By Bike (☑ 055 4 8 89 92; www.florencebybike.it; adult/reduced €83/75; ⊙ daily Mar-Oct)

I Bike Italy (☑ 342 9352395; www.ibikeitaly.com; road/electric bike €450/550; ⊙ Mon, Wed & Fri mid-Mar–Oct)

I Bike Tuscany (☑ 335 812 07 69; www.ibiketuscany.com; €120-160)

differently, and what a wonderful difference it is. Greve's famous *macelleria* (butcher) and gourmet-provision shop opened this cafeteria attached to the *macelleria* in 2013, and it was an instant success with both locals and tourists. Choose from the range of *taglieri* (tasting boards), *panini* and bruschette on offer, and order a glass of wine (€4), too.

La Castellana TUSCAN €€
(☑ 055 8 5 31 34; www.ristorantelacastellana.it; Via di Montefioralle 2, Montefioralle; meals €40; ⊙ noon-2pm & 7.30-9.30pm Tue-Sun summer, hours vary winter) Make your way to this hamlet above Greve to enjoy wonderful home-style Tuscan cooking – perhaps handmade ravioli stuffed with mushrooms and truffles, or succulent sliced, rosemary-studded beef. The wine list reads like a map of Chianti's highlights. Sit at one of the six indoor tables or on the hillside terrace with its panorama of cypresses, olive trees and vines.

La Castellana is in the hilltop village of Montefioralle, a 2km walk uphill from Greve.

ℹ Information

The **tourist office** (☑ 390 55853606, 0558 54 52 71; www.helloflorence.net; Piazza Matteotti 10; ⊙ 10.30am-1.30pm late Mar–mid-Oct, to 6.30pm Easter-Aug) is located in Greve's main square.

ℹ Getting There & Around

BUS
Buses travel between Greve in Chianti and Florence (€3.30, one hour, hourly) and between Greve and Panzano in Chianti (€1.30, 15 minutes,

frequent). The bus stop is on Piazza Trento, 100m from Piazza Giacomo Matteotti.

CAR & MOTORCYCLE
Greve is on the Via Chiantigiana (SR222). Find parking in the two-level, open-air car park on Via Luca Chini, on the opposite side of the main road to Piazza Matteotti (this is free on the top level). On Fridays, don't park overnight in the paid spaces in Piazza Matteotti – your car will be towed away to make room for Saturday market stalls.

Badia a Passignano

Chianti doesn't get much more atmospheric than Badia a Passignano, a Benedictine Vallombrosan abbey set amid vineyards run by the legendary Antinori dynasty. Head here to visit the historic church and abbey buildings, admire the views over the vineyards and taste Antinori wines in the classy *osteria* (casual tavern).

⊙ Sights & Activities

Chiesa di San Michele Arcangelo CHURCH
(Abbey of Passignano; Via di Passignano; admission by donation; ⊙ guided tours in Italian 10am-noon & 3-5.30pm Fri, Sat & Mon-Wed summer, 3-5.30pm Sun, reduced hours winter) An 11th-century church on this site was destroyed in the 13th century and replaced by this structure, which was subsequently heavily altered over the centuries. Dedicated to St Michael the Archangel (look for the 12th-century statue of him slaying a dragon next to the high altar), it is home to frescoes and paintings of varying quality – the best are by Domenico Cresti (known as 'Il Passignano') in the central chapel in the apse.

Monastery MONASTERY

(☑ 0558 07 23 41 (English), 0558 07 11 71 (Italian); Abbey of Passignano, Via di Passignano; admission by donation; ☺ guided tours in Italian 10am-noon & 3-5.30pm Fri, Sat & Mon-Wed summer, 3-5.30pm Sun, reduced hours winter) The four Vallombrosan monks who call this medieval abbey home open their quarters to visitors on regular guided tours. The highlight is the refectory, which was remodelled in the 15th century and is presided over by Domenico Ghirlandaio's utterly marvellous, recently restored 1476 fresco *The Last Supper*. The tours also visit the monastery's garden cloister and historic kitchen. It's best to book in advance.

La Bottega di Badia a Passignano WINE

(☑ 0558 07 12 78; www.osteriadipassignano.com; Via di Passignano 33; ☺ 10am-7.30pm Mon-Sat) Taste or purchase Antinori wine in this *enoteca* beside the prestigious Osteria di Passignano restaurant. A tasting of three wines by the glass will cost between €25 and €55 and there is a variety of guided tours of the cellars and vineyards on offer – check the website for details.

🛏 Sleeping & Eating

⭐ **L'Antica Scuderia** TUSCAN €€

(☑ 335 8252669; www.ristorolanticascuderia.com; Via di Passignano 17; meals €45, pizza €8-12; ☺ 12.30-2.30pm & 7.30-10.30pm Wed-Mon; 🚲) The large terrace at this ultra-friendly restaurant overlooks one of the Antinori vineyards and is perfect for summer dining. In winter, the elegant dining room comes into its own. Lunch features antipasti, pastas and traditional grilled meats, while dinner sees plenty of pizza-oven action. Kids love the playground set; adults love the fact that it keeps the kids occupied.

⭐ **Fattoria di Rignana** AGRITURISMO €€

(☑ 0558 5 20 65; www.rignana.it; Via di Rignana 15, Rignana; d from €95; ☺ Apr–mid-Dec; 🅿@🛜🏊🐕) The historic farmhouse of this wine estate has its very own chapel and bell tower, which reveal themselves after you brave a long, rutted access road. You'll also find glorious views, a large swimming pool and a nearby eatery. You'll sleep in rustic rooms in the estate's *fattoria* (farmhouse). It's 4km from Badia a Passignano.

Osteria di Passignano MODERN ITALIAN €€€

(☑ 055 807 12 78; www.osteriadipassignano.com; Via di Passignano 33; meals €85, tasting menus

€80-90, with wine €100-140; ☺ 12.15-2.15pm & 7.30-10pm Mon-Sat; 🅿) Badia a Passignano sits amid a landscape scored by row upon row of vines, and the elegant Michelin-starred eatery in the centre of the hamlet has long been one of Tuscany's best-loved dining destinations. Intricate, Tuscan-inspired dishes fly the local-produce flag and the wine list is mightily impressive, with Antinori offerings aplenty (by the glass €7 to €35).

ℹ Getting There & Away

There is no public transport connection to Badia a Passignano. The easiest road access is via Strada di Badia off the SP94.

San Casciano in Val di Pesa

POP 17,100

Almost totally destroyed by Allied bombs in 1944, San Casciano in Val di Pesa, to the south of Florence, was fully rebuilt and is now a busy hub for the local wine and olive-oil industries. There are no sights of note within the town itself, but the surrounding countryside is home to a number of impressive *agriturismi* (farm-stay accommodation) and villas.

🏃 Activities

⭐ **Antinori nel Chianti Classico** WINE

(☑ 0552 35 97 00; www.antinorichianticlassico.it; Via Cassia per Siena 133, Località Bargino; tour & tasting €25-50, bookings essential; ☺ 10am-5pm Mon-Fri, to 5.30pm Sat & Sun winter, to 6.30pm Sat & Sun summer) Marco Casaminti's sculptural building set into the hillside is a landmark sight on the autostrada just south of Florence, and is one of the world's most impressive examples of contemporary winery design. Daily guided tours (in English and Italian) visit the wine-making and fermentation areas before heading to one of the glass tasting rooms cantilevered over the barriques in the cathedral-like ageing cellar for a tutored tasting of Antinori wines. Tours (90 minutes/1½ hours) cost €30/50 for three/five wines; bookings essential.

The Antinori family has been in the wine-making business since 1180. At the bar beside the shop you can taste 16 of their recent vintages (€4 to €15 per tasting) or have a sommelier-led 'guided tasting' of three wines (€9 or €12). Afterwards, you can also enjoy lunch or a glass of wine in the Rinuccio 1180 restaurant (p528). Alternatively, book for the 2½-hour wine tour and lunch (€150), which includes tastings of seven cru wines.

DON'T MISS

TUSCANY'S CELEBRITY BUTCHER

The small town of Panzano in Chianti, 10km south of Greve in Chianti, is known throughout Italy as the location of **L'Antica Macelleria Cecchini** (☑ 0558 5 20 20; www.dariocecchini.com; Via XX Luglio 11; ⊙ 9am-4pm), a butcher's shop owned and run by the ever-extroverted Dario Cecchini. This Tuscan celebrity has carved out a niche for himself as a poetry-spouting guardian of the *bistecca* (steak) and other Tuscan meaty treats, and he operates three eateries clustered around the *macelleria*: **Officina della Bistecca** (☑ 0558 5 21 76; www.dariocecchini.com; Via XX Luglio 11; set menu adult/child under 10 €50/10; ⊙ sittings at 1pm & 8pm), with a set menu built around the famous *bistecca*; **Solociccia** (☑ 0558 5 27 27; www.dariocecchini.com; Via XX Luglio; set meat menus €30 & €50; ⊙ sittings at 1pm, 7pm & 9pm), where guests sample meat dishes other than steak; and **Dario DOC** (☑ 0558 5 21 76; www.dariocecchini.com; Via XX Luglio 11; burgers €10 or €15, meat sushi €20; ⊙ noon-3pm Mon-Sat), his casual lunchtime-only eatery. Book ahead for the Officina and Solociccia. When we last visited, Cecchini had plans to add a fourth eatery to his empire – check the website for an update.

Don't leave Panzano in Chianti without visiting one of Chianti's most beautiful churches, Romanesque **Pieve di San Leolino** (Strada San Leolino, Località San Leolino; ⊙ 7.30am-noon), on a hilltop just outside Panzanoin Chianti. Artworks inside the church include a 1421 polyptych behind the high altar by Mariotto di Nardo (1421), two glazed terracotta tabernacles by Giovanni della Robbia, and a luminous 13th-century triptych by the master of Panzano depicting the Virgin and Child next to saints including St Catherine of Alexandria, the patron saint of philosophers.

Bargino is 7km south of San Casciano in Val di Pesa and 20km northwest of Greve.

🛏 Sleeping

⭐ Il Paluffo
AGRITURISMO €€

(☑ 0571 66 42 59; www.paluffo.com; Via Citerna 144, Località Fiano; B&B r €160, 2-/7-person apt €160-420; P ✳ @ 🛜 🐾 🐕) ❧ Hidden in the hills 14km southwest of San Casciano, this clever conversion of a centuries-old olive farm has seen the former fermentation room transformed into a comfortable guest lounge, farm buildings into self-catering apartments, and upstairs rooms of the frescoed farm villa into elegant B&B rooms with modern bathrooms. Views from the terraces stretch as far as San Gimignano's towers.

Staff can arrange wine tasting and truffle hunting, cookery courses cover everything from pasta making to Tuscan dinner parties. Add a luscious bio-filtered swimming pool, an honesty bar stacked with Tuscan wines and a delicious breakfast featuring organic local produce (included in B&B room cost, adult/child €12/3 for apartment guests). There's a two-night minimum stay in winter, three nights in summer.

⭐ Villa I Barronci
HOTEL €€

(☑ 0558 2 05 98; www.ibarronci.com; Via Sorripa 10; s/d/ste €100/170/200; P ✳ @ 🛜 🐾) Exemplary service, superb amenities and high comfort levels ensure this country hotel on the northwestern edge of San Casciano is one to remember. You can relax in the bar, rejuvenate in the spa, laze by the pool, dine in the excellent **restaurant** (meals €35) or take day trips to Pisa, Lucca, Florence, Volterra, San Gimignano and Siena. Amazing low-season rates.

🍴 Eating & Drinking

⭐ L'Osteria di Casa Chianti
TUSCAN €€

(☑ 0571 66 96 88; www.osteriadicasachianti.it; Località Case Nuove 77, Fiano; meals €38; ⊙ 7-10pm Tue-Sat, 12.30-2.30pm & 7-10pm Sun) The type of restaurant that fuels fantasies of moving permanently to Tuscany, this eatery bakes its own bread, makes pasta by hand, grills *bistecca* on a wood fire, specialises in truffle and porcini mushroom dishes, and has an exceptional wine list. It also imparts the secrets of its delectable cooking in 4½-hour classes (€95 including lunch). Book ahead.

You'll find it on the SP79 between Fiano and Certaldo, 14km southwest of San Casciano in Val di Pesa.

Rinuccio 1180
TUSCAN €€

(☑ 0552 35 97 20; www.antinorichianticlassico.it; Via Cassia per Siena 133, Bargino; meals €40, tasting platters €14-15; ⊙ noon-4pm) Built on the rooftop of the sleek Antinori winery, this restaurant seats diners on an expansive outdoor terrace with a 180-degree Dolby-esque surround of hills, birdsong and pea-green vines. In cooler weather, the dining action moves into a glass dining space. Cuisine is Tuscan, modern, seasonal and sassy (Chianti burger, anyone?) and the wine list is (naturally) fabulous. Book ahead.

ℹ Getting There & Away

San Casciano is on the SP92, just off the Florece–Siena autostrada. **Busitalia/Autolinee Chianti Valdarno (ACV)** (☑ 800 373760; www.acvbus.it) operates services between San Casciano and Florence (€2.30, 20 minutes, 10 daily) and between San Casciano and Greve in Chianti (€2.30, 30 minutes, three daily).

Castellina in Chianti

POP 2900

Established by the Etruscans and fortified by the Florentines in the 15th century as a defensive outpost against the Sienese, sturdy Castellina in Chianti is now a major centre of the wine industry, as the huge silos brimming with Chianti Classico on the town's approaches attest. The town's location on the SR222 makes it a convenient overnight or meal stop for those travelling between Florence and Siena.

◉ Sights & Activities

Museo Archeologico del Chianti Senese   MUSEUM
(☑ 0577 74 20 90; www.museoarcheologicochianti.it; Piazza del Comune 17; adult/reduced €5/3; ⊙ 10am-6pm daily Apr, May, Sep & Oct, 11am-7pm Jun-Aug, 10am-5pm Sat & Sun Nov-Mar) Etruscan archaeological finds from the local area are on display at this museum in the town's medieval *rocca* (fortress). Room 4 showcases artefacts found in the 7th-century BC **Etruscan Tombs of Montecalvario** (Ipogeo Etrusco di Monte Calvario; ⊙ 24hr) FREE, which are on the northern edge of town off the SR222.

🛏 Sleeping & Eating

Il Colombaio   B&B €
(☑ 0577 74 04 44; www.albergoilcolombaio.it; Via Chiantigiana 29; s/d/tr €90/100/130; P🕸🐾) A tasteful conversion has turned this 14th-century farmhouse on the edge of Castellina into a welcoming *albergo* (hotel) with 15 rooms and a rich heritage feel: tapestry-covered chairs frame lace curtains and oil paintings; wood-beamed ceilings and iron bedheads add plenty of

character. Breakfast is served in the vaulted wine cellar or in the garden, where there is also a pool.

Ristorante Taverna Squarcialupi   TUSCAN €€
(☑ 0577 74 14 05; www.tavernasquarcialupi.it; Via Ferruccio 26; meals €38; ⊙ noon-3pm & 7-10pm Thu-Mon & noon-3pm Tue) Interesting and highly successful flavour combinations characterise the menu at this huge *taverna* in the centre of Castellina. The handmade pasta dishes are delicious – grab a seat on the panoramic rear terrace enjoy one with a glass or two of wine from the nearby La Castellina wine estate.

ℹ Information

Castellina's **tourist office** (☑ 0577 74 13 92; www.amocastellinainchianti.it; Via Ferruccio 40; ⊙ 10am-1pm Apr-Jun, 10am-1pm & 4-7 Tue-Fri Jul-Sep) can book visits to wineries and cellars. It also provides maps, accommodation suggestions and other information.

ℹ Getting There & Away

Tiemme (☑ 0577 20 41 11; www.tiemmespa.it) bus 125 links Castellina in Chianti with Radda in Chianti (€1.60, 10 minutes, three to five daily Monday to Saturday) and with Siena (€3.40, 40 minutes, seven daily Monday to Saturday). The most convenient bus stops are on the main road near Via delle Mura.

Radda in Chianti

POP 1600

The age-old streets in pretty Radda in Chianti fan out from its central square, where the shields and escutcheons of the 16th-century Palazzo del Podestà add a touch of drama to the scene. A historic wine town, it's the home of the Consorzio di Chianti Classico and is an appealing if low-key base for visits to some classic Tuscan vineyards.

◉ Sights & Activities

Casa Chianti Classico   MUSEUM
(☑ 0577 73 81 87; www.chianticlassico.com; Monastery of Santa Maria al Prato, Circonvallazione Santa Maria 18; ⊙ museum 11.30am-1pm & 3-6pm Mon-Sat Apr-Oct) FREE Occupying an 18th-century convent complex attached to a 10th-century church, this facility is operated by the Consorzio di Chianti Classico and pays homage to the region's favourite product. Book to visit the **Wine Museum** on the 1st floor to learn all about the history of the denomination, purchase a glass of wine (€5) and then compare your tasting notes to an expert's in a clever

530

4 DAYS Wine Tour of Chianti

Tuscany has more than its fair share of highlights, but few can match the glorious indulgence of a leisurely drive through Chianti. On offer is an intoxicating blend of scenery, acclaimed restaurants and ruby-red wine.

From **Florence** (p478), take the *superstrada* (expressway) towards Siena, exit at Bargino and follow the signs to **Antinori nel Chianti Classico** (p527), a state-of-the-art wine estate featuring an architecturally innovative ageing cellar. Take a tour, prime your palate with a wine tasting and enjoy lunch in the estate's Rinuccio 1180 restaurant.

Head southeast along the SS2, SP3 and SS222 (Via Chiantigiana) towards Greve in Chianti. Stop at historic **Castello di Verrazzano** (p525) for a tasting en route.

On the next day, make your way to **Greve in Chianti** (p525) to test your new-found knowledge over a self-directed tasting at Enoteca Falorni. For lunch, eat a Tuscan-style burger at Dario DOC in **Panzano in Chianti** (p528). Your destination in the afternoon should be **Badia a Passignano** (p526), an 11th-century, still-functioning Vallombrosian abbey surrounded by an Antinori wine estate. Enjoy a tasting in the *enoteca* (wine bar) and consider staying for an early pizza dinner at L'Antica Scuderia opposite the abbey, where you'll be able to watch the sun set over the vineyards.

On day three, pop into the pretty hilltop hamlet of **Volpaia** (p532) near **Radda in Chianti** (p529) and take a tour of the **Castello di Volpaia** (p532) cellars before relaxing over lunch at the innovative Ristorante Taverna Squarcialupi in **Castellina in Chianti** (p529).

On the final day, head towards **Siena** (p516). Along the way, take a guided tour of the **Castello di Brolio** (p533), ancestral home of the aristocratic Ricasoli family. Their wine estate is the oldest in Italy, so be sure to sample some Baron Ricasoli Chianti Classico at the estate's *cantina* (cellar) or over lunch in its *osteria* (casual tavern). Afterwards, investigate award-winning wines and contemporary art at **Castello di Ama** (p532).

Top: Vineyards near Radda in Chianti (p529)
Bottom: Castello di Brolio (p533)

VOLPAIA

Wines, olive oils and vinegars have long been produced at wine estate **Castello di Volpaia** (☑0577 73 80 66; www.volpaia.it; Località Volpaia), 7km north of Radda in Chianti in the medieval hamlet of Volpaia (the name is misleading, as there's no actual castle here). Book ahead to enjoy a tasting and tour of the cellars (price on application), or purchase from the *enoteca* (noon to 7pm Thursday to Tuesday) inside the hamlet's main tower.

Post estate-visit, consider a light lunch of salami made by the owner's father and a glass of Volpaia's Chianti Classico or Riserva at **Bar Ucci** (☑0577 73 80 42; www.bar-ucci. it; Piazza della Torre 9, Volpaia; snacks €4-8, meals €18; ⊙8am-9pm Tue-Sun); modern Tuscan cuisine using herbs and veg from the estate's organic garden at the highly regarded **Osteria Volpaia** (☑0577 73 80 66; www.osteriavolpaia.com; Vicolo della Torre 2, Volpaia; meals €36; ⊙12.30-3pm & 7.30-9.30pm Thu-Tue) 🍃; or *cucina contadina* (food from the farmers' kitchen) on a tree-shaded terrace with sweeping views of the Chianti hills at family-run **Ristorante La Bottega** (☑0577 73 80 01; www.labottegadivolpaia.it; Piazza della Torre 1, Volpaia; meals €28; ⊙noon-2.30pm & 7.30-9.30pm Wed-Mon Easter-Jan).

multimedia quiz. Or sign up for a 90-minute **wine class** (Italian or English; €35).

The complex also has a **restaurant** (meals €35; ⊙12.30-2.30pm & 7.30-9.30pm Tue-Sat, 12.30-2.30pm Sun Mar-Dec) and a well-stocked *enoteca*. The latter has a lovely terrace overlooking vineyards – perfect for a leisurely lunch or late-afternoon glass of wine. To find it, head downhill from Radda in Chianti's main piazza.

🛏 Sleeping & Eating

Palazzo Leopoldo   HOTEL €€
(☑0577 73 56 05; www.palazzoleopoldo.it; Via Roma 33; r €190-230, ste €370; P✳🛜🐕) Like the idea of staying in a luxury hotel in an elegant 15th-century building but fear your budget won't stretch that far? This meticulously presented hotel may well be the answer. Well-equipped rooms and suites are located in the main building and an annex; many have valley views. There's an indoor pool, outdoor hot tubs and a **restaurant** (meals €35).

Enoteca Casa Chianti Classico   WINE BAR
(☑0577 73 81 87; www.chianticlassico.com; Monastery of Santa Maria al Prato, Circonvallazione Santa Maria 18; antipasti €8-16, pastas €10-13; ⊙11.30am-6pm Tue-Sat & 11.30-2.30pm Sun Mar-Dec) The rear terrace of the *enoteca* inside this wine complex is one of the best lunch or *aperitivo* spots in the Chianti Senese, sporting lovely views over the wine country. The pasta is handmade, antipasto platters are replete with local produce, and wines by the glass include a house Chianti Classico (€5), Riserva (€7) or Gran Selezione (€9).

ⓘ Information

Tourist Office (☑0577 73 84 94; www.chianti radda.it; Piazza del Castello 2; ⊙10am-1pm & 3-6.30pm summer, 10.30am-12.30pm winter)

ⓘ Getting There & Away

Tiemme (☑0577 20 41 11; www.tiemmespa. it) buses link the town with Castellina (€1.60, 10 minutes, three to five daily Monday to Saturday) and with Siena (€4.20, one hour, four daily Monday to Saturday). There are also services to/from Florence (€4, 95 minutes, two to four daily Monday to Saturday); you'll need to change at Lucarelli on some of these. Buses stop on Via XX Settembre (SR429) near the Monte dei Paschi di Siena bank.

Gaiole in Chianti

POP 2800

Surrounded by majestic medieval castles and atmospheric *pievi* (rural churches), this small town has few attractions but is sometimes visited en route to Castello di Brolio or Castello di Ama.

⊙ Sights & Activities

⭐**Castello di Ama**   SCULPTURE, WINE
(☑0577 74 60 69; www.castellodiama.com; Località Ama; guided tours adult/child under 16yr €15/free; ⊙by appointment) At Castello di Ama, centuries-old wine-making traditions meet cutting-edge contemporary art in a 12th-century *borgo* (agricultural estate). As well as vineyards and a winery producing internationally acclaimed wines such as 'L'Apparita' merlot, the estate also features a boutique hotel, a restaurant and a sculpture park showcasing 14 impressive

site-specific pieces by artists including Louise Bourgeois, Chen Zhen, Anish Kapoor, Kendell Geers and Daniel Buren. This can be visited on a guided tour; advance bookings essential.

Castello di Brolio CASTLE
(☑ 0577 73 02 80; www.ricasoli.it; Località Madonna a Brolio; garden, chapel & crypt €5, guided tours €8; ◷ 10am-5.30pm mid-Mar–Nov, guided tours 10.30am-12.30pm & 2.30-5pm Tue-Sun) The ancestral estate of the aristocratic Ricasoli family dates from the 11th century and is the oldest winery in Italy. Currently home to the 32nd baron, it opens its formal garden, panoramic terrace and museum to day trippers, who often adjourn to the excellent on-site *osteria* for lunch after a guided tour of the castle's small but fascinating museum.

Occupying three rooms in the castle's tower, the museum is dedicated to documenting the life of the extravagantly mustachioed Baron Bettino Ricasoli (1809–80), the second prime minster of the Republic of Italy and a true polymath (scientist, farmer, winemaker, statesman and businessman). A leading figure in the Risorgimento, one of his other great claims to fame is inventing the formula for Chianti Classico that is enshrined in current DOC regulations.

The *castello*'s chapel dates from the early 14th century; below it is a crypt where generations of Ricasolis are interred. The estate produces wine and olive oil, and the huge terrace commands a spectacular view of the vineyards and olive groves.

The Classic Tour (€28, two hours) takes in the wine-making facilities and features a tasting; it runs daily from Friday to Wednesday (book online). The Vineyard Tour (€45, two hours, 3.30pm Thursday) sees you exploring three of the estate's different terroirs and sampling vintages beside the vines; advance bookings are essential.

A *bosco inglese* (English garden) surrounds the estate; in it (near the car park) you'll find the estate's **Osteria del Castello** (☑ 0577 73 02 90; osteria@ricasoli.it; meals €40; ◷ noon-2.30pm & 7-9.30pm Fri-Wed Apr-Oct; noon-2.30pm Sun-Wed plus 7-9.30pm Fri & Sat 2nd half of Mar, Nov & Dec). Just outside the estate's entrance gates, on the SP484, is a modern **cantina** (◷ 10am-7pm Apr-Oct), or cellar, where you can taste the Castello di Brolio's well-regarded Chianti Classico.

❶ Getting There & Away

Gaiole is on the SP408 between Siena and Montevarchi. **Tiemme** (☑ 0577 20 41 11; www.tiemmespa.it) bus 127 travels between Gaiole and Via Lombardi behind Siena's railway station (€1.60, 40 minutes, nine daily Monday to Saturday). The bus stop is on the main road, opposite the elementary school.

San Gimignano

POP 7800

As you crest the nearby hills, the 14 towers of the walled town of San Gimignano rise up like a medieval Manhattan. Originally an Etruscan village, the settlement was named after the bishop of Modena, San Gimignano, who is said to have saved the city from Attila the Hun. It became a *comune* (local government) in 1199, prospering in part because of its location on the Via Francigena. Building a tower taller than their neighbours' (there were originally 72) became a popular way for prominent families to flaunt their power and wealth. In 1348 plague wiped out much of the population and weakened the local economy, leading to the town's submission to Florence in 1353. Today, not even the plague would deter the swarms of summer day trippers, who are lured by a palpable sense of history, intact medieval streetscapes and enchanting rural setting.

◉ Sights

★**Collegiata** CHURCH
(Duomo; Basilica di Santa Maria Assunta; ☑ 0577 94 01 52; www.duomosangimignano.it; Piazza del Duomo; adult/reduced €4/2; ◷ 10am-7pm Mon-Sat, 12.30-7pm Sun summer, 10am-4.30pm Mon-Sat, 12.30-4.30pm Sun winter) Parts of San Gimignano's Romanesque cathedral were built in the second half of the 11th century, but its remarkably vivid frescoes, depicting episodes from the Old and New Testaments, date from the 14th century. Look out, too, for the Cappella di Santa Fina, near the main altar – a Renaissance chapel adorned with naive and touching frescoes by Domenico Ghirlandaio depicting the life of one of the town's patron saints. These featured in Franco Zeffirelli's 1999 film *Tea with Mussolini*.

San Gimignano

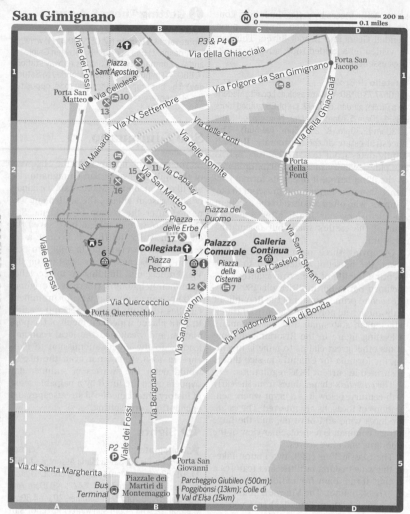

★ **Palazzo Comunale**　　　　　MUSEUM
(☎ 0577 99 03 12; www.sangimignanomusei.it; Piazza del Duomo 2; combined Civic Museums ticket adult/reduced €9/7; ☺ 10am-7.30pm summer, 11am-5.30pm winter) The 13th-century Palazzo Comunale has always been the centre of San Gimignano's local government; its magnificently frescoed **Sala di Dante** is where the great poet addressed the town's council in 1299 and its **Camera del Podestà** and **Pinacoteca** (Art Gallery) once housed government offices – now they are home to wonderful artworks. Be sure to climb the 218 steps of the *palazzo*'s 54m **Torre Grossa**

for a spectacular view over the town and surrounding countryside.

**Chiesa di
Sant'Agostino**　　　　　CHURCH
(Piazza Sant'Agostino; ☺ 10am-noon & 3-7pm summer, to 6pm & closed Mon morning winter) **FREE**
This late-13th-century church is best known for Benozzo Gozzoli's charming fresco cycle (1464–65) illustrating the life of St Augustine. You'll find it in the choir behind the altar. Gozzoli also painted the fresco featuring San Sebastian on the north wall, which shows the saint protecting the citizens of

San Gimignano

San Gimignano during the 1464 plague. What makes the image highly unusual is that he's helped by a bare-breasted Virgin Mary; this symbolises her maternal love for humanity.

★ **Galleria Continua**   GALLERY
(☑ 0577 94 31 34; www.galleriacontinua.com; Via del Castello 11, ⊙ 10am-1pm & 2-7pm) **FREE** It may seem strange to highlight contemporary art in this medieval time capsule of a town, but there's good reason to do so. This is one of the best commercial art galleries in Europe, showing the work of big-name artists such as Ai Weiwei, Daniel Buren, Antony Gormley and Mona Hatoum. Spread over four venues (an old cinema, a medieval tower, a vaulted cellar and an apartment on Piazza della Cisterna), it's one of San Gimignano's most compelling attractions.

Vernaccia Wine Experience   MUSEUM
(☑ 0577 94 12 67; www.sangimignanomuseovernaccia.com; Via della Rocca 1; ⊙ 11.30am-6.30pm Apr-Oct) **FREE** San Gimignano's famous wine, Vernaccia, is celebrated in this small museum next to the **rocca** (fortress; Via della Rocca; ⊙ 24hr) **FREE**. Interactive exhibits

on the 1st floor trace the history of the product and the surrounding land; there's also a ground-floor *enoteca* where you can taste Vernaccia and other varietals produced in the region (per taste €1 to €6) or buy a glass to enjoy on a terrace with a panoramic view.

☞ Tours

★ **Vernaccia Master Class**   WINE
(Via della Rocca 1; €25; ⊙ noon, 4pm & 6pm) Organised by the Vernaccia Wine Experience, these daily master classes include a guided tour of the 1st-floor Vernaccia exhibition and a tasting of four wines accompanied by typical local foods. Book through the tourist office (p536).

★ **Vernaccia di San Gimignano Vineyard Visit**   WINE
(€30; ⊙ 5-7pm Tue & Thu Apr-Oct) These highly enjoyable tastings of local foods and wines are delivered by English-language guides. Book at the tourist office (p536) at least a day in advance.

🛏 Sleeping

Il Pino   D&D €
(☑ 0577 94 04 15; www.locandailpino.it; Via Cellolese 6; s/d €55/80; ☎) Exposed rafters and well-worn terracotta floors enhance the atmosphere at this good-value *locanda* (inn) on the floor above the **restaurant** (www.ristoranteilpino; ⊙ noon-2.30pm & 7-9.30pm Fri-Wed, closed Mon winter) of the same name. Rooms at the rear are dark – opt for front room number 11 if possible. The location near Sant'Agostino is relatively quiet despite being inside the historic walls.

Foresteria del Monastero di San Girolamo   HOSTEL €
(☑ 0577 94 05 73; www.monasterosangirolamo.it; Via Folgore da San Gimignano 26; s/tw/tr €35/60/90; Ⓟ) This is a first-rate backpacker choice. Run by friendly Benedictine Vallumbrosan nuns, it has basic but comfortable and impeccably clean rooms sleeping two to four people in single beds; all have attached bathrooms. Parking costs €2 per night, breakfast costs €3 and there are two rooms set up for guests in wheelchairs (a rarity in town). Sadly, no wi-fi.

If you don't have a reservation, arrive between 9am and noon or between 3.30pm and 5.30pm and ring the monastery bell (the one closer to the town centre), rather than the Foresteria one, which is never answered.

Al Pozzo dei Desideri APARTMENT €
(☑370 3102538, 0577 90 71 99; www.alpozzodei
desideri.it; Piazza della Cisterna 32; s €70 d €85-
120, tr €120; ✳🐕) Three rooms-with-a-view
(two over the countryside and one over
San Gimignano's main piazza) are on offer
in this 13th-century building; though well
worn, they are comfortable and relatively
well priced. There's no breakfast, but this
is town-centre Tuscany: there are plenty of
cafes close by.

Hotel L'Antico Pozzo BOUTIQUE HOTEL €€
(☑0577 94 20 14; www.anticopozzo.com; Via San
Matteo 87; s €90, d €120-140, ste €180; ⊘closed
mid-Jan–mid-Feb; ✳@🐕) The sense of heritage here is palpable: stone arches and
winding stairs lead to a handsome breakfast
salon, a sun-drenched rear courtyard and
room types named after Italian poets – those
in the Boccaccio category are cramped but
the Dante suites are – unsurprisingly – elegant and extremely desirable.

✘ Eating & Drinking

Many of San Gimignano's restaurants are
solely geared to the tourist trade and serve
mediocre food at inflated prices. Those that
have higher standards tend to focus on fresh
local produce, including the town's famous
zafferano (saffron). You can purchase meat,
vegetables, fish and takeaway food at the
Thursday morning market (Piazza delle Erbe;
⊘8am-1.30pm) held in and around Piazzas
Cisterna, Duomo and Erbe.

★ Gelateria Dondoli GELATO €
(☑0577 94 22 44; www.gelateriadipiazza.com; Piazza della Cisterna 4; gelato €2.20-6; ⊘9am-11pm
summer, to 7.30pm winter, closed mid-Dec–mid-
Feb) Think of it less as ice cream, more as
art. Former gelato world champion Sergio
Dondoli is a member of Italy's Ice Cream
World Championship team and among his
most famous creations are Crema di Santa
Fina (saffron cream) gelato and Vernaccia
sorbet. His creations are so delicious that
some devotees even sign up for a two-hour
gelato-making workshop (€400).

Dal Bertelli SANDWICHES €
(☑348 3181907; Via Capassi 30; panini €4-
6, glasses of wine €3; ⊘1-7pm Apr-Dec) The
Bertelli family has lived in San Gimignano since 1779, and its current patriarch
is fiercely proud of both his heritage and
his sandwiches. Salami, cheese, bread
and wine are sourced from local artisan-

producers and is sold in generous portions
in a determinedly un-gentrified space with
marble work surfaces, wooden shelves and
curious agricultural implements dangling
from stone walls.

★ Ristorante La Mandragola TUSCAN €€
(☑348 3023766; www.locandalamandragola.it; Via
Diaccetto 26; meals €35; ⊘noon-3pm & 7-10pm;
🐕) Nestled beneath the crumbling walls of
the *rocca*, La Mandragola (The Mandrake)
is deservedly popular – book ahead, especially if you're keen to dine in the gorgeous
courtyard. It's not exactly tourist-free, but
the welcome is genuine and the food is
delicious, especially the handmade pasta
dishes, which feature unusual sauces and
stuffings. The set menus (€15 to €25) offer
excellent value.

Locanda Sant'Agostino TUSCAN €€
(☑0577 94 31 41; Piazza Sant'Agostino 15; meals
€35, pizza €8-10; ⊘noon-3pm & 7-10pm Thu-Tue)
It's a bit like eating in an Italian grandmother's kitchen: there's a family vibe, knick-
knacks stack the shelves and the food is
tasty. Homemade *pici* (thick, hand-rolled
pasta) and tomato-slathered pizza are popular choices. In summer, seating on the piazza
is hotly contested.

Olivieri Bistrot MODERN ITALIAN €€
(☑0577 94 07 90; Via San Matteo 55; meals €30;
⊘11am-10pm Tue-Sun, closed Tue winter) There's
nothing traditional about this newcomer to
the San Gimignano dining scene. Located
on the major pedestrian spine, it has an attractive modern interior, friendly staff and
a menu incorporating plenty of twists on
Tuscan favourites. We love the homemade
bread served with good-quality olive oil, and
we like the fact that it serves *merende* (afternoon snacks) between meal services.

❶ Information

Tourist Office (☑0577 94 00 08; www.
sangimignano.com; Piazza del Duomo 1;
⊘10am-1pm & 3-7pm summer, 10am-1pm &
2-6pm winter)

❶ Getting There & Around

BUS

San Gimignano's **bus station** (Piazzale dei Martiri di Montemaggio) is next to the Carabinieri
(Police Station) at Porta San Giovanni. The tourist office sells bus tickets.

Florence (€6.80, 1¼ to two hours, 14 daily)
Change at Poggibonsi.

Siena (€6, one to 1½ hours, 10 daily Monday to Saturday)

Monteriggioni (€4.20, 55 minutes, eight daily Monday to Saturday)

Head to Colle di Val d'Elsa (€3.40, 35 minutes) to take a connecting bus to Volterra (€2.75, 50 minutes). These run four times daily from Monday to Saturday.

CAR & MOTORCYCLE

Parking is expensive. The cheapest option (€1.50/6 per hour/24 hours) is at Parcheggio Giubileo (P1) on the southern edge of town; the most convenient is at Parcheggio Montemaggio (P2) next to Porta San Giovanni (€2/20 per hour/24 hours).

TRAIN

The closest train station to San Gimignano is Poggibonsi (by bus €2.50, 30 minutes, frequent).

Volterra

POP 10,500

Volterra's well-preserved medieval ramparts give the windswept town a proud, forbidding air that author Stephenie Meyer deemed ideal for the discriminating tastes of the planet's principal vampire coven in her wildly popular *Twilight* series. Fortunately, the reality is considerably more welcoming, as a wander through the winding cobbled streets attests.

⊙ Sights

★ Museo Etrusco Guarnacci   MUSEUM
(☑ 0588 8 63 47; Via Don Minzoni 15; adult/reduced €8/6; ⊙ 9am-7pm summer, 10am-4.30pm winter) The vast collection of artefacts exhibited here makes this one of Italy's most impressive Etruscan collections. Found locally, they include some 600 funerary urns carved mainly from alabaster and tufa – perhaps the pick is the Urn of the Sposi, a strikingly realistic terracotta rendering of an elderly couple. The finds are displayed according to subject and era; the best examples (those dating from later periods) are on the 2nd and 3rd floors.

Cattedrale di Santa Maria Assunta   CATHEDRAL
(Duomo di Volterra; Piazza San Giovanni; ⊙ 8am-noon & 2-6pm summer, to 5pm winter) A handsome coffered ceiling is the most striking single feature of Volterra's *duomo*, which was built in the 12th and 13th centuries and remodelled in the 16th. The **Chapel of Our Lady of Sorrows**, on the first chapel to the left as you enter from Piazza San Giovanni, has two sculptures by Andrea della Robbia and a small fresco of the *Procession of the Magi* by Benozzo Gozzoli. In front of the *duomo*, is a 13th-century **baptistry** featuring a Sansovino font (1502).

Pinacoteca Comunale   GALLERY
(☑ 0588 8 75 80; Via dei Sarti 1; adult/reduced €8/6; ⊙ 9am-7pm summer, 10am-4.30pm winter) Local, Sienese and Florentine art holds sway in this modest collection in the Palazzo Minucci Solaini. Taddeo di Bartolo's *Madonna Enthroned with Child* (1411) is exquisite, while Rosso Fiorentino's *Deposition from the Cross* (1521) appears strikingly modern. The gallery shares an entrance with the Ecomuseo dell'Alabastro.

Ecomuseo dell'Alabastro   MUSEUM
(☑ 0588 8 63 47; Via dei Sarti 1; adult/reduced €8/6; ⊙ 9am-7pm summer, 10am-4.30pm winter) As befits a town that's hewn the precious material from nearby quarries since Etruscan times, Volterra is the proud possessor of an alabaster museum. It's an intriguing exploration of everything related to the rock, from production and working to commercialisation. Contemporary creations feature strongly; there are also choice examples from Etruscan times onwards, as well as a re-created artisan's workshop. The museum shares an entrance with the Pinacoteca Comunale.

Roman Theatre   ARCHAEOLOGICAL SITE
(☑ 0588 8 63 47; Via Francesco Ferrucci; adult/reduced €5/3; ⊙ 10.30am-5.30pm summer, 10am-4.30pm Sat & Sun winter) The grassy ranks of seating and towering columns of Italy's finest and best-preserved Roman theatre makes this a particularly evocative archaeological site. It was commissioned in the 1st century BC and could hold up to 2000 spectators. Today the *cavea* (sloping seating area), orchestra pit and stage are still clearly discernible. Note that there's also a great – and free – view of the theatre from Via Lungo Le Mura del Mandorlo.

᠅ Festivals & Events

Volterra AD 1398   CULTURAL
(www.volterra1398.it; day pass adult/reduced €10/6; ⊙ 3rd & 4th Sun Aug) The citizens of Volterra roll back the calendar some 600 years, take to the streets in period costume and celebrate all the fun of a medieval fair.

FLORENCE & TUSCANY VOLTERRA

Volterra

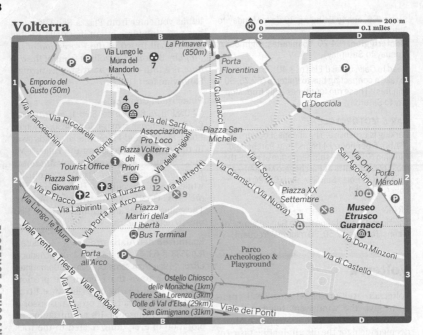

Volterra

◎ Top Sights

◎ Sights

✖ Eating

🛍 Shopping

🛏 Sleeping

★ Podere San Lorenzo
AGRITURISMO €

(☎0588 3 90 80; www.agriturismo-volterra.it; Via Allori 80; B&B d €100, 2-/3-/4-bed apt without breakfast €105-165; 🛜🐕) In this tranquil model of slow tourism you dip straight into a rural idyll. An alluring spring-fed swimming pool is located next to an enviable veggie garden; apartments sleep between two and four (some have private terraces) and rooms have a heritage feel. Gourmet dinners (per person €30 including wine) are served in a former 12th-century chapel.

Walking, biking and hands-on olive-oil production opportunities are available, as are cooking classes given by chef Jeta (per person €100 including dinner and wine). It's set on an olive farm some 3km outside Volterra and accessed via a narrow, almost hidden road that is signed off the SS68 (right-hand-side) as you drive up to the town from the direction of Siena, Florence and San Gimignano. Staff are happy to drop or pick up guests from a bus stop a short distance away, making trips to and from town easy.

★ La Primavera
B&B €

(☎0588 8 72 95; www.affittacamere-laprimave ra.com; Via Porta Diana 15; s/d/tr €50/75/100; ⊘mid-Apr–mid-Nov; 🅿🛜) This home-style B&B in a former alabaster workshop is a cosy affair, with a knick-knack-adorned lounge, pretty garden, polished parquet floors and meticulously presented bedrooms featuring soothing pastel colour schemes. It's in an excellent location just outside the city walls, a 10-minute walk from Piazza dei Priori. The free on-site parking is a definite plus. No credit cards.

Ostello Chiosco delle Monache HOSTEL€
(📞0588 8 66 13; www.ostellovolterra.it; Via del Teatro 4, Località San Girolamo; dm €20-22, B&B s/d €65/75; ☺mid-Mar–Oct; 🅿🙍🛜) This excellent hostel occupies a 13th-century monastery complete with a frescoed refectory where breakfast is served. Airy rooms overlook the cloisters and have good beds and bathrooms; dorms sleep up to six. Breakfast (for those in dorms) costs €6. It's 1km from the centre of Volterra. Local bus 1 from Piazza Martiri della Libertà stop, right outside the entrance (€1.10).

🍴 Eating & Drinking

⭐ L'Incontro CAFE€
(📞0588 8 05 00; Via Matteotti 18; panini €1.80 3.50, biscuits €1.50-2.50; ☺6am-midnight, closed Wed winter; 🛜) L'Incontro's rear *salone* is a top spot to grab a quick antipasto plate or *panino* for lunch, and its front bar area is always crowded with locals enjoying a coffee or *aperitivo*. The house-baked biscuits are noteworthy – try the nutty *brutti mai buoni* ('ugly but good') or their alabaster-coloured cousin, *ossi di morto* (bones of the dead).

La Carabaccia TUSCAN €€
(📞0588 8 62 39; www.lacarabacciavolterra.it; Piazza XX Settembre 4-5; meals €25; ☺12.30-2.30pm & 7.30-9pm Tue-Sat summer, 12.30-2.30pm Tue-Thu & Sun & 12.30-2.30pm & 7.30-9pm Fri & Sat winter; 🛜🍴) Mother and daughters Sara, Ilaria and Patrizia have put their heart and soul into this charming trattoria with a country style interior and attractive front terrace. Named after a humble Tuscan vegetable soup (one of the specialities of the house), it's the city's best lunch option. The small seasonal menu changes daily and always features fish on Fridays.

🛍 Shopping

Volterra's centuries-old heritage of alabaster mining and working ensures plenty of shops specialise in hand-carved alabaster items. The Società Cooperativa Artieri Alabastro (📞0588 8 61 35; www.artierialabastro.it; Piazza dei Priori 4-5; ☺10am-7pm) showcases the impressive work of 23 local alabaster artisans in a roomy town-centre

shop. To watch alabaster being carved, head to Alab'Arte (📞340 7187189, 340 9816908; www.alabarte.com; Via Orti di San Agostino 28; ☺10am-12.30pm & 3-6pm Mon-Sat).

For more information about artisans in Volterra, see www.arteinbottegavolterra.it.

Boutique del Tartufo FOOD
(📞348 7121883; www.boutiquedeltartufo.it; Vicolo Ormanni 1; ☺10.30am-7.30pm Wed-Mon summer, 10.30am-12.30pm & 2.30-6.30pm winter) Stefania Socchi's husband is a professional truffle hunter, and sources the tasty fungi that are used to produce the products sold in her shop just off Piazza XX Settembre. Purchase whole truffles or opt for honey, polenta, pasta, oil or pastes made or infused with them. You can also order a *panino* made with truffle paste or truffle-infused cheese.

Email trufflehunting@boutiquedeltartufo.it to enquire about the possibility of going on a truffle hunt with Stefania's husband and his dog – this is sometimes possible.

ℹ Information

Volterra's extremely efficient **tourist office** (📞0588 8 60 99; www.volterratur.it; Piazza dei Priori 19; ☺9.30am-1pm & 2-6pm) provides free maps, offers a free hotel-booking service and rents out an audioguide tour of the town (€5).

The equally helpful, volunteer-run **Associazione Pro Loco Volterra** (📞0588 8 61 50; www.provolterra.it; Piazza dei Priori 10; ☺9am-12.30pm & 3-6pm Mon-Sat, 9am-12.30pm Sun) gives tourist advice, sells bus tickets and provides **luggage storage** (2hr/extra hr/day €3/1/6).

ℹ Getting There & Around

BUS
Volterra's **bus station** (Piazza Martiri della Libertà) is in Piazza Martiri della Libertà. Buy tickets at *tabacchi* or the volunteer-run

---

ℹ CENT SAVER

The Volterra Card (adult/reduced/family €14/12/22, valid 72 hours) gives admission to Volterra's Museo Etrusco Guarnacci (p537), the Pinacoteca Comunale (p537), Ecomuseo dell'Alabastro (p537), Palazzo dei Priori (Piazza dei Priori; adult/reduced €5/3; ☺10.30am-5.30pm summer, 10am-4.30pm Sat & Sun winter), Acropoli and Teatro Romano. It's available at all of the museums.

WORTH A TRIP

A GARDEN ESCAPADE

Built in four stages between 1924 and 1939, the formal gardens of **La Foce** (📞0578 6 91 01; www.lafoce.com; Strada della Vittoria 61, off SP40; adult/child under 12yr €10/free; ⏰tour & entry 3pm, 4pm, 5pm & 6pm Wed, 11.30am, 3pm & 4.30pm Sat & Sun last weekend Mar–1 Nov) were commissioned by Anglo-American expat Iris Ortiga and her Italian husband Antonio. Designed by English architect Cecil Pinsent (1884–1963), who created many splendid gardens around Florence in the early decades of the 20th century, they surround a 16th-century former pilgrims' inn that was converted into a residence by the Ortigas after they purchased the La Foce estate in 1924. Visits are by 45-minute guided tour in English or Italian.

Post-guided tour, indulge in a long and lazy lunch al fresco at **Dopolavoro La Foce** (📞0578 75 40 25; www.dopolavorolafoce.it; Strada della Vittoria (SP40) 90; meals €28, sandwiches €4-5; ⏰8am-11pm; 🅿🛜🍷), a textbook exercise in Tuscan chic with its idyllic back garden for summer dining and on-trend menu featuring vegetarian pastas, burgers, flatbread sandwiches, craft beers and organic juices.

Associazione Pro Loco Volterra office. Note bus services are greatly reduced on Sundays.

CTT (📞800 570530; www.pisa.cttnord.it) buses connect Volterra with Pisa (€5.50, two hours, up to 10 Monday to Saturday) via Pontedera (€3.85).

You'll need to go to Colle di Val d'Elsa (€2.75, 50 minutes, four Monday to Saturday) to catch one of four connecting **Tiemme** (📞0577 20 41 11; www.tiemmespa.it) services (Monday to Saturday) to San Gimignano (€3.40, 35 minutes), Siena (€3.40, two hours) or Florence (€5.60, two hours).

CAR & MOTORCYCLE

A ZTL (Limited Traffic Zone) applies in the historic centre. The most convenient car park is beneath Piazza Martiri della Libertà (€1.80/15 per hour/day).

Val d'Orcia

The picturesque agricultural valley of Val d'Orcia is a Unesco World Heritage site, as is the town of Pienza on its northeastern edge. Its distinctive landscape features flat chalk plains, out of which rise almost conical hills topped with fortified settlements and magnificent abbeys that were once important staging points on the Via Francigena.

Montalcino

POP 5100

Known globally as the home of one of the world's great wines, Brunello di Montalcino, the attractive hilltop town of Montalcino has a remarkable number of *enoteche* lining its medieval streets, and is surrounded by hugely picturesque vineyards. There's history to explore too: the town's efforts to hold out against Florence even after Siena had fallen earned it the title 'the Republic of Siena in Montalcino', and there are many well-preserved medieval buildings within the historic city walls.

⊙ Sights

To save a couple of euros for your wine fund, purchase a combined ticket (adult/reduced €6/4.50) for entry to the Fortezza's ramparts and the Museo Civico e Diocesano d'Arte Sacra. These are available from the tourist office (p542).

Fortezza   HISTORIC BUILDING
(Piazzale Fortezza; courtyard free, ramparts adult/reduced €4/2; ⏰9am-8pm Apr-Oct, 10am-6pm Nov-Mar) This imposing 14th-century structure was expanded under the Medici dukes and now dominates Montalcino's skyline. You can sample and purchase local wines in its *enoteca* (p541) and also climb up to the fort's ramparts. Buy a ticket for the ramparts at the bar.

Museo Civico e
Diocesano d'Arte Sacra   MUSEUM
(📞0577 84 60 14; Via Ricasoli 31; adult/reduced €4.50/3; ⏰10am-1pm & 2-5.30pm Tue-Sun) Occupying the former convent of the neighbouring **Chiesa di Sant'Agostino**, this collection of religious art from the town and surrounding region includes a triptych by Duccio and a *Madonna and Child* by Simone Martini. Other artists represented include the Lorenzetti brothers, Giovanni di Paolo and Sano di Pietro.

★ Abbazia di Sant'Antimo
ABBEY

(☎ 0577 28 63 00; www.antimo.it; Castelnuovo dell'Abate; ⏰ 10am-1pm & 3-7pm summer, till 5pm winter) **FREE** The beautiful Romanesque Abbazia di Sant'Antimo lies in an isolated valley just below the village of Castelnuovo dell'Abate, 11km from Montalcino. Its Romanesque exterior features stone carvings of various fantastical animals. Inside, there it is an intense polychrome 13th-century *Madonna and Child* and a 12th-century Crucifixion above the main altar.

It's a two- to three-hour walk from Montalcino to the abbey. The route starts next to the police station near the main roundabout in town; many visitors choose to walk to the abbey and return by bus (€1.50) – check the timetable with the tourist office.

☆ Activities

★ Poggio Antico
WINE

(☎ restaurant 0577 84 92 00, 0577 84 80 44; www.poggioantico.com; Località Poggio Antico, off SP14; ⏰ cantina 10am-6pm, restaurant noon-2.30pm & 7-9.30pm Tue-Sun, closed Sun evening winter) Located 5km outside Montalcino on the road to Grosseto, Poggio Antico is a superb foodie one-stop hop. It makes award-winning wines (try its Brunello Altero or Riserva), conducts free cellar tours in Italian, English and German, offers paid tastings (approximately €25 depending on wines) and has an on-site restaurant (p542). Book tours in advance.

Enoteca La Fortezza
WINE

(☎ 0577 84 92 11; www.enotecalafortezza.com; Piazzale Fortezza; ⏰ 9am-8pm, reduced hours winter) The *enoteca* in Montalcino's medieval fortress offers a range of paid tastings, stocks a huge range of wine for sale and will ship overseas. Start with a tasting of two/three/five Brunellos (€9.50/13.50/19.50) and then consider graduating to two/three/five Riserva and Gran Selezioni vintages (€19/27/39). Designated drivers can limit themselves to one Rosso and one Brunello (€8).

🛏 Sleeping

★ Podere Brizio
AGRITURISMO €€

(☎ 0577 04 10 72; www.poderebrizio.it; Località Podere Brizio, near Tavernelle; r €170-220; ⏰ closed Dec-Easter; P ❄ 🛜 ⛱ 🐕) A huge amount of thought has gone into the design and construction of this splendid hotel on a wine estate 8km southwest of Montalcino. Room rates are remarkably restrained considering comfort and amenity levels in the spacious rooms and the wide array of facilities (huge swimming pool, restaurant, tennis court, spa). Breakfast is delicious but dinner is disappointing – dine elsewhere.

★ Hotel Vecchia Oliviera
HOTEL €€

(☎ 0577 84 60 28; www.vecchiaoliviera.com; Via Landi 1; s €85, d €150-170; P ❄ 🛜 ⛱) Chandeliers, elegant armchairs, polished wooden floors and rich rugs lend this converted oil mill a refined air. The 11 rooms have comfortable beds and satellite TV – opt for one in the superior category as these have great views (number 9 is best). The pool is in an attractive garden setting and the terrace has wraparound views.

✕ Eating & Drinking

★ Enoteca
Osteria Osticcio
WINE BAR

(☎ 0577 84 82 71; www.osticcio.it; Via Giacomo Matteotti 23; antipasto & cheese plates €7-17, meals €40; ⏰ noon-4pm & 7-11pm Fri-Wed, plus noon-7pm Thu summer) In a town overflowing with *enoteche,* this is definitely one of the best. Choose a bottle from the huge selection of Brunello and its more modest sibling Rosso di Montalcino to accompany a meal, or opt for a tasting of three Brunelli (€16) or a Brunello and Rosso (€9). The panoramic view, meanwhile, almost upstages it all.

DON'T MISS

THE PERFECT BASE
....

Sophisticated urban style melds with stupendous scenery at **La Bandita** (☎ 333 4046704; www.la-bandita.com; Podere La Bandita, Località La Foce; r €250-395, self-contained ste €550; ⏰ Apr-Dec; P ❄ @ 🛜 ⛱), a rural retreat in one of the most stunning sections of the Val d'Orcia. Owned and operated by a former NYC music executive and his travel-writer wife (non-Lonely Planet, we hasten to add), it offers spacious rooms, amenities galore (we love the Ortigia toiletries), wonderful meals and impressive levels of personalised service.

Put simply, this is the type of retreat we all fantasise about owning, but probably can't afford. It's also the perfect base for exploring nearby Pienza, Montepulciano and Montalcino.

IL LECCIO

Sometimes simple dishes are the hardest to perfect. And perfection is the only term to use when discussing **Il Leccio** (📞0577 84 41 75; www.illeccio.net; Via Costa Castellare 1/3, Sant'Angelo in Colle; meals €30, 4-course set menu €36; ⊗noon-2.30pm & 7-9pm Thu-Tue; 🖊) trattoria in Brunello heartland. Watching the chef make his way between his stove and kitchen garden to gather produce for each order puts a whole new spin on the word 'fresh', and both the results and the house Brunello are spectacular.

Be sure to order the *grande antipasti* (it's large enough for two to share) and always ask about daily specials.

Sant'Angelo in Colle is 10km southwest of Montalcino along Via del Sole (or 10km west of the Abbazia di Sant'Antimo along an unsealed but signed road through vineyards).

⭐ **Trattoria L'Angelo**   TUSCAN €
(📞0577 84 80 17; Via Ricasoli 9; meals €20; ⊗noon-3pm Wed-Mon Sep-Jun, noon-3pm & 7-11pm Wed-Mon Jul & Aug) We thought about keeping shtum about this place (everyone loves to keep a secret), but it seemed selfish not to share our love for its pasta dishes with our loyal readers. Be it vegetarian (ravioli stuffed with ricotta and truffles) or carnivorous (*pappardelle* with wild-boar sauce), the handmade *primi* (first courses) here are uniformly excellent. *Secondi* aren't as impressive.

Ristorante di Poggio Antico   MODERN ITALIAN €€€
(📞0577 84 92 00; www.poggioantico.com; Località Poggio Antico, off SP14; meals €50, tasting menus €50-80; ⊗noon-2.30pm & 7-9.30pm Tue-Sun, closed Sun dinner winter; 🖊) The fine-dining restaurant on this highly regarded wine estate (p541) is one of the best in the area, serving a menu of creative, contemporary Italian cuisine. Order à la carte, or opt for a tasting menu – there are four, one of which is vegetarian. You'll dine inside a converted barn building or on the scenic terrace.

ℹ Information

Montalcino's **tourist office** (📞0577 84 93 31; www.prolocomontalcino.com; Costa del Municipio 1; ⊗10am-1pm & 2-5.50pm, closed Mon winter) is just off the main square. It can supply free copies of the *Consorzio del Vino Brunello di Montalcino* map of wineries and also books cellar-door visits and winery accommodation.

ℹ Getting There & Away

Tiemme (📞0577 20 41 11; www.tiemmespa.it) buses run between Montalcino and Siena (€4.50, 75 minutes, six daily Monday to Saturday). The bus stop is near the Hotel Vecchia Oliviera.

Pienza

POP 2100

Once a sleepy hamlet, pretty Pienza was transformed when, in 1459, Pope Pius II began turning his home village into an ideal Renaissance town. The result is magnificent – the church, papal palace, town hall and accompanying buildings in and around Piazza Pio II went up in just three years and haven't been remodelled since. In 1996 Unesco added the town to its World Heritage list, citing the revolutionary vision of urban space. On weekends, Pienza draws big crowds; come midweek if you possibly can.

🅞 Sights

⭐ **Duomo**   CATHEDRAL
(Piazza Pio II; ⊗8.30am-1pm & 2.15-6.30pm) Pienza's *duomo* was built on the site of the Romanesque Chiesa di Santa Maria, of which little remains. The Renaissance church with its handsome travertine facade was commissioned by Pius II, who was so proud of the building that he issued a papal bull in 1462 forbidding any changes to it. The interior is a strange mix of Gothic and Renaissance styles and contains a superb marble tabernacle by Rossellino housing a relic of St Andrew the Apostle, Pienza's patron saint.

Piazza Pio II   PIAZZA
Stand in this magnificent square and spin 360 degrees. You've just taken in an overview of Pienza's major monuments. Gems of the Renaissance constructed in a mere three years between 1459 and 1462, they're arranged according to the urban design of Bernardo Rossellino, who applied the principles of Renaissance town planning devised by his mentor, Leon Battista Alberti.

★ **Palazzo Piccolomini** PALACE

(☑0577 28 63 00; www.palazzopiccolominipien za.it; Piazza Pio II; adult/reduced with guided tour €7/5; ⊙10am-6.30pm Tue-Sun summer, to 4.30pm winter, closed early Jan–mid-Feb & 2nd half Nov) This magnificent palace was the residence of Pope Pius II, and is considered Bernardo Rossellino's masterpiece. Built on the site of the pope's family houses, it features a fine courtyard, handsome staircase and the former papal apartments, which are filled with period furnishings and minor art. To the rear, a three-level loggia offers a spectacular panorama over the Val d'Orcia far below. Guided tours leave at 30-minute intervals but not between 12.30pm and 2pm; peeking into the courtyard is free.

🛏 Sleeping

★ **La Bandita Townhouse** BOUTIQUE HOTEL €€€

(☑0578 74 90 05; www.la-bandita.com/town house; Corso il Rossellino 111; r €350-395, ste €550; ❄@🅟) Aiming to provide their guests with a taste of Tuscan village life and give Pienza a world-class boutique hotel, La Bandita's American owners purchased and renovated a Renaissance-era convent close to Piazza Pio – the result is both sensitive and supremely stylish. Facilities include a communal lounge with honesty bar, spa (€50 per hour) and restaurant with a garden terrace.

🍴 Eating

Osteria Sette di Vino TUSCAN €

(☑0578 74 90 92; Piazza di Spagna 1; meals €16; ⊙noon-2.30pm & 7.30-10pm Thu-Tue) Known for its *zuppa di pane e fagioli* (bread and white-bean soup), *bruschette* and range of local *pecorino* (sheep's-milk cheese), this simple place is run by the exuberant Luciano, who is immortalised as Bacchus in a copy of Caravaggio's famous painting hanging above the main counter. There's a clutch of tables inside and a scattering outside – book ahead.

★ **Townhouse Caffè** MODERN ITALIAN €€

(☑0578 74 90 05; www.la-bandita.com/town house/the-restaurant; Via San Andrea 8; meals €40; ⊙noon-2.30pm Tue-Sun, 7-10pm daily early Apr–early Jan) The menu at this chic eatery is pared back in more ways than one: there are around four choices per course, presentation is minimalist and the emphasis is on the quality of the produce rather than clever culinary tricks – bravo! In summer, guests dine in an atmospheric medieval courtyard; in winter, the action moves into a two-room space with open kitchen.

★ **La Terrazza del Chiostro** MODERN ITALIAN €€€

(☑0578 74 81 83, 349 5676148; www.laterrazza delchiostro.it; Via del Balzello; meals €50; ⊙12.30-2.30pm & 7.30-10pm Thu-Tue, closed mid-Nov–mid-Mar, open Wed in high summer) Chef Alessandro Rossi was one of the youngest-ever recipients of an Italian Michelin star and clearly has ambitions to reprise his success here. Dining on the gorgeous terrace with its panoramic view is the stuff of which lasting travel memories are made, and the food has plenty of pizzazz – to fully appreciate it, opt for a set menu (four/six/nine courses €50/75/125).

ℹ Information

Tourist Office (☑0578 74 99 05; info.turismo@ comune.pienza.si.it; Corso il Rossellino 30; ⊙10.30am-1.30pm & 2.30-6pm Wed-Mon summer, 10am-4pm Sat & Sun winter)

ℹ Getting There & Away

Two **Tiemme** (☑0577 20 41 11; www.tiemme spa.it) buses run Monday to Saturday between Siena and Pienza (€5.50, 70 minutes) and nine travel to/from Montepulciano (€2.50, 20 minutes). The bus stops are just off Piazza Dante Alighieri. Buy tickets at one of the nearby bars.

OFF THE BEATEN TRACK

BAGNI SAN FILIPPO

Medieval pilgrims walking the Via Francigena from Canterbury to Rome loved pausing in this part of central Tuscany to enjoy a long therapeutic soak in its thermal springs. If you're keen to do the same, consider avoiding the famous thermal institute in Bagno Vignoni and instead head to the open-air cascades (⊙24hr) FREE in this tiny village 16km southwest of Pienza. You'll find them just uphill from Hotel Le Terme – follow signs to 'Fosso Bianco' down a lane for about 150m. Your destination is a series of mini pools, fed by hot, tumbling cascades of water. A free al fresco spa.

Montepulciano

POP 14,100

Exploring the medieval town of Montepulciano, perched on a reclaimed narrow ridge of volcanic rock, will push your quadriceps to failure point. When this happens, self-medicate with a generous pour of the highly reputed Vino Nobile while also drinking in the spectacular views over the Val di Chiana and Val d'Orcia.

◎ Sights

★ Museo Civico & Pinocoteca Crociani
ART GALLERY, MUSEUM

(☑ 0578 71 73 00; www.museocivicomonte pulciano.it; Via Ricci 10; adult/reduced €5/3; ☺ 10.30am-6.30pm Wed-Mon summer, reduced hours winter) It was a curatorial dream come true: in 2011 a painting in the collection of this modest art gallery was attributed to Caravaggio. The work, *Portrait of a Man*, is thought to portray Cardinal Scipione Borghese, the artist's patron. It's now accompanied by a touchscreen interpretation that allows you to explore details of the painting, its restoration and diagnostic attribution. Other works here include two terracottas by Andrea Della Robbia and Domenico Beccafumi's painting of the town's patron saint, Agnese.

Palazzo Comunale
PALACE

(Piazza Grande; terrace & tower adult/reduced €5/2.50, terrace only €2.50; ☺ 10am-6pm) Built in the 14th century in Gothic style and remodelled in the 15th century by Michelozzo, the Palazzo Comunale still functions as Montepulciano's town hall. Head up the 67 narrow stairs to the tower to enjoy extraordinary views – you'll see as far as Pienza, Montalcino and even, on a clear day, Siena.

🏃 Activities

★ Enoliteca Consortile
WINE

(www.consorziovinonobile.it; Fortezza di Montepulciano, Via San Donato 21; ☺ 11am-5pm Mon-Thu, noon-7pm Fri & Sat) Operated by Montepulciano's consortium of local wine producers, this recently opened showcase of Vino Nobile on the ground floor of the Medicean fortress has a modern tasting room offering over 70 wines for tasting and purchase. Buy a €10 or €15 card, use it to pour the tipples of your choice and direct your own tasting.

★ Cantina de' Ricci
WINE

(☑ 0578 75 71 66; www.cantinadericci.it; Via Ricci 11; per tasting €3; ☺ 10.30am-7pm mid-Mar–early Jan, Sat & Sun only early Jan–mid-Mar) **FREE** The most evocative of Montepulciano's wine cellars, this *cantina* lies at the foot of a steep winding staircase in the Renaissance-era **Palazzo Ricci** (www.palazzoricci. com; Via Ricci 9-11). Immense vaulted stone encasements surround two-storey-high barrels. Dimly lit and hushed, it's like a cathedral of wine. Entry is free, but tastings are charged.

★ Palazzo Vecchio Winery
WINE

(☑ 0578 72 41 70; palazzovecchio@vinonobile. it; Via Terra Rossa 5, Valiano) Idyllic is the first word that comes to mind when describing this wine estate. Its large 14th-century stone farmhouse is surrounded by fruit trees, the winery is in converted outbuildings, and 25 hectares of vineyards planted with Sangiovese, Canaiolo and Mammolo grapes cascade down the hillsides. Visits are by reservation only; tastings cost €20 and a five-course lunch with wine €80.

You'll find the estate atop a hill outside the town of Valiano, 15km northeast of Montepulciano. The excellent La Dogana (p545) *enoteca,* part of the same estate, is nearby.

👉 Tours

Strada del Vino Nobile di Montepulciano e dei Sapori della Valdichianna Senese
TOURS

(☑ 0578 75 78 12; www.stradavinonobile.it; Piazza Grande 7; ☺ 9.30am-1.30pm & 2.30-6pm Mon-Fri, 10am-1pm & 2-5pm Sat, 10am-1pm Sun) This office organises a huge range of tours and courses, including cooking courses (€59 to €90), vineyard tours (€49 to €115) and walking tours in the vineyards culminating in a wine tasting (€29 to €49). Book in advance online or at its information office on Piazza Grande.

🎊 Festivals & Events

Bravio delle Botti
CULTURAL

(www.braviodellebotti.com; ☺ Aug) Members of Montepulciano's eight *contrade* (districts) push 80kg wine barrels uphill in this race held on the last Sunday in August. There are also Renaissance-themed celebrations during the week before.

🛏 Sleeping

Camere Bellavista
HOTEL €

(📞0578 75 73 48; Via Ricci 25; r €90; 🅿🛜) As this excellent budget hotel is four storeys tall and sits on the edge of the old town, the views live up to its name. The styling is heritage rustic with exposed beams, hefty wooden furniture, brass bedsteads and smart new bathrooms. The owner isn't resident, so phone ahead to be met with the key. No breakfast; cash only.

★Locanda San Francesco
B&B €€

(📞0578 75 87 25; www.locandasanfrancesco.it; Piazza San Francesco 3; r €200-260; 🅿❄@🛜) There's only one downside to this four-room luxury B&B: once you check in, you might never want to leave. The feel is elegant but also homey: refined furnishings meet well-stocked bookshelves; restrained fabrics are teamed with fluffy bathrobes. The best room has superb views over the Val d'Orcia on one side and Val di Chiana on the other.

🍴 Eating

★La Dogana
MODERN ITALIAN €€

(📞339 5405196; Strada Lauretana Sud 75, Valiano; meals €32, cheese & salumi platter €9; ⏱10am-10.30pm Wed-Sun, closed Jan) Chef and cookbook writer Sunshine Manitto presides over the kitchen of this *enoteca* overlooking the Palazzo Vecchio Winery. Windows frame vistas of vines and cypress trees, but the best seats in the house are on the grassed rear terrace. The menu showcases seasonal produce and offers both snacks and full meals.

★La Grotta
RISTORANTE €€€

(📞0578 75 74 79; www.lagrottamontepulciano.it; Via di San Biagio 15; meals €40; ⏱12.30-2pm & 7.30-10pm Thu-Tue, closed mid-Jan–mid-Mar) The dishes here may be traditional, but their flavour and presentation is refined – artfully arranged Parmesan shavings and sprigs of herbs crown delicate towers of pasta, vegetables and meat. The service is exemplary and the courtyard garden divine. It's just below town, overlooking the Renaissance splendour of the Chiesa di San Biago.

🍷 Drinking & Nightlife

★Caffè Poliziano
CAFE

(📞0578 75 86 15; www.caffepoliziano.it; Via di Voltaia 27; ⏱7am-8pm Mon-Fri, to 11pm Sat, to 9pm Sun; 🛜) Established as a cafe in 1868, Poliziano was lovingly restored to its original form 20 years ago and is the town's favourite cafe. A sit-down coffee is expensive, but is worth the outlay – especially if you score one of the tiny, precipitous balcony tables.

★E Lucevan Le Stelle
WINE BAR

(📞0578 75 87 25; www.lucevanlestelle.it; Piazza San Francesco 5; ⏱11.30am-11.30pm mid-Mar–Dec; 🛜) The decked terrace of this ultra-friendly *osteria* is the top spot in Montepulciano to watch the sun go down. Inside, squishy sofas, modern art and jazz on the sound system give the place a chilled-out vibe. Its food (antipasto plates €4.50 to €8, *piadine* €6, pasta €6.50 to €9) isn't a strength – stick to a glass or two of Nobile (€5 to €7).

ℹ Information

Tourist Office (📞0578 75 73 41; www.prolocomontepulciano.it; Piazza Don Minzoni 1; ⏱9am-1pm)

ℹ Getting There & Around

BUS

The Montepulciano **bus station** (Piazzo Pietro Nenni) is next to Car Park No 5. **Tiemme** (📞0577 20 41 11; www.tiemmespa.it) runs four buses daily to/from Siena's train station (€6.60, 1½ hours) stopping at Pienza (€2.50, 20 minutes) en route.

CAR & MOTORCYCLE

A 24-hour ZTL (Limited Traffic Zone) applies in the historic centre between May and September; in October and April it applies from 8am to 8pm, and from November to March it applies from 8am to 5pm. Check whether your hotel can supply a permit. Otherwise, there are plenty of paid car parks circling the historic centre.

SOUTHERN TUSCANY

With its landscape of dramatic coastlines, mysterious Etruscan sites and medieval hilltop villages, this little-visited pocket of Tuscany offers contrasts galore. It's a region created for the Italy connoisseur.

Massa Marittima

POP 8400

Drawcards at this tranquil hill town include an eccentric yet endearing jumble of museums, an extremely handsome central piazza and largely intact medieval streets that are blessedly bereft of tour groups.

Briefly under Pisan domination, Massa Marittima became an independent *comune* (city-state) in 1225 but was swallowed up by Siena a century later. A plague in 1348 was followed by the decline of the region's lucrative mining industry, reducing the town to the brink of extinction, a situation made even worse by the prevalence of malaria in surrounding marshlands. Fortunately, the draining of marshes in the 18th century and the re-establishment of mining shortly afterwards brought it back to life.

The town is divided into three districts: the Città Vecchia (Old Town), Città Nuova (New Town) and Borgo (Borough). Entry to the Città Vecchia is via the massive Arco Senese.

◎ Sights

A cumulative ticket (€10) gives access to all of Massa Marittima's museums and monuments.

★ Cattedrale di San Cerbone   CATHEDRAL
(Piazza Garibaldi; ◷8am-noon & 3-7pm summer, to 6pm winter) Presiding over photogenic Piazza Garibaldi (aka Piazza Duomo), Massa Marittima's asymmetrically positioned 13th-century *duomo* is dedicated to St Cerbonius, the town's patron saint, who's always depicted surrounded by a flock of geese. Inside, don't miss the free-standing *Maestà* (Madonna and Child enthroned in majesty; 1316), attributed by some experts to Duccio di Buoninsegna.

★ Museo di Arte Sacra   MUSEUM
(Complesso Museale di San Pietro all'Orto; ☑0566 90 22 89; www.museiartesacra.net; Corso Diaz 36; adult/reduced €5/3; ◷10am-1pm & 4-7pm Tue-Sun summer, 11am-1pm & 3-5pm Tue-Sun winter) In the former monastery of San Pietro all'Orto, this museum houses a splendid *Maestà* (c 1335–37) by Ambrogio Lorenzetti as well as sculptures by Giovanni Pisano that originally adorned the facade of the *duomo*. The collection of primitive grey alabaster bas-reliefs also came from the *duomo*, but originally date from an earlier era.

★ Torre del Candeliere   TOWER
(Candlestick Tower; Piazza Matteotti; adult/reduced €3/2; ◷10.30am-1.30pm & 3-6pm Tue-Sun summer, 11am-1pm & 2.30-4.30pm Tue-Sun winter) Climb to the top of this 13th-century, 74m-high tower for stupendous views over the old town.

⌷ Sleeping

★ Casa della Pia   B&B €
(☑333 9777614; www.casadellapia.eu; Via della Libertà 15; r €95, apt per week €400; ☏) The marital home of tragic Pia dei Tolomei, immortalised in Dante's *Divine Comedy*, this one-room B&B in a 13th-century *palazzo* just off Piazza Garibaldi is run by the charming Costanza, who goes out of her way to make guests feel at home. The room is spacious and well equipped, providing extremely comfortable accommodation.

★ Conti di San Bonifacio   AGRITURISMO €€€
(☑0566 8 00 06; www.contidisanbonifacio.com; Località Casteani 1; r €380-450, ste €580-830; ℗☀☏☲) There are plenty of wine resorts in Tuscany, but few – if any – are this impressive. Accommodation is in elegant rooms and super-luxurious suites, but guests spend little time in them, instead opting to laze by the saltwater swimming pool, dine in the excellent restaurant, relax on the vineyard-facing terrace or sign up for one of the many activities on offer.

The resort is on the wine estate, 18km southeast of Massa Marittima.

✕ Eating & Drinking

★ Taverna del Vecchio Borgo   TUSCAN €€
(☑0566 90 21 67; taverna.vecchioborgo@libero.it; Via Norma Parenti 12; meals €32; ◷7.30-10pm Tue-Sun summer, 7.30-10pm Tue-Sat, 12.30-2.30pm Sun winter) Massa's best restaurant is as atmospheric as it is delicious. You'll sit in a dimly lit brick-vaulted wine cellar dating from the 16th century and dine on top-quality beef grilled on the wood-fired oven, or unusual dishes such as *testaroli* pasta with a pistachio sauce. The set four-course menu (€30) is a steal.

★ Il Bacchino   WINE BAR
(☑0566 94 02 29; Via Moncini 8; ◷10am-1pm & 4-7.30pm, closed Mon Nov-Feb) Owner Magdy Lamei may not be a local (he's from Cairo), but it would be hard to find anyone else as knowledgeable and passionate about local artisanal produce. Come to this classy *enoteca* he runs with his wife, Monica, to taste and buy local wines (€3.50 to €25 per glass), or to stock up on picnic provisions including jams, cheese and cured meats.

ⓘ Information

Tourist Office (☑0566 90 65 54; www.turismo
massamarittima.it; Via Todini 3; ⊙10am-1pm
& 3-5pm Wed-Fri, to 6pm Sat & Sun Apr-Jun &
Oct, 10am-1pm & 4-7pm Wed-Mon Jul & Aug,
10am-1pm & 3-5pm Fri-Mon Nov-Mar)

ⓘ Getting There & Away

BUS

The bus station is near the hospital on Piazza
del Risorgimento, 1km down the hill from Piazza
Garibaldi. **Tiemme** (www.tiemmespa.it) operates two buses to Grosseto (€5.20, 80 minutes,
Monday to Saturday) and one to Siena (€6, two
hours, Monday to Saturday) at 7.10am. To get to
Volterra you'll need to change at Monterotondo
Marittimo. **Massa Veternensis** (Piazza Garibaldi
18) sells bus and train tickets.

CAR & MOTORCYCLE

There's a convenient car park (€1 per hour
during the day, free at night) close to Piazza
Garibaldi; head up the hill and you'll find it on
your left.

TRAIN

The nearest train station is in Follonica, 22km
southwest of Massa; it's served by a regular
shuttle bus (€2.60, 25 minutes, 10 daily).

Città del Tufo

The picturesque towns of Pitigliano, Sovana
and Sorano form a triangle enclosing a dramatic landscape where local buildings have
been constructed from the volcanic porous
rock called tufo since Etruscan times. This
area is known as the Città del Tufo (City of
the Tufo) or, less commonly, the Paese del
Tufo (Land of the Tufo).

Pitigliano

POP 3800

Organically sprouting from a volcanic
rocky outcrop towering over the surrounding country, this spectacularly sited hilltop
town is surrounded by gorges on three sides,
constituting a natural bastion completed to
the east by a fort. Within the town, twisting
stairways disappear around corners, cobbled alleys bend tantalisingly out of sight
beneath graceful arches, and reminders of
the town's once-considerable Jewish community remain in the form of a 16th-century
synagogue and a unique Jewish-flavoured
local cuisine.

WORTH A TRIP

SATURNIA HOT SPRINGS

The sulphurous thermal baths at **Terme
di Saturnia** (☑0564 60 01 11; www.
termedisaturnia.it; day €25, after 2pm €20;
⊙9.30am-7pm summer, to 5pm winter) are
some 2.5km downhill from the village
of the same name, which is 35km from
Sorano and 26km from Pitigliano. You
can happily replicate the Romans and
spend a whole day indulging in hot pools
and spa treatments at this luxury resort,
or take the econo-bather option and
track down the springs themselves. Just
south of the Terme di Saturnia turn-
off, look for the telltale sign of bathers'
cars parked beside the road (or spy the
Cascate del Gorello signs), then forage
down the dirt path until you find this
cluster of gratis, open-air pools, where
temperatures are a constant 37.5°C.
Alternatively, overnight in the **Hotel
Saturno Fonte Pura** (☑0564 60 13 13;
www.hotelsaturnofontepura.com; Località
la Croce; r from €110; P❉☂☎), a spa
resort with its own thermal pool overlooking the terme.

◎ Sights & Activities

For Etruscan heritage savings, buy the combined ticket (adult/reduced €6/3) giving
entry to the Museo Civico Archeologico
di Pitigliano and the Museo Archeologico
all'Aperto 'Alberto Manzi' outside town.

**Museo Civico
Archeologico di Pitigliano**   MUSEUM
(☑0564 61 40 67; Piazza della Fortezza; adult/
reduced €3/2; ⊙10am-7pm Mon, Thu & Fri, to
6pm Sat & Sun Jun-Aug, 10am-5pm Sat & Sun
Easter-May) Head up the stone stairs to this
small but well-run museum, which has
rich displays of finds from local Etruscan
sites. Highlights include some huge intact
bucchero (black earthenware pottery) urns
dating from the 6th century BC and a collection of charming pinkish-cream clay oil
containers in the form of small deer.

La Piccola Gerusalemme   MUSEUM
(Little Jerusalem; ☑0564 61 42 30; www.lapicco
lagerusalemme.it; Vicolo Manin 30; adult/reduced
€5/4; ⊙10am-1pm & 2.30-6pm Sun-Fri summer,
10am-noon & 3-5pm Sun-Fri winter) Head down
Via Zuccarelli and turn left at a sign indicating 'La Piccola Gerusalemme' to visit

VIE CAVE

There are at least 15 *vie cave* (sunken roads) hewn out of tufo in the valleys below Pitigliano. These enormous passages – up to 20m deep and 3m wide – are popularly believed to be sacred routes linking Etruscan necropolises and other religious sites. A more mundane explanation is that these strange ancient corridors were used to move livestock or as some kind of defence, allowing people to flit from village to village unseen. The **Torciata di San Giuseppe** (19 March) is a procession through the Via Cava di San Giuseppe marking the end of winter.

Two particularly good examples of *vie cave*, the **Via Cava di Fratenuti** and the **Via Cava di San Giuseppe**, are found 500m west of Pitigliano on the road to Sovana. Fratenuti has high vertical walls and Etruscan markings, and San Giuseppe passes the **Fontana dell'Olmo**, a fountain carved out of solid rock. From it stares the sculpted head of Bacchus, the god of wine and fertility.

There's a fine **walk** from Pitigliano to Sovana (8km) that incorporates parts of the *vie cave*. For a description and map, go to www.trekking.it and download the pdf in the Maremma section. There's also an enjoyable 2km walk from the small stone bridge in the gorge below Sorano along the **Via Cava San Rocco** to the **Necropoli di San Rocco**, another Etruscan burial site.

The open-air **Museo Archeologico all'Aperto 'Alberto Manzi'** (Alberto Manzi Open-Air Archaeology Museum; ☑ 0564 61 40 67; Strada Provinciale 127 Pantano, off SS74; adult/reduced €4/2; ☺10am-7pm Tue-Sun Apr-Oct), south of Pitigliano on the road to Saturnia, contains sections of *vie cave* and several necropolises.

this fascinating time capsule of Pitigliano's rich but sadly near-extinct Jewish culture. It incorporates a tiny, richly adorned synagogue (established in 1598 and one of only five in Tuscany), ritual bath, kosher butcher, bakery, wine cellar and dyeing workshops.

🛏 Sleeping & Eating

Il Tufo Rosa PENSION €
(☑ 333 9701148, 0564 61 70 19; www.iltuforosa.com; Piazza Petruccioli 97-101; s/d €48/75; ❋🐾) There's an old-fashioned feel to these appealing bedrooms which are set in a bastion of the fortress on Piazza Petruccioli, on the edge of the old town. Each room is named after an Aldobrandeschi, Orsini or Medici countess and features silky throws, dainty cushions and filmy fabrics. No breakfast, and air-con is only available in a few rooms.

★**La Casa Degli Archi** APARTMENT €€
(☑ 349 4986298; www.lacasadegliarchi.com; Vicolo Antico Pretorio 22; q apt €338) In our view, this is one of the best apartment rentals in Tuscany. At the edge of the town, perched on the edge of a picturesque precipice, it has a modern kitchen/laundry, two good-sized bedrooms and two attractive lounges with antique furnishings, comfy couches and open fireplaces. Views from a tiny balcony and the second lounge are simply spectacular.

★**Il Tufo Allegro** TUSCAN €€
(☑ 0564 61 61 92; www.iltufoallegro.com; Vicolo della Costituzione 5; meals €42; ☺noon-2.30pm & 7.30-9.30pm Wed-Sun) The aromas emanating from the kitchen door off Via Zuccarelli should be enough to draw you down the stairs and into the cosy dining rooms, which are carved out of tufo. Chef Domenico Pichini's menu ranges from traditional to modern and all of his creations rely heavily on local produce for inspiration. It's near La Piccola Gerusalemme.

❶ Information

The **tourist office** (☑ 0564 61 71 11; www.comune.pitigliano.gr.it; Piazza Garibaldi 12; ☺10am-12.30pm & 3-5.30pm Tue-Sat, 10am-12.30pm Sun summer, 10am-12.30pm & 3-5.30pm Sat, 10am-12.30pm Sun winter) is in the piazza just inside the Old City's main gate.

❶ Getting There & Away

Tiemme (www.tiemmespa.it) buses leave from Via Santa Chiara, just off Piazza Petruccioli. They tend to operate Monday to Saturday only; buy tickets at Bar Guastini in Piazza Petruccioli. Services include the following:

Grosseto (€7.90, two hours, three daily)

Siena (€10.10, three hours, one daily)

Sorano (€1.50, 10 to 20 minutes, one to three daily)

Sovana (€1.50, 10 to 20 minutes, two daily)

Sovana

The main attractions at this postcard-pretty town are a cobbled main street that dates from Roman times, two austerely beautiful Romanesque churches and a museum showcasing a collection of ancient gold coins.

Sights

★ **Parco Archeologico 'Città del Tufo'** ARCHAEOLOGICAL SITE
(Necropoli di Sovana; www.leviecave.it; €5; ⊙10am-7pm summer, to 6pm Oct, to 5pm Sat & Sun Nov-Mar) At Tuscany's most significant Etruscan tombs, 1.5km east of town, signs in Italian and English guide you around four elaborate burial sites. The headline exhibit is the **Tomba Ildebranda**, named after Gregory VII, which preserves traces of its carved columns and stairs. The **Tomba dei Demoni Alati** (Tomb of the Winged Demons) features a recumbent headless terracotta figure.

Sleeping & Eating

Sovana Hotel & Resort HOTEL €€
(☑3385 802977, 0564 61 70 30; www.sovanahotel.it; Via del Duomo 66; s €110, d €130 140; [P][❄][☷][❄]) The huge garden surrounding this hotel is nothing less than extraordinary, featuring a maze, Etruscan ruin, olive grove and swimming pool grand enough for a Roman emperor's villa. Rooms aren't quite as swish, but they are perfectly comfortable and offer good value. There's also a bar, restaurant and communal lounge with open fire. Low-season prices are considerably lower.

★ **Vino al Vino** TUSCAN €
(☑0564 61 71 08; vinoalvino@virgilio.it; Via del Duomo 10; cheese & salumi plates €14; ⊙10.30am-9pm Wed Mon mid-Mar–Dec, 10.30am-9pm Sat & Sun Jan–mid-Mar) Mellow jazz plays on the soundtrack, art adorns every wall and the vibe is friendly at this hybrid cafe and *enoteca* on Sovana's main street. The speciality-roast coffee is good; cakes (sourced in Pitigliano) are even better. At lunch or dinner, glasses of wine and tasting plates of local produce reign supreme.

Information

The extremely helpful **tourist office** (☑0564 61 40 74; ⊙10am-1pm & 3-7pm Wed-Mon mid-Mar-Oct, 10am-1pm & 2-5pm Sat & Sun Nov & Dec) is in the Palazzo Pretorio on the main piazza.

Getting There & Away

Between Monday and Saturday, **Tiemme** (www.tiemmespa.it) buses (www.tiemmespa.it) travel to/from Pitigliano (€1.50, 10 to 20 minutes, two daily) and Sorano (€1.50, 15 minutes, once or twice daily).

Sorano

POP 3400

Sorano's setting is truly dramatic – sitting astride a rocky outcrop, its weatherworn stone houses are built along a ridge overlooking the Lente river and gorge. Below the ridgeline are *cantine* (cellars) dug out of tufo, as well as a tantalising series of terraced gardens, many part-hidden from public view.

Sights & Activities

Fortezza Orsini FORT
(☑0564 63 34 24; adult/reduced €4/2; ⊙10am-1pm & 3-7pm Tue-Sun summer, 10am-1pm & 2-5pm Sat & Sun Nov & Dec) Work on this massive fortress started in the 11th century. Today it still stands sentinel over the town, its sturdy walls linking two bastions surrounded by a dry moat. The highlight of any visit is undoubtedly a guided tour of the evocative **subterranean passages** (⊙11am, 3.30pm, 4.30pm & 5.30pm summer, 11am & 3pm Nov & Dec), which are noticeably chilly even in the height of the Tuscan summer.

Area Archeologica di Vitozza ARCHAEOLOGICAL SITE
(⊙10am-dusk) [FREE] More than 200 caves pepper a high rock ridge here, making it one of the largest troglodyte dwellings in Italy. The complex was first inhabited in prehistoric times. To explore the site, you'll need two hours and sturdy walking shoes. It's 4km due east of Sorano; there's a signed walking path between Sorano and the site.

Sleeping & Eating

★ **Sant'Egle** AGRITURISMO €€
(☑329 4250285; www.santegle.it; Case Sparse Sant'Egle 18; s €90, d €112-125, ste €154-171; ⊙closed mid-Jan–mid-Mar; [P][❄][☷][❄]) ✔ If only all accommodation could be as sustainable and comfortable as this. Set on an organic multi-crop farm, it offers individually designed bedrooms in a carefully renovated 17th-century customs house and a wonderfully tranquil garden environment in which to de-stress and relax.

Almost everything here is organic, from the bedding and the toiletries (made with

WORTH A TRIP

PARCO REGIONALE DELLA MAREMMA

The spectacular **Parco Regionale della Maremma** (☑ 0564 39 32 38; www.parco-maremma.it; adult/reduced from €6/4; ⊙ 8.30am-4pm Apr–mid-Jun, to 6pm mid-Jun–Oct, to 2pm Nov-Mar) incorporates the Uccellina Mountain Range, a 600-hectare pine forest, marshy plains and 20km of unspoiled coast. Park access is limited to 13 signed walking trails ranging in length from 2.5km to 13km; the most popular is A2 ('Le Torri'), a 5.8km walk to the beach. From mid-June to mid-September you can only visit on a guided tour because of possible bushfires; call ahead to check times. An entry fee is paid at the main, Alberese **visitor centre** (☑ 0564 39 32 38; Via del Bersagliere 7-9, Alberese; ⊙ 8am-6pm mid-Jun–mid-Sep, to 4pm mid-Sep–mid-Nov, to 2pm mid-Nov–mid-Jun).

There are also **bicycle, horse-riding** and **canoe trails** within the park; the visitor centre can supply plenty of information about these.

extra virgin olive oil) to the gourmet breakfast buffet. There's also a tiny bio-pool, a yoga pavilion and two al fresco hot tubs.

Ristorante Fidalma   TUSCAN €€
(☑ 0564 63 30 56; www.ristorantefidalma.com; Piazza Busatti 5; meals €26; ⊙ 12.30-3.30pm & 7.30-10.30pm Thu-Tue; ❋) There's a lot to like at this barn-like restaurant just off Sorano's main piazza. The menu is dominated by home-style Maremmese dishes (expect lots of meat), the pasta is handmade by nonna, and the family members waiting on tables are incredibly friendly. There's even a well-priced set menu of two courses, *contorno* (side dish) and a coffee for €20.

❶ Information

Tourist Office (☑ 0564 63 30 99; Fortezza; ⊙ 10am-1pm & 3-7pm Thu-Sun mid-Mar–Oct, 10am-1pm & 2-5pm Sat & Sun Nov-Dec)

❶ Getting There & Away

From Monday to Saturday, **Tiemme** (www.tiemme spa.it) operates services to/from Pitigliano (€1.50, 10 to 20 minutes, one to three daily) and Sovana (€1.50, 15 minutes, two daily).

CENTRAL COAST & ELBA

Despite possessing the types of landscapes that dreams are made of, much of this part of Tuscany feels far away from well-beaten tourist trails.

Livorno

POP 159,200

Tuscany's third-largest city is a quintessential port town with a colourful history and cosmopolitan heritage. Declared a free port in the 17th century, Livorno (Leghorn in English) attracted traders from across the globe, who brought with them new customs and habits, exotic goods, slaves and foreign forms of worship. The result was a city famed throughout Europe for its multiculturalism. Today its seafood is the best on the Tyrrhenian coast, its shabby historic quarter threaded with Venetian-style canals is full of character, and its elegant belle-époque buildings offer evocative reminders of a prosperous past. An easy train trip from Florence, Pisa and Rome, it makes an understated but undeniably worthwhile stop on any Tuscan itinerary.

◉ Sights & Activities

The city's beach clubs open from May to September.

Piccola Venezia   AREA
Piccola Venezia (Little Venice) is a tangle of small canals built during the 17th century using Venetian methods of reclaiming land from the sea. At its heart sits the remains of the Medici-era **Fortezza Nuova** (New Fort; ⊙ 24hr) FREE. Canals link this with the slightly older waterfront **Fortezza Vecchia** (Old Fort; infofortezzavecchia@portolivorno. it; ⊙ 9am-7pm Tue-Sun) FREE. The waterways can be explored by canal-side footpaths but a boat tour is the best way to see its shabby-chic panoramas of faded, peeling apartments draped with brightly coloured washing, interspersed with waterside cafes and bars.

Terrazza Mascagni   STREET
(Viale Italia; ⊙ 24hr) FREE No trip to Livorno is complete without a stroll along this seafront terrace with its dramatic black-and-white chessboard-style pavement. When it was built in the 1920s, it was called Terrazza Ciano after the leader of the Livorno fascist movement; it now bears the name of Livorno-

born opera composer Pietro Mascagni (1863–1945).

Livorno in Battello

BOATING

(☑ 333 1573372; www.livornoinbattello.it; adult/child €12/5) Three local companies offer daily one-hour guided tours of Livorno's Medicean waterways by boat, but this is the only one that operates year-round (up to four departures daily in summer, limited departures December to February). Boats leave from Scali Finocchietti in summer and from Piazza Giuseppe Micheli in winter. Buy tickets and check schedules/departure points at the tourist office.

Acquario di Livorno

AQUARIUM

(☑ 0586 26 91 11; www.acquariodilivorno.com; Piazzale Mascagni 1; adult/child €14/8; ⏱ 10am-6pm Apr-Jun & Sep, to 7.30pm Jul & Aug, tour 4pm) The main attraction here is a 45-minute 'Behind the Tanks' tour that visits the aquarium's kitchen, laboratory and tanks. Offered daily, it is unexpectedly fascinating (who knew that a turtle eats kilos of salad every day?). Front of house, the stars of the show are reef sharks, seahorses and huge green sea turtles Ari and Cuba. The Napoleon fish with their prominent and familiar profiles provide a laugh. Upstairs there's a reptile area featuring a chameleon and gloriously green iguana.

🛏 Sleeping

Camping Miramare

CAMPGROUND €

(☑ 0586 58 04 02; www.campingmiramare.it; Via del Littorale 220; camping 2 people, car & tent €76; P🛜📶🏖) Be it tent pitch beneath trees or deluxe version with wooden terrace and sunloungers on the stony beach, this campground – open year-round thanks to its village of mobile homes, maxi caravans and bungalows – has it all. Rates outside of summer are at least 50% lower. Find the site 8km south of town in Antignano, near Montenero.

Hotel al Teatro

BOUTIQUE HOTEL €€

(☑ 0586 89 87 05; www.hotelalteatro.it; Via Mayer 42; s/d €90/130; P❄🛜) The eight rooms in this hotel opposite the Goldoni Theatre are comfortable and clean, but the real draw is the gravel garden out back where guests can lounge on wicker furniture beneath a breathtakingly beautiful, 300-year-old magnolia tree.

⭐ Grand Hotel Palazzo

HISTORIC HOTEL €€€

(☑ 0586 26 08 36; www.grandhotelpalazzo.com; Viale Italia 195; s €360, d €375-400, ste €575; P❄@🛜📶🏖) Recently acquired by Sofitel, the grand dame of Livorno's hotels faces the seafront and many of its spacious, elegant rooms enjoy sea views. Guests are treated to a generous dose of belle-époque style in common areas and can also enjoy thoroughly modern facilities including a rooftop infinity pool and restaurant-bar with panoramic balcony – perfect for a sunset *aperitivo*.

✖ Eating

Livornese cuisine – particularly traditionally prepared seafood – is known throughout Italy for its excellence. Indeed, sampling the city's signature dish of *cacciucco* (pronounced kar-*choo*-ko), a mixed seafood stew, is reason enough to visit the city. Preferably made using the local Slow Food–accredited San Vincenzo tomatoes, it packs more than its fair share of flavour.

Mercato Centrale

MARKET €

(Mercato Centrale detto Vettovaglie; Via Buontalenti; ⏱ 6am-2pm Mon-Sat) The largest covered market in Italy, this 95m-long neoclassical building miraculously survived Allied WWII bombing. Arresting both gastronomically and architecturally, it has a particularly

---

DON'T MISS

FESTA DEL MADONNA

The story goes like this: in 1345, the Virgin Mary appeared to a shepherd, who led her to black mountain (*monte nero*), a haven of brigands. Needless to say, the brigands immediately saw the error of their ways and built a chapel on the mountain. Soon pilgrims arrived and the chapel was extended in stages; it reached its present form in 1774. Rooms and corridors surrounding Santuario della Madonna di Montenero (☑ 0586 57 96 27; www.santuariomontenero.org; Piazza di Montenero 9; ⏱ 8.30am-12.30pm & 2.30-6pm summer, 8.30am-5pm Mon-Fri & 7.30am-5.30pm Sat & Sun winter) house a fascinating collection of 20,000 historic ex-votos thanking the Virgin for miracles.

The best time to visit is on 8 September, for the Festa del Madonna. To get here by public transport, take the LAM Rosso bus (direction: Montenero) and get off at the last stop, Piazza delle Carrozze in Montenero Basso. From there, take the historic funicular (€2, every 10 to 20 minutes) up to the sanctuary.

Livorno

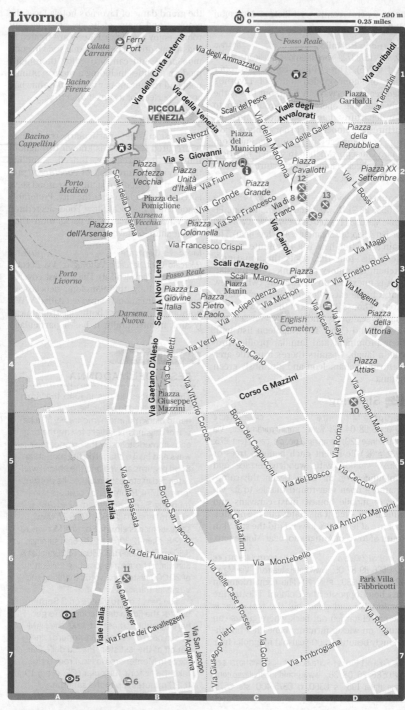

N 0 ——————— 500 m
0 ——————— 0.25 miles

Ferry Port

Calata Carrara

Via della Cinta Esterna

Via degli Ammazzatoi

Fosso Reale

Via Garibaldi

2

Bacino Firenze

P

Via della Venezia

Piazza Garibaldi

Via Terrazzini

PICCOLA VENEZIA

4

Scali del Pesce

Viale degli Avvalorati

Bacino Cappellini

Via Strozzi

Piazza del Municipio

Via delle Galere

Piazza della Repubblica

3

Via S Giovanni

CTT Nord

Via della Madonna

Piazza Cavallotti

Piazza XX Settembre

Via L Bossi

Porto Mediceo

Scali della Darsena

Piazza Fortezza Vecchia

Piazza Unità d'Italia

Via Fiume

Piazza Grande

12

8

13

Piazza del Pomiglione

Via Grande

Via San Francesco

Via di Franco

9

Darsena Vecchia

Piazza Colonnella

Via Cairoli

Piazza dell'Arsenale

Via Francesco Crispi

Via Maggi

Porto Livorno

Scali A Novi Lena

Fosso Reale

Scali d'Azeglio

Scali Manzoni

Piazza Cavour

Via Ernesto Rossi

Via Magenta

Co

Darsena Nuova

Piazza La Giovine Italia

Piazza SS Pietro e Paolo

Piazza Manin

Via Independenza

Via Michon

7

Via Ricasoli

Via Mayer

Piazza della Vittoria

Via Gaetano D'Alesio

Via Cavalletti

Via Verdi

Via San Carlo

English Cemetery

Piazza Attias

4

Piazza Giuseppe Mazzini

Via Vittorio Corcos

Corso G Mazzini

Via Roma

Via Giovanni Maradi

10

Via della Bassata

Borgo San Jacopo

Borgo dei Cappuccini

Via del Bosco

Via Cecconi

5

Viale Italia

Via Antonio Mangini

Via dei Funaioli

Via delle Case Rossee

Via Montebello

Park Villa Fabbricotti

6

11

Via Carlo Meyer

Via Roma

1

Viale Italia

Via Forte dei Cavalleggeri

Via San Jacopo In Acquaviva

Via Giuseppe Pietri

Via Goito

Via Ambrogiana

7

5

6

FLORENCE & TUSCANY LIVORNO

Livorno

impressive fish hall that has recently undergone a sensitive restoration. Famed Italian painter Amedeo Modigliani (1184–1920) once had an atelier on the upper floor (now offices).

★ **Antica Torteria Al Mercato Da Gagarin** SANDWICHES €

(☑ 0586 88 40 86; Via del Cardinale 24; ☺ 8am-2pm & 4.30-8.30pm Mon-Sat) There's only one treat on offer here: a simply sensational sandwich known as a *cinque e cinque* (five and five) that is filled with scrumptious *torta di ceci* (chickpea pancake). When ordering, choose between bread or focaccia and consider adding the traditional accompaniment of a *spuma bionda* (traditional carbonated drink).

★ **Antica Friggitoria** SWEETS €

(☑ 0586 88 45 71; www.anticafriggitoria.it; Piazza Cavalotti 9; ☺ 8.30am-12.30pm & 4-7.30pm Mon-Sat) It's rare to encounter a Livornese who isn't a fan of the delectable *frati* (doughnuts) and *scagliozzi* (fried polenta) that have been made at this simple place on the city's major market square since 1920. In the lead-up to the Festival of San Giuseppe in March, customers flock here to buy *frittelle di riso* (sweet fried rice balls)

★ **Gelateria Populare 2** GELATO €

(☑ 0586 26 03 54; www.gelateriapopolare2.it; Via Carlo Meyer 11; gelato €2.20-3.70; ☺ 8am-1am Tue-Sun summer, to 8pm winter; ☎) Many locals stop at this local institution for a sugar hit after enjoying a late-afternoon *passeggiata* (stroll) on the Terrazza Mascagni, and we strongly recommend you do the same. Made fresh each day, its gelato is undoubtedly the best in town. Also serves crepes, frappés and hot chocolate (the latter in winter only).

★ **Cantina Nardi** TUSCAN €

(☑ 0586 80 80 06; Via Cambini 6-8; bar snacks from €1, meals €22; ☺ 10am-3.30pm & 4.45-9.30pm Mon-Thu, to 11pm Fri & Sat) They've been in business since 1965, so the friendly Nardis know how to keep their customers happy. As much an *enoteca* as Slow Food–hailed eatery, Cantina Nardi has a 400-bottle wine list (an amazing 100 wines are offered by the glass) and is one of the city's best *aperitivo* spots. Sit between bottle-filled shelves inside, or at a streetside table.

★ **La Barrocciaia** OSTERIA €

(☑ 0586 88 26 37; www.labarrocciaia.it; Piazza Cavallotti 13; meals €24, panini €5-7; ☺ 11am-3pm & 6-11pm Tue-Sat, 6-11pm Sun) Locals speak of La Barrocciaia with great fondness – partly because of a homey interior that's alive with banter, but also because of its simple but flavour-packed food. Stews fluctuate between wild boar and *cacciucco*, there's always a choice of *mare* (sea) or *terra* (land) antipasti and it's perfectly acceptable to drop in for a simple *panino* and glass of wine.

ℹ Information

Tourist Office (☑ 0586 09 42 30; www.comune. livorno.it/portaleturismo; Via Pieroni 18; ☺ 9am-4pm summer, to 3pm Apr & Oct-Dec, to 1pm Jan-Mar) Hands out free maps and books boat tours.

ℹ Getting There & Away

BOAT

Livorno is a major port. Regular ferries for Sardinia and Corsica depart from the **ferry port** (Calata Carrara); and ferries to Capraia use the smaller **Porto Mediceo** (Via del Molo Mediceo) near Piazza dell'Arsenale. Boats to Spain use Porto Nuovo, 3km north of the city.

Corsica Ferries (☑ 825 095095 per min €0.15; www.corsica-ferries.co.uk) Two to seven services per week to Bastia, Corsica (from €33, four hours) and Golfo Aranci, Sardinia (from €61, 9½ hours).

Grimaldi Lines (☑ 081 49 64 44; www.grimaldi -ferries.com) Daily sailings to/from Olbia, Sardinia (from €25, nine hours) and Palermo, Sicily (from €43, 18 hours).

FLORENCE & TUSCANY LIVORNO

GIULIANO DEL MORETTO/SHUTTERSTOCK ©

1. Duomo (p478), Florence

The city's most iconic landmark took almost 150 years to complete.

2. Lucca (p565)

At nearly every turn there is a pavement terrace to dine alfresco.

3. Tuscan landscapes

Tuscany rolls out gently undulating hills and sun-kissed vineyards surrounding medieval and Renaissance villages.

4. Panforte

Tuscany is a paradise for foodies, especially those with a sweet tooth.

ROMAN BABAKIN/SHUTTERSTOCK ©

Moby (www.moby.it) Year-round it runs at least two services a day to Olbia, Sardinia (from €48, seven to 10 hours). Plus in the summer, several crossings a week to Bastia, Corsica (from €30, four hours).

Toremar (www.toremar.it) Several crossings per week, year-round to Capraia (€17, 2¾ hours).

TRAIN

From the **main train station** (Piazza Dante) walk westwards (straight ahead) along Viale Carducci, Via de Larderel and Via Grande to access Piazza Grande, Livorno's central square.

Services include the following:

Florence (*regionale veloce* from €9.60, 1¼ hours, hourly).

Pisa (€2.60, 15 minutes, frequent).

Rome (*regionale veloce* from €22.75, three to four hours, at least seven daily).

A taxi between the train station and the centre of town costs €16.

❶ Getting Around

LAM Blu buses operated by **CTT Nord** (www. livorno.cttnord.it; Via Bellatalla 1) travel from the main train station into the city centre, stopping at Piazza Grande before continuing to Porto Mediceo and then along the seafront (€1.20, on board €1.70, valid for 75 minutes). If you're catching a ferry to Sardinia or Corsica, take bus 1 to Piazza Grande then bus 5 from Via Cogorano, just off Piazza Grande.

Isola d'Elba

Napoleon would think twice about fleeing Elba today. Dramatically more congested than when the emperor was exiled here in 1814 (he managed to engineer an escape within a year), the island is an ever-glorious paradise of beach-laced coves, vineyards, azure waters, hairpin-bend motoring, a 1018m mountain (Monte Capanne) and mind-bending views. It's all supplemented by a fine seafaring cuisine, lovely island wines, and land and seascapes just made for hiking, biking and sea kayaking.

With the exception of high season (actually only August), when the island's beaches and roads are jam-packed, Elba is something of a Robinson Crusoe paradise. In springtime, early summer and autumn, when grapes and olives are harvested, there are plenty of tranquil nooks on this stunningly picturesque, 28km-long, 19km-wide island.

There is a wealth of information about the island at www.infoelba.com.

❶ Getting There & Around

Elba is a one-hour ferry crossing from Piombino on the mainland to Portoferraio (at least hourly, passenger/car and driver €17/50). Unless it's August or a summer weekend, there's no need to book tickets in advance.

Car is the easiest way to get around Elba, except in August when roads are jammed; **TWN Rent** (☑ 0565 91 46 66; www.twn-rent.it; Viale Elba 32, Portoferraio) rents cars, scooters and electric bikes. The island's southwest coast offers the most dramatic and scenic motoring.

Portoferraio

POP 12,000

Known to the Romans as Fabricia and later Ferraia (an acknowledgement of its important role as a port for iron exports), this small harbour was acquired by Cosimo I de' Medici in the mid-16th century, when its distinctive fortifications took shape.

Portoferraio can be a hectic place, especially in August when holidaymakers pour off the ferries from Piombino on the mainland every 20 minutes or so. But wandering the streets and steps of the historic centre, indulging in the exceptional eating options and haggling for sardines with fishermen more than makes up for the squeeze.

◉ Sights & Activities

The Old Town's spiderweb of narrow streets and alleys staggers uphill from the old harbour to Portoferraio's defining twinset of forts, **Forte Falcone** and **Forte Stella** (☑ 0565 91 69 89; Via della Stella; adult/reduced €2/1.50; ☺ 9am-7pm Easter-Sep), revealing deserted 16th-century ramparts to wander and seagulls freewheeling overhead.

From waterside square **Piazza Cavour** head uphill along Via Garibaldi to the foot of the monumental **Scalinata Medici**, a fabulous mirage of 140 wonky stone steps cascading up through every sunlit shade of amber to the dimly lit, 17th-century **Chiesa della Misericordia** (Via della Misericordia; ☺ 8am-5pm). Inside is Napoleon's death mask. Continue to the top of the staircase to reach the forts and **Villa dei Mulini**, where Napoleon lived when in Portoferraio.

Museo Nazionale della Residenze Napoleoniche MUSEUM

(Villa dei Mulini; ☑ 0565 91 58 46; Piazzale Napoleone; adult/reduced €5/2.50; ☺ 8.30am-7pm Mon & Wed-Sat, to 1pm Sun) Villa dei Mulini was home to Napoleon during his stint in exile

PORTOFERRAIO SUBURBS

So close to Portoferraio that they are generally considered to be its suburbs, Schiopparello, Magazzini and Otone cluster around pebbled coves and rich agricultural land east of the ferry docks. The settlements date to the Roman period when powerful owners of the island's iron mines built ornate seaside villas here. These days, the coves shelter some of the island's accommodation, at home between olive groves, vineyards, lemon groves and golden fields of wheat.

Agriturismo Due Palme (☑ 0565 93 30 17, 338 7433736; www.agriturismoelba.it; Via Schiopparello 28, Schiopparello; d €120, tr & q €130; P) Utterly tranquil despite being just a few minutes from the Portoferraio–Magazzini road, this *agriturismo* is part of the only olive plantation on Elba to produce quality-stamped IGP olive oil. Its six simple but well-maintained self-catering cottages are dotted amid flowerbeds, citrus trees and 100-year-old olive groves. Tree-shaded deckchairs, a barbec and a tennis court heighten the charm. Guests and visitors can taste and buy the silky fresh-green oil (€20 per litre). No breakfast.

Ristoro Agricolo Montefabbrello (☑ 339 8296298; www.montefabbrello.it; Località Schiopparello 30; meals €38; ☺ 7.30-10pm Jun-Sep, 7.30-10pm Fri & Sat, noon-3pm Sun Oct–May) A model of sustainable cuisine, this rustic restaurant on the Montefabbrello farm grows its own wheat to make pasta, grapes to make wine and olives to produce oil. Fruit and veggies are homegrown too. Tasty pasta dishes, homemade bread and plenty of meat and game choices (unusual on Elba) make it an essential stop on every foodie itinerary.

on this small isle. With its Empire style furnishings, splendid library, fig-tree-studded Italianate gardens and unbeatable sea view, the emperor didn't want for creature comforts – contrast this with the simplicity of the camp bed and travelling trunk he used when on campaigns. While that history lesson is nice, the dearth of actual Napoleonic artefacts here is a tad disappointing.

★**Museo Villa Napoleonica di San Martino** MUSEUM
(☑ 0565 91 58 46; San Martino; adult/reduced €5/2.50; ☺ 8.30am-7pm Tue-Sat, to 1pm Sun summer, 9am-3pm Tue-Sat, to 1pm Sun winter) Napoleon personally supervised the transformation of what had been a large farmhouse in the hills 5km southwest of Portoferraio into an elegant villa where he could escape the summer heat. Romanticism and hubris both came into play as he sought to give his new residence a Parisian sheen – the pretty **Room of the Love Knot** and grand **Egyptian Room** were particular triumphs. In the 1850s, a Russian nobleman purchased the villa and built a grandiose gallery at its base.

Bus 1 travels between the port at Portoferraio and San Martino at least eight times per day (€1, 15 minutes). The car park near the villa charges a whopping €3.50.

🛏 Sleeping

There aren't all that many accommodation options in Portoferraio, and those that do exist are lacklustre – you're better off sleeping elsewhere on the island.

Rosselba Le Palme CAMPGROUND €
(☑ 0565 93 31 01; www.rosselbalepalme.it; Località Ottone; campsites adult €15.50, child €11.50, tent €18.50, car €5.50; ☺ late-Apr–Sep; P) Set around a botanical garden backed by Mediterranean forest, few campgrounds are as leafy or large. The beach is a 400m walk between trees while accommodation ranges from simple pitches to 'glamping' tents with bathtubs, cute wooden chalets to villa apartments. Find the ground 9km east of Portoferraio near Ottone.

Porta del Mare PENSION €
(☑ 328 8261441; www.bebportadelmarelba.com; Piazza Cavour 34; r €140, tr €170; ☺) If you like being in the heart of things, the 4th-floor rooms in this elegant townhouse could work a treat. Light, bright bedrooms have tall ceilings and filmy drapes; two have cracking harbour views. It's right in the middle of Portoferraio's main square (so expect some night-time noise). Owners Rossella and Bruno are gracious hosts.

Eating

Il Castagnacciao
PIZZA €

(☑0565 91 58 45; www.ilcastagnacciaio.com; Via del Mercato Vecchio 5; pizza €5-8; ⊙10.30am-2.30pm & 4.30-10.30pm) They work the pizza chef so hard here the dining room sometimes has a smoky tinge. To go local, start with a lip-smacking plate of *torta di ceci* (chickpea 'pizza'), then watch your rectangular, thin-crust supper go in and out of the wood-fired oven. But save space for dessert – *castagnaccio* (chestnut 'cake') baked over the same flames.

Osteria Libertaria
TUSCAN €€

(☑0565 91 49 78; Calata Giacomo Matteotti 12; meals €35; ⊙noon-2.30pm & 7-10.30pm summer) Fish drives the menu of this traditional *osteria* – no wonder, as the boats that land it are moored right outside. Traditional dishes such as fried calamari or *tonno in crosta di pistacchi* (pistachio-encrusted tuna fillet) are super-fresh and very tasty. Dine at one of two tile-topped tables on the traffic-noisy street or on the back-alley terrace.

Bitta 20
SEAFOOD €€€

(☑0565 93 02 70; ristorantebitta20@gmail.com; Calata Mazzini 20; meals €50; ⊙noon-2.30pm & 7-11pm Tue-Sun Easter–mid-Oct) A Portoferraio favourite, this harbourside eatery has a long terrace overlooking a string of bobbing yachts. White napery and efficient service combine with fresh fish and seafood to make it a good choice for lunch or dinner. Book for the latter.

ℹ Information

Parco Nazionale dell'Arcipelago Toscana Office (Info Park; ☑0565 90 82 31; www.parcoarcipelago.info; Calata Italia 4; ⊙9am-7pm Apr-Oct, to 10pm Tue & Thu Aug, 9am-4pm Mon-Sat, to 3pm Sun Nov-Mar) Helpful staff have abundant information on walking and biking on the island. Find the office on the seafront, near the ferry docks

---

LOCAL KNOWLEDGE

ELBA'S BEST BEACHES

Given the wide range of bays on Elba's 147km-long coast, it pays to know your *spiagge* (beaches) - the quietest, prettiest beaches are tucked in bijou rocky coves and often involve a steep clamber down. Find sandy strands on the south coast, in the Golfo della Biodola and on the western side of Capo d'Enfola; **La Biodola** is Portoferraio's closest sandy beach. Parking is invariably roadside and scant.

Colle d'Orano & Fetovaia

The standout highlight of these two gorgeous swathes of golden sand on Elba's western coast is the dramatic drive between the two. Legend has it Napoleon frequented Colle d'Orano to sit and swoon over his native Corsica, which is visible across the water. A heavenly scented promontory covered in *maquis* (herbal scrubland) protects sandy Fetovaia, where nudists flop on nearby granite rocks known as Le Piscine.

Enfola

Just 6km west of Portoferraio, it's not so much the grey pebbles as the outdoor action that lures crowds to this tiny fishing port. There are pedalos to rent, a beachside diving school, and a family-friendly 2.5km-long circular **hiking trail** around the green cape.

Morcone, Pareti & Innamorata

Find this trio of charming sandy-pebble coves framed by sweet-smelling pine trees some 3km south of Capoliveri in southeast Elba. Rent a **kayak** and paddle out to sea on Innamorata, the wildest of the three; or fine-dine and overnight on Pareti beach at **Hotel Stella Maris** (☑0565 96 84 25; www.albergostellamaris.it; Località Pareti; d €145-190; P ❄ 🤶), one of the few three-star hotels to be found on the sand.

Sansone & Sorgente

This twinset of cliff-ensnared, white-shingle and pebble beaches stands out for crystal-clear, turquoise waters just made for **snorkelling**. By car from Portoferraio, follow the SP27 towards Enfola. Parking is challenging.

Marciana Marina, Marciana & Poggio

POP 2000

Unlike many modern cookie-cutter marinas, the attractive resort of Marciana Marina has character and history to complement its pleasant pebble beaches. The port is 18km west along the coast from Portoferraio. From it, a twisting 9km mountain road winds inland up to Marciana, the island's oldest and highest village (375m).

Marciana's stone streets, arches and stone houses with flower boxes and petite balconies are as pretty as a picture, and it's worth exploring them before heading uphill from the village to Elba's most important pilgrimage site: the Santuario della Madonna del Monte.

Between the two Marcianas, along a precipitous road, is the mountain village of Poggio. Set on the SP25, it's famous for its spring water and has steep cobblestone alleys and stunning coastal views.

⊙ Sights & Activities

★**Cabinovia Monte Capanne**   FUNICULAR
(Cableway; ☑0565 90 10 20; www.cabinovia-isoladelba.it; Località Pozzatello; adult/reduced/child return €18/13/9; ☺10am-1pm & 2.20-5pm mid-Apr–mid-Oct) Elba's famous cable car transports passengers up to the island's highest point, Monte Capanne (1018m), in open, barred baskets – imagine riding in a canary-yellow parrot cage and you'll get the picture. After a 20-minute ride, passengers alight and can scramble around the rocky peak to enjoy an astonishing, 300-degree panorama of Elba, the Tuscan Archipelago, Etruscan Coast and Corsica 50km away. Keen hikers can buy a cheaper one-way ticket and take the 90-minute walk back down a rocky path.

Santuario della Madonna del Monte   CHAPEL
(☺24hr) **FREE** To enjoy an invigorating 40-minute hike, head up through Marciana along Via della Madonna to reach this much-altered hilltop chapel with its 13th-century fresco of the Madonna painted on a slab of granite. A remarkable coastal panorama unfolds as you make your way here past scented parasol pines, chestnut trees, wild sage and thyme. Once you reach the chapel (627m), emulate Napoleon and drink from the old stone fountain across from the church – a plaque commemorates his visit in 1814.

✕ Eating

★**La Svolta**   GELATO €
(☑0565 9 94 79; www.gelaterialasvolta.it; Via Cairoli 6, Marciana Marina; ☺10.30am-late Tue-Sun Apr-Oct) The philosophy here is laudable: use fresh local produce (organic where possible), ensure that the flavours are as natural as possible, and serve the almost inevitably delectable result in cones or in biodegradable cups. Love it.

★**Ristorante Salegrosso**   SEAFOOD €€
(☑0565 99 68 62; salegrossoristo@hotmail.com; Piazza della Vittoria 14, Marciana Marina; meals €40; ☺12.30-2.30pm & 7.30-10pm Tue-Sun Mar-Dec) Those on the hunt for Elba's best fish dish need look no further – the fish stew here is a flavoursome pile of shellfish, tomato and saffron topped by a garlicky slice of bruschetta. Delicious! Dine on it or other fishy treats, including excellent homemade pasta, while watching locals take their evening *passeggiata* along the waterfront.

★**Osteria del Noce**   SEAFOOD €€
(☑0565 90 12 84; www.osteriadelnoce.it; Via della Madonna 19, Marciana; meals €30; ☺noon-2pm & 7.30-9.30pm late-Mar–Sep) This family-run bistro in hilltop Marciana is the type of place where the bread is homemade and flavoured with fennel, chestnut flour and other seasonal treats. The pasta and seafood dishes and the sweeping views from the terrace are truly memorable. To find it, follow the Madonna del Monte walking signs to the top of the village.

ⓘ Getting There & Away

Bus 116 links Marciana Marina and Marciana with Portoferraio at least eight times per day (€2.50).

NORTHWESTERN TUSCANY

There is more to this green corner of Tuscany than Italy's iconic Leaning Tower. Linger over lunches of rustic regional specialities, and meander through medieval hilltop villages and along ancient pilgrim routes. Even the largest towns – university hub Pisa and 'love at first sight' Lucca – have an air of tranquillity and tradition that positively beg the traveller to stay for a few days of cultural R&R. This is snail-paced Italy, impossible not to love.

Pisa

POP 89,200

Once a maritime power to rival Genoa and Venice, Pisa now draws its fame from an architectural project gone terribly wrong. But the world-famous Leaning Tower is just one of many noteworthy sights in this compelling city. Education has fuelled the local economy since the 1400s, and students from across Italy compete for places in its elite university. This endows the centre of town with a vibrant cafe and bar scene, balancing an enviable portfolio of well-maintained Romanesque buildings, Gothic churches and Renaissance piazzas with a lively street life dominated by locals rather than tourists – a charm you will definitely not discover if you restrict your visit to Piazza dei Miracoli.

◉ Sights

Many visitors to Pisa arrive by train at Pisa San Rossore and don't get any further than neighbouring Piazza dei Miracoli; those in the know arrive or depart using Stazione Pisa Centrale, allowing casual discovery of the *centro storico* (historic centre).

◉ Piazza Miracoli

★**Leaning Tower**   TOWER

(Torre Pendente; ☐ 050 83 50 11; www.opapisa.it; Piazza dei Miracoli; €18; ☉ 8am-8pm Apr-Sep, 9am-7pm Oct, to 6pm Mar, 10am-5pm Nov-Feb) One of Italy's signature sights, the Torre Pendente truly lives up to its name, leaning a startling 3.9 degrees off the vertical. The 56m-high tower, officially the Duomo's *campanile* (bell tower), took almost 200 years to build, but was already listing when it was unveiled in 1372. Over time, the tilt, caused by a layer of weak subsoil, steadily worsened until it was finally halted by a major stabilisation project in the 1990s.

Building began in 1173 under the supervision of architect Bonanno Pisano, but his plans came a cropper almost immediately. Only three of the tower's seven tiers had been built when he was forced to abandon construction after it started leaning. Work resumed in 1272, with artisans and masons attempting to bolster the foundations but failing miserably. They kept going, though, compensating for the lean by gradually building straight up from the lower storeys. But once again work had to be suspended – this time due to war – and construction wasn't completed until the second half of the 14th century.

Over the next 600 years, the tower continued to tilt at an estimated 1mm per year. By 1993 it stood 4.47m out of plumb, more than five degrees from the vertical. To counter this, steel braces were slung around the 3rd storey and joined to steel cables attached to neighbouring buildings. This held the tower in place as engineers began gingerly removing soil from below the northern foundations. After some 70 tonnes of earth had been extracted from the northern side, the tower sank to its 18th-century level and, in the process, rectified the lean by 43.8cm. Experts believe that this will guarantee the tower's future for the next three centuries.

Access to the Leaning Tower is limited to 45 people at a time – children under eight are not allowed in/up and those aged eight to 10 years must hold an adult's hand. To avoid disappointment, book in advance online or go straight to a ticket office when you arrive in Pisa to book a slot for later in the day. Visits last 35 minutes and involve a steep climb up 251 occasionally slippery steps. All bags, handbags included, must be deposited at the free left-luggage desk next to the central ticket office – cameras are about the only thing you can take up.

★**Duomo**   CATHEDRAL

(Duomo di Santa Maria Assunta; ☐ 050 83 50 11; www.opapisa.it; Piazza dei Miracoli; ☉ 10am-8pm Apr-Sep, to 7pm Oct, to 6pm Nov-Mar) FREE Pisa's magnificent Romanesque Duomo was begun in 1064 and consecrated in 1118. Its striking tiered exterior, with cladding of green-and-cream marble bands, gives onto a vast columned interior capped by a gold wooden ceiling. The elliptical dome, the first of its kind in Europe at the time, was added in 1380.

Admission is free but you need a ticket from another Piazza dei Miracoli sight to get in or a fixed-timed free pass issued by **ticket offices** (☐ 050 83 50 11; www.opapisa.it; Piazza dei Miracoli; ☉ 8.30am-7.30pm summer, to 5.30pm winter) behind the Leaning Tower or inside Museo delle Sinopie.

★**Battistero**   CHRISTIAN SITE

(Battistero di San Giovanni; ☐ 050 83 50 11; www.opapisa.it; Piazza dei Miracoli; €5, combination ticket with Camposanto or Museo delle Sinopie €7, Camposanto & Museo €8; ☉ 8am-8pm Apr-Sep, 9am-7pm Oct, to 6pm Mar, 10am-5pm Nov-Feb)

Pisa's unusual round baptistry has one dome piled on top of another, each roofed half in lead, half in tiles, and topped by a gilt bronze John the Baptist (1395). Construction began in 1152, but it was remodelled and continued by Nicola and Giovanni Pisano more than a century later and finally completed in the 14th century. Inside, the hexagonal marble pulpit (1260) by Nicola Pisano is the highlight.

The lower level of arcades is Pisan-Romanesque; the pinnacled upper section and dome are Gothic.

Pisan scientist Galileo Galilei (who, so the story goes, came up with the laws of the pendulum by watching a lamp in Pisa's cathedral swing), was baptised in the octagonal font (1246). Don't leave without climbing to the **Upper Gallery** to listen to the custodian demonstrate the double dome's remarkable acoustics and echo effects, every half-hour on the hour/half-hour.

Camposanto   CEMETERY
(📞050 83 50 11; www.opapisa.it; Piazza dei Miracoli; €5, combination ticket with Battistero or Museo delle Sinopie €7, Battistero & Museo €8; ⊙8am-8pm Apr-Sep, 9am-7pm Oct, to 6pm Mar, 10am-5pm Nov-Feb) Soil shipped from Calvary during the Crusades is said to lie within the white walls of this hauntingly beautiful, final resting place for many prominent Pisans, arranged around a garden in a cloistered quadrangle. During WWII, Allied artillery destroyed many of the cloisters' frescoes, but a couple were salvaged and are now displayed in the **Sala Affreschi** (Frescoes Room). Most notable is the Triumph of Death (1336–41), a remarkable illustration of Hell attributed to 14th-century painter Buonamico Buffalmacco.

Museo
delle Sinopie   MUSEUM
(📞 050 83 50 11; www.opapisa.it; Piazza dei Miracoli; €5, combination ticket with Battistero or Camposanto €7, Battistero & Camposanto €8; ⊙ 8am-8pm Apr-Sep, 9am-7pm Oct, to 6pm Mar, 10am-5pm Nov-Feb) Home to some fascinating frescoes, this museum safeguards several *sinopie* (preliminary sketches), drawn by the artists in red earth pigment on the walls of the Camposanto in the 14th and 15th centuries before frescoes were painted over them. The museum is a compelling study in fresco painting, with short films and scale models filling in the gaps.

ℹ️ TOWER & COMBO TICKETS

Buy tickets for the Leaning Tower from one of two well-signposted ticket offices: the main ticket office behind the tower or the smaller office inside Museo delle Sinopie. To guarantee your visit to the tower and cut the long queue in high season, buy tickets in advance online (note tickets can only be bought 20 days before visiting).

Ticket offices in Pisa also sell combination tickets covering admission to the Battistero, Camposanto and Museo delle Sinopie: buy a ticket covering one/two/three sights for €5/7/8 (reduced €3/4/5). Admission to the Duomo is free, but you need to show a ticket valid for another Piazza dei Miracoli sight or a fixed-time free pass issued at ticket offices.

👁️ Along the Arno

Palazzo Blu   GALLERY
(www.palazzoblu.it; Lungarno Gambacorti 9; ⊙10am-7pm Tue-Fri, to 8pm Sat & Sun) **FREE** Facing the river is this magnificently restored 14th-century building with a striking dusty-blue facade. Inside, its over-the-top 19th-century interior decoration is the perfect backdrop for the Foundation Pisa's art collection – predominantly Pisan works from the 14th to the 20th centuries on the 2nd floor, plus various temporary exhibitions (adult/reduced €6/4) on the ground floor. Admission also includes an **archaeological area** in the basement and the noble **residence** of this aristocratic palace, furnished as it would have been in the 19th century, on the 1st floor.

Museo Nazionale di San Matteo   MUSEUM
(📞050 54 18 65; Piazza San Matteo in Soarta 1; adult/reduced €5/2.50; ⊙8.30am-7.30pm Tue-Sat, to 1.30pm Sun) This inspiring repository of medieval masterpieces sits in a 13th-century Benedictine convent on the Arno's northern waterfront boulevard. The museum's collection of paintings from the Tuscan school (c 12th to 14th centuries) is notable, with works by Lippo Memmi, Taddeo Gaddi, Gentile da Fabriano and Ghirlandaio. Don't miss Masaccio's *St Paul,* Fra' Angelico's *Madonna of Humility* and Simone Martini's *Polyptych of Saint Catherine.*

Pisa

FLORENCE & TUSCANY PISA

Map labels:

Via Contessa Matilde

9

Piazza Santa Caterina 4

V Andrea Pisano

Piazza Manin

11

Battistero 1

2 **Duomo** 3

Leaning Tower

5

Piazza Arcivescovado

Via Cardinale Maffi

Via Carducci

ViaCapponi

10

Via S.Apollonia

Via Bonanno

Via Savi

15 Piazza Cavallotti

Via Corsica

Via Don G Boschi

Via della Faggiola

Via Savi

Orto Botanico 7

Via Volta

Via Roma

Via Santa Maria

Via Paoli

Via San Frediano

Piazza dei Cavalieri

Via dei Consoli del Mare

Via Oberdan

Via Risorgimento

Piazza Dante Alighieri

16

Borgo Stretto

Piazza Sant'Omobono

Piazza delle Vettovaglie

13

19 12 18

Lungarno Pacinotti

Piazza Garibaldi

Ponte di Mezzo

Piazza XX Settembre

Lungarno Gambacorti

8

Via Mazzini

Lungarno Simonelli

Ponte Solferino

Arno

Via Sant'Antonio

Viale Crispi

Via San Martino

Corso Italia

Lungarno Sonnino

Stazione Pisa Centrale (530m)

CPT (220m)

Keith (220m)

Sleeping

★ Hotel Di Stefano
HOTEL €

(☏ 050 55 35 59; www.hoteldistefanopisa.com; Via Sant'Apollonia 35; d €89-139; P ✳ @ ☏) This three-star hotel has been in business since 1969 for good reason. Partly tucked in a medieval townhouse, it fuses vintage charm with no-frills functionality and a warm, family-run ambience. Deluxe rooms have beamed ceilings, exposed brickwork and a balcony overlooking the small back garden. The rooftop terrace, with armchairs and stunning sunset views, is accessible – fabulously so – to all.

Hostel
Pisa Tower
HOSTEL €

(☏ 050 520 24 54; www.hostelpisatower.it; Via Piave 4; dm €20-25; @ ☏) This super-friendly hostel occupies a suburban villa that is situated a couple of minutes' walk from Piazza dei Miracoli. It's bright and cheery, with colourful decor, female and mixed dormitories, communal kitchen, and a summer-friendly terrace overlooking a small grassy garden. Dorms are named, meaning you can sleep with Galileo, Mona Lisa, Leonardo or Michelangelo.

Pisa

⊙ Top Sights
1 Battistero	B1
2 Duomo	B1
3 Leaning Tower	C1

⊙ Sights
4 Camposanto	B1
5 Museo delle Sinopie	B1
6 Museo Nazionale di San Matteo	F5
7 Orto e Museo Botanico	B3
8 Palazzo Blu	D4

🛏 Sleeping
9 Hostel Pisa Tower	C1
10 Hotel Di Stefano	D2
11 Hotel Pisa Tower	A1
12 Royal Victoria Hotel	D4

⊗ Eating
13 Gelateria De' Coltelli	D4
14 Ir Tegame	E4
15 L'Ostellino	C2
16 Pizzeria Il Montino	D3
17 Ristorante Galileo	E5

⊙ Drinking & Nightlife
18 Bazeel	D4
19 La Stafetta	D4
20 Sottobosco	E4

Royal Victoria Hotel HOTEL €€

(☑ 050 94 01 11; www.royalvictoria.it; Lungarno Pacinotti 12; d €65-130, tr €100-180; ❄ 🤶) This doyen of Pisan hotels, run by the Piegaja family since 1837, offers old-world luxury accompanied by warm, attentive service. Its 38 rooms exude a shabby-chic spirit with their Grand Tour antiques – some peep out onto the murky river. Don't miss an *aperitivo* flopped on a sofa on the 4th-floor terrace, packed with potted plants. Garage parking per day €20.

✗ Eating

L'Ostellino SANDWICHES €

(Piazza Cavallotti 1; panini €3.50-7; ⊙ noon-4.30pm Mon-Fri, to 6pm Sat & Sun) For a gourmet *panino* wrapped in crunchy waxed paper, this minuscule deli and *panineria* delivers. Take your pick from dozens of different combos written by hand on the blackboard (*lardo di colonnata* with figs or cave-aged *pecorino* with honey and walnuts are sweet favourites), await construction, then hit the green lawns of Piazza dei Miracoli to picnic with the crowds.

★Hotel Pisa Tower HOTEL €€

(☑ 050 520 00 19; www.hotelpisatower.com; Via Andrea Pisano 23; d €115-125, tr €140-145, q €150-160; 🅿 ❄ 🤶) Superb value for money, a superlative location, and spacious, high-ceilinged rooms – this polished three-star is one of Pisa's best deals. Chandeliers, marble floors and old framed prints adorn the classically attired interiors, while out back, a pristine lawn adds a soothing dash of green. Check the website for cheaper, last-minute deals.

Ir Tegame
ITALIAN €

(☑ 050 57 28 01; www.facebook.com/irtegamepisa; Piazza Cairoli 9; meals €10-20; ⊗noon-2.30pm & 7.45-11.15pm) When the urge for a swift bowl of pasta strikes, hit this stylish *spaghetteria* on one of Pisa's buzziest squares. A riot of faux flowers, strung on red and white ladders, decorate the low ceiling and the menu only features *primi* (first courses) – pasta *primi* to be precise, all fresh and handmade. The *taglioni* with black truffle shavings is spot on. The 'Giro Pasta' menu (€20), comprising four different pasta dishes brought to the tables in pans, plus dessert, water and house wine, is unbeatable value.

Pizzeria Il Montino
PIZZA €

(☑ 050 59 86 95; www.pizzeriailmontino.com; Vicolo del Monte 1; pizza €6-8.50, foccacine €2.50-5; ⊗10.30am-3pm & 5-10pm Mon-Sat) There's nothing fancy about this down-to-earth pizzeria, an icon among Pisans, students and sophisticates alike. Take away or order at the bar then grab a table, inside or out, and munch on house specialities such as *cecina* (chickpea pizza), *castagnaccio* (chestnut cake) and *spuma* (sweet, nonalcoholic drink). Or go for a *focaccine* (small flat roll) filled with salami, pancetta or *porchetta* (suckling pig).

It's hidden in a back alley; the quickest way to find Il Montino is to head west along Via Ulisse Dini from the northern end of Borgo Stretto (opposite the Lo Sfizio cafe at Borgo Stretto 54) to Piazza San Felice where

ESCAPE THE CROWDS

For a Zen respite from the Piazza dei Miracoli crowd, explore the peaceful **Orto e Museo Botanico** (Botanical Garden & Museum; ☑ 050 221 13 10; Via Roma 56; adult/reduced/family €4/2/6; ⊗8.30am-8pm Apr-Sep, 9am-5pm Mon-Sat, to 1am Sun Oct-Mar) laced with centurion palm trees, flora typical to the Apuane Alps, a fragrant herb garden, vintage greenhouses and 35 orchid species. Showcasing the botanical collection of Pisa University, the garden dates to 1543 and was Europe's first university botanical garden, tended by the illustrious botanist Luca Ghini (1490–1556). The museum, inside **Palazzo della Conchiglie**, explores the garden's history, with exquisite botanical drawings, catalogues, maquettes etc.

it is easy to spot, on your left, a telling blue neon 'Pizzeria' sign.

Ristorante Galileo
TUSCAN €€

(☑ 050 2 82 87; www.ristorantegalileo.com; Via San Martino 6-8; meals €25; ⊗12.30-2.30pm & 7.30-10.30pm Wed-Mon) For good, honest, unpretentious Tuscan cooking, nothing beats this classical old-timer. From the cork-covered wine list to the complimentary plate of warm homemade focaccia and huge platters of tempting *cantuccini* (almond-studded biscuits), Galileo makes you feel welcome. Fresh pasta is strictly hand- and homemade, and most veggies are plucked fresh that morning from the restaurant's veggie garden.

⚲ Drinking & Nightlife

Sottobosco
CAFE

(☑ 050 314 20 84; www.facebook.com/sottobosco. libricafe; Piazza San Paolo all'Orto 3; ⊗noon-3pm & 6pm-midnight Tue-Fri, 6pm-1am Sat, to midnight Sun summer, reduced hours winter) This creative book-cafe is a breath of fresh air. Tuck into a sugar doughnut and cappuccino or an early-evening *aperitivo* at a glass-topped table filled with artists' crayons, or a button collection. Salads, *panini,* salami or cheese *taglieri* (tasting boards) and oven-baked cheese are simple and home-made. Come dark, jazz bands play or DJs spin tunes.

Bazeel
BAR

(☑ 349 088 06 88; www.bazeel.it; Lungarno Pacinotti 1; ⊗7am-1am Sun-Thu, to 2am Fri & Sat) A dedicated all-rounder, Bazeel is a hot spot from dawn to dark. Laze over breakfast, linger over a light buffet lunch or hang out with the A-list crowd over a generous *aperitivo* spread, live music and DJs. Its chapel-like interior is nothing short of fabulous, as is its pavement terrace out the front. Check its Twitter feed for what's on.

La Stafetta
CRAFT BEER

(www.lastaffetta.com; Lungarno Pacinotti 24; ⊗5pm-1am, to 2am Fri & Sat) Squat on a bench outside or grab a pew inside this funky riverside tap room, the creation of three ale-loving Pisan students: Matteo, Davide and Francesco. Inside, order one of the small microbrewery's own brews: taste English hops in Wilson (a dark-red bitter with hints of coffee, chocolate and liquorice) or go for a light and golden May Ale.

Keith
CAFE

(☑ 050 50 31 35; www.facebook.com/keithcafe; Via Zandonai 4; ⊗7am-11pm summer, to 9pm winter; ☎) This trendy cafe stares face to face with *Tuttomondo* (1989), a mural on the facade of a Pisan church – and the last mural American pop artist Keith Haring painted just months before his death. Sip a coffee or cocktail on the terrace and lament the fading, weather-beaten colours of Haring's 30 signature prancing dancing men.

❶ Information

Tourist Office (☏050 55 01 00; www.turismo. pisa.it/en; Piazza dei Miracoli 7; ⊗9.30am-5.30pm) Provides city information, free maps and various services including guided tours, left luggage (€3/4 per small/large bag per day), bicycle rental (€3/15 per hour/day), and a computer terminal to check train times and sign up for city bike-sharing scheme **Ciclopi** (☏800 005 640; www.ciclopi.eu; Piazza Vittorio Emanuele II; 1st hr free, 2nd/3rd/4th half-hour €0.90/1.50/2.50; ⊗9.30am-1pm). Also sells public transport tickets.

❶ Getting There & Away

AIR

Pisa International Airport (Galileo Galilei Airport; ☏050 84 93 00; www.pisa-airport. com) Tuscany's main international airport, a 10-minute drive south of Pisa; has flights to most major European cities.

BUS

From its **bus station** (Piazza Sant'Antonio 1) hub, Pisan bus company **CPT** (☏050 50 55 02; www.cpt.pisa.it; ⊗ticket office 7am-8.15pm Mon-Fri, to 8pm Sat & Sun) runs buses to/from Volterra (€6.10, two hours, up to 10 daily with change of bus in Pontedera).

TRAIN

There is a handy **left-luggage counter** (Deposito Bagagli; ☏050 261 52; www.deposito bagaglipisa.it; Pisa Centrale; bag per day €5; ⊗6am-9pm) at **Pisa Centrale** (Piazza della Stazione) train station – not to be confused with north-of-town **Pisa San Rossore** (Via Giunta) station. Regional train services to/from Pisa Centrale include the following:

Florence (€8.40, 1¼ hours, frequent)

Livorno (€2.60, 15 minutes, frequent)

Lucca (€3.50, 30 minutes, every 30 minutes)

Viareggio (€3.50, 15 minutes, every 20 minutes)

❶ Getting Around

TO/FROM THE AIRPORT

Fully automated, super-speedy **PisaMover** (http://pisa-mover.com) trains link Pisa International Airport with Pisa Centrale train station

(€2.70, five minutes, every five minutes from 6am to midnight).

The LAM Rossa (red) bus line (€1.20, 10 minutes, every 10 to 20 minutes) run by CPT passes through the city centre and by the train station en route to/from the airport. Buy tickets from the blue ticket machine, next to the bus stops to the right of the train station exit.

A taxi between the airport and city centre should cost no more than €10. To book, call **Radio Taxi Pisa** (☏050 54 16 00; www.cotapi.it).

CAR & MOTORCYCLE

Parking costs around €2 per hour; don't park in the historic centre's Limited Traffic Zone (ZTL). There's a free car park outside the zone on Lungarno Guadalongo, near Fortezza di San Gallo on the south side of the Arno.

Lucca

POP 89,000

Lovely Lucca endears itself to everyone who visits. Hidden behind imposing Renaissance walls, its cobbled streets, handsome piazzas and shady promenades make it a perfect destination to explore by foot – as a day trip from Florence or in its own right. At the day's end, historic cafes and restaurants tempt visitors to relax over a glass or two of Lucchesi wine and a slow progression of rustic dishes prepared with fresh produce from nearby Garfagnana.

If you have a car, the hills to the east of Lucca demand exploration. Home to historic villas and belle-époque Montecatini Terme where Puccini lazed in warm spa waters, they are easy and attractive day-trip destinations from Lucca.

◎ Sights

Stone-paved **Via Fillungo**, with its fashion boutiques and car-free mantra, threads its way through the medieval heart of the old city. East is one of Tuscany's loveliest piazzas, oval cafe-ringed **Piazza Anfiteatro**, named for the amphitheatre that was here in Roman times. Spot remnants of the amphitheatre's brick arches and masonry on the exterior walls of the medieval houses ringing the piazza.

★**City Wall**　　　　　　HISTORIC SITE

Lucca's monumental *mura* (wall) was built around the old city in the 16th and 17th centuries and remains in almost perfect condition. It superseded two previous walls, the first built from travertine stone blocks as early as the 2nd century BC. Twelve metres

Lucca

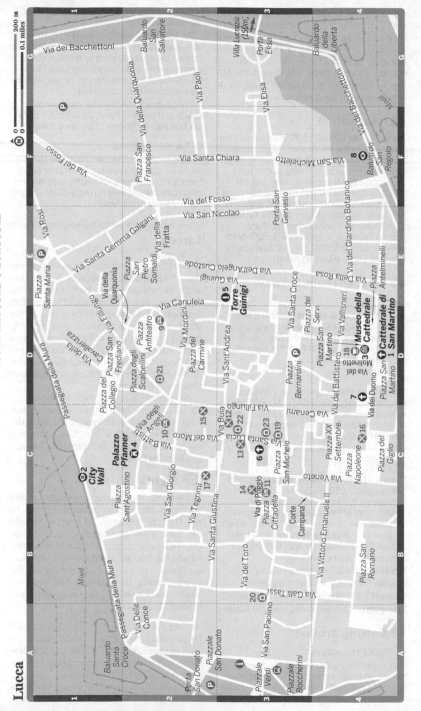

200 m
0.1 miles

Via dei Bacchettoni

Baluardo San Salvatore

Villa Lucrezia (150m);

Porta Elisa

Baluardo della Libertà

Via dei Bacchettoni

Moat

Via del Fosso

Via Rosi

Piazza San Francesco

Via della Quarquonia

Via Paoli

Via Elisa

Via San Regolo

Via Santa Chiara

Via San Michele

8

Baluardo San Regolo

Via del Fosso

Porta San Gervasio

Via San Nicolao

Via Santa Gemma Galgani

Via del Giardino Botanico

Piazza Santa Maria

Via della Fratta

Via della Quarquonia

Piazza San Pietro Somaldi

Via Dell'Angelo Custode

Via Della Rosa

Piazza Antelminelli

Via della Cavallerizza

Via della Quarquonia

Via Canuleia

Via Guinigi

5

Torre Guinigi

Via Santa Croce

Via Fillungo

Via dei Fossi

Piazza del Collegio

Piazza degli Scalpellini

Piazza San Frediano

Piazza Anfiteatro

9

Via Mordini

Piazza del Carmine

Via Sant'Andrea

Piazza dei Servi

Piazza San Martino

Via Vallisneri

Museo della Cattedrale

Cattedrale di San Martino

3

1

Passeggiata della Mura

21

Via degli Angeli

Via Battisti

10

Via del Moro

15

Via Buia

Via Lucia

12

22

23

13

Via Santa Lucia

19

Piazza San Michele

Via Cenami

Piazza San Martino

Via del Battistero

18

Via del Molinetto

Piazza San Martino

7

Via del Duomo

Palazzo Pfanner

4

2

City Wall

Piazza Sant'Agostino

Via San Giorgio

Via Tegrimi

17

14

Via di Poggio

Piazza Cittadella

11

6

Piazza XX Settembre

Piazza Napoleone

16

Piazza del Giglio

Moat

Baluardo Santa Croce

Porta San Donato

Via Delle Conce

Passeggiata della Mura

Via San Giustina

Via del Toro

Corte Campana

Piazza San Michele

Piazza Vittorio Emanuele II

Via Veneto

Piazza San Romano

Via Galli Tassi

20

Via San Paolino

Piazza San Donato

Piazzale Verdi

Piazzale Boccherini

Lucca

high and 4.2km long, today's ramparts are crowned with a tree-lined footpath looking down on the historic centre and – by the **Baluardo San Regolo** (San Regolo Bastion) – the city's vintage **Orto Botanico** (Botanical Garden; ☑0583 44 21 61; Casermetta San Regolo; adult/reduced €4/3; ⊙10am-7pm Jul-Sep, to 6pm May & Jun, to 5pm Mar, Apr & Oct) with its magnificent centurion cedar trees.

★**Cattedrale di San Martino**   CATHEDRAL
(☑0583 49 05 30; www.museocattedralelucca. it; Piazza San Martino; adult/reduced €3/2, incl Museo della Cattedrale & Chiesa e Battistero dei SS Giovanni & Reparata €9/5; ⊙9.30am-6pm Mon-Fri, to 6.45pm Sat, noon-6pm Sun summer, 9.30am-5pm Mon-Fri, to 6.45pm Sat, noon-6pm Sun winter) Lucca's predominantly Romanesque cathedral dates from the 11th century. Its stunning facade was constructed in the prevailing Lucca-Pisan style and designed to accommodate the pre-existing *campanile* (bell tower). The reliefs over the left doorway of the portico are believed to be by Nicola Pisano, while inside, treasures include the **Volto Santo** (literally, Holy Countenance) crucifix sculpture and a wonderful 15th-century tomb in the **sacristy**. The cathedral interior was rebuilt in the 14th and 15th centuries with a Gothic flourish.

★**Museo della Cattedrale**   MUSEUM
(Cathedral Museum; ☑0583 49 05 30; www.museo cattedralelucca.it; Piazza San Martino; adult/reduced €4/3, with cathedral sacristy & Chiesa e Battistero dei SS Giovanni e Reparata €9/5; ⊙10am-6pm summer, to 5pm Mon-Fri, to 6pm Sat & Sun winter) The cathedral museum safeguards gold and silver decorations made for the cathe-

dral's Volto Santo, including a 17th-century crown and a 19th-century sceptre.

★**Torre Guinigi**   TOWER
(Via Sant'Andrea 45; adult/reduced €4/3; ⊙9.30am-7.30pm Jun-Sep, to 6.30pm Apr & May, to 5.30pm Oct & Mar) The bird's-eye view from the top of this medieval, 45m-tall red-brick tower adjoining 14th-century **Palazzo Guinigi** is predictably magnificent. But what impresses even more are the seven oak trees planted in a U-shaped flower bed at the top of the tower. Legend has it that upon the death of powerful Lucchese ruler Paolo Guinigi (1372–1432) all the leaves fell off the trees. Count 230 steps to the top.

Chiesa e Battistero dei SS Giovanni e Reparata   CHURCH
(☑0583 49 05 30; www.museocattedralelucca. it; Piazza San Giovanni; adult/reduced €4/3, with cathedral sacristy & Museo della Cattedrale €9/5; ⊙10am-6pm summer, to 5pm Mon-Fri, to 6pm Sat & Sun winter) The 12th-century interior of this deconsecrated church is a hauntingly atmospheric setting for summertime opera and **concert recitals** (www.puccinielasua lucca.com), staged daily at 7pm; buy tickets (adult/reduced €20/16) in advance inside the church. In the north transept, the Gothic baptistry crowns an **archaeological area** comprising five building levels going back to the Roman period. Don't miss the hike up the red-brick **bell tower**.

★**Palazzo Pfanner**   PALACE
(☑0583 95 21 55; www.palazzopfanner.it; Via degli Asili 33; palace or garden adult/reduced €4.50/4, both €6/5; ⊙10am-6pm Apr-Nov) Fire the

romantic in you with a stroll around this beautiful 17th-century palace where parts of *Portrait of a Lady* (1996), starring Nicole Kidman and John Malkovich, were shot. Its baroque-styled garden – the only one of substance within the city walls – enchants with ornamental pond, lemon house and 18th-century statues of Greek gods posing between potted lemon trees. Summertime chamber-music concerts hosted here are absolutely wonderful.

Chiesa di San Michele in Foro CHURCH
(Piazza San Michele; ☉ 7.40am-noon & 3-6pm summer, 9am-noon & 3-5pm winter) One of Lucca's many architecturally significant churches, this glittering Romanesque edifice marks the spot where the city's Roman forum was. The present building with its exquisite wedding-cake facade was constructed over 300 years on the site of its 8th-century precursor, beginning in the 11th century. Crowning the structure is a figure of the archangel Michael slaying a dragon. Inside the dimly lit interior, don't miss Filippino Lippi's 1479 painting of Sts Helen, Jerome, Sebastian and Roch (complete with plague sore) in the south transept.

🛏 Sleeping

Piccolo Hotel Puccini HOTEL €
(☑ 0583 5 54 21; www.hotelpuccini.com; Via di Poggio 9; s/d/t €75/95/120; ❄ 🛜) In a brilliant central location, this welcoming three-star hotel hides behind a discreet brick exterior. Its small guest rooms are attractive with wooden floors, vintage ceiling fans and colourful, contemporary design touches. Breakfast, optional at €3.50, is served at candlelit tables behind the small reception area. Rates are at least 30% lower in winter.

★ Villa Lucrezia B&B €€
(☑ 0583 95 42 86; www.luccainvilla.it; Viale Luigi Cadorna 30; d/q €120/140; 🅿 🛜) A particularly handy address for those arriving by car, this 10-room B&B is a two-minute walk from the city walls, inside a graceful 19th-century villa with a jasmine-scented garden. Rooms

are spacious and light-filled, with big windows, contemporary design furnishings and sharp en-suite bathrooms. Complimentary tea, coffee and cakes are at hand throughout the day in the basement breakfast room.

The villa also lends guests free bicycles to pedal into town. Free courtyard parking.

2italia APARTMENT €€
(☑ 392 996 02 71; www.2italia.com; Via della Anfiteatro 74; apt for 2 adults & up to 4 children per night/week €190/1050; 🛜) Not a hotel but several family-friendly self-catering apartments overlooking Piazza Anfiteatro, with a communal kids' playroom in the attic. Available on a nightly basis (minimum two nights), the project is the brainchild of well-travelled parents-of-three, Kristin (English) and Kaare (Norwegian). Spacious apartments sleep up to six, have a fully equipped kitchen and washing machine, and come with sheets and towels.

Kristin and Kaare have several other apartments and villas to rent in and around Lucca. They also organise cycling tours, cooking courses, wine tastings and olive pickings for guests.

Alla Corte degli Angeli BOUTIQUE HOTEL €€€
(☑ 0583 46 92 04; www.allacortedegliangeli. com; Via degli Angeli 23; d €240-270; ❄ @ 🛜) This boutique hotel sits in a couple of 15th-century townhouses, with a stylish beamed lounge leading to 21 sunny rooms adorned with frescoed ceilings, patches of exposed brick and landscape murals. Every room is named after a different flower, and up-to-the-minute bathrooms have hot tubs and power-jet showers.

🍴 Eating

★ Gustevole GELATO €
(☑ 366 896 03 46; www.facebook.com/gelateria gustevolelucca; Via di Poggio Seconda 26; cones & tubs €2.30-3; ☉ 1.30-7pm Tue-Thu, noon-7pm Fri, to 8pm Sat) With enticing flavours like liquorice and mint, ricotta with fig and walnut, or pine kernel made with local Pisan kernels (nuts in sweet, crunchy caramelised clumps), the most recent addition to Lucca's artisan gelato scene is pure gold. Gelato is organic, natural and gluten-free. The key to entering gelato heaven: ask for a dollop of thick whipped cream on top.

L'Hamburgheria di Eataly BURGERS €
(☑ 0583 42 92 16; www.facebook.com/hamburghe riadieatalylucca; Via Fillungo 91a; burgers €9.80-

---

> ℹ **CENT SAVER**
>
> If you plan to visit the Museo della Cattedrale, Chiesa de SS Giovanni e Reparata and the sacristy at Cattedrale di San Martino, buy a cheaper combined ticket (adult/reduced €9/5) at any of the sights.

A WALLTOP PICNIC

When in Lucca, picnicking atop its city walls – on grass or at a wooden picnic table – is as lovely (and typical) a Lucchesi lunch as any.

Buy fresh-from-the-oven pizza and focaccia with a choice of fillings and toppings from fabulous bakery **Forno Amedeo Giusti** (☑0583 49 62 85; www.facebook.com/Panificio Giusti; Via Santa Lucia 20; pizzas & filled focaccias per kg €10-15; ⊘7am-7.30pm Mon-Sat, 4-7.30pm Sun), then nip across the street for a bottle of Lucchesi wine and Garfagnese *biscotti al farro* (spelt biscuits) at **La Bodega di Prospero** (Via Santa Lucia 13; ⊘9am-7pm); look for the old-fashioned shop window stuffed with sacks of beans and other local pulses.

Complete the perfect picnic with a slice of *buccellato*, a traditional sweet bread loaf with sultanas and aniseed seeds, baked in Lucca since 1881. Devour the rest at home, with butter, dipped in egg and pan-fried, or dunked in sweet Vin Santo. Buy it at pastry shop **Taddeucci** (☑0583 49 49 33; www.buccellatotaddeucci.com; Piazza San Michele 34; buccellato loaf per 300/600g €4.50/9; ⊘8.30am-7.45pm, closed Thu winter). Or seduce taste buds with truffles, white-chocolate spread and other artisanal chocolate creations almost too beautiful to eat from **Caniparoli** (www.caniparolicioccolateria.it; Via San Paolino 96; ⊘9.30am-1pm & 3.30-7.30pm), the finest chocolate shop in town.

Swill down the picnic with your pick of Italian craft beers at microbrewery **De Cervesia** (☑0583 49 30 81; www.decervesia.it; Via Fillungo 90; ⊘10.30am-1pm & 3.30-7.30pm Tue-Sat), which has a small shop on Lucca's main shopping street and a tap room for serious tasting (open 5pm to 10pm Tuesday to Sunday) a few blocks away at Via Michele Rosi 20. Should a shot of something stronger be required to aid digestion, nip into historic pharmacy **Antica Farmacia Massagli** (☑0583 49 60 67; Piazza San Michele 36, ⊘9am-7.30pm Mon-Sat) for a bottle of China elixir, a heady liqueur of aromatic spices and herbs first concocted in 1855 as a preventive measure against the plague. Lucchese typically drink the natural alcoholic drink (no colouring or preservatives) at the end of a meal.

13.80; ⊘11am-midnight Mon, 8.30am-midnight Tue-Sat, 9.30am-midnight Sun; ▣) A clever mix of fast and slow food, this modern Eataly eatery cooks up gourmet burgers crafted from Tuscany's signature Chianina beef alongside a tantalising mix of hot dogs, grilled meats and *taglieri* (wooden chopping boards) loaded with salami, cold meats and cheeses. Begin with a focaccia (€9.50 to €19.50) to share beneath red-brick vaults inside or among potted lemon trees in the courtyard.

Trattoria da Leo   TRATTORIA €
(☑0583 49 22 36; http://trattoriadaleo.it/; Via Tegrimi 1; meals €25; ⊘12.30-2pm & 7.30-10.30pm Mon-Sat) A much-loved veteran, Leo is famed for its friendly ambience and cheap food – ranging from plain-Jane acceptable to grandma delicious. Arrive in summer to snag one of 10 tables covered with chequered tablecloths and crammed beneath parasols on the narrow street outside. Otherwise, it's noisy dining inside among typically nondescript 1970s decor. No credit cards.

Da Felice   PIZZA €
(☑0583 49 49 86; www.pizzeriadafelice.it; Via Buia 12; focaccia €1-3, pizza slices €1.30; ⊘11am-8.30pm Mon, 10am-8.30pm Tue-Sat) This buzz-ing spot behind Piazza San Michele is where the locals come for wood-fired pizza, *cecina* (salted chickpea pizza) and *castagnacci* (chestnut cakes). Eat in or take away, *castagnaccio* comes wrapped in crisp white paper, and my, it's good married with a chilled bottle of Moretti beer.

★ **Ristorante Giglio**   TUSCAN €€
(☑0583 49 40 58; www.ristorantegiglio.com; Piazza del Giglio 2; meals €40; ⊘noon-2.30pm & 7.30-10pm Thu-Mon, 7.30-10pm Wed) Splendidly at home in the frescoed 18th-century Palazzo Arnolfini, Giglio is stunning. Dine at white-tableclothed tables, sip a complimentary *prosecco*, watch the fire crackle in the marble fireplace and savour traditional Tuscan with a modern twist: think fresh artichoke salad served in an edible parmesan-cheese wafer 'bowl', or risotto simmered in Chianti. End with Lucchesi *buccellato* (sweet bread) filled with ice cream and berries. Tasting menus (€40 and €60) are the best value.

🍷 Drinking & Nightlife

★ **Bistrot Undici Undici**   CAFE
(☑0583 189 27 01; www.facebook.com/und1c1 und1c1; Piazza Antelminelli 2; ⊘10am-8pm Tue-Thu,

to 1am Fri-Sun) With one huge cream-coloured parasol providing shade and a tinkling fountain providing an atmospheric soundtrack, cafe terraces don't get much better than this. And then there is the view at this bucolic cafe (the only cafe) on Piazza San Miniato of the almighty facade of Lucca's lovely cathedral. Live music sets the place rocking after dark.

ℹ Information

Tourist Office (☑ 0583 58 31 50; www.turismo.lucca.it; Piazzale Verdi; ☺9am-7pm Apr-Sep, to 5pm Mar-Oct) Free hotel reservations, left-luggage service (two bags €1.50/4.50/7 per hour/half-day/day) and guided city tours in English departing at 2pm daily in summer and on Saturdays and Sundays in winter. The two-hour tour is €10/free per adult/child under 15 years.

ℹ Getting There & Away

BUS

From the bus stops around Piazzale Verdi, **Vaibus Lucca** (www.lucca.cttnord.it) runs services throughout the region, including to the following destinations:

Bagni di Lucca (€3.40, 50 minutes, eight daily)

Castelnuovo di Garfagnana (€4.20, 1½ hours, eight daily)

Pisa airport (€3.40, 45 minutes to one hour, 30 daily)

TRAIN

The train station is south of the city walls: take the path across the moat and through the (dank and grungy) tunnel under Baluardo San Colombano. Regional train services:

Florence (€7.50 to €9.60, 1¼ to 1¾ hours, hourly)

Pietrasanta (€4.40 to €6.10, 50 minutes, hourly)

Pisa (€3.50, 30 minutes, half-hourly)

Pistoia (€5.50, 45 minutes to one hour, half-hourly)

Viareggio (€3.50, 25 minutes, hourly)

ℹ Getting Around

BICYCLE

Rent wheels (ID required) to pedal the 4.2km circumference of Lucca's romantic city walls:

Biciclette Poli (☑ 0583 49 37 87; www.biciclettepoli.com; Piazza Santa Maria 42; per hr/day €3/15; ☺9am-7pm summer) Just across from the city walls, this seasonal bike-rental outfit has regular city bikes as well as mountain bikes (€4/20 per hour/day), racing bikes (€7/35 per hour/day) and tandems (€6.50/32.50 per hour/day). Kids' bikes too.

Cicli Bizzarri (☑ 0583 49 66 82; www.ciclibizzarri.net; Piazza Santa Maria 32; per hr/day €3/15; ☺8.30am-7.30pm summer, to 12.30pm & 2-7.30pm winter) Every type of bike imaginable for rent – tandems and e-bikes included.

Tourist Center Lucca (☑ 338 821 39 52, 0583 49 44 01; www.touristcenterlucca.com; Piazzale Ricasoli 203; bike per 3hr/day €8/12; ☺9am-7pm) Exit the train station and bear left to find this handy bike-rental outlet, with kids' bikes, tandems, trailers and various other gadgets. It also has left-luggage facilities (€3/5 per bag up to three hours/day).

CAR & MOTORCYCLE

In Lucca it's easiest to park at Parcheggio Carducci, just outside Porta Sant'Anna. Within the walls, most car parks are for residents only, indicated by yellow lines. Blue lines indicate where anyone, including tourists, can park (€2 per hour). If you are staying within the city walls, contact your hotel ahead of your arrival and enquire about the possibility of getting a temporary resident permit during your stay.

Pietrasanta

POP 24,000

Often overlooked by Tuscan travellers, this refined art town sports a bijou historic heart (originally walled) peppered with tiny art galleries, workshops and fashion boutiques – perfect for a day's amble broken only by lunch.

Founded in 1255 by Guiscardo da Pietrasanta, the *podestà* (governing magistrate) of Lucca, Pietrasanta was seen as a prize by Genoa, Lucca, Pisa and Florence, all of which jostled for possession of its marble quarries and bronze foundries. Florence won out and Leo X (Giovanni de' Medici) took control in 1513, putting the town's quarries at the disposal of Michelangelo, who came here in 1518 to source marble for the facade of Florence's San Lorenzo. Artists continue to work here, including internationally lauded Colombian-born sculptor Fernando Botero (b 1932), whose work can be seen here.

Pietrasanta is a great base for exploring the Apuane Alps and a lovely day trip from Pisa or Viareggio.

◉ Sights & Activities

From Pietrasanta train station on Piazza della Stazione head straight across Piazza Carducci, through the Old City gate and onto Piazza del Duomo, the main square, which doubles as an outdoor gallery for sculptures and other large works of art.

Duomo di San Martino CATHEDRAL
(Piazza del Duomo; ⊙ hours vary) It is impossible to miss Pietrasanta's attractive cathedral, dating from 1256, on the central square. Its distinctive 36m-tall, red-brick bell tower is actually unfinished; the red brick was meant to have a marble cladding.

Via Garibaldi STREET
This quaint pedestrian strip is peppered with chic fashion boutiques and stylish art galleries. Highlights guaranteed to tempt include fashion designer **Paolo Milani** (☑ 0584 79 07 29; Via Garibaldi 11; ⊙ hours vary), whose studio is a riot of bold vibrant prints and a wild mix of textures covering the whole sombre-to-sequin spectrum; multibrand fashion queen and trendsetter **Zoe** (☑ 0424 52 21 25; www.zoecompany.eu; Via Garibaldi 29-33 & 44-46; ⊙ 10am-1pm & 4-8pm); vintage furniture design boutique Lei; and concept store **Dada** (☑ 0584 7 04 37; www.dadaconcept.it; Via Garibaldi 39; ⊙ 10am-1pm & 3.30-7.30pm Tue-Sun).

✖ Eating & Drinking

★ Filippo Mud Bar TUSCAN €€
(☑ 0584 7 00 10; www.facebook.com/filippomud; Via Barsanti 45; 3-/5-course menu €35/55; ⊙ 12.30-2.15pm & 7pm-1am Wed-Sun, 7pm-1am Tue) Completely on trend, this chic open-plan space is part lounge, part cocktail bar (stunning paprika-roasted almonds) and part formal restaurant with a sensational industrial-meets-lime green-velour interior. Its menu, an ode to fusion cuisine, is equally fabulous: order a three- or five-course menu, or try the 'sensual experience for provocative souls' (€25) – aka a cocktail perfectly paired with a surprise dish. Reservations essential.

La Brigata di Filippo TUSCAN €€
(☑ 0584 7 00 10; http://ristorantefilippo.com; Via Stagio Stagi 22; meals €40; ⊙ 12.30-2.30pm & 7.30pm-2am, closed Mon winter) 🌡 This exceptional foodie address never disappoints. From the homemade bread and focaccia brought warm to your table throughout the course of your meal to the contemporary fabric on the walls, to giant wicker lampshades and modern open kitchen, this bistro is chic. Cuisine is seasonal modern Tuscan and is perfect for a lazy lunch (two-/three-/four-course menus €25/35/45) inside or out.

★ L'Enoteca Marcucci WINE BAR
(☑ 0584 79 19 62; www.enotecamarcucci.it; Via Garibaldi 40; ⊙ 10am-1pm & 5pm-1am Tue-Sun) Taste fine Tuscan wine on bar stools at high wooden tables or beneath big parasols on the street outside. Whichever you pick, the distinctly funky, artsy spirit of Pietrasanta's best-loved *enoteca* enthrals.

❶ Getting There & Away
Regional train services:
Pisa (€4.40, 30 minutes, every 30 minutes)
Viareggio (€2.60, 10 minutes, every 10 minutes)
Lucca (with change of train in Pisa or Viareggio; €6.10, one hour, every 30 minutes)

EASTERN TUSCANY
The eastern edge of Tuscany is beloved by film directors who've immortalised its landscape and hilltop towns in several critically acclaimed and visually splendid films. Yet the region remains refreshingly bereft of tourist crowds and offers uncrowded trails for those savvy enough to explore here.

Arezzo
POP 99,500
Arezzo may not be a Tuscan centretold, but those parts of its historic centre that survived merciless WWII bombings are as compelling as any destination in the region – the city's central square is as beautiful as it appears in Roberto Benigni's classic film *La vita è bella* (Life is Beautiful).

Once an important Etruscan trading post, Arezzo was later absorbed into the Roman Empire. A free republic as early as the 10th century, it supported the Ghibelline cause in the violent battles between pope and emperor and was eventually subjugated by Florence in 1384.

Today, the city is known for its churches, museums and fabulously sloping **Piazza Grande**, across which a huge antiques fair (p573) spills each month. Come dusk, Arentini (locals of Arezzo) spill along the length of shop-clad Corso Italia for the ritual late-afternoon *passeggiata* (stroll).

◉ Sights
A combined ticket (adult/reduced €15/12) covers admission to Cappella Bacci, Museo Archeologico Nazionale and Museo di Casa Vasari.

★ Cappella Bacci CHURCH
(☑ 0575 35 27 27; www.pierodellafrancesca.it; Piazza San Francesco; adult/reduced €8/5;

Arezzo

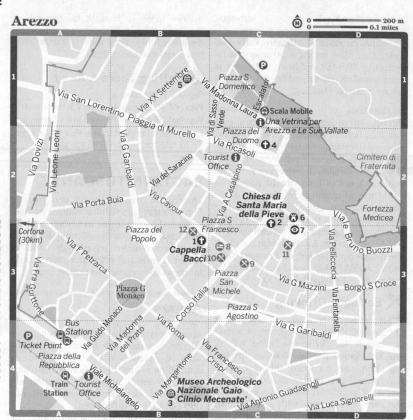

⊙9am-6pm Mon-Fri, to 5.30pm Sat, 1-5.30pm Sun) This chapel, in the apse of 14th-century **Basilica di San Francesco**, safeguards one of Italian art's greatest works: Piero della Francesca's fresco cycle of the *Legend of the True Cross*. Painted between 1452 and 1466, it relates the story of the cross on which Christ was crucified. Only 25 people are allowed in every half hour, making advance booking (by telephone or email) essential in high season. The ticket office is down the stairs by the basilica's entrance.

★ Chiesa di Santa Maria della Pieve   CHURCH

(Corso Italia 7; ⊙8am-12.30pm & 3-6.30pm) FREE This 12th-century church – Arezzo's oldest – has an exotic Romanesque arcaded facade adorned with carved columns, each uniquely decorated. Above the central doorway are 13th-century carved reliefs called *Cyclo dei Mesi* representing each month of the year.

The plain interior's highlight – removed for restoration work at the time of writing – is Pietro Lorenzetti's polyptych *Madonna and Saints* (1320–24), beneath the semidome of the apse. Below the altar is a 14th-century silver bust reliquary of the city's patron saint, San Donato.

★ Museo Archeologico Nazionale 'Gaio Cilnio Mecenate'   MUSEUM

(Gaius Cilnius Maecenas Archeological Museum; ☎0575 2 08 82; www.facebook.com/archeologico arezzo; Via Margaritone 10; adult/reduced €6/3, 1st Sunday each month free; ⊙8.30am-7.30pm, to 1.30pm Nov) Overlooking the remains of a Roman amphitheatre that once seated up to 10,000 spectators, this museum – named after Gaius Maecenas (68–8 BC), a patron of the arts and trusted advisor to Roman Emperor Augustus – exhibits Etruscan and Roman artefacts in a 14th-century convent building. The highlight is the *Cratere di Euphronios*, a

Arezzo

◉ Top Sights
1 Cappella Bacci B3
2 Chiesa di Santa Maria della
   Pieve C2
3 Museo Archeologico Nazionale
   'Gaio Cilnio Mecenate' B4

◉ Sights
4 Duomo di Arezzo C2
5 Museo di Casa Vasari B1
6 Palazzo della Fraternità dei
   Laici C2
7 Piazza Grande C3

◉ Activities, Courses & Tours
Fiera Antiquaria di Arezzo .... (see 7)
Giostra del Saracino .... (see 7)

◉ Sleeping
8 Graziella Patio Hotel C3

◉ Eating
9 Antica Osteria Agania C3
10 Creml C3
11 La Bottega di Gnicche C3
12 Le Chiavi d'Oro B3

6th-century-BC Etruscan vase decorated with vivid scenes showing Hercules in battle.

Duomo di Arezzo　　　　　　　CATHEDRAL
(Cattedrale di SS Donato e Pietro; Piazza del Duomo; ☉ 7am-12.30pm & 3.30-6.30pm) **FREE** Construction started in the 13th century but Arezzo's cathedral wasn't completed until the 15th century. In the northeast corner, next to the vestry door left of the intricately carved main altar, is Piero della Francesca's exquisite fresco, *Mary Magdalene* (c 1459), unfortunately dwarfed somewhat by the 13m-tall cenotaph of Arezzo bishop Guido Tarlati (moved to its current spot in 1783). Also notable are five glazed terracottas by Andrea della Robbia and his studio in the **Cappella della Madonna del Conforto**.

Palazzo della Fraternità dei Laici　　PALACE
(☎ 0575 2 46 94; www.fraternitadeilaici.it; Piazza Grande; adult/child €3/free; ☉ 10am-6pm Thu-Mon, 11.30am-5.30pm Tue & Wed) This *palazzo*, with its churchlike facade, was started in 1375 in the Gothic style and finished in the late 1550s after the onset of the Renaissance. Delve into its small museum to admire portraits of grand dukes and benefactors of the Fraternità dei Laici, a fraternity set up in 1262 to help the poor, and artworks collected by local sculptor Ranieri

Bartolini (1794–1856). Don't leave without scaling the staircase to the rooftop astronomical clock (1552).

Museo di Casa Vasari　　　　　MUSEUM
(Vasari House Museum; ☎ 0575 29 90 71; www.museistataliarezzo.it/museo-casa-vasari; Via XX Settembre 55; adult/reduced €4/2; ☉ 8.30am-7.30pm Mon & Wed-Sat, to 1.30pm Sun) Built and sumptuously decorated by Arezzo-born painter, architect and art historian Giorgio Vasari (1511–74), this museum is where Vasari lived and worked, and where the original manuscript of his *Lives of the Most Excellent Painters, Sculptors and Architects* (1550) – still in print under the title *The Lives of the Artists* is kept. End on the bijou, Renaissance-style roof garden with flower beds, box hedges and a fountain in its centre. To access the museum, ring the bell.

✰ Festivals & Events

Giostra del Saracino　　　　　CULTURAL
(Joust of the Saracino; www.giostradelsaracinoarezzo.it, ☉ Jun & Sep) This medieval jousting competition, held on Piazza Grande on the third Saturday of June and first Sunday of September, sees each of the city's four *quartieri* (quarters) put forward a team of 'knights'.

Fiera Antiquaria di Arezzo　　　　FAIR
(Arezzo Antique Fair; www.fieraantiquaria.org) Tuscany's most famous antiques fair is held in Piazza Grande on the first Sunday and preceding Saturday of every month.

⬛ Sleeping

Casa Volpi　　　　　　　　　HOTEL €
(☎ 0575 35 43 64; www.casavolpi.it; Via Simone Martini 29; s/d/tr €75/90/120; ℗ ⊛ @ ☎) This 18th-century manor is an easy, scenic 4km bicycle ride away from the cobbled streets of downtown Arezzo (the hotel lends guests wheels). Its 15 rooms are decorated in a classical style, with plenty of charming original features – beamed ceilings, red-brick flooring, parquet. Family run, the hotel restaurant expands its seating into the pretty garden in summer.

Graziella Patio Hotel　　BOUTIQUE HOTEL €€
(☎ 0575 40 19 62; www.hotelpatio.it; Via Cavour 23; s/d from €120/150; ⊛ @ ☎) A delightful mix of ancient (15th-century cellars) and contemporary design, this 10-room hotel has themed rooms inspired by Bruce Chatwin's travel books – with decor to match. Pink-kissed Arkady is the 'Australia room', Fillide

exudes a distinctly Moroccan air and Cobra Verde is a green Amazon-inspired loft. Every room has a MacBook for guests to go online and service is first class.

✗ Eating

★ Cremì
GELATO €

(☑333 976 63 36; www.facebook.com/gelateria artigianalecremi; Corso Italia 100; cones & tubs €1.80-5; ☺10am-7.30pm Tue-Sun) Follow the locals to this bright, modern *gelateria artigianale* (artisan gelato shop) on Arezzo's main *passeggiata* (late-afternoon strolling) strip. Enticing seasonal flavours include pear and vanilla, strawberry cheesecake, peanut, and walnut and fig. Or opt for the luscious and wildly popular house speciality – *mousse di nutella* (a creamy, light-as-air chocolate- and hazelnut-flavoured mousse-like ice cream).

La Bottega di Gnicche
SANDWICHES €

(☑0575 182 29 26; www.bottegadignicche.com; Piazza Grande 4; panini €3.50-7; ☺11am-8pm Thu-Tue) Choose from a delectable array of artisan meats and cheeses to stuff in a *panino* at this old-fashioned *alimentari* (grocery store) on Arezzo's main piazza. Check the day's handwritten menu for hot dishes too, such as *ribollita* (traditional Tuscan veg-and-bread soup). Eat inside, between shelves of canary-yellow bags of Martelli pasta, or on the wooden terrace with a sweeping piazza view.

Antica Osteria Agania
TUSCAN €

(☑0575 29 53 81; www.agania.com; Via G Mazzini 10; meals €20; ☺noon-3pm & 6-10.30pm Tue-Sun) Agania has been around for years and her fare is die-hard traditional; the tripe and *grifi con polenta* (lambs' cheeks with polenta) are sensational. Indeed it's timeless, welcoming restaurants like this, potted herbs on the doorstep, that remain the cornerstone of Tuscan dining. Begin with *antipasto misto* (mixed appetisers), then choose your *primo* (first course) from the six pasta types and eight sauces on offer. Agania's *pici* (fat spaghetti) with wild boar sauce is legendary. Arrive by 1pm to beat the crowd of regulars, or join the crowd waiting outside.

★ Le Chiavi d'Oro
ITALIAN €€

(☑0575 40 33 13; www.ristorantelechiavidoro.it; Piazza San Francesco 7; meals €45; ☺12.30-2.30pm & 7.30-10.30pm Tue-Sun) Contemporary Italian cooking is on offer at this game-changing restaurant in central Arezzo. Design lovers are wooed by the minimalist interior with part-resin, part-parquet floor and stylish 1960s Danish chairs, while foodies are quickly won over by the simplistic menu that reads something like a shopping list of ingredients. Bream with artichokes, saffron, breadcrumbs and lime anyone?

ℹ Information

Tourist Office (☑0575 40 19 45; Piazza della Libertà; ☺2-4pm) Find another branch of the **tourist office** (☑0575 2 68 50; Piazza della Repubblica 22-23; ☺10.30am-12.30pm) to the right as you exit the train station.

Una Vetrina per Arezzo e Le Sue Vallate (☑0575 182 27 70; www.arezzoturismo. it; Emiciclo Giovanni Paolo II, Scale Mobili di Arezzo; ☺9am-6pm Mon-Fri, to 7pm Sat & Sun) Private tourist office on the *scala mobile* (escalator) leading up to Piazza del Duomo; it has toilet facilities (€0.50).

ℹ Getting There & Away

BUS

Buses operated by **Siena Mobilità** (www.siena mobilita.it) serve Siena (€7, 1½ hours, seven daily). **Etruria Mobilità** (www.etruriamobilita. it) buses serve Sansepolcro (€4.40, one hour, hourly) and Cortona (€3.50, one hour, frequent). Buy tickets from the **ticket point** (Via Piero della Francesca 1; ☺6.10am-8pm Mon-Sat year-round, 6.30am-noon Sun summer, 8am-12.30pm Sun winter) to the left as you exit the train station; buses leave from the **bus bay** (Via Piero della Francesca) opposite.

TRAIN

Arezzo is on the Florence–Rome train line, and there are frequent services to Florence (*Regionale* €8.50, one to 1½ hours) and Rome (Intercity €27.50, 2¼ hours; *Regionale* €14.50, 2¾ hours). There are twice-hourly regional trains to Camucia–Cortona (€3.50, 20 minutes).

Cortona

POP 22,500

Rooms with a view are the rule rather than the exception in this spectacularly sited hilltop town. In the late 14th century Fra' Angelico lived and worked here, and fellow artists Luca Signorelli and Pietro da Cortona were both born within the walls – all three are represented in the Museo Diocesano's small but sensational collection. Large chunks of *Under the Tuscan Sun*, the soap-in-the-sun film of the book by Frances Mayes, were shot here.

⊙ Sights

★ Museo dell'Accademia Etrusca e della Città di Cortona   MUSEUM

(MAEC; www.cortonamaec.org; Piazza Signorelli 9; adult/reduced €10/7; ⊙ 10am-7pm Apr-Oct, to 5pm Tue-Sun Nov-Mar) In the 13th-century Palazzo Casali, this fascinating museum displays substantial local Etruscan and Roman finds, Renaissance globes, 18th-century decorative arts and contemporary paintings. The Etruscan collection is the highlight, particularly those objects excavated from the tombs at Sodo, just outside town. The *palazzo*'s plain facade was added in the 17th century.

★ Museo Diocesano   MUSEUM

(Piazza del Duomo 1; adult/reduced €5/3; ⊙ 10am-7pm Apr-Oct, to 5pm Tue-Sun Nov-Mar) Little is left of the original Romanesque character of Cortona's cathedral (Piazza del Duomo, ⊙ hours vary), rebuilt several times in a less-than-felicitous fashion. Fortunately, its artworks have been saved and displayed in this museum. Highlights include *Crucifixion* (1320) by Pietro Lorenzetti and two beautiful works by Fra' Angelico: *Annunciation* (1436) and *Madonna with Child and Saints* (1436–37). Room 1 features a remarkable Roman sarcophagus decorated with a frenzied battle scene between Dionysus and the Amazons.

Fortezza del Girifalco   LANDMARK

(⌨ 0575 164 53 07; www.fortezzadelgirifalco.it; Via di Fortezza; adult/reduced €5/3; ⊙ 10am-8pm mid-Jun–Aug, to 7pm mid-Apr–mid-Jun & Sep, to 6pm Oct, Nov & Mar–mid-Apr, 10am-6pm Sat & Sun Dec-Feb) Lap up the stupendous view over the Val di Chiana to Lago Trasimeno in Umbria from the remains of this Medici fortress, atop the highest point in town – count on a good 15 minutes for the steep hike up. Check the website for its fabulous season of events including yoga workshops, falconry shows, theatre performances, collective picnics, dinner concerts, DJ sets and dancing after dark.

🛏 Sleeping & Eating

★ La Corte di Ambra   B&B €€

(⌨ 0575 178 82 66; www.cortonaluxuryrooms.com; Via Benedetti 23; d €150-300; ❄ @ 🕸) Tucked away in Palazzo Fierli-Petrella, this contemporary guesthouse has five luxurious rooms with whitewashed beamed ceilings, chandelier lighting and beautiful linens in mellow neutral tones. En-suite bathrooms are up to the minute and the B&B has a lift; one room is genuinely wheelchair friendly.

Villa Marsili   HOTEL €€

(⌨ 0575 60 52 52; www.villamarsili.net; Viale Cesare Battisti 13; s/d from €85/115; ❄ @ 🕸) Service is the hallmark at this attractive four-star villa, wedged against the city walls and a short walk downhill from Cortona centre. Guests rave about the helpful staff, lavish breakfast buffet and early-evening *aperitivo* served in the garden. Pricier suites have Jacuzzis and wonderful views across the Val di Chiana to Lago Trasimeno. The cheapest rates are nonrefundable online.

★ Beerbone Artburger   BURGERS €

(⌨ 0575 60 17 90; www.facebook.com/cortona burger; Via Nazionale 55; burgers €9-14; ⊙ 11am-midnight Mon & Thu-Sun, 9am-5pm & 6pm-midnight Wed; 🕸) The feisty burgers cooked up at this contemporary restaurant on Cortona's main pedestrian drag are no ordinary burgers. Select your Tuscan meat – Chianina beef or *cinta senese* pork, smoked over applewood – and choose between lavish toppings: truffles with truffle cream, fried egg and lettuce perhaps, or *pecorino* cheese with homemade syrah mayonnaise. Craft beer completes the tasty ensemble.

★ La Bucaccia   TUSCAN €€

(⌨ 0575 60 60 39; www.labucaccia.it; Via Ghibellina 17; meals €35; ⊙ 12.45-3pm & 7-10.30pm Tue-Sun) Cortona's finest address, this gourmet gem resides in the medieval stable of a Renaissance *palazzo*. Cuisine is Tuscan and Cortonese – much meat and handmade pasta (chestnut ravioli!) – and the cheese course is superb, thanks to owner Romano Magi who ripens his own. Dedicated gourmets won't be able to resist the six *pecorino* types with fruit sauces, homemade salsas and honeys. Reservations essential. Cooking classes and cheese-making workshops are offered too.

ℹ Information

Tourist office (⌨ 0575 63 72 21; www.comune dicortona.it; Piazza Signorelli 9; ⊙ 9am-1pm & 2-6pm Mon-Fri, 9.30am-1pm Sat)

ℹ Getting There & Away

The nearest train station is 6km southwest in Camucia, accessible via bus (€1.40, 15 minutes, hourly). Camucia train station has no ticket office, only machines. If you need assistance purchasing tickets, go to the station at Terontola, 6.7km south of Camucia, instead. Destinations include:

Arezzo (€3.50, 25 minutes, hourly)

Florence (€10.70, 1¾ hours, hourly)

Rome (€11.55, 2¾ hours, eight daily)

Umbria & Le Marche

Best Places to Eat

➜ Vespasia (p609)

➜ Il Lampone (p608)

➜ DivinPeccato (p590)

➜ Antica Osteria da la Stella (p624)

➜ Osteria La Piazzetta dell'Erba (p599)

Best Places to Sleep

➜ Castello di Monterone (p584)

➜ Agriturismo il Bastione (p600)

➜ La Cuccagna (p601)

➜ Misia Resort (p613)

➜ Alla Madonna del Piatto (p598)

Why Go?

For years Italophiles have waxed lyrical about Tuscany's natural, artistic and culinary wonders, without so much as a passing nod to its neighbours, Umbria and Le Marche. How they have missed out! This phenomenally beautiful yet unsung region is Italy in microcosm: olive groves, vineyards, sun-ripened wheat fields stippled with wildflowers and hills plumed with cypress trees rolling gently west to the snow-dusted Apennines and east to the glittering Adriatic. In between, castle-topped medieval hill towns await, glowing like honey in the fading light of sundown.

The region scores highly on the artistic front, too, as the birthplace of Renaissance masters Raphael and Perugino, and sprightly composer Rossini. St Francis of Assisi, St Benedict and St Valentine all hail from here and make a spiritual pilgrimage to this area a profound one. So next time you glance at the map and your eyes alight on old favourite Tuscany, why not press on east? You won't regret it.

When to Go
Perugia

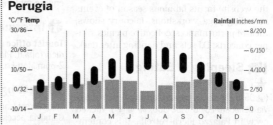

Feb Celebrate all things truffle at Norcia's Mostra Mercato del Tartufo Nero festival.

May Hit Le Marche's beaches, as wildflowers bloom on the Piano Grande.

Jun & Jul Get lost in music at the Spoleto Festival and Perugia's Umbria Jazz.

UMBRIA

Italy's green heart, Umbria is a land unto itself, the only Italian region that borders neither the sea nor another country. Removed from outside influences, it has kept alive many of Italy's old-world traditions. You'll see grandmothers in aprons making pasta by hand and front doors that haven't been locked in a century.

Separated from Le Marche by the jagged spine of the Monti Sibillini, it contrasts wild, in-your-face beauty with the gentle fall and rise of overlapping hills and wildflower-flecked meadows. The Etruscans, Romans and medieval feuding families have left their indelible imprint on its pretty hill towns, where history seems to creep up on you at every corner – from the Gothic wonder of Orvieto to Assisi's saintly calling.

Foodies are in their element here, with the rich earthiness of the *tartufo* (truffle), fine cured meats from Norcia and full-bodied local wines finding their way onto menus.

History

Umbria is named in honour of its first inhabitants, the Umbri tribe, who settled east of the Tiber around 1000 BC, establishing the towns of Spoleto, Gubbio and Assisi. They jockeyed for regional supremacy with the Etruscans to the west of the river – the founders of Perugia and Orvieto – until the 3rd century BC, when the Romans came marching through, conquering them both.

Following the collapse of the Western Roman Empire, the region spent much of the Middle Ages being fought over by Holy Roman Empire advocates (Ghibellines) and supporters of the Pope (Guelphs). Intriguingly, it was during this turbulent period that peace-loving St Francis came to prominence in Assisi.

Eventually the region became one of the Papal States, though this was not to its long-term benefit. Indeed, historians like to say that time stopped in Umbria in 1540 when the pope imposed a salt tax. The resulting war brought Umbrian culture to a standstill, which is partly why the medieval hearts of Umbrian towns are so well preserved.

Perugia has a strong artistic tradition. In the 15th century it was home to fresco painters Bernardino Pinturicchio and his master Pietro Vannucci (known as Perugino), who would later teach Raphael. Its cultural tradition continues to this day in the form of the University of Perugia and the famous

Università per Stranieri (University for Foreigners; p583), which teaches Italian, art and culture to thousands of students from around the world.

ⓘ Getting Around

While having your own wheels certainly makes it easier to reach those off-the-radar hill towns and rural corners of Umbria, it is possible to get to many places by public transport with a little pre-planning.

Buses head from Perugia to most towns in the area; check at the tourist office or the bus station for exact details. **Trenitalia** (www.trenitalia.com) sparsely criss-crosses Umbria, but **Busitalia** (www.fsbusitalia.it) fills in the blanks with bus and ferry services.

Your first port of call for mountain biking and road-cycling itineraries should be **Bike in Umbria** (http://bikeinumbria.it).

Perugia

POP 162,100

Lifted by a hill above a valley patterned with fields, where the River Tiber runs swift and clear, Perugia is Umbria's petite and immediately likeable capital. Its *centro storico* (historic centre) rises in a helter-skelter of cobbled alleys, arched stairways and piazzas framed by magnificent *palazzi* (mansions). History seeps through every shadowy corner of these streets and an aimless wander through them can feel like time travel.

Back in the 21st century, Perugia is a party-loving, pleasure-seeking university city, with students pepping up the nightlife and filling cafe terraces. The hopping summer event line-up includes one of Europe's best jazz festivals.

USEFUL WEBSITES ON UMBRIA

Bella Umbria (www.bellaumbria.net) Accommodation and restaurant listings for Umbria. Search for festivals and events by location or date.

Regione Umbria (www.umbriatourism.it) The official Umbrian tourist website.

Sistema Museo (www.sistemamuseo.it) Get the inside scoop on Umbria's museums and upcoming events.

Umbria Online (www.umbriaonline.com) Find information on accommodation, events and itineraries.

Umbria & Le Marche Highlights

1 **Basilica di San Francesco** (p593) Make the spiritual pilgrimage in the footsteps of a peace-seeking saint to Assisi's fresco-peppered Unesco World Heritage cathedrals.

2 **Parco del Conero** (p621) Swim, chill and eat just-caught shellfish by the Adriatic at some of Central Italy's most gorgeous and wild beaches.

3 **Funivia Colle Eletto** (p601) Savour towering views on a rickety ride up Monte Ingino aboard Gubbio's soaring birdcage-like cableway.

4 **Casa del Cioccolato Perugina** (p581) Cash in your golden ticket for a tour of Perugia's world-renowned chocolate factory.

5 **Lago Trasimeno** (p589) Slip into the relaxed groove of lake life: swimming, cycling and sipping locally grown wines at Italy's fourth-largest lake.

6 **Spello** (p600) Lazily wander the colourful, floral-potted wonderland of one of Umbria's prettiest and most pristinely-preserved villages.

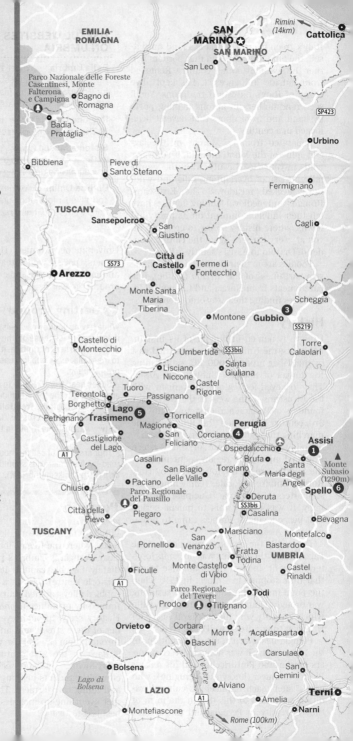

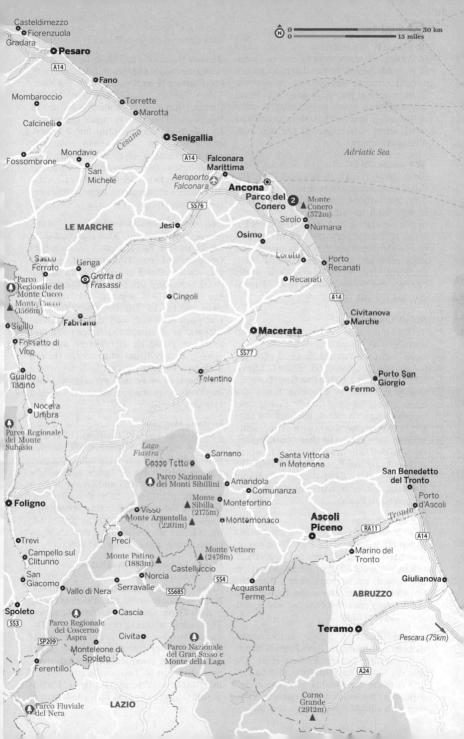

⊙ Sights

★ Piazza IV Novembre   PIAZZA

In Perugia all roads seem to lead to Piazza IV Novembre, once the meeting point for the ancient Etruscan and Roman civilisations. In the medieval period, it was the political centre of Perugia. Now people from all walks of life gather here to chat, slurp gelato and watch street entertainers or the odd budding opera singer.

★ Palazzo dei Priori   PALACE

(Corso Vannucci 19) Flanking Corso Vannucci, this Gothic palace, constructed between the 13th and 14th centuries, is architecturally striking with its tripartite windows, ornamental portal and fortress-like crenellations. It was formerly the headquarters of the local magistracy, but now houses the city's main art gallery, the Galleria Nazionale dell'Umbria, the Nobile Collegio del Cambio, the Nobile Collegio della Mercanzia and the Sala dei Notari.

Nobile Collegio del Cambio   HISTORIC BUILDING

(Exchange Hall; www.collegiodelcambio.it; Palazzo dei Priori, Corso Vannucci 25; €4.50, incl Nobile Collegio della Mercanzia €5.50; ⊗9am-12.30pm & 2.30-5.30pm Mon-Sat, 9am-1pm Sun) Perugia's money exchange in medieval times, the extravagantly adorned Nobile Collegio del Cambio has three rooms: the **Sala dei Legisti** (Lawyers Chamber), with 17th-century wooden stalls carved by Giampiero Zuccari; the **Sala dell'Udienza** (Audience Chamber), with outstanding Renaissance frescoes by Perugino; and the **Chapel of San Giovanni Battista**, painted by a student of Perugino's, Giannicola di Paolo.

Nobile Collegio della Mercanzia   HISTORIC BUILDING

(Merchant's Hall; Palazzo dei Priori, Corso Vannucci 15; €1.50, incl Nobile Collegio del Cambio €5.50; ⊗9am-1pm & 2.30-5.30pm Tue-Sat & 9am-1pm Sun summer, shorter hours winter) The Nobile Collegio della Mercanzia showcases a 14th-century audience chamber with exquisite wood panelling.

Sala dei Notari   HISTORIC BUILDING

(Notaries' Hall; Palazzo dei Priori, Piazza IV Novembre; ⊗9am-1pm & 3-7pm Tue-Sun) FREE The Sala dei Notari was built from 1293 to 1297 and is where the nobility met. The arches supporting the vaults are Romanesque, covered with vibrant frescoes depicting biblical scenes and Aesop's fables. To reach the hall, walk up the steps from Piazza IV Novembre.

Galleria Nazionale dell'Umbria   GALLERY

(www.gallerianazionaleumbria.it; Palazzo dei Priori, Corso Vannucci 19; adult/reduced €8/4; ⊗8.30am-7.30pm Tue-Sun, noon-7.30pm Mon Apr-Oct) Umbria's foremost art gallery is housed in Palazzo dei Priori on Perugia's main strip. Its collection, one of central Italy's richest, numbers almost 3000 works pleasantly distributed among 40 rooms, ranging from Byzantine-inspired 13th-century paintings to Gothic works by Gentile da Fabriano and Renaissance masterpieces by hometown heroes Pinturicchio and Perugino.

Cattedrale di San Lorenzo   CATHEDRAL

(Piazza IV Novembre; ⊗7.30am-12.30pm & 3.30-6.45pm Mon-Sat, 8am-12.45pm & 4-7.30pm Sun) Overlooking Piazza IV Novembre is Perugia's stark medieval cathedral. A church has stood here since the 900s, but the version you see today was begun in 1345 from designs created by Fra Bevignate. Building continued until 1587, although the main facade was never completed. Inside you'll find dramatic late-Gothic architecture, an altarpiece by Signorelli and sculptures by Duccio. The steps in front of the facade are where seemingly all of Perugia congregates; they overlook the piazza's centrepiece, Fontana Maggiore.

Fontana Maggiore   FOUNTAIN

(Great Fountain; Piazza IV Novembre) The centrepiece of Piazza IV Novembre, the delicate pink-and-white marble Fontana Maggiore was designed by Fra Bevignate and built by father-son team Nicola and Giovanni Pisano between 1275 and 1278. Bas-relief statues grace the polygonal basin, representing scenes from the Old Testament, the founding of Rome, the seven 'liberal arts', the signs of the zodiac, and a griffin and lion.

Museo Archeologico Nazionale dell'Umbria   MUSEUM

(MUNA; http://polomusealeumbria.beniculturali.it; Piazza Giordano Bruno 10; adult/reduced €5/2.50; ⊗10am-7.30pm Sat & Sun, 8.30am-7.30pm Mon) The convent adjoining the Chiesa di San Domenico is home to a superior collection of Etruscan and prehistoric artefacts – carved funerary urns, coins and Bronze Age statuary – dating as far back as the 16th century BC. The *Cippo Perugino* (Perugian Memorial Stone) has the longest Etruscan-language engraving ever found, offering a rare window into this obscure culture.

Casa del Cioccolato Perugina
MUSEUM

(📞800 434434; www.perugina.it; Van San Sisto 207, Loc San Sisto; adult/reduced €9/7; ⊙9am-1pm & 2-5.30pm Mon-Fri, plus 10am-4pm Sat Mar-May, Aug & Oct-Dec; 🚗) **FREE** To visit the Wonka-esque world of Perugian chocolate, call ahead to latch onto a 1¼-hour guided tour (in Italian or English, times vary). After visiting the museum, you'll wend your way through an enclosed sky bridge, watching as the white-outfitted Oompa Loompas, er, factory workers, go about their chocolate-creating business.

Basilica di San Pietro
BASILICA

(www.sanpietroperugia.it; Borgo XX Giugno 74; ⊙7am-noon & 3-5pm Nov-Jan, to 6pm Feb-Apr & Oct, to 6.30pm May-Sep) South of the town centre, past the Porta di San Pietro, this 10th-century basilica's interior is an absolutely stunning mix of gilt and marble that's quite expletive-inducing on first sight, and contains a *Pietà* (a painting of the dead Christ supported by the Madonna) by Perugino. For a glimpse into gardens past, take a stroll or picnic at the serene **Orto Medievale** (www.sanpietroperugia.it/orto-medievale; ⊙8am-5pm Mon-Fri) **FREE** gardens, behind the basilica.

Rocca Paolina
FORT, GARDENS

(Piazza Italia; ⊙6.15am-2am) **FREE** Built by Pope Paolo III Farnese in the 1540s, this fortress wiped out entire sections of a formerly wealthy neighbourhood. Now used as the throughway for the *scale mobili* (escalators), its fascinating nooks and crannies are venues for art exhibits, and the last weekend of the month sees Perugia's **antiques market** held here. Up above is a small park, **Giardini Carducci** (Corso Pietro Vannucci; ⊙24hr).

Casa Museo di Palazzo Sorbello
MUSEUM

(www.casamuseosorbello.org; Piazza Piccinino 9; adult/reduced €4/3, with Pozzo Etrusco €6; ⊙guided tours 10.30am-2pm & 3-6pm, shorter hours winter) A few steps from the Piazza IV Novembre, this exquisite 17th-century mansion, once owned by the noble Sorbello family, has recently been restored to its frescoed, gilt-clad, chandelier-lit 18th-century prime. Guided tours (in Italian and English) let you admire the family's almost ludicrously opulent collection of art, porcelain, embroidery and manuscripts.

Capella di San Severo
CHAPEL

(Piazza Raffaello; adult/reduced €3/2; ⊙11am-1pm & 2.30-5.30pm Tue-Sun Jan-Mar & Nov-Dec, 10am-1.30pm & 2.30-6pm Apr & Aug, 10am-1.30pm & 2.30-6pm Tue-Sun May-Jul & Sep-Oct) Walking for a couple of minutes northeast from Piazza IV Novembre brings you to this rather bland, boxy-looking church. Your efforts will be rewarded, however, once you step inside and find the tiny chapel decorated with Raphael's lush *Trinity with Saints* (thought by many to be his first fresco), painted during the artist's residence in Perugia (1505–08).

Ipogeo dei Volumni
HISTORIC SITE

(www.archeopg.arti.beniculturali.it; Via Assisana 53, Località Ponte San Giovanni; adult/reduced €3/1.50; ⊙9am-6.30pm Sep-Jun, 9am-7pm Jul-Aug) About 5km southeast of the city, the Ipogeo dei Volumni is a 2nd-century-BC underground Etruscan burial site, holding the funerary urns of the Volumni, a local noble family. The surrounding grounds are a massive expanse of partially unearthed burial chambers, with several buildings housing the artefacts that haven't been stolen over the years.

Pozzo Etrusco
HISTORIC SITE

(Etruscan Well; www.casamuseosorbello.org; Piazza Danti 18; adult/reduced €3/2, with Casa Museo di Palazzo Sorbello €6; ⊙10am-1.30pm & 2.30-6pm Tue-Sun summer, 11am-1.30pm & 2.30-5pm winter) Just north of Piazza IV Novembre, you can venture down into a 37m-deep well. Dating from the 3rd century BC, it was the main water reservoir of the Etruscan town, and, more recently, a source of water during WWII bombing raids.

Chiesa di San Domenico
CHURCH

(Piazza Giordano Bruno; ⊙7.30am-6pm Mon-Sat, to 7pm Sun) Erected in the early 14th century, Umbria's largest church is an imposing

Perugia

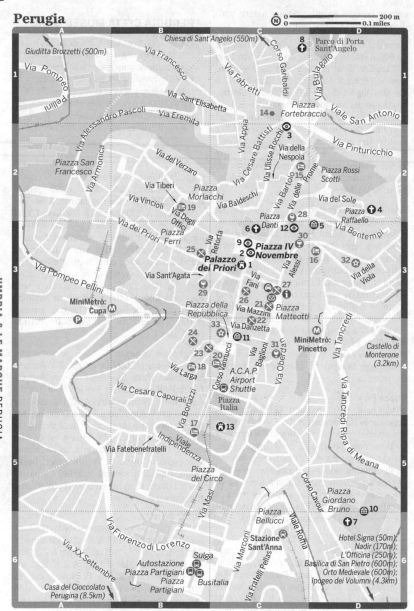

N 0 ——— 200 m
0 ——— 0.1 miles

vision, with a 17th-century interior lit by immense stained-glass windows. The church's pride and joy is the Gothic **tomb of Pope Benedict XI**, who died after eating poisoned figs in 1304.

Arco Etrusco HISTORIC SITE
(Etruscan Arch; Piazza Fortebraccio) At the end of Via Ulisse Rocchi, facing Piazza Fortebraccio and the Università per Stranieri, are the ancient city's Etruscan gates, dating from the

Perugia

3rd century BC. The upper part is Roman and bears the inscription 'Augusta Perusia'.

Chiesa di Sant'Agostino CHURCH
(Piazza Lupattelli; ⊙10am-1pm & 5.30-7pm Mon-Sat, 8am-12.30pm Sun) North of the Università per Stranieri, along Corso Garibaldi, this formerly magnificent church still boasts a beautiful 16th-century choir by sculptor Baccio d'Agnolo. However, small signs forlornly mark the places where artworks once hung before they were carried off to France by Napoleon's troops.

Chiesa di Sant'Angelo CHURCH
(Templio di San Michele Arcangelo; Via Sant'Angelo; ⊙9am-6pm) North along Corso Garibaldi, Via del Tempio branches off to one of Italy's oldest churches, the Romanesque Chiesa di Sant'Angelo, parts of which date back to the 5th century.

Palazzo Baldeschi al Corso MUSEUM
(www.fondazionecariperugiaarte.it; Corso Vannucci 66; adult/reduced €6/4; ⊙3-7.30pm Tue-Fri, 11am-7.30pm Sat) This eclectic museum has a lot going for it: temporary exhibitions occupy a series of palatial 14th-century rooms with stunning Murano chandeliers and frescoes dating to the 1850s, including Mariano Piervittori's intricate Sala della Muse. The permanent collection is two-fold: the donated private collection of famed art historian Alessandro Marabottini consisting of mostly paintings and sculptures spanning the 16th to 20th centuries; and Italy's most heralded collection of Renaissance ceramics, a 200-piece exhibition from all over central Italy.

Courses

Università per Stranieri LANGUAGE
(☑075 574 62 11; www.unistrapg.it; Piazza Fortebraccio 4) Italy's foremost academic institution for foreigners offers courses in language, literature, history, art, music, opera and architecture. One-, three- and six-month language courses start at €400 a month; intensive courses in summer cost €600 a month.

Festivals & Events

Check www.bellaumbria.net for details on Perugia's gazillions of festivals, concerts, summertime outdoor film screenings and *sagre* (traditional festivals).

Eurochocolate FOOD & DRINK
(www.eurochocolate.com) Perugia celebrates the cocoa bean over 10 days in mid-October. More than a million chocolate lovers flock here for choc-crazy exhibitions, cookery classes, giant chocolate sculptures and – the

DON'T MISS

ALL THAT JAZZ

Ever since making its debut in 1973, Perugia's swinging 10-day festival, **Umbria Jazz** (www.umbriajazz.com; ⊙ Jul), has put the city firmly on the world jazz map, with such headline acts as BB King, Van Morrison, James Brown, Sting, Chet Baker, Diana Krall and, more recently, Kraftwerk and Brian Wilson.

real reason everyone is here – to hoover up the free samples.

🛏 Sleeping

★ B&B San Fiorenzo   B&B €

(📞 393 3869987; www.sanfiorenzo.com; Via Alessi 45; d/qd €70/120; 🖻) Buried in Perugia's medieval maze of a centre is this charming 15th-century *palazzo*, where Luigi and Monica make you welcome in one of three unique rooms, all with independent entrances.

Hotel Fortuna   HISTORIC HOTEL €

(📞 075 573 50 40; www.hotelfortunaperugia.com; Via Luigi Bonazzi 19; s €58-88, d €77-140, tr €134-186; 🕸 @ 🖻) Behind a gorgeous, weathered facade draped in ivy, this historic, great-value three-star hotel hides 12th-century walls and secrets like its former past as a love motel. Past the friendly and welcoming front desk, you'll find original 15th-century frescoes and Murano chandeliers (in the breakfast room); and classic decor that instils a sense of place (in the 51 guest rooms).

Alla Maison di Alessia   B&B €

(📞 345 0784208; www.allamaisondialessia.it; Via Bartolo 55-61; d €60-100, r per week €350-450; 🖻) Alessia and Enrico have waved magic wands over this historic house, where rooms are rented mostly by the week. There are just four spacious, great-value rooms – three doubles with kitchenettes and one single – but each has been lovingly dressed in chalk-box pastel shades and plenty of artistic renditions of musicians and actors. Breakfast is a sweet affair playing up Italian produce.

Hotel Signa   HOTEL €

(📞 075 572 41 80; www.hotelsigna.it; Via del Grillo 9; s €34-59, d €49-99, tr €69-104, q €69-135; 🕸 🖻 🖻) Slip down an alley off Corso Cavour to reach Signa, one of Perugia's best budget picks. The petite rooms are simple, bright and well kept (some boast modernised bathrooms); many

have balconies with cracking views of the city and countryside. Rooms at the cheaper end of the scale forgo minibars and air-con. The owner, Mario, hands out maps and tips freely.

Hotel Morlacchi   GUESTHOUSE €

(📞 075 572 03 19; www.hotelmorlacchi.it; Via Tiberi 2; s €45-50, d €65-85, tr €95-105; 🖻) This is a friendly, old-school guesthouse near Piazza IV Novembre. The 14 cosy, low-ceilinged rooms, spread over several floors of a 17th-century townhouse carved from a former convent, are modest but comfortable, with antiques and original artworks.

Locanda della Posta   BOUTIQUE HOTEL €€

(📞 075 572 89 25; www.locandadellapostahotel. it; Corso Vannucci 97; d €130-280, ste €200-500; 🕸 @ 🖻) Perugia's oldest hotel dates to 1786, but a complete 2017 makeover has turned it into one of the city's sleekest digs. Stunning 18th century frescoes now juxtapose post-modernly with glistening marble flooring, funky contemporary art and grey-toned minimalist touches. None of the 17 rooms is the same, but modish elements like hardwood flooring and textured shower walls feature in several.

★ Castello di Monterone   HOTEL €€€

(📞 075 572 42 14; www.castellomonterone.com; Strada Montevile 3; s €100-190, d €110-290; 🅿 🕸 @ 🖾) Ever fancied spending the night in a medieval castle? This is the real McCoy, with all the turreted, ivy-clad, vaulted trappings you would imagine. The individually designed rooms have been finished to great effect, with exposed stone, custom wooden furniture, handmade wrought-iron beds, antiques and occasional but extraordinary Etruscan and medieval artefacts.

Hotel Brufani Palace   HERITAGE HOTEL €€€

(📞 075 573 25 41; www.brufanipalace.com; Piazza Italia 12; s €110-400, d €140-450, ste €340-1000; 🅿 🕸 @ 🖻 🖾) From its hilltop perch, this five-star hotel has captivating views of the valley below and hills beyond. The hotel itself matches this initial impression with frescoed public rooms, impeccably decorated bedrooms with marble bathrooms, a garden terrace for summer dining, and helpful multilingual staff. Swim over Etruscan ruins in the subterranean fitness centre. Parking is €20.

🍴 Eating

Perugia has a staggering number of places to eat. The first days the mercury rises above

15°C or so (usually in March), dozens of open-air locales spring up along and around Corso Vannucci, while Via Sant'Ercolano and Borgo XX Giugno have blossomed into somewhat gourmet corridors.

Antica Salumeria
Granieri Amato
SANDWICHES €

(www.anticasalumeriagranieri.it; Piazza Matteotti; sandwiches €3; ⊙9am-8pm Mon-Sat, hours vary Sun) Sitting inconspicuously in a no-fanfare green cart next to the post office (p587) is this Perugian street-food classic that has done but a single item since 1916: succulent *porchetta* (roast pork) served – crispy skins and all – on a toasted roll for €3. Get in line!

Sandri
CAFE €

(www.sandridal1860.it; Corso Vannucci 32; pastries from €2.50; ⊙7.30am-11pm) This Perugia institution has been serving coffee and cake since 1860. Its delicately frescoed, chandelier-lit interior provides the perfect backdrop for exquisite-looking pastries, chocolates and cakes, enticingly presented in floor-to-ceiling cabinets.

Testone
UMBRIAN €

(www.magnatestone.it; Piazza Matteotti 24; meals €5-15; ⊙7.30am-noon & 4-7pm; ☎) The fateful flock to Testone for *torta al testa*, Umbria's thick and savoury flat bread pies. These are cooked in the traditional way dating back to Etruscan times: on a coal-fired circular cast-iron plate called a *testo*, complete with a coating of fiery ashes (don't worry, they shake them off before serving).

Società Anonima
GASTROPUB €

(www.societaanonimaperugia.it; Via Bartolo 25; ⊙6.30pm-midnight Sun-Tue & Thu, to 1am Fri-Sat; ☎) Local food-and-wine enthusiasts Paolo Baldelli and Antonio Boco are striving for something different at this trendy newcomer, easily the city's most sophisticated spot for a tipple – the long, black bar feels like an escape to the city for pining urbanites.

Six carefully chosen craft-beer taps and monthly featured Umbrian wines are complemented by gourmet bites (€2.50 to €19) from a team of under-30s chefs who hail from Perugia but have all lived and cooked abroad (both age and travel experience are requirements). Fried cod, pickled eggs and beef tartare highlight the chef-driven pub-grub menu.

★L'Officina
UMBRIAN €€

(☑075 572 16 19; www.l-officina.net; Borgo XX Giugno 56; meals €25-35, 6-course tasting menus €25-40; ⊙12.30-3.30pm & 6.30-midnight; ☎) Passionate Greek owner Yannis harbours 30 years of Italian food and wine enthusiasm under his belt at L'Officina, his cozy and meandering restaurant and emporium set inside a former scales factory now teaming with bottles of wine in every nook and cranny. His passion? Gourmet food and wine without the price tag.

★La Taverna
ITALIAN €€

(☑075 572 41 28; www.ristorantelataverna.com; Via delle Streghe 8; meals €30-40; ⊙12.30-3pm & 7.30-11pm; ☎) Way up there on the Perugia dining wish list, La Taverna consistently wins the praise of local foodies. Chef Claudio

---

TOP FIVE UMBRIAN EATS

Umbria was once something of a culinary backwater, but much of the world is now playing catch up with its Slow Food commitment in a region where three-hour dinners, organic produce and locavore dining have long been part of daily life. Eat like an Umbrian by sampling these dishes on your travels:

Cinghiale Richly gamey but tender, wild boar is often served over pasta or stewed in sauce.

Tartufi Umbrian black truffles (preferably the stronger *nero* variety) give menus earthy edge, especially in the autumn harvest months.

Lenticchie These small, thin lentils from Castelluccio are at their best in a thick soup topped with bruschetta and virgin olive oil.

Piccione Umbrians readily order pigeon, often from the highest-end restaurants. The delicate poultry was a mainstay for townsfolk under siege in the Middle Ages.

Farro Emmer wheat still graces tables today. Classic *zuppa di farro* is rich, nutty and distinctly Umbrian, perfect for a warm lunch on a cold, misty day in the hills.

Brugolossi cooks market-fresh produce with flair and precision, while waiters treat you like one of the *famiglia*.

Nadir
MEDITERRANEAN €€

(☑ 388 4831430; www.ristorantenadir.it; Via Benedetto Bonfigli 11; meals €25-30; ◷ 7pm-1am) 🖉 Buried under Perugia's oldest cinema, this former cinema club has yielded to this local favourite where a melange of Mediterranean and Italian fare with a biological bent draws an alternative crowd in the know. Ingredients are so fresh, they don't even bother editing the menu – they just go over all the changes all at the table.

Osteria a Priori
OSTERIA €€

(☑ 075 572 70 98; www.osteriaapriori.it; Via dei Priori 39; meals €30; ◷ 12.30-2.30pm & 7.30-10pm Mon-Sat; 🖥) 🖉 Located above an *enoteca* (wine bar), this fashionable *osteria* (casual tavern) specialises in local wines and fresh regional cuisine prepared with seasonal ingredients. Umbrian cheeses and cured meats feature alongside truffles, roast meats and autumnal mushrooms. Weekday lunch is a snip at €10. Reservations are recommended.

🍷 Drinking & Nightlife

Much of Perugia's nightlife parades outside the cathedral and around Fontana Maggiore, where local and foreign students gather to chat, flirt and play guitars and drums. Grab a gelato and go for a people-watching *passeggiata* (evening stroll) to watch the street theatre unfold.

Caffè Morlacchi
CAFE

(www.facebook.com/caffemorlacchi; Piazza Morlacchi 6/8; ◷ 7.30am-10pm Mon, to midnight Tue-Sat, 4-10pm Sun; 🖥) Students, professors and all comers flock to this vibrantly coloured, blissfully relaxed hang-out for coffee by day and cocktails to the backbeat of DJ tunes by night.

Elfo Pub
CRAFT BEER

(www.facebook.com/elfopubperugia; Via Sant'Agata 20; pints from €5; ◷ 8pm-2am; 🖥) Hophead central in Perugia, this snug pub rife with 14th-century brick dates to 1989 but turned to craft a decade ago and never looked back. Artsy beer geeks sip from 10 taps or choose from a 200-strong bottle menu; and knowledgable and passionate staff will enthusiastically guide you to a local Belgian-style ale or Scandinavian IPA suiting your tastes.

Kundera
BAR

(www.facebook.com/KunderaCaffeBistrot; Via Guglielmo Oberdan 23; ◷ 6.30pm-midnight Tue-Thu, to 1am Fri-Sat, to 11pm Sun; 🖥) Follow the lead of students and clued-up locals by heading to this artsy little bar for *aperitivo* time, when cocktails starting from €4.50 get you a deal on three sizes of tasty appetiser platters (€1.50 to €5) – you can even ask for vegetarian and gluten-free options. Snag a table on the terrace when it's warm.

Fríttole
WINE BAR

(www.facebook.com/frittolevineri; Via Alessi 30; wine by the glass €3.50-10; ◷ 5.30pm-1.30am) Lilla and Lillo are wonderful hosts at this intimate wine bar offering 200 or so bottles democratically spread across Italy's inventory – any of which you can try by the glass. They work closely with boutique and small-production wineries only, and pour alongside local artisanal *salumi* (cured meats), house-made pâtés and local cheeses.

Bottega del Vino
WINE BAR

(Via del Sole 1; wine by the glass from €3.50; ◷ 7pm-midnight Mon, noon-3pm & 7pm-midnight Tue-Sat; 🖥) A fire or candles burn romantically on the skinny terrace, while inside live jazz (Wednesdays at 10pm) and hundreds of bottles of wine lining the walls add to the romance of the setting. You can taste dozens of Umbrian wines, which you can purchase with the help of sommelier-like experts.

☆ Entertainment

When Perugia's student population grows, some of the clubs on the outskirts of town run a bus to Palazzo Gallenga, starting around 11pm. Students hand out flyers on Corso Vannucci, so check with them or ask at the steps. Most clubs get going around midnight, so it's worth remembering that the *scale mobili* (escalators) stop running at 2am.

Balù
LIVE MUSIC

(www.facebook.com/baluperugialive; Via Cartolari 26; ◷ 7pm-2am) An artsy, alternative bar for live music or just hanging out with the bohemian crowd.

Cinema Teatro del Pavone
CINEMA

(☑ 075 572 81 53; Corso Vannucci 67) Dating back to 1717, this grand theatre plays host to not only films but also musical performances and special events.

🔒 Shopping

Perugia's Via Oberdan, the main boulevard Corso Vannucci and the steep Via Sant'Ercolano, wedged between the high townhouses of the *centro storico*, are dotted with boutiques, music shops, bookstores and jewellers.

Giuditta Brozzetti　　ARTS & CRAFTS
(📞 075 4 02 36; www.brozzetti.com; Via Tiberio Berardi 5; ⏰ 8.30am-12.30pm & 3-6pm Mon-Fri, tours by appt Sat) Inside Perugia's oldest Franciscan church, fourth-generation weaver Marta Cucchia is Italy's last surviving artisan working with Jacquard looms. Her extraordinary and fascinating workshop resurrects previously lost medieval and Renaissance textile styles and patterns – some seen in Leonardo da Vinci's *The Last Supper* – weaving them into everything from cocktail napkins (€6) to table runners (€350) and custom-priced tablecloths.

ℹ️ Information

Informazione e Accoglienza Turistica (IAT)
(Tourist Information; 📞 075 573 64 58; http://turismo.comune.perugia.it; Piazza Matteotti 18; ⏰ 9am-6pm) Housed in the 14th-century Loggia dei Lanari, Perugia's main tourist office has stacks of info on the city, maps (€0.50) and up-to-date bus and train timetables.

Poste Italiane (Post Office; www.poste.it; Piazza Matteotti 1; ⏰ 8.20am-7.05pm Mon-Fri, 8am-12.35pm Sat)

Ospedale Perugia (📞 075 57 81; www.ospedale.perugia.it; Piazzale Menghini 1; ⏰ 24hr)

ℹ️ Getting There & Away

AIR

Aeroporto Internazionale dell'Umbria – Perugia San Francesco d'Assisi (PEG; 📞 075 59 21 41; www.airport.umbria.it; Via dell'Aeroporto, Sant'Egidio), 12km east of the city, is small and easy to navigate, with flights from London Stansted and Brussels with Ryanair, and Bucharest with Wizzair, among others.

BUS

Busitalia (📞 075 963 76 37; www.fsbusitalia.it; Piazza Partigiani; ⏰ 6.15am-8pm Mon-Sat, 7.30am-7.30pm Sun) now operates all of Perugia's intercity buses (though many buses still say Umbria Mobilità). They all leave from **Autostazione Piazza Partigiani** (📞 075 506 78 94; Piazza Partigiani; ⏰ ticket office 6.15am-8pm Mon-Sat, 7.30am-7.30pm Sun), in the city's south (take the *scale mobili* through the Rocca Paolina from Piazza Italia) except for Florence, buses which leave from 2.30pm

at the train station (note that it's better to travel to Florence by train). Services go to the following destinations (with additional services possible in summer):

TO	FARE (€)	DURATION	FREQUENCY (DAILY)
Assisi	4.20	45min	6-7
Castiglione del Lago	6.10	1hr	6
Deruta	3.60	30min	6-7
Florence	23	2hr	1
Gubbio	5.50	1¼hr	8
Todi	6.30	1¼hr	6-7
Torgiano	2.50	30min	4

CAR & MOTORCYCLE

To reach Perugia from Rome, leave the A1 at the Orte exit and follow the signs for Terni. Once there, take the SS3bis/E45 for Perugia. From the north, exit the A1 at Valdichiana and take dual-carriageway SS75 for Perugia. The SS75 to the east connects the city with Assisi.

Rental companies have offices at the airport and train station.

TRAIN

In the southwest of town, Perugia's main **train station** (Perugia Fontivegge; 📞 075 963 78 91; www.trenitalia.com; Piazza Vittorio Veneto) has trains running to the following destinations:

TO	FARE (€)	DURATION	FREQUENCY
Arezzo	7.45-13	1hr	every 2hr
Assisi	2.60	20min	hourly
Florence	14.55-19.50	2hr	every 2hr
Fossato di Vico-Gubbio	5.85-12.60	1½hr	7 daily
Orvieto	7.60-16.10	1¾-3hr	10 daily
Rome	11.70-19.10	2¼-3½hr	17 daily
Spello	3.30	30min	hourly

ℹ️ Getting Around

If you're not carrying too much luggage, the simplest way of getting from Perugia's intercity bus station to the town centre is by hopping aboard the *scale mobili* linking Piazza Partigiani with **Piazza Italia** (www.fsbusitalia.it; ⏰ 6.15am-1.45pm). Alternatively, you can catch buses TS and TD to the centre (€1.50). There are also *scale*

GOING TO ROME?

Blue-and-white **Sulga** (☑ 800 099661; www.sulga.it; Piazza Partigiani) buses link the bus station on Piazza Partigiani with Terminal 3 at Rome's Fiumicino (FCO) airport (€22, 3¼ hours, 8am, 9am, 2.30pm and 5.30pm from Monday to Saturday, 7.30am, 8.30am, 2.30pm and 5.30pm on Sunday) and Rome's Tiburtina train station (€17, 2½ hours).

mobili from the car park at the **Piazzale della Cupa** (www.fsbusitalia.it; ⏰ 6.45am-1.45am) outside the city walls up to the Via dei Priori.

TO/FROM THE AIRPORT

The easiest way to Perugia's airport is the **ACAP** (☑ 075 501 67 35; www.acap.perugia.it; cnr Corso Vanucco & Piazza Italia) shuttle bus (€8), which leaves from Piazza Italia for the airport about two hours before each flight, stopping at the train station. The tourist office has exact timetables, which vary according to flight schedules. From the airport, buses leave once everyone is on board. A taxi between the centre and the airport costs approximately €30.

Drive time is approximately 25 minutes.

BUS

It's a steep 1.5km climb from Perugia's train station, so a bus is highly recommended (and essential for those with luggage). The bus takes you to Piazza Italia. Tickets cost €1.50 from the train-station kiosk or €2 on board. Validate your ticket on board to avoid a fine. A 10-ticket pass costs €12.90.

CAR & MOTORCYCLE

Perugia is notoriously difficult to navigate and most of the city centre is only open to residential or commercial traffic. The city has several fee-charging car parks (€0.80 to €1.60 per hour, 24 hours). Piazza Partigiani and the Mercato Coperto are the most central and convenient. There's also a free car park at Piazzale della Cupa.

MINIMETRÒ

These single-car people movers traverse the route between Perugia's train station and Pincetto (just off Piazza Matteotti) every minute. A €1.50 ticket works for the bus and **Minimetrò** (www.minimetrospa.it). From the train station facing the tracks, head right up a long platform.

TAXI

Available from 6am to 2am (24 hours from July to September); call **Happy Taxi** (☑ 075 500 48 88; www.happytaxiperugia.it; Via Fani) to

arrange pick-up. A ride from the city centre to the main train station will cost about €10 to €15. Tack on €1 for each suitcase.

Torgiano

POP 6510

Vineyards and olive groves sweep up to the medieval walled town of Torgiano, on a hilltop perch overlooking the confluence of the Chiascio and Tiber Rivers. The town has an irresistible draw for gastronomes: it's renowned for its thick, green extra-virgin olive oil and spicy, peppery red wines, such as Rubesco Rosso DOC, produced with 70% Sangiovese grapes.

⊙ Sights

Museo del Vino   MUSEUM

(Wine Museum; www.lungarotti.it/fondazione/muvit; Corso Vittorio Emanuele 31; adult/reduced incl Museo dell'Olivo e dell'Olio €7/5; ⏰ 10am-1pm & 3-5pm Tue-Sun Oct-Mar, 10am-1pm & 3-6pm Tue-Sun Apr-Jun, 10am-6pm daily Jul-Sep) The Museo del Vino takes a thematic romp through viticulture in a 20-room, 17th-century mansion. Greek, Etruscan and Roman ceramics, jugs and vessels, glassware and various wine-making implements race you from the Bronze Age to the present, covering topics such as wine as medicine and its role in mythology. A wine tasting and audio guide are included in the ticket price.

Museo dell'Olivo e dell'Olio   MUSEUM

(www.lungarotti.it/fondazione/moo; Via Garibaldi 10; adult/reduced incl Museo del Vino €7/5; ⏰ 10am-1pm & 3-5pm Tue-Sun Oct-Mar, 10am-1pm & 3-6pm Tue-Sun Apr-Jun, 10am-6pm daily Jul-Sep) Showcasing mills, presses and crafts, the Museo dell'Olivo e dell'Olio is an ode to olive oil and its symbolic, medicinal and dietary uses.

🛏 Sleeping & Eating

Al Grappolo d'Oro   HOTEL €

(☑ 075 98 22 53; www.algrappolodoro.net; Via Principe Umberto 24; s €50-70, d €90; ⓟ ❄ 🛜 ⛱) The view across vineyards from the tree-rimmed pool is soothingly beautiful at this bijou hotel in the centre of town. Smartly furnished 19th-century rooms are bright, serene and kept spotlessly clean; and common areas are chock-full of local character and wine-country kitsch. Breakfast is included.

Ristorante Siro   ITALIAN €€

(☑ 075 98 20 10; www.hotelsirotorgiano.it; Via Giordano Bruno 16; meals €20-30; ⏰ noon-2.30pm

& 7-10pm; 🛜) Overflowing with regulars, this convivial, picture-plastered restaurant is big on old-school charm. The mixed antipasti starter for two would feed a small family. Next, loosen a belt notch for *gnocchetti* with radicchio cooked in Rubesco wine sauce, and mains like wild-boar stew and butter-soft steaks.

ℹ️ Getting There & Away

Torgiano sits around 2.3km east of the E45, about 16km south of Perugia. **Busitalia** (p587) *extraurbano* buses head from Torgiano to Perugia (€2.50, 30 minutes, at least four daily).

Lago Trasimeno

A splash of inky blue on the hilly landscape, Lago Trasimeno is where Umbria spills over into Tuscany. Italy's fourth-largest lake is a prime spot if you want to tiptoe off the well-trodden trail for a spell and slip into the languid rhythm of lake life. Around this 128-sq-km lake, silver-green olive groves, vines, woods of oak and cypress and sunflower fields frame castle-topped medieval towns, such as **Castiglione del Lago** and **Passignano**, which are draped along its shores like a daisy chain. A gentle and unhurried ambience hangs over the lake's trio of islands – Maggiore, Minore and Polvese – all wonderfully relaxing escapes.

Hannibal destroyed the Roman army here in 217 BC, and the lake's numerous fortifications attest to its strategic position and turbulent past.

👁️ Sights & Activities

Lago Trasimeno's main inhabited island – **Isola Maggiore**, near Passignano – was reputedly a favourite with St Francis. The hilltop **Chiesa di San Michele Arcangelo** contains a crucifixion painted by Bartolomeo Caporali dating from around 1460. You can also visit the mostly uninhabited island and environmental lab at **Isola Polvese** on a day trip with Fattoria Il Poggio.

Dotted with nature reserves and crisscrossed with well-signposted trails, Lago Trasimeno begs outdoor escapades. For the inside scoop on activities from hiking and cycling to sailing and wine tasting, visit www.lagotrasimeno.net.

Ask at any of the tourist offices around the lake or in Perugia for a booklet of walking and horse-riding tracks. Horse-riding centres offering beautiful hacks into the surrounding countryside include **Le Case Rosse dei Montebuono** (☑️ 075 528 85 56; www.lecaserosse.com; Via Case Sparse di Monte Buono 15, Magione; 2hr ride €50), inland to the southeast of the lake.

One of the best places to base yourself is Castiglione del Lago, which has a fine beach where you can lounge, swim, windsurf, or hire a pedalo or kayak, as well as a sprinkling of cultural attractions.

Palazzo della Corgna   PALACE
(www.palazzodellacorgna.it; Piazza Gramsci; adult/reduced incl Rocca del Leone €8/5; ⊙ 9.30am-7pm, shorter hours winter) Castiglione del Lago's attractions include the Palazzo della Corgna, a 16th-century ducal palace housing frescoes by Giovanni Antonio Pandolfi Mealli and Salvio Savini. A covered passageway connects the palace with the 13th-century **Rocca del Leone** fortress, a stellar example of medieval military architecture.

🛏️ Sleeping

⭐ **Fattoria Il Poggio**   HOSTEL €
(☑️ 075 965 95 50; www.fattoriaisolapolvese.com; Isola Polvese; dm/d/apt/q €20/60/100/100, meals €16; ⊙ Mar-Oct; 📶🛜) 🍃 Nestled in gardens on the tranquil islet of Isola Polvese, this eco-minded farmstead has bright, spick-and-span rooms and gorgeous lake views. If you don't mind catching a ferry back each evening by 7pm, you'll be rewarded handsomely with a family-style meal prepared with organic produce and home-grown herbs and superb morning lake views. Prices include breakfast.

La Casa sul Lago   HOSTEL €
(☑️ 075 840 00 42; www.lacasasullago.com; Via del Popolo 8, Torricella di Magione; dm €15-18, s €30-50, d €40-80, meals €15; 🅿️📶🛜♿) This is one of central Italy's top-rated hostels. The private rooms could be in a three-star hotel – some boast four-poster beds, new bathrooms and parquet floors – and guests have access to every amenity known to hostelkind: bicycles, games, home-cooked meals, an outdoor pool and a garden with hammocks – all within 50m of the lake.

Il Torrione   B&B €
(☑️ 075 95 32 36; www.iltorrionetrasimeno.com; Via delle Mura 4, Castiglione del Lago; s €60, d & apt €80-110; ❄️🛜) Romance abounds at this artistically minded, tranquil retreat. Each room is decorated with artworks painted by a former owner, and a private flower-filled garden – complete with a 16th-century

tower and chaise longues from which to watch the sun set – overlooks the lake. Rent the tower room (up a flight of pirate-ship stairs) for an intimate private apartment.

Camping Badiaccia   CAMPGROUND €
(📞075 965 90 97; www.badiaccia.com; Via Pratovecchio 1, Badiaccia; camping 2 people, car & tent €24-28; 🅿🛜🏊) Right on the lakefront, this tree-shaded campground is kid heaven, with a playground, pizzeria, tennis courts, a private beach, two pools, minigolf and loads of activities to keep the *bambini* (and their parents) amused. Bikes are available for hire.

🍴 Eating

Restaurants line Lago Trasimeno with the best concentration along and around Via Vittorio Emanuele in Castiglione del Lago. Specialities of the Trasimeno area include *fagiolina* (little white beans), carp in *porchetta* (cooked in a wood oven with garlic, fennel and herbs) and *tegamaccio,* a kind of soupy stew of the best varieties of local fish, cooked in olive oil, white wine and herbs.

⭐ DivinPeccato   TRATTORIA €€
(📞075 528 02 34; www.ristorantedivinpeccato. com; Strada Pievaiola 246, Capanne; meals €30-35; ⏰7.30-10pm Tue-Sat, 12.30-2pm & 7.30-10pm Sun; 🛜) Chef Nicola works culinary magic at this wonderful trattoria, well worth the 27km trek southeast of Castiglione del Lago. The menu fizzes with seasonal oomph – the red Cannara onion starter baked with Parmesan and tomato is a total stunner. From there, think *primi* like *tagliolini* with octopus

and cherry tomatoes, and *secondi* like duck breast with strawberry sauce.

Ristorante Monna Lisa   UMBRIAN €€
(📞075951071; www.facebook.com/ristorantemonna lisa; Via del Forte 2, Castiglione del Lago; meals €25-40; ⏰12.30-2.30pm & 7.30-10.30pm Thu-Tue; 🛜) You can imagine Mona Lisa giving a wry smile of approval to the food served at this intimate, art-strewn restaurant in the heart of town. You, too, will be smiling about specialities like *fagiolina*, carpaccio of wild boar on rocket and fresh Trasimeno lake fish. The *spaghetti alle vongole* (spaghetti with clams) deserves a gold star, too.

La Cantina   UMBRIAN €€
(📞075 965 24 63; www.ristorantecantina.it; Via Vittorio Emanuele 93, Castiglione del Lago; meals €20-30; ⏰noon-3.30pm & 6.45-11pm; 🛜) Sunset is the prime time for lake-viewing from the flowery terrace of this old-town restaurant, housed in a converted 17th-century olive mill. A fire warms the brick-vaulted interior in the cooler months. It does wood-oven pizza for pocket-money prices, as well as local carp and perch, but it's really about the views.

🍷 Drinking & Nightlife

Cafes, restaurants and bars line Via Vittorio Emanuele in Castiglione del Lago (considered the main drag of Lago Trasimeno). Be sure to try the town's best winery, **Poggio Bertaio** (red fans will love their Stucchio and Cimbolo Sangioveses); and sample Lake, a Belgian-style blonde ale brewed with *fagiolina* (beans).

WINE & OLIVE-OIL TASTING

Vines and olives thrive in the microclimate of Lago Trasimeno, which yields some top-quality DOC (Denominazione di origine controllata) red and white wines, as well as gold-green DOP (Denominazione d'origine protetta) olive oils. You can pick up a bottle anywhere, but you'll get more out of a tasting at one of the *cantine* (cellars) that open their doors to visitors.

Cantine Giorgio Lungarotti (📞075 988 66 49; http://lungarotti.it; Viale Giorgio Lungarotti 2; tastings from €12; ⏰9am-1pm & 3-7pm Mon-Fri, 9.30am-1pm & 3.30-6pm Sat) The Lungarottis, who operate most of the wineries around here, are the closest thing Umbria has to a ruling noble family these days. At their Tor giano wine estate, Cantine Giorgio Lungarotti, you can take a spin of their cellars and taste the fruits of their labours.

Strada del Vino Colli del Trasimeno (📞333 9854593; www.stradadelvinotrasimeno.it; Piazza Trento e Trieste, Passignano) The Strada del Vino (Wine Route) of the Colli del Trasimeno (Trasimeno Hill district) is made for slow touring, taking in *cantine* and cellars offering tastings (you almost always need to call ahead), farms and *agriturismi* (farmstays), where you can sleep off the overindulgence.

★ **L'Angolo del Buon Gustaio** WINE BAR
(📱 329 3168456; www.angolodelbuongustaio.com;
Via Vittorio Emanuele 40, Castiglione del Lago;
wines by the glass €3-12; ⊙ 8am-1am, closed Tue
winter; 🛜) The most consistently packed
spot along Castiglione del Lago's main drag
and for good reason. Ricardo, armed with a
wealth of wine knowledge, assembles epic
taglieri (cheese and charcuterie plates with
onion jam) and expertly pairs them with local wines like Poggio Beltraio or any number
of the 75 or so in his gourmet shop's inventory. Definitely reserve ahead.

ℹ Information

Informazione e Accoglienza Turistica (IAT)
(Tourist Office; 📱 075 965 24 84; www.lago
trasimeno.net; Piazza Gramsci 1, Castiglione
del Lago; ⊙ 8.30am-1pm & 3.30-7pm Mon-Fri,
8.30am-1pm Sat) Located directly underneath
Palazzo della Corgna; advises on *agriturismi*
and activities like cycling and water sports, and
has an impressive collection of maps.

ℹ Getting There & Around

BICYCLE

You can hire bikes at most campgrounds around
Lago Trasimeno or at **Cicli Valentini** (📱 075
95 16 63; www.ciclivalentini.it; Via Firenze 68b,
Castiglione del Lago; per day/week €10/49;
⊙ 9am-1pm & 3.30-7.30pm Mon-Sat).

BUS

Busitalia (www.fsbusitalia.it) bus E017 links
Perugia with Passignano (€4.20, one hour, four
daily in summer) and E018 with Castiglione del
Lago (€6.10, one hour, six daily in summer).
Services are scaled back in winter.

CAR & MOTORCYCLE

Two major highways skirt Lago Trasimeno: the
SS71, which heads from Chiusi to Arezzo on
the west side (in Tuscany); and SS75bis, which
crosses the north end of the lake, heading from
the A1 in Tuscany to Perugia.

FERRY

Busitalia (www.fsbusitalia.it) ferry services
run only from late March to late September
(frequencies here represent the highest season, from 2 July to 27 August). Hourly ferries
head from San Feliciano (in front of Ristorante I
Bonci) to Isola Polvese (return €6, 10 minutes,
eight per day), Tuoro to Isola Maggiore (return
€6, 10 minutes, 12 per day), Castiglione del
Lago to Isola Maggiore (return €8.10.10, 30
minutes, seven per day) and Passignano to
Isola Maggiore (return €7.30, 25 minutes).
Ferries stop running around 7pm.

ALL SAINTS

As saintly performances go, Umbria
has a star-studded cast. Besides being
the much-venerated birthplace of St
Francis of Assisi, the region has given
rise to two other greats: St Benedict
and the Casanova of the saint world, St
Valentine. St Benedict, founder of the
Benedictine rule and western monas-
ticism, was born in 480 AD in Norcia
(p608). St Valentine, meanwhile, was
a bishop from **Terni**, allegedly martyred
on 14 February 273 AD. His remains
are entombed in the **Basilica di San
Valentino**, now a much-loved wedding
venue and the scene of a great feast
on St Valentine's Day. Want to impress
someone special? You could draw back
your cupid bow and bring them here for
a romantic weekend – it sure beats a
bunch of petrol-station roses. For inspiration, visit www.sanvalentinoterni.it.

TRAIN

Services run roughly hourly from Perugia to Passignano (€3.30, 28 minutes) and Castiglione del
Lago (€4.75 to €13.45, 65 minutes to 1½ hours).

Todi

POP 16,900

A collage of soft-stone houses, *palazzi* and
belfries pasted to a hillside, Todi looks freshly minted for a fairy tale. Wandering its
steeply climbing backstreets is like playing
a game of medieval snakes and ladders. The
pace of life inches along, keeping time with
the wildflowers and vines that seasonally
bloom and ripen in the valley below.

Like rings around a tree, Todi's history can
be read in layers: the interior walls show Todi's Etruscan and even Umbrian influence,
the middle walls are an enduring example of
Roman know-how, and the 'new' medieval
walls boast of Todi's economic stability and
prominence during the Middle Ages.

⊙ Sights

Piazza del Popolo PIAZZA
Just try to walk through the Piazza del Popolo without feeling compelled to sit on
the medieval building steps and write a
postcard home. The 13th-century Palazzo
del Capitano links to the Palazzo del Popolo
to create what is now the **Museo Civico e**

WORTH A TRIP

NARNI: THE MAGICAL HEART OF ITALY

Like Greenwich or the North Pole, Narni is a place best known for where it is, almost slap-bang at the geographical centre of Italy. You can walk to a stone marking the exact spot just outside the town. But Narni has a lot more going for it than merely being the answer to a trivia question. It boasts one of the finest medieval town centres in Umbria, with a collection of churches, piazzas, *palazzi* and fortresses that are quite magical – and fittingly so, given that CS Lewis used the Roman name for the town (plucked at random from an ancient atlas) for his own fictional magical kingdom of Narnia.

Narni lies 21km south of Todi, just east of the A1 autostrada (from the south take the Magliano Sabina exit; from the north the Orte exit). Narni is well served by **Busitalia** (☑ 0744 40 29 00) buses, mostly to Terni (€2.50, 30 minutes, four to seven per day).

Pinacoteca Comunale (www.sistemamuseo.it; adult/reduced €5/2.50; ☑ 10am-1.30pm & 3-6pm Tue-Sun, shorter hours in winter). The **cathedral** (☑ 9.30am-7.30pm), at the northwestern end of the square, has a magnificent rose window.

Tempio di San Fortunato   CHURCH
(www.sistemamuseo.it; Via San Fortunato; ☑ 9am-1pm & 3-7pm Tue-Sun, shorter hours winter) The lofty medieval Tempio di San Fortunato has frescoes by Masolino da Panicale, and contains the tomb of Beato Jacopone, Todi's beloved patron saint. Inside, make it a point to climb the **Campanile di San Fortunato** (www.sistemamuseo.it; Via San Fortunato; adult/reduced €2/1.50; ☑ 10am-1pm & 3-6.30pm Tue-Sun), where views of the hills and castles surrounding Todi await.

**Chiesa di Santa Maria
della Consolazione**   CHURCH
(Via della Consolazione; ☑ 9.30am-12.30pm & 3-6.30pm Wed-Mon, shorter hours winter) The postcard home you've just written most likely features Todi's famed church, the late-Renaissance masterpiece Chiesa di Santa Maria della Consolazione. Inside, architecture fans can admire its geometrically perfect Greek-cross design, and outside, its soaring cupola-topped dome.

🎆 Festivals & Events

Todi Festival   CULTURAL
(www.todifestival.it) Held for 10 days each August/September, this festival brings together a mix of classical and jazz concerts, theatre, ballet and art exhibitions.

🛏 Sleeping

San Lorenzo Tre   B&B €
(☑ 075 894 45 55; www.sanlorenzo3.it; Via San Lorenzo 3; d €75-110, ste €130-150; @ 🛜) Five generations of the same family have lived at this 17th-century abode. Awaiting guests are rooms full of character, with polished brick floors, delicately painted beams and carefully chosen antiques. There's no TV, but there are books to browse, in keeping with the blissfully laid-back vibe. Breakfasts are home cooked and the garden terrace has magical views. There's no lift.

★ **Il Ghiottone Umbro**   B&B €€
(☑ 075 894 84 44, 339 1321509; www.ilghiottone umbro.com; Frazione San Giorgio 45, Vocabolo Molino; r €95-130; P🐾🛜) Danish duo Thomas and Lisbeth bring together old-stone farmhouse charm with Scandi cool at their gorgeous boutique B&B. The rooms combine historic features like beams and tiles with bursts of original detail: canopy beds, free-standing tubs and Nordic designer furnishings. Breakfast is a second-to-none spread of muesli, fresh fruits and juices, homemade pastries and other imaginative treats.

Fonte Cesia   BOUTIQUE HOTEL €€
(☑ 075 894 37 37; www.fontecesia.it; Via Lorenzo Leonj 3; s €75-130, d €85-170, ste €175-220; P🐾) Just south of the main square, this renovated 17th-century *palazzo* has great old-world charm. The rooms are a bit small, but come with elegant antique touches, and some have views of the surrounding hills. The suites step up the romance – all with tubs are Jacuzzi style, one has a half-canopy bed.

🍴 Eating

★ **Vineria San Fortunato**   UMBRIAN €
(☑ 075 372 11 80; www.vineriasanfortunato.it; Piazza Umberto I 5; meals €25; ☑ 10am-2am Thu-Tue) Wine lovers are in their element at this slick, vaulted wine bar, where Umbrian and Tuscan wines are perfectly matched with delicious tasting platters of *salumi e formaggi* (cured meats and cheeses) and season-

driven day specials, simple as tender lamb and olive stew or *scafata* (a seasonal stew of broad beans, peas and artichokes).

Bar Pianegiani
GELATO €

(www.barpianegiani.it; Corso Cavour 40; small/medium/large €2/2.50/3; ⊙7am-midnight Tue-Sun; ⊙) Around 50 years of tradition has created one of the world's most perfect gelato. Try the *amarena* (black cherry), *nocciola* (hazelnut) or the house specialty: cream with pine nuts.

Pizzeria Ristorante Cavour
PIZZA €€

(✆075 894 37 30; www.ristorantecavour-todi.com; Corso Cavour 21; meals €20-30, pizza €3.50-9; ⊙noon-3.30pm & 7-2am) If it's a fine day, bypass the brick-vaulted interior and head straight outside to the terrace for towering views. Try the thin-crust pizza or house specialities like guinea-fowl-stuffed *tortelloni* with Sargentino wine, raisins and sausage.

ℹ Information

Informazione e Accoglienza Turistica (IAT) (Tourist Information, ✆075 895 62 67; www.regioneumbria.eu; Piazza del Popolo 38, ⊙9.30am-1pm & 3-6pm Mon-Fri, 10am-1pm & 3-6pm Sat, 10am-1pm Sun) Helpful tourist office on Todi's main square.

Poste Italiane (Post Office; www.poste.it; Piazza Garibaldi 4; ⊙8.20am-1.35pm Mon-Fri, 8.20am-12.35pm Sat)

ℹ Getting There & Away

By car, Todi is easily reached on the SS3bis-E45, which runs between Perugia and Terni, or take the Orvieto turn-off from A1 (the Milan–Rome–Naples route).

Busitalia (p587) operates buses between Todi and Perugia (€6.30, 1¼ hours, at least 4 daily).

Although the Todi Ponte Rio station is 3km away, city bus C (€2, eight minutes) coincides with arriving trains (you may wait a few minutes for it to turn up).

Assisi

POP 27,400

As if cupped in celestial hands, with the plains spreading picturesquely below and Monte Subasio rearing steep and wooded above, the mere sight of Assisi in the rosy glow of dusk is enough to send pilgrims' souls spiralling to heaven. It is at this hour, when the pitter-patter of day tripper footsteps have faded and the town is shrouded in saintly silence, that the true spirit of St Francis of Assisi, born here in 1181, can be felt most keenly. Though certainly at its heart a religious destination, Assisi's striking beauty and pristinely preserved medieval *centro storico* and Unesco-listed Franciscan structures are a fabled haven that will compel and electrify visitors of any motive.

⊙ Sights

★ Basilica di San Francesco
BASILICA

(www.sanfrancescoassisi.org; Piazza di San Francesco; ⊙upper church 8.30am-6.50pm, lower church & tomb 6am-6.50pm) **FREE** Visible for miles around, the Basilica di San Francesco is the crowning glory of Assisi's Unesco World Heritage ensemble. It's divided into the **Basilica Superiore** (Upper Church; www.sanfrancescoassisi.org; ⊙8.30am-6.50pm), with a celebrated cycle of Giotto frescoes, and beneath, the older **Basilica Inferiore** (Lower Church; www.sanfrancescoassisi.org; ⊙6am-6.50pm), where you'll find frescoes by Cimabue, Pietro Lorenzetti and Simone Martini. Also here, in the **Cripta di San Francesco**, is St Francis' elaborate and monumental tomb.

The Basilica Superiore, which was built immediately after the lower church between 1230 and 1253, is home to one of Italy's most famous works of art – a series of 28 frescoes depicting the life of St Francis. Vibrant and colourful, they are generally attributed to a young Giotto, though some art historians contest this, claiming that stylistic discrepancies suggest that they were created by several different artists.

From outside the upper church, stairs lead down to the Romanesque Basilica Inferiore, whose half-light and architectural restraint beautifully embody the ascetic, introspective spirit of Franciscan life. Divine works by Giotto and fellow Sienese and Florentine masters Cimabue, Lorenzetti and Martini decorate the main body of the church and side chapels, representing an artistic weathervane for stylistic developments across the ages.

The basilica has its own **information office** (✆075 819 00 84; www.sanfrancescoassisi.org; Piazza di San Francesco 2; ⊙9am-5.30pm Mon-Sat), opposite the entrance to the lower church, where you can pick up an audio guide in 10 languages (€4). Groups of 10 or more can schedule an hour-long tour in English or Italian, led by a resident Franciscan friar. To avoid disappointment at busy times, either call ahead or reserve online.

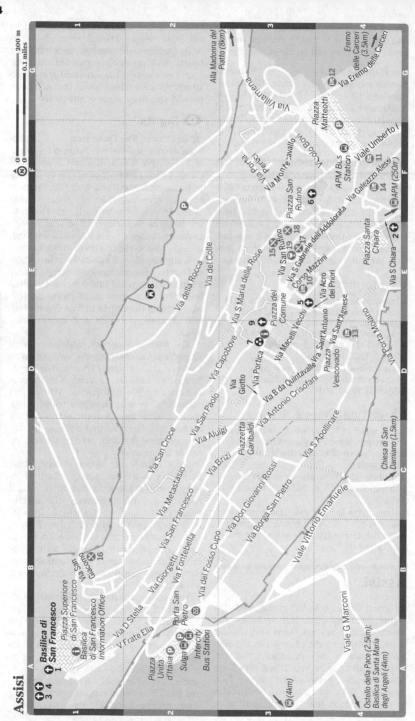

UMBRIA & LE MARCHE ASSISI

Assisi

Basilica di San Francesco

Basilica Superiore di San Francesco

Basilica di San Francesco Information Office

Piazza Unità d'Italia

Sulga

Intercity Bus Station

Porta San Pietro

V. Frate Elia

Via D Stella

Via Giorgetti

Via San Francesco

Via Fontebella

Via del Fosso Cupo

Via San Croce

Via Metastasio

Via Brizi

Piazzetta Garibaldi

Via Don Giovanni Rossi

Via Borga San Pietro

Viale Vittorio Emanuele

Viale G Marconi

Via San Paolo

Via Aluigi

Via Giotto

Via B da Quintavalle

Via Antonio Crisofani

Via S Apollinare

Via Capobove

Via S Maria delle Rose

Via S Maria delle Rose

Via Portica

Via Macelli Vecchi

Via Sant'Antonio

Piazza Vescovado

Via Sant'Agnese

Via Arco dei Priori

Corso Mazzini

Via S Gabriele

Via San Rufino

Piazza del Comune

Piazza San Rufino

Via Monte:avallo

V:olo Bovi

Via Porta Perlici

Via Villamena

Alla Madonna del Piatto (8km)

Eremo delle Carceri (3.5km)

Via Eremo delle Carceri

Piazza Matteotti

Viale Umberto I

APM BLs Station

Via Galeazzo Ales

APM (250m)

Piazza Santa Chiara

Via S Chiara

Via Porta Moiano

Chiesa di San Damiano (1.5km)

Ostello della Pace (2.5km); Basilica di Santa Maria degli Angeli (4km)

Via della Rocca

Via del Colle

200 m
0.1 miles

Rocca Maggiore FORT
(www.sistemamuseo.it; Via della Rocca; adult/reduced €5.50/3.50; ⊙10am-7pm, shorter hours winter) Dominating the city is the massive 14th-century Rocca Maggiore, an often-expanded, pillaged and rebuilt hill-fortress offering 360-degree views of Perugia to the north and the surrounding valleys below. Walk up winding staircases and claustrophobic passageways to reach the archer slots that served Assisians as they went medieval on Perugia.

Basilica di Santa Chiara BASILICA
(www.assisisantachiara.it; Piazza Santa Chiara; ⊙6.30am-noon & 2-7pm summer, to 6pm winter) Built in a 13th-century Romanesque style, with steep ramparts and a striking pink-and-white facade, this church is dedicated to St Clare, a spiritual contemporary of St Francis and founder of the *Sorelle Povere di Santa Chiara* (Order of the Poor Ladies), now known as the Poor Clares. She is buried in the church's crypt, alongside the revered **Crocifisso di San Damiano**, a Byzantine cross before which St Francis was praying when he heard from God in 1205.

Assisi

⊚ **Top Sights**

⊚ **Sights**

⊜ **Sleeping**

⊗ **Eating**

⊚ **Drinking & Nightlife**

Basilica di Santa Maria degli Angeli CHURCH
(www.porziuncola.org; Piazza Porziuncola 1, Santa Maria degli Angeli; ⊙6.15am-12.50pm & 2.30-7.30pm) That enormous domed church you can see as you approach Assisi along the Tiber Valley is the 16th-century Basilica di Santa Maria degli Angeli some 4km west and several hundred metres further down the hill from old Assisi.

Eremo delle Carceri CHRISTIAN SITE
(www.eremodellecarceri.it; Via Eremo delle Carceri; ⊙6.30am-7pm summer, to 6pm winter) FREE In around 1205 St Francis chose these caves above Assisi as his hermitage where he could retire to contemplate spiritual matters and be at one with nature. The *carceri* (isolated places, or 'prisons') along Monte Subasio's forested slopes are as peaceful today as in St Francis' time, even though they're now surrounded by various religious buildings. It's a claustrophobic walk down to Francesco's **Grotta** (cave), where he prayed and slept on a stone bed in his later years.

Chiesa di San Damiano CHURCH
(www.sanfrancescoassisi.org; Via San Damiano; ⊙10am-noon & 2-6pm summer, to 4.30pm winter) It's a 1.5km olive-tree-lined stroll southeast of Assisi's centre to the church where St Francis first heard the voice of God and where he wrote his *Canticle of the Creatures*. You walk through the church's various fresco-slathered rooms, small Canticle museum and gorgeous cloister following an Italian/English signposted step-by-step guide. A copy of the *Crocifisso di San Damiano* can be seen here.

Foro Romano ARCHAEOLOGICAL SITE
(Roman Forum; www.sistemamuseo.it; Via Portica; adult/reduced €4/2.50, with Rocca Maggiore €8/5; ⊙10am-1pm & 2.30-6pm summer, to 5pm winter) On Piazza del Comune, just around the corner from the tourist office, is the entrance to the town's partially excavated Roman Forum, while on the piazza's northern side is the well-preserved facade of a 1st-century Roman temple, the **Tempio di Minerva** (Temple of Minerva; ⊙7.30am-noon & 2-7pm Mon-Sat, 8.30am-noon & 2-7pm Sun) FREE, hiding a rather uninspiring 17th-century church.

Duomo di San Rufino CHURCH
(Piazza San Rufino; ⊙8am-1pm & 2-7pm summer, to 6pm winter) The 13th-century Romanesque church, remodelled by Galeazzo Alessi in the 16th century, contains the fountain where St Francis and St Clare were baptised. The

The Saint of Assisi

That someone could found a successful movement based on peace, love, compassion, charity and humility in any age is remarkable; that Francis Bernardone was able to do it in war-torn 13th-century Umbria was nothing short of a miracle. But then again, in his early years Francis was very much a man of the times – and anything but saintly.

Not-So-Humble Beginnings

Born in Assisi in 1181, the son of a wealthy cloth merchant and a French noblewoman, Francis was a worldly chap: he studied Latin, spoke passable French, had a burning fascination with troubadours and spent his youth carousing. In 1202 Francis joined a military expedition to Perugia and was taken prisoner for nearly a year until his father paid ransom. Following a spate of ill health, he enlisted in the army of the Count of Brienne and was Puglia-bound in 1205 when a holy vision sparked his spiritual awakening.

Life & Death

Much to the shock, horror and ridicule of his rich, pleasure-seeking friends, Francis decided to renounce all his possessions in order to live a humble, 'primitive' life in imitation of Christ, preaching and helping the poor. He travelled widely around Italy and beyond, performing miracles such as curing the sick, communicating with animals, spending hermit-like months praying in a cave, and founding monasteries. Before long, his wise words and good deeds had attracted a faithful crowd of followers.

St Francis asked his followers to bury him in Assisi on a hill known as Colle

1

d'Inferno (Hell Hill), where people were executed at the gallows until the 13th century, so as to be in keeping with Jesus, who had died on the cross among criminals and outcasts.

Saintly Spots

Today various places claim links with St Francis, including Greccio in Lazio where he supposedly created the first (live) nativity scene in 1223; Bevagna in Umbria where he is said to have preached to the birds; and La Verna in Tuscany where he received the stigmata shortly before his death at the age of 44. He was canonised just two years later, after which the business of 'selling' St Francis began in earnest. Modern Assisi, with its glorious churches and thriving souvenir industry, seems an almost wilfully ironic comment on Francis' ascetic and spiritual values.

TOP ST FRANCIS SITES

Assisi (p593) His home town and the site of his birth and death, his hermitage, his chapel, the first Franciscan monastery and the giant basilica containing his tomb.

Gubbio (p601) Where the saint supposedly brokered a deal between the townsfolk and a man-eating wolf – Francis tamed the wolf with the promise that it would be fed daily.

Rome Francis was given permission by Pope Innocent III to found the Franciscan order at the Basilica di San Giovanni in Laterano (p93).

1. Basilica di San Francesco (p593), Assisi **2.** Mosaic floor, Basilica di San Giovanni in Laterano (p93), Rome **3.** View of Assisi (p593)

facade is festooned with grotesque figures and fantastic animals.

Chiesa Nuova
CHURCH

(Piazza Chiesa Nuova; ⊘8am-7pm, 6pm in winter) Just southeast of the Piazza del Comune, this domed church is a peaceful place for contemplation. It was built by King Philip III of Spain in 1615 on the spot reputed to be the house of St Francis' family. A bronze statue of the saint's parents stands outside.

🏃 Activities

To really feel the spirituality of Assisi, do as St Francis did and make the pilgrimage into the surrounding wooded hills. Many make the trek to Eremo delle Carceri (p595) or Chiesa di San Damiano (p595) on foot. The tourist office has several maps, including a route that follows in St Francis' footsteps to Gubbio (18km). A popular spot for hikers is nearby **Monte Subasio**. Local bookshops sell walking and mountain-biking guides and maps for the area.

Bicycle rentals are available at **Angelucci Cicli** (☑075 804 25 50; www.angeluccicicli.it; Via Risorgimento 54a; bike rental per hr/day €5/20; ⊘8.30-12.30pm & 3.30-7.30pm Mon-Sat) in Assisi's suburb of Santa Maria degli Angeli.

🎉 Festivals & Events

The **Festa di San Francesco** falls on 3 and 4 October and is the main religious event in Assisi. **Settimana Santa** (Easter Week) is celebrated with processions and performances.

Festa di Calendimaggio
CULTURAL

(www.calendimaggiodiassisi.com; ⊘May) This festival sees Assisi take a joyous leap into spring with flamboyant costumed parades, jousting and other medieval fun. It starts the first Wednesday after 1 May.

🛏 Sleeping

Keep in mind that in Assisi's peak periods such as Easter, August and September, and during the Festa di San Francesco, you will need to book accommodation well in advance. The tourist office has a list of private rooms, religious institutions (of which there are 22), flats and *agriturismi* (farm stay accommodation) in and around Assisi.

★ Alla Madonna del Piatto
AGRITURISMO €

(☑075 819 90 50; www.incampagna.com; Via Petrata 37, Petrata; s/d €75/90; ⊘Mar-Nov; P) 🍃

Waking up to views of meadows and olive groves sweeping up to Assisi is bound to put a spring in your step at this ecofriendly *agriturismo*, less than 15 minutes' drive from the basilica. Each of the six rooms has been designed with care, love and character, with wrought-iron beds, antique furnishings and intricate handmade fabrics.

St Anthony's Guesthouse
B&B €

(☑075 81 25 42; atoneassisi@tiscali.it; Via Galeazzo Alessi 10; s/d/tr €50/70/90; ⊘Mar-mid-Nov; P🛜) Look for the iron statue of St Francis feeding the birds and you've found your Assisian oasis – a peaceful convent run by sweet sisters. Rooms are spartan but welcoming and six have balconies with breathtaking views. Olive-tree-shaded gardens and an 800-year-old breakfast room make this a heavenly choice. There is a two-night minimum stay and an 11pm curfew.

Ostello della Pace
HOSTEL €

(☑075 81 67 67; www.assisihostel.com; Via di Valecchie 4; dm €18, d without bathroom €40-44, d €50; ⊘1 Mar-8 Nov & 27 Dec-6 Jan; P🛜) Snug below the city walls and housed in a beautifully converted 17th-century farmhouse, this hostel is a charmer. The dorms and handful of private rooms are kept spick and span and the well-tended gardens have magical views of Assisi, crowned by the dome of its famous basilica. Find it just off the road coming in from Santa Maria degli Angeli.

Hotel Alexander
HOTEL €

(☑075 81 61 90; www.hotelalexanderassisi.it; Piazza Chiesa Nuova 6; s €50-75, d €75-108; ❄🛜) On a small cobbled piazza by the Chiesa Nuova, Hotel Alexander offers eight spacious rooms and a communal terrace with wonderful rooftop views. The modern decor – pale wooden floors and earthy brown tones – contrasts well with the wood-beamed ceilings and carefully preserved antiquity all around.

Hotel Ideale
B&B €€

(☑075 81 35 70; www.hotelideale.it; Piazza Matteotti 1; s €50-60, d €95-160; P❄🛜) Ideal indeed (and recently renovated), this welcoming family-run B&B sits plumb on Piazza Matteotti. Many of the bright, high-ceilinged rooms open onto balconies with uplifting views over the rooftops to the valley beyond. Breakfast is done properly, with fresh pastries, fruit, cold cuts and frothy cappuccino, and is served in the garden when the weather's fine.

Nun Assisi
BOUTIQUE HOTEL €€€

(☑ 075 815 51 50; www.nunassisi.com; Via Eremo delle Carceri 1a; s €280-360, d €340-420, ste €440-750; P ❄ ⑤ ≋) This former convent has been reborn as a superstylish boutique hotel, with a clean, modern aesthetic and whisper-quiet gardens planted with olive trees. Stone arches and beams provide flair in pared-down rooms with virginal white walls and flat-screen TVs. The restaurant puts a contemporary spin on seasonal Umbrian fare, and the gorgeous subterranean spa is snuggled within 1st-century Roman ruins.

Residenza D'Epoca
San Crispino
HISTORIC HOTEL €€€

(☑075 815 51 24; www.assisibenessere.it; Via Sant'Agnese 11; s €99-149, d €139-309; ❄⑤) Big on medieval charm, this 14th-century mansion has soul-stirring views of Assisi from its gardens and a shuttle is available to whisk you to its private spa. Each generously sized suite is different, but all have oodles of character, with original vaulting and eye-catching features such as fireplaces, four-poster beds and antique trappings. Basilica di Santa Chiara is close by. Breakfast is included.

✗ Eating & Drinking

★ Osteria La Piazzetta dell'Erba
OSTERIA €

(☑075 81 53 52; www.osterialapiazzetta.it; Via San Gabriele dell'Addolorata 15a; meals €30-35; ⊙12.30-2.30pm & 7.30-10.30pm Tue-Sun; ⑤) Snag one of the few coveted tables set up on a small, flower-strewn square a few steps from rambunctious Piazza del Comune and you'll feel a world away at this local favourite. The seasonally changing menu is flecked with Asian and Mediterranean touches (hummus, tzatziki and wasabi pop up) and complemented with daily specials – all priced to wow.

Hostaria Terra Chiama
OSTERIA €

(☑ 075 819 90 51; www.hostariaterrachiama.it; Via San Rufino 16; meals €25-35; ⑤) Annarita is a consummate host at this delightful *osteria* and *enoteca*, where enquiries for a glass of local red are met with a barrage of tasting options. The Km0 (eat local, buy local) menu might tempt you with simple but honed-in preparations like white *ragù* with IGP-certified veal from the Apennine Mountains or baked chicken *all'arrabbiata*.

Pizzeria da Andrea
PIZZA €

(Via San Rufino 26; pizza & snacks €1.30-5.50; ⊙8.30am-9pm) The go-to place on the square for perfectly thin, crisp *pizza al taglio* (by

the slice) and *torta al testo* (filled Umbrian flatbread) for a fistful of change.

Osteria Eat Out
UMBRIAN €€

(☑075 81 31 63; www.eatoutosteriagourmet.it; Via Eremo delle Carceri 1a; meals €40-50; ⊙7.30-10.30pm daily & 12.30-2.30pm Sat & Sun; ⑤) With such astounding views and minimalist-chic interiors, you might expect the glass-fronted restaurant of the Nun Assisi hotel to prefer style over substance. Not so. Polished service and an exciting wine list are well matched with seasonal Umbrian cuisine flavoured with home-grown herbs.

La Locanda del Podestà
UMBRIAN €€

(☑075 81 65 53; www.locandadelpodesta.it; Via San Giacomo 6; meals €20-30; ⊙12.30-2.30pm & 7-9.30pm Thu-Tue) This inviting cubby hole of a restaurant is big on old world charm, with low arches and stone walls. Distinctly Umbrian dishes such as *torta al testo* with pork sausage and Umbrian pastas like *strangozzi* are expertly matched with regional wines. Friendly service adds to the familiar vibe.

Bibenda Assisi
WINE BAR

(☑339 8615152; www.bibendaassisi.it; Vicolo Nepis 9; wines by the glass €3.50-10; ⊙11.30am-11pm Wed-Mon; ⑤) This rustic-chic wine bar is Assisi's best for exploring wines and beyond. Nila, a highly knowledgable Ukrainian transplant, will talk you through a wine list she has assembled from small, boutique producers and tiny appellations – all served in proper Riedel glassware – and paired with tasting plates of local *salumi e formaggi*. Call ahead to reserve one of two outside tables.

★ Umami Beer
CRAFT BEER

(☑392 2043500; www.umamibeer.it; Via Los Angeles 145, Santa Maria degli Angeli; pints €4.50-7; ⊙7pm midnight Sun-Thu, to 1am Fri-Sat; ⑤) You'll need to head down to Santa Maria degli Angeli, 4.3km from the *centro storico* as the crow flies, to get your craft-beer fix in Assisi, but it's worth the haul for more reasons than that. Massive, creative burgers forged with top Chianina beef (or nearly 10 vegie and vegan options) are outrageously good by Italian standards (€9 to €15).

❶ Information

Informazione e Accoglienza Turistica (IAT)
(Tourist Office; ☑ 075 813 86 80; www.visit-assisi.it; Piazza del Comune 22; ⊙9am-6pm Mon-Fri, to 7pm Sat, to 6pm Sun, shorter hours winter) Stop by here for maps, leaflets and info on accommodation.

Poste Italiane (www.poste.it; Porta San Pietro; ⊙8.20am-1.45pm Mon-Fri, to 12.45pm Sat)

ⓘ Getting There & Around

BUS

Busitalia (www.fsbusitalia.it) runs buses from Assisi to Perugia (€4.20, 45 minutes, six daily) from Piazza Matteotti. **Sulga** (⌨ 075 500 96 41; www.sulga.eu; iazza Giovanni Paolo II) buses leave from Porta San Pietro for Naples (€25, 5¼ hours, 1.45pm) and Rome's Stazione Tiburtina (€18.50, 3¼ hours, 1.45pm and 4.30pm).

CAR & MOTORCYCLE

To reach Assisi from Perugia take the SS75, exit at Ospedalicchio and follow the signs. In town, daytime parking is all but banned. Central car parks for the old town include **Piazza Giovanni Paolo II** (www.sabait.it; first 1-2hr/per hr after/day €1.05/1.45/12), the closest to the basilica; and **Piazza Matteotti** (www.sabait.it; first 1-2hr/per hr after/day €1.05/1.45/12).

TAXI

For a taxi, call **Radio Taxi Assisi** (⌨ 075 81 31 00; www.radiotaxiassisi.it).

TRAIN

Assisi is on the Foligno–Terontola train line with regular services to Perugia (€2.60, 24 minutes, hourly). You can change at Terontola or Perugia for Florence (€15.70 to €19.90, two to three hours, 10 daily) and at Foligno or Terontola for Rome (€10.40 to €22.65, two to three hours, 10 daily).

Assisi's train station is 4km west in Santa Maria degli Angeli; shuttle bus C (€1.30, 13 minutes) runs between the train station and Piazza Matteotti every 30 minutes. Buy tickets from the station *tabaccaio* (tobacconist) or in town.

Spello

POP 8620

Sometimes it seems like it's just not possible for the next Umbrian town to be prettier than the last. And then you visit Spello, a higgledy-piggledy ensemble of honey-coloured houses spilling down a hillside, guarded by three stout Roman gates and chess-piece towers.

Come summer, the green-fingered locals try to outdo each other with their billowing hanging baskets and flowerpots, filling the streets with a riot of colour and scent.

⊙ Sights

A leisurely stroll is the best way to click into Spello's easygoing groove. Begin at Porta Consolare, which dates from Roman times,

then head towards Piazza Matteotti, the heart of Spello.

Chiesa di Santa Maria Maggiore CHURCH
(Piazza Matteotti; Cappella Baglioni €2; ⊙9.30am-12.30pm & 3.30-6.30pm Mon-Fri, 9.30am-12.30pm & 3-6pm Sat-Sun) The impressive 12th-century Chiesa di Santa Maria Maggiore houses the town's real treat. In its **Cappella Baglioni**, Pinturicchio's beautiful frescoes of the life of Christ are in the right-hand corner as you enter. Even the floor, dating back to 1566, is a masterpiece.

Belvedere Cappuccini VIEWPOINT
(near the Arco Romano) To see the view of all views, head up past Spello's Arco Romano near the Chiesa di San Severino (an active Capuchin monastery that's closed to the public) for a living postcard view across the bucolic countryside below.

Chiesa di Sant'Andrea CHURCH
(Piazza Matteotti; ⊙8am-7pm) You can admire Pinturicchio's *Madonna with Child and Saints* in the gloomy Chiesa di Sant'Andrea.

✯ Festivals & Events

Corpus Domini RELIGIOUS
The people of Spello celebrate this feast in May or June (the Sunday 60 days after Easter) by skilfully decorating the main street with fresh flowers in colourful designs. Come on the Saturday evening before the Sunday procession to see the floral fantasies being laid out (from about 8.30pm). The Corpus procession begins at 11am on Sunday.

⤒ Sleeping

★ **Agriturismo il Bastione** AGRITURISMO €
(⌨ 340 5973402; www.agriturismoilbastione.it; Via Fontemonte 3; d €90-120, incl half-board €140-170; ℙ☀@ⓢ) What a delight this medieval farmstead is! On the slopes of 1290m Monte Subasio and surrounded by olive trees, the *agriturismo* has stirring views over patchwork plains and hills. The six rooms and suites have a cosily rustic flavour, with wrought-iron beds, beams and 1000-year-old stone walls. Dinner, served in the barrel-vaulted restaurant, is a feast of home-grown produce.

La Residenza dei Cappuccini APARTMENT €
(⌨ 331 4358591; www.residenzadeicappuccini.it; Via Cappuccini 5; s €45-55, d €55-65; ⓢ) Up a steep, winding lane lies this little gem of an *affittacamere* (offering rooms for rent), which plays up the historic charm with its

atrium of exposed stone and beams. All rooms come with kitchenettes and a DIY breakfast basket. Additional apartments are found in two other annexes around town.

Palazzo Bocci   HISTORIC HOTEL **€€**
(📞0742 30 10 21; www.palazzobocci.com; Via Cavour 17; s €80-100, d €100-120, ste €130-150; P❋☎) Within the walls of this 17th-century *palazzo*'s lavishly frescoed salon, you get a real sense of Spello's history. Quarters are understated yet elegant, with tiled floors and beams or ceiling murals. There's a garden terrace with soothingly lovely country views and a restaurant, ensconced in a 14th-century mill, that makes the most of Umbrian produce such as Norcia truffles.

✖ Eating & Drinking

Osteria del Buchetto   OSTERIA **€€**
(📞0742 30 30 52; www.osteriadelbuchetto.it; Via Cappuccini 19; meals €25-30; ⊘1-3pm & 7.30-11pm Thu-Sat, 1-3pm Sun) You eat on a raised platform with romantic views of the valley towards Assisi at this *osteria* right at the top of town near the Roman arch. The food is proudly local, and lingering is positively encouraged. Perhaps start with the *tagliatelli* pasta with crunchy truffles (or, if in season, asparagus), and move on to the speciality – expertly grilled steaks.

Enoteca Properzio   WINE BAR
(📞0742 30 15 21; www.enotecaproperzio.com; Palazzo dei Canonici, Piazza Matteotti 8; sharing plates from €10; ⊘10am-10pm; ☎) At the most charming *enoteca* in Spello, you can mingle among 8th-generation owners and master sommeliers while trying five or so Umbrian wines and snacking on cheese, prosciutto and bruschetta, then stock up on an enticing array of regional specialities (*salumi*, Spello olive oil, *strangozzi* pasta and the like) and over 3000 wines by the bottle.

ℹ Information

Pro Loco (Tourist Office; 📞0742 30 10 09; www.prospello.it; Piazza Matteotti 3; ⊘10am-noon & 3-5pm Thu-Fri & Sun, 10am-noon & 3-5pm Sat) Has Spello town maps, a list of accommodation options and walking maps, including an 8km walk across the hills to Assisi.

ℹ Getting There & Away

Spello is on the SS75 between Perugia and Foligno.

There are services from the **train station** (www.trenitalia.com; Via Pasciana) at least hourly from Spello to Perugia (€3.30, 30 minutes)

and Assisi (€1.75, 10 minutes). If the station is unstaffed, buy your tickets at the self-service ticket machine. It's a 10-minute walk into town from the station.

Gubbio
POP 32,400

While most of Umbria feels soft, warm and rounded by the millennia, Gubbio is angular, sober, imposing and medieval through and through. Perched on the steep slopes of Monte Ingino, the Gothic buildings wend their way up the hill towards Umbria's closest thing to a theme-park ride: its open-air *funivia* (cable car). The town's stunning preservation will floor you, and wandering its evocative streets, alleyways and staircases elicit textbook Italian dreaming.

◉ Sights

★ Funivia Colle Eletto   CABLE CAR
(www.funiviagubbio.it; adult/reduced return €6/5; ⊘9am-8pm daily summer, 10am-1.15pm & 2.30-5pm Thu-Tue winter) Although the Basilica di Sant'Ubaldo (p602), perched high up on Monte Ingino, is a perfectly lovely church, the real adventure is reaching it on the *funivia*, as exhilarating as any roller coaster. The word *funivia* suggests an enclosed cable car, but it's actually a ski lift of sorts, whisking visitors up the mountain in precarious-looking metal baskets.

OFF THE BEATEN TRACK

A GREAT RURAL ESCAPE

You'll find it tough to drag yourself away from the spirit-lifting views from the garden patio and olive-tree-fringed pool at high-on-a-hill B&B **La Cuccagna** (📞348 7792330; http://lacuccagna.com; Frazione Santa Cristina 22; s €80-140, d €100-140; P☎⊠). Sarah and Salvatore's beautifully restored country home is pin-drop peaceful and big on rustic charm, with rooms fitted out with original beams and stone walls. Organic produce makes its way onto the breakfast table. They also arrange everything from pizza nights to pasta classes and olive-picking holidays and will do everything in their power to ensure you have an authentic experience. The B&B is midway between Perugia and Gubbio – see the website for precise directions.

Gubbio

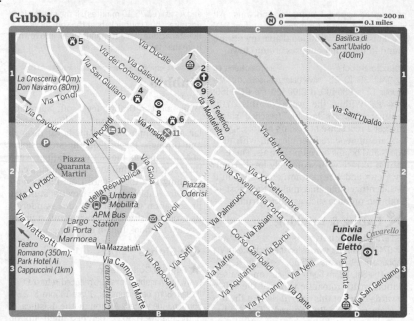

Basilica di Sant'Ubaldo

BASILICA

(Via Monte Ingino 5; ⊙8am-7.30pm) **FREE**
Perched high up on Monte Ingino and
reached by Gubbio's funivia, the basilica
displays the body of St Ubaldo, the 12th-
century bishop of Gubbio, in a glass coffin
above the altar. It also has a small **museum**
dedicated to the Corsa dei Ceri, the town's
most popular festival, where you can see the
massive statues carried through the streets
during the *corsa* (race).

Piazza Grande

PIAZZA

Gubbio's medieval showpiece is Piazza
Grande, where the Corsa dei Ceri festival
takes place. The piazza is dominated by the
14th-century **Palazzo dei Consoli** and the
Palazzo del Podestà.

Museo Civico

MUSEUM

(Piazza Grande; adult/reduced €5/3; ⊙10am-
1.30pm & 3-6pm Apr-Octr, 10am-1pm & 2-5pm Nov-
Mar) Housed within the Palazzo dei Consoli,
this museum displays the Eugubian Tablets, which were discovered in 1444. Dating
from between 300 and 100 BC, these seven
bronze tablets are the best existing example of the ancient Umbrian script. Situated
upstairs is a picture and ceramics gallery
featuring works from the Gubbian school
and panoramic viewpoint while downstairs

– and accessed around the back – is a small
archaeological gallery.

Via Federico da Montefeltro

AREA

Walk up Via Ducale to the Via Federico da
Montefeltro where you'll encounter a triumvirate of ancientness, beginning at the
13th-century pink **cathedral** (donations welcome; ⊙10am-5pm), the 15th-century **Palazzo
Ducale** (http://polomusealeumbria.beniculturali.
it; adult/reduced €5/2.50; ⊙8.30am-7.30pm) and
the 12th-century **Museo Diocesano** (www.
museogubbio.it; adult/reduced €5/3; ⊙10am-6pm
Tue-Sun Mar-Oct, 10am-6pm Thu-Sun Nov-Feb).

Palazzo del Bargello

PALACE

(Via Consoli 35; adult/reduced €3/1; ⊙10.30am-
1pm & 3-6pm Tue-Sun, shorter hours winter) The
14th-century Palazzo del Bargello, once the
city's police station and prison in medieval
times, is now home to the Society of Crossbow-
men, who host a small **museum** dedicated to
the ancient weapon and Palio della Balestra
festival. It is Gubbio's only medieval residence
that has never been altered inside or out.

Museo della Maiolica a Lustro

MUSEUM

(www.museoportaromana.it; Via Dante 24; €5;
⊙9am-1pm & 3.30-7pm) Just below the Funivia Colle Eletto (p601), this museum is dedicated to the *a lustro* ceramic style, which

Gubbio

◎ **Top Sights**
1 Funivia Colle Eletto D3

◎ **Sights**
2 Cattedrale di Gubbio............................B1
   Museo Civico ....(see 4)
3 Museo della Maiolica a Lustro D3
   Museo Diocesano ....(see 2)
4 Palazzo dei Consoli B1
5 Palazzo del Bargello............................A1
6 Palazzo del Podestà.............................B1
7 Palazzo Ducale B1
8 Piazza Grande.......................................B1
9 Via Federico da Montefeltro B1

🛌 **Sleeping**
10 Residenza di Via Piccardi B2

🍴 **Eating**
11 Taverna del Lupo................................. B2

has its origins in 11th century Muslim Spain. Up in the tower, on the 2nd floor, ceramics from prehistoric times share space with medieval and Renaissance pieces.

🎊 Festivals & Events

★ **Corsa dei Ceri**   CULTURAL
(www.ceri.it; ⊙ 15 May) The 'Ceri Race' is a centuries-old event held each year to celebrate Gubbio's patron saint, Sant'Ubaldo. It starts at 5.30am and involves three teams, each carrying a *cero* (massive wooden pillars weighing about 300 to 400kg) each bearing a statue of of a different saint – Sant'Ubaldo, St George and St Antony – and racing through the city's streets.

Palio della Balestra   CULTURAL
On the last Sunday in May, Gubbio gets out its medieval crossbows for its annual archery competition with regional rival Sansepolcro. The festival carries over all year into tourist shops alive with rather scary-looking crossbow paraphernalia.

🛏 Sleeping

While Gubbio's *centro storico* is dominated by hotels (25) and B&Bs (15), the *comune* of Gubbio counts 115 *agriturismo* options in the surrounding area – check those countryside views from the *funivia* and it's not hard to figure out why. Expect 300% price gouging on May 15 for the Corsa dei Ceri. There is a €1 per person per night tourism tax chargeable for up to five nights.

Residenza di Via Piccardi   HISTORIC HOTEL €
(☑ 075 927 61 08; www.residenzadiviapiccardi.it; Via Piccardi 12; s €25-30, d €45-60; ☎) Step through the arched gate into the romantic garden of this period residence. Family owned, the medieval stone building has five cosy rooms decorated in cheery florals, with all the basic comforts.

Park Hotel Ai Cappuccini   BOUTIQUE HOTEL €€€
(☑ 075 92 34; www.parkhotelaicappuccini.it; Via Tifernate; s €130-190, d €170-270, meals €40-50; ⓟ✳🅟📶♨) Silence still hangs like a monk's habit over this stunningly converted 17th-century monastery, which skillfully intertwines history with contemporary comfort. Rooms are classically elegant, with fine fabrics and lots of polished wood. Its own art gallery, an excellent restaurant serving Mediterranean cuisine, an indoor pool and spa and beautiful gardens all make this one of the top places to stay in Gubbio.

🍴 Eating & Drinking

Don't miss *crescia*, the town's version of Umbria's *torta al testo* (a savoury stuffed flatbread similar to Perugia's *torta al testa*), and *friccò*, a hearty stew-like concoction of chicken, rabbit and lamb flavoured with garlic, rosemary and white wine. *Brustengo*, a fried bread served with prosciutto, will also likely find its way to your table.

La Crescerla   UMBRIAN €
(www.lacrescerla.net; Via Cavour 23; meals €10; ⊙ noon-3pm & 6.30pm-midnight; ☎) A trendy spot for digging into *crescia*, stuffed with all manner of locally sourced goodness (prosciutto, *porchetta*, pancetta, *scamorza* – you name it!). The €10 meal deal includes a DOC glass of wine and dessert!

Taverna del Lupo   UMBRIAN €€€
(☑ 075 927 43 68; www.tavernadellupo.it; Via Ansidei 21; meals €35-55; ⊙ noon-3pm & 7-11pm; 📶🍴) Soft light casts flattering shadows

---

ⓘ **GUBBIO TURISTICARD**

The **tourist office** (p604) sells the Gubbio Turisticard, which comes in three versions. For €6, you get an audio guide (in Italian or English), reductions on the *funivia* and a 50% discount on key museums and discounts in various shops. For €3, you can choose the same as above minus the audio guide, or an audio guide minus the museum discounts.

PARCO REGIONALE DEL MONTE CUCCO

A memorable road trip on the Umbria-Le Marche border, just 13km east of Gubbio, is the SS3 that wends along the eastern fringes of **Parco Regionale del Monte Cucco** (🕿 075 91 72 71; www.discovermontecucco.it; Corso Mazzini, Costacciaro) **FREE**, a gorgeous swathe of wildflower-speckled meadows, gentle slopes brushed with beech, yew and silver fir trees, deep ravines splashed by waterfalls and karst cave systems, all topped off by the oft snowcapped hump of 1566m Monte Cucco.

The winding road affords mood-lifting views on almost every corner, passing quaint mountain hamlets and woods where wolves, lynx and wild boar roam. The park beckons outdoor escapades and the website gives the low-down on everything from its 120km of marked hiking trails to mountain biking, horse riding, hang-gliding and cross-country skiing.

The big deal for spelunkers is **Grotta Monte Cucco** (🕿 075 917 10 46; www.grotta montecucco.umbria.it; Via Valentini 39, Costacciaro; tour adult/reduced from €12/10; ⊙ info point 9am-12.30pm & 3-5pm daily summer, shorter hours spring & autumn), one of Europe's most spectacular limestone caves, with a 30km maze of galleries reaching up to 900m deep. Those up for a challenge can delve into its underground forest of stalactites and stalagmites on a guided two-to-three hour discovery tour. For more details on the caves and park, stop by the info point in the nearby village of Costacciaro.

across the barrel-vaulted interior of Gubbio's most sophisticated restaurant, serving Umbrian cuisine with a pinch of creativity and a dash of medieval charm. It's a class act, with tables draped in white linen and polished service. Flavours ring true in specialities like pork with Sargentino wine and Cannara onions or guinea fowl with juniper berries and mushrooms.

Don Navarro   CRAFT BEER
(www.facebook.com/aldonsepuede; Piazza Bosone 2; ⊙ 8am-2am Tue-Sun; 🛜) On Piazza Bosone, this craft-beer bar named after a legendary rum kingpin has 16 taps and one hand pump, from which flows a surprisingly eclectic mix of international and Italian brews. At the 6pm to 9.30pm *aperitivo*, you'll get a selection of their excellent pizza with your beer, making it very easy to call it a night here.

ℹ Information

Informazione e Accoglienza Turistica (IAT) (Tourist Infomation; 🕿 075 922 06 93; www. comune.gubbio.pg.it; Via della Repubblica 15; ⊙ 8.30am-1.45pm & 3.30-6.30pm Mon-Fri, 9am-1pm & 3-6.30pm Sat & Sun) Sells the Gubbio Turisticard and rents multilingual audio guides (€3 to €6).

Poste Italiane (Post Office; www.poste.it; Via Cairoli 11; ⊙ 8.20am-7.05pm Mon-Fri, 8.20am-12.35pm Sat)

ℹ Getting There & Away

To reach Gubbio by car, take the SS298 from Perugia or the SS76 from Ancona, and follow the signs.

Gubbio has no train station but **Umbria Mobilità** (www.umbriamobilita.it) buses run to Perugia (€5.50, 1¼ hours, 10 daily) from Piazza Quaranta Martiri.

Spoleto

POP 39,300

Presided over by a formidable medieval fortress and backed by the broad-shouldered Apennines, their summits iced with snow in winter, Spoleto is visually stunning. The hill town is also something of a historical picnic: the Romans left their mark in the form of grand arches and an amphitheatre; and the Lombards made it the capital of their duchy in 570, building it high and mighty and leaving it with a parting gift of a Romanesque cathedral in the early 13th century.

Today, the town has winged its way into the limelight with its mammoth Spoleto Festival (Festival dei Due Mondi), a 17-day summer feast of opera, dance, music and art.

◉ Sights

Rocca Albornoziana   FORT
(Piazza Campello; adult/reduced €7.50/3.75; ⊙ 9.30am-7pm Tue-Sun, to 1.30pm Mon) High on a hilltop above Spoleto, the Rocca, a glowering 14th-century former papal fortress, is now a fast, scenic escalator ride from **Via della Ponzianina** (Via Ponzianina 3; per hr €1; ⊙ 24hr). The fortress contains the **Museo Nazionale del Ducato**, which traces the history of the Spoleto duchy through a series

of Roman, Byzantine, Carolingian and Lombard artefacts, from 5th-century sarcophagi to Byzantine jewellery.

Museo Archeologico   MUSEUM
(http://polomusealeumbria.beniculturali.it; Via Sant'Agata 18; adult/reduced €4/2; ☉8.30am-7.30pm) Down in the centre of town, Spoleto's pride and joy is its archaeological museum, located on the western edge of Piazza della Libertà. It showcases a well-curated collection of Roman and Etruscan bits and bobs from the area, spread over four floors. You can step outside to view the mostly intact 1st-century **Teatro Romano** (Via delle Terme 2; ☉adult/reduced €4/2 with Museo Archeologico).

Palazzo Collicola Arte Visive   MUSEUM
(www.palazzocollicola.it; Piazza Collicola; adult/reduced €6.50/4; ☉10.30am-1pm & 3.30-7pm Wed-Mon) Spoleto's premier collection of modern art is named after its late former director and noted art critic, Giovanni Carandente, and has been significantly revamped. The collection includes works of late-20th-century Italian artists, including the sculptor Leonardo Leoncillo, painter/sculptor Alexander Calder and painter Alberto Burri. The 2nd floor is dominated by the 18th-century noble apartment, designed by Sienese architect Sebastiano Cipriani and once home to Carlo di Borbone – the future Charles III of Spain.

Casa Romana   HISTORIC BUILDING
(Roman House; Via di Visiale 6; adult/reduced €3/2; ☉10.30am-1.30pm & 2-7pm) This excavated Roman house isn't exactly Pompeii, but it gives visitors a peek into what a typical home of the area would have looked like in the 1st century BC.

Arco di Druso e
Germanico   ARCHAEOLOGICAL SITE
(Arch of Drusus and Germanicus; Via Arco di Druso 19) Near the Piazza Fontana are the remains of the Arco di Druso e Germanico (named for the sons of Emperor Tiberius), which once marked the entrance to the Roman forum.

Duomo di Spoleto   CATHEDRAL
(Piazza del Duomo; ☉8.30am-6pm) A flight of steps sweeps down to Spoleto's pretty pale-stone cathedral, originally built in the 11th century using huge blocks of salvaged stones from Roman buildings for its slender bell tower. A 17th-century remodelling saw a striking Renaissance porch added. The rainbow swirl of mosaic frescoes in the domed apse was executed by Filippo Lippi and his assistants.

Museo del Tessile e
del Costume   MUSEUM
(Museum of Textiles and Costumes; www.sistema museo.it; Via delle Terme; adult/reduced €3/2; ☉3.30-7pm Fri-Sun) Housed in the Palazzo Rosari-Spada, this museum holds a collection of antique noble finery from the 15th to the 20th century donated from the wardrobes of some of the area's leading families.

Ponte delle Torri   BRIDGE
(Via Giro del Ponte) Many people gasp the first time they glimpse the medieval Ponte delle Torri, a 10-arch bridge that leaps spectacularly across a steeply wooded gorge – a scene beautifully captured by Turner in his 1840 oil painting. The bridge was erected in the 14th century on the foundations of a Roman aqueduct, but was damaged in the August 2016 earthquake. It was closed at time of research with expectations of reopening by the end of 2018.

Chiesa di San Pietro   CHURCH
(Località San Pietro; ☉9am-4pm) An 1.4km stroll can be made along the Via del Ponte to the Ponte delle Torri. If the bridge has reopened, cross it and follow the lower path, Strada di Monteluco, to reach Chiesa di San Pietro, where the 13th-century facade is liberally bedecked with sculpted animals.

⭐ Festivals & Events

Spoleto Festival   PERFORMING ARTS
(Festival dei Due Mondi; www.festivaldispoleto.it; Via Filitteria 1; ☉late Jun–mid-Jul, box office 10am-1pm & 3-6pm 23 Apr-22 Jul, 10am-7pm 23 Jun-16 Jul) The Italian-American composer Gian Carlo Menotti conceived the Festival dei Due Mondi (Festival of Two Worlds) in 1958.

DON'T MISS

A WALK WITH A VIEW

Beginning near Rocca fort, the 6km **Giro dei Condotti** walk is an irresistible draw for photographers, keen walkers and anyone who appreciates a jaw-dropping view. It begins just after the ramparts and the staggering 10-arch Ponte delle Torri, and takes you along sun-dappled woodland trails to a lookout with a classic postcard view of the bridge, valley and fortress-crowned hilltop. Be sure to wear flat, comfortable shoes.

Spoleto

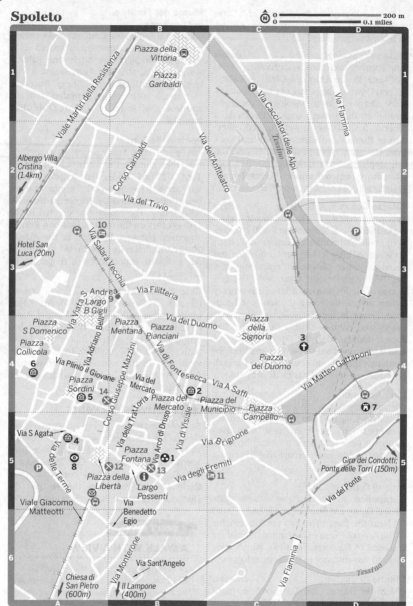

Now simply known as the Spoleto Festival, it has given the town a worldwide reputation. Events at the 17-day festival range from opera and theatre performances to ballet and art exhibitions. For details and tickets, visit the website.

🛏 Sleeping

Stop by the tourist office for info on *affitta-camere* (rooms for rent), hostels, campsites and *agriturismi* (farm stay accommodation) in the surrounding area. Prices rocket during the festival and drop considerably

Spoleto

Sights

1 Arco di Druso e Germanico ... B5
2 Casa Romana ... B4
3 Duomo di Spoleto ... C4
4 Museo Archeologico ... A5
5 Museo del Tessile e del Costume ... A4
6 Palazzo Collicola Arte Visive ... A4
7 Rocca Albornoziana ... D4
8 Teatro Romano ... A5

Activities, Courses & Tours

9 Spoleto Festival ... B3

Sleeping

10 L'Aura ... A3
11 Palazzo Leti ... C5

Eating

12 Bar Canasta ... B5
13 Il Tempio del Gusto ... B5
14 Sabatini ... A4

during low season; good deals can often be snapped up by prebooking online. Much of the pedestrianised old town is off limits to traffic – hotels generally give you a free pass to park outside the medieval walls.

★ L'Aura B&B €
(☎347 2210013; Piazza Torre dell'Olio 5; s €50-60, d €70-80; P@) You'll feel as snug as an Italian bug at this cute one-room B&B on the top floor of a 200-year-old *palazzo*. Claudia makes you welcome and gives excellent tips on Spoleto. It's a tidy, homey place, with bright, wood-beamed rooms and a terrace overlooking rooftops to the hills beyond. There's no lift, so be prepared to schlep your bags up the stairs (there are a few flights).

Albergo Villa Cristina GUESTHOUSE €
(☎0743 4 80 36; www.albergovillacristina.com; Via Collerisana 15, Collerisana; s €40-70, d €58-90; P) Anna Maria is the little ray of sunshine brightening up this guesthouse, lodged in a lovingly restored 18th-century country home, with dreamy views out over cypress-plumed hillsides from its garden terrace. Traditional-style, tiled-floor rooms are kept spick and span. Homemade cakes and honey are served with bread, ricotta and fresh coffee at breakfast.

Hotel San Luca BOUTIQUE HOTEL €€
(☎0743 22 33 99; www.hotelsanluca.com; Via Interna delle Mura 21; s €70-130, d €90-240, ste €190-300; P@) Once a tannery and now a heavenly boutique hotel, the San Luca has polished service and refined interiors to rival any of the five-stars in Umbria, yet the atmosphere is relaxed enough to cater to cyclists and walkers. Pastel tones and antique furnishings inside complement the manicured 17th-century garden. The homemade cakes are the stars of the breakfast buffet.

Palazzo Leti GUESTHOUSE €€€
(☎0743 22 49 30; www.palazzoleti.com; Via degli Eremiti 10; s €80-180, d €120-250; P) In the southeast part of town facing the hills, this beautifully converted 13th-century noble palace exudes romance and charm down to the last detail, from the delicate breakfast china to the historical oak and wrought-iron furnishings. With the view and perfect silence, you'll feel like you're staying in the country, but you're a three-minute walk from the centre of Spoleto.

Eating

Strangozzi alla spoletina, a thin fettuccine-like pasta with tomato, garlic and chilli pepper, is the local dish of choice in Spoleto. You'll also see *attorta*, a sweet pastry filled with apples and chocolate.

Bar Canasta ITALIAN €
(Piazza della Libertà 14; meals €20-45; kitchen 12.30-3pm & 7.30-10.30pm Thu-Tue;) This simple spot with prime Piazza della Libertà patio seating has a well-rounded menu evenly distributed among meat and seafood (no fish Sunday through Tuesday) but locals in the know come for one thing and one thing only: what they consider to be the best *spaghetti alla carbonara* in the region. It is indeed fantastically good and perfectly rich.

Sabatini ITALIAN €€
(☎0743 4 72 30; www.ristorantesabatinispoleto.it; Corso Mazzini 52-54; meals €25-40; 11am-midnight Tue-Sun;) Forget studying the menu – just go for one of the tasting menus (€25 to €30) and loosen a belt notch for dish after delectable dish. This is home cooking at its best with a pinch of seasonality – as simple as 24-month dry-cured prosciutto sliced by hand, black pork fillet cooked with Sagrantino and red onion, and wild boar stew with porcini and juniper berries.

Il Tempio del Gusto ITALIAN €€
(☎0743 4 71 12; www.iltempiodelgusto.com; Via Arco di Druso 11; meals €25-40; 12.30-3pm & 7-11pm Fri-Wed;) Intimate, inventive and unmissable, Tempio del Gusto is fine dining without the Michelin-starred price

ⓘ SPOLETO CARD

Valid for seven days, the **Spoleto Card** (www.spoletocard.it; adult/reduced €9.50/8) offers significant savings, giving you access to six of the town's main museums for less than a tenner. You can pick one up from either of the tourist information points in the city or purchase online at the website.

tag. The food here speaks volumes about a chef who believes in sourcing, cooking and presenting with real pride and purpose. Eros Patrizi is the whiz behind the stove. Freshly made pasta, a trio of smoked fish, or herb-crusted pork – every dish strikes a perfect balance.

★**Il Lampone**   UMBRIAN

(☏0743 84 01 35; www.ristorantelampone.it; Via Strada Romana 8; meals €30-40; ◷12.30-2.30pm & 7.30-10.30pm; ☎) Behind a 350-year-old facade in a nondescript parking lot on the town outskirts is where you'll find Spoleto's best meal, a rustic-chic, whimsical and contemporary culinary retreat overseen by a husband-wife culinary tag team. Dive straight into the tasting menus (€25 to €35, including a vegetarian option) for a Michelin-approaching, seasonal ride through Umbrian feast and folly without the wallet-emptying prices.

ⓘ Information

Informazione e Accoglienza Turistica (IAT) (Tourist Office; ☏ 0743 21 86 20; www. comunespoleto.gov.it/turismo-e-cultura; Via Brigone 14; ◷ 9am-1.30pm & 2.30-6.15pm Mon-Sat, 9.30am-1pm & 3-5pm Sun)

Poste Italiane (Post Office; www.poste.it; Viale Giacomo Matteotti 2; ◷ 8.20am-7.05pm Mon-Fri, to 12.35pm Sat)

ⓘ Getting There & Around

Busitalia (www.fsbusitalia.it) buses run frequently to Norcia (€6.10, 50 minutes, five daily) from the train station, stopping a few minutes later in Piazza della Vittoria.

Trains from the **main station** (Piazzale Giovanni Polvani) connect with Rome (€8.85 to €14.65, 1½ hours, hourly), Perugia (€5.15, one hour, every 30 minutes) and Assisi (€4, 40 minutes, hourly).

By car, the city lies on the E45 and is an easy connection via the SS209 to the Valnerina. Vehicle traffic in Spoleto's *centro storico* is heavily restricted. Parking in the city lots costs between €1 and €1.20 per hour.

Spoleto is compact and best explored on foot.

Norcia & the Valnerina

After the thigh-challenging hill towns of western and northern Umbria, the flatter, less elevated prospects of Norcia can come as a relief, but it is the town itself which needs relief these days. Devastated by the October 2016, magnitude 6.6 earthquake – the largest in Italy since the 1980 Irpinia shake – Norcia lost its precious medieval Basilica di San Benedetto (only the facade survived) and numerous buildings around town. Down but not out, however, things were looking up at the time of research as Norcia – and the surrounding Valnerina river valley – was slowly coming back to life.

Lured by its *tartufo nero* (black truffle) and slew of gourmet delights, foodies have begun returning to Norcia, keen to take in the crisp mountain air and picture-book medieval views between bites of *prosciutto di Norcia IGP* (dry-cured ham) and *salame di cinghiale* (spicy wild-boar sausage). The town's spiritual claim to fame as the birthplace of St Benedict is another reason for lingering here.

◎ Sights

Devastated by earthquakes all too often, the city's petite, walled centre is a joy to explore on foot. Its medieval buildings have been seriously patched up over the years (although broken and bruised once again), but the town has preserved its charm and was roaring back to life at the time of research.

Norcia's other great draw is its proximity to the rugged, exhilarating wilderness of Monti Sibillini. With access to towns like Visso, Castelluccio and Arquata del Tronto still restricted as of mid-2017, Norcia is one of the best and easiest-to-reach park bases until the situation improves. Check ahead.

Almost as scenic is Norcia's own valley, the steep-sided Valnerina valley, freckled with wildflowers in summer, is best explored on a meandering drive along the SS209 (which was unaffected by the 2016 earthquake).

Piazza San Benedetto   PIAZZA

On the centrepiece Piazza San Benedetto, a statue of Norcia's famous son, St Benedict, with hand outstretched in blessing, stands proud. The saint and his twin sister, St Scholastica, were born here to a well-to-do family in 480 AD. Next to the ruins of the Basilica di San Benedetto is the 14th-century **Palazzo Comunale** – intact, but not without 2016 earthquake damage – with a striking portico and belfry, while opposite lies the **Castellina**, a 16th-century papal fortress that now houses a (currently closed) museum.

Basilica di San Benedetto
CHURCH

(Piazza San Benedetto) St Benedict and St Scholastica were apparently born in the Roman crypt of this 13th-century church. The church's pale, delicate facade – all that survived the devastating 2016 earthquake – once gave way to a calm, contemplative interior, where monks often shuffled past bearing prayer books. Filippo Napoletano's early-17th-century frescoes depicted scenes from the life of San Benedetto. No word what, if anything, besides the facade, will be salvaged. Furious efforts to rebuild are already underway, but expect it to be closed for some time.

🛏️ Sleeping & Eating

The merest mention of Norcia sends Italian gastronomes into raptures about the earthy delights of its *tartufo nero* (black truffle) and the prized *salumi* from its acorn-fed pigs, both of which feature prolifically on restaurant menus and in shop windows. Pear-shaped savoury ricotta cheese is also a renowned Norcia speciality.

★ Palazzo Seneca
HISTORIC HOTEL €€€

(📞 0743 81 74 34; www.palazzoseneca.com; Via Cesare Battisti 12; s €128-176, d €160-220, ste €400-800; 🅿 ❄ 🐕 📶) In family hands since 1850, Relais & Châteaux Palazzo Seneca gives guests a tantalising glimpse of the high life. You can truly feel like you're living in a palace here, even if just for a night or two, playing chess in a leather chair in front of the fireplace or having a soothing aromatherapy massage in the subterranean spa.

Trattoria dal Francese
TRATTORIA €€

(📞 0743 81 62 90; www.trattoriadalfrancese.it; meals €30) Once a staple in many of the Italian 'best restaurant' guides and boasting a kitchen that was a cut above most places even in this renowned foodie town, Trattoria dal Francese was closed at the time of research – it falls within a post-2016 earthquake red zone – but was planning to reopen outside the city walls as early as summer 2017.

★ Vespasia
ITALIAN €€€

(📞 0743 81 74 34; www.palazzoseneca.com; Via Cesare Battisti 10; tasting menus €70-130; ☯ noon-3pm & 7-10pm) Set in a 16th-century *palazzo* among contemporary lighting and modern art, everything was bright when Vespasia's understated gourmet cuisine earned its first Michelin star before the 2016 earthquake. We all know what happened next. But Napoletano chef Valentino Palmisano returned to Italy from a lengthy stint in Kyoto not only to conduct a gastronomic experience, but for social good as well.

Ansuini do Maestro Peppe
FOOD & DRINKS

(www.norcineriaansuini.it; Via Anicia 105; ☯ 7.30am-7.30pm) You can't miss the wild boar flanking the entrance to this classic gourmet deli, the best spot in Norcia for local *salume*, cheeses and other gourmet goodies, including craft beer from Amatrice. If you're nice, they'll invite you behind the counter to watch the *salume*-stuffing process.

HUNTERS & GATHERERS

Gastronomically speaking, Norcia is a town of hunters and gatherers. As the country's cured-meat capital, its shops brim with delectable pork and wild boar prosciutto, salami and sausages. In fact, the word 'Norcineria' has become synonymous with 'butcher' throughout Italy.

Pigs aren't the only animals that like to snuffle around in the undergrowth of the surrounding oak woods, however. The area is also one of the region's largest producers of the elusive *tartufo nero* (black truffle), unearthed by dogs led by a *cavatore*, or truffle hunter. Should you wish to embark on your own tuber treasure hunt, Palazzo Seneca offers **truffle-hunting** packages, or ask the tourist office (p610) in Cascaia (Norcia's tourist office was temporarily shut down at the time of research) to put you in touch with local guides heading out in search of culinary gold.

If you're here on the last weekend in February or the first weekend in March, you're in for a treat at the **Nero Norcia festival** (www.neronorcia.com; ☯ Feb/Mar), where thousands turn out to taste and buy wonderful truffles and *salumi* direct from the producers.

PIANO GRANDE

What sounds like a finely tuned instrument is in fact a lyrical landscape. Tucked in the far-eastern corner of Umbria, between Castelluccio and Norcia, the Piano Grande is a 1270m-high plain flanked by the bare-backed peaks of the Apennines. When the snow melts, it gives way to a springtime eruption of wildflowers more beautiful than any Monet painting, its canvas embroidered red, gold, violet and white with poppies, cornflowers, wild tulips, daisies, crocuses and narcissi. It's a florist's heaven, a hay-fever sufferer's hell and an endless source of camera-clicking fascination for walkers, who flock here for serendipitous strolls through the meadows.

❶ Information

Informazione e Accoglienza Turistica (IAT)
(Tourist Office; ☑ 0743 714 01; www.lavalnerina.it; Piazza Garibaldi 1, Cascia; ⊙9am-1pm & 3.30-6.30pm)

❶ Getting There & Away

To reach Norcia and the Valnerina by car from Spoleto, take the SS209 to the SS396. The closest train station is in Spoleto (p608).

Buses run to and from Spoleto (€6.30, 50 minutes, 9am, 11.30am, 5pm and 6.20pm) and Perugia (€7.50, two hours, 6.30am). Buses depart from Porta Masari (aka Porta Ascolana), stopping at Porta Romana as well before leaving town.

Orvieto

POP 21,100

Sitting astride a volcanic plug of rock above fields streaked with vines, and olive and cypress trees, Orvieto is visually stunning from the first. Like the love child of Rome and Florence and nestled midway between the two cities, history hangs over the cobbled lanes, medieval piazzas and churches of this cinematically beautiful city. And few churches in Italy can hold a candle to its wedding cake of a Gothic cathedral, which frequently elicits gasps of wonder at its layers of exquisite detail.

⊙ Sights

★ **Duomo di Orvieto**   CATHEDRAL
(www.opsm.it; Piazza Duomo 26; €4, with Museo dell'Opera del Duomo di Orvieto €5; ⊙9.30am-7pm

Mon-Sat, 1-5.30pm Sun summer, shorter hours winter) Nothing can prepare you for the visual feast that is Orvieto's soul-stirring Gothic cathedral. Dating to 1290, it sports a black-and-white banded exterior fronted by what is perhaps the most astonishing facade to grace any Italian church: a mesmerising display of rainbow frescoes, jewel-like mosaics, bas-reliefs and delicate braids of flowers and vines.

The building took 30 years to plan and three centuries to complete. It was started by Fra Bevignate and later additions were made by Sienese master Lorenzo Maitani, Andrea Pisano (of Florence Cathedral fame) and his son Nino Pisano, Andrea Orcagna and Michele Sanmicheli.

Of the art on show inside, it's Luca Signorelli's magnificent *Giudizio Universale* that draws the crowds. The artist began work on the vast fresco in 1499 and over the course of the next four years covered every inch of the **Cappella di San Brizio** with a swirling and at times grotesque, depiction of the Last Judgment. Michelangelo is said to have taken inspiration from the work. Indeed, to some, Michelangelo's masterpiece runs a close second to Signorelli's creation.

On the other side of the cathedral's transept, the **Cappella del Corporale** houses a 13th-century altar cloth stained with blood that miraculously poured from the communion bread of a priest who doubted the transubstantiation.

Museo dell'Opera del Duomo di Orvieto   MUSEUM
(www.museomodo.it; Piazza Duomo 26; €4, with Duomo di Orvieto €5; ⊙9.30am-7pm) Housed in the former papal palace, this museum contains a fine collection of religious relics from the cathedral, paintings by artists such as Arnolfo di Cambio and the three Pisanos (Andrea, Nino and Giovanni), and a separate permanent exhibit on sculptor and medallist Emilio Greco (1913–95).

Orvieto Underground   HISTORIC SITE
(www.orvietounderground.it; Piazza Duomo 23; adult/reduced €6/5) The coolest place in Orvieto (literally), this series of 440 caves (out of 1200 in the system) has been used for millennia by locals for various purposes, including WWII bomb shelters, refrigerators, wine storage, wells and, during many a pesky Roman or barbarian siege, as dovecotes to trap the usual one-course dinner: pigeon (still seen on local restaurant menus as *palombo*).

Museo Claudio Faina e Civico
MUSEUM

(www.museofaina.it; Piazza Duomo 29; adult/reduced €4.50/3; ⊗9.30am-6pm summer, shorter hours winter) Stage your own archaeological dig at this fantastic museum opposite the Duomo di Orvieto. It houses one of Italy's foremost collections of Etruscan artefacts, including plenty of stone sarcophagi and terracotta pieces and some amazing bronze, as well as some significant Greek ceramic works.

Torre del Moro
HISTORIC BUILDING

(Moor's Tower; Corso Cavour 87; adult/reduced €2.80/2; ⊗10am-8pm summer, shorter hours winter) From the Piazza Duomo, head northwest along Via del Duomo to Corso Cavour and the 13th-century Torre del Moro. Climb all 250 steps for sweeping views of the city.

Chiesa di San Giovenale
CHURCH

(Piazza San Giovenale; ⊗9am-12.30pm & 3.30-6pm) At the western end of town is this stout little church, constructed in the year 1000. Its Romanesque-Gothic art and frescoes from the later medieval Orvieto school are an astounding contrast. Just to the north, you can enjoy towering views of the countryside from the town walls.

Museo Archeologico Nazionale
MUSEUM

(Palazzo Papale, Piazza Duomo; adult/reduced €4/2; ⊗8.30am-7.30pm) Ensconced in the medieval Palazzo Papale, the archaeological museum holds plenty of interesting artefacts, some over 2500 years old. Etruscan ceramics, necropolis relics, bronzes and frescoed chamber tombs are among the items on display.

Chiesa di Sant'Andrea
CHURCH

(☎328 1911316; www.parrocchiadisantandrea-it.it; Piazza della Repubblica; ⊗8.30am-12.30pm & 3.30-7.30pm) This 12th-century church, with its curious decagonal bell tower, presides over the Piazza della Repubblica, once Orvieto's Roman forum and now lined with cafes. It lies at the heart of what remains of the medieval city. Call ahead for an archaeologist-led tour of ancient Etruscan and Roman buildings and an Early Christian church in the basement (€5).

✺ Festivals & Events

Umbria Jazz Winter
MUSIC

(www.umbriajazz.com; ⊗late Dec-early Jan) This celebration of cool musical styles jazzes up the dull patches of Orvieto's winter, with a great feast and party on New Year's Eve.

Palombella
RELIGIOUS

(⊗Pentecost Sun) For traditionalists, this rite has celebrated the Holy Spirit and good luck since 1404. For animal rights activists, the main event celebrates nothing more than scaring the life out of a poor bewildered dove. Take one dove, cage it, surround the cage with a wheel of exploding fireworks, and hurtle the cage 300m down a wire towards the cathedral steps. If the dove lives (it usually does), the couple most recently married in the cathedral becomes its caretakers.

🛏 Sleeping

It's always a good idea to book ahead in Orvieto for summer, on weekends, or if you're planning to come over New Year, when the Umbria Jazz Winter festival is in full swing.

★ B&B Ripa Medici
B&B €

(☎0763 34 13 43; www.ripamedici.it; Vicolo Ripa Medici 14; s/d from €50/75; ❄🔊) Hugging the cliff walls on the edge of Orvieto's old town, this B&B takes the concept of 'room with a view' to a whole new level, gazing longingly out across undulating countryside. The rooms have been given a pinch of romance, with antique furnishings, while the beamed apartment offers even more space and a kitchen. Welcoming owner Sabrina is a total angel.

B&B Michelangeli
B&B €

(☎0763 39 38 62; www.bbmichelangeli.com; Via Saracinelli 20; s €60-100, d €70-160; P🔊) A spacious guesthouse, with bright, nicely kept rooms scattered with homey trinkets, plus

---

MORE FOR YOUR EURO

The **Carta Unica Orvieto** (adult/reduced €20/17) permits entry to the town's nine main attractions, including the Duomo and its Cappella di San Brizio, Museo Claudio Faina e Civico, Orvieto Underground, Torre del Moro and Museo dell'Opera del Duomo. It also includes one round trip on the funicular (p615) and another on a city bus. It can be most easily purchased at the museums. Also available at the Orvieto Underground/Carta Unica office next to the tourist office and the **Orvieto Città Narrante tourist office** (Via Postierla; ⊗10am-2.30pm summer) on Piazza Cahen.

Orvieto

200 m
0.1 miles

Funicular Station

Piazza Cahen

Via Roma

Via Belisario

Corso Cavour

Via San Stefano

Via Postierla

Via Montemarte

Via Porcari

Via Soliana

Piazza
Angelo da
Orvieto

Via da Orvieto

Corso Cavour

Via Nebbia

Piazza
Marconi

Parco
delle
Grotte

14

Piazza
XXIX Marzo

Via Cavallotti

19

13

6 4

Duomo di 1
Orvieto

Piazza
Duomo

Carta
Unica
Orvieto

Via degli Orti

Via San
Leonardo
Fracassini

Piazza
Fracassini

11

7

Informazione e
Accoglienza
Turistica (IAT)

Via di Loreto

Viale G Carducci

Via del Popolo

16

Piazza del
Popolo

Via Gualtieri

Via del Duomo

5

Via Lorenzo Maitani

Piazza
di Febei

18

Via Angelico

8

Via della Misericordia

Via Luca
Signorelli

Via Saracinelli

Piazza
Clementini

3

17

9

Via Pecorelli

Piazza della
Repubblica

Via Magalotti

Vicolo Ripa
Medici

Via Garibaldi

Via dell'Olmo

Via Loggia
dei Mercanti

12

10

15

Piazza San
Giovenale

Via Malabranca

Via della Cava

Via Ripa
Serancia

2

Locanda
Palazzone
(4.7km);
Misia Resort
(5.3km)

a well-stocked kitchen where you can knock up a speedy pasta dish should you so wish. We love the beautiful woodcarvings and wrought-iron beds.

★ **Misia Resort** BOUTIQUE HOTEL €€
(☏0763 34 23 36; www.misiaresort.it; Località Rocca Ripesena 51/52; s €70-80, d €110-130, ste €130-160; P❋✿) You won't regret going the extra mile to this boutique hotel on the rocks, with fabulous views of Orvieto from its hilltop hamlet perch surrounded by 500 planted roses. This stunning country-house conversion has been designed with the utmost taste. The light, spacious rooms in soft, earthy tones come with stylish vintage touches – a chesterfield sofa here, a distressed wood beam there.

Hotel Duomo HOTEL €€
(☏0763 34 18 87; www.orvietohotelduomo.com; Vicolo di Maurizio 7; s €70-90, d €100-130, ste €120-150; P❋@✿) Orvieto's captivating Duomo is almost close enough to touch at Hotel Duomo, where the church bells will most likely be your wake-up call. This Liberty-style *palazzo* – where Orvieto-born artist Livio Orazio Valentini has left his bold, abstract imprint on all of the 17 refined, neutral-hued rooms (all have marble bathrooms) – has service both discreet and polite.

✖ Eating

Umbrichelli, a thick, spaghetti-like pasta, served *all'arrabbiata* (with spicy tomato sauce), stews of wild boar and – like most of Umbria truffled *everything* are just a few of the delicacies that will pair quite nicely with what the *comune* of Orvieto is far more famous for than food: Orvieto DOC wines.

A TASTE OF ORVIETO

If you're keen to slip on an apron, sip some wine and get behind the stove, **Decugnano dei Barbi** (☏0763 30 82 55; www.decugnanodeibarbi.com; Località Fossatello 50) 🍴 estate, perched above vineyards 18km east of Orvieto, offers unique tastings and four-hour cookery classes. The winery can trace its viticultural lineage back 800 years and the lovely master sommelier Anna Rita will guide you through its cellars and talk you through a tasting of its minerally whites and full-bodied Orvieto Classico reds. Or sign up in advance to assemble a four-course meal together with Rosanna, paired (naturally) with home-grown wines and served in the atmospheric surrounds of a converted chapel.

Di Pasqualetti GELATO €
(www.facebook.com/PasqualettiSrl; Piazza Duomo 14; cones €2.50-5; ⊙11am-10pm, to midnight Sat) This gelateria serves mouth-watering gelato, plus there are plenty of tables on the piazza for you to gaze at the magnificence of the cathedral while you gobble.

Trattoria La Palomba UMBRIAN €
(☏0763 34 33 95; Via Cipriano Menente 16; meals €20-30; ⊙12.30-2.15pm & 7.30-10pm Thu-Tue; ✿) Ask a local about Orvieto's best traditional restaurant and inevitably La Palomba jumps into the conversation. Wood panelling and old-school house wine labels abound. The food – heavy on various versions of *umbrichelli* (the *alla matriciana* is perfect!) and hearty meat dishes (the wild boar with

Orvieto

UMBRIA & LE MARCHE ORVIETO

ORVIETO'S WINE COUNTRY

Now famed for its white DOC vintages, Orvieto's wine-growing potential was first spotted by the Etruscans more than 2000 years ago. They were attracted not just by the ideal soil and climate, but also by the soft tufa rock that underpins much of the landscape from which deep cool cellars could be (and indeed still are) cut to allow the grapes to ferment. From the Middle Ages onwards, Orvieto became known across Italy and beyond for its super-sweet gold-coloured wines. Today these have largely given way to drier vintages, such as Orvieto DOC and Orvieto Classico.

To really immerse yourself in the world of viticulture, spend a night or two at the **Locanda Palazzone** (📋0763 39 36 14; www.locandapalazzone.com; Località Rocca Ripesena; suite d €159-350, q €340-410; 🅿️🛜❄️), a highly respected winery a few kilometres outside Orvieto. Dreamy vineyard landscapes unfurl before your eyes from rather stylish suites in a restored papal pilgrim's house.

tomatoes and hot peppers was the best that graced our plates in Umbria) – excels.

⭐ Al Pozzo Etrusco   UMBRIAN €€

(📋0763 34 10 50; www.alpozzoetruscodagiovanni.it; Piazza dei Ranieri 1a; meals €23-35; ⏱️12.30-2.30pm & 7.30-9.30pm Wed-Mon; 🛜) Named after an ancient Etruscan well and silo that graces its basement, this fan favourite has drawn quite a following in just a few short years. Your host, Giovanni, will guide you through his seasonal menu of Umbrian delights, best enjoyed alfresco on the charming candlelit patio.

Trattoria del Moro Aronne   TRATTORIA €€

(📋0763 34 27 63; www.trattoriadelmoro.info; Via San Leonardo 7; meals €25-30; ⏱️12.30-3pm & 7-10pm Wed-Mon; 🛜) This welcoming trattoria has a convivial feel, authentic food and honest prices. The focus is on traditional cooking and strong regional flavours. Warm up with a goat cheese and fig marmalade starter before hitting your stride with a house speciality *bucatini* carbonara with fava and *baffo* (guanciale) and/or a healthy cut of grilled beef.

Le Grotte del Funaro   UMBRIAN €€

(📋0763 34 32 76; www.grottedelfunaro.it; Via Ripa Serancia 41; pizza €4-8.50, meals €25-35; ⏱️noon-3pm & 7pm-midnight; 🛜) What could be more romantic – well, at least in a *Snow White* fairy-tale kind of way – than dining in a proper underground grotto? But this restaurant has more going for it than novelty factor alone. Alfredo and Sandra make a cracking kitchen duo, preparing wood-oven pizzas alongside Umbrian dishes like truffle-ridden *ombrichelli* and braised Chianina beef.

 ## Drinking & Nightlife

Bottega Vera   WINE BAR

(www.casaveraorvieto.it; Via del Duomo 36; wines by the glass €3-7; ⏱️9am-8pm Mon-Thu, 8.30am-10pm Fri-Sun; 🛜) It's no easy task sussing out a non-touristy *enoteca* (wine bar) in Orvieto, but this stylish gourmet deli and wine shop has been at it since 1938, when it was started by the grandmother of current host Cesare, who will expertly guide you – and mostly Italians! – through his daily changing offerings by the glass. Of Cesare's 120 wines or so, half are from Orvieto.

Febo   BAR

(www.facebook.com/officinafebo; Via Gualverio Michelangeli 7; ⏱️noon-2am Tue-Sat, 5.30pm-2am Sun; 🛜) Tucked away down a narrow, tree-draped alley lined with sculpted wooden horses with a story to tell, this is the bar where you'll find Orvieto's coolest crowd, including a seemingly disproportionate amount of young hipster couples with newborns! You'll find six taps of craft beer, local wines by the glass and a small but fresh selection of *aperitivo* bites. Go early – the few alley tables are snatched up fast. But it's just as cool to drink inside, where roped herbs are suspended from the ceiling, creating the town's funkiest, most creative vibe.

☆ Entertainment

Teatro Mancinelli   THEATRE

(📋0763 34 04 93; www.teatromancinelli.com; Corso Cavour 122; adult/reduced €2/1, show tickets €15-60; ⏱️theatre visits 10am-8pm) This theatre plays host to Umbria Jazz (p611) in winter but offers everything from ballet and opera to folk music and Pink Floyd tributes throughout the year. If you're not able to catch a performance, it's worth a visit to see the allegorical frescoes and tufa walls.

ⓘ Information

Informazione e Accoglienza Turistica (IAT)
(Tourist Office; ☑0763 34 17 72; www.inorvieto.it; Piazza Duomo 24; ⊗8.15am-1.50pm & 4-7pm Mon-Fri, 10am-1pm & 3-6pm Sat & Sun) Helpful tourist information near the Duomo.

Poste Italiane (Post Office; www.posteitaliane.it; Via Largo M Ravelli; ⊗8.20am-7.05pm Mon-Fri, to 12.35pm Sat)

ⓘ Getting There & Away

BUS

Buses depart from Orvieto's station near Piazza Cahen, stopping at the train station, and include services to Todi (€6.30, two hours, one daily Sep-Jun) and Terni (€6.90, two hours, 6.35am, 5.20pm & 7.40pm).

CAR & MOTORCYCLE

Orvieto is on the Rome–Florence A1, while the SS71 heads north to Lago Trasimeno. There's plenty of metered parking on Piazza Cahen and in designated areas outside the city walls, including **Parcheggio Campo della Fiera** (Via Belisario 10; per hr €1-1.50).

TRAIN

Orvieto's **train station** (Via Antonio Gramsci) is west of the *centro storico* (historic centre) in Orvieto Scalo. Hourly connections include Rome (€7.80 to €9.90, 1¼ hours), Florence (€11.80 to €16.10, 1½ to 2½ hours) and Perugia (€7.60 to €13.95, 1¾ to 2½ hours).

ⓘ Getting Around

A century-old **funicular** (tickets €1.30; ⊗every 10min 7.20am-8.30pm Mon-Sat, every 15min 8am-8.30pm Sun) creaks up the wooded hill from Orvieto's train station (west of the centre) to Piazza Cahen. The fare includes a bus ride from Piazza Cahen to Piazza Duomo. Outside of funicular hours, bus 1 runs up to the old town from the train station (€1.30). An elevator connects Parcheggio Campo della Fiera with the old town on the western end.

Bus A (€1.30) connects Piazza Cahen with Piazza Duomo and bus B (€1.30) runs to Via Garibaldi.

LE MARCHE

From the white-pebble, cliff-backed bays along the Adriatic to sloped hill towns and the high-rise mountain ranges of Monti Sibillini, Le Marche is one of Italy's little-known treasures.

It's inland where Le Marche really shines. Urbino, Raphael's hometown, presents a smorgasbord of Renaissance art and history up and down its vertical streets. Pale but lovely Ascoli Piceno has beauty and history in bounds and is one of the region's coolest and trendiest cities. Equally walkable is Macerata, with a famous open-air opera theatre and festival. Covering its western reaches, and bleeding over into neighbouring Umbria, is the wild and wonderful Parco Nazionale dei Monti Sibillini. Although the park's towns and villages suffered greatly in the 2016 Central Italian earthquakes, the area is slowly rebuilding and rebounding.

History

The first well known settlers of Le Marche were the Piceni tribe, whose 3000-year-old artefacts can be seen in the Museo Archeologico in Ascoli Piceno (p629). The Romans invaded the region early in the 3rd century BC, and dominated it for almost 700 years. After they fell, Le Marche was sacked by the Goths, Vandals, Ostrogoths and, finally, the Lombards.

In the 8th century AD, Pope Stephen II decided to call upon foreigners to oust the ungodly Lombards. First to lead the charge of the Frankish army was Pepin the Short, but it was his rather tall son Charlemagne who finally took back control from the Lombards for good. On Christmas Day in 800, Pope Leo III crowned him Emperor of the Holy Roman Empire.

After Charlemagne's death, Le Marche entered into centuries of war, anarchy and general Dark Ages mayhem. In central Italy, two factions developed: the Guelphs (who backed papal rule) and the Ghibellines (who supported the emperor). The Guelph faction eventually won out and Le Marche became part of the Papal States. It stayed that way until Italian unification in 1861.

ⓘ Getting There & Away

Drivers have two options on the Marche coastline: the A14 autostrada (main highway) or the SS16 *strada statale* (state highway). Inland roads are either secondary or tertiary and much slower. Regular trains ply the coast on the Bologna–Lecce line and spurs head to Macerata and Ascoli Piceno. Marche Airport (p619) in Ancona is the main aerial gateway.

Ancona

POP 102,500

Often brushed aside as being just another of Italy's bolshie, gritty port towns, Ancona is no beauty at first glance from the ferry, it's true. But there's more to Ancona than meets the superficial eye, and to simply bypass it is to miss much. In the old town, crowned by the *duomo*, you can peel back layers of history of the city founded by Greek settlers from Syracuse around 387 BC, admiring Roman ruins, the rich stash of its archaeological museum and its Renaissance *palazzi*, which glow softly in the evening light. Linger long enough in its hilltop parks overlooking the Adriatic and lively boulevards and cafe-rimmed piazzas and you will see a more likeable side to Le Marche's seafront capital, we promise.

◉ Sights

★ Museo Archeologico Nazionale delle Marche
MUSEUM

(www.archeomarche.beniculturali.it; Via Ferretti 6; adult/reduced €5/2.50; ⊙8.30am-7.30pm Tue-Sun) Housed in the beautiful 16th-century **Palazzo Ferretti**, where the ceilings are covered with original frescoes and bas reliefs, this museum presents a fascinating romp through time, from the Palaeolithic period to the Middle Ages. Although not as well curated as it could be (English information is sorely lacking), persevere, as this museum holds real treasures.

★ Pinacoteca Comunale di Ancona
MUSEUM

(www.facebook.com/PinacotecaAncona; Palazzo Bosdari Vicolo Foschi 4; adult/reduced €6/3; ⊙11am-6pm Thu, to 8pm Fri, 10am-1pm & 5-8pm Sun) Reopened after an extensive 4½-year renovation, Ancona's fascinating civic art

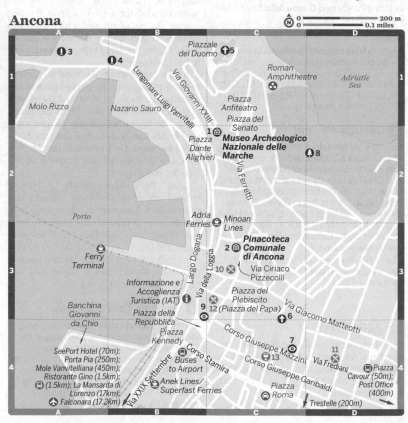

Ancona

gallery houses Le Marche's most important art collection. Among 7th- to 9th-century city fortification walls and spread over two former palaces, the new museum juxtaposes the modern and antiquated with raging success, arranging galleries by theme, not chronology, and is daringly curated without regard for tradition or expectation. Unmissable masterpieces include Titian's *Pala Gozzi* (made the more special by unusually displayed backside) and Carlo Crivelli's absolutely flooring *Madonna and Child*.

Chiesa di San Domenico CHURCH
(Piazza del Plebiscito; ⊙10am-noon & 4-8pm) Flanked by cafes, the elegant Piazza del Plebiscito has been Ancona's meeting spot since medieval times. It's dominated by this baroque church, though the church is closed indefinitely due to earthquake damage. Its prized possessions – the superb *Crucifixion* by Titian and *Annunciation* by Guercino – have temporarily moved to Pinacoteca Comunale di Ancona. The gigantic statue in front is Pope Clement XII, who was honoured by the town for giving it free port status, hence the alternative name of 'Piazza del Papa'.

Cattedrale di San Ciriaco CATHEDRAL
(Piazzale del Duomo; ⊙8am-noon & 3-7pm summer, to 6pm winter) A stiff but scenic climb up from the old town, Ancona's perkily domed cathedral commands sweeping views of the city and port from its hilltop perch. Guard-

DON'T MISS

HIGH ABOVE ANCONA

The din of central Ancona fades to a distant hum from **Parco del Cardeto** (www.parcodelcardeto.it; ⊙8.30am-8.30pm summer, 8am-5.30pm winter), straddling the hill behind the city, with broad views across the rooftops of the old town to the port and the Adriatic. The pine shade and sea breezes up here are refreshing in summer. Fortifications, a 19th-century lighthouse and a Napoleonic-era cemetery can be found in its grounds.

ed by two marble lions, the cathedral sits grandly atop the site of an ancient pagan temple and is an architectural potpourri of Byzantine, Romanesque and Gothic features. Wandering downhill from here along Piazza Anfiteatro, you will glimpse the remains of the city's **Roman amphitheatre**, believed to have been built during the reign of Emperor Augustus.

Fontana del Calamo FOUNTAIN
(Corso Mazzini) Head along Corso Mazzini to see the 16th-century Fontana del Calamo, its 13 masked spouts supposedly representing effigies of those who have been beheaded.

Teatro delle Muse THEATRE
(☎071 5 25 25; www.teatrodellemuse.org; Via della Loggia) On Piazza della Repubblica, this ornate theatre was built in 1826 and has a neoclassical facade that melds with Greek friezes portraying Apollo and the Muses.

🛏 Sleeping

★ **La Mansarda di Lorenzo** APARTMENT €
(☎333 5051307, 333 4199279; www.facebook. com/LaMansardaDiLorenzo; Via Cuneo 1, Falconara Marittima; apt €50-60; P❄🛜) Handily placed near the airport yet still peaceful, this penthouse apartment is a delight – spacious, immaculate, homey and run by the affable Lorenzo. It's kitted out with lounge and dining areas, the comfiest of beds, a huge terrace and a proper kitchen with breakfast goodies. Give Lorenzo a call and he'll even pick you up from the airport.

Trestelle B&B €
(☎345 4562337; www.bbtrestelle.it; Via San Martino 10; s/d/tr €35/60/90; ❄🛜) This welcoming

MONUMENTAL ANCONA

North of Piazza Dante Alighieri, at the far end of the port, is the **Arco di Traiano** (Trajan's Arch; Banchina Nazario Sauro), erected in 115 BC by Apollodorus of Damascus in honour of the Roman Emperor Trajan. Luigi Vanvitelli's grand **Arco Clementino** (Clementine's Arch; Molo Nord), inspired by Apollodorus' arch and dedicated to Pope Clement XII, is further on, near Molo Rizzo.

Head south along the coastal road and, after about 750m, you'll come across the enormous **Mole Vanvitelliana** (www.museoomero.it; Banchina Nazario Sauro 28; ☺5-8pm Tue-Thu & Sat, 10am-8pm Fri, 10am-1pm & 5-8pm Sun, shorter hours winter) **FREE**, designed by Luigi Vanvitelli in 1732 for Pope Clementine. Just past the pentagonal building, on Via XXIX Settembre, is the baroque **Porta Pia** (Largo Caduti sul Mare 27), built as a monumental entrance to the town in the late-18th century at the request of Pope Pius VI.

B&B is right in the thick of things in Ancona, a three-minute amble from Piazza Roma. Four rooms are simple yet modern and immaculately kept, with tiled floors and the odd burst of colour.

SeePort Hotel BOUTIQUE HOTEL €€
(☏071 971 51 00; www.seeporthotel.com; Rupi di Via XXIX Settembre 12; d €84-159, ste €189-229) A breath of fresh air to Ancona's hotel scene, the SeePort gazes wistfully out across the harbour and the Adriatic. Housed in a clever conversion of a 1950s concrete block, the crisp minimalist interiors have subtle nods to the sea, and the light-drenched, parquet-floored rooms are among Marche's most stylish. The highly regarded **restaurant** dishes up Le Marche cuisine.

Grand Hotel Passetto HOTEL €€
(☏071 3 13 07; www.hotelpassetto.it; Via Thaon de Revel 1, Passetto; s €84-162, d €106-205, ste €190-257; P❄@🛜🏊) Near Ancona's white-shingle beach, a 1.3km walk east of the centre, this hotel has a genteel atmosphere, a relaxing pool area and occasional incredible sea views. The light rooms are done out with hardwood floors and crisp white linen; the best have four-poster beds and the suite

has its own Jacuzzi. Substantial discounts are offered on winter weekends and around holidays.

 Eating

The city's culinary claim to fame is *stoccafisso all'anconetana* (wind-dried stockfish – similar to salted cod but somewhat milder – with potatoes, tomatoes, *verdicchio* wine and a boatload of olive oil).

Ristorante Gino ITALIAN €
(☏071 4 33 10; www.albergogino.it; Piazza Carlo e Nello Rosselli 26; meals €20-30) Locals swear by the *stoccafisso all'anconetana* at this old school *anconetano* joint across from the railway station. Other local delicacies pop up here as well, such as fish lasagna and *brodetto di pesce all'anconetana* (a fish soup).

Mercato delle Erbe MARKET €
(Piazza dell'Erbe; ☺7.30am-12.45pm & 5-8pm) Going strong since 1926, this market hall does a brisk trade in fresh produce, pastries and bread, cheese, *salumi* and other picnic goodies.

Osteria del Pozzo OSTERIA €€
(☏071 207 39 96; www.osteriadelpozzo.net; Via Bonda 2; meals €25-35; ☺noon-2.30pm & 7.30-10pm Mon-Sat; 🛜) Unless you've booked ahead, you'll be lucky to grab one of the cheek-by-jowl tables at this inviting *osteria* teeming with regulars. Spot-on seafood – generous helpings of pasta (seabass ravioli is a good bet), a beautiful shellfish *ciavattoni* (a tubular pasta served in an epic copper pot) and the like – are all washed down with inexpensive house wine and mostly unsympathetic service.

🍷 **Drinking & Nightlife**

Piazza del Plebiscito – referred to by Ancona's locals by its original name, Piazza del Papa – is one of the most relaxed spots for an al fresco drink, with tables set up on the pretty square.

Bar Torino COCKTAIL BAR
(www.facebook.com/bartorinoancona1860; Corso Giuseppe Garibaldi 49; cocktails €7.50; ☺6.30pm-midnight, shorter hours winter) Boasting a righteously retro font and slinging cocktails since 1860, this is one of Ancona's liveliest spots for a tipple, especially during the nightly *aperitivo* (from 6.30pm), which feeds a mid-sized army. The Americano and Ne-

groni *Marchigiano* (Vermouth traded for verdicchio wine) are fantastic, but the Torino Special – red Vermouth, Campari, vanilla liqueur and bitter orange – is world-class.

Amarillo Tap Room CRAFT BEER
(www.facebook.com/amarillo.ancona.birreria; Piazza del Plebiscito 19; pints €5-6; ☺6pm-2am Tue-Sun; 🖥) Enjoying privileged Piazza del Plebiscito position, Ancona's hophead central is this welcomed newcomer (named after a type of hops, not a Spanish colour) with eight taps built from imported New York water piping. Grab a *birra* and monopolize an outdoor table for a boozy afternoon of pints and people-watching.

Keep an eye out for owner Francesco's own strong ale and double Imperial Pale Ale on draught.

ℹ Information

Informazione e Accoglienza Turistica (IAT)
(Tourist Office; ☑071 207 64 31; www.turismo.marche.it; Banchina Sauro 50; ☺9am-2pm Mon, 9am-6pm Tue-Fri) Opposite the ferry terminal, this is the tourist office for Ancona Le Marche province. Stop by for leaflets, maps, itineraries and more.

Poste Italiane (www.poste.it; Largo XXIV Maggio; ☺8.20am-7.05pm Mon-Fri, 8.20am-12.35pm Sat)

ℹ Getting There & Away

AIR
Marche Airport (☑071 2 82 71; www.aeroporto marche.it; Piazzale Sandro Sordoni, Falconara Marittima) Lufthansa, Alitalia, Vueling and Ryanair (with daily flights to London Stansted), among others, fly into Marche Airport, about 18km west of Ancona.

SAILING THE ADRIATIC SEA

The port of Ancona is a jumping off point for three countries: Greece, Croatia and Albania (there were no longer direct ferries to Turkey at the time of research). Information and prices below are examples from the highest season (generally a variety of dates between June and August) – check ferry websites for a comprehensive list of schedules and prices. Ferry companies generally charge a 50% surcharge for single occupancy in private cabins.

Greece

Anek Lines/Superfast Ferries (☑071 207 23 46; www.anekitalia.com; Via XXIX Settembre 29) heads to Igoumenitsa (8¼ hours) and Patras (22½ hours) daily at 1.30pm and Saturday at 4.30pm. An additional 4.30pm departure Tuesday and Thursday stops first in Corfu (seven hours). Fares per person range from €85 for standing on deck to €379 (based on double occupancy) for a luxe cabin. **Minoan Lines** (☑071 20 17 08; www.minoan.it; Lungomare Vanvitelli 18) sails to Igoumenitsa and Patras daily at daily-changing times (check the website for specifics). Fares range from €79 on deck to €219 (based on double occupancy) for a luxe cabin (prices spike slightly over those listed on a few select days in August).

Croatia

Snav (☑081 428 55 55; www.snav.it) heads to Split (11 hours) Monday, Tuesday, Wednesday and Thursday at 10pm (with an additional Sunday departure at 11am). Fares per person range from €50 for deck passage to €85 (based on double occupancy) for a sea-view cabin (tack on an additional €25 for a pet-friendly cabin berth). **Jadrolinija** (www.jadrolinija.hr) also goes to Split (from €63) as well as Zadar (from €63, 10pm, 8½ hours). Split ferries often make a stop in Stari Grad (from €63, 7.45pm Friday, 10 hours) as well.

Albania

Adria Ferries (☑071 5021 1621; www.adriaferries.com; Lungomare Vanvitelli 18) sails to Durrës (20 hours) on Tuesday, Thursday and Friday at 7pm; Saturday at 5pm and Wednesday at 1pm. Fares per person range from €95 for desk passage to €215 (based on double occupancy) for a luxe suite. **Fritelli Maritime** (www.frittellimaritime.it) handles bookings in Ancona.

BASILICA DELLA SANTA CASA

Straddling a hilltop south of Ancona and visible from afar, **Loreto** is absorbed entirely by its bauble-domed **Basilica della Santa Casa** (http://santuarioloreto. it; Piazza della Madonna; ☉7.15am-7.30pm summer, to 7pm winter). While the original basilica started in 1468 was Gothic, Renaissance additions (including some savvy engineering by Bramante) have made today's imposing Basilica della Santa Casa an architectural masterpiece. Inside, gold-leafed halos, impressive frescoes and religious triptychs create viewing opportunities worth braving the schlock shops. Plus, whether you've sinned in Italian, English, Japanese or German, you're in luck: in addition to several daily masses, visitors can take advantage of multilingual confessionals throughout the day.

Inside stands the elaborate marble Santa Casa di Loreto, or the Holy House shrine, where pilgrims flock to glimpse a bejewelled black statue of the Virgin and pray in the candlelit twilight. The chapel is allegedly where Jesus was raised as a child. Legend has it a host of angels winged the chapel over from Nazareth in 1294 after the Crusaders were expelled from Palestine.

Loreto sits 3km or so west of the A14 autostrada from Ancona (exit Loreto–Porto Recanati). It's easily reached by train from Ancona (€2.90, 20 minutes, hourly).

BUS

Most buses leave from Ancona's Piazza Cavour, inland from the port (it's a five-minute walk east of the seafront along Corso Giuseppe Garibaldi), except for Portonovo, whose services originate at the train station (in summer only).

TO	FARE (€)	DURATION	FREQUENCY
Jesi	3.20	45min	21 daily
Marche Airport	5	45min	hourly
Macerata	3.85	1½hr	13 daily
Numana	2.60	45min	16 daily
Portonovo	1.25	30min	13 daily Jun-Aug
Recanati	3.40	1¼hr	15 daily
Senigallia	2.90	1hr	11 daily

CAR & MOTORCYCLE

Ancona is on the A14, linking Bologna with Bari. The SS16 coastal road runs parallel to the autostrada and is a pleasant, toll-free alternative if you're not looking to get anywhere fast. The SS76 connects Ancona with Perugia and Rome.

There's plenty of parking in Ancona, which gets steadily more expensive the closer to the centre you get (€1.20 to €2.70 per hour). The multistorey **Parcheggio Degli Archi** (www. anconaparcheggi.it; Via Terenzio Mamiani; all day €2) near the train station has economical all-day parking.

You'll find all the major car hire companies at the airport, including **Europcar** (☐071 916 22 40; www.europcar.it; Marche Airport), **Avis** (☐071 5 22 22; www.avis.com; Marche Airport) and **Hertz** (☐071 207 37 98; www.hertz.com; Marche Airport); **Maggiore** (☐071 918 88 05; www.maggiore.it; Piazza Carlo e Nello Rosselli) is by the train station.

FERRY

Direct ferries operate from Ancona to Greece, Croatia and Albania (see p619).

TRAIN

Ancona is on the Bologna–Lecce line. Check whether you're taking a Eurostar service, as there can be a substantial supplement.

TO	FARE (€)	DURATION	FREQUENCY
Bari	23.30-46.50	3¾-4¾hr	hourly
Bologna	13.30-33.50	1¾-2¾hr	twice hourly
Florence	30.30-60.50	2¾-3¼hr	hourly
Milan	29.30-66.40	3¼-4hr	hourly
Pesaro	4.75-9.90	27-56min	twice hourly
Rome	17.75-32.50	3-4hr	every 2hr

❶ Getting Around

TO/FROM THE AIRPORT

There is a frequent train service between Castel-ferreti station, opposite the terminal, and Ancona (15 to 25 minutes, €1.90).

Alternatively, Conero bus runs the **Aerobus Raffaelo** roughly hourly from Piazza Cavour and Piazza Kennedy, among other stops, to Marche Airport from 7am to 10.30pm Monday to Saturday (shorter hours on Sunday). The trip costs €5.50 one way and takes around 30 minutes. The **Airport Taxi Service** (☑ 071 91 82 21) can take you to central Ancona (around €35, from 30 minutes).

BUS

Conero Bus (☑ 071 283 74 11; www.conerobus. it) services, including bus 1/3 and 1/4, connect Ancona's main train station with the centre (Piazza Cavour), while bus 12 connects the main station with the ferry port (€1.20); look for the bus stop with the big signpost displaying Centro and Porto.

TAXI

Ancona Taxi (town centre ☑ 071 20 28 95, train station ☑ 071 4 33 21; Corso Stamira)

Parco del Conero

Only minutes from Ancona but a world unto itself, Parco del Conero (aka Parco Regionale del Conero) is stunning, with limestone cliffs razoring above the cobalt blue Adriatic, and crescent-shaped, white pebble bays backed by fragrant woods of pine, oak, beech, broom and oleander trees. Walking trails thread through the 60 sq km park, which is a conservation area. Remarkably still off the radar for many travellers, the park retains a peaceful, unspoilt air found nowhere else along Le Marche's coastline. Its highest peak is 572m Monte Conero, which takes a spectacular nosedive into the sea. The vineyards that taper down its slopes produce the excellent, full-bodied Rosso Conero red wine.

Parco del Conero encompasses the cliff-backed seaside resorts of **Portonovo**, **Sirolo** and **Numana**, all of which make fine bases for exploring. Boat trips from Portonovo and Sirolo are the best way to cove- or beach-hop.

🛏 Sleeping

Camping Internazionale CAMPGROUND €
(☑ 071 933 08 84; www.campinginternazionale. com; Via San Michele 10, Sirolo; camping 2 people, car & tent €22-50, for sea view add €4-10, bungalows €50-200; ☺ mid-May–mid-Sep; @ 🛜 ☲) Shaded in the trees just a few metres from the scenic beaches below Sirolo, this full-service campground is replete with swimming pool, pizzeria, bar, grocery store and children's club with plenty of activities to keep the little ones amused. The views from here – and the two beaches above which it sits – are spectacular.

★ **Acanto Country House** GUESTHOUSE €€
(☑ 071 933 11 95; www.acantocountryhouse.com; Via Ancarano 18, Sirolo; s €70, d €90-140, ste €100-150; 🅿 ❄ 🛜 ☲) Set back from Sirolo's beaches and surrounded by cornfields, meadows and olive groves, this converted farmhouse is a gorgeous country escape, taking in the full sweep of the coast. Named after flowers like peony and rose, rooms have been designed with the utmost attention to detail, with gleaming wood floors, exposed stone, embroidered bedspreads and two with steamroom showers.

🍴 Eating

★ **Ristorante da Giacchetti** SEAFOOD €€
(☑ 071 80 13 84; www.ristorantedagiacchetti. it; Via Portonovo 171, Portonovo; meals €30-50; ☺ 12.30-3pm & 8-10pm Apr-Oct) The best of Portonovo's wildly popular seaside restaurants, Ristorante da Giacchetti has been dishing up the freshest of Marche's sea treasures since 1959. Hand-harvested mussels and *raguse* (sea snails), doused in a secret spicy sauce, are obvious starting points, paired with a long list of Marche whites like *verdicchio*. *Secondi* specialties include *stoccafisso all'anconetana* (stockfish stew) and monkfish for two.

La Torre SEAFOOD €€
(☑ 071 933 07 47; www.latorrenumana.it; Via la Torre 1, Numana; meals €30-40; ☺ 12.30-2.30pm & 7.30-10.30pm Mon-Sat, 12.30-3pm Sun) Floor-to-ceiling glass walls maximise the wraparound sea views from this sleek, industrial-chic restaurant, with bare wood floors, crisp white tablecloths and exposed silver pipework. Go for artistically presented antipasti and mains, mostly – surprise, surprise – with a seafood slant. It's hugely popular with the locals.

ℹ Information

Centro Visite (Visitor Centre; ☑ 071 933 11 61; www.parcodelconero.org; Via Peschiera 30a, Sirolo)

ⓘ Getting There & Away

Conero (p621) buses to Portonovo (€1.25, ½ hour, 13 daily) from Ancona operate in the summer from Ancona's train station, but the area is much easier to explore with your own set of wheels.

Urbino

POP 15,500

Raphael's Renaissance 'hood, the vibrant university town of Urbino is often the first stop on a trip to Le Marche and understandably so. The patriarch of the Montefeltro family, Duca Federico da Montefeltro, created the hippest art scene of the 15th century here, gathering the great artists, architects and scholars of his day to create a sort of think tank. The town's splendour was made official by Unesco, which deemed the entire city centre a World Heritage Site in 1998.

⊙ Sights

Palazzo Ducale PALACE

(www.palazzoducaleurbino.it; Piazza del Rinascimento 13; ⊙8.30am-7.15pm Tue-Sun, to 2pm Mon) A microcosm of Renaissance architecture, art and history, the Palazzo Ducale contains the Galleria Nazionale delle Marche, housed within Federico da Montefeltro's palace. The duke enlisted the foremost artists and architects of the age to create this whimsically turreted masterpiece. From Corso Garibaldi you get the best view of the complex, with its unusual **Facciata dei Torricini**, a three-storey loggia in the form of a triumphal arch, flanked by circular towers.

Galleria Nazionale delle Marche MUSEUM

(www.gallerianazionalemarche.it; Piazza Duca Federico; adult/reduced €6.50/4; ⊙8.30am-7.15pm Tue-Sun, to 2pm Mon) The Galleria

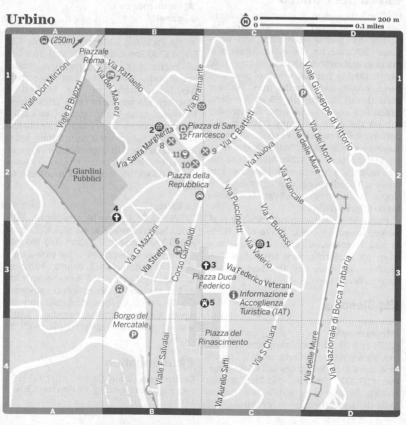

Urbino

Nazionale delle Marche lodges inside the striking Renaissance Palazzo Ducale. A monumental staircase, which was one of Italy's first, leads to the *piano nobile* (literally 'noble floor') and the Ducal Apartments. Piero della Francesca was one of the artists employed by the duke, and his work, *The Flagellation*, adorns the wall of the duke's library. The collection also includes a large number of drawings by Federico Barocci, as well as some stunning Renaissance works by Raphael, Titian and Signorelli.

Duomo di Urbino   CATHEDRAL
(Piazza Duca Federico; ⊙7.30am-1pm & 2-8pm) Rebuilt in the early 19th century in neoclassical style, the interior of Urbino's *duomo* commands much greater interest than its austere facade. Particularly memorable is Federico Barocci's *Last Supper*. The basilica's **Museo Diocesano Albani** (www.museodiocesanourbino.it; Piazza Pascoli 1; €3.50; ⊙9.30am-1pm & 2.30-6.30pm Wed-Mon) is still operating and contains religious artefacts, vestments and more paintings, including Andrea da Bologna's *Madonna del Latte* (Madonna Breastfeeding).

Earthquake damage, however, has closed the cathedral to visits for what could be as long as through 2018.

Urbino

⊚ **Sights**

Casa Natale di Raffaello   MUSEUM
(www.palazzoducaleurbino.it; Via Raffaello 57; €3.50; ⊙9am-1pm & 3-7pm Mar-Oct, 9am-2pm Nov-Feb) North of the Piazza della Repubblica you'll find the 15th-century house where Raphael was born in 1483 and spent his first 16 years. On the 1st floor is possibly one of Raphael's first frescoes, a Madonna with child. The museum takes a touching look at Raphael's family life.

Oratorio di San Giovanni   CHURCH
(Via Barocci 31; €2.50; ⊙10am-1pm & 3-6pm Mon-Sat, 10am-1pm Sun) This 14th-century church features brightly coloured frescoes by Lorenzo and Giacomo Salimbeni.

Casa della Poesia   MUSEUM
(www.casadellapoesiaurbino.blogspot.it; Palazzi Odasi, Via Valerio 1; ⊙3-7pm Mon & Thu, 9am-1pm Wed & Fri, 10.30am-6.30pm Sat & Sun) FREE South of the piazza, this brand new cultural space in the Renaissance Palazzo Odasi is dedicated to expat American poet Ezra Pound, a seminal figure in the early modernism movement (and a controversial proponent of Mussolini and Hitler). Centered on a lovely arcaded inner courtyard, it hosts everything from art and photography exhibitions to readings and talks.

✦ Festivals & Events

The city swings into summer at the **Urbino Jazz Festival** in June, with performances held all over town, followed by the **International Festival of Ancient Music** in July and the **Festa dell'Aquilone**, a kite festival, on the first weekend in September.

Festa dell'Duca   CULTURAL
(www.urbinofestadelduca.it; ⊙2nd or 3rd Sun Aug) Urbino time-travels back to the Middle Ages, with medieval fun hitting the streets in the shape of a costumed procession and the re-enactment of a tournament on horseback.

🛏 Sleeping

Urbino charges a tourist tax ranging from €1.50 to €2.50 (depending on number of stars) per person per night for up to five nights. The town teams with hotels, *alberghi* and B&Bs in the historic centre, and *agriturismo* farm stays in the surrounding countryside.

UMBRIA & LE MARCHE URBINO

★**Locanda della Valle Nuova** FARMSTAY €
(☎0722 33 03 03; www.vallenuova.it; La Cappella 14, Sagrata di Fermignano; d €56, apt €90-150, half-board per person €30; ☺ late May-early Nov; P@🖥🛜🏊) ✆ What a delight this organic farm is, with bright, immaculate rooms and lovely, soothing views across wooded hills to the mountains beyond. Whether you want to rustle up an Italian feast with a cookery class, go horse riding or learn basket weaving, friendly owner Giulia will oblige. She is also a terrific cook and dinners are a feast of homegrown goodies.

B&B Albornoz B&B €
(☎347 2987897; www.bbalbornoz.com; Via dei Maceri 23; s/d €50/80; 🛜) Wedged in a quiet old-town corner, this B&B has boutique flavour for a pinch of the price. A spiral staircase links three studios full of designer touches, with murals, funky lighting and bold artworks, from the monochromatic *You and Me* to the floral, lilac-kissed romance of *Osaka*. Rain-style showers are dreamy. All come with kitchenettes and espresso machines.

Tenuta Santi Giacomo e Filippo AGRITURISMO €€
(☎0722 58 03 05; www.tenutasantigiacomoefilippo.it; Via San Giacomo in Foglia 7, Pantiere; s €79-149, d €99-189, ste €109-209, meals €30-40; P🌑🛜🏊) ✆ And relax... You can't help but unwind the minute you check into this gorgeous country abode, surrounded by vineyards and gardens fragrant with flowers and herbs. Spread across six stylishly converted stone farm buildings, the wood-floored rooms are individually designed – some are decorated in soothing pastels with Laura Ashley fabrics, others are slick and contemporary.

Albergo Italia HOTEL €€
(☎0722 27 01; www.albergo-italia-urbino.it; Corso Garibaldi 32; s €50-75, d €85-130; 🌑@🛜) Set behind the Palazzo Ducale, the Italia could not be better positioned. Modern and well designed, the shuttered townhouse is restfully quiet and staff are genuinely friendly. In warmer months, take breakfast on the balcony.

✕ **Eating & Drinking**

Urbino's ubiquitous local speciality is *crescia sfogliata*. Similar to Emilia-Romagna's *piadina* (flatbread), the *urbinate* version is enhanced with eggs, salt and pepper, then stuffed with all sorts of goodness, of which the most common combo is prosciutto and local *pecorino* cheese.

Sorbetto del Duca GELATO
(www.facebook.com/sorbettodelDuca; Via Raffaello 1; small/medium/large €2.20/2.70/3.20; ☺11.30am-midnight) Urbino's best gelateria is set on prime Piazza della Repubblica real estate. The seasonally alternating flavour of the house flips between pomegranate and fig, but we fell hard for the *crema di nocciole bianca* (white hazelnut cream).

La Trattoria del Leone TRATTORIA €
(☎0722 32 98 94; www.latrattoriadelleone.it; Via Battisti 5; meals €20-25; ☺12.30-2.30pm & 6.30-10.30pm Mon-Sat) ✆ This homey, rustic basement trattoria raids Le Marche's larder for the best regional produce. *Olive all'ascolana* (stuffed olives fried in breadcrumbs) whet appetites for dishes such as ravioli with the local Casciotta d'Urbino cheese and baked rabbit with wild fennel and olives, with true depth of flavour. Save an inch for the excellent chocolate cake.

★**Antica Osteria da la Stella** OSTERIA €€
(☎0722 32 02 28; www.anticaosteriadalastella.com; Via Santa Margherita 1; meals €30-40; ☺12.30-2.15pm & 7.30-10.30pm Tue-Sat, 7.30-10.30pm Mon; 🛜) Duck down a quiet side street to this rustically elegant, beamed 15th-century inn once patronised by the likes of Piero della Francesca. Legendary in these parts, Osteria de la Stella puts its own inventive twist on seasonal food. Every dish pops with flavour and the *strozzapreti* (tubular pasta) with asparagus, artichokes, sausage and tomatoes topped with toasted almonds is worth a trip.

Caffè Raffaello WINE BAR
(www.raffaellodegusteria.it; Via Raffaello 41; wines by the glass €2.50-4.50; ☺6am-8pm Mon-Sat; 🛜) A mixed crowd of students and middle-aged urbanites spill out into Via Raffaello during Urbino's best wine bar's nightly *aperitivo*. There's an ever-changing, superbly curated selection of *marchigiana* wines by the glass; and the outdoor tables a tad down the street are in prime Piazza della Repubblica people-watching position.

This is also a good spot to try Birrificio Le Fate, a craft beer from Monti Sibillini.

🛍 Shopping

★Raffaello Degusteria FOOD & DRINKS
(www.raffaellodegusteria.it; Via Bramante 6/8/10; ⊙9-1pm & 4-8pm Mon-Sat, 10.20-6pm Sun) The best spot in town for local products bar none. With the selection here – Casciotta d'Urbina DOC cheese, *salumi*, biscotti, wine, craft beer, honey, grappa, olive oil, truffles, there's even local saffron!– you could stock up for a WWIII bomb shelter and still not be hungry after three years of fallout. At least 90% of their inventory counts as *marchigiana*.

ℹ Information

Informazione e Accoglienza Turistica (IAT) (Tourist Information; ☑ 0722 26 31; Via Puccinotti 37; ⊙ 9am-1pm Mon & Wed-Thu, 9am-1pm & 3-5.45pm Tue & Fri-Sun) Urbino's main tourist information office is across from Palazzo Ducale.

Poste Italiane (Post Office; www.poste.it; Via Donato Bramante 22; ⊙ 8.20am-7.05pm Mon-Fri, 8am-12.35pm Sat)

ℹ Getting There & Around

BUS

Adriabus (☑ 0722 376738, 800 664332; www.adriabus.eu; Viale Antonio Gramsci) runs a half-hourly service daily between Urbino's new **bus station** (☑ 800 664332; Viale Antonio Gramsci) and Pesaro, from where you can pick up a train for Bologna.

CAR

Most vehicles are banned from Urbino's walled city. There are car parks outside the city gates, including the main one at Borgo del Mercatale. Parking costs €1.20 per hour.

TAXI

Taxi Urbino (☑ 0722 25 50; Piazza della Repubblica)

Pesaro

POP 94,600

Look beyond the concrete high-rise hotels and the crowds of bronzed holidaymakers jostling for towel space on the beach in August, and you'll find a lot to like about Pesaro. The town's setting is perfect, with beaches of fine golden sand fringing the Adriatic, a backdrop of undulating hills, and a pretty old town centred on the cafe-rimmed Piazza del Popolo, where the Renaissance Palazzo

Ducale stands proud. The composer Rossini was so fond of his home town that he left it all of his possessions when he died (be sure to check out Casa Rossini while you're here).

◉ Sights

Pesaro has four major beach areas – the Blue Flag-awarded **Levante, Ponente, Baia Flaminia** and the **free beach**. Levante and Ponente are the jam-packed hotel-fronted beaches, so for more elbow room head to the *spiaggia libera* (free beach) to the south of the city, under Monte Ardizio.

Musei Civici MUSEUM
(www.pesaromusei.it; Piazza Toschi Mosca 29; combined ticket incl entry to Casa Rossini adult/reduced €10/6; ⊙10am-1pm & 4.30-7.30pm Tue-Sun, shorter hours winter) Opened in the 1860s, just after Italian reunification, the town's original art gallery is now the Musei Civici, which also showcases Pesaro's stunning 700-year-old pottery tradition with one of Italy's best collections of majolica ceramics.

Casa Rossini MUSEUM
(www.pesaromusei.it; Via Rossini 34; combined ticket incl entry to Musei Civici adult/reduced €10/6; ⊙10am-1pm & 4.30-7.30pm Tue-Sun, shorter hours winter) In 1792 famous composer Rossini was born in a typical Pesaro townhouse that is now the Casa Rossini. His mother was a singer, his father a horn player and the young lad was composing when he was knee-high to a grasshopper. Prints, personal items and portraits provide an insight into the life of the virtuoso and his operas, such as the jaunty *Barber of Seville*.

🎭 Festivals & Events

Rossini Opera Festival MUSIC
(☑0721 380 02 94; www.rossinioperafestival.it; Via Rossini 24; ⊙Aug; box office during festival 10am-noon & 4-6.30pm) This two-week festival is a love letter to Pesaro's local legend. Productions of Rossini's operas and concerts are staged at the Teatro Rossini and Adriatic Arena. Tickets go for anything from €20 to €180, with substantial student and last-minute discounts.

🛏 Sleeping & Eating

Most Pesaro hotels close from October to Easter. Though many places are uninspiring 1960s concrete blocks, you can find some charmers if you look hard enough. The

Associazione Pesarese di Albergatori (☑ 0721 6 79 59; www.apahotel.it) can help.

Campeggio Marinella
CAMPGROUND €

(☑ 0721 5 57 95; www.campingmarinella.it; SS16 km244; camping 2 people, car & tent €26.50-39.50; ☺ Easter-Sep; 🛜) Drift off in your seaside tent to the sound of waves breaking on the beach. A pizzeria is on site, as well as a minimarket, beach volleyball and lots of child-friendly activities.

Hotel Clipper
HOTEL €€

(☑ 0721 3 09 15; www.hotelclipper.it; Viale Guglielmo Marconi 53; s €34-220, d €39-220, tr €54-257; P ✳ 🛜) In the capable hands of the friendly Gasparini family, Clipper is literally steps from the beach and a five-minute stroll from the Pesaro centre. The bright and breezy rooms, all with balconies, were completely modernised in 2017 and now feature trendy earth-toned bedding and nature-centric headboard images. And those funky blue sinks! Rates include bike rental and beach towels.

L'Angolo di Mario
SEAFOOD, PIZZA €€

(☑ 0721 6 58 50; http://angolodimario.it; Via Nazario Sauro; pizza €2.50-11, meals €25-35; ☺ noon-3pm & 7-11pm; 🛜) L'Angolo di Mario couples sea views with contemporary decor, pleasant service and great food. Bag a table on the terrace to gaze out across the Adriatic as you dig into well-heaped plates of mussels and clams or seafood pasta (especially *strozzapreti pasta* with fresh tuna, pistachio pesto and julienne zucchini) before mains of grilled fish or beef.

☆ Entertainment

Teatro Rossini
THEATRE

(☑ 0721 38 76 20; www.teatridipesaro.it; Piazza Lazzarini 1; ☺ box office 10am-1pm & 3.30-6.30pm) This theatre was renamed in the composer's honour, and its grand ceiling and ornate box seats make it a breathtaking spot to catch a concert, especially during the Rossini Opera Festival.

ℹ Information

Informazione e Accoglienza Turistica (IAT) (Tourist Office; ☑ 0721 6 93 41; www.turismo pesaro.it; Piazzale della Libertà 11; ☺ 9am-1pm Mon, Wed & Fri, 9am-1pm & 2.30-5.30pm Tue & Thu) Has excellent information in English, with maps, bike path info, hotels and sights, and is extra friendly to boot.

ℹ Getting There & Around

BUS

Pesaro's main **bus station** (☑ 0722 37 67 38, 800 664332) is next to the train station on Piazzale Giovanni Falcone e Paolo Borsellino, about 1.5km southwest of the beach. **Adriabus** (☑ 0722 37 67 38, 0800 664332; www. adriabus.eu; Piazzale Giovanni Falcone e Paolo Borsellino) operates a daily 5.40am departure to Rome (€35, 4¾ hours), with an additional departure at 3pm on weekdays, and half-hourly buses to Urbino.

TRAIN

Pesaro's **train station** (www.trenitalia.com; Viale del Risorgimento) is on the Bologna–Lecce train line and you can reach Rome (€20.70 to €47.50, 3½ to 5¾ hours, 10 daily) directly twice daily.

Macerata

POP 42,000

Straddling low-rise hills, Macerata combines charming hilltown scenery with the verve of student life – its university is one of Europe's oldest, dating to 1290. Its old town, a jumbled maze of cobblestone streets and honey-coloured *palazzi,* springs to life in summer for a month-long opera festival.

◉ Sights & Activities

Arena Sferisterio
THEATRE

(☑ 0733 23 07 35; www.sferisterio.it; Piazza Mazzini 10; adult/reduced €3/2, incl guided tour €5/4; ☺ 9am-4pm Mon, 9am-1pm & 3-7pm Tue-Sun summer, 10am-5pm Mon, to 6pm Tue-Sun winter) One of Europe's most stunning outdoor theatres is the neoclassical Arena Sferisterio, a grand colonnaded affair resembling an ancient Roman arena, which was built between 1820 and 1829. Its acoustics are second to none, most notably enjoyed during the city's important Macerata Opera Festival (www. sferisterio.it; Arena Sferisterio; ☺ Jul-Aug) every summer.

Torre Civica
HISTORIC BUILDING

(Piazza della Libertà) Conceived as early as 1492 but not completed until 1653, Macerata's 64m-tall civic tower looms over Piazza della Libertà. It houses a recently restored replica of the astronomical clock (originally removed in 1882) that was once a banner of Renaissance cosmology. It features an immense blue dial with concentric circles that

UMBRIA & LE MARCHE MACERATA

indicate the hour, the moon phases and the movement of celestial bodies.

Musei Civici di Palazzo Buonaccorsi
MUSEUM
(☑0733 25 63 61; www.maceratamusei.it; Via Don Minzoni 24; adult/reduced €3/2; ☺10am-6pm Tue-Sun, to 7pm Jul-Aug) Macerata's museums cluster in the Musei Civici di Palazzo Buonaccorsi. On the bottom floor is the **Museo delle Carozza**, a beautifully displayed and extensive collection of 18th- to 20th-century coaches in a modern setting. The 1st floor brings you to the city's **Arte Antica** collection, with works dating from the 13th to the 19th centuries, while the 2nd floor is dedicated to **Arte Moderna**, with several rooms given over to Macerata born painter Ivo Pannaggi, a driving force behind Italian futurism in the 1920s and '30s.

Loggia dei Mercanti
LANDMARK
(Piazza della Libertà) The historic centre is presided over by the Renaissance Loggia dei Mercanti on Piazza della Libertà. Built in 1505 for Cardinal Alessandro Farnese, the soon-to-be Pope Paul III, the arcaded building housed travelling merchants selling their wares.

🛏 Sleeping

Hotel Arcadia
HOTEL €
(☑0733 23 59 61; www.harcadia.it/dove.htm; Via Matteo Ricci 134; s/d/tr €50/70/90; P❋☎) On a quiet lane not far from the cathedral, the Arcadia gives three-star comfort and a genuinely warm welcome at wallet-friendly prices. The pick of the rooms sport a contemporary look, with warm hues, parquet floors and flat-screen TVs. Light sleepers should be aware that the walls are quite thin.

Albergo Arena
HOTEL €
(☑0733 23 09 31; www.albergoarena.com; Vicolo Sferisterio 16; s €40-85, d €55-130; P❋@☎) Bang in the heart of Macerata's old town, this shuttered stone house offers modest, spotlessly kept rooms, some of which have newly modernised bathrooms. It's a welcoming base for exploring the historic centre.

Le Case
AGRITURISMO €€
(☑0733 23 18 97; www.ristorantelecase.it; Via Mozzavinci 16/17; s/d/ste Mon-Fri €75/100/200, Sat & Sun €85/120/230; P❋☎⛱) 🍃 A drive lined with cypress trees sweeps up to this country manor and organic farm, nestled in glorious

isolation 9km west of Macerata. The pale-hued, wood-floored rooms combine an air of discreet luxury with original trappings like beams, flagstone floors and antique furnishings, and you'll sleep like a log given the pin-drop peace here.

🍴 Eating & Drinking

Macerata's regional version of lasagna, *vincisgrassi alla maceratese*, features prominently on menus and differs from the usual in that the *ragù* contains a mix of pork, beef and lamb. Don't miss *ciauscolo*, either, a soft, spreadable *salume* that is wonderful slathered on bread.

Da Secondo
ITALIAN €
(☑0733 26 09 12; www.dasecondo.com; Via Pescheria Vecchia 26/28; ☎) One of Macerata's longest-running restaurants and apparently one of the few open on Sunday, Da Secondo is both welcoming – Giacomo wins Marche Server of the Year! – and an excellent spot for *maceratese* specialities like *vincisgrassi*, *ciauscolo* and *frittura mista* (fried veggies, beef-stuffed olives and other goodies).

Trattoria da Ezio
TRATTORIA €€
(☑0733 23 23 66; www.trattoriadaezio.eu; Via Giovanni Mario Crescimbeni 65; meals €25-30; ☺noon-2.30pm & 7.30-9.30pm Tue-Sat; 🍽) A trattoria in the classic mould, da Ezio has been bubbling and stirring since 1957. The look and homey vibe have changed little since then and neither has the Slow Food menu – making the most of freshly made pasta and farm-fresh meat and veggies. There are good vegetarian options.

Osteria dei Fiori
OSTERIA €€
(☑0733 26 01 42; www.osteriadeifiori.it; Via Lauro Rossi 61; meals €25-30; ☺noon-3.30pm & 7-10.30pm Mon-Sat; 🍽) This *osteria* has a homey, low-key vibe and al fresco seating in summer. The cuisine is season focused, but the creative menu might include, say, spaghetti with spring chicory and hazelnuts, followed by roasted rabbit with fennel and coffee-aniseed gelato. Kids and vegetarians are well catered for.

Beer Bang
CRAFT BEER
(☑6pm-2am; www.facebook.com/beerbangmacerata; Via Francesco Crispi 41; beers €2-5; ☺6pm-2am; ☎) An atmospheric pub for local and international craft beer under historic

arched ceilings. There are eight beers on draught (plus one hand-pump) and a refrigerator full of mostly Belgium and German choices in bottles.

☆ Entertainment

Teatro Lauro Rossi　　　　THEATRE
(☎0733 23 35 08; Piazza della Libertà) Teatro Lauro Rossi is an elegant theatre built in 1774 for the musical enjoyment of the nobility. It now also allows well-dressed riff-raff to attend. It stages everything from classical music concerts to comedies, contemporary plays and dance productions.

ℹ Information

Informazione e Accoglienza Turistica (IAT) (Tourist Office; ☎0733 23 48 07; www.turismo. provinciamc.it; Corso della Repubblica 32; ⊙9am-1pm Mon, 9am-1pm & 3-6pm Tue-Sat) Pick up info on Macerata and its surrounds and book tours here.

Poste Italiane (Post Office; www.poste.it; Via Gramsci 44; ⊙8.20am-7.05pm Mon-Fri, 8.20am-12.35pm Sat)

ℹ Getting There & Around

BUS

Roma Marche (☎call centre Civitanova Marche 0733 81 86 38; www.romamarchelinee. it) connects Macerata with Rome (€24, four hours, 1.30am, 5am, 6.15am, 8.30am, 10.45am, & 4.15pm) and Naples (€34, 6½ hours, 5am). Timetables for local **Contram** (☎0733 23 08 75; www.contram.it; Piazza Piazzarello) buses are available at the **bus terminal** (☎0733 23 08 75; Piazza Piazzarello).

CAR & MOTORCYCLE

The SS77 connects the city of Macerata with the A14 to the east and roads for Rome in the west. There is paid parking (€1.20 per hour) from 8am to 8pm skirting the city walls and free parking at the Giardini Diaz, where the long-distance buses arrive.

TRAIN

From Macerata's **train station** (☎0733 24 03 54; www.trenitalia.com; Piazza XXV Aprile 8/10) there are good connections to Ancona (€6.10, 1¼ hours, hourly) and Rome (€17.20 to €26, four to five hours, eight daily). To reach Ascoli Piceno (€8.25, 1¾ to 2¼ hours, 10 daily), change trains at Civitanova Marche-Montegranaro.

Bus 6 links the train station with the Piazza della Libertà in the Macerata city centre.

Ascoli Piceno

POP 49,900

With a continuous history dating from the Sabine tribe in the 9th century, Ascoli (as it's known locally) is like the long-lost cousin of ancient Rome and a small *Marchigiani* village, heavy on history and food. Weary legs will appreciate its lack of hills and all travellers will appreciate its historical riches, excellent *pinacoteca* (art gallery), trendy bars and restaurants, one of Italy's unsung perfect piazzas and the calorific treat, *olive all'ascolana* – veal-stuffed fried olives. Welcome to the hippest town in Le Marche.

◉ Sights

Ascoli Piceno's Vecchio Quartiere (Old Quarter) stretches from Corso Mazzini (the main thoroughfare of the Roman-era settlement) to the Castellano river. Its main street is the picturesque Via delle Torri, which eventually becomes Via Solestà; it's a perfect spot to wander round.

A museum card is purportedly on the way for Ascoli Piceno's civic museums. Check at the tourist office (p631).

★ Piazza del Popolo　　　　PIAZZA

The harmonious and simply lovely Piazza del Popolo has been Ascoli's *salotto* (sitting room) since Roman times. The rectangular square is flanked on the west by the 13th-century **Palazzo dei Capitani del Popolo**. Built in the same famed travertine stone used throughout the region for centuries, the 'Captain's Palace' was the headquarters for the leaders of Ascoli. The statue of Pope Paul III above the main entrance was erected in recognition of his efforts to bring peace to the town.

Chiesa di San Francesco　　　　CHURCH
(Via del Trivio 49; ⊙7am-12.30pm & 3.30-8pm) This beautiful church was started back in 1262 as an homage to a visit from St Francis himself. In the left nave is a 15th-century wooden cross that miraculously made it through a 1535 fire at the **Palazzo dei Capitani**, and has since reputedly spilled blood twice.

Pinacoteca　　　　MUSEUM
(www.ascolimusei.it; Piazza Arringo; adult/reduced €8/5; ⊙10am-7pm Tue-Sun summer, to 5pm winter) Gathered around a tree-shaded courtyard, the second-largest art gallery

in Le Marche sits inside the 17th-century **Palazzo Comunale**. It boasts an outstanding display of art, sculpture and religious artefacts; there are 400 works in total, including paintings by Titian, Crivelli and Reni, and a stunning embroidered 13th-century papal cape worn by Ascoli-born Pope Nicholas IV.

Galleria d'Arte Contemporanea Oswaldo Licini
GALLERY

(www.ascolimusei.it; Corso Mazzini 90; adult/reduced €3/2; ⊙10am-1pm & 3-6pm Tue-Sun, guided tours 11am & 3pm, shorter hours winter) This gallery is the small personal collection of Oswaldo Licini's Italian contemporary art, including a number of graphic works. The collection is highlighted by several 1950s era paintings by the museum's namesake himself, one of Italy's best-known abstract artists.

Museo dell'Arte Ceramica
MUSEUM

(☑0736 29 82 13; www.ascolimusei.it; Piazza San Tommaso; adult/reduced €3/2; ⊙10am-1pm & 3-6pm Tue-Sun, guided tours 11am & 3pm, shorter hours in winter) The Museo dell'Arte Ceramica has displays on the major Italian pottery towns, including Deruta, Faenza and Genoa, among others. Don't miss Libero Grue's 18th-century framed pictorials, a sort of Old World comic strip.

Duomo
CATHEDRAL

(Piazza Arringo; ⊙8am noon & 4-8pm) Topped by a pair of mismatched towers, Ascoli's *duomo* was built in the 16th century over a medieval building and dedicated to St Emidio, patron saint of the city. In the **Cappella del Sacramento** is the three-section *Polyptych of San Emidio*, Venetian painter Carlo Crivelli's 1473 masterpiece. It is still in its original frame and is an extraordinarily rare example of 15-th century pictorial art. It has never once left this spot.

The elaborate **crypt of Sant'Emidio** has a set of mosaics any ceramicist will appreciate.

Museo Archeologico
MUSEUM

(www.archeomarche.beniculturali.it; Piazza Arringo 28; adult/reduced €4/2; ⊙8.30am-7.30pm Tue-Sun, free 1st Sun of the month) Ascoli's archaeological museum holds a small collection of tribal artefacts from the Piceni and other European peoples dating back to the first centuries AD, as well as a fantastic mosaic floor featuring a stunning and fascinating centrepiece: a dual-sided depiction of an old/young Roman God Janus (an optical illusion depending on your viewpoint).

Torre degli Ercolani
HISTORIC BUILDING

(Via dei Soderini) This 40m-high tower, west of the Chiesa di San Pietro Martire, is closed to the public but is the tallest of the town's medieval towers. **Palazzetto Longobardo**, a 12th-century Lombard-Romanesque defensive position and now the **Ostello dei Longobardi youth hostel**, abuts the tower. Just to the north is the well-preserved **Ponte Romano**, a single-arched Roman bridge.

★ Festivals & Events

Quintana
CULTURAL

(www.quintanadiascoli.it; ⊙late Jul/early Aug) This is one of Italy's most famous medieval festivals, and for good reason. Expect thousands of locals dressed in typical medieval garb: knights in armour, flag throwers and ladies in flamboyant velvet robes. Processions and flag-waving contests take place throughout July and August, but the big draw is the Quintana joust, when the town's six *sestieri* (districts) face off.

Fritto Misto all'Italiana
FOOD & DRINK

(www.frittomistoallitaliana.it; ⊙late Apr) This four-day festival of fried food aims to 'debunk the prejudice that it's unhealthy'. After a few hours spent grazing stalls packed with heavy-duty treats – *cannoli* from Sicily, *panzerotti* from Puglia and, of course, *olive all'ascolana* (fried stuffed Ascoli olives) your body may not agree, although your taste buds will have had a blast.

🛏 Sleeping

For a town of such modest proportions, Ascoli Piceno has an extraordinary number of charming hotels, many of which offer early-booking discounts. Stop by the tourist office (p631) for lists of apartments, *agriturismi* (farm stay accommodation) and B&Bs.

★ Villa Fortezza
B&B €

(☑328 413 16 56; www.villafortezza.it; Via Fortezza Pia 5; s €50-80, d €60-100, q €120, 3br house €250; P❄🤶) On its hilltop perch above Ascoli's old town near the fort, and reached by a seemingly never-ending flight of steps, this villa is a delight. Salvatore, your kindly host, does his best to welcome you in his art-strewn home, where individually designed, parquet-floored rooms swing from classic to contemporary.

Hotel Palazzo dei Mercanti   HISTORIC HOTEL €€

(☑0736 25 60 44; www.palazzodeimercanti.it; Corso Trento e Trieste 35; d €75-150, ste €120-200; P🕯🉐) This 16th-century *palazzo* was once part of the Sant'Egido convent. Today you'll count your blessings in rooms done out in soothing pastel tones and hand-crafted furniture, with nice touches like tea and coffee and bathrobes (handy for the spa's whirlpool, sauna and hammam). The *palazzo* manages the delicate task of combining original stone-vaulted interiors with a fresh, contemporary aesthetic.

Palazzo Guiderocchi   BOUTIQUE HOTEL €€

(☑0736 25 97 10; www.palazzoguiderocchi.com; Via Cesare Battisti 3; s €69-129, d €89-149, ste €119-190; P✳@🉐) Not many places offer the history, atmosphere and comfort of this 16th-century *palazzo*. Beautifully gathered around an inner courtyard, it retains the romance of vaulted ceilings on the 1st floor, low wood-beamed ceilings on the 2nd, and frescoes and several original doors throughout.

🍴 Eating & Drinking

★ Degusteria 25 Doc & Dop   ITALIAN €

(☑0736 31 33 24; Via Panichi 3; meals €15; ⊙noon-12.30pm & 7pm-midnight Tue, Thu & Sat-Sun, 7pm-midnight Wed & Fri) Strings of garlic and chilli dangle from the ceiling of this convivial deli-*enoteca,* where the locals squeeze in or spill out onto the terrace for fine wines and tasting plates of regional *salumi,* cheese and, of course, *olive all'ascolana.* Decent daily specials are rustled up for €6.

Siamo Fritti   CAFE €

(www.siamofritti.ap.it; Piazza Simonetti 87; snacks €3-4.50; ⊙11am-3pm & 5.30pm-midnight) A great little cafe specialising in both the city's famed fried-and-stuffed olives (there's a vegetarian version for non-carnivores) and local wines. The perfect initiation to this local delicacy is the €6 *olive con vino* package deal, which includes a portion of *olive*

EARTHQUAKE UPDATE: MONTI SIBILLINI NATIONAL PARK

Straddling the Le Marche–Umbria border in rugged splendour, the Parco Nazionale dei Monti Sibillini never looks less than extraordinary, whether visited in winter, when its peaks – 10 of which tower above 2000m – are dusted with snow, or in summer, when its meadows are carpeted with poppies and cornflowers.

At the time of research, access to many towns in the park was highly restricted, as this region took the brunt of central Italy's two devastating 2016 earthquakes. Many of the park's glacier-carved valleys and beautifully preserved hilltop hamlets are now strewn with rubble and devastation, traversed only by uniformed firefighters, public rescue and civil defence authorities rather than hikers and outdoor enthusiasts.

So, what *can* you do in the park during this extremely painful healing process? The northeast side of the park fared better. Two visitor centres remain open – Centro Visite del Parco Nazionale dei Monti Sibillini e Museo della Sibilla (☑0736 85 64 62; www.sibillini.net; Via Trieste 11, Montemonaco; ⊙9.30am-12.30pm & 3.30-6.30pm July & Aug, shorter hours rest of year) in Montemonaco and Centro il Chirocefalo e il Lago di Pilato in Foce in Foce di Montemonaco – while temporary centres were in the works at most other places where permanent ones previously operated. Il Giardino delle Farfalle (www.prolococessapalombo.it), the butterfly garden at Cessapalombo, is open.

The majority of trekking routes through the park can also be accessed, including the 124km Grande Anello dei Sibillini (two *rifugi* remain open as well as some alternative accommodation along the route) and hiking routes E10 (Monte Sibilla), E2 (Lame Rosse), E6 and E1, among others. Additionally, all the ski slopes on the Sarnano side of the park are operating normally.

It's hard to say how long repairs and reconstruction will take, but park officials estimate one to two years for the park to return to normal operating status and 10 to 15 years for restoration of historic structures in the area (though some say the park will never be quite like it was pre-earthquake). Of course, all of these conditions remain extremely fluid – check the park's website for the most up-to-date conditions.

all'ascolana and a glass of wine – try it with the Fiori di Seta *passerina frizzante* (a fizzy local white).

Piccolo Teatro
ITALIAN €€

(☑0736 26 15 74; Via Goldoni 2; meals €25-35; ☺7.30-10pm Tue & Fri, 12.30-2.30pm & 7.30-10.30pm Wed-Thu & Sun, 12.30-2.30pm & 7.30-11pm Sat) This barrel-vaulted restaurant blends historic charm with a dash of style and a strong sense of place. Tables draped in white linen set the scene for wonderfully light pasta and season-driven dishes – from *stringoni* pasta carbonara modified with black truffles to pork ribs with Sibillini pink apples.

Il Desco
MEDITERRANEAN €€

(☑0736 25 07 57; www.ildescoristorante.it; Via Vidacilio 10; meals €30-40; ☺12.30-2.30pm & 7.30-10.30pm Tue-Sat, 12.30-2.30pm Sun; ☂) Funky chandeliers, high vaults and white distressed wood create a country-chic backdrop at this gorgeously styled *palazzo*. When the weather warms, diners spill out into the garden courtyard, lit by tealights. A clever use of herbs elevates seasonal specialities, from homemade *paccheri di gragnano* with artichokes and bacon, to grilled calamari with chickpea purée and rosemary. It's all delicious.

Vincè Fa La Carita A Lu Dome
WINE BAR

(www.vincefalacaritaaludome.it; Piazza Arringo 18; white/red by the glass €3.50/4) An Ascoli meeting point on pretty Piazza Arringo, this cheekily named cafe/wine bar draws a fun, artsy crowd for its nightly *aperitivo*. Great local wines can be sunk here on the cheap – especially when you pair them with the setting. The name literally means 'Vincenzo is giving out money to the cathedral for charity' and is a not so subtle dig at the Catholic church. Next door, the same owners at **Ariafritta** do a good *olive all'ascolana*.

ℹ Information

Centro Informazioni Turistiche (Tourist Office; ☑0736 28 83 34; www.visitascoli.it; Piazza Arringo 7; ☺9am-7pm Mon-Sat, 10am-7pm Sun) Ascoli's *comune* tourist office is stocked with maps and leaflets on Ascoli's sights and hiking in the surrounds and Monti Sibillini. It also rents out bikes for €2/4 per half/full day.

Poste Italiane (Post Office; www.poste.it; Via Crispi 2; ☺8.20am-7.05pm Mon-Fri, 8.20am-12.35pm Sat)

ℹ Getting There & Away

BUS

Services leave from **Piazzale della Stazione** (Via Venezia 5), in front of the train station in the new part of Ascona, east of the Castellano river. **Start** (☑0736 23 55; www.startspa.it; Piazzale della Stazione) runs buses to Rome (€17.50, three hours, eight daily) and Civitanova Marche (€4.70, two hours, 10 daily).

TRAIN

Connections to Ancona (€9.05, two hours, 10 daily) occasionally involve a change in Porto d'Ascoli. Trains to Macerata (€8.25, 2¼ hours, 12 daily) require one or two changes. The **train station** (www.trenitalia.com; Piazza Stazione) is a 1.2km walk east of the centre.

Sarnano
POP 3270

Spilling photogenically down a hillside, its medieval heart a maze of narrow cobbled lanes, Sarnano looks every inch the Italian hilltown prototype, particularly when its red-brick facades glow warmly in the late-afternoon sun. It is a charming, hospitable base for exploring the Monti Sibillini range and home to 11km of ski slopes.

The medieval town centre made it through the October 2016 central Italy earthquake relatively unscathed, but a few businesses – including several restaurants and the tourist office – have been relocated.

🛏 Sleeping & Eating

Typical local eats include *ciauscolo di Sarnano* (a soft, spreadable salami) and *crosta-ta al torroncino* (a typical pie made with dried fruit, cocoa and shortcrust pastry).

★ Agriturismo Serpanera
AGRITURISMO €€

(☑334 122 02 42; www.serpanera.com; Contrada Schito 447; apt €79-169, per week €500-1200; P❄🞱🏊) ✿ Quite the rural idyll, this 17th-century farmhouse snuggles deep among 10 hectares of orchards, vines and woodlands. Besides its spotless apartments, the eco-savvy *agriturismo* invites lingering with its gorgeous views of Sarnano to Monti Sibillini beyond, a pool overlooking rolling hills, a spa, barbecue area, nature trails and horse riding. Your affable hosts, Marco and Cristiana, whip up delicious breakfasts with farm-fresh produce.

Le Clarisse

(☑ 345 4959389; www.osterialeclarisse.it; Contrada Brill, Camping Quattro Stagioni; meals €15-40; ⊙ noon-3pm & 7.30-10pm daily summer, Wed-Sun winter) Once right in the centre of town, Le Clarisse was forced to move due to to an unstable post-earthquake structure it shared with neighbours. Unfortunately, it traded atmospheric medieval walls for a cruddy campground outside town. But the food and kitchen remain the same: it serves whatever is fresh and seasonal (with an emphasis on regional truffles).

ℹ Information

Informazione e Accoglienza Turistica (IAT)
(Tourist Office; www.sarnanoturismo.it; Piazzale Bottoni; ⊙ 9am-1pm Mon-Fri, plus 3-6pm Tue & Thu) The Sarnano tourist office has walking and climbing information and details of accommodation in the park. Earthquake damage has forced a temporary move to a small wooden house on Piazzale Bottoni (between the temporary police station and UBI bank), with no estimate of its return to its original location at Largo Ricciardi 1.

ℹ Getting There & Away

Sarnano sits about 20km south of the Caldarola exit off the SS71, about halfway between Foligno and Civitanova Marche.

Buses depart from a stop on SP78 on the north side of Piazza della Libertà. **SASP** (www.autolineesasp.it; Piazza della Libertà) connects Sarnano with Macerata (€3.40, one hour, every 30 to 60 minutes). To Ascoli Pisceno, **Madebus** (www.madebus.it; Piazza della Libertà) runs buses to Comunanza (€3.15), from where you can switch for a SASP bus on to Ascoli Piceno (€2.60, 45 minutes, seven daily).

Abruzzo & Molise

Best Places to Eat

➔ Ristorante Gino (p639)

➔ Ristorante da Paolino (p641)

➔ Osteria dei Sabatini (p646)

➔ Locanda Sotto gli Archi (p636)

➔ Nabucco Osteria Verdi (p650)

Best Places to Sleep

➔ Sextantio (p636)

➔ Albergo La Rua (p641)

➔ Legacy Casa Residencia (p638)

➔ Il Palazzo (p644)

➔ Albergo Antico Borga La Torre (p645)

Why Go?

Bisected by the spinal Apennine mountains, Abruzzo and Molise make up Italy's forgotten quarter, blessed more with natural attractions than cultural colossi. A major national park building effort in the 1990s created an almost unbroken swath of protected land that stretches from the harsh, isolated Monti della Laga in the north to the round-topped Majella mountains further south.

Dotted in their midst are some of Italy's most unspoilt, picturesque mountain villages. Sometimes, a visit here feels like a trip back to the 1950s – a world of wheezing trains, ruined farmhouses and poppy-filled pastures. All this is good news for prospective walkers, who share the region's ample paths with sheepdogs, mountain goats, abundant bird life and the odd, rarely sighted, human being.

Sulmona is the best base for mountain excursions, Pescara on the Adriatic coast satisfies those with traditional beach urges, while diminutive Molise hides vestiges of the Roman past.

When to Go

L'Aquila

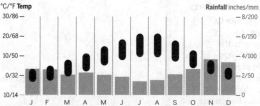

Jan & Feb Grab some skis and head for one of the Abruzzo-Molise ski areas.

Jul Sulmona holds its medieval festival, while Pescara hosts a major jazz festival.

May, Jun & Sep Spring wildflowers, summer sun or autumn leaves – perfect conditions for hiking.

Abruzzo & Molise Highlights

1 **Parco Nazionale d'Abruzzo, Lazio e Molise** (p644) Keeping an eye out for rare Marsican bears while hiking in this fabulous wilderness.

2 **Saepinum** (p649) Pacing the wildflower-strewn foundations of one of Italy's most complete provincial Roman towns.

3 **Sulmona** (p637) Joining the *passeggiatta* (evening stroll) to scope out which Abruzzese trattoria you'll eat in that night.

4 **Museo Archeologico Nazionale d'Abruzzo** (p647) Coming face to face with masterpieces of pre-Roman Italy in this museum in Chieti.

5 **Pescocostanzo** (p641) Breathing in the pure mountain air of this small town with stately foundations.

6 **Parco Nazionale della Majella** (p640) Taking a walk through history on the Sentiero della Libertà.

7 **Isernia La Pineta** (p650) Digging to the 700,000-year-old roots of European humankind at this intriguing archaeological site.

8 **Gole di Sagittario** (p642) Driving the winding switchbacks of this ravishingly beautiful gorge, between Sulmona and Scanno.

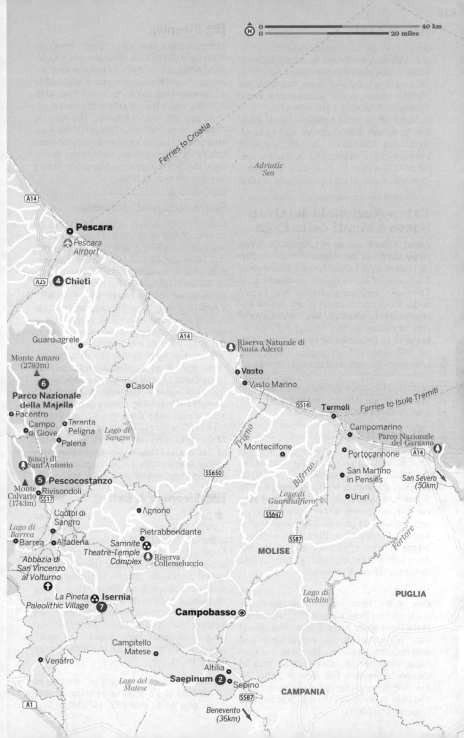

ABRUZZO

Best known for its dramatic mountain scenery, Abruzzo's landscape is surprisingly diverse. A vast plain extends east of Avezzano, the coastline is flat and sandy, and there are ancient forests in the mountainous Parco Nazionale d'Abruzzo, Lazio e Molise.

Many towns retain a medieval look, while the numerous hilltop castles and isolated, sometimes abandoned, *borghi* (medieval towns) exude a sinister charm, lending credence to Abruzzo's fame as an ancient centre of magic, and the land of a thousand castles.

Parco Nazionale del Gran Sasso e Monti della Laga

About 20km northeast of L'Aquila, the Gran Sasso massif is the centrepiece of the Parco Nazionale del Gran Sasso e Monti della Laga, one of Italy's largest national parks. The park's predominant feature is its jagged rocky landscape, through which one of Europe's southernmost glaciers, the Calderone, cuts its course. It's also a haven for wildlife, home to an estimated 40 wolves, 350 chamois and six pairs of royal eagles. Hiking trails criss-cross the park, and atmospheric castles and medieval hill towns crown the foothills. Some towns within the park, such as Santo Stefano di Sessanio, are making slow recoveries from the 2009 earthquake.

🏃 Activities

The small village of Fonte Cerreto near Assergi is the main gateway to the Gran Sasso. From here a funivia (cable car; ☑ 0862 40 00 07; www.ilgransasso.it; weekday/weekend €10/15; ⏰ 8am-5pm Mon-Sat, to 6pm Sun, closed May) runs up to Campo Imperatore (2117m), a high windswept plateau 27km long that is known as Italy's 'Little Tibet'. Up top, there's hiking in summer and skiing in winter. For more information, contact the visitor centre in Santo Stefano di Sessanio.

Corno Grande HIKING
One of the most popular trekking routes leads up to Corno Grande (2912m), which is the Apennines' highest peak, and should only be attempted by experienced and well-prepared climbers. The 9km *via normale* starts in the main parking area at Campo Imperatore and ascends 782m. Allow five to seven hours for the round trip, and bear in mind that the trail is graded EE (experienced hiker).

🛏 Sleeping

The park has a network of *rifugi* (mountain huts) for walkers. Otherwise, there is a handful of hotels near the *funivia* base station, including Hotel Nido dell'Aquila (☑ 0862 60 68 40; www.nidodellaquila.it; Fonte Cerreto; d from €133; 🅿 🛜 🏊), which has a pool and restaurant.

At the top of the *funivia*, the Rifugio Campo Imperatore (☑ 0862 40 00 00; www.ilgransasso.it; Campo Imperatore; half-/full-board €59/79; 🛜 🏊) has been welcoming guests since the 1930s (including Mussolini, briefly imprisoned here in 1943).

Santo Stefano di Sessanio

Known as Sextantio in Roman times, this atmospheric hilltop village has a commanding position overlooking two valleys. Although the 2009 earthquake that struck L'Aquila damaged a number of buildings in Santo Stefano, including the iconic 18m-high watchtower (which completely collapsed), a stroll through the *centro storico* (historic centre) reveals why the village is regarded as one of the *borghi più belli d'Italia* (one of the most beautiful towns in Italy).

The town flourished in the 16th century under the rule of the Medici family, and the Medici coat of arms can still be seen on the entrance portal to the main piazza. Subsequently left behind by history, Santo Stefano was untouched by development, making it a perfect place for radical eco-restorer Daniele Kihlgren to carry out his work. He invested in the town, following an agreement with the authorities that no unsympathetic and ugly development would mar his vision.

🛏 Sleeping & Eating

⭐ **Sextantio** DESIGN HOTEL €€
(☑ 0862 89 91 12; www.sextantio.it; Via Principe Umberto; d from €171; 🛜) This enchanting *albergo diffuso* has 28 distinctive rooms and suites scattered throughout the village. Designed to 'breathe life into forgotten places' without scrimping on luxury, they marry traditional handmade bedspreads and rustic furniture with under-floor heating, mood lighting and divinely deep bathtubs. The hotel's restaurant, Locanda Sotto gli Archi, serves quality regional fare in a 16th-century dining room.

⭐ **Locanda Sotto gli Archi** ABRUZZESE €€
(☑ 0862 89 91 16; http://santostefano.sextantio. it; Via degli Archi; meal €35; ⏰ 7.30-11pm Mon,

Thu-Sun & noon-2pm Sun) Sextantio hotel's restaurant makes imaginative use of an arched, 16th-century dining room. Furniture and crockery is designed to recreate the austere quality of bygone times, and the excellent food uses time-honoured ingredients and techniques native to the region. Expect simple, handmade food such as *maccheroni alla chitarra con patate, noci e pepe nero* (pasta with potato, nuts and pepper).

ⓘ Information

Centro Visite (☑ 0862 89 91 17, 347 3159855; www.centrovisitesantostefanodisessanio.it; Via del Municipio; ⊙10am-7pm summer, to 3pm Sat & Sun winter) The main visitor centre for the national park, it also houses the Museo della Baronia, a museum exploring the environment, history and culture of the region.

ⓘ Getting There & Away

Taking the SS17, Santo Stefano di Sessanio is 27km from L'Aquila, but a more scenic route takes you through Fonte Cerreto on the main 17bis road and across the grand plateau of Campo Imperatore before turning south to Santo Stefano (about 50km).

Sulmona

POP 24,500

An underappreciated city of fantastic restaurants, medieval charm and half-discovered mountain magic, Sulmona sits strategically on a plateau surrounded by three national parks, making it the ideal base for outdoor excursions in Abruzzo. It's easy to reach from Pescara or Rome, and simple to navigate once you arrive (trails fan out from the city limits). The city can trace its history back to the Roman town of Sulmo, where the poet Ovid (of *Metamorphoses* fame) was born in 43 BC. It is also known within Italy for its *confetti* – the almond sweets, not the coloured paper scattered at weddings.

◉ Sights

Most sights are on or near the main street, Corso Ovidio, which runs southeast from the Villa Comunale park to Piazza Garibaldi, Sulmona's main square. A five-minute stroll away is Piazza XX Settembre, with its statue of Ovid – a popular meeting point.

Piazza Garibaldi   PIAZZA
The large town square is home to Sulmona's extensive Wednesday and Saturday morning market: you'll find fresh fish, veg, fruit and flowers, as well as the ubiquitous *porchetta* van, selling pork in a roll. Along Corso Ovidio is a striking series of arches, all that remains of a 13th century aqueduct. In the centre of the piazza, the Renaissance Fontana del Vecchio (Fountain of the Old One) is said by some to depict Solimo, the founder of Sulmona.

REBUILDING L'AQUILA

Nearly a decade on from 2009's devastating 6.3-magnitude earthquake that killed 309 people and rendered 65,000 homeless, L'Aquila's skyline is still dotted with cranes and scaffolding. The city's precious *centro storico* remains a building site, with cordoned-off streets and impassable 'red zones', though a sprinkling of new bars and restaurants has breathed new life into some areas. Not surprisingly, L'Aquila's historic buildings have taken second place to rehousing its residents.

Putting a time frame on the rest of L'Aquila's revival is difficult. An estimated 485 historical buildings were damaged in the quake and forecasters are suggesting that a minimum of €600 million will be required to restore them to their former glory. The notoriously sluggish revival has been dogged by squabbling and scandal; given the financial deadlock to date, it's unlikely the city will return to anything like business as usual before 2021.

L'Aquila's finest sight, the Basilica di Santa Maria di Collemaggio (www.basilica collemaggio.it; Piazzale di Collemaggio) remains closed, although you can admire its two-tone jewel-box walls from the outside.

The Basilica di San Bernardino (www.basilicasanbernardino.it; Via San Bernardino; ⊙7am-12.30pm & 3-7.30pm) reopened in May 2015, six years after sustaining major damage in the 2009 earthquake. Also open for viewing is the city's impressive Fontana delle 99 Cannelle (Fountain of 99 Spouts; Piazza San Vito).

To the northeast, the 14th-century **Chiesa di San Filippo Neri** displays its impressive Gothic portal against a backdrop of often snow-covered mountains. To the southwest, beyond the aqueduct, lies the **Rotonda**, once the monumental entrance and apse of the Chiesa di San Francesco della Scarpa, but cut off from the functional church when salvaged from the 1706 earthquake. It's used for exhibitions and other events.

Palazzo dell'Annunziata   PALACE

(Corso Ovidio; ⊙ 9am-1pm & 3.30-6.30pm Tue-Sun) The most impressive of Sulmona's *palazzi* (mansions), founded as a hospital in 1320 but rebuilt many times over, sits above the remains of a 1st-century-BC Roman *domus* (villa). The building has a harmonious blend of Gothic and Renaissance architecture. Inside is the Museo Civico and in the same complex is the heavily baroque **Chiesa della SS Annunziata**.

Museo Civico   MUSEUM

(⌨ 0864 21 02 16; Palazzo Annunziata, Corso Ovidio; €3.15, incl Museo Diocesano di Arte Sacra €5.25; ⊙ 9am-1pm & 3.30-6.30pm Tue-Sun) Inside the Palazzo dell'Annunziata is the four-in-one Museo Civico, with sections dedicated to archaeology, religious art, Abruzzese-Molisiano culture and the remains of the Roman *domus* (villa) over which the *palazzo* stands. The brilliant Abruzzese-Molisiano folk costumes are particularly worth seeing. Signs are in Italian.

Cattedrale di San Panfilo   CATHEDRAL

(Piazza del Duomo; ⊙ 7.30am-noon & 3-7pm) Slightly out of the centre, the Gothic-meets-baroque cathedral is like many things in Sulmona: understated and underrated. The fantastically restored interior guards some precious old artefacts, including a 14th-century wooden crucifix. The highlight, however, is a subterranean room (opened in 2009) containing the relics of hermit turned pope, Pietro da Morrone (1215–96), including his slippers and a piece of his heart. The original church built here deliberately replaced a temple of Apollo and Vesta.

Museo dell'Arte Confettiera   MUSEUM

(⌨ 0864 21 00 47; www.pelino.it; Via Stazione Introdacqua 55; ⊙ 8.30am-12.30pm & 3-7pm Mon-Sat) FREE This museum is housed in the **Fabbrica Confetti Pelino** (established 1783), Sulmona's most famous manufacturer of *confetti*. With its antique sweet-making equipment, the reconstructed laboratory looks more like an old-time science lab than a sweet-making plant.

★☆ Festivals & Events

Giostra Cavalleresca di Sulmona   CULTURAL

(www.giostrasulmona.it; ⊙ Jul) On the last weekend in July, gaily caparisoned horse riders gallop around Piazza Garibaldi in this spectacular display of pageantry and horsemanship, revived from Renaissance times. There are a series of jousts between different neighbourhoods, then between Italy's most beautiful villages, and lastly between riders from across Europe in the **Giostra Cavalleresca d'Europa**. A daily procession accompanies the tourneys.

🛏 Sleeping

Excellent, charismatic *locandas* (inns) and *albergo diffusos* are easily found in Sulmona's medieval heart.

★ Legacy Casa Residencia   B&B €

(⌨ 377 9766036; www.legacycasaresidencia.com; Vico dell'Ospedale 54; d/apt €75/135; P ✳ 🗢) A beautifully curated and professionally run B&B right in the centre of Sulmona with a choice of double rooms or mini-apartments. All the accommodation skillfully combines convenience and comfort with the distinct sense that you're in the heart of traditional Italy. The apartments can be let on self catering and (discounted) weekly bases and cooking and hiking packages are available.

La Locanda di Gino   B&B €

(⌨ 0864 5 22 89; www.lalocandadigino.it; Via Serafini 1; s/d/tr/q €80/90/130/140; 🗢) Above the Ristorante Gino, one of Sulmona's best, this handsome family-run *locanda* has two double and two quadruple rooms. Blond wood, white walls and bedspreads and tall windows with great views of the Chiesa di Santa Maria della Tomba and old city provide a bright and stylish bolthole in the centre of Sulmona.

Albergo Stella   HOTEL €

(⌨ 0864 5 26 53; www.albergostella.info; Via Panfilo Mazara 18; s/d/ste €70/85/130; P ✳ @ 🗢) A bright little three-star place in the *centro storico* (historic centre), the Stella offers nine airy, modern rooms and a smart, ground-floor restaurant-wine bar (meals €25). Discounts of around 20% are available for stays of more than one night, and for small groups, there's a nearby apartment that sleeps up to eight.

✖ Eating & Drinking

Gelateria La Rotonda
GELATO €

(Corso Ovidio 161; medium cone or cup €3; ⊙9am-11pm) Sulmona's favourite place for a mid-afternoon gelato, this busy little gelataria takes its name from the Rotonda, the monumental remains of the original Chiesa di San Francesco della Scarpa, next door.

★ Ristorante Gino
ABRUZZESE

(☑0864 5 22 89; www.lalocandadigino.it; Piazza Plebiscito 12; ⊙12.30-2.30pm) Occupying handsome arched chambers that have been used as an inn or wine shop for centuries, the restaurant of La Locanda di Gino is up there with Sulmona's best. Proudly advertising the provenance of its produce (red garlic of Sulmona, lentils from Santo Sefano di Sessanio, saffron from an Abruzzese collective), the menu is a paean to the best of Abruzzo.

★ La Cantina di Biffi
ABRUZZESE €€

(☑0864 3 20 25; Via Barbato 1; meal €33; ⊙12.30-2.30pm & 8-11pm Tue-Sun) Dedicated to the food and wine of Abruzzo, this stone-walled *cantina* (wine cellar) features an open kitchen and daily blackboard of lip-smacking temptations. Seasonal treats such as new-season asparagus on poached egg with *grana* cheese share space with classics such as spaghetti carbonara with thick lardons of *guanciale* (cured pig's cheek).

Il Vecchio Muro
ABRUZZESE €€

(☑0864 5 05 95; Via M D'Eramo 20; meal €28; ⊙12.45-2.30pm & 7.45-10.30pm, closed Wed Oct-Apr) One of Sulmona's best restaurants, the 'old wall' is notable for spot-on Abruzzese fare such as wholewheat pasta with lentils and *guanciale*. The rest of the menu – especially the bits involving sausage and mushroom – is delicious, and even the pizza is well above average. You can eat inside, or outside in a covered garden.

Nin-Harra
PUB

(☑347 7198184; Corso Ovidio 139; ⊙6pm-1am Sun-Thu, to 2.30am Fri & Sat) Great tunes (either playlists pieced together by the affable bar staff or live performances) meet great draught beer and great atmosphere at this beer garden/pub tucked behind Sulmona's main drag.

SULMONA'S SACRED SURROUNDS

Located 5km north of Sulmona at the foot of the Monte Morrone, the village of **Badia** and its environs are filled with religious significance.

Eremo di Sant'Onofrio al Morrone (Contrada Morrone) This cliff-clinging hermitage with its 15th-century ceiling, 13th-century frescoes, narrow oratory and arched porticoes cowers under a massive rock face in the Morrone mountains. It was here in a grotto beneath the present church that Pietro da Morrone was apparently told he was to become pope in 1294. It's a steep 20-minute walk from a car park just outside Badia to reach the hermitage. The views of Sulmona and the Valle Peligna below are superb. Opening hours vary; check ahead with the tourist office (p640) in Sulmona.

Santuario di Ercole Curino Sitting below the Sant'Onofrio hermitage, this sanctuary was originally thought to be the house of Sulmona-born poet Ovid when it was first uncovered in the 1950s, but statues later found confirmed it as a Roman-era shrine to Hercules. The sanctuary's former foundations cover a couple of mountainside terraces and include a preserved mosaic floor sheltered in a wooden hut. Precious votive offerings found here are kept at Chieti's Museo Archeologico Nazionale – Villa Frigerj (p647).

Abbazia di Santo Spirito Al Morrone (☑0864 3 28 49; www.santospiritoalmorrone. beniculturali.it; Badia; adult/reduced €4/2; ⊙9am-1pm Mon-Fri) It's hard to miss this massive 13th-century Celestine abbey in Badia, close to the sheer western slopes of the Morrone mountains. Notable for its monumental staircase, religious frescoes and old pharmacy, its main sights can be seen on English- and Italian-language tours. Damaged in an earthquake in 1706, it has been restored several times, done time as a prison and now houses local government offices, the HQ of Majella national park, and regular art expos and music concerts.

ℹ️ Information

Tourist Office (☎ 0864 21 02 16; www.comune.sulmona.aq.it; Corso Ovidio 208, Palazzo Annunziata; ⏰ 9am-1pm & 3.30-7.30pm) *Molto* helpful staff. The office also sells local bus tickets.

ℹ️ Getting There & Away

BUS

Buses leave from a confusing array of points, including Villa Comunale, the hospital and beneath Ponte Capograssi. The tourist office will point you in the right direction.

ARPA (☎ 800 762622; www.arpaonline.it) buses go to and from L'Aquila (€13, 1½ hours, up to eight daily) and Pescara €6, one hour, four daily).

TRAIN

Trains link Sulmona with L'Aquila (€5.80, 1¼ hours, frequent), Pescara (€5.80, 1¼ hours, frequent) and Rome (€11, 2¾ hours, 10 daily). The train station is 2km northwest of the historic centre; the half-hourly bus A runs between the two.

Parco Nazionale della Majella

History, geology and ecology collide in 750-sq-km Parco Nazionale della Majella, Abruzzo's most diverse park, where wolves roam in giant beech woods, ancient hermitages speckle ominous mountains, and 500km of criss-crossing paths and a handful of ski areas cater to the hyperactive. Monte Amaro, the Apennines' second-highest peak, surveys all around it from a lofty 2793m vantage point. From Sulmona the two easiest access points are **Campo di Giove** (elevation 1064m), a small skiing village 18 tortuous kilometres to the southeast, and the lovely town of Pescocostanzo, 33km south of Sulmona along the SS17.

OFF THE BEATEN TRACK

THE FREEDOM TRAIL

During WWII, with the Allies advancing swiftly through southern Italy, the inmates at one of the country's most notorious POW camps – **Fonte d'Amore (Campo 78)**, 5km north of Sulmona – began to sniff freedom.

Their excitement wasn't unfounded. When the Italian government surrendered in September 1943, the camp's Italian guards deserted their posts and promptly disappeared. Their boots were quickly filled by German soldiers invading Italy from the north but, in the confusion of the changeover, many POWs escaped.

Using the Apennines as a natural refuge, the prisoners fanned out into the surrounding mountains. With the help of local partisans, most fled east across the Majella range from German-occupied Sulmona to Casoli on the Sangro river, which had been held by the Allies since September 1943. The rugged and dangerous escape route – nicknamed the **Sentiero della Libertà** (Freedom Trail; www.ilsentierodellaliberta.it) – was used multiple times by escaped Allied POWs during the exceptionally cold winter of 1943–44, when the Allied advance was temporarily halted by German troops dug in along the Gustav Line (a fortified defensive line built by the Germans across central Italy in 1943 to stem the Allied advance).

Having to negotiate well-guarded checkpoints and rugged, mountainous terrain, not all the escapees made it. On a windswept mountain pass known as Guado di Coccia, halfway between Campo di Giove and the small mountain village of Palena, a stone monument memorialises Ettore De Conti, an Italian partisan captured and executed by the Germans in September 1943. It acts as an enduring symbol of the underground resistance.

Today, the Sentiero della Libertà has been turned into a historic **long-distance hiking trail** that cuts across the peaks and plateaus of the Parco Nazionale della Majella. Well-signposted with red and white markers, the 60km-long path starts at the eastern suburbs of Sulmona and is usually tackled over three to four days with stops in Campo di Giove and Taranta Peligna. Since 2001, a commemorative communal march along the trail has been held in late April attracting up to 700 people. See the Sentiero della Libertà website (Italian only) for entry details.

The foreboding fences and watchtowers of the now disused Campo 78 still rise above the village of Fonte d'Amore.

ℹ️ Getting There & Away

ARPA (📱 800 762622; www.arpaonline.it) buses run from Sulmona to Roccaraso (€4, one hour, three daily), near Pescocostanzo, via Castel di Sangro, and to Campo di Giove (€2.30, 45 minutes, four daily).

Pescocostanzo

POP 1110 / ELEV 1395M

Set amid verdant highland plains, Pescocostanzo is practically alpine. It's a surprisingly grand hilltop town, whose historical core has changed little in more than 500 years. Much of the cobbled centre dates from the 16th and 17th centuries when it was an important town on the 'Via degli Abruzzi', the main road linking Naples and Florence.

👁 Sights & Activities

Of particular note is the **Collegiata di Santa Maria del Colle**, an atmospheric church that combines a superb Romanesque portal with a lavish baroque interior. Nearby, **Piazza del Municipio** is flanked by a number of impressive *palazzi*, including **Palazzo Comunale**, with its distinctive clock tower, and **Palazzo Fanzago**, designed by the great baroque architect Cosimo Fanzago in 1624; look out for the carved wooden dragons under the roof.

History apart, Pescocostanzo also offers skiing on **Monte Calvario** and summer hiking in the **Bosco di Sant'Antonio**, a nature reserve characterised by its beech forest, 9km northwest of town.

🛏 Sleeping

⭐ **Albergo La Rua**　　　　　　HOTEL €

(📱 0864 64 00 83; www.larua.it; Via Rua Mozza 1/3; d €85; 🛜) Hikers should head straight for this charming little hotel in Pescocostanzo's historic centre. The look is country cosy, with low, wood-beamed ceilings, parquet floors and stone walls and fireplaces. Super-friendly owner Giuseppe is a mine of local knowledge on the town's distinctive domestic architecture, fine jewellery and dialect, while his brother Luigi is an experienced guide who can organise treks.

🍴 Eating

⭐ **Ristorante da Paolino**　　ABRUZZESE €€

(📱 0864 64 00 80; www.ristorantedapaolino.com; Strada Vulpes 34; meal €35; ⏲ 1-3pm & 8pm-

midnight Tue-Sun) Be sure to book ahead at this bustling and popular little inn-restaurant in the heart of Pescocostanzo. Pasta dishes make expert use of local ingredients in season, such as truffles and chestnuts. Follow up with *secondi* of rabbit, veal or beef, and perhaps a creamy pudding to finish.

Il Gallo di Pietra　　　　ABRUZZESE €€

(📱 0864 64 20 40; www.ilgallodipietra.it; Via del Vallone 4; meal €40; ⏲ 11am-2pm & 7-11pm Mon-Sat) Attached to **Le Torri Hotel** (📱 0864 64 20 40; www.letorrihotel.it; Via del Vallone 4; s/d/tr €160/180/230; ✳@🛜), this classy restaurant offers cosy indoor dining or alfresco dining in the garden. The food is Abruzzese rustic-refined, featuring meaty *primi* and *secondi* such as *polenta con ragu di maialino* (polenta with young pork stew) and *agnello speziato al Trebbiano d'Abruzzo* (spicy lamb cooked in Abruzzese white wine).

ℹ️ Information

Tourist Office (Pro Loco Pescocostanzo; 📱 0864 64 10 54; www.visit-pescocostanzo.it; Via delle Carceri 6; ⏲ 9am-1pm & 3-6pm Mon-Fri Sep-Jun, 9am-1pm & 4-7pm daily Jul & Aug) Off the central Piazza del Municipio. Also see the Parco Nazionale della Majella's comprehensive website (www.parcomajella.it).

ℹ️ Getting There & Away

ARPA buses run from Sulmona to Roccaraso, 6km south of Pescocostanzo.

Pacentro

POP 1140

Set on a knoll above the Sulmona plateau in the foothills of the Parco Nazionale della Majella, Pacentro is a gorgeous hill town, its three slim Renaissance towers evoking those of Tuscany's San Gimignano. It has never expanded far beyond its medieval boundaries and remains free of the unsightly modern sprawl that encircles some of its bigger neighbours. Largely off the standard tourist circuit and – unlike Pescocostanzo and Scanno – not affiliated with a ski resort, its pleasantly tangled streets remain quiet and authentic. It's a good place to mingle with the locals, taste home cooking in low-key trattorias, or use as a base for some nearby national park walks.

Of interest to modern visitors are the 14th-century **Cantelmo Castle** with its famous three towers, the mannerist-meets-baroque **Chiesa Santa Maria della**

TAKE TO THE PISTES

Abruzzo and Molise might lack the glamour of the northern Alps, but skiing is enthusiastically followed and there are numerous resorts in the high places of Abruzzo (and, to a lesser extent, Molise). Bank on about €38 for a daily lift pass.

Campitello Matese In Molise's Monti del Matese, Campitello offers 40km of pistes, including 15km for cross-country skiers.

Campo di Giove At the foot of the Parco Nazionale della Majella, this resort offers Abruzzo's highest skiing, at 2360m.

Campo Felice A small resort 40km south of L'Aquila with 40km of pistes (30km downhill, 10km cross-country).

Campo Imperatore Twenty-two kilometres of mainly downhill pistes and more than 60km of cross-country trails in the Parco Nazionale del Gran Sasso e Monti della Laga.

Ovindoli Monte Magnola One of Abruzzo's biggest ski resorts, with 30km of downhill pistes and 50km of cross-country trails.

Pescasseroli A popular outpost deep in the Parco Nazionale d'Abruzzo with 30km of downhill slopes.

Pescocostanzo Good for ski hiking as well as downhill skiing. It's celebrated for its medieval architecture.

Roccaraso-Rivisondoli Near Pescocostanzo, this is one of the best-equipped resorts, with 28 ski lifts, two cable cars and more than 100km of ski slopes.

Misericordia, and a slew of grand nobles' houses that beautify the lanes between Piazza del Popolo and Piazza Umberto I.

🛏 Sleeping

B&B In Centro a Pacentro   B&B €
(☏ 349 7841697; www.incentroapacentro.it; Via San Marco 5; s/d from €35/60; �) This lovely family-run B&B is, as the name suggests, right in the medieval heart of Pacentro. The immaculate interior teems with photos and mementoes of the owner's parents and grandparents, and the breakfast terrace offers stunning views across Pacentro to the mountains beyond.

ⓘ Information

Centro Informazioni Parco Nazionale Majella (Majella National Park Information Centre; ☏ 0864 4 13 04; www.parcomajella.it; Piazza del Popolo 7, Palazzo Tonno; ⏱ 9am-1pm & 4-8pm Jul & Aug, shorter hours rest of year)

ⓘ Getting There & Away

Pacentro lies 10km east of Sulmona along the SS487. Regular **ARPA** (☏ 800 762622; www.arpaonline.it) buses run between the two towns (€2.40, 35 minutes, nine daily).

Scanno

POP 1820

A tangle of steep alleyways and sturdy, greystone houses, Scanno is a dramatic and atmospheric *borgo* (medieval town), known for its finely worked filigree gold jewellery. For centuries a centre of wool production, it is one of the few places in Italy where you can still see women wearing traditional dress – especially during the week-long costume festival held at the end of April.

Be sure to take the exhilarating drive or bus ride up to Scanno from Sulmona through the rocky **Gole di Sagittario**, a World Wildlife Fund reserve and gorge, and past tranquil **Lago di Scanno**, where there's a scattering of bars and cafes, and you can hire boats in summer.

🎉 Festivals & Events

Costume Festival   CULTURAL
(www.costumediscanno.org; ⏱ Apr) Traditional Abruzzese dress is on show during Scanno's annual costume festival towards the end of April. It comprises a full black skirt and bodice with puffed sleeves, a headdress of braided fabric topped with an angular cap, and filigree jewellery including star-shaped

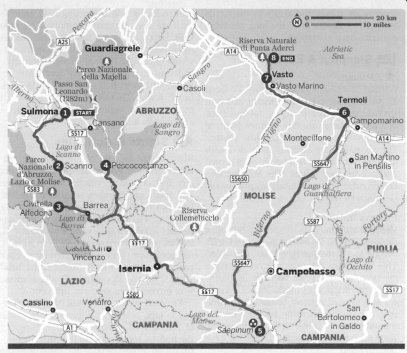

Driving Tour
Cut to the Heart

START SULMONA
END RISERVA NATURALE DI PUNTA ADERCI
LENGTH 245KM TO 310KM; ONE WEEK

A cobbled oasis of food, culture and history in mountainous southern Abruzzo, **1 Sulmona** is the place to start. With its attractive historic centre, welcoming vibe and great trattorias, it's an undemonstrative gem of central Italy. Check out the market on Piazza Garibaldi (Wednesday and Saturday mornings) then join the locals on their *passeggiata* (evening stroll) along Corso Ovidio. After a night in Sulmona, push on southward to hilltop **2 Scanno**. It's a slow, scenic drive that takes you through the breathtaking Gole di Sagittario, a rocky gorge that squeezes the road like a natural vice, and up past the beautiful Lago di Scanno. Scanno's dramatic appearance has made it something of a tourist attraction, but visit outside summer and you'll find it a tranquil spot.

From Scanno, the next leg takes you into the national parks. From Lago di Barrea you can head deep into the magnificent Parco Nazionale d'Abruzzo, Lazio e Molise, the most popular of Abruzzo's three national parks, and set up camp in **3 Civitella Alfedena**. Or you can head north and take the long way round to pretty **4 Pescocostanzo** in the Parco Nazionale della Majella. Either way, spend a couple of days exploring the surrounding mountains. Once you've recharged your batteries, continue on past Isernia to the well-preserved Roman ruins at **5 Saepinum** (p649).

After the mountains, it's time to hit the coast and top up your tan at **6 Termoli**, or further up the road at **7 Vasto**, both popular Adriatic resorts. From Termoli the Isole Tremiti, three gorgeous islands in the Adriatic, are just a day trip away. But if the crowds get too much (and they might in summer), go north to the Spiaggia di Punta Penna, a lovely beach in the **8 Riserva Naturale di Punta Aderci**.

charms, given as betrothal gifts by shepherds before they departed on the long *transhumanza* (sheep migration).

🛏 Sleeping & Eating

★ Il Palazzo
B&B €

(☑0864 74 78 60; www.ilpalazzobb.it; Via Ciorla 25; s/d €55/100; 🅿🛜) This elegant and gently welcoming B&B occupies the 2nd floor of Casa Parente, an 18th-century *palazzo* in Scanno's *centro storico* (historic centre). The six rooms are stylishly decorated with antique furnishings, and breakfast is served under a frescoed ceiling. The building was commandeered for a military hospital by the Germans in WWII.

Pizzeria Trattoria Vecchio Mulino
TRATTORIA €

(☑0864 74 72 19; Via Silla 50; pizza/meal €8/28; ⏰noon-3pm & 7pm-midnight, closed Wed winter) This old-school eatery is a good bet for a classic wood-fired pizza, lentil soups, pastas (perhaps ravioli with mushroom and ricotta) and roasted *salsicce* (sausage). In summer the pretty streetside terrace provides a good perch from which to people-watch. Keep an eye out for seasonal treats like fresh porcini salad.

❶ Information

Tourist Office (☑0864 7 43 17; Piazza Santa Maria della Valle 12; ⏰9am-1pm Mon-Fri & 5-8pm Tue & Thu yr-round, & 9am-1pm & 3-6pm Sat & Sun Jul-Sep) In the village centre.

❶ Getting There & Away

ARPA (☑800 762622; www.arpaonline.it) Buses run to and from Sulmona (€3.20, one hour, seven daily).

Parco Nazionale d'Abruzzo, Lazio e Molise

Italy's second-oldest national park is also one of its most ecologically rich. Established by royal decree in 1923, it began as a modest 5-sq-km reserve that, little by little, morphed into the 440-sq-km protected area it is today. The evolution wasn't easy. The park was temporarily abolished in 1933 by the Mussolini government. It returned to the fold in 1950 only to face further encroachment from housing construction, road building and ski developers.

The park has managed to remain at the forefront of Italy's conservation movement,

reintroducing and protecting wild animals such as the Abruzzo chamois, Apennine wolf, lynx, deer and – most notably – Marsican bear (the park has Italy's largest surviving enclave of these threatened animals).

Today the park extends over three regions, with over half of it covered in thick beech forest. Thanks to its long history, it receives more visitors than other parks – around two million annually.

◉ Sights & Activities

Right in the middle of the park, the redroofed town of **Pescasseroli** has the open, airy feel of a large village. Narrow streets and medieval churches suggest a rich history, but the lure of the wilderness is never far away. The **Centro di Visita di Pescasseroli** (☑0863 911 32 21; www.parcoabruzzo.it; Viale Colli dell'Oro, Pescasseroli; adult/reduced €6/4; ⏰10am-5.30pm) is interesting, but for a better rundown of the park's flora and fauna, head 17km southeast to Civitella Alfedena, whose wolf museum doubles as an info centre.

Situated on a hilltop 6km from Pescasseroli is **Opi**, a *borgo più bella d'Italia* (one of Italy's most beautiful towns). It's one of the highest settlements in the park (1250m), makes an attractive base and is home to the little **Centro Visita del Camoscio** (www.parcoabruzzo.it; Via Affacciata, Opi; ⏰9am-1pm & 3.30-7.30pm summer, 10am-1pm & 3.30-6.30pm winter) 𝐅𝐑𝐄𝐄, a wildlife sanctuary that studies the Apennine chamois. On the park's eastern edge and about 17km from Opi is the picturesque **Lago di Barrea**, with the venerable and handsome town of **Barrea** positioned on a rocky spur above the lake.

At nearby **Civitella Alfedena**, a seductive hamlet reached via a bridge across the lake, you can learn about the Appenine wolf and other fauna (and flora) at the **Museo del Lupo Appenninico** (Appenine Wolf Museum; ☑0864 890141; Via Santa Lucia, Civitella Alfedena; adult/reduced €3/2; ⏰10am-1.30pm & 3-6.30pm Apr-Sep, to 5.30pm Oct-Mar).

Hiking opportunities abound, whether you want to go it alone or with an organised group. There are numerous outfits, including **Ecotur** (☑0863 91 27 60; www.ecotur.org; Via Piave 9, Pescasseroli; ⏰9am-1pm & 4-7.30pm), offering guided excursions. Between May and October, there are horse treks with **Centro Ippico Vallecupa** (☑0863 91 04 44; www.agriturismomaneggiovallecupa.it; Via della Difesa Monte Tranquillo, Pescasseroli; rides 1hr/full day €20/80).

🛏 Sleeping & Eating

⭐ La Fattoria di Morgana
AGRITURISMO €

(☎334 1564908; www.lafattoriadimorgana.it; Via Fonte Dei Cementi Snc, Opi; per person €40) It's hard to imagine a lovelier place in which to base yourself than this *agriturismo* below the stunning village of Opi. Surrounded by forest-clad mountains, you'll not only have gregarious farmers Simon and Claudia for company, but also their menagerie of ducks, goats, pigs, horses and adorable Abruzzo sheepdogs, usually including litters of puppies. It's worth the extra €20 for Claudia's excellent cooking.

⭐ Albergo Antico Borga La Torre
HOTEL €

(☎0864 89 01 21; www.albergolatorre.com; Via Castello 3, Civitella Alfedena; half-board per person €50; P 🛜) Housed in an atmospheric *palazzo* incorporating Civitella Alfedena's oldest (medieval) tower, this attractive and spotless hotel is deservedly popular with hikers. Also in-house is the Ristorante La Torre, serving delicious Abruzzese food, after which the owner might treat you to his homemade (and eye-wateringly strong) *digestivo*.

Il Duca degli Abruzzi
ITALIAN €€

(☎0863 91 10 75; Piazza Duca degli Abruzzi 5, Pescasseroli; meal €25; ⏱lunch & dinner) This handsome hotel-restaurant is located on a quiet square in Pescasseroli's *centro storico*. Everything is homemade and utterly delicious: try the truffle pasta or potato gnocchi, and follow up with baked cod or grilled pork, washed down with Montepulciano d'Abruzzo.

ℹ Getting There & Away

Pescasseroli, Civitella Alfedena and other villages in the national park are linked by **ARPA** (☎800 762622; www.arpaonline.it) buses to Avezzano (€5, 1½ hours, six daily) from where you can change for L'Aquila, Pescara and Rome. Buses also head to Castel di Sangro, where there are connections to Sulmona and Naples.

Pescara

POP 120,400

Abruzzo's largest city is a heavily developed seaside resort with one of the biggest marinas on the Adriatic. The city was heavily bombed during WWII, reducing much of the centre to rubble. It's a lively place with

---

WALKING & WILDLIFE

With about 150 well-marked routes, signalled by white and red marks daubed on trees and rocks, the Parco Nazionale d'Abruzzo, Lazio e Molise is a mecca for hikers. Trails range from easy family jaunts to multi-day hikes over rocky peaks and exposed highlands. The best time to go is between June and September, although access to some of the busier routes around Pescasseroli is often limited in July and August. To book entry to trails, contact the Centro di Visita in Pescasseroli or the Museo del Lupo Appenninico in Civitella Alfedena.

Don't set off without the official hiking map (€12), available at all local tourist offices. Note that the time estimates given are one way only.

Two of the area's most popular hikes are the climbs up Monte Amaro di Opi (1862m; Route F1) and Monte Tranquillo (1841m; Route C3). The **Monte Amaro di Opi route**, a 2¼-hour hike, starts from a car park 7km southeast of Pescasseroli (follow the SS83 for about 2km beyond Opi) and rises steeply up to the peaks, where you're rewarded with stupendous views over the Valle del Sangro. There's quite a good chance of spotting a chamois on this walk.

The **Monte Tranquillo route** takes about 2½ hours from a starting point 1km south of Pescasseroli (follow signs for the Hotel Iris and Centro Ippico Vallecupa). If you still have your breath at the top, you can continue northwards along the Rocca ridge before descending down to Pescasseroli from the north. This beautiful but challenging 19.5km circuit takes six or seven hours.

You may be lucky enough to spot an Apennine wolf or a Marsican brown bear on your hike: this might sound like a scary prospect, but the animals are extremely shy, the only possible threat being from a female bear protecting her cubs. Lynx, chamois, roe deer, wild boar, golden eagles and peregrine hawks also inhabit the park, and flora includes the rare lady's slipper orchid.

an animated seafront, especially in summer, but unless you're coming for the 16km of sandy beaches, there's no great reason to hang around. One attraction not to miss is the Museo delle Genti d'Abruzzo, which has plenty that will appeal to kids too.

◎ Sights

Pescara's main attraction is its long stretch of beachfront, and the shopping precinct around pedestrianised **Corso Umberto**. From **Piazzale della Repubblica**, the beach is a short walk down Corso Umberto. The only vaguely old streets in Pescara are on the south side of the Aterno-Pescara river, occupying the site of the former Roman town of Aternum.

Museo delle Genti d'Abruzzo   MUSEUM
(🖉 085 451 00 26; Via delle Caserme 24; adult/reduced €6/3; ⊘ 8.30am-2pm Mon-Sat) Located on a quiet road parallel to the river on the opposite bank from the centre, this wonderful museum illustrates Abruzzo peasant culture. The information is mainly in Italian, but the objects in the 16 themed rooms speak eloquently for themselves. There are shepherds' capes, carnival masks, outlandish silver saddle pommels and even a conical stone hut, and the section on Scanno costume and jewellery is outstanding. Hours can vary; call ahead.

**Museo Casa Natale
Gabriele D'Annunzio**   MUSEUM
(🖉 085 60391; www.proloco.pescara.it/arte_cultura.php; Corso Manthonè 116; €2; ⊘ 9am-1pm Tue-Sat & 3-5.30pm Tue & Thu) The birthplace of controversial fascist poet Gabriele D'Annunzio is small but excellently curated, with nine rooms displaying furniture, documents, photos and his death mask displayed in a polished glass case.

✯✦ Festivals & Events

Pescara Jazz   MUSIC
(🖉 box office 085 454 09 69; www.pescarajazz.com; tickets from €15; ⊘ mid-Jul) This international jazz festival is held over nearly two weeks in mid-July at the Teatro D'Annunzio and Porto Turistico. Previous highlights have included big-name stars such as Keith Jarrett, Herbie Hancock and Stan Getz.

⊨ Sleeping

Villa del Pavone   B&B €
(🖉 085 421 17 70; www.villadelpavone.it; Via Pizzoferrato 30; s/d/tr €60/80/100; 🅿 ❄ 🛜) You'll

find this lovely home away from home on a quiet residential street, about 300m behind the train station. A model of old-fashioned pride, it's laden with gleaming antiques and chichi knick-knacks. Outside, the lush garden, presided over by a resident peacock, is the setting for excellent breakfasts in the warmer months.

Hotel Victoria   HOTEL €€
(🖉 085 37 41 32; www.victoriapescara.com; Via Piave 142; s/d €95/124; 🅿 ❄ @ 🛜) A top-notch hotel in a handsome building in the city centre, the Victoria is a memorable place with Impressionist paintings etched onto bedroom doors, curvaceous balconies and an excellent downstairs cafe. Best of all, though, is the service, which goes above and beyond the call of duty. Bonuses include a fitness centre and a spa.

✗ Eating & Drinking

Head to Corso Manthonè and the surrounding streets for the greatest density of interesting bars.

Caffè Letterario   CAFE €
(🖉 085 6 42 43; Via delle Caserme 62; lunch buffet €10; ⊘ 9am-6pm Sun-Wed, to 3am Thu-Sat) This popular lunchtime spot has huge floor-to-ceiling windows and exposed-brick walls. The menu changes daily, or you can do as the locals do, and enjoy the fabulous value of the lunchtime buffet (€10 with starter, water and coffee; it includes poached veal, greens, cold cuts, baked vegetables and much more). There's live music Thursday to Saturday nights.

★**Osteria dei Sabatini**   ABRUZZESE €€
(🖉 380 6463551; Via Piave 61; meal €30; ⊘ 12.30-3pm & 7.30-11.30pm Tue-Sat, 12.30-2.30pm Sun) Bringing Abruzzo's mountain cuisine to the coast, this *osteria* serves some of Pescara's best food. Hearty simplicity is to the fore in dishes such as *pasta alla gricia* (pasta with cured pork jowl and *pecorino*) *frittatina alle ortiche di montagna* (mountain-nettle frittata) and *filetto di maiale al ginepro del Gran Sasso* (pork fillet in Gran Sasso juniper). There are great Abruzzese wines, too.

ⓘ Information

Tourist Office (🖉 085 42 90 01, 800 502520; www.proloco.pescara.it; Corso Emanuele II 301; ⊘ 9am-1pm & 4-7pm Jun-Sep, 9am-1pm & 3-6pm Oct-May) Run by Abruzzo Turismo.

❶ Getting There & Around

AIR

Abruzzo International Airport (☑ 895 8989512; www.abruzzoairport.com; Via Tiburtina Km 229) Pescara's airport is 3km out of town and easily reached by bus 38 (€1.10, 20 minutes, every 15 minutes) from in front of the train station. Ryanair flies to London Stansted, and Alitalia flies to Milan and Rome-Fiumicino.

BOAT

Ferries leave from the **Marina di Pescara** (☑ 085 45 46 81; www.marinape.com; Via Papa Giovanni XXIII), immediately south of the Ponte del Mare (the footbridge over the mouth of the Pescara river).

SNAV ferries run several times per week between Pescara and two destinations on the Croatian island of Hvar.

Contact **Agenzia Sanmar** (☑ 085 451 08 73; www.sanmar.it; 1 Località Porto Turistico) at the port for ferry information and tickets to Croatia.

BUS

ARPA (☑ 800 762622; www.arpaonline.it) Buses connect Pescara with Rome (€17, three hours, 11 daily), Naples (€26, four hours, five daily), Sulmona (€6, one hour, 11 daily), L'Aquila (€8, 1½ hours, 10 daily) and towns throughout Abruzzo and Molise.

Pescara has a local bus system, but its attractions are closely clustered enough to explore on foot.

TRAIN

Direct trains run from Pescara Centrale to Ancona (from €11, 1¼ to 2¼ hours, frequent), Bari (from €20, 2¾ to 4¾ hours, frequent), Rome (from €15, 3½ to 5½ hours, seven daily) and Sulmona (€5.80, 1¼ hours, 20 daily).

Chieti

POP 51,300

Overlooking the Aterno valley, Chieti is a sprawling hilltop town with roots dating back to pre-Roman times when, as capital of the Marrucini tribe, it was known as Teate Marrucinorum. Later, in the 4th century BC, it was conquered by the Romans and incorporated into the Roman Republic.

The *comune* of Chieti splits into two parts: Chieti Scalo is the new commercial district, while hilltop Chieti Alta is of more interest to travellers thanks to two fine archaeology museums and handsome streets lined with dignified buildings and dotted with Roman remains.

◉ Sights

★ **Museo Archeologico Nazionale d'Abruzzo – Villa Frigerj** MUSEUM
(☑ 0871 40 43 92; www.archeoabruzzo.beniculturali.it; Via Costanzi 2, Villa Comunale; adult/reduced €4/2; free 1st Sun of month; ◐ 9am-8pm Tue-Sun) Housed in a neoclassical villa in the Villa Comunale park, Abruzzo's chief archaeological museum displays a comprehensive collection of local finds, illuminating Chieti's three millennia of existence. While the primary focus is on the vanished worlds of the Marrucini, Aequi, Marsi, Sabini and other tribes that inhabited central Italy prior to Roman expansion, there are also plenty of Roman artefacts. Of particular note are impressive coin hoards and classical sculpture – including a colossal seated Hercules from the 1st century BC.

Museo Archeologico Nazionale d'Abruzzo – La Civitella MUSEUM
(☑ 0871 6 31 37; www.archeoabruzzo.beniculturali.it; Via Pianell; adult/reduced €4/2; free 1st Sun of month; ◐ 8.30am-7.30pm Tue-Sat, to 1.30pm Sun) 'La Civitella' is a modern museum curled around a Roman amphitheatre, built at the city's highest point in the first century AD, and restored in 2000. Exhibits charting the history of Chieti and the area since Palaeolithic times include relics of the pre-Roman Marrucini and statuary and everyday items from early Imperial Rome.

🍽 Sleeping & Eating

Chieti is oddly under-supplied with restaurants, although street food such as focaccia stuffed with *porchetta* (roast pork) is cheap and excellent.

Agriturismo Il Quadrifoglio AGRITURISMO €
(☑ 0871 6 34 00; www.agriturismoilquadrifoglio.com; Strada Licini 22; s/d/tr €40/50/70; ℗ 🛜 ⛱) About 3km downhill from Chieti's historic centre, this picturesque *agriturismo* is set in a farmhouse with rustic rooms, panoramic views over surrounding woods and farmlands and a lovely, rambling garden. Meals are around €20. To get here, follow signs to Colle Marcone.

Grande Albergo Abruzzo HOTEL €
(☑ 0871 4 19 40; www.albergoabruzzo.it; Via Herio 20; d from €59; ℗ 🛜) Well located on the lip of Chieti Alta, this flamingo-pink *albergo* offers panoramic views of coast and mountains. The Grande's rooms are more dusty

than grand these days, but there are other perks – such as the outdoor terrace, left-luggage facility, on-site restaurant and bar, and free parking.

ℹ Information

Tourist Office (Abruzzo Promozione Turismo; ☑ 0871 6 59 67; Via Spaventa 47; ☺ 8am-1pm & 4-7pm Mon-Sat Jul-Sep, shorter hours rest of year) Chieti's tourist office can provide information and accommodation listings for the town and surrounding area.

ℹ Getting There & Away

ARPA (☑ 800 762622; www.arpaonline.it) buses link Chieti Scalo with Pescara (€2.20, 20 minutes, frequent).

Vasto & Around

On Abruzzo's southern coast, the hilltop town of Vasto has an atmospheric medieval quarter and superb sea views. Much of the *centro storico* (historic centre) dates from the 15th century, a period in which the city was known as 'the Athens of the Abruzzi'; it's also distinguished as the birthplace of the poet Gabriele Rossetti.

Two kilometres downhill is the blowzy resort of **Vasto Marina**, a strip of hotels, restaurants and campgrounds fronting a long sandy beach. About 5km north of town along the coast is the beautiful **Spiaggia di Punta Penna** and the **Riserva Naturale di Punta Aderci** (www.puntaderci.it).

In summer the action is on the beach at Vasto Marina. In the old town, interest revolves around the small historic centre, with its landmark **Castello Caldoresco**, located on Piazza Rossetti, and the low-key Romanesque Cattedrale di San Giuseppe. The Renaissance Palazzo d'Avalos hosts four museums, including the Museo Archeologico.

◎ Sights

Palazzo d'Avalos   MUSEUM
(☑ 0873 36 77 73; www.museipalazzodavalos.it; Piazza Pudente; palazzo & museums adult/reduced €5/3.50; ☺ 10am-1pm & 6-11pm Jul & Aug, shorter hours rest of year) The Renaissance Palazzo d'Avalos houses four museums: the **Museo Archeologico** (adult/reduced €3/1.50), with its eclectic collection of ancient bronzes, glasswork and paintings; the **Pinacoteca Comunale** (€4/2), featuring paintings by the Palizzi brothers and other 19th-century artists; the **Galleria d'Arte Contempora-**

nea (€3/1.50) with 80 works by contemporary Italian and Spanish artists; and the **Museo del Costume** (€3/1.50), with donated Abruzzese folk outfits dating back to the early 19th century.

Cattedrale di San Giuseppe   CATHEDRAL
(☑ 0873 36 71 93; Piazza Pudente; ☺ 8.30am-noon & 4.30-7pm) The facade is a lovely low-key example of 13th-century Romanesque architecture; the rest of the building was destroyed in 1566 when the city was sacked by the Turks, and later rebuilt.

⎸ Sleeping & Eating

★ **Residenza Amblingh**   HOTEL €€
(☑ 0873 36 27 02; www.amblingh.it; Via Portone Panzotto 13, Loggia Amblingh; ste €190; ☏) Central Vasto's most stylish accommodation, this *residenza* offers beautifully decorated suites, some with sea views and all making luxurious use of the stone-walled rooms of a handsome 18th-century palazzo. It's on the Loggia Amblingh, Vasto's scenic Adriatic-facing promenade.

Sunrise Agri Food   ITALIAN €€
(☑ 0873 6 93 41; Loggia Amblingh 51; meal €25; ☺ noon-3pm & 7.30pm-midnight Wed-Mon) This friendly, slightly brash little place offers swoonworthy sea views and delicious home cooking, with seafood particularly recommended (and apt, with the Adriatic spread out before you). The *frittura mista* (mixed fried seafood) is a good bet. To get here, follow the *passeggiata* (evening stroll) sign to the right of the Museo Civico.

ℹ Getting There & Away

The train station (Vasto-San Salvo) is about 2km south of Vasto Marina. Trains run frequently to Pescara (€4.80, one hour) and Termoli (from €2.60, 15 minutes). From the station take bus 1 or 4 for Vasto Marina and the town centre (€1.10).

MOLISE

Of Italy's 20 regions, Molise probably ranks 20th in terms of name recognition. In fact, until 1970, it was part of Abruzzo, the adjacent region it closely resembles. Mountains and hills rather than people crowd the interior, while flatter plains guard a short 35km stretch of Adriatic coast. Although Campobasso is the largest city, its brightest

SAEPINUM

....

Molise's hidden treasure, the Roman ruins of **Saepinum** (⊘9am-7pm), are among the best preserved and least visited in the country. Unlike Pompeii and Ostia Antica, which were both major ports, Saepinum was a small provincial town of no great importance. It was originally established by the Samnites but the Romans conquered it in 293 BC, paving the way for an economic boom in the 1st and 2nd centuries AD. Some 700 years later, it was sacked by Arab invaders.

The walled town retains three of its four original gates and its two main roads, the *cardusmaximus* and the *decamanus*. Highlights include the forum, basilica and theatre – where you'll find the **Museo Archeologico Vittoriano** (adult/reduced €2/1; ⊘8.30am-2pm & 2.30-5pm Tue-Sun).

It's not easy to reach Saepinum by public transport, but the bus from Campobasso to Sepino (€1.20, six daily weekdays) generally stops near the site at Altilia, although it's best to ask the driver.

---

attractions are Termoli, a higgledy-piggledy coastal town characterised by its *trabucchi* (fishing platforms), and Isernia and Saepinum, for glimpses of the Palaeolithic and Roman past. Molise has suffered steady depopulation since the late 19th century, adding to its sense of isolation.

ⓘ Getting There & Away

Molise has no international airport. Typically, visitors arrive by road from Campania, Puglia or Abruzzo.

Campobasso

POP 49,300

Molise's regional capital and main transport hub is a sprawling, uninspiring city with little to recommend it. However, if you do find yourself passing through, the pocket-sized *centro storico* (historic centre) is worth a quick look.

Although rarely open, the Romanesque churches of **San Bartolomeo** (Salita San Bartolomeo) and **San Giorgio** (Salita San Bartolomeo) are fine examples of their genre. Further up the hill, at the top of a steep tree-lined avenue, sits Castello Monforte, while below is the small Museo Sannitico.

◉ Sights

Castello Monforte CASTLE
(✆0874 6 32 99; www.incima.eu; Viale delle Rimembranze; ⊘9am-1pm yr-round & 3.30-7.30pm Apr-Sep, 3-5pm Oct-Mar) FREE At the top of a steep tree-lined avenue sits this squat, quadrangular tower, much of which was built in the 15th and 16th centuries after the original Norman castle was damaged by earthquake

in 1456. The views towards the Appenines are spectacular.

Museo Sannitico MUSEUM
(Samnite Museum; ✆0874 41 22 65; Via Chiarizia 12; adult/reduced €4/2; ⊘9.30am-7pm Wed-Mon) FREE Samnite ceramics found in Castello Monforte are now on show at this museum, along with weapons, armour and sculptures from local archaeological sites. The Samnites were the pre-Roman nation that once controlled the area around Campobasso.

⏁ Sleeping & Eating

Most travellers pass through Campobasso. If you do need to overnight here, there are good B&Bs and hotels to be found in the old town, near the junction of Vias Ziccardi and Cannavina.

**Trattoria La Grotta di
Zi Concetta** TRATTORIA €€
(✆0874 31 13 78; Via Larino 9; meal €28; ⊘noon-2pm & 7.30-10.30pm Mon-Fri) Equally good for a spot of lunch or dinner, this old-school stone-walled trattoria serves some delicious homemade pasta and superb meat dishes.

ⓘ Information

Tourist Office (Chamber of Commerce; ✆0874 41 56 62; Piazza della Vittoria 14; ⊘8.30am-12.30pm Mon-Fri & 3.30-4.30pm Mon & Wed)

ⓘ Getting There & Away

Trains run to/from Isernia (€3.10, 50 minutes, up to 14 daily) and Termoli (€4.40, 1¾ hours, five daily).

Buses fun to/from Termoli (€3.20, 1¼ hours, 10 daily), Naples (€10, 2¾ hours, four daily on weekdays) and Rome (€12.10, three hours, five daily).

ABRUZZO & MOLISE CAMPOBASSO

Isernia

POP 21,800

With roots stretching back to the pre-Roman Samnites and beyond (to our proto-human ancestors), the city known to the Romans as *Aesernia* is historically rich. This may not be immediately apparent, as earthquakes and a massive WWII bombing raid have spared little of its original *centro storico*. But spend some time and you'll discover an undemonstrative old town harbouring sights such as the **Fontana Fraterna**, a 19th-century fountain built of ancient Roman stones; the 14th-century **Cattedrale di San Pietro Apostolo**, and various Roman and medieval arches and statuary. Among all that, you'll also stumble across some wonderful trattorias doing real Molisan food for the locals.

But the main historical draw is **La Pineta**, a 700,000 year-old archaeological site that is one of Europe's oldest proto-human links and has an intriguing museum.

◉ Sights

The hills surrounding Isernia are peppered with sights rich in history, from Pietrabbondante's ancient **Samnite theatre-temple complex** (📞0865 7 61 29; http://archeologica molise.beniculturali.it; Località Calcatello, Pietrabbondante; adult/reduced €2/1; ⊙10am-7.30pm May-Aug, to 3.30pm Sep-Apr, closed Mon) to **Abbazia di San Vicenzo al Volturno** (📞0865 95 52 46; www.sanvincenzoalvolturno.it; ⊙9am-2pm Tue-Sun), an ancient abbey graced by precious 9th-century frescoes.

★ **Museo Paleolitico di Isernia**   MUSEUM
(📞0865 29 06 87; Contrada Ramiera Vecchia; adult/reduced €4/2; ⊙8am-7pm Tue-Sun) Built around the adjacent 730,000-year-old archaeological site of **La Pineta**, this intriguing museum includes piles of elephant and rhino bones, the remains of ancient lions, fossils, and stone tools left by our ancestor, *Homo erectus*. Uncovered by road workers in 1978, La Pineta is basically a huge abattoir, in which butchered kills were hidden from predators in the mud. Excavations are ongoing, and in 2014 archaeologists found the tooth of a young child dated to around 586,000 years ago.

🛏 Sleeping & Eating

Isernia's outstanding, great-value trattorias are one of its foremost attractions.

Residenze Portacastello Graffolus   B&B €
(📞0865 23 45 79; www.residenzeportacastello.
it; Vico Storto Castello 42; s/d/apt €55/65/75) A renovated, early-17th-century stone building in Isernia's historic heart is the setting for this welcoming and well-run B&B. Spread over three floors, the seven rooms and two apartments (with kitchenettes) feature parquet floors, whitewash and stone walls, good-quality beds and (in some) fireplaces.

Nabucco Osteria Verdi   OSTERIA €
(📞0865 41 34 58; Corso Marcelli 160; meal €23; ⊙noon-11pm Tue-Sat, to 2.30pm Sun) Typical of the generosity and unabashed home-style cooking of Isernia's best *osterie*, this friendly place is a great way to experience the food of Molise. *Secondi* (perhaps *tagliata di manzo*, strips of beef with rocket and parmesan) are mainly meaty, but *primi* such as gnocchi in rosemary sauce or *paccheri* with gorgonzola and porcini gives vegetarians enough to work with.

O'Pizzaiuolo   OSTERIA €
(📞0865 41 27 76; www.ristoranteopizzaiuolo.it; Corso Marcelli 253; pizza/meal €7/23; ⊙noon-3.30pm & 7.30pm-midnight) For dinner hit Osteria O'Pizzaiuolo in the old town for epic *cavatelli* (small pasta shells) with sausage and broccoli, or beef with black truffles.

ℹ Information

Tourist Office (📞338 3976081; www.proloco isernia.com; Piazza San Pietro Celestino V; ⊙9am-6pm Mon-Sat) Includes a small civic museum.

ℹ Getting There & Away

BUS

From the **bus station** (Piazza della Repubblica) next to the train station, ATM runs buses to Campobasso (€3.50, one hour, three daily), Termoli (€4.90, 1½ hours, one daily), and Castel San Vincenzo (€1.50, 35 minutes, three daily), a 1km walk from Abbazia di San Vincenzo al Volturno. Get tickets from Bar Ragno d'Oro on Piazza della Repubblica.

From Isernia, SATI buses serve Pietrabbondante (€1.65, 35 minutes, three or four daily) and Agnone (€2.05, one hour, three to four daily).

TRAIN

Trains connect Isernia with Sulmona (from €8.35, three to four hours, one to two changes, two daily), Campobasso (€3.10, one hour, 14 daily), Naples (€6.75, two hours, four direct services daily) and Rome (€11.30, 2¼ hours, seven direct services daily).

Termoli

POP 33,700

Despite its touristy trattorias and brassy bars, Molise's top beach resort retains a winning, low-key charm. At the eastern end of the seafront, the pretty *borgo antico* (old town) juts out to sea like a massive pier, dividing the sandy beach from Termoli's small harbour. From the sea wall you'll see several typical Molisan *trabucchi* (fishing platforms).

◉ Sights

Cattedrale di Santa Maria della Purificazione
CATHEDRAL

(☑ 0875 70 80 25; Piazza Duomo; ⊙ 7.30-11.50am & 4.30-8pm) Termoli's majestic 12th-century cathedral is a masterpiece of Puglian Romanesque architecture. The cream-coloured facade features a striking round-arched central portal. The remains of an earlier basilica and a pagan temple (to Castor and Pollux) lie beneath the current structure.

Castello Svevo
CASTLE

(Swabian Castle; ☑ 0875 71 23 54; Largo Castello; ⊙ by request) Termoli's most famous landmark, Frederick II's 13th-century Castello Svevo guards the entry to the tiny *borgo*.

⌂ Sleeping & Eating

Locanda Alfieri
B&B €

(☑ 0875 70 81 13; www.locandalfieri.com; Via Duomo 39; s/d/tr €53/99/130; ❉ ☎) An *albergo diffuso* with rooms scattered throughout the *centro storico* (historic centre), this is a great base from which to explore Termoli, the Isole Tremiti and Molise. Room styles vary from 'creative' traditional to modern-chic (some with ubercool showers with mood lighting).

★ Residenza Sveva
HOTEL €€

(☑ 0875 70 68 03; www.residenzasveva.com; Piazza Duomo 11; r from €129; ❉ ☎) This elegant *centro storico albergo diffuso* has its reception on Piazza Duomo, near the cathedral,

but the 21 rooms are squeezed into several *palazzi* in the *borgo*. The style is summery with plenty of gleaming blue tiles and traditional embroidery. There's also an excellent, elegant seafood restaurant, Svevia (☑ 0875 55 02 84; www.svevia.it; ⊙ 12.30-2.30pm & 8-10.30pm Tue-Sun), on site.

Ristorante Da Nicolino
SEAFOOD €€

(☑ 0875 70 68 04; Via Roma 13; meal €35; ⊙ 12.30-3pm & 7.30-11pm Fri-Wed) Well regarded by locals, this discreet restaurant near the entrance to the old town serves some of the best seafood in town. Highly recommended is the *brodetto alla termolese* (fish soup of Termoli) and the stuffed squid.

❶ Information

Tourist Office (☑ 0875 70 39 13; www.termoli. net; 1st fl, Piazza Bega 42; ⊙ 8am-2pm & 3-6pm Mon & Wed, 8am-2pm Tue, Thu & Fri) Helpful but hard to find, Termoli's tourist office is tucked away in a dodgy-looking car park behind a small shopping galley, 100m east of the train station.

❶ Getting There & Away

BOAT

Termoli is the only port with year-round ferries to the Isole Tremiti. **Tirrenia Navigazione** (☑ 049 61114020; www.tirrenia.it) runs a year-round ferry and **Navigazione Libera del Golfo** (☑ 0875 70 48 59; www.nuvlib.it; ⊙ Apr-Sep) operates a quicker hydrofoil in summer. Buy tickets online or at the port (east of the old town).

BUS

Termoli's **bus station** is beside Via Martiri della Resistenza. Various companies have services to/from Campobasso (€3.20, 1¼ hours, 10 daily), Isernia (€4.90, 1½ hours, five daily), Pescara (from €5.40, 1¾ hours, up to nine daily) and Rome (from €16, 3½ to five hours, up to five daily).

TRAIN

Direct trains serve Bologna (from €46, four to 5½ hours, 10 daily), Lecce (from €42, 3½ to 4½ hours, 10 daily) and stations along the Adriatic coast.

Naples & Campania

Best Places to Eat

➡ Casa Mele (p707)

➡ Da Salvatore (p711)

➡ La Cantina del Feudo (p714)

➡ Salumeria (p670)

➡ Soul & Fish (p701)

Best Places to Sleep

➡ Atelier Ines (p670)

➡ Casa Mariantonia (p679)

➡ Albergo il Monastero (p683)

➡ Hotel Piazza Bellini (p670)

➡ Palazzo Marziale (p700)

Why Go?

Campania is the Italy of your wildest dreams; a rich, intense, hypnotic *ragù* of Arabesque street life, decadent palaces, pastel-hued villages and aria-inspiring vistas.

Few corners of Europe can match the cultural conundrums here. Should you spend the morning waltzing through chandeliered Bourbon bedrooms or the frescoed villa of a Roman emperor's wife? And which of Caravaggio's canvases shouldn't you miss: the multi-scene masterpiece inside Naples' Pio Monte della Misericordia, or the artist's brooding swansong inside the city's belle époque Palazzo Zevallos?

Mother Nature let loose in Italy's south, creating a thrilling playground of rugged mountains, steaming fumaroles, and ethereal coastal grottoes. Horse ride the slopes of Mt Vesuvius, sail the Amalfi Coast or simply soak at a thermal beach on Ischia. Afterwards, local feasts await; bubbling, wood-fired pizza in Naples, long lunches at Cilento *agriturismi* (farm stays), and lavish pastries at celebrity-status Amalfi Coast *pasticcerie* (pastry shops).

When to Go
Naples

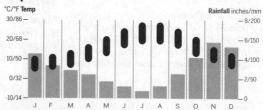

May Best month to visit the region. Warm days, with many special events on.

Jun & Sep Generally deliver summer heat without the August crowds and traffic.

Aug Hottest month; many shops and restaurants close while locals go on holiday.

NAPLES

081 / POP 970,200

Italy's third-largest city is one of its oldest, most artistic and most appetising. Naples' *centro storico* (historic centre) is a Unesco World Heritage Site, its archaeological treasures are among the world's most important, and its palaces, castles and churches make Rome look positively provincial.

Then there's the food. Blessed with rich volcanic soils, a bountiful sea, and centuries of culinary know-how, the Naples region is one of Italy's epicurean heavyweights, serving up the country's best pizza, pasta and coffee, and many of its most celebrated seafood dishes, street snacks and sweet treats.

Certainly, Naples' urban sprawl can feel anarchic, tattered and unloved. But look beyond the grime, graffiti and occasional gruffness and you'll uncover a city of breathtaking frescoes, sculptures and panoramas, of unexpected elegance, of spontaneous conversations and profound humanity. Welcome to Italy's most unlikely masterpiece.

History

After founding nearby Cuma in the 8th century BC, the ancient Greeks settled the city in around 680 BC, calling it Parthenope. Under the Romans, the area became an ancient Miami of sorts: a sun-soaked spa region that drew the likes of Virgil. Dampening the bonhomie was Mt Vesuvius' eruption in AD 79.

Naples fell into Norman hands in 1139 before the French Angevins took control a century later, boosting the city's cred with the mighty Castel Nuovo. By the 16th century, Naples was under Spanish rule and riding high on Spain's colonial riches. By 1600, it was Europe's largest city and a burgeoning baroque beauty adorned by artists like Luca Giordano, Giuseppe de Ribera and Caravaggio.

Despite a devastating plague in 1656, Naples' ego soared under the Bourbons (1734–1860), with epic constructions such as the Teatro San Carlo and the Reggia di Caserta sealing the city's showcase reputation.

An ill-fated attempt at republican rule in 1799 was followed by a short stint under the French and a final period of Bourbon governance before nationalist rebel Giuseppe Garibaldi inspired the city to snip off the puppet strings and join a united Italy in 1860.

Although the Nazis took Naples in 1943, they were quickly forced out by a series of popular uprisings between 26 and 30 September, famously known as the *Quattro giornate di Napoli* (Four Days of Naples). Led by locals, especially by young *scugnizzi* (Neapolitan for 'street urchins') and ex-soldiers, the street battles paved the way for the Allies to enter the city on 1 October.

Despite setting up a provisional government in Naples, the Allies were confronted with an anarchic mass of troops, German prisoners of war and bands of Italian fascists all competing with the city's starving population for food. Overwhelmed, Allied authorities turned to the underworld for assistance. As long as the Allies agreed to turn a blind eye to their black-market activities, the Mafia was willing to help. And so the Camorra (Neapolitan Mafia) was given a boost.

On 23 November 1980, a devastating earthquake struck the mountainous area of Irpinia, 100km east of Naples. The quake, which left more than 2700 people dead and thousands more homeless, caused extensive damage in Naples. It is believed that US$6.4 billion of the funds poured into the region to assist the victims and rebuilding ended up in the pockets of the Camorra.

In 2011, Neapolitan voters elected the city's current mayor, Luigi de Magistris, a youthful former public prosecutor and vocal critic of both the mafia and government corruption. Determined to improve the city's liveability, de Magistris has pushed through a number of initiatives, including the transformation of the Lungomare from a traffic-clogged thoroughfare into a pedestrian and bike-friendly waterfront strip.

◉ Sights

◉ Centro Storico

★ **Complesso Monumentale di Santa Chiara**   BASILICA

(Map p658; 081 551 66 73; www.monastero disantachiara.com; Via Santa Chiara 49c; basilica free, Complesso Monumentale adult/reduced €6/4.50; ⊙basilica 7.30am-1pm & 4.30-8pm, Complesso Monumentale 9.30am-5.30pm Mon-Sat, 10am-2.30pm Sun; Ⓜ Dante) Vast, Gothic and cleverly deceptive, the mighty **Basilica di Santa Chiara** stands at the heart of this tranquil monastery complex. The church was severely damaged in WWII: what you see today is a 20th-century recreation of Gagliardo Primario's 14th-century original. Adjoining it are the basilica's **cloisters**, adorned with brightly coloured 17th-century majolica tiles and frescoes.

Naples & Campania Highlights

1 **Pompeii** (p691) Channelling the ancients on the ill-fated streets of this erstwhile Roman city.

2 **Grotta Azzurra** (p678) Being bewitched by Capri's ethereal blue cave.

3 **Sentieri degli Dei** (p709) Walking with the gods on the Amalfi Coast.

4 **Cappella Sansevero** (p656) Re-evaluating artistic ingenuity in Naples.

5 **Procida** (p685) Lunching by lapping waves on the Bay of Naples' pastel-hued smallest island

6 **Negombo** (p682) Indulging in a little thermal therapy on Ischia.

7 **Villa Rufolo** (p710) Attending a concert at this dreamy Ravello villa and its cascading gardens.

8 **Reggia di Caserta** (p697) Pretending you're royalty at this monumental Unesco-listed palace complex.

9 **Paestum** (p715) Admiring ancient Hellenic ingenuity in the colossal ruins of Magna Graecia.

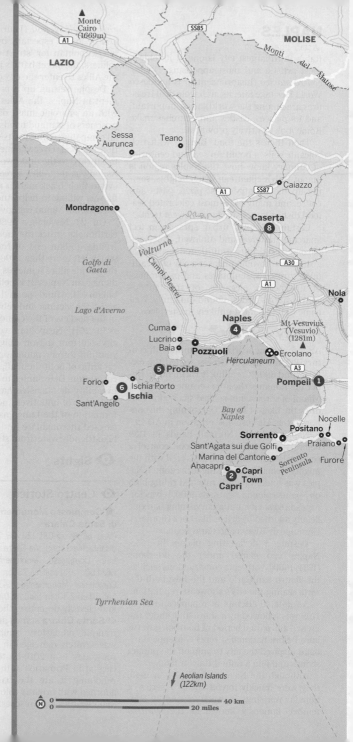

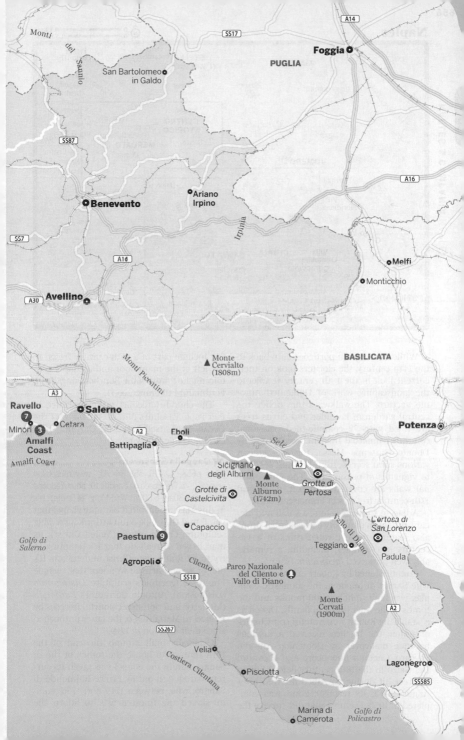

Naples

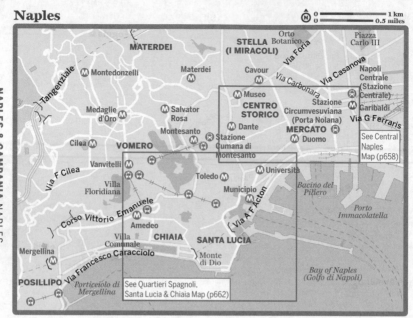

While the Angevin porticoes date back to the 14th century, the cloisters took on their current look in the 18th century thanks to the landscaping work of Domenico Antonio Vaccaro. The walkways that divide the central garden of lavender and citrus trees are lined with 72 ceramic-tiled octagonal columns connected by benches. Painted by Donato Giuseppe Massa, the tiles depict various rural scenes, from hunting sessions to vignettes of peasant life. The four internal walls are covered with soft, whimsical 17th-century frescoes of Franciscan tales.

Adjacent to the cloisters, a small and elegant **museum** of mostly ecclesiastical props also features the excavated ruins of a 1st-century spa complex, including a remarkably well-preserved *laconicum* (sauna).

Commissioned by Robert of Anjou for his wife Sancia di Maiorca, the monastic complex was built to house 200 monks and the tombs of the Angevin royal family. Dissed as a 'stable' by Robert's ungrateful son Charles of Anjou, the basilica received a luscious baroque makeover by Domenico Antonio Vaccaro, Gaetano Buonocore and Giovanni Del Gaizo in the 18th century before taking a direct hit during an Allied air raid on 4 August 1943. Its reconstruction was completed in 1953. Features that did survive the fire include part of a 14th-century fresco to the left of the main door and a chapel containing the tombs of the Bourbon kings from Ferdinand I to Francesco II.

The church forecourt makes a cameo in Pier Paolo Pasolini's film *Il Decameron* (The Decameron), itself based on Giovanni Boccaccio's 14th-century novel.

★ **Cappella Sansevero**   CHAPEL
(Map p658; ☑ 081 551 84 70; www.museosan severo.it; Via Francesco de Sanctis 19; adult/reduced €7/5; ⊗ 9.30am-6.30pm Wed-Mon; M Dante) It's in this Masonic-inspired baroque chapel that you'll find Giuseppe Sanmartino's incredible sculpture, *Cristo velato* (Veiled Christ), its marble veil so realistic that it's tempting to try to lift it and view Christ underneath. It's one of several artistic wonders that include Francesco Queirolo's sculpture *Disinganno* (Disillusion), Antonio Corradini's *Pudicizia* (Modesty) and riotously colourful frescoes by Francesco Maria Russo, the latter untouched since their creation in 1749.

Originally built around the end of the 16th century to house the tombs of the di Sangro family, the chapel was given its current baroque fit-out by Prince Raimondo di Sangro, who, between 1749 and 1766, commissioned the finest artists to adorn the interior. In Queirolo's *Disinganno,* the man trying to untangle himself from a net represents Raimondo's father, Antonio, Duke of Torremaggiore. After the premature death of his wife, Antonio abandoned the young Raimondo, choosing instead a life of travel and hedonistic pleasures. Repentant in his later years, he returned to Naples and joined the priesthood, his attempt to free himself from sin represented in Queirolo's masterpiece.

Even more poignant is Antonio Corradini's *Pudicizia,* whose veiled female figure pays tribute to Raimondo's mother, Cecilia Gaetani d'Aquila d'Aragona. Raimondo was only 11 months old when she died, and the statue's lost gaze and broken plaque represent a life cruelly cut short.

The chapel's original polychrome marble flooring was badly damaged in a major collapse involving the chapel and the neighbouring Palazzo dei di Sangro in 1889. Designed by Francesco Celebrano, the flooring survives in fragmentary form in the passageway leading off from the chapel's right side. The passageway leads to a staircase, at the bottom of which you'll find two meticulously preserved human arterial systems – one of a man, the other of a woman. Debate still circles the models: are the arterial systems real or reproductions? And if they are real, just how was such an incredible state of preservation achieved? More than two centuries on, the mystery surrounding the alchemist prince lives on.

Queues here can be notoriously long so consider purchasing your ticket online in advance for fast-track entry into the chapel; it's worth the extra €2 booking fee, especially during peak holiday periods.

Chiesa del Gesù Nuovo
CHURCH

(Map p658; ☎081 551 86 13; Piazza del Gesù Nuovo; ⊙7.30am-1pm & 4-8pm Mon-Sat, 7.30am-2pm & 4-9pm Sun; Ⓜ Dante) The extraordinary Chiesa del Gesù Nuovo is an architectural Kinder Surprise. Its shell is the 15th-century, Giuseppe Valeriani–designed facade of Palazzo Sanseverino, converted to create the 16th-century church. Inside, piperno-stone sobriety gives way to a gob-smacking blast of baroque that could make the Vatican blush: a vainglorious showcase for the work of top-tier artists such as Francesco Solimena, Luca Giordano and Cosimo Fanzago.

The church is the final resting place of much-loved local saint Giuseppe Moscati (1880–1927), a doctor who served the city's poor. Adjacent to the right transept, the Sale di San Giuseppe Moscati (Rooms of St Joseph Moscati) include a recreation of the great man's study, complete with the armchair in which he died. Scan the walls for *ex-votos,* gifts offered by the faithful for miracles purportedly received. The church itself received a miracle of sorts on 4 August 1943, when a bomb dropped on the site failed to explode. Its shell is aptly displayed beside the *ex-votos.*

The church flanks the northern side of beautiful **Piazza del Gesù Nuovo**, a favourite late-night hang-out for students and lefties. At its centre soars Giuseppe Genuino's lavish **Guglia dell'Immacolata** (Map p658; Ⓜ Dante), an obelisk built between 1747 and 1750. On 8 December, the Feast of the Immacolata, firemen scramble up to the top to place a wreath of flowers at the Virgin Mary's feet.

Via San Gregorio Armeno
STREET

(Map p658; ☐ E1, E2 to Via Duomo) Dismissed by serious collectors, this narrow street remains famous across Italy for its *pastori* (Christmas crib figurines) nonetheless. Connecting Spaccanapoli with Via dei Tribunali, the *decumanus maior* (main road) of ancient Neapolis, its clutter of shops and workshops peddle everything from doting donkeys to kitsch celebrity caricatures. At No 8 you'll find the workshop of **Giuseppe Ferrigno**, whose terracotta figurines are the most famous and esteemed on the strip.

★ Complesso Monumentale di San Lorenzo Maggiore
ARCHAEOLOGICAL SITE

(Map p658; ☎081 211 08 60; www.sanlorenzomaggiorenapoli.it; Via dei Tribunali 316; church admission free, excavations & museum adult/reduced €9/7; ⊙church 8am-7pm, excavations & museum 9.30am-5.30pm; ☐ E1, E2 to Via Duomo) The **basilica** at this richly layered religious complex is deemed one of Naples' finest medieval buildings. Aside from Ferdinando Sanfelice's facade, the Cappella al Rosario and the Cappellone di Sant'Antonio, its baroque makeover was stripped away last century to reveal its austere, Gothic elegance. Beneath the basilica is a sprawl of extraordinary Graeco-Roman **ruins**, best explored on one of the regular one-hour guided tours (€1).

To better understand the ruins, start your explorations in the **Museo dell'Opera di San Lorenzo Maggiore**, which includes a model of the area as it appeared in ancient times. The museum also includes an intriguing collection of local archaeological finds, including Graeco-Roman sarcophagi, ceramics

Central Naples

400 m
0.2 miles

Corso Novara

Corso G Garibaldi

Via C Carmignano
Via Sopramuro

Via Firenze
Alibus Bus
(Stazione
Centrale stop)

Napoli
Centrale
(Stazione
Centrale)

Stazione
Circumvesuviana
(Piazza Garibaldi)

Terminal Bus
Metropark

Eccellenze Campane (1km)

Piazza
Garibaldi

Garibaldi

Piazza
Garibaldi

Garibaldi

Via G Pica

Via S Cosmo Fuori Porta Nolana

Stazione
Circumvesuviana
(Porta Nolana)

Via E Cosenz

Vico S Giovanni

Via Amerigo Vespucci

Calata della Marinella

Piazza
G Pepe

Piazza Principe Umberto

Via C M Vico

Via Carbonara

Via Duchesca

Via PS Mancini

Via Ranieri

Via dell'Annunziata

Via A de Pace

Via G Savarese

Via Nolana

Via Lavinaio

Piazza del Mercato

Piazza
Masaniello

Via Sant'Eligio

Via Nuova Marina

Calata Villa del Popolo

MERCATO

Via Duca di San Donato

Via D Carmine

22

Via P Colletta

Corso Umberto I

Via S Nicola dei Caserti

Via del Tribunali

Vico della Pace

Via S Nicola della Misericordia

6 Pio Monte della Misericordia

Via Vicaria Vecchia

CENTRO STORICO

Piazza Nicola Amore

Duomo

Via Duomo

Piazza del Duomo

Via Scialoia

See Quartieri Spagnoli; Santa Lucia & Chiala Map (p662)

Piazzetta Orefici

Via Sedile di Porto

MADRE (50m)

Vicolo Sedil Capuano

Duomo 4

9

Via SS Apostoli

Via Santissimi Apostoli

Complesso Monumentale di San Lorenzo Maggiore 2

Via San Gregorio Armeno

11

Via San Biagio dei Librai

Via d'Alagno

Via dei Cimbri

Via Duomo

Ceraselo B&B (350m)

Vico Giganti

Via Anticaglia

Via San Paolo

13

10 24

17 19

Vico Zuroli

Vico S Severino

Vico S Nicola al Nilo

Via B Capasso

Via G Paladino

Catacombe di San Gennaro (1km);
Palazzo Reale di Capodimonte (2km)

Piazza Museo Nazionale

Museo

Museo Archeologico Nazionale 5

Via S Gaudioso

Via S Pisanelli

Via Atri

Via F del Giudice

Via del Sole

Cappella Sansevero 1

Piazza San Domenico Maggiore

20

Vico Donnaromita

Via Mezzocannone

Largo Giusso

Via Donnalbina

Via del Porto

12

Via Tommasi

Via Santa Maria di Costantinopoli

Via Broggia

Via Bellini

Piazza Luigi Miraglia

Piazza Bellini

21

15

Via Port'Alba

Dante

Piazza Dante

Via San Sebastiano 23

Vico San Domenico Maggiore

Complesso Monumentale di Santa Chiara 3

7

Via Benedetto Croce

8

16

18

Via Santa Chiara

14

Vico San Geronimo

Piazza del Gesù Nuovo

Via Enrico Pessina

Via S Anna dei Lombardi

Via D Lioy

Piazza Sant'Anna dei Lombardi

Via Toledo

Piazza Carità

Via Pignasecca

Via G Brombeis

Central Naples

and crockery from the digs below. Other treasures include vivacious 9th-century ceramics, Angevin frescoes, paintings by Giuseppe Marullo and Luigi Velpi, and fine examples of 17th- and 18th-century ecclesiastical vestments.

The ruins themselves will see you walking past ancient bakeries, wineries, laundries and barrel-vaulted rooms that once formed part of the city's two-storey *macellum* (market).

Above them, the basilica itself was commenced in 1270 by French architects, who built the apse. Local architects took over the following century, recycling ancient columns in the nave. Catherine of Austria, who died in 1323, is buried here in a beautiful mosaiced tomb. Legend has it that this was where Boccaccio first fell for Mary of Anjou, the inspiration for his character Fiammetta, while the poet Petrarch called the adjoining convent home in 1345.

★ Pio Monte
della Misericordia   CHURCH, MUSEUM
(Map p658; ☎ 081 44 69 44; www.piomontedella misericordia.it; Via dei Tribunali 253; adult/reduced €7/5; ☉ 9am-6pm Mon-Sat, to 2.30pm Sun; ▣ E1, E2 to Via Duomo) The 1st floor gallery of this octagonal, 17th-century church delivers a small, satisfying collection of Renaissance and baroque art, including works by Francesco de Mura, Giuseppe de Ribera, Andrea Vaccaro and Paul van Somer. It's also home to contemporary artworks by Italian and foreign artists, each inspired by Caravaggio's masterpiece *Le sette opere di Misericordia*

(The Seven Acts of Mercy). Considered by many to be the most important painting in Naples, you'll find it above the main altar in the ground-floor chapel.

Magnificently demonstrating the artist's chiaroscuro style, which had a revolutionary impact in Naples, *Le sette opere di Misericordia* was considered unique in its ability to illustrate the various acts in one seamlessly choreographed scene. On display in the 1st-floor gallery is the *Declaratoria del 14 Ottobre 1607*, an original church document acknowledging payment of 400 ducats to Caravaggio for the masterpiece. The painting itself is best viewed from the 1st-floor gallery's Sala del Coretto (Coretto Room), where the lighting used to illuminate the canvas is less glary.

On the opposite side of the street stands the Guglia di San Gennaro (Map p658; Piazza Riario Sforza; ▣ C55 to Via Duomo). Dating back to 1636, with stonework by Cosimo Fanzago and a bronze statue by Tommaso Montani, the obelisk is a soaring *grazie* (thank you) to the city's patron saint for protecting Naples from the 1631 eruption of Mt Vesuvius.

★ Duomo   CATHEDRAL
(Map p658; ☎ 081 44 90 97; Via Duomo 149; cathedral/baptistry free/€2; ☉ cathedral 8.30am-1.30pm & 2.30-7.30pm Mon-Sat, 8am-1pm & 4.30-7.30pm Sun, baptistry 8.30am-12.30pm & 4-6.30pm Mon-Sat, 8.30am-1pm Sun; ▣ E1, E2 to Via Duomo) Whether you go for Giovanni Lanfranco's fresco in the Cappella di San Gennaro (Chapel of St Janarius), the 4th-century mosaics

in the baptistry, or the thrice-annual miracle of San Gennaro, do not miss Naples' cathedral. Kick-started by Charles I of Anjou in 1272 and consecrated in 1315, it was largely destroyed in a 1456 earthquake, with copious nips and tucks over the subsequent centuries.

Among these is the gleaming neo-Gothic facade, only added in the late 19th century. Step inside and you'll immediately notice the central nave's gilded coffered ceiling, studded with late-mannerist art. The high sections of the nave and the transept are the work of baroque overachiever Luca Giordano.

Off the right aisle, the 17th-century Cappella di San Gennaro (also known as the Chapel of the Treasury) was designed by Giovanni Cola di Franco and completed in 1637. The most sought-after artists of the period worked on the chapel, creating one of Naples' greatest baroque legacies. Highlights here include Giuseppe de Ribera's gripping canvas *St Gennaro Escaping the Furnace Unscathed* and Giovanni Lanfranco's dizzying dome fresco. Hidden away in a strongbox behind the altar is a 14th-century silver bust in which sit the skull of San Gennaro and the two phials that hold his miraculously liquefying blood.

The next chapel eastwards contains an urn with the saint's bones and a cupboard full of femurs, tibias and fibulas. Below the high altar is the **Cappella Carafa**, a Renaissance chapel built to house yet more of the saint's remains.

Off the left aisle lies the 4th-century **Basilica di Santa Restituta**, subject to an almost complete makeover after the earthquake of 1688. From it you can access the **Battistero di San Giovanni in Fonte**. Western Europe's oldest baptistry, it's encrusted with fragments of glittering 4th-century mosaics. The Duomo's subterranean **archaeological zone**, which includes fascinating remains of Greek and Roman buildings and roads, remains closed indefinitely.

MADRE
GALLERY

(Museo d'Arte Contemporanea Donnaregina; ☑081 1931 3016; www.madrenapoli.it; Via Settembrini 79; adult/reduced €7/3.50, Mon free; ⊙10am-7.30pm Mon & Wed-Sat, to 8pm Sun; 🚊E1, E2 to Via Duomo, Ⓜ️Piazza Cavour) When *Madonna and Child* overload hits, reboot at Naples' museum of modern and contemporary art. Start on level three – the setting for temporary exhibitions – before hitting level two's permanent collection of painting, sculpture, photography and installations from prolific 20th- and 21st-century artists. Among these are Andy Warhol, Gilbert & George and Cindy Sherman, as well as Italian heavyweights Mario Merz and Michelangelo Pistoletto. Specially commissioned installations from the likes of Anish Kapoor and Rebecca Horn round things off on level one.

★ Museo Archeologico Nazionale
MUSEUM

(Map p658; ☑848 80 02 88, from mobile 06 3996 7050; www.museoarcheologiconapoli.it; Piazza Museo Nazionale 19; adult/reduced €12/6; ⊙9am-7.30pm Wed-Mon; Ⓜ️Museo, Piazza Cavour) Naples' National Archaeological Museum serves up one of the world's finest collections of Graeco-Roman artefacts. Originally a cavalry barracks and later seat of the city's university, the museum was established by the Bourbon king Charles VII in the late 18th century to house the antiquities he inherited from his mother, Elisabetta Farnese, as well as treasures looted from Pompeii and Herculaneum. Star exhibits include the celebrated *Toro Farnese* (Farnese Bull) sculpture and a series of awe-inspiring mosaics from Pompeii's Casa del Fauno.

Before tackling the collection, consider investing in the *National Archaeological Museum of Naples* (€12), published by Electa; if you want to concentrate on the highlights, audio guides (€5) are available in English. It's also worth calling ahead to ensure that the galleries you want to see are open, as staff shortages often mean that sections of the museum close for part of the day.

Downstairs is the impressive, recently revamped Borgia collection of Egyptian epigraphs and relics, organised around themes including Tombs and Grave Goods, Mummification and Magic. The ground-floor **Farnese collection** of colossal Greek and Roman sculptures features the *Toro Farnese* and a muscle-bound *Ercole* (Hercules). Sculpted in the early 3rd century AD and noted in the writings of Pliny, the *Toro Farnese,* probably a Roman copy of a Greek original, depicts the humiliating death of Dirce, Queen of Thebes. Carved from a single colossal block of marble, the sculpture was discovered in 1545 near the Baths of Caracalla in Rome and was restored by Michelangelo, before eventually being shipped to Naples in 1787. *Ercole* was discovered in the same Roman excavations, albeit without his legs. When they turned up at a later dig, the Bourbons had them fitted.

If you're short on time, take in both these masterpieces before heading straight to the

CATACOMBA DI SAN GENNARO

Naples' oldest and most sacred catacombs, **Catacombe di San Gennaro** (☎081 744 37 14; www.catacombedinapoli.it; Via Capodimonte 13; adult/reduced €9/5; ⊙1hr tours every hour 10am-5pm Mon-Sat, to 2pm Sun; 🚌R4, 178 to Via Capodimonte), became a Christian pilgrimage site when San Gennaro's body was interred here in the 5th century. The carefully restored site allows visitors to experience an evocative other world of tombs, corridors and broad vestibules, its treasures including 2nd-century Christian frescoes, 5th-century mosaics and the oldest known portrait of San Gennaro.

The catacombs are home to three types of tomb, each corresponding to a specific social class. The wealthy opted for the open-room *cubiculum*, originally guarded by gates and adorned with colourful wall frescoes. One *cubiculum* to the left of the entrance features an especially beautiful funerary fresco of a mother, father and child: it's made up of three layers of fresco, one commissioned for each death. The smaller, rectangular wall niches, known as *loculum*, were the domain of the middle classes, while the *forme* (floor tombs) were reserved for the poor.

Further ahead you'll stumble upon the *basilica minore* (minor basilica), home to the tombs of San Gennaro and 5th-century archbishop of Naples Giovanni I. Sometime between 413 and 431, Giovanni I accompanied the martyr's remains from Pozzuoli to Naples, burying them here before Lombard prince Sico I of Benevento snatched them in the 9th century. The *basilica minore* also harbours fragments of a fresco depicting Naples' first bishop, Sant'Aspreno. The city's bishops were buried here until the 11th century.

Close to the *basilica minore* is a 3rd-century tomb whose Pompeiian-hued artwork employs both Christian and pagan elements. In the image of three women building a castle, the figures represent the three virtues, while the castle symbolises the Church.

The lower level is even older, dating back to the 2nd century and speckled with typically pagan motifs like fruit and animals. The painting on the side of San Gennaro's tomb – depicting the saint with Mt Vesuvius and Mt Somma in the background – is the first known image of San Gennaro as the protector of Naples. Also on the lower level is the Basilica di Agrippino, named in honour of Sant'Agrippino. The sixth bishop of Naples, Agrippino was also the first Christian to be buried in the catacombs, back in the 3rd century.

Tours of the catacombs are run by the Cooperativa Sociale Onlus 'La Paranza' (p668), whose ticket office is to the left of the **Chiesa di Madre di Buon Consiglio** (☎081 741 00 06; Via Capodimonte 13; ⊙8am-noon & 5-7pm Mon-Sat, 9am-1pm & 5-7pm Sun; 🚌R4, 178 to Via Capodimonte), a snack-sized replica of St Peter's in Rome completed in 1960. The co-operative also runs a fascinating Sunday morning walking tour called Il Miglio Sacro (The Holy Mile; adult/reduced €15/13), which explores the neighbouring Sanità district. It must be pre-booked; see its website for details.

The catacombs themselves also host occasional theatrical and live-music performances; see the website for upcoming events.

mezzanine floor, home to an exquisite collection of **mosaics**, mostly from Pompeii. Of the series taken from the Casa del Fauno, it is *La battaglia di Alessandro contro Dario* (The Battle of Alexander against Darius) that really stands out. The best-known depiction of Alexander the Great, the 20-sq-metre mosaic was probably made by Alexandrian craftsmen working in Italy around the end of the 2nd century BC.

Beyond the mosaics, the **Gabinetto Segreto** (Secret Chamber) contains a small but much-studied collection of ancient erotica. Pan is caught in the act with a nanny goat in the most famous piece – a small and

surprisingly sophisticated statue taken from the Villa dei Papiri in Herculaneum. You'll also find a series of nine paintings depicting erotic positions – a menu for brothel patrons.

Originally the royal library, the **Sala Meridiana** (Great Hall of the Sundial) on the 1st floor is home to the *Farnese Atlante,* a statue of Atlas carrying a globe on his shoulders, as well as various paintings from the Farnese collection. Look up to find Pietro Bardellino's colourful 1781 fresco depicting the (short-lived) triumph of Ferdinand IV of Bourbon and Marie Caroline of Austria in Rome.

The rest of the 1st floor is largely devoted to fascinating discoveries from Pompeii,

Quartieri Spagnoli, Santa Lucia & Chiaia

VOMERO

Vanvitelli

Via Tito Angelini

Largo San Martino

🏛 9

1 Certosa e Museo di San Martino

Via Annibale Caccavello

Piazza Fuga

Via Gaetano Donizetti

Via G Puccini

Via Luigia Sanfelice

Via G Toma

Via F Palizzi

Corso Vittorio Emanuele

Via de Deo

QUARTIERI SPAGNOLI

Vico della Tofa

Piazzetta Cariati

24

Via Santa Caterina da Siena

Via G Nicotera

Corso Vittorio Emanuele

Funicolare di Chiaia

Via del Parco Margherita

Amedeo

Piazza Amedeo

Via F Crispi

Via Vittorio Colonna

15

Vico Vetriera

Via dei Mille

Via G Filangieri

Vico Sergente Maggiore

Vico Cario de Cesare

13

Piazza Santa Maria degli Angeli

Vico Santo Spirito

Galleria Borbonica

2

Via Egiziaca a Pizzofalcone

Via G Martucci

Via G Piscicelli

Via Santa Teresa a Chiaia

Via G Bausan

Via Ascensione

Via S Pasquale a Chiaia

Piazza Amendola

Via Cavalerizza a Chiaia

Via V Imbriani

Vico Belledonne a Chiaia

Via V Cuoco

CHIAIA

Via Ferrigni

Via Alabardieri

16

22

Piazza dei Martiri

Via Domenico Morelli

Monte Echia

Vico Santa Maria a Cappella Vecchia

Via Monte di Dio

Largo Principessa R Pignatelli

Via C Poerio

Riviera di Chiaia

Vico Satriano

Vico Calabritto

26

Viale Anton Dohrn

Vico Ischitella

Villa Comunale

Piazza Vittoria

Via G Arcoleo

Largo Nunziatella

Via Francesco Caracciolo

PIZZOFALCONE

Via Partenope

Monte di Dio

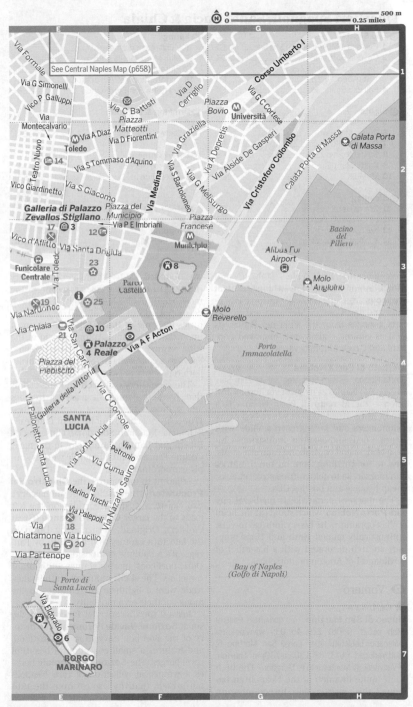

NAPLES & CAMPANIA

Quartieri Spagnoli, Santa Lucia & Chiaia

Herculaneum, Boscoreale, Stabiae and Cuma. Among them are whimsical wall **frescoes** from the Villa di Agrippa Postumus and the Casa di Meleagro, extraordinary bronzes from the Villa dei Papiri, as well as ceramics, glassware, engraved coppers and Greek funerary vases.

Mercato di Porta Nolana MARKET
(Porta Nolana; ⏰8am-6pm Mon-Sat, to 2pm Sun; Ⓜ Garibaldi) Naples at its most vociferous and intense, the Mercato di Porta Nolana is a heady, gritty street market where bellowing fishmongers and greengrocers collide with fragrant delis and bakeries, industrious Chinese traders and contraband cigarette stalls. Dive in for anything from buxom tomatoes and mozzarella to golden-fried street snacks, cheap luggage and bootleg CDs.

The market's namesake is medieval city gate **Porta Nolana**, which stands at the head of Via Sopramuro. Its two cylindrical towers, optimistically named Faith and Hope, support an arch decorated with a bas-relief of Ferdinand I of Aragon on horseback.

◉ Vomero

★ Certosa e
Museo di San Martino MONASTERY, MUSEUM
(Map p662; ☏081 229 45 03; www.polomusealenapoli.beniculturali.it; Largo San Martino 5; adult/reduced €6/3; ⏰8.30am-7.30pm Thu-Tue; Ⓜ Vanvitelli, 🚋 Montesanto to Morghen) The high point (quite literally) of the Neapolitan baroque, this charterhouse-turned-museum

was founded as a Carthusian monastery in the 14th century. Centred on one of the most beautiful cloisters in Italy, it has been decorated, adorned and altered over the centuries by some of Italy's finest talent, most importantly Giovanni Antonio Dosio in the 16th century and baroque master Cosimo Fanzago a century later. Nowadays, it's a superb repository of Neapolitan artistry.

The monastery's **church** and the rooms that flank it contain a feast of frescoes and paintings by some of Naples' greatest 17th-century artists, among them Francesco Solimena, Massimo Stanzione, Giuseppe de Ribera and Battista Caracciolo. In the nave, Cosimo Fanzago's inlaid marble work is simply extraordinary.

Adjacent to the church, the **Chiostro dei Procuratori** is the smaller of the monastery's two cloisters. A grand corridor on the left leads to the larger **Chiostro Grande** (Great Cloister). Originally designed by Dosio in the late 16th century and added to by Fanzago, it's a sublime composition of Tuscan-Doric porticoes, marble statues and vibrant camellias. The skulls mounted on the balustrade were a lighthearted reminder to the monks of their own mortality.

Just off the Chiostro dei Procuratori, the small **Sezione Navale** documents the history of the Bourbon navy from 1734 to 1860, and features a small collection of beautiful royal barges. The **Sezione Presepiale** houses a whimsical collection of rare Neapolitan *presepi* (nativity scenes) from the 18th and 19th centuries, including the colossal

18th-century Cuciniello creation, which covers one wall of what used to be the monastery's kitchen. The **Quarto del Priore** in the southern wing houses the bulk of the picture collection, as well as one of the museum's most famous pieces, Pietro Bernini's tender *Madonna col Bambino e San Giovannino* (Madonna and Child with the Infant John the Baptist).

A pictorial history of Naples is told in **Immagini e Memorie di Napoli** (Images and Memories of Naples). Here you'll find portraits of historic characters; antique maps, including a 35-panel copper map of 18th-century Naples in Room 45; and rooms dedicated to major historical events such as the Revolt of the Masaniello (Room 36) and the plague (Room 37). Room 32 boasts the beautiful *Tavola Strozzi* (Strozzi Table); its fabled depiction of 15th-century maritime Naples is one of the city's most celebrated historical records.

It's worth noting that some sections of the museum are only open at various times of the day; see the website for specific times.

Below the Certosa is the imposing **Sotterranei Gotici** (Gothic basement). The austere vaulted space harbours circa 150 marble sculptures and epigraphs, including a statue of St Francis of Assisi by 18th-century master sculptor Giuseppe Sanmartino. Guided tours (in Italian) of the Sotterranei Gotici usually take place at 11.30am on Saturday and Sunday and must be reserved about two weeks in advance by emailing accoglienza. sanmartino@beniculturali.it. Unfortunately, tours were suspended indefinitely in 2017; contact the museum for updates.

Castel Sant'Elmo CASTLE
(Map p662; ☑081 558 77 08; www.coopculture. it; Via Tito Angelini 22, adult/reduced €5/2.50 Wed-Mon, €2.50/1.25 Tue; ⊙castle 8.30am-7.30pm daily, museum 9.30am-5pm Wed-Mon; Ⓜ Vanvitelli, 🚠 Montesanto to Morghen) Star-shaped Castel Sant'Elmo was originally a church dedicated to St Erasmus. Some 400 years later, in 1349, Robert of Anjou turned it into a castle before Spanish viceroy Don Pedro de Toledo had it further fortified in 1538. Used as a military prison until the 1970s, it's now famed for its jaw-dropping panorama, and for its **Museo del Novecento**, dedicated to 20th-century Neapolitan art.

The museum's collection of paintings, sculpture and installations documents major influences in the local art scene, including Futurism and the Nuclear Art movement. Standout works include Eugenio Viti's sensual *La schiena* (The Back) in Room 7, Raffaele Lippi's unnerving *Le quattro giornate di Napoli* (The Four Days of Naples) in Room 9, and Giuseppe Desiato's magnetic photograph *Monumento* in Room 18. In Room 17, Salvatore Cotugno's untitled sculpture of a bound, wrapped, muted figure strangely recalls Giuseppe Sanmartino's *Cristo velato* (Veiled Christ) in the Cappella Sansevero (p656).

◉ Via Toledo & Quartieri Spagnoli

★ Galleria di Palazzo Zevallos Stigliano GALLERY
(Map p662; ☑081 42 50 11; www.palazzozevallos. com; Via Toledo 185; adult/reduced €5/3; ⊙10am-6pm Tue-Fri, to 8pm Sat & Sun; Ⓜ Municipio) Built for a Spanish merchant in the 17th century and reconfigured in belle époque style by architect Luigi Platania in the early 20th century, Palazzo Zevallos Stigliano houses a compact yet stunning collection of Neapolitan and Italian art spanning the 17th to early-20th centuries. Star attraction is Caravaggio's mesmerising swansong, *The Martyrdom of St Ursula* (1610). Completed weeks before the artist's lonely death, the painting depicts a vengeful king of the Huns piercing the heart of his unwilling virgin bride-to-be, Ursula.

Positioned behind the dying martyr is a haunted Caravaggio, an eerie premonition of his own impending fate. The tumultuous history of both the artist and the painting is documented in the free and highly informative tablet audio guide.

Caravaggio's masterpiece is one of around 120 works on display in the *palazzo's* sumptuous rooms. Among the numerous standouts are Luca Giordano's robust *The Rape of Helen*, a graphic *Judith Beheads Holophernes* attributed to Louis Finson, Francesco Solimena's *Hagar and Ishmael in the Desert Confronted by the Angel* and a series of bronze and terracotta sculptures by Vincenzo Gemito. A fine collection of landscape paintings includes Gasper van Wittel's *View of Naples with Largo di Palazzo*, which offers a fascinating early-18th-century depiction of what is now Piazza del Plebiscito. The triple-arched fountain in the bottom right corner of the painting is the Fontana dell'Immacolatella. Designed by Michelangelo Naccherini and Pietro Bernini in 1601, the fountain is now located at the corner of Via Partenope and Via Nazario Sauro, beside Borgo Marinaro.

Gaspar van Wittel was the father of celebrated Neapolitan architect Luigi Vanvitelli.

⊙ Santa Lucia & Chiaia

★ **Palazzo Reale**   PALACE
(Royal Palace; Map p662; ☑ 081 40 05 47; Piazza del Plebiscito 1; adult/reduced €4/3; ☺ 9am-8pm Thu-Tue; ☑ R2 to Via San Carlo, Ⓜ Municipio) Envisaged as a 16th-century monument to Spanish glory (Naples was under Spanish rule at the time), the magnificent Palazzo Reale is home to the **Museo del Palazzo Reale**, a rich and eclectic collection of baroque and neoclassical furnishings, porcelain, tapestries, sculpture and paintings, spread across the palace's royal apartments.

Among the many highlights is the Teatrino di Corte, a lavish private theatre created by Ferdinando Fuga in 1768 to celebrate the marriage of Ferdinando IV and Marie Caroline of Austria. Incredibly, Angelo Viva's statues of Apollo and the Muses set along the walls are made of papier mâché.

Sala (Room) VIII is home to a pair of vivid, allegorical 18th-century French tapestries representing earth and water respectively. Further along, Sala XII will leave you sniggering at the 16th-century canvas *Gli esattori delle imposte* (The Tax Collectors). Painted by Dutch artist Marinus Claesz Van Reymerswaele, it confirms that attitudes to tax collectors have changed little in 500 years. Sala XIII used to be Joachim Murat's study in the 19th century but was used as a snack bar by Allied troops in WWII. Meanwhile, what looks like a waterwheel in Sala XXIII is actually a nifty rotating reading desk made for Marie Caroline by Giovanni Uldrich in the 18th century.

The Cappella Reale (Royal Chapel) houses an 18th-century *presepe napoletano* (Neapolitan nativity crib). Fastidiously detailed, its cast of *pastori* (crib figurines) were crafted by a series of celebrated Neapolitan artists, including Giuseppe Sanmartino, creator of the *Cristo velato* (Veiled Christ) sculpture in the Cappella Sansevero.

The palace is also home to the **Biblioteca Nazionale** (National Library; Map p662; ☑ 081 781 91 11; www.bnnonline.it; ☺ 8.30am-7pm Mon-Fri, to 2pm Sat, papyri exhibition 8.30am-2pm Mon-Fri, Sezione Lucchesi Palli 8.30am-6.45pm Mon-Thu, to 3.30pm Fri; ☑ R2 to Via San Carlo, Ⓜ Municipio) **FREE**, its own priceless treasures including at least 2000 papyri discovered at Herculaneum and fragments of a 5th-century Coptic Bible. The National Library's beautiful **Biblioteca Lucchesi Palli** (Lucchesi Palli Library) – designed by some of Naples' most celebrated 19th-century craftspeople – is home to fascinating artistic artefacts, including letters by composer Giuseppe Verdi. Bring photo ID to enter the Biblioteca Nazionale.

SUBTERRANEAN NAPLES
....

Mysterious shrines, secret passageways, forgotten burial crypts: it might sound like the set of an Indiana Jones film, but it's actually what lurks beneath Naples' loud and greasy streets. Subterranean Naples is one of the world's most thrilling urban wonderlands; a silent, mostly undiscovered sprawl of cathedral-like cisterns, pin-thin conduits, catacombs and ancient ruins.

Speleologists (cave specialists) estimate that about 60% of Neapolitans live and work above this network, known in Italian as the *sottosuolo* (underground). Since the end of WWII, some 700 cavities have been discovered, from original Greek-era grottoes to palaeo-Christian burial chambers and royal Bourbon escape routes. According to the experts, this is simply a prelude, with another 2 million sq metres of troglodytic treats to unfurl.

Naples' dedicated caving geeks are quick to tell you that their underworld is one of the largest and oldest on earth. Sure, Paris might claim a catacomb or two, but its subterranean offerings don't come close to this giant's 2500-year history.

And what a history it is. Naples' most famous saint, San Gennaro, was interred in the Catacombe di San Gennaro in the 5th century. A century later, in 536, Belisario and his troops caught Naples by surprise by storming the city through the city's ancient tunnels. According to legend, Alfonso of Aragon used the same trick in 1442, undermining the city walls by using an underground passageway leading into a tailor's shop and straight into town. Even the city's dreaded Camorra has got in on the act. In 1992 the notorious Stolder clan was busted for running a subterranean drug lab, with escape routes heading straight to the clan boss's pad.

★ **Galleria Borbonica**   HISTORIC SITE
(Map p662; ☎081 764 58 08, 366 2484151; www.
galleriaborbonica.com; Vico del Grottone 4; 75min
standard tour adult/reduced €10/5; ⊗standard tour
10am, noon, 3.30pm & 5.30pm Fri-Sun; ☒R2 to Via
San Carlo) Traverse five centuries along Naples' engrossing Bourbon Tunnel. Conceived
by Ferdinand II in 1853 to link the Palazzo
Reale to the barracks and the sea, the never-
completed escape route is part of the
17th-century Carmignano Aqueduct system,
itself incorporating 16th-century cisterns.
An air-raid shelter and military hospital
during WWII, this underground labyrinth
rekindles the past with evocative wartime
artefacts. The standard tour doesn't require
pre-booking, though the Adventure Tour
(80 minutes; adult/reduced €15/10) and
adults-only Speleo Tour (2½ hours; €30) do.

Tours also depart from Galleria Borbonica's second entrance, reached through the
Parcheggio Morelli (Via Domenico Morelli
40) parking complex in Chiaia.

MeMus   MUSEUM
(Museum & Historical Archive of the Teatro San
Carlo; Map p662; http://memus.squarespace.com;
Palazzo Reale, Piazza del Plebiscito; adult/reduced
€6/5; ⊗9am-7pm Mon, Tue & Thu-Sat, to 3pm
Sun; ☒R2 to Via San Carlo, Ⓜ Municipio) Located
inside the Palazzo Reale (purchase tickets
at the palace ticket booth), MeMus documents the history of Europe's oldest working
opera house, the Teatro San Carlo (p673).
The collection includes costumes, sketches,
instruments and memorabilia, displayed in
annually changing themed exhibitions. One
interactive, immersive exhibit allows visitors
to enjoy the music of numerous celebrated
composers with accompanying visuals by
artists who have collaborated with the opera
house, among them William Kentridge.

Castel Nuovo   CASTLE
(Map p662; ☎081 795 77 22; Piazza Municipio;
adult/reduced €6/3, free Sun; ⊗9am-7pm Mon-
Sat, to 1.30pm Sun; Ⓜ Municipio) Locals know
this 13th-century castle as the Maschio
Angioino (Angevin Keep) and its Cappella
Palatina is home to fragments of frescoes
by Giotto; they're on the splays of the Gothic windows. You'll also find Roman ruins
under the glass-floored Sala dell'Armeria
(Armoury Hall). The castle's upper floors
(closed on Sunday) house a collection of
mostly 17th- to early-20th-century Neapolitan paintings. The top floor houses the more
interesting works, including landscape

paintings by Luigi Crisconio and a watercolour by architect Carlo Vanvitelli.

The history of the castle stretches back
to Charles I of Anjou, who upon taking over
Naples and the Swabians' Sicilian kingdom
found himself in control not only of his new
southern Italian acquisitions but also of
possessions in Tuscany, northern Italy and
Provence (France). It made sense to base the
new dynasty in Naples, rather than Palermo
in Sicily, and Charles launched an ambitious
construction program to expand the port
and city walls. His plans included convert-
ing a Franciscan convent into the castle that
still stands in Piazza Municipio.

Christened the Castrum Novum (New
Castle) to distinguish it from the older Castel
dell'Ovo and Castel Capuano, it was completed in 1282, becoming a popular hang-out for
the leading intellectuals and artists of the day
– Giotto repaid his royal hosts by painting
much of the interior. Of the original structure, however, only the Cappella Palatina
remains; the rest is the result of Aragonese
renovations two centuries later, as well as a
meticulous restoration effort prior to WWII.

The two-storey Renaissance triumphal
arch at the entrance – the **Torre della
Guardia** – commemorates the victorious
entry of Alfonso I of Aragon into Naples in
1443, while the stark stone **Sala dei Baro-
ni** (Hall of the Barons) is named after the
barons slaughtered here in 1486 for plotting against King Ferdinand I of Aragon. Its
striking ribbed vault fuses ancient Roman
and Spanish late-Gothic influences.

Castel dell'Ovo   CASTLE
(Map p662; ☎081 795 45 93; Borgo Marinaro;
⊗8am-7pm Mon-Sat, to 1.45pm Sun; ☒128 to Via
Santa Lucia) **FREE** Built by the Normans in
the 12th century, Naples' oldest castle owes
its name (Castle of the Egg) to Virgil. The
Roman scribe reputedly buried an egg on the
site where the castle now stands, warning that
when the egg breaks, the castle (and Naples)
will fall. Thankfully, both are still standing,
and walking up to the castle's ramparts will
reward you with a breathtaking panorama.

Used by the Swabians, Angevins and Alfonso of Aragon, who modified it to suit his
military needs, the castle sits on the rocky,
restaurant-lined 'island' of Borgo Marinaro
(Map p662). According to legend, the heart-
broken siren Partenope washed ashore here
after failing to seduce Ulysses with her song.
It's also where the Greeks first settled the
city in the 7th century BC, calling the island

Megaris. Its commanding position wasn't wasted on the Roman general Lucullus, either, who had his villa here long before the castle hit the skyline. Views aside, the castle is also the setting for temporary art exhibitions, special events, and no shortage of posing brides and grooms.

⊙ Capodimonte & La Sanità

★ Palazzo Reale di Capodimonte MUSEUM
(☑ 081 749 91 11; www.museocapodimonte. beniculturali.it; Via Miano 2; adult/reduced €8/4; ⊙ 8.30am-7.30pm Thu-Tue; ⊡ R4, 178 to Via Capodimonte, shuttle bus Shuttle Capodimonte) Originally designed as a hunting lodge for Charles VII of Bourbon, this monumental palace was begun in 1738 and took more than a century to complete. It's now home to the **Museo Nazionale di Capodimonte**, southern Italy's largest and richest art gallery. Its vast collection – much of which Charles inherited from his mother, Elisabetta Farnese – was moved here in 1759 and ranges from exquisite 12th-century altarpieces to works by Botticelli, Caravaggio, Titian and Andy Warhol.

The gallery is spread over three floors and 160 rooms; for most people, a full morning or afternoon is enough for an abridged best-of tour. The 1st floor includes works by greats such as Michelangelo, Raphael and Titian, with highlights including Masaccio's *Crocifissione* (Crucifixion; Room 3), Botticelli's *Madonna col Bambino e due angeli* (Madonna with Child and Angels; Room 6), Bellini's *Trasfigurazione* (Transfiguration; Room 8) and Parmigianino's *Antea* (Room 12). The floor is also home to the royal apartments, a study in regal excess. The **Salottino di Porcellana** (Room 52) is an outrageous example of 18th-century chinoiserie, its walls and ceiling dense with whimsically themed porcelain 'stucco'. Originally created between 1757 and 1759 for the Palazzo Reale in Portici, it was transferred to Capodimonte in 1867.

Upstairs, the 2nd-floor galleries display work by Neapolitan artists from the 13th to the 19th centuries, including de Ribera, Giordano, Solimena and Stanzione. It's also home to some striking 16th-century Belgian tapestries. The piece that many come to see, however, is Caravaggio's *Flagellazione* (Flagellation; 1607–10), which hangs in reverential solitude in Room 78.

If you have any energy left, the small gallery of modern art on the 3rd floor is worth a quick look, if for nothing else than Andy Warhol's poptastic *Mt Vesuvius*.

Once you've finished in the museum, the **Parco di Capodimonte** – the palace's 130-hectare estate – provides a much-needed breath of fresh air.

In 2017, the museum launched a convenient, hourly shuttle bus service that runs between central Naples and the museum. Buses depart from Piazza Trieste e Trento (opposite Teatro San Carlo) and stop outside the Museo Archeologico Nazionale and Catacombe di San Gennaro en route. Return tickets (adult/reduced €12/6) include museum entry and can be purchased directly on the bus.

★ Cimitero delle Fontanelle CEMETERY
(☑ 081 1970 3197; www.cimiterofontanelle.com; Via Fontanelle 80; ⊙ 10am-5pm; ⊡ C51 to Via Fontanelle) **FREE** Holding about eight million human bones, the ghoulish Fontanelle Cemetery was first used during the 1656 plague, before becoming Naples' main burial site during the 1837 cholera epidemic. At the end of the 19th century it became a hotspot for the *anime pezzentelle* (poor souls) cult, in which locals adopted skulls and prayed for their souls. Lack of information at the site makes joining a tour much more rewarding; reputable outfits include Cooperativa Sociale Onlus 'La Paranza'. Avoid guides offering tours at the entrance.

⌒ Tours

★ Cooperativa Sociale Onlus 'La Paranza' TOURS
(☑ 081 744 37 14; www.catacombedinapoli.it; Via Capodimonte 13; ⊙ information point 10am-5pm Mon-Sat, to 2pm Sun; ⊡ R4, 178 to Via Capodimonte) Runs tours of the Catacombe di San Gennaro and a fascinating walking tour called Il Miglio Sacro (The Holy Mile), which explores the earthy Sanità district. The walking tour must be pre-booked; see website for details. The ticket office is to the left of the Chiesa di Madre di Buon Consiglio (Via Capodimonte 13).

Napoli Sotterranea ARCHAEOLOGICAL SITE
(Underground Naples; Map p658; ☑ 081 29 69 44; www.napolisotterranea.org; Piazza San Gaetano 68; adult/reduced €10/8; ⊙ English tours 10am, noon, 2pm, 4pm & 6pm; ⊡ E1, E2 to Via Duomo) This evocative guided tour leads you 40m below street level to explore Naples' ancient labyrinth of aqueducts, passages and cisterns.

The passages were originally hewn by the Greeks to extract tufa stone used in construction and to channel water from Mt Vesuvius. Extended by the Romans, the network of conduits and cisterns was more recently used as an air-raid shelter in WWII. Part of the tour takes place by candlelight via extremely narrow passages – not suitable for expanded girths!

✯ Festivals & Events

Maggio dei Monumenti
CULTURAL
(⊘ May) A month-long cultural feast, with a bounty of concerts, performances, exhibitions, guided tours and other events across Naples.

Napoli Teatro Festival
THEATRE
(www.napoliteatrofestival.it; ⊘ Jun/Jul) One month of local and international theatre and performance art, staged in conventional and unconventional venues

Wine & The City
WINE
(www.wineandthecity.it; ⊘ May) A three-week celebration of regional *vino*, with free wine tastings and cultural events in palaces, museums, boutiques and eateries throughout the city.

Festa di San Gennaro
RELIGIOUS
The faithful flock to the Duomo to witness the miraculous liquefaction of San Gennaro's blood on the Saturday before the first Sunday in May. Repeat performances take place on 19 September and 16 December.

🛏 Sleeping

Where to slumber? The *centro storico* is studded with important churches and sights, artisan studios and student-packed bars. Seafront Santa Lucia delivers grand hotels, while sceney Chiaia is best for fashionable shops and *aperitivo* bars. The lively, laundry-strung Quartieri Spagnoli is within walking distance of all three neighbourhoods.

B&B Arte e Musei
B&B €
(Map p658; ☑ 333 6962469; www.facebook. com/bnbarteemusei; Via Salvator Rosa 345; s €40-50, d €60-100, tr €90-120; ❉ 🖥; Ⓜ Museo, Cavour) Close to the Museo Archeolgico Nazionale, this quiet, artful B&B is adorned with Neapolitan-themed paintings and ceramics by gracious owner and artist Federica. Both the double and triple room include a small balcony and spotless en suite bathroom, while the smaller single room (with double bed) has its private bathroom in the hallway.

All three simple, tasteful rooms are whitewashed and clean, with high ceilings and upbeat accents in pistachio and blue. Breakfast is served at a communal table in the dining room, set with colourful crockery made by Federica herself.

Nardones 48
APARTMENT €
(Map p662; ☑ 338 8818998; www.nardones48. it; Via Nardones 48; small apt €65-74, large apt €85-140; ❉ 🖥; 🚇 R2 to Via San Carlo) White-on-white Nardones 48 serves up seven smart mini-apartments in a historic Quartieri Spagnoli building. The five largest apartments, each with mezzanine bedroom, accommodate up to four; the two smallest, each with sofa bed, accommodate up to two. Three apartments boast a panoramic terrace, and all have modern kitchenette, flat-screen TV and contemporary bathroom with spacious shower.

Stays of one week or longer enjoy discounted rates and complimentary laundry service, and the apartment offers nearby parking (€20 per 24 hours).

Casa Latina
B&B €
(Map p658; ☑ 338 9264453; www.casalatina.it; Vico Cinquesanti 47; s €40 55, d €55 75, tr €70 90, q €85-100; ❉ 🖥; Ⓜ Piazza Cavour, Museo) Creativity and style flow through this crisp new B&B, accented with eclectic lighting, boho photography, a fully equipped kitchen and a tranquil terrace. All four rooms are soothing and contemporary, with original architectural detailing and fetching bathrooms with recycled terracotta basins. One upper-level room features a tatami style bed and banquettes, the latter transforming into extra bed space (ideal for young families).

Cerasiello B&B
B&B €
(☑ 081 033 09 77, 338 9264453; www.cerasiello. it; Via Supportico Lopez 20; s €40-85, d €60-100, tr €75-110, q €90-125; ❉ 🖥; Ⓜ Piazza Cavour, Museo) This gorgeous B&B consists of four rooms with private bathrooms, an enchanting communal terrace and an ethno-chic look melding Neapolitan art with North African furnishings. The stylish kitchen offers a fabulous view of the Certosa di San Martino, a view shared by all rooms (or their bathroom) except Fuoco (Fire), which looks out at a beautiful church cupola.

Although technically in the Sanità district, the B&B is a short walk from Naples' *centro storico* (historic centre). Bring €0.20 for the lift.

Sui Tetti di Napoli
B&B €

(Map p662; ☑338 9264453, 081 033 09 77; www.
suitettidinapoli.net; Vico Figuerelle a Montecalvario
6; s €35-60, d €45-80, tr €60-95, q €80-105; ✳🔁;
Ⓜ Toledo) A block away from Via Toledo, this
well-priced B&B is more like four apartments atop a thigh-toning stairwell. While
two apartments share a small terrace, the
rooftop option boasts its own, complete
with mesmerising views. Recently refurbished, all apartments include a kitchenette
(the cheapest two share a kitchen), simple,
crisp, modern furnishings and comfy, new,
memory-foam mattresses.

★Atelier Ines
B&B €€

(☑349 4433422; www.atelierinesgallery.com; Via
Cristallini 138; d €125-150; ✳🔁) A stylish, eclectic oasis in the heart of the earthy Sanità district, this three-suite B&B is a homage to the
late Neapolitan sculptor and designer Annibale Oste, whose workshop shares a leafy
courtyard. Everything from the lamps and
spiral towel racks to the one-of-a-kind sculptural bedheads are Oste's whimsical designs,
complimented by heavenly mattresses, a
choice of pillows, and Vietri-ceramic bathrooms with satisfying hot water.

Multilingual host Ines and her partner
Vincenzo (Annibale's son) are gracious and
passionate about their city, while breakfast
is a mostly made-from-scratch affair, with
house-made jams, yoghurt and cakes, as
well as farm-fresh scrambled eggs and organic fruit. Guests are welcome to explore
Oste's workshop and archive.

★La Ciliegina
Lifestyle Hotel
BOUTIQUE HOTEL €€

(Map p662; ☑081 1971 8800; www.cilieginahotel.
it; Via PE Imbriani 30; d €160-300, junior ste €200-
400; ✳🔁; Ⓜ Municipio) An easy walk from
the hydrofoil terminal, this chic, contemporary slumber spot is a hit with fashion-
conscious urbanites. Spacious white rooms
are splashed with blue and red accents, each
with top-of-the-range Hästens beds, flat-
screen TVs and marble-clad bathrooms with
a water-jet Jacuzzi shower (one junior suite
has a Jacuzzi tub).

Breakfast in bed, or on the rooftop terrace, which comes with sunbeds, hot tub
and a view of Vesuvius. Complimentary iPad
use is a nice touch.

★Hotel Piazza Bellini
BOUTIQUE HOTEL €€

(Map p658; ☑081 45 17 32; www.hotelpiazza
bellini.com; Via Santa Maria di Costantinopoli 101;

d €58-170; ✳@🔁; Ⓜ Dante) Only steps from
buzzing Piazza Bellini, this sharp, contemporary hotel occupies a 16th-century *palazzo* (mansion), its mint white spaces spiked
with original majolica tiles and the work of
emerging artists. Rooms offer pared-back
cool, with designer fittings, chic bathrooms
and mirror frames drawn straight onto the
wall. Rooms on the 5th and 6th floors feature panoramic terraces. Check the hotel
website for decent discounts.

Decumani Hotel
de Charme
BOUTIQUE HOTEL €€

(Map p658; ☑081 551 81 88; www.decumani.it;
Via San Giovanni Maggiore Pignatelli 15; s €99-124,
d €99-164; ✳@🔁; Ⓜ Università) This classic
boutique hotel occupies the former *palazzo* of Cardinal Sisto Riario Sforza, the last
bishop of the Bourbon kingdom. Its simple, stylish 42 rooms feature high ceilings,
parquet floors, 19th-century furniture, and
modern bathrooms with spacious showers.
Deluxe rooms crank up the *dolce vita* with
personal hot tubs. The *pièce de résistance*,
however, is the property's breathtaking
baroque salon.

Grand Hotel Vesuvio
HOTEL €€€

(Map p662; ☑081 764 00 44; www.vesuvio.it; Via
Partenope 45; s/d €280/310; ✳@🔁; 🚍128 to Via
Santa Lucia) Known for hosting legends – past
guests include Rita Hayworth and Hum-
phrey Bogart – this five-star heavyweight is
a decadent melange of dripping chandeliers,
period antiques and opulent rooms. Count
your lucky stars while drinking a martini at
the rooftop restaurant.

✖ Eating

Naples is one of Italy's gastronomic darlings, and the bonus of a bayside setting
makes for some seriously memorable meals.
While white linen, candlelight and €50 bills
are readily available, some of the best bites
await in the city's spit-and-sawdust trattorias, where two courses and house wine can
cost under €20. Even cheaper is Naples'
plethora of top-notch pizzerias and *friggi-
torie* (fried-food kiosks). On the downside,
many eateries close for two weeks in August,
so call ahead if visiting then.

★Salumeria
BISTRO €

(Map p658; ☑081 1936 4649; www.salumeria
upnea.it; Via San Giovanni Maggiore Pignatelli 34/35;
sandwiches from €4.90, charcuterie platters from €8,
meals around €22; ⊗noon-5.30pm & 7pm-midnight

Mon, Tue & Thu, 7pm-midnight Wed, 7pm-12.30am Fri, 10am-12.30am Sat, 10am-midnight Sun; ⓢ; ⓂDante) Small producers, local ingredients and contemporary takes on provincial Campanian recipes drive bistro-inspired Salumeria. Nibble on quality charcuterie and cheeses or fill up on artisanal *panini*, hamburgers and daily specials that might include pasta with a rich *ragù napoletano* sauce slow-cooked over two days. Even the ketchup here is made in-house, using DOP Piennolo tomatoes from Vesuvius.

On weekend mornings, don't miss the *polacca*, a cornetto-like pastry filled with custard and cherries. Libations include Campanian craft beers and the venue hosts rotating exhibitions of contemporary, Neapolitan-themed art.

★ Pizzeria Starita
PIZZA €

(ⓩ 081 557 36 82; Via Materdei 28; pizzas from €3.50; ⓉⒽnoon-3.30pm & 7pm-midnight Tue-Sun; ⓂMaterdei) The giant fork and ladle hanging on the wall at this historic pizzeria were used by Sophia Loren in *L'Oro di Napoli*, and the kitchen made the *pizze fritte* sold by the actress in the film. While the 60-plus pizza varieties include a tasty *fiorilli e zucchine* (zucchini, zucchini flowers and *provola*), our allegiance remains to its classic *marinara*.

★ Muu Muuzzarella Lounge
NEAPOLITAN €

(Map p662; ⓩ 081 40 53 70; www.muumuuzzarella lounge.It; Vico II Alabardieri 7; dishes €7-16; ⓉⒽ12.30pm-midnight Tue-Sun; ⓢ; ⓆC24 to Riviera di Chiaia) Pimped with milking-bucket lights and cow-hide patterned cushions, playful Muu is all about super-fresh Campanian mozzarella, from cheese and charcuterie platters to creative dishes like buffalo bocconcini with creamy pesto and crunchy apple. Leave room for the chef's secret recipe white-chocolate cheesecake, best paired with a glass of Guappa (buffalo-milk liqueur).

Serafino
SICILIAN €

(Map p658; ⓩ 081 557 14 33; Via dei Tribunali 44; arancini €2.50, cannoli €2.50; ⓉⒽ11.30am-10pm) A veritable porthole to Sicily, this takeaway stand peddles authentic island street food. Savoury bites include various types of *arancini* (deep-fried rice balls), among them *al ragù* (with meat sauce) and *alla Norma* (with fried eggplant and ricotta). The real reason to head here, however, is for the crisp, flawless cannoli, filled fresh with silky Sicilian ricotta and sprinkled with pistachio crumbs. Bliss.

Pizzeria Gino Sorbillo
PIZZA €

(Map p658; ⓩ 081 44 66 43; www.sorbillo.it; Via dei Tribunali 32; pizzas from €3; ⓉⒽnoon-3.30pm & 7-11.30pm Mon-Thu, to midnight Fri & Sat; ⓢ; ⓂDante) Day in, day out, this cult-status pizzeria is besieged by hungry hordes. While debate may rage over whether Gino Sorbillo's pizzas are the best in town, there's no doubt that his giant, wood-fired discs – made using organic flour and tomatoes – will have you licking fingertips and whiskers. Head in super early or prepare to wait.

Pintauro
PASTRIES €

(Map p662; ⓩ 081 41 73 39; Via Toledo 275; sfogliatelle €2; ⓉⒽ9am-8pm, closed mid-Jul–early Sep; ⓆR2 to Via San Carlo, ⓂMunicipio) Of Neapolitan *dolci* (sweets), the cream of the crop is the *sfogliatella*, a shell of flaky pastry stuffed with creamy, scented ricotta. This local institution has been selling *sfogliatelle* since the early 1800s, when its founder supposedly brought them to Naples from their culinary birthplace on the Amalfi Coast. The pastry comes in two versions: *frolla* (shortcrust pastry) and *riccia* (filo-style pastry).

★ Benvenuti al Sud
NEAPOLITAN €€

(ⓩ 081 1934 9334; Corso Vittorio Emanuele 9; pizzas from €4.50, meals around €25; ⓉⒽnoon-3.30pm & 6.30pm-midnight Tue-Sat, noon-3.30pm Sun; ⓂMergellina) Its walls splashed with technicolour murals of market produce and Neapolitan vistas, this friendly, upbeat pizzeria-cum-trattoria flips great Neapolitan pie, from simple *marinara* (tomato, oregano, garlic and olive oil) to lesser-known classic *montanara*, which sees the base lightly fried before being topped and baked in the oven for a lovely sheen and crackle. Beyond the pizzas are some fantastic seafood pasta dishes.

★ Eccellenze Campane
NEAPOLITAN €€

(ⓩ 081 20 36 57; www.eccellenzecampane.it; Via Benedetto Brin 49; pizza from €6, meals around €30; ⓉⒽcomplex 7am-11pm Sun-Fri, to 12.30am Sat, restaurants 12.30-3.30pm & 7.30-11pm Sun-Fri, to 12.30am Sat; ⓢ; Ⓠ192, 460, 472, 475) This is Naples' answer to Turin-based food emporium Eataly, an impressive, contemporary showcase for top-notch Campanian comestibles. The sprawling space is divided into various dining and shopping sections, offering everything from beautifully charred pizzas and light *fritture* (fried snacks) to finer-dining seafood, lust-inducing pastries, craft beers and no shortage of take-home pantry treats. A must for gastronomes.

★ **L'Ebbrezza di Noè** NEAPOLITAN €€
(Map p662; ☑ 081 40 01 04; www.lebbrezza
dinoe.com; Vico Vetriera 9; meals around €37;
⊙ 6pm-midnight Tue-Thu, to 1am Fri & Sat, noon-
3pm Sun; ☎; Ⓜ Piazza Amedeo) A wine shop by
day, 'Noah's Drunkenness' transforms into
an intimate culinary hotspot by night. Slip
inside for *vino* and conversation at the bar,
or settle into one of the bottle-lined dining
rooms for seductive, market-driven dishes
such as house special *paccheri fritti* (fried
pasta stuffed with eggplant and served with
fresh basil and a rich tomato sauce).

Topping it off are circa 2800 wines, artfully selected by sommelier owner Luca Di
Leva. Book ahead.

★ **Ristorantino dell'Avvocato** NEAPOLITAN €€
(Map p662; ☑ 081 032 00 47; www.ilristorantino
dellavvocato.it; Via Santa Lucia 115-117; meals
€40-45; ⊙ noon-3pm daily, also 7-11pm Tue-Sat;
☎; ☐ 128 to Via Santa Lucia) This elegant yet
welcoming restaurant is a favourite of Neapolitan gastronomes. Apple of their eye is
affable lawyer turned head chef Raffaele
Cardillo, whose passion for Campania's
culinary heritage merges with a knack for
subtle, refreshing twists – think coffee pa-
pardelle served with mullet ragù.

The degustation menus (€45 to €60) are
good value, as is the weekday 'three courses
on a plate' lunch special. Book ahead Thursday to Saturday.

La Taverna di Santa Chiara NEAPOLITAN €€
(Map p658; ☑ 081 048 49 08; Via Santa Chiara
6; meals €25; ⊙ 1-2.30pm & 8-10.30pm Mon, Wed
& Thu, to 3pm Fri-Sun, 8-10.30pm Mon-Sat; ☎;
Ⓜ Dante) Gragnano pasta, Agerola pork, *con-
cato romano*: this modest, two-level eatery is
healthily obsessed with small, local producers and Slow Food ingredients. The result is a
beautiful, seasonal journey across Campania.

For an inspiring overview, order the
rustic *antipasto di terra* (an antipasto of
cheese and cured meats), then tuck into
lesser-known dishes like *genovese di polipo*
(a rich onion and octopus pasta dish) with
wine from a lesser-known regional winemaker or a Campanian craft brew.

Trattoria San Ferdinando NEAPOLITAN €€
(Map p662; ☑ 081 42 19 64; Via Nardones 117;
meals €25-32; ⊙ 12.30-3.30pm Mon-Sat, 7.30-
11pm Tue-Fri; ☐ R2 to Via San Carlo, Ⓜ Municipio)
Hung with theatre posters, cosy San Ferdinando pulls in well-spoken theatre types
and intellectuals. For a Neapolitan taste

trip, ask for a rundown of the day's antipasti
and choose your favourites for an *antipasto
misto* (mixed antipasto). Seafood standouts
include a delicate *seppia ripieno* (stuffed
squid), while the homemade desserts make
for a satisfying dénouement.

🍷 Drinking & Nightlife

Neapolitans aren't big drinkers, and in the
centro storico many people simply buy a
bottle of beer from the nearest bar and hang
out on the streets. Here, drinking hotspots
include Piazza Bellini and Calata Trinità
Maggiore off Piazza del Gesù Nuovo, where
a high concentration of students, artists
and bohemians lend an energetic, live-and-
let-live vibe. Those after fashion-conscious
prosecco sessions should aim for Chiaia's
sleek bars, famed for their *aperitivo* spreads
(gourmet nibbles for the price of a drink,
nightly from around 6.30pm to 9.30pm).
Popular strips include Via Ferrigni, Via
Bisignano and Vico Belledonne a Chiaia.

★ **Ba-Bar** BAR
(Map p662; ☑ 081 764 35 25; www.ba-bar.it; Via
Santa Lucia 169; ☐ 128 to Via Santa Lucia) Don't be
fooled by the faux British-pub exterior. With
its muted colour palette, soft lighting and subtle nautical motif, Ba-Bar sets a sophisticated
scene for well-crafted cocktails made using
fresh ingredients. A short, detail-orientated
food menu includes the likes of sesame
baguette stuffed with Campanian *provola*
cheese, *culatello* (air-cured ham) and hazelnuts, not to mention regional staple *parmigiana di melanzane* (eggplant parmigiana).

★ **Donna Romita** BAR
(Map p658; ☑ 081 1851 5074; www.donnaromi
ta.it; Vico Donnaromita 14; ⊙ 6pm-2am Mon-Sat,
from 11am Sun; ☎) Part of Napoli's new guard
of genuinely hip, on-point drinking holes,
Donna Romita eschews video screens, un-
flattering lighting and tacky decor for an architecturally designed combo of minimalist
concrete, industrial lighting, sculptural furniture and well-crafted drinks. Not surprisingly, it's a hit with arty, cosmopolitan *centro
storico* (historic centre) types.

Food options include artisan cheeses and
salumi (charcuterie), and there's a sleek dining room downstairs serving gorgeous, locavore fare with competent modern tweaks.

Caffè Gambrinus CAFE
(Map p662; ☑ 081 417 75 82; www.grancaffegambrinus.
com; Via Chiaia 1-2; ⊙ 7am-1am Sun-Thu, to 2am Fri

& Sat; R2 to Via San Carlo, MMunicipio) Grand, chandeliered Gambrinus is Naples' oldest and most venerable cafe. Oscar Wilde knocked back a few here and Mussolini had some of the rooms shut to keep out left-wing intellectuals. The prices may be steep, but the *aperitivo* nibbles are decent and sipping a *spritz* or a *cioccolata calda* (hot chocolate) in its belle époque rooms is something worth savouring.

Spazio Nea
CAFE

(Map p658; 081 45 13 58; www.spazionea.it; Via Constantinopoli 53; 9am-2am, to 3am Fri & Sat; ; MDante) Aptly skirting bohemian Piazza Bellini, this whitewashed gallery features its own cafe-bar speckled with books, flowers, cultured crowds and alfresco seating at the bottom of a baroque staircase. Eye up exhibitions of contemporary Italian and foreign art, then kick back with a *caffè* or a *spritz*. Check Nea's Facebook page for upcoming readings, live music gigs or DJ sets. Bites include bountiful salads.

☆ Entertainment

Although Naples is no London, Milan or Melbourne on the entertainment front, it does offer some top after-dark options, from opera and ballet to thought-provoking theatre and cultured classical ensembles. To see what's on, scan daily papers like *Corriere del Mezzogiorno* or *La Repubblica* (Naples edition), click onto www.napoliunplugged.com, or ask at the tourist office. In smaller venues you can usually buy your ticket at the door; for bigger events try the box office inside **Feltrinelli** (Map p662; 081 032 23 62; www.azzurroservice.net; Piazza dei Martiri 23; 11am-2pm & 3-8pm Mon-Sat; C24 to Piazza dei Martiri), or **Box Office** (Map p662; 081 551 91 88; www.boxofficenapoli.it; Galleria Umberto I 17; 9.30am-8pm Mon-Fri, 10am-1.30pm & 4.30-8pm Sat; R2 to Piazza Trieste e Trento, MMunicipio).

★ Teatro San Carlo
OPERA, BALLET

(Map p662; 081 797 23 31; www.teatrosancarlo.it; Via San Carlo 98; box office 10am-5.30pm Mon-Sat, to 2pm Sun; R2 to Via San Carlo, MMunicipio) San Carlo's opera season usually runs from November or December to June, with occasional summer performances. Reckon on €50 for a place in the sixth tier, €100 for a seat in the stalls or – if you're under 30 (with ID) – €30 for a place in a side box. The ballet season generally runs from late October to April or early May. Ballet tickets range from €35 to €80, with €20 tickets for those under 30.

★ Lanificio 25
LIVE MUSIC

(Map p658; www.lanificio25.it; Piazza Enrico De Nicola 46; free-€10; varies; MGaribaldi) This Bourbon-era wool factory and 15th-century cloister is now a burgeoning party and culture hub, strung with coloured lights and awash with video projections. Live music and performances are the mainstay, ranging from cabaret acts to mostly Italian outfits playing indie, rock, world music and electronica to an easy, arty, cosmopolitan crowd. Check the website or Facebook page for upcoming events.

★ Stadio San Paolo
FOOTBALL

(Piazzale Vincenzo Tecchio; MNapoli Campi Flegrei) Naples' football team, Napoli, is the third most supported in Italy after Juventus and Milan, and watching it play in the country's third-largest stadium is a rush. The season runs from late August to late May; seats cost from around €20 to €100. Tickets are available from selected tobacconists, the agency inside Feltrinelli, or Box Office; bring photo ID. On match days, tickets are also available at the stadium itself.

Centro di Musica Antica Pietà de' Turchini
CLASSICAL MUSIC

(Map p662; 081 40 23 95; www.turchini.it; Via Santa Caterina da Siena 38; Centrale to Corso Vittorio Emanuele) Classical-music buffs are in for a treat at this beautiful deconsecrated church, an evocative setting for concerts of mostly 17th- to 19th-century Neapolitan works. Tickets usually cost €10 (reduced €7), and upcoming concerts are listed on the venue's website. Note that some concerts are held at the elegant Palazzo Zevallos Stigliano (p665) on Via Toledo.

🛍 Shopping

Bottega 21
FASHION & ACCESSORIES

(Map p658; 081 033 55 42; www.bottegaventuno.it; Vico San Domenico Maggiore 21; 9.30am-8pm Mon-Sat) Top-notch Tuscan leather and traditional, handcrafted methods translate into coveted, contemporary leather goods for sale at Bottega 21. Block colours and clean, simple designs underline the range, which includes stylish totes, handbags, backpacks and duffel bags, as well as wallets and coin purses, unisex belts, notebook covers and tobacco pouches. A solid choice for those who prefer to shop local and independent.

La Scarabattola
ARTS & CRAFTS

(Map p658; ☑ 081 29 17 35; www.lascarabattola.it; Via dei Tribunali 50; ⊙ 10.30am-2pm & 3.30-7.30pm Mon-Fri, 10am-6pm Sat; ☐ E1, E2 to Via Duomo) Not only do La Scarabattola's hand-made sculptures of *magi* (wise men), devils and Neapolitan folk figures constitute Jerusalem's official Christmas crèche, the artisan studio's fans include fashion designer Stefano Gabbana and Spanish royalty. Figurines aside, sleek ceramic creations (think Pulcinella-inspired place-card holders) inject Neapolitan folklore with refreshing contemporary style.

E. Marinella
FASHION & ACCESSORIES

(Map p662; ☑ 081 764 32 65; www.marinella napoli.it; Via Riviera di Chiaia 287; ⊙ 7am-8pm Mon-Sat, 9am-1pm Sun; ☐ C25 to Riviera di Chiaia, C24 to Piazza dei Martiri) One-time favourite of Luchino Visconti and Aristotle Onassis, this pocket-sized, vintage boutique is *the* place for prêt-à-porter and made-to-measure silk ties in striking patterns and hues. Match them with an irresistible selection of luxury accessories, including shoes, vintage colognes, and scarves for female style queens.

❶ Information

MEDICAL

Loreto Mare Hospital (Ospedale Maria di Loreto Nuovo; ☑ 081 254 21 11; www.asl napoli1centro.it/818; Via Vespucci 26; ☐ 154) Central-city hospital with an emergency department.

Pharmacy (Stazione Centrale; ⊙ 7am-9.30pm Mon-Sat, 8am-9pm Sun) Pharmacy inside the main train station.

POST

Main Post Office (Map p662; ☑ 081 552 44 10; www.posteitaliane.it; Piazza Matteotti 2) Naples' curvaceous main post office is famous for its Fascist-era architecture.

TOURIST INFORMATION

Tourist Information Office (Map p658; ☑ 081 26 87 79; Stazione Centrale; ⊙ 9am-8pm; ☐ Garibaldi) Tourist office inside Stazione Centrale (Central Station).

Tourist Information Office (Map p658; ☑ 081 551 27 01; www.inaples.it; Piazza del Gesù Nuovo 7; ⊙ 9am-5pm Mon-Sat, to 1pm Sun; ☐ Dante) Tourist office in the *centro storico*.

Tourist Information Office (Map p662; ☑ 081 40 23 94; www.inaples.it; Via San Carlo 9; ⊙ 9am-5pm Mon-Sat, to 1pm Sun; ☐ R2 to Via San Carlo, ☐ Municipio) Tourist office at Galleria Umberto I, directly opposite Teatro San Carlo.

❶ Getting There & Away

AIR

Naples International Airport (Capodichino; ☑ 081 789 62 59; www.aeroportodinapoli.it), 7km northeast of the city centre, is southern Italy's main airport, linking Naples with most Italian and several other European cities, as well as New York. Budget carrier easyJet operates several routes to/from Capodichino, including London, Paris, Brussels and Berlin.

BOAT

Fast ferries and hydrofoils for Capri, Ischia, Procida and Sorrento depart from **Molo Beverello** (Map p662) in front of Castel Nuovo; hydrofoils for Capri, Ischia and Procida also sail from Mergellina.

Ferries for Sicily, the Aeolian Islands and Sardinia sail from **Molo Angioino** (Map p662) (right beside Molo Beverello) and neighbouring **Calata Porta di Massa** (Map p662).

BUS

Most national and international buses leave from **Terminal Bus Metropark** (Map p658; ☑ 800 65 00 06; Corso Arnaldo Lucci; ☐ Garibaldi), located on the southern side of Stazione Centrale. The bus station is home to **Biglietteria Vecchione** (☑ 331 88969217, 081 563 03 20; www.biglietteriavecchione.it; ⊙ 6.30am-9.30pm Mon-Fri, to 7.30pm Sat & Sun), a ticket agency selling national and international bus tickets.

Terminal Bus Metropark serves numerous bus companies offering regional and inter-regional services, among them **FlixBus** (www.flixbus.com). The bus stop for **SITA Sud** (☑ 344 1031070; www.sitasudtrasporti.it) services to the Amalfi Coast is just around the corner on Via Galileo Ferraris (in front of the hulking Istituto Nazionale della Previdenza Sociale office building).

CAR & MOTORCYCLE

Naples is on the north–south Autostrada del Sole, the A1 (north to Rome and Milan) and the A3 (south to Salerno and Reggio di Calabria).

TRAIN

Naples is southern Italy's rail hub and on the main Milan–Palermo line, with good connections to other Italian cities and towns.

National rail company **Trenitalia** (☑ 892 021; www.trenitalia.com) runs regular services to Rome (2nd class €12 to €45, 70 minutes to three hours, up to 69 daily). High-speed private rail company **Italo** (☑ 892 020; www.italotreno.it) also runs daily services to Rome (2nd class €15 to €39, 70 minutes, up to 17 daily). Most Italo services stop at Roma Termini and Roma Tiburtina stations.

OPLONTIS

Buried beneath the unappealing streets of Torre Annunziata, **Oplontis** (☑ 081 857 53 47; www.pompeiisites.org; Via dei Sepolcri, Torre Annunziata; adult/reduced incl Boscoreale & Stabiae €5.50/2.75, incl Pompeii & Herculaneum €22/12; ⊘ 9am-7.30pm, last entry 6pm Apr-Oct, to 5pm, last entry 3.30pm Nov-Mar; ⊠ Circumvesuviana to Torre Annunziata) was once a blue-ribbon seafront suburb under the administrative control of Pompeii. First discovered in the 18th century, only two of its houses have been unearthed, and only one, Villa Poppaea, is open to the public. This villa is a magnificent example of an *otium* villa (a residential building used for rest and recreation), thought to have belonged to Sabina Poppaea, Nero's second wife.

Particularly outstanding are the richly coloured 1st-century wall paintings in the *triclinium* (dining room) and *calidarium* (hot bathroom) in the west wing. Marking the villa's eastern border is a garden with an envy-inducing swimming pool (17m by 61m). The villa is a straightforward 300m walk from Torre Annunziata Circumvesuviana train station.

ℹ Getting Around

BUS

A much cheaper alternative to a taxi, airport shuttle **Alibus** (☑ 800 639525; www.anm.it) connects the airport to **Via Novara** (Map p658; Corso Novara) (in front of the Deutsche Bank branch opposite Stazione Centrale) and the ferry port **Molo Angioino** (Map p662) (€4, 45 minutes, every 15 to 20 minutes). Buy tickets on board or from selected tobacconists.

ANM (☑ 800 639525; www.anm.it) buses serve the city and its periphery. Many routes pass through Piazza Garibaldi.

FUNICULAR

Three services connect central Naples to Vomero, while a fourth connects Mergellina to Posillipo.

Funiculare Centrale (www.anm.it; ⊘ 6.30am-10pm Mon & Tue, to 12.30am Wed-Sun & holidays) Travels from Piazzetta Augusteo to Piazza Fuga. Expected to reopen in early 2018.

Funiculare di Chiaia (www.anm.it; ⊘ 7am-10pm Wed & Thu, to 12.30am Sun-Tue, to 2am Fri & Sat) Travels from Via del Parco Margherita to Via Domenico Cimarosa.

Funiculare di Montesanto (⊘ 7am-10pm) Travels from Piazza Montesanto to Via Raffaele Morghen.

Funiculare di Mergellina (⊘ 7am-10pm) Connects the waterfront at Via Mergellina with Via Manzoni.

METRO

Metro Line 1 (Linea 1; www.anm.it) runs from Garibaldi (Stazione Centrale) to Vomero and the northern suburbs via the city centre. Useful stops include Duomo and Università (southern edge of the *centro storico*), Municipio (hydrofoil and ferry terminals), Toledo (Via Toledo and Quartieri Spagnoli), Dante (western edge of the *centro storico*) and Museo (National Archaeological Museum).

Metro Line 2 (Linea 2; www.trenitalia.com) runs from Gianturco to Garibaldi (Stazione Centrale) and on to Pozzuoli. Useful stops include Piazza Cavour (La Sanità and northern edge of *centro storico*), Piazza Amedeo (Chiaia) and Mergellina (Mergellina ferry terminal). Change between lines 1 and 2 at Garibaldi or Piazza Cavour (known as Museo on Line 1).

Metro Line 6 (Linea 6; www.anm.it) is a light-rail service running between Mergellina and Mostra.

TAXI

Official fares from the airport are as follows: €23 to a seafront hotel or to Mergellina hydrofoil terminal; €19 to Piazza del Municipio or Molo Beverello ferry terminal; and €16 to Stazione Centrale and the *centro storico* (historic centre).

Book a taxi by calling any of the following companies:

Consortaxi (☑ 081 22 22; www.consortaxi.com)

Taxi Napoli (☑ 081 88 88; www.taxinapoli.it)

Radio Taxi La Partenope (☑ 081 01 01; www.radiotaxilapartenope.it)

BAY OF NAPLES

Capri

☑ 081 / POP 14,200

Capri's fabled beauty and refined hedonism has charmed them all, from Roman rulers and Russian revolutionaries to Hollywood legends. It's a perfect microcosm of Mediterranean appeal, a fusion of glittering grottoes and coves, Roman ruins and chi-chi piazzas.

Capri

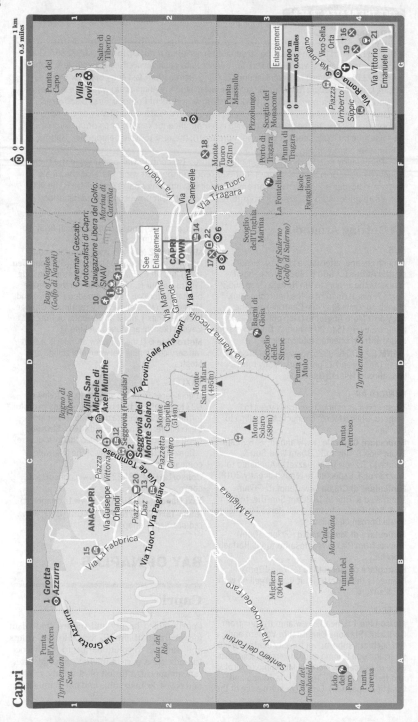

Tyrrhenian Sea

Punta dell'Arcera

1 Grotta Azzurra ⊙

Via Grotta Azzurra

Cala del Rio

Cala del Tombesiello

Sentiero dei Fortini

Via Nuove del Faro

Lido del Faro

Punta Carena

Punta del Thono

Cala Marmolata

Punta Ventroso

Via Migliera

Migliera (304m)

Via Tuoro Via Pagliaro

ANACAPRI

15

Via La Fabbrica

Piazza Diaz 20 13

Via de Tommaso

Piazza Vittoria 23 12 2

Via Giuseppe Orlandi

4 Villa San Michele di Axel Munthe ⊙

Seggiovia del Monte Solaro

Seggiovia (Funicular)

Monte Cappello (514m)

Piazzetta Cimitero

Monte Solaro (589m)

Monte Santa Maria (495m)

Bagno di Tiberio

Villa San Michele di Axel Munthe

Via Provinciale Anacapri

Via Marina Grande

Via Marina Piccola

Via Roma

Bay of Naples (Golfo di Napoli)

Caremar; Gescab; Motoscafisti di Capri; Navigazione Libera del Golfo; SNAV

10

11

See Enlargement

Marina di Guterola

Via Tiberio

Via Camerelle

Via Tuoro

Via Tragara

14 22

CAPRI TOWN

17 8 6

Bagni di Gioia

Scoglio delle Sirene

Punta di Mulo

Tyrrhenian Sea

Gulf of Salerno (Golfo di Salerno)

Scoglio dell'Unghia Marina

La Fontelina

Isole Faraglioni

Punta di Tragara

Porto di Tragara

Scoglio del Monacone

Pizzolungo

Punta Massullo

Monte Tuoro (261m)

18

5

Punta del Capo

Salto di Tiberio

Villa Jovis ⊙ 3

Punta del Capo

Via Longano

Vico Sella Orta

19 16

21

7

9

Via Roma

Via Vittorio Emanuele III

Piazza Umberto I/ Sippic

Piazza Umberto I

Capri

Already inhabited in the Palaeolithic pe-riod, the island was briefly occupied by the Greeks before Emperor Augustus made it his private playground and Tiberius retired here in AD 27. Its modern incarnation as a tourist centre dates from the early 20th century.

It's also a favourite day-trip destination and a summer favourite of holidaying VIPs. Inevitably, the two main centres, Capri Town and its uphill rival Anacapri, are almost en-tirely given over to tourism, with the high prices that follow. But explore beyond the designer boutiques and cafes and you'll find that Capri retains an unspoilt charm, with grand villas, overgrown vegetable plots, sun-bleached, peeling stucco and banks of bril-liantly coloured bougainvillea.

◎ Sights

◎ Capri Town & Around

With its whitewashed stone buildings and tiny, car-free streets, Capri Town exudes a cinematic air. A diminutive model of upmar-ket Mediterranean chic, it's a well-tended playground of luxury hotels, expensive bars, smart restaurants and high-end bou-tiques. In summer the centre swells with crowds of camera-wielding day trippers and yacht-owning playboys (and girls), but don't be put off from exploring the atmospheric and ancient side streets, where the crowds quickly thin. The walk west out of town to Villa Jovis is especially wonderful.

★ **Villa Jovis**   RUINS
(Jupiter's Villa; Via A Maiuri; adult/reduced €4/2; ◎10am-6pm Wed-Mon Jun, to 7pm Jul & Aug, re-duced hours rest of year, closed Jan–mid-Mar) A 45-minute walk east of Capri along Via Ti-berio, Villa Jovis was the largest and most sumptuous of the island's 12 Roman villas and Tiberius' main Capri residence. A vast pleasure complex, now reduced to ruins, it famously pandered to the emperor's sup-posedly debauched tastes, and included im-perial quarters and extensive bathing areas set in dense gardens and woodland.

The villa's spectacular location posed ma-jor headaches for Tiberius' architects. The main problem was how to collect and store enough water to supply the villa's baths and 3000-sq-metre gardens. The solution they eventually hit upon was to build a complex canal system to transport rainwater to four giant storage tanks, whose remains you can still see today.

Beside the ticket office is the 330m-high **Salto di Tiberio** (Tiberius' Leap), a sheer cliff from where, as the story goes, Tiberi-us had out-of-favour subjects hurled into the sea. True or not, the stunning views are real enough; if you suffer from vertigo, tread carefully.

A shortish but steep walk from the vil-la, down Via Tiberio and Via Matermània, is the **Arco Naturale** – an imposing, Palaeolithic-era rock arch formed by the pounding sea; you can time this walk to take in lunch at nearby Le Grotelle (p680).

DON'T MISS

GROTTA AZZURRA

Capri's single most famous attraction is the **Grotta Azzurra** (Blue Grotto; €14; ⊙9am-5pm), a stunning sea cave illuminated by an other-worldly blue light. The easiest way to visit is to take a **tour** (☑081 837 56 46; www.motoscafisticacapri.com; Private Pier 0, Marina Grande; €15) from Marina Grande; tickets include the return boat trip but the rowing boat into the cave and admission are paid separately. Allow a good hour.

The grotto had long been known to local fishermen when it was rediscovered by two Germans – writer Augustus Kopisch and painter Ernst Fries – in 1826. Subsequent research, however, revealed that Emperor Tiberius had built a quay in the cave around AD 30, complete with a *nymphaeum* (shrine to the water nymph). Remarkably, you can still see the carved Roman landing stage towards the rear of the cave.

Measuring 54m by 30m and rising to a height of 15m, the grotto is said to have sunk by up to 20m in prehistoric times, blocking every opening except the 1.3m-high entrance. And this is the key to the magical blue light. Sunlight enters through a small underwater aperture and is refracted through the water; this, combined with the reflection of the light off the white sandy seafloor, produces the vivid blue effect to which the cave owes its name.

The grotto is closed if the sea is too choppy and swimming in it is forbidden, although you can swim outside the entrance – get a bus to Grotta Azzurra, take the stairs down to the right and dive off the small concrete platform. When visiting, keep in mind that the singing 'captains' are included in the price, so don't feel any obligation if they push for a tip.

Giardini di Augusto GARDENS
(Gardens of Augustus; €1; ⊙9am-7.30pm Apr-Oct, 9.30am-5.30pm Nov-Mar) As their name suggests, these gardens near the Certosa di San Giacomo were founded by Emperor Augustus. Rising in a series of flowered terraces, they lead to a lookout point offering breathtaking views over to the **Isole Faraglioni**, a group of three limestone stacks rising out of the sea.

Measuring 109m, 81m and 104m respectively, the *isole* are home to a rare blue lizard that was once thought to be unique to the Faraglioni but has since been found on the Sicilian coast.

From the gardens, pretty, hairpin **Via Krupp** winds down to Marina Piccola and past a bust of Lenin overlooking the road from a nearby platform. The Russian revolutionary visited Capri in 1908, during which time he was famously snapped engaged in a game of chess with fellow revolutionary Alexander Bogdanov. Looking on in the photograph is Russian writer Maxim Gorki, who called the island home between 1906 and 1909.

Certosa di San Giacomo MONASTERY
(☑081 837 62 18; Viale Certosa 40; adult/reduced €4/2; ⊙10am-7pm Tue-Sun Apr-Aug, to 5pm Sep-Dec, to 2pm Jan-Mar) Founded in 1363, this picturesque monastery is generally considered to be the finest remaining example of Caprese architecture and today houses a school, a library, a temporary exhibition space and a museum with some evocative 17th-century paintings. Be sure to look at the two cloisters, which have a real sense of faded glory (the smaller is 14th century, the larger 16th century).

To get here take Via Vittorio Emanuele III, east of Piazza Umberto I, which meanders down to the monastery.

The monastery's history is a harrowing one: it became the stronghold of the island's powerful Carthusian fraternity and was viciously attacked during Saracen pirate raids in the 16th century. A century later, monks retreated here to avoid the plague and were rewarded by an irate public (whom they should have been tending), who tossed corpses over the walls. There are some soothing 17th-century frescoes in the church, which will hopefully serve as an antidote as you contemplate the monastery's dark past.

Piazza Umberto I PIAZZA
Located beneath the 17th-century clock tower and framed by see-and-be-seen cafes, this showy, open-air salon is central to your Capri experience, especially in the evening when the main activity in these parts is dressing up and hanging out. Be prepared for the cost of these front-row seats – the moment you sit down for a drink, you're going to pay handsomely for the grandstand views (around €6 for a cappuccino and €16 for a couple of glasses of white wine).

Chiesa di Santo Stefano CHURCH
(☑ 081 837 23 96; Piazza Umberto I; ⊙ 9am-7pm Apr-Oct, 10am-2pm rest of year) Overlooking Piazza Umberto I, this baroque 17th-century church boasts a well-preserved marble floor (taken from Villa Jovis) and a statue of San Costanzo, Capri's patron saint. Note the pair of languidly reclining patricians in the chapel to the south of the main altar, who seem to mirror some of the mildly debauched folk in the cafes outside. Beside the northern chapel is a reliquary with a saintly bone that reputedly saved Capri from the plague in the 19th century.

👁 Anacapri & Around

Traditionally Capri Town's more subdued neighbour, Anacapri is no stranger to tourism. The focus is largely limited to Villa San Michele di Axel Munthe and the souvenir stores on the main streets. Delve further, though, and you'll discover that Anacapri is still, at heart, the laid-back, rural village that it's always been.

⭐ Seggiovia del Monte Solaro CABLE CAR
(☑ 081 837 14 38; www.capriseggiovia.it; single/return €8/11; ⊙ 9.30am-5pm May-Oct, to 4pm Mar & Apr, to 3.30pm Nov-Feb) A fast and painless way to reach Capri's highest peak, Anacapri's Seggiovia del Monte Solaro chairlift whisks you to the top of the mountain in a tranquil, beautiful ride of just 13 minutes. The views from the top are outstanding – on a clear day, you can see the entire Bay of Naples, the Amalfi Coast and the islands of Ischia and Procida.

⭐ Villa San Michele di Axel Munthe MUSEUM, GARDENS
(☑ 081 837 14 01; www.villasanmichele.eu; Via Axel Munthe 34; €8; ⊙ 9am-6pm May-Sep, reduced hours rest of year) The former home of Swedish doctor, psychiatrist and animal-rights advocate Axel Munthe, San Michele di Axel Munthe should be included on every visitor's itinerary. Built on the site of the ruins of a Roman villa, the gardens make a beautiful setting for a tranquil stroll, with pathways flanked by immaculate flowerbeds. There are also superb views from here, plus some fine photo props in the form of Roman sculptures.

🏃 Activities

⭐ Banana Sport BOATING
(☑ 348 5949665; Marina Grande; 2hr/day rental €90/220; ⊙ May-mid-Oct) Located on the eastern edge of the waterfront, Banana Sport hires out five-person motorised dinghies, allowing you to explore secluded coves and grottoes. You can also visit the popular swimming spot **Bagno di Tiberio** (€10), a small inlet west of Marina Grande; it's said that Tiberius once swam here.

⭐ Capri Whales BOATING
(☑ 081 837 58 33; www.capriwhales.it; Marina Grande 17; 2hr rental €90, 3hr tour €200; ⊙ May-Oct; 🖬) These dinghies are well equipped for families, with coolers, snorkelling gear, floats and water toys. The outfit also run tours around the island and to the mainland.

🛏 Sleeping

This island is all about lemon trees, pavement cafes, sultry summer evenings and wearing the largest pair of shades you can get your hands on. In other words, accommodation is strictly seasonal, which means bed space is tight and, in general, costly. Always book well ahead in the summer.

⭐ Casa Mariantonia BOUTIQUE HOTEL €€
(☑ 081 837 29 23; www.casamariantonia.com; Via Giuseppe Orlandi 80; d €120-280; ⊙ Apr-Oct; 🅿✳🐾🛜) This fabulous boutique retreat counts Jean-Paul Sartre and Alberto Moravia among its past guests, which may well give you something to muse over while you are enjoying the tranquil beauty of the surroundings. Rooms deliver restrained elegance in soothing tones and there are private terraces with garden views. The in-house restaurant is set in a lemon grove, *naturally*.

⭐ Hotel Villa Eva HOTEL €€
(☑ 081 837 15 49; www.villaeva.com; Via La Fabbrica 8; d €120-200, tr €150-220, apt per person €60-90; ⊙ Apr-Oct; ✳@🛜🏊) Nestled amid fruit and olive trees in the countryside near Anacapri, Villa Eva is an idyllic retreat, complete with swimming pool, lush gardens and sunny rooms and apartments. Whitewashed domes, terracotta floors, stained-glass windows and vintage fireplaces add character, while the location ensures peace and quiet.

Capri Palace HOTEL €€€
(☑ 081 978 01 11; www.capripalace.com; Via Capodimonte 2b; d/ste from €500/1000; ⊙ Apr-Oct; ✳🛜🏊) A VIP favourite (Gwyneth Paltrow, Liz Hurley and Naomi Campbell have all relaxed here), the super-chic Capri Palace takes *dolce vita* to dizzying levels. Its stylish

Mediterranean interior is enlivened with eye-catching contemporary art and its guest rooms are never less than lavish – some even have their own terraced garden and private plunge pool.

Grand Hotel Quisisana

HOTEL €€€

(☑ 081 837 07 88; www.quisi.com; Via Camerelle 2; r/ste from €330/850; ⊘ Easter-Oct; ❄ 🖃 🌊) Boasting a five-star luxury rating, the Quisisana is Capri's most prestigious address and is just few espadrille-clad steps from La Piazzetta (Piazza Umberto I). A slumber palace since the 19th century, it's a bastion of unashamed opulence, with two swimming pools, a fitness centre and spa, restaurants, bars and subtropical gardens. Rooms are suitably palatial, with cool colour schemes and mostly classic, conservative furniture.

Eating

Traditional Campanian food served in traditional trattorias is what you'll mainly find on Capri. Prices are high but drop noticeably the further you get from Capri Town.

The island's culinary gift to the world is *insalata caprese,* a salad of fresh tomatoes, basil and silky mozzarella drizzled with olive oil. Look out for *caprese* cheese, a cross between mozzarella and ricotta, and *ravioli caprese,* ravioli stuffed with *cacciota* cheese and herbs. For a local sugar high, sink your teeth into *torta caprese,* a dense, flourless cake made with chocolate and almonds and best paired with a glass of Strega liqueur.

Many restaurants, like the hotels, close over winter and only reopen at Easter.

★ Raffaele Buonacore

FAST FOOD €

(☑ 081 837 78 26; Via Vittorio Emanuele III 35; snacks €2-10, gelato from €2.50; ⊘ 8am-9pm, closed Tue Oct-Jun; 👶) Ideal for a quick fill-up, this popular, down-to-earth snack bar does a roaring trade in savoury and sweet treats. Hit the spot with *frittate, panini* (sandwiches), *focaccie,* stuffed peppers, waffles and legendary ice cream. Hard to beat, though, are the delicious *sfogliatelle* (cinnamon-infused ricotta in a puff-pastry shell, €2.50) and the feather-light speciality *caprilu al limone* (lemon and almond cakes).

★ È Divino

ITALIAN €€

(☑ 081 837 83 64; www.edivinocapri.com/divino; Vico Sella Orta 10a; meals €30-35; ⊘ 8pm-1am daily Jun-Aug, 12.30-2.30pm & 7.30pm-midnight Tue-Sun rest of the year; 🛜) Look hard for the sign: this Slow-Food restaurant is a well-kept secret. Whether dining among lemon trees in the garden or among antiques, chandeliers, contemporary art (and a bed) inside, expect a thoughtful, regularly changing menu dictated by what's fresh from the garden or market. Favourites include a sultry pasta dish of *paccheri* with tuna, olives, capers and *datterini* tomatoes.

Le Grottelle

ITALIAN €€

(☑ 081 837 57 19; Via Arco Naturale 13; meals €27-40; ⊘ noon-3pm & 7-11pm Jul & Aug, noon-2.30pm & 7-11pm Fri-Wed Jun & Sep, noon-3pm Fri-Wed Apr, May & Oct; 🛜) This is a great place to impress someone – not so much for the food, which is decent enough, but for the dramatic setting. Close to the Arco Naturale, its two dining areas are set in a cave and on a hillside terrace with sea views. Dishes are rustic and honest, from homemade *fusilli* pasta with shrimps and zucchini to rabbit with onions, garlic and rosemary.

★ Il Geranio

SEAFOOD €€€

(☑ 081 837 06 16; www.geraniocapri.com; Via Matteotti 8; meals €45-50; ⊘ noon-3pm & 7-11pm mid-Apr–mid-Oct) Time to pop the question or quell those pre-departure blues? The terrace at this sophisticated spot offers heart-stealing views over the pine trees to the Isole Faraglioni rocks. Seafood is the house speciality, particularly the salt-baked fish. Other fine choices include the octopus salad and linguine with saffron and mussels. Book at least three days ahead for a terrace table in high season.

Drinking & Nightlife

Capri's nightlife is a showy business. The main activity is styling up and hanging out, ideally at one of the cafes on La Piazzetta (Piazza Umberto I). Aside from the cafes, the nightlife here is fairly staid, with surprisingly few clubs. The most famous late-night party spot remains Taverna Anema e Core.

Taverna Anema e Core

CLUB

(☑ 329 4742508; www.anemaecore.com; Vico Sella Orta 39E, Capri Town; ⊘ 11pm-late Tue-Sun) Lying beyond a humble exterior is one of the island's most famous nightspots, run by the charismatic Guido Lembo. This smooth and sophisticated bar-club attracts an appealing mix of super-chic and casually dressed punters, here for the relaxed atmosphere and regular live music, including unwaveringly authentic Neapolitan guitar strumming and singing.

Caffè Michelangelo   CAFE
(Via Giuseppe Orlandi 138, Anacapri; ⊗ 8am-2am
Jul & Aug, to 1am Sep-Jun, closed Thu Nov & Dec;
☎) On a street flanked by tasteful shops and
near two lovely piazzas, this modest, friendly
corner cafe is a sound spot for a fix of people
watching. Rate the passing parade over a
spritz con Cynar, a less-sweet take on the
classic Aperol *spritz*, made using a herbacious Italian bitter liqueur.

🛍 Shopping

Limoncello di Capri   DRINKS
(✒ 081 837 29 27; www.limoncello.com; Via Capodimonte 27, Anacapri; ⊗ 9am-7.30pm) Don't be
put off by the gaudy yellow display; this historic shop stocks some of the island's best
limoncello. In fact, it was here that the drink
was first concocted (or at least that is the
claim...). Apparently, the grandmother of
current owner Massimo made the tot as an
after-dinner treat for the guests in her small
guesthouse.

**Carthusia I
Profumi di Capri**   COSMETICS
(✒ 081 837 53 93; www.carthusia.it; Viale Matteotti
2d, Capri Town; ⊗ 9am-8pm Apr-Sep, to 5pm rest
of year) Allegedly, Capri's famous floral perfume was established in 1380 by the prior
of the Certosa di San Giacomo. Caught un-
awares by a royal visit, he displayed the island's most beautiful flowers for the queen.
Changing the water in the vase, he discovered a floral scent. This became the base of
the classic perfume now sold at this smart
laboratory outlet.

ℹ Information

Post Office (www.poste.it; Via Roma 50;
⊗ 8.20am-7pm Mon-Fri, to 12.30pm Sat)
Located just west of the bus terminal in Capri
Town.

Tourist Office (✒ 081 837 06 34; www.
capritourism.com; Banchina del Porto, Marina
Grande; ⊗ 8.30am-4.15pm daily Jun–mid-Sep,
8.30am-2.30pm Mon-Sat rest of year) Can
provide a map of the island, plus accommodation listings, ferry timetables and other useful
information.

ℹ Getting There & Away

The two major ferry routes to Capri are from
Naples and Sorrento, although there are also
seasonal connections with Ischia and the Amalfi
Coast (Amalfi, Positano and Salerno).

Caremar (✒ 081 837 07 00; www.caremar.it)
operates hydrofoils and ferries to/from Naples
(€12.10 to €20, 40 minutes to 1¼ hours, up to
seven daily) and hydrofoils to/from Sorrento
€13.50 to €16, 25 minutes, four daily).

Gescab (✒ 081 428 55 55; www.gescab.it) runs
hydrofoils to/from Naples (€20 to €22.50, 40
minutes, up to 17 daily) and to/from Sorrento
(€17.70 to €20.20, 20 minutes, up to 19 daily).

Navigazione Libera del Golfo (NLG; ✒ 081
552 07 63; www.navlib.it) operates hydrofoils
to/from Naples (from €18.70 to €22.50, 45
minutes, eight daily).

SNAV (✒ 081 428 55 55; www.snav.it) also
operates hydrofoils to/from Naples (€22.20 to
€23.50, 45 minutes, seven daily).

ℹ Getting Around

BUS

Sippic (✒ 081 837 04 20; Bus Station, Via
Roma, Capri Town; tickets €1.80, day tickets
€8.60) Runs regular buses between Marina
Grande and Anacapri, as well as between
Anacapri and Capri Town.

Staiano Autotrasporti (✒ 081 837 24 22;
www.staianotourcapri.com; Bus Station, Via
Tommaso, Anacapri; tickets €2) These buses
serve the Grotta Azzurra and Punta Carena *faro*
(lighthouse).

FUNICULAR

Funicular (tickets €1.80; ⊗ 6.30am-9.30pm)
The first challenge facing visitors is how to get
from Marina Grande to Capri Town. The most
enjoyable option is the funicular, if only for
the evocative en-route views over the lemon
groves and surrounding countryside. The ticket
booth in Marina Grande is not at the funicular
station itself; it's behind the tourist office (turn
right onto Via Marina Grande from the ferry
port). Note that the funicular usually closes
from January through March for maintenance;
a substitute bus service is in place during this
period.

SCOOTER

Ciro dei Motorini (✒ 338 3606918, 081
362 00 83; www.capriscooter.com; Via Marina Grande 55, Marina Grande; per 2/24hr
€30/65) If you're looking to hire a scooter at
Marina Grande, stop here.

TAXI

Taxi (✒ in Anacapri 081 837 11 75, in Capri
Town 081 837 66 57) From Marina Grande, a
taxi costs from €17 to Capri and from €22 to
Anacapri; from Capri to Anacapri costs from
€18. These rates include one bag per vehicle.
Each additional bag (with dimensions exceed-
ing 40cm x 20cm x 50cm) costs an extra €2.

Ischia

📱 081 / POP 64,000

The volcanic outcrop of Ischia is the most developed and largest of the islands in the Bay of Naples. It's an intriguing concoction of sprawling spa towns, abundant gardens, buried necropolises and spectacular scenery, with forests, vineyards and picturesque small towns.

Most visitors head straight for the north-coast towns of Ischia Porto, Ischia Ponte, Casamicciola Terme, Forio and Lacco Ameno. Of these, Ischia Porto boasts the best bars, Casamicciola the worst traffic and Ischia Ponte and Lacco Ameno the most appeal. On the calmer south coast, the car-free perfection of Sant'Angelo offers a languid blend of a cosy harbour and nearby bubbling beaches. In between the coasts lies a less-trodden landscape of dense chestnut forests, loomed over by Monte Epomeo, Ischia's highest peak.

◉ Sights

★ Castello Aragonese   CASTLE
(Aragon Castle; 📱 081 99 28 34, 081 99 19 59; www.castelloaragoneseischia.com; Rocca del Castello, Ischia Ponte; adult/reduced €10/6; ⊙ 9am-sunset) The elegant 15th-century Ponte Aragonese connects Ischia Ponte to Castello Aragonese, a magnificent, sprawling castle perched high and mighty on a rocky islet. While Syracusan tyrant Gerone I built the site's first fortress in 474 BC, the bulk of the current structure dates from the 1400s, when King Alfonso of Aragon gave the older Angevin fortress a thorough makeover, building the fortified bastions, current causeway and access ramp cut into the rock.

★ La Mortella   GARDENS
(Place of the Myrtles; 📱 081 98 62 20; www.lamortella.it; Via F Calese 39, Forio; adult/reduced €12/10; ⊙ 9am-7pm Tue, Thu, Sat & Sun Apr-Oct) Designed by Russell Page and inspired by the Moorish gardens of Spain's Alhambra, La Mortella is recognised as one of Italy's finest botanical gardens and is well worth a couple of hours of your time. Stroll among terraces, pools, palms, fountains and more than 1000 rare and exotic plants from all over the world. The lower section of the garden is humid and tropical, while the upper level features Mediterranean plants and beautiful views over Forio and the coast.

Ischia's veritable Eden was established by the late British composer Sir William Walton and his Argentine wife, Susana (who died in March 2010, aged 83), who made it their home in 1949, entertaining such venerable house guests as Sir Laurence Olivier, Maria Callas and Charlie Chaplin. Walton's life is commemorated in a small museum and his music wafts over the loudspeakers at the elegant cafe. The gardens host chamber-music recitals in the spring and autumn, as well as symphonic concerts in the summer.

🏃 Activities

★ Negombo   SPA
(📱 081 98 61 52; www.negombo.it; Baia di San Montano, Lacco Ameno; admission all day €33, from 1.30pm/3.30pm/5.30pm €26/22/8; ⊙ 8.30am-7pm mid-Apr–Oct) This is the place to come for a dose of pampering. Part spa resort, part botanical wonderland, with more than 500 exotic plant species, Negombo's combination of Zen-like thermal pools, hammam, contemporary sculpture and private beach on the Baia di San Montano tends to draw a younger crowd than many other Ischian spa spots.

There's a Japanese labyrinth pool for weary feet, a decent *tavola calda* (snack bar), and a full range of massage and beauty treatments. Those arriving by car or scooter can park all day on site (car €5, scooter €3). For a free dip in the bay, follow the signs to the *spiaggia* (beach) out the front of Negombo.

Monte Epomeo   WALKING
Lace up those hiking boots and set out on a roughly 2.5km (50-minute) uphill walk from the village of Fontana, which will bring you to the top of Monte Epomeo (788m). Formed by an underwater eruption, it boasts superlative views of the Bay of Naples.

The little church near the top is the 15th-century **Cappella di San Nicola di Bari**, where you can check out the pretty majolica floor. The adjoining hermitage was built in the 18th century by an island governor who, after narrowly escaping death, swapped politics for poverty and spent the rest of his days here in saintly solitude. Have a peek inside, then head back down the hill, thankful that your saintliness doesn't exclude good wining and dining, Capri style.

Ischia Diving   DIVING
(📱 081 98 18 52; www.ischiadiving.net; Via Iasolino 106, Ischia Porto; single dive €40) This well-established diving outfit offers some

LOCAL KNOWLEDGE

ISCHIA'S BEST BEACHES

Baia di Sorgeto (Via Sorgeto; ⊙ Apr–Oct) Catch a water taxi from Sant'Angelo (€5 one way) or reach the beach on foot from the town of Panza. Waiting at the bottom is an intimate cove complete with bubbling thermal spring. Perfect for a winter dip.

Spiaggia dei Maronti Long, sandy and very popular; the sand here is warmed by natural steam geysers. Reach the beach by bus from Barano, by water taxi from Sant'Angelo (€3 one way) or on foot along the path leading east from Sant'Angelo.

Spiaggia dei Pescatori (Fishermen's Beach) Wedged between Ischia Porto and Ischia Ponte is the island's most down to earth and popular seaside strip; it's perfect for families.

Baia di San Montano Due west of Lacco Ameno, this gorgeous bay is the place for warm, shallow, crystal-clear waters. You'll also find the Negombo spa park here.

Punta Caruso Located on Ischia's northwestern tip, this secluded rocky spot is perfect for a swim in clear, deep water. To get here, follow the walking path that leads off Via Guardiola down to the beach. Not suitable for children or when seas are rough.

attractively priced dive packages, such as five dives including equipment for €180.

🛏 Sleeping

Camping Mirage　　　CAMPGROUND €
(☑ 081 99 05 51; www.campingmirage.it; Via Maronti 37, Spiagga dei Maronti, Barano d'Ischia; camping per 2 people, car & tent €34-46; ⊙ Easter–Oct; P) Located on Spiagga dei Maronti, one of Ischia's best beaches, and within walking distance of Sant'Angelo, this shady campground offers 50 places, showers, laundry facilities, a bar and a restaurant dishing up local special *tubettoni, cozze e pecorino* (pasta with mussels and sheep cheese).

Hotel Noris　　　HOTEL €
(☑ 081 99 13 87; www.norishotel.it; Via A Sogliuzzo 2, Ischia Ponte; d €50-90; ⊙ Easter–mid-Oct; ❄ 🐾) This place has a great price and a great position within easy strolling distance of the Ponte sights. Some of the comfy, decent-sized rooms have small balconies. Breakfast is the standard, albeit slightly more expensive, continental buffet. Bonus points are due for the special parking deal (€10 per night) with the public car park across the way.

★ Semiramis Hotel de Charme　　HOTEL €€
(☑ 081 90 75 11; www.hotelsemiramisischia.it; Spiaggia di Citara, Forio; d €140-185; ⊙ mid-Apr–Oct; P ❄ 🐾 🏊) A few minutes' walk from the Poseidon spa complex, this bright hotel has a tropical-oasis feel with its outdoor thermal pool surrounded by lofty palms. Rooms are large and beautifully tiled in the traditional yellow-and-turquoise pattern, and the garden is glorious, with fig trees, vineyards and sea views.

★ Albergo
Il Monastero　　　HOTEL €€
(☑ 081 99 24 35; www.albergoilmonastero.it; Castello Aragonese, Rocca del Castello, Ischia Ponte; s €80-90, d €140-200; ⊙ Easter–mid-Oct; ❄ 🐾) The former monks' cells still have a certain appealing sobriety about them, with their dark-wood furniture, white walls, vintage terracotta tiles and no TV (the views are sufficiently prime time). Elsewhere, the hotel exudes a pleasing sense of space and style, with vaulted ceilings, plush sofas, antiques and contemporary art by the late owner and artist Gabriele Mattera. The hotel restaurant has an excellent reputation.

🍴 Eating

★ Il Focolare　　　ITALIAN €€
(☑ 081 90 29 44; www.trattoriailfocolare.it; Via Creajo al Crocefisso 3, Barano d'Ischia; meals €30; ⊙ 12.30-2.45pm Thu-Sun & 7.30-11.30pm daily Jun-Oct, closed Wed Nov-Jan & Mar-May, closed Feb) A good choice for those seeking a little turf instead of surf, this is one of the island's best-loved restaurants. Family run, homey and rustic, it has a solidly traditional meat-based menu with steaks, lamb cutlets and specialities including *coniglio all'Ischitana* (typical local rabbit dish with tomatoes, garlic and herbs). On the sweet front, the desserts are homemade and exquisite.

Owner Riccardo D'Ambra (who runs the restaurant together with his son, Agostino) is a leading local advocate of the Slow Food movement. If you want seafood, coffee or soft drinks, you'll have to go elsewhere; they're not on the menu here.

ISCHIA ON A FORK

Ischian restaurateur Carlo Buono of **Da Ciccio** (☑ 081 199 13 14; www.bardaciccio.it; Via Porto 1, Ischia Porto; snacks from €1; ⊙ 8am-midnight) gives the low-down on his cherished classic island cuisine:

'Fresh, seasonal ingredients are the cornerstone of Ischian cooking, from silky olive oil to plump *pomodorini* (cherry tomatoes). Like Neapolitan cooking, the emphasis is on simple, uncomplicated home cooking. Traditionally, there are two types of Ischian cuisine: coastal and mountain. For centuries, fishermen would barter with farmers, who'd offer wine, vegetables, pork and rabbit in exchange for the catch.

'Rabbit is a typical Ischian meat and we're seeing a revival of the traditional *fossa* (pit) breeding method, where rabbits are bred naturally in deep *fosse* instead of in cages. The result is a more tender, flavoursome meat. Leading this renaissance is local Slow Food advocate Riccardo D'Ambra, whose famous trattoria Il Focolare (p683) is well known for its rabbit and rustic mountain dishes. Definitely worth eating on the island is a popular Sunday dish called *coniglio all'ischitana* (Ischia-style rabbit), prepared with olive oil, unpeeled garlic, chilli, tomato, basil, thyme and white wine.

'Typical local fish include *pesce bandiera* (sailfish), the flat *castagna, lampuga* and *palamide* (a small tuna). A popular way of cooking it is in *acqua pazza* (crazy water). Traditionally prepared on the fishing boats, it's a delicate sauce made with *pomodorini*, garlic and parsley. Fried fish is also very typical; a fresh serve of *frittura di mare* (mixed fried seafood) drizzled with lemon juice is just superb. May to September is *totano* (squid) season and a great time to try *totani imbotti* (squid stuffed with olives, capers and breadcrumbs, and stewed in wine).

'Equally wonderful is fresh, wood-fired *casareccio* bread – it's perfect for doing the *scarpetta* (wiping your plate clean) or for filling with salami or *parmigiano* cheese. If you have any room left, track down a slice of *torta caprese*, a moist chocolate and almond cake. *Buon appetito.*'

★**Ristorante Pietratorcia**   ITALIAN €€
(☑ 081 90 72 32; www.ristorantepietratorcia.it; Via Provinciale Panza 401, Forio; meals around €30; ⊙ 11am-2pm & 5.30pm-midnight Easter-Oct; 🖘)
Enjoying a bucolic setting among tumbling vines, wild fig trees and rosemary bushes, this A-list winery is a foodie's nirvana. Tour the old stone cellars, sip a local drop (wine degustations from €20) and eye up a competent, seasonal turf-and-surf menu that might include artichoke parmigiana or *baccalà* (salted cod) with *scarole* (escarole) and toasted pine nuts. Consider booking ahead in high season. The CD and CS buses stop within metres of the winery's entrance; ask the driver to advise you when to alight.

Montecorvo   ITALIAN €€
(☑ 081 99 80 29; www.montecorvo.it; Via Montecorvo 33, Forio; meals €30; ⊙ 7.30pm-midnight daily, also 12.30-3pm Sun, closed Wed Dec-Mar; 🖘)
Part of the dining room at hillside Montecorvo is tunnelled into a cave, while the verdant terrace offers magnificent sunset views. Hidden amid lush foliage outside Forio, the place is owned by Giovanni, who prides himself on the special dishes he makes daily.

There's an emphasis on grilled meat and fish, and an especially popular dish of local rabbit, cooked in a woodfired oven.

Despite its sneaky location, Montecorvo is well signposted along the side street that leads to it.

ℹ Information

Tourist Office (☑ 081 507 42 31; www.info ischiaprocida.it; Corso Sogliuzzo 72, Ischia Porto; ⊙ 9am-2pm & 3-8pm Mon-Sat) A slim selection of maps and brochures.

ℹ Getting There & Away

Caremar (☑ 081 98 48 18; www.caremar.it) operates up to six hydrofoils daily each way between Naples and Ischia Porto (€17.60, 45 minutes).

Alilauro (☑ 081 497 22 42; www.alilauro.it) operates up to 12 hydrofoils daily each way between Naples and Ischia Porto (€18.90 to €19.80, 50 minutes). It also runs up to six hydrofoils daily between Forio and Naples (€20.10 to €21.10).

SNAV (☑ 081 428 55 55; www.snav.it) operates hydrofoils between Naples and Casamicciola (€19.90 to €20.90, one hour), up to eight times daily.

ℹ️ Getting Around

Ischia's main circular highway can get clogged with traffic in the height of summer. This, combined with the penchant the local youth have for overtaking on blind corners and the environmental impact of just too many cars, means that you may want to consider riding the excellent network of buses (cheap!) or hopping in a taxi (not cheap!) to get around. The distance between attractions and the lack of pavements on the busy roads makes walking unappealing.

The island's main **bus station** is a one-minute walk west of the **pier**, at Ischia Porto, with buses servicing all other parts of the island.

Procida

📍 081 / POP 10,500

The Bay of Naples' smallest island is also its best-kept secret. Mercifully off the mass-tourist radar, Procida is like the Portofino prototype and is refreshingly real. August aside – when beach bound mainlanders flock to its shores – its narrow, sun-bleached streets are the domain of the locals: young boys clutch fishing rods, mothers push prams and old seamen swap yarns. Here, the hotels are smaller, fewer waiters speak broken German and the island's welcome is untainted by too much tourism.

If you have the time, Procida is an ideal place to explore on foot. The most compelling areas (and where you will also find most of the hotels, bars and restaurants) are Marina Grande, Marina Corricella and Marina di Chiaiolella. Beaches are not plentiful here, apart from the Lido di Procida, where, aside from August, you shouldn't have any trouble finding some towel space.

👁 Sights

Isola di Vivara　　　　NATURE RESERVE
(www.visitprocida.it; adult/reduced €10/5; ⊙ guided tours 10am & 3pm Fri-Sun) Linked to Procida by pedestrian bridge, pocket-sized Vivara is what remains of a volcanic crater dating back some 55,000 years. The island is home to unique flora and abundant bird life, while archaeological digs have uncovered traces of a Bronze-Age Mycenaean settlement as well as pottery fragments dating back to early Greek colonisation. Guided tours (including in English) of Vivara are run Friday to Sunday and must be booked two to three days in advance via the Visit Procida website.

Abbazia di San Michele Arcangelo　　　CHURCH, MUSEUM
(📞 334 8514028, 334 8514252; www.abbaziasanmicheleprocida.it; Via Terra Murata 89, Terra Murata; ⊙ 10am-12.45pm & 3-5pm) FREE Soak in the dizzying bay views at the belvedere before exploring the adjoining Abbazia di San Michele Arcangelo. Built in the 11th century and remodelled between the 17th and 19th centuries, this one-time Benedictine abbey houses a small museum with some arresting pictures created in gratitude by shipwrecked sailors, plus a church with a spectacular coffered ceiling and an ancient Greek alabaster basin converted into a font. On our last visit, the museum was closed indefinitely for maintenance.

The church apse features four paintings by Neapolitan artist Nicola Russo. Dating back to 1690, these works include a depiction of St Michael the Archangel protecting Procida from Saracen attack on 8 May 1535. The painting is especially fascinating for its depiction of Marina Grande in the 16th century.

🏃 Activities

Blue Dream Yacht Charter Boating　　　BOATING
(📞 339 5720874, 081 896 06 79; www.bluedreamcharter.com; Via Vittorio Emanuele 14, Marina Grande; 4/8-person yacht per week from €1300/2200) If you have 'champagne on the deck' aspirations, you can always charter your very own yacht or catamaran from here.

Procida Rent a Bike　　　CYCLING
(📞 081 896 00 60, 338 1329102; Via Roma, Marina Grande; 1/4hr €10/15; 🚲) The bicycles for hire here are one of the best ways to explore the island. Small, open micro-taxis can also be hired for two to three hours for around €35, depending on your bargaining prowess.

👣 Tours

Cesare Boat Trips　　　BOATING
(📞 333 4603877; 2½hr tour per person €25; ⊙ Mar-Oct) On the harbour at Marina Corricella, ask for friendly Cesare in your best Italian. Check at one of the beach bars or by La Gorgonia restaurant – he won't be far away. Cesare runs some great boat trips as well as half-day trips in a traditional galleon for €100 (minimum 25 people).

✻ Festivals & Events

**Procession
of the Misteri**   RELIGIOUS

Good Friday sees a colourful procession when a wooden statue of Christ and the Madonna Addolorata, along with life-size plaster and papier-mâché tableaux illustrating events leading to Christ's crucifixion, are carted across the island. Men dress in blue tunics with white hoods, while many of the young girls dress as the Madonna.

🛏 Sleeping

Bed & Breakfast La Terrazza   B&B €

(📱 081 896 00 62; Via Faro 26, Marina Grande; s €50-70, d €75-90; ⊙ Easter-Oct; 🛜) An extremely attractive budget option, where the rooms are decked out with paintings, metal lamps, tiles and antiques. Take time out on the terracotta-floored terrace – thus the B&B's name – where you can lie back on a lounger and enjoy the sunset. Homemade breakfasts are served up here.

★ Hotel La Vigna   BOUTIQUE HOTEL €€

(📱 081 896 04 69; www.albergolavigna.it; Via Principessa Margherita 46, Terra Murata; d €150-180, ste €180-230; ⊙ Easter-Oct; 🅿 ✻ @ 🛜 ⛱) Enjoying a discreet cliff-side location, this 18th-century villa is a gorgeous retreat, complete with rambling garden, vines and a brand-new swimming pool. Five of the spacious, simply furnished rooms offer direct access to the garden. Superior rooms (€180 to €200) feature family-friendly mezzanines, while the main perk of the suite is the bedside hot tub: perfect for romancing couples.

The small in-house spa has wine-therapy treatments.

★ Casa Sul Mare   HOTEL €€

(📱 081 896 87 99; www.lacasasulmare.it; Salita Castello 13, Marina Corricella; r €125-170; ⊙ Mar-Oct; ✻ 🛜) A crisp, white-washed place with the kind of evocative views that helped make *The Talented Mr Ripley* such a memorable film. Overlooking the pastel-hued fishing village of Marina Corricella, near the ruined Castello d'Avalos, its rooms are simple yet elegant, with fetching tiled floors, wrought-iron bedsteads and the odd piece of antique furniture.

The hotel treats its guests well: during summer there's a boat service to the nearby Spiaggia della Chiaia (Chiaia Beach), and the morning cappuccino, courtesy of Franco, may be the best you've ever had.

✗ Eating

Da Giorgio   TRATTORIA €

(📱 081 896 79 10; Via Roma 36, Marina Grande; meals €24; ⊙ noon-3pm & 7-11.30pm Mar-Oct, closed Tue Nov-Feb) A retro, no-frills neighbourhood eatery close to the port. The menu holds few surprises, but the ingredients are fresh; try the *spaghetti con frutti di mare* (seafood spaghetti) or the *soutè di cozze e lupini* (sauté of mussels and small clams), the latter a perfect match for Da Giorgio's wonderfully spongy *casareccio* (homestyle) bread.

Fammivento   SEAFOOD €€

(📱 081 896 90 20; Via Roma 39, Marina Grande; meals €25; ⊙ noon-3.30pm & 8-11pm Tue-Sat, noon-3.30pm Sun, closed Dec-Feb) Get things going with the *frittura di calamari* (fried squid), then try the *fusilli carciofi e calamari* (pasta with artichokes and calamari). For a splurge, go for the house speciality of *zuppa di crostaci e moluschi* (crustacean and mollusc soup).

ℹ Information

Pro Loco (📱 344 1162932; www.facebook.com/proloco.procida.3; Via Roma, Stazione Marittima, Marina Grande; ⊙10am-1pm daily, also 3-5pm Sat & Sun) Located at the Ferry & Hydrofoil Ticket Office, this modest office has sparse printed information but should be able to advise on activities, accommodation and the like.

ℹ Getting There & Away

The **Ferry & Hydrofoil Terminal** is in Marina Grande.

Caremar (📱 081 896 72 80; www.caremar.it) operates up to eight daily hydrofoils to/from Naples (€16.70, 25 minutes).

SNAV (📱 081 428 55 55; www.snav.it) operates up to four hydrofoils daily to/from Naples (€17.30 to €18.80, 25 minutes).

SOUTH OF NAPLES

Herculaneum (Ercolano)

Ercolano is an uninspiring Neapolitan suburb that's home to one of Italy's best-preserved ancient sites: Herculaneum. A superbly conserved fishing town, the site is smaller and less daunting than Pompeii, allowing you to visit without the nagging feeling that you're bound to miss something.

◉ Sights

★ Ruins of Herculaneum
ARCHAEOLOGICAL SITE

(☏ 081 857 53 47; www.pompeiisites.org; Corso Resina 187, Ercolano; adult/reduced €11/5.50, incl Pompeii €22/12; ☺ 8.30am-7.30pm Apr-Oct, to 5pm Nov-Mar; ℞ Circumvesuviana to Ercolano-Scavi) Upstaged by its larger rival, Pompeii, Herculaneum harbours a wealth of archaeological finds, from ancient advertisements and stylish mosaics to carbonised furniture and terror-struck skeletons. Indeed, this superbly conserved Roman fishing town of 4000 inhabitants is easier to navigate than Pompeii, and can be explored with a map and audio guide (€8).

To reach the ruins from Ercolano-Scavi train station, walk downhill to the very end of Via IV Novembre and through the archway across the street. The path leads down to the ticket office, which lies on your left. Ticket purchased, follow the walkway around to the actual entrance to the ruins, where you can also hire audio guides.

Herculaneum's fate runs parallel to that of Pompeii. Destroyed by an earthquake in AD 62, the AD 79 eruption of Mt Vesuvius saw it submerged in a 16m-thick sea of mud that essentially fossilised the city. This meant that even delicate items, such as furniture and clothing, were discovered remarkably well preserved. Tragically, the inhabitants didn't fare so well; thousands of people tried to escape by boat but were suffocated by the volcano's poisonous gases. Indeed, what appears to be a moat around the town is in fact the ancient shoreline. It was here in 1980 that archaeologists discovered some 300 skeletons, the remains of a crowd that had fled to the beach only to be overcome by the terrible heat of clouds surging down from Vesuvius.

The town itself was rediscovered in 1709 and amateur excavations were carried out intermittently until 1874, with many finds carted off to Naples to decorate the houses of the well-to-do or ending up in museums. Serious archaeological work began again in 1927 and continues to this day, although with much of the ancient site buried beneath modern Ercolano it's slow going. Indeed, note that at any given time some houses will invariably be shut for restoration.

➡ Casa d'Argo

(Argus House) This noble house would originally have opened onto Cardo II (as yet unearthed). Its porticoed garden opens onto a *triclinium* (dining room) and other residential rooms.

➡ Casa dello Scheletro

(House of the Skeleton) The modest Casa dello Scheletro features five styles of mosaic flooring, including a design of white arrows at the entrance to guide the most disorientated of guests. In the internal courtyard, don't miss the skylight, complete with the remnants of an ancient security grill. Of the house's mythically themed wall mosaics, only the faded ones are originals; the others now reside in Naples' Museo Archeologico Nazionale (p660).

➡ Terme Maschili

(Men's Baths) The Terme Maschili were the men's section of the **Terme del Foro** (Forum Baths). Note the ancient latrine to the left of the entrance before you step into the *apodyterium* (changing room), complete with bench for waiting patrons and a nifty wall shelf for sandal and toga storage.

While those after a bracing soak would pop into the *frigidarium* (cold bath) to the left, the less stoic headed straight into the *tepadarium* (tepid bath) to the right. The sunken mosaic floor here is testament to the seismic activity preceding Mt Vesuvius' catastrophic eruption. Beyond this room lies the *caldarium* (hot bath), as well as an exercise area.

➡ Decumano Massimo

Herculaneum's ancient high street is lined with shops, and fragments of advertisements – listing everything from the weight of goods to their price – still adorn the walls. Note the one to the right of the Casa del Salone Nero. Further east along the street, a crucifix found in an upstairs room of the Casa del Bicentenario (Bicentenary House) provides possible evidence of a Christian presence in pre-Vesuvius Herculaneum.

➡ Casa del Bel Cortile

(House of the Beautiful Courtyard) Closed on our last visit, the Casa del Bel Cortile is home to three of the 300 skeletons discovered on the ancient shore by archaeologists in 1980. Almost two millennia later, it's still poignant to see the forms of what are understood to be a mother, father and young child huddled together in the last, terrifying moments of their lives.

➡ Casa di Nettuno e Anfitrite

(House of Neptune and Amphitrite) This aristocratic pad takes its name from the extraordinary mosaic in the *nymphaeum* (fountain and bath). The warm colours in which the

1. Tempio di Cerere (p715), Paestum 2. Villa dei Misteri (p969), Pompeii 3. Herculaneum (p686) 4. Complesso Monumentale di San Lorenzo Maggiore (p657), Naples

Historical Riches

Few Italian regions can match Campania's historical legacy. Colonised by the ancient Greeks and loved by the Romans, it's a sun-drenched repository of A-list antiquities, from World Heritage wonders to lesser-known archaeological gems.

Paestum

Great Greek temples never go out of vogue and those at Paestum (p715) are among the greatest outside Greece itself. With the oldest structures stretching back to the 6th century BC, this place makes Rome's Colosseum feel positively modern.

Herculaneum

A bite-sized Pompeii, Herculaneum (p686) is even better preserved than its nearby rival. This is the place to delve into the details, from once-upon-a-time shop advertisements and furniture, to vivid mosaics, even an ancient security grille.

Pompeii

Short of stepping into the Tardis, Pompeii (p691) is your best bet for a little time travel. Locked in ash for centuries, its excavated streetscapes offer a tangible encounter with the ancients and their daily lives, from luxury homes to a racy brothel.

Subterranean Naples

Eerie aqueducts, mysterious burial crypts and ancient streetscapes: beneath Naples' hyperactive streets lies a wonderland of Graeco-Roman ruins. For a taste, head below the Complesso Monumentale di San Lorenzo Maggiore (p657) or follow the leader on a tour of the evocative Catacombe di San Gennaro (p661).

sea god and his nymph bride are depicted hint at how lavish the original interior must have been.

→ Casa del Tramezzo di Legno

(House of the Wooden Partition) Unusually, this house features two atria, which very likely belonged to two separate dwellings that were merged in the 1st century AD. The most famous relic here is a wonderfully well-preserved wooden screen, which separates the atrium from the *tablinum*, where the owner talked business with his clients. The second room off on the left side of the atrium features the remains of an ancient bed.

→ Casa dell'Atrio a Mosaico

(House of the Mosaic Atrium) An ancient mansion, the House of the Mosaic Atrium harbours extensive floor tile-work, although time and nature have left the floor buckled and uneven. Particularly noteworthy is the black-and-white chessboard mosaic in the atrium. Closed for restoration at the time of research.

→ Casa del Gran Portale

(House of the Large Portal) Named after the elegant brick Corinthian columns that flank its main entrance, the House of the Large Portal is home to some well-preserved wall paintings.

→ Casa dei Cervi

(House of the Stags) Closed indefinitely on our last visit, the Casa dei Cervi is an imposing example of a Roman noble family's house that, before the volcanic mud slide, boasted a seafront address. Constructed around a central courtyard, the two-storey villa contains murals and some beautiful still-life paintings. Waiting for you in the courtyard is a diminutive pair of marble deer assailed by dogs, and an engaging statue of a drunken, peeing Hercules.

→ Villa dei Papiri

(Villa of the Papyri) The Villa dei Papiri was the most luxurious villa in Herculaneum. Owned by Lucius Calpurnius Piso Caesoninus, Julius Caesar's father-in-law, it was a vast four-storey, 245m-long complex stretching down to the sea; there were swimming pools, fountains and a collection of up to 80 sculptures. There was also an important library, whose 1800 papyrus scrolls lend the villa its name. Most of the carbonised scrolls are now in Naples' Museo Archeologico Nazionale.

→ Terme Suburbane

(Suburban Baths) Marking Herculaneum's southernmost tip is the 1st-century-AD Terme Suburbane, one of the best-preserved Roman bath complexes in existence, with deep pools, stucco friezes and bas-reliefs looking down upon marble seats and floors. This is also one of the best places to observe the soaring volcanic deposits that smothered the ancient coastline.

MAV   MUSEUM

(Museo Archeologico Virtuale; ☑081 1777 6843; www.museomav.com; Via IV Novembre 44; adult/reduced €7.50/6, with 3D documentary €11.50/10; ⊙9am-5.30pm daily Mar-May, 10am-6.30pm daily Jun-Sep, 10am-4pm Tue-Sun Oct-Feb; 🚻; 🚃 Circumvesuviana to Ercolano-Scavi) Using computer-generated recreations, this 'virtual archaeological museum' brings ruins such as the forum at Pompeii and Capri's Villa Jovis back to virtual life. Unfortunately, several of the panels are out of order and some of the displays are in Italian only. The short, optional documentary gives an overview of the history of Mt Vesuvius and its infamous eruption in AD 79...in rather lacklustre 3D. The museum is on the main street linking Ercolano-Scavi train station to the ruins of Herculaneum.

✗ Eating

Viva Lo Re   NEAPOLITAN €€

(☑081 739 02 07; www.vivalore.it; Corso Resina 261; meals €32; ⊙noon-4pm & 7-11pm Tue-Sat, noon-4pm Sun) Located 500m southeast of the Herculaneum ruins on Corso Resina – dubbed the Miglio d'Oro (Golden Mile) for its once glorious stretch of 18th-century villas – Viva Lo Re is a stylish *osteria* (casual tavern), where vintage prints and bookshelves meet a superb wine list and competent regional cooking made using quality ingredients. On the downside, service can be a little patchy and portions somewhat small (ask before ordering).

ℹ Information

Tourist Office (Via IV Novembre 44; ⊙9am-5.30pm Mon-Fri; 🚃 Circumvesuviana to Ercolano-Scavi) Ercolano's tourist office is located in the same building as MAV, between the Circumvesuviana Ercolano-Scavi train station and the Herculaneum *scavi* (ruins).

ℹ Getting There & Away

If travelling by Circumvesuviana train (€2.20 from Naples or €2.90 from Sorrento), get off at Ercolano-Scavi station and walk 500m downhill to the ruins – follow the signs for the *scavi* down the main street, Via IV Novembre.

If driving from Naples, the A3 runs southeast along the Bay of Naples. To reach Herculaneum, exit at Ercolano Portico and follow the signs to car parks near the site. From Sorrento, head north along the SS145, which spills onto the A3.

From mid-April to mid-October, tourist train Campania Express runs four times daily between Naples (Porta Nolana and Piazza Garibaldi Circumvesuviana stations) and Sorrento, stopping at Ercolano-Scavi and Pompei-Scavi-Villa dei Misteri en route. One-day return tickets from Naples to Ercolano (€7) or from Sorrento to Ercolano (€11) can be purchased at the stations or online at www.eavsrl.it.

Mt Vesuvius

Rising formidably beside the Bay of Naples, Mt Vesuvius forms part of the Campanian volcanic arch, a string of active, dormant and extinct volcanoes that include the Campi Flegrei's Solfatara and Monte Nuovo, and Ischia's Monte Epomeo. Infamous for its explosive Plinian eruptions and surrounding urban sprawl, it's also one of the world's most carefully monitored volcanoes. Another full-scale eruption would be catastrophic. More than half a million people live in the so called 'red zone', the area most vulnerable to pyroclastic flows and crushing pyroclastic deposits in a major eruption. Yet, despite government incentives to relocate, few residents are willing to leave.

◎ Sights

Mt Vesuvius VOLCANO
(crater adult/reduced €10/8; ☺ crater 9am-6pm Jul & Aug, to 5pm Apr-Jun & Sep, to 4pm Mar & Oct, to 3pm Nov-Feb, ticket office closes 1hr before crater) Since exploding into history in AD 79, Vesuvius has blown its top more than 30 times. What redeems this slumbering menace is the spectacular panorama from its crater, which takes in Naples, its world-famous bay, and part of the Apennine mountains. Vesuvius is the focal point of the Parco Nazionale del Vesuvio, with nine nature walks around the volcano – download a simple map from the park's website. **Horse Riding Tour Naples** (☎345 8560306; www.horseriding naples.com; guided tour €60) also runs three daily horse-riding tours (€60).

The mountain is widely believed to have been higher than it currently stands, claiming a single summit rising to about 3000m rather than the 1281m of today. Its violent outburst in AD 79 not only drowned Pompeii in pumice and pushed the coastline back several kilometres but also destroyed much of the mountain top, creating a huge caldera and two new peaks. The most destructive explosion after that of AD 79 was in 1631, while the most recent was in 1944.

❶ Getting There & Away

Vesuvius can be reached by bus from Pompeii and Ercolano.

The cheapest option is to catch the public **EAV bus** (☎800 211388; www.eavsrl.it) service from Piazza Anfiteatro in Pompeii. Buses depart every 50 minutes from 8am to 3.30pm and take around 50 minutes to reach the summit car park. Once here, purchase your entry ticket to the summit area (€10) and follow the 860m path (best tackled in trainers and with sweater in tow) up to the crater (roughly a 25-minute climb). In Pompeii, ignore any touts telling you that the public bus only runs in summer; they are merely trying to push private tours. Bus tickets cost €2.70 one-way and can be purchased on board.

If you do want to use a private company, **Busvia del Vesuvio** (☎081 878 21 03; www.busvia delvesuvio.com; Via Villa dei Misteri, Pompeii; return incl entry to summit adult/reduced €22/7; ☺ hourly from 9am-4pm) runs hourly shuttle buses from outside Pompeii-Scavi-Villa dei Misteri Circumvesuviana train station, travelling to Boscoreale Terminal Interchange. From here, it's a 25-minute journey up the national park in a 4WD-style bus. Bookings are not required.

In Ercolano, private company **Vesuvio Express** (☎081 739 36 66; www.vesuvioexpress. it; Piazzale Stazione Circumvesuviana, Ercolano; return incl admission to summit €20; ☺ every 40min, 9.30am-4pm) runs buses to the summit car park from Piazzale Stazione Circumvesuviana, outside Ercolano-Scavi train station. A word of warning: this company has received very mixed reviews, with numerous claims of unreliability from travellers.

When the weather is bad the summit path is shut and bus departures are suspended.

If travelling by car, exit the A3 at Ercolano Portico and follow signs for the Parco Nazionale del Vesuvio.

Pompeii

Modern-day Pompeii (Pompei in Italian) may feel like a nondescript satellite of Naples, but it's here that you'll find Europe's most compelling archaeological site: the ruins of Pompeii. Sprawling and haunting, the site is a stark reminder of the malign forces that lie deep inside Vesuvius.

◉ Sights

★ Ruins of Pompeii   ARCHAEOLOGICAL SITE

(📞 081 857 53 47; www.pompeiisites.org; entrances at Porta Marina, Piazza Esedra & Piazza Anfiteatro; adult/reduced €13/7.50, incl Herculaneum €22/12; ⊙ 9am-7.30pm, last entry 6pm Apr-Oct, to 5pm, last entry 3.30pm Nov-Mar) The ghostly ruins of ancient Pompeii make for one of the world's most engrossing archaeological experiences. Much of the site's value lies in the fact that the town wasn't simply blown away by Vesuvius in AD 79 but buried under a layer of *lapilli* (burning fragments of pumice stone). The result is a remarkably well-preserved slice of ancient life, where visitors can walk down Roman streets and snoop around millennia-old houses, temples, shops, cafes, amphitheatres, and even a brothel.

The origins of Pompeii are uncertain, but it seems likely that it was founded in the 7th century BC by the Campanian Oscans. Over the next seven centuries, the city fell to the Greeks and the Samnites before becoming a Roman colony in 80 BC.

In AD 62, a mere 17 years before Vesuvius erupted, the city was struck by a major earthquake. Damage was widespread and much of the city's 20,000-strong population was evacuated. Fortunately, many had not returned by the time Vesuvius blew, but 2000 men, women and children perished nevertheless.

After its catastrophic demise, Pompeii receded from the public eye until 1594, when the architect Domenico Fontana stumbled across the ruins while digging a canal. Exploration proper, however, didn't begin until 1748. Of Pompeii's original 66 hectares, 44 have now been excavated. Of course that doesn't mean you'll have unhindered access to every inch of the Unesco-listed site – expect to come across areas cordoned off for no apparent reason, a noticeable lack of clear signs, and the odd stray dog. Audio guides are a sensible investment (€8, cash only) and a good guidebook will also help – try *Pompeii*, published by Electa Napoli.

Maintenance work is ongoing, but progress is beset by political, financial and bureaucratic problems.

➡ Terme Suburbane

Just outside ancient Pompeii's city walls, this 1st-century-BC bathhouse is famous for several erotic frescoes that scandalised the Vatican when they were revealed in 2001.

The panels decorate what was once the *apodyterium* (changing room). The room leading to the colourfully frescoed *frigidarium* (cold bath) features fragments of stuccowork, as well as one of the few original roofs to survive at Pompeii. Beyond the *tepadarium* (tepid bath) and *caldarium* (hot bath) rooms are the remains of a heated outdoor swimming pool.

➡ Porta Marina

The ruin of Pompeii's main entrance is at Porta Marina, the most impressive of the seven gates that punctuated the ancient town walls. A busy passageway now, as it was then, it originally connected the town with the nearby harbour, hence the gateway's name. Immediately on the right as you enter the gate is the **Antiquarium** and the 1st-century-BC **Tempio di Venere** (Temple of Venus), formerly one of the town's most opulent temples.

➡ Foro

(Forum) A huge rectangle flanked by limestone columns, the *foro* was ancient Pompeii's main piazza, as well as the site of gladiatoral battles before the Anfiteatro was constructed. The buildings surrounding the forum are testament to its role as the city's hub of civic, commercial, political and religious activity.

➡ Basilica

The basilica was the 2nd-century-BC seat of Pompeii's law courts and exchange. Their semicircular apses would later influence the design of early Christian churches.

➡ Tempio di Apollo

(Temple of Apollo) The oldest and most important of Pompeii's religious buildings, the Tempio di Apollo largely dates to the 2nd century BC, including the striking columned portico. Fragments remain of an earlier version dating to the 6th century BC.

➡ Tempio di Giove

(Temple of Jupiter) One of the two flanking triumphal arches of the Tempio di Giove still remains.

➡ Granai del Foro

(Forum Granary) The Granai del Foro is now used to store hundreds of amphorae and a number of body casts that were made in the late 19th century by pouring plaster into the hollows left by disintegrated bodies. Among these casts is a pregnant slave; the belt

Old Pompeii

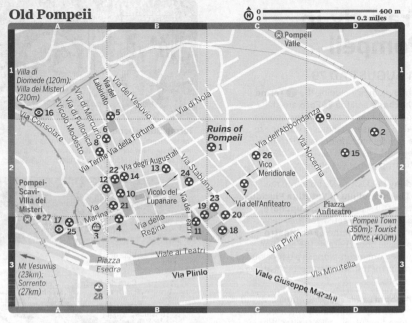

Old Pompeii

around her waist would have displayed the name of her owner.

➡ Macellum

The *macellum* was the city's main produce market. The circular area in the centre was the *tholos*, a covered space in which fish and seafood were sold. Surviving market frescoes reveal some of the goods for sale, including prawns.

➡ Lupanare

Ancient Pompeii's only dedicated brothel, Lupanare is a tiny two-storey building with five rooms on each floor. Its collection of raunchy frescoes was a menu of sorts for clients. The walls in the rooms are carved with graffiti – including declarations of love and hope written by the brothel workers – in various languages.

Tragedy in Pompeii

24 AUGUST AD 79

8am Buildings including the **①Terme Suburbane** and the **②Foro** are still undergoing repair after an earthquake in AD 63 caused significant damage to the city. Despite violent earth tremors overnight, residents have little idea of the catastrophe that lies ahead.

Midday Peckish locals pour into the **③Thermopolium di Vetutius Placidus**. The lustful slip into the **④Lupanare**, and gladiators practise for the evening's planned games at the **⑤Anfiteatro**. A massive boom heralds the eruption. Shocked onlookers witness a dark cloud of volcanic matter shoot some 14km above the crater.

3pm–5pm Lapilli (burning pumice stone) rains down on Pompeii. Terrified locals begin to flee; others take shelter. Within two hours, the plume is 25km high and the sky has darkened. Roofs collapse under the weight of the debris, burying those inside.

25 AUGUST AD 79

Midnight Mudflows bury the town of Herculaneum. Lapilli and ash continue to rain down on Pompeii, bursting through buildings and suffocating those taking refuge within.

4am–8am Ash and gas avalanches hit Herculaneum. Subsequent surges smother Pompeii, killing all remaining residents, including those in the **⑥Orto dei Fuggiaschi**. The volcanic 'blanket' will safeguard frescoed treasures like the **⑦Casa del Menandro** and **⑧Villa dei Misteri** for almost two millennia.

Terme Suburbane
The *laconicum* (sauna), *caldarium* (hot bath) and large, heated swimming pool weren't the only sources of heat here; scan the walls of this suburban bathhouse for some of the city's raunchiest frescoes.

VIACHESLAV LOPATIN / SHUTTERSTOCK ©

Villa di Diomede

Casa del Poeta Tragico

Porta Ercolano

Casa del Fauno

Basilica

Tempio di Apollo

Porta Marina

①

②

④

Terme del Foro

Macellum

Teatro Grande

Quadriportico dei Teatri

Porta di Stabia

Teatro Piccolo

Foro
An ancient Times Square of sorts, the forum sits at the intersection of Pompeii's main streets and was closed to traffic in the 1st century AD. The plinths on the southern edge featured statues of the imperial family.

PHOOEY / GETTY IMAGES ©

TOP TIPS

➡ Visit in the afternoon.
➡ Allow three hours.
➡ Wear comfortable shoes and a hat.
➡ Bring drinking water.
➡ Don't use flash photography.

Villa dei Misteri

Home to the world-famous *Dionysiac Frieze* fresco. Other highlights at this villa include *trompe l'oeil* wall decorations in the *cubiculum* (bedroom) and Egyptian-themed artwork in the *tablinum* (reception).

Lupanare

The prostitutes at this brothel were often slaves of Greek or Asian origin. Mattresses once covered the stone beds and the names engraved in the walls are possibly those of the workers and their clients.

Thermopolium di Vetutius Placidus

The counter at this ancient snack bar once held urns filled with hot food. The *lararium* (household shrine) on the back wall depicts Dionysus (the god of wine) and Mercury (the god of profit and commerce).

Casa del Vettii

Porta del Vesuvio

Porta di Nola

Casa della Venere in Conchiglia

Porta di Sarno

Grande Palestra

Tempio di Iside

EYEWITNESS ACCOUNT

Pliny the Younger (AD 61–c 112) gives a gripping, first-hand account of the catastrophe in his letters to Tacitus (AD 56–117).

Orto dei Fuggiaschi

The Garden of the Fugitives showcases the plaster moulds of 13 locals seeking refuge during Vesuvius' eruption – the largest number of victims found in any one area. The huddled bodies make for a moving scene.

Anfiteatro

Magistrates, local senators and the games' sponsors and organisers enjoyed front-row seating at this veteran amphitheatre, home to gladiatorial battles and the odd riot. The parapet circling the stadium featured paintings of combat, victory celebrations and hunting scenes.

Casa del Menandro

This dwelling most likely belonged to the family of Poppaea Sabina, Nero's second wife. A room to the left of the atrium features Trojan War paintings and a polychrome mosaic of pygmies rowing down the Nile.

➡ Foro Triangolare

The Foro Triangolare would originally have overlooked the sea.

➡ Teatro Grande

The 2nd-century-BC Teatro Grande was a huge 5000-seat theatre carved into the lava mass on which Pompeii was originally built.

➡ Quadriportico dei Teatri

Behind the Teatro Grande's stage, the porticoed Quadriportico dei Teatri was initially used for the audience to stroll between acts and later as a barracks for gladiators.

➡ Teatro Piccolo

Also known as the Odeion, the Teatro Piccolo was once an indoor theatre renowned for its acoustics.

➡ Tempio di Iside

(Temple of Isis) The pre-Roman Tempio di Iside was a popular place of cult worship.

➡ Casa del Menandro

Better preserved than the larger Casa del Fauno, luxurious Casa del Menandro has an outstanding, elegant peristyle (a colonnade-framed courtyard) beyond its beautifully frescoed atrium. On the peristyle's far right side a doorway leads to a private bathhouse, lavished with exquisite frescoes and mosaics. The central room off the far end of the peristyle features a striking fresco of the ancient Greek dramatist Menander, after which the rediscovered villa was named.

➡ Via dell'Abbondanza

(Street of Abundance) The Via dell'Abbondanza was ancient Pompeii's main street. The elevated stepping stones allowed people to cross the street without stepping into the waste that washed down the thoroughfare.

➡ Terme Stabiane

At this typical 2nd-century-BC bath complex, bathers would enter from the vestibule, stop off in the vaulted *apodyterium* (changing room), and then pass through to the *tepidarium* (warm baths) and *caldarium* (hot baths). Particularly impressive is the stuccoed vault in the men's changing room, complete with whimsical images of *putti* (winged babies) and nymphs.

➡ Casa della Venere in Conchiglia

(House of the Venus Marina) Casa della Venere in Conchiglia harbours a lovely peristyle looking onto a small, manicured garden. It's here in the garden that you'll find the large, striking Venus fresco after which the house is named.

➡ Anfiteatro

(Amphitheatre) Gladiatorial battles thrilled up to 20,000 spectators at the grassy *anfiteatro*. Built in 70 BC, it's the oldest known Roman amphitheatre in existence.

➡ Palestra Grande

Lithe ancients kept fit at the Palestra Grande, an athletics field with an impressive portico dating to the Augustan period. At its centre lie the grassy remains of a swimming pool. The site is now occasionally used to host temporary exhibitions.

➡ Casa del Fauno

(House of the Faun) Covering an entire *insula* (city block) and boasting two atria at its front end (humbler homes had one), Pompeii's largest private house is named after the delicate bronze statue in the *impluvium* (rain tank). It was here that early excavators found Pompeii's greatest mosaics, most of which are now in Naples' Museo Archeologico Nazionale (p660). Valuable on-site originals include a beautiful, geometrically patterned marble floor.

➡ Casa del Poeta Tragico

(House of the Tragic Poet) The Casa del Poeta Tragico features the world's first known 'beware of the dog' – *cave canem* – warnings, visible through a protective glass panel.

➡ Casa dei Vettii

The Casa dei Vettii is home to a famous depiction of Priapus with his gigantic phallus balanced on a pair of scales...much to the anxiety of many a male observer.

➡ Villa dei Misteri

(Villa of the Mysteries) This restored, 90-room villa is one of the most complete structures left standing in Pompeii. The **dionysiac frieze**, the most important fresco still on site, spans the walls of the large dining room. One of the biggest and most arresting paintings from the ancient world, it depicts the initiation of a bride-to-be into the cult of Dionysus, the Greek god of wine.

A farm for much of its life, the villa's *vino*-making area is still visible at the northern end.

Follow Via Consolare out of the town through **Porta Ercolano**. Continue past **Villa di Diomede**, turn right, and you'll come to Villa dei Misteri.

NAPLES & CAMPANIA POMPEII

REGGIA DI CASERTA

The one compelling reason to visit the town of Caserta, 30km north of Naples, is to gasp at the colossal, World Heritage–listed **Reggia di Caserta** (Palazzo Reale; ☑ 0823 27 71 11; www.reggiadicaserta.beniculturali.it; Viale Douhet 22, Caserta; adult/reduced €12/6; ⊙ palace 8.30am-7.30pm Wed-Mon, park & Giardino Inglese 8.30am-1hr before sunset Wed-Mon; ℞ Caserta). Italy's swansong to the baroque, the complex began life in 1752 after Charles VII ordered a palace to rival Versailles. Not one to disappoint, Neapolitan architect Luigi Vanvitelli delivered a palace bigger than its French rival. With its 1200 rooms, 1790 windows, 34 staircases and 250m-long facade, it was reputedly the largest building in 18th-century Europe.

Vanvitelli's immense staircase leads up to the royal apartments, lavishly decorated with frescoes, art, tapestries, period furniture and crystal.

The restored back rooms off the Sala di Astrea (Room of Astraea) house an extraordinary collection of historic wooden models of the Reggia, along with architectural drawings and early sketches of the building by Luigi Vanvitelli and his son, Carlo. The apartments are also home to the Mostra Terrea Motus, an underrated collection of international modern art commissioned after the region's devastating earthquake in 1980. Among the contributors are US heavyweights Cy Twombly, Robert Mapplethorpe and Keith Haring, as well as local luminaries like Mimmo Paladino and Jannis Kounellis.

The complex has appeared in numerous films, including *Mission: Impossible 3*, *Star Wars Episode 1: The Phantom Menace* and *Star Wars Episode 2: Attack of the Clones*, moonlighting as Queen Amidala's palace in the latter two.

To clear your head afterwards, explore the elegant landscaped park, which stretches for some 3km to a waterfall and a fountain of Diana. Within the park is the famous Giardino Inglese (English Garden), a romantic oasis of intricate pathways, exotic flora, pools and cascades. Bicycle hire (from €4) is available at the back of the palace building, as are pony-and-trap rides (€50 for 30 minutes, up to five people). Ignore the illegal souvenir hawkers roaming the grounds.

If you're feeling peckish, consider skipping the touristy palace cafeteria for local cafe Martucci, located 250m east of the complex. Great coffee aside, the counters here heave with freshly made *panini* (sandwiches), salads, vegetable dishes, pastries and substantial cooked-to-order meals.

Regular trains connect Naples to Caserta (€3.10, 30 to 50 minutes); always plan ahead and check times online before hitting the station. Caserta train station is located directly opposite the palace grounds. If you're driving, follow signs for the Reggia.

☞ Tours

Walks of Italy TOURS
(www.walksofitaly.com; 3hr Pompeii guided tour per person €59) This American-based tour company specialises in tours of Italy, including walking tours of Pompeii.

🛏 Sleeping & Eating

Although the town of Pompeii has a number of nondescript hotels, you're better off basing yourself in Sorrento or Naples and exploring the ruins as an easy day trip.

★President CAMPANIAN €€€
(☑ 081 850 72 45; www.ristorantepresident.it; Piazza Schettini 12; meals from €40, tasting menus €65-90; ⊙ noon-3.30pm & 7pm-late Tue-Sun; ℞ FS to Pompei, ℞ Circumvesuviana to Pompei-Scavi-

Villa dei Misteri) At the helm of this Michelin-starred standout is charming owner-chef Paolo Gramaglia, whose passion for local produce, history and culinary creativity translates into bread made to ancient Roman recipes, slow-cooked snapper paired with tomato purée and sweet-onion gelato, and deconstructed *pastiera* (sweet Neapolitan tart).

The menu's creative and visual brilliance is matched by sommelier Eulalia Buondonno's swoon-inducing wine list, which features around 600 drops from esteemed and lesser-known Italian winemakers; best of all, the staff are happy to serve any bottle to the value of €100 by the glass.

A word of warning: if you plan on catching a *treno regionale* (regional train) back to Naples from nearby Pompei station (a closer, more convenient option than the Pompei-Scavi-Villa dei Misteri station on the Circumvesuviana train line), check train times first as the last service from Pompei can depart as early as 9.40pm.

❶ Information

Tourist Office (☏ 081 1951 7589; Via Sacra 16; ⊘ 8.30am-6pm) Located in the centre of the modern town.

❶ Getting There & Away

To reach the *scavi* (ruins) by Circumvesuviana train (€2.80 from Naples, €2.40 from Sorrento), alight at Pompei-Scavi-Villa dei Misteri station, located beside the main entrance at Porta Marina. Regional trains (www.trenitalia.com) stop at Pompei station in the centre of the modern town.

From mid-April to mid-October, tourist train Campania Express runs four times daily between Naples (Porta Nolana and Piazza Garibaldi Circumvesuviana stations) and Sorrento, stopping at Ercolano-Scavi and Pompei-Scavi-Villa dei Misteri en route. One-day return tickets from Naples to Pompeii (€11) or from Sorrento to Pompeii (€7) can be purchased at the stations or online at www.eavsrl.it.

If driving from Naples, head southeast on the A3, using the Pompei exit and following the signs to Pompei Scavi. Car parks (about €5 all day) are clearly marked and vigorously touted. Among them is **Camping Spartacus** (☏ 081 862 40 78; Via Plinio 127), conveniently located opposite the ruins. From Sorrento, head north along the SS145, which connects to the A3 and Pompeii.

Sorrento

☏ 081 / POP 16,700

An unashamed resort, Sorrento is nonetheless a civilised and beautiful town. Even the souvenirs are a cut above the norm, with plenty of fine old shops selling the ceramics, lacework and *intarsio* (marquetry items) that are famously produced here. The main drawback is the lack of a proper beach: the town straddles the cliffs overlooking the water to Naples and Mt Vesuvius.

Sorrento makes a good base for exploring the region's highlights: to the south is the best of the peninsula's unspoilt countryside, to the east is the Amalfi Coast, to the north lie Pompeii and other archaeological sites, and offshore lies the fabled island of Capri.

◉ Sights

★ Museo Correale di Terranova MUSEUM

(☏ 081 878 18 46; www.museocorreale.it; Via Correale 50; €8; ⊘ 9.30am-6.30pm Tue-Sat, to 1.30pm Sun Apr-Oct, 9.30am-1.30pm Tue-Sun Nov-Mar) East of the city centre, this engaging museum is well worth a visit whether you're a clock collector, an archaeological egghead or into delicate ceramics. In addition to the rich assortment of 16th- to 19th-century Neapolitan art and crafts (including extraordinary examples of marquetry), you'll discover Japanese, Chinese and European ceramics, clocks, fans and, on the ground floor, ancient and medieval artefacts. Among these is a fragment of an ancient Egyptian carving uncovered in the vicinity of Sorrento's Sedile Dominova.

Chiostro di San Francesco COURTYARD

To the left of the Chiesa di San Francesco are its beautiful cloisters, featuring an Arabic portico and interlaced arches supported by octagonal pillars. Surrounded by bougainvillea and birdsong, the cloisters are built on the ruins of a 7th-century monastery. Upstairs lies the **Sorrento International Photo School** (☏ 344 0838503; www.raffaelecelentano.com; adult/reduced €2.50/free; ⊘ 10am-8pm Mar-Dec), a gallery space showcasing evocative black-and-white photographs of Italian life and landscapes by contemporary local photographer Raffaele Celentano.

Museo Bottega della Tarsia Lignea MUSEUM

(☏ 081 877 19 42; www.museomuta.it; Via San Nicola 28; adult/reduced €8/5; ⊘ 10am-6.30pm Apr-Oct, to 5.30pm Nov-Mar) Since the 18th century, Sorrento has been famous for its *intarsio* (marquetry) furniture, made with elaborately designed inlaid wood. Some wonderful examples can be found in this museum, housed in an 18th-century palace, complete with beautiful frescoes. There's also an interesting collection of paintings, prints and photographs that depict the town and surrounding area in the 19th century.

If you're interested in purchasing a new *intarsio* piece, visit **Gargiulo & Jannuzzi** (☏ 081 878 10 41; www.gargiulo-jannuzzi.it; Viale Enrico Caruso 1; ⊘ 8am-8pm May-Oct, 9am-7pm Nov, Dec & Mar-Apr), one of the longest-established specialist shops in town; they are happy to ship.

Sorrento

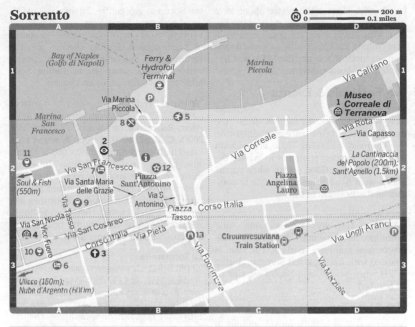

Sorrento

⊙ Top Sights
1 Museo Correale di Terranova................D1

⊙ Sights
2 Chiostro di San Francesco....................A2
3 Duomo...A3
Gallery Celentano........................(see 2)
4 Museo Bottega della Tarsia Lignea......A3

⊕ Activities, Courses & Tours
5 Sic Sic...B1

⊜ Sleeping
6 Casa Astarita.......................................A3
7 Palazzo Marziale..................................A2

⊗ Eating
8 Acqu' e Sale...B2

⊙ Drinking & Nightlife
9 Bollicine..A2
10 Cafè Latino..A3
11 La Pergola...A2

⊙ Entertainment
12 Teatro Tasso.......................................B2

⊜ Shopping
13 Gargiulo & Jannuzzi.............................B3

Duomo   CATHEDRAL

(☑081 878 22 48; Corso Italia; ⊙8am-12.30pm & 4.30-9pm) Sorrento's cathedral features a striking exterior fresco, triple-tiered bell tower, four classical columns and an elegant majolica clock. Inside, take note of the marble bishop's throne (1573), as well as both the wooden choir stalls and stations of the cross, decorated in the local *intarsio* (marquetry) style. Although the cathedral's original structure dates from the 15th century, the building has been altered several times, most recently in the early 20th century when the current facade was added.

🏃 Activities

★ Sic Sic   BOATING

(☑081 807 22 83; www.nauticasicsic.com; Marina Piccola; ⊙May-Oct) Seek out the best beaches by rented boat, with or without a skipper. This outfit rents a variety of motor boats, starting at around €50 per hour or from €150 per day. It also organises boat excursions, wedding shoots and similar.

Bagni Regina Giovanna   SWIMMING

Sorrento lacks a decent beach, so consider heading to Bagni Regina Giovanna, a rocky beach with clear, clean water about 2km west of town, set among the ruins of the Roman Villa Pollio Felix. It's possible to walk here (follow Via Capo), although you'll save your strength if you get the SITA Sud bus headed for Massa Lubrense.

⚡ Festivals & Events

Settimana Santa RELIGIOUS
(Holy Week) Famed throughout Italy; the first procession takes place at midnight on the Thursday preceding Good Friday, with robed and hooded penitents in white; the second occurs on Good Friday, when participants wear black robes and hoods to commemorate the death of Christ.

Sant'Antonino RELIGIOUS
(⊙14 Feb) The city's patron saint, Sant' Antonino, is remembered annually with processions and huge markets. The saint is credited with having saved Sorrento during WWII when Salerno and Naples were heavily bombed.

🛌 Sleeping

Accommodation is thick on the ground in this town, although if you're arriving in high summer (July and August), you'll need to book ahead. Most of the big city-centre hotels are geared towards package tourism and prices are correspondingly high. There are, however, some excellent choices, particularly on Via Capo, the coastal road west of the centre. This area is within walking distance of the city centre, but if you're carrying luggage it's easier to catch a SITA Sud bus for Sant'Agata or Massa Lubrense.

★ Ulisse HOTEL €
(✆081 877 47 53; www.ulissedeluxe.com; Via del Mare 22; dm €20-35, d €60-150; P❋🐾🛜🏊) Although it calls itself a hostel, the Ulisse is about as far from a backpackers' pad as a hiking boot from a stiletto. Most rooms are plush, spacious affairs with swish if rather bland fabrics, gleaming floors and large ensuite bathrooms. There are two single-sex dorms, and quads for sharers. Breakfast is included in some rates but costs €10 with others.

Nube d'Argento CAMPGROUND €
(✆081 878 13 44; www.nubedargento.com; Via Capo 21; camping per 2 people, car & tent €27-43, 2-person bungalows €65-90, 4-person bungalows €95-125; ⊙Mar-Dec; @🏊) This inviting campground is an easy 1km drive west of

the Sorrento city centre. Pitches and wooden chalet-style bungalows are spread out beneath a canopy of olive trees – a source of much-needed summer shade – and the facilities are excellent. Kids in particular will enjoy the open-air swimming pool, table-tennis table, slides and swings.

★ Hotel Cristina HOTEL €€
(✆081 878 35 62; www.hotelcristinasorrento.it; Via Privata Rubinacci 6, Sant'Agnello; s €130, d €150-200, tr €220, q €240; ⊙Mar-Oct; P❋🛜🏊) Located high above Sant'Agnello, this hotel has superb views, particularly from the swimming pool. The spacious rooms have seaview balconies and combine inlaid wooden furniture with contemporary flourishes like Philippe Starck chairs. There's an in-house restaurant and a free shuttle bus to/from Sorrento's Circumvesuviana train station.

La Tonnarella HOTEL €€
(✆081 878 11 53; www.latonnarella.com; Via Capo 31; d €120-140, ste €240-350; ⊙Apr-Oct & Christmas; P❋@🛜) A splendid choice – but not for minimalists – La Tonnarella is a dazzling canvas of majolica tiles, antiques, chandeliers and statues. Rooms, most with their own balcony or small terrace, continue the sumptuous classical theme with traditional furniture and discreet mod cons. The hotel also has its own private beach, accessible by lift, and a highly regarded terrace restaurant.

Casa Astarita B&B €€
(✆081 877 49 06; www.casastarita.com; Corso Italia 67; d €70-140, tr €95-165; ❋🛜) Housed in an 18th-century *palazzo* (mansion) on Sorrento's main strip, this charming B&B has a colourful, eclectic look with original vaulted ceilings, brightly painted doors and majolica-tiled floors. Its six simple but well-equipped rooms surround a central parlour, where breakfast is served on a large rustic table.

★ Palazzo Marziale BOUTIQUE HOTEL €€€
(✆081 807 44 06; www.palazzomarziale.com; Largo San Francesco 2; d/ste from €199/459; ❋🛜) From cascading vines, Chinese porcelain urns and Persian rugs in the lobby lounge, to antique furniture, *objets* and artworks in the hallways and inlaid wood in the lift, this sophisticated, eleven-room hideaway is big on details. The family's elegant tastes extend to the rooms, resplendent with high ceilings, chaise longues and high-end mattresses and linens.

Eating

The centre of town heaves with bars, cafes, trattorias, restaurants and even the odd kebab takeaway shop. Many places, particularly those with waistcoated waiters stationed outside (or the ones displaying sun-bleached photos of the dishes), are tourist traps serving bland food at inflated prices. Thankfully, not all are and it's perfectly possible to eat very well.

★ La Cantinaccia del Popolo
NEAPOLITAN €

(📞 366 1015497; Vico Terzo Rota; meals €21; ⊙ 11am-3pm & 7-11pm Tue-Sun) Its small, rustic interiors festooned with garlic and prosciutto, this down-to-earth favourite proves that top-notch produce and simplicity are the keys to culinary success. A case in point is the *spaghetti al pomodoro*, a basic dish of pasta and tomato that bursts with flavour, vibrancy and balance. Charcuterie options include La Cantinaccia's own cured meats as well as some interesting Campanian cheeses. Outdoor seating available.

★ Acqu' e Sale
NEAPOLITAN €€

(📞 081 1900 5967; http://acquesale.it; Piazza Marina D'Italia 2; pizzas from €6, meals around €37) Despite its proximity to the ferry terminal, Acqu' e Sale is popular among fastidious locals. Heading the open kitchen is chef Antonino Esposito, who turns glistening fresh fish into beautiful, thoughtfully presented dishes. The Neapolitan-style pizzas are gorgeous, with a creative choice of bases that include a very local *al limone* (lemon-flavoured). There's an outdoor patio, numerous gluten-free dishes and fine coffee to boot.

★ Soul & Fish
SEAFOOD €€€

(📞 081 878 21 70; www.soulandfish.com; Marina Grande; meals €30-42; ⊙ noon-2.30pm & 7-10.30pm, closed Nov-Easter; 🐾) Soul & Fish is arguably the best of the waterfront eateries at Marina Grande. While we love the beach shack–chic design and complimentary glass of *prosecco*, it's the beautiful, intriguing dishes that seal the deal. If it's on the menu, start with the *caponatina*, a fresh salad of cuttlefish, rocket, orange pistachio and wholemeal bread. Fresh fish aside, the kitchen also cooks impressive risottos.

🍷 Drinking & Nightlife

Bollicine
WINE BAR

(📞 081 878 46 16; Via Accademia 9; ⊙ 6.30pm-late) The wine list at this unpretentious bar with a dark, woody interior includes all the big Italian names and a selection of interesting local labels. If you can't decide what to go for, the amiable bar staff will advise you. There's also a small menu of *panini* (sandwiches), bruschettas and one or two pasta dishes.

Cafè Latino
BAR

(📞 081 877 37 18; http://cafelatinosorrento.it; Vico Fuoro 4a; ⊙ 10am-1am Mar-Dec) Think locked-eyes-over-cocktails time. This is the place to impress your date with cocktails (from €7) on the terrace, surrounded by orange and lemon trees. Sip a Mary Pickford (rum, pineapple, *grenadino* and maraschino) or a glass of chilled white wine. If you can't drag yourselves away, you can also eat here (meals around €35).

La Pergola
BAR

(📞 081 878 10 24; www.bellevue.it; Hotel Bellevue Syrene, Piazza della Vittoria 5) When it's time for romance (or simply time to treat yourself), style up and indulge with a pre-dinner libation at the Hotel Bellevue Syrene's swoon-inducing terrace bar/restaurant. The clifftop view across the Bay of Naples is breathtaking, taking in soaring Mt Vesuvius and, in the distance, Naples. Not cheap but utterly unforgettable.

☆ Entertainment

Teatro Tasso
THEATRE

(📞 081 807 55 25; www.teatrotasso.it; Piazza Sant'Antonino; incl cocktail €25; ⊙ Sorrento Musical 9.30pm Apr-Oct) The southern-Italian equivalent of a London old-time music hall, Teatro Tasso is home to the *Sorrento Musical,* a sentimental 75-minute revue of Neapolitan classics such as 'O Sole Mio' and 'Trona a Sorrent'.

ℹ Information

Post Office (www.poste.it; Corso Italia 210; ⊙ 8.20am-7pm Mon-Fri, to 12.30pm Sat) Just north of the train station.

Main Tourist Office (📞 081 807 40 33; www. sorrentotourism.com; Via Luigi de Maio 35; ⊙ 8.30am-7.30pm Mon-Fri Jun-Oct, to 4pm Nov-May) In the Circolo dei Forestieri (Foreigners' Club), lists ferry and train times. Ask for the useful publication *Surrentum*.

❶ Getting There & Away

BOAT

Sorrento is the main jumping-off point for Capri and also has ferry connections to Naples and Amalfi coastal resorts during the summer months from its **Ferry & Hydrofoil Terminal** (Via Luigi de Maio).

Caremar (☏ 081 807 30 77; www.caremar.it) runs hydrofoils to Capri (€16, 25 minutes, four daily).

Gescab (☏ 081 807 18 12; www.gescab.it) also runs hydrofoils to Capri (€19, 20 minutes, 17 to 19 daily).

Navigazione Libera del Golfo (p681) runs one daily hydrofoil to Naples (€12.90, 20 minutes).

BUS

SITA Sud (www.sitasudtrasporti.it) buses serve Naples, the Amalfi Coast and Sant'Agata, leaving from the **bus station** (Piazza Giovanna Battista de Curtis) across from the entrance to the Circumvesuviana train station. Buy tickets at the station or from shops bearing the blue SITA sign.

TRAIN

Sorrento is the last stop on the **Circumvesuviana** (☏ 800 21 13 88; www.eavsrl.it) train line from Naples. Train services run every half-hour for Naples (€3.90, 70 minutes), via Pompeii (€2.40, 30 minutes) and Ercolano (€2.90, 50 minutes).

THE AMALFI COAST

Deemed an outstanding example of a Mediterranean landscape by Unesco, the Amalfi Coast is one of Italy's most piercing destinations. Here, mountains plunge into the sea in a nail-biting vertical scene of precipitous crags, cliff-clinging abodes and verdant woodland.

Its string of fabled towns read like a Hollywood cast list. There's jet-set favourite Positano, a pastel-coloured cascade of chic boutiques, *spritz*-sipping pin-ups and sunkissed sunbathers. Further east, ancient Amalfi lures with its Arabic-Norman cathedral, while mountaintop Ravello stirs hearts with its cultured villas and Wagnerian connection. To the west lies Amalfi Coast gateway Sorrento (p698), a handsome cliff-top resort that has miraculously survived the onslaught of package tourism.

Turquoise seas and postcard-perfect piazzas aside, the region is home to some of Italy's finest hotels and restaurants. It's also one of the country's top spots for hiking, with well-marked trails providing the chance to escape the star-struck coastal crowds.

❶ Getting There & Away

BOAT

Year-round hydrofoil services run between Naples and Sorrento, as well as between Sorrento and Capri. From around May to October, regular ferry services connect Sorrento to Positano and Amalfi, from where ferries continue to Salerno.

BUS

The Circumvesuviana train has services that run from Naples' Piazza Garibaldi to Sorrento, from where there is a regular and efficient **SITA Sud** (p704) bus service to Positano, Amalfi and Salerno.

TRAIN

The **Circumvesuviana** runs every half-hour between Naples' Garibaldi station (beside Napoli Centrale station) and Sorrento. Trains stop in Ercolano (Herculaneum) and Pompeii en route. **Trenitalia** (p674) runs frequent services between Napoli Centrale station and Salerno.

Amalfi

☏ 089 / POP 5150

It is hard to grasp that pretty little Amalfi, with its sun-filled piazzas and small beach, was once a maritime superpower with a population of more than 70,000. For one thing, it's not a big place – you can easily walk from one end to the other in about 20 minutes. For another, there are very few historical buildings of note. The explanation is chilling: most of the old city, and its populace, simply slid into the sea during an earthquake in 1343.

Despite this, the town exudes a sense of history and culture, most notably in its breathtaking cathedral and fascinating paper museum. And while the permanent population is a fairly modest 5000 or so these days, the numbers swell significantly during summer.

Just around the headland, neighbouring **Atrani** is a picturesque tangle of whitewashed alleys and arches centred on a lively, lived-in piazza and popular beach; don't miss it.

⊙ Sights

★ Cattedrale di Sant'Andrea CATHEDRAL

(☑089 87 10 59; Piazza del Duomo; ⊙7.30am-7.30pm) A melange of architectural styles, Amalfi's cathedral, one of the few relics of the town's past as an 11th-century maritime superpower, makes a striking impression at the top of its sweeping flight of stairs. Between 10am and 5pm entrance is through the adjacent Chiostro del Paradiso (☑089 87 13 24; Piazza del Duomo; adult/reduced €3/1; ⊙9am-7.45pm Jul-Aug, reduced hours rest of year), a 13th-century cloister.

The cathedral dates in part from the early 10th century and its striped facade has been rebuilt twice, most recently at the end of the 19th century. Although the building is a hybrid, the Sicilian Arabic-Norman style predominates, particularly in the two tone masonry and the 13th-century bell tower. The huge bronze doors also merit a look – the first of their type in Italy, they were commissioned by a local noble and made in Syria before being shipped to Amalfi. While the baroque interior is less impressive, indoor highlights include fine statues at the altar and some interesting 12th- and 13th-century mosaics.

★ Museo della Carta MUSEUM

(☑089 830 45 61; www.museodellacarta.it; Via delle Cartiere 23; €4; ⊙10am-6.30pm daily Mar-Oct, 10am-3.30pm Tue, Wed & Fri-Sun Nov-Feb) Amalfi's paper museum is housed in a rugged, cave-like 13th-century paper mill (the oldest in Europe). It lovingly preserves the original paper presses, which are still in full working order, as you'll see during the 30-minute guided tour (in English), which explains the original cotton-based paper production and the later wood-pulp manufacturing. Afterwards you may well be inspired to pick up some of the stationery sold in the gift shop, alongside calligraphy sets and paper pressed with flowers.

Grotta dello Smeraldo CAVE

(€5; ⊙9am-4pm) Four kilometres west of Amalfi, this grotto is named after the eerie emerald colour that emanates from the water. Stalactites hang down from the 24m-high ceiling, while stalagmites grow up to 10m tall. Buses regularly pass the car park above the cave entrance (from where you take a lift or stairs down to the rowing boats). Alternatively, Coop Sant'Andrea (☑089 87 31 90; www.coopsantandrea.com; Lungomare dei Cavalieri 1) runs boats from Amalfi

(€10 return, plus cave admission). Allow 1½ hours for the return trip.

🏃 Activities

Amalfi Marine BOATING

(☑338 3076125; www.amalfiboatrental.com; Spiaggia del Porto, Lungomare dei Cavalieri) Amalfi Marine hires out boats (without a skipper from €150 per day, per boat excluding petrol; maximum six passengers). Private day-long tours with a skipper start from €300.

🛏 Sleeping

★ Albergo Sant'Andrea HOTEL €

(☑089 87 11 45; www.albergosantandrea.it; Via Costanza d'Avalos 1; s/d €60/100; ⊙Mar-Dec; ❄🛜) Enjoy the atmosphere of busy Piazza del Duomo from the comfort of your own room. This modest two-star has basic rooms with brightly coloured tiles and coordinating fabrics. Double glazing has helped cut down the piazza hubbub, which can reach fever pitch in high season – this is one place to ask for a room with a (cathedral) view.

Residenza del Duca HOTEL €€

(☑089 873 63 65; www.residencedelduca.it; Via Duca Mastalo II 3; r €70-175; ⊙Mar-Oct; ❄🛜) This family-run hotel has just six rooms, all of them light, sunny, and prettily furnished with antiques, majolica tiles and the odd chintzy cherub. The Jacuzzi showers are excellent. Call ahead if you are carrying heavy bags, as it's a seriously puff-you-out-climb up some steps to reach here and a luggage service is included in the price.

Hotel Lidomare HOTEL €€

(☑089 87 13 32, www.lidomare.it; Largo Duchi Piccolomini 9; s/d €65/115; ❄🛜) Family run, this gracious, old-fashioned hotel has no shortage of character. The large, luminous rooms have an air of gentility, with their appealingly haphazard decor, vintage tiles and fine antiques. Some have spa baths, others have sea views and a balcony, some have both. Rather unusually, breakfast is laid out on top of a grand piano.

Hotel Centrale HOTEL €€

(☑089 87 26 08; www.amalfihotelcentrale.it; Largo Duchi Piccolomini 1; d €100-120; ⊙year-round; ❄🛜) This is one of the best-value hotels in Amalfi. The entrance is on a tiny little piazza in the *centro storico* (historic centre), but many of the small yet tastefully decorated rooms overlook Piazza del Duomo. The aquamarine ceramic tiling lends a fresh, summery feel and the views from the rooftop terrace are magnificent.

 Hotel Luna Convento   HOTEL €€€

(089 87 10 02; www.lunahotel.it; Via Pantaleone Comite 33; s €270-370, d €290-390, ste €490-590; Easter-Oct; P✳@⚡☎) This former convent was founded by St Francis in 1222 and has been a hotel for some 170 years. Rooms in the original building are in the former monks' cells, but there's nothing poky about the bright tiles, balconies and seamless sea views. The newer wing is equally beguiling, with religious frescoes over the bed. The cloistered courtyard is magnificent.

✗ Eating

La Pansa   CAFE €

(089 87 10 65; www.pasticceriapansa.it; Piazza del Duomo 40; cornetti from €1, pastries from €4.50; 7.30am-11pm, closed early Jan-early Feb) A marbled and mirrored 1830 cafe on Piazza del Duomo where black-bow-tied waiters serve a great Italian breakfast: freshly made *cornetti* (croissants), full-bodied espresso and deliciously frothy cappuccino. Standout pastries include the crisp, flaky *coda di aragosta con crema di limone*, a lobster tail–shaped concoction filled with a rich yet light lemon custard cream.

Le Arcate   ITALIAN €€

(089 87 13 67; www.learcate.net; Largo Orlando Buonocore, Atrani; pizzas from €6, meals €30; 12.30-3.30pm & 7.30-11.30pm Tue-Sun Sep-Jun, daily Jul & Aug; ☎) On a sunny day, it's hard to beat Le Arcate's dreamy location: at the far eastern point of the harbour overlooking the beach, with Atrani's ancient rooftops and majolica-tiled domes before you. Huge parasols shade the sprawl of tables, while the dining room is a stone-walled natural cave. The food is fine, if not exceptional, with decent pizzas and pasta dishes, including gluten-free options.

★ **Marina Grande**   SEAFOOD €€€

(089 87 11 29; www.ristorantemarinagrande.com; Viale della Regione 4; tasting menu €70, meals €50; noon-3pm & 6.30-10.30pm Wed-Mon Mar-Oct; ☎) Run by the third generation of the same family, this savvy beachfront favourite serves fish so fresh it's almost flapping. It prides itself on the use of locally sourced organic produce, which, in Amalfi, means superlative seafood. Reservations recommended.

❶ Information

Post Office (www.poste.it; Corso delle Repubbliche Marinare 31; 8.20am-7pm Mon-Fri, to 12.30pm Sat) Next door to the tourist office.

Tourist Office (089 87 11 07; www.amalfi touristoffice.it; Corso delle Repubbliche Marinare 27; 8.30am-1pm & 2-6pm Mon-Sat Apr-Oct, 8.30am-1pm Mon-Sat Nov-Mar) Just off the main seafront road.

❶ Getting There & Away

BOAT

Between May and October there are daily sailings from Amalfi's **ferry terminal** east to Salerno and west to Positano, Sorrento and Capri.

BUS

From the **bus station** (Lungomare dei Cavalieri) in Piazza Flavio Gioia, **SITA Sud** (344 103 10 70; www.sitasudtrasporti.it; Piazza Flavio Gioia) runs up to 27 buses daily to Ravello (€1.30, 25 minutes).

Eastbound, it runs up to 20 buses daily to Salerno (€2.40, 1¼ hours) via Maiori (20 minutes). Westbound, it runs up to 25 buses daily to Positano (€2, 40 minutes) via Praiano (€1.30, 25 minutes). Many continue to Sorrento (€2.90, 1¾ hours).

You can buy tickets from the *tabacchi* (tobacconist) on the corner of Piazza Flavio Gioia and Via Duca Mansone I (the side street that leads to Piazza del Duomo).

Nocelle

089 / POP 140

A tiny, still relatively isolated mountain village, located beyond Montepertuso, Nocelle (450m) commands some of the most spectacular views on the entire coast. A world apart from touristy Positano, it's a silent place where not much ever happens and where the few residents are happy to keep it that way. Hikers tackling the Sentiero degli Dei might want to stop off as they pass through.

⌂ Sleeping

Villa della Quercia   B&B €

(089 812 34 97; www.villadellaquercia.com; Via Nocelle 5; r €75-85; Apr-Oct; ☎) This simple, delightful B&B is located in a former hilltop monastery with a tranquil garden and spectacular, bird's-eye views of the coast. All six rooms come with a terrace or balcony for blissful, languid lounging. To reach the property, catch a local bus (€1.30) from Amalfi to Nocelle. The B&B is about a 10-minute walk from the bus stop.

Eating

Trattoria
Santa Croce ITALIAN €€

(☑089811260; www.ristorantesantacrocepositano. com; Via Nocelle 19; meals €22; ☺noon-3.30pm & 7-9.30pm Apr-Oct) Service here can be woefully inattentive, but this modest trattoria offers spectacular views over the coast. The menu is short and traditional, with a mix of good (if not memorable) surf and turf dishes like rustic lentil soup, *tagliatelle alla genovese* (pasta with a rich, onion-based Neapolitan sauce) and freshly caught fish with local herbs.

❶ Getting There & Away

From Piazza dei Mulini in Positano, a local bus runs up to Nocelle (€1.30, 30 minutes) via Montepertuso around 14 times daily.

If you're driving, follow the signs from Positano. A taxi from Positano costs an extortionate €35 to €40 – avoid.

Positano

☑089 / POP 3960

Positano is the Amalfi Coast's most photogenic (and expensive) town, with vertiginous houses tumbling down to the sea in a cascade of sun-bleached peach, pink and terracotta. No less colourful are its steep streets and steps, flanked by wisteria-draped hotels, smart restaurants and fashionable retailers.

Look beyond the facades and the fashion, however, and you will find reassuring signs of everyday reality: crumbling stucco, streaked paintwork and even, on occasion, a faint whiff of drains. There's still a southern-Italian holiday feel about the place, with sunbathers eating pizza on the beach, kids pestering parents for gelato and chic *signore* from Milan browsing the boutiques. The fashionista history runs deep – *moda Positano* was born here in the '60s and the town was the first in Italy to import bikinis from France.

◉ Sights

Positano's most memorable sight is its pyramidal townscape, with pastel-coloured houses arranged down the slope to **Spiaggia Grande**, the main beach. Although it isn't anyone's dream beach, with greyish sand covered by legions of bright umbrellas, the water's clean and the setting is memorable. Hiring a chair and umbrella in the

fenced-off areas costs around €20 per person per day, but the crowded public areas are free.

Getting around town is largely a matter of walking. If your knees can take the slopes, there are dozens of narrow alleys and stairways that make walking relatively easy and joyously traffic-free. The easy option is to take the local bus to the top of the town for the best views, and wind your way down on foot, via steps and slopes, enjoying the memorable vistas en route.

Chiesa di Santa Maria
Assunta CHURCH

(☑089 87 54 80; Piazza Flavio Gioia; ☺8am-noon & 4-9pm) This church, with its colourful majolica-tiled dome, is the most famous and – let's face it – pretty much the only sight in Positano. If you are visiting at a weekend you will probably have the added perk of seeing a wedding; it's one of the most popular churches in the area for exchanging vows.

Step inside to see a delightful classical interior, with pillars topped with gilded Ionic capitals and winged cherubs peeking from above every arch.

🏃 Activities

★ Blue Star BOATING

(☑089 81 18 88; www.bluestarpositano.it; Spiaggia Grande; ☺8.30am-9pm) Operating out of a kiosk on Spiaggia Grande, Blue Star hires out small motorboats (half-day/full day €250/350). Consider heading for the archipelago of Li Galli, the four small islands where, according to Homer, the sirens lived. The company organises popular yacht group excursions to Capri (€75) and along the Amalfi Coast (€65), as well as a private sunset *aperitivo* cruise (from €220).

L'Uomo e il Mare BOATING

(☑089 81 16 13; www.escursioniluomoeilmare.it; ☺9am-8pm Easter-Oct) Offers a range of tours, including Capri and Amalfi day trips (from €60), out of a kiosk near the ferry terminal. They also offer private sunset tours to Li Galli, complete with champagne (from €200 for up to 12 people). Private tours should be organised at least a day in advance.

🛏 Sleeping

Positano is a glorious place to stay, but be aware that prices are, overall, high. Like everywhere on the Amalfi Coast, it gets very busy in summer, so book ahead, particularly on weekends and in July and August. Ask at

Positian

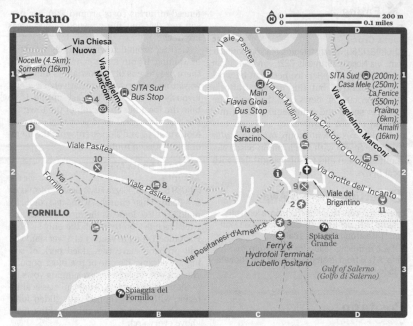

Positano

◉ Sights

◉ Activities, Courses & Tours

◉ Sleeping

◉ Eating

◉ Drinking & Nightlife

the tourist office about rooms or apartments in private houses.

★ **Villa Nettuno** HOTEL €

(☏ 089 87 54 01; www.villanettunopositano.it; Viale Pasitea 208; d €80-140; ☉ year-round; ☀ ☎) Hidden behind a barrage of perfumed foliage, lofty Villa Nettuno is not short on charm. Go for one of the original rooms in the 300-year-old part of the building, decked out in robust rustic decor and graced with a communal terrace. Rooms in the renovated part of the villa lack the same character.

Hostel Brikette HOSTEL €

(☏ 089 87 58 57; www.hostel-positano.com; Via Marconi 358; dm €24-50, d €65-145, apt €80-220;

☉ mid-Mar–mid-Oct; ☀ ☎) The Brikette is a cheerful place with wonderful views and a range of sleeping options, from dorms to doubles and apartments. Some of the dorms have recently been revamped, with handy bunk-side USB sockets and reading lights. Pod-style bunks are expected to replace the tired current bunks in 2018. Breakfast – not included in the price – includes options like pancakes and cold-pressed juices.

Pensione Maria Luisa PENSION €

(☏ 089 87 50 23; www.pensionemarialuisa.com; Via Fornillo 42; r €55-160; ☉ Mar-Oct; ☀ @ ☎) The Maria Luisa is a friendly, old-school *pensione*. Rooms are lined with shiny tiles and simple, no-frills decor; those with private balconies are well worth the extra euros for the bay views. If you can't bag a room with a vista, there's a small communal terrace offering the same sensational panorama. Breakfast is an additional €8.

★**La Fenice** B&B €€

(☏089 87 55 13; www.lafenicepositano.com; Via Guglielmo Marconi 8; d €170; ☺Easter-Oct; ✳🛜🏊) With hand-painted Vietri tiles, high ceilings and the odd piece of antique furniture, the rooms at this friendly, family-run place are simple but smart; most have their own balcony or terrace with dreamy views. As with everywhere in Positano, you'll need to be good at stomping up and down steps to stay here.

★**Hotel California** HOTEL €€

(☏089 87 53 82; www.hotelcaliforniapositano.it; Via Cristoforo Colombo 141; d €160-205; ☺Easter-Oct; ▣🛜🏊) Ignore the incongruous name: this Hotel California is housed in a grand 18th-century palace, its facade washed in soothing pinks and yellows. The rooms in the older part of the house are magnificent, with original ceiling friezes; new rooms are simply decorated though tasteful, spacious and airy.

★**Hotel Palazzo Murat** HOTEL €€€

(☏089 87 51 77; www.palazzomurat.it; Via dei Mulini 23; d €180-290; ☺May–mid-Jan; ✳@🛜🏊) Hidden behind an ancient wall from the tourists who surge along its pedestrian thoroughfare daily, this magnificent hotel occupies the 18th-century *palazzo* (mansion) that the one-time king of Naples used as his summer residence. Rooms – five (more expensive) in the original part of the building, 25 in the newer section – are decorated with sumptuous antiques, original oil paintings and gleaming marble.

✖ Eating

Take note that, overall, the nearer you get to the seafront, the more expensive everything becomes. Many places close over winter, making a brief reappearance for Christmas and New Year.

★**La Cambusa** SEAFOOD €€

(☏089 87 54 32; www.lacambusapositano.com; Piazza Vespucci 4; meals €40; ☺noon-11pm, closed Nov-early Dec; 🛜) Sporting summery pastel hues and a seafront terrace, La Cambusa is on the front line, which, given the number of cash-rich tourists in these parts, could equal high prices for less than average food. Happily, that is not the case. Ingredients are top

notch and shine brightly in dishes such as homemade *scialatelli* pasta with seafood or risotto with shrimp and asparagus.

★**Donna Rosa** ITALIAN €€

(☏089 81 18 06; www.drpositano.com; Via Montepertuso 97-99, Montepertuso; meals from €40; ☺11am-2pm & 5.30-9.30pm Wed-Mon Apr-Dec, closed lunch Aug) This is one of the coast's top restaurants, located in Montepertuso, above Positano. Once a humble trattoria and now run by Rosa's daughter Raffaella, the lineage is set to continue with Raffaella's daughter Erika, who studied with Jamie Oliver in London. The celebrity chef dined here on his honeymoon and declared it one of his favourite restaurants. Dinner reservations are highly recommended and obligatory at lunch.

★**Casa Mele** ITALIAN €€€

(☏089 81 13 64; www.casamele.com; Via Guglielmo Marconi 76; tasting menu €60-75; ☺7pm-midnight Tue-Sun Apr-early Dec) Clever, contemporary Casa Mele celebrates the region's culinary traditions with refreshing innovation. The open kitchen is run by a competent young team, who offer both a traditional and contemporary degustation menu. The latter offers the most thrills, with dishes that might see *triglia* (mullet) caramelised with orange and served with a pesto and almond cream. Traditional and creative pizzas are also offered.

★**Next2** ITALIAN €€€

(☏089 812 35 16; www.next2.it; Viale Pasitea 242; meals €50; ☺6.30-11.30pm Apr-Oct) Understated elegance meets subtle culinary twists at this contemporary set-up. Local and organic ingredients are put to impressive use in dishes such as grilled octopus with potato puree and snow peas, or ravioli stuffed with bluefish and fennel seeds. Desserts are wickedly delicious, and the alfresco sea-facing terrace is summer perfection.

🍷 Drinking & Nightlife

Music on the Rocks CLUB

(☏089 87 58 74; www.musicontherocks.it; Via Grotte dell'Incanto 51; cover €10-30; ☺10pm-late Easter-Oct; 🛜) This is one of the town's few genuine nightspots and one of the best clubs on the coast. The venue is dramatically carved into the tower at the eastern end of Spiaggia Grande. Join a flirty, eye-candy crowd and some of the region's top DJs spinning mainstream house and reliable disco.

ℹ Information

Post Office (www.poste.it; Via Marconi 318; ⊕8.20am-1.45pm Mon-Fri, to 12.45pm Sat) On the main highway passing through town.

Tourist Office (☑089 87 50 67; www.azienda turismopositano.it; Via Regina Giovanna 13; ⊕8.30am-8pm Mon-Sat, to 2pm Sun May-Sep, reduced hours rest of year) Provides lots of information, from sightseeing and tours to transport information. Also supplies a free hiking map.

ℹ Getting There & Away

BOAT

Positano has excellent ferry service connections to the coastal towns and islands from around May to October from its Ferry & Hydrofoil Terminal.

TraVelMar (☑089 87 29 50; www.travelmar. it) sails to numerous coastal destinations in season, including Amalfi (€8, 25 minutes, around six daily) and Salerno (€12, 70 minutes, around seven daily). Those wanting to reach Minori (€11), Maiori (€11) and Cetara (€11) will need to transfer in Amalfi.

Lucibello Positano (☑089 87 50 32; www. lucibello.it) operates three daily services to Capri (€19.50, 50 minutes).

BUS

Situated about 16km west of Amalfi and 18km from Sorrento, Positano is on the main SS163 coastal road. There are two main bus stops: coming from Sorrento and the west, the first stop you come to is **SITA Sud** (Via Guglielmo Marconi), opposite Bar Internazionale; arriving from Amalfi and the east, the **SITA Sud** (Via Guglielmo Marconi) stop is at the top of Via Cristoforo Colombo. To get into town from the former, follow Viale Pasitea; from the latter (a far shorter route), take Via Cristoforo Colombo. When departing, buy bus tickets at either **Bar Internazionale** (Via Marconi 306; ⊕7am-1am) or (if it's still closed for renovations) the *tabaccheria* (tobacconist) across the road. If headed east, buy your tickets from the **tabaccheria** (☑089 81 21 33; Via Cristoforo Colombo 5; ⊕9.30am-9pm) at the bottom of Via Cristoforo Colombo.

SITA Sud (p704) runs up to 28 daily buses to Sorrento (€2, one hour). It also runs up to 25 daily services to Amalfi (€2, 50 minutes) from where buses continue east to Salerno.

Flavia Gioia (☑089 81 18 95; www.flavio gioia.com) runs local buses following the lower ring road every half-hour. Stops are clearly marked and you can buy your ticket at tobacconists (€1.30) or on board. The **main bus stop** (Via Cristoforo Colombo) in central

Positano is on the corner of Viale Pasitea and Via dei Mulini. Flavia Gioia buses also pass by both SITA Sud bus stops. The company also runs around 14 daily buses up to Montepertuso and Nocelle.

Praiano

☑089 / POP 2050

An ancient fishing village, a low-key summer resort and, increasingly, a popular centre for the arts, Praiano is a delight. With no centre as such, its whitewashed houses pepper the verdant ridge of Monte Sant'Angelo as it slopes towards Capo Sottile. Formerly an important silk-production centre, it was a favourite of the Amalfi doges (dukes), who made it their summer residence.

🏃 Activities

Praiano is 120m above sea level, and exploring involves lots of steps. There are also several trails that start from town, including a scenic walk – particularly stunning at sunset – that leaves from beside the San Gennaro church, descending due west to the **Spiaggia della Gavitelli** beach (via 300 steps), and carrying on to the medieval defensive Torre di Grado. The town is also a starting point for the Sentiero degli Dei.

🛏 Sleeping

Hotel Onda Verde HOTEL €€€
(☑089 87 41 43; www.hotelondaverde.com; Via Terramare 3; d €150-300; ⊕Apr-Oct; 🅿❄🛜❄) The 'Green Wave' enjoys a stunning cliffside position overlooking picturesque Marina de Praiano. The interior is tunnelled into the stone cliff face, which makes it wonderfully cool in the height of summer. Rooms have lashings of white linen, satin bedheads, Florentine-inspired furniture and majolica-tiled floors. Some spoil guests with terraces and deckchairs for panoramic contemplation. The restaurant comes highly recommended.

🍴 Eating

Fish and seafood dominate the menus in this old fishing town. Its most famous traditional dish is *totani e patate alla praianese*, a soulful combination of soft calamari rings, sliced potato, *datterini* tomatoes, garlic, croutons, *peperoncino* (chilli) and parsley.

WALK OF THE GODS

By far the best-known walk on the Amalfi Coast is the three-hour, 12km Sentiero degli Dei, which follows the high ridge linking Praiano to Positano. The walk commences in the heart of **Praiano**, where a thigh-challenging 1000-step start takes you up to the path itself. An easier alternative is to opt for the bus to **Bomerano**, near Agerola in the mountains between Sorrento and Amalfi: take the SITA bus to the Agerola turnoff, then another bus to Agerola. Bomerano is located immediately south of Agerola. Do consider the stepped route, though, which winds through well-tended gardens and makes for a charming start.

The route proper is not advised for vertigo sufferers: it's a spectacular, meandering trail along the top of the mountains, with caves and terraces set dramatically in the cliffs and deep valleys framed by the brilliant blue of the sea. It can sometimes be cloudy in the dizzy heights, but that somehow adds to the drama, with the cypresses rising through the mist like dark, shimmering sword blades and shepherds herding their goats through fog-wreathed foliage. Bring a rucksack and plenty of water and wear proper walking shoes, as the going is rough and the descents are steep. You may want to pack swimming gear, too, and end the walk with a refreshing plunge into the sea.

The Praiano tourist office (p710) can provide maps and guidance. Just downhill and on the same side is Alimentari Rispoli (p710), where you can buy *panini*, cheeses, meat, drinks and fruit for the hike (take a penknife for cheese and so on, as they don't make up rolls). The steps out of town begin at Via Degli Ulivi, which leads off the main road almost opposite Hotel Smereldo. Brace yourself for the long climb to come, and be sure to follow the brown arrows placed at regular intervals along the flower-edged paths. After around 45 minutes you'll emerge at **Fontanella**, at Chiesa di Santa Maria a Castro, a lovely whitewashed chapel with a 15th-century fresco of the Madonna. You can also explore the spare chambers of the Convento San Domenico.

Just beyond you'll see a natural rock arch over the path to the right – don't go through it but continue uphill, where after around 20 minutes of steep terrain and craggy rock steps you'll come to the path proper, where you should take the turning to the left, signed 'Positano Nocelle'. It's a long, delightful, gentle descent from here to Nocelle: if there's cloud cover the combination of this and the glimpses of dizzying views is unforgettable. The route is marked by red and white stripes daubed on rocks and trees and is easy to follow.

You eventually emerge at **Nocelle**, where cold drinks and coffee are served at a terraced kiosk with flowers on the tables. Or head a little further through the village to Piazza Santa Croce, where a stall dispenses fantastic freshly squeezed orange and lemon juice.

Continue down through the village and a series of steps will take you through the olive groves and deposit you on the road just east of Positano. A nicer though longer option – especially if you're weary of steps at this point – is to continue on the path that leads west out of Nocelle towards **Montepertuso**. Don't miss the huge hole in the centre of the cliff at Montepertuso, where it looks as though some irate giant has punched through the slab of limestone. From here the route winds its way to the northern fringes of **Positano**. From here you can dip down through town to the beachfront bars and balmy sea.

The CAI (Club Alpino Italiano; Italian Alpine Club) has a website dedicated to the Monti Lattari area (www.caimontilattari.it), with useful information on various trails and downloadable maps. If you prefer a guided hike, there are a number of reliable local guides, including American Frank Carpegna (www.positanofrankcarpegna.com), a longtime resident here, and Zia Lucy (www.zialucy.it).

Drinking & Nightlife

★**Africana** CLUB
(☑089 81 11 71; www.africanafamousclub.com; Via Terramare 2; €10-35; ⊗9pm-3am Sun-Thu, to 5am Fri & Sat May-Sep; ☎) This club near Marina di Praia makes for a memorable boogie – though beware the pricey drinks.

Africana has been going since the '60s, when Jackie Kennedy was just one of the famous VIP guests. It has an extraordinary cave setting, complete with natural blowholes, a mix of DJs and live music, not to mention a glass dance floor with fish swimming under your feet.

Shopping

Alimentari Rispoli　　　FOOD & DRINKS
(☑089 87 40 18; Via Nazionale 82; ⊘8am-1pm & 4-9pm) Sells cheese and cold cuts, as well as fruit and drinks; a useful spot to stock up before embarking on the Sentieri degli Dei hiking trail.

ℹ Information

Tourist Office (☑089 87 45 57; www.praiano. org; Via G Capriglione 116b; ⊘9am-1pm & 4-8pm Mon-Sat) Can provide maps and information for those wanting to hit the area's hiking trails.

ℹ Getting There & Away

SITA Sud (p704) runs up to 27 daily buses to Sorrento (€2.40, 1¼ hours). It also runs up to 25 daily services to Amalfi (€1.30, 25 minutes) from where buses continue east to Salerno. Reduced services on Sunday.

Ravello

☑089 / POP 2490

Sitting high in the hills above Amalfi, Ravello is a refined and polished town almost entirely dedicated to tourism (and increasingly popular as a wedding venue). Boasting impeccable bohemian credentials – Wagner, DH Lawrence and Virginia Woolf all spent time here – it's today known for its ravishing gardens and stupendous views, the best in the world according to former resident Gore Vidal, and certainly the best on the coast.

Most people visit on a day trip from Amalfi – a nerve-tingling 7km drive up the Valle del Dragone – although, to best enjoy its romantic, otherworldly atmosphere, you'll need to stay here overnight. On Tuesday morning there's a lively street market in Piazza Duomo, where you'll find wine, mozzarella and olive oil, as well as discounted designer clothes.

◎ Sights

★**Villa Rufolo**　　　GARDENS
(☑089 85 76 21; www.villarufolo.it; Piazza Duomo; adult/reduced €7/5; ⊘9am-9pm May-Sep, reduced hours rest of year, tower museum 11am-4pm) To the south of Ravello's cathedral, a 14th-century tower marks the entrance to this villa, famed for its beautiful cascading gardens. Created by a Scotsman, Francis Neville Reid, in 1853, they are truly magnificent, commanding divine panoramic views packed with exotic colours, artistically crumbling towers and luxurious blooms. Note that the gardens are at their best from May till October; they don't merit the entrance fee outside those times.

The villa was built in the 13th century for the wealthy Rufolo dynasty and was home to several popes as well as king Robert of Anjou. Wagner was so inspired by the gardens when he visited in 1880 that he modelled the garden of Klingsor (the setting for the second act of the opera *Parsifal*) on them.

The 13th-century Torre Maggiore (Main Tower) now houses the **Torre-Museo**, an interactive museum that sheds light on the villa's history and characters. Among the latter is Sir Francis Neville Reid, the Scottish botanist who purchased and extensively restored the property in the 19th century. The museum also showcases art, archaeological finds and ceramics linked to the villa. Stairs inside the tower lead up to an outdoor viewing platform, affording knockout views of the villa and Amalfi Coast.

Today Villa Rufolo's gardens stage world-class concerts during the town's classical music festival.

★**Villa Cimbrone**　　　GARDENS
(☑089 85 74 59; www.hotelvillacimbrone.com/ gardens; Via Santa Chiara 26; adult/reduced €7/4; ⊘9am-sunset) Some 600m south of Piazza Duomo, the Villa Cimbrone is worth a wander, if not for the 11th-century villa itself (now an upmarket hotel), then for the shamelessly romantic views from the delightful gardens. They're best admired from the Belvedere of Infinity, an awe-inspiring terrace lined with classical-style statues and busts and overlooking the impossibly blue Tyrrhenian Sea.

Camo　　　MUSEUM
(☑089 85 74 61; www.museodelcorallo.com; Piazza Duomo 9, Ravello; ⊘10am-noon & 3-5pm Mon-Sat) This very special place is ostensibly a cameo shop – and exquisite they are, too, crafted primarily out of coral and shell – but there's a treasure trove of a museum beyond the showroom. Even more of a treat is if cameo creator and shop founder Giorgio Filocamo is here to explain the background to such pieces as a 16th-century crucifix on a crystal cross, a mid-16th-century Madonna, a 3rd-century-AD Roman amphora, gorgeous

tortoiseshell combs and some exquisite oil paintings.

✹ Festivals & Events

★ Ravello Festival
PERFORMING ARTS
(☑089 85 84 22; www.ravellofestival.com; ⏱Jul–Sep) Between early July and September, the Ravello Festival – established in 1953 – turns much of the town centre into a stage. Events range from orchestral concerts and chamber music to ballet performances, film screenings and exhibitions. The festival's most celebrated (and breathtaking) venue is the overhanging terrace in the Villa Rufolo gardens.

🛏 Sleeping

Agriturismo
Monte Brusara
AGRITURISMO €
(☑089 85 74 67; www.montebrusara.com; Via Monte Brusara 32; d €94-100; ⏱year-round; 🕸) A working farm, this mountainside *agriturismo* (farm stay) is located a tough half-hour walk of about 1.5km from Ravello's centre (call ahead to arrange to be picked up). It is especially suited to families or those who simply want to escape the crowds and drink in the bucolic views.

★ Villa Casale
APARTMENT €€
(☑089 85 74 12; www.ravelloresidence.it; Via Orso Papice 4; apt €90-186, ste €180-250; ❄🕸🌊) A short, easy walk from Piazza Duomo, Villa Casale consists of two elegant suites and five apartments. Top billing goes to the suites, graced with antiques and occupying the original 14th-century building. All the suites and apartments come with a self-contained kitchen and the property's tranquil terraced gardens include a smart, inviting pool with hypnotic views of the coastline.

★ Belmond
Hotel Caruso
HOTEL €€€
(☑089 85 88 01; www.grandluxuryhotels.com; Piazza San Giovanni del Toro 2; s €605-770, d €748-990; ⏱Apr-Oct; 🅿❄🕸🌊) There can be no better place to swim than the Caruso's sensational infinity pool. Seemingly set on the edge of a precipice, its blue waters merge with sea and sky to magical effect. Inside, the sublimely restored 11th-century *palazzo* (mansion) is no less impressive, with Moorish arches doubling as window frames, 15th-century vaulted ceilings and high-class ceramics.

✕ Eating

★ Babel
CAFE €
(☑089 85 86 215; Via Trinità 13; meals €20; ⏱11.30am-3.30pm & 7-11pm Thu-Tue mid-Jun–mid-Sep, closed Jan & Feb; 🕸) A cool little deli-cafe with a compact menu of high-quality, affordable bites, from Campanian *salumi* (charcuterie) and cheeses, to bruschetta, dry polenta and creative salads with combos like lemon and orange with goat's cheese and chestnut honey. There's an excellent range of local wines, smooth jazz on the sound system, plus an assortment of unique, stylish ceramics for sale.

★ Da Salvatore
ITALIAN €€
(☑089 85 72 27; www.salvatoreravello.com; Via della Republicca 2; meals around €40; ⏱12.30-3pm & 7.30-10pm Tue-Sun Easter-Nov) Located just before the bus stop, Da Salvatore doesn't merely rest on the laurels of its spectacular terrace views. This is one of the coast's best restaurants, serving arresting dishes that showcase local produce with creativity, flair and whimsy; your pre-meal *benvenuto* (welcome) may include an '*aperitivo*' of Negroni encased in a white-chocolate ball. Wines by the glass include knockout super-reds such as Amarone and Barolo.

ⓘ Information

Tourist Office (☑089 85 70 96; www.ravellotime.it; Via Roma 18; ⏱10am-8pm) Provides brochures, maps and directions, and can also assist with accommodation.

ⓘ Getting There & Away

From Amalfi's Piazza Flavio Gioia, SITA Sud (p704) runs up to 27 buses daily to Ravello (€1.30, 25 minutes).

SALERNO & THE CILENTO

Salerno

☑089 / POP 135.300
Salerno may initially seem like a bland big city, but the place has a charming, if gritty, individuality, especially around its vibrant *centro storico* (historic centre), where medieval churches share space with neighbourhood trattorias, trendy wine bars and boutiques. The city has invested in various urban-regeneration programs centred on this historic neighbourhood, which features

NAPLES & CAMPANIA SALERNO

Salerno

0 — 400 m
0 — 0.2 miles

Piazza Sedile del Campo

Piazza Amendola

Amalfi (26km);
Positano (42km)

Vicolo della Neve

8

Via del Canali

5

Piazza Alfano

1 Duomo

Via Mercanti

Via Duomo

Via S Michele

2 Via Iannelli

3

Piazza Matteotti

Via San Benedetto

6

Via Velia

Via Roma

Via Volpe

Via Nizza

Piazza XXIV Maggio

4

Corso Vittorio Emanuele II

Via Cilento

7

Via Diaz

Lungomare Trieste

Gulf of Salerno
(Golfo di Salerno)

Molo Manfredi

Via Dalmazia

Irno

Piazza Vittorio Veneto

Via Luigi Barrella

Piazza Corso Garibaldi
Giuseppe Mazzini

Busitalia Campania

Piazza della Concordia

Via Torrione

Lungomare Guglielmo Marconi

A3 (Southbound);
Paestum (36km)

Porto Turistico

Ferry & Hydrofoil Terminal

Salerno

⊙ **Top Sights**
  1 Duomo C1

⊙ **Sights**
  2 Museo Archeologico Provinciale........C1
  3 Museo Virtuale della Scuola
      Medica Salernitana C1

⊟ **Sleeping**
  4 Hotel Montestella...............................D2
  5 Ostello Ave Gratia Plena.....................B1

⊗ **Eating**
  6 La Cantina del Feudo D2
  7 Pizza Margherita D2
  8 Vicolo della Neve B1

a tree-lined seafront promenade widely considered to be one of the most beautiful in Europe.

⊙ Sights

★**Duomo**   CATHEDRAL
(Piazza Alfano; ⊗8.30am-8pm Mon-Sat, 8.30am-1pm & 4-8pm Sun) You can't miss the looming presence of Salerno's impressive cathedral, widely considered to be the most beautiful medieval church in Italy. Built by the Normans in the 11th century and later remodelled in the 18th century, it sustained severe damage in a 1980 earthquake. It is dedicated to San Matteo (St Matthew), whose remains were reputedly brought to the city in 954 and now lie beneath the main altar in the vaulted crypt.

Take special note of the magnificent main entrance, the 12th-century **Porta dei Leoni**, named after the marble lions at the foot of the stairway. It leads through to a beautiful, harmonious courtyard, surrounded by graceful arches and overlooked by a 12th-century bell tower. Carry on through the huge bronze doors (similarly guarded by lions), which were cast in Constantinople in the 11th century. When you come to the three-aisled interior, you will see that it is largely baroque, with only a few traces of the original church. These include parts of the transept and choir floor and the two raised pulpits in front of the choir stalls. Throughout the church you can see extraordinarily detailed and colourful 13th-century mosaic work.

In the right-hand apse, don't miss the **Cappella delle Crociate** (Chapel of the

Crusades), containing stunning frescoes and more wonderful mosaics. It was so named because crusaders' weapons were blessed here. Under the altar stands the tomb of 11th-century pope Gregory VII.

**Museo Archeologico
Provinciale**   MUSEUM
(☑089 23 11 35; www.museoarcheologicosalerno.it; Via San Benedetto 28; adult/reduced €4/2; ⊗9am-7.30pm Tue-Sun) The province's restored and revitalised main archaeological museum is an excellent showcase for a collection of mesmerising grave goods from the surrounding area, dating back to cave dwellers and the colonising Greeks. Seek out the 4th-century-BC bronze candelabra topped with the figures of a warrior and a woman, his arm around her shoulder.

Castello di Arechi   CASTLE
(☑089 296 40 15; www.ilcastellodiarechi.it; Via Benedetto Croce; adult/reduced €4/2; ⊗9am-5pm Tue-Sat, to 3.30pm Sun) Hop on bus 19 from Piazza XXIV Maggio to visit Salerno's most famous landmark, the forbidding Castello di Arechi, dramatically positioned 263m above the city. Originally a Byzantine fort, it was built by the Lombard duke of Benevento, Arechi II, in the 8th century and subsequently modified by the Normans and Aragonese, most recently in the 16th century.

**Museo Virtuale della
Scuola Medica Salernitana**   MUSEUM
(☑089 257 61 26; www.museovirtualescuola medicasalernitana.beniculturali.it; Via Mercanti 74, adult/reduced €3/2, ⊗9.30am-1pm Tue-Wed, 9.30am-1pm & 5-8pm Thu-Sat, 10am-1pm Sun; ⊕) In Salerno's historic centre, this small, slightly forlorn museum deploys videos and touch-screen technology to explore the teachings and wince-inducing procedures of Salerno's once-famous, now-defunct medical institute. Established around the 9th century, the school was the most important centre of medical knowledge in medieval Europe, reaching the height of its prestige in the 11th century. It was closed in the early 19th century.

⊨ Sleeping

**Ostello Ave
Gratia Plena**   HOSTEL €
(☑089 23 47 76; www.ostellodisalerno.it; Via dei Canali; dm/s/d €16/45/65; ⊗year-round; @⊗) Housed in a 16th-century convent, Salerno's

excellent HI hostel is right in the heart of the *centro storico*. Inside there's a charming central courtyard and a range of bright rooms, from dorms to great bargain doubles with private bathroom. The 2am curfew is for dorms only.

Hotel Montestella HOTEL €€
(☏089 22 51 22; www.hotelmontestella.it; Corso Vittorio Emanuele II 156; d €80-120, tr €90-150; ✳@🛜) Within walking distance of just about anywhere worth going to, the fresh, modern Montestella is on Salerno's main pedestrian thoroughfare, halfway between the *centro storico* and train station. Although some rooms are quite tight, all are light and contemporary, with firm beds and patterned feature walls. Staff are friendly and helpful, and the breakfast spread is decent.

 Eating

Vicolo della Neve ITALIAN €
(☏089 22 57 05; www.vicolodellaneve.it; Vicolo della Neve 24; meals €20-25; ⊙7.15pm-midnight Mon, Tue & Thu-Sat, 12.30-3.30pm Sun) A city institution on a scruffy street, this is the archetypal *centro storico* trattoria, with brick arches, fake frescoes and walls hung with works by local artists. The menu is unwaveringly authentic, with pizzas and *calzoni, peperoni ripieni* (stuffed peppers) and a top-notch *parmigiana di melanzane* (baked eggplant). It can get incredibly busy: book in advance, especially later in the week.

Pizza Margherita ITALIAN €
(☏089 22 88 80; Corso Garibaldi 201; pizzas/buffet from €3/4, lunch menu €8.50; ⊙12.30-3.30pm & 7.30pm-midnight; 🚸) It looks like a bland, modern canteen, but this is, in fact, one of Salerno's most popular lunch spots. Locals regularly queue for the lunchtime buffet that, on any given day, might include buffalo mozzarella, salami, mussels in various guises and a range of salads.

If that selection doesn't appeal, the daily lunch menu (offering pasta, main course and half a litre of bottled water) is chalked up on a blackboard, or there's the regular menu of pizzas, pastas, salads and main courses.

★**La Cantina del Feudo** ITALIAN €€
(☏089 25 46 96; Via Velia 45; meals around €28; ⊙12.30-3.30pm & 7pm-midnight Thu-Tue; 🚸) Frequented by locals in the know, this restaurant is run by a charming Puglian family. The culinary traditions of their home region are evident on the well-executed menu, which includes *cozze gratinate* (mussels with breadcrumbs) and gorgeous vegetable dishes (try the vegetable antipasto). The interior offers a sophisticated take on the rural trattoria and there's a terrace on the pedestrianised street for al fresco noshing.

❶ Information

Post Office (Piazza Vittorio Veneto 7; ⊙8.20am-1.30pm Mon-Fri, to 12.30pm Sat) Beside the train station.
Tourist Office (☏089 23 14 32; Lungomare Trieste 7; ⊙9am-1pm & 3-7pm Mon-Sat) Has limited information.

❶ Getting There & Away

BOAT

TraVelMar (p708) sails seasonally to Amalfi (€8, 35 minutes, around 12 daily) and Positano (€12, 70 minutes, around seven daily), as well as to Cetara (€5, 15 minutes, around six daily), Maiori (€7, 30 minutes, around six daily) and Minori (€7, 40 minutes, around six daily).

Alicost (☏089 87 14 83; www.alicost.it) runs one daily seasonal ferry service to Capri (€25, 2¼ hours) via Minori (€7), Amalfi (€8) and Positano (€12).

Navigazione Libera del Golfo (p681) runs one daily hydrofoil service to Capri (€25.50) from Easter to mid-October.

TraVelMar services depart from the Porto Turistico, 200m down the pier from Piazza della Concordia. You can buy tickets from the booths by the embarkation point. Alicost and Navigazione Libera del Golfo services depart from Molo Manfredi, 1.8km further west.

BUS

SITA Sud (www.sitasudtrasporti.it) buses for Amalfi depart at least hourly from the **bus station** (Piazza Vittorio Veneto) on Piazza Vittorio Veneto, beside the train station, stopping en route at Vietri sul Mare, Cetara, Maiori and Minori. For Pompeii, take **Busitalia Campania** (☏089 48 72 70; www.fsbusitaliacampania.it) bus 4 from nearby Corso Garibaldi (at the corner of Via Luigi Barrella). For the south coast and Paestum, take the hourly bus 34 from Piazza della Concordia near the Porto Turistico ferry terminal.

CAR & MOTORCYCLE

Salerno is on the A3 between Naples and Reggio di Calabria; the A3 is toll-free from Salerno south. Take the Salerno exit and follow signs to the *centro* (city centre). If you want to hire a car, there's a **Europcar** (🖵 089 258 07 75; www.europcar.com; Via Clemente Mauro 18; ⊙ 8.30am-1pm & 2.30-6.30pm Mon-Fri, 8.30am-1pm Sat) agency not far from the train station.

TRAIN

Salerno is a major stop on southbound routes to Calabria, and the Ionian and Adriatic coasts. From the station in Piazza Vittorio Veneto there are regular trains to Naples (from €4.30, 35 to 45 minutes) and Rome (Intercity from €30.50, three hours).

Cilento Coast

While the Cilento stretch of coastline lacks the sophistication of the Amalfi Coast, it too has its string of craggy, sun-bleached towns, among them popular Agropoli, Palinuro and especially charming Castellabate. The Cilento can even afford to have a slight air of superiority when it comes to its beaches: a combination of secluded coves and long stretches of golden sand with fewer overpriced ice creams and sunbeds. Yet, Campania's southern bookend is more than its waterside appeal. It's here that you'll find the ancient Greek temples of Paestum and the hiking paradise of the Parco Nazionale del Cilento e Vallo di Diano. Together with the monumental Certosa San Lorenzo in Padula, they form one of Italy's Unesco World Heritage sites.

Paestum

Paestum is home to one of Europe's most glorious archaeological zones. Deemed a World Heritage Site by Unesco, the site includes three of the world's best-preserved ancient Greek temples, as well as an engrossing museum crammed with millennia-old frescoes, ceramics and daily artefacts. Among these is the iconic *Tomba del Truffatore* (Tomb of the Diver) funerary fresco.

Paestum, or Poseidonia as the city was originally called (in honour of Poseidon, the Greek god of the sea), was founded in the 6th century BC by Greek settlers and fell under Roman control in 273 BC. Decline later set in following the demise of the Roman Empire. Savage raids by the Saracens and periodic outbreaks of malaria forced the steadily dwindling population to abandon the city altogether.

Today, it offers visitors a vivid, to-scale glimpse of the grandeur and sophistication of the area's past life.

◉ Sights

★ **Paestum's Temples**   ARCHAEOLOGICAL SITE
(Area Archeologica di Paestum; 🖵 0828 81 10 23; www.museopaestum.beniculturali.it; adult/reduced incl museum €9/4.50; ⊙ 8.30am-7.30pm, last entry 6.50pm) These temples are among the best-preserved monuments of Magna Graecia, the Greek colony that once covered much of southern Italy. Rediscovered in the late 18th century, the site as a whole wasn't unearthed until the 1950s. Lacking the tourist mobs that can sully better-known archaeological sites, the place has a wonderful serenity. Take sandwiches and prepare to stay at least three hours. In spring the temples are particularly stunning, surrounded by scarlet poppies.

Buy your tickets in the museum, just east of the site, before entering from the main entrance at the northern end. The first structure is the 6th-century-BC **Tempio di Cerere** (Temple of Ceres); originally dedicated to Athena, it served as a Christian church in medieval times.

As you head south, you can pick out the basic outline of the large rectangular forum, the heart of the ancient city. Among the partially standing buildings are the vast domestic housing area and, further south, the amphitheatre; both provide evocative glimpses of daily life here in Roman times. In the former houses you'll see mosaic floors, and a marble *impluvium* that stood in the atrium and collected rainwater.

The **Tempio di Nettuno** (Temple of Neptune), dating from about 450 BC, is the largest and best preserved of the three temples at Paestum; only parts of its inside walls and roof are missing. The two rows of double-storied columns originally divided the outer colonnade from the *cella*, or inner chamber, where a statue of the temple deity would have been displayed. Despite its commonly used name, many scholars believe that temple was actually dedicated to the Greek goddess Hera, sister and wife of Greek god Zeus.

Almost next door, the so-called **basilica** (in fact, a temple to the goddess Hera) is Paestum's oldest surviving monument. Dating from the middle of the 6th century BC, it's a magnificent sight, with nine columns across and 18 along the sides. Ask someone to take your photo next to one of the columns: it's a good way to appreciate the scale.

Save time for the **museum** (⌨0828 81 10 23; ⊙8.30am-7.30pm, last entry 6.50pm, closes 1.40pm 1st & 3rd Mon of month), which covers two floors and houses a collection of fascinating, if weathered, metopes (bas-relief friezes). This collection includes original metopes from the Tempio di Argiva Hera (Temple of Argive Hera), situated 9km north of Paestum, of which virtually nothing else remains. The most famous of the museum's numerous frescoes is the 5th-century-BC *Tomba del Tuffatore* (Tomb of the Diver), thought to represent the passage from life to death with its frescoed depiction of a diver in mid-air. The fresco was discovered in 1968 inside the lid of the tomb of a young man, alongside his drinking cup and oil flasks, which he would perhaps have used to oil himself for wrestling matches. Rare for the period in that it shows a human form, the fresco expresses pure delight in physicality, its freshness and grace eternally arresting. Below the diver, a symposium of men repose languidly on low couches and brandish drinking cups.

🛏 Sleeping

⭐**Casale Giancesare** B&B €€
(⌨0828 72 80 61, 333 1897737; www.casale-giancesare.it; Via Giancesare 8; s €50-140, d €60-140, apt per week €600-1300; 🅿✳@🛜🏊) A 19th-century former farmhouse, this elegantly decorated, stone-clad B&B is run by the delightful Voza family, who will happily ply you with their homemade wine, *limoncello* and marmalades (they even make their own olive oil). It's located 2.5km from the glories of Paestum and surrounded by vineyards and olive and mulberry trees; views are stunning, particularly from the swimming pool.

🍴 Eating

Nonna Sceppa ITALIAN €€
(⌨0828 85 10 64; Via Laura 53; meals €35; ⊙12.30-3pm & 7.30-11pm Fri-Wed; 🚼) Seek out the superbly prepared, robust dishes at Nonna Sceppa, a family-friendly restaurant that's gaining a reputation throughout the region for excellence. Dishes are firmly seasonal and, during summer, concentrate on fresh seafood like the refreshingly simple grilled fish with lemon. Other popular choices include risotto with zucchini and artichokes, and spaghetti with lobster.

ℹ Information

Tourist Office (⌨0828 81 10 16; www.info paestum.it; Via Magna Grecia 887; ⊙9am-1pm & 3-5pm Apr-Sep, 9am-1pm & 2-4pm Oct-Mar) Across the street from the archaeological site, this helpful tourist office offers a map of the archaeological site, plus information on the greater Cilento region.

ℹ Getting There & Away

Trains run around 16 times daily from Salerno to Paestum (€2.70, 30 minutes).

Busitalia Campania (⌨089 48 72 70; www. fsbusitaliacampania.it) Bus 34 goes to Paestum from Piazza della Concordia in Salerno (€2.70, one hour). Buses run roughly every hour to two hours Monday to Saturday and four times on Sunday.

Parco Nazionale del Cilento e Vallo di Diano

Proving the perfect antidote to the holiday mayhem along the coast, the stunning Parco Nazionale del Cilento e Vallo di Diano (Cilento National Park and the Valley of Diano) combines dense woods and flowering meadows with dramatic mountains, streams, rivers and waterfalls. A World Heritage Site, it is the second-largest national park in Italy, covering a staggering 1810 sq km, including 80 towns and villages. To get the best out of the park, you will, unfortunately, need a car. Allow yourself a full day to visit the park's highly regarded grottoes and more if you're intending to hike some of the area's beautiful nature trails.

◉ Sights

⭐**Grotte di Castelcivita** CAVE
(⌨0828 77 23 97; www.grottedicastelcivita. it; Piazzale N Zonzi, Castelcivita; adult/reduced €10/8; ⊙standard tours 10.30am, noon, 1.30pm & 3pm Mar & Oct, plus 4.30pm & 6pm Apr-Sep; 🅿🚼) The grottoes are fascinating otherworldly caves that date from prehistoric times: excavations have revealed that they were inhabited 42,000 years ago, making them the oldest known settlement in Europe. Don't forget a jacket, and leave the high heels at home, as paths are wet and slippery. Hard hats, and a certain level of fitness and mobility, are required. Located 40km southeast of Salerno, the complex is refreshingly non-commercial.

Although it extends over 4800m, only around half of the complex is open to the public. The one-hour tour winds through a route surrounded by extraordinary stalagmites and stalactites, and a mesmerising play of colours, caused by algae, calcium and iron that tint the naturally sculpted rock shapes.

The tour culminates in a cavernous lunar landscape – think California's Death Valley in miniature – called the Caverna di Bertarelli (Bertarelli Cavern). The caves are still inhabited – by bats – and visitors are instructed not to take flash photos for fear of blinding them.

Certosa di San Lorenzo   MONASTERY
(☑0975 77 74 45; www.polomusealecampania.be niculturali.it; Viale Certosa, Padula; adult/reduced €4/2; ☺9am-7pm Wed-Mon) One of the largest monasteries in southern Europe, the Certosa di San Lorenzo dates from 1306 and covers 250,000 sq metres. Numerologists can swoon at the following: 320 rooms and halls, 2500m of corridors, galleries and hallways, 300 columns, 500 doors, 550 windows, 13 courtyards, 100 fireplaces, 52 stairways and 41 fountains – in other words, it is *huge*.

As it is unlikely you will have time to see everything, be sure to visit the highlights, including the vast central courtyard (a venue for summer classical-music concerts), the magnificent wood-panelled library, frescoed chapels, and the kitchen with its grandiose fireplace and famous tale: apparently this is where the legendary 1000-egg omelette was made in 1534 for Charles V. Unfortunately, the historic frying pan is not on view – just how big was it, one wonders?

Within the monastery you can also peruse the modest collection of ancient artefacts at the **Museo Archeologico Provinciale della Lucania Occidentale** (☑0975 7 71 17; ☺9am-6.45pm Wed-Mon; 🚻) FREE.

Grotte di Pertosa   CAVE
(☑0975 39 70 37; www.grottedipertosa-auletta. it; Pertosa; guided visits adult/reduced 100min €20/15, 60min €13/10; ☺tour times vary, see website; P 🚻) (Re)discovered in 1932, the Grotte di Pertosa date back 35 million years. Used by the Greeks and Romans as places of worship, the caves burrow for some 2500m, with long underground passages and lofty grottoes filled with stalagmites and stalactites. The first part of the tour is a boat (or raft) ride on the river; you disembark just before the waterfall (phew!) and continue on foot for around 800m, surrounded by marvellous rock formations and luminous crystal accretions.

🏃 Activities

The park has 15 well-marked **nature trails** that vary from relatively easy strolls to serious hikes requiring stamina and good knees. The countryside in the park is stunning and dramatic and, in spring, you'll experience real flower power: delicate narcissi, wild orchids and tulips hold their own among blowsier summer drifts of brilliant yellow ox-eye daisies and scarlet poppies.

Thickets of silver firs, wild chestnuts and beech trees add to the sumptuous landscape, as do the dramatic cliffs, pine-clad mountains and fauna, including wild boars, badgers and wolves and, for bird watchers, the increasingly rare golden eagle.

Even during the busier summer season, the sheer size of the park means that hikers are unlikely to meet others on the trail to swap tales and muesli bars so getting lost could become a lonely, not to mention dangerous, experience if you haven't done some essential planning before striding out. In theory, the tourist offices should be able to supply you with a guide to the trails. In reality, they frequently seem to have run out of copies. Failing this, you can buy the *Parco Nazionale del Cilento e Vallo di Diano: Carta Turistica e dei Sentieri* (Tourist and Footpath Map; €7) or the excellent *Monte Stella: Walks & Rambles in Ancient Cilento* published by the Comunita' Montana Alento Monte Stella (€3). Most of the *agriturismi* (farm stays) in the park can also organise guided treks.

A popular self-guided hike, where you are rewarded with spectacular views, is a climb of Monte Alburno (1742m). There's a choice of two trails, both of which are clearly marked from the centre of the small town of Sicignano degli Alburni and finish at the mountain's peak. Allow approximately four hours for either route. The less experienced may prefer to opt for a guide.

There are some excellent *agriturismi* here that offer additional activities, including **guided hikes**, **painting courses** and **horse riding**.

🛌 Sleeping

★**Agriturismo i Moresani**   AGRITURISMO €
(☑0974 90 20 86; www.imoresani.com; Località Moresani; d €90-110; ☺Mar-Oct; ❊🔊🐾) If you are seeking utter tranquillity, head to this *agriturismo* 1.5km west of Casal Velino. The setting is bucolic: rolling hills in every direction, interspersed with grapevines, grazing pastures and olive trees. Family run, the

18-hectare farm produces its own *caprino* goat's cheese, wine, olive oil and preserves. Rooms have cream- and earth-coloured decor and surround a pretty private garden.

Eating

Trattoria degli Ulivi
ITALIAN €

(☎334 2595091; www.tavolacaldadegliulivi.it; Viale Certosa, Padula; set menu €12; ☺11am-4pm Wed-Mon, also 7pm-midnight Thu-Sun) If you've worked up an appetite walking the endless corridors of the Certoza di San Lorenzo then this restaurant – located just 50m to the west – is the place to come. The decor is canteen-like, but the daily specials are affordable, tasty and generously proportioned. It serves snacks as well as four-course blowout lunches.

Vecchia Pizzeria Margaret
PIZZA €

(☎0975 33 00 00; Via Luigi Curto, Polla; pizza from €3; ☺7.30pm-midnight Tue-Sun; 🐾) Fabulous wheels of pizza, cooked in a wood-fired oven; it also dishes up antipasti and pasta dishes. Service is fast and friendly, and prices are low. You'll find the restaurant just east of the river, near the hospital. It's great for a fill-up after a walk in the national park.

❶ Information

Paestum's **tourist office** (p716) also has some information on the Parco Nazionale del Cilento.

Alpine Rescue (☎118) For emergencies.

Sicignano degli Alburni Pro Loco (☎0828 97 37 55; www.scoprisicignano.it; Piazza Plebiscito 13, Sicignano degli Alburni; ☺9am-1.30pm & 2.30-5pm Mon-Sat) Tourist information.

Parks.it (www.parks.it/parco.nazionale. cilento/Eindex.html) Useful online information about the national park.

❶ Getting There & Away

Curcio Viaggi (☎800 122012, 0975 39 12 13; www.curcioviaggi.it) operates three to four daily buses each way between Salerno and Polla on weekdays, and one daily service each way on Saturday. **SITA Sud** (p714) runs three daily services between Salerno and Pertosa Monday to Saturday, two of which continue to Polla. It also runs two daily buses from Polla and Pertosa to Salerno Monday to Saturday.

Puglia, Basilicata & Calabria

Best Places to Eat

➡ Dedalo (p763)

➡ Al Trabucco da Mimì (p734)

➡ Trattoria Il Rifugio della Buona Stella (p747)

➡ Trattoria Terra Madre (p737)

➡ Paglionico Vini e Cucina (p724)

➡ La Cantina del Macellaio (p776)

Best Places to Sleep

➡ Hotel Il Belvedere (p761)

➡ Locanda delle Donne Monache (p767)

➡ Palazzo Rollo (p746)

➡ Relais Parallelo 41 (p729)

➡ Il Frantoio (p740)

Why Go?

The Italian boot's heel (Puglia), instep (Basilicata) and toe (Calabria) are where the 'Mezzogiorno' (southern Italy) shows all its throbbing intensity. Long stereotyped as the poorer, more passionate cousins of Italy's sophisticated northerners, these regions are finally being appreciated for their true richness. You *will* see washing on weather-worn balconies, scooters speeding down medieval alleys and ancient towns crumbling under Mediterranean suns. But look past the pasta-advert stereotypes and you'll find things altogether more complex and wonderful: gritty, unsentimental cities with pedigrees stretching back thousands of years; dramatically broken coastlines that have harboured fisherfolk and pirates for millennia; and above all, proud and generous people, eager to share these delights with you.

Puglia is defined by its coast, the longest in Italy; little Basilicata touches two seas, but is known for forests and mountains; while Calabria, last stop before Sicily, is a hodgepodge of Greek, Latin, African and Norman influences.

When to Go
Bari

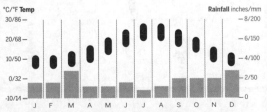

Apr–Jun Spring wildflowers are blooming: perfect for hiking in the Pollino National Park.	**Jul & Aug** Summer is beach weather and festivals blossom in towns such as Lecce and Matera.

Sep & Oct Crowds have thinned, the weather is mild, and mushrooms are emerging in Sila National Park.

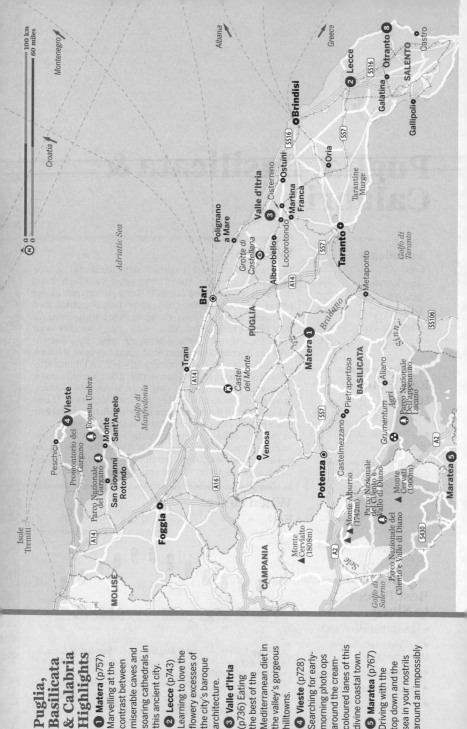

Puglia, Basilicata & Calabria Highlights

① Matera (p757)
Marvelling at the contrast between miserable caves and soaring cathedrals in this ancient city.

② Lecce (p743)
Learning to love the flowery excesses of the city's baroque architecture.

③ Valle d'Itria (p736) Eating the best of the Mediterranean diet in the valley's gorgeous hilltowns.

④ Vieste (p728)
Searching for early-morning photo ops around the cream-coloured lanes of this divine coastal town.

⑤ Maratea (p767)
Driving with the top down and the sea in your nostrils around an impossibly

beautiful string of coastal towns.

6 Parco Nazionale dell'Aspromonte (p774) Rambling in the wild, lonely uplands of this mysterious Calabrian wilderness.

7 Museo Nazionale di Reggio Calabria (p775) Getting up close and personal with the godlike Riace Bronzes.

8 Otranto Cathedral (p752) Viewing macabre skulls and magnificent mosaics in this unique Norman basilica.

Ionian Sea

Crotone
Capo Colonna
Le Castella

San Giovanni in Fiore

Lago di Cecita
C. Mucone

Parco Nazionale della Sila

Camigliatello Silano
S.bar

Monte Pollino (2248m)
Parco Nazionale del Pollino

CALABRIA

Cosenza
Paola

Tyrrhenian Coast

Golfo di Squillace

Ionian Coast

Golfo di Sant'Eufemia

Pizzo
Tropea

Capo Vaticano

Golfo di Gioia

South Tyrrhenian Coast

Scilla
Villa San Giovanni

Messina

SICILY

6 Parco Nazionale dell'Aspromonte

Gerace
Locri

7 Reggio di Calabria

North Tyrrhenian Coast

Tortora
Ajeta

Golfo di Policastro
Praia a Mare

Monti di Orsomarso (1987m)

Diamante

Tyrrhenian Sea

Aeolian Islands

PUGLIA

Puglia can surely now take its place in the first rank of Italy's famous regions. Clearly, everything the Italophile craves is there in abundance: ancient towns heavy with the tangible past; extravagant churches dreamt up by Europe's finest architects; the footprints of an endless procession of conquerors and cultures, stamped in stone, gold and marble; seas of olives; olive-green seas; and food the equal of any in Italy. Travellers bored or worn down by the crowds of Campania and Tuscany can find still release in the baroque splendour of Lecce, 'Florence of the South', or one of many lesser (but no less beautiful) Puglian towns.

But it's perhaps outside of its cities that Puglia shines brightest. From the ancient Forest of Umbra in the north to the fruitful Valle d'Itria and sun-baked Salento, Puglia's countryside has always been its foundation – the source of its food, its wealth and its culture.

Bari

POP 324,200

If Lecce is the south's Florence, Bari is its Bologna, a historic but forward-looking town with a high percentage of young people and migrants lending it vigour. More urban than Lecce and Brindisi, with grander boulevards and better nightlife, Bari supports a large university, an opera house and municipal buildings that shout confidence.

Most travellers skip Bari on their way to Puglia's big-hitter, Lecce (the towns have a long-standing rivalry, especially over football), but Bari doesn't lack history or culture. The old town contains the bones of St Nicholas (aka Santa Claus) in its Basilica di San Nicola, along with a butch castle and plenty of unfussy trattorias that have the local nosh – *cucina barese* – down to a simple art.

The second-largest town in southern Italy, Bari is a busy port with connections to Greece, Albania and Croatia, and sports an international airport with connections to much of Europe.

ℹ Dangers & Annoyances

Once notorious for petty crime, Bari has cleaned up its act of late. Nonetheless, take all of the usual precautions: don't leave anything in your car; don't display money or valuables; and watch out for bag-snatchers on scooters.

◉ Sights

Most sights are in or near the atmospheric old town, Bari Vecchia, a medieval labyrinth of tight alleyways and graceful piazzas. It fills a small peninsula between the new port to the west and the old port to the southeast, cramming in 40 churches and more than 120 shrines.

★ **Basilica di San Nicola**   BASILICA
(📋 0805 73 71 11; www.basilicasannicola.it; Piazza San Nicola; ⊘ 7am-8.30pm Mon-Sat, to 10pm Sun) Bari's signature basilica was one of the first Norman churches to be built in southern Italy, and is a splendid (if square and solid) example of Puglian-Romanesque architecture. Dating to the 12th century, it was originally constructed to house the relics of St Nicholas (better known as Father Christmas), which were stolen from Turkey in 1087 by local fishing folk. Today, it is an important place of pilgrimage for both Catholics and Orthodox Christians.

St Nicholas' remains, which are said to emanate a miraculous myrrh with special powers, are ensconced in a shrine in the beautiful, vaulted crypt. Above, the interior is huge and simple with a gilded 17th-century wooden ceiling. The magnificent 13th-century *ciborium* over the altar is Puglia's oldest. Other items related to the basilica, including chalices, vestments and crests, are displayed in the **Museo Nicolaiano** (📋 0805 23 14 29; Largo Papa Urbano II; ⊘ 11am-6pm Thu-Tue) FREE, adjacent.

Cathedral   CATHEDRAL
(📋 080 521 06 05; www.arcidiocesibaribitonto.it; Piazza dell'Odegitria; ⊘ 8am-7pm Mon-Sat, 8-10am & 11am-7pm Sun) Built over the original Byzantine church, the 12th- to 13th-century Romanesque cathedral, dedicated to San Sabino, is technically Bari's most important church, although its fame pales alongside San Nicola. Inside, the plain walls are punctuated with deep arcades and the eastern window is a tangle of plant and animal motifs. The highlight lies in the subterranean **Museo del Succorpo della Cattedrale** (adult/reduced €3/2; ⊘ 9.30am-4pm Mon, Wed, Sat & Sun, to 12.30pm Tue, Thu & Fri), where recent excavations have revealed remnants left over from an ancient Christian basilica and various Roman ruins.

Bari

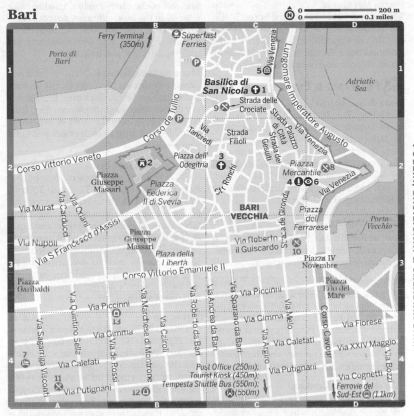

Bari

◉ Top Sights
1 Basilica di San Nicola C1

◎ Sights
2 Castello Svevo B2
3 Cathedral C2
4 Colonna della Giustizia C2
Museo del Succorpo della
Cattedrale ....(see 3)
5 Museo Nicolaiano C1
6 Piazza Mercantile D2

⊜ Sleeping
7 B&B Casa Pimpolini A4

✖ Eating
8 La Locanda di Federico D2
9 Maria delle Sgagliozze C1
10 Paglionico Vini e Cucina C3
11 Terranima A4

🛍 Shopping
12 Enoteca Vinarius de Pasquale B4
13 Il Salumaio B4

Castello Svevo   CASTLE
(Swabian Castle; ☎ 080 521 37 04; Piazza Federico II di Svevia; adult/reduced/under 18yr €8/4/free; ⊘8.30am-7.30pm Thu-Tue) Roger the Norman originally built this castle, in the 12th century, over the ruins of a Byzantine structure. Later, Frederick II of Swabia built over the existing castle, incorporating it into his design and leaving intact the the two towers of the Norman structure that still stand. The bastions, with corner towers overhanging the moat, were added in the 16th century during Aragonese rule, when the castle was a magnificent residence. Excavation is ongoing, uncovering more rich layers of elite Barese history.

Piazza Mercantile PIAZZA
This beautiful piazza is fronted by the Sedile, the headquarters of Bari's Council of Nobles. In the square's northeast corner is the Colonna della Giustizia (Column of Justice), where debtors were once tied and whipped.

✦ Festivals & Events

Festa di San Nicola RELIGIOUS
(☉7-9 May) The Festival of St Nicholas is Bari's biggest annual shindig, celebrating the 11th-century arrival of St Nicholas' relics from Turkey. On the first evening a procession leaves Castello Svevo for the Basilica di San Nicola. The next day there's a deafening fly-past and a fleet of boats carries the statue of St Nicholas along the coast.

🛏 Sleeping

Most of Bari's hotels tend to be bland and overpriced, aimed at business clientele. B&Bs are generally a better option.

B&B Casa Pimpolini B&B €
(☑0805 21 99 38, 333 9580740; www.casapimpolini.com; Via Calefati 249; s/d €60/80; ❋🛜) This lovely B&B in Bari's new town is within easy walking distance to shops, restaurants and Bari Vecchia (the old town). The two rooms are warm and welcoming, and the homemade breakfast is a treat. Great value.

Villa Romanazzi Carducci HOTEL €
(☑0805 42 74 00; www.villaromanazzi.com; Via Capruzzi 326; s/d from €59/99; 🅿❋🛜🏊) Run by the French Accor group, the Villa Romanazzi shows flair that transcends its workaday (if convenient) location, near the train station. Businesslike rooms are modern and clean-lined, but the real bonuses are in the extras: statue-embellished gardens, picturesque swimming pool (summer only), enormous fitness centre, free bikes, a spa and a decent restaurant with excellent breakfasts.

🍴 Eating

One of the best things about Bari is its trattorias, and the simple, delightful seafood and *cucina barese* they serve.

★ Paglionico Vini e Cucina OSTERIA €
(☑338 2120391; Strada Vallisa 23; meals €27; ☉noon-3pm daily & 7-11pm Mon-Sat) Dishing up what the locals like since 1870, this 100% Barese *osteria* (casual tavern) is an absolute classic. There's no menu, just a chalkboard displaying what's cooking that day. It's all fine salt-of-the-earth Puglian cuisine, with seafood to the fore – the *riso, patate e cozze* (oven-baked rice, potatoes and mussels) is particularly good. The owners/waiters are undemonstrative, and brilliant.

Maria delle Sgagliozze PUGLIAN €
(Strada delle Crociate 13; snacks €1; ☉from 5pm) Octogenarian Maria dispenses the legendary Barese street food *sgagliozze* (deep-fried polenta cubes) from the front of her house. Sprinkle them with a pinch of salt and Bob's your uncle!

La Locanda di Federico PUGLIAN €€
(☑0805 22 77 05; www.lalocandadifederico.com; Piazza Mercantile 63; meals €35; ☉noon-3.30pm & 7pm-midnight) With domed ceilings, archways and medieval-style artwork on the walls, this restaurant oozes atmosphere, and a quiet (justified) confidence in its classic Puglian fare. The menu is proudly studded with regional staples such as *orecchiette* ('little ears' of pasta) *con le cime di rape* (with turnip tops) and even *al ragù di cavallo* (with horsemeat sauce).

Terranima PUGLIAN €€
(☑0805 21 97 25; www.terranima.com; Via Putignani 213; meals €32; ☉noon-3pm daily & 7-11pm Mon-Sat) Peep through the lace curtains into the cool interior of this rustic trattoria, where worn flagstone floors and period furnishings make you feel like you're dining in someone's front room. The menu features fabulous regional offerings such as veal, lemon and caper meatballs, and *sporcamuss*, a sweet flaky pastry.

🛍 Shopping

Il Salumaio FOOD & DRINKS
(☑0805 21 93 45; www.ilsalumaio.it; Via Piccinni 168; ☉8.30am-2pm & 4.30-9pm Mon-Sat) Breathe in the delicious smells of Puglia's best produce at this venerable delicatessen.

Enoteca Vinarius de Pasquale WINE
(☑0805 21 31 92; Via Marchese di Montrone 87; ☉8am-1.30pm & 4-8.30pm Mon-Sat) Stock up on Puglian drops such as Primitivo di Manduria at this gorgeous old wine shop, founded in 1911.

ℹ Information

From Piazza Aldo Moro, in front of the main train station, streets heading north will take you to Corso Vittorio Emanuele II, which separates the old and new parts of the city.

Tourist Office (☑ 0805 82 14 11; Piazza Aldo Moro 32; ⊙ 9am-1pm & 3-7pm Mon-Sat) This kiosk, convenient to Bari's central station, is packed with information on the city and Puglia generally.

Police Station (☑ 0805 29 11 11; Via Murat 4)

Post Office (☑ 0805 25 01 50; Piazza Umberto I 33a; ⊙ 8.30am-7pm Mon-Fri, to 12.30pm Sat)

Policlinico di Bari (☑ 800 34 93 49; Piazza Cesare 11) Bari's main hospital has a 24-hour emergency room.

ⓘ Getting There & Away

AIR

Bari's **Karol Wojtyła Airport** (☑ 0805 80 02 00; www.aeroportidipuglia.it; Viale Ferrari), 10km northwest of the city centre, is served by a host of international and budget airlines, including easyJet, Alitalia and Ryanair.

Pugliairbus (www.aeroportidipuglia.it) connects Bari airport with Foggia and Brindisi airports. It also has services to Matera, Vieste, and Taranto.

BOAT

Ferries run from Bari to Albania, Croatia, Greece and Montenegro. All boat companies have offices at the **ferry terminal**, accessible on bus 20 from the main train station. Fares vary considerably among companies and it's easier to book with a travel agent such as **Morfimare** (☑ 0805 7 98 15; www.morfimare.it; Corso de Tullio 36-40).

The main companies and their routes:

Jadrolinija (☑ 0805 27 54 39; www.jadrolinija. hr; Nuova Stazione Marittima di Bari) For Dubrovnik (Croatia).

Montenegro Lines (☑ 382 30 31 11 64; www. montenegrolines.net; Corso de Tullio 36) For Bar (Montenegro) and Dubrovnik (Croatia).

Superfast (☑ 0805 28 28 28; www.superfast. com; Corso de Tullio 6) For Corfu, Igoumenitsa and Patras (Greece).

Ventouris Ferries (☑ Albania 0808 496685, Greece 0808 761451; www.ventouris.gr; Nuova Stazione Marittima di Bari) For Corfu, Cephalonia and Igoumenitsa (Greece) and Durrës (Albania).

BUS

Intercity buses leave from two main locations. From Via Capruzzi, south of the main train station, **SITA** (☑ 0805 79 01 11; www.sitabus.it) covers local destinations. **Ferrovie Appulo-Lucane** (☑ 0805 72 52 29; http://ferrovie appulolucane.it) buses serving Matera (€4.90, 1¾ hours, six daily) also depart from here, plus **Marozzi** (☑ 0805 79 02 11; www.marozzivt.it) buses for Rome (from €34.50, 4½ hours to 5½ hours, six daily – note that the overnight bus departs

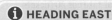

from Piazza Moro) and other long-distance destinations.

Buses operated by **Ferrovie del Sud-Est** (FSE; ☑ 0805 46 21 11; www.fseonline.it) leave from Largo Ciaia, south of Piazza Aldo Moro and service the following places:

Alberobello (€4.90, 1½ hours, hourly); continues to Locorotondo (€5.60, 1¾ hours) and Martina Franca (€5.60, two hours)

Grotte di Castellana (€2.80, one hour, frequent)

Taranto (€8.40, three hours with change, four per day)

TRAIN

A web of train lines spreads out from Bari. Note that there are fewer services on the weekend.

From the **Bari Centrale Station** (☑ 0805 24 43 86), Trenitalia trains go to Puglia and beyond:

Brindisi (from €8.40, one hour, frequent)

Foggia (from €9.10, one hour, frequent)

Milan (from €59, 6¾ to eight hours, frequent)

Rome (from €40, four hours, four per day)

Ferrovie Appulo-Lucane serves two main destinations:

Matera (€4.90, 1¾ hours, 12 daily)

Potenza (€11, 3¾ hours, four daily)

Ferrovie del Sud-Est trains leave from the southern side of the station where they have their own separate ticket office:

Alberobello (€4.90, 1¾ hours, hourly)

Martina Franca (€5.60, 3¼ hours, five per day)

Taranto (from €8.40, 2½ hours, nine daily)

ⓘ Getting Around

Central Bari is compact – a 15-minute walk will take you from Piazza Aldo Moro to the old town.

For the ferry terminal, take bus 20 (tickets €1.50) from Piazza Moro.

Street parking is migraine-inducing. There's a large parking area (€1) south of the main port entrance; otherwise, there's a large multi-storey car park between the main train station and the FSE station. Another car park is on Via Zuppetta, opposite Hotel Adria.

TO/FROM THE AIRPORT

For the airport, take the **Tempesta shuttle bus** (www.autoservizitempesta.it) from the main train station (€4, 30 minutes, hourly), with pickups at Piazza Garibaldi and the corner of Via Andrea da Bari and Via Calefati. Alternatively, normal city bus 16 covers the same route and a trip is much cheaper (€1), though marginally slower (40 minutes). A taxi trip from the airport to town costs around €25.

Around Bari

The *Terra di Bari* (Land of Bari) surrounding the capital is rich in olive groves and orchards, and the region has an impressive architectural history with some magnificent cathedrals, an extensive network of castles along its coastline, charming seaside towns such as Trani and, inland, the mysterious Castel del Monte.

Trani

POP 56,100

Known as the 'Pearl of Puglia', beautiful Trani has a sophisticated feel, particularly in summer when well-heeled visitors pack the array of marina-side bars. The marina is the place to promenade and watch the white yachts and fishing boats in the harbour, while the historic centre, with its medieval churches, glossy limestone streets, historic Jewish quarter and faded yet charming *palazzi* is an enchanting area to explore. But it's the cathedral, pale against the deep-blue sea, that is the town's most arresting sight.

👁 Sights

Cathedral
CATHEDRAL

(www.cattedraletrani.it; Piazza del Duomo; campanile €5; ⊙ 8.30am-12.30pm & 3.30-7pm Mon-Sat, 9am-12.30pm & 4-9pm Sun Apr-Oct, shorter hours Nov-Mar) This dramatic seafront cathedral is dedicated to St Nicholas the Pilgrim, a Greek Christian who wandered through Puglia crying '*Kyrie eleison*' ('Lord, have mercy'). First thought to be a simpleton, he was posthumously revered after several miracles attrib-

uted to him occurred. Below the church is the **crypt**, a forest of ancient columns that predates the current structure, and where the bones of St Nicholas are kept beneath the altar. You can also visit the **campanile** (bell tower).

Castle
CASTLE

(☑ 080 528 52 49; www.castelloditrani.beniculturali.it; Piazza Manfredi 16; adult/reduced €5/2.50; ⊙ 8.30am-7.30pm) Two hundred metres north of the cathedral is one of Trani's major landmarks, the vast, almost modernist Swabian castle built by Frederick II in 1233. Charles V later strengthened the fortifications and it was used as a prison from 1844 to 1974. While the moat is now dry, the ingenious engineers originally devised a system allowing the level of seawater in it to be precisely controlled.

Scolanova Synagogue
SYNAGOGUE

(☑ 0883 48 17 99; Via Scolanova 23; ⊙ hours vary) This synagogue, one of four once established in Trani's ancient Jewish quarter, has been reborn after over 600 years. Persecutions, forced conversions and confiscations periodically beset the Jews of Trani, culminating in their forced expulsion in 1510. This 13th-century synagogue was converted to a Christian church in an earlier wave of hate, around 1380. Abandoned by the mid-20th century, it has been deconsecrated and returned to life as the Jewish house of worship it originally was.

Ognissanti Church
CHURCH

(http://chiesadiognissanti.it; Via Ognissanti; ⊙ hours vary) Traditionally (but controversially) thought to be built by the Knights Templar in the 12th century, this church became a place of blessing for those setting out on Crusade. Legend has it that it was in this austere and dignified building that the knights of the First Crusade swore allegiance to their leader, Bohemond I of Antioch, before setting off to 'liberate' the Holy Lands. Whatever the truth, it's a treasured example of Puglian-Romanesque architecture of the period.

🛏 Sleeping

B&B Centro Storico Trani
B&B €

(☑ 0883 50 61 76; www.bbtrani.it; Via Leopardi 28; s/d €40/60; 🐾) This simple, old-fashioned B&B inhabits the 14th-century Palazzo Morola in the old Jewish quarter, and is run by a lovely elderly couple. It's basic, but the

WORTH A TRIP

FREDERICK II'S TOY CASTLE

You'll see **Castel del Monte** (☑ 0883 56 99 97; www.casteldelmonte.beniculturali.it; adult/reduced €10/6; ⊗ 10.30am-7.30pm Apr-Sep, 9am-6.30pm Oct-Mar), an inhumanly exact geometric shape on a hilltop, from miles away. Mysterious and perfectly octagonal, it's one of southern Italy's most talked-about landmarks and a Unesco World Heritage Site. No one knows why Frederick II built it – there's no nearby town or strategic crossroads. It was not built to defend anything, as it has no moat or drawbridge, no arrow slits, and no trapdoors for pouring boiling oil on invaders.

Some theories claim that, according to mid-13th-century beliefs in geometric symbolism, the octagon represented the union of the circle and square, of God-perfection (the infinite) and human-perfection (the finite). The castle was therefore nothing less than a celebration of the relationship between humanity and God.

The castle has eight octagonal towers. Its interconnecting rooms have decorative marble columns and fireplaces, and the doorways and windows are framed in corallite stone. Many of the towers have washing rooms with what are thought to be Europe's first flushing loos – Frederick II, like the Arab world he admired, set great store by cleanliness.

To get to the castle without a car, take the Ferrovia Bari-Nord train from Bari to Andria, then bus number 6 from Andria station to the castle (35 minutes, five daily, April to October only). The castle is about 35km from Trani; there's no parking, but a nearby site charges €5 for a car, and €1 for a shuttle up the short, steepish 500m to the castle.

rooms are large and 'Mama' makes a mean *crostata* (jam tart). There's a terrace, laundry and wi-fi in communal areas.

Hotel Regia HOTEL €€
(☑ 0883 58 44 44; www.hotelregia.it; Piazza Addazi 2; s/d/tr €120/130/170; ❄ 🐾) A lone, lovely building facing the cathedral and the Adriatic, the 18th-century Palazzo Filisio houses this charmingly understated grand hotel. Rooms are sober and stylish, and the location is stupendous. Half- and full-board packages are available, and the in-house restaurant (meals €40) maintains the upmarket vibe with dishes such as risotto with prawns, asparagus and black truffle.

✖ Eating

★ Corteinfiore SEAFOOD €€
(☑ 0883 50 84 02; www.corteinfiore.it; Via Ognissanti 18; meals €40; ⊗ 1-2.15pm Tue-Sun, 8-10.15pm Tue-Sat) The decking, stiff tablecloths and marquee setting of this famed Trani seafood restaurant set hopes racing, and the food, wine and service deliver in full. Expect lots of seafood, and expect it to be excellent: try the *frutti di mari antipasti*, or the Gallipoli prawns with candied lemon. Also rents delightful rooms (double €120) decked out in pale colours.

La Darsena SEAFOOD €€
(☑ 0883 48 73 33; Via Statuti Marittimi 96; meals €32; ⊗ noon-3pm & 8-11.30pm Tue-Sun)

Renowned for its seafood, swish La Darsena is housed in a waterfront *palazzo*. Outside tables overlook the port while inside, photos of old Puglia cover the walls beneath a huge wrought-iron dragon chandelier. Dishes such as *cavatelli* (pasta) with mussels and salted ricotta just sing with unabashed flavour.

ℹ Information

Tourist Office (☑ 0883 58 88 30; www.traniweb.it; 1st fl, Palazzo Palmieri, Piazza Trieste 10; ⊗ 10.30am 12.30pm & 5.30 7.30pm Mon-Sat) Located 200m south of the cathedral. Offers free guided walking tours most days at 8pm.

ℹ Getting There & Away

STP (☑ 0883 49 18 00; www.stpspa.it) has frequent bus services to Bari. Services depart from **Bar Stazione** (Piazza XX Settembre 23), which also has timetables and tickets.

Trani is on the main train line between Bari (€3.10, 30 to 45 minutes, frequent) and Foggia (€6.30, 40 to 50 minutes, frequent).

Polignano a Mare

POP 18,000

Dip into this spectacularly positioned small town if you can. Located around 34km south of Bari on the S16 coastal road, Polignano a Mare is built on the edge of a craggy ravine pockmarked with caves. The town is thought to be one of the most important ancient settlements in Puglia and was later inhabited by successive invaders ranging from the Huns to the Normans. On Sunday the *logge* (balconies) are crowded with day trippers from Bari who come here to view the crashing waves, visit the caves and crowd out the *cornetterias* (shops specialising in Italian croissants) in the atmospheric c*entro storico*.

🏃 Activities

Dorino
BOATING

(☑ 329 6465904; www.dorinogb.it; Lungomare Domenico Modugno; adult/child 11-15yr/under 11yr €25/10/free) For excursions into the dramatic sea caves and under the looming coast around Polignano, make a booking with this laid-back operation. Call ahead, as opening hours aren't fixed.

🛏 Sleeping & Eating

B&B Santo Stefano
B&B €

(☑ 0804 24 95 63, 345 1686043; www.santostefano.info; Vico Santo Stefano 9-13; d from €89; 🛜) Santo Stefano offers six attractive rooms located in an ancient tower in the old part of Polignano, complete with tufa walls, antique furniture and bright bathrooms. There's a terrace facing the sea, and activities such as biking and trekking can be organised, for a fee.

Antiche Mura
PUGLIAN €€

(☑ 0804 24 24 76; www.ristoranteantichemura.it; Via Roma 11; meals €30; ☻ noon-2.30pm & 7.30-11.30pm Wed-Mon) Huddled against the eponymous 'Old Walls' of Polignano, this delightful little restaurant features a vaulted cave-like interior with lanterns and bells adorning the walls. Unsurprisingly, fish is a speciality, with sea bass, octopus and lobster making an appearance in simple yet memorable dishes such as linguine with baby lobster and sea bass from Orbetello (Tuscany) with potatoes and zucchini.

Promontorio del Gargano

The coast surrounding this expansive promontory seems permanently bathed in a pink-hued, pearly light, providing a painterly contrast to the sea, which softens from intense to powder blue as the evening draws in. It's one of Italy's most beautiful corners, encompassing white limestone cliffs, fairy-tale grottoes, sparkling sea, ancient forests, rare orchids and tangled, fragrant maquis (dense scrub vegetation).

Once connected to what is now Dalmatia (in Croatia), the 'spur' of the Italian boot has more in common with the land mass across the sea than with the rest of Italy. Creeping urbanisation was halted in 1991 by the creation of the **Parco Nazionale del Gargano** (www.parcogargano.gov.it) FREE. Aside from its magnificent national park, the Gargano is home to pilgrimage sites and the lovely seaside towns of Vieste and Peschici.

Vieste

POP 13,950

Clinging to a spectacular headland jutting into the Adriatic, Vieste resembles nothing so much as a cross between Naples and Dubrovnik, with a bit of Puglian magic mixed in. The narrow alleys of the old town, draped with lines of drying clothes and patrolled by slinking cats and the odd friendly dog, are an atmospheric place, day or night, high or off-season. Wedged up against the old town is the equally unpretentious new town, ghostly in winter, but packed with holidaying humanity in summer, especially during the *passeggiata* (evening stroll).

👁 Sights

Cathedral
CATHEDRAL

(Via Duomo; ☻ 7.30am-noon & 4-11pm) Built by the Normans on the ruins of a Vesta temple, this 11th-century 'co-cathedral' (so called because its bishopric is shared with another) is in Puglian-Romanesque style with a fanciful tower that resembles a cardinal's hat. Of note are its beautiful paintings, swirling interior columns and Latin-inscribed altar.

La Salata
CEMETERY

(☑ 0854 70 66 35; Strada Provinciale 52; adult/child €5/free; ☻ 5.30pm & 6.15pm Mon-Fri Jul & Aug, fewer days Jun & Sep, by appointment Oct-May) This palaeo-Christian graveyard dating from the 4th to 6th centuries AD is 9km out of town. Inside the cave, tier upon tier of narrow tombs are cut into the rock wall; others form shallow niches in the cave floor. Guided tours are mandatory.

Chianca Amara
HISTORIC SITE

(Bitter Stone; Via Cimaglia) Vieste's most gruesome sight is this worn and polished stone where thousands were beheaded when Turks sacked Vieste in the 16th century.

⚡ Activities

Superb sandy beaches surround the town: in the south are **Spiagga del Castello**, **Cala San Felice** and **Cala Sanguinaria**; due north, head for the area known as **La Salata**. Diving is popular around the promontory's rocky coastline, which is filled with marine grottoes.

From May to September fast boats zoom to the **Isole Tremiti**.

For hiking ideas, pick up a *Guida al Trekking sul Gargano* brochure from the tourist office. A section of walk 4 is doable from Vieste. It starts 2.5km south of town off the Lungomare Enrico Mattei, where a track cuts up through olive groves into increasingly wild terrain.

Centro Ormeggi e Sub   BOATING
(✆ 0884 70 79 83; Scalo Marittimo 3ud 18/19) Offers diving courses and rents out sailing boats and motorboats.

⚓ Tours

Several companies offer tours of the caves that pock the Gargano coast – a three-hour tour costs around €15.

Motobarca Desirèe   BOATING
(✆ 360 262386; www.grottemarinegargano.com; Lungomare Vespucci; adult/child €20/10; ☉ Apr-Oct) Boat tours of the various caves, arches and *trabucchi* (Puglian fishing structures) that characterise the Gargano coast. Trips are spectacular, though the boats can get crowded. Two departures a day (9am and 2.30pm); buy tickets port-side.

Explora Gargano   CYCLING
(✆ 0884 70 22 37, 340 7136 864; www.explora gargano.it; Vieste-Peschici km 5.5; tours from €50) To get off the beach for a day or two, take one of the many tours on offer at Explora Gargano. As well as hiking and mountain biking (half-day from €70) in the Foresta Umbra, it offers quad tours and jeep safaris (from €50 per day).

🛏 Sleeping

Campeggio Capo Vieste   CAMPGROUND €
(✆ 0884 70 63 26; www.capovieste.it; Vieste-Peschici km 8; 2 adults & campsite/1-bedroom cottage €38/164; ☉ Mar-Oct; ☀) This tree-shaded campground is right by a sandy beach at La Salata, around 8km from Vieste and accessible by bus. Activities include tennis, a sailing school, beach volleyball and treks in the Gargano.

B&B Rocca sul Mare   B&B €
(✆ 0884 70 27 19; www.roccasulmare.it; Via Mafrolla 32; per person €45; 🐾) In a former convent in the old quarter, this is a popular, charming and reasonably-priced place, with comfortable high-ceilinged rooms. There's also a rooftop terrace with panoramic views, a suite with a steam bath and simple, tasty meals (€22 for four courses). Bike hire is available and it can arrange fishing trips and cook your catch that evening.

★ Relais Parallelo 41   B&B €€
(✆ 0884 35 50 09; www.bbparallelo41.it; Via Forno de Angelis 3; r €138; ☉ Mar-Oct; ❄ 🐾) This beautiful small B&B in an updated *palazzo* in the midst of the old town has five renovated rooms, decorated with hand-painted ceilings, luxurious beds and super modern bathrooms. Breakfasts consist of a substantial buffet, and the reception area acts as a mini information centre for local activities. Note that there are minimum stays in July and August.

🍴 Eating

★ Vecchia Vieste   PUGLIAN €
(✆ 0884 70 70 83; Via Mafrolla 32; meals €25; ☉ noon-3pm & 7-11pm) Look beyond the stony, cavernous interior of this modest-seeming restaurant to find what is possibly the best homemade, hand-shaped *orecchiette* in Puglia (and that's saying something). Try it topped with the obligatory *cima di rape* (rapini – a bitter green leafy veg – with anchovies, olive oil, chilli peppers, garlic and *pecorino*).

Osteria Al Duomo   OSTERIA €€
(✆ 0884 70 82 43; www.osterialduomo.it; Via Alessandro III 23; meals €32; ☉ noon-3pm & 7-11pm Mar-Nov) Tucked away in a picturesque narrow alley in the heart of the old town, this welcoming *osteria* has a cosy cave-like interior and outdoor seating under a shady arbour. And it's not relying on its plum position to get diners through the door: real care and innovation goes into experimental-yet-pleasing creations such as *tagliolini* with fish skin, clams and pistachios.

ℹ Information

Post Office (✆ 0884 70 28 49; Via Vittorio Veneto 7; ☉ 8.30am-7pm Mon-Sat)

Tourist Office (✆ 0884 70 88 06; Piazza Kennedy; ☉ 8am-8pm Mon-Sat) You can weigh yourself down with useful brochures in this office, housed in the old fish market.

Surprises of the South

In the Mezzogiorno, the sun shines on a magical landscape: dramatic cliffs and sandy beaches fringed with turquoise seas; wild rocky mountains and gentle forested slopes; rolling green fields and flat plains. Sprinkled throughout are elegant *palazzi* (mansions), *masserias* (working farms), ancient cave-dwellings and gnome-like stone huts.

Promontorio del Gargano

Along with its charming seaside villages, sandy coves and crystalline blue waters, the Gargano (p728) is also home to the Parco Nazionale del Gargano. It's perfect for hikers, nature trippers and beach fiends alike.

Valle d'Itria

In a landscape of rolling green hills, vineyards, orchards and picture-pretty fields, conical stone huts called *trulli* sprout from the ground en masse in the Disneyesque towns of Alberobello (p737) and Locorotondo (p738).

Salento

In Salento, hot, dry plains covered in wildflowers and olive groves reach toward the gorgeous beaches and waters of the Ionian and Adriatic Seas. It's the unspoilt 'heel' of Italy, with Lecce (p743) as its sophisticated capital.

Matera

The ancient cave city of Matera (p757) has been inhabited since Palaeolithic times. Explore the tangled alleyways, admire frescoes in rock churches, and sleep in millennia-old *sassi* (former cave dwellings).

Parco Nazionale dell'Aspromonte

In this wild park (p774), narrow roads lead to hilltop villages such as spectacularly sited Bova. Waterfalls, wide riverbeds, jagged cliffs and sandstone formations form the backdrop to a landscape made for hiking.

1. Conical *trulli* houses, Alberobello (p737), Valle d'Itria 2. Bova (p774), Parco Nazionale dell'Aspromonte 3. Matera (p757) 4. Lecce (p743), Salento

ℹ️ Getting There & Around

BOAT

Vieste's port is to the north of town, about a five-minute walk from the tourist office. In summer, several companies, including **Linee Marittime Adriatico** (📞 0884 96 20 23; www.collegamentiisoletremiti.com; Corso Garibaldi 32), head to the Isole Tremiti. Tickets can be bought port-side.

BUS

From Piazzale Manzoni, where intercity buses terminate, a 10-minute walk along Viale XXIV Maggio, which becomes Corso Fazzini, brings you into the old town and the Marina Piccola's attractive promenade. In summer buses terminate at Via Verdi, a 300m walk from the old town down Via Papa Giovanni XXIII.

SITA (📞 0881 35 20 11; www.sitabus.it) buses run between Vieste and Foggia via Manfredonia. There are also services to Monte Sant'Angelo (€5) via Macchia Bivio Monte.

From May to September, **Pugliairbus** (📞 080 580 03 58; http://pugliairbus.aeroportidipuglia.it) runs a service to the Gargano, including Vieste, from Bari airport.

Monte Sant'Angelo

POP 12,550

One of Europe's most important pilgrimage sites, this isolated mountain-top town has an extraordinary atmosphere. Pilgrims have been coming here for centuries – and so have the hustlers, pushing everything from religious kitsch to parking spaces.

The object of devotion is the Santuario di San Michele. Here, in AD 490, St Michael the Archangel is said to have appeared in a grotto to the Bishop of Siponto.

During the Middle Ages, the sanctuary marked the end of the Route of the Angel, which began in Mont St-Michel (in Normandy) and passed through Rome. In 999 the Holy Roman Emperor Otto III made a pilgrimage to the sanctuary to pray that prophecies about the end of the world in the year 1000 would not be fulfilled. His prayers were answered, the world staggered on and the sanctuary's fame grew.

The sanctuary has been a Unesco World Heritage Site since 2011.

THE RICH FLAVOURS OF LA CUCINA POVERA

In Italy's less wealthy 'foot', traditional recipes evolved through economic necessity rather than experimental excess. Local people used whatever ingredients were available to them, plucked directly from the surrounding soil and seas, and kneaded and blended using recipes passed down through generations. The result is called *cucina povera* (literally 'food of the poor'), which, thanks to a recent global obsession with farm-to-table purity, has become increasingly popular.

If there is a mantra for *cucina povera*, it is 'keep it simple'. Pasta is the south's staple starch. Made with just durum wheat and water (and no eggs, unlike some richer northern pastas) it is most commonly sculpted into *orecchiette* ('little ears') and used as the starchy platform on which to serve whatever else might be growing readily and inexpensively. For the same reasons, vegetables feature prominently: eggplants, mushrooms, tomatoes, artichokes, olives and many other staple plants grow prodigiously in these climes and are put to good use in the dishes.

Meat, though present in *cucina povera*, is used more sparingly than in the north. Lamb and horsemeat predominate and are usually heavily seasoned. Unadulterated fish is more common, especially in Puglia, which has a longer coastline than any other mainland Italian region. Popular fish dishes incorporate mussels, clams, octopus (in Salento), swordfish (in northern Calabria), cod and prawns.

A signature Puglian *primi* (first course) is *orecchiette con cima di rape*, a gloriously simple blend of rapini (a bitter green leafy veg with small broccoli-like shoots) mixed with anchovies, olive oil, chilli peppers, garlic and *pecorino*. Another popular *orecchiette* accompaniment is *ragù di carne di cavallo* (horsemeat), sometimes known as *ragù alla barese*. Bari is known for its starch-heavy *riso, patate e cozze*, a surprisingly delicious marriage of rice, potatoes and mussels that is baked in the oven. Another wildly popular vegetable is wild chicory, which, when combined with a fava bean purée, is reborn as *fave e cicorie*.

Standard cheeses of the south include *burrata*, which has a mozzarella-like shell and a gooey centre, and *pecorino di filiano*, a sheep's-milk cheese from Basilicata. There are tons of bread recipes, but the horn-shaped crusty bread from Matera is king.

◉ Sights

The town's serpentine alleys and jumbled houses are perfect for a little aimless ambling. Look out for the different shaped *cappelletti* (chimney stacks) on top of the neat whitewashed houses.

★**Santuario di San Michele** CAVE
(☑0884 56 11 50; www.santuariosanmichele.it; Via Reale Basilica; ⊙7.30am-7.30pm Jul-Sep, shorter hours rest of year) FREE Over the centuries this sanctuary has expanded to incorporate a large complex of religious buildings that overlay its original shrine. The double-arched entrance vestibule at street level stands next to a distinctive octagonal bell tower built by Carlo I of Naples in 1282. As you descend the staircase inside, look for the 17th-century pilgrims' graffiti. The grotto/shrine where St Michael is said to have left a footprint in stone is located at the bottom of the staircase.

Because of St Michael's footprint, it became customary for pilgrims to carve outlines of their feet and hands into the stone. Etched Byzantine bronze and silver doors, cast in Constantinople in 1076, open into the grotto itself. Inside, a 16th-century statue of the Archangel Michael covers the site of St Michael's footprint. Audio guides cost €3, and it's €5 to get into the museum (or €7 for both together).

Tomba di Rotari TOMB
(☑0884 56 11 50; Largo Tomba di Rotari; €1; ⊙9am-noon & 3-7pm Apr-Oct, to 4.30pm Nov-Mar) A short flight of stairs opposite the Santuario di San Michele leads to a 12th-century baptistry with a deep sunken basin for total immersion. You enter the baptistry through the facade of the **Chiesa di San Pietro** with its intricate rose window squirming with serpents – all that remains of the church, destroyed in a 19th-century earthquake. The Romanesque portal of the adjacent 11th-century **Chiesa di Santa Maria Maggiore** has some fine bas-reliefs.

Castle CASTLE
(☑0884 56 54 44; Largo Roberto Giuscardo 2; €2; ⊙9am-1pm & 2-6pm) At the highest point of Monte Sant'Angelo is this rugged fastness, first built by Orso I, who later became Doge of Venice, in the 9th century. One 10th-century tower, Torre dei Giganti, survives, but most of what you can see are Norman, Swabian and Aragonese additions. The views alone are worth the admission.

⏝ Sleeping & Eating

Hotel Michael HOTEL €
(☑0884 56 55 19; www.hotelmichael.com; Via Reale Basilica 86; s/d €60/80; ☞) A small hotel with shuttered windows, located on the main street across from the Santuario di San Michele, this traditional place has spacious rooms, some with with extremely pink bedspreads, and walls spruced up with devotional art. Ask for a room with a view, or just enjoy it as you breakfast on the rooftop terrace.

Casa li Jalantuúmene TRATTORIA €€
(☑0884 56 54 84; www.li-jalantuumene.it; Piazza de Galganis 5; meals €42; ⊙noon-3pm & 7.30-10.30pm Wed-Mon) This renowned restaurant has a well-known chef, Gegè Mangano, and serves excellent fare. Vegetarians are looked after (try the pasta with wild fennel, cherry tomatoes and ricotta cream), the setting is intimate, there's a select wine list and, in summer, tables spill onto the piazza. There are also four suites on site (from €100), decorated in traditional Puglian style.

❶ Getting There & Away

SITA (☑0881 35 20 11; www.sitasudtrasporti.it) buses run from Foggia (€4.50, 1¾ hours, four daily) and Vieste via Macchia Bivio Monte.

Peschici
POP 4500

Perched above a turquoise sea and tempting beach, Peschici, like Vieste, is another cliff-clinging Amalfi lookalike. Its tight-knit old walled town of Arabesque whitewashed houses acts as a hub to a wider resort area. The small town gets crammed in summer, so book in advance. Boats zip across to the Isole Tremiti in high season.

⏝ Sleeping & Eating

Peschici's ample accommodation stocks can come under stress when it seems half of Puglia heads to Gargano in August.

Baia San Nicola CAMPGROUND €
(☑0884 96 42 31; www.baiasannicola.it; Localita Punta San Nicola; 2 adults & tent/2-person bungalow per week €33/720; ⊙mid-May–mid-Oct) The best campground in the area, 2km south of Peschici towards Vieste, Baia San Nicola is on a pine-shaded beach, offering camping, bungalows, apartments and myriad amenities.

Locanda al Castello B&B €€

(☑0884 96 40 38; www.peschicialcastello.it; Via Castello 29; s/d €70/120; P❋🛜) Staying here is like entering a large, welcoming family home. It's by the cliffs with fantastic views and it's air-conditioned, should you visit in the height of summer. Enjoy hearty home cooking in the restaurant (meals €23) while the owners' kids run around playing football – indoors!

⭐ **Al Trabucco da Mimì** SEAFOOD €€

(☑0884 96 25 56; www.altrabucco.it; Localita Punta San Nicola; meals €40; ☺12.30-2pm & 7-11pm Easter-Oct) Mimì sadly passed away in 2016, but his daughter and grandsons keep this delightful place ticking. Sitting on wooden trestles beneath the eponymous *trabucco* (a traditional Puglian wooden fishing platform) you'll eat the freshest seafood, prepared with expertise but no fuss, as you watch the sun sink behind Peschici. The raw seafood antipasti and grilled mullet are stunning. There are three simple rooms for rent, at €50 per person. There's also occasional live music (usually jazz) and *aperitivo* in summer.

⭐ **Porta di Basso** ITALIAN €€€

(☑0884 35 51 67; www.portadibasso.it; Via Colombo 38; menus €45-60; ☺noon-2.30pm & 7-11pm, closed Jan & Feb) 🍴 Superb views of the ocean drop away from the floor-to-ceiling windows beside intimate alcove tables at this adventurous and stylish clifftop restaurant. Choose from one of three degustation menus, and prepare to be delighted by dishes such as smoked bluefish with Jerusalem artichokes, fois gras and honey vinegar.

ℹ️ Information

Tourist Office (☑0884 96 49 66; Via Magenta 3; ☺10am-1pm & 4.30-7.30pm Mon-Sat) Friendly staff give you the lowdown on Peschici and the Gargano.

ℹ️ Getting There & Away

The bus terminal is beside the sportsground, uphill from the main street, Corso Garibaldi.

From April to September, ferry companies, including **Linee Marittime Adriatico** (p732), serve the Isole Tremiti.

Foresta Umbra

The 'Forest of Shadows' is the Gargano's enchanted interior – thickets of tall, epic trees interspersed with picnic spots bathed in dappled light. It's the last remnant of Puglia's ancient forests: Aleppo pines, oaks, yews and beech trees cloak the hilly terrain. More than 65 different types of orchid have been discovered here, and the wildlife includes roe deer, wild boar, foxes, badgers and the increasingly rare wild cat. Walkers and mountain bikers will find plenty of well-marked trails within the forest's 5790 sq km.

You'll need your own transport to get in and out of the forest.

👁 Sights & Activities

The small visitor centre in the middle of the forest houses a **museum and nature centre** (SP52bis, Foresta Umbra; €1.50; ☺9.30am-6.30pm mid-Apr–mid-Oct, 4-10pm Easter) where you can buy maps, hire bikes and join guided hikes.

There are 15 official trails in the park ranging from 0.5km to 13.5km in length. Several of them start near the visitor centre and the adjacent Laghetto Umbra, including path 9, which can be done as a loop returning on a military road. A park leaflet provides a map and trail descriptions.

🛏 Sleeping

Rifugio Sfilzi B&B €

(☑338 3345544; www.rifugiosfilzi.com; SP528; adult €45, incl half-/full board €85/100, child 4-12 incl full board €50) In the middle of the Foresta Umbra, five kilometres north of the visitor centre on the way to Vico di Gargano, this cosy *rifugio* (mountain hut) offers eight rooms with three- and four-bed configurations, making them ideal for groups or families. It also has a small shop selling locally made products such as jams and oils, and a cafe-restaurant with fantastic homemade cake and coffee.

Isole Tremiti

POP 500

This beautiful archipelago of three islands, 36km offshore, is a picturesque composition of ragged cliffs, sandy coves and thick pine woods, surrounded by the glittering dark-blue sea.

Unfortunately, the islands are no secret, and in July and August some 100,000 holidaymakers head over. If you want to savour the islands in tranquillity, visit during the shoulder season. In the low season most tourist facilities close down and the few permanent residents resume their quiet and isolated lives.

Driving Tour
Italy's Authentic South

START VIESTE
END MARATEA
LENGTH 650KM TO 700KM; ONE WEEK

Consider a gentle start in lovely, laid-back **1 Vieste**, with its white sandy beaches and medieval backstreets, but set aside half a day to hike or bike in the lush green forests of the **2 Parco Nazionale del Gargano**. Follow the coastal road past dramatic cliffs, salt lakes and flat farming land to **3 Trani**, with its impressive seafront cathedral and picturesque port, before spending a night in **4 Bari**, where you'll find boisterous bars and salt-of-the-earth trattorias. The next day head to **5 Alberobello**, home to a dense neighbourhood of Puglia's extraordinary cone-shaped stone homes, called *trulli*; consider an overnight *trulli* stay.

Stroll around one of the most picturesque *centro storicos* (historic centres) in southern

Italy at **6 Locorotondo**. Hit the road and cruise on to lively baroque **7 Lecce**, where you can easily chalk up a full day exploring the sights, shops and flamboyantly fronted *palazzi* and churches, including the Basilica di Santa Croce.

Day five will be one to remember. Nothing can prepare you for Basilicata's **8 Matera**, where *sassi* (former cave dwellings) are a dramatic reminder of the town's poverty-stricken past. After days of pasta, *fave* beans and *cornetti* (Italian croissants), it's high time for some exercise on the trails of the spectacular **9 Parco Nazionale del Pollino**. Finally, wind up the trip with more walking or a day of beach slothing at the spread out coastal town of **10 Maratea** with its surrounding seaside resorts, medieval village and cosmopolitan harbour, offset by a thickly forested and mountainous interior.

The islands' main facilities are on San Domino, the largest and lushest island, formerly used to grow crops. It's ringed by alternating sandy beaches and limestone cliffs; inland grows thick maquis flecked with rosemary and foxglove. The centre harbours a nondescript small town with several hotels.

Small San Nicola island is the traditional administrative centre; a castle-like cluster of medieval buildings rises up from its rocks. The third island, Capraia, is uninhabited.

◉ Sights & Activities

San Domino ISLAND

Head to San Domino for walks, grottoes and coves. It has a pristine, marvellous coastline and the islands' only sandy beach, **Cala delle Arene**. Alongside the beach is the small cove **Grotta dell'Arene**, with calm clear waters for swimming. You can also take a boat trip (around €15 from the port) around the island to explore the grottoes: the largest, Grotta del Bue Marino, is 70m long. A tour of all three islands costs around €20.

Diving in the translucent sea is another option with **Tremiti Diving Center** (☑337 648917; www.tremitidivingcenter.com; Via Federico II, Villaggio San Domino; 1-tank day-/night-dive €40/50). There's an undemanding, but enchanting, walking track around the island, starting at the far end of the village.

San Nicola ISLAND

Medieval buildings thrust out of San Nicola's rocky shores, the same pale-sand colour as the barren cliffs. In 1010, Benedictine monks founded the **Abbazia e Chiesa di Santa Maria** here; for the next 700 years the islands were ruled by a series of abbots who accumulated great wealth.

Although the church retains a weatherworn Renaissance portal and a fine 11th-century floor mosaic, its other treasures have been stolen or destroyed throughout its troubled history, which has seen various religious orders come and go including the Benedictines, the Cistercians and the Lateran Canons. The only exceptions are a painted wooden Byzantine crucifix brought to the island in AD 747 and a black Madonna, probably transported here from Constantinople in the Middle Ages.

Capraia ISLAND

The third of the Isole Tremiti, Capraia (named after the wild caper plant) is uninhabited. Bird life is plentiful, with impressive flocks of seagulls. There's no organised transport, but trips can be negotiated with local fishing folk.

🛏 Sleeping & Eating

La Casa di Gino B&B €€

(☑0882 46 34 10; www.hotel-gabbiano.com; Via dei Forni, San Nicola; s/d from €110/170; ✿) A tranquil accommodation choice on San Nicola, away from the frenzy of San Domino, this B&B run by the Hotel Gabbiano has stylish white-on-white rooms. Great views and quiet space to amble or relax are two of its most delightful aspects.

Hotel Gabbiano HOTEL €€

(☑0882 46 34 10; www.hotel-gabbiano.com; Via Garibaldi 5, Villaggio San Domino; d from €123; ✿🖥) An established icon on San Nicola and run for decades by the same Neapolitan family, this smart hotel has pastel-coloured rooms with balconies overlooking the town and the sea. It also has a seafood restaurant, spa and gym.

Architiello SEAFOOD €€

(☑0882 46 30 54; Via Salita delle Mura 5, San Nicola; meals €30; ⊙noon-3pm & 7.30-11pm Apr-Oct) A class act with a sea-view terrace, this place specialises in – what else? – fresh fish.

ⓘ Getting There & Away

Boats for the Isole Tremiti depart from several points on the Italian mainland: Manfredonia, Vieste and Peschici in summer, and Termoli in nearby Molise year-round. Most boats arrive at San Domino. Small boats regularly make the brief crossing to San Nicola (€6 return) in high season; from October to March a single boat makes the trip after meeting the boat from the mainland.

Valle d'Itria

Between the Ionian and Adriatic coasts rises the great limestone plateau of the Murgia (473m). It has a strange karst geology: the landscape is riddled with holes and ravines through which small streams and rivers gurgle, creating what is, in effect, a giant sponge. At the heart of the Murgia lies the idyllic Valle d'Itria.

The rolling green valley is criss-crossed by dry-stone walls, vineyards, almond and olive groves, and winding country lanes. This is the part of Puglia most visited by foreign tourists and is the best served by hotels and luxury *masserias* (working farms) or manor farms.

Alberobello

POP 10,750

Unesco World Heritage Site Alberobello resembles an urban sprawl – for gnomes. The *zona dei trulli* on the westernmost of the town's two hills is a dense mass of 1500 beehive-shaped houses, white-tipped as if dusted by snow. These dry-stone buildings are made from local limestone; none are older than the 14th century. Inhabitants do not wear pointy hats, but they do sell anything a visitor might (or might not) want, from miniature *trulli* to woollen shawls.

The town is named after the primitive oak forest Arboris Belli (beautiful trees) that once covered this area. It's an amazing place, but also something of a tourist trap – from May to October busloads of tourists pile into *trullo* homes, drink in *trullo* bars and shop in *trullo* shops.

If you park in Lago Martellotta, follow the steps up to Piazza del Popolo, where the Belvedere Trulli lookout offers fabulous views over the whole higgledy-piggledy picture.

⊙ Sights

Rione Monti   AREA

Within the old town quarter of Rione Monti more than 1000 *trulli* cascade down the hillside, many of which are now souvenir shops. The area is surprisingly quiet and atmospheric in the late evening, once the gaudy stalls have been stashed away.

Rione Aia Piccola   AREA

On the eastern side of Via Indipendenza is Rione Aia Piccola. This neighbourhood is much less commercialised than Rione Monti, with 400 *trulli*, many still used as family dwellings. You can climb up for a rooftop view at many shops, although most do have a strategically located basket for donations.

Trullo Sovrano   MUSEUM

(☑080 432 60 30; www.trullosovrano.eu; Piazza Sacramento 10; adult/reduced €1.50/1; ⊙10am-1.30pm & 3.30-7pm Apr-Oct, to 6pm Nov-Mar) Trullo Sovrano dates in parts to the early 17th century, and is Alberobello's only two-floor *trullo*. Built by a wealthy priest's family, it's now a small 'living' museum recreating *trullo* life, with sweet, rounded rooms that include a recreated bakery, bedroom and kitchen. The souvenir shop here has a wealth of literature on the town and surrounding area, plus Alberobello recipe books.

🛏 Sleeping

Casa Albergo Sant'Antonio   HOTEL €

(☑080 432 29 13; www.santantonioalbergo.it; Via Isonzo 8a; s/d/tr/q €50/78/95/110; 🖄) Excellent value right in the heart of the Rione Monti neighbourhood, this simple hotel is in an old monastery and located next to a unique *trulli*-style church with a conical roof. The tiled rooms are relatively monastic and spartan, but will do the trick for the unfussy.

Camping dei Trulli   CAMPGROUND €

(☑080 432 36 99; www.campingdeitrulli.com; Via Castellana Grotte km 1.5; camping 2 people & car €19.50, bungalows per person €20, trulli €40; P@🖄) This campground 1.5km out of town has some nice tent sites, a restaurant, a market, two swimming pools, tennis courts and bicycle hire. You can also rent *trulli* off the grounds. It has 120 pitches, 90 for camper vans, lots of pines for shade and good shower blocks.

Trullidea   RENTAL HOUSE €€

(☑080 432 38 60; www.trullidea.it; Via Monte Sabotino 24; trulli from €120; 🖄) Trullidea has numerous renovated, quaint, cosy and atmospheric *trulli* in Alberobello's historic centre available on a self-catering, B&B, or half- or full-board basis. Half-board is €25 person, and the buffet breakfast is included in the price.

🍴 Eating

Trattoria Amatulli   TRATTORIA €

(☑080 432 29 79; Via Garibaldi 13; meals €20; ⊙12.30-3pm & 7.30-11.30pm Tue-Sun) The cheerily cluttered interior of this excellent trattoria is papered with photos of smiley diners, obviously put in the best mood by dishes like *orecchiette scure con cacioricotta pomodoro e rucola* ('little ears' pasta with cheese, tomato and rucola). Wash it down with the surprisingly drinkable house wine, only €4 a litre. It won't add much to an invariably reasonable bill.

★ Trattoria Terra Madre   VEGETARIAN €€

(☑080 432 38 29; www.trattoriaterramadre.it; Piazza Sacramento 17; meals €30; ⊙12.15-2.45pm & 7.15-9.45pm Tue-Sat, 12.15-2.45pm Sun; 🖄) Vegetables take pride of place in Italian kitchens, especially at this enthusiastic vegetarian-ish (some meat is served) restaurant. The farm-to-table ethos rules – most of what you eat comes from the organic garden outside. Start with the huge vegetable antipasti and save room for *primi* like *capunti* 'Terra Madre' (pasta with eggplant, zucchini and peppers) and the perfect house-baked desserts.

Il Poeta Contadino
ITALIAN €€€

(☎ 080 432 19 17; www.ilpoetacontadino.it; Via Indipendenza 23; menu €65; ⊙ noon-2.30pm & 7-10.30pm Tue-Sun Feb-Dec; ⚲) Vegetarians can be pleased here, as vegetables step timidly out of the *contorni* shadow, into the *primi* limelight. Alongside the swordfish, shrimp and clams that predominate, you'll find a flan of cave-aged cheese, celery and potato cream with turnip and ricotta, and other good, imaginative things. The dining room has a medieval feel, with its sumptuous decor and chandeliers.

ℹ Information

Tourist Information Office (☎ 080 432 28 22; www.prolocoalberobello.it; Monte Nero 1; ⊙ 9am-7pm) Local office in the *zona dei trulli*.

ℹ Getting There & Away

Alberobello is easily accessible from Bari (€4.90, 1½ hours, hourly) on the FSE Bari–Taranto train line. From the station, walk straight ahead along Via Mazzini, which becomes Via Garibaldi, to reach Piazza del Popolo.

Locorotondo

POP 14,200

Locorotondo is endowed with a whisper-quiet pedestrianised *centro storico*, where everything is shimmering white aside from the blood-red geraniums that tumble from the window boxes. Situated on a hilltop on the Murge Plateau, it's a *borgo più bella d'Italia* (www.borghipiubelliditalia.it) – that is, it's rated as one of the most beautiful towns in Italy. There are few 'sights' as such – rather, the town itself is a sight. The streets are paved with smooth ivory-coloured stones, with the church of **Santa Maria della Graecia** as their sunbaked centrepiece.

From **Villa Comunale**, a public garden, you can enjoy panoramic views of the surrounding valley. You enter the historic quarter directly across from here.

Not only is this deepest *trulli* country, it's also the liquid heart of the Puglian wine region. Sample some of the local *verdeca* at Controra.

🛏 Sleeping

Locorotondo and the surrounding country are blessed when it comes to quality accommodation. If you're going to stay on a *masseria* or in a *trullo* while in Puglia, this is the place to do it.

Truddhi
AGRITURISMO €

(☎ 080 443 13 26; www.trulliresidence.it; Contrada Trito 161; d/tr per week from €450/624; P ✿) This charming cluster of 11 self-catering *trulli* in the hamlet of Trito near Locorotondo is surrounded by olive groves and vineyards. It's a tranquil place and you can take cooking courses (per day €80) with Mino, a lecturer in gastronomy. The *trulli* sleep between two and six people, depending on size.

★ Sotto le Cummerse
APARTMENT €€€

(☎ 0804 31 32 98; www.sottolecummerse.it; Via Vittorio Veneto 138; apt incl breakfast from €200; ✴ 🛜) At this *albergo diffuso* (dispersed hotel) you'll stay in one of 13 tastefully furnished apartments scattered throughout Locorotondo's *centro storico*. The apartments are traditional buildings that have been beautifully restored and furnished, and you can book activities such as horse riding, cooking classes and historical tours. A delightful base for exploring the Valle d'Itria.

🍴 Eating & Drinking

★ Quanto Basta
PIZZA €

(☎ 080 431 28 55; Via Morelli 12; pizza €7; ⊙ 7.30-11pm Tue-Sun; 🛜) Craft beer and pizza make an excellent combination, no more so than at Quanto Basta, a quietly stylish old-town restaurant with wooden tables, soft lighting and stone floors. It's hard to stop at *quanto basta* ('just enough') when the pizza, carpaccio, salads and antipasti are so good, to say nothing of the lovely Itrian wines.

La Taverna del Duca
TRATTORIA €€

(☎ 080 431 30 07; www.tavernadelducascatigna.it; Via Papatodero 3; meals €35; ⊙ noon-3pm & 7.30pm-midnight Tue-Sat, noon-3pm Sun & Mon) In a narrow side street off Piazza Vittorio Emanuele, this well-regarded trattoria serves robust Itrian fare such as pork cheek in a primitivo reduction and donkey stew. If they sound daunting, there's always Puglia's favourite pasta (*orecchiette* 'little ears' pasta), thick vegetable soup and other more comforting foods.

WORTH A TRIP

GROTTE DI CASTELLANA

The spectacular limestone caves of **Grotte di Castellana** (☏ 080 499 82 21; www.grotte dicastellana.it; Piazzale Anelli; short/full tour €12/16; ⊗ 9am-6pm Aug, shorter hours other months, by appointment Jan & Feb), 40km southeast of Bari, are Italy's longest natural subterranean network. The interlinked galleries, first discovered in 1938, contain an incredible range of underground landscapes, with extraordinary stalactite and stalagmite formations – look out for the jellyfish, the bacon and the stocking. The highlight is the **Grotta Bianca** (White Grotto), an eerie alabaster cavern hung with stiletto-thin stalactites. 'Speleonights' take small torch-wieding groups into the caves after dark, among the bats, beetles, and crustacea that live there.

There are two tours in English: a 1km, 50-minute tour that doesn't include the Grotta Bianca (€12, on the half-hour); and a 3km, two-hour tour (€16, on the hour) that does include it. The staff like you to assemble in good time before your scheduled tour, and remember that temperatures inside the cave average 18°C, so take a light jacket.

In the same complex, you'll also find a speleology **museum** (☏ 080 499 82 30; www. grottedicastellana.it; ⊗ 9.30am-1pm & 3.30-6.30pm mid-Mar–Oct, 10am-1pm Nov–mid-Mar) and an **observatory** (☏ 080 499 82 13; www.osservatorio.grottedicastellana.it; adult/child 6-14yr €5/3; ⊗ tours by appointment Jul & Aug).

Grotte di Castellana can be reached by rail from Bari on the FSE Bari–Taranto train line (€3.20, 1¼ hours, roughly hourly).

Controra   WINE BAR
(☏ 339 6874169; Via Nardelli 67) Treat this laidback little place either as a sandwich shop or wine bar, sampling *prosit* (sparkling rose), *verdeca* and other niche wines of the Valle d'Itria, all over amazing sandwiches, platters of regional produce and Locorotondo's uniformly stunning views.

ℹ️ Information

Tourist Office (☏ 080 431 30 99; www.prolo colocorotondo.it; Piazza Emanuele 27; ⊗ 9am-1pm & 5 7pm) Offers free internet access and multilingual tourist information.

ℹ️ Getting There & Away

Locorotondo is easily accessible via frequent trains from Bari (€5.60, 1½ to two hours) on the FSE Bari–Taranto train line.

Cisternino

POP 11,600

An appealing, whitewashed, hilltop town, slow-paced Cisternino has a charming *centro storico* beyond its bland modern outskirts; with its kasbah-like knot of streets, it has been designated as one of the country's *borghi più belli* (most beautiful towns). Beside its 13th-century **Chiesa Matrice** and **Torre Civica** there's a pretty communal garden with rural views. If you take Via Basilioni next to the tower you can amble along an elegant route right to the central piazza, Vittorio Emanuele.

🍴 Eating

Micro   VEGETARIAN €
(☏ 340 5315463; Via Santa Lucia 53; meals €20; ⊗ 10am-3pm & 6-11pm Wed-Mon; 🌿) This tiny, charismatic little juice bar/lunch spot is the necessary counterbalance to the meaty excesses Cisternino is famous for. Boxloads of fresh vegetables and herbs arrive each morning, whatever's in the market, and are turned into soups, salads, torte, vegetarian sushi and more. There are some choices for carnis, but for once it's they who are the afterthought.

Rosticceria L'Antico Borgo   BARBECUE €€
(☏ 080 444 64 00; www.rosticceria-lanticoborgo. it; Via Tarantini 9; meals €30; ⊗ 6.30-11pm daily summer, Mon-Sat winter) A classic *fornello pronto* (half butcher's shop, half trattoria), this is the place for a cheerful, no-frills meat fest. The menu is brief, listing a few simple pastas and various meat options (priced per kilo), including Cisternino's celebrated *bombette* (skewered pork wrapped around a piece of cheese). Choose your roast meat and eat it with red wine, chips and salad.

ℹ️ Getting There & Away

Cisternino is accessible by regular trains from Bari (€5.80, 45 minutes). STP Brindisi runs hourly buses between Cisternino and Ostuni.

MASSERIAS: LUXURY ON THE FARM

Masserias are unique to southern Italy. Modelled on the classical Roman villa, these fortified farmhouses – equipped with oil mills, cellars, chapels, storehouses and accommodation for workers and livestock – were built to function as self-sufficient communities. These days, they still produce the bulk of Italy's olive oil, but many have been converted into luxurious hotels, *agriturismi* (farm-stay accommodation), holiday apartments or restaurants. Staying in a *masseria* is a unique experience, especially when you can dine on home-grown produce.

Il Frantoio (☎0831 33 02 76; www.masseriailfrantoio.it; SS16 km 874, Ostuni; d €216; P ❋ @ ❖) Stay at this charming, whitewashed farmhouse, where the owners still live and work producing high-quality organic olive oil (a *frantoio* is an oil-press). Owner Armando takes guests for a tour of the farm each evening in his 1949 Fiat, and local producers are regularly invited to share their produce and the love they have for it.

Masseria Torre Maizza (☎080 482 78 38; www.masseriatorremaizza.com; Contrada Coccaro, Fasano; d/ste €568/696; ❋ ❖ ☀) Definitely at the high end of the *masseria* experience is this luxurious *agriturismo*. You won't get your hands dirty, but you will destress – playing golf, riding horses, getting a massage, sweating it all out in the hammam or just lolling by the pool, drink in hand. There are two restaurants on site and little expense has been spared in the suites.

Masseria Torre Coccaro (☎080 482 93 10; www.masseriatorrecoccaro.com; Contrada Coccaro 8, Fasano; d/ste €453/650; P ❋ ❖ ☀) For pure luxury, stay at this super chic yet countrified *masseria*. There's a glorious spa set in a cave, a beach-style swimming pool, cooking courses on offer and a restaurant (meals €90) dishing up home-grown produce. It's around 10km from Locorotondo.

Borgo San Marco (☎080 439 57 57; www.borgosanmarco.it; Contrada Sant'Angelo 33, Fasano; ste €210; P ❋ ❖ ☀) Once a *borgo* (medieval town), this *masseria* has 16 rooms and a spa in the orchard, and manages to be traditional while also showing a bohemian edge. Nearby are some frescoed rock churches. Note: there's a four-night minimum stay in July, and seven-night minimum in August.

Martina Franca

The old quarter of this town is a picturesque scene of winding alleys, blinding white houses and blood-red geraniums. There are graceful baroque and rococo buildings here too, plus airy piazzas and curlicue ironwork balconies that almost touch above the narrow streets.

This town is the highest in the Murgia, and was founded in the 10th century by refugees fleeing the Arab invasion of Taranto. It only started to flourish in the 14th century when Philip of Anjou granted tax exemptions (*franchigie,* hence Franca); the town became so wealthy that a castle and defensive walls complete with 24 solid bastions were built.

◉ Sights & Activities

The best way to appreciate Martina Franca's beauty is to wander around the *centro storico*'s narrow lanes and alleyways.

Passing under the baroque **Arco di Sant'Antonio** at the western end of pedestrianised Piazza XX Settembre, you emerge into Piazza Roma, dominated by the imposing, 17th-century rococo **Palazzo Ducale** (☎080 480 57 02; Piazza Roma 28; ⊙9am-8pm Mon-Fri, from 10am Sat & Sun mid-Jun–Sep, shorter hours rest of year) **FREE**, whose upper rooms have semi-restored frescoed walls and host temporary art exhibitions.

From Piazza Roma, follow the fine Corso Vittorio Emanuele, with baroque townhouses, to reach Piazza Plebiscito, the centre's baroque heart. The piazza is overlooked by the 18th-century **Basilica di San Martino**, its centrepiece a statue of city patron, St Martin, swinging a sword and sharing his cloak with a beggar.

Walkers can ask for the free *Carta dei Sentieri del Bosco delle Pianelle* brochure at the tourist office, which maps out 10 walks in the nearby **Bosco delle Pianelle** (around 10km west of town). This lush woodland is part of the larger 1206-hectare **Riserva**

Naturale Regionale Orientata, populated with lofty trees, wild orchids, and a rich and varied bird life, including kestrels, owls, buzzards, hoopoe and sparrow hawks. There's a small museum dedicated to the park in the Palazzo Ducale.

★ Festivals & Events

Festival della Valle d'Itria
MUSIC

(☑080 480 51 00; www.festivaldellavalleditria.it; single-event tickets from €15; ☺ Jul & Aug) Festival della Valle d'Itria is a summer music festival that takes over Martina Franca's venues from mid-July to early August. Musical theatre, especially opera, tops the bill, but concertos and other recitals also abound. For information, contact the Centro Artistico Musicale Paolo Grassi in the Palazzo Ducale.

⌂ Sleeping

Villaggio In
APARTMENT €

(☑080 480 59 11; www.villaggioincasesparse.it; Via Arco Grassi 8; studio/apt/ste €75/90/100; 🅟🅰) These charming apartments are located in original *centro storico* homes. Arched stone ceilings, large pastel-coloured rooms and antique furniture are common features of the various apartments, which sleep two to six people. There's a self-serve laundry and vouchers for breakfast in a local cafe, but unfortunately the wi-fi only really works near reception.

B&B San Martino
B&B €

(☑080 48 56 01; http://xoomer.virgilio.it/bed-and-breakfast-sanmartino; Via Abate Fighera 32; s/d from €50/80, 🅟🅰) A stylish B&B in a historic palace with rooms overlooking gracious Piazza XX Settembre. The rooms have exposed stone walls, shiny parquet floors, wrought-iron beds and small kitchenettes (only one has a working cooker) and there's a pool to take a dip when it's hot.

✕ Eating

Don't miss the chance to try the *capocollo* – cured pork neck – that Martina Franca is famous for.

Gran Caffè
CAFE €

(☑080 480 54 91; Via Santoro 7a; snacks €2-3; ☺7.30am-2am) With a broad communal bar, ever-hissing espresso machines and outdoor tables aligned towards busy Piazza XX Settembre, this is the quintessential Italian cafe. Sit. People-watch. Sip coffee. Nibble *cornetto*. Repeat.

Nausikaa
ITALIAN €€

(☑080 485 82 75; Vico Arco Fumarola 2; meals €30; ☺noon-3pm Tue-Sun, 7.30-11.30pm Tue-Sat) Tucked away down a dogleg alley off Martina Franca's main pedestrian drag is this lovely little modern Italian, run by brothers Francesco and Martino. Tradition is not sacrificed to forward-thinking, and vice versa – a 'caprese' salad, for instance, is stuffed inside a silky pasta bundle, anointed with 'basil pearls'. The Puglia-focused wine list is a joy, too.

Osteria Garibaldi
OSTERIA €€

(☑080 430 49 00; Via Garibaldi 17; meals €28; ☺noon-3pm & 7.30pm-midnight Thu-Tue) A highly recommended green-shuttered *osteria* in the *centro storico*. Delicious aromas entice you into the cave-like interior and the *cucina tipica* menu of typical Pugliese food doesn't disappoint. Worthy of a long lunch.

ⓘ Information

Tourist Office (☑080 480 57 02; www.agenziapugliapromozione.it; Piazza XX Settembre 3; ☺10.30am-1.30pm & 4.30-7pm Jul & Aug, shorter hours rest of year) The tourist office is to the right of the Arco di Sant'Antonio, just before you enter the old town.

ⓘ Getting There & Away

The FSE train station is downhill from the historic centre. From the train station, go right along Viale della Stazione, continue along Via Alessandro Fighera to Corso Italia, then continue to the left along Corso Italia to Piazza XX Settembre.

FSE (☑080 546 21 11; www.fseonline.it) trains run to/from Bari (€5.60, 2¼ hours, hourly) and Taranto (€2.50, 50 minutes, four per day).

FSE buses run to Alberobello (€1.10, 20 minutes, frequent).

Ostuni

POP 31,150

Chic Ostuni shines like a pearly white tiara, extending across three hills with the magnificent gem of a cathedral as its sparkling centrepiece. It's the end of the *trulli* region and the beginning of the hot, dry Salento. With some excellent restaurants, stylish bars and swish yet intimate places to stay, it's packed in summer.

Ostuni is surrounded by olive groves, so this is the place to buy some of the region's DOC 'Collina di Brindisi' olive oil – either delicate, medium or strong – direct from producers.

◉ Sights & Activities

The surrounding countryside is perfect for cycling. Ciclovagando (www.ciclovagando. com), based in Mesagne, 30km south of Ostuni, organises guided tours. Each tour covers approximately 20km and departs daily from various towns in the district, including Ostuni and Brindisi. For an extra €15, you can sample typical Puglian foods on the tour.

Museo di Civiltà Preclassiche
della Murgia   MUSEUM
(✐ 0831 33 63 83; www.ostunimuseo.it; Via Cattedrale 15; adult/reduced €5/3; ◷ 10am-1pm & 6-10pm Jul–mid-Sep, shorter hours rest of year) Located in the Convento delle Monacelle, the museum's most famous exhibit is Delia, a 25,000-year-old expectant mother. Pregnant at the time of her death, her well-preserved skeleton was found in a local cave. Many of the finds here come from the Palaeolithic burial ground, now the Parco Archeologico e Naturale di Arignano (✐ 0831 30 39 73; ◷ 9.30am-1pm Sun, or by appointment).

Cathedral   CATHEDRAL
(Piazza Beato Giovanni Paolo II; €1; ◷ 9am-noon & 3.30-7pm) Dedicated to the Assumption of the Virgin Mary, Ostuni's dramatic 15th-century cathedral has an unusual Gothic-Romanesque-Byzantine facade with a frilly rose window and an inverted gable. The 18th-century sacred art covering the ceiling and altars is well worth stepping inside to see.

✯✯ Festivals & Events

La Cavalcata   RELIGIOUS
Ostuni's annual feast day is held on 26 August. Processions of horsemen dressed in glittering red-and-white uniforms (resembling Indian grooms on their way to be wed) follow the statue of Sant'Oronzo around town.

⊨ Sleeping

Le Sole Blu   B&B €
(✐ 0831 30 38 56; www.webalice.it/solebluostuni; Corso Vittorio Emanuele II 16; s/d €40/80) Located in the 18th-century (rather than medieval) part of town, Le Sole Blu only has one room available: fully renovated, it's large with a separate entrance, but the bathroom is tiny. However, the two self-catering apartments nearby are excellent value.

★ La Terra   HOTEL €€
(✐ 0831 33 66 51; www.laterrahotel.it; Via Petrarolo 16; d from €170; ᴘ ✳ ☎) This former 13th-century palazzo offers atmospheric and stylish accommodation with original niches, dark-wood beams and furniture, and contrasting light stonework and whitewash. There's a colonnaded terrace, wi-fi throughout, a more-than-decent restaurant and a truly cavernous bar – tunnelled out of a cave.

✗ Eating

Osteria del Tempo Perso   PUGLIAN €€
(✐ 0831 30 33 20; www.osteriadeltempoperso. com; Via Vitale 47; meals €35; ◷ 12.30-3pm & 7.30-11pm Tue-Sun, open Mon Jul & Aug) A wonderful temple of Puglian cuisine in a cavernous former bakery, this laid-back place makes masterful use of the best of the region's produce, from Martina Franca's capocollo (cured pork neck) to whatever's been hauled from the nearby sea. If you're in Ostuni for a while, and want to get deeper into Puglia's food, consider the cooking courses the osteria offers.

Osteria Piazzetta Cattedrale   OSTERIA €€
(✐ 0831 33 50 26; www.piazzettacattedrale.it; Largo Arcidiacono 7; meals €40; ◷ 12.30-3pm & 7pm-12.30am Wed-Mon; ✐) This compact osteria serves up great food in a setting that manages to keep it classy, despite a kitsch chandelier and muzak soundtrack competing with more tasteful mise-en-scene. While lovers of fish, fowl and flesh won't be disappointed, the menu includes plenty of vegetarian options, making great use of local mushrooms, cheeses and greens.

★ Porta Nova   ITALIAN €€€
(✐ 0831 33 89 83; www.ristoranteportanova.com; Via Petrarolo 38; meals €50; ◷ 1-3.30pm & 7-11pm) Scenically installed in the Aragonese fortifications, this terraced restaurant is a special occasion charmer. Seafood is wonderful here, with a whole section of the menu devoted to crudo mare (raw fish). Ease into what will be a splendid hour or so of indulgence with seabass carpaccio, then ramp it up with rosemary-scented Gallipoli prawns on beech-smoked potato.

ⓘ Information

Tourist Office (✐ 0831 33 96 27, 0831 30 12 68; Corso Mazzini 6; ◷ 8am-2pm & 3-8pm) Located off Piazza della Libertà, this helpful office can organise guided visits of the town in summer, and bike rental.

ⓘ Getting There & Away

STP Brindisi (p751) buses run to Brindisi (€3.10, 50 minutes, six daily) and to Martina

Franca (€2.10, 45 minutes, three daily), leaving from Piazza Italia in the newer part of Ostuni.

Trains run frequently to Brindisi (€4, 25 minutes) and Bari (€9, 50 minutes). A half-hourly local bus covers the 2.5km between the station and town.

Salento

The Penisola Salentina, better known simply as Salento, is hot, dry and remote, retaining a flavour of its Greek past. It stretches across Italy's heel from Brindisi to Taranto and down to Santa Maria di Leuca. Here the lush greenery of Valle d'Itria gives way to flat, ochre-coloured fields hazy with wildflowers in spring, and endless olive groves.

Lecce

POP 95,000

If Puglia were a movie, Lecce would be cast in the starring role. Bequeathed with a generous stash of baroque buildings by its 17th century architects, the city has a completeness and homogeneity that other southern Italian metropolises lack. Indeed,

so distinctive is Lecce's architecture that it has acquired its own moniker, *barocco leccese* (Lecce baroque), an expressive and hugely decorative incarnation of the genre replete with gargoyles, asparagus columns and cavorting gremlins. Swooning 18th-century traveller Thomas Ashe thought it 'the most beautiful city in Italy', but the less-impressed Marchese Grimaldi said the facade of Basilica di Santa Croce made him think a lunatic was having a nightmare.

Either way, it's a lively, graceful but relaxed university town with some upmarket boutiques, decent Puglian restaurants, and a strong tradition for papier-mâché making. Both the Adriatic and Ionian Seas are within easy access and it's a great base from which to explore the Salento.

◉ Sights

Lecce has more than 40 churches and at least as many *palazzi*, all built or renovated between the 17th and 18th centuries, giving the city an extraordinary cohesion. Two of the main proponents of *barocco leccese* (the craziest, most lavish decoration imaginable)

LECCE'S NOTABLE CHURCHES

Lecce's unique baroque style is perhaps best seen in its churches; the city harbours dozens of them.

Chiesa dei Santi Nicolò e Cataldo (Via Cimitero; ⊙9am-noon & 5-7pm Jun-Aug, shorter hours rest of year) The beautiful church of Saints Nicolò and Cataldo, located in the monumental cemetery outside the city walls, was built by the Normans in 1180. It got caught up in the city's baroque frenzy and was revamped in 1716 by the prolific Giuseppe Cino, who retained the Romanesque rose window and portal. The 18th-century fresco cycles inside tell stories from the saints' lives.

Chiesa di Santa Chiara (Piazzetta Vittorio Emanuele II; ⊙9am-1pm & 4.30-6.30pm) A notable 15th-century church given a baroque makeover between 1687 and 1691, Santa Chiara is one of the most important and admired churches in Lecce. Inside, every niche and surface swirls with twisting columns and ornate statuary. The ceiling is 18th-century Leccese *cartapesta* (papier-mâché) masquerading as wood.

Chiesa di Sant'Irene (Corso Vittorio Emanuele II; ⊙7.30-11am & 4-6pm) Dedicated to Lecce's former patron saint and modelled on Rome's Basilica di Sant'Andrea della Valle, this church was completed in 1639. Inside you'll find a magnificent pair of mirror-image baroque altarpieces, facing each other across the transept.

Chiesa di San Matteo (Via dei Perroni 29; ⊙8.30am-1pm & 5-8pm) Known by the locals as Santa Maria della Luce, this graceful little church bears the fingerprints of Giuseppe Zimbalo, as much of baroque Lecce does. The famed architect completed the building, with its elaborate facade and more restrained interior, when the original architect died before completion.

Chiesa del Rosario (Via Libertini 5; ⊙8.30-11.30am & 5-6pm) Also known as the Chiesa di San Giovanni Battista (Church of John the Baptist), this elaborately fronted church was prodigious Leccese architect Giuseppe Zimbalo's last commission. He died before it was completed, and a quick-fix wooden roof was put up, instead of the dome he had intended.

Lecce

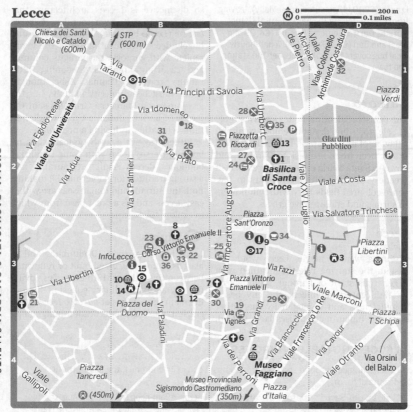

were brothers Antonio and Giuseppe Zimbalo, who both had a hand in the fantastical Basilica di Santa Croce.

⭐ **Basilica di Santa Croce**   BASILICA
(☎ 0832 24 19 57; Via Umberto I; ⓘ 9am-noon & 5-8pm) **FREE** It seems that hallucinating stonemasons have been at work on the basilica. Sheep, dodos, cherubs and beasties writhe across the facade, a swirling magnificent allegorical feast. Throughout the 16th and 17th centuries, a team of artists under Giuseppe Zimbalo laboured to work the building up to this pitch. The interior is more conventionally baroque, and deserves a look, once you've drained your camera batteries outside. Spare a thought for the expelled Jewish families whose land the basilica was built on.

Zimbalo also left his mark in the former Convento dei Celestini, just north of the basilica, which is now the **Palazzo del Governo** (Via Umberto I), the local government headquarters. Look for his profile on the facade of the basilica.

Piazza del Duomo   PIAZZA
Piazza del Duomo is a baroque feast, the city's focal point and a sudden open space amid the surrounding enclosed lanes. During times of invasion the inhabitants of Lecce would barricade themselves in the square, which has conveniently narrow entrances. Lecce's 12th-century cathedral, episcopal palace and **museum of sacred art** (☎ 0832 24 47 64; http://museo.diocesilecce. org; Piazza del Duomo 5; €4; ⓘ 9.30am-12.30pm & 4-7pm Mon-Fri) face one another in silent dignity across the square.

Cathedral   CATHEDRAL
(☎ 0832 30 85 57; Piazza del Duomo; crypt €1; ⓘ 7am-noon & 4-6.30pm) Giuseppe Zimbalo's 1659 reconstruction of Lecce's original 12th-century cathedral is recognised as

Lecce

being among his finest work. Zimbalo, Lecce's famous 17th-century architect, was also responsible for the thrusting, tiered **bell tower**, 72m high. The cathedral is unusual in that it has two facades, one on the western end and the other, more ornate, facing the piazza. It's framed by the 17th-century **Palazzo Vescovile** (Episcopal Palace) and the 18th-century **Seminario**, designed by Giuseppe Cino.

Palazzo Vescovile   PALACE
(Episcopal Palace; Piazza del Duomo) Facing Lecce's cathedral is the arched arcade loggia of the 15th-century Palazzo Vescovile, one time residence of Neapolitan royalty and one of Lecce's baroque masterpieces.

★ **Museo Faggiano**   MUSEUM
(☑ 0832 30 05 28; www.museofaggiano.it; Via Grandi 56/58; €3; ⊙ 9.30am-8pm) Descend through Lecce's rich historical strata in this fascinating home-turned-museum, where sewerage excavations led to the chance discovery of an archaeological treasure trove. The deepest finds take you all the way back to the Messapii culture of the 5th century BC; you then ascend through Roman crypts, medieval walls, Jewish insigna and Knights Templar symbols in the rooftop tower.

Castello di Carlo V   CASTLE
(☑ 0832 24 65 17; www.castellocarlov.it; Via XXV Luglio; adult/reduced/child 6-12yr €3/2/1; ⊙ 9am-8.30pm Mon-Fri, from 9.30am Sat & Sun, closes later in summer) While the Normans built the original castle in the 12th century, it became associated with the Spanish Holy Roman Emperor Charles V, who enlarged it extensively in the 16th century. Bound within enormous trapezoidal walls cornered with stout bastions, it is Puglia's largest castle, and has been used as a prison, court, military barracks and now the headquarters of Lecce's cultural authorities. You can wander around inside, catch a recital, and visit the on-site **papier-mâché museum**.

Museo Provinciale Sigismondo Castromediano   MUSEUM
(☑ 0832 68 35 03; Viale Gallipoli 30; ⊙ 8.30am-7.30pm Mon-Sat, 9am-1pm Sun) FREE This museum stylishly covers 10,000 years of history, from Palaeolithic and Neolithic bits and bobs to a handsome display of Greek and Roman jewels, weaponry and ornaments. The stars of the show are the Messapians, whose jaunty Mycenaean-inspired jugs and bowls date back 2500 years. There's also an interesting collection of 15th- to 18th-century paintings.

Roman Amphitheatre
AMPHITHEATRE

(Piazza Sant'Oronzo; ⊙ tours 10.15am-7.15pm Fri-Wed) Below the ground level of the piazza is this restored 2nd-century-AD amphitheatre, discovered in 1901 by construction workers. It was excavated in the 1930s to reveal a perfect horseshoe with seating for 15,000. A little colonised by weeds, it's nonetheless an impressive centrepiece to Lecce's main communal square. Book tickets for tours (€2, 10.15am, 12.15pm, 5.15pm and 7.15pm) at the neighbouring tourist office (p748).

MUST
GALLERY

(Museo Storico Citta di Lecce; ☑ 0832 24 10 67; www.mustlecce.it; Via degli Ammirati 11; adult/reduced €4.50/2.50; ⊙ noon-7pm Tue-Sun) The beautifully restored 15th-century Monastery of Santa Chiara houses this civic museum and gallery, and has a great view of the Roman theatre from the back window. Exhibits focus on the history of Lecce, from the Messapians of 2500 years ago to the present day, while the work of modern Leccese artists hangs in the ground-floor gallery.

Colonna di Sant'Oronzo
MONUMENT

(Piazza Sant'Oronzo) Two Roman columns once marked the end of the Appian Way in Brindisi. When one of them crumbled in 1582 some of the pieces were rescued and subsequently donated to Lecce (the base and capital remain in Brindisi). The old column was rebuilt in 1666 with a statue of Lecce's patron saint placed on top. Sant'Oronzo is venerated for supposedly saving the city of Brindisi from a 1656 plague.

Museo Teatro Romano
MUSEUM

(☑ 0832 27 91 96; Via degli Ammirati 5; adult/reduced €3/2; ⊙ 9.30am-1pm Mon-Sat) Exhibiting artefacts revealed excavating the adjacent Roman theatre, this museum also has displays recreating classical Roman life, including a reconstruction of Roman Lupiae (Lecce). The museum is housed in a handsome 17th-century *palazzo*.

Porta Napoli
GATE

The main city gate, Porta Napoli, was erected in 1548 in anticipation of a state visit from Charles V. It's a typically bombastic effort by Gian dell'Acaja (builder of Lecce's fortified walls), who modelled it on a Roman triumphal arch and gave it a pointy pediment carved with toy weapons and an enormous Spanish coat of arms.

Courses

Awaiting Table
COOKING

(☑ 334 7676970; www.awaitingtable.com; Via Idomeneo 41; day/week €195/1895) Silvestro Silvestori's splendid culinary- and wine-school provides day- or week-long courses with market shopping, tours, tastings, noteworthy lecturers – and lots of hands-on cooking. Week-long courses are held in Silvestro's home, but you'll need to arrange your own accommodation. Book well in advance as courses fill up rapidly.

🛏 Sleeping

★ Palazzo Rollo
B&B, APARTMENT €

(☑ 0832 30 71 52; www.palazzorollo.it; Corso Vittorio Emanuele II 14; s/d €75/90; P ❄ @) This tastefully restored 17th-century *palazzo* – the Rollo family seat for more than 200 years – makes a delightful base from which to explore Lecce. The grand B&B suites (with kitchenettes) have high curved ceilings and chandeliers while, downstairs, the contemporary-chic studios open onto an ivy-hung courtyard. There are also self-catering apartments (€75 per person) and a rooftop garden with wonderful views.

B&B Idomeneo 63
B&B €

(☑ 333 9499838; www.bebidomeneo63.it; Via Idomeneo 63; d/ste €85/120; ☎) You'll be looked after like a VIP at this wonderfully curated B&B in the midst of Lecce's baroque quarter, complete with six colour-coded rooms and a funky entrance lounge. Decked out boutique-hotel style, it manages to seamlessly incorporate older features like stone ceiling arches. The two 'apartments', with kitchenettes, are great value.

Azzurretta B&B
B&B €

(☑ 0832 24 22 11; www.hostelecce.com; Via Vignes 2; d/tr/apt €72/87/105; P ☎) Tullio runs this arty B&B located in an historic *palazzo*. Of the four rooms, ask for the large double with a balcony, wooden floors and vaulted ceiling. Massage is available in your room or on the roof terrace – also a splendid place to take a sundowner. You get a cafe voucher for breakfast.

B&B Prestige
B&B €

(☑ 349 7751290; www.bbprestige-lecce.it; Via Libertini 7; s/d/q €70/100/140; P @ ☎) On the corner of Via Santa Maria del Paradiso in the historic centre, the rooms at this lovely B&B are light, airy and beautifully finished. The communal sun-trap terrace has views over

San Giovanni Battista church. Breakfast is an extra €5 per day.

Centro Storico B&B
B&B €

(☑0832 24 27 27, 328 8351294; www.centros toricolecce.it; Via Vignes 2; s/d/ste €60/70/90; P❄🛜) This friendly and efficient B&B located in the 16th-century Palazzo Astore features big rooms, double-glazed windows and pleasantly old-fashioned decor. The huge rooftop terrace has sun loungers and views. Cafe vouchers are provided for breakfast, and there are also coffee- and tea-making facilities.

Palazzo Belli B&B
B&B €€

(☑0832 169 05 05, 348 0946802; Corso Vittorio Emanuele II 33; d €110; ❄🛜) A wonderfully central, elegant and well-priced option located in a handsome *palazzo* near the cathedral. Rooms have marbled floors and wrought-iron beds, and breakfast is served in your room.

Patria Palace Hotel
HOTEL €€

(☑0832 24 51 11; http://patriapalace.com; Piazzetta Riccardi 13; d from €114; P❄@🛜) This sumptuous hotel is traditionally Italian with large mirrors, dark wood furniture and wistful murals. The location is wonderful, the bar gloriously art deco with a magnificent carved ceiling, and the shady roof terrace has views over the Basilica di Santa Croce. The attached restaurant, Atenze (https://patriapalace.com/it/ristorante-atenze; Piazzetta Riccardi; meals €50; ⊙12.30-3pm & 7-11pm), is one of Lecce's finest.

Risorgimento Resort
HOTEL €€€

(☑0832 24 63 11; www.risorgimentoresort.it; Via Imperatore Augusto 19; d/ste €220/355; P❄@🛜) A warm welcome awaits at this stylish five-star hotel in the centre of Lecce. The rooms are spacious and refined with high ceilings, modern furniture and contemporary details reflecting the colours of the Salento. The bathrooms are enormous, too. There's a restaurant, wine bar and rooftop garden.

🍴 Eating

⭐ Baldo Gelato
GELATO

(☑328 0710290; Via Idomeneo 78; medium cone or cup €3; ⊙11am-8pm Mon-Thu, to midnight Fri-Sun) The couple behind Baldo Gelato make the best gelato in Lecce, hands down. The dark chocolate may be the most intensely chocolatey thing you've ever put in your mouth.

⭐ Trattoria Il Rifugio della Buona Stella
PUGLIAN €

(☑0832 181 05 11; www.ilrifugiodellabuonastella.it; Via Prato 28; meals €23; ⊙noon-3pm & 7-11.45pm Wed-Mon) A third-generation family restaurant in a gorgeous Leccese building with sandy stone walls and medieval decor, this wonderful trattoria serves utterly delicious Pugliese food at more-than-reasonable prices. Start off with the homemade bread, proceed to pasta with swordfish and rapini (turnip tops), and round off a happy evening's gluttony with the grilled sausages with mushrooms.

⭐ Trattoria le Zie – Cucina Casareccia
TRATTORIA €€

(☑0832 24 51 78; Viale Costadura 19; meals €30; ⊙12.30-2.30pm Tue-Sun & 7.30-10.30pm Tue-Sun) Where better to eat *cucina casareccia* (home cooking) than a place that feels like a private home, with patterned cement floor tiles, paper-strewn desk and a welcoming hostess (Carmela Perrone)? Known locally as simply 'le Zie' (the aunt) it's here you'll taste true *cucina povera*, such as horse meat in *salsa piccante* (spicy sauce). Booking is a must.

La Torre di Merlino
PUGLIAN €€

(☑0832 24 20 91; Via Giambattista del Tufo 10; meals €45; ⊙12-2.30pm & 7.30-11.30pm) This sweet courtyard restaurant is dependably one of Lecce's best eating options. There are pizzas, but why would you, when the seafood's so good? Try the *antipasti di crude di mare* (spanking-fresh raw scallops, red Gallipoli prawns, and whatever else that day's market suggested).

Alle due Corti
PUGLIAN €€

(☑0832 24 22 23; www.alleduecorti.com; Via Prato 42; meals €30; ⊙12.30-2pm & 7.30-11pm Mon-Sat, closed Jan) Rosalba de Carlo, a noted repository of Salento gustatory wisdom, is the presiding authority in this authentic-as-it gets Puglian kitchen. 'The Two Courts' keeps it strictly seasonal and local, dishing up classics such as *ciceri e tria* (crisply fried pasta with chickpeas) and *turcineddhi* (offal of kid) in a relaxed, traditional restaurant environment.

La Cucina di Mamma Elvira
PUGLIAN €€

(☑331 5795127; www.mammaelvira.com; Via Maremonti 33; meals €30; ⊙12.30pm-midnight) An offshoot of the stylish Enoteca Mamma Elvira, 'The Kitchen' makes use of a bigger space than that available to its older sibling to deliver more ambitious and substantial food. There's still the same focus on Puglian wine, simply augmented by a menu that offers seafood antipasti, lovely vegetarian options (try the eggplant fritters), robust Puglian pastas and more.

🍷 Drinking & Nightlife

Via Umberto I, just north of the Palazzo del Governo, is now an unbroken stretch of stylish bars, spilling out onto the pavement.

★ Enoteca Mamma Elvira
WINE BAR

(☑ 0832 169 20 11; www.mammaelvira.com; Via Umberto I 19; ☺ 8am-3am; 🖭) All you need to know about emerging Salento wine will be imparted by the hip but friendly staff at this cool new joint near the Santa Croce church. Taster glasses are dispatched liberally if you order a few snacks. You'll need to order a few if you're going to properly research the 250+ Puglian wines it stocks.

All'Ombra del Barocco
WINE BAR

(☑ 0832 24 55 24; Corte dei Cicala 1; ☺ 7am-midnight) Open throughout the day, this cool restaurant/cafe/wine bar has most needs covered, offering a range of teas, cocktails and *aperitivi*. It's open for breakfast, hosts musical events and the modern cooking is

---

LECCE'S PAPIER-MÂCHÉ ART

Lecce is famous for its papier-mâché art *(cartapesta)*. Statues and figurines are sculpted out of a mixture of paper and glue before being painted and used to adorn churches and other public buildings. Lecce's *cartapesta* culture originated in the 17th century when glue and paper offered cheap raw materials for religious artists who couldn't afford expensive wood or marble. Legend has it that the first exponents of the art were Leccese barbers who shaped and chiseled their statues in between haircuts.

These days the art is still practiced in Lecce and you'll see a number of traditional workshops such as **Cartapesta Riso** (☑ 0832 24 34 10; www.cartapesta riso.it; Corso Emanuele II 27; ☺ 9.30am-7.30pm) scattered around the old town centre. Also worth perusing are the papier-mâché museum inside the Castello di Carlo V (p745) and the decorative papier-mâché ceiling inside the Chiesa di Santa Chiara (p743).

---

well worth a try. Tables fill the little square outside, an ideal place from which to watch the *passeggiata*.

Caffè Alvino
CAFE

(☑ 0832 24 67 48; Piazza Sant'Oronzo 30; ☺ 7am-2am Wed-Mon; 🖭) Treat yourself to great coffee and *pasticciotto* (custard pie) at this iconic chandeliered cafe in Lecce's main square. And try to get past the lavish display of cakes without at least having second thoughts.

ℹ Information

Hospital (Ospedale Vito Fazzi; ☑ 0832 66 11 11; Piazza Filippo) Has a 24-hour emergency room.

InfoLecce (☑ 0832 52 18 77; www.infolecce. it; Piazza del Duomo 2; ☺ 9.30am-1.30pm & 3.30-7.30pm Mon-Fri, 10am-1.30pm & 3.30-7pm Sat & Sun) Independent and helpful tourist information office. Has guided tours and bike rental (per hour/day €3/15).

Police Station (☑ 0832 69 11 11; Viale Otranto 1)

Post Office (Piazza Libertini 5; ☺ 8.30am-7pm Mon-Fri, to 12.30pm Sat)

Puglia Blog (www.thepuglia.com) An informative site run by Fabio Ingrosso with articles on culture, history, food, wine, accommodation and travel in Puglia.

Tourist Office (☑ 0832 68 29 85; Corso Vittorio Emanuele II 16; ☺ 10am-1pm & 4-6pm) One of three main government-run offices. The others are in **Castello di Carlo V** (☑ 0832 24 65 17; ☺ 9am-8.30pm Mon-Fri, 9.30am-8.30pm Sat & Sun, closes later in summer) and **Piazza Sant'Oronzo** (☑ 0832 24 20 99; ☺ 10am-1pm & 4-6pm).

ℹ Getting There & Away

BUS

The city bus terminal is located to the north of Porta Napoli.

Pugliairbus (http://pugliairbus.aeroportidi puglia.it) Connects with Brindisi airport.

STP (☑ 0832 35 91 42; www.stplecce.it) STP runs buses to Brindisi, Gallipoli and Otranto from the **STP bus station** (☑ 800 43 03 46; Viale Porta D'Europa).

TRAIN

The main **train station**, 1km southwest of Lecce's historic centre, runs frequent services.

Bari from €9, 1½ to two hours

Bologna from €59.50, 7½ to 9½ hours

Brindisi from €2.80, 30 minutes

Naples from €53.10, 5½ hours (transfer in Caserta)

Rome from €66, 5½ to nine hours

FSE trains head to Otranto, Gallipoli and Martina Franca; the ticket office is located on platform 1.

Brindisi

POP 87,800

Like all ports, Brindisi has its seamy side, but it's also surprisingly slow paced and balmy, particularly along the palm-lined Corso Garibaldi, which links the port to the train station, and the promenade stretching along the interesting *lungomare* (seafront).

The town was the end of the ancient Roman road Via Appia, down whose length trudged weary legionnaires and pilgrims, crusaders and traders, all heading to Greece and the Near East. These days little has changed except that Brindisi's pilgrims are now sun-seekers rather than soul-seekers.

◉ Sights

Museo Archeologico
Provinciale Ribezzo MUSEUM
(☑0831 56 55 01; Piazza del Duomo 6; adult/reduced €5/3; ⊙9.30am-1.30pm Tue-Sat, plus 3.30-6.30pm Tue) This superb museum covers several floors with well-documented exhibits (in English), including some 3000 bronze sculptures and fragments in Hellenistic Greek style. There are also terracotta figurines from the 7th century, underwater archaeological finds, and Roman statues and heads (not always together).

Roman Column MONUMENT
(Via Colonne) The gleaming white column above a sweeping set of sun-whitened stairs leading to the waterfront promenade marks the terminus of the Roman Via Appia at Brindisi. Originally there were two columns, but one was presented to the town of Lecce back in 1666 as thanks to Sant'Oronzo for having relieved Brindisi of the plague.

Tempio di San Giovanni
al Sepolcro CHURCH
(☑0831 52 30 72; Piazzetta San Giovanni al Sepolcro) This 12th-century church, a brown bulk of Norman stone conforming to the circular plan the Templars so loved, is a wonderfully evocative structure, austere and bare. You'll see vestigial medieval frescoes on the walls, and glimpses of the crypt below.

Palazzo Granafei-Nervegna MUSEUM
(Via Duomo 20; ⊙10am-1pm & 5-8pm Tue-Sun) FREE A 16th-century Renaissance-style palace named for the two different families who owned it. The building is of interest because it houses the huge ornate capital that used to sit atop one of the Roman columns that marked the end of the Appian Way (the rest of the column is in Lecce). Also on site are a pleasant cafe, a bookshop, exhibition spaces and the archaeological remains of a Roman *domus* (house).

Cathedral CATHEDRAL
(Piazza del Duomo; ⊙8am-9pm Mon-Fri & Sun, to noon Sat) This 12th-century cathedral was substantially remodelled after an earthquake in 1743. You can see how the original Romanesque structure may have looked by studying the nearby **Porta dei Cavalieri Templari**, a fanciful portico with pointy arches – all that remains of a medieval Knights Templar's church that once also stood here.

🛏 Sleeping

Grande Albergo
Internazionale HISTORIC HOTEL €€
(☑0831 52 34 73; www.albergointernazionale.it; Viale Regina Margherita 23; s/d €100/160; P ✳ 🛜) Built in 1869 for English merchants en route to India, the Internazionale definitely offers grandeur, albeit of the rather faded variety. It has great harbour views, large rooms with grandly draped curtains, and stately common areas. There are mod cons, but gadgetry takes second place to history here (wi-fi is available only in public areas). Check for off-season deals online.

Hotel Orientale HOTEL €€
(☑0831 56 84 51; www.hotelorientale.it; Corso Garibaldi 40; r €130; P ✳ 🛜) This sleek, modern hotel overlooks the long palm-lined *corso*. Rooms are pleasant, the location is good and it has a small fitness centre, private car park and (rare) cooked breakfast option.

🍴 Eating

Il Giardino PUGLIAN €€
(☑0831 52 49 50; Via Tarantini 14-18; meals €30; ⊙12.30-2.30pm & 8-10.30pm Tue-Sat, 12.30-2.30pm Sun) Established more than 40 years ago in a restored 15th-century *palazzo*, sophisticated Il Giardino serves refined seafood and meat dishes in a delightful garden setting. You won't be disappointed with the pizza, but try something a little different, like the pasta with *bottarga* (dried mullet roe).

Brindisi

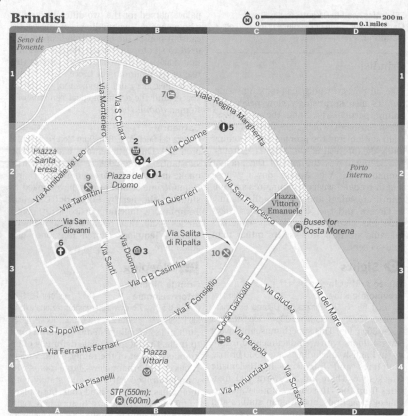

Trattoria Pantagruele   TRATTORIA €€
(📞 0831 56 06 05; Via Salita di Ripalta 1; meals €30; ⏰ 12.30-2.30pm Mon-Sat, 7.30-10.30pm Mon-Fri) Named after the Rabelaisian giant Pantagruel, this charming trattoria three blocks from the waterfront serves up excellent fish and grilled meats. Expect fresh anchovies in season, and lovely homemade pasta in all seasons.

ℹ Information

Antonio Perrino Hospital (📞 0831 53 71 11; Strada Statale 7 per Mesagne) Has an emergency room. Southwest of the centre; take the SS7 for Mesagne.

Post Office (📞 0831 22 55 95; Piazza Vittoria 10; ⏰ 8am-6.30pm Mon-Fri, to 1pm Sat)

Tourist Office (📞 0831 52 30 72; www.viag giareinpuglia.it; Viale Regina Margherita 44; ⏰ 10am-6pm Mon, 8am-8pm Tue-Sun) Has a wealth of information and brochures on the area. If you are interested in pedal power, pick up *Le Vie Verdi* map, which shows eight bicycling routes in the Brindisi area, ranging from 6km to 30km.

ℹ Getting There & Away

AIR

From **Salento Airport** (BDS; 📞 0831 411 74 06; www.aeroportidipuglia.it; Contrada Baroncino), Brindisi's small airport, there are domestic flights to Rome, Naples and Milan. Airlines include Alitalia and easyJet. There are also direct flights from London Stansted with Ryanair.

BOAT

Ferries, all of which take vehicles, leave Brindisi for Greece and Albania.

Ferry companies have offices at Costa Morena (the newer port), which is 4km from the train station. A free minibus connects the two.

Grimaldi Lines (📞 0831 54 81 16; www.grimal di-lines.com; Costa Morena Terminal) Frequent

Brindisi

year-round ferries to Igoumenitsa and Patras in Greece.

Red Star Ferries (☑ 0831 57 52 89; www. directferries.co.uk/red_star_ferries.htm; Costa Morena Terminal) To Vlorë in Albania, once a day.

BUS

Pugliairbus (www.aeroportidipuglia.it) has services to Bari airport and Lecce from Brindisi's airport.

Ferrovie del Sud-Est buses serving local towns leave from Via Bastioni Carlo V, in front of the train station.

Marozzi (☑ 0831 52 16 84; www.marozzivt.it) Runs to Rome's Stazione Tiburtina from Viale Arno.

STP Brindisi (www.stpbrindisi.it) Buses go regularly to Ostuni, Lecce and other towns throughout the Salento. Most leave from Via Bastioni Carlo V, in front of the train station.

TRAIN

Brindisi train station has regular services to the following destinations:

Bari from €8.40, 1¼ hours
Lecce from €2.80, 30 minutes
Milan from €99.50, 8½ to 11 hours
Rome from €70, eight to 12 hours
Taranto from €4.90, one hour

ⓘ Getting Around

Major and local car-rental firms are represented at the airport. To reach the airport by bus, take the STP-run **Cotrap** (☑ 800 232 042; www. stpbrindisi.it; single ticket €1) bus from Via Bastoni Carlo V.

A free minibus connects the train station and old ferry terminal with Costa Morena. It departs two hours before boat departures. You'll need a valid ferry ticket.

Galatina

POP 27,100

With a charming historic centre, Galatina, 18km south of Lecce, is at the core of the Salentine Peninsula's Greek past. It is almost the only place where the ritual *tarantismi* (Spider Music) is still practised. The tarantella folk dance evolved from this ritual, and each year on the feast day of St Peter and St Paul (29 June), it is performed at the (now deconsecrated) church.

⊙ Sights

**Basilica di Santa Caterina
d'Alessandria**   BASILICA
(Piazzetta Orsini; ⊙ 4-6.30pm daily & 8.30am-12.30pm Mon-Sat Apr-Sep, shorter hours rest of year) Most people come to Galatina to see the incredible 14th-century Basilica di Santa Caterina d'Alessandria. Its interior is a kaleidoscope of frescoes and is absolutely beautiful, with a pure-white altarpiece set against the frenzy of frescoes. It was built by the Franciscans, whose patron was Frenchwoman Marie d'Enghien de Brienne.

🛏 Sleeping

Samadhi   AGRITURISMO €€
(☑ 0836 60 02 84; www.agricolasamadhi.com; Via Stazione 116, Zollino; d €130; P ❋ 🛜 ☒) 🐾 Soothe the soul with a stay at Samadhi, located around 7km east of Galatina in tiny Zollino. It's on a 10-hectare organic farm and the owners are multilingual. As well as Ayurvedic treatments, shiatsu and yoga courses, there's a vegan restaurant offering organic meals. Check the website for upcoming retreats and courses.

ⓘ Getting There & Away

Ferrovie del Sud runs frequent trains between Lecce and Galatina (€2.10, 30 minutes), and Galatina and Zollino (€1, eight minutes).

Otranto

POP 5750

Bloodied and bruised by an infamous Turkish massacre in 1480, Otranto is best appreciated in its amazing cathedral, where the bones of 813 martyrs are displayed in a glass case behind the altar. Less macabre is the cathedral's other jaw-dropper, its medieval mosaic floor, which rivals the famous early

Christian mosaics of Ravenna in its richness and historical significance.

Lying deep in Italy's stiletto, Otranto has back-heeled quite a few invaders over the centuries and been brutally kicked by others – most notably the Turks. Sleuth around its compact old quarter and you can peel the past off in layers – Greek, Roman, Turkish and Napoleonic. These days the town is a generally peaceful place, unless you're fighting for beach space at the height of summer.

👁 Sights

★ Cathedral
CATHEDRAL

(☎ 0836 80 27 20; Piazza Basilica; ⏱ 7am-noon & 3-8pm, shorter hours in winter) Mosaics, skulls, crypts and biblical-meets-tropical imagery: Otranto's cathedral is like no other in Italy. It was built by the Normans in the 11th century, incorporating Romanesque, Byzantine and early Christian styles with their own, and has been given a few facelifts since. Covering the entire floor is its pièce de résistance, a vast 12th-century mosaic of a stupendous tree of life balanced on the back of two elephants.

Castello Aragonese Otranto
CASTLE

(☎ 0836 21 00 94; Piazza Castello; adult/reduced/under 17yr €5/2/free; ⏱ 10am-7pm summer, shorter hours rest of year) Built in the late 15th century, when Otranto was more populous and important than today, and not long after the calamitous Ottoman raid that resulted in the execution of hundreds for refusing Islam, the castle is a blunt and grim structure, well preserved internally and offering splendid views from the outer walls. It is famous,

---

SCENIC DRIVE: OTRANTO TO CASTRO

For a scenic road trip, the drive south from Otranto to Castro takes you along a wild and beautiful coastline. The coast here is rocky and dramatic, with cliffs falling down into the sparkling, azure sea; when the wind is up you can see why it is largely treeless. Many of the towns here started life as Greek settlements, although there are few monuments to be seen. Further south, the resort town of Santa Maria di Leuca is the tip of Italy's stiletto and the dividing line between the Adriatic and Ionian Seas.

---

among other things, from Horace Walpole's *The Castle of Otranto* (1764), recognised as the first Gothic novel. Last tickets are sold an hour before closing.

Chiesa di San Pietro
CHURCH

(Via San Pietro; ⏱ 10am-noon & 4-8pm Jun-Sep, by request rest of year) The origins of this cross-shaped Byzantine church are uncertain, but some think they may be as remote as the 5th century. The present structure seems to be a product of the 10th century, to which the oldest of the celebrated frescoes decorating its three apses dates.

🏃 Activities

There are some great beaches north of Otranto, especially **Baia dei Turchi**, with its translucent blue water. South of Otranto a spectacular rocky coastline makes for an impressive drive down to Castro. To see what goes on underwater, speak to **Scuba Diving Otranto** (☎ 0836 80 27 40; www.scubadiving.it; Via del Porto 1; 1-/2-tank dive incl equipment €48/75; ⏱ 7am-10pm).

🛏 Sleeping

Palazzo de Mori
B&B €€

(☎ 0836 80 10 88; www.palazzodemori.it; Bastione dei Pelasgi; s/d €105/140; ⏱ Apr-Oct; ❄ @) ⏺ In Otranto's historic centre, this charming B&B serves fabulous breakfasts on the sun terrace overlooking the port. The rooms are decorated in soothing white on white.

★ Palazzo Papaleo
HOTEL €€€

(☎ 0836 80 21 08; www.hotelpalazzopapaleo.com; Via Rondachi 1; r from €200; P ❄ @ 🛜) ⏺ Located next to the cathedral, this sumptuous hotel, the first to earn the EU Eco-label in Puglia, has magnificent rooms with original frescoes, exquisitely carved antique furniture and walls washed in soft greys, ochres and yellows. Soak in the panoramic views while enjoying the rooftop spa, or steam yourself pure in the hammam. The staff are exceptionally friendly.

🍴 Eating

La Bella Idrusa
PIZZA €

(☎ 0836 80 14 75; Lungomare degli Eroi 1; pizza €7; ⏱ 7pm-midnight) You can't miss this pizzeria right by the huge Porta Terra as you enter the historic centre. Despite the tourist-trap location, the food doesn't lack authenticity. Pizza's the main event, but there is support: seafood, grilled meat, vegetarian *contorni* (side dishes) and pasta are all there to lend a hand.

★ L'Altro Baffo
SEAFOOD €€

(☑0836 80 16 36; www.laltrobaffo.com; Via Cenobio Basiliano 23; meals €40; ☉12-2.30pm & 7.30pm-midnight Tue-Sun) This elegant modern restaurant near the castle stands out in Otranto's competitive dining scene. It stays in touch with basic Pugliese and Italian principles, but ratchets things up several notches: the 'carbonara' made with sea-urchin roe is a daring instant classic. The menu is mainly seafood, but there are a few vegetarian dishes that are anything but afterthoughts.

❶ Information

Tourist Office (☑0836 80 14 36; Via del Porto; ☉9am-1pm & 3-6pm) Down in the new port area.

❶ Getting There & Away

Otranto can be reached from Lecce by FSE train (€3.50, 1½ hours). It is on a small branch line, which necessitates changing in Maglie and sometimes Zollino too. Services are reduced on Sundays.

Castro
POP 2450

One of Salento's most striking coastal settlements, the walled commune of Castro has a pedigree that predates the Romans, who gave it the name *Castrum Minervae*, or 'Minerva's Castle'. The castle and walls that remain today date to the 16th-century rule of the Aragonese, who built atop foundations laid by the Angevins and Byzantines before them. The charming old town, which also boasts a 12th century cathedral, the re mains of a Byzantine church and a cliff-top piazza with delightful sea views, sits above a marina (which really comes alive in summer) and terraced olive groves leading to a limestone coast riddled with spectacular caves.

◉ Sights

Grotta Zinzulusa
CAVE

(☑0836 94 38 12; Via Zinzulusa; adult/reduced €6/3; ☉9.30am-7pm Jul & Aug, shorter hours rest of year; ℗) An aperture on the Ionian coast below Castro leads into the magnificent sta-lactite-festooned Cave of Zinzulusa, one of the most significant coastal limestone karst formations in Italy. The portion accessible to the public stretches hundreds of metres back from the cliff face, terminating in a chamber grand enough to justify the sobriquet 'Il Duomo'. Divided into three distinct geomorphological sections, Zinzulusa is home to endemic crustacea and other 'living fossils' known nowhere else on the planet.

Castello Aragonese
CASTLE

(☑0836 94 70 05; Via Sant Antonio 1; adult/reduced €2.50/2; ☉10am-1pm & 3-7.30pm) Primarily the work of the Aragonese who ruled southern Italy in the 16th century, this sturdy redoubt retains elements built by the Angevins in previous centuries, on earlier Byzantine foundations. Partly ruinous by the 18th century, it's been thoroughly restored, and now houses the small Antonio Lazzari Civic Museum, exhibiting Messapian, Greek and Roman archaeology uncovered in Castro and the surrounding area. Its prize piece is a torso of the goddess Minerva (Athena), buried at the ancient city gates.

❶ Getting There & Away

STP Lecce runs a daily bus between Castro and Lecce (€4, 90 minutes).

Gallipoli
POP 20 700

Like Taranto (p754), Gallipoli is a two-part town: the modern hub is based on the mainland, while the older *centro storico* inhabits a small island that juts out into the Ionian Sea. With a raft of serene baroque architecture usurped only by Lecce, it is, arguably, the prettiest of Salento's smaller settlements.

The old town, ringed by the remains of its muscular 14th-century walls, is the best place to linger. It's punctuated by several baroque chapels, a traditional fishing port, a windswept sea drive, and narrow lanes barely wide enough to accommodate a Fiat *cinquecento* (500).

◉ Sights

Gallipoli has some fine beaches, including the Baia Verde, just south of town. Nature enthusiasts will want to take a day trip to Parco Regionale Porto Selvaggio, about 20km north – a protected area of wild coastline with walking trails among the trees and diving off the rocky shore.

Cattedrale di Sant'Agata
CATHEDRAL

(www.cattedralegallipoli.it; Via Duomo 1; ☉hours vary) On the island, Gallipoli's 17th-century

PUGLIA, BASILICATA & CALABRIA SALENTO

cathedral is a baroque beauty that could compete with anything in Lecce. Not surprisingly, Giuseppe Zimbalo, who helped beautify Lecce's Santa Croce basilica, worked on the facade. Inside, it's lined with paintings by local artists.

Frantoio Ipogeo
HISTORIC SITE

(☑ 0833 26 42 42; Via Antonietta de Pace 87; €3; ⊙ 10am-mindnight Jul & Aug, shorter hours rest of year) This is only one of some 35 olive presses buried in the tufa rock below the town. It was here, between the 16th and early 19th centuries, that local workers pressed Gallipoli's olive oil, which was then stored in one of the 2000 cisterns carved beneath the old town.

🛏 Sleeping

Insula
B&B €€

(☑ 329 8070056, 0833 20 14 13; www.bbinsulagallipoli.it; Via Antonietta de Pace 56; s/d €80/150; ⊙ Apr-Oct; ❄ @) A magnificent 16th-century building houses this memorable B&B. The five rooms are all different but share the same princely atmosphere with exquisite antiques, vaulted high ceilings and cool pastel paintwork. Directly adjacent to the cathedral, it couldn't be any more central.

Hotel Palazzo del Corso
HOTEL €€€

(☑ 0833 26 40 40; www.hotelpalazzodelcorso.it; Corso Roma 145; r/ste €239/389; P❄@ 🛜🏊) It's worth forking out a bit extra for this beautiful new town hotel, if you fancy a bit of luxury. The rooms are furnished distinctively enough to avoid looking too corporate, there's a gym and a fantastic terrace (complete with a small swimming pool), and there's also a fine terrace restaurant, La DolceVita, serving lots of seafood (meals €40).

🍴 Eating

Gallipoli is famous for its red prawns and its soothing *spumone* layered ice cream.

Baguetteria de Pace
SANDWICHES €

(Via Sant'Angelo 8; baguettes from €5; ⊙ 11am-2.30pm & 7-11pm) The Italian art of making truly exceptional sandwiches is practised assiduously here. Choose the dense Italian bread (or a baguette if you're feeling fluffy) and have the friendly staff stuff it with topnotch smallgoods, cheeses, vegetables and whatever else takes your fancy. It also sells craft beer and Salento wines.

Caffè Duomo
CAFE €

(☑ 0833 26 44 02; Via Antonietta de Pace 72; desserts €9; ⊙ 7.30am-1am) For good Gallipoli *spumone* (layered ice cream with candied fruit and nuts) and refreshing *granite* (ices made with coffee, fresh fruit or locally grown pistachios and almonds), head to Caffè Duomo. The tables set up in the lee of the cathedral make a good place to people-watch as you refresh yourself.

⭐ La Puritate
SEAFOOD €€€

(☑ 0833 26 42 05; Via Sant'Elia 18; meals €50; ⊙ 12.30-3pm & 7.30-10.30pm, closed Wed winter) Book ahead to ensure your table at *the* place for fish in this seafood-loving town. Follow the practically obligatory seafood *antipasti* with delicious *primi* (first courses). Anything fishy is good (especially the prawns, swordfish and tuna) and the picture windows allow splendid views of the waters whence it came.

ℹ Information

Tourist Office (☑ 0833 26 25 29; Via Antonietta de Pace 86; ⊙ 8am-9pm summer, 8am-1pm & 4-9pm Mon-Sat winter) Near the cathedral in the old town.

ℹ Getting There & Away

FSE (www.fseonline.it) buses and trains head direct to Lecce.

Taranto

The once-mighty Greek-Spartan colony of Taras is, today, a city of two distinct parts – a mildewed *centro storico* on a small artificial island protecting a lagoon (the Mar Piccolo), and a swankier new city replete with wide avenues laid out in a formal grid. The contrast between the two is sudden and sharp: the diminutive old town with its muscular Aragonese castle harbours a downtrodden, almost derelict air, while the larger new city is busier, plusher and bustling with commerce.

Not generally considered to be on the tourist circuit, Taranto is rimmed by modern industry, including a massive steelworks, and is home to Italy's second biggest naval base after La Spezia. Thanks to an illustrious Greek and Roman history, it has been bequeathed with one of the finest Magna Graecia museums in Italy. For this reason alone, it's worth a stopover.

Taranto

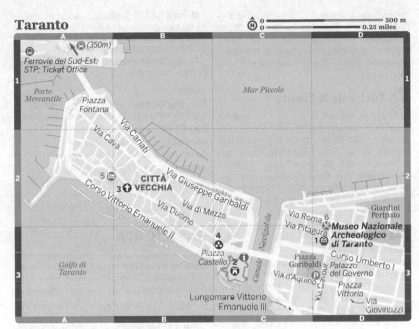

Sights

★ Museo Nazionale
Archeologico di Taranto   MUSEUM

(☎099 453 21 12; www.museotaranto.org; Via
Cavour 10; adult/reduced €5/2.50; ◷8.30am-
7.30pm) Sitting unassumingly in a side street
in Taranto's new town is one of Italy's most
important archaeological museums, chief-
ly dedicated to the archaeology of ancient
Taras (Taranto). It houses, among other
artefacts, the largest collection of Greek
terracotta figures in the world. Also on display are fine collections of 1st-century BC
glassware, classic black-and-red Attic vases
and stunning gold and jewellery from Magna Grecia (Italy's ancient Greek cities), such
as a 4th-century BC bronze and terracotta
crown.

Cathedral   CATHEDRAL

(Piazza Duomo; ◷4.30-7.30pm daily & 7.30am-
noon Sat & Sun) The 11th-century cathedral is
one of Puglia's oldest Romanesque buildings
and an extravagant treat. It's dedicated to
San Cataldo, an Irish monk who lived and
was buried here in the 7th century. Within,
the Capella di San Cataldo is a baroque
riot of frescoes and polychrome marble
inlay.

Taranto

◉ **Top Sights**
1 Museo Nazionale Archeologico
   di Taranto..D3

◉ **Sights**
2 Castello Aragonese.................................C3
3 Cathedral...B2
4 Temple of Poseidon...............................C3

🛏 **Sleeping**
5 Hotel Akropolis...A2

🍴 **Eating**
6 Trattoria al Gatto Rosso.......................D3

Castello Aragonese   CASTLE

(☎0997 75 34 38; www.castelloaragonesetaranto.
it; Piazza Castello; ◷9.30am-1.30am summer,
shorter hours rest of year) **FREE** Guarding the
swing bridge that joins the old and new
parts of town, this impressive 15th-century
structure, built on Norman and Byzantine
predecessors, was once a prison and is currently occupied by the Italian navy, which
has restored it. Multilingual and free guided
tours, mandatory to get inside, are led by naval officers throughout the day. Opposite are
the two remaining columns of the ancient
Temple of Poseidon (Piazza Castello).

Palazzo del Governo NOTABLE BUILDING
(Via Anfiteatro 4) The gigantic rust-red 1930s Palazzo del Governo, inaugurated by Mussolini, is a forbidding and masculine structure, expressive of the fascist ideas of strength then current.

Festivals & Events

Le Feste di Pasqua RELIGIOUS
Taranto is famous for its Holy Week celebrations – the biggest in the region – when bearers in Ku Klux Klan–style robes carry icons around the town. There are three processions: the Perdoni, celebrating pilgrims; the Addolorata (lasting 12 hours but covering only 4km); and the Misteri (even slower at 14 hours to cover 2km).

Sleeping & Eating

Hotel Akropolis HOTEL €€
(☎099 470 41 10; www.hotelakropolis.it; Vico Seminario 3; s/d €105/145; ❄@🛜) If Taranto's richly historic yet crumbling old town is ever to be reborn, it will be due to businesses such as this hotel – a converted medieval *palazzo* with a heavy Greek theme. It offers 13 stylish cream-and-white rooms, beautiful majolica-tiled floors, a panoramic rooftop terrace and an atmospheric bar and restaurant, decked out in stone, wood and glass.

Trattoria al Gatto Rosso TRATTORIA €€
(☎340 5337800, 099 452 98 75; www.ristorantegattorosso.com; Via Cavour 2; meals €35; ⏰noon-3pm & 7.30-11pm Tue-Sun) Unsurprisingly, seafood is the thing at the Red Cat. Relaxed and unpretentious, its heavy tablecloths, deep wine glasses and solid cutlery set the scene for full enjoyment of dishes such as spaghetti with local clams and slow-cooked swordfish with eggplant *caponata* (sweet-and-sour vegetable salad).

Information

Tourist Office (☎334 2844098; Castello Aragonese; ⏰9am-8pm summer, shorter hours rest of year)

Getting There & Away

BUS

Buses heading north and west depart from Porto Mercantile. **FSE** (☎080 546 21 11; www.fseonline.it) buses go to Bari; **STP** (☎080 975 26 19) buses go to Lecce, with a change at Monteparano.

Marozzi (☎080 5799 0211; www.marozzivt.it) has express services serving Rome's Stazione Tiburtina; **Autolinee Miccolis** (☎099 470 44 51; www.miccolis-spa.it) serves Naples.

The bus **ticket office** (⏰6am-1pm & 2-7pm) is at Porto Mercantile.

TRAIN

From **Bari Centrale** (Piazza Moro), Trenitalia and FSE trains go to the following destinations:

Bari €8.40, 1¼ hours, frequent

Brindisi €4.90, one hour, frequent

Rome from €50.50, six hours, five daily

AMAT (☎099 452 67 32; www.amat.taranto.it) buses run between the train station and the new city.

BASILICATA

Much of Basilicata is an otherworldly landscape of mountain ranges, trackless forests and villages that seem to sprout organically from the granite. Not easily penetrated, it is strategically located, and has been dominated by the Lucanians, Greeks, Romans, Germans, Lombards, Byzantines, Saracens, Normans and others. Being the plaything of such powers has not been conducive to a quiet or happy fate.

In the north the landscape is a fertile zone of gentle hills and deep valleys; the interior is dominated by the Lucanian Apennines and the Parco Nazionale del Pollino. The Tyrrhenian coast is a fissured wonderland of rocky coves and precariously sited villages. Here, Maratea is one of Italy's most charming seaside resorts.

But it is inland Matera, where primitive *sassi* (caves) lurk under grand cathedrals, that is Basilicata's most precious gem. The third-oldest continuously inhabited city in the world, it's intriguing, breathtaking and tragic in equal measures.

History

Basilicata spans Italy's 'instep', and is landlocked apart from slivers of Tyrrhenian and Ionian coastline. It was known to the Greeks and Romans as Lucania, after the Lucani tribe who lived here as far back as the 5th century BC. Their name survives in the 'Lucanian Dolomites', 'Lucanian cooking' and elsewhere. The Greeks also prospered in ancient Basilicata, possibly settling along the coastline at Metapontum and Erakleia as far back as the 8th century BC. Roman power came next, and the Punic Wars between that expanding power and Carthage. Hannibal, the ferocious Carthaginian general, rampaged through the region, making the city of Grumentum his base.

In the 10th century, the Byzantine Emperor Basil II (976–1025) bestowed his title, 'Basileus', on the region, overthrew the Saracens in southern Italy and reintroduced Christianity. The pattern of war and overthrow continued throughout the Middle Ages right up until the 19th century, as the Normans, Hohenstaufens, Angevins and Bourbons ceaselessly tussled over this strategic location. As talk of the Italian unification began to gain ground, Bourbon-sponsored loyalists took to Basilicata's mountains to oppose political change. Ultimately, they became the much-feared bandits of local lore who make scary appearances in writings from the late 19th and early 20th centuries. In the 1930s, Basilicata was used as a kind of open prison for political dissidents – most famously the painter, writer and doctor Carlo Levi – sent into exile to remote villages by the fascists.

The rugged region's hardscrabble history is perhaps best expressed in Levi's superb 1945 memoir, *Christ Stopped at Eboli* – a title suggesting Basilicata was beyond the hand of God, a place where pagan magic still existed and thrived.

Matera

POP 60,350

Matera, Basilicata's jewel, may be the third-longest continuously inhabited human settlement in the world. Natural caves in the tufa limestone, exposed as the Gravina cut its gorge, attracted the first inhabitants perhaps 7000 years ago. More elaborate structures were built atop them. Today, looking across the gorge to Matera's huddled *sassi* (cave dwellings) it seems you've been transported back to the ancient Holy Land. Indeed, the 'Città Sotterranea' (Underground City) has often been used for biblical scenes in films and TV.

Old Matera is split into two sections – the Sasso Barisano and the Sasso Caveoso – separated by a ridge upon which sits Matera's gracious *duomo* (cathedral). The *sassi*, many little more than one-room caves, once contained such appalling poverty and

PUGLIA, BASILICATA & CALABRIA MATERA

WORTH A TRIP

CRIPTA DEL PECCATO ORIGINALE

A fascinating Benedictine site dating to the Lombard period, the **Cripta del Peccato Originale** (Crypt of Original Sin; ☑320 3345323; www.zetema.org; Contrada Pietrapenta; adult/child 7-17yr/child under 7yr €10/8/free; ⊙10am-1pm & 4-7.30pm Tue-Sun Apr-Sep, shorter hours rest of year) houses well-preserved 8th-century frescoes – depicting vivid scenes from both Old and New Testaments – that have earned it a reputation as the 'Sistine Chapel' of Matera's cave churches. It's 7km south of Matera: group visits must be booked through the website, then joined at the ticket office (at Azienda Agricola Dragone on Contrada Pietrapenta) 30 minutes prior to the scheduled starting time.

---

unthinkable living conditions that in the 1950s Matera was denounced as the 'Shame of Italy', and the *sassi*-dwellers were moved on. Only in later decades has the value of this extraordinarily built environment been recognised.

◉ Sights

The two *sassi* districts – the more restored, northwest-facing **Sasso Barisano** and the more impoverished, northeast-facing **Sasso Caveoso** – are both extraordinary, riddled with serpentine alleyways and staircases, and dotted with frescoed *chiese rupestri* (cave churches) created between the 8th and 13th centuries. Modern Matera still contains some 3000 habitable caves.

The *sassi* are accessible from several points. There's an entrance off Piazza San Francisco, or take Via delle Beccherie to Piazza del Duomo and follow the tourist itinerary signs to enter either Barisano or Caveoso. Sasso Caveoso is also accessible from Via Ridola.

For a great photograph, head out of town for about 3km on the Taranto–Laterza road and follow signs for the *chiese rupestri*. This takes you up on the Murgia Plateau to the **belvedere** (Contrada Murgia Timone), from where you have fantastic views of the plunging ravine and Matera.

Matera

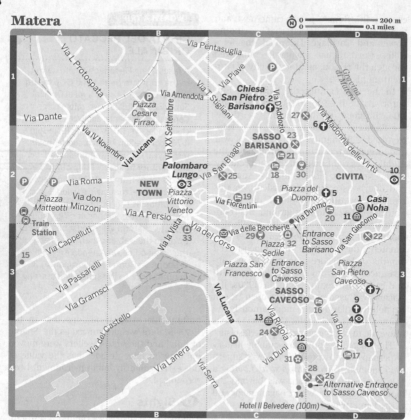

◉ Sasso Barisano

**Chiesa di Madonna delle Virtù &
Chiesa di San Nicola del Greci** CHURCH
(☑ 377 4448885; www.caveheritage.it; Via Madonna delle Virtù; ☺ 10am-8pm Jun-Sep, shorter hours rest of year) **FREE** This monastic complex, one of the most important monuments in Matera, comprises dozens of chambers carved into the tufa limestone over two floors. Chiesa di Madonna delle Virtù was built in the 10th or 11th century and restored in the 17th century. Above it, the simple Chiesa di San Nicola del Greci is rich in frescoes. The complex was used in 1213 by Benedictine monks of Palestinian origin.

★ Chiesa San Pietro Barisano CHURCH
(☑ 342 0319991; www.oltrelartematera.it; Piazza San Pietro Barisano; adult/reduced €3/2, incl Chiesa di Santa Lucia alle Malve & Chiesa di Santa Maria €6/4.50; ☺ 10am-7pm Apr-Oct, to 4pm

Nov-Mar) Dating in its earliest parts to the 12th-century Saint Peter's, the largest of Matera's rupestrian churches, overlays an ancient honeycomb of niches where corpses were placed for draining. At the entrance level can be found 15th- and 16th-century frescoes of the Annunciation and a variety of saints. The empty frame of the altarpiece graphically illustrates the town's troubled recent history: the church was plundered when Matera was partially abandoned in the 1960s and '70s.

◉ Sasso Caveoso

★ Casa Noha MUSEUM
(☑ 0835 33 54 52; www.visitfai.it/casanoha; Recinto Cavone 9; adult/reduced €5/3; ☺ 9am-7pm Apr-Oct, shorter hours rest of year) Highly recommended as a precursor to visiting the *sassi* themselves, this wonderful 25-minute multimedia exhibit, spread across three rooms of a 16th-century family home donated to the

Matera

Fondo Ambiente Italiano, relates the astonishing and often painful social history of the town and its *sassi*. Your appreciation of Matera's unique history and renaissance, and the tribulations of the *sassi* dwellers, will be transformed.

Chiesa di San Pietro Caveoso CHURCH
(☑0835 31 15 10; Piazza San Pietro Caveoso 1; ☺mass 7pm Mon-Sat, 11am & 7pm Sun) FREE The only church in the *sassi* not dug into the tufa rock, Chiesa di San Pietro Caveoso was originally built in 1300 and has a 17th-century Romanesque-baroque facade and frescoed timber ceiling.

Chiesa di Santa Maria di Idris CHURCH
(☑344 2763197; www.oltrelartematera.it; Piazza San Pietro Caveoso; adult/reduced €3/2, incl Chiesa San Pietro Barisano & Chiesa di Santa Lucia alle Malve €6/4.50; ☺10am-7pm Apr-Oct, to 4pm Nov-Mar) Dug into the Idris rock, this church has an unprepossessing facade, but the narrow corridor communicating with the recessed church of San Giovanni in Monterrone is richly decorated with 12th- to 17th-century frescoes.

Chiesa di Santa Lucia alle Malve CHURCH
(☑342 0919624; www.oltrelartematera.it; Rione Malve; adult/reduced €3/2, incl Chiesa San Pietro Barisano & Chiesa di Santa Maria €6/4.50; ☺10am-7pm Apr-Oct, to 4pm Nov-Mar) Dating to the 8th century, when it was built as the Benedictine Order's first foothold in Matera, this cliff-face church has a number of 13th-century frescoes, including an unusual breastfeeding Madonna. The church originally comprised three aisles, with two later adapted as dwellings.

Casa-Grotta di Vico Solitario HISTORIC SITE
(€3; ☺9.30am-late) For a glimpse of life in old Matera, visit this historic *sasso* off Via Bruno Buozzi. There's a bed in the middle, a loom, a room for manure and a section for a pig and a donkey. You also have access to a couple of neighbouring caves: in one, a black-and-white film depicts gritty pre-restoration Matera.

**Museo della Scultura
Contemporanea** MUSEUM
(MUSMA; ☑366 9357768; www.musma.it; Via San Giacomo; adult/reduced €5/3.50; ☺10am-2pm & 4-8pm Tue-Sun Apr-Sep, shorter hours rest of year) The setting of this fabulous museum of contemporary sculpture – deeply recessed caves and the frescoed rooms of the 16th-century Palazzo Pomarici – is as extraordinary as the exhibits. Italian sculpture from the

late 19th century to the present day is the principal focus, but you can also see beautiful examples of graphic art, jewellery and ceramics.

◉ New Town

The nucleus of the new town is **Piazza Vittorio Veneto**, an excellent, bustling meeting point for a *passeggiata* (sociable evening stroll). It's surrounded by elegant churches and richly adorned *palazzi* with their backs deliberately turned on the *sassi*: an attempt by the bourgeois to block out the shameful poverty the *sassi* once represented.

★ Palombaro Lungo   HISTORIC SITE
(🗷 339 3638332; Piazza Vittorio Veneto; guided tour €3; ⊙10am-1pm & 3-6pm) This giant cistern, arguably as magnificent as a subterranean cathedral, is one of Matera's great sights. Lying under the city's main square with arches carved out of the existing rock, it is mind-boggling in its scale and ingenuity, and was still supplying water to Materans within living memory. Book ahead for a 25-minute tour with the multilingual guides, who explain its conception and history (English-language tours generally leave at 10.30am, 12.30pm, 3.30pm and 5.30pm).

Museo Nazionale d'Arte Medievale e Moderna della Basilicata   MUSEUM
(🗷 0835 25 62 11; Piazzetta Pascoli 1, Palazzo Lanfranchi; adult/18-25yr/child €3/1.50/free; ⊙9am-8pm Thu-Tue) The Palazzo Lanfranchi, built as a seminary incorporating an earlier church in the 17th century, now houses this intriguing museum of sacred and contemporary art. The stars of the show here are Carlo Levi's paintings, including the panoramic mural *Lucania '61* depicting peasant life in biblical Technicolor. There are also some centuries-old sacred art from the *sassi*.

Cathedral   CATHEDRAL
(🗷 0835 33 29 08; www.matera-irsina.chiesacattolica.it; Piazza del Duomo; ⊙9am-1pm & 4-7pm) Set high up on a spur between the two natural bowls of the *sassi*, the wan, graceful exterior of the 13th-century Puglian-Romanesque cathedral makes the neobaroque excess within all the more of a surprise. Following 13 years of renovation, it's possible once again to admire the ornate capitals, sumptuous chapels, 17th-century frescoes, 13th-century Byzantine Madonna and two 12th-century frescoed crypts, uncovered in the works. Note the pediments mounted on the cathedral's altars, which come from Greek temples at Metaponto.

Museo Nazionale Ridola   MUSEUM
(🗷 0835 31 00 58; www.beniculturali.it; Via Ridola 24; adult/reduced €2.50/1.25; ⊙9am-8pm Tue-Sun, 2-8pm Mon) This impressive collection includes local Neolithic finds and some remarkable Greek pottery, such as the *Cratere Mascheroni*, a huge urn more than 1m high.

EXPLORING THE GRAVINA GORGE

In the picturesque landscape of the Murgia Plateau, the **Matera Gravina** cuts a rough gouge in the earth, a 200m-deep canyon pockmarked with abandoned caves and villages and roughly 150 mysterious *chiese rupestri* (cave churches). The area is protected as the **Parco della Murgia Materana**, an 80-sq-km wild park formed in 1990 and, since 2007, included in Matera's Unesco World Heritage site. You can hike from the *sassi* into the gorge; steps lead down from the parking place near the **Monasterio di Santa Lucia** (Via Madonna delle Virtù; ⊙7.30am-1pm & 5-8.30pm). At the bottom of the gorge you have to ford a river and then climb up to the belvedere (p757) on the other side; this takes roughly two hours.

Cave churches accessible from the belvedere include San Falcione, Sant'Agnese and Madonna delle Tre Porte. The belvedere is connected by road to the **Jazzo Gattini** (🗷 0835 33 22 62; www.ceamatera.it; Contrada Murgia Timone; ⊙9.30am-2.30pm & 4-6.30pm Apr-Oct, shorter hours rest of year) visitor centre, housed in an old sheepfold. Guided hikes can be organised here, as can walks to the nearby Neolithic village of **Murgia Timone**. For longer forays into the park, including a long day trek to the town of Montescaglioso, consider a guided hike with **Ferula Viaggi** (🗷 0835 33 65 72; www.ferulaviaggi.it; Via Cappelluti 34; ⊙9am-1.30pm & 3.30-7pm Mon-Sat).

Beware: paths and river crossings in the park can be treacherous during and after bad weather.

☞ Tours

There are plenty of official guides for the *sassi* – find one to suit you at www.sassiweb.it.

Altieri Viaggi   TOURS
(☑346 6453440, 0835 31 43 59; www.altieriviaggi.it; Via Ridola 61; ⊙9am-9pm) Runs tours around the *sassi* and rupestrian churches of Matera and the Parco della Murgia, starting from €15 for a 50-minute tour (minimum four people). Altieri also offers plenty of other trips, including hiking and *sassi* tours by *ape calessino* (auto rickshaw). Tours usually end with a tasting of typical local products.

✤ Festivals & Events

Sagra della Madonna
della Bruna   RELIGIOUS
(⊙2 Jul) This week-long celebration of Matera's patron saint has 14th-century roots. The culminating day, 2 July, begins at dawn with the colourful 'Procession of Shepherds', in which an image of the Virgin is carried through Matera's neighbourhoods. The finale is the *assalto al carro*, when the crowd descends on the ornately decorated main float and tears it to pieces.

Gezziamoci   MUSIC
(☑331 4711589; www.onyxjazzclub.it; ⊙summer) Run by the Onyx Jazz Club since 1987, the Jazz Festival of Basilicata brings music to diffuse venues around Matera: not only bars, but the cavernous, acoustically rich *sassi* and the surrounding Parco della Murgia Materana.

🛏 Sleeping

Matera's unique appeal has seen accommodation options mushroom, across the *sassi* and the new town. Take your pick: a smartly refurbished *sasso*, a room in a repurposed *palazzo*, or something more modern in the new town. Cheaper options can still be found.

La Dolce Vita B&B   B&B €
(☑328 7111121, 0835 31 03 24; www.ladolcevitamatera.it; Rione Malve 51; r €80; ☎) ✐ This delightful, ecofriendly B&B in Sasso Caveoso comprises two self-contained apartments with solar panels, rainwater recycling, a scenic terrace and cool, comfortable furnishings. Owners Vincenzo and Carla are passionate about Matera and are mines of information on the *sassi*.

Il Vicinato   B&B €
(☑380 1828935; www.ilvicinato.com; Piazzetta San Pietro Caveoso 7; s/d €60/90; ❉☎) Run by Luigi and Teresa, 'The Neighbourhood' is wonderfully located in Sasso Caveoso, in a building dating in parts to around 1600. Rooms are decorated in clean modern lines, with views across to the Murgia Plateau. As well as the standard rooms, there's a room with a balcony and a small apartment, each with an independent entrance.

Locanda di San Martino   HOTEL €€
(☑0835 25 66 00; www.locandadisanmartino.it; Via Fiorentini 71; d from €134; ❉☎❊) The main lure of this Sasso Caveoso hotel is its subterranean *termae romanae* (Roman baths). Cave accommodation, with niches and rustic brick floors, is set around a warren of cobbled paths and courtyards. Featuring a *tepidarium* (warm pool), *caldarium* (steam bath) and other basics of classical Roman baths, the spa is open only to adults, and costs €20.

★ Hotel Il Belvedere   HOTEL €€
(☑0835 31 17 02; www.hotelbelvedere.matera.it; Via Casalnuovo 133; d from €134; ☎) This cave boutique looks unremarkable from its street-side perch on the edge of the Sasso Caveoso, but you'll feel your jaw start to drop as you enter its luxurious entrails and spy the spectacle of Old Matera sprawling below a jutting terrace. Cavernous rooms sport mosaics, mood lighting and curtained four-poster beds. Two-night minimums apply in August.

Sassi Hotel   HOTEL €€
(☑0835 33 10 09; www.hotelsassi.it; Via San Giovanni Vecchio 89; d/ste from €119/165; ❉☎) Established in 1996 (making it the first hotel in the *sassi*), the Sassi Hotel is set in a rambling edifice dating in parts to the 16th century. Some of the 35 rooms are set into the rock, and some built above it. Singles are smallish but doubles are gracefully furnished and those with balconies have superb views of the cathedral.

L'Hotel in Pietra   BOUTIQUE HOTEL €€
(☑0835 34 40 40; www.hotelinpietra.it; Via San Giovanni Vecchio 22; s/d/ste from €70/115/230; ❉☎) The lobby of this hotel in Sasso Barisano makes sensitive use of a former 13th-century chapel complete with soaring arches, while the nine rock-cut rooms combine soft golden stone with the natural cave

THE RESURRECTION OF LA CITTÀ SOTTERRANEA

Named 2019 European City of Culture, Matera has taken huge strides in burying the unpleasant ghosts of its past. In the 1950s and '60s, the town and its ancient cave-houses were ingloriously considered to be the shame of Italy, a giant slum where malaria was rampant and a desperate populace subsisted on or below the breadline. After years of political squabbling, Matera's inhabitants were eventually evacuated (some forcibly) and resettled in a burgeoning new town higher up the gorge. Neglected and uncared for, the old town and its *sassi* (former cave dwellings) fell into a steep decline. By the 1980s old Matera was a virtual ghost town, an unholy mess of unlivable abodes.

Help came with a three-pronged attack of film-making, tourism and Unesco intervention. Italian director, Pier Paolo Pasolini was one of the first to put Matera on the map, making use of the town's biblical landscapes in his 1964 film, *The Gospel According to St Matthew*. The success of the film and its eerie backdrops inspired others, including Hollywood heavyweights such as Mel Gibson, who arrived in Matera in 2004 to film *The Passion of the Christ*.

Celluloid fame led to a trickle of curious tourists and this, in turn, fuelled an increasing desire among Italians to clean up the once-dilapidated *sassi* and showcase their historical value for future generations. In 1993, Unesco gave the town an extra boost when it named Matera's *sassi* and rupestrian churches a World Heritage Site. Progress has been rapid since. Bars and restaurants now inhabit once abandoned cave-houses and meticulous restoration work has saved ancient frescoes from almost certain decay.

Priming itself for 2019, Matera meticulously restored its 13th-century cathedral and opened the interactive museum, Casa Noha, which tells the story of Matera's recent past in blunt, uncensored detail. In 2015, the *sassi* provided a backdrop for the remaking of the movie *Ben Hur*, starring Morgan Freeman and Jack Huston.

interior. Furnishings are Zen-style with low beds, and the bathrooms are super stylish and include vast sunken tubs.

★ **Palazzo Gattini** HOTEL €€€
(✆0835 33 43 58; www.palazzogattini.it; Piazza del Duomo 13; d/ste from €300/480; P🛜❄) The Gattini is the Matera's plushest hotel, located in the former palatial home of the city's most noble family. And if the nobility of yesteryear could see the palace's 20 luxuriously refurbished rooms today, with their smooth stone walls, quality furnishings and intricate detailing, they'd surely still feel right at home. Prices drop during the week.

✖ Eating

I Vizi degli Angeli GELATO €
(✆0835 31 06 37; www.ivizidegliangeli.it; Via Ridola 36; medium cone €2.50; ⊙noon-11pm Thu-Tue) 'The Angels' Vices', an artisinal gelato 'laboratory' on the busy promenade of Via Domenico Ridola, is Matera's best. Alongside classics such as pistachio, you'll find experimental flavours such as grapefruit with pink pepper and thyme and mallow, which taste even better than they read.

★ **Soul Kitchen** ITALIAN €€
(✆0835 31 15 68; www.ristorantesoulkitchen.it; Via Casalnuovo 27; meals €35; ⊙12.15-2.45pm & 7.30-11pm Fri-Wed) If you thought Basilicata was somehow lagging behind the rest of Italy in the food stakes, correct your prejudice with pleasure at Soul Kitchen: this cavernous restaurant with sharp colour accents epitomises Matera's ambitious drive to reinvent its image. Grab a pew on the mezzanine and tuck into recognisably Basilicatan dishes that have been given modern twists, and presented with artistic aplomb.

Osteria al Casale OSTERIA €€
(✆329 8021190; www.osterialcasale.it; Via Casale 24; meals €30; ⊙1-3pm & 8-11pm Thu-Tue; ✐) While al Casale's *secondi* are uniformly meaty, this charming *osteria* does offer more vegetarian options than most. *Antipasti* such as *sformatino* (a 'mis-shapen' dumpling) of eggplant with tomato and basil and *primi* such as truffle ravioli with Parmesan and toasted pinenuts provide enough options to piece together an excellent non-carnivorous meal.

Dedalo
ITALIAN €€

(☑0835 197 30 60; www.dedalomatera.it; Via D'Addozio 136-140; meals €40; ☺12.30-2.30pm & 7.30-10.30pm Wed-Mon) Dedalo's motto *'sensi sommersi'* (submerged senses) will either hint at pretension, or indicate the lengths this classy fine diner goes to to wow its clientele. Surrounded by modern art in a softly lit and impeccably stylish cave, you can expect top-notch service and divine dishes such as eggplant agnolotti with tender *scottona* (yearling beef).

La Grotta nei Sassi
ITALIAN €€

(☑0835 33 48 91; www.ristorantesassidimatera. com; Via Rosario 73; meals €40; ☺12.30-3pm & 7.30-11.30pm Tue-Sun) This welcoming little cave restaurant is a great bet for Materan classics and spanking fresh seafood. Try the tuna tagliata, stuffed mussels or *orecchiette* with turnip-tops, but leave room for dessert. In good weather, choose the small terrace overlooking Sasso Barisano over the cosy twin-chambered interior.

L'Abbondanza Lucana
ITALIAN €€

(☑0835 33 45 74; Via Buozzi 11; meals €35; ☺noon-3pm Tue-Sun, 7-11pm Tue-Sat) The paradoxical bounty of Lucania's *cucina povera* is laid out before you in this stone cellar in Sasso Caveoso. For a fantastic introduction to a range of *prodotti tipici* (typical products) from the region, start with the Lucanian tasting plate, laden with delights such as wild boar, baked ricotta and a soup of chestnuts with Sarconi's famous beans.

Baccanti
ITALIAN €€€

(☑0835 33 37 04; www.baccantiristorante.com; Via Sant'Angelo 58-61; meals €50; ☺1-3.30pm & 8-11.30pm Tue Sat, 1-4pm Sun) Baccanti is as classy as a cave can be. The design is simple glamour against the low arches of the cavern; the dishes – perhaps ash-baked potato with stracciatella cheese and crumbled *taralli* (crackers) or ravioli with *pezzente* (pork sausage) and beans – make refined use of robust local ingredients; and the gorge views are sublime.

🍷 Drinking & Entertainment

Options for drinking and socialising have mushroomed, along with Matera's renaissance. You'll find wine bars, pubs and *enotecas* along Via Domenico Ridola, Via Fiorentina, Via San Biagio and Via delle Beccherie, and dotted throughout the *sassi*.

★ Vicolo Cieco
WINE BAR

(☑338 8550984; Via Fiorentini 74; ☺6pm-2am Tue-Thu, from noon Fri-Sun) Matera's renaissance and new-found relaxed vitality come to the fore at this wine-bar in a typical cave-house off Sasso Barisano's main drag. The eccentric decor signals its friendly, upbeat spirit – retro jukeboxes, a wall-mounted Scalextric track, chairs cut in half and glued to the wall in the name of art, and a chandelier of repurposed cutlery.

Birrificio 79
MICROBREWERY

(☑328 3587369; Via delle Beccherie 54; ☺noon-3pm & 7pm-1am) This diminutive microbrewery spills out onto the adjoining piazza, providing tables, occasional live music and permanent good cheer to help the Black Lake stout and Little John English ale down. Hearty plates (perhaps lasagna with artichokes, or roast-beef carpaccio) provide ballast for longer sessions.

Area 8
CINEMA, LIVE MUSIC

(☑333 3369788; http://area8.it; Via Casalnuovo 15; ☺7.30pm midnight Thu & Sun, to 3am Fri & Sat) This unusual cafe/bar and 'nano-theatre' is a production agency by day, but comes alive four nights a week to host film screenings, live music, product launches and other events beneath its beautiful creamy arches.

🛍 Shopping

Il Buongustaio
FOOD & DRINKS

(☑0835 33 19 82; www.ilbuongustaiomatera.it; Piazza Veneto 1; ☺8.30am-1.30pm Mon-Sat & 5-8.30pm Fri, Sat & Mon-Wed) With walls and deli cabinets bursting with preserves, pasta, cheeses, sweetmeats and smallgoods, this is the place to stock up on Matera's *prodotti tipici*.

Geppetto
ARTS & CRAFTS

(☑0835 33 18 57; Piazza Sedile 19; ☺9.30am-1pm & 3.30-8pm) This craft shop stands out among the tawdrier outlets selling tufa lamps and tiles. Its speciality is the *cuccù*, a brightly painted ceramic whistle in the shape of a cockerel, which was once prized by Matera's children. The whistles were traditionally considered a symbol of good luck and fertility.

ℹ Information

Basilicata Turistica (www.aptbasilicata.it) is the official tourist website with useful information on history, culture, attractions and sights. Sassiweb (www.sassiweb.it) is another informative website on Matera. Quite a few private operators also advertise themselves as tourist infomation offices. They're there to sell tours, generally, but can still give good (if not impartial) advice.

The maps *Carta Turistica di Matera* and *Matera: Percorsi Turistici* (€1.50), available from various travel agencies, bookstores and hotels around town, describe a number of itineraries through the *sassi* and the gorge.

Presidio Ospedaliero Madonna delle Grazie (☑ 0835 25 31 11; Contrada Cattedra Ambulante; ⏱ 24hr) About 1km southeast of the centre.

Parco Archeologico Storico Naturale delle Chiese Rupestri del Materano (☑ 0835 33 61 66; www.parcomurgia.it; Via Dolori 10; ⏱ 9.30am-6.30pm) Materan office of the Parco della Murgia Materana.

Police Station (☑ 0835 37 81 11; Via Gattini 12)

Post Office (☑ 0835 25 70 40; Via del Corso 15; ⏱ 8am-1.30pm Mon-Fri, to 12.30pm Sat; 🖥)

🛈 Getting There & Away

BUS

The bus station is north of Piazza Matteotti, next to the subterranean train station.

Grassani (☑ 0835 72 14 43; www.grassani.it) For Potenza

Marino (www.marinobus.it) For Naples

Marozzi (☑ 06 225 21 47; www.marozzivt.it) For Rome

Pugliairbus (☑ 080 579 02 11; www.aeroporti dipuglia.it) For Bari airport

SITA (☑ 0835 38 50 07; www.sitabus.it) For Taranto and Metaponto

TRAIN

Ferrovie Appulo-Lucane (FAL; ☑ 800 050500; http://ferrovieappulolucane.it) For Bari.

Metaponto

POP 1050

In stark contrast to the dramatic Tyrrhenian coast, Basilicata's Ionian coast is undistinguished and dotted with large tourist resorts. Metaponto, once a Greek Achaean colony known as Metapontum, is an exception. A sprawling archaeological site, all that remains of a prosperous city of tens of thousands, is twinned with a museum built expressly to house the archaeology the site keeps giving up. Together they bring alive the ancient civilisation of Magna Graecia in southern Italy.

Archaeologists studying the undisturbed ruins have managed to map the entire ancient urban plan. Settled by Greeks in the 8th and 7th centuries BC, Metaponto's most famous resident was Pythagoras (he of the theorem), who founded a school here after being ban-ished from Crotone (in Calabria) in the 6th century BC. After Pythagoras died, his house and school were incorporated into the Temple of Hera (known as the Tavole Palatine), whose elegantly ruined columns remain.

⊙ Sights

Museo Archeologico Nazionale   MUSEUM
(☑ 0835 74 53 27; Via Aristea 21; €2.50; ⏱ 9am-8pm Tue-Sun, 2-8pm Mon) This small but important museum is a real throwback to the days when precious artefacts of the past sat soberly behind glass, accompanied only by simple interpretative cards. Mirrors, ceramics, votive offerings and other relics of the area's Greek and Roman past are laid out for quiet contemplation. Signage is in Italian.

Parco Archeologico   ARCHAEOLOGICAL SITE
(☑ 0835 74 53 27; ⏱ 9am-1hr before sunset) FREE Not to be confused with the Tavole Palatine, the Parco Archeologico is a larger, if less immediately impressive collection of Metaponto ruins that contains the remains of a Greek theatre and the Doric Tempio di Apollo Licio. The classical coastal Greek colony that once flourished here can be readily imagined, walking through the quiet fields and shin-high remains. It's especially interesting to see where the artefacts displayed in the Museo Archeologico Nazionale, 2km northwest, came from.

Tavole Palatine   ARCHAEOLOGICAL SITE
(Palatine Tables; Strada Statale 106 Jonica; ⏱ 9am-1hr before sunset) FREE The remains of the 6th-century Temple of Hera – 15 columns and sections of pavement – are Metaponto's most impressive sight. They're known as the Tavole Palatine (Palatine Tables), since knights, or paladins, are said to have gathered here before heading to the Crusades. The ruins are 3km north of town, just off the highway – to find them, follow the slip road for Taranto onto the SS106.

🛏 Sleeping

Palazzo Margherita   HOTEL €€€
(☑ 0835 54 90 60; www.coppolaresorts.com/palaz zomargherita; Corso Umberto I 64; d/ste from €520/1000; 🖥) Located near the birthplace of director Francis Ford Coppola's grandfather, this 19th-century *palazzo* has been thoughtfully resurrected as a boutique hotel, complete with colourful frescoes and tiles. There are a number of bars scattered about the property and guests can learn from the chefs as they prepare lip-smacking Basilicatan fare.

Potenza

POP 67,200

Basilicata's regional capital, Potenza, has been ravaged by earthquakes (the last in 1980) and, as the highest town in the region, broils in summer and shivers in winter. You may find yourself passing through as it's a major transport hub.

Potenza's few sights are in the old centre, at the top of the hill. To get there, take the elevators from Piazza Vittorio Emanuele II. The ecclesiastical highlight is the cathedral, erected in the 12th century and rebuilt in the 18th. The elegant Via Pretoria, flanked by a boutique or two, makes a pleasant traffic-free stroll, especially during the *passeggiata*.

The town centre straddles a high ridge, east to west. To the south lie the Trenitalia and Ferrovie Appulo-Lucane train stations, connected to the centre by buses 1 and 10.

⊙ Sights

Cathedral CATHEDRAL
(☑ 0971 2 74 88; Via Scafarelli 6; ☺ 7.30am–1pm & 5–8pm) Potenza's Cattedrale di San Gerardo is the town's ecclesiastical highlight. Originally erected in the 12th century but rebuilt in the 18th (since then it has survived bombs and earthquakes) it houses the remains of Saint Gerard, Potenza's patron saint.

⊨ Sleeping

B&B Al Convento B&B €
(☑ 348 3307693; http://alconventopotenza.it; Vicolo San Michele Arcangelo; s/d €55/80; ⊞ ⊕) In central Potenza, Al Convento is a great accommodation choice. It's in an early 19th century building (funnily enough, once a convent), housing a mix of polished antiques and design classics.

❶ Getting There & Away

Grassani (☑ 0835 72 14 43; www.grassani.it) has buses to Matera (€8, 1¾ hours, five daily). Buses leave from Via Appia 185 and also stop near the Scalo Inferiore Trenitalia train station. **Liscio** (☑ 0971 5 46 73; www.autolineeliscio. it) buses serve various cities including Rome (€25, 4½ hours).

There are regular train services from Potenza to Foggia (€6, 2¼ hours), Salerno (from €6, 1¾ hours) and Taranto (€8.20, 2¼ hours). For Bari (from €15, four hours, four daily), take the **Ferrovie Appulo-Lucane** (☑ 800 050500; http://ferrovieappulolucane.it) train at Potenza Superiore station.

Appennino Lucano

The Appennino Lucano (Lucanian Apennines) bite Basilicata in half like a row of jagged teeth. Sharply rearing up south of Potenza, they protect the lush Tyrrhenian coast and leave the Ionian shores gasping in the semi-arid heat. Much of the area is protected by the **Parco Nazionale Dell'Appennino Lucano**, inaugurated in 2007 and the second-youngest of Italy's 25 national parks .

Aside from its gorgeous mountain terrain, the park's most iconic site is the abandoned Roman town of Grumentum (p766), 75km south of Potenza and just outside the town of Grumento Nova. In the granite eyries of Pietrapertosa and Castelmezzano, it can also lay claim to two of Italy's most strikingly situated hill towns.

Castelmezzano & Pietrapertosa

The two mountaintop villages of Castelmezzano (elevation 985m) and Pietrapertosa (elevation 1088m), ringed by the Lucanian Dolomites, are spectacular. Basilicata's highest villages, they're often swathed in cloud, making you wonder why anyone would build here – in territory best suited to goats.

Castelmezzano is surely one of Italy's most theatrical villages: the houses huddle along an impossibly narrow ledge that falls away in gorges to the Rio di Caperrino. Pietrapertosa is possibly even more amazing: the Saracen fortress at its pinnacle is difficult to spot as it is carved out of the mountain. Despite difficulties of access, the towns can be swarmed by Italian tourists on weekends and holidays. Foreign visitors are scarcer.

You can 'fly' between these two dramatic settlements courtesy of Il Volo dell'Angelo, two heart-in-mouth ziplines across the void.

⚹ Activities

★ Il Volo dell'Angelo ADVENTURE SPORTS
(Angel's Flight; ☑ Castelmezzano 0971 98 60 20, Pietrapertosa 0971 98 31 10; www.volodellangelo. com; singles €35-40, couples €63-72; ☺ 9.30am–6.30pm May-Oct) The extraordinary situation of Pietrapertosa and Castelmezzano, two steepling Basilicatan hill towns, is the inspiration behind 'Angel's Flight', two ziplines running over 1400m between the peaks, dropping over 100m and reaching speeds of up to 120kmh. Tandem flights are possible, providing the couple's combined weight

WORTH A TRIP

GRUMENTUM

The **Parco Archeologico di Grumentum** (☑0975 6 50 74; Contrada Spineta, Grumento Nova; incl museum €2.50; ☉9am-1hr before sunset; P) – sometimes known as Basilicata's 'Little Pompeii' – contains remains of a theatre, an amphitheatre, Roman baths, a forum, two temples and a *domus* (villa) with mosaic floors. Knowing something of its history ratchets up the interest: among its illustrious inhabitants numbers Hannibal, who made it his headquarters in the 3rd century BC. Its swansong came when the Saracen invasions of the 10th century forced its abandonment in favour of Grumento Nova, on a nearby hill.

Many of the artefacts found here are on display at the nearby **Museo Nazionale dell'Alta Val d'Agri** (www.beniculturali.it; incl archaeological site €2.50; ☉9am-8pm Tue-Sun, 2-8pm Mon; P).

doesn't exceed 150kg. It's only open daily in August; check the website for details.

🛏 Sleeping & Eating

La Casa di Penelope e Cirene B&B €
(☑338 3132196; Via Garibaldi 32, Pietrapertosa; d €90) This delightful B&B, the 'House of Penelope and Cirene', offers just two handsomely furnished rooms in the heart of Pietrapertosa. There's a sitting room, kitchenette, and great views over the Lucanian Dolomites.

Al Becco della Civetta RISTORANTE €€
(☑0971 98 62 49; Vico I Maglietta 7, Castelmezzano; meals €35; ☉1-3pm & 8-10pm) Don't miss the authentic Lucano restaurant Al Becco della Civetta in Castelmezzano, which serves excellent regional cuisine based on seasonal local ingredients. It also offers 22 traditionally furnished, simple whitewashed rooms (doubles €90), some with lots of dark wood, others with vivid murals, and many with fabulous views. Booking recommended.

ℹ Getting There & Away

SITA SUD (☑0971 50 68 11; www.sita sudtrasporti.it) bus 102 runs twice a day between Potenza and Castelmezzano (€5, 80 minutes) but you'll probably want your own wheels to explore properly.

Venosa

POP 11,850

About 70km north of Potenza, unassuming Venosa was once the thriving Roman colony of Venusia, which owed much of its prosperity to its position on the Appian Way. It was also the birthplace of the poet Horace (65 BC). The main reason to come here is to see the remains of Basilicata's largest monastic complex.

Venosa's main square, **Piazza Umberto I**, is dominated by a 15th-century Aragonese castle; within is the small **Museo Archeologico** (☑0972 3 60 95; Piazza Umberto I 49; adult/reduced €2.50/1.25; ☉9am-8pm Wed-Mon, from 2pm Tue), while to the northeast of the centre lie Venosa's two other principal attractions, the ruins of the **Roman settlement** (☉9am-1hr before dusk Wed-Mon, from 2pm Tue) and the graceful later ruins of **Abbazia della Santissima Trinità** (☑0972 3 42 11).

🛏 Sleeping

Hotel Orazio HOTEL €
(☑0972 3 11 35; www.hotelorazio.it; Vittorio Emanuele II 142; s/d/tr €45/65/85) Named for Venosa's most famous son, the Roman poet Horace, this hotel occupies a 17th-century palace complete with antique majolica tiles, frescoes, marble floors and a terrace with beautiful views. The Lacolla family and their staff do all they can to make your stay comfortable.

ℹ Getting There & Away

Venosa can be reached by taking highway S658 north from Potenza and exiting at Barile onto the S93. Buses run Monday to Saturday from Potenza (€3.30, two hours, two daily).

Basilicata's Western Coast

Resembling a mini Amalfi, Basilicata's Tyrrhenian coast is short but sweet. Squeezed between Calabria and Campania's Cilento peninsula, it shares the same beguiling characteristics: hidden coves and pewter sandy beaches backed by majestic coastal cliffs. The SS18 threads a spectacular route along the mountains to the coast's star attraction: the charming seaside settlements of Maratea.

Maratea

POP 5150

A sparkling, sun-drenched contrast to Basilicata's rugged interior, Maratea is a pure delight. In fact a disparate collection of placid coastal villages, rather than a single place, it's the centrepiece of Basilicata's Tyrrhenian coast. Embellished with lush vegetation, riven by rock-walled coves below well-tended hillside villages, Maratea's joys might be compared to those of the Amalfi. Perhaps the biggest, most welcome disparity is the number of tourists – far fewer here, and notably fewer non-Italians. You can climb the steep hill above Maratea to see the ruins of the prior settlement, take boat cruises and fishing trips, poke around venerable hilltop churches (44 of them), or just kick back with a coffee in a perfectly photogenic piazza, watching the sun play on the waters below.

◉ Sights & Activities

The deep green hillsides that encircle this tumbling conurbation offer excellent walking trails, providing a number of easy day trips to the surrounding hamlets of Acquafredda and Fiumicello, with its small sandy beach. The tourist office (p769) in Maratea Borgo's main square can provide an excellent map.

Maratea Superiore   RUINS
FREE The ruins of the original settlement of Maratea, supposedly founded by the Greeks, are situated at a higher elevation than the current village on a rocky escarpment just below the Christ the Redeemer statue. Abandoned houses with trees growing in their midst, some thought to be over 1000 years old, have long been given over to nature.

Statue of Christ the Redeemer   STATUE
The symbol of Maratea, visible from multiple vantage points along the coast, this 22m-high statue of Christ faces inland towards the Basilica di San Biagio. Slightly smaller than Rio's Christ the Redeemer, it's made of concrete faced with Carrara marble and sits atop 644m-high Monte San Biagio. A dramatic winding asphalt road leads to the top, although it's more fun to walk the steep path (number 1) that starts off Via Cappuccini in Maratea Borgo.

Marvin Escursioni   BOATING
(📋 338 8777899; Porto di Maratea; half-day boat trips €25; ⊙9am-1pm & 2.30-6pm) This operator based in the Porto di Maratea offers half-day boat tours that include visits to surrounding grottoes and coves.

🛏 Sleeping

★ Locanda delle Donne Monache   HOTEL €€
(📋0973 87 61 39; www.locandamonache.com; Via Mazzei 4, Maratea Borgo; d/ste €175/335; ⊙Apr-Oct; P✱@🅿🛜) Overlooking the medieval *borgo*, this exclusive hotel is in a converted 18th-century convent with a suitably lofty setting. It's a hotch-potch of vaulted corridors, terraces and gardens fringed with bougainvillea and lemon trees. The rooms are elegantly decorated in pastel shades and there's a fitness centre, Jacuzzi and a stunning panoramic outdoor pool.

Hotel Villa Cheta Elite   HOTEL €€€
(📋0973 87 81 34; www.villacheta.it; Via Canonica 48, Acquafredda; r from €224; ⊙Apr-Oct; P✱🛜🅿) Set in an art nouveau villa in Acquafredda, this hotel is like a piece of plush Portofino towed several hundred kilometres south. Enjoy a broad terrace with spectacular views of the Gulf of Policastro, a fabulous restaurant (1pm to 2pm and 8pm to 9.30pm), a pool and large rooms where antiques mix seamlessly with modern

---

ⓘ ORIENTATION
....

What is usually referred to as Maratea is actually a collection of small settlements split into several parts, some of them walkable if you're relatively fit and the weather cooperates. Maratea's main train station sits roughly in the middle.

The **Porto** is clustered around a small harbour and is about a 10-minute walk below the station (towards the sea). The 'village' of **Fiumicello** is in the same direction, but reached by turning right rather than left once you've passed under the railway bridge. The main historic centre, known as **Maratea Borgo**, is perched in the hills behind. A bus leaves every 30 minutes or so from the station, or you can walk up a series of steps and paths (approximately 5km; the town is always visible). It has plenty of cafes and places to eat. The **Marina di Maratea** is located 5km south along the coast and has its own separate train station. The village of **Acquafredda** is 8km in the other direction, kissing the border of Campania.

amenities. Bright Mediterranean foliage fills sun-dappled terraced gardens.

 Eating

Il Sacello MODERN ITALIAN **€€**
(☑ 0973 87 61 39; www.locandamonache.com; Via Mazzei 4, Maratea Borgo; meals €35; ☺ 12.30-2.30pm & 7.30-10pm; ☎) The in-house *risto-* *rante* of the Locanda delle Donne Monache hotel, Il Sacello serves wonderful Lucanian fare and seafood, overlooking the red rooftops of Maratea Borgo. Try the pasta with local sausage, the beef tartare or delicately wrought desserts such as the buffalo-ricotta souffle. Il Sacello sometimes closes on Monday or Tuesday night in June.

PARCO NAZIONALE DEL POLLINO

The **Pollino National Park** (www.parcopollino.it), Italy's largest, straddles Basilicata and Calabria and covers 1960 sq km. It acts like a rocky curtain separating the region from the rest of Italy and has the richest repository of flora and fauna in the south.

The park's most spectacular areas are **Monte Pollino** (2248m), **Monti di Orsomarso** (1987m) and the canyon of the Gole del Raganello. The mountains, often snowbound, are blanketed by forests of oak, alder, maple, beech, pine and fir. The park is most famous for its ancient *pino loricato* trees, which can only be found here and in the Balkans. The oldest specimens reach 40m in height.

Your own vehicle is needed to explore within Pollino. To get there, however, there's a daily **SLA Bus** (☑ 0973 2 10 16; www.slasrl.it) between Naples and Rotonda, while **SAM Autolinee** (☑ 0973 66 38 35; www.samautolinee.com) buses operate around some of Pollino's Basilicatan villages.

Basilicata

In Basilicata the park's main centre is **Rotonda** (elevation 626m), which houses the official park office, **Ente Parco Nazionale del Pollino** (☑ 0973 66 93 11; Via delle Frecce Tricolori, Rotonda, Complesso Monumentale Santa Maria della Consolazione; ☺ 9am-1pm & 2-4pm Mon-Fri). Interesting villages to explore include the unique Albanian villages of **San Paolo Albanese** and **San Costantino Albanese**. These isolated and unspoilt communities fiercely maintain their mountain culture and the Greek liturgy is retained in the main churches. For local handicrafts, visit the town of **Terranova di Pollino** for wooden crafts, **Latronico** for alabaster, and **Sant'Arcangelo** for wrought iron.

The chalet-style **Picchio Nero** (☑ 0973 9 31 70; www.hotelpicchionero.com; Via Mulino 1, Terranova di Pollino; s/d €65/78; ℗) in Terranova di Pollino, with its Austrian-style wooden balconies and recommended restaurant, is a popular hotel for hikers.

Two highly recommended restaurants include **Luna Rossa** (☑ 0973 9 32 54; www.fed ericovalicenti.it; Via Marconi 18, Terranova di Pollino; meals €35; ☺ noon-3pm & 7-10pm Thu-Tue) in Terranova di Pollino and **Da Peppe** (☑ 0973 66 12 51; Corso Garibaldi 13, Rotonda; meals €30; ☺ noon-3pm & 7.30-11pm Tue-Sun) in Rotonda.

Calabria

Civita was founded by Albanian refugees in 1746. Other towns worth visiting are **Castrovillari**, with its well-preserved 15th-century Aragonese castle, and **Morano Calabro** (look up the beautiful MC Escher woodcut of this town). Naturalists should also check out the wildlife museum **Centro Il Nibbio** (☑ 0981 3 07 45; www.ilnibbio.it; Vico Il Annunziata 11, Morano Calabro; €4; ☺ 9am-6pm Jul & Aug, shorter hours rest of year) in Morano, which explains the Pollino ecosystem.

White-water rafting down the spectacular Lao river is popular in the Calabrian Pollino. **Centro Lao Action Raft** (☑ 0985 9 10 33; www.laoraft.it; Via Lauro 10/12, Scalea) in Scalea can arrange rafting trips as well as canyoning, trekking and mountain-biking. **Ferula Viaggi** (p760) in Matera runs mountain-bike excursions and treks into the Pollino.

The park has a number of *agriturismi*. Tranquil **Agriturismo Colloreto** (☑ 347 3236914, 0981 3 12 55; www.colloreto.it; Contrada Colloreto, Morano Calabro; half pension per person €56) near Morano Calabro, and **Locanda di Alia** (☑ 0981 4 63 70, 339 8346881; www.alia.it; Via Ietticelle 55, Castrovillari; s/d from €76/86; ℗ ❄ ☎ ▣) in Castrovillari are noteworthy.

Lanterna Rossa
SEAFOOD €€

(☑ 0973 87 63 52; Via Arenile, Maratea Porto; meals €40; ⏱ 11am-3pm & 7-11.30pm) This terrace restaurant, sitting above the Bar del Porto overlooking the marina, has been knocking out delightful Lucanian seafood for over 20 years. Sit either in the tastefully art-strewn interior or on the terrace to enjoy dishes such as *zuppa di pesce* (fish soup) and octopus with wild beans and fennel. Bookings are advised, especially in July and August.

ℹ Information

Maratea Porto Tourist Office (☑ 371 1446350, 0973 87 71 15; Via Arenile 35, Maratea Porto; ⏱ 8am-1pm & 3-7pm Jun-Oct, shorter hours rest of year)

Tourist Office (☑ 0973 03 03 66; Piazza Vitolo 1, Maratea Borgo; ⏱ 10am-1pm & 5-10pm Mon-Fri, daily Jul & Aug)

ℹ Getting There & Around

Maratea is easily accessed via the coastal train line. InterCity and regional trains on the Rome–Reggio line stop at Maratea train station. Some slower trains stop at Marina di Maratea.

Local buses (€1.10) connect the coastal towns and Maratea train station with Maratea Borgo, running more frequently in summer. Some hotels offer pick-ups from the station.

CALABRIA

If a Vespa-riding, siesta-loving, unapologetically chaotic Italy still exists, it's in Calabria. Rocked by recurrent earthquakes and lacking a Matera or Lecce to give it high-flying tourist status, this is a corner of Italy less globalised and homogenised. Its wild mountain interior and long history of poverty, Mafia activity and emigration have all contributed to its distinct culture. Calabria is unlikely to be the first place in Italy you'd visit. But if you're intent on seeing a candid and uncensored version of *la dolce vita* that hasn't been dressed up for tourist consumption, look no further, *ragazzi* (guys).

Calabria's gritty cities are of patchy interest. More alluring is its attractive Tyrrhenian coastline, broken by several particularly lovely towns (Tropea and Scilla stand out). The mountainous centre is dominated by three national parks, none of them particularly well-explored. Its museums, collecting the vestiges of rich classical past are probably its greatest treasure.

History

Traces of Neanderthal, Palaeolithic and Neolithic life have been found in Calabria, but the region only became internationally important with the arrival of the Greeks in the 8th century BC. They founded a colony at what is now Reggio di Calabria. Remnants of this colonisation, which spread along the Ionian coast with Sibari and Crotone as the star settlements, are still visible. However, the fun didn't last forever, and in 202 BC the cities of Magna Graecia all came under the control of Rome, the rising power in Italy. The Romans did irreparable environmental damage, destroying the countryside's handsome forests. Navigable rivers became fearsome *fiumare* (torrents) dwindling to wide, dry, drought-stricken riverbeds in high summer.

Post-Rome, Calabria's fortified hilltop communities weathered successive invasions by the Normans, Swabians, Aragonese and Bourbons, and remained largely undeveloped. Although the late 18th-century Napoleonic incursion and the later arrival of Garibaldi and Italian unification inspired hope for change, Calabria remained a disappointed, feudal region and, like the rest of the south, was racked by malaria.

A by-product of this tragic history was the growth of banditry and organised crime. Calabria's Mafia, known as the 'ndrangheta (from the Greek for heroism/virtue), inspires fear in the local community, but tourists are rarely the target of its aggression. For many, the only answer has been to get out and, for at least a century, Calabria has seen its young people emigrate in search of work.

Northern Tyrrhenian Coast

The good, the bad and the ugly all jostle check-by-jowl along Calabria's northern Tyrrhenian coast. The *Autostrada del Mediterraneo* (A2), one of Italy's great coastal drives, ties them all together. It twists and turns through mountains, past huge swathes of dark-green forest and flashes of cerulean-blue sea. But the Italian penchant for cheap summer resorts has taken its toll here and certain stretches, particularly in the south, are blighted by shoddy hotels and soulless stacks of flats.

A 30km stretch of wide, pebbly beach runs south from the border with Basilicata, from the popular and not-too-garish resort town of Praia a Mare to Diamante, a fashionable seaside town famed for its chillis and bright murals painted by local and foreign artists. Inland are the precariously perched, otherworldly villages of Aieta and Tortora, reached by a tortuously twisted but rewarding mountain drive. Further south, Paola is worth a stop to see its holy shrine.

◉ Sights

Santuario di San Francesco di Paola CAVE (☑ 0984 47 60 32; www.santuariopaola.it; Via San Francesco di Paola, Paola; ☺ 6am-1pm & 2-6pm Oct-Mar, 6am-1pm & 2-8pm Apr-Sep) FREE Watched over by a crumbling castle, the Santuario di San Francesco di Paola is a curious, empty cave with tremendous significance to the devout. The saint lived and died in Paola in the 15th century and the sanctuary that he and his followers carved out of the bare rock has attracted pilgrims for centuries. The cloister is surrounded by naive wall paintings depicting the saint's truly incredible miracles. The original church contains an ornate reliquary of the saint.

Isola di Dino ISLAND
Visible from the Praia a Mare seafront is an intriguing rocky chunk off the coast, the Isola di Dino. The **tourist office** (Tyrrhenian Tourist Consortium; ☑ 0985 77 76 37; Via Amerigo Vespucci 4, Praia a Mare; ☺ 9am-noon Mon-Fri) has information on the island's sea caves; alternatively, expect to pay around €10 for a guided tour from the old boys who operate from the beach.

❶ Getting There & Away

Paola is the main train hub for Cosenza, about 25km inland. From Praia a Mare, **Autolinee Preite** (☑ 0984 41 30 01; www.autoservizipreite.it) buses go to Cosenza via Diamante and to Aieta and Tortora, (6km and 12km from Praia respectively). **SITA** (☑ 0971 50 68 11; www.sitabus.it) buses run to Maratea and regular trains also pass through for Paola and Reggio di Calabria.

Cosenza

POP 67,600
Cosenza epitomises the unkempt charm of southern Italy. It is a no-nonsense workaday town where tourists are incidental and local life, with all its petty dramas, takes centre stage. The modern city centre is a typically chaotic Italian metro area that serves as a transport hub for Calabria and a gateway to

the nearby mountains of Sila National Park. The old town, stacked atop a steep hill, has a totally different atmosphere. Time-warped and romantically dishevelled, its dark weathered alleys are full of drying clothes on rusty balconies, old curiosity shops and the freshly planted shoots of an arty renaissance.

◉ Sights

In the new town, pedestrianised Corso Mazzini serves as an **open-air museum** with numerous sculptures lining the corso, including Saint George and the Dragon by Salvador Dalí.

In the old town, head up the winding, charmingly dilapidated Corso Telesio, which has a raw Neapolitan feel to it and is lined with ancient tenements and antiquated shopfronts. At the top is Cosenza's 12th-century **cathedral** (☑ 0984 7 78 64; www.cattedraledicosenza.it; Piazza del Duomo 1; ☺ 8am-noon & 3-7.30pm), rebuilt in restrained Baroque style in the 18th century after devastating earthquakes.

Head further along the corso to Piazza XV Marzo, an appealing square fronted by the Palazzo del Governo and the handsome neoclassical **Teatro Rendano** (☑ 0984 81 32 27; Piazza XV Marzo; adult/reduced €3/2), a leading Calabrian venue for opera and classical music.

From Piazza XV Marzo, follow Via Paradiso, then Via Antonio Siniscalchi for the route to the restored Norman **castle** (☑ 0984 181 12 34; www.castellocosenza.it; Piazza Frederico II; adult/reduced €4/2; ☺ 9.30am-6pm Tue-Sat, from 10am Sun).

Cosenza's culture is low-key, but you can see a noteworthy collection of southern-Italian paintings at the **Galeria Nazionale** (☑ 0984 79 56 39; Via Gravina; ☺ 10am-6pm Tue-Sun) FREE, or spend an hour in the **Museo dei Brettii e degli Enotri** (☑ 0984 2 33 03; www.museodeibrettiiedeglienotri.it; Salita Agostino 3; adult/reduced €4/3; ☺ 9am-1pm & 3.30-6.30pm Tue-Fri, 10am-1pm & 3.30-6.30pm Sat & Sun), which displays finds from the Bronze Age Enotri culture, and the Brettii people who founded Cosenza in the 4th century BC.

🛏 Sleeping

B&B Via dell'Astrologo B&B €
(☑ 338 9205394; www.viadellastrologo.com; Via Rutilio Benincasa 16; r from €65; ☜) A gem in the historic centre, this small B&B is tastefully decorated with polished wooden floors, white bedspreads and good-quality artwork. Brothers Mario and Marco, the venue's own-

ers, are a mine of information on Cosenza and Calabria in general.

Royal Hotel
HOTEL €

(☑0984 41 21 65; www.hotelroyalcosenza.it; Via delle Medaglie d'Oro 1; s/d/ste from €56/69/75; P ✳ ☎) Probably the best all-round hotel central Cosenza can provide, the four-star Royal is a short stroll from Corso Mazzini right in the heart of town. Rooms are fresh and businesslike, and there's a bar, restaurant and parking on site.

✗ Eating

Il Paesello
CALABRIAN €

(☑349 4385786; Via Rivocati 95; meals €25; ⊙7-11pm Mon-Sat, noon-3pm Sun) Beloved of the locals, this unpretentious trattoria is one of Cosenza's best. Simple, robust dishes such as *fagioli con cozze* (beans with mussels), tagliatelle with porcini mushrooms and anything plucked from the sea are executed with care and skill

Gran Caffè Renzelli
CAFE €

(www.renzelli.com; Corso Telesio 46; cakes from €1.20; ⊙7am-9pm; ☎) This venerable cafe behind the *duomo* has been run by the same family since 1803 when the founder arrived from Naples and began baking gooey cakes and desserts. Sink your teeth into *torroncino torrefacto* (a confection of sugar, spices and hazelnuts) or *torta telesio* (made from almonds, cherries, apricot jam and lupins).

Ristorante Calabria Bella
CALABRIAN €€

(☑0984 79 35 31; www.ristorantecalabriabella.it; Piazza del Duomo 20; meals €28; ⊙noon-3pm & 7pm-midnight) Traditional Calabrian cuisine, such as *cavatelli con cozze e fagioli* (pasta with mussels and beans) and *grigliata mista di carne* (mixed grilled meats), is dished up with aplomb at this cosy restaurant in the old town.

❶ Orientation

The main drag, Corso Mazzini, runs south from Piazza Bilotti (formerly known as Piazza Fera), near the bus station, and intersects Viale Trieste before meeting Piazza dei Bruzi. Head further south and cross the Busento river to reach the old town.

❶ Getting There & Away

AIR
Lamezia Terme Airport (Sant'Eufemia Lamezia, SUF; ☑0968 41 43 85; www.sacal.it; Via Aeroporto 40, Lamezia Terme), 63km south of Cosenza, at the junction of the A3 and SS280

motorways, links the region with major Italian cities. The airport is served by Ryanair, easyJet and charters from northern Europe. A shuttle leaves the airport every 20 minutes for the airport train station, where **Autolinee Romano** (☑0962 2 17 09; www.autolineeromano.com) runs two buses a day to Cosenza.

BUS
Cosenza's main **bus station** (☑0984 41 31 24) is northeast of Piazza Bilotti. Services leave from here for Catanzaro and towns throughout La Sila. **Autolinee Preite** (☑0984 41 30 01; www.autoservizipreite.it) has buses heading daily along the north Tyrrhenian coast; **Autolinee Romano** serves Crotone as well as Rome and Milan.

TRAIN
Stazione Nuova (Via Vaglio Lise) is about 2km northeast of the centre. Regular trains go to Reggio di Calabria (from €14.60, 2¾ hours) and Rome (from €52.10, four to six hours) both usually with a change at Paola, and Naples (from €16.90, three to four hours), as well as most destinations around the Calabrian coast

Regular buses link the centre and the main train station, although they follow a roundabout route.

Parco Nazionale della Sila

'La Sila' is a big landscape, where wooded hills stretch to endless rolling vistas. Dotted with hamlets, it's cut through with looping roads that make driving a test of your digestion.

The park's 130 sq km are divided into three areas: the **Sila Grande**, with the highest mountains; the strongly Albanian **Sila Greca** (to the north); and the **Sila Piccola** (near Catanzaro), with vast forested hills.

The highest peaks, covered with tall Corsican pines, reach 2000m – high enough to generate enough winter snow to attract skiers. In summer the climate is coolly Alpine; spring sees carpets of wildflowers; and there's mushroom hunting in autumn. Gigantic firs grow in the **Bosco di Gallopane** (Forest of Gallopane). There are several beautiful lakes, the largest of which is **Lago di Cecita o Mucone** near Camigliatello Silano. There is plenty of wildlife here, including the light-grey Apennine wolf, a protected species.

◉ Sights & Activities

La Sila's main town, **San Giovanni in Fiore** (1049m), is named after the founder of its beautiful medieval **abbey**. Today, the abbey houses a home for the elderly and the **Museo Demologico** (☑ 0984 97 00 59; Abbazia Forense; adult/reduced €1.50/1; ☉ 8.30am-6.30pm Mon-Sat year round & 9.30am-12.30pm Sun mid-Jun–mid-Sep). San Giovanni's handsome old centre is famous for its Armenian-style handloomed carpets and tapestry. See how it's done at the studio and shop of master carpet maker **Domenico Caruso** (☑ 0984 99 27 24; http://carusotessiture.it; Via Gramsci 195; ☉ 8.30am-8pm Mon-Sat).

A popular ski-resort town with 6km of slopes, **Camigliatello Silano** (1272m) looks much better under snow. A few lifts operate on Monte Curcio, about 3km to the south. Around 5.5km of slopes and a 1500m lift can be found near **Lorica** (1370m), on gloriously pretty **Lago Arvo** – the best place to camp in summer.

Scigliano (620m) is a small hilltop town located west of the Sila Piccola section of the park and 75km south of Cosenza.

✯✯ Festivals & Events

During August, **Sila in Festa** takes place, featuring traditional music. Autumn is mushroom season, when you'll be able to frequent mushroom festivals, including the **Sagra del Fungo** in Camigliatello Silano.

🛏 Sleeping & Eating

★ **B&B Calabria**   B&B €

(☑ 349 8781894; www.bedandbreakfastcalabria.it; Via Roma 7, Scigliano; s/d €40/60; ☉ Apr-Nov; 🅿) This B&B in the mountains has five clean, comfortable and characterful rooms, all with separate entrances. Owner Raffaele is a great source of information on the region and can recommend places to eat, visit and go hiking. There's a wonderful terrace overlooking endless forested vistas. Mountain bikes are available. and there's wi-fi in public areas. Cash only.

Albergo San Lorenzo   HOTEL €

(☑ 0984 57 08 09; www.sanlorenzosialberga.it; Campo San Lorenzo, near Camigliatello Silano; d/tr/q €110/130/160; 🅿 ✳ 🛜) Above their famous restaurant, the owners of La Tavernetta have opened the area's most stylish sleep, with 21 large, well-equipped rooms done up in colourful, modernist style.

★ **La Tavernetta**   CALABRIAN €€€

(☑ 0984 57 90 26; www.sanlorenzosialberga.it; Campo San Lorenzo, near Camigliatello Silano; meals €50; ☉ 12.30-3pm & 7.30-11pm Tue-Sun)

Among Calabria's best eats, La Tavernetta marries rough country charm with citified elegance in warmly colourful dining rooms. The food is first-rate and based on the best local ingredients, from wild anise seed and mushrooms to mountain-raised lamb and kid. Reserve ahead on Sundays and holidays.

🛍 Shopping

★ **Antica Salumeria Campanaro**   FOOD

(☑ 0984 57 80 15; Piazza Misasi 5, Camigliatello Silano; ☉ 9am-9pm) Even among Italian delicatessens, this long-established *salumeria* is something special. It's a temple to all things fungoid (get your Sila porcini here) as well as an emporium of fine meats, cheeses, pickles, sweetmeats and wines.

ℹ Information

Good-quality information in English is scarce. You can try the national park **visitors centre** at Cupone, 10km from Camigliatello Silano, or the **Pro Loco tourist office** (☑ 0984 57 81 59; www.prolococamigliatello.it; Via Roma, Camigliatello Silano; ☉ 9.30am-6.30pm Tue-Sun) in Camigliatello Silano. A useful internet resource is the official park website (www.parcosila.it). The people who run B&B Calabria in the park are extremely knowledgeable and helpful.

For a map, you can use *La Sila: Carta Turistico-Stradale ed Escurionistica del Parco Nazionale* (€7). *Sila for 4* is a mini-guide in English that outlines a number of walking trails in the park. The map and booklet are available at tourist offices.

Visitors Centre (☑ 0984 53 71 09; www.parcosila.it; Via Nazionale, Lorica)

ℹ Getting There & Away

You can reach the park's two main hubs, Camigliatello Silano and San Giovanni in Fiore, via regular **Ferrovie della Calabria** buses from Cosenza or Crotone.

Ionian Coast

With its flat coastline and wide sandy beaches, the Ionian coast has some fascinating stops from **Sibari** to **Santa Severina**, with some of the best beaches around **Soverato**. However, it has borne the brunt of some ugly development and is mainly a long, uninterrupted string of resorts, thronged in the summer months and mothballed from October to May.

It's worth taking a trip inland to visit Santa Severina, a spectacular mountain-top town, 26km northwest of Crotone. The town is dominated by a **Norman castle** and is home to a beautiful **Byzantine church**. But the true glories of this long stretch of coast are its museums and archaeological sites, preserving what remains of the pre-Roman cities of Magna Graecia (Greater Greece).

Le Castella

This town is named for its impressive 16th-century Aragonese **castle** (☏ 0965 36 21 11; €3; ⏰ 9am-midnight Jul & Aug, shorter hours

FOOTPRINTS OF MAGNA GRAECIA

Long before the Romans colonised Greece, the Greeks were colonising southern Italy. Pushed out of their homelands by demographic, social and political pressures, the nebulous mini-empire they created between the 8th and 3rd centuries BC was often referred to as Magna Graecia by the Romans in the north. Many Greek-founded cities were located along the southern coast of present-day Puglia, Basilicata and Calabria. They included (west to east) Locri Epizephyrii, Kroton, Sybaris, Metapontum and Taras (now known, respectively, as Locri, Crotone, Sibari, Metaponto and Taranto).

Magna Graecia was more a loose collection of independent cities than a coherent state with fixed borders, and many of these cities regularly raged war against each other. The most notable conflict occurred in 510 BC when the athletic Krotons attacked and destroyed the hedonistic city of Sybaris (from which the word 'sybaritic' is derived).

Magna Graecia was the 'door' through which Greek culture entered Italy, influencing its language, architecture, religion and culture. Though the cities were mostly abandoned by the 5th century AD, the Greek legacy lives on in the Griko culture of Calabria and the Salento peninsula, where ethnic Greek communities still speak Griko, a dialect of Greek.

Remnants of Magna Graecia can be seen in numerous museums and architectural sites along Calabria's Ionian coast.

Locri

Museo Nazionale di Locri Epizephyrii (☏ 0964 39 00 23; www.locriantica.it; Contrada Marasà, Locri; adult/reduced €4/2; ⏰ 9am-8pm; P ♿) Situated 3km south of modern-day Locri, the Greek colony of Locri Epizephyrii was founded in 680 BC, later subsumed by Rome and finally abandoned following Saracen raids in the 10th century AD. The archaeological site is sprawling and full of interest, including harbour structures, the *centocamere* (hundred rooms) and the Casino Macri – a Roman bathhouse later repurposed as a farming villa. The attached museum is well curated, and includes artefacts found in the numerous nearby necropoli.

Sibari

Museo Archeologico Nazionale delle Sibaritide (☏ 0981 7 93 91; Località Casa Bianca, Sibari; €3; ⏰ 9am-8pm Tue-Sun) Founded around 730 BC and destroyed by the Krotons in 510 BC, Sybaris was rebuilt twice: once as Thurii by the Greeks in 444 BC, and again in 194 BC by the Romans, who called it Copia. Prehistoric artefacts and evidence of all three cities are displayed at this important (if underpatronised) museum, 5km southeast of the modern beach resort of Sibari. The nearby archaeological park has been affected by flooding in the past: check ahead to ensure it's open.

Crotone

Museo Archeologico Nazionale di Crotone (☏ 0962 2 30 82; Via Risorgimento 14, Crotone; €2; ⏰ 9am-8pm) Founded in 710 BC, the powerful city state of Kroton was known for its sobriety and high-performing Olympic athletes. Crotone's museum is located in the modern town, while the main archaeological site is at Capo Colonna, 11km to the southeast. Votive offerings and other remnants of the famous Hera Lacinia Sanctuary at Cape Colonna are a highlight.

rest of year, closed Mon Oct-Mar), a vast edifice linked to the mainland by a short causeway. Evidence shows it was begun in the 4th century BC, designed to protect Crotone in the wars against Pyrrhus.

Le Castella is situated south of a rare protected area along this coast, Capo Rizzuto, rich not only in nature but also in Greek history. For further information on the park, try www.riservamarinacapo rizzuto.it.

With around 15 campgrounds near Isola di Capo Rizzuto to the north, this is the Ionian coast's prime camping area. Try **La Fattoria** (☑ 0962 79 11 65; Via del Faro, Isola di Capo Rizzuto; camping 2 people, car & tent €25, bungalow €60; ☻ Jun-Sep), 1.5km from the sea. Otherwise, **Da Annibale** (☑ 0962 79 50 04; Via Duomo 35; s/d €50/70; P ✱ @ ☎) is a pleasant hotel in town with a splendid fish **restaurant** (☑ 0962 79 50 04; Via Duomo 35; meals €40; ☻ noon-3pm & 7.30-11pm).

For expansive sea views dine at bright and airy **Ristorante Micomare** (☑ 0962 79 50 82; Via Vittoria 7; meals €35; ☻ noon-3pm & 7.30-11pm).

Gerace

POP 2650

A spectacular medieval hill town, Gerace is worth a detour for the views alone – it's dramatically sited on a rocky fastness rearing up from the inland plain, culminating in the photogenic ruin of a Norman castle that seems to grow from the stone itself.

Gerace is graced by numerous handsome churches – some dating back to the Byzantine 9th century – and has Calabria's largest Romanesque **cathedral** (Via Duomo 28; ☻ 9.30am-12.30pm & 3-6.30pm). Dating to 1045, later alterations have not robbed it of its majesty.

For a taste of traditional Calabrian cooking, **Ristorante A Squella** (☑ 0964 35 60 86; Via Ferruccio 21; meals €25; ☻ 12.30-2.30pm daily & 7.30-10.30pm Mon-Sat) serves reliably good seafood and Calabrian dishes. Afterwards you can wander down the road and admire the views.

Further inland is **Canolo**, a small village seemingly untouched by the 20th century. Buses connect Gerace with Locri and also Canolo with Siderno, both of which link to the main coastal railway line. To explore these quiet hills properly, you'll need your own transport.

Parco Nazionale dell'Aspromonte

Most Italians think of the Parco Nazionale dell'Aspromonte (www.parcoaspromonte. gov.it) as a hiding place used by Calabrian kidnappers in the 1970s and '80s. It's still rumoured to contain 'ndrangheta strongholds, but as a tourist you're unlikely to encounter any murky business.

The park, Calabria's second-largest, is dramatic, rising sharply inland from Reggio. Its highest peak, **Montalto** (1955m), is dominated by a huge bronze statue of Christ and offers sweeping views across to Sicily.

Subject to frequent mudslides and carved up by torrential rivers, the mountains are nonetheless awesomely beautiful. Underwater rivers keep the peaks covered in coniferous forests and ablaze with flowers in spring. It's wonderful walking country and is crossed by several colour-coded trails.

Extremes of weather and geography have resulted in some extraordinary villages, such as **Pentidàttilo** and **Roghudi**, clinging limpet-like to the craggy, rearing rocks and now all but deserted. It's worth the drive to explore these eagle-nest villages. Another mountain eyrie with a photogenic ruined castle is **Bova**, perched at 900m above sealevel. The drive up the steep, dizzying road to Bova is not for the faint-hearted, but the views are stupendous.

Maps are scarce. Try the **national park office** (☑ 0965 74 30 60; www.parcoaspromonte. gov.it; Via Aurora 1, Gambarie; ☻ 10.30am-12.30pm Mon & Fri & 3-6pm Tue) in **Gambarie**, the Aspromonte's main town and the easiest approach to the park. The roads are good and many activities are organised from here – you can ski and it's also the place to hire a 4WD; ask around in the town.

It's also possible to approach from the south, but the roads aren't as good. The cooperative **Naturaliter** (☑ 347 3046799; www. naturaliterweb.it), based in Condofuri, is an excellent source of information, and can help arrange walking and donkey treks or place you in B&Bs throughout the region. **Co-operativa San Leo** (☑ 347 3046799), based in Bova, also provides guided tours and accommodation. In Reggio di Calabria, you can book treks and tours with **Misafumera** (☑ 347 0804515, 0965 67 70 21; Via Nazionale 306d, Reggio di Calabria Bocale 2; treks €260-480).

Hotel Centrale (☑0965 74 31 33; www. hotelcentrale.net; Piazza Mangeruca 22, Gambarie; s/d €50/100; P ✳ ☏) in Gambarie is a large, all-encompassing place reminiscent of a ski hotel in the Italian Dolomites. It has a decent restaurant, a comprehensive modern spa, wood-finished rooms and the best cafe in town. It's located right at the bottom of the ski lift.

To reach Gambarie, take ATAM (p777) city bus 319 from Reggio di Calabria (€1, 1½ hours, up to six daily). Most of the roads inland from Reggio eventually hit the SS183 road that runs north to the town.

Reggio di Calabria

POP 182,550

Port, transport nexus and the main arrival and departure point for Sicily, Reggio seems more functional than fascinating. That is up until the point you set foot inside its fabulous national museum, custodian of some of the most precious artefacts of Magna Graecia known.

The city's architectural eclecticism is a result of its tectonic liveliness: in 1908 the last big earthquake triggered a tsunami that killed over 100,000. By Italian standards, little of historical merit remains, although the *lungomare,* with its views across the Messina Strait to smouldering Mt Etna is, arguably, one of the most atmospheric places in Italy for an evening *passeggiata.*

Fortunately, there's no need to doubt the food. Reggio hides some of Calabria's best salt-of-the-earth restaurants. You can work up an appetite for them by hiking in the nearby Parco Nazionale dell'Aspromonte, or exploring the coastline at nearby seaside escapes along the Tyrrhenian and Ionian coasts.

◉ Sights

★ **Museo Nazionale
di Reggio Calabria** MUSEUM
(☑0965 81 22 55; http://sabap-rc.beniculturali.it; Piazza de Nava 26; adult/reduced €8/5; ◷9am-8pm Tue-Sun; ⊕) Partly closed during years of renovation from 2009, southern Italy's finest museum is now fully reopened. Over several floors you'll descend through millennia of local history, from Neolithic and palaeolithic times through Hellenistic, Roman and beyond. The undoubted crown jewels are, probably, the world's finest

examples of ancient Greek sculpture: the Bronzi di Riace, two extraordinary bronze statues discovered on the seabed near Riace in 1972 by a snorkelling chemist from Rome.

You'll have to stand for three minutes in a decontamination chamber to see the bronzes, but they're more than worth the wait. Larger than life, they depict the Greek obsession with the body; inscrutable, determined and fierce, their perfect form is more godlike than human. The finest of the two has ivory eyes and silver teeth parted in a faint *Mona Lisa* smile. No one knows who they are – whether human or god – and even their provenance is a mystery. They date from around 450 BC, and it's believed they're the work of two artists.

In the same room as the bronzes is the 5th-century-BC bronze *Philosopher's Head,* the oldest-known Greek portrait in existence. Also on display are impressive exhibits from Locri, including statues of Dioscuri falling from his horse.

Castle Ruins RUINS
(Piazza Castello) Only two towers, restored in 2000, remain of the Aragonese Castle damaged by earthquake and partially demolished in 1922. The site is used for events and performances today.

⇱ Sleeping

Finding a room should be easy, even in summer, since most visitors pass straight through en route to Sicily

B&B Casa Blanca B&B €
(☑340 9032992; www.bbcasablanca.it; Via Arcovito 24; s/d/tr €55/75/85; P ✳ ☏) A little gem in Reggio's heart, this 19th-century *palazzo* has three floors of spacious rooms gracefully furnished with white-on-white decor. There's a self-serve breakfast nook, a small breakfast table in each room and two apartments available. Breakfast is a celebration of fresh pastries.

Hotel Continental HOTEL €
(☑0965 81 21 81; www.hotelcontinentalrc.it; Via Vincenzo Florio 10; r from €69; P ✳ ☏) Right next to the port, the Continental does a brisk trade in overnight travellers bound for Sicily. The decor holds no surprises, but the service is exceedingly polite and professional. A breakfast buffet can be procured for €10, and a room with a view to Sicily for another €20.

Reggio di Calabria

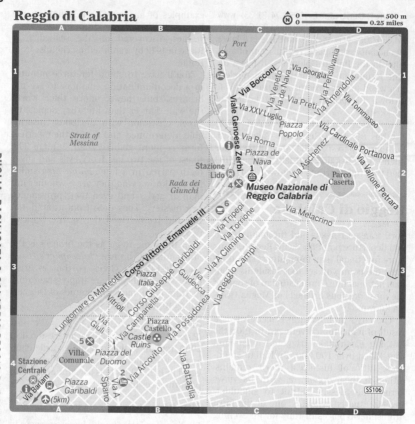

Reggio di Calabria

◎ Top Sights
1 Museo Nazionale di Reggio Calabria...C2

🛏 Sleeping
2 B&B Casa Blanca.....................................B4
3 Hotel Continental....................................C1

✖ Eating
4 Cèsare...C2
La Cantina del Macellaio...............(see 2)
5 Le Nasse U Bais.....................................A4

🍷 Drinking & Nightlife
6 Gelateria Matteotti.................................C2

✖ Eating

Reggio's well stocked with no-nonsense trattorias serving Calabrian classics the way the locals demand they should be. You'll struggle to eat badly here.

Cèsare GELATO €
(Piazza Indipendenza 2; gelato from €2.40; ⊗6am-1am) The most popular gelateria in town is in a modest green kiosk at the end of the *lungomare* (seafront promenade). Try the Kinder Egg flavour.

La Cantina del Macellaio TRATTORIA €€
(☑0965 2 39 32; www.lacantinadelmacellaio.com; Via Arcovito 26/28; meals €30; ⊗12.30-3pm & 7.30-11.30pm Wed-Mon) One of the best restaurants in Reggio, serving *fagioli cu l'oghiu bonu* (Sicilian beans), *maccheroni al ragù di maiale* (handmade pasta with pork sauce) and *involtini di vitello* (veal rolls) in an open, tiled dining room with exposed stonework and green flasks on the walls. The mostly Calabrian wines are equally impressive, as is the service.

Le Nasse U Bais SEAFOOD €€
(☑0965 89 72 66; www.ubais.it; Via Lemos 6; meals €40; ⊗noon-3pm & 7.30-11pm Tue-Sun)

Offering a long wine list and locally caught seafood such as *pesce spada* (swordfish), this restaurant looks like a sophisticated version of a fisherman's whitewashed shack. The food follows the same theme – quality, fresh ingredients, served up with care and intelligence.

Gelateria Matteotti CAFE
(☑ 0965 89 11 61; www.caffematteotti.it; Corso Vittorio Emanuele III 39; ⊙ 7am-2am Mon-Fri, to 4am Sat & Sun) This gelateria/cafe is one of the prime people-watching spots on Reggio's *lungomare* (seafront). Across from the main premises you'll find a sea-facing terrace furnished with stylish white tables and chairs, perfect for your *aperitivi*.

ℹ Information

Tourist Information Kiosk (☑ 0965 2 11 71; Via Roma 3; ⊙ 9am-noon & 4-7pm) There are also information kiosks at both the airport (☑ 0965 64 32 91; ⊙ 9am-5pm) and the Stazione Centrale (☑ 0965 2 71 20; ⊙ 9am-5pm).

Police Station (☑ 0965 41 11; Corso Garibaldi 442)

Grande Ospedale Metropolitano Bianchi Melacrino Morelli (☑ 800 19 86 29, emergency 118; www.ospedalerc.it; Via Melacrino; ⊙ 24hr) Reggio di Calabria's main hospital has a 24-hour *pronto soccorso* (emergency department).

ℹ Getting There & Away

AIR
Reggio's **airport** (REG; ☑ 0965 64 05 17; www.aeroportodellostretto.it) is at Ravagnese, about 5km south. It has Alitalia flights to Rome and Milan.

BUS
Most bus services terminate at the **Piazza Garibaldi bus station** (Piazza Garibaldi), situated in front of the Stazione Centrale. Several different bus companies operate services to towns in Calabria and beyond. Regional trains are more convenient than bus services to Scilla and Tropea.

ATAM runs bus 127 to Gambarie in the Aspromonte National Park.

Lirosi (☑ 0966 5 79 01; www.lirosiautoservizi.com) has two daily buses to Rome.

CAR & MOTORCYCLE
The A2 ends at Reggio, via a series of long tunnels. If you are continuing south, the SS106/F90 hugs the coast around the 'toe', then heads north along the Ionian Sea.

TRAIN
Trains stop at **Stazione Centrale** (☑ 0965 32 41 91; Via Barlaam 1), the main train station at the town's southern edge. Of more use to ferry foot passengers and those visiting the Museo Nazionale is the **Stazione Lido** (Viale Zerbi), near the harbour. There are frequent trains to Milan, Rome and Naples. Regional services run along the coast to Scilla and Tropea, and also to Catanzaro and less frequently to Cosenza and Bari.

ℹ Getting Around

Orange local bus services run by **ATAM** (☑ 800 43 33 10; www.atam-rc.it) cover most of the city area including regular buses that run between the port and Piazza Garibaldi outside Stazione Centrale. The Università–Aeroporto bus, bus 27, runs from Piazza Garibaldi to the airport and vice versa (15 minutes, hourly). Buy your ticket at ATAM offices, tobacconists or news stands.

ℹ ONWARD TO SICILY

Reggio is the gateway to Sicily, via the island's main port, Messina. There are also boats to the Aeolian Islands.

Note that there are two main departure ports for Sicily: the **Stazione Marittima** in Reggio di Calabria, and the ferry port in the town of Villa San Giovanni, 14km north of Reggio and easily accessible by train.

The main car ferry from Reggio's Stazione Marittima is operated by **Meridiano** (☑ 0965 81 04 14; www.meridianolines.net), which runs a dozen ferries a day on weekdays (three to four on weekends).

The other main ferry company operating is **Liberty Lines** (☑ 0923 87 38 13; http://eng.libertylines.it), which runs passenger-only ferry services to Messina, Stromboli and Vulcano.

The car ferries from Villa San Giovanni are run by **Caronte & Tourist** (☑ 800 62 74 14; www.carontetourist.it). This is also the port used by Trenitalia's train-ferry – carriages are pulled directly onto the ferry.

Southern Tyrrhenian Coast

North of Reggio di Calabria, along the coast-hugging **Autostrada del Mediterraneo (A2)**, the scenery rocks and rolls to become increasingly beautiful and dramatic, if you can ignore the shoddy holiday camps and unattractive developments that sometimes scar the land. Like the northern part of the Tyrrhenian coast, it's mostly quiet in winter and packed in summer.

Scilla

POP 4900

In Scilla, cream-, ochre- and earth-coloured houses cling on for dear life to the jagged promontory, ascending in jumbled ranks to the hill's summit, which is crowned by a castle and, just below, the dazzling white confection of the **Chiesa Arcipretale Maria Immacolata**. Lively in summer and serene in low season, the town is split in two by the tiny port. The fishing district of Scilla Chianalea, to the north, harbours small hotels and restaurants off narrow lanes, lapped by the sea. It can only be visited on foot.

Scilla's high point is a rock at the northern end, said to be the lair of Scylla, the mythical six-headed sea monster who drowned sailors as they tried to navigate the Strait of Messina. Swimming and fishing off the town's glorious white sandy beach is somewhat safer today. Head for **Lido Paradiso** from where you can squint up at the castle while sunbathing on the sand.

Sights

Castello Ruffo CASTLE

(☎0965 70 42 07; Piazza San Rocco; admission €2; ⏲8.30am-7.30pm) An imposing fortress surmounting the headland commanding Scilla, this castle has at times been a lighthouse and a monastery. It houses a *luntre*, the original boat used for swordfishing, and on which the modern-day *passarelle* (a special swordfish-hunting boat equipped with a 30m-high metal tower) is based.

Sleeping

The old fishing village of Chianalea, on Scilla's eastern flank, holds some delightful sea-facing B&Bs.

Hotel Principe di Scilla HOTEL €€

(☎0965 70 43 24; www.ubais.it; Via Grotte 2; ste from €150; ❄📶) Get lulled to sleep by the sound of lapping waves in this grand old family residence on Scilla's seafront. Two suits of armour guard the front door while inside six individually themed suites are stuffed with countless antiques. In warm weather throw the windows open onto lovely views of the fishing village of Chianalea and, beyond, the sparkling Tyrrhenian.

Le Piccole Grotte B&B €€

(☎338 2096727, 0965 75 48 81; www.lepiccolegrotte.it; Via Grotte 10; d €120; ❄📶) In the picturesque Chianalea district, 'The Small Caves' is a sweet B&B housed in a 19th-century fisherman's house beside steps leading to the lapping Tyrrhenian. Rooms have small balconies facing the cobbled alleyway or the sea.

Eating & Drinking

Bleu de Toi SEAFOOD €€

(☎0965 79 05 85; www.bleudetoi.it; Via Grotte 40; meals €35; ⏲noon-3pm & 8pm-midnight Wed-Mon) Soak up the atmosphere at this lovely little restaurant, where blue lampshades, a Blue Note soundtrack and glimpses of the blue Tyrrhenian set the mood. It has a terrace over the water and excellent seafood dishes, made with local ingredients such as Scilla's renowned swordfish, perhaps with fresh pasta and eggplant. Ask for the homemade Amaro (herbal liqueur) to finish.

Dali City Pub BAR

(☎347 5541586; Via Porto 6; ⏲noon-midnight) On the beach in Scilla town, this popular bar has a Beatles tribute corner (appropriately named the Cavern) and has been going strong since 1972.

Getting There & Away

Scilla is on the main coastal train line. Frequent trains run to Reggio di Calabria (€2.40, 30 minutes). The train station is a couple of blocks from the beach.

Tropea

POP 6400

Tropea, a puzzle of lanes and piazzas, is famed for its beauty, dramatic cliff's-edge site and spectacular sunsets. It sits on the Promontorio di Tropea, which stretches from Nicotera in the south to Pizzo in the north. The coast alternates between dramatic cliffs and icing sugar–soft sandy beaches, all edged by translucent sea. Unsurprisingly, hordes of Italian holidaymakers descend here in summer. If you hear English being spoken, it is probably from Americans visiting relatives: enormous numbers left to forge better lives in America in the early 20th century.

Despite the legend that Hercules founded the town, it seems this area has been settled as far back as Neolithic times. Tropea has been occupied by the Arabs, Normans, Swabians, Anjous and Aragonese, as well as being attacked by Turkish pirates. Perhaps they were all after the town's famous red onions, so sweet they can be turned into marmalade?

🧿 Sights

Cathedral
CATHEDRAL

(Largo Duomo 12; ⊙7am-noon & 4-8pm) The beautiful Norman cathedral has two undetonated WWII bombs near the door: it's believed they didn't explode due to the protection of the town's patron saint, Our Lady of Romania. A Byzantine icon (1330) of the Madonna hangs above the altar – she is also credited with protecting the town from the earthquakes that have pummelled the region.

Santa Maria dell'Isola
CHURCH

(☎347 2541232; www.santuarlosantamariadelliso latropea.it; garden & museum €2; ⊙9am-1pm & 3-7.30pm Apr-Jun, 9am-8.30pm Jul & Aug, shorter hours rest of year) Tropea's number one photo opp is Santa Maria dell'Isola, a medieval monastic church given several facelifts over centuries of wear and tear (mainly attributable to earthquakes). Sitting on what was once its own rocky little island, it's now joined to the mainland by a causeway created by centuries of silt, and is reached via a flight of steps up the cliff-face. Access to the church is free, but the small museum and garden costs €2.

🛏️ Sleeping

⭐ Donnaciccina
B&B €€

(☎0963 6 21 80; www.donnaciccina.com; Via Pelliccia 9; s/d/ste €75/150/240; ✴️🛜) Look for the sign of a bounteous hostess bearing fruit and cake to find this delightful B&B, overlooking the main *corso*. The 17th-century *palazzo* retains a tangible sense of history with carefully selected antiques, canopy beds and terracotta tiled floors. There are nine restful rooms, a nearby suite (itself dating to the 15th century) and a chatty parrot at reception.

Residenza il Barone
B&B €€

(☎0963 60 71 81; www.residenzailbarone.it; Largo Barone; ste from €180; ✴️🛜) This graceful *palazzo* has six suites that are decorated in masculine neutrals and tobacco browns, with dramatic modern paintings by the owner's brother adding pizzazz to the walls. There's a computer available in each suite and you can eat breakfast on the small roof terrace with views over the old city and out to sea.

🍴 Eating

Al Pinturicchio
ITALIAN €

(☎0963 60 34 52; Via Dardono 2; meals €22; ⊙7.30pm-midnight) Recommended by the locals, this restaurant in a smartly whitewashed cellar in the old town has a romantic ambience, candlelit tables and a solid repertoire of Calabrian dishes.

Osteria del Pescatore
SEAFOOD €€

(☎0963 60 30 18; Via del Monte 7; meals €26; ⊙noon-2.30pm & 8pm-midnight Wed-Mon) Swordfish (*spada*) is a speciality on this part of the coast and it rates highly on the menu at this simple seafood place tucked away in the backstreets. Also arranges fishing trips in good weather.

ℹ️ Information

Tourist Office (☎0963 6 14 75, 347 5318989; www.prolocotropea.eu; Piazza Ercole; ⊙9am-1pm & 4-8pm) In the old town centre.

WORTH A TRIP

CAPO VATICANO

There are spectacular views from this rocky cape, around 7km south of Tropea, with its beaches, ravines and limestone sea cliffs. Birdwatchers' spirits should soar. There's a lighthouse, built in 1885, which is close to a short footpath from where you can see as far as the Aeolian Islands. Capo Vaticano beach is one of the balmiest along this coast.

❶ Getting There & Away

Trains run to Pizzo-Lamezia (€2.40, 30 minutes, 12 daily), Scilla (€4.60, 1¼ hours, frequent) and Reggio (from €6.40, 1¾ hours, frequent). **Ferrovie della Calabria** (📞 0961 89 62 39; www.ferroviedellacalabria.it) buses connect with other towns on the coast.

Pizzo

POP 9300

Stacked high up on a sea cliff, pretty little Pizzo is the place to go for *tartufo*, a death-by-chocolate ice-cream ball, and to see an extraordinary rock-carved grotto church. It's a popular and cheerful tourist stop. Piazza della Repubblica is the heart, set high above the sea with great views. Settle here at one of the many gelateria terraces for an ice-cream fix.

◉ Sights

Castello Murat   CASTLE

(📞 0963 53 25 23; www.castellomurat.it; Scesa Castello Murat; adult/reduced €2.50/1.50; ⊙ 9am-11pm Jul & Aug, to 7pm Apr-Jun, Sep & Oct, shorter hours rest of year) This neat little 15th-century castle is named for Joachim Murat, brother-in-law of Napoleon Bonaparte and briefly King of Naples, captured in Pizzo and sentenced to death for treason in 1815. Inside the castle, you can see his cell and the details of his grisly end by firing squad, which is graphically illustrated with waxworks. Although Murat was the architect of enlightened reforms, the locals showed no great concern when he was executed.

**Chiesa Matrice
di San Giorgio**   CHURCH

(Via San Giorgio 1; ⊙ hours vary) In town, the 16th-century Chiesa Matrice di San Giorgio, with its splendid Baroque facade and dressed-up Madonnas, houses the tomb of Joachim Murat, the French-born former king of Naples and brother-in-law of Napoleon.

Chiesetta di Piedigrotta   CHURCH

(📞 0963 53 25 23; Via Riviera Prangi; adult/reduced €2.50/1.50; ⊙ 9am-1pm & 3-7.30pm Jul & Aug, shorter hours rest of year) The Chiesetta di Piedigrotta is an underground cave full of carved stone statues. It was carved into the tufa rock by Neapolitan shipwreck survivors in the 17th century. Other sculptors added to it and it was eventually turned into a church. Later statues include the less-godly figures of Fidel Castro and John F Kennedy. It's a bizarre, one-of-a-kind mixture of mysticism, mystery and kitsch, especially transporting when glowing in the setting sun.

🛏 Sleeping

Armonia B&B   B&B €

(📞 0963 53 33 37; www.casaarmonia.com; Vico II Armonia 9; s/d €60/85; @) Run by the charismatic Franco in his 16th-century family home, this B&B has three relaxing rooms and spectacular sea views.

Piccolo Grand Hotel   BOUTIQUE HOTEL €€

(📞 0963 53 32 93; www.piccolograndhotel.com; Via Chiaravalloti 32; s/d €110/158; ❈ 🅿 🛜) This pleasant four-star boutique hotel is hidden on an unlikely and rather dingy side street. But its exuberant blue-and-white design, upscale comforts and panoramic rooftop breakfasts make it one of Pizzo's top sleeps. There's also a small fitness area and e-bikes to rent.

🍽 Eating

Bar Gelateria Ercole   GELATO €

(📞 0963 53 11 49; Piazza della Repubblica 18; tartufo €5; ⊙ 8am-midnight) Pizzo enjoys something of a reputation for its gelato, and, on the main square, Ercole is reckoned by many to serve the best in town. The most admired flavours include *tartufo* (chocolate and hazelnut) and *cassata* (egg cream with candied fruit).

Ristorante Don Diego di Pizzo   PIZZA €

(📞 340 8924469; www.dondiegoristorante.com; Via Salomone 243; meals/pizza €25/7; ⊙ noon-3pm & 7pm-midnight Thu-Tue; 🖪) You'll earn your carbs walking uphill from central Pizzo to reach this welcoming restaurant, but be amply recompensed with fantastic views from a panoramic terrace and food to match. Don Diego is particularly known for its pizza.

❶ Getting There & Away

Pizzo is just off the major A3 autostrada. There are two train stations. Vibo Valentia-Pizzo is located 4km south of town on the main Rome–Reggio di Calabria line. A bus service connects you to Pizzo. Pizzo-Lamezia is south of the town on the Tropea–Lamezia Terme line. Shuttle buses (€2) connect with trains or you can walk for 20 minutes along the coast road.

Sicily

Best Places to Eat

➜ Accursio (p832)

➜ Il Barcaiolo (p812)

➜ Ristorante Crocifisso (p830)

➜ Osteria La Bettolaccia (p844)

➜ Punta Lena (p809)

Best Places to Stay

➜ Hotel Ravesi (p806)

➜ B&B Crociferi (p817)

➜ Stanze al Genio Residenze (p791)

➜ Villa Quartarella (p831)

➜ Pensione Tranchina (p841)

Why Go?

More of a sugar-spiked espresso than a milky cappuccino, Sicily rewards visitors with an intense, bittersweet experience. Overloaded with art treasures and natural beauty, undersupplied with infrastructure, and continuously struggling against Mafia-driven corruption, Sicily's complexities sometimes seem unfathomable. To really appreciate this place, come with an open mind – and a healthy appetite. Despite the island's perplexing contradictions, one factor remains constant: the uncompromisingly high quality of the cuisine.

After 25 centuries of foreign domination, Sicilians are the heirs to an impressive cultural legacy, from the refined architecture of Magna Graecia to the Byzantine splendour and Arab craftwork of the island's Norman cathedrals and palaces. This cultural richness is matched by a startlingly diverse landscape that includes bucolic farmland, smouldering volcanoes and kilometres of island-studded aquamarine coastline.

When to Go
Palermo

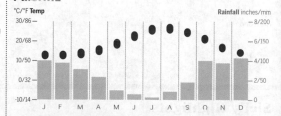

| **Easter** Colourful religious processions and marzipan lambs in every bakery window. | **May** Wildflowers, dreamy coastal walking and Syracuse's festival of classic drama. | **Sep** Warm weather and seaside fun without summer prices. |

N 0 ——————— 50 km
0 ——————— 25 miles

Ferries to Genoa;
Livorno

Ferries to
Naples

Ustica

*Tyrrhenian
Sea*

Falcone-
Borsellino **Mondello**

Riserva
Naturale dello
Zingaro

Trapani   **Erice**   Scopello   **Monreale**   ❶ **Palermo**

A29

A20

Marettimo

Favignana

Birgi
Airport

❸ **Segesta**

SS121

Egadi Islands

Marsala

Corleone

A29

Mazara del Vallo

SS189

Selinunte

Sciacca

Mediterranean Sea

Agrigento   Valley of the
Temples

Pantelleria

Ferries to
Pelagic Islands

Sicily Highlights

❶ **Teatro Massimo** (p791)
Joining the ranks of impeccably
dressed opera-goers at this
elegant theatre in Palermo.

❷ **Catania** (p814) Bargaining
with fish vendors at dawn,

climbing Europe's most active
volcano in the afternoon, and
returning to buzzing nightlife.

❸ **Segesta** (p846)
Marvelling at the majesty of the
5th-century ruins, whose Doric

temple sits in splendid isolation
on a windswept hillside.

❹ **Taormina** (p809)
Watching international stars
perform against Mt Etna's
backdrop at summer festivals.

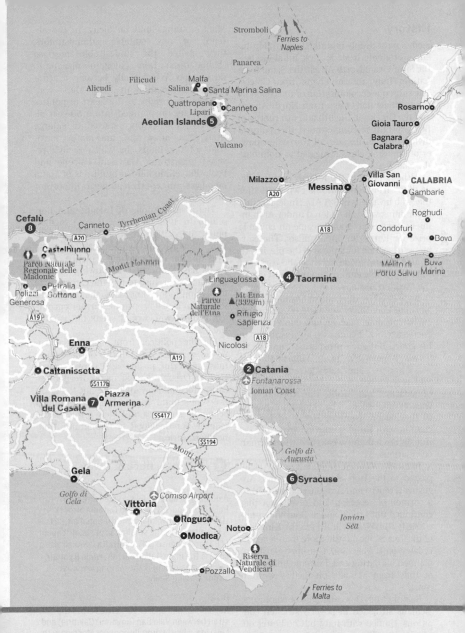

5 Aeolian Islands (p798)
Observing Stromboli's volcanic
fireworks and hiking on these
stunningly scenic islands.

6 Syracuse (p823)
Wandering in Ortygia's

atmospheric alleys or stepping
back in time at an Ancient
Greek theatre performance.

7 Villa Romana del Casale
(p833) Admiring prancing
wild beasts and dancing bikini-

clad gymnasts on the mosaic
floors.

8 Cefalù (p796) Being
dazzled by Byzantine mosaics
and splendid coastal sunsets.

History

Sicily's most deeply ingrained cultural influences originate from its first inhabitants – the Sicani from North Africa, the Siculi from Latium (Italy) and the Elymni from Greece. The subsequent colonisation of the island by the Carthaginians (also from North Africa) and the Greeks, in the 8th and 6th centuries BC respectively, compounded this cultural divide through decades of war when powerful opposing cities struggled to dominate the island.

Although part of the Roman Empire, Sicily didn't truly come into its own until after the Arab invasions of 831 AD. Trade, farming and mining were all fostered under Arab influence and Sicily soon became an enviable prize for European opportunists. The Normans, desperate for a piece of the pie, invaded in 1061 and made Palermo the centre of their expanding empire and the finest city in the Mediterranean.

Impressed by the cultured Arab lifestyle, Norman king Roger squandered vast sums on ostentatious palaces and churches and encouraged a hedonistic atmosphere in his court. But such prosperity – and decadence (Roger's grandson, William II, even had a harem) – inevitably gave rise to envy and resentment and, after two centuries of pleasure and profit, the Norman line was extinguished. The kingdom passed to the austere German House of Hohenstaufen with little opposition from the seriously eroded and weakened Norman occupation.

In the centuries that followed, Sicily passed to the Holy Roman Emperors, Angevins (French) and Aragonese (Spanish) in a turmoil of rebellion and revolution that continued until the Spanish Bourbons united Sicily with Naples in 1734 as the Kingdom of the Two Sicilies. Little more than a century later, on 11 May 1860, Giuseppe Garibaldi planned his daring and dramatic unification of Italy from Marsala on Sicily's western coast.

Reeling from this catalogue of colonisers, Sicilians struggled in poverty-stricken conditions. Unified with Italy, but no better off, nearly one million men and women emigrated to the US between 1871 and 1914 before the outbreak of WWI.

Ironically, the Allies (who were seeking Mafia help in America for the re-invasion of Italy) helped in establishing the Mafia's stranglehold on Sicily. In the absence of any suitable administrators, they invited the undesirable *mafioso* (Mafia boss) Don Calógero Vizzini to do the job. When Sicily became a semi-autonomous region in 1948, Mafia control extended right to the heart of politics and the region plunged into a 50-year silent civil war. It only started to emerge from this after the anti-Mafia maxi-trials of the 1980s, in which Sicily's revered magistrates Giovanni Falcone and Paolo Borsellino hauled hundreds of Mafia members into court, leading to important prosecutions.

The assassinations of Falcone and Borsellino in 1992 helped galvanise Sicilian public opposition to the Mafia's inordinate influence, and while organised crime lives on, the thuggery and violence of the 1980s has diminished. A growing number of businesses refuse to pay the extortionate protection money known as the *pizzo*, and important arrests continue, further encouraging those who would speak out against the Mafia.

On the political front, anti-Mafia crusaders currently serve in two of the island's most powerful positions: Palermo mayor Leoluca Orlando and Sicilian governor Rosario Crocetta. Nowadays the hot topics on everyone's mind are the island's continued economic struggles and Sicily's role as the gateway for the flood of immigrants from northern Africa.

ⓘ Getting There & Away

AIR

A number of airlines fly services direct to Palermo airport (PMO) and Catania airport (CTA), Sicily's two main international airports. A few also serve the smaller airports of Trapani (TPS) and Comiso (CIY). **Alitalia** (www.alitalia.com) is the main Italian carrier, while **Ryanair** (www.ryanair.com) is the leading low-cost airline serving Sicily.

BOAT

Regular car and passenger ferries cross the strait between Villa San Giovanni (Calabria) and Messina, while hydrofoils connect Messina with Reggio di Calabria.

Sicily is also accessible by ferry from Naples, Genoa, Civitavecchia, Livorno, Salerno, Cagliari, Malta and Tunis. Prices rise between June and September, when advanced bookings may also be required.

Sicily Ferry & Hydrofoil Crossings

ROUTE	COST PER ADULT FROM (€)	DURATION
Genoa–Palermo	80	20hr
Malta–Pozzallo	70	1¾hr
Naples–Catania	45	11hr
Naples–Palermo	45	10hr
Naples–Trapani	108	7hr
Reggio di Calabria–Messina	3.50	35min
Tunis–Palermo	49	10hr

BUS

SAIS Trasporti (☏ 091 617 11 41; www.sais trasporti.it) runs long-haul services to Sicily from Rome and Naples.

TRAIN

For travellers originating in Rome and points south, InterCity trains cover the distance from mainland Italy to Sicily in the least possible time, without a change of train. If coming from Milan, Bologna or Florence, your fastest option is to take the ultra-high-speed Frecciarossa as far as Naples, then change to an InterCity train for the rest of the journey.

All trains enter Sicily at Messina, after being transported by ferry from Villa San Giovanni at the toe of Italy's boot. At Messina, trains branch west along the Tyrrhenian coast to Palermo, or south along the Ionian coast to Catania.

❶ Getting Around

AIR

Mistral Air (www.mistralair.it) offers direct flights to the offshore islands of Pantelleria (from Palermo and Trapani) and Lampedusa (from Palermo and Catania).

BUS

Bus services within Sicily are provided by a variety of companies. Buses are usually the fastest option if your destination involves travel through the island's interior; trains tend to be cheaper (and sometimes faster) on the major coastal routes. In small towns and villages tickets are often sold in bars or on the bus.

CAR & MOTORCYCLE

Having your own vehicle is advantageous in the interior, where public transport is often slow and limited. Autostradas connect the major cities and are generally of good quality, especially the A18 and A20 toll roads, running along the Ionian and Tyrrhenian coasts, respectively. Even so, the island's highways have suffered some high-profile problems in recent years – most notably the landslide-induced collapse of a key section of the A19 between Catania and Palermo in 2015. Drive defensively; Sicilian drivers are some of Italy's most aggressive, with a penchant for overtaking on blind corners, while holding a mobile phone in one hand and gesticulating wildly with the other!

TRAIN

Sicily's train service is very efficient along the north and east coasts. Services to towns in the interior tend be infrequent and slow, but the routes can be very picturesque. InterCity trains are the fastest and most expensive, while the *regionale* is the slowest.

PALERMO

POP 657,000

Palermo is a city of both decay and splendour, and – provided you can handle its raw energy, deranged driving and chaos – has plenty of appeal. Unlike Florence or Rome, many of the city's treasures are hidden, rather than scrubbed up for endless streams of tourists.

At one time an Arab emirate and the seat of a Norman kingdom, Palermo became Europe's grandest city in the 12th century, then underwent a further round of aesthetic transformations during 500 years of Spanish rule. The resulting treasure trove of palaces, castles and churches has a unique architectural fusion of Byzantine, Arab, Norman, Renaissance and baroque gems.

While some of the crumbling *palazzi* (mansions) bombed in WWII are being restored, others remain dilapidated, turned into shabby apartments, the faded glory of their ornate facades just visible behind strings of brightly coloured washing. The evocative history of the city remains very much part of the daily life of its inhabitants, and the dusty web of backstreet markets in the old quarter has a Middle Eastern feel.

The flip side is the modern city, a mere 15-minute stroll away, parts of which could be neatly jigsawed and slotted into Paris, with a grid system of wide avenues lined by seductive shops and handsome 19th-century apartments.

◉ Sights & Activities

Via Maqueda is the main street, running north from the train station, changing names to Via Ruggero Settimo as it passes the landmark Teatro Massimo, then finally widening into leafy Viale della Libertà north of Piazza Castelnuovo, the beginning of the city's modern district.

Palermo

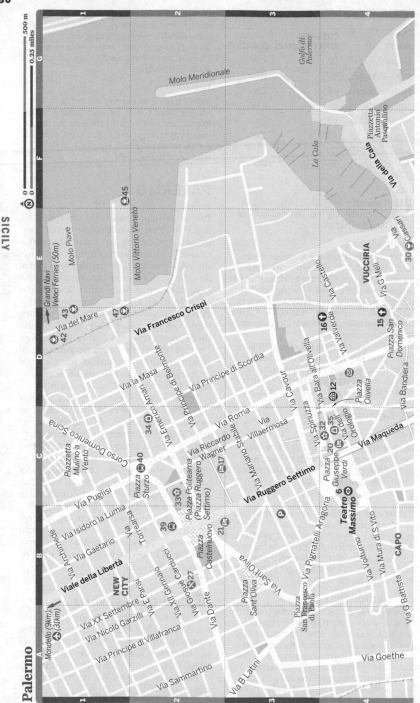

Map labels:

- 500 m
- 0.25 miles
- Mondello (9km)
- (31km)
- NEW CITY
- Viale della Libertà
- Via XX Settembre
- Via Nicolò Garzilli
- Via Principe di Villafranca
- Via Sammartino
- Via Dante
- Via B Latini
- Via Goethe
- Via E Parisi
- Via XII Gennaio
- Via Giosuè Carducci
- Via Archimede
- Via Isidoro la Lumia
- Via Gaetario
- Via Puglisi
- Piazzetta Mulino a Vento
- Corso Domenico Scinà
- Via Torrearsa
- Piazza Sturzo
- Piazza Castelnuovo
- Piazza Sant'Oliva
- Via Sant'Oliva
- Via San Francesco di Paola
- Via Pignatelli Aragona
- Piazza San Francesco di Paola
- Piazza Politeama (Piazza Ruggero Settimo)
- Via Ruggero Settimo
- Teatro Massimo
- CAPO
- Via Volturno
- Via Mura di S Vito
- Via G Battista
- Via Maqueda
- Piazza Giuseppe Verdi
- Via dell' Orologio
- Via Spinuzza
- Via Mariano Stabile
- Via Villaermosa
- Via Roma
- Via Emerico Amari
- Via Principe di Belmonte
- Via la Masa
- Via Principe di Scordia
- Via Riccardo Wagner
- Via Cavour
- Via Bara all'Olivella
- Piazza Olivella
- Via Valverde
- Via Castello
- Piazza San Domenico
- Via Bandiera
- Piazza Olivella
- VUCCIRIA
- Via G Meli
- Via G Cassari
- Via della Cala
- Piazzetta Antonio Pasqualino
- La Cala
- Golfo di Palermo
- Molo Meridionale
- Molo Vittorio Veneto
- Molo Piave
- Via del Mare
- Grandi Navi Veloci Ferries (50m)
- Via Francesco Crispi

Numbered locations: 6, 12, 15, 16, 17, 20, 21, 27, 30, 32, 33, 34, 35, 39, 40, 42, 43, 45, 47

SICILY

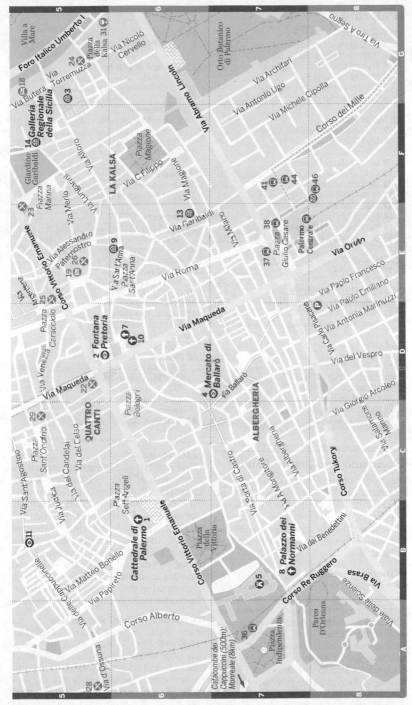

Villa a
Mare

Foro Italico Umberto I

Via Nicoló
Cervello

31 Piazza
della Kalsa

Via
24 Torremuzza

18 Via Butera

3

14 Galleria
Regionale
della Sicilia

Via Vittorio

Via Lungarini

Via Merlo

Giardino
Garibaldi

Piazza
Garibaldi

Piazza
Marina

23

Via Alessandro
Paternostro

26
19

Corso Vittorio Emanuele

Piazza
25 Caracciolo

A2

Via Venezia

Via Maqueda

22

29

Piazza
Sant'Onofrio

Via Sant'Agostino

Via dei Candelai

Via Judica

Via del Celso

QUATTRO
CANTI

Piazza
Bologni

11

Via delle Cappuccinelle

Via Matteo Bonello

Via Papireto

Piazza
Sett'Angeli

Cattedrale di
Palermo 1

Corso Vittorio Emanuele

Catacombe dei
Cappuccini (500m);
Monreale (8km)

28

Via d'Ossuna

Corso Alberto

LA KALSA

Piazza
Magione

Via C Filippo

Via Magione

13

Via Garibaldi

Via Sant'Anna

9

Via Sant'Anna

Via Roma

2 Fontana
Pretoria

7

10

Via Maqueda

4 Mercato di
Ballarò

Via Ballarò

ALBERGHERIA

Via Porta di Castro

Via A Mongitore

Via Albergheria

Piazza
della
Vittoria

5

8 Palazzo dei
Normanni

Via del Benedettini

36

Piazza
Indipendenza

Orto Botanico
di Palermo

Via Archifari

Via Antonlo Ugo

Via Michele Cipolla

Corso dei Mille

41

44

38

Piazza
Giulio Cesare

37

Palermo
Centrale

46

Via Oreto

Via Paolo Francesco

Via Paolo Emiliano

Via Carlo Pisacane

Via Antonia Marinuzzi

Via del Vespro

Via Giorgio Arcoleo

Via S Amore

Via Matteo

Corso Tukory

Corso Re Ruggero

Via Brasa

Viale delle Scienze

Parco
D'Orleans

Via a Tiro a Segno

Via Abramo Lincoln

Palermo

◉ Around the Quattro Canti

The busy intersection of Corso Vittorio Emanuele and Via Maqueda is known as the Quattro Canti. Forming the civic heart of Palermo, this crossroads neatly divides the historic nucleus into four traditional quarters – Albergheria, Capo, Vucciria and La Kalsa.

★ Fontana Pretoria   SQUARE
(Piazza Pretoria) This huge, ornate fountain, with tiered basins and sculptures rippling in concentric circles, forms the centrepiece of **Piazza Pretoria**, a spacious square just south of the Quattro Canti. The city bought the fountain in 1573; however, the flagrant nudity of the provocative nymphs proved too much for Sicilian churchgoers attending Mass next door, and they prudishly dubbed it the Fountain of Shame.

La Martorana   CHURCH
(Chiesa di Santa Maria dell'Ammiraglio; Piazza Bellini 3; adult/reduced €2/1; ⊙9.30am-1pm & 3.30-5.30pm Mon-Sat, 9-10.30am Sun) On the southern side of Piazza Bellini, this luminously beautiful 12th-century church was endowed by King Roger's Syrian emir, George of Antioch, and was originally planned as a mosque. Delicate Fatimid pillars support a domed cupola depicting Christ enthroned amid his archangels. The interior is best appreciated in the morning, when sunlight illuminates magnificent Byzantine mosaics.

Chiesa Capitolare di San Cataldo   CHURCH
(Piazza Bellini 3; adult/reduced €2.50/1.50; ⊙9.30am-12.30pm & 3-6pm) With its dusky-pink bijou domes, solid square shape, blind arcading and delicate tracery, this 12th-century church perfectly embodies the synthesis of Arab and Norman architectural

styles. The interior, while more austere, has a lovely inlaid floor and some fine stone- and brickwork.

⊙ Albergheria

Southwest of the Quattro Canti, Albergheria is a rather shabby, rundown district once inhabited by Norman court officials, now home to a growing number of immigrants who are attempting to revitalise its dusty backstreets. The top tourist draws here are the Palazzo dei Normanni (Norman Palace) and its exquisite chapel, both at the neighbourhood's far western edge.

★ Palazzo dei Normanni   PALACE

(Palazzo Reale; ☑ 091 626 28 33; www.federico secondo.org; Piazza Indipendenza 1; adult/reduced Fri-Mon €12/10, Tue-Thu €10/8, ⊙ 8.15am-5pm Mon-Sat, to 12.15pm Sun) This venerable palace dates to the 9th century but owes its current look (and name) to a major 12th-century Norman makeover, during which spectacular mosaics were added to its **Royal Apartments** and priceless jewel of a chapel, the **Cappella Palatina**. Designed by Roger II in 1130, the chapel glitters with stunning gold mosaics, its aesthetic harmony further enhanced by the inlaid marble floors and wooden *muqarnas* ceiling, a masterpiece of Arab-style honeycomb carving that reflects Norman Sicily's cultural complexity.

The chapel is Palermo's top tourist attraction. Note that queues are likely, and that you'll be refused entry if you're wearing shorts, a short skirt or a low cut top. The top level of the palace's three-tiered loggia houses Sicily's regional parliament and the Royal Apartments, including the mosaic-lined Sala dei Venti, and Sala di Ruggero II, King Roger's magnificent 12th century bedroom These latter attractions are only open to visitors from Friday to Monday.

Chiesa di San Giovanni degli Eremiti   CHURCH

(☑ 091 651 50 19; Via dei Benedettini 20; adult/reduced €6/3; ⊙ 9am-6.30pm Mon-Sat, to 1pm Sun) Surrounded by a garden of citrus trees, palms, cacti and ruined walls, this remarkable, five-domed remnant of Arab-Norman architecture is hidden away in an otherwise rather squalid neighbourhood. It's built atop a mosque that itself was superimposed on an earlier chapel. The peaceful Norman cloisters outside offer lovely views of the Palazzo dei Normanni.

★ Mercato di Ballarò   MARKET

(⊙ 7.30am-8pm Mon-Sat, to 1pm Sun) Snaking for several city blocks southeast of Palazzo dei Normanni is Palermo's busiest street market, which throbs with activity well into the early evening. It's a fascinating mix of noises, smells and street life, and the cheapest place for everything from Chinese padded bras to fresh produce, fish, meat, olives and cheese – smile nicely for a taste.

⊙ Capo

Northwest of Quattro Canti is the Capo neighbourhood, a densely packed web of interconnected streets and blind alleys.

★ Cattedrale di Palermo   CATHEDRAL

(☑ 091 33 43 73; www.cattedrale.palermo.it; Corso Vittorio Emanuele; cathedral free, tombs €1.50, treasury & crypt €2, roof €5, all-inclusive ticket adult/reduced €7/5; ⊙ cathedral 7am-7pm Mon-Sat, 8am-1pm & 4-7pm Sun, royal tombs, treasury & roof 9am-5.30pm Sat, tombs only 10am-1pm Sun) A feast of geometric patterns, ziggurat crenellations, maiolica cupolas and blind arches, Palermo's cathedral has suffered aesthetically from multiple reworkings over the centuries, but remains a prime example of Sicily's unique Arab-Norman architectural style. The interior, while impressive in scale, is essentially a marble shell whose most interesting features are the **royal Norman tombs** (to the left as you enter) and the **treasury**, home to Constance of Aragon's gem-encrusted 13th-century crown.

Mercato del Capo   MARKET

(Via Sant'Agostino; ⊙ 7am-8pm Mon, Tue, Thu-Sat, to 1pm Wed & Sun) Capo's street market, running the length of Via Sant'Agostino, is a seething mass of colourful activity during the day, with vendors selling fruit, vegetables, meat, fish, cheese and household goods of every description.

Catacombe dei Cappuccini   CATACOMB

(www.catacombepalermo.it; Piazza Cappuccini; adult €3, child under 8yr free; ⊙ 9am-1pm & 3-6pm, closed Sun afternoon Nov-Mar) These catacombs house the mummified bodies and skeletons of some 8000 Palermitans who died between the 17th and 19th centuries. Earthly power, gender, religion and professional status are still rigidly distinguished, with men and women occupying separate corridors, and virgins set aside in a first-class section. From Piazza Indipendenza, it's a 15-minute walk.

⊙ Vucciria

Once a notorious den of Mafia activity, the Vucciria retains a grungy, authentic edge. In the evenings it becomes a destination for bar-hopping and seriously down-to-earth street food. It's also home to some of Palermo's finest baroque artwork.

Museo Archeologico Regionale   MUSEUM
(☑ 091 611 68 07; www.regione.sicilia.it/bbccaa/ salinas; Piazza Olivella 24; ⊙ 9.30am-6.30pm Tue-Sat, to 1.30pm Sun) Situated in a converted Renaissance monastery, this splendid, wheelchair-accessible museum has been undergoing renovations since 2010, and has partially reopened, with attractive new exhibition spaces spread around its gracious courtyard. It houses some of Sicily's most valuable Greek and Roman artefacts, including the museum's crown jewel, a series of original decorative friezes from the temples at Selinunte.

Oratorio di Santa Cita   CHAPEL
(www.ilgeniodipalermo.com; Via Valverde; admission €4, incl Oratorio di San Domenico €6; ⊙ 9am-6pm Mon-Sat) This 17th-century chapel showcases the breathtaking stucco work of Giacomo Serpotta, who famously introduced rococo to Sicilian churches. Note the elaborate *Battle of Lepanto* on the entrance wall. Depicting the Christian victory over the Turks, it's framed by stucco drapes held by hundreds of naughty cherubs modelled on Palermo's street urchins. Serpotta's virtuosity also dominates the side walls, where sculpted white stucco figures hold gilded swords, shields and a lute, and a golden snake (Serpotta's symbol) curls around a picture frame.

Oratorio di San Domenico   CHAPEL
(www.ilgeniodipalermo.com; Via dei Bambinai 2; admission €4, incl Oratorio di Santa Cita €6; ⊙ 9am-6pm Mon-Sat) Dominating this small chapel is Anthony Van Dyck's fantastic blue-and-red altarpiece, *The Virgin of the Rosary with St Dominic and the Patronesses of Palermo*. Van Dyck completed the work in Genoa in 1628, after leaving Palermo in fear of the plague. Also gracing the chapel are Giacomo Serpotta's amazingly elaborate stuccoes (1710–17), vivacious and whirling with figures. Serpotta's name meant 'lizard' or 'small snake', and he often included these signature reptiles in his work; see if you can find one!

⊙ La Kalsa

Due to its proximity to the port, La Kalsa was subjected to carpet bombing during WWII, leaving it derelict and run down. Mother Teresa considered it akin to the shanty towns of Calcutta and established a mission here. Certain areas of La Kalsa, especially the part nearest the Quattro Canti, have undergone extensive renovation in recent years – for example, the former stock exchange has been converted into a high-end hotel. However, the neighbourhood still feels scruffy around the edges, with a decaying ambience that some will find intriguing, others off-putting.

★ Galleria Regionale della Sicilia   MUSEUM
(Palazzo Abatellis; ☑ 091 623 00 11; Via Alloro 4; adult/reduced €8/4; ⊙ 9am-6.30pm Tue-Fri, to 1pm Sat & Sun) Housed in the stately 15th-century Palazzo Abatellis, this fine museum features works by Sicilian artists from the Middle Ages to the 18th century. Its greatest treasure is *Triunfo della Morte* (Triumph of Death), a magnificent fresco in which Death is represented as a demonic skeleton mounted on a wasted horse, brandishing a wicked-looking scythe while leaping over his hapless victims.

Museo dell'Inquisizione   MUSEUM
(Palazzo Chiaramonte-Steri; ☑ 091 2389 3788; Piazza Marina 61; adult/reduced €8/3; ⊙ 10am-6pm Tue-Sun) Housed in the lower floors and basements of the 14th-century Palazzo Chiaramonte-Steri, this unique museum offers a chilling but fascinating look at the legacy of the Inquisition in Palermo. Thousands of 'heretics' were detained here between 1601 and 1782; the honeycomb of former cells has been painstakingly restored to reveal multiple layers of their graffiti and artwork (religious and otherwise). Excellent guided visits of the prison and the palace itself are available in English with advance notice.

Galleria d'Arte Moderna   MUSEUM
(☑ 091 843 16 05; www.gampalermo.it; Via Sant'Anna 21; adult/reduced €7/5; ⊙ 9.30am-6.30pm Tue-Sun) This wheelchair-accessible museum is housed in a sleekly renovated 15th-century *palazzo* and former convent. The wide-ranging collection of 19th- and 20th-century Sicilian art is beautifully displayed on three floors, along with regular modern-art exhibitions. There's an excellent bookshop and gift shop. English-language audio guides cost €4.

◉ New City

North of Piazza Giuseppe Verdi, Palermo elegantly slips into cosmopolitan mode. Here you'll find fabulous neoclassical and art nouveau buildings hailing from the last golden age of Sicilian architecture, along with late 19th-century mansion blocks lining the broad boulevard of Viale della Libertà.

★ **Teatro Massimo**   THEATRE
(⌨ tour reservations 091 605 32 67; www.teatro massimo.it; Piazza Giuseppe Verdi; guided tours adult/reduced €8/5; ◷ 9.30am-6pm) Palermo's grand neoclassical opera house (built 1875-97) took more than 20 years to complete and has become one of the city's iconic landmarks. The closing scene of *The Godfather: Part III*, with its visually stunning juxtaposition of high culture, crime, drama and death, was filmed here. Guided 25-minute tours are offered throughout the day in English, Spanish, French, German and Italian.

✵ Festivals & Events

Festino di Santa Rosalia   RELIGIOUS
(U Fistinu; www.festinodisantarosaliapalermo.it; ◷ 10-15 Jul) Palermo's biggest annual festival celebrates patron saint Santa Rosalia, beloved for having saved the city from a 17th-century plague. The most colourful festivities take place on the evening of 14 July, when the saint's relics are paraded aboard a grand chariot from the Palazzo dei Normanni through the Quattro Canti to the waterfront, where fireworks and general merriment ensue.

🛏 Sleeping

Budget options can be found around Via Maqueda and Via Roma in the vicinity of the train station. Midrange and top-end hotels are concentrated further north. Parking usually costs an extra €10 to €15 per day.

★ **Stanze al Genio Residenze**   B&B €
(⌨ 380 3673773; www.stanzealgeniobnb.it; Via Garibaldi 11; r €75-98; ✻ 🛜) Speckled with Sicilian antiques, this B&B offers four gorgeous bedrooms, three with 19th-century ceiling frescoes. All four are spacious and thoughtfully appointed, with Murano lamps, old wooden wardrobes, the odd balcony railing turned bedhead, and top-quality, orthopaedic beds. That the property features beautiful maiolica tiles is no coincidence; the B&B is affiliated with the wonderful **Museo delle**

Maioliche (Stanze al Genio; ⌨ 340 0971561; www.stanzealgenio.it; adult/reduced €7/5; ◷ by appointment), downstairs.

B&B Amélie   B&B €
(⌨ 328 8654824, 091 33 59 20; www.bb-amelie.it; Via Prinicipe di Belmonte 94; s €40-60, d €60-90, tr €90-100; ✻ @ 🛜) On a pedestrianised New City street a stone's throw from Teatro Politeama, the affable, multilingual Angela has converted her grandmother's spacious 6th-floor flat into a cheery B&B. Rooms are colourfully decorated, and the corner triple has a sunny terrace. Angela, a native Palermitan, generously shares her local knowledge and serves a tasty breakfast featuring homemade cakes and jams.

Palazzo Pantaleo   B&B €
(⌨ 091 32 54 71; www.palazzopantaleo.it; Via Ruggero Settimo 74h; s/d/ste €80/100/150; P 🛜) Offering unbeatable comfort and a convenient location, Giuseppe Scaccianoce's classy B&B occupies the top floor of an old *palazzo* half a block from Piazza Politeama, hidden from the busy street in a quiet courtyard with free parking. Five rooms and one spacious suite feature high ceilings, marble, tile or wooden floors, soundproof windows and modern bathrooms.

Butera 28   APARTMENT €€
(⌨ 333 3165432; www.butera28.it; Via Butera 28; apt per day €70-220, per week €450-1500; ✻ 🛜 👝) Delightful multilingual owner Nicoletta rents 12 comfortable apartments in the 18th-century Palazzo Lanzi Tomasi, the last home of Giuseppe Tomasi di Lampedusa, author of *The Leopard*. Units range from 30 to 180 sq metres, most sleeping a family of four or more. Four apartments face the sea; most have laundry facilities; and all have well-equipped kitchens.

Massimo Plaza Hotel   HOTEL €€
(⌨ 091 32 56 57; www.massimoplazahotel.com; Via Maqueda 437; r €100-250; P ✻ 🛜) Boasting a prime location along Palermo's pedestrianised Via Maqueda, this older hotel is a Palermo classic. Seven of the 15 rooms boast full-on views of the iconic Teatro Massimo across the street. The included breakfast (continental or American) can be delivered directly to your room at no extra charge, and enclosed parking costs €15 per day.

Grand Hotel Piazza Borsa   HOTEL €€€
(⌨ 091 32 00 75; www.piazzaborsa.com; Via dei Cartari 18; s/d/ste from €154/208/454; P ✻ @ 🛜)

Grandly situated in Palermo's former stock exchange, this four-star hotel encompasses three separate buildings housing 127 rooms. Nicest are the high-ceilinged suites with jacuzzis and windows facing Piazza San Francesco. Parking costs €18 per 24-hour period.

 Eating

Restaurants rarely start to fill up before 9pm. Many places close on Sundays, especially in the evening. For cheap eats, wander the tangle of alleys east and south of Teatro Massimo, or snack with locals at the street-food carts in Palermo's markets.

★**Trattoria al Vecchio Club Rosanero** SICILIAN €
(☑ 091 251 12 34; Vicolo Caldomai 18; meals €15; ☺ 1-3.30pm Mon-Sat & 8-11pm Thu-Sat; ☏) A veritable shrine to the city's football team (*rosa nero* refers to the team's colours, pink and black), cavernous Vecchio Club scores goals with its bargain-priced, flavour-packed grub. Fish and seafood are the real fortes here; if it's on the menu, order the *caponata e pesce spada* (sweet-and-sour vegetable salad with swordfish), a culinary victory. Head in early to avoid a wait.

★**Bisso Bistrot** BISTRO €
(☑ 091 33 49 99, 328 1314595; Via Maqueda 172; meals €14-18; ☺ 9am-11.30pm Mon-Sat) Frescoed walls, high ceilings and reasonably priced appetisers, *primi* and *secondi* greet diners at this historic Liberty-style bookstore at the northwest corner of the Quattro Canti, which has been converted into a classy but casual bistro. Lunch and dinner menus range from traditional Sicilian pasta, meat and fish dishes to sardine burgers, with cafe service in the mornings and afternoons.

DON'T MISS

PALERMO'S STREET FOOD

If you were taught that it is bad manners to eat in the street, you can break the rule in good company here. The mystery is how Palermo is not the obesity capital of Europe, given how much eating goes on. Palermitans are at it all the time: when they're shopping, commuting, discussing business, romancing...basically at any time of the day. What they're enjoying is the *buffitieri* – little hot snacks prepared at stalls and meant to be eaten on the spot.

Kick off the morning with *pane e panelle*, Palermo's famous chickpea fritter sandwich – great for vegetarians and a welcome change from a sweet custard-filled croissant. If you like, ask for it with a few *crocchè*, potato croquettes flavoured with fresh mint, also cheekily nicknamed *cazzilli* (little penises). Then again, you might want to go for some *sfincione* (a spongy, oily pizza topped with onions and *caciocavallo* cheese). In summer, locals also enjoy a freshly baked brioche filled with gelato or a *granita* (crushed ice mixed with fresh fruit, almonds, pistachios or coffee).

From 4pm onwards the snacks become decidedly more carnivorous, and you may wish you hadn't read the following translations: how about some barbecued *stigghiola* (goat intestines filled with onions, cheese and parsley), for example? Or a couple of *pani ca meusa* (bread rolls stuffed with sautéed beef spleen)? You'll be asked if you want your roll *schietta* (single) or *maritata* (married). If you choose *schietta*, the roll will only have ricotta in it before being dipped into boiling lard; choose *maritata* and you'll get the beef spleen as well.

You'll find street-food stalls all over town. Classic spots include Piazza Caracciolo in the Vucciria district, **Francu u Vastiddaru** (Corso Vittorio Emanuele 102; sandwiches €1.50-3.50; ☺ 8am-1am) and **Friggitoria Chiluzzo** (Piazza della Kalsa; sandwiches €1.50-2; ☺ 8am-5pm Mon-Sat) in the Kalsa, and the no-name *pane e panelle* cart on Piazza Carmine in Ballarò market.

For expert guidance, check out the low-key tours offered by **Palermo Street Food** (www.palermostreetfood.com; 3hr tours per person €30) and **Streaty** (www.streaty.com; 3/4hr tours per person €30/39). Both offer the chance to wander Palermo's backstreets with a knowledgable local guide, stopping for a taste (or two, or three) at the city's most authentic hang-outs.

Trattoria Ai Cascinari   SICILIAN €

(📞091 651 98 04; Via d'Ossuna 43/45; meals €20-25; ⊙12.30-2.30pm Tue-Sun, plus 8-10.30pm Wed-Sat) Yes, it's a bit out of the way, but this friendly neighbourhood trattoria, 1km north of the Cappella Palatina, is a long-standing Palermitan favourite, and deservedly so. It's especially enjoyable on Sunday afternoons, when locals pack the labyrinth of back rooms and waiters perambulate nonstop with plates of scrumptious seasonal antipasti, fresh seafood and desserts.

Pasticceria Cappello   PASTRIES €

(📞091 611 37 69; www.pasticceriacappello.it; Via Nicolo Garzilli 19; desserts from €1.70; ⊙7.30am-9.30pm Thu-Tue) One of Palermo's finest bakeries, Cappello is famous for its *setteveli* (seven-layer chocolate-hazelnut cake), invented here and long since copied all over Palermo. Its display case brims with countless other splendid pastries and desserts, including the dreamy *delizia di pistacchio* (a granular pistachio cake topped with creamy icing and a chocolate medallion) and ricotta-filled treats such as *cannoli* and *sfogliatelle*.

Il Maestro del Brodo   TRATTORIA €€

(📞091 32 95 23; Via Pannieri 7; meals €22-31; ⊙noon-3pm Tue-Sun, plus 7.30-11pm Fri & Sat) This trattoria in the Vucciria offers delicious soups, an array of ultrafresh seafood and a sensational antipasto buffet (€8) featuring a dozen-plus homemade delicacies: *sarde a beccafico* (stuffed sardines), eggplant *involtini* (roulades), smoked fish, artichokes with parsley, sun-dried tomatoes, olives and more.

Osteria Ballarò   SICILIAN €€

(📞091 32 64 88; www.osteriaballaro.it; Via Calascibetta 25; meals €30-45; ⊙noon-3.15pm & 7-11.15pm) This classy restaurant-cum-wine bar marries an atmospheric setting with fantastic island cooking. Bare stone columns, exposed brick walls and vaulted ceilings set the stage for delicious seafood *primi*, local wines and memorable Sicilian *dolci* (sweets). Reservations recommended. For a faster eat, you can snack on street food at the bar or take away from the hole-in-the-wall counter outside.

🍷 Drinking & Nightlife

Palermo's liveliest clusters of bars can be found along Via Chiavettieri in the Vucciria neighbourhood (just northwest of Piazza Marina) and in the Champagneria district east of Teatro Massimo, centred on Piazza Olivella, Via Spinuzza and Via Patania. Higher-end bars and dance venues are concentrated in the newer part of Palermo. In summer, many Palermitans decamp to Mondello by the sea.

Bocum Mixology   COCKTAIL BAR

(📞091 33 20 09; www.bocum.it; Via dei Cassari 6; ⊙6pm-1.30am Tue-Sun) All hail Bocum, Palermo's first proper cocktail bar. While the ground-floor cantina is a fine spot for cognoscenti wines and DOP (Denominazzione di Origine Protetta; Protected Designation of Origin) *salumi* (charcuterie), the real magic happens upstairs. Here, on your right, lies the mixology lounge, where skilled hands shake and stir seamless, nuanced libations. Add flickering candlelight and crackling jazz, and you have yourself one rather bohemian Palermo evening.

Kursaal Kalhesa   BAR

(📞340 1573493; www.facebook.com/kursaalkalhesa; Foro Umberto I 21; ⊙8pm-12.30am Tue & Wed, to 2am Thu, to 3am Fri-Sun) Restyled Kursaal Kalhesa has long been a noted city nightspot. Touting itself as a restaurant, wine bar and jazz club, it draws a cool, in-the-know crowd who come to hang out over *aperitivi*, dine alfresco or catch a gig under the high vaulted ceilings. It's in a 15th-century *palazzo* on the city's massive sea walls.

☆ Entertainment

The daily paper *Il Giornale di Sicilia* (http://gds.it/articoli/cultura) has a listing of what's on. If you can read some Italian, www.balarm.it is another excellent resource.

★Teatro Massimo   OPERA

(📞box office 091 605 35 80; www.teatromassimo.it; Piazza Giuseppe Verdi) Ernesto Basile's six-tiered art nouveau masterpiece, with lions flanking its grandiose columned entrance and an interior gleaming in red and gold, is Europe's third-largest opera house and one of Italy's most prestigious, right up there with La Scala in Milan, San Carlo in Naples and La Fenice in Venice. The theatre stages opera, ballet and music concerts from September to June.

Teatro dei Pupi di Mimmo Cuticchio   THEATRE

(📞091 32 34 00; www.figlidartecuticchio.com; Via Bara all'Olivella 95; adult/reduced €10/5) This puppet theatre is a charming low-tech choice for children (and adults), staging

SICILIAN PUPPET THEATRE

Since the 18th century, the Opera dei Pupi (traditional Sicilian puppet theatre) has been enthralling adults and children alike. The shows are a mini theatrical performance, with some puppets standing 1.5m high – a completely different breed from the popular glove puppet. These characters are intricately carved from beech, olive or lemon wood and have realistic-looking features; flexible joints ensure they have no problem swinging their swords or beheading dragons.

Effectively the soap operas of their day, Sicilian puppet shows expounded the deepest sentiments of life – unrequited love, treachery, thirst for justice, and the anger and frustration of the oppressed. The swashbuckling tales centre on the legends of Charlemagne's heroic knights, Orlando and Rinaldo, with an extended cast including the fair Angelica, the treacherous Gano di Magonza and forbidding Saracen warriors. Puppeteers are judged on the dramatic effect they can create – lots of stamping feet and a gripping running commentary – and on their speed and skill in directing the battle scenes.

traditional shows with fabulous handcrafted puppets.

Teatro Politeama Garibaldi
PERFORMING ARTS

(☏ 091 607 25 11; Piazza Ruggero Settimo) This grandiose theatre is a popular venue for opera, ballet and classical music, staging afternoon and evening concerts. It's home to Palermo's symphony orchestra, the Orchestra Sinfonica Siciliana.

Shopping

Via Bara all'Olivella is good for arts and crafts.

Il Laboratorio Teatrale
ARTS & CRAFTS

(☏ 091 32 34 00; Via Bara all'Olivella 40; ⊙10am-1pm & 4-7pm Tue-Sat) A true artists' workshop, this enchanting space is where the Cuticchio family constructs puppets for its famous theatre across the street. High-quality puppets dating from the late 19th century to the present are displayed here, and are available for purchase by serious enthusiasts.

Gusti di Sicilia
FOOD & DRINKS

(www.gustidisicilia.com; Via Emerico Amari 79; ⊙8.30am-11pm) Stock up on beautifully packaged Sicilian edibles, from tins of tuna to jars of *caponata* (sweet-and-sour vegetable salad), capers and marmalade, and bottles of wine and olive oil.

ℹ Information

EMERGENCY
For an ambulance, call ☏118 or ☏091 666 55 28. **Police** (Questura; ☏ 091 21 01 11; Piazza della Vittoria 8) Main police station.

MEDICAL SERVICES
Hospital (Ospedale Civico; ☏ 091 666 11 11; www.arnascivico.it; Piazza Nicola Leotta; ⊙24hr) Emergency facilities.

TOURIST INFORMATION
Municipal Tourist Office (☏ 091 740 80 21; http://turismo.comune.palermo.it; Piazza Bellini; ⊙8.30am-6.30pm Mon-Fri, from 9.30am Sat) The most reliable of Palermo's city-run information booths. Others, located at Piazza Castelnuovo, Teatro Massimo, the Port of Palermo and Mondello, keep shorter hours.

Tourist Information – Falcone-Borsellino Airport (☏ 091 59 16 98; www.gesap.it/tourist-information-office; ⊙8.30am-7.30pm Mon-Fri, to 6pm Sat) Downstairs in the Arrivals hall.

ℹ Getting There & Away

AIR
Falcone-Borsellino Airport (☏ 800 541880, 091 702 02 73; www.gesap.it) is at Punta Raisi, 31km west of Palermo.

Alitalia and other major airlines such as Air France, Lufthansa and KLM fly from Palermo to destinations throughout Europe. Several cut-rate carriers also offer flights to/from Palermo, including Ryanair, Volotea, Vueling and easyJet. Falcone-Borsellino is the hub airport for regular domestic flights to the islands of Pantelleria and Lampedusa.

BOAT
The ferry terminal is located just east of the corner of Via Francesco Crispi and Via Emerico Amari.

Grandi Navi Veloci (☏ 010 209 45 91, 091 6072 6162; www.gnv.it; Calata Marinai d'Italia) Runs ferries to Civitavecchia (from €59, 14 hours), Genoa (from €100, 19½ hours), Naples (from €48, 10 hours) and Tunis (from €49, 9½ hours).

Grimaldi Lines (☑ 091 611 36 91, 081 49 64 44; www.grimaldi-lines.com; Via del Mare) Runs ferries twice weekly to Salerno (from €40, 9½ hours) and Tunis (from €56, 11 hours), and thrice weekly to Livorno (from €65, 18 hours).

Liberty Lines (☑ 0923 87 38 13; www.liberty lines.it; Molo Vittorio Veneto) From late June to early September, Liberty operates one daily hydrofoil to Lipari (€57.30, four hours), Stromboli (€75.10, 5½ hours) and other points in the Aeolian Islands.

Tirrenia (☑ 892123; www.tirrenia.it; Calata Marinai d'Italia) Ferries to Cagliari (from €50, 12 hours, once or twice weekly) and Naples (from €45, 10¼ hours, daily).

BUS

Offices for all bus companies are located within a block or two of Palermo Centrale train station. The two main departure points are the **Piazzetta Cairoli bus terminal** (Piazzetta Cairoli, just south of the train station's eastern entrance, and **Via Paolo Balsamo**, due east of the train station.

AST (Azienda Siciliana Trasporti; ☑ 091 680 00 11; www.aziendasicilianatrasporti.it; New Bus Bar, Via Paolo Balsamo 32) Services to southeastern destinations including Ragusa (€13.50, four hours, four daily Monday to Saturday, two on Sunday).

Autoservizi Tarantola (☑ 0924 310 20; www.tarantolabus.it; New Bus Bar, Via Paolo Balsamo 32) Buses to Segesta (one way/return €8/12.70, 80 minutes) run once daily, with two buses returning daily to Palermo.

Cuffaro (☑ 091 616 15 10; www.cuffaro.info; Via Paolo Balsamo 13) Services to Agrigento (€9, two hours, three to seven daily).

SAIS Autolinee (☑ 800 211020, 091 616 60 28; www.saisautolinee.it; Piazzetta Cairoli bus station) To/from Catania (€13.50, 2¾ hours, nine to 13 daily) and Messina (€14, 2¾ hours, four to six daily).

SAIS Trasporti (☑ 091 617 11 41; www.saistrasporti.it; Via Paolo Balsamo 20) Thrice-weekly overnight service to Rome (€34, 12 hours).

Salemi (☑ 091 772 03 47; www.autoservizi salemi.it; Piazzetta Cairoli bus station) Several buses daily to Marsala (€11, 2½ hours) and Trapani's Birgi Airport (€11, 1¾ hours).

CAR & MOTORCYCLE

Palermo is accessible on the A20-E90 toll road from Messina and the A19-E932 from Catania via Enna. Trapani and Marsala are also easily accessible from Palermo by motorway (A29), while Agrigento and Palermo are linked by the SS121 and SS189, good state roads through the island's interior.

Most major auto-hire companies are represented at the airport; you'll often save money by booking online before leaving home. Given the city's chaotic traffic and expensive parking, and the excellent public transport from Palermo's airport, it's generally best to postpone rental car pick-up until you're ready to leave the city.

TRAIN

From Palermo Centrale station, just south of the centre at the foot of Via Roma, regular trains leave for the following destinations:

Agrigento €9, 2¼ hours, eight to 10 daily

Catania €13.50, 2¾ hours, three to six daily

Cefalù €5.60, 45 minutes to one hour, hourly

Messina from €12.80, 2¾ to 3½ hours, hourly

From Messina, InterCity trains continue to Reggio di Calabria, Naples and Rome.

ⓘ Getting Around

TO/FROM THE AIRPORT

Prestia e Comandè (☑ 091 58 63 51; www.prestiaecomande.it; one way/return €6.30/11) runs a half-hourly bus service from the airport to the centre of town, making stops outside Teatro Politeama Garibaldi (35 minutes) and Palermo Centrale train station (50 minutes). Buses are parked to the right as you exit the airport Arrivals hall. Buy tickets at the kiosk adjacent to the bus stop. Return journeys to the airport run with similar frequency, picking up at the same points.

Service on Trenitalia's Trinacria Express train, which normally runs half-hourly between Palermo Centrale and the airport (Punta Raisi station) was indefinitely suspended as of 2017 due to construction. Check www.trenitalia.com for current status.

A taxi from the airport to downtown Palermo costs €40 to €45.

BUS

Palermo's orange, white and blue city buses, operated by **AMAT** (☑ 848 800817, 091 35 01 11; www.amat.pa.it), are frequent but often crowded and slow. The free map handed out at Palermo tourist offices details all the major bus lines; most stop at the train station. Tickets, valid for 90 minutes, cost €1.40 if pre-purchased from *tabaccherie* (tobacconists) or AMAT booths, or €1.80 if purchased on board the bus. A day pass costs €3.50.

Especially useful for visitors is AMAT's Navetta Centro Storico, a free orange shuttle bus that makes a circular loop connecting Palermo's main downtown landmarks, including the train station, the Palazzo dei Normanni, the cathedral and Teatro Massimo.

CAR & MOTORCYCLE

Driving is frenetic in the city and best avoided, if possible. Use one of the staffed car parks around town (from €12 to €20 per day) if your hotel lacks parking.

WORTH A TRIP

AROUND PALERMO

A few kilometres outside Palermo's city limits, the beach town of Mondello and the dazzling cathedral of Monreale are both worthwhile day trips. Just offshore, Ustica makes a great overnight or weekend getaway.

Monreale

In the hills 8km southwest of Palermo, **Cattedrale di Monreale** (☎ 091 640 44 03; Piazza del Duomo; admission to cathedral free, north transept, Roano chapel & terrace €4, cloisters adult/reduced €6/3; ⊙ cathedral 8.30am-12.45pm & 2.30-5pm Mon-Sat, 8-10am & 2.30-5pm Sun, cloisters 9am-6.30pm Mon-Sat, to 1pm Sun) is considered the finest example of Norman architecture in Sicily, incorporating Norman, Arab, Byzantine and classical elements. Inspired by a vision of the Virgin, it was built by William II in an effort to outdo his grandfather, Roger II, who was responsible for the cathedral in Cefalù and the Cappella Palatina in Palermo. The interior, completed in 1184 and executed in shimmering mosaics, depicts 42 Old Testament stories. Outside the cathedral, the **cloister** is a tranquil courtyard with a tangible oriental feel. Surrounding the perimeter, elegant Romanesque arches are supported by an exquisite array of slender columns alternately decorated with mosaics. To reach Monreale, take AMAT bus 389 (€1.40, 35 minutes, every 1¼ hours) from Piazza Indipendenza in Palermo or AST's Monreale bus (one way/return €1.90/3, 40 minutes, hourly Monday to Saturday) from in front of Palermo Centrale train station.

Mondello

Tucked between dramatic headlands 12km north of Palermo, Mondello is home to a long, sandy beach that became fashionable in the 19th century, when people came to the seaside in their carriages, prompting the construction of the huge art nouveau pier that still graces the waterfront. Most of the beaches near the pier are private (two sun loungers and an umbrella cost from €10 to €20); however, there's a wide swath of public beach opposite the centre of town with all the requisite pedalos and jet skis for hire. Given its easygoing seaside feel, Mondello is an excellent base for families. To get here, take bus 806 (€1.40, 30 minutes) from Piazza Sturzo in Palermo.

Ustica

A 90-minute boat trip from downtown, the 8.7-sq-km island of Ustica was declared Italy's first marine reserve in 1986. The surrounding waters are a playground of fish and coral, ideal for snorkelling, diving and underwater photography. To enjoy Ustica's wild coastline and dazzling grottoes without the crowds, try visiting in June or September. There are numerous dive centres, hotels and restaurants on the island, as well as some nice hiking. To get here from Palermo, take the once-daily car ferry (€18.85, three hours) operated by **Siremar** (☎ 090 36 46 01; www.siremar.it) or the faster, more frequent hydrofoils (€27.60, 1½ hours) operated by Liberty Lines (p795). For more details on Ustica, see Lonely Planet's *Sicily* guide.

TYRRHENIAN COAST

The coast between Palermo and Milazzo is studded with popular tourist resorts attracting a steady stream of holidaymakers, particularly between June and September. The best of these is Cefalù, a resort second only to the Ionian coast's Taormina in popularity. Just inland lie the two massive natural parks of the Madonie and Nebrodi mountains.

Cefalù

POP 14,300

This popular holiday resort wedged between a dramatic mountain peak and a sweeping stretch of sand has the lot: a great beach, a truly lovely historic centre with a grandiose cathedral, and winding medieval streets lined with restaurants and boutiques. Avoid the height of summer when prices soar, beaches are jam packed and the charm of the place is tainted by bad-tempered drivers trying to find a car park.

◎ Sights

★ Duomo di Cefalù
CATHEDRAL

(☑ 092 192 20 21; www.cattedraledicefalu.com; Piazza del Duomo; cloisters adult/reduced €3/2; ⊙ duomo 8.30am-6.30pm Apr-Oct, 8.30am-1pm & 3.30-5pm Nov-Mar, cloisters 10am-1pm & 3-6pm daily Apr-Oct, 10am-1pm Mon-Fri & by arrangement Sat Nov-Mar) Cefalù's cathedral is one of the jewels in Sicily's Arab-Norman crown, equalled in magnificence only by the Cattedrale di Monreale (southwest of Palermo) and Palermo's Cappella Palatina. Filling the central apse, a towering figure of Christ All Powerful is the focal point of the elaborate Byzantine mosaics – Sicily's oldest and best preserved, pre-dating those of Monreale by 20 or 30 years.

★ La Rocca
VIEWPOINT

(adult/reduced €4/2, ⊙ 8am-7pm May-Sep, 9am-4pm Oct-Apr) Looming over the town, this imposing rocky crag is the site where the Arabs built their citadel, occupying it until the Norman conquest in 1061 forced them down to the port below. To reach the summit, follow signs for Tempio di Diana from the corner of Corso Ruggero and Vicolo Saraceni. The 30- to 45-minute route climbs the **Salita Saraceno**, a winding staircase, through three tiers of city walls before emerging onto rock-strewn upland slopes with spectacular coastal views.

✤ Activities

Cefalù's crescent-shaped **beach**, just west of the medieval centre, is lovely, but in the summer get here early to find a patch for your umbrella and towel.

You can escape with a boat tour along the coast during the summer months, through agencies along Corso Ruggero, including **Visit Sicily Tours** (☑ 0921 92 50 36; www.visitsicilytours.com; Corso Ruggero 83; boat tours €30-80; ⊙ Apr-Oct), right next door to the tourist office.

⌂ Sleeping

Bookings are essential in summer.

Dolce Vita
B&B €

(☑ 0921 92 31 51; www.dolcevitabb.it; Via Bordonaro 8; s €35-60, d €50-110) This popular B&B has one of the loveliest terraces in town, complete with deckchairs overlooking the sea and a barbecue for those warm balmy evenings. Rooms are airy and light, with comfy beds, though the staff's lackadaisical attitude can detract from the charm.

Scirocco Bed & Breakfast
B&B €

(☑ 0392 644 41 31; www.sciroccobeb.com; Piazza Garibaldi 8; s €50-70, d €70-110; ☀ �☎) Convenient location and spectacular views are the two big selling points at this B&B halfway between the train station and the cathedral. Four comfortable and bright upper-floor guest rooms are crowned by a rooftop terrace that's perfect for watching the sun set over the Tyrrhenian Sea, or for monitoring cafe life on Piazza Garibaldi, directly below.

Hotel Kalura
HOTEL €€

(☑ 0921 42 13 54; www.hotelkalura.com; Via Vincenzo Cavallaro 13; s €100-134, d €157-200, 4-person apt €215-259; P ☀ @ ☎ ♣) East of town on a rocky outcrop, this German-run, family-oriented hotel has its own pebbly beach, a restaurant and a fabulous pool. Most rooms have sea views, and the hotel staff can arrange loads of activities, including mountain biking, hiking, canoeing, pedalos, diving and dance nights. It's a 20-minute walk into town.

✕ Eating & Drinking

Ti Vitti
SICILIAN €€

(☑ 0921 92 15 71; www.ristorantetivitti.com; Via Umberto I 34; meals €35-45; ⊙ noon-3pm & 6.30-11pm Wed-Mon) Named after a Sicilian card game, this restaurant serves up fresh-from-the-market fish dishes, locally sourced treats such as *basilisco* mushrooms from nearby Monte Madonie, and scrumptious *cannoli* (pastry shells filled with ricotta or custard) for dessert. For something more casual, head to its affiliated pizzeria, **Bottega Ti Vitti** (☑ 0921 92 26 42; www.bottegativitti.com; Lungomare Giardina 7; pizza, salads & burgers €5-12; ⊙ 10am-midnight, closed Tue Nov-Apr), whose waterfront setting is perfect for sunset *aperitivi* (pre-dinner drinks).

La Galleria
SICILIAN, CAFE €€

(☑ 0921 42 02 11; www.lagalleriacefalu.it; Via Mandralisca 23; meals €30-40; ⊙ noon-3pm & 7-11pm Wed-Mon) This is about as hip as Cefalù gets. Functioning as a restaurant, cafe and occasional gallery space, La Galleria has an informal vibe, a bright internal courtyard and an innovative menu that mixes standard *primi* and *secondi* with a range of all-in-one dishes (€14 to €16) designed to be meals in themselves.

WORTH A TRIP

THE MADONIE MOUNTAINS: CEFALÙ'S BACKYARD GETAWAY

Due south of Cefalù, the 400sq-km **Parco Naturale Regionale delle Madonie** incorporates some of Sicily's highest peaks, including the imposing Pizzo Carbonara (1979m). The park's wild, wooded slopes are home to wolves, wildcats, eagles and the near-extinct ancient Nebrodi fir trees that have survived since the last ice age. Ideal for hiking, cycling and horse trekking, the park is also home to several handsome mountain towns, including **Castelbuono**, **Petralia Soprana** and **Petralia Sottana**.

The region's distinctive rural cuisine includes roasted lamb and goat, cheeses, grilled mushrooms, and aromatic pasta with *sugo* (meat sauce). A great place to sample these specialties is **Nangalarruni** (☑ 0921 67 12 28; www.hostariananagalarruni.it; Via delle Confraternite 7; fixed menus €28-35; ◷ 12.30-3pm & 7-10pm, closed Wed Nov-Mar) in Castelbuono.

For information, contact the **park headquarters** (☑ 0921 68 40 11; www.parcodellemadonie.it; Corso Paolo Agliata 16) in Petralia Sottana or the **branch office** (☑ 0921 92 33 27; www.parcodellemadonie.it; Corso Ruggero 116; ◷ 8am-6pm Mon-Sat) in Cefalù.

Bus service to the park's main towns is limited; to fully appreciate the Madonie, you're better off hiring a car for a couple of days.

Locanda del Marinaio   SEAFOOD €€
(☑ 0921 42 32 95; Via Porpora 5; meals €30-40; ◷ noon-2.30pm & 7-11pm Wed-Mon) Fresh seafood rules the chalkboard menu at this eatery along the old town's main waterfront thoroughfare. Depending on the season, you'll find dishes such as red tuna carpaccio with toasted pine nuts, shrimp and zucchini on a bed of velvety ricotta, or grilled octopus served with thyme-scented potatoes, all accompanied by an excellent list of Sicilian wines.

❶ Information

Hospital (☑ 0921 92 01 11; www.fondazionesanraffaelegiglio.it; Contrada Pietrapollastra; ◷ 24hr) On the main road out of town in the direction of Palermo.

Tourist Office (☑ 0921 42 10 50; strcefalu@regione.sicilia.it; Corso Ruggero 77; ◷ 9am-7.30pm Mon-Fri, 8am-2pm Sat) English-speaking staff, lots of leaflets and good maps.

❶ Getting There & Away

The best way to get to and from Cefalù is by rail. Hourly trains go to Palermo (€5.60, 50 minutes) and virtually every other town on the coast.

AEOLIAN ISLANDS

The Aeolian Islands are a little piece of paradise. Stunning cobalt sea, splendid beaches, some of Italy's best hiking and an awe-inspiring volcanic landscape are just part of the appeal. The islands also have a fascinating human and mythological history that

goes back several millennia: the Aeolians figured prominently in Homer's *Odyssey*, and evidence of the distant past can be seen everywhere, most notably in Lipari's excellent archaeological museum.

The seven islands of Lipari, Vulcano, Salina, Panarea, Stromboli, Alicudi and Filicudi are part of a huge 200km volcanic ridge that runs between the smoking stack of Mt Etna and the threatening mass of Vesuvius above Naples. Collectively, the islands exhibit a unique range of volcanic characteristics, which earned them a place on Unesco's World Heritage List in 2000. The islands are mobbed with visitors in July and August, but out of season things remain delightfully tranquil.

❶ Getting There & Away

Liberty Lines (☑ 0923 87 38 13; www.libertylines.it) runs hydrofoils year-round from Milazzo, the mainland city closest to the islands. Almost all boats stop first at Vulcano and Lipari, then continue to the ports of Santa Marina and Rinella on Salina island. Beyond Salina, boats either branch off east to Panarea and Stromboli, or west to Filicudi and Alicudi. Liberty Lines also operates limited year-round service to Lipari from Messina and summertime service from Reggio Calabria.

Frequency of service on all routes increases in the summer. Note that hydrofoils are sometimes cancelled due to heavy seas.

Both **Siremar** (☑ 090 36 46 01; www.siremar.it) and **NGI Traghetti** (☑ 090 928 40 91; www.ngi-spa.it) run year-round car ferries from Milazzo to the islands; these are slightly cheaper but slower and less regular than the hydrofoils. Siremar also runs twice-weekly overnight ferries from Naples to the Aeolians, docking first at Stromboli before continuing to the other islands.

Additional seasonal services include Liberty Lines hydrofoils from Palermo (once daily late June to early September) and **SNAV** (☑ 081 428 55 55; www.snav.it) hydrofoils from Naples (daily July to early September, plus weekends in June).

❶ Getting Around

BOAT
Liberty Lines operates year-round, inter-island hydrofoil services, while Siremar offers inter-island ferries. Ticket offices with posted timetables can be found close to the docks on all islands.

CAR & SCOOTER
You can take your car to Lipari, Vulcano or Salina by ferry, or garage it at Milazzo or Messina on the mainland from €12 per day. The islands are small, with narrow, winding roads. You'll often save money (and headaches) by hiring a scooter on-site, or better yet, exploring the islands on foot.

Lipari

POP 11,200 / ELEV 602M

Lipari is the Aeolians' thriving hub, both geographically and functionally, with regular ferry and hydrofoil connections to all other islands. Lipari town, the largest urban centre in the archipelago, is home to the islands' only tourist office and most dependable banking services, and has enough restaurants, bars and year-round residents to offer a bit of cosmopolitan buzz. Meanwhile, the island's rugged shoreline offers excellent opportunities for hiking, boating and swimming.

As evidenced by its fine archaeological museum and the multilayered ruins strewn about town, Lipari has been inhabited for some 6000 years. The island was settled in the 4th millennium BC by Sicily's first

known inhabitants, the Stentinellians, who developed a flourishing economy based on obsidian, a glassy volcanic rock. Commerce subsequently attracted the Greeks, who used the islands as ports on the east–west trade route, and pirates such as Barbarossa (or Redbeard), who sacked the city in 1544.

Lipari's two harbours, Marina Lunga (where ferries and hydrofoils dock) and Marina Corta (700m south, used by smaller boats) are linked by a bustling main street, Corso Vittorio Emanuele, which is flanked by shops, restaurants and bars. Overlooking the colourful snake of day-trippers is Lipari's clifftop citadel, surrounded by 16th-century walls.

◉ Sights & Activities

★ Museo Archeologico
Regionale Eoliano   MUSEUM
(☑ 090 988 01 74, www.regionesicilia.it/benicul turali/museoeolipari; Via Castello 2; adult/reduced €6/3; ⊙ 9am-6.30pm Mon-Sat, to 1pm Sun) A must-see for Mediterranean history buffs, Lipari's archaeological museum boasts one of Europe's finest collections of ancient finds. Especially worthwhile are the Sezione Preistorica, devoted to locally discovered artefacts from the neolithic and Bronze Age periods to the Graeco-Roman era, and the Sezione Classica, whose highlights include ancient shipwreck cargoes and the world's largest collection of miniature Greek theatrical masks.

★ Quattrocchi   VIEWPOINT
Lipari's best coastal views are from a celebrated viewpoint known as Quattrocchi (Four Eyes), 3km west of town. Follow the road for Pianoconte and look to your left. Stretching off to the south, great grey cliffs plunge into the sea, while in the distance plumes of sinister smoke rise from neighbouring Vulcano.

HYDROFOILS TO THE AEOLIAN ISLANDS

FROM	TO	COST (€)	DURATION	FREQUENCY
Messina	Lipari	27.80	1½-2¾hr	4 daily in summer, 1 daily in winter
Milazzo	Alicudi	34.20	3hr	2-3 daily
Milazzo	Filicudi	28.75	2½hr	2-3 daily
Milazzo	Lipari	22.30	1hr	13-17 daily
Milazzo	Panarea	24.30	1½-2½hr	3-7 daily
Milazzo	Salina	22.05	1½hr	12 daily
Milazzo	Stromboli	27.45	1¼-3hr	3-7 daily
Milazzo	Vulcano	21.50	45min	12-16 daily

Lipari Town

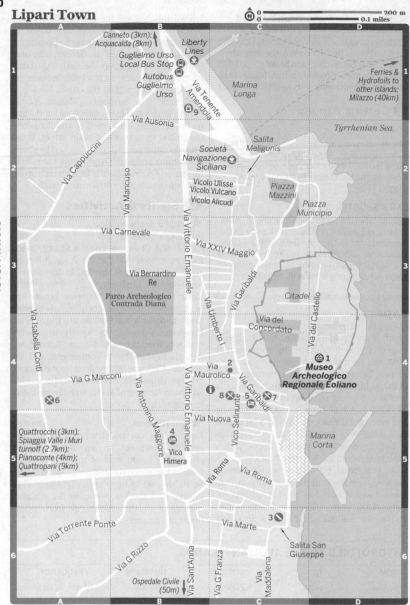

★ **Spiaggia Valle i Muria**   BEACH
Lapped by clean waters and surrounded by sheer cliffs, this dark, pebbly beach on Lipari's southwestern shore is a dramatically beautiful swimming and sunbathing spot. From the signposted turn-off, 3km west of Lipari town towards Pianoconte, it's a steep 15-minute downhill walk; come prepared with water and sunscreen. In good weather, Lipari resident **Barni** (☏ 349 1839555, 339 8221583) sells refreshments from his rustic cave-like beach bar, and provides scenic boat transfers to and from Lipari's Marina Corta (€5/10 one way/return).

Lipari Town

Diving Center La Gorgonia   DIVING
(☎090 981 26 16; www.lagorgoniadiving.it; Salita San Giuseppe; per dive with own/rented equipment €35/55, courses €70-750) This outfit offers courses, boat transport, equipment hire and general information about scuba diving and snorkelling around Lipari. See the website for a complete price list.

☞ Tours

Numerous agencies in town, including the dependable **Da Massimo/Dolce Vita** (☎090 981 30 86; www.damassimo.it; Via Maurolico 2), offer boat tours to the surrounding islands. Prices are around €25 for a circuit around Vulcano; €30 for a tour of Salina; €40 to visit Filicudi and Alicudi; €40 for a day trip to Panarea and Stromboli; and €75 to €80 for a late-afternoon trip to Stromboli, including a guided hike up the mountain at sunset and a late-night return to Lipari.

🛏 Sleeping

Lipari is the Aeolians' best-equipped base for island-hopping, with plenty of places to stay, eat and drink. Note that prices soar in summer; avoid August if possible.

★**Diana Brown**   B&B €
(☎090 981 25 84, 338 6407572; www.dianabrown.it; Vico Himera 3; s €35-65, d €50-80, tr €65-105; ❄🛜) Tucked down a narrow alley, South African Diana's delightful rooms sport tile floors, abundant hot water and welcome extras such as kettles, fridges, clothes-drying racks and satellite TV. Units downstairs are

darker but have built-in kitchenettes. There's a sunny breakfast terrace and a solarium with deckchairs, plus a book exchange and laundry service. Optional breakfast costs €5 extra per person.

Enzo Il Negro   GUESTHOUSE €
(☎090 981 31 63; www.enzoilnegro.com; Via Garibaldi 29; s €40-50, d €60-90; ❄🛜) Family-run for decades, this down-to-earth guesthouse near picturesque Marina Corta offers spacious, tiled, pine-furnished rooms with fridges. Two panoramic terraces overlook the rooftops, the harbour and the castle walls.

★**B&B Al Salvatore di Lipari**   B&B €€
(☎335 8343222; www.facebook.com/BBAlSalvatore; Via San Salvatore, Contrada al Salvatore; d €80-100; ◔Apr-Oct; 🛜) It's a trek to reach this hillside oasis 2km south of town, but once here, you'll never want to leave. Artist Paola and physicist Marcello have transformed their Aeolian villa into a green B&B that works at all levels, from dependable wi-fi to a panoramic terrace where guests enjoy one of Sicily's best breakfasts, featuring home-marinated tuna, omelettes and housemade marmalade.

Pre-arrange pick-up at the hydrofoil dock or take the 'Linea Bianca' bus from Marina Lunga to Capistello (€1.30, 10 minutes) and walk 200m steeply uphill.

✕ Eating & Drinking

Fish abound in the waters of the archipelago and include tuna, mullet, cuttlefish and sole, all of which end up on local menus. Try *pasta all'eoliana,* a simple blend of the island's excellent capers with olives, olive oil, anchovies, tomatoes and basil.

Bars are concentrated along Corso Vittorio Emanuele and down by Marina Corta.

Gilberto e Vera   SANDWICHES €
(☎090 981 27 56; www.gilbertoevera.it; Via Garibaldi 22; half/full sandwich €3.50/5; ◔8am-2.30pm & 4pm-midnight mid-Mar–mid-Nov) This straightforward shop sells two dozen varieties of sandwiches, served with a smile. Sicilian ingredients such as capers, olives, eggplant and tuna all make frequent appearances. Long hours make this the perfect spot to purchase early-morning hiking or beach-hopping provisions, or to sip a mid-afternoon or late-evening glass of wine on the streetside terrace.

WORTH A TRIP

COASTAL HIKES AROUND LIPARI

Lipari's rugged northwestern coastline offers excellent walking opportunities. Most accessible is the pleasant hour-long stroll from Quattropani to Acquacalda along Lipari's north shore, which affords spectacular views of Salina and a distant Stromboli. Take the bus to Quattropani (€2.40, 25 minutes), then simply proceed downhill on the main road 5km to Acquacalda, where you can catch the bus (€1.55) back to Lipari.

More strenuous, but equally rewarding in terms of scenery, is the three- to four-hour hike descending steeply from Pianoconte (€1.90, 15 minutes by bus) down past the old Roman baths of Terme di San Calogero to the western shoreline, then skirting the clifftops along a flat stretch before climbing steeply back to Quattropani.

Kasbah
MODERN SICILIAN, PIZZA €€

(☑090 981 10 75; www.kasbahlipari.it; Vico Selinunte 45; pizzas €6-8, meals €33-35; ⊙7-11.30pm Apr-Oct) Tucked down a narrow alleyway, with a window where you can watch the chefs at work, this place serves everything from fancy pasta, fish and meat dishes to simple wood-fired pizzas. The stylish dining room with its grey linen tablecloths is complemented by a more casual outdoor terrace.

E Pulera
MODERN SICILIAN €€

(☑090 981 11 58; www.pulera.it; Via Isabella Conti; meals €30-45; ⊙7pm-midnight late Apr–mid-Oct) With its serene garden setting, low lighting, tile-topped tables and exquisite food – from tuna carpaccio with blood oranges and capers to *cassata* (sponge cake, ricotta, marzipan, chocolate and candied fruit) served with sweet Malvasia wine for dessert – E Pulera makes an upmarket but relaxed choice for a romantic dinner.

🔒 Shopping

La Formagella
FOOD & DRINKS

(☑090 988 07 59; Corso Vittorio Emanuele 250; ⊙8am-8.30pm Mar-Oct) You simply can't leave the Aeolian Islands without a small pot of capers and a bottle of sweet Malvasia wine.

You can get both, along with meats, cheeses and other delicious goodies, at this gourmet grocery-deli just around the corner from the hydrofoil dock.

ℹ️ Information

Corso Vittorio Emanuele is lined with ATMs. The other islands have relatively few facilities, so it's best to sort out your finances here before moving on.

Ospedale Civile (☑090 988 51 11; Via Sant'Anna) First-aid and emergency services.

Tourist Office (☑090 988 00 95; infopoint eolie@regione.sicilia.it; Via Maurolico 17; ⊙9am-1pm & 4.30-7pm Mon, Wed & Fri, 9am-1pm Tue & Thu) Lipari's sporadically staffed tourist office provides information covering all of the Aeolian Islands.

ℹ️ Getting There & Around

BOAT

Lipari is the Aeolians' transport hub. The main port is Marina Lunga, where you'll find the hydrofoil jetty to the north and the ferry docks to the south. Timetable information is displayed at the adjacent ticket offices.

Year-round ferries and hydrofoils serve Milazzo and all the other Aeolian Islands; less frequent services include year-round hydrofoils to Messina and ferries to Naples, and summer-only hydrofoil services to Palermo. Websites for **Liberty Lines** (☑090 981 24 48; www.libertylines.it), **Siremar** (☑090 981 10 17; www.siremar.it) and NGI Traghetti (p798) have complete schedules and price details.

BUS

Autobus Guglielmo Urso (☑090 981 10 26; www.ursobus.com/orariursobus.pdf) runs buses around the island roughly hourly from its bus stop adjacent to Marina Lunga. The Linea Urbana follows the eastern shoreline, making stops at Canneto (€1.30) and Acquacalda (€1.55), while the Linea Extraurbana climbs to the splendid Quattrocchi viewpoint (€1.90) and the western highland settlements of Pianoconte (€1.90) and Quattropani (€2.40). Discounts are available for round-trip journeys or multiple rides (six-/10-/20-ride tickets from €7/10.50/20.50).

CAR & MOTORCYCLE

Several places around town rent bicycles (€10 to €15 per day), scooters (€15 to €50) and cars (€30 to €80), including **Da Marcello** (☑090 981 12 34; www.noleggiodamarcello.com; Via Sottomonastero), down by the ferry dock.

Vulcano

POP 720 / ELEV 500M

Vulcano is a memorable place, not least because of the vile smell of sulphurous gases. Once you escape the drab and dated tourist centre, Porto di Levante, the island has a delightfully tranquil, unspoilt quality. Beyond the well-marked trail to the looming Fossa di Vulcano, the landscape gives way to rural simplicity, with vineyards, birdsong and a surprising amount of greenery. The island is worshipped by Italians for its therapeutic mud baths and hot springs, and its black beaches and weird steaming landscape make for an interesting day trip.

Boats dock at Porto di Levante. To the right, as you face the island, are the mud baths and the small Vulcanello peninsula; to the left is the volcano. Straight ahead is Porto di Ponente, 700m west, where you will find the Spiaggia Sabbia Nera (Black Sand Beach).

◉ Sights & Activities

At Porto di Ponente, on the far side of the peninsula from Porto di Levante, the dramatic and only mildly commercialised black-sand beach of **Spiaggia Sabbia Nera** curves around a pretty bay. It is one of the few sandy beaches in the archipelago. A smaller, quieter black-sand beach, **Spiaggia dell'Asino** (Donkey Beach), can be found on the island's southern side near Gelso.

★ Fossa di Vulcano   HIKING

Vulcano's top attraction is the straightforward trek up its 391m volcano (no guide required). Start early if possible and bring a hat, sunscreen and water. Follow the signs south along Strada Provinciale, then turn left onto the zigzag gravel track that leads to the summit. It's about an hour's scramble to the lowest point of the crater's edge (290m).

Laghetto di Fanghi   HOT SPRINGS

(€3, shower/towel €1/2.60; ⊙ 7am-10pm Jul & Aug, 9am-6.30pm late Mar-Jun & Sep-early Nov) Backed by a *faraglione* (rock tower) and stinking of rotten eggs, Vulcano's harbourside pool of thick, coffee-coloured sulphurous gloop isn't exactly a five-star beauty farm. But the warm (28°C) mud is considered an excellent treatment for rheumatic pains and skin diseases, and rolling around in it can be fun if you don't mind smelling funny for a few days. Keep the mud away from your eyes

(and hair), as the sulphur is acidic and can damage your cornea.

Sicily in Kayak   WATER SPORTS

(☏ 329 5381229; www.sicilyinkayak.com) This outfit offers kayaking tours around Vulcano and the other Aeolians, along with sailing and stand-up paddleboarding excursions.

🛏 Sleeping & Eating

Unless you're here for the walking and the mud baths, Vulcano isn't a great place for an extended stay; the town is pretty soulless and the sulphurous fumes really do smell. However, there are some good options for those who choose to stick around.

★ Casa delle Stelle   B&B €

(☏ 334 9804104, 347 3626282; Contrada Gelso; s €30-45, d €50-90; 🅿) This lovely hideaway, high in the hills above the island's south shore, is run by former Gelso lighthouse keeper Sauro and his wife, Maria. The two guest rooms share a living room, a fully equipped kitchen, and a panoramic terrace with spectacular views of the Mediterranean and a distant Mt Etna. In summer, local buses will drop you at the gate.

La Forgia Maurizio   SICILIAN €€

(☏ 334 7660069; www.laforgiamaurizio.it; Strada Provinciale 45, Porto di Levante; meals €30-35; ⊙ 12.30-3pm & 7-11pm; 🍴) The owner of this devilishly good restaurant spent 20 winters in Goa, India; Eastern influences sneak into the menu of Sicilian specialties, and several items are vegan- and/or vegetarian-friendly. Don't miss the *liquore di kumquat e cardamom*, Maurizio's homemade answer to *limoncello* (lemon liqueur). The multicourse tasting menu is an excellent deal at €30 including wine, water and dessert.

ℹ Getting There & Around

BOAT

Vulcano is an intermediate stop between Milazzo and Lipari; both Liberty Lines and Siremar run multiple vessels in both directions throughout the day. The hydrofoil journey to or from Lipari takes only 10 minutes, making Vulcano an easy and popular day trip destination.

CAR & MOTORCYCLE

Sprint da Luigi (☏ 347 7600275, 090 985 22 08; www.nolosprintdaluigi.com; Porto di Levante; bicycle/scooter/car rental per day from €7/25/50) Rent some wheels from this well-signposted outfit near the port.

Delightful Desserts

From citrus-scented pastries filled with ricotta, to ice cream served on brioche, to the marzipan fruits piled in every confectioner's window, Sicily celebrates the joys of sugar morning, noon and night.

Multicultural Roots

People from the Arabs to the Aztecs have influenced Sicily's culture of sweets: the former introduced sugar cane; the latter's fiery hot chocolate so impressed the Spaniards that they brought it to Sicily. The land also supplied inspiration, from abundant citrus, almond and pistachio groves to Mt Etna's snowy slopes, legendary source of the first *granita*.

Sweet Sicilian Classics

The all-star list of Sicilian desserts starts with *cannoli,* crunchy pastry tubes filled with sweetened ricotta, garnished with chocolate, crumbled pistachios or a spike of candied citrus. Vying for the title of Sicily's most famous dessert is *cassata,* a coma-inducing concoction of sponge cake, cream, marzipan, chocolate and candied fruit. Feeling more adventurous? How about an *'mpanatigghiu,* a traditional Modican pastry stuffed with minced meat, almonds, chocolate and cinnamon?

A SUGAR-FUELLED ISLAND SPIN

➡ **Pasticceria Cappello** Renowned for its *setteveli,* a velvety seven-layer chocolate cake. (p793)

➡ **Da Alfredo** Dreamy *granita* made with almonds and wild strawberries. (p807)

➡ **Ti Vitti** Divine *cannoli* featuring fresh-from-the-sheep ricotta from the Madonie Mountains. (p797)

➡ **Dolceria Bonajuto** Aztec-influenced chocolate with vanilla and hot peppers. (p832)

➡ **Gelati DiVini** Outlandish ice-cream flavours including Marsala wine, wild fennel and olive oil. (p833)

➡ **Maria Grammatico** Marzipan fruit, almond pastries and toasted-nut *torrone* (nougat).(p846)

2

ENKI PHOTO/SHUTTERSTOCK ©

1. Display of marzipan fruit 2. Almond nougat 3. Cannoli and cassata 4. Strawberry granita

4

GIOVANNI BOSCHERINO/SHUTTERSTOCK ©

Multilingual owners Luigi and Nidra offer tips for exploring the island and also rent out an apartment (€40 to €70) in Vulcano's tranquil interior.

Salina

POP 2200 / ELEV 962M

Ah, green Salina! In stark contrast to sulphur-stained Vulcano and lava-blackened Stromboli, Salina's twin craters of Monte dei Porri and Monte Fossa delle Felci – nicknamed *didyme* (twins) by the ancient Greeks – are lushly wooded and invitingly verdant, a result of the numerous freshwater springs on the island. Wildflowers, thick yellow gorse bushes and serried ranks of grapevines carpet the hillsides in vibrant colours and cool greens, while its high coastal cliffs plunge dramatically towards beaches. The famous Aeolian capers grow plentifully here, as do the grapes used for making Malvasia wine.

◎ Sights & Activities

There are numerous wineries outside Malfa where you can try the local Malvasia wine. Signposted off the main road 1km east of town is award-winning **Fenech** (☑090 984 40 41; www.fenech.it; Via Fratelli Mirabito 41). About 3km further east, another important Malvasia is produced at the luxurious Capofaro resort on the 13-acre Tasca d'Almerita estate between Malfa and Santa Marina.

Pollara   VILLAGE

Don't miss a trip to sleepy Pollara, sandwiched dramatically between the sea and the steep slopes of an extinct volcanic crater on Salina's western edge. The gorgeous beach here was used as a location in the 1994 film *Il Postino*, although the land access route to the beach has since been closed due to landslide danger.

You can still descend the steep stone steps at the northwest end of town and swim across to the beach, or simply admire the spectacular view, with its backdrop of volcanic cliffs.

★ Monte Fossa delle Felci   HIKING

For jaw-dropping views, climb to the Aeolians' highest point, Monte Fossa delle Felci (962m). The two-hour ascent starts from the **Santuario della Madonna del Terzito**, an imposing 19th-century church at Valdichiesa, in the valley separating the island's two volcanoes. From the top, gorgeous perspectives unfold on the symmetrically arrayed

volcanic cones of Monte dei Porri, Filicudi and a distant Alicudi.

🛏 Sleeping & Eating

The island remains relatively undisturbed by mass tourism, yet offers some of the Aeolians' finest hotels and restaurants. Accommodation can be found in Salina's three main towns: Santa Marina Salina on the east shore, Malfa on the north shore and Rinella on the south shore, as well as in Lingua, a village adjoining ancient salt ponds 2km south of Santa Marina. Note that many hotels have their own excellent restaurants.

★ Hotel Ravesi   HOTEL €€

(☑090 984 43 85; www.hotelravesi.it; Via Roma 66, Malfa; d €90-240, ste €160-300; ◎mid-Apr–mid-Oct; ✳❄☏⛱) Star attractions at this peach of a hotel in a converted family home beside Malfa's town square include the delightful grassy lounge and bar area, the chiming of church bells next door, and the outdoor deck with an infinity pool overlooking Panarea, Stromboli and the sea. Especially nice are the brand-new honeymoon suite with private terrace and the corner room 12 upstairs.

Homemade bar snacks during the sunset *aperitivi* hour, and freshly made jams from the fruit trees in the hotel garden are icing on the cake.

A Cannata   PENSION €€

(☑090 984 30 57; www.hotelacannata.it; Via Alfieri 9, Lingua; d €80-180, ste €120-200; ☏) Remodelled in classic Aeolian style, with peach-coloured stucco, cheerful blue doors and reproduction historic tiles, this family-run *pensione* offers 25 spacious units, many of which (along with the breakfast terrace) overlook Lingua's picturesque salt lagoon. The adjacent **restaurant** (☑090 984 31 61; Via Umberto I 13, Lingua; meals €30-35; ◎12.30-2.30pm & 7.30-10pm) features menus built around freshly caught seafood and home-grown veggies and herbs. Half board costs €35 extra per person.

Hotel Mamma Santina   BOUTIQUE HOTEL €€

(☑090 984 30 54; www.mammasantina.it; Via Sanità 40, Santa Marina Salina; d €140-250; ◎Apr-Oct; ✳@☏⛱) A labour of love for its architect owner, this boutique hotel has inviting rooms decorated with pretty tiles in traditional Aeolian designs. Many of the sea-view terraces come with hammocks, and on warm evenings the attached restaurant (meals from €35 to €40) has outdoor seating overlooking the glowing blue pool and landscaped garden.

⭐**Hotel Signum**   BOUTIQUE HOTEL **€€€**
(📞090 984 42 22; www.hotelsignum.it; Via Scalo 15, Malfa; d €250-600, ste €500-750; ❉🛜🏊) Hidden in Malfa's hillside lanes is this alluring labyrinth of antique-clad rooms, peach-coloured stucco walls, tall blue windows and vine-covered terraces with full-on views of Stromboli. The attached wellness centre, Signum Spa (Salus Per Aquam; €30, treatments extra; ⊘10am-8pm Apr-Sep), a stunning pool and one of the best-regarded restaurants on the island make this the perfect place to unwind for a few days in utter comfort.

Capofaro   BOUTIQUE HOTEL **€€€**
(📞090 984 43 30; www.capofaro.it; Via Faro 3; d €290-570, ste €490-780; ⊘May-mid-Oct; ❉@🛜🏊) Immerse yourself in luxury at this five-star boutique resort halfway between Santa Marina and Malfa, surrounded by well-tended Malvasia vineyards and a picturesque lighthouse. The 20 rooms all have sharp white decor and terraces looking straight out to smoking Stromboli. Tennis courts, poolside massages, wine tasting and vineyard visits complete this perfect vision of island chic.

⭐**Da Alfredo**   SANDWICHES **€**
(Piazza Marina Garibaldi, Lingua; granite €2.60, sandwiches €9-13; ⊘8am-11pm Jun-Sep, 10am-6pm Oct-May) Salina's most atmospheric option for an affordable snack, Alfredo's place is renowned all over Sicily for its *granite:* ices made with coffee, fresh fruit or locally grown pistachios and almonds. It's also worth a visit for its *pane cunzatu* (open-faced sandwiches piled high with tuna, ricotta, eggplant, tomatoes, capers and olives); split one with a friend – they're huge!

ℹ Getting There & Around

BOAT

Hydrofoils and ferries serve Santa Marina Salina and Rinella from Lipari and the other islands. You'll find ticket offices in both ports.

BUS

CITIS (📞090 984 41 50; www.trasportisalina. it) runs buses every hour or two in low season (more frequently in summer) from Santa Marina Salina to Lingua and Malfa. In Malfa, make connections for Rinella, Pollara, Valdichiesa

and Leni. Fares cost from €1.90 to €2.90 depending on your destination. Timetables are posted online, and at ports and bus stops.

CAR & MOTORCYCLE

Above Santa Marina Salina's port, **Antonio Bongiorno** (📞338 3791209; www.rentbongiorno. it; Via Risorgimento 222, Santa Marina Salina) rents bikes (per day from €8), scooters (€25 to €30) and cars (€60 to €70). Several agencies in Rinella offer similar services – look for signs at the ferry dock.

Stromboli

POP 400 / ELEV 924M

Stromboli's perfect triangle of a volcano juts dramatically out of the sea, its permanently active cone attracting a steady stream of visitors like moths to a giant flame. Volcanic activity has scarred and blackened the northwest side of the island, while the eastern side is untamed, ruggedly green and dotted with low-rise whitewashed houses.

The youngest of the Aeolian volcanoes, Stromboli was formed a mere 40,000 years ago and its gases continue to send up an almost constant spray of liquid magma, a process defined by vulcanologists as *attività stromboliana* (Strombolian activity). The volcano's most dramatic recent activity involved major lava flows that burst forth between June and December 2014, creating a new mass of hardened lava rock below the volcano's northeast crater and cancelling tours to the summit for several months. Several other significant eruptions have occurred in recent time; on 27 February 2007, two new craters opened on the volcano's summit; on 5 April 2003, the village of Ginostra was showered with rocks up to 4m wide; and on 30 December 2002, a tsunami caused damage to Stromboli town, injuring six people and closing the island to visitors for a few months.

Boats arrive at Porto Scari, downhill from the main town of Stromboli at the island's northeastern corner. Accommodation is concentrated within a 2km radius of the port, while San Vincenzo church, the meeting point for guided hikes up the volcano, is a short walk up the Scalo Scari to Via Roma.

◉ Sights

⭐**Stromboli Crater**   VOLCANO
For nature lovers, climbing Stromboli is one of Sicily's not-to-be-missed experiences. Since 2005 access has been strictly regulated:

you can walk freely to 400m but will need a guide to continue any higher. Organised treks depart daily (between 3.30pm and 6pm, depending on the season), timed to reach the summit (924m) at sunset and to allow 45 minutes to observe the crater's fireworks.

The climb itself takes 2½ to three hours, while the descent back to Piazza San Vincenzo is shorter (1½ to two hours). All told, it's a demanding five- to six-hour trek to the top and back; you'll need to have proper walking shoes, a backpack that allows free movement of both arms, clothing for cold and wet weather, a change of T-shirt, a handkerchief to protect against dust (wear glasses not contact lenses), a torch (flashlight), 1L to 2L of water and some food. If you haven't got any of these, **Totem Trekking** (☑090 986 57 52; www.totemtrekkingstromboli.com; Piazza San Vincenzo 4; ⏲9.30am-1pm & 3.30-7pm) hires out all the necessary equipment, including backpacks (€5), windbreakers (€5), boots (from €5), hiking poles (from €3) and torches (from €2).

★ **Sciara del Fuoco Viewpoint**   VIEWPOINT

(Path of Fire) An alternative to scaling Stromboli's summit is the hour-long climb to this viewpoint (400m, no guide required), which directly overlooks the Sciara del Fuoco (the blackened laval scar running down Stromboli's northern flank) and offers fabulous if more-distant views of the crater's explosions. Bring plenty of water, and a torch if walking at night. The trail (initially a switchbacking road) starts in Piscità, 2km west of Stromboli's port; halfway up, you can stop for pizza at L'Osservatorio.

🏃 **Activities**

Stromboli's black sandy beaches are among the best in the Aeolian archipelago. The most accessible and popular swimming and sunbathing is at **Ficogrande**, a strip of rocks and black volcanic sand about a 10-minute walk northwest of the hydrofoil dock. Further-flung beaches worth exploring are at **Piscità** to the west and **Forgia Vecchia**, about 300m south of the port.

La Sirenetta Diving   DIVING

(☑331 2545288; www.lasirenettadiving.it; Via Mons di Mattina 33; ⏲late May–mid-Sep) This outfit, opposite the beach at La Sirenetta Park Hotel, offers diving courses and accompanied dives.

 Tours

Magmatrek (☑090 986 57 68; www.magmatrek. it; Via Vittorio Emanuele) has experienced, multilingual vulcanological guides who lead regular treks (maximum group size 20) up to the crater every afternoon (per person €28). It can also put together tailor-made treks for individual groups. Other agencies charging identical prices include **Stromboli Adventures** (☑339 5327277; www.stromboli adventures.it; Via Vittorio Emanuele), **Quota 900** (☑090 98 62 51; www.quota900stromboli.it; Via Roma) and **Il Vulcano a Piedi** (☑090 98 61 44; www.ilvulcanoapiedi.it; Via Pizzillo).

Società Navigazione Pippo (☑338 9857883, 090 98 61 35; pipponav.stromboli@libero. it; Porto Scari) is among the numerous boat companies at Porto Scari offering 2½-hour daytime circuits of the island (€25), 1½-hour sunset excursions to watch the Sciara del Fuoco from the sea (€20) and evening trips to Ginostra village on the other side of the island for dinner or *aperitivi* (€25).

🍴 **Sleeping & Eating**

More than a dozen places offer accommodation, including B&Bs, guesthouses and fully fledged hotels.

★ **Casa del Sole**   GUESTHOUSE €

(☑090 98 63 00; www.casadelsolestromboli.it; Via Cincotta; dm €25-35, s €30-55, d €60-110) This cheerful Aeolian-style guesthouse is only 100m from a sweet black-sand beach in Piscità, the tranquil neighbourhood at the west end of town. Dorms, private doubles and a guest kitchen all surround a sunny patio, overhung with vines, fragrant with lemon blossoms, and decorated with the masks and stone carvings of sculptor-owner Tano Russo. It's a pleasant 25-minute walk or a €10 taxi ride from the port, 2km away.

Pensione Aquilone   GUESTHOUSE €

(☑090 98 60 80; www.aquiloneresidence.it; Via Vittorio Emanuele 29; d €50-110) A short distance west of Stromboli's hilltop church square, this cheerful place has a sunny central garden patio and views up to the volcano. Three rooms come with cosy cooking nooks; otherwise, friendly owners Adriano and Francesco provide breakfast.

L'Osservatorio   PIZZA €

(☑090 958 69 91; www.facebook.com/osservato riostromboli; pizzas €7-12; ⏲10.30am-late) Sure, you could eat a pizza in town, but come on

– you're on Stromboli! Make the 45-minute, 2km uphill trek west of town to this pizzeria and you'll be rewarded with exceptional volcano views from an expansive panoramic terrace, best after sundown.

★ **Punta Lena** SICILIAN €€
(☎090 98 62 04; Via Marina 8; meals €35-40; ☯12.15-2.30pm & 7-10.30pm early May–mid-Oct) For a romantic outing, head to this family-run waterfront restaurant with cheerful blue decor, fresh flowers, lovely sea views and the soothing sound of waves lapping in the background. The food is as good as you'll get anywhere on the island, with signature dishes including fresh seafood and spaghetti *alla stromboliana* (with wild fennel, cherry tomatoes and breadcrumbs).

Pardès SICILIAN €€
(☎337 1505194; www.facebook.com/pardes. stromboli; Via Vittorio Emanuele 81; meals €25-35; ☯noon-2.30pm & 6-10pm Easter-Oct; ⓢ) A 10-minute walk west of San Vincenzo church, this wine bar–cafe has pleasant seating both indoors and on an outdoor terrace where you can sip coffee or wine while using the wi-fi (it's one of the few places on the island with reliable internet access).

ⓘ Information

Bring enough cash for your stay on Stromboli. Many businesses don't accept credit cards, and the village's lone ATM on Via Roma is sometimes out of service. Internet access is limited and slow.

ⓘ Getting There & Away

Liberty Lines (☎090 98 60 03; www.liberty lines.it) offers hydrofoil service to/from Lipari (€19.30, 50 minutes to 1¾ hours), Salina (€20.80, one hour) and all the other Aeolian Islands, as well as one direct early-morning hydrofoil from Milazzo (€27.45, 1¼ hours). **Siremar** (☎090 98 60 16; www.siremar.it) offers twice-weekly ferry service to Naples (€53.40, 10 hours) and the other Aeolians. Ticket offices for both companies are at Stromboli's port. Another option is to visit Stromboli on an all-inclusive day trip from Lipari.

IONIAN COAST

Magnificent, overdeveloped, crowded – and exquisitely beautiful – the Ionian coast is among Sicily's most popular tourist destinations and home to 20% of the island's

WORTH A TRIP

SICILY'S OFFSHORE ISLANDS

Sicily is an island lover's paradise, with more than a dozen offshore islands scattered in the seas surrounding the main island. Beyond the major Aeolian Islands of **Lipari**, **Vulcano**, **Stromboli** and **Salina**, you can detour to the smaller Aeolians: **Panarea**, **Filicudi** and **Alicudi**. Alternatively, cast off from Trapani on Sicily's western coast to the slow-paced **Egadi Islands** or the remote, rugged volcanic island of **Pantelleria**. South of Agrigento, the sand-sprinkled **Pelagic Islands** of Lampedusa, Linosa and Lampione offer some fantastic beaches. **Liberty Lines** (☎0923 87 38 13; www.libertylines.it) and Siremar (p796) provide hydrofoil and/ or ferry services to all of these islands. For complete information about the Egadi Islands and the lesser Aeolian Islands, including where to sleep and eat, see Lonely Planet's *Sicily* guide.

population. Moneyed entrepreneurs have built their villas and hotels up and down the coastline, eager to bag a spot on Sicily's version of the Amalfi Coast. Above it all towers the muscular peak of Mt Etna (3329m), puffs of smoke billowing from its snow-covered cone.

Taormina

POP 11,100 / ELEV 204M

Spectacularly situated on a terrace of Monte Tauro, with views westwards to Mt Etna, Taormina is a beautiful small town, reminiscent of Capri or an Amalfi coastal resort. Over the centuries, Taormina has seduced an exhaustive line of writers and artists, aristocrats and royalty, and these days it's host to a summer arts festival that packs the town with international visitors.

Perched on its eyrie, Taormina is sophisticated, chic and comfortably cushioned by some serious wealth – far removed from the banal economic realities of other Sicilian towns. But the charm is not manufactured. The capital of Byzantine Sicily in the 9th century, Taormina is an almost perfectly preserved medieval town, and, if you can tear yourself away from the shopping and

Taormina

0 _____ **200 m**
0 _____ **0.1 miles**

Lido Mazzarò (800m);
Nike Diving Centre (1.1km);
Isola Bella (1.2km)

Interbus (150m);
Lido Mazzarò (4km);
(4km)

Lumbi Car
Park (700m)

Teatro
Greco 1

Via Luigi Prandello

Fumivia

Porta
Messina

Via Timeo

Via di
Giovanni

Via Teatro Greco

Via Timoleone

Via Ginnasio

Parco Duchi di Cesarò
(Villa Comunale)

Via Bagnoli Croce

8

4

Isoco Guest
House (200m)

10

Palazzo Corvaja

Piazza
Santa
Caterina

Piazzetta
Filea

Via Naumachie

Via Giardinazzo

Corso Umberto I

16

Via A Marziani

Via Roma

Via Scesa Bastione

14

3

Via Don Bosco

Via Circonvallazione

9

6

Salita dei Gracchi

Piazza
IX Aprile

2

Torre dell'
Orologio

Via Rotabile Per Castelmola

Autostrada Messina-Catania

Castelmola
(4km)

Via Leonardo da Vinci

Via Fazzello

Palazzo
Ciampoli

Corso Umberto I

Piazza del
Duomo

Piazza
Garibaldi

Piazza
Paladini

13

Paladini

11

Piazza San
Domenico

Porta Catania Car Park (100m);
(3km)

12

15

5

Palazzo Duca di
Santo Stefano

Via Pietro Rizzo

Taormina

⊙ Top Sights
1 Teatro Greco G3

⊙ Sights
2 Chiesa San Giuseppe C3
3 Corso Umberto I D3
4 Villa Comunale F4

🛏 Sleeping
5 Casa Cuseni... A2
6 Casa Turchetti... D3
7 Hostel Taormina D2
8 Hotel Villa Belvedere G4
9 Villa Nettuno.. F1

⊗ Eating
10 L'Arco dei Cappuccini............................ E1
11 Osteria Nero D'Avola B4
12 Osteria RossoDivino A4
13 Tischi Toschi.. B4

☕ Drinking & Nightlife
14 Morgana.. D3

⊙ Shopping
15 Dieffe... A4
16 La Torinese.. D2

sunbathing, it has a wealth of small but perfect tourist sites. Taormina is also a popular resort with gay men.

Be warned that in July and August the town and its surrounding beaches swarm with visitors.

⊙ Sights & Activities

A short walk uphill from the bus station brings you to Corso Umberto I, a pedestrianised thoroughfare that traverses the length of the medieval town and connects its two historic town gates, Porta Messina and Porta Catania.

★ Teatro Greco   RUINS
(☑ 0942 2 32 20; www.parconaxostaormina.it/en; Via Teatro Greco; adult/reduced €10/5; ⊙ 9am-1hr before sunset) Taormina's premier sight is this perfect horseshoe-shaped theatre, suspended between sea and sky, with Mt Etna looming on the southern horizon. Built in the 3rd century BC, it's the most dramatically situated Greek theatre in the world and the second largest in Sicily (after Syracuse). In summer, it's used to stage international arts and film festivals.

Corso Umberto I   STREET
Taormina's chief delight is wandering this pedestrian-friendly thoroughfare, lined with stylish boutiques and Renaissance palaces. Midway down, pause to revel in stunning panoramic views of Mt Etna and the coast from Piazza IX Aprile and admire the charming rococo Chiesa San Giuseppe (Piazza IX Aprile; ⊙ usually 8.30am-8pm). Continue west through Torre dell'Orologio, the 12th-century clock tower, into Piazza del Duomo, home to an ornate baroque fountain (1635) that sports Taormina's symbol,

a two-legged centaur with the bust of an angel.

Villa Comunale   PARK
(Parco Duchi di Cesarò; Via Bagnoli Croce; ⊙ 9am-midnight summer, 9am-sunset winter) To escape the crowds, wander down to these stunningly sited public gardens. Created by Englishwoman Florence Trevelyan, they're a lush paradise of tropical plants and delicate flowers. There's also a children's play area.

Castelmola   VILLAGE
For eye-popping views of the coastline and Mt Etna, head for this hilltop village above Taormina, crowned by a ruined castle. Either walk (one hour) or take the hourly Interbus service (one way/return €1.90/3, 15 minutes). While you're up here, stop in for almond wine at Bar Turrisi (☑ 0942 2 81 81, www.barturrisi.com; Piazza Duomo; ⊙ 9am-2am daily, ◨), a four-level bar with some rather cheeky decor.

Isola Bella   ISLAND
(adult/reduced €4/2) Southwest of Lido Mazzaro is the minuscule Isola Bella, set in a stunning cove with fishing boats. You can walk here in a few minutes but it's more fun to rent a small boat from Mazzarò and paddle round Capo Sant'Andrea.

Lido Mazzarò   BEACH
Many visitors to Taormina come only for the beach scene. To reach Lido Mazzarò, directly beneath Taormina, take the funivia (Cable Car; Via Luigi Pirandello; one way/day pass €3/10; ⊙ every 15min 9am-1.30am Mon, from 8am Tue-Sun summer, 7.45am-8pm Tue-Sun winter). This beach is well serviced with bars and restaurants; private operators charge a fee for umbrellas and deckchairs (usually about €10 per person per day).

SICILY TAORMINA

Nike Diving Centre DIVING
(☑ 339 1961559; www.diveniketaormina.com; Spiaggia dell'Isola Bella) Opposite Isola Bella, this dive centre offers a wide range of courses for children and adults.

⚜ Festivals & Events

Taormina FilmFest FILM
(www.taorminafilmfest.it; ☺ Jun or Jul) Hollywood big shots arrive for a week of film screenings, premieres and press conferences at Teatro Greco.

Taormina Arte PERFORMING ARTS
(☑ 0942 2 11 42; www.taormina-arte.com; ☺ Jun-Sep) This festival features opera, dance, theatre and music concerts with an impressive list of international names.

🛏 Sleeping

Taormina has plenty of luxurious accommodation, but some less expensive places can be found. Many hotels offer discounted parking (from €10) at Taormina's two public car parks.

Hostel Taormina HOSTEL €
(☑ 0942 62 55 05; www.taorminahostel.net; Via Circonvallazione 13; dm €17-23, r €58-85; ❄ ⑦) Friendly and laid-back, this year-round hostel occupies a house with pretty tiled floors and a roof terrace commanding panoramic sea views. It's a snug, homey set-up with accommodation in three brightly coloured dorms and one private room. Facilities are basic but the owners are helpful and there's a small communal kitchen for DIY catering. Locks are also provided for the lockers.

Villa Nettuno PENSION €
(☑ 0942 2 37 97; www.hotelvillanettuno.it; Via Luigi Pirandello 33; s €38-44, d €60-78, breakfast €4; ❄ ⑦) A throwback to another era, this conveniently located salmon-pink *pensione* has been run by the Sciglio family for seven decades. Its low prices reflect a lack of recent updates, but the pretty gardens, complete with olive trees and potted geraniums, and the sea views from the breakfast terrace, offer a measure of charm you won't find elsewhere at this price. Breakfast costs €4.

Isoco Guest House GUESTHOUSE €€
(☑ 0942 2 36 79; www.isoco.it; Via Salita Branco 2; r €130-220; ☺ Mar-Nov; ℙ ❄ @ ⑦) Each room at this welcoming, LGBT-friendly guesthouse is dedicated to an artist, from Botticelli to Keith Haring. While the older rooms are highly eclectic, the newer suites are chic and subdued, each with a modern kitchenette. Breakfast is served around a large table, and a pair of terraces offer stunning sea views and a hot tub. Multi-night or prepaid stays earn the best rates.

★ Casa Turchetti B&B €€€
(☑ 0942 62 50 13; www.casaturchetti.com; Salita dei Gracchi 18/20; d €220-260, junior ste €360. ste €470; ❄ @ ⑦) Every detail is perfect at this painstakingly restored former music school turned luxurious B&B, on a back alley near Piazza IX Aprile. Vintage furniture and fixtures (including a giant four-poster bed in the suite), handcrafted woodwork and fine homespun sheets exude a quiet elegance. Topping it off is a breathtaking rooftop terrace and the warmth of Sicilian hosts Pino and Francesca.

★ Casa Cuseni B&B €€€
(☑ 0942 2 87 25; www.casacuseni.com; Via Leonardo da Vinci 5; r €175-270; ℙ ❄ ⑦) Pre-booking is essential at this early 20th-century villa once frequented by Tennessee Williams, DH Lawrence, Greta Garbo and Bertrand Russell. Converted to a B&B in 2012, it positively drips with period character and comes surrounded by a seven-tiered garden with views out to the Ionian Sea and Mt Etna. It's only five minutes from Porta Catania but feels a world apart.

Hotel Villa Belvedere HOTEL €€€
(☑ 0942 2 37 91; www.villabelvedere.it; Via Bagnoli Croce 79; s €328-540, d €375-610; ☺ Mar-late-Nov; ❄ @ ⑦ ☼) Built in 1902, the jaw-droppingly pretty Villa Belvedere was one of the original grand hotels, well positioned with fabulous views and luxuriant gardens, which are a particular highlight. There is also a swimming pool with a 100-year-old palm tree rising from a small island in the middle.

🍴 Eating

Eating out in Taormina comes at a cost, and goes hand in hand with posing. Overpriced, touristy places abound.

★ Il Barcaiolo SICILIAN €€
(☑ 0942 62 56 33; www.barcaiolo.altervista.org; Via Castellucci 43, Spiaggia Mazzarò; meals €33-45; ☺ 1-2.30pm & 7-10.45pm May-Sep, to 10pm rest of year) You'll need to book five days ahead come summer, when every *buongustaio* (foodie) and hopeless romantic longs for a table at this fabulous trattoria. Set snugly in a boat-fringed cove at the northern end

of Lido Mazzarò, it's celebrated for its sublimely fresh seafood, from sweet *gamberi rossi marinati agli agrumi* (raw Mazzara shrimps served with citrus fruits) to *sarde a beccaficu* (stuffed sardines). Leave room for the homemade *cassata* or deliciously naughty chocolate-and-orange mousse.

★ **Osteria Nero D'Avola**   SICILIAN €€
(☑ 0942 62 88 74; Piazza San Domenico 2b; meals €40; ⊙ 12.30-3pm & 7-11pm Tue-Sun Sep-Jun, 7pm-midnight Jul & Aug) Not only does affable owner Turi Siligato fish, hunt and forage for his smart *osteria*, he'll probably greet you at your table, share anecdotes about the day's bounty and play a few tunes on the piano. Here, seasonality, local producers and passion underscore arresting dishes like the signature *cannolo di limone Interdonato* (thinly sliced Interdonato lemon with roe, tuna, tomato and chives).

An impressive wine list showcases local drops, with staff usually happy to open most bottles, even if you're only after a glass.

Tischi Toschi   SICILIAN €€
(☑ 339 3642088; www.tischitoschitaormina.com; Via Paladini 3; meals €30-45; ⊙ 12.30-2.30pm & 7.30-10.30pm, closed Mon lunch May-Oct, closed Mon Nov-Apr) This family-run, Slow Food acclaimed trattoria with its charming front patio offers a level of creativity and attention to detail that's generally lacking in touristy Taormina. The limited menu of six *primi* and six *secondi* changes regularly based on what's in season.

L'Arco dei Cappuccini   SICILIAN €€
(☑ 0942 2 48 93; Via Cappuccini 5; meals €30-45; ⊙ 5-11.30pm mid-Jul–Aug, 12.30-2.30pm & 5-11.30pm rest of year, closed Nov–mid-Dec & early Jan–mid Mar) If you demand your seafood ridiculously fresh, reserve a table at this superlative local favourite. The *crudo* (raw fish) antipasto makes for a show-stopping prologue, followed by beautifully balanced dishes such as *fettuccine cernia* (pasta with grouper) and an earthy *pasta con le sarde* (spaghetti with sardines, raisins, pine nuts and fennel) in which every ingredient sings. Service is kind and gracious.

Osteria RossoDivino   SICILIAN €€€
(☑ 0942 62 86 53; www.osteria-rosso-divino.com; Vico Spuches 8; meals €37-55; ⊙ 7pm-2am Jul-Sep, noon-3pm & 7pm-midnight Wed-Mon Oct-Jan & Mar-Jun) With seating in an intimate, candle-lit courtyard, this coveted nosh spot (book ahead!) is the passion project of siblings Jacqueline and Sara Ragusa. The day's offerings – written on a blackboard – are dictated by the season, the local fishers' catch, and the siblings' own morning market trawl. Expect anything from heavenly anchovy tempura (the secret: mineral water in the batter) to fragrant seafood couscous.

 Drinking & Nightlife

★ **Morgana**   COCKTAIL BAR
(☑ 0942 62 00 56; www.morganataormina.it; Scesa Morgana 4; ⊙ 7.30pm-late Apr-Oct, closed Tue Nov & Dec) This so-svelte cocktail lounge sports a new look every year, with each concept inspired by Sicilian culture, artisans and landscape. It's the place to be seen, whether on the petite dance floor or among the prickly pears and orange trees in the dreamy, chi-chi courtyard. Fuelling the fun are gorgeous libations, made with local island ingredients, from wild fennel and orange to sage.

🅱 **Shopping**

Taormina is a window-shopper's paradise, especially along Corso Umberto I. The quality in most places is high, but don't expect any bargains.

La Torinese   FOOD & DRINKS
(☑ 0942 2 31 43; Corso Umberto I 59; ⊙ 9.30am-1pm & 4-8.30pm) Stock up on local olive oil, capers, marmalade, honey and wine. Smash-proof bubble wrapping helps to bring everything home in one piece.

Dieffe   FASHION & ACCESSORIES
(www.dioffetaormina.com; Corso Umberto I 226; ⊙ 10am-10pm summer, 10.30am-8pm rest of year) A bastion of 'Made in Italy', this easy-to-miss boutique offers sharp edits of men's threads, shoes and accessories from unique local and mainland designers. Expect anything from hand-painted leather belts from Sicilian artist Salvatore Montanucci, to handcrafted shoes from Le Marche's Galizio Torresi and beautifully detailed linen shirts from Tuscany's Osvaldo Trucchi. A must for lovers of idiosyncratic Italian style.

ℹ **Information**

Hospital (Ospedale San Vincenzo; ☑ 0942 57 91; Contrada Sirina) Downhill, 2km from the centre.

Tourist Office (☑ 0942 2 32 43; Palazzo Corvaja, Piazza Santa Caterina; ⊙ 8.30am-2.15pm & 3.30-6.45pm Mon-Fri year-round, also 8.30am-2.15pm & 3.30-6.45pm Sat & Sun summer) Has plenty of practical information.

ℹ️ Getting There & Around

BUS

Bus is the easiest way to reach Taormina. **Interbus** (www.interbus.it; Via Luigi Pirandello) goes to Messina (€4.30, 50 minutes to 1¾ hours, four daily Monday to Saturday, one on Sunday) and Catania (€5.10, 1¼ hours, hourly), the latter continuing to Catania's Fontanarossa Airport (€8.20, 1½ hours).

CAR & MOTORCYCLE

Taormina is on the A18 autostrada and the SS114 between Messina and Catania. Driving near the historic centre is a complete nightmare and Corso Umberto is closed to traffic. The most convenient places to leave your car are the **Porta Catania car park** (per 24hr €15), at the western end of Corso Umberto, or the **Lumbi car park** (per 24hr €13.50) north of the centre, connected to Porta Messina (at Corso Umberto's eastern end) by a five-minute walk or a free yellow shuttle bus.

TRAIN

There are frequent trains to and from Messina (€4.30, 45 minutes to 1¼ hours) and Catania (€4.30, 35 minutes to one hour), but the awkward location of Taormina's station (a steep 4km below town) is a strong disincentive. If you arrive this way, catch a taxi (€15) or an Interbus coach (€1.90, 20 minutes, half-hourly) up to town.

Catania

POP 296,000

Sicily's second-biggest metropolis, Catania is a city of grit and raw energy, a thriving, entrepreneurial centre with a large university and a cosmopolitan urban culture. Yes, it has its rough edges, but it's hard not to love a city with a smiling elephant gracing its central square and gorgeous snowcapped Mt Etna floating on the horizon. Catania is a true city of the volcano; much of it is constructed from the lava that poured down the mountain and engulfed the city in Etna's massive 1669 eruption. It is also lava-black in colour, as if a fine dusting of soot permanently covers its elegant buildings, most of which are the work of baroque master Giovanni Vaccarini.

In recent years, Catania has made steady moves to pedestrianise its historic centre, which you'll appreciate as you stroll the streets between Via Crociferi, Via Etnea and Piazza del Duomo, where most of the city's attractions are concentrated.

👁️ Sights

If you're visiting multiple attractions or travelling frequently by bus and metro, consider picking up a **Catania Pass** (www.cataniapass.it; 1-/3-/5-day pass individual €12.50/16.50/20, family €23/30.50/38), which offers free museum admissions and unlimited use of public transport, including the Alibus service between downtown and Fontanarossa Airport.

Piazza del Duomo   SQUARE

A Unesco World Heritage Site, Catania's central piazza is a set piece of contrasting lava and limestone, surrounded by buildings in the unique local baroque style and crowned by the grand Cattedrale di Sant'Agata . At its centre stands **Fontana dell'Elefante** (Piazza del Duomo), an 18th-century fountain built around a naive, smiling black-lava elephant dating from Roman times, surmounted by an improbable Egyptian obelisk. Another fountain at the piazza's southwest corner, **Fontana dell'Amenano**, marks the entrance to Catania's fish market.

★ La Pescheria   MARKET

(Via Pardo; ⏰7am-2pm Mon-Sat) Catania's raucous fish market, which takes over the streets behind Piazza del Duomo every workday morning, is street theatre at its most thrilling. Tables groan under the weight of decapitated swordfish, ruby-pink prawns and trays full of clams, mussels, sea urchins and all manner of mysterious sea life. Fishmongers gut silvery fish and women in high heels step daintily over pools of blood-stained water. It's absolutely riveting. Surrounding the market are a number of good seafood restaurants.

Parco Archeologico Greco Romano   RUINS

(📋095 715 05 08; Via Vittorio Emanuele II 262; adult/reduced incl Casa Liberti €6/3; ⏰9am-7pm) West of Piazza del Duomo lie Catania's most impressive ancient ruins: the remains of a 2nd-century Roman theatre and its small rehearsal theatre, the Odeon. The ruins are evocatively sited in the thick of a crumbling residential neighbourhood, with vine-covered buildings that appear to have sprouted organically from the half-submerged stage. Adjacent to the main theatre is the **Casa Liberti**, an elegantly restored 19th-century apartment now home to two millennia worth of artefacts discovered during the excavation of the site.

DON'T MISS

SICILIAN CUISINE

Eating is one of the great joys of any trip to Sicily. In addition to the island's ubiquitous street food, you'll encounter countless uniquely Sicilian specialties that reflect Sicily's multicultural heritage while making abundant use of local ingredients, such as sardines, wild fennel, eggplant (aubergine), ricotta, lemons, almonds and pistachios. Here's a quick primer on the island's most classic dishes:

Busiate con pesto alla trapanese A mainstay of western Sicilian menus, these hollow, corkscrew-shaped pasta tubes come served with a sauce of chopped almonds, garlic and fresh tomatoes.

Caponata The quintessential Sicilian appetiser, made with eggplant, olives, capers and celery marinated in a sweet-and-sour sauce.

Couscous alla trapanese Reflecting the island's Arab roots, this signature dish of western Sicily features couscous with mixed seafood topped with a delicious sauce of tomatoes, garlic and parsley.

Involtini di pesce spada Thinly sliced swordfish fillets, rolled up and filled with bread-crumbs, capers, tomatoes and olives.

Pasta alla Norma A specialty of Catania, Sicily's most famous pasta dish comes topped with fresh ricotta, eggplant, tomatoes and basil.

Pasta con le sarde This Palermitan original features pasta topped with sardines, wild fennel, pine nuts, raisins and toasted breadcrumbs.

Sarde a beccafico A classic Sicilian appetiser or main course of sardines, stuffed with breadcrumbs, pine nuts, raisins, garlic and parsley, then fried or baked to a golden brown colour.

★**Teatro Massimo Bellini** THEATRE
(📞095 730 61 35; www.teatromassimobellini.
it; Via Perrotta 12; guided tours adult/reduced
€6/4; ⊙tours 9am-noon Tue-Thu) A few blocks
northeast of the *duomo*, this gorgeous opera house forms the centrepiece of Piazza Bellini. Square and opera house alike were named after composer Vincenzo Bellini, the father of Catania's vibrant modern musical scene.

Cattedrale di Sant'Agata CATHEDRAL
(📞095 32 00 44; Piazza del Duomo; ⊙7am-noon & 4-7pm Mon-Sat, 7.30am-12.30pm & 4.30-7pm Sun) Inside the vaulted interior of this cathedral, beyond its impressive marble facade sporting two orders of columns taken from the Roman amphitheatre, lie the relics of the city's patron saint. The **Museo Diocesano** (📞095 28 16 35; www.museodiocesanocatania. com; Piazza del Duomo; adult/reduced museum only €7/4, museum & baths €10/6; ⊙9am-2pm Mon, Wed & Fri, 9am-2pm & 3-6pm Tue & Thu, 9am-1pm Sat), next door, grants access to the Roman baths directly underneath the church and fine views from the roof terrace beneath the cathedral's dome.

Castello Ursino CASTLE
(Piazza Federico II di Svevia) Catania's forbidding 13th-century castle once guarded the city from atop a seafront cliff. The 1669 eruption of Mt Etna changed the landscape, however, and the whole area to the south was reclaimed by lava, leaving the castle completely landlocked. The castle now houses the **Museo Civico** (📞095 34 58 30; adult/reduced €6/3; ⊙9am-7pm Mon-Fri, to 8.30pm Sat & Sun), home to the valuable archaeological collection of the Biscaris, Catania's most important aristocratic family. Exhibits include colossal classical sculpture, Greek vases and some fine mosaics.

Museo Belliniano MUSEUM
(📞095 715 05 35; Piazza San Francesco 3; adult/reduced €5/2; ⊙9am-7pm Mon-Sat, to 1pm Sun) One of Italy's great opera composers, Vincenzo Bellini (1801–35) was born in Catania. His childhood home, now a museum, boasts an interesting collection of memorabilia, including original scores, photographs, pianos once played by Bellini, and the maestro's death mask.

Catania

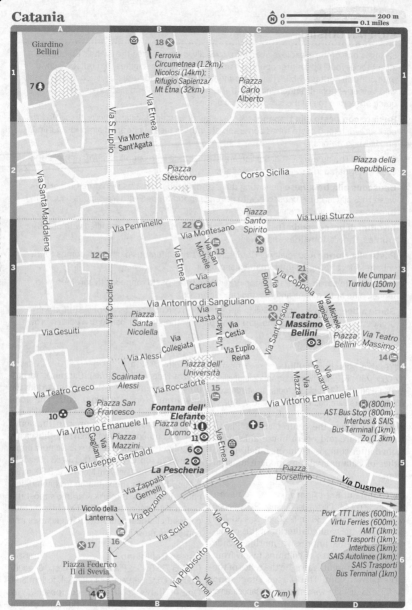

SICILY CATANIA

N 0 ——— 200 m
0 ——— 0.1 miles

Giardino
Bellini

7

18

Ferrovia
Circumetnea (1.2km);
Nicolosi (14km);
Rifugio Sapienza/
Mt Etna (32km)

Piazza
Carlo
Alberto

Via S. Euplio

Via Etnea

Via Monte
Sant'Agata

Via Santa Maddalena

Piazza
Stesicoro

Corso Sicilia

Piazza della
Repubblica

Via Penninello

22

Via Montesano

Via San Michele

13

Piazza
Santo
Spirito

19

Via Luigi Sturzo

12

Via Etnea

Via
Carcaci

Via
Biondi

Via Coppola

21

Me Cumpari
Turridu (150m)

Via Crociferi

Via Antonino di Sangiuliano

Via
Vasta

20

Via Michele Rapisardi

**Teatro
Massimo
Bellini**

Via Gesuiti

Piazza
Santa
Nicolella

Via
Collegiata

Via Mancini

Via
Cestia

Via
Sant'Orsola

3

Piazza
Bellini

Via Teatro
Massimo

14

Via Alessi

Via Euplio
Reina

Via Leonardi

Via
Mazza

Via Teatro Greco

Scalinata
Alessi

Piazza dell'
Università

Via Roccaforte

15

i

Via Vittorio Emanuele II

(800m);
AST Bus Stop (800m);
Interbus & SAIS
Bus Terminal (1km);
Zo (1.3km)

8 Piazza San
Francesco

10

Via Vittorio Emanuele II

**Fontana dell'
Elefante**

Piazza del
Duomo

1

11

5

Via Gagliani

Via
Mazzini

6

2

9

Via Giuseppe Garibaldi

La Pescheria

Via Etnea

Piazza
Borsellino

Via Dusmet

Via Zappalà
Gemelli

Via Bozomo

Vicolo della
Lanterna

16

17

Via Scuto

Via Colombo

Port, TTT Lines (600m);
Virtu Ferries (600m);
AMT (1km);
Etna Trasporti (1km);
Interbus (1km);
SAIS Autolinee (1km);
SAIS Trasporti
Bus Terminal (1km)

Piazza Federico
II di Svevia

Via Plebiscito

Via
Formai

4

(7km)

Giardino Bellini   PARK
(☉ 6am-11pm summer, to 10pm spring & autumn, to
9pm winter) Escape the madding crowd and
enjoy fine views of Mt Etna from these lovely
gardens along Via Etnea.

✥ Festivals & Events

If visiting Catania in February or early
March, don't miss **Carnevale** (www.carnevale
acireale.com) in nearby Acireale, one of Sicily's most colourful festivals.

Catania

Festa di Sant'Agata RELIGIOUS
(www.festadisantagata.it; ⊙3-5 Feb) In what is Catania's biggest religious festival, one million Catanians follow the Fercolo (a silver reliquary bust of St Agatha) along the main street of the city, accompanied by spectacular fireworks.

🛏 Sleeping

Catania is served by a good range of reasonably priced accommodation, making it an excellent base for exploring the Ionian coast and Etna.

★ B&B Crociferi B&B €
(☑095 715 22 66; www.bbcrociferi.it; Via Crociferi 81; d €75-85, tr €100-110, apt €110-170; ❋ 🖎) Perfectly positioned on pedestrianised Via Crociferi, this B&B in a beautifully decorated family home affords easy access to Catania's historic centre. Three palatial rooms (each with private bathroom across the hall) feature high ceilings, antique tiles, frescoes and artistic accoutrements from the owners' travels. The B&B also houses two apartments, the largest (called Leela) with a leafy panoramic terrace. Book ahead.

★ Palazzu Stidda APARTMENT €
(☑095 34 88 26, 338 6505133; www.palazzu-stidda.com; Vicolo della Lanterna 5; d €80-100, q €120-140; ❋ 🖎 🚗) Multilingual hosts Giovanni and Patricia have poured their hearts into creating these three family-friendly apartments (two with kitchens and washing machines) on a peaceful dead-end alley, with all the comforts of home, plus a host of whimsical touches. Each has a flowery mini balcony, and all are decorated with the owners' artwork, handmade furniture, family heirlooms and vintage finds.

B&B Faro B&B €
(☑349 4578856; www.bebfaro.it; Via San Michele 26; s/d/tr €50/80/100, apt €130-150; ❋ @) Polished-wood floors, double-glazed windows, modern bathroom fixtures and antique tiles set a stylish tone at this cosy B&B, owned by artist couple Anna and Antonio. Suites can sometimes be booked for the price of a double during slower periods; free bikes are provided; and there's a studio downstairs at number 30 where visiting artists are invited to come and paint.

Ostello degli Elefanti HOSTEL €
(☑095 226 56 91; www.ostellodeglielefanti.it; Via Etnea 28; dm €19-25, s €40-45, d €60-70; ❋ 🖎) Housed in a 17th-century *palazzo* a stone's throw from the *duomo*, this hostel offers incredible location and value. Three dorms and one private room have frescoed high ceilings and panoramic balconies, and there are reading lights, USB ports and curtains for every bed. The marble-floored former ballroom doubles as a restaurant-lounge, while the rooftop terrace-bar offers incomparable Etna vistas.

★ B&B Habitat B&B €€
(☑095 826 67 55; www.bbhabitatcatania.it; Via Teatro Massimo 29; s €84-117, d €95-140; ❋ 🖎 🚗) Fit for the pages of *Domus* magazine, this 19th-century factory turned B&B is the work of two young architects. Smart, minimalist rooms feature high-quality mattresses and

linen, coffee machines and custom-made furniture in wood and steel. Superior rooms add warmth with wooden floors. The seasonal breakfast buffet is served in a striking communal lounge, lined with floor-to-ceiling jars filled with Sicilian ingredients.

✖ Eating

Popular street snacks in Catania include *arancini* (deep-fried rice balls stuffed with meat, cheese, tomatoes and/or peas) and *seltz* (fizzy water with freshly squeezed lemon juice and natural fruit syrup). Don't leave town without trying *pasta alla Norma* (pasta with basil, eggplant, ricotta and tomato), a Catania original named after Bellini's opera *Norma*.

★ Da Antonio   TRATTORIA €
(🖉 095 218 49 38; www.facebook.com/Trattoria DaAntonio; Via Castello Ursino 59; meals €20; ⊙ 7.30-11pm daily, plus 12.30-3pm Tue-Sun) Humble yet quietly sophisticated, Da Antonio spoils food lovers with well-priced, beautifully cooked dishes served by knowledgable waitstaff. Despite having crept onto the tourist radar, it's still the kind of place where well-dressed local families come for Sunday lunch. The antipasti (to sample various offerings ask for an *assaggio*) and *primi* are particularly good, especially those showcasing local seafood.

Trattoria di De Fiore   TRATTORIA €
(🖉 095 31 62 83; Via Coppola 24/26; meals €15-25; ⊙ 7pm-12.30am Mon, 1pm-12.30am Tue-Sun) For more than 50 years, septuagenarian chef Rosanna has been re-creating her great-grandmother's recipes, including the best *pasta alla Norma* you'll taste anywhere in Sicily. Service can be excruciatingly slow, but for patient souls this is a rare chance to experience classic Catanian cooking from a bygone era. Don't miss Rosanna's trademark *zeppoline* (sugar-sprinkled ricotta-lemon fritters) at dessert time.

FUD Bottega Sicula   BURGERS €
(🖉 095 715 35 18; www.fud.it; Via Santa Filomena 35; burgers, panini & pizzas €5-10; ⊙ noon-3pm & 7pm-1am; 🛜) With sharp service and pavement seating on trendy Via Santa Filomena, this hip, back-alley eatery epitomises youthful Catania's embrace of 'Sicilian fast food', all made with high-quality, locally sourced ingredients, from Sicilian cheeses to Nebrodi black pork. With wry humour, every burger and *panino* on the menu is spelled

using Italian phonetics, from the 'cis burgher' (cheeseburger) to the rustic 'cauntri' (country) sandwich.

Millefoglie   VEGETARIAN €
(🖉 331 2505331; Via Sant'Orsola 12; dishes €6-8; ⊙ 12.45-3pm Mon-Sat, closed Sat May-Oct; 🛜🖉) Delicious, flesh-free grub awaits at little Millefoglie, a shabby-chic, whitewashed eatery with wooden floors, communal tables and an open kitchen. The morning's market produce dictates the menu, which might feature vibrant wholewheat *casarecce* (twisted pasta) with zucchini, fava beans, peas, *pecorino* (sheep's milk cheese), lemon zest and basil, or chocolate mousse with chilli and strawberries. A few vegan dishes usually dot the menu.

★ Mè Cumpari Turiddu   SICILIAN €€
(🖉 095 715 01 42; www.mecumparituriddu.it; Piazza Turri Ferro 36-38; meals €22-30; ⊙ bistro 11am-1am, restaurant noon-12.30am; 🛜) Old chandeliers, recycled furniture and vintage mirrors exude a nostalgic air at this quirky bistro–restaurant–providore, where tradition and modernity meet to impressive effect. Small producers and Slow Food sensibilities underline sophisticated, classically inspired dishes such as ricotta and marjoram ravioli in a pork sauce, soothing Ustica lentil stew or a playful 'deconstructed' *cannolo*. There's a fabulous selection of Sicilian cheeses, lighter bistro fare and cakes.

Le Tre Bocche   TRATTORIA €€€
(🖉 095 53 87 38; Via Mario Sangiorgi 7; meals €35-45; ⊙ two sittings daily, 8.30pm & 10.30pm, plus 1-3pm Sun) A fantastic Slow Food-recommended trattoria that takes pride in the freshest seafood and fish – so much so, it has a stand at La Pescheria market. Short pasta comes with wonderful sauces such as *bottarga* (mullet roe) and artichoke; spaghetti is soaked in sea urchins or squid ink; and risotto is mixed with courgette and king prawns.

🍶 Drinking & Nightlife

Not surprisingly for a busy university town, Catania has a reputation for its effervescent nightlife. Areas that bustle with activity after dark include Via Montesano, Via Teatro Massimo, the steps at the western end of Via Alessi, and Via Santa Filomena.

★ Ritz   COCKTAIL BAR
(www.facebook.com/ritzcatania; Via Pantano 54; ⊙ 7.30pm-2am Tue-Sun) Ritz is a svelte, clued-

up spot that takes its libations seriously. Divided into Aperitif, Anytime, Dinner, After Dinner and Long Drink & Muddle, cocktails are made with passion and precision, from the punchy Aviations to a very local Etna Kir (spumante Brut rosé, Etna cherry liqueur and hazelnut crust). There's a small, interesting selection of craft beer and a range of bites, including decent pizzas.

★ **Razmataz**   BAR
(☑ 095 31 18 93; Via Montesano 17; ☺ 9am-late Mon-Sat, 5pm-late Sun; ☜) Wines by the glass, draught and bottled beer, and an ample cocktail list are offered at this delightful wine bar with tables invitingly spread out across the tree-shaded flagstones of a sweet backstreet square. It doubles as a cafe in the morning, but really gets packed with locals from *aperitivo* time onward.

☆ Entertainment

For a current calendar of music, theatre and arts events around Catania, check the website www.lapisnet.it/catania.

Teatro Massimo Bellini   THEATRE
(☑ 095 730 61 11; www.teatromassimobellini. it; Via Perrotta 12) Catania's premier theatre is named after the city's most famous son, composer Vincenzo Bellini. Sporting the full red-and-gilt fit out, it stages a year-round season of opera and an eight-month program of classical music from November to June. Tickets, which are available online, start at around €20 and can rise to more than €100 for a seat in the stalls.

Zo   PERFORMING ARTS
(☑ 095 816 89 12; www.zoculture.it; Piazzale Asia 6; ☜) Housed in Catania's former sulphur works, Zo serves up contemporary art and performance from Italy and beyond. Its eclectic program of events ranges from club nights, concerts and dance performances, to installations, theatre workshops and the occasional film screening. The venue also houses a hip bar serving decent drinks and bites (including vegetarian dishes). Check the website for upcoming events.

ℹ Information

Hospital (Ospedale Santo Bambino; ☑ 095 743 63 06; www.policlinicovittorioemanuele.it/ ospedale-santo-bambino; Via Tindaro 2) Has a 24-hour emergency doctor.
Tourist Office (☑ 095 742 55 73; www.co mune.catania.it/la-citta/turismo; Via Vittorio Emanuele 172; ☺ 8am-7.15pm Mon-Sat, 8.30am-1.30pm Sun) Very helpful city-run tourist office.

ℹ Getting There & Away

AIR
Catania's airport, **Fontanarossa** (☑ 095 723 91 11; www.aeroporto.catania.it), is 7km southwest of the city centre. Alitalia, Ryanair and two dozen other airlines fly from Catania to destinations throughout Italy and Europe.

BOAT
The ferry terminal is located southwest of the train station along Via VI Aprile.
TTT Lines (☑ 800 627414, 095 34 85 86; www. tttlines.com) Runs nightly ferries from Catania to Naples (from €45, 11 hours).
Virtu Ferries (☑ 095 703 12 11; www.virtu-ferries.com) From May through September, Virtu runs daily ferries from Pozzallo (south of Catania) to Malta (1¾ hours). Fares vary depending on length of stay in Malta (same-day return €88 to €139; open return €116 to €164 depending on season). Coach transfer between Catania and Pozzallo (€12 each way) adds 2½ to three hours to the journey.

BUS
All long-distance buses leave from a terminal 250m north of the train station. Ticket offices for **Interbus** (☑ 095 53 27 16; www.interbus.it; Via d'Amico 187), **SAIS Trasporti** (☑ 090 601 21 36; www.saistrasporti.it; Via d'Amico 181) and **SAIS Autolinee** (☑ 095 53 61 68, 800 211020; www. saisautolinee.it; Via d'Amico 181) are across the street on Via d'Amico.

Interbus services include the following:
Piazza Armerina €9.20, 1¾ hours, two to five daily
Ragusa €8.60, two hours, eight to 13 daily
Syracuse €6.20, 1½ hours, hourly Monday to Friday, fewer on weekends
Taormina €5.10, 1¼ hours, hourly

SAIS Trasporti services go to **Agrigento** (€13.40, three hours, 10 to 14 daily) and **Rome** (€42, 10½ hours overnight). Its sister company SAIS Autolinee has services to **Messina** (€8.40, 1½ hours, hourly) and **Palermo** (€13.50, 2¾ hours, nine to 13 daily).

CAR & MOTORCYCLE
Catania is easily reached from Messina on the A18 autostrada and from Palermo on the A19. From either autostrada, signs for the centre of Catania will bring you to Via Etnea.

TRAIN
Frequent trains run from Catania Centrale station on Piazza Papa Giovanni XXIII.

SICILY CATANIA

Messina €7.60, 1½ to two hours, hourly

Palermo €13.50, three hours, six daily, three on Sunday

Syracuse €6.90, 1¼ hours, nine daily, four on Sunday

The private **Ferrovia Circumetnea** train circles Mt Etna, stopping at towns and villages on the volcano's slopes.

❶ Getting Around

TO/FROM THE AIRPORT

Alibus 457, operated by AMT, runs every 25 minutes from 4.40am to midnight from the airport to Catania Centrale train station (€4, 30 minutes). **Etna Transporti/Interbus** (p819) also runs a regular shuttle from the airport to Taormina (€8.20, 1½ hours, hourly 7.15am to 8.45pm). Stops for both buses are to the right as you exit the Arrivals hall.

All the main car-hire companies are represented at the airport.

CAR & MOTORCYCLE

Drivers should note that there are complicated one-way systems around the city, and the centre is increasingly pedestrianised, which means parking is scarce.

PUBLIC TRANSPORT

Several useful **AMT** (☑ 095 751 91 11, 800 018696; www.amt.ct.it) city buses terminate in front of Catania Centrale train station, including bus 1-4 (which runs hourly from the station to Via Etnea) and Alibus 457 (running from the station to the airport every 25 minutes from 4.40am to midnight). Also useful is bus D, which runs from Piazza Borsellino (just south of the *duomo*) to the local beaches.

Catania's slowly expanding metro system is currently limited to one line and nine stops, most on the periphery of town. Most useful for visitors are the newly opened Giovanni XXIII and Stesicoro stations, the former located near the train and bus stations, the latter near the heart of town; and the Borgo station, which is a transfer point for the Ferrovia Circumetnea train.

A 90-minute ticket for either bus or metro costs €1. A two-hour combined ticket for both costs €1.20.

TAXI

For a taxi, call **Radio Taxi Catania** (☑ 095 33 09 66; www.radiotaxicatania.org).

Mt Etna

ELEV 3329M

Dominating the landscape of eastern Sicily and visible from the moon (if you happen to be there), Mt Etna is Europe's largest

volcano and one of the world's most active. Eruptions occur frequently, both from the volcano's four summit craters and from its slopes, which are littered with fissures and old craters. The volcano's most devastating eruptions occurred in 1669, killing 15,000 people and lasting 122 days. Lava poured down Etna's southern slope, engulfing much of Catania and dramatically altering the landscape. The volcano's most destructive recent eruption came in 2002, when lava flows caused an explosion in Sapienza, destroying two buildings and temporarily halting the cable-car service. Less destructive eruptions continue to occur regularly, and locals understandably keep a close eye on the smouldering peak.

Enshrined as a Unesco World Heritage Site in 2013, the volcano is surrounded by the huge Parco dell'Etna, the largest unspoilt wilderness remaining in Sicily. The park encompasses a remarkable variety of environments, from the severe, almost surreal, summit to deserts of lava and alpine forests.

◎ Sights & Activities

The southern approach to Mt Etna presents the easier ascent to the craters. The AST bus from Catania drops you off at Rifugio Sapienza (1923m) from where the Funivia dell'Etna (☑095 91 41 41; www.funiviaetna.com; return €30, incl bus & guide €63; ⊙9am-4.15pm Apr-Nov, to 3.45pm Dec-Mar) cable car runs up the mountain to 2500m. From the upper cable-car station it's a 3½- to four-hour return trip up the winding track to the authorised crater zone (2920m). Make sure you leave enough time to get up *and* down before the last cable car leaves at 4.45pm. You can pay an extra €33 for a guided 4WD tour to take you up from the cable car to the crater zone, but the guides provided by the Funivia tend to be perfunctory at best, and you'll have more freedom to explore if you go it alone.

An alternative ascent is from Piano Provenzano (1800m) on Etna's northern flank. This area was severely damaged during the 2002 eruptions, as is still evidenced by the bleached skeletons of the surrounding pine trees. To reach Piano Provenzano you'll need a car, as there's no public transport beyond Linguaglossa, 16km away.

☞ Tours

Several Catania-based companies offer private excursions up the mountain, as do

Gruppo Guide Alpine Etna Sud (🖉 389 3496086, 095 791 47 55; www.etnaguide.eu) and Gruppo Guide Alpine Etna Nord (🖉 095 777 45 02; www.guidetnanord.com), official guide agencies based on Etna's slopes.

🛏 Sleeping & Eating

There's plenty of B&B accommodation around Mt Etna, particularly in the small, pretty town of Nicolosi. Contact Nicolosi's **tourist information office** (🖉 095 791 70 31; Piazza Vittorio Emanuele) for a full list.

Agriturismo San Marco   AGRITURISMO €
(🖉 389 4237294; www.agriturismosanmarco.com; Rovittello; per person B&B/half board/full board €35/53/68; 🛜 🕸 🐾) Get back to basics at this delightful *agriturismo* (farm-stay accommodation) near Rovittello, on Etna's northern flank. The bucolic setting, rustic rooms, a swimming pool, a kids' play area and superb country cooking make it a relaxed place to kick back for a couple of days. Call ahead for directions.

Rifugio Sapienza   CHALET €
(🖉 095 91 53 21; www.rifugiosapienza.com; Piazzale Funivia; s/d €46/70; 🅿 🛜) Offering comfortable accommodation with a good restaurant, this place adjacent to the cable car is the closest lodging to Etna's summit.

ℹ Information

Catania's downtown tourist office (p819) provides information about Etna, as does the office of **Parco dell'Etna** (🖉 095 82 11 11; www.parcoetna.ct.it; Via del Convento 45, Nicolosi; ☉ 9am-2pm & 4-7.30pm), 1km from the centre of Nicolosi on the mountain's southern flank.

ℹ Getting There & Away

BUS

AST (🖉 095 723 05 11; www.aziendasicilianatrasporti.it) runs one bus daily from Catania to Rifugio Sapienza (one way/return €4/6.60, two hours), leaving the car park opposite Catania's train station at 8.15am and arriving at Rifugio Sapienza at 10.15am. The return journey leaves Rifugio Sapienza at 4.30pm, arriving in Catania at 6.30pm.

TRAIN

You can circle Etna on the private **Ferrovia Circumetnea** (FCE; 🖉 095 54 11 11; www.circumetnea.it; Via Caronda 352a, Catania) train line, departing from Catania. From Catania's main train station catch the metro to the FCE station at Via Caronda (metro stop Borgo) or take bus 429 or 432 going up Via Etnea and ask to be let off at the Borgo metro stop.

The train follows a 114km route around the base of the volcano, providing lovely views. It also passes through many of Etna's unique towns, such as Adrano, Bronte and Randazzo. See the website for fares and timetables.

SYRACUSE & THE SOUTHEAST

Home to Sicily's most beautiful baroque towns and Magna Graecia's most magnificent ancient city, the southeast is one of Sicily's most compelling destinations. The classical charms of Syracuse are reason enough to visit, but once you leave the city behind you'll find an evocative checkerboard of river valleys and stone-walled citrus groves dotted with handsome towns.

Shattered by a devastating earthquake in 1693, the towns of Noto, Ragusa and Modica

---

DON'T MISS

NECROPOLI DI PANTALICA

On a huge plateau above the Valle dell'Anapo (Anapo Valley), the **Necropoli di Pantalica** (Via Pantalica) is Sicily's most important Iron and Bronze Age necropolis, with more than 5000 tombs of various shapes and sizes honeycombed along the limestone cliffs. The site is incredibly ancient, dating to between the 13th and 8th centuries BC, and its origins are largely mysterious, although it is thought to be the Siculi capital of Hybla, which gave the Greeks Megara Hyblaea in 664 BC.

Enshrined by Unesco as a World Heritage Site, Pantalica's ruins are surrounded by the beautifully wild and unspoilt landscape of the Valle dell'Anapo, a deep limestone gorge laced with walking trails. Maps posted at the archaeological site's entrance allow you to find your way, but the site is remote, with no services; wear sensible hiking shoes and bring plenty of water. Agencies in Syracuse also offer guided trips.

You'll need your own wheels to get here. From Syracuse, head northwest on the SS124 towards Palazzolo Acreide. After about 36km, turn right towards Ferla; the Necropoli di Pantalica is 11km beyond the town.

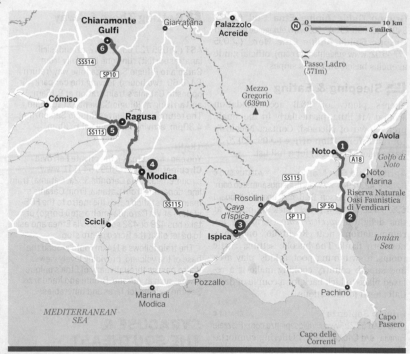

🏃 Driving Tour
Baroque Towns

START NOTO
END CHIARAMONTE GULFI
LENGTH 71KM; TWO DAYS

A land of remote rocky gorges, sweeping views and silent valleys, Sicily's southeastern corner is home to the 'baroque triangle', an area of Unesco-listed hilltop towns famous for their lavish baroque architecture. This tour takes in some of the finest baroque towns in Sicily, all within easy driving distance of each other.

Located just over 35km south of Syracuse, ❶ **Noto** is home to what is arguably Sicily's most beautiful street – Corso Vittorio Emanuele, a pedestrianised boulevard lined with golden baroque *palazzi* (mansions). From Noto, head 12km south along the SP19 to the ❷ **Riserva Naturale Oasi Faunistica di Vendicari**, a coastal preserve whose trails, wetlands and beaches are prime territory for walking, birdwatching and swimming. Next, head 23km southwest along the SP56, SP11 and SS115 to ❸ **Ispica**, a hilltop town

overlooking a huge canyon, the Cava d'Ispica, riddled with prehistoric tombs. Continuing up the SS115 for a further 18km brings you to ❹ **Modica**, a bustling town set in a deep rocky gorge. There's excellent accommodation here and a wealth of great restaurants, so the town makes a good place to overnight. The best of the baroque sights are up in Modica Alta, the high part of town, but save some energy for the *passeggiata* (evening stroll) on Corso Umberto I in the lower town.

Next morning, a short, winding, up-and-down drive through rock-littered hilltops leads to ❺ **Ragusa**, one of Sicily's nine provincial capitals. The town is divided in two – it's the lower town, Ragusa Ibla, that you want; it's a claustrophobic warren of grey stone houses and elegant *palazzi* that opens up onto Piazza Duomo, a superb example of 18th-century town planning. Although you can eat well in Ragusa, consider lunching in ❻ **Chiaramonte Gulfi**, a tranquil hilltop town some 20km to the north along the SP10, famous for its olive oil and delicious pork.

are the superstars here, rebuilt in the ornate and much-lauded Sicilian baroque style that lends the region a cohesive aesthetic appeal. Writer Gesualdo Bufalino described the southeast as an 'island within an island'; indeed, this pocket of Sicily has a remote, genteel air – a legacy of its Greek heritage.

Syracuse

POP 124,000

A dense tapestry of overlapping cultures and civilisations, Syracuse is one of Sicily's most appealing cities. Settled by colonists from Corinth in 734 BC, this was considered to be the most beautiful city of the ancient world, rivalling Athens in power and prestige. Under the demagogue Dionysius the Elder, the city reached its zenith, attracting luminaries such as Livy, Plato, Aeschylus and Archimedes, and cultivating the sophisticated urban culture that was to see the birth of comic Greek theatre.

Arriving in today's drab modern downtown by train or bus, you could be excused for wondering what all the fuss is about. But cross the bridge to the ancient island neighbourhood of Ortygia, and Syracuse's irresistible appeal quickly becomes manifest; in the Ancient Greek temple columns peeking out from the baroque walls of Ortygia's cathedral; the throngs of locals and tourists mingling in the reflected evening glow of Piazza del Duomo's vast marble pavements; the flash of fish swimming amid the papyrus plants in the Fontana Aretusa, and the splash of sunbathers plunging off rocks into the blue Ionian Sea. Adding to the city's magic is Syracuse's annual theatre festival, where classical Greek dramas are staged in one of the Mediterranean's greatest surviving ancient theatres.

Add to this the city's ambitious and enlightened moves towards pedestrian friendliness and environmental sustainability (including the recent launch of a fleet of electric minibuses), and you'll begin to understand why this has become Sicily's number one tourist destination and a city to savour.

◉ Sights

◉ Ortygia

★ **Duomo** CATHEDRAL
(Map p826; Piazza del Duomo; adult/reduced €2/1; ⊙9am-6.30pm Mon-Sat Apr-Oct, to 5.30pm Nov-Mar) Built on the skeleton of a 5th-century

BC Greek temple to Athena (note the Doric columns still visible inside and out), Syracuse's cathedral became a church when the island was evangelised by St Paul. Its most striking feature is the columned baroque facade (1728–53) added by Andrea Palma after the 1693 earthquake. A statue of the Virgin Mary crowns the rooftop, in the same spot where a golden statue of Athena once served as a beacon to homecoming Greek sailors.

Miqwe JEWISH SITE
(Ritual Bath; Map p826; ☑0931 2 22 55; Via Alagona 52; tours in English & Italian €5; ⊙tours 9am-7pm late-Mar–Oct, reduced hours rest of year) Buried 20m beneath the Alla Giudecca hotel in Ortygia's old Jewish ghetto (known as the Giudecca) is an extraordinary ancient Jewish *miqwe* (ritual bath), reputedly Europe's oldest. The baths were once connected to a synagogue, but were blocked by members of the Jewish community when they were expelled from the island in 1492. Regularly scheduled tours are offered in English and Italian.

Fontana Aretusa FOUNTAIN
(Map p826; Largo Aretusa) Stop to relax among papyrus plants and swans at this lovely spring, where fresh water still bubbles up just as it did in ancient times when it was the city's main water supply. Legend has it that the goddess Artemis transformed her beautiful handmaiden Aretusa into the spring to protect her from the unwelcome attention of the river god Alpheus.

Castello Maniace CASTLE
(Map p826; Piazza Federico di Svevia; adult/reduced €4/2; ⊙9am-1.30pm) Guarding the island's southern tip, Ortygia's 13th-century castle is a lovely place to wander, gaze out over the water and contemplate Syracuse's past glories. The castle grounds house two exhibitions, one shedding light on the fortress' evolution through the centuries, the other displaying archaeological finds from the site.

Galleria Regionale di Palazzo Bellomo GALLERY
(Map p826; ☑0931 6 95 11; www.regione.sicilia.it/beniculturali/palazzobellomo; Via Capodieci 16; adult/reduced €8/4; ⊙9am-7pm Tue-Sat, 2-7.30pm Sun) Housed in a 13th-century Catalan-Gothic palace, this art museum's eclectic collection ranges from early Byzantine and Norman stonework to 19th-century Caltagirone ceramics to a beautiful *Annunciation* by Antonello da Messina.

Syracuse

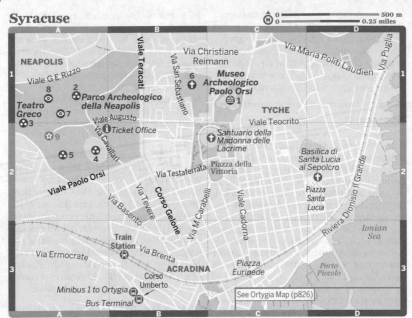

Syracuse

Museo del Papiro   MUSEUM
(Map p826; ☑ 0931 2 21 00; www.museodelpapiro.
it; Via Nizza 14; adult/reduced €5/2; ⊘10am-7pm
Tue-Sat, to 2pm Sun May-Sep, 9.30am-2pm Tue-Sun
Oct-Apr) This museum exhibits a fine collection of boats, papyrus documents and products, and an English-language film about the
nifty material's history. The papyrus plant
grows in abundance around the nearby Ci-
ane river, and was used to make paper in the
18th century.

◎ Mainland Syracuse

★ Parco Archeologico
della Neapolis   ARCHAEOLOGICAL SITE
(Map p824; ☑0931 6 62 06; Viale Paradiso 14;
adult/reduced €10/5, incl Museo Archeologico
€13.50/7; ⊘9am-1hr before sunset Mon-Sat,
9am-1pm Sun) For the classicist, Syracuse's

real attraction is this archaeological park
and its pearly white 5th-century-BC **Teatro
Greco.** Hewn out of the rocky hillside, this
16,000-capacity amphitheatre staged the
last tragedies of Aeschylus (including *The
Persians*), which were first performed here
in his presence. In late spring it's brought
to life with an annual season of classical
theatre.

Beside the theatre is the mysterious **La-
tomia del Paradiso** (Garden of Paradise),
a deep, precipitous limestone quarry out of
which stone for the ancient city was extracted. Riddled with catacombs and filled with
citrus and magnolia trees, it's also where
7000 survivors of the war between Syracuse
and Athens in 413 BC were imprisoned.
The **Orecchio di Dionisio** (Ear of Dionysius), a 23m-high grotto extending 65m back
into the cliffside, was named by Caravaggio

after the tyrant Dionysius, who is said to have used the almost perfect acoustics of the quarry to eavesdrop on his prisoners.

Back outside this area you'll find the entrance to the 2nd-century **Anfiteatro Romano**, originally used for gladiatorial combat and horse races. The Spaniards, little interested in archaeology, largely destroyed the site in the 16th century, using it as a quarry to build Ortygia's city walls. West of the amphitheatre is the 3rd-century-BC **Ara di Gerone II** (Altar of Hieron II), a monolithic sacrificial altar to Hieron II where up to 450 oxen could be killed at one time.

To reach the park, take Sd'A Trasporti's *linea rossa* minibus ('red' minibus No 2; €1, 15 minutes) from Molo Sant'Antonio, on the west side of the main bridge into Ortygia. Alternatively, walking from Ortygia will take about 30 minutes. If driving, park on Viale Augusto (tickets are available at the nearby souvenir kiosks).

The **ticket office** is located near the corner of Via Cavallari and Viale Augusto, opposite the main site.

★ Museo Archeologico Paolo Orsi
MUSEUM

(Map p824; ☏ 0931 48 95 11; www.regione.sicilia.it/beniculturali/museopaoloorsi; Viale Teocrito 66; adult/reduced €8/4, incl Parco Archeologico €13.50/7; ⊙ 9am-6pm Tue-Sat, to 1pm Sun) About 500m east of the archaeological park, this modern museum contains one of Sicily's largest and most interesting archaeological collections. Allow plenty of time to investigate the four sectors charting the area's prehistory, as well as Syracuse's development from foundation to the late Roman period.

Basilica & Catacombe di San Giovanni
CHURCH, CATACOMB

(Map p824; ☏ 0931 6 46 94; www.kairos-web.com; Via San Sebastiano; guided tour adult/reduced €8/5; ⊙ 9.30am-12.30pm & 2.30-5.30pm Tue-Sun) Beneath the Basilica di San Giovanni – a pretty, truncated church that served as the city's cathedral in the 17th century – lie these eerie, extensive catacombs, accessible on 30- to 40-minute guided tours (available in English).

☂ Activities

In midsummer, when Ortygia steams like a cauldron, people flock to the beach south of town at **Lido Arenella**; take bus 23 from Piazza della Posta.

Also a favourite local hang-out for swimming and sunbathing in the summer months is the **platform** (Map p826) along Ortygia's eastern waterfront, surrounded by flat rocks and flanked by the crenellated walls of Forte Vigliena.

★ Festivals & Events

Ciclo di Rappresentazioni Classiche
THEATRE

(Festival of Greek Theatre; www.indafondazione.org; ⊙ mid-May–Jun) Syracuse boasts the only school of classical Greek drama outside Athens, and in May and June it hosts live performances of Greek plays (in Italian) at the Teatro Greco, attracting Italy's finest performers. Tickets (€26 to €68) are available online, from the **Fondazione Inda ticket office** (Map p826; ☏ office 0931 48 72 00, tickets 800 542644Corso Matteotti 29; ⊙ 10am-1pm Mon-Sat) in Ortygia or at the **ticket booth** (⊙ 10am-6.30pm) outside the theatre.

Festa di Santa Lucia
RELIGIOUS

(⊙ 13 Dec) The enormous silver statue of the city's patron saint wends its way from the cathedral to Piazza Santa Lucia, accompanied by fireworks.

☐ Sleeping

Stay on Ortygia for atmosphere. Cheaper accommodation is located around the train station.

B&B Aretusa Vacanze
B&B €

(Map p826; ☏ 0931 48 34 84; www.aretusavacanze.com; Vicolo Zuccalà 1; d €59-90, tr €70-120, q €105-147; ☑❄☏) This great budget option, elbowed into a tiny pedestrian street in a 17th-century building, has large rooms and apartments with kitchenettes, wi-fi, satellite TV and small balconies from where you can shake hands with your neighbour across the way. Parking costs €7 per day.

★ Hotel Gutkowski
HOTEL €€

(Map p826; ☏ 0931 46 58 61; www.guthotel.it; Lungomare Vittorini 26; d €90-140, tr €140; ❄@☏) Book well in advance for one of the sea-view rooms at this stylish, eclectic hotel on the Ortygia waterfront, at the edge of the Giudecca neighbourhood. Divided between two buildings, its rooms are simple yet chic, with pretty tiled floors, walls in teals, greys, blues and browns, and a mix of vintage and industrial details.

Ortygia

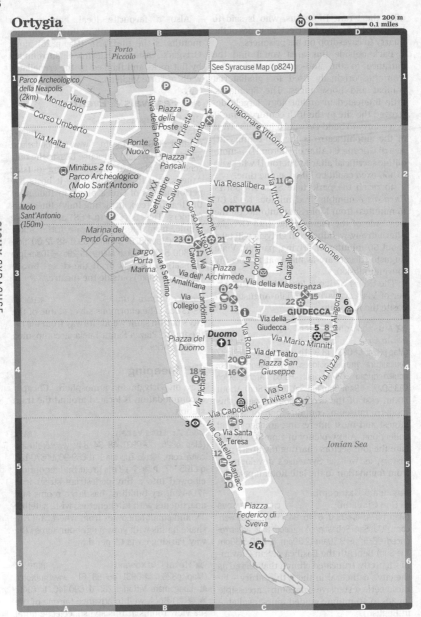

N 0 ——————— 200 m
   0 ——————— 0.1 miles

See Syracuse Map (p824)

SICILY SYRACUSE

Porto Piccolo

Parco Archeologico
della Neapolis
(2km)
Viale Montedoro
Corso Umberto
Via Malta

Minibus 2 to
Parco Archeologico
(Molo Sant'Antonio
stop)

Molo
Sant'Antonio
(150m)

Marina del
Porto Grande

Largo
Porta
Marina

Riva della Posta
Piazza
della
Poste
Ponte
Nuovo
Piazza
Pancali
Via XX Settembre
Via Savoia
Via Trieste
Via Trento
14
Lungomare Vittorini

Via Resalibera
Via Vittorio Veneto
11
ORTYGIA

Corso Matteotti
Via Drone
Via del Tolomei

23
17
Cavour
21
Via S Coronati
Via Gargallo
Via della Maestranza
15
22
GIUDECCA
6

Via dell'
Amalfitana
Piazza
Archimede
24
19 13
Via Landolina
Via Collegio
Via della
Giudecca
5 8
Via Mario Minniti
Via Alagona

Piazza del
Duomo
Duomo
1
Via Roma
Via del Teatro
Piazza San
Giuseppe
Via Nizza

18
4
16
20
Via Pichieli
Via Capodieci
Via S
Privitera
7

3
9
12
10
Via Castello Maniace
Via Santa
Teresa

Ionian Sea

Piazza
Federico di
Svevia

2

---

ments await in this *palazzo* owned by a Milanese art collector. The larger is decadent,
with luxurious sofas, king-size bed, dining
table, precious artworks and a vaulted stone
ceiling. There's a sea-view terrace and the
bathroom has original stonework and a

Ortygia

SICILY SYRACUSE

hydro-massage shower. The smaller apartment wows with floor-to-ceiling artwork and a romantic four-poster bed. Both have kitchenettes and can accommodate up to four. Minimum three nights.

Alla Giudecca   HOTEL €€

(Map p826; ☑0931 2 22 55; www.allagiudecca.it; Via Alagona 52; d €135-220; ❄@❄) Located in the old Jewish quarter, this charming hotel offers 21 suites with warm terracotta-tiled floors, exposed wood beams and lashings of heavy white linen. The communal areas are a warren of vaulted rooms full of museum-quality antiques and enormous tapestries, and feature cosy sofas gathered around a huge fireplace. A few more expensive rooms have sea views.

Henry's House   HOTEL €€€

(Map p826; ☑0931 2 13 61; www.hotelhenrys house.com; Via del Castello Maniace 68; s €160-200, d €190-230, ste €290-330; ❄❄) Directly overlooking Ortygia's waterfront, with three communal sun terraces perfect for lounging and soaking up the views, this gorgeous 17th-century *palazzo* was lovingly restored by antique collector Signor Corsaro before opening as a hotel in 2014. If money isn't an issue, book one of the two upstairs suites (one with terrace, both with water views). Complimentary bikes are available to guests.

✖ Eating

Ortygia is the best place to eat. Its narrow lanes are chock-full of trattorias, restaurants, cafes and bars, and while some are obvious tourist traps, there are plenty of quality options in the mix. Most places specialise in seafood.

★ Caseificio Borderi   SANDWICHES €

(Map p826; www.caseificioborderi.eu; Via Benedictis 6; sandwiches €5; ⊙7am-4pm Mon-Sat) No visit to Syracuse's market is complete without a stop at this colourful deli near Ortygia's far northern tip. Veteran sandwich-master Andrea Borderi stands out front with a table full of cheeses, olives, greens, herbs, tomatoes and other fixings, and engages in non-stop banter with customers while creating free-form sandwiches big enough to keep you fed all day.

Sicilia in Tavola   SICILIAN €

(Map p826; www.siciliaintavolo.eu; ☑392 4610889; Via Cavour 28; meals €20-30; ⊙12.30-2.30pm & 7.30-10.30pm Tue-Sun) One of the longest-established and most popular eateries on Via Cavour, this snug, simple trattoria has built its reputation on delicious homemade pasta and seafood. To savour both at once, tuck into the *fettuccine allo scoglio* (pasta ribbons with mixed seafood) or the equally fine prawn ravioli, paired with sweet cherry tomatoes and chopped mint. Reservations recommended

★ Moon   VEGAN €€

(Map p826; ☑0931 44 95 16; www.moonortigia. com; Via Roma 112; meals €18-30; ⊙6-11.30pm; ❄�𝄞) If vegan fare usually makes you yawn, subvert your thinking at boho-chic Moon. A cast of mostly organic and biological ingredients beam in decadent, intriguing dishes that might see a tower of thinly sliced pears interlayered with a rich, soy-based cashew cream cheese, or chickpea and tofu conspiring in a smokey *linguine alla carbonara* as wicked as the original.

Moon also doubles as a performance space, serving up weekly theatre and music performances on its small backstage.

★ A Putia delle Cose Buone SICILIAN €€
(Map p826; ☎334 3524585, 0931 44 92 79; www.aputiadellecosebuone.it; Via Roma 8; meals €18-30; ⊗12.45-3pm & 7-11pm; ☑) From the whimsical lanterns to the benches draped in colourful pillows, this little bolthole feels welcoming from the word go. Then there's the food: creative, reasonably priced Sicilian dishes that make ample use of local seafood, veggies and extra-virgin olive oil (labelled EVO on the menu). Salads, vegan and vegetarian options also abound. Service is friendly, and there's pavement seating in warm weather.

★ Don Camillo MODERN SICILIAN €€€
(Map p826; ☎0931 6 71 33; www.ristorantedoncamillo.it; Via Maestranza 96; degustation menus €35-70; ⊗12.30-2.30pm & 8-10.30pm Mon-Sat; ☎☑) One of Ortygia's most elegant restaurants, Don Camillo specialises in sterling service and innovative Sicilian cuisine. Pique the appetite with mixed shellfish in a thick soup of Noto almonds; swordfish with orange-blossom honey and sweet-and-sour vegetables; or outstanding *tagliata di tonno* (tuna steak) with red-pepper 'marmalade'. A must for Slow Food gourmands.

🍷 Drinking & Nightlife

Syracuse is a vibrant university town, which means plenty of life on the streets after nightfall. Many places are clustered near Piazza del Duomo.

Barcollo BAR
(Map p826; www.facebook.com/barcollosiracusa; Via Pompeo Picherali 10; ⊗7pm-3am; ☎) Hidden away in a flamboyant baroque courtyard, sultry Barcollo lures with its fresh flowers, flickering tealights and chi-chi outdoor deck. *Aperitivo* is served daily between 7pm and 10pm (there's a buffet on Sundays), with DJ sets Fridays and Sundays, and live music Saturdays.

Biblios Cafè CAFE
(Map p826; www.biblioscafe.it; Via del Consiglio Reginale 11; ⊗noon-9pm Wed-Mon Apr-Oct, 10am-2pm & 5-10pm Wed-Mon Nov-Mar) This beloved bookshop-cafe organises a whole range of cultural activities, including wine tasting, literary readings and language courses. It's a great place to drop in any time of day, for coffee or *aperitivi* or just to mingle.

Solaria Vini & Liquori WINE BAR
(Map p826; ☎0931 46 30 07; www.vini-siciliani.it; Via Roma 86; ⊗11.30am-2.30pm & 6pm-1am Mon-Sat; ☎) Thi is a wonderfully old-school *enoteca* (wine bar), with rows of rustic wooden tables and dark bottles lined up on floor-to-ceiling shelves. Stop by for a glass of wine or two, and pair with *vino*-friendly bites including cheese, olives, prosciutto, anchovies, sardines and *crocchè* (potato croquettes). The wine list is extensive and predominantly local, with French vintages and Champagnes thrown in for Gallic flair.

☆ Entertainment

Piccolo Teatro dei Pupi THEATRE
(Map p826; ☎0931 46 55 40; www.pupari.com; Via della Giudecca 17; ⊗6 times weekly Apr-Oct, fewer Nov-Mar) Syracuse's beloved puppet theatre hosts regular performances; see its website for a calendar. You can also buy puppets made at the family's workshop across the street and visit the affiliated puppet museum.

🛍 Shopping

Browsing in Ortygia's quirky boutiques is great fun.

Massimo Izzo JEWELLERY
(Map p826; ☎0931 2 23 01; www.massimoizzo.com; Piazza Archimede 25; ⊗4-8pm Mon, 9am-1pm & 4-8pm Tue-Sat) The flamboyant jewellery of Messina-born Massimo Izzo is not for the faint-hearted. Featuring bold idiosyncratic designs and made with Sciacca coral, gold and precious stones, his handmade pieces are often inspired by themes close to the Sicilian heart: the sea, theatre and classical antiquity.

Fish House Art ARTS & CRAFTS
(Map p826; ☎339 7771364; www.fishhouseart.it; Via Cavour 29-31; ⊗10am-1pm & 4-8pm Mon-Sat) This quirky gallery and shop is swimming with whimsical, beautifully crafted objects inspired by the sea. It's a showcase for both emerging and established Italian artisans, whose wares span richly hued fish made of

hand-blown glass to curious, recycled-metal creatures and wearable art.

ℹ Information

Hospital (Ospedale Umberto I; ☑ 0931 72 41 11; Via Testaferrata 1) Hospital between the centre and Parco Archeologico.

Tourist Office (Map p826; ☑ 0931 46 29 46; http://turismo.provsr.it; Via Roma 31; ⊘ 9am-12.30pm Mon-Fri) City maps and lots of good information.

ℹ Getting There & Away

Syracuse's train and bus stations are a block apart from each other, halfway between Ortygia and the archaeological park.

BUS

Long-distance buses operate from the bus stop along Corso Umberto, just east of Syracuse's train station.

Interbus (☑ 0931 6 67 10; www.interbus.it) runs buses hourly on weekdays (less frequently on weekends) to Catania (€6.20, 1½ hours) and Catania's Fontanarossa Airport (€6.20, 1¼ hours). Other Interbus destinations include Noto (€3.60, 55 minutes, two to four daily) and Palermo (€13.50, 3¼ hours, two to three daily).

AST (☑ 0931 46 27 11; www.aziendasicil ianatrasporti.it) offers service to Ragusa (€7.50, 3¼ hours, five daily except Sunday), with intermediate stops in Noto (€4, 55 minutes) and Modica (€6.40, 2¾ hours).

CAR & MOTORCYCLE

The modern A18 and SS114 highways connect Syracuse with Catania and points north, while the SS115 runs south to Noto and Modica. Arriving by car, exit onto the eastbound SS124 and follow signs to Syracuse and Ortygia.

Traffic on Ortygia is restricted; you're better off parking and walking once you arrive on the island. Most convenient is the **Talete parking garage** (Parcheggio Talete) at Ortygia's northern tip, which charges a 24-hour maximum of €10 (payable by cash or credit card at the machine when you leave). **Molo Sant'Antonio** on the mainland, just across the bridge from Ortygia, is another option.

TRAIN

From Syracuse's **train station** (Via Francesco Crispi), several trains depart daily for Messina (€10.50, 2½ to 3¼ hours) via Catania (€6.90, 1¼ hours). Some go on to Rome, Turin and Milan as well as other long-distance destinations. For Palermo, the bus is a better option. There are also local trains from Syracuse to Noto (€3.80, 30 minutes, eight daily except Sunday) and Ragusa (€8.30, two to 2½ hours, two daily except Sunday).

ℹ Getting Around

Syracuse's most convenient and ecofriendly public transport option is the fleet of electric minibuses operated by **Sd'A Trasporti** (www.siracusadamare.it; one way/day pass/week pass €1/3/10). To reach Ortygia from the bus and train stations, hop aboard the *linea blu* ('blue' minibus No 1), which loops around the island every half-hour or so, making stops at more than a dozen convenient locations. To reach Parco Archeologico della Neapolis, take the *linea rossa* ('red' minibus No 2) from Molo Sant'Antonio, just west of the bridge to Ortygia. For route maps, see Sd'A Trasporti's website.

Noto

POP 23,800 / ELEV 160M

Flattened by the devastating earthquake of 1693, Noto was grandly rebuilt by its nobles into the finest baroque town in Sicily. Now a Unesco World Heritage Site, the town is especially impressive in the early evening, when its golden-hued sandstone buildings seem to glow with a soft inner light, and at night when illuminations accentuate the beauty of its intricately carved facades. The baroque masterpiece is the work of Rosario Gagliardi and his assistant, Vincenzo Sinatra, local architects who also worked in Ragusa and Modica.

◉ Sights

Two piazzas break up the long Corso Vittorio Emanuele: Piazza dell'Immacolata to the east and Piazza XVI Maggio to the west. The latter is overlooked by the beautiful **Chiesa di San Domenico** and the adjacent **Dominican monastery**, both designed by Rosario Gagliardi. On the same square, Noto's elegant 19th-century **Teatro Comunale** is worth a look. For sweeping views of Noto's baroque splendour, climb to the rooftop terrace at **Chiesa di Santa Chiara** (adult/reduced €2/1; ⊘ 10am-1pm & 3-6.30pm Mar-Jul, Sep & Oct, 9.30am-midnight Aug, 10am-noon Nov-Jan, closed Feb) or the *campanile* (bell tower) of **Chiesa di San Carlo al Corso** (campanile €2; ⊘ 10am-1pm & 3-6.30pm Mar-Jul, Sep & Oct, 9.30am-midnight Aug, 10am-noon Nov-Jan, closed Feb).

★ **Cattedrale di San Nicolò**   CATHEDRAL
(Piazza Municipio; ⊘ 8am-1pm & 4-8pm) Pride of place in Noto goes to San Nicolò cathedral, a baroque beauty that had to undergo extensive renovation after its dome collapsed during a 1996 thunderstorm. The ensuing decade saw

the cathedral scrubbed of centuries of dust and dirt before reopening in 2007. Today the dome, with its peachy glow, is once again the focal point of Noto's skyline.

Piazza Municipio
PIAZZA

About halfway along Corso Vittorio Emanuele is the graceful Piazza Municipio, flanked by Noto's most dramatic buildings. To the north, sitting in stately pomp at the head of Paolo Labisi's monumental staircase, is the Cattedrale di San Nicolò, surrounded by a series of elegant palaces. To the left (west) is Palazzo Landolina, once home to the powerful Sant'Alfano family.

Palazzo Nicolaci di Villadorata
PALACE

(📞 338 7427022; www.comune.noto.sr.it/palazzo -nicolaci; Via Corrado Nicolaci; €4; ⏱10am-1.30pm & 2.30-7pm) The striking facade of this 18th-century palace features wrought-iron balconies supported by a swirling pantomime of grotesque figures. Inside, the *palazzo*'s richly brocaded walls and frescoed ceilings offer an idea of the sumptuous lifestyle of Sicilian nobles.

✦ Festivals & Events

Infiorata
CARNIVAL

(www.infioratadinoto.it; ⏱mid-May) Noto's big annual jamboree, the Infiorata is celebrated over three days around the third Sunday in May, with parades, historical re-enactments and the decoration of Via Corrado Nicolaci with designs made entirely of flower petals.

🛏 Sleeping & Eating

B&Bs are plentiful in Noto; the tourist office keeps a list.

Locals are serious about their food, so take time to enjoy a meal and follow it up with a visit to one of the town's excellent gelaterie (ice-cream shops).

★ Nòtia Rooms
B&B €€

(📞 366 5007350, 0931 83 88 91; www.notiarooms. com; Vico Frumento 6; d €130-150, tr €150-170; 🖥) In Noto's historic workers' quarter, this sophisticated B&B is owned by the gracious Giorgio and Carla, who gave up the stress of northern Italian life to open this three-room beauty. Crisp white interiors are accented with original artworks, Modernist Italian lamps and upcycled vintage finds. Rooms seduce with sublimely comfortable beds and polished modern bathrooms. Gorgeous breakfasts maintain the high standards.

La Corte del Sole
INN €€

(📞 0931 82 02 10; www.lacortedelsole.it; Contrada Bucachemi, Eloro, Lido di Noto; d €152-226, q €261-390; 🅿❄@🛜🏊) Overlooking the green fields of Eloro is this stylish hotel housed in a traditional Sicilian *masseria* (farmstead). A delightful place to stay, it also offers a range of activities, including cooking lessons (3hr lesson per guest/nonguest €75/90; ⏱9.30am-12.30pm Tue-Sat, closed Aug) run by the hotel chef and, in winter, tours to study the 80 or so types of wild orchid found in the area.

★ Caffè Sicilia
GELATO €

(📞 0931 83 50 13; Corso Vittorio Emanuele 125; desserts from €2; ⏱8am-10pm Tue-Sun) Dating from 1892 and especially renowned for its *granite,* this beloved place vies with its next-door neighbour, Dolceria Corrado Costanzo, for the honours of Noto's best dessert shop. Frozen desserts are made with the freshest seasonal ingredients (wild strawberries in spring, for example), while the delicious *torrone* (nougat) bursts with the flavours of local honey and almonds.

★ Ristorante Crocifisso
SICILIAN €€

(📞 0931 57 11 51; www.ristorantecrocifisso.it; Via Principe Umberto 48; meals €30-40; ⏱12.30-2.15pm Thu-Tue, plus 7.30-10pm Tue & Thu-Sat) Up in Noto Alta, this Slow Food–acclaimed restaurant with an extensive wine list is widely regarded as Noto's best. Sicilian classics such as *macco di fave* (fava bean purée with wild fennel), garnished with ricotta and toasted breadcrumbs, and *casarecce alla palermitana* (short handmade pasta with sardines and wild fennel) are complemented by juicy roast lamb, Marsala-glazed pork and pistachio- and sesame-crusted tuna.

★ Ristorante Vicari
MODERN SICILIAN €€€

(📞 0931 83 93 22; www.ristorantevicari.it; Ronco Bernardo Leanti 9; 5-/7-course degustation menu €50/60; ⏱12.30-2pm & 7-10pm Tue-Sun, closed lunch Wed & Sun Jun-Sep) Low-slung lamps spotlight linen-clad tables at Vicari, and rightfully so. In the kitchen is up-and-coming chef Salvatore Vicari, who thrills with his whimsical takes on Sicilian produce: think sea urchin spaghetti with white-bean cream and *selicornia* (sea asparagus), tender rabbit decadently stuffed with liver pâté, or ridiculously succulent octopus barbecued and smoked to perfection. Book ahead.

ℹ️ Information

Infopoint Noto (☑ 339 4816218; www.notoin forma.it; Corso Vittorio Emanuele 135; ⊘ 10am-10pm Jul & Aug, to 6pm Apr-Jun & Sep, to 5pm Oct-Mar) A useful tourist office, with maps, brochures and enthusiastic, multilingual staff who can also organise excursions.

ℹ️ Getting There & Away

BUS

From Largo Pantheon on the eastern edge of Noto's historic centre, **AST** (☑ 840 000323; www.aziendasiciliatrasporti.it) and **Interbus** (☑ 0935 2 24 60, 091 34 20 55; www.interbus. it) serve Catania (€8.40, 1½ hours) and Syracuse (€3.60 to €4, 55 minutes). Service is less frequent on Sundays.

TRAIN

Trains run to Syracuse (€3.80, 30 minutes, eight daily except Sunday), but Noto's station is inconveniently located 1km downhill from the centre.

Modica

POP 54,700 / ELEV 296M

A powerhouse in Grecian times, Modica remains a superbly atmospheric town, with its medieval and baroque buildings climbing steeply up either side of a deep gorge. The multilayered town is divided into Modica Alta (Upper Modica) and Modica Bassa (Lower Modica). A devastating flood in 1902 resulted in the wide avenues of Corso Umberto and Via Giarrantana (the river was dammed and diverted), which remain the main axes of the town, lined by *palazzi* and tiled stone houses.

👁 Sights

Aside from simply wandering the streets and absorbing the atmosphere, make time to visit Modica's extraordinary churches. Highlights include **Chiesa di San Giorgio** (Corso San Giorgio, Modica Alta; ⊘ 8am-12.30pm & 3.30-6.30pm), Gagliardi's masterpiece, a butter-coloured vision of pure rococo splendour perched on a majestic 250-step staircase. Its counterpoint in Modica Bassa is the **Cattedrale di San Pietro** (Corso Umberto I, Modica Bassa; ⊘ 9am-1pm & 3.30-7.30pm Mon-Sat, 9.30am-12.30pm & 4-7.30pm Sun), another impressive church atop a rippling staircase lined with life-sized statues of the Apostles. Up the hill in Modica Alta, the big draw is the **Chiesa di San Giovanni Evangelista** (off Piazza San Giovanni, Modica Alta; ⊘ hours vary), with its sweeping staircase, elliptical

interior and beautiful, neoclassical stucco work. Nearby, at the end of Via Pizzo, a viewing balcony offers arresting views over the old town.

🛏 Sleeping

Modica's quality-to-price ratio is generally excellent.

⭐ **Villa Quartarella** AGRITURISMO €
(☑ 360 654829; www.quartarella.com; Contrada Quartarella Passo Cane 1; s €40, d €75-80, tr €85-100, q €90-120; 🅿❄🛜🏊) Spacious rooms, welcoming hosts and ample breakfasts make this converted villa in the countryside about 7km south of Modica an appealing choice for anyone travelling by car. Owners Francesco and Francesca are generous in sharing their love and encyclopaedic knowledge of local history, flora and fauna, and can suggest a multitude of driving itineraries in the surrounding area.

Palazzo Failla HOTEL €
(☑ 0932 94 10 59; www.palazzofailla.it; Via Blandini 5, Modica Alta; s €55-99, d €80-125; ❄@🛜) Smack in the heart of Modica Alta, this four-star hotel in an exquisitely restored 18th-century palace has retained much of its historical splendour, with original frescoed ceilings, hand-painted Caltagirone floor tiles and elegant drapes. Start the day with the generous breakfast buffet and end it at the well-regarded restaurant down the lane, run by the hotel's management.

⭐ **Casa Gelsomino** APARTMENT €€
(☑ 335 8087841; www.casedisicilia.com; Via Raccomandata, Modica Bassa; per night €180-200, per week €1000-1260; ❄🛜) It's easy to pretend you're a holidaying celebrity in this stunning abode, the balconies and private terrace of which serve up commanding views over Modica. Incorporating an airy lounge, a fully equipped kitchen, stone-walled bathroom, laundry room, sitting room and separate bedroom, the apartment's combination of vaulted ceilings, antique floor-tiles, original artworks and plush furnishings take self-catering to sophisticated highs. Start planning that swank, sunset soirée.

🍴 Eating & Drinking

La Locanda del Colonnello SICILIAN €€
(☑ 0932 75 24 23; www.locandadelcolonnello.it; Vico Biscari 6, Modica Alta; meals €30-35; ⊘ 12.30-2pm & 7.30-10pm Wed-Mon; 🛜) Book ahead for a table at this Slow Food darling, hidden away

in Modica Alta. Seasonality steers a menu that gives classic Sicilian flavours subtle, elegant twists. Succulent shrimps give earthy *zuppetta di ceci* (chickpea soup) added intrigue, while ricotta and marjoram-stuffed ravioli seduce in a rich pork *sugo* (meat sauce). Finish with a smooth *gelo di limone* (lemon jelly).

★ **Accursio**   MODERN SICILIAN €€€
(✆0932 94 16 89; www.accursioristorante.it; Via Grimaldi 41, Modica Bassa; meals €65, tasting menus €100; ⊙12.30-2.30pm Wed-Sat, 7.30-10pm daily) While we love the modernist furniture and vintage Sicilian tiles, the food is the real thrill at this fine-dining maverick, which was honoured in 2016 with its first Michelin star. Head chef Accursio Craparo specialises in boldly creative, nuanced dishes inspired by childhood memories and emblematic of new Sicilian thinking. For a well-rounded adventure, opt for a tasting menu.

Rappa Enoteca   WINE BAR
(Corso Santa Teresa 97-99, Modica Alta; ⊙5pm-midnight Mon-Sat) High ceilings, antique mouldings, tiled floors and chandeliers create a delightful backdrop at this atmospheric *enoteca* in the upper town. Sample a wide range of Sicilian wines, along with cheese and meat platters.

🛍 Shopping

Dolceria Bonajuto   FOOD
(✆0932 94 12 25; www.bonajuto.it; Corso Umberto I 159, Modica Bassa; ⊙9am-8.30pm Sep-Jul, to midnight Aug) Sicily's oldest chocolate factory is the perfect place to taste Modica's famous chocolate. Flavoured with cinnamon, vanilla, orange peel and even hot peppers, it's a legacy of the town's Spanish overlords who imported cocoa from their South American colonies. Leave room for Bonajuto's *'mpanatigghi,* sweet local biscuits filled with chocolate, spices...and minced beef!

ⓘ Information

Tourist Office (✆346 6558227; www.comune.modica.rg.it; Corso Umberto I 141, Modica Bassa; ⊙8am-1.30pm & 3.30-7pm Mon-Fri, 9am-1pm & 3.30-7pm Sat) City-run tourist office in Modica Bassa.

ⓘ Getting There & Away

BUS
AST (✆0932 76 73 01; www.aziendasicil ianatrasporti.it) runs frequent buses from

Monday to Saturday, departing Piazzale Falcone-Borsellino at the top of Corso Umberto I, to Syracuse (€6.40, 2¾ hours), Noto (€4, 1¾ hours) and Ragusa (€2.70, 30 minutes). Service is limited on Sundays: two buses each to Noto and Ragusa, none to Syracuse.

TRAIN
From Modica's station, 600m southwest of the centre, five trains daily (except Sunday) head to Syracuse (€7.60, 1¾ hours) and seven to Ragusa (€2.50, 20 to 25 minutes).

Ragusa

POP 72,800 / ELEV 502M
Ragusa is a dignified and well-aged provincial town. Like every other in the region, it collapsed after the 1693 earthquake; a new town called Ragusa Superiore was built on a high plateau above the original settlement. But the old aristocracy was loath to leave their tottering *palazzi*, and so rebuilt Ragusa Ibla on the original site. The two towns were only merged in 1927.

Ragusa Ibla remains the heart and soul of the town, and has all the best restaurants and the majority of sights. A sinuous bus ride or some very steep and scenic steps connect the lower town to its modern sibling up the hill.

⊙ Sights

Grand churches and *palazzi* line the twisting, narrow streets of Ragusa Ibla, interspersed with gelaterie and delightful piazzas where the local youth stroll and the elderly gather on benches. Palm-planted Piazza del Duomo, the centre of town, is dominated by 18th-century **Cattedrale di San Giorgio** (Piazza Duomo; ⊙10am-12.30pm & 4-7pm Jun-Sep, reduced hours rest of year), which features a magnificent neoclassical dome and stained-glass windows.

At the eastern end of the old town is the **Giardino Ibleo** (✆0932 65 23 74; ⊙9am-10pm Mon-Thu, to 1am Fri & Sat), a pleasant public garden laid out in the 19th century. It's the perfect spot for a picnic lunch.

🛏 Sleeping & Eating

L'Orto Sul Tetto   B&B €
(✆0932 24 77 85; www.lortosultetto.it; Via Tenente di Stefano 56; s €45-60, d €70-110; ❄🛜) This sweet little B&B behind Ragusa's *duomo* offers an intimate experience, with just three rooms and a lovely roof terrace where breakfast is served.

THE MOSAICS OF VILLA ROMANA DEL CASALE

Near the town of Piazza Armerina in central Sicily is the stunning 3rd-century Roman **Villa Romana del Casale** (☑ 0935 68 00 36; www.villaromanadelcasale.it; adult/reduced €10/5; ⊙ 9am-6pm Apr-Oct, to 4pm Nov-Mar), a Unesco World Heritage Site and one of the few remaining sites of Roman Sicily. This sumptuous hunting lodge is thought to have belonged to Diocletian's co-emperor Marcus Aurelius Maximianus. Buried under mud in a 12th-century flood, it remained hidden for 700 years before its magnificent floor mosaics were discovered in the 1950s. Visit out of season or early in the day to avoid the hordes of visitors.

The mosaics cover almost the entire floor (3500 sq metres) of the villa and are considered unique for their narrative style, the range of subject matter and variety of colour – many are clearly influenced by African themes. Along the eastern end of the internal courtyard is the wonderful **Corridor of the Great Hunt**, vividly depicting chariots, rhinos, cheetahs, lions and the voluptuously beautiful Queen of Sheba. Across the corridor is a series of apartments, where floor illustrations reproduce scenes from Homer's *Odyssey*. But perhaps the most captivating of the mosaics is the so-called **Room of the Ten Girls in Bikinis**, with depictions of sporty girls in bikinis throwing a discus, using weights and throwing a ball; they would blend in well on a Malibu beach. These most famous of Piazza Armerina's mosaics were fully reopened to the public in 2013 after years of painstaking restoration and are among Sicily's greatest classical treasures.

Travelling by car from Piazza Armerina, follow signs south of town to the SP15, then continue 5km to reach the villa. Getting here by public transport is more challenging. Buses operated by Interbus (p819) run from Catania to Piazza Armerina (€9.20, 1¾ hours); from here catch a local bus (€1, 30 minutes, summer only) or a taxi (€20) for the remaining 5km.

Gelati DiVini   GELATO €
(☑ 0932 22 89 89; www.gelatidivini.it; Piazza Duomo 20, gelato from €2; ⊙ 10am-late) This exceptional gelateria makes wine-flavoured gelato such as Marsala, *passito* and muscat, plus other unconventional offerings such as pine nut, watermelon, ricotta, and chocolate with spicy peppers.

A Rusticana   SICILIAN €€
(☑ 0932 22 79 81; www.arusticana-ibla.it; Via Domenico Morelli 4; meals €20-32; ⊙ 12.30-2.30pm & 7.30pm-midnight Wed-Mon) Fans of the *Montalbano* TV series will want to eat here, as it's where scenes set in the fictional Trattoria San Calogero were filmed. In reality, it's a cheerful, boisterous trattoria, where generous portions and a relaxed vine-covered terrace ensure a loyal clientele. The food is defiantly *casareccia* (home-style), so expect no-frills pasta and uncomplicated cuts of grilled meat.

★ **Ristorante Duomo**   MODERN SICILIAN €€€
(☑ 0932 65 12 65; www.cicciosultano.it; Via Capitano Bocchieri 31; lunch menus from €60, dinner tasting menus €135-195; ⊙ 12.30-4pm Tue-Sat, plus 7.30-11pm Mon-Sat) Widely regarded as one of Sicily's finest restaurants, behind its stained-glass door Duomo comprises a cluster of small rooms outfitted like private parlours, ensuring a suitably romantic ambience for chef Ciccio Sultano's refined creations. The menu abounds in classic Sicilian ingredients such as pistachios, fennel, almonds and Nero d'Avola wine, combined in imaginative and unconventional ways. Booking is essential.

ⓘ Information

Tourist Office (☑ 0932 68 47 80; www.comune.ragusa.gov.it; Piazza San Giovanni; ⊙ 9am-7pm Mon-Fri, plus 9am 2pm Sat & Sun Easter–mid-Oct) Ragusa's main tourist office, with friendly, helpful staff.

ⓘ Getting There & Around

BUS

Long-distance and municipal buses share a terminal on Via Zama in the upper town. Buy tickets at the Interbus/Etna kiosk in the main lot or at cafes around the corner. **Interbus** (www.interbus.it; Via Zama) runs to Catania (€8.60, two hours, eight to 13 daily). **AST** (☑ 0932 76 73 01; www.aziendasicilianatrasporti.it; Via Zama) serves Syracuse (€7.20, 2¾ to 3¼ hours, three daily except Sunday) with intermediate stops in Modica (€2.70, 30 minutes) and Noto (€6, 2¼ hours).

Monday through Saturday, AST's city buses 11 and 33 (€1.20) run hourly between the Via Zama bus terminal and Giardino Ibleo in Ragusa Ibla. On Sundays, bus 1 makes a similar circuit.

TRAIN

From the station in the upper town, there are three direct trains daily except Sunday to Syracuse (€8.30, two hours) via Noto (€6.20, 1½ hours).

CENTRAL SICILY & THE MEDITERRANEAN COAST

Central Sicily is a land of vast panoramas, undulating fields, severe mountain ridges and hilltop towns not yet sanitised for tourism. Moving towards the Mediterranean, the perspective changes, as ancient temples jostle for position with modern high-rise apartments outside Agrigento, Sicily's most lauded classical site and also one of its busier modern cities.

Agrigento

POP 59,100 / ELEV 230M

Seen from a distance, modern Agrigento's rows of unsightly apartment blocks loom incongruously on the hillside, distracting attention from the splendid Valley of the Temples below, where the ancient Greeks once built their great city of Akragas. Never fear: once you get down among the ruins, their monumental grace becomes apparent, and it's easy to understand how this remarkable complex of temples became Sicily's preeminent travel destination, first put on the tourist map by Goethe in the 18th century.

Three kilometres uphill from the temples, Agrigento's medieval core is a pleasant place to pass the evening after a day exploring the ruins. The InterCity bus and train stations are both in the upper town, within a few blocks of Via Atenea, the medieval city's main thoroughfare.

◉ Sights

◉ Valley of the Temples

★ **Valley of the Temples**   ARCHAEOLOGICAL SITE
(Valle dei Templi; www.parcovalledeitempli.it; adult/reduced €10/5, incl Museo Archeologico €13.50/7; ⊙8.30am-7pm year-round, plus 7.30-10pm Mon-Fri, 7.30-11pm Sat & Sun mid-Jul–mid-Sep) Sicily's most enthralling archaeological site encompasses the ruined ancient city of Akragas, highlighted by the well-preserved **Tempio della Concordia** (Temple of Concordia), one of several ridge-top temples that once served as beacons for homecoming sailors. The 13-sq-km park, 3km south of Agrigento, is split into eastern and western zones. Ticket offices with car parks are at the park's southwestern corner (the main Porta V entrance) and at the northeastern corner near the Temple of Hera (eastern entrance).

★ **Museo Archeologico**   MUSEUM
(☑0922 40 15 65; Contrada San Nicola 12; adult/reduced €8/4, incl Valley of the Temples €13.50/7; ⊙9am-7.30pm Tue-Sat, to 1.30pm Sun & Mon) North of the temples, this wheelchair-accessible museum is one of Sicily's finest, with a huge collection of clearly labelled artefacts from the excavated site. Of note are the dazzling displays of Greek painted ceramics and the awe-inspiring reconstructed *telamon*, a colossal statue recovered from the nearby Tempio di Giove.

◉ Medieval Agrigento

Roaming the town's lively, winding streets is relaxing after a day among the temples.

Chiesa di Santa Maria dei Greci   CHURCH
(www.museodiocesanoag.it; Salita Santa Maria dei Greci; ⊙10am-1.30pm & 3.30-7pm Apr-Oct, 10am-1pm Nov-Mar, closed Mon) This small church stands on the site of a 5th-century Doric temple dedicated to Athena. Inside are some badly damaged Byzantine frescoes, the remains of a Norman ceiling and traces of the original Greek columns.

Monastero di Santo Spirito   CONVENT
(☑0922 20664; www.monasterosantospirito.com; Cortile Santo Spirito 9; ⊙9am-7pm) At the top of a set of steps off Via Atenea, this convent was founded by Cistercian nuns around 1290. A handsome Gothic portal leads inside, where nuns are still in residence, praying, meditating and baking heavenly sweets, including *cuscusu* (sweet couscous made with local pistachios), *dolci di mandorla* (almond pastries) and *conchiglie* (shell-shaped sweets filled with pistachio paste). Press the doorbell and say '*Vorrei comprare qualche dolce*' ('I'd like to buy a few sweets').

Agrigento

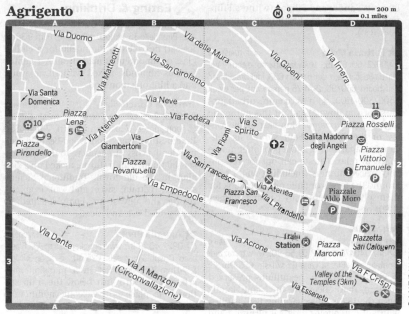

Agrigento

☞ Tours

Associazione Guide Turistiche Agrigento   WALKING
(📞345 8815992; www.agrigentoguide.org) Agrigento's official tour-guide association offers guided visits of the Valley of the Temples, Agrigento and the surrounding area, in English and eight other languages.

Temple Tour Bus   BUS
(📞331 8313720; www.templetourbusagrigento.com; adult/child day ticket €15/8, night ticket €10/6, combo ticket €20/10) This open-roofed bus offers hop-on, hop-off tours both day and night between Agrigento and the Valley of the Temples.

🛏 Sleeping

★ PortAtenea   B&B €
(📞349 093 74 92; www.portatenea.com; Via Atenea, cnr Via C Battisti; s €39-50, d €59-75, tr €79-95; ❄🗐) This five-room B&B wins plaudits for its panoramic roof terrace overlooking the Valley of the Temples, and its unbeatable location at the entrance to the old town, just five minutes' walk from the train and bus stations. Best of all is the generous advice about Agrigento offered

by hosts Sandra and Filippo (witness Filippo's amazing Google Earth tour of nearby beaches!).

★ Fattoria Mosè
AGRITURISMO €

(☏0922 60 61 15; www.fattoriamose.com; Via Mattia Pascal 4a; r per person €50, incl breakfast/half board €60/90, 2-/4-/6-person apt per week €500/800/1100; ☀) If Agrigento's urban jungle's got you down, head for this authentic organic *agriturismo*, 6km east of the Valley of the Temples. Four suites, six self-catering apartments and a pool offer ample space to relax. Guests can opt for reasonably priced dinners (including wine) built around the farm's organic produce, cook for themselves or even enjoy cooking courses (€80) onsite.

Terrazze di Montelusa
B&B €

(☏347 7404784, 0922 59 56 90; www.terrazzedimontelusa.it; Piazza Lena 6; s/d/ste €50/75/85; ❉❄⊛) Occupying a beautifully preserved *palazzo* that's been in the same family since the 1820s, this charming B&B is filled with antique photos, original furniture and period details. As the name implies, it also boasts an inspiring collection of panoramic terraces, the most ample of which is reserved for the upstairs suite (well worth the extra €10).

Camere a Sud
B&B €

(☏349 6384424; www.camereasud.it; Via Ficani 6; s €40, d €50-70, tr €70-100, q €90-120; ❉@⊛) This lovely B&B situated in the medieval centre has three guest rooms that are decorated with style and taste, where traditional decor and contemporary textiles are matched with bright colours and modern art. Breakfast is served on the terrace in warmer months.

★ Villa Athena
HISTORIC HOTEL €€€

(☏0922 59 62 88; www.hotelvillaathena.it; Via Passeggiata Archeologica 33; d €423-577, ste €505-1165; P❉@⊛☀) With the Tempio della Concordia lit up in the near distance and palm trees lending an exotic *Arabian Nights* feel, this historic five-star hotel in an aristocratic 18th-century villa offers the ultimate luxury experience. The cavernous Villa Suite, floored in antique tiles with a free-standing jacuzzi and a vast terrace overlooking the temples, might well be Sicily's most dramatic hotel room.

✗ Eating & Drinking

On a hot day, head for **Caffè Concordia** (Piazza Pirandello 36; almond milk €2; ⊙6am-9.30pm Tue-Sat) near Teatro Pirandello for a chilled glass of almond milk made from Agrigento's famous almonds, mixed with sugar, water and a hint of lemon rind.

Trattoria Concordia
TRATTORIA €

(☏0922 2 26 68; Via Porcello 8; meals €18-30; ⊙noon-3pm & 7-10.30pm Mon-Fri, 7-11pm Sat) Rough stone walls and wood-beamed ceilings lend a cosy atmosphere to this quintessential family-run trattoria, tucked up a side alley in the old town. Traditional Sicilian starters (frittata, sweet-and-sour eggplant, ricotta and olives) are complemented by tasty grilled fish and meats.

★ Aguglia Persa
SEAFOOD €€

(☏0922 40 13 37; www.agugliapersa.it; Via Francesco Crispi 34; meals €25-40; ⊙noon-3.30pm & 7-11pm Wed-Mon) Set in a mansion with a leafy courtyard, just below the train station, this place is a welcome addition to Agrigento's fine-dining scene. Opened in 2015 by the owners of Porto Empedocle's renowned Salmoriglio restaurant, it specialises in fresh-caught seafood in dishes such as citrus-scented risotto with shrimp and wild mint, or marinated salmon with sage cream and fresh fruit.

★ Kalòs
MODERN SICILIAN €€

(☏0922 2 63 89; www.ristorantekalos.it; Piazzetta San Calogero; meals €30-45; ⊙12.30-3pm & 7-11pm Tue-Sun) At this 'smart' restaurant which is situated just outside the historic centre, five cute tables on little balconies offer a pleasant setting to enjoy homemade pasta *all'agrigentina* (with fresh tomatoes, basil and almonds), grilled lamb chops, citrus shrimp or *spada gratinata* (baked swordfish covered in breadcrumbs). Superb desserts, including homemade *cannoli* and almond *semifreddi*, round out the menu.

☆ Entertainment

Teatro Pirandello
THEATRE

(☏0922 59 02 20; www.teatroluigipirandello.it; Piazza Pirandello; tickets €18-23) This city-run theatre is Sicily's third largest, after Palermo's Teatro Massimo and Catania's Teatro Massimo Bellini. Works by local hero, dramatist and writer Luigi Pirandello (1867–1936), figure prominently. The program runs from November to early May.

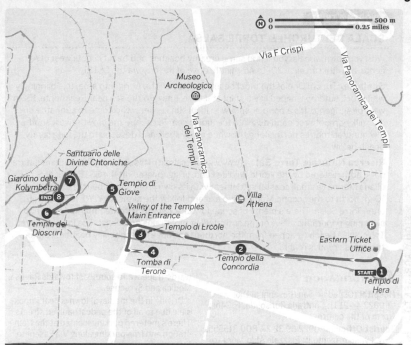

Archaeological Walking Tour
Valley of the Temples

START TEMPIO DI HERA
END GIARDINO DELLA KOLYMBETRA
LENGTH 3KM; THREE HOURS

Begin your exploration in the so-called Eastern Zone, home to Agrigento's best-preserved temples. From the eastern ticket office, a short walk leads to the 5th-century BC **① Tempio di Hera**, perched on the ridge top. Though partly destroyed by an earthquake, the colonnade remains largely intact, as does a long sacrificial altar. Traces of red are the result of fire damage likely dating to the Carthaginian invasion of 406 BC.

Next, descend past a gnarled 500-year-old olive tree and a series of Byzantine tombs to the **② Tempio della Concordia**. This remarkable edifice is the model for Unesco's logo. It has survived almost entirely intact since its construction in 430 BC, partly due to its conversion into a Christian basilica in the 6th century, and partly thanks to the shock-absorbing, earthquake-dampening qualities of the soft clay underlying its hard rock foundation.

Further downhill, the **③ Tempio di Ercole** is Agrigento's oldest, dating from the end of the 6th century BC. Down from the main temples, the miniature **④ Tomba di Terone** dates to 75 BC. Cross the pedestrian bridge into the western zone, stopping at the **⑤ Tempio di Giove**. This would have been the world's largest Doric temple had its construction not been interrupted by the Carthaginian sacking of Akragas. A later earthquake reduced it to the ruin you see today. Lying on his back amid the rubble is an 8m-tall *telamon* (a sculpted figure of a man with arms raised), originally intended to support the temple's weight. It's actually a copy; the original is in Agrigento's archaeological museum.

Take a brief look at the ruined 5th-century BC **⑥ Tempio dei Dioscuri** and the 6th-century BC complex of altars and small buildings known as the **⑦ Santuario delle Divine Chtoniche**, before ending your visit in the **⑧ Giardino della Kolymbetra**, a lush garden in a natural cleft near the sanctuary,

WORTH A TRIP

SCALA DEI TURCHI & TORRE SALSA

With your own wheels, you'll find some dreamy beaches and beauty spots west of Agrigento, all within an easy 30- to 45-minute drive of the city via the SS115.

Scala dei Turchi One of the most beautiful sights in the Agrigento area, this blindingly white rock outcrop, shaped like a giant staircase, juts into the sea near Realmonte, 15km west of Agrigento. It's a popular spot with local sun seekers who come to sunbathe on the milky-smooth rock and dive into the indigo sea. To escape the crowds, walk another few hundred metres north along the white rocky shelf, and descend to the long sandy beach below.

Riserva Naturale Torre Salsa (www.wwftorresalsa.it) This stunning 761-hectare natural park, administered by the World Wildlife Fund, is signposted off the SS115. Exit at Siculiana Marina (a small coastal settlement with its own great sandy beach) or continue 10km north to the second Montallegro exit and follow the signs for WWF Riserva Naturale Torre Salsa. There's plenty of scope for walkers here, with well-marked trails and sweeping panoramic views of the surrounding mountains and coast. The long, deserted Torre Salsa beach (reached from the northern entrance) is especially beautiful, although the access road is rough.

ℹ Information

Hospital (Ospedale San Giovanni di Dio; ☑ 0922 44 21 11; Contrada Consolida; ⊙24hr) North of the centre.

Tourist Office (☑ 0922 59 32 27, 800 315555; www.livingagrigento.it; Piazzale Aldo Moro 1; ⊙8am-1pm & 2-7pm Mon-Fri, to 1pm Sat) In the provincial government building.

ℹ Getting There & Away

BUS

The **InterCity bus station** and ticket booths are located on Piazza Rosselli.

Autoservizi Camilleri (☑ 0922 47 18 86; www.camilleriargentoelattuca.it) Runs to Palermo (€9, two hours) four to five times daily Monday to Saturday, once on Sunday.

Cuffaro (☑ 091 616 15 10; www.cuffaro.info) Operates seven buses to Palermo (€9, two hours) Monday to Friday, six on Saturday and three on Sunday.

Lumia (☑ 0922 2 04 14; www.autolineelumia.it) Has departures to Trapani and its Birgi Airport (€11.90, 2½ to 3½ hours) three times daily Monday to Saturday, one on Sunday).

SAIS Trasporti (☑ 0922 2 60 59; www.saistrasporti.it) Runs buses to Catania (€13.40, three hours, 11 to 15 daily).

SAL (Società Autolinee Licata; ☑ 0922 40 13 60; www.autolineesal.it) Offers direct service to Palermo's Falcone-Borsellino Airport (€12.60, 2¾ hours, four daily except Sunday).

CAR & MOTORCYCLE

The SS189 links Agrigento with Palermo, while the SS115 runs along the coast, northwest towards Trapani and southeast towards Ragusa, Modica and Syracuse.

Driving in the medieval town is near impossible due to all of the pedestrianised streets. There's metered parking located at the train station and free parking along Via Esseneto, just below.

TRAIN

From Agrigento Centrale station (Piazza Marconi), direct trains run regularly to Palermo (€9, two hours, six to 10 daily). Service to Catania (from €11.30, 3¼ to six hours) is less frequent and requires a change of trains; for this and most other destinations, you're better off taking the bus.

ℹ Getting Around

City bus 1, operated by **TUA** (Trasporti Urbani Agrigento; ☑ 0922 41 20 24; www.trasportiurbaniagrigento.it), runs half-hourly services from Agrigento's bus and train stations to the archaeological museum (15 minutes) and the Porta V entrance to the temples (20 minutes). Bus 2/ (as distinct from bus 2, which has a different route – watch out for the hard-to-spot forward slash) runs services every hour or so to the temples' eastern entrance near the Tempio di Hera (10 to 15 minutes). Tickets cost €1.20 if they are bought in advance from a tobacconist, or €1.70 on board the bus. A day ticket costs €3.40.

The *linea verde* (green line) departs every 50 minutes from the train station, running the length of Via Atenea and looping through the medieval town centre.

WESTERN SICILY

Situated directly across the water from North Africa and still retaining vestiges of the Arab, Phoenician and Greek cultures that once prevailed here, western Sicily has a bit of the Wild West about it. There is plenty to stir the senses, from Trapani's savoury fish couscous to the dazzling views from hilltop Erice and the wild coastal beauty of the Riserva Naturale dello Zingaro.

Marsala & Around

POP 82,300

Best known for its sweet dessert wines, Marsala revolves around a lovely, elegant core of stately baroque buildings within a perfect square of walls. To the east and north lie less attractive modern outskirts that gradually peter out into the surrounding vineyards.

The city was originally founded by Phoenician escapees from the Roman onslaught at nearby Mozia. Not wanting to risk a second attack, they fortified their new home with 7m-thick walls, ensuring that it was the last Punic settlement to fall to the Romans. In 830 AD it was conquered by the Arabs, who gave it its current name, Marsa Allah (Port of God).

It was here in 1860 that Giuseppe Garibaldi, leader of the movement for Italian unification, landed in his rickety old boats with his 1000 strong army – a claim to fame that finds its way into every tourist brochure.

⊙ Sights & Activities

For a taste of local life, take a stroll at sunset around pretty **Piazza della Repubblica**, heart of the historic centre.

Whitaker Museum MUSEUM
(☑ 0923 71 25 98; www.fondazionewhitaker.it; San Pantaleo; adult/reduced €9/5; ⊙ 9.30am-6.30pm Apr-Oct, 9am-3pm Nov-Mar) This museum on San Pantaleo island, 10km north of Marsala, houses a unique collection of Phoenician artefacts assembled over decades by amateur archaeologist Joseph Whitaker. Its greatest treasure (returned to Sicily in 2014 after two years at London's British Museum and Los Angeles' Getty) is *Il Giovinetto di Mozia*, a 5th-century-BC Carthaginian-influenced marble statue of a young man.

To get here, drive or cycle to the Mozia dock 10km north of Marsala and catch one of the half-hourly ferries operated by **Mozia Line** (☑ 338 7860474, 0923 98 92 49; www.mozialine.com; round trip adult/reduced €5/2.50; ⊙ 9.15am-6.30pm) for the 10-minute crossing.

Museo Archeologico
Baglio Anselmi MUSEUM
(☑ 0923 95 25 35; Lungomare Boeo 30; adult/reduced €4/2; ⊙ 9am-6.30pm Wed-Sat, to 1.30pm Tue & Sun) Reopened to the public in 2017 after a multi-year renovation, this museum revolves around the partially reconstructed remains of a Carthaginian *liburna* (warship) sunk off the Egadi Islands during the First Punic War. Displayed alongside objects from its cargo, the ship's bare bones provide the only remaining physical evidence of the Phoenicians' seafaring superiority in the 3rd century BC, offering a glimpse of a civilisation extinguished by the Romans.

SICILY MARSALA & AROUND

WORTH A TRIP

SALINE DI TRAPANI

Along the coast between Trapani and Marsala, the Saline di Trapani present an evocative landscape of *saline* (shallow salt pools) and decommissioned *mulini* (windmills). The salt from these marshes is considered Italy's finest and was big business for centuries; today, only a cottage industry remains, providing for Italy's more discerning dinner tables. The best time to visit is summer, when the sun turns the saltpans rosy pink and makes the salt heaps shimmer. In winter, the heaps – covered with tiles and plastic tarpaulins to keep out the rain – are considerably less picturesque.

The most attractive stretches of coast are protected within two wetland preserves: **Riserva Naturale Saline di Trapani e Paceco** (☑ 0923 86 77 00, 327 5621529; www.salineditrapani.it), to the north near Trapani, and **Riserva Naturale di Stagnone**, to the south near Marsala. The latter encompasses Isola San Pantaleo – home to the noted archaeological site of Mozia – and the larger Isola Lunga, which protects the shallow waters of Stagnone lagoon.

Cantine Florio   WINE
(🖉0923 78 13 05; www.duca.it/en/ospitalita/
cellar-tours; Via Vincenzo Florio 1; tours adult/
reduced €13/5; ⊙9am-6pm Mon-Fri, to 1pm Sat,
English-language tours 10am & 4pm Mon-Fri, 10am
Sat) These venerable wine cellars just east
of town open their doors to visitors to explain the Marsala-making process and the
fascinating history of local viticulture. Afterwards, visitors can sample the goods in
Florio's spiffy tasting room (tasting of four
wines accompanied by hors d'oeuvres included in tour price). Book in advance for
English-language tours. Take bus 16 from
Piazza del Popolo. Other producers in the
same area include Pellegrino, Donnafugata,
Rallo, Mavis and Intorcia.

🛏 Sleeping & Eating

Marsala has few hotels within the historic
centre.

★**Il Profumo del Sale**   B&B €
(🖉0923 189 04 72; www.ilprofumodelsale.it; Via
Vaccari 8; s/d €35/60; 🕸) Perfectly positioned
in Marsala's historic city centre, this B&B
offers three attractive rooms – including a
palatial front unit with cathedral views from
its small balcony – enhanced by welcoming
touches such as almond cookies, fine soaps
and ample breakfasts featuring homemade
bread and jams. Sophisticated owner Celsa
is full of helpful tips about Marsala and the
surrounding area.

Hotel Carmine   HOTEL €€
(🖉0923 71 19 07; www.hotelcarmine.it; Piazza Carmine 16; s €75-105, d €105-125; 🅿🕸@🕸) This
lovely hotel in a converted 16th-century
monastery has elegant rooms with vintage
touches such as original blue-and-gold
maiolica tiles, stone walls, antique furniture
and lofty beamed ceilings. Enjoy your corn-
flakes in the baronial-style breakfast room
with its historic frescoes and over-the-top
chandelier, or sip your drink by the roaring
fireplace in winter. Modern perks include a
rooftop solarium.

Quimera   SANDWICHES €
(🖉349 6783243; www.facebook.com/quimerapub;
Via Sarzana 34-36; sandwiches & salads from €5;
⊙noon-3pm & 6.30pm-2am Mon-Sat, 6.30pm-2am
Sun) Smack in the middle of the pedestrianised centre, this is Marsala's hot spot for
artisanal beers, gourmet sandwiches and
meal-sized salads, all served with a smile by
the friendly young owners.

San Lorenzo Osteria   SICILIAN €€
(SLO; 🖉0923 71 25 93; www.osteriasanlorenzo.
com; Via Garraffa 60; meals €30-40; ⊙7.30-11pm
daily, plus 12.30-2.30pm Sun; 🕸) This stylish
eatery is a class act all round – from the ever-
changing menu of fresh seafood scrawled
daily on the blackboard to the interior's
sleek modern lines to the gorgeous presentation of the food. The wine list, updated regularly, features some local choices you won't
find elsewhere.

❶ Information

Tourist Office (🖉0923 71 40 97, 0923 99 33
38; ufficioturistico.proloco@comune.marsala.
tp.it; Via XI Maggio 100; ⊙8.30am-1.30pm &
3-8pm Mon-Fri, to 1.30pm Sat) Spacious office
with comfy couches right off the main square;
provides a wide range of maps and brochures.

❶ Getting There & Away

From Marsala, bus operators include **Lumia**
(www.autolineelumia.it), which goes to Agrigento (€10.10, 2½ to three hours, one to three daily),
and **Salemi** (🖉0923 98 11 20; www.autoservizi
salemi.it) to Palermo (€11, 2¼ to 2½ hours, at
least 10 daily).

Train is the best way to get to Trapani (€3.80,
30 minutes, 10 daily Monday to Saturday, four
on Sunday).

Selinunte

The **Ruins of Selinunte** (🖉0924 4 62 77;
adult/reduced €6/3; ⊙9am-6pm Apr-Oct, to 5pm
Nov-Mar) are the most impressively sited in
Sicily. The huge city was built in 628 BC
on a promontory overlooking the sea, and
over the course of two-and-a-half centuries
became one of the richest and most powerful in the world. It was destroyed by the
Carthaginians in 409 BC and finally fell to
the Romans about 350 BC, at which time
it went into rapid decline and disappeared
from historical accounts.

The city's past is so remote that the names
of the various temples have been forgotten
and they are now identified by the letters A to
G, M and O. The most impressive, **Temple E**,
has been partially rebuilt, its columns pieced
together from their fragments with part of its
tympanum. Many of the carvings, particularly from **Temple C**, are now in the archaeological museum in Palermo. Their quality is on
par with the Parthenon marbles and clearly
demonstrates the high cultural levels reached
by many Greek colonies in Sicily.

The ticket office and entrance to the ruins is located near the eastern temples. Try to visit in spring when the surroundings are ablaze with wildflowers.

Escape the mediocre restaurants near the ruins by heading for **Lido Zabbara** (☑ 0924 4 61 94; Via Pigafetta, Marinella di Selinunte; buffet per person €12; ⊘ noon-3pm Mar-early Nov, plus 7.30-10.30pm Jun-Sep), a beachfront eatery in nearby Marinella di Selinunte that serves good grilled fish and a varied buffet. Alternatively, drive 15km east to **Da Vittorio** (☑ 0925 7 83 81; www.ristorantevittorio.it; Via Friuli Venezia Giulia, Porto Palo; meals €30-45; ⊘ 12.30-2.30pm & 7-10pm) in Porto Palo, another wonderful spot to enjoy seafood, sunset and the sound of lapping waves.

ⓘ Getting There & Away

Selinunte is midway between Agrigento and Trapani, about 10km south of the junction of the A29 and SS115 near Castelvetrano. **Autoservizi Salemi** (☑ 0924 8 18 26; www.autoservizi salemi.it/tratte/selinunte) runs seven buses daily except Sunday from Selinunte to Castelvetrano (€1.50, 25 to 35 minutes), where you can make onward bus connections with **Lumia** (☑ 0922 2 04 14; www.autolineelumia.it) to Agri-

gento (€8.60, two hours), or train connections to Marsala (€4.30, 35 to 45 minutes), Trapani (€6.20, one to 1¼ hours) and Palermo (€8.30, three hours).

Trapani

POP 70,600

The lively port city of Trapani makes a convenient base for exploring Sicily's western tip. Its historic centre is filled with atmospheric pedestrian streets and some lovely churches and baroque buildings, although the heavily developed outskirts are rather bleak.

Once situated at the heart of a powerful trading network that stretched from Carthage to Venice, Trapani's sickle-shaped spit of land hugs the precious harbour, nowadays busy with a steady stream of tourist traffic to and from Pantelleria and the nearby Egadi Islands.

◉ Sights

Trapani's pedestrianised historic centre is a Moorish labyrinth; its main thoroughfare, Corso Vittorio Emanuele, is lined with 18th-century baroque gems such as the

---

WORTH A TRIP

SCOPELLO & RISERVA NATURALE DELLO ZINGARO

Saved from development and road projects by local protests, the tranquil **Riserva Naturale dello Zingaro** (☑ 0924 3 51 08; www.riservazingaro.it; adult/reduced €5/3; ⊘ 7am-7.30pm Apr-Sep, 9am-5pm Oct-Mar) is the star attraction on the Golfo di Castellammare, halfway between Palermo and Trapani. Founded in 1981, this was Sicily's first nature reserve. Zingaro's wild coastline is a haven for the rare Bonelli's eagle, along with 40 other species of bird. Mediterranean flora dusts the hillsides with wild carob and bright yellow euphorbia, and hidden coves, such as Capreria and Marinella Bays, provide tranquil swimming spots. The main entrance to the park is 2km north of the village of Scopello. Several walking trails are detailed on maps available for free at the entrance or downloadable from the park website. The main 7km trail along the coast passes by the visitor centre and five museums that document everything from local flora and fauna to traditional fishing methods.

Once home to tuna fishers, tiny **Scopello** now mainly hosts tourists. Its port, 1km below town and reachable by a walking path, has a picturesque **beach** (www.tonnaradis copello.com; €3; ⊘ 9am-7pm), backed by a rust-red *tonnara* (tuna-processing plant) and dramatic *faraglioni* (rock towers) rising from the water.

Pensione Tranchina (☑ 0924 54 10 99; www.pensionetranchina.com; Via Diaz 7; B&B per person €36-48, half board per person €55-75; ❋ ⎙) is the nicest of several accommodation options clustered around the cobblestoned courtyard at Scopello's village centre. Friendly hosts Marisin and Salvatore offer comfortable rooms, a roaring fire on chilly evenings and superb home-cooked meals featuring local fish and home-grown fruit and olive oil. If you're just here on a day trip, the terrace at nearby **Bar Nettuno** (☑ 0924 54 13 62; Baglio Isonzo 13; meals €30-40; ⊘ 9am-late) makes another brilliant end-of-day destination for seafood and sundowners.

DEAGOSTINI/GETTY IMAGES ©

1. Room of the Ten Girls in Bikinis (p833), Villa Romana del Casale
2. Duomo (p823), Ortygia, Syracuse 3. Teatro Greco (p811),
Taormina 4. Valle dei Templi (p834), Agrigento

2

PETR JILEK/SHUTTERSTOCK ©

A Graeco-Roman Legacy

As the crossroads of the Mediterranean since the dawn of time, Sicily has seen countless civilisations come and go. The island's classical treasure trove includes Greek temples and amphitheatres, Roman mosaics and a host of fine archaeological museums.

Valle dei Templi

Crowning the craggy heights of Agrigento's Valley of the Temples (p834) are five Doric temples – including stunning Tempio della Concordia, one of the best preserved in all of Magna Graecia. Throw in the superb archaeological museum and you've got Sicily's most cohesive and impressive collection of Greek treasures.

Villa Romana del Casale

Bikini-clad gymnasts and wild African beasts prance side by side in remarkable floor decorations in this ancient Roman hunting lodge (p833). Buried under mud for centuries and now gleaming from restoration work completed in 2013, they're the most extensive mosaics in Sicily and a Unesco World Heritage Site.

4

Segesta

Segesta's perfect Doric temple (p846) perches on a windswept hilltop above a rugged river gorge.

Taormina

With spectacular views of snowcapped Mt Etna and the Ionian Sea, Taormina's Teatro Greco (p811) makes the perfect venue for the town's summer film and arts festivals.

Selinunte

Selinunte's vast ruins (p840) poke out of wildflower-strewn fields beside the sparkling Mediterranean.

Syracuse

Once the most powerful city in the Mediterranean, Syracuse (p823) brims with reminders of its ancient past, from the Greek columns supporting Ortygia's cathedral to the annual festival of classical Greek drama, staged in a 2500-year-old amphitheatre.

Cattedrale di San Lorenzo (Corso Vittorio Emanuele; ⊙ 8am-4pm) and the **Palazzo Senatorio** (cnr Corso Vittorio Emanuele & Via Torrearsa). The best time to stroll here is in the early evening (around 7pm) when the *passeggiata* is in full swing.

Chiesa del Purgatorio CHURCH
(☑ 0923 56 28 82; Via San Francesco d'Assisi; voluntary donation requested; ⊙ 7.30am-noon & 4-7pm Mon-Sat, 10am-noon & 4-7pm Sun) Just off Corso Vittorio Emanuele in the heart of the city, this church houses the impressive 18th-century *Misteri,* 20 life-sized wooden effigies depicting the story of Christ's Passion, which take centre stage during the city's dramatic Easter Week processions each year. Explanatory panels in English, Italian, French and German help visitors understand the story behind each figure.

Museo Nazionale Pepoli MUSEUM
(☑ 0923 55 32 69; www.comune.trapani.it/turismo/pepoli.htm; Via Conte Pepoli 180; adult/reduced €6/3; ⊙ 9am-5.30pm Tue-Sat, to 12.30pm Sun) In a former Carmelite monastery, this museum houses the collection of Conte Pepoli (1796–1881), who devoted his life to salvaging Trapani's local arts and crafts – most notably the garish coral carvings that were once all the rage in Europe before Trapani's offshore coral banks were decimated. The museum also has a good collection of Gagini sculptures, silverwork, archaeological artefacts and religious art.

✸ Festivals & Events

Local culinary treasure couscous is the centrepiece of two annual festivals: Trapani's newer addition **Cuscusu** (www.cuscusu.it; ⊙ Jun) and the well-established **Cous Cous Fest** (www.couscousfest.it; ⊙ mid-late Sep) in nearby San Vito Lo Capo.

I Misteri RELIGIOUS
(www.processionemisteritp.it) Sicily's most venerated Easter procession is a four-day festival of extraordinary religious fervour. Nightly processions, bearing life-sized wooden effigies, make their way through the old quarter to a specially erected chapel in Piazza Lucatelli. The high point is on Good Friday when the celebrations reach fever pitch.

🛏 Sleeping & Eating

The most convenient and attractive places to stay and eat are in Trapani's pedestrianised historic centre, just north of the port.

Sicily's Arab heritage and Trapani's unique position on the sea route to Tunisia have made couscous (or *'cuscusu'* as it's sometimes spelt around here) a local specialty.

Ai Lumi B&B B&B €
(☑ 0923 54 09 22; www.ailumi.it; Corso Vittorio Emanuele 71; s €53-70, d €85-106, tr €111-132, q €138-159; ❋ 🛜) Housed in an 18th-century *palazzo,* this centrally located B&B offers 13 rooms of varying size. Best are the spacious apartments (numbers 32, 34 and 35), with kitchenettes and balconies overlooking Trapani's most elegant pedestrian street. Upstairs apartment 23 is also lovely, with a private balcony reached by a spiral staircase. Guests get discounts at the hotel's atmospheric restaurant next door.

La Gancia HOTEL €€
(☑ 0923 43 80 60; www.lagancia.com; Piazza Mercato del Pesce; s €75-85, d €110-164, q €179-280; ❋ 🛜) Well positioned on the waterfront at the north end of Trapani's historic centre, this immaculate hotel offers 20 comfortable kitchenette-equipped rooms, ranging from lower-priced interior-facing units to a spacious 4th-floor junior suite with its own sea-view terrace. The breakfast room enjoys pretty views of the water, and the port is just a five-minute walk away.

La Rinascente PASTRIES €
(☑ 0923 2 37 67; Via Gatti 3; cannoli €2; ⊙ 9am-1.30pm & 3-7pm Mon, Tue, Thu & Fri, 7.30am-2pm Sat & Sun) When you enter this bakery through the side door, you'll feel like you've barged into someone's kitchen – and you have! Thankfully, owner Giovanni Costadura's broad smile will quickly put you at ease, as will a taste of his homemade *cannoli,* which he'll create for you on the spot.

★ **Osteria La Bettolaccia** SICILIAN €€
(☑ 0923 2 59 32; www.labettolaccia.it; Via Enrico Fardella 25; meals €35-45; ⊙ 12.45-3pm Mon-Fri, plus 7.45-11pm Mon-Sat) Unwaveringly authentic, this perennial Slow Food favourite just two blocks from the ferry terminal is the perfect place to try *cous cous con zuppa di mare* (couscous with mixed seafood in a spicy fish sauce, with tomatoes, garlic and parsley). Due to its great popularity, it's wise to book ahead.

Caupona Taverna di Sicilia SEAFOOD €€
(☑ 0923 54 66 18, 340 3421335; Piazza Purgatorio 32; meals €25-36; ⊙ 1-2.15pm & 8-11.30pm Wed-

Mon) Fresh fish rules the menu at this fabulous family-run spot two blocks from the port. Chef Rosi cooks and husband Claudio works the tables, serving up superb couscous and colourful seafood classics such as *pesce spada alla pantesca* (swordfish in a sauce of tomatoes, garlic, parsley, olives and capers). Save room for the monster-sized *cannoli* (enough to feed two people easily).

❶ Information

Hospital (Ospedale Sant'Antonio Abate; ☑ 0923 80 91 11; www.asptrapani.it; Via Cosenza) Five kilometres east of the centre.

Tourist Office (☑ 0923 54 45 33; sport.turismo.spettacolo@comune.trapani.it; Piazzetta Saturno; ⊙ 9am-9pm Jun-Sep, to 5.30pm Mon & Thu, to 2pm Tue, Wed & Fri Oct-May) Just north of the port, Trapani's tourist office offers city maps and information.

❶ Getting There & Around

The ferry and hydrofoil docks straggle along Via Ammiraglio Staiti at the peninsula's southern edge. **Egatour** (☑ 0923 2 17 54; www.egatour viaggi.it; Via Ammiraglio Staiti 13), a travel agency opposite the port, offers one-stop shopping for bus, plane and ferry tickets. The bus and train stations lie about 1km east of the centre.

AIR

Trapani's small **Vincenzo Florio Airport** (Birgi Airport; TPS; ☑ 0923 61 01 11; www.airgest.it) is 1/km south of town at Birgi. **Ryanair** (☑ 899 018880; www.ryanair.com) offers direct flights to two dozen Italian and European cities, while Alitalia goes to Rome and Mistral Air flies to the Mediterranean island of Pantelleria. **AST** (Azienda Siciliana Trasporti; ☑ 0923 2 10 21; www.astsicilia.it) operates hourly buses from 5.30am to 12.30am connecting the airport with downtown Trapani (€4.90, 45 minutes).

BOAT

Ferry ticket offices are located inside Trapani's ferry terminal, opposite Piazza Garibaldi. Hydrofoil ticket offices are 350m further east along Via Ammiraglio Staiti.

Liberty Lines (☑ 0923 87 38 13; www.liberty lines.it; Via Ammiraglio Staiti) Operates hydrofoils year-round to the Egadi Islands ports of Favignana (€12.80, 25 to 40 minutes), Levanzo (€11.80, 25 to 40 minutes) and Marettimo (€18.80, 1¼ hours), along with summer-only service to Pantelleria (€47, 2¼ hours), Ustica (€32.50, 2½ hours) and Naples (€108, seven hours). The latter two services run on Saturdays only.

Siremar (☑ 090 36 46 01; www.siremar.it; Ferry Terminal) Offers year-round ferry service to Pantelleria (€36.50, six to seven hours) and the Egadi Islands ports of Favignana (€10.70, one to 1½ hours), Levanzo (€9.70, one to 1½ hours) and Marettimo (€14.60, three hours).

Traghetti delle Isole (☑ 0923 2 24 67; www. traghettidelleisole.it) Runs ferries to Pantelleria (€34.50, six to 7¼ hours) daily in July and August, three to five times weekly rest of year.

BUS

InterCity buses arrive and depart from the terminal 1km east of the centre (just southeast of the train station).

Segesta (☑ 0923 2 84 04, 0923 2 19 56; www. buscenter.it) runs express buses to Palermo (€9.60, two hours, hourly). Board at the bus stop across the street from Egatours or at the bus station. **Lumia** (☑ 0922 2 04 14, 0923 2 17/ 54; www.autolineelumia.it) serves Agrigento (€11.90, 2¾ to 3¾ hours, one to three daily).

ATM (Azienda Trasporto e Mobilità; ☑ 0923 55 95 75; www.atmtrapani.it) operates two free city buses (Nos 2 and 10), which make circular trips through Trapani, connecting the bus station, the train station and the port. Tickets for ATM's other local buses – valid for 90 minutes – cost €1.20 at *tabacchi* (tobacco shops) or €1.40 if purchased on board the bus.

CAR & MOTORCYLE

To bypass Trapani's vast suburbs and avoid the narrow streets of the city centre, follow signs from the A29 autostrada directly to the port, where you'll find abundant paid parking along the broad waterside avenue Via Ammiraglio Staiti, within walking distance of most attractions.

TRAIN

From Trapani's station on Piazza Umberto I, Trenitalia offers efficient connections to Marsala (€3.80, 30 minutes, 10 daily Monday to Saturday, five on Sunday). For Palermo and most other destinations, the bus is a better option.

Erice

POP 28,800 / ELEV 751M

One of Italy's most spectacular hill towns, Erice combines medieval charm with astounding 360-degree views. It sits on the legendary Mt Eryx (750m); on a clear day, you can see Cape Bon in Tunisia. The town has a seductive history as a centre for the cult of Venus. Settled by the mysterious Elymians, the town followed the peculiar ritual of sacred prostitution, with the prostitutes themselves accommodated in the Temple of Venus. Despite countless invasions, the temple remained intact – no guesses why.

These days, the greatest pleasure here is simply wandering Erice's medieval tangle of streets interspersed with churches, forts and tiny cobbled piazzas. Posted throughout town, you'll find bilingual (Italian–English) informational displays, and town maps providing suggested walking routes.

◉ Sights

The best views can be had from **Giardino del Balio**, which overlooks the turrets and wooded hillsides south to Trapani's salt-pans, the Egadi Islands and the sea. Looking north, there are equally staggering views of San Vito Lo Capo's rugged headlands.

Castello di Venere   CASTLE
(☑ 366 6712832; www.fondazioneericearte.org/castellodivenere.php; Via Castello di Venere; adult/reduced €4/2; ◷ 10am-1hr before sunset daily Apr-Oct, 10am-4pm Sat, Sun & holidays Nov-Mar) The Norman Castello di Venere was built in the 12th and 13th centuries over the Temple of Venus, long a site of worship for the ancient Elymians, Phoenicians, Greeks and Romans. The views from up top, extending to San Vito Lo Capo on one side and the Saline di Trapani on the other, are spectacular. To arrange visits in winter, phone at least 24 hours in advance.

⬛ Sleeping & Eating

Hotels, many with their own restaurants, are scattered along Via Vittorio Emanuele, Erice's main street. After the day-trippers have gone, the town assumes a beguiling medieval air.

Erice has a tradition of *dolci ericini* (Erice sweets) made by local nuns. There are numerous pastry shops in town, the most famous being **Maria Grammatico** (☑ 0923 86 93 90; www.mariagrammatico.it; Via Vittorio Emanuele 14; pastries from €2; ◷ 9am-10pm May, Jun & Sep, to 1am Jul & Aug, to 7pm Oct-Apr), revered for its *frutta martorana* (marzipan fruit) and almond pastries. If you like what you taste, you can even stick around and take cooking classes from Signora Grammatico herself.

Hotel Elimo   HOTEL €€
(☑ 0923 86 93 77; www.hotelelimo.it; Via Vittorio Emanuele 75; s €80-110, d €90-130, ste €150-170; ✲ ☏) Communal spaces at this atmospheric historic house are filled with tiled beams, marble fireplaces, intriguing art, knick-knacks and antiques. The bedrooms are more mainstream, although many (along with the hotel terrace and restaurant) have

breathtaking vistas south and west towards the Saline di Trapani, the Egadi Islands and the shimmering sea.

ⓘ Information

Up near the Castello di Venere, **Pro Loco Erice** (☑ 329 0658244; www.prolocoerice.it; Via Castello di Venere; ◷ 10am-6pm) provides a wealth of tourist information.

ⓘ Getting There & Away

AST (p845) runs six buses daily (four on Sunday) between Erice and Trapani's bus terminal (€2.90, 40 minutes). Alternatively, catch the **funicular** (Funivia; ☑ 0923 86 97 20, 0923 56 93 06; www.funiviaerice.it; one way/return €5.50/9; ◷ 1-8pm Mon, 8.10am-8pm Tue-Fri, 9am-9pm Sat, 10am-8pm Sun) opposite the car park at the foot of Erice's Via Vittorio Emanuele; the 10-minute descent drops you in Trapani near Ospedale Sant'Antonio Abate, where you can catch local bus 21 or 23 (€1.40) into the centre of Trapani.

Segesta

ELEV 304M

Set on the edge of a deep canyon in the midst of wild, desolate mountains, the 5th-century BC **Ruins of Segesta** (☑ 0924 95 23 56; adult/reduced €6/3; ◷ 9am-7.30pm Apr-Sep, to 6.30pm Mar & Oct, to 5pm Nov-Feb) are a magical site. On windy days the 36 giant columns of its magnificent temple are said to act like an organ, producing mysterious notes.

The city, founded by the ancient Elymians, was in constant conflict with Selinunte in the south, whose destruction it sought with dogged determination and singular success. Time, however, has done to Segesta what violence inflicted on Selinunte; little remains now, save the **theatre** and the never-completed **Doric temple**, the latter dating from around 430 BC and remarkably well preserved. A shuttle bus (€1.50) runs every 30 minutes from the temple entrance 1.5km uphill to the theatre.

Tarantola (☑ 0924 3 10 20; www.tarantolabus.com) buses run to Segesta three times daily (except Sunday) from Trapani (one way/return €4/6.60, 45 minutes) and once daily (except Sunday) from Via Balsamo near Palermo's train station (one way/return €8/12.70, 80 minutes); all buses stop just outside the archaeological site's entrance. If driving, exit the A29dir at Segesta and follow signs 1.5km uphill to the site.

Sardinia

Best Places to Eat

➡ Trattoria Lo Romani (p871)

➡ La Pola (p855)

➡ Dolceacqua (p877)

➡ Il Portico (p883)

➡ Locanda di Corte (p868)

Best Places to Sleep

➡ Casa Solotti (p883)

➡ B&B Domus de Janas (p880)

➡ Angedras Hotel (p870)

➡ Hotel Nautilus (p854)

➡ B&B Lu Pastruccialeddu (p878)

➡ Agriturismo Codula Fuili (p889)

Why Go?

As DH Lawrence so succinctly put it: 'Sardinia is different'. Indeed, where else but on this 365-village, four-million-sheep island could you travel from shimmering bays to near-alpine forests, granite peaks to snow-white beaches, rolling vineyards to one-time bandit towns – all in the space of a day? Sardinia baffles with its unique prehistory at 7000 nuraghic sites, dazzles with its kaleidoscopic blue waters, and whets appetites with island treats like spit-roasted suckling pig, sea urchins, crumbly *pecorino* cheese, Vermentino whites and Cannonau reds.

Over millennia islanders have carved out a unique identity, cuisine, culture and language. And whether you're swooning over the mega-yachts in the Costa Smeralda's fjord-like bays or kicking back at a rustic *agriturismo* (farm stay accommodation), you can't help but appreciate this island's love of the good life. Earthy and glamorous, adventurous and blissfully relaxed, Sardinia delights in being that little bit different.

When to Go
Cagliari

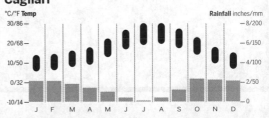

Feb Pre-Lenten shenanigans, from Carnivale madness to medieval jousting at Oristano's Sa Sartiglia.	**Mar-May** Spring wildflowers, Easter parades, and hiking without the heat and crowds.	**Jun-Aug** Sun-kissed beaches, open-air festivals and folksy fun at Nuoro's Sagra del Redentore.

Sardinia Highlights

1 Gola Su Gorropu
(p885) Walking on the wild side in Sardinia's most spectacular gorge.

2 Costa Verde
(p861) Feeling the lure of the sea on the windswept beaches of Sardinia's southwest coast.

3 Il Castello
(p851) Wandering the medieval backstreets of Cagliari's rocky citadel.

4 Costa Smeralda
(p878) Rubbing bronzed shoulders with the rich and super-famous.

5 Nuraghe Su Nuraxi (p861) Boning up on prehistory at Sardinia's sole World Heritage Site.

6 Golfo di Orosei
(p888) Dropping anchor in brilliant

Piombino

Genoa;
Livorno

Civitavecchia

TYRRHENIAN
SEA

Marseille;
Toulon

Genoa

Îles
Lavezzi

Bouches de
Bonifacio

Bonifacio

Santa Teresa
di Gallura

Costa Paradiso

Golfo dell'Asinara

Parco Nazionale
dell'Asinara

Torre
Pelosa

Spiaggia
della
Pelosa

Stintino

Isola della
Maddalena

Palau

Porto
Pollo

Caprera

Baia
Sardinia

Parco Nazionale
dell'Arcipelago
di La Maddalena **9**

Spiaggia
del Principe **3**

Costa
Romazzino

4 Costa
Smeralda

Porto
Rotondo

Golfo Aranci

Aeroporto Olbia
Costa Smeralda

Olbia

Golfo di
Olbia

SS125

San Pantaleo

Coddu Ecchju

Arzachena

Tempio
Pausania

Monti

SS389

SS133

Valle della Luna

Lago del
Coghinas

Coghinas

SS199

Castelsardo

SS200

Marina
di Sorso

Sorso

Platamona

Porto
Torres

Sassari

Basilica della
Santissima Trinità
di Saccargia

Ozieri

Torralba

Nuraghe
Santu Antine

SS131

Valle dei Nuraghi

Valle dei Nuraghi

Siniscola

Orosei

Cala
Cartoe

Cala Gonone

6 Golfo di
Orosei

Caletta
Fuili

Cala
Sisine

7 Dorgali

Valle di Lanaittu

Serra
Orrios

Tomba dei
Giganti S'Ena
e Thomes

Monte Albo

Oliena

1 Gola Su
Gorropu

Orgosolo

Mamoiada

Nuoro

Orune

Monte
Ortobene
(955m)

Parco Nazionale
del Golfo di Orosei e
del Gennargentu

SS131d

Macomer

Cuglieri

Torre

Bosa

Mare di
Sardegna

Villanova
Monteleone

SS292

Alghero

7 Alghero

Cala
Bona

Fertilia

Alghero
Airport

Porto
Ferro

Monte
Timidone
(361m)

Grotta di
Nettuno **10**

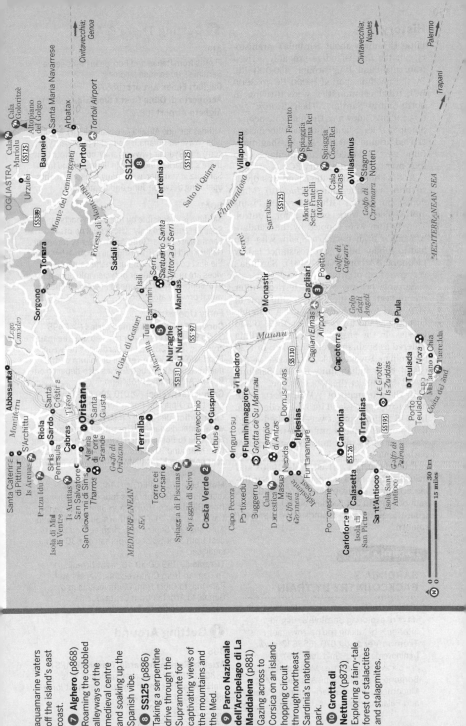

aquamarine waters off the island's east coast.

7 Alghero (p868)
Roaming the cobbled alleyways of the medieval centre and soaking up the Spanish vibe.

8 SS125 (p886)
Taking a serpentine drive through the Supramonte for captivating views of the mountains and the Med.

9 Parco Nazionale dell'Arcipelago di La Maddalena (p881)
Gazing across to Corsica on an island-hopping circuit through northeast Sardinia's national park.

10 Grotta di Nettuno (p873)
Exploring a fairy-tale forest of stalactites and stalagmites.

History

Little is known about Sardinia's prehistory, but the first islanders probably arrived from mainland Italy around 350,000 BC. By the neolithic period (8000 BC to 3000 BC), tribal communities were thriving in north-central Sardinia. Their Bronze Age descendants, known as the nuraghic people, dominated the island until the Phoenicians arrived around 850 BC. The Carthaginians came next, followed by the Romans, who took over in the 3rd century BC.

In the Middle Ages, the island was divided into four independent *giudicati* (kingdoms), but by the 13th century the Pisans and Genoese were battling for control. They in turn were toppled by the Catalan-Aragonese from northern Spain, who also had to subdue bitter Sard resistance led by Eleonora d'Arborea (1347-1404), Sardinia's very own Joan of Arc.

Sardinia became Spanish territory after the unification of the Spanish kingdoms in 1479, and today there remains a tangible Hispanic feel to towns such as Alghero and Iglesias. In the ensuing centuries, Sardinia suffered as Spain's power crumbled; in 1720 the Italian Savoys took possession of the island. After Italian unity in 1861, Sardinia found itself under the boot of Rome.

In the aftermath of WWII, efforts were made to drag the island into the modern era. In 1946 a huge project was launched to rid the island of malaria and in 1948 Sardinia was granted its own autonomous regional parliament.

Coastal tourism arrived in the 1960s and has since become a mainstay of the Sardinian economy. Environmentalists breathed a sigh of relief in 2008 when NATO withdrew from the Maddalena islands after a 35-year sojourn.

WORTH A TRIP

SARDINIA'S BACKCOUNTRY BY TRAIN

If you're not in a rush, one of the best ways of exploring Sardinia's rugged interior is by taking the narrow-gauge **Trenino Verde** (☑ 070 265 76 12; www.treninoverde.com; ☉ mid-Jun–Sep). There are six available routes: Mandas–Isili–Sorgono, Mandas–Seui, Arbatax–Gairo, Macomer–Bosa, Sassari–Tempio–Palau and Palau–Tempio.

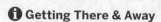

❶ Getting There & Away

AIR

Flights from Italian and European cities serve Sardinia's three main airports:

Cagliari Elmas Airport (p857)
Aeroporto di Olbia Costa Smeralda (p877)
Alghero Airport (p872)

Airlines include Alitalia (www.alitalia.it), Meridiana (www.meridiana.it), easyJet (www.easyjet.com) and Ryanair (www.ryanair.com). Note that there's a marked increase in flights to and from Sardinia in summer, with many seasonal flights operating between June and September.

BOAT

Sardinia is accessible by ferry from ports in Spain, France and Italy. The arrival points in Sardinia are Olbia, Golfo Aranci, Santa Teresa di Gallura and Porto Torres in the north; Arbatax on the east coast; and Cagliari in the south. Services are most frequent between mid-June and mid-September. Book ahead at www.traghettiweb.it or www.aferry.co.uk.

Ferry Operators

Corsica Ferries, Sardinia Ferries (☑ 0495 32 95 95; www.corsica-ferries.co.uk) The main crossing from Corsica to Sardinia is between Bonifacio and Santa Teresa di Gallura on the northern coast, though ferries also depart from Bastia, Ajaccio and Propriano.

Grandi Navi Veloci (☑ 010 209 45 91; www.gnv.it) To Olbia and Porto Torres from Genoa.

La Méridionale (☑ in France 0970 83 20 20; www.lameridionale.fr) Operates ferries from Marseille to Porto Torres (via Corsica). Crossing time is around 10 hours. Tickets for a reclinable seat cost roughly €44 and for a small car €98 in high season.

Moby Lines (☑ +49 (0)611-14020; www.mobylines.com) Operates four daily crossings from Bonifacio on Corsica to Santa Teresa di Gallura on Sardinia's northern tip between mid-April and late September. High-season tickets cost from about €22 per person or €30 with a small car.

Tirrenia (☑ 199 30 30 40; www.tirrenia.it) To Cagliari from Civitavecchia, Naples and Palermo; to Olbia from Civitavecchia and Genoa; to Arbatax from Civitavecchia and Genoa; to Porto Torres from Genoa.

❶ Getting Around

BUS

Azienda Regionale Sarda Trasporti (ARST; ☑ 800 865042; www.arst.sardegna.it) is Sardinia's main bus company running most local and long-distance services.

CAR & MOTORCYCLE

Sardinia is best explored by road. There are rental agencies at all airports, along with downtown branches in Cagliari and other cities.

TRAIN

Trenitalia (☑ 892021; www.trenitalia.com) services link Cagliari with Oristano, Sassari, Porto Torres, Olbia and Golfo Aranci. Services are slow but generally reliable. Slow ARST trains serve Sassari, Alghero and Nuoro. Between mid-June and early September, ARST also operates a scenic tourist train service, the Trenino Verde.

CAGLIARI

Forget flying: the best way to arrive in Sardinia's historic capital is by sea, the city rising in a helter-skelter of golden-hued *palazzi*, domes and facades up to the rocky centrepiece, Il Castello. Although Tunisia is closer than Rome, Cagliari is the most Italian of Sardinia's cities. Vespas buzz down tree-fringed boulevards and locals hang out at busy cafes tucked under arcades in the seafront Marina district.

Like many Italian cities, Cagliari wears its history on its sleeve and everywhere you go you come across traces of its rich past: ancient Roman ruins, museums filled with prehistoric artefacts, centuries-old churches and elegant *palazzi*.

Edging east of town brings you to Poetto beach, the hub of summer life with its limpid blue waters and upbeat party scene.

◎ Sights

★ Il Castello
AREA

This hilltop citadel is Cagliari's most iconic image, its domes, towers and *palazzi*, once home to the city's aristocracy, rising above the sturdy ramparts built by the Pisans and Aragonese. Inside the battlements, the old medieval city reveals itself like Pandora's box. The university, cathedral, museums and Pisan palaces are wedged into a jigsaw of narrow high-walled alleys. Sleepy though it may seem, the area harbours a number of boutiques, bars and cafes popular with visitors, students and hipsters.

★ Museo Archeologico Nazionale
MUSEUM

(☑ 070 6051 8245; http://museoarcheocagliari. beniculturali.it; Piazza Arsenale; adult/reduced €5/2.50, incl Pinacoteca Nazionale €7/3.50; ☻9am-8pm Tue-Sun) Of the four museums

SAND IN THE CITY

An easy bus ride from the centre, Cagliari's fabulous **Poetto beach** extends for 7km beyond the green Promontorio di Sant'Elia, nicknamed the Sella del Diavola (Devil's Saddle). In summer much of the city's youth decamps here to sunbathe and party in the restaurants and bars that line the sand. Water sports are big and you can hire canoes at the beach clubs. To get to the beach, take bus PF or PQ from Piazza Matteotti.

at the **Cittadella dei Musei**, this is the undoubted star. Sardinia's premier archaeological museum showcases artefacts spanning thousands of years of history, from the early Neolithic, through the Bronze and Iron Ages to the Phoenician and Roman eras. Highlights include a series of colossal figures known as the Giganti di Monte Prama and a superb collection of *bronzetti* (bronze figurines), which, in the absence of any written records, are a vital source of information about Sardinia's mysterious nuraghic culture.

★ Cattedrale di Santa Maria
CATHEDRAL

(☑ 070 864 93 88, www.duomodicagliari.it; Piazza Palazzo 4; ☻8am-noon & 4-8pm Mon Sat, 8am-1pm & 4.30-8.30pm Sun) Cagliari's graceful 13th-century cathedral stands proudly on Piazza Palazzo. Except for the square based bell tower, little remains of the original Gothic structure: the clean Pisan-Romanesque facade is a 20th-century imitation, added between 1933 and 1938. Inside, the once-Gothic church has all but disappeared beneath a rich icing of baroque decor, the result of a radical late-17th-century makeover. Bright frescoes adorn the ceilings, and the side chapels spill over with exuberant sculptural whirls.

Torre dell'Elefante
TOWER

(www.beniculturalicagliari.it; Via Santa Croce, cnr Via Università; adult/reduced €3/2; ☻10am-7pm summer, 9am-5pm winter) One of only two Pisan towers still standing, the Torre dell'Elefante was built in 1307 as a defence against the threatening Aragonese. Named after the sculpted elephant by the vicious-looking portcullis, the 42m-high tower became something of a horror show, thanks to the severed heads the city's Spanish rulers used to adorn it with. The crenellated storey was added in 1852 and used as a prison for political detainees. Climb to the top for far-reaching views over the city's rooftops to the sea.

Bastione di Saint Remy   VIEWPOINT

This vast neoclassical structure, comprising a gallery space, monumental stairway and panoramic terrace, was built into the city's medieval walls between 1899 and 1902. The highlight is the elegant Umberto I terrace, which commands sweeping views

Cagliari

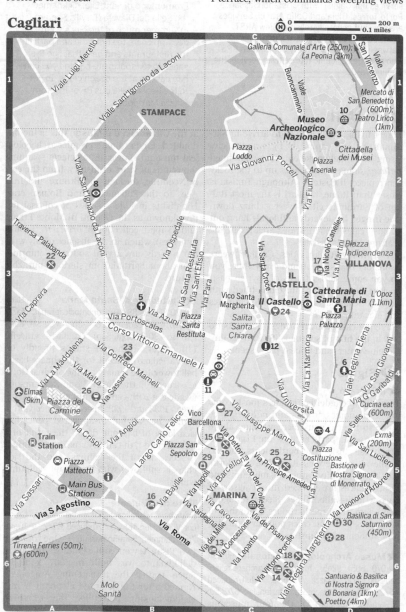

200 m
0.1 miles

over Cagliari's jumbled rooftops to the sea and distant mountains. To reach the terrace, which was recently reopened after a two-year restoration, you can try the stairway (closed at the time of research) on Piazza Costituzione or take the elevator from the **Giardino Sotto Le Mure** (Viale Regina Elena; ☉7am-9pm winter, longer hours summer).

Pinacoteca Nazionale
GALLERY

(☑070 65 69 91; www.pinacoteca.cagliari.beni culturali.it; Piazza Arsenale; adult/reduced €3/1.50, incl Museo Archeologico Nazionale €7/3.50; ☉9am-8pm Tue-Sun) Cagliari's principal gallery showcases a prized collection of 15th- to 17th-century art. Many of the best works are *retablos* (grand altarpieces), painted by Catalan and Genoese artists. Of those by known Sardinian painters, the four 16th-century works by Pietro Cavaro, father of the so-called Stampace school and arguably Sardinia's most important artist, are outstanding. They include a moving *Deposizione* (Deposition) and portraits of St Peter, St Paul and St Augustine.

Orto Botanico
GARDENS

(Botanic Gardens; ☑070 675 35 22; www.ccb-sardegna.it; Viale Sant'Ignazio da Laconi 11; adult/reduced €4/2; ☉9am-6pm Tue-Sun summer, to 2pm winter) Established in 1858, the Orto Botanico is one of Italy's most famous botanical gardens. Today it extends over 5 hectares and nurtures 2000 species of flora.

Leafy arches lead to trickling fountains and gardens bristling with palm trees, cacti and *ficus* trees with huge snaking roots.

Galleria Comunale d'Arte
GALLERY

(☑070 677 75 98; www.museicivicicagliari.it; Giardini Pubblici; adult/reduced €6/2.50; ☉10am-9pm Wed-Mon summer, to 6pm winter) Housed in a neoclassical villa in the Giardini Pubblici (Public Gardens) north of the Castello, this gallery focuses on modern and contemporary art. Works by many of Sardinia's top artists are on show, alongside paintings and sculptures from the Collezione Ingrao, a formidable collection of 20th-century Italian art.

Chiesa di San Michele
CHURCH

(Via Ospedale 2; ☉8-11am & 7-8.30pm Mon-Sat, 9am-noon & 7-9pm Sun) Although consecrated in 1538, this Jesuit church is best known for its lavish 18th-century decor, considered the finest example of baroque styling in Sardinia. The spectacle starts outside with the ebullient triple-arched facade and continues through the vast colonnaded atrium into the magnificent octagonal interior. Here six heavily decorated chapels radiate out from the centre, capped by a grand, brightly frescoed dome. Also of note is the sacristy, with its vivid frescoes and intricate inlaid wood.

★ Santuario & Basilica di Nostra Signora di Bonaria
CHURCH

(☑070 30 17 47; Piazza Bonaria 2; donations welcome; ☉6.30-11.45am & 4.30-8pm summer,

SARDINIA CAGLIARI

Cagliari

6.30-11.45am & 4-7pm winter) Crowning the Bonaria hill, around 1km southeast of Via Roma, this religious complex is a hugely popular pilgrimage site. Devotees come from all over the world to visit the 14th-century Gothic church (sanctuary) and pray to *Nostra Signora di Bonaria,* a statue of the Virgin Mary and Christ that supposedly saved a ship's crew during a storm. To the right of the sanctuary, the towering basilica still acts as a landmark to returning sailors.

Piazza Yenne
PIAZZA

The focal point of the Marina district, and indeed of central Cagliari, is Piazza Yenne. The small square is adorned with a statue of **King Carlo Felice** to mark the beginning of the SS131 cross-island highway, the project for which the monarch is best remembered. On summer nights, the piazza heaves as a young crowd flocks to its bars, gelaterie and pavement cafes.

Museo del Tesoro e Area Archeologica di Sant'Eulalia
MUSEUM

(☑ 070 66 37 24; www.mutseu.org; Vico del Collegio 2; adult/reduced €5/2.50; ⊙10am-1pm & 4-7pm Tue-Sun) In the heart of the Marina district, this museum contains a rich collection of religious art, as well as an archaeological area beneath the adjacent **Chiesa di Sant' Eulalia**. The main drawcard is a 13m section of excavated Roman road (constructed between the 1st and 2nd centuries AD), which archaeologists think would have connected with the nearby port.

🎊 Festivals & Events

Cagliari puts on a good show for Carnevale, and during the Easter Holy Week, when hooded processions pass by its historic churches. The city's headline event is the **Festa di Sant'Efisio** (www.festadisantefisio. com; ⊙1-4 May), dating back to 1657, during which Cagliari's patron saint gets paraded through the streets on a bullock-drawn carriage.

🛏 Sleeping

Il Cagliarese
B&B €

(☑339 6544083; www.ilcagliarese.com; Via Vittorio Porcile 19; s €45-60, d €60-75; ❋@🛜) Bang in the heart of the Marina district, this snug B&B is a real find. It has three immaculate rooms, each with homey touches such as embroidered fabrics and carved wooden furnishings. Breakfast is scrumptious, and

Mauro, your welcoming host, bends over backwards to please.

Residenza Kastrum
B&B €

(☑348 0012280; www.kastrum.eu; Via Nicolò Canelles 78; s €45-60, d €55-85, q €120-160; ❋🛜) Escape the hurly-burly of the centre at this cosy B&B in the hilltop Castello district. Its simple white rooms are comfortable enough, with parquet floors and classic dark wood furniture, but what sets it apart are the memorable views from the small rooftop terrace. The quad rooms are ideal for families.

Marina di Castello
B&B €

(☑335 8125881; www.bedandbreakfastcagliari city.it; Via Roma 75a; d €75-120; ❋🛜) Sabrina makes you feel instantly at ease at this B&B on Cagliari's main seafront boulevard. There's a clean, modern feel about the place with rooms tastefully done out in silver, bronze and gold, while patches of exposed brick and artistic flourishes add a boutique touch. Up top, the roof terrace overlooking the marina is a panoramic spot for a summer sundowner.

Maison Savoia
GUESTHOUSE €

(☑334 2088478, 070 67 81 81; www.maisonsavoia. it; Piazza Savoia 2; s €60-70, d €80-90; ❋🛜) This discreet guesthouse is brilliantly placed right in the heart of the action. It's surrounded by restaurants, bars and shops, yet its decently sized rooms are quiet. Decor is old school with parquet floors, framed prints and heavy wood furniture. Note that breakfast is not always included in your room rate.

⭐ Hotel Nautilus
HOTEL €€

(☑070 37 00 91; www.hotelnautiluspoetto.com; Viale Poetto 158; d €150-210, tr €170-225; ❋🛜) Nothing shouts holiday as much as the sight of sea and sand on your doorstep. This gleaming three-star hotel is one of the best on the Poetto beachfront, offering summery blue and white rooms, balconies and sea views. Rates plummet in the low season, meaning there are some real off-season bargains to be had.

⭐ Hotel Miramare
BOUTIQUE HOTEL €€€

(☑070 66 40 21; www.hotelmiramarecagliari.it; Via Roma 59; r €195-500; ❋🛜) A fashion magazine spread waiting to happen, this boutique four-star hotel exudes effortless chic with its artistic interiors and classy rooms. Located on sea-facing Via Roma, it has individually styled rooms whose decor ranges from pared-down contemporary cool to full-on belle-époque glamour, with crimson walls, zebra-print chairs, pop art and art-deco furniture.

✖ Eating

It's not difficult to eat well in Cagliari. The city offers everything from classy fine-dining restaurants to humble neighbourhood trattorias, pizzerias, bars and takeaways. Marina is chock-full of places, some of which are obviously touristy but many that are not and are popular with locals. Other good eat streets include Via Sassari and Corso Vittorio Emanuele.

Pizzeria Nansen   PIZZA €
(070 667 03 35; Corso Vittorio Emanuele II 269; pizzas €5-10; 11.30am-2.30pm & 6.30-11.30pm Tue-Sun) For a slice of *deltzloso* pizza and a cool bottle of Ichnusa (Sardinian beer), head to this super-friendly pizzeria. The pizzas, served ready cut on a tray, are finger-lickingly good with light fluffy bases and flavour-packed toppings, and the setting – high stools, paper napkins and framed Roma football shirts (!) – is suitably relaxed.

★ La Pola   SEAFOOD €€
(070 65 06 04; Vico Barcellona 10; meals €30; 7-11pm Mon-Sat, plus 1-3pm Sat & Sun) There are many seafood restaurants in the Marina district but few bring in the crowds like this local favourite. To look at, it's nothing out of the ordinary with its murals and orange and yellow walls, but once the food starts arriving you'll appreciate why it's so often packed: multi-dish starters, luxurious lobster mains, beautifully seared tuna.

★ Luigi Pomata   SEAFOOD €€
(070 67 20 58; www.luigipomata.com; Viale Regina Margherita 14; meals restaurant €40-50, bistro €25-30; 1-3pm & 8-11pm Mon-Sat) There's always a buzz at chef Luigi Pomata's minimalist seafood restaurant, with pared-down decor and chefs skillfully preparing super-fresh sushi. For a more casual eating experience, try the Pomata Bistrot, beneath the main restaurant, where you can dine on dishes such as stuffed squid with broccoli cream in a tranquil, relaxed setting.

Ristorante Ammentos   SARDINIAN €€
(070 65 10 75; Via Sassari 120; fixed-price menu €15-30; 1-3pm & 8-11pm Wed-Mon) Dine on authentic southern Sardinian fare in rustic surrounds at this traditional old-school trattoria. *Malloreddus* (typical Sardinan gnocchi) with gorgonzola cheese is a delicious lead to succulent meat dishes such as wild pork and sausages.

Martinelli's   ITALIAN €€
(070 65 42 20; www.martinellis.it; Via Principe Amedeo 18; meals from €35; 8.30pm-midnight Mon-Sat) Simplicity is the ethos underpinning this intimate, subtly lit bistro in the Marina district. Service is friendly without being overbearing, and the menu plays up seasonal, winningly fresh seafood along the lines of *tagliolini* (flat spaghetti) with octopus ink and sea bass cooked in Vernaccia wine.

Dal Corsaro   RISTORANTE €€€
(070 66 43 18; www.stefanodeidda.it; Viale Regina Margherita 28; fixed-price menus €70-80; 7.45-11pm Tue-Sun) One of only two Michelin-starred restaurants in Sardinia, Dal Corsaro has long been a bastion of high-end culinary creativity. Calling the shots is chef Stefano Deidda whose artistic brand of cuisine marries technical brilliance with a passion for seasonal Sardinian ingredients. Typical of his style is his *maialino da latte, topinambur e aglio* (roast pork with Jerusalem artichoke and garlic). Bookings required.

🍸 Drinking & Nightlife

★ Cucina eat   WINE BAR
(070 099 10 98; www.shopcucina.it; Piazza Gallileo Galilei 1; 10.30am-11.30pm Mon-Sat) A bookshop, a bar, a bistro? Cucina eat is pretty much all these things with its central bar and ceiling-high shelves stocked with wines, olive oils, cookbooks and kitchen gadgets, all of which are available to buy. Cool and relaxed, it's a fine spot to spend an evening over a bottle of wine and a light meal (around €20 to €25).

★ Caffè Libarium Nostrum   BAR
(346 5220212; Via Santa Croce 33; 7.30am-2am Tue-Sun) Offering some of the best views in town, this modish Castello bar has panoramic seating on top of the city's medieval ramparts. If the weather's being difficult, make for the brick-lined interior and order yourself an Alligator, a formidable cocktail of Calvados and Drambuie created in honour of the hero of Massimo Carlotto's novels.

Inu   WINE BAR
(070 667 04 14; www.inusardinianwinebar.it; Via Sassari 50; 7pm-1am Tue-Sun) Get versed in

SARDINIA CAGLIARI

Sardinian wine at this contemporary, high ceilinged wine bar, which pairs throaty Cannonau reds and tangy Vermentino whites with platters of top-quality Sardinian cured meats and cheeses, prepared at the well-stocked counter.

Hop Corner   PUB
(☑070 67 31 58; www.hopcornerbirreria.com; Via Principe Amedeo 14; ☉7pm-1am Tue-Sat) This vaulted pub carved out of rock is an atmospheric spot for specialty craft beers and ales, which pair nicely with the excellent hamburgers and platters of Sardinian cured meats and cheeses. It hosts occasional live music evenings with a retro vibe.

Tiffany   CAFE
(☑070 732 47 87; Via Baylle 133; ☉6am-9pm Mon-Sat) The outside tables at this handsome brick-vaulted cafe are *the* place to be for an early evening aperitif. Come around 6.30pm and you'll find every seat taken as Cagliari's fashionable drinkers congregate to catch up on gossip, sip on *spritz* and look beautiful.

☆ Entertainment

Cagliari has a lively performance scene, comprising classical music, dance, opera and drama. The season generally runs from October to May, although some places also offer a summer line-up of events. For information on up-coming events ask at the tourist office, check online at **Box Office Tickets** (☑070 65 74 28; www.boxofficesardegna.it; Viale Regina Margherita 43; ☉10am-1pm & 5-8pm Mon-Fri winter, plus 10am-1pm Sat summer), or pick up a copy of the local newspaper *L'Unione Sarda*.

Teatro Lirico   THEATRE
(☑070 408 22 30; www.teatroliricodicagliari.it; Via Sant'Alenixedda) This is Cagliari's premier venue for classical music, opera and ballet. The line-up is fairly traditional but quality is high and concerts are well attended. Tickets range range from €10 to €35 for concerts, from €15 to €75 for opera and ballet.

🛍 Shopping

Cagliari has a refreshing absence of overtly touristy souvenir shops, although they do exist. Style-conscious shoppers will find plenty to browse on Via Giuseppe Manno and Via Giuseppe Garibaldi. Nearby Via Sulis is another good area with several fashion boutiques and jewellery stores. You'll also find various artisanal shops tucked away,

particularly in the Marina district. Sunday is best for flea market and antique finds.

★ Durke   FOOD
(☑347 2246858; www.durke.com; Via Napoli 66; ☉10.30am-1.30pm & 4.30-8pm Mon-Sat) In Sardinian, *durke* means 'sweet', and they don't come sweeter than this delightful old-fashioned store. Its *dolci* (sweets) are all made according to age-old recipes, often with nothing more than sugar, egg whites and almonds. Indulge in fruit-and-nut *papassinos*, moist *amaretti di sardegna* biscuits and *pardulas* (delicate ricotta cheesecakes flavoured with saffron).

★ Mercato di San Benedetto   MARKET
(Via San Francesco Cocco Ortu; ☉7am-2pm Mon-Sat) Cagliari's historic morning food market is exactly what a thriving market should be – busy, noisy and packed with fresh, fabulous produce: fish, salami, heavy clusters of grapes, *pecorino* the size of wagon wheels, steaks, sushi, you name it.

Enoteca Biondi 1959   WINE
(☑070 667 04 26; www.enotecabiondi.it; Viale Regina Margherita 83; ☉10am-1.30pm daily & 5-9.30pm Mon-Sat) One of Cagliari's best stocked bottle shops, Enoteca Biondi sells wine and beer from all over the world, as well as a selection of Italian gourmet specialties: balsamic vinegar from Modena, Sicilian *torrone* (nougat), conserves, cheeses and truffles.

ℹ Information

Virtually all hotels and B&Bs offer free wi-fi, as do many bars and cafes. The city is dotted with free wi-fi zones, but you'll need an Italian SIM card to log on (the password is sent to your mobile phone).

Banks and ATMs are widely available, particularly around the port and train station, on Largo Carlo Felice and Corso Vittorio Emanuele.

InfoPoint (☑070 3791 9201; www.parcomolentargius.it; Edificio Sali Scelti, Via La Palma; ☉8.30am-8pm Mon-Fri, 9am-8.30pm Sat & Sun) Learn about the Parco Naturale Regionale Molentargius at its information point on the eastern fringes of town.

Ospedale Brotzu (☑070 53 92 10; www.aobrotzu.it; Piazzale Ricchi 1) Hospital with accident and emergency department. It's located northwest of the city centre; take bus 1 from Via Roma if you need to make a non-emergency visit.

Tourist Office (☑070 677 81 73; www.cagliariturismo.it; Via Roma 145, Palazzo Civico;

⊙ 9am-8pm summer, 10am-1pm & 2-5pm Mon-Sat winter) Helpful English-speaking staff can provide city information and maps. The office is just inside Palazzo Civico's main entrance, on the right.

ⓘ Getting There & Away

AIR

Cagliari Elma Airport (☑ 070 21 12 11; www.cagliariairport.it) is 9km northwest of the city centre, near Elmas. Flights connect with mainland Italian cities, including Rome, Milan, Bergamo, Bologna, Florence, Naples, Rome, Turin and Venice. There are also flights to/from European destinations including Barcelona, London, Paris and Frankfurt. In summer, there are additional charter flights.

BOAT

Cagliari's ferry port is located just off Via Roma. **Tirrenia** (☑ 892 123, agency 070 66 95 01; www.tirrenia.it; Via Riva di Ponente 1; ⊙ agency 9am-noon Mon-Sat, plus 4-7pm Mon-Wed, 5-8pm Thu, 4.30-7.30pm Fri, 5-7pm Sat) is the main ferry operator, with year-round services to Civitavecchia, Naples and Palermo. Book tickets at the port agency, online or at travel agencies.

BUS

From the **main bus station** (Piazza Matteotti), **ARST** (Azienda Regionale Sarda Trasporti; ☑ 800 865042; www.arst.sardegna.it) buses serve Pula (€3.10, 50 minutes, hourly), Chia (€3.70, 1¼ hours, up to 10 daily) and Villasimius (€4.30, 1½ hours, at least six daily), as well as Oristano (€6.70, two hours, two daily), Nuoro (€12.50, 2¾ hours, two daily) and Iglesias (€4.30, 1½ hours, daily weekdays).

Turmo Travel (☑ 0789 2 14 87; www.gruppoturmotravel.com) has services to Olbia (€16.50, 4½ hours, twice daily) and Santa Teresa di Gallura (€19.50, 5½ hours, daily).

CAR & MOTORCYCLE

The island's main dual-carriage, the SS131 'Carlo Felice', links the capital with Porto Torres via Oristano and Sassari; a branch road, the SS131dcn, runs from Oristano to Olbia via Nuoro. The SS130 leads west to Iglesias.

TRAIN

The main train station is located on Piazza Matteotti. Direct trains serve Iglesias (€4.30, one hour, 11 daily), Sassari (€16.50, 2¾ hours, three daily), Oristano (€6.70, 50 minutes to 1½ hours, 15 daily) and Olbia (€18, 3¼ hours, three daily).

ⓘ Getting Around

BUS

CTM (Consorzio Trasporti e Mobilità; ☑ 800 078870; www.ctmcagliari.it; single/daily ticket €1.30/3.30) bus routes cover the city and surrounding area. You might use the buses to reach a handful of out-of-the-way sights, and they come in handy for Calamosca and Poetto beaches. Tickets are valid for 1½ hours.

CAR & MOTORCYCLE

Driving in the centre of Cagliari is a pain, although given the geography of the town (one big hill), you might consider renting a scooter for a day or two.

Parking in the city centre from 9am to 1pm and 4pm to 8pm Monday to Saturday means paying. On-street metered parking (within the blue lines) costs €1 per hour. Alternatively, there's a 24-hour car park next to the train station, which costs €1 per hour or €10 for 24 hours. There's no maximum stay.

TAXI

Many hotels and guesthouses arrange airport pick-ups. There are taxi ranks at Piazza Matteotti (Via Sassari), Piazza Repubblica and on Largo Carlo Felice (Piazza Yenne). Otherwise you can call the radio taxi firms **Radio Taxi 4 Mori** (☑ 070 40 01 01; www.cagliaritaxi.com) and **Rossoblù** (☑ 070 66 55; www.radiotaxirossoblu.com).

AROUND CAGLIARI

The Sarrabus, the triangular-shaped territory that covers Sardinia's southeastern corner, is one of the island's least-populated and least-developed areas. It might only be an hour or two by car from Cagliari but it feels like another world with its remote, thickly wooded mountains and snaking, silent roads. Its high point, Monte dei Sette Fratelli (1023m), is a miraculously unspoilt wilderness, home to some of the island's last remaining deer. The coastal scenery is every bit as impressive, featuring high cliff bound coves and endless swathes of sand fronted by transparent azure waters.

DON'T MISS

TOP FIVE BEACHES IN SARDINIA

➡ Chia (p859)

➡ Spiaggia del Principe (p879)

➡ Spiaggia della Pelosa (p873)

➡ Is Aruttas (p866)

➡ Cala Goloritzè (p889)

Villasimius & Capo Carbonara

Once a quiet fishing village surrounded by pines and *macchia* (Mediterranean scrubland), Villasimius has grown into one of Sardinia's most popular southern resorts. The town is 1.5km inland but makes a handy base for exploring the fabulous beaches and transparent waters that sparkle on the nearby coast.

◎ Sights & Activities

★ Capo Carbonara　　　NATURE RESERVE
(www.ampcapocarbonara.it) If you embark on just one excursion from Villasimius, make it the 15-minute drive south to Capo Carbonara, a protected marine park. The promontory dips spectacularly into the crystal-clear waters of the Med. Besides perfect conditions for divers, the area has some gorgeously secluded bays with white quartz sand, backed by cliffs cloaked in *macchia* and wildflowers. Walking trails teeter off in all directions.

★ Cala Giunco　　　BEACH
The pick of Villasimius' *spiagge* (beaches), Cala Giunco is a vision of beach perfection: a long strip of silky white sand sandwiched between tropical azure waters and a silvery lagoon, the **Stagno Notteri**, where pink flamingos congregate in winter. To the north, *macchia*-clad hills rise on the blue horizon.

Fiore di Maggio　　　BOATING
(☑ 345 6032042; www.fioredimaggio.eu; per adult/child incl lunch €45/35) These daily boat tours are a superb way to see the hidden bays and islands of the Capo Carbonara marine reserve. Take your bathers if you fancy a dip.

⌂ Sleeping & Eating

Hotel Mariposas　　　HOTEL €€
(☑ 070 79 00 84; www.hotelmariposas.it; Via Mar Nero 1; s €75-190, d €100-250, ste €125-280; P ❄ ⓢ ☒) Situated about halfway between the town centre and Spiaggia Simius, this lovely stone-clad hotel is set in glorious flower-strewn gardens. Its sunny spacious rooms all have their own terrace or balcony, and there's an attractive pool for whiling away those lazy afternoons.

Ristorante Le Anfore　　　MEDITERRANEAN €€
(☑ 070 79 20 32; www.hotelleanfore.com; Via Pallaresus 16; meals €30-40; ⊙ noon-2.30pm Tue-Sun & 7.30-10.30pm daily) The chef's love of fresh local produce shines through in Sardinian dishes such as *bottarga di muggine* (mullet roe) and *fregola con le vongole* (couscous-like pasta with clams) at this highly regarded hotel-restaurant. Adding to the experience is the alfresco verandah overlooking the hotel gardens.

❶ Getting There & Away

ARST buses run to and from Cagliari (€4.30, 1½ hours, at least six daily) throughout the year.

Costa Rei

Stretching along Sardinia's southeastern seafront, the Costa Rei extends from Cala Sinzias, about 25km north of Villasimius, to a rocky headland known as Capo Ferrat. Its lengthy beaches are stunning with soft, pearly-white sands and glorious azure waters.

Approaching from Villasimius, the first beach you hit is Cala Sinzias, a pretty sandy strip some 6km south of the main Costa Rei resort. The resort is typical of many in Sardinia, a functional holiday village of villas, shops, bars and eateries that's dead in winter but packed in the summer holiday months.

North of the resort, the beaches continue up to the road's end at Capo Ferrato, beyond which drivable dirt trails lead north.

◎ Sights

Spiaggia Costa Rei　　　BEACH
In front of the eponymous resort, the Spiaggia Costa Rei is a lengthy strip of dazzling white sand lapped by astonishingly clear blue-green waters.

Spiaggia Piscina Rei　　　BEACH
To the north of Costa Rei, this fabulous beach impresses with its blinding-white sand and turquoise water. A couple more beaches fill the remaining length of coast up to Capo Ferrato.

⌂ Sleeping

**Villaggio Camping
Capo Ferrato**　　　CAMPGROUND €
(☑ 070 99 10 12; www.campingcapoferrato.it; Località Costa Rei; 2 people, car & tent €17-45; ⊙ Apr-Oct; P ⓢ) Pitch a tent under eucalyptus and mimosa trees at this well-organised campground by the southern entrance to Capo Rei. Facilities include a small food shop, ten-

nis court, kids' playground and direct access to the adjacent beach.

❶ Getting There & Away

Throughout the year, three weekday ARST buses connect the Costa Rei with Villasimius (€1.90, 45 minutes). In summer, there are at least a couple more services.

Costa del Sud & Chia

Extending from Porto di Teulada to Chia, the Costa del Sud is one of southern Sardinia's most beautiful coastal stretches. The main hub is Chia, a popular summer hang-out centred on two glorious beaches. Elsewhere, you'll find several swimming spots on the Strada Panoramica della Costa del Sud, the stunning road that dips and twists its way along the rocky coastline.

◉ Sights & Activities

★ **Strada Panoramica della Costa del Sud**   SCENIC DRIVE

Running the 25km length of the Costa del Sud, this panoramic road – known more prosaically as the SP71 – snakes along the spectacular coastline between Porto di Teulada and Chia. It's a stunning drive whichever way you do it, with jaw-dropping views at every turn and a succession of bays capped by Spanish-era watchtowers.

Starting in Porto di Teulada, the first stretch twists past several coves as it rises to the high point of **Capo Malfatano**. Along the way, **Spiaggia Piscinni** is a great place for a dip with incredible azure waters.

Beyond the cape, the popular **Cala Teuradda** beach boasts vivid emerald-green waters, summer snack bars and a conveniently situated bus stop.

From here the road climbs inland away from the water. For great coastal views, turn off along the narrow side road at Porto Campana and follow the dirt track to the lighthouse at **Capo Spartivento**. From here a series of beaches stretch north – watch out for signposts off the main coastal road to **Cala Cipolla** (a gorgeous spot backed by pine and juniper trees), **Spiaggia Su Giudeu** and **Porto Campana**.

At the end of this stretch you'll see another Spanish watchtower presiding over Chia, the small resort that marks the end of the road.

OFF THE BEATEN TRACK

THE ANCIENT CITY OF NORA

About 30km southwest of Cagliari, the ruins of **Nora** (☎070 920 91 38; http://nora.beniculturali.unipd.it; adult/reduced €7.50/4.50; ◷10.30am-7pm Apr-Sep, 10.30am-5.30pm Oct, 10am-4pm Nov–mid-Feb, 8.30am-5pm mid-Feb–Mar) are all that's left of a once-powerful ancient city. Founded by Phoenicians in the 8th century BC, Nora later became an important Punic centre, and in the 3rd century AD, the island's Roman capital. It was eventually abandoned in the 8th century as the threat of Arab raids got too much for its nervous citizens. Highlights of the site, which is accessible by guided tour only, include a Roman theatre and an ancient baths complex.

From Cagliari, take a bus to Pula (€3.10, 50 minutes, hourly), then catch one of the regular Nora shuttles from Pula's Piazza Municipio.

Chia   VILLAGE

More a collection of hotels, holiday homes and campgrounds than a traditional village, Chia is surrounded by rusty-red hills tufted with tough *macchia*. Its beaches are hugely popular, drawing an annual influx of sun-seekers, windsurfers and water-sports enthusiasts. To see what all the fuss is about, head up to the Spanish watchtower and look down on the **Spiaggia Sa Colonia**, the area's largest and busiest beach, to the west, and the smaller **Spiaggia Su Portu** to the east.

🛏 Sleeping

Campeggio Torre Chia   CAMPGROUND €
(☎070 923 00 54; www.campeggiotorrechia.it; Via del Porto 21, Chia; 2 people, car & tent €24-32, 4-person cottage €65-130; ◷May-Oct) At the popular summer resort of Chia, this busy campground enjoys a prime location near the beach. It's fairly spartan with minimal facilities, tent pitches under pine trees and basic four-person cottages.

❶ Getting There & Away

Chia is located off the SS195, the main road that runs between Cagliari and Teulada. Regular ARST buses connect Cagliari with Chia (€4.30, 1¼ hours).

IGLESIAS & THE SOUTHWEST

Iglesias

Surrounded by the skeletons of Sardinia's once-thriving mining industry, Iglesias is a historic town that bubbles in the summer and slumbers in the colder months. Its historic centre, an appealing ensemble of lived-in piazzas, sun bleached buildings, churches and Aragonese-style wrought-iron balconies, creates an atmosphere that's as much Iberian as Sardinian – a vestige of its time as a Spanish colony. Visit at Easter to experience the city's extraordinary Settimana Santa (Holy Week) processions, featuring trains of sinister, white-robed celebrants parading through the skinny lanes of the *centro storico*.

Iglesias' focal square, **Piazza Quintino Sella**, throngs with people during the *passeggiata* (evening stroll).

◎ Sights

Cattedrale di Santa Chiara   CATHEDRAL
(Duomo; Piazza del Municipio; ⊗9am-12.30pm & 3-8pm) Dominating the eastern flank of Piazza del Municipio, the Cattedrale di Santa Chiara boasts a lovely Pisan-flavoured facade and a checkerboard stone bell tower. The church was originally built in the late 13th century, but it was given a comprehensive makeover in the 16th century, which accounts for its current Catalan Gothic look.

Inside, the highlight is a gilded retable that once held the relics of St Antiochus.

Museo dell'Arte Mineraria   MUSEUM
(☏347 5176886; www.museoartemineraria.it; Via Roma 47; adult/reduced €5/4; ⊗6.30-8.30pm Sat & Sun summer, by appointment rest of year) Just outside the historic centre, Iglesias' main museum is dedicated to the town's mining heritage. It displays up to 70 extraction machines, alongside tools and a series of thought-provoking B&W photos. But to get a real taste of the claustrophobic conditions in which the miners worked, duck down into the recreated tunnels. These were dug by mining students and were used to train senior workers until WWII when they were used as air-raid shelters.

⎘ Sleeping

★**B&B Mare Monti Miniere**   B&B €
(☏348 3310585, 0781 4 17 65; www.maremonti miniere-bb.it; Via Trento 10; s €35-40, d €45-50, tr €65-75; ❋⊛) A warm welcome awaits at this cracking B&B. Situated in a quiet side street near the historic centre, it has two cheery and immaculately kept rooms in the main house and an independent studio with its own kitchen facilities. Thoughtful extras include beach towels and a regular supply of home-baked cakes and biscuits.

❶ Getting There & Away

Twice-daily ARST buses run to Cagliari (€4.50, one to 1½ hours).

WORTH A TRIP

ISOLE DI SANT'ANTIOCO & SAN PIETRO
....

The southwest's two islands, Isola di Sant'Antioco and Isola di San Pietro, display very different characters. The larger and more developed of the two, Isola di Sant'Antioco boasts little of the obvious beauty that you'd ordinarily associate with small Mediterranean islands, but it hides a rich history – it was founded by the Phoenicians in the 8th century BC, and its historic hilltop centre is littered with necropolises.

Barely half an hour across the water, Isola di San Pietro presents a prettier picture with its pastel houses and bobbing fish boats. A mountainous trachyte island measuring about 15km long and 11km wide, it's named after St Peter, who, legend has it, was marooned here during a storm on the way to Karalis (now Cagliari). Its main town, **Carloforte**, is the very image of Mediterranean chic, with graceful *palazzi*, crowded cafes, palm trees along the waterfront and quaint cobbled streets. The island's restaurants dish up the world-famous local tuna.

Regular **Delcomar** (☏0781 85 71 23; www.delcomar.it) ferries sail from Portovesme on the Sardinian 'mainland' to Carloforte (per person/midsize car €4.90/13.70, 30 minutes) and Calasetta (per person/midsize car €4.50/10.80, 13 daily) on Sant'Antioco. Alternatively, Sant'Antioco town is accessible by the SS126 road bridge.

NURAGHE SU NURAXI

In the heart of the voluptuous green countryside near Barumini, the **Nuraghe Su Nuraxi** (☑ 070 936 81 28; www.fondazionebarumini.it; adult/reduced €11/7; ⊘ 9am-7pm summer, to 4pm winter) is Sardinia's sole World Heritage Site and the island's most visited *nuraghe*. The focal point is the 1500 BC tower, which originally stood on its own but was later incorporated into a fortified compound. Many of the settlement's buildings were erected in the Iron Age, and it's these that constitute the beehive of circular interlocking buildings that tumble down the hillside.

Visits are by guided tour only (usually in Italian, with explanatory printouts in English). Queues are the norm in summer when it can get extremely hot outside on the exposed site.

Costa Verde

Extending from Capo Pecora in the south to the small resort of Torre dei Corsari in the north, the Costa Verde (Green Coast) is one of Sardinia's great untamed coastlines, an unspoilt stretch of wild, exhilarating sands and windswept dunes. Inland, woods and *macchia* (Mediterranean scrubland) cover much of the mountainous hinterland.

The area's main drawcards are its two magnificent beaches – Spiaggia di Scivu and Spiaggia di Piscinas – and the former mining complex of Montevecchio. Elsewhere, keen hikers can summit Monte Arcuentu (785m), one of the last preserves of the *cervo sardo* (Sardinian deer), and lovers of quirky museums can learn about Sardinian knives at **Arbus**, a small mountain town sprawled along the slopes of Monte Linas.

◎ Sights

★ **Spiaggia di Piscinas**   BEACH
This magnificent beach is a picture of unspoilt beauty. A broad band of golden sand, it's sandwiched between a windswept sea and a vast expanse of dunes flecked by hardy green *macchia*. These towering dunes, known as Sardinia's desert, rise to heights of up to 60m. The beach is signposted off the SS126 and accessible via Ingurtosu and a 9km dirt track.

Spiaggia di Scivu   BEACH
A 3km lick of fine sand backed by towering dunes and walls of sandstone, Spiaggia Scivu is the most beautiful of the Costa Verde's beaches. To get there take the SS126 and head towards Arbus (if heading north) or Fluminimaggiore (if heading south) and follow the signs about 12km south of Arbus.

⊨ Sleeping & Eating

Agriturismo L'Oasi del Cervo   AGRITURISMO €
(☑ 347 3011318; www.oasidelcervo.com; Località Is Gennas, Montevecchio; d €60-70; half-board per person €55-60; ℙ 🤶) With 12 modest rooms and a remote location in the midst of *macchia*-cloaked hills, this working farm is a genuine country hideaway. It's all very down to earth but the rooms are comfortable enough, the views are uplifting, and the homemade **food** (meals €25-30) is delicious. You'll see a sign for the *agriturismo* off the SP65 between Montevecchio and Torre dei Corsari.

❶ Getting There & Away

Travelling in this area is difficult without a car. You can get to Arbus by bus from Cagliari (€5.50, two hours) or Oristano (€4.90, 1¼ hours), but beyond that you're pretty much on your own. Access to the area by road is via the inland SS126.

ORISTANO & THE WEST

Oristano

☑ 0783 / POP 31,600

With its elegant shopping streets, ornate piazzas, popular cafes and some good restaurants, Oristano's refined and animated centre is a lovely place to hang out. Though there's not a huge amount to see beyond some churches and an interesting archaeological museum, the city makes a good base to explore the surrounding area.

◎ Sights

★ Piazza Eleonora d'Arborea   PIAZZA

Oristano's elegant outdoor salon sits at the southern end of pedestrianised Corso Umberto I. An impressive, rectangular space, it comes to life on summer evenings when townsfolk congregate and children blast footballs against the glowing *palazzi*. The city's central square since the 19th century, it's flanked by grand buildings, including the neoclassical **Municipio**. In the centre stands an ornate 19th-century **statue of Eleonora**, raising a finger as if about to launch into a political speech.

Cattedrale di Santa Maria Assunta   CATHEDRAL

(Duomo; Piazza del Duomo; ⊗9am-7pm summer, to 6pm winter) Lording it over Oristano's skyline, the Duomo's onion-domed bell tower is one of the few remaining elements of the original 14th-century cathedral, itself a reworking of an earlier church damaged by fire

Oristano

Oristano

in the late 12th century. The free-standing *campanile* (bell tower), topped by its conspicuous majolica-tiled dome, adds an exotic Byzantine feel to what is otherwise a typical 18th-century baroque complex.

Museo Antiquarium Arborense   MUSEUM
(☑0783 79 12 62; www.antiquariumarborense.it; Piazza Corrias; adult/reduced €5/2.50; ⊙9am-8pm Mon-Fri, 9am-2pm & 3-8pm Sat & Sun) Oristano's principal museum boasts one of the island's major archaeological collections, with prehistoric artefacts from the Sinis Peninsula and finds from Carthaginian and Roman Tharros. There's also a small collection of *retabli* (painted altarpieces), including the 16th-century *Retablo del Santo Cristo,* by the workshop of Pietro Cavaro, which depicts a group of apparently beatific saints. But look closer and you'll see they all sport the instruments of their torture slicing through their heads, necks and hearts.

Festivals & Events

★ **Sa Sartiglia**   CARNIVAL
(⊙Feb) Oristano's carnavale is the most colourful on the island. It is attended by hundreds of costumed participants and involves a medieval joust, horse racing and incredible, acrobatic riding.

Sleeping

★ **Eleonora B&B**   B&B €
(☑347 4817976, 0783 7 04 35; www.eleonora-bed-and-breakfast.com; Piazza Eleonora d'Arborea 12; s €40-60, d €70-90, tr €80-110; ❀🖧) This charming B&B scores on all counts: location – it's in a medieval *palazzo* on Oristano's central piazza; decor – rooms are tastefully decorated with a mix of antique furniture, exposed brick walls and gorgeous old tiles; and hospitality – owners Andrea and Paola are helpful and hospitable hosts. All this and it's excellent value for money.

★ **Hotel Regina d'Arborea**   BOUTIQUE HOTEL €€
(☑0783 30 21 01; www.hotelreginadarborea.com; Piazza Eleonora 4; r €130-180) Palatial elegance and prime location are the twin attractions at this relative newcomer on Oristano's main square. Four of the seven rooms are downright magnificent, with 7m-high ceilings, restored ceiling frescoes and original patterned floors. Book ahead for the Sofia room, crowned with a hexagonal cupola and wraparound windows that offer a bird's-eye view of Oristano's famous Eleonora d'Arborea statue.

Eating & Drinking

★ **DriMcafè**   CAFE €
(☑078 330 37 50; Via Cagliari 316; light snacks & meals €4-9; ⊙8.30am-8pm Mon-Sat; 🖧🍴) This laid-back hang-out brings a slice of boho warmth to Oristano, with its rust-red walls, mishmash of vintage furnishings, book shelves and chipper service. Besides specialty teas (including Moroccan mint) and homemade cakes, it rustles up day specials – from vegetarian and vegan offerings to rosemary-rubbed lamb with seasonal vegetables.

★ **Trattoria Gino**   TRATTORIA €€
(☑0783 7 14 28; Via Tirso 13; meals €25-33; ⊙12.30-3pm & 8-11pm Mon-Sat) For excellent food and a bustling, authentic vibe, head to this old-school trattoria. Since the 1930s, locals and visitors alike have been squeezing into Gino's simple dining room to feast on tasty seafood and classic pastas. Don't miss the seafood antipasto, the butter-soft roast *seppie* (cuttlefish) and the scrumptious *seadas* (fried dough pockets with fresh *pecorino*, lemon and honey) for dessert.

La Brace   SARDINIAN €€
(☑0783 7 33 28; Via Figoli 41; lunch specials €15-20, meals €25-35; ⊙1-3pm & 8-11pm Tue-Sun) This restaurant's name refers to the glowing embers of a wood fire, and grilled meats and fish are indeed its specialty – but you'll also find a full range of Sardinian appetisers, homemade pastas and desserts. The weekday lunch special is a big draw at €15 for two courses, or €20 for three.

Information

Tourist Office (☑0783 368 32 10; www.gooristano.com; Piazza Eleonora d'Arborea 18; ⊙9am-1pm Mon-Fri, plus 3-6pm Mon & Wed) Oristano's tourist office is helpful and centrally located on the main square.

Getting There & Away

From the main **bus station** (Via Cagliari), direct buses run to/from Santa Giusta (€1.30, 15 minutes, half-hourly), Cagliari (€6.70, two hours, two daily), Bosa (€4.90, two hours, five daily) and Sassari (€8.10, two hours, three daily).

The main train station is on Piazza Ungheria, east of the town centre. Up to 15 daily trains, some of which involve a change, run between Oristano and Cagliari (€6.70, 50 to 80 minutes). Direct trains serve Sassari (€11, two to 2¼ hours, two to three daily) and Olbia (€12.50, 2½ hours, two to three daily); there are additional services but they require a change at Ozieri-Chilivani.

IVAN HLOBE/SHUTTERSTOCK ©

SHEVCHENKO ANDREY/SHUTTERSTOCK ©

TOR.65/SHUTTERSTOCK ©

1. Cagliari (p851)
Golden-hued palazzi, domes and facades lead up to the castle battlements.

2. Hiking, Gola Su Gorropu (p885)
This spectacular gorge is flanked by 500m vertical rock walls.

3. Grotta di Ispinigoli (p886)
A fairy-tale-like cave full of glittering rock formations and giant stalagmites.

4. Cala Mariolu (p888)
One of the most beautiful spots on the Golfo di Orosei, a stunning stretch of limestone cliffs, pretty beaches, caves and grottoes.

Tharros & the Sinis Peninsula

Spearing into the Golfo di Oristano, the Sinis Peninsula feels like a world apart. Its limpid lagoons – the Stagno di Cabras, Stagno Sale Porcus and Stagno Is Benas – and snow-white beaches lend it an almost tropical air, while the low-lying green countryside appears uncontaminated by human activity. In fact, the area has been inhabited since the 5th century BC. *Nuraghi* litter the landscape and the compelling Punic-Roman site of Tharros stands testament to the area's former importance. Sports fans will enjoy great surfing, windsurfing and some fine diving.

◉ Sights

★ **Area Archeologica di Tharros**   ARCHAEOLOGICAL SITE

(☑0783 37 00 19; www.tharros.sardegna.it; adult/reduced €5/4, incl tower €6/5, incl Museo Civico Cabras $8/6; ☺9am-7pm Jun, Jul & Sep, to 8pm Aug, to 6pm Apr, May & Oct, to 5pm Nov-Mar) The choppy blue waters of the Golfo di Oristano provide a magnificent backdrop to the ruins of ancient Tharros. Founded by the Phoenicians in the 8th century BC, the city thrived as a Carthaginian naval base and was later taken over by the Romans. Much of what you see today dates to the 2nd and 3rd centuries AD, when the basalt streets were laid and the aqueduct, baths and other major monuments were built.

★ **Museo Civico**   MUSEUM

(☑0783 29 06 36; www.museocabras.it; Via Tharros 121; adult/reduced €5/4; ☺9am-1pm & 4-8pm daily Apr-Oct, 9am-1pm & 3-7pm Tue-Sun Nov-Mar) Cabras' cultural highlight is the Museo Civico, and the real superstars here are the so-called Giants of Monte Prama, a series of towering nuraghic figures depicting archers, wrestlers and boxers. Also of interest are finds from Tharros and the prehistoric site of Cuccuru Is Arrius, along with obsidian and flint tools said to date back to the Neolithic cultures of Bonu Ighinu and Ozieri. As of 2017, the museum was expanding to accommodate additional finds from the Monte Prama excavations.

Chiesa di San Giovanni di Sinis   CHURCH

(☺9am-5pm) Near the southern tip of the Sinis Peninsula, just beyond the car park at the foot of the Tharros access road, you'll see the sandstone Chiesa di San Giovanni di Sinis, one of the two oldest churches in Sardinia (Cagliari's Basilica di San Saturnino is older). It owes its current form to an 11th-century makeover, although elements of the 6th-century Byzantine original remain, including the characteristic red dome. Inside, the bare walls lend a sombre and surprisingly spiritual atmosphere.

WORTH A TRIP

EXPLORING THE SINIS PENINSULA

One of the peninsula's most famous beaches, **Is Aruttas** is a pristine arc of white sand fronted by translucent aquamarine waters. For years its quartz sand was carted off to be used in aquariums and on beaches on the Costa Smeralda, but it's now illegal to take the sand away. From San Salvatore on the main Oristano–Tharros road, follow signs 2km north along the SP7 then continue 5km west on the SP59 to reach the beach.

Backed by a motley set of holiday homes and beach bars, **Putzu Idu's** beach is situated near the north of the peninsula. It's a picturesque strip of sand that's something of a water-sports hot spot with excellent surfing, windsurfing and kitesurfing. To the north, the **Capo Mannu** promontory is scalloped with a tantalising array of more secluded beaches – and battered by some of the Mediterranean's biggest waves.

In business for more than 20 years, the Sinis Peninsula's top surf school, **Is Benas Surf Club** (☑0783 192 53 63; www.isbenas.com; Lungomare S'Arena Scoada, Putzu Idu), has it all – from lessons to equipment to accommodation to professional advice – for surfers, kitesurfers and stand-up paddleboarders. The main branch is just south of Putzu Idu at Arena Scoada beach, while the affiliated Capo Mannu Kite School is a few kilometres northwest at Sa Rocca Tunda.

🛏 Sleeping & Eating

Agriturismo Sinis
AGRITURISMO €€

(📋 328 9312508, 0783 39 26 53; www.agriturismo
ilsinis.it; Località San Salvatore; half-board per
person €52-65; ❋) This working farm offers
12 guest rooms (including six constructed
in 2017) and serves wonderful earthy food.
Rooms are frill-free but clean and airy, and
views of the lush garden can be enjoyed
from chairs on the patio.

★ Hotel Lucrezia
HOTEL €€

(📋 0783 41 20 78; www.hotellucrezia.it; Via Roma
14a, Riola Sardo; r €164-184, ste €264-284; ❋ @)
Housed in a 17th-century *cortile* (courtyard
house), this elegant hideaway has rooms
surrounding an inner garden complete
with wisteria-draped pergola, fig and citrus
trees. The decor is rustic-chic, with high
18th-century antique beds, period furniture
and eye-catching tiled bathrooms. Bikes are
provided, and the welcoming staff regularly
organise cooking classes. Note that there's a
three-night minimum stay in August.

Sa Pischera 'e Mar 'e Pontis
SEAFOOD €€

(📋 0783 39 17 74; www.consorziopontis.it; Strada Provinciale 6; menus €27-32; ⏲ 1-2.30pm &
8-9.30pm) Fronting the Pontis fishing cooperative on the waterfront between Cabras
and Tharros, this is an atmospheric spot to
sample fresh seafood. The menu changes
according to the daily catch, but pride of
place goes to the local *muggine* (mullet)
and prized *bottarga* (mullet roe). Booking is
recommended.

Bosa

📋 0785 / POP 7930

Bosa is one of Sardinia's most attractive
towns. Seen from a distance, its rainbow
townscape resembles a vibrant Paul Klee
canvas, with pastel houses stacked on a
steep hillside, tapering up to a stark, grey
castle. In front, moored fishing boats bob
on a glassy river elegantly lined with palm
trees.

Bosa was established by the Phoenicians
and thrived under the Romans. During the
early Middle Ages it suffered repeat raids by
Arab pirates, but in the early 12th century a
branch of the noble Tuscan Malaspina family moved in and built their huge castle. In
the 19th century, the Savoys established lucrative tanneries here, but these have since
fallen by the wayside.

At the mouth of the Fiume Temo, about
2.5km west of Bosa proper, Bosa Marina is
the town's seaside satellite, a busy summer
resort set on a wide, 1km-long beach overlooked by a 16th-century Aragonese defensive tower.

◉ Sights

★ Castello Malaspina
CASTLE

(📋 0785 37 70 43; adult/reduced €4/3; ⏲ 10am-
1hr before sunset Apr-Oct, 10am-1pm Sat & Sun Nov-
Mar) Commanding huge views, this hilltop
castle was built in the 12th and 13th centuries by the Tuscan Malaspina family. Little
remains of the original structure except for
its skeleton – imposing walls and a series of
stone towers. Inside, a humble 14th-century
chapel, the Chiesa di Nostra Signora di
Regnos Altos, is adorned with an extraordinary 14th-century fresco cycle depicting
saints ranging from St George slaying the
dragon to St Lawrence in the middle of his
martyrdom on the grill.

★ Museo Casa Deriu
MUSEUM

(📋 0785 37 70 43; Corso Vittorio Emanuele 59;
adult/reduced €4.50/3; ⏲ 10.30am-1pm & 3-5pm
Tue-Fri, to 6pm Sat & Sun) Housed in an elegant
19th-century townhouse, Bosa's main museum showcases local arts and artisanal crafts.
Each of the three floors has a different theme
relating to the city and its past: the 1st floor
hosts temporary exhibitions and displays of
traditional hand embroidery; the 2nd floor
displays the *palazzo*'s original 19th-century
decor and furnishings; and the top floor is
dedicated to Melkiorre Melis (1889–1982),
a local painter and one of Sardinia's most
important modern artists.

🛏 Sleeping

★ La Torre di Alice
B&B €

(📋 347 6671785, 329 8570064; www.latorredi
alice.it; Via del Carmine 7; s/d/tr €60/75/95;
❋ 🛜) This great budget choice is set in a
wonderful old tower house in Bosa's medieval centre, within easy walking distance
of everything. Its five rooms are neat and
comfortable, with low brick-vaulted ceilings,
wrought-iron beds and electric kettles. Owners Alice and Marco offer oodles of local information and serve a tasty breakfast at the
rustic communal table downstairs.

Hotel Sa Pischedda
HOTEL €€

(📋 0785 37 30 65; www.hotelsapischedda.com; Via
Roma 8; d €95-170; ❋ @ 🛜) The apricot facade

WORTH A TRIP

THE SACRED WELL OF SANTA CRISTINA

Signposted off the SS131 about 25km northeast of Oristano, the extraordinary **Nuraghe di Santa Cristina** (www.archeotour.net; adult/reduced incl Museo Archeologico-Etnografico Paulilatino €5/2.50; ⊙8.30am-sunset) is Sardinia's finest example of a nuraghic *tempio a pozzo* (well temple). The worship of water was a fundamental part of nuraghic religious practice, and there are reckoned to be about 40 such sacred wells across the island.

Dating back to the late Bronze Age (11th to 9th century BC), the temple is accessible through a finely cut keyhole entrance and a flight of 24 superbly preserved steps. When you reach the bottom you can gaze up at the perfectly constructed tholos (conical tower), through which light enters the dark well shaft. Every 18 years, one month and two days, the full moon shines directly through the aperture into the well. Otherwise you can catch the yearly equinoxes in March and September, when the sun illuminates the stairway down to the well.

of this restored 1890s hotel greets you just south of the Ponte Vecchio. Several rooms retain original frescoed ceilings, some are split-level, and a few (such as 305) have terraces overlooking the river. Additional perks include friendly staff, an excellent restaurant and thoughtful touches for families (witness the 4th-floor suite with its own elevator for easy stroller access).

🍴 Eating & Drinking

⭐**Locanda di Corte**   SARDINIAN €€
(☑340 2474823; www.facebook.com/LocandaDi Corte; Via del Pozzo 7; meals €30-35; ⊙12.30-2.30pm & 7.30-10pm Wed-Mon) Wriggle through Bosa's backstreets to discover this sweet local trattoria on a secluded cobblestoned square. Owners Angelo and Angela work the small collection of tables adorned with red-and-white-checked cloths, while their son Nicola cooks up scrumptious Sardinian classics such as *fregola* pasta with mussels, clams and cherry tomatoes, or pork chops in Cannonau wine.

Cantina G Battista Columbu   WINE BAR
(☑339 5731677; www.malvasiacolumbu.com; Via del Carmine 104; ⊙10.30am-1.30pm & 5.30-9pm) A wonderful venue for sampling Bosa's renowned Malvasia, this attractive cantina is operated by the Columbu family, which has been producing wine in the region for three generations. Sip glasses (€3 to €4) of their smooth-as-silk, sherry-like Malvasia di Bosa and aromatic Alvariga along with wines from other Sardinian vintners, accompanied by local *salumi* and *formaggi* (cold cuts and cheeses).

ℹ Getting There & Away

There are weekday services from the bus stops (Piazza Zanetti) to Alghero (€3.70, 55 minutes, two daily), Sassari (€4.30, 2¼ hours, three daily) and Oristano (€5.50, two hours, five daily). Buy tickets at **Edicola da Oscar** (Corso Vittorio Emanuele 80; ⊙6am-8pm Mon-Sat, to 1pm Sun).

ALGHERO & THE NORTHWEST

Alghero

☑079 / POP 44,000

One of Sardinia's most beautiful medieval cities, Alghero is the main resort in the northwest. Although largely given over to tourism – its population can almost quadruple in July and August – the town retains a proud and independent spirit. Its animated historic centre is a terrific place to hang out, and with so many excellent restaurants and bars, it makes an ideal base for exploring the beaches and beauty spots of the nearby Riviera del Corallo.

The main focus of attention is the picturesque *centro storico* (historic centre), one of the best preserved in Sardinia. Enclosed by robust, honey-coloured sea walls, it's a tightly knit enclave of cobbled lanes, Gothic *palazzi* and cafe-lined piazzas. Below, yachts crowd the marina and long, sandy beaches curve away to the north. Presiding over everything is a palpable Spanish atmosphere, a hangover from the city's past as a Catalan colony.

Alghero

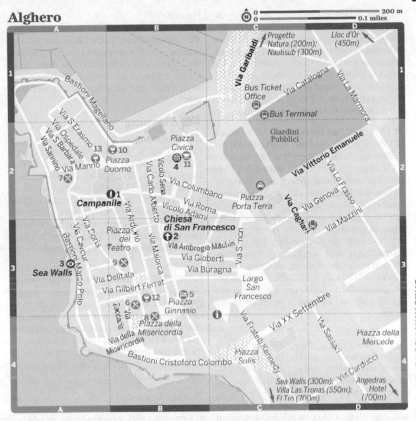

Alghero

◎ Top Sights
1 Campanile	B2
2 Chiesa di San Francesco	B3
3 Sea Walls	A3

◉ Sights
4 Palazzo d'Albis	B2
Piazza Civica	(see 4)

⊟ Sleeping
5 B&B Benebbenniu	B3

⊗ Eating
6 La Botteghina	B3
7 Mabrouk	A2
8 Prosciutteria Sant Miquel	B4
9 Trattoria Lo Romaní	B3

⊖ Drinking & Nightlife
10 Cafè Latino	B2
11 Caffè Costantino	B2
12 l'altra vineria	B3
13 SardOa	A2

◉ Sights

★ **Sea Walls**   WALLS
(Bastioni) Alghero's golden sea walls, built around the *centro storico* by the Aragonese in the 16th century, are a highlight of the town's historic cityscape. Running from Piazza Sulis in the south to Porta a Mare and the marina in the north, they're crowned by a pedestrianised path that commands superb views over to Capo Caccia on the blue horizon. Restaurants and bars line the walkway, providing the perfect perch to sit back and lap up the holiday atmosphere.

★ **Campanile**   TOWER
(Bell Tower; ☏ 079 973 30 41; Via Principe Umberto; adult/reduced €2.50/free; ⊙ 11am-1pm & 7-9pm Mon & Fri Jul & Aug, 11am-1pm Mon, Tue, Thu & Fri & 4-7pm Thu & Fri May, Jun, Sep & Oct, by request

Dec & Jan, closed Feb-Apr) Rising above the historic centre, the Cattedrale di Santa Maria's 16th-century *campanile* (bell tower) is one of Alghero's signature landmarks. The tower, accessible through a Gothic doorway on Via Principe Umberto, is a fine example of Catalan Gothic architecture with its elegant octagonal structure and short pyramid-shaped spire. Climb to the top for amazing views.

★ **Chiesa di San Francesco**　CHURCH
(☑ 079 97 92 58; Via Carlo Alberto; ☺ 9.15am-12.30pm Mon-Sat & 5-6.30pm Mon, Wed, Thu & Sat, 4.30-6.30pm Tue & Fri, 9.15-10.30am & 5-6.30pm Sun) Alghero's finest church is a model of architectural harmony. Originally built to a Catalan Gothic design in the 14th century, it was later given a Renaissance facelift after it partially collapsed in 1593. Inside, interest is focused on the 18th-century polychrome marble altar and a strange 17th-century wooden sculpture of a haggard Christ tied to a column. Through the sacristy you can enter a beautiful 14th-century cloister, where the 22 columns connect a series of round arches.

Piazza Civica　PIAZZA
Just inside Porta a Mare, Piazza Civica is Alghero's showcase square. In a former life it was the administrative heart of the medieval city, but where Spanish aristocrats once met to debate affairs of empire, tourists now converge to browse jewellery displays in elegant shop windows, eat gelati and drink at the city's grandest cafe – **Caffè Costantino** (☑ 079 98 29 29; Piazza Civica 31; ☺ 7.30am-1.30am, closed Mon winter). It occupies the ground floor of the Gothic **Palazzo d'Albis** (Palazzo de Ferrera; Piazza Civica), where the Spanish emperor Charles V famously stayed in 1541.

🏃 Activities

Progetto Natura　TOURS
(☑ 392 1404069; www.progettonaturasardegna.com; Lungomare Barcellona; tours adult/reduced €37/25) Take to Alghero's seas with a crew of marine biologists and environmental guides. Summer day tours, which run from June to October, combine dolphin watching with snorkelling in the protected waters of the Area Marina Protetta Capo Caccia-Isola Piana; winter tours, from November to May, are dedicated to dolphin watching. Note, its seafront kiosk is only operative May through October.

Nautisub　DIVING
(☑ 079 95 24 33; www.nautisub.com; Via Garibaldi 45; ☺ 9am-1pm daily, plus 4-7.30pm Tue-Sat) Operating out of a dive shop on the seafront, this year-round outfit organises dives (from €45 or €60 with kit hire), snorkelling excursions (€35) and boat tours (€50 including lunch).

🛌 Sleeping

B&B Benebenniu　B&B €
(☑ 380 1746726; www.benebenniu.com; Via Carlo Alberto 70; r €50-105; ❉ 🛜) A home away from home, this laid-back B&B exudes warmth and familiarity. It's wonderfully located on a lively *centro storico* piazza and has three generously sized rooms with simple furnishings and plenty of natural light. Hosts Katya and Valeria are more than happy to share their local tips and recommendations.

Lloc d'Or　B&B €
(☑ 391 1726083; www.llocdor.com; Via Logudoro 26; s €45-55, d €60-80; ❉ 🛜) A cute budget B&B just a couple of minutes' walk from the seafront and harbour. Its two rooms and apartment are bright and simply furnished, and hosts Gemma and Giovanni go that extra mile to make you feel welcome – be it with beach towels, delicious breakfasts or tips on getting about town.

★ **Angedras Hotel**　HOTEL €€
(☑ 079 973 50 34; www.angedras.it; Via Frank 2; s €74-110, d €90-200; 🅿 ❉ 🛜) A 15-minute walk from the historic centre, the Angedras – Sardegna backwards – is a model of whitewashed Mediterranean elegance. Rooms, which come with their own small balcony, are decorated in an understated Sardinian style with cool white tiles and aquamarine blue touches. There's also an airy terrace, good for iced drinks on hot summer evenings.

★ **Villa Las Tronas**　HERITAGE HOTEL €€€
(☑ 079 98 18 18; www.hotelvillalastronas.it; Via Lungomare Valencia 1; s €227-297, d €257-519; 🅿 ❉ 🛜 🏊) Live like royalty at this palatial seafront hotel. Housed in a 19th-century palace once used by holidaying royals, it's set in its own lush gardens on a private headland. The individually styled rooms are pure fin de siècle, with elegant antiques, oil paintings and glorious sea views. A spa with an indoor pool, sauna, hydro-massage and gym invites lingering.

PREHISTORIC WONDERS

The strange *nuraghi* (prehistoric stone structures) that litter Sardinia's interior provide compelling windows into the world of the island's mysterious Bronze Age people. There are said to be up to 7000 *nuraghi* across the island, most built between 1800 and 500 BC. No one is absolutely certain what they were used for, although most experts think they were defensive watchtowers.

Even before they started building *nuraghi*, the Sardinians were busy digging tombs into the rock, known as **domus de janas** (fairy houses). More elaborate were the common graves fronted by stele called **tombe dei giganti** (giants' tombs).

Evidence of pagan religious practices is provided by **pozzi sacri** (well temples). Built from around 1000 BC, these were often constructed to capture light at the yearly equinoxes, hinting at a naturalistic religion as well as sophisticated building techniques.

✖ Eating

Eating out is a joy in Alghero. There are a huge number of restaurants, trattorias, pizzerias and takeaways, many in the historic centre, and standards are generally high. Menus feature the full range of Sardinian staples, but seafood is the star. A local specialty is Catalan-style lobster, *aragosta alla catalana,* served with tomato and onion.

Prosciutteria Sant Miquel   SARDINIAN €
(🗹 348 4694434; Via della Misericordia 20; meals €20; ⊙11.30am-1am summer, shorter hours winter) A model wine bar complete with wood en ceiling, hanging hams and a menu of delicious Sardinian charcuterie and cheeses. Grab a table in the tiny, usually packed, interior and tuck into wafer-thin slices of ham and salami, wedges of aged *pecorino* and bowls of plump, glistening olives, all served on thick wooden boards

⭐ Trattoria Lo Romani   SARDINIAN €€
(🗹 079 973 84 79; Via Principe Umberto 29; meals €35; ⊙12.30-2.30pm Tue-Sun & 7.30-10.30pm daily) Many of Alghero restaurants serve *porcetto*, Sardinia's classic spit-roasted pork, but few places cook it to such buttery perfection. The crackling is spot on and the meat is sweet and packed with flavour. *Porcetto* apart, it's a delightful trattoria. Exposed sandstone walls and soft lighting create a warm, elegant atmosphere, service is attentive and the fresh island food is terrific.

⭐ La Botteghina   SARDINIAN €€
(🗹 079 973 83 75; www.labotteghina.biz; Via Principe Umberto 63; meals €35; ⊙7-11.30pm Wed-Fri, noon-3pm & 7-11.30pm Sat & Sun) Cool, casual dining in a stylish *centro storico* setting – think blond-wood decor and low sandstone arches – is what La Botteghina is all about.

In keeping with the upbeat, youthful vibe, the food is simple, seasonal and local, so expect steaks of *bue rosso* beef, cured meats and Sardinian cheeses, alongside inventive pizzas and Sardinian wines and craft beers.

Mabrouk   SEAFOOD €€
(🗹 079 97 00 00; http://mabroukalghero.com; Via Santa Barbara 4; meals €40; ⊙6pm-midnight Tue-Sat, 1-3.30pm Sun) Reserve a table at this cosy, low-ceilinged stone restaurant and you never know what you're going to get. What you do know is that it'll be fish, it'll be fresh, and it'll be excellent. Dinner, which is served as a set menu, depends on the day's catch, but with several antipasti, three pasta dishes and three main courses included, you won't go hungry.

🍷 Drinking & Nightlife

⭐ l'altra vineria   CRAFT BEER
(🗹 079 601 49 54; Via Principe Umberto 66-68; ⊙7pm-late) A newcomer to Alghero's drinking scene, l'altra vineria is all about the pleasures of craft beer and island wine. The bar, run with warmth and infectious enthusiasm by Luca and Sonia, is a small, cosy place with barrels doubling as tables and a selection of terrific beers, including Sassari-brewed Speed.

⭐ SardOa   WINE BAR
(🗹 349 2212055; Piazza Duomo 4; ⊙6pm-late daily summer, noon-2.30pm & 6pm-late Sat & Sun winter) The Basque country lands in Alghero at this chilled wine bar. Under a vaulted stone ceiling, happy punters sit on wooden crates and sip Basque and Sardinian wines while munching on *pintxos* (Basque-style tapas) made with glistening anchovies and Iberic ham.

WORTH A TRIP

TOP DROP

Sardinia's top wine producer **Sella e Mosca** (☑ 079 99 77 00; www.sellaemosca.com; Località I Piani; guided tour free, tasting depends on wines; ☺ tour & tasting 10am & 4pm Mon-Fri, guided tour 5.30pm Mon-Sat summer, by request rest of year) has been based on this 650-hectare estate since 1899. To learn more about its history and production methods, join the free afternoon tour of the estate's historic cellars and lovingly tended museum. Afterwards, stock up at the beautiful **enoteca** (☑ 079 99 77 19; ☺ 8.30am-8pm Mon-Sat summer, to 6pm winter). Private tastings can also be organised.

From Alghero, three weekday buses pass by the turn-off for Sella e Mosca (€1.90, 25 minutes).

Cafè Latino   BAR
(☑ 079 97 65 41; Bastioni Magellano 10; ☺ 9am-2am daily summer, to 9.30pm Wed-Mon winter) Revel in romantic harbour views over an evening *aperitivo* at this chic bar on the sea walls. Overlooking the marina, it has outside tables and an ample menu of drinks and snacks.

ℹ Information

Airport Tourist Office (☑ 079 93 50 11; ☺ 9am-11pm) In the arrivals hall.

InfoAlghero Office (☑ 079 97 90 54; www.algheroturismo.eu; Largo Lo Quarter; ☺ 9am-1pm & 3.30-6.30pm Mon-Fri, 9am-1pm & 4-7pm Sat year-round, plus 10am-1pm Sun summer only) The helpful English-speaking staff can provide information on the city and environs. Note that there's a possibility the office will relocate to the Giardini Pubblici.

Ospedale Civile (☑ 079 995 51 11; Via Don Minzoni) Alghero's main hospital.

Police Station (☑ 079 972 00 00; Via Fratelli Kennedy; ☺ 8am-8pm Mon-Fri, to 2pm Sat & Sun)

ℹ Getting There & Away

AIR

Alghero airport (Fertilia; ☑ 079 93 50 11; www.aeroportodialghero.it) is 10km northwest of town in Fertilia. It's served by **Alitalia** (☑ 892010; www.alitalia.com) and a number of low-cost carriers, including **Ryanair** (☑ 895 589 5509; www.ryanair.com), which operates flights to mainland Italy and destinations across Europe, including Brussels, Eindhoven, Frankfurt, London and Munich.

BUS

Intercity buses serve the **bus terminal** (Via Catalogna) by the Giardini Pubblici. Note, however, that it's not much of a terminal, more a series of bus stops with a small **ticket office** (Via Catalogna; ☺ 6.25am-7.15pm Mon-Sat). Up to 11 daily **ARST** (☑ 800 865042; www.arst.sardegna.it) buses run to Sassari (€3.10, one hour), where you can pick up connections to Olbia. ARST also offers direct service to/from Bosa (€3.70, 1¼ hours, two daily with extra services in summer). **Logudoro Tours** (☑ 079 28 17 28; www.logudorotours.it) runs two daily buses from Alghero airport to Cagliari (€20, 3½ hours), via Oristano (€16, 2¼ hours). **Redentours** (☑ 0784 3 03 25; www.redentours.com) operates two daily buses from the airport to Nuoro (€18, 2¼ hours).

CAR & MOTORCYCLE

The fast-running SS291 connects with Sassari, 40km to the northeast, where you can pick up the SS131, the island's main north–south artery. Snaking along the west coast, the scenic SP105 runs 46km southwards to Bosa.

TRAIN

The train station is 1.5km north of the old town on Via Don Minzoni. There are up to 12 daily trains to/from Sassari (€3.10, 35 minutes).

ℹ Getting Around

From the bus stop (Via Cagliari), bus line AF runs along the seafront and up to Fertilia. Tickets, available at newspaper stands and tabacchi (tobacconists), cost €1, although you can also buy them on board for €1.50.

Operating out of a hut on the seaward side of Via Garibaldi, **Cicloexpress** (☑ 079 98 69 50; www.cicloexpress.com; Via Garibaldi; ☺ 9am-1pm & 4-7.30pm Mon-Sat, 9.30am-noon Sun) hires out cars (from €60 per day), scooters (from €30) and bikes (from €5).

There's a taxi rank by the Giardini Pubblici at Via Vittorio Emanuele 1. Otherwise you can call for one by phoning **Alghero Radio Taxi** (☑ 079 989 20 28; www.taxialghero.it).

Riviera del Corallo

The Riviera del Corallo (Coral Riviera), named after the red coral for which the area is famous, encompasses Alghero's northwest coast and hinterland. The main focus of interest is Porto Conte, a scenic bay sprinkled with hotels and discreet villas, and Capo

Caccia, a rocky headland famous for its cave complex, the Grotta di Nettuno. Along the way are several great beaches and a couple of interesting archaeological sites.

Sights & Activities

★ Grotta di Nettuno
CAVE

(☑ 079 94 65 40; adult/reduced €13/7; ☺ 9am-7pm May-Sep, 10am-4pm Apr & Oct, 10am-2pm Jan-Mar, Nov & Dec) Capo Caccia's principal crowd-puller is the Grotta di Nettuno, a haunting fairyland of stalactites and stalagmites. The easiest way to get to the caves is to take a ferry from Alghero, but for those with a head for heights, there's a vertiginous 654-step staircase, the Escala del Cabirol, that descends 110m of sheer cliff from the car park at the end of the Capo Caccia road. To get to the caves by public transport, a daily ARST bus departs from Via Catalogna (€2.50, 50 minutes) in Alghero at 9.15am and returns at midday. From June to September, there are two extra runs at 3.10pm and 5.10pm, returning at 4.05pm and 6.05pm.

★ Le Prigionette
Nature Reserve
NATURE RESERVE

(☑ 079 94 21 11; Località Prigionette; on foot or by bike €3, per person in car €5; ☺ 9am-6pm summer, to 4pm winter) This reserve, just west of Porto Conte at the base of Monte Timidone (361m), is a beautiful pocket of uncontaminated nature. Encompassing 12 sq km of woodland, aromatic *macchia* (Mediterranean scrub) and rocky coastline, it offers wonderful scenery and excellent walking with a network of well-marked tracks, suitable for hikers and cyclists. Wildlife flourishes – deer, albino donkeys, Giara horses and wild boar roam the woods, while griffon vultures and falcons fly the skies.

Nuraghe di Palmavera
ARCHAEOLOGICAL SITE

(☑ 329 4385947; www.coopsilt.it; Località Monte Palmavera; adult/reduced €6/4, incl Necropoli di Anghelu Ruju €8/6; ☺ 9am-7pm Mon-Fri summer, 10am-2pm daily winter) A few kilometres west of Fertilia on the SS127bis road to Porto Conte, the Nuraghe di Palmavera is a 3500-year-old nuraghic village. At its centre stands a limestone tower and an elliptical building with a secondary sandstone tower. The ruins of smaller towers and fortified walls surround the central edifice, beyond which are the packed remnants of circular dwellings, of which there may originally have been about 50.

Between April and September a single weekday bus runs to the site from Alghero (€1.30); otherwise you'll need a bike or car to get there.

Spiaggia Mugoni
BEACH

The main focus of Porto Conte is Spiaggia Mugoni, a hugely popular beach that arcs around the bay's northeastern flank. With its fine white sand and protected waters, it makes an excellent venue for beginners to try their hand at water sports. The Club della Vela (☑ 338 1489583; www.clubdellavelaalghero.it; Località Mugoni) offers windsurfing, canoeing, kayaking and sailing courses, and also rents out boats.

Getting There & Away

You can get to most places in this area by ARST bus from Alghero. That said, there might only be two or three weekday buses, and even fewer on Sundays and in winter. To explore the area in any depth, you'll really need your own transport.

Stintino & Isola dell'Asinara

Sardinia's remote northwestern tip boasts wild, unspoiled countryside and one of the island's most celebrated beaches, the stunning Spiaggia della Pelosa.

The only town of any note is Stintino, a former tuna-fishing village turned breezy summer resort and the main gateway to the Isola dell'Asinara. This small island, now a national park and wildlife haven, was for years home to one of Italy's most notorious prisons.

North of Stintino, the road continues to Capo Falcone, a rugged headland peppered with hotels and holiday homes, and the fabled Pelosa beach.

Outside of summer, the area is pretty deserted. Silence hangs over the empty landscape and the cold *maestrale* (northwesterly) wind blows through, blasting the tough *macchia* (Mediterranean scrubland) and bare rocks.

Sights & Activities

★ Spiaggia della Pelosa
BEACH

About 2.5km north of Stintino, the Spiaggia della Pelosa is a dreamy image of beach perfection: a salt-white strip of sand lapped by shallow, turquoise seas and fronted by strange, almost lunar, licks of rocky land. Completing the picture is a Catalan-Aragonese watchtower on the craggy Isola Piana. The beach gets extremely busy in July and August, but is popular throughout the year, especially with wind- and kitesurfers, who take to its waters when the *maestrale* wind whips through.

★ Parco Nazionale dell'Asinara
NATIONAL PARK

(www.parcoasinara.org) Named after its resident *asini bianchi* (albino donkeys), the Isola dell'Asinara encompasses 51 sq km of *macchia* (Mediterranean scrub), rocky coastline and remote sandy beaches. The island, Sardinia's second largest, is now a national park, but for years it was home to one of Italy's toughest maximum-security prisons. The only way to reach it is with a licensed boat operator from Stintino or Porto Torres. Once there, you can explore independently, although there's no public transport and access is restricted to certain areas.

Windsurfing Center Stintino
WINDSURFING

(☑ 079 52 70 06; www.windsurfingcenter.it; Località l'Approdo, Le Saline) On the beach at Pelosa, this outfit rents out windsurf rigs (from €18 per hour) and canoes (from €10 per hour), as well as offering windsurfing and sailing courses. If that all sounds far too energetic, it can also sort you out with an umbrella and sunloungers (€17 to €33 per day).

Asinara Scuba Diving
DIVING

(☑ 079 52 71 75; www.asinarascubadiving.com; Viale la Pelosa, Località Porto dell'Ancora) Just before Pelosa beach, near the Club Hotel Ancora, this diving centre offers a range of dives around Capo Falcone and the protected waters of the Parco Nazionale dell'Asinara. Reckon on €45-plus for a dive and €20 for kit hire.

Agenzia La Nassa
TOURS

(☑ 079 52 00 60; www.agenzialanassa.it; Via Sassari 39; tours per person €18-65; ⊙8.30am-1pm & 4.30-8pm daily summer, Mon-Sat winter) This agency runs a number of tours around Parco Nazionale dell'Asinara. The cheapest option, available between June and September, covers your ferry passage only, leaving you free to walk or cycle on designated paths on the island – you can download a map from the agency's website. More expensive packages include boat tours and visits with 4WD or bus transport.

🛏 Sleeping & Eating

Albergo Silvestrino
HOTEL €

(☑ 079 52 30 07; www.hotelsilvestrino.it; Via Sassari 14; s €45-70, d €60-130; ⊙ closed Dec & Jan; ❈ ☎) Stintino's oldest hotel is still one of its best. Housed in a hard-to-miss red villa at the sea end of the main street, it offers summery rooms with cool aquamarine tiled floors, colourful paintings and unfussy furniture; some also have their own terrace. Downstairs, the excellent in-house restaurant specialises in local seafood.

Skipper
ITALIAN €€

(☑ 079 52 34 60; Lungomare Cristoforo Colombo 57; panini €5, meals €25; ⊙11am-11pm daily summer, 10.30am-8pm Tue-Sun winter) A long-standing favourite, this casual bar-restaurant is a jack of all trades. You can sit down on the waterfront terrace and order anything from coffee and cocktails to *zuppa di cozze* (mussel soup), hamburgers, salads and *panini*.

ℹ Getting There & Away

Between June and mid-September, **Sardabus** (☑ 079 51 05 54; www.sardabus.it) operates five daily buses to Stintino from Alghero and Alghero airport (€7, 50 minutes).

There are at least four weekday ARST buses (two on Sunday) to Stintino from Porto Torres (€2.50, 45 minutes) and Sassari (€3.70, 70 minutes). Services increase between June and September.

From May to October daily boats sail for the Isola dell'Asinara from the Porto Turistico in Stintino. Departures are generally around 9am to 9.30am, returning 5pm to 6pm. A simple return costs €18. Services are much reduced between November and April.

Sassari

Sassari, Sardinia's second-largest city, is a proud and cultured university town with a handsome historic centre and an unpretentious, workaday vibe.

Like many Italian towns it hides its charms behind an outer shell of drab apartment blocks and confusing, traffic-choked roads. But once through to the inner sanctum it opens up, revealing a grand centre of wide boulevards, impressive piazzas and stately *palazzi*. In the evocative and slightly run-down *centro storico* (historic centre), medieval alleyways hum with Dickensian activity as residents run about their daily business amid grimy facades and hidden churches.

◎ Sights

★ Museo Nazionale Sanna   MUSEUM
(☑ 079 27 22 03; www.museosannasassari.beni
culturali.it; Via Roma 64; adult/reduced €3/2,
1st Sun of month free; ⊙ 9am-8pm Tue-Sat & 1st
Sun of month, to 1pm Sun) Sassari's premier
museum, housed in a grand Palladian villa,
boasts a comprehensive archaeological collection and an ethnographical section dedicated to Sardinian folk art. The highlight
of the collection is the nuraghic bronze-
ware, including weapons, bracelets, votive
boats and figurines depicting humans and
animals.

★ Piazza Italia   PIAZZA
Sassari's largest piazza is one of Sardinia's
most impressive public spaces. Covering
about a hectare, it is surrounded by imposing 19th-century buildings, including the
neoclassical **Palazzo della Provincia** (Piazza Italia), seat of the provincial government
and, opposite, the neo-Gothic **Palazzo
Giordano** (Piazza Italia), now home to the
Banca Intesa SanPaolo. Presiding over
everything is a statue of King Vittorio
Emanuele II.

Duomo   CATHEDRAL
(Cattedrale di San Nicola; Piazza Duomo; ⊙ 8.45am-
noon Mon-Sat & 4.30-7pm Tue-Sat, 9-11.30am &
5-7pm Sun) Sassari's principal cathedral dazzles with its 18th century baroque facade, a
giddy free-for-all of statues, reliefs, friezes
and busts. It's all a front, though, because
inside the cathedral reverts to its true Gothic character. The facade masks a late-15th-
century Catalan Gothic body, which was
itself built over an earlier Romanesque
church. Little remains of this, except for the
13th-century bell tower.

🛏 Sleeping

★ Tanina B&B   B&B €
(☑ 346 1812404; www.taninabandb.com; Viale
Trento 14; s/d/tr €30/50/70; 🛜) Situated
about 500m from Piazza Italia, this is a
model B&B. Its three large guest rooms
are lovingly maintained and decked out in
old-school Italian style with original tiled
floors, antique furniture and floral motifs.
Each has its own external bathroom and
there's a fully equipped communal kitchen
for guest use.

Hotel Vittorio Emanuele   HOTEL €€
(☑ 079 23 55 38; www.hotelvittorioemanuele.ss.it;
Corso Vittorio Emanuele II 100-102; s €44-54, d €54-

SADDLE UP FOR FESTIVAL FUN

Cavalcata Sarda, one of Sardinia's
highest-profile festivals, is held in
Sassari on the second-last Sunday of
May. Thousands of people converge
on the city to participate in costumed
processions, to sing and dance and
watch fearless horse riders exhibit their
acrobatic skills.

150; ✳ @ 🛜) Occupying a renovated medieval *palazzo* (historic mansion), this friendly three-star provides corporate comfort at
reasonable rates. Rooms are decent enough,
if anonymous, and the location, on the main
drag in the historic centre, is convenient for
pretty much everywhere.

🍴 Eating

Fainè alla Genovese Sassu   SARDINIAN €
(☑ 079 23 64 02; Via Usai 17; meals €10-15;
⊙ 7.30-11.30pm Mon-Sat) Modest, no-frills and
much loved locally, this bare, white-tiled
eatery is the place to try Sassari's famous
fainè, thick pancakes made with chickpea
flour and cooked like pizzas. There's nothing else on the menu, but with various
types to choose from – sausage, onions,
mushrooms, anchovies – they're ideal for a
cheap, tasty fill-up.

L'Antica Hostaria   RISTORANTE €€
(☑ 079 20 00 66; www.lanticahostaria.eu; Via
Cavour 55; meals €40; ⊙ 1-3pm & 8-11.30pm
Mon-Sat) Hidden behind a chipped, low-key
exterior, L'Antica Hostaria is a consistently
top restaurant. In intimate, homey surroundings you're treated to inventive dishes
rooted in Italian culinary traditions. Desserts are also impressive, and there's an excellent list of island and Italian wines.

ⓘ Information

Ospedale Civile SS Annunziata (☑ 079 206
10 00; Via De Nicola 14) Hospital south of the
city centre.

Tourist Office (☑ 079 200 80 72; www.turismo
sassari.it; Via Sebastiano Satta 13; ⊙ 9am-
1.30pm & 3-6pm Tue-Fri, 9am-1.30pm Sat) The
helpful staff can provide information on Sassari
and the surrounding area.

ℹ Getting There & Away

Sassari shares Alghero airport (p872), about 28km west of the city at Fertilia. Up to nine daily buses run from the airport to Via Padre Zirano (€3.10, 30 minutes).

Intercity buses depart from and arrive at Via Padre Zirano. Services run to/from Alghero (€3.10, one hour, up to 10 daily), Porto Torres (€1.90, 30 minutes, hourly) and Castelsardo (€3.10, one hour, 11 weekdays, four Sunday). Further afield, there are also buses to Nuoro (€8.10, 1¾ hours, six daily) and Oristano (€8.10, two hours, two daily).

The main train station is just beyond the western end of the old town on Piazza Stazione. Direct trains run to Cagliari (€16.50, three to four hours, three daily), Oristano (€11, two to 2½ hours, four daily) and Olbia (€8.10, 1¾ hours, four daily).

OLBIA, THE COSTA SMERALDA & GALLURA

The Costa Smeralda evokes Sardinia's classic images: pearly-white beaches and weird, wind-whipped licks of rock tapering into emerald seas. The dazzling coastal strip that the Aga Khan bought for a pittance is today the playground of millionaires and A-listers. Come summer, scandal-hungry paparazzi haunt the marinas, zooming in on oligarchs cavorting with bikini-clad beauties on yachts so big they eclipse the sun.

A few kilometres inland, a very different vision of the good life emerges. Here, vine-striped hills roll to deeply traditional villages and mysterious *nuraghi* (Bronze Age fortified settlements), silent cork-oak woods and granite mountains. Immune to time and trends, the hinterland offers a refreshing contrast to the coast, best appreciated during a multiday getaway at a country *agriturismo* (farm-stay).

Further north the Gallura coast becomes wilder, the preserve of the dolphins, divers and windsurfers who splash around in the startlingly blue waters of La Maddalena marine reserve.

Olbia

📞 0789 / POP 59.370

Often ignored in the mad dash to the Costa Smeralda, Olbia has more to offer than first meets the eye. Look beyond its industrial outskirts and you'll find a fetching city with a *centro storico* (historic centre) crammed with boutiques, wine bars and cafe-rimmed piazzas. Olbia is a refreshingly authentic and affordable alternative to the purpose-built resorts stretching to the north and south.

◉ Sights

★ **Museo Archeologico**   MUSEUM
(Isolotto di Peddone; ◷10am-1pm & 5-8pm Wed-Sun) **FREE** Architect Vanni Macciocco designed Olbia's strikingly contemporary museum near the port. The museum spells out local history in artefacts, from Roman amulets and pottery to nuraghic finds. The highlight is the relic of a Roman vessel discovered in the old port. A multimedia display recreates the scene of the Vandals burning and sinking such ships in 450 AD. Free audio guides are available in English.

Chiesa di San Simplicio   CHURCH
(Via San Simplicio; ◷7.30am-1pm & 3.30-8pm) Considered to be Gallura's most important medieval monument, this Romanesque granite church was built in the late 11th and early 12th centuries on what was then the edge of town. It is a curious mix of Tuscan and Lombard styles with little overt decoration other than a couple of 13th-century frescoes depicting medieval bishops.

🛏 Sleeping

★ **Porto Romano**   B&B €
(📱349 1927996; www.bedandbreakfastportoromano.it; Via A Nanni 2; d €65-90; ✳🛜) We love the chilled vibe and the heartfelt *benvenuto* at this welcoming B&B in an old family home near the train station. Light, spacious and well kept, the rooms have tiled floors and wood furnishings, and some come with balconies. Homey touches include the shared kitchen and barbecue area, and the friendly reception from owner Simonetta and her lovable dog, Lilly.

Hotel Panorama   HOTEL €€
(📱0789 2 66 56; www.hotelpanoramaolbia.it; Via Giuseppe Mazzini 7; s €95-140, d €110-200, ste €170-300; ℙ✳🛜) The name says it all: the roof terrace and 5th-floor superior rooms at this friendly, central hotel enjoy peerless views over the rooftops of Olbia to the sea and Monte Limbara. Even the standard rooms are fresh and elegant, with gleaming wooden floors and marble bathrooms, and there's a whirlpool and sauna for quiet moments.

La Locanda del Conte Mameli

BOUTIQUE HOTEL €€

(☑0789 2 30 08; www.lalocandadelcontemameli. com; Via delle Terme 8; r €89-159; P❄🖘) Raising the style stakes is this boutique hotel, which is housed in an 18th-century *locanda* (inn) built for Count Mameli. A wrought-iron balustrade twists up to chic caramel-cream rooms with Orosei marble bathrooms. The vaulted breakfast room boasts a pair of unique treasures: an original Roman well and a 1960s-vintage Lambretta motorcycle.

✕ Eating & Drinking

★ Dolceacqua

ITALIAN €€

(☑0789 196 90 84; http://ristorantedolceacqua. com; Via Giacomo Pala 4; meals €30-40; ⊗12.30-2pm & 7.30-10.30pm Tue-Sun, 7.30-10.30pm only mid-Jun–mid-Sep) This smart, intimate bistro entices with a laid-back vibe, warm service and an appetising mix of Sardinian and Ligurian cuisine. Start with its decadent sampler of five seafood antipasti, then move on to Sardinian classics such as *culurgiones* or creative alternatives like *millefoglie di orata alla ligure* (bream cooked in oil, garlic, olives and wine, served between thin pastry layers).

★ Agriturismo Agrisole

SARDINIAN €€

(☑349 0848163; www.agriturismo-agrisole.com; Via Sole Ruiu 7, Località Casagliana; menu incl drinks €30; ⊗dinner daily by reservation Apr-Sep) Tucked serenely away in the countryside around 10km north of Olbia, this Gallurese *stazzo* (farmhouse) dishes up a feast of home cooking. Monica, your charming host, brings dish after marvellous dish to the table – antipasti, *fregola* (granular pasta), *porceddu* (roast suckling pig) and ricotta sweets. From Olbia, take the SS125 towards Arzachena/Palau, turning left at the signs to Km 327.800.

★ Movida Lounge

BAR

(Via Porto Romano 4; ⊗10am-2am) Olbia's coolest new lounge bar draws locals for cocktails, wine, excellent food, DJs and live music. The vast space encompasses three distinct environments: a slick brick- and stone-walled resto-bar, a spacious courtyard under the palm trees out back (complete with sofas and a little AstroTurf terrace) and an underground wine bar in a vaulted cellar dating to the 17th century.

ℹ Information

Tourist Office (☑0789 5 22 06; www.olbia turismo.it; Piazza Terranova Pausania; ⊗9am-8pm Apr-Sep, reduced hours Oct-Mar) This helpful tourist office should be your first port of call for info on Olbia.

ℹ Getting There & Away

AIR

Olbia's **Aeroporto di Olbia Costa Smeralda** (☑0789 56 34 44; www.geasar.it) is about 5km southeast of the centre and handles flights from major Italian and European airports. It's the home airport for Meridiana, which flies to two dozen cities. Low-cost operators include Air Berlin, easyJet and Volotea. Destinations served include most mainland Italian airports as well as London, Paris, Madrid, Barcelona, Berlin, Amsterdam and Zurich.

BOAT

Olbia's ferry terminal, Stazione Marittima, is on Isola Bianca, an island connected to the town centre by the 1km Banchina Isola Bianca causeway. All the major ferry companies have counters here, including **Moby Lines** (☑199 30 30 40; www.moby.it), **Grimaldi Lines** (☑0789 183 55 64; www.grimaldi-lines.com) and **Tirrenia** (☑199 30 30 40; www.tirrenia.it). There are frequent services, especially during the summer months, to Civitavecchia, Genoa, Livorno and Piombino.

You can book tickets at any travel agent in town, or directly at the port.

BUS

ARST (☑0789 5 53 00, 800 865042; www. arst.sardegna.it) buses run to Arzachena (€2.50, 45 minutes), Porto Cervo (€2.50, 1½ hours), Nuoro (€8.10, 2½ hours), Santa Teresa di Gallura (€4.30, 1½ hours) and Sassari (€8.10, 1½ hours). Get tickets from **Bar della Caccia** (Corso Vittorio Veneto 28; ⊗5.30am-8pm Mon-Sat), just opposite the main bus stops on Corso Vittorio Veneto, or from the self-service machine (Corso Umberto 166E) behind Olbia's train station.

Turmo Travel (☑0789 2 14 87; www.gruppo turmotravel.com) runs two daily buses from Olbia to Cagliari (€19, 4½ hours), while **Sun Lines** (☑348 2609881, 0789 5 08 85; www.sunlines eliteservice.com) offers service between Olbia and various destinations on the Costa Smeralda.

TRAIN

The station is off Corso Umberto. There are direct trains to Cagliari (€18, 3¼ hours, three daily), Oristano (€12.50, 2¼ hours, three daily), Sassari (€8.10, 1¾ hours, four daily) and Golfo Aranci (€2.50, 25 minutes, six daily).

Costa Smeralda & Around

Back in 1962, flamboyant millionaire Karim Aga Khan established a consortium to buy a strip of unspoiled coastline in northeastern Sardinia. Each investor paid roughly US$25,000 for a little piece of paradise, and the coast was christened Costa Smeralda (Emerald Coast) for its brilliant green-blue waters.

These days billionaire jet-setters cruise into Costa Smeralda's marinas in megayachts like floating mansions, and models, royals, Russian oligarchs and balding media moguls come to frolic in its waters.

Starting at the Golfo di Cugnana, 17km north of Olbia, the Costa stretches 55km northwards to the Golfo di Arzachena. The 'capital' is the yachtie haven of Porto Cervo, although Porto Rotondo, a second marina developed in 1963, attracts plenty of paparazzi with its Silvio Berlusconi connections and its attractive seafront promenade.

Inland from the Costa Smeralda, the mountain communities of San Pantaleo and Arzachena offer a low-key counterpoint to the coastline's glitz and glamour.

◎ Sights

The Costa Smeralda's beaches are among the loveliest in the entire Mediterranean region. Inland, a mix of nuraghic sites, wineries and mountain scenery vie for your attention.

Coddu Ecchju ARCHAEOLOGICAL SITE
(€3; ⊙9am-7pm) Taking the Arzachena–Luogosanto road south, you can follow signs to one of the most important *tombe dei giganti* in Sardinia. The most visible part of it is the oval-shaped central stele (standing stone). Both slabs of granite, one balanced on top of the other, show an engraved frame that apparently symbolises a door to the hereafter, closed to the living. On either side of the stele stand further tall slabs of granite that form a kind of semicircular guard of honour around the tomb.

Tempio di Malchittu ARCHAEOLOGICAL SITE
(€3; ⊙9am-7pm) Accessible via a signposted track from the Nuraghe di Albucciu ticket office, 2km south of Arzachena, this temple dating back to 1500 BC is one of a few of its kind in Sardinia. Experts can only guess at its original purpose, but it appears it had a timber roof and was closed with a wooden door. Just as engaging as the ruins is the trail to get here, which affords lovely views over the surrounding countryside, strewn with granite boulders.

Cantine Surrau WINE
(☎0789 8 29 33; www.vignesurrau.it; Località Chilvagghja; ⊙10am-10pm May-Sep, to 9pm Apr & Oct, to 8pm Nov-Mar) Cantine Surrau takes a holistic approach to winemaking. Take a spin of the cellar and the gallery showcasing Sardinian art before tasting some of the region's crispest Vermentino white and beefiest Cannonau red wines.

⊨ Sleeping

B&B La MeSenda B&B €
(☎0789 8 19 50; www.lamesenda.com; Loc Malchittu; d €70-100) Immersed in peaceful countryside along the Tempio di Malchittu trail, this converted stone and stucco farmhouse makes an idyllic spot for an overnight stay. Simple rooms with exposed beams face onto a courtyard with a 500-year-old olive tree, a hot tub and comfortable spaces for lounging. Owners Judith (from French Polynesia) and Mario (from Sardinia) serve a delicious homemade breakfast.

★**B&B Lu Pastruccialeddu** B&B €€
(☎0789 8 17 77; www.pastruccialeddu.com; Località Lu Pastruccialeddu, Arzachena; s €70-100, d €90-120, ste €120-150; Ⓟ⌘) This is the real McCoy, a smashing B&B housed in a typical stone farmstead, with pristine rooms, a beautiful pool and two resident donkeys. It's run by the ultra-hospitable Caterina Ruzittu, who prepares the sumptuous breakfasts – a vast spread of biscuits, yoghurt, freshly baked cakes, salami, cheese and cereals.

★**Ca' La Somara** B&B €€
(☎0789 9 89 69; www.calasomara.it; s €58-98, d €80-148; Ⓟ⌘) Follow the donkey signs to Laura Lagattolla's welcoming rural retreat, 1km north of San Pantaleo. A relaxed, ramshackle farm, it offers simple guest rooms and endless opportunities for downtime: swinging in a hammock, strolling the gardens, or lounging poolside surrounded by rocky crags. Marvellous breakfasts featuring home-grown produce are served in the rustic dining room.

B&B Smeralda B&B €€
(☎0789 9 98 11; www.bbsmeralda.com; Villaggio Faras; d €80-140; ✳@☎) Straddling a steep hillside 1km above Poltu Quatu's fjord-like harbour, this charming B&B offers three comfortable bedrooms with pretty tiled

COSTA SMERALDA BEACH CRAWL

You'll need your own set of wheels to hop between the most sublime beaches on the Costa Smeralda, but it's worth the effort. They're super-busy in July and August, so avoid peak summer season if you want these bays to yourself. The following (listed from north to south) are all between Porto Cervo and Porto Rotondo.

Spiaggia del Grande & Piccolo Pevero This twinset of stunning bays, 3km south of Porto Cervo, fulfil the Sardinian paradise dream with their floury sands and dazzlingly blue, shallow water. There's a small beach bar, too.

Spiaggia Romazzino Less busy than some, this curving sandy bay has remarkably clear water and is named after the rosemary bushes that grow in such abundance. Look beyond the main bay to smaller coves for more seclusion.

Spiaggia del Principe Also known as Portu Li Coggi, this magnificent crescent of white sand is bound by unspoiled *macchia* and startlingly clear blue waters. Apparently it's the Aga Khan's favourite. It's around 2.5km northeast of Capriccioli.

Spiaggia Capriccioli Dotted with granite boulders and backed by fragrant *macchia*, this gorgeous half-moon bay has water that goes through the entire spectrum of blues and is shallow enough for tots. Umbrellas and sunbeds are available to rent.

Spiaggia Liscia Ruia Though busy in peak season, this beach is a beauty – a long arc of pale, fine sand and crystal-clear water. It's close to the neo-Moorish fantasy that is Hotel Cala di Volpe.

bathrooms. The real stars here are the outdoor whirlpool tub surrounded by sculpted rocks and the tantalising sea views from the verandah, where you can enjoy Luciana's freshly made breads and pastries at breakfast.

✕ Eating & Drinking

Aruanà Churrascaria BRAZILIAN €€
(📞 0789 90 60 85; www.aruana.it; Via Degli Oleandri; buffet €40; ⏰ 8pm-1am) With romantically lit tables set amid garden terraces that cascade down from a boulder-strewn hillside, this Brazilian steakhouse offers that rare combination of classy setting and top notch food. Relocated to Poltu Quatu in 2017, Aruanà specialises in Brazilian-style grilled meats. Serve yourself at will from the all-you-can-eat buffet; drinks cost extra.

Ristorante La Rocca SARDINIAN €€
(📞 0789 93 30 11; www.ristorante-larocca.com; Loc Pulicinu; ⏰ 12.30-2.30pm & 7pm-midnight) With black-clad waiters and impeccably fresh seafood ('choose any shellfish living in the aquarium'), La Rocca offers dependable quality with a resolutely old-school vibe. It's the kind of place where you'll find Sardinian families lingering over a long lunch or celebratory dinner. Look for it southwest of town along the main road towards Cannigione.

Spinnaker MODERN ITALIAN €€€
(📞 0789 9 12 26; www.ristorantespinnaker.com; Liscia di Vacca; meals €40-55; ⏰ 12.30-2.30pm & 7.30-10pm daily Jun-Sep, closed Wed Apr, May & Oct) This fashionable restaurant buzzes with a good-looking crowd, who come for the stylish ambience and fabulous seafood. Pair dishes such as calamari with fresh artichokes or rock lobster with a local Vermentino white. The restaurant is on the road between Porto Cervo and Baia Sardinia.

ℹ Getting There & Away

ARST and Sun Lines operate buses from Olbia to the Costa Smeralda, but to properly explore all the nooks and crannies of this beautiful coastline, you'll want your own wheels. The main coastal road changes names a time or two as you make your way along the coast: known as SP73 near Porto Redondo, it becomes SP94 closer to Porto Cervo, and SP59 as you continue west through Poltu Quatu to Baia Sardinia.

Santa Teresa di Gallura

📞 0789 / POP 5230

Bright and breezy Santa Teresa di Gallura occupies a prime seafront position on Gallura's north coast. The resort gets extremely busy during high season, yet somehow manages to retain a distinct local character, making it an agreeable alternative to the more soulless resorts on the Costa Smeralda.

The town was established by Savoy rulers in 1808 to help combat smugglers, but the modern town grew up as a result of the tourism boom since the early 1960s. Santa Teresa's history is caught up with Corsica as much as it is with Sardinia. Over the centuries plenty of Corsicans have settled here, and the local dialect is similar to that of southern Corsica.

◎ Sights & Activities

Spiaggia Rena Bianca   BEACH
The 'just like the Caribbean' comments come thick and fast when it comes to this bay – a glorious sweep of pale sand lapped by shallow, crystal-clear aquamarine water. From the eastern tip, a trail threads along the coastline past granite boulders and formations that fire the imagination with their incredible shapes.

★ Capo Testa   WALKING, SWIMMING
Four kilometres west of Santa Teresa, this extraordinary lighthouse-topped headland resembles a vast sculptural garden. Giant boulders lie strewn about the grassy slopes, their weird and wonderful forms the result of centuries of wind erosion. The Romans quarried granite here, as did the Pisans centuries later.

A couple of beaches lie to either side of the narrow isthmus that leads out to the headland: **Rena di Levante** and **Rena di Ponente**, where you can rent surfing gear, beach umbrellas and sunloungers.

Consorzio delle Bocche   BOATING
(☑0789 75 51 12; www.consorziobocche.com; Piazza Vittorio Emanuele; ☺9am-1pm & 5pm-7.30pm May, Jun & Sep, to 12.30am Jul & Aug) This outfit runs various excursions, including trips to the Maddalena islands and down the Costa Smeralda (summer only). These cost around €45/25 per adult/child and include lunch (excluding drinks).

🛏 Sleeping & Eating

★ B&B Domus de Janas   B&B €€
(☑338 4990221; www.bbdomusdejanas.it; Via Carlo Felice 20a; s €70-100, d €80-150, q €130-170; ☀🖤) Daria and Simone are your affable hosts at this sumptuous six-room B&B located smack in the centre of town (as photos on the wall attest, the rambling

home has belonged to Daria's family since her great-great-grandmother's days). The colourfully decorated rooms are spacious and regally comfortable, the rooftop terrace enjoys cracking sea views, and guests rave about the varied, abundant self-service breakfast.

Hotel Moderno   HOTEL €€
(☑393 9177814, 0789 75 42 33; www.moderno hotel.eu; Via Umberto 39; s €65-80, d €75-150, tr €105-180; ☀) This is a homey, family-run pick near the piazza. Rooms are bright and airy with little overt decor but traditional blue-and-white Gallurese bedspreads and tiny balconies.

Il Grottino   MEDITERRANEAN €€
(☑0789 75 42 32; Via del Mare 14; pizzas €5-14, meals €35-45; ☺noon-3pm & 7-11.30pm summer) Il Grottino sets a rustic picture with bare, grey stone walls and warm, low lighting. In keeping with the look, the food is wholesome and hearty with no-nonsense pastas, fresh seafood, juicy grilled meats and wood-fired pizzas.

La Locanda dei Mori   SEAFOOD €€
(☑0789 75 51 68; www.locandadeimori.com; SP90, Km 5; menus €33-43; ☺8-11pm Jun-Sep) Immersed in a country setting just off the main road 6km south of Santa Teresa, this lovely *agriturismo* spreads a sea of tables onto its open-air terrace each summer. Guests come from miles around for the Locanda's multicourse menu of fresh seafood. Wine, water, coffee and after-dinner drinks are all included in the price.

★ Agriturismo Saltara   SARDINIAN €€€
(☑0789 75 55 97; www.agriturismosaltara.it; Località Saltara; meals €40-60; ☺7-11pm; 🅿) Natalia and Gian Mario welcome you warmly at this *agriturismo*, situated 10km south of town off the SP90 (follow the signs up a dirt track). Tables are scenically positioned under the trees for a home-cooked feast. Wood-fired bread and garden-vegetable antipasti are a delicious lead to dishes such as *pulilgioni* (ricotta-filled ravioli with orange zest) and roast suckling pig or wild boar.

❶ Information

Tourist Office (☑0789 75 41 27; www. comunesantateresagallura.it; Piazza Vittorio Emanuele 24; ☺9am-1pm & 4-6pm) Very helpful, with loads of information.

❶ Getting There & Away

Moby Lines (☑ 0789 75 14 49, 199 30 30 40; www.mobylines.it) and **Blu Navy** (☑ 0789 75 55 70; www.blunavytraghetti.com) each run three to four car ferries daily from Santa Teresa to Bonifacio, Corsica (adult/car €25/55, 50 minutes). Between November and March services are drastically reduced.

Departing from the bus terminus on Via Eleonora d'Arborea, ARST buses run to/from Arzachena (€3.10, 1¼ hours, five daily), Olbia (€4.30, two hours, seven daily), Castelsardo (€4.90, 1½ hours, two daily) and Sassari (€6.70, 2½ hours, three daily). **Turmo Travel** (☑ 0789 2 14 87; www.gruppoturmotravel.com) operates a daily service to/from Cagliari (€19.50, six hours), as well as a summer service to Olbia airport (€4.30, 1½ hours, six daily) via Arzachena and Palau.

Palau & Arcipelago di La Maddalena

Off Sardinia's northeastern tip, Palau is a lively summer resort crowded with surf shops, boutiques, bars and restaurants. It's also the main gateway to the wind-sculpted granite islands and jewel-coloured waters of Arcipelago di La Maddalena.

The only town of any size on the islands is La Maddalena, which makes a good base with its bustling core of guesthouses, restaurants and cafes. The adjacent Isola Caprera, reached by a causeway just east of La Maddalena, was the longtime home of 19th-century Italian revolutionary Giuseppe Garibaldi. To visit the archipelago's uninhabited smaller islands, check out the daily boat tours from Palau or La Maddalena, which stop in at some of Sardinia's most idyllic coves and beaches.

◎ Sights & Activities

★ **Parco Nazionale dell'Arcipelago di La Maddalena** NATIONAL PARK
(www.lamaddalenapark.it) Established in 1996, Parco Nazionale dell'Arcipelago di La Maddalena consists of seven main islands and several smaller granite islets off Sardinia's northeastern coast. Over the centuries the prevailing *maestrale* (northwesterly wind) has helped mould the granite into the bizarre natural sculptures that festoon the archipelago. The spectacular seascapes of La Maddalena's outer islands are best explored by boat, although the two main islands have plenty of charm with their sun-baked ochre buildings, cobbled piazzas and infectious holiday atmosphere.

Roccia dell'Orso VIEWPOINT
(trail adult/reduced €3/2, parking €3; ☉ 9am-sunset; 🅿) This weather-beaten granite sculpture sits on a high point 6km east of Palau. The Roccia dell'Orso (Bear Rock) looks considerably less bearlike up close, resembling more – dare we say it? – a dragon. Analogies aside, the granite formations are extraordinary, as are the far-reaching views of the coast from up here. From the parking lot it's a 10- to 15-minute climb.

Fortezza di Monte Altura FORT
(adult/reduced €5/2.50; ☉ guided tours 9.15am-12.15pm & 5.15-7.15pm Jun-Aug, 10.15am-12.15pm & 3.15-5.15pm Apr, May & Sep–mid-Oct) Standing sentinel on a rocky crag, this sturdy 19th-century bastion was built to help defend the north coast and Arcipelago di La Maddalena from invasion – something it was never called on to do. A guided 45-minute tour leads you to watchtowers and battlements with panoramic views out to sea. The fortress is signposted off the SS125, 3km west of town.

Sardinia Island Tours/ Natour Sardinia BOATING
(☑ Kevin 391 7327232, Rodolfo 339 4774472; www.sardiniaislandtours.com; Via Guerrazzi 4; full-day tour €60) Sharing an office near the port, these two companies work in tandem to provide excellent multilingual tours of the Maddalena archipelago. In addition to visiting local beaches, guides Kevin and Rodolfo offer hikes to local fortresses dating back to WWII and Napoleon's ill-fated attempt to take over Isola Maddalena in 1793. Lunch, wine and water are included in the tour price.

Nautilus DIVING
(☑ 340 6339006, 0789 70 90 58; www.divesardegna.com; Piazza Fresi 8) There's some excellent diving in the marine park. This PADI five-star dive centre runs dives to 40 sites, with single dives starting at around €55. Kids' Bubblemaker courses are available.

🛏 Sleeping & Eating

★ **B&B Petite Maison** B&B €
(☑ 0789 73 84 32, 340 6463722; www.lapetitmaison.net; Via Livenza 7, La Maddalena; d €85-110; 🔊) Liberally sprinkled with paintings and

art-deco furnishings, this B&B is a five-minute amble from the main square. Miriam's artistically presented breakfasts, with fresh homemade goodies, are served in a bougainvillea-draped garden. Credit cards not accepted.

L'Orso e Il Mare   B&B €
(📞331 2222000; www.orsoeilmare.com; Vicolo Diaz 1; d €55-110, tr €85-145; ❈) Pietro gives his guests a genuinely warm welcome at this two-room B&B, just steps from Piazza Fresi. The spacious rooms sport cool blue-and-white colour schemes and homey amenities such as fridges, kettles and corkscrews in each room. Breakfast is a fine spread of cakes, biscuits and fresh fruit salad.

Del Porticciolo   SARDINIAN €
(📞0789 70 70 51; Via Omero; pizzas €4-9, meals €25-35; ⏱12.15-2pm & 7.15-10.30pm Sat-Thu) Locals swear by the authentic antipasti, pasta and fresh fish at this no-frills restaurant just south of the harbour. Stop by for a good-value lunch, or in the evening when chefs fire up the pizza ovens.

❶ Getting There & Away

BOAT
Car ferries to Isola Maddalena are operated by **Delcomar** (📞0789 70 92 28; www.delcomar. it) and **Maddalena Lines** (📞0789 73 91 65; www.maddalenalines.it). Boats run every 15 to 30 minutes during daylight hours, then roughly hourly from midnight to 5.30am, with Delcomar offering the most frequent service. The 15-minute crossing costs between €3.40 and €5 per passenger and €7.30 to €12.50 per car (one way).

BUS
ARST buses connect Palau with Olbia (€3.10, 1¼ hours, eight daily), Santa Teresa di Gallura (€2.50, 45 minutes, five daily) and Arzachena (€1.90, 30 minutes, five daily).

NUORO & THE EAST

Nowhere else in Sardinia is nature such an overwhelming force as in the wild, wild east, where the Supramonte's imperious limestone mountains roll down to the Golfo di Orosei's cliffs and startling aquamarine waters. Who knows where that winding country road might lead you? Perhaps to deep valleys concealing prehistoric caves and Bronze Age *nuraghi*, to the lonesome

villages of the Barbagia steeped in bandit legends, or to forests where wild pigs snuffle amid centuries-old holm oaks. Neither time nor trend obsessed, this region is refreshingly authentic.

Outdoor action is everywhere: along the coast where you can drop anchor in a string of pearly white bays, upon the cliffs where you can multi-pitch climb above the sea, on old mule trails best explored by mountain bike, and atop peaks and ravines only reachable on foot. True, the Costa Smeralda attracts more celebrities, but the real rock stars and rolling stones are right here.

Nuoro

📞0784 / POP 37,100
Once an isolated hilltop village and a byword for banditry, Nuoro had its cultural renaissance in the 19th and early 20th centuries when it became a hotbed of artistic talent. Today museums in the historic centre pay homage to local legends including Nobel Prize–winning author Grazia Deledda, acclaimed poet Sebastiano Satta, novelist Salvatore Satta and sculptor Francesco Ciusa. Further enhancing Nuoro's modern-day cultural vitality are the local university, with its graduate program in environmental studies and sustainable development, and the city's recently renovated ethnographic museum.

Nuoro's spectacular backdrop is the granite peak of Monte Ortobene (955m), capped by a 7m-high bronze statue of the Redentore (Christ the Redeemer). The thickly wooded summit commands dress-circle views of the valley below and the limestone mountains enshrouding Oliena opposite.

◉ Sights

★**Museo Etnografico Sardo**   MUSEUM
(Museo del Costume; www.isresardegna.it; Via Antonio Mereu 56; adult/reduced €5/3; ⏱10am-1pm & 3-8pm Tue-Sun mid-Mar–Sep, 10am-1pm & 3-7pm Oct–mid-Mar) Beautifully renovated in 2016, this museum zooms in on Sardinian folklore, harbouring a peerless collection of filigree jewellery, carpets, tapestries, rich embroidery, musical instruments, weapons and masks. The highlight is the traditional costume display – the styles, colours and patterns speaking volumes about the people and their villages. Look out for fiery red skirts from the fiercely inde-

FESTIVALS OF NUORO'S INTERIOR

Nuoro province boasts some of Sardinia's most colourful and characteristic festivals. Topping the list is the **Festa di Sant'Antonio Abate**, held In mid-January in the town of Mamoiada, 20km south of Nuoro. Bonfires rage throughout town for two nights starting on 16 January, as half-human, half-animal *mamuthones* parade through the streets – clad in sheepskins and shaking heavy bells – accompanied by white-masked, red-jacketed *issohadores* who go about town lassoing young women.

The rest of the year, you can get a vicarious taste of Mamoiada's festivities at the small but engaging **Museo delle Maschere Mediterranee** (www.museodellemaschere. it; Piazza Europa 15; adult/reduced €5/3; ⊘9am-1pm & 3-7pm). Film footage documents the making of masks and bells, along with the processions and bonfires that mark Mamoiada's big event. A second room displays masks and costumes from three of Nuoro province's most traditional carnivals (Mamoiada, Ovodda and Ottana).

pendent mountain villages, the Armenian-influenced dresses of Orgosolo and Desulo finished with a blue-and-yellow silk border, and the burkalike headdresses of Ittiri and Osilo.

Museo Ciusa   MUSEUM
(Museo Tribu; Piazza Santa Maria della Neve; adult/reduced €3/2; ⊘10am-8pm Tue-Sun Jun-Sep, 10am-1pm & 3-7pm Tue-Sun Oct-May) This recently reopened space has an entire wing devoted to the works of renowned Nuoro-born sculptor Francesco Ciusa (1883-1949). It also houses the permanent collection of Nuoro's excellent art museum, displaying works by the island's top 20th-century artists, including painters Antonio Ballero, Giovanni Ciusa-Romagna and Mario Delitalia, abstract artist Mauro Manca and sculptor Costantino Nivola.

Museo Deleddiano   MUSEUM
(www.isresardegna.it; Via Grazia Deledda 44; adult/reduced €3/2; ⊘9am-1pm & 3-6pm Tue-Sun) Up in the oldest part of town, the birthplace of Grazia Deledda (1871-1936) has been converted into this lovely little museum. The rooms, full of Deledda memorabilia, have been carefully restored to show what a well-to-do 19th-century Nuorese house looked like. Best of all is the material relating to her Nobel Prize – a congratulatory telegram from Italian king Vittorio Emanuele III and photos of the prize-giving ceremony, which show her, proud and tiny, surrounded by a group of stiffly suited men.

⭐ Festivals & Events

Sagra del Redentore   RELIGIOUS
(Festa del Redentore; ⊘Aug) The Sagra del Redentore (Feast of Christ the Redeemer), in

the last week of August, is Nuoro's main event and one of Sardinia's most exuberant folkloric festivals, attracting costumed participants from across the island for parades, music-making and dancing. On the evening of 28 August a torchlit procession, starting at the **Chiesa della Solitudine** (Viale della Solitudine), winds its way through the city.

🛏 Sleeping & Eating

⭐ Casa Solotti   B&B €
(☑328 6028975, 0784 3 39 54; www.casasolotti. it; Località Monte Ortobene; per person €26-35; 🅿🐾🖭) This B&B reclines in a rambling garden amid woods and walking trails near the top of Monte Ortobene, 5km from central Nuoro. Decorated with stone and beams, the elegantly rustic rooms have tremendous views of the surrounding valley and the Golfo di Orosei in the distance. Staying here is a delight.

Nothing is too much trouble for your hosts, Mario and Frédérique, who can arrange everything from horse riding to packed lunches and guided hikes in the Supramonte.

Silvia e Paolo   B&B €
(☑0784 3 12 80; www.silviaepaolo.it; Corso Garibaldi 58; s €33-40, d €55-65, tr €77; 🖭🖭) Silvia and Paolo run this sweet B&B in the historic centre. Cheerful family decor makes you feel right at home in the bright, spacious rooms, while up top there's a roof terrace for observing the action on Corso Garibaldi by day and stargazing by night. Note that two of the three guest rooms share a bathroom.

⭐ Il Portico   SARDINIAN €€
(☑0784 21 76 41, 331 9294119; www.ilportico nuoro.it; Via Monsignor Bua 13; meals €35-45;

12.30-2.30pm & 8-10.30pm Tue-Sat, 12.30-2.30pm Sun) You'll receive a warm welcome at this restaurant, where abstract paintings grace the walls and jazzy music plays. Behind the scenes, the talented Graziano and Vania rustle up a feast of local fare such as *spaghetti ai ricci* (spaghetti with sea urchins) and fresh gnocchi with lamb *ragù*. Save room for the delectable caramel-nougat semifreddo.

🛈 Information

Tourist Office (📞 0784 44 18 23; www.provincia.nuoro.it; Piazza Italia 8; ⊙ 8.30am-2pm Mon-Fri, plus 3.30-7pm Tue) Multilingual staff provide plenty of useful information on Nuoro and environs.

🛈 Getting There & Away

ARST (📞 0784 29 08 00; www.arst.sardegna.it) buses run from the bus station on Viale Sardegna to destinations throughout the province and beyond. These include Dorgali (€2.50, 45 minutes, six daily), Olbia (€8.10, 2¾ to 3½ hours, three daily), Oliena (€1.90, 20 minutes) and Cagliari (€12.50, 2¾ hours).

The train station is west of the town centre at the corner of Via Lamarmora and Via G Ciusa Romagna. ARST operates trains from Nuoro to Macomer (€4.90, 70 minutes, six daily Monday to Saturday), where you can connect with mainline Trenitalia trains to Cagliari, Olbia and Sassari.

Supramonte

Southeast of Nuoro rises the great limestone massif of the Supramonte, its sheer walls like an iron curtain just beyond Oliena. Despite its intimidating aspect, it's actually not as high as it seems – its peak, Monte Corrasi, only reaches 1463m – but it is impressively wild, the bare limestone plateau pitted with ravines and ragged defiles. The raw, uncompromising landscape is made all the more thrilling by its one-time notoriety as the heart of Sardinia's bandit country.

The Supramonte provides some magnificent hiking. But because much of the walking is over limestone, there are often few discernible tracks to follow, and in spring and autumn you should carefully check the weather conditions. You can engage a local guide in towns throughout the region, including Oliena, Dorgali and Baunei.

Oliena & Around

📞 0784 / POP 7140

Few images in Sardinia are as arresting as the magnificent peak of Monte Corrasi (1463m) when the dusky light makes its limestone summit glow. From Nuoro you can see Oliena's multicoloured rooftops cupped in the mountain's palm. The village itself is an unassuming place with a grey-stone centre, and is a handy base for exploring the Supramonte.

Oliena was probably founded in Roman times, although its name is a reference to the Ilienses people, descendants of a group of Trojans who supposedly escaped Troy and settled in the area. The arrival of the Jesuits in the 17th century was better documented and set the scene for the village's modern fame. The eager fathers helped promote the local silk industry and encouraged farmers to cultivate the surrounding slopes. The lessons were learnt well, and now Oliena is famous for its beautiful silk embroidery and its blood-red Cannonau wine, Nepente di Oliena. Oliena is also the home town of Gianfranco Zola, English football's favourite Sardinian import, who was born here in 1966.

OFF THE BEATEN TRACK

VALLE DI LANAITTU

Immerse yourself in the karst wilderness of the Supramonte by hiking, cycling or driving through this enchanting 7km valley south of **Su Gologone**, signposted off the Oliena–Dorgali road. Towering limestone mountains, cliffs and caves lord it over the narrow valley, scattered with natural and archaeological wonders. Rosemary and mastic, grapes and olives flourish here, along with wildlife such as martens, birds of prey, wild boar and goats. Near the valley's southern end it's possible to visit a pair of caves – **Grotta di Sa Ohe** (€2; ⊙ 9am-6pm Apr-Sep) and **Grotta Corbeddu** (€5; ⊙ 9am-7pm Apr-Sep) – and the nuraghic site of **Sa Sedda 'e Sos Carros** (📞 333 5808844; €5; ⊙ 9am-7pm Apr-Sep), with its unique circular Temple of the Sacred Well.

ℹ GET A GUIDE

If you fancy striking out into the Supramonte, here's our pick of the best guides:

Corrado Conca (☑ 347 2903101; www.corradoconca.it; Via Barzini 15, Sassari) A brilliant companion for Sardinia's legendary seven-day Selvaggio Blu trek.

Cooperativa Gorropu (☑ Franco 347 4233650, Sandra 333 8507157; www.gorropu.com; Passo Silana SS125, Km 183, Urzulei) Sandra and Franco offer trekking, canyoning and caving excursions in the Supramonte.

Cooperative Ghivine (☑ 338 8341618; www.ghivine.com; Via Lamarmora 31) A one-stop action shop, arranging treks to classic destinations like Tiscali and Gola Su Gorropu.

Sardegna Nascosta (☑ 349 4434665, 0784 28 85 50; www.sardegnanascosta.it; Via Masiloghi 35) Organises trekking, canoeing, climbing and caving excursions with a cultural focus.

◉ Sights & Activities

★ Su Gologone   SPRING
(www.sorgentisugologone.it;   adult/reduced
€2/1.50; ☉9am-7pm) Tucked beneath sheer limestone cliffs, this gorgeous mountain spring is the final outflow point for Italy's largest underground river system. Water percolating through the countless fissures and sinkholes in the Supramonte's high country eventually gathers here and flows out to join the Cedrino river. The spring is beautiful any time, but try to catch it around 1pm when the sun passes directly overhead, turning the water brilliant green. Afterwards, the adjacent tree-shaded park is perfect for a picnic or an afternoon swim.

To get here from Oliena, follow the SP46 east 6km towards Dorgali, then turn right following signs for Su Gologone until the road dead ends into a parking lot.

Cooperativa Enis   ADVENTURE SPORTS
(☑ 0784 28 83 63; www.coopenis.it; Località Monte Maccione) This highly regarded adventure sports company offers guided treks and 4WD excursions into the Supramonte and along the Golfo di Orosei. Destinations include Tiscali, Gola Su Gorropu, Cala Luna and the Supramonte di Orgosolo and Murales, with prices starting at €37 for a half-day trek or €43 for a full day. A packed lunch bumps up the cost by €5.

🛏 Sleeping & Eating

★ Agriturismo Guthiddai   AGRITURISMO €
(☑ 0784 28 60 17; www.agriturismoguthiddai.com; Nuoro-Dorgali bivio Su Gologone; d €98-115, half-board per person €70-80; ❄ 🛜) Situated on the road to Su Gologone, this bucolic, whitewashed farmstead sits at the foot of rugged mountains, surrounded by fig, olive and fruit trees. Olive oil, Cannonau wine and fruit and vegetables are all home produced. Rooms are tiled in pale greens and cobalt blues. From Oliena, head to Dorgali, taking the turn-off right towards Valle di Lanaittu.

Su Gologone   HOTEL €€€
(☑ 0784 28 75 12; www.sugologone.it; Località Su Gologone; d incl half-board €254-392; 🅿 ❄ 🛜 ▧) Treat yourself to a spot of rural luxury at Su Gologone, nestled in glorious countryside situated 7km east of Oliena. Rooms are decorated with original artworks and handicrafts, and the facilities are top notch it has a pool, a spa, a wine cellar and a **restaurant** (meals €35-45; ☉12.30-3pm & 8-10pm), which is considered one of Sardinia's best.

Dorgali & Around
☑ 0784 / POP 8550

Dorgali is a down-to-earth town with a grandiose backdrop, nestled at the foot of Monte Bardia and framed by vineyards and olive groves. Limestone peaks rear above the centre's pastel-coloured houses and steep, narrow streets, luring hikers and climbers to their summits.

For more outdoor escapades, the dramatic Golfo di Orosei and spectacularly rugged Supramonte are within easy striking distance.

◉ Sights & Activities

★ Gola Su Gorropu   CANYON
(☑ 328 8976563; www.gorropu.info; adult/reduced €5/3.50; ☉10.30am-5pm) Sardinia's most spectacular gorge is flanked by limestone walls towering up to 500m in height. The en-

WORTH A TRIP

ROAD TRIPPING THROUGH THE SUPRAMONTE

It's well worth getting behind the wheel to drive the 60km stretch from Dorgali to Santa Maria Navarrese. Serpentine and at times hair-raising, the SS125 threads through the mountain tops where the scenery is distractingly lovely: to the right the ragged limestone peaks of the Supramonte rear above wooded valleys and deep gorges; to the left mountains tumble down to the bright-blue sea. The first 20km to the Genna 'e Silana pass (1017m) are the most breathtaking.

demic (and endangered) *Aquilegia nuragica* plant grows here, and at quieter times it's possible to spot mouflon and golden eagles. From the Rio Flumineddu riverbed you can wander about 1km into the boulder-strewn ravine without climbing gear; follow the markers. Near the narrowest point (just 4m wide) you reach the formidable **Hotel Supramonte**, a tough 8b multi-pitch climb up a vertical 400m rock face.

To hike into the gorge, you'll need sturdy shoes and sufficient water. There are two main routes. The most dramatic begins from the car park opposite Hotel Silana at the **Genna 'e Silana** pass on the SS125 at Km 183. The mostly easygoing descent of the 8km trail takes 1½ to two hours, while the climb back up is considerably tougher; allow at least four hours for the return trek.

The second and slightly easier hiking route to Gorropu is via the **Sa Barva bridge**, about 15km south of Dorgali. Take the SS125 and look for signs for Gola Su Gorropu and Tiscali between Km 200 and Km 201. Follow this road for 10.5km until the asphalt finishes (about 20 minutes). Park here and cross the Sa Barva bridge, after which you'll see the trail signposted off to the left. From here it's a scenic two-hour hike along the Rio Flumineddu to the mouth of the gorge (14km return).

★**Tiscali**   ARCHAEOLOGICAL SITE
(www.museoarcheologicodorgali.it/wp/Reperto_Sito/tiscali; adult/reduced €5/2; ⊘9am-7pm daily May-Sep, to 5pm Oct-Apr, closed in rainy weather) Hidden in a mountain-top cave deep in the Valle Lanaittu, the mysterious nuraghic village of Tiscali is one of Sardinia's must-

see archaeological highlights. Dating from the 6th century BC and populated until Roman times, the village was discovered in the late 19th century. At the time it was relatively intact, but since then grave robbers have done a pretty good job of looting the place, stripping the conical stone-and-mud huts down to the skeletal remains that you see today.

Despite the fragmentary condition of the ruins themselves, Tiscali is an awe-inspiring sight: jumbled stone foundations amid holm oak and turpentine trees huddled in the eerie twilight of the limestone overhang. The inhabitants of the nearby nuraghic site Sa Sedda 'e Sos Carros used it as a hiding place from the Romans, and its inaccessibility ensured that the Sards were able to hold out here until well into the 2nd century BC.

The hike to Tiscali is pure drama, striking into the heart of the limestone Supramonte. The trailhead is at the Sa Barva bridge over the green Rio Flumineddu, the same starting point as the route to Gola Su Gorropu. The 7km trail is signposted and takes between 1½ and two hours; allow five hours for the return hike, including breaks and a visit to Tiscali. You can go it alone, or join one of the guided tours offered by companies in Oliena, Dorgali and Cala Gonone (around €40 per person).

Grotta di Ispinigoli   CAVE
(adult/reduced €7.50/3.50; ⊘hourly tours 10am-6pm Jul & Aug, to 5pm Jun & Sep, 10am-noon & 3-5pm Apr, May & Oct) A short drive north of Dorgali, the fairy-tale-like Grotta di Ispinigoli is a veritable forest of glittering rock formations, including the world's second-tallest stalagmite (the highest is in Mexico and stands at 40m). Unlike most caves of this type, which you enter from the side, here you descend 60m inside a giant 'well', at whose centre stands the magnificent 38m-high stalagmite. You can admire the tremendous rock formations, many of them sprouting from the walls like giant mushrooms and broccoli.

🛏 Sleeping & Eating

Sa Corte Antica   B&B €
(☏349 8401371; www.sacorteantica.it; Via Mannu 17; d €50-60, tr €75-90; ❇🐱) Gathered around an old stone courtyard, this B&B housed in an 18th-century townhouse oozes charm from every brick and beam. The rooms are

traditional and peaceful, with reed ceilings and wrought-iron bedsteads. Enjoy home-made bread and *biscotti* at breakfast.

★ Ristorante Ispinigoli · SARDINIAN €€

(☎0784 9 52 68; www.hotelispinigoli.com; meals €30-36; ⊙12.30-2.30pm & 7.30-9.30pm) Linger for dinner and panoramic sunset views at the Ristorante Ispinigoli, just below the entrance to the Grotta di Ispingoli. Located in Hotel Ispinigoli, the well-known restaurant rolls out local delights such as stone bass-stuffed black ravioli with mullet roe, herb-infused roast kid and a waistline-expanding selection of *formaggi*.

❶ Getting There & Away

ARST buses serve Nuoro (€2.50, 50 minutes, eight daily Monday to Saturday, four Sunday). Up to seven (four on Sunday) shuttle back and forth between Dorgali and Cala Gonone (€1.30, 20 minutes). You can pick up buses at several stops along Via Lamarmora. Buy tickets at the bar at the junction of Via Lamarmora and Corso Umberto.

By car or motorcycle, Dorgali is 15 minutes from Cala Gonone via the SP26, 35 minutes from Orosei via the SS125, and 45 minutes from Nuoro via the SP46 or SS129.

Baunei & the Altopiano del Golgo

Clinging to a precipitous rocky ridge on the long, tortuous road between Arbatax and Dorgali, the old stone shepherd's village of Baunei is an agreeable mountain outpost and a welcome oasis in the middle of the rugged Supramonte. Whether or not you linger in town, be sure not to miss the region's uncontested highlight: the 10km detour up to the Altopiano del Golgo, a strange, other-worldly plateau where goats, pigs and donkeys graze in the *macchia* (Mediterranean scrub) and woodland. From here, one of Sardinia's best hiking trails descends to the coast at Cala Goloritzè, while a hardscrabble road snakes down to the rock spike of Pedra Longa, a natural monument and also the starting point for Sardinia's star coastal trek, the Selvaggio Blu.

◉ Sights & Activities

Cala Goloritzè Trail · HIKING

(€6; ⊙trailhead 7.30am-4pm, beach to 6pm) Few experiences in Sardinia compare with this thrilling trek to Cala Goloritzè (p889), one of the Mediterranean's most spectacular beaches. Suitable for families, the easygoing, well-signposted (if rocky and occasionally steep) hike along an old mule trail takes you through a gorgeous limestone canyon shaded by juniper and holm oaks, passing cliffs honeycombed with caves, dramatic rock arches, overhangs and pinnacles. From the trailhead at Bar Su Porteddu on the Altopiano del Golgo, it's 3.5km down to the beach (about 1¼ hours). To reach the trailhead from Baunei, drive up Via San Pietro, following signs for the Altopiano. After travelling 8.4km north on pavement, turn east 1.2km on a signposted dirt road to the parking lot.

Il Golgo · LANDMARK

FREE Follow the signs from Baunei up a 2km climb of impossibly steep switchbacks to the plateau, then continue 6km north on pavement before taking the signposted turn-off for the final unpaved 1km to Su Sterru (Il Golgo). From the car park, walk five minutes to this remarkable feat of nature – a 270m abyss just 40m wide at its base. Its funnel-like opening is now fenced off, but just peering into the dark opening is enough to bring on vertigo.

Cooperativa Goloritzè · HIKING

(☎368 7028980; www.coopgoloritze.com; Località Golgo) This highly regarded cooperative organises excursions ranging from trekking to 4WD trips. Many treks involve a descent through canyons to the Golfo di Orosei's dreamy beaches. Staff at the refuge also arrange guides and logistical support for walkers attempting Sardinia's once-in-a-lifetime Selvaggio Blu trek.

SARDINIA SUPRAMONTE

DON'T MISS

SELVAGGIO BLU

Selvaggio Blu (www.selvaggioblu.it) is the big one: an epic four- to seven-day 45km trek along the Golfo di Orosei's dramatic coastline, traversing wooded ravines, cliffs and caves. A guide is recommended as the trail is not well sign-posted and there's no water en route. If you are going it alone, be aware that it involves scrambling, fixed-rope routes and abseiling, so some alpine mountaineering experience is necessary. Visit the website, or get a copy of Enrico Spanu's *Book of Selvaggio Blu*.

🛏 Sleeping & Eating

Lemon House
B&B €

(📞 333 3862210; www.lemonhouse.eu; Via Dante 19, Lotzorai; r per person €33-43; 🛜) New owners Riky and Elena have kept the same great vibe alive at this long-time favourite for hikers, climbers and cyclists. The lime-hued B&B makes a terrific base for outdoor escapades, with a bouldering wall, a relaxing roof terrace, a great library of outdoors-themed guidebooks, and plenty of invaluable tips on hiking, climbing, mountain biking and kayaking in the area.

Hotel Bia Maore
B&B €€

(📞 0782 61 10 33; www.biamaore.it; Via San Pietro 19, Baunei; s €55-85, d €82-130, tr €107-150; 🅿🌀🛜) Perched like an eyrie above Baunei, this B&B has compelling views of the mountains and coast. The warm-hued rooms are decked out with handmade furnishings and Sardinian fabrics – the pick of them with a balcony overlooking the mountains and the Gulf of Ogliastra.

Locanda Il Rifugio
SARDINIAN €€

(📞 368 7028980; www.coopgoloritze.com; Località Golgo; meals €25-35; ⏰12.30-3pm & 7.30-11pm Easter-Oct) Managed by Cooperativa Goloritzè, this converted farmstead puts on a generous spread of regional fare such as *ladeddos* (potato gnocchi) and spit-roasted kid and suckling pig, washed down with local Cannonau red. Afterwards, spare yourself the nail-biting drive back down to Baunei by camping (per person €7) or staying in one of the refuge's simple rooms (double including breakfast €60).

ℹ Getting There & Away

Baunei sits astride the SS125, about 20km north of Tortolì/Arbatax and 48km south of Dorgali. Several daily ARST buses run south to Tortolì (€1.90, 35 minutes), but for travel north to Dorgali or up to the Altopiano del Golgo, you're much better off with your own wheels.

Golfo di Orosei

For sheer stop-dead-in-your-tracks beauty, there's no place like this gulf, forming the seaward section of the **Parco Nazionale del Golfo di Orosei e del Gennargentu** (www.parcogennargentu.it). Here the high mountains of the Gennargentu abruptly meet the sea, forming a crescent of dramatic cliffs riven by false inlets, scattered with horseshoe-shaped bays and lapped by exquisitely aquamarine waters. Beach space is at a premium in summer, but there's room for everyone, especially in the rugged, elemental hinterland.

Cala Gonone
📞 0784 / POP 1280

Climbers, divers, sea kayakers, beachcombers and hikers all find their thrill in Cala

---

DON'T MISS

THE BLUE CRESCENT

If you do nothing else in Sardinia, you should try to make an excursion along the 20km southern stretch of the Golfo di Orosei by boat. Intimidating limestone cliffs plunge headlong into the sea, scalloped by pretty beaches, coves and grottoes. With an ever-changing palette of sand, rocks, pebbles, seashells and crystal-clear water, the unfathomable forces of nature have conspired to create a sublime taste of paradise. The colours are at their best until about 3pm, when the sun starts to drop behind the higher cliffs.

From the port of Cala Gonone you head south to the Grotta del Bue Marino. The first beach after the cave is **Cala Luna**, a crescent-shaped strand closed off by high cliffs to the south. **Cala Sisine** is the next beach of any size, also a mix of sand and pebbles and backed by a deep, verdant valley. **Cala Biriola** quickly follows, and then several enchanting spots where you can bob below the soaring cliffs – look out for the patches of celestial-blue water.

Cala Mariolu is arguably one of the most sublime spots on the coast. Split in two by a cluster of bright limestone rocks, it has virtually no sand. Don't let the smooth white pebbles put you off, though. The water that laps these beaches ranges from a kind of transparent white at water's edge through every shade of light and sky blue and on to a deep purplish hue.

Gonone. Why? Just look around you: imperious limestone peaks frame grandstand views of the Golfo di Orosei, sheer cliffs dip into the brilliant-blue sea, trails wriggle through emerald-green ravines to pearly-white beaches. It is quite magnificent. Even getting here is an adventure, with each hairpin bend bringing you ever closer to a sea that spreads out before you like a giant liquid mirror.

Gathered along a pine-shaded promenade, this seaside resort still has the low-key, family-friendly vibe of the small fishing village it once was. August aside, the beaches tend to be uncrowded and the room rates affordable. Bear in mind that the resort slumbers in winter, closing from October until Easter.

◎ Sights & Activities

Boat tour and adventure sports operators are clustered down by the port, including **Prima Sardegna** (☑0784 9 33 67; www.primasardegna.com; Viale Lungomare Palmasera 32; ☺9am-1pm & 4-8pm summer), **Cielomar** (☑0784 92 00 14; www.ciclomar.it; Piazza del Porto 6), **Dolmen** (☑347 6698192; www.sardegnadascoprire.it; Piazza del Porto 3) and **Nuovo Consorzio Trasporti Marittimi** (☑0784 9 33 05; www.calagononecrociere.it; Piazza del Porto 1).

Cala Fuili BEACH
About 3.5km south of town (follow Viale del Bue Marino) is this captivating rocky inlet backed by a deep green valley. From here you can hike over the cliff tops to Cala Luna, about two hours (4km) away on foot. The trail cuts a scenic path through juniper and mastic trees and is easy to navigate, with triangle-circle symbols marking handy rocks. The coastal views are breathtaking as you approach Cala Luna.

**Grotta del
Bue Marino** CAVE
(adult/reduced €8/5; ☺guided tours hourly 10am-noon & 3-5pm summer, 11am-3pm winter, groups only Oct-Mar) It's a scenic 40-minute hike from Cala Fuili, or a speedy boat ride from Cala Gonone, to this enchanting grotto. It was the last island refuge of the rare monk seal ('*bue marino*' or 'sea ox' as it was known by local fishermen). The watery gallery is impressive, with shimmering light playing on the strange shapes and Neolithic petroglyphs within the cave. Guided visits

take place up to seven times a day. In peak season you may need to book.

★**Cala Goloritzè** BEACH
The last beachette of the gulf, Cala Goloritzè rivals the best. At the southern end, bizarre limestone formations soar away from the cliffside. Among them is jaw-dropping Monte Caroddi or the **Aguglia**, a 148m-high needle of rock beloved of climbers. Many boat trips will take you here, or you can hike in from the Altopiano del Golgo on the beautiful, 3.5km Cala Goloritzè Trail (p887). Note that the beach itself is rather small and can get crowded in summer.

🛏 Sleeping & Eating

★**Agriturismo Codula Fuili** AGRITURISMO €
(☑340 2546208, 328 7340863; www.codulafuili.com; r per person incl breakfast €35-60, half-board €65-90, camping 2 people, car & tent €16-20) You could be excused for fainting when you first see the spellbinding views from this end-of-the-road *agriturismo*. Perched high on the slopes above Nuraghe Mannu and Cala Fuili, it offers four rooms, campsites, a bungalow and a panoramic terrace. Dinners (€30) feature cheese from the family's free-ranging goats, plus homegrown olives, olive oil, meats and veggies.

**Agriturismo
Nuraghe Mannu** AGRITURISMO €
(☑0784 9 32 64, 328 8685824; www.agriturismonuraghemannu.com; Località Pranos; r per person incl breakfast €28-35, half-board €46-53, camping 2 people, car & tent €10-24) 🖋 Immersed in greenery and with blissful sea views, this is an authentic, ecofriendly working farm with five simple rooms, a restaurant open to all, and home-produced bread, milk, ricotta and sweets at breakfast. For campers, there are also five tent pitches available.

**Hotel Bue
Marino** HOTEL €€
(☑0784 92 00 78; www.hotelbuemarino.it; Via Vespucci 8; s €82-108, d €108-180) Conveniently located just steps above the port, this blindingly white hotel has pleasant, cool blue rooms done up in traditional Sardinian fabrics. Adding to its appeal are friendly staff and magnificent sea views from many guest rooms, as well as from the upper-floor breakfast area, solarium and hot tub.

Hotel L'Oasi
B&B €€

(☑ 0784 9 31 11; www.loasihotel.it; Via Garcia Lorca 13; s €60-102, d €75-138; P ❋ 🛜) Perched on the cliffs above Cala Gonone and nestling in flowery gardens, this B&B offers enticing sea views from many of its breezy rooms. The friendly Carlesso family can advise on activities from climbing to diving. L'Oasi is a 700m uphill walk from the harbour.

Il Pescatore
SEAFOOD €€

(☑ 0784 0 31 74; www.ristoranteilpescatorecalagonone.com; Via Acqua Dolce 7; meals €30-45; ⊙ noon-2.30pm & 7-10.30pm; �︎) Fresh seafood is what this authentic place is about. Sit on the terrace for sea breezes and fishy de-lights, such as pasta with *ricci* (sea urchins), and spaghetti with clams and *bottarga* (mullet roe). It also does a kids' menu (€15).

❶ Information

Tourist Office (☑ 0784 9 36 96; www.dorgali.it; Viale del Bue Marino 1a; ⊙ 9am-1pm & 3-7pm May-Sep, to 1pm Oct-Apr) A very helpful office in the small park off to the right as you enter town.

❶ Getting There & Away

Buses run to Cala Gonone from Dorgali (€1.30, 20 minutes, seven daily Monday to Saturday, four Sunday) and Nuoro (€3.10, 1¼ hours, six daily Monday to Saturday, three Sunday).

Understand Italy

Italy Today

Despite the approach of the 2020s, many of Italy's problems have remained unchanged for years. High unemployment and nepotism continue to drive ambitious young Italians out of the country, while ever-increasing numbers of refugees risk their lives to reach Italian shores. Meanwhile, geological instability has rattled central Italy with a string of destructive earthquakes. Thankfully, it's not all doom and gloom, with positive developments including cutting-edge urban renewal in Milan and hints of a southern Italian revival.

Best Blogs

Becoming Italian Word by Word (http://becomingitalianwordbyword.typepad.com) Italian language.
Parla Food (www.parlafood.com) Savvy food blogger Katie Parla.
Italian Food Forever (www.italianfoodforever.com) Umbria-based, delicious recipes.

Best on Film

La Grande Bellezza (Great Beauty; 2013) Paolo Sorrentino's Fellini-esque tribute to Italy.
La Dolce Vita (The Sweet Life; 1960) Federico Fellini capturing Italy's 1950s zeitgeist.
The Leopard (1963) Luchino Visconti's portrayal of the decaying Sicilian nobility.
Ladri di Biciclette (Bicycle Thieves; 1948) Vittorio De Sica's moving portrait of post-WWII Italy.

Best in Print

The Italians: A Full Length Portrait Featuring Their Manners and Morals (Luigi Barzini; 1964) Revealing portrait of the Italian character.
The Leopard (Giuseppe Tomasi di Lampedusa; 1958) Masterpiece about tumultuous 19th-century changes.
The Italians (John Hooper; 2015) Italy correspondent assesses modern Italy.
Gomorrah (Roberto Saviano; 2006) Unputdownable epic about the Neapolitan Camorra (mafia).

Regions Rattled

Between August 2016 and January 2017, eight major earthquakes rattled the Appenine areas of Lazio, Le Marche, Umbria and Abruzzo in central Italy. The deadliest was a 6.2-magnitude quake on 24 August 2016. The earthquake caused close to 300 fatalities. Most of these were in the Lazio town of Amatrice, where the collapse of buildings deemed seismically sound exposed a lax approach to building codes. Four strong earthquakes struck Abruzzo on 18 January 2017. Of the 34 people killed, 29 perished when a post-quake avalanche slammed into a luxury mountain resort.

According to Italy's Civil Protection Agency (Dipartimento Protezione Civile), the damage bill from the eight quakes exceeds €23 billion. The tremors have delivered a particular blow to the regions' tourism and agricultural industries, considered backbones of their local economies. While both the Italian government and the EU have poured millions of euros into recovery efforts, some of Italy's fashion giants are also pitching in. Among these is luxury footwear company Tod's, whose new factory in Le Marche plans to boost employment in the local area. Meanwhile in Umbria, fashion mogul Brunello Cucinelli announced plans to finance the restoration of the Benedictine monastery flanking Norcia's medieval basilica.

Italexit?

While the UK's Brexit vote has solidified support for the Europe Union across much of the continent, Italy is bucking the trend. Figures released by the Pew Research Centre in 2017 revealed Italy to be the only EU nation where support for the bloc weakened over the previous year. A significant 35% of Italians are now in favour of leaving the EU, compared to 11% in Germany and 22% in France. Italy's figure matches that of Greece, making the two Mediterranean countries the most likely to file for divorce from Brussels. Italy's slipping support has been blamed on growing pessimism about the country's economic performance and criticism of the EU's general management of economic issues and Brussels' management of the ongoing refugee crisis. In line with other European nations, pro-EU sentiment in Italy remains strongest among younger generations and the political left.

Refugees & Rhetoric

In the first third of 2017, 46,000 asylum seekers reached Italian shores from Africa, an increase of 30% from the previous year. The figure constituted more than 80% of all refugees who had entered Europe in that period. Indeed, since the EU and Turkey made a pact to block the flow of refugees from Turkey into Greece in 2016, Italy has become the continent's main gateway for asylum seekers.

To many Italians, this influx is merely exacerbating the country's already high unemployment and general economic uncertainty. Similar anxieties have been voiced by some of Italy's political figures. In 2017, the District Attorney of Catania, Carmelo Zuccaro, suggested that the very NGOs rescuing refugees at sea could be receiving funding from organised crime syndicates set on flooding Italy with immigrants to destabilise the economy. The accusations have been vehemently refuted by the NGOs, including the Italian branch of Doctors Without Borders.

Cultural Revivals

Despite its enduring political, economic and social challenges, Italy continues to inspire, impress and reinvent. In the north, Milan is back on the global hot list with revamped museums, electric car-sharing schemes and a slew of fresh, contemporary buildings from visionaries like Stefano Boeri, Herzog & de Meuron and the late Zaha Hadid. Parts of southern Italy are also finding their groove. Tourist numbers are soaring in Naples, where improved museums and youth-led cultural initiatives are injecting the city with newfound pride and optimism. Among the city's believers is US tech giant Apple, which opened its first iOS Developer Academy there in 2016.

Further south in Basilicata, Matera is drawing greater tourist numbers in the lead-up to its role as Europe's Capital of Culture in 2019. Matera is also one of five Italian cities slated for a 5G mobile network aimed at attracting high-tech research and innovation companies. Across the Tyrrhenian Sea in Sicily, Palermo is slowly but determinedly moving forward from its dark, mafia-riddled past with a string of urban-renewal projects. In 2018, the city is also set to host Manifesta, Europe's top biennial of contemporary art.

POPULATION: **61 MILLION**

AREA: **302,073 SQ KM**

UNEMPLOYMENT: **11.1%**

ANNUAL PASTA CONSUMPTION: **24KG PER CAPITA**

ANNUAL FOREIGN TOURISTS: **56 MILLION**

if Italy were 100 people

92 would be Italian
2 would be Romanian
1 would be Albanian
1 would be Maghrebi and/or Arabic
4 would be other

belief systems
(% of population)

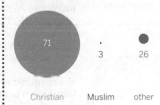

71   •
     3   26

Christian   Muslim   other

population per sq km

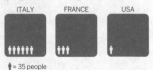

ITALY   FRANCE   USA

🚶 ≈ 35 people

History

Italy has only been a nation since 1861, prior to which it was last unified as part of the Roman Empire. It has wielded powerful influence as the headquarters of Catholicism, and Italy's dynamic city-states set the modern era in motion with the Renaissance. Italian unity was won in blood, fusing north and south in a dysfunctional yet enduring marriage. Even today, Italy still feels like a powerfully distinct collection of regions, existing in a present that has deep roots in the past.

Etruscans, Greeks & Wolf-Raised Twins

Bordered by Emilia-Romagna and Le Marche, the Republic of San Marino was established in AD 301. The wealthy microstate is home to the world's oldest continuous constitution and is the only country on Earth with more cars than people.

Of the many tribes that emerged from the millennia of the Stone Age in ancient Italy, it was the Etruscans who dominated the peninsula by the 7th century BC. Etruria was based on city-states mostly concentrated between the Arno and Tiber rivers. Among them were Caere (modern-day Cerveteri), Tarquinii (Tarquinia), Veii (Veio), Perusia (Perugia), Volaterrae (Volterra) and Arretium (Arezzo). The name of their homeland is preserved in the name Tuscany, where the bulk of their settlements were (and still are) located.

Most of what we know of the Etruscan people has been deduced from artefacts and paintings unearthed at their burial sites, especially at Tarquinia, near Rome. Argument persists over whether the Etruscans had migrated from Asia Minor. They spoke a language that today has barely been deciphered. An energetic people, the Etruscans were redoubtable warriors and seamen, but lacked cohesion and discipline.

At home, the Etruscans farmed and mined metals. Their gods were numerous, and they were forever trying to second-guess them and predict future events through such rituals as examining the livers of sacrificed animals. They were also quick to learn from others. Much of their artistic tradition (which comes to us in the form of tomb frescoes, statuary and pottery) was influenced by the Greeks.

Indeed, while the Etruscans dominated the centre of the peninsula, Greek traders settled in the south in the 8th century BC, setting up a series of independent city-states along the coast and in Sicily that together were known as Magna Graecia. They flourished until the 3rd century BC

TIMELINE	c 700,000 BC	2000 BC	474 BC
	Primitive tribes lived in caves and hunted elephants, rhinoceroses, hippopotamuses and other hefty wild beasts on the Italian peninsula.	The Bronze Age reaches Italy. Hunter-gatherers have settled as farmers. The use of copper and bronze to fashion tools and arms marks a new sophistication.	The power of the Etruscans in Italy is eclipsed after Greek forces from Syracuse and Cumae join to crush an Etruscan armada off the southern Italian coast in the Battle of Cumae.

and the ruins of magnificent Doric temples in Italy's south (at Paestum) and on Sicily (at Agrigento, Selinunte and Segesta) stand as testimony to the splendour of Greek civilisation in Italy.

Attempts by the Etruscans to conquer the Greek settlements failed and accelerated the Etruscan decline. The death knell, however, would come from an unexpected source – the grubby but growing Latin town of Rome.

The origins of the town are shrouded in myth, which says it was founded by Romulus (who descended from Aeneas, a refugee from Troy whose mother was the goddess Venus) on 21 April 753 BC on the site where he and his twin brother, Remus, had been suckled by a she-wolf as orphan infants. Romulus later killed Remus and the settlement was named Rome after him. At some point, legend merges with history. Seven kings are said to have followed Romulus and at least three were historical Etruscan rulers. In 509 BC, disgruntled Latin nobles turfed the last of the Etruscan kings, Tarquinius Superbus, out of Rome after his predecessor, Servius Tullius, had stacked the Senate with his allies and introduced citizenship reforms that undermined the power of the aristocracy. Sick of monarchy, the nobles set up the Roman Republic. Over the following centuries, this piffling Latin town would grow to become Italy's major power, sweeping aside the Etruscans, whose language and culture disappeared by the 2nd century AD.

The Roman Republic

Under the Republic, *imperium*, or regal power, was placed in the hands of two consuls who acted as political and military leaders and were elected for non-renewable one-year terms by an assembly of the people. The Senate, whose members were appointed for life, advised the consuls.

Although from the beginning monuments were emblazoned with the initials SPQR (Senatus Populusque Romanus, or the Senate and People of Rome), the 'people' initially had precious little say in affairs. (The initials are still used and many Romans would argue that little has changed.) Known as plebeians (literally 'the many'), the disenfranchised majority slowly wrested concessions from the patrician class in the more than two centuries that followed the founding of the Republic. Some plebeians were even appointed as consuls, and by about 280 BC most of the distinctions between patricians and plebeians had disappeared. That said, the apparently democratic system was largely oligarchic, with a fairly narrow political class (whether patrician or plebeian) vying for positions of power in government and the Senate.

The Romans were a rough-and-ready lot. Rome did not bother to mint coins until 269 BC, even though the neighbouring (and later conquered or allied) Etruscans and Greeks had long had their own currencies. The

Ancient Artefacts

Vatican Museums
(Rome)

Capitoline
Museums
(Rome)

Museo
Archeologico
Nazionale
(Naples)

Museo
Archeologico
Paolo Orsi
(Syracuse)

Museo
Nazionale Etrusco
di Villa Giulia
(Rome)

HISTORY THE ROMAN REPUBLIC

396 BC	264–241 BC	218–146 BC	133 BC
Romans conquer the key Etruscan town of Veio, north of Rome, after an 11-year siege. Celebrations are short-lived, as invading Celtic tribes sweep across Italy and sack Rome in 390 BC.	War rages between Rome and the empire of Carthage, stretching across North Africa and into Spain, Sicily and Sardinia. By the war's end Rome is the western Mediterranean's prime naval power.	Carthage sends Hannibal to invade Italy overland from the north in the Second Punic War. Rome invades Spain, Hannibal fails, and Carthage is destroyed in a third war from 149–146 BC.	Rome gains control of Sardinia, Sicily, Corsica, mainland Greece, Spain, most of North Africa and part of Asia Minor.

Etruscans and Greeks also brought writing to the attention of Romans, who found it useful for documents and technical affairs but hardly glowed in the literature department. Eventually, the Greek pantheon of gods formed the bedrock of Roman worship. Society was patriarchal and its prime building block was the household (familia). The head of the family (pater familias) had direct control over his wife, children and extended family. He was responsible for his children's education. Devotion to household gods (eg Panes, the spirits of the kitchen) was as strong as devotion to the pantheon of state gods, led at first by the Capitoline Triad of Jupiter (the sky god and chief protector of the state), Juno (the female equivalent of Jupiter and patron goddess of women) and Minerva (patron goddess of craftsmen). An earlier version of the triad included Mars (god of war) instead of Juno.

Slowly at first, then with gathering pace, Roman armies conquered the Italian peninsula. Defeated city-states were not taken over directly; they were instead obliged to become allies. They retained their government and lands but had to provide troops on demand to serve in the Roman army. This relatively light-handed touch was a key to success. Increasingly, the protection offered by Roman hegemony induced many cities to become allies voluntarily. Wars with Carthage and other rivals in the east led Rome to take control of Sardinia, Sicily, Corsica, mainland Greece, Spain, most of North Africa and part of Asia Minor by 133 BC.

As the empire grew, so did its ancient system of 'motorways'. With the roads came other bright concepts: postal services and wayside inns. Messages could be shot around the empire in a matter of days or weeks by sending dispatch riders. At ancient 'truck stops', the riders would change mounts, have a bite and continue on their way (more efficient than many modern European postal systems).

By the second half of the 2nd century BC, Rome was the most important city in the Mediterranean, with a population of 300,000. Most were lower-class freedmen or slaves living in often precarious conditions. Tenement housing blocks (mostly of brick and wood) were raised alongside vast monuments. Among the latter was the Circus Flaminius, the stage of some of the spectacular games held each year. These became increasingly important events for the people of Rome, who flocked to see gladiators and wild beasts in combat.

Seizing the Day

Born in 100 BC, Gaius Julius Caesar would prove to be one of Rome's most masterful generals and capable administrators, but his hunger for power was probably his undoing.

He was a supporter of the consul Pompey (later known as Pompey the Great), who in 78 BC had become a leading figure in Rome after

46 BC	30 BC	AD 79	100–138
Julius Caesar assumes dictatorial powers, alienating pro-republican senators. Cassius and Brutus orchestrate Caesar's assassination on 15 March 44 BC. This sparks civil wars that lead to the Republic's dissolution.	Octavian (Augustus) invades Egypt, Antony and Cleopatra commit suicide and Egypt becomes a province of Rome. Three years later, Octavian becomes the first emperor of the newly formed Roman Empire.	Mt Vesuvius showers molten rock and ash upon Pompeii and Herculaneum. Pliny the Younger later describes the eruption in letters, and the towns are only rediscovered in the 18th century.	The Roman Empire reaches its greatest extent, during the reign of Hadrian.

putting down rebellions in Spain and eliminating piracy. Caesar himself had been in Spain for several years dealing with border revolts; on his return to Rome in 60 BC, he formed an alliance with Pompey and another important commander and former consul, Crassus. They backed Caesar's candidacy as consul.

To consolidate his position in the Roman power game, Caesar needed a major military command. This he received with a mandate to govern the province of Gallia Narbonensis, a southern swathe of modern France stretching from Italy to the Pyrenees, in 59 BC. Caesar raised troops and in the following year entered Gaul proper (modern France) to head off an invasion of Helvetic tribes from Switzerland and subsequently to bring other tribes to heel. What started as a defensive effort soon became a full-blown campaign of conquest. In the next five years, he subdued Gaul and made forays into Britain and across the Rhine. In 51 BC he stamped out the last great revolt in Gaul, led by Vercingetorix. Caesar was generous to his defeated enemies and consequently won over the Gauls. Indeed, they became his staunchest supporters in coming years.

By now, Caesar also had a devoted veteran army behind him. Jealous of the growing power of his one-time protégé, Pompey severed his political alliance and joined like-minded factions in the Senate to outlaw Caesar in 49 BC. On 7 January, Caesar crossed the Rubicon river into Italy and civil war began. His three-year campaign in Italy, Spain and the eastern Mediterranean proved a crushing victory. Upon his return to Rome in 46 BC, he assumed dictatorial powers.

He launched a series of reforms, overhauled the Senate and embarked on a building program (of which the Curia and Basilica Giulia remain). By 44 BC it was clear Caesar had no plans to restore the Republic, and dissent grew in the Senate, even among former supporters like Marcus Junius Brutus, who thought he had gone too far. A small band of conspirators led by Brutus finally stabbed him to death in a Senate meeting on the Ides of March (15 March), two years after he had been proclaimed dictator for life.

In the years following Caesar's death, his lieutenant, Mark Antony (Marcus Antonius), and nominated heir, great-nephew Octavian, plunged into civil war against Caesar's assassins. Things calmed down as Octavian took control of the western half of the empire and Antony headed to the east, but when Antony fell head over heels for Cleopatra VII in 31 BC, Octavian went to war and finally claimed victory over Antony and Cleopatra at Actium, in Greece. The following year Octavian invaded Egypt, Antony and Cleopatra committed suicide and Egypt became a province of Rome.

Medieval Towns

Gubbio (Umbria)

Bologna (Emilia-Romagna)

Perugia (Umbria)

Assisi (Umbria)

Scanno (Abruzzo)

476	568	754–56	902
Germanic tribal leader Odovacar proclaims himself king in Rome. The peninsula sinks into chaos and only the eastern half of the empire survives intact.	Lombards invade and occupy northern Italy, leaving just Ravenna, Rome and southern Italy in the empire's hands. Other tribes invade Balkan territories and cut the eastern empire off from Italy.	Frankish king Pepin the Short enters Italy at the request of Pope Stephen II, defeats the Lombards and declares the creation of the Papal States.	Muslims from North Africa complete the occupation of Sicily, encouraging learning of the Greek classics, mathematics and other sciences. Agriculture flourishes and Sicily is relatively peaceful for two centuries.

Augustus & the Glories of Empire

At its height, the Roman Empire stretched from Portugal in the west to Syria in the east, and from Britain in the north to the North African deserts across the Mediterranean. It covered an area two-thirds the size of the US and had a population of around 120 million people.

Octavian was left as sole ruler of the Roman world and by 27 BC had been acclaimed Augustus (Your Eminence) and the Senate had conceded to him virtually unlimited power. In effect, he had become emperor.

Under Augustus, the arts flourished – his contemporaries included the poets Virgil, Horace and Ovid, as well as the historian Livy. He encouraged the visual arts, restored existing buildings and constructed many new ones. During his reign the Pantheon was raised and he boasted that he had 'found Rome in brick and left it in marble'. The long period of comparatively enlightened rule that he initiated brought unprecedented prosperity and security to the Mediterranean.

By AD 100, the city of Rome was said to have had more than 1.5 million inhabitants and all the trappings of an imperial capital – its wealth and prosperity were obvious in the rich mosaics, marble temples, public baths, theatres, circuses and libraries. People of all races and conditions converged on the capital. Poverty was rife among an often disgruntled lower class. Augustus had created Rome's first police force under a city prefect (*praefectus urbi*) to curb mob violence, which had long gone largely unchecked.

Augustus carried out other far-reaching reforms. He streamlined the army, which was kept at a standing total of around 300,000 men. Military service ranged from 16 to 25 years, but Augustus kept conscription to a minimum, making it a largely volunteer force. He consolidated Rome's three-tier class society. The richest and most influential class remained the senators. Below them, the so-called equestrians filled posts in public administration and supplied officers to the army (control of which was essential to keeping Augustus' position unchallenged). The bulk of the populace filled the ranks of the lower class. The system was by no means rigid and upward mobility was possible.

A century after Augustus' death in AD 14 (at age 75), the Roman Empire reached its greatest extent. Under Hadrian (76–138), it stretched from the Iberian Peninsula, Gaul and Britain to a line that basically followed the Rhine and Danube rivers. All of the present-day Balkans and Greece, along with the areas known in those times as Dacia, Moesia and Thrace (considerable territories reaching to the Black Sea), were under Roman control. Most of modern-day Turkey, Syria, Lebanon, Palestine and Israel were occupied by Rome's legions and linked up with Egypt. From there a deep strip of Roman territory stretched along the length of North Africa to the Atlantic coast of what is today northern Morocco. The Mediterranean was a Roman lake.

962	1130	1202–03	1271
Otto I is crowned Holy Roman Emperor in Rome, the first in a long line of Germanic rulers. His meddling in Italian affairs leads to clashes between papacy and empire.	Norman invader Roger II is crowned King of Sicily, a century after the Normans landed in southern Italy, creating a united southern Italian kingdom.	Venice leads the Fourth Crusade to the Holy Land on a detour to Constantinople in revenge for attacks on Venetian interests there. The Crusaders topple the Byzantine emperor, installing a puppet ruler.	Venetian merchant Marco Polo embarks on a 24-year journey to Central Asia and China with his father and uncle. His written travel accounts help enlighten Europeans about Asia.

This situation lasted until the 3rd century. By the time Diocletian (245–305) became emperor, attacks on the empire from without and revolts within had become part and parcel of imperial existence. A new religious force, Christianity, was gaining popularity and persecution of Christians became common. This policy was reversed in 313 under Constantine I (c 272–337) in his Edict of Milan.

Inspired by a vision of the cross, Constantine defeated his own rival, Maxentius, on Rome's Ponte Milvio (Milvian Bridge) in 312, becoming the Roman Empire's first Christian leader and commissioning Rome's first Christian basilica, San Giovanni in Laterano.

The empire was later divided in two, with the second capital in Constantinople (founded by Constantine in 330), on the Bosphorus in Byzantium. It was this, the eastern empire, which survived as Italy and Rome were overrun. This rump empire stretched from parts of present-day Serbia and Montenegro across to Asia Minor, a coastal strip of what is now Syria, Lebanon, Jordan and Israel down to Egypt and a sliver of North Africa as far west as modern Libya. Attempts by Justinian I (482–565) to recover Rome and the shattered western half of the empire ultimately came to nothing.

IMPERIAL INSANITY

Bribes? *Bunga bunga* parties? Think they're unsavoury? Spare a thought for the ancient Romans, who suffered their fair share of eccentric leaders. We salute some of the Roman Empire's wackiest, weirdest and downright kinkiest rulers.

Tiberius (14–37) – A steady governing hand but prone to depression, Tiberius had a difficult relationship with the Senate and withdrew in his later years to Capri, where, they say, he devoted himself to drinking, orgies and fits of paranoia.

Gaius (Caligula; 37–41) – 'Little Shoes' made grand-uncle Tiberius look tame. Sex (including with his sisters) and gratuitous, cruel violence were high on his agenda. He emptied the state's coffers and suggested making a horse consul, before being assassinated.

Claudius (41–54) – Apparently timid as a child, he proved ruthless with his enemies (among them 35 senators), whose executions he greatly enjoyed watching. According to English historian Edward Gibbon, he was the only one of the first 15 emperors not to take male lovers (unusual at the time).

Nero (54–68) – Augustus' last descendant, Nero had his pushy stage mum murdered, his first wife's veins slashed, his second wife kicked to death and his third wife's ex-husband killed. The people accused him of playing the fiddle while Rome burned to the ground in 64. He blamed the disaster on the Christians, executed the evangelists Peter and Paul and had others thrown to wild beasts in a grisly public spectacle.

1282	1309	1321	1348
Charles of Anjou creates enemies in Sicily with heavy taxes on landowners, who rise in the Sicilian Vespers revolt. They hand control of Sicily to Peter III, King of Aragón.	Pope Clement V shifts the papacy to Avignon, France, for almost 70 years. Clement had been elected pope four years earlier but refused to rule in a hostile Rome.	Dante Alighieri completes his epic poem *La divina commedia* (The Divine Comedy). The Florentine poet, considered Italy's greatest literary figure, dies the same year.	The Black Death (bubonic plague) wreaks havoc across Italy and much of the rest of western Europe. Florence is said to have lost three-quarters of its populace.

Papal Power & Family Feuds

Ironically, the minority religion that Emperor Diocletian had tried so hard to stamp out saved the glory of the city of Rome. Through the chaos of invasion and counter-invasion that saw Italy succumb to Germanic tribes, the Byzantine reconquest and the Lombard occupation in the north, the papacy established itself in Rome as a spiritual and secular force. It invented the Donation of Constantine, a document in which Emperor Constantine I had supposedly granted the Church control of Rome and surrounding territory. What the popes needed was a guarantor with military clout. This they found in the Franks and a deal was done.

In return for formal recognition of the popes' control of Rome and surrounding Byzantine-held territories henceforth to be known as the Papal States, the popes granted the Carolingian Franks a leading (if ill-defined) role in Italy and their king, Charlemagne, the title of Holy Roman Emperor. He was crowned by Leo III on Christmas Day 800. The bond between the papacy and the Byzantine Empire was thus broken and political power in what had been the Western Roman Empire shifted north of the Alps, where it would remain for more than 1000 years.

The stage was set for a future of seemingly endless struggles. Similarly, Rome's aristocratic families engaged in battle for the papacy. For centuries, the imperial crown was fought over ruthlessly and Italy was frequently the prime battleground. Holy Roman emperors sought time and again to impose their control on increasingly independent-minded Italian cities, and even on Rome itself. In riposte, the popes continually sought to exploit their spiritual position to bring the emperors to heel and further their own secular ends.

The clash between Pope Gregory VII and Emperor Henry IV over who had the right to appoint bishops (who were powerful political players and hence important friends or dangerous foes) in the last quarter of the 11th century showed just how bitter these struggles could become. They became a focal point of Italian politics in the late Middle Ages, and across the cities and regions of the peninsula two camps emerged: Guelphs (Guelfi, who backed the pope) and Ghibellines (Ghibellini, in support of the emperor).

Europe's first modern banks appeared in Genoa in the 12th century. The city claims the first recorded public bond (1150) and the earliest known exchange contract (1156). Italy's Banca Monte dei Paschi di Siena is the world's oldest surviving bank, counting coins since 1472.

The Wonder of the World

The Holy Roman Empire had barely touched southern Italy until Henry, son of the Holy Roman Emperor Frederick I (Barbarossa), married Constance de Hauteville, heir to the Norman throne in Sicily. The Normans had arrived in southern Italy in the 10th century, initially as pilgrims en route from Jerusalem, later as mercenaries attracted by the money to be made fighting for rival principalities and against the Arab Muslims in

1506	1508–12	1534	1582
Work starts on St Peter's Basilica, to a design by Donato Bramante, on the site of an earlier basilica in Rome. Work would continue on Christendom's showpiece church until 1626.	Pope Julius II commissions Michelangelo to paint the ceiling frescoes in the Sistine Chapel. Michelangelo decides the content, and the central nine panels recount stories from Genesis.	The accession of Pope Paul III marks the beginning of the Counter-Reformation.	Pope Gregory XIII replaces the Julian calendar (introduced by Julius Caesar) with the modern-day Gregorian calendar. The new calendar adds the leap year to keep in line with the earth's rotation.

A WHIFF OF HELLFIRE

Politics in Italy's mercurial city-states could take a radical turn. When Florence's Medici clan rulers fell into disgrace (not for the last time) in 1494, the city's fathers decided to restore an earlier republican model of government.

Since 1481, the Dominican friar Girolamo Savonarola had been in Florence preaching repentance. His blood-curdling warnings of horrors to come if Florentines did not renounce their evil ways somehow captured everyone's imagination and the city submitted to a fiery theocracy. He called on the government to act on the basis of his divine inspiration. Drinking, whoring, partying, gambling, flashy fashion and other signs of wrongdoing were pushed well underground. Books, clothes, jewellery, fancy furnishings and art were burned on 'bonfires of the vanities'.

Pleasure-loving Florentines soon began to tire of this fundamentalism, as did Pope Alexander VI (possibly the least religious pope of all time) and the Dominicans' rivals, the Franciscan religious order. The local economy was stagnant and Savonarola seemed increasingly out to lunch. The city government, or signoria, finally had the fiery friar arrested. After weeks at the hands of the city rack-master, he was hanged and burned at the stake as a heretic, along with two supporters, on 22 May 1498.

Sicily. Of Henry and Constance's match was born one of the most colourful figures of medieval Europe, Frederick II (1194–1250).

Crowned Holy Roman Emperor in 1220, Frederick was a German with a difference. Having grown up in southern Italy, he considered Sicily his natural base and left the German states largely to their own devices. A warrior and scholar, Frederick was an enlightened ruler with an absolutist vocation. A man who allowed freedom of worship to Muslims and Jews, he was not to everyone's liking, as his ambition was to finally bring all of Italy under the imperial yoke.

A poet, linguist, mathematician, and philosopher, Frederick founded a university in Naples and encouraged the spread of learning and translation of Arab treatises. Having reluctantly carried out a crusade (marked more by negotiation than the clash of arms) in the Holy Land in 1228 and 1229 on pain of excommunication, Frederick returned to Italy to find papal troops invading Neapolitan territory. Frederick soon had them on the run and turned his attention to gaining control of the complex web of city-states in central and northern Italy, where he found allies and many enemies, in particular the Lombard League. Years of inconclusive battles ensued, which even Frederick's death in 1250 did not end. Campaigning continued until 1268 under Frederick's successors, Manfredi (who fell in the bloody Battle of Benevento in 1266) and Corradino (captured and

1600	1714	1805	1814–15
Dominican monk and proud philosopher Giordano Bruno is burned alive at the stake in Rome for heresy after eight years of trial and torture at the hands of the Inquisition.	The end of the War of the Spanish Succession forces the withdrawal of Spanish forces from Lombardy. The Spanish Bourbon family establishes an independent Kingdom of the Two Sicilies.	Napoleon is proclaimed king of the newly constituted Kingdom of Italy, comprising most of the northern half of the country. A year later he takes the Kingdom of Naples.	After Napoleon's fall, the Congress of Vienna is held to re-establish the balance of power in Europe. The result for Italy is largely a return of the old occupying powers.

executed two years later by French noble Charles of Anjou, who had by then taken over Sicily and southern Italy).

Rise of the City-States

While the south of Italy tended to centralised rule, the north was heading the opposite way. Port cities such as Genoa, Pisa and especially Venice, along with internal centres such as Florence, Milan, Parma, Bologna, Padua, Verona and Modena, became increasingly hostile towards attempts by the Holy Roman Emperors to meddle in their affairs.

The cities' growing prosperity and independence also brought them into conflict with Rome. Indeed, at times Rome's control over some of its own Papal States was challenged. Caught between the papacy and the emperors, it was not surprising that these city-states were forever switching allegiances in an attempt to best serve their own interests.

Between the 12th and 14th centuries, they developed new forms of government. Venice adopted an oligarchic, 'parliamentary' system in an attempt at limited democracy. More commonly, the city-state created a *comune* (town council), a form of republican government dominated at first by aristocrats but then increasingly by the wealthy middle classes. The well-heeled families soon turned their attentions from business rivalry to political struggles, in which each aimed to gain control of the *signoria* (government).

In some cities, great dynasties, such as the Medici in Florence and the Visconti and Sforza in Milan, came to dominate their respective stages.

War between the city-states was constant and eventually a few, notably Florence, Milan and Venice, emerged as regional powers and absorbed their neighbours. Their power was based on a mix of trade, industry and conquest. Constellations of power and alliances were in constant flux, making changes in the city-states' fortunes the rule rather than the exception. Easily the most stable and long the most successful of them was Venice.

In Florence, prosperity was based on the wool trade, finance and general commerce. Abroad, its coinage, the *firenze* (florin), was king.

In Milan, the noble Visconti family destroyed its rivals and extended Milanese control over Pavia and Cremona, and later Genoa. Giangaleazzo Visconti (1351–1402) turned Milan from a city-state into a strong European power. The policies of the Visconti (up to 1450), followed by those of the Sforza family, allowed Milan to spread its power to the Ticino area of Switzerland and east to the Lago di Garda.

The Milanese sphere of influence butted up against that of Venice. By 1450 the lagoon city had reached the height of its territorial greatness. In addition to its possessions in Greece, Dalmatia and beyond, Venice had

Despite the Italians claiming it as their own, it was the Arabs who first introduced spaghetti to Italy, where 'strings of pasta' were documented by the Arab geographer Al-Idrissi in Palermo, Sicily, in 1150.

1848	1860	1861	1889
European revolts spark rebellion in Italy, especially in Austrian-occupied Milan and Venice. Piedmont's King Carlo Alberto joins the fray against Austria, but within a year Austria recovers Lombardy and Veneto.	In the name of Italian unity, Giuseppe Garibaldi lands with 1000 men, the Red Shirts, in Sicily. He takes the island and lands in southern Italy.	By the end of the Franco-Austrian War (1859–61), Vittorio Emanuele II controls Lombardy, Sardinia, Sicily, southern Italy and parts of central Italy and is proclaimed king of a newly united Italy.	Raffaele Esposito invents pizza margherita in honour of Queen Margherita, who takes her first bite of the Neapolitan staple on a royal visit to the city.

expanded inland. The banner of the Lion of St Mark flew across north-east Italy, from Gorizia to Bergamo.

These dynamic, independent-minded cities proved fertile ground for the intellectual and artistic explosion that would take place across northern Italy in the 14th and 15th centuries – an explosion that would come to be known as the Renaissance and the birth of the modern world. Of them all, Florence was the cradle and launch pad for this fevered activity, in no small measure due to the generous patronage of the long-ruling Medici family.

A Nation Is Born

The French Revolution at the end of the 18th century and the rise of Napoleon awakened hopes in Italy of independent nationhood. Since the glory days of the Renaissance, Italy's divided mini-states had gradually lost power and status on the European stage. By the late 18th century, the peninsula was little more than a tired, backward playground for the big powers and a Grand Tour hot spot for the romantically inclined.

Napoleon marched into Italy on several occasions, finishing off the Venetian republic in 1797 (ending 1000 years of Venetian independence) and creating the so-called Kingdom of Italy in 1805. That kingdom was in no way independent, but the Napoleonic earthquake spurred many Italians to believe that a single Italian state could be created after the emperor's demise. But it was not to be so easy. The reactionary Congress of Vienna restored all the foreign rulers to their places in Italy.

Count Camillo Benso di Cavour (1810–61) of Turin, the prime minister of the Savoy monarchy, became the diplomatic brains behind the Italian unity movement. Through the pro-unity newspaper *Il Risorgimento* (founded in 1847) and the publication of a parliamentary *Statuto* (Statute), Cavour and his colleagues laid the groundwork for unity.

Cavour conspired with the French and won British support for the creation of an independent Italian state. His 1858 treaty with France's Napoleon III foresaw French aid in the event of a war with Austria and the creation of a northern Italian kingdom, in exchange for parts of Savoy and Nice.

The bloody Franco-Austrian War (also known as the Second Italian War of Independence; 1859–61), unleashed in northern Italy, led to the occupation of Lombardy and the retreat of the Austrians to their eastern possessions in the Veneto. In the meantime, a wild card in the form of professional revolutionary Giuseppe Garibaldi had created the real chance of full Italian unity. Garibaldi took Sicily and southern Italy in a military blitz in the name of Savoy king Vittorio Emanuele II in 1860. Southern Italy was thus conquered, rather than willingly forming a union with the north.

America was named after Amerigo Vespucci, a Florentine navigator who, from 1497 to 1504, made several voyages of discovery in what would one day be known as South America.

Italy lays claim to numerous revolutionary inventions. Istrian Santorio Santorio invented the first clinical thermometer in 1612. Como's Alessandro Volta introduced the electric battery in 1800, while Bologna's Guglielmo Marconi shook up global communications by introducing the world's first practical wireless telegraphy transmitters and receivers in the mid-1890s.

1908	1915	1919	1922
On the morning of 28 December, Messina and Reggio di Calabria are struck by a 7.5-magnitude earthquake and a 13m-high tsunami. More than 80,000 lives are lost.	Italy enters WWI on the side of the Allies to win Italian territories still in Austrian hands after Austria's offer to cede some of the territories is deemed insufficient.	Former socialist journalist Benito Mussolini forms a right-wing militant group, the Fasci Italiani di Combattimento (Italian Combat Fasces), precursor to his Fascist Party.	Mussolini and his Fascists stage a march on Rome in October. Doubting the army's loyalty, a fearful King Vittorio Emanuele III entrusts Mussolini with the formation of a government.

Giuliano Procacci's *History of the Italian People* is one of the best general histories of the country in any language. It covers the period from the early Middle Ages until 1948.

Spotting the chance, Cavour and the king moved to take parts of central Italy (including Umbria and Le Marche) and so were able to proclaim the creation of a single Italian state in 1861. In the following nine years, Tuscany, the Veneto and Rome were all incorporated into the fledgling kingdom. Unity was complete and parliament was established in Rome in 1871. However, Italy is a collection of discrete regions rather than a nation, and this is perhaps where many of its contemporary problems lie. As one of the architects of unification, Massimo d'Azeglio, said in his memoirs, 'we made a nation, now we have to make the Italians.'

The turbulent new state saw violent swings between socialists and the right. Giovanni Giolitti, one of Italy's longest-serving prime ministers (heading five governments between 1092 and 1921), managed to bridge the political extremes and institute male suffrage. Women, however, were denied the right to vote until after WWII.

From Trenches to Hanged Dictator

When war broke out in Europe in July 1914, Italy chose to remain neutral despite being a member of the Triple Alliance with Austria and Germany. Italy had territorial claims on Austrian-controlled Trento (Trentino), southern Tyrol, Trieste and even in Dalmatia (some of which it had tried and failed to take during the Austro-Prussian War of 1866). Under the terms of the Triple Alliance, Austria was due to hand over much of this territory in the event of occupying other land in the Balkans, but Austria refused to contemplate fulfilling this part of the bargain.

The Italian government was divided between non-interventionists and a war party. The latter, in view of Austria's intransigence, decided to deal with the Allies. In the London pact of April 1915, Italy was promised the territories it sought after victory. In May, Italy declared war on Austria and thus plunged into a 3½-year nightmare.

Italy and Austria engaged in a weary war of attrition. The Austro-Hungarian forces collapsed in November 1918, after which the Austrian Empire ceded the South Tyrol, Trieste, Trentino and Istria to Italy in the postwar Paris Peace Conference. However, Italy failed to obtain additional territorial claims upon Dalmatia and Albania in the Treaty of Versailles, which left many Italians bitterly disappointed.

These were slim pickings after such a bloody and exhausting conflict. Italy lost 600,000 men and the war economy had produced a small concentration of powerful industrial barons while leaving the bulk of the civilian populace in penury. This cocktail was made all the more explosive as hundreds of thousands of demobbed servicemen returned home or shifted around the country in search of work. The atmosphere was perfect for a demagogue, who was not long in coming forth.

1929	1935	1940	1943
Mussolini and Pope Pius XI sign the Lateran Pact, which declares Catholicism Italy's sole religion and the Vatican an independent state. Satisfied, the papacy acknowledges the Kingdom of Italy.	Italy seeks a new colonial conquest through the invasion of Abyssinia (Ethiopia) from Eritrea. The League of Nations condemns the invasion and imposes limited sanctions on Italy.	Italy enters WWII on Nazi Germany's side and invades Greece, which quickly proves to be a mistake. Greek forces counter-attack and enter southern Albania. Germany saves Italy in 1941.	Allies land in Sicily. King Vittorio Emanuele III sacks Mussolini. He is replaced by Marshall Badoglio, who surrenders after Allied landings in southern Italy. German forces free Mussolini.

Benito Mussolini (1883–1945) was a young war enthusiast who had once been a socialist newspaper editor and one-time draft dodger. This time he volunteered for the front and only returned, wounded, in 1917. The experience of war and the frustration shared with many at the disappointing outcome in Versailles led him to form a right-wing militant political group that by 1921 had become the Fascist Party, with its black-shirted street brawlers and Roman salute. These were to become symbols of violent oppression and aggressive nationalism for the next 23 years. After his march on Rome in 1922 and victory in the 1924 elections, Mussolini, who called himself Il Duce (the Leader), took full control of the country by 1926, banning other political parties, trade unions not affiliated to the party, and the free press.

By the 1930s, all aspects of Italian society were regulated by the party. The economy, banking, a massive public works program, the conversion of coastal malarial swamps into arable land and an ambitious modernisation of the armed forces were all part of Mussolini's grand plan.

On the international front, Mussolini at first showed a cautious hand, signing international cooperation pacts (including the 1928 Kellogg Pact solemnly renouncing war) and until 1935 moving close to France and the UK to contain the growing menace of Adolf Hitler's rapidly re-arming Germany.

That all changed when Mussolini decided to invade Abyssinia (Ethiopia) as the first big step to creating a 'new Roman empire'. This aggressive side of Mussolini's policy had already led to skirmishes with Greece over the island of Corfu and to military expeditions against nationalist forces in the Italian colony of Libya.

The League of Nations condemned the Abyssinian adventure (King Vittorio Emanuele III was declared Emperor of Abyssinia in 1936) and

GOING THE DISTANCE FOR THE RESISTANCE

In 1943 and 1944, the Assisi Underground hid hundreds of Jewish Italians in Umbrian convents and monasteries, while the Tuscan Resistance forged travel documents for them – but the refugees needed those documents fast, before they were deported to concentration camps by Fascist officials. Enter the fastest man in Italy: Gino Bartali, world-famous Tuscan cyclist, Tour de France winner and three-time champion of the Giro d'Italia. After his death in 2003, documents revealed that during his 'training rides' throughout the war years, Bartali had carried Resistance intelligence and falsified documents to transport Jewish refugees to safe locations. Bartali was interrogated at the dreaded Villa Triste in Florence, where suspected anti-Fascists were routinely tortured – but he revealed nothing. Until his death, the long distance hero downplayed, even to his children, his efforts to rescue Jewish refugees, saying, 'One does these things, and then that's that.'

1944	1946	1957	1966
Mt Vesuvius explodes back into action on 18 March. The eruption is captured on film by USAAF (United States Army Air Forces) personnel stationed nearby.	Italians vote in a national referendum to abolish the monarchy and create a republic. King Umberto II leaves Italy and refuses to recognise the result.	Italy joins France, West Germany and the Benelux countries to sign the Treaty of Rome, which creates the European Economic Community (EEC). The treaty takes effect on 1 January 1958.	A devastating flood inundates Florence in early November, leaving around 100 people dead, 5000 families homeless and 14,000 movable artworks damaged. The flood is the city's worst since 1557.

Roberto Rossellini's *Roma città aperta* (Rome: Open City), starring Anna Magnani, is a classic of Italian neorealist cinema and a masterful look at wartime Rome. The film is the first in his Trilogy of War, followed by *Paisà* and *Germania anno zero* (Germany: Year Zero).

from then on Mussolini changed course, drawing closer to Nazi Germany. Italy backed the rebel General Franco in the three-year Spanish Civil War and in 1939 signed an alliance pact.

WWII broke out in September 1939 with Hitler's invasion of Poland. Italy remained aloof until June 1940, by which time Germany had overrun Norway, Denmark, the Low Countries and much of France. It seemed too easy and so Mussolini entered on Germany's side in 1940, a move Hitler must have regretted later. Germany found itself pulling Italy's chestnuts out of the fire in campaigns in the Balkans and North Africa and could not prevent Allied landings in Sicily in 1943.

By then, the Italians had had enough of Mussolini and his war and so the king had the dictator arrested. In September, Italy surrendered and the Germans, who had rescued Mussolini, occupied the northern two-thirds of the country and reinstalled the dictator.

The painfully slow Allied campaign up the peninsula and German repression led to the formation of the Resistance, which played a growing role in harassing German forces. Northern Italy was finally liberated in April 1945. Resistance fighters caught Mussolini as he fled north in the hope of reaching Switzerland. They shot him and his lover, Clara Petacci, before stringing up their corpses (along with others) in Milan's Piazzale Lotto. This was a far cry from Il Duce's hopes for a glorious burial alongside his ancient imperial idol, Augustus, in Rome.

The Grey & Red Years

In the aftermath of war, the left-wing Resistance was disarmed and Italy's political forces scrambled to regroup. The USA, through the economic largesse of the Marshall Plan, wielded considerable political influence and used this to keep the left in check.

Immediately after the war, three coalition governments succeeded one another. The third, which came to power in December 1945, was dominated by the newly formed right-wing Democrazia Cristiana (DC; Christian Democrats), led by Alcide De Gasperi. Italy became a republic in 1946 and De Gasperi's DC won the first elections under the new constitution in 1948, and remained prime minister until 1953.

Paul Ginsborg's *A History of Contemporary Italy: Society and Politics, 1943–1988* remains one of the most readable and insightful books on postwar Italy.

Until the 1980s, the Partito Comunista Italiano (PCI; Communist Party), at first under Palmiro Togliatti and later the charismatic Enrico Berlinguer, played a crucial role in Italy's social and political development, despite being systematically kept out of government.

The popularity of the party led to a grey period in the country's history, the *anni di piombo* (years of lead) in the 1970s. Just as the Italian economy was booming, Europe-wide paranoia about the power of the communists in Italy fuelled a secretive reaction, that, it is said, was largely directed by the CIA and NATO. Even today, little is known about

1970	1980	1980	1999
Parliament approves the country's first-ever divorce legislation. Unwilling to accept this 'defeat', the Christian Democrats call a referendum to annul the law in 1974. Italians vote against the referendum.	A bomb in Bologna kills 85 and injures hundreds more. The Red Brigades and a Fascist cell both claim responsibility. Analysis later points to possible para-state terrorism in Operation Gladio.	At 7.34pm on 25 November, a 6.8–Richter scale earthquake strikes Campania. The quake kills almost 3000 people and causes widespread damage, including in the city of Naples.	Italy becomes a primary base in NATO's air war on Yugoslavia. Air strikes are carried out from the Aviano airbase from 24 May until 8 June.

Operation Gladio, an underground paramilitary organisation supposedly behind various unexplained terror attacks in the country, apparently designed to create an atmosphere of fear in which, should the communists come close to power, a right-wing coup could be quickly carried out.

The 1970s were thus dominated by the spectre of terrorism and considerable social unrest, especially in the universities. Neo-fascist terrorists struck with a bomb blast in Milan in 1969. In 1978, the Brigate Rosse (Red Brigades, a group of young left-wing militants responsible for several bomb blasts and assassinations), claimed their most important victim – former DC prime minister Aldo Moro. His kidnap and murder some 54 days later (the subject of the 2003 film *Buongiorno, notte*) shook the country.

Despite the disquiet, the 1970s was also a time of positive change. In 1970, regional governments with limited powers were formed in 15 of the country's 20 regions (the other five, Sicily, Sardinia, Valle d'Aosta, Trentino-Alto Adige and Friuli Venezia Giulia, already had strong autonomy statutes). In the same year, divorce became legal and eight years later abortion was also legalised.

From Clean Hands to Berlusconi

A growth spurt in the aftermath of WWII saw Italy become one of the world's leading economies, but by the 1970s the economy had begun to falter, and by the mid-1990s a new and prolonged period of crisis had set in. High unemployment and inflation, combined with a huge national debt and mercurial currency (the lira), led the government to introduce draconian measures to cut public spending, allowing Italy to join the single currency (euro) in 2001.

The 1990s saw the Italian political scene rocked by the Tangentopoli ('kickback city') scandal. Led by a pool of Milanese magistrates, including the tough Antonio di Pietro, investigations known as Mani Pulite (Clean Hands) implicated thousands of politicians, public officials and businesspeople in scandals ranging from bribery and receiving kickbacks to blatant theft.

The old centre-right political parties collapsed in the wake of these trials and from the ashes rose what many Italians hoped might be a breath of fresh political air. Media magnate Silvio Berlusconi's Forza Italia (Go Italy) party swept to power in 2001 and again in April 2008 (after an inconclusive two-year interlude of centre-left government under former European Commission head Romano Prodi from 2006). Berlusconi's carefully choreographed blend of charisma, confidence, irreverence and promises of tax cuts appealed to many Italian voters, and he has enjoyed political success and longevity that is incomprehensible to many outsiders.

Published in 2004, Paul Ginsborg's book *Silvio Berlusconi: Television, Power and Patrimony* reveals the power and influence of Italy's highly controversial former prime minister. Equally disturbing is the 2009 film *Videocracy*, which offers a disturbing take on the nature of celebrity and Berlusconi's TV empire.

2001	2005	2006	2011
Silvio Berlusconi's right-wing Casa delle Libertà (Liberties House) coalition wins an absolute majority in national polls. The following five years are marked by economic stagnation.	Pope John Paul II dies at age 84, prompting a wave of sorrow and chants of *santo subito* (sainthood now). He is succeeded by Benedict XVI, the German Cardinal Ratzinger.	Juventus, AC Milan and three other top Serie A football teams receive hefty fines in a match-rigging scandal that also sees Juventus stripped of its 2005 and 2006 championship titles.	Berlusconi stands trial in Milan in April on charges of abuse of power and paying for sex with under-aged Moroccan prostitute Karima El Mahroug (aka Ruby Heartstealer).

However, Berlusconi's tenure saw the economic situation go from bad to worse, while a series of laws were passed that protected his extensive business interests, for example, granting the prime minister immunity from prosecution while in office. In 2011, Berlusconi was finally forced to resign due to the deepening debt crisis. A government of technocrats, headed by economist Mario Monti, took over until the inconclusive elections of February 2013. After lengthy post-electoral negotiations, Enrico Letta, a member of the Partito Democratico (PD), was named prime minister, steering a precarious right-left coalition.

Renzi & Renewal

The downfall of former prime minister Silvio Berlusconi ushered in a new era in Italian politics. In 2014, 39-year-old Matteo Renzi, former mayor of Florence, took over as leader of a right-left coalition, making him the third unelected prime minister since Berlusconi's fall (following Mario Monti and Enrico Letta). Renzi's cabinet became the youngest in Italian history and the first with an even gender balance.

Under his leadership, the government introduced a number of reforms, including the legalisation of same-sex civil unions and a relaxation of labour laws aimed at stimulating economic growth. The latter measures included temporary tax breaks for companies willing to hire workers on permanent contracts. Much to the ire of the country's powerful trade unions, they also granted employers more freedom to monitor their workers' performance and to fire those who under-performed. Some critics of Renzi's labour reforms argued that the new rules failed to touch the country's massive, inefficient public sector or the employment contracts of those already in a job.

Renzi also proposed a highly contentious amendment to the Italian constitution that he argued would provide the country with greater political stability. The amendment would have reduced the size and power of the Senate, which currently wields as much influence as the lower house. According to Renzi, the change would allow the ruling government to pass legislation with greater efficiency. Critics of the change, however, argued that it would give the government too much power and threaten the very concept of democracy. The proposal was put to voters in a national referendum on 4 December 2016. The proposal was rejected, leading Renzi to honour his promise to resign as prime minister in the case of a 'No' vote. On 12 December 2016, Foreign Affairs Minister Paolo Gentiloni became Italy's new prime minister. After resigning as PD leader in February 2017, Renzi won his party's primary election by a landslide on 1 May the same year, returning Renzi as PD leader and reinvigorating the young Tuscan's political ambitions.

Italy has hosted the Olympic Games three times to date. The 1956 Winter Olympics were held in the northern ski resort of Cortina d'Ampezzo, while the 1960 Summer Olympics took place in Rome. In 2006, the Winter Olympics took over the Piedmontese city of Turin.

2011	2014	2016	2018
Berlusconi is forced to step down as the prime minister of Italy. Northern Italian economist Mario Monti is put in charge, heading a government of technocrats.	Matteo Renzi becomes the youngest prime minister in the republic's history and the third PM in succession to take control without an election. He resigns in 2016 after losing a referendum to change the constitution.	Central Italy is rocked by a series of powerful earthquakes. The deadliest, measuring 6.2 on the Richter scale, hits the mountainous northeastern corner of Lazio on 24 August. Almost 300 people die.	Palermo is crowned Italian Capital of Culture. The Sicilian capital hosts a number of special cultural events, including the 12th edition of Manifesta, Europe's most important biennial exhibition of contemporary art.

Italian Art & Architecture

The art and architecture of Italy has seduced visitors for hundreds of years. This rich legacy stretches back to before Roman times and continues today in the country's thriving, evolving contemporary scenes. While all periods across this long history have their treasures and devotees, it's the Renaissance that is the most stunning, from Florence's elegant streetscapes and the otherworldly beauty of Venice's *palazzi* to the dizzying caches of works that line galleries and churches like the Uffizi in Florence, the Brera in Milan and St Peter's Basilica in Rome.

Art

Italian art's long history underpins that of all Western art, from the classical, Renaissance and baroque to the explosive doctrine of the Futurists and the conceptual play of Arte Povera in the 20th century. A roll call of Italian artists – Giotto, Botticelli, da Vinci, Michelangelo, Raphael, Caravaggio and Bernini – forged their vision into some of the greatest bodies of work of the millennia and are, centuries after their deaths, still household names the world over.

The Ancient & the Classical

Greek colonists settled many parts of Sicily and southern Italy as early as the 8th century BC, naming it Magna Graecia and building great cities such as Syracuse and Taranto. These cities were famous for their magnificent temples, many of which were decorated with sculptures modelled on, or inspired by, masterpieces by Praxiteles, Lysippus and Phidias. In art, as in so many other realms, the ancient Romans looked to the Greeks for inspiration.

Sculpture flourished in southern Italy into the Hellenistic period. It also gained popularity in central Italy, where the art of the Etruscans was greatly refined by the contribution of Greek artisans, who arrived to trade.

In Rome, sculpture, architecture and painting flourished first under the Republic and then the empire. But the art that was produced here during this period differed in key ways from the Greek art that influenced it. Essentially secular, it focused less on ideals of aesthetic harmony and more on accurate representation, taking sculptural portraiture to new heights of verisimilitude, as innumerable versions of Pompey, Titus and Augustus showing a similar visage attest.

The Roman ruling class understood art could be used as a political tool, one that could construct a unified identity and cement status and power. As well as portraiture, Roman narrative art often took the form of relief decoration recounting the story of great military victories – the Colonna di Traiano (Trajan's Column) and the Ara Pacis Augustae (Altar of Peace) in Rome exemplify this tradition. Both are magnificent, monumental examples of art as propaganda, exalting the emperor and Rome in a form that no Roman citizen could possibly ignore.

Italy has more World Heritage–listed sites than any other country in the world; many of its 51 listings are repositories of great art.

Italy's dedicated art police, the Comando Carabinieri Tutela Patrimonio Culturale, tackle the looting of priceless heritage. It's estimated that over 100,000 ancient tombs have been ransacked by *tombaroli* (tomb raiders) alone; contents are sold to private and public collectors around the world.

Wealthy Roman citizens also dabbled in the arts, building palatial villas and adorning them with statues looted from the Greek world or copied from Hellenic originals. Today, museums in Rome burst at the seams with such trophies, from the Capitoline Museums' 'Made in Italy' *Galata morente* (Dying Gaul, c 240–200 BC) to the Vatican Museums' original Greek *Laocoön and His Sons* (c 160–140 BC).

And while the Etruscans had used wall painting – most notably in their tombs at centres like Tarquinia and Cerveteri in modern-day Lazio, it was the Romans who refined the form, refocusing on landscape scenes to adorn the walls of the living. A visit to Rome's Museo Nazionale Romano: Palazzo Massimo alle Terme or to Naples' Museo Archeologico Nazionale offers sublime examples of the form.

The Glitter of Byzantine

Emperor Constantine, a convert to Christianity, made the ancient city of Byzantium his capital in 330 and renamed it Constantinople. The city became the great cultural and artistic centre of early Christianity and it remained so up to the time of the Renaissance, though its influence was not as fundamental as the art of ancient Rome.

The Byzantine period was notable for its sublime ecclesiastical architecture, its extraordinary mosaic work and – to a lesser extent – its ethereal painting. Drawing inspiration from the symbol-drenched decoration of the Roman catacombs and the early Christian churches, the Byzantine de-emphasised the naturalistic aspects of the classical tradition and exalted the spirit over the body, glorifying God rather than humanity or the state. This was infused with the Near East's decorative traditions and love of luminous colour.

In Italy, the Byzantine virtuosity with mosaics was showcased in Ravenna, the capital of the Byzantine Empire's western regions in the 6th century. The Basilica di Sant'Apollinare (in nearby Classe) and the Basilica di San Vitale and Basilica di Sant'Apollinare Nuovo house some of the world's finest Byzantine art, their hand-cut glazed tiles *(tesserae)* balancing extraordinary naturalness with an epic sense of grandeur and mystery.

The Byzantine aesthetic is also evident in Venice, in the exoticism of the Basilica di San Marco, and in the technicolored interior of Rome's Chiesa di San Prassede. Byzantine, Norman and Arab influences in Sicily fused to create a distinct regional style showcased in the mosaic-encrusted splendour of Palermo's Cappella Palatina, as well as the cathedrals of Monreale and Cefalù.

The Not-so-Dark Ages

Italy, and Italian art, were born out of the so-called Dark Ages. The barbarian invasions of the 5th and 6th centuries began a process that turned a unified empire into a land of small independent city-states, and it was these states – or rather the merchants, princes, clergy, corporations and guilds who lived within them – that created a culture of artistic patronage that engendered the great innovations in art and architecture that would define the Renaissance.

Clarity of religious message continued to outweigh the notion of faithful representation in the art of the medieval period. To the modern eye, the simplicity and coded allegorical narrative of both the painting and sculpture of this period can look stiff, though a closer look usually reveals a sublimity and grace, as well as a shared human experience, that speaks across the centuries.

Gothic Refinement

The Gothic style was much slower to take off in Italy than in the rest of Europe. But it did, marking the transition from medieval restraint to the Renaissance, and seeing artists once again drawing inspiration from life itself rather than concentrating solely on religious themes. Occurring at the same time as the development of court society and the rise of civic culture in the city-states, its art was both sophisticated and elegant, highlighting attention to detail, a luminous palette and an increasingly refined technique. The first innovations were made in Pisa by sculptor Nicola Pisano (c 1220–84), who emulated the example of the French Gothic masters and studied classical sculpture in order to represent nature more convincingly, but the major strides forward occurred in Florence and Siena.

Giotto & the 'Rebirth' of Italian Art

The Byzantine painters in Italy knew how to make use of light and shade and had an understanding of the principles of foreshortening (how to convey an effect of perspective). It only required a genius to break the spell of their conservatism and to venture into a new world of naturalism. Enter Florentine painter Giotto di Bondone (c 1266–1337), whose brushstrokes focused on dramatic narrative and the accurate representation of figures and landscape. The Italian poet Giovanni Boccaccio wrote in his *Decameron* (1350–53) that Giotto was 'a genius so sublime that there was nothing produced by nature...that he could not depict to the life; his depiction looked not like a copy, but the real thing.'

Many Renaissance painters included self-portraits in their major works. Giotto didn't, possibly due to the fact that friends such as Giovanni Boccaccio described him as the ugliest man in Florence. With friends like those...

ITALIAN ART & ARCHITECTURE ART

ART, ANGER & ARTEMESIA

Sex, fame and notoriety: the life of Artemesia Gentileschi (1593–1652) could spawn a top-rating soap opera. One of the early baroque's greatest artists, and one of the few females, Gentileschi was born in Rome to Tuscan painter Orazio Gentileschi. Orazio wasted little time introducing his young daughter to the city's working artists. Among her mentors was Michelangelo Merisi da Caravaggio, whose chiaroscuro technique would deeply influence her own style.

At the tender age of 17, Gentileschi produced her first masterpiece, *Susanna and the Elders* (1610), now in the Schönborn Collection in Pommersfelden, Germany. Her depiction of the sexually harassed Susanna proved eerily foreboding: two years later Artemesia would find herself at the centre of a seven-month trial, in which Florentine artist Agostino Tassi was charged with her rape.

Out of Gentileschi's fury came the gripping, technically brilliant *Judith Slaying Holofernes* (1612–13). While the original hangs in Naples' Museo di Capodimonte, you'll find a larger, later version in Florence's Uffizi. Vengeful Judith would make a further appearance in *Judith and her Maidservant* (c 1613–14), now in Florence's Palazzo Pitti. While living in Florence, Gentileschi completed a string of commissions for Cosimo II of the Medici dynasty, as well as becoming the first female member of the prestigious Accademia delle Arti del Disegno (Academy of the Arts of Drawing).

After separating from her husband, Tuscan painter Pietro Antonio di Vincenzo Stiattesi, Gentileschi headed south to Naples sometime between 1626 and 1630. Here her creations would include *The Annunciation* (1630), also in Naples' Museo di Capodimonte, and her *Self-Portrait as the Allegory of Painting* (1630), housed in London's Kensington Palace. The latter work received praise for its simultaneous depiction of art, artist and muse, an innovation at the time. Gentileschi's way with the brush was not lost on King Charles I of England, who honoured the Italian talent with a court residency from 1638 to 1641.

Despite her illustrious career, Gentileschi inhabited a man's world. Nothing would prove this more than the surviving epitaphs commemorating her death, focused not on her creative brilliance, but on the gossip depicting her as a cheating nymphomaniac.

The Renaissance

Of Italy's countless artistic highs, none surpass the Renaissance. The age of Botticelli, da Vinci and Michelangelo is defined by a rediscovery of classical learning and humanist philosophy, driven by the spirit of scientific investigation. It also marks a seismic shift of the artists' own role; once considered a mere craftsman, the Renaissance artist is reborn as intellectual and philosopher.

Florence, Classicism & the Quattrocento

Giotto and the painters of the Sienese school introduced many innovations in art: the exploration of proportion, a new interest in realistic portraiture and the beginnings of a new tradition of landscape painting. At the start of the 15th century (Quattrocento), most of these were explored and refined in one city – Florence.

Sculptors Lorenzo Ghiberti (1378–1455) and Donatello (c 1382–1466) replaced the demure robe-clad statues of the Middle Ages with anatomically accurate figures evoking ancient Greece and Rome. Donatello's bronze *David* (c 1440–50) and *St George* (c 1416–17), both in Florence's Museo del Bargello, capture this spirit of antiquity.

Ghiberti's greatest legacy would be his bronze east doors (1424–52) for the baptistry in Florence's Piazza del Duomo. The original 10 relief panels heralded a giant leap from the late-Gothic art of the time, not only in their use of perspective, but also in the individuality bestowed upon the figures portrayed.

When the neighbouring Duomo's dome was completed in 1436, author, architect and philosopher Leon Battista Alberti called it the first great achievement of the 'new' architecture, one that equalled or even surpassed the great buildings of antiquity. Designed by Filippo Brunelleschi (1377–1446), the dome was as innovative in engineering terms as the Pantheon's dome had been 1300 years before.

A New Perspective

While Brunelleschi was heavily influenced by the classical masters, he was able to do something that they hadn't – discover the mathematical rules by which objects appear to diminish as they recede. In so doing, Brunelleschi gave artists a whole new visual perspective.

The result was a new style of masterpiece, including Masaccio's *Trinity* (c 1424–25) in Florence's Basilica di Santa Maria Novella and Leonardo da Vinci's fresco *The Last Supper* (1495–98) in the refectory of Milan's Chiesa di Santa Maria delle Grazie. Andrea Mantegna (1431–1506) was responsible for the painting that is the most virtuosic of all perspectival experiments that occurred during this period – his highly realistic *Dead Christ* (c 1480), now in Milan's Pinacoteca di Brera.

These innovations in perspective were not always slavishly followed, however. Sandro Botticelli (c 1444–1510) pursued a Neoplatonic concept of ideal beauty that, along with his penchant for luminous decoration, resulted in flat linear compositions and often improbable

1. Cupola del Brunelleschi (p478), Duomo, Florence
2. Michelangelo's *Pietà*, St Peter's Basilica (p110), Rome

poses. *The Birth of Venus* (c 1485), now in Florence's Uffizi, is a deft and daring synthesis of poetry and politics, eroticism and spirituality, contemporary Florentine fashion and classical mythology.

High Renaissance Masters

By the early 16th century (Cinquecento), the epicentre of artistic innovation shifted from Florence to Rome and Venice. This reflected the political and social realities of the period, namely the transfer of power in Florence from the Medicis to the moral-crusading, book-burning friar Girolamo Savonarola (1452–98), and the desire of the popes in Rome to counter the influence of Martin Luther's Reformation through turning the city into a humbling showpiece. While the age delivered a bounty of talent, some of its luminaries shone exceedingly bright.

Donato Bramante

Donato Bramante (1444–1514) knew the power of illusion. In Milan's Chiesa di Santa Maria presso San Satiro, he feigned a choir using the trompe l'œil technique. In Rome, his classical obsession would shine through in his perfectly proportioned Tempietto of the Chiesa di San Pietro in Montorio, arguably the pinnacle of High Renaissance architecture. The Urbino native would go on to design St Peter's Basilica, though his Greek-cross floor plan would never be realised.

Leonardo da Vinci

Leonardo da Vinci (1452–1519), the quintessential polymath Renaissance man, took what some critics have described as the decisive step in the history of Western art – abandoning the balance that had previously been maintained between colour and line in painting and choosing to modulate his contours using colour. This technique, called sfumato, is perfectly displayed

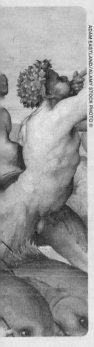

1. Raphael's *Triumph of Galatea* in the Villa Farnesina (p101), Rome **2.** Detail of Donatello's *David*, Museo del Bargello (p490), Florence

in his *Mona Lisa* (now in the Louvre in Paris). In Milan's Chiesa di Santa Maria delle Grazie, his *The Last Supper* bestowed dramatic individuality to each depicted figure.

Raphael Santi

Raphael Santi (1483–1520) would rise to the aforementioned challenge faced by the Quattrocento painters – achieving harmonious and accurate (in terms of perspective) arrangement of figures – in works such as *Triumph of Galatea* (c 1514) in Rome's Villa Farnesina and *La Scuola d'Atene* (The School of Athens) in the Vatican Museums' Stanza della Segnatur. Other inspiring works include his enigmatic *La Fornarina* in Rome's Galleria Nazionale d'Arte Antica: Palazzo Barberini, and *Portrait of Alessandro Farnese* in Naples' Palazzo Reale di Capodimonte.

Michelangelo Buonarroti

Michelangelo Buonarroti (1475–1564) saw himself first and foremost as a sculptor, creating incomparable works like the *Pietà* in St Peter's Basilica and *David* (1504) in Florence's Galleria dell'Accademia. As a painter, he would adorn the ceiling of Rome's Sistine Chapel, creating figures that were not just realistic, but emotive visual representations of the human experience. A true Renaissance Man, Michelangelo's talents extended to architecture – the dome atop St Peter's Basilica is another Michelangelo creation.

Andrea Palladio

Bramante's Tempietto would influence Andrea Palladio (1508–80) when he was designing . Like Bramante, northern Italy's greatest Renaissance architect was enamoured of classicism. His Palladian villas, such as the Brenta Riviera's Villa Foscari, radiate an elegant mathematical logic, perfectly proportioned and effectively accentuated with pediments and loggias. Classical influences also inform his Chiesa di San Giorgio Maggiore in Venice.

Boccaccio wasn't the only prominent critic of the time to consider Giotto revolutionary – the first historian of Italian art, Giorgio Vasari, said in his *Lives of the Artists* (1550) that Giotto initiated the 'rebirth' *(rinascità or renaissance)* in art. Giotto's most famous works are all in the medium of the fresco (where paint is applied on a wall while the plaster is still damp), and his supreme achievement is the cycle gracing the walls of Padua's Cappella degli Scrovegni. It's impossible to overestimate Giotto's achievement with these frescoes, which illustrate the stories of the lives of the Virgin and Christ. Abandoning popular conventions such as the three-quarter view of head and body, he presented his figures from behind, from the side or turning around, just as the story demanded. Giotto had no need for lashings of gold paint and elaborate ornamentation either, opting to convey the scene's dramatic tension through a naturalistic rendition of figures and a radical composition that created the illusion of depth.

Giotto's oeuvre isn't limited to the frescoes in the Cappella degli Scrovegni. His Life of St Francis cycle in the Upper Church of the Basilica di San Francesco in Assisi is almost as extraordinary and was to greatly influence his peers, many of whom worked in Assisi during the decoration of the church. One of the most prominent of these was the Dominican friar Fra' Angelico (c 1395–1455), a Florentine painter who was famed for his mastery of colour and light. His *Annunciation* (c 1450) in the convent of the Museo di San Marco in Florence is arguably his most accomplished work.

The Sienese School

Giotto wasn't the only painter of his time to experiment with form, colour and composition and create a radical new style. The great Sienese master Duccio di Buoninsegna (c 1255–1319) successfully breathed new life into the old Byzantine forms using light and shade. His preferred medium was panel painting and his major work is probably his *Maestà* (Virgin Mary in Majesty; 1311) in Siena's Museo dell'Opera Metropolitana.

It was in Siena, too, that two new trends took off: the introduction of court painters and the advent of purely secular art.

The first of many painters to be given ongoing commissions by one major patron or court, Simone Martini (c 1284–1344) was almost as famous as Giotto in his day. His best-known painting is the stylised *Maestà* (1315–16) in Siena's Museo Civico, in which he pioneered his famous iridescent palette (one colour transformed into another within the same plane).

Also working in Siena at this time were the Lorenzetti brothers, Pietro (c 1280–1348) and Ambrogio (c 1290–1348), who are considered the greatest exponents of what, for lack of a better term, can be referred to as secular painting. Ambrogio's magnificent *Allegories of Good and Bad Government* (1337–40) in the Museo Civico lauds the fruits of good government and the gruesome results of bad. In the frescoes, he applies the rules of perspective with an accuracy previously unseen, as well as significantly developing the Italian landscape tradition. In *Life in the Country,* one of the allegories, Ambrogio successfully depicts the time of day, the season, colour reflections and shadows – a naturalistic depiction of landscape that was quite unique at this time.

In *M: The Man Who Became Caravaggio,* Peter Robb gives a passionate personal assessment of the artist's paintings and a colourful account of Caravaggio's life, arguing he was murdered for having sex with the pageboy of a high-ranking Maltese aristocrat.

The Venetians

While Byzantine influence lingered longer in Venice than in many other parts of Italy, its grip on the city loosened by the early to mid-15th century. In *Polyptych of St James* (c 1450) by Michele Giambono (c 1400–62) in Venice's Gallerie dell'Accademia, the luscious locks and fair complexion of the archangel Michael channel the style of early Renaissance master Pisanello (c 1395–1455). The winds of change blow even stronger in fel-

ITALIAN ARTISTS: THE EXCLUSIVE SCOOP

Painter, architect and writer Giorgio Vasari (1511–74) was one of those figures rightly described as a 'Renaissance Man'. Born in Arezzo, he trained as a painter in Florence, working with artists including Andrea del Sarto and Michelangelo (he idolised the latter). As a painter, he is best remembered for his floor-to-ceiling frescoes in the Salone dei Cinquecento in Florence's Palazzo Vecchio. As an architect, his most accomplished work was the elegant loggia of the Uffizi (he also designed the enclosed, elevated corridor that connected the Palazzo Vecchio with the Uffizi and Palazzo Pitti and was dubbed the 'Corridoio Vasariano' in his honour). But posterity remembers him predominantly for his work as an art historian. His *Lives of the Most Excellent Painters, Sculptors and Architects, from Cimabue to Our Time,* an encyclopaedia of artistic biographies published in 1550 and dedicated to Cosimo I de' Medici, is still in print (as *The Lives of the Artists*). It's full of wonderful anecdotes and – dare we say it – gossip about his artistic contemporaries in 16th-century Florence. Memorable passages include his recollection of visiting Donatello's studio one day only to find the great sculptor staring at his extremely lifelike statue of the *Prophet Habakkuk* and imploring it to talk (we can only assume that Donatello had been working too hard). Vasari also writes about a young Giotto (the painter whom he credits with ushering in the Renaissance) painting a fly on the surface of a work by Cimabue that the older master then tried to brush away. The book makes wonderful pre-departure reading for anyone planning to visit Florence and its museums.

low Accademia resident *Madonna with Child* (c 1455) by Jacopo Bellini (c 1396–1470). Featuring a bright-eyed baby Jesus and a patient, seemingly sleep-deprived Mary, it's an image any parent might relate to. Relatable emotions are equally strong in the biblical scenes of Andrea Mantegna (1431–1506); one can almost hear the sobbing in his *Lamentation over the Dead Christ* (c 1480) in Milan's Pinacoteca di Brera.

Tuscan painter Gentile da Fabriano (c 1370–1427) worked in Venice during the early stages of his transition to Renaissance realism, and his evolving style reputedly influenced Venetian Antonio Vivarini (c 1415–80), the latter's *Passion* polyptych in radiating tremendous pathos. Antonio's brother, Bartolomeo Vivarini (c 1432–99) created a delightful altarpiece in Venice's I Frari, in which a baby Jesus wriggles out of the arms of his mother, squarely seated on her marble Renaissance throne.

In 1475, visiting Sicilian painter Antonello da Messina (c 1430–79) introduced the Venetians to oil paints, and their knack for layering and blending colours made for a luminosity that would ultimately define the city's art. Among early ground-breakers was Giovanni Bellini (c 1430–1516). The son of Jacopo Bellini, his Accademia *Annunciation* (1500) deployed glowing reds and ambers to focus attention on the solitary figure of the kneeling Madonna, the angel Gabriel arriving in a rush of geometrically rumpled drapery.

Bellini's prowess with the palette was not lost on his students, among them Giorgione (1477–1510) and Titian (c 1488–1576). Giorgione preferred to paint from inspiration without sketching out his subject first, as in his enigmatic *La Tempesta* (The Storm; 1500), also in the Accademia. The younger Titian set himself apart with brushstrokes that brought his subjects to life, from his early and measured *St Mark Enthroned* (1510) in Venice's Chiesa di Santa Maria della Salute to his thick, textured swansong *Pietà* (1576) in the Accademia.

Titian raised the bar for a new generation of northern Italian masters, including Jacopo Robusti, aka Tintoretto (1518–94). Occasionally enhancing his palette with finely crushed glass, Tintoretto created action-packed biblical scenes that read like a modern graphic novel. His wall and ceiling paintings in Venice's Scuola Grande di San Rocco are nail-bitingly spectacular, laced with holy superheroes, swooping angels, and deep, ominous shadows. Paolo Caliari, aka Veronese (1528–88) was another 16th-century star, the remarkable radiance of his hues captured in *Feast in the House of Levi* (1573), another Accademia must-see.

From Mannerism to Baroque

Michelangelo's *David* is no stranger to close calls. In 1527, the lower part of his arm was broken off in a riot. In 1843, a hydrochloric 'spruce-up' stripped away some of the original surface, while in 1991 a disturbed, hammer-wielding Italian painter smashed the statue's second left toe.

By 1520, artists such as Michelangelo and Raphael had pretty well achieved everything that former generations had tried to do and, alongside other artists, began distorting natural images in favour of heightened expression. This movement – which reached its heights in Titian's luminous *Assunta* (Assumption, 1516–18), in Venice's I Frari, and in Raphael's *La trasfigurazione* (Transfiguration, 1517–20), in the Vatican Museums' Pinacoteca – was derided by later critics, who labelled it mannerism. Pejorative as the term once was, the stylish artificiality of Agnolo Bronzino's Florentine court portraits has an almost 21st-century seductiveness.

Milanese-born enfant terrible Michelangelo Merisi da Caravaggio (1573–1610) had no sentimental attachment to classical models and no respect for 'ideal beauty'. He shocked contemporaries in his relentless search for truth and his radical, often visceral, realism. But even his most ardent detractors could not fail to admire his skill with the technique of chiaroscuro (the bold contrast of light and dark) and his employment of tenebrism, where dramatic chiaroscuro becomes a dominant and highly effective stylistic device. One look at his *Conversion of St Paul* and the *Crucifixion of St Peter* (1600–01), both in Rome's Chiesa di Santa Maria del Popolo, or his *Le sette opere di Misericordia* (The Seven Acts of Mercy) in Naples' Pio Monte della Misericordia, and the raw emotional intensity of his work becomes clear.

This creative intensity was reflected in the artist's life. Described by the writer Stendhal as a 'great painter [and] a wicked man', Caravaggio fled to Naples in 1606 after killing a man in a street fight in Rome. Although his sojourn in Naples lasted only a year, it had an electrifying effect on the city's younger artists. Among these artists was Giuseppe (or Jusepe) de Ribera (1591–1652), an aggressive, bullying Spaniard whose *capo lavoro* (masterpiece), the *Pietà*, hangs in the Museo Nazionale di San Martino in Naples. Along with the Greek artist Belisiano Crenzio and Naples-born painter Giovanni Battista Caracciolo (known as Battistello), Ribera formed a cabal to stamp out any potential competition. Merciless in the extreme, they shied from nothing in order to get their way. Ribera reputedly won a commission for the Cappella del Tesoro in the Duomo by poisoning his rival Domenichino (1581–1641) and wounding the assistant of a second competitor, Guido Reni (1575–1642). Much to the relief of other nerve-racked artists, the cabal eventually broke up when Caracciolo died in 1642.

North of Rome, Annibale Caracci (1560–1609) was the major artist of the baroque Bolognese school. With his painter brother Agostino he worked in Bologna, Parma and Venice before moving to Rome to work for Cardinal Odoardo Farnese. In works such as his magnificent frescoes of mythological subjects in Rome's Palazzo Farnese, he employed innovative illusionistic elements that would prove inspirational to later baroque painters such as Cortona, Pozzo and Gaulli. However, Caracci never let the illusionism and energy of his works dominate the subject matter, as these later painters did. Inspired by Michelangelo and Raphael, he continued the Renaissance penchant for idealising and 'beautifying' nature.

Arguably the best known of all baroque artists was the sculptor Gian Lorenzo Bernini (1598–1680), who used works of religious art such as his *Ecstasy of St Theresa* in Rome's Chiesa di Santa Maria della Vittoria to arouse feelings of exaltation and mystic transport. In this and many other works he achieved an extraordinary intensity of facial expression and a totally radical handling of draperies. Instead of letting these fall in dignified folds in the approved classical manner, he made them writhe and whirl to intensify the effect of excitement and energy.

While creative boundary pushing was obviously at play, the baroque was also driven by the Counter-Reformation, with much of the work commissioned in an attempt to keep hearts and minds from the clutches of the Protestant church. Baroque artists were early adopters of the sex sells mantra, depicting Catholic spirituality, rather ironically, through worldly joy, exuberant decoration and uninhibited sensuality.

The New Italy
Discontent at years of foreign rule – first under Napoleon and then under the Austrians – may have been good for political and philosophical thinkers, but there was little innovation in art. The most notable product of this time was, ironically, the painting and engraving of views, most notably in Venice, to meet the demand of European travellers wanting Grand Tour souvenirs. The best-known painters of this school are Francesco Guardi (1712–93) and Giovanni Antonio Canaletto (1697–1768).

WHO'S WHO IN RENAISSANCE & BAROQUE ART
•••

Giotto di Bondone (c 1266–1337) Said to have ushered in the Renaissance; two masterworks: the Cappella degli Scrovegni (1304–06) in Padua and the upper church (1306–11) in Assisi.

Donatello (c 1382–1466) Florentine born and bred; his *David* (c 1440–50) in the collection of the Museo del Bargello in Florence was the first free-standing nude sculpture produced since the classical era.

Fra' Angelico (1395–1455) Made a saint in 1982; his best-loved work is the *Annunciation* (c 1450) in the convent of the Museo di San Marco in Florence.

Sandro Botticelli (c 1444–1510) *Primavera* (c 1482) and *The Birth of Venus* (c 1485) are among the best-loved of all Italian paintings; both in the Uffizi.

Domenico Ghirlandaio (1449–94) A top Tuscan master; his frescoes include those in the Tornabuoni Chapel in Florence's Basilica di Santa Maria Novella.

Michelangelo Buonarroti (1475–1564) The big daddy of them all; everyone knows *David* (1504) in the Galleria dell'Accademia in Florence and the Sistine Chapel ceiling (1508–12) in Rome's Vatican Museums.

Raphael Sanii (1483–1520) Originally from Urbino; painted luminous Madonnas and fell in love with a baker's daughter, immortalised in his painting *La Fornarina*, in Rome's Galleria Nazionale d'Arte Antica: Palazzo Barberini.

Titian (c 1490–1576) Real name Tiziano Vecelli; seek out his *Assumption* (1516–18) in the Chiesa di Santa Maria Gloriosa dei Frari (I Frari), Venice.

Tintoretto (1518–1594) The last great painter of the Italian Renaissance, known as 'Il Furioso' for the energy he put into his work; look for his *Last Supper* in Venice's Chiesa di Santo Stefano.

Annibale Caracci (1560–1609) Bologna-born and best known for his baroque frescoes in Rome's Palazzo Farnese.

Michelangelo Merisi da Caravaggio (1573–1610) Baroque's bad boy; his most powerful work is the *St Matthew Cycle* in Rome's Chiesa di San Luigi dei Francesi.

Gian Lorenzo Bernini (1598–1680) The sculptor protégé of Cardinal Scipione Borghese; best known for his *Rape of Persephone* (1621–22) and *Apollo and Daphne* (1622–25) in Rome's Museo e Galleria Borghese.

Despite all the talk of unity, the 19th-century Italian cities remained as they had been for centuries – highly individual centres of culture with sharply contrasting ways of life. Music was the supreme art of this period and the overwhelming theme in the visual arts was one of chaste refinement.

The major artistic movement of the day was neoclassicism and its greatest Italian exponent was the sculptor Antonio Canova (1757–1822). Canova renounced movement in favour of stillness, emotion in favour of restraint and illusion in favour of simplicity. His most famous work is a daring sculpture of Paolina Bonaparte Borghese as a reclining *Venere vincitrice* (Conquering Venus), in Rome's Museo e Galleria Borghese.

Canova was the last Italian artist to win overwhelming international fame. Italian architecture, sculpture and painting had played a dominant role in the cultural life of Europe for some 400 years, but with Canova's death in 1822, this supremacy came to an end.

Modern Movements

Italy entered the turbulent days of the early 20th century still in the throes of constructing a cohesive national identity. Futurism, led by poet Filippo Tommaso Marinetti (1876–1944) and painter Umberto Boccioni (1882–1916), grew out of this sense of urgent nationalism and, as Italy's north rapidly industrialised, sought new ways to express the dynamism of the machine age. Futurists demanded a new art for a new world and denounced every attachment to the art of the past. Marinetti's *Manifesto del futurismo* (Futurist Manifesto, 1909) was reinforced by the publication of a 1910 futurist painting manifesto by Boccioni, Giacomo Balla (1871–1958), Luigi Russolo (1885–1947) and Gino Severini (1883–1966). The manifesto declared that 'Everything is in movement, everything rushes forward, everything is in constant swift change.' Boccioni's *Rissa in galleria* (Brawl in the Arcade, 1910) in the collection of Milan's Pinacoteca di Brera, clearly demonstrates the movement's fascination with frantic movement and with modern technology. After WWI, a number of the futurist painters, including Mario Sironi (1885–1961) and Carlo Carrà (1881–1966), became aligned with fascism, sharing a common philosophy of nationalism and violence. Milan's Museo del Novecento along with Trentino's Museo d'Arte Moderna e Contemporanea di Trento e Rovereto (MART) have the world's best collection of futurist works.

Paralleling futurism's bullying bluster, the metaphysical movement of Giorgio de Chirico (1888–1978) produced paintings notable for their stillness and sense of foreboding. He and Carlo Carrà depicted disconnected images from the world of dreams, often in settings of classical Italian architecture, as in the *The Red Tower* (1913), now in Venice's Peggy Guggenheim Collection. Like futurism, the movement was short lived, but held powerful attraction for the French surrealist movement in the 1920s.

As Italy's north flourished in the 1950s, so did the local art scene. Artists such as Alberto Burri (1915–95) and the Argentine-Italian Lucio Fontana (1899–1968) experimented with abstraction. Fontana's punctured canvases were characterised by *spazialismo* (spatialism) and he also experimented with 'slash paintings', perforating his canvases with actual holes or slashes and dubbing them 'art for the space age'. Burri's assemblages were made of burlap, wood, iron and plastic and were avowedly anti-traditional. *Grande sacco* (Large Sack) of 1952, housed in Rome's Galleria Nazionale d'Arte Moderna e Contemporanea, caused a major controversy when it was first exhibited.

Piero Manzoni (1933–63) created highly ironic work that questioned the nature of the art object itself, such as his canned *Artist's Shit* (1961), directly prefiguring conceptual art and earning him posthumous membership of the radical new movement of the 1960s, *Arte Povera* (Poor

---

British art critic Andrew Graham-Dixon has written three authoritative books on Italian art: *Michelangelo and the Sistine Chapel*, *Caravaggio: A Life Sacred & Profane*; and *Renaissance*, the companion book to the BBC TV series.

Exibart (www.exibart.com) and My Art Guides (http://myartguides.com) have up-to-date listings of art exhibitions throughout Italy, as well as exhibition reviews, articles and interviews.

Art). Often using simple, everyday materials in installation or performance work, artists such as Mario Merz (1925–2003), Michelangelo Pistoletto (b 1933), Giovanni Anselmo (b 1934), Luciano Fabro (1936–2007), Giulio Paolini (b 1940) and Greek-born Jannis Kounellis (b 1936) sought to make the art experience more 'real', and to attack institutional power.

The 1980s saw a return to painting and sculpture in a traditional (primarily figurative) sense. Dubbed 'Transavanguardia', this movement broke with the prevailing international focus on conceptual art and was thought by some critics to signal the death of avant-garde. The artists who were part of this movement include Sandro Chia (b 1946), Mimmo Paladino (b 1948), Enzo Cucchi (b 1949) and Francesco Clemente (b 1952).

While global interest in contemporary art and the art market has shown exponential growth over the last two decades, Italian art-world insiders bemoan the country's art scene, citing a dearth of institutional support, no real market to speak of and a backward-gazing population. That said, Italy does have a number of innovative, engaged contemporary-art champions, from museums such as Rome's MAXXI, Turin's Castello di Rivoli, Bologna's MAMbo and Museion in Bolzano. They are joined in Milan by a growing number of *fondazione* – private foundation collections, from the new Fondazione Feltrinelli to the sprawling Fondazione Prada (and its recently opened city photography gallery) and the edgy Hangar Bicocca, along with the magnificent Palazzo Grassi in Venice, and the broadly roaming Museo Ettore Fico and small but astutely curated Fondazione Sandretto Re Rebaudengo, both in Turin. Gagosian has set up a Roman gallery and Milan's dealers continue to flourish. Naples and Turin also have a small but significant number of contemporary galleries.

Due to the influence of superstar Italian curators such as Francesco Bonami and Massimiliano Gioni, Italian contemporary artists are often celebrated as much, if not more, on the international stage as at home. Italian artists to watch both at home and abroad include Rudolf Stingel (b 1956), Paolo Canevari (b 1963), Maurizio Cattelan (b 1960), Vanessa Beecroft (b 1969), Rä di Martino (b 1975), Paola Pivi (b 1971), Pietro Roccasalva (b 1970), Francesco Vezzoli (b 1971) and Venice Biennale 2017 poster boy, Giorgio Andreotta Calò (b 1979) – variously working in painting, sculpture, photography, installation, video and performance.

Architecture

Italian architecture has an enduring obsession with the 'classical', a formula that pleases the eye and makes the soul soar. The Greeks, who established the style, employed it in the southern cities they colonised; the Romans refined and embellished it; Italian Renaissance architects rediscovered and tweaked it; and the Fascist architects of the 1930s returned to it in their powerful modernist buildings. Even today, architects such as Richard Meier are designing buildings in Italy that clearly reference classical prototypes.

8th–3rd Century BC Magna Graecia

Greek colonisers grace southern Italy with Stoic temples, sweeping amphitheatres and elegant sculptures that later influence their Roman successors.

6th Century BC– 4th Century AD Roman

Epic roads and aqueducts spread from Rome, alongside proud basilicas, colonnaded markets, sprawling thermal baths and frescoed villas.

4th–6th Century Byzantine

Newly Christian and based in Constantinople, the Roman Empire turns its attention to the construction of churches with exotic, Eastern mosaics and domes.

8th–12th Century Romanesque

Attention turns from height to the horizontal lines of a building. Churches are designed with a stand-alone bell tower and baptistry.

13th & 14th Century Gothic

Northern European Gothic gets an Italian makeover, from the Arabesque spice of Venice's Cá d'Oro to the Romanesque flavour of Siena's cathedral.

Late 14th–15th Century Early Renaissance

Filippo Brunelleschi's elegant dome graces the Duomo in Florence, heralding a return to classicism and a bold new era of humanist thinking and rational, elegant design.

CAPITAL SCANDALS: CONTROVERSIAL ART IN ROME

The Last Judgment (1537–41), Michelangelo There were more than just arms and legs dangling from Michelangelo's Sistine Chapel fresco in Rome's Vatican Museums. The depiction of full-frontal nudity on the chapel's altar horrified Catholic Counter-Reformation critics. No doubt Michelangelo turned in his grave when the offending bits were covered up.

Madonna and Child with St Anne (1605–06), Caravaggio St Anne looks more 'beggar woman' than 'beatified grandmother', but it's Mary who made the faithful blush on Caravaggio's canvas, her propped-up cleavage a little too 'flesh-and-bone' for the mother of God. The boxed-up scene was too much for the artist's client, who offered a 'Grazie, but no grazie'. The painting now hangs in Rome's Museo e Galleria Borghese.

St Matthew and the Angel (1602), Caravaggio In the original version, personal space (or the sheer lack of it) was the main problem for Caravaggio's client Cardinal del Monte. It features a sensual, handsome angel snuggling up to St Matthew – exactly what kind of inspiration the winged visitor was offering the saint was anybody's guess. And so Caravaggio went back to his easel, producing the prime-time version now gracing the Chiesa di San Luigi dei Francesi in Rome.

Conquering Venus (1805–08), Antonio Canova When asked whether she minded posing nude, Paolina Bonaparte Borghese provocatively replied 'Why should I?'. Given her well-known infidelities, this marble depiction of Napoleon's wayward sister as the Roman goddess of love merely confirmed her salacious reputation. This fact was not lost on her husband, Italian prince Camillo Borghese, who forbade the sculpture from leaving their home. You'll find it at the Museo e Galleria Borghese.

Classical

Only one word describes the buildings of ancient Italy: monumental. The Romans built an empire the size of which had never before been seen and went on to adorn it with buildings cut from the same pattern. From Verona's Roman Arena to Pozzuoli's Anfiteatro Flavio, giant stadiums rose above skylines. Spa centres like Rome's Terme di Caracalla were veritable cities of indulgence, boasting everything from giant marble-clad pools to gymnasiums and libraries. Aqueducts like those below Naples provided fresh water to thousands, while temples such as Pompeii's Tempio di Apollo provided the faithful with awe-inspiring centres of worship.

Having learned a few valuable lessons from the Greeks, the Romans refined architecture to such a degree that their building techniques, designs and mastery of harmonious proportion underpin much of the world's architecture and urban design to this day.

And though the Greeks invented the architectural orders (Doric, Ionic and Corinthian), it was the Romans who employed them in bravura performances. Consider Rome's Colosseum, with its ground tier of Doric, middle tier of Ionic and penultimate tier of Corinthian columns. The Romans were dab hands at temple architecture too. Just witness Rome's exquisitely proportioned Pantheon, a temple whose huge but seemingly unsupported dome showcases the Roman invention of concrete, an ingredient as essential to the modern construction industry as Ferrari is to the F1 circuit.

Byzantine

After Constantine became Christianity's star convert, the empire's architects and builders turned their talents to the design and construction of churches. The emperor commissioned a number of such buildings in Rome, but he also expanded his sphere of influence east, to Constantinople in Byzantium. His successors in Constantinople, most notably Justinian and his wife, Theodora, went on to build churches in the style that became known as Byzantine. Brick buildings built on the Roman basilican plan but with domes, they had sober exteriors that formed a stark contrast to their magnificent, mosaic-encrusted interiors. Finding its way back to Italy in the mid-6th century, the style expressed itself on a grand scale in Venice's Basilica di San Marco, as well as more modestly in buildings like the Chiesa di San Pietro in Otranto, Puglia. The true stars of Italy's Byzantine scene, however, are the Basilica di San Vitale in Ravenna and the Basilica di Sant'Apollinare in nearby Classe, both built on a cruciform plan.

Romanesque

The next development in ecclesiastical architecture in Italy came from Europe. The European Romanesque style became momentarily popular in four regional forms the Lombard, Pisan, Florentine and Sicilian Norman. All displayed an emphasis on width and the horizontal lines of a building rather than height, and featured churches where the bell tower (*campanile*) and baptistry (*battistero*) were separate to the church.

The use of alternating white and green marble defined the facades of the Florentine and Pisan styles, as seen in iconic buildings like Florence's Basilica di Santa Maria Novella and Duomo baptistry, as well as in Pisa's cathedral and baptistry.

The Lombard style featured elaborately carved facades and exterior decoration featuring bands and arches. Among its finest examples are the Lombard cathedral in Modena, Pavia's Basilica di San Michele and Brescia's unusually shaped Duomo Vecchio.

Down south, the Sicilian Norman style blended Norman, Saracen and Byzantine influences, from marble columns to Islamic-inspired pointed arches to glass tesserae detailing. One of the greatest examples of the form is the Cattedrale di Monreale, located just outside Palermo.

Gothic

The Italians didn't wholeheartedly embrace the Gothic: its verticality, flying buttresses, grotesque gargoyles and over-the-top decoration were just too far from the classical ideal that seems to be integral to the Italian psyche. The local version was generally much more restrained, a style beautifully exemplified by Naples' simple, elegant Basilica di San Lorenzo Maggiore. There were, of course, exceptions. The Venetians used the style in grand *palazzi* (mansions) such as the Ca' d'Oro and on the facades of high-profile public buildings like the Palazzo Ducale. The Milanese employed it in their flamboyant Duomo, and the Sienese came up with a distinctive melange in Siena's beautiful cathedral.

Baroque

Unlike the gradual, organic spread of the styles that preceded it, Renaissance architecture's adoption was a highly conscious and academic affair, helped along by

---

15th & 16th Century High Renaissance

Rome ousts Florence from its status as the centre of the Renaissance, its newly created wonders including Il Tempietto and St Peter's Basilica.

Late 16th–Early 18th Century Baroque

Renaissance restraint gives way to theatrical flourishes and sensual curves as the Catholic Church uses spectacle to upstage the Protestant movement.

Mid-18th–Late 19th Century Neoclassical

Archaeologists rediscover the glories of Pompeii and Herculaneum and architects pay tribute in creations like Vicenza's La Rotonda and Naples' Villa Pignatelli.

19th Century Industrial

A newly unified Italy fuses industrial technology, consumer culture and ecclesial traditions in Milan's cathedral-like Galleria Vittorio Emanuele II and Naples' Galleria Umberto I.

Late 19th–Early 20th Century Liberty

Italy's art nouveau ditches classical linearity for whimsical curves and organic motifs.

Early–Mid-20th Century Modernism

Italian modernism takes the form of futurism (technology-obsessed and anti-historical) and rationalism (seeking a middle ground between a machine-driven utopia and Fascism's fetish for classicism).

Architectural Wonders

Italy is Europe's architectural overachiever, bursting at its elegant seams with triumphant temples, brooding castles and dazzling basilicas. If you can't see it all in one mere lifetime, why not start with five of the best?

LEUCHEN66/SHUTTERSTOCK ©

Duomo, Milan

A forest of petrified pinnacles and fantastical beasts, Italy's ethereal Gothic glory (p243) is pure Milan: a product of centuries of pillaging, trend spotting, one-upmanship and mercantile ambition. Head to the top for a peek at the Alps.

Duomo, Florence

Florence's most famous landmark (p478) is more than a monumental spiritual masterpiece. It's a living, breathing testament to the explosion of creativity, artistry, ambition and wealth that would define Renaissance Florence.

Piazza dei Miracoli, Pisa

Pisa (p560) promises a threesome you won't forget: the Duomo, the Battistero and the infamous Leaning Tower. Together they make up a perfect Romanesque trio, artfully arranged like objets d'art on a giant green coffee table.

Colosseum, Rome

Almost 2000 years on, Rome's mighty ancient stadium (p70) still has the X factor. Once the domain of gladiatorial battles and ravenous wild beasts, its 50,000-seat magnitude radiates all the vanity and ingenuity of a once-glorious, intercontinental empire.

Basilica di San Marco, Venice

It's a case of East–West fusion at this Byzantine beauty (p340), founded in AD 829 and rebuilt twice since. Awash with glittering mosaics and home to the remains of Venice's patron saint, its layering of eras reflects the city's own worldly pedigree.

2

1. Duomo (p243), Milan 2. Duomo (p478), Florence
3. Colosseum (p70), Rome 4. Leaning Tower (p560), Pisa

4

The Italian equivalent of French Impressionism was the Macchiaioli movement based in Florence. Its major artists were Telemaco Signorini (1835–1901) and Giovanni Fattori (1825–1908). See their socially engaged and light-infused work in the Palazzo Pitti's Galleria d'Arte Moderna in Florence.

the invention of the printing press. The Florentine Filippo Brunelleschi and the Venetian Andrea Palladio spread a doctrine of harmonic geometry and proportion, drawing on classical Roman principles.

This insistence on restraint and purity was sure to lead to a backlash, and it's no surprise that the next major architectural movement in Italy was noteworthy for its exuberant – some would say decadent – form. The baroque took its name from the Portuguese word *barroco,* used by fishermen to denote a misshapen pearl. Compared to the pure classical lines of Renaissance buildings, its output could indeed be described as 'misshapen' – Andrea Palma's facade of Syracuse's cathedral, Guarino Guarini's Palazzo Carignano in Turin, and Gian Lorenzo Bernini's baldachin in St Peter's in Rome are dramatic, curvaceous and downright sexy structures that bear little similarity to the classical ideal.

The baroque's show-stopping qualities were not lost on the Catholic Church. Threatened by the burgeoning Reformation to the north of the Alps, the Church commissioned a battalion of grandiose churches, palaces and art to dazzle the masses and reaffirm its authority. Rome soon became a showcase of this baroque exuberance, its impressive new statements including Giacomo della Porta's Chiesa del Gesù. Commissioned to celebrate the newly founded Jesuit order, the church's hallucinatory swirl of frescoes and gilded interiors was produced by baroque greats such as Battista Gaulli (aka Il Baciccio), Andrea Pozzo and Pietro da Cortona.

Even more prolific was Gian Lorenzo Bernini, who expressed the popes' claim to power with his sweeping new design of St Peter's Square, its colonnaded arms 'embracing' the faithful with a majesty that still moves visitors today. Yet not everyone was singing Bernini's praise, especially the artist's bitter rival, Francesco Borromini (1599–1667). Reclusive and tortured, Borromini looked down on his ebullient contemporary's lack of architectural training and formal stone-carving technique. No love was lost: Bernini believed Borromini 'had been sent to destroy architecture'. Centuries on, the rivalry lives on in the works they left behind, from Borromini's Chiesa di San Carlo alle Quattro Fontane and Bernini's neighbouring Chiesa di Sant'Andrea al Quirinale to their back-to-back creations in Piazza Navona.

For a Blast of Baroque

....

Lecce, Puglia

....

Noto, Sicily

....

Rome, Lazio

....

Naples, Campania

....

Catania, Sicily

Glowing in the wealth of its Spanish rulers, 16th-century Naples also drew driven, talented architects and artists in search of commissions and fame. For many of Naples' baroque architects, however, the saying 'it's what's inside that counts' had a particularly strong resonance. Due in part to the city's notorious high density and lack of show-off piazzas, many invested less time on adorning hard-to-see facades and more on lavishing interiors. The exterior of churches like the Chiesa e Chiostro di San Gregorio Armeno gives little indication of the opulence inside, from cheeky cherubs and gilded ceilings to polychromatic marble walls and floors. The undisputed meister of this marble work form was Cosimo Fanzago, whose pièce de résistance is the church inside the Museo Nazionale di San Martino in Naples – a mesmerising kaleidoscope of inlaid colours and patterns.

Considering the Neapolitans' weakness for all things baroque, it's not surprising that the Italian baroque's grand finale would come in the form of the Palazzo Reale in Caserta, a 1200-room royal palace designed by Neapolitan architect Luigi Vanvitelli to upstage France's Versailles.

The Industrial & the Rational

Upstaged by political and social upheaval, architecture took a back seat in 19th-century Italy. One of the few movements of note stemmed directly from the Industrial Revolution and saw the application of industrial innovations in glass and metal to building design. Two monumental examples of the form are Galleria Vittorio Emanuele II in Milan and its southern sibling Galleria Umberto I in Naples.

By century's end, the art nouveau craze sweeping Europe inspired an Italian version, called *lo stile floreale* or 'Liberty'. It was notable for being more extravagant than most, evidenced in Giuseppe Sommaruga's Casa Castiglione (1903), a large block of flats at Corso Venezia 47 in Milan.

Italy's take on European modernism was rationalism, which strove to create an indigenous style that would fuse classical ideals with the charged industrial-age fantasies of the futurists. Its founding group was Gruppo 7, seven architects inspired by the Bauhaus; their most significant member, Giuseppe Terragni, designed the 1936 Casa del Fascio (now called Casa del Popolo) in Como. MIAR (Movimento Italiano per l'Architettura Razionale, the Italian Movement for Rational Architecture), a broader umbrella organisation, was led by Adalberto Libera, the influential architect best known for his Palazzo dei Congressi in EUR, a 20th-century suburb of Rome. EUR's most iconic building is the Palazzo della Civiltà del Lavoro (Palace of the Workers), designed by Giovanni Guerrini, Ernesto Bruno La Padula and Mario Romano, its arches and gleaming travertine skin graphically referencing the Colosseum and ancient Rome's glory. With most of these commissions at the behest of Mussolini's government, rationalism is often known simply as 'Fascist Architecture', although the architects' uncompromising modernism eventually fell out of favour as the regime turned to a theatrical pastiche of classical styles. A rare example of rationalism on a domestic scale (and, rarer still, one that is open to the public) is Piero Portaluppi's Villa Necchi in Milan.

Into the Future

Italy's post-war boom may have driven an internationally acclaimed and deliciously cutting-edge design industry, but this was not reflected in its built environment. One of the few high points came in 1956, when architect Giò Ponti and engineer Pier Luigi Nervi designed Milan's slender Pirelli Tower. Ponti was the highly influential founding editor of the international architecture and design magazine *Domus*, which had begun publication in 1928; Nervi's innovations in reinforced concrete changed the face of modern architecture.

Mid–Late 20th Century Modern

Industrialised and economically booming, mid-century Italy shows off its wealth in commercial projects like Giò Ponti's slim-lined Pirelli skyscraper.

21st Century Contemporary

Italian architecture gets its groove back with the international success of starchitects like Renzo Piano, Massimiliano Fuksas and Gae Aulenti.

TOP FIVE: ARCHITECTS

Filippo Brunelleschi (1377–1446) Brunelleschi blazed the neoclassical trail; his dome for Florence's Duomo announcing the Renaissance's arrival.

Donato Bramante (1444–1514) After a stint as court architect in Milan, Bramante went on to design the tiny Tempietto and huge St Peter's Basilica in Rome.

Michelangelo (1475–1564) Architecture was but one of the many strings in this great man's bow; his masterworks are the dome of St Peter's Basilica and the Piazza del Campidoglio in Rome.

Andrea Palladio (1508–80) Western architecture's single-most influential figure, Palladio turned classical Roman principles into elegant northern Italian villas.

Gian Lorenzo Bernini (1598–1680) The king of the Italian baroque is best known for his work in Rome, including the magnificent baldachin, piazza and colonnades at St Peter's.

Architects such as Carlo Scarpa, Aldo Rossi and Paolo Portoghesi then took Italian architecture in different directions. Veneto-based Scarpa was well known for his organic forms, most particularly the Brion Tomb and Sanctuary at San Vito d'Altivole. Writer and architect Rossi was awarded the Pritzker Prize in 1990, and was known for both his writing (eg *The Architecture of the City* in 1966) and design work. Rome-based Paolo Portoghesi is an architect, academic and writer with a deep interest in classical architecture. His best-known Italian building is the Central Mosque (1974) in Rome, famed for its luminously beautiful interior.

Italy's most brilliant starchitect is, however, Renzo Piano, whose international projects include London's scene-stealing Shard skyscraper and the Centre Culturel Tjibaou in Nouméa, New Caledonia. At home, recent projects include Turin's rather uninteresting Intesa Sanpaolo tower (166m) and his far more bold Museo delle Scienze (MUSE) in Trento. Composed of a series of voids and volumes that seemingly float on water, its striking design echoes its dramatic mountain landscape. Further south in Rome, Piano's 2002 Auditorium Parco della Musica is considered one of his greatest achievements to date. He was also asked to help in earthquake reconstruction efforts and in developing anti-earthquake building codes. Piano's stature is so great, he was appointed as 'senator for life' in 2013.

Piano's heir apparent is Massimiliano Fuksas, whose projects are as whimsical as they are visually arresting. Take, for instance, his brand new Nuovo Centro Congressi (New Congress Center) in Rome's EUR, dubbed the 'Nuvola' (Cloud) for its 'floating', glass-encased auditorium. Other Fuksas highlights include the futuristic Milan Trade Fair Building and the San Paolo Parish Church in Foligno.

High-profile foreign architects have also shaken things up. In Venice, David Chipperfield extended the Isola di San Michele's cemetery, while Tadao Ando oversaw the city's acclaimed Punta della Dogana and Palazzo Grassi renovation. In Rome, Richard Meier divided opinion with his 2006 Ara Pacis pavilion. The first major civic building in Rome's historic centre in more than half a century, the travertine, glass and steel structure was compared to a petrol station by popular art critic Vittorio Sgarbi. A little more love was given to Zaha Hadid's bold, sinuous MAXXI art gallery in northern Rome, which earned the Iraqi-British starchitect the prestigious RIBA (Royal Institute of British Architects) Sterling prize in 2010. One of Hadid's final works, the Messner Mountain Museum Kronplatz, opened in 2016, now also graces a stunning Dolomiti site.

Meanwhile, Milan's skyline has had a 21st-century makeover, with the ambitious redevelopment of its Porta Nuova district. Home to Italy's tallest building (the 231m César Pelli–designed UniCredit tower), the project also features Stefano Boeri's Bosco Verticale (Vertical Forest), a pair of eco-conscious apartment towers covered in the equivalent of a hectare of woodland. The city's ambitious CityLife project, a commercial, residential and parkland development, revolves around three experimental skyscrapers by Zaha Hadid, Arata Isozaki and Daniel Libeskind. Hadid's low-rise housing project welcomed its first residents in 2015 and the three towers are finally complete, with Allianz staff already working in Arata Isozaki's 202m tower and Hadid's and Libeskind's opening before 2019.

Modern-Art Musts

Galleria Nazionale d'Arte Moderna e Contemporanea, Rome

....

Peggy Guggenheim Collection, Venice

....

Museo del Novecento, Milan

....

Fondazione Prada, Milan

....

Castello di Rivoli, Turin

....

MADRE, Naples

....

MAMbo, Bologna

....

Museion, Bolzano

The Italian Way of Life

Imagine you wake up tomorrow and discover you're Italian. How would life be different, and what could you discover about Italy in just one day as a local? Read on...

A Day in the Life of an Italian

Sveglia! You're woken not by an alarm but by the burble and clatter of the *caffettiera*, the ubiquitous stovetop espresso-maker. You're running late, so you bolt down your coffee scalding hot (an acquired Italian talent) and pause briefly to ensure your socks match before dashing out the door. Yet still you walk blocks out of your way to buy your morning paper from Bucharest-born Nicolae, your favourite news vendor and (as a Romanian) part of Italy's largest migrant community. You chat briefly about his new baby – you may be late, but at least you're not rude.

On your way to work you scan the headlines: another 24-hour transport strike, more coalition-government infighting and an announcement of new EU regulations on cheese. Outrageous! The cheese regulations, that is; the rest is to be expected. At work, you're buried in paperwork until noon, when it's a relief to join friends for lunch and a glass of wine. Afterwards you toss back another scorching espresso at your favourite bar and find out how your barista's latest audition went – turns out you went to school with the sister of the director of the play, so you promise to put in a good word.

Back at work by 2pm, you multitask Italian-style, chatting with co-workers as you dash off work emails, text your schoolmate about the barista on your *telefonino* (mobile phone) and surreptitiously check *l'Internet* for employment listings – your work contract is due to expire soon. After a busy day like this, *aperitivi* are definitely in order, so at 6.30pm you head directly to the latest happy-hour hot spot. Your friends arrive, the decor is *molto design* and the vibe *molto fashion*, until suddenly it's time for your English class – everyone's learning it these days, if only for the slang.

By the time you finally get home, it's already 9.30pm and dinner will have to be reheated. *Peccato!* (Shame!) You eat, absent-mindedly watching the latest episode of *MasterChef Italia* while recounting your day and complaining about cheese regulations to whoever's home – no sense giving reheated pasta your undivided attention. While brushing your teeth, you dream of a vacation in Anguilla, though without a raise, it'll probably be Abruzzo again this year.

Finally you make your way to bed and check Facebook one last time; your colleague Marco seems to be acclimatising to life in Sydney. He's the third person you know who has moved to Australia in recent years. You wonder what it would be like to live in a nation so young and booming. They say hard work pays over there. Marco has already been promoted,

> There are 12 minority languages officially recognised in Italy, consisting of native languages Friulian, Ladin and Sardinian, and the languages of neighbouring countries, including French, Franco-Provençal, German, Catalan, Occitan, Slovene, Croatian, Albanian and Greek.

without the need of favours or influential contacts. Once again you entertain the thought of following in his footsteps, but then ponder the distance and start to pine for your *famiglia e amici* (family and friends). As you drift off, you console yourself in the knowledge that while it mightn't be perfect, they don't call Italy the *bel paese* (beautiful country) for nothing.

Being Italian

The People

Who are the people you'd encounter every day as an Italian? Just over 19% of your fellow citizens are smokers and around 61% drive (or are driven) to work, compared to only 3.3% who cycle. The average Italian is 44.9 years old, up 0.2 years since 2015. The percentage of Italians aged over 65 is 22.3%, the highest ratio in the European Union. This explains the septuagenarians you'll notice on parade with dogs and grandchildren in parks, affably arguing about politics in cafes, and ruthlessly dominating bocce tournaments.

You might also notice a striking absence of children. Italy's birth rate is one of the lowest in Europe; an average of 1.43 births per woman compared to 1.89 in the UK, 1.98 in Ireland and 2.07 in France.

North v South

In his film *Ricomincio da tre* (I'm Starting from Three; 1980), acting great Massimo Troisi comically tackles the problems faced by Neapolitans forced to head north for work. Punchlines aside, the film reveals Italy's north–south divide; a divide that still lingers almost 40 years on. While the north is known for its fashion empires and moneyed metropolises, Italy's south (dubbed the 'Mezzogiorno') is often spotlit for its higher unemployment, poorer infrastructure and mafia-related police raids. To many Italians, the terms *settentrionale* (northern Italian) and *meridionale* (southern Italian) remain weighed down by crude stereotypes: while the former is often considered modern, sophisticated and successful, the latter is still often seen as lazy, traditional and somewhat unrefined. From the Industrial Revolution to the 1960s, millions of southern Italians fled to the industrialised northern cities for factory jobs. Disparagingly nicknamed *terroni* (literally meaning 'of the soil'), these in-house 'immigrants' were often exposed to discriminatory attitudes from their northern cousins. Decades on, the overt discrimination may have dissipated but some prejudices remain. It's not uncommon to find northerners who resent their taxes being used to 'subsidise' the south – a sentiment that has been well exploited by the Lega Nord (Northern League) political party.

Today, people of Italian origin account for more than 40% of the population in Argentina and Uruguay, more than 10% in Brazil, more than 5% in Switzerland, the US and Venezuela, and more than 4% in Australia and Canada.

From Emigrants to Immigrants

From 1876 to 1976, Italy was a country of net emigration. With some 30 million Italian emigrants dispersed throughout Europe, the Americas and Australia, remittances from Italians abroad helped keep Italy's economy afloat during economic crises after independence and WWII.

The tables have since turned. Political and economic upheavals in the 1980s brought new arrivals from Central Europe, Latin America and North Africa, including Italy's former colonies in Tunisia, Somalia and Ethiopia. More recently, waves of Chinese and Filipino immigrants have given Italian streetscapes a Far Eastern twist. While immigrants account for just over 8% of Italy's population today, the number is growing. In 2001, the country's foreign population (a number that excludes foreign-born people who take Italian citizenship) was 1.3 million. By 2016, that number had almost quadrupled to over five million.

From a purely economic angle, these new arrivals are vital for the country's economic health. While most Italians today choose to live and work within Italy, the country's population is ageing and fewer young Italians are entering blue-collar agricultural and industrial fields. Without immigrant workers to fill the gaps, Italy would be sorely lacking in tomato sauce and shoes. From kitchen hands to hotel maids, it is often immigrants who take the low-paid service jobs that keep Italy's tourism economy afloat.

Despite this, not everyone is rolling out the welcome mat. In 2010, the shooting of an immigrant worker in the town of Rosarno, Calabria, sparked Italy's worst race riots in years. In 2013, a top-level football match between AC Milan and Roma was suspended after fans chanted racist abuse at Mario Balotelli, AC Milan's black, Italian-born striker. In 2017, Pescara midfielder Sulley Muntari walked off the field in response to racist chants during a Serie A game against Cagliari. The Ghanaian-born footballer was consequently penalised, receiving one yellow card for protesting about the abuse and another for leaving the field without following procedures. The Italian Football Federation subsequently withdrew the penalty (which equalled a one-match ban) in the face of widespread condemnation, including from the UK's Kick It Out anti-discrimination organisation.

Religion, Loosely Speaking

While almost 80% of Italians identify as Catholics, only around 15% of Italy's population regularly attends Sunday Mass. That said, the Church continues to exert considerable influence on public policy and political parties, especially those of the centre- and far-right.

But in the land of the double park, even God's rules are up for interpretation. Sure, *mamma* still serves fish on Good Friday, but while she might consult *la Madonna* for guidance, chances are she'll get a second opinion from the *maga* (fortune-teller) on channel 02. It's estimated that around 13 million Italians use the services of psychics, astrologers and fortune tellers. While the uncertainties stirred up by Italy's still-stagnant economy help drive these numbers, Italians have long been a highly superstitious bunch. From not toasting with water to not opening umbrellas inside the home, the country offers a long list of tips to keep bad luck at bay.

Superstitious beliefs are especially strong in Italy's south. Here *corni* (horn-shaped charms) adorn everything from necklines to rear-view mirrors to ward off the *malocchio* (evil eye) and devotion to local saints takes on an almost cultish edge. Every year in Naples, thousands cram into the *duomo* to witness the blood of San Gennaro miraculously liquefy in the phial that contains it. When the blood liquefies, the city breathes a sigh of relief – it symbolises another year safe from disaster. When it didn't in 1944, Mt Vesuvius erupted, and when it failed again in 1980, an earthquake struck the city that year. Coincidence? Perhaps. Yet even the most cynical Neapolitans may have wondered what the future holds when the miracle failed once more in December 2016.

It's Not What You Know...

From your day as an Italian, this much you know already: conversation is far too important to be cut short by tardiness or a mouthful of toothpaste. All that chatter isn't entirely idle, either: in Europe's most ancient, entrenched bureaucracy, social networks are essential to get things done. Putting in a good word for your barista isn't just a nice gesture, but an essential career boost. According to Italy's Ministry of Labour, over 60% of Italian firms rely on personal introductions for recruitment. Indeed,

According to the OECD's 2016 Better Life Index, 91% of Italians surveyed knew of someone they could rely on in a time of need, more than the OECD average of 88%. On a scale from 0 to 10, general life satisfaction ranked 5.8, below the OECD average of 6.5.

In 2017, Italy's Interior Ministry and the country's nine major Islamic associations signed an unprecedented agreement that would see Muslim organisations create a registry of their imams and to require them to preach in Italian. In return, the government promised to move towards officially recognising Islam in Italy.

THE ITALIAN WAY OF LIFE BEING ITALIAN

clientelismo (nepotism) is as much a part of the Italian lexicon as *caffè* (coffee) and *tasse* (taxes); a fact that is satirised in Massimiliano Bruno's film *Viva l'Italia* (2012), about a crooked, well-connected senator who secures jobs for his three children, among them a talentless TV actress with a speech impediment.

In 2016, Raffaele Cantone – president of the Autorità Nazionale Anti-corruzione (ANAC) – sparked a national debate after claiming that nepotism in Italian universities played a major role in the country's ongoing 'brain drain'. It's a sentiment echoed in a 2011 study conducted by the University of Chicago Medical Center. The study found an unusually high recurrence of the same surnames among academic staff at various Italian universities.

Currently, over 100,000 Italians leave the country annually in search of better opportunities abroad, including a growing number of people from wealthy northern regions like Lombardy and the Veneto. Despite the fact that these northern regions enjoy a high per-capita GDP, a growing number of its people believe that better employment opportunities and quality of life can be found elsewhere. The most popular destina-

FASHION FAMILY SAGAS
....

Tight as they may be, Italian families are not always examples of heart-warming domesticity. Indeed, some of Italy's most fashionable *famiglie* (families) prove that every clan has its problems, some small, some extra, extra large.

Consider the Versace bunch, fashion's favourite catwalking Calabrians. One of Italy's greatest exports, the familial dynasty was founded by Gianni, celebrity BFF and the man who single-handedly made bling chic. But not even the fashion gods could save the bearded genius, inexplicably shot dead outside his Miami mansion by serial killer Andrew Cunanan in 1997. With Gianni gone, creative control was passed to Donatella, Gianni's larger-than-life little sister. The subject of Anna Wintour's most unusual fashion memory – full-body spandex on horseback – the former coke-addled party queen flew herself to rehab on daughter Allegra's 18th birthday.

Then there are the Florentine fashion rivals, the Gucci clan. Established by Guccio Gucci in 1904, the family firm reads like a bad Brazilian soap – power struggles between Rodolfo and Aldo (Guccio's sons) in the 1950s; assault charges by Paolo (Aldo's son) against siblings Roberto and Giorgio, and cousin Maurizio Gucci, in 1982; and a major fallout between Paolo and father Aldo over the offshore siphoning of profits.

The last Gucci to run the company was Maurizio, who finally sold his share to Bahrain investment bank Investcorp in 1993 for a healthy US$170 million. Two years later, Maurizio was dead, gunned down outside his Milan office on the order of ex-wife, Patrizia Reggiani. Not only had Reggiani failed to forgive her then ex-husband's infidelity, she was far from impressed with her US$500,000 annual allowance. After all, this was the woman who famously quipped that she'd rather weep in a Rolls Royce than be happy on a bicycle. Offered parole in 2011 from Milan's San Vittore prison on condition of finding employment, Reggiani stayed true to form, stating: 'I've never worked a day in my life; I'm certainly not going to start now'. Despite the now-infamous quip, fashion's 'black widow' did find herself a gig while on day release, working part-time in a Milanese jewellery store. Reggiani's most famous accessory while strutting Milan's upmarket streets was a live macaw, perched on her shoulder.

Having served only 18 years of her 26-year sentence, Reggiani was released early from custody in late 2016 for good behaviour. The widow's lucky streak continued in 2017 when an appeals court in Milan ruled that despite her conviction, Gucci's ex-wife remained entitled to an annual allowance of just over €1 million, a deal agreed to by Maurizio in 1993. The court also ruled that Reggiani was owed over €18 million in back payments accrued during her time behind bars. No doubt the windfall will fuel Reggiani's infamous spending, which reputedly includes €10,000 a month on orchids.

tions for Italian expats are Germany, the UK, Switzerland and France, with almost 70% of departing Italians remaining in Europe. The most popular non-European destination is North America.

Hotel Mamma

If you're between the ages of 18 and 34, there's a 67% chance that's not a roommate in the kitchen making your morning coffee: it's mum or dad. The number of young Italian adults living at home is almost 20% higher than the European average, with only Slovakia claiming more young adults slumming it under their parents' roof.

This is not because Italy is a nation of pampered *bamboccioni* (big babies) – at least, not entirely. With a general unemployment rate of 11.7% and a youth unemployment rate hovering around 35% in mid-2017, it's no wonder that so many refuse to cut those apron strings. Yet high unemployment is only part of the picture. In general, Italians tend to graduate later than most Europeans. Once they do graduate, many end up in low-paying jobs or voluntary internships. It's a reality that has coined the term *milleuristi* to describe the many young, qualified Italian adults living on a paltry *mille euro* (€1000) or less a month.

While Italy's family-based social fabric provides a protective buffer for many during these challenging economic times, inter-generational solidarity has always been the basis of the Italian family. According to the time-honoured Italian social contract, you'd probably live with your parents until you start a career and a family of your own. Then after a suitable grace period for success and romance – a couple of years should do the trick – your parents might move in with you to look after your kids, and be looked after in turn.

As for those who don't live with family members, chances are they're still a quick stroll away, with over 50% living within a 30-minute walk of close relatives. All this considered, it's hardly surprising to hear that famous mobile phone chorus at evening rush hour: *'Mamma, butta la pasta!'* (Mum, put the pasta in the water!).

What it Feels Like for a Girl

It might score straight As in fashion, food and design, but Italy's performance in the gender-equality stakes leaves much room for improvement. Despite the fact that many of Italy's current cabinet ministers are women – a conscious effort on the part of former prime minister Matteo Renzi to redress the country's male-dominated parliament – sexism remains deeply entrenched in Italian society.

According to the European Commission's *2017 Report on Equality Between Women and Men in the EU*, only 52% of Italian women are in the workforce, compared to 80% in Sweden, 75% in Denmark and 66% in France. On average, Italian women earn about 33% less than their male counterparts. And though successful Italian businesswomen do exist – among them Poste Italiane chairperson Bianca Maria Farina and Eni chairperson Emma Marcegaglia – almost 95% of public company board members in Italy remain male, and of these, approximately 80% of them are older than 55.

Italian women fare no better on the domestic front. OECD figures reveal that Italian men spend 103 minutes per day cooking, cleaning or caring, less than a third as long as Italian women, who spend an average of 315 minutes per day on what the OECD labels unpaid work.

Italian Passions

Co-ordinated wardrobes, strong espresso and general admiration are not the only things that make Italian hearts sing. And while Italian passions are wide and varied, few define Italy like football and opera.

The World Economic Forum's 2016 Global Gender Gap Report ranked Italy 50th worldwide in terms of overall gender equality, down from 41st position in 2015. It ranked 117th in female economic participation and opportunity, 56th in educational attainment and 25th in political empowerment.

Italian Style Icons

Bialetti (coffee-maker)

Cinzano (vermouth)

Acqua di Parma (cologne)

Piaggio (Vespa)

Olivetti 'Valentine' (typewriter)

Better Living by Design

As an Italian, you actually did your co-workers a favour by being late to the office to give yourself a final once-over in the mirror. Unless you want your fellow employees to avert their gaze in dumbstruck horror, your socks had better match. The tram can wait as you *fare la bella figura* (cut a fine figure).

Italians have strong opinions about aesthetics and aren't afraid to share them. A common refrain is *Che brutta!* (How hideous!), which may strike visitors as tactless. But consider it from an Italian point of view – everyone is rooting for you to look good, so who are you to disappoint? The shop assistant who tells you with brutal honesty that yellow is *not* your colour is doing a public service, and will consider it a personal triumph to see you outfitted in orange instead.

If it's a gift, you must allow 10 minutes for the sales clerk to *fa un bel pacchetto,* wrapping your purchase with string and an artfully placed sticker. This is the epitome of *la bella figura* – the sales clerk wants you to look good by giving a good gift. When you do, everyone basks in the glow of *la bella figura:* you as the gracious gift-giver and the sales clerk as savvy gift consultant, not to mention the flushed and duly honoured recipient.

As a national obsession, *la bella figura* gives Italy its undeniable edge in design, cuisine, art and architecture. Though the country could get by on its striking good looks, Italy is ever mindful of delightful details. They are everywhere you look and many places you don't: the intricately carved cathedral spire only the bell-ringer could fully appreciate, the toy duck hidden inside your chocolate *uova di pasqua* (Easter egg), the absinthe-green silk lining inside a sober grey suit sleeve. Attention to such details earns you instant admiration in Italy – and an admission that, sometimes, non-Italians do have style.

Calcio (Football): Italy's Other Religion

Catholicism may be your official faith, but as an Italian your true religion is likely to be *calcio* (football). On any given weekend from September to May, chances are that you and your fellow *tifosi* (football fans) are at the *stadio* (stadium), glued to the TV or checking the score on your mobile phone. Come Monday, you'll be dissecting the match by the office water cooler.

Like politics and fashion, football is in the very DNA of Italian culture. Indeed, they sometimes even converge. Silvio Berlusconi first found fame as the owner of AC Milan and cleverly named his political party after a well-worn football chant. Fashion royalty Dolce & Gabbana declared football players 'the new male icons', using five of Italy's hottest on-field stars to launch its 2010 underwear collection. Decades earlier, 1960s singer Rita Pavone topped the charts with 'La partita di pallone' (The Football Match), in which the frustrated pop princess laments being left alone by her lover, who has gone to watch a football match. It's no coincidence that in Italian *tifoso* means both 'football fan' and 'typhus patient'. When the ball ricochets off the post and slips fatefully through the goalie's hands, when half the stadium is swearing while the other half is euphorically shouting *Goooooooooooooooal!,* 'fever pitch' is the term that comes to mind.

Nothing quite stirs Italian blood like a good (or bad) game. Nine months after Italy's 2006 World Cup victory against France, hospitals in northern Italy reported a baby boom. In February the following year, rioting at a Palermo-Catania match in Catania left one policeman dead and around 100 injured. Blamed on the Ultras – a minority group of hard-core football fans – the violence shocked both Italy and the world,

Italy's culture of corruption and *calcio* (football) is captured in *The Dark Heart of Italy,* in which English expat author Tobias Jones wryly observes, 'Footballers or referees are forgiven nothing; politicians are forgiven everything.'

MUSIC FOR THE MASSES

Most of the music you'll hear booming out of Italian cafes to inspire sidewalk singalongs is Italian *musica leggera* (popular music), a term covering home-grown rock, jazz, folk, hip hop and pop ballads. The scene's annual highlight is the Sanremo Music Festival (held at San Remo's Teatro Ariston and televised on RAI1), a Eurovision-style song comp responsible for launching the careers of chart-topping contemporary acts like Eros Ramazzotti, Giorgia, Laura Pausini and, more recently, singer-songwriter Marco Mengoni. In 2013, Mengoni won Sanremo for his ballad 'L'essenziale', using the same song later that year to represent Italy at Eurovision. Two years later, operatic pop trio Il Volo took their winning hit 'Grande amore' to Eurovision, the soaring anthem winning Italy third place. The trend was continued in 2017, when Sanremo champion Francesco Gabbani took 'Occidentale's Karma' to Europe's campy song comp. While the Italian hit only managed sixth place, it did win the competition's affiliated OGAE Award, voted by a network of over 40 Eurovision fan clubs that together make up the Organisation Générale des Amateurs de l'Eurovision (OGAE).

In the early 1960s, Sanremo helped launch the career of living music legend, Mina Mazzini. Famed for her powerful, three-octave voice and a musical versatility spanning pop, soul, blues, R&B and swing, the songstress dominated the charts throughout the 1960s and 1970s, her emancipated image and frank tunes about love and sex ruffling a few bourgeois feathers. Equally controversial was the late Fabrizio de André, an Italian Bob Dylan celebrated for his poetic lyrics, musing monotone and cutting criticism of religious hypocrisy. Sharp social observation and bittersweet sentiments also underpin the work of late singer-songwriter Pino Daniele, whose style fused Neapolitan music with blues and world music influences.

---

leading to a temporary ban of all matches in Italy and increased stadium security. A year earlier, the match-fixing 'Calciopoli' scandals resulted in revoked championship titles and temporary demotion of Serie A (top-tier national) teams, including the mighty Juventus.

Yet, the same game that divides also unites. You might be a Lazio-loathing supporter of AS Roma, but when the national *Azzurri* (The Blues) swag the World Cup, you are nothing but a heart-on-your-sleeve *italiano* (Italian). In his book *The 100 Things Everyone Needs to Know About Italy,* Australian journalist David Dale writes that Italy's 1982 World Cup win 'finally united twenty regions which, until then, had barely acknowledged that they were part of the one country.'

Opera: Let the Fat Lady Sing

At the stadium, your beloved *squadra* (team) hits the field to the roar of Verdi. OK, so you might not be first in line to see *Rigoletto* at La Fenice, but Italy's opera legacy remains a source of pride. After all, not only did you invent the art form, you gave the world some of its greatest composers and compositions. Gioachino Rossini (1792–1868) transformed Pierre Beaumarchais' *Le Barbier de Séville* (The Barber of Seville) into one of the greatest comedic operas, Giuseppe Verdi (1813–1901) produced the epic *Aida,* while Giacomo Puccini (1858–1924) delivered staples such as *Tosca, Madama Butterfly* and *Turandot.*

Lyrical, intense and dramatic – it's only natural that opera bears the 'Made in Italy' label. Track pants might be traded in for tuxedos, but Italy's opera crowds can be just as ruthless as their pitch-side counterparts. A centuries-old tradition, the dreaded *fischi* (mocking whistles) still possess a mysterious power to blast singers right off stage. In December 2006, a substitute in street clothes had to step in for Sicilian-French star tenor Roberto Alagna when his off-night aria met with vocal disapproval at Milan's legendary La Scala. Best not to get them started about musicals and 'rock opera', eh?

The word *diva* was invented for legendary sopranos such as Parma's Renata Tebaldi and Italy's adopted Greek icon Maria Callas, whose rivalry peaked when *Time* quoted Callas saying that comparing her voice to Tebaldi's was like comparing 'champagne and Coca-Cola'. Both were fixtures at La Scala, along with the wildly popular Italian tenor to whom others are still compared, Enrico Caruso. Tenor Luciano Pavarotti (1935–2007) remains beloved for attracting broader public attention to opera, while best-selling blind tenor Andrea Bocelli became a controversial crossover sensation with what critics claim are overproduced arias sung with a strained upper register. Newer generations of stars include soprano Fiorenza Cedolins, who performed a requiem for the late Pope John Paul II, recorded *Tosca* arias with Andrea Bocelli and scored encores in Puccini's iconic *La Bohème* at the Arena di Verona Festival. Younger still is celebrated tenor Francesco Meli, a regular fixture at many of the world's great opera houses. Much sadder, however, was the fate of promising tenor Salvatore Licitra. Famed for stepping in for Pavarotti on his final show at New York's Metropolitan Opera, the 43-year-old died tragically after a motorcycle accident in 2011.

In 2017, Genoa airport introduced a partial relaxation of its restrictions on liquids allowed in cabin luggage. Tourists flying out of the airport are now able to carry up to 500g of pesto on board. The exception is only made for the region's famous basil and pine-nut sauce.

Italy on Page & Screen

From ancient Virgil to modern-day Eco, Italy's literary canon is awash with world-renowned scribes. The nation's film stock is equally robust, packed with visionary directors, iconic stars and that trademark Italian pathos.

Literature

Latin Classics

Roman epic poet Virgil (aka Vergilius) spent 11 years and 12 books tracking the outbound adventures and inner turmoil of Trojan hero Aeneas, from the fall of Troy to the founding of Rome. Virgil died in 19 BC with just 60 lines to go in his *Aeneid*, a kind of sequel to Greek epic poet Homer's *Iliad* and *Odyssey*. As Virgil himself observed: 'Time flies'.

Fellow Roman Ovid (Ovidius) was also skilled at telling a ripping tale. His *Metamorphoses* chronicled civilisation from murky mythological beginnings to Julius Caesar, and his how-to seduction manual *Ars amatoria* ('The Art of Love') inspired countless Casanovas. Despite his popularity, Ovid was banished to the ancient Black Sea settlement of Tomis by Augustus in 8 AD. The emperor's motive remains a mystery to this day, with theories ranging from Ovid's association with people opposed to his rule, to the poet's knowledge of a supposedly incestuous relationship between Augustus and his daughter or granddaughter.

Timeless Poets

Some literature scholars claim that Shakespeare stole his best lines and plot points from earlier Italian playwrights and poets. Debatable though this may be, the Bard certainly had stiff competition from 13th-century Dante Alighieri as the world's finest romancer. Dante broke with tradition in *La divina commedia* (The Divine Comedy; c 1307–21) by using the familiar Italian, not the formal Latin, to describe travelling through the circles of hell in search of his beloved Beatrice. Petrarch (aka Francesco Petrarca) added woo to Italian woo with his eponymous sonnets, applying a strict structure of rhythm and rhyme to romance the idealised Laura.

If sonnets aren't to your taste, try 1975 Nobel laureate Eugenio Montale, who wrings poetry out of the creeping damp of everyday life, or Ungaretti, whose WWI poems hit home with a few searing syllables.

Cautionary Fables

The most universally beloved Italian fabulist is Italo Calvino, whose titular character in *Il barone rampante* (The Baron in the Trees; 1957) takes to the treetops in a seemingly capricious act of rebellion that makes others rethink their own earthbound conventions. In Dino Buzzati's *Il deserto dei Tartari* (The Tartar Steppe; 1940), an ambitious officer posted to a mythical Italian border is besieged by boredom, thwarted expectations and disappearing youth while waiting for enemy hordes to materialise – a parable drawn from Buzzati's own dead-end newspaper job.

Over the centuries, Niccolo Machiavelli's *Il principe* (The Prince; 1532) has been referenced as a handy manual for budding autocrats, but also as a cautionary tale against unchecked 'Machiavellian' authority.

Any self-respecting Italian bookshelf features one or more Roman rhetoricians. To *fare la bella figura* (cut a fine figure) among academics, trot out a phrase from Cicero or Horace (Horatio), such as 'Where there is life there is hope' or 'Whatever advice you give, be brief'.

For Dante with a pop-culture twist, check out Sandow Birk and Marcus Sanders' satirical, slangy translation of *The Divine Comedy*, which sets *Inferno* in hellish Los Angeles traffic, *Purgatorio* in foggy San Francisco and *Paradiso* in New York.

Crime Pays

Italy's most coveted literary prize, the Premio Strega, is awarded annually to a work of Italian prose fiction. Its youngest recipient to date is physicist-cum-writer Paolo Giordano, who, at 26, won for his debut novel *La solitudine dei numeri primi* (The Solitude of Prime Numbers; 2008).

Crime fiction and *gialli* (mysteries) dominate Italy's best-seller list, and one of its finest writers is Gianrico Carofiglio, the former head of Bari's anti-Mafia squad. Carofiglio's novels include the award-winning *Testimone inconsapevole* (Involuntary Witness; 2002), which introduces the shady underworld of Bari's hinterland. The scribe's latest novel is *L'estate fredda* (The Cold Summer; 2016), a hard-hitting tale set against the especially gruesome mafia violence that marked 1992.

Art also imitates life for judge-cum-novelist Giancarlo de Cataldo, whose best-selling novel *Romanzo criminale* (Criminal Romance; 2002) spawned both a TV series and film. Another crime writer with page-to-screen success is Andrea Camilleri, his savvy Sicilian inspector Montalbano starring in capers like *Il gioco degli specchi* (Game of Mirrors; 2011).

Umberto Eco gave the genre an intellectual edge with his medieval detective tale *Il nome della rosa* (The Name of the Rose; 1980) and *Il pendolo di Foucault* (Foucault's Pendulum; 1988). In Eco's *Il cimitero di Praga* (The Prague Cemetery; 2010), historical events merge with the tale of a master killer and forger.

Historical Epics

Set during the Black Death in Florence, Boccaccio's *Decameron* (c 1350–53) has a visceral gallows humour that foreshadows Chaucer and Shakespeare. Italy's 19th-century struggle for unification parallels the story of star-crossed lovers in Alessandro Manzoni's *I promessi sposi* (The Betrothed; 1827, definitive version released 1842), and causes an identity crisis among Sicilian nobility in Giuseppe Tomasi di Lampedusa's *Il gattopardo* (The Leopard; published posthumously in 1958).

Wartime survival strategies are chronicled in Elsa Morante's *La storia* (History; 1974) and in Primo Levi's autobiographical account of Auschwitz in *Se questo è un uomo* (If This Is a Man; 1947). WWII is the uninvited guest in *Il giardino dei Finzi-Contini* (The Garden of the Finzi-Continis; 1962), Giorgio Bassani's tale of a crush on a girl whose aristocratic Jewish family attempts to disregard the rising tide of anti-Semitism. In Margaret Mazzantini's *Venuto al mondo* (Twice Born; 2008), it's the Bosnian War that forms the backdrop to a powerful tale of motherhood and loss.

Social Realism

Italy's north–south divide is the focus of Luca Miniero's comedy smash *Benvenuti al Sud* (Welcome to the South; 2010). An adaptation of the French film *Bienvenue chez les Ch'tis* (Welcome to the Sticks; 2008), it tells the tale of a northern postmaster posted to a small Campanian town, bullet-proof vest in tow.

Italy has always been its own sharpest critic and several 20th-century Italian authors captured their own troubling circumstances with unflinching accuracy. Grazia Deledda's *Cosima* (1937) is her fictionalised memoir of coming of age and into her own as a writer in rural Sardinia. Deledda became one of the first women to win the Nobel Prize for Literature (1926) and set the tone for such bittersweet recollections of rural life as Carlo Levi's *Cristo si è fermato a Eboli* (Christ Stopped at Eboli; 1945).

Jealousy, divorce and parental failings are grappled with by pseudonymous author Elena Ferrante in her brutally honest *I giorni dell'abbandono* (The Days of Abandonment; 2002). In 2014, Ferrante published *Storia della bambina perduta* (The Story of the Lost Child), the final installment in her so-called Neapolitan series, four novels exploring the life-long friendship of two women born into a world of poverty, chaos and violence in Naples.

Confronting themes also underline Alessandro Pipero's *Persecuzione* (Persecution; 2010), which sees an esteemed oncologist accused of child molestation. Its sequel, *Inseparabili* (2012), won the 2012 Premio Strega literature prize.

Cinema

Neorealist Grit

Out of the smouldering ruins of WWII emerged unflinching tales of woe, including Roberto Rossellini's *Roma, città aperta* (Rome: Open City; 1945), a story of love, betrayal and resistance in Nazi-occupied Rome. In Vittorio De Sica's Academy-awarded *Ladri di biciclette* (The Bicycle Thieves; 1948), a doomed father attempts to provide for his son without resorting to crime in war-ravaged Rome, while Pier Paolo Pasolini's *Mamma Roma* (1962) revolves around an ageing prostitute trying to make an honest living for herself and her deadbeat son. More recently, Gianfranco Rosi's Oscar-nominated documentary *Fuocoammare* (Fire at Sea; 2016) has drawn comparisons to the neorealist movement in its confronting, moving exploration of the European refugee crisis as played out on the island of Lampedusa.

Crime & Punishment

Italy's acclaimed contemporary dramas combine the truthfulness of classic neorealism, the taut suspense of Italian thrillers and the psychological revelations of Fellini. Among the best is Matteo Garrone's brutal Camorra exposé *Gomorra* (2008). Based on Roberto Saviano's award-winning novel, the film won the Grand Prix at the 2008 Cannes Film Festival before inspiring a successful spin-off TV series.

Paolo Sorrentino's *Il divo* (2008) explores the life of former prime minister Giulio Andreotti, from his migraines to his alleged mafia ties. The entanglement of organised crime and Rome's political class is at the heart of Stefano Sollima's neo-noir *Suburra* (2015), while mafiosi also appear in the deeply poignant *Cesare deve morire* (Caesar Must Die; 2012). Directed by octogenarian brothers Paolo and Vittorio Taviani, this award-winning documentary tells the story of maximum-security prisoners preparing to stage Shakespeare's *Julius Caesar*. Italy's political and social ills drive Gabriele Mainetti's acclaimed film *Lo chiamavano Jeeg Robot* (They Call Me Jeeg; 2015), which gives Hollywood's superhero genre a gritty local twist.

Italian acting greats Sophia Loren and the late Marcello Mastroianni appeared together in 13 films, including Vittorio De Sica's classics *Ieri, oggi, domani* (Yesterday, Today, Tomorrow; 1963) and *Matrimonio all'italiana* (Marriage Italian Style; 1964). Their last on-screen union was in Robert Altman's catwalk comedy *Prêt-à-Porter* (1994).

LOCATION! LOCATION!

Italy's cities, hills and coastlines set the scene for countless celluloid classics. Top billing goes to Rome, where Bernardo Bertolucci uses the Terme di Caracalla in the oedipal *La luna* (1979), Gregory Peck gives Audrey Hepburn a fright at the Bocca della Verità in William Wyler's *Roman Holiday* (1953) and Anita Ekberg cools off in the Trevi Fountain in Federico Fellini's *La dolce vita* (The Sweet Life; 1960). Fellini's love affair with the Eternal City culminated in his silver-screen tribute, *Roma* (1972). More recent tributes include Woody Allen's romantic comedy *To Rome with Love* (2012) and Italian director Paolo Sorrentino's sumptuous, decadent *La grande bellezza* (Great Beauty; 2013).

Florence's Piazza della Signoria recalls James Ivory's *Room with a View* (1985). Further south, Siena's Piazza del Palio and Piazza della Paglietta stir fantasies of actor Daniel Craig – both featured in the 22nd James Bond instalment, *Quantum of Solace* (2008).

Venice enjoys a cameo in *The Talented Mr Ripley* (1999), in which Matt Damon and Gwyneth Paltrow also tan and toast on the Campanian islands of Procida and Ischia. Fans of *Il postino* (The Postman; 1994) will recognise Procida's pastel-hued Corricella, while on the mainland, Naples' elegant *palazzi*, fin-de-siècle cafes and tailors are flaunted in Gianluca Migliarotti's fashion documentary film *E poi c'è Napoli* (And Then There is Naples; 2014). The city also stars in Turkish-Italian director Ferzan Özpetek's much-anticipated thriller, *Napoli velata* (2018).

Further south, the cavernous landscape of Basilicata's Matera moonlights as Palestine in Mel Gibson's *Passion of the Christ* (2004).

Romance all'italiana

It's only natural that a nation of hopeless romantics should provide some of the world's most tender celluloid moments. In Michael Radford's *Il postino* (The Postman; 1994), exiled poet Pablo Neruda brings poetry and passion to a drowsy Italian isle and a misfit postman, played with heartbreaking subtlety by the late Massimo Troisi. Another classic is Giuseppe Tornatore's Oscar-winning *Nuovo cinema paradiso* (Cinema Paradiso; 1988), a bittersweet tale about a director who returns to Sicily and rediscovers his true loves: the girl next door and the movies. In Silvio Sordini's *Pane e tulipani* (Bread and Tulips; 2000), a housewife left behind at a tour-bus pit stop runs away to Venice, where she befriends an anarchist florist, an eccentric masseuse and a suicidal Icelandic waiter – and gets pursued by an amateur detective. Equally contemporary is Ferzan Özpetek's *Mine vaganti* (Loose Cannons; 2010), a situation comedy about two gay brothers and their conservative Pugliese family.

> Crueller and bloodier than their American counterparts, Italian zombie films enjoy international cult status. One of the best is director Lucio Fulci's *Zombi 2* (aka Zombie Flesh Eaters; 1979). Fulci's other gore classics include *City of the Living Dead* (1980), *The Beyond* (1981) and *The House by the Cemetery* (1981).

Spaghetti Westerns

Emerging in the mid-1960s, Italian-style Westerns had no shortage of high-noon showdowns featuring flinty characters and Ennio Morricone's terminally catchy whistled tunes (*doodle-oodle-ooh, wah wah wah...*). Top of the directorial heap was Sergio Leone, whose Western debut *Per un pugno di dollari* (A Fistful of Dollars; 1964) helped launch a young Clint Eastwood's movie career. After Leone and Clintwood teamed up again in *Il buono, il brutto, il cattivo* (The Good, the Bad, and the Ugly; 1966), it was Henry Fonda's turn in Leone's *C'era una volta il West* (Once Upon a Time in the West; 1968), a story about a revenge-seeking widow.

Tragicomedies

Italy's best comedians pinpoint the exact spot where pathos intersects with the funny bone. A group of ageing pranksters turn on one another in Mario Monicelli's *Amici miei* (My Friends; 1975), a satire reflecting Italy's own postwar midlife crisis. Midlife crisis also underscores Paolo Sorrentino's Oscar-winning *La grande bellezza* (The Great Beauty; 2013), a Fellini-style tale that evolves around Jep Gambardella, an ageing, hedonistic bachelor haunted by lost love and memories of the past.

> A one-man Abbott and Costello, Antonio de Curtis (1898–1967), aka Totò, famously depicted the Neapolitan *furbizia* (cunning). Appearing in over 100 films, including *Miseria e nobilità* (Misery and Nobility; 1954), his roles as a hustler living on nothing but his quick wits have guaranteed him cult status in Naples.

Contemporary woes feed Massimiliano Bruno's biting *Viva l'Italia* (2012), its cast of corrupt politicians and nepotists cutting close to the nation's bone. Italy is slapped equally hard by Matteo Garrone's *Reality* (2012), a darkly comic film revolving around a Neapolitan fishmonger desperately seeking fame through reality TV. The foibles of modern Italian life are also pulled into sharp focus in Paolo Genovese's *Perfetti sconosciuti* (Perfect Strangers; 2016), an award-winning comedy-drama in which three couples and a bachelor disclose each other's private text messages and phone calls in an attempt to prove they have nothing to hide.

Darkest of all, however, remains actor-director Roberto Benigni's Oscar-winning *La vita è bella* (Life is Beautiful; 1997), in which a father tries to protect his son from the brutalities of a Jewish concentration camp by pretending it's all a game.

Shock & Horror

Sunny Italy's darkest dramas deliver more style, suspense and falling bodies than Prada platform heels on a slippery Milan runway. In Michelangelo Antonioni's *Blow-Up* (1966) a swinging-'60s fashion photographer spies dark deeds unfolding in a photo of an elusive Vanessa Redgrave. Gruesome deeds unfold at a ballet school in Dario Argento's *Suspiria* (1977), while in Mario Monicelli's *Un borghese piccolo piccolo* (An Average Little Man; 1977), an ordinary man goes to extraordinary lengths for revenge. The latter stars Roman acting great Alberto Soldi in a standout example of a comedian nailing a serious role.

The Italian Table

One of the world's most revered cuisines, Italian food is a handy umbrella term for the country's cache of regional cuisines. Together they reflect Italy's extraordinary geographic and cultural diversity. The common thread between all is an indelible link between food and the locals' sense of identity. From the quality of the produce to the reverence for tradition, eating here is all about passion, pride and *godere la vita* (enjoying life).

Tutti a Tavola

'Everyone to the table!' Traffic lights are merely suggestions and queues are fine ideas in theory, but this is one command every Italian heeds without question. To disobey would be unthinkable – what, you're going to eat your pasta cold? And insult the cook? Even anarchists wouldn't dream of it. You never really know Italians until you've broken a crusty loaf of *pagnotta* with them – and once you've arrived in Italy, jump at any opportunity to do just that.

Morning Essentials

In Italy, *colazione* (breakfast) is a minimalist affair. Eggs, pancakes, ham, sausage, toast and orange juice are only likely to appear at weekend *brr-runch* (pronounced with the rolled Italian *r*), an American import popular at many trendy urban eateries. Expect to pay upwards of €20 to graze a buffet of hot dishes, cold cuts, pastries and fresh fruit, usually including your choice of coffee, juice or cocktail.

Italy's breakfast staple is *caffè* (coffee). Scalding-hot espresso, cappuccino (espresso with a dollop of foamed milk) or *caffè latte* – the hot, milky espresso beverage Starbucks mistakenly shortened to *latte*, which will get you a glass of milk in Italy. An alternative beverage is *orzo*, a slightly nutty, noncaffeinated roasted-barley beverage that looks like cocoa. With a *tazza* (cup) in one hand, use the other for that most Italian of breakfast foods – a pastry. Some especially promising options include the following:

Cornetto The Italian take on the French croissant is usually smaller, lighter, less buttery and slightly sweet, with an orange-rind glaze brushed on top. Fillings might include *cioccolato* (chocolate), *cioccolato bianco* (white chocolate), *crema* (custard) or varying flavours of *marmelata* (jam).

Crostata The breakfast tart with a dense, buttery crust is filled with your choice of fruit jam, such as *amarena* (sour cherry), *albicocca* (apricot) or *frutti di bosco* (wild berry). You may have to buy an entire tart instead of a slice, but you won't be sorry.

Doughnuts Chow down a *ciambella* (also called by its German name, *krapfen*), the fried-dough treat rolled in granulated sugar and sometimes filled with jam or custard. Join the line at kiosks and street fairs for *fritole*, fried dough studded with golden raisins and sprinkled with confectioners' sugar, and *zeppole* (also called *bignè di San Giuseppe*), chewy doughnuts filled with ricotta or *zucca* (pumpkin), rolled in sugar, and handed over in a paper cone to be devoured dangerously hot.

Viennoiserie Italy's colonisation by the Austro-Hungarian Empire in the 19th century had its upside: a vast selection of sweet buns and other rich baked goods. Standouts include cream-filled brioches and *strudel di mele,* an Italian adaptation of the traditional Viennese *apfelstrudel.*

For a comprehensive yet easy-to-use guide to Italian cooking, hunt down Marcella Hazan's award-winning *Essentials of Classic Italian Cooking* (1992), which incorporates two of her cult-status cookbooks.

Lunch & Dinner

A nation prone to perpetual motion with Vespas, Ferraris and Bianchis pauses for *pranzo* (lunch) – hence the term *la pausa* to describe the midday break. In the cities, power-lunchers settle in at their favourite *ristoranti* and *trattorie*, while in smaller towns and villages, workers often head home for a two- to three-hour midday break, devouring a hot lunch and resting up before returning to work fortified by espresso.

Where *la pausa* has been scaled back to a scandalous hour and a half, *rosticcerie* (rotisseries) or *tavole calde* (literally 'hot tables') keep the harried sated with steamy, on-the-go options like roast chicken and *supplì* (fried risotto balls with a molten mozzarella centre). Bakeries and bars are also on hand with *focaccia, panini* and *tramezzini* (triangular, stacked sandwiches made with squishy white bread) providing a satisfying bite.

Traditionally, *cena* (dinner) is lunch's lighter sibling and cries of 'Oh, I can hardly eat anything tonight' are still common after a marathon weekend lunch. 'Maybe just a bowl of pasta, a salad, some cheese and fruit...'. Don't be fooled: even if you've been invited to someone's house for a 'light dinner', wine and elastic-waisted pants are always advisable.

But while your Italian hosts may insist you devour one more ricotta-filled *cannolo*, your waiter will usually show more mercy. Despite the Italians' 'more is more' attitude to food consumption, restaurant diners are rarely obliged to order both a *primo* and *secondo,* and antipasti and dessert are strictly optional. That said, a lavish dinner at one of Italy's fine-dining hot spots, such as Modena's Osteria Francescana (p450) or Alba's Piazza Duomo (p220), is a highlight few will want to skip.

Many top-ranked restaurants open only for dinner, with a set-price *degustazione* meal that leaves the major menu decisions to your chef and frees you up to concentrate on the noble quest of conquering four to six tasting courses. *Forza e coraggio!* (Strength and courage to you!)

Italian Menu 101

The *cameriere* (waiter) leads you to your table and hands you the menu. The scent of slow-cooked *ragù* (meat and tomato sauce) lingers in the air and your stomach rumbles in anticipation. Where might this culinary encounter lead you? Order a glass of *prosecco,* unfurl that *tovagliolo* (napkin) and read on...

Antipasti (Appetisers)

The culinary equivalent of foreplay, antipasti are a good way to whet the appetite and sample a number of different dishes. Tantalising offerings on the antipasti menu may include the house bruschetta (grilled bread with a variety of toppings, from chopped tomato and garlic to black-truffle spread) or regional treats like *mozzarella di bufala* (buffalo mozzarella) or *salatini con burro d'acciughe* (pastry sticks with anchovy butter). Even if it's not on the menu, it's always worth requesting an *antipasto misto* (mixed antipasto), a platter of morsels including anything from *olive fritte* (fried olives) and *prosciutto e melone* (cured ham and cantaloupe) to *friarielli con peperoncino* (Neapolitan broccoli with chilli). At this stage, bread (and sometimes *grissini* – Turin-style breadsticks) are also deposited on the table as part of your €1 to €3 *pane e coperto* ('bread and cover' or table service).

Primo (First Course)

Starch is the star in Italian first courses, from pasta and gnocchi to risotto and polenta. You may be surprised how generous the portions are – a *mezzo piatto* (half-portion) might do the trick for kids.

Primi menus usually include ostensibly vegetarian or vegan options, such as pasta *con pesto* – the classic Ligurian basil paste with *parmigiano reggiano* (Parmesan) and pine nuts – or Sicilian *alla norma* (with

THE BIG FORK MANIFESTO

The year is 1987. McDonald's has just begun expansion into Italy and lunch outside the bun seems to be fading into fond memory. Enter Carlo Petrini and a handful of other journalists from small-town Bra, Piedmont. Determined to buck the trend, these *neo-forchettoni* ('big forks', or foodies) created a manifesto. Published in the like-minded culinary magazine *Gambero Rosso*, they declared that a meal should be judged not by its speed, but by its pure pleasure.

The organisation they founded would soon become known worldwide as Slow Food (www.slowfood.com), and its mission to reconnect artisanal producers with enthusiastic, educated consumers has taken root with around 100,000 members in over 160 countries – not to mention Slow Food *agriturismi* (farm-stay accommodation), restaurants, farms, wineries, cheesemakers and revitalised farmers' markets across Italy.

Held on even-numbered years in venues across Turin, Italy's top Slow Food event is the biennial Salone del Gusto & Terre Madre (www.salonedelgusto.com). Slow Food's global symposium, it features Slow Food producers, chefs, activists, restaurateurs, farmers, scholars, environmentalists and epicureans from around the world...not to mention the world's best finger food. Thankfully, odd years don't miss out on enlightened epicureans either, with special events such as Slow Fish (http://slowfish.slowfood.it) in Genoa and Cheese (www.cheese.slowfood.it) in Bra.

basil, eggplant, ricotta and tomato), *risotto ai porcini* (risotto with pungent, earthy porcini mushrooms) or the extravagant *risotto al Barolo* (risotto with high-end Barolo wine, though actually any good dry red will do). But even if a dish sounds vegetarian in theory, before you order you may want to ask about the stock used in that risotto or polenta, or the ingredients in that suspiciously rich tomato sauce – there may be beef, ham or ground anchovies involved.

Carnivores will rejoice in such legendary dishes as pasta *all'amatriciana* (Roman pasta with a spicy tomato sauce, *pecorino* cheese and *guanciale*, or bacon-like pigs' cheeks), *osso bucco con risotto alla milanese* (Milanese veal shank and marrow melting into saffron risotto), Tuscan speciality *pappardelle alle cinghiale* (ribbon pasta with wild boar sauce) and northern favourite *polenta col ragù* (polenta with meat sauce). Near the coasts, look for seafood variations like *risotto al nero* (risotto cooked with black squid ink), *spaghetti allo vongole* (spaghetti with clam sauce) or *pasta ai frutti di mare* (pasta with seafood).

Secondo (Second Course)

Light lunchers usually call it a day after the *primo*, but *buongustai* (gourmands) pace themselves for meat, fish or *contorni* (side dishes, such as cooked vegetables) in the second course. These options may range from the outrageous *bistecca alla fiorentina*, a 3in-thick steak served on the bone in a puddle of juice, to more modest yet equally impressive *fritto misto di mare* (mixed fried seafood), *carciofi alla romana* (Roman artichokes stuffed with mint and garlic) or *pollo in tegame con barbe* (chicken casserole with salsify).

Even if your waiter does not tell you the day's specials, follow the Italians' lead and always ask *'Cosa c'è di buono oggi?'* (What's good today?). Daily specials often feature the best of the morning's market produce or may include a rarer dish. Just because it's not on the menu doesn't mean it's not on offer. Also, as a general rule of thumb, opt for fish and seafood dishes in coastal areas and earthier meats and vegetables further inland and in mountainous regions. This way you're more likely to eat local specialities made with the freshest produce. When eating fish and seafood, always ask if it's *surgelato* (frozen) or *fresco* (fresh) – it's the latter you want to be eating.

Less is more; most of the recipes in Ada Boni's classic *The Talisman Italian Cookbook* have fewer than 10 ingredients, yet her robust flavours of her osso bucco, polenta and wild duck with lentils are anything but simple.

APERITIVI: BUDGET FEASTING

Aperitivi are often described as a 'before-meal drink and light snacks'. Don't be fooled. Italian happy hour can easily turn into a budget-friendly dinner disguised as a casual drink. This is particularly true of *aperitivi* accompanied by a buffet of antipasti, pasta salads, cold cuts and some hot dishes (this may include your fellow diners: *aperitivi* is prime time for hungry singles). You can methodically pillage buffets in cities including Milan, Turin, Rome, Naples and Palermo from about 5pm or 6pm to 8pm or 9pm for the price of a single drink – which crafty diners nurse for the duration – while Venetians enjoy *ombre* (half-glasses of wine) and bargain seafood *cicheti* (Venetian tapas).

Favourite *aperitivo* libations include the spritz, a mix of *prosecco*, soda water and either Aperol, Campari or the more herbacious Cynar. Not surprisingly, *aperitivi* are wildly popular among the many young Italians who can't afford to eat dinner out, but still want a place to enjoy food while schmoozing with friends – leave it to Italy to find a way to put the glam into budget.

When it comes to *contorni*, Italians prefer to keep things simple, with common options including seasonal *verdure alla griglia* (grilled vegetables), usually dressed in little more than olive oil. The classic *insalata mista* (mixed green salad) typically consists of unadorned greens with vinegar and oil on the side; croutons, crumbled cheeses, nuts, dried fruit and other frou-frou ingredients have no business in a classic (some may say bland) Italian salad.

Frutti e dolci (Fruit & Dessert)

'Siamo arrivati alla frutta' ('We've arrived at the fruit') is an idiom roughly meaning 'we've hit rock bottom' – but hey, not until you've had one last tasty morsel. Your best bets on the fruit menu are local and seasonal. *Formaggi* (cheeses) are another option, but only diabetics or the French would go that route when there's room for *dolci* (sweets). *Biscotti* (twice-baked biscuits) made to dip in wine make for a delicious closure to the meal, but other great desserts include *zabaglione* (egg and marsala custard), *torta di ricotta e pera* (pear and ricotta cake), cream-stuffed profiteroles or *cannoli siciliani,* ricotta-stuffed shell pastry. Cannoli worthy of the pickiest Sicilian palates will only be filled fresh to order, ensuring that the *cialda* (shell) retains its satisfying crunch.

Caffè (Coffee)

Don't believe the hype about espresso: one diminutive cup packs less of a caffeine wallop than a large cup of French-pressed or American-brewed coffee, and leaves drinkers less jittery.

Most Italian mornings start with a creamy, frothy cappuccino, which is rarely taken after about 11am and usually served not too hot. Otherwise it's espresso all the way, though you could ask for a tiny stain of milk in a *caffè macchiato* or a cheeky *caffè corretto* (espresso 'corrected' with a splash of grappa or brandy). On the hottest days of summer, a *granita di caffè* (coffee with shaved ice and whipped cream) is ideal. An ever-growing number of Italian bars in both northern and southern Italy now also offer alternatives to cow's milk, making that cappuccino *con latte di soia* (soy-milk cappuccino) or *latte di mandorla* (almond milk) less of an odd request.

Vino (Wine)

A sit-down meal without *vino* (wine) in Italy is as unpalatable as pasta without sauce. Not ordering wine at a restaurant can cause consternation – was it something the waiter said? Italian wines are considered among the most versatile and 'food friendly' in the world, specifically cultivated over the centuries to elevate regional cuisine. Here, wine is a consideration as essential as your choice of dinner date. Indeed, while the country's perfectly quaffable pilsner beers and occasional red ale pair well with roast meats, pizza and other quick eats, *vino* is considered appropriate for a proper meal – and since many wines cost less than a pint in Italy, this is not a question of price, but a matter of flavour.

Some Italian wines will be as familiar to you as old flames, including pizza-and-a-movie Chianti or reliable summertime fling pinot grigio. But you'll also find some captivating Italian varietals and blends for which there is no translation (eg Brunello, Vermentino, Sciacchetrá), and intriguing Italian wines that have little in common with European and New World cousins of the same name, from merlot and pinot nero (aka pinot noir) to chardonnay.

Many visitors default to carafes of house reds or whites, which in Italy usually means young, fruit-forward reds to complement tomato sauces and chilled dry whites as seafood palate-cleansers. But with a little daring, you can pursue a wider range of options by the glass or half-bottle.

Sparkling wines Franciacorta (Lombardy), *prosecco* (Veneto), Asti (aka Asti Spumante; Piedmont), Lambrusco (Emilia-Romagna)

Light, citrusy whites with grassy or floral notes Vermentino (Sardinia), Orvieto (Umbria), Soave (Veneto), Tocai (Friuli), Frascati (Lazio)

Dry whites with aromatic herbal or mineral aspect Cinque Terre (Liguria), Lugana (Lake Garda), Gavi (Piedmont), Falanghina (Campania), Est! Est!! Est!!! (Lazio)

Versatile, food-friendly reds with pleasant acidity Barbera d'Alba (Piedmont), Montepulciano d'Abruzzo (Abruzzo), Valpolicella (Veneto), Chianti Classico (Tuscany), Bardolino (Lombardy), Sangiovese (Tuscany)

Although some producers find Italy's official appellations costly and creatively constraining, the DOCG (Denominazione di origine controllata e garantita) and DOC (Denominazione di origine controllata) titles are awarded to wines that meet regional quality-control standards.

THE ITALIAN TABLE VINO (WINE)

FIVE MUST-TRY CHEESES

Cheese fiends can expect soaring spirits (and cholesterol levels) in Italy, home to some of the world's most esteemed *formaggi* (cheeses). While there are hundreds of regional creations to nibble on, start with these prized heavyweights:

Parmigiano reggiano A grainy, nutty DOP cheese high in calcium and relatively low in fat. Produced in the northern provinces of Parma, Reggio Emilia, Modena, Bologna and Mantua, it's made using milk from free-range cows on a prized grass or hay diet. *Parmigiano reggiano* is available *fresco* (aged less than 18 months), *vecchio* (aged 18 to 24 months) and *stravecchio* (aged 24 to 36 months). Beautiful with a bubbly Franciacorta or lighter, fruit-forward red.

Gorgonzola Gloriously pungent, this washed-rind, blue-veined DOC cheese is produced in Lombardy and Piedmont. Made using whole cow's milk, it's generally aged three to four months. Varieties include the younger, sweeter *gorgonzola dolce* and the sharper, spicier *gorgonzola piccante* (also known as *stagionato* or *montagna*). To crank up the decadence, pair it with a sticky dessert wine.

Mozzarella A chewy, silky cheese synonymous with Campania and Puglia and best eaten the day it's made. Top of the range is luscious, porcelain-white DOP *mozzarella di bufala* (buffalo mozzarella), produced using the whole milk of black water buffaloes. Variations include *burrata*, buffalo-milk mozzarella filled with cream. Mozzarella made using cow's milk is called *fior di latte*. Match all types with a dry, crisp white.

Provolone Its roots in Basilicata, this semi-hard, wax-rind staple is now commonly produced in Lombardy and the Veneto. Like mozzarella, it's made using the *pasta filata* method, which sees the curd heated until it becomes stringy (*filata*). Aged two to three months, *provolone dolce* is milder and sweeter than the more piquant *provolone piccante*, itself aged for over four months. Pair with pinot grigio or a medium-bodied red.

Asiago Hailing from the northern provinces of Vicenza, Trento, Padua and Treviso, pungent, full-flavoured Asiago DOP uses unpasteurised cow's milk from the Asiago plateau. Choose between milder, fresh *pressato* and strong, crumbly, aged *d'allevo*. The latter can be enjoyed at various stages of maturation, from sweeter *mezzano* (aged four to six months) and more bitter *vecchio* (aged over 10 months), to spicy *stravecchio* (aged for over two years). Wash it down with an earthy, tannin-heavy red.

Well-rounded reds, balancing fruit with earthy notes Brunello di Montalcino (Tuscany), Refosco dal Pedulunco Rosso (Friuli), Dolcetto (Piedmont), Morellino di Scansano (Tuscany), Oltrepò Pavese Rosso (Lombardy)

Big, structured reds with velvety tannins Amarone (Veneto), Barolo (Piedmont), Sagrantino di Montefalco secco (Umbria), Sassicaia and other 'super-Tuscan' blends (Tuscany)

Fortified and dessert wine Sciacchetrá (Liguria), Colli Orientali del Friuli Picolit (Friuli), Vin Santo (Tuscany), Moscato d'Asti (Piedmont)

Liquori (Liqueurs)

Failure to order a postprandial espresso may shock your server, but you may yet save face by ordering a *digestivo* (digestive). Among these is grappa, a potent grape-derived pomace brandy that is offered *bianca* (white, or clear) or *barricata* (cask aged). The latter variety – aged in oak, acacia, ash or cherrywood casks – is golden in colour and has a mellower, more rounded flavour than *grappa bianca*. Flavoured grappa is also produced, offering anything from hints of almond or honey to hints of blueberry and citrus. Another popular digestivo is *amaro*. Literally translating as 'bitter', this dark, bittersweet liqueur is prepared from herbs, roots, flowers and, in some cases, citrus peel. Citrus underscores southern Italy's iconic *limoncello*, a sweet, lemon liqueur most famously associated with the region of Campania.

Festive Favourites

In Italy, culinary indulgence is the epicentre of any celebration, and major holidays are defined by their specialities. Lent is heralded by Carnevale (Carnival), a time for *migliaccio di polenta* (a casserole of polenta, sausages, *pecorino* and *parmigiano reggiano*), *sanguinaccio* ('blood pudding' made with dark chocolate and cinnamon), *chiacchiere* (fried biscuits sprinkled with icing sugar) and Sicily's *mpagnuccata* (deep-fried dough tossed in soft caramel).

If you're here around 19 March (St Joseph's Feast Day), expect to eat *bignè di San Giuseppe* (fried doughnuts filled with cream or chocolate) in Rome, *zeppole* (fritters topped with lemon-scented cream, sour cherry and dusting sugar) in Naples and Bari, and *crispelle di riso* (citrus-scented rice fritters dipped in honey) in Sicily.

Lent specialities like Sicilian *quaresimali* (hard, light almond biscuits) give way to Easter bingeing with the obligatory lamb, *colomba* (dove-shaped cake) and *uove di pasqua* (foil-wrapped chocolate eggs with toy surprises inside). The dominant ingredient at this time is egg, also used to make traditional regional specialities like Genoa's *torta pasqualina* (pastry tart filled with ricotta, *parmigiano,* artichokes and hard-boiled eggs), Florence's *brodetto* (egg, lemon and bread broth) and Naples' legendary *pastiera* (shortcrust pastry tart filled with ricotta, cream, candied fruits and cereals flavoured with orange water).

Christmas means stuffed pasta, seafood dishes and one of Milan's greatest inventions: *panettone* (a yeasty, golden cake studded with raisins and dried fruit). Equally famous are Verona's simpler, raisin-free *pandoro* (a yeasty, star-shaped cake dusted with vanilla-flavoured icing sugar) and Siena's *panforte* (a chewy, flat cake made with candied fruits, nuts, chocolate, honey and spices). Further south, Neapolitans throw caution (and scales) to the wind with *raffioli* (sponge and marzipan biscuits), *struffoli* (tiny fried pastry balls dipped in honey and sprinkled with colourful candied sugar) and *pasta di mandorla* (marzipan), while their Sicilian cousins toast to the season with *cucciddatu* (ring-shaped cake made with dried figs, nuts, honey, vanilla, cloves, cinnamon and citrus fruits).

Survival Guide

Directory A–Z

Accommodation

Accommodation in Italy is incredibly varied, with everything from family-run *pensioni* and *agriturismi* (farm stays) to idiosyncratic B&Bs, designer hotels, serviced apartments, and even *rifugi* (mountain huts) for weary mountain trekkers. Capturing the imagination even more are options that span from luxurious country villas and castles to tranquil convents and monasteries. Book ahead for the high season, especially in popular tourist areas or if visiting cities during major events.

When considering where to slumber, note the following tips:

➡ It pays to book ahead in high season, especially in popular coastal areas in the summer and popular ski resorts in the winter. In the urban centres you can usually find something if you leave it to luck, though reserving a room is essential during key events (such as the furniture and fashion fairs in Milan) when demand is extremely high.

➡ Accommodation rates can fluctuate enormously depending on the season, with Easter, summer and the Christmas/New Year period being the typical peak tourist times. Seasonality also varies according to location. Expect to pay top prices in the mountains during the ski season (December to March) or along the coast in summer (July and August). Conversely, summer in the parched cities can equal low season; in August especially, many city hotels charge as little as half price.

➡ Price also depends greatly on location. A bottom-end budget choice in Venice or Milan will set you back the price of a decent midrange option in, say, rural Campania. Where possible, we present the high-season rates for each accommodation option. Half-board equals breakfast and either lunch or dinner; full board includes breakfast, lunch and dinner.

➡ Some hotels, in particular the lower-end places, barely alter their prices throughout the year. In low season there's no harm in bargaining for a discount, especially if you intend to stay for several days.

➡ Most hotels offer breakfast, though this can vary from bountiful buffets to more modest offerings of pastries, packaged yoghurt and fruit. The same is true of B&Bs, where morning food options can sometimes be little more than pre-packaged *cornetti* (Italian croissants), biscuits, jam, coffee and tea.

➡ Hotels usually require that reservations be confirmed with a credit-card number. No-shows will be docked a night's accommodation.

B&Bs

B&Bs are a burgeoning sector of the Italian accommodation market and can be found throughout the country in both urban and rural settings. Options include everything from restored farmhouses, city *palazzi* (mansions) and seaside bungalows to rooms in family houses. In some cases, a B&B can also refer to a self-contained apartment with basic breakfast provisions provided. Tariffs for a double room cover a wide range, from around €60 to €140.

Booking Services

From hotels and B&Bs, to farm stays and campgrounds, you'll find a huge

---

BOOK YOUR STAY ONLINE

For more accommodation reviews by Lonely Planet authors, check out http://lonelyplanet.com/hotels. You'll find independent reviews, as well as recommendations on the best places to stay. Best of all, you can book online.

list of accommodation offerings at Lonely Planet (lonelyplanet.com/italy/hotels). Other booking websites worth exploring include the following:

HOTELS & PENSIONI

Great Small Hotels (www.greatsmallhotels.com/italy)

Secret Places (www.secretplaces.com/italy/guide)

In Italia (www.initalia.it)

B&BS

BBItalia.it (www.bbitalia.it)

Bed-and-Breakfast.it (www.bed-and-breakfast.it)

HOSTELS

Associazione Italiana Alberghi per la Gioventù (www.aighostels.com)

Hostel World (www.hostelworld.com)

APARTMENTS, HOMES & VILLAS

Cuendet (www.cuendet.com)

Essential Italy (www.essentialitaly.co.uk)

Interhome (www.interhome.co.uk)

Ilios Travel (www.iliostravel.com)

Owners Direct (www.ownersdirect.co.uk)

Holiday Lettings (www.holidaylettings.co.uk)

Homelidays (www.homelidays.com)

Interhome (www.interhome.co.uk)

Porta Portese (www.portaportese.it)

The Thinking Traveller (www.thethinkingtraveller.com)

Long Travel (www.long-travel.co.uk)

Wanted in Rome (www.wantedinrome.com)

AGRITURISMI (FARM STAYS)

Agriturismo.it (www.agriturismo.it)

Agriturismo-Italia.net (www.agriturismo-italia.net)

Agriturismo.com (www.agriturismo.com)

Agriturist (www.agriturist.com)

Agriturismo Vero (www.agriturismovero.com)

CAMPGROUNDS

Campeggi.com (www.campeggi.com)

Camping.it (www.camping.it)

Italcamping.it (www.italcamping.it)

Eurocamp (www.eurocamp.co.uk)

Canvas Holidays (www.canvasholidays.co.uk)

CONVENTS & MONASTERIES

MonasteryStays.com (www.monasterystays.com)

MOUNTAIN HUTS

Club Alpino Italiano (www.cai.it)

Camping

Most campgrounds in Italy are major complexes with swimming pools, restaurants and supermarkets. They are graded according to a star system. Charges usually vary according to the season, peaking in July and August. Note that some places offer an all-inclusive price, while others charge separately for each person, tent, vehicle and/or campsite. Typical high-season prices range from around €10 to €20 per adult, up to €12 for children under 12, and from €5 to €25 for a site.

Italian campgrounds are generally set up for people travelling with their own vehicle, although some are accessible by public transport. In the major cities, grounds are often a long way from the historic centres. Most but not all have space for RVs. Tent campers are expected to bring their own equipment, although a few grounds offer tents for hire. Many also offer the alternative of bungalows or even simple, self-contained (self-catering) flats. In high season, some only offer deals for a week at a time.

Convents & Monasteries

Some Italian convents and monasteries let out cells or rooms as a modest revenue-making exercise and happily take in tourists, while others only take in pilgrims or people who are on a spiritual retreat. Many impose a fairly early curfew, but prices tend to be quite reasonable.

Two useful if ageing publications are Eileen Barish's *The Guide to Lodging in Italy's Monasteries* and Charles M Shelton's *Beds and Blessings in Italy: A Guide to Religious Hospitality*. Online, St Patrick's Church (https://stpatricksamericanrome.org) lists convent and monastery accommodation in Rome, Assisi and Venice. Some of these are simply residential accommodation run by religious orders and not necessarily big on monastic atmosphere. The website doesn't handle bookings; to request a spot, you'll need to contact each individual institution directly. Another website with useful information on monastery stays is In Italy Online (www.initaly.com/agri/convents.htm).

Farm Stays

Live out your bucolic fantasies at one of Italy's growing number of *agriturismi* (farm stays). A long-booming industry in Tuscany and Umbria, farm stays are spreading across the country like freshly churned butter.

While all *agriturismi* are required to grow at least one of their own products, the farm stays themselves range from rustic country houses with a handful of olive trees to elegant country estates with sparkling pools or fully functioning farms where guests can pitch in.

Hostels

Ostelli per la gioventù (youth hostels) are run by the **Associazione Italiana Alberghi per la Gioventù** (AIG; ☑06 487 11 52; www. aighostels.it; Via Nicotera 1, entrance Via Settembrini 4, Rome; ⊗8am-5.30pm Mon-Fri; ⬛Viale delle Milizie), affiliated with Hostelling International (www.hihostels.com). A valid HI card is required in all associated youth hostels in Italy. You can get this in your home country or directly at many hostels.

A full list of Italian hostels, with details of prices and locations, is available online or from hostels throughout the country. Nightly rates in basic dorms vary from around €15 to €50, which usually includes a buffet breakfast. You can often get lunch or dinner for roughly an extra €10 to €15.

Many hostels also offer singles and doubles, with prices ranging from around €30/50 in cheaper parts of the country to as high as €80/100 in major tourist centres like Rome. Some also offer family rooms. Be aware that some hostels have a curfew of 11pm or midnight

A growing contingent of independent hostels offers alternatives to HI hostels. Many are barely distinguishable from budget hotels.

Hotels & Pensioni

While the difference between an *albergo* (hotel) and a *pensione* is often minimal, a *pensione* will generally be of one- to three-star quality while an *albergo* can be awarded up to five stars. *Locande* (inns) long fell into much the same category as *pensioni*, but the term has become a trendy one in some parts and reveals little about the quality of a place. *Affittacamere* are rooms for rent in private houses. They are generally quite simple affairs.

Quality can vary enormously and the official star system gives limited clues. One-star hotels/*pensioni* tend to be basic and usually do not offer private bathrooms. Two-star places are similar, but rooms will generally have a private bathroom. Three-star options usually offer reasonable standards. Four- and five-star hotels offer facilities such as room service, laundry and dry-cleaning.

Prices are highest in major tourist destinations. They also tend to be higher in northern Italy. A *camera singola* (single room) costs from around €40, and from around €60 in more expensive cities like Milan. A *camera doppia* (twin beds) or *camera matrimoniale* (double room with a double bed) will cost from around €60 or €70, even more in places like Milan.

Tourist offices usually have booklets with local accommodation listings. Many hotels are also signing up with (steadily proliferating) online accommodation-booking services.

OFFBEAT ACCOMMODATION

Looking for something out of the ordinary? Italy offers a plethora of sleeping options that you won't find anywhere else in the world.

➡ Down near Italy's heel, rent a *trullo*, one of the characteristic whitewashed conical houses of southern Puglia.

➡ Ancient *sassi* (cave dwellings) have found new life as boutique hotels in otherworldly Matera, a Unesco World Heritage–listed town in the southern region of Basilicata.

➡ Cruise northern Italy on the **Avemaria** (☑0444 127 84 30; www.avemariaboat.com; Via Conforto da Costozza 7, Vicenza; 7 days per person €990; 🔊) 🏊, a river barge that sails from Mantua to Venice over seven leisurely days, with cultural and foodie pit stops, and the chance to cycle between locations.

➡ In Friuli Venezia Giulia, experience village life in an *albergo diffuso*, an award-winning concept in which self-contained (self-catering) apartments in neighbouring houses are rented to guests through a centralised hotel-style reception.

➡ In Naples, spend a night or two slumbering in the aristocratic *palazzo* of a Bourbon bishop. Now the **Decumani Hotel de Charme** (☑081 551 81 88; www.decumani.it; Via San Giovanni Maggiore Pignatelli 15; s €99-124, d €99-164; ◙🔊; ⓜUniversità), the property comes complete with a sumptuous baroque salon.

THE SLUMBER TAX

Italy's *tassa di soggiorno* (accommodation tax) sees visitors charged an extra €1 to €7 per night.

Exactly how much you're charged may depend on several factors, including the type of accommodation (campground, guesthouse, hotel), a hotel's star rating and the number of people under your booking. Depending on their age and on the location of the accommodation, children may pay a discounted rate or be completely exempt from the tax. In Florence and Siena, for instance, children under 12 are exempt from paying, while in Venice, children aged 10 to 16 pay half-price. It's also worth noting that the maximum number of nights that the tax is charged can vary between cities and regions.

Most of our listings do not include the hotel tax, although it's always a good idea to confirm whether taxes are included when booking.

Mountain Huts

The network of *rifugi* in the Alps, Apennines and other mountains is usually only open from June to late September. While some are little more than rudimentary shelters, many *rifugi* are more like Alpine hostels. Accommodation is generally in dormitories, but some of the larger *rifugi* have doubles. Many *rifugi* also offer guests hot meals and/or communal cooking facilities. Though mattresses, blankets and duvets are usually provided, most *rifugi* will require you to bring your own sleeping bag or travel sheet. Some places offer travel sheets for hire or purchase.

The price per person (which typically includes breakfast) ranges from €20 to €30 depending on the quality of the *rifugio* (it's more for a double room). A hearty post-walk single-dish dinner will set you back another €10 to €15.

Rifugi are marked on good walking maps. Those close to chair lifts and cable-car stations are usually expensive and crowded. Others are at high altitude and involve hours of hard walking. It is important to book in advance. Additional information can be obtained from the local tourist offices.

The Club Alpino Italiano (www.cai.it) owns and runs many of the mountain huts. Members of organisations such as the New Zealand Alpine Club, Fédération Française des Clubs Alpins et de Montagne and Deutscher Alpenverein can enjoy discounted rates for accommodation and meals. See the International Mountaineering and Climbing Federation website (www.theuiaa.org) for details.

Rental Accommodation

Finding rental accommodation in the major cities can be difficult and time-consuming; rental agencies (local and foreign) can assist, for a fee. Rental rates are higher for short-term leases. A studio or one-bedroom apartment anywhere near the centre of Rome will cost around €900 per month and it is usually necessary to pay a deposit (generally one month in advance). Expect to spend similar amounts in cities such as Florence, Milan, Naples and Venice.

Search online for apartments and villas for rent. Another option is to share an apartment; check out university noticeboards for student flats with vacant rooms. Tourist offices in resort areas (coastal towns in summer, ski towns in winter) also maintain lists of apartments and villas for rent.

Customs Regulations

On leaving the EU, non-EU citizens can reclaim any Value Added Tax (VAT) on any purchases over €154.94. For more information, visit www.italia.it.

Visitors coming into Italy from non-EU countries can import the following items duty free:

spirits & liqueurs	1L
wine	4L (or 2L of fortified wine)
perfume	60mL
cigarettes	200
other goods	up to a value of €300/430 (travelling by land/sea)

Discount Cards

Free admission to many galleries and cultural sites is available to those under 18 and over 65 years old; and visitors aged between 18 and 25 often qualify for a discount. In some cases, these discounts only apply to EU citizens.

Some cities or regions offer their own discount passes, such as Roma Pass (three days €38.50), which offers free use of public transport and free or reduced admission to Rome's museums.

In many places around Italy, you can also save money by purchasing a *biglietto cumulativo*, a ticket that allows admission to a number of associated sights for less than the combined cost of separate admission fees.

Electricity

**Type F
230V/50Hz**

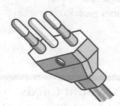

**Type L
220V/50Hz**

Embassies & Consulates

For foreign embassies and consulates in Italy not listed here, look under 'Ambasciate' or 'Consolati' in the telephone directory. Some countries also run honorary consulates in other cities.

Australian Embassy Rome (☑06 85 27 21, emergencies 800 877790; www.italy.embassy.gov.au; Via Antonio Bosio 5; ☺9am-5pm Mon-Fri; ☐Via Nomentana)

Austrian Embassy Rome (☑06 844 01 41; www.aussenministerium.at/rom; Via Pergolesi 3; ☺9am-noon Mon-Fri; ☐Via Pinciana)

Canadian Embassy Rome (☑06 8 5444 2911; www.canadainternational.gc.ca/italy-italie; Via Zara 30; ☺9am-noon Mon-Fri; ☐Via Nomentana)

French Embassy Rome (☑06 68 60 11; www.ambafrance-it.org; Piazza Farnese 67)

German Embassy Rome (☑06 49 21 31; www.rom.diplo.de; Via San Martino della Battaglia 4)

Irish Embassy Rome (☑06 585 23 81; www.ambasciata-irlanda.it; Via Giacomo Medici 1, Villa Spada)

Japanese Embassy Rome (☑06 48 79 91; www.it.emb-japan.go.jp; Via Quintino Sella 60)

Netherlands Embassy Rome (☑06 3228 6001; www.olanda.it; Via Michele Mercati 8; ☺9am-noon Mon-Wed & Fri, 10am-noon & 2-4pm Thu; ☐Via Ulisse Aldrovandi)

New Zealand Embassy Rome (☑06 853 75 01; www.mfat.govt.nz/en/countries-and-regions/europe/italy/new-zealand-embassy; Via Clitunno 44; ☺8.30am-12.30pm & 1.30-5pm Mon-Fri; ☐Corso Trieste)

Slovenian Embassy Rome (☑06 8091 4310; www.rim.veleposlanistvo.si; Via Leonardo Pisano 10; ☺9.30am-12.30pm Mon & Thu, 9.30am-12.30pm & 1.30 3.30pm Wed; ☐Via Archimede)

Swiss Embassy Rome (☑06 80 95 71; www.eda.admin.ch/roma; Via Barnaba Oriani 61; ☺9am-noon Mon-Fri; ☐Viale dei Parioli)

UK Embassy Rome (☑06 4220 0001; www.ukinitaly.fco.gov.uk; Via XX Settembre 80a)

US Embassy Rome (☑06 4 67 41; www.italy.usembassy.gov; Via Vittorio Veneto 121)

Food & Drink

For detailed information on eating and drinking in Italy see Eat & Drink Like a Local (p39) and The Italian Table (p941).

Health

Before You Go

HEALTH INSURANCE

Italy has a public health system that is legally bound

EATING PRICE RANGES

The following price ranges refer to a meal of two courses (antipasto/*primo* and *secondo*), a glass of house wine, and *coperto* (cover charge) for one person.

€ under €25

€€ €25-45

€€€ over €45

These figures represent a halfway point between expensive cities such as Milan and Venice and the considerably cheaper towns across the south. Indeed, a restaurant rated as midrange in rural Sicily might be considered dirt cheap in Milan. Note that most eating establishments add *coperto* of around €2 to €3. Some also include a service charge (*servizio*) of 10% to 15%.

YOUTH, STUDENT & TEACHER CARDS

CARD	WEBSITE	COST	ELIGIBILITY
European Youth Card (Carta Giovani)	www.eyca.org	€10	under 30yr
International Student Identity Card (ISIC)	www.isic.org	US$26, UK£12, AUD$30, €10-15	full-time student
International Teacher Identity Card (ITIC)		US$20, UK£12, AUD$30, €10-18	full-time teacher
International Youth Travel Card (IYTC)		US$20, UK£12, AUD$30, €10-15	under 31yr

to provide emergency care to everyone. EU nationals are entitled to reduced cost, sometimes free, medical care with a European Health Insurance Card (EHIC), which is available from your home health authority; non-EU citizens should take out medical insurance.

If you do need health insurance, make sure you get a policy that covers you for the worst possible scenario, such as an accident requiring an emergency flight home. Find out in advance if your insurance plan will make payments directly to providers or reimburse you later for overseas health expenditures.

It's also worth finding out if there is a reciprocal arrangement between your country and Italy. If so, you may be covered for essential medical treatment and some subsidised medications while in Italy. Australia, for instance, has such an agreement; carry your Medicare card.

VACCINATIONS
No jabs are required to travel to Italy, though the World Health Organization (WHO) recommends that all travellers should be covered for diphtheria, tetanus, the measles, mumps, rubella, polio and hepatitis B.

In Italy
AVAILABILITY & COST OF HEALTH CARE
Health care is readily available throughout Italy, but standards can vary significantly. Public hospitals tend

to be less impressive the further south you travel. Pharmacists (farmacisti) can give you valuable advice and sell over the counter medication for minor illnesses. They can also advise you when more-specialised help is required and point you in the right direction. In major cities you are likely to find English-speaking doctors or a translator service available.

Pharmacies generally keep the same hours as other shops, closing at night and on Sundays. A handful, however, remain open on a rotation basis (farmacie di turno) for emergency purposes. These are usually listed in newspapers. Closed pharmacies display a list of the nearest open ones.

If you need an ambulance anywhere in Italy, call ☑118. For emergency treatment, head straight to the pronto soccorso (casualty) section of a public hospital, where you can also get emergency dental treatment.

TAP WATER
Tap water in Italy is safe to drink. The only exception is where a tap is marked 'Acqua non potabile' (Water not suitable for drinking).

Insurance
A travel-insurance policy to cover theft, loss and medical problems is a very good idea. It may also cover you for cancellation or delays to your travel arrangements. Paying for your ticket with a

credit card can often provide limited travel accident insurance and you may be able to reclaim the payment if the operator doesn't deliver. Ask your credit-card company what it will cover.

Worldwide travel insurance is available at www.lonelyplanet.com/travel-insurance. You can buy, extend and claim online any time – even if you're already on the road.

Internet Access
➜ Numerous Italian cities and towns offer public wi-fi hotspots, including Rome, Bologna and Venice. To use them, you will need to register online using a credit card or an Italian mobile number. An easier option (no need for a local mobile number) is to head to a cafe or bar offering free wi-fi.

➜ Most hotels, B&Bs, hostels and agriturismi (farm stays) offer free wi-fi to guests, though signal quality can vary. There will sometimes be a computer for guest use.

Legal Matters
Italy is generally a safe country to travel in. The most likely reason for a brush with the law is to report a theft. If you have something stolen and you want to claim it on insurance, you must make a statement to the police, as insurance companies won't pay up without official proof of a crime.

Drugs & Alcohol

➜ If you're caught with what the police deem to be a dealable quantity of hard or soft drugs, you risk prison sentences of between two and 20 years.

➜ Possession for personal use is punishable by administrative sanctions, although first-time offenders might get away with a warning.

➜ The legal limit for blood-alcohol when driving is 0.05% and random breath tests do occur.

Police

The Italian police force is divided into three main bodies: the *polizia*, who wear navy-blue jackets; the *carabinieri*, in a black uniform with a red stripe; and the grey-clad *guardia di finanza* (fiscal police), responsible for fighting tax evasion and drug smuggling. If you run into trouble, you're most likely to end up dealing with the *polizia* or *carabinieri*.

To contact the police in an emergency, dial 🕿112 or 113.

Your Rights

➜ You should be given verbal and written notice of the charges laid against you within 24 hours by arresting officers.

➜ You have no right to a phone call upon arrest, though the police will inform your family with your consent. You may also ask the police to inform your embassy or consulate.

➜ The prosecutor must apply to a magistrate for you to be held in preventive custody

awaiting trial (depending on the seriousness of the offence) within 48 hours of arrest.

➜ You also have the right to a lawyer. If you do not know of any local lawyers, the police should ask the local bar council for a state-appointed lawyer (*difensore di ufficio*) to be appointed.

➜ You have the right not to respond to questions without the presence of a lawyer.

➜ If the magistrate orders preventive custody, you have the right to then contest this within the following 10 days.

Gay & Lesbian Travellers

Homosexuality is legal (over the age of 16) and even widely accepted, but Italy is notably conservative in its attitudes, largely keeping in line with those of the Vatican. Overt displays of affection by LGBT couples can attract a negative response, especially in smaller towns.

There are gay venues in Rome, Milan and Bologna, and a handful in places such as Florence and Naples. Some coastal towns and resorts (such as the Tuscan town of Viareggio or Taormina in Sicily) are popular gay holiday spots in the summer.

Online resources include the following (mostly Italian-language) websites:

Arcigay (www.arcigay.it) Bologna-based national organisation for the LGBT community.

Circolo Mario Mieli (www.mariomieli.org) Rome-based cultural centre that organises debates,

cultural events and social functions, including Gay Pride.

Coordinamento Lesbiche Italiano (CLR; www.clrbp.it) The national organisation for lesbians, holding regular conferences, literary evenings and other cultural special events.

Gay.it (www.gay.it) Website featuring LGBT news, feature articles and gossip.

Pride (www.prideonline.it) Culture, politics, travel and health with an LGBT focus.

Maps

The city maps provided by Lonely Planet, combined with the good, free local maps available at most Italian tourist offices, will be sufficient for many travellers. For more-specialised maps, browse the good selection at national bookshop chain Feltrinelli (www.lafeltrinelli.it), or consult the websites of the following organisations:

Touring Club Italiano (www.touringclub.com) Italy's largest map publisher offers a comprehensive 1:200,000, 592-page road atlas of Italy (€54.90), as well as 1:400,000 maps of northern, central and southern Italy (€8.50). It also produces 15 regional maps at 1:200,000 (€8.50), as well as a series of walking guides with maps (€14.90).

Tabacco (www.tabaccoeditrice.com) Publishes an excellent 1:25,000 scale series of walking maps (€8.50), covering an area from Livigno in the west to the Slovenia border in the east.

Kompass (www.kompass-italia.it) Publishes 1:25,000 and 1:50,000 scale hiking maps of

ITALIAN POLICE ORGANISATIONS

Polizia statale (state police)	Thefts, visa extensions and permits
Carabinieri (military police)	General crime, public order and drug enforcement (often overlapping with the *polizia statale*)
Vigili urbani (local traffic police)	Parking tickets, towed cars
Guardia di finanza	Tax evasion, drug smuggling
Corpo forestale	Environmental protection

various parts of Italy, plus a nice series of 1:70,000 cycling maps.

Stanfords (www.stanfords.co.uk) Excellent UK-based shop that stocks many useful maps, including cycling maps.

Money

ATMs are widespread in Italy. Major credit cards are widely accepted, but some smaller shops, trattorias and hotels might not take them.

ATMs

➡ ATMs (known as 'Bancomat' in Italy) are widely available throughout Italy, and most will accept cards tied into the Visa, MasterCard, Cirrus and Maestro systems.

➡ Beware of transaction fees. Every time you withdraw cash, you'll be hit by charges – typically your home bank will charge a foreign-exchange fee (usually around 1%) as well as a transaction fee of around 1% to 3%. Fees can sometimes be reduced by withdrawing cash from banks affiliated with your home banking institution; check with your bank.

➡ If an ATM rejects your card, try another one before assuming the problem is with your card.

➡ If your card is lost, stolen or swallowed by an ATM, you can telephone toll-free to have an immediate stop put on its use:

American Express (Amex; ☎06 7290 0347)

Diners Club (☎800 393939)

MasterCard (☎800 870866)

Visa (☎800 819014)

Credit Cards

➡ Major cards such as Visa, MasterCard, Eurocard, Cirrus and Eurocheques are widely accepted. Amex is also recognised, although it's less common than Visa or MasterCard.

PRACTICALITIES

Smoking Smoking is banned in enclosed public spaces, which includes restaurants, bars, shops and public transport.

Newspapers Key national dailies include centre-left *La Repubblica* (www.repubblica.it) and right-wing rival *Corriere della Sera* (www.corriere.it). For the Vatican's take on affairs, *L'Osservatore Romano* (www.osservatoreromano.va) is the Holy See's official newspaper.

Radio As well as the principal Rai channels (Radiouno, Radiodue, Radiotre), there are hundreds of commercial radio stations operating across Italy. Popular Rome-based stations include Radio Capital (www.capital.it) and Radio Città Futura (www.radiocittafutura.it).

TV The main terrestrial channels are RAI 1, 2 and 3 which are run by Rai (www.rai.it), Italy's state-owned national broadcaster, and Canale 5, Italia 1 and Rete 4 run by Mediaset (www.mediaset.it), the commercial TV company founded and still partly owned by Silvio Berlusconi.

Weights & Measures Italy uses the metric system.

➡ Virtually all midrange and top-end hotels accept credit cards, as do most restaurants and large shops. Some cheaper *pensioni*, trattorias and pizzerias only accept cash.

➡ Do not rely on credit cards at museums or galleries.

➡ Note that using your credit card in ATMs can be costly. On every transaction there's a fee, which can reach US$10 with some credit-card issuers, as well as interest per withdrawal. Check with your issuer before leaving home.

➡ Always inform your bank of your travel plans to avoid your card being blocked for payments made in unusual locations.

Currency

Italy's currency is the euro. The seven euro notes come in denominations of €500, €200, €100, €50, €20, €10 and €5. The eight euro coins are in denominations of €2 and €1, then 50, 20, 10, five, and two cents, and finally one cent.

Money Changers

➡ You can change money in banks, at post offices or in a *cambio* (exchange office). Post offices and banks tend to offer the best rates, exchange offices keep longer hours, but watch for high commissions and inferior rates.

➡ Take your passport or photo ID when exchanging money.

Taxes & Refunds

A 22% value-added tax known as IVA (Imposta sul Valore Aggiunta) is included in the price of most goods and services. Tax-free shopping is available at some shops.

Non-EU residents who spend more than €155 at one shop at a single time can claim a refund when leaving the EU. The refund only applies to purchases from stores that display a 'Tax Free' sign. When making the purchase, ask for a tax-refund voucher, to be filled in with the date of the purchase and its value. When leaving the EU, get this voucher stamped at customs and take it to the nearest tax-refund counter where you'll get an immediate refund, either in cash or charged to your credit card. For more information, see www.taxrefund.it.

Tipping

Italians are not big tippers. Use the following as a rough guide:

Taxis Optional, but most people round up to the nearest euro

Hotels Tip porters about €5 at high-end hotels.

Restaurants Service (*servizio*) is generally included in restaurants – if it's not, a euro or two is fine in pizzerias, 10% in restaurants.

Bars Optional, though many Italians leave small change on the bar when ordering coffee (usually €0.10 per coffee). If drinks are brought to your table, a small tip is generally appreciated.

Opening Hours

Opening hours vary throughout the year. We've provided high-season opening hours; hours will generally decrease in the shoulder and low seasons. 'Summer' times generally refer to the period from April to September or October, while 'winter' times generally run from October or November to March.

Banks 8.30am–1.30pm and 2.45–4.30pm Monday to Friday

Restaurants noon–3pm and 7.30–11pm or midnight

Cafes 7.30am–8pm, sometimes until 1am or 2am

Bars and clubs 10pm–4am or 5am

Shops 9am–1pm and 4–8pm Monday to Saturday, some also open Sunday

Post

Called **Poste Italiane** (☑803 160; www.poste.it), Italy's postal system is reasonably reliable, though parcels do occasionally go missing.

Francobolli (stamps) are available at post offices and authorised tobacconists (look for the big white-on-black 'T' sign). Since letters often need to be weighed, what you get at the tobacconist for international airmail will occasionally be an approximation of the proper rate. Tobacconists keep regular shop hours.

The cost of sending a letter by *aerea* (airmail) depends on its weight, size and where it is being sent. Most people use *posta prioritaria* (priority mail), Italy's most efficient mail service, guaranteed to deliver letters sent to Europe within three working days and to the rest of the world within four to nine working days. Using *posta prioritaria*, mail up to 50g costs €3.50 within Europe, €4.50 to Africa, Asia and the Americas, and €5.50 to Australia and New Zealand. Mail weighing 51g to 100g costs €4.30 within Europe, €5.20 to Africa, Asia and the Americas, and €7.10 to Australia and New Zealand.

Public Holidays

Most Italians take their annual holiday in August, with the busiest period occurring around 15 August, known locally as Ferragosto. As a result, many businesses and shops close for at least part of that month. Settimana Santa (Easter Holy Week) is another busy holiday period for Italians.

National public holidays include the following:

Capodanno (New Year's Day) 1 January

Epifania (Epiphany) 6 January

Pasquetta (Easter Monday) March/April

Giorno della Liberazione (Liberation Day) 25 April

Festa del Lavoro (Labour Day) 1 May

Festa della Repubblica (Republic Day) 2 June

Ferragosto (Feast of the Assumption) 15 August

Festa di Ognisanti (All Saints' Day) 1 November

Festa dell'Immacolata Concezione (Feast of the Immaculate Conception) 8 December

Natale (Christmas Day) 25 December

Festa di Santo Stefano (Boxing Day) 26 December

Telephone

Mobile Phones

➡ Italian mobile phones operate on the GSM 900/1800 network, which is compatible with the rest of Europe and Australia but not always with the North American GSM or CDMA systems – check with your service provider.

➡ The cheapest way of using your mobile is to buy a prepaid (*prepagato*) Italian SIM card. TIM (www.tim.it), Wind (www.wind.it), Vodafone (www.vodafone.it) and Tre (www.tre.it) all offer SIM cards and have retail outlets in most Italian cities and towns. All SIM cards must be registered in Italy, so make sure you have a passport or ID card with you when you buy one.

➡ You can easily top up your Italian SIM with a recharge card (*ricarica*), available from most tobacconists, some bars, supermarkets and banks.

Domestic Calls

➡ Italian telephone area codes all begin with ☑0 and consist of up to four digits. The area code is followed by anything from four to eight digits. Area codes are an integral part of all Italian phone numbers and must be dialled even when calling locally.

➡ Mobile-phone numbers begin with a three-digit prefix starting with a ☑3.

➡ Toll-free (free-phone) numbers are known as

numeri verdi and usually start with ☑800.

➜ Nongeographical numbers start with ☑840, 841, 848, 892, 899, 163, 166 or 199.

➜ Some six-digit national rate numbers are also in use (such as those for Alitalia and Trenitalia).

International Calls

➜ To call Italy from abroad, call your international access number, then Italy's country code (☑39) and then the area code of the location you want, including the leading 0.

➜ Avoid making international calls from a hotel, as rates are high.

➜ The cheapest options are free or low-cost apps such as Skype and Viber, connecting by using the wi-fi at your accommodation or at a cafe or other venue offering free wi-fi.

➜ Another cheap option is to use an international calling card. Note, however, that there are very few public payphones left, so consider a pre-paid card that allows you to call from any phone. Cards are available at newsstands and tobacconists.

➜ To call abroad from Italy dial ☑00, then the country and area codes, followed by the telephone number.

➜ To make a reverse-charge (collect) international call from a public telephone, dial ☑170. All phone operators speak English.

Information

National and international phone numbers can be requested at ☑1254 (or online at www.1254.it).

Phonecards

Although public payphones still exist across Italy, their numbers continue to decrease. Those that are still working take telephone cards (*schede telefoniche*), which are available from tobacconists and newsstands.

Time

➜ All of Italy occupies the Central European Time Zone, which is one hour ahead of GMT. When it is noon in London, it is 1pm in Italy.

➜ Daylight-saving time (when clocks move forward one hour) starts on the last Sunday in March and ends on the last Sunday in October.

➜ Italy operates on a 24-hour clock, so 3pm is written as 15:00.

Toilets

Beyond museums, galleries, department stores and train stations, there are few public toilets in Italy. If you're caught short, the best thing to do is to nip into a cafe or bar. The polite thing to do is to order something at the bar. You may need to pay to use public toilets at some venues (usually €0.50 to €1.50).

Tourist Information

Four tiers of tourist office exist: local, provincial, regional and national.

Local & Provincial Tourist Offices

Despite their different names, provincial and local offices offer similar services. All deal directly with the public and most will respond to written and telephone requests for information. Staff can usually provide a city map, lists of hotels and information on the major sights. In larger towns and major tourist areas, English is generally spoken, along with other languages, depending on the region (for example, German in Alto Adige, French in Valle d'Aosta).

Main offices are generally open Monday to Friday; some also open on weekends, especially in urban areas or during peak summer season. Affiliated information booths (at train stations and airports, for example) may keep slightly different hours.

Regional Tourist Boards

Regional offices are generally more concerned with planning, budgeting, marketing and promotion than with offering a public information service. However, they still maintain some useful websites. In some cases you'll need to look for the Tourism or Turismo link within the regional site. (Note that

TOURIST OFFICES

OFFICE NAME	DESCRIPTION	MAIN FOCUS
Azienda di Promozione Turistica (APT)	Main provincial tourist office	Information on the town and its surrounding province
Azienda Autonoma di Soggiorno e Turismo (AAST) or Informazione e Assistenza ai Turisti (IAT)	Local tourist office in larger towns and cities	Town-specific information only (bus routes, museum opening times etc)
Pro Loco	Local tourist office in smaller towns and villages	Similar to AAST and IAT

Campania currently has no official regional tourism website.)

Abruzzo (www.abruzzoturismo.it)

Basilicata (www.aptbasilicata.it)

Calabria (www.turiscalabria.it)

Emilia-Romagna (www.emiliaromagnaturismo.it)

Friuli Venezia Giulia (www.turismo.fvg.it)

Lazio (www.visitlazio.com)

Le Marche (www.le-marche.com)

Liguria (www.turismoinliguria.it)

Lombardy (www.turismo.regione.lombardia.it)

Molise (www.regione.molise.it/turismo)

Piedmont (www.piemonteitalia.eu)

Puglia (www.viaggiareinpuglia.it)

Sardinia (www.sardegnaturismo.it)

Sicily (www.regione.sicilia.it/turismo)

Trentino-Alto Adige (www.visittrentino.it)

Tuscany (www.turismo.intoscana.it)

Umbria (www.regione.umbria.it)

Valle d'Aosta (www.lovevda.it)

Veneto (www.veneto.eu)

Travellers with Disabilities

Italy is not an easy country for travellers with disabilities, and getting around can be a problem for wheelchair users. Even a short journey in a city or town can become a major expedition if cobblestone streets have to be negotiated. Although many buildings have lifts, they are not always wide enough for wheelchairs. Not a lot has been done to make life easier for the hearing or vision impaired either.

The Italian National Tourist Office in your country may be able to provide advice on Italian associations for travellers with disabilities and

information on what help is available.

If travelling by train, ring the national helpline ☏199 303060 to arrange assistance (6.45am to 9.30pm daily). Airline companies should be able to arrange assistance at airports if you notify them of your needs in advance. Alternatively, contact ADR Assistance (www.adrassistance.it) for help at Fiumicino or Ciampino airports. Some taxis are equipped to carry passengers in wheelchairs; ask for a taxi for a *sedia a rotelle* (wheelchair).

Italy's official tourism website (www.italia.it) offers a number of links for travellers with disabilities.

Accessible Italy (www.accessibleitaly.com) A San Marino–based company that specialises in holiday services for people with disabilities. This is the best first port of call.

Sage Traveling (www.sagetraveling.com) A US-based agency offering advice and tailor-made tours to assist mobility-impaired travellers in Europe.

Resources

Download Lonely Planet's free Accessible Travel guide from http://shop.lonelyplanet.com/accessible-travel. Another online resource is Lonely Planet's Travel for All community on Google+, worth joining for information sharing and networking.

Visas

➡ Italy is a signatory of the Schengen Convention, an agreement whereby participating countries abolished customs checks at common borders. EU citizens do not need a Schengen tourist visa to enter Italy. Nationals of some other countries, including Australia, Canada, Israel, Japan, New Zealand, Switzerland and the USA, do not need a tourist visa for

stays of up to 90 days. To check the visa requirements for your country, see www.schengenvisainfo.com/tourist-schengen-visa.

➡ All non-EU and non-Schengen nationals entering Italy for more than 90 days or for any reason other than tourism (such as study or work) may need a specific visa. See http://vistoperitalia.octori.it or contact an Italian consulate for details.

➡ Ensure your passport is valid for at least six months beyond your departure date from Italy.

Electronic Authorisation

The European Commission has outlined plans for an electronic vetting system for travellers to the Schengen area.

Under the proposed terms of the European Travel Information & Authorisation System (ETIAS), all non-EU travellers would be required to complete an online form and pay a €5 fee before travelling to the Schengen block.

If approved by the European Parliament, the system may come into force in 2020.

For further details, see www.etiaseurope.eu.

Permesso di Soggiorno

➡ A *permesso di soggiorno* (permit to stay, also referred to as a residence permit) is required by all non-EU nationals who stay in Italy longer than three months. In theory, you should apply for one within eight days of arriving in Italy.

➡ EU citizens do not require a *permesso di soggiorno*, but are required to register with the local registry office (Ufficio Anagrafe) if they stay for more than three months.

➡ Check exact requirements on www.poliziadistato.it – click on the English tab and then follow the links.

➜ The main office dealing with permits is the Ufficio Immigrazione (https://questure.poliziadistato.it).

Volunteering

Concordia International Volunteer Projects (www.concordiavolunteers.org.uk) Short-term community-based projects covering the environment, archaeology and the arts.

European Youth Portal (http://europa.eu/youth) Has various links suggesting volunteering options across Europe. Navigate to the Volunteering page.

Legambiente (http://international.legambiente.it) Offers numerous environmentally focussed opportunities for volunteering.

World Wide Opportunities on Organic Farms (www.wwoof.it) For a membership fee of €35 this organisation provides a list of farms looking for volunteer workers.

Women Travellers

Italy is not a dangerous country for women to travel in. That said, in some parts of the country, solo women travellers may be subjected to a high level of unwanted attention. Eye-to-eye contact is the norm in Italy's daily flirtatious interplay. Eye contact can become outright staring the further south you travel.

If ignoring unwanted male attention doesn't work, politely tell your interlocutor that you're waiting for your *marito* (husband) or *fidanza-*to (boyfriend), and if necessary, walk away.

If you feel yourself being groped on a crowded bus or metro, a loud '*che schifo!*' (how disgusting!) will draw attention to the incident. Otherwise take all the usual precautions you would in any other part of the world.

You can report incidents to the police, who are required to press charges.

Work

Citizens of the European Union (EU), Norway, Iceland, Switzerland and Liechtenstein are legally entitled to work in Italy. Those wanting to stay in the country for more than three months are simply required to register with the local *anagrafe* (Register Office) in their Italian municipality of residence.

Working longer-term in Italy is trickier if you are a non-EU citizen. Firstly, you will need to secure a job offer. Your prospective employer will then need to complete most of the work visa application process on your behalf. If your application is successful, your employer will be given your work authorisation. Your local Italian embassy or consulate will then be informed and should be able to provide you with an entry visa within 30 days. It's worth noting that Italy operates a visa quota system for most occupations, meaning that you will only be offered a visa if the relevant quota has not been met by the time your application is processed. Non-EU citizens planning to stay in Italy for more than 90 days must also apply for a *permesso di soggiorno* (permit to stay) within eight working days of their entry into Italy. Applications for the permit should be made at their nearest *questura* (police station). General information on the permit is available on the Italian State Police website (www.poliziadistato.it).

Italy does have reciprocal, short-term working-holiday agreements with a handful of countries, including Canada, Australia and New Zealand. These visas are generally limited to young adults aged between 18 and 30 or 35 and allow the visa holder to work a limited number of months over a set period of time. Contact your local Italian embassy (www.esteri.it) for more information.

Popular jobs for those permitted to work in Italy include teaching English, either through a language school or as a private freelancer. While some language schools do take on teachers without professional language qualifications, the more reputable (and better-paying) establishments will require you to have a TEFL (Teaching of English as a Foreign Language) certificate. Useful job-seeker websites for English-language teachers include ESL Employment (www.eslemployment.com) and TEFL (www.tefl.org.uk/tefl-jobs-centre). Au pairing is another popular work option; click onto www.aupairworld.com for more information on work opportunities and tips.

Transport

GETTING THERE & AWAY

A plethora of airlines link Italy with the rest of the world, and cut-rate carriers have significantly driven down the cost of flights from other European countries. Excellent rail and bus connections, especially with northern Italy, offer efficient overland transport, while car and passenger ferries run to ports throughout the Mediterranean.

Flights, cars and tours can be booked online at lonelyplanet.com/bookings.

Entering the Country

Entering Italy from most other parts of the EU is generally uncomplicated, with no border checkpoints and no customs thanks to the Schengen Agreement. Document and customs checks remain standard if arriving from (or departing to) a non-Schengen country.

Air

Airports & Airlines

Italy's main intercontinental gateway airports are Rome's **Leonardo da Vinci** (Fiumicino; ☑06 6 59 51; www.adr.it/fiumicino) and Milan's **Aeroporto Malpensa** (MXP; ☑02 23 23 23; www.milanomalpensa-airport.com; ℝMalpensa Express). Both are served by non-stop flights from around the world. Venice's **Marco Polo Airport** (☑flight information 041 260 92 60; www.veniceairport.it; Via Galileo Gallilei 30/1, Tessera) is also served by a handful of intercontinental flights.

Dozens of international airlines compete with the country's revamped national carrier, Alitalia, rated a three-star airline by UK aviation research company Skytrax.

If you're flying from Africa or Oceania, you'll generally need to change planes at least once en route to Italy.

Intra-European flights serve plenty of other Italian cities; the leading mainstream carriers include Alitalia, Air France, British Airways, Lufthansa and KLM.

Cut-rate airlines, led by Ryanair and easyJet, fly from a growing number of European cities to more than two dozen Italian destinations, typically landing in smaller airports such as Rome's **Ciampino** (☑06 6 59 51; www.adr.it/ciampino).

Departure Tax

Departure tax is included in the price of a ticket.

Land

There are plenty of options for entering Italy by train, bus or private vehicle.

CLIMATE CHANGE & TRAVEL

Every form of transport that relies on carbon-based fuel generates CO_2, the main cause of human-induced climate change. Modern travel is dependent on aeroplanes, which might use less fuel per kilometre per person than most cars but travel much greater distances. The altitude at which aircraft emit gases (including CO_2) and particles also contributes to their climate change impact. Many websites offer 'carbon calculators' that allow people to estimate the carbon emissions generated by their journey and, for those who wish to do so, to offset the impact of the greenhouse gases emitted with contributions to portfolios of climate-friendly initiatives throughout the world. Lonely Planet offsets the carbon footprint of all staff and author travel.

Border Crossings

Aside from the coastal roads linking Italy with France and Slovenia, border crossings (p20) into Italy mostly involve tunnels through the Alps (open year-round) or mountain passes (seasonally closed or requiring snow chains).

The list below outlines the major points of entry.

Austria From Innsbruck to Bolzano via A22/E45 (Brenner Pass); Villach to Tarvisio via A23/E55

France From Nice to Ventimiglia via A10/E80; Modane to Turin via A32/E70 (Fréjus Tunnel); Chamonix to Courmayeur via A5/E25 (Mont Blanc Tunnel)

Slovenia From Sežana to Trieste via SR58/E70

Switzerland From Martigny to Aosta via SS27/E27 (Grand St Bernard Tunnel); Lugano to Como via A9/E35

Bus

Buses are the cheapest over land option to Italy, but services are less frequent, less comfortable and significantly slower than the train.

Eurolines (☑0861 199 19 00; www.eurolines.it) A consortium of coach companies with offices throughout Europe. Italy-bound buses head to Milan, Rome, Florence, Venice and other Italian cities. It offers a bus pass valid for 15/30 days that costs €320/425 (reduced €270/350) in high season and €225/340 (reduced €195/265) in low season. This pass allows unlimited travel between 47 European cities, including Milan, Venice, Florence and Rome.

FlixBus (www.flixbus.com) German-owned company offering both inter-regional and international routes. Direct international routes to/from Italy include Milan to Paris, Lyon, Nice, Zurich, Geneva, Basel and Munich. From Venice, direct routes include Ljubljana, Vienna, Budapest, Zurich, Lyon and Paris. Its InterFlix bus pass (€99) allows travel on five FlixBus routes across Europe. The pass is valid for three months from the time of activation.

Car & Motorcycle

FROM CONTINENTAL EUROPE

➡ Every vehicle travelling across an international border should display the nationality plate of its country of registration.

➡ Always carry proof of vehicle ownership and evidence of third-party insurance. If driving an EU-registered vehicle, your home country insurance is sufficient. Ask your insurer for a European Accident Statement (EAS) form, which can simplify matters in the event of an accident. The form can also be downloaded online at http://cartraveldocs.com/european-accident-statement.

➡ A European breakdown assistance policy is a good investment and can be obtained through the Automobile Club d'Italia.

➡ Italy's scenic roads are tailor-made for motorcycle touring, and motorcyclists swarm into the country every summer. With a motorcycle you rarely have to book ahead for ferries and can enter restricted-traffic areas in cities. Crash helmets and a motorcycle licence are compulsory.

➡ The US-based Beach's Motorcycle Adventures (www.bmca.com) offers a number of two-week tours from April to October, with destinations including the Alps, Tuscany and Umbria and Sicily. For campervan and motorhome hire, check IdeaMerge (www.ideamerge.com).

FROM THE UK

You can take your car to Italy, via France, by ferry or via the Eurotunnel Shuttle rail service (www.eurotunnel.com). The latter runs up to four times per hour between

DIRECT TRAINS TO ITALY FROM CONTINENTAL EUROPE

FROM	TO	FREQUENCY	DURATION (HR)	COST (€)
Geneva	Milan	4 daily	4	86
Geneva	Venice	1 daily	7	120
Munich	Florence	1 nightly	11	99
Munich	Rome	1 nightly	14	99
Munich	Venice	1-2 daily/1 nightly	6½/8¾	95/79
Paris	Milan	3 daily/1 nightly	7½/10¼	104/95
Paris	Turin	3 daily	5½-6½	104
Paris	Venice	1 nightly	14½	115
Vienna	Milan	1 nightly	14	49
Vienna	Rome	1 nightly	14	79
Zurich	Milan	7-8 daily	3½	77

Folkestone and Calais (35 minutes) in peak times.

For breakdown assistance, both the AA (www.theaa.com) and the RAC (www.rac.co.uk) offer comprehensive cover in Europe.

Train

Regular trains on two western lines connect Italy with France (one along the coast and the other from Turin into the French Alps). Trains from Milan head north into Switzerland and on towards the Benelux countries. Further east, two main lines head for the main cities in Central and Eastern Europe. Those crossing the Brenner Pass go to Innsbruck, Stuttgart and Munich. Those crossing at Tarvisio proceed to Vienna, Salzburg and Prague. The main international train line to Slovenia crosses near Trieste.

Depending on distances covered, rail can be highly competitive with air travel. Those travelling from neighbouring countries to northern Italy will find it is frequently more comfortable, less expensive and only marginally more time-consuming than flying.

INTERNATIONAL FERRY ROUTES FROM ITALY

DESTINATION COUNTRY	DESTINATION PORT(S)	ITALIAN PORT(S)	COMPANY
Albania	Durrës	Bari	Ventouris, SNAV
	Durrës	Bari, Ancona, Trieste	Adria Ferries
Croatia	Dubrovnik	Bari	Jadrolinija
	Hvar	Pescara	SNAV
	Split	Ancona, Pescara	SNAV
	Split, Zadar	Ancona	Jadrolinija
	Umag, Poreč, Rovinj, Pula	Venice	Venezia Lines
	Vela Luka	Pescara	SNAV
France (Corsica)	Bastia	Livorno, Genoa	Moby Lines
	Bonifacio	Santa Teresa di Gallura	Moby Lines
Greece	Corfu, Igoumenitsa, Patras	Bari	Superfast, Anek Lines
	Igoumenitsa, Patras	Brindisi	Grimaldi Lines
	Igoumenitsa, Patras	Ancona	Superfast, Anek Lines, Grimaldi Lines, Minoan Lines
	Igoumenitsa, Patras	Venice	Superfast, Anek Lines, Grimaldi Lines, Minoan Lines
Malta	Valletta	Pozzallo	Virtu Ferries
Montenegro	Bar	Bari	Montenegro Lines, Jadrolinija
Morocco	Tangier	Genoa	GNV, SNAV
	Tangier	Livorno	Grimaldi Lines
Slovenia	Piran	Venice	Venezia Lines
Spain	Barcelona	Genoa	GNV
	Barcelona	Civitavecchia, Livorno, Savona, Porto Torres	Grimaldi Lines
Tunisia	Tunis	Genoa, Civitaveccchia, Palermo	GNV, SNAV
	Tunis	Civitavecchia, Palermo, Salerno	Grimaldi Lines

Those travelling longer distances (say, from London, Spain, northern Germany or Eastern Europe) will doubtless find flying cheaper and quicker. Bear in mind, however, that the train is a much greener way to go – a trip by rail can contribute up to 10 times fewer carbon dioxide emissions per person than the same trip by air.

Voyages-sncf (http://uk.voyages-sncf.com) is an online booking service for rail journeys across Europe.

FROM CONTINENTAL EUROPE

➜ The comprehensive European Rail Timetable (UK£16.99, digital version UK£11.99), updated monthly, is available for purchase online at www.europeanrailtimetable.co.uk, as well as at a handful of bookshops in the UK and continental Europe (see the website for details).

➜ Reservations on international trains to/from Italy are always advisable, and sometimes compulsory.

➜ Some international services include transport for private cars.

➜ Consider taking long journeys overnight, as the supplemental fare for a sleeper costs substantially less than Italian hotels.

FROM THE UK

➜ High-velocity passenger train Eurostar (www.eurostar.com) connects London to Lille and Brussels, as well as to Paris, Lyon, Avignon and Marseille. Direct trains to Italy run from Paris, Lyon and Marseille. Alternatively, you can get a train ticket that includes crossing the Channel by ferry.

➜ For the latest fare information on journeys to Italy, contact International Rail (www.internationalrail.com).

Sea

Multiple ferry companies connect Italy with countries throughout the Mediterranean. Many routes only operate during the summer months, when ticket prices also increase in cost. Prices for vehicles vary according to their size.

The helpful website www.directferries.co.uk allows you to search various ferry routes and compare prices between the numerous international ferry companies servicing Italy. Another useful resource for ferries from Italy to Greece is the website www.ferries.gr.

International ferry companies that operate services to Italy:

Adria Ferries (071 5021 1621; www.adriaferries.com)

Anek Lines (071 207 23 46; www.anekitalia.com)

GNV (Grandi Navi Veloci; 010 209 45 91; www.gnv.it)

Grimaldi Lines (081 49 64 44; www.grimaldi-lines.com)

Jadrolinija (Ancona 071 20 45 16, Bari 080 521 28 40; www.jadrolinija.hr)

Minoan Lines (071 20 17 08; www.minoan.it)

Moby Lines (199 30 30 40; www.moby.it)

Montenegro Lines (Bar 382 3030 3469; www.montenegrolines.net)

SNAV (081 428 55 55; www.snav.it)

Superfast (Athens 30 210 891 97 00; www.superfast.com)

Venezia Lines (041 847 09 03; www.venezialines.com)

Ventouris (Albania 0808 496685, Greece 0808 761451; www.ventouris.gr; Nuova Stazione Marittima di Bari)

Virtu Ferries (Catania 095 703 12 11; www.virtuferries.com)

GETTING AROUND

Air

Italy offers an extensive network of internal flights. The privatised national airline, Alitalia, is the main domestic carrier, and numerous low-cost airlines also operate across the country. Useful search engines for comparing multiple carriers' fares (including those of cut-price airlines) are www.skyscanner.com, www.kayak.com and www.azfly.it. Airport taxes are included in the price of your ticket.

Airlines in Italy

Alitalia (89 20 10; www.alitalia.com)

Blue Panorama (06 9895 6666; www.blu-express.com)

easyJet (www.easyjet.com)

Etihad Regional (www.etihadregional.com)

Meridiana (89 29 28; www.meridiana.it)

Ryanair (www.ryanair.com)

Volotea (www.volotea.com)

Bicycle

Cycling is very popular in Italy. The following tips will help ensure a pedal-happy trip:

➜ If bringing your own bike, you'll need to disassemble and pack it for the journey, and may need to pay an airline surcharge.

➜ Make sure to bring tools, spare parts, a helmet, lights and a secure bike lock.

➜ Bikes are prohibited on Italian *autostrade* (motorways).

➜ Bikes can be wheeled onto regional trains displaying the bicycle logo. Simply purchase a separate bicycle ticket (*supplemento bici*), valid for 24 hours (€3.50). Certain international trains, listed on Trenitalia's

'Travelling with Your Bike' page, also allow transport of assembled bicycles for €12, paid on board. Bikes dismantled and stored in a bag can be taken for free, even on night trains.

➜ Most ferries also allow free bicycle passage.

➜ In the UK, Cycling UK (www.cyclinguk.org) can help you plan your tour or organise a guided tour. Membership costs £43 for adults, £28.50 for seniors and £21.50 for students and under-18s.

➜ Bikes are available for hire in most Italian towns. City bikes start at €10/50 per day/week; mountain bikes a bit more. A growing number of Italian hotels offer free bikes for guests.

Boat

Craft *Navi* (large ferries) service Sicily and Sardinia, while *traghetti* (smaller ferries) and *aliscafi* (hydrofoils) service the smaller islands. Most ferries carry vehicles; hydrofoils do not.

Routes Main embarkation points for Sicily and Sardinia are Genoa, Livorno, Civitavecchia and Naples. Ferries for Sicily also leave from Villa San Giovanni and Reggio Calabria. Main arrival points in Sardinia are Cagliari, Arbatax, Olbia and Porto Torres; in Sicily they're Palermo, Catania, Trapani and Messina.

Timetables and tickets Comprehensive website Direct Ferries (www.directferries.co.uk) allows you to search routes, compare prices and book tickets for ferry routes in Italy.

Overnight ferries Travellers can book a two- to four-person cabin or a *poltrona*, which is an airline-type armchair. Deck class (which allows you to sit/sleep in lounge areas or on deck) is available only on some ferries.

Bus

Routes Everything from meandering local routes to fast, reliable InterCity connections is provided by numerous bus companies.

Timetables and tickets Available on bus-company websites and from local tourist offices. Tickets are generally competitively priced with the train and are often the only way to get to smaller towns. In larger cities most of the InterCity bus companies have ticket offices or sell tickets through agencies. In villages and even some good-sized towns, tickets are sold in bars or on the bus.

Advance booking Generally not required, but advisable for overnight or long-haul trips in high season.

Car & Motorcycle

Italy's extensive network of roads spans numerous categories. The main ones include the following:

➜ Autostradas – An extensive, privatised network of motorways, represented on road signs by a white 'A' followed by a number on a

ROAD DISTANCES (KM)

	Bari	Bologna	Florence	Genoa	Milan	Naples	Palermo	Perugia	Reggio di Calabria	Rome	Siena	Trento	Trieste	Turin	Venice
Bologna	681														
Florence	784	106													
Genoa	996	285	268												
Milan	899	218	324	156											
Naples	322	640	534	758	858										
Palermo	734	1415	1345	1569	1633	811									
Perugia	612	270	164	432	488	408	1219								
Reggio di Calabria	490	1171	1101	1325	1389	567	272	816							
Rome	482	408	302	526	626	232	1043	170	664						
Siena	714	176	70	296	394	464	1275	103	867	232					
Trento	892	233	339	341	218	874	1626	459	1222	641	375				
Trieste	995	308	414	336	420	948	1689	543	1445	715	484	279			
Turin	1019	338	442	174	139	932	1743	545	1307	702	460	349	551		
Venice	806	269	265	387	284	899	799	394	1296	567	335	167	165	415	
Verona	808	141	247	282	164	781	1534	377	1139	549	293	97	250	295	120

Note

Distances between Palermo and mainland towns do not take into account the ferry from Reggio di Calabria to Messina. Add an extra hour to your journey time to allow for this crossing green background. The main north–south link is the A1. Also known as the Autostrada del Sole (the 'Motorway of the Sun'), it extends from Milan to Naples. The main link from Naples south to Reggio di Calabria is the A3. There are tolls on most motorways, payable by cash or credit card as you exit.

➡ *Strade statali* (state highways) – Represented on maps by 'S' or 'SS'. Vary from toll-free, four-lane highways to two lane main roads. The latter can be extremely slow, especially in mountainous regions.

➡ *Strade regionali* (regional highways connecting small villages) – Coded 'SR' or 'R'.

➡ *Strade provinciali* (provincial highways) – Coded 'SP' or 'P'.

➡ *Strade locali* – Often not even paved or mapped.

For information in English about distances, driving times and fuel costs, see https://en.mappy.com. Additional information, including traffic conditions and toll costs, is available at www. autostrade.it.

Automobile Associations

The **Automobile Club d'Italia** (ACI; ☑803116, from a foreign mobile 800 116800; www.aci.it) is a driver's best resource in Italy. Foreigners do not have to join to get 24-hour roadside emergency service but instead pay a per-incident fee.

Driving Licences

All EU driving licences are recognised in Italy. Travellers from other countries should obtain an International Driving Permit (IDP) through their national automobile association.

Fuel & Spare Parts

Italy's petrol prices vary from one service station (*benzinaio, stazione di servizio*) to another. At the time of writing, unleaded petrol (*senza piombo*; 95 octane) was averaging €1.44 per litre, with diesel (*gasolio*) costing €1.29 per litre.

Spare parts are available at many garages or via the 24-hour ACI motorist assistance number ☑803 116 (or 800 116800 if calling with a non-Italian mobile-phone account).

Hire

CAR

➡ Pre-booking via the internet often costs less than hiring a car once in Italy. Online booking agency Rentalcars.com (www.rentalcars.com) compares the rates of numerous car-rental companies.

➡ Renters must generally be aged 21 or over, with a credit card and home-country driving licence or IDP.

➡ Consider hiring a small car, which will reduce your fuel expenses and help you negotiate narrow city lanes and tight parking spaces.

➡ Check with your credit-card company to see if it offers a Collision Damage Waiver, which covers you for additional damage if you use that card to pay for the car. The following companies have pick-up locations throughout Italy:

Auto Europe (www.autoeurope.com)

Avis (www.avis.com)

Budget (www.budget.com)

Europcar (www.europcar.com)

Hertz (www.hertz.it)

Italy by Car (www.italybycar.it)

Maggiore (www.maggiore.it)

Sixt (www.sixt.com)

MOTORCYCLE

Agencies throughout Italy rent motorbikes, ranging from small Vespas to larger touring bikes. Prices start at around €35/150 per day/week for a 50cc scooter, or upwards of €80/400 per day/week for a 650cc motorcycle.

Road Rules

➡ Cars drive on the right side of the road and overtake on the left. Unless otherwise indicated, always give way to cars entering an intersection from a road on your right.

➡ Seatbelt use (front and rear) is required by law; violators are subject to an on-the-spot fine. Helmets are required on all two-wheeled vehicles.

➡ Day and night, it is compulsory to drive with your headlights on outside built-up areas.

➡ It's obligatory to carry a warning triangle and fluorescent waistcoat in case of breakdown. Recommended accessories include a first-aid kit, spare-bulb kit and fire extinguisher.

➡ A licence is required to ride a scooter – a car licence will do for bikes up to 125cc; for anything over 125cc you'll need a motorcycle licence.

➡ Motorbikes can enter most restricted traffic areas in Italian cities, and traffic police generally turn a blind eye to motorcycles or scooters parked on footpaths.

➡ The blood alcohol limit is 0.05%; it's zero for drivers under 21 and those who have had their licence for less than three years.

Unless otherwise indicated, speed limits are as follows:

➡ 130km/h on autostradas

➡ 110km/h on all main, non-urban roads

➡ 90km/h on secondary, non-urban roads

➡ 50km/h in built-up areas

Local Transport

Major cities all have good transport systems, including bus and underground-train networks. In Venice, the main public transport option is *vaporetti* (small passenger ferries).

Bus & Metro

➡ Extensive *metropolitane* (metros) exist in Rome, Milan, Naples and Turin, with smaller metros in Genoa and Catania. The *Minimetrò* in Perugia connects the train station with the city centre.

➡ Cities and towns of any size have an efficient *urbano* (urban) and *extraurbano* (suburban) bus system. Services are generally limited on Sundays and holidays.

➡ Purchase bus and metro tickets before boarding and validate them once on board. Passengers with unvalidated tickets are subject to a fine (between €50 and €110). Buy tickets from a *tabaccaio* (tobacconist's shop), newsstands, ticket booths or dispensing machines at bus and metro stations. Tickets usually cost around €1 to €2. Many cities offer good-value 24-hour or daily tourist tickets.

Taxi

➡ You can catch a taxi at the ranks outside most train and bus stations, or simply telephone for a radio taxi. Radio taxi meters start running from when you've called rather than when you're picked up.

➡ Charges vary somewhat from one region to another. Most short city journeys cost between €10 and €15. Generally, no more than four people are allowed in one taxi.

Train

Trains in Italy are convenient and relatively cheap compared with other European countries. The better train categories are fast and comfortable.

Trenitalia (☎892021; www.trenitalia.com) is the national train system that runs most services. Its privately owned competitor **Italo** (☎89 20 20; www.italotreno.it) runs high-velocity trains between Turin and Salerno, Venice and Naples, and Brescia and Naples. All three routes stop in Bologna, Florence and Rome. The Turin line also stops in Milan.

Train tickets must be stamped in the green machines (usually found at the head of rail platforms) just before boarding. Failure to do so usually results in fines.

Italy operates several types of trains:

Regionale/interregionale Slow and often cheaper, stopping at all or most stations.

EURAIL & INTERRAIL PASSES

Generally speaking, you'll need to cover a lot of ground to make a rail pass worthwhile. Before buying, consider where you intend to travel and compare the price of a rail pass to the cost of individual tickets on the Trenitalia website (www.trenitalia.com).

InterRail (www.interrail.eu) passes, available online and at most major stations and student-travel outlets, are for people who have been a resident in Europe for more than six months. A Global Pass encompassing 30 countries comes in seven versions, ranging from five days' travel within a 15-day period to a full month's unlimited travel. There are four price categories: youth (12 to 27), adult (28 to 59), senior (60+) and family (one adult and up to two children), with different prices for 1st and 2nd class.

The InterRail one-country pass for Italy can be used for three, four, six or eight days in one month. See the website for full price details. Cardholders have access to various discounts and special deals, including on selected accommodation.

Eurail (www.eurail.com) passes, available for non-European residents, are good for travel in 28 European countries (not including the UK). They can be purchased online or from travel agencies outside Europe.

The original Eurail pass, now known as the **Global Pass**, offers a number of options, from five days of travel within a one-month period to three months of unlimited travel.

Youth aged 12 to 27 are eligible for a 2nd-class pass; all others must buy the more expensive 1st-class pass (the family ticket allows up to two children aged 0 to 11 to travel free when accompanied by a paying adult).

Eurail offers several alternatives to the traditional Global Pass:

➡ The **Select Pass** allows four to 10 days of travel within a two-month period in two to four bordering countries of your choice.

➡ The two-country **Regional Pass** (France/Italy, Switzerland/Italy, Spain/Italy, Greece/Italy, Croatia & Slovenia/Italy) allows four to 10 days of travel within a two-month period.

➡ The **One Country Pass** allows three to eight days of travel in Italy within a one-month period.

POPULAR HIGH-VELOCITY ROUTES

FROM	TO	DURATION (HR)	PRICE FROM (€)
Turin	Naples	5½- 6	50
Milan	Rome	3-3¼	70
Venice	Florence	2	25
Rome	Naples	1¼	17
Florence	Bologna	35min	15

InterCity (IC) Faster services operating between major cities. Their international counterparts are called Eurocity (EC).

Alta Velocità (AV) State-of-the-art, high-velocity trains, including Frecciarossa, Frecciargento, Frecciabianca and Italo trains, with speeds of up to 300km/h and connections to the major cities. Marginally more expensive than some InterCity express trains, but journey times are cut by almost half.

Classes & Costs

Prices vary according to the class of service, time of travel and how far in advance you book. Most Italian trains have 1st- and 2nd-class seating; a 1st-class ticket typically costs from a third to half more than 2nd-class.

Travel on Trenitalia's Inter-City and Alta Velocità (Frecciarossa, Frecciargento, Frecciabianca) trains means paying a supplement, included in the ticket price, determined by the distance you are travelling. If you have a standard ticket for a slower train and end up hopping on an IC train, you'll have to pay the difference on board. (You can only board an Alta Velocità train if you have a booking, so the problem does not arise in those cases.)

Reservations

➡ Reservations are obligatory on AV trains. On other services they're not, and outside peak holiday periods, you should be fine without them.

➡ Reservations can be made on the Trenitalia and Italo websites, at railway station counters and self-service ticketing machines, or through travel agents.

➡ Both Trenitalia and Italo offer a variety of advance purchase discounts. Basically, the earlier you book, the greater the saving. Discounted tickets are limited, and refunds and changes are highly restricted. For all ticket options and prices, see the Trenitalia and Italo websites.

Train Passes

Trenitalia offers various discount passes, including the Carta Verde for youth and Carta d'Argento for seniors, but these are mainly useful for residents or long-term visitors, as they only pay for themselves with regular use over an extended period.

More interesting for short-term visitors are Eurail and InterRail passes.

Language

Standard Italian is taught and spoken throughout Italy. Regional dialects are an important part of identity in many parts of the country, but you'll have no trouble being understood anywhere if you stick to standard Italian, which we've also used in this chapter.

The sounds used in spoken Italian can all be found in English. If you read our coloured pronunciation guides as if they were English, you'll be understood. The stressed syllables are indicated with italics. Note that ai is pronounced as in 'aisle', ay as in 'say', ow as in 'how', dz as the 'ds' in 'lids', and that r is a strong and rolled sound. Keep in mind that Italian consonants can have a stronger, emphatic pronunciation – if the consonant is written as a double letter, it should be pronounced a little stronger, eg *sonno son*·no (sleep) versus *sono so*·no (I am).

BASICS

Hello.	*Buongiorno.*	bwon·*jor*·no
Goodbye.	*Arrivederci.*	a·ree·ve·*der*·chee
Yes./No.	*Sì./No.*	see/no
Excuse me.	*Mi scusi.* (pol)	mee *skoo*·zee
	Scusami. (inf)	*skoo*·za·mee
Sorry.	*Mi dispiace.*	mee dees·*pya*·che
Please.	*Per favore.*	per fa·*vo*·re
Thank you.	*Grazie.*	*gra*·tsye
You're welcome.	*Prego.*	*pre*·go

WANT MORE?

For in-depth language information and handy phrases, check out Lonely Planet's *Italian Phrasebook*. You'll find it at **shop.lonelyplanet.com**, or you can buy Lonely Planet's iPhone phrasebooks at the Apple App Store.

How are you?
Come sta/stai? (pol/inf)	*ko*·me sta/stai

Fine. And you?
Bene. E lei/tu? (pol/inf)	*be*·ne e lay/too

What's your name?
Come si chiama? (pol)	*ko*·me see *kya*·ma
Come ti chiami? (inf)	*ko*·me tee *kya*·mee

My name is ...
Mi chiamo ...	mee *kya*·mo ...

Do you speak English?
Parla/Parli	*par*·la/*par*·lee
inglese? (pol/inf)	een·*gle*·ze

I don't understand.
Non capisco.	non ka·*pee*·sko

ACCOMMODATION

campsite	*campeggio*	kam·*pe*·jo
guesthouse	*pensione*	pen·*syo*·ne
hotel	*albergo*	al·*ber*·go
youth hostel	*ostello della gioventù*	os·*te*·lo de·la jo·ven·*too*
Do you have a ... room?	*Avete una camera ...?*	a·*ve*·te oo·na *ka*·me·ra ...
double	*doppia con letto matrimoniale*	*do*·pya kon *le*·to ma·*tree*·mo·*nya*·le
single	*singola*	*seen*·go·la
How much is it per ...?	*Quanto costa per ...?*	*kwan*·to *kos*·ta per ...
night	*una notte*	oo·na *no*·te
person	*persona*	per·*so*·na
air-con	*aria condizionata*	*a*·rya kon·dee·tsyo·*na*·ta
bathroom	*bagno*	*ba*·nyo
window	*finestra*	fee·*nes*·tra

DIRECTIONS

Where's ...?
Dov'è ...?   do·ve ...

What's the address?
Qual'è l'indirizzo?   kwa·le leen·dee·ree·tso

Could you please write it down?
Può scriverlo,   pwo skree·ver·lo
per favore?   per fa·vo·re

Can you show me (on the map)?
Può mostrarmi   pwo mos·trar·mee
(sulla pianta)?   (soo·la pyan·ta)

EATING & DRINKING

What would you recommend?
Cosa mi consiglia?   ko·za mee kon·see·lya

What's the local speciality?
Qual'è la specialità   kwa·le la spe·cha·lee·ta
di questa regione?   dee kwe·sta re·jo·ne

Cheers!
Salute!   sa·loo·te

That was delicious!
Era squisito!   e·ra skwee·zee·to

Please bring the bill.
Mi porta il conto,   mee por·ta eel kon·to
per favore?   per fa·vo·re

I'd like to	*Vorrei*	vo·ray
reserve a	*prenotare un*	pre·no·ta·re oon
table for ...	*tavolo per ...*	ta·vo·lo per ...
(eight) o'clock	*le (otto)*	le (o·to)
(two) people	*(due) persone*	(doo·e) per·so·ne

I don't eat ...	*Non mangio ...*	non man·jo ...
eggs	*uova*	wo·va
fish	*pesce*	pe·she
nuts	*noci*	no·chee

Key Words

bar	*locale*	lo·ka·le
bottle	*bottiglia*	bo·tee·lya
breakfast	*prima colazione*	pree·ma ko·la·tsyo·ne
cafe	*bar*	bar
dinner	*cena*	che·na
drink list	*lista delle bevande*	lee·sta de·le be·van·de
fork	*forchetta*	for·ke·ta
glass	*bicchiere*	bee·kye·re
knife	*coltello*	kol·te·lo

To get by in Italian, mix and match these simple patterns with words of your choice:

When's (the next flight)?
A che ora è   a ke o·ra e
(il prossimo volo)?   (eel pro·see·mo vo·lo)

Where's (the station)?
Dov'è (la stazione)?   do·ve (la sta·tsyo·ne)

I'm looking for (a hotel).
Sto cercando   sto cher·kan·do
(un albergo).   (oon al·ber·go)

Do you have (a map)?
Ha (una pianta)?   a (oo·na pyan·ta)

Is there (a toilet)?
C'è (un gabinetto)?   che (oon ga·bee·ne·to)

I'd like (a coffee).
Vorrei (un caffè).   vo·ray (oon ka·fe)

I'd like to (hire a car).
Vorrei (noleggiare   vo·ray (no·le·ja·re
una macchina).   oo·na ma·kee·na)

Can I (enter)?
Posso (entrare)?   po·so (en·tra·re)

Could you please (help me)?
Può (aiutarmi),   pwo (a·yoo·tar·mee)
per favore?   per fa·vo·re

Do I have to (book a seat)?
Devo (prenotare   de·vo (pre·no·ta·re
un posto)?   oon po·sto)

lunch	*pranzo*	pran·dzo
market	*mercato*	mer·ka·to
menu	*menù*	me·noo
plate	*piatto*	pya·to
restaurant	*ristorante*	ree·sto·ran·le
spoon	*cucchiaio*	koo·kya·yo
vegetarian	*vegetariano*	ve·je·ta·rya·no

Meat & Fish

beef	*manzo*	man·dzo
chicken	*pollo*	po·lo
herring	*aringa*	a·reen·ga
lamb	*agnello*	a·nye·lo
lobster	*aragosta*	a·ra·gos·ta
mussels	*cozze*	ko·tse
oysters	*ostriche*	o·stree·ke
pork	*maiale*	ma·ya·le
prawn	*gambero*	gam·be·ro
salmon	*salmone*	sal·mo·ne
scallops	*capasante*	ka·pa·san·te

shrimp	gambero	gam·be·ro
squid	calamari	ka·la·ma·ree
trout	trota	tro·ta
tuna	tonno	to·no
turkey	tacchino	ta·kee·no
veal	vitello	vee·te·lo

Fruit & Vegetables

apple	mela	me·la
beans	fagioli	fa·jo·lee
cabbage	cavolo	ka·vo·lo
capsicum	peperone	pe·pe·ro·ne
carrot	carota	ka·ro·ta
cauliflower	cavolfiore	ka·vol·fyo·re
cucumber	cetriolo	che·tree·o·lo
grapes	uva	oo·va
lemon	limone	lee·mo·ne
lentils	lenticchie	len·tee·kye
mushroom	funghi	foon·gee
nuts	noci	no·chee
onions	cipolle	chee·po·le
orange	arancia	a·ran·cha
peach	pesca	pe·ska
peas	piselli	pee·ze·lee
pineapple	ananas	a·na·nas
plum	prugna	proo·nya
potatoes	patate	pa·ta·te
spinach	spinaci	spee·na·chee
tomatoes	pomodori	po·mo·do·ree

Other

bread	pane	pa·ne
butter	burro	boo·ro
cheese	formaggio	for·ma·jo
eggs	uova	wo·va
honey	miele	mye·le
jam	marmellata	mar·me·la·ta

Signs

Closed	Chiuso
Entrance	Entrata/Ingresso
Exit	Uscita
Men	Uomini
Open	Aperto
Prohibited	Proibito/Vietato
Toilets	Gabinetti/Servizi
Women	Donne

noodles	pasta	pas·ta
oil	olio	o·lyo
pepper	pepe	pe·pe
rice	riso	ree·zo
salt	sale	sa·le
soup	minestra	mee·nes·tra
soy sauce	salsa di soia	sal·sa dee so·ya
sugar	zucchero	tsoo·ke·ro
vinegar	aceto	a·che·to

Drinks

beer	birra	bee·ra
coffee	caffè	ka·fe
juice	succo	soo·ko
milk	latte	la·te
red wine	vino rosso	vee·no ro·so
tea	tè	te
water	acqua	a·kwa
white wine	vino bianco	vee·no byan·ko

EMERGENCIES

Help!
Aiuto! · a·yoo·to

Leave me alone!
Lasciami in pace! · la·sha·mee een pa·che

I'm lost.
Mi sono perso/a. (m/f) · mee so·no per·so/a

Call the police!
Chiami la polizia! · kya·mee la po·lee·tsee·a

Call a doctor!
Chiami un medico! · kya·mee oon me·dee·ko

Where are the toilets?
Dove sono i gabinetti? · do·ve so·no ee ga·bee·ne·tee

I'm sick.
Mi sento male. · mee sen·to ma·le

SHOPPING & SERVICES

I'd like to buy ...
Vorrei comprare ... · vo·ray kom·pra·re ...

I'm just looking.
Sto solo guardando. · sto so·lo gwar·dan·do

Can I look at it?
Posso dare un'occhiata? · po·so da·re oo·no·kya·ta

How much is this?
Quanto costa questo? · kwan·to kos·ta kwe·sto

It's too expensive.
È troppo caro. · e tro·po ka·ro

There's a mistake in the bill.
C'è un errore nel conto. · che oo·ne·ro·re nel kon·to

ATM	*Bancomat*	ban·ko·mat
post office	*ufficio postale*	oo·*fee*·cho pos·*ta*·le
tourist office	*ufficio del turismo*	oo·*fee*·cho del too·*reez*·mo

TIME & DATES

What time is it?
Che ora è?   ke o·ra e

It's (two) o'clock.
Sono le (due).   so·no le (*doo*·e)

Half past (one).
(L'una) e mezza.   (*loo*·na) e me·dza

in the morning	*di mattina*	dee ma·*tee*·na
in the afternoon	*di pomeriggio*	dee po·me·*ree*·jo
in the evening	*di sera*	dee se·ra
yesterday	*ieri*	ye·*ree*
today	*oggi*	o·jee
tomorrow	*domani*	do·*ma*·nee

Monday	*lunedì*	loo·ne·*dee*
Tuesday	*martedì*	mar·te·*dee*
Wednesday	*mercoledì*	mer·ko·le·*dee*
Thursday	*giovedì*	jo·ve·*dee*
Friday	*venerdì*	ve·ner·*dee*
Saturday	*sabato*	*sa*·ba·to
Sunday	*domenica*	do·*me*·nee·ka

TRANSPORT

boat	*nave*	*na*·ve
bus	*autobus*	*ow*·to·boos
ferry	*traghetto*	tra·*ge*·to
metro	*metropolitana*	me·tro·po·lee·*ta*·na
plane	*aereo*	a·*e*·re·o
train	*treno*	*tre*·no
bus stop	*fermata dell'autobus*	fer·*ma*·ta del *ow*·to·boos
ticket office	*biglietteria*	bee·lye·te·*ree*·a
timetable	*orario*	o·*ra*·ryo
train station	*stazione ferroviaria*	sta·*tsyo*·ne fe·ro·*vyar*·ya
... ticket	*un biglietto ...*	oon bee·*lye*·to
one way	*di sola andata*	dee so·la an·*da*·ta
return	*di andata e ritorno*	dee an·*da*·ta e ree·*tor*·no

Numbers		
1	*uno*	*oo*·no
2	*due*	*doo*·e
3	*tre*	tre
4	*quattro*	*kwa*·tro
5	*cinque*	*cheen*·kwe
6	*sei*	say
7	*sette*	*se*·te
8	*otto*	*o*·to
9	*nove*	*no*·ve
10	*dieci*	*dye*·chee
20	*venti*	*ven*·tee
30	*trenta*	*tren*·ta
40	*quaranta*	kwa·*ran*·ta
50	*cinquanta*	cheen·*kwan*·ta
60	*sessanta*	se·*san*·ta
70	*settanta*	se·*tan*·ta
80	*ottanta*	o·*tan*·ta
90	*novanta*	no·*van*·ta
100	*cento*	*chen*·to
1000	*mille*	*mee*·lel

Does it stop at ...?
Si ferma a ...?   see *fer*·ma a ...

Please tell me when we get to ...
Mi dica per favore quando arriviamo a ...   mee *dee*·ka per fa·vo·re *kwan*·do a·ree·*vya*·mo a ...

I want to get off here.
Voglio scendere qui.   *vo*·lyo *shen*·de·re kwee

I'd like to hire a ...	*Vorrei noleggiare una ...*	vo·*ray* no·le·*ja*·re *oo*·na ...
bicycle	*bicicletta*	bee·chee·*kle*·ta
car	*macchina*	*ma*·kee·na
motorbike	*moto*	*mo*·to
bicycle pump	*pompa della bicicletta*	*pom*·pa *de*·la bee·chee·*kle*·ta
child seat	*seggiolino*	se·jo·*lee*·no
helmet	*casco*	*kas*·ko
mechanic	*meccanico*	me·*ka*·nee·ko
petrol	*benzina*	ben·*dzee*·na
service station	*stazione di servizio*	sta·*tsyo*·ne dee ser·*vee*·tsyo

Is this the road to ...?
Questa strada porta a ...? *kwe*·sta *stra*·da *por*·ta a ...

Can I park here?
Posso parcheggiare qui? *po*·so par·ke·*ja*·re kwee

GLOSSARY

abbazia – abbey

agriturismo – farm-stays

(pizza) al taglio – (pizza) by the slice

albergo – hotel

alimentari – grocery shop

anfiteatro – amphitheatre

aperitivo – pre-dinner drink and snack

APT – Azienda di Promozione Turistica; local town or city tourist office

autostrada – motorway; highway

battistero – baptistry

biblioteca – library

biglietto – ticket

borgo – archaic name for a small town, village or town sector

camera – room

campo – field; also a square in Venice

cappella – chapel

carabinieri – police with military and civil duties

Carnevale – carnival period between Epiphany and Lent

casa – house

castello – castle

cattedrale – cathedral

centro storico – historic centre

certosa – monastery belonging to or founded by Carthusian monks

chiesa – church

chiostro – cloister; covered walkway, usually enclosed by columns, around a quadrangle

cima – summit

città – town; city

città alta – upper town

città bassa – lower town

colonna – column

comune – equivalent to a municipality or county; a town or city council; historically, a self-governing town or city

contrada – district

corso – boulevard

duomo – cathedral

enoteca – wine bar

espresso – short black coffee

ferrovia – railway

festa – feast day; holiday

fontana – fountain

foro – forum

funivia – cable car

gelateria – ice-cream shop

giardino – garden

golfo – gulf

grotta – cave

isola – island

lago – lake

largo – small square

lido – beach

locanda – inn; small hotel

lungomare – seafront road/promenade

mar, mare – sea

masseria – working farm

mausoleo – mausoleum; stately and magnificent tomb

mercato – market

monte – mountain

necropoli – ancient name for cemetery or burial site

nord – north

nuraghe – megalithic stone fortress in Sardinia

osteria – casual tavern or eatery

palazzo – mansion; palace; large building of any type

palio – contest

parco – park

passeggiata – evening stroll

pasticceria – cake/pastry shop

pensione – guesthouse

piazza – square

piazzale – large open square

pietà – literally 'pity' or 'compassion'; sculpture, drawing or painting of the dead Christ supported by the Madonna

pinacoteca – art gallery

ponte – bridge

porta – gate; door

porto – port

reale – royal

rifugio – mountain hut; accommodation in the Alps

ristorante – restaurant

rocca – fortress

sala – room; hall

salumeria – delicatessen

santuario – sanctuary; 1. the part of a church above the altar; 2. an especially holy place in a temple (antiquity)

sassi – literally 'stones'; stone houses built in two ravines in Matera, Basilicata

scalinata – staircase

scavi – excavations

sestiere – city district in Venice

spiaggia – beach

stazione – station

stazione marittima – ferry terminal

strada – street; road

sud – south

superstrada – expressway; highway with divided lanes

tartufo – truffle

tavola calda – literally 'hot table'; pre-prepared meals, often self-service

teatro – theatre

tempietto – small temple

tempio – temple

terme – thermal baths

tesoro – treasury

torre – tower

trattoria – simple restaurant

Trenitalia – Italian State Railways; also known as Ferrovie dello Stato (FS)

trullo – conical house in Perugia

vaporetto – small passenger ferry in Venice

via – street; road

viale – avenue

vico – alley; alleyway

villa – town house; country house; also the park surrounding the house

Behind the Scenes

SEND US YOUR FEEDBACK

We love to hear from travellers – your comments keep us on our toes and help make our books better. Our well travelled team reads every word on what you loved or loathed about this book. Although we cannot reply individually to your submissions, we always guarantee that your feedback goes straight to the appropriate authors, in time for the next edition. Each person who sends us information is thanked in the next edition – the most useful submissions are rewarded with a selection of digital PDF chapters.

Visit **lonelyplanet.com/contact** to submit your updates and suggestions or to ask for help. Our award-winning website also features inspirational travel stories, news and discussions.

Note: We may edit, reproduce and incorporate your comments in Lonely Planet products such as guidebooks, websites and digital products, so let us know if you don't want your comments reproduced or your name acknowledged. For a copy of our privacy policy visit lonelyplanet.com/privacy.

OUR READERS

Many thanks to the travellers who used the last edition and wrote to us with helpful hints, useful advice and interesting anecdotes: Brian Feldman, Carmel Mackin, Craig Elliott, Deborah Santomero, Erika Passerini, Haley Sewell, Jonathan Del Mar, Jonathan Keohane, Kerry Poole, Matt Anness, Neil Harris, Paul Fisher, Rob McDonald, Robert Fairchild, Rolf Wrelf, Stefano Boffetta, Suzanne Tillor

WRITER THANKS

Gregor Clark

Sincere thanks to the many Sardinians who so generously shared their time, insights and love of place, particularly Mario and Frédérique in Nuoro, Daria in Santa Teresa, Simonetta in Olbia, Riky in Lotzorai, Laura in San Pantaleo, and Kevin and Rodolfo in Palau. Finally, hugs to my wife Gaen and daughters Meigan and Chloe, who always make coming home the best part of the trip.

Peter Dragicevich

It turns out that it's not hard to find willing volunteers to keep you company on an extended research assignment in Venice, especially when it coincides with Carnevale. Many thanks to my Venice crew of Christine Henderson, Hamish Blennerhassett and Sarah Welch for much masked fun and many good meals. Special thanks to Christine for the unpaid but much appreciated translation services.

Hugh McNaughtan

Thanks for the patience and support of Tasmin, Anna, my girls, the Lonely Planet tech team and the kind people I met in Italy, who made the research not just possible, but a pleasure.

Donna Wheeler

Thanks to Wayne Young, Elena Ciurletti, Gianluca Cannizzo, Emanuela Grandi, Stefano Libardi and the ultra-helpful Duparc Suites team for inspiring local knowledge. To Kathrin Mair, Verena Hut, Caroline Willeit, Antonella Arlotti, Virginia Ciraldo, Elena Boggio, Matteo Paini and Laura Sailis, *grazie* for gracious, warm hospitality. *Soprattutto, molto amore a Giuseppe Giuseppe Guario.*

Nicola Williams

Grazie mille to those who shared their love and insider knowledge with me: in Rome Linda Martinez (The Beehive), Elyssa Bernard, tour guide Fiona Brewer, Sian Lloyd and Lorna Davidson (Roman Guy), Gina Tringali and Eleonora Baldwin at Casa Mia. In Tuscany, Manuele Giovanelli and Zeno Fioravanti, Doreen and Carmello at Florence's Hotel Scoti, Georgette Jupe, Coral Sisk, Nardia Plumridge, Molly McIlwrath, Cailin Swanson and Betti Soldi. Finally, kudos to my expert, trilingual, family-travel research team: Niko, Mischa and Kaya.

Cristian Bonetto

Mille grazie to Raffaele e Silvana, Joe Brizzi, Alfonso Sperandeo, Carmine Romano, Sylvain Bellenger, Federica Rispoli, the team at Cooperativa La Paranza, Vincenzo Mattiucci, Marcantonio Colonna and the many other friends and locals who offered invaluable tips and insight. At Lonely Planet, many thanks to Anna Tyler and my ever-diligent Italy writing team.

Kerry Christiani

Mille grazie to all the Sardinian locals, experts and tourism officials who made the road to research smooth and provided such valuable insight for the Planning and Understand chapters. Big thanks, too, go to my fellow authors – Duncan Garwood and Gregor Clark – for being such stars to work with.

Marc Di Duca

A big *grazie mille* goes to the many tourist offices around the Veneto, especially those in Verona, Vicenza, Padua and Mantua, as well as to Antonio in Belluno. Also huge thanks to Ukrainian grandma and grandpa for looking after my two sons while I was in Italy, and to my wife for suffering my lengthy absences.

Duncan Garwood

A big thank you to Giacomo Bassi for his brilliant tips and suggestions. In Sardinia, *grazie* to everyone who helped and offered advice, in particular Luisa Besalduch, Agostino Rivano, Marianna Mascalchi, Valentina Sanna, Marco Vacca, and the tourist office teams at Alghero, Sassari and Castelsardo. At Lonely Planet, thanks to Anna Tyler for all her support. And, as always, a big, heartfelt hug to Lidia and the boys, Ben and Nick.

Paula Hardy

Grazie mille to all the fun and fashionable Venetians and Milanese who spilled the beans on their remarkable cities: Paola dalla Valentina, Costanza Cecchini, Sara Porro, Lucia Cattaneo, Monica Cesarato, Francesca Giubilei, Luca Berta, Marco Secchi and Nan McElroy. Thanks, too, to coauthors Regis and Marc for their contributions, and to Anna Tyler for all the support. Finally, much love to Rob for sharing the beauty of the *bel paese*.

Virginia Maxwell

So many locals assisted me in my research for this trip. Many thanks to Tiziana Babbucci, Fernando Bardini, Maricla Bicci, Niccolò Bisconti, Enrico Bracciali, Rita Ceccarelli, Cecilia in Massa Marittima, Stefania Colombini, Ilaria Crescioli, Martina Dei, Paolo Demi, Federica Fantozzi, Irene Gavazzi, Francesco Gentile, Francesca Geppetti, Maria Guarriello, Benedetta Landi, Freya Middleton, Alessandra Molletti, Sonai Pallai, Luigi Pagnotta, Valentina De Pamphilis, Franco Rossi, Fabiana Sciano, Maria Luisa Scorza, Raffaella Senesi, Coral Sisk, Carolina Taddei and Luca Ventresca. Many thanks, too, to my travelling companions: Peter Handsaker, Eveline Zoutendijk, Max Handsaker, Elizabeth Maxwell, Matthew Clarke and Ella Clarke.

Kevin Raub

Thanks to my wife, Adriana Schmidt Raub, who probably can't remember who I am at this point! Anna Tyler, Gregor Clark and all at Lonely Planet. On the road, Alice Brignani (always willing to wave her magic wand), Emanuela Boni, Barbara Candolfini, Francesca Soffici, Michela Iorio, Stefania Sala, Jen Wittman, Giovanni Pellegrini, Errica Dall'Ara, Claudia Valentini, Franca Rastelli, Sara Laghi, Maria Marini, Beatrice Morlunghi and Sviluppumbria, Ubaldo Casoli, Marta Paraventi, Lia Sciarra, Sabrina Pasqualoni, Valeria Giroldini and Maria Talamè.

Regis St Louis

I'm grateful to the countless tourist office staff, innkeepers, chefs, baristas, market vendors, store clerks, students and many other locals who provided helpful tips and advice along the way. Warm thanks to Cassandra and daughters Magdalena and Genevieve, who make this enterprise all the more worthwhile.

ACKNOWLEDGEMENTS

Climate map data adapted from Peel MC, Finlayson BL & McMahon TA (2007) 'Updated World Map of the Köppen-Geiger Climate Classification', Hydrology and Earth System Sciences, 11, 1633–44.

Cover photograph: Manarola, Cinque Terre, ronnybas/Getty ©

Illustrations pp76-7, pp356-7, pp486-7, pp694-5 by Javier Martinez Zarracina.

THIS BOOK

This 13th edition of Lonely Planet's *Italy* guidebook was researched and written by Gregor Clark, Peter Dragicevich, Hugh McNaughton, Brendan Sainsbury, Donna Wheeler, Nicola Williams, Cristian Bonetto, Kerry Christiani, Marc Di Duca, Duncan Garwood, Paula Hardy, Virginia Maxwell, Kevin Raub and Regis St Louis.

This guidebook was produced by the following:

Destination Editor
Anna Tyler

Product Editors
Alison Ridgway, Anne Mason

Senior Cartographer
Anthony Phelan

Book Designer
Clara Monitto

Assisting Editors Sarah Bailey, Andrew Bain, Carolyn Bain, James Bainbridge, Bridget Blair, Katie Connolly, Michelle Coxall, Samantha Forge, Carly Hall, Gabrielle Innes, Kate James, Jodie Martire, Kate Morgan, Kristin Odijk, Monique Perrin, Sarah Reid, Gabrielle Stefanos, Saralinda Turner, Fionnuala Twomey, Simon Williamson

Assisting Cartographers Julie Dodkins, Mick Garrett, Corey Hutchison, Rachel Imeson

Assisting Book Designer
Nicholas Colicchia

Cover Researcher
Naomi Parker

Thanks to Imogen Bannister, Carolyn Boicos, Grace Dobell, Sasha Drew, Lauren Keith, Anne Mason, Catherine Naghtan, Claire Naylor, Lauren O'Connell, Martine Power, Kirsten Rawlings, Tony Wheeler

Index

SORINA CHIRITA

LONELY PLANET IN THE WILD

Send your 'Lonely Planet in the Wild' photos to social@lonelyplanet.com
We share the best on our Facebook page every week!

Map Legend

Sights

- Beach
- Bird Sanctuary
- Buddhist
- Castle/Palace
- Christian
- Confucian
- Hindu
- Islamic
- Jain
- Jewish
- Monument
- Museum/Gallery/Historic Building
- Ruin
- Shinto
- Sikh
- Taoist
- Winery/Vineyard
- Zoo/Wildlife Sanctuary
- Other Sight

Activities, Courses & Tours

- Bodysurfing
- Diving
- Canoeing/Kayaking
- Course/Tour
- Sento Hot Baths/Onsen
- Skiing
- Snorkelling
- Surfing
- Swimming/Pool
- Walking
- Windsurfing
- Other Activity

Sleeping

- Sleeping
- Camping
- Hut/Shelter

Eating

- Eating

Drinking & Nightlife

- Drinking & Nightlife
- Cafe

Entertainment

- Entertainment

Shopping

- Shopping

Information

- Bank
- Embassy/Consulate
- Hospital/Medical
- Internet
- Police
- Post Office
- Telephone
- Toilet
- Tourist Information
- Other Information

Geographic

- Beach
- Gate
- Hut/Shelter
- Lighthouse
- Lookout
- Mountain/Volcano
- Oasis
- Park
- Pass
- Picnic Area
- Waterfall

Population

- Capital (National)
- Capital (State/Province)
- City/Large Town
- Town/Village

Transport

- Airport
- Border crossing
- Bus
- Cable car/Funicular
- Cycling
- Ferry
- Metro station
- Monorail
- Parking
- Petrol station
- S-Bahn/Subway station
- Taxi
- T-bane/Tunnelbana station
- Train station/Railway
- Tram
- Tube station
- U-Bahn/Underground station
- Other Transport

Routes

- Tollway
- Freeway
- Primary
- Secondary
- Tertiary
- Lane
- Unsealed road
- Road under construction
- Plaza/Mall
- Steps
- Tunnel
- Pedestrian overpass
- Walking Tour
- Walking Tour detour
- Path/Walking Trail

Boundaries

- International
- State/Province
- Disputed
- Regional/Suburb
- Marine Park
- Cliff
- Wall

Hydrography

- River, Creek
- Intermittent River
- Canal
- Water
- Dry/Salt/Intermittent Lake
- Reef

Areas

- Airport/Runway
- Beach/Desert
- Cemetery (Christian)
- Cemetery (Other)
- Glacier
- Mudflat
- Park/Forest
- Sight (Building)
- Sportsground
- Swamp/Mangrove

Note: Not all symbols displayed above appear on the maps in this book

Kevin Raub

Emilia-Romagna & San Marino; Umbria & Le Marche Atlanta native Kevin started his career as a music journalist in New York, working for *Men's Journal* and *Rolling Stone* magazines. He ditched the rock 'n' roll lifestyle for travel writing and has written nearly 50 Lonely Planet guides, focused mainly on Brazil, Chile, Colombia, USA, India, the Caribbean and Portugal. Raub also contributes to a variety of travel magazines in both the USA and UK. Along the way, the self-confessed hophead is in constant search of wildly high IBUs in local beers.

Regis St Louis

Milan & the Lakes Regis grew up in a small town in the American Midwest – the kind of place that fuels big dreams of travel – and he developed an early fascination with foreign dialects and world cultures. He spent his formative years learning Russian and a handful of Romance languages, which served him well on journeys across much of the globe. Regis has contributed to more than 50 Lonely Planet titles, covering destinations across six continents. When not on the road, he lives in New Orleans.

Nicola Williams

Rome & Lazio; Florence & Tuscany Border-hopping is way of life for British writer, runner, foodie, art aficionado and mum-of-three Nicola Williams, who has lived in a French village on the southern side of Lake Geneva for more than a decade. Nicola has authored more than 50 guidebooks on Paris, Provence, Rome, Tuscany, France, Italy and Switzerland for Lonely Planet and covers France as a destination expert for the *Telegraph*. Nicola also wrote the Travel with Children chapter.

Cristian Bonetto

Naples & Campania Cristian has contributed to more than 30 Lonely Planet guides to date, including *New York City*, *Italy*, *Venice & the Veneto*, *Naples & the Amalfi Coast*, *Denmark*, *Copenhagen*, *Sweden* and *Singapore*. Lonely Planet work aside, his musings on travel, food, culture and design appear in numerous publications around the world, including *The Telegraph* (UK) and *Corriere del Mezzogiorno* (Italy). Cristian also wrote chapters for Plan, Understand and Survival.

Kerry Christiani

Sardinia Kerry is an award-winning travel writer, photographer and Lonely Planet author, specialising in Central and Southern Europe. Based in Wales, she has authored more than a dozen Lonely Planet titles. An adventure addict, she loves mountains, cold places and true wilderness. Kerry's insatiable wanderlust has taken her to all seven continents – from the frozen wilderness of Antarctica to the Australian Outback – and shows no sign of waning. Her writing appears regularly in publications such as *Adventure Travel* magazine, and she is a *Telegraph* Travel expert for Austria and Wales. Kerry also wrote the Outdoor Activities chapter.

Marc Di Duca

Milan & the Lakes; Venice & the Veneto A travel author for the last decade, Marc has worked for Lonely Planet in Siberia, Slovakia, Bavaria, England, Ukraine, Austria, Poland, Croatia, Portugal, Madeira and on the Trans-Siberian Railway, as well as writing and updating tens of other guides for other publishers. When not on the road, Marc lives between Sandwich, Kent and Mariánské Lázně in the Czech Republic with his wife and two sons.

Duncan Garwood

Rome & Lazio; Sardinia From facing fast bowlers in Barbados to sidestepping hungry pigs in Goa, Duncan's travels have thrown up many unique experiences. These days he largely dedicates himself to Italy, his adopted homeland where's he's been living since 1997. From his base in the Castelli Romani hills outside Rome, he's clocked up endless kilometres exploring the country's well-known destinations and far-flung reaches, working on guides to *Rome*, *Sardinia*, *Sicily*, *Piedmont*, and *Naples & the Amalfi Coast*.

Paula Hardy

Milan & the Lakes; Venice & the Veneto Paula Hardy is an independent travel writer and editorial consultant, whose work for Lonely Planet and other publications has taken her from nomadic camps in the Danakil Depression to Seychellois beach huts and the jewel-like bar at the Gritti Palace on the Grand Canal. Over two decades, she has authored more than 30 Lonely Planet guidebooks and spent five years as commissioning editor of Lonely Planet's bestselling Italian list. These days you'll find her hunting down new hotels, hip bars and up-and-coming artisans primarily in Milan, Venice and Marrakesh.

Virginia Maxwell

Florence & Tuscany Though based in Melbourne, Australia, Virginia spends at least three months of every year in Europe and the Middle East researching guidebooks and other travel-related content for a variety of publishers. She caught the travel bug during her first overseas trip to London, where she lived for a couple of years after finishing an Arts degree at university, and she's been travelling regularly ever since. For the past 13 years Virginia has been working full-time as a travel writer and occasional book reviewer.

OUR STORY

A beat-up old car, a few dollars in the pocket and a sense of adventure. In 1972 that's all Tony and Maureen Wheeler needed for the trip of a lifetime – across Europe and Asia overland to Australia. It took several months, and at the end – broke but inspired – they sat at their kitchen table writing and stapling together their first travel guide, *Across Asia on the Cheap*. Within a week they'd sold 1500 copies. Lonely Planet was born.

Today, Lonely Planet has offices in Franklin, London, Melbourne, Oakland, Dublin, Beijing and Delhi, with more than 600 staff and writers. We share Tony's belief that 'a great guidebook should do three things: inform, educate and amuse'.

OUR WRITERS

Gregor Clark

Sardinia, Sicily Gregor is a US-based writer whose love of foreign languages and curiosity about what's around the next bend have taken him to dozens of countries on five continents. Chronic wanderlust has also led him to visit all 50 states and most Canadian provinces on countless road trips through his native North America. Since 2000, Gregor has regularly contributed to Lonely Planet guides, with a focus on Europe and the Americas.

Peter Dragicevich

Venice & the Veneto After a career in niche newspaper and magazine publishing, both in his native New Zealand and in Australia, Peter finally gave into Kiwi wanderlust, giving up staff jobs to chase his diverse roots around much of Europe. Over the last decade he's written dozens of guidebooks for Lonely Planet on an oddly disparate collection of countries, all of which he's come to love.

Hugh McNaughtan

Abruzzo & Molise; Puglia, Basilicata & Calabria A former English lecturer, Hugh swapped grant applications for visa applications, and turned his love of travel into a full-time thing. Having done a bit of restaurant-reviewing in his home town (Melbourne) he's now eaten his way across four continents. He's never happier than when on the road with his two daughters.

Brendan Sainsbury

Born and raised in the UK in a town that never merits a mention in any guidebook (Andover, Hampshire), Brendan spent the holidays of his youth caravanning in the English Lake District and didn't leave Blighty until he was nineteen. Making up for lost time, he's since squeezed 70 countries into a sometimes precarious existence as a writer and professional vagabond. In the last 11 years, he has written more than 40 books for Lonely Planet from Castro's Cuba to the canyons of Peru.

Donna Wheeler

Turin, Piedmont & the Italian Riviera, Trentino & South Tyrol; Friuli Venezia Giulia Donna has written guidebooks for Lonely Planet for more than 10 years, covering regions across Italy, Norway, Belgium, Africa, Tunisia, Algeria, France, Austria and Australia. She is the author of *Paris Precincts*, a curated photographic guide to the city's best bars, restaurants and shops, and is reporter for Italian contemporary art publisher My Art Guides. Donna also wrote the Art & Architecture chapter.

OVER PAGE MORE WRITERS

Published by Lonely Planet Global Limited
CRN 554153
13th edition – Feb 2018
ISBN 978 1 78657 351 3
© Lonely Planet 2018   Photographs © as indicated 2018
10 9 8 7 6 5 4 3 2 1
Printed in China

Although the authors and Lonely Planet have taken all reasonable care in preparing this book, we make no warranty about the accuracy or completeness of its content and, to the maximum extent permitted, disclaim all liability arising from its use.